SEVENTEENTH EDITION

SCHROEDER'S
ANTIQUES
PRICE GUIDE

Edited by Sharon & Bob Huxford

COLLECTOR BOOKS
A Division of Schroeder Publishing Co., Inc.

The current values in this book should be used only as a guide. They are not intended to set prices, which vary from one section of the country to another. Auction prices as well as dealer prices vary greatly and are affected by condition as well as demand. Neither the Editors nor the Publisher assumes responsibility for any losses that might be incurred as a result of consulting this guide.

Searching For A Publisher?

We are always looking for knowledgable people considered experts within their fields. If you feel that there is a real need for a book on your collectible subject and have a large comprehensive collection, please contact Collector Books.

COLLECTOR BOOKS
P.O. Box 3009
Paducah, Kentucky 42002-3009

Introduction

As the editors and staff of *Schroeder's*, our goal is to compile the most useful, comprehensive, and accurate background and pricing information possible. Our guide encompasses nearly 500 categories, many of which you will not find in other price guides. Our sources are varied; we use auction results and dealer lists, and we consult with national collectors' clubs, recognized authorities, researchers, and appraisers. We have by far the largest advisory board of any similar publication on the market. Each year we add several new advisors and now have over 450 who cover almost all our categories. They go over our computer print-outs line by line, deleting listings that are misleading or too vague to be of merit; they often send background information and photos. We appreciate their assistance very much. Only through their expertise and experience in their special fields are we able to offer with confidence what we feel are useful, accurate evaluations that provide a sound understanding of the dealings in the market place today. Correspondence with so large an advisory panel adds months of extra work to an already monumental task, but we feel that to a very large extent this is the foundation that makes *Schroeder's* the success that it has become.

Our Directory, which you will find in the back of the book, lists each contributor by state. These are people who have allowed us to photograph various examples of merchandise from their show booths, sent us pricing information, or in any way have contributed to this year's book. If you happen to be traveling, consult the Directory for shops along your way. We also list clubs who have worked with us and auction houses who have agreed to permit us the use of photographs from their catalogs.

Our Advisory Board lists only names and home states, so check the Directory for addresses and telephone numbers should you want to correspond with one of our experts. Remember, when you do, **always** enclose a self-addressed, stamped envelope (SASE). Thousands of people buy our guide, and hundreds contact our advisors. The only agreement we have with our advisors is that they edit their categories. They are in no way obligated to answer mail. Some are dealers who do many shows a month. The time they spend at home may be very limited, and they may not be open to contacts. There's no doubt that the reason behind the success of our book is their assistance. We regret seeing them become more and more burdened by phone and mail inquiries. We have lost some of our good advisors for this reason, and when we do, the book suffers and consequently, so do our readers. Many of our listed reference sources report that they constantly receive long distance calls (at all hours) that are really valuation requests. If they are registered appraisers, they make their living at providing such information and expect a fee for their service and expertise.

If you find you need more information than *Schroeder's* provides, there are other sources available to you. Go to your local library; check their section on reference books. Museums are public facilities that are willing and able help you establish the origin and possibly even the value of your particular treasure. Check the yellow pages of your phone book. Other cities' phone books are available from either your library or from the telephone company office. Look under the heading *Antique Dealers*. Those who are qualified appraisers will mention this credit in their advertisement. But remember that if you sell to a dealer, he will expect to buy your merchandise at a price low enough that he will be able to make an appreciable profit when he sells it. Once you decide to contact one of these appraisers, unless you intend to see them directly, you'll need to take photographs. Don't send photos that are under or over exposed, out of focus, or shot against a background that detracts from important details you want to emphasize. It is almost impossible for them to give you a value judgement on items they've not seen when your photos are of poor quality. Shoot the front, top, and the bottom; describe any marks and numbers (or send a pencil rubbing), explain how and when you acquired the article, and give accurate measurements and any further background information that may be helpful.

The auction houses listed in the Directory nearly all have a staff of appraisal experts. If the item you're attempting to research is of the caliber of material they deal with, they can offer extremely accurate evaluations. Of course, most have a fee. Be sure to send them only professional-quality photographs. Tell them if you expect to consign your item to their auction.

If you disagree with the value they suggest, you are under no obligation to do so.

We have organized our topics alphabetically, following the most simple logic, usually either by manufacturer or by type of product. If you have difficulty in locating your subject, consult the index. Our guide is unique in that much more space has been allotted to background information than in any other publication of this type. Our readers tell us that these are features they enjoy. To be able to do this, we have adopted a format of one-line listings wherein we describe the items to the fullest extent possible by using several common-sense abbreviations; they will be easy to read and understand if you will first take the time to quickly scan through them.

The Editors

Editorial Staff

Editors
Sharon and Bob Huxford

Research and Editorial Assistants
Michael Drollinger, Nancy Drollinger, Linda Holycross, Donna Newnum, Loretta Woodrow

Layout
Beth Ray, Terri Stalions, Donna Ballard

Cover Design
Beth Summers

On the cover
Front: K & R bride doll, 19", $1,700.00.
Tiffany Favrile glass and patinated bronze lotus lamp, 20", $15,400.00.
Pepsi-Cola cardboard fan with wooden handle, 1940, $95.00.
Van Briggle vase, 6", $1,375.00.
I'm Looking For A Girl Like Mother sheet music, 1916, $15.00.
Mickey Mouse Story Book, 1930s, $150.00.
Royal Vienna charger, 16", $2,750.00.
Back: Hand-painted Nippon vase, 11", $935.00.

Listing of Standard Abbreviations

The following is a list of abbreviations that have been used throughout this book in order to provide you with the most detailed descriptions possible in the limited space available. No periods are used after initials or abbreviations. When two dimensions are given, height is noted first. If only one dimension is listed, it will be height, except in the case of bowls, dishes, plates, or platters, when it will be diameter. The standard two-letter state abbreviations apply.

For glassware, if no color is noted, the glass is clear. Hyphenated colors, for example blue-green, olive-amber, etc., describe a single color tone; colors divided by a slash mark indicate two or more colors, i.e. blue/white. Teapots, sugar bowls, and butter dishes are assumed to be 'with cover.' Condition is extremely important in determining market value. Common sense suggests that art pottery, china, and glassware values would be given for examples in pristine, mint condition, while suggested prices for utility wares such as Redware, Mocha, and Blue and White Stoneware, for example, reflect the probability that since such items were subjected to everyday use in the home they may show minor wear (which is acceptable) but no notable damage. Values for other categories reflect the best average condition in which the particular collectible is apt to be offered for sale without the dealer feeling it necessary to mention wear or damage. For instance, advertising items are assumed to be in excellent condition since mint items are scarce enough that when one is offered for sale the dealer will most likely make mention of that fact. The same holds true for toys, banks, coin-operated machines, and the like. A basic rule of thumb is that an item listed as VG (very good) will bring 40% to 60% of its mint price — a first-hand, personal evaluation will enable you to make the final judgement; EX (excellent) is a condition midway between mint and very good, and values would correspond.

Am....................American	dvtl....................dovetail	litho....................lithograph	rfn....................refinished
appl....................applied	emb............embossed, embossing	lt....................light	rnd....................round
att....................attributed to	embr....................embroidered	M....................mint	rpl....................replaced
bbl....................barrel	Emp....................Empire	mahog....................mahogany	rpr....................repaired
bk....................back	eng............engraved, engraving	mc....................multicolor	rpt....................repainted
bl....................bl	EPNS...electroplated nickel silver	MIB....................mint in box	rstr....................restored
blk....................black	EX....................excellent	MIG............Made in Germany	rtcl....................reticulated
brn....................brown	Fed....................Federal	MIP....................mint in package	rvpt............reverse painted
bulb....................bulbous	fr....................frame, framed	mk....................mark	s&p............salt and pepper
bsk....................bisque	Fr....................French	MOC....................mint on card	sgn....................signed
b3m....................blown 3-mold	ft, ftd............foot, feet, footed	MOP............mother-of-pearl	SP....................silverplated
C....................century	G....................good	mt, mtd............mount, mounted	sq....................square
c....................copyright	gr....................green	NE....................New England	std....................standard
ca....................circa	grad....................graduated	NM....................near mint	str....................straight
cb....................cardboard	grpt....................grain painted	NP....................nickel plated	sz....................size
Chpndl....................Chippendale	H....................high, height	opal....................opalescent	trn............turned, turning
CI....................cast iron	Hplwht....................Hepplewhite	orig....................original	turq....................turquoise
compo....................composition	hdl, hdld............handle, handled	o/l....................overlay	uphl....................upholstered
cr/sug............creamer and sugar	HP....................hand painted	o/w....................otherwise	VG....................very good
c/s....................cup and saucer	illus......illustration, illustrated by	Pat....................patented	Vict....................Victorian
cvd....................carved	imp....................impressed	pc....................piece	W....................width
cvg....................carving	ind....................individual	ped....................pedestal	wht....................white
dbl....................double	int....................interior	pk....................pink	w/....................with
decor....................decoration	Invt T'print..Inverted Thumbprint	pkg....................package	w/o....................without
dk....................dark	irid....................iridescent	pnt....................paint	X, Xd............cross, crossed
Dmn Quilt........Diamond Quilted	L....................length, long	porc....................porcelain	yel....................yellow
drw....................drawer	lav....................lavender	prof....................professional	(+)............has been reproduced
dtd....................dated	ldgl....................leaded glass	re....................regarding	

A B C Plates

Children's plates featuring the alphabet as part of the design were popular from as early as 1820 until after the turn of the century. The earliest English creamware plates were decorated with embossed letters and prim moralistic verses, but the later Staffordshire products were conducive to a more relaxed mealtime atmosphere, often depicting playful animals and riddles or scenes of pleasant leisure-time activities. They were made around the turn of the century by American potters as well. All featured transfer prints, but color was sometimes brushed on by hand to add interest to the design.

Be sure to inspect these plates carefully for damage, since condition is a key price-assessing factor, and aside from obvious chips and hairlines, even wear can substantially reduce their values.

For further information we recommend *A B C Plates & Mugs, Identification and Value Guide,* by Irene and Ralph Lindsay (Collector Books). Our advisor for this category is Dr. Joan George; she is listed in the Directory under New Jersey.

Ceramic

Abraham Lincoln, brn transfer, 7½"	600.00
Aesop's Fables, Fox & Grapes transfer, Staffordshire, 7½"	175.00
Am Sports Base Ball Running to First Base, blk transfer, 7"	225.00
B Is for Bobby's Breakfast, bl transfer, Staffordshire	110.00
Birds on branch, Staffordshire transfer, dtd 1884	115.00
Blind Girl, blk transfer w/mc, unmk, 5¾"	125.00
Blood Relations, 2 puppies in basket, red transfer, unmk, 7"	125.00
Boy selling newspapers, red transfer, Staffordshire, 1870s	135.00
Brighton Beach-Bathing Pavilion, brn transfer, unmk, 6¾"	135.00
Children feed dog & parrot, mc transfer, Elsmore & Foster, 5½"	170.00
Children's toys w/flowers, Germany	100.00
Clown & dog doing hat tricks, Germany	125.00
Conundrum Pear (pr), 6½"	300.00
Crusoe at Work, Staffordshire, EX	185.00
Crusoe Finding the Footprints, 7¼"	130.00
Crusoe Viewing Island, Staffordshire	170.00
Cup, Robin, ABCs	165.00
Dr Franklins's Maxims, blk transfer, 8¼"	180.00
Frolics of Youth-The Young Artist, blk w/mc, unmk, 8"	140.00
Gathering Cotton, Blacks in cotton field, ABC rim, 6"	425.00
Girl playing piano, mc transfer, Elsmore & Foster, 7⅛"	150.00
Horsebk scene w/hunting dogs, purple transfer, Staffordshire, 7½"	100.00
Horses jumping, bl transfer, Staffordshire	125.00
Hunters, hounds & rabbit, brn transfer w/mc, Staffordshire, 5¾"	100.00
Lion, brn transfer w/mc, BPCo, 7¼"	200.00
Mug, I&J, blk w/red & yel, 2¾"	165.00
Mug, jungle animals, ABC rim	48.00
Mug, K Is a Kitten, purple transfer, 2¾x2½"	150.00
Nations of the World, BPCo	150.00
No Morning Sun Lasts..., blk transfer, Staffordshire, 6⅝"	100.00
Now I Have a Cow & Sheep..., gr transfer, Staffordshire	100.00
Peacock, blk transfer w/mc, unmk, 7¼"	150.00
Pride of the Barnyard, blk transfer, Staffordshire, 7"	110.00
Red Riding Hood & Her Supposed Grandmother, BPCo, 7¼"	190.00
Rooster, hens & chicks, ABC rim w/gold, Germany, 7"	75.00
Rooster & hens, pk border w/gold, Germany, 6½"	75.00
Rugby scene, brn transfer, CA & Sons, England, 6¾"	160.00
Sign Language Owl School, 6⅜"	300.00
Sioux Indian Chief, brn transfer, CA & Sons, England, 7"	160.00
Tom & Harry Playing at Horses, blk transfer w/mc, unmk, 6"	145.00
Uncle Tom's Cabin, Buyer & Seller..., brn transfer, 7½"	275.00
Village Blacksmith, blk transfer w/mc, unmk, 5¼"	145.00

Glass

Christmas Eve, Santa climbing down chimney in frosted center, 6⅛", $175.00.

Clock face, Arabic numbers, ABC rim, clear, 7"	50.00
Ducks in center, cobalt, ABC rim, 6"	40.00
Girl's head, amber	30.00
Little Bo-Peep, 3-compartment, ABC rim	75.00
President Garfield, ABC rim interspersed w/stars, 6¾"	80.00
Sancho Panza & Dapple, frosted, 6"	60.00

Tin

Alphabet rim, 4½"	65.00
Brownies, Up the Table See Them..., ABC rim, 8¾"	110.00
Geo Washington (bust) & 13 stars, emb ABC rim, 6"	170.00
Hi Diddle Diddle, emb ABC rim, 8¾"	100.00
Horse in center, ABC rim, 5½"	170.00
Horse standing in center, emb ABC rim, 5½"	140.00
Jumbo, elephant in center, emb ABC rim, 6⅛"	125.00
Kittens, litho, ABC rim	55.00
Little Red Riding Hood, wolf dressed as grandmother, 8"	175.00
Mary Had a Little Lamb, emb ABC rim, 7¾"	135.00
Simple Simon, Tudor Plate, 6"	90.00
Up the Table See Them Climb..., Brownies, ABC rim, 9"	135.00
Who Killed Cock Robin..., ABC rim, 7¾", NM	120.00

Abingdon

From 1934 until 1950, the Abingdon Pottery Co. of Abingdon, Illinois, made a line of art pottery with a white vitrified body decorated with various types of glazes in many lovely colors. Novelties, cookie jars, utility ware, and lamps were made in addition to several lines of simple yet striking art ware. Fern Leaf, introduced in 1937, featured molded vertical feathering. La Fleur, in 1939, consisted of flowerpots and flower-arranger bowls with rows of vertical ribbing. Classic, 1939 – 40, was a line of vases, many with evidence of Chinese influence. Several marks were used, most of which employed the company name. In 1950 the company reverted to the manufacture of sanitary ware that had been their mainstay before the Art Ware Division was formed.

Highly decorated examples and those with black, bronze, or red glaze usually command at least 25% higher prices.

#116, vase, Classic, 10", from $18 to	22.50
#117, vase, Classic, gr, 10"	35.00
#151, flowerpot, 5"	22.00
#321, bookends, Cossack/Russian, blk, 6½" or 8½", pr	85.00
#363, bookends, colt, color other than blk, 5¾", pr	85.00
#370, bookends, cactus, 6", pr	70.00
#388, pouter pigeon, 4½"	40.00
#3906, shepherdess & faun, blk, 11½"	250.00

#393, bowl, Morning Glory, 7"	35.00
#400, tea tile, geisha, sq, 5"	50.00
#408, bowl, leaf, beige, 1937, 6½"	40.00
#412, vase, Volute, wht, 1937-40, 15½"	125.00
#416, peacock, 7"	95.00
#422, vase, Fern Leaf, wht, 10"	30.00
#428, bookends, Fern Leaf, 5½", pr	45.00
#429, vase/candle holder, Fern Leaf, 8"	25.00
#435, wall pocket, Tri-Fern, 9", minimum value	135.00
#444, bookend/planter, dolphin, decor, 5¾", pr	50.00
#450, bowl, Asters, flared rim, oval	50.00
#452, bowl, Asters, 9x14½"	45.00
#453, vase, Asters, 8"	25.00
#460, bowl, Panel, 8"	25.00
#463, vase, Star, 7"	18.00
#474, cornucopia, yel, 5½"	18.00
#476, window box	20.00
#484, fan vase, wht, 8"	20.00
#486, vase, Acanthus, silver o/l birds on peach, 11"	300.00
#487, floor vase, Egret, 14"	150.00
#497, Blackamoor, w/decor, 7½"	95.00
#501, bowl, Shell, pk, sm	20.00
#505, candle holder, Shell, dbl, 4"	20.00
#507, vase, Shell, oval, wht, 7½"	25.00
#509, ashtray, elephant, 5½"	50.00
#510, ashtray, donkey, 5½"	50.00
#512, vase, Swirl, gr, 9"	20.00
#513, vase, Swirl, 9", from $15 to	25.00
#514, vase, Swirl, chartreuse, 11"	25.00
#520, vase, gr, 9"	25.00
#522, vase, Barre, 9"	35.00
#532, bowl, console; gold trim, 14½" L	25.00
#532, bowl, console; lt bl, 14½" L	25.00
#533, bowl, Shell, yel, 12"	22.00
#552, vase, squatty	40.00
#563, urn, 9"	30.00
#564, bowl, Scallop, pk, 11"	18.00
#568, mint compote, pk, ftd, 1942-47, 6" dia	28.00
#569D, cornucopia, bl w/decor, 10" L	27.50
#571, goose, blk, 5"	40.00
#573, penguin, decor, 5½"	40.00
#576, window box, gr, 12¼" L	25.00
#593, vase, bowknot, bl, 9"	35.00
#610, bowl, Shell, 9"	25.00

#616, vase, Cactus, with sleeping Mexican man, 6½x7", $30.00.

#629, vase, Poppy, 6½"	30.00
#640, wall pocket, Triad, 5½"	40.00
#652, planter, puppy, decor, 6¾"	25.00
#654, vase, Tulip, 6½"	20.00
#659, vase, Hackney, 8½"	30.00

#667, planter, gourd, 5½"	20.00
#669, planter, donkey, 7½"	25.00
#675D, wall pocket, match box form, 5½"	50.00
#676D, wall pocket, book form, 6½"	48.00
#681/#682, sugar bowl & creamer, Daisy	30.00
#699, wall pocket, apron, 6"	50.00
#711, wall vase, carriage lamp, 10"	25.00
#714, candle holders, Star, 4¼", pr	30.00
Cookie jar, #471, Old Lady, plain, 1942 (+)	210.00
Cookie jar, #471, Old Lady, rare gr	195.00
Cookie jar, #495, Fat Boy	250.00
Cookie jar, #549, Hippo, decor, 1942	225.00
Cookie jar, #561, Baby, Black decor	300.00
Cookie jar, #588, Money Bag, 1947	70.00
Cookie jar, #602, Hobby Horse (+)	185.00
Cookie jar, #611, Jack-in-Box	275.00
Cookie jar, #622, Miss Muffet (+)	205.00
Cookie jar, #651, Choo Choo (Locomotive) (+)	150.00
Cookie jar, #653, Clock, 1949	100.00
Cookie jar, #663, Humpty Dumpty, decor (+)	250.00
Cookie jar, #664, Pineapple	95.00
Cookie jar, #665, Wigwam, minimum value	300.00
Cookie jar, #674, Pumpkin, 1949	300.00
Cookie jar, #677, Daisy, 1949	45.00
Cookie jar, #678, Windmill	185.00
Cookie jar, #692, Witch, minimum value	350.00
Cookie jar, #693, Little Girl	60.00
Cookie jar, #694, Bo Peep (+)	240.00
Cookie jar, #695, Mother Goose (+)	295.00
Cookie jar, #696, Three Bears	90.00

Adams

Wm. Adams, whose potting skills were developed under the tutelage of Josiah Wedgwood, founded the Greengates Pottery at Tunstall, England, in 1769. Many types of wares including basalt, ironstone, parian, and jasper were produced; and various impressed or printed marks were employed. Until 1800 'Adams Co.' or 'Adams' impressed in block letters identified the company's earthenwares and a fine type of jasper similar in color and decoration to Wedgwood's. The latter mark was used again from 1845 to 1864 on parian figures. Most examples of their product found on today's market are transfer-printed dinnerwares with ornate backstamps which often include the pattern name and the initials 'W.A. & S.' This type of product was made from 1820 until about 1920. After 1890 the word 'England' was included in the mark; 'Tunstall' was added after 1896. From 1914 through 1940, a printed crown with 'Adams, Estbd 1657, England' identified their products. From 1900 to 1965, they produced souvenir plates with transfers of American scenes, many of which were marketed in this country by Roth Importers of Peoria, Illinois. In 1965 the company affiliated with Wedgwood. Although there were other Adams potteries in Staffordshire, their marks incorporate either the first name initial or a partner's name and so are easily distinguished from those of this company. See also Spatter; Staffordshire; Adams Rose.

Plate, Bologna, lt bl transfer, 10¾"	70.00
Plate, Caledonia, purple transfer, 10⅝", NM	100.00
Plate, Caledonia, purple transfer, 8½", 3 for	200.00
Plate, Dr Syntax Bound to a Tree, pearlized rim, 9½"	55.00
Plate, Oliver Twist Amazed at Dodger's Mode of Work	130.00
Platter, Lake George, red transfer, 13¼", EX	325.00
Platter, pearlware, bl feathered edge, 17x13½", EX	60.00

Adams, Matthew

In the 1950s a trading post located in Alaska contacted Sascha Brastoff to design a line of porcelain with scenes of Eskimos, Alaskan motifs and animals indigenous to that country. These items were to be sold in Alaska to the tourist trade.

Brastoff selected Matthew Adams to design the Alaska series. Pieces from the line he produced have the Sascha B mark on the front; some have a pattern number on the reverse. They did not have the rooster backstamp. (See the Sascha Brastoff category for information on this mark.)

After the Alaska series was introduced and proved to be successful, Matthew Adams left the employment of Sascha Brastoff and opened his own studio. Pieces made in his studio are signed Matthew Adams in script and may have the word Alaska on the front. Where his studio (or studios) was is unknown at the present time, but a 'Made in Alaska' paper label has been found, suggesting that he may have worked from that location. Our advisor for this category is Marty Webster; he is listed in the Directory under Michigan. Feel free to contact Mr. Webster if you have any further information.

Ashtray, Eskimo family, 8½" 48.00
Ashtray, hollow star shape, full Eskimo, 13" 75.00
Ashtray, star shape, walrus, 10x12" 95.00
Ashtray, walrus on gr, 6" dia 25.00
Bowl, console; glacier on bl, 12x20" 165.00
Bowl, Eskimo on blk, 9" 45.00
Bowl, grizzly bear on brn, free-form, 6½" L 55.00
Bowl, polar bear on gr, free-form, 7½" L 60.00
Bowl, ram on gr, free-form, 7" 55.00
Bowl, seal, oval, 9" 60.00
Bowl, seal on blk, free-form, w/lid, #145, 7½" L 75.00
Bowl, walrus, yel, w/lid, 7" 75.00
Bowl, walrus & glacier on brn, free-form, 8" 65.00
Bowl, walrus on blk, free-form, #104, 6½" L 50.00
Box, glacier on bl, w/lid, 12" 95.00
Charger, caribou on dk bl, 18" 150.00
Charger, walrus, dk bl, 17" 150.00
Coffeepot, ram on gr, 11½", +6 4½" mugs 180.00
Compote, grizzly bear on brn, tall, 8½" dia 70.00
Cracker jar, Eskimo mother & child on brn, 7" 80.00
Cup & saucer, sled on bl 25.00
Dish, Eskimo lady on gr, elbow shape, 12" 50.00
Humidor, seal on gr, #025, 5¾" 85.00
Jar, Eskimo on ice bl, 6" 30.00
Jar, Eskimo woman on brn, w/lid, 7½" 50.00
Jar, polar bear on gr, w/lid, 7" 65.00
Jar, walrus on lt bl, w/lid, #1492, 7½" 50.00
Lighter, glacier, 6" 50.00
Pitcher, Eskimo, 13" 90.00
Pitcher, Eskimo mother & child, 13", +6 5½" mugs 195.00
Pitcher, grizzly bear, 11", +6 4" tumblers 200.00
Pitcher, Husky dog, wht on teal, bulbous, 5" 65.00
Plate, Eskimo girl, #162, 7½" 30.00
Platter, house, 12" 50.00
Pot, walrus, w/lid, 12" 55.00
Shakers, rams on gr, 4", pr 40.00
Tankard, man on brn, 19", +6 mugs 250.00
Tankard, polar bear on blk, w/lid, 13" 235.00
Teapot, walrus on ice bl, 6½" 85.00
Tile, mountains & glacier on blk, 10x8½" 85.00
Tile, walrus on bl, 10x8½" 95.00
Tumbler, cabin 24.00
Vase, glacier on gray, #143, 5½" 50.00
Vase, house on yel, 11½" 125.00
Vase, iceberg on gray, 7" 40.00
Vase, mother & child on teal, cylindrical, 17" 185.00
Vase, mountain & glacier on blk, #114, 12" 80.00
Vase, polar bear on gr, 10" 140.00
Vase, reindeer, 4½" 45.00
Vase, sea lion & seaweed, oval, #128, 8" 95.00
Vase, seal & glacier on brn, free-form, #911, 11" 155.00
Vase, walrus on ice on bl, 10" 110.00

Adams Rose, Early and Late

In the second quarter of the 19th century, the Adams and Son Pottery produced a line of hand-painted dinnerware decorated in large, red brush-stroke roses with green leaves on whiteware, which collectors call Adams Rose. Later, G. Jones and Son (and possibly others) made a similar ware with less brilliant colors on a gray-white surface.

Our values are for items in mint condition or nearly so; be sure to discount prices for damage.

Coffeepot with rare domed lid, hairlines, repairs, early, 12", $600.00; Pitcher, scrolled handle and rim, 9", early, VG, $235.00; Platter, scalloped rim, early, 20x16½", rare, $2,075.00.

Bowl, late, 2¾x5⅝" 50.00
Bowl, late, 3x6¼" 70.00
Bowl, sauce; early, 1⅛x4⅞" 150.00
Bowl, vegetable; late, oval, 1⅝x8x6" 170.00
Bowl, vegetable; late, oval, 2x9¾x7", EX 90.00
Coffeepot, late, 8¼" 875.00
Creamer, late, scalloped rim, 4⅝" 210.00
Creamer, late, scalloped rim, 5⅝", EX 200.00
Cup & saucer, handleless; early 330.00
Cup & saucer, handleless; mk Adams 220.00
Cup & saucer, handleless; red spatter rim 440.00
Pitcher, late, scalloped rim, 6½" 235.00
Pitcher, milk; late, scalloped rim, 7½" 375.00
Pitcher, water; late, scalloped rim, 7⅜" 400.00
Pitcher, water; late, scalloped rim, 8½" 500.00
Plate, early, lt stains, 9⅛" 220.00
Plate, early, mk Adams, 10½" 140.00
Plate, early, plain rim, mk Adams, 7⅛" 75.00
Plate, early, scalloped rim, Adams, 7" 60.00
Plate, late, England, 7" 20.00
Plate, late, mk Adams, 9½" 90.00
Plate, late, 10" 95.00
Platter, early, mk Adams, 13½" 385.00

Platter, late, 10⅞x7¾" 100.00
Platter, late, 12x8½" 135.00
Platter, late, 13⅛x9¼" 190.00
Platter, late, 14⅛x10" 250.00
Platter, late, 16⅜x11½" 525.00
Soup plate, late, 9" dia 150.00
Sugar bowl, late, w/lid, 6" 340.00
Waste bowl, early, gr spatter rim, 2¾x5" 550.00

Advertising

The advertising world has always been a fiercely competitive field. In an effort to present their product to the customer, every imaginable gimmick was put into play. Colorful and artfully decorated signs and posters, thermometers, tape measures, fans, hand mirrors, and attractive tin containers (all with catchy slogans, familiar logos, and often-bogus claims) are only a few of the many examples of early advertising memorabilia that are of interest to today's collectors.

Porcelain signs were made as early as 1890 and are highly prized for their artistic portrayal of life as it was then . . . often allowing amusing insights into the tastes, humor, and way of life of a bygone era. As a general rule, older signs are made from a heavier gauge metal. Those with three or more fired-on colors are especially desirable.

Tin containers were used to package consumer goods ranging from crackers and coffee to tobacco and talcum. After 1880 can companies began to decorate their containers by the method of lithography. Though colors were still subdued, intricate designs were used to attract the eye of the consumer. False labeling and unfounded claims were curtailed by the Pure Food and Drug Administration in 1906, and the name of the manufacturer as well as the brand name of the product had to be printed on the label. By 1910 color was rampant with more than a dozen hues printed on the tin or on paper labels. The tins themselves were often designed with a second use in mind, such as canisters, lunch boxes, even toy trains. As a general rule, tobacco-related tins are the most desirable, though personal preference may direct the interest of the collector to peanut butter pails with illustrations of children, or talcum tins with irresistible babies or beautiful ladies. Coffee tins are popular, as are those made to contain a particularly successful or well-known product.

Perhaps the most visual of the early advertising gimmicks were the character logos, the Fairbank Company's Gold Dust Twins, the goose trademark of the Red Goose Shoe Company, Nabisco's ZuZu Clown and Uneeda Kid, the Campbell Kids, the RCA dog Nipper, and Mr. Peanut, to name only a few. Many early examples of these bring high prices on the market today.

Our listings are alphabetized by product name or, in lieu of that information, by word content or other pertinent description. When no condition is indicated, the items listed below are assumed to be in excellent condition, except glass and ceramic items, which are assumed mint. Remember that condition greatly affects value (especially true for tin items). For instance, a sign in excellent or mint condition may bring twice as much as the same one in only very good condition, sometimes even more. On today's market, items in good to very good condition are slow to sell, unless they are extremely rare. Mint (or near-mint) examples are high.

We have several advertising advisors; see specific subheadings. For further information we recommend *Zany Characters of the Ad World* by Mary Jane Lamphier, *Advertising Character Collectibles* by Warren Dotz, *Value Guide to Advertising Memorabilia* by B.J. Summers, *The World of Beer Memorabilia* by Herb and Helon Haydock, and *Huxford's Collectible Advertising* by Sharon and Bob Huxford. All of these books are available at your local bookstore or from Collector Books. See also Advertising Dolls; Advertising Cards; Automobilia; Coca-Cola; Banks; Calendars; Cookbooks; Paperweights; Posters; Sewing Items.

Key:
cb — cardboard
cl — celluloid
lcs — litho on canvas sign
pp — pre-prohibition
ps — porcelain sign
sf — self-framed
tc — tin container
ts — tin sign

Admiral Cigarettes, paper sign, lady w/binoculars, 22½x16", EX ..150.00
After Lunch Snuff, tc, man in chair, 2x2½x5", NM 200.00
Air Float Baby Powder, tc, baby reserve, sm top, EX 135.00
Aircraft Ginger Ale, menu brd, tin litho sign, 14x20", NM 60.00
Alka-Seltzer, dispenser, chrome/tin, 15", EX 120.00
Amocat Mace, tc, reserve on red, scarce, EX 80.00
Anona Tea, tc, brn version, sample sz, EX 60.00
Armour's Veribest Peanut Butter, pail, tin litho, 12-oz, EX 200.00
Arrow Beer, tray, Gambrinus King of Lager, post-pro, EX+ 68.00
Aunt Jemima Buckwheat...& Wheat Flour, cb box, 1911, 13x9x14", EX .105.00
B-1 Lemon-Lime, thermometer, emb tin, 16½x4½", NM 65.00
Baby Stuart Breakfast Cocoa, tc, portrait, 6x3½x2½", EX 125.00
Baby Stuart Butter Scotch Patties, tc, pry lid, 1-lb, EX 55.00
Bagdad Coffee, tc, tin litho, scene on gold, 5-lb, EX 160.00
Barbarossa Premium Beer, sign, sf paper on compo, 14x11", NM .50.00
Bauer & Black Baby Talc, tc, animal silhouettes, sample sz, EX ...85.00
Beacon Coal, ts, lighthouse by ocean, 14", NM 125.00
Belar Cigars, sf ts, 2 cigars on yel, easel bk, 7½x10", NM 90.00
Betty Zane Ohio Super Yel Popcorn, tc, EX- 165.00
Beverly Peanut Better, tc, boy & girl, Canadian, 48-oz 105.00
Big Master Cocoa, cb container, man w/sword, 2-lb, NM 110.00
Billiard Chalk, tc, w/striker plate for cue tip, 3x2x1", EX 100.00
Black Cat Stove & Polish, bill hook, NM 145.00
Blue Bird Coffee, pail, tin litho, bl/red/wht, 5-lb, EX 440.00
Blue Ribbon Baking Powder, tc, 3-lb, NM 50.00
Bond Street Tobacco, pocket tin, vertical, sample sz, EX 70.00
Borden's Malt Drink, tc, pry lid, Canadian, 1-lb, EX 35.00
Borden's Malted Milk, tc, red/wht/bl, screw cap, 1915, 5-lb, EX+ ..75.00
Boston Pipe Tobacco, canister, tin litho, slip lid, EX 40.00
Boston Slice Cut Cavendish, lunch box, tin litho, dome top, EX 300.00
Brilliant Mixture, tc, Blacks in field, 2x4x3", EX 225.00
Brischoff's Breakfast Cocoa, tc, early ¼-lb sample sz, EX+ 55.00
Brown's Jumbo Bread, ts, litho elephant diecut, 13x15", NM 800.00
Buckingham Cut Plug Smoking Tobacco, pocket tin, vertical, EX ...70.00
Buckingham Tobacco, tin canister, slip lid, NM 90.00
Buddha Talc, tc, red & gold, 1-lb, EX 80.00
Budweiser, paper sign, foaming mug on red, 1920, 11x21", VG 40.00

Buster Brown

Buster Brown was the creation of cartoonist Richard Felton Outcault; his comic strip first appeared in the *New York Herald* on May 4, 1902. Since then Buster and his dog Tige (short for Tiger) have adorned sundry commercial products but are probably best known as the trademark for the Brown Shoe Company established early in this century. Today hundreds of Buster Brown premiums, store articles, and advertising items bring substantial prices from many serious collectors.

Banner, multicolor printed scene on white cloth, some discoloration at creases, 35x58", VG, $40.00.

Airline glider, yel styrofoam, VG 10.00
Bank, BB & Tige, pnt CI, Canada, 5½", VG 200.00
Bank, BB & Tige, pnt CI, gold w/red, AC Williams, 5½", EX ...230.00
Bank, Good Luck Horseshoe, BB & Tige, pnt CI, 4¼x4¾", VG ..230.00
Bowl, baby's; Stop Smiling...We'll Get Some Cake, BB & Tige .535.00
Calendar/postcard, BB & Tige, Outcault, 1913 ....18.00
Clicker, mc portrait & BB Shoes, 1920s, NM 38.00
Comic book, Adventures of BB & His Wristsquirter, 1976, EX ...12.00
Comic book, 1959, EX 25.00
Compass, Moon Mission Agent, for wrist, EX 25.00
Creamer, BB & Tige drinking tea, china 85.00
Cup & saucer, BB & Mary Jane, tea party, ca 1910, EX 110.00
Figure, Buster Brown, bsk, ca 1915, 2¾", EX 800.00
Flicker ring 40.00
Lunar Space Phones, w/decoder, complete, 1950s, MIP 65.00
Mannequin, vinyl, 26", NM 125.00
Nature Scope, clear plastic w/built-in lenses, EX 9.00
Pocket mirror, BB & Tige, 1946 ....75.00
Postcard, auto race series, ca 1907, EX, set of 3 ....55.00
Postcard, Buster Brown Coffee, Outcault 12.00
Postcard, Months of the Year (July & August), Outcault, 1908, pr 40.00
Rug, BB & Tige, wool, red/gold/bl, oval, 53" 425.00
Shirt box, EX illus, NM 20.00
Shoe box, games on sides, NM 40.00
Shoe box, suitcase style w/Daffyland graphics & trade cards, EX ..35.00
Shoes, boy's, 1950s, MIB 35.00
Sign, bas-relief plaster, BB & Tige, 1940s, 17" dia, NM 325.00
Sign, tin, BB Bread, BB w/Tige, 28x22" 695.00
Sign, tin diecut, BB in shoe w/Tige, 39x25", G 1,900.00
Whistle, BB & Tige, rectangular, EX+ 32.00
Yo-Yo, metal, NM 58.00

C.D. Kenny

C.D. Kenny was determined to be a successful man, and he was. Between 1890 and 1934, he owned seventy-five groceries in fifteen states. He realized his success in two ways: fair business dealings and premium giveaways. These ranged from trade cards and advertising mirrors to tin commemorative plates and kitchen items. There were banks and toys, clocks and tins. Today's collectors are finding scores of these items, all carrying Kenny's name.

Doll, pnt bsk, premium, printed mk, 4", NM 98.00
Match holder, elephant figural 30.00
Plate, boy w/dog, holly/mistletoe border, tin litho, 9¾" 80.00
Plate, child in snow scene, tin, NM 95.00
Plate, Santa w/toys, sleeping child, 9⅝", NM 150.00

Salt shaker, Geisha girl, $20.00.

Sign, sf tin, 2 girls (having tea) & rabbits (Easter), 13x9", VG ..250.00
Tape measure, retractable 50.00

Tin container, Tea Party scene, oval 155.00
Tip tray, America's Pride, sailor & soldier, 4¼" dia, VG 275.00
Tip tray, Geo Washington, rnd, sm 50.00
Tip tray, lady in woods, flower border, M 125.00

Canadian Club Cigars, cb sign, man in oval, 13½x21", NM 50.00
Candee Shoes, cb sign, children & kittens, 1910, 12½x10", EX ...165.00
Canova Mace, tc, red/wht/gold, rare, EX 55.00
Cashmere Bouquet, sampler, NM in orig Cinderella box 105.00
Castle Hall Twins Cigars, cb sign, stork w/twins, 10x12", NM 60.00
Ceresota, match holder, bbl version, lt fading, 6x3", EX 200.00
Champagne Velvet, tip tray, That Ever Welcome..., cherubs, EX .110.00
Charm of West, pocket tin, horse scene, flat, EX 300.00
Chase & Sanborn, tc, gold & wht on red, sample sz, NM 38.00
Checkers Tobacco, pocket tin, gold version, EX- 160.00
Choisa Coffee, tc, SS Pierce Co, full, NM 110.00
Cincinnati Burger Brau, ts, Vas You Efer..., 9½x13½", NM 100.00
Clark B&B, thermometer, bevel-edged wood, rare, VG+ 50.00
Clark's Zagnut Candy Bars, display case decals, 9x5", pr 30.00
Climax Plug Tobacco, tip tray, enamel on tin, EX 50.00
Colgate Baby Talc, tc, baby reserve, sample sz, NM w/orig wrap ...165.00
Collins Axes, cb sign, axe head, hangs, 1915, 20x10", NM 55.00
Comrade Steel Cut Coffee, tc, slip lid, EX 100.00
Conquest Mustard Seed, tc, reserve on lt bl, EX 90.00
Consolidated Biscuits, biscuit box, cb house, 1932, 9x8½" 85.00
Consumer's Beer, sf ts, Ask Father, hangs, 14", EX 88.00
Copley Coffee, tc, 4-color, full, NM 60.00
Cork Distilleries, sf ts, bottle & case, 12½x16", EX- 95.00
Corona Coffee, store canister, tin litho, key-wind, 15-lb, EX 175.00
Cottage Cigars, cigar box, children & cottage, EX 85.00
Country Club Cigars, cigar box, golfer/canoeists/etc, EX+ 85.00
Covered Wagon Cigars, cigar box, NM 95.00
Crush, thermometer, aluminum fr & plastic bubble, 1950s, 12½", NM ..37.50
Cudahy's Dmn C Ham, sign, cb, boy reaching, 13x10", VG+ 120.00
Cunningham's Ice Cream, tray, factory scene, 1917, rstr to EX ..110.00
Cuticura Talcum powder, tc, red & blk, sm lid, NM 50.00
Dairylea Ice Cream, fan, cow & moon diecut, cone hdl, NM 155.00
Dalmatian Blk Dmn Brand Insect Powder, tc, sm top, 10-lb, EX ..60.00
Dan Patch Cut Plug, pocket tin, NM 125.00
Davis of Baltimore Paint, sample holder, matchbox type, 4x8", EX ..55.00
DeLaval, match holder, separator diecut, 6½x4", EX 275.00
Dennison's Coffee Pennant, felt, wht letters in red, 25", NM 80.00
Derby Peanut Butter, tc, Free Sample, 2-oz, EX 100.00
DeWitt's Tonic Pills, cb sign, fisherman, easel bk, 21x13", VG .235.00
Dining Car Cloves, tc, dining car scene, EX 165.00
Dining Car Coffee, tc, dining car scene on turq, rare, EX 385.00
Dixie Kid Cut Plug, tc, Black baby, Nall & Williams, EX 335.00
Dixie Queen Plug Cut, canister, tin litho, sm top, EX 300.00
Dixie Queen Plug Cut, lunch box, tin litho, flat lid, EX+ 150.00
Dolly Varden Coffee, tc, paper label, slip lid, VG 25.00
Donald Duck Beverages, sf ts, Walt Disney Productions, 28x20", EX ...365.00
Dove Brand Allspice, tc, cream on brn, EX 95.00

Dr. Pepper

A young pharmacist, Charles C. Alderton, was hired by W.B. Morrison, owner of Morrison's Old Corner Drug Store in Waco, Texas, around 1884. Alderton, an observant sort, noticed that the drugstore's patrons could never quite make up their minds as to which flavor of extract to order. He concocted a formula that combined many flavors, and Dr. Pepper was born. The name was chosen by Morrison in honor of a beautiful young girl with whom he had once been in love. The girl's father, a Virginia doctor by the name of Pepper, had discouraged the relationship due to their youth, but Morrison had never forgotten her. On December 1, 1885, a U.S. patent was issued to the creators of Dr. Pepper. Our advisors for Dr. Pepper are Craig and Donna Stifter; they are listed in the Directory under Illinois.

Bottle, seltzer; Cheerio-Memphis 180.00
Bottle carrier, cb, for 6-pack bottles, 1940s, EX 100.00
Bottle carrier, tin, for 6-pack bottles, 1930s 125.00
Bottle opener, wall mt, emb letters, NM 25.00
Calendar, 1944, complete, EX 250.00
Calendar, 1964, complete, EX 50.00
Clock, compo fr w/glass front, 1930s, 15", EX 225.00
Clock, Pam, lights up, 1971, 15½" sq 100.00
Fan, cb, 1950s, EX 70.00
Match holder, tin, 1930s, EX 100.00
Matchbook, 1930s-40s, ea, from $10 to 15.00
Pencil, mechanical; 1940s, EX 40.00
Radio, wooden cooler shape, 8½x12x8", working, EX 1,200.00
Sign, aluminum, Energy UP! At 10, 2 & 4, hangs, 1930s, 10", EX ..375.00

Sign, cardboard, We Redeem Coupons, 14x15½", NM, $40.00.

Sign, cb, 1940s, 15x25", NM, ea, from $225 to 375.00
Sign, paper, Frosty Man Frosty!, chef, 1950s, 15x25", NM 30.00
Sign, paper, mc, 1963, 15x25", M 12.50
Sign, paper in aluminum fr, Try Frosty Pepper, 1950s, 17x22", EX ..66.00
Sign, porc, Drink...Good for Life, 1930s, 9x21", EX 200.00
Sign, porc, wht/blk/gr, 27" L, VG 140.00
Sign, tin, Drink...Distinctively..., wht on red, 12x29", NM ..135.00
Street marker, Safety First...Birmingham, brass, VG+ 150.00
Thermometer, tin, bottle shape w/logo & 10-2-4 at top, 1930s, EX+ ..350.00
Thermometer, 1960s, 18" dia, M 180.00
Tray, Drink a Bite to Eat, girl w/2 bottles, 1939, EX 275.00
Trophy, horse show; SP, eng, 1940s 275.00
Watch fob, Billiken, brass, EX 120.00

Dunbar's Pitcher Syrup, tc, litho pitcher shape, 5½", EX 175.00
Elephant Salted Peanuts, tc, Good Enuf For Me, 2x4" sq, EX ...315.00
Epicure Coffee, tc, man serving, red/wht/gr, 1923, EX 280.00
Estabrooks' Red Rose Coffee, ts, can on yel, 15" sq, NM 200.00
Eveready Batteries & Mazda Lamps, counter display, 11x9x11½", EX ..200.00
Fairway Ginger, cb container, children, early version, EX 60.00
Fairway Pepper, cb container, children, 1½-oz, EX 60.00
Fashion Cut Plug Tobacco, lunch box, tin litho, flat top, EX ..110.00
Federal Cartridge Co, ts on cb, ducks, 16x23", NM 170.00
Fidelio Brewery, tray, men drinking, ca 1936, EX 70.00
Fort Henry Brand Lard, tin pail, Fort Henry litho, 8-lb, EX ...22.00
Fort Western Rolled Oats, canister, tin litho, 3-lb, EX 135.00
Foster Hose Supporters, cl sign, lady, bright, 17x9", EX 360.00
Fox Point Coffee, tc, red & wht, VG+ 55.00
Franklin Life Insurance, tip tray, portrait, EX 20.00
Free Lance Cigars, cb sign, Independent..., 11x9½", EX 70.00
Frontenac Peanut Butter, pail, tin litho, w/bail, NM 55.00

Full Dress Tobacco, tin canister, man in tux, Sears Roebuck, EX 180.00
G Krueger Brewing, tip tray, 1858 serving man silhouette logo, EX ...30.00
Galat Lard, pail, tin litho, dog, 4-lb, EX 60.00
Game Fine Cut, store bin, game birds, 7x8x12", EX 750.00
Gargoyle Mobiloil B, tc, early pour spout, VG+ 80.00
Gillett's Cloves, tc, owl on moon, NM 60.00
Glancy's Popcorn, cb container, w/tin lid & bottom, NM 60.00
Goebel Bantam Beer, cb sign, heavy rooster diecut, 11x9", EX ..30.00
Gold Dust Twins, shipping crate panel, wooden, 7½x8", EX 45.00
Gold Dust Washing Powder, cb container, sample sz, NM 55.00
Gold Shore Cut Plug, lunch box, tin litho, flat lid, NM 295.00
Golden Drip Tumeric, tc, blk & red on yel, EX 55.00
Great Majestic Ranges, sign, gesso bas-relief, 1915, 37x49", EX ..3,000.00
Great West Cut Plug, lunch box, tin litho, flat top, VG+ 85.00
Green Turtle Cigars, lunch box, tin litho, flat top, EX 325.00
Hampden Brewing, tray, none-too-handsome waiter, 12", NM ..140.00
Harlequin Tobacco, tobacco caddy label, Harlequin & ballerina, NM ..35.00
Hatchet Brand Toasted Corn Flakes, cb box, 8-oz, NM 180.00
Heineken's Holland Beer, sign, tin on cb, 1950s, EX 45.00
Hellick's Allspice, tc, ship silhouette, 3-oz, EX 25.00
Helmbold's Bologna & Frankfurters, ts on cb, 9x13", EX 60.00
Hendler's Ice Cream, festoon, paper, 5-pc, NM in envelope 150.00
Hendler's Ice Cream, tc, diecut display, cones, 1950s, 23x36", NM .45.00
Hi-Plane Tobacco, canister, tin litho, jet on red, pry lid, EX 45.00
Hi-Plane Tobacco, pocket tin, 2-engine plane, vertical, VG+ 95.00
Hills Bros Coffee, tc, red litho, key-wind, ½-lb, EX 10.00

Hires

    Charles E. Hires, a drugstore owner in Philadelphia, became interested in natural teas. He began experimenting with roots and herbs and soon developed his own special formula. Hires introduced his product to his own patrons and began selling concentrated syrup to other soda fountains and grocery stores. Samples of his 'root beer' were offered for the public's approval at the 1876 Philadelphia Centennial. Today's collectors are often able to date their advertising items by observing the Hires boy on the logo. From 1891 to 1906, he wore a dress. From 1906 until 1914, he was shown in a bathrobe; and from 1915 until 1926, he was depicted in a dinner jacket. The apostrophe may or may not appear in the Hires name; this seems to have no bearing on dating an item. Our advisors for Hires are Craig and Donna Stifter; they are listed in the Directory under Illinois.

Ashtray, glass, bottle shape, EX+ 15.00
Belt buckle, ugly kid, 3", EX 150.00
Booklet, How To Make Hires Root Beer at Home, EX 15.00
Bottle, syrup; paper label, w/measuring cap, 12", EX 425.00
Calendar, 1947, man w/frosty mug & 8-pack carton, complete 25.00
Checkerboard, Exhilarating..., Hires boy, blk/yel, 12", VG ...350.00
Clock, plastic, 1960s, 15" sq 50.00
Decal, Drink Hires Root Beer on bottle cap, EX 15.00
Diecut, Hire's Ugly Kid, fr, 1897 ....150.00
Dispenser, ceramic, hourglass shape, orig pump, 13½", VG 700.00
Dispenser, name on pump, NM 1,400.00
Dispenser, stainless w/medallions on bl porc base, 1940s, EX .650.00
Display, cb diecut, baby crawling, 2-pc, 14x11", G 150.00
Menu board, Drink..., w/blackboard, 29x16" 125.00
Mug, Drink..., child w/mug, ceramic, Crush Internat'l, 4½" 85.00
Mug, glass, appl label in script on slanted band, M 35.00
Opener, over-the-top, NM 15.00
Pocket mirror, girl w/mug & ugly kid, 1907, VG 300.00
Pocketknife, metal eng boot-shaped hdl, Remington, EX 110.00
Scoop, plastic, Only 1 Taste Says Hires to You 10.00
Sign, cb, Hires w/food specials, 1950s, 8x24", NM, from $36 to ..60.00

Sign, cb diecut, girl w/telephone, new old stock, 33½x14½" **250.00**
Sign, cb diecut, Hires Root Beer, woman **300.00**
Sign, cb diecut w/easel bk, boy w/pkg, 1892, 7x5", NM **175.00**
Sign, cl, Drink...Root Beer, 1950s, 9", EX **100.00**
Sign, cl, 2 ladies, Haskel Coffin artwork, 1918, 7x10", EX **725.00**
Sign, paper, So Good w/Food, 1940s, 34x58", NM, from $250 to ...**400.00**
Sign, tin, Enjoy..., w/bottle, emb, 1927, 11x28", EX **350.00**
Sign, tin, girl w/glass, EX color, 19½x13½", VG **500.00**
Sign, tin, Hires to You!, bottle, '40s, 13½x42", from $125 to **200.00**
Sticker, boy pointing, NM **50.00**
Trade card, Hire's Root Beer ad **22.50**
Tray, lady in oval, 13x11", VG **85.00**
Tray, tin, Haskell Coffin artwork, 1917, 10½x13½" **375.00**

Holiday Pipe Mixture, can, tin litho, EX **10.00**
Holleb's Supreme Brownie Toasted Corn flakes, cb box, 11-oz, NM .**55.00**
Honeymoon Rum Flavored Tobacco, pocket tin, EX **365.00**
Hoosier Boy Coffee, tc, paper label, pry lid, EX+ **660.00**
Hope Crackers & Biscuits, shipping box, paper label, 21" L, EX ..**250.00**
Hyroler Whiskey, tip tray, well-dressed man, NM **20.00**
IGA Gold-Tost Wheat Puffs, cb box, 5-oz, EX **35.00**
Imperial Bird's Eye, tc, rectangular, Allen & Ginter, early, EX **95.00**
Jack Sprat Cream of Tarter, cb container, 1½-oz, EX **40.00**
Jap Rose Talcum, tc, Oriental lady in reserve w/gold, EX **75.00**
Jap Rose Talcum, tc, Oriental lady reserve, sample sz, EX **100.00**
Japp's Hair Rejuvenator, ts, missing hair samples, 9x13", EX **35.00**
Jayne's Hair Tonic, sign, paper on paperbrd, 1880s, 15x12", EX .**150.00**
Jergen's Rose de Lorme Talcum Powder, tc, sm top, 15-oz, EX **90.00**
Jersey Cream, sign, girls on swing, string hanger, EX **45.00**
Jersey Ice Cream, porc sign, 2-sided, Everybody..., 28x20", VG+ .**120.00**
Jewel T Allspice, tc, orange version, EX **60.00**
Jewel T Baking Powder, tc, tin litho, 1-lb, NM **75.00**
Jewel T Instant Cocoa Mix, tc, full, 12-oz, NM **75.00**
Jolly Time Popcorn, tc, full, EX+ **35.00**
JP Alley's Hambone Cigar, 2-sided cb sign, airplane, 7½", NM .**125.00**
Juno Tumeric, tc, goddess, NM **50.00**
Just Suits Cut Plug, tin canister, sm top, EX+ **100.00**
Kalsomine, sign, cb, lady & painter, hangs, 1909, 15x11", EX **50.00**
Kamo Thyme, tc, duck reserve, scarce, EX **110.00**
Kellogg's Corn Flakes, transitional cb box, 8-oz, EX **165.00**
Kellogg's Toasted Corn Flakes, cb box, dtd 1911, 8-oz, EX **275.00**
Kibbe Bros Cough Drops, tc, early Sommers sample sz, EX **75.00**
Kibbe's Peanut Butter, pail, tin litho, bail hdl, 1-lb, EX **55.00**
Kimbo Cut Plug Tobacco, cb container, lady on gr, sealed, NM ...**215.00**
King Cole Coffee, tc, King being served, tall, EX **220.00**
King's Puremalt, tip tray, barmaid & Pan-Am awards, 6" **65.00**
Knickerbocker Beer, tip tray, Beer Drinker's Beer, EX+ **25.00**
La Valla Rosa Cigars, cigar box, lady's portrait, VG **22.00**
Lambert & Butlers Waverly Mixture, pocket tin, horizontal, EX ..**30.00**
Lee Boys' Overalls, sign, cb easel bk, boy diecut, 10", EX+ **60.00**
Lee Riders, cb light-up display, boy/horse diecut, 22x13x6", EX .**480.00**
Lift Beverage, sign, porc, Drink..., bottle, red/wht/gr, 24x12", NM ..**200.00**
Liquid Peptnoids, cb sign, McKinley portrait, fr, 16x13", EX **20.00**
Little Buster Popcorn, tc, full, NM **155.00**

Log Cabin Syrup

Log Cabin Syrup tins have been made since the 1890s in variations of design that can be attributed to specific years of production. Until about 1914, they were made with paper labels. These are quite rare and highly prized by today's collectors. Tins with colored lithographed designs were made after 1914. When General Foods Purchased the Towle Company in 1927, the letters 'GF' were added.

A Cartoon series, illustrated with a mother flipping pancakes in the cabin window and various children and animals declaring their appreciation of the syrup in voice balloons, was introduced in the 1930s. A Frontier Village series followed in the late 1940s. A schoolhouse, jail, trading post, doctor's office, blacksmith shop, inn, and private homes were also available. Examples of either series today often command prices of $75.00 to $200.00 and up.

Bank, glass cabin shape, EX **40.00**
Bank, tin cabin, mother/children in doorway & window, 12-oz, EX+ **75.00**
Container, plastic wigwam, yel letters, 1950, 2x2" dia **9.00**
Pull toy, tin cabin, Log Cabin Express, 5x4½x3½", VG **350.00**
Spoon, SP, log cabin on tree trunk stem, ca 1910, NM **65.00**
Syrup tin, bear in door, cartoon ends, Towle's, 5-lb **160.00**
Syrup tin, blacksmith, 33-oz **200.00**
Syrup tin, boy w/lasso, 1-lb **125.00**
Syrup tin, cartoon all sides, sm **125.00**
Syrup tin, cartoon ends, goose & boy, 1930s, table sz, EX **155.00**

Syrup tin, child in doorway, 1-pint, EX, $125.00.

Syrup tin, children, man by pump, Towle's, 33-oz **165.00**
Syrup tin, dog at door, 12-oz **70.00**
Syrup tin, Dr RU Well, cartoon style, rare, EX+ **300.00**
Syrup tin, Express Office, coach, Towle's, 33-oz, NM **200.00**
Syrup tin, Frontier Inn, cowboys & horse, 5-lb, NM **275.00**
Syrup tin, Frontier Jail, 12-oz **165.00**
Syrup tin, hand w/finger pointing on top, Towle's, med **175.00**
Syrup tin, Home Sweet Home, 12-oz **165.00**
Syrup tin, pancakes, VG **25.00**
Syrup tin, paper label, sample sz, 2x1½" **400.00**
Syrup tin, red, 5-lb **65.00**
Syrup tin, red w/wht lettering, w/lid, 12-oz, EX **50.00**
Syrup tin, Stockade School, Towle's, 33-oz **170.00**
Syrup tin, wigwam, 2-lb, very rare, 4x3¼x3½" **550.00**

Long Island Oysters, paper sign, yel ground, 1950s, 11x21", EX ...**15.00**
Lorenz Bros Macaroni, mirror/paperweight, 4", NM **65.00**
Lubri-Gas, sign, cb, 2-sided, fr, 38x25", VG **60.00**
Lulu Gal Cigars, cigar box, impressed text, 5x4", VG **25.00**
Lux Soap, tc, offer for 15" inflatable Beatles dolls, 1967, M **120.00**
Madison Cigars, paper sign, Indian maiden, 1906, 30x15", NM .**725.00**
Mail Pouch Sweet Tobacco, sample packet, unopened, NM **20.00**
Marvel Coffee & Food, decal, cup on table, 1925, 11x8½", EX **80.00**
Mayo's Cut Plug, milk pail, paper label on tin, scarce, VG+ **135.00**
McColloch Chain Saws, thermometer, rvpt bubble, 1950s, 14", NM .**100.00**
McLaughlin's Manor House Coffee, tc, gr & wht, EX+ **165.00**
Medaglia D'Oro Coffee, tc, red/yel/gr, key-wind, ½-lb, NM **32.00**
Mennen's Violet Talcum, tc, man's portrait reserve, EX **58.00**
Mike Conroy Cigars, canister, paper on tin, boxing champ, EX .**170.00**
Miner Puddlers, pail, tin litho, bail hdl, NM **210.00**

Monarch Marshmallows, tc, emb paper label, pry lid, 1-lb, EX ...**100.00**
Monarch Peanut Butter, pail, tin litho, w/bail, 1-lb, EX **295.00**
Morning Glory Oats, cb box, flower on red, 3-lb, EX **35.00**
Moses Cough Drops, sample tin, Sommers litho, 2½x2¼x1¾", EX **85.00**
Nebia Brand Oysters, tc, paper litho, EX- **105.00**
Necco Mints, counter dispenser, tin litho, 7x6x5", NM **20.00**
Newly Wed Sugar Stick Candy, pennant, couple, 25", NM **125.00**
Niggerhair Tobacco, lunch pail, brn version, EX+ **325.00**
Ojibwa Fine Cut, canister, cb w/tin lid & base, 7x11x8", EX **140.00**
Old Crow, chocolate mold, rare **225.00**
Old Crow, highball glass, 1950s-60s, 4½x2½" **5.00**
Old Crow, mug, ceramic, yel, Broken Leg, Hall **15.00**
Old Crow, phone dialer, crow figural, NM **10.00**
Old Crow, pitcher, avocado gr, McCoy **40.00**
Old Crow, plaque, molded compo, 1950s, 15½" dia, M **300.00**
Old Crow, playing cards, M, scarce **35.00**
Old Crow, wooden sign, 3-Bird Toast, 14x19" **70.00**
Old Reliable Coffee, cb sign, trolley card sz, 11x21", NM **97.50**
Old Southern Coffee, tc, lady on yel, screw lid, tall, VG+ **30.00**
Ology Cigars, cb sign, golfer diecut, easel bk, 37x25", EX **145.00**
Orange-Crush, cb sign, lady & puppy, 19x13½", NM **190.00**
Orioles Cigars, cigar box, early stone litho, EX **85.00**
Orphan Boy Tobacco, cb sgn, package diecut, hanging, 17x12", NM ...**100.00**
Pabst, cb sign, lady drinking wine, 1899, 15x11½", VG+ **27.50**
Pace's Electric Mixture, tc, vertical box, EX- **250.00**
Pacific Beer, tray, Mt Tacoma, EX **60.00**
Patterson-Sargent PBS Paint, porc sign, 2-sided, 24x33", EX **40.00**
Peachy Double Cut Tobacco, tc, 3-color, EX+ **130.00**
Peerless Tobacco, canister, tin litho, NM **110.00**
Pennzoil, tc, We Oil Wise, no lid, 5-qt, EX+ **60.00**

Pepsi-Cola

Pepsi-Cola was first served in the early 1890s to customers of Caleb D. Bradham, a young pharmacist who touted his concoction to be medicinal as well as delicious. It was first called 'Brad's Drink' but was renamed Pepsi-Cola in 1898. Various logos have been registered over the years. The familiar oval was first used in the early 1940s. At about the same time, the two 'dots' between the words Pepsi and Cola became one, though more recent items may carry the double-dot logo as well, especially when they're designed to be reminiscent of the old ones. The bottle cap logo came along in 1943 and with variations was used through the early '60s. Our advisors for Pepsi are Craig and Donna Stifter; they are listed in the Directory under Illinois.

Ashtray, enameled bottle cap on smoked glass, 1950s, 3½" dia, NM ..**75.00**
Baseball score card, Milton Spring Beverages, NM **18.00**
Blotter, Pepsi & Pete the Pepsi-Cola Cops, 1939, EX+ **80.00**
Bottle carrier, wood w/wire & wood grip hdl, Buy..., G **100.00**
Bottle opener, metal, Am's Biggest Nickel's Worth, 3", EX **15.00**
Calendar, Am Art Series, complete, 1943, 24x18", EX+ **85.00**
Charm, gold-tone metal, logo on shamrock w/horseshoe on chain, NM **60.00**
Clock, rectangular, Say...Please, lights up, 1960s, 18x12", EX **80.00**
Clock, rnd, Drink...Light Refreshment, plastic, 1950s, 17", EX ..**350.00**
Clock, rnd, glass front metal fr, lights up, Telechron, 1940s, NM ..**300.00**
Clock, rnd, rvpt front, metal fr, bl numbers, 15" dia, NM+ **450.00**
Clock, sq, Drink...Now! on bottle cap, List-O-Matic, 14", EX ...**275.00**
Clock, sq, glass front, metal fr, Sessions, 1930s, 14", EX+ **250.00**
Cooler, wooden 4-leg box w/CI opener & tin sign, 32x35x19", VG ...**350.00**
Cup, paper, Pepsi Cops/ruler, Bigger-Better, G- **70.00**
Dispenser, stainless, metal & plastic, counter-top, 1960s, VG+ ..**250.00**
Display, cb 3-D diecut, Treat the..., girl at window, 27x28", EX ...**75.00**
Fountain glass, flared, etched logo, 1910-15, 4", NM **350.00**
Fountain pen, bottle-shaped metal clip, 1930s, 6", NMIB **200.00**

Matchbook cover, Bigger & Better, tilted bottle, EX **10.00**
Menu board, tin, Drink...Bigger-Better, w/chalkbrd, 30x20", VG ..**250.00**
Pencil, mechanical; bottle cap, NM **30.00**
Pin-bk button, Refresh w/o Filling, EX **35.00**
Pocket lighter, bottle-cap logo, Super Automatic..., Japan, EX+ ..**75.00**
Push bar, porc, Enjoy...Iced, red on wht w/yel, 3x32", EX **150.00**
Rack sign, Take Home a Carton, logo ea end, 5x17", EX+ **150.00**

Sign, cardboard, Gibson Girl, 24½x19½", G, $300.00.

Photo courtesy Gary Metz

Sign, cb stand-up diecut, picnic couple, 23x17", EX **200.00**
Sign, glass, free-standing wooden base, 1950s-60s, 12x17", NM .**200.00**
Sign, masonite, bottle cap, 48" dia, EX+ **325.00**
Sign, masonite, 2-sided, Jaycees/Dormeyer, 24x8", EX **35.00**
Sign, paper, Bigger & Better...12-oz/5¢, 6x20", NM **175.00**
Sign, porc, Drink...Now!, bottle cap, 2-sided, 42" dia, VG+ **500.00**
Sign, sf cb, Certified Quality, lady, 1940s, 22x28", EX+ **650.00**
Sign, sf cb stand-up, skater in Santa suit, 1930s, 31x21", EX ...**1,600.00**
Sign, tin, bottle cap, dtd 7-68, 19" dia, NM **280.00**
Sign, tin, bottle cap, wht ground, 25" dia, EX+ **225.00**
Sign, tin, bottle cap, 1950s, 20" dia, NM+ **375.00**
Sign, tin, bottle diecut, 5¢, 1930s-40s, 45", G+ **400.00**
Sign, tin, Have a..., cap on wht, 18x58", NM **175.00**
Sign, tin flange, Buy...Here, red/wht/bl, 12x16", VG+ **550.00**
Sign, trolley; Something To Hoe For, 3 girls, 1940s, 11x28", EX **650.00**
Thermometer, tin, Any Weather's..., bottle cap above, 1951, EX ..**130.00**
Tray, Bigger & Better/Coast-To-Coast, US map, 1930s, EX+ **350.00**
Tray, Enjoy...Hits the Spot, musical notes, 11x14", NM+ **55.00**

Pet Cigarettes, sign, cb, Allen & Gintner, 9¼x4", EX **80.00**
Peter Pan Bread, broom holder, tin & wood, EX **350.00**
Peter Pan Peanut Butter, tc, EK Pond, 12-oz, NM **175.00**
Peters Firearms & Ammunition, paper sign, metal fr, 35x24", EX ..**175.00**
Peters High Velocity Shells, box, 410-gauge, w/some shells, EX ...**45.00**
Pickwick Rolled Oats, tc, mc tin litho, 3-lb 7-oz, EX **120.00**
Pittsburg Paint, sf ts, product can, bright colors, 27x38", NM **390.00**

Planters Peanuts

The Planters Peanut Co. was founded in 1906. Mr. Peanut, the dashing peanut man with top hat, spats, monocle and cane, has represented Planters since 1916. He took on his modern-day appearance after the company was purchased by Standard Brands in 1961. He remains perhaps the most highly recognized logo of any company in the world. Mr. Peanut has promoted the company's products by appearing in ads; on product packaging; on or as store displays, novelties and premiums; and even in character at promotional events (thanks to a special Mr. Peanut costume).

Among the favorite items of collectors today are the glass display jars which were sent to retailers nationwide to stimulate 'point-of-sale' trade. They come in a variety of shapes and styles. The first, distributed in the early 1920s, was a large universal candy jar (round covered bowl on a pedestal) with only a narrow paper label affixed at the neck to identify it as 'Planters.' In 1924 an octagonal jar was produced, all eight sides embossed, with Mr. Peanut on the narrow corner panels. On a second octagon jar, only seven sides were embossed, leaving one of the large panels blank to accomodate a paper label.

In late 1929 a fishbowl jar was introduced, and in 1932 a beautiful jar with a blown-out peanut on each of the four corners was issued. The football shape was also made in the 1930s, as were the square jar, the large barrel jar, and the hexagon jar with yellow fired-on designs alternating on each of the six sides. All of these early jars had glass lids which after 1930 had peanut finials.

In 1937 jars with lithographed tin lids were introduced. The first of these was the slant-front streamline jar, which is also found with screened yellow lettering. Next was a squat version, the clipper jar, then the upright rectangular 1940 leap year jar, and last, another upright rectangular jar with a screened, fired-on design similar to the red, white, and blue design on the cellophane 5¢ bags of peanuts of the period. This last jar was issued again after WWII with a plain red tin lid.

In 1959 Planters first used a stock Anchor Hocking one-gallon round jar with a 'customer-special' decoration in red. As the design was not plainly evident when the jar was full, the decoration was modified with a white under-panel. The two jars we've just described are perhaps the rarest of them all due to their limited production. After Standard Brands purchased Planters, they changed the red-on-white panel to show their more modern Mr. Peanut and in 1963 introduced this most plentiful, thus very common, Planters jar. In 1966 the last counter display jar was distributed: the Anchor Hocking jar with a fired-on large four-color design such as those that appeared on peanut bags of the period. Prior to this, a plain jar with a transfer decal in an almost identical but smaller design was used.

Some Planters jars have been reproduced: the octagon jar (with only six of the sides embossed), a small version of the barrel jar, and the four peanut corner jar. Some of the first were made in clear glass with 'Made in Italy' embossed on the bottom, but most have been made in Asia, many in various colors of glass (a dead giveaway) as well as clear, and carrying only small paper stickers, easily removed, identifying the country of origin. At least two reproductions of the Anchor Hocking jar with four-color designs have been made, one circa 1978, the other in 1989. Both, using the stock jar, are difficult to detect, but there are small differences between them and the original that will enable you to make an accurate identification. With the exception of several of the earliest and the Anchor Hocking, all authentic Planters jars have 'Made in USA' embossed on the bottom, and all, without exception, are clear glass. Unfortunately, several paper labels have also been reproduced, no doubt due to the fact that an original label or decal will greatly increase the value of an original jar.

In the late 1920s, the first premiums were introduced in the form of story and paint books. Late in the 1930s, the tin nut set (which was still available into the 1960s) was distributed. A wood jointed doll was available from Planters Peanuts Stores at that time. Many post-WWII items were made of plastic: banks, salt and pepper shakers, cups, cookie cutters, small cars and trucks, charms, whistles, various pens and mechanical pencils, and almost any other item imaginable. In recent years the company, now a division of Nabisco, has continued to distribute a wide variety of novelties.

Note that there are many unauthorized Planters/Mr. Peanut items. Although several are reproductions or 'copycats,' most are fantasies and fakes. Our advisors for Planters Planters are Judith and Robert Walthall; they are in the Directory under Alabama.

Key:
al — aluminum   pfl — peanut finial lid

cc — common colors   pl — plastic
(green, light blue, red, tan)   pnut — peanut
MrP — Mr. Peanut

Apron, wht w/colorful pnut bag design, navy trim	15.00
Ashtray, MrP, 3 pnuts behind, bsk, EX	75.00
Ashtray, MrP w/gr pants, 2 pnuts, ceramic, EX	400.00
Backpack, natural duck cloth w/lg MrP, 1974, EX	15.00
Backpack, vinyl-bkd bl denim w/allover MrPs, EX	15.00
Ball, beach; inflatable, bl & yel w/MrP, 1974, EX	10.00
Ball, tennis; yel w/blk MrP, 1989, EX	3.00
Baseball, blk MrP, Canadian, Cooper, 1989, M	10.00
Baseball, yel/blk/wht MrP, 1992, M	3.00
Baseball bat, wood w/blk MrP, 1992, M	30.00
Bookmark, diecut MrP, orange, 1950s, M	15.00
Box, cb w/MrP diecut, orange w/bl & wht, 1930, EX	600.00
Box, Clean Crisp, 72 1¢ Bars, wood, 1910-18, VG	200.00
Jar, Streamline, Planters emb, tin lid, 1937, EX	75.00
Jar, 6-Sides w/yel MrP & Planters alternating, pfl	90.00
Lighter, al w/emb MrP, Firefly, 1948, 1x2½x½", MIB	350.00
Lighter, in 6.75 oz Cocktail Pnut tin, 1960s, EX	50.00
Lighter, mini Cocktail Pnut tin, 1950s, M	100.00
Lighter, pnut shape, tan, compo, 2½", EX	90.00
Lunch tote, MrP, ABCs, days, months, vinyl, 1979	35.00

Nodder, Mr. Peanut body on spring, removable plastic cane, clayware by LEGO, Japan, 6½", $120.00.

Photo courtesy Judith and Robert Walthall

Nodder, MrP on spring, LEGO, clayware, 6½", EX	120.00
Note pad, cube type, MrP, 1990s	5.00
Pin, wooden MrP, 1939 or 1940 World's Fair, MOC	100.00
Pin, wooden MrP, 1940s, 1¾", MOC	75.00
Pin-bk button, Operation Friend, 1973, M (+)	10.00
Plaque, ceramic MrP head, ltd ed of 300, 1982, 12"	100.00
Plate, Wilton Armetele, ltd ed of 2,000, 6", M	75.00
Plate, Wilton Armetele, Super Bowl XIII, 11", M	100.00
Radio, bkpack, Munch 'N Go, 1991, M	25.00
Radio, Cocktail Pnut tin, 1978, 3½x3¼", MIB	55.00
Radio, Cocktail Pnut tin, 1980s, 4x2⅝", MIB	40.00
Radio, 2-D figural MrP, yel pl, 1978, 10", MIB	70.00
Sleeping bag, pnut bag design	125.00
Spoon, measuring; 4-in-1 w/MrP hdl, pl, EX	8.00
Towel set, w/MrP on bk of whale, 1980, 3-pc	20.00
Toy, pnut-shaped roadster, cc, pl, 1950s, 5¼", EX	500.00
Toy, truck, MrP's Express, pl, PYRO, 1950s, 5", NM	350.00
Toy, truck, stake trailer, pl, PYRO, 5½", M	250.00
Vendor, bl pl w/MrP relief, Bdwy Toys, 1997, MIB	10.00
Vendor, bl pl w/MrP relief, Tarco, 1978, MIB (+)	25.00
Vendor-bank, MrP's hat holds can of nuts, 7", MIB	500.00

POC Beer, cb sign, bowlers, easel bk, 20x15", EX	60.00
Poll Parrot Shoes, cb sign, boy w/bird, wood fr, 21x13", EX	80.00

Pomco Coffee, tc, tin litho, red/wht/blk, key-wind, NM **40.00**

Possom Red Tobacco, canister, tin litho, slip lid, EX **200.00**

Postmaster Cigars, canister, tin litho, EX **66.00**

Postum General, tc, blk & red on wht, sample sz, VG **15.00**

President Suspenders, tip tray, renaissance lady, EX **120.00**

Pride of Arabia Coffee, horseman, ½-lb, EX **140.00**

Puffenjoy Tobacco, tc, paper label on tin, pry lid, 1940s, NM **100.00**

Puritan Tobacco, pocket tin, vertical, EX **220.00**

RCA Victor

Nipper, the RCA Victor trademark, was the creation of Francis Barraud, an English artist. His pet's intent fascination with the music of the phonograph seemed to him a worthy subject for his canvas. Although he failed to find a publishing house who would buy his work, the Gramophone Co. in England saw its potential and adopted Nipper to advertise their product. The painting was later acquired and trademarked in the United States by the Victor Talking Machine Co., which was purchased by RCA in 1929. The trademark is owned today by EMI in England and by General Electric in the U.S. Nipper's image appeared on packages, accessories, ads, brochures, and in three-dimensional form. You may find a life-size statue of him; but all are not old. They have been manufactured for the owner throughout RCA history and are marketed currently by licensees, BMG Inc. and Thomson Consumer Electronics (dba RCA). Except for the years between 1968 and 1976, Nipper has seen active duty, and with his image spruced up only a bit for the present day, the ageless symbol for RCA still listens intently to 'His Master's Voice.' Our advisor for RCA Victor is Roger R. Scott; he is listed in the Directory under Oklahoma.

Bank, Nipper, felt over pot metal, mk Radio Corp of Am, 6", NM .**125.00**

Bank, Nipper figural, flocked metal, 1940s **125.00**

Buckle, His Master's Voice, brass, Nash Tiffany London **25.00**

Chair, NP-pipe fr w/armrest, plastic bk/seat, logo on bk, M **100.00**

Chair, plastic bk & seat, on NP pipe fr w/arms, logo on bk **100.00**

Curtains, RCA **40.00**

Doll, Radio Man, jtd wood, Maxfield Parrish, M **900.00**

Figure, Nipper, chalk, Victor, 4" **40.00**

Figure, Nipper, crystal, Fenton, 4" **50.00**

Figure, Nipper, felt over pot metal, 6", NM **125.00**

Figure, Nipper, molded plastic, 36", EX **235.00**

Figure, Nipper, papier-mache, 41", minimum value **1,000.00**

Figure, Nipper, plaster, 12½x7½x5", VG **200.00**

Necktie, Nipper, M **20.00**

Needle tin, Nipper, 3-color, NM, from $25 to **50.00**

Pin-bk button, I Support Nipper, 1930s, ½", EX **45.00**

Plate, Nipper, collector's edition **50.00**

Puzzle record, Victor, MIP **250.00**

Record brush, Lucite hdl, in faux leather snap case **30.00**

Record brush, Nipper, 5½" **25.00**

Record display, dog & phonograph, chalk **150.00**

Shakers, dog & RCA phonograph, plastic, pr **45.00**

Shakers, Nipper, Lenox, 3", pr **55.00**

Shakers, Radio Corp of Am, 1940s, pr **40.00**

Sign, cb, blk & wht w/maroon label, hanging, faded, 20" dia **350.00**

Sign, plastic/metal, lights up, 1940s, 15x37", EX **200.00**

Sign, porc, Authorized Dealer..., 1940s, 18x24", EX **165.00**

Sign, porc, His Master's Voice, mc on blk, oval, 19x25", NM .**1,500.00**

Sign, porc, record shape w/trademark image on red label, 24", VG **300.00**

Sign, tin, Nipper Listening, fr, 13½x19", G **500.00**

Sign, tin, Victor Talking Machines, dog & Victrola, 13½x19", VG ...**500.00**

Thermometer, porc, NM **485.00**

Watch fob, EX **30.00**

Red Goose Shoes

Realizing that his last name was difficult to pronounce, Herman Giesecke, a shoe company owner resolved to give the public a modified, shortened version that would be better suited to the business world. The results suggested the use of the goose trademark with the last two letters, 'ke,' represented by the key that this early goose held in his mouth. Upon observing an employee casually coloring in the goose trademark with a red pencil, Giesecke saw new advertising potential and renamed the company Red Goose Shoes. Although the company has changed hands down through the years, the Red Goose emblem has remained. Collectors of this desirable fowl increase in number yearly, as do prices. Beware of reproductions; new chalkware figures are prevalent.

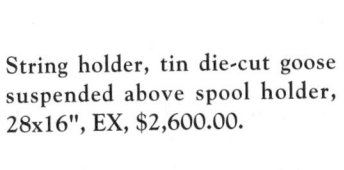
String holder, tin die-cut goose suspended above spool holder, 28x16", EX, $2,600.00.

Baseball bat, Red Goose Shoes **35.00**

Blotter, circus illus & Red Goose on cb **85.00**

Booklet, Cream of Wheat, Rastus on cover, w/recipes **20.00**

Candy, Red Goose Shoes giveaway, unopened roll **45.00**

Clicker, Red Goose logo on yel, 1950s, M **15.00**

Clock, rnd, glass front, metal fr, Telechron, 1930s-40s, NM **400.00**

Dispenser, Golden Egg, cb & papier-mache goose, w/sign, EX ...**325.00**

Egg, plastic, w/ring inside, shoe premium **35.00**

Erasers, set of 24, MIB **245.00**

Figure, chalkware goose, red w/emb name, gr base, 12", NM+ **400.00**

Golden Egg machine, cb/papier-mache/pressed cb, mechanical, EX ...**325.00**

Pencil, mechanical; Red Goose Shoes, red, Bakelite **35.00**

Rug, Half the Fun of Having Feet..., goose, 50x38", EX **325.00**

Sign, Red Goose, dbl-sided, neon, 1930s-40s, 24x12", NM **3,750.00**

Sign, tin, For Boys & Girls, goose on yel, 13x19", VG **110.00**

String holder, CI, goose figural, rare, 16", NM **3,000.00**

Red Raven, tip tray, lady hugging lg red raven, rnd, EX **150.00**

Rexall Baby Talcum, tc, baby in reserve, VG+ **80.00**

Richardson Root Beer, ts, blk/wht/red, 1950, 14x10", NM **57.00**

Rivals Tobacco, tobacco caddy label, lady at station, 1875, NM ..**38.00**

Roly Poly

The Roly Poly tobacco tins were patented on November 5, 1912, by Washington Tuttle and produced by Tindeco of Baltimore, Maryland. There were six characters in all: Satisfied Customer, Storekeeper, Mammy, Dutchman, Singing Waiter, and Inspector. Four brands of tobacco were packaged in selected characters; some tins carry a printed tobacco box on the back to identify their contents. Mayo and Dixie Queen Tobacco were packed in all six; Red Indian and U.S. Marine Tobacco in only Mammy, Singing Waiter, and Storekeeper. Of the set, the Inspector is considered the rarest and in excellent/near mint condition may fetch more than $1,100.00 on today's market.

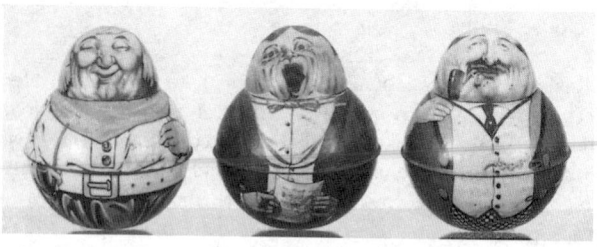

Dutchman, Mayo, EX, $500.00; Singing Waiter, Mayo, VG+, $600.00; Satisfied Customer, Mayo, VG+, $600.00.

Dutchman, Dixie Queen, EX 400.00
Dutchman, Mayo, NM 675.00
Inspector, Dixie Queen, VG 500.00
Mammy, Mayo, NM+ 750.00
Mammy, Red Indian, EX+ 750.00
Storekeeper, Mayo, EX 500.00

Rosy Morn, tc, paper label, pry lid, EX 40.00
Royal Crown Cola, thermometer, tin litho, 13½x5¾", EX 105.00
Salada Tea, door push, porc, red on wht, 30", EX 60.00
San Alto Cigars, cb sign, men in clubhouse, 30x14", EX 230.00
Sanders Candy, tin litho, children at play, 1930s, 6x5", NM 340.00
Scandanavian-Am Lines, sf ts, ocean liner, 37x41", EX 875.00
School Days Peanut Butter, pail, tin litho, w/bail, 14-oz 450.00
Scotch Brand Oats, tc, Scotsman on yel, 18-oz, NM 60.00
Seal of N Carolina, canister, tin litho, sm top, EX+ 325.00
Sealtest, menu board, metal fr w/10-slot cb inserts, 22x10", NM ..30.00
Search Light, matchbox holder, Dmn Match Co, MIB 150.00
Silver Buckle Coffee, tc, pry lid, EX+ 80.00
Sir Walter Raleigh, change receiver, brass/wood/glass, EX 50.00
Sir Walter Raleigh Tobacco, emb ts, 4-color, 26x17", EX 100.00
Smith Bros Cough Drops, cb box, sample sz, NM 30.00
Smith Bros Cough Drops, sign, paperbrd, 2 portraits, 16x24", EX ...98.00
Southbend Watches, ts, pocketwatch in ice cube, 13x19", NM .190.00
Spear Head Plug Tobacco, ts, 2-sided, hangs, 6", EX+ 80.00
Stag Tobacco, pocket tin, vertical, complimentary trial sz, EX 65.00
Stag Tobacco, tc, stag in reserve on red, short, EX 50.00
Standard Varnish Works, sf ts, Man Who Knows..., 10½x16½", EX ..235.00
Star Soap, litho-on-linen sign, lady w/fan, 1910, 14x11", NM ...180.00
Stewart Clipping Machine, cb sgn, man w/horse, 1900s, 18x15", NM ..825.00
Strong Heart Coffee, tc, Indian portrait, tall, EX 820.00
Summer-Time Tobacco, canister, tin litho, pry lid, NM 140.00
Summit Shirts, pennant, man putting on cuff links, 25", EX 100.00
Sun Light Axle Grease, tc, Shonk litho of winking sun, 5x5", EX ..100.00
Sunset Brand Wheat Flakes, cb box, Montgomery Ward, 8-oz, NM .450.00
Sunshine Cigarettes, ts, emb package, 18x14", EX 135.00
Super-Superb Typewriter Ribbons, tc, beaver gnawing tree, EX ...35.00
Sure Shot, store bin, tin litho, EX 825.00
Swedish Spritz Cookies, tc, tin litho, key wind, EX+ 35.00
Sweet Mist, canister, cb w/tin lid & base, NM 150.00
Sykes Comfort Powder, tc, girls in reserve, 4½x1½" dia, NM 245.00
Sylvan Violet Talcum, tc, scenic reserve, EX 75.00
Tiger Chewing Tobacco, canister, cb w/tin lid & base, EX+ 110.00
Tobacco Girls Cigars, cigar box, lady's portrait, EX 75.00
Tower Root Beer, ts, Like Mother..., 19½x9", EX 100.00
Tucket's Orinoco, tc, Black man fishing, 4x6", NM ..100.00
Turf Cigarettes, porc sign, Pegasus, red/wht/bl, 30x20", NM 165.00
Tuxedo Tobacco, pocket tin, Indian logo, vertical, full, NM 65.00
Twin Cola, cb sign, diecut, easel bk, 9x6", NM 30.00
Uncle Sam Oat Flakes, tc, mc on wht, 20-oz, NM+ ...395.00
Union Commander Cut Plug, lunch box, tin litho, flat lid, EX ..300.00

Union Stamps, ts, We Give & Redeem..., red/wht, 8½x20", VG+ ..35.00
US Marine Flake Cut, pocket tin, yel/blk/wht on red, VG+ 100.00
Viking Snuff, dispenser, tin litho, NM 58.00
War Eagle Cigars, tin canister, eagle, dk gr, EX 175.00
Warner's Gilt Edge Brassieres, ts on cb, easel bk, 1915, 12x6", EX 300.00
Washington Crisps Corn Flakes, cb box, eagle & cameo, 7-oz, NM .250.00
Watkins Egyptian Bouquet, tc, Sphinx reserve, NM 175.00
Weideman Boy Brand Coffee, tc, key-wind, EX 80.00
Wellsbach Lighting, tip tray, lady reading, NM 160.00
Weyman's Cutty Pipe, canister, tin litho, red/yel/gr, 14", EX 375.00
Whistle Soda, cb sign, bottle & elf diecut, easel bk, 1951, EX 80.00
White Clover Peanut Butter, pail, tin litho, w/bail, 1-lb, EX 550.00
White House Coffee, tc, bl, key-wind, NM 45.00
White House Coffee, tc, copper version, key-wind, EX 40.00
White King Washing Machine Soap, ts, 1930s, 14x10", EX 120.00
White Orchid Cigars, cigar box, EX 35.00
White Rock, tip tray, World's Best..., Psyche, 6½x4½", EX 120.00
Wigwam Tumeric, cb container, Indian camp, EX 28.00
Wilco Allspice, tc, 3-color on wht, NM 22.00
Williams La Tosca Rose Talc, tc, rose on cream, sample sz, EX 75.00
Wish Bone Coffee, tc, red/bl/blk/wht, key-wind, NM 40.00
Worker Cut Plug, lunch box, gr version, EX 75.00
Wright Ditson Tennis Balls, tc, key-wind, Spalding, NM 115.00
Yale Coffee, tc, gold on bl, sample sz, 2½x2¼", EX- 75.00
Yeast Foam, paper sign, w/metal strips, 15x10", NM 75.00
Yellow Bonnet Coffee, girl on red, earlier version, full, EX 40.00
Yellow Creek Lard, bucket, tin litho, reserve on bl, 5", EX 50.00
Yellow Kid, cigar box, ad for Sunday NY Journal, EX 1,000.00
Yellow Kid, plate, HP YK w/parrot & cat, dtd 1897, 7" 125.00
Yellow Kid, postcard, Over the Bounding Main, VG 30.00

7-Up

The Howdy Company of St. Louis, Missouri, was founded in 1920 by Charles L. Grigg. His first creation was an orange drink called Howdy. In the late 1920s Howdy's popularity began to wane, so in 1929, Grigg invented a lemon-lime soda called Seven-Up as an alternative to colas. Grigg's Seven-Up became a widely accepted favorite. Our advisors for this category are Craig and Donna Stifter; they are listed in the Directory under Illinois.

7-Up, place mat, American Lace Paper Co., copyright 1959, 9¾x14½", M, $15.00.

Bottle carrier, cb, You'll Like It..., 3-hole hdl, EX 35.00
Calendar, 1942, pinup girl, complete, 12x7", NM 185.00
Calendar, 1943, General McArthur, complete, 12x7", EX+ 70.00
Door pull plate, tin, 12x3", NM 20.00
Drinking glass, str sides, appl gold lettering, syrup line, NM 65.00
Menu board, tin, Fresh Up/Nothing Does It..., EX 60.00
Picnic cooler, Fresh Up w/7-Up, wht w/gr straps, vinyl, NM 17.00
Sign, cb, Real...Sold Here, Fresh Up, 1930s, 13x20", EX 40.00
Sign, cb diecut, Morning Noon & Night..., 1930s, 8½x10½", EX 50.00
Sign, cb diecut stand-up, Here's Your Family..., 1948, 12x9", NM ..65.00
Sign, compo, 2-sided, Service Bar, 1945, 5½x11½", EX 50.00
Sign, glass shield w/light, shows bottle, wood base, 1930s, NM ...1,100.00

Sign, tin, hand holds bottle, 1947, 19½x27", EX 275.00
Sign, tin, sf button, red/wht/gr, 1940s, 8½" dia, EX 70.00
Sign, tin, Take Some Home, for corner, 1930s, 8x10½", EX, pr .165.00
Sign, tin, 6-pack, All family Drink, Canada, 1950s, 60x36", NM .600.00
Thermometer, porc, bottle on wht, 15x6", EX 130.00
Thermometer, porc, You Like It..., 1950s, 14", EX 100.00
Thermometer, tin, Ca Ravigote..., lg bottle, 15", G 40.00

Advertising Cards

Advertising trade cards enjoyed great popularity during the last quarter of the 19th century when the chromolithography printing process was refined and put into common use. The purpose of the trade card was to aquaint the public with a business, product, service, or event. Most trade cards range in size from 2" x 3" to 4" x 6"; however, many are found in both smaller and larger sizes.

There are two classifications of trade cards: 'private design' and 'stock.' Private design cards were used by a single company or individual; the images on the cards were designed for only that company. Stock cards were generics that any individual or company could purchase from a printer's inventory. These cards usually had a blank space on the front for the company to overprint with their own name and product information. Values are given for cards in near-mint condition.

Four categories of particular interest to collectors are:

Mechanical — a card which achieves movement through the use of a pull tab, fold-out side, or movable part.

Hold-to-light — a card that reveals its design only when viewed before a strong light.

Diecut — a card in the form of something like a box, a piece of clothing, etc.

Metamorphic — a card that by folding down a flap shows a transformed image, such as a white beard turning black after use of a product.

For a more thorough study of the subject, we recommend *Reflections 1* and *Reflections 2* by Kit Barry; his address can be found in the Directory under Vermont.

Photo courtesy Kit Barry

The Enterprise Lawn Mower, Both Worlds Happy!, $45.00.

Alaska Down Bustle, woman facing right & inset 45.00
Alexandra Exhibition Co, fireworks display over water 100.00
Asbestos Packed Steam Cocks, rooster on steam cock 60.00
Aultman Hay Binder, mechanical, slide pc & finder folds up 125.00
Belding Thread, Blaine/Logan & Cleveland/Hendricks 75.00
Belding Thread, burning building & rescue 75.00
Belding Thread, loading silk bale onto steamship 75.00
Belding Thread, train & Indians 75.00
Blair Hog Rings, 6 pigs watching, 2 pigs pulling 65.00
Buffalo Scale Co, 2 men using scales 35.00
California Silk Co, Cliff House & tightrope walker 75.00
Chase & Sanborn Coffee, Montreal winter carnival 45.00
Chicago Daily News, newsboy hawking papers 35.00

David's Ink, dressed monkey writing at desk 75.00
Diamond Polishing Powder, girl cleaning window w/elf 45.00
Eclipse Halter, Black man & donkey at tether post 35.00
Feigenspan Brewery, photographic image of building 50.00
G&S silhouette, L Prang, 'And we are his sisters...' 35.00
G&S silhouette, L Prang, 'But when the breezes blow...' 35.00
G&S silhouette, L Prang, 'Fair moon, to thee I sing' 35.00
G&S silhouette, L Prang, 'Fairwell, my own...' 35.00
G&S silhouette, L Prang, 'For I hold that...' 35.00
G&S silhouette, L Prang, 'He is an Englishman' 35.00
G&S silhouette, L Prang, 'I'm called Little Butt...' 35.00
G&S silhouette, L Prang, 'My gallant crew...' 35.00
G&S silhouette, L Prang, 'Over the bright bl sea...' 35.00
G&S silhouette, L Prang, 'We sail the ocean blue...' 35.00
Genessee Hotel, Buffaly NY, bl & wht image of building 35.00
Gloss Paint, paint can diecut 35.00
Hawley & Hoops, girl facing left drinking cocoa 35.00
Henry's Premium Minstrels, 'Great baseball contest...' 50.00
Hires Root Beer, girl w/glass diecut 25.00
Imperial Egg Food, boy pulling sled on ice 20.00
Imperial Egg Food, rooster riding eggshell on water 20.00
Imperial Egg Food, 10 poultry birds in barnyard 20.00
Jackson's Best Chewing tobacco, Stanley, rhino, hippo 45.00
Jackson wagon held aloft by air balloon 150.00
Knickerbocker Life Insurance, George Washington 45.00
Knickerbocker Life Insurance, Martha Washington 45.00
L May Co, Santa Claus' Headquarters, Santa in crowd 100.00
Lamb Knitting Machine Co, factory, machine images 100.00
Lamb Wire Fence Co, 'Nothing gets off the farm' 45.00
Lancaster Watches, skeleton w/scythe on watch 50.00
Lang's Beer, cherub in flowers w/butterfly 45.00
Larus Bros 'Fair Play' Plug Tobacco, policeman & 2 boys 50.00
Lautz Marseilles White Soap, girl w/soap on bike 45.00
Lautz Snow Boy Wash Powder, boy w/soap on sled 45.00
Levi Strauss, closed-front & open-front jumper jackets 200.00
Levi Strauss, engineer holding tools, 7-pocket overalls 200.00
Levi Strauss, engineer's coat & combination coat 200.00
Levi Strauss, man w/cigar, spring bottom pants 200.00
Levi Strauss, minor w/shovel & pick, blouse/overalls 200.00
Lillian Russell Cigars, standing caped woman 60.00
Maillard Chocolate School, woman cooking chocolate 45.00
Manhattan Life Insurance, boy painting Indian 50.00
Manhattan Life Insurance, lady holding picture 50.00
Manhattan Life Insurance, 2 children in a tub 50.00
Marburg Tobacco, Black man & woman over pack 45.00
Mason & Pollard Pills, cherub & sick man 45.00
McClain Horse Collar, 1 horse w/ & 1 w/o collar 35.00
Montserrat Lime Fruit Juice, bottle, drinks on table 35.00
Nigger Head Tobacco, Black w/bow & cow 75.00
Nigger Head Tobacco, Black w/bow & target 75.00
Nigger Head Tobacco, Black w/bow shooting apple 75.00
Nigger Head Tobacco, Black w/target, arrow in nose 75.00
Nigger Head Tobacco, Black w/target on his bk 75.00
Palmer Cox Brownies (13) at table eating, L Prang printer 75.00
Palmer Cox Brownies (5) band, L Prang printer 75.00
Palmer Cox Brownies (5) running, L Prang printer 75.00
Palmer Cox Brownies (6) dancing, L Prang printer 75.00
Palmer's Dewey Bouquet Perfume, US flag 35.00
Parshley Beer & Lunch Rooms, 2 men shooting pool 35.00
Pierce's Invalid's Hotel, bl & wht image of hotel 40.00
Pierce's Invalid's Hotel & Dispensary, images of both 45.00
Planet Jr, image of dbl-wheel hoe cultivator 40.00
Red Raven Water, nude child on box by dresser 45.00
Reeves Hay Stacker, Palmer Cox-type Brownies & stacker 45.00

Rentchlers IXI Grain Drill, woman driving drill 60.00
Richmond Cedar Works, cylinder-churn woman w/cows 45.00
Rieger Lemon Sugar, 3 children on giant glass 50.00
Salzgeber Coffee Roaster, image of machine 45.00
Schuttler & Holtz wagon w/Echard prize steer 65.00
Schuttler & Holtz wagon w/Tom Brown prize steer 65.00
Spencerian Pens, girl writing, w/collie dog 45.00
Standard Screw Fastened Boots, 'Dat's de firsted pegged...' 45.00
Standard Screw Fastened Boots, man reading paper 25.00
Standard Screw Fastened Boots, shoe on air balloon 20.00
Stearns Lawn Mower, girl mowing, gear insert 45.00
Stollwerk 1893 Chocolate, statue of Germania 45.00
Suit Co Capitol Whiskey, image of capitol building 75.00
Suit Co Congress Whiskey, image of congress 75.00
Suite Co Senate Whiskey, scene of senate 75.00
Taylor's Cherokee Remedy, girl by mullein plant 35.00
Taylor's Premium Cologne, girl riding butterfly 25.00
Uncle Sam's Condition Powder, horses, cattle & sheep 25.00
Van Houten Cocoa, crowd around base of air balloon 35.00
Weber Wagon Co, wagon facing right 50.00

Advertising Dolls and Figures

Whether your interest in ad dolls is fueled by nostalgia or strictly because of their amusing, often clever advertising impact, there are several points that should be considered before making your purchases. Condition is of utmost importance; never pay book price for dolls in poor condition, whether they are cloth or of another material. Restoring fabric dolls is usually unsatisfactory and involves a good deal of work. Seams must be opened, stuffing removed, the doll washed and dried, and then reassembled. Washing old fabrics may prove to be disastrous. Colors may fade or run, and most stains are totally resistant to washing. It's usually best to leave the fabric doll as it is.

Watch for new dolls as they become available. Save related advertising literature, extra coupons, etc., and keep these along with the doll to further enhance your collection. Old dolls with no marks are sometimes challenging to identify. While some products may use the same familiar trademark figures for a number of years (the Jolly Green Giant, Pillsbury's Poppin' Fresh, and the Keebler Elf, for example) others appear on the market for a short time only and may be difficult to trace. Most libraries have reference books with trademarks and logos that might provide a clue in tracking down your doll's identity. Children see advertising figures on Saturday morning cartoons that are often unfamiliar to adults, or other ad doll collectors may have the information you seek.

Some advertising dolls are still easy to find and relatively inexpensive, ranging in cost from $1.00 to $100.00. The hard plastic and early composition dolls are bringing the higher prices. Advertising dolls are popular with children as well as adults. For a more thorough study of the subject, we recommend *Advertising Dolls* by Joleen Robison and Kay Sellers, and *Advertising Dolls with Values* by Myra Yellin Outwater (Schiffer). Our advisor for this category is Jim Rash; he is listed in the Directory under New Jersey. Values are for dolls in near mint condition; be sure to discount prices for soil, missing parts, wear, or damage of any type.

Adam's Black Jack Gum, rabbit, cloth, 11" 175.00
Alka Seltzer, Speedy, vinyl, bank, 1950s, 5½" 250.00
Am Beauty Macaroni Co, Roni Mac, cloth, 1937, 11" 150.00
Arbuckle Bros, Jack or Jill, cotton, 1931, 14½", ea 200.00
Arkadelphia Milling Co, Dolly Dimple, flour sack, 18" 150.00
Aunt Jemima Pancake Flour, Aunt Jemima, cloth, 1905, 15" 200.00
Baker's Chocolate, La Belle, metal pencil sharpener, 2" 40.00
Beach-Nut's Fruit Stripe Gum, zebra, cloth, 1972, 12" 20.00

Bewley's Yeast, Little Red Riding Hood, cloth, 11" 150.00
Big Boy Restaurant, Big Boy, plastic, 1974-78, 10" 7.00
Blatz Beer, baseball player, CI, 10½" 150.00
Campbell Soup Co, Campbell Kid, cloth, 1910, 15½" 225.00
Carnation Milk Co, Cry Baby, jointed vinyl, Horsman, 1962, 18" ..50.00
Cheer Detergent, girl, vinyl, 1960s, 10" 5.00
Chesty Potato Chip Co, Chesty Boy, rubber squeak toy, 1950, 8" ..250.00
Chocks Vitamins, Charley Chocks, cloth, 1970s, 20" 20.00
Chrysler Corp, Mr Fleet, plastic bank, 1973, 10" 300.00
Corn Products Refining Co, Indian Princess, compo, 1930s, 10" .450.00
Cox Gelatine Co, girl, cloth cutout for stuffing, 1973 ....175.00
Cream of Wheat Corp, Chef, cloth, 1930s, 20" 200.00
Derby Oil Co, Derby Man, cloth, 1960s, 17" 20.00
Dodge, Little Profit, papier-mache/plaster, nodder, 1960s, 6" 30.00
Exxon, tiger, plastic bank, 1960s, 8½" 40.00
Fels-Naptha Soap, Anty Drudge, fabric for stuffing, 1933, 11" ...175.00
Frostie Root Beer, Frostie Man, cloth, 1970s, 16" 20.00
GE, Bandy, jointed wood, Cameo, 1929, 18" 500.00
Glenmore Distilleries, Colonel Glenmore, cloth, 1940s, 22" 175.00
Green Giant Co, Sprout, inflatable vinyl, 1976, 24" 15.00
Hawaiian Punch, Punchy, cloth, 1965, 13" 15.00
Hostess Bakery Co, Happy Ho Ho, inflatable plastic, 1970s, 48" ..25.00
Imperial Granum, girl, cloth cutout for stuffing, 1918 ....175.00
Junior Mints, Fonzie, cloth, 1976, 16" 15.00
Pepto Bismol, 24-Hour Bug, vinyl, bank, Niagara Plastic, 7" 75.00
Pine Sol, bear, fur/fabric, 1978, 15x15" 25.00
Plymouth/Chrysler Corp, Roadrunner, inflatable, 7½" 10.00
Poll Parrot Shoes, girl, compo/cloth, 20" 150.00
Post Cereals, Sugar Bear, cloth, 1972, 12½" 15.00
Puritan Flour, pilgrim, cloth, 1920, 15½" 175.00
Quaker Oats, Cap'n Crunch, cloth, Animal Fair Inc, 1978, 15½" ..20.00
Ralston Purina Co, raisin doll, cloth, 1973, 15" 25.00
RCA, Sellin' Fool, wood/compo, Cameo Doll Co, 1926, 15½" ..600.00
RCA, Service Man, bank, plastic, 1960, 5" 30.00
Red Barn Restaurant, Hamburger Hungry, cloth, R&R Toys, 1970 ...30.00

Renk Seed Company, Kernel Renk, Dakin, 1970, 8", $200.00.

Photo courtesy Jim Rash

Rodkey's Flour, Rag Darling, printed on flour sack 150.00
Royal Gelatin, King Royal, vinyl bank, 9½" 135.00
Sambo's Restaurant, tiger, velvet, Dakin, 1978 ....25.00
Scott Paper Co, Scottie, plush fabric, A&L Novelty, 1976, 7" 10.00
Seiko Watches, robot, inflatable plastic, 1977, 21" 15.00
Shakey's Pizza, Shakey Chef, cloth, 18" 50.00
Sinclair Refining Co, Dino the Dinosaur, plastic, 1978, 14" 15.00
Snoboy Apples, Snuggle Snoboy, plush fabric, Princess, 12" 20.00
So-Lo, Pudgie, plastic, hand puppet, 1972 ....3.00
Sony Corp, Sony Boy, plastic, 1960s, 8" 475.00
Star-Kist Tuna, Charlie, talking pillow, Mattel, 1970, 15" 35.00

Stoney's Beer, bartender, plastic, Sculpture Promotions, 8" **65.00**
Sunshine Animal Crackers, elephant, cloth, 5½x6½" **140.00**
Texaco, Cheerleader, jointed vinyl, Hong Kong, 1973, 11½" **30.00**
Tillamook Cheese Co, Tillie the Cow, rubber, Remple, 1958, 4x9" .**45.00**
Travelodge, Sleepy Bear, plush fabric, 1967, 12" **15.00**
Tru Test Paint, girl, compo head, cloth body, 1940s, 12" **50.00**
Victor's Eucalyptus Cough Drops, Koala Twins, fur/fabric, 1975, 15" .**15.00**
Western Union, Congratulations, Editions Limited, 1975, 6" **15.00**
Wurlitzer, Funmaker, cloth, 15" **25.00**
Yukon Flour Mills, Peter Rabbit, cloth, ca 1915, 7" **80.00**
7-Up, Fresh Up Freddie, cloth, 1958, 24" **100.00**

African Art

African Art does not consist of a single class of objects. Rather, these often powerful sculptures are carved by many varying African tribes and groups across the central continent; each item represents specific cultural and spiritual functions and meanings. Many kinds of materials are used including wood, metal, fiber, ivory, and bone. Large numbers of these items are now being produced and sold to the tourist trade, but 'authentic' African art is generally considered to consist of objects which were used in cultural and/or religious activities. The items listed here are authentic, in good condition, without provenance, and considered to be of average aesthetic quality. Scott Nelson, a collector of African art, is our advisor; his address is listed in the Directory under District of Columbia.

Basket, Nigeria, open, fiber w/cowrie shells, 8x10" **125.00**
Beads, trade, ceramic, string of 20..**100.00**
Bracelet, Ashanti, bronze, knobs..**30.00**
Cloth, Kuba, geometric design, 18" sq **175.00**
Comb, Ashanti, bird's head surmount, 4" **200.00**
Container, Luba, gourd, wooden figural stopper **60.00**
Container, Warega, ivory tusk, 15"...**500.00**
Divination board, Yoruba, animals, 20" dia **475.00**
Doll, Ewe, pnt figure, 5" **175.00**
Doll, Mossi, abstract human figure...**275.00**
Door, Dogan, granary, human figures, 26" **1500.00**
Drum, Hemba, geometric designs, 22" **275.00**
Earrings, Masai, beaded, 6"..**275.00**
Figure, Baule, standing female, 14" **250.00**
Figure, Dogon, crouched male, 10" **650.00**
Figure, Yoruba, pnt Colonial, 12" **175.00**
Goldweight, Ashanti, bronze turtle..**125.00**
Hat, Kuba, fiber, blk pnt..**175.00**
Headdress, Bamana, Tchi-wara (antelope), horizontal................**475.00**
Headrest, Luba, supporting human figure, 5"...........................**375.00**
Heddle pulley, Senufo, bird surmount, 5" **375.00**
Ibejis, Yoruba, 9", pr..**375.00**
Knife, Kuba throwing, str blade, 14" **125.00**
Lock, Bamana, door, 2 figural surmounts, 14" **575.00**
Mask, Bamana, N'Tomo, 14"..**275.00**
Mask, Dan, human face, 15"..**375.00**
Mask, Dogon, Kanaga, 26"..**800.00**
Mask, Karumba, polychrome, antelope, 21" **475.00**
Mask, Mende, helmet, female initiation, 12".............................**675.00**
Mask, Pende, human face, 8"..**275.00**
Pendant, Yoruba, ivory human figure, 4" **800.00**
Pipe, Cameroons, elephant, brass, 14" **275.00**
Ring, Dogon, bronze, horse & rider **275.00**
Slingshot, Baule, animal head, 5"...**85.00**
Stool, Lega, human figural supports, 13".................................**475.00**
Whisk, Yoruba, human figure, wood & horsehair, 12" **275.00**

Agata

Agata is New England peachblow (the factory called it 'Wild Rose') with an applied metallic stain which produces gold tracery and dark blue mottling. The stain is subject to wear, and the amount of remaining stain greatly affects the value. It is especially valuable (and rare) when found on peachblow of intense color. Caution! Be sure to use only gentle cleaning methods.

Currently rare types of art glass have been realizing erratic prices at auction; until they stablize, we can only suggest an average range of values. In the listings that follow, examples are glossy unless noted otherwise. A condition rating of 'EX' indicates that the stain shows a slight amount of wear. Our advisors for this category are Betty and Clarence Maier; they are listed in the Directory under Pennsylvania. See also Green Opaque.

Bowl, finger; shiny, EX gold & mottling, 2½x5¼" **675.00**
Celery vase, scalloped, VG mottling, 6½" **975.00**
Celery vase, sqd/scalloped rim, M mottling, 6½" **1,950.00**
Creamer, sq rim, mottled reed hdl, M mottling **1,800.00**
Cruet, NM mottling **2,000.00**

Pitcher, reeded handle, 7½", $3,000.00, M mottling.

Pitcher, sq rim, sparce mottling, 6¼" **725.00**
Pitcher, sq rim, tapered, M mottling, 6" **2,750.00**
Punch cup, NM mottling **500.00**
Spooner, EX mottling, sq top, 4½" **865.00**
Toothpick holder, sqd rim, EX color & mottling, 2¼" **1,000.00**
Toothpick holder, tricorner, worn mottling, 2½" **525.00**
Tumbler, EX color & mottling, 3¾" **1,000.00**
Vase, lily; EX color & mottling **950.00**
Vase, satin, M blk tracery, waisted, 10" **1,450.00**
Vase, scalloped top, EX color & mottling, 5x6" **2,900.00**
Vase, scalloped top, M mottling, 6½x3½" **1,200.00**

Akro Agate

The Akro Agate Co., founded in 1914 primarily as a marble maker, operated in Clarksburg, West Virginia, until 1951. Their popular wares included children's dishes, powder jars, flowerpots, and novelty items along with the famous 'Akro Aggies.' Much of their glass was produced in the distinctive marbleized colors they called Red Onyx, Blue Onyx, etc.; solid opaque and transparent colors were also produced. Most of the wares are marked with their trademark, a crow flying through the letter 'A' holding an Aggie in its beak and one in each claw. Other marks include 'J.P.' on children's pieces, 'J.V. Co., Inc.,' 'Braun & Corwin,' 'N.Y.C. Vogue Merc Co. U.S.A.,' 'Hamilton Match Co.,' and 'Mexicali Pickwick Cosmetic Corp.' on novelty items. In 1936 Akro obtained the molds from the Balmer-Westite Co. of Weston, West Virginia. Westite produced a similar line of products for several years. Their ware is drab in color when compared to Akro and is generally unmarked. The embossed Westite logo does appear occasionally on the bottoms of some pieces. Westite is commonly accepted as a companion collectible of Akro.

For more information we recommend *The Collector's Encyclopedia of Children's Dishes* by Margaret and Kenn Whitmyer, available at your local bookstore. Our advisor for miscellaneous Akro Agate is Albert Morin; he is listed in the Directory under Massachusetts.

Chiquita

Chiquita, 12-piece set, cobalt transparent, MIB, $100.00.

Creamer, baked-on color, 1½"	8.00
Cup, cobalt transparent, 1½"	8.00
Plate, gr opaque, 3¾"	3.00
Saucer, opaque color other than gr, 3⅛"	5.00
Set, baked-on color, 16-pc, MIB	84.00
Set, gr opaque, 16-pc, MIB	58.00
Set, gr opaque, 22-pc, MIB	78.00
Set, opaque color other than gr, 12-pc, MIB	150.00
Sugar bowl, cobalt, 1½"	16.00
Teapot, baked-on color, w/lid, 3"	22.00

Concentric Rib

Creamer, sm, opaque colors other than gr or wht, 1¼"	16.00
Cup, sm, gr or wht opaque, 1¼"	5.00
Plate, sm, opaque colors other than gr or wht, 3¼"	7.00
Set, sm, gr or wht opaque, 8-pc, MIB	33.00
Sugar bowl, sm, opaque gr or wht, 1¼"	10.00
Teapot, opaque colors other than gr or wht, w/lid, 3⅜"	18.00

Concentric Ring

Cereal, lg, cobalt, 3⅜"	35.00
Creamer, sm, bl marbleized, 1¼"	40.00
Cup, lg, bl marbleized, 1⅜"	40.00
Cup, sm, solid opaque color, 1¼"	10.00
Plate, lg, solid opaque color, 4¼"	7.00
Plate, sm, cobalt, 3¼"	20.00
Saucer, lg, cobalt, 3⅛"	10.00
Set, lg, cobalt, 21-pc, MIB	560.00
Set, sm, solid opaque color, 16-pc, MIB	160.00
Sugar bowl, sm, bl marbleized, 1¼"	40.00
Teapot, lg, bl marbleized, w/lid, 3¾"	125.00

Interior Panel, Stippled Interior Panel

Cereal, lg, pk or gr lustre, 3⅜"	25.00
Cereal, lg, red & wht marbleized, 3⅜"	37.00
Creamer, lg, lemonade & oxblood, 1⅜"	40.00
Creamer, sm, pk lustre, 1¼"	27.00
Cup, lg, azure bl or yel opaque, 1⅜"	35.00
Cup, lg, gr & wht marbleized, 1⅜"	25.00
Cup, sm, red & wht marbleized, 1¼"	27.00
Pitcher, sm, gr, topaz or gr lustre, 2⅞"	14.00
Plate, lg, gr, 4¼"	6.00
Plate, lg, pk or gr lustre, 4¼"	9.00
Plate, sm, azure bl or yel, 3¾"	10.00
Saucer, lg, bl & wht marbleized, 3⅛"	10.00
Saucer, sm, gr & wht marbleized, 2⅜"	6.00
Set, lg, azure bl or yel opaque, 21-pc, MIB	475.00
Set, lg, lemonade & oxblood, 21-pc, MIB	500.00
Set, sm, azure bl or yel, 16-pc, MIB	300.00
Set, sm, red & wht marbleized, 8-pc, MIB	148.00
Sugar bowl, lg, pk or gr lustre, w/lid, 1⅞"	35.00
Sugar bowl, lg, topaz, w/lid, 1⅞"	27.00
Sugar bowl, sm, pk lustre, 1¼"	27.00
Teapot, lg, red & wht marbleized, w/lid, 3¾"	145.00
Teapot, sm, bl & wht marbleized, w/lid, 3⅜"	50.00
Tumbler, sm, gr lustre, 2"	55.00

J.P. (Made for J. Pressman Company)

Cereal, lg, baked-on colors	11.00
Creamer, lg, gr transparent, 1½"	45.00
Creamer, lt bl or crystal, 1½"	32.50
Cup, lg, cobalt w/ribs, 1½"	10.00
Plate, lt bl or crystal, 4¼"	10.00
Saucer, lg, baked-on colors, 3¼"	1.50
Set, lg, baked-on colors, 21-pc, MIB	150.00
Set, lg, lt bl or crystal, 17-pc, MIB	245.00
Sugar bowl, lg, red or brn transparent, w/lid, 1½"	65.00
Teapot, lg, baked-on colors, w/lid, 2¾"	22.00
Teapot, lg, gr transparent, w/lid, 2¾"	70.00

Miss America

Creamer, wht, 1¼"	60.00
Cup, orange & wht, 1⅝"	65.00
Cup, wht w/decal, 1⅝"	50.00
Plate, forest gr, 4½"	45.00
Plate, wht, 4½"	25.00
Set, forest gr, 17-pc, MIB	650.00
Set, wht, 17-pc, MIB	515.00
Sugar bowl, wht, w/lid, 2"	85.00
Teapot, forest gr, w/lid, 3¼"	150.00
Teapot, orange & wht, w/lid, 3¼"	95.00

Octagonal

Octagonal, small: Cup, pumpkin, $25.00; Saucer, yellow, $4.00; Plate, green, $5.00.

Cereal, lg, gr, wht or dk bl, 3⅜" 10.00
Cereal, lg, lemonade & oxblood, 3⅜" 27.00
Creamer, lg, pk, yel or other opaques, closed hdl, 1½" 10.00
Creamer, sm, dk gr, bl or wht, 1¼" 16.00
Cup, lg, beige, pumpkin or lt bl, closed hdl, 1½" 15.00
Pitcher, sm, dk gr, bl or wht, 2¾" 18.00
Plate, lg, pk, yel or other opaques, 4¼" 6.50
Saucer, lg, gr, wht or dk bl, 3⅜" 3.00
Saucer, sm, pumpkin, yel or lime gr, 2¾" 3.50
Set, lg, gr, wht, or dk bl, 21-pc, MIB 140.00
Set, lg, pk, yel or other opaques, 17-pc, MIB 130.00
Set, sm, dk gr, bl or wht, 21-pc, MIB 200.00
Sugar bowl, lg, lemonade & oxblood, closed hdl, w/lid, 1½" 50.00
Teapot, lg, beige, pumpkin or lt bl, w/lid, closed hdl, 3⅝" 30.00
Tumbler, sm, dk gr, bl or wht, 2" 12.00

Raised Daisy

Creamer, sm, yel, 1¾" 50.00
Cup, sm, bl, 1¾" 45.00
Plate, sm, bl, 3" 14.00
Saucer, sm, beige, 2½" 9.00
Sugar bowl, sm, yel, 1¾" 50.00
Teapot, sm, gr, 2⅜" 35.00
Teapot, sm, yel, 2⅜" 45.00
Tumbler, sm, beige, 2" 35.00
Tumbler, sm, bl, 2" 60.00

Stacked Disc

Creamer, sm, any opaque color other than gr or wht, 1¼" 14.00
Cup, sm, gr or wht, 1¼" 6.00
Pitcher, sm, any opaque color other than gr or wht, 2⅞" 16.00
Plate, sm, gr or wht, 3¼" 3.00
Saucer, sm, any other opaque color than gr or wht, 2¾" 4.00
Set, sm, gr or wht, 21-pc, MIB 130.00
Sugar bowl, sm, gr or wht, 1¼" 10.00
Teapot, sm, any opaque color other than gr or wht, w/lid, 3⅜" 16.00
Tumbler, sm, gr or wht, 2" 8.50

Stacked Disc and Interior Panel

Stacked Disc, small: Teapot,
cobalt with custard lid, 3⅜",
$32.50.

Cereal, lg, solid opaque color, 3⅜" 25.00
Creamer, lg, bl marbleized, 1⅜" 45.00
Creamer, lg, gr, 1⅜" 27.00
Creamer, sm, solid opaque color, 1¼" 18.00
Cup, lg, bl marbleized, 1⅜" 40.00
Cup, lg, solid opaque color, 1⅜" 22.00
Cup, sm, bl marbleized, 1¼" 37.00
Pitcher, sm, gr, 2⅞" 18.00
Plate, lg, cobalt, 4¾" 15.00

Plate, lg, gr, 4¾" 12.00
Plate, sm, cobalt, 3¼" 14.00
Saucer, lg, cobalt, 3¼" 10.00
Saucer, lg, solid opaque color, 3¼" 6.00
Saucer, sm, solid opaque color, 2¾" 5.00
Set, lg, bl marbleized, 21-pc, MIB 685.00
Set, lg, gr, 21-pc, MIB 370.00
Set, sm, bl marbleized, 8-pc, MIB 275.00
Set, sm, solid opaque color, 16-pc, MIB 220.00
Sugar bowl, lg, bl marbleized, w/lid, 1⅞" 60.00
Sugar bowl, lg, gr, w/lid, 1⅞" 40.00
Sugar bowl, sm, bl marbleized, 1¼" 45.00
Teapot, lg, cobalt, w/lid, 3¾" 75.00
Teapot, lg, solid opaque color, w/lid, 3¾" 50.00
Teapot, sm, gr, w/lid, 3⅜" 35.00
Tumbler, sm, cobalt, 2" 18.00
Water set, sm, gr, 7-pc, MIB 100.00

Stippled Band

Creamer, lg, amber, 1¼" 22.00
Creamer, sm, gr, 1¼" 30.00
Cup, lg, gr, 1½" 8.00
Cup, sm, amber, 1¼" 8.00
Pitcher, sm, gr, 2⅞" 15.00
Plate, lg, azure, 4¼" 16.00
Plate, sm, amber, 3¼" 6.00
Saucer, lg, gr, 3¼" 2.50
Set, lg, azure, 17-pc, MIB 360.00
Set, sm, amber, 16-pc, MIB 145.00
Set, sm, gr, 28-pc, MIB 175.00
Set, sm, gr, 7-pc, MIB 70.00
Sugar bowl, lg, amber, w/lid, 1⅞" 30.00
Sugar bowl, sm, amber, 1¼" 30.00
Teapot, lg, gr, w/lid, 3¾" 40.00
Teapot, sm, gr, w/lid, 3⅜" 20.00
Tumbler, sm, amber, 1¾" 11.00

Miscellaneous

Ashtray, gr, Hotel Lincoln, w/matchbook holder 65.00
Ashtray, gr/wht, hexagonal, 4½" 28.00
Ashtray, Gypsy Smoker Set, MIB 125.00
Ashtray, orange, Hotel Edison 75.00
Ashtray, oxblood/wht, 3" sq 18.00
Ashtray, Texas Centennial, 1936, rare 750.00
Basket, gr/wht, 1-hdl 325.00
Basket, orange/wht, 2-hdl 40.00
Bell, gr 350.00
Bell, wht 50.00
Bowl, Dart, orange/wht, #340 ....30.00
Bowl, fruit; cobalt, ftd 350.00
Bowl, Graduated Dart, ice bl transparent, #320 ....350.00
Bowl, Stacked Disc, bl/wht, no ft 95.00
Candlesticks, crystal, lamp parts, pr 25.00
Candlesticks, gr, 3¼", pr 200.00
Candlesticks, ivory, lamp parts, pr 40.00
Candlesticks, orange/wht, 3¼", pr 250.00
Cornucopia, crystal, Vogue Merc NYC 50.00
Cornucopia, gr/wht, #765 ....12.00
Cornucopia, Niagara Falls 35.00
Creamer & sugar bowl, mk w/crow trademk, rare, 3", ea 300.00
Flowerpot, Banded Dart, orange, #300 ....40.00
Flowerpot, gr, #1309 ....165.00

Flowerpot, Graduated Dart, gr/wht, scalloped top, #307 ....**45.00**
Flowerpot, Ribbed Top, blk, #294 ....**75.00**
Flowerpot, Ribs & Flutes, gr, #296 ....**15.00**
Flowerpot, Ribs & Flutes, yel, #305 ....**28.00**
Flowerpot, Thumbpots, marbleized, #290 ....**28.00**
Flowerpot stand, gr/wht, #740 ....**100.00**
J Vivaudou, apothecary jar, pk, #329 ....**95.00**
J Vivaudou, mortar & pestle jar, wht, #331 ....**12.00**
J Vivaudou, shaving mug, beige, rare **200.00**
Jardiniere, Graduated Dart, orange/wht, scalloped rim, #306 ....**50.00**
Jardiniere, Graduated Dart, yel, narrow ledge, #314 ....**38.00**
Jardiniere, Ribs & Flutes, bl, #306CF **45.00**
Knife, crystal, grid style, #739 ....**45.00**
Knife, forest gr transparent, grid style, #739 ....**300.00**
Lamp, crystal, 5-pc **45.00**
Lamp, ivory, 3-pc **28.00**
Lamp shade, marbleized **165.00**
Marble box, Akro Chinese Checkers **35.00**
Marble box, Akro Solitary Checkers **50.00**
Marble box, 100 #0 Hero marbles **350.00**
Marble box, 100 #00 glassies **150.00**
Marble box, 100 #1 moss agates **500.00**
Milk bottle cover, wht, mk w/Crow trademk, rare **650.00**
Mirror/brush hdls, crystal, many designs, ea **38.00**
Pitcher, milk; bl, X-14, rare **800.00**

Photo courtesy
Albert Morin

Lily planter, #657, with period floral arrangement, $28.00.

Planter, bl, rectangular, #653 ....**35.00**
Planter, gr/wht, #658, 5¼" lily **12.00**
Planter, orange/wht, oval, #654 ....**12.00**
Powder jar, apple form, ivory **400.00**
Powder jar, Colonial lady figural, pk **80.00**
Powder jar, Mexicali, bl/wht **45.00**
Powder jar, sawtooth, crystal **75.00**
Powder jar, Scottie dog figural, gr **250.00**
Tire ashtray, marbleized, Goodrich **50.00**
Tire ashtray, marbleized, US Rubber **95.00**
Urn, floral, NYC Vogue Merc, bl **18.00**
Urn, Grecian, Niagara Falls, #764 ....**35.00**
Vase, Graduated Dart, dk gr, #316 ....**150.00**
Vase, Ribs & Flutes, orange/wht, #311 ....**250.00**
Westite, ashtray, bl, hexagonal **28.00**
Westite, cigar ashtray, NASM **75.00**
Westite, flowerpot, gr, #301 ....**40.00**

Alexandrite

Alexandrite is a type of art glass introduced around the turn of the century by Thomas Webb and Sons of England. It is recognized by its characteristic shading, pale yellow to rose and blue at the edge of the item. Although other companies produced glass they called alexandrite, only examples made by Webb possess all the described characteristics and command premium prices. Amount and intensity of blue determines value. Our advisors for this category are Betty and Clarence Maier; they are listed in the Directory under Pennsylvania.

Compote, mint; Honeycomb, canary yel wafer stem/ft, 1¾x5" ..**1,400.00**
Stem, wine; wafer base, faint vertical ribs, 4½x2½" **1,650.00**
Toothpick holder, crimped rim, 2x2¾", w/5" underplate **2,975.00**
Toothpick holder, Peacock Feathers, ruffled rim, 2" **1,400.00**

Almanacs

The earliest evidence indicates that almanacs were used as long ago as ancient Egypt. Throughout the Dark Ages they were circulated in great volume and were referred to by more people than any other book except the Bible. *The Old Farmer's Almanac* first appeared in 1793 and has been issued annually since that time. Usually more of a pamphlet than a book (only a few have hard covers), the almanac provided planting and harvesting information to farmers, weather forecasts for seamen, medical advice, household hints, mathematical tutoring, postal rates, railroad schedules, weights and measures, 'receipts,' and jokes. Before 1800 the information was unscientific and based entirely on astrology and folklore. The first almanac in America was printed in 1639 by William Pierce Mariner; it contained data of this nature. One of the best-known editions, Ben Franklin's *Poor Richard's Almanac*, was introduced in 1732 and continued to be printed for twenty-five years.

By the 19th century, merchants saw the advertising potential in a publication so widely distributed, and the advertising almanac evolved. These were distributed free of charge by drug stores and mercantiles and were usually somewhat lacking in information, containing simply a calendar, a few jokes, and a variety of ads for quick remedies and quack cures.

Today their concept and informative, often amusing, text make almanacs popular collectibles that may usually be had at reasonable prices. Because they were printed in such large numbers and often saved from year to year, their prices are still low. Most fall within a range of $4.00 to $15.00. Very common examples may be virtually worthless; those printed before 1860 are especially collectible. Quite rare and highly prized are the Kate Greenaway 'Almanacks,' printed in London from 1883 to 1897. These are illustrated with her drawings of children, one for each calendar month.

1808, Middlebrook's, printed on laid paper, twine ties **10.00**
1840, Freeman's...for the Year..., Dwelle, Cincinnati **10.00**
1849, Moral, Phila, G **5.00**
1855, Farmer's, wear **17.50**
1858, Wright's Pictorial Family, many illus/cartoons, 26-pg, EX **6.50**
1867, Rush's, health guide, bl illus wraps, 32-pg, NM **21.00**
1881, Rush's, mc wraps, many illus, 34-pg, EX **10.00**
1881, Simons Liver Regulator, EX **25.00**
1885, NY State, mc illus, orig wraps, 31-pg, EX **6.50**
1886, Merchant's Gargling Oil, EX **18.00**
1888, NY Medical, mc illus, 32-pg, NM **9.50**
1897, The Household, NM **14.00**
1905, Reverend R Hicks, many illus, 192-pg, NM **10.00**
1909, Abe Martin..., hardbound, EX **30.00**
1916, Armour's Maid on the Farm, EX **16.00**
1958, Herbalist, EX **9.50**

Aluminum

Aluminum, though being the most abundant metal in the earth's crust, always occurs in combination with other elements. Before a practical method for its refinement was developed in the late 19th century, articles made of aluminum were very expensive. After the process for commercial smelting was perfected in 1916, it became profitable to adapt the ductile, non-tarnishing material to many uses.

By the late '30s, novelties, trays, pitchers, and many other tableware items were being produced. They were often handcrafted with elaborate decoration. Russel Wright designed a line of lovely pieces such as lamps, vases, and desk accessories that are becoming very collectible. Many who crafted the ware marked it with their company logo, and these signed pieces are attracting the most interest. Wendell August Forge (Grove City, Pennsylvania) is a mark to watch for; this firm produced some particularly nice examples and upwardly mobile market values reflect their popularity with today's collectors. In general, 'spun' aluminum is from the '30s or early '40s, and 'hammered' aluminum is from the '50s.

For further information, refer to *Hammered Aluminum, Hand Wrought Collectibles*, Dannie Woodard (listed in the Directory under Clubs and Newsletters), and *Collectible Aluminum, An Identification and Value Guide* (Collector Books, 1997 updated values), by Everett Grist.

Purse, embossed mums on rectangular form, 8½" long, $50.00.

Basket, angelfish among plant on hammered ground, 7x12" **40.00**
Basket, emb roses in 2 panels on 2 sides, floral hdl, 4x9x5" **10.00**
Basket, hammered, beaded rim, twist hdl, Buenilum, 5x9" **20.00**
Bowl, chrysanthemums, fluted rim, Continental, 1x5½" **12.00**
Bowl, fruit; fruit & flowers, knives held in center, unmk, 4x11" ...**25.00**
Bowl, hammered, serrated rim, 3-loop hdls, Buenilum, 2x12" **10.00**
Bowl, pine cones & needles, serrated rim, Everlast, 2x10" **15.00**
Bowl, spun, no decor, flared rim, 3½x11" **12.50**
Bowl, vintage on hammered background, rolled rim, 2x14¼" **15.00**
Bowl, wild roses/geometrics, scalloped rim, Continental, 3x11" ...**35.00**
Buffet cart, hammered, tooled florals, Everlast, 42" L **1,045.00**
Candelabrum, hammered, 3-socket, unmk, 21" **50.00**
Candy dish, fruit & flowers, coiled hdl, 3-compartment, 9" **15.00**
Candy dish, fruit & flowers, 2 joined bowls, center hdl, 13" L **25.00**
Casserole, pea vines, pea pod finial, Everlast, 4x7" **20.00**
Casserole, tomatoes, flower finial, Everlast, 5x9" **20.00**
Casserole holder, wheat & vegetables, 4-ftd, w/lid, unmk, 6x8" ...**25.00**
Compote, wild roses, Continental, 5x5" **20.00**
Creamer & sugar bowl w/lid & tray, dbl-loop hdls, Buenilum **35.00**
Ice bucket, dogwood decor, August Wendell Forge **125.00**
Ice bucket, hammered, beaded lip, twisted hdl, Buenilum, 6x5" ...**25.00**

Ice bucket, tulips, flat ribbon decor lid, unmk, 7x8" **40.00**
Ice bucket, Wendell August Forge **125.00**
Lamp, hurricane; twisted center hdl, 2-socket, Buenilum, 10x9" ..**30.00**
Lazy susan, fruit & flowers, serrated edge, Cromwell, 16" **10.00**
Lazy susan, Rodney Kent, 18" dia **20.00**
Mug, hammered, rolled lip, ear hdl, copper color, unmk, 3" **1.00**
Parfait set, 1950s, 8-pc, MIB **65.00**
Pitcher, hammered, ice lip, ear hdl, Everlast, 8x6" **20.00**
Pitcher, tulips, ice lip, Rodney Kent, 9x5" **35.00**
Plaque, butterflies, scalloped rim, unmk, 10" **3.00**
Platter, well & tree; tulips & scrolls, 4-leg, unmk, 18x13" **15.00**
Shakers & toothpick holder on triangular base w/center hdl, unmk ..**15.00**
Silent butler, berries, Everlast, 6" **20.00**
Silent butler, fruit, Everlast **30.00**
Silent butler, wild roses, Continental, 8" **30.00**
Snack server, Ferris-wheel type, bamboo pattern, glass inserts **65.00**
Syrup, hammered, blk plastic hdl, Stratford-On-Avon, 6x4" **15.00**
Tray, bar; tulips, Rodney Kent **40.00**
Tray, bread; chrysanthemums, scrolled rim, Forman, 12x7" **15.00**
Tray, bread; grapes, unmk, 12x6" **10.00**
Tray, crumb; tulips, Rodney Kent, w/brush **45.00**
Tray, dogwood & leaves, ftd, low, Wendell August, #810, 12x6½" ..**45.00**
Tray, floral, hammered, ball ft, Everlast, M **65.00**
Tray, fruit band, oblong, Cromwell, 19x13" **22.00**
Tray, larkspur, Wendell August Forge, 20x13" **75.00**
Tray, leaping gazelles on hammered ground, unmk, 15" **25.00**
Tray, sandwich; Oriental scene, unmk, 11" dia **10.00**
Tray, tulips, Rodney Kent, 14x20" **38.00**
Tray, 4 flying ducks on hammered ground, Everlast, 12x10" **25.00**
Wastebasket, emb floral, Everlast, 11x11" dia **60.00**

AMACO, American Art Clay Co.

AMACO is the logo of the American Art Clay Co. Inc., founded in Indianapolis, Indiana, in 1919, by Ted O. Philpot. They produced a line of art pottery from 1931 through 1938. The company is still in business but now produces only supplies, implements, and tools for the ceramic trade.

Values for AMACO have risen sharply, especially those for figurals, items with Art Deco styling, and pieces with uncommon shapes. Our advisor for this category is Virginia Heiss; she is listed in the Directory under Indiana.

Ewer, gold spray/rose, #70, 10½" **185.00**
Figurine, geisha girl, kneeling, wht, #199, 6½" **125.00**
Figurine, mountain goat, wht gloss, ink stamp, 6¾" **135.00**
Temple jar, bl gloss, #131, w/lid, 9" **135.00**
Vase, baluster, Deco style, blended gr, rose & bl, #68, 6¾" **185.00**
Vase, cobalt gloss, urn shape w/hdls, early mk, #10, 8" **195.00**
Vase, dk bl matt, hdls, #2, 4½" **40.00**
Vase, dk red gloss, Deco w/hdls, #1, 8½" **125.00**
Vase, wht gloss, #129, 9" **150.00**
Vase, yel gloss, #S-5, 4½" **35.00**

Amberina

Amberina, one of the earliest types of art glass, was developed in 1883 by Joseph Locke of the New England Glass Company. The trademark was registered by W.L. Libbey, who often signed his name in script within the pontil.

Amberina was made by adding gold powder to the batch, which produced glass in the basic amber hue. Part of the item, usually the top, was simply reheated to develop the characteristic deep red or fuchsia shading. Early amberina was mold-blown, but cut and pressed amberina was also produced. The rarest type is plated amberina, made by New England for a short time after 1886. It has been estimated that less than 2,000 pieces were ever produced. Other companies, among them Hobbs and Brockunier, Mt. Washington Glass Company, and Sowerby's Ellison Glassworks of England, made their own versions, being careful to change the name of their product to avoid infringing on Libbey's patent. Prices realized at auction seem to be erratic, to say the least, and dealers appear to be 'testing the waters' with prices that start out very high only to be reduced later if the item does not sell at the original asking price. Lots of amberina glassware is of a more recent vintage — look for evidence of an early production, since the later wares are worth much less than glassware that can be attributed to the older makers. Generic amberina with hand-painted flowers will bring lower prices as well. Our values are taken from auction results and dealer lists, omitting the extremely high and low ends of the range. Our advisor is Debby Maggard; she is listed in the Directory under Ohio. See also Libbey.

Basket, amber wishbone decor, rare loop hdl, NE Glass, 7x5½" ..1,100.00
Basket, Swirl, egg form w/invt wishbone hdl, 12½x5" 400.00
Basket, Swirl w/gold roses & fence, amber rigaree hdl, 15x10" ...450.00
Basket vase, mc florals, amber hdl & ft, 9x4" 425.00
Bowl, centerpc; Daisy & Button, boat form, Hobbs & Brockunier, 14" ..950.00
Bowl, Daisy & Button, Hobbs, 2⅛x7⅛" sq 575.00
Bowl, Hobnail, sq, 3x4" 60.00
Bowl, oblong, Mt WA, 1½x5x4½" 425.00
Bowl, ruffled rim, NE Glass, 3x5½" 375.00
Bowl, sauce; Daisy & Button, sq ruffled rim, 1⅝x5" 125.00
Bowl, Swirl, bl swirl bands, Mt WA, 2¾x4½" 295.00
Bowl, Venetian Dmn, tricorner, 2¼x4½" 325.00
Cracker jar, Invt T'print, amber knob finial, Hobbs, 8x5¾" 825.00
Cruet, Invt T'print, amber stopper & hdl, 5½" 500.00
Cruet, Invt T'print, clear hdl/stopper, 6¾" 275.00
Cruet, Invt T'print, trifold rim, NE Glass, 6¾" 850.00
Cruet, purple opal collar, tricorn spout, amber hdl, 7" 3,000.00
Cruet, Swirl, amber faceted stopper, NE Glass, 6" 535.00
Cruet, Swirl, amber hdl & bubble stopper, 8⅝x4¼" 225.00
Cup, custard; Dmn Quilt, amber reeded hdl, 2¾x2⅝" 175.00
Cup, punch; Dmn Quilt, amber reeded hdl, 2½x3½" 75.00
Cup, punch; Honeycomb, reeded hdl, eng name in script 95.00
Finger bowl, Hobnail, 2⅞x4¼" sq 85.00
Finger bowl, ruffled rim, 2¾x6" 125.00
Goblet, water; internal ribs, 6⅛x3⅜" 300.00
Mug, amber spun rope hdl, 2⅝x2⅞" 55.00
Mug, Swirl, bbl shape, wafer ft, amber rope hdl, 4¾x2⅝" 65.00
Mug, Swirl, florals, appl amber rope hdl, 5½x2½" 165.00
Mug, Swirl, pnt decor, amber smooth hdl, 3¾x3" 150.00
Nut dish, Daisy & Button, Gillinder, 1¾x6⅛x4¼" 375.00
Pitcher, Daisy & Button, Hobbs, 5" 425.00
Pitcher, Dmn Optic, ruffled rim, clear reeded hdl, 7¼" 295.00
Pitcher, Invt Bull's Eye, sq rim, amber reeded hdl, 7½" 300.00
Pitcher, Invt T'print, bulbous, amber reeded hdl, 8½x6" 300.00
Pitcher, Invt T'print, dimpled sides, amber hdl, 5¾x4½" 175.00
Pitcher, Invt T'print, ruffled rim, amber loop hdl, 6¾x4" 150.00
Pitcher, tankard; amber smooth hdl, 4⅝x3" 425.00
Pitcher, tankard; 10-panel, amber reeded hdl, 6¾" 645.00
Salt yacht, Daisy & Button, Hobbs Brockunier & Co, 2x4½x2" 300.00
Sauce boat, Daisy & Button, scalloped, Hobbs & Brockunier, 6" L ..150.00
Shade, Dmn Quilt, 2" opening, 4¼x5" 575.00
Shaker, Baby T'print, bulbous, mold blown, 2-pc lid, 2½" 235.00
Shaker, Dmn Quilt, orig metal lid 225.00
Shaker, Invt T'print, 2-pc lid, NE Glass, 4" 195.00
Shakers, ribbed, 3¾", pr 350.00

Spooner, Dmn T'print, petticoat shape, Mt WA, 4" 850.00
Toothpick holder, Invt Baby T'print, NE Glass, 1½x2¼" 295.00
Toothpick holder, Invt Baby T'print, sq top, NE Glass, 2¼" 295.00
Toothpick holder, Invt T'print, tricorner 275.00
Toothpick holder, Invt T'print, waisted, flared rim 295.00
Toothpick holder, Venetian Dmn, tricorner, NE Glass, 2¼x3" .450.00
Tray, ice cream; Daisy & Button, 5½" dia 85.00
Tumbler, amber reeded hdl, 3¾x2½" 400.00
Tumbler, bulge at base, 4⅞x2¾" 45.00
Tumbler, Dmn Quilt, NE Glass, 3¾" 175.00
Tumbler, gold scrolls & fans, 3⅞x2¼" 65.00
Tumbler, Invt Baby T'print, sq rim, 4" 105.00
Tumbler, Swirl, 3⅞x2⅝" 150.00
Tumbler, Venetian Dmn, NE Glass or Mt WA, 4" 135.00
Vase, Dmn Quilt, reversed color, clear ft, 3¾x2¼" 75.00
Vase, florals, serpentine amber trim at base, crimped rim, 12" 350.00
Vase, HP florals, cylindrical, ground pontil, 6⅞x3⅞" 195.00
Vase, Invt T'print, bulbous, short neck, 4x3" 395.00
Vase, Invt T'print, sq rim, dbl reeded hdls, 4¼" 400.00
Vase, Invt T'print, 3x2¼" 350.00
Vase, jack-in-pulpit; Invt T'print, amber ruffled rim, 13½" 325.00
Vase, lily; faint vertical ribs, NE Glass, 15½x6" 975.00
Vase, lily; NE Glass, 8" 650.00
Vase, lily; trifold rim, NE Glass, 10x4" 700.00
Vase, mc floral w/gold, amber ft, crimped rim, 12⅜x3⅝" 350.00
Vase, ribbed stem, flared rim w/pie-crust edge, amber ft, 7" 250.00

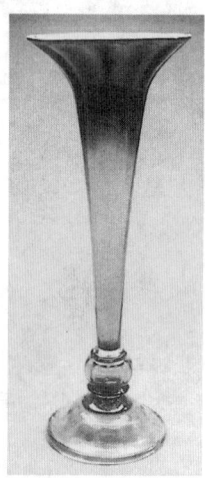

Vase, ribbed trumpet on bulb stem, pedestal foot, 23¾", $900.00.

Vase, trumpet form, fold-over appl amber rim, 20" 950.00
Whiskey taster, Baby Dmn Quilt, 2¾" 200.00

Plated Amberina

Cruet 8,500.00
Mug, amber hdl 2,300.00
Pitcher, bulbous w/tricorn rim, dk amber hdl, 6¼" 10,000.00
Pitcher, tankard, amber hdl, 7" 12,000.00
Plate, ruffled, 6⅜" 1,300.00
Tumbler, 4", M 2,450.00
Vase, lav to red to yel, NE Glass, 3½" 3,200.00
Vase, lily; slight swirl at 3-fold rim, 9½" 5,000.00

American Bisque

The American Bisque Pottery operated in Williamstown, West Virginia, from 1919 to 1982. The company was begun by Mr. B.E.

Allen and remained an Allen-family business until its sale in 1982. Figural pottery was produced from approximately 1937 until about the time the pottery sold.

American Bisque pottery is often identified by the 'wedges' or dry-footed cleats on the bottom of the ware. Many cookie jar designs are unique to the American Bisque Company, such as cookie jars with blackboards and magnets, cookie jars with lids that doubled as serving trays, and cookie jars with 'action pieces' which show movement. American Bisque pieces are very collectible and are available in a broad variety of color schemes; some items are decorated with 22 – 24k gold. Many items are modeled after highly popular copyrighted characters.

For further information, we recommend *American Bisque, Collector's Guide With Prices*, by our advisor Mary Jane Giacomini; she is listed in the Directory under California.

Ashtray, free-form triangle, Marietta Modern line, #715-A 20.00
Ashtray, shaped like state of OH 20.00
Bank, Attitude Pig Baby, unmk, 7" 65.00
Bank, Boy/Girl Turnabout, factory-fused lid, unmk, 9" 175.00
Bank, Chicken Feed, hen beside lg sack, unmk, 4½" 25.00
Bank, For Your Rainy Day, pig beside bank, unmk, 6¼x7½" 75.00
Bank, Humpty Dumpty, mk Alice in Philcoland, 6" 120.00
Bank, Little Audrey, holds lollipop, unmk, 8¼" 775.00
Bank, Mr Pig, unmk, 6" 35.00
Cookie jar, Blackboard Girl, Musn't Forget, 13" (+)..............350.00

Cookie jar, Boy Lamb, sitting, marked USA, 13", $165.00.

Photo courtesy Mary Jane Giacomini

Cookie jar, Cookie Barrel, wood grain, mk USA, 9½" 30.00
Cookie jar, Daisy Cylinder, mk USA, 9½" 40.00
Cookie jar, Liberty Bell, USA, 9¾" 125.00
Cookie jar, Pig in a Poke, mk USA, 12½" 85.00
Cookie jar, Puppy in Pot, Cookies on base, mk USA, 11½" 70.00
Cookie jar, Rabbit & Log (Tortoise & Hare), #803 USA, 9¾" ..775.00
Cookie jar, Rooster, airbrushed, 10¾" 85.00
Cookie jar, Sack of Cookies, mk USA, 10" 45.00
Cookie jar, Sad Clown, I Want Some Cookies, mk Cardinal, 9½" ..140.00
Cookie jar, Strawberry, Sears...Pending, 8¾" 35.00
Cookie jar, Sweet Pea, 8¼x6½" 2,500.00
Cookie jar, Tall Train, mk USA, 12" 200.00
Head vase, lady's head & shoulders, 24k gold allover, unmk, 6" ...48.00
Mug, Santa, U-shaped ft, unmk, 4" 25.00
Pitcher, Apple, gold hdl, mk USA, 6" 75.00
Pitcher, cream; chick figural, mk USA, 7¾" 25.00
Pitcher, milk; kitten beside lg ball of yarn (pitcher), 8¼" 250.00
Planter, Bird of Paradise, unmk, 5¼" 20.00
Planter, Bird w/Blossom, much gold, unmk, 4" 30.00
Planter, Boy Davy Crockett, c-in-circle mk, 4½" 50.00
Planter, Dalmatians, unmk, 5½" 32.00

Planter, Elephant in Basket, unmk, 3¾" 12.00
Planter, Happy Fish, unmk, 4¾" 25.00
Planter, Mallard Duck, gold trim, unmk, 4¾" 26.00
Planter, Poodle, unmk, 7" 20.00
Planter, Rabbit in the Log, unmk, 5¾" 24.00
Planter, Reclining Deer, made by APCO, unmk, 5¾" 14.00
Planter, Reclining Elf, beside stump, unmk, 2¾" 10.00
Planter, Southern Belle, unmk, 7½" 26.00
Planter, Stork w/Cradle, mk USA, 6½" 10.00
Planter, Wailing Kitten, 5¾" 22.00
Planter, Yarn Doll w/House, unmk, 5¼" 20.00
Shakers, Dancing Pigs, shamrocks, unmk, 4", pr 24.00
Shakers, Strawberries, 5", pr, from $75 to 85.00
Sprinkler bottle, cat, marble eyes, 8¼" 195.00
Vase, cornucopia; emb rose, gold trim, unmk, 5" 24.00
Vase, emb rose, red & gr on ivory, unmk, 6½" 16.00

American Encaustic Tiling Co.

A.E. Tile was organized in 1879 in Zanesville, Ohio. Until its closing in 1935, they produced beautiful ornamental and architectural tile equal to the best European imports. They also made vases, figurines, and novelty items with exceptionally fine modeling and glazes.

Bookends, putti play w/rabbit, matt blk & silver, mk 325.00
Bowl, eagle on rock w/wings out at side, gr, high glaze, mk 285.00
Inkwell, matt blk & silver, dbl, w/logo 255.00
Plaque, lion & lioness, dusty rose, 12x6", pr 695.00
Tile, bl, 1892, 4½x4½" 70.00
Tile, clown jester, 4½x4½" 170.00
Tile, elegant couple in high relief on bl, 6x18", pr 675.00
Tile, Hamlet & Orphelia, pale mottled creams & grs, fr, 6", pr ..595.00
Tile, squirrel, 4½x4½" 170.00
Tile, 1892 dedication 100.00

American Indian Art

That time when the American Indian was free to practice the crafts and culture that was his heritage has always held a fascination for many. They were a people who appreciated beauty of design and colorful decoration in their furnishings and clothing; and because instruction in their crafts was a routine part of their rearing, they were well accomplished. Several tribes developed areas in which they excelled. The Navajo were weavers and silversmiths, the Zuni, lapidaries. Examples of their craftsmanship are very valuable. Today even the work of contemporary Indian artists — weavers, silversmiths, carvers, and others — is highly collectible. Unless otherwise noted, values are for items with no obvious damage or excessive wear (EX/NM). For a more thorough study we recommend *Arrowheads and Projectile Points*, *Indian Axes*, and *Indian Artifacts of the Midwest*. All three have been written by our advisor, Lar Hothem; you will find his address in the Directory under Ohio.

Key:
bw — beadwork   S — Southern
dmn — diamond   s-s — sinew sewn
E — Eastern   W — Western
NE — Northeastern   x — cross
p-h — prehistoric

Apparel and Accessories

Before the white traders brought the Indian women cloth from which to sew their garments and beads to use for decorating them, clothing was made from skins sewn together with sinew, usually made of animal tendon. Porcupine quills were dyed bright colors and woven into bags and armbands and used to decorate clothing and moccasins. Examples of early quillwork are scarce today and highly collectible.

Early in the 19th century, beads were being transported via pony pack trains. These 'pony' beads were irregular shapes of opaque glass imported from Venice. Nearly always blue or white, they were twice as large as the later 'seed' beads. By 1870 translucent beads in many sizes and colors had been made available, and Indian beadwork had become commercialized. Each tribe developed its own distinctive methods and preferred decorations, making it possible for collectors today to determine the origin of many items. Soon after the turn of the century, the craft of beadworking began to diminish.

Arm bands, Sioux, parfleche, bw disks, quill drops, 1900, 23" **200.00**
Belt, Crow, full bw tacked panel on leather w/drop, 1910s, 68" ..**200.00**
Belt, Plateau, bw hourglass design on leather panel, 1920s **75.00**
Breech-clout, Osage, leather w/mc ribbonwork, 1940s, 16x3" **25.00**
Cap, Santee Sioux, leather, quillwork/pictorial birds, 1880s, sm ...**900.00**
Cuffs, Nez Perce, lined leather w/bw/brass snaps, 1910s, 12", pr .**110.00**
Dress, Cheyenne, ornate bw on buckskin w/long fringe, 1920s, 54" **3,100.00**
Dress, Nez Perce, wht buckskin w/cutouts & fringe, 1900s, 43" ..**290.00**
Gauntlets, Athabasca, embr florals on buckskin, 1920s, 13", pr .**100.00**
Gauntlets, Blackfoot, tanned moosehide w/bw stars, 1920s, 11", pr ..**100.00**
Gauntlets, E Woodlands, mc bw, leather fringe, 12", pr **250.00**
Gauntlets, embr florals on buckskin, high-top, 1920s, 15", pr **275.00**
Gauntlets, ornate floral bw, tanned buckskin, fringe, 1920s, pr ..**275.00**
Hat, Great Lakes, bw on Fr velvet, 19th C, 11" **225.00**
Hat, Yakima, fez w/full-cut bw eagles/salmon/flags, 20th C, 8" ..**550.00**
Jacket, Crow scout, pony/seed bw on Mountie red wool, 19th C ..**3,250.00**
Leggings, Nez Perce, trade cloth w/red stroud bw panels, 1900s **400.00**
Leggings, Sioux, antelope hide w/much quillwork, 1870s, 32" ..**4,100.00**
Leggings, Sioux boy's, bw strip on trade cloth, 1890s, 12x8" **250.00**
Moccasins, Apache child's, antelope leather, high-top, 1930s **500.00**
Moccasins, Arikira, s-s hide, Maltese Cross bw on toe, 1900s **400.00**
Moccasins, Cheyenne, fine bw, high-top, rawhide soles, 1890s ..**750.00**
Moccasins, Cheyenne, s-s, full mc bw on wht, 1920s, 10" **250.00**
Moccasins, Cree, moosehide w/fine silk floral embr **150.00**
Moccasins, Crow lady's, high-top style, mainly pk bw, 1900s **400.00**
Moccasins, Flathead, classic full bw, soft soles, 1890s, 11" **1,650.00**
Moccasins, Iroquois, classic floral bw/puckered toes, 1880, 10" ..**200.00**
Moccasins, Kiowa child's, bw w/yel ochred high tops, 1900s **125.00**
Moccasins, Kootaenai, soft-soled buckskin w/mc line bw, 1930s .**145.00**
Moccasins, Nez Perce, full geometric bw, soft sole, 1920s, 10" ...**175.00**
Moccasins, Plains, full geometric bw, late 19th C, 9½", VG **225.00**

Moccasins, Sioux, multi-color geometric beadwork, 1880s, NM, $1,100.00.

Moccasins, Sioux child's burial, full bw (includes soles), 1930s ..**400.00**
Moccasins, Woodlands, gathered/bw toes, velvet cuffs, 1890s, sm **1,250.00**
Robe, tanned buffalo hide w/pnt sunburst, 20th C, 56x61" **500.00**
Shirt, muslin Ghost Dance style w/fetish/ermines/etc, 20th C **100.00**
Vest, Flathead, floral designs on blk trade cloth, 1900, 21x18" ..**135.00**
Vest, Kiowa, bw stars & geometrics on blk cloth, 1900s, 27" **150.00**

Arts and Crafts

Canoe, Chippewa, birchbark model, fine detail, 1930s, 26x7" ...**125.00**
Carving, Salish, wooden spindle whorl w/abalone inlay, 1940s, 7" ..**75.00**
Painting, Hopi, Wolf Kachina, sgn Kaye, 1970, 13x10" **150.00**
Painting, Navajo, End of Long Trail, R Naha, 1960, 16x19" **250.00**
Parfleche, Crow, pnt geometrics, Sharp Studio, 1870s, 20x11" ..**1,250.00**
Tapestry, 2 Grey Hills, Priscilla Taugelchee, 1974, 27x16" **4,500.00**
Watercolor, Indian spears buffalo, J Martinez, 1930s, 11x14" ..**1,150.00**
Weaving, Navajo, blk/red dmns & whirling logs, 1900, 60x37" **700.00**
Weaving, Navajo, mc vertical design on red, 1920, 52x84", NM ...**825.00**

Bags and Cases

The Indians used bags for many purposes, and most display excellent form and workmanship. Of the types listed below, many collectors consider the pipe bag to be the most desirable form. Pipe bags were long, narrow, leather and bead or quillwork creations made to hold tobacco in a compartment at the bottom and the pipe, with the bowl removed from the stem, in the top. Long buckskin fringe was used as trim and complemented the quilled and beaded design to make the bag a masterpiece of Indian Art.

Apache, awl case, mc bw w/tin cone dangles, 1920s, 17" **500.00**
Arapaho, awl case, s-s w/mc bw, bw flap & drops, 20th C, 18" ...**350.00**
Assiniboine, pouch, hide w/geometric bw/Civil War braid, 1900, 6" **400.00**
Blackfoot, knife case, full mc bw, w/strap & dangles, 1910s, 8" ..**450.00**
Blackfoot, pipe case, floral bw, quilled fringe, 1920s, 24x5" **475.00**
Cheyenne, pipe bag, hourglass design bw, fringed, 1910s, 32x5" ..**1,250.00**
Cheyenne, strike-a-lite bag, full bw, tin cones, 1900, 5x3" **300.00**
Chippewa, bandolier, full floral bw, ca 1890, lg **1,200.00**
Chippewa, shoulder bag, full floral bw, 1890s, 47x19" **1,750.00**
Comanche, awl case, mc bw, w/awl, ca 1880, 10" **700.00**
Crow, awl case, orange w/red/bl stripes, tin cones, 1920s, 12" **325.00**
Crow, awl case, s-s, full bw w/flap & drops, w/awl, 20th C, 12" ..**300.00**
Crow, knife sheath, s-s, full bw, w/handmade knife, 1870, 14" ...**1,100.00**
Kiowa, geometric cut bw on fringed leather, 1960, 14x7" **125.00**
Menominee, otter bag, bw ft & tail, ca 1900, 28x6", NM **775.00**
Navajo, medicine man's, leather w/silver decor, 1930s, 35x6" **700.00**
Nez Perce, bonnet case, pnt parfleche w/fringe, 1920s, 26x7" **700.00**
Nez Perce, corn husk, hourglass symbols/dmns/arrow points, 18x11" **350.00**
Nez Perce, twined corn husk w/intricate decor, 1900s, 11x9" **725.00**
Nez Perce, twined corn husks, design ea side, 1900s, 19x14" ...**1,000.00**
Plains, knife case, bw on buckskin, rawhide lined, 20th C, 11" **85.00**
Plateau, bw animals on bl, trade bead hdl, fringe, 1890s, 9x5" **600.00**
Plateau, bw stylized florals/foliage, fringed, 1940, 22x14" **170.00**
Plateau, full eagle-in-flight bw, 1950s, 11" dia **100.00**
Seminole, shoulder bag, full bw on stroud cloth, 20th C, 67" ..**2,600.00**
Sioux, knife case, fine full-cut bw on leather, 1965, 9x2" **65.00**
Sioux, knife case, s-s hide w/full bw geometrics, 1880s, 12" **450.00**
Sioux, pipe case, s-s, bw tabs/quill drops/tin cones, 20th C, 32" **1,600.00**
Sioux, strike-a-lite pouch, s-s, 1880s, 3½x4" **750.00**
Sioux, teepee, s/s, full bw on buffalo hide, tin cone drops, 20x13" .**2,500.00**
Wasco, belt pouch, hard leather w/bw symbols, 19th C, 8x9" .**1,000.00**

Baskets

In the following listings, examples are basket form and coiled unless noted otherwise.

Athabascan, cvd bark, ca 1850, 3x11" L **125.00**
Hopi, 2nd Mesa, plaque, ca 1920, 16" dia **200.00**
Karok, mc geometrics, sm knob finial, ca 1910, 5x5" **850.00**
Kern, finely coiled, rattlesnake bands, 1890s, 10x6" **1,500.00**

Makah, treasure box, 2 butterflies, w/lid, 1910s, 3x3½" 150.00
Makah, 4 birds & bands, colored finial, w/lid, 3½x4", G 150.00
Mission, bowl, oval coils w/triangular design, 1910s, 4x13" 700.00
Mission, rnd coils w/Thunderbird design, 1910s, 3x6" 400.00
Navajo, medicine, 3-color, ca 1950, 10" dia 75.00
Navajo, wedding, braided rim, 1950s, 10½" dia 85.00
Ojibway, bark w/cvd quill decor, cvd beaver on lid, 1920, 3x5" ...250.00
Panamint, ped style w/arrowhead & dmn motif, 1920, 7x4" 1,450.00
Papago, 3 brn dogs circle body, brn borders, 2¾x4¾", EX 125.00
Pima, blossom & fret design, braided rim, 1920s, 4½x12" 1,600.00
Pima, bowl, dbl squash & dmn pattern, braided rim, 1916, 2x10" ...550.00
Pima, bowl, striking geometrics, 1920s, 7x17" 775.00
Pima, tray, brn geometrics & center, 4x18", EX 1,000.00
Pomo, boat-style, fine weave, stair-step design, 1900s, 2x4" 225.00
Pomo, gift basket, feather coiled w/shell beads, 1975, 6x10" 1,150.00
Salish, embricated geometrics, trunk form w/lid/hdls, 1900, 25" L...350.00
Salish, embricated trunk w/lid, buckskin hdls, 1900s, 8x16x8" ...250.00
Salish, embricated trunk w/star & cross motif, lid/hdls, 21" L 500.00
Salish, red & blk human forms, w/lid, ca 1910, 4x5" 175.00
Tlingit, mc geometrics & arrows, 8¾x10", VG 800.00
Tlingit, tight weave, blk & brn geometrics, 5½x6", EX 275.00
Ute, bowl, pnt V decor, 1920s, 5x13" 125.00
Ute, medicine man's, ca 1900, 4x10" 115.00
W Apache, brn geometrics, 4x15", EX 1,400.00
Wht Mtn Apache, olla, blk humans & animals, 10x8", EX 2,000.00
Yavapai, tray, woven figures, 20th C, 25" dia 375.00

Blades and Points

Relics of this type usually display characteristics of a general area, time period, or a particular location. With study, those made by the Plains Indians are easily discerned from those of the West Coast. Because modern man has imitated the art of the Indian by reproducing these artifacts through modern means, use caution before investing your money in 'too good to be authentic' specimens.

Adena, stemmed, mottled gray chert, KY, 4½x2¼" 350.00
Archaic, pentagonal type, brn & gray flint, OH, 4½" 160.00
Clovis-like, wht chert w/some gray, unfluted, IL, 2½" 125.00
Corner notch, wht flint, sm serrations on edges, MO, 3⅛" 550.00
Dalton, blk flint, basal-thinning scars, IL, 2½" 100.00
Dalton, Breckenridge variety, gray mottled flint, IN, 2½" 145.00
Diagonal notch, red chert, MO, 3x1¼" 225.00
Dovetail/St Charles, dk flint, beveled/serrated edges, KY, 4⅜" ...275.00
Hardin, tan flint, shallow basal grinding, barbed, MO, 3¼x1½" ...225.00
Hopewell, dk Upper Mercer flint, IN, 3" 125.00
Hopewell, milky wht flint, MO, 3x1⅜" 50.00
Lanceolate, stemmed & shouldered, gray chert, OH, 3½" 90.00
Scottsbluff, sugar quartz, MO, 2⅝" 100.00
Snyders, red & pk chert, IN, 4x2½" 275.00
Stanfield, wht Burlington chert or flint, MO, 5¼" 200.00
Stilwell, blk & gray chert, IN, 4x1¼" 225.00

Ceremonial Items

Dance belt & drops, Sioux, loom beaded geometrics, 35x3" 150.00
Dance wand, Hopi, HP decor on wood, ca 1920, 20", pr 225.00
Dance wand, wooden hdld dbl horn w/full bw, 20th C, 26x10" ..175.00
Drum, Crow, hide-covered hand type, pnt traces, 1910s, 16" dia 200.00
Drum, Peyote, CI kettle water drum w/hide cover, 1910s, 6½x10" ...350.00
Drum, Plains, hide covered, pnt geometrics, 1890s, 9x2", G 150.00
Fetish, Cheyenne, full bw umbilical cord lizard form, 1900s, 6x2" ..350.00
Fetish, Sioux, umbilical cord, full bw/tin cones, 1920s, 6x2½" ...220.00
Leggings, Stomp Dance, turtle shell rattles on leather, 1890s, 11" ...450.00

Mask, Iroquois, False Face Society, cvd/pnt, 1920s, 12", pr 1,300.00
Stick, Horse Dance, cvd wood w/quillwork, hoof end, 1890s, 22" ..1,200.00

Dolls

Kachina, cvd & pnt wood w/birds on tabletta, 20th C, 18x5" 200.00
Kachina, Hemis, cottonwood w/mc tabletta, 20th C, 21x12" 325.00
Kachina, Hemis, handmade cottonwood root, 20th C, 16" 350.00
Kachina, Hopi, cvd/pnt, flat bk, ca 1900, 15x4" 500.00
Kachina, Hopi, Swaying Man, body pnt, kilt, rattle, 1956, 16" ..150.00
Kachina, Mana w/colorful tabletta, 20th C, 21x10" 275.00
Kachina, Mana w/whirling logs & Xs, 20th C, 23" 300.00
Kachina, Zuni, cvd wood, EX detail, ca 1940, 10" 300.00
Nez Perce, buckskin, fully outfitted, much bw, 1890s, 12" 1,850.00
Sioux, full bw, w/moccasins/belt/ear drops, 1920s, 9½" 450.00

Domestics

Box, NE Woodlands, pine/hardwood, oval, hdls, rpt, 11x28x19" ..350.00
Container, carrying; Woodlands, birch w/scratch decor, 7x5x6" ...400.00
Container, Penobscot, birchbark cylinder w/decor, 1880s, 7x8" .325.00
Cradle, Hupa, twined basketry, 1880s, mini, 17x7" 200.00
Cradle, Seneca, wood w/dbl floral bw velvet covers, 1890s, 19" .200.00
Cradle, Shoshone, basketry w/bw & buckskin trim, 1940s, 28x13" ..100.00
Cradle, Umatilla, yel hide w/floral bw, sunshade, 1900, 15" 700.00
Cradle board, Athabascan, birchbark w/bw strip, 1950s, 22" 195.00
Cradle board, Great Lakes, 6 Nations, ash fr w/leather & bw, 33" 250.00
Cradle board, Sioux, pnt hide, covered bkbrd, 1940s, 42", M 900.00

Cradle cover, Sioux, beaded hide, sinew sewn, glass tube beads, brass bells, muslin lining, Reservation period, 30", EX, $2,300.00.

Spoon, bent horn w/bead-wrapped hdl, 20th C, 14" 75.00
Spoon, Haida, cvd wood w/bear track design, 1930s, 9x3" 60.00
Spoon, Plains, bent horn, beaded bird effigy hdl, 20th C, 17" 175.00
Spoon, Woodlands, curly maple, vine-cvd hdl, 5" bowl, 11½" L ...300.00
Teepee, Colville, old style, canvas, ca 1900, lg 175.00
Teepee, Plateau, old canvas, pnt chief & woman, 1920s, lg 225.00

Jewelry and Adornments

As early as 500 A.D., Indians in the Southwest drilled turquoise nuggets and strung them on cords made of sinew or braided hair. The Spanish introduced them to coral, and it became a popular item of jewelry; abalone and clam shells were favored by the Coastal Indians. Not until the last half of the 19th century did the Indians learn to work with silver. Each tribe developed its own distinctive style and preferred design, which until about 1920 made it possible to determine tribal origin with some degree of accuracy. Since that time, because of modern means of communication and travel, motifs have become less distinct.

Quality Indian silver jewelry may be antique or contemporary. Age, though certainly to be considered, is not as important a factor as fine workmanship and good stones. Pre-1910 silver will show evidence of hammer marks, and designs are usually simple. Beads have sometimes been shaped from coins. Stones tend to be small; when silver wire was used, it is usually square. To insure your investment, choose a reputable dealer.

Bracelet, Navajo, silver w/4 inset turq pcs, 1¾" W **150.00**
Bracelet, Navajo, turq & silver cluster, sgn VMB, 1980, 6½x3" .**170.00**
Bracelet, Navajo, 3-strand turq & silver, 1950, 6" **75.00**
Bracelet, Zuni, turq w/4 circles of inset turq, 3¼" W **200.00**
Bracelet, Zuni, 10-row petit-point turq (160 stones), 1958, 2" ...**450.00**
Breastplate, Crow woman's, red bkground bw, 1930s, sm **275.00**
Breastplate, Plains, buffalo bone/bl beads/leather fringe, 38" **500.00**
Breastplate, Sioux, bone hair pipe w/trade bead dangles, 19th C ...**950.00**
Hair drop, Kiowa, German silver w/spreader w/engr bird, 1870s, 51" ...**900.00**
Hair drop, Osage, cloth/ribbons/otter fur/mirrors/bells, 1900s **800.00**
Hair drops, Sioux, quilled medicine wheel w/tin cones, 1920s, pr **35.00**
Necklace, Hupa Yurok, 2-strand dentalium wampum, 19th C, 22" ...**325.00**
Necklace, Navajo, silver, naja w/1 turq stone, 1940s, 30" **200.00**
Necklace, Navajo, silver w/pendant cross & turq stone, 1940, 34" .**375.00**

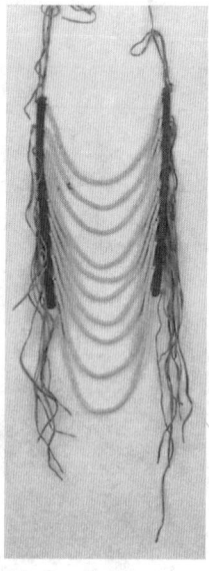

Necklace, Northern Plains, 10 strands of white mandril-wound glass disk beads strung on rawhide, harness leather supports, 18", $1,400.00.

Necklace, Zuni, silver/turq, dbl-bead strand, 26"+earrings **400.00**
Necklace, Zuni, silver/turq, w/pendant/tassles, 16"+earrings **750.00**
Pendant, Wasco, cvd human face on stone, p-h, 2½x½" **75.00**
Squash blossom, silver pomegranate w/turq stones, 1940s, 30" ...**175.00**
Squash blossom, silver praying hands w/turq stones, 1940s, 30" .**145.00**
Squash blossom, silver Rainbow Man w/turq stone, 1940s, 29" ...**175.00**
Trade beads, brick red, Venetian, ca 1840, 24" **55.00**
Trade beads, faceted cobalt, Russian, rare, ca 1800, 35" **150.00**
Trade beads, Hudson Bay robin's egg bl & cobalt bl, 19th C, 36" ...**100.00**
Trade beads, mixed Venetian of Lewis & Clark type, 1840s, 24" .**120.00**

Pipes

Pipe bowls were usually carved from soft stone, such as catlinite or red pipestone, an argilaceous sedimentary rock composed mainly of

clay. Steatite was also used. Some ceremonial pipes were simply styled, while others were intricately designed naturalistic figurals, sometimes in bird or frog forms called effigies. Their stems, made of wood and often covered with leather, were sometimes nearly a yard in length.

Blackfoot, catlinite elbow w/orig beaded stem, 1870s, 16x2" **400.00**
Catlinite L-bowl, wooden stem w/cvd animals, 1920s, 24x2x4" .**325.00**
Pipe tomahawk, brass head, pewter inlay wood hdl, dtd 1898, 21" ..**750.00**
Plains, blk stone T-bowl w/pewter inlay, beaded stem, 20th C, 21" .**150.00**
Plains, red catlinite T-bowl, long stem, 1880s, 26x3" **600.00**
Sioux, catlinite dragon-head bowl, 1920s, 6x4" **100.00**
Sioux, catlinite horse effigy, EX patina, 20th C, 4½x8" **250.00**
Sioux, catlinite snake & frog effigy, snake stem, 20th C, 32" **400.00**
Sioux, red catlinite T-bowl, wood stem/plaited quillwork, 28x4x2" ...**1,000.00**
Trade, E Woodlands, covered w/basketry, 1850s, 6½x1" **125.00**

Pottery

Indian pottery is nearly always decorated in such a manner as to indicate the tribe that produced it or the pueblo in which it was made. For instance, the designs of Cochiti potters were usually scattered forms from nature or sacred symbols. The Zuni preferred an ornate repetitive decoration of a closer configuration. They often used stylized deer and bird forms, sometimes in dimensional applications.

Acoma, olla, ca 1910, no rstr, 12" **1,000.00**
Anasazi, bowl, Four Mile, mc geometrics int/ext, p-h, 5x10" **500.00**
Anasazi, bowl, jeddito blk on red w/pnt geometrics, p-h, 6x3" ...**350.00**
Anasazi, pitcher, blk on wht, p-h, 5x5" **350.00**
Casas Grandes, pot, blkware, rabbit, M Ortiz, 1996, 5x6" **125.00**
Hohokam, olla, red on buff w/shoulder, p-h, 5x6" **350.00**
Hohokam, olla, water storage; redware, p-h, 19x21" **300.00**
Homolobi, bowl, blk on orange int decor, p-h, 4x8" **200.00**
Hopi, bowl, mc bird & X-hatch design, L Nampeyo, 1970, 5x6" ..**500.00**
Hopi, dough bowl, lg int design, sgn, ca 1970, 6x13" **160.00**
Maricopa, canteen, turtle design, 1880s, 7x4" **400.00**
Matsaki, bowl, stylized bird decor, p-h, 5x10" **425.00**
Mound Builder, jar, human face & bear track effigy, p-h, 8x6" ...**300.00**
Salado, bowl, blk int geometrics on wht, p-h, 4x8" **100.00**
Santa Ana, bowl, blk & wht on red, ca 1910, 7x13", EX **225.00**
Santa Clara, bowl, blk w/Avenu, sgn Rosalie & Joe, 1950, 4x8" ...**450.00**
Santa Clara, jar, blkware, fingerprints at rim, 1890s, 7x10½" **400.00**
Santo Domingo, dough bowl, classic pnt designs, 1980s, 6x14" ..**250.00**
Santo Domingo, olla, Arthur & Hilda Coriz, 1985, 10x11" **500.00**
Zia, olla, birds decor, sgn H Gachupin, 1975, 15x15" **1,100.00**
Zia, olla, mc birds & geometrics, sgn Sofia Medina Zia, 9x11" ...**900.00**
Zuni, bowl, frog effigy, 20th C, 4x8½" **900.00**

Pottery, San Ildefonso

The pottery of the San Ildefonso pueblo is especially sought after by collectors today. Under the leadership of Maria Martinez and her husband Julian, experiments began about 1918 which led to the development of the 'black-on-black' design achieved through exacting methods of firing the ware. They discovered that by smothering the fire at a specified temperature, the carbon in the smoke that ensued caused the pottery to blacken. Maria signed her work (often 'Marie') from the late teens to the 1960s; she died in 1980. Today a piece with her signature may bring prices in the $500.00 to $4,500.00 range.

Jar, blkware, feather, Marie & Julian, ca 1925, 5x6" **1,600.00**
Olla, blkware, polished, Carmelita Dunlap, 1976, 3x4" **250.00**
Olla, 3-color, shouldered form, Maria Martinez, 1930s, 8½x9" ..**1,300.00**
Pot, blkware, bear claw, Blue Corn, 1954, 4" **195.00**

Pot, blkware, feathers, Carmelita Dunlap, 1950, 5x6½" 375.00
Pot, blkware, sea serpent, sgn, 7½" 200.00
Pot, blkware w/sculpted bear claw, Blue Corn, 1954, 4" 195.00

Rugs, Navajo

Regional, 5-color, geometric design, 63x35", EX, $375.00 at auction.

Center dmn w/cross, serrated triangles at end, 4-color, 76x44" ..300.00
Dbl dmn center w/red swastikas, 4-color, 72x52" 500.00
Eye Dazzler type, blk/wht/red, 60x35", EX 400.00
Ganado, dmns/terraces, gray/blk/red/wht, 1900s, 39x52" 385.00
Ganado transitional, dmns, 5-color, natural/blk borders, 34x48" ..330.00
Geometrics/lizards/snakes, fret border, 4-color, 73x54", EX 2,100.00
Germantown Eye Dazzler, mc dmns on red w/blk/wht, 1890s, 23x23" ...550.00
Klagetoh, geometrics, 3-color on wht w/blk border, 1950s, 77x36" ..700.00
Klagetoh, Sunrise, 4-color, West Reservation edge, 32x49" 200.00
Klagetoh, triple dmn w/blk & wht stripes, 4-color, 38x68" 440.00
Transitional, red central lozenge, 1910s, 126x54" 700.00
Yei, handwoven by Mae Yazzie, 1950, 49x30", M w/orig tag 275.00
Yei, 4 wht Rainbow Man figures on copper ground, 1940s, 23x22" ..175.00
2 geometric forms connected w/bows & arrows, 4-color, 71x45" ..1,300.00
2 Grey Hills, natural wool, brn/wht/gray, 1920s, 88x58" 550.00

Shaped Stone Artifacts

Bannerstone, dbl-knobbed, gr glacial slate, IN, 4⅞x3⅜" 1,800.00
Bannerstone, winged butterfly type, gr banded slate, KY, 4x2⅞" ..400.00
Birdstone, Adena/Woodland, bust type, hardstone, OH, 1¾" .1,000.00
Birdstone, animal type, lt banded glacial slate, IN, 2⅝" 300.00
Boatstone, Woodland, lt granite gneiss w/dk spots, KY, 5⅜" 500.00
Discoidal, Late Woodland, Jersey Bluff type, quartz, 4¼x2½" 500.00
Discoidal, Salt River/Woodland, blk & cream mottle, MO, 4x1" ..650.00
Discoidal, Woodland, Jersey Bluff type, dk hardstone, MO, 3" ...500.00
Gorget, Adena Early Woodland, quadriconcave, IN, 3⅜" 215.00
Gorget, Adena/Early Woodland, expanded center, gr slate, 4½" ..600.00
Gorget, Hopewell/Middle Woodland, boat shape, slate, 4½" 600.00
Gorget, knobbed, 2 drill holes, tan glacial slate, 4x2½" 1,000.00
Gorget, Woodland, rectangular, banded slate, IN, 3¼" 150.00
Pendant, Adena/Early Woodland, trapezoidal, banded slate, 3¼" ..225.00
Pendant, Red Ochre/Early Woodland, dmn shape, dk slate, 3½" ..100.00
Plummet, grooved top, gray hematite, IL 300.00
Plummet, mottled red, blk & gray, p-h, 1x½" 50.00

Tools

Adz, chert, MO, 6½x3", from $75 to 100.00
Axe, full groove, red stone, age unknown, 8x4" 95.00
Axe, full groove, tan stone, age unknown, 7x3" 35.00
Axe, ¾-groove, gray-gr granite, IN, 3¾x2¾" 135.00

Axe, ¾-groove, streaked hardstone, IN, 4¼" 300.00
Celt, gr slate, IL, 2⅛x1¾" 20.00
Celt, gr slate, IL, 4⅜x2⅛" 25.00
Celt, Woodland, dk hardstone, IN, 2x1⅜" 40.00
Club, stone, dbl-pointed head, full bw hdl, 10th C, 20x6½" 125.00
Drill, Dalton based, milky wht chert, MO, 1⅛x2" 50.00
Drill, wht chert, unusually fine, IL, 5⅛x1", from $400 to 600.00
Drill, Woodland, chert, IN, 2½x⅞", from $30 to 45.00
Drill/perforator, dk gray flint, IL, 3x⅞" 100.00
Hook, halibut; Haida, all wood, ca 1870, 5x3" 175.00
Hook, halibut; Haida, cvd wooden eagle effigy, 1870s, 10x4" 550.00
Knife, Dalton, cream w/brn swirls, IL, 4½", from $150 to 250.00
Knife, wht flint, lance shape, IL, 4x1¼" 75.00
Pestle, knobbed type, brn to lt orange quartzite, polished, OH, 7" ...1,000.00

Weapons

Bow, Yurok, cvd/pnt, from Klamath River, 1850s, 52x3" 400.00
Club, Great Lakes, wood ball head w/iron blade, 1900s, 21x5" ...250.00
Club, Plains, egg shape, bw on hide-wrapped hdl, 1880s, 26x4" .250.00
Club, Plains, hide-covered flop knob type, bw hdl, 20th C, 25" .250.00
Dagger, Tlingit, copper w/leather-wrapped hdl, 1920, 23x3" 600.00
Lance, hand-forged steel point, trade cloth cover, 1880s, 80" .1,100.00
Tomahawk, Crow, brass pipe, tacked stem, bw/quilled drop, 53x9" ..1,950.00
Tomahawk, spike-bk trade, Indian War era, ca 1800, 10x5" 60.00
War club, Penobscot, root w/pnt/cvd eagle & Indian, 26" 325.00

Miscellaneous

Canteen, Apache, hide cover w/bw, 1880s, 11" dia 400.00
Canteen, tobacco; Navajo, wrought silver w/9 turq, 20th C, 4" dia ..225.00
Cigar box cover, Cree, buffalo hide w/floral bw, 1900s, 9" L 275.00
Holster, bw stars/crosses/geometrics allover, 1900s, 11" 1,050.00
Kayak, NW Coast, sealskin on wood fr, ca 1900, model, 22" 400.00
Peace medal, silver, Geo Washington, dtd 1801, 3" dia 325.00
Peace medal, silver, WH Harrison/Eel River Nation, 1803, 3x3½" ..400.00
Photo, Jack Red Cloud, sgn Billy Walker, WY, 1908, 7x9" 550.00
Photo, White Swan, Crow, orig Rhinehart, ca 1900, 11x14" 150.00
Photogravure, Cayuse woman, sgn ES Curtis, 1910, 6x9" 75.00
Saddle, Flathead, wooden pack type, 1880s, 20x14" 100.00
Shield, Pueblo, rnd disk buffalo hide w/pnt traces, 1890s, 19" .1,500.00
Totem pole, cvd wood, 2-figure, Canada, 1920, 13x2" 85.00
Trade token, NY Co, beaver/king, ca 1820, 1" dia 300.00

American Painted Porcelain

    The American china-painting movement can be traced back to an extracurricular class attended by art students at the McMicken School of Design in Cincinnati. These students, who were the wives and daughters of the city's financial elite, managed to successfully paint numerous porcelains for display in the Woman's Pavilion of the 1876 United States Centennial Exposition held in Philadelphia — an amazing feat considering the high technical skill required for proficiency, as well as the length of time and multiple firings necessary to finish pieces. From then until 1917 when the United States entered World War I, china painting was a profession as well as a popular amateur pursuit for many people, particularly women. In fact, over 20,000 people were involved in this artform at the turn of the last century.

    Collectors and antique dealers have only recently 'discovered' American hand-painted porcelain, and they are just becoming aware of its history, beauty, and potential value. Until now, there was no all-inclusive source to turn to for information on this subject. *American Painted Porcelain: Collector's Identification & Value Guide* by Dorothy

Kamm is the culmination of nearly a decade of research; we recommend it highly for further study.

Though American pieces are of high quality and commensurate with their European counterparts, they are much less costly today. Generally, you will pay as little as $10.00 for a 6" plate and less than $50.00 for many other items. Values are based on aesthetic appeal, quality of the workmanship, size, rarity of the piece and of the subject matter, and condition. Age is the least important factor, because most American painted porcelains are not dated. (Factory backstamps are helpful in establishing the approximate time period an item was decorated, but they aren't totally reliable.) See Clubs and Newsletters for information regarding *Dorothy's Kamm's Porcelain Collector's Companion*, each issue of which contains comprehensive material expounding on artists, patterns, dating, and functions of china.

Our advisor for this category is Dorothy Kamm; she is listed in the Directory under Florida.

Below are some examples of what you can expect to pay for American painted porcelain.

Bonbon dish, from $18 to 45.00
Bowl, fruit; from $60 to 80.00
Box, 4¾" dia, from $50 to 60.00
Cake plate, from $35 to 55.00
Candlestick, from $45 to 60.00
Celery tray, from $35 to 45.00
Cruet, from $50 to 60.00
Cup & saucer, bouillon; from $35 to 45.00
Cup & saucer, from $15 to 30.00
Ewer (depends on sz), from $100 to 250.00
Gravy boat, from $35 to 65.00
Hatpin holder, from $88 to 98.00
Jardiniere (depends on sz), from $65 to 250.00

Lemonade pitcher, signed C.N. Patterson, 1908, from $175.00 to $225.00; Jam jar, ca 1880, from $30.00 to $40.00; Stein, signed Mabel Carlson, 1917, from $75.00 to 95.00.

Mug, from $30 to 70.00
Napkin ring, from $10 to 25.00
Nappy, from $20 to 35.00
Pin tray, from $30 to 50.00
Plate, 6", from $10 to 20.00
Plate, 8", from $25 to 45.00
Salt cellar, from $20 to 40.00
Shakers, pr, from $20 to 30.00
Tea set or coffee set, ea, from $175 to 250.00
Vase, 6-7", ea, from $45 to 65.00

Amethyst Glass

The term amethyst simply describes the rich color of this glassware made by many companies both here and abroad since the 19th century.

Ashtray, 1x3¼" 5.00
Bonbon dish, hdls, 6" 20.00
Bowl, hdls, 2½x6" 25.00
Bowl, serving; center hdl, LE Smith, 9" sq 35.00
Box, HP florals, brass mts & ft, 3⅞x3½" dia 195.00
Decanter, HP florals, amethyst bubble stopper, 13x3⅜" 165.00
Decanter, Optic pattern, flattened bulb, clear hdl, stoppèr, 8½" ...175.00
Server, dbl hdld, 12" 30.00
Vanity lamp, pancake type, w/etched chimney & base, Jefferson ...95.00
Vase, gold leaves & mc flowers, bl dots, 4⅜x2⅞" 85.00
Vase, HP decor, pillow form on ped base, scalloped rim, 13" 125.00
Vase, HP jonquils w/gold, cylindrical, 8x3⅜" 145.00

Amphora

The Amphora Porcelain Works in the Teplitz-Turn area of Bohemia produced Art Nouveau-styled vases and figurines during the latter part of the 1800s through the first few decades of the 20th century. They marked their wares with various stamps, some incorporating the name and location of the pottery with a crown or a shield. Because Bohemia was part of the Austro-Hungarian empire prior to WWI, some examples are marked Austria; items marked with the Czechoslovakia designation were made after the war. All decoration described in the listings that follow is hand painted unless otherwise indicated. Our advisor for this category is Jack Gunsaulus; he is listed in the Directory under Michigan.

Vases, all with Art Nouveau lady with flowers in her hair, forest background, marked Amphora Turn 1326: Rounded form with 3-lobed lip, 6x5½", $650.00; Broad based organic form, 13½", $1,800.00; Broad shouldered twisted form, 7", $700.00.

Basket, apples & leaves on branch, 9x6" 395.00
Basket, Deco florals, cobalt trim, 7x5½", EX 95.00
Basket, lg pk flowers, 3 stems form high hdl, Stellmacher 800.00
Basket, vintage on basketweave, mc w/lustre, sgn, 12" 285.00
Basket vase, flowers & basketweave, mc w/gold rope hdls, 12" ...550.00
Compote vase, Nouveau decor w/jewels, 4 buttress hdls, mk, 9¼" ..150.00
Ewer, floral bosses on shoulder, disk panels, mc on tan, 17" 350.00
Ewer, forest scene, gr/bl w/gold, slim dragon forms hdl, 9½" 450.00
Ewer, gold flowers, gr jewels, gold spout & 3 hdls, 7½x5" 375.00
Ewer, swan & lady's portrait reserves, 2-spout, 10", EX 150.00
Figurine, peasant lady empties apron, gold trim, crown mk, 18½" ...550.00
Figurine, peasant lady w/basket on bk, gold trim, 16¼" 650.00
Jar, goose reserves, fox finial, 10½" 600.00
Jardiniere, grapes & leaves, 3 low hdls, 6½" 350.00
Jug, ladies' portraits, mc enameling, 2-spout, 7" 895.00
Lamp, world base, rpl shade, 8½" 500.00

Pitcher, floral w/gold & jewels, Wahliss, 2-spout, 4½" **145.00**
Planter, Deco florals, ram's head hdl, 4 hooved ft, 3¾" **450.00**
Planter, Deco style, 3 low hdls, 7" **500.00**
Planter, Nouveau flowers w/gold on gold-tan irid, 5x14x9", NM ..**700.00**
Vase, blackberries appl on cream basketweave, hdls, 10x9½" **650.00**
Vase, coiled dragon sends steam up side & rim, mc on olive, 26" .**3,000.00**
Vase, Deco ladies (3), cobalt, 3-hdld, 1920s, 7" **425.00**
Vase, Egyptian reserves, tan/brn/wht, 13⅝" **550.00**
Vase, floral emb on gold matt, 3-D florals at neck, #3128, 14" ...**400.00**
Vase, flowers & vines in relief, mk, 13x10½" **475.00**
Vase, geometric fired-on gold on wht, #2023/41, 11¾" **600.00**
Vase, grapes, purple on bl to purple w/gold, 7x4", EX **525.00**
Vase, grapes appl to wide centerpc base, hdls, 14½" **1,100.00**
Vase, hops appl, mc on Nouveau gr-beige, 14½x7½" **1,100.00**
Vase, hunter in chariot/hunter w/bow & arrow, mk, 17x10", EX ..**400.00**
Vase, jewels, mc on cobalt, 4¾x3¾", EX **125.00**
Vase, lady in sheer pk stands by floral teardrop form, 18" **2,500.00**
Vase, lady's portrait, long blk hair & flowers, w/jewels, 6" **325.00**
Vase, lady's portrait reserve among trees & sky w/gold, mk, 14½" .**1,400.00**
Vase, man's portrait, 3 openings, prof rpr, 9" **265.00**
Vase, Nouveau floral in matt & glossy, hdls, #11663/46, 10", pr **225.00**
Vase, octopus forms neck & rim, 2 tentacle hdls, #4545/50, 8¾" ...**600.00**
Vase, octopus w/2 legs circling cylindrical vase, gr to tan, 20" .**2,000.00**
Vase, paisley body, caryatid hdls, drilled, 25", pr **550.00**
Vase, pierced protruding bulbs, dk gr, 4-hdld, MK, 12½", pr **200.00**
Vase, roses on yel w/gold, 4 buttress hdls, #3883/42, 10⅜" **225.00**
Vase, rtcl gr & wht dmn bands on pitted teal bl, ftd, 6¾" **375.00**
Vase, The Onion, gold/grs/grays, Paul Dashell, 9" **295.00**
Vase, women harvesting wheat, brn/tan/gold, #44/11563, 10⅛" ...**350.00**

Animal Dishes with Covers

Covered animal dishes have been produced for nearly two centuries and are as varied as their manufacturers. They were made in many types of glass (slag, colored, clear, and milk glass) as well as china and pottery. On bases of nests and baskets, you will find animals and birds of every sort. The most common was the hen.

Some of the smaller versions made by McKee, Indiana Tumbler and Goblet Company, and Westmoreland Specialty Glass of Pittsburgh, Pennsylvania, were sold to food-processing companies who filled them with prepared mustard, baking powder, etc. Occasionally one will be found with the paper label identifying the product and processing company still intact.

Many of the glass versions produced during the latter part of the 19th century have been recently reproduced. As early as the 1960s, the Kemple Glass Company made the rooster, fox, lion, cat, lamb, hen, horse, turkey, duck, dove, and rabbit on split-ribbed or basketweave bases. They were made in amethyst, blue, amber, and milk glass, as well as a variegated slag. It is sometimes necessary to compare items in question to verified examples of older glass in order to recognize reproductions. Reproduction is continued today.

For more information, we recommend *Covered Animal Dishes* by our advisor, Everett Grist, whose address is in the Directory under Tennessee. In the listings below, when only one dimension is given, it is the greater one, usually length.

Bull's head, milk glass, spoon tongue (missing), mk **175.00**
Chick in vertical egg, milk glass, 3¾" **125.00**
Chicks in oblong basket, milk glass, pnt details, 2¼x4¼" **325.00**
Dog (Pekingese) on base, milk glass, att Sandwich, 4¾" **800.00**
Dolphin on sauce dish, milk glass, att Westmoreland, 7¼" **100.00**
Dolphin on sawtooth base, milk glass, Kemple or St Clair repro ...**75.00**
Duck, Pintail; on dmn basketweave base, Westmoreland, 5½" **55.00**

Duck on cattail base, milk glass, unmk, 5½" **120.00**
Duck soap dish, clear, pnt bill **15.00**
Eagle mother, milk glass, Westmoreland reissue w/WG mk **100.00**
Elephant w/rider, milk glass, Vallerysthal, 7" **350.00**
Fish, Flat; bl opaque **165.00**
Fish on collared base, clear frosted, unmk **150.00**

Fox on lacy base, milk glass,
dated 1889, 7½", **$175.00**.

Hand & Dove, milk glass, lacy rectangular base, Atterbury, dtd .**125.00**
Hen, amberina, LE Smith, 5½" **75.00**
Hen, Straight Headed; clear, att Indiana Glass, 5½" **15.00**
Hen on basketweave base, milk glass, Vallerysthal, 2" **35.00**
Hen on lacy base, marbled bk, bl opaque, 6¼" L **300.00**
Hen w/chicks, milk glass, pnt comb, ea pc mk McKee, 5½" **450.00**
Hen w/chicks on split-rib base, milk glass, unmk McKee, 5½" ...**300.00**
Lamb on picket fence, milk glass w/bl opaque head, Westmoreland .**125.00**
Lamb on split-rib base, amber, recent, 5½" **45.00**
Lion, British; milk glass, unmk, 6¼" **195.00**
Quail on scroll base, milk glass, unmk, 5½" **85.00**
Rabbit, Atterbury; bl opaque, glass eyes, dtd base, 6" **425.00**
Rabbit emerging from horizontal egg, milk glass, worn pnt **125.00**
Rabbit on wheat base, milk glass, Flaccus **350.00**
Robin on ped base, bl opaque, unmk Westmoreland late repro **45.00**
Rooster, goofus on milk glass base, att Westmoreland, 5½" **65.00**
Rooster on wide rib base, milk glass, Westmoreland, 5¼" **85.00**
Setter on sq base, bl opaque, att Vallerysthal **210.00**
Steer's head, milk glass, Challinor Taylor, 7½" **2,200.00**
Swan, Block; milk glass, Challinor Taylor, 7" **200.00**
Swan, Block; on basketweave base, milk glass **150.00**
Swan, clear frosted, Vallerysthal, 5½" **65.00**
Swan, Raised Wing; milk glass, molded eyes, Westmoreland **150.00**
Swan on knobby basketweave base, amber, Pat Applied For, 7" .**165.00**
Turtle, amber transparent, lg **100.00**
Turtle, milk glass, knobby bk, unmk, lg **150.00**

Antiquities

The ancient Egyptians, Romans, and the early craftsmen of India and China have left us with exquisite treasures bearing mute witness of their esthetic convictions that even a water carrier, a knife, or a rug should be a thing of beauty. Though time and the elements have taken their toll on the more fragile works of these ancient artisans, it is incredible that many remain intact to this day. The thin-walled tear and scent bottles blown by Roman artisans from the last century A.D. and examples of the red or black predynastic potteries of Egypt, though understandably quite rare, can yet occasionally be found on the market today. Jewelry, often interred with the dead, has survived the centuries well; figures of marble and terra cotta, ceremonial masks, earthenware vessels, and other relics such as these offer us of the 20th century the only tangible link possible to the ancient world. Our advisor for this category is Alex G. Malloy; he is listed in the Directory under New York.

Key
cyl — cylinder   Mil — millenium
Dy — Dynasty

Amulets

Coptic Period, 4th-6th C AD, bird pr, MOP, ½x⅞" 250.00
Late Period, 1085-333 BC, gr faience Isis, 2", VG 200.00
Ptolemaic, 332-30 BC, ivory figure of Harpocrates, nude, 1⅜" ...400.00
Roman Period, 1st-4th C AD, Isis, bl/gr faience, 2½", EX 125.00
Sumerian, 3rd Mil BC, bronze serpentine bird, ⅞" 85.00
XVIIth Dy, 1567-1320 BC, glass heart, bl w/wht opaque 175.00
XXVI-XXX Dys, 664-343 BC, papyrus sceptre, gr faience, ⅞" 100.00

Bronze Objects

Assyrian, 8th C BC, human arm fibula, 1½x⅞" 125.00
Hasanlu, 3rd Mil BC, rattle bell, openwork, ¾" 45.00
Luristan, 10th-7th C BC, brooch of antelope's head, 1⅜" 60.00
Parthian, 300-200 BC, bell, horse form, iron clapper, 1⅛" 65.00
Urartu, 800 BC, bell, truncated, suspension loop, 2⅛" 165.00
1st-3rd C AD, sewing pin, needle w/2 holes, 5⅛" 150.00

Cuneiform Tablet Fragments

Akkadian, 2334-2145 BC, red terra cotta, economic text, 1¼" W ..150.00
Old Babylonian, 1900-1600 BC, economic text w/names 350.00
Syrian, 1200 BC, sale contract, w/seal impression, 1¾x1¼" 200.00

Glass

Early Roman midnight blue flask, 1st – 2nd centuries AD, purple/silver iridescence, repaired chip, 4½", $875.00.

Byzantine, 4th-5th C AD, flask, gr sq shape, 2¾", VG 200.00
Late Roman/Byzantine, 4th-5th C AD, gold glass amulet, 1⅛" 80.00
Roman/Byzantine, 4th-6th C AD, mirror, in terra cotta fr, 3" dia ..750.00

Jewelry and Adornments

Greek, 6th-5th C BC, silver ring, Zeus intaglio, VG 75.00
Greek/Hellenistic, 1st C BC-1st C AD, gold earrings, loops, pr .500.00
Late Roman, 5th-6th C AD, bronze bracelet, incised decor 110.00
Roman, 2nd-34d C AD, bronze ring, cvd bezel of Helios 145.00
Visigothic, 6th-7th C AD, bronze bracelet, bird designs 135.00
Visigothic, 6th-7th C AD, bronze buckle, oval, 1" W 50.00

Pottery

Apulian, 4th C BC, dish, blk slip, thick rim, 1¼x3⅞" 125.00
Attic, 520-510 BC, blk figure amphora fragment, satyr head, 1¼" ..275.00
Attic/Corinth, 5th-4th C BC, lekythos, glazed, rstr, 2⅞x3⅛" 225.00
Corinth, 575-550 BC, cothon, orange & slip w/blk, ⅞x5¼" 350.00
Early Roman Period, 1st-2nd C, cooking pot, wheel made, hdls, 6" ...475.00
Iron Age, 731-530 BC, Ammonite mug, wheel made, buffware, 2½" .200.00
Ptolemaic, 3rd-1st C BC, votive lamp, terra cotta, mini, 1¼" 50.00
W Asia Minor, 4th-3rd C BC, bowl, red slip traces, hdls, 5½" ...100.00
586-300 BC, jar, wheel made, wide mouth, brn slip, 2½" 175.00
600-300 BC, flask, wheel made, ovoid, grayware, 3¾" 150.00
800-586 BC, bowl, wheel made, pale redware, 5½" dia 175.00

Scarabs/Seals

Libyan Dy, 935-730 BC, scarab of Shashanq V, ⅞x1⅜" 175.00
Middle Kingdom, 2050-1786 BC, glazed/cvd steatite plaque, ⅝x⅜" .85.00
XIXth Dy, 1320-1200 BC, cvd steatite hedgehog w/pharoah 500.00
XVIIth Dy, 1567-1320 BC, bl faience scarab, crude, ¾" 65.00
XXIInd Dy, 935-730 BC, steatite scarab, lion/gazelles, 1⅜" 75.00
XXVIth Dy, 664-525 BC, steatite scarab of Psemthek I, ⅜" 150.00

Stamp and Cylinder Seals

Early Dynastic, 2600-2500 BC, limestone cyl, animals, 1⅛x½" .225.00
Jemdet Nasr, Peripheral Period, hematite, 10-sided star, ½" 75.00
Mesopotamia, 3500-3000 BC, gray serpentine, crisscrossing, ½" ..65.00
Neo-Assyrian, 9th-8th C BC, bl faience, hunting contest, ⅞" 75.00
Old Babylonia, 2nd Mil BC, alabaster cyl, relief cvd king, 1¼" ..500.00
1800-1650 BC, blk goethite cyl, seated diety, ⅞", EX 275.00
1900-1600 BC, blk hematite, cyl, robed figures, 1" 300.00

Appliances, Electric

Antique electric appliances represent a diverse field and are always being sought after by collectors. There were over one hundred different companies manufacturing electric appliances in the first half of the twentieth century, some were making over ten different models under several different names at any given time in all fields: coffeepots, toasters, waffle irons, etc., while others were making only one or two models for extended periods of time. Today collectors and decorators alike are seeking those items to add to a collection or to use as accent pieces in a period kitchen.

Always check the cord before using and make sure the appliance is in good condition, free of rust and pitting. The prices below are for appliances in good to excellent condition. Prices may vary around the country.

If you have any questions regarding antique appliances, feel free to contact our advisor, Jim Barker; he is listed in the Directory under Pennsylvania. (Please include SASE.)

Bottle warmer, Sunbeam, chrome w/plastic knobs, 1950s, 13" 95.00
Coffee urn, chrome & yel Bakelite, Manning-Bowman, 14x11", VG ...70.00
Egg boiler, El Eggo, Pacific Electric Heating Co, late 1890s, NM .50.00
Egg poacher, 4-egg, EX 25.00
Fan, Emerson, #6250-D, 10" blades, 1939, NM 55.00
Fan, Emerson, #79646-AT, 12" blades, 1941, EX 35.00
Fan, Emerson Electric, 4-blade, 1930s, 8½" dia 45.00
Fan, Emerson Junior, 10" blades, CI base, 1925-28", EX 45.00
Fan, General Electric, #174948, 9" blades, 1917, EX 75.00
Fan, General Electric, #34017, 12" blades, 1922, NM 85.00
Fan, General Electric, #55X165B, 9" blades, 1932, EX 45.00
Fan, General Electric, Type D, 12" blades, ca 1903, EX 350.00

Fan, Peerless, #G-1, 12" blades, 1905, VG 600.00
Fan, Wagner Electric, #52603, 10" blades, ca 1939, EX 35.00
Fan, Westinghouse, #1381675, 10" blades, ca 1958, NM 23.00
Fan, Westinghouse, #60673, 12" blades, 1912, EX 500.00
Mixer, Dormeyer, chrome, 1950s 85.00
Mixer, General Electric, #139DM6 ....85.00
Mixer, General Electric, #49X390 ....65.00
Mixer, Hamilton Beach, Model C, 1930s 75.00
Mixer, Sears' Powermaster DeLuxe, cast-metal base, 1930s, EX ...55.00
Mixer, Sunbeam Mixmaster, Model 9 ....75.00
Toaster, American Electric Htr 75.00
Toaster, Beardsley & Wolcott, Torrid, chrome, 1930s 100.00
Toaster, Bersted, #66 ....50.00
Toaster, Bersted, #72 ....45.00
Toaster, Bersted, #85 ....55.00
Toaster, Challenge, #307, Deco design 55.00
Toaster, Delta Pop-Down Automatic, chrome/Bakelite, 1940s ..300.00
Toaster, Electrahot, chrome/blk enamel, 1920s, 7⅜" 55.00
Toaster, General Electric, #119T38 ....45.00
Toaster, General Electric, #119T46 ....75.00
Toaster, General Electric, #119T48, late 1930s, 7⅝" 50.00
Toaster, General Electric, #139T77 ....65.00
Toaster, General Electric, D-12 ....395.00
Toaster, Heatmaster, #307, chrome, Bakelite hdls, 1930s, 7½" 55.00
Toaster, Helion 175.00
Toaster, Hold Heat 65.00
Toaster, Hotpoint, #1Z6T33 ....95.00
Toaster, Kenmore, #344-63321, chrome/Bakelite, 1940s 145.00
Toaster, Landers, Frary & Clark, #E3412, NP, blk hdls, 1920s 65.00
Toaster, Malda, #84, chrome, blk pulls, 1930s, 6⅝" 45.00
Toaster, Manning-Bowman, #108 ....90.00
Toaster, Manning-Bowman, #85 ....55.00
Toaster, Reddy, horizontal 75.00
Toaster, Samson, #198, Bakelite base 95.00

Toaster, Security #220, EX, $75.00.

Toaster, Simplex, #211 ....225.00
Toaster, Simplex, #212 ....85.00
Toaster, Superior Electric, #66 ....150.00
Toaster, Tamco, horizontal 95.00
Toaster, Toastmaster, #1B2 ....65.00
Toaster, Toastswell, #791 ....65.00
Toaster, Torrid, horizontal 85.00
Toaster, Universal, #E7211 ....65.00
Toaster, Universal, #E7812 ....95.00
Toaster, Universal, #E941, wire doors 85.00
Toaster, Universal, #E943 ....275.00
Universal, White Cross, #230 ....65.00
Waffle iron, Bersted, #212 ....35.00
Waffle iron, Dominion, #377 ....35.00

Waffle iron, Electra Hot, #705 ....55.00
Waffle iron, Hotpoint, #116Y53 ....45.00
Waffle iron, Thermax, #3931 ....35.00
Waffle iron, Universal, #9314 ....45.00
Waffle iron, Westinghouse, #284186 ....65.00
Waffle iron, Westinghouse, WD-2 ....65.00
Waffle iron, White Cross, #255 ....40.00

Arequipa

The Arequipa Pottery operated from 1911 until 1918 at a sanitorium near Fairfax, California. Its purpose was twofold: therapy for the patients and financial support for the institution. Frederick H. Rhead was the originator and director. The ware, made from local clays, was often hand thrown, simply styled and decorated. Marks were varied but always incorporated the name of the pottery and the state. A circular arrangement encompassing the negative image of a vase beside a tree is most common.

Examples are evaluated according to quality of artwork; size and shape are less important. Those done by Rhead himself are most desirable.

Bowl, bl gloss, yel int, mk, 2½x9" 170.00
Bowl, blk gloss, bl mottle int, mk, 3x8½" 190.00
Bowl, primrose in relief, dk gr matt, sgn HBL, 2½x5" 1,200.00
Vase, floral (cvd/incised), gr & brn matt, sgn EM, 8½" 220.00
Vase, floral (squeezebag), 4-color, att F Rhead, 8¾x6" 3,100.00
Vase, floral cvg, gr & brn matt, sgn EM, mk, 8½" 220.00
Vase, flower w/leaves (deeply cvd) brn matt, MIW, rpr, 5½" 425.00
Vase, spade-shaped pk squeezebag florals on gr, 3¾x3¼" 2,000.00

Argy-Rousseau, G.

Gabriel Argy-Rousseau produced both fine art glass and quality commercial ware in Paris, France, in 1918. He favored Art Nouveau as well as Art Deco and in the '20s produced a line of vases in the Egyptian manner, made popular by the discovery of King Tut's tomb. One of the most important types of glass he made was pate-de-verre. Most of his work is signed. Items listed below are pate-de-verre unless noted otherwise.

Bowl, Lotus, amber/clear mottle w/brn, 4" H 3,750.00
Bowl, raspberry vines, clear/purple frost, 4" 2,100.00
Charger, sea gulls HP on smoke, gold scallops, 12¼" 700.00
Vase, floral on wht w/amber & gr, cylindrical, 5¼" 4,800.00
Vase, Les Rainures, gr/bl streaks, pate-de-crystal, mk, 8¼" 3,165.00
Veilleuse, floral on gray, wrought fr, 8½" 7,000.00

Art Deco

To the uninformed observer, 'Art Deco' evokes images of chrome and glass, streamlined curves and aerodynamic shapes, mirrored prints of pink flamingos, and statues of slender nudes and greyhound dogs. Though the Deco movement began in 1925 at the Paris International Exposition and lasted to some extent into the 1950s, within that period of time the evolution of fashion and taste continued as it always has, resulting in subtle variations.

The French Deco look was one of opulence — exotic inlaid woods, rich material, lush fur and leather. Lines tended toward symmetrical curves. American designers adapted the concept to cover every aspect of fashion and home furnishings from small inexpensive picture frames, cigarette lighters, and costume jewelry to high-fashion designer clothing and exquisite massive furniture with squared or circular lines. Vinyl was a popular covering, and chrome-plated brass was used for chairs, cocktail shakers, lamps, and tables. Dinnerware, glassware, theaters, and train stations were designed to reflect the new 'Modernism.'

The Deco movement made itself apparent into the '50s in wrought iron lamps with stepped pink plastic shades and Venetian blinds. The sheer volume of production during those twenty-five years provides collectors today with fine examples of the period that can be bought for as little as $10.00 or $20.00 up to the thousands. Chrome items signed 'Chase' are prized by collectors, and blue glass radios and tables with blue glass tops are high on the list of desirability in many areas.

Those interested in learning more about this subject will want to read *Collector's Guide to Art Deco* by our advisor, Mary Frank Gaston. See also Bronzes; Chase; Frankart; Furniture; Jewelry; Lalique; Radios; etc.

Ashtray, nude on pillar, Nuart **135.00**
Ashtray, seated gold-pnt cast figure holds amber tray, Nuart **150.00**
Belt buckle, enameled crescent moons w/gold trim, Germany **25.00**
Bookends, nude w/man at ft, Bronzmet, dtd 1924, pr **125.00**
Box, powder; Windsor Diamond, Jeannette Glass, 1930s, 3½" dia ..**30.00**
Candle holders, sterling on bronze, Heintz, 5", pr **250.00**
Cigarette dispenser, wht plastic, sliding lid, Ziegfield, 6" L **150.00**
Cigarette holder, bl plastic w/silver trim, 2" **35.00**
Cigarette holder, blk plastic, 6" **20.00**
Cigarette holder, celluloid, 5" **18.00**
Clock, boudoir; plastic base, bl glass fr, Teletron **225.00**
Clock, mantel; gold-pnt dog on gr ceramic base, 11½x10" L **150.00**
Clock, mantel; Verde Antico marble/rose quartz, 8-day, Swiss, 8" .**1,150.00**
Clock, marble, shape-on-shape form, Fr, 13", +2 side panels **325.00**
Consoles, D-shaped marble top/wrought strapwork bases, 47x45", pr ..**4,885.00**
Cup & saucer, demi; HP mc dots on cream w/blk, Ivory Ware **25.00**
Curling iron, electric, gr Bakelite hdl, M in Deco box **25.00**
Door knocker, brass, Egyptian decor, 6½" **75.00**
Figurine, draped dancing nude, bronzed wht metal, Fayral, 21" .**1,800.00**
Figurine, lady w/dog & pheasant, patinated metal, Arisse, 18" ..**2,185.00**
Figurine, Pan & nymph, alabaster, Continental, rstr, 17½" **1,100.00**
Figurine, Russian wolfhounds, ceramic, B Kopecki, 1940s, 13" L ..**300.00**
Figurine, seminude lady w/bowl, ceramic, Kent Art Ware, 11" ...**175.00**
Flower frog, nude holding long veil, ceramic, Coronet, 13½" **140.00**
Frame, beveled glass w/etched floral, 1940s, 14½x17" **100.00**

Gates, wrought iron with stylized bud and vine decoration, four brackets, French, ca 1925, 54x45½", $800.00.

Hors d'oeuvres server, chrome, 4 trays, Bakelite hdl, 11½" **150.00**
Lamp, dancer, spelter & ivorene, on alabaster globe, 15" **335.00**
Lamp, frosted glass circle shade; chrome & Bakelite, 14", pr **200.00**
Lamp, patinated copper streamline form, 11x10" dia, VG **150.00**
Lamp, Pierrot, maiden & crescent moon, alabaster/onyx, 25" **600.00**

Lamp, SP bird in flight, marble base, millefiori globe, 11x9" **300.00**
Lamp base, flamingo, pk on blk base, ceramic, pr **325.00**
Mirror, vanity; pot-metal nude on faux marble base **200.00**
Mirror, wrought iron & polished steel, stepped corners, 50x32" .**400.00**
Mirror, 8-sided w/wrought flower-head fr, 37x22" **1,600.00**
Night light, German shepherd on rocks, clear & opaque glass **195.00**
Planter, plaster & wood, nude frieze, gold on plum, 22x21" dia ..**345.00**
Sconce, 3 chrome tiers, Fr, 14½" **350.00**
Statuette, dancer, silver metal & ivorene, blk marble base, 12" ..**575.00**
Table, 8-sided marble top, scrolled wrought base, 28x32" **3,750.00**
Table lighter, nude lady, Parker **45.00**
Tea set, chrome w/Bakelite hdls, Manning-Bowman, 3-pc on tray ...**300.00**
Torchiere, 3-flare shade, blk shaft w/metal base, 1930s, 66", pr ..**400.00**
Tumbler, sterling siver, flared mouth, ftd, Cartier, 3" **125.00**
Vase, pottery, leaves, mc on wht w/blk stripes, Catteau, 10" **550.00**
Vase, red enamel on brn-pnt metal, ovoid, 20¼" **140.00**
Vase, sterling floral on bronze stick form, Heintz, 12" **225.00**
Wash bowl & pitcher, Rose Marie (geometric), Keller & Guerin ..**300.00**
Watch pendant, gr/blk enamel w/silver trim, pentagon, Broel **250.00**

Art Glass Baskets

Popular novelty and gift items during the Victorian era, these one-of-a-kind works of art were produced in just about any type of art glass in use at that time. They were never marked. Many were not true production pieces but 'whimsies' made by glassworkers to relieve the tedium of the long work day. Some were made as special gifts. The more decorative and imaginative the design, the more valuable the basket. Our advisor for this category is Deborah Maggard; she is listed in the Directory under Ohio.

Amberina rose-bowl shape w/HP florals, amber hdl, 8x5" **325.00**
Amberina w/HP daisies, amber hdl, ribbed int, 6x5" **325.00**
Bl o/l w/amber edge & thorn hdl, 10-Row Hobnail, 6x7" **250.00**
Bl o/l w/silver mica, clear briar hdl, 9¼x5¾" **325.00**
Bl opal to crystal, melon ribs, ruffled, clear hdl, 10½x11" **365.00**
Bl satin w/15 melon ribs, crimped rim, thorn hdl, 8¾x7¾x7" .**295.00**
Bl to wht MOP Dmn Quilt, sq loop hdl, Mt WA, 7½x4½" **550.00**
Clear w/pk/wht latticinio striped hdl, 3-ftd, 8¾x7½" **850.00**
Clear w/3 rows appl rigaree, dbl Xd hdl w/rigaree, 12x10" **450.00**
Cranberry, amber cased w/aventurine, amber ft & hdl, 9x5" **295.00**
Cranberry Dmn Quilt rose bowl shape, wishbone hdl, 8½x5" ...**250.00**
Cranberry opal w/wht opal stripes & silver mica, twist hdl, 4x5" ..**175.00**
Cranberry to amber w/wht opal stripes & threads, pk hdl, 8x7" .**175.00**
Cranberry w/clear ruffle, rolled-over rim, shell ft, 6x6½" **150.00**
Cranberry w/swirled paneled body, clear thorn hdl, 6¼" W **150.00**
Dk to lt bl w/silver mica, clear rope hdl, crimped rim, 9x10" **175.00**
Emerald gr, 6 rows appl glass openwork, silver o/l, 5x7½" **500.00**
Emerald gr w/crystal flower-petal top & twist hdl, 6¾x4⅝" **150.00**
Gold & pk pull-ups on wht, frosted rim, Northwood, 4½x9" ..**1,250.00**
Gr crackle w/2 yel leaves at base, clear hdl, 7½" **125.00**
Mahog red to cherry to lt yel cased, clear hdl, crimped rim, 8x8" ..**295.00**
Mahog to red to gr, wht cased, clear rope hdl, 8x8½" **250.00**
Mc spatter, clear thorn hdl, scalloped/ruffled rim, 6x7x6" **250.00**
Mc spatter w/pk int, ruffled rim, thorn hdl, 6" dia **250.00**
Mc spatter w/silver mica, clear rope hdl & ruffle, 9½x10x9" **325.00**
Mc spatter w/3 rows of hobnails, thorn hdl, 6x6" **150.00**
Mc tortoise-shell spatter, gold-decor loop hdl, 8x13x8" **275.00**
Millefiori canes/wht opal cased w/butterscotch, pk hdl, 11x7" ...**250.00**
Peach satin w/lt gr int, frosted thorn hdl, ruffled, 9½x10" **250.00**
Peach to gold w/gold mica, pk int, rnd w/sq rim, 6½x5½" **325.00**
Pk & bl striped satin, wht int, ruffled rim, 7x5½" **175.00**
Pk & wht candy stripe, wht int, frosted thorn hdl, 8½x8½" **250.00**

Pk & wht spatter w/air traps, thorn hdl, star-shaped top, 6x8" ...250.00
Pk MOP, frosted thorn V-shaped hdl, thorn ft, 11¾x8½" 600.00
Pk nailsea loops on wht, appl frosted hdl & ft, 5½x5" 425.00
Pk o/l, melon ribs, crimped/ruffled, frosted hdl/ft, 15x11" 300.00
Pk o/l w/amber ruffled rim, twisted thorn hdl, 6¾x5¼" 145.00
Pk o/l w/hobnails, frosted thorn hdl, 9½" dia 150.00
Pk o/l w/mc mottle, custard hdl, HP Turkish decor, 9x7" 225.00
Pk o/l w/mica, ruffled rim, amber casing & thorn hdl, 8x9¾" 250.00
Pk opal, crimped rim, pk hdl, 6½x4⅞" 95.00
Pk to aqua o/l w/mc spatter & mica, 10½x10x8" 345.00
Pk to wht w/HP florals, crystal thorn hdl, 11¼" 865.00
Pk w/silver mica, melon ribs, 7½x7" 150.00
Robin's-egg bl satin, wht int, ribbed/ruffled/crimped, 8x7" 100.00
Sapphire bl, emb swirls, ruffled, clear hdl, 6x5½" 135.00
Vaseline & satin stripe w/floral etch, 8" 65.00
Vaseline opal to pk, petal edge, twisted pk hdl, 6½x8" 250.00
Vaseline opal w/vaseline hdl, appl leaves, 6x2¾" 150.00
Wht crackle w/bl int, crystal V-shaped thorn hdl, 7½x6" 150.00
Wht opal Coin Spot, pie-crust edge, clear hdl, 9x10½" 150.00
Wht opaque w/blown hobnails, bl int, amber rim/hdl, 6½x7" 275.00
Wht satin w/frosted hobnails, yel satin int, frosted hdl, 5" 145.00

Art Nouveau

From the famous 'L'Art Nouveau' shop in the Rue de Provence in Paris, 'New Art' spread across the continent and belatedly arrived in America in time to add its curvilinear elements and asymmetrical ornamentations to the ostentatious remains of the Rococo revival of the 1800s. Nouveau manifested itself in every facet of decorative art. In glassware Tiffany turned the concept into a commercial success that lasted well into the second decade of this century and created a style that inspired other American glassmakers for decades. Furniture, lamps, bronzes, jewelry, and automobiles were designed within the realm of its dictates. Today's market abounds with lovely examples of Art Nouveau, allowing the collector to choose one or several areas that hold a special interest. Our advisor for this category is Steven Whysel; he is listed in the Directory under Florida. See also Bronzes; Galle; Jewelry; Loetz; Tiffany; Silver; specific manufacturers.

Pitcher, bronze, nude maiden handle joins baluster form with molded fish decoration, Ledru, Susse Freres Foundry mark, 15½", $1,600.00.

Buckle, SP over brass, lady's head, for sash, 4" 80.00
Candelabrum, gilt bronze, nymph stands on lily pad, 10" 200.00
Candlestick, gilt brass, lady figural, 12" 125.00
Clock, gilt on wht metal, lady's head, Ansonia, 9" 350.00
Curio, 2-drw w/glass panes, mahog w/marquetry, VG 3,800.00
Dish, brass, water nymph stands at side, C Kauba, 3½x8⅜" 300.00
Dish, bronze, nymph on rim of poppy-cast leaf, 5" 300.00
Frame, gilt metal, nymph/flower in openwork border, 11x8" 255.00

Inkwell, gilt bronze, nude kneels between 2 wells, 9" L 865.00
Lamp, caramel blown-out panels w/metal o/l shade, metal std, 15" ..400.00
Lamp, SP water bird w/fish in its beak, sgn MC, 22½" 625.00
Letter opener, brass, stylized flower, 7" 95.00
Pitcher, metal, frog/crab/bee in relief, 9" 245.00
Plaque, SP over pewter, lady w/flowing hair, rstr, 20" 625.00
Sculpture, draped ladies (2), unmk pottery, 28", EX 5,000.00
Tray, cast copper, draped nude w/flowing hair, 5" 115.00
Vase, glass, floral, mc on clear, cylindrical, Fr, 11x3½" 675.00
Vase, pottery, winged lizard coils gr-blk bottle form, 12" 425.00
Vase, silver, iris w/pierced rims, appl details, Shreve, 23" 2,500.00
Vase, SP pewter, maid/nymph/frog in full relief, 22" 1,500.00

Arts and Crafts

The Arts and Crafts movement began in England during the last quarter of the 19th century, and its influence was soon felt in this country. Among its proponents in America were Elbert Hubbard (see Roycroft) and Gustav Stickley (see Stickley). They rebelled against the mechanized mass production of the Industrial Revolution and against the cumulative influence of hundreds of years of man's changing taste. They subscribed to a theory of purification of the styles: that designs be geared strictly to necessity. At the same time they sought to elevate these basic ideals to the level of accepted 'art.' Simplicity was their virtue; to their critics it was a fault.

The type of furniture they promoted was squarely built, usually of heavy oak, and so simple was its appearance that as a result many began to copy the style which became known as 'Mission.' Soon factories had geared production toward making cheap copies of their designs. In 1915 Stickley's own operation failed, a victim of changing styles and tastes. Hubbard lost his life that same year on the ill-fated *Lusitania*. By the end of the decade the style had lost its popularity.

Metalware was produced by numerous crafts people, from experts such as Dirk van Erp and Albert Berry to unknown novices. Prices for Arts and Crafts accessories rose dramatically in 1988, but by the beginning of 1991 leveled off and (in some cases) dropped. Metal items or hardware should not be scrubbed or scoured; to do so could remove or damage the rich, dark patina typical of this period. Our advisor for this category is Bruce Austin; he is listed in the Directory under New York. See also Furniture; Roycroft; Silver; Stickley; specific manufacturers.

Key: h/cp — hammered copper

Andirons, circular brass disk finial, hammered iron base, 24" 325.00
Bookends, Albert Berry, h/cp w/tooling, EX patina, 4½", pr 250.00
Bookends, Forest Craft Guild, h/cp, geometric cutouts, 4½x6" ..150.00
Bookends, Frost, h/cp w/emb tulips & vines, 5x6", EX 350.00
Bookends, h/cp, radial hammering, EX patina, 5x6" 150.00
Bowl, Handicraft Guild, h/cp, orig patina, mk, 3x7" 500.00
Bowl, Harry Dixon, h/cp, waisted, EX patina, 1920, 2½x5", EX .375.00
Bowl, Heintz, bronze w/silver floral o/l, mk, 3x9" dia, VG 200.00
Bowl, Jarvie, h/cp, cleaned patina, 1x7¼" 100.00
Bowl, van Erp, h/cp, closed form, dk brn patina, 3x7" 800.00
Bowl, van Erp, h/cp, closed-in rim, G new patina, 4½x11" 850.00
Bowl, van Erp, h/cp, dk brn orig patina, 2½x7" 500.00
Box, cigarette; Heintz, verdigris w/silver o/l, 2x4x4" 225.00
Box, cigarette; Silver Crest, gold dore w/silver o/l, 3x6x5" 100.00
Box, h/cp chest form w/iron strap hinges, EX patina, 14x20x13" ..1,100.00
Box, h/cp w/tooled leather sections, lined, unmk, 2x4x3" 850.00
Box, Heintz, bronze w/silver floral o/l, 1¼x4¼x3¼" 500.00
Box, mahog, copper lined, HP ship cartouch on lid, 6x13x7" 600.00
Box, stamp; Art Craft Chop, copper w/enamel decor, 2x4x3" 550.00
Candlesticks, ET Hurley, bronze, 3-light, EX patina, 15", pr 750.00

Candlesticks, Heintz, verdigris w/silver floral o/l, 5½", pr 600.00
Candlesticks, Jarvie style, bronze, orig patina, 12", VG, pr 425.00
Candlesticks, Jessie Preston, bronze, bobeche, 14½", pr 900.00
Desk set, Carence Crafters, copper w/floral design, 3-pc 325.00
Desk set, Heintz, verdigris w/silver o/l, 7-pc, EX 500.00

Frame, leather covered with copper overlay decoration of leaves and pods, hook on back for hanging, 9½x8", EX, $750.00.

Handbag, leather, floriform tooling, w/change purse, 5½x8" 150.00
Humidor, Benedict, h/cp, riveted brass straps form 4 ft, 6½" 300.00
Humidor, Jarvie, h/cp, riveted lid, EX patina, #24, 6¾x7" 2,700.00
Inkwell, Forest Craft Guild, h/cp, geometric cutouts, 2½x5" 375.00
Inkwell, Heintz, copper w/silver o/l, glass insert, 2½x4" 150.00
Lamp, ET Hurley, sea horse metal std, paneled shell shade, 13" ..1,000.00
Lamp, Heintz, bronze helmet w/silver o/l, harp base, 10" 800.00
Lamp, Heintz, NP helmet shade w/silver o/l, harp base, 10" 325.00
Lamp, table; Prairie School, bl slag pyramid shade, 2-socket, 25" ...800.00
Lamp, table; slag 14" shade w/riveted o/l, wrought base, 23" ...2,000.00
Lamp, van Erp, h/cp, 13" conical shade w/mica panels, 15" 5,000.00
Letter opener, Carence Crafters, hammered brass, unmk, 8" 100.00
Tray, Carence Crafters, brass, bamboo relief, 9x5", EX 170.00
Tray, Carence Crafters, brass w/emb floral, orig patina, 9x5" 325.00
Tray, Jarvie, h/cp, undulating rim, EX patina, 6x8" 300.00
Tray, van Erp, h/cp, recessed center, EX patina, 19x13" 425.00
Tray, van Erp, h/cp w/raised edge, recent patina, 18" dia, VG ...1,000.00
Vase, h/cp, tooled stylized branches, unmk, 2½" 150.00
Vase, Harry Dixon, h/cp, fluted neck, EX patina, 1925, 4" 350.00
Vase, Heintz, bronze w/silver cattails, 8x3½" 300.00
Vase, Redlands, emb frogs/grasses, bronze/copper lustre, 3¼" ...7,750.00
Vase, trophy; Jarvie, tooled/hammered silver #1029/1916, 10" ..12,000.00
Vase, van Erp, h/cp, fine patina, 5½" 950.00
Vase, van Erp, h/cp, orig patina, lt scratches, 8½x8", VG 1,500.00
Vase, van Erp, h/cp, radial hammering near base, mk, 7" 900.00
Vase, van Erp, h/cp, rolled rim, orig patina, 7x5½", VG 850.00
Vase, van Erp, h/cp, shouldered, EX patina, mks, 6½" 900.00
Vase, Zark, lilies, wht on gr matt, shouldered, 7", NM 2,500.00
Woodblock print, CA mtn scene, Lydia Cooley, 5¾x4½", EX ..400.00
Woodblock print, children w/dragon, H Hyde, 1914, 8" dia 160.00
Woodblock print, Go-Cart, Helen Hyde, 1913, 4½x4", EX 475.00
Woodblock print, Twins (trees), HE Thompson, 8x10"+fr, VG ...250.00

Attwell, Mabel Lucie

Born in London in 1879, Mabel Lucie Attwell put her talent in illustration and design toward many outlets. Merchandise ranging from children's books and dinnerware, postcards, advertising, dolls, calendars, and greeting cards were marketed under her direction. She also designed a line of china called Nursery Ware for the Shelley China Company (see also Shelley). Our advisor for this category is David Ehrhard; he is listed in the Directory under California.

Book, Alice in Wonderland, L Carroll, Tuck & Sons, 12 plates .150.00

Book, Children's Stories by Lucie Attwell, Whitman 70.00
Calendar, Never Forget If the World Goes Wry...Standing By ...135.00
Creamer & sugar bowl, BooBoo 150.00
Figurine, BooBoo on a puppy, Shelley, 4" 400.00
Figurine, BooBoo w/mushroom 500.00
Figurine, Little Mermaid 500.00
Handkerchief set, Lucie Attwell's Picture Hankys, M 75.00
Magazine cover, Pictorial Review, Who's Afraid, Nov 1913 ....75.00
Nursery Ware, bowl, Look at This Wee Jolly..., Shelley 185.00
Nursery Ware, cake plate, If I Had a Fairy, Shelley 120.00
Nursery Ware, plate, Bobby Bear Went to Moon..., Shelley, 5" ...75.00
Nursery Ware, saucer, Oh! Mr Rabbit Do Put Up..., Shelley 75.00
Nursery Ware, teapot, flying plane scene & verse, Shelley 160.00
Plaque, This Is Home Not an Ashtray, Valentine/Sons of Dundee ..95.00
Print, Fairies Are Mischiefing Dorothy Dell, 4x6" 50.00
Print, False Perjured Clarence, Tatler, Jan 1921 ....70.00
Print, Working on the Act, 8x10" 45.00
Tea set, mushroom house pot/toadstool sugar/BooBoo creamer ..650.00
Tin container, Little Friends, Huntley Palmers, 1 of 6, 5" dia 30.00
Tray, Mischief, I'm Nuts About You, Wright's Biscuits 175.00

Austrian Ware

From the late 1800s until the beginning of WWI, several companies were located in the area known at the turn of the century as Bohemia. They produced hard-paste porcelain dinnerware and decorative items primarily for the American trade. Today examples bearing the marks of these firms are usually referred to by collectors as Austrian ware, indicating simply the country of their origin. Of those various companies, these marks are best known: M.Z. Austria; Victoria, Carlsbad, Austria (Schmidt and Company); and O. & E.G. (Royal) Austria.

Though most of the decorations were transfer designs which were sometimes signed by the original artist, pieces marked Royal Austria were often hand painted and so indicated alongside the backstamp.

Of these three companies, Victoria, Carlsbad, Austria, is the most highly valued. Collectors should note that in our listings transfer decorations showing 'signatures' (sgn), such as 'Wagner,' 'Kauffmann,' 'LeBrun,' etc., were not actually painted by those artists but were merely based on their original paintings.

Photo courtesy Monsen and Baer

Cologne bottle, painted daisies on porcelain, gold ball stopper, 5", $120.00.

Bone dish, mc roses w/gold, scrolled blank, Carlsbad, 6¼" 65.00
Bowl, ladies & child w/instruments, cobalt & gold, rtcl, 11½" ...195.00
Bowl, 3 maidens w/cherub, cobalt & gold, Carlsbad, 9" 110.00
Chocolate set, pk & wht roses, pot+5 c/s 425.00
Ewer, gold/yel swirls on cobalt, ornate gold mouth, mk, 16" 260.00
Ewer, pk & yel wild roses w/gold, gold scroll hdl, ftd, 11¾" 125.00
Ewer, wild roses w/gold, gold hdl, 4-ftd, mk, 11¾x6" 130.00

Figurine, aristocrat & dog, sgn EW (Wahliss), crown mk, 20¾" ..**2,500.00**
Fish set, fish among seaweed, boat w/attached plate, +6 plates ...**300.00**
Nappy, pk daisies w/gold, Carlsbad, 5⅜", 4 for **10.00**
Plate, chariot w/Cupid & 3 maidens, Angelica Kauffmann, 8⅝" ..**550.00**
Plate, floral, scalloped rim, Austrian China, 9½", NM **20.00**
Platter, roses w/gold, mk, 12⅝x8⅝" **50.00**
Sauce boat, fish at sea, open hdls, attached underplate, 9" **95.00**
Tray, ice cream; yel roses, scalloped, oval, 15½" **65.00**
Vase, flowers & berries w/gold, dolphin hdls, mk, 10x9¾" **135.00**
Vase, flowers & holly w/gold hdls, Carlsbad, 13⅜x6½", pr **400.00**
Vase, gold florals, dolphin hdls, divided 2-spout rim, 10" **125.00**
Vase, lady w/embr cap, dragon hdls, Royal Wettina, 20" **300.00**
Vase, peacock on balcony, ped ft, rtcl hdls, Carlsbad, 10½" **265.00**
Vase, poppies & butterfly w/gold, 4-ftd, twig hdls, 12¾x5" **120.00**

Autographs

Autograph collecting, also known as 'philography' or 'love of writing,' used to be a hobby shared by a few thousand dedicated collectors. But in recent years, autograph collecting has become a serious pursuit for more than 2,000,000 collectors worldwide. And in the past decade, more investors are adding rare and valuable autograph portfolios to their traditional investments. One reason for this sudden interest in autograph investing relates to the simple economic law of supply and demand. Rare autographs have a 'fixed' supply, meaning that unlike diamonds, gold, silver, stock certificates, etc., no more are being produced. There are only so many Abraham Lincoln, Marilyn Monroe, and Charles Lindbergh autographs available. In the meantime, it's estimated that more than 20,000 new collectors enter the market each year, thus creating an ever-increasing demand. Hence, the rare autographs generally rise steadily in value each year. Because of this scarcity, a serious collector will pay over $10,000.00 for a photograph signed by both Wilbur and Orville Wright, or as much as $25,000.00 for a handwritten letter of George Washington.

But by far, the majority of autograph collectors in the country do it for the love of the hobby. A polite letter and self-addressed, stamped envelope sent to a famous person will often bring the desired result. And occasionally one receives not only an autograph but a nice handwritten letter thanking the fan as well!

In terms of value, there are five general types of autographs: 1) mere signatures on an album page or card; 2) signed photographs; 3) signed documents; 4) typed letters signed; and 5) handwritten letters. The signatures are the least valuable, and handwritten letters the most valuable. The reasoning here is simple: with a handwritten letter, not only do you get an autograph but the handwritten message of the person as well. And this content can sometimes increase the value many times over. A handwritten letter of Babe Ruth thanking a fan for a gift might fetch a few thousand dollars. But if the letter were to mention Ruth's feelings on the day he retired, it could easily sell for $10,000.00 or more.

There are several major autograph collector organizations where members can exchange celebrity addresses or buy, sell, and trade their autographed wares. Philography can be a fun and rewarding hobby. And who knows! In ten or twenty years, those autographs you got for free could be worth a small fortune!

In the listings below, photos are assumed black and white unless noted color. Our advisor for autographs is Tim Anderson; he is listed in the Directory under Utah.

Key:
ALS — handwritten letter signed
ANS — handwritten note signed
DS — document signed
ISP — inscribed signed photo
LS — signed letter, typed or written by someone else
sig — signature
SP — signed photo

Abbott, Bud; SP, w/Lou Costello, blk & wht, 8x10" **160.00**
Anderson, Brad; sig on Marmaduke sketch on 3x5" card **18.00**
Armstrong, Louis 'Satchmo'; ISP, 1930s, 6¾x4¼" **275.00**
Arthur, Chester A; lg bold sig on White House card **350.00**
Ball, Lucille; SP, orig color still **100.00**
Bradley, Wm F; sig on cabinet photo as general, EX **865.00**
Brynner, Yul; SP, from King & I, 8x10" **75.00**
Buck, Fran; sig on World's Fair souvenir booklet, 1939-40, 9x12" ...**65.00**
Bush, Barbara, LS, dtd 1982, on Vice President's stationery **60.00**
Chancellor, John; SP, 8x10" **25.00**
Clapton, Eric; SP, 4x6" **65.00**
Coolidge, Calvin; DS, appointment of officer, 1927, 16x20" **200.00**
Craig, Yvonne; SP, as Batgirl, 8x10" **20.00**
Crawford, Joan; SP, 17x14" in fr **175.00**
Curtis, BR; ALS, 1-pg, 1849 (2 yrs from entering Supreme Court) ...**100.00**
Darnell, Linda; SP, 8x10" glossy **65.00**
Darwin, Charles; ANS, on eng letterhead, contribution, 1-pg ...**600.00**
Davis, Bette; sig on press photo **75.00**

**Deana Durbin, signed 8x10"
black and white photo, $30.00.**

Dickinson, Anna E; ALS on personal stationery, scheduling, 1872 ..**90.00**
Dietrich, Marlene; sig on portrait magazine, EX **45.00**
Donovan, Gen Wild Bill; SP in uniform, matted/fr **275.00**
Douglas, Wm O; LS on Supreme Court letterhead, 1960 ....**120.00**
Eddy, Nelson; LS **40.00**
Eisenhower, Dwight D; ISP, head & shoulders, 13½x10½" **275.00**
Eisenhower, Mamie; LS, thanks for gifts, 1954, 1-pg **75.00**
Gish, Lillian; ANS w/sm photo on 4x6" card **40.00**
Gleason, Jackie; SP, 8x10" **65.00**
Goodman, Benny; LS on personal letterhead, NY, 1966, 1-pg **75.00**
Harrison, Caroline Scott; sig on White House card **250.00**
Hayes, Rutherford B; DS, as notary public, sgn twice, 1853 ....**300.00**
Henie, Sonia; SP, sepia, sm **60.00**
Hitchcock, Alfred; sales receipt from LA store, undtd **200.00**
Huston, Angelica; SP, blk & wht glossy, 8x10" **12.50**
Jackson, Andrew; DS, land grant, bold sig/presidential seal **550.00**
John, Elton; SP, 8x10" glossy **65.00**
Kelly, Gene; SP, scene from Singin' in the Rain **75.00**
Lamour, Dorothy; sig on sheet music, photo cover (in sarong) **35.00**
Lantz, Walter; sig on card w/sketch of Woody Woodpecker **100.00**
LaRue, Lash; SP, 8x10" **75.00**
Lauck, Charles 'Lum'; check written to Max Factor **85.00**
Lindbergh, Charles A; sig on book We (published 1927), VG .**1,200.00**
Lombardi, Vince; sig on Gr Bay Packer check, as general manager ...**325.00**

Longfellow, Henry W; ALS, invitation to dinner, 1851, VG 435.00
Madison, James; DS as President, land grant, 1813, EX 600.00
Mays, Willie; SP, 8x10" glossy 50.00
McCormick, Cyrus H; sig on bank draft, 1879 ....250.00
Nixon, Richard; ISP, blk & wht, as Vice President, 8x10" 150.00
Nixon-Cox, Tricia, sig on wedding photo 30.00
Nureyev, Rudolf; bold sig on Fr magazine cover, 1977, 7x10" 55.00
Ott, Mell; sig on 8x10" batting still 375.00
Pearl, Minnie; SP, 8x10" 40.00
Power, Tyrone; SP, early sepia still 100.00
Randolph, Geo W; DS, transfer request, as Secretary of War 550.00
Redford, Robert; bold sig on 3x5" card 15.00
Robinson, Edward G; SP, 5x7" 85.00
Rockefeller, John D; sig on stock certificate, MO KS TX Ry, 1891 ..1,155.00
Rogers, Ginger; ISP, head & shoulders, blk & wht glossy, 8x10" ..95.00
Rommel, Erwin; DS, lists soldiers to receive medals, 1941, 1-pg .1,200.00
Roosevelt, Eleanor; LS on personal stationery, 1-pg, 1947 ....150.00
Roosevelt, Theodore; sig on card as Governor of NY, EX 250.00
Schmelling, Max; sig on card w/Joe Louis stamp 15.00
Shearer, Norma; SP, 8x10" 75.00
Skelton, Red; SP, 8x10" 25.00
Starr, Ringo; SP, 4x6" 100.00
Taylor, Maxwell D; LS, to student on education, 1-pg 50.00
Truman, Bess; ANS, excuse for absence, 1-pg 200.00
Truman, Harry; LS, on personal stationery, dtd Dec 1964 ....275.00
Wagner, Robert; SP, 8x10" glossy 15.00
Webster, Daniel; ALS, note of introduction, 1849, 1-pg 220.00
West, Mae; SP, 8x10" glossy 100.00
Williams, Ted; SP, 4x6" 100.00
Williams, Tennessee; DS, literary agreement, 1943, 3-pg 550.00
Wilson, Woodrow; LS, dtd 1912 ....395.00
Yeager, Chuck; sig on plain wht 3x5" card 12.50

Automobilia

While some automobilia buffs are primarily concerned with restoring vintage cars, others concentrate on only one area of collecting. For instance, hood ornaments were often quite spectacular. Made of chrome or nickel plate on brass or bronze, they were designed to represent the 'winged maiden' Victory, flying bats, sleek greyhounds, soaring eagles, and a host of other creatures. Today they often bring prices in the $75.00 to $200.00 range. R. Lalique glass ornaments go much higher!

Horns, radios, clocks, gear shift knobs, and key chains with company emblems are other areas of interest. Generally, items pertaining to the classics of the '30s are most in demand. Paper advertising material, manuals, and catalogs in excellent condition are also collectible.

License plate collectors search for the early porcelain-on-cast-iron examples. First year plates (e.g., Massachusetts, 1903; Wisconsin, 1905; Indiana, 1913) are especially valuable. The last of the states to issue regulation plates were South Carolina and Texas in 1917, and Florida in 1918. While many northeastern states had registered hundreds of thousands of vehicles by the 1920s making these plates relatively common, those from the southern and western states of that period are considered rare. Naturally, condition is important. While a pair in mint condition might sell for as much as $100.00 to $125.00, a pair with chipped or otherwise damaged porcelain may sometimes be had for as little as $25.00 to $30.00.

For more information we recommend *American Automobilia: An Illustrated History and Price Guide* by Jim and Nancy Schaut. See also Gas Globes and Panels.

Ashtray, Castrol 75th Anniversary, porc 10.00
Badge, chauffeur's, MI, 1919 ....110.00

Badge, chauffeur's, NY, brass, 1927 ....45.00
Badge, chauffeur's, NY, 1925 ....50.00
Badge, chauffeur's, NY, 1928 ....80.00
Banner, Edsel, New Nifty Thrifty...1960, 36x48" 150.00
Book, 100 Years on the Road, Studebaker history, 1952, EX 35.00
Booklet, Motor Magazine, advertising, 8-pg, 1908, 3½x5" 150.00
Booklet, promo; Dodge, Lawrence Welk, 1956 ....8.00
Brochure, Alfa Romeo, full color, 20-pg, 8½x11" 25.00
Brochure, Chalmers Motors, 1911 ....65.00
Brochure, 1932 Studebaker, 5 color full-pg pictures, EX 35.00
Brochure, 1936 Oldsmobile, 14 color pgs, VG 30.00
Brochure, 1937 Graham Super Charger, color fold-out, VG 20.00
Brochure, 1939 Hudson, color, 23-pg 45.00
Brochure, 1940 Dodge Luxury Liner, fold-out, EX 20.00
Brochure, 1951 Dodge HD trucks 10.00
Brochure, 1968 Mercedes, prices for pickup at Stuttgart factory ...25.00
Brochure, 1976 Ford Mustang, EX 15.00
Bumper sticker, Buick, 1940s, M 20.00
Catalog, Buick, 1913 ....20.00
Clock, Buick, cloisonne diecut of radiator w/logo, 4x5½", EX ...350.00
Clock, desk, GMAC award, 1950 ....18.00
Decal, AMA Motorcycle Classics, Daytona Beach, ca 1950 ....10.00
Decal, St Louis vehicle tax, 1954, unused 8.00
Display, Get a Fisk, animated boy w/tire & candle, lights up ..5,500.00
Display case, oak fr, AC Standard Spark Plug..., 2-shelf, 35" 325.00
Emblem, Packard 8, cloisonne shield logo, EX 40.00
First-aid kit, Ford, 1962, unused 8.00
Flag holder bracket, for 1920s car 45.00
Gauge, tire pressure; Cadillac-LaSalle, plated case, 3¼", NM 210.00
Gauge, tire pressure; Ford Model A, celluloid face, 3¼", EX 225.00
Handbook, Ferrari 346GT 25.00
Helmet, motorcycle; soft style, blk leather, 1950s 125.00
Hood ornament, 1956 Ford 25.00
Hubcaps, Nash, 1947-51, lg, pr 27.50
Key fob, Oldsmobile, eng medallion logo, 1930s 25.00
License plate, PA, 1915 ....90.00
License plate attachment, Chicago Motor Club, celluloid/tin, 4x5" ..50.00
License plate attachment/insert, Hudson 6, tin, 4¼x14", NM ...110.00
List, Model-T Ford parts & accessories, 1922 ....16.00
Magazine, Auto Comfort, shows Sharp Arrow, 1909 ....45.00
Manual, owner's, 1919 Ford 18.00
Manual, owner's, 1947 Ford HD truck, EX 10.00
Manual, owner's, 1951 Chrysler, EX 25.00
Manual, service; Jaguar, form Mk 2, w/supplement 50.00
Manual, shop; Desoto, 1948 ....25.00
Motometer, Boyce/Packard logo, gr pnt patina, 3¼", VG 90.00
Order blank, Harley-Davidson, shows 5 models, 1924, EX 45.00
Paper cup & plate, 1955 Chevrolet 365.00
Pipe wrench, emb Ford, 9" 98.00

Photo courtesy
Nancy Schaut

Pocket mirror, Invincible Oil, celluloid, 1910s, $75.00.

Promotional car, 1953 Chevy Bel Air, bank, 2-door hardtop, EX+ ...90.00

Promotional car, 1963 Ford Galaxie Convertible, beige, 8½", EX ...50.00
Promotional car, 1965 Plymouth Barracuda, friction, 7¾", EX 60.00
Promotional car, 1968 Lincoln Continental, 4-door sedan, MIB ..65.00
Promotional car, 1972 Chevy Fleetside Pickup, MIB 165.00
Radiator mascot, griffin figural, lt wear, 4", EX 250.00
Saddle bags, Indian Motorcycle, leather, pr, VG 675.00
Sign, BMW Dealership, porc, convex, 1950s, 24" dia, M 925.00
Sign, Chevrolet, masonite diecut, chain-hung, 1950s, 9½x21", EX ..220.00
Sign, Dodge Dependable Service, 2-sided porc, 42" dia, NM 875.00
Sign, Ferrari, porc, blk & wht w/red stripe, 17½x34", EX 1,100.00
Sign, Ford Genuine Parts, porc, oval, NM 650.00
Sign, Mercedes-Benz, porc, convex, 23¼" dia, NM 450.00
Sign, Pontiac Factory Engineered Parts, porc, 2-sided, 24" dia, NM ..1,300.00
Steering wheel knob, wooden, red, swivel 16.00
Tie tack, Ford emblem 10.00
Token, GM Motorama of 1954, brass 10.00
Token, Pontiac, Indian Chief, brass 20.00
Weather vane, Pontiac Indian head w/feathers on roof rig & base ..895.00
Wings, Harley-Davidson, brass, 1⅝" 225.00
Wings, Harley-Davidson, brass, 3" 340.00
Wrench, adjustable, Indian Motor Cycle, 1930s 100.00
Wrench, Ford emblem, lg 12.50

Autumn Leaf

In 1933 the Hall China Company designed a line of dinnerware for the Jewel Tea Company, who offered it to their customers as premiums. Although you may hear the ware referred to as 'Jewel Tea,' it was officially named 'Autumn Leaf' in the 1940s. In addition to the dinnerware, frosted Libbey glass tumblers, stemware, and a melmac service with the orange and gold bittersweet pod were available over the years, as were tablecloths, plastic covers for bowls and mixers, and metal items such as cake safes, hot pads, coasters, wastebaskets, and canisters. Even shelf paper and playing cards were made to coordinate. In 1958 the International Silver Company designed silverplated flatware in a pattern called 'Autumn' which was to be used with dishes in the Autumn Leaf pattern. A year later, a line of stainless flatware was introduced. These accessory lines are prized by collectors today.

One of the most fascinating aspects of collecting the Autumn Leaf pattern has been the wonderful discoveries of previously unlisted pieces. Among these items are two different bud-ray lid one-pound butter dishes; most recently a one-pound butter dish in the 'Zephyr' or 'Bingo' style; a miniature set of the 'Casper' salt and pepper shakers; coffee, tea, and sugar canisters; a pair of candlesticks; an experimental condiment jar; and a covered candy dish. All of these china pieces are attributed to the Hall China Company. Other unusual items have turned up in the accessory lines as well and include a Libbey frosted tumbler in a pilsner shape, a wooden serving bowl, and an apron made from the oilcloth (plastic) material that was used in the 1950s tablecloth. These latter items appear to be professionally done, and we can only speculate as to their origin. Collectors believe that the Hall items were sample pieces that were never meant to be distributed.

Hall discontinued the Autumn Leaf line in 1978. At that time the date was added to the backstamp to mark ware still in stock in the Hall warehouse. A special promotion by Jewel saw the reintroduction of basic dinnerware and serving pieces with the 1978 backstamp. These pieces have made their way into many collections. Additionally, in 1979 Jewel released a line of enamel-clad cookware and a Vellux blanket made by Martex which were decorated with the Autumn Leaf pattern. They continued to offer these items for a few years only, then all distribution of Autumn Leaf items was discontinued.

It should be noted that the Hall China Company has produced several limited edition items for the National Autumn Leaf Collectors Club (NALCC): a New York-style teapot (1984); an Edgewater vase (1987, different than the original shape); candlesticks (1988); a Philadelphia-style teapot, creamer and sugar set (1990); a tea-for-two set and a Solo tea set (1991), a donut jug, and a large oval casserole. New items for the NALCC: small ball jug, 1-cup French teapot, and a set of four chocolate mugs. The NALCC has also given their club members special items over the past few years made for them by Hall China: a sugar packet holder, a chamberstick, and an oyster cocktail. Other items are scheduled for production. All of these are plainly marked as having been made for the NALCC and are appropriately dated. A few other pieces have been made by Hall as limited editions for an Ohio company, but these are easily identified: the Airflow teapot and the Norris refrigerator pitcher (neither of which was previously decorated with the Autumn Leaf decal), a square-handled beverage mug, and the new-style Irish mug. A production problem with the square-handled mugs halted their production. The company then issued a regular conic-style mug with a round handle. Additional items available now are a covered onion soup, tall bud vase, china kitchen memo board, and egg drop-style salt and pepper shakers with a mustard pot. They have also issued a deck of playing cards and Libbey tumblers. See *The Garage Sale & Flea Market Annual* (Collector Books) for suggested values for club pieces. Our advisor for this category is Gwynne Harrison; she is listed in the Directory under California.

Pitcher, ball jug style, 1938 – 76, $40.00.

Baker, French; 2-pt, from $150 to 175.00
Baker, French; 3-pt 20.00
Baker, oval, Fort Pitt, 12-oz ind 225.00
Baker/souffle, 4½" 50.00
Baker/souffle, 4⅛" 12.00
Bean pot, 1-hdl 1,000.00
Bean pot, 2-hdl, 2¼-qt 250.00
Bowl, cereal; 6½" 12.00
Bowl, cream soup; 2-hdl 35.00
Bowl, flat soup; 8½" 20.00
Bowl, fruit; 5½" 6.00
Bowl, mixing; set of 3: 6¼", 7½", 9" 65.00
Bowl, refrigerator, metal w/plastic lids, 3 for 275.00
Bowl, Royal Glas-Bake, set of 4 ....200.00
Bowl, salad; 9" 20.00
Bowl, vegetable; divided, 10½", from $90 to 125.00
Bowl, vegetable; oval, w/lid, 10" 75.00
Bowl, vegetable; oval, 10½" 25.00
Bowl, vegetable; rnd, 9" 150.00
Bowl cover set, plastic, 8-pc: 7 assorted covers in pouch 90.00
Bread box, metal 400.00
Butter dish, 1-lb, regular, ruffled top 500.00
Butter dish, ¼-lb, regular, ruffled top 250.00
Butter dish, ¼-lb, Square Top, rare 1,200.00
Butter dish, ¼-lb, Wings 1,800.00
Cake plate, 9½" 28.00
Cake safe, metal, motif on top & sides, 5" 50.00
Cake safe, metal, side decor only, 4½x10½", from $35 to 45.00

Cake stand, metal base, orig box, $150 to 225.00
Candy dish, metal base, from $450 to 500.00
Canister, metal, rnd, w/coppertone lid, set of 4, from $200 to 500.00
Canister, metal, rnd, w/ivory plastic lid 10.00
Canister, metal, rnd, w/matching lids, set of 3, from $200 to 300.00
Canister, metal, sq, set of 4, from $250 to 350.00
Casserole, Royal Glas-Bake, rnd, w/clear glass lid 90.00
Casserole, Tootsie-hdl, w/lid 22.00
Cleanser can, metal, sq, 6", M 1,400.00
Coaster, metal, 3⅛" 8.00
Coffee dispenser/canister, metal, wall type, 10½x19" dia 400.00
Coffee maker, 9-cup, w/metal dripper, 8" 45.00
Coffee percolator, Douglas, w/warmer base, MIB 300.00
Coffee percolator, electric, all china, 4-pc 350.00
Cookie jar, Zeisel 300.00
Creamer, New Style 25.00
Creamer, Old Style, 4¼" 45.00
Cup & saucer, regular 10.00
Cup & saucer, St Denis 30.00
Custard cup 10.00
Drip jar, w/lid 20.00
Flatware, silverplate, ea 35.00
Flatware, stainless, ea 30.00
Fruit cake tin, metal 10.00
Gravy boat, w/underplate (pickle dish) 55.00
Hot pad, metal, red or gr felt-like bking, rnd 20.00
Hot pad, oval, 10¾", from $12 to 15.00
Hurricane lamp, Douglas, w/metal base, pr 600.00
Marmalade jar, 3-pc 100.00
Mug, beverage 60.00
Mug, Irish coffee 125.00
Mustard jar, 3½", 3-pc 100.00
Napkin, ecru muslin, 16" sq 50.00
Pickle dish or gravy liner, oval, 9" 25.00
Picnic thermos, metal 375.00
Pie baker, 9½" 35.00
Pie plate, Heatflow, clear glass, Mary Dunbar 70.00
Pitcher, utility; 2½-pt, 6" 25.00
Place mat, paper, scalloped, from $35 to 40.00
Place mat, set of 8, M in orig package 325.00
Plate, 10" 18.00
Plate, 6" 8.00
Plate, 7¼" 10.00
Plate, 8" 18.00
Plate, 9" 12.00
Platter, 11½" 28.00
Platter, 13½", from $25 to 28.00
Playing cards, regular or Pinochle, dbl deck, from $150 to 200.00
Sauce dish, serving; Douglas, Bakelite hdl, w/warmer base 600.00
Shakers, Casper, regular, pr 30.00
Shakers, range, hdl, pr 30.00
Sugar bowl, New Style 30.00
Sugar bowl, Old Style, 3½" 40.00
Tablecloth, cotton sailcloth w/gold stripe, 54x54", from $100 to .150.00
Tablecloth, cotton sailcloth w/gold stripe, 54x72", from $125 to .150.00
Tablecloth, ecru muslin, 56x81" 300.00
Tablecloth, plastic 150.00
Teakettle, metal enamelware 250.00
Teapot, Aladdin 70.00
Teapot, long spout, 1935-42 ....70.00
Teapot, Newport, dtd 1978, from $175 to 200.00
Teapot, Newport, from $175 to 200.00
Toaster cover, plastic, fits 2-slice toaster 50.00
Towel, dish; pattern & clock motif 60.00

Towel, tea; cotton, 16x33" 60.00
Trash can, metal, red 400.00
Tray, glass, wood hdl, 19½x11¼", from $100 to 130.00
Tray, metal, oval 100.00
Tray, tidbit; 3-tier 100.00
Tumbler, Brockway, 13-oz 45.00
Tumbler, Brockway, 16-oz 45.00
Tumbler, Brockway, 9-oz 45.00
Tumbler, frosted, 14-oz, 5½" 20.00
Tumbler, frosted, 9-oz, 3¾" 32.00
Tumbler, gold frost etched, flat, 10-oz 65.00
Tumbler, gold frost etched, flat, 15-oz 65.00
Tumbler, gold frost etched, ftd, 10-oz 65.00
Tumbler, gold frost etched, ftd, 6½-oz 65.00
Vase, bud; sm or regular decal, 6" 225.00
Warmer base, oval 200.00
Warmer base, rnd 160.00

Aviation

Aviation buffs are interested in any phase of flying, from early developments with gliders, balloons, airships, and flying machines to more modern innovations. Books, catalogs, photos, patents, lithographs, ad cards, and posters are among the paper ephemera they treasure alongside models of unlikely flying contraptions, propellers and rudders, insignia and equipment from WWI and WWII, and memorabilia from the flights of the Wright Brothers, Lindbergh, Earhart, and the Zeppelins. See also Militaria. Our advisor for this category is John R. Joiner; he is listed in the Directory under Georgia.

Bag, 1st class complimentary, Pan Am, w/toiletries 5.00
Bank, Delta Airlines Credit Union, rocket, vertical, mechanical ...110.00
Beret, Eastern Airlines, Golden Falcon, blk velvet 18.50
Blanket, Mohawk Airlines, lt bl w/blk lettering, 40x56", EX 65.00
Blanket, Pan Am, gray wool, herringbone design, 59x80", EX 95.00
Blanket, Transcontinental Airlines, blk w/bl edge, 55x62", G 80.00
Book, NASA, Exploring Space w/Camera, 1968 ....12.00
Book, Science of Preflight Aeronautics, bronze, 1978 ....130.00
Book, We, Charles Lindbergh, 48 illus, NY, 1927, EX 50.00
Brochure, Predictions of Future, Spirit on St Louis cover, 1950s ..35.00
Brochure, Super Constellation, 1955 ....20.00
Calendar, Am Air, 1945, lg 65.00
Calendar, TWA, 1949, M 65.00
Candle, vigil; Amelia Earhart, on orig glass base 385.00
Coffee cup, Delta Airlines, gold at rim, 4" dia 4.00
Cup & saucer, United Airlines, china, mk THC 35.00
Desk model plane, Ozark Airlines DC-9 McDonnel Douglas, VG ..650.00
Envelope, Hindenburg stamps, dtd 1936, EX 32.00
Flight bag, BOAC 20.00

Gravy boat, United Airlines, silverplated, 3½x7½", $48.00.

Hatpin, Eastern Airlines flight attendant 25.00
Helmet & goggles, barnstorming-era pilot's, EX 350.00
Ice hammer, TWA 25.00
Map, Pan Am, routes of China Clipper, N & S America, 1930s ..65.00
Map, Western Air, wood, early, lg 1,500.00
Medal, TWA, emb plane on bronze, 1940s, 1½" 60.00
Model, DC-3, chrome 175.00
Oven, Ozark Airlines, w/food trays 65.00
Patch, Apollo II, embr, recovery fleet, M 25.00
Pen set, Hughes Air West, Cross 28.00
Photo, Amelia Earhart w/plane, 1939, M 20.00
Pinball game, Air Ways, 1930s, EX 55.00
Pitcher, coffee; TWA, silver, 1950s 135.00
Plane, Ford tri-motor, Schieble, 28" L, EX 850.00
Plate, Delta Airlines, gold band at rim, 6" 4.00
Program, Detroit Nat'l Air Races, 1951, EX 150.00
Program, souvenir; Amelia Earhart, Prof Women's Club, 1932 ..195.00
Propellor, wooden, over 72", VG 395.00
Ring, Am Airline Jr Pilot 15.00
Throw, KLM Dutch Airlines, 56x74", EX 35.00
Timetable, Northwest Orient, 1958, 4x8" 12.00
Timetable, TWA, Mediterranean & Far East, Egypt cover, 1962 ...9.00
Wings, Pan Am Junior Clipper Pilot, metal 8.00

Avon Works

In 1902 a firm based in Wheeling, West Virginia, absorbed several small local potteries; the Vance Avon Faience Co. of Tiltonville, Ohio, was one of them. They continued in operation at Tiltonville until 1905, when Avon moved to the Wheeling location. The production of artware was discontinued in an effort to produce a more commercially profitable semiporcelain ware; but even that proved to be unsuccessful, and the Wheeling department closed in 1907. For more information on the earlier pottery, see Vance Avon.

Teapot, squeezebag trees, wht/bl on cobalt/gr, rstr, #1217, 5¼" ...1,500.00
Vase, squeezebag trees, blk on gr & orange, gourd shape, 5½" 650.00

Baccarat

The Baccarat Glass company was founded in 1765 near Luneville, France, and continues to this day to produce quality crystal tableware, vases, perfume bottles, and figurines. The firm became famous for the high-quality millefiori and caned paperweights produced there from 1845 until about 1860. Examples of these range from $300.00 to as much as several thousand. Since 1953 they have resumed the production of paperweights on a limited edition basis. Our advisors for this category are Randall Monsen and Rod Baer; their address is listed in the Directory under Virginia. See also Bottles, Commercial Perfume; Paperweights.

Bottles: Dresser, Rose Tiente Pinwheel, $795.00; Barber, Rose Tiente Swirl, $325.00.

Bottle, Arys, 4-tier pyramid shape, #802, 1945, 3⅜" 120.00
Bottle, Mry, 6 curving sides, red flashed, #339, 1917, 4⅜" 165.00
Bottle, Parfise, long vertical facets, w/stopper, #563, 1925, 4" 55.00
Bottle, scent; Rose Tiente Swirl, 7x3" 85.00
Bottle, Violet, amber urn form, #650, 1927, 6¾" 600.00
Figurine, elephant, trumpeting, sgn ft, 6¼" 125.00
Jar, dresser; floral, cranberry cut to gr, sterling lid, 2½x4½" 450.00
Lamp, peg; Rose Tiente Swirl 375.00
Lamp, perfume; amberina, emb scrolls on global form, 5" 145.00

Badges

The breast badge came into general usage in this country about 1840. Since most are not marked and styles have changed very little to the present day, they are often difficult to date. The most reliable clue is the pin and catch. One of the earliest types, used primarily before the turn of the century, involved a 't-pin' and a 'shell' catch. In a second style, the pin was hinged with a small square of sheet metal, and the clasp was cylindrical. From the late 1800s until about 1940, the pin and clasp were made from one continuous piece of thin metal wire. The same type, with the addition of a flat back plate, was used a little later. There are exceptions to these findings, and other types of clasps were used as well. Hallmarks and inscriptions may also help pinpoint an approximate age.

Badges have been made from a variety of materials, usually brass or nickel silver; but even solid silver and gold were used for special orders. They are found in many basic shapes and variations — stars with five to seven points, shields, disks, ovals, and octagonals being most often encountered. Of prime importance to collectors, however, is that the title and/or location appear on the badge. Those with designations of positions no longer existing (City Constable, for example) and names of early western states and towns are most valuable.

Badges are among the most commonly reproduced (and faked) types of antiques on the market. At any flea market, ten fakes can be found for every authentic example. Genuine law badges start at $30.00 to $40.00 for recent examples (1950 – 1970); earlier pieces (1910 – 1930) usually bring $50.00 to $90.00. Pre-1900 badges often sell for more than $100.00. Authentic gold badges are usually priced at a minimum of scrap value (karat, weight, spot price for gold); fine gold badges from before 1900 can sell for $400.00 to $800.00, and a few will bring even more. A fire badge is usually valued at about half the price of a law badge from the same circa and material. Our advisor for this category is Gene Matzke; he is listed in the Directory under Wisconsin.

Am Express, celluloid hat badge, orig brass fr 475.00
Deputy Sheriff, Albany Co (WY), SP 50.00
Deputy Sheriff, Queen's Co, 1892, gold-plated 75.00
Employee's, First Liberty Loan, Statue of Liberty, rare 165.00
Fargo ND Police, silver, for hat 20.00
Fire Police Terryville, SP 15.00
Honorary Deputy Sheriff, MS, gold star, wallet type 20.00
IL State Police, 6-point star, gold-plated 75.00
Jackson MS Police Patrolman, silver shield, 2" 30.00
Kansas City Special Police, silver-tone, 1922 ....50.00
Military Aide, blk metal w/gold & blk seal, 1977, 4x2" 125.00
NY & Coney Island RR Police, 1890s 250.00
Pinkerton Special Services, winged eagle, hallmk 350.00
Pleasantville NY, silver shield, mini, 1" 15.00
Public Defender Investigator, Hillsborough Co FL, gold, wallet ...25.00
Special Police, State of Maine, SP 30.00
Union Stockyards, South Omaha #46, SP 95.00

US Post Office Dept, SP **35.00**

Banks

As is always true, the continuing impact of auctions shows in the listings. Again, condition, condition, condition is what is driving the market. The spread between a bank in good condition and an excellent or original condition example continues to widen. It is imperative that you realize the importance of paint and the completeness of a bank. Also some banks have a wide margin of value based on color variations. It becomes more and more important that you attend as many shows and auctions as possible. Direct contact with collectors and knowledgeable dealers is the only way you can get a feel for prices and the desirability of banks, both mechanical and still. Banks continue to hold their value. However, it is becoming extremely important for collectors to understand the market.

Let's take a look at the price variations possible on an Uncle Sam mechanical bank. If you find one with considerable paint missing but with some good color showing, the price would be around $1,000.00. If it has repairs or restoration, the value would drop to something like $800.00 or less. If you had another example, and it had two thirds of its original paint and no repairs, it would be priced around $1,800.00. One with minor nicks and 90% of the original paint could go as high as $3,500.00. Or if you find one that is in near-original paint and has no repairs, $5,000.00 would not be out of line. This should help you see what causes price variations. After considering all of these factors, remember the final price is always determined by what a willing buyer and seller agree on for a specific bank.

The category of mechanical banks is unique. Along with cast-iron toys, they are among the most outstanding products of the Industrial Revolution and are recognized as some of the most successful of the mass-produced products of the 19th century. The earliest mechanicals were made of wood or lead; but when John Hall introduced Hall's Excelsior, a cast-iron mechanical bank, it was an immediate success. J. & E. Stevens produced the bank for Hall and soon began to make their own designs. Several companies followed suit, most of which were already in the hardware business. They used newly developed iron-molding techniques to produce these novelty savings devices for the emerging toy market. Mechanical banks reflect the social and political attitudes of the times, racial prejudices, the excitement of the circus, and humorous everyday events. Their designers made the most of simple mechanics to produce banks with captivating actions that served not only to amuse but to promote the concept of thrift to the children. The quality of detail in the castings are truly remarkable. The most collectible examples were made during the period of 1870 to 1900; however, they continued to be made until the early days of World War II. J. & E. Stevens, Shepard Hardware, and Kyser and Rex are some of the more well-known manufacturers; most made still banks as well.

Still banks are widely collected, and you can literally choose from thousands of banks. No one knows exactly how many different banks were made, but at least three thousand have been identified in the various books published on the subject. Cast-iron examples still dominate the market, but the lead banks from Europe are growing in value. Tin and early pottery banks are drawing more interest as well. American pottery banks which were primarily collected by Americana collectors are becoming more important in the still bank field. This market has not been as volatile as the mechanical banks, but the number of collectors is growing. The auction market on still banks is not as extensive as with the mechanicals, but some nice examples do turn up. Collectors and dealers are still the best source.

Book of Knowledge Banks were produced by John Wright (Pennsylvania) from circa 1950 until 1975. Of the thirty models they made during those years, a few continued to be made in very limited numbers until the late 1980s; these they referred to as the 'Medallion' series. (Today the Medallion banks command the same prices as the earlier Book of Knowledge series.) Each bank was a handcrafted, hand-painted duplicate of an original as was found in the collection of The Book of Knowledge, the first children's encyclopedia in this country. Because the antique banks are often priced out of the range of many of today's collectors, these banks are being sought out as affordable substitutes for their very expensive counterparts.

As both value and interest continue on the increase, it becomes even more important to educate one's self to the fullest extent possible. We recommend these books for your library: *The Dictionary of Still Banks* by Long and Pitman, *The Penny Bank Book* by Moore, and *The Bank Book* by Norman. If you are primarily interested in mechanicals, *Penny Lane*, a book by Davidson, is considered the most complete reference available. It contains a cross-reference listing of numbers from all other publications on mechanical banks.

In the listings that follow, banks are identified by L for Long, G for Griffith, M for Moore, N for Norman, D for Davidson, and W for Whiting.

Our advisors for this category are Diane Patalano, listed in the Directory under New Jersey, and Dan Iannotti (for Book of Knowledge), listed under Michigan.

Key:
CI — cast iron   NPCI — nickel-plated cast iron
EPCI — electroplated cast iron

Advertising

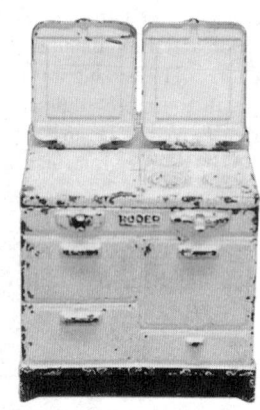

Roper Stoves, stove form, cast iron and sheet metal, Arcade, 1920s, 3¾", EX, $145.00.

Campbell's Beans, Model-T Ford, MIB **50.00**
Campbell's Vegetable Garden, tin w/paper label, 4½", EX **35.00**
Colonel Harland Sanders, plastic, 1970s, NMIP **45.00**
Eze-Orange truck, plastic w/rubber wheels, 1950s, EX **55.00**
Florida Orange Bird, vinyl, 1970s, EX **20.00**
Green Giant's Little Sprout, compo figure, musical, 8½", $50 to .**65.00**
Howard Johnson's Restaurants, plastic, 1950s, EX **28.00**
Ice Cream Freezer, CI, ...Buy a Steel..., Grey Iron, 4¼", G **220.00**
Minute Man, M-327, wht metal, worn bronze pnt, bank ad, 8⅛" .**40.00**
Peter's Weatherbird, CI, mc pnt, yel base, Arcade, 4¼", M **990.00**
Robin Hood Shoes, 1930s, EX **50.00**
Save w/Torchy, torch figure beside pig, pnt wht metal, 6⅝", EX ..**55.00**
Shoney's Bear, vinyl, 1993, MIP **15.00**
Sinclair Power X Super Fuel, tin litho gas pump form, EX **40.00**
Strat-O-Bank, space theme w/bank advertisement, cast, 1954, VG+ ..**100.00**
Western Savings, owl figural, M **15.00**

Book of Knowledge Banks

Artillery Bank, M **350.00**
Boy on Trapeze, NM **550.00**

Bulldog, M 325.00
Butting Buffalo, NM 385.00
Cabin Bank, M 315.00
Cat & Mouse, NM 425.00
Creedmoor Bank, M 395.00
Dentist, M 315.00
Eagle & Eaglets, M 425.00
Humpty Dumpty, M 335.00
Indian & Bear, M 425.00
Jonah & the Whale, M 325.00
Leap Frog, M 395.00
Magician Bank, NM 425.00
Milking Cow, NM 345.00
Organ Bank, Boy & Girl, M 335.00
Owl Turns Head, M 275.00
Paddy & the Pig, M 385.00
Punch & Judy Bank, M 375.00
Spise a Mule, Boy on Bench, M 395.00
Spise a Mule, Jockey Over, M 325.00
Tammany Bank, NM 295.00
Teddy & the Bear, NM 315.00
Trick Pony, w/orig box & documents, NM 345.00
Uncle Remus, NM 450.00
Uncle Sam, M 375.00
US & Spain, M 325.00
William Tell, M 340.00

Mechanical

Artillery Bank, EX paint on cast iron, Shepard Hardware, Pat 1892, EX, $2,100.00.

Afghanistan, N-1020, pnt CI, Mechanical Novelty Works, 1885, G ..1,540.00
Always Did 'Spise a Mule, Bench; N-2940, J&E Stevens, 1897, EX+ .1,500.00
Always Did 'Spise a Mule, Jockey; N-2950, pnt CI, Stevens, VG ..1,150.00
Bad Accident, N-1150, pnt CI, EX 1,200.00
Bad Accident, N-1150-A, pnt CI, J&E Stevens, ca 1891, EX 2,400.00
Bad Accident, N-1150-A, pnt CI, J&E Stevens, ca 1891, VG ..1,100.00
Bank of Education & Economy, NP CI, crank, Proctor-Raymond, VG 415.00
Billy Goat, N-1240-A, pnt CI, J&E Stevens, M 2,850.00
Bird on Roof, G-16, pnt CI, J&E Stevens, VG 1,595.00
Boy on Trapeze (Gray Pants), pnt CI, Barton & Smith, VG 2,200.00
Boy Robbing Bird's Nest, rpt CI, J&E Stevens 1,540.00
Bulldog, N-1430, pnt CI, J&E Stevens, 1880, EX 1,300.00
Cabin, N-1610, pnt CI, J&E Stevens, 1885, M 1,485.00
Cat & Mouse, N-1700-A, pnt CI, J&E Stevens, 1891, EX 4,300.00
Cat & Mouse, N-1700-B, pnt CI, J&E Stevens, 1891, EX 5,170.00
Circus, pnt CI, pony & clown in ring, Shepard Hdw, 1887, EX ..15,000.00
Circus Ticket Collector, N-1830-B, pnt CI, Judd, EX+ 2,400.00
Clown on Globe, N-1930-A, pnt CI, J&E Stevens, 1890, VG ..1,540.00

Creedmore, N-2000-B, pnt CI, J&E Stevens, EX 800.00
Darktown Battery, N-2080-A, CI, worn mc pnt, rpr, 10", VG 2,200.00
Dog on Turntable, N-2170, copper-bronze plated, Judd, 1870s, EX 950.00
Dog on Turntable, N-2170-A, pnt CI, Judd Mfg, 1870s, M ...1,425.00
Eagle & Eaglets, N-2230-B, pnt CI, J&E Stevens, NM 1,800.00
Eagle & Eaglets, N-2230-B, pnt CI, J&E Stevens, 1883, EX ...1,500.00
Elephant Pull Tail, N-2300-B, pnt CI (wht), Hubley, 1930s, VG ..330.00
Feed the Kitty, modern, CI, w/mc pnt, 10¼", EX 990.00
Fortune Teller, N-2460-B, pnt CI, fortune in window, G 145.00
Frog on Rnd Base, N-2530, pnt CI, J&E Stevens, 1870s, EX ..1,000.00
Frog on Rnd Base, N-2530, pnt CI, J&E Stevens, 1870s, VG 525.00
Giant Standing, electroplated, swallows coin, rare, M 25,000.00
Girl in Victorian Chair, N-2630-A, pnt CI, Reed, EX 12,000.00
Give Me a Penny, N-2650, pnt CI, Friend W Smith Jr, EX 5,000.00
Hall's Excelsior, N-2710-C, pnt CI, J&E Stevens, 1869, M 2,200.00
Hall's Liliput, (Gray Pants), pnt CI, J&E Stevens, Pat 1877, VG .550.00
Hall's Liliput, (Yel & Red), pnt CI, J&E Stevens, Pat 1877, EX ..1,200.00
Hen & Chick, N-2790-B, pnt CI, J&E Stevens, 1901, EX 4,000.00
Home, N-2860, pnt CI, J&E Stevens, 1870s, VG 2,500.00
Hoopla Bank, pnt CI, John Harper, VG, A, ...1,200.00
Humpty Dumpty, N-2900, CI, mc pnt w/touchup, 7¾", VG ..1,000.00
Humpty Dumpty, N-2900, pnt CI, Ohio Mfg, EX+ 3,500.00
Humpty Dumpty, N-2900, pnt CI, Shepard Hdw, EX 2,750.00
Indian & Bear, N-2980-A, pnt CI, J&E Stevens, ca 1900, EX ..2,800.00
Initiating Bank, 1st Degree; pnt CI, Pat 1880, EX 9,570.00
Initiating Bank, 2nd Degree; N-3010, pnt CI, EX 1,500.00
Joe Socko, pnt tin, Straits Corp, M 770.00
Jolly Joe, tin litho, lever op, Saalheimer & Strauss, VG 900.00
Jolly N, N-3370, CI, old worn rpt, trap missing, 6⅝", G- 200.00
Jolly N, N-3370, pnt CI, J&E Stevens, EX 910.00
Jolly N Figure, aluminum, bright mc pnt, Austrian (?), M 3,850.00
Jonah & Whale, N-3490, pnt CI, Shepard Hdw, Pat 1890, VG ...3,000.00
Leap Frog, N-3490, pnt CI, Shepard Hdw, 1890, G 1,980.00
Lion & Monkeys, N-3650, 1 peanut, pnt CI, Kyser & Rex, 1883, EX ..2,200.00
Lion & Monkeys, N-3650, 1 peanut, pnt CI, Kyser & Rex, 1883, VG .1,100.00
Lion Hunter, N-3660, pnt CI, J&E Stevens, M 10,600.00
Magic, N-3730-C, pnt CI, J&E Stevens, EX 2,500.00
Mason, N-3800, pnt CI, Shepard Hdw, 1887, EX 4,000.00
Minstrel, tin litho, lever op, Saalheimer & Strauss, G 525.00
Monkey & Coconut, N-3940, pnt CI, J&E Stevens, 1886, VG ..2,650.00
Mule Entering Barn, N-4030, pnt CI, J&E Stevens, 1880, M ..2,860.00
National Savings, NP CI, ornate casting, M 3,500.00
New Bank, N-4210-A, pnt CI, J&E Stevens, 1870s, EX 1,485.00
Novelty, N-4260, pnt CI, J&E Stevens, 1873, EX 1,200.00
Octagonal Fort, N-4280, pnt CI, lever op, G 1,700.00
Organ Bank, N-4310, boy & girl, pnt CI, Kyser & Rex, 1882, NM ...3,400.00
Organ Bank, N-4340-B, pnt CI, Kyser & Rex, 1881, mini, EX ..1,300.00
Owl Turns Head, N-4380-A, pnt CI, J&E Stevens, 1880, VG ...415.00
Owl Turns Head, N-4380-B, pnt CI (wht), J&E Stevens, 1880, EX ..2,200.00
Panorama, N-4410-A, pnt CI, J&E Stevens, 1876, NM 8,800.00
Pay Phone, N-4470-A, NP CI, J&E Stevens, G 715.00
Peg-Leg Begger, pnt CI, Judd, 2nd casting 330.00
Picture Gallery, N-4560, pnt CI, Shepard Hdw, ca 1885, VG ..13,750.00
Pig in Highchair, N-4570, pnt CI, J&E Stevens, 1897, G 660.00
Professor Pug Frog, N-4690-A, pnt CI, J&E Stevens, 1886, EX .6,800.00
Punch & Judy, N-4740-A, pnt CI, Shepard Hdw, 1884, EX ...2,500.00
Punch & Judy, N-4740-C, pnt CI, Shepard Hdw, EX 4,000.00
Punch & Judy, N-4740-C, pnt CI, Shepard Hdw, G 725.00
Rabbit in Cabbage, N-4790-A, pnt CI, Kilgore, ca 1925, G- 275.00
Reclining Chinaman, N-4830-B, pnt CI, J&E Stevens, 1885, EX ..4,950.00
Saluting Sailor, tin litho, lever op, Germany, VG 1,100.00
Santa Claus, N-5010, CI, worn mc pnt, 5⅞", VG 1,100.00
Speaking Dog, CI, worn mc w/touchup on base, 7", VG 1,425.00
Stump Speaker (Gr Jacket), pnt CI, Shepard Hdw, VG 2,300.00

Tammany, N-5420, pnt CI, J&E Stevens, 1873, VG 400.00
Tammany, N-5420-B, pnt CI, J&E Stevens, 1873, M 2,000.00
Teddy & Bear, pnt CI, J&E Stevens, Pat 1907, EX 2,100.00
Trick Dog, N-5620, CI, worn mc pnt, trap missing, 8¾", G 385.00
Trick Dog (Bl Base), pnt, CI, Hubley, NM 800.00
Trick Dog (Red & Gr Base), pnt CI, Shepard Hdw, NM 2,900.00
Trick Dog (Yel & Brn Base), pnt CI, Hubley, EX 900.00
Trick Pony, N-5640, CI, Shepard Hdw, mc pnt, 7⅞", EX 1,200.00
Trick Pony, N-5640, CI, worn dk mc pnt, 7¾", G 415.00
Tricky Pig, similar to N-1280, old rpt/rpl teller, 7½" 415.00
Uncle Sam, N-5740, pnt CI, Shepard Hdw, 1886, EX+ 3,300.00
Uncle Tom w/Star, pnt CI, Kyser & Rex, Pat 1882, EX 525.00
United States, N-5790, pnt CI, J&E Stevens, 1880s, VG 660.00
Vending Bank, tin litho w/glass view, Hatwig & Vogel, EX 195.00
William Tell, pnt CI, J&E Stevens, Pat 1896, NM 2,000.00
Zoo, N-6070, pnt CI, Kyser & Rex, ca 1894, VG 990.00

Registering

Benjamin Franklin Thrift Bank, tin litho, 4", $100.00.

Bean Pot, Nickel Register 5¢, pnt CI, G 150.00
Beehive, NP CI, bees in flowers, 5⅜x6½", EX 65.00
Boy & Girl, polished chrome, dime register, 3" dia, EX 100.00
Captain Kidd, US, CI, rpt, 5⅝" 150.00
Daily Dime, tin itho circus scene w/clown & monkey, EX 65.00
Daily Dime Piggy, Kalon, metal box w/canted corners, 2⅝" sq, NM .90.00
Jackie Robinson, tin litho, dime register, 2⅝", VG 465.00
Popeye Daily Dime, tin litho, 1956, EX 65.00
Prince Valiant, M-231, tin litho, 3", EX 230.00
Superman, tin litho, CDC, 2½" sq, VG 275.00
Transvaal Money Box, England, pnt CI, mc roly-type figure, 6", EX ..200.00

Still

Alligator, lead, mc pnt, Germany, 2⅞", VG 550.00
American Trust Safe, CI, emb all sides, 6x6½", G- 85.00
Andy Gump, pnt CI, Arcade, 4⅜x2⅞", EX 900.00
Apple, CI, red & gr pnt, Kyser & Rex, ca 1882, 3x5¼", G 660.00
Arabian Safe, CI, japanned, Kyser & Rex, 4¾x4¼", M 360.00
Aunt Jemima (w/spoon), CI, mc pnt, AC Williams, 5⅞", EX 200.00
Auto, CI, red w/NP wheels, 4-passenger model, Williams, 6", VG ..580.00
Auto, M-1494, pnt lead, 2", VG 150.00
Battleship Kentucky, M-1439, CI, mc pnt w/gold, 10¼", EX 350.00
Battleship Maine, CI, japanned w/gold, Grey Iron, 4⅝x4½", VG ..225.00
Battleship Maine, M-1440, pnt CI, 4⅝", EX 350.00
Battleship Oregon, CI, japanned w/gold, Stevens, 3⅞x4⅞", EX ...165.00
Bay Window Building, M-1213, pnt CI, 4⅞", NM 4,500.00
Bear Stealing Pig, CI, gold pnt, 5½", G 525.00
Bennett & Fish Mulligan, M-179 variant, pnt CI, 5¾", EX 800.00
Bismark Pig w/Rider, CI, japanned, ca 1883, 6½x7¼", EX 6,500.00
Black Boy, 2-Faced; CI, blk w/gold pnt, AC Williams, 3⅛", G ..145.00
Blackpool Tower, CI, japanned, Chamberlain & Hill, 7⅛", M ..325.00
Boston Bull Terrier, CI, mc CI, Vindex Toys, 5¼" L, EX 300.00
Building w/Belfry, CI, gold highlights, Am, rare, 8", M 3,500.00
Bungalow, CI, mc pnt, Grey Iron, 3¾x3x3¼", EX 440.00
Camel Kneeling, CI, japanned, Kyser & Rex, 1889, 2½x4¾", EX ..825.00
Castle w/2 Towers, M-1114, pnt CI, 7", EX 750.00
Circus Elephant (seated), CI, mc pnt, Hubley, 3⅞", M 360.00
Circus Horse, M-509, on tub, CI, mc pnt, 5⅜", EX 140.00
Clown w/Black Face, M-232, pnt lead, 3⅞", NM 750.00
Columbia, CI, wht pnt, Kenton, 5¾", EX 495.00
Columbia, M-1077, CI, gold traces, rust, rpl base, 7¼" 250.00
County Bank, M-1110, pnt CI, 4¼", EX 250.00
Crosley Radio, M-820, pnt CI & tin, 4¼", NM 700.00
Cruise Ship, silvered lead, Souvenir Chicago, 8¼", EX 770.00
Cupola, CI, HP brns w/gr trim, J&E Stevens, ca 1870s, 5½", EX ..470.00
Cupola, CI, yel & red pnt, J&E Stevens, ca 1872, 4⅛", EX 330.00
Cupola, M-1145, pnt CI, 5½", VG 175.00
Czar Safe, NP CI/tin, combo trap on front panel, 3½", M 400.00
Darkey Sharecropper, pnt CI, toes visible, US, 1900s, 5¾", M ..300.00
Domed Mosque, CI, gold pnt, Grey Iron, 5⅛", M 500.00
Double-Decker Bus, aluminum, slot on roof, 3½", EX 95.00
Dresser (drawer), redware, Savings Bank on front, lg, VG 600.00
Duck on Tub, CI, red/wht/blk pnt, Hubley, 5⅜", M 330.00
Dutch Boy on Barrel, CI, mc suit, wht bbl, Hubley, 5⅝", NM ...525.00
Eiffel Tower, M-1074, pnt CI, 8⅜", EX 775.00
Elephant, Art Deco; CI, red pnt, trunk up, US, 4⅜", M 250.00
Elephant w/Raised Slot, CI, gray pnt, trunk moves, 4½", EX 230.00
Every Copper Helps, aluminum, gr pnt, New Zealand, 4¾", M ..220.00
Ferdinand the Bull, pnt compo, Crown, ca 1938, 5⅛", EX 300.00
Fidelity Trust Vault Counting House, M-903, CI, worn pnt, 6⅝" ..360.00
Fido, CI, wht w/red & blk pnt, Hubley, 5", M 275.00
Flat-Iron Building, M-1161, CI, silver pnt w/gold, 5¼", EX 200.00
Floral Safe, CI, mc pnt, Kyser & Rex, 4⅛x4⅝", M 385.00
Foxy Grandpa, pnt CI, Wing, 5½", VG 300.00
General Pershing, bronze-plated CI, Grey Iron, 7¾", VG 75.00
General Sherman on Base, CI, old gold pnt, Arcade, 6", G 330.00
Globe Savings Fund, CI, japanned, Kyser & Rex, ca 1889, 7⅛", M .3,500.00
Graf Zeppelin, CI, silver pnt, AC Williams, 6⅝", VG 120.00
Grandpa's Hat, CI, blk & red pnt, US, 2¼x3⅞", EX 400.00
Guardian, HP tin, Bergman, rare, VG 6,000.00
Hansel & Gretel, M-1016, tin litho, 2¼", EX 220.00
Hen House w/Rabbit, lead, mc pnt, ca 1908, 4⅜", EX 1,200.00
Home, NP CI, Wing, 6½x5", G- 40.00
Horn of Plenty Safe, NP CI, EM Roche, 4x3⅝", EX 470.00
House That Jack Built, paper litho, 5¼x6¼", EX 770.00
House w/Basement, CI, red & blk pnt, Ohio Foundry, 1893, 4⅝", EX ...2,400.00
Independence Hall Tower Bank, M-1205, pnt CI, 9½", NM ..2,600.00
Indiana Silo, CI, emb lettering, 3½x2", G 1,100.00
Iron Master's House, CI, mc pnt, Kyser & Rex, 1884, 4½", M ...1,375.00
Lamb, M-595, CI, worn pnt, 3¼" 270.00
Lindy-Bank By G&T 1928, M-124, wht metal w/gold pnt, 6½" .150.00
Log Cabin, CI, brn pnt, sm ped ft, 5½x7⅜", EX 1,700.00
Log Cabin, CI, chimney in center of roof, US, 2¾x3½", EX 275.00
Log Cabin, M-1023 variant, pnt CI, 2½", EX 250.00
Main Street Trolley (no people), CI, gold pnt, Williams, 3x6¾", VG ..300.00
Main Street Trolley (people), CI, gold pnt, Williams, 3x6¾", VG .250.00
Mammy w/Basket, wht metal, mc pnt 5¼", EX 200.00
Mammy w/Hands on Hips, CI, mc pnt, Hubley, 5¼", NM 350.00
Mary & Lamb, M-164, CI, wht w/red & gold, worn/flaked, 4½" ...495.00
Mascot (Am Nat'l League on Baseball), NP CI, Hubley, 5¾", EX ..1,045.00
McKinley/Roosevelt, emb on sides of elephant, CI, 1900s, 4⅜", M 1,200.00
Metropolitan Bank, CI, J&E Stevens, ca 1872, 5⅞x4⅛", G 150.00

Mickey Mouse, Hands on Hips, CI, mc pnt, 8", EX **4,400.00**
Middy, CI, 5¼", VG **110.00**
Moon & Star Safe, CI, blk w/gold pnt, 5⅛x3⅞", EX **140.00**
Mutt & Jeff, CI, gold pnt, AC Williams, 4¼x3½", VG **155.00**
Mutt & Jeff, M-157, CI, worn gold pnt, 5⅛" **105.00**
Mutual Clock, brass, Time & Money, Save Both, EX **220.00**
National Safe, NP CI, emb figures, 4¾x3½", M **165.00**
Newfoundland Dog, M-440, pnt CI, 3⅝", EX **225.00**
Old Abe w/Shield, CI, gold pnt, 1880s, 3⅞", G **550.00**
Old Volunteer (fire hydrant), CI, blk & red pnt, early, EX **1,870.00**
Owl, M-597, pnt CI, 4¼", NM **400.00**
Parlor Stove, NP CI, early floor model stove, 6¼", EX **275.00**
Pelican (Mammy), N-4510, pnt CI, NM **1,050.00**
Piano, CI, rpt, detailed casting, 5¾x7½" **330.00**
Pingree Potato, CI, emb letters, Mary Martin, 5¼" L, VG **825.00**
Polar Bear, M-716, CI, worn wht pnt, 5¼" **385.00**
Put Money in Thy Purse, CI, ca 1886, 3⅝x4¼", VG **385.00**
Rabbit Lying Down, CI, gold pnt, scarce, 2⅛x5⅛", M **650.00**
Rabbit on Base, CI, mc pnt, dtd 1884, 2¼x3¾", G- **450.00**
Radio Bank (2 dials), CI/metal, Kenton, 3⅜x4½x3¼", VG **385.00**
Recessed Door Filigree Safe, CI, copper pnt, 7⅝", EX **130.00**
Recording Bank, NP CI, Pat 1891, 6⅝x4¼", EX **350.00**
Rocking Chair, CI, gold pnt, CJ Manning, ca 1898, 6¾", EX .**2,750.00**
Santa Claus, CI, mc pnt, Wing, rpl pin, 5⅞", EX **470.00**
Save for a Rainy Day, M-616, CI, mc pnt, lt wear, 5¼", VG+ **200.00**
Seal on Rock, M-732, pnt CI, 3½", NM **1,300.00**
Share Cropper, M-173, CI, blk/gold/red pnt, lt wear, 5½" **190.00**
Shell Out (conch shell), CI, wht pnt, Stevens, 1882, 2½x4¾", G ..**385.00**
Ship, silvered lead, emblem: Hamburg, tin trap, 4x3⅞", M **360.00**
Ship on Base, HP tin, 2-mast, 2-stack, 9¼" L, EX **2,800.00**
Singer Sewing Machine, pnt tin w/decal, Germany, 5¼x4¼", VG **600.00**
Spirit of Saving Airplane, aluminum, monoplane, 10" wingspan, EX ..**525.00**
Squirrel w/Nut, CI, old gold pnt, rpl screw, US, 4⅛", VG **525.00**
St Bernard, M-437, CI, blk w/gold pnt, lt wear, 7¾" **130.00**
Standard Safe, CI, blk pnt, 7x5", EX **200.00**
State Bank, CI, japanned w/gold, Am, ca 1897, 5⅞x4⅝", EX **250.00**
State Bank, CI, japanned w/gold, Am, 4⅛", M **220.00**
State Bank, M-1080, NP w/worn brn japanning, key lock door, 6" ...**115.00**
Statue of Liberty, CI, gr & gold pnt, Kenton, 6⅜", EX **415.00**
Statue of Liberty, CI, silver w/gold trim, 9⅜", M **635.00**
Steamboat, CI, bl w/red stacks, AC Williams, 2½x7⅝", M **495.00**
Street Clock, CI/steel, red w/gold face, AC Williams, 6", VG **580.00**
Submarine, HP lead, removable top, emb waves, 5¼" L, EX **360.00**
Tabernacle Savings, CI, copper pnt, Keyless, 2¼x5x2½", M ..**3,400.00**
Teepee, lead, mc pnt, EX **250.00**
Tower, CI, japanned, John Harper, 9¼x3⅞", G **265.00**
Tower, CI, japanned w/red & gold, Kyser & Rex, 6⅞", EX **770.00**
Trader's Bank, CI, Canada, casting break, 8½x9½", EX **1,200.00**
Trolley Car, CI, silver pnt, Kenton, scarce, 2¾x5¼", G **275.00**
Turkey, M-587, pnt CI, 4¾", EX **150.00**
US Bank (eagle finial), CI, blk pnt, ca 1890, 9¼", VG **415.00**
Villa Bank, M-959, pnt CI, 5⅞", EX **150.00**
Washington Monument, CI, gold pnt, AC Williams, 6⅛", VG **195.00**
Western Reserve Trust & Savings, M-965 variant, pnt CI, 5", EX ..**550.00**
Westminster Abbey, CI, japanned, England, ca 1908, 6⅜", M ...**360.00**
Westminster Abbey, M-973, CI, worn bronze pnt, 6¼", VG+ **250.00**
White City Puzzle Barrel, NP CI, 1894, 5", EX **220.00**
White City Puzzle No 12, NP CI, Nichol, ca 1893, 4⅞x3⅝", M ...**360.00**
Wire-Haired Terrier, M-422, CI, worn pnt, 4⅝", G **110.00**
Yel Cab, CI, yel & blk pnt, Arcade, 7¾", EX **935.00**
2 Kids, CI, mc pnt, Harper, 4½x4½", EX **950.00**
2-Faced Boy, M-83, CI, worn pnt, 4⅛" **350.00**
4-Gable Roof Bank, CI, silver pnt, 3½", VG **250.00**
4-Tower Bank, CI, japanned, J&E Stevens, 5¾x4¼", VG **275.00**

$100,000 Money Bag, chrome-plated CI, scarce, 3⅝x4¼", NM ..**450.00**

Barber Shop Collectibles

Even for the stranger in town, the local barber shop was easy to find, its location vividly marked with the traditional red and white striped barber pole that for centuries identified such establishments. As far back as the 12th century, the barber has had a place in recorded history. At one time he not only groomed the beards and cut the hair of his gentlemen clients but was known as the 'blood-letter' as well, hence the red stripe for blood and the white for the bandages. Many early barbers even pulled teeth! Later, laws were enacted that divided the practices of barbering and surgery.

The Victorian barber shop reflected the charm of that era with fancy barber chairs upholstered in rich wine-colored velvet; rows of bottles made from colored art glass held hair tonics and shaving lotion. Backbars of richly carved oak with beveled mirrors lined the wall behind the barber's station. During the late 19th century, the barber pole with a blue stripe added to the standard red and white as a patriotic gesture came into vogue.

Today the barber shop has all but disappeared from the American scene, replaced by modern unisex salons. Collectors search for the barber poles, the fancy chairs, and the tonic bottles of an era gone but not forgotten. See also Bottles; Razors; Shaving Mugs.

Bowl, tin w/stamped floral pinwheel center, 10⅞" dia **220.00**
Chair, Archer, CI, pierced & raised reliefs, Pat 1878 ....**1,200.00**
Chair, child's, Odell, Pluto figure on seat w/CI base, 1930s, EX ...**1,250.00**
Chair, gargoyle heads, walnut & oak, early, rstr **950.00**
Chair, Koken, oak, brn uphl bk & seat **1,000.00**
Chair, Koken, recliner, orange crushed velour, 1901, EX orig **600.00**
Jar, Pixcresol Antiseptic, milk glass, metal lid, 6" dia **150.00**
Kit, traveling barber's, case w/scissors/razors/etc, 1890s **175.00**
Pole, leaded glass, Koken, Victorian, 48" **1,600.00**
Pole, porc, Look Better, Feel..., ½-rnd, wall mt, 48x8" **265.00**
Pole, porc, red/wht/bl, Genuine Paidar Chicago USA, rstr, 79" .**600.00**
Pole, porc, red/wht/bl stripes, gr porc base, 84", G **400.00**
Pole, trn wood, old red & wht rpt, 59" **465.00**
Rack, shaving mug; oak, floor type, lg **3,500.00**
Shoe shine stand, cast brass, 1835-1930, 14¾" **75.00**
Sign, curved porc, red/wht/bl, 14½x24", EX **325.00**
Sign, curved porc, red/wht/bl stripes, 24x15½", VG **165.00**
Sign, Hair Bobbing Our Specialty, 1930s, M **250.00**
Sign, Journeyman's Barber's Union Shop, metal, 1920s **35.00**
Sign, pole design w/name, pnt wood, early, 36x9½", VG **150.00**

Sign, porcelain flange, red, white, and blue, minor chips,
12x24", $200.00.

Sign, Vigorator Hair Tonic, man washing hair, tin, 7-color, 9x5" ..**145.00**
Stone, razor sharpening, Koken's Moor, in aluminum holder, M .**100.00**
Strop, Kriss Kross, rotates w/crank, Pat 6-30-21, NMIB **35.00**

Barometers

Barometers are instruments designed to measure the weight or pressure of the atmosphere in order to anticipate approaching weather changes. They have a glorious history. Some of the foremost thinkers of the 17th century developed the mercury barometer, as the discovery of the natural laws of the universe progressed. Working in 1644 from experiments by Galileo, Evangelista Torrecelli used a glass tube and a jar of mercury to create a vacuum and therefore prove that air has weight. Four years later, Rene Descartes added a paper scale to the top of Torrecelli's mercury tube and created the basic barometer. Blaise Pascal, working with Descartes, used it to determine the heights of mountains; indeed, only later was the correlation between changes in air pressure and changes in the weather observed and the term 'weatherglass' applied. Robert Boyle introduced it to England, and Robert Hook modified the form and designed the wheel barometer.

The most common type of barometer is the wheel or banjo type. Second is the stick type. Modifications of the plain stick would be the marine gimballed type, followed by the laboratory or Kew or Fortin type. Others are the Admiral Fitzroys of which there are twelve or more types. The above all have mercury contained in either glass tubing or wood-box cisterns.

Another type of barometer is the aneroid, working on atmospheric pressure changes. They come in all sizes ranging from 1" in diameter to 12" or larger. They may be in metal or wood cases. There is a Barograph which records on a graph that rotates around a drum powered by a 7-day clock mechanism. Pocket barometers (altimeters) vary in sizes from 1" diameter up to 6" diameter. One final type of barometer is the symphisometer, a modification of the stick barometer used for a limited time and not as accurate as a conventional marine barometer. Our advisor for this category is Bob Elsner; he is listed in the Directory under Florida.

American

B Pike & Sons, NY, silvered scale, 14" thermometer, 1880s **2,450.00**
Charles Wilder, Peterboro NH, rosewood, Woodruff/Pat **950.00**
DE Lent, Rochester NY **950.00**
EO Spooner Storm King, Boston MA **1,250.00**
FD McKay Jr, Elmira NY, dbl-trn wood columns **3,100.00**
Simmons & Sons, Fulton NY **950.00**

English

Wheel or banjo type, A. Columba 37 Charles St. Hatton Gard. London, Regency style, mahogany wheel with flame veneered case, 43", $900.00.

Admiral Fitzroy, various styles, ea, from $500 up to **3,000.00**
Angle barometer, right, John Whitehurst, ca 1790 ....**12,000.00**
Fortin-type (Kew or laboratory), metal on brd w/milk glass **750.00**
Marine gimballed, Walker, London **4,000.00**
Stick, bow-front mahog urn-shape cistern cover, Troutman/Simms ..**5,000.00**
Stick, rosewood, L Casella, London **1,650.00**
Symphisometer, Adie **3,850.00**
Wheel, 10", heavy cvg, Angelenetta & Bregazzi, London **1,650.00**
Wheel, 10", MOP, Spelzini, London **1,250.00**
Wheel, 10", sgn J Smith...London..to King George IV..., mahog .**1,250.00**
Wheel, 6", Stanley, Peterborough, silvered scale/thermometer ..**1,450.00**
Wheel, 8", F Molten, Norwich **1,150.00**

Other Barometer Types

Aneroid, w/½-rnd thermometer **250.00**
Aneroid, 4-6" dia, brass case **150.00**
Barograph reading barometer, mahog, Negretti & Zambra **950.00**
Pocket barometer (altimeter), w/case, from $200 to **300.00**

Barware

Back in the '30s when social soirees were very elegant affairs thanks to the influence of Hollywood in all its glamour and mistique, cocktails were often served up in shakers styled as miniature airplanes, zeppelins, skyscrapers, lady's legs, penguins, roosters, bowling pins, etc. Some were by top designers such as Norman Bel Geddes and Russel Wright. They were made of silverplate, glass, and chrome, often trimmed with colorful Bakelite handles. Today these are hot collectibles, and even the more common Deco-styled chrome cylinders are often priced at $25.00 and up. Ice buckets, trays, and other bar accessories are also included in this area of collecting.

For further information we recommend *Vintage Bar Ware Identification & Value Guide* by Stephen Visakay, our advisor for this category; he is listed in the Directory under New Jersey.

Book, The Savoy Cocktail Book, H Craddock, 1930, M **150.00**
Bottle, syphon; Norman Bel Geddes Soda King, chrome, bl top ...**160.00**
Dispenser, Black bartender, France, 6½x6", NM **750.00**
Dispenser, seltzer; N Bel Geddes, Soda King, chrome/blk, 10" **50.00**
Dispenser, seltzer; Soda King Syphon, ca 1938, 9½x3⅞" **200.00**
Ice bucket, aluminum, emb penguins, West Bend Alum Co, 1944 ....**35.00**
Ice bucket, chrome w/Bakelite trim, Keystone Ware, 10½x6¼" ...**75.00**
Ice bucket, chrome-plated copper, Keystone, 1930s, +tray **95.00**
Ice bucket, red anodized aluminum, apple form, Italy, 1950s **35.00**
Ice chopper, cobalt glass w/silk-screened recipes, 11½" **75.00**
Mixer, chrome, jade Catalin mts, Manning-Bowman, K-128, 10¾" **225.00**
Rack, tumbler; gyroscopic, chrome, 20x8½" dia, +4 tumblers **200.00**
Shaker, aluminum, Chicago Century of Progress, 1933 ....**45.00**
Shaker, chrome, Connoisseur, ivory knob, Manning-Bowman, 12" ...**95.00**
Shaker, chrome, cylinder w/blk bands, w/4 tumblers & 16" tray .**175.00**
Shaker, chrome, penguin form, unmk, 11" **350.00**
Shaker, chrome, vintage etch, slim form, unmk, 12" **50.00**
Shaker, chrome & plastic w/glass insert, mk Ritz, 1930s **75.00**
Shaker, chrome w/Catalin lid, Revere, 1937, 12⅛" **350.00**
Shaker, clear glass, w/strainer, horse's head lid, Heisey **200.00**
Shaker, clear glass w/chrome, hourglass form, Maxwell Phillip **75.00**
Shaker, clear glass w/emb dmns, plastic lid, 1928, 12½" **40.00**
Shaker, clear glass w/silver o/l hunt scene, Heisey, 14" **250.00**
Shaker, cobalt glass, w/SP trim, chrome lid, 1935, +6 tumblers ..**450.00**
Shaker, cobalt glass w/silver o/l, 1920s, 11", +8 tumblers **350.00**
Shaker, cobalt glass w/wht angelfish, chrome top, Hazel Atlas, 10" ..**28.00**
Shaker, cobalt glass w/wht silk-screened recipes, 10½" **38.00**

Shaker, frosted glass dumbbell w/SP trim, Nat'l, +12 martinis 500.00
Shaker, hammered/plain NP, 3-hdld, Expressware NY..., 17½" ..150.00
Shaker, nickel/SP brass/plastic, F Arstrom, 1935, 8½x3½" 700.00
Shaker, polished aluminum, skyscraper-inspired, 13x3½" 95.00
Shaker, ruby glass w/silver hunt scene, chrome lid, 1-qt 175.00
Shaker, ruby glass w/silver roosters, SP lid, 1-qt 175.00
Shaker, SP, penguin figural, Napier, ca 1936, 12" 850.00
Shaker/cooler, aluminum & silver hammertone, 1930s, 10¾" 75.00
Travel bar, SP plane breaks apart for shaker, etc, '28, 17½" 5,000.00
Tray, clear glass w/cut/etched olives, Lucite hdls, 1950s, 18" 85.00
Tray, flappers w/drinks, Here's How, rectangular, NM 100.00
Tray, gyroscopic, glass/chrome, 24" dia, +shaker & 8 tumblers ...750.00

Baskets

Basket weaving is a craft as old as ancient history. Baskets have been used to harvest crops, for domestic chores, and to contain the catch of fishermen. Materials at hand were utilized, and baskets from a specific region are often distinguishable simply by analyzing the natural fibers used in their construction. Early Indian baskets were made of corn husks or woven grasses. Willow splint, straw, rope, and paper were also used. Until the invention of the veneering machine in the late 1800s, splint was made by water-soaking a split log until the fibers were softened and flexible. Long strips were pulled out by hand and, while still wet and pliable, woven into baskets in either a cross-hatch or hexagonal weave.

Most handcrafted baskets on the market today were made between 1860 and the early 1900s. Factory baskets with a thick, wide splint cut by machine are of little interest to collectors. The more popular baskets are those designed for a specific purpose, rather than the more commonly found utility baskets that had multiple uses. Among the most costly forms are the Nantucket Lighthouse baskets, which were basically copied from those made there for centuries by aboriginal Indians. They were designed in the style of whale-oil barrels and named for the South Shoal Nantucket Lightship where many were made during the last half of the 19th century. Cheese baskets (used to separate curds from whey), herb-gathering baskets, and finely woven Shaker miniatures are other highly-prized examples of the basket-weaver's art.

In the listings that follow, assume that each has a center bentwood handle (unless handles of another type are noted) that is not included in the height. Unless another type of material is indicated, assume that each is made of splint. Conditions described as 'EX,' 'VG,' or 'G' indicate some measure of damage.

For further information we recommend *Collector's Guide to Country Baskets* by Don and Carol Raycraft, available from Collector Books. See also American Indian; Eskimo; Sewing; Shaker.

Blk stacked cube/eye design, star decor base, w/lid, 2½x3¼" 450.00
Buttocks, brn stain, minor damage, 13x21x14" 150.00
Buttocks, crossed hdl supports, wide rib at rim, 5x10x8" 800.00
Buttocks, crossed hdl supports, 1¾x3⅜x3⅛" 350.00
Buttocks, crossed hdl supports, 3½x6½x5½" 275.00
Buttocks, crossed hdl supports, 7x12x12" 175.00
Buttocks, crossed hdl supports, 8x15x14" 300.00
Buttocks, early twig hdl, 18x16½" 165.00
Buttocks, Eye-of-God hdls, 2⅜x4¾x4½" 300.00
Buttocks, old patina, 6x10x10" 125.00
Buttocks, 7-rib, Eye-of-God hdls, EX color, 6½x16½x15" 120.00
Buttocks, 21-rib, old dk finish, wear, 3½x8x8" 100.00
Buttocks, 24-rib, 4x6¾x6¼" 200.00
Buttocks, 24-rib, 9x19x15" 145.00
Buttocks, 28-rib, well made, EX color, lt damage, 6x12x10" 165.00
Buttocks, 32-rib, worn/weathered, 8x12½x13½" 100.00
Buttocks, 34-rib, old varnish, EX detail, 6½x11x11½" 140.00
Buttocks, 56-rib, well made, med patina, 4¾x8x7" 330.00
Coiled form w/vertical interlacing, finial on lid, 8x8", G 150.00
Coiled rye straw, bound w/splint, flat bottom, 5¾x14x11" 250.00
Coiled rye straw, bound w/splint, 3x7⅜" 175.00
Coiled rye straw, woven-in hdls, 9⅜x18½" dia, EX 375.00
Coiled rye straw, woven-in loop hanger on rim, 4⅛x12½" 275.00
Courses in 4 colors & natural, bentwood rim hdls, 8x14x15½" ..220.00
Cvd hdl w/name, 8x13x12", G 100.00
Dbl hdl, 12 rows of curled splint decorating side, 5x8" dia 300.00
Gathering, gr pnt bentwood staves, wire bands, 1890s, 9x15" 225.00
Gathering, sq bottom, rnd rim, 3½x7½x6¾" 300.00
Gathering, turned-up sides, 22" L 125.00
Gathering, vertical ribs, flat bottom, 3⅝x6⅝" 450.00
Goose feather, oblong, brushed blk pnt, dbl lids, 9x18x14" 250.00
Half, rib type, stationary hdl, 5x7⅝x4⅝" 130.00
Hdl attached on outside in last 4 rows of splint, w/lid, 13" sq 200.00
Herb drying, openwork sides, EX age & color, 5¼x11x11" 195.00
Laundry, G age & color, lt wear, 14x27x20" 150.00
Linear decor, attached ring at shoulder for lid, 1860s, 15x18" 450.00
Market, vertical ribs, flat bottom, 8¼x12½" dia 250.00
Market, vertical ribs, solid wood bottom, 7½x13½x10⅝" 350.00
Melon, brass rivets at hdls, 2⅝x4¼x5" 375.00
Melon, Eye-of-God hdls, 4x6x5½" 400.00
Melon, gr pnt, sgn H on hdl, 14x16x15", EX 350.00
Melon, wrapped rim, cvd wood hdl, 3x5½" 200.00
Melon, 20-rib, EX age & patina, 4¼x8½x8", EX 150.00
Mini, wide rib around rim, crossing hdl supports, 2x3⅝x3⅛" 275.00
Mini vegetable, stapled rim, rectangular, 1½x3¼x2½" 60.00

Nantucket, swing handle with brass ears, turned wooden bottom, early 20th century, 5x7¼", $550.00.

Nantucket, trn wood base w/woven cane & splint, 4x9", VG 165.00
Nantucket, trn wooden bottom, swivel hdl, 5½x10" 880.00
Picket-fence style, wood & wire, wire bail hdls, oblong, 33x17" .300.00
Pie, lid slides on hdl, 6x12" dia, VG 250.00
Rectangular, w/lid, 9½x14x9½", EX 225.00
Sewing, coiled rye straw bound w/splint, flat bottom, 3x15x7" 95.00
Sewing, coiled rye straw w/openwork design at rim, 3x12x6½" ..400.00
Shaker type, rnd hdl fastens through to bottom, 5x10½" dia 250.00
Storage, flat bottom, flat lid, 10⅜x16¾" dia 850.00
Swing hdl, pnt decor, 5x8½", VG 250.00
Trug, oblong, wooden ft/rim/hdl, dk patina, English 120.00
Trug, old gr pnt, English, 5½x20½x11½" 200.00

Batchelder

Ernest A. Batchelder was a leading exponent of the Arts and Crafts movement in the United States. His influential book, *Design in Theory and Practice,* was originally published in 1910. He is best known, however, for his artistic tiles which he first produced in Pasedena, California, from 1909 to 1916. In 1916 the business was relocated to Los Angeles where it continued until 1932, closing because of the Depression.

In 1938 Batchelder resumed production in Pasedena under the name of 'Kinneola Kiln.' Output of the new pottery consisted of delicately cast bowls and vases in an Oriental style. This business closed in 1951. Tiles carry a die-stamped mark; vases and bowls are hand incised. Our advisor for this category is Jack Chipman, author of *Collector's Encyclopedia of California Pottery*; he is listed in the Directory under California.

Ashtray, lt bl matt, hexagonal w/emb advertising, 4½", EX 275.00
Bowl, bl, flared rim, incised mk, 3¼x7½" 95.00
Bowl, dk teal, rose int, Pasadena mk, 2x7" 85.00
Tile, artichoke, gold & bl patina, 3" 85.00
Tile, Evangelist series, bl engobe, 9" sq, set of 6, M 5,700.00
Tile, feathery bird, bl patina, thick, 4" sq 185.00
Tile, mythical bird & animal, unglazed gray, mk, 6" 265.00
Tile, peacocks, pk & yel, 3" sq 85.00
Vase, gray, cylindrical, 9½" 225.00
Vase, yel, flared rim, 6" 155.00
Vase, yel, sq, 7" 145.00

Battersea

Battersea is a term that refers to enameling on copper or other metal. Though originally produced at Battersea, England, in the mid-18th century, the craft was later practiced throughout the Staffordshire district. Boxes are the most common examples. Some are figurals, and many bear an inscription. Values are given for examples with only minimal damage, which is normal. Our advisor for this category is John Harrigan; he is listed in the Directory under Minnesota.

**Plaque, England, 1700s, gilt frame,
12x15" overall, $935.00.**

Bonbonniere, European scene on underside, 1½x2¾", EX 625.00
Bonbonniere, florals/pnt-on 'hdls,' basketweave ground, 2" L 650.00
Box, bluebird on foliage, hinged lid, 1½" 285.00
Box, Esteem the Giver, bird on nest, ca 1780, 2¼" 260.00
Box, grisaille classical scene w/gold, 3½" dia 500.00
Box, maid & lamb, bk: cherubs & lady w/fan, 1¾" dia 500.00
Box, patch; lady's torso form, head forms lid, 3" 1,600.00
Box, snuff; French/English naval battle, 2" L 750.00
Box, Trifle From London, floral garland, 1½" L, EX 350.00
Candlesticks, floral, scalloped drip pans, 9", pr 1,250.00
Curtain tie-bk/mirror knob, Comre Truxton (Naval officer), 2" ...450.00
Mirror holder, eagle/E Pluribus Unum, mc, rpr, 2", VG, pr 450.00
Needle case, floral & insects on yel, rstr, 4¾" L 550.00
Opera glasses, children hunting & fishing, 4" W, in case 425.00
Tray, card; 4-suit decor, pr 950.00

Bauer

Originally founded in Paducah, Kentucky, in 1885, the J.A. Bauer Company moved to Los Angeles where it was re-established in 1910. Until the 1920s, their major products were terra cotta gardenware, flowerpots, and stoneware and yellow ware bowls. During prohibition they produced crocks for home use. A more artful form of product began to develop with the addition of designer Louis Ipsen to the staff circa 1915. Some of his work, a line of molded vases, flowerpots, bowls, etc., was awarded a bronze medal at the Pacific International Exposition in 1916.

In 1930 the first of many dinnerware lines was tested on the market. Their initial pattern, Plain Ware, was well accepted and led the way to the introduction of the most popular dinnerware in their history and with today's collectors, Ring Ware. It was produced from 1932 into the early 1960s in solid colors of jade green, royal blue, dusty burgundy, ivory, Chinese yellow, Delph blue, orange-red, and (in very limited quantities) black or white. Its simple pattern was a design of closely-spaced concentric ribs, either convex or concave. Over the years, more than one hundred shapes were available. Some were made in limited quantities, resulting in rare items to whet the appetites of Bauer buffs today. Other patterns were La Linda, produced during the 1940s and 1950s, and Monterey Moderne, introduced in 1948 and remaining popular into the 1950s (made in pink, black, gray, brown, and green).

After WWII a flood of foreign imports and loss of key employees drastically curtailed their sales, and the pottery began a steady decline that ended in failure in 1962. Prices listed below reflect the California market. For more information we recommend *Collector's Encyclopedia of Bauer Pottery: Identification & Values* (Collector Books) and *The Collector's Encyclopedia of California Pottery*, both by Jack Chipman, our advisor for this category. Mr. Chipman's address may be found in the Directory under California.

In the lines of Ring and Plain ware, pricing depends to some extent on color. Use the low end of our range of values for light brown, Chinese Yellow, orange-red, jade green, red-brown, olive green, light blue, turquoise, and gray; the high end colors are delph blue, ivory, dusty burgundy, cobalt, chartreuse, papaya, and burgundy. Black is 50% higher than the high end; to evaluate white, double the high side. Use the low end of the range to evaluate Monterey items in all colors but Monterey blue, burgundy, and white — those are high-end colors. You'll need to double the high end for black in this line as well as Monterey Moderne. An in-depth study of colors and values may be found in the books referenced above.

Art Pottery

Bookends, CA bear emb on dome shape, mossy gr, pr, minimum 1,500.00
Carnation jar, gr satin matt w/dk specks, 24", minimum 1,500.00
Flower bowl, dark gr overdrip, low, 10", minimum value 800.00
Jardiniere, emb filigree, mossy gr, 10" 500.00
Vase, Rebekah, gr matt w/blk specks, hdls, 15", minimum value ..1,500.00

Brusche Alfresco and Contempo

Bowl, divided vegetable; Al Fresco, Hemlock Gr, 9¼" 30.00
Cup, Contempo, Spicy Gr 12.00
Pitcher, Al Fresco, Dubonnet, w/ice lip, 2-qt 75.00
Pitcher, Contempo, Indio Brn, 1-pt 30.00
Plate, bread & butter; Al Fresco, pk speckled, 6" 6.00
Plate, dinner; Al Fresco, Lime, 11½" 12.00
Teapot, Contempo, Desert Beige, 6-cup 45.00

Cal-Art Pottery

Figurine, Madonna, wht matt, praying, 8", minimum value 125.00

Flower bowl, bl matt, oval, 10" 45.00
Miniature, duck, orange-red (rare color), minimum value 100.00
Vase, cream matt, 6-lobe shape, hdls, 7" 80.00

Matt Carlton

Basket (uncommon shape), orange-red, 8", minimum value ...1,500.00
Bowl, jade gr, ruffled rim, 3½x7" 85.00
Bowl, orange-red, sq, 2½x6" 75.00
Vase, carnation; jade green, waisted, 10" 350.00
Vase, Chinese Yel, ruffled rim, 3" 75.00
Vase, Chinese Yel, smooth sides, ruffled rim, 12", minimum 500.00
Vase, fan; wht (scarce color), striations, 6x8", minimum value ..500.00
Vase, orange-red, ribbed, ruffled rim, 12", minimum value 450.00
Vase, royal bl, twist hdls, flared rim, 9½", minimum value 1,200.00

Florist and Garden Pottery

Jardiniere, Cal-Art swirl, gr, 5" 35.00
Jardiniere, Hi-Fire Ring style, yel, 5" 40.00
Pinnacle pot, olive gr, glossy, 10" 85.00
Planter, oblong, gr, 4x24" 95.00
Pot, stepped dmn shape, early, scarce, from $150 to 225.00
Stock vase, Chinese Yel, 18" 150.00
Strawberry pot, burgundy, 8-cup, 9" 185.00

Hi-Fire Pottery

Dog dish, emb DOG on chartreuse, scarce, 7" 150.00
Pitcher, red-brn, ewer form, Fred Johnson, 11½", minimum 450.00
Rose bowl, Monterey Bl, 4" 55.00
Vase, turq, waisted cylinder, 12½" 225.00
Vase, wht, flared rim, 9½" 165.00

La Linda

Bowl, fruit; 5" 18.00
Cup 18.00
Plate, bread & butter; 6" 7.50
Plate, dinner; 9" 15.00
Platter, oval, 10" 22.50
Shakers, pr 12.00
Tumbler, clip-on metal hdl 5.00

Monterey

Bowl, oval vegetable; 10", from $55 to 80.00
Candle holder, from $45 to 65.00
Cup & saucer, from $24 to 34.00
Gravy boat, lg, from $40 to 60.00
Plate, dinner; 10½", from $30 to 45.00
Plate, salad; 7½", from $10 to 15.00

Monterey Moderne and Related Kitchenware

Bowl, serving; chartreuse, 7" 25.00
Bowl, serving; yel, 10½" 35.00
Bowl, soup; any color but blk, 5¼", from $15 to 20.00
Butter dish, pk, rnd 65.00
Canister/cookie jar, ceramic lid, chartreuse, 8" 95.00
Pitcher, chartreuse, 2½-qt 85.00
Pitcher, olive gr, 6½" 45.00
Plate, bread & butter; olive gr, 6½" 8.00
Plate, dinner; pk, 10½" 25.00

Teapot, yel, 6-cup 65.00

Plain Ware

Bean pot, 2-qt, from $75 to 100.00
Mug, 4", from $50 to 75.00
Plate, dinner; 11½", from $65 to 95.00
Plate, salad; 8½", from $35 to 50.00
Pudding dish, 10¼", from $80 to 120.00
Ramekin, any color but blk, from $15 to 20.00
Sugar bowl, w/lid, from $50 to 75.00

Red, White, and Yellow Ware

Churn, redware, shiny glaze, 2-gal, w/lid 125.00
Porch pot, redware, laurel wreath relief, marked, 10" 150.00
Sanitary chick fount, whtware, 2-pc, mk on tray, 1-gal 65.00
Spice jar, yelware, 4½" 75.00

Ring Ware

Photo courtesy Roger Gass/Jack Chipman

Beer pitcher, from $350.00 to $525.00;
Beer mug, from $150.00 to $225.00.

Batter bowl, 2-qt, from $85 to 125.00
Bowl, divided vegetable; from $150 to 225.00
Bowl, mixing; #18, from $45 to 65.00
Bowl, mixing; #9, from $100 to 120.00
Bowl, nappy, #9, from $65 to 95.00
Bowl, vegetable; oval, 8", from $85 to 125.00
Butter dish, oblong, ¼-lb, from $175 to 250.00
Candle holder, 2½", from $45 to 65.00
Coffeepot, drip; from $300 to 400.00
Cookie jar, from $400 to 600.00
Mug, bbl shape, from $100 to 150.00
Pitcher, beer; from $350 to 525.00
Pitcher, orig shape, 2-qt, from $85 to 125.00
Plate, dinner; 10½", from $65 to 95.00
Plate, salad; 7½", from $30 to 45.00
Platter, oval, 12", from $50 to 75.00
Platter, oval, 9", from $30 to 45.00
Sugar bowl, w/lid, from $45 to 65.00
Sugar shaker, from $200 to 300.00
Teapot, any color but blk, 6-cup, from $100 to 150.00
Teapot, 2-cup, from $75 to 100.00
Tumbler, bbl shape, metal hdl, from $100 to 150.00

Bavaria

Bavaria, Germany, was long the center of that country's pottery industry; in the 1800s, many firms operated in and around the area.

Chinaware vases, novelties, and table accessories were decorated with transfer prints as well as by hand by artists who sometimes signed their work. The examples listed here are marked with 'Bavaria' and the logos of some of the various companies which were located there.

Ashtray, flower medallion w/gold tracery, maroon border, 4x3" **7.50**
Bowl, chrysanthemums & roses w/gold, emb scrolls, 3x10½" **42.00**
Bowl, mc flowers w/gold, ZS&Co, lg **85.00**
Bowl, mixed flowers w/gold, scrolled blank, 3x11" **65.00**
Coffee set, floral w/gold, melon ribs, mk, 9½" pot+cr/sug **95.00**
Cup & saucer, demi; floral, pk w/gold on pk to bl, mk **10.00**
Cup & saucer, roses, pk on wht w/gold scalloped, ftd **50.00**
Pickle dish, mc floral w/gold on elongated leaf form, 11x4½" **30.00**
Pitcher, rose medallions on gr to orange, emb scrolls/leaves, 6½" .**35.00**
Plate, classical figures medallion w/gold, Kauffmann, 6¼" **12.00**
Plate, mc flowers/game birds, Schumann, rtcl rim, 10-sided, 10" ..**25.00**
Plate, mc roses w/gold lattice & swag trim, scalloped, 6" **5.00**
Plate, roses, mc on pastel w/gold, ZS&Co, 12⅜" **70.00**
Tea/coffee set, florals w/gold, tea/coffeepots+10 plates+cr/sug **200.00**

Beer Cans

When the flat-top can was first introduced in 1934, it came with printed instructions on how to use the triangular punch opener. Cone-top cans, which are rare today, were patented in 1935 by the Continental Can Company. By the 1960s, aluminum cans with pull tabs had made both types obsolete.

Condition is an important consideration when evaluating market price. Grade 1 must be in like-new condition with no rust. However, the triangular punch hole is acceptable. Grade 2 cans may have slight scratches or dimples but must be free of rust. For Grade 3, light rust, minor scratching, and some fading may be acceptable. When these defects are more pronounced, a can is defaulted to Grade 4. Those in less-than-excellent condition devaluate sharply. In the listings that follow, cans are arranged alphabetically by brand name, not by brewery. Unless noted otherwise, values are for 11- to 12-oz. cans in Grade 1 condition.

All cone tops with original caps, ca 1930: Clyde Cream Ale, EX, $60.00; Old Tap Ale, man in reserve, EX, $225.00; Old Tap Ale, EX, $200.00; Old Tap Beer, VG, $150.00.

Acme, wht label, flat top **20.00**
Atlas Prager, red & wht, flat top **12.50**
Bohemian Wiedeman Beer, bl & red letters on wht, cone top **28.00**
Bull Dog Malt Liquor, red/wht/bl/gold, flat top **12.00**
Butte Special, cone top **78.00**
Champagne Velvet, Heileman, pull top **1.50**
Clear Lake Beer, lake scene, red label, flat top **135.00**
Country Club Malt Liquor, wht, pull top **1.00**
Drewery's Extra Dry Beer, bl label on wht, flat top **5.00**
Duquesne, boy waving from w/in red circle on wht, flat top **32.00**

Erin Brew, Standard, flat top **34.00**
Fallstaff, gold & blk on wht, pull top, 16-oz **2.00**
Fischer's Light Dry Beer, red/wht/bl, flat top **22.50**
Fitger's Rex, cone top **37.50**
Fitgerald's Burgomaster, bl & ivory, crown top **48.00**
Fort Pitt Special, cone top **50.00**
Gettelman, brn label on ivory, flat top **24.00**
Golden Crown, General, pull top **3.00**
Hampten Beer, bl & wht, flat top **7.50**
Hauenstein, red & white, cone top **55.00**
Highlander, gold, low cone top **165.00**
Iron City, red on wht, pull top, 16-oz **4.00**
James Bond 007 Special Blend, pull top, 1 of series **220.00**
Lucky Lager, flat top, 7-oz **12.00**
Maier Select Beer, red/wht/bl, flat top **12.00**
Mile Hi, red/wht/bl, Tivoli, flat top **42.50**
Milwaukee Club Beer, brn & yel, cone top **40.00**
National Bohemian, red on wht, pull top, 8-oz **8.00**
Old Topper Ale, man in top hat silhouette, crown top **165.00**
Old Vienna, red/wht/tan, cone top **95.00**
Olympia Light, red & wht, pull top, 16-oz **3.50**
POC, gold label on bl, cone top **130.00**
Prima Ale, red & wht on bl, cone top **160.00**
Ranier Ale, yel oval, flat top **10.00**
Ranier Club, blk w/red label, cone top **85.00**
Regency, red & wht on yel, Maier, flat top **34.00**
Royal Pilsner Beer, yel on red, crown top **175.00**
Ruppert Knickerbocker Beer, red & gold on wht, flat top **12.50**
Schell's Deer Brand Beer, blk/yel/red, cone top **100.00**
Schlitz, gold w/red & wht label, cone top **85.00**
Schmidt's First Premium, man in bl jacket, cone top **80.00**
Texas A&M Football 1975, brn & wht **4.00**
Tuborg, Carling, pull top, 10-oz **8.00**
Weber, red & wht on gr, flat top **45.00**
Yusay Pilsner Premium Beer, wht bird, red & wht, flat top **22.00**

Bellaire, Marc

Marc Bellaire, originally Donald Edmund Fleischman, was born in Toledo, Ohio, in 1925. He studied at the Toledo Museum of Art under Ernest Spring while employed as a designer for the Libbey Glass Company. During World War II, while serving in the Navy, he travelled extensively throughout the Pacific resulting in his enriched sense of design and color.

Marc settled in California in the 1950s where his work attracted the attention of national buyers and agencies who persuaded him to create ceramic lines of his own, employing hand-decorating techniques throughout. This resulted in the building of a studio in Culver City. He produced high-quality ceramics, often decorated with ultramodern figures or geometric patterns and executed with a distinctive flair. His most famous line was Mardi Gras, decorated with slim dancers in spattered and striped colors of black, blue, pink and white. Other major patterns were Jamaica, Balinese, Beachcomber, Friendly Island, Cave Painting, Hawaiian, Bird Isle, Oriental, Jungle Dancer, and Kashmir. Kashmir usually has the name Ingle on the front and Bellaire on the reverse.

It should be noted that Marc was employed by Sascha Brastoff during the 1950s. Many believe that he was hired for his creative imagination and style.

During the period of 1951 – 1956, Marc was named one of the top ten artware designers by *Giftwares Magazine*. After 1956 he taught and lectured on art, design, and ceramic decorating techniques from coast to coast. Many pieces were one of a kind, commissioned throughout the United States.

During the 1970s he set up a studio in Marin County, California, and eventually moved to Palm Springs where he opened his final studio/gallery. There he produced large pieces with a Southwestern style. Mr Bellaire died in 1994. Our advisor for this category is Marty Webster; he is listed in the Directory under Michigan.

Ashtray, Bird Isle, blk birds on cream, 8" 85.00
Ashtray, Clown, mc on cream, 7" 65.00
Ashtray, Jamaica, musicians on brn, 10x14" 85.00
Ashtray, Mardi Gras, figures on blk, rolled rim, 9" 100.00
Ashtray, Mardi Gras, figures on blk, 14x14" 225.00
Ashtray, Still Life, matt fruits & leaves, 10x15" 100.00
Box, Jamaica, man w/guitar, free-form, B46, 8" 155.00
Box, Mardi Gras, 10" dia 200.00
Compote, Cave Painting, 4-ftd, 6x12" 125.00
Compote, Woman w/Blue Bird, 4-ftd, 8x17" 225.00
Cookie jar, Stick People, wooden lid, 10" 150.00
Ewer, Mardi Gras, figures on blk, hdl, 18" 400.00
Figurine, Mardi Gras, man reclining, very slim, 18" 1,000.00
Figurine, Mardi Gras, man standing, very slim, 24" 1,000.00
Figurine, Polynesian man standing, 12" 500.00
Lamp, Mardi Gras, long-neck vase, wooden base, 28" 450.00

Platter, multicolored angels on gray, signed and dated 1958, 14" diameter (believed to be a personal presentation piece), $400.00.

Platter, Friendly Island, 10" 135.00
Platter, Hawaiian, 3 figures on orange, 7x13" 125.00
Platter, Mardi Gras, figures on blk, 12x18" 250.00
Platter, Polynesian Dancer, egg shaped, 11x15" 250.00
Tray, Jungle Dancer, figure on blk & gr, 12" dia 200.00
Vase, Balinese Women, hourglass shape, 8" 125.00
Vase, Black Cats, hourglass shape, 8" 125.00
Vase, Mardi Gras, hourglass shape on 3 ft, 11" 125.00
Vase, Polynesian Woman, 9" 125.00

Belleek, American

From 1883 until 1930, several American potteries located in New Jersey and Ohio manufactured a type of china similar to the famous Irish Belleek soft-paste porcelain. The American manufacturers identified their porcelain by using 'Belleek' or 'Beleek' in their marks. American Belleek is considered the highest achievement of the American porcelain industry. Production centered around artistic cabinet pieces and luxury tablewares. Many examples emulated Irish shapes and decor with marine themes and other naturalistic styles. While all are highly collectible, some companies' products are rarer than others. The best-known manufacturers are Ott and Brewer, Willets, The Ceramic Art Company (CAC), and Lenox. You will find more detailed information in those specific categories. Our advisor for this category is Mary Frank Gaston.

Key:
AAC — American Art China Company
ABC — American Beleek Works
CAP — Columbian Art Pottery Works

Bell, Independence Hall bl transfer, CAP, 4½" 600.00
Cream soup, Bouquet, Coxon, w/underplate 230.00
Cup & saucer, demitasse; Tridacna, gold trim, CAP 140.00
Plate, peacocks & mixed florals w/gold, Gordon, 7" 65.00
Shell dish, pk lustre int, ABC mk, 4x5" 180.00
Teapot, dragon form, gold past leaves, CAP, 7½x9" 1,550.00
Teapot, Turkish design w/ornate gold & jewels 350.00
Vase, florals on wht, gold emb hdls, AAC, 12", pr 1,650.00

Belleek, Irish

Belleek is a very thin translucent porcelain that takes its name from the village in Ireland where it originated in 1859. The glaze is a creamy ivory color with a pearl-like lustre. The tablewares, baskets, figurines, and vases that have always been made there are being crafted yet today. Shamrock, Tridacna, Echinus, and Thorn are but a few of the many patterns of tableware which have been made during some period of the pottery's history. Throughout the years, their most popular pattern has been Shamrock.

It is possible to date an example to within twenty to thirty years of crafting by the mark. Pieces with an early stamp often bring prices nearly triple that of a similar but current item. With some variation, the marks have always incorporated the Irish wolfhound, Celtic round tower, harp, and shamrocks. The first three marks (usually in black) were used from 1863 to 1946. A series of green marks identified the pottery's offerings from 1946 until the seventh mark (in gold/brown) was introduced in 1980 (it was discontinued in 1992). The most current mark, the eighth, is blue. Belleek Collector's International Society limited edition pieces are designated with a special mark in red. In the listings below, numbers designated with the prefix 'D' relate to the book *Belleek, The Complete Collector's Guide and Illustrated Reference, Second Edition*, published by Wallace-Homestead Book Company, One Chilton Way, Radnor, PA 19098-0230. The author, Richard K. Degenhardt, is our advisor for Belleek; he is listed in the Directory under North Carolina.

Key:
A — plain (glazed only)
B — cob lustre
C — hand tinted
D — hand painted
E — hand-painted shamrocks
F — hand gilted
G — hand tinted and gilted
H — hand-painted shamrocks and gilted
J — mother-of-pearl
K — hand painted and gilted
L — bisque and plain
M — decalcomania
N — special hand-painted decoration
T — transfer design

I — 1863 – 1890
II — 1891 – 1926
III — 1926 – 1946
IV — 1946 – 1955
V — 1955 – 1965
VI — 1965 – 3/31/1980
VII — 4/1/1980 – 12/22/1992
VIII — 1/4/1993 – current

Further information concerning Periods of Crafting (Baskets):
1 — 1865 – 1890, BELLEEK (three-strand)
2 — 1865 – 1890, BELLEEK CO. FERMANAGH (three-strand)

3 — 1891 – 1920, BELLEEK CO. FERMANAGH IRELAND (three-strand)
4 — 1921 – 1954, BELLEEK CO. FERMANAGH IRELAND (four-strand)
5 — 1955 – 1979, BELLEEK® CO. FERMANAGH IRELAND (four-strand)
6 — 1980 – 1985, BELLEEK® IRELAND (four-strand)
7 — 1985 – 1989, BELLEEK® IRELAND 'ID NUMBER' (four-strand)
8-12 — 1990 to present (Refer to *Belleek, The Complete Collector's Guide and Illustrated Reference*, 2nd Edition, Chapter 5)

Aberdeen Vase, floral, D58-IV, D, med 300.00
Artichoke Tea Ware Breakfast Saucer, D1462-I, F, 7" 200.00
Basket, oval, floral, D11804, 4-strand, lg, 12" 1,700.00
Belleek Flowerpot, floral, D47-II, A, sm 250.00
Boat Ashtray, D229-IV, B, 4⅝" L 40.00
Celtic Cross, D1740-VI, B, lg, 12" 350.00
Chinese Tea Ware Cream, D486-I, K 550.00
Christmas Plate, 1970, D1850-VI, A 125.00
Coral Bell, D2078-VI, D, 5½" 65.00
Double Shell Cream & Sugar, D288-VI/D1301-VI, B 110.00
Echinus Tea Ware Teapot, D646-I, F, med 800.00
Erne Tea Ware Tea & Saucer, D445-II, C 250.00
Figurine, Crouching Venus, D16-I, F, 17" 9,000.00
Figurine, Meditation, D20-VII, 7th gold mk, L, 14½" 575.00
Florence Jug, D813-VII, G, med 90.00

Flowerpot, footed, D51-II, $2,600.00.

Photo courtesy Richard Degenhardt

Grass Tea Ware Honey Pot on Stand, D755-I, K, 6½" 800.00
Heart Basket, No 3, D1258-4, 4-strand, D, 6½" 475.00
Hexagon Cake Plate, D1263-4, 4-strand, 10" 500.00
Hexagon Tea & Saucer, D391-II, C 200.00
Hexagon Tea Ware Tea & Saucer, D622-II, N 350.00
Irish Pot, D204-II, A, sz 5, 6" 250.00
Ivy Tea Ware Plate, D1413-III, B, 7" 85.00
Lifford Cream, D301-I, B, 3¼" 250.00
Limpet Tea Ware Plate, D447-VI, B, 6¼" 35.00
Lithophane, Girl at Wall, D1538-III, A, 8x6½" 3,500.00
Mask Tea Ware Cream, tall shape, D1484-III, A, sm 100.00
Nautilus Cream, D279-II, A, 4" 275.00
Neptune Plate, D411-I, C, 6" 85.00
Neptune Tea Ware Tea & Saucer, D414-II, C 150.00
Neptune Tea Ware Tray, D418-II, C, 17¼x14" 1,250.00
Prince of Wales Ice Pail, D3-I, F 8,000.00
Ribbon Vase, flowered, D1220-III, A, 8" 300.00
Scroll Tea Ware Tea & Saucer, D502-II, G 250.00
Shamrock, basket, 3-strand, D109-3 ....450.00
Shamrock Ware Box, oval, D604-II, E&D, 3¾" 375.00
Shamrock Ware Coffeepot, D1319-V, H, 7" 295.00
Shamrock Ware Kettle, D387-II, E, sm 525.00
Shamrock Ware Tea & Saucer, low shape, D366-II, E 175.00

Shamrock Ware Teapot, D384-III, E, lg 350.00
Shell Biscuit Jar, D599-VI, B, 7" 125.00
St Matthew Gospel Plate, D1811-VI, M&F, ltd ed, 1979 ....125.00
Swan, D254-I, A, lg, 4½" 350.00
Table Centre, D56-IV, D 1,500.00
Thorn Scent Bottle, D335-I, K 385.00
Tridacna Tea Ware Coffee & Saucer, D462-II, B 135.00
Tridacna Tea Ware Plate, D464-VI, B, 6" 40.00
Tridacna Tea Ware Plate, D465-III, C, 6" 65.00
Tridacna Tea Ware Tea & Saucer, D454-IV, B 80.00
Undine Cream, D305-VI, B, 5" dia 45.00
Wild Irish Rose Thimble, D2110-VII, D 30.00

Bells

Some areas of interest represented in the study of bells are history, religion, and geography. Since Biblical times, bells have announced morning church services, vespers, deaths, christenings, school hours, fires, and community events. Countries have used them en masse to peal out the good news of Christmas, New Year's, and the endings of World Wars I and II. They've been rung in times of great sorrow, such as the death of Abraham Lincoln.

Dorothy Malone Anthony is the author of a series of ten books entitled *World of Bells*. Her address is in the Directory under Kansas. All have over two hundred colored pictures covering many bell categories. See also Nodders; Schoolhouse Collectibles.

Brace (Conestoga), 3 4" cast metal bells in 13x15" wrought fr, pr ...275.00
Brass, Becky Sharp from Fanity Fair figural, 5¼" 80.00
Brass, cherub holding up bell, tap style, 10x3½" 135.00
Brass, Dutch boy w/umbrella & jug, 4¼x2" 55.00
Brass, Jacobean head finial, emb figures around sides, heavy, 4" .110.00
Brass, lady w/hat & fan, full gown, EX detail, 6x2⅝" 75.00
Bronze, iron maiden torture device shape, 4" 65.00
Bronze, Robin Hood hdl, emb deer at sides, Ballantyne, 6½" 225.00
Ceramic, Little Red Riding Hood, 1950s, 4½" 37.50
China, cherub figural hdl, emb floral on wht, unmk Italy 38.00
China, Colonial lady figural, Germany, 3" 48.00
China, lady figural, pk lustre w/yel trim, Germany, 5½" 85.00
Glass, Dmn Daisy, pressed, 1800s, 5¾" 88.00
Glass, 1893 Columbian Expo, Libbey, 5" 135.00
Sleigh, 17 brass graduated bells on orig leather strap 240.00
Sleigh, 21 bell-metal bells on new 86" leather strap 350.00
Sleigh, 29 brass #d graduated bells on new leather strap 275.00
Sleigh, 3 2½" bells on metal strap 32.00
Sleigh, 37 graduated NP-steel bells on orig 80" leather strap 140.00
Sterling, man in top hat & coat figural, Gorham 75.00

Bennington

Although the term has become a generic one for the mottled brown ware produced there, Bennington is not a type of pottery, but rather a town in Vermont where two important potteries were located. The Norton Company, founded in 1793, produced mainly redware and salt-glazed stoneware; only during a brief partnership with Fenton (1845 – 47) was any Rockingham attempted. The Norton Company endured until 1894, operated by succeeding generations of the Norton family. Fenton organized his own pottery in 1847. There he manufactured not only redware and stoneware, but more artistic types as well — graniteware, scroddled ware, flint enamel, a fine parian, and vast amounts of their famous Rockingham. Though from an esthetic standpoint his work rated highly among the country's finest ceramic achievements, he was economically unsuccessful. His pottery closed in 1858.

It is estimated that only one in five Fenton pieces were marked; and although it has become a common practice to link any fine piece of Rockingham to this area, careful study is vital in order to be able to distinguish Bennington's from the similar wares of many other American and Staffordshire potteries. Although the practice was without the permission of the proprietor, it was nevertheless a common occurrence for a potter to take his molds with him when moving from one pottery to the next, so particularly well-received designs were often reproduced at several locations. Of eight known Fenton marks, four are variations of the '1849' impressed stamp: 'Lyman Fenton Co., Fenton's Enamel Patented 1849, Bennington, Vermont.' These are generally found on examples of Rockingham and flint enamel. A raised, rectangular scroll with 'Fenton's Works, Bennington, Vermont,' was used on early examples of porcelain. From 1852 to 1858, the company operated under the title of the United States Pottery Company. Three marks — the ribbon mark with the initials USP, the oval with a scrollwork border and the name in full, and the plain oval with the name in full — were used during that period.

Among the more sought-after examples are the bird and animal figurines, novelty pitchers, figural bottles, and all of the more finely modeled items. Recumbent deer, cows, standing lions with one forepaw on a ball, and opposing pairs of poodles with baskets in their mouths and 'coleslaw' fur were made in Rockingham, flint enamel, and occasionally in parian. Numbers in the listings below refer to the book *Bennington Pottery and Porcelain* by Barret. Our advisors for Bennington (except for parian and stoneware) are Barbara and Charles Adams; they are listed in the Directory under Massachusetts.

Key: c/s — cobalt on salt glaze

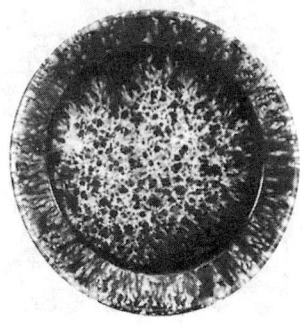

Pie plate, Rockingham, marked, 9", NM, $500.00 (value for unmarked example, $135.00).

Baking dish, flint enamel, 8-sided, 1849 mk, 2¼x11x8¾", VG ..**500.00**
Book flask, Bennington Battle, flint enamel, unmk, 8" **1,200.00**
Book flask, Hermit's Companion, flint enamel, mk, pt, EX **1,200.00**
Book flask, Life of Kossuth, flint enamel, unmk, 5½" **800.00**
Book flask, Parted Spirits, flint enamel, sm chip, 8" **440.00**
Book flask, Parted Spirits, flint enamel, 8", NM **1,200.00**
Book flask, scroddleware, rstr, 5½" **800.00**
Bottle, Coachman, Rockingham, 1849 mk, 10¾", EX **900.00**
Bottle, Toby Barrel, flint enamel, 1849 mk, 10½", EX+ **3,300.00**
Cake mold, Rockingham, 4½x10" **175.00**
Candlestick, Rockingham, B 197-C, 8", M **750.00**
Cuspidor, scroddleware, scalloped ribs, 9" dia **1,250.00**
Doorknob, flint enamel, 8-sided, 2" dia, EX **200.00**
Frame, Rockingham, emb decor, prof rstr, 10½" **1,000.00**
Goblet, Rockingham, w/hdl, 4½", M **625.00**
Lamp, flint enamel, 8-sided step-ftd baluster std, prisms, 26" ...**12,000.00**
Pie plate, Rockingham, 1849 mk, wear, 9¾" **450.00**
Pitcher, flint enamel, Alternate Rib, 1849 mk, 10½" **1,200.00**
Pitcher, flint enamel, Alternate Rib, 1849 mk, 8", EX **400.00**

Pitcher, flint enamel, Alternate Rib, 6", M **500.00**
Pitcher, flint enamel, Tulip & Heart, 1849 mk, 6½", EX **775.00**
Pitcher, Rockingham, bbl shape, unmk, 6", EX **225.00**
Pitcher, Rockingham parian, emb ribs & flowers, mini, 1⅝" **130.00**
Snuff jar, Toby, gr flint enamel, 1849 mk, 4¼" **1,200.00**
Snuff jar, Toby, nonflint, 4½" **875.00**
Soap dish/toilet box, red-brn/gr flint enamel, 3¾x7¾" **1,300.00**
Sugar bowl, flint enamel, Alternate Rib, 1849 mk, 6½" **1,400.00**
Teapot, Rockingham, Alternate Rib, unmk, 9", EX **800.00**
Tiebacks, Rockingham, petal-form top, 4", pr, EX **400.00**
Toothbrush holder, scroddleware, emb dmns, w/lid, att, 8" L **800.00**
Wash bowl, flint enamel, mk, rare sm sz, B 169, 13½" **600.00**
Wash bowl & pitcher, flint enamel, 1849 mk, 4¼x14", 12" ...**3,250.00**

Stoneware

Cake crock, stylized flower, c/s, J&E Norton, 7½", EX **415.00**
Churn, dotted leaf, c/s, E&LP Norton, ca 1870, 13½", EX **550.00**
Churn, peacock & tree, c/s, J Norton & Co, rstr, 18" **2,200.00**
Crock, bird on plume, c/s, E&LP Norton, ca 1870, rstr, 12" **385.00**
Crock, dotted deer/pine/fence, c/s, J&E Norton, rstr, 10½" **4,400.00**
Crock, dotted floral, c/s, E&LP Norton, 3-gal, crack, 10" **80.00**
Crock, dotted leaf, c/s, E&LP Norton, hairline, 8¾" **100.00**
Crock, floral (ornate), c/s, J&E Norton, 11¼", EX **1,200.00**
Crock, flower, ochre on cinnamon, L Norton & Son, rstr, 14½" ..**250.00**
Crock, flowers in vase, c/s, J&E Norton, flakes, 11" **715.00**
Crock, leaf & dot, c/s, J Norton & Co, ca 1861, 7", EX **175.00**
Crock, plume, slip & c/s, E&LP Norton, 1-gal, 1870s, 9", VG ...**110.00**
Crock, rabbit running, c/s, Norton & Fenton, rstr, 1840s, 14½" ...**660.00**
Jar, dotted leaf, c/s, E&LP Norton, ca 1870, rstr, 13" **175.00**
Jar, floral (heavy), c/s, J&E Norton, ca 1855, 11½", EX **275.00**
Jar, peacocks (2) in tree, c/s, J&E Norton, 3-gal, EX **4,300.00**
Jar, triple flower, c/s, Julius Norton, rstr, 13½" **100.00**
Jug, bird on branch, c/s, J&E Norton, ca 1859, rstr, 1-gal, 12" **220.00**
Jug, bird on lg floral branch, c/s, J&E Norton, 3-gal, 15½", EX ...**4,850.00**
Jug, bird on plume, c/s, E&LP Norton, ca 1870, 13½", VG **360.00**
Jug, bird on stump, c/s, J&E Norton, 2-gal, 13½", EX **1,600.00**
Jug, dbl floral, c/s, Norton & Fenton, 2-gal, ca 1845, 11½", EX .**725.00**
Jug, dotted bird on branch, c/s, J&E Norton, 2-gal, 13½", EX .**1,980.00**
Jug, leaf, c/s, E&LP Norton, ca 1870, 1-gal, 11½", EX **165.00**
Jug, long-tailed bird on plume, c/s, E&LP Norton, rstr, 14" **400.00**
Jug, LWC in script, c/s, Norton & Co, ca 1870, 13½", EX **175.00**
Jug, triple floral plume, c/s, J&E Norton, ca 1855, 14½", EX **415.00**
Jug, triple flower, c/s, Norton & Fenton, 13½", EX **275.00**
Pitcher, flower basket, c/s, J&E Norton, 12", EX **2,035.00**

Beswick

In the early 1890s, James Wright Beswick operated a pottery in Longston, England, where he produced fine dinnerware as well as ornamental ceramics. Today's collectors are most interested in the figurines made since 1936 by a later generation Beswick firm, John Beswick, Ltd. They specialize in reproducing accurately detailed bone-china models of authentic breeds of animals. Their Fireside Series includes dogs, cats, elephants, horses, the Huntsman, and an Indian figure, which measure up to 14" in height. The Connoisseur line is modeled after the likenesses of famous racing horses. Beatrix Potter's characters and some of Walt Disney's are charmingly re-created and appeal to children and adults alike. Other items, such as character Tobys, have also been produced. The Beswick name is stamped on each piece. The firm was absorbed by the Doulton group in 1973. Our advisor for this category is Nicki Budin; she is listed in the Directory under New York.

Cheese dish, floral, emb/pnt on gr, flower finial **55.00**
Figurine, Alice in Wonderland **385.00**
Figurine, Aunt Pettitoes, Beatrix Potter, gold mk, #2276 ....**200.00**
Figurine, Barnaby Rudge, #1121 ....**50.00**
Figurine, cat, orange Tabby **35.00**
Figurine, cat, recumbent, #1559 ....**52.00**
Figurine, cat, wht, standing, 5½x5¼" **75.00**
Figurine, Cheshire Cat, Alice series **550.00**
Figurine, deer, bl, #721 ....**90.00**
Figurine, Dodo, Alice series **285.00**
Figurine, Duchess, Beatrix Potter, 3rd mk, #2601 ....**175.00**
Figurine, Felia Cat, David Hand, rare **550.00**
Figurine, Fierce Bad Rabbit, Beatrix Potter, 1st brn mk **150.00**
Figurine, Fish Footman, Alice series **285.00**
Figurine, Flopsy, Mopsy, & Cottontail, Beatrix Potter, gold mk .**225.00**
Figurine, Foxy Whiskered Gentleman, Beatrix Potter, gold mk .**250.00**
Figurine, girl w/doll, JW Anglund, 1958 ....**125.00**
Figurine, Gryphon, Alice series **165.00**
Figurine, Hunca Munca, Beatrix Potter, brn mk **65.00**
Figurine, Hunca Munca, Beatrix Potter, gold mk **200.00**
Figurine, King or Queen of Heats, Alice series, ea **95.00**
Figurine, Kitty MacBride Racegoer **55.00**
Figurine, Mad Hatter, Alice series **265.00**
Figurine, Miss Moppet, Beatrix Potter, 1st gold mk **250.00**
Figurine, Mock Turtle, Alice series **195.00**
Figurine, Mr Alderman Ptolemy, Beatrix Potter, brn mk **80.00**
Figurine, Mrs Tiggywinkle, Beatrix Potter, gold mk **200.00**
Figurine, Old English Sheepdog, #453 ....**150.00**
Figurine, Old Mr Brown, Beatrix Potter, gold mk **160.00**
Figurine, Old Woman in Shoe, Beatrix Potter, gold mk **200.00**
Figurine, Old Woman in Shoe, brn mk **50.00**
Figurine, penguin chick, #2398 ....**220.00**
Figurine, Persian cat, gray, #1867, lg **72.00**
Figurine, Pig-Wig, Beatrix Potter, brn mk **450.00**
Figurine, Pigling Bland, Beatrix Potter, 1st brn mk **200.00**
Figurine, Pigling Bland, Beatrix Potter, 1st paper label **390.00**
Figurine, shepherd boy, #914 ....**750.00**
Figurine, Siamese kittens, #1296 ....**45.00**
Figurine, Tailor of Gloucester, Beatrix Potter, gold mk **195.00**
Figurine, Tony Weller, #281 ....**50.00**
Figurine, trout, #1390 ....**115.00**
Figurine, Welsh Cob, rearing horse, #1014 ....**150.00**
Plate, Christmas in Mexico **45.00**
Toby mug, Sairey Gamp, #372, MIE, 6⅝" **50.00**
Toby mug, Scrooge, #372, MIE, 6¾" **25.00**

Big Little Books

The first Big Little Book was published in 1933 and copyrighted in 1932 by the Whitman Publishing Company of Racine, Wisconsin. Its hero was Dick Tracy. The concept was so well accepted that others soon followed Whitman's example; and though the 'Big Little Book' phrase became a trademark of the Whitman Company, the formats of his competitors (Saalfield, Goldsmith, Van Wiseman, Lynn, and World Syndicate) were exact copies. Today's Big Little Book buffs collect them all.

These hand-sized sagas of adventure were illustrated with full-page cartoons on the right-hand page and the story narration on the left. Colorful cardboard covers contained hundreds of pages, usually totaling over an inch in thickness. Big Little Books originally sold for 10¢ at the dime store; as late as the mid-1950s when the popularity of comic books caused sales to decline signaling an end to production, their price had risen to a mere 20¢. Their appeal was directed toward the pre-teens who bought, traded, and hoarded Big Little Books. Because so many were

stored in attics and closets, many have survived. Among the super heroes are G-Men, Flash Gordon, Tarzan, the Lone Ranger, and Red Ryder; in a lighter vein, you'll find such lovable characters as Blondie and Dagwood, Mickey Mouse, Little Orphan Annie, and Felix the Cat.

In the early to mid-'30s, Whitman published several Big Little Books as advertising premiums for the Coco Malt Company, who packed them in boxes of their cereal. These are highly prized by today's collectors, as are Disney stories and super-hero adventures. For more information see *Big Little Books* by Larry Jacobs (Collector Books). Our advisor for this category is Ron Donnelly; he is listed in the Directory under Alabama.

Note: At the present time, the market for these books is fairly stable — values for common examples are actually dropping. Only the rare, character-related titles are increasing.

Ace Drummond, Whitman #1177, 1935, NM **40.00**
Alley Oop in Jungles of Moo, Whitman #1473, EX **24.00**
Arizona Kid on the Bandit Trail, Whitman #1192, 1936, NM **36.00**
Believe It or Not by Ripley, Whitman #760, hardcover, 1931, EX ..**25.00**
Betty Boop in Snow White, Whitman #1119, hardcover, EX **75.00**
Big Chief Wahoo & Lost Pioneers, Whitman #1432, G **10.00**
Blondie & Dagwood Everybody's Happy, Whitman #1438, EX+ .**35.00**
Blondie or Life Among the Bumsteads, Whitman #1466, NM **40.00**
Bobby Benson on the H-Bar-O Ranch, Whitman #1108, EX **25.00**
Brer Rabbit, Song of the South, Whitman #1426, NM **75.00**
Buck Jones in Ride 'Em Cowboy, Whitman #1116, EX **25.00**
Buck Rogers & the Planetoid Plot, #1197, EX **80.00**
Buck Rogers in War w/Planet Venus, Whitman #1437, EX **70.00**
Buck Rogers 25th Century AD, Whitman #742, NM **100.00**
Buffalo Bill Plays a Lone Hand, Whitman #1194, EX **10.00**

Captain Midnight and the Moon Woman, Better Little Book, Whitman #1452, EX, $75.00.

Chester Gump Finds Hidden Treasure, Whitman #766, G **15.00**
Clyde Beatty Daredevil Lion & Tiger Trainer, Whitman #1410, NM ..**45.00**
Cowboy Lingo, #1457, 1938, VG **15.00**
Detective Higgins of the Racket Squad, Whitman #1482, NM **25.00**
Dick Tracy & His G-Men, Whitman #1439, NM **45.00**
Dick Tracy & Man w/No Face, Whitman #1491, EX **32.00**
Dick Tracy Out West, Whitman #723, EX **50.00**
Dick Tracy Solves the Penfield Mystery, #1137, 1934, VG **35.00**
Don Winslow of Navy & Great War Pilot, Whitman #1489, NM ..**35.00**
Donald Duck Lays Down the Law, Whitman #1449, EX **45.00**
Erik Noble & the Forty Niners, Whitman #772, 1934, EX **24.00**
Felix the Cat, Whitman #1439, 1943, NM **95.00**
Flash Gordon & the Witch Queen of Mongo, 1936, EX+ **90.00**
Flash Gordon in Forest...of Mongo, Whitman #1492, 1938, VG ..**35.00**
Freckles & Lost Dmn Mine, Whitman #1164, EX **22.50**
G-Man Vs the Red X, Whitman #1147, VG **15.00**
Gene Autry & Red Bandit's Ghost, Whitman #1461, EX+ **35.00**
Gene Autry Special Ranger, Whitman #1428, NM **65.00**
Jack Swift & His Rocket Ship, #1102, M **80.00**

Jane Arden the Vanished Princess, Whitman #1498, NM **45.00**

Jungle Jim, Whitman #1138, 1936, EX **40.00**

Jungle Jim & Vampire Woman, Whitman #1139, EX **38.00**

Junior Nebb on Dmn Bar Ranch, Whitman #1422, EX **22.50**

Kazan King of the Pack, #1471, EX **15.00**

Ken Maynard & Gun Wolves of Gila, Whitman #1442, EX **25.00**

Little Annie Rooney & the Orphan House, #117, EX **25.00**

Little Annie Rooney on Highway to Adventure, Whitman #1406, EX ..**32.00**

Little Orphan Annie, Whitman #708, EX **70.00**

Little Orphan Annie & Ghost Gang, Whitman, softcover, rare, EX **120.00**

Lone Ranger on Barbary Coast, Whitman #1421, EX **28.00**

Mandrake Magician & Midnight Monster, Whitman #1431, VG .**20.00**

Mickey Mouse, Whitman #717, 2nd version, EX+ **480.00**

Mickey Mouse & Bat Bandit, Whitman #1153, EX **45.00**

Mickey Mouse & the Magic Lamp, 1942, G **15.00**

Mickey Mouse & 7 Ghosts, Whitman #1475, NM **70.00**

Mickey Rooney Himself, Whitman #1427, EX **38.00**

Moby Dick, #710, EX **35.00**

Nancy & Sluggo, Whitman #1400, VG **25.00**

Oswald the Rabbit Plays G-Man, Walter Lantz, 1937, G **20.00**

Peggy Brown & Secret Treasure, Whitman #1423, NM **35.00**

Phantom & Desert Justice, Whitman #1421, EX **45.00**

Popeye, Whitman #1406, NM **65.00**

Popeye & Deep Sea Mystery, Whitman #1499, NM **45.00**

Prairie Bill & Covered Wagon, Whitman #758, 1954, NM **32.00**

Red Ryder & Code of West, Whitman #1427, NM **45.00**

Red Ryder & the Squaw-Tooth Rustlers, 1946, EX **22.00**

Reg'lar Fellers, Whitman #754, VG **15.00**

Scrappy, Whitman #1122, 1934, NM **40.00**

Silver Streak, Whitman #1155, EX **35.00**

Skeezix at the Military Academy, #1408, 1938, EX **39.00**

Smilin' Jack & Escape From Death Rock, Whitman #1445, G **12.00**

Smokey Stover All Pictures Comics, Whitman #1413, 1942, NM.....**45.00**

Speed Douglas & Mole Gang, #1455, 1941, EX **30.00**

Steve Hunter of the Coast Guard, 1942, EX **15.00**

Tailspin Tommy Hunting for Pirate Gold, Whitman #1172, EX ..**32.00**

Terry Lee Flight Officer USA, Whitman #1492, NM **32.00**

Tim McCoy in Westerner, Whitman #1193, EX **32.00**

Two-Gun Montana, Whitman #1104, EX+ **25.00**

Uncle Don's Strange Adventures, Whitman #1114, NM **42.50**

Walt Disney's Bambi, Whitman #1489, NM **70.00**

West Point of the Air, Whitman #1164, NM **35.00**

Wimpy the Hamburger Eater, #1458, EX **30.00**

Zane Gray's King of Royal Mounted, Whitman #1103, M **50.00**

Bing and Grondahl

In 1853 brothers M.H. and J.H. Bing formed a partnership with Frederick Vilhelm Grondahl in Copenhagen, Denmark. Their early wares were porcelain plaques and figurines designed by the noted sculptor Thorvaldsen of Denmark. Dinnerware production began in 1863, and by 1889 their underglaze color 'Copenhagen Blue' had earned them worldwide acclaim. They are perhaps most famous today for their Christmas plates, the first of which was made in 1895. See also Limited Edition Plates.

Cake plate, dolphin hdls, gold decor **60.00**

Coffeepot, Sea Gull **195.00**

Cup & saucer, demitasse; #106 ....**50.00**

Cup & saucer, demitasse; Empire **35.00**

Cup & saucer, demitasse; floral, wht on bl **40.00**

Cup & saucer, demitasse; Sea Gull **35.00**

Dealer sign **40.00**

Figurine, boy seated on book, #1742E **145.00**

Figurine, cat, wht, sitting, #1876 ....**80.00**

Figurine, chicken, #2194 ....**75.00**

Figurine, girl w/arm raised, #2273 ....**135.00**

Figurine, Headache, wht, #2206, 4½" **25.00**

Figurine, lamb, #2171 ....**50.00**

Figurine, Love Refused, #1614 ....**155.00**

Figurine, lovebird, #2341 ....**55.00**

Figurine, parrot on limb, bl & mauve, #2019, 5½" **140.00**

Figurine, St Bernard, #1926, 4½" **65.00**

Planter, Snow Flower **40.00**

Shell dish, #347 ....**95.00**

Sugar bowl, Blue Flute, basketweave border, #94, w/lid **55.00**

Binoculars

There are several types of binoculars, and the terminology used to refer to them is not consistent or precise. Generally, 'field glasses' refer to simple Galilean optics, where the lens next to the eye (the ocular) is concave and dished away from the eye. By looking through the large lens (the objective), it is easy to see that the light goes straight through the two lenses. These are lower power, have a very small field of view, and do not work nearly as well as prism binoculars. In a smaller size, they are opera glasses, and their price increases if they are covered with mother-of-pearl (fairly common but very attractive), abalone shell (more colorful), ivory (quite scarce), or other exotic materials. Field glasses are not valuable unless very unusual or by the best makers, such as Zeiss or Leitz. Prism binoculars have the objective lens offset from the eyepiece and give a much better view. This is the standard binocular form, called Porro prisms, and dates from around 1900. Another type of prism binocular is the roof prism, which at first resembles the straight-through field glasses, with two simple cylinders or cones, here containing very small prisms. These can be distinguished by the high quality views they give and by a thin diagonal line that can be seen when looking backwards through the objective. In general, German binoculars are the most desirable, followed by American, English, and finally French, which can be of good quality but are very common unless of unusual configuration. Japanese optics of WWII or before are often of very high quality. 'Made in Occupied Japan' binoculars are very common, but collectors prize those by Nippon Kogaku (Nikon). Some binoculars are center focus (CF), with one central wheel that focuses both sides at once. These are much easier to use but more difficult to seal against dirt and moisture. Individual focus (IF) binoculars are adjusted by rotating each eyepiece and tend to be cleaner inside in older optics. Each type is preferred by different collectors. Very large binoculars are always of great interest. All binoculars are numbered according to their magnifying power and the diameter of the objective in millimeters. 6 x 30 optics magnify six times and have 30-millimeter objectives.

Prisms are easily knocked out of alignment, requiring an expensive and difficult repair. If severe, this misalignment is immediately noticeable on use by the double-image scene. Minor damage can be seen by focusing on a small object and slowly moving the binoculars away from the eye, which will cause the images to appear to separate. Overall cleanliness should be checked by looking backwards (through the objective) at a light or the sky, when any film or dirt on the lenses or prisms can easily be seen. Pristine binoculars are worth far more than when dirty or misaligned, and broken or cracked optics lower the value far more. Cases help keep binoculars clean but do not add materially to the value. The following listings assume a very good overall condition, with generally clean and alligned optics.

Our advisor for this category is Peter Abrahams, who studies and collects binoculars and other optics. Please contact, especially to exchange reference material. Mr. Abrahams is listed in the Directory under Oregon.

Field Glasses

Fernglas 08, German WWI, 6x39, military gr, many makers 50.00
Folding, modern, hinged flat case, oculars outside 10.00
Folding or telescoping, no bbls, old 125.00
Ivory covered, various sm szs & makers 180.00
LeMaire, bl leather/brass, various szs & makers 25.00
Metal, emb hunting scene, various sm szs & makers 45.00
Pearl covered, various sm szs & makers 90.00
Porc covered, delicate painting, various szs & makers 175.00
US Naval Gun Factory Optical Shop 6x30 ....75.00
Zeiss 'Galan' 2.5x34, modern design look, early 1920s 100.00

Prism Binoculars (Porro)

Barr & Stroud, 7x50, Porro II prisms, IF, WWII 110.00
Bausch & Lomb, 6x30, IF, WWI, Signal Corps 50.00
Bausch & Lomb, 7x50, IF, WWII, other makers same 80.00
Bausch & Lomb Zephyr, 7x35 & others, CF 150.00
Bausch & Lomb/Zeiss, Pat 1897, 8x17, CF 140.00
Crown Optical, 6x30, IF, WWI, filters 45.00
France, various makers & szs, if not unusual 30.00
German WWII 10x80, eyepcs at 45 degrees, 3-letter code (makers) ..450.00
German WWII 6x30, 3-letter code for various makers 60.00
Goertz Trieder Binocle, various szs, unusual adjustment 90.00
Huet, Paris 7x22, other sm szs, unusual shapes 80.00
Leitz 6x30 Dienstglas, IF, good optics 65.00
Leitz 8x30 Binuxit, CF, 1950s 150.00
M19, US military 7x50, ca 1980 ....150.00
Nikon 9x35, 7x35, CF, 1950s 95.00
Nippon Kogaku, 7x50, IF, Made in Occupied Japan 150.00
Ross Stepnada, 7x30, CF, wide angle, 1930s 250.00
Ross 6x30, standard British WWI issue 50.00
Sard, 6x42, IF, very wide angle, WWII 800.00
Toko (Tokyo Opt Co) 7x50, IF, Made in Occupied Japan 45.00
Universal Camera 6x30, IF, WWII, other makers same 50.00
US Naval Gun Factory Optical Shop 6x30, IF, filters, WWI 70.00
US Naval Gun Factory Optical 10x45, IF, WWI 180.00
US Navy, 20x120, various makers, WWII & later 3,000.00
Warner & Swasey (important maker) 8x20, CF, 1902 ....250.00
Wollensak 6x30, ca 1940 ....50.00
Zeiss, Starmobi 12/23/42x60, turret eyepcs, 1920s 2,000.00
Zeiss Deltrintem 8x30, CF, 1930s 95.00
Zeiss DF 95, 6x18, sq shoulder, very early 150.00
Zeiss Teleater 3x13, CF, bl, leather 100.00
Zeiss 15x60, CF or IF, various models 600.00
Zeiss 8x40 Delactis, CF or IF, 1930s 200.00

Roof Prism Binoculars

Hensoldt, Dialyt, various szs, long tapered bbl, 1930s-80s 110.00
Hensoldt Universal Dialyt, 6x26, 3.5x26, cylindrical, 1920s 80.00
Leitz Trinovid, 7x42 & other, CF, 1960s-80s, EX 375.00
Zeiss Dialyt, 8x30, CF, 1960s 400.00

Birdcages

Birdcages can be found in various architectural styles and in a range of materials such as wood, wicker, brass, and gilt metal with ormolu mounts. Those that once belonged to the wealthy are sometimes inlaid with silver or jewels. In the 1800s, it became fashionable to keep birds, and some of the most beautiful examples found today date back to that era. Musical cages that contained automated bird figures became popular;

today these command prices of several thousand dollars. In the latter 1800s, wicker styles came into vogue. Collectors still appreciate their graceful lines and find they adapt easily to modern homes.

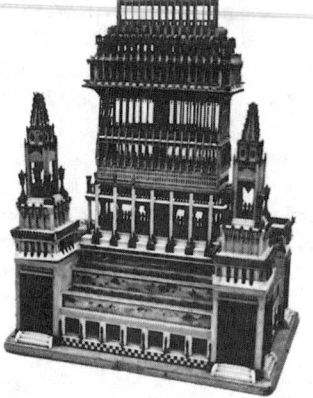

Victorian cage from the Chicago World's Fair Exposition, electrified, 72x40x55", EX, $1,750.00.

Brass & steel, chinoiserie ivory pnt/decor, 1900s, w/stand, 70" ...330.00
Folk art w/domed wire top, orig red pnt 110.00
Paddle-wheeler boat design, red/wht/bl pnt, w/flags/captain/etc ..6,875.00
Tin & wire, common type, from $50 to 60.00
Tin straps form cylinder, old gr pnt traces, rprs, 20" 110.00
Wicker, crescent moon floor stand 800.00
Wire & wood, domed top, rpr, 23", EX 275.00
Wood & wire, ornate, wht rpt w/bl trim, 25" 115.00
Wooden, China, 1840s 335.00
3-story house w/7 compartments, ring perches, glass doors 2,225.00

Bisque

Bisque is a term referring to unglazed earthenware or porcelain that has been fired only once. During the Victorian era, bisque figurines became very popular. Most were highly decorated in pastels and gilt and demonstrated a fine degree of workmanship in the quality of their modeling. Few were marked. See also Heubach; Nodders; Dolls; Piano Babies.

Baby in armchair, pastels w/gold, Continental, 11½", EX 85.00
Black African princess, mc & gold, Fr, 11x3½" 495.00
Boy & girl at beach w/toys, pastels, Germany, 16", pr 750.00
Bust, lady w/draped bodice, curls, Copeland, Owen Hale, 18" ...2,500.00
Candle holder, boy & girl in front, gold beads, 7½x4" 50.00
Country couple, searching poses, mc, Continental, 24", pr 1,300.00
Lamp, boy & girl, dancing bear on balcony, Germany, 11" 145.00
Nouveau nude on rocks w/stream below, artist sgn, 11" 500.00
Planter, fox in clothes beside open stump, Germany 135.00
Vase, boy in lederhosen/Alpine cap sits on on log w/zither, 8¾" ..65.00
Vase, cherub before flower form w/3 openings, mc w/gold, 7¼" ...65.00
Victorian boy & girl, ornate costumes, German, 12", pr 350.00
Wall pocket, boy & girl w/basket lean from balcony, 6⅞x5" 65.00
Youth w/flower baskets, mc w/gold, Japan, 9¾" 15.00
18th-C gentleman w/threshing implement, mc/gilt, Germany, 36" ..2,500.00

Black Americana

Black memorabilia is without a doubt a field that encompasses the most widely exploited ethnic group in our history. But within this field there are many levels of interest: arts and achievements such as folk music and literature, caricatures in advertising, souvenirs, toys, fine art, and legitimate research into the days of their enslavement and enduring struggle for equality. The list is endless.

In the listings below are some with a derogatory connotation. Thankfully, these are from a bygone era and represent the mores of a culture that existed nearly a century ago. They are included only to convey the fact that they are a part of this growing area of collecting interest. Black Americana catalogs featuring a wide variety of items for sale are available; see the Directory under Clubs, Newsletters, and Catalogs for more information. We also recommend *Black Collectibles* by P.J. Gibbs; and *Black Dolls, Books I* and *II*, by Myla Perkins, all published by Collector Books. See also Cookie Jars; Postcards; Posters; Sheet Music.

Advertising page, Aunt Jemima, in fr **25.00**
Alarm clock, Gold Dust, ca 1940, NM **550.00**
Book, Black Alice, hardcover, 1968, M **25.00**
Book, Ezekiel, Elvira Gardner, 1937, EX **110.00**
Book, Little Black Sambo, Fern Peat illus, w/jacket, 1943 ....**125.00**
Book, Little Black Sambo, H Bannerman, 1965, EX **65.00**
Book, Little Black Sambo, Tell-A-Tale, 1950s, EX **35.00**
Book, Little Pick A Ninnies, Ida M Chubb, Whitman, 1929, EX **160.00**
Book, Naughty Amelia Jane, hardcover, 1939, EX **70.00**
Book, Ol' Man Adam & His Chillun, Bradford, Harper Bros, 1928 ..**100.00**
Book, Sambo's Family Funbook, M **48.00**
Book, Swanee River, hardcover, 1890, VG **65.00**
Book, The Little Washingtons at School, hardcover, 1920, EX ...**40.00**
Book, Three Golliwogs, hardcover, 1968, NM **55.00**
Book, Topsy Turvy & the Easter Bunny, hardcover, 1936, VG **45.00**
Bottle, shoe polish; Champ, Muhammad Ali, M **17.50**
Bowl, Aunt Jemima's Kitchen, ceramic, Wellsville, 6½" **75.00**
Box, Original Cream of Wheat Cereal, unopened, NM **65.00**
Button, Topsy Club, Safety First, 1940s **45.00**
Can, Sambo Axle Grease, 1-lb, EX **125.00**
Coffee mug, Sambo's, china **30.00**
Cookie jar, Aunt Jemima, F&F **400.00**
Creamer, Uncle Mose, F&F, EX **80.00**
Creamer & sugar bowl, Aunt Jemima & Uncle Mose, F&F **175.00**
Dancing figure, Strutting Sam, tin man on tin ped, MIB **575.00**
Dexterity puzzle, tin litho of woman, BBs go in teeth, Germany ...**125.00**
Doll, Aunt Jemima, cloth, 1920, 16", NM **125.00**
Doll, bsk baby, jointed, 3" **45.00**
Doll, golliwog, felt, 1940s, 20", EX **65.00**
Doll, golliwog, googly eyes, cloth, 12" **60.00**
Dolls, Aunt Jemima & family, cloth, 1948, set of 4, M in mailer ..**375.00**
Fan, Gold Dust, twins, St Louis 1904 World's Fair, rare, NM **450.00**
Figurine, man w/basket, pot metal w/brass basket, 1890s, 5⅜" ...**145.00**
Game, Golli Ring Toss, Chad Valley, England **165.00**

Photo courtesy P.J. Gibbs

Game, Twin Target, Milton Bradley, 1920 – 25, M in 13" square box, $350.00.

Hot pad, Aunt Jemima **20.00**
Jar, dresser, Butler, heart shape, rare **375.00**
Jar, Lucky Brown Hair Dressing, couple illus, 1940s **8.50**

Lapel pin, boy playing saxophone, mc enameling **45.00**
Map, Amos & Andy, Weber City **65.00**
Mask, Black-faced Al Jolson style, gauze, EX **30.00**
Menu, Coon Chicken Inn, sm **75.00**
Money clip, Coon Chicken Inn, brass **175.00**
Napkin, Plantation Grill, chef saying: Chicken What Am! **35.00**
Pancake mold, Aunt Jemima, aluminum **185.00**
Pancake shaker, Aunt Jemima, yel bottom, ceramic, 9½", EX **100.00**
Pancake turner, Aunt Jemima, metal **45.00**
Paper plate, Aunt Jemima, lg face **50.00**
Pencil, mechanical; boy in alligator **150.00**
Pincushion, Mammy w/watermelon, satin, ca 1920-30s, 5" **65.00**
Pitcher, Mandy, Omnibus **175.00**
Place mat, Coon Chicken Inn **85.00**
Planter, native boy in canoe, Hollywood Ceramics **35.00**
Plate, Aunt Jemima, china, restaurant ware, sm **75.00**
Plate, dinner; Coon Chicken Inn, Incaware **250.00**
Plate, Sambo's, china, 9¾" **85.00**
Plate, Topsy's, pigtail girl, Shenango, 7", rare **300.00**
Platter, Coon Chicken Inn, M **300.00**
Pomade tin, Sweet Georgia Brown, sm **15.00**
Postcard, Gold Dust Twins, twins walking clothesline **20.00**
Postcard, lady w/basket of cotton, 1922, unused **10.00**
Poster, Martin Luther King, 1968, 22x28" **225.00**
Print, Martin Luther King, on canvas, ca 1968, 27x23" **175.00**
Program, Josephine Baker, many pictures, European, 1932, EX ..**125.00**
Recipe box, Mammy litho on tin, pull-out drw, Mah Bestest... ..**155.00**
Recipe cards, Aunt Jemima, 16+promotional card, 1940s, M **295.00**
Record, Little Black Sambo, 78 rpm, mc sleeve, 1948, NM **55.00**
Records, Amos & Andy, set of 3 in box **35.00**
Scarf, Sambo's, knit, M **45.00**
Scour pad holder, Mammy, ceramic, 1940s **185.00**
Shakers, Aunt Jemima & Uncle Mose, F&F, 3½", pr **65.00**
Shakers, Aunt Jemima & Uncle Mose, F&F, 5", pr **75.00**
Shakers, boy & whale, pr **85.00**
Shakers, boy lying in alligator's mouth, ceramic, pr **115.00**
Shakers, Salty & Peppy, Pearl China, lg, pr **225.00**
Shakers, Valentine couple, gray hair, ceramic, pr **195.00**
Sheet music, Alabama Bound, 1911 ....**25.00**
Sheet music, High Brown Babies Ball, 1919 ....**22.50**
Sheet music, 4 Little Blackberries, 1907 ....**28.00**
Sign, Gold Dust Twins, ca 1910, 69x24"+fr **1,900.00**
Spice jar, Aunt Jemima, plastic figural, F&F, from set of 6, ea **50.00**
Spoon, soup; Coon Chicken Inn, SP **75.00**
Spoon rest, Chef, ceramic, Japan **135.00**
Spoon rest, Chef nodder **225.00**
Sugar bowl, Aunt Jemima, plastic figural, w/lid, F&F, 1950s, EX ..**90.00**
Sugar bowl, Chef, Cameo china **285.00**
Syrup, Aunt Jemima, F&F, 5½" **70.00**
Tablecloth, printed family tending garden, sq **90.00**
Thermometer, boy figural, ceramic, 1940s **75.00**
Tin, Aunt Dinah Orleans Molasses, Mammy pictured **100.00**
Toy, stuffed tiger, Sambo's Restaurant **25.00**
Wall plate/spoon rest, Mammy, Rockingham **165.00**

Black Cats

Made in Japan during the '50s, these novelty cats may be found bearing the labels of several different importers, all with their own particular characteristics. The best known and most collectible of these cats are from the Shafford line. Even when unmarked, they are easily identified by their red bows, green eyes, and white whiskers, eyeliners, and eyebrows. Relco/Royal Sealy cats are tall and slender, and their bow ties are gold with red dots. Wales is a wonderful line with yellow eyes and gold detailing; Enesco cats have blue eyes, and there are other lines as well. When evaluating your black cats, be sure to inspect their paint and judge them accordingly. 50% paint should relate to 50% of our suggested values, which are given for cats in mint (or nearly mint) paint.

Ashtray, flat face shape, Shafford, 4½x4½"	18.00
Ashtray, 3-D head, open mouth w/cigarette rest, Shafford	18.00
Bank, seated, gr eyes, bl whiskers/eyelashes, Shafford, rare, 6"	125.00
Cigarette lighter, Shafford, 5½"	175.00
Condiment, cojoined heads, M or J on lids w/spoons, Shafford	75.00
Cookie jar, lg cat head, Shafford	85.00
Creamer & sugar bowl, Shafford, pr	45.00
Cruets, he w/O eyes, she w/V eyes & hair bow, Shafford, pr	60.00
Decanter, upright cat holds bottle w/cork stopper, Shafford	50.00
Demitasse pot, tail hdl, bow finial, Shafford, 7½"	95.00
Egg cup, cat face on bowl, ped ft, Shafford	30.00
Fork, emb cat face, gr eyes, from wall-hanging utensil set, Shafford	90.00
Grease jar, sm cat head, Shafford	75.00
Measuring cups, 4 on wood rack w/cat's face, Shafford	300.00
Mug, Shafford, rare lg sz, 4¼"	65.00
Mug, Shafford, 3½"	50.00
Pitcher, milk; upright, Shafford	100.00
Planter, upright, gr eyes, Shafford, 6"	20.00
Pot holder caddy, 'teapot' cat, 3-hook, Shafford	125.00
Shaker, long cat, salt in 1 end, pepper in other end, Shafford	85.00
Shakers, rnd-bodied teapot cat, Shafford, pr	50.00
Shakers, seated, 1 w/head tilted, gr eyes, Shafford, 3¾", pr	25.00
Shakers, seated, 1 w/head tilted, gr eyes, Shafford, 5", pr	50.00
Spice rack, wireware face w/marble eyes, 4 shakers, Shafford	350.00
Spice set, 3-tier, emb faces, triangular wood rack, Shafford	350.00
Spice set, 6 sq shakers w/emb faces in wood rack, Shafford	145.00
Strainer, w/cat face, long wood hdl, Shafford	90.00
Sugar bowl, seated red bow, gr eyes, Shafford, 4⅞"	22.00
Teapot, ball-shaped body, gr eyes, Shafford, 5¼"	45.00
Teapot, bulbous body, head lid, gr eyes, Shafford, 7"	75.00
Teapot, head w/2 spouts & chambers, wrapped hdl, Shafford, 5"	125.00
Teapot, upright, ovoid body (not ball-shaped), Shafford, 8"	175.00
Tray, head shaped, wicker hdl, Shafford, rare	125.00
Wall pocket, flattened 'teapot' cat, Shafford, scarce	95.00
Wall rack, long flat cat w/hooks for utensils, Shafford	90.00
Wine, emb cat's face, gr eyes, Shafford, sm	20.00

Black Glass

Black glass is a type of colored glass that when held to strong light usually appears deep purple, though since each glasshouse had its own formula, tones may vary. It was sometimes etched or given a satin finish; and occasionally it was decorated with silver, gold, enamel, coralene, or any of these in combination. The decoration was done either by the glasshouse or by firms that specialized in decorating glassware. Crystal, jade, colored glass, or milk glass was sometimes used with the black as an accent. Black glass has been made by many companies since the 17th century. Contemporary glasshouses produced black glass during the Depression, seldom signing their product. It is still being made today.

To learn more about the subject, we recommend *A Collector's Guide to Black Glass*, written by our advisor, Marlena Toohey; she is listed in the Directory under Colorado. Look for her newly updated value guide. See also Tiffin; and other specific manufacturers.

Ashtray, hat shape, emb DOBBS on brim, 2½"	28.00
Batter set, jug & syrup w/clear lids on tray, Paden City	80.00
Bottle, scent; figural stem, metal mts, ca 1930s, 6"	75.00

Bowl, hdls, ftd, ca 1937, 8"	45.00
Bowl, shallow, cupped, 1920-25, 10¼"	35.00
Bowl, silver flowers & scrolls, 3-ftd, 3x12½"	75.00
Bowl, 12-sided, ftd, 9"	35.00
Bowl, 6-scallop, 12¾"	66.00
Candlestick, crimped ft, ca 1925-35, 3"	20.00
Candlestick, Ellen, unknown mfg, pr	30.00
Cheese dish, clear glass lid, 5" dia	28.00
Comport, scalloped edge, HP florals, McKee, #157	40.00
Creamer & sugar bowl, Greensburg, #5029/#5029-2	40.00
Creamer & sugar bowl, Octagon Scroll, US Glass, 1930s	25.00
Creamer & sugar bowl, Ovide, Hazel-Atlas	25.00
Cup & saucer, Dmn Quilt	18.00
Flower cart, Viking, #772, ca 1940s	50.00
Goblet, clear bowl w/blk ft, 8-oz	18.00
Ice bucket, Decagon, #851, ca 1928-40	70.00
Paper cup holder, 2½"	12.00
Paperweight, ca 1930, 2x2"	85.00
Shakers, red plastic lids, Hazel-Atlas, #1533, 1930s, 3", pr	18.00
Sugar server, red plastic lid, att Duncan & Miller, 1930s, 6"	35.00
Tumbler, Allegheny, 10-scallop ft, ftd, Seneca, 8-oz	18.00
Tumbler, clear bowl, blk domed ft, 1929-35, 12-oz	14.00
Vase, bottle form, unknown mfg, 10½"	22.00
Vase, fan form, rnd ft, LE Smith, #1000	45.00
Vase, flared rim, hdls, ftd, LE Smith, #1900, 7¼"	28.00

Vase, loving cup form with classic figures in heart reserve, 7½", $30.00.

Wall vase, Crackle, US Glass, 1920s, 5¾"	50.00

Blown Glass

Blown glass is rather difficult to date; 18th and 19th century examples vary little as to technique or style. It ranges from the primitive to the sophisticated, but the metallic content of very early glass caused tiny imperfections that are obvious upon examination, and these are often indicative of age.

In America, Stiegel introduced the English technique of using a patterned, part-size mold, a practice which was generally followed by many glasshouses after the Revolution. From 1820 to about 1850, glass was blown into full-size three-part molds. In the listings below, glass is assumed clear unless color is mentioned. Numbers refer to a standard reference book, *American Glass* by George and Helen McKearin. See also Bottles and specific manufacturers. Our advisor for this category is Mark Vuono; he is listed in the Directory under Connecticut.

Bellows, clear w/wht loopings, appl rigaree/mouth/ft, 11⅜"	90.00
Bowl, aquamarine, galleried rim, polished pontil, 5½x10½"	90.00
Bowl, cobalt, 16 vertical ribs, appl ft, pontil, 4⅜x5½"	100.00

Bowl, red-amber to yel-amber, pontil, folded rim, 4¾x14⅜" ..2,050.00
Bowl, sapphire bl, 15 vertical ribs, hollow ft, wht lip, 4½" 220.00
Bowl, wine glass rinsing; apple gr opaque, 4¾" 140.00
Bowl, 16-dmn, cobalt, sm appl ft, pontil, 2¼x4¼" 300.00
Candlestick, olive-amber, folded edges on lip/ft, att Keene, 4¾" ...850.00
Celery vase, 10-panel, flared rim, 7⅝" 155.00
Creamer, cobalt, tooled rim, appl hdl, pontil, mini, 1⅞" 220.00
Creamer, dk violet, pinched spout, tooled ft, pontil, 4¾" 70.00
Creamer, tooled rim, appl hdl & ft, pontil, 3¾" 85.00
Creamer/pitcher, red/honey amber, tooled mouth, solid hdl, 5¾" ..7,000.00
Cruet, cobalt, lily pad base w/swirled ribs, appl hdl, 5¼" 95.00
Cruet, Pillar Mold, solid hdl, pewter lid, 8" 425.00
Fly trap, bl-aqua, tooled base, appl ft, German, 1870s, 6½" 175.00
Fly trap, deep yel-gr, tooled base, w/chain, 1900s, 6" 110.00
Fly trap, lt turq w/t'prints, open base, 6¼" 1,050.00
Fly trap, med yel-gr, tooled base, appl ft, 7⅜" 190.00
Fly trap, sun-colored amethyst, tooled base, appl lip, 5¾" 90.00
Goblet, baluster stem, 8 arched panels & ribs in bowl 55.00
Goblet, etched floral & monogram, pontil, 6⅜" 100.00
Mug, appl ribbed hdl, threaded lip, 6¼" 330.00
Mug, bbl shape w/wheel-eng floral decor, appl hdl, w/lid 475.00
Pan, cobalt, pontil, smooth rim, 1¾" H 170.00
Pan, lt gr, 25 ribs, terminal ring, 1¼x5⅞" 30.00
Pitcher, cobalt, appl ft & hdl, 6½" 165.00
Pitcher, forest gr, tooled rim, solid hdl, pontil, 5¼" 120.00
Pitcher, Pillar Mold, 8 red-striped vertical ribs, 5" 375.00
Plate, 17 dmn mold, petaled base w/pontil, 5⅝" 50.00
Salt cellar, cobalt-violet, flared rim, pontil, 1½" 250.00
Salt cellar, folded rim, knop stem, pontil, 3¼" 225.00
Salt cellar, lt aquamarine, pontil on inside, appl base, 2" 400.00
Salt cellar, lt to deep swirled amethyst, 24 vertical ribs, 2" 550.00
Sweetmeat, domed & ribbed foot, knop stem, ribbed bowl 525.00
Tumbler, flip; aquamarine, 16 vertical ribs, att Mantua, 3¾" 375.00
Tumbler, molded panels, eng rim, 6¼" 155.00
Tumbler, Sheaf of Wheat cutting, 3¾", pr 140.00
Tumbler, wheel-eng basket w/flowers, 7¼" 185.00
Tumbler, wheel-eng flower, 6" 150.00
Wine, air-twist stem, flared trumpet bowl, 6¼" 220.00
Wine, dbl wht opaque twist stem w/latticinio, eng bowl, 6" 220.00
Wine, red & wht twist stem w/wht latticinio, 4⅝" 250.00
Wine, wht opaque dbl-twist stem, eng bowl, 6" 165.00
Wine, wht twist stem, 8-rib bowl, 5⅜" 250.00

Blown Three-Mold Glass

A popular collectible in the 1920s, '30s, and '40s, blown three-mold glass has again gained the attention of many. Produced from approximately 1815 to 1840 in various New York, New England, and Midwestern glasshouses, it was a cheaper alternative to the expensive imported Irish cut glass.

Distinguishing features of blown three-mold glass are the three distinct mold marks and the concave-convex appearance of the glass. For every indentation on the inner surface of the ware, there will be a corresponding protuberance on the outside. Blown three-mold glass is most often clear with the exception of inkwells and a few known decanters. Any colored three-mold glass commands a premium price.

The numbers in the listings that follow refer to the book *American Glass* by George and Helen McKearin. Our advisor for this category is Mark Vuono; he is listed in the Directory under Connecticut.

Bottle, condiment; GII-37, 4"+matching stopper 250.00
Bottle, ink; GII-18, dk olive gr, 2¾" 160.00
Bottle, ink; GII-2, dk olive gr, 2¼" 180.00
Bottle, ink; GII-38, olive-amber, lt wear, 2¼" 200.00
Bottle, toilet water; GI-3, cobalt, pontil, 5⅝" 130.00
Bottle, toilet water; GI-3, type 4, cobalt, 5½" 60.00
Bottle, toilet water; GI-7, violet, folded lip, rayed base, 7" 225.00
Creamer, GI-29, flared mouth, ringed base w/pontil, 4¼" 600.00
Creamer, GIII-21, appl ribbed hdl, 2⅞" 275.00
Decanter, GI-29, flared rim, pressed wheel stopper, 10¾" 100.00
Decanter, GII-18, 3 appl rings, 8"+rpl stopper 110.00
Decanter, GII-43, lt ice bl-aqua, pontil, 8" 2,200.00
Decanter, GII-6, lt sea gr, 1824-30s, 8¾", NM 2,400.00

Decanter, GIII-2 type 1, olive green, flared lip, pontiled base, ca 1830, 7", $2,400.00.

Decanter, GIII-16, med amber w/olive tone, pontil, 7" 375.00
Decanter, GIII-6, flared lip, rayed base w/pontil, 9½" 100.00
Decanter, GIV-5, flared rim, pressed wheel stopper, 9" 170.00
Decanter, GIV-7, emb Rum, rayed base, lt haze, 9½" 200.00
Flip hat, GII-23 (pattern like), cobalt, pontil, 2⅜" 950.00
Hat, GII-18, dk sapphire bl, dmn base w/pontil, 2¼" 70.00
Mustard, GI-24, flared mouth, plain base w/pontil, stopper, 4¼" ..160.00
Mustard, GII-4, rayed base w/pontil, swirl rib stopper, 5" 140.00
Pan, GII-21, Dmn-type XI base w/pontil, folded rim, 5", NM 65.00
Pitcher, GI-29, flared tooled mouth, ringed base w/pontil, 4½" .300.00
Pitcher, GII-18, type XV base w/pontil, tooled rim, 6¾" 800.00
Salt cellar, GII-18, hat shape w/folded rim, 2⅛" 140.00
Shaker, GI-10, cobalt, sheared lip, 5¼", NM 800.00
Syrup, GV-11, Dmn type II base, flake, 6¼" 50.00
Tumbler, GII-18, bbl form, Dmn-type XII base w/pontil, 2¾" ...155.00
Tumbler, GII-18, 5¼" 140.00
Tumbler, GII-19, Dmn-type XII base w/pontil, 2½" 150.00
Tumbler, GII-22 (like pattern), pontil scar, tooled rim, 4¾" 80.00
Wine, GII-19, bladed stem, pontil, 4", NM 150.00

Blue and White Stoneware

Salt glaze or molded stoneware was most commonly produced in a blue and white coloration, much of which was also decorated with numererous 'in-mold' designs (some 150 plus patterns). It was made by practically every American pottery from the turn of the century until the mid-1930s. Crocks, pitchers, wash sets, rolling pins, and other household wares are only a few of the items that may be found in this type of 'country' pottery, now one of today's popular collectibles.

Logan, Brush-McCoy, Uhl Co., and Burley Winter were among those who produced it; but very few pieces were ever signed. Naturally, condition must be a prime consideration, especially if one is buying for resale; pieces with good, strong color and fully molded patterns bring premium prices. Normal wear and signs of age are to be expected, since this was utility ware and received heavy use in busy households. In the listings that follow, crocks, salts and butter holders are assumed to be without lids unless noted otherwise. For further information we recommend *Blue and White Stoneware* (1981) by Kathryn McNerny and *Collector's Encyclopedia of Salt Glaze Stoneware* (1997) by Terry Taylor (our advisor for this category) and Terry and Kay Lowrance. See also specific manufacturers.

Bank w/Money Bank stencil, coin slot, break to open, 4x3" **1,000.00**
Batter jar, Wildflower, appl wood & wire hdl, 5x7" **275.00**
Bean pot, Boston Baked Beans, Swirl, heavy diffused pattern **450.00**
Bowl, Apricot, 9½" **95.00**
Bowl, Daisy on Waffle, 10¾" **95.00**
Bowl, mixing; Flying Bird, 4x7½" **300.00**
Bowl, Reverse Pyramids w/Reverse Picket Fence, 2½x4½" **95.00**
Bowl, Wedding Ring, 6 szs, $150 ea, or set of 6 for **800.00**
Bowl, Wildflower, 4½x7" **125.00**
Bowl (milk crock), Apricot, w/hdl **175.00**
Box, powder; Wildflower & Fishscale, w/lid **325.00**

Butter crock, Apricot With Honeycomb, dark blue, replaced wire handle, 4x7", $250.00.

Butter crock, Basketweave & Morning Glory, w/lid, 4x7½" **400.00**
Butter crock, Butterfly, orig lid & bail, 6½" **225.00**
Butter crock, Cows, appl wood & wire hdl, w/lid, 4½x7¼" **500.00**
Butter crock, Daisy & Trellis, orig lid & bail, 4½" **200.00**
Butter crock, Daisy & Waffle, 4x8", NM **175.00**
Butter crock, Draped Windows, 4½x8" **225.00**
Butter crock, Eagle, orig lid & bail, M **750.00**
Butter crock, Grapes & Leaves, dbl ring around rim, 3x6½" **175.00**
Butter crock, Lovebirds, w/lid, 5½x6", M **500.00**
Butter crock, Peacock, w/lid, 6x6" **550.00**
Canister, Basketweave, Cloves, orig lid, 4½" **200.00**
Canister, Basketweave, Coffee, orig lid, 7½" **350.00**
Canister, Basketweave, Pepper, orig lid, 4½" **200.00**
Canister, Basketweave, Put Your Fist In, orig lid, 7½" **750.00**
Canister, Basketweave, Salt, orig lid, 7½" **350.00**
Canister, Basketweave, Sugar, orig lid, 7½" **350.00**
Canister, Basketweave, Tobacco, orig lid, 7½" **750.00**
Canister, Snowflake, rpl lid, 6½x5¾" **150.00**
Canister set, Basketweave, 9-pc **4,000.00**
Chamberpot, Fishscale & Wild Rose, no lid, 5½x9¼" **200.00**
Chamberpot, Wildflower, stenciled pattern, 6x11" **135.00**
Chamberpot, Wildflower & Fishscale, w/lid **450.00**
Coffeepot, Oval, Diffused Bl, bl-tipped knob, str sides, 11x4" .**1,500.00**
Coffeepot, Peacock, patterned sloped sides, 7x10" **2,500.00**
Coffeepot, Swirl, 'spurs' on hdl, acorn finial, 11½x6" **1,000.00**
Cookie jar, Brickers, flat button finial, 8x8" **500.00**
Cookie/biscuit jar, Flying Bird, orig lid, 9x6¾" **1,200.00**
Cooler, iced tea; Bl Band, flat lid, complete, 13x11" **295.00**
Cooler, water; Apple Blossom, brass spigot, 17x15" **2,000.00**
Cooler, water; Bl Band, orig lid **250.00**
Cooler, water; Cupid, brass spigot, patterned lid, 15x12" **700.00**
Cooler, water; Polar Bear, brass NP spigot, rare, 2-gal, 17x15" ...**4,000.00**

Cooler, water; Polar Bear, Ice Water, no lid, 15¼" **385.00**
Crock, Lovebird, rstr bail & handgrip, 5½x9" **400.00**
Crock, Peacock, rstr bail & handgrip, 5½x9" **500.00**
Cup, measuring; Spearpoint & Flower Panels, 6x6¾" **400.00**
Cup, Wildflower w/emb Ribbon & Bow, 4½x2½" **85.00**
Cuspidor, Basketweave & Morning Glory, 5x7½" **125.00**
Cuspidor, Butterfly & Shield, 6x7½" **175.00**
Cuspidor, Flower Panels & Arches, 7x7½" **250.00**
Custard cup, Fishscale, 5x2½" **125.00**
Egg storage crock, Barrel Staves, bail hdl, 5½x6" **235.00**
Foot warmer, Diffused Bl, A Warm Friend, 12½x6½" **275.00**
Grease jar, Flying Bird, orig lid, 4x4½" **900.00**
Ice crock, Barrel Staves, rope/tongs/ice block emb, 4½x6" **225.00**
Jardiniere, Flowers, hairline, 7⅞" (complete w/stand & crock) ..**800.00**
Mug, Basketweave & Flower, 5x3" **150.00**
Mug, beer; advertising, Diffused Bl, sqd hdl **150.00**
Mug, Cattails **150.00**
Mug, Flying Bird, 5x3" **200.00**
Mug, plain **65.00**
Mug, Windy City (Fannie Flagg), Robinson Clay Products **200.00**
Pie plate, Bl Walled Brick-Edge, star-emb base, 10½" **200.00**
Pitcher, Acorns, stenciled, 8x6½" **150.00**
Pitcher, American Beauty Rose, 10" **500.00**
Pitcher, Apricot, 8" **250.00**
Pitcher, Avenue of Trees, allover bl, 9x7" **200.00**
Pitcher, Barrel, +6 mugs **395.00**
Pitcher, Basketweave & Morning Glory, 9" **300.00**
Pitcher, Bl Band, plain **200.00**
Pitcher, Bl Band Scroll, emb design **300.00**
Pitcher, Bluebird, 9x7" **450.00**
Pitcher, Butterfly, 9x7" **450.00**
Pitcher, Castle & Fishscale, 8" **195.00**
Pitcher, Cattails, 10" **300.00**
Pitcher, Cattails, 7" **250.00**
Pitcher, Cattails, 9½" **275.00**
Pitcher, Cherries & Leaves, w/printing, 9½" **385.00**
Pitcher, Cherry Cluster, 7½" **650.00**
Pitcher, Cherry Cluster & Basketweave, 10" **350.00**
Pitcher, Daisy Cluster, 7x7" **700.00**
Pitcher, Doe & Fawn, EX color **250.00**
Pitcher, Doe & Fawn, sparce bl, 8½" **185.00**
Pitcher, Dutch Boy & Girl by Windmill, 9" **175.00**
Pitcher, Dutch Landscape, stenciled, Diffused Bl, tall **275.00**
Pitcher, Eagle w/Shield & Arrows, rare, 8" **800.00**
Pitcher, Fishscale & Wild Rose (part of wash set), 10" **160.00**
Pitcher, Flying Bird, 9" **600.00**
Pitcher, Garden Rose, 9", NM **500.00**
Pitcher, Girl & Dog, regular bl, 9" **675.00**
Pitcher, Girl & Dog, sponge, 9" **800.00**
Pitcher, Grape & Shield, 8½x5" **150.00**
Pitcher, Grape Cluster on Trellis, allover bl, 7x7" **225.00**
Pitcher, Grape w/Rickrack, any sz **250.00**
Pitcher, Grazing Cows, 6½" **500.00**
Pitcher, Grazing Cows, 7½" **400.00**
Pitcher, Grazing Cows, 8" **250.00**
Pitcher, hot water; Wildflower & Fishscale **150.00**
Pitcher, Indian Boy & Girl, 6" **300.00**
Pitcher, Indian Good Luck (Swastika), 8½" **200.00**
Pitcher, Indian Head in War Bonnet, dk bl, waffled body, 9" **350.00**
Pitcher, Iris, 9" **300.00**
Pitcher, Leaping Deer, sponge, 8" **1,200.00**
Pitcher, Leaping Deer, 8½" **350.00**
Pitcher, Leeping Deer in 1 oval, Swan in other (mfg error), 8" ..**1,200.00**
Pitcher, Lincoln, allover deep bl, 10x7" **600.00**

Photo courtesy Terry Taylor

Pitcher, Lincoln, allover deep bl, 4¾x4¾" 175.00
Pitcher, Lincoln, allover deep bl, 6x4" 250.00
Pitcher, Lincoln, allover deep bl, 7x5" 300.00
Pitcher, Lincoln, allover deep bl, 8x6" 350.00
Pitcher, Lovebird, arc bands, deep color, 8½", EX 450.00
Pitcher, Lovebird, pale color, 8½" 300.00
Pitcher, Monk, dk cobalt 350.00
Pitcher, Peacock, 7¾x6½" 800.00
Pitcher, Pine Cone, 9½" 500.00
Pitcher, Poinsettia, 6½" 275.00
Pitcher, Rose on Trellis, 8x5½" 225.00
Pitcher, Scroll & Leaf, advertising, 8" 450.00
Pitcher, Shield, prof rpr, 8" 150.00
Pitcher, Stag & Pine Trees, 9" 300.00
Pitcher, Swan, in oval, deep color, 8½", EX 400.00
Pitcher, Swan, lt bl, 8½" 300.00
Pitcher, Tulip, 8x4" 350.00
Pitcher, Wild Rose, solid bl, 9x6" 450.00
Pitcher, Wild Rose, sponged bands, 9" 450.00
Pitcher, Wildflower, stenciled 200.00
Pitcher, Windmill & Bush, 9" 225.00
Pitcher, Windmills, 7¼", EX 195.00
Pitcher, Windy City (Fannie Flagg), Robinson Clay, 8½" 450.00
Roaster, Diffused Bl, appl hdls, flat finial, 9x19" 225.00
Roaster, Wildflower, domed lid, 8½x12" 195.00
Rolling pin, Bl Band, advertising, 14x4" 550.00
Rolling pin, Bl Band, no advertising, 14x4" 400.00
Rolling pin, Swirl, baker's sz, 16" 1,200.00
Rolling pin, Swirl, orig wooden hdls, 13" 1,200.00
Rolling pin, Wildflower, advertising, Analomink PA, dtd 1905 ......700.00
Rolling pin, Wildflower, plain 350.00
Rolling pin, Wildflower, w/advertising, 15x4½" 500.00
Salt crock, Apricot, orig lid 225.00
Salt crock, Butterfly, orig lid 250.00
Salt crock, Daisy on Snowflakes, orig lid, 6½x6" 250.00
Salt crock, Eagle, w/lid 575.00
Salt crock, Grapevine on Fence, pale bl, orig lid, 6½x6¾" 300.00
Salt crock, Lovebirds, orig lid, 9" 450.00
Salt crock, Peacock, w/lid 550.00
Soap dish, Beaded Rose 150.00
Soap dish, cat's head 200.00
Soap dish, Indian in War Bonnet 250.00
Soap dish, Wildflower & Fishscale 150.00
Spice set, Basketweave, 6-pc 1,750.00
Teapot, Swirl, dbl wire bail hdl, ball shape, 9x6½" 1,200.00
Toothbrush holder, Bow Tie, stenciled flower 50.00
Toothbrush holder, Wildflower & Fishscale 150.00
Vase, Swirl, cone shape 250.00
Vinegar cruet, 4½x3" 300.00
Wash bowl & pitcher, Rose on Trellis 300.00
Wash bowl & pitcher, Wildflower & Fishscale 500.00
Wash set, Wildflower & Fishscale, complete, 7-pc 1,775.00
Water bottle, Diffused Bl Swirl, stopper w/cork, 10x5½" 500.00
Whipped cream jar, 4¾x6¾" 475.00

Blue Ridge

Blue Ridge dinnerware was produced by Southern Potteries of Erwin, Tennessee, from the late 1930s until 1956 in twelve basic styles and two thousand different patterns, all of which were hand decorated under the glaze. Vivid colors lit up floral arrangements of seemingly endless variation, fruit of every sort from simple clusters to lush assortments, barnyard fowl, peasant figures, and unpretentious textured pat-

terns. Although it is these dinnerware lines for which they are best known, collectors prize the artist-signed plates from the '40s and the limited line of character jugs made during the '50s most highly. Examples of the French Peasant pattern are valued at double the prices listed below; very simple patterns will bring 25% to 50% less.

Our advisors, Betty and Bill Newbound, have compiled three lovely books, *Blue Ridge Dinnerware, Revised Third Edition*, and *The Collector's Encyclopedia of Blue Ridge, Volumes I and II*, both with beautiful color illustrations and current market values. They are listed in the Directory under North Carolina. For information concerning the National Blue Ridge Newsletter, see the Clubs, Newsletters, and Catalogs section of the Directory.

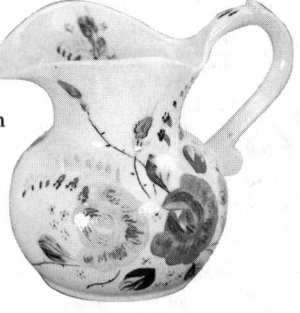

Pitcher, Sally, 6", from $170.00 to $180.00.

Ashtray, advertising, w/rest 75.00
Ashtray, ind 22.00
Basket, aluminum edge, 10" 25.00
Bonbon, flat shell 75.00
Bowl, cereal/soup; 6" 12.00
Bowl, divided, 9" 25.00
Bowl, fruit; 5" 8.00
Bowl, mixing; sm 20.00
Bowl, salad; 10½" 70.00
Bowl, vegetable; Premium, w/lid 125.00
Bowl, vegetable; rnd, 8" 20.00
Box, candy; rnd w/lid, rare 150.00
Box, cigarette 80.00
Box, Dancing Nudes, rare 850.00
Box, powder; rnd 175.00
Box, Seaside 170.00
Butter dish, Woodcrest 50.00
Cake tray, Maple Leaf 65.00
Casserole, w/lid 50.00
Celery, leaf chape, china 55.00
Child's feeding dish 150.00
Child's mug 85.00
Child's plate 120.00
Chocolate pot 225.00
Coffeepot 125.00
Creamer, Colonial shape, no hdls 15.00
Creamer, demitasse 75.00
Creamer, Fifties shape 15.00
Creamer, regular 15.00
Cup, dessert; glass 12.00
Cup & saucer, demitasse 45.00
Cup & saucer, Premium 60.00
Cup & saucer, regular 15.00
Custard cup 14.00
Deviled egg dish 60.00
Dish, baking; 13x8", w/metal stand 40.00
Gravy boat 25.00
Jug, batter; w/lid 85.00
Jug, character; china, rare 750.00

Lamp, china 250.00
Lazy susan, complete 700.00
Leftover, w/lid, lg 35.00
Pitcher, Abbey, china 175.00
Pitcher, Chick 110.00
Pitcher, Milady, china 190.00
Pitcher, Spiral shape, 7" 95.00
Plate, aluminum edge, 12" 45.00
Plate, Christmas Tree 75.00
Plate, dinner; 10½" 25.00
Plate, divided, heavy 40.00
Plate, party; w/cup well & cup 45.00
Plate, sq, novelty pattern, 6" 100.00
Plate, 11½" 50.00
Platter, Turkey w/Acorns 90.00
Platter, 12½" 120.00
Platter, 15" 35.00
Ramekin, w/lid, 5" 30.00
Relish, Charm House 150.00
Relish, heart shape, sm 90.00
Relish, loop handle, china 85.00
Relish, Mod Leaf, china 70.00
Relish, shell shape, deep, china 85.00
Relish, T-hdl 70.00
Salad fork 50.00
Sconce 75.00
Shakers, Blossom Top, pr 50.00
Shakers, bud top, pr 50.00
Shakers, Charm House, pr 150.00
Shakers, ftd, china, tall, pr 80.00
Shakers, mallards, pr 350.00
Shakers, Palisades, pr 25.00
Sherbet 25.00
Sugar bowl, Charm House, china 75.00
Sugar bowl, ped ft, w/lid 60.00
Sugar bowl, Rope hdl, w/lid 20.00
Sugar bowl, Woodcrest, w/lid 20.00
Teapot, ball shape 150.00
Teapot, Chevron hdl 165.00
Teapot, Colonial 125.00
Teapot, Fine Panel, china 150.00
Teapot, Good Housekeeping 175.00
Teapot, Piecrust 100.00
Tidbit, 2-tier 25.00
Tidbit, 3-tier 35.00
Tile, rnd or sq, 3" 45.00
Tray, snack; Martha 160.00
Vase, boot, 8" 95.00
Vase, bud 160.00
Vase, hdld 95.00

Bluebird China

Made from 1910 to 1934, Bluebird China is lovely ware decorated with bluebirds flying among pink flowering branches. It was inexpensive dinnerware and reached the height of its popularity in the second decade of this century. Several potteries produced it; shapes differ from one manufacturer to another, but the decal remains basically the same. Among the backstamps you'll find W.S. George; Cleveland; Carrolton; Homer Laughlin; Knowles, Taylor, Knowles; Limoges China of Sebring, Ohio; and there are others.

Because examples of this line are relatively scarce, we seldom find new listings. If you have some to add, let us hear from you.

Bowl, berry; Cleveland, ind 12.50
Bowl, deep, Deerwood, WS George, 4¾" 25.00
Bowl, deep, Homer Laughlin, 5½" 35.00
Bowl, gravy; w/saucer, Hopewell China 50.00
Bowl, sauce; SP Co, 4½" 12.50
Bowl, soup; PMC Co, 8" 30.00
Bowl, vegetable; Cleveland, 9¾" 45.00
Butter dish, 4½" holder w/in 7" dish, Steubenville 85.00
Butter pat, unmk 15.00
Casserole, Ostro China, 10½" dia 95.00
Casserole, Royal China Internat'l, 7x11½" 125.00
Creamer, Deerwood, WS George 15.00
Creamer & sugar bowl, Knowles Taylor Knowles 45.00
Creamer & sugar bowl, w/lid, Homer Laughlin 45.00
Cup, chocolate; ftd, 3½" 35.00
Cup, coffee; unmk, 3½" 25.00
Cup, tea; unmk 15.00
Dish, oval, mk Hudson, Homer Laughlin, 1x5¼x4" 20.00
Ladle, sauce; gold scrolling 40.00
Pitcher, water; Salem China, 10" 125.00
Plate, dessert; Limoges, 6" 8.00
Plate, dinner; Knowles Taylor Knowles, 9¾" 22.50
Plate, Homer Laughlin, 8½" 15.00
Plate, National China, 8" 15.00
Plate, rtcl, sq, unmk, 9" 35.00
Plate, scalloped, Homer Laughlin, 7¼" 15.00
Plate, Steubenville China, 9" 15.00

Platter, 14¾x11", $85.00.

Platter, Hopewell China, 13x10" 75.00
Platter, Hopewell China, 17½x13" 100.00
Platter, sqd oval, Carrolton, 17¾x12¾" 95.00
Platter, unmk, 9x7" 45.00
Saucer, Homer Laughlin 5.00
Syrup, unmk, 4" 35.00
Teapot, Carrolton 125.00
Teapot, ELP Co, 8½x8½" 125.00

Boch Freres

Founded in the early 1840s in La Louviere, Boch Freres Keramis became the foremost producer of art pottery in Belgium. Though primarily they served a localized market, in 1844 they earned worldwide recognition for some of their sculptural works on display at the International Exposition in Paris.

In 1907 Charles Catteau of France was appointed head of the art department. Before that time, the firm had concentrated on developing glazes and perfecting elegant forms. The style they pursued was traditional, favoring the re-creation of established 18th-century ceramics. Catteau brought with him to Boch Freres the New Wave (or Art Nouveau) influence in form and decoration. His designs won him international acclaim at the Exhibition d'Art Decoratif in Paris in 1925, and it is for his work that Boch Freres is so highly regarded today. He occasionally signed his work as well as that of others who under his direct supervision carried out his preconceived designs. He was associated with the company until 1950 and lived the remainder of his life in Nice, France, where he died in 1966. The Boch Freres Keramis factory continues to operate today, producing bathroom fixtures and other utilitarian wares. A variety of marks have been used, most incorporating some combination of 'Boch Freres,' 'Keramis,' 'BFK,' or 'Ch Catteau.' A shield topped by a crown and flanked by a 'B' and an 'F' was used as well.

Vase, incised and painted three-color geometrics on crackled yellow, Catteau, 12", $650.00; Vase, three-color stylized birds on white crackle, Keramis, 8", $900.00.

Bowl, geometrics, bl/cobalt on wht crackle, #10L9/#1187, 10" ...435.00
Vase, floral, mc/incised on crackle, 12", EX 225.00
Vase, lg floral sprays on wht crackle, spherical, 8" H 775.00
Vase, lg wht cranes stand in water, red bsk ground, 10x10" 1,100.00
Vase, wavy bars & ovals, aqua/blk on wht crackle, 9½x9" 400.00
Vase, wide/scalloped floral top over vertical stripes, 11" 450.00

Boehm

Boehm sculptures were the creation of Edward Marshall Boehm, a ceramic artist who coupled his love of the art with his love of nature to produce figurines of birds, animals, and flowers in lovely background settings accurate to the smallest detail. Sculptures of historical figures and those representing the fine arts were also made and along with many of the bird figurines, have established secondary-market values many times their original prices. His first pieces were made in the very early 1950s in Trenton, New Jersey, under the name of Osso Ceramics. Mr. Boehm died in 1969, and the firm has since been managed by his wife. Today known as Edward Marshall Boehm, Inc., the private family-held corporation produces not only porcelain sculptures but collector plates as well. Both limited and non-limited editions of their works have been issued. Examples are marked with various backstamps, all of which have incorporated the Boehm name since 1951. 'Osso Ceramics' in upper case lettering was used in 1950 and 1951.

Arctic Tern 2,750.00
Baby Robin, #437 ....175.00
Canada Goose w/3 goslings, #408, 4½x6" 625.00
Chrysanthemums 1,850.00
Deer Mouse, #400-89 ....100.00
Hummingbird, on cactus, #440 ....600.00
Madonna, sm 110.00
Madonna on stand, lg, EX 155.00
Mallards, in flight, #406, 11", pr 1,600.00
Non-Pariel Bunting, #466 ....625.00
Panda, #40237, 5" 300.00
Pascali Rose, #30093 ....1,450.00
Pope Pius 135.00
Ptarmigans, #463 ....1,800.00
Red-Shouldered Hawk, #40251, 1954, 26½" 900.00

Trumpeter Swan, sgn edition, 1958, 14¼" 450.00
Wht-Throated Sparrow, yel flower, #430, 9" 300.00
Yel-Throated Warbler, flower & bud base, #431, 9" 395.00

Bohemian Glass

The term 'Bohemian glass' has come to refer to a type of glass developed in Bohemia in the late 16th century at the Imperial Court of Rudolf II, the Hapsburg Emperor. The popular artistic pursuit of the day was stone carving, and it naturally followed to transfer familiar procedures to the glassmaking industry. During the next century, a formula was discovered that produced a glass with a fine crystal appearance which lent itself well to deep, intricate engraving, and the art was further advanced.

Although many other kinds of art glass were made there, collectors today use the term 'Bohemian glass' to most often indicate clear glass overlaid or stained with color through which a design is cut or etched. (Unless otherwise described, the items in the listing that follows are of this type.) Red or yellow on clear glass is common, but other colors may also be found. Another type of Bohemian glass involves cutting through and exposing two layers of color in patterns that are often very intricate. Items such as these are sometimes further decorated with enamel and/or gilt work.

Beaker, amber, 3 eng spa scenes, late 19th C, 5" 175.00
Beaker, gr, enameled crest, ca 1900, 7" 150.00
Beaker, red, cut pattern, 19th C, 5½" 150.00
Bottle, scent; red, deer & castle, cut/faceted stopper, 1890s, 6" ..175.00
Bowl, red, good luck symbols, cut ft, late 19th C, 8x6" 175.00
Decanter, red, vintage, pattern stopper, 9", +4 cordials 150.00
Lustres, red, forest/fox/stag, vintage base, prisms, 10", pr 350.00
Pokal, bl, gilt man & woman, ca 1900, 9" 290.00
Plate, cobalt, draped couple among flowers, 12" dia 125.00
Stein, red, eng spa scenes, late 19th C, 6" 275.00
Vase, amber, stag & foliage, 7x2½" 195.00
Vase, bl opal, wht enamel & gilt flowers, ca 1860s, 9" 250.00
Wine, red, outdoor scenes/scrolls, 4½", 4 for 110.00

Bookends

Though a few were produced before 1880, bookends became a necessary library accessory and a popular commodity after the printing industry was revolutionized by Mergenthaler's invention, the linotype. Books became abundantly available at such affordable prices that almost every home suddenly had need for bookends. They were carved from wood, cast in iron, bronze, or brass, or cut from stone. Today's collectors may find such designs as ships, animals, flowers, and children. Patriotic themes, art reproductions, and those with Art Nouveau and Art Deco styling provide a basis for a diverse and interesting collection.

Currently, figural cast-iron pieces are in demand, especially examples with good original polychrome paint. This has driven the value of painted cast-iron bookends up considerably.

For further information we recommend *Collector's Guide to Bookends, Identification and Values,* by Louis Kuritzky, our advisor for this category; he is listed in the Directory under Florida. See also Arts and Crafts; Bradley and Hubbard.

Amish man w/harness & lady sewing, Hubley, 4¾" 165.00
Amos & Andy, pnt chalkware, 9", 9½", EX 225.00
Angelus Call to Prayer, gray metal, K&O, 4¼" 200.00
Aviator, CI, Conn Foundry, 1928, 6" 125.00
Bear chained to post, metal on marble base 135.00

Beethoven at piano, gilded gray metal on polished stone base 250.00
Buccaneer, CI, Conn Foundry, 1930, 7¼" 125.00
Charioteer, gray metal on polished stone base, 5" 275.00
Dancing girls, bronze, Gorham, Ziegler, 1921, 6¾" 595.00
Deco female bust, gray metal, Frankart, 6" 225.00
Deco lady, mc pnt on CI, 8" 175.00
Deer, stylized, ball ft, CI 95.00

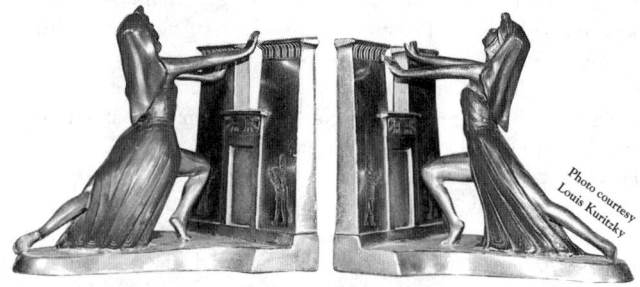

Photo courtesy Louis Kuritzky

Egyptian woman at wall, gray metal, Ronson, 1924, 6", $375.00.

Elk logo in relief, Hartford Fire Ins Co, bronze, 1935 ....65.00
Eve, CI, Verona Foundry, 6¾" 175.00
Fisherman, bronzed metal, Jennings Bros, 8" 200.00
Flamingos, gray metal, JB, #2034, 6½" 125.00
Flamingos, silver over copper, Everstyle, 6¼x3¼" 145.00
Goddess on pillar, bronze, Austria, 6⅞" 595.00
Golden retriever profile, Bruce Fox 60.00
Great Emancipator, gray metal, Pompeian Bronze, 5½" 225.00
Hammered copper, mk Apollo Studios NY #341, 4x6" 75.00
Hammered copper rectangles, Apollo Studios NY #341, 4x6" 75.00
Indian chief in full headdress, CI 160.00
Kneeling nude in circle, CI, #17, 5¼" 195.00
Lazy Pedro, bronze pnt CI, Hubley 150.00
Lincoln bust, bronze-plated CI 80.00
Lion, bronze on blk marble base, Fr 460.00
March Girl, windblown girl, cat & dog, bronze, 7" 225.00
Mexican seated, pnt CI, att Hubley, EX 185.00
Minerva, CI, Judd Co, #9726, 5¾" 85.00
Nude on tiptoes, bronze, Glauber, 9" 595.00
Nude w/tambourine, CI, Gift House, 1926, 5¼" 110.00
Pioneer woman & child, gray metal, JB, #8355, 8½" 300.00
Pirate sitting on treasure chest, CI 70.00
Pirate w/ft on trunk beside open coin bag, pnt CI, 5¾x4" 155.00
Rooster, CI, blown-out figure incorporated in solid base 100.00
Sailing ship, brass-plated CI, 3-masted, EX details 45.00
Sailing ship, bronze, mk Silvercrest, 5½x5" 80.00
Sea captain at wheel, bronzed metal, Ronson, 6½" 100.00
Sleeping man reading book in chair, gray metal, K&O, 4¼" 150.00
Three Musketeers on book, gray metal, JB, 5¾" 275.00
Whistler's Mother, pnt metal w/celluloid face 225.00
Winged woman w/Comedy/Tragedy, gray metal, JB, #1529, 5" ..250.00
3 semicircular steps lead to arched door, bronze, 7½" 200.00

Bootjacks and Bootscrapers

Bootjacks were made from metal or wood. Some were fancy figural shapes, others strictly business! Their purpose was to facilitate the otherwise awkward process of removing one's boots. Bootscrapers were handy gadgets that provided an effective way to clean the soles of mud and such. Our advisor for this category is Louis Picek; he is listed in the Directory under Iowa.

Bootjacks

Am Bull Dog, pistol shaped, CI, blk pnt, 8" 75.00
Beetle, CI, openwork bk, 11¾x5x2", EX 110.00
Beetle, CI, orig worn pnt, Reading PA, 4x11x3", EX 120.00
Boss emb on shaft, lacy CI, 15" L 135.00
CI, openwork between hexagonal supports, blk pnt, 6" L 65.00
Cricket, CI, no pnt, Webster Bros, Reading PA, 11" 55.00
Heart figural, scalloped sides, CI, 13" L 225.00
Hickory, bentwood hdl, hinged/folds, use w/out bending over 85.00
Naughty Nellie, CI, EX pnt, no rust, 11x5x2½", EX 250.00
Pine w/sq nails, early, lg 150.00
Try Me, CI, openwork, no pnt, ca 1890s, 12x4x1¾" 100.00
V-shaped, ornate CI, VG 48.00

Bootscrapers

Aunt Jemima figure atop, CI, rpt, 14½" 250.00
CI, scrolled harp shape, 7⅞x7¼" 75.00
Dachshund, CI, old worn wht pnt, 1900s, 7x22x5" 250.00
Dog, cast steel, blk pnt, simple tooling, 13" 140.00
Duck, full bodied, scraper on bk, CI, 14½" L 350.00
Griffins jtd at wings & tails, CI, marble base, 18" 880.00
Lyre on oval scalloped base, CI, 9x11" 125.00
Pointer on 'bridge,' brushes in base at 1 time, CI/rpt, 16" 330.00
Scottie dog, CI, orig pnt, EX 65.00
Scottie silhouette w/edge tooling, cast steel, pnt, 9" 110.00
Wrought iron, ribbon curls at top of ea end, 7x7", EX 40.00
Wrought iron, twisted posts w/star-emb faceted knobs, 12x8" 150.00
Wrought iron w/detailed scroll finial, 21x24" 500.00
2 quail ea end, CI, rectangular pan, pnt traces, 7x16" 275.00

Boru, Sorcha

Sorcha Boru was the professional name used by California ceramist Claire Stewart. She was a founding member of the Allied Arts Guild of Menlo Park (California) where she maintained a studio from 1932 to 1938. From 1938 until 1955, she operated Sorcha Boru Ceramics, a production studio in San Carlos. Her highly acclaimed output consisted of colorful, slip-decorated figurines, salt and pepper shakers, vases, wall pockets, and flower bowls. Most production work was incised 'S.B.C.' by hand.

Bowl, maroon, appl peony on lid, 6" 85.00
Cup, 3 dinosaur hdls 75.00
Figurine, Penelope, fawn, 6" 85.00
Pitcher, pk lustre florals w/gold centers, beading, 6½" 80.00
Shakers, sailor boy & girl, pr 85.00
Sugar shaker, lady figural, 6" 95.00
Vase, appl florals & leaves, 8" 70.00

Bossons Artware

In December 1996 the W.H. Bossons, Ltd., Congleton, England, announced the closing of their operation for the 'purpose of restructuring.' Since then and of this date (spring 1998), they have permanently ceased operations, and it is this author's (Dr. Don Hardisty) understanding there are no plans to reopen. (Rumors regarding a fire and pilfering of molds are unfounded.) All authenic molds not already officially destroyed are safely stored and preserved, and though they have received several offers, there are currently no plans to sell the molds or the business. Some limited production and distribution may be initiated and may be announced through the International Bossons

Collectors Society. During the past few years, all of the molds and plaster patterns for several popular Bossons were officially destroyed as 'obsolete models' — in '92: Bretonne Lady, Rumanian, Sardinian, Cheyenne, Pancho, Old Timer, and all 8" Scenic Plaques, e.g., Village Pub; and in 1994: Mozart, King Henry VIII, Catherine of Aragon, Anne Boleyn, Punjabi, and Fijian.

All Bossons are now categorized as discontinued, and as current stock holdings are depleted, it is expected most Bossons will continue to appreciate in value. With few exceptions, the earliest models (1958 – 63, e.g., Caspian Man and Caspian Woman, veiled and unveiled; all pottery products; and Paul Kruger) and the most recent released (1990 – 96, e.g., Rolf, King Olaf, and Cossack) will be in increasingly short supply, thus they will command higher prices. Keep in mind that without written records (and few were kept), it is impossible to know how many of each were produced. As an example, Bengali once thought to have been made in a limited quantity of only fifty at one time commanded prices in excess of $5,200.00; now the estimate is nearer one hundred, and today values range from $2,200.00 to $4,000.00 for a perfect condition Bengali.

Bossons were originated in Congleton, Cheshire, England, in 1944 by the Senior Mr. W.H. Bossons, an accredited potter. In 1946 he was joined by his son Ray. Early on they experimented with other mediums including pottery and lead for soldiers and other toys. Their first high-relief wall plaques depicting English scenes and floral subjects were released in 1948. Though they continued to make the floral plaques (in sizes ranging from 3" to 14"), it is Bossons' character wall masks (life-like sculptures) and figurines, conceived and developed in 1948 by Mr. W. Ray Bossons and his associates, that have become so collectible. Ray Bossons has sculpted several extremely popular Bossons including Don Quixote and Sancho Panza, Rolf, Sir Lancelot, Blackbeard, Pierre le Grand, The Parson, The Bossons Santa Claus, Shakespearean Collection, and The Briar Rose Collection of comical animal studies.

Most often the 'wall masks' (called 'heads') are subjects of men from all nations and walks of life. The early (1959) Women masks are rare. Some of the larger wall figurines include an animal (Desert Hawks, Desert Hunters with dog, and Deccan Hunters with cheetah). The most popular Bossons are made of a special gypsum (plaster) medium that is easily chipped or scuffed. Therefore mint or mint-in-box discontinued Bossons are few.

Since the mid-1960s, in nearly every case Bossons have the mask name incised under the collar (Smuggler, Tibetan, and Tyrolean, illustrated here, are three recent exceptions; and Snake Charmer, Bengali, Nigerian Women, Mexican, and Caspians are early exceptions). Nearly all pottery items have no name. Those figurines with names at their bases also carry a copyright date indicating when the mold was created. Also, on the reverse side of most Bossons sculptures will appear the following incision: 'Bossons Copyright Reserved,' and usually 'Congleton, England,' with date. **Those dates will not change though that model may be issued for years,** but collectors seek out the variations in color and sculptural changes that occur during the mask's span of production. Nine pottery dogs were released in 1960 (three each of Pooch, Mac, and Patch), and four 6" shelf ornaments in 1963 (Sikh, Himalayan, Moroccan, and Serbian), all of which were unmarked. Beware of copies (including Pancho, Punjabi, Syrian, Rawhide, Chef, Military Masks [six originals]) and numerous fakes and look-alikes cast in everything from plaster, rubber, or even metal.

There are other English character masks and hand-painted gypsum artware products of fine quality produced by NatureCraft and the Legend Company that look very much like Bossons, no doubt because Fred Wright, principal Bossons sculptor from 1957 to 1972, also did free-lance work for Legend (1950 – 1980). Other English 'heads' may be incised simply 'Made in England,' however, in addition, NatureCraft masks may carry an incised name and date.

As early as 1952, Mrs. Alice Brindley (or Miss Wilde as she was then known), sculpted some of the most outstanding Bossons ever created, including the three much loved 'Aboriginal Plaques.' She free-lanced until 1971 when she became an exclusive employee of Bossons, remaining there until

1995. She modeled nearly one hundred Bossons, including many Wildlife Figurines, Scrooge, Victorian Bobby and Fireman, King Henry VIII, Catherine of Aragon and Anne Boleyn, Country-side Collection, The Americans, Seafarers, many of the Europeans, Tulip Time, Zapata, and Mozart. She now has her own 'AB Sculpture Studio' and is modeling, producing, and distributing her own work including the Seafarers, a new version of Sherlock Holmes, and her most recent models, Josephine and Napoleon.

Molded in plaster, Bossons are frequently found in deplorable condition, and **avid collectors only pay the premium prices here for the most perfect examples,** either in factory 'mint' condition or perfectly returned to their original structural and coloring beauty by a recognized restoration artist recommended by Bossons.

In addition to a series of both domestic animals and wildlife in plaster, some Bossons were made of a hard plastic called 'Stonite.' Produced in this Fraser-Art Division of Bossons were the wildlife series of nine limited editions known as the 'Crown Collection,' including 'Bears and Bees,' all modeled by Alice Brindley. Nearly indestructible, Fraser-Art works are also hand painted and therefore, in most cases, they are preserved in excellent condition. Produced from 1966 to 1995, they include Pony and Horse Heads, many Bird and Fish Studies, and the Copper Collection. A limited number of Bossons collectors seek the clocks, mirrors, and other decorative items released during the late 1950s and early 1960s. In 1980 Bossons produced their 'Ivorex' plaques, formerly Osborne Editions, a collection of over fifty high-relief plaques of English scenes, two American Revolutionary subjects (extremely rare), and those including the popular 1994 editions of 'Fisherman-Waiting for the Tide' and 'Cornish Fishwife - Unloading the Boat.'

Our advisor for this category is Dr. Don Hardisty; since 1984 he has been recommended by Bossons to restore their products. He is listed in the Directory under New Mexico. The items below are all plaster products unless noted otherwise.

Key:
AC — American Collection	MMD — Men of Mountains and Desert
BR — Briar Rose Collection	NNUC — no name under collar
CB — commonly found Bossons	OE — original edition
CE — Collectors Edition	OEBR — older edition, becoming rare
CS — Country-side Collection	OEC — older edition, common
DC — Dickensian Collection	PP — pottery products
DCS — Dogs and Cats	RB — rare Bossons
DS — Dogs of Distinction	RE — recent editions
EC — European Collection	Sa — Series A
ER — extremely rare	Sb — Series B
FA — Fraser-Art (Stonite Products)	SE — Second Edition
FAC — Fraser-Art Crown Collection	SF — Seafarers Collection
FP — floral plaques	VC — Victorian Collection
FP14 — floral plaques, 14" dia	VLWF — very large wall figures
LRE — less recent edition	VRB — very rare Bossons
LWF — larger wall figure	WL — Wild Life
MD — mold destroyed by Bossons	

Photo courtesy Dr. Don Hardisty

Smuggler, Tibetan, Tyrolean, $65.00 to $85.00. See listings for full descriptions.

Abduhl, EC, Sb, OEC, from $125 to 165.00
Aboriginal plaques, PP, ER, ea, from $200 to 425.00
Anemones, FP, OE & RE, 12" dia, ea, $75 to 100.00
Anemones & Daffodils, rococo style, OE, ER, from $100 to 150.00
Anemones & Daffodils, rococo style, RE, from $45 to 85.00
Anne Hathaway's Cottage, 14" plaque, RB, from $60 to 100.00
Aruj Barbarossa, SF, Sb, RE, from $65 to 85.00
Autumn Gold, FP, OE & RE, 14" dia, from $100 to 125.00
Bargee, SF, Sb, LRE, from $85 to 125.00
Bears & Bees, FAC, LRE, from $500 to 750.00
Beefeater, EC, OEC, from $85 to 125.00
Betsey Trotwood, bl collar, DC, RB, from $100 to 150.00
Betsey Trotwood, pk collar, DC, OEBR, from $45 to 85.00
Bill Sikes, DC, OEBR, from $45 to 85.00
Black Panther (Golden Puma mold), SE, VLWF, RB, $325 to ...400.00
Blackbeard, SF, Sb, RE, from $85 to 125.00
Boatman, SF, Sb, OEC, from $45 to 85.00
Bossons Ivorex Plaque, Waiting for the Tide, RE, RB, 8", $125 to ...150.00
Boxer, DCS, OEC, from $75 to 100.00
Boxer, DS, OEC, from $20 to 35.00
Bretonne Lady, OEBR, Sb, from $95 to 150.00
Bruin, BR, OEC, unmk, from $75 to 125.00
Buccaneer, SF, LWF, OEC, from $100 to 125.00
Carnation (1 of 6), FP, OE, RE, 6" dia, from $40 to 60.00
Caspian Man, thick or thin sideburn, Sb, EC, RB, from $150 to ...175.00
Cheyenne Indian, red-fringed jacket, SE, VLWF, OEC, MD, $140 to ...175.00
Coolie, Sa, CB, LWF, from $125 to 175.00
Corsican (early examples have NNUC), Sb, CB, from $85 to 125.00
Cossack, EC, RE, Sa, from $115 to 145.00
Coxswain, SF, LRE, from $95 to 145.00
Deccan Hunters, brn or gr-eyed cat, LWF, RB, from $185 to 295.00
Desert Hunters, dog's mouth closed, OE, MMD, RB, from $225 to ...285.00
Desert Hunters, dog's mouth open, SE, MMD, OEBR, from $175 to ...185.00
Dogs (Mac, Pooch, Patch), PP, unmk, VRB, ea, from $400 to ...600.00
Don Quixote-Sancho Panza (composite), CE, LWF, RE (ltd), $125 to 175.00
Double Terriers, DCS, Series II, OEBR, from $75 to 125.00
Engineer, AC, RE, Sa, from $85 to 115.00
Eskimo, Sa, AC, OEBR, from $125 to 145.00
Evzon, EC, RE, Sa, from $115 to 145.00
Fisherwoman/Fisherman, Sb, RE, from $85 to 125.00
Floral Spray, FP, RE, 10" dia 96.00
French Military Masks, RE (3 w/eyes), EC, from $100 to 150.00
Golden Puma, OE, VLWF, RB, from $275 to 375.00
Horatius Cocles, FA Copper Collection, LWF, RB, from $175 to ...225.00
Horse Heads, FA, OEBR, from $100 to 150.00
King Olaf, LRE, from $85 to 100.00
Kurd, Sb, OEC, from $40 to 60.00
Mozart, EC, RE, Sa, from $140 to 175.00
Mr Wang, CE, Sb, RE, RB, from $200 to 300.00
Nigerian Man, OE, Sb, RB, from $165 to 185.00
Nuvolari, RE, from $85 to 145.00
Owl, WL, VRB, from $250 to 375.00
Owlet, WL, OEC, from $65 to 95.00
Owlets & Squirrel, WL, RE, from $85 to 125.00
Pancho, Sa, AC, OEBR, MD, from $125 to 150.00
Peon, LWF, full length, OEBR, from $300 to 375.00
Pony Girl, part of 3 Children Studies, LWF, RB, from $600 to ..750.00
Pony Heads, FA, OEC, from $100 to 125.00
Punjabi, MMD, OEC, Sb, MD (1994), from $75 to 140.00
Rawhide, Sa, AC, OEC, from $85 to 110.00
Robin Hood, EC, Sb, CB, from $125 to 140.00
Romany, VLWF, SE, CB, from $150 to 175.00
Romany (Scandali w/gr or yel collar), LWF, OEBR, $200 to 315.00
Saracen, wht or yel hat, Sb, OEC, from $165 to 185.00

Shakespearean Collection (Malvilio, etc), RE, CE, RB, ea, $75 to .150.00
Shelf Ornaments, unmk, RB, all 6", ea, from $175 to 325.00
Shepherd, CS, RE, from $125 to 150.00
Sherlock Holmes, VC, CB, from $125 to 140.00
Sherpa, LWF, full length, RB, from $375 to 425.00
Smuggler, NNUC, Sb, CB, from $65 to 85.00
Snake Charmer (thick or thin sideburns), NNUC, LWF, RB, $175 to 350.00
Squirrel, BR, ER, from $275 to 415.00
Squirrel, WI, OEC, LWF, from $95 to 135.00
Stag's Head, FA, WL, ER, unmk, from $350 to 500.00
Syrian, EC, MMD, Sb, OEC, from $45 to 85.00
Teals, RB, 14" plaque, from $125 to 140.00
The Bossons Santa Claus, RE, from $65 to 85.00
Tibetan, NNUC, EC, Sb, OEBR, from $65 to 85.00
Tulip Time, Composite ed, RE, Sa, RB, from $125 to 185.00
Tyrolean, EC, Sb, OEC, from $65 to 85.00
USAF Fighter Pilot, AC, LWF, RE, from $140 to 175.00
Warrior Panels, RB, 17x11" plaques, ea, from $350 to 500.00
Winston Churchill, CE, Sb, RB, from $185 to 300.00
Wood Anemones, 1 of 4, FP, RE, 4" dia, from $40 to 60.00
York, coonskin hat, yel shirt, AC, SE, from $85 to 125.00
York, hat w/brim, bl shirt, AC, OEBR, from $185 to 300.00
Zapata, AC, LWF, RE, from $85 to 125.00

Bottle Openers

Around the turn of the century, manufacturers began to seal bottles with a metal cap that required a new type of bottle opener. Now the screw cap and the flip top have made bottle openers nearly obsolete. There are many variations, some in combination with other tools. Many openers were used as means of advertising a product. Various materials were used including silver and brass.

A figural bottle opener is defined as a figure designed for the sole purpose of lifting a bottle cap. The actual opener must be an integral part of the figure itself. A base-plate opener is one where the lifter is a separate metal piece attached to the underside of the figure. The major producers of iron figurals were Wilton Products, John Wright Inc., Gadzik Sales, and L & L Favors. Openers may be free standing and three dimensional, wall hung or flat. They can be made of cast iron (often painted), brass, bronze, or aluminum.

Numbers within the listings refer to a new reference book printed by the FBOC (Figural Bottle Opener Collectors) organization. Those seeking additional information are encouraged to contact FBOC, whose address can be found in the Directory under Clubs, Newsletters, and Catalogs.

Volstead, nickel-plated cast iron with light wear and tarnish, ca 1933, 9⅝", $100.00.

Alligator, CI, F-136, VG 70.00
Alligator & boy, CI, J Wright, F-133, EX 200.00
Alligator & boy, Wilton Pdts, F-134, VG 175.00
Bulldog head, CI, F-425, ca 1900, 4x3¾x1½", NM 75.00
Canada goose, CI, mc pnt, Wilton Pdts, F-105, EX 80.00
Cockatoo, CI, mc pnt, J Wright, F-121, 1947, VG 190.00
Dachshund, brass, F-83 ....80.00

Donkey, pnt CI, J Wright, F-61, EX **40.00**
Elephant, CI, pk pnt, J Wright, F-49, EX **50.00**
Flamingo, CI, hollow, Wilton Pdts, F-120 ....**100.00**
Foundryman, pnt CI, J Wright, F-29, EX **80.00**
Miss 4-Eyes, pnt CI, Wilton Pdts, F-408, VG **80.00**
Nude native girl kneeling, CI, 1950s **70.00**
Parrot, long bl tail, pnt CI, J Wright, F-108, 5¼" **50.00**
Parrot, Wilton Pdts, F-112, sm, VG **65.00**
Rooster, pot metal, old wht pnt, hollow, J Wright, F-98, VG **70.00**
Salted Pretzel, F-230 ....**40.00**
Sea gull, CI, worn pnt, Wright, F-123, VG **50.00**
Skunk, CI, orig blk & wht pnt, J Wright, F-92 ....**130.00**
4-eyed lady, pnt CI, J Wright, F-407, EX **100.00**

Bottles and Flasks

As far back as the 1st century B.C., the Romans preferred blown glass containers for their pills and potions. Though you're not apt to find many of those, you will find bottles of every size, shape, and color made to hold perfume, ink, medicine, soda, spirits, vinegar, and many other liquids. American business firms preferred glass bottles in which to package their commercial products and used them extensively from the late 18th century on. Bitters bottles contained 'medicine' (actually herb-flavored alcohol), and judging from the number of these found today, their contents found favor with many! Because of a heavy tax imposed on the sale of liquor in 17th-century England by King George who hoped to curtail alcohol abuse among his subjects, bottlers simply added 'curative' herbs to their brew and thus avoided taxation. Since gin was taxed in America as well, the practice continued in this country. Scores of brands were sold; among the most popular were Dr. H.S. Flint & Co. Quaker Bitters, Dr. Kaufman's Anti-Cholera Bitters, and Dr. J. Hostetter's Stomach Bitters. Most bitters bottles were made in shades of amber, brown, and aquamarine. Clear glass was used to a lesser extent, as were green tones. Blue, amethyst, red-brown, and milk glass examples are rare. (Please note that color is a strong factor when pricing bottles. For example, an amber Hostetter's bitters sells for $25.00 or less, but a green variant can bring hundreds of dollars. An aqua scroll flask may bring $50.00, but a cobalt blue variation will command over $1,000.00.)

Perfume or scent bottles were produced abroad by companies all over Europe from the late 16th century on. Perfume making became such a prolific trade that as a result beautifully decorated bottles were fashionable. In America they were produced in great quantities by Stiegel in 1770 and by Boston and Sandwich in the early 19th century. Cologne bottles were first made in about 1830 and toilet-water bottles in the 1880s. Rene Lalique produced fine scent bottles from as early as the turn of the century. The first were one-of-a-kind creations done in the cire perdue method. He later designed bottles for the Coty Perfume Company with a different style for each Coty fragrance. Prices for commercial perfumes hinge on condition. Their values appreciate according to these factors: are they still sealed or full; do they retain all factory labels; is the original box or packing included? Deluxe versions bring premium prices.

Spirit flasks from the 19th century were blown in specially designed molds with varied motifs including political subjects, railroad trains, and symbolic devices. The most commonly used colors were amber, dark brown, and green.

From the 20th century, early pop and beer bottles are very collectible as is nearly every extinct commercial container. Dairy bottles are a relatively new area of interest; look for round bottles in good condition with both city and state as well as a nice graphic relating to the farm or the dairy.

Bottles may be dated by the methods used in their production. For instance, a rough pontil indicates a date before 1845. After the bottle was blown, a pontil rod was attached to the bottom, a glob of molten glass acting as the 'glue.' This allowed the glassblower to continue to manipulate the extremely hot bottle until it was finished. From about 1845 until approximately 1860, the molten glass 'glue' was omitted. The rod was simply heated to a temperature high enough to cause it to afix itself to the bottle. When the rod was snapped off, a metallic residue was left on the base of the bottle; this is called an 'iron pontil.' (The presence of a pontil scar thus indicates early manufacture and increases the value of a bottle.) A seam that reaches from base to lip marks a machine-made bottle from after 1903, while an applied or hand-finished lip points to an early mold-blown bottle. The Industrial Revolution saw keen competition between manufacturers, and as a result, scores of patents were issued. Many concentrated on various types of closures; the crown bottle cap, for instance, was patented in 1892. If a manufacturer's name is present, consulting a book on marks may help you date your bottle.

Among our advisors for this category are Madeleine France (see the Directory under Florida), Mark Vuono (Connecticut), Steve Ketcham (Minnesota), Monsen and Baer (Virginia), and John Tutton (Virginia). In the listings that follow (most of which have been taken from auction catalogs), glass is assumed to be clear unless color is indicated. Numbers refer to a standard reference book, *American Glass,* by George and Helen McKearin. See also Advertising, various companies; Avon; Barber Shop Collectibles; Blown Glass; Blown Three-Mold Glass; California Perfume Company; Czechoslovakia; De Vilbiss; Fire Fighting; Lalique; Medical Collectibles; Steuben.

Key:

am — applied mouth	grd — ground pontil
bbl — barrel	GW — Glass Works
bt — blob top	ip — iron pontil
b3m — blown 3-mold	ps — pontil scar
cm — collared mouth	rm — rolled mouth
fl — filigree	sb — smooth base
fm — flared mouth	sl — sloping
gm — ground mouth	sm — sheared mouth
gp — graphite pontil	tm — tooled mouth

Apothecary (Druggist)

Blk amethyst w/3-color pnt label, gp, orig stopper, 11¾" **400.00**
Cobalt, 2-color label under glass, pontil, tm, stopper, 4½" **110.00**
Cobalt, 3-color label under glass, ps, tm, blown stopper, 11⅜" ...**400.00**
Cobalt, 3-color label under glass, sb, tm, 7⅝" **160.00**
Cobalt, 4-color label under glass, sb, tm, haze, 7⅝" **125.00**
Owl Drug Co (owl/mortar & pestle) San Francisco, lt teal, 9½" ..**180.00**
Turq, gold & blk porc label, polished pontil, tm, Fr, 9¾" **180.00**
Yel-gr, 3-color label under glass, sb, tm, blown stopper, 8" **95.00**

Barber Bottles

Cobalt with vertical ribs, white and green enameling, pontil scar, 1885 – 1925, 7½", $140.00; Cobalt with vertical ribs and white enameling, pontil scar, 1885 – 1925, 7⅝", $130.00.

AH Seely Bay Rum, cobalt w/mc florals/gold, 10¾" stopper 350.00
Brilliantine, dk red, sb, tm, metal stopper, 4" 155.00
Clear irid w/purple amethyst decor, sb, gm, chip, 7⅝" 180.00
Cobalt w/wht flower band, ftd, ps, rm, 7⅛" 175.00
Coin Spot, pale straw yel w/wht Nouveau cameo decor, ps, 8" ...250.00
Coin Spot, sapphire bl w/melon ribs, sb, rm, metal stopper, 8½" ...100.00
Coin Spot, yel-amber, mc enameling, ps, rm, 8⅛" 75.00
Cranberry opal, melon ribs w/wht stripes, sb, rm, 7¼" 120.00
Emerald gr bell form w/mc thistles, ps, sm, 7⅝" 350.00
Gold & purple Loetz style, sb, gm, 1885-1925, 8⅛" 375.00
Hobnail, med gr, sb, tm, 7" 75.00
Hobnail, purple amethyst, sb, rm, 7" 125.00
Hobnail, turq, polished pontil, rm, 6½", NM 80.00
Jade frost w/Nouveau floral, ps, sm, 8" 250.00
Mary Gregory-style boy on emerald gr, vertical ribs, ps, 7⅞" 300.00
Mary Gregory-style grist mill & Bay Rum, dk amethyst, ps, 8" ...325.00
Mary Gregory-style lady & Vegederma, dk amethyst, ps, 7⅝" 400.00
Med pk-amethyst, ribbed bbl form w/mc florals, ps, sm, 7⅝" 325.00
Purple amethyst frost, ribbed, pnt floral, ps, 7⅞" 240.00
Purple amethyst w/wht pnt grist mill & Bay Rum, ps, 7⅝" 210.00
Red cased w/wht & gold Nouveau decor, ps, 8⅜", NM 425.00
Shampoo, milk glass w/mc florals, ps, rm, 7" 170.00
Spanish Lace, clear opal, polished pontil, rm, 7⅛" 90.00
Stars & Stripes, turq opal, sb, rm, 6⅞" 210.00
Yel-gr, mc water lilies, ribbed, ps, sm, 6¾" 110.00
Yel-gr crackle, 4 indents, sb, gm, metal stopper, flakes, 7¾" 125.00
Yel-gr frost w/Nouveau floral, vertical ribs, 7¾" 300.00
Yel-gr frost w/ribs, heavy mc floral, polished pontil, 7⅞" 200.00

Bitters Bottles

Jacob Pinkerton Wahoo & Calisaya Bitters..., yellow-amber, semicabin, 9⅞", NM, $475.00.

African Stomach..., yel-olive, sb, am, cooling cracks, 9⅜" 120.00
AR Thayer's Iron...Lansing MI, dk bl-aqua, sb, am, 7" 650.00
Big Bill Best..., med amber to yel-amber, sb, tm, 12" 100.00
Brown's Celebrated Indian Herb...1868, yel-amber, queen, 12" ...1,500.00
Burton's Ginger Wine..., aqua sample, sb, tm, 4⅛" 500.00
Canteen...For All Disorders...John Hart..., med bl-gr, sb, 10" ...1,450.00
CH Swain's Bourbon..., yel-amber, sb, sl cm, 9¼" 150.00
Clarke's Sherry Wine..., aqua, sb, am, 90% orig label, 8¼" 170.00
Colburg Stomach...Blood Purifier, med amber, tm, sb, 10¼" 150.00
Dr Banker's Home...NY, aqua, sb, sl cm, 9" 100.00
Dr Campbell's Scotch, golden yel-amber, strap-side, sb, 6¼" 250.00
Dr CW Roback's Stomach..., yel-amber, sb, sl cm, 10⅛", NM ...170.00
Dr Jacob's...SA Spencer...CT, aqua, open pontil, cm, 8⅜" 220.00
Dr Jas Graves Tonic...KY, aqua, sb, sl cm, semicabin, 9⅞" 325.00
Dr John Bull's Cedron...Patented, golden amber, semicabin, 10¼" 625.00
Dr John Bull's Compound Cedron..., yel-olive gr, sb, sl cm, 9⅜" ...800.00
Dr Lawrence's Wild Cherry Family..., yel-amber, sb, cm, 8½" 110.00

Dr M Smith's Stomach...KY, root beer amber, semicabin, 9½" ..500.00
Dr Planett's..., aqua, ip, sl cm, lt haze, 9¾" 825.00
Dromgoole English Female...KY, aqua, sb, tm, 8⅜" 110.00
E Bull's Luxury...Louisville KY, amber, lady's leg, 9⅛" 200.00
Edward Wilder's Stomach (5-story building), semicabin, 10⅜" ..325.00
Established 1845 Schroeder's..., amber, lady's leg, 5⅝" 300.00
German Hop Bitters 1872...MI, yel-amber, semicabin, 9⅜" 170.00
Graves & Son Tonic...KY, lt ice bl, sb, sl cm, semicabin, 10¼" .375.00
Greer's Eclipse, amber, sb, sl cm, 8¾" 170.00
Greer's Eclipse...KY, med amber, sb, am, 9⅜" 95.00
H&K Stomach Tonic, amber, sb, sl cm, ca 1880, 8¾" 125.00
Johnson's Calisaya...VT, dk reddish-puce w/amber tone, 9¾" 450.00
Ko-Hi...Koehler & Hinrichs St Paul, amber, sb, tm, 9" 240.00
Old Dr Townsend's Magic Stomach..., dk bl-aqua, sb, cm, 9¾" .825.00
Professor EE Mann's Oriental..., med amber, sb, semicabin, 10" .775.00
RL Egerton's Stomach...KY, med honey amber, sb, am, 10½" 275.00
Sazerac Aromatic...PHC&Co, med olive gr, lady's leg, 10⅛" 825.00
Schroeder's (rooster)...Louisville KY, amber, lady's leg, 4½" 450.00
Schroeder's Stomach..., golden yel-amber, sb, sl cm, 9¾", EX 190.00
Schroeder's...Louisville KY, amber, lady's leg, 5¼" 300.00
Schroeder's...Louisville KY, golden amber, lady's leg, 12" 300.00
Snyder's Celebrated...Cordial...PA, amber, sb, dbl cm, 9⅝" 130.00
St Drake's 1860 Plant'n X Pat 1862, copper puce, 6-log, 10" 210.00
St Drake's 1860 Plant'n X Pat 1862, smoky yel-olive, 6-log, 10" ...775.00
St Drake's 1860 Plant'n X Pat 1862, strawberry puce, 6-log, 10" ...275.00
Warner's Safe Tonic...NY, amber, sb, dbl cm, potstone, 9½" 275.00

Black Glass Bottles

Many early European and American bottles are deep, dark green, or amber in color. Collectors refer to such coloring as black glass. Before held to light, the glass is so dark it appears to be black.

Apothecary, dk olive-amber, ps, rm, gold-flashed clear lid, 12½" ..325.00
Kidney shape, olive gr, ps, am, 7⅜" 525.00
Mallet, dk olive-amber, ps, string lip, dull, 8⅛" 110.00
Onion, yel olive-amber, ps, am, 1720-30, magnum, 11x6¾" ...1,200.00
Pancake onion, olive-amber, ps, am, sm chip, 5½x5¾" 275.00
Seal: John Winn Jr, dk olive-amber, ps, am, b3m, 8⅞" 160.00
Seal: JW Boot, olive-amber, ps, am, squatty, 7¾" 250.00
Seal: SW 1816, olive gr, cylindrical, appl string rim, 12" 300.00

Blown Glass Bottles and Flasks

Club, aqua, 16 vertical ribs, ps, am w/pour spout, 8⅛" 160.00
Club, aqua, 24 right-swirl ribs, ps, rm, 7⅞" 100.00
Ludlow, olive gr, am, 9" 150.00
Pitkin flask, med olive gr, 36 broken swirl ribs, 5⅛" 350.00
Storage, bl-aqua, ps on pointed kick-up base, wide rm, 10½" 80.00
Storage, lt bl-gr, ps, wide dbl folded rim, bubbles, 13½" 90.00

Cologne, Perfume, and Toilet Water Bottles

Bl to clear, cut/polished panels, clear spear-point top, 6" 95.00
Bl-gray opaque, column on ped, ps, tm, 8½" 400.00
Cobalt, 8-sided, waisted, fm, sb, 5⅞" 375.00
Cranberry w/gold leaves, matching stopper, 6x3" 165.00
Double-ended, teal gr, 2 cylindrical necks, hex body, 2⅞" 60.00
Fiery opal, hexagonal, pewter cap, 2¾" 20.00
Lav & wht striated, 8-sided, waisted, pewter cap, 2½" 170.00
Loop, golden amber, flanged lip, polished ps, 4" 90.00
Lt amethyst, 12-sided, thick tm, sb, 9½" 375.00
Monument, cobalt w/EX label, rm, sb, 6½" 725.00
Monument, lav opal, beaded urn on dolphin stem, ps, 4¾" 400.00

Napoleon on ped w/falcon & wreaths, bl opaque fiery opal, 5" ..**2,350.00**
Poodle on hassock figural, fiery opal milk glass, ps, 7" **750.00**
Sea horse w/sm curled base, clear, ps, 2½" **25.00**
Stars & Stripes, milk glass, sb, fm, 7½" **100.00**
Steel bl to med sapphire bl, 12-sided, fm, sb, 6⅜" **140.00**
Turq opal, tapered cylinder, rm, rough pontil, 8½" **170.00**
8-panel, cobalt, waisted, rm, rough pontil, 7⅛" **600.00**
8-panel, flattened flanged lip & pontil, 2⅜" **50.00**
8-rib Pillar Mold, canary, flanged lip, polished pontil, 6" **400.00**
12-panel, aqua, rm, ps, 4¾" **60.00**
12-panel, cobalt bl, rm, sb, 6¼" **225.00**
12-panel, emerald gr, flanged lip, sb, 7½" **275.00**
12-panel, wht opal opaque, flattened flanged lip, sb, 5½" **900.00**
20-panel, teal gr, flattened flanged lip, sb, 4" **150.00**

Commercial Perfume Bottles

Asuma, Coty, frosted ball w/emb flowers, 2¼", +EX box **500.00**
Bouquet de Faune, Guerlain, frosted urn w/emb decor, 4¼" **835.00**
Chantilly, Houbigant, gold metal ball shape, 1¼", +box **55.00**
Coq d'Or, Guerlain, gold bow-tie form, Baccarat, 2⅛" **470.00**
Dans La Nuit, Worth, bl ball, crescent stopper, 1¾" **65.00**
Diorissimo, C Dior, gold metal encased, flacon, 2¼", MIB **66.00**
Ecusson, Jean d'Albret, horse medallion, gold cap, 1¾", MIB **165.00**
Ellen's Secret, Deleith, pressed to resemble Czech cut, 7" **55.00**
Fringed Orchis/Misu, M Porter, gold caps, 1⅛", pr in pouch **145.00**
Gardenia, Charbet, rectangular, 5", MIB **65.00**
Gerlain Misouko, Baccarat, orig label, 4x2½" **65.00**
Incanto, Simonato, enameled crown, gold label, 1950s, MIB **230.00**
Indescret, Lucien Lelong, octagon, gold label, blk cap, 2", MIB .**120.00**
Indigo, Dorothy Gray, clear/frosted sq, figural stopper, 3½" **275.00**
Le Pois de Senteur, Corday, octagon, Baccarat, 4¾" **145.00**
Nuit de Longchamps, Lubin, plume stopper, empty, 6" **155.00**
Old Paris, Legrain, lady in cape & muff, 6¼" **600.00**
On the Wind, Bourjois, orange cap, gold label, 1¾" **145.00**
Renommee, Sophie Nerval, gold label, fan stopper, 4¼", MIB ...**100.00**
Replique, Raphael Paris, orig seal & label, 5x2½" **65.00**
Rose d'Ispahan, Coryse, clear/frosted urn, red traces, 5" **210.00**
Souvenir d'un Soir, Mary Chess, clear/frosted fountain, 3½" **715.00**
Strategy, Mary Chess, as knight chess pc, empty, 4¼", MIB **75.00**
Violette, Houbigant, oval, gold stopper, 2¾", +box **77.00**

Dairy Bottles

Athletes Train on Milk & basketball player, blk pyro, rnd, qt **20.00**
Balance Your Diet & seal, red pyro, rnd, qt **40.00**
Borden's & Elsie, red pyro, sq, lg cap, ½-pt **12.00**
Buy More War Bonds, red pyro, rnd, qt **35.00**
Cloverleaf, Stockton CA, red pyro, modern top, qt **28.00**
Cloverleaf Dairy...OH & barn, gr pyro, rnd, qt **35.00**
Country Fresh Milk & milkmaid, gr pyro, rnd, qt **25.00**
Crane Dairy, Buy War Bonds & Stamps..., red pyro, rnd, qt **45.00**
Heiss & Sons Dairy & scene, orange pyro, rnd, qt **12.50**
Indiana Dairy...PA, blk pyro on milk glass, wide mouth, pt **35.00**
It's Pure-We're Sure & child w/bottle, 2-color pyro, qt **25.00**
Old King Cole w/verse, red pyro, rnd, qt **50.00**
Schwenk Dairy, Southampton LI, maroon pyro, tall, qt **12.00**
Sparta Dairy w/poem, red pyro, rnd, qt **50.00**
Sunnydale Farms & cow, red & blk pyro, rnd, qt **45.00**
Waynesburg Sanitary Dairy, red pyro, wide mouth, pt **20.00**

Figural Bottles

African boy on bbl holding bottle, amber, Deponiert, 9" **1,750.00**

Bear, deep amber, appl snout, sb, 1875-85, 10¾" **950.00**
Clown, frosted clear, ps, gm, clear head stopper, 12⅞" **50.00**
Coal chunk, blk amethyst, sb, gm, metal screw cap, Am, 3½" **80.00**
Columbus, frosted clear bust lid on column, 1892, 6½", NM **325.00**
Columbus on column, milk glass w/metal statue, 18⅛" **600.00**
Dice (single), fiery wht opal, sb, gm, w/stopper, 5⅛" **140.00**
Ear of corn, clear, sb, tm, 1880-1910, 10¾" **95.00**
Flamingo, clear, hand blown, Apricot Liqueur label, 20th C, 5¾" ..**50.00**
Grant's Tomb, milk glass, sb, gm, no closure, 8" **150.00**

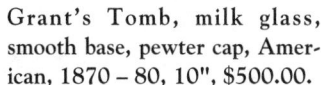
Grant's Tomb, milk glass, smooth base, pewter cap, American, 1870 – 80, 10", $500.00.

Hand holding bottle, ice bl, Depose emb near base, ps, 9⅝" **60.00**
Hand holding dagger, frosted turq, Depose S at base, 11¼" **145.00**
Hand holding dagger, gr, sb, ca 1910-20, 14½" **75.00**
John Bull on stump, golden amber, cm, sb, 12" **270.00**
La Tsarine, milk glass, La Tsarine Bonbons..., tin lid, 13⅛" **375.00**
Life preserver, frosted clear w/blk enameling, sb, 6¾" **35.00**
Lorraine DD Depose DD, lady, milk glass, sb, 1900-15, 13" **500.00**
Milk bottles in basket, milk glass, sb, tm, 3⅞" **85.00**
Nude in foliage, clear, sb, tm, Am, 1890-1910, 13⅜" **30.00**
Pickle, lt bl-gr, rm, ca 1885-1900, 4½" L **130.00**
Pig, clear, sb, tm, Am, ca 1880-90, 9½" L **230.00**
Polar bear & lamppost, milk glass, Depose, 11" **600.00**
Policeman, cobalt, orig pnt, nightstick stopper, 18⅝" **110.00**
Rabbit, clear, sitting, sb, tm, 1880-1910, 9" **95.00**
Revolver, amber, Dmn Revolver on bk of hdl, metal screw cap, 8" ..**70.00**
Shoe, turq, Depose across heel, ps, tm, 10¾", EX **70.00**
Wise man, frosted clear bust, base opening, tin lid, 11⅛" **550.00**

Flasks

All Seeing Eye/Bent Arm Inside Star, GIV-143, yel-amber, 1-pt ..**160.00**
Columbia w/Liberty Cap/Eagle, GI/121, aqua, ps, sm, 1-pt, NM ..**150.00**
Corn for World/Ear of Corn, GVI-6, aqua, ps, sm, 1-pt **220.00**
Cornucopia/Urn, GIII-16, med bl-gr, ip, sm, 1-pt **375.00**
Eagle w/HS/Masonic, GIV-2, dk olive gr, am, bubbly, 7½" **3,025.00**
Eagle/Cornucopia, GII-73, dk olive gr, 6¾", 1-pt **140.00**
Eagle/Dyottville GW Philada, GII-38, aqua, ps, sm, 1-pt **300.00**
Eagle/HS & Masonic, GIV-2, dk olive gr, am, 7⅜", 1-pt **2,365.00**
Eagle/Indian, GII-142, dk bl-aqua, sb, am, 1-qt, NM **190.00**
Eagle/Masonic Arch, GIV-1, lt bl-gr, ps, sm, 1-pt **230.00**
Eagle/Masonic Arch, GIV-18, med olive-amber, sm, 1-pt **130.00**
Eagle/Masonic Arch, GIV-24, yel olive-amber, ps, sm, 1-pt **120.00**
Eagle/Masonic Arch, GIV-32, golden amber, ps, sm, 1-pt **475.00**
Eagle/Prospector, GII-21, dk bl-aqua, sb, am, 1-pt **130.00**
For Pike's Peak Prospector/Eagle, GXI-8, dk bl-aqua, sb, 1-qt **85.00**
Grant/Eagle, GI-79a, aqua, sb, am, flake/stain, 1-pt **80.00**
Hunter/Hounds, GXIII-7, aqua, ps, dbl cm, bubbles, 1-pt **180.00**
Jenny Lind/Glass House, GI-102, dk bl-aqua, ps, calabash **160.00**
Jenny Lind/Glass Works, GI-99, aqua, ip, sl cm, calabash **90.00**
Lowell RR Horse Drawn Cart/Eagle, GV-10, yel-olive gr, ps, ½-pt ..**140.00**

Ringold/Taylor, GI-72, smoky amethystine tint, ps, sm, 1-pt 400.00
Scroll, GIX-10b, med amber, sp, sm, 1-pt 750.00
Scroll, GIX-34, golden amber, ½-pt 400.00
Sheaf of Wheat/Cluster of Grapes, GX-3, lt apple-gr, ½-pt 350.00
Sheaf of Wheat/Westford, GXIII-35, dk root beer-amber, 1-pt ..110.00
Soldier/Daisy, GXIII-15, dk bl-aqua, ip, sl cm, calabash 275.00
Success to RR/Horse Pulling Cart, GV-5, med to dk gr, 1-pt 350.00
Success to RR/Success to RR, GV-3, olive-amber, ps, stain, 7" 200.00
Sunburst, GVIII-16, med yel-olive gr, ps, sm, ½-pt 275.00
Sunburst Keen/Sunburst P&W, GVIII-9, yel-amber, ps, 5⅞" 235.00
Traveler's Companion/Railroad Guide, GXIV-27, lt bl-gr, ps, ½-pt .160.00
Washington/Eagle, GI-1, gr-aqua, ps, sm, 1-pt 230.00
Washington/Tree, GI-36, aqua, open pontil, cm, calabash 150.00
Willington/Eagle, GII-61, olive gr, sb, am, bubbles, 1-qt 130.00
Willington/Eagle, GII-63, olive gr, sb, sm, 6⅛" 125.00

Food Bottles and Jars

Blueberry, med gr, 10 lobed flutes, sb, cm, 11" 160.00
Peppersauce, cathedral, dk aqua, open pontil, am, 8⅜" 425.00
Pickle, aqua, tm, mc label: Arrow Brand Pickles, 7¼" 150.00
Pickle, cathedral, dk emerald gr, ip, rm, 11¾" 725.00
Pickle, cathedral, med emerald gr, open ps, rm, 9¼" 525.00
Pickle, med emerald gr, sq w/beveled edges, ip, 11¾" 625.00
Pickle, Skilton Foote...Bunker Hill, yel-amber, lighthouse, 11" ..170.00
Pickle, W Numsen & Son..., aqua, open pontil, rm, whittled, 10½" ..650.00

Ink Bottles

Carter's, medium sapphire blue, six-sided, multicolor labels, original red-painted wood cap, 3", M, $200.00.

Carter's, cathedral, cobalt, st, tm, NM label, 6¼" 240.00
J&IEM, turtle, lt citron, lt haze, 1870s, 1¾" 300.00
Log cabin, sb, gm, 1865-1875, 3⅛" 800.00
Teakettle, blk amethyst bbl w/gold highlights, sb, gm, 2⅛" 500.00
Teakettle, cobalt, 8-sided, gilt traces, sb, sm, haze, 2⅜" 400.00
Teakettle, cobalt w/emb florals, sb, gm, 2" 650.00
Teakettle, gr fiery opal, 8-sided, bl & gold floral, sb, 2⅝" 325.00
Teakettle, lav opaque, pear shape w/ribs, sb, gm, 2⅜" 350.00
Teakettle, med purple amethyst, bbl form, sb, sm, 2¼" 1,500.00
Teakettle, mint gr opaque, pear shape w/ribs, sb, sm, 2½", NM .350.00
Teakettle, robin's egg bl fiery opal, 8-sided, sb, stain, 2⅝" 400.00
Teakettle, sapphire bl, bbl form, sb, gm, flake, 2⅛" 600.00
Teakettle, sapphire bl, beehive form, star-topped dome, 2¼" ..1,050.00
Teakettle, wht fiery opal, pear shape w/ribs, sb, sm, 2¾", NM 300.00
Turtle, lt yel-apple gr, sb, tm, 1⅝" 225.00
Umbrella, lt to med emerald gr, 8-sided, open pontil, rm, 2½" 80.00
Umbrella, med root beer-amber, 8-sided, NM label, 2¼" 400.00

Medicine Bottles

Warner's bottles listed below are not American versions and so are valued higher than those from Rochester, New York.

AJ White/The Shaker Family Pills..., amber, sb, tm, label, 2¼" .120.00
Allan's Anti-Fat Botanic, dk teal bl (rare), sb, am, haze, 7⅝" 400.00
Bettison's English Horse Liniment..., open pontil, rm, 4" 375.00
Burkhardt's Fever & Ague Remedy Louisville KY, aqua, ps, 6¾" ..375.00
Cocoa Nut Oil C Toppan, aqua, ps, disc am, 6" 130.00
Costar's NY, smoky pinkish puce, sb, rm, 4", NM 80.00
Daily's Pain Extractor Louisville, deep bl-aqua, ps, 4⅝" 75.00
Dr C Crooke's Never Fail..., aqua, ps, rm, 4¼" 300.00
Dr Grave's Worm Syrup Louisville KY, tm, semicabin, 4½" 95.00
Dr J Blackman's Genuine...Balsam, smoky clear, 8-sided, 5⅝" 60.00
Dr Lane's Headache & Liver Regulator..., aqua, ps, 5⅛", EX 55.00
Dr NM Nutt's Cough Mixture, aqua, rectangular, open pontil, 6" ...210.00
Dr Pinkham's Emmenagogue, dk aqua, open pontil, am, 5¾" 90.00
Dr WW Brown Louisville, bl-aqua, ps, rm, sm stain, 4½" 35.00
Duff Gordon Sherry Medical..., dk olive-amber, sb, 9¾" 325.00
Guide to Health Avery & Co, med amber, book form, 9¼" 300.00
GW Merchant Chemist Lockport NY, Lockport gr, sb, cm, 7¼" ..200.00
GW Merchant Lockport NY, dk bl-gr, ps, sl cm, 5¼" 200.00
Mother's Worm Syrup (5-story building), sb, tm, semicabin, 4¾" ...130.00
Rohrer's Expectoral Wild Cherry...PA, golden amber, sb, 10⅝" 300.00
Schenck's Seaweed Tonic, bl-aqua, ip, sl dbl cm, haze, 8⅞" 150.00
Smith's Green Mtn Renovator..., yel olive-amber, ps, am, 7" ...1,300.00
Stern's Chemist (mortar & pestle) Detroit, cobalt, sb, tm, 4½" .180.00
Strong Cobb & Co...Cleveland O, cobalt, sb, am, 10⅜" 140.00
Sutcliffe & Hughes Druggists Louisville KY, gr-aqua, ip, 10¼" ..160.00
Tippecanoe/HH Warner & Co, amber log, sb, am, 9⅛", NM 70.00
Warner's Safe Cure (safe) Frankfort A/M, yel-olive gr, sb, 9" 235.00
Warner's Safe Rheumatic...London, yel-topaz, sb, 9¼" 170.00
Warner's Safe Rheumatic...Melbourne, red-amber, sb, 9½" 160.00
Wilder's Vermifuge, bl-aqua, open pontil, rm, lt stain, 6" 160.00

Mineral Water and Soda Bottles

Adirondack Spring Co...NY, dk emerald gr, sb, dbl cm, 9⅜" ..1,000.00
AW Cudworth & Co San Francisco CA, gr, ip, am, haze, 7¼" ..100.00
Blount Springs...Sulphur Water..., cobalt, sb, am, 9" 170.00
Boardman, dk sapphire bl, red ip, am, lt haze, 7¼" 190.00
CA...Works F Hicken SF (eagle/snake), aqua, sb, am, 7" 250.00
Clark & White/NY, med olive gr, ps, sl dbl cm, 9½" 90.00
Congress Spring...NY/Congress Water, yel-gr, sb, sl dbl cm, 8" 55.00
Crystal...Water Co Patented Nov 12 1872, bright aqua, sb, 7¾" 50.00
Fred Goosmann...Cincinnati..., bl-aqua, 10-sided, ip, am, 7¼" ..350.00
Geo Eagle (in banner w/twisted ribs allover), bl-gr, ip, 7" 575.00
Herve & Carbon, aqua, sb, am, hutch, 6⅞" 60.00
Massena Spring (monogram) Water, golden amber, sb, tm, 9¾" ...120.00
Matthews HM NY Soda... & Apparatus, med emerald gr, ps, 7⅞" 350.00
Missisquoi A Springs, yel-lime gr, sb, sl dbl cm, chip, 9⅜" 125.00
Napa Soda/Natural...TAW, emerald gr, sb, am, lt haze, 7¼" 110.00
Phoenix Bottling Works Phoenix AZ, dk bl, hutch, 6⅞" 75.00
Poland Water...H Ricker & Sons..., aqua, man figural, 11⅛" 150.00
Poland Water/Poland Mineral...PMSW..., aqua, Moses figural, sb, 11" .165.00
Strumatic Mineral...N PSMCo, dk red-amber, st, sl dbl cm, 7⅜" 500.00
Syracuse Springs...NY, golden yel-amber, sb, sl cm, 7¾" 400.00
Syracuse Springs/Excelsior, dk red-amber, sb, sl dbl cm, 7⅞", NM ..130.00
Victoria Springs...Canada, dk bl-aqua, sb, sl dbl cm, 9½" 850.00
Washington Spring Saratoga NY, emerald gr, sb, sl dbl cm, 8" ...200.00
WHH Chicago IL, lt sapphire bl, fluted panels, 7" 60.00

Poison Bottles

Chester A Baker/Boston, cobalt, irregular hexagon, sb, 4⅛" 250.00
Dmn & lattice pattern, cobalt, sb, tm, Poison stopper, 5⅛" 110.00
Jacob's Bichloride Tablet, skull & Xbones, honey amber, 2¼" ...850.00
Lattice & Dmn pattern, cobalt, sb, tm, Poison stopper, 11¼" 425.00

Owl Drug Co (owl/mortar & pestle) San Francisco, lt teal, 9½" ...**180.00**
Poison, cobalt coffin, sb, tm, M orig label, 3⅜" **200.00**
Poison (skull & Xbones)/Demert Drug..., cobalt, sb, tm, 4¼" **1,500.00**
Poison (star, skull & Xbones)/Poison, yel-amber, sb, tm, 4¾" **675.00**
Poison Not To Be Taken, cobalt, sb, tm, 13¼" **170.00**
Poison Not To Be Taken/The Martin..., aqua, sb, tm, 6½" **160.00**
Poison-Pat Appl'd For, med cobalt skull form, tm, flakes, 4¼" ..**1,150.00**
Poison/Owl Drug Co (mortar & pestle)/TODCo..., cobalt, sb, 9⅝" **550.00**
Poison/Poison, med bl cobalt coffin, sb, w/label, 7⅝" **875.00**
Poison/Poison, triangular, sb, tm, NM label, 5½" **165.00**
Poison/The Martin Poison Bottle Patented, aqua, sb, 4½" **130.00**
Registered No 336907 emb on cobalt submarine form, sb, 3x4⅝" ...**400.00**

Sarsaparilla Bottles

John Bull Extract of...KY, aqua, open pontil, 6½" **250.00**
John Bull Extract of...KY, bl-aqua, open pontil, sl cm, 9¾" **125.00**
Thos A Hurley Compound Syrup...KY, bl-aqua, ip, am, 9½" **825.00**
Turner's...Buffalo NY, dk bl-aqua, sb, sl cm, potstone, 12¼" **475.00**

Spirits Bottles

AM Bininger...NY, frost gr jug, sb, appl hdl, 7¾" **1,250.00**
Bear Grass (bear head) Bourbon..., clear, sb, tm, 10⅞" **220.00**
Bininger's Peep-o-Day...NY, yel-amber, sb, am, 7¾" **350.00**
Davy Crockett...Pure Old Bourbon, deep amber, sb, tm, 12⅜" ...**100.00**
Hard To Beat Extra...Bourbon Loew Bros..., amethystine, 12" ...**800.00**
I Got My Fill (drunk/dog), pumkin-seed flask, lt amethyst, 6⅜" ...**235.00**
JF Cutter Extra Trade Old Bourbon, med yel-amber, 1-pt, 7⅜" ..**700.00**
Jos Melczer...Liquor Dealers...CA, clear, st, tm, 11¾" **65.00**
Kolberg & Cavagnaro Stockton CA, clear, sb, tm, 11½" **80.00**
Naber, Alfs & Brune...San Francisco, amber, sb, am, 11½" **1,350.00**
Oak Valley Distilling (griffin in triangle), clear, sb, tm, 10" **60.00**
Old Bourbon Castle Whiskey..., bright yel-amber, sb, 12" **350.00**
Rothenberg Co Old Judge..., med yel-amber to red-amber, sb, 11½" ..**80.00**
Trade Mark N Van Bergen (horse) Gold Dust..., aqua, sb, 12" ...**750.00**
Wm H Spears...Pioneer Whiskey...SF, clear, sb, tm, 11¾" **325.00**
Wm H Spears...Whiskey (bear)..., med orange-amber, sb, crude, 12" ..**1,650.00**
Wolf Wreden & Co San Francisco, med yel-amber, sb, tm, 11¾" ...**300.00**

Miscellaneous

Lavender Salts, Goetting & Co, See California Perfume Co
Pure Food Cigar Mfg By Hettermann Bros..., yel-amber, sb, 6⅝" ..**140.00**

Boxes

Boxes have been used by civilized man since ancient Egypt and Rome. Down through the centuries, specifically designed containers have been made from every conceivable material. Precious metals, papier-mache, Battersea, Oriental lacquer, and wood have held riches from the treasuries of kings, snuff for the fashionable set of the last century, China tea, and countless other commodities. In the following descriptions, when only one dimension is given, it is length. See also Toleware; specific manufacturers.

Bentwood, old dk gr pnt, 11x15¼" **385.00**
Bentwood, oval Shaker type, solid wood bottom, 4-finger, 4x3x2" ..**60.00**
Bentwood, 2 tiered compartments, orig dk pnt w/stencil, 8x12" .**415.00**
Bible, pine w/alligatored red, turnip ft, dvtl, 17" **880.00**
Bible, walnut w/brass mts, dvtl, 19th C, 7½x14⅛x10⅝" **125.00**
Bird's-eye maple & walnut w/ivory inlay, dvtl, 13" **195.00**
Book, gr-pnt pine w/gilt, silk lining, 11½" **165.00**

Book stack form, cvd/pnt wood, w/secret lock, 1910s, 9½" **200.00**
Bride's, couple pnt on pine, laced seams, Germany, 18" **550.00**
Burl, elongated oval, some age, 11⅛" **195.00**
Butternut, appl base & lid moldings, bkwards dvtls, 12" **100.00**
Candle, birch w/old blk pnt, dvtl drw, 23x12x6" **935.00**
Candle, pine/poplar w/worn yel pnt, slide lid, 12" **210.00**
Candle, soft wood, mustard & red pnt, slide lid, 9¼x12⅜", EX ..**600.00**
Candle, soft wood, orange red PA pnt, 1800s, 4x12x5⅝" **525.00**
Cherry, sm ogee ft, brass escutcheon, 10" **225.00**
Chip cvd, wooden pegs, sliding lid, 2¾x3½" dia **155.00**
Document, leather-covered w/brass studs, 1900s, 11½" **110.00**
Dome top, pine w/wallpaper covering, 1812 newspaper lining, 9" ..**250.00**
Dome top, poplar w/old brn grpt, dvtl & nailed, 8" **330.00**

Dues box, folk-carved and applied doves and acorns, slide lid, probably Pennsylvania, ca 1800s, EX, $850.00.

Figured mahog w/exotic wood inlay, hidden drw, rpr, 12" **255.00**
Figured walnut veneer w/corner banding, dtd 1856, 11" **200.00**
Glass, cobalt w/HP birds & flowers, hinged, 3¾x4⅜" dia **245.00**
Glass, emerald gr w/HP flowers & gold, 3⅝x5⅛" **175.00**
Glass, lime gr w/HP flowers & gold, 4⅝x4" dia **195.00**
Grpt on pine, sliding lid, 4¾x5⅝x6⅞" **275.00**
Hat, mc flower paper, wooden base, oval, 9x5½" **500.00**
Hat, sponged-pnt softwood, bentwood bands, 1800s, 12x17x15" ..**2,000.00**
Knife, English Hplwht mahog veneer, hinged slant lid, 14½" **250.00**
Mahog w/lt wood inlay, locking mechanism, 10" **150.00**
PA German wallpaper on cb, w/lid, dtd 1831, 2⅛x2¾" dia **400.00**
PA German wallpaper on cb w/wood top & int, 1820s, 4¼x5¾" ..**2,450.00**
Pine, old red finish, brass bail hdl & lock, dvtl, 13⅜" **165.00**
Pine w/mc pnt houses, wire hinges, partial hasp, 4¾" **275.00**
Poplar, orig red flame grpt, compartments, dvtl, 14" **220.00**
Sewing, walnut w/maple inlay star, dvtl, sq nails, 9" **250.00**
Spice, bentwood, rnd w/tin bands, 8 containers inside **375.00**
Spice, tin, oblong, w/6 containers **85.00**
Toiletry, rosewood, brass bound, fitted int, English, EX **300.00**
Utensil, pnt soft wood, dvtl, compartments, 1800s, 8x14x9", EX ..**1,550.00**
Utensil, soft wood, PA mustard pnt, nailed, 19th C, 5x12x8½" .**325.00**
Writing, Country pine, red pnt w/blk stripes, 15½" **150.00**
Writing, red-pnt soft wood, slant lid, gallery, 9½x10½x8" **1,200.00**

Boyd Crystal Art Glass

This small but productive glasshouse has more than 300 molds and has produced more than 350 colors. They are very collector oriented and alter their mark every five years. In 1978 they used a simple B in a diamond. Today, with three changes behind them, the original mark is now emcompassed by three additional lines, and 1998 should see yet another change. Vaseline collectors have increased in number, and many of Boyd's Vaseline pieces (variations include Firefly and Citron) are increasing in value rapidly. Many of Boyd's colors — Golden Delight, Peridot, Pippin Green, and others — fluoresce under black light.

In the near future, watch for price increases for Joey the Horse, as the mold has recently been converted to a carousel horse, preventing further production. Li'l Joe the Horse and Sammy Squirrel have met the same fate and are now very limited. As always, satins and hand-painted pieces are commanding 10 – 50% more than the same items in the regular finish. (N) indicates new for 1997; (R) indicates retired. Our advisor for this category is Joyce Pringle; she is listed in the Directory under Texas.

Airplane, Banana Cream	17.50
Airplane, Carnival Red	20.00
Airplane, Vaseline	32.50
Amish Couple, Capri Blue (N)	14.00
Angel, Green Bouquet	18.00
Angel, Spring Surprise	18.00
Angel, Vaseline	28.00
Angel, Vaseline Carnival	21.00
Artie the Penguin, Banana Cream (R)	8.00
Artie the Penguin, Cobalt (R)	12.50
Artie the Penguin, Vaseline (R)	18.00
Bow Slipper, Capri Blue	9.00
Bow Slipper, Rubina	18.00
Boyd Special, HP Christmas Train, 1995	110.00
Boyd Special, 6-pc Train, Cobalt	85.00
Boyd Special, 6-pc Train, Nile Green	58.00
Brian Bunny, Cashmire Pink (R)	9.25
Brian Bunny, Sunflower (R)	8.50
Cat Slipper, Cobalt	20.00
Cat Slipper, Spinnaker Blue	12.00
Chick Salt, Mirage	7.00
Chick Salt, Pocono Blue	21.00
Chick Salt, Ruby Gold	130.00
Chick Salt, Silver Fox	7.75
Duck Salt, Classic Black	8.00
Elizabeth Doll, Classic Black (R)	8.50
Elizabeth Doll, Crown Tuscan Carnival (R)	9.50
Hand Dish, Lemon Ice	12.50
Hand Dish, Vaseline Carnival	15.00
JB Scotty, Buckeye (R)	45.00
JB Scotty, Cashmire Pink (R)	15.00
JB Scotty, Cobalt (R)	50.00
JB Scotty, Cobalt Carnival (R)	20.00
JB Scotty, Cornsilk (R)	10.00
JB Scotty, Mirage (R)	10.00
JB Scotty, Ruby (R)	70.00
JB Scotty, Spring Surprise (R)	45.00
JB Scotty, Sunburst (R)	18.00
Jeremy Frog, Nile Green	9.50
Jeremy Frog, Sunkist Carnival	9.00
Jeremy Frog, Vanilla Corral	8.50
Joey the Horse, Caramel (R)	27.50
Joey the Horse, Chocolate (R)	28.50
Joey the Horse, Cobalt Carnival (R)	50.00
Joey the Horse, Persimmon (R)	22.50
Joey the Horse, Zak Boyd Slag (R)	18.00
Kewpie, Cobalt (N)	8.00
Kewpie, Vaseline (N)	10.00
Kitten on a Pillow, Delphinium (R)	18.00
Kitten on a Pillow, Firefly (R)	32.00
Kitten on a Pillow, Golden Delight (R)	20.00
Lil Joe, Cobalt (R)	12.50

Lil Joe, Country Red (R)	10.00
Lil Luck the Unicorn, Orange Calico (R)	9.00
Lil Luck the Unicorn, Rosewood (R)	8.50
Louise Doll, Delphinium (R)	20.00
Louise Doll, Ice Blue (R)	65.00
Louise Doll, Sandpiper (R)	18.00
Lucky the Unicorn, Bermuda	8.00
Lucky the Unicorn, Peridot	15.00
Mabel the Cow, Vaseline (N)	10.50
Owl, Firefly	22.00
Owl, Katydid	10.00
Owl Bell, Classic Black Slag	11.00
Owl Bell, Pippen Green	10.00
Patrick the Balloon Bear, Enchantment (R)	28.00
Patrick the Balloon Bear, Spinnaker Blue (R)	10.00
Salt, Bunny, Banana Cream	8.00
Salt, Bunny, Confetti	35.00
Salt, Turkey, Cobalt	11.00
Salt, Turkey, Sunkist Carnival	11.00
Salt Signature Series, Chick, Cobalt (N)	7.50
Salt Signature Series, Chick, Vaseline (N)	8.00
Sammy Squirrel, Alexandrite (R)	15.00
Sammy Squirrel, Crown Tuscan Carnival (R)	12.00
Sammy Squirrel, Vaseline (R)	18.00
Sonny the Gorilla, Chocolate (N)	8.00
Sonny the Gorilla, Vaseline (N)	10.50
Willie the Mouse, Buckeye	7.00
Willie the Mouse, Primrose	7.00
Zak the Elephant, Alice Blue	22.50
Zak the Elephant, Flame	50.00
Zak the Elephant, Sunburst (R)	18.00

Bradley and Hubbard

The Bradley and Hubbard Mfg. Company was a firm which produced metal accessories for the home. They operated from about 1860 until the early part of this century, and their products reflected both the Arts and Crafts and Art Nouveau influence. Their logo was a device with a triangular arrangement of the company name containing a smaller triangle and an Aladdin lamp.

Lamps

Aquarium lamp, reverse painted, framed by nautical gilt metal holder, faux marble base, 11x14", $2,875.00.

Banquet, HP flowers on pk globe; fancy rtcl base, 27"	650.00
Banquet, HP holly globe; cast metal & brass mk fr, 31"	500.00
Banquet, HP magnolia globe; wht onyx base, gilt cast fr, 30"	450.00
Gone w/the Wind, chrysanthemum globe & base, electrified, 22"	400.00
Hanging, HP lilies & leaves, ornate mk fr	825.00
Piano, mesh decor shade; ornate base/font holder, 52" w/o shade	200.00
Table, oil lamp style, 6-sided metal & glass shade, 11½", VG	700.00

Table, 20" ldgl honeycomb dome shade; emb brass mk std, 22", EX **1,600.00**

Miscellaneous

Bookends, Egyptian man-faced lion & columns, bronze, 4¾" **100.00**
Bookends, emb ship, bronze/gold/silver, 5⅛x4⅛" **200.00**
Bookends, rural scene relief, CI, brass finish, 3½x5" **55.00**
Bookends, Shakespeare, bronzed, pr **140.00**
Inkwell, Nouveau foliage, brass, single ornate glass bottle **195.00**
Inkwell, stag & hound figural, brass w/2 glass bottles **325.00**
Inkwell, winged lions, marbleized enamel **385.00**
Letter holder, ornate pierced brass, 7x10x6" **265.00**
Letter holder, stag & hounds, brass, mk, 6½x9x5" **210.00**
Smoking stand, brass, stepped shelf w/tray & match holder, 25½" ..**250.00**
Thermometer, cherub, ornate, easel bk, 13" **225.00**
Thermometer, lady's head, ornate, easel bk, 11" **195.00**

Brass

Brass is an alloy consisting essentially of copper and zinc in variable proportions. It is a medium that has been used for both utilitarian items and objects of artistic merit. Today, with the inflated price of copper and the popular use of plastics, almost anything made of brass is collectible, though right now, at least, there is little interest in items made after 1950. Our advisor, Mary Frank Gaston, has compiled a lovely book, *Antique Brass and Copper*, with full-color photos. See also Candlesticks.

Bowl, rnd bottom, wrought-iron rim hdls, 10¾" **40.00**
Candle snuffer, scissors style, 6⅛", w/9¼x4" brass tray **65.00**
Clock jack, w/CI spit wheel, Geo Salter, working, 17" **440.00**
Kettle, Am Brass Kettle Mfg, iron bail hdl, ca 1950s, 15" dia **60.00**
Kettle, Am Brass Kettle Mfg, iron bail hdl, 9x13½" **100.00**
Kettle, flared to rolled rim, CI hdl, 1850s, 5½x9¾" **75.00**
Kettle, rolled rim, arched iron hdl, 13" dia, +wrought tripod **110.00**
Kettle, rolled rim, stationary arched iron hdl, 6⅝x14½" **50.00**
Kettle, rolled rim, wrought-iron hdl mts & bail hdl, 9x14" **150.00**
Kettle, spun, iron bail hdl, dents, 14" dia **60.00**
Kettle shelf, rtcl top & apron, English, 14x12½" **250.00**
Ladle, skimmer; flattened hooked hdl, ca 1800, 2" dia, 9" L **475.00**
Ladle, skimmer; wrought-iron hdl, J Schmidt, 1842, 20" **250.00**
Ladle, tasting; wrought-iron hdl, 1¾" dia, 8½" L **250.00**
Ladle, tasting; wrought-iron hdl w/hook, 1¾" dia, 6½" hdl **400.00**
Ladle, 4¾" dia w/17" wrouht-iron hdl **30.00**
Plant stand, gilt brass w/onyx inserts, 31" **200.00**
Plate, pierced band w/griffin heads, toothed rim, 10¼" **36.00**
Pot, rnd bottom w/tripod ft, 7⅝x11½" dia+12" hdl **55.00**
Table, tea; tripod base, rtcl top w/horse, 8½x8" **140.00**
Tazza, baluster stem, rtcl top, 10x9" **140.00**
Teapot, tin lined, copper rivets, gooseneck spout, 8½" **225.00**
Tray, desk; emb decor, ftd, w/2 inkwells & letter rack **550.00**
Tray, nude w/flowing hair at rim, 3¾x7½" **125.00**
Tray, smoking; 3 removable wells, swan neck hdls, 1870s **75.00**
Warming pan, chased tulips & fruit, 19th C, 42" L **300.00**
Warming pan, pierced & eng lid, long wrought-iron hdl, 41" L .**125.00**

Brastoff, Sascha

The son of immigrant parents, Sascha Brastoff was encouraged to develop his artistic talents to the fullest, encouragement that was well taken, as his achievements aptly attest. Though at various times he was a dancer, sculptor, Hollywood costume designer, jeweler, and painter, it is his ceramics that are today becoming highly regarded collectibles.

Sascha began his career in the United States in the late 1940s. In a beautiful studio built for him by his friend and mentor, Winthrop Rockefeller, he designed innovative wares that even then were among the most expensive on the market. All designing was done personally by Brastoff; he also supervised the staff which at the height of production numbered approximately 150. Wares signed with his full signature (not merely backstamped 'Sascha Brastoff') were personally crafted by him and are valued much more highly than those signed 'Sascha B.,' indicating work done under his supervision. Until his death in 1993, he continued his work in Los Angeles, in his latter years producing 'Sascha Holograms,' which were distributed by the Hummelwerk Company.

Though the resin animals signed 'Sascha B.' were neither made nor designed by Brastoff, collectors of these pieces value them highly. According to the book cited in the last paragraph, after he left the factory in the 1960s, the company retained the use of the name to be used on reissues of earlier pieces or merchandise purchased at trade shows.

In the listings that follow, items are ceramic and signed 'Sascha B.' unless 'full signature' or another medium is indicated.

For further information we recommend *The Collector's Encyclopedia of Sascha Brastoff* by Steve Conti, A. DeWayne Bethany, and Bill Seay; available from Collector Books or your local book store. Our advisor for this category is Jack Chipman, author of *Collector's Encyclopedia of California Pottery*, another source of valuable information for Brastoff collectors. Mr. Chipman is listed in the Directory under California.

Figurine, bird, amber resin, 6½", $225.00.

Ashtray, Chi Chi Birds, #07, 10" **80.00**
Ashtray, teepee shape, gold w/underglaze decor, 7x6" **45.00**
Ashtray/incense burner, fireplace w/chimney, bronze/gold, 7" **75.00**
Bowl, wht shell, Mayan **95.00**
Box, Ballet, 7x4½" **125.00**
Box, Jewel Bird, #020, 7" **60.00**
Candle holders, gr/bl resin, 6", pr **50.00**
Candlestick, Star Steed, 8" **75.00**
Chop plate, abstract design, #053, 17" **110.00**
Curtains, dancers, wht/blk/pk on teal, 82x20" panels, pr **950.00**
Dish, fish form, Rooftops, 3-ftd, 8¼x8¼" **95.00**
Dish, floral, enamel on copper, 4" **40.00**
Dish, Vanity Fair, ovoid, 7" **75.00**
Figurine, hippopotamus, resin, bl **400.00**
Figurine, musk ox, resin, gold **350.00**
Lighter, floral, bl on gr, enamelware, w/6½" ashtray **100.00**
Mug, stylized horse **40.00**
Plate, Abstract, pierced for hanging, 10½" **85.00**
Plate, African dancer, full signature, 12" **575.00**
Plate, enamel on copper, cobalt & gold, 10" **75.00**
Plate, Merbaby, 9", from $75 to **85.00**
Plate, Persian, free-form, #103/4 ....**150.00**

Tray, Chi Chi Birds, #052, 15", from $125 to 150.00
Vase, grapes on wht matt, cylindrical, 5½" 75.00
Vase, stylized lion in ochre over bl, swooping rim, 8x6" 135.00

Brayton Laguna

Durlin E. Brayton made handcrafted vases, lamps, and dinnerware in a small kiln at his Laguna Beach, California, home in 1927. He soon married, and with his wife, Ellen Webster Grieve, as his partner, the small business became a successful commercial venture. They are most famous for their amusing, well-detailed figurines, some of which were commissioned by Walt Disney Studios. Though very successful even through the Depression years, with the influx of imported novelties that deluged the country after WWII, business began to decline. By 1968 the pottery was closed. For more information on this as well as many other potteries in the state, we recommend *The Collectors Encyclopedia of California Pottery* by Jack Chipman; he is listed in the Directory under California.

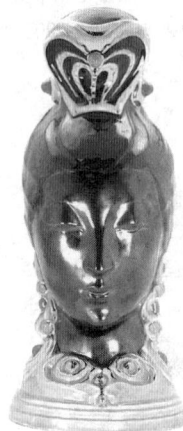

Bust, Kame Kameha, Hawaiian ruler, iridescent with pastel, rare, 14½", minimum value $500.00.

Ashtray, HP ducks, mk, 7" sq 30.00
Bowl, burgundy, wavy lip, handmade, 4" 65.00
Box, Fr peasants, rnd 50.00
Candle holders, Blackamoor, mc w/gold trim, 5", pr 150.00
Cookie jar, Calico Dog 595.00
Cookie jar, Christina (Swedish Maiden) 425.00
Cookie jar, Gingerbread House 250.00
Cookie jar, Mammy, burgundy base, turq bandana, not repro .1,300.00
Cookie jar, Provincial Lady, yel scarf & apron 375.00
Cookie jar, Ringmaster, from Pinocchio series 3,100.00
Cookie jar, Wedding Ring Granny (Grandma), not repro 500.00
Figurine, abstract man & woman w/cat, blk, 21", pr 750.00
Figurine, Blackamoor w/bowl, gold & jewels, 8" 75.00
Figurine, Chinese girl w/baby on bk, mc, Childhood series, 7" 90.00
Figurine, Chinese man, gr & violet, rare, #535, 17" 375.00
Figurine, Dopey, Disney 325.00
Figurine, duck, brn bsk, wht crackle, 5x5½" 55.00
Figurine, Gay Nineties, bartender trio 145.00
Figurine, horse, abstract, blk, 9½" 250.00
Figurine, horses, fighting, yellow & gr, Carol Safholm, pr 275.00
Figurine, horses, Pa & Ma, pr 225.00
Figurine, Jamaican man & lady dancers, C Safholm, 16", pr 750.00
Figurine, matador & bull, mc & woodtone 250.00
Figurine, Miranda, bl plaid, Childhood series 100.00
Figurine, Olga, red & blk, Childhood series 90.00
Figurine, panther, blk, jeweled collar, pacing, 20", NM 225.00
Figurine, Pluto, sniffing 125.00
Figurine, quails, B-40/B-41, pr 225.00

Figurine, ringmaster, 8" 85.00
Figurine, toucan, mc, 9" 150.00
Figurine, zebra, sm 100.00
Flower holder, Frances, bl & wht 60.00
Flower holder, girl in pk w/2 wolfhounds, 10½" 75.00
Flower holder, peasant lady, 8" 85.00
Flower holder, Sally 50.00
Pitcher, men in cityscape, bls & grays, B2 Laguna Beach, 8¼" ...195.00
Planter, rabbit, sm 75.00
Planter, silver, 10x5", w/pr of candlesticks 100.00
Shakers, Calico Cat & Gingham Dog, pr 85.00
Shakers, Provincial, peasant couple, pr 65.00
Sugar bowl, Gingham Dog 75.00
Teapot, Provincial, brn, tulip stand 125.00
Teapot, woman figural, rare 650.00
Toothbrush holder, Gingham Dog 125.00
Vase, Dutch man leaning on basket (vase), 9½" 125.00
Vase, Modern, thin, 18", & 12", pr 245.00
Wall hanger w/flowerpot, caballero, maroon & wht 95.00

Bread Plates and Trays

Bread plates and trays have been produced not only in many types of glass but in metal and pottery as well. Those considered most collectible were made during the last quarter of the 19th century from pressed glass with well-detailed embossed designs, many of them portraying a particularly significant historical event. A great number of these plates were sold at the 1876 Philadelphia Centennial Exposition by various glass manufacturers who exhibited their wares on the grounds. Among the themes depicted are the Declaration of Independence, the Constitution, McKinley's memorial 'It Is God's Way,' Rememberance of Three Presidents, the Purchase of Alaska, and various presidential campaigns, to mention only a few.

'L' numbers correspond with a reference book by Lindsey; 'S' refers to a book by Stuart. Our advisor for this category is Darlene Yohe; she is listed in the Directory under Arkansas.

American Flag, 38 stars, L-51, 11x8" 235.00
Balky Mule 85.00
Bishop, L-201 ....200.00
Black Builders of Bicentennial, 1776-1976 ....35.00
Columbia, shield shape, bl, L-54, 11½x9½" 165.00
Columbus, amber, L-54 ....165.00
Constitution 55.00
Cupid & Venus, 10½" dia 40.00
Double Hands w/Grapes, milk glass 45.00
Eggs in Sand, 12¼x7¾" 50.00
GAR, L-505, 11" L 90.00
Garfield 101, frosted, L-300 ....85.00
Give Us This Day, Sheaf of Wheat, 13" L 75.00
Grant Memorial, amber, L-288 ....48.00
Kansas, motto 48.00
Last Supper 40.00
Liberty Bell, John Hancock, oval, 13" 50.00
Lotus & Serpent 55.00
Maltese Cross, 10" 26.00
Maple Leaf, vaseline, oval, 13x9½" 85.00
McCormick's Reaper 160.00
McKinley, His Will Be Done, clear/frosted 55.00
Memorial Hall 65.00
Niagara Falls, clear/frosted, L-489, 16" L 135.00
One Hundred Years Ago, Centennial 45.00
Polar Bear, ship, L-486, 16" 165.00

Retriever, milk glass **80.00**
Rock of Ages, milk glass center, dtd, 8¾" **180.00**
Shield (Columbia), vaseline **295.00**
Teddy Roosevelt, dancing bears, L-357, 10" L **145.00**
Three Presidents, In Remembrance, 12½x10" **95.00**
US Grant, Let Us Have Peace, gr maple leaf, L-289 ....**195.00**
Virginia Dare, rare **135.00**
Washington, First in War/First in Peace, L-27, 12x8½" ...**100.00**
Wildflower, sq **28.00**
William J Bryan, milk glass **45.00**

Bride's Baskets and Bowls

Victorian brides were showered with gifts, as brides have always been; one of the most popular gift items was the bride's basket. Art glass inserts from both European and American glasshouses, some in lovely transparent hues with dainty enameled florals, others of Peachblow, Vasa Murrhina, satin or cased glass, were cradled in complementary silverplated holders. While many of these holders were simply engraved or delicately embossed, others (such as those from Pairpoint and Wilcox) were wonderfully ornate, often with figurals of cherubs or animals. The bride's basket was no longer in fashion after the turn of the century.

Watch for 'marriages' of bowls and frames. To warrant the best price, the two pieces should be the original pairing. If you can't be certain of this, at least check to see that the bowl fits snuggly into the frame. Beware of later-made bowls (such as Fenton's) in Victorian holders.

Our advisor for this category is Deborah Maggard; she is listed in the Directory under Ohio. In the listings that follow, if no frame is described, the price is for a bowl only.

Amber Dmn Quilt w/appl fruits & HP flowers; SP 11x12" fr **650.00**
Amber w/bl int, HP dragonfly/leaves; SP mk fr, 9½x9" dia **325.00**
Amber w/pk & bl HP berries; orig SP ftd fr **475.00**
Bl MOP Dmn Quilt, crimped edge, Mt WA; SP fr, 14½" **400.00**
Bl o/l, crimped/folded rim, gold florals, 4½x11" **100.00**
Bl o/l satin w/gold flowers; rstr SP fr w/branch hdls, 8x10½" **495.00**
Bl opaque, ruffled rim; ornate openwork brass fr, 1900s, mini **295.00**
Bl satin w/lacy gold foliage/lav flowers; rstr SP fr, 13½x14" **1,100.00**
Burmese, HP spider mums, Mt WA; orig SP Wilcox ft, 10x15" ...**2,500.00**
Clear to bl, Invt Honeycomb, ruffled, HP floral; SP fr **375.00**
Clear w/rose decor, oval; orig SP fr, mini, 5½x5½x3½" **245.00**
Lt gr satin, ruffled/folded rim, HP floral w/gold, 3x11" **155.00**
Maroon o/l, clear ruffle, HP florals; SP Rockford fr, 13x8" **450.00**
Orange satin w/wht HP decor; SP Meriden fr, lg **800.00**
Pale mauve to deeper at border, emb lattice on border, Mt WA, 12" **350.00**
Peachblow, crimped/folded rim, gold florals, 4½x11" **275.00**
Peachblow w/HP florals & scrolls; ornate SP fr, 12" dia **395.00**
Peachblow w/swirls & hobnails, camphor trim; SP fr, 12x6" **195.00**
Pigeon blood, Drapery & Dot; ornate SP fr, 12x10" **450.00**
Pigeon blood to cranberry to custard cased; ftd SP fr, 14x12" **395.00**
Pk cased w/mc decor; SP Benedict fr, 15x12" **250.00**
Pk Dmn Quilt MOP, Mt WA; orig SP Pairpoint fr, 6½x11" **950.00**
Pk frosted Hobnail w/bl rim, oblong; in SP Derby holder **500.00**
Pk Herringbone MOP w/yel int, HP chrysanthemums; cherub SP fr .**2,500.00**
Pk MOP Dmn Quilt, rectangular, Mt WA; mk SP fr, 11x10½" .**495.00**
Pk MOP Dmn Quilt; ornate Tufts SP fr, 14¾x8" **495.00**
Pk o/l, ruffled rim; Wilcox SP fr, 8¼" dia **125.00**
Pk o/l w/gr ruffled/crimped rim; ornate SP Columbia fr **300.00**
Pk o/l w/HP gold & silver florals, ruffled, 3⅛x8" **175.00**
Pk o/l w/wht flowers & gold, frilly rim; SP fr, 14x11x12" **495.00**
Pk satin w/HP florals & melon ribs, Mt WA; SP cherub fr, 15½" **950.00**
Pk to wht satin, pleated rim w/gold enamel, Webb, 4½x11" **350.00**
Pk to wht w/amber apples & leaves, 4x11" **275.00**

Pk to wht w/lime gr int, HP decor w/gold; Webster fr, 15x10" ...**695.00**
Pk to wht w/portrait & decor; ornate SP fr, 13½x11½" **450.00**
Purple to pale lav satin o/l, HP orchids, 3¼x10¼" **350.00**
Raspberry w/turq int, HP decor, ruffled; ornate SP fr, 13x13" **700.00**
Rubena frosted satin; grapes on SP fr, 8½x9½" **450.00**
Rubena verde Hobnail opal; SP Tufts #107 fr, 12½x8" sq ...**775.00**
Sapphire bl, ruffled; ornate SP fr, 10x14" **450.00**
Sapphire bl w/HP bird & floral; SP fr, 7¾x6" **350.00**
Vaseline cased w/HP florals; ornate Meriden SP fr, 10½x11" **300.00**
Wht opaque w/mc & gold flowers; SP Wallace fr **385.00**
Wht satin w/gold, scalloped; ornate SP fr **500.00**
Wht satin w/hobnails & HP decor, Mt WA; mk SP fr, 14½" H .**395.00**
Wht satin w/mc decor & gold, ruffled, Mt WA; SP fr, 15x13" ...**350.00**
Yel o/l w/griffin birds/flowers, Mt WA, 3¾x9½" **900.00**
Yel o/l w/HP decor; bronzed fr w/berries & bird, 12x13x12" **550.00**
Yel o/l w/lav edge, gold decor, 4x10x10⅝" **295.00**

Bristol Glass

Bristol is a type of semi-opaque opaline glass whose name was derived from the area in England where it was first produced. Similar glass was made in France, Germany, and Italy. In this country, it was made by the New England Glass Company and to a lesser extent by its contemporaries. During the 18th and 19th centuries, Bristol glass was imported in large amounts and sold cheaply, thereby contributing to the demise of the earlier glasshouses here in America. It is very difficult to distinguish the English Bristol from other opaline types. Style, design, and decoration serve as clues to its origin; but often only those well versed in the field can spot these subtle variations.

Box, wht, children building snowman, 2⅜x4½" **145.00**
Decanter, wht w/mc floral & gold, bottle form, ball top, 11" **70.00**
Jar, pk w/mc floral & wht dots, w/lid, 8⅜" **50.00**
Sweetmeat jar, bl, HP floral, rst SP lid/rim/hdl, 5½x3" **145.00**
Sweetmeat jar, gr, HP birds, SP lid/rim/hdl, 4⅜x3¼" **125.00**
Teapot, cream opaque, water birds in grasses, 5¼x4½" **295.00**

Vase, blue to white with painted floral decor, 10", $75.00.

Vase, caramel w/mc floral, red flashing at rim, 8¾x4¼" **45.00**
Vase, custard, HP floral w/gold, 9¾" **50.00**
Vase, pk cased w/HP floral, 9x3½", pr **95.00**
Vase, ruby w/HP floral, blown baluster, scalloped rim, 12x6" **125.00**
Vase, turq bl w/HP florals & gold, 10½x4", pr **225.00**
Vase, wht w/pnt church scene, ruffled rim, 10" **75.00**
Vase, yel, HP floral, tapered cylinder, 13" **85.00**

British Royalty Commemoratives

Royalty commemoratives have been issued for royal events since Edward VI's 1547 coronation through modern-day events, so it's possible to start collecting at any period of history. Many collectors begin with Queen Victoria's reign, collecting examples for each succeeding monarch and continuing through modern events.

Some collectors identify with a particular royal personage and limit their collecting to that era, ie., Queen Elizabeth's life and reign. Other collectors look to the future, expanding their collection to include the heir apparents Prince Charles and his first-born son, Prince William.

Royalty commemorative collecting is often further refined around a particular type of collectible. Nearly any item with room for a portrait and a description has been manufactured as a souvenir. Thus royalty commemoratives are available in glass, ceramic, metal, fabric, plastic, and paper. This wide variety of material lends itself to any pocketbook. The range covers expensive limited edition ceramics to inexpensive souvenir key chains, puzzles, matchbooks, etc.

Many recent royalty headline events have been commemorated in a variety of souvenirs. Buying some of these modern commemoratives at the moderate issue prices could be a good investment. After all, today's events are tomorrow's history.

For further study we recommend *British Royal Commemoratives* by our advisor for this category, Audrey Zeder; she is listed in the Directory under California.

Key:
anniv — anniversary	ILN — Illustrated London News
chr — christening	inscr — inscribed
com — commemorative	jub — jubilee
cor — coronation	LE — limited edition
EPNS — electro-plated nickel silver	mem — memorial
	wed — wedding

Baby dish, Geo VI cor, mc portrait, Baby Plate rim lip, inscr **125.00**
Bank, Edward VIII 1937, red w/mc portrait, ad for OXO Cubes ...**60.00**
Bank, Elizabeth II jub, mc picture, plastic, triangular **20.00**
Beaker, Edward VII 1902 King's Dinner, gr, Doulton **150.00**
Beaker, Elizabeth II jub, mc, lion-head hdls, Caverswall **80.00**
Beaker, George VI cor, sepia portrait, mc design, gold rim, 3⅝" **40.00**
Beaker, Victoria 1897 jub, enamel w/portrait, 3¾" **195.00**
Bell, Charles/Diana wed, mc portrait, Royal Grafton, 7½" **55.00**
Bell, Prince William birth/chr, mc w/gold, bone china, 6¼" **60.00**
Book, Elizabeth II, Princesses at Home, 1st edition **20.00**
Book, George V jub, given to Portsmouth School children **20.00**
Book, Royal Family Pop-Up, Patrick Montague Smith **40.00**
Book, Victoria 1897, Queen's Resolve, some wear **65.00**
Booklet, Charles/Diana wed, IPC Magazine Ltd **20.00**
Booklet, Elizabeth II cor, Our Queen & Her Consort, Pitkins **15.00**
Booklet, George V jub, Story of Our King & Queen **30.00**
Booklet, Prince of Wales 1926 Luton visit, 20-pg **30.00**
Booklet, Victoria 1901, Queen Victoria Life & Times, set of 16 ...**300.00**
Bottle, scent; Charles/Diana wedding, mc portrait, ceramic **45.00**
Bust, Charles 1981, wht, Coalport, 5" **65.00**
Bust, Elizabeth II cor, wht bsk, rose dress, Foley, 6" **125.00**
Button, Victoria 1872, brass, ¾" **50.00**
Calendar, George VI 1939 Canada Visit, unused **45.00**
Child's toy dish, Princess Elizabeth 1937, sepia portrait, 4½" **60.00**
Child's toy dish, Victoria 1858, children w/cart, Prattware, 4¼" ...**295.00**
Coin, William IV 1830, 4 pence, silver groat **45.00**
Compact, George V jub, mc portrait, cor robes, hinged, 2¼" **80.00**
Covered dish, George VI cor, mc transfer, blk cat finial, 5" **150.00**
Cup & saucer, Edward VII cor, mc portrait & decor, fluted edge ..**175.00**

Cup & saucer, George V cor, mc portrait, fluted rim, registry mk .**175.00**
Doll, Charles/Diana wed, vinyl, Goldberger, 12", MIB **195.00**
Doll, Charles/Diana wed, vinyl, Peggy Nisbett, ea 8¼", MIB **350.00**
Doll, Prince William birth, cloth, Nottingham lace gown, 3", MIB ...**50.00**
Egg cup, George VI 1937 cor, mc portrait, ftd **50.00**
Ephemera, George III 1761, 8-pg Act of Parliament **75.00**
Ephemera, George V 1910, trade cards, Robin Hood Lollies, 25 for ..**25.00**
Ephemera, George V 1935 visit, invitation to watch procession ...**15.00**
Ephemera, George VI cor, stickers Victoria/George VI, 1½x1⅛" .**45.00**
Ephemera, George VI 1939 visit, stickers: king/queen/2 princesses ..**45.00**
Ephemera, George VI 1949, invitation to Buckingham Palace party ..**45.00**
Ephemera, Victoria 1897 jub, matchbox label, 3½x2½" **15.00**
Ephemera, Victoria 1901 mem, ad card by Lever Bros, 3x2" **30.00**
First Day cover, Elizabeth II cor, w/decorated envelope **20.00**
Goblet, Elizabeth II jub, bl crystal w/jasper insert, Wedgwood, pr ..**220.00**
Goblet, Elizabeth II jub, blk w/14k gold lining, Prinknash **35.00**
Jewelry, Elizabeth II cor, crown earrings, MOC **25.00**
Jewelry, George IV pendant, 1835 shilling in silver bezel **100.00**
Jewelry, George VI stickpin, cut-out profile, brass **20.00**
Jug, George III, emb portrait, Westerwald, late 18th C **425.00**
Loving mug, Charles/Diana wed, bl portrait, Adams, 3½x5¾" **50.00**
Loving mug, Elizabeth II jub, gold Coat Arms, Royal Stafford, 3x6" .**40.00**
Magazine, Elizabeth II cor, ILN, cor week, dbl number, 1953 ....**35.00**
Magazine, George V jub, ILN, May 4, 1935 ....**35.00**
Magazine, George V mem, The Sphere, February 1, 1936 ....**45.00**
Magazine, George VI cor, Weekly Illustrated Cor Souvenir **25.00**
Magazine, Princess Elizabeth wed, ILN, 1947 ....**45.00**
Matchbook, George V jub, blk & wht portrait, inscr, unused **25.00**
Medal, Charles/Diana wed, emb portrait, bronze, Tower Mint, MIB **50.00**
Medal, Diana 1997 mem, emb portrait, cupronickel, 1½" **45.00**
Medal, Duke of York 1893 wed, brass, 1⅝" **60.00**
Medal, George III 1761 cor, emb cor scene, 1⅝" **195.00**
Medal, George V cor, relief portrait, brass, Elect Cococa, 1" **45.00**
Medal, Victoria 1897 jub, bronze, Royal Mint design, 2¼" **125.00**
Medal, Victoria cor, profile & cor scene, pierced, 2" **160.00**
Medal, Victoria 1897 jub, 5-star shape w/relief portrait, 2" **45.00**
Miniature, Elizabeth II cor, book, gold metal, w/photos, 1x1" **35.00**
Miniature, Elizabeth II cor, coach w/horses, Lesney, 4¾" L **55.00**
Miniature, Prince Henry chris, teapot, mc family portrait, 3" **75.00**
Mug, Charles/Diana wed, mc allover portrait/design, Wedgwood, 3½" **50.00**
Mug, Edward VII, king's profile, Art Deco decor & shape **45.00**
Mug, Edward VII cor, bl & gr portrait, bbl shape, CTM **165.00**
Mug, Elizabeth II cor, queen looking over shoulder, Tuscan **45.00**
Mug, George V cor, mc portrait in robes, presentation pc **150.00**
Mug, George VI cor, blk portrait on maize, bbl shape **50.00**
Mug, George VI cor, emb portrait w/HP decor, Art Deco, Burleigh ..**55.00**

Mug, Queen Victoria coronation, portrait and inscription purple transfers, Swansea, 3¼", NM, $800.00.

Mug, Victoria 1897 jub, bl & gray overall transfer, JCN **195.00**
Napkin rings, George VI cor, blk & wht portrait, plastic, pr **35.00**

New Testament, Edward VII cor, blk cover w/gold, mc picture **75.00**
New Testament, Elizabeth II cor, bl cover w/gold inscr, 4x3" **50.00**
New Testament, George VI cor, red cover w/silver seal **55.00**
Newspaper, Evening Sentinel 1936, Edward VIII abdicates **50.00**
Newspaper, Fort Dodge Messenger 1937, Vicar To Marry Edward ..**30.00**
Newspaper, Gleason's Pictorial 1862, royal coverage inside **20.00**
Newspaper, Illustrated Mail 1902, Edward VI cor **45.00**
Newspaper, ILN 1855, Queen meets Emperor of France at Windsor .**45.00**
Photograph, Duke of Windsor 1940 radio broadcast, blk/wht, 5x7" ...**45.00**
Picture, Elizabeth II jub needlepoint, in wooden fr, 15x13" **60.00**
Pillbox, Elizabeth II cor, emb metal portrait, brass **45.00**
Pitcher, Victoria 1897 jub, Queen/Prince Edward, Balmoral, 4" ...**270.00**
Pitcher, Victoria 1897 jub, sponged royal bl, gold portrait, 4" **175.00**
Plaque, Elizabeth II, blk basalt, wht portrait, Wedgwood, 4¼" ...**110.00**
Plaque, George VI cor, king/queen/children, tin, 7¼x6" **45.00**
Plate, Charles/Diana wed, mc portrait, Crown Staffordshire, 9" .**250.00**
Plate, Charles/Diana 1981, royal bl, LE, Bing & Grondahl, 10½" ..**190.00**
Plate, Edward VII cor, mc portrait, emb/scalloped rim, 8½" **165.00**
Plate, Edward VII cor, 6 circles w/mc portrait, Blair, 9" **195.00**
Plate, Edward VIII 1972 mem, blk basalt, Wedgwood, 6½" **150.00**
Plate, Elizabeth II cor, profile, sq w/extended hdls, 10" **45.00**
Plate, Elizabeth II 1991 Visit...Bush, LE 250, Chown, 10¼" **100.00**
Plate, George V cor, mc portrait, pierced rim for ribbon, 7½" **150.00**
Plate, George VI cor, mc design w/gold rim, 6½" **30.00**
Plate, George VI cor, portrait, Sovereign of Canada, 10" **40.00**
Plate, George VI 1939 Canada, w/queen & princesses, Wedgwood ..**150.00**
Plate, Princess Margaret 1930 birth, bird design, Paragon, 7" **120.00**
Plate, Victoria 1837, mc young Queen, emb edge, gold rim, 9½" ...**695.00**
Postcard, Diana 21st birthday, portrait w/gold, LE, Veldale **15.00**
Postcard, Edward VII mem, blk/wht inscr, blk border, Rotary **25.00**
Postcard, George V cor, mc portrait in cor robes, Tuck **25.00**
Poster, Charles/Diana wed, mc portrait, line of descent, 32x23" ...**35.00**
Pot lid, Prince Albert 1860, mc portrait/study scene, Pratt, 4" ...**295.00**
Pot lid, Victoria 1850, mc portrait/balcony scene, 5½" **350.00**
Print, Marriage Princess Louise/Marquis of Lorne 1871, blk & wht ..**20.00**
Program, Elizabeth II cor, Church of England Services, 16-pg **20.00**
Program, Elizabeth Order of Garter procession & installation **25.00**
Program, Windsor Castle, town & neighborhood guide, 1934 ......**15.00**
Puzzle, Elizabeth II cor, wood, Valentine, MIB (sealed) **60.00**
Scrapbook, Elizabeth II cor, w/newspaper clippings, 15x10" **50.00**
Spoon, Elizabeth II cor, HP mc portrait on bowl, SP, MIB **35.00**
Spoon, Elizabeth II jub, emb portrait, EPNS, set of 6, MIB **60.00**
Spoon, George VI cor, emb portrait, EPNS, Birks of Canada **45.00**
Spoon, George VI 1939 Canada visit, emb portrait, SP **45.00**
Spoon, Victoria 1897, emb portrait/design, Sterling hallmk **150.00**
Stamp album, Charles/Diana wed, 50 1st day covers in album ...**350.00**
Tape measure, George V cor, retractable, Butt Bros ad **105.00**
Tea caddy, Elizabeth II cor, emb inscr, copper/brass, Purity Tips ..**75.00**
Teapot, Edward VII, mc portrait, pk lustre, 2-cup **265.00**
Teapot, Victoria 1887 jub, blk w/gold enameling, 2-cup **325.00**
Teapot, 4 generation 1994, mc portrait, 1-cup **55.00**
Textile, Charles/Diana wed, tea towel, mc portrait, Irish linen **35.00**
Textile, Edward VIII cor, tablecloth, bl portrait w/mc, 46x44" **50.00**
Textile, Geo V 1934 Mersey Tunnel opening, handkerchief **45.00**
Thimble, Elizabeth II 1987 wed anniv, silhouettes, appl ruby **40.00**
Thimble, Prince William birth, mc enamel portrait on metal **35.00**
Tile, Victoria 1887 jub, emb portrait/design on gr, Minton **320.00**
Tin, Charles/Diana wed, royal bl w/4 mc portraits, 5½" **40.00**
Tin, Edward VII cor, mc portrait, Cadbury, 3½x2½" **60.00**
Tin, George V 1910, mc portrait w/generals, 4x3" **95.10**
Tin, Prince of Wales 1930, mc portrait, hinged, Throne's, 4x2½" ..**65.00**
Tin, Princess Elizabeth 1952 Trooping Colors, on horse, 9x6" **75.00**
Tin, Victoria 1890s, emb portrait, for salve, 1½" dia **50.00**
Tray, Victoria 1897 jub, 4 generations, mc, 12" **250.00**

Broadmoor

In October of 1933, the Broadmoor Art Pottery was formed and space rented at 217 East Pikes Peak Avenue, Colorado Springs, Colorado. Most of the pottery they produced would not be considered elaborate and only a handful was decorated. Many pieces were signed by P.H. Genter, J.B. Hunt, Eric Hellman, and Cecil Jones. It is reported that this plant closed in 1936, and Genter moved his operations to Denver.

Broadmoor pottery is marked in several ways: a Greek or Egyptian-type label depicting two potters (one at the wheel and one at a tile-pressing machine) and the word Broadmoor; an ink-stamped 'Broadmoor Pottery, Colorado Springs (or Denver), Colorado'; and an incised version of the latter.

The bottoms of all pieces are always white and can be either glazed or unglazed. Glaze colors are turquoise, green, yellow, cobalt blue, light blue, white, pink, pink with blue, maroon red, black, and a copper lustre. Both matt and high gloss finishes were used.

The company produced many advertising tiles, novelty items, coasters, ashtrays, and vases for local establishments around Denver and as far away as Wyoming. An Indian head was incised into many of the advertising items, which also often bear a company or a product name. A series of small animals (horses, dogs, elephants, lamb, squirrels, a toucan bird, and a hippo), each about 2" high, are easily recognized by the style of their modeling and glaze treatments, though all are unmarked. Our advisors for this category are Carol and Jim Carlton, authors of *Collector's Encyclopedia of Colorado Pottery*; they are listed in the Directory under Colorado.

Photo courtesy Carol and Jim Carlton

Vase, embossed Indian portrait on maroon, marked Plains Hotel, Cheyenne, Wyoming, dated 1935, 17", $500.00 minimum value.

Ashtray, bl w/wht dog center **45.00**
Creamer & sugar bowl, bl, curved hdls, ind, 2" **35.00**
Figurine, elephant, brn, stamp, 2" **45.00**
Figurine, squirrel on sq base, brn, stamp, 2" **40.00**
Lamp base, swirled cream-wht, sgn Cecil Jones, 15", minimum ..**200.00**
Pitcher, gr w/gold floral, hand-thrown cylinder, Hellman, 15" ...**200.00**
Planter, frog figural, red, open mouth **65.00**
Planter, turq flared pot form w/saucer, orig sticker, 18" **125.00**
Vase, brn w/honeycomb panel, ftd, 12" **140.00**
Vase, cornucopia; bl to mauve, 6" **45.00**
Vase, lt bl, bulbous, trumpet neck, rim-to-waist hdls, 11" **95.00**
Vase, Mongol red, flared rim, sm ft, 4" **35.00**
Vase, Mongol red, waisted, 8" **75.00**
Vase, red, hand-thrown hdls, sgn E Heilman, 8" **125.00**
Vase, turq, shouldered cylinder, 8" **55.00**

Broadsides

Webster defines a broadside as simply a large sheet of paper printed on one side. During the 1880s, they were the most practical means of mass communication. By the middle of the century, they had become elaborate and lengthy with information, illustrations, portraits, and fancy border designs. Those printed on coated stock are usually worth more.

Boston Museum broadside, Mr. Wm. Warren starring in My Son, Boston, 1880, 25½x9", fair, $135.00.

Administrators sale of restaurant items, 1866, 9x12", EX **55.00**
Christy's Minstrels, 1861 ....**350.00**
Death of Daniel Webster, 2 columns, eulogy, bl stock, 7x10" **25.00**
Eloquent & Humorous Speech of ...Mars, Esq..., London, 1820 ....**50.00**
Farewell Address...A Jackson to...US, silk, 1840, 22x17" **500.00**
German Regiment in Phila, volunteers sought, in German, 9x14" ...**75.00**
Much Ado About Nothing, lists players, Sept 1855, VG **45.00**
Old Style Minstrel Show..., Dec 1928, 20x14", VG **70.00**
Pizarro (play) starring Mr Burgess, 1848, 7x13½" **45.00**
Religious verses, German language, PA, GS Peters, 1800s, 16x11" ..**40.00**
Republican Rallying Song, Union patriotic song, 1865, 11x5½" ..**90.00**
Revolutionary War call for men, 2-sided, 1778, 8½x13", EX **775.00**
Suffragette info, Every Woman Should Join..., London, 1915, 9x11" **80.00**
To Firemen, lists hose & carriages, RI, 1858, 20x14"+mat/fr **325.00**
Water Witch drama to be shown, ship vignette, ca 1850s, 7x14" .**50.00**

Bronzes

Thomas Ball, George Bessell, and Leonard Volk were some of the earliest American sculptors who produced figures in bronze for home decor during the 1840s. Pieces of historical significance were the most popular, but by the 1880s a more fanciful type of artwork took hold. Some of the fine sculptors of the day were Daniel Chester French, Augustus St. Gaudens, and John Quincy Adams Ward. Bronzes reached the height of their popularity at the turn of the century. The American West was portrayed to its fullest by Remington, Russell, James Frazier, Hermon MacNeil, and Solon Borglum. Animals of every species were modeled by A.P. Proctor, Paul Bartlett, and Albert Laellele, to name but a few.

Art Nouveau and Art Deco influenced the medium during the '20s, evidenced by the works of Allen Clark, Harriet Frismuth, E.F. Sanford, and Bessie P. Vonnoh.

Be aware that recasts abound. While often esthetically satisfactory, they are not original and should be priced accordingly. In much the same manner as prints are evaluated, the original castings made under the direction of the artist are the most valuable. Later castings from the original mold are worth less. A recast is not made from the original mold. Instead, a rubber-like substance is applied to the bronze, peeled away, and filled with wax. Then, using the same 'lost wax' procedure as the artist uses on completion of his original wax model, a clay-like substance is formed around the wax figure and the whole fired to vitrify the clay. The wax, of course, melts away, hence the term 'lost wax.' Recast bronzes lose detail and are somewhat smaller than the original due to the shrinkage of the clay mold.

Aubert, Archimedes, G patina, late 19th C, 10½x12" **825.00**
Austria, nude seated on cvd marble base, 14½" **800.00**
Austria, topless dancer in short skirt & ballet slippers, 12" **7,600.00**
Barbedienne Foundry, Wrestlers, lt brn patina, 12" **425.00**
Belleuse, Festival Bound, lady w/basket & 2 children, 27" **3,000.00**
Boux, mythical warrior, braided hair, marble base, 22" **5,750.00**
Brooks, Richard; Boxer, orig blk patina, 12" **1,500.00**
Buschelberge, Runner, dk brn patina, marble base, 13½" **600.00**
Callender, Anita, ivory inlay, onyx base, 16¾" **6,325.00**
Charol, Pierrot, ivory face & hands, oval marble base, 12⅜" ..**1,400.00**
Charol, Tennis Player, orig brn patina, marble base, 13" **400.00**
Chiparus, costumed dancing lady, cold pnt, marble base, 18" .**3,000.00**
Chiparus, nude dancer & 2 seated nudes w/horns, 1930s, 20x20" **5,750.00**
Chiparus, Russian dancers, cold pnt/ivory, 1925, 14¾" **20,700.00**
Clark, Balinese dancer, nude w/headdress, 8⅞" **5,175.00**
Colinet, Danseuse Hindoue, cold pnt/gilt/ivory, 15" **4,300.00**
Colinet, Handkerchief Dance, cold pnt/gilt/ivory, 13" **5,465.00**
Coran, Shot Putter, stamped Susse Frere, Paris..., 24" **3,000.00**
Cormier, lady in long tunic on sofa, brn patina, 19x25" **2,600.00**
Epheres, Archer, orig blk patina, rpr, 23" **550.00**
Erte, Gala, 1920s lady in evening gown, patinated, 15" **2,300.00**
Erte, L'Amour, lady w/heart on body suit, patinated, 20¾" **2,000.00**
Erte, La Coquette, lady w/mirror, patinated, 18¼" **1,600.00**
Erte, lady among butterflies, stepped base, 20½" **1,850.00**
Erte, lady in exotic costume, patinated, 17⅞" **2,300.00**
Erte, lady in ornate costume & headdress, patinated, 23¾" **2,875.00**
Erte, lady w/fan, long draped gown, patinated, 18½" **2,185.00**
Erte, lady w/shawl, fur-lined dress, patinated, gilt, 16" **2,300.00**
Fremiet, Emmanuel; Cavalier Romain, horseman, 16x10" **1,650.00**
Frishmuth, nude reaching skyward, #311, 1918, 19" **8,000.00**
Guirad-Riviere, Bacchante head, 15"+marble plinth **2,875.00**
Krusha, buffalo, slightly stylized, 1910s, 9x9" **250.00**
Laurent, nymph kneeling w/Aladdin-type lamp, oval base, 9" **350.00**
Maindron, Velleda, garland in hair, beside stump, sq base, 18" ..**6,325.00**
Meier, lady w/flowers, ivory face, HP details, 8" **600.00**
Messina, Dying Gaul, marble base, 17¾" **850.00**
Meyer, Salome, orig brn patina, stamped C93, 24" **2,600.00**
Neopolitan, Narcissus, old gr patina, 19th C, 25x10" **1,650.00**
Philippe, Russian dancer, pnt details, onyx base, 17" **4,600.00**
Pillig, after; Swordsman, orig dk brn to blk patina, 24" **4,260.00**
Poertzel, Butterfly Dancers, ivory inlay, 1930s, 17" **8,000.00**
Poertzel, Serpentina, lady dancer, ivory mts, marble base, 23" ...**6,325.00**
Poertzel, snake charmer, ivory inlay, ca 1930, 21" **9,200.00**
Schliepstein, German Shepherd, on blk marble plinth, 10x13" .**385.00**
Tereszczuk, lady dancer, ivory inlay, marble base, 18" **3,165.00**
Thai, Shaky Amuni Buddha, 17th C, 9¼" **150.00**
Trodoux, pheasants (2) in underbrush, on wood stand, 23½" **650.00**
Vallanis, Hostage, lt brn patina, 21" **2,100.00**
Valton, La Lionne Blesse, wounded lion, 13x17" **770.00**
Villanis, bust of woman in turban, agate base, 5½" **185.00**
Villanis, maiden reclining on palette on rock, 61" **6,325.00**
Villanis, Sapho in draped gown, holding lyre, 35⅝" **3,200.00**
Vonnoh, draped nude, hands at breast, gr marble base, 21" **7,500.00**
West, moose, oval naturalistic base, 12x17" **600.00**
Zach, Amazon on horse by tree, ivory inlay, 33" **5,750.00**

Brouwer

Theophilis A. Brouwer, an accomplished artist even before his interests turned to the medium of pottery, started a small one-man operation in 1894 in East Hampton, New York. Two years later he relocated in Westhampton, where he perfected the technique of fire painting, learning to control the effects of the kiln to produce the best possible results. In 1925 he founded the Ceramic Flame Company in New York, but it is for his earlier work that he is best known. Brouwer died in 1932.

Pitcher, stylized bird, bl gloss on blk matt, mks, 5", NM 350.00
Vase, flame-pnt mc lustre, whalebone mk, 4x4" 1,000.00
Vase, gr irid crackle drips on gold-leaf base, mk, 8x6" 3,100.00
Vase, orange/yel/metallic brn, bottle form, 7x3½", NM 1,200.00

Brownies by Palmer Cox

Created by Palmer Cox in 1883, the Brownies charmed children through the pages of books and magazines, as dolls, on their dinnerware, in advertising material, and on souvenirs. Each had his own personality, among them The Bellhop, The London Bobby, The Chairman, and Uncle Sam. But the oversized, triangular face with the startled expression, the protruding tummy, and the spindlelegs were characteristics of them all. They were inspired by the Scottish legends related to Cox as a child by his parents, who were of English descent. His introduction of the Brownies to the world was accomplished by a poem called *The Brownies Ride*. Books followed in rapid succession, thirteen in the series, all written as well as illustrated by Palmer Cox.

By the late 1890s, the Brownies were active in advertising. They promoted such products as games, coffee, toys, patent medicines, and rubber boots. 'Greenies' were the Brownies' first cousins, created by Cox to charm and to woo through the pages of the advertising almanacs of the G.G. Green Company of New Jersey. Perhaps the best-known endorsement in the Brownies' career was for the Kodak Brownie, which became so popular and sold in such volume that their name became synonymous with this type of camera. Our advisor for this category is Anne Kier; she is listed in the Directory under Ohio.

Ashtray, Brownie scene, RS Germany 1913 ....65.00
Book, Another Brownie Book, Appleton Century, 1942, w/jacket ...35.00
Book, Brownie Year Book, Cox illus, Century, 1895, EX 100.00
Book, Brownies at Home, Cox illus, Century, 1893, EX 150.00
Book, Brownies Round the World, Cox illus, Unwin, 1894, EX ...100.00
Book, Brownies: Their Book, Cox illus, Century, 1895, EX 150.00
Book, Little Goody Two Shoes, 1903, EX 40.00
Book, Queer Animals, EX 45.00
Book, Queer People, Palmer Cox illus, 1894, EX 60.00
Book, Queerie Queers, color plates, EX 125.00
Brownie Blocks, McLoughlin, litho decor, wood box, 13½x11" .260.00
Calendar, Ramon's Pills advertising, EX 75.00
Candlestick, Bobby, majolica, 7½" 275.00
Candlestick, Sailor, majolica, 7½" 260.00
Chocolate mold, 2-pc 120.00
Cloth, 6 printed dolls to stuff, uncut, NM 450.00
Crate label, 1930s, 10x12", NM 15.00
Creamer, Little Boy Blue verse & 4 Brownies, gold trim, china 85.00
Creamer, Scotsman head, majolica, 3¼" 75.00
Dish, child's, SP, 19 Brownies, 8½" 125.00
Figurine, Chinaman, papier-mache head, 9", EX 450.00
Game, Brownie Horseshoes, early, complete in box 85.00
Hand mirror, pewter fr w/emb Brownies 195.00

Handkerchief, linen, action Brownies, Arnold Print Works, 1894 ..125.00
Ice cream bag, Cox illus, 5¢ orig value, 1930s, M 20.00
Inkwell, majolica 135.00
Needle book, Brownies, 1892 World's Fair, rare 50.00
Nodder, compo figure, wooden legs, Germany, ca 1900, 7⅝", EX ...275.00
Paper doll, Lion Coffee, Indian Brownie, EX 40.00
Paperweight, 3 intaglio-cut Brownies in glass base, gold pnt, 3" .145.00
Pencil box, rolling-pin shape, 15 Brownies in boat 90.00
Pin dish, artist Brownie w/palette, Limoges, gold rim, 3½x3" 125.00
Plate, porc, mk La Francaise, 7" 85.00
Plate, SP, Brownies on rim, 8½" 50.00
Puzzle, Brownies skating, 20-pc, early, fr, 10½x12½" 65.00
Sheet music, Brownie Rag, Brownie cover, 1907 ....35.00
Sheet music, Dance of the Brownies 25.00
Spoon, SP 60.00
Spoon, sterling w/enameled Brownie man finial, demitasse 60.00
Table set, brass, emb Brownies, 3-pc (knife/fork/spoon), no box ..45.00
Table set, brass, emb Brownies, 6", in orig box 90.00
Tea tile, 6 dancing Brownies, 6¼" 95.00
Whiskey taster, German head, majolica, 3¼" 85.00

Brush

George Brush began his career in the pottery industry in 1901 working for the J.B. Owens Pottery Co. in Zanesville, Ohio. He left the company in 1907 to go into business for himself, only to have fire completely destroy his pottery less than one year after it was founded. Brush became associated with J.W. McCoy in 1909 and for many years served in capacities ranging from general manager to president. (From 1911 until 1925, the firm was known as The Brush-McCoy Pottery Co.; see that section for information.) After McCoy died, the family withdrew their interests, and in 1925 the name of the firm was changed to The Brush Pottery. The era of hand-decorated art pottery had passed for the most part and would soon be completely replaced by the production of commercial lines. Of all the wares bearing the later Brush script mark, their figural cookie jars are the most collectible, and several have been reproduced.

For additional information we recommend *The Collector's Encyclopedia of Brush-McCoy Pottery* (recently revised) by Sharon and Bob Huxford. Information on Brush cookie jars (as well as confusing reproductions) can be found in *The Collector's Encyclopedia of Cookie Jars, Books I, II*, and *III* by Joyce and Fred Roerig; they are listed in the Directory under South Carolina. See also Brush-McCoy for information on a second reference book.

Cookie Jars

Photo courtesy Ermagene Westfall

Davy Crockett, gold trim, marked USA, $800.00 minimum value.

Antique Touring Car, minimum value 700.00
Boy w/Balloons, minimum value 850.00
Chick in Nest (+)..400.00
Cinderella Pumpkin, #W32 ....250.00
Circus Horse, gr (+)..950.00
Clown, yel pants 250.00
Clown Bust, #W49, minimum value 325.00
Cookie House, #W31 ....125.00
Covered Wagon, dog finial, #W30, minumum value (+)............550.00
Cow w/Cat on Bk, purple, minimum value (+)....................1,000.00
Cow w/Cat on Bk, brn, #W10 (+) 125.00
Davy Crockett, no gold, mk USA (+) 300.00
Dog & Basket 300.00
Donkey w/Cart, ears down, #W33, gray 400.00
Donkey w/Cart, ears up, #W33, minimum value 800.00
Elephant w/Baby Bottle & Ice Cream Cone (+) 500.00
Elephant w/Monkey on Bk, minimum value 5,000.00
Fish, #W52 (+) 500.00
Formal Pig, gr hat & coat (+) 300.00
Gas Lamp, #K1 ....75.00
Granny, pk apron, bl dots on skirt 325.00
Granny, plain skirt, minimum value (+)................................400.00
Happy Bunny, wht, #W25 ....225.00
Hen on Basket, unmk 125.00
Hillbilly Frog, minimum value (+) 4,500.00
Humpty Dumpty, w/beany & bow tie (+)............................275.00
Humpty Dumpty, w/peaked brn hat & shoes 250.00
Laughing Hippo, #W27 (+) 750.00
Little Angel (+)..800.00
Little Boy Blue, gold trim, #K25, sm 700.00
Little Boy Blue, #K24 Brush USA, lg (+) 800.00
Little Girl, #017 (+) 550.00
Little Red Riding Hood, gold trim, mk, lg, minimum value (+) ..850.00
Little Red Riding Hood, no gold, #K24 USA, sm 550.00
Night Owl 125.00
Old Clock, #W10 ....165.00
Old Shoe, #W23 (+) 125.00
Panda, #W21 (+)..250.00
Peter, Peter Pumpkin Eater, #W24 ....300.00
Peter Pan, gold trim, lg (+) 800.00
Peter Pan, sm 550.00
Puppy Police (+)..585.00
Raggedy Ann, #W16 ....350.00
Sitting Pig (+)..400.00
Smiling Bear, #W46 (+) 350.00
Squirrel on Log, #W26 ....100.00
Squirrel w/Top Hat, blk coat & hat 275.00
Squirrel w/Top Hat, gr coat 250.00
Stylized Owl 350.00
Stylized Siamese, #W41 ....400.00
Teddy Bear, ft apart 250.00
Teddy Bear, ft together 200.00
Treasure Chest, #W28 ....150.00

Miscellaneous

Carafe, Bronze Line, palette mk #928, 9" 50.00
Flowerpot, Rockcraft, gr-brn, 1933, 8" 140.00
Lawn ornament, rooster, brn w/red comb & waddle, 1956 ....300.00
Nursery light, rabbit figural, 10" 30.00
Planter, bird beside flower-form planter, USA #246, 1957 ....25.00
Planter, dbl cornucopia; Bittersweet, 1945, 4½" 75.00
Planter, horse & foal beside trough planter, 1958 ....45.00
Planter, Madonna praying, planter at bk, ivory 25.00

Planter, rooster figural, gr, 1956 ....40.00
Plaques, African masks, USA, 1958, 10½", pr 150.00
Vase, emb rose, pillow form, #13, 1950s, 5x6" 15.00
Vase, Glo Art, ivory, #773, 1939, 9" 85.00
Vase, ivory, waisted, hdls, #579, 1939, 6" 20.00
Vase, V form w/emb V & flying eagle, early 1940s, 8" 80.00
Wall pocket, dog in doghouse, 1952 ....100.00
Wall pocket, fish figural, 1958 ....95.00

Brush-McCoy

The Brush-McCoy Pottery was formed in 1911 in Zanesville, Ohio, an alliance between George Brush and J.W. McCoy. Brush's original pottery had been destroyed by fire in 1907; McCoy had operated his own business in Roseville, Ohio, since 1899. After the merger, the company expanded and produced not only their staple commercial wares but also fine artware. Lines such as Navarre, Venetian, Oriental, and Sylvan were of fine quality equal to that of their larger competitors. Because very little of the ware was marked, it is often mistaken for Weller, Roseville, or Peters and Reed.

In 1918 after a fire in Zanesville had destroyed the manufacturing portion of that plant, all production was contained in their Roseville (Ohio) plant #2. A stoneware type of clay was used there; and as a result, the artware lines of Jewel, Zuniart, King Tut, Florastone, Jetwood, Krakle-Kraft, and Panelart are so distinctive that they are more easily recognizable. Examples of these lines are unique and very beautiful, also quite rare and highly prized!

The Brush-McCoy Pottery operated under that name until after 1925 when it became the Brush Pottery. The Brush-Barnett family retained their interest in the pottery until 1981 when it was purchased by the Dearborn Company. For more information we recommend *The Collector's Encyclopedia of Brush-McCoy Pottery* by Sharon and Bob Huxford and *Sanford's Guide to Brush-McCoy Pottery, Books I and II*, written by Martha and Steve Sanford and edited by David P. Sanford, our advisors for this category. They are listed in the Directory under California. See also Brush.

Vase, Zuniart, Native American designs in both matt and gloss glazes, #049, 7", $750.00.

Birdbath ornament, 2 frogs on base, 1920s-30s, 7½" 200.00
Bookends, Venetian, Indian chief, Ivotint, 1929, 5x5½", pr 250.00
Bowl, Jetwood, incurvate rim, #01, 2½x7½" 500.00
Candlestick, Vogue, blk geometrics on wht, 12" 325.00
Candlestick, Zuniart, Indian-style decor, #032, 1923, 10", pr ..1,100.00
Candlesticks, Amaryllis KolorKraft, #026, 9", pr 250.00
Cuspidor, emb frog & lily pads on brn, 1910, 5½" 215.00
Jardiniere, Blue Birds, 1915, 7½" 350.00
Jardiniere, Egyptian, bl, 1923, 5½" 200.00
Jardiniere, Jewel, geometrics on tan, 1923, 7½" 700.00
Jardiniere, Stonecraft, #241, 1923, 6" 150.00
Jardiniere & pedestal, Athenian, 1928, 39" overall 900.00

Lamp base, Wise Bird (owl) figural, 1927, 9" 225.00
Ornament, frog figural, 1967, 11½" 250.00
Vase, King Tut, scarb, 12" **1,850.00**
Vase, King Tut, walking figures, 12" **2,500.00**
Vase, Onyx (bl), #1050, 6½" 75.00
Vase, Onyx (bl), swan hdls, #747, 5" 65.00
Vase, Onyx (brn), hdls, #22, 9" 85.00
Vase, Onyx (brn), shouldered, 4" 45.00

Buffalo Pottery

The founding of the Buffalo Pottery in Buffalo, New York, in 1901, was a direct result of the success achieved by John Larkin through his innovative methods of marketing 'Sweet Home Soap.' Choosing to omit 'middle-man' profits, Larkin preferred to deal directly with the consumer and offered premiums as an enticement for sales. The pottery soon proved a success in its own right and began producing advertising and commemorative items for other companies, as well as commercial tableware. In 1905 they introduced their Blue Willow line after extensive experimentation resulted in the development of the first successful underglaze cobalt achieved by an American company. Between 1905 and 1909, a line of pitchers and jugs were hand decorated in historical, literary, floral, and outdoor themes. Twenty-nine styles are known to have been made. These have been found in a wide array of color variations.

Their most famous line was Deldare Ware, the bulk of which was made from 1908 to 1909. It was hand decorated after illustrations by Cecil Aldin. Views of English life were portrayed in detail through unusual use of color against the natural olive green cast of the body. Today the 'Fallowfield Hunt' scenes are more difficult to locate than 'Scenes of Village Life in Ye Olden Days.' A Deldare calendar plate was made in 1910. These are very rare and are highly valued by collectors. The line was revived in 1923 and dropped again in 1925. Every piece was marked 'Made at Ye Buffalo Pottery, Deldare Ware Underglaze.' Most are dated, though date has no bearing on the value. Emerald Deldare, made with the same olive body and on standard Deldare Ware shapes, featured historical scenes and Art Nouveau decorations. Most pieces are found with a 1911 date stamp. Production was very limited due to the intricate, time-consuming detail. Needless to say, it is very rare and extremely desirable.

Abino Ware, most of which was made in 1912, also used standard Deldare shapes, but its colors were earthy and the decorations more delicately applied. Sailboats, windmills, and country scenes were favored motifs. These designs were achieved by overpainting transfer prints and were often signed by the artist. The ware is marked 'Abino' in hand-printed block letters. Production was limited; and as a result, examples of this line are scarce today. Prices only slightly trail those of Emerald Deldare Ware.

The many uncataloged items that have been found over the years indicate that Buffalo Pottery decorators were free to use their own ideas and talents to create many beautiful one-of-a-kind pieces.

Our advisors for this category are Fred and Lila Shrader; they are listed in the Directory under California.

Key:
C — commercial ware marked   RW — Rouge Ware
    Buffalo China   TL — top logo
BS — bottom stamp   BW — Blue Willow
FH — Fallowfield Hunt   TM — top mark

Abino

Bowl, sailing vessels underway, choppy seas, 9" 875.00

Candlestick, lg full-masted sailing vessel, 9" 825.00
Mug, seascape w/distant lighthouse, 4½" 510.00
Pitcher, sailing vessels underway, choppy seas, 7" 950.00
Plate, sailboat in foreground, windmills on distant shore, 6" 335.00
Plate, windmill & boat scene, 9¼" 380.00
Plate, windmill & distant figures, finely detailed, 10" 475.00
Toothpick holder, shoreline w/distant buildings 375.00
Tray, dresser; coastal scene w/boats, sea gulls, clouds, 9x12" ...**1,125.00**

Deldare

Jardiniere and stand, Ye Lion Inn, 9x12", 14x14", $4,200.00.

Bowl, cereal; FH, The Start, 6¼" 295.00
Bowl, flat rim soup; FH, Breaking Cover, 9" 450.00
Bowl, flat rim soup; Ye Village Street, 8¾" 425.00
Bowl, fruit; Emerald, Dr Syntax Reading His Tour, 9" **1,000.00**
Bowl, fruit; Ye Village Tavern, 9" 425.00
Bowl, sauce; FH, Breaking Cover, 5" 175.00
Candle holder, untitled Village scenes, shield bk, 6¾" **1,185.00**
Candlestick, Emerald, butterfly, grapes & geometric design **1,050.00**
Candlestick, untitled Village Scene, 9" 475.00
Chamberstick, untitled village scenes, w/finger ring 500.00
Chocolate pot, Emerald, Art Nouveau decor, 10" **2,800.00**
Chocolate pot, Ye Village Scene, 10" 675.00
Creamer, Emerald, Dr Syntax w/the Dairy Maid, 3" 375.00
Creamer, Scenes of Village Life in Ye Olden Days, 2¾" 175.00
Cup & saucer, Emerald, Dr Syntax at Liverpool 395.00
Cup & saucer, FH 275.00
Cup & saucer, Ye Olden Days 185.00
Egg cup, untitled FH decor 550.00
Hair receiver, Emerald, Art Nouveau, 4" **1,200.00**
Hair receiver, Ye Village Street, 4" 425.00
Humidor, There Was an Old Sailor..., 7¾" **1,400.00**
Ink container, Emerald, Art Nouveau decor, no cap, 3¼" 750.00
Mug, FH, At 3 Pigeons, tankard style, 4¼" 450.00
Mug, FH, mini, 2¼" 550.00
Mug, shaving; Ye Razor, ftd base, 3¾" **1,100.00**
Mug, Ye Lion Inn, 4½" 175.00
Pitcher, Emerald, Dr Syntax Amused..., 7" **1,300.00**
Pitcher, FH, Breaking Cover, 6" 510.00
Pitcher, FH, Breaking Cover, 9" 800.00
Pitcher, tankard; FH, The Hunt Supper, 12" **1,600.00**
Pitcher, tankard; Ye Village Scenes, drilled/capped for lamp, 12" ..**1,200.00**
Pitcher, To Spare an Old Broken Soldier..., 7" 400.00
Plaque, An Evening at Ye Lion Inn, 13½" 350.00
Plaque, Emerald, Dr Syntax Sketching the Lake..., 12" **1,900.00**
Plaque, FH, Breakfast at the 3 Pigeons, 12" 550.00
Plate, advertising; HP Deldare Ware underglaze, 6½" **1,800.00**
Plate, At Ye Lion Inn, 6¼" 150.00
Plate, cake; Ye Village Gossips, open fancy hdls, 10½" 480.00
Plate, chop; An Evening at Ye Lion Inn, 13¾" 375.00
Plate, chop; FH, The Start, 14" 550.00
Plate, Emerald, Dr Syntax Sililoquising..., 7¼" 425.00

Plate, Emerald, Introduction to Courtship...(Dr Syntax), 9" 650.00
Plate, FH, The Start, 9½" 275.00
Plate, Ye Town Crier, 8½" 150.00
Plate, Ye Village Gossips, 10" 165.00
Powder bowl, Ye Village Street, w/lid, 4⅛" 350.00
Sugar bowl, Emerald, Dr Syntax, hdls, w/lid, 4" 800.00
Sugar bowl, FH, Breaking Cover, 2-hdld, w/lid, 4" 250.00
Sugar bowl, Scenes of Village Life, 6-sided, 3½" 300.00
Sugar bowl, Ye Village Scenes, 2-hdld, w/lid, 4" 195.00
Teapot, FH, Breaking Cover, 4½" 700.00
Teapot, Scenes of Village Life, 5½" 510.00
Tile, tea; Emerald, Dr Syntax Taking Possession..., 6" 600.00
Tile, tea; Traveling in Ye Olden Days, 6" 175.00
Tray, ad for Reopening of Waldorf...on Ye Minuet scene, 12" ...1,700.00
Tray, card; Emerald, Dr Syntax Robbed of His Property, 7¾" 450.00
Tray, card; FH, 7¾" 475.00
Tray, card; Ye Lion Inn, 7¾" 300.00
Tray, dresser; Dancing Ye Minuet, 9x12" 550.00
Tray, pin; Ye Olden Days, 6¼x3½" 345.00
Vase, Emerald, Kingfisher, Dragonflies & Iris, 7¾" 2,900.00
Vase, untitled, lovely ladies on Village Scenes ground, 8" 1,100.00
Vase, Ye Village Schoolmaster-Ye Village Parson, 8½" 650.00

Miscellaneous

Advertising cup plate, Wanamaker Store, 1861-1911, 4¼" 95.00
Ashtray, Blue Lune, cowboy-hat shape, 5¾" 45.00
Bowl, flat rim soup; Gaudy Willow, 9½" 175.00
Butter pat, BAC, TL, blk w/bl & gold striping, C 18.00
Butter pat, BW, 3¼" 45.00
Butter pat, Congregational Church, bl script/blk pinstripe, TL, C ..18.00
Butter pat, Gaudy Willor, 3¼" 165.00
Butter pat, May's, TM in gray script w/bl/blk pinstriping, C 35.00
Butter pat, Park Lane, TL, BS: Park Lane, New York, C 15.00
Butter pat, pine trees, lakeside lodge, fine pinstripe, C 24.00
Butter pat, SRCC, TL, in blk w/dotted border, C 15.00
Butter pat, The Tacoms, TM, shades of gray & gr, C 25.00
Butter pat, Vienna, dk bl w/gold trim, 3¼" 55.00
Chamber pot, lg pk roses w/greenery & gold touches, w/lid 145.00
Child's feeding dish, Blue Bird decor, 7½" 105.00
Child's feeding dish, Campbell Kids scene w/ABC rim, 7½" 135.00
Chop plate, Morgan's Red Coach Tavern w/FH scene, on RW, 11" ..325.00
Creamer, Boos Bros, brn w/yel flowers, w/hdl, C, ind 45.00
Creamer, BW, 5" 145.00
Creamer, HH superimposed on football w/blk pinstripe, 3¾" 35.00
Cup, red devil, ped ft, C, 5¼" 35.00
Cup & saucer, demitasse; BW 95.00
Jug, Bluebird, Chicago-style 7" 145.00
Jug, BW, Chicago-style, 7" 295.00
Jug, BW, rnd Buffalo-style, 6" 225.00
Jug, Cinderella, mc, 6" 690.00
Jug, George Washington, 7¾" 490.00
Jug, Geranium, gr-bl, cobalt, or mc, 4½" 265.00
Jug, Landing of Roger Williams, 6" 650.00
Jug, The Gunner, Buffalo-style, gr-bl w/speckled gold, 6" 1,000.00
Jug, Triumph, cobalt poppies & gold accents, 7" 325.00
Jug, Whaling, whaling ship & whaling scenes, 6" 600.00
Jug, Wild Ducks, Buffalo-style, gr-bl w/speckled gold, 6" 500.00
Mug, Celebration, Vacation, Expectation, etc, 4½" 72.00
Pitcher, Gloriana, gr-bl or cobalt, 9" 610.00
Pitcher, Roosevelt Bears, 8" 2,600.00
Pitcher, tankard; hooded friar holding mug, 12", +3 5" mugs 850.00
Pitcher, Whirl of the Town, 7" 1,000.00
Plate, Airport Cafe, mc single-propeller airplane, C, 7" 42.00
Plate, BW, BS, First Old Willow Ware, scalloped, 10½" 185.00
Plate, BW, scalloped, 10½" 135.00
Plate, calendar; for Bing & Nathan, Buffalo NY, 1911, 7" 200.00
Plate, Gaudy Willow, 9½" 145.00
Plate, Geranium, mc, 10" 175.00
Plate, Hotel Rob't Fulton, BS, ship on HP waves w/cobalt, 10" .175.00
Plate, Lincoln reviewing troops on horsebk, cobalt, 12x14" 1,200.00
Plate, Mandalay, mc floral, C, 9½" 45.00
Plate, Roosevelt Bears, scalloped, 7¼" 480.00
Plate, RW Willow, blk transfer on RW body, 9" 100.00
Platter, Dr Syntax Advertisement for a Wife, bl & wht, 11x14" ...420.00
Sauce boat w/underplate, BW, 8½" 185.00
Shaker, Roycroft Pepper, tabered w/Roycroft logo, 1926, 2¾" ...150.00
Sugar bowl, BW, sq w/hdls, w/lid, 6" 110.00
Teapot, Argyle, bl & wht, w/orig metal tea ball, C 235.00
Toaster, BW, ceramic fr att to Buffalo china, 6¾x7¼" 1,000.00
Vase, FH scene on Ye Old Ivory body, bulbous, 8" 250.00
Vase, rose bowl; Geranium, mc, 3¼" 265.00
Vase, rose clusters w/gold, 2 delicate hdls, slim, tall 45.00
Wash set, Chrysanthemum, pitcher+bowl+soap dish w/lid+4x6" tray ..465.00

Buggy Steps

New and younger buggy step collectors have created a demand for original cast-iron buggy steps. They seek steps with design and pattern. 'Name' steps still command good prices. The buggy era (1864 – 1910) produced vehicles from over forty-six different manufactures. What remains are treasured reminders of a past era. The listings that follow describe unmarked steps with multiple designs. However, there are numerous 'name' steps shown in previous editions. (Prices shown are for original steps, mint to good. Rusty, broken, and pitted condition reduces the value.) Our advisor for this category is John Waddell; he is listed in the Directory under Texas.

Open sq w/toe shield, 2-hole mt, 3x3½" 24.00
Oval pad, raised checks, 2-hole mt, 3x4½" 24.00
Rectangular pad, raised checks, 2-hole mt, 3½x4½" 25.00
Rectangular pad, 22 raised lines, 2-hole mt, 3½x4½" 28.00
Rectangular pad, 3 raised lines/12 holes, 2-hole mt, 3½x4½" 35.00
Rnd pad, open toe pad, 6 lines w/checks, 2-hold mt, 4½x4½" 35.00
Rnd pad w/toe shield, Hesse & Son, 3-hole mt, 4½" dia 45.00
Shield pad, open cross lattice, 3-hole mt, 3½x3½" 30.00
Spade pad, raised checks, 2-hole mt, 3x4" 22.00
Sq pad w/toe shield, open circles, 2 top bolts, 3½x3½" 30.00
Sq pad w/toe shield, open lattice, 3-hole mt, 3½x4" 30.00
Sq pad w/toe shield, raised lines, 3-hole mt, 3¼x3¼" 22.00
Sq w/toe shield, Aztec in circle, 2-hole mt, 3¼x3¼" 35.00
Sq w/toe shield, raised Ys, 2-hole mt, 3¼x3½" 27.00

Burmese

Burmese glass was patented in 1885 by the Mount Washington Glass Co. It is typically shaded from canary yellow to a rosy salmon color. The yellow is produced by the addition of uranium oxide to the mix. The salmon color comes from the addition of gold salts and is achieved by reheating the object (partially) in the furnace. It is thus called 'heat sensitive' glass. Thomas Webb of England was licensed to produce Burmese and often added more gold, giving an almost fuchsia tinge to the salmon in some cases. They called their glass 'Queen's Burmese,' and this is sometimes etched on the base of the object. This is not to be confused with Mount Washington's 'Queen's Design,' which refers to the design painted on the object. Both companies added decoration to many pieces. Mount Washington-Pairpoint produced some Burmese in the late 1920s and Gundersen and Bryden in the '50s and '70s, but the color and shapes are different. Our advisors for this category are Dolli and Wilfred Cohen; they are listed in the Directory under California. In the listings that follow, examples are assumed to have the satin finish unless noted 'shiny.' See also Lamps, Fairy.

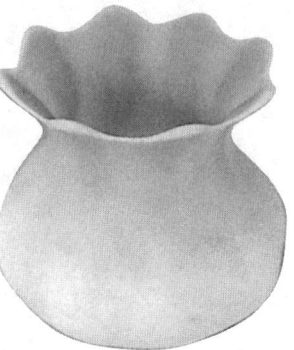

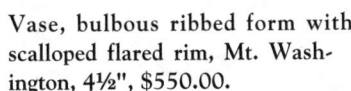

Vase, bulbous ribbed form with scalloped flared rim, Mt. Washington, 4½", $550.00.

Basket, burmese rope hdl, Gundersen, 8x5" 300.00
Bonbon, optic ribs, inverted rim, Mt WA, 2x5¼x4½" 350.00
Bowl, berry; crimped rim, Mt WA, 2¾x9" 950.00
Bowl, berry; Mt WA, 1x6½" 225.00
Bowl, console; Mt WA, 3½x11½" 1,500.00
Bowl, floral, appl rim, Webb, 3¾x6¼" 1,100.00
Bowl, rectangular top, Mt WA, 2x5¼x4½" 425.00
Bowl, ruffled rim, Gundersen, 2½x6" 385.00
Bowl, ruffled rim, lg ft, Mt WA, 6x7¼" 1,500.00
Bowl, ruffled rim, 3 appl burmese feathers, 7x9" 1,250.00
Bowl, ruffled top, 3 shell ft, berry pontil, Mt WA, 7¼" 425.00
Candle holders, shiny, pk flanged/ruffled rims, 5½", pr 600.00
Compote, wafer base, Pairpoint, 4½x7" 550.00
Creamer, appl burmese hdl, Mt WA, 2½x1⅜" 550.00
Creamer & sugar bowl, shiny, Pairpoint, 1920s, 3¾x3" 415.00
Cruet, vertical ribs, appl yel hdl, Mt WA, 6⅛x3¾" 1,150.00
Cup, custard; shiny, yel hdl, 2⅞x2½" 350.00
Cup, Dmn Quilt, appl hdl, 3¼" 330.00
Cup & saucer, yel hdl, Mt WA, 2½", 5½" 600.00
Ewer/creamer, long spout, loop hdl, appl base, Mt WA, 6" 950.00
Finger bowl, scalloped rim, 2½x4¾" 225.00
Jar, florals, w/lid, 5¼" 1,200.00
Lamp, fairy; ruffled rim, Gundersen, 5⅞" 200.00
Match holder, shiny, lav 5-petal florals, Webb, 3x2½" dia 350.00
Pitcher, Egyptian style, sq hdl, Mt WA, 7", w/6 4" tumblers ..2,250.00
Pitcher, milk; shiny, roses w/bl enameled verse, Mt WA, 7x7" ..3,500.00
Pitcher, milk; tankard, loop hdl, Mt WA, 7¼x4" 950.00
Pitcher, petticoat form, loop hdl, Mt WA, 11x9½" 1,385.00
Pitcher, yel hdl, Mt WA, 7x6½" 1,100.00
Plate, Gundersen, 9" 650.00
Plate, shiny, Pairpoint, 1930s, 8" 225.00
Rose bowl, crimped rim, gold prunus decor, mini, 2x2¾" 525.00
Rose bowl, Webb, 2¼" 295.00
Shakers, floral, orig SP cart-form fr, pr 675.00
Shakers, Ribbed Pillar, floral, Mt WA, pr 395.00
Sherbet, ftd, Mt WA, 2½x2⅞" 395.00
Sugar bowl, wishbone ft, berry prunt, Mt WA, 3½x4½" 595.00
Sugar shaker, floral, unfired, egg form, orig lid, 4½x4" 750.00
Sugar shaker, forget-me-nots, 4" 750.00
Toothpick holder, bulbous w/sq rim, Mt WA, 2½x2" 375.00
Toothpick holder, HP chrysanthemums, sq rim, Mt WA, 2½" 595.00
Toothpick holder, pine cones/branches/needles, Mt WA, 3" 675.00
Toothpick holder, ruffled rim, 2⅞" 450.00

Tumbler, juice; English ivy, Mt WA, 3¾" 395.00
Tumbler, juice; rim refired yel, Mt WA, 3¾x2¾" 275.00
Tumbler, juice; yel roses, Mt WA, 3¾" 465.00
Tumbler, lemonade; Dmn Quilt, loop hdl, 4¾" 450.00
Vase, bell form, mc floral, crimped rim, 4½" 250.00
Vase, bud; Webb, SP hdld fr, 8¼" 515.00
Vase, bulbous, ruffled rim, Webb, 3½x2½" 225.00
Vase, bulbous, shiny, Mt WA, 6" 350.00
Vase, bulbous w/6-sided top, gr ivy decor, Webb, 3⅝x3¾" 550.00
Vase, chalice form, dbl-knob stem, Pairpoint, 10¼x6½" 850.00
Vase, dbl-gourd form, Mt WA, 10¼x5½" 750.00
Vase, dbl-gourd form, Mt WA, 7x4" 650.00
Vase, dbl-gourd form, Mt WA, 8¾x5" 695.00
Vase, dbl-gourd form, roses & forget-me-nots, Mt WA, 8" 1,250.00
Vase, gourd form, barn swallows, Mt WA, 8" 1,350.00
Vase, gourd form, Mt WA, 12x6½" 825.00
Vase, gourd form, Mt WA, 8x4" 650.00
Vase, gourd form w/bamboo, Mt WA, 11½x6½" 1,875.00
Vase, jack-in-pulpit; folded/crimped rim, Mt WA, 9¾" 490.00
Vase, jack-in-pulpit; ruffled rim, Mt WA, 6½x3" 425.00
Vase, jack-in-pulpit; shiny, Pairpoint, 1920s, 5¼x6¾" 575.00
Vase, lily or Tappan; Gundersen, 1940s, 9½" 375.00
Vase, lily; Mt WA, 12¼" 750.00
Vase, lily; Mt WA, 14" 875.00
Vase, lily; Mt WA, 15" 950.00
Vase, lily; Mt WA, 18" 800.00
Vase, lily; Mt WA, 8" 450.00
Vase, lily; shiny, Mt WA, 6" 495.00
Vase, lily; shiny, Mt WA, 9¾" 750.00
Vase, Queen's, dbl-gourd form, daisies w/gold, 8" 2,600.00
Vase, Queen's, gold berries & leaves w/mc, Webb, 8¾" 1,250.00
Vase, Queen's, stick neck, gold trim, 8" 2,950.00
Vase, Queen's, w/ivy decor on bottle shape, Webb, 10¼x5" 895.00
Vase, shiny, in SP fr w/3 ball ft, 15" 650.00
Vase, shiny, Mt WA, 6" 350.00
Vase, shiny, scalloped rim, Webb, 2½" 395.00
Vase, stick neck, bamboo, much gold, 10½" 1,850.00
Vase, stick neck, daisies & ivy, gold rings, Mt WA, 10¾" 1,950.00
Vase, stick neck, Mt WA, 5½" 550.00
Vase/rose bowl, Honeycomb, 3 reeded ft, Mt WA, 8" 1,200.00
Whiskey taster, Webb, 2⅞x2½" 335.00
Whiskey taster, 2⅞x2½", +4" saucer 450.00

Butter Molds and Stamps

The art of decorating butter began in Europe during the reign of Charles II. This practice was continued in America by the farmer's wife who sold her homemade butter at the weekly market to earn extra money during hard times. A mold or stamp with a special design, hand carved either by her husband or a local craftsman, not only made her product more attractive but also helped identify it as hers. The pattern became the trademark of Mrs. Smith, and all who saw it knew that this was her butter. It was usually the rule that no two farms used the same mold within a certain area, thus the many variations and patterns available to the collector today. The most valuable are those which have animals, birds, or odd shapes. The most sought-after motifs are the eagle, cow, fish, and rooster. These works of early folk art are quickly disappearing from the market.

Molds

Berries, wood w/iron hinge, 3¼x4½"+hdl 160.00
Cherries on stem w/leaves, 2½" sq 110.00

Cornflower, EX cvg, rnd case w/plunger, 4¾" dia 95.00
Cow, rectangular w/hinged box, Continental, 11" L 165.00
Floral reserve w/geometric border, 4⅝x8¾" 150.00
Geometric, deep cvg, cherry wood, 4½x7", EX 120.00
Hex sign & hearts, 3½x5" 225.00
Pomegranate, rnd case, 4¾" dia 95.00
Sheaf of wheat, dbl, 2½x3¾" L 85.00
Sheaf of wheat (2), notch design at rim, nailed, 2¾x7x4⅛" 100.00
Strawberries & leaves, natural patina, 5" L 100.00
Swan, detailed, 5" dia 125.00
Tulips (2) & circular designs, walnut box, 2¾x5⅞x4¼" 125.00

Stamps

Acorn & 2 lg leaves, lathe-trn, 1-pc, 4⅛" dia 250.00
Bud & leaves w/X-hatching, incised border, 1-pc, 3½" dia 110.00
Chicken among foliage, linear border, 1-pc, 4⅜" dia 600.00
Cow, 1-pc, trn hdl, 4⅜" dia 200.00
Cow w/lg horns & sm rail fence, coggled rim, 1-pc, 3¼" dia 825.00
Dbl pomegranate w/X-hatching & leaves, knob hdl, 3¼x6" 230.00
Dbl 3-leaf clover w/EX cvg, rectangular, 4x5¼" 130.00
Eagle, semicircular, inserted hdl, 7" 220.00
Eagle w/wings wide, olive branch in beak, 1-pc, 4¼" dia 225.00
Flower & foliage, inserted hdl, 3½" dia 125.00
Heart & fleur-de-lis w/leaves, 3¼" dia 175.00
Heart w/X-hatching, 1-pc, knob-shaped hdl, 4⅜" dia 250.00
Heart-shaped leaf w/leaf border, 1-pc, 4¼" dia 180.00
Pineapple, semicircular, EX old patina, inserted hdl, 7" 220.00
Pineapple w/X-hatching, 1-pc, age crack, 3⅞" dia 100.00
Radial dbl-sided design w/4 lobes & 8-point star, 5" dia, EX ...1,000.00
Radial design w/incised herringbone designs, flat bk, 3⅛" dia 85.00
Radial design w/3 lobes, lollipop style, 1-pc, 3⅝" dia 500.00
Radial design w/4 lobes, notched rim, 2-pc, 2¼" dia 60.00
Radial design w/6 lobes, dtd 1846, 3¾" dia 375.00
Radial design w/6 lobes, lollipop style, 4⅛" dia 425.00
Radial design w/6 lobes, plain rim, 4" dia 100.00
Star w/5 points, incised lines, 3" dia 80.00
Star w/5 points, sawtooth border, 1-pc, 4½x4¾" 150.00
Sunburst floral, semicircular, inserted hdl, 7", pr 350.00
Swirl design, lathe-trn & cvd, rnded base, 3¾x3¾" dia 475.00
Thistles, 1-pc, 3⅛" dia+2¾" hdl 85.00
Tulip, EX color, 1-pc w/trn hdl, 3⅞" dia 165.00
Tulip, sawtooth border, 1-pc oval, 4½x5" 300.00
Tulip & stars, primitive w/natural growth hdl, 3⅛x3¾" 150.00
Tulips (lg amid 2 sm) w/star border, 1-pc, 4¾" dia 350.00

Buttonhooks

The earliest known written reference to buttonhooks (shoe hooks, glove hooks, or collar buttoners) is dated 1611. They became a necessary implement in the 1850s when tight-fitting high-button shoes became fashionable. Later in the 19th century, ladies' button gloves and men's button-on collars and cuffs dictated specific types of buttoners, some with a closed wire loop instead of a hook end. Both shoes and gloves used as many as twenty-four buttons each. Usage began to wane in the late 1920s following a fashion change to low-cut laced shoes and the invention of the zipper. There was a brief resurgence of use following the 1948 movie *High Button Shoes*. For a simple, needed utilitarian device, buttonhook handles were made from a surprising variety of materials: natural wood, bone, ivory, agate, and mother-of-pearl to plain steel, celluloid, aluminum, iron, lead and pewter, artistic copper, brass, silver, gold, and many other materials, in lengths that varied from under 2" to over 20". Many designs folded or retracted, and button-

hooks were often combined with shoehorns and other useful implements. Stamped steel buttonhooks often came free with the purchase of shoes, gloves, or collars. Material, design, workmanship, condition, and relative scarcity are the primary market value factors. Prices range from $1.00 to over $100.00. Buttonhooks are fairly easy to find, and they are interesting to display. Our advisor for this category is Richard Mathes; he is listed in the Directory under Ohio.

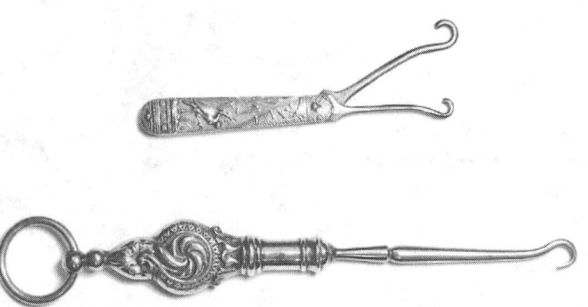

Glove hook, brass, double, folds, $40.00; Shoe hook, sterling, $45.00.

Buttonhook/penknife, ivory side plates, man's 40.00
Glove hook, gold plated, rectractable, 3" 75.00
Glove hook, loop end, agate hdl, 2½" 45.00
Shoe hook, colored celluloid hdl, 8" 12.00
Shoe hook, lathe-trn hardwood hdl, dk finish, 8" 12.00
Shoe hook, stamped steel, advertising, 5" 8.00
Shoe hook, sterling, floral & geometrics 45.00
Shoe hook, sterling, Nouveau lady's face, 6½" 75.00
Shoe hook, sterling, W w/arrow, hammered Florentine decor, mk .45.00
Shoe hook/shoehorn combination, steel & celluloid, 9" 25.00

Bybee

The Bybee Pottery was founded in 1809 in the small town of Bybee, Kentucky. Their earliest wares were primarily stoneware churns and jars. Today the work is carried on by sixth-generation Cornelison potters who still use the same facilities and production methods to make a more diversified line of pottery. From a fine white clay mined only a few miles from the potting shed itself, the shop produces vases, jugs, dinnerware, and banks in a variety of colors, some of which are shipped to the larger cities to be sold in department stores and specialty shops. The bulk of their wares, however, is sold to the thousands of tourists who are attracted to the pottery each year.

Bowl, batter; brn, unsgn, 1966, 3¾x10x12", NM 45.00
Bowl, tan gloss, ca 1981, rstr chip, 2¾x7¼" 25.00
Pot, storage; turq gloss, script mk, w/lid, 4½" 40.00
Vase, 3 hdls, 5½x7" 65.00

Cabat

From beginning experimentation with pottery in New York City around 1940, through several different types of clay, designs, and glazes, and relocation to Arizona, the Rose Cabat 'Feelie,' so named because 'it feels so good,' evolved into present forms and glazes in the late 1950s. Rose was aided and encouraged through the years by her late husband Erni. Their small 'weed pots' are readily recognizable by their light weight, tiny thin necks, and soft glazes. Pieces are marked with a hand-incised 'Cabat' on the bottom.

Vase, Feelie, bl matt w/gold crystals, 3¼" 300.00
Vase, Feelie, lime to med gr w/gray crystals, 3" 300.00
Vase, Feelie, striated brn to tan w/copper dust crystals, 2¼" 175.00

Calendar Plates

Calendar plates were advertising giveaways most popular from about 1906 until the late '20s. They were decorated with colorful underglaze decals of lovely ladies, flowers, animals, birds and, of course, the twelve months of the year of their issue. During the 1950s they came into vogue again but never to the extent they were originally. Those with exceptional detailing, or those with scenes of a particular activity are most desirable, so are any from before 1906.

1904, Happy New Year, Cupid & bell, 8" 50.00
1908, dog, 8½" 48.00
1908, lady, Detroit MI 38.00
1908, pk rose border 30.00
1909, Friars w/fruit & goose, Sterling China, 9¼", EX 45.00
1909, fruit & flowers, 7" 25.00
1909, rose center, 8½" 35.00
1909, roses, Price Hill Fuel Co, WV 30.00
1909, scenic, 8½" 30.00
1910, Betsy Ross, Jersey City 38.00
1910, horseshoe encircles hunter w/gun 40.00
1910, Indian Chief's portrait, Imperial China, 8" 25.00
1910, lighthouse & sailboats 35.00
1910, sailboats on water 35.00
1910, setter dog, Binghampton NY 30.00
1911, hunter w/dog & quail 40.00
1911, Old Acquaintance 30.00
1911, 4-leaf clover 35.00
1912, biplane, Cincinnati grocery 68.00
1912, flowers & cherubs, 8½" 25.00
1912, Indian maiden 40.00
1912, owl, Augusta IL 35.00
1913, farm boy 40.00
1914, automobile 42.00
1914, deer at stream, 7" 35.00
1914, 3 plums & 1 pear, 7¼" 25.00
1915, Panama Canal, w/Am flag, 6" 50.00
1916, flag, 7½" 28.00
1918, flag, 8" 27.50
1921, dove & 5 Allied flags, 7½" 40.00
1930, Dutch boy & dog, 9" 70.00
1930, parrot, Schultz Produce, Spencer NE 65.00

Calendars

Calendars are collected for their colorful prints, often attributed to a well-recognized artist of the period. Advertising calendars from the turn of the century often have a double appeal when representing a company whose tins, signs, store displays, etc., are also collectible. See also Parrish, Maxfield.

1888, Farmers Fire Ins Co, girl w/fruit, full pad, 10x7", NM 280.00
1888, Hood's Sarsaparilla, girl in bl bonnet, EX 80.00
1889, Hood's Sarsaparilla, girl in bonnet, EX 80.00
1890, Hibard's Rheumatic Syrup, lady w/baby, 5x7", EX 90.00
1890, Sulphur Bitters, boy eating fruit, 9x7", VG+ 40.00
1890, Victorian girls, Horsford Bread, 4-pg, EX 65.00
1892, Singer Sewing Machines, pretty lady, 9x6"+mat & fr, EX ..135.00

1894, Clay Robinson & Co, country scene w/sheep, may only, fr .15.00
1894-95, Nestle's Food, babies, May 1894-April 1895, 2-sided 50.00
1898, Hood's Sarsaparilla, coupon calendar, complete, NM 70.00
1899, Grit America's Greatest Family Newspaper, cb, 12x9", EX .110.00
1900, draped nude, Varga, incomplete pad, postcard sz 20.00
1900, Hood's Sarsaparilla, 2 girls arm in arm, March, EX 125.00
1900, Hoods' Sarsaparilla, 2 baby girls, EX 95.00
1901, Hoods Sarsaparilla, Patience, full pad, 20x7", NM 100.00
1902, Lambertville Rubber Co, Brownies in boots, complete, VG .75.00
1903, Bel-Cap-Sic Plaster, girl & puppy, 10x13", EX 50.00
1903, Hood's Sarsaparilla, girl, dogs & donkey, EX 120.00
1903, Yale, Sports Illustrated, complete, EX 60.00
1904, Metropolitan Life Ins, lady w/holly, Am Litho, 20x7", NM .150.00
1904, Pabst Extracts, different baby ea month, 28x10", EX+ 375.00
1905, Bauder, children in wagon, candies/nuts/etc, 13½x10½", EX ...175.00
1905, Dr AC Daniel's Veterinary Medicines, complete, EX 200.00
1906, child & puppy, Nat'l Stoves & Ranges, 13x9¾", EX 145.00
1906, Deering Cream Separators, beautiful lady, complete, NM ...325.00
1906, Hiawatha, Indian scenes, 36x7½", EX 125.00
1906, Lambertville Rubber Co, Lambertville Girl, complete, EX ...200.00
1906, Life's Calendar, Charles Dana Gibson art, partial pad 15.00
1907, Capewell Horse Nails, 13", matted & fr 150.00
1907, Pabst Extract, Yard Long Girl, 27x10", NM 330.00
1908, Pabst Extract, Jewel, 41x10", EX 575.00
1909, cowgirl on horse, North British & Mercantile, 12x17", EX ...85.00
1909, Independent Tea Co, girl & lilacs, complete, 20x15", NM .300.00
1910, Dr Simmon's Squaw Vine Liver Medicine, complete, NM ..120.00
1910, Pabst Extract, lady in wht dress/plumed hat, 35x10", NM ..250.00
1911, Iowa's Successful Farmer, dogs & months, 25x11", VG+ 50.00
1912, Champion Harvesting Machines, farmer/child, 20x12", EX ..175.00
1912, Sunbonnet babies fishing, 6x8", EX 75.00
1914, Hood's Sarsaparilla, mother in red cape w/baby, NM 145.00
1914, Westinghouse Mazda, lady, complete, NM 425.00
1915, Hood's Sarsaparilla, schoolgirl w/books, NM 165.00
1915, Pabst Extract, Panama Girl, 36x10", VG+ 155.00
1918, Dmn Dyes, salesman's, NM 100.00
1918, Fidelity-Phoenix Fire Ins Co, hockey, complete, 10x8", EX ..65.00
1919, Djer-Kiss, Parrish-like art, EX 20.00
1919, Hood's Sarsaparilla, mother & child, WWI, complete, NM ..195.00
1921, McCormick-Deering, girl on fence by wheat field, 232x1", VG ...30.00
1923, EJ Myers Garage, auto w/roses, complete, 10x15", EX 145.00
1923, Winona, Indian princess on cliff, FA Rettke, full pad, VG .50.00
1927, Seneca Cameras, Indian princess, complete, VG+ 350.00
1930, Kist Beverages, girl w/bottle at fence, complete, NM 100.00
1933, Fairbank's Gold Dust Washing Powder, complete, NM 55.00
1935, Keen Kutter, hunting dogs, complete, 17x12", EX+ 150.00
1936, Hercules Powder Co, Day's End, EX 70.00
1936, Jacob Ruppert Beer, elves pushing keg, full pad, EX 25.00

1937, Dr. Miles Weather Calendar, Owl Drug Co., EX+, $55.00.

1939, Earl Christy art, NM 125.00
1939, Erie Club Beverages, pinup girl in swing, complete, EX 150.00
1939, Poll Parrot, Anna Benson Mueller color illus, EX 55.00
1940, Keen Kutter, winter scene/open scissors, complete, NM 50.00
1942, Mission Orange, complete, NM 145.00
1944, John Eichler Brewing Co, eagle & name, complete, VG+ ...100.00
1946, Kist Beverages, girl in flower garden, complete, NM 130.00
1947, Earl Moran pinup art, NM 70.00
1947, Petty pinup art, NM 70.00
1948, Esquire Glamour Gallery, NM 60.00
1948, Man of Tomorrow, Rockwell, VG 17.50
1948, Morrell Fairy Tales, complete 30.00
1950, Pal Ade, Babe Ruth From the Heavens/boy at bat, NM+ .525.00
1951, Modern Venus, Elvgren nude, M 70.00
1954, Mission Orange, 1954, EX 65.00
1955, Speedy Muffler, Marilyn Monroe pinup, 1955, EX 375.00
1957, North Shore Foundry, Joe DiMaggio, complete, 33x16", EX .55.00

Caliente

Caliente was a line of colored dinnerware made by the Paden City Pottery Company in Paden City, West Virginia. It was produced during the 1930s and 1940s in tangerine, yellow, blue, green, and cobalt blue.

Creamer, $14.00; Sugar bowl with lid, $18.00.

Bowl, salad; 10" 25.00
Bowl, 5¼" 10.00
Bowl, 9" 20.00
Candle holder 15.00
Cup & saucer 15.00
Plate, dinner; 10" 17.50
Plate, 6" 5.00
Plate, 9½" 10.00
Platter, 12" 20.00
Platter, 14" 25.00
Teapot 45.00

California Faience

California Faience was the tradename used by William V. Bragdon and Chauncy R. Thomas on vases, bowls, and other artware produced at their pottery known as 'The Tile Shop' in Berkeley, California, from 1920 to 1930. Faience tile was the principal product of the business during these years and is the favorite with today's collectors. Items in a glossy glaze are rare and therefore more valuable. Tiles were marked 'California Faience' with a die stamp.

Bowl, floral band, mc on yel, closed rim, 2¾x4¼" 1,400.00
Tile, basket of fruit, red/celadon/yel/bl, 5½" dia 295.00

Tile, raised pinwheel, bl on maroon, 5½" sq 350.00
Tile, sailing ship in rough sea, brn/lt & dk bl/yel, 5½" sq 450.00
Vase, bl gloss on red clay, invt rim, 4⅝" 200.00
Vase, deep rose matt, mk, 4½" 240.00
Vase, floral band, mc on bl, bulbous, 2½x4" 600.00
Vase, turq, 4x3" 145.00

California Perfume Company

D.H. McConnell, Sr., founded the California Perfume Company (C.P. Company; C.P.C.) in 1886 in New York City. He had previously been a salesman for a book company, which he later purchased. His door-to-door sales usually involved the lady of the house, to whom he presented a complimentary bottle of inexpensive perfume. Upon determining his perfume to be more popular than his books, he decided that the manufacture of perfume might be more lucrative. He bottled toiletries under the name 'California Perfume Company' and a line of household products called 'Perfection.' In 1928 the name 'Avon' appeared on the label, and in 1939 the C.P.C. name was entirely removed from the product. The success of the company is attributed to the door-to-door sales approach and 'money back' guarantee offered by his first 'Depot Agent,' Mrs. P.F.E. Albee, known today as the 'Avon Lady.'

The company's containers are quite collectible today, especially the older, hard-to-find items. Advanced collectors seek 'go with' items labeled Goetting & Co., New York; Goetting's; or Savoi Et Cie, Paris. Such examples date from 1871 to 1896. The Goetting Company was purchased by D.H. McConnell; Savoi Et Cie was a line which they imported to sell through department stores. Also of special interest are packaging and advertising with the Ambrosia or Hinze Ambrosia Company label. This was a subsidiary company whose objective seems to have been to produce a line of face creams, etc., for sale through drugstores and other such commercial outlets. They operated in New York from about 1875 until 1954. Because very little is known about these companies and since only a few examples of their product containers and advertising material have been found, market values for such items have not yet been established. Other items sought by the collector include products marked Gertrude Recordon, Marvel Electric Silver Cleaner, Easy Day Automatic Clothes Washer, pre-1915 catalogs, and California Perfume Company 1909 and 1910 calendars.

There are hundreds of local Avon Collector Clubs throughout the world that also have C.P.C. collectors in their membership. If you are interested in joining, locating, or starting a new club, contact the National Association of Avon Collectors, Inc., listed in the Directory under Clubs, Newsletters, and Catalogs. Those wanting a National Newsletter Club or price guides may contact Avon Times, listed in the same section. See also Avon. Inquiries concerning California Perfume Company items and the companies or items mentioned in the previous paragraphs should be directed toward our advisor, Dick Pardini, whose address is given under California. (Please send a large SASE and be sure to request clearly the information you are seeking; not interested in Avons, 'Perfection' marked C.P.C.'s, or Anniversary Keepsakes.)

American Ideal Box 'C' Set, perfume+powder sachet, 1911, M ..300.00
Army & Navy Kit, 6 grooming items, 1918, MIB 210.00
Atomizer Set, atomizer +3 perfumes, ca 1900, M 375.00
Baby Set, oil+powder+soap+boric acid, 1925, M in yel box 300.00
Baking Powder 'California,' 16-oz, 1-lb or 5-lb szs, M, ea 80.00
Bay Rum, came in 4-, 8- & 16-oz, 1890s, M, ea 150.00
Daphne Set, 1-oz perfume, face powder, rouge, 1918, M 200.00
Easy Day/Simplex Automatic Clothes Washer, 1918, MIB 100.00
Flavoring Extract Set, 20 1-oz bottles in blk case, 1912, M 1,100.00
Gentleman's Shaving Set, 7 items, 1923, MIB 310.00
Gertrude Recordon's Facial Treatment Set, 4-pc, 1929, MIB 250.00

Gift Box Set #1, ½-oz perfume+powder sachet, 1915, MIB **175.00**
Holly Set, pr ½-oz perfumes, 1912, M in holly-pattern box **260.00**
Little Folks Set, 4 sm perfumes, 1915, MIB **300.00**
Manicure Set, holds 8 different items, 1912, M **250.00**
Marvel Electric Silver Cleaner, 1918, MIB **100.00**
Memories That Linger Set, 3 different perfumes, 1913, M **325.00**
Mission Garden Perfume, Bavarian glass, 1½-oz, MIB **200.00**
Natoma Rose Talcum, triangular tin container, 1914, 4-oz, M ...**150.00**
Shoe White, 5-oz sack of powder, 1915, MIB **75.00**
Supreme Huile D'Olive Oil, 1-pt or 1-qt can, 1923, M, ea **50.00**
Trailing Arbutus Gift Box 'T,' 3-pc, 1915, M in mc box **300.00**
Vernafleur Threesome Gift Set, 3-pc, 1928, MIB **200.00**
Violet Gift Set 'H,' 1-oz perfume+talc+sachet+atomizer, M **325.00**

Calling Cards, Cases, and Receivers

The practice of announcing one's arrival with a calling card borne by the maid to the mistress of the house was a social grace of the Victorian era. Different messages (condolences, a personal visit, or a good-bye) were related by turning down one corner or another. The custom was forgotten by WWI. Fashionable ladies and gents carried their personally engraved cards in elaborate cases made of such materials as embossed silver, mother-of-pearl with intricate inlay, tortoise shell, and ivory. Card receivers held cards left by visitors who called while the mistress was out or 'not receiving.' Calling cards with fringe, die-cut flaps that cover the name, or an unusual decoration are worth about $3.00 to $4.00, while plain cards usually sell for around $1.00.

Cases

Abalone & pearl harlequin design w/tortoise & ivory edge, 4" **55.00**
Coin silver w/presentation eng, 3½", w/chain **82.50**
MOP, cvd cameo & monogram, 3⅝" **92.50**
Silver filigree, lobed/scalloped sides **110.00**
Sterling, chinoiserie relief, grapevines, 3¾" **225.00**
Sterling, w/floral eng, jade at clasp, 4", w/chain **110.00**
Tortoise shell, ivory mts, English, 1800s **92.50**
Tortoise shell w/detailed emb florals, 4" **92.50**
Tortoise shell w/silver/gold/MOP inlay, book style **300.00**

Receivers

Brass, Black male figure on base holding basket **450.00**
Bronze, monkey figural, Victorian, 7" **135.00**
Bronze, Nouveau lady overlooks lily pond, 6x7" **150.00**
NP CI, peacock, Richmond Stove Co...CT, EX **115.00**
Pottery, Nouveau scene of Hotel Astor, German mk, 6¼" **75.00**
SP, Cupid riding goat emb at bk of tray **350.00**
SP, stag's head hdl, Middleton **195.00**
Sterling, inscr 1887-1907 ....**45.00**

Camark

The Camden Art and Tile Company (commonly known as Camark) of Camden, Arkansas, was organized in the fall of 1926 by Samuel J. 'Jack' Carnes. Using clays from Arkansas, John Lessell, who had been hired as art director by Carnes, produced the initial lustre and iridescent Lessell wares for Camark ('CAM'den, 'ARK'ansas) before his death in December 1926. Before the plant opened in the spring of 1927, Carnes brought John's wife, Jeanne, and stepdaughter Billie to oversee the art department's manufacture of Le-Camark. Production by the Lessell family included variations of J.B. Owens' Soudanese and Opalesce

and Weller's Marengo and Lamar. Camark's version of Marengo was called Old English. They also made wares identical to Weller's LaSa. Pieces made by John Lessell back in Ohio were signed 'Lessell,' while those made by Jeanne and Billie in Arkansas during 1927 were signed 'Le-Camark.' By 1928 Camark's production centered on traditional glazes. Drip glazes similar to Muncie Pottery were produced, in particular the green drip over pink. In the 1930s commercial castware with simple glossy and matt finishes became the primary focus and would continue so until Camark closed in the early 1960s. Between the 1960s and 1980s the company operated mainly as a retail store selling existing inventory, but some limited production occurred. In 1986 the company was purchased by the Ashcraft family of Camden, but no pottery has yet been made at the factory.

Our advisor for this category is David Edwin Gifford. He is listed in the Directory under Arkansas. Mr. Gifford is the author of *Collector's Encyclopedia of Camark Pottery, Volume I*, and the editor of the *National Society of Arkansas Pottery Collectors Newsletter*.

Ashtray, brn stipple, circular mold mk #400, 2", from $30 to **40.00**
Ball jug, rose w/gr overflow, 1st block letter, 6¼", $100 to **120.00**
Ball pitcher, brn stipple, ink stamp, 6½", from $180 to **200.00**
Charger, wht matt, 1st block letter, 12¼", from $100 to **120.00**
Flower bowl, Aztec red mottle, die stamp, 5¼", $160 to **180.00**

Photo courtesy Weldi-Skinner collection

**Ginger jar, white 6-sided, 13",
from $300.00 to $350.00.**

Ginger jar, ivory crackle matt, gold ink stamp, 9", $300 to **350.00**
Jug, Pure Arkansas Corn, blk ink stamp, 5¼", from $60 to **80.00**
Lamp base, olive gr w/lt overflow, unmk, 6", from $160 to **180.00**
Leaf dish, bl matt, 1st block letter, 13", from $100 to **120.00**
Vase, Autumn, flower shape, 1st block letter, 10", from $80 to ..**100.00**
Vase, Barcelona/Spano Ware, sea gr, folded rim, stamped, 7" **150.00**
Vase, bl & wht stipple, gourd shape, unmk, 3", from $20 to **30.00**
Vase, bl crackle, shouldered, flared rim, ink stamp, 10½" **600.00**
Vase, bl stippled matt, trumpet neck, 1st block letter, 9" **250.00**
Vase, bl to gr, ring hdls, unmk, 4", from $140 to **160.00**
Vase, cornucopia; yel matt, 1st block letter, 6½", $40 to **60.00**
Vase, gr frosted fan form, unmk, 5¾", from $40 to **60.00**
Vase, gr w/orange overflow, angle hdls, #420, 10", from $400 to .**500.00**
Vase, gray & bl mottle, Deco style w/stepped sides, unmk, 9" **225.00**
Vase, olive gr w/lt overflow, brn sticker, 4½", from $80 to **100.00**
Vase, swirl, shouldered, 1st block letter, 4½", from $80 to **100.00**
Water jug, brn stipple, gold ink stamp, 6¼", from $200 to **250.00**

Cambridge Glass

The Cambridge Glass Company began operations in 1901 in Cambridge, Ohio. Primarily they made crystal dinnerware and well-designed accessory pieces until the 1920s when they introduced the concept of color that was to become so popular on the American dinnerware market. Always maintaining high standards of quality and elegance, they produced many lines that became bestsellers; through the '20s and '30s they were recognized as the largest manufacturer of this type of glassware in the world.

Of the various marks the company used, the 'C in triangle' is the most familiar. Production stopped in 1958. For a more thorough study of the subject, we recommend *Colors in Cambridge Glass* by the National Cambridge Collectors, Inc.; their address may be found in the Directory under Clubs. *Glass Animals and Figural Flower Frogs of the Depression Era* by Lee Garmon and Dick Spencer is a wonderful source for an in-depth view of their particular aspect of glass collecting. They are both listed in the Directory under Illinois. See also Carnival Glass; Glass Animals. In the listings below items are crystal unless noted otherwise. Caprice listings with an (*) at the end of the lines are made from moulds now owned by Summit Art Glass, with many of those pieces having been reproduced.

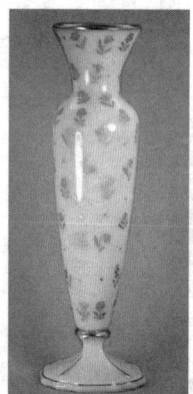

Crown Tuscan, vase, gold flowers (chintz), $150.00.

Apple Blossom, crystal, ashtray, heavy, 6" 35.00
Apple Blossom, crystal, bowl, oval, 4-ftd, 12" 40.00
Apple Blossom, crystal, cheese compote w/11½" plate 40.00
Apple Blossom, crystal, mayonnaise, w/liner & ladle, 4-ftd bowl ..35.00
Apple Blossom, crystal, plate, dinner; sq 39.00
Apple Blossom, crystal, plate, 8½" 12.00
Apple Blossom, crystal, shakers, pr 37.50
Apple Blossom, crystal, stem, parfait; #1066 ....65.00
Apple Blossom, crystal, stem, water; #3130, 8-oz 15.00
Apple Blossom, crystal, tray, sandwich; center hdl, 11" 25.00
Apple Blossom, pk or gr, bowl, finger; #3130, w/plate 45.00
Apple Blossom, pk or gr, bowl, fruit; saucer-like, 5½" 20.00
Apple Blossom, pk or gr, bowl, low ftd, 11" 90.00
Apple Blossom, pk or gr, candelabrum, keyhole; 3-light 60.00
Apple Blossom, pk or gr, stem, sherbet; #3130, low, 6-oz 15.00
Apple Blossom, pk or gr, tray, relish; hdls, 7" 30.00
Apple Blossom, pk or gr, tumbler; #3135, ftd, 5-oz 28.00
Apple Blossom, pk or gr, vase, rippled sides, 6" 75.00
Apple Blossom, yel or amber, bowl, baker; 10" 70.00
Apple Blossom, yel or amber, bowl, bonbon; hdls, 5¼" 25.00
Apple Blossom, yel or amber, creamer, ftd 50.00
Apple Blossom, yel or amber, pitcher, ball shape, 80-oz 165.00
Apple Blossom, yel or amber, saucer, AD 12.00
Apple Blossom, yel or amber, tumbler, #3130, ftd, 8-oz 25.00
Apple Blossom, yel or amber, tumbler, #3400, ftd, 2½-oz 50.00
Apple Blossom, yel or amber, vase, keyhole base w/neck indent, 12" ..150.00
Candlelight, crystal, bottle, oil; #3900/100, 6-oz 75.00
Candlelight, crystal, bowl, #3400/160, 4-ftd, oblong, 12" 75.00

Candlelight, crystal, bowl, #3900/54, flared, 4-toed, 10" 60.00
Candlelight, crystal, candle, #3900/72, 2-light, 6" 45.00
Candlelight, crystal, candlestick, #1338, 3-light, 6", ea 55.00
Candlelight, crystal, comport, cheese; #3900/135, 5" 35.00
Candlelight, crystal, cup, #3900/17 ....30.00
Candlelight, crystal, lamp, hurricane; #1617 ....165.00
Candlelight, crystal, plate, #900/166, rolled edge, 14" 70.00
Candlelight, crystal, relish, #3900/125, 3-part, 9" 47.50
Candlelight, crystal, stem, claret; #3776, 4½-oz 65.00
Candlelight, crystal, stem, cocktail; #3111, 3-oz 35.00
Candlelight, crystal, stem, cordial; #3776, 1-oz 95.00
Candlelight, crystal, stem, sherbet; #3776, tall, 7-oz 20.00
Candlelight, crystal, tumbler, iced tea; #3111, ftd, 12-oz 30.00
Candlelight, crystal, tumbler, juice; #3111, ftd, 5-oz 22.00
Caprice, crystal, bonbon, #154, hdls, sq, 6" 12.00
Caprice, crystal, bowl, #54, belled, 4-ftd, 10½" 35.00
Caprice, crystal, bowl, #61, crimped, 4-ftd, 12½" 35.00
Caprice, crystal, butterdish, #52, ¼-lb (*) 295.00
Caprice, crystal, candlestick, #1338, 3-light, ea 35.00
Caprice, crystal, candlestick, #67, 2½", ea 15.00
Caprice, crystal, candy dish, #168, divided, w/lid, 6" 55.00
Caprice, crystal, cigarette box, #207, w/lid, 3½x2¼" 20.00
Caprice, crystal, comport, #136, tall, 7" 30.00
Caprice, crystal, mayonnaise, #106, 3-pc set, 8" (*) 50.00
Caprice, crystal, pitcher, #183, ball shape, 80-oz 100.00
Caprice, crystal, plate, #30, 16" 50.00
Caprice, crystal, plate, dinner; #24, 9½" (*) 45.00
Caprice, crystal, stem, cordial; #300, blown, 1-oz 50.00
Caprice, crystal, stem, fruit cocktail; #7, 4½-oz 35.00
Caprice, crystal, tumbler, #188, flat, 2-oz (*) 22.00
Caprice, crystal, tumbler, #9, ftd, 12-oz 22.50
Caprice, crystal, vase, #238, ball shape, 6½" 65.00
Caprice, crystal, vase, #252, blown, 4½" 55.00
Caprice, crystal, vase, ivy bowl; #232, 5" 60.00
Caprice, pk or bk, bonbon, #133, ftd, sq, 6" 50.00
Caprice, pk or bl, bottle, w/stopper, 3-oz (*) 90.00
Caprice, pk or bl, bowl, #58, 4-ftd, sq, 10" 130.00
Caprice, pk or bl, bowl, #65, oval, 4-ftd, hdls, 11" (*) 125.00
Caprice, pk or bl, bowl, relish; #124, 3-part, 8" (*) 45.00
Caprice, pk or bl, bowl, salad; #84, shallow, 15" 225.00
Caprice, pk or bl, candlestick, #70, w/prism, 7", ea 65.00
Caprice, pk or bl, celery/relish; #124, 3-part, 8½" 45.00
Caprice, pk or bl, decanter, #187, w/stopper, 35-oz 425.00
Caprice, pk or bl, ice bucket, #201 ....200.00
Caprice, pk or bl, plate, cabaret; #26, 11½" 70.00
Caprice, pk or bl, shakers, #90, ball shape, ind, pr 145.00
Caprice, pk or bl, stem, sherbet; #4, low, 5-oz 85.00
Caprice, pk or bl, stem, wine; #300, blown, 2½-oz 60.00
Caprice, pk or bl, tumbler, #10, ftd, 10-oz (*) 40.00
Caprice, pk or bl, tumbler, #180, flat, 5-oz 65.00
Caprice, pk or bl, tumbler, tea; #310, flat, 12-oz 125.00
Caprice, pk or bl, tumbler, water; #300, ftd, 10-oz 40.00
Caprice, pk or bl, vase, #343, crimped top, 8½" 325.00
Caprice, pk or bl, vase, rose bowl; #235, ftd, 6" 150.00
Cascade, crystal, bowl, flared, 4-ftd, 10" 22.00
Cascade, crystal, buffet set, 21" plate w/8" ashtray 70.00
Cascade, crystal, punch bowl liner, 21" 50.00
Cascade, crystal, shakers, pr 18.00
Cascade, gr or yel, candlestick, 5", ea 27.50
Cascade, gr or yel, creamer 18.00
Cascade, gr or yel, mayonnaise, w/liner 50.00
Cascade, gr or yel, sugar bowl 18.00
Cascade, milk white, vase, 9½" 40.00
Chantilly, crystal, bowl, tab hdls, ftd, 11½" 35.00

Chantilly, crystal, butter dish, ¼-lb 225.00
Chantilly, crystal, cocktail icer, 2-pc 60.00
Chantilly, crystal, creamer 14.50
Chantilly, crystal, decanter, ftd 155.00
Chantilly, crystal, hurricane lamp, keyhole base w/prisms 175.00
Chantilly, crystal, mayonnaise, w/liner & ladle 37.50
Chantilly, crystal, pitcher, upright 195.00
Chantilly, crystal, plate, dinner; 10½" 85.00
Chantilly, crystal, shakers, flat, pr 35.00
Chantilly, crystal, stem, claret; #3600, 4½-oz 50.00
Chantilly, crystal, stem, claret; #3775, 4½-oz 50.00
Chantilly, crystal, stem, sherbet; #3779, tall, 6-oz 17.50
Chantilly, crystal, stem, water; #3625, 10-oz 25.00
Chantilly, crystal, stem, wine; #3779, 2½-oz 32.00
Chantilly, crystal, tumbler, juice; #3625, ftd, 5-oz 18.00
Chantilly, crystal, tumbler, 13-oz 24.00
Cleo, bl, bowl, almond; ind, 2½" 95.00
Cleo, bl, bowl, bonbon; 2-hdld, Decagon, 5½" 30.00
Cleo, bl, bowl, finger; #3077, w/liner 50.00
Cleo, bl, bowl, 2-hdld, Decagon, 8½" 55.00
Cleo, bl, creamer, Decagon 27.50
Cleo, bl, cup, Decagon 25.00
Cleo, bl, salt cellar, 1½" 110.00
Cleo, bl, stem, sherbet; #3077, tall, 6-oz 35.00
Cleo, bl, tumbler, #3077, ftd, 5-oz 50.00
Cleo, colors other than bl, bouillon cup, w/saucer, 2-hdld 35.00
Cleo, colors other than bl, bowl, cranberry; 6½" 30.00
Cleo, colors other than bl, candlestick, 2-light, ea 35.00
Cleo, colors other than bl, ice tub 60.00
Cleo, colors other than bl, pitcher, #804, w/lid, 60-oz 250.00
Cleo, colors other than bl, plate, hdls, Decagon, 11" 30.00
Cleo, colors other than bl, stem, cordial; #3077, 1-oz 135.00
Cleo, colors other than bl, syrup pitcher, drip-cut 160.00
Cleo, colors other than bl, wafer tray 225.00
Decagon, pastel colors, basket, hdls, upturned sides, 7" 15.00
Decagon, pastel colors, bowl, bonbon; hdls, 6¼" 12.00
Decagon, pastel colors, bowl, vegetable; oval, 10½" 20.00
Decagon, pastel colors, comport, tall, 7" 22.00
Decagon, pastel colors, ice bucket 45.00
Decagon, pastel colors, plate, service; 12½" 9.00
Decagon, pastel colors, stem, sherbet; low, 6-oz 10.00
Decagon, red or bl, bowl, almond; ind, 2½" 38.00
Decagon, red or bl, bowl, cereal; belled, 6" 25.00
Decagon, red or bl, bowl, soup; flat rim, 8½" 35.00
Decagon, red or bl, comport, 5¾" 22.00
Decagon, red or bl, creamer, scalloped edge 18.00
Decagon, red or bl, plate, grill; 10" 25.00
Decagon, red or bl, salt cellar, ftd, 1½" 25.00
Decagon, red or bl, stem, cordial; 1-oz 75.00
Decagon, red or bl, sugar bowl, lightning-bolt hdls 20.00
Diane, crystal, bottle, oil; w/stopper, 6-oz 125.00
Diane, crystal, bowl, #3122 ....25.00
Diane, crystal, bowl, baker; 10" 45.00
Diane, crystal, bowl, berry; 5" 20.00
Diane, crystal, bowl, celery/relish; 5-part, 12" 37.50
Diane, crystal, bowl, relish; 2-part, 7" 22.00
Diane, crystal, bowl, relish; 3-part, 6½" 25.00
Diane, crystal, bowl, 4-ftd, 11" 45.00
Diane, crystal, bowl, 4-ftd, 12" 42.00
Diane, crystal, candelabrum, keyhole base, 3-light 45.00
Diane, crystal, cigarette urn 45.00
Diane, crystal, cocktail icer, 2-pc 65.00
Diane, crystal, comport, 5½" 27.50
Diane, crystal, decanter, ftd, lg 175.00

Diane, crystal, ice bucket, w/chrome hdl 65.00
Diane, crystal, pitcher, martini 550.00
Diane, crystal, plate, torte; 4-ftd, 13" 40.00
Diane, crystal, platter, 13½" 70.00
Diane, crystal, stem, cordial; #1066, 1-oz 60.00
Diane, crystal, stem, cordial; #3122, 1-oz 60.00
Diane, crystal, stem, sherbet; #3122, tall, 7-oz 18.00
Diane, crystal, tumbler, ftd, 8-oz 25.00
Diane, crystal, vase, globe shape, 5" 35.00
Elaine, crystal, bowl, flared, 4-ftd, 12" 40.00
Elaine, crystal, bowl, pickle/relish; 7" 25.00
Elaine, crystal, bowl, tab hdld, 11" 40.00
Elaine, crystal, candlestick, 3-light, 6" 40.00
Elaine, crystal, comport, blown, 5⅜" 42.00
Elaine, crystal, ice bucket, w/chrome hdl 65.00
Elaine, crystal, pitcher, ball shape 150.00
Elaine, crystal, plate, salad; 8" 15.00
Elaine, crystal, stem, claret; #1402, 5-oz 27.50
Elaine, crystal, stem, parfait; #3500, low stem, 5-oz 30.00
Elaine, crystal, stem, pousse-cafe; #3104, 1-oz 150.00
Elaine, crystal, stem, roemer; #3104, 5-oz 85.00
Elaine, crystal, stem, water; #3500, 10-oz 25.00
Elaine, crystal, tumbler, tea; #1402, tall, ftd, 12-oz 30.00
Elaine, crystal, tumbler, tea; #3500, ftd, 12-oz 30.00
Gloria, crystal, bottle, oil; w/stopper, hdld, ftd, tall 90.00
Gloria, crystal, bowl, #118, oblong, crimped, 12" 32.50
Gloria, crystal, bowl, celery/relish; 5-part, 12" 35.00
Gloria, crystal, bowl, cream soup; w/sq saucer 22.00
Gloria, crystal, bowl, nut; ind, 4-ftd, 3" 50.00
Gloria, crystal, comport, fruit cocktail; 4" 13.00
Gloria, crystal, comport, 4-ftd, 6" 20.00
Gloria, crystal, creamer, #4, ind 10.00
Gloria, crystal, plate, service; sq 22.00
Gloria, crystal, shakers, ftd, metal lids, pr 50.00
Gloria, crystal, stem, water; #3135, 8-oz 18.00
Gloria, crystal, tray, relish; center hdld, 4-part 30.00
Gloria, crystal, vase, 4 indents, oval, 9" 85.00
Gloria, gr, pk or yel, bowl, bonbon; ftd, crimped edge, 5" 34.00
Gloria, gr, pk or yel, bowl, cereal; rnd, 6" 32.00
Gloria, gr, pk or yel, bowl, console; 4-ftd, 12" 65.00
Gloria, gr, pk or yel, candlestick, 6", ea 35.00
Gloria, gr, pk or yel, comport, tall, 7" 75.00
Gloria, gr, pk or yel, pitcher, middle indent, 67-oz 275.00
Gloria, gr, pk or yel, plate, chop/salad; 14" 75.00
Gloria, gr, pk or yel, plate, salad; tab hdls, 10" 35.00
Gloria, gr, pk or yel, shakers, short, pr 75.00
Gloria, gr, pk or yel, stem, cocktail; #3035, 3-oz 28.00
Gloria, gr, pk or yel, tumbler, #3035, high ft, 12-oz 30.00
Gloria, gr, pk or yel, tumbler, #3130, ftd, 5-oz 20.00
Gloria, gr, pk or yel, vase, squarish top, 12" 130.00
Imperial Hunt Scene, colors, bowl, finger; #3085, w/plate 40.00
Imperial Hunt Scene, colors, candlestick, keyhole, 3-light, ea 65.00
Imperial Hunt Scene, colors, stem, parfait; #3085, 5½-oz 60.00
Imperial Hunt Scene, crystal, bowl, 8" 35.00
Imperial Hunt Scene, crystal, cup 45.00
Imperial Hunt Scene, crystal, stem, #1402, 14-oz 50.00
Imperial Hunt Scene, crystal, stem, wine; #1402, 2½-oz 45.00
Imperial Hunt Scene, crystal, sugar bowl, flat, w/lid 75.00
Imperial Hunt Scene, crystal, tumbler, #1402, flat, 5-oz 20.00
Mt Vernon, amber or crystal, bonbon, #10, ftd, 7" 12.50
Mt Vernon, amber or crystal, bowl, #126, shallow, 11½" 30.00
Mt Vernon, amber or crystal, bowl, #43, deep, 10½" 30.00
Mt Vernon, amber or crystal, bowl, #44, flared, 12½" 35.00
Mt Vernon, amber or crystal, bowl, fruit; #6, 5¼" 10.00

Mt Vernon, amber or crystal, box, #17, sq, w/lid, 4" 30.00
Mt Vernon, amber or crystal, cake stand, #150, ftd, 10½" 35.00
Mt Vernon, amber or crystal, candlestick, #110, 2-light, 5", ea 20.00
Mt Vernon, amber or crystal, cigarette box, #69, oval, w/lid, 6" ...30.00
Mt Vernon, amber or crystal, coaster, #70, ribbed, 3" 5.00
Mt Vernon, amber or crystal, comport, #77, hdls, 5½" 15.00
Mt Vernon, amber or crystal, comport, #96, belled, 6½" 22.50
Mt Vernon, amber or crystal, decanter, #52, w/stopper, 40-oz 70.00
Mt Vernon, amber or crystal, mug, #84, 14-oz 30.00
Mt Vernon, amber or crystal, pitcher, #90, 50-oz 80.00
Mt Vernon, amber or crystal, pitcher, #91, 86-oz 115.00
Mt Vernon, amber or crystal, rose bowl, #106, 6½" 18.00
Mt Vernon, amber or crystal, shaker, #102, hdls, oval 12.00
Mt Vernon, amber or crystal, stem, claret; #25, 4½-oz 13.50
Mt Vernon, amber or crystal, stem, wine; #27, 3-oz 13.50
Mt Vernon, amber or crystal, tumbler, #21, ftd, 5-oz 12.00
Mt Vernon, amber or crystal, tumbler, #58, tall, 10-oz 12.00
Mt Vernon, amber or crystal, tumbler, cordial; #87, ftd, 1-oz 22.00
Mt Vernon, amber or crystal, vase, #46, ftd, 10" 50.00
Nude stem, amber, brandy 90.00
Nude stem, amber, bud vase 800.00
Nude stem, amber, cocktail 90.00
Nude stem, amber, comport, cupped, 7" 250.00
Nude stem, amber, cordial 650.00
Nude stem, amber, mint dish 750.00
Nude stem, amber, wine 250.00
Nude stem, amethyst, brandy 90.00
Nude stem, amethyst, bud vase 900.00
Nude stem, amethyst, cigarette box, tall 650.00
Nude stem, amethyst, claret 175.00

Nude stem, amethyst, comport with Farberware stem, $75.00.

Nude stem, amethyst, goblet, water 250.00
Nude stem, amethyst, mint dish 900.00
Nude stem, amethyst, sweetmeat 1,100.00
Nude stem, carmen, cigarette box, tall 550.00
Nude stem, carmen, claret 225.00
Nude stem, carmen, comport, short 550.00
Nude stem, carmen, comport, tall 600.00
Nude stem, carmen, cordial 900.00
Nude stem, cobalt, ashtray 550.00
Nude stem, cobalt, brandy 150.00
Nude stem, cobalt, bud vase 1,250.00
Nude stem, cobalt, candlestick 750.00
Nude stem, cobalt, cigarette box, short 750.00
Nude stem, cobalt, cigarette box, tall 650.00
Nude stem, cobalt, claret 225.00
Nude stem, cobalt, cocktail 125.00
Nude stem, cobalt, comport, flared 425.00

Nude stem, cobalt, comport, cupped, tall 500.00
Nude stem, cobalt, cordial 950.00
Nude stem, cobalt, goblet, water 175.00
Nude stem, cobalt, hoch 750.00
Nude stem, cobalt, ivy ball 550.00
Nude stem, cobalt, sauterne 700.00
Nude stem, cobalt, Tulip cocktail 650.00
Nude stem, cobalt, V cocktail 650.00
Nude stem, cobalt, wine 325.00
Nude stem, cobalt w/frost stem, comport, cupped 425.00
Nude stem, Crown Tuscan, candlesticks, w/locking bobeche, pr 1,300.00
Nude stem, Crown Tuscan, comport, gold trim, silk screen stamp ..1,300.00
Nude stem, crystal, ashtray 200.00
Nude stem, crystal, bud vase 500.00
Nude stem, crystal, candlestick 350.00
Nude stem, crystal, cigarette box, tall 375.00
Nude stem, crystal, cigarette holder w/ashtray ft 595.00
Nude stem, crystal, claret 175.00
Nude stem, crystal, comport, flared, tall, 7" 175.00
Nude stem, crystal, comport, shell top, 7" 175.00
Nude stem, crystal, cordial 500.00
Nude stem, crystal, mint dish 800.00
Nude stem, crystal frost/wheel-cut stem, cigarette box, short 350.00
Nude stem, crystal Optic, brandy 90.00
Nude stem, crystal Optic, ivy ball 220.00
Nude stem, crystal Optic bowl/Pearl Mist stem, cordial, rare 750.00
Nude stem, crystal/Apple Blossom etch, goblet, water 1,050.00
Nude stem, crystal/Art Deco etch, wine 695.00
Nude stem, crystal/Chintz etch, claret 700.00
Nude stem, crystal/Diane etch, comport, cupped 1,200.00
Nude stem, crystal/Diane etch, comport, tall 1,355.00
Nude stem, crystal/Gloria etch, comport, 7" 1,200.00
Nude stem, crystal/Vichy etch, hoch 1,250.00
Nude stem, dk gr, ashtray 225.00
Nude stem, dk gr, brandy 90.00
Nude stem, dk gr, cigarette box, short 300.00
Nude stem, dk gr, cigarette box, tall 450.00
Nude stem, dk gr, claret 160.00
Nude stem, dk gr, cocktail 95.00
Nude stem, dk gr, comport, cupped, 7" 200.00
Nude stem, dk gr, cordial 650.00
Nude stem, emerald gr, champagne 225.00
Nude stem, emerald gr, claret 190.00
Nude stem, emerald gr/frosted, cigarette holder w/ashtray ft 750.00
Nude stem, Heatherbloom, brandy 250.00
Nude stem, Heatherbloom, champagne 800.00
Nude stem, Heatherbloom, claret 450.00
Nude stem, Heatherbloom, goblet, water 1,000.00
Nude stem, honey mocha, brandy 90.00
Nude stem, Moonstone, candlestick, w/bobeche 900.00
Nude stem, Moonstone, comport, Flying Nude 800.00
Nude stem, Moonstone, comport, tall 400.00
Nude stem, pistachio, cocktail, tall, rare 575.00
Nude stem, pk, ashtray 750.00
Nude stem, pk, brandy 180.00
Nude stem, pk, champagne 590.00
Nude stem, pk, cocktail, tall 550.00
Nude stem, pk, comport, short 700.00
Nude stem, smoke, ashtray 600.00
Nude stem, smoke, cocktail, tall 560.00
Nude stem, smoke, goblet, water 600.00
Nude stem, smoke, ivy ball 800.00
Nude stem, smoke crackle, cocktail 700.00
Nude stem, smoke crackle, goblet, water 700.00

Nude stem, Windsor bl, comport, shell top, sgn **1,200.00**
Nude stem, yel, brandy **90.00**
Nude stem, yel, candlestick **500.00**
Nude stem, yel, cocktail **90.00**
Nude stem, yel, hoch **675.00**
Portia, crystal, basket, 2-hdld, uptrn sides **20.00**
Portia, crystal, bottle, oil; loop hdld, w/stopper, 6-oz **75.00**
Portia, crystal, bowl, cranberry; sq, 3½" **25.00**
Portia, crystal, bowl, finger; #3124, w/liner **35.00**
Portia, crystal, bowl, relish; 2-part, 7" **22.00**
Portia, crystal, bowl, 2-hdld, 11" **37.50**
Portia, crystal, candlestick, 3-light, 6", ea **45.00**
Portia, crystal, cocktail icer, 2-part **65.00**
Portia, crystal, cologne, hdld, w/stopper, 2-oz **100.00**
Portia, crystal, hurricane lamp, keyhole base, w/prisms **165.00**
Portia, crystal, plate, torte; 4 ftd, 13" **40.00**
Portia, crystal, stem, cocktail; #3121, 3-oz **20.00**
Portia, crystal, stem, goblet; #3130, 9-oz **22.50**
Portia, crystal, stem, sherbet; #3121, tall, 6-oz **15.00**
Portia, crystal, stem, wine; #3126, 2½-oz **35.00**
Portia, crystal, sugar bowl, ftd **12.00**
Portia, crystal, tumbler, #3124, 3-oz **15.00**
Portia, crystal, tumbler, #3126, 2½-oz **35.00**
Portia, crystal, vase, flower; 13" **110.00**
Rosalie, amber, bowl, finger; w/liner **30.00**
Rosalie, amber, bowl, oval, 15½" **75.00**
Rosalie, amber, bowl, soup; 8½" **30.00**
Rosalie, amber, icer, w/liner **45.00**
Rosalie, amber, salt cellar, ftd, 1½" **40.00**
Rosalie, amber, tray, for sugar bowl & creamer, center hdl **14.00**
Rosalie, amber, vase, ftd, 5½" **30.00**
Rosalie, bl, pk or gr, bowl, basket, hdls, 11" **40.00**
Rosalie, bl, pk or gr, bowl, Decagon; 14" **235.00**
Rosalie, bl, pk or gr, bowl, 10" **40.00**
Rosalie, bl, pk or gr, candy dish, w/lid, 6" **110.00**
Rosalie, bl, pk or gr, nut dish, ftd, 2½" **60.00**
Rosalie, bl, pk or gr, plate, 8¾" **15.00**
Rosalie, bl, pk or gr, relish, 2-part, 9" **25.00**
Rosalie, bl, pk or gr, tumbler, #3077, ftd, 8-oz **25.00**
Rose Point, crystal, ashtray, #1715, stack set on metal pole **225.00**
Rose Point, crystal, ashtray, #3500/130, oval, 4" **85.00**
Rose Point, crystal, basket, #3500/51, hdld, 5" **275.00**
Rose Point, crystal, bowl, #1351, crimped edge, 10½" **85.00**
Rose Point, crystal, bowl, #1402/89, hdls, 6" **42.00**
Rose Point, crystal, bowl, #221, 3-part, 8½" **165.00**
Rose Point, crystal, bowl, #3400/34, hdls, 9½" **67.50**
Rose Point, crystal, bowl, #3500/49, hdls, 5" **35.00**
Rose Point, crystal, bowl, #3900/28, ftd, w/tab hdl, 11½" **75.00**
Rose Point, crystal, bowl, #993, 4-ftd, 12½" **90.00**
Rose Point, crystal, bowl, bonbon; #3400/1180, hdls, 5½" **32.00**
Rose Point, crystal, bowl, finger; #3106, w/liner **110.00**
Rose Point, crystal, candlestick, #499, Calla Lily, 6½" **110.00**
Rose Point, crystal, candy box, #3500/78, ram's head, w/lid, 6" ..**295.00**
Rose Point, crystal, celery, #3400/67, 5-part, 12" **80.00**
Rose Point, crystal, coaster, #1628, 3½" **55.00**
Rose Point, crystal, cocktail shaker, #101, w/stopper, 32-oz **195.00**
Rose Point, crystal, comport, #3500/111, 6" **150.00**
Rose Point, crystal, creamer, #3400/68 ....**20.00**
Rose Point, crystal, cup, punch; #488, 5-oz **37.50**
Rose Point, crystal, decanter, #1380, sq, 26-oz **425.00**
Rose Point, crystal, dressing bottle, #1261, ftd **325.00**
Rose Point, crystal, ice tub, #671, Pristine **225.00**
Rose Point, crystal, mustard, #151, 3-oz **150.00**
Rose Point, crystal, oil, #3400/99, ball shape, w/stopper, 6-oz **125.00**

Rose Point, crystal, pitcher, #3900/115, 76-oz **195.00**
Rose Point, crystal, plate, bread & butter; #3400/60, 6" **13.50**
Rose Point, crystal, plate, service; #3900/26, 4-ftd, 12" **70.00**
Rose Point, crystal, plate, torte; #3500/38, 13" **185.00**
Rose Point, crystal, punch bowl, #478, Martha, 15" **3,500.00**

Rose Point, crystal three-part relish, 11", $65.00.

Rose Point, crystal, shakers, #1471, glass base, rnd, lg, pr **85.00**
Rose Point, crystal, stem, cocktail; #3104, 3½-oz **275.00**
Rose Point, crystal, stem, cocktail; #7801, 4-oz **45.00**
Rose Point, crystal, stem, parfait; #3121, low ft, 5-oz **75.00**
Rose Point, crystal, stem, water; #3500, 10-oz **32.50**
Rose Point, crystal, sugar bowl, #3500/14 ....**20.00**
Rose Point, crystal, tray, #3900/37, for sugar & creamer **25.00**
Rose Point, crystal, tumbler, #3106, ftd, 12-oz **40.00**
Rose Point, crystal, vase, #1242, flat, 10" **135.00**
Square, crystal, candy box, #3797/165, w/lid **30.00**
Square, crystal, icer, cocktail; #3797/18, w/liner **35.00**
Square, crystal, plate, dessert/salad; #3797, 7" **12.00**
Square, crystal, tumbler, cocktail; #3797, low **12.00**
Square, crystal, vase, #3797/80, ftd, 8" **20.00**
Square, crystal, vase, #3797/91, belled, 5½" **25.00**
Valencia, crystal, basket, #3500/55, hdls, ftd, 6" **22.00**
Valencia, crystal, bowl, #3500/115, hdls, ftd, 9½" **38.00**
Valencia, crystal, bowl, finger; #3500, ftd **30.00**
Valencia, crystal, decanter, #3400/119, ball shape, 12-oz **125.00**
Valencia, crystal, plate, breakfast; #3500/5, 8½" **12.00**
Valencia, crystal, relish, #3500/68, 2-part, 5½" **20.00**
Valencia, crystal, stem, wine; #1402 ....**35.00**
Valencia, crystal, stem, wine; #3500, 2½-oz **32.00**
Valencia, crystal, tumbler, #3500, ftd, 16-oz **22.00**
Wildflower, crystal, bowl, #3400/4, flared, 4-ftd, 12" **40.00**
Wildflower, crystal, bowl, #3900/54, flared, 4-ftd, 10" **37.50**
Wildflower, crystal, bowl, bonbon; #3400/1180, hdls, 5¼" **18.00**
Wildflower, crystal, bowl, relish; #3900/124, 2-part, 7" **22.00**
Wildflower, crystal, butter dish, #3400/52, 5" **125.00**
Wildflower, crystal, candy box, #3900/165, w/lid, rnd **70.00**
Wildflower, crystal, creamer, #3900/41 ....**15.00**
Wildflower, crystal, ice bucket, #3900/671, w/chrome hdl **95.00**
Wildflower, crystal, plate, cake; #3900/35, hdls, 13½" **40.00**
Wildflower, crystal, shakers, #3900/1177, pr **37.50**
Wildflower, crystal, stem, water; #3121, 10-oz **30.00**
Wildflower, crystal, stem, wine; #3121, 3½-oz **35.00**
Wildflower, crystal, vase, #1238, keyhole ftd, 12" **110.00**

Cameo

     The technique of glass carving was perfected 2,000 years ago in ancient Rome and Greece. The most famous ancient example of cameo glass is the Portland Vase, made in Rome around 100 A.D. After glass blowing was developed, glassmakers devised a method of casing several layers of colored glass together, often with a light color over a darker base, to enhance the design. Skilled carvers meticulously worked the fragile glass to produce incredibly detailed classic scenes. In the 18th and 19th centuries Oriental and Near-Eastern artisans used the technique more extensively. European glassmakers revived the art during the last quarter of the 19th century. In France, Galle and Daum produced some of the finest examples of modern times, using as many as five layers of glass to develop their designs, usually scenics or subjects from nature. Hand carving was supplemented by the use of a copper engraving wheel, and acid was used to cut away the layers more quickly.

In England, Thomas Webb and Sons used modern machinery and technology to eliminate many of the problems that plagued early glass carvers. One of Webb's best-known carvers, George Woodall, is credited with producing over four hundred pieces. Woodall was trained in the art by John Northwood, famous for reproducing the Portland Vase in 1876. Cameo glass became very popular during the late 1800s, resulting in a market that demanded more than could be produced, due to the tedious procedures involved. In an effort to produce greater volume, less elaborate pieces with simple floral or geometric designs were made, often entirely acid etched with little or no hand carving. While very little cameo glass was made in this country, a few pieces were produced by James Gillinder, Tiffany, and the Libbey Glass Company. Though some continued to be made on a limited scale into the 1900s (and until about 1920 in France), for the most part, inferior products caused a marked reduction in its manufacture by the turn of the century. Beware of new 'French' cameo glass from Romania and Taiwan. Some of it is very good and may be signed with 'old' signatures. Watch for stencil-cut designs that are 'disconnected' and segmented. Know your dealer! Our advisor for this category is Don Williams; he is listed in the Directory under Missouri. See also specific manufacturers.

Key: fp — fire polished

English

Bottle, scent; floral, wht/clear/citron, screw-on lid, 2" 700.00
Bottle, scent; florals/ferns, wht on yel, ball shape, 6" 900.00
Plaque, carnation-like flowers, wht on citron, 3½x5½" 1,275.00
Sweetmeat, plants ea indented side, wht on bl, 5¾x3½" sq 1,825.00
Vase, cyclamens/leafy sprigs, wht on citron, 5" 1,300.00
Vase, floral w/butterfly, wht on cranberry, waisted, 7x5" 1,700.00
Vase, floral/berry panels, wht on citron, Woodall style, 3½" 3,500.00
Vase, floral/butterfly, corseted, wht on cranberry, 7x5" 1,750.00
Vase, fuchsias/morning glories, wht on citron, 7" 850.00
Vase, lg poppies w/leafy stems, wht on red, 10" 2,750.00
Vase, morning glories/vines/butterfly, red/wht on citron, 6" 2,000.00
Vase, trumpet flowers/dragonfly, wht on amber, 5½x6" 1,750.00

French

Vase, daisy-like flowers with many leaves, orange and amethyst on white frost, Degue, 8¾x6", $400.00.

Bowl, berry ovals, gold on amethyst, Lamon, #20B, 3¼x8" 475.00
Lamp, lady/children shade: blk/gr/orange/opal frost, 15x8" 2,300.00
Lamp, perfume; sailing scene, maroon/gold-red, Berger, 6½" 900.00
Lamp, snowy woods w/marmalade sky, Maison Marcus, 14x7½" ..5,000.00
Night light, camel scene, maroon/peach/orange, Degue, 6½x3" .795.00
Pin tray, floral branches, gr/brn on yel frost, 1x3¾" 200.00
Tumbler, wisteria, bl on yel/opal, Weiss, 4" 500.00
Vase, Arab & camel scene, maroon/peach/orange, Degue, 6½" .750.00
Vase, birds & floral shrubs, blk on gr w/gold, bottle form, 8" 350.00
Vase, chrysanthemums/butterflies, brick red on red, 14" 400.00
Vase, dandelions, gr on frost, Graveur, 9½" 1,000.00
Vase, elm leaves/seed pods, wht to orange, Weiss, 1¾x1" 295.00
Vase, floral, mahog/red/yel mottle, bottle form, D'Aurys, 4½" ...350.00
Vase, floral, orange/brn on lemon yel, ftd, Degue, 16½" 2,300.00
Vase, floral/leaves, red on citron mottle, Barz, 6" 225.00
Vase, grape pods/vines, brn/olive gr on citron, Arsall, 7½" 300.00
Vase, house/trees/mtns, brn to orange, Degue, 6¼x3" 645.00
Vase, leafy branches w/catkins, dk/lt brn on lt bl, 6¼" 120.00
Vase, nasturtiums/pod leaves, pk-olive/gr frost, P Rigot, 3" 250.00
Vase, patriot/rabbit/raptor/trees/bird, pk on wht, oviform, 9" 300.00
Vase, sailboats on lake, maroon/yel, Michel Paris, 7½x4⅜" 950.00
Vase, sailing ship/lighthouse, bl/orange/yel, Michel, 10¼" 1,220.00
Vase, trees/lake, gold-brn/lilac-pk, gondola shape, 7x5" 1,000.00
Vase, valley/mtn/bridge, olive/pk/opal/purple, Lamartine, 12" ...2,000.00

Canary Ware

Canary ware was produced from the late 1700s until about the mid-19th century in the Staffordshire district of England. It was potted of yellow clay and the overglaze was yellow as well. More often than not, copper or silver lustre trim was added. Decorations were usually black-printed transfers, though occasionally hand-painted polychrome designs were also used.

Flowerpot, HP floral, red rim on pot & saucer, 5¼x4½" 650.00
Garniture set, mc flowers & foliage, brn stripes, 3-pc, 5", 4¼" ...1,430.00
Mug, child's, boy fishing, red transfer, 2½" 550.00
Mug, child's, flower in red & gr, leaf hdl, 2¼" 195.00
Mug, child's, man running from bull, red transfer, 2½", EX 200.00
Mug, child's, My Sin..., red-brn transfer, leaf hdl, 2⅜" 415.00
Mug, child's, My Soul If Sinners..., red transfer, 2½", VG 100.00
Mug, child's, New Carriage for Ann, blk transfer, 2", NM 400.00
Mug, child's, Present for My Dear Girl, rstr, 2¼" 200.00
Mug, child's, red transfer w/in wreath, 2¼" 400.00
Mug, Werger Going To Shoot Himself..., red transfer, rpr, 6¼" .550.00
Pitcher, Application, blk transfer, rpr, 5½" 110.00
Pitcher, stylized brn flowers, feather edge decor, 7¼", EX 500.00
Plate, child's, sheep transfer, imp name, 4¾" 200.00
Plate, child's, turkey in relief center, 4" 85.00
Plate, men fishing, brn transfer, wear, 6¼" 300.00
Whistle, bird form, 3", EX 350.00

Candle Holders

The earliest type of candlestick, called a pricket, was constructed with a sharp point on which the candle was impaled. The socket type, first used in the 16th century, consisted of the socket and a short stem with a wide drip pan and base. These were made from sheets of silver or other metal; not until late in the 17th century were candlesticks made by casting. By the 1700s, styles began to vary from the traditional fluted column or baluster form and became more elaborate. A Rococo style with scrolls, shellwork, and naturalistic leaves and flowers came into vogue that afforded the individual silversmith the opportunity to exhibit his skill and artistry. The last half of the 18th century brought a return to fluted columns with neoclassic motifs. Because they were made of thin sheet silver, weighted bases were used to add stability. The Rococo styles of the Regency period were heavily encrusted with applied figures and flowers. Candelabra with six to nine branches became popular. By the Victorian era when lamps came into general use, there was less innovation and more adaptation of the earlier styles. See also Silver; Tinware; specific manufacturers.

Brass, beehive style, slush-molded base, mini, 4⅛x1⅞", pr 45.00
Brass, beehive style, sq base, mini, 4¼x2⅛", pr 30.00
Brass, cylindrical w/saucer base, ca 1800, w/tray & snuffer 140.00
Brass, neoclassic, rpr lip, 9¼", pr 225.00
Brass, Nouveau vasiform molded shaft, quatrelobed base, 14", pr ..110.00
Brass, push-ups, Victorian, 8¼" 140.00
Brass, push-ups, w/ejectors, early 19th C, 10", pr 200.00
Brass, push-ups & scalloped bases, old solder, early, 6½", pr 385.00
Brass, Queen Anne, scalloped base, early, 7¼" 880.00
Brass, Queen Anne, scalloped base w/floral some age, 9", pr 660.00
Brass, reeded columns on triangular bases, late, 13½", pr 65.00
Brass, scalloped base, segmented stem, drip pan, late, 9" 40.00
Brass, spring loaded, Cornelius & Baker, Phila, 9½" 100.00
Brass, sq base, stem not seamed, early, 6" 220.00
Brass, urn & trn shafts, early 1800s, 6", pr 175.00
Brass, winged dragon form, late, 6½", pr 50.00
Brass & marble, Fr 2nd Emp, cherubs w/torches, 22", pr 1,950.00
Bronze, cut glass prisms from arched floral mts, 9", pr 350.00
Candelabra, brass, 5 scroll arms, wht marble plinth, 15", pr 350.00
Candelabra, brass, 5-arm, pineapple center to top, 30", pr 800.00
Candelabra, brass, 5-arm on urn-form shaft, 1880s, 21", pr 350.00
Candelabra, SP, Georgian style, 5-arm, wax pan, 18", pr 660.00
Candelabrum, Emp blk-patinated/gilt metal mtd, 4-arm, 25" 1,100.00
Candelabrum, gilt bronze, Continental neoclassical, 7-arm, 21" ...575.00
Girondole set, gilt bronze, warrior motif, prisms, 3-pc 495.00
Hogscraper, sheet iron, cylindrical, w/ejector, 9¾x5" 225.00
Hogscraper, sheet iron, cylindrical w/rnd base, 1800s, 7½" 110.00
Rush light, wrought iron, spring-type adjustment, 30" 75.00
Sconce, brass Hplwht style, mirror bk, 2-arm, 23", pr 200.00
SP, Geo III style in Rococo taste, scrollwork base, 13⅝", pr 165.00
Torchere, bronze, Classical Fr, 3-light, 19th C, 26", pr 770.00
Wrought iron, sticking tommy, 12½" 140.00
Wrought support w/twist & beam hook, 10¼" 55.00

Candlewick

Candlewick crystal was made by the Imperial Glass Corporation, a division of Lenox Inc., Bellaire, Ohio. It was introduced in 1936, and though never marked except for paper labels, it is easily recognized by the beaded crystal rims, stems, and handles inspired by the tufted needlework called candlewicking, practiced by our pioneer women. During its production, more than 741 items were designed and produced. In September 1982 when Imperial closed its doors, thirty-four pieces were still being made.

Identification numbers and mold numbers used by the company help collectors recognize the various styles and shapes. Most of the pieces are from the #400 series, though other series numbers were also used. Stemware was made in eight styles — five from the #400 series made from 1941 to 1962, one from #3400 series made in 1937, another from #3800 series made in 1941, and the eighth style from the #4000 series made in 1947. In the listings that follow, some #400 items lack the mold number because that information was not found in the company files.

A few pieces have been made in color or with a gold wash. At least two lines, Valley Lily and Floral, utilized Candlewick with floral patterns cut into the crystal. These are scarce today. Other rare items include gifts such as the desk calendar made by the company for its employees and customers; the dresser set comprised of a mirror, clock, puff jar, and cologne; and the chip and dip set.

Party tray, center handle, #400/68D, etching, 11½", $85.00.

Ashtray, #400/174, heart shape, 6½" 15.00
Ashtray, #400/19, rnd, 2¾" 9.00
Ashtray, #400/651, sq, 3¼" 35.00
Basket, #400/40/0, hdld, 6½" 30.00
Bottle, bitters; #400/117, w/tube, 4-oz 60.00
Bowl, #400/113A, 2-hdld, deep, 10" 115.00
Bowl, #400/182, 3-ftd, 8½" 110.00
Bowl, #400/183, 3-ftd, 6" 60.00
Bowl, #400/42B, hdls, rnd, 4¾" 12.00
Bowl, #400/74SC, fancy crimped edge, 4-ftd, sq, 9" 70.00
Bowl, #400/92B, rnd, 12" 40.00
Bowl, pickle/celery; #400/57, 7½" 27.50
Bowl, relish; #400/234, divided, sq, 7" 125.00
Bowl, salad; #400/75B, 10½" 40.00
Bowl, sauce; #400/243, deep, 5½" 37.50
Butter & jam set, #400/204, 5-pc 295.00
Cake stand, #400/67D, low ftd, 10" 52.50
Calender, desk; 1947 ....175.00
Candle holder, #400/207, 3-toed, 4½", ea 60.00
Candle holder, #400/40F, flared w/6 petalled rim, rnd, 6", ea 25.00
Candle holder, #400/79, rolled edge, 3½", ea 12.00
Candy box, #400/259, w/lid, 7" 135.00
Cigarette box, #400/134, w/lid 35.00
Cigarette holder, #400/44, bead ft, 3" 35.00
Clock, rnd, 4" 265.00
Coaster, #400/226, w/spoon rest 16.00
Compote, #400/220, 3-bead stems, 5" 70.00
Creamer, #400/30, bead hdl, 6-oz 8.00
Cup, punch; #400/211 ....7.50
Decanter, #400/163, w/stopper, 26-oz 295.00
Hurricane lamp, #400/76, candle base, hdld, 2-pc 150.00
Icer, seafood/fruit cocktail; #400/53/3, 2-pc 95.00
Knife, butter; #4000 ....295.00
Mirror, standing, rnd, 4½" 110.00
Oil, #400/166, bead base, 6-oz 65.00
Pitcher, #400/16, no ft, 16-oz 175.00
Pitcher, #400/424, plain, 80-oz 55.00
Plate, #400/266, triangular, 7½" 85.00
Plate, #400/50, w/indent, 8" 11.00
Plate, #400/72C, crimped, 2-hdld, 10" 30.00
Plate, bread & butter; #400/1D, 6" 8.00
Plate, salad; #400/5D, 8½" 10.00
Plate, service; #400/13D, 12" 30.00
Plate, torte; #400/17D, 14" 42.50
Punch ladle, #400/91 ....30.00
Salt cellar, #400/19, 2¼" 11.00

Salt spoon, #400/616, w/ribbed bowl **11.00**
Snack jar, #400/139/1, beaded ft, w/lid **425.00**
Stem, claret; #3800 ....**30.00**
Stem, oyster cocktail; #3400, 4-oz **14.00**
Stem, parfait; #3400, 6-oz **16.00**
Stem, tea; #4000, 12-oz **25.00**
Stem, wine; #400/190, 5-oz **21.00**
Sugar bowl, #400/18, domed ft **115.00**
Tidbit, #400/18TB, 3-pc **195.00**
Tumbler, #3400, ftd, 9-oz **16.00**
Tumbler, #400/19, 10-oz **12.00**
Tumbler, juice; #400/18, 5-oz **37.50**
Tumbler, old-fashion; #400/18, 7-oz **35.00**
Tumbler, tea; #400/18, 12-oz **47.50**
Vase, #400/193, ftd, 10" **165.00**
Vase, bud; #400/107, bead ft, 5¾" **55.00**
Vase, fan; #400/287, 6" **30.00**
Vase, rose bowl; #400/142K, 7" **210.00**

Candy Containers

Figural glass candy containers were first created in 1876 when ingenious candy manufacturers began to use them to package their products. Two of the first containers, the Liberty Bell and Independence Hall, were distributed for our country's centennial celebration. Children found these toys appealing, and an industry was launched that lasted into the mid-1960s.

Figural candy containers include animals, comic characters, guns, telephones, transportation vehicles, household appliances, and many other intriguing designs. The oldest (those made prior to 1920) were usually hand painted and often contained extra metal parts in addition to the metal strip or screw closures. During the 1950s these metal parts were replaced with plastic, a practice that continued until candy containers met their demise in the 1960s. While predominately clear, they are found in nearly all colors of glass including milk glass, green, amber, pink, emerald, cobalt, ruby flashed, and light blue. Usually the color was intentional, but leftover glass was used as well and resulted in unplanned colors. Various examples are found in light or ice blue, and new finds are always being discovered. Production of the glass portion of candy containers was centered around the western Pennsylvania city of Jeannette. Major producers include Westmoreland Glass, West Bros., Victory Glass, J.H. Millstein, J.C. Crosetti, L.E. Smith, Jack Stough, and T.H. Stough. While 90% of all glass candies were made in the Jeannette area, other companies such as Eagle Glass, Play Toy, and Geo. Borgfeldt Co. have a few to their credit as well.

Buyer beware! Many candy containers have been reproduced. Some, including the Camera and the Rabbit Pushing Wheelbarrow, come already painted from distributors. Others may have a slick or oily feel to the touch. The following list may also alert you to possible reproductions:

E&A #149/L #12 Chicken on Nest
E&A #184/L #17 Scottie Dog (repro has a ice-like color and is often slick and oily)
E&A #180/L #24 Dog (clear and cobalt)
E&A #566/L #37, Owl (original in clear only, often painted; repro found in clear, blue, green, and pink with a higher threaded base and less detail)
E&A #539/L #38 Mule and Waterwagon (original marked Jeannette, PA)
E&A #601/L #47 Rabbit Pushing Wheelbarrow (eggs are speckled on the repro; solid on the original)
E&A #618/L #55 Peter Rabbit
E&A #651/L #58 Rocking Horse (original in clear only)
E&A #342/L #76 Independence Hall (original is rectangular; repro has offset base with red felt-lined closure)

E&A #137/L #83 Charlie Chaplin (original has 'Geo. Borgfeldt' on base; reproduction comes in pink and blue)
E&A #208/L #89 Happifats on Drum (no notches on repro for closure to hook into)
E&A #345/L #90 Jackie Coogan (marked inside 'B')
E&A #349/L #91 Kewpie (must have Geo. Borgfeldt on base to be original)
E&A #546/L #94 Naked Child
E&A #674/L #103 Santa (original has plastic head; repro is all glass and opens at bottom)
E&A #162/L #114 Mantel Clock (originally in ruby flashed, milk glass, clear, and frosted only)
#144 Amber Pistol (first sold full in the 1970s, not listed in E&A)
E&A #303/L #168 Uncle Sam's Hat
E&A #111/L #233 Santa's Boot
E&A #121/L #238 Camera (original says 'Pat Apld For' on bottom, reproduction says 'B. Shakman' or is ground off)
E&A #132/L #242 Carpet Sweeper (currently being sold with no metal parts)
E&A #133/L #243 Carpet Sweeper (currently being sold with no metal parts)
E&A #177/L #246 Display Case (original should be painted silver and brown)
E&A #521/L #254 Mailbox
E&A #543/L #255 Drum Mug
E&A #661/L #268 Safe (original in clear, ruby flashed, and milk glass only)
E&A #577/L #289 Piano (original in only clear and milk glass, both painted)
E&A #60/L #356 Auto
E&A #33/L #377 Auto
E&A #56/L #378 Station Wagon
E&A #213/L #386 Fire Engine (repros in green and blue glass)

Others are possible. If in doubt, do not buy without a guarantee from the dealer and return privilege in writing.

1997 was a record year for candy container collectors with two notable collections being sold (by Old Barn Auction in Findlay, Ohio) — Mary Louise Stanley's (in April) and Jennie Long's (in September). Both were very important, as both ladies had written books on candy containers. Several new records were set, and some drastic differences in prices realized were noted between the two sales. For example, in April a Flossie Fisher Bed brought $5,100.00 (without buyer's premium), but in September the same piece in similar condition brought only $3,600.00. Other pieces, like the Soldier by the Tent were closer at $3,000.00 and $2,600.00 respectively (not including buyer's premium). The prices in this column have taken into consideration both auctions, dealer lists, and show prices, and represent an average of all. Values are given for undamaged examples with original paint and metal parts when applicable or unless noted otherwise. Repaired pieces (often repainted) are worth only a small fraction of one that is perfect. The symbol (+) at the end of some of the following lines was used to indicate items that have been reproduced.

Our advisor for glass containers is Jeff Bradfield; he is listed in the Directory under Virginia. You may contact him with questions, if you will include an SASE. See Clubs, Newsletters, and Catalogs for the address of the Candy Container Collectors of America. A bimonthly newsletter offers insight into new finds, reproductions, updates, and articles from over four hundred collectors and members, including all authors of books on candy containers. Dues are $18.00 yearly. The club holds an annual convention in June in Reading, Pennsylvania, for collectors of candy containers.

'L' numbers used in this guide refer to a standard reference series, *An Album of Candy Containers*, Vols 1 and 2, by Jennie Long. 'E&A'

numbers correlate with *The Compleat American Glass Candy Containers Handbook* by Eikelberner and Agadjanian, revised by Adele Bowden. For more information we recommend *The Collector's Guide to Candy Containers* by Doug Dezso and Leon and Rose Poirier, published by Collector Books.

Acorn, L #221 ....375.00
Airplane, Army Bomber; w/paper label prop, L #328 (E&A #6) ..32.00
Airplane, P-51; L #327 (E&A#5) 45.00
Airplane, Spirit of Goodwill; gray pnt, L #320 (E&A #8) 160.00
Airplane, Spirit of St Louis; tin wings, L #321 (E&A #9) 350.00
Angeline Coach, L #398 (E&A #166) 450.00
Auto w/Tassels #2, L #361 (E&A #64) 150.00
Automobile, Streamlined; no closure, L #377 (E&A #33) 15.00
Automobile, Streamlined; w/cb closure, L #377 (E&A #33) 30.00
Baseball Player w/Glove, L #81 (E&A #78) 800.00
Basket, flower design, L #223 (E&A #81) 30.00
Bear on Circus Tub, orig blades, L #1 (E&A #83) 450.00

Bottle, Round Nurser; L #72 (E&A #549), $25.00.

Bus, Jitney; closure, L #340 (E&A #114) 365.00
Bus, Rapid Transit; no pnt, L #345 (E&A #116) 550.00
Bus, Victory Lines Special; bl pnt, L #347 (E&A #115) 40.00
Camera, orig tripod & closure, L #238 (E&A #121) (+) 300.00
Cannon, Rapid Fire; L #143 (E&A #129) 335.00
Carpet Sweeper (Baby), orig tin parts, L #242 (E&A #32) (+) ..300.00
Charlie Chaplin by Barrel, G pnt, L #83 (E&A #137) (+) 150.00
Chick in Eggshell Auto, G pnt, L #7 (E&A #144) 350.00
Chicken, fancy closure, L #9 ....500.00
Chicken on Nest, JH Millstein, L #12 (E&A #149) 20.00
Coal Car, orig closure, L #402 (E&A #170) 350.00
Coupe, Long Hood; #1, L #357 (E&A #50) 150.00
Decorettes, L #655 ....125.00
Dog, Scotty, L #17 (E&A #184) 15.00
Duck, rectangular basket, L #27 (E&A #198) 80.00
Felix on Pedestal, no pnt, L #87 (E&A #211-1) 3,000.00
Felix on Pedestal, orig blk pnt, L #87 (E&A #211-1) 4,000.00
Fire Engine, orig closure, L #388 (E&A #212) 25.00
Flossie Fisher Bed, L #127 (E&A #234 ....3,800.00
Flossie Fisher Side Board, L #130 (E&A #237) 1,800.00
Flossie Fisher Table, all orig tin, L #131 (E&A #233) 1,800.00
Grocery Truck, L #458 (E&A #783) 700.00
Helicopter, DX7; mk TH Stough Co - Patented, 1⅛x4¾" 3,000.00
Horn, 3-valve, no mouthpc, L #281 (E&A #312) 75.00
Horn, 3-valve, w/mouthpc, L #281 (E&A #312) 175.00
House of Glass, L #75 (E&A #324) 175.00
Jackie Coogan, L #521 (E&A #345), frosted or clear, ea 800.00
Jeep Scout Car, L #390 (E&A #350) 35.00
Lamp, high base, L #189 ....30.00
Lamp, Hurricane; mini, L #211 (E&A #366) 75.00

Lantern, barn type, #2, L #178 (E&A #427-B) 75.00
Lantern, domed closure, L #576 ....45.00
Lantern, Japanese paper type, L #572 (E&A #389) 300.00
Lantern, Victory Glass #1, L #191 (E&A #443)(+ by Avon) 20.00
Liberty Bell, various colors, screw closure, L #229 (E&A #85) 35.00
Locomotive, dbl sq windows, no closure, L#414 (E&A #497) 60.00
Locomotive, dbl sq windows, orig closure, L #414 (E&A #497) ...90.00
Locomotive, Little Gem, L #587 (E&A #474) 500.00
Locomotive 888, no wheels, L #395 (E&A #485) 45.00
Man on Motorcycle w/Side Car, L #392 (E&A #522) 500.00
Mantel Clock #1, w/paper face, L #115 (E&A #164) 150.00
Model Cruiser, orig closure, L #339 (E&A #98) 22.00
Mounted Policeman, G pnt, L #551 ....2,600.00
Naked Child, Victory Glass, L #94 (E&A #546) 40.00
Opera Glasses, celluloid fr, L #625 ....250.00
Owl, glass eyes, closure, L #37 (E&A #566) (+) 110.00
Phonograph w/Glass Record & Tin Horn, L #288 (E&A #574) .250.00
Pocket Watch, 'Jeannette' on paper face, L #457 (E&A #825) ..400.00
Rabbit, aluminum ears, L #487 ....425.00
Rabbit, no ears, L #487 ....125.00
Rabbit Begging, orig pnt, closure, L #50 (E&A #611) 90.00
Rabbit Family, G pnt, L #43 (E&A 604) 825.00
Rabbit on Dome, gold pnt, L #46 (E&A #607) 300.00
Rabbit Running on Log, G pnt, L #42 (E&A #603) 250.00
Rabbit w/Layed-Back Ears, EX pnt, L #40 (E&A 616) 100.00
Radio, Tune In; orig pnt, L #290 (E&A #643) 150.00
Santa Claus, banded coat, L #97 (E&A #669) 225.00
Santa w/Plastic Head, L #103, (E&A #674) 60.00
Sedan, 4-door, orig tin wheels, no pnt, L #370 (E&A #57) 100.00
Soldier by Tent, G orig pnt, L #688 (E&A #108) 3,000.00
Soldier on Monument, L #107 (E&A #682) 825.00
Statue of Liberty, gold gilted, L #110 (E&A #700) 1,900.00
Suitcase, clear, L #217 (E&A #707) 35.00
Tank, 2-Gun; cb closure, L #438 (E&A #723) 25.00
Telephone, Pewter Top; (E&A #735) 75.00
Telephone, Victory Glass #6, L #303 (E&A #739) 45.00
Train, Overland Limited, L #394 (E&A #778), 4-pc, EX 1,200.00
Ugly Duckling, L #28 (E&A #199) 150.00
Valise, L #220 (E&A #599) 350.00
Village, 2-Story House; tin, no liner, L #76-I (E&A #807) 25.00
Wheelbarrow, lg wheel, L #610 (E&A #832) 100.00
Wheelbarrow, tin, L #611 ....65.00
Windmill, Stough's 1915, orig blades, L #445 (E&A #842) 350.00

Papier-Mache, Composition

These types of candy containers are generally figural. Many are holiday-related. Our advisor for this category is Jenny Tarrant; she is listed in the Directory under Missouri. See also Christmas; Halloween.

Key: pm — papier-mache

Cherry tree box w/ax beside, pm, Germany, 6x12" 95.00
Chick cart, celluloid, Irwin 48.00
Clown rabbit, pm, opens at neck, 6", EX 325.00
Duck, cotton, wing lifts 165.00
Duck, pm & wood, jtd neck, lead ft, 6", VG 195.00
Geo Washington, pm, 3", G 95.00
Geo Washington bust, compo, plug at bottom, Germany, 4" 165.00
Geo Washington bust, pm, curly hair w/pigtail, Germany, 3¾", EX ...150.00
Geo Washington monument, compo, plug on bottom, Germany, 4" .240.00
Geo Washington on boat, compo, plug at bottom, Germany, 3½" .225.00
Golf bunny, pm, wood base, Germany, 6½", EX 225.00

Rabbit, cotton, w/carrot, Occupied Japan 25.00
Rabbit, pm, emerging from egg, Germany, 5", EX 250.00
Rabbit, pm, glass eyes, Germany, EX 175.00
Rabbit, pm, in tin car, 6½", VG 395.00
Rabbit, pm, pnt details, glass eyes, Germany, 5" 110.00
Rabbit, pm, pulling wooden cart, glass eyes, 10½", EX 240.00
Rabbit, porc, on haunches, cabbage cache pot 115.00
Rabbit, winking, pm, Germany, 5", EX 155.00
Rabbits (2), pm, carrying litter w/lg egg, 13x16" 250.00
Rooster, pm, rnd base, 3½" 75.00
Stork, cotton batting/paper/wire, full bodied, 6x4½" 85.00
Turkey, pm, HP, wht metal ft, glass eyes, rpr, 10" 525.00
Turkey, pm, W Germany, 2" 35.00
Turkey, pm, W Germany, 3" 50.00
Turkey (hen), pm, W Germany, 5½" 175.00
Turkey (Tom), pm, Germany, 3" 75.00
Turkey (Tom), pm, W Germany, 4½" 65.00

Canes

Fancy canes and walking sticks were once the mark of a gentleman. Hand-carved examples are collected and admired as folk art from the past. The glass canes that never could have been practical are unique whimseys of the glass-blower's profession. Gadget and container sticks, which were produced in a wide variety, are highly desirable. Character, political, and novelty types are also sought after as are those with handles made of precious metals.

For more information we recommend *American Folk Art Canes, Personal Sculpture*, by George H. Meyer, Sandringham Press, 100 West Long Lake Rd., Suite 100, Bloomfield Hills, MI 48304. Other possible references are *Canes in the United States* by Catherine Dike and *Canes From the 17th – 20th Century* by Jeffrey Snyder. Our advisor for this category is Bruce Thalberg.

Am Indian, 4-color allover beadwork, EX 525.00
Bambo w/dragon cvgs, Japanese characters, etc, 1-pc 200.00
Bamboo fishing rod, brass ferrule, 2-pc rod, Japan, 1910s 250.00
Bamboo shaft/knob, silver cap, Toledo steel etch sword, 1900s ..500.00
Bamboo w/str sword hdl, ivory cap, brass ferrule, 1880s 275.00
Bloodstone ball hdl, gilt collar dtd 1913, partridge shaft 250.00
Boxwood cvd rabbit hdl, metal ferrule, 1-pc, ca 1890 ....375.00
Brass eagle-head hdl, silver collar, baleen shaft, ca 1850 ....375.00
Brass lady's leg 4" hdl, metal ferrule, bamboo shaft, ca 1890 ....200.00

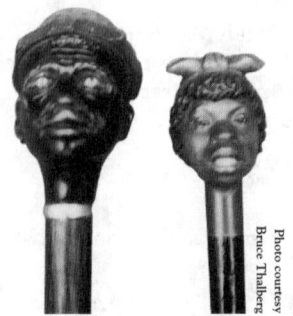

Carved Black man's head, glass eyes, some wear on hat, oak shaft, ca 1870, $850.00; Black lady's head, glass eyes, ivory teeth, dark-stained hair, ebony shaft, ca 1880, $800.00.

Photo courtesy
Bruce Thalberg

Cast metal mtn climber's, ice pick & ax on hazelwood shaft 250.00

Cast pewter German soldier hdl, fabric-covered shaft, 1930s 200.00
Celluloid horse & jockey hdl w/silver, hardwood shaft, G 225.00
Celluloid tau dog hdl, brass collar, hardwood shaft 100.00
Ebony, cvd ivory lion hdl, 35½", EX 330.00
Ebony w/elephant hdl & ivory decor, 1-pc, G 250.00
Faceted agate hdl, silver collar, hardwood shaft 250.00
Flashlight in crook hdl, sterling cap/band, Am, 1920s 325.00
Folk art, Black man w/top hat, polychrome, 1-pc, ca 1865 ....650.00
Folk art, cvd hand & snake, mahoganized shaft, 19th C, VG 400.00
Fruitwood cvd seal, 1-pc, glass eyes, ca 1880 ....450.00
German porc, male/female faces, HP malacca shaft, ca 1895 ......350.00
Gold-filled crook, 5½" partridge wood hdl, London, 1901 ....300.00
Gold-filled half-crook on ebony, metal ferrule, dtd 1899, 33" 200.00
Horn cvd dog's-head whistle hdl w/silver, wood shaft, 1890s 475.00
Horn cvd horse-head hdl w/silver bridle, malacca shaft, 36" 575.00
Horse measure in silver hdl, malacca shaft, England, 1880 ....550.00
Ivory cvd classical lady/flowers hdl, vulcanized rubber shaft 700.00
Ivory cvd dog's-head hdl, horn ferrule, malacca shaft, Am, 1890s ..375.00
Ivory cvd lioness & snake 5" hdl, horn ferrule, malacca shaft 450.00
Ivory elephant ball hdl, brass eyelets, ebonized shaft, 1850s 300.00
Ivory L-hdl w/silver mt & bronze stag head, cherry shaft 350.00
Ivory L-hdl w/silver mts, bamboo shaft 275.00
Lizard-skin hdl, malacca shaft 150.00
Long pipe type, cvd ivory hdl, silver bowl, ebony shaft, 1900 .....750.00
Maple shaft, whale-oil stick, wick in hdl, w/blade, 1860s 750.00
Nouveau silver hdl w/greyhound, rosewood shaft, ca 1890, 37" 1,100.00
Pepper-box Fellstchutz gun hdl w/5" blade, hardwood hdl, 1880s .3,700.00
Pewter molded bear 4" hdl, brass ferrule, hardwood shaft, Am ...500.00
Rhino horn hdl w/gold mts, exotic figured wood shaft, EX 300.00
Rosewood crook w/sterling mts/lapiz stones, metal ferrule, '20s ..600.00
Scrimshaw ivory hdl, island wood shaft, 36" 175.00
Shark vertebra shaft w/wood cvd hdl w/MOP inlay, 1860s 200.00
Shepherd's crook hdl w/cvd thistle, 1-pc 75.00
Silver & MOP hdl on horn ring shaft, VG 375.00
Silver village scene crook hdl, cvd ebony shaft, Philippines 200.00
Snake-skin covered, crook type, pnt wood ferrule, ca 1920 , ...250.00
SP bbl hdl w/sm holes to emit fragrance, malacca shaft, 1884 ....500.00
Staghorn w/silver o/l & snake, brass ferrule, malacca shaft 700.00
Sterling wolf's head, gold collar, ruby eyes, lady's, ca 1880 ....475.00
Tortoise shell crook w/silver collar, malacca shaft 200.00
Umbrella crook hdl, horn ferrule, telescoping shaft, Am, 1900 ..250.00
Walrus ivory L-shaped hdl w/silver collar, hardwood shaft 200.00
Whale tooth hdl, cvd sawtooth whalebone shaft, Am, 1850s 675.00
Whalebone, overall cvg, dmn baleen inlay, ca 1850 ....400.00
Wood cvd lion w/brass ring in mouth hdl, chestnut shaft 225.00
Wood w/burned stylized bird & snake, 1-pc 200.00
14k gold-chased knob on ebony shaft, ca 1910 ....750.00

Canton

Canton is a blue and white porcelain that was first exported in the 1790s by clipper ships from China to the United States, a practice that continued into the 1920s. Canton became very popular along the East coast where the major ports were located. Its popularity was due to several factors: it was readily available, inexpensive, and (due to the fact that it came in many different forms) appealing to the housewife.

The porcelain's blue and white color and simple motif (teahouse, trees, bridge, and a rain-cloud border) have made it a favorite of people who collect early American furniture and accessories. Buyers of Canton should shop at large outdoor shows and up-scale antique shows. Collections are regularly sold at auction. Collectors usually prefer a rich, deep tone rather than a lighter blue. Cracks, large chips, and major repairs will substantially affect values. Prices of Canton have escalated sharply over the last twenty years, and rare forms are highly sought after by advanced collectors. Our advisor for this category is Hobart D. Van Deusen; he is listed in the Directory under Connecticut.

Basket, fruit; rtcl rim, end hdls, hairline, 10¾" 825.00
Basket, fruit; rtcl rim, 19th C, 8½", w/mismatched tray 600.00
Basket, fruit; rtcl rim, 9¼" 500.00
Bowl, scalloped rim, 2¼x9½", EX 500.00
Bowl, scalloped rim, 4½x10¼" 900.00
Bowl, scalloped rim, 8¼", NM 400.00
Bowl, serving; 10½x8½" 275.00
Bowl, vegetable; almond shape, w/lid, 11" 325.00
Bowl, vegetable; almond shape, w/near-match lid, 10¼" 300.00
Bowl, vegetable; fruit finial on lid, 10¼" L 450.00
Bowl, vegetable; w/lid, 9x8", VG 400.00
Creamer, flat spout, 3½" 150.00
Creamer, helmet shape, rpr, 4½x6½" 300.00
Creamer, U-shaped spout, 3¼" 130.00
Dish, leaf shape, minor roughness, 8x6" 275.00
Ginger jar, w/lid, 7" 125.00
Pitcher, intertwined hdl & lid w/foo dog finial (mismatched) 550.00
Pitcher, 7¼", EX 500.00
Plate, hot water; std form, 11", pr 400.00
Platter, mk Made in China, 14½x11½" 300.00
Platter, pierced drip tray, 19th C, 17½" 900.00
Platter, 12¼x9½" 200.00
Platter, 19th C, 15¾x13¾" 400.00
Platter, 19th C, 17½", EX 600.00
Tea caddy, w/lid, 6½", EX+ 990.00
Teapot, domed lid, hairline in hdl, 8x9¼" 550.00
Tray, oval w/rtcl rim, 10⅞", EX 470.00
Tray, quatrefoil, 10¾x8", VG 300.00
Tureen, gravy; boar-head hdls, w/lid, hairline, 7¼" L 315.00
Tureen, soup; boar-head hdls, prof rpr, 8½x12" 450.00

Capodimonte

The relief style, highly colored and defined porcelain pieces in this listing are commonly called and identified in our current market place as Capo-di-Monte. It was King Ferdinand IV, son of King Charles who opened a factory in Naples in 1771 and began to use the mark of the blue crown N (BCN). When the factory closed in 1834, the Ginori family at Doccia near Florence, Italy, acquired what was left of the factory and continued using its mark. The factory continued until 1896 when it was then combined with Societa Ceramica Richard of Milan which continues today to manufacture fine porcelain pieces marked with a crest and wreaths under a blue crown with R. Capodimonte.

As more collectors recognize and appreciate the quality of the older ware, buyer demand drives prices higher. Our advisor for this category is James Highfield; he is listed in the Directory under Indiana.

Photo courtesy James Highfield

Tureen, figural pediment and winged female handles, BCN, 11½x11½", $900.00; Stein, cherub finial, screaming mask handle, BCN, 11½", $700.00.

Box, armor-making scene, mc w/gilt, gilt brass mts, 9" 400.00
Box, cherubs ride goat in landscape, quatrefoil shape, 4" 150.00
Box, mythological figures on lid, masks etc on base, 9" L 375.00
Compote, raised border, crest center, maidens/trunk std, 10¼" ..200.00
Cup & saucer, Triumph of Flora & Judgment of Paris, BCN 150.00
Figurine, Bird of Paradise, Armani, 21" 395.00
Figurine, Buccaneer, gr pants, red cape, sgn Cole, 12x6" 250.00
Figurine, lady w/fan, ruffled bl & red bonnet, purple dress, 4" 175.00
Inkwell, dbl, cherubs & satyrs, BCN, 7½" sq 400.00
Lamp, cherubs, gr & pk ribbing 75.00
Plaque, draped nude on winged horse, 1880s, in 8-sided fr, 17x19" ..1,800.00
Plate, armorial, sgn Rusconi, 10½" 225.00
Plate, crest in center, molded border, 7½", set of 12 ....950.00
Salt shaker & pepper grinder, recent, 4", 4½", pr 35.00
Stein, battle scene, helmet finial, 1-litre, M 900.00
Stein, battle scene, porc lid w/brass mt, 1-litre, NM 695.00
Tureen, winged maid hdls, putti surmount, 13" L, +tray 1,250.00
Urn, cherubs, gold hdls, cherub w/wreath finial, 4-ftd, 21" 595.00
Urn, frolicking cherubs & sea gods, BCN, 7¼", pr 190.00
Vase, battle scene, mc w/gold, BCN, 4½" 155.00

Carlton Ware

Carlton Ware was the product of Wiltshaw and Robinson, who operated in the Staffordshire district of England from about 1890. During the 1920s, they produced ornamental ware with enameled and gilded decorations such as flowers and birds, often on a black background. In 1958 the firm was renamed Carlton Ware Ltd. Their trademark was a crown over a circular stamp with 'W & R, Stoke on Trent' surrounding a swallow. 'Carlton Ware' was sometimes added by hand.

Vase, fantasy garden and butterflies on dark blue, #1689G on base, 6", $225.00.

Ashtray, Rouge Royale, chinoiserie w/willow 135.00
Bowl, Deco tree, mc on cream, scalloped rim, ftd, 3¼x7⅛" 350.00
Bowl, ducks & iris w/much gold on blk, 6½x13¼x6½" 920.00
Bowl, floral, mc on gr w/gold, mk, 3¼x12⅜" 395.00
Bowl, Oriental landscape, mc trim & dots, much gold, 3⅞x8⅝" ..350.00
Bowl, Rouge Royale, bird/butterflies/etc w/gold, peg ft, 3x10" 485.00
Bowl, Rouge Royale, chinoiserie w/willow, oval, 10" 260.00
Cookie jar, Water Lily, yel w/emb flowers, flower finial, 6½" 185.00
Cup & saucer, demi; Royal Lustre, storks in marsh w/gold 75.00
Figurine, cat, wht, 2¼" 25.00
Inkwell/pen tray, Egyptian Fan on cobalt bl, 2¼x8" 600.00
Jar, ginger; Rouge Royale, pagoda/people/etc, gold trim 195.00
Jar, Oriental couple w/fans in landscape w/gold, 9x4½" 450.00
Jar, Oriental scene on bl lustre, gold trim, mk, 9⅜x3⅝" 395.00
Jar, Rouge Royale Lustre, birds & flowers, 4x3⅝" 165.00
Pitcher, Rouge Royale, scenic, 6x6" 195.00
Tazza, floral, mc on gr w/gold, 2½x7¼" 225.00
Tazza, gum nut decor, ped ft, 2½x7" 195.00
Teapot, Buttercup, yel 450.00
Teapot, Wedgwood style, wht w/pastel classical figures, 1894 mk ..650.00

Tray, bird w/grapes & flowers in red lustre, Rouge Royale, 10¼" ..**175.00**
Vase, bird & exotic landscape on bl lustre w/gold, MOP int, 7⅝" ..**450.00**
Vase, floral branches on bl mottled, Handcraft, 9x3¼" **395.00**
Vase, flowers on fan of colored panels, gold trim, #d, 7½" **900.00**
Vase, Oriental scenes, bl lustre, 12½x4½" **395.00**
Vase, Oriental scenes on bl lustre, w/lid, 9¼x3¾" **395.00**
Vase, Oriental scenes on bl lustre w/gold, w/lid, 7⅜x3" **275.00**
Vase, Rouge Royale, no enameling, 5" **70.00**

Carnival Collectibles

Carnival items from the early part of this century represent the lighter side of an America that was alternately prospering and sophisticated or devastated by war and domestic conflict. But whatever the country's condition, the carnival's thrilling rides and shooting galleries were a sure way of letting it all go by — at least for an evening.

For further information on chalkware figures, we recommend *The Carnival Chalk Prize* by our advisor, Thomas G. Morris, who is listed in the Directory under Oregon.

In the shooting gallery target listings below, items are rated for availability from 1 (commonly found) to 10 (rarely found) and all are made of cast iron. Our advisors for shooting gallery targets are Richard and Valerie Tucker; their address is listed in the Directory under Texas.

**Cat w/bull's eye, worn pnt, Wurfflein,
5, 14¼x19", minimum $1,000.00.**

Photo courtesy Richard and Valerie Tucker

Chalkware figure, Alice the Goon, 1940-45, 10" **145.00**
Chalkware figure, Apache Babe, 1936-45, 15" **75.00**
Chalkware figure, Betty Boop, 1930-40, 14½" **295.00**
Chalkware figure, Bugs Bunny, flat bk, 1940-45, 9¼" **60.00**
Chalkware figure, Capt Marvel, 1940-50, 14½" **125.00**
Chalkware figure, Felix the Cat, 1922-40, 12½" **245.00**
Chalkware figure, Frenchie, by Jenkins, 1924, 15" **225.00**
Chalkware figure, I Love Me Girl, 1915-30, 11¼" **85.00**
Chalkware figure, lighthouse, 1935-40, 12¼" **45.00**
Chalkware figure, Lone Ranger, 1938-50, 14½" **85.00**
Chalkware figure, Maggie & Jiggs, 1920-35, 8¼" & 9½", pr **265.00**
Chalkware figure, majorette, 1949, 12" **50.00**
Chalkware figure, Mexican girl, 1925, 14½" **170.00**
Chalkware figure, Ming Toy, by Jenkins, 1924, 13" **170.00**
Chalkware figure, Miss Malibu, by Jenkins, jtd, 1933, 25½" **125.00**
Chalkware figure, piano baby, 1910-25, 10½" **120.00**
Chalkware figure, Pinocchio, ca 1940-50, 15" **175.00**
Chalkware figure, reading girl, 1910-25, 12x8½" **85.00**
Chalkware figure, sailor girl, by Jenkins, 1934, 13½" **70.00**
Chalkware figure, Sheba doll, 1923-30, 13½" **95.00**
Chalkware figure, Shirley Temple, 1935-40, 10" **95.00**
Chalkware figure, Snow White, 1937-50, 14" **85.00**
Chalkware figure, Snuffy Smith, 1934-45, 9¼" **90.00**

Chalkware figure, Sugar, by Jenkins, 1948, 13" **165.00**
Chalkware figure, windmill, 1935-40, 10¾" **25.00**

Shooting Gallery Targets

Battleship, worn wht pnt, Mangels, 5, 6¼x11⅜", $200 to **300.00**
Birds (8) on bar, worn pnt, Mangels, 9, 1½x41½, $700 to **800.00**
Bull's eye w/pop-up duck, old pnt, Quackenbush, 5, 12" dia, $300 to **400.00**
Dbl star spinner, worn mc pnt, Mangels, 3, 8x2¾", $100 to **200.00**
Dog running, worn wht pnt, Smith or Evans, 5, 6x11", $100 to ..**200.00**
Duck, detailed feathers, old pnt, Parker, 4, 3¾x5½", $100 to **200.00**
Duck, detailed feathers, worn pnt, Evans, 4, 5½x8½", $100 to ..**200.00**
Eagle w/wings wide, mc pnt, Smith or Evans, 5, 14¾", $500 to ..**600.00**
Greyhound, bull's eye, old patina, Parker, 8, 26" W, minimum ..**1,000.00**
Harlequin w/bull's eye, worn pnt, Hoffman, 9, 20½", minimum ..**1,000.00**
Monkey, standing, worn rpt, 10, 9¾x8½", from $300 to **400.00**
Owl, bull's eye, wht traces, Evans, 6, 10¾x5⅛", $400 to **500.00**
Pipe, old patina, Smith, 1, 5⅜x1¾", value less than **50.00**
Rabbit running, old patina, Parker, 8, 12x25x1¼", minimum ..**1,000.00**
Rabbit standing, worn red/wht pnt, Smith, 9, 18x10", $900 to .**1,000.00**
Reindeer (elk), worn rpt over wht, 5, 10x9", from $300 to **400.00**
Saber-tooth tiger, old patina, Mangels, 10, 7¾x13", $500 to **600.00**
Soldier w/rifle, pnt traces/old patina, Mueller, 5, 9x5", $100 to ..**200.00**
Squirrel running, old patina, Smith, 4, 5⅛x9¼", $100 to **200.00**
Swan, worn wht pnt, Mueller, 7, 5¾x5", $200 to **300.00**

Carnival Glass

Carnival glass is pressed glass that has been coated with a sodium solution and fired to give it an exterior lustre. First made in America in 1905, it was produced until the late 1920s and had great popularity in the average American household; for unlike the costly art glass produced by Tiffany, carnival glass could be mass produced at a small cost. Colors most found are marigold, green, blue, and purple; but others exist in lesser quantities and include white, clear, red, aqua opalescent, peach opalescent, ice blue, ice green, amber, lavender, and smoke.

Companies mainly responsible for its production in America include the Fenton Art Glass Company, Williamstown, West Virginia; the Northwood Glass Company, Wheeling, West Virginia; the Imperial Glass Company, Bellaire, Ohio; the Millersburg Glass Company, Millersburg, Ohio; and the Dugan Glass Company (Diamond Glass), Indiana, Pennsylvania. In addition to these major manufacturers, lesser producers included the U.S. Glass Company, the Cambridge Glass Company, the Westmoreland Glass Company, and the McKee Glass Company.

Carnival glass has been highly collectible since the 1950s and has been reproduced for the last twenty-five years. Several national and state collectors' organizations exist, and many fine books are available on old carnival glass, including *The Standard Encyclopedia of Carnival Glass* by Bill Edwards and Mike Carwile.

Acorn (Fenton), bowl, amethyst, 7-8½", ea **140.00**
Acorn Burrs (Northwood), punch bowl & base, gr **850.00**
Adam's Rib (Dugan/Diamond), pitcher, marigold **160.00**
Amaryllis (Northwood), compote, bl, sm **275.00**
Apple Blossoms (Dugan), plate, wht, 8¼" **300.00**
Apple Tree (Fenton), pitcher, water; marigold **350.00**
Arcadia Lace, rose bowl, marigold **155.00**
Arcs (Imperial), compote, amethyst **90.00**
Asters, bowl, marigold **60.00**
Australian Diamond (Crystal), sugar bowl, amethyst **85.00**
Autumn Acorns (Fenton), plate, bl, rare **1,500.00**
Balloons (Imperial), compote, smoke **90.00**
Band of Roses, pitcher, marigold **250.00**

Banded Diamond & Fan (English), toothpick holder, marigold ...80.00
Banded Diamonds (Crystal), tumbler, amethyst, rare 400.00
Banded Drape (Fenton), tumbler, bl 50.00
Banded Panels (Crystal), sugar bowl, amethyst 60.00
Barbella (Northwood), tumbler, vaseline 225.00
Basketweave (Fenton), bowl, wht, open edge, 5" 100.00
Basketweave (Fenton), plate, bl, open edge, 10" 1,600.00
Beaded Hearts (Northwood), bowl, gr 90.00
Beaded Shell (Dugan), bowl, amethyst, ftd, 9" 95.00
Beaded Shell (Dugan), butter dish, amethyst 150.00
Beaded Stars (Fenton), plate, marigold, 9" 110.00
Beaded Swirl (English), compote, bl 60.00
Bells & Beads (Dugan), nappy, peach opal 100.00
Big Basketweave (Dugan), basket, amethyst, sm 60.00
Big Fish (Millersburg), banana bowl, gr, rare 2,000.00
Bird of Paradise (Northwood), bowl, amethyst, advertising 395.00
Birds & Cherries (Fenton), compote, bl 60.00
Black Bottom (Fenton), candy jar, marigold 60.00
Blackberry (Fenton), spittoon whimsey, bl, rare 3,600.00
Blackberry Banded (Fenton), hat shape, gr 55.00
Blackberry Block (Fenton, tumbler, vaseline 300.00
Blackberry Spray (Fenton), compote, bl 50.00
Blocks & Arches (Crystal), tumbler, amethyst 90.00
Blossoms & Band (Imperial), wall vase, marigold, complete 45.00
Blueberry (Fenton), pitcher, bl, scarce 900.00
Booker, cider pitcher, marigold 600.00
Border Plants (Dugan), bowl, peach opal, flat, 8½" 180.00
Bow & English Hob (English), nut bowl, bl 60.00
Briar Patch, hat shape, amethyst 50.00
Brocaded Summer Gardens, dome bowl, pastel 95.00
Broken Arches (Imperial) bowl, gr, 8½-10", ea 75.00
Bubble Berry, shade, pastel 75.00
Bull's Eye & Leaves (Northwood), bowl, gr, 8½" 50.00
Bunny, bank, marigold 35.00
Butterfly, pin tray, marigold 40.00
Butterfly (Northwood), bonbon, gr, regular 100.00
Butterfly (US Glass), tumbler, marigold, rare 5,800.00
Butterfly & Berry (Fenton), butter dish, bl 225.00
Butterfly & Berry (Fenton), vase, wht, rare 500.00
Butterfly & Fern (Fenton), pitcher, gr 650.00

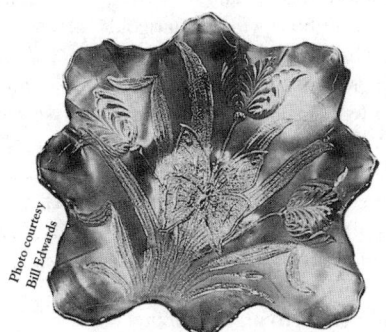

**Butterfly and Tulip (Dugan), bowl,
marigold, footed, 10½", $320.00.**

Buttermilk, Plain (Fenton), goblet, gr 80.00
Buzz Saw, shade, marigold 45.00
Cane (Imperial), pickle dish, marigold 32.00
Capitol (Westmoreland), mug, marigold, sm 140.00
Carnival Honeycomb (Imperial), bonbon, gr 60.00
Carolina Dogwood (Westmoreland), bowl, amethyst, 8½" 110.00
Cartwheel #411 (Heisey), compote, marigold 50.00

Cathedral (Sweden), flower holder, marigold 75.00
Chain & Star (Fostoria), tumbler, marigold, rare 900.00
Checkerboard (Westmoreland), tumbler, marigold, rare 750.00
Checkers, ashtray, marigold 47.00
Cherry (Dugan), bowl, peach opal, flat, 5" 90.00
Cherry (Millersburg), bowl, gr, rare, 7" 130.00
Cherry (Millersburg), milk pitcher, marigold, rare 1,700.00
Cherry & Cable (Northwood), bowl, marigold, scarce, 9" 125.00
Cherry Chain (Fenton), bonbon, bl 60.00
Cherry Circles (Fenton), compote, amethyst 80.00
Cherry Smash (US Glass), tumbler, marigold 190.00
Chrysanthemum (Fenton), bowl, bl, flat, 9" 80.00
Circle Scroll (Dugan), creamer or spooner, amethyst, ea 225.00
Cleopatra, bottle, marigold 110.00
Cleveland Memorial (Millersburg), ashtray, amethyst, rare 8,000.00
Coin Dot (Fenton), tumbler, gr, rare 265.00
Coin Spot (Dugan), goblet, ice gr 390.00
Colonial (Imperial), toothpick holder, gr 95.00
Columbia (Imperial), cake plate, amber pastel, rare 170.00
Concave Flute (Westmoreland), rose bowl, gr 65.00
Cone & Tie (Imperial), tumbler, amethyst, rare 950.00
Coolie Hat, hatpin, amethyst 100.00
Coral (Fenton), bowl, wht, 9" 50.00
Cornucopia (Fenton), candlesticks, marigold, 5", pr 80.00
Coronation (English), vase, marigold, Victoria Crown design, 5" ..250.00
Cosmos & Cane, chop plate, marigold, rare 1,450.00
Cosmos & Cane, spooner, wht 195.00
Cosmos VT (Fenton), bowl, bl, 9-10", ea 75.00
Country Kitchen (Millersburg), bowl, marigold, rare, 9" 595.00
Crab Claw (Imperial), bowl, smoke, 10"5" 70.00
Crackle (Imperial), candy jar, marigold, w/lid 30.00
Crackle (Imperial), tumbler, gr, dome base 30.00
Curtain Optic (Fenton), pitcher, vaseline 450.00
Cut Arcs (Fenton), vase whimsey (from bowl), gr 150.00
Cut Ovals (Fenton), candlesticks, marigold, pr 175.00
Dahlia (Dugan), tumbler, amethyst, rare 145.00
Daisy & Cane (English), vase, marigold 75.00
Daisy & Plume (Northwood-Dugan), candy dish, bl, ftd 100.00
Daisy Cut Bell (Fenton), bell, marigold, rare 500.00
Daisy Squares, goblet, marigold 700.00
Dandelion (Northwood), pitcher, bl 900.00
Deep Grape (Millersburg), compote, amethyst, rare 1,500.00
Diamond & Daisy Cut (US Glass), compote, bl 75.00
Diamond & File, banana bowl, marigold 65.00
Diamond & Sunburst (Imperial), decanter, gr 150.00
Diamond Checkerboard, cracker jar, marigold 85.00
Diamond Lace (Imperial), bowl, marigold, 10-11", ea 65.00
Diamond Ovals (English), compote (open sugar), marigold 40.00
Diamond Point, rose bowl, marigold 700.00
Diamond Point Columns (Imperial-Fenton), vase, amethyst 55.00
Diamond Ring (Imperial), bowl, smoke, 9" 55.00
Diamonds (Millersburg), pitcher, gr 350.00
Diving Dolphins (English), bowl, bl, ftd, 7" 270.00
Dolphins (Millersburg), compote, bl, rare 6,000.00
Double Diamonds, puff box, marigold 50.00
Double Dolphins (Fenton), candy dish, pastel, ftd, w/lid 80.00
Double Dutch (Imperial), bowl, gr, ftd, 9" 75.00
Double Star (Cambridge), pitcher, gr, scarce 500.00
Double Stem Rose (Dugan), bowl, amethyst, dome base, 8½" 90.00
Dragon's Tongue (Fenton), shade, peach opal 115.00
Drapery (Northwood), candy dish, aqua 200.00
Dugan's Many Ribs, hat shape, peach opal 100.00
Dutch Mill, plate, marigold, 8" 50.00
Egg & Dart, candlesticks, marigold, pr 90.00

Elephant, paperweight, marigold **1,250.00**
Elks (Fenton), plate, gr, Parkersburg, rare **1,450.00**
Embroidered Mums (Northwood), bowl, bl, 9" **525.00**
Enameled Panel, goblet, marigold **190.00**
English Hobstar, bowl, marigold, oval, 6", in holder **150.00**
Engraved Grapes (Fenton), candy jar, marigold, w/lid **85.00**
Estate (Westmoreland), mug, marigold, rare **75.00**
Etched Vine, tumbler, marigold **40.00**
Faceted Spearhead, hatpin, marigold **150.00**
Fan-Tail (Fenton), compote, bl **195.00**
Fancy Cut (English), pitcher, marigold, rare, mini **225.00**
Fans (English), pitcher, marigold **185.00**
Fashion (Imperial), tumbler, amethyst **225.00**
Feather & Heart (Millersburg), spittoon whimsey, marigold ...**7,000.00**
Feather Swirl (US Glass), vase, marigold **65.00**
Fenton's Basket (Fenton), basket, marigold, open edge **45.00**
Fentonia, bowl, gr, ftd, 9½" **75.00**
Fentonia Fruit (Fenton), pitcher, marigold, rare **575.00**
Fern (Northwood), compote, gr **85.00**
Field Flower (Imperial), pitcher, bl, scarce **400.00**
Field Thistle (US Glass), breakfast set, ice bl, 2-pc, rare **350.00**
Filigree (Dugan), vase, amethyst, rare **1,350.00**
Fine Cut Rings (English), creamer, marigold **145.00**
Firefly (Moth), candlesticks, marigold, pr **90.00**
Fishscales & Beads (Dugan), bowl, peach opal, 6-8", ea **150.00**
Flared Panel, shade, milk glass opal **75.00**
Fleur-De-Lis (Millersburg), bowl, clambroth, flat, 8½" **240.00**
Flora (English), float bowl, bl **175.00**
Florabell, pitcher, ice gr **600.00**
Floral & Grape (Dugan), pitcher, marigold **145.00**
Floral & Optic (Imperial), cake plate, peach opal, ftd **180.00**
Floral Sunburst, vase, marigold **175.00**
Flower & Beads, plate, marigold, rnd, 8½" **95.00**
Flowering Dill (Fenton), hat, bl **40.00**
Flowering Vine (Millersburg), compote, amethyst, tall, rare ...**8,500.00**
Flute (Millersburg), vase, bl, rare **2,750.00**
Flute (Northwood), pitcher, marigold, rare **395.00**
Flute & Cane (Imperial), wine, marigold **50.00**
Flute #3 (Imperial), butter dish, gr **210.00**
Flute #3 (Imperial), pitcher, bl **450.00**
Folding Fan (Dugan), compote, bl **85.00**
Footed Rib (Northwood), vase, pastel **110.00**
Formal (Dugan), vase, jack-in-pulpit; marigold, rare **700.00**
Four Flowers, plate, peach opal, 6½" **150.00**
Four Flowers VT, bowl, gr, 9-11", ea **70.00**
French Knots (Fenton), hat, amethyst **50.00**
Frolicking Bears (US Glass), tumbler, gr, rare **8,000.00**
Frosted Block (Imperial), bowl, marigold, sq, rare **50.00**
Fruit & Berries (English), bean pot, bl, w/lid, rare **425.00**
Fruit & Flowers (Northwood), plate, marigold, 9½" **235.00**
Fruit Salad (Westmoreland), punch bowl & base, amethyst, rare ...**700.00**
Garden Path (Dugan), bowl, peach opal, 5" **60.00**
Garland (Fenton), rose bowl, amethyst, ftd **170.00**
Georgia Bell (Dugan), compote, peach opal, ftd **140.00**
Gibson Girl, toothpick holder, marigold **60.00**
Goddess of Harvest (Fenton), bowl, bl, 9½", rare **6,500.00**
Golden Grapes (Dugan), bowl, pastel, 7" **50.00**
Golden Thistle, tray, pastel, 5", rare **350.00**
Goodyear, ashtray in tire, marigold **60.00**
Graceful (Northwood), vase, bl **135.00**
Grape, Heavy (Dugan); bowl, amethyst, 10" **295.00**
Grape, Heavy (Imperial); plate, gr, 6" **170.00**
Grape (Imperial), fruit bowl, gr, 8¾" **55.00**
Grape (Imperial), pitcher, amethyst **350.00**

Grape (Northwood's Grape & Cable), centerpc bowl, gr, ftd ...**1,100.00**
Grape (Northwood's Grape & Cable), compote, pastel, open ...**750.00**
Grape (Northwood's Grape & Cable), sugar bowl, marigold, w/lid ...**70.00**
Grape & Gothic Arches (Northwood), bowl, bl, 10" **80.00**
Grape Delight (Dugan), rose bowl, amethyst, ftd, 6" **80.00**
Grape Leaves (Northwood), bowl, gr, 8¼" **85.00**
Grape Wreath VT (Millersburg), bowl, gr, 5" **70.00**
Grapevine Lattice (Fenton), pitcher, wht, rare **850.00**
Grecian Urn, perfume, marigold, 6" **45.00**

Greek Key (Northwood), bowl,
amethyst, 8½", $120.00.

Greek Key (Northwood), pitcher, gr, rare **1,650.00**
Hamilton Souvenir, vase, marigold, 6¼" **70.00**
Harvest Flower (Dugan), tumbler, gr **365.00**
Harvest Poppy, compote, bl **450.00**
Hawaiian Moon, tumbler, cranberry flashed **90.00**
Heart & Horseshoe (Fenton), plate, marigold, rare, 9" ...**1,150.00**
Heart Band Souvenir (McKee), mug, gr, sm **140.00**
Heavy Diamond, nappy, marigold **40.00**
Heavy Heart (Higbee), tumbler, marigold **150.00**
Heavy Prisms (English), celery vase, bl, 6" **95.00**
Heavy Web (Dugan), plate, peach opal, rare, 11" **1,800.00**
Heisey Colonial (Heisey), perfume (cologne), marigold **90.00**
Heisey Set, creamer & tray, marigold **150.00**
Herringbone & Beaded Oval, compote, marigold, rare **600.00**
Hex Base, candlesticks, gr, pr **110.00**
Hobnail (Millersburg), tumbler, bl, rare **950.00**
Hobnail Panels (McKee), vase, clambroth, 8¾" **70.00**
Hobstar (Imperial), fruit bowl w/base, marigold **50.00**
Hobstar & Arches (Imperial), bowl, marigold, 9" **50.00**
Hobstar & Feather (Millersburg), dessert, marigold, stemmed ...**650.00**
Hobstar & Feather (Millersburg), punch cup, amethyst, scarce ...**40.00**
Hobstar & Fruit (Westmoreland), bowl, aqua opal, rare, 6" ...**300.00**
Hobstar & Shield, pitcher, marigold **195.00**
Hobstar Band (Imperial), celery, marigold **85.00**
Hobstar Panels (English), creamer, marigold **45.00**
Holly, Panelled (Northwood); bonbon, amethyst, ftd **90.00**
Holly (Fenton), compote, bl, 5" **50.00**
Holly Sprig or Whirl (Millersburg), compote, marigold, rare ...**450.00**
Holly Wreath Multi-Star VT (Millersburg), bowl, gr, 7" ...**130.00**
Honeybee (Jeannette), pot, pastel **85.00**
Honeycomb & Clover (Fenton), compote, bl **50.00**
Horses' Heads (Fenton), rose bowl, marigold, ftd **170.00**
Hourglass, bud vase, marigold **50.00**
Ice Crystals, bowl, pastel, ftd **85.00**
Idyll (Fenton), vase, bl **850.00**
Imperial #9 (Imperial), compote, marigold **40.00**
Imperial Basket (Imperial), basket, marigold, rare **65.00**
Intaglio Daisy (English), bowl, marigold, 7½" **50.00**
Interior Flute, creamer, marigold **50.00**

Interior Rib, vase, smoke 50.00
Inverted Coin Dot (Northwood-Fenton), pitcher, bl 400.00
Inverted Feather (Cambridge), cracker jar, gr, w/lid 395.00
Inverted Strawberry, bowl, gr, 9-10½", ea 295.00
Inverted Strawberry, candlesticks, marigold, pr, rare 300.00
Inverted Thistle (Cambridge), box, bl, rare 400.00
Inverted Thistle (Cambridge), sugar bowl, amethyst, rare 400.00
Jack-in-the-Pulpit (Dugan), vase, peach opal 110.00
Jacob's Ladder VT (US Glass), rose bowl, marigold 90.00
Jewel Box, inkwell, marigold 150.00
Jewels (Imperial-Dugan), vase, amber pastel 195.00
Kingfisher & Variant (Australian), bowl, amethyst, 5" 125.00
Kitten, mini paperweight, marigold, rare 250.00
Kittens (Fenton), plate, bl, scarce, 4½" 500.00
Kokomo (English), rose bowl, marigold, ftd 45.00
Lacy Dewdrop (Westmoreland), pitcher, pastel 650.00
Late Enameled Bleeding Hearts, tumbler, marigold 175.00
Late Enameled Strawberry, tumbler, marigold, tall 175.00
Lattice & Daisy (Dugan), pitcher, bl 285.00
Lattice & Grape (Fenton), pitcher, wht 850.00
Lattice & Leaves, vase, bl, 9½" 295.00
Lattice Heart (English), bowl, bl, 10" 70.00
Laurel Leaves (Imperial), plate, smoke 60.00
Leaf & Beads (Northwood-Dugan), rose bowl, bl, ftd 190.00
Leaf & Little Flowers (Millersburg), compote, amethyst, mini ..495.00
Leaf Swirl (Westmoreland), compote, amber pastel 70.00
Leaf Tiers (Fenton), pitcher, bl, ftd, rare 695.00
Lined Lattice, vase, bl, 5-14", ea 180.00
Little Barrel (Imperial), barrel, gr 195.00
Little Fishes (Fenton), bowl, gr, flat of ftd, 5½", ea 280.00
Little Stars (Millersburg), bowl, gr, rare, 9" 575.00
Loganberry (Imperial), vase, amethyst, scarce 525.00
Long Leaf (Dugan), bowl, peach opal, ftd 165.00
Long Thumbprint (Dugan), bowl, amethyst, 8¾" 40.00
Lotus & Grape (Fenton), plate, gr, rare, 9½" 2,100.00
Louisa (Westmoreland), nut bowl, amethyst, rare 350.00
Lucille, pitcher, bl, rare 1,300.00
Lustre & Clear (Imperial), creamer or sugar bowl, marigold, ea 40.00
Lustre & Flute (Northwood), bonbon, amethyst 60.00
Lustre Rose (Imperial), bowl, marigold, flat, 7-11", ea 35.00
Lustre Rose (Imperial), pitcher, milk; marigold 60.00
Magnolia Drape, pitcher, marigold 275.00
Malaga (Dugan), plate, amethyst, rare, 10" 650.00
Many Fruits (Dugan), cup, bl 45.00
Many Prisms, perfume w/stopper, marigold 75.00
Maple Leaf (Dugan), creamer or spooner, amethyst, ea 65.00
Marilyn (Millersburg), pitcher, gr, rare 1,350.00
Mary Ann (Dugan), loving cup, marigold, 3-hdld, rare 800.00
Mayflower, bowl, pastel, 7½" 50.00
Maypole, vase, gr, 6¼" 60.00
Memphis (Northwood), fruit bowl, ice gr, w/base 3,750.00
Mexican Bell, goblet, marigold flashed 40.00
Milady (Fenton), pitcher, bl 975.00
Miller Furniture (Fenton), basket, gr, open edge 65.00
Miniature Intaglio (Westmoreland), nut cup, wht, stemmed, rare ...700.00
Minnesota (US Glass), mug, marigold 100.00
Mirrored Lotus (Fenton), bonbon, marigold 85.00
Mitered Ovals (Millersburg), vase, amethyst, rare 7,500.00
Moon & Star (Westmoreland), compote, pearl 385.00
Moonprint (English), candlestick, marigold, rare 50.00
Morning Glory (Imperial), funeral vase, amethyst 300.00
Multi-Fruits & Flowers (Millersburg), punch bowl w/base, bl ..3,700.00
Napoleon, bottle, pastel 85.00
Nell (Higbee), mug, marigold 75.00

Night Stars (Millersburg), bonbon, gr, rare 500.00
Nola (Scandanavian), pitcher, marigold, squat 350.00
Northwood Jack-in-the-Pulpit, vase, bl, any sz 50.00
Northwood's Poppy, pickle dish, ice bl, oval 450.00
Nu-Art (Homestead)(Imperial), plate, marigold, scarce 850.00

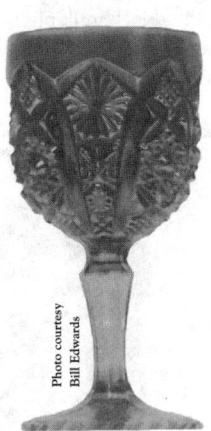

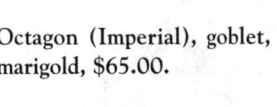
Octagon (Imperial), goblet, marigold, $65.00.

Photo courtesy Bill Edwards

Number 2176 (Sowerby), lemon squeezer, marigold 55.00
Octagon (Imperial), pitcher, pastel 200.00
Ohio Star (Millersburg), compote, marigold, rare 1,100.00
Omnibus, tumbler, gr, rare 795.00
Open Rose (Imperial), bowl, bl, flat, 9" 50.00
Optic & Buttons (Imperial), salt cellar, marigold 850.00
Optic VT, bowl, amethyst, 6" 65.00
Orange Tree (Fenton), mug, red, 2 szs, ea 650.00
Orange Tree Orchard (Fenton), pitcher, bl 600.00
Oval & Round (Imperial), plate, amber pastel, 10" 90.00
Oxford, mustard pot, marigold, w/lid 70.00
Palm Beach (US Glass), bowl, pastel, 9" 75.00
Paneled Dandelion (Fenton), tumbler, bl 70.00
Paneled Hobnail (Dugan), vase, peach opal, 5-10", ea 85.00
Paneled Prism, jam jar, marigold, w/lid 55.00
Paneled Thistle (Higbee), tumbler, marigold 100.00
Panels & Ball (Fenton), bowl, wht, 11" 175.00
Pansy (Imperial), plate, gr, ruffled, rare 120.00
Panther (Fenton), bowl, red, ftd, 5" 1,450.00
Parlor, ashtray, bl 95.00
Pastel Panels (Imperial), tumbler, pastel 75.00
Peach (Northwood), spooner, wht 150.00
Peaches, wine bottle, marigold 45.00
Peacock (Millersburg), ice cream bowl, bl, 5" 390.00
Peacock & Dahlia (Fenton), plate, bl, rare, 8½" 585.00
Peacock & Urn (Fenton), goblet, amethyst, rare 100.00
Peacock & Urn & VTs (Millersburg), ice cream bowl, bl, 6" 750.00
Peacock at the Fountain (Dugan), tumbler, amethyst 90.00
Peacock at the Fountain (Northwood), tumbler, amethyst 50.00
Peacock Tail (Fenton), bowl, peach opal, 4-10", ea 650.00
Peacocks (on Fence) (Northwood), plate, marigold, 9" 500.00
Pearl & Jewels (Fenton), basket, wht, 4" 200.00
Penny, match holder, amethyst, rare 250.00
Perfection (Millersburg), pitcher, amethyst, rare 4,000.00
Persian Garden (Dugan), chop plate, peach opal, 13!", rare 4,800.00
Persian Medallion (Fenton), bowl, marigold, 5" 48.00
Persian Medallion (Fenton), punch cup, gr 40.00
Petal & Fan (Dugan), plate, amethyst, ruffled, 6" 750.00
Petal Band, compote vase, marigold, 6" 85.00
Petals (Dugan), compote, gr 175.00
Peter Rabbit (Fenton), plate, amber, rare, 10" 1,800.00

Pinched Swirl (Dugan), vase, peach opal 115.00
Pine Cone (Fenton), plate, gr, 6½" 275.00
Pineapple (English), compote, bl 58.00
Pinwheel (English), bowl, marigold, rare, 8" 50.00
Plaid (Fenton), plate, marigold, rare, 9" 350.00
Plain Petals (Northwood), nappy, gr, scarce 90.00
Plume Panels, vase, gr, 7-12", ea 110.00
Poinsettia (Imperial), milk pitcher, marigold 170.00
Pony (Dugan), bowl, amethyst, 8½" 310.00
Poppy & Fish Net (Imperial), vase, red, rare, 6" 750.00

Poppy Show (Northwood), bowl, blue, 8½", $1,700.00.

Portland (US Glass), bowl, pastel, 8½" 170.00
Premium Imperial, candlesticks, amethyst, pr 90.00
Pretty Panels (Fenton), pitcher, red, w/lid 500.00
Primrose (Millersburg), bowl, clambroth, ruffled, 8¾" 160.00
Primrose & Fishnet (Imperial), vase, red, rare, 6" 750.00
Princely Plumes, candle holder, amethyst 300.00
Prism, shakers, marigold, pr 60.00
Prism & Daisy Band (Imperial), bowl, marigold, 5" 18.00
Prism Band (Fenton), pitcher, marigold, w/decor 175.00
Prisms (Westmoreland), compote, gr, scarce, 5" 100.00
Proud Puss (Cambridge), bottle, marigold 85.00
Pulled Loop (Dugan), vase, Celeste Blue 650.00
Puzzle (Dugan), compote, peach opal 90.00
Quarter Block, creamer, marigold 60.00
Question Marks (Dugan), cake plate, marigold, stemmed, rare ..150.00
Quill (Dugan), pitcher, amethyst 3,500.00
Radiance, pitcher, marigold 240.00
Rainbow (Northwood), compote, gr 150.00
Ranger (Mexican), creamer, marigold 40.00
Raspberry (Northwood), bowl, gr, 9" 75.00
Rays (Dugan), bowl, gr, 9" 90.00
Red Panels (Imperial), shade, red 200.00
Regal Swirl, candlestick, marigold 75.00
Ribbed Panels, mustard pot, marigold 350.00
Ribbon Tie (Fenton), bowl, bl, 8¾" 335.00
Ribs (Czechoslovakia), soap dish, marigold 60.00
Rising Sun (US Glass), tumbler, bl, rare 600.00
Rock Crystal (McKee), punch bowl w/vase, amethyst 600.00
Roll, tumbler, marigold 40.00
Rolled Ribs (New Martinsville), bowl, marigold opal ...150.00
Rosalind (Millersburg), bowl, gr, rare, 5" 575.00
Rose, bottle, pastel 130.00
Rose Bouquet, creamer, marigold 60.00
Rose Garden (Sweden), pitcher, communion; marigold, rare 600.00
Rose Show (Northwood), bowl, amethyst, 8¾" 850.00
Rose Spray (Fenton), compote, Celeste Blue 190.00

Roses & Fruit (Millersburg), bonbon, gr, ftd, rare ...1,100.00
Round-Up (Dugan), bowl, peach opal, 8¾" 300.00
Ruffled Rib (Northwood), spittoon whimsey, marigold, rare 225.00
S-Repeat (Dugan), cup, marigold, rare 120.00
Six-Sided (Imperial), candlestick, gr 250.00
Ski-Star (Dugan), banana bowl, amethyst 125.00
Small Blackberry (Northwood), compote, marigold 60.00
Small Rib (Dugan), compote, gr 45.00
Smooth Panels (Imperial), tumbler, pastel marigold 46.00
Smooth Rays (Westmoreland), compote, gr 75.00
Soda Gold (Imperial), pitcher, marigold 240.00
Soda Gold Spears (Dugan), bowl, clear, 4½" 30.00
Soutache (Dugan), plate, peach opal, rare, 10½" 375.00
Sowerby File & Shell, candle lamp, marigold, 9¼" 350.00
Sowerby Wide Panel (Sowerby), bowl, blk amethyst 75.00
Spiderweb (Northwood-Dugan), vase, pastel, 8" 80.00
Spiralex (English), vase, gr, various szs, ea 70.00
Spring Basket (Imperial), basket, marigold, 5" 50.00
Square Daisy & Button (Imperial), toothpick holder, pastel, rare ..125.00
Stag & Holly (Fenton), bowl, bl, ftd, 9-13", ea 425.00
Standard, vase, marigold, 5½" 50.00
Star & Diamond Point, hatpin, amethyst 75.00
Star & Fan (English), decanter, marigold, +4 cordials/tray ...1,500.00
Star & File (Imperial), rose bowl, amethyst 100.00
Star & Nearcut, hatpin, amethyst 60.00
Star Medallion (Imperial), compote, marigold 45.00
Star Medallion (Imperial), tumbler, pastel 55.00
Starburst Lustre (Northwood), compote, marigold 50.00
Starfish (Dugan), bonbon, peach opal, hdld, rare 160.00
Stars & Bars, rose bowl, marigold 130.00
Stippled Diamond Swag (English), compote, marigold 45.00
Stippled Petals (Dugan), bowl, peach opal, 9" 90.00
Stippled Rays (Fenton), bonbon, gr 55.00
Stippled Rays (Imperial), creamer, red, stemmed 500.00
Stippled Strawberry (Jenkins), syrup, marigold, rare 250.00
Stork & Rushes (Dugan), creamer, amethyst, rare 90.00
Strawberry (Millersburg), compote, gr, rare 450.00
Strawberry (Northwood), bowl, gr, 5" 70.00
Strawberry Scroll (Fenton), tumbler, marigold, rare ...275.00
Stretched Diamond (Northwood), tumbler, marigold, rare ...175.00
Stretched Diamonds & Dots, tumbler, marigold 175.00
Sunflower (Northwood), plate, gr, rare 400.00
Sunflower & Diamond, vase, bl, 2 szs, ea 110.00
Swan, Pastel (Dugan-Fenton); swan, bl 190.00
Swirl Variant (Imperial), dessert, marigold, stemmed ...30.00
Swirled Flute (Fenton), vase, red, 7-12", ea 485.00
Swirled Threads, goblet, marigold 95.00
Taffeta Lustre (Fostoria), bowl, console; gr, rare, 11" 150.00
Target (Fenton), vase, amethyst, 7-11", ea 55.00
Ten Mums (Fenton), bowl, gr, 8-11", ea 260.00
Thin & Wid Rib (Northwood), vase, amethyst, ruffled 130.00
Thistle (English), vase, marigold, 6" 45.00
Thistle & Thorn (English), creamer, marigold 60.00
Three Fruits (Northwood), bowl, bl, 9" 180.00
Three Fruits Medallion (Northwood), bowl, bl, ftd, 8-10½", ea ..285.00
Three Row (Imperial), vase, amethyst, rare 1,200.00
Three-In-One (Imperial), banana bowl whimsey, marigold 100.00
Thumbprint & Oval (Imperial), vase, amethyst, rare, 5½" ...850.00
Thunderbird (Australian), bowl, amethyst, 9½" 395.00
Tiered Thumbprint, candlesticks, marigold, pr 120.00
Tiger Lily (Imperial), pitcher, bl 185.00
Tobacco Leaf (US Glass), champagne, clear 160.00
Top o' the Morning, hatpin, amethyst 160.00
Tornado (Northwood), vase, bl, ribbed, 2 szs, ea ...1,150.00

Tornado VT (Northwood), vase, marigold, rare 1,450.00
Tracery (Millersburg), bonbon, gr, rare 650.00
Tree Bark (Imperial), candlesticks, marigold, 7", pr 50.00
Tree Bark VT, candle holder, marigold, on stand 85.00
Tree Trunk (Northwood), vase, aqua opal, 7-12", ea 1,200.00
Triplets (Dugan), bowl, amethyst, 6-8", ea 40.00
Trout & Fly (Millersburg), plate, amethyst, rare, 9" 7,500.00
Tulip Scroll (Millersburg), vase, amethyst, rare, 6-12", ea 400.00
Turbin, hatpin, amethyst 100.00
Twins (Imperial), bowl, gr, 5" 30.00
Two Flowers (Fenton), bowl, marigold, ftd, 5-8", ea 60.00
Umbrella Prisms, hatpin, amethyst, sm 45.00
US Diamond Block (US Glass), compote, marigold, rare 65.00
Venetian (Cambridge), creamer, marigold, rare 550.00
Vineyard (Dugan), pitcher, peach opal 950.00
Vining Leaf & VT (English), spittoon, marigold 350.00
Vining Twigs (Dugan), plate, wht, rare, 7" 750.00
Vintage (Fenton), whimsey fernery, amethyst 200.00
Vintage (Millersburg), bowl, gr, rare, 5" 1,000.00
Vintage Banded (Dugan), mug, marigold 35.00
Vintage Leaf (Fenton), bowl, amethyst, 8½" 75.00
Vintage VT (Dugan), plate, amethyst 400.00
Virginia Blackberry (US Glass), pitcher, bl, rare, sm 950.00
Waffle Block (Imperial), basket, marigold, 10" 50.00
Waffle Block & Hobstar (Imperial), basket, smoke 265.00
Washboard, creamer, marigold, 5½' 45.00
Water Lily (Fenton), bowl, blk amethyst, ftd, 10" 175.00
Water Lily & Cattails (Fenton), bonbon, bl 90.00
Water Lily & Cattails (Northwood), pitcher, marigold 400.00
Western Daisy (Westmoreland), bowl, amethyst 60.00
Wheat (Northwood), sweetmeat, gt, w/lid, rare 9,500.00
Whirling Hobstar, cup, marigold 20.00
White Elephant, ornament, wht, rare 350.00
Wide Panel (Northwood-Fenton-Imperial), goblet, marigold 40.00
Wide Panel Cherry, pitcher, wht, sm 195.00
Wide Rib (Dugan), vase, peach opal 90.00
Wild Blackberry (Fenton), bowl, amethyst, scarce, 8½" 115.00
Wild Loganberry (Westmoreland), cider pitcher, moonstone irid .520.00
Wild Rose, light shade, marigold 95.00
Wild Rose (Northwood), bowl, marigold, ftd, open edge, 6" 60.00
Wild Strawberry (Northwood), bowl, amethyst, rare, 6" 140.00
Wildflower (Millersburg), compote, gr, ruffled, rare 1,500.00
Wildflower (Northwood), compote, bl, plain int 450.00
Windflower (Dugan), nappy, bl, hdls 185.00
Windmill (Imperial), bowl, gr, 9" 40.00
Windsor (Imperial), flower arranger, marigold, rare 90.00
Wine & Roses (Fenton), wine, vaseline 100.00
Wishbone (Northwood), plate, amethyst, flat, rare, 10" 1,875.00
Wishbone & Spades (Dugan), plate, peach opal, rare, 10½" ...1,350.00
Wisteria (Northwood), bank whimsey, wht, rare 2,500.00
Woodpecker (Dugan), wall vase, marigold 55.00
Wreath of Roses (Dugan/Diamond), rose bowl whimsey, marigold .70.00
Wreath of Roses (Fenton), compote, bl 45.00
Wreathed Cherry (Dugan), butter dish, amethyst 160.00
Zig Zag (Millersburg), card tray, gr, rare 900.00
Zip Zip (English), flower frog holder, marigold 60.00
Zipper VT (English), sugar bowl, marigold, w/lid 50.00
Zippered Heart, bowl, amethyst, 5" 50.00
49er, atomizer, marigold 90.00

Carousel Figures

For generations of Americans, visions of carousel horses revolving majestically around lively band organs rekindle wonderful childhood experiences. These nostalgic memories are the legacy of the creative talent from a dozen carving shops that created America's carousel art. Skilled craftsmen brought their trade from Europe where American carvers took the carousel animal from a folk art creation to a true art form. The 'Golden Age of Carousel Art' lasted from 1880 to 1929.

There are two basic types of American carousels. The largest and most impressive is the 'park style' carousel built for permanent installation in major amusement centers. These were created in Philadelphia by Gustav and William Dentzel, Muller Brothers, and E. Joy Morris who became the Philadelphia Toboggan Company in 1902. A more flamboyant group of carousel animals was carved in Coney Island, New York, by Charles Looff, Marcus Illions, Charles Carmel, and Stein & Goldstein's Artistic Carousel Company. These park-style carousels were typically three, four, and even five rows with forty-five to sixty-eight animals on a platform. Collectors often pay a premium for the carvings by these men. The outside row animals are larger and more ornate and command higher prices. The horses on the inside rows are smaller, less decorated, and of lesser value.

The most popular style of carousel art is the 'country fair style.' These carousels were portable affairs created for mobility. The horses are smaller and less ornate with leg and head positions that allow for stacking and easy loading. These were built primarily for North Tonawanda, New York, near Niagara Falls, by Armitage Herschell Company, Herschell Spillman Company, Spillman Engineering Company, and Allen Herschell. Charles W. Parker was also well known for his portable merry-go-rounds. He was based in Leavenworth, Kansas. Parker and Herschell Spillman both created a few large park-style carousels as well, but they are better known for their portable models.

Horses are by far the most common figure found, but there are two dozen other animals that were created for the carousel platform. Carousel animals, unlike most other antiques, are oftentimes worth more in a restored condition. Figures found with original factory paint are extraordinarily rare and bring premium amounts. Typically, carousel horses are found in garish, poorly applied 'park paint' and often are missing legs or ears. Carousel horses are hollow. They were glued up from several blocks for greater strength and lighter weight. Bass and poplar woods were used extensively.

If you have an antique carousel animal you would like to have identified, send a clear photograph and description along with a LSASE to our advisor, William Manns, who is listed in the Directory under New Mexico. Mr. Manns is the author of *Painted Ponies*, containing many full-color photographs, guides, charts, and directories for the collector.

Key:
IR — inside row
MR — middle row
OR — outside row
PTC — Philadelphia Toboggan Company

Coney Island-Style Horses

Carmel, IR, jumper, unrstr 4,800.00
Carmel, MR jumper, unrstr 8,900.00
Carmel, OR jumper w/cherub, rstr 34,000.00
Illions, IR jumper, rstr 4,500.00
Illions, MR stander, rstr 9,800.00
Looff, IR jumper, unrstr 5,000.00
Looff, OR jumper, unrstr 21,500.00
Stein & Goldstein, IR jumper, unrstr 5,000.00
Stein & Goldstein, MR jumper, rstr 11,000.00
Stein & Goldstein, OR stander w/bells, unrstr 39,000.00

European Horses

Anderson, English, unrstr 3,500.00

Bayol, French, unrstr **3,000.00**
Heyn, German, unrstr **3,500.00**
Hubner, Belgian, unrstr **2,800.00**
Savage, English, unrstr **3,500.00**

Menagerie Animals (Non-Horses)

Dentzel, bear, unrstr **28,000.00**
Dentzel, cat, unrstr **35,000.00**
Dentzel, lion, unrstr **45,000.00**
Dentzel, pig, unrstr **9,000.00**
Dentzel, rabbit, unrstr **35,000.00**
E Joy Morris, deer, unrstr **10,000.00**
Herschell Spillman, cat, unrstr **12,500.00**
Herschell Spillman, chicken, portable, unrstr **7,000.00**
Herschell Spillman, dog, portable, unrstr **6,500.00**
Herschell Spillman, frog, unrstr **24,000.00**
Looff, camel, unrstr **9,000.00**
Looff, goat, rstr **15,000.00**
Muller, tiger, rstr **25,000.00**

Philadelphia-Style Horses

Dentzel, IR 'topknot' jumper, unrstr **5,500.00**
Dentzel, MR jumper, unrstr **14,000.00**

Dentzel, outside row stander, with female carving on shoulder, ca 1915, restored, from $30,000.00 to $35,000.00.

Dentzel, prancer, rstr **9,500.00**
Morris, IR prancer, rstr **7,000.00**
Morris, MR stander, unrstr **9,500.00**
Morris, OR stander, rstr **20,000.00**
Muller, IR jumper, rstr **6,900.00**
Muller, MR jumper, rstr **12,000.00**
Muller, OR stander, rstr **40,000.00**
Muller, OR stander w/military trappings **75,000.00**
PTC, chariot (bench-like seat), rstr **8,900.00**
PTC, IR jumper, rstr **4,000.00**
PTC, MR jumper, rstr **15,500.00**
PTC, OR stander, armored, rstr **52,000.00**
PTC, OR stander, unrstr **29,500.00**

Portable Carousel Horses

Allan Herschell, all aluminum, ca 1950 ....**750.00**
Allan Herschell, half & half, wood & aluminum head **1,500.00**
Allan Herschell, IR Indian pony, unrstr **2,500.00**
Allan Herschell, OR, rstr **3,200.00**
Allan Herschell, OR Trojan-style jumper **3,800.00**
Armitage Herschell, track-machine jumper **2,600.00**
Dare, jumper, unrstr **2,800.00**

Herschell Spillman, chariot (bench-like seat) **3,000.00**
Herschell Spillman, IR jumper, unrstr **2,400.00**
Herschell Spillman, MR jumper, unrstr **2,900.00**
Herschell Spillman, OR, eagle decor **4,500.00**
Herschell Spillman, OR, park machine **10,000.00**
Parker, MR jumper, unrstr **3,000.00**
Parker, OR jumper, park machine, unrstr **7,500.00**
Parker, OR jumper, rstr **5,800.00**

Cartoon Art

Collectors of cartoon art are interested in many forms of original art — animation cels, sports, political or editorial cartoons, syndicated comic strip panels, and caricature. To produce even a short animated cartoon strip, hundreds of original drawings are required, each showing the characters in slightly advancing positions. Called 'cels' because those made prior to the 1950s were made from a celluloid material, collectors often pay hundreds of dollars for a frame from a favorite movie. Prices of Disney cels with backgrounds vary widely. Background paintings, model sheets, storyboards, and preliminary sketches are also collectible — so are comic book drawings executed in India ink and signed by the artist. Daily 'funnies' originals, especially the earlier ones portraying super heroes, and Sunday comic strips, the early as well as the later ones, are collected. Cartoon art has become recognized and valued as a novel yet valid form of contemporary art. In the listings below all cells are gouache on celluloid unless noted otherwise.

Key:
ab — airbrushed
HB — Hanna-Barbera
WB — Warner Brothers
WD — Walt Disney
KFS — King Features Syndicate

Animation Cel, Full Color

Alice in Wonderland, WD, Tweedledum/Tweedledee, 1951, 7½x5" ..**800.00**
Bambi, WD, Flower, pnt bkground, rstr, 1942, 3x3" **2,070.00**
Deputy Droopy, MGM, Droopy & Slim, 7½x6", pr **1,100.00**
Foghorn Leghorn, WB, hand-inked, rstr, 1960, 5x8" & 7x12", pr .**1,380.00**
Fox & Hound, WD, Big Mama (owl) w/Fox, 1981, fr, 7½x10" ..**490.00**
Hush My Mouse, WB, Sniffles, master bkground, rstr, 1946, 6x3" .**1,495.00**
Jumpin' Jupiter, WB, Sylvester & Porky Pig, 1955, 7½x8" **3,220.00**
Jungle Book, WD, boy & bear, 1967, untrimmed, fr, 7x7" **2,185.00**
Peter Pan, WD, full figure of Peter, untrimmed, fr, 3x4" **1,380.00**
Pinocchio, WD, Jiminy Cricket, ab bkground, 1940, 2½x3½" .**2,300.00**
Plute, WD, full figure, from theatrical short, 4x5" **750.00**
Prince & Pauper, WD, Mickey Mouse as prince, w/seal, 6x4" **750.00**
Roller Coaster Rabbit, WD, Roger Rabbit w/dart, 8x10" **635.00**
Royal Cat Nap, MGM, Tom as Cardinal's guard, 1958, 6x4½" ..**700.00**
Sleeping Beauty, Merryweather & flora, mat/sticker, 5x8½" **700.00**
Sleeping Beauty, WD, King's lackey (full figure), 1959, 7½x6" ..**400.00**
Sleeping Beauty, WD, King Stefan portrait, 1959, 5x6½" **450.00**
Winnie Pooh & Honey Tree, WD, Pooh stuck in door, 1966, 6x8" ..**485.00**

Animation Drawing

Bambi, WD, pencil & crayon, set of 14 from 2x6" to 11x14", VG .**1,265.00**
Bambi, WD, Thumper, conte crayon, 1942, fr, 6x8" **1,100.00**
Bugs Bunny, WB, red/blk pencil, 1940s, 6x4" **1,035.00**
Canine Caddy, WD, golfer & Pluto, mc pencil, 1941, 6x6", pr ..**1,500.00**
Fantasia, WD, Yen Sid, colored pencil, 1940, 9½x6½" **1,700.00**
Fishin' Around, WD, Mickey & Pluto, pencil, 1931, 2½x10" .**1,265.00**
Mail Pilot, WD, Mickey delivering mail, 1933, 1½x5" **865.00**
Snow White & 7 Dwarfs, WD, Bashful full figure, 1937, 7x5" ..**1,500.00**

Whoopy Party, WD, Minnie Mouse/Clarabelle Cow, 1932, 7x9½" ...**2,750.00**
Ye Olden Days, WD, Mickey & Minnie, bl/blk pencil, 1933, 3x3½" ..**575.00**

Miscellaneous

Drawing, Brave Little Tailor, Mickey & Minnie, WD, 1950s, 8x9" ..**850.00**
Illustration, Mickey as cowboy, WD, pencil, 1980s, 6½x7¼" **375.00**
Oil on bkground sheet, WD, Pete & Donald Duck, 8x10½" **800.00**
Pencil sketches, Drag-A-Long Droopy, MGM, 1954, 9½x11" **975.00**
Poster, Food for Feudin', WD, Pluto, Chip & Dale, 1950, 41x27" ..**865.00**
Production drawing, Bambi & Faline, WD, dk red pencil, 7x8" .**357.00**
Production drawing, Blk Cauldron, WD, Taran w/apple, 6x5½" ..**130.00**
Production drawing, Mickey's Mellerdrammer, WD, w/Minnie, 4x8" ..**900.00**
Silkscreened serigraph, Belle & Beast, WD, 1991 ....**275.00**
Storyboard, Bernard & Bianca, WD, 15 frames, 15x15" **425.00**
Tempera on bkground sheet, Dough for Do-Do, WB, 4 scenes, 9x11" **1,500.00**
Tempera on bkground sheet, Roadrunner/Coyote, WB, '60s, 10x13" ..**925.00**
Wc on bkbround sheet, Sky Trooper, WD, Donald & Pete, 8x11" ..**1,000.00**
Wc on story sheet, Dumbo, WD, w/Timothy, 5½x7½" **1,150.00**

Cartoon Books

'Books of cartoons' were printed during the first decade of the 20th century and remained popular until the advent of the modern comic book in the late '30s. Cartoon books, printed in both color and black and white, were merely reprints of current newspaper comic strips. The books, ranging from thirty to seventy pages and in sizes from 3½" x 8" up to 11" x 17", were usually bound with cardboard covers and were often distributed as premiums in exchange for coupons saved from the daily paper. One of the largest of the companies who printed these books was Cupples and Leon, producer of nearly half of the two hundred titles on record. Among the most popular sellers were *Mutt and Jeff*, *Bringing Up Father*, and *Little Orphan Annie*.

The Gumps, #2, Cupples and Leon, 1925, EX, $45.00.

Angelic Angelina, Cupples & Leon, 1909, EX **150.00**
Barnie Google & Spark Plug, #2, Cupples & Leon, 1924, VG **50.00**
Bringing Up Father, #4, Cupples & Leon, EX **105.00**
Bringing Up Father, #11, Cupples & Leon, scarce, EX **115.00**
Bringing Up Father, #15, VG **85.00**
Daffydills, Cupples & Leon, 1911, EX **90.00**
Foxy Grandpa & Little Brother, Donohue, EX **150.00**
Henry, McKay, 1935, EX **100.00**
Mutt & Jeff #6, Cupples & Leon, 1919, EX **125.00**
Smitty at Ballgame, Cupples & Leon, 1929, EX **80.00**
Tarzan, Grosset & Dunlap, 1929, EX **75.00**
Tillie the Toiler, #6, Cupples & Leon, EX **65.00**

Cash Registers

By 1970 antique cash registers had risen to become blue chip collectibles, joining the ranks of fine paintings, bronzes, firearms, clocks, and other categories having permanent, established worth. Some extremely scarce and elegant cash registers will command up to $25,000.00 on today's market.

Register prices are determined by make, model, size, desirability of pattern, and accessories such as add-on clocks, topsigns, and personalized nameplates (which may be cast as topsigns or 'lid ovals' and on occasion cast into the register's front or back plates). Of immense consideration is the register's condition.

This column uses 'mint' condition (M) to indicate registers which have been cleaned, oiled, polished, and lacquered by a professional and have perfect glass, keytops, and indicators. Some restorers will replace the velvet underneath the lid (where applicable), which is an added touch of elegance. 'Very good' condition (VG) describes unrestored, unpolished registers which are complete and operating. For registers not listed, use this basic equation to arrive at an approximate evaluation: A) M restored = 2X G/VG; B) EX original = 1½X G/VG. All prices may vary as much as 20%, depending on geography and demand.

For further information we recommend the highly informative books *Antique Cash Registers, 1880 – 1920,* by Bartsch and Sanchez (Mr. Bartsch's address may be found in our Directory under Oregon); and *The Incorruptible Cashier,* Vols. I & II, currently available from our other advisor, John Apple, listed in our Directory under Wisconsin.

Dial, emb brass, emb pattern on drw, 25", EX **6,500.00**
NCR #1, American detail adder, VG **2,650.00**
NCR #1, w/rare topsign **2,800.00**
NCR #1054, glass autographic w/box attachment, 1910-16, M .**1,200.00**
NCR #129-130, bronze, VG **850.00**
NCR #13 or #14, Ionic CI, 1899, G **750.00**
NCR #130, Art Nouveau cabinet, M **1,600.00**
NCR #135, Art Nouveau pattern, CI, 31-key, 1905, VG **600.00**
NCR #2 or #3, detail adder, scroll pattern, VG **900.00**
NCR #2 or #3, inlaid oak or mahog, scarce **2,250.00**
NCR #215 or #216, bronze fleur-de-lis, VG **950.00**
NCR #226, rare bilingual topsign, EX orig **900.00**
NCR #250 or #251, bronze, VG **900.00**
NCR #3, mahog inlay, deep wood drw, ca 1886 ....**4,500.00**
NCR #30, bronze, total adder, VG **1,400.00**
NCR #312, #313, or #317, dolphin pattern, VG **800.00**
NCR #322, #323, or #327, marble 3 sides, extended base, M ..**1,800.00**
NCR #322, #323, or #327, marble 3 sides, extended base, VG .**1,050.00**
NCR #324, EX orig **700.00**
NCR #324 or #325, Woolworth sz, M **1,050.00**
NCR #33, $5 maximum, CA, 1903, VG **900.00**
NCR #332, #333, #349, or #356, orig topsign, M **1,150.00**
NCR #332, #333, #349, or #356, orig topsign, VG **550.00**
NCR #336, brass, rstr **950.00**
NCR #337, dolphin design, M **950.00**
NCR #338, dogwood pattern, English numerals, CA, 1910-16, VG ..**475.00**
NCR #360, 37 keys, rings to $60, 1908-09, M **1,500.00**
NCR #441, #442, Empire design w/quartered-oak base, M **1,750.00**
NCR #441-#452, Empire pattern, M **1,750.00**
NCR #441-#452, Empire pattern, VG **800.00**
NCR #441E-#452E, electric, M **2,250.00**
NCR #441E-#452E, electric, VG **950.00**
NCR #442E-L, EX orig **1,400.00**
NCR #47, oak or mahog inlay, up to $6, VG **2,250.00**
NCR #5, narrow scroll, glass topsign, EX orig **2,750.00**
NCR #50, Renaissance design, orig clock, EX orig **2,500.00**
NCR #52, Renaissance design, orig clock, extended base, M ..**3,800.00**
NCR #52 or #52¼, Renaissance design, extended base, VG ...**2,900.00**
NCR #522, 2-drw, electric bar model, 1910-16, M **2,500.00**
NCR #522, 2-drw, electric bar model, 1910-16, VG **1,800.00**
NCR #64, Bohemian pattern, iron, 25-key, 1901, VG **600.00**

NCR #7 or #8, detail adder, fleur-de-lis, VG 850.00
NCR #711-#717, mahog-grain finish on steel, M 275.00
NCR #78, custom built to eliminate bk window, NP, 1902, VG .950.00

Cast Iron

In the mid-1800s, the cast-iron industry was raging in the United States. It was recognized as a medium extremely adaptable for uses ranging from ornamental architectural filigree to actual building construction. It could be cast from a mold into any conceivable design that could be reproduced over and over at a relatively small cost. It could be painted to give an entirely versatile appearance. Furniture with open-work designs of grapevines and leaves and intricate lacy scrollwork was cast for gardens as well as inside use. Figural doorstops of every sort, bootjacks, trivets, and a host of other useful and decorative items were made before the 'ferromania' had run its course. See also Kitchen, Cast-Iron Bakers and Kettles; and other specific categories.

Garden seat, ornate casting with seated female medallion in back, 63", fine condition, $1,000.00.

Architectural pc, cowboy on horse, hollow, ca 1890, 13x12x2" .225.00
Bank, pig form, Granite City Pig Iron, 3¾" 95.00
Bench, ornate 3-part bk, old wht rpt, welded rpr, 47" 380.00
Bullet mold, hinged, makes ball-shaped bullet, 4⅞" L 30.00
Croquet wickets, jockey figurals, old rpt, 17½", set of 9 ....2,475.00
Figurine, rooster, old finish, 6¼" 180.00
Foot scraper, AK & Sons 486, sq supports, wide blade, pnt, 7¾" ..45.00
Heat vent cover, openwork, old wht pnt, 16" dia 75.00
Hitching post, Black jockey boy, mc rpt, 38", G 250.00
Kettle, gypsy, 3-legged, hinged arched hdl, 6½x5¾" 75.00
Kettle, gypsy, no hdl, 17½" 75.00
Kettle, rendering; firebox base, Kenwood...Newark O, 45-gal .1,100.00
Paperweight, pig figural, worn yel rpt, 2⅛" 80.00
Sconces, gilded, beveled mirror bks, cut prisms, 23", pr 220.00
Settee, vintage castings, cleaned to bare iron, 38" 250.00
Strong box, w/key & bail hdl, 5⅝" L 220.00
Teakettle, Pat July 14, 1868, E Ripleys, wrought hdl, 7½" 85.00
Umbrella stand, Art Nouveau floral details, old rpt, 29" 140.00
Umbrella stand, heron w/lily pads & fish in base, old rpt, 21" 275.00
Urn, CE Walbridge, Pat Jan 26, 1873, old wht rpt, 34¼" 250.00
Urn, on sq plinth, rpl bolts, old blk rpt, 25" 165.00

Castor Sets

Castor sets became popular during the early years of the 18th century and continued to be used through the late Victorian era. Their purpose was to hold various condiments for table use. The most common type was a circular arrangement with a center handle on a revolving pedestal base that held three, four, five, or six bottles. Some had extras;

a few were equipped with a bell for calling the servant. Frames were made of silverplate, glass, or pewter. Though most bottles were of pressed glass, some of the designs were cut, and on rare occasion, colored glass with enameled decorations was used as well. To maintain authenticity and value, castor sets should have matching bottles. Prices listed below are for those with matching bottles and in frames with plating that is in excellent condition (unless noted otherwise). Note: Watch for new frames and bottles in both clear and colored glass; these have recently been appearing on the market. Our advisor for this category is Deborah Maggard; she is listed in the Directory under Ohio.

3-bottle, Gothic Arch, blown, orig stoppers; pewter fr 115.00
3-bottle, rubena, cut Dmns; SP fr, 5½x4" 295.00
4-bottle, amberina w/eng decor; orig fr 985.00
4-bottle, Banded Ring; orig pewter fr, child sz 125.00
4-bottle, cranberry, orig stoppers; pressed glass holder 350.00
4-bottle, cut; SP Walker & Hall fr, Sheffield 135.00
4-bottle, King's Crown, ruby stain; orig glass stand 350.00
4-bottle, ribbed band; pewter fr, mini 150.00
5-bottle, b3m, GI-24; orig SP fr 70.00
5-bottle, etched amberina, cut amberina stoppers; gilt fr, EX ..2,200.00
5-bottle, Honeycomb; ornate Wilcox fr, EX 285.00
6-bottle, Bellflower, metal lids; 13½" pewter fr mk Gleason 300.00
6-bottle, cut vintage; SP Rogers Smith & Co fr 250.00
6-bottle, Daisy & Button; ornate rstr Wilcox fr, revolves 375.00
6-bottle, Honeycomb; ornate Tufts fr, 18", EX 335.00
6-bottle, Sawtooth; ornate Meriden fr, call bell, dtd 1888, EX ...495.00
7-bottle, Chrysanthemum, cut; Gleason ftd fr w/movable doors ...1,600.00
7-bottle, cut crystal; gadrooned/shell-border Geo III fr 525.00

Catalina Island

Catalina Island pottery was made on the island of the same name, which is about twenty-six miles off the coast of Los Angeles. The pottery was started in 1927 at Pebble Beach, by Wm. Wrigley, Jr., who was instrumental in developing and using the native clays. Its principal products were brick and tile to be used for construction on the island. Garden pieces were first produced, then vases, bookends, lamps, ashtrays, novelty items, and finally dinnerware. The ware became very popular and was soon being shipped to the mainland as well.

Some of the pottery was hand thrown; some was made in molds. Most pieces are marked Catalina Island or Catalina with a printed incised stamp or handwritten with a pointed tool. Cast items were sometimes marked in the mold, a few have an ink stamp, and a paper label was also used. The most favored colors in tableware and accessories are 1) black (rare), 2) Seafoam and Monterey Brown (uncommon), 3) Toyon Red (orange), 4) other brights, and 5) pastels with a matt finish.

The color of the clay can help to identify approximately when a piece was made: 1927 to 1932, brown to red (Island) clay (very popular with collectors, tends to increase values); 1931 to 1932, an experimental period with various colors; 1932 to 1937, mainly white clay, though tan to brown clays were also used on occasion.

Items marked Catalina Pottery are listed in Gladding McBean. For further information we recommend *The Collector's Encyclopedia of California Pottery* by our advisor, Jack Chipman; he is listed in the Directory under California.

Dinnerware

Carafe, red, early red clay 195.00
Carafe, turq 145.00
Catalina Island, bowl, berry 45.00

Catalina Island, bowl, cereal 75.00
Catalina Island, bowl, fruit; ftd, sq, 13" 180.00
Catalina Island, bowl, vegetable; rnd, 8½" 145.00
Catalina Island, candle holder, low 95.00
Catalina Island, coffee server, slanted opening, w/lid, rare 300.00
Catalina Island, coffeepot, Deco style, rare 325.00
Catalina Island, compote, ftd, lg 225.00
Catalina Island, cup, coffee/tea 55.00
Catalina Island, cup mug, demi 45.00
Catalina Island, custard cup 50.00
Catalina Island, mug, 6" 55.00
Catalina Island, pitcher, squat base, 9" 250.00
Catalina Island, plate, bread & butter; coupe design, 6" 25.00
Catalina Island, plate, chop; #622, 17½" 200.00
Catalina Island, plate, dinner; wide rim, 10½" 75.00
Catalina Island, plate, rolled rim, 12½" 100.00
Catalina Island, plate, salad; 7" 45.00
Catalina Island, salt cellar 50.00
Catalina Island, saucer, 6½" 20.00
Catalina Island, sugar bowl, w/lid 80.00
Catalina Island, teapot, traditional English style 275.00
Catalina Island, tumbler, 4" 35.00
Catalina Island, wine cup, hdld 35.00
Charger, Dutch lady, sgn Graham, #d, 14" 750.00
Charger, swordfish, ivory 265.00
Coaster, plain, bl, red clay 35.00
Coaster, yel, red clay 35.00
Rope Edge, casserole, w/lid 95.00
Rope Edge, chop plate, 13½" 85.00
Rope Edge, creamer 30.00
Rope Edge, cup & saucer 45.00
Rope Edge, plate, dinner; 10½" 30.00
Rope Edge, plate, salad; 8½" 25.00
Rope Edge, sugar bowl 35.00
Rope Edge, teapot 200.00
Shakers, cactus, early red clay, 4½", pr 200.00
Shakers, Senorita & Peon, red & yel, pr 150.00

Miscellaneous

Ashtray, cowboy hat form, Catalina Blue, red clay 195.00
Ashtray, cowboy hat form, yel on wht clay 150.00
Ashtray, Mexican sleeping, cold pnt on gr matt 325.00
Ashtray, seal, wht, mk, 4" 165.00
Bowl, fruit; gr, 3-ftd, 11" 325.00
Bowl, ovoid w/flared rim, red, w/frog, sm 300.00
Bowl, pearly wht, #703 ....125.00
Bowl, pearly wht, fluted, 9x14" 175.00
Bowl, Starlight, #710, 13" 100.00
Bowl, wht, flared, 14x9½" 150.00
Candle flower holders, #606, pr 150.00
Candlesticks, bl, 3¼", pr 295.00
Candlesticks, turq, 5½", pr 350.00
Flower frog, red, ovoid, lg 75.00
Planter, Cat-Lina, turq 250.00
Tray, yel, fluted, 9½" 150.00
Vase, bl matt, #601, 7" 200.00
Vase, bud; red 295.00
Vase, cafe-au-lait, #618, 8" 225.00
Vase, ivory satin, wht clay, #609, 5½" 175.00
Vase, ivory satin, wht clay, #610, 7½" 225.00
Vase, ivory satin, wht clay, 3627, 7½" 250.00
Vase, red, #322 ....325.00
Vase, Starlight, #616, 7½" 225.00

Vase, Toyon Red, hdls, 8" 350.00

Catalogs

Catalogs are not only intriguing to collect on their own merit, but for the collector with a specific interest, they are often the only remaining source of background information available, and as such they offer a wealth of otherwise unrecorded data. The mail-order industry can be traced as far back as the mid-1800s. Even before Aaron Montgomery Ward began his career in 1872, Laacke and Joys of Wisconsin and the Orvis Company of Vermont, both dealers in sporting goods, had been well established for many years. The E.C. Allen Company sold household necessities and novelties by mail on a broad scale in the 1870s. By the end of the Civil War, sewing machines, garden seed, musical instruments, even medicine, were available from catalogs. In the 1880s Macy's of New York issued a 127-page catalog; Sears and Spiegel followed suit in about 1890. Craft and art supply catalogs were first available about 1880 and covered such varied fields as china painting, stenciling, wood burning, brass embossing, hair weaving, and shellcraft. Today some collectors confine their interests not only to craft catalogs in general but often to just one subject. There are several factors besides rarity which make a catalog valuable: age, condition, profuse illustrations, how collectible the field is that it deals with, the amount of color used in its printing, its size (format and number of pages), and whether it is a manufacturer's catalog verses a jobber's catalog (the former being the most desirable). Our advisor for this category is Richard M. Bueschel; he is listed in the Directory under Illinois.

Key: hdw — hardware

Spiegel Home Coming Bargain Book, spring 1917, 15x11", EX, $30.00.

Acme Road Machinery Co, quarry equipment, 1927, 112-pg, NM ..58.00
AJ Hopewells' Turbine Water Wheel, 1884, 121-pg, EX 65.00
Am Ironing Machine, laundering equipment, 1923, 20-pg, VG ...54.00
Am Separator Co, cream separator info, 1910, 72-pg, VG 124.00
AMF Harley-Davidson, motorcycle accessories, 1973, 22-pg, EX ..38.00
B Heller & Co, guide for ice-cream makers, 1918, 154-pg, EX ...124.00
B&H Model Railroad Supply, 1948, 68-pg, VG 42.00
Belcher & Talor, agricultural implements, 80-pg, 1901 ....75.00
Belnap Hardware, misc tools/equipment, 1950, 3,548-pg, VG+ .140.00
Brewer-Titchener Corp, buggy irons, 1918, 521-pg, VG+ 148.00
Brigg & Co, piano specialties, 1889, 24-pg, VG+ 73.00
Buchanan, photographic materials, Philadelphia, 1899, 105-pg .150.00
Butterick Pattern Service, fashion patterns, 1975, 208-pg, VG 45.00
Cash Buyers Union Baby Carriages, 1900, 64-pg, VG+ 90.00
Chas Wm Stores, general merchandise, 1926-27, 526-pg, VG+ ...70.00
Chicago Mail Order Co, fashions, 1932, 312-pg, G 60.00
Clark & Barlow Hdw Co, industrial items, 1953, 498-pg, NM 35.00
Columbus Show Case Co, display equipment, 1930, 36-pg, VG ..126.00
Cullen & Newman...Bargain House, housewares, 1897, 24-pg, VG ...35.00

Deering Farm Equipment, 1895, 32-pg 60.00
Eagle Lock Co, 1930, 773-pg, EX 275.00
EJ Willis Co, boat supplies, 1936, 264-pg, NM- 118.00
Elite Furniture Co, 1928, 64-pg, VG 42.00
ET Barnum Iron & Wire Works, eng items, 1927, 66-pg, VG 76.00
Eugene Dietzgen Co, drafting/surveying, 1928, 496-pg, EX 80.00
F Debski, willow furniture, 1916, 57-pg, VG 100.00
Fowler-Howard, uphl wood furniture, Boston/1880s, 48-pg 75.00
Francis Bannerman Sons, military goods, 1945, 306-pg, VG 80.00
Geo W Claflin & Co, guns & sporting goods, 1887, 32-pg, EX ..185.00
Gifford-Wood Co, tools, 1923, 88-pg, EX 124.00
Graham Mfg, Peerless Mission furniture, 29-pg 65.00
Henry Disston & Sons, Inc, saws, 1917, 86-pg, VG 55.00
Hertzler & Zook & Co, sawing equipment, 1934-35, 40-pg, VG ..58.00
Hewood Bros & Co, children's carriages, etc, 1897, 118-pg, VG ..96.00
Hibbard..., Bartlett & Co, hdw, 1932, 1800-pg, VG+ 165.00
HP Coffee Co, coffee supplies, 1934, 14-pg, VG 39.00
International Harvester, cream separators, 1928, 31-pg, VG+ 65.00
International Harvester of Am, auto buggies & wagons, 24-pg, EX ..276.00
International Merchandise, misc, 1942, 190-pg, VG 90.00
Jim Brown's Bargain Book, poultry to heaters, 1930, 128-pg, NM ...38.00
John Plain & Co, gifts & homewares, 1955, 668-pg, EX 52.00
John Wanamaker Fashion, ladies' mail order, 1920, 96-pg, VG ...45.00
Johnson Bros, general merchandise, 1900, 144-pg, VG 75.00
JS Shields & Co, hats & caps, 1902, 44-pg, EX- 55.00
JW Pepper & Son, musical equipment, 1920s, 64-pg, EX 74.00
Keuffel & Esser, drafting & surveying tools, 1921, 482-pg, VG 70.00
Keystone, farm machines, PA, 1900s, 127-pg 65.00
Kingsford Machine Works, water wheels, 1871, 96-pg 55.00
Larkin Co, houseware supplies, 1922, 240-pg+supplements, VG ..95.00
LM Rumsey Mfg Co, agricultural implements, 1884, 512-pg, VG ..674.00
Lyon Bros, stationery & sporting goods, 1901, 80-pg, VG 93.00
Marshall Field, Christmas, 1985, 74-pg, EX 30.00
Marshall Field, kid's Christmas gifts, 1974, 52-pg, VG 30.00
Marta Lane Adams, ladies'/children's clothes, 1923, 192-pg, VG .55.00
Max Geisler Bird Co, pet supplies, 1910, 64-pg, VG 123.00
McCormick Harvesting Machines, mc illus, 1897, 42-pg 200.00
McCray Refrigerator...Corp, cooling systems, 1927, 48-pg, NM+ ..155.00
Moore's Toy & Gift..., 1965, 72-pg, VG+ 28.00
National Bellas Hess, Christmas book, 1957, 119-pg, VG 54.00
National Cloak & Suit Co, family clothing, 1923, 352-pg, VG+ .65.00
Norton Jewelry Co, 1918, 518-pg, VG 178.00
OH Berry & Co, men & boys clothing, 1900, 64-pg, EX 35.00
Peck, Stow & Wilcox Co, tinsmith's items, 1911, 168-pg, VG ..154.00
Pelton-Crane, dental equipment, Detroit, 1914, 52-pg 35.00
Pick's General Cat, wartime hotel supplies, 1945, 32-pg, VG 35.00
Quality Stove & Range Co, 1927, 84-pg, VG 80.00
Rawlings, farm implements & vehicles, Baltimore, 1900, 80-pg ...75.00
Rouss Wholesale, general merchandise, 1914, 402-pg, VG 125.00
Safe Padlock & Hdw, 1942, 158-pg, NM 110.00
Sears, Roebuck & Co, bicycles, 1898, 36-pg, EX 275.00
Sears, Roebuck & Co, bicycles, 1902, 20-pg, EX 185.00
Sears, Roebuck & Co, cameras & supplies, 1939, 22-pg, EX- 38.00
Sears, Roebuck & Co, grocery items, 1914, 64-pg, VG 75.00
Sears, Roebuck & Co, mens clothing, 1928-29, 20-pg, VG 96.00
Shakespeare Co, fishing equipment, 1950, 32-pg, EX 75.00
Siegel Copper Co, artist supplies, ca 1900, 32-pg, VG 58.00
Silver Mfg Co, silos & ensilage, 1892, 64-pg, EX 65.00
Simplicity Pattern Co, Oct 1975, 12½x13¾x1½", VG 55.00
Southern Baptist...Board, Bible school supplies, 1957, 16-pg, EX .24.00
Spencer Fireworks, Spring 1936, 32-pg, EX 226.00
Stickley of Fayetteville, furniture, 1928, 100-pg, EX 150.00
Taylor Instrument Co, thermometers, 1922, 24-pg, EX 64.00
Victor Safe Co, 1927, 23-pg, VG 54.00

Wallace Sterling, 1928, 95-pg, 9x12" 100.00
Wm Poole Residential Design, showcase of homes, 1969, 27-pg, VG .32.00
Wmsburg Restoration Repros, 18th C repros, 1942, 32-pg, VG 42.00
Wolf Co, mill machinery, 1922, 128-pg, EX 72.00
Yawman & Erbe Mfg Co, filing/record systems, 1904, 82-pg, VG ..124.00
Zebco Division Brunswick Corp, fishing goods, 1967, 32-pg, EX ..18.00

Caughley Ware

The Caughley Coalport Porcelain Manufactory operated from about 1775 until 1799 in Caughley, near Salop, Shropshire, in England. The owner was Thomas Turner, who gained his potting experience from his association with the Worcester Pottery Company. The wares he manufactured in Caughley are referred to as 'Salopian.' He is most famous for his blue-printed earthenwares, particularly the Blue Willow pattern, designed for him by Thomas Minton. For a more detailed history, see Coalport.

Bowl, scenic, gray-gr transfer w/mc, floral border, 8", EX, pr 160.00
Cup & saucer, Stag, mc w/bl-striped rims, 2¼", 5⅜", EX 200.00
Plate, Stag, mc w/bl-striped rim, 7¼", pr 600.00
Saucer, 3 pheasants in shrub, bl transfer, mk S, 1780, 4¾" 200.00
Sugar bowl, Stag, mc w/bl-striped lid, 4⅞", EX 250.00
Teapot, Acorn & Floral, brn transfer w/mc, rpr, 10⅜" 150.00

Ceramic Art Company

Jonathan Coxon, Sr., and Walter Scott Lenox established the Ceramic Art Company in 1889 in Trenton, New Jersey, where they produced fine belleek porcelain. Both were experienced in its production, having previously worked for Ott and Brewer. They hired artists to hand paint their wares with portraits, scenes, and lovely florals. Today artist-signed examples bring the highest prices. Several marks were used, three of which contain the 'CAC' monogram. A green wreath surrounding the company name in full was used on special-order wares, but these are not often encountered. Coxon eventually left the company, and it was later reorganized under the Lenox name. See also Lenox. Our advisor for this category is Mary Frank Gaston.

Photo courtesy Mary Frank Gaston

Vase, gold-paste floral decor on creamy matt, circular branch-style handles, lavender mark, 11", $350.00.

Bowl, floral w/gold & pastel sponge decor, ruffled, 2x4½" 135.00
Candy/nut bowl, leaf form, wht w/gold, pk int, CAC mk, 2x6¼" ...120.00

Cream soup & saucer, wht Irish-style Tridacna form w/gold, CAC mk ..120.00
Cup & saucer, demi; pk & bl w/gold, shell shape 160.00
Inkwell, mums (non-factory) w/gold on wht, sq, CAC mk, 4½" H ...200.00
Loving cup, floral, gold child's head atop ea hdl, CAC, 8½" 600.00
Mug, holly leaves & berries w/gold, factory decor, ca 1894, 5¾" ...200.00
Pitcher, strawberries & flowers w/gold, sgn Leroy, 9" 335.00
Tankard, floral & scenic, sgn Heidrich, CAC (unmk), 13" 840.00
Vase, irises, mc on salmon, 8" 225.00
Vase, mums (professional art), urn form, gold hdls, CAC, 18" ...600.00

Ceramic Arts Studio, Madison

The Ceramic Arts Studio Company began operations sometime prior to the 1940s, but it was about then that Betty Harrington started marketing her goods through this company. Betty Harrington was the designer primarily responsible for creating the line of figurines and knick-knacks that has become so popular with collectors. There were two others — Ulli Rebus, who not only designed several of the animals and various other pieces but taught Betty the art of mold making as well; and Ruth Planter, who's work may have been very limited. About 65% of these items are marked, but even unmarked items become easily recognizable after only a brief study of their distinctive styling and glaze colors. At least eight different marks were used, among them the black ink stamp and the incised mark: 'Ceramic Arts Studio, Madison, Wisc.' A paper sticker was used in the early years.

After the 1955 demise of the company in Madison, the owner (Ruben Sand) went to Japan where he continued production under the same name using many of the same molds. After a short time, the old molds were retired, and new and quite different items were produced. Most of the Japan pieces can be found with a Ceramic Arts Studio backstamp. The Japan identification was often on a paper label and can be missing. Japan pieces are never marked Madison, Wisc., but not all Madison pieces are either. Red or blue backstamps are exclusively Japanese.

Another company that also produced figurines operated at about the same time as the Madison studio. It was called Ceramic Art (no 's') Studio; do not confuse the two.

A second and larger building in the C.A.S. complex in Madison was for the exclusive production of metal accessories. The creator and designer of this related line was Zona Liberace, Liberace's stepmother, who was art director for the line of figurines as well. These pieces are rising fast in value and because they weren't marked can sometimes be found at bargain prices. They were so popular that other ceramic companies bought them to complement their own lines, so they may also be found with ceramic figures other than C.A.S.'s.

Our advisor for this category is BA Wellman; his address can be found under Massachusetts. Mr. Wellman encourages collectors to write him with any new information concerning company history and/or production. He sends Jeff, Rosie, and Vera a 'thank you' for helping us with this year's updates. See also Clubs, Newsletters, and Catalogs.

Note: We must regretfully inform you that Betty Harrington passed away on Good Friday, 1997.

Figurine, Autumn Andy, 5", and Summer Sally, 3½", $95.00 each.

Ashtray, hippo, 3½" 165.00
Bank, Mr Blankety Blank, 4½" 90.00
Bell, Summer Bell, 5¼" 90.00
Candle holder, Hear No Evil, angel on cloud, 5" 125.00
Figurine, Accordion Lady, 8½" 250.00
Figurine, Alice & Rabbit, 4½", 6", pr 400.00
Figurine, Archibald Dragon, 8" 260.00
Figurine, Bali Hai & Bali Lao, 8", 8½", pr 200.00
Figurine, Balinese Man & Woman, pr 275.00
Figurine, Bedtime Girl, 4¾" 75.00
Figurine, Beth, 5" 50.00
Figurine, boy & girl running, 3½", 3¼", pr 100.00
Figurine, Bright Eyes, cat, gr bow, 3" 38.00
Figurine, Carmen & Carmelita, 7¼", 4¼", pr 135.00
Figurine, chipmunk, 2" 45.00
Figurine, Cinderella & Prince, 6½", pr 150.00
Figurine, Colonel Jackson & Lucindy, 7¼", 7", pr 135.00
Figurine, Daisy Ballerina, 5½" 110.00
Figurine, Daisy Donkey, 4¾" 125.00
Figurine, Drummer Girl 75.00
Figurine, Dutch Love Couple, pr 75.00
Figurine, Elsie Elephant, 5" 75.00
Figurine, Fire Man & Woman, 11¼", pr 650.00
Figurine, Frisky lamb, garland, 3" 28.00
Figurine, Gay '90s Man & Woman, 6¾", 6½", pr 130.00
Figurine, Guitar Boy, 5" 70.00
Figurine, Hansel & Gretel 100.00
Figurine, Harry & Lillibeth, 6½", 6", pr 100.00
Figurine, Inky & Dinky, skunks, 2¼", 2", pr 50.00
Figurine, Isaac & Rebekah, 10", pr 275.00
Figurine, lion & lioness, 6½" L, 5" L, pr 450.00
Figurine, Little Bo Peep, 5½" 28.00
Figurine, Little Boy Blue, 4½" L 28.00
Figurine, Little Miss Muffet #1, rare, 4½" 125.00
Figurine, Manchu & Lotus, wht & gold, w/lanterns, pr 145.00
Figurine, panda w/hat, 2½" 145.00
Figurine, Petrov & Petruskha, 5", 5¼", pr 100.00
Figurine, Pioneer Susie, 5" 45.00
Figurine, Pioner Sam & Suzie, 5", 5½", pr 95.00
Figurine, Polish Boy & Girl, 6½", pr 100.00
Figurine, Pomeranian sitting 50.00
Figurine, Praise Angel, hand up, 6" 80.00
Figurine, Santa & evergreen, 2¼", 2½", pr 500.00
Figurine, sea horse & coral, snuggle, 3½", 3", pr 70.00
Figurine, Shepherd & Shepherdess, 8½", 8", pr 175.00
Figurine, Sooty & Taffy, Scotties, 5¼", 5", pr 150.00
Figurine, Square Dance Boy & Girl, 6½", 6", pr 175.00
Figurine, Swedish Dance Couple, 7", pr 275.00
Figurine, Swish & Swirl, fish, pr 110.00
Figurine, Tembo & Tembino elephants, 6½", 2½", pr 650.00
Figurine, Violet Ballerina, 3" 125.00
Figurine, Water Man & Woman, 11½", pr 495.00
Figurine, Zulu Man & Woman, 6, 7¼", pr 600.00
Head vase, African Man & Woman, pr 650.00
Head vase, Barbie & Bonnie, 7", pr 300.00
Head vase, Lotus 125.00
Head vase, Svea & Sven, pr 300.00
Lamps, Manchu & Lotus, pr 650.00
Lamps, Zor & Zorina, Lucite bases, pr 500.00
Pitcher, Adam & Eve 60.00
Pitcher, Ballerina (ewer) 75.00
Pitcher, Horse Head (saucer boat) 50.00
Pitcher, Pine Tree 50.00
Planter, Bamboo 22.00

Plaque, Comedy & Tragedy masks, pr 225.00
Plaque, Greg & Grace, pr 135.00
Plate, Paul Bunyon, 6" 150.00
Shakers, bear & mother & cub, brn, snuggle, pr 90.00
Shakers, Black boy & alligator, pr 275.00
Shakers, Blackamoors, 4¾", pr 110.00
Shakers, boy in chair, snuggle, pr 75.00
Shakers, Calico Cat & Gingham Dog, pr 125.00
Shakers, Chirp & Twirp, parakeets, 4", pr 250.00
Shakers, cow & calf, snuggle, 5½", 2½", pr 190.00
Shakers, Dem & Rep (donkey & elephant), 6", pr 395.00
Shakers, dog & doghouse, snuggle, pr 150.00
Shakers, Dutch Boy & Girl, 4", pr 50.00
Shakers, elf & mushroom, pr 65.00
Shakers, Eskimo Boy & Girl, sm, pr 125.00
Shakers, fighting cocks, pr 80.00
Shakers, fish up on tails, 4", pr 70.00
Shakers, frog & mushroom, 2", 3", pr 75.00
Shakers, horses' heads, pr 65.00
Shakers, monkey & baby, snuggle, pr 75.00
Shakers, mouse & cheese, pr 38.00
Shakers, Mr & Mrs Penguin, pr 95.00
Shakers, Siamese mother & kitten, pr 110.00
Shakers, Thai & Thai-Thai, 5" L, pr 145.00
Shakers, Wee Chinese Boy & Girl, sm, pr 45.00
Shakers, Wee Dutch Boy & Girl, 3", pr 45.00
Shelf sitters, Farm Girl & Boy, w/fish pole & fish, pr 100.00
Shelf sitters, Pudgie & Budgie (parakeets), 5½", pr 125.00
Shelf sitters, Sun-Li & Lu-Lin, chubby, 5½", pr 70.00
Shelf sitters, Young Love Girl & Boy, pr 100.00
Teapot, swan form, open, mini 50.00

Metal Accessories

Arched window for Madonna & Child, 14" 75.00
Artist palette w/shelves, left & right, 13" across 95.00
Bean stalk for Jack, rare 95.00
Birdcage w/perch for birds, 14" 65.00
Diamond shadow box, for Attitude & Arabesque, 15½x13¾" 55.00
Frame w/shelf, 22" sq 55.00
Holder for planter 45.00
Pocket step shelf, w/planter, rnd, 8" 75.00
Pyramid shelf 75.00
Sofa, for Maurice & Michele, 10x3¾" 65.00
Triple ring shelves 125.00

Chalkware

Chalkware figures were a popular commodity from approximately 1860 until 1890. They were made from gypsum or plaster of Paris formed in a mold and then hand painted in oils or watercolors. Items such as animals and birds, figures, banks, toys, and religious ornaments modeled after more expensive Staffordshire wares were often sold door to door. Their origin is attributed to Italian immigrants. Today regarded as a form of folk art, 19th century American pieces bring prices in the hundreds of dollars. Carnival chalkware from this century is also collectible, especially figures that are personality related. For those, see Carnival Collectibles.

Bird on spherical plinth, old mc pnt, 7⅞" 165.00
Cat on base, mc pnt, ca 1850, 5¼x3½x2½", EX, pr 1,300.00
Cherry Boy, removable arm, holds 3 cherries, mc pnt, early, 27" ..150.00
Dog, seated, worn 4-color pnt, damage/rpr, 6½" 110.00

Dog, seated, 4-color, lt wear/soil, early, 9" 140.00
Dog, spaniel on stepped base, worn pnt, ca 1850, 8x6⅛x3⅛" 180.00
Dog, stands w/legs open, worn mc pnt, rpr, 7⅞" 250.00

Horse, hollow, original paint, $450.00; Dove, hollow, original paint, $450.00.

Parrot on ped w/sq base, realistic pnt, 8¼x3x3½", EX 1,500.00
Rabbit w/bobbing head, splotchy pnt, 1850s, 3x5½x2½", EX 400.00
Sheep w/lamb, mc pnt, rpr, 6¼x8¾x4" 320.00
Squirrel, worn orig mc pnt, on closed base, 6½", pr 330.00
Stag on base, smoked pnt, ca 1850, 10¼x8½x3¾", pr, EX 6,200.00

Champleve

Champleve, enameling on brass, differs from cloisonne in that the design is depressed or incised into the metal, rather than being built in with wire dividers as in the cloisonne procedure. The cells, or depressions, are filled in with color, and the piece is then fired.

Box, arabesque decor, florals, ca 1900, 6" dia 600.00
Clock, bronze w/faux dmns & enamel dial, Fr, 6½" 650.00
Compote, florals & geometrics in bands, blk patina, 7x8¼" 135.00
Teapot, dragon form w/3 monkey ft, monkey finial, rpr, 12" 450.00
Vase, immortals, 6-sided, late, Japan, 20⅛" 260.00
Vase, stylized floral, figural hdls, bronze, Japan, late, 12" 275.00

Chase Brass & Copper Company

Americans were shocked in 1923 when an invitation to stage an exhibit at the first major postwar fair, *The 1925 Exposition des Arts Decoratifs et Industriels*, was declined by the American government because the U.S. could not comply with the exposition's requirement that only original work would be exhibited. Even though American industry produced a vast quantity of varied goods, there was very little 'original American' to show, since most design ideas were being brought in from Europe.

This blow to American prestige and the uproar that resulted prompted a dispatch of designers (among them Donald Deskey, Walter Dorwin Teague, and Russel Wright) to the Paris exhibition. They were to determine what steps would be necessary in order for U.S. designs to compete with European standards. They returned championing the new modernist style. By the mid-1930s, products were being designed and marketed that were attractive to the reluctant consumer insistent upon buying a streamline style that was uniquely American. During the decade of the '30s, the Chase Brass & Copper Company offered lamps, smoking acessories, and housewares similar to those Americans were seeing on the Hollywood screen at prices the average buyer could afford. These products are highly valued today not only because of their superior quality but also because of those who created them. Walter von Nessen, Gerth & Gerth, Rockwell Kent, Russel Wright, Lurelle Guild, and Dr. A. Reimann were some of Chases' well-known designers. Emily Post, who served as a spokesperson for Chase, promoted a trend away from expensive silver and toward chromium serving pieces.

Besides chromium, Chase manufactured many products in brass, copper, nickel plate, or a combination of these metals; all are equally collectible. Some items had glass inserts which collectors also seek. A few items can even be found in silver plate.

Nearly all Chase products were marked, either on the item itself or on a screw or rivet. However, a few authentic pieces were not, for reasons that remain unknown, and because Chase sold screws, rivets, nails, etc., with their own logo, not all items having those Chased-marked componets were actually made by them. It should also be noted that during the 1930s, China produced good quality plated-ware copies; so when you're not absolutely positive an item is Chase, buy it if you like it, understanding that its authenticity may be in question. But be cautious. Check unmarked items to make sure they measure up to Chase's standard of quality; lighting fixtures that are unmarked may be compared with pictures of verified examples.

For safety's sake, replace both cords and internal wiring before attempting to use any electrical product. Not only will you be protected against possible loss from fire, but you will enhance the value of your collectible as well.

Prior to 1933, Chase made smoking accessories for the Park Sherman Co. Some are marked 'Park Sherman Co., Chicago, Illinois, Made in Chase Brass.' Others carry a Park Sherman logo. It is believed that the 'heraldic emblem' ensignia of Park Sherman was also used during this period. Many items are identical or very similar to Chase-marked pieces. Produced in the 1950s, National Silver Co.'s 'Emerald-Glo' pieces look very much like Chase, but Chase did not make them. (It is very possible that the company purchased Chase Tooling after the Chase Specialties Line was discontinued.)

For more thorough study we recommend *Art Deco Chrome, The Chase Era*, and *Art Deco Chrome, Book 2, A Collector's Guide, Industrial Design in the Chase Era*. Both are authored by Richard J. Kilbride; his wife is listed in the Directory under Connecticut. In the listings that follow, examples are polished unless noted satin. For further information contact the Chase Collector's Society, listed in the Directory under Clubs, Newsletters, and Catalogs. Our advisor for this category is Barbara Endter; she is listed in the Directory under New York.

Bell, Ming, copper, #13007	60.00
Bookends, Sentinel, soldier, Bakelite, by brass ball, #17109	350.00
Canape plate, #27001 & cup #2600	40.00
Cigarette box, Bacchus, Rockwell Kent, bronze, #847	1,000.00
Cigarette holder, open chrome sphere, ped ft, mk, #860, 2½"	30.00
Cigarette lighter, table; chrome, #825	35.00
Coaster tray, bl glass, from pancake & corn set #28003	100.00
Cocktail mixer, Von Nessen, #17049	125.00
Cocktail shaker, Blue Moon, rnd dk bl knob, #90066, 1936	125.00
Cocktail shaker, Gaeity, chrome w/blk rings, #90034, from $20 to	25.00
Cocktail shaker, Gaeity, chrome w/colored rings, from $70 to	90.00
Coffee set, Continental, #17054, 3-pc w/ring tray	195.00
Flower holder, bl glass bubble, #17065	30.00
Newspaper rack, #27027 (chrome more expensive), from $50 to	60.00
Pitcher, water; Sparta, chrome w/wht plastic hdl, #90055, 8"	75.00
Pretzel Man, copper, #90038	75.00
Relish/jelly, 2-part, hdl, mk, #9002, 5½" dia	40.00
Sauce bowl, Viking, #17046, w/ladle & undertray	90.00
Silent butler, chrome w/Bakelite hdl, mk, #17111, 11½", $65 to	75.00
Syrup, Sparta, #90056	50.00

Vase, Ring, chrome w/blk rings, #17039, 9½"	75.00
Vase, Ring, golden triangle w/bl rings, 9½"	100.00

Chelsea Dinnerware

Made from about 1830 to 1880 in the Staffordshire district of England, this white dinnerware is decorated with lustre embossings in the grape, thistle, sprig, or fruit and cornucopia patterns. The relief designs vary from lavender to blue, and the body of the ware may be porcelain, ironstone, or earthenware. Because it was not produced in Chelsea as the name would suggest, dealers often prefer to call it 'Grandmother's Ware.'

Grape, bowl, 8"	30.00
Grape, coffeepot, stick hdl, 2-cup, 7"	65.00
Grape, creamer	35.00
Grape, cup & saucer	25.00
Grape, egg cup	25.00
Grape, pitcher, milk; 40-oz	50.00
Grape, plate, 6"	12.00
Grape, plate, 7"	18.00
Grape, plate, 8"	20.00
Grape, sauce boat	30.00
Grape, sugar bowl, w/lid	50.00
Grape, teacup	25.00
Grape, teapot, octagonal, 10"	30.00
Grape, teapot, 2-cup	65.00
Grape, waste bowl	40.00
Sprig, cake plate, 9"	40.00

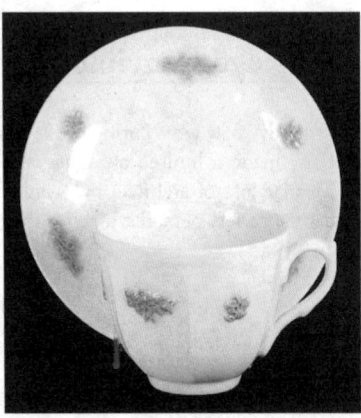

Sprig, cup and saucer, $40.00.

Sprig, pitcher, milk	45.00
Sprig, plate, dinner	25.00
Sprig, plate, 7"	18.00
Thistle, butter pat	15.00
Thistle, cup & saucer	35.00
Thistle, plate, 7"	15.00
Thistle, sugar bowl, 8-sided, w/lid, 7½"	45.00

Chelsea Keramic Art Works

The Chelsea Keramic Art Works Robertson and Sons Pottery was established in 1872 in Chelsea, Massachusetts, by several members of the Robertson family, including Hugh C. Robertson who later formed the Dedham Pottery. Though their very early artware utilized a redware body, by the late 1870s it was replaced with yellow or buff burning clay. A line called Bourg-la-Reine (underglazed slip-decorated ware with primarily blue and green backgrounds) was produced, though not to any great extent. Other pieces were designed in imitation of Asian metalware, even to the extent that surfaces were 'hammered' to further enhance the effect. Occasionally live flora was pressed into the damp vessel walls to leave a decorative impression. They also made glazed plaques and tiles. Hugh C. Robertson ran the pottery alone after 1884 and labored to re-create the ancient Ming-era blood-red glaze. Although world acclaim greeted his rediscovery of what he then called 'Robertson's Blood,' his red-glazed vases cost too much to produce and bankruptcy followed in 1889. Supported by wealthy Boston art patrons, Hugh's pottery reopened in 1891 as the Chelsea Pottery U.S., and began using his other 1880s rediscovery, the crackle glaze, producing cobalt blue-decorated dinnerware. When this firm moved to Dedham in 1895 the ware became known as Dedham Pottery. From 1875 to 1880 the pottery was marked Chelsea Keramic Art Works Robertson and Sons in either two or three impressed lines. Earlier pieces were not marked. The impressed mark CKAW in a diamond formation was also used between 1875 and 1889. From 1891 through 1895 the impressed letters CPUS in a clover leaf was utilized for the new firm. After the move to Dedham, only new Dedham Pottery marks were used. See also Dedham Pottery.

Figurine, poodle w/pup, gold anchor mk, ca 1832 ....75.00
Pitcher, Greek Key design, feathered bl-gray, CKAW, 8x6½" .1,400.00
Planter, birds/fish in panels, 4-sided, CKAW, 5¾x6", EX 350.00
Plate, Upside Down Dolphin & Baby, CPUS & clover mk, 10¼" .1,000.00
Salt cellar, walnut shell shape on leaf, bsk int, CKAW 350.00
Vase, cvd flowers/2 appl frogs on gr sq, 3-line mk, 7½x3½" 800.00
Vase, dk red metallic sang-de-boeuf, bottle form, 8x3¼" 1,300.00
Vase, gr & brn glossy flambe, tapered w/'torn' rim, 7¼x6" 1,300.00
Vase, lava wht crackle on brn gloss & wht, shaved top, 6x4¼" ..275.00
Vase, red oxblood to gunmetal w/irid, bulbous, mk, 4" 800.00

Chicago Crucible

For only a few years during the 1920s, the Chicago (Illinois) Crucible Company made a limited amount of decorative pottery in addition to their regular line of architectural wares. Examples are very scarce today; they carry a variety of marks, all with the company name and location.

Vase, green matt, flared bottom, two angular handles, 10½", $600.00.

Bookend/paperweight, gold glazed figure on 5-color rug 450.00
Vase, brn & gr mottle, hdls, 11x5" 475.00
Vase, gr & brn mottle, long neck, twisted body, 8" 300.00
Vase, turq & olive gr matt, 4-lobed, bottle neck, 5x3½" 400.00

Children's Books

Children's books, especially those from the Victorian era, are charming collectibles. Colorful lithographic illustrations that once

delighted little boys in long curls and tiny girls in long stockings and lots of ribbons and lace have lost none of their appeal. Some collectors limit themselves to a specific subject, while others may be far more interested in the illustrations. First editions are more valuable than later issues, and condition and rarity are very important factors to consider before making your purchase. For further information we recommend *Collector's Guide to Children's Books, 1850 – 1950*, by Diane McClure Jones and Rosemary Jones; and *Whitman Juvenile Books Reference & Value Guide* by David and Virginia Brown. Both are available from Collector Books or your local bookstore.

Aesop's Fables, Coates, Tenniel illus, 1848 ed, EX 150.00
Alice in Wonderland, Carroll, illus, Whitman #1616, 1970, M 5.00
Alphabet of Animals, linen, 1885, VG 20.00
Ann Sheridan & Sign of Sphinx, Heisenfelt, Whitman #2390, EX .15.00
Babes in Toyland, AA Chapin, Betts illus, Dodd, 1924, EX 200.00
Baby Book, Maud Humphrey, 3 color plates, 1898, EX 200.00
Baby's Record..., Maud Humphrey, 12 mc plates, 1898, MIB 495.00
Bat Masterson, Lee, Whitman #1550, photo cover, 1960, EX 12.00
Beloved Belindy, Gruelle, illus, Volland, 1926, EX 100.00
Beverly Hillbillies Saga of Wildcat Creek, Whitman #1572, M ...15.00
Black Beauty, Sewell, Whitman Classics #1604, 1955, EX 6.00
Blue Book of Children's Stories, Whitman #4059, 1934, EX 10.00
Bobby Blake at Rockledge School, Whitman #2300, 1915, NM ..12.00
Brenda Starr Girl Reporter, Messic, Whitman #2383, 1943, EX ...22.50
Call of Wild, London, Whitman #1635, 1970, 210-pg, M 4.00
Captains Courageous, Kipling, Taber illus, Macmillan, 1897, EX ..150.00
Corny Cornpicker Finds a Home, John Deere, 1959 ....25.00
Cross Creek, Rawlings, 1st edition, ex-library, VG 7.00
Defiant Heart, Michelson, Whitman #2310, 1964, M 4.00
Dimsie Moves Up, DF Bruce, London, 1921, EX 15.00
Donna Parker in Hollywood, Martin, Whitman #1593, 1956, M .10.00
Dr Suess Cat in the Hat, 1957, w/dust jacket, EX 35.00
Ernestine Takes Over, WR Brooks, 1935, EX 15.00
Fairy Tales, Anderson, Nielson illus, Doran, 1914, EX 250.00
Famous Fairy Tales, Whitman #1609, 1971, 210-pg, EX 12.00
Father Goose: His Book, Baum, Donohue, 1913 ed, EX 150.00
Five Little Pigs, McLaughlin, 1890, EX 40.00
Freckles, Porter, Whitman Classics #2713, 1961, EX 3.00
Garden of Verses, Bessie Pease Gutmann, 20 mc pictures, EX 100.00
Gene Autry & Golden Stallion, Fannin, Whitman #1511:49, 1954, NM 18.00
Goblins of Haubeck, Bancroft, Sichel illus, McBride NY, 1925, EX .15.00
Good Shepherd, Gunnarson illus, Bobbs Merrill, '40, EX 20.00
Heels of the Gale, Grant, Quinn illus, Little Brown, 1937, EX 15.00
Henry Huggins, Cleary, Darling illus, Morrow, 1st ed, 1950, EX ..35.00
I Spy Message From Moscow, Keith, Whitman #1542, 1966, NM .22.00
Jane Withers & Phantom Violin, Snell, Whitman #2389, VG 8.00
Janet Lennon Adventure at 2 Rivers, Meyers, Whitman #1536, M ..12.00
Jo's Boys, Alcott, Grosset Dunlap, 8 color plates, 1947, EX 20.00
Jolly Animal ABC, linen, 1888, VG 25.00
Jungle Tales of Tarzan, Burroughs, Gossett-Dunlap, EX 25.00
Katy Kruse Dolly Book, Fyleman, illus, Doran, 1927, EX 65.00
Kim, Kipling, JL Kipling illus, Macmillan, London, 1st ed, EX ...100.00
Kim Aldrich...Silent Partner, McDonnell, Whitman #1596, 1972, M ...4.00
Kitty Carter Canteen Girl, Radford, Whitman #2305, 1944, EX ..18.00
Little Buffalo Robe, Beck, DeCora illus, Holt, 1st ed, 1914, EX ...20.00
Little Men, Alcott, Whitman #2135, 1940, w/dust jacket, NM 10.00
Lucy & Madcap Mystery, Fannin, Whitman TV ed #1505, 1963, EX ..22.50
Lucy Locket Doll w/the Pocket, John Ray, Volland, 1928, MIB .195.00
Many Moons, Thurber, Slobodkin illus, Harcourt, 1943, EX 65.00
Maude Humphrey's Book of Fairy Tales, mc illus, Stokes, 1892, EX ...220.00
Melindy's Medal, Faulkner, Fox illus, Messner, 1945, EX 10.00
Milestone Summer, Meridith, Whitman Teen Novel #2311, 1962, M ..8.00
Munster's Last Resort, Johnston, Whitman TV Adventure #1567, NM 22.50

Mystery Rides Trail, Lathrop, Goldsmith, 1937, EX **10.00**
Night Before Christmas, Moore, Saalfield, 1940s, oversz, EX **35.00**
Nobody's Boy, Malot, Gruell illus, Cupples, 1916, EX **45.00**
Over the Polar Ice, Andy Lane Story; Adams, Grosset, 1928, EX ..**10.00**
Pee-Wee Harris on Trail, Fitzhugh, Whitman #2307, w/jacket, NM **10.00**
Penelope's Progress, Wiggin, Grosset Dunlap, 1907, EX **20.00**
Peter Rabbit's Easter, Almond, Altemus, color illus, 1921, EX **40.00**
Pinocchio, Collodi, Whitman Classics #1916, plain tan, NM **12.00**
Pinto Pony, Birney, Lee illus, Penn, 1930, EX **15.00**
Power Boys...Flying Skeleton, Lyle, Whitman #1524, 1964, M **10.00**
Prince & Pauper, Twain, Booth illus, 1917 ed, EX **45.00**
Rebecca of Sunnybrook Farm, Wiggin, Whitman #2734, 1960, NM **5.00**
Red Ryder & ...Lucky Mine, Smith, Whitman #2334, w/jacket, M ..**20.00**
Restless Gun, Meyers, Whitman TV Ed #1559, 1959, NM **22.50**
Robinson Crusoe, Defoe, Whitman #2124, w/jacket, M **10.00**
Roy Rogers King of Cowboys, Fannin, Whitman #1503, 1956, M .**10.00**
Sand Dune Pony, Nesbit, Whitman #1544:49, 1954, M **8.00**
Seventeeth Summer, Daly, Dodd, 1st ed, 1942, EX **35.00**
Six Who Were Left in a Shoe, Volland, 1st ed, 1923, EX **110.00**
Songs of Father Goose, L Frank Baum, Denslow illus, 1909, VG .**275.00**
Space Cadet, Heinlein, Scribner, 1st edition, 1948, EX **45.00**
Swiss Family Robinson, Wyss, Whitman #1935, plain gr cover, M .**4.00**
Tales of Peter Rabbit, Potter, Altemus, 1904, EX **45.00**
Tammy...in Hollywood, Wellman, Whitman #2322, 1965, EX **15.00**
Tarzan Twins, Burroughs, Grant illus, Volland, 1927, EX **40.00**
Terry & the Pirates, Shipwrecked, pop-up, Caniff, 20-pg, NM ...**600.00**
That Certain Girl, Snow, Whitman #1558, 1964, M **5.00**
Timber Trail Riders Long Trail North, Murray, Whitman #1593, M ..**8.00**
Toad of Toad Hall, Milne, Longmans, 1st trade ed, 1929, EX **125.00**
Trixie Belden...Off Glenn Road, Campbell, Whitman #1563, EX .**10.00**
Tuckers Trouble on Valley View, Mendel, Whitman #2303, 1956, NM **7.00**
Walt Disney's Bedknobs & Broomsticks, Whitman #1570, 1971, M **12.00**
Walt Disney's Gnome-Mobile, Carey, Whitman #1577, 1967, M ...**12.00**
War of the Worlds, Wells, Whitman #1628, 1964, NM **10.00**
Wonderful Wizard of Oz, Baum, Whitman #1620, 1970, EX **3.00**

Children's Things

Nearly every item devised for adult furnishings has been reduced to child size — furniture, dishes, sporting goods, even some tools. All are very collectible. During the late 17th and early 18th centuries, miniature china dinnerware sets were made both in China and in England. They were not intended primarily as children's playthings, however, but instead were made to furnish miniature rooms and cabinets that provided a popular diversion for the adults of that period. By the 19th century, the emphasis had shifted, and most of the small-scaled dinnerware and tea sets were made for children's play.

Late in the 19th century and well into the 20th, toy pressed glass dishes were made, many in the same pattern as full-scale glassware. Today these toy dishes often fetch prices in the same range as those for the 'grown-ups'!

Authorities Margaret and Kenn Whitmyer have compiled a lovely book, *The Collector's Encyclopedia of Children's Dishes*, with full-color photos and current market values; you will find their address in the Directory under Ohio. We also recommend *Children's Glass Dishes, China, and Furniture*, by Doris Anderson Lechler, and *ABC Plates & Mugs* by Irene and Ralph Lindsay available at your local bookstore or public library. Examples with no dimensions given are child size unless noted doll size. See also A B C Plates; Canary Ware; Clothing; Stickley; Willow Ware; etc.

Key:
ds — doll size   Fr — French
Emp — Empire

China

Bowl, covered vegetable; Fishers, gr/cream, CE&M (England), 5½" ...**50.00**
Bowl, covered vegetable; Kite Flyers, bl on wht, England, 3½" ..**110.00**
Bowl, Fishers, gr on cream, oval, C&EM (England), 3" **22.00**
Bowl, Myrtle Wreath, bl on wht, oval, JM&S (England), 5" **27.00**
Bowl, soup; Dimity, gr on cream, England, 4¼" **10.00**
Bowl, soup; Fern & Floral, gr on wht, Livesley Powell, 4¼" **25.00**
Bowl, soup; Gaudy Floral, England, 4" **20.00**
Bowl, soup; Twin Flower, flow bl, England **45.00**
Bowl, Twin Flower, flow bl, deep, oval, England, 3¾" **100.00**
Canister, Blue Banded, Germany, 2½" **25.00**
Canister, Rice, tan lustre, Japan, 3⅛" **22.00**
Casserole, floral, pk on wht, Japan, w/lid **8.00**
Casserole, floral w/geometric band, Moritace, w/lid, 6" **30.00**
Casserole, Pagodas, bl on wht, w/lid, England, 5½" **55.00**
Casserole, Pembroke, red on cream, England, 5¼" **45.00**
Compote, Blue Banded Ironstone, England, 3¼" **35.00**
Creamer, Blue Banded, Dimmock, 2¾" **25.00**
Creamer, Bridesmaid, decal on wht, Germany, 3⅜" **22.00**
Creamer, Chinaman (figural), Japan, 2¼" **35.00**
Creamer, clown w/duck, bl lustre rim, Japan, 1¾" **9.00**
Creamer, Father Christmas & Children, Germany, 3½" **35.00**
Creamer, floral band on cream, Nippon, 2¼" **10.00**
Creamer, Humphrey's Clock, bl on wht, Ridgway's **35.00**
Creamer, Mary Had Little Lamb, Warwick China, 2¾" **10.00**
Creamer, Pink Rose, Eggshell, Homer Laughlin, 2¼" **15.00**
Creamer, Whirligig, floral, gr edge, Southern Potteries, 3" **28.00**
Creamer, 3 Little Pigs on tan lustre, Japan **15.00**
Creamer & sugar bowl, Merry Christmas, pk lustre, Germany, w/lid **75.00**
Cup & saucer, Basket, flow bl, England, 1½", 4¼" **40.00**
Cup & saucer, Hunter w/Dog, Canonsburg Pottery **11.00**
Cup & saucer, Merry Christmas, gr lustre, Germany, 2⅛", 4½" ...**30.00**
Cup & saucer, Mickey Mouse, Disney, Japan, 1⅜", 3¾" **25.00**
Cup & saucer, Old Mother Hubbard, mc, ca 1900, 2¾x2¾" **55.00**
Cup & saucer, Pagoda, on wht, Japan **3.00**
Cup & saucer, Sunset, water landscape, MIJ, 1¼", 3⅜" **8.00**
Cup & saucer, Water Hen, bl on wht, England, 2", 4⅜" **22.50**
Gravy boat, Blue Marble, bl & wht, England, 1½" **55.00**
Gravy boat, Fancy Loop, gr on cream, England, 4½" **25.00**
Gravy boat, floral, pk on wht, Japan **7.00**
Pitcher, Robin Hood & Sheriff...Butcher, brn transfer, 4¼" **60.00**
Pitcher & bowl, floral on wht, 5⅛", 2⅛" H **125.00**
Plate, Basket, tapestry look on wht, Salem China, 6¼" **5.00**
Plate, Flow Blue Dogwood, Minton, 4" **22.00**
Plate, Forget-Me-Not, bl on wht, England, 3¾" **35.00**
Plate, Holly, decal on wht, Germany **10.00**
Plate, House That Jack Built, Germany, 5¼" **8.00**
Plate, Humphrey's Clock, bl on wht, Ridgway's, 3⅞" **12.00**
Plate, Kite Fliers, bl on wht, England, 2¾" **48.00**
Plate, Playful Cats, decal on wht w/pk at rim, 5¼" **14.00**
Plate, Pot Boys, boys complaining, star & flower border, 5½" **100.00**
Plate, Punch & Judy, bl on wht, England, 5¾" **25.00**
Plate, Scenes From House That Jack Built, Florence Cook, 6" **10.00**
Plate, Snow White character on wht, Disney, Japan, ca 1937, 4⅜" ..**10.00**
Platter, Athens, bl on wht, Davenport, mid-1800s, 5½" **27.00**
Platter, Blue Acorn, England, 5¼" **18.00**
Platter, Blue Banded Ironstone, England, 6" **25.00**
Platter, Embossed Leaf, burgundy, MIJ, 5½" **5.00**
Platter, Fancy Loop, gr on cream, oblong, England, 6" **26.00**
Platter, Gaudy Floral, England, 4" **35.00**
Sugar bowl, Barnyard Animals, decal on wht, Germany, w/lid, 4" ...**18.00**
Sugar bowl, butterflies on wht, Japan, w/lid, 3⅛" **12.00**
Sugar bowl, dog on ball, bl lustre rim, Japan, w/lid, 2⅝" **14.00**

Sugar bowl, Dutch figures, bl on wht, Japan, w/lid 16.00
Sugar bowl, Playful Zoo Animals, Edwin M Knowles, w/lid, 2¾" .16.00
Tea service, Smitty, Germany, 23-pc 1,200.00
Tea set, bl dragon on wht, Japan, ds, 17-pc 85.00
Tea set, Blue Banded, Dimmock, 6-place 310.00
Tea set, Butterfly, mc on wht, Japan, 4-place 95.00
Tea set, girl w/fruit in apron on wht, Staffordshire, 16-pc 200.00
Tea set, Happifats, Germany, 23-pc 425.00
Tea set, Kewpies in military helmets, sgn, 6-place 1,575.00
Tea set, Little Bo Peep (Victory), Salem, 4-place 160.00
Tea set, Nursery Scenes, decal on wht, Germany, 6-place 175.00
Tea set, Pink Rose, decal on wht, unmk, 6-place 185.00
Tea set, Sunbonnet Babies, semiporc, Am, 4-place 750.00
Tea set, tan & gray lustre, Japan, 4-place 97.00
Teapot, Buster Brown, decal on wht, Germany, 5⅞" 165.00
Teapot, Circus, Edwin M Knowles China, w/lid, 4½" 35.00
Teapot, Colonial American, Am Ceramic Co, late 1930s, w/lid ..35.00
Teapot, Dutch Children, on lustre, Japan, w/lid 27.00
Teapot, Dutch Windmill, decal on wht to pk, w/lid, 6½" 80.00
Teapot, elephant figural, tan lustre w/mc, Japan, 3¼" 60.00
Teapot, Silhouette, w/lid, Japan, 4⅛" 30.00
Tray, Dimity, gr on cream, England, 4½" dia 18.00
Tureen, Athens, bl on wht, Davenport, mid-1800s, 3½" 45.00
Tureen, Dogwood, flow bl, Minton, 4½" 85.00
Tureen, Myrtle Wreath, bl on wht, JM&S (England), 4½" 70.00
Underplate, Blue Marble, bl & wht, England, 5½" 35.00
Underplate, Forget-Me-Not, bl on wht, England, 4" 35.00

Furniture

Rocking cradle, scrolled rod-iron base and cradle, decorative fabric and padding, complete with laced head drape, doll size, 27x19", EX, $200.00.

Armchair, arrowbk, brn rpt w/mc fruit, 23¾" 165.00
Armchair, crest rail/plank seat, brn grpt w/mc florals, 19" 275.00
Armchair, mahog Sheraton, slip seat over potty cutout, 21" 200.00
Armchair, 3-slat ladder-bk, rfn hardwood, splint seat 100.00
Armchair rocker, arched crest, grpt w/cream striping, 24", VG ..100.00
Armchair rocker, oak Mission style 110.00
Armchair rocker, old stencil on blk, 26" 165.00
Armchair rocker, orig gr pnt w/floral decor on crest, rpr, 16½" ..145.00
Armchair rocker, 3-slat ladder-bk, splint seat, red pnt, 32" 500.00
Armchair rocker, 3-slat ladder-bk, splint seat, 25", EX 220.00
Bed, birch w/cannonball trn posts, bold details, 17x27x18" 660.00
Bed, cannonball rope; birch, old natural, rpr, 19½x12¼" 250.00

Bed, curly maple Sheraton, trn posts & spindles, rprs, 53" L 660.00
Bed, hardwood, trn posts, +quilt/mattress/bolster, 29x28x14" 300.00
Bed, sleigh bed form w/panel ends, old finish, 40½" L 175.00
Bed, walnut Victorian, trn details, stripped of pnt, 21" 200.00
Bed, walnut Victorian, trn posts/spindles, disassembles, 34x38" .140.00
Bench, poplar w/worn blk & wht pnt, cut-out cats in bk, 25" 330.00
Cabinet, kitchen; paneled doors, old gray rpt, 39x23x16" 200.00
Carriage, Victorian style, wood wheels/hdl, leather canopy, 38" ...500.00
Chair, Arts & Crafts, sq cut-out design in bk, 38", VG 200.00
Chair, bamboo Windsor, mustard pnt w/mc floral & name, 34" .400.00
Chair, bamboo Windsor, old rfn, 25½" 110.00
Chair, cane seat, bentwood bk, 25x12x13" 115.00
Chair, cvd walnut, pk reuphl, early 20th C, 30" 120.00
Chair, hickory, rnd bk, caned seat, 1920s 175.00
Chair, ladder-bk, splint seat, incised decor, gr pnt, 23" 200.00
Chair, oak, trn/pressed details, cane seat, adjusts to rock, rfn 275.00
Chair, plank seat, flat crest rail, mustard pnt, ca 1800, 16" 2,500.00
Chair, plank seat, spindle-bk, blk w/yel decor, 1850s, 17" 250.00
Chair, side; 2 graduated slats, splint seat, 26½", EX 150.00
Chairs, curved crest/plank seat, yel pnt w/smoke decor, 18", pr 3,500.00
Chest, mahog/oak/hardwoods, 2 half-drw over 2 drws, 15x14x10" ..1,300.00
Chest, pine, dvtl, 2 short drws over 3, brn pnt, 14x14½" 185.00
Chest, step-down type, 2 short drw over 3, lt bl pnt, 24" 200.00
Chest, walnut, 3 dvtl drw, brass hdw, ca 1900, 15x14x8", EX 350.00
Chest, walnut Emp, 3-drw, dvtl, 1850s, 18x7x12" 1,500.00
Chest, 3 dvtl drw, orig grpt, early 19th C, 23x20x13", EX 675.00
Cradle, cherry, dvtl, EX details, rprs, 17" L, 9½" rockers 250.00
Cradle, cherry, dvtl, rprs to rockers, 43" 220.00
Cradle, curly maple, canted sides, scalloped top, 41", EX 525.00
Cradle, mahog, dvtl, hooded, age cracks, VA, 40" L 400.00
Cradle, pine w/oak grpt, gr int, blk stenciled initials, 17" L 330.00
Cradle, poplar, dvtl, shaped rockers, cut-out sides, 42" 295.00
Cradle, softwood, grpt, str bk, hooded, 1800s, 27x39x21" 425.00
Cradle, splint, w/hood, butterfly rockers, buttermilk red 515.00
Cradle, wicker, hooded, wht pnt, ds 55.00
Cradle, wood, in fr to swing, old bl pnt, ds 110.00
Cupboard, pewter, hardwood w/old gr rpt, wire nails, 13", VG 30.00
Cupboard, pine & oak, old dk red pnt, 19" 495.00
Cupboard, step-bk, oak, open top, 2 doors below, EX, 22x17" 300.00
Cupboard, step-bk, pine w/porc knobs, sq nails, 19" 415.00
Cupboard, step-bk, pine/poplar, old pnt, wire nails, 18x14x8" ...195.00
Desk, schoolmaster's, grpt pine, slant lid, 3-drw, 12x14x9" 415.00
Dresser, oak, 3 sm over 3 lg drws, swivel mirror, 22½" 350.00
Dresser, poplar, 3-drw, high-bk mirror w/shelves, red pnt, 23" 300.00
Dresser, serpentine top drw, tilt mirror, brass pulls, 26" 625.00
Highchair, Country ladder-bk, splint seat, rstr, 33" 150.00
Highchair, ladder-bk, old splint seat, rfn, rstr, 36" 200.00
Highchair, Limbert, vertical slat-bk, tray missing, rfn, VG 220.00
Highchair, oak, trn/pressed details, cane seat, CI wheels, rfn 300.00
Highchair, walnut Eastlake Victorian w/burl veneer, rprs, 36" ...175.00
Highchair, wht wicker/wood, 2 tray szs, EX 175.00
Highchair, Windsor spindle bow-bk, worn blk rpt, rprs, 31" 850.00
Highchair, 3 arched slats, splint seat, pnt traces, 1790s, 39" 1,900.00
Highchair/stroller, folding, hardwood, cane seat, 24"+hdl 300.00
Lowboy, hardwood QA w/mahog finish, handmade repro, 18½" ..200.00
Screen, oak & brass w/shirred fabric, Victorian, 3 panels 825.00
Settle, Limbert #1937, 2-slat bk, orig solid seat, 38" L 900.00
Settle, spindle bk, weathered/rprs/red rpt, 74" L 360.00
Stand, curly maple, handmade repro, 14¼x8x14" 165.00
Stroller, metal & canvas, folding, 1928, EX 45.00
Table, pine drop-leaf, star & circle, rnd top, sq legs, 15" 155.00
Table, pnt softwood drop-leaf, late 1800s, 16x25x18", EX 1,100.00
Table, walnut drop-leaf Hplwht style, rpr, 13x18x8"+leaves 400.00
Table, walnut drop-leaf Sheraton, dvtl drw, 19x23"+leaves 1,100.00

Glass

All Over Star, mug, bl, 3⅛"	48.00
Amazon, creamer	50.00
Amazon, spooner	40.00
Amazon, sugar bowl, w/lid	85.00
Arrowhead in Ovals, butter dish	45.00
Arrowhead in Ovals, cake stand	35.00
Arrowhead in Ovals, creamer	25.00
Arrowhead in Ovals, spooner	25.00
Austrian, creamer, vaseline	140.00
Balder, butter dish, worn gold	100.00
Balder, spooner, gold trim	45.00
Beaded Swirl, butter dish	55.00
Beaded Swirl, creamer	30.00
Beaded Swirl, spooner	40.00
Beaded Swirl, sugar bowl, w/lid	40.00
Begging Dog, mug	40.00
Block & Daisy, mug, amber, 3¼"	35.00
Bucket, creamer	75.00
Buzz Saw, creamer	25.00
Buzz Saw, spooner	25.00
Condiment set, 4 clear bottles in pewter fr	135.00
Cup & saucer, squirrel decal, Hammersley	24.00
Dewdrop, mug, bl, 3¼"	72.00
Diamond & Sunburst, butter dish	25.00

Fine Cut Star and Fan, banana stand, $40.00.

Fine Cut Star & Fan, banana stand	40.00
Fine Cut Star & Fan, butter dish	35.00
Fine Cut Star & Fan, cake stand	35.00
Fine Cut Star & Fan, creamer	25.00
Fine Cut Star & Fan, sugar bowl, w/lid	35.00
Flattened Diamond & Sunburst, butter dish	35.00
Flattened Diamond & Sunburst, creamer, bl	10.00
Flattened Diamond & Sunburst, punch bowl	35.00
Flattened Diamond & Sunburst, spooner	25.00
Fuchsia Flower, mug, clear, 1"	45.00
Galloway, pitcher	32.00
Grape, mug, amber, 3"	28.00
Grape, mug, bl, 3"	28.00
Grapevine w/Ovals, mug	35.00
Hawaiian Lei, creamer	20.00
Hawaiian Lei, sugar bowl	30.00
Hobnail w/T'print Band, butter dish, amber	115.00
Hobnail w/T'print Band, creamer, bl	45.00
Inverted Strawberry, punch bowl	50.00
Lamb, creamer	85.00
Lamb, spooner	125.00
Lamb, sugar bowl, w/lid	150.00

Liberty Bell, mug	150.00
Louisiana, cake stand	45.00
Martyrs, mug	40.00
Menagerie, spooner, bl	140.00
Menagerie, sugar bowl, slotted lid	240.00
Michigan, creamer	45.00
Michigan, spooner	45.00
Monk, stein, milk glass, 4"	35.00
Nursery Rhyme, butter dish	110.00
Nursery Rhyme, pitcher	120.00
Nursery Rhyme, sugar bowl, w/lid	90.00
Nursery Rhyme, tumbler	25.00
Oval Star, bowl, berry; sm	11.00
Oval Star, pitcher, lemonade	55.00
Oval Star, punch bowl	50.00
Oval Star, punch bowl w/4 mugs	90.00
Oval Star, punch cup	11.00
Oval Star, tumbler	11.00
Pennsylvania, butter dish, gr w/gold	245.00
Prism Panel, mug, Sandwich	25.00
Prism Panel, tumbler, Sandwich	15.00
Rex (Fancy Cut), creamer	28.00
Rex (Fancy Cut), tumbler	18.00
Sawtooth, butter dish	50.00
Sawtooth Band, creamer	65.00
Sawtooth Band, spooner	85.00
Squirrel, mug	25.00
Sweetheart, butter dish, Cambridge	25.00
Sweetheart, creamer, Cambridge	15.00
Sweetheart, spooner, Cambridge	20.00
Tulip & Honeycomb, bowl, oval, hdls	55.00
Tulip & Honeycomb, butter dish	45.00
Tulip & Honeycomb, punch bowl	30.00
Tulip & Honeycomb, punch bowl w/6 mugs	85.00
Waterfowl, mug, amber	45.00
Wheat Sheaf, punch bowl w/6 mugs	90.00
Wheat Sheaf, tumbler	15.00
Whirligig, punch bowl	35.00
Whirligig, punch bowl w/4 cups	70.00
Whirligig, spooner	18.00

Miscellaneous

Baby basket, Windsor type, wood bottom, splint weaving, 36" L	750.00
Bicycle, wooden rims, fenders & guards, girl's, 1906, EX	1,000.00
Carpet sweeper, Bissell's Little Queen, rpl hdl	65.00
Ice skates, leather & CI, brass at heels, Wheeler, EX	135.00
Noah's ark, pnt wood w/orig 24 cvd/pnt figures, Germany, 12" L	200.00
Rattle, celluloid, man in moon, winking	175.00
Rattle, celluloid, 3 cats in basket form, EX	150.00
Rattle, coral & 5 bells w/whistle, sterling, England, 1860s	325.00
Rattle, MOP, Little Jack Horner, 2 sterling bells	60.00
Rattle, MOP, oval ring w/3 brass bells	60.00
Rattle, MOP ring w/Webster sterling bell	45.00
Rocking horse, old rpt w/rpl yarn mane & tail, vinyl saddle, 46"	300.00
Rocking horse, pine w/dapple gray pnt, homemade, good age, 43"	385.00
Rocking horse, wood, roan pnt, 19th C, rprs, 23x42x12", VG	1,100.00
Rocking horse, wood w/dapple gray pnt, orig saddle, 34x40"	580.00
Sled, wood w/mc stencil & orig varnish, steel-tipped runners, 34"	525.00
Sleigh, wood w/cvd/trn details, pnt scenes, European, 38", EX	770.00
Tea set, Girl in Bonnet, tin litho, Germany, 13-pc	475.00
Tea set, graniteware, cream w/gold bands, pot+cr/sug+5 c/s	225.00
Tea set, Red Riding Hood, tin litho, Germany, 13-pc	535.00
Wheel, letters & numbers, Cress Board, 1912	50.00

Chintz

'Chintz' is the generic name for English china with an allover floral transfer design. This eye-catching china is reminiscent of chintz dress fabric. It is colorful, bright, and cheery with its many floral designs and reminds one of an English garden in full bloom. It was produced in England during the first half of this century and stands out among other styles of china. Pattern names often found with the manufacturer's name on the bottom of pieces include Anemone, Chelsea, Chintz, Delphinium Chintz, June Roses, Mayfair, Hazel, Eversham, Royalty, Sweet Pea, Summertime, Springtime, and Welbeck, among others.

The older patterns tend to be composed of larger flowers, while the later, more popular lines can be quite intricate in design. And while the first collectors preferred the earthenware lines, many are now searching for the bone china dinnerware made by such firms as Shelley. Prices are already formidable and rising. You can concentrate on reassembling a favorite pattern, or you can mix two or more designs together for a charming, eclectic look. Another choice may be to limit your collection to teapots (the stacking ones are especially nice), breakfast sets, or cups and saucers. For further information we recommend *Chintz Ceramics* by Joan Welsh (Schiffer). See also Shelley. Our advisor is Mary Jane Hastings; she is listed in the Directory under Illinois.

Teapots: Beeston, Countess shape, Royal Winton, 6-cup, 5½", hard to find, $1,200.00; Evesham, Ascot shape, Royal Winton, 6-cup, 6½", hard to find, $1,200.00.

Ascot, creamer & sugar bowl, Royal Winton	225.00
Ascot, plate, Royal Winton, 8"	225.00
Ascot, plate, 8-sided, Crown Ducal, 9"	90.00
Begonia, creamer & sugar bowl, Shelley	78.00
Black Beauty, butter dish, Lord Nelson	225.00
Black Beauty, creamer & sugar bowl, on tray, Lord Nelson	225.00
Black Beauty, cup & saucer, Lord Nelson	165.00
Cheadle, bonbon, Royal Winton	175.00
Cheadle, compote, ftd, Royal Winton	150.00
Cheadle, tray	210.00
DuBarry, creamer, James Kent	60.00
Eleanor, bowl, fruit; Royal Winton, sm	50.00
Estelle, creamer & sugar bowl, Royal Winton	135.00
Estelle, egg cup, Royal Winton	140.00
Estelle, plate, Royal Winton, 6"	75.00
Esther, creamer & sugar bowl, Royal Winton	145.00
Gold Leaves, bonbon, ftd, Royal Winton	75.00
Green Tulip, cake plate, Lord Nelson	200.00
Green Tulip, cake server, 3-tier, Lord Nelson	225.00
Julia, ashtray, Royal Winton, 4"	160.00
Julia, cup & saucer, Royal Winton	195.00
June Festival, creamer & sugar bowl, w/tray, Royal Winton	145.00
Lorna Doone, plate, Midwinter, 7"	70.00
Lorna Doone, plate, Midwinter, 9"	125.00

Lorna Doone, sugar shaker, Midwinter	200.00
Marina, cheese dish, Lord Nelson	295.00
Marina, cup & saucer, Lord Nelson	65.00
Marina, pitcher, Lord Nelson, 5½"	175.00
Marina, plate, Lord Nelson, 8"	60.00
May Festival, candy dish, Royal Winton	150.00
May Festival, coaster, Royal Winton	35.00
May Festival, creamer & sugar bowl, Royal Winton	195.00
Maytime, creamer & sugar bowl, Shelley	160.00
Maytime, cup & saucer, demi; Shelley	115.00
Maytime, cup & saucer, Shelley	125.00
Maytime, pin dish, Shelley	50.00
Melody, plate, Shelley, 8"	125.00
Old Cottage, bowl, oval vegetable; Royal Winton	195.00
Old Cottage, cup & saucer, Royal Winton	85.00
Old Cottage, plate, Royal Winton, 6"	55.00
Old Cottage, plate, Royal Winton, 8"	90.00
Old Cottage, relish, 4-part, Royal Winton	245.00
Pansy, cheese keeper, Lord Nelson	225.00
Pansy, creamer & sugar bowl, on tray, Lord Nelson	140.00
Pansy, plate, Lord Nelson, 4"	35.00
Royal Brocade, creamer, Lord Nelson	60.00
Royal Brocade, creamer & sugar bowl, Lord Nelson	125.00
Royal Brocade, cup & saucer, farmer's; Lord Nelson	275.00
Royal Brocade, shakers, pr, on tray, Lord Nelson	160.00
Summertime, bowl, 8-sided, Royal Winton, 5"	65.00
Summertime, charger, Royal Winton, 12"	395.00
Summertime, coffeepot, Royal Winton	950.00
Summertime, cup & saucer, Royal Winton	85.00
Summertime, nut dish, Royal Winton	85.00
Summertime, plate, Royal Winton, 5½"	50.00
Summertime, sauce bowl, Royal Winton	50.00
Summertime, teapot, Royal Winton	650.00
Sunshine, canoe, Royal Winton	265.00
Sunshine, creamer & sugar bowl, Royal Winton	145.00
Sunshine, tray, Royal Winton, 7x12"	195.00
Sweet Pea, jam dish, Royal Winton, w/lid & liner	325.00
Sweet Pea, plate, Royal Winton, 6"	100.00
Tapestry, plate, James Kent, 9"	85.00
Tapestry, plate, sandwich; James Kent	95.00
Tiger Lily, celery dish, Royal Winton, lg	75.00
Tiger Lily, toast rack, 3-bar, Royal Winton	100.00

Chocolate Glass

Jacob Rosenthal developed chocolate glass, a rich shaded opaque brown sometimes referred to as caramel slag, in 1900 at the Indiana Tumbler and Goblet Company of Greentown, Indiana. Later, other companies produced similar ware. Only the latter is listed here. See also Greentown. Our advisors for this category are Jerry and Sandi Garrett; they are listed in the Directory under Indiana.

Bowl, Aldine, oval, w/lid	1,650.00
Bowl, Geneva, oval, 9⅜x5⅞"	210.00
Bowl, 5-fluted	350.00
Box, Aurora, rectangular, open, 9x5½"	1,500.00
Butter dish, child's, Wild Rose w/Scrolling	675.00
Butter dish, File	2,500.00
Butter dish, Fleur-de-lis	700.00
Butter dish, Wild Rose w/Bowknot	550.00
Candle holder, griffin	2,000.00
Celery holder, Fleur-de-lis, 5¾"	365.00
Celery vase, Chrysanthemum Leaf, 6"	875.00

Compote, Melrose, 7¼" dia 300.00
Covered dish, chick, 2-headed 3,000.00
Covered dish, lamb (+) 2,000.00
Cracker jar, Chrysanthemum Leaf, w/lid 2,500.00
Creamer, Cattail & Waterlily 600.00
Creamer, Touching Squares 1,300.00
Cuff box, 4½" H 500.00
Dish, Honeycomb, rectangular, 7⅝x5" 475.00
Hatpin holder, Orange Tree, w/irid finish 3,000.00
Mug, Serenade, 4¾" 175.00
Mug, Swirl 600.00
Nappy, Masonic, triangular, 5" 175.00
Orange bowl, Grape & Cable 3,500.00
Pitcher, Chrysanthemum Leaf 3,000.00
Pitcher, File 2,000.00
Pitcher, Fleur-de-lis 1,200.00
Pitcher, Rose Garland 3,000.00
Plate, Serenade, 6¼" 250.00
Sauce dish, Wild Rose w/Bowknot 125.00
Shaker, Beaded Triangle 475.00
Shaker, Geneva 300.00
Sugar bowl, Chrysanthemum Leaf, w/lid 1,000.00
Sugar bowl, Fleur-de-lis, w/lid 265.00
Toothpick holder, Chrysanthemum Leaf 850.00
Tray, Venetian, 8x10" 450.00

Christmas Collectibles

Christmas past . . . lovely mementos from long ago attest to the ostentatious Victorian celebrations of the season.

St. Nicholas, better known as Santa, has changed much since 300 A.D. when the good Bishop Nicholas showered needy children with gifts and kindnesses. During the early 18th century, Santa was portrayed as the kind gift-giver to well-behaved children and the stern switch-bearing disciplinarian to those who were bad. In 1822 Clement Clark Moore, a New York poet, wrote his famous *Night Before Christmas*, and the Santa he described was jolly and jovial — a lovable old elf who was stern with no one. Early Santas wore robes of yellow, brown, blue, green, red, white, or even purple. But Thomas Nast, who worked as an illustrator for *Harper's Weekly*, was the first to depict Santa in a red suit instead of the traditional robe and to locate him the entire year at the North Pole headquarters.

Today's collectors prize early Santa figures, especially those in robes of fur or mohair or those dressed in an unusual color. Some early examples of Christmas memorabilia are the pre-1870 ornaments from Dresden, Germany. These cardboard figures — angels, gondolas, umbrellas, dirigibles, and countless others — sparkled with gold and silver trim. Late in the 1870s, blown glass ornaments were imported from Germany. There were over 6,000 recorded designs, all painted inside with silvery colors. From 1890 through 1910, blown glass spheres were often decorated with beads, tassels, and tinsel rope.

Christmas lights, made by Sandwich and some of their contemporaries, were either pressed or mold-blown glass shaped into a form similar to a water tumbler. They were filled with water and then hung from the tree by a wire handle; oil floating on the surface of the water served as fuel for the lighted wick.

Kugels are glass ornaments that were made as early as 1820 and as late as 1890. Ball-shaped examples are more common than the fruit and vegetable forms and have been found in sizes ranging from 1" to 14" in diameter. They were made of thick glass with heavy brass caps, in cobalt, green, gold, silver, red, and occasionally in amethyst.

Although experiments involving the use of electric light bulbs for the Christmas tree occured before 1900, it was 1903 before the first

manufactured socket set was marketed. These were very expensive and often proved a safety hazard. In 1921 safety regulations were established, and products were guaranteed safety approved. The early bulbs were smaller replicas of Edison's household bulb. By 1910 G.E. bulbs were rounded with a pointed end, and until 1919 all bulbs were hand blown. The first figural bulbs were made around 1910 in Austria. Japan soon followed, but their product was never of the high quality of the Austrian wares. American manufacturers produced their first machine-made figurals after 1919. Today figural bulbs (especially character-related examples) are very popular collectibles. Bubble lights were popular from about 1945 to 1960 when miniature lights were introduced. These tiny lamps dampened the public's enthusiasm for the bubblers, and manufacturers stopped providing replacement bulbs.

Feather trees were made from 1850 to 1950. All are collectible. Watch for newly manufactured feather trees that have been reintroduced.

For further information concerning Christmas collectibles, we recommend these highly informative books: *Christmas Collectibles* by Margaret and Kenn Whitmyer; and *Christmas Ornaments, Lights, and Decorations, A Collector's Identification and Value Guide, Volumes I through III*, by George Johnson. All are available from Collector Books or your local bookstore.

Note: values are given for bulbs that are in good paint, with no breaks or cracks, and in working order. Examples termed 'mini' measure no more than 1½".

Bulbs

Photo courtesy
George Johnson

Woman, short redhead, pre-1940, 2½", from $60.00 to $70.00; Wooden doll, pre-1940, 2½", from $90.00 to $100.00.

Angel, clear, standing, Japan, ca 1925, 2½" 70.00
Apple, milk glass, oval shape, Japan, 2½" 12.50
Baby in clown suit, milk glass, Japan, 3¼" 80.00
Ball w/holly leaves & berries, milk glass, Japan, 1950s, 1¾" 12.50
Ball w/indent, silvered, 1¾" 18.00
Bear, sitting on haunches, milk glass, Japan, 1950s, 2¾" 80.00
Beaver on log, milk glass, Japan, 3" 165.00
Bell, milk glass, emb Christmas Greetings, Japan, 1950, mini 12.50
Bell w/Santa face, milk glass, long/narrow, Japan, 2¼" 15.00
Betty Boop, milk glass, strapless gown, Japan, 2¼" 65.00
Bird in birdhouse, milk glass, Japan, 1935-50, mini, 1½" 18.00
Canary, clear, exhaust tip beak, Germany, 4¾" 30.00
Cat, begging, lg eyes, milk glass, Japan, 1930s, 2½" 25.00
Cat in evening gown, milk glass, Japan, ca 1950, 3" 120.00
Cat w/ball, milk glass, Japan, 2¼" 75.00
Chick, clear, mini 30.00
Chrysanthemum, milk glass, Japan, 2" 30.00
Church w/bell, milk glass, Japan, 2½" 55.00
Clarabell, milk glass, Japan, 2" 325.00
Clown head w/tall hat, milk glass, Japan, 2½" 40.00

Clown horn player, clear, exhaust tip, European, 2¾" 70.00
Cottage in hillside, milk glass, Japan, 1950s, 2¼" 55.00
Crown, clear, Am, mini 70.00
Deep sea diver, milk glass, Japan, 2¼" 190.00
Dick Tracy, milk glass, Japan, 2¾" 75.00
Dog, dressed up on dmn shape, milk glass, Japan, 2½" 140.00
Dog in polo outfit w/mallet, milk glass, Japan, ca 1950, 2¾" 32.00
Dog in stocking, milk glass, short & fat, 2¾" 45.00
Dopey, milk glass, Disney, Japan, 1940s, 2¼" 115.00
Dragon on lantern, milk glass, Japan, 2¼" 12.50
Dutch man w/pipe, milk glass, Japan, ca 1950, 3¼" 115.00
Eggplant, clear, Mazda, ca 1940, 2½" 55.00
Fiddler pig (of 3 pigs), milk glass, Japan, 1970s, 2½" 17.50
Fish in fishbowl, milk glass, Japan, 1¾" 35.00
Flapper girl, milk glass, slim, Japan, 1950s, 2¾" 60.00
Flower, generic, clear or milk glass, Japan, 1920-50, mini, ea 10.00
Flower in seashell, milk glass, 10-petal, Japan, 2¼" 80.00
Girl in pumpkin dress, milk glass, Japan, ca 1950, 2¾" 90.00
Gourd man, milk glass, Japan, 2½" 28.00
Hippo girl in dress, milk glass, Japan, 4½" 185.00
Humpty Dumpty on wall, clear, Germany, 3" 115.00
Indian head, clear, Japan, mini 70.00
Indian head, frosted glass, full headdress, Japan, mini 70.00
Indian princess, milk glass, Japan, 3" 165.00
Jack-o'-lantern, clear, type I, ribbed body rnd eyes, 1½" 18.00
Kewpie, milk glass, nude, Japan, 2½" 35.00
Kewpie girl w/hat, milk glass, 2½" 30.00
Lantern, clear, cylindrical, Germany, 3" 45.00
Lantern, clear, rectangular, Japan, 2¾" 18.00
Lion on dmn shape, milk glass, unmk, 2½" 135.00
Little Boy Blue, milk glass, Japan, 2¼" 38.00
Log cabin, milk glass, Japan, 1950s, 2" 12.50
Man w/lg tuba, milk glass, Japan, ca 1950, 2¼" 165.00
Matchless Star, dbl row, frosted, standard 250.00
Matchless Star, single row, sm 25.00
Minnie Mouse, milk glass, Disney, Japan, 3" 220.00
Miss Liberty, clear, Germany, 3¼" 235.00
Monkey holding orange, milk glass, Japan, 1950s, 1¾" 115.00
Monkey holding stick, milk glass, Perma-lite, Japan, 2¼" 75.00
Moon Mullins, frosted glass, Japan, 2¾" 42.50
Mushroom, milk glass, thick stalk, 2" 25.00
Mushroom man, clear, Germany, ca 1910, 2¾" 225.00
Ocean liner, milk glass, Japan, ca 1950, 2¾" 90.00
Old woman in shoe, milk glass, 2¼" 70.00
Owl, standing, clear, Am, 1950s, mini, 1½" 70.00
Owl-head girl, frosted glass, Japan, ca 1950, 2½" 85.00
Parrot, clear, Am, ca 1950, mini 70.00
Peach, clear, ca 1920, 2" 22.50
Peacock w/wedge-shaped tail feathers, milk glass, Japan, 2¼" 45.00
Pig in hooded basket, clear, Japan, 2" 115.00
Pig playing drum, milk glass, Japan, ca 1950, 2¾" 185.00
Pine cone, generic, clear, Japan, 1¾" 8.00
Polar bear, standing, clear, Japan, mini, 1½" 22.50
Rabbit in suit, clear, Japan, mini 32.00
Raspberry, clear, exhaust tip, mini, 1½" 25.00
Red Riding Hood, milk glass, Paramount, 2¾" 20.00
Ribbed heart, silvered, Japan, 2" 80.00
Rooster in tub, milk glass, Japan, 2¼" 45.00
Rosebud, milk glass, Japan, 1½" 7.50
Santa, milk glass, common, standing, Japan, 2½" 12.00
Santa face on lantern, milk glass, Japan, ca 1950, 2½" 55.00
Santa on housetop, milk glass, Japan, 2½" 85.00
Santa w/bag, milk glass, Japan, 3¾" 15.00
Santa w/umbrella, milk glass, Japan, 1950s, 2½" 12.00

Scotty mother & pup, milk glass, Japan, ca 1950, 2" 60.00
Seashell, milk glass, Japan, 2" 45.00
Skull & Crossbones on ball, milk glass, Japan, 2" 15.00
Songbird, common, milk glass, Japan, ca 1920-55, 4" 12.50
Squirrel, milk glass, Japan, ca 1950, 2" 22.50
Star, clear, 5-point, mini 32.00
Star, common, milk glass, 5-point, Japan, 1950s, 1¾" 5.00
Star w/smiling face, milk glass, 5-point, Japan, 1950s, 2" 30.00
Strawberry, clear, Japan, 1⅝" 7.00
Sun face, milk glass, 1¾" 22.00
Uncle Sam, clear, standing, Germany, 1910, 3 14" 325.00
Witch, clear, Germany, 3" 195.00
Wolf head, milk glass, Japan, 2¾" 50.00

Candy Containers

Belsnickle Santas: Olive green coat with white trim, base missing, 8", VG, $525.00; Yellow coat with blue trim, base missing, 5¾", VG, 180.00.

Antelope head, Dresden, 3-D, natural colors, 3¾" 400.00
Bull's head, Dresden, 3-D, gold or silver, 3" 525.00
Carp, Dresden, 3-D, natural colors, 3¾x7¼" 475.00
Clown's hat, mc paper w/appl Dresden stars, fabric bag, 3¼" 215.00
Cockateel head, Dresden, 3-D, gold or silver, 2½" 385.00
Cow head, Dresden, 3-D, natural colors, 2¾" 485.00
Dog's head, Dresden, 3-D, gold or silver, 2½" 525.00
Hatbox, printed paper on lt cb, 1920s, 2½" dia 35.00
Horse's head, Dresden, 3-D, natural colors, 3" 365.00
Liberty shield, Dresden, dbl, gold or silver, 2¼x1¾" 115.00
Liberty Shield, fabric over heavy paper, 1920s, 3" 35.00
Loaf of French bread, Dresden, 3-D, gold or silver, 2½" 200.00
Lobster, Dresden, 3-D, red, 4½" 285.00
Mouse, Dresden, 3-D, gold or silver, 2½" L+tail 350.00
Santa, compo w/fur beard, on wood/twig sleigh, 1910s, 15", EX 650.00
Santa, papier-mache, fur beard, red cloth coat, Germany, 7½" 65.00
Santa, papier-mache, fur beard, wire neck, Germany, 9" 35.00
Santa, pressed cb w/mica flakes, HP face/beard, 1940s, 12", NM 275.00
Santa on dmn-shaped box, paper, Russia, 1930s, 4" 65.00
Santa on skis, plastic, Am, ca 1955, 3½" 15.00
Santa waving, plastic, NE Plastic...MA, ca 1960, 3½" 12.50
Snowman, papier-mache, glass eyes, mk Germany, 5" 38.00
Stork, Dresden, 3-D, natural colors, 4" 265.00
Turkey, Dresden, 3-D, natural colors, 4x3½" 235.00
Water can, cb cylinder w/printed paper, opens at bottom, 2½" 215.00

Ornaments

Alarm clock, Dresden, 3-D, gold or silver, 2½" 265.00
Anchor, Dresden, flat, gold or silver, 2⅜" 45.00
Angel, scrap w/spun glass skirt & body, 4¾" 80.00
Angel boy w/tree & ax, scrap w/tinsel, 5x2½" 35.00
Angel doll, celluloid, jtd, tinsel dress/foil wings, '20s, 4" 30.00

Angel head w/wings, Dresden, flat, gold or silver, 3¼" 135.00
Angel in ring, colored or silvered hard plastic, 1950s, 3¾" 4.00
Angel on cloud praying, scrap, 7" 35.00
Angel w/cornucopia & book, scrap w/tinsel, 5" 35.00
Baby in bathtub, celluloid, 3" 80.00
Baby w/bottle, scrap w/cotton batting gown, 15" 18.00
Ball, filigree w/holly leaves, plastic, Bradford, 1955, 3" 2.00
Ball, shapes inside, acrylic, 1930s, 2" 7.00
Ball w/filigree scenes, plastic, Bradford, 1955, 2¾" 2.00
Beads, plastic, rnd or oval, Japan, 1960s-70s, 108" 3.00
Bear, Dresden, dbl, natural, 2¼" 275.00
Bell, Dresden-style, 3-D, Berhardt Wilmsen, ca 1935, 1¼" 12.50
Bird on branch, Dresden, 3-D, natural, appl feathers, 3" L 285.00
Boy clown, celluloid, coin-shaped hat, 5" 80.00
Buffalo, Dresden, dbl, natural colors, 2¼" 235.00
Butterfly, Dresden, flat, gold or silver, 2" W 50.00
Butterfly w/Venetian dew, cb layers, 3-D, 3" 30.00
Carriage, Dresden, flat, gold or silver, 6½" 70.00
Champagne bottle, Dresden, 3-D, gold or silver, 3½" 365.00
Cherries on heart, Dresden-like, 3-D, mc pnt, 2½" 45.00
Cow w/milk pail, Dresden, flat, gold or silver, 3x5¼" 110.00
Cowboy boot w/spur, Dresden, dbl, gold or silver, 6" 260.00
Deer, celluloid, Japan, 6" 7.50
Donkey, Dresden, dbl, natural colors, 2½x2½" 185.00
Duck, Dresden, 3-D, natural colors, 3" 265.00
Duck, Glow-in-the-Dark, fluorescent plastic, 1940s-50s, 3¾" 16.00
Eagle on branch, Dresden, flat, wings wide, gold, 5½" L 100.00
Elephant, Dresden, dbl, natural colors, 1½x2" 135.00
Fan, Dresden, flat, gold & mc pnt, 2x3½" 35.00
Flounder, Dresden, dbl, gold or silver, 3½" 300.00
Flower basket w/hdl, Dresden, flat, gold or silver, 4¾" 130.00
Garland, honeycomb paper, red or gr, various szs, from $6 to 7.00
Gecko on branch, Dresden, 3-D, natural colors, 4" 400.00
Girl w/cornucopia, celluloid, 4" 80.00
Girl w/doll, scrap, cotton batting dress, tinsel bow, 10x8" 90.00
Grapes, Dresden, dbl, gold or silver, 3¼" L 120.00
Greek warrior, Dresden, flat, gold or silver, 4¾" 135.00
Harp, Dresden, flat, gold or silver, 3¼" 70.00
Heart w/ivy, Dresden, flat, gold or silver, 2½" 50.00
Icicle, 3-flanged, plastic w/molded hook, Am, ca 1960, 5½" 50
Lantern, colored/pnt tissue paper, Japan, 1915-30, 4-10", ea 5.00
Lion, Glow-in-the-Dark, fluorescent plastic, Am, 1940s-50s, 3¼" ..7.50
Man in moon, Dresden, dbl, gold or silver, 3" 215.00
Nanny goat, Dresden, 3-D, natural colors, 4" 400.00
Nativity scene, scrap, generic type, 3" 4.00
Opera glasses (lorgnette), dbl, gold or silver, 8½" 285.00
Owl, Dresden, 3-D, natural colors, detailed feathers, 3¼" 450.00
Palm in urn, Dresden, flat, gold or silver, 3x1½" 45.00
Patriotic shield, paper on cb, flat, 1880-1910, sm 30.00
Peacock, Dresden, flat, gold or silver, trailing feathers, 7" 125.00
Pine cone, Dresden-like, 3-D, wht pnt, 3½" 115.00
Rabbit, Dresden, flat, gold or silver, 6¼" L 100.00
Rooster, Dresden, dbl, natural colors, 3⅞x3½" 285.00
Salamander, Dresden, 3-D, natural colors, 4" 315.00
Santa head, scrap, 2" 5.00
Santa in airplane, cb, 3-D, glitter covered, M Ward, 1920s, 5" ..95.00
Santa in short coat, Dresden, flat, gold or silver, 4½" 165.00
Santa in wht fur coat w/cane, scrap w/tinsel, 4½" 55.00
Santa w/girl & lamb, scrap, 6" 17.50
Santa w/tree, toys & fruit plate, scrap, 9¼" 40.00
Sleigh, paper on cb, flat, 1880-1910, lg 100.00
Snow girl w/primroses, scrap, 5¾x2½" 15.00
Snowflake, jeweled plastic, 1940s-70, 4 to 4¼" 2.00
Spaniel tracking, Dresden, 3-D, natural colors, 3" L 400.00

Star, plastic, 16 spikes, ca 1960, 4¾" 2.00
Swan, celluloid, 3½" 50.00
Swan, Dresden, flat, gold or silver, 7" 90.00
Tiger, Dresden, 3-D, natural colors, 2½" 265.00

Miscellaneous

Plaque, Santa face, painted chalkware, some chipping and scuffing, 22", VG, $150.00.

Bubble light, Good-Light or Peerless Shooting Star, ca 1948 ....70.00
Bubble light, Noma, clear base, ca 1988 ....1.50
Bubble light, Noma, flat, 1948-49 ....5.00
Bubble light, Noma Biscuit, common form, 1946-60, EX 5.00
Bubble light, Noma Tulip, common, 1948-60 ....7.00
Bubble light, Paramount Biscuit, ca 1951-72 ....4.00
Bubble light, Reliance, Spark-L-Light, 1949-51 ....8.00
Bubble light, World Wide, ca 1970 ....5.00
Candle holder, litho on metal, angel on cloud, 1890-1915, 2" ...110.00
Candle holder, litho on metal, flowers, 1890-1915, 2" 70.00
Candle holder, metal clip-on type, emb butterfly, 1920s, 3x2" 65.00
Candle holder, metal clip-on type, emb parrot, 1920s, 1¾" 50.00
Candle holder, pendulum-weighted, glass apples, 1880s, 3" 50.00
Candle holder, pendulum-weighted, standard type, ca 1880s, 5½" ..15.00
Candle holder, pendulum-weighted, tin/lead star, 1880s, 6½" 50.00
Candle shade, arched windows, glass, 1895-1920, 3½" 120.00
Candle shade, boy in nightcap, molded glass, 1890s-1920, 3" 400.00
Candle shade, witch's face, molded glass, 1890s-1920s, 4" 365.00
Decoration, Santa in sleigh, cb & glitter, Japan, 2½x10" 95.00
Fence, red & gr pnt wooden 4¾" pickets, 6" end posts, 37" sq ...250.00
Figure, reindeer, celluloid, hollow, glitter trim, 5" 25.00
Figure, sheep, papier-mache, wood legs, Germany, 1920s, 3-4" 45.00
Figure, sheep, woolly, German, 3½", 3 for 75.00
Kugel, ball, gold, 3-5", from $35 to 45.00
Kugel, ball, mc spatter, 3", from $350 to 450.00
Kugel, ball, silver, 2" 25.00
Kugel, ball w/pike, gr, 2" 40.00
Kugel, ball w/ribs, bl, 1-2", from $90 to 100.00
Kugel, ball w/zigzag pattern, amethyst, 2" 350.00
Kugel, berries in ball cluster, cobalt, 4", from $350 to 400.00
Kugel, berries in ball cluster, silver, 3" 125.00
Kugel, grape cluster, gr, 4-6", from $225 to 250.00
Kugel, grapes in oval cluster, amethyst, 5-7", from $750 to 950.00
Kugel, grapes w/emb leaves, various colors, Indian repro, 4" 8.00
Kugel, oval, cranberry, 3" 300.00
Kugel, pine cone w/leaves, silver, 4¼" 550.00
Kugel, strawberry, cobalt, 4¼" 650.00
Kugel, teardrop, bl, 5-10", from $150 to 225.00
Lantern, pierced metal, 6-sided, 1930s, Germany, 4¼" 70.00
Light, Bust of King Edward, gr-aqua, smooth base, 4" 300.00
Light, Daisy, lt gr, 3¾" 65.00
Light, Dmn Quilt, cobalt, smooth base, 3½", NM 65.00
Light, Dmn Quilt, dk teal gr, smooth base, 3½" 85.00

Light, Dmn Quilt, lt sapphire bl, smooth base, 3½" 95.00
Light, Dmn Quilt, ruby, 3¾" 105.00
Light, Dot & Dash, amber, 3¾" 55.00
Light, Fern, lt aqua, smooth base, 3⅜" 100.00
Light, grapes, clear, 4" 145.00
Light, grapes, dk amethyst, smooth base, 3⅞" 230.00
Light, Hobnail, dk gr, bottom resembles chrysanthemum, 3¾" 90.00
Light, Honeycomb, cranberry, 3¾" 95.00
Light, Queen Mary's head, amber, 4" 325.00
Light, Queen Victoria cameo, cobalt, 4 ovals, 3¾" 325.00
Light, Starburst, amber, smooth base, 3⅞" 95.00
Light, Starburst, clear, smooth base, 3⅞" 40.00
Mug, Father Christmas transfer, Germany, 3x3½" 85.00
Santa, cb diecut, w/bell & toys, glitter trim, Germany, 20x8" 100.00
Santa, celluloid, red & wht, Irwin, 8¼" 75.00
Santa, celluloid on tin base, spring limbs, Japan 155.00
Santa, chalk face, cotton body, felt suit, Japan, 5" 60.00
Santa, compo face, felt clothes, squeaker, Germany, 12" 475.00
Santa, figure, chalk face, cotton body, Japan, 5½" 65.00
Santa, nodder, compo, Japan 50.00
Santa in sleigh, compo face, cb & mica, Germany, 1½x5", VG ...65.00
Tree, feather; gr w/compo berries, 11" 65.00
Tree, feather; gr w/red berries, sq red base, 1930s, 37" 300.00
Tree, feather; gr w/red compo berries, mk Germany, 26" 190.00
Tree, feather; gr w/red holly, wht sq base, 1920s-30s, 29" 250.00
Tree, feather; gr w/wht base, 72" 275.00
Tree, feather; many branches, candle clips, 1930s, 26" 200.00
Tree stand, CI, geometrics, mk Harras Germany, 11¾" 40.00
Tree stand, CI, rnd w/Christ Child relief, Germany, 10½" 115.00
Tree stand, CI, Tree Roots, 3-leg, Austrian, ca 1911, lg 75.00
Tree stand, musical, Cameo, 1960s, 13" 25.00
Tree stand, tin w/5 plug outlets, copper-plated CI ft, 13¼" 165.00
Tree topper, angel, compo/fabric, non-electric, Noma, 1950, 8¼" ..15.00
Tree topper, angel, wax, purple fabric, Germany, 12" 190.00
Tree topper, angel in cloud wreath, plastic, Am, 1958, 8" 6.00
Tree topper, angel w/cornucopia, paper, Germany, 8x5" 60.00
Tree topper, point, glass w/plastic figure, Germany, 1950s, 10" 30.00
Tree topper, star, free-blown spikes, Germany, 8" 50.00
Tree topper, star, plastic/metal, Noma, 9½" 20.00
Tree topper, star, tin, 7-arm w/indents, Rigby, 1880s, 7¾" 225.00
Tree topper, storks at fountain, glass, Italy, ca 1950, 15¾" 165.00

Chrysanthemum Sprig, Blue

This is the blue opaque version of Northwood's popular pattern, Chrysanthemum Sprig. It was made at the turn of the century and is today very rare, as its values indicate. Prices are influenced by the amount of gold remaining on the raised designs. Our advisors for this category are Betty and Clarence Maier; they're listed in the Directory under Pennsylvania.

Bowl, berry; sm 325.00
Bowl, master fruit; 10½" W 600.00
Butter dish 1,250.00
Celery 1,495.00
Compote, jelly 600.00
Condiment tray, rare, VG gold 750.00
Creamer 385.00
Cruet, EX gold, from $975 to 1,200.00
Pitcher, water 1,100.00
Spooner, from $300 to 350.00
Sugar bowl, w/lid 600.00
Toothpick holder 450.00

Tumbler 350.00

Circus Collectibles

The 1890s — the golden age of the circus. Barnum and Bailey's parades transformed mundane city streets into an exotic never-never land inhabited by trumpeting elephants with jeweled gold headgear strutting by to the strains of the calliope that issued from a fine red- and gilt-painted wagon extravagantly decorated with carved wooden animals of every description. It was an exciting experience. Is it any wonder that collectors today treasure the mementos of that golden era? See also Posters.

Key:
B&B — Barnum & Bailey

Photo courtesy Aston Macek Auctioneers & Appraisers

Wagon crest, highly-carved eagle with lioness and dolphins (1 lioness missing), $650.00.

Bicycle, chimpanzee; wood & steel, 24x36", EX 700.00
Cardboard punch-out premium, B&B, Lever Bros, 35-pc, M in mailer 135.00
Costume, clown; baggy pants/hat/tie/shoes/etc, '38, +makeup kit ..250.00
Pin-bk button, Cole Bros, Clyde Beatty, 1930s 25.00
Popcorn wagon, Cretors, EX 3,995.00
Program, B&B, Wizard Prince of Arabia, 1914, EX 165.00
Schedule, B&B, color graphics, 1924, EX 75.00

Clambroth

Clambroth is a term that refers to a type of glass popular in the Victorian period. It was semi-opaque and gray-white in color, said to resemble the broth of the clam. See also Sandwich.

Bowl, scalloped, 3x12" 38.00
Candlestick, sq base, fluted std, petal socket, 8¾" 100.00
Candlesticks, crucifix form, 9¾", pr, NM 65.00
Candlesticks, hexagonal, 6⅞", pr, EX 145.00
Cruet, lt bl cuttings in paneled body, step-cut lip, 7" 725.00
Epergne, 1-lily, ftd/ruffled bowl: 6¼x4½" 135.00
Ewer, appl cranberry rim & hdl, 10¼", NM 120.00
Ladle, 9½" 52.00
Spill holder, ltly sanded, Dmn Quilt, 3 bull's-eye dmns, 4½" 185.00
Toothpick holder, Button Arches 24.00
Toothpick holder, floral at rim, Sandwich, 2" 100.00
Vase, blk horizontal lines, 9x4¾" 35.00

Clarice Cliff

Between 1928 and 1935 in Burslem, England, as the director and part owner of Wilkinson and Newport Pottery Companies, Clarice Cliff and her 'paintresses' created a body of hand-painted pottery whose influence is felt to the present time.

The name for the oevre was Bizarre Ware, and the predominant sensibility, style, and appearance was Deco. Almost all pieces are signed and include the pattern names. There were over 160 patterns and more than 400 shapes, all of which are illustrated in *A Bizarre Affair — the Life and Work of Clarice Cliff,* published by Harry N. Abrams, Inc., written by Len Griffen and Susan and Louis Meisel.

Note: Non-hand-painted work (transfer printed) was produced after World War II and into the 1950s. Some of the most common names are 'Tonquin' and 'Charlotte.' These items, while attractive and enjoyable to own, have little value in the collector market. Our advisors for this category are Wilfred and Dolli Cohen; they are listed in the Directory under California.

Cup & saucer, Gay Day, yel/orange/gr, 4 for 635.00
Jug, Fantasque, orange & blk flowers, 7¾x7" 1,150.00
Jug, Lotus; Autumn, house & landscape, 11¾x8" 1,295.00
Teapot, Harvest, fruit & florals, orange/yel/gr, 6½x9" 745.00
Vase, Coral Firs, trees & landscape, 8¼x6" 850.00
Vase, Delicia Citrus, blk & gr drips among oranges/lemons, 7¾" ..795.00
Vase, floral sprays on brn stems, corseted, 9¼x8" 950.00
Vase, Inspiration, floral bouquets, w/frog, 4¾x9" 650.00
Vase, Inspiration Lily, purple lilies on bl-gr, 7x3" 795.00
Vase, orange/yel/blk bands, 8x5½" 650.00
Vase, Windbells, tree bands, mc on gr, 8x6" 850.00

Cleminson

A hobby turned to enterprise, Cleminson is one of several California potteries whose clever hand-decorated wares are attracting the attention of today's collectors. The Cleminsons started their business at their El Monte home in 1941 and were so successful that eventually they expanded to a modern plant that employed more than 150 workers. They produced not only dinnerware and kitchen items such as cookie jars, canisters, and accessories, but novelty wall vases, small trays, plaques, etc., as well. Though nearly always marked, Cleminson wares are easy to spot as you become familiar with their distinctive glaze colors. Their grayed-down blue and green, berry red, and dusty pink say 'Cleminson' as clearly as their trademark. Unable to compete with foreign imports, the pottery closed in 1963. Our advisor for this category is Jack Chipman, author of *The Collector's Encyclopedia of California Pottery;* he is listed in the Directory under California.

Ashtray, fish, 2 rests at bottom edge, 2¾x7½" 28.00
Ashtray, stylized fruit, ftd, 7" 32.00
Bowl, Distlefink, duck's head forms hdl, oblong, 12" 45.00
Butter dish, Distlefink 25.00
Cookie jar, Carrot Head 165.00

Cookie jar, Cottage House, $210.00.

Cookie jar, Potbellied Stove 200.00
Cookie jar, Way to a Man's Heart 175.00
Cookie jar, 6-sided shape, tulip finial 185.00
Creamer, rooster 20.00
Creamer & sugar bowl, chicken 40.00

Cup & saucer, Gramma's 35.00
Cup & saucer, My Old Man, lg 35.00
Dinner bell, Fancy Pants maid, bl dress/fancy leggings, w/tag 85.00
Drip jar, Cherry, w/lid 40.00
Egg cup, lady in apron figural, early 36.00
Egg cup, man w/blk coat & striped pants 36.00
Hairpin holder, soldier 30.00
Mug, Morning After, w/ice bag lid 35.00
Oyster dish, World Is Our... on easel shape, 6½" dia 25.00
Pancake server, Big Top Circus, juvenile 75.00
Pie bird, mc on wht, Betty Cleminson's initials in mold, 4½" 32.00
Pitcher, Cherry, oil-can shape 55.00
Pitcher, Distlefink, 9½" 35.00
Plaque, boy & girl profiles, oval, 4x3", pr 45.00
Plaque, gardener w/rake, 6x8" 35.00
Plaque, girl's face on heart form, Stay As Sweet As You Are 22.00
Plaque, grapes, 6½x6½" 35.00
Plaque, man w/scissors, lady w/basket, 4x5", pr 55.00
Plate, florals, molded scalloped rim, 7" 30.00
Plate, rooster crowing, yel decor in rim, 9½" 35.00
Recipe holder, hearts & flowers on ftd/rectangular base, 4" L 28.00
Ring holder, bulldog 25.00
Shakers, Cherry, 6", pr 40.00
Shakers, Gala Gray, stylized woman, 6¼" 40.00
Shakers, kangaroos, w/orig label, pr 50.00
Shakers, Katrina, pr 40.00
Spoon rest, Cherry, 6x8" 36.00
Spoon rest, floral, 3-lobed, 8½" 27.00
Spoon rest, fruit 27.00
Sprinkler, Chinese boy 40.00
String holder, heart form 45.00
Tankard, Proud Papa 85.00
Tray, Distlefink, 12" 30.00
Wall pocket, chef's head, stamped mk, 7¼" 75.00
Wall pocket, coffee grinder 45.00
Wall pocket, frying pan 45.00
Wall pocket, scoop w/pnt flowers, 9" 40.00
Wall pocket, teapot, Penny Saved Is a Penny 40.00

Clewell

Charles Walter Clewell was a metal worker who perfected the technique of plating an entire ceramic vessel with a thin layer of copper or bronze treated with an oxidizing agent to produce a natural deterioration of the surface. Through trial and error, he was able to control the degree of patina achieved. In the early stages, the metal darkened and if allowed to develop further formed a natural turquoise-blue or green corrosion. He worked alone in his small Akron, Ohio, studio from about 1906, buying undecorated pottery from several Ohio firms, among them Weller, Owens, and Cambridge. His work is usually marked. Clewell died in 1965, having never revealed his secret process to others.

Prices for Clewell have advanced rapidly during the past few years along with the Arts and Crafts market in general. Right now, good examples are bringing whatever the traffic will bear.

Humidor, gr/brn patina, riveted design on body & finial, 4" 350.00
Jardiniere, gr/brn patina, flared, bulbous, 5½" 525.00
Mug, copper clad w/external rivets, mk Clewell Coppers, 4⅛" ...125.00
Mug, gr/brn patina, mk, 4" 130.00
Vase, crusty gr on orange-copper, #321-24, 6¼" 700.00
Vase, gr patina, mk, #321, 7" 500.00
Vase, gr/brn patina, broad shoulders, #369-2, 5½" 550.00
Vase, gr/brn patina, ear of corn design, Weller blank, 10" 1,000.00

Vase, gr/brn patina, flared petal rim, ftd, 6½" 425.00
Vase, gr/brn patina, mk, 10½" 650.00
Vase, gr/brn patina, stylized leaves & geometrics, 9¾" 600.00
Vase, gr/brn patina, tapered form, #345-2-6, 6½" 425.00
Vase, gr/brn patina, waisted, 15½" 1,700.00
Vase, gr/brn patina, 4-ftd, jewels, orig label, 9" 1,100.00

Clews

Brothers Ralph and James Clews were potters who operated in Cobridge in the Staffordshire district from 1817 to 1835. They are best known for their blue and white transfer-printed earthenwares, which included American Views, Moral Maxims, Picturesque Views, and English Views. A series called *Three Tours of Dr. Syntax* contained thirty-one different scenes with each piece bearing a descriptive title. Another popular series was *Pictures of Sir David Wilkie* with seven prints. (Though we once thought that the Don Quixote series was made by Clews, new information seems to indicate that it was made instead by Davenport.) Both printed and impressed marks were used, often incorporating the pattern name as well as the pottery. See also Staffordshire, Historical.

Plate, Christmas Eve, dk bl transfer, 10½", EX 170.00
Plate, Christmas Eve, dk bl transfer, 8¾", M 285.00
Plate, Dr Syntax Reading His Tour, dk bl transfer, 8⅞" 165.00
Plate, man w/donkey, dk bl transfer, flake, 10" 120.00
Plate, Mosaic Tracery, dk bl transfer, 10⅛", EX 45.00
Plate, Valentine, dk bl transfer, 9" 100.00

Clifton

Clifton Art Pottery of Clifton, New Jersey, was organized ca 1903. Until 1911 when they turned to the production of wall and floor tile, they made artware of several varieties. The founders were Fred Tschirner and William A. Long. Long had developed the method for underglaze slip painting that had been used at the Lonhuda Pottery in Steubenville, Ohio, in the 1890s. Crystal Patina, the first artware made by the small company, utilized a fine white body and flowing, blended colors, the earliest a green crystalline. Indian Ware, copied from the pottery of the American Indians, was usually decorated in black geometric designs on red clay. (On the occasions when white was used in addition to the black, the ware was often not as well executed; so even though two-color decoration is very rare, it is normally not as desirable to the collector.) Robin's Egg Blue, pale blue on the white body, and Tirrube, a slip-decorated matt ware, were also produced.

Vase, Indian Ware, geometric decoration in dark brown and beige on brick red, #241, 10½x12", $750.00.

Vase, Crystal Patina, caramel to buff matt, can neck, 5x4" 325.00
Vase, Crystal Patina, celadon, gourd shape, 1906, 7x3" 325.00
Vase, Crystal Patina, fish/waves on gr, spherical, 1906, 3½x4" ...700.00
Vase, Crystal Patina, gr & beige on lt gr flambe, 1906, 8x7" 375.00

Vase, Crystal Patina, poppies emb on turq, 1905, 7x5", NM 400.00
Vase, Crystal Patina, silver o/l on gr, hdls, 1906, 4½x5" 300.00
Vase, Crystal Patina, silver o/l trellis, bulbous, 1906, 5x4" 400.00
Vase, Indian Ware, blk/tan on red, #160, 5½x7½" 350.00
Vase, Indian Ware, interlocking waves, 2-color on red, 2⅝" 150.00

Clocks

In the early days of our country's history, clock makers were influenced by styles imported from Europe. They copied the European's cabinets and reconstructed their movements — needed materials were in short supply; modifications had to be made. Of necessity was born mainspring motive power and spring clocks. Wooden movements were made on a mass-production basis as early as 1808. Before the middle of the century, metal movements had been developed.

Today's collectors prefer clocks from the 18th and 19th centuries with pendulum-regulated movements. Bracket clocks made during this period utilized the shorter pendulum improvised in 1658 by Fromentiel, a prominent English clock maker. These smaller square-face clocks usually were made with a dome top fitted with a handle or a decorative finial. The case was usually walnut or ebony and was sometimes decorated with pierced brass mountings. Brackets were often mounted on the wall to accommodate the clock, hence the name. The banjo clock was patented in 1802 by Simon Willard. It derived its descriptive name from its banjo-like shape. A similar but more elaborate style was called the lyre clock.

The first electric novelty clocks were developed in the 1940s. Lux, who was the major producer, had been in business since 1912, making wind-up novelties during the '20s and '30s. Another company, Mastercrafter Novelty Clocks, first obtained a patent to produce these clocks in the late 1940s. Other manufacturers were Keebler, Westclox, and Columbia Time. The cases were made of china, Syroco, wood, and plastic; most were animated and some had pendulettes. Prices vary according to condition and rarity.

Except for the novelty clocks whose values are on the increase, clock prices have been stable for several years. Unless noted otherwise, values are given for clocks in excellent condition. Clocks that have been altered, damaged, or have had parts replaced are worth considerably less.

Our advisor is Bruce A. Austin; he is listed in the Directory under New York. Our novelty clock advisors is Anita Levi (Allegheny Mountain Antiques Gallery); she is listed in the Directory under Pennsylvania.

Key:
br — brass   reg — regulator
dl — dial   rswd — rosewood
esc — escapement   T — time only
mcr — mercury   t & s — time & strike
mvt — movement   wt — weight
og — ogee   vnr — veneer
pnd — pendulum   2nds — seconds

Calendar Clocks

Fashion #4, dbl-dl, walnut case, Seth Thomas mvt 1,800.00
G Maranville, office drop, 8-day, walnut case, 12" dl, 34" 1,100.00
Ithaca, walnut Gothic Revival, rpt face, w/pnd & key, 29" 700.00
Ithaca, 8-day, t&s, 8" dls, walnut case, 33", EX 1,200.00
Ithaca #10, dbl-dl, farmer's, walnut case 750.00
Ithaca #11, dbl-dl, octagon, walnut case 750.00
Ithaca #7, dbl-dl, cottage, walnut case 750.00
Ithaca #9, dbl-dl, cottage, walnut case 1,000.00
New Haven, oak, dbl-dl, wall 1,295.00

New Haven, time & calendar, short drop 495.00
New Haven-Jerome & Co Register, 8-day, spring mvt, dbl-dl, EX ...825.00
Seth Thomas, dbl-dl, rfn walnut case, Pat...1876, 20" 385.00
Seth Thomas #3, dbl-dl, parlor 895.00
Seth Thomas Office #4, 8-day, t&s, walnut vnr case, 28" 950.00
Waterbury, time & calendar, short drop 495.00
Waterbury #44, dbl-dl, walnut 995.00
Welch Spring & Co #2, upside-down mvt, 12" dl, walnut case, 36" 1,500.00

Novelty Clocks

Antique auto, Mastercrafters, electric 125.00
Ballerina, musical, wood & metal w/plastic face, United 160.00
Band leader (guitar), US Clock Co 325.00
Bird in cage, Mastercrafters 150.00
Black cat, blinking eye, 30-hour T, Lux, EX 250.00
Boy fishing, metal, United 150.00
Bulldog, Lux, EX 150.00
Chef's head, Sessions 125.00
Coach & driver w/horses, United, electric 135.00
Coffeepot perking, Mastercrafters, electric, EX 90.00
Couple swinging, United, fancy case 225.00
Cuckoo, red bird, Lux, EX orig 30.00
Dachshund, rolling eyes, Oswold, NM 300.00
Davy Crockett fighting bear, Haddon 420.00
Deco fish swimming, Sessions, electric 250.00
Elephant swinger, Junghan, old & orig 1,295.00
Fireplace, plastic, Mastercrafters, 1950s 90.00
Girl swinging, marbleized case, Mastercrafters 125.00
Granny rocking, Haddon, electric 125.00
Lighthouse & moving ships, electric, United, EX 120.00
Lighthouse w/sailboats, United 250.00
Majorette twirling baton, United, electric 150.00
Popeye, Aerolux, glow bulb, w/base 350.00
Potbelly stove, United 160.00
Roosevelt, Man of the Hour, animated 195.00
Sally Rand, Lux 495.00
See-Saw, Haddon, electric 175.00
Ship's wheel & fish, United, electric 135.00
Statue of Liberty w/NY harbor scene, United 395.00
Water running, German mantel style, mini 1,298.00

Shelf Clocks

Birge and Fuller, Bristol, Connecticut, Gothic double-steeple mantel clock, ca 1840, 27½", EX, $1,200.00.

Ansonia, br & glass, scrolled urn top, mcr pnd, 15½" 225.00
Ansonia, fancy gr marble w/urn 450.00
Ansonia, outside esc, crystal reg 450.00
Ansonia, rswd Gothic Revival, paper face, pnd, 19" 250.00
Ansonia, steeple, 8-day, t&s, walnut case, 20", VG 225.00
Birge Mallory & Co, 30-hr br mvt, fruit crest, rstr, 26" 225.00

Bronze B Franklin w/Declaration of Independence, 1850s, 22" ..950.00
Bronze bell form, cast florals, winged cat ft, 12⅜" 275.00
E Terry & Sons, Empire w/mahog vnr, wooden works, 30", EX ..275.00
E&GW Bartholomew, Bristol CT, Empire mahog vnr, pnd, 30", VG 275.00
English, gilt-metal pineapple finial, mahog case, 1800s, 21" ...2,400.00
English skeleton, 2-train, walnut/beveled glasses, 1871, 25½" ..2,225.00
English skeleton, 8-day, wood base/br columns/dome, 15½" ...1,200.00
Fr, Amazon bronze figure, marble case, 4 claw ft, 21", VG 150.00
Fr, bronze maiden w/dove by palm, dl in base, 1850s, 22" 950.00
Fr, gilt bronze eagle above Pegasus panel w/columns, 1880s, 20" .1,250.00
Fr, Shakespeare figure, patinated metal & marble, 8-day, 1880s .525.00
German cuckoo, 8-day t&s, dbl fusee, walnut case, 24", EX ...,1,825.00
Gilbert, Amphion model, walnut case 1,100.00
Gillette skeleton, 2-train, br columns/marble base, 8-day 2,000.00
Gilt bronze maiden on slate base w/cvg, 1880s, 25¼" 900.00
Kitchen, Gilbert, rfn walnut w/Eastlake cvg, pnd, 19½" 165.00
Kitchen, rfn walnut w/relief cvgs, br works, pnd, 21", VG 165.00
Kitchen, Seth Thomas, rfn oak w/br ornaments, pnd, 22½" 150.00
Lefebvre & Fils..., marble & br, figural finial, pnd, 20" 1,000.00
M Welton, NY, ogee w/figured vnr, pnt wooden face, 25x15" 250.00
Mark Leavenworth & Son, mahog pillar & scroll, 1825, 30" 900.00
New Haven Ivanhoe, seated figure, bronzed metal, 16x20", EX .365.00
Paris, Louis XV design, florals on gr, cartouch shape, 32" 1,750.00
Peerless Blk Forest, mahog w/br face, chimes/pnd, 13½" 300.00
PH Mourey, wht alabaster w/gilt cast youth & cottage, rprs, 12" .250.00
Pillar & scroll, rfn mahog/curly maple vnr, pnd, 31" 1,250.00
Pinchon a Paris, br & cast metal, maiden detail, pnd, 20" 800.00
Quarter-sawn Mission Oak, Fr br works, pnd, 12½" 250.00
Riley Whiting, mahog vnr Emp w/ebonized trim & gold, 36" 525.00
Rouge marble & ormolu bust of maiden, rnd face, 19th C, 18" ..550.00
Samuel Terry, Emp, rfn mahog, gold stencil, pnd, 33" 195.00
Seth Thomas, cottage, 8-day, strike, walnut case, 14½", NM 135.00
Seth Thomas, mahog Gothic style, br works, pnd, 13" 125.00
Seth Thomas, mahog w/bird transfer on glass, pnd, 16⅜" 265.00
Seth Thomas, og w/figured vnr, wts/pnd, 25x15" 140.00
Seth Thomas, presentation crystal reg 1,295.00
Seth Thomas, rswd vnr, br works, pnd, 9", EX 100.00
Seth Thomas, rswd vnr Emp triple decker, 33" 300.00
Seth Thomas Bee Hive, 8-day, t&s, porc dl, ebony case w/cvd bee 225.00
Villardry Paris, wht marble w/enameled ormolu, pnd, 17" 700.00
Walnut/mirrored case w/2 gilt-metal cherubs, 1870s, 21½" 160.00
Waterbury, og w/rswd vnr facade, rvpt, pnd, 19x12" 165.00
Welch, walnut, lg lion heads, parlor 600.00
Welch Spring & Co Italian #3, 20" walnut vnr case, EX 575.00
2nd Emp Fr ormolu w/2 putti & goat, 1950s, 20¼" 2,500.00

Tall Case Clocks

Butternut Chpndl, man's face w/moving eyes in arch, 1780s, 95" ...4,000.00
Cherry, trn columns, scrolled apron, ball ft, pnd, 92" 1,600.00
Cherry w/old varnish, broken arch pediment w/cvg, pnd, 91" 5,000.00
Cherry/mahog/bird's-eye maple, broken arch pediment, pnd, 97" ...4,000.00
Curly maple w/figure, detailed dvtl bonnet, pnt face, pnd, 90" ...5,600.00
Martin & Broswell 1631 Anderston, mahog vnr w/inlay, pnd, 82" ...1,900.00
S Hoadley Plymouth, pine w/grained finish, dvtl base, pnd, 83" ...1,875.00
Sam Stevens, London, marquetry, 8-day t & s, br mvt, rstr, 87" 15,000.00
Scottish, mahog w/flame vnr, Gothic-like crest, rfn, 86" 1,900.00
Silas Hoadley, dk stained pine, 31-day dl, 83", VG 800.00
Wm Sellers, japanned case, 8-day, early wts, 88", rstr 14,000.00

Wall Clocks

Ansonia Capitol, mahog 1,000.00
Art Deco mahog case w/ebonized cvd florals, pnd, 28" 300.00

Atkins, jeweler's reg, dbl fusee, rswd vnr, 1856, EX 2,000.00
Banjo, mahog vnr w/br, br finial, pnd, 40½" 900.00
Banjo, mahog vnr w/inlay, lyre shape, eagle finial, pnd, 38" 1,300.00
Banjo, mahog w/banded vnr facade, 20th C repro, 40½" 600.00
Chelsea, oak, 1-wt, reg 1,400.00
Daniel Balch...MA, br mvt, wag-on-wall, 12½" dl, G 400.00
Federal banjo, mahog, pnt dl, rvpt tablet, 8-day, 1820s, 34" 1,600.00
Gilbert No 5, walnut, 1-wt, reg 2,500.00
H Tifft Pat, banjo, mahog vnr, rpl rvpt glass, eagle finial, 32" 825.00
Ingraham Treasure Island, banjo, 8-day, t&s, mahog case, 39", EX ...400.00
Lenzkirsch Reg #5, 8-day, porc dl, pnd, mahog case, 1877, 49" ..975.00
Morbier, br, 8-day repeater 500.00
Regulator, ebonized case w/enameled face, pnd, 33" 400.00
Regulator, oak w/br works, pnd & key, rstr, 38x19" 175.00
Regulator, rfn walnut w/pnd & key, minor vnr damage, 32" 325.00
Samuel Whiting, mahog banjo w/gilt, rvpt at waist, pnd, 34" 1,200.00
Seth Thomas Gallery, mahog, 14" dl 1,700.00
Seth Thomas King Jewett, kitchen, 8-day t&s/cathedral gong, EX ...460.00
Vienna reg, ebonized case, w/pnd & key, 33" 435.00
Vienna reg, 2-toned wood, Minerva head crest, pnd, 47" 300.00
Waltham, rope front, 8-day, mini banjo 600.00
Waterbury, oak, t&s, Cincinnati model 695.00
Waterbury, oak, t&s, mini schoolhouse 495.00
Waterbury, oak, 2-wt, reg 1,495.00

Cloisonne

Cloisonne is a method of decorating metal with enameling. Fine metal wires are soldered onto the metal body following the lines of a predetermined design. The resulting channels are filled in with enamels of various colors, and the item is fired. The final step is a smoothing process that assures even exposure of the wire pattern. The art is predominately Oriental and has been practiced continuously, except during war years, since the 16th century. The most excellent examples date from 1865 until the turn of the century. The early 20th century export variety is usually lightweight and the workmanship inferior. Modern wares are of good quality and are produced in Taiwan as well as China.

Several variations of the basic art include plique-a-jour, achieved by removing the metal body after firing, leaving only the transparent enamel work; foil cloisonne, using transparent or semitranslucent enameling over a layer of embossed silver covering the metal body of the vessel; wireless cloisonne, made by removing the wire dividers prior to firing; and cloisonne executed on ceramic, wood, or lacquer rather than metal.

Vase, two large carp swimming on blue-gray, morning-glory border, Japanese signature, 15", $1,100.00.

Box, ho-ho & kiro on red, navy bands, sq, w/lid, Meiji, 4½" 250.00
Censer, dragons/phoenixes/etc, elephant finial, 19th C, 23" ...1,800.00
Charger, birds & flowering bamboo, mc on bl, 18" dia 200.00

Vase, peacocks/mums on cream crackle, gold rim, Nagoya, 7" 80.00
Vase, sparrows between brocade bands on gr, w/lid, Meiji, 12" ...300.00

Clothing and Accessories

'Second-hand' or 'vintage?' It's all a matter of opinion. But these days it's considered good taste (downright fashionable) to wear clothing from Victorian to styles from the '60s. Jackets with padded shoulders from the '30s are 'trendy.' Jewelry from the Art Deco era is just as beautiful and often less expensive than current copies. But why settle for new when the genuine article can be bought for the same price with exquisite lace that no reproduction can rival! When once the 'style' of the day was so strictly obeyed, today, in New York and the larger cities of California and Texas, in particular, nothing well designed and constructed is out of style. And though costumes by such designers as Chanel, Fortuny, and Lanvin may bring four-figure prices at fine auction houses, as a general rule, prices are very modest considering the wonderful fabrics one may find in vintage clothing, many of which are no longer available. Cashmere coats, elegant furs, and sequined or beaded gowns can be bought for only a small fraction of today's retail. Though some are strictly collectors, many do buy their clothes to wear. Care must be given to alterations, and gentle cleaning methods employed to avoid damage that would detract from their value. For any valuable garment requiring more than minimal repair, consult a professional restorer.

Prices in vintage clothing depend on condition, basic materials, trims, label (if available), construction, where found, scarcity of type, and desirability as a collectible item or a wearable historic artifact. For further information read *Antique & Vintage Clothing* by Diane Snyder-Haug, and *Vintage Hats & Bonnets* by Susan Langley available from Collector Books or your local bookstore. Our advisor for this category is Maryanne Dolan, author of *Value Guide to Vintage Clothing, 1880 – 1960* (which we highly recommend); she is listed in the Directory under California.

Key:
embr — embroidery   n/s — no sleeves
l/s — long sleeves   s/s — short sleeves

Blazer, boy's, linen, w/matching short trousers 40.00
Blazer, lady's, Ralph Lauren, 1972, M 500.00
Blouse, lace Gibson-girl style, NM 55.00
Bustle, bedspring type, EX 55.00
Bustle, Crinolette, long wires 52.00
Bustle, wire mesh, EX 85.00
Cape, child's, flannel wool w/silk cord embr 45.00
Cape, lady's, blk jet, Victorian, long, EX 95.00
Cape, lady's, blk silk, Victorian, long, NM 500.00
Cape, lady's, wht corded cotton, embr ruffled trim 45.00
Coat, baby christening; ivory wool w/much crochet, w/hood 90.00
Coat, lady's, blk velvet w/silver fox collar, full-length 275.00
Coat, lady's, brn wool w/chinchilla fur collar/cuffs/front, 1940s .275.00
Coat, man's, leather, Harley-Davidson, knee-length, 1930s, EX ..300.00
Coat, toddler's, Edwardian lace 65.00
Collar, sequin & net 12.50
Dress, blk rayon top w/silk blk & wht skirt, s/s, 1950s 35.00
Dress, blk silk taffeta, full-length, s/s, 1890s, EX 250.00
Dress, brn satin, lace insert at neck, l/s, 1920s 120.00
Dress, child's, dotted Swiss, hand smocking, full skirt, s/s 25.00
Dress, child's, net w/silk lining, ruffles at neck & /s, rosettes 120.00
Dress, christening; pin-tucked lace, ca 1890, EX 65.00
Dress, christening; wht w/embr, lg collar, Victorian, 28" L 35.00
Dress, cocktail; blk w/satin trim, n/s, str skirt, 1950s 40.00
Dress, cocktail; jet beaded top, n/s, blk taffeta skirt 275.00

Dress, dinner; lace w/beaded sleeves, ca 1914, EX **65.00**
Dress, fitted bodice, s/s, full skirt, late 1940s, NM **35.00**
Dress, floral gauze w/blk lace inserts, pk sash, Edwardian **150.00**
Dress, pk dotted Swiss, s/s, ca 1918 ....**55.00**
Dress, red wool, full skirt, collar, l/s, w/cotton petticoat, 1900s ..**150.00**
Dress, silk, full skirt, blk dots on gr, l/s, 1950s **35.00**
Dress, toddler's, wht corded material w/some embr & cutwork **25.00**
Dress, wht lawn, simple drop waist, s/s, 1920s **60.00**
Duster, cotton, s/s, 1950s **15.00**
Fur, blouse collar, mink, 18" **5.00**
Fur, cape, lady's, ocelot, 1940s, 27" **165.00**
Fur, coat, lady's, Persian lamb w/mink trim, full-length, EX **65.00**
Fur, coat, lady's, seal, heavy, full-length, EX **225.00**
Fur, coat, man's, bear, mid-length w/sheep collar, EX **750.00**
Fur, collar, lady's, raccoon, 36" **10.00**
Fur, hat, lady's, mink pillbox **10.00**
Fur, hat, lady's, ranch mink **25.00**
Fur, jacket, lady's, mink, 4 skins w/heads, EX **25.00**
Fur, jacket, lady's, monkey, l/s, wide collar, short **850.00**
Fur, jacket, lady's, natural red fox, cowl collar, tail trim, NY **250.00**
Fur, jacket, lady's, sheared beaver, hip-length **55.00**
Gloves, wht cotton, 1950s, pr **5.00**
Gloves, wht kid, pr **10.00**
Gown, christening; heavily embr eyelet, 47", +matching bonnet .**85.00**
Gown, christening; wht embr net w/silk slip, 44" **150.00**
Hat, child's, gable bonnet style, 1880s, EX **145.00**
Hat, child's, gold/bl silk spoon bonnet, 1860s, EX **135.00**
Hat, child's, woven straw, elaborate weaving, 1880s, EX **95.00**
Hat, lady's, blk crepe (mourning), 1880s **65.00**
Hat, lady's, boudoir, satin w/ribon trim **65.00**
Hat, lady's, brn satin flapper style w/amber-tone ornament **30.00**
Hat, lady's, chip straw w/velvet rose, 1870s, EX **88.00**
Hat, lady's, cloche, Deco style w/Bakelite ornament, EX **48.00**
Hat, lady's, cloche, felt flowers, 1920s **55.00**
Hat, lady's, cloche, navy straw, 1920s **45.00**
Hat, lady's, crinoline, orig ribbons, 1860s, EX **125.00**
Hat, lady's, flowered pancake style, 1900s, EX **110.00**
Hat, lady's, gold lace, lavishly trimmed, 1890s **85.00**
Hat, lady's, gr cloth w/plum trim, 1870s **82.00**
Hat, lady's, lace & velvet, wide brim, 1916, EX **225.00**
Hat, lady's, maroon smocked velvet w/huge rose, ca 1900, NM ..**110.00**
Hat, lady's, mourning bonnet, w/lace weepers, ca 1830 ....**250.00**
Hat, lady's, plush w/plumes & coral flowers, Edwardian **250.00**
Hat, lady's, rubber bathing cap, 1930s-40s **35.00**
Hat, lady's, straw, bl w/ribbon, 1870s **65.00**
Hat, lady's, straw, flowers along wide brim, 1930s **48.00**
Hat, lady's, straw, rolled rim, Lilly Dache **35.00**
Hat, lady's, straw, work type w/full-wing feathers as trim **300.00**
Hat, lady's, straw bonnet, wht mums, 1880s **75.00**
Hat, lady's, straw bonnet w/brn plume, 1860s, EX **80.00**
Hat, lady's, straw w/wht glass grapes, 1890s **125.00**
Hat, lady's, toque, rosebuds & lg bow, Edwardian, EX **75.00**
Hat, lady's, turq & blk velvet, cloche **75.00**
Hat, lady's, velvet, wide brim, 1918 ....**110.00**
Hat, lady's, wht straw, forget-me-nots, ca 1900 ....**110.00**
Hat, lady's, wool felt w/sequins & beads, 1920s **55.00**
Hat, man's, bowler, M **50.00**
Hat, man's, Derby **45.00**
Hat, man's, Harley-Davidson, all leather, early **200.00**
Hat, man's, Panama fedora, 1930s, MIB **75.00**
Hat, man's, snap brim, wool felt, grosgrain band, 1930-40 ....**35.00**
Hat, man's, Stetson, felt, full sz, in ornate orig box, NM **50.00**
Hat, man's, Stetson Hombert, w/label, 1930s **50.00**
Hat, man's, top hat, beaver, designer label, blk ribbons **450.00**

Hat, man's, top hat, beaver, dk, no label **85.00**
Hat, man's, top hat, brn felt w/blk ribbons **600.00**
Hat, man's, top hat, silk, collapsible **65.00**
Hat, man's, top hat, stove-pipe style, beaver, w/label **295.00**
Hat, teenage girl's, velvet w/gold lame & circular feathers **95.00**
Jacket, lady's, plush, l/s, Victorian, EX **65.00**
Jacket, Lee Storm Rider, bl denim, fully lined, NM **100.00**
Jacket, man's, motorcycle, blk leather, Wilson, 1950s, EX **250.00**
Jacket, man's, wht silk mandarin style w/embr, l/s, pre-1940s **75.00**
Jeans, Levi Big Bells, 1970, M unused, from $25 to **35.00**
Kimono, red silk w/embr dragon, pre-1940, lt wear **125.00**
Kimono jacket, silk w/bamboo pattern, l/s, pre-1940s **125.00**
Mantilla, Spanish lace, blk, sm **20.00**
Mittens, lady's, lace, long, 1860s, pr **45.00**
Mittens, man's, leather, fleece lined, Harley-Davidson tag, pr **225.00**
Night cap, net & lace, silk roses **45.00**
Pantaloons, wht cotton **25.00**
Parasol, bl damask, much trim, ca 1830, EX **145.00**
Parasol, chintz w/bamboo shaft/ivory tip, Victorian, 36", EX **135.00**
Parasol, silk, folding hdl, Victorian, sm **65.00**
Parasol, teen's, gold fabric & tassel, wood hdl **75.00**
Peignoir, ecru lace w/satin lining, 1920s **85.00**
Petticoat, embr trim, 32" **12.50**
Petticoat, wht, 3 rows crochet trim **40.00**
Robe, bl w/blk valenciennes on skirt, silk ribbon, Victorian **155.00**
Shawl, Deco design on silk, open weave, 1930s, 68"+12" fringe .**185.00**
Shawl, machine woven in paisley pattern, 68x69" **115.00**
Shirt, man's work; Big Yank Union Made, tan, l/s, M **75.00**
Shirtwaist, bl watered silk, l/s, 1860s **50.00**
Shoes, baby's, high-button style, lt bl leather **88.00**
Shoes, baby's, wht leather, ca 1900 ....**75.00**

Shoes, black suede and leather Oxfords, 2½" heels, 1930s, $55.00 for the pair.

Shoes, lady's, blk leather pumps, Cuban heels, 1920s **35.00**
Shoes, lady's, blk patent leather, pointed toes, 3½" heel, pr **55.00**
Shoes, lady's, leather high-button style, EX **50.00**
Shoes, lady's, open toe, ankle strap, 3" heel, NM **45.00**
Shoes, lady's, purple suede, pointed toes, 2½" heel, pr **50.00**
Shoes, lady's wedding; wht satin **40.00**
Skirt, hoop; crinoline, Civil War era, EX **135.00**
Skirt & blouse, lace & net, l/s, high collar, ca 1918 ....**100.00**
Stole, embr silk, knotted fringe, 6x22x72" **95.00**
Sweater, beadwork on wool, l/s, NM **45.00**
Tie, HP horse, 1940s, NM **20.00**
Undersleeves, much embr, Civil War era, pr **55.00**
Veil, bridal; orange blossoms & buds on headpc, ca 1900 ....**120.00**
Veil, bridal; tulle w/orange blossoms on headpc, long, '50s **45.00**
Vest, child's, blk velvet w/blk jet bead trim, Victorian **150.00**
Vest, denim w/sheepskin lining, 1950s, M **24.00**
Waist, blk w/blk beads, Victorian, l/s, EX **125.00**
Waist, taffeta w/lace & velvet trim, l/s, Victorian **60.00**

Cobalt Glass

Cobalt glass is characterized by its deep transparent blue color obtained by mixing cobalt oxide and alumina to the batch. It may be found in free-blown, mold-blown, and pressed glassware. See Blown Glass.

Bowl, blown, 15 swirled ribs, flared lip, appl ft, 3⅝x5" **440.00**
Bowl, Expanded Dmn, blown, appl ft, 3⅛x4¼" **250.00**
Box, HP birds & flowers, 3¾x4¾" dia **265.00**
Box, wht fleur-de-lis amid crisscross pattern, hinged, 5x5" dia ...**325.00**
Creamer, Expanded Dmn, appl hdl, 3½" **165.00**
Sugar bowl, emb flowers, ped ft, resilvered hdls, 7½x6¾" **275.00**
Sugar bowl, paneled, flakes on ft, 5⅝" **200.00**
Sugar bowl, paneled, sm flakes, 8¾" **660.00**
Vase, gold beading & jewels, 9" **200.00**
Vase, urn form, ftd, flared rim, 7x6¾" **25.00**

Coca-Cola

J.S. Pemberton, creator of Coca-Cola, originated his world-famous drink in 1886. From its inception, the Coca-Cola Company began an incredible advertising campaign which has proven to be one of the most successful promotions in history. The quantity and diversity of advertising material put out by Coca-Cola in the last one hundred years is literally mind-boggling. From the beginning, the company has projected an image of wholesomeness and Americana. Beautiful women in Victorian costumes, teenagers and schoolchildren, blue- and white-collar workers, the men and women of the Armed Forces, even Santa Claus have appeared in advertisements with a Coke in their hands. Some of the earliest collectibles include trays, syrup dispensers, gum jars, pocket mirrors, and calendars. Many of these items fetch prices in the thousands of dollars. Later examples include radios, signs, lighters, thermometers, playing cards, clocks, and toys — particularly toy trucks.

In 1970 the Coca-Cola Company initialed a multimillion-dollar 'image-refurbishing campaign' which introduced the new 'Dynamic Contour' logo, a twisting white ribbon under the Coca-Cola and Coke trademarks. The new logo often serves as a cut-off point to the purist collector. Newer and very ardent collectors, however, relish the myriad of items marketed since that date, as they often cannot afford the high prices that the vintage pieces command. For more information we recommend *Petretti's Coca-Cola Collectibles Price Guide*, 1994 edition (available from Nostalgia Publications whose address you will find under Auctions in the Directory); *Huxford's Collectible Advertising, Third Edition*; *BJ Summers' Guide to Coca-Cola*; and *Collectible Coca-Cola Toy Trucks* by Gael deCourtivron. You may wish to call our advisors for this category, Craig and Donna Stifter, at 630-789-5780; they are listed in the Directory under Illinois.

Key:
CC — Coca-Cola   tm — trademark

Reproductions and Fantasies

Beware of reproductions! Prices are given for the genuine original articles, but the symbol (+) at the end of some of the following lines indicate items that have been reproduced. Warning! The 1924, 1925, and 1935 calendars have been reproduced. They are identical in almost every way; only a professional can tell them apart. These are *very* deceiving! Watch for frauds: genuinely old celluloid items ranging from combs, mirrors, knives, and forks to doorknobs that have been recently etched with a new double-lined trademark. Still another area of concern deals with reproduction and fantasy items. A fantasy item is a novelty made to appear authentic with inscriptions such as 'Tiffany Studios,' 'Trans Pan Expo,' 'World's Fair,' etc. In reality, these items never existed as originals. For instance, don't be fooled by a Coca-Cola cash register; no originals are known to exist! Large mirrors for bars are being reproduced and are often selling for $10.00 to $50.00.

Of the hundreds of reproductions (designated 'R' in the following examples) and fantasies (designated 'F') on the market today, these are the most deceiving.

Belt buckle, no originals thought to exist (F), up to **10.00**
Bottle, dk amber, w/arrows, heavy, narrow spout (R) **10.00**
Bottle carrier, wood, yel w/red logo, holds 6 bottles (R) **10.00**
Clock, Gilbert regulator, battery op, ¾-sz, NM+ (R) **175.00**
Cooler, Glascock Jr, made by Coca-Cola USA (R) **350.00**
Doorknob, glass etched w/tm (F) **3.00**
Knife, bottle shape, 1970s, many variations (F), ea **5.00**
Knife, fork, or spoon w/celluloid hdl, newly etched tm (F) **5.00**
Letter opener, stamped metal, Coca-Cola for 5¢ (F) **3.00**
Pocket watch, often old watch w/new face (R) **10.00**
Pocketknife, yel & red, 1933 World's Fair (F) **2.00**
Sign, cb, lady w/fur, dtd 1911, 9x11" (F) **3.00**
Soda fountain glass holder, word 'Drink' not orig (R) **5.00**
Thermometer, bottle form, DONASCO, 17" (R) **10.00**
Trade card, copy of 1905 'Bathtub' foldout, emb 1978 (R) **25.00**

The following items have been reproduced and are among the most deceptive of all:
Pocket mirrors from 1905, 1906, 1908, 1909, 1910, 1911, 1916, and 1920
Trays from 1899, 1910, 1913, 1914, 1917, 1920, 1923, 1925, 1926, 1934, and 1937
Tip trays from 1907, 1909, 1910, 1913, 1914, 1917, and 1920
Knives: many versions of the German brass model
Cartons: wood versions, yellow with logo
Calendars: 1924, 1925, and 1935

These items have been marketed:
Brass thermometer, bottle shape, Taiwan, 24"
Cast-iron toys (none ever made)
Cast-iron door pull, bottle shape, made to look old
Poster, Yes Girl (R)
Button sign, has 1 round hole while original has 4 slots, most have bottle logo, 12", 16", 20" (R)
Bullet trash receptacles (old cans with decals)
Paperweight, rectangular, with Pepsin Gum insert
1930 Bakelite radio, 24" tall, repro is lighter in weight than the original, of poor quality and cheaply made
1949 cooler radio (reproduced with tape deck)
Tin bottle sign, 40"
Fishtail die-cut tin sign, 20" long
Straw holders (no originals exist)
Coca-Cola bicycle with cooler, fantasy item: the piece has been totally made-up, no such original exists
1914 calendar top, reproduction, 11¼x23¾", printed on smooth-finish heavy ivory paper
Countless trays — most unauthorized (must read 'American Artworks; Coshocton, OH.')

Centennial Items

The Coca-Cola Company celebrated its 100th birthday in 1986, and amidst all the fanfare came many new collectible items, all sporting the 100th-anniversary logo. These items are destined to become an important part of the total Coca-Cola collectible spectrum. The following pieces are among the most popular centennial items.

Bottle, gold-dipped, in velvet sleeve, 6½-oz **60.00**
Bottle, Hutchinson, amber, Root Co, ½-oz, 3 in case **375.00**
Bottle, International, set of 9 in plexiglas case **450.00**

Bottle, leaded crystal, 100th logo, 6½-oz, MIB 150.00
Medallion, bronze, 3" dia, w/box 100.00
Pin set, wood fr, 101 pins 300.00
Scarf, silk, 30x30" 40.00
Thermometer, glass cover, 14" dia, M 35.00

Coca-Cola Originals

Ashtray, 1950s, ruby glass, set of 4 in card suit shapes, MIB 425.00
Bank, 1950s, Marx, red battery-op vending machine form, EX ..400.00
Baseball counter, 1907, keeps runs, hits & errors, VG+ 130.00

Blotter, 1906, Restores Energy, 4x9¼", EX, $150.00.

Blotter, 1927, So Refreshing...On Ice, couple at cooler, M 50.00
Blotter, 1931, Pause That Refreshes, lady w/bottle, M 150.00
Blotter, 1935, Delicious/Wholesome..., Canadian, NM 100.00
Blotter, 1940, Greatest Pause on Earth, clown, red disk, NM 80.00
Book, Wonderful World of CC, soft cover, blk/wht photos, NM ..75.00
Bookmark, 1900, celluloid heart, Drink...Delicious..., lady, EX+ .525.00
Bottle, 1900s, amber, str sides, w/arrow 100.00
Bottle, 1910s, clear, str sides, Rochester NY, NM 75.00
Bottle carrier, 1940s, wooden w/wood hdl, wings on side, EX 125.00
Bottle carrier, 1950s, aluminum, 6 for 25¢, NM 80.00
Bowl, 1930s, gr w/emb Drink CC Ice Cold, Vernonware, 4x10", NM ..525.00
Calendar, 1922, girl in pk at ballpark, complete, EX 1,200.00
Calendar, 1925, girl in bl turban, wht stole, complete, EX+ 1,300.00
Calendar, 1932, Old Oaken Bucket, boy & dog, complete, EX+ ...450.00
Calendar, 1940, Pause That Refreshes, girl w/bottle, EX+ 600.00
Calendar, 1946, Sprite boy cover, complete, NM 850.00
Calendar, 1952, Coke Adds Zest, complete, NM 125.00
Calendar holder, 1950s, tin w/button, Drink...in Bottles, NM ...250.00
Calendar holder, 1960s, tin diecut, ...Refreshes You..., 13", NM ...300.00
Can, 1960s, red & wht alternating dmns, VG+ 50.00
Change purse, 1919, Drink...In Bottles..., gold stamped, VG 65.00
Clock, 1905-07, Ingraham, store regulator, wood case, VG 1,000.00
Clock, 1910, Gilbert regulator, Gibson girl decal, VG 4,000.00
Clock, 1939-42, metal fr, ...In Bottles on red dot, 15" dia, VG ...550.00
Clock, 1940s-50s, rocking bottle, Drink..., 20" dia, EX+ 3,000.00
Clock, 1950s, light-up, rnd, #d 1-12, metal fr, EX+ 600.00
Clock, 1960s, Things Go Better w/..., plastic, sq, NM 110.00
Coupon, 1930s, Drink...In Bottles..., 6-pack, M 20.00
Decal, 1950s, Drink...In Bottles, red rectangle, 9x15", NM 45.00
Decal, 1960s, Things Go Better..., NM 25.00
Dispenser, 1940s, Drink...Ice Cold on red, Have a Coke on tap, EX .375.00
Display, carton; 1950s, cb, Shop Here..., 2-tier, 38x14x20", EX+ ..200.00
Display, window; 1922, tri-fold, girl on surfboard, EX 2,600.00
Display bottle, 1948, hard rubber, 48", VG 600.00
Display bottle, 1961, styrofoam, 42", VG+ 210.00
Door plate, 1930s, porc, Thanks Call..., 3-color, 13½x3½", NM ..325.00
Festoon, 1922, Autumn Leaves, 5-pc, EX+ 1,300.00
Festoon, 1939, Petunia, Thirst Stops..., 5-pc, EX 1,000.00

Festoon, 1948, Bathing Beauties, 5-pc, EX 1,800.00
Festoon, 1957, Square Dance, 5-pc, VG+ in orig envelope 1,000.00
Manual/parts catalog, 1950s, VMC machines, leatherette, 9x8", EX+ 250.00
Menu board, 1929, tin, Specials To-Day, rope border, 28x20", G ..150.00
Menu board, 1930s, tin w/blkboard, mc, Canada, 24", NM 650.00
Menu board, 1930s-40s, plywood, 11 slots, Drink CC, 24x14", EX+ ..325.00
Menu board, 1940s, silver-tone metal, red disk, Kay Displays, VG+ ...400.00
Menu board, 1960s, light-up, EX 115.00
Mirror, 1930s, Drink...In Bottles... at top, 12x8", VG 130.00
Napkin, 1914, rice paper, girl w/bottle, EX+ in fr 50.00
Opener, 1910-20, brass w/blk & red enamel, NM 100.00
Opener/spoon, 1930, Happy Days stamped on spoon, EX+ 220.00
Pencil box, 1948, Sprite Boy, cork removes, NM 150.00
Pin, 15 Yrs of Service, 10k gold, oval, NM 50.00
Plate, Vienna Art, girl facing left, gold fr, G (EX+ fr) 575.00
Plate, 1931, Drink...Refresh Yourself, Knowles China, 7", EX 475.00
Playing cards, 1958, Ice Man, VG+ IB 65.00
Playing cards, 1963, Things Go Better..., couple & tree, MIB 70.00
Pocket mirror, 1906, Juanita w/glass, oval, G+ 85.00
Pocket mirror, 1911, girl in wide-brimmed hat, oval, EX+ 225.00
Pocket mirror, 1916, girl leaning on hand w/bottle, EX 200.00
Pocketknife, 1915-25, Drink...In Bottles..., bone hdl, VG+ 95.00
Poster, 1930s, cb, Dancing Lady, Joan Crawford & Clark Gable, EX 1,700.00
Push bar, 1950s, porc, Ice Cold...In Bottles, 3-color, 34", NM ...525.00
Push bar, 1950s, porc, Take Some...Home..., wht on red, 34", NM ...525.00
Push bar, 1970s-80s, pnt steel, Coke Adds Life..., NM 35.00
Radio, 1950, red cooler form, wht letters, rstr, NM 625.00
Roller skates, 1914 (Pat), clamp-on, leather straps, VG+ 900.00
Sheet music, 1906, Nearer My God..., Juanita cover, 13x11", NM ...700.00
Sign, 1910s, porc, Drink CC, wht on red, 18x45", EX+ 1,000.00
Sign, 1913, cb diecut, girl & flower garland, trifold, 34x60", VG 5,200.00
Sign, 1914, tin, Drink CC..., str-sided bottle, 14x39", VG 1,865.00
Sign, 1920s, cb trolley, Drink..., bordered, matted/fr, G- 135.00
Sign, 1920s, paper, Drink..., flapper girl & bottle, 20x12", G- 175.00
Sign, 1920s, tin, arrow, Ice Cold..., 2-sided hanger, 8x30", VG ..200.00
Sign, 1930s, flange, Refresh..., Colonial-style emblem, mc, EX+ .575.00
Sign, 1930s, paper, Cold..., iceberg, 20x58½", EX 600.00
Sign, 1930s, porc, Drink..., wht/yel/gr, self-fr, 48x106", NM ...1,300.00
Sign, 1930s, tin, Drink... below bottle, mc on wht, 18x5", NM ..625.00
Sign, 1930s, tin, Drink...Ice Cold, w//bottle, 20x28, NM 800.00
Sign, 1930s, tin, Refresh Yourself!..., mc, 29x28", NM 1,400.00
Sign, 1930s, tin diecut, Drink... on triangle, 2-sided hanger, EX+ ..600.00
Sign, 1930s, wood, Drink..., 2 bell glasses, metal top, 11x9", M .850.00
Sign, 1935, porc, Fountain Service..., 14x27", NM 1,800.00
Sign, 1936, cb, lady in wht w/glass, 50x30", EX+ 1,900.00
Sign, 1938, Drink...Ice Cold, bottle on yel dot, 36x60", VG+ 400.00
Sign, 1939, cb hanger, Buvez..., girl drinking, Canada, 22x15", EX ..1,200.00
Sign, 1939, neon, Drink...In Bottles, chrome trim, 14x17", VG+ ...1,700.00
Sign, 1939, wood, arrow & disk, appl silver bottle, 17" dia, G+ .400.00
Sign, 1940, cb, Inviting You..., girl at table, horizontal, VG+ 450.00
Sign, 1940s, cl, Delicious..., red w/gold, 9" dia, EX 180.00
Sign, 1940s, paper, Home Refreshment, 6-pack, 3-pc, NM 200.00
Sign, 1940s, tin, Real Drink, boy w/straw, self-fr, 35x11", EX+ ..275.00
Sign, 1940s, wood, Ye Who Enter..., w/bottle, Kay, 11x29", EX+ ..675.00
Sign, 1940s-50s, paper, bottle in snow bank, 18x57, EX 275.00
Sign, 1940s-50s, plastic, wooden block, Canada, 9x11", NM 260.00
Sign, 1941, cb, Entertain Your..., lady singing, 20x36", VG 425.00
Sign, 1942, cb, 2 ballerinas w/bottles, Entertain..., 27x16", G ..125.00
Sign, 1942, tin, Drink..., bottle far right, self-fr, 12x34", NM 700.00
Sign, 1942, tin flange, Drink CC, bottle on yel dot, 20x24", NM ..525.00
Sign, 1944, cb, boy suprises girl w/bottle, 20x36", G 325.00
Sign, 1944, cb, Yes!, girl eyes bottle, 20x36", EX+ 500.00
Sign, 1947, cb, Refreshing, girl w/sunglasses, 20x36", NM 1,350.00
Sign, 1948, cb, ...For Hospitality, barbecue scene, 20x36", G+ ...375.00

Sign, 1948, glass, Please Pay..., invt trapezoid, hangs, EX+ 700.00
Sign, 1948, light-up counter, Please Pay..., trapezoid, 12x20", EX ...2,200.00
Sign, 1948-50s, light-up, cash-register topper, 6x11", NM 400.00
Sign, 1950s, button, Drink CC...Sign of..., red, 36", EX 300.00
Sign, 1950s, button, 2-sided, electric, 16" dia, EX 300.00
Sign, 1950s, porc, bottle diecut, 16", NM 260.00
Sign, 1950s, porc, Drink..., dispenser w/full glass, 28x28", EX 650.00
Sign, 1950s, tin, bottle on wht, 36x18", EX+ 225.00
Sign, 1950s, tin, It's a Natural..., bottle, 16" dia, EX+ 675.00
Sign, 1950s, tin diecut, 6-pack on red, NM 750.00
Sign, 1950s, wood, Sundaes Malts, Sprite Boy, 12x78", EX ...1,050.00
Sign, 1951, tin, bottle diecut, 108", EX 500.00
Sign, 1951, tin, bottle diecut, 72", EX+ 525.00
Sign, 1951, tin, Take Home a Carton, 6-pack, Canada, 54x36", EX 475.00
Sign, 1951, tin flange, Drink...Ice Cold, disk/arrow, 22x18", EX ...575.00
Sign, 1953, cb diecut, elves w/bottles in snow, 20x12", EX 180.00
Sign, 1954, cb die-cut standup, Eddie Fisher, 19", EX 375.00
Sign, 1954, tin, bottle diecut, appears wet, 72", NM 575.00
Sign, 1955, cb, Coke Time, cowgirl w/triangle, 27x16", NM 650.00
Sign, 1955, cb, Now Family Sz Too..., Sprite Boy, 20x36", NM .500.00
Sign, 1960s, tin, Enjoy...New Feeling, w/bottle, 12x32", NM 200.00
Sign, 1960s, tin, Sign of Good Taste, fishtail, 18x54", EX+ 240.00
Sign, 1960s, tin diecut, King-Size, wht fishtail, 36x30", NM 425.00
Stamp holder, 1900, cl, w/calendar, 1½x2½", EX+ 1,200.00
Syrup can, 1940s-50s, red/wht/gr paper label, 1-gal, EX 275.00
Syrup jug, 1900s, stoneware, paper label, cork stopper, 10", VG+ ..2,000.00
Thermometer, 1939, porc, Thirst Knows..., girl silhouette, 18", NM ...875.00
Tip tray, 1901, Hilda Clark w/roses, 6" dia, G- 400.00
Tip tray, 1906, Juanita w/glass, 4" dia, VG+ 550.00
Tip tray, 1913, Drinks..., girl in wide-brimmed hat, 6x4", EX+ ..525.00
Toy shopping cart, 1950s, masonite basket, metal wheels, EX+ .375.00
Toy truck, 1956-57, Marx #1090, tin, yel w/red, 5-tier, 17", M ..650.00
Toy truck, 1970s, Buddy L #5215, Ford, 7½", NM 35.00
Toy truck, 1978, Matchbox, Super King, tractor-trailer, NMIB ...35.00
Watch fob, 1911, Duster Girl, VG 400.00
Whistle, 1930s, wooden cylinder shape, Pure As..., EX+ 130.00

Trays

Values are given for trays in excellent plus condition (C8+). Those that have been reproduced are marked with a (+). The 1934 Weismuller and O'Sullivan tray has been reproduced at least three times. To be original, it will have a black back and must say 'American Artworks, Coshocton, Ohio.' It was not reproduced by Coca-Cola in the 1950s.

All 10½x13½" original serving trays produced from 1910-42 are marked with a date, Made in USA and the American Artworks Inc., Coshocton Ohio. All original trays of this format (1910-40) had REG TM in the tail of the C.

1897, Victorian lady, 9¼" dia, VG 12,500.00
1901, Hilda Clark, 9¾" dia, VG 4,000.00
1903, Hilda Clark, oval, 18½x15", EX 6,000.00
1905, Lillian Russell, glass or bottle, 10½x13¼", EX 3,500.00
1906, Juanita, glass or bottle, oval, 13¼x10½", EX 2,200.00
1907, Relieves Fatigue, 10½x13¼", NM 3,000.00
1907, Relieves Fatigue, 13½x16½", EX 3,600.00
1908, Topless, Ginger Ale, 12¼" dia, NM 6,500.00
1909, St Louis Fair, 10½x13¼", EX 1,800.00
1909, St Louis Fair, 13½x16½", NM 3,000.00
1910, Coca-Cola Girl, Hamilton King, 10½x13¼", VG 850.00
1913, Girl in Lg Hat, Hamilton King, oval, 12¼x15¼", EX 650.00
1914, Betty, oval, 12¼x15¼", EX+ 575.00
1914, Betty, 10½x13¼", EX 600.00
1916, Elaine, 8½x19", NM 300.00

1920, Garden Girl, oval, 12¼x15¼", EX+ 800.00
1921, Autumn Girl, oval, 12¼x15¼", EX+ 800.00

Photo courtesy Gary Metz

**Tray, 1922, Summer Girl,
10½x13¼", NM, $950.00**

1923, Flapper Girl, 10½x13¼", NM 400.00
1924, Smiling Girl, brn rim, 10½x13¼", EX 650.00
1924, Smiling Girl, maroon rim, 10½x13¼", EX 850.00
1925, Party, 10½x13¼", NM 400.00
1926, Golfers, 10½x13¼", VG 700.00
1927, Curbside Service, 10½x13¼", EX 750.00
1928, Bobbed Hair, 10½x13¼", EX+ 650.00
1929, Girl in Swimsuit w/Glass, 10½x13¼", EX+ 450.00
1930, Swimmer, 10½x13¼", EX 425.00
1930, Telephone, 10½x13¼", NM 400.00
1931, Boy w/Sandwich & Dog, 10½x13¼", NM 750.00
1932, Girl in Swimsuit on Beach, Hayden, 10½x13¼", EX+ 625.00
1933, Francis Dee, 10½x13¼", NM 500.00
1934, Weismuller & O'Sullivan, 10½x13¼", NM 900.00
1935, Madge Evans, 10½x13¼", NM 375.00
1936, Hostess, 10½x13¼", NM 350.00
1937, Running Girl, 10½x13¼", NM 300.00
1938, Girl in the Afternoon, 10½x13¼", NM 275.00
1939, Springboard Girl, 10½x13¼", EX 285.00
1940, Sailor Girl, 10½x13¼", NM 350.00
1941, Ice Skater, 10¼x13¼", NM 300.00
1942, Roadster, 10½x13¼", NM+ 350.00
1950, Girl w/Wind in Hair, screened bkground, 10½x13¼", M ..85.00
1950, Girl w/Wind in Hair, solid bkground, 10½x13¼", NM 150.00
1955, Menu, 10½x13¼", M 65.00
1957, Birdhouse, 10½x13¼", NM 100.00
1957, Rooster, 10½x13¼", NM 175.00
1957, Umbrella Girl, 10½x13¼", M 325.00
1961, Pansy Garden, 10½x13¼", NM 20.00

Machines

Though interest in Coca-Cola machines of the 1949-1959 era rose dramatically over the last few years, values currently seem to have leveled off and actually dropped 15% to 20%. The major manufacturers of these curved-top, 5¢ and 10¢ machines were Vendo (V), Vendorlator (VMC), Cavalier (C or CS), and Jacobs. Prices are for machines in excellent or better condition, complete and working. They vary greatly according to geographical location.

Cavalier, model #CS72, EX orig 1,200.00
Cavalier, model #CS72, M rstr 2,800.00
Cavalier, model #C27, EX orig 1,200.00
Cavalier, model #C27, M rstr 2,700.00

Cavalier, model #C51, EX orig 850.00
Cavalier, model #C51, M rstr 1,800.00
Jacobs, model #26, EX 1,200.00
Jacobs, model #26, M rstr 2,500.00
Vendo, model #23, EX orig 550.00
Vendo, model #23, M rstr 1,800.00
Vendo, model #39, EX orig 800.00

Vendo, model #44, late
1950s, 58x16", EX original,
$1,700.00.

Vendo, model #39, M rstr 2,000.00
Vendo, model #44, M rstr 3,750.00
Vendo, model #56, EX orig 1,200.00
Vendo, model #56, M rstr 3,200.00
Vendo, model #80, EX orig 500.00
Vendo, model #80, M rstr 1,250.00
Vendo, model #81, EX orig 1,200.00
Vendo, model #81, M rstr 3,200.00
Vendorlator, model #27, EX orig 1,200.00
Vendorlator, model #27, rstr (w/stand) 2,750.00
Vendorlator, model #27A, EX orig 800.00
Vendorlator, model #27A, M rstr 2,000.00
Vendorlator, model #33, EX orig 800.00
Vendorlator, model #33, M rstr 2,250.00
Vendorlator, model #44, EX orig 1,500.00
Vendorlator, model #44, M rstr 3,200.00
Vendorlator, model #72, EX orig 800.00
Vendorlator, model #72, M rstr 1,700.00

Coffee Grinders

The serious collector of kitchenwares and country store items rank coffee mills high on their want lists. A trend is developing toward preferring examples whose manufacturers are easily identifiable. Names to look for include Arcade, Daisy, Elgin National, Enterprise, Sun, Parker, Swift, Landers, Frary and Clark, Simmons Gardware Co., Logan and Strobridge, Bronson-Walton, Russel & Erwin, Wrightsville Hardware Co, and there are others. While some of these are from the 20th century, many are earlier.

Side mills usually have a brass tag located on the tin hopper. If the hopper was cast iron, the name was usually cast into the metal. Some of the less expensive versions had no identification. Paper labels were often used on the front of lap mills and table styles, though sometimes you will find these labels in a drawer or even inside the mill. Because decals and labels are prone to flake off and fade, when they are still legible, they contribute considerably to a mill's value. Canister mills had

names and patent dates molded into the cast-iron housing or on the canister itself. Commercial mills used in country and general stores were made of cast iron. Important information such as manufacturer and patent dates were usually cast into the housing, base, or wheels. Such identification helps determine date of manufacture.

To evaluate a coffee mill, remember that it should be complete, with original decals or labels. Missing or broken parts decrease the value considerably as do incorrect replacemant parts. Excellent examples of early coffee mills are rapidly becoming difficult to find. Beware of many imported impostors that are on the market today. A high-quality, authentic restoration of a cast-iron or wooden box mill will serve to enhance their values as long as the correct decals and labels are used.

Key: adj — adjustment

A Kendrick & Sons No 1, lap, CI w/brass hopper, CI drw 175.00
AK & Sons #237707, CI, octagon base, rnd hopper, heavy 285.00
American Duplex No 47, electric, working, VG 65.00
American Duplex No 50, electric, working, VG 65.00
Arcade, Favorite No 47, wood box, CI hopper, EX 160.00
Arcade, Favorite No 7, side, CI w/orig lid, grind adj front 85.00
Arcade, Imperial No 200, lap, CI hopper w/eagle, Pat 88, 89 .....155.00
Arcade, IXL, table, ornate CI hopper, hdl on side, 1-lb, EX 225.00
Arcade, Our Baby, G label, mini, EX 85.00
Arcade, Queen, glass canister & receiver, CI works, EX 295.00
Arcade, Sunbeam, CI w/glass hopper, orig lid & cup, EX 145.00
Arcade, Telephone, canister, CI front, Pat Sept 25 '88, EX 575.00
Arcade Crystal No 40, canister, orig lid & catcher, EX 285.00
Arcade No 147, lap, fancy CI closed hopper, wood box, EX 95.00
Arcade No 4, canister, CI, glass hopper, orig lid, wall mt 285.00
Arcade No 700, lap, w/dust cover, Sears 1908 catalog, EX 155.00
Blacksmith-made, funnel shape, 1-hdl, open hopper, wall mt 275.00
Blacksmith-made, funnel shape, 2-hdl, wall mt to 2x4" 295.00
Bronson-Walton Monitor, table, tin, ca 1909, NM 95.00
C Ibach stamp on hdl, dvtl walnut, CI hopper, orig drw 165.00
Caravan, canister, CI works, tin hopper, ca 1910, VG/EX 125.00
Cavanaugh Bros, table, front fill, 1-lb, EX 225.00
Citizen's Golden Rule, coffee bin 275.00
Clark & Clawson No 1, CI, dbl grind, Pat 1886, 6" wheel 495.00
Coles Mfg No 7, counter, CI, Pat 1887, 16" wheels, 27", EX 825.00
Common unmk, table, orig drw, screw cap on top, VG 75.00
Crescent, table, wood, top fill, cylinder, 13", EX 235.00
Dazey, gr-pnt tin, side crank, wall or shelf model 125.00
Dwinel Wright Co, coffee bin, VG 250.00
Elgin Nat'l No 40, counter, CI, red pnt, 2 wheels, orig, VG 575.00
Elma No 0, CI, single wheel, 9¼" 125.00
Elma No 1, CI, single wheel, 11" 155.00
Enterprise, Baby No 2, orig pnt & decals, 2 wheels, 7½" 795.00
Enterprise, counter, CI, brass hopper, Pat 1873, 6" wheels, EX ..575.00
Enterprise, floor, CI, CI hopper, Pat 1898, 39" wheels, VG 2,500.00
Enterprise No 1, counter, open hopper, hdl, Pat 1873, 11", VG ..225.00
Enterprise No 16, floor, CI, orig pnt, CI hopper 4,100.00
Enterprise No 212, floor, CI, 2 wheels, orig pnt, 30½" 2,900.00
Enterprise No 7, counter, CI, w/eagle, orig pnt, 17" wheels 825.00
Enterprise Pioneer, floor, CI, Pat 1873, 34" wheels, 65", VG ..2,795.00
Golden Rule, canister, w/orig glass, CI front, wood box, EX 425.00
Golden Rule Blend Coffee, tin, gr & gold pnt, 10-lb, EX 125.00
Griswold, coffee bean roaster, rnd, CI, wood hdl, 3-pc, EX 595.00
Griswold, counter, CI, 2 wheels, Pat 1897, EX 895.00
Husqvrna No 7, Swedish made, single wheel, 16½" 525.00
J Fisher Warranted, lap, dvtl walnut, pewter hopper, unique 245.00
K&M, lap, maple, aluminum closed hopper, clips on drw side 55.00
L'il Tot, mini, CI hopper & drw front, wood box 85.00
Landers, Frary & Clark, CI, rnd, sq base, ornate, Pat 1875 ....495.00

Landers, Frary & Clark, lap, fancy, CI top, wood box, VG/EX ...**125.00**
Landers, Frary & Clark, Regal, canister, wall mt **150.00**
Landers, Frary & Clark, Standard, lap, 1878 ....**145.00**
Landers, Frary & Clark, table, CI, Pat Feb 14, 1905, EX **125.00**
Landers, Frary & Clark, Universal No 14, table, Pat 1905, VG **85.00**
Landers, Frary & Clark No 50, counter, CI, 12" wheels, EX+ **675.00**
Leslir & Krater, table, wood, Pat Oct 5, 1886, rare, NM **575.00**
Lightning, canister, CI works, tin hopper, 1-lb, EX **145.00**
Luther, side, CI, tin hopper, brass plate, Pat 1843 ....**175.00**
Mimosa, table mt, CI, open hopper, heavy **85.00**
Nat'l, coffee & spice counter, CI, 17" wheels, 28", VG **625.00**
Nat'l, counter, CI works, covered hopper, wood drw, 1-wheel **125.00**
Nat'l Specialty...Philadelphia, CI, 25" wheels, VG **625.00**
New Home, table, CI top, enclosed hopper, wood box, 1-lb, EX+ ..**80.00**
Parker, Charles; table, tall/thin, CI & tin top, hdl on top **125.00**
Parker No 260, table, CI top & hdl, side grind, EX **275.00**
Parker No 260 Columbia, table, side grind, 1-lb **225.00**
Parker No 446, wall mt **320.00**
Parker No 449, canister, CI works, rnd glass hopper, VG **85.00**
Parker No 5005, counter, CI, 12½" wheels, 17", EX **875.00**
Parker No 555, Challenge Fast Grind, table, 1-lb, orig, EX **125.00**
Parker Union, side, CI, gear drive, Pat 1855, EX **125.00**
Parker Victor No 535, table, wood/tin hopper, hdl **135.00**
Persepolis, table, CI & brass, unique **275.00**
Primitive, lap, cherry, brass hopper, handmade/unique, 4x4" **195.00**
PS&W Standard No 31, lap, CI open hopper, wood box **125.00**
PSW&Co No 6, side, orig CI lid, EX **75.00**
Rock Hard, Garant-Sewaarborge, lap, imported **55.00**
Royal, side, CI w/CI cup, open hopper, Pat Apr 15, 1890, VG **85.00**
Russell & Erwin, Diamond, lap, CI, sloped sides **350.00**
Russell & Erwin Mfg Co No 1008, CI hopper, wood box **90.00**
Selsor, Cook & Co, lap, name on hdl, Pat 1859 ....**165.00**
Silvers No 1, CI, dbl-grind, w/cup, EX **475.00**
Standard Cabinet Co, spice cabinet w/mill **565.00**
Star, canister, tin w/CI works, Pat 1910, VG **75.00**
Star No 7, counter, CI, w/pan, 2-wheel, VG **475.00**
Strobridge, Brighton No 5, lap, open hopper, ca 1877 ....**135.00**
Sun No 1050 Improved, lap, wood, tin hopper **85.00**
Swift, drug mill, CI, open hopper, Pat June 30, 1874 ....**525.00**
Swift No 13, counter, orig tin drw, red pnt, 12" wheels, 19" **475.00**
Swift No 15, counter, orig decals/pnt, Pat 1875, 19" wheels **875.00**
Turkish, brass cylinder, seal of sultan, folding hdl, old **75.00**
Turkish, primitive, table, lg sq box on 28" brd, ornate, old **225.00**
Waddel, lap, wood box **160.00**
Walton, Bronson, canister, tin & CI, Pat 1911` **85.00**
Wright's Hdwe Co, Brighton, table, w/label, 1-lb, 8", EX **95.00**
Wrightsville Hdwe Co, Peerless No 200, canister, CI/glass **125.00**

Coin-Operated Machines

Coin-operated machines may be the fastest-growing area of collector interest in today's market. Many machines are bought, restored, and used for home entertainment. Older examples from the turn of the century and those with especially elaborate decoration and innovative features are most desirable.

The coin-operated phonograph of the early 1900s paved the way for the jukeboxes of the '20s. Seeburg was first on the market with an automatic 8-tune phonograph. By the 1930s Wurlitzer was the top name in the industry with dealerships all over the country. As a result of the growing ranks of competitors, the '40s produced the most beautiful machines made. Wurlitzers from this era are probably the most popularly sought-after models on the market today. The model #1015 of 1946 is considered the all-time classic and often brings prices in excess of $7,000.00.

The http://GameRoomAntiques.com web site and *Antique Amusements, Slot Machine, and Jukebox Gazette* are excellent sources of information for those interested in coin-operated machines; see the Clubs, Newsletters, and Catalogs section of the Directory for publishing information. Jackie and Ken Durham are our advisors; they are listed in the Directory under the District of Columbia.

Arcade Machines

Atlas 5¢ Tilt Test, flat top game, rstr **350.00**
Automatic Novelty Dumbbell Strength Tester, EX orig **2,950.00**
Bat a Penny, CI w/wood base, flip penny, rstr **1,300.00**
Bennett Drop Card, floor model, rstr **1,500.00**
Big Game Hunter 5¢, shooting game, rstr **750.00**
Buckley Treasure Chest Digger, rstr **2,200.00**
Caille Bros Cail-o-Scope, floor model, 72", EX rstr **3,500.00**
Chester Pollard Football, EX **2,500.00**
Chester Pollard Golf, EX **3,500.00**
Clown Maze 1¢, rstr **500.00**
Duck Penny Pistol Shoot, rstr **465.00**
Exhibit Arcadian, claw machine, floor model, 27", EX orig **1,000.00**
Exhibit Knotty Peek, counter top, G orig **895.00**
Exhibit Supply Hercules Grip Tester, EX **2,100.00**
Exhibit Supply Kiss-O-Meter, EX **975.00**
Exhibit Supply Lighthouse Strength Tester, rstr **2,300.00**
Exhibit Supply Merchant Man, electric crane, 1920s, 70", EX ...**2,500.00**
Exhibit Supply Punching Bag, rstr **2,500.00**
Exhibit Supply Rotary Merchandiser, rstr **950.00**
Exhibit Supply 1¢ Cupid's Post Office, old rstr, 74" **2,500.00**
Exhibit 1¢ Striking Clock, strength tester, rstr **2,800.00**
Gatter Novelty strength tester, floor model, oak case, 76", EX ...**850.00**
Gatter Striking Clock, strength tester, rstr **2,300.00**
Genco Gypsy Grandma Fortune Teller, floor model, 1950s, EX **3,500.00**
Grandma Fortune Teller, oak case, wax hands & head, rstr, M ...**7,000.00**
Indoor 1¢ Striker, cast front, rstr **900.00**
International Mutoscope, rnd metal cabinet, 1926, 8" dia, G .**1,200.00**

Jennings Comet 1¢ fortune teller and gum ball vendor, ca 1930, EX original, $3,500.00.

Jr League Bat a Ball 1¢, kicker-catcher type, rstr **1,200.00**
Kissen Kupids 5¢ Fortune Teller, lights up, rstr **1,400.00**
Lindy Striker 1¢, 1929, rstr **3,000.00**
Love Meter 1¢, rstr **600.00**
Male/Female Barrel, peep show on stand, 62", G **1,200.00**
Mercury 1¢ Grip Tester, orig decal, rstr **500.00**
Mills Drop Card Peep Show, EX **1,400.00**
Mills Horoscope Fortune Teller, 4-column, on stand, EX orig ...**2,400.00**

Mills Punching Bag, EX 3,000.00
Mills 1¢ Electricity Is Life, strength tester, 80", M rstr 5,500.00
Mills 1¢ Wizard Fortune Teller, ornate, rstr 1,500.00
Miniature 1¢ Baseball, cast front, wood base, rstr 1,200.00
Munves Strength Tester (striking clock), floor model, 76", EX ..850.00
Mutoscope Atomic Bomber, EX 500.00
Mutoscope Clam Shell, CI, EX 4,500.00
Mutoscope Love Pilot, EX 975.00
Mutoscope Magic Finger, digger type 2,200.00
Oomph 1¢ Lung Tester, rare, EX orig 2,500.00
Pete's Penny Ante, 1934, EX orig 500.00
Poker Skill 5¢, mini pinball-type game, rstr 500.00
Smilin Sam Voo Doo Man 1¢, fortune teller, rstr 4,500.00
Vest Pocket 1¢ Basketball, rstr 1,200.00
Whiz Ball 1¢, rstr 500.00

Jukeboxes

AMI #200, 1957, NM 2,000.00
AMI F-120, 1954, EX orig 1,000.00
Mills Empress 2,000.00
Rockola #1422, rstr 4,000.00
Rockola #1426, rstr 4,350.00
Rockola #1428, EX orig 3,800.00
Rockola #1434 Rocket, 1951, EX orig 2,000.00
Rockola #1454, 1956, EX orig 1,500.00
Seeburg #147MA, rstr 3,300.00
Seeburg A, plays 45s, 1948, VG orig 2,000.00
Seeburg G, 1953, EX orig 2,000.00
Wurlitzer #1015, rstr 8,500.00
Wurlitzer #1100, EX orig 5,500.00
Wurlitzer #1100, M rstr 8,500.00
Wurlitzer #2150, 1957, EX orig 4,000.00
Wurlitzer #2510, EX orig 1,700.00
Wurlitzer #500, EX 2,700.00
Wurlitzer #600, 1938, EX 3,000.00
Wurlitzer #61, table-top, EX orig 4,500.00
Wurlitzer #700, EX 3,500.00
Wurlitzer #750, G orig 6,000.00
Wurlitzer #780, EX 7,000.00
Wurlitzer #800, EX 6,000.00

Pinball Machines

Gottlieb Baffle-Ball, mechanical counter-top style, 10 balls for a penny, ca 1931, 11x27½x16", VG original, $550.00.

Mills Post Time Payout, 53x46", G 700.00
Mills Redman, w/unusual pay-out mechanism, 1937, 52x45x24", EX ...700.00
Ritz, Stoner Mfg Corp of Aurora IL, floor model, 53", VG 400.00

Rock-Ola Jig Saw, ca 1933, 38", G 1,600.00
Rock-Ola World Series, ca 1934, 40x38", G- 1,400.00

Slot Machines

Big Bertha $1, 96", EX orig 3,500.00
Buckley 5¢ Track Odds, console model, 1930s, EX 900.00
Caille Quintette, rare, NM 75,000.00
Caille 25¢ Big 6, EX orig 12,900.00
Caille 5¢ Center Pull, w/vendor, EX orig 4,600.00
Caille 5¢ Jockey, rare, NM 5,000.00
Caille 5¢ Our Baby, 1-wheel, cherry counter-top cabinet, rstr ...3,500.00
Caille 5¢ Silver Cup, CI case, dbl dial, cash pay, old rstr 10,000.00
Caille 5¢/25¢ Double, rare, NM 31,500.00
Caille 5¢/25¢ Twin Centaur, ca 1910, 68", EX orig 27,500.00
Cricket 5¢, rare, NM 14,200.00
Fey 5¢ Silver Cup, rare, NM 28,000.00
HC Evans Galloping Dominoes, electric console floor model, EX 900.00
Jennings $1 Standard Chief, EX orig 2,500.00
Jennings $1 Sun Chief, rstr 2,695.00
Jennings Today, 4-column front vendor & jackpot, 1926, G ..2,000.00
Jennings 10¢ Tic-Tac-Toe Chief, chrome front, post WWII, rstr ..2,500.00
Jennings 25¢ Operator Bell, counter-top, EX orig 1,450.00
Jennings 25¢ Standard Chief, rstr 2,500.00
Jennings 25¢ Sun Chief, rstr 2,500.00
Jennings 5¢ Dutch boy & girl, rstr 1,800.00
Mills Dewey 2 Bits Jackpot, upright, 1-wheel, ca 1905, 70", EX ...6,500.00
Mills Vest Pocket, rstr 450.00
Mills 10¢ Diamond Front, EX orig 1,600.00
Mills 10¢ Standard Chief, rstr 1,595.00
Mills 25¢ Castle, rstr 1,795.00
Mills 25¢ Golden Falls, EX orig 1,700.00
Mills 25¢ Hi Top, EX orig 1,700.00
Mills 25¢ Lion Front, rstr 1,795.00
Mills 25¢ Money Honey, rstr 1,500.00
Mills 5¢ Black Cherry, EX orig 1,600.00
Mills 5¢ Bursting Cherry, EX orig 1,800.00
Mills 5¢ C OK, w/side vendor & future payout, EX orig 1,450.00
Mills 5¢ Castle Front, EX orig 1,600.00
Mills 5¢ Dewey, upright, EX orig 7,800.00
Mills 5¢ Futurity, EX orig 3,395.00
Mills 5¢ Golden Falls, EX orig 2,000.00
Mills 5¢ Golden Falls, M rstr 2,395.00
Mills 5¢ Hi Top, VG orig 1,600.00
Mills 5¢ Judge, upright, rstr 6,500.00
Mills 5¢ Judge, 2-wheel, upright, ca 1899, 65x22", EX orig 7,000.00
Mills 5¢ Liberty Bell, rare, NM 9,000.00
Mills 5¢ Liberty Bell, 3-reel, CI case, toed ft, marque, rstr 6,000.00
Mills 5¢ Liberty Bell Front, w/gum vendor, on stand, NM ...20,000.00
Mills 5¢ Lion Front, 3-reel, ca 1931, EX orig 2,000.00
Mills 5¢ Owl, rstr 6,800.00
Mills 5¢ Scarab, rare, NM 15,000.00
Mills 5¢ Silent Mystery, oak cabinet, 1930s, EX orig 1,600.00
Mills 5¢ Silent Sales, w/side vendor, ca 1925, 24x19", EX orig ..1,500.00
Mills 5¢ Skyscraper, rstr 1,800.00
Mills 5¢ War Eagle, EX orig 1,595.00
Mills 5¢/25¢ Double Dewey, upright, 66", rstr 25,000.00
Mills 50¢ Diamond, 3-reel, chrome front, ca 1950, EX orig 1,500.00
Mysterious Eye 5¢, NM 2,900.00
New Century 5¢ Puck, NM 12,500.00
Pace $1, EX orig 1,800.00
Pace 5¢ Chrome Deluxe, rstr 1,400.00
Watling 10¢ Roll-A-Top Bird, EX orig 3,395.00
Watling 25¢ Detroit, NM 14,500.00

Watling 25¢ Roll-A-Top Coin Front, rare, NM 3,295.00
Watling 5¢ Blue Seal, rstr 1,595.00
Watling 5¢ Golden Gate, rare, NM 25,000.00
Watling 5¢ Little 6, NM 25,000.00
Watling 5¢ Operator Bell Fey, Nm 15,000.00
Watling 5¢ Roll-A-Top, gold-plated, rstr 4,000.00
Watling 5¢ Roll-A-Top, ornate front, oak cabinet, 1930s, rstr ..2,600.00
Watling 5¢ Roll-A-Top Coin Front, rstr 3,995.00
Watling 5¢ Torch Front, rstr 1,695.00

Trade Stimulators

Automatic 1¢ Dice Popper, CI, ca 1892, 12x6", G 875.00
Bally 1¢ Baby, 3-reel, mini 500.00
Bally 5¢ Skipper, roulette style, wood case, 24x11x6", EX orig ...600.00
Banner 1¢ Leader, penny drop, NM 500.00
Buckley 1¢ Ball Gum, fruit reels, NM 500.00
Buckley 1¢ Pilgrim, 5-reel, EX 600.00
Caille Puritan Bell, CI, EX orig 950.00
Cal the New Deal, w/gum vendor, ca 1934, EX orig 800.00
Churchill 1¢ Bingo, flip ball w/gum vendor, EX orig 600.00
Daval Bell Slide, ca 1938, EX orig 600.00
Daval Cent a Pack, w/gum vendor, 1936, NM 525.00
Daval Clearing House, w/gum vendor, ca 1937, EX orig 600.00
Daval Joker, w/gum vendor, ca 1940, 13x12", EX orig 600.00
Daval Reel Dice, 1936 ....600.00
Daval 1¢ Chicago Club House, w/gum vendor, EX orig 600.00
Daval 1¢ Jiffy Cigarette, 3-reel, w/gum vendor, EX orig 300.00
Daval 1¢ Smokes Reels, radio style, cvd wood cabinet, 1938, NM ..400.00
Daval 5¢ Free Play, w/gum vendor, NM 425.00
Daval 5¢ Liberty, gumballs, 1930s, 10x11x9", EX orig 400.00
Daval 5¢ 21, blackjack game, NM 450.00
Decatur Fairest Wheel, ca 1910, 25", EX orig 900.00
Exhibit Select Em Dice Spinner, 1934, EX orig 225.00
Exhibit Sweet Sally, w/gum vendor, ca 1935, EX orig 400.00
Exhibit 1¢ Play Ball, penny flip, EX orig 1,500.00
Garden City 1¢ Bar Boy, beer motif, EX 700.00
Goeldner/Caille 1¢ Bowling, 21x8", EX orig 1,100.00
Gottlieb 1¢ Indian Dice, 1937, EX orig 950.00
Groetchen Klix 21, w/gum vendor, ca 1945, 7x7", EX orig 400.00
Groetchen Royal Flush, w/gum vendor, 1939, EX orig 500.00
Groetchen 1¢ Ginger, Deco style w/girl on front, 1937, NM 500.00
Groetchen 1¢ Liberty, 3-reel, token vendor, ca 1945, G 400.00
Groetchen 1¢ Roto-Matic, dice vendor, 1934, sm, NM 600.00
Groetchen 21, w/gum vendor, ca 1937, rpt, EX 600.00
Groetchen 5¢ Punchette, NM 500.00
Groetchen 5¢ 21 Blackjack Vendor, NM 600.00
Jennings 1¢ Favorite, horse race game, EX 1,595.00
Jennings 1¢ Target, Indian decor, penny flip, NM 600.00
Keeney's 5¢ Spinner Winner, NM 600.00
Marvel 5¢ Slugger, ca 1950, EX orig 600.00
Mills New Target Practice, 1925, VG 600.00
Mills 5¢ Midget, dice game, EX 1,295.00
Pente Ante 1¢ Draw Poker, NM 400.00
Pick a Pack 1¢/5¢ Windmill, Deco style, EX 895.00
Pierce Whirlwind, disk model, 1933, EX orig 1,300.00
Pierce 1¢ Hit Me, EX 900.00
Puritan 1¢ Baby Bell w/jackpot, EX 700.00
Rockola 5¢ Hold & Draw, 1933, NM 700.00
Scramball Gambling, mc balls on ramps, 19", EX 300.00
Sparky 5¢ Poker, 6½x15x11", EX orig 150.00
Western Tot, w/fruit reel strips, ca 1940, 7x7", EX orig 300.00
Whitney Seven Grand, ca 1939, EX orig 700.00
Windmill 1¢, penny drop, catcher feature, NM 700.00

Zoom 1¢, ball flip, ca 1940s, rstr 900.00

Vendors

Vending machines sold a product or a service. They were already in common usage by 1900 selling gum, cigars, matches, and a host of other commodities. Peanut and gumball machines are especially popular today. The most valuable are those with their original finish and decals. Older machines made of cast iron are especially desirable, while those with plastic globes have little or no collector value. When buying unrestored peanut machines, beware of salt damage.

B Madorsky Football Novelty, gum, ca 1930, 24", EX orig 1,650.00
Baby, peanuts, table-top, 1940s, EX 200.00
Black man figural, pnt CI, cigar vendor, 32", VG 12,500.00

Bull's Head perfume vendor, cast iron and glass, original paint and paper directions, rare, 15", EX, $3,200.00.

Columbus Dart Gambling, gumball, porc w/bbl locks, NM 1,700.00
Columbus Model A, CI, all orig w/globe, EX 275.00
Columbus Model A, gum, 1930s, w/stand, EX 400.00
Columbus Model A, 1910s, EX orig 375.00
Crippen 1¢, gumball, 1930s, EX 225.00
EZ Gambling, gum, 1908, EX 600.00
Ford, gumball, CI, 1930s, EX 150.00
Freeport Goo-Goo Gum, ca 1899, 16½", VG 5,500.00
Gillette 15¢/25¢, razor blades, 7x13", EX orig 65.00
Glasco Coke slider, EX orig 850.00
Gooseneck 1¢/5¢, gum, porc, 1931, EX 450.00
Hance-Coleman Chicago, peanuts, 1905, M 5,500.00
Hershey's 5¢, candy kisses 250.00
Hoskins 5¢, gum & mints, 7-column, 15x10", EX orig 325.00
Ideal 55 Pepsi dbl-dot, rstr 1,400.00
Ideal 55 Seven-Up, complete 550.00
Mystic Swami Fortune Teller, Mutoscope, 1950s, EX orig 7,500.00
Northwestern Tri-Selector, EX orig 425.00
Perk-Up, w/decal, 1940s, EX 225.00
Popmatic 5¢ Corn Popper, dispensed into bag, EX orig 600.00
Pulver, Cop, gum, red, EX working 900.00
Pulver, Yel Kid, gum, bl, rstr 700.00
Pulver Clark 1¢ Get Hot Gum, 3-column, ca 1950, 32", EX orig ..850.00
Pulver 1¢ Kola-Pepsin Happy Hooligan, orange case, EX orig ...5,000.00
Silver King, hot nuts, NM 225.00
Square Deal 5¢, gum, rare, NM 2,000.00
Stampmasters 10¢, postage stamps, 14x8", EX 50.00
Standard, peanuts & gum, 1923, EX orig 450.00
Stanley, peanuts, 1918, NM 3,000.00
Stollwerk Volkman 1¢ Automat-Sweet, chocolates, 1890s, EX orig ..1,600.00
Topper 1¢, gum, rstr 125.00
True Blue, gum, 2-column, glass dome, side lever, CI base, 1906 ..5,500.00
Vendo #3 Standard, complete 650.00

Walter, peanuts, 1930, EX orig **250.00**
Wildroot 5¢ Hair Oil, ca 1950, 15x10", EX orig **350.00**

Miscellaneous

Hotel Radio 25!, EX orig **200.00**
Mutoscope, sheet metal on wood & iron ped, w/marque, 74", EX **1,400.00**
National Shoe Shine, rstr **1,650.00**
Peerless 1¢ weighing machine, lollipop floor model, 1930s, EX orig **1,200.00**
Slezak, height machine, porc base, 77", G **1,000.00**

Cole, A. R.

A second generation North Carolina potter, Arthur Ray Cole opened his own shop in 1926, operating under the name Rainbow Pottery until 1941 when he adopted his own name for the title of his business. He remained active until he died in 1974. He was skilled in modeling the pottery and highly recognized for his fine glazes.

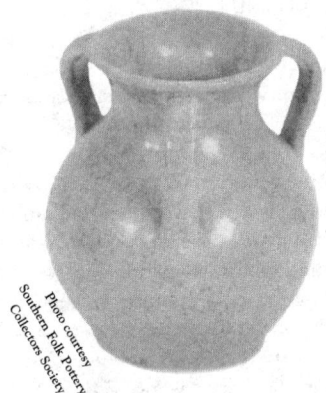

Vase, speckled turquoise lead glaze, three-handled, early 1930s, circular ink stamp, 5⅛", $105.00.

Bowl, 4-color splotches, looped hdls, mk, 5x9" **150.00**
Vase, bl w/mc runs, pear shape, sgn/Rainbow Pottery, 5½" **85.00**
Vase, blk gloss w/yel band, ftd cone, 1930s, 9½" **225.00**
Vase, gr w/mustard brn splotches, 8" **65.00**
Vase, mc mottle, cylindrical, sgn, pre-1962, 9⅛" **200.00**

Comic Books

For almost sixty years, the American public has been thrilled by the monthly adventures of everyone's favorite comic book heroes such as Superman, Captain Marvel, and Spiderman. Each 10¢ comic book issue, featuring a new saga of adventure and mystery, were usually met with excitement and anticipation by the youngsters who eagerly purchased them from their neighborhood candy store or newsstand. Unfortunately, the vast majority of these comic books were eventually discarded in favor of other worldly pursuits. Due to this fact, most comic books from the '30s and '40s did not survive, making them a very scarce and desirable collectible in today's world. Many comic books are worth very little, a few of the better examples are listed here.

Adventures of Bob Hope, #28, EX **36.00**
Adventures of the Jaguar, #1, VG **35.00**
Adventures of the Jaguar, #7, 1962, NM **30.00**
Annie Oakley & Tagg, #575, EX **25.00**
Avengers, Marvel #1, 1963, G+ **225.00**

Bionic Woman, Carlton #1, 1977, EX, from $15 to **25.00**
Brave & Bold, DC Comics #28, 1960, G+ **370.00**
Bugaloos, Charlton #1, 1971, EX **15.00**
Bugs Bunny Christmas Funnies, Dell Giant #4, EX **30.00**
Bullwinkle, Gold Key #1, 1962, EX **35.00**
Bullwinkle & Rocky, Whitman #5, 1972, EX **10.00**
Captain Midnight, Fawcett #37, NM **150.00**
Cat, The; Dell #1, EX **10.00**
Christmas w/Mother Goose, Dell #201, EX **35.00**
Comic Cavalcade, #16, 1946, Green Lantern, Flash & others, NM **500.00**
Daredevil, Marvel #1, 1964, VG **155.00**
Doc Savage, #12, 1943, NM **300.00**
Donald & Mickey in Disneyland, Dell Giant #1, EX **30.00**
Donald Duck's Beach Party, Dell Giant #6, 1959, EX **35.00**
Donald Duck the Crocodile Collector, Dell, 1951, VG+ **25.00**
Dr Who & the Daleks, Dell #1, 1966, photo cover, VG **15.00**
Felix the Cat, Dell #6, 1964, EX **20.00**
Felix the Cat, Toby Press #58, 1954, VG **25.00**
Flintstones, Dell #6, 1962, EX **20.00**
Flintstones, March of Comics #243, 1963, NM **50.00**
Gang Busters, DC Comics #58, VG **14.00**
Get Smart, Dell #1, 1965, VG+ **20.00**
Hardy Boys, Dell Four-Color #760, 1956, photo cover, EX **25.00**
Hardy Boys, Gold Key #2, 1970, photo cover, NM **8.00**
Hennesey, Dell Four-Color #1200, 1961, VG+ **15.00**
Honey West, Gold Key #1, 1966, NM **70.00**
Horse Soldiers, Dell Four-Color #1048, 1959, photo cover, G **45.00**
HR Pufnstuf, Gold Key #2, 1971, photo cover, NM **40.00**
Huckleberry Hound, Dell #3, EX+ **15.00**
I Dream of Jeannie, Dell #1, photo cover, EX+ **60.00**
I Love Lucy, Dell Four-Color #559, EX **100.00**
Incredible Hulk, Marvel #6, 1963, VG+ **200.00**
Jetsons, Gold Key #6, 1963, VG+ **15.00**
King of Kings, Dell Four-Color #1236, 1961, EX **30.00**
Lancer, Gold Key #1, EX **10.00**
Little Lulu, Dell #209, EX+ **3.00**
Lone Ranger, Dell #6, 1948, EX+ **60.00**
Marvel Super Heroes Tales Annual, #1, 1964, EX **65.00**
Mary Poppins, Gold Key, 1964, EX **18.00**
Mickey Mouse Birthday Party, Dell Giant #1, VG+ **60.00**
Munsters, Gold Key #1, VG+ **45.00**
Nancy & Sluggo, Dell #145, EX+ **15.00**
Pat Boone, DC Comics #4, 1960, rare, EX **80.00**
Peter Potamus, Gold Key #1, 1964, G **15.00**
Playful Little Audry, Dell #1, 1957, EX+ **60.00**
Queen of the West, Dale Evans, Dell #5, NM **50.00**
Rawhide, Dell Four-Color #1097, 1960, photo cover, VG **22.00**
Red Ryder, Dell #69, 1949, EX **20.00**
Roy Rogers, Dell #139, 1950s, NM **35.00**
Savage Sword of Conan, Marvel #1, NM **65.00**
Secret Agent, Gold Key #1, 1966, NM **100.00**
Star Trek, Gold Key #19, 1969, EX, from $30 to **35.00**
Super Duck in Cockeyed Wonder, MLJ comics #1, 1944, VG **80.00**
Superboy, Dell #22, 1952, VG **50.00**
Tales From the Crypt, Dell #28, VG, from $70 to **80.00**
Tarzan, Dell #28, 1952, photo cover, EX **45.00**
Tarzan's Jungle World, Dell Giant #25, VG **22.00**
That Darn Cat, Movie Comics, NM, from $40 to **50.00**
Three Stooges, Gold Key #32, 1967, photo cover, NM **45.00**
Tom & Jerry Back to School, Dell Giant #1, 1956, EX+ **120.00**
Tom Mix, Fawcett #10, 1948, VG **35.00**
Uncle Scrooge, Dell #13, EX, 1956, from $35 to **40.00**
Underworld Crime, Dell #3, 1952, EX **35.00**
Vacation in Disneyland, Dell Giant #1, 1959, NM **150.00**

Voyage to the Bottom of the Sea, Gold Key #2, 1965, EX 10.00
Wings of Eagles, Dell #790, VG 30.00
Woody Woodpecker, Dell Four-Color #288, 1950, EX 20.00
Young Men, Atlas #27, 1954, EX+ 225.00
Zorro, Gold Key #3, 1966, EX+ 15.00

Compacts

The use of cosmetics before WWI was looked upon with disdain. After the war women became liberated, entered the work force, and started to use makeup. The compact, a portable container for cosmetics, became a necessity. The basic compact contains a mirror and a powder puff.

The vintage compacts were fashioned in a myriad of shapes, styles, materials, and motifs. They were made of precious metals, fabrics, plastics, and in almost any other conceivable medium. Commemorative, premium, patriotic, figural, Art Deco, plastic, and gadgetry compacts are just a few of the most sought-after types available today. Those that are combined with other accessories (music/compact, watch/compact, cane/compact) are also very much in demand. Vintage compacts are an especially desirable collectible since the workmanship, design, techniques, and materials used in their execution would be very expensive and virtually impossible to duplicate today.

Our advisor, Roselyn Gerson, has written four highly informative books: *Ladies' Compacts of the 19th and 20th Centuries, Vintage Vanity Bags and Purses, Vintage and Contemporary Purse Accessories,* and *Vintage Ladies' Compacts.* She is listed in the Directory under the state of New York. See Clubs, Newsletters, and Catalogs for information concerning the compact collectors' club and their periodical publication, *The Powder Puff.*

Photo courtesy Roselyn Gerson

Miniature gold-tone compact modeled as a fan; yellow, pink, silver-tone, and gold-tone flowers on lid; pearl twist lock; interior mirror and powder well; 2½x2½", $60.00.

Art-Deco plastic w/flashlight above mirror, 1⅜x3¼" 125.00
Atomette, gold-tone suitcase w/leather covers, 3x2⅛" 100.00
Bakelite, blk shield shape w/gold/silver/rhinestones, 3¼x5¼" 425.00
Bakelite, brn w/rhinestones & cvd flowers, tassel, 2" dia 175.00
Bakelite, gr marbleized acorn w/silver & stones, tassel, 2" dia 300.00
Bakelite, yel w/pnt floral, tube in tassel, 1¾" dia 175.00
Britain, Scottie w/movable head (plastic) on gold-tone, 3" dia ..125.00
Brn leather suitcase w/stickers, leather hdls, 2¾x2½" 165.00
Celluloid hand-mirror shape, exterior mirror, 5x2¾" dia 125.00
Ciner, blk & gilt egg-shape minaudiere, finger ring, 3x2" dia 300.00
Copper-tone w/emb blk cat on lid, finger ring chain, 1½" dia 100.00
David Webb...NY, birth of Venus scene w/gilt silver, 4x3" 375.00
Dorothy Gray, brushed gold-tone Savoire Fair w/blk mask, 3¾x3" .115.00
Dorothy Gray, silver-tone wide-brimmed hat form, 3⅞" dia 150.00
Dresser vanity, Tangee, wht enamel w/red pnt lips, 5x5" 100.00
E Arden, eng silver-tone powder-sifter type, 2½" dia 80.00
Elgin Am, brushed gold-tone, w/music box, lyre closure, 2¾" L .135.00
Elgin Am, Eastern Star emblem on gold-tone, 3" dia 50.00

Elgin Am, gold-tone w/Queen For a Day & scene, 3½x2¾" 125.00
Elgin Am, gold-tone w/red/wht/bl stripes, 2¾" sq 65.00
Faux leather hat box form w/faux zipper, 3x2¾" 100.00
Flato, gold-tone w/bl leather, eng lipstick tube, 2½x3" 225.00
Flato, gold-tone w/pear-shaped stones, 2½x1⅛", +lipstick 175.00
France, gold-tone w/mc intaglio & purple stones, 1900s, mini ...150.00
France, Lucite, lady on swing pnt in marbleized irid, 2½" dia 200.00
Gold-tone pocket watch form w/rhinestones, 3" dia 50.00
Gold-tone w/Deco-like flowers on fan form, 2½x1½" 50.00
Gr enameled telephone dial w/gold center cartouch, 3½" 175.00
Hattie Carnegie, gold-tone w/mc stones, w/lipstick, 3¾x2¼" 200.00
Italy, champleve, red & gold-tone hand mirror form, ca 1900 ....350.00
Italy, gold-tone cat's face shape w/jewel eyes 300.00
Italy, snakeskin & gold-tone, 1½" dia, w/attached key chain 90.00
Italy, Vermeil silver w/bl enamel, ca 1900 ....325.00
Ivorene celluloid w/mc sparkles, 8-sided, w/chain & tassel, 2½" ...175.00
Le Rage, gold-tone dial-a-date, 2 movable dials, 4" dia 235.00
Lucite, photo placed behind removable mirror, 3¼" sq 75.00
Lucite, sterling repousse doves medallion on lid, 2⅞" sq 165.00
Marbleized metal w/portrait transfer, 2¾" sq 50.00
Mc striped glitter plastic, rnd, 1920s 65.00
Paloma Piccaso, silver & gold-tone w/red stone, dome lid, 2½" .150.00
Parisian Novelty, Christo Cola logo on gr, 2¼" dia 90.00
Petit-point triangle shape w/swivel mirror 165.00
Pk Lucite-rimmed sterling silver w/sterling hinge & catch 175.00
Pygmalion, gold-tone ball w/eng floral, plastic int, 2⅛" dia 175.00
Red plastic oval w/rhinestones, cord & tassel, 1920s 300.00
Rex, brushed silver w/gold-tone flowers, tango chain, 3½" dia ...200.00
Rex, gold-tone band on bl enamel ½-moon shape, 5¼x2½" 85.00
Roger & Gallet, Lucite sunburst medallion appl to lid, 4x4" 200.00
Schiaparelli, enamel figure on gold-tone, triangular, 2" 85.00
Silver-tone heart shape w/WA DC attractions on lid, souvenir, 3" ..50.00
Souvenir, Statue of Liberty on pearloid w/rhinestones 65.00
Sterling mini ball-shaped pendant w/eng, 1" dia 225.00
Stratton, MOP lid w/G clef & notes, w/music box, 3¼x2¾" 165.00
Tan snakeskin w/enameled stripes on 2 sides, 3" sq 85.00
Turq enamel w/foliate gilt o/l, HP portrait, 2¾x2¼" 300.00
Vanity, antique gold-tone filigree w/mc stones, tassel, 2x1¼" 400.00
Vanity, antique gold-tone filigree w/pearls & stones, 3x1½" 325.00
Vanity, antique gold-tone w/mc stones, mesh chain, 2¼x2½" ...175.00
Vanity, Bakelite, blk triangle w/silver pnt/rhinestones, tassel 200.00
Vanity, blk suede & brass cone shape w/pull-out lipstick, 6½" ...350.00
Vanity, Coty, blk & wht enamel domino shape w/gold-tone, 3¾" L ..200.00
Vanity, DFB Co, bl enamel w/windmill scene, Pat'd...1926, 3x2" 225.00
Vanity, Evans, bl enamel, pnt cloisonne lid, tango chain 175.00
Vanity, Evans, bl enamel w/mesh bottom, 2¼" dia 50.00
Vanity, gilt-metal horseshoe w/mc intaglio & bl stones, 1900s ...250.00
Vanity, gold-tone & MOP book form, tube in spine, 2x2½" 85.00
Vanity, Mondaine, mc Deco decor on book form, 1⅞x2¾" 100.00
Vanity, petit-point & gold-tone ½-moon shape, 1930s 125.00
Vanity, purple & blk fabric saddle bag form, w/tube & comb, 4" L ...175.00
Vanity, R Hudnut, Deauville, bl cloisonne, tango chain, 1920s .225.00
Vanity, R Hudnut, orchids on wht, cigarette case combo, 4½" L .165.00
Vanity, Raquel, emb leather resembles book, 2x3" 100.00
Vanity, Richard Hudnut, Le Debut, gr w/gold enamel octagon, 2" ..200.00
Vanity, SP bullet shape w/cartouch on side, 3½x1" dia 200.00
Vanity, Venine bl plastic w/gold-tone filigree lid 75.00
Vanity, Zanadu, gold-tone w/Deco enamel, mini lipstick, 3½" L ...115.00
Volupte, gold-tone hand shape w/enamel lace mitt, 4½" L 300.00
Volupte, mc on gold-tone artist's palette form, 3x2¾" 150.00
Volupte, red enameled apple form, 3x3" 200.00
W Germany, blk enamel/gold-tone saddle bag form, 5x2¾" 200.00
Wadsworth, Bon Bon, gold-tone necessaire w/tassel, 4¾x1¾" ...165.00
Wadsworth, Crystelle, mc butterfly form, 4¼x2¾" 200.00

Wadsworth, gold-tone ball & chain, lipstick on chain, 2" dia **165.00**
Zell, gold-tone pocket watch design, MIB **45.00**
Zell, maroon hatbox form w/gold-tone hardware, USN emblem, 3" dia **165.00**
Zell, tan leather football shape w/laces on lid 4½x3½" **85.00**

Computing Devices

Computing, calculating, and adding devices come in many shapes, sizes, and weights. Some are complex machines with many moving parts while others, such as slide rules, are quite simple in construction. These devices were used by scientists, accountants, engineers, and many other professionals when mathematical computations and exactness were required. Exampes of devices and machines with early patent dates are usually of greatest interest to collectors. Our advisor for this category is Dale Beeks; he is listed in the Directory under Iowa.

Adder, Addometer, 7 numbered wheels, EX in case **35.00**
Adder, Gem, chain drive, pocket sz, EX **65.00**
Adder, Webb, Pat 1867, wooden base, EX **600.00**
Adder, Webb, Pat 1889, all metal, EX **165.00**
Adder, Webb type, unsgn, all metal, EX **110.00**
Curta, pepper-grinder type, EX in case **450.00**
Machine, Brunsviga midget, wooden cover, EX **200.00**
Machine, Burroughs, push button, glass sides, lg **125.00**
Machine, Comptometer, copper case, push buttons **45.00**
Machine, Comptometer, wooden case, G **900.00**
Machine, Millionaire, metal case, heavy, lg, VG **750.00**
Slide rule, beginner's, EX in case **12.00**
Slide rule, circular, Gilson, EX in case **45.00**
Slide rule, demonstration, Picket, 84" L, EX **250.00**
Slide rule, Keuffel & Esser NY, typical, EX **22.00**
Slide rule, Thachers, cylindrical, Pat 1882, EX in case **1,200.00**

Consolidated Lamp and Glass

The Consolidated Lamp and Glass Company of Coraopolis, Pennsylvania, was incorporated in 1894. For many years their primary business was the manufacture of lighting glass such as oil lamps and shades for both gas and electric lighting. The popular 'Cosmos' line of lamps and tableware was produced from 1894 to 1915. (See also Cosmos.) In 1926 Consolidated introduced their Martele line, a type of 'sculptured' ware closely resembling Lalique glassware of France. (Compare Consolidated's 'Lovebirds' vase with the Lalique 'Perruches' vase.) It is this line of vases, lamps, and tableware which is often mistaken for a very similar type of glassware produced by the Phoenix Glass Company, located nearby in Monaca, Pennsylvania. For example, the so-called Phoenix 'Grasshopper' vases are actually Consolidated's 'Katydid' vases.

Items in the Martele line were produced in blue, pink, green, crystal, white, or custard glass decorated with various fired-on color treatments or a satin finish. For the most part, their colors were distinctively different from those used by Phoenix. Although not foolproof, one of the ways of distinguishing Consolidated's wares from those of Phoenix is that most of the time Consolidated applied color to the raised portion of the design, leaving the background plain, while Phoenix usually applied color to the background, leaving the raised surfaces undecorated. This is particularly true of those pieces in white or custard glass.

In 1928 Consolidated introduced their Ruba Rombic line, which was their Art Deco or Art Moderne line of glassware. It was only produced from 1928 to 1932 and is quite scarce. Today it is highly sought after by both Consolidated and Art Deco collectors.

Consolidated closed its doors for good in 1964. Subsequently a few of the molds passed into the hands of other glass companies that later reproduced certain patterns; one such reissue is the 'Chickadee' vase, found in avocado green, satin-finish custard, or milk glass. Our advisor for this category is Jack D. Wilson, author of *Phoenix and Consolidated Art Glass, 1926 – 1980*; he is listed in the Directory under Illinois.

Key: mg — milk glass

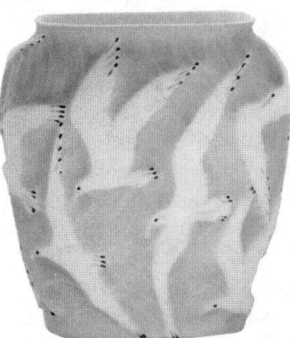

Sea Gulls, vase, reverse blue highlighting on milk glass, 11", $500.00.

Bird of Paradise, fan vase, yel wash, rare sz, 10" **275.00**
Bird of Paradise, plate, gr wash, 12" **95.00**
Bird of Paradise, vase, lt bl, ornate ormolu mts, 9" **275.00**
Bittersweet, vase, red, 9½" **450.00**
Bittersweet, vase, tricolor on satin mg, 9½" **150.00**
Bittersweet, vase, turq highlights on satin mg, 9½" **135.00**
Catalonian, candlestick, yel **45.00**
Catalonian, triangle vase, amethyst, 10" **85.00**
Chickadee, vase, gr wash on crystal, 6½" **145.00**
Chickadee, vase, sepia wash on crystal, 6½" **175.00**
Chrysanthemum, vase, reverse ruby stain on clear, 12" **200.00**
Con-Cora, cookie jar, violets on mg, 9" **145.00**
Dancing Girls, vase, straw opal, 12" **550.00**
Dancing Nymph, bowl, frosted, 8" **175.00**
Dancing Nymph, goblet, pk frosted **125.00**
Dancing Nymph, plate, Fr crystal, 6" **65.00**
Dancing Nymph, platter, gr wash, place sz, 18" **1,300.00**
Dogwood, vase, tricolor highlights on satin custard, 11" **185.00**
Dogwood, vase, yel cased, 11" **300.00**
Dragon-Fly, vase, gold on glossy custard, 7" **175.00**
Fish, bowl, gr wash w/frosted design, 15" **375.00**
Five Fruits, cocktail, gr wash **15.00**
Five Fruits, goblet, yel wash **30.00**
Five Fruits, snack set (tray & sundae), yel wash **40.00**
Florentine, vase, gr, 6½" **185.00**
Foxglove, vase, bicolor highlights on satin custard, &" **145.00**
Hummingbird, powder jar, purple wash, 5" **75.00**
Iris, candlestick, yel wash, low **75.00**
Iris, jug, purple wash **275.00**
Iris, tumbler, gr transparent over wht cased **90.00**
Jonquil, vase, gold highlights on mg, 6¼" **110.00**
Jonquil, vase, red, 6¼" **250.00**
Jonquil, vase, yel & gr on satin custard, 6¼" **275.00**
Katydid, ashtray, yel wash, rare **135.00**
Katydid, fan vase, bl on ivory satin **285.00**
Katydid, vase, amber/crysal, 8¼" **185.00**
Katydid, vase, bl on satin mg, ovoid, 7" **165.00**
Lamp, elk figural, chocolate brn, bl clock between horns, 13" ..**1,000.00**
Lamp, flower basket form, mc stain, on blk glass base, 8" **300.00**
Lamp, lovebirds figural, mc on brn & yel stump, blk base, 10½" ..**350.00**
Lamp, owl figural, brn w/blk eyes, blk glass base, 8½" **400.00**
Line 700, fruit bowl, bl, 10" **175.00**
Line 700, lamp, red slag on satin bkground, made from 7" vase ..**300.00**

Line 700, vase, gold highlights on custard, 10" **495.00**
Line 700, vase, rvpt bl highlights on crystal, 7" **175.00**
Lovebirds, banana boat, rvpt bl on crystal **400.00**
Lovebirds, powder jar, yel wash **80.00**
Lovebirds, vase, ruby stain on crystal, decor surmount, 11" **475.00**
Olive, bowl, purple wash, 4" **125.00**
Orchids, console bowl, gray wash, rare **275.00**
Pine Cone, vase, ruby stain on crystal, 6½" **150.00**
Pine Cone, vase, straw opal, 6½" **185.00**
Poppy, vase, bl wash, rare, 10½" **275.00**
Regent Line, vase, ash-rose pk over wht opal, #1174-B, 4½" **125.00**
Regent Line/Florette, cookie jar, pk satin **250.00**
Ruba Rombic, ashtray, wht opal **450.00**
Ruba Rombic, bowl, lav, oblong, 12" **1,200.00**
Ruba Rombic, nut dish, jungle gr, rare **175.00**
Ruba Rombic, perfume, jungle gr **1,400.00**
Ruba Rombic, service plate, jungle gr, 10" **150.00**
Ruba Rombic, sugar bowl, lav **250.00**
Ruba Rombic, vase, jungle gr, rare, 9½" **1,200.00**
Screech Owls, vase, bl on ivory satin, 5¾" **195.00**
Screech Owls, vase, orange w/gr reeds on satin custard, 5¾" **145.00**
Sea Gulls, vase, blk & gold irid on glossy custard, rare, 11" **500.00**
Sea Gulls, vase, gold highlights on red, rare, 11" **550.00**
Sea Gulls, vase, rose & bl wash on mg, 10¾" **425.00**
Spanish Knobs, sundae, yel **30.00**
Tropical Fish (Gold Fish), vase, brn wash on satin mg, 9" **195.00**
Tropical Fish (Gold Fish), vase, orange on gr satin, 9" **185.00**
Tropical Fish (Gold Fish), vase, rvpt ruby stain on clear, 9" **225.00**

Cookbooks

Cookbooks from the 19th century, though often hard to find, are a delight to today's collectors both for their quaint formats and printing methods as well as for their outmoded, often humorous views on nutrition. Recipes required a 'pinch' of salt, butter 'the size of an egg' or a 'walnut,' or a 'handful' of flour. Collectors sometimes specialize in cookbooks issued as advertising premiums. Especially desirable are the figurals that were shaped like a jar, a slice of bread, or some other form relative to the product. Others with unique features such as illustrations by well-known artists or references to famous people or places are priced in accordance. Cookbooks written earlier than 1874 are the most valuable and when found command prices as high as $200.00; figurals usually sell in the $10.00 to $15.00 range.

As is true with all other books, if the original dust jacket is present and in nice condition, a cookbook's value goes up by at least $5.00. Right now, books on Italian cooking from before 1940 are in demand, and bread-baking is important this year. For further information we recommend *A Guide to Collecting Cookbooks* by Col. Bob Allen and *Price Guide to Cookbooks and Recipe Leaflets* by Linda Dickinson. Our advisor for this category is Charlotte Safir; she is listed in the Directory under New York.

Key:
CB — cookbook   dj — dust jacket

Backpack Cookery, Ruth Dyar Mendenhall, 1966, 40-pg, VG **6.50**
Betty Crocker's 42 Hot Potato Ideas, Gen Mills, 1967, 15-pg, EX ..**5.50**
Blue Ribbon Cookies, M Robbins, paperbk, 1988, 134-pg, EX **7.50**
Boys' CB, H&P Brown, hardbk, 1959, 285-pg, EX **10.00**
Brer Rabbit's...Molasses Recipes, Penick & Ford, 1948, 48-pg, VG ..**12.50**
Cake Bible, Rose Beranbaum, hardbk, 1988, 556-pg, EX, w/dj **17.50**
Cake Decorating Yearbook, Wilton, paperbk, 1979, 198-pg, EX **8.50**
Celebrity CB, Johnna Blinn, paperbk, 1981, 511-pg, VG **17.50**

Chocolate Cooking, J Ridgway, hardbk, 1981, 77-pg, EX **8.00**
Clam Lover's CB, Wm Flagg, paperbk, 1983, 143-pg, EX **7.50**
Colonial Cooking, Caruba, hardbk, 1975, 128-pg, VG, w/dj **8.00**
Cooking for the Crowd, Carnation, 1963, 23-pg, EX **5.00**
Cooking Texas Style, Wagner/Marquez, hardbk, 1984, 193-pg, VG ...**10.00**
Cooking w/o a Kitchen, Berland, hardbk, 1978, 229-pg, VG, w/dj **10.00**
Country Goodness CB, Groff, hardbk, 1981, 320-pg, VG, w/jd **15.00**
Country Kitchen Party Dishes, Hatfield, 1993, 48-pg, EX, w/dj **7.50**

Cream of Rice, ca 1890, $30.00.

Cross Creek Cookery, Rawlings, 1942, 1st ed, EX **75.00**
Cross Creek Cookery, Rawlings, 1942, 1st ed, EX w/VG dj **125.00**
Del Monte Dried Fruit Family CB, 1959, 20-pg, EX **9.00**
Dishes Men Like, Lea & Perrins, 1952, 62-pg, EX **8.00**
Fabulous Pies From Pillsbury, 1961, 24-pg, EX **7.50**
Fleischmann Treasury of Yeast Baking, Std Brand, 1962, 61-pg, VG ..**7.50**
Fondue Magic, A Pritchard, hardbk, 1969, 192-pg, EX, w/dj **9.00**
Foxfire Book of Appalachian Cookery, Page, paperbk, '84, VG **12.50**
Frigidaire Frozen Delights, Frigidaire Corp, 1929, 47-pg, EX **12.50**
Gifts From Your Kitchen, Woman's Day, hardbk, 1982, 221-pg, EX ..**8.00**
Good Housekeeping CB, Marsh, Rhinehart, hardbk, 1945, 760-pg, EX ...**15.00**
Good Things To Eat, Commercial Milling, 1934, 64-pg, EX **8.00**
Gourmet's Menu CB, Gourmet Magazine, hardbk, 1964, 652+ pgs, EX **22.50**
Great Fast Breads, Carol Cutler, hardbk, 1985, 216-pg, VG, w/dj ..**8.00**
Housewife's Year Book of Health &..., Kellogg, 1937, 36-pg, VG .**14.00**
How To Have...Fun w/Cake Mixes, General Mills, 1956, 35-pg, EX ...**8.50**
In Kitchen w/Rosie, Rosie Daley, 1994, 129-pg, EX, w/dj **12.00**
Japanese Cooking, Martin, hardbk, 1970, 192-pg, VG, w/dj **8.00**
Kosher Gourmet CB, Miller/Snyder, hardbk, 1974, 313-pg, VG, w/dj **10.00**
Mazola Salad Bowl, Corn Products...Co, 1938, 31-pg, EX **14.00**
Mirro All-Purpose CB, Wilson, hardbk, 1954, 304-pg, VG **10.00**
Money-Saving Meals..., Pet Milk, 1940, 32-pg, VG **10.00**
NY's Master Chefs, Sax, paperbk, 1985, 120-pg, EX **9.00**
PA Dutch CB, Culinary Arts Press, 1936, 48-pg, VG **10.00**
Parade of Brazil Nut Recipes, Brazil Nut Assoc, 1940s, 31-pg, VG .**3.50**
Pearl's Kitchen, Pearl Bailey, hardbk, 1973, 211-pg, VG, w/dj **16.00**
Pillsbury's Butter Cookie Booklet, leaflet, 1961, 22-pg, EX **4.00**
Pillsbury's Let's Have a Barbecue, paperbk, 9x6", VG **3.50**
Pillsbury's Recipes You'll Use Over & Over Again, leaflet **10.00**
Pillsbury's 100 New Bundt Ideas, softcover, 1977, 90-pg, EX **4.00**
Pillsbury's 100 Prize-Winning..., 2nd Grand Nat'l, 1951 ....**20.00**
Pillsbury's 1950 Grand Nat'l Recipe & Baking Contest **75.00**
Pillsbury's 1950s Grand Nat'l Recipe & Baking..., #3-10, ea **20.00**
Pillsbury's 1960s Grand Nat'l Recipe & Baking..., #11-20, ea **8.00**
Pillsbury's 1970s Grand Nat'l Recipe & Baking..., #21-30, ea **5.00**
Popular Chinese Cookery, Burt, hardbk, 1972, 128-pg, EX **8.00**
Prince Golden Macaroni Recipes, 1951, 31-pg, VG **7.50**

Prudence Penny Regional CB, Berolzheimer, hardbk, '47, 752-pg, EX ..**18.00**
Quick Cuisine, Ann Clark, hardbk, 1993, 275-pg, VG, w/dj **12.00**
Redbook Timesaver CB, hardbk, 1972, 328-pg, VG, w/dj **10.00**
Rodale Herb Book, Wm Hylton, hardbk, 1975, 653-pg, EX w/dj ..**12.50**
Royal CB, Standard Brands, 1932, 45-pg, EX **14.00**
Rumford New Use CB, Rumford Co, 1935, 32-pg, EX **15.00**
Simple Family Favorites, Shepard, hardbk, 1970, EX, w/dj **8.00**
Sourdough Jack's Cookery, Mabee, comb bound, 1967, 48-pg, EX .**7.50**
Southern & Southwestern CB, Culinary Arts, 1956, 68-pg, EX **6.50**
Step-By-Step Cookery, Patten, 1963, 300-pg, EX, w/dj **16.00**
Versatile Salads, Michigan State University, 1964, 15-pg, EX **5.00**
Wonder Book of Good Meals, World's Fair Ed, 1934, 32-pg, EX ..**28.00**
Young Cook's Bake-A-Bun Book, Std Brands, 1967, 5-pg, NM **7.50**
250 Ways of Serving Potatoes, Culinary Arts, 1949, 48-pg, EX **6.00**

Cookie Cutters

Early hand-fashioned cookie cutters have recently been commanding stiff prices at country auctions, and the ranks of interested collectors are growing steadily. Especially valuable are the figural cutters; and the more complicated the design, the higher the price. A follow-up of the carved wooden cookie boards, the first cutters were probably made by itinerant tinkers from leftover or recycled pieces of tin. Though most of the 18th-century examples are now in museums or collections, it is still possible to find some good cutters from the late 1800s when changes in the manufacture of tin resulted in a thinner, less expensive material. The width of the cutting strip is often a good indicator of age; the wider the strip, the older the cutter. While the very early cutters were 1" to 1½" deep, by the '20s and '30s, many were less than ½" deep. Crude, spotty soldering indicates an older cutter, while a thin line of solder usually tends to suggest a much later manufacture. The shape of the backplate is another clue. Later cutters will have oval, round, or rectangular backs, while on the earlier type the back was cut to follow the lines of the design. Cookie cutters usually vary from 2" to 4" in size, but gingerbread men were often made as tall as 12". Birds, fish, hearts, and tulips are common; simple versions can be purchased for as little as $12.00 to $15.00. The larger figurals, especially those with more imaginative details, often bring $75.00 and up. The cookie cutters listed here are tin and handmade unless noted otherwise.

Bird, flat bk, 3½x6½" **80.00**
Bird, standing, flat bk, 5x5½" **55.00**
Cat running, 4¾" **50.00**
Duck, flat bk, folded rim, 3½x4¼" **75.00**
Eagle on nest, flat bk, 5x5" **85.00**
Eagle w/wings spread, no hdl, 4⅝x4¾" **80.00**
Hand, flat bk, 4¾" **45.00**
Hatchet, flat bk, 6¼" **60.00**
Heart, figural hdl, sgn Fries, 4x3¾" **45.00**
Heart, flat hdl, handmade, ca 1900, 4½" **36.00**
Heart, folded rim, flat bk, 2½x3⅛" **65.00**
Horse, detailed shape, flat bk, 5x7" **225.00**
Horse, flat bk, 6" **60.00**
Horse, flat bk, 9" **85.00**
Horse, no hdl, 5⅜x7⅜" **75.00**
Lady's high-top shoe, flat bk, 4¼x3" **90.00**
Man waving, hdl missing, 5¼x3¾" **70.00**
Peafowl, lg tail, flat bk, folded rim, 5x6¼" **225.00**
Pig, flat bk, 6" **65.00**
Rabbit w/inset eye, flat bk, 4x8" **275.00**
Reindeer, rnd cylindrical hdl, folded rim, 6¼x5½" **525.00**
Rocking horse, flat bk, 4½" **75.00**

Rooster, flat bk, 4⅛x1¾" **110.00**

Cookie Jars

The appeal of the cookie jar is universal; folks of all ages, both male and female, love to collect 'em! The early '30s heavy stoneware jars of a rather nondescript nature quickly gave way to figurals of every type imaginable. Those from the mid to late '30s were often decorated over the glaze with 'cold paint,' but by the early '40s underglaze decorating resulted in cheerful, bright, permanent colors and cookie jars that still have a new look fifty years later.

Stimulated by the high prices commanded by desirable cookie jars, a broad spectrum of 'new' cookie jars are flooding the marketplace in three categories: 1) Manufactures have expanded their lines with exciting new designs specifically geared toward attracting the collector market. 2) Limited editions and artist-designed jars have proliferated. 3) Reproductions, signed and unsigned, have pervaded the market, creating uncertainty among new collectors and inexperienced dealers. One of the most troublesome reproductions is the Little Red Riding Hood jar marked McCoy. Several Brush jars are being reproduced, and because the old molds are being used, these are especially deceptive. In addition to these reproductions, we've also been alerted to watch for cookie jars marked Brush-McCoy made from molds that Brush never used. Remember that none of Brush's cookie jars were marked Brush-McCoy, so any bearing the compound name is fraudulent. For more information on cookie jars and reproductions, we recommend *The Collector's Encyclopedia of Cookie Jars, I, II,* and *III* by Fred and Joyce Roerig; they are listed in the Directory under South Carolina. Another good source is *An Illustrated Value Guide to Cookie Jars, I* and *II* by Ermagene Westfall. Our advisors for this category are Charlie and Rose Snyder; they are listed in the Directory under Kansas.

The examples listed below were made by companies other than those found elsewhere in this book; see also specific manufacturers.

Airplane, dbl prop, North Am Ceramics **525.00**
Bambi, basket hdl, Japan, Disney **450.00**
Baseball, Vandor, from $40 to **45.00**
Beany & Cecil, Bob Clampett, Kellams of Pasadena, 1953, from $600 to **650.00**
Bear, decor, #2648, CA Originals, from $50 to **75.00**

Betty Boop, King Features Syndicate, 1985, $850.00.

Betty Boop Kitchen, Vandor, from $50 to **60.00**
Boy w/Baseball Glove, brn wood-tone stain, Treasure Craft **45.00**
Buick Convertible, wht, Appleman, from $850 to **900.00**
Bulldog Cafe, Disney **175.00**
Bunny Bloomers, Fitz & Floyd **175.00**
Car w/Flat Tire, Fitz & Floyd **275.00**

Chef, Pearl China 575.00
Chicken Racer, Clay Art, from $50 to 65.00
Cinderella Fairy Godmother, Applause 75.00
Cinderella Fairy Godmother, Fitz & Floyd 175.00
Circus Wagon, Century Bros; Enesco 150.00
Clown w/Umbrella, Lane 200.00
Clown w/Umbrella, Yona 165.00
Cook w/Spoon, Otagiri, from $20 to 25.00
Cookie Monster, CA Originals 65.00
Daffy Duck, Certified Internat'l, from $40 to 50.00
Disney Bus, Disney, from $700 to 900.00
Ernie, blk hair, Newcor 75.00
Ernie, CA Originals, from $55 to 75.00
Fire Truck, red, CA Originals, from $175 to 225.00
Frog, Maurice of CA 195.00
Froggy Went a-Courtin' 350.00
Gibson Greetings Clown Bust (Clarabell), from $150 to ...200.00
Gingerbread House, Enesco, from $30 to 40.00
Gone w/the Wind Mammy, Hamilton Gifts, 1st edition 310.00
Gone w/the Wind Mammy, Hamilton Gifts, 2nd edition 150.00
Halloween Witch w/Pumpkin, Fitz & Floyd 140.00
Hampshire Hog, Fitz & Floyd 175.00
Hi Diddle Diddle, Robinson Ransbottom, no gold 275.00
Hi Diddle Diddle, Robinson Ransbottom, w/gold, from $300 to ..350.00
Hound Hound, brn & wht, Doranne of CA, mk J1 USA 50.00
Humpty Dumpty, brn, CA Originals 100.00
Humpty Dumpty, Clay Art 135.00
Humpty Dumpty, Omnibus, from $100 to 130.00
James Dean, Happy Memories, from $325 to 375.00
Jungle Elephant, Fitz & Floyd, from $200 to 250.00
Katrina, Treasure Craft, from $450 to 475.00
Kermit on TV, Sigma 425.00
Ketchup Bottle, Doranne of CA, from $70 to 90.00
Kliban Cat w/Kiss on Cheek, full-bodied, Sigma, from $275 to ..325.00
Kliban Mama, Sigma 350.00
Koala Bear, CA Originals, from $250 to 300.00
Little Red Riding Hood, Napco, from $275 to 300.00
Mammy, Googly Eyed; basket hdld, Japan 975.00
Mammy, Mosaic Tile, yel 495.00
Mammy, Pearl China, from $700 to 800.00
Mammy, plaid dress, basket hdl, Japan, from $900 to 950.00
Mickey Mouse in Car, Disney, from $350 to 375.00
Mother Goose, decor, Gilner 350.00
Mother Goose, plain, Gilner, from $200 to 250.00
Mother Goose Bus 750.00
Mrs Potato Head, JD James Pottery, Hasbro, from $200 to ..250.00
Mrs Potts, Disney, from $75 to 100.00
Mrs Tiggywinkle, Sigma 150.00
Napco Spaceship-Cookies Out of This World, from $650 to ..750.00
Noah's Ark, CA Originals, from $50 to 75.00
Noah's Ark, Starns, from $250 to 300.00
Nun, DeForest 350.00
Ol' King Cole, red coat, Robinson Ransbottom 700.00
Ol' King Cole, yel coat, Robinson Ransbottom 300.00
Old MacDonald's Cow, Fitz & Floyd 95.00
Old World Santa, Home Collection, from $85 to 100.00
Olympic Torch, Warner Bros, from $100 to 135.00
Parking Garage, Cardinal 95.00
Peter Max, Sigma, from $350 to 400.00
Petting Zoo Hippo, Fitz & Floyd, from $150 to 175.00
Pig Waiter, Sigma 465.00
Pinocchio Head, Enesco 325.00
Pinocchio, holding glass bowl, Disney 65.00
Popeye Head, Vandor, from $450 to 500.00

Prunella Pig, Fitz & Floyd 125.00
Raccoon, Fitz & Floyd, from $125 to 150.00
Red Corvette, N Am Ceramics, from $125 to 150.00
Red Van, CA Original, #843 USA, from $150 to 175.00
Rio Rita, Fitz & Floyd 125.00
Roly Dalmatian, Disney 75.00
Rose-Pedal Coach (PD Centipede), Treasure Craft 575.00
R2-D2, Roman Ceramics 250.00
Santa in Chair, Fitz & Floyd 125.00
Santa in Rolls Royce (Christmas Car), Fitz & Floyd 895.00
Santa on Motorcycle, Fitz & Floyd (sgn), from $850 to 900.00
Santa on Motorcycle, Fitz & Floyd (unsgn), from $450 to ..500.00
Scarecrow, CA Originals 250.00
Scarlett O'Hara, Fitz & Floyd, from $150 to 160.00
Sheriff, Lane, from $650 to 700.00
Shirt Tales Penguin Cool Cookie, Hallmark 550.00
Shirt Tales Ricky Raccoon, Hallmark, from $190 to 200.00
Smokey Bear Head, Norcrest 900.00
Snow White & 7 Dwarfs, Enesco 825.00
Sock Hoppers, Fitz & Floyd, from $400 to 450.00
Southwest Santa, Fitz & Floyd, from $500 to 575.00
Strawberry Jar, CA Originals 35.00
Sugarplum Castle, from Nutcracker Sweets series, Fitz & Floyd .115.00
Superman, brn booth, CA Originals, from $375 to 425.00
Taxi Cab, CA Originals, from $175 to 200.00
Taxi Cab, Expressive Designs 75.00
WC Fields, Cumberland Ware, from $850 to 950.00
Wile E Coyote, Certified Internat'l, from $40 to 50.00
Winnie the Pooh, lg honey pot, #909, CA Originals, from $175 to ...200.00
Winnie the Pooh, sm honey pot, #900, CA Originals, from $125 to .150.00
Woody Woodpecker Head, Walter Lantz 700.00
Woody Woodpecker in Stump, CA Originals, full color 1,000.00
Ziggy on Stack of Cookies 325.00

Cooper, Susie

A 20th-century ceramic designer whose works are now attracting the attention of collectors, Susie Cooper was first affiliated with the A.E. Gray Pottery in Henley, England, in 1922 where she designed in lustres and painted items with her own ideas as well. (Examples of Gray's lustreware is rare and costly.) By 1930 she and her brother-in-law, Jack Beeson, had established a family business. Her pottery soon became a success, and she was subsequently offered space at Crown Works, Burslem. In 1940 she received the honorary title of Royal Designer for Industry, the only such distinction ever awarded by the Royal Society of Arts solely for pottery design. Miss Cooper received the Order of the British Empire in the New Year's Honors List of 1979. She was the chief designer for the Wedgwood group from 1966 until she resigned in 1972. After 1980 she worked on a free-lance basis until her death in July 1995. Our advisor is J. David Ehrhard; he is listed in the Directory under California.

Bowl, bouillon; red/brown lines w/X's, 2" H w/plate 40.00
Bowl, floral on bl, ftd, 8" dia 50.00
Casserole, Wedding Ring, #817, running deer bkstamp, w/lid 75.00
Cheese dish, red-brn, slant lid, 4½" H 170.00
Chocolate pot, Crayon Line, red & brn, Kestrel shape, 7" 175.00
Coffeepot, Sea Anemone, 7¾" 170.00
Cream soup, Wedding Ring, running deer bkstamp 30.00
Cup & saucer, Black Fruit, 2½" 35.00
Cup & saucer, lily, gold bands, Doric shape 45.00
Cup & saucer, red & cream shaded bands, earthenware, 1930s 40.00
Cup & saucer, Wedding Ring 65.00
Dish, gr & blk sgraffito design, 8½" L 75.00

Grapefruit dish, lime-gr sgraffito panel, mc stripes, 4" dia **55.00**
Jam pot, Nosegay, bl wash, 4" H **70.00**
Jug, tulips emb on olive gr, 6½" **155.00**
Mug, prancing unicorn, silver lustre w/gr-wash Kestrel shape **350.00**
Plate, fruits, yel band, 8½" **65.00**
Plate, Leaf & Vine, bl scroll border, 9" **40.00**
Plate, Pear in Pompadour, gr/blk/red/yel, 6" **35.00**
Plate, Tiger Lily, red & gr, gray wash band, 10" **45.00**
Platter, Dresden Spray, gr-wash border, 14" L **100.00**
Platter, Wedding Ring, mk, 14" **100.00**
Teapot, orange w/blk lines, 6½" **150.00**

Vase, tulips and leaves, olive green, 4", $350.00; Vase, pink and gray tubelined design, 8", $500.00.

Photo courtesy
J. David Ehrhard

Coors

The firm that became known as Coors Porcelain Company in 1920 was founded in 1908 by John J. Herold, originally of the Roseville Pottery in Zanesville, Ohio. Though still in business today, they are best known for their artware vases and Rosebud dinnerware produced before 1939.

Coors vases produced before the late '30s were made in a matt finish; by the latter years of the decade, high-gloss glazes were also being used. Nearly fifty shapes were in production, and some of the more common forms were made in three sizes. Typical colors in matt are white, orange, blue, green, yellow, and tan. Yellow, blue, maroon, pink, and green are found in high gloss. All vases are marked with a triangular arrangement of the words 'Coors Colorado Pottery' enclosing the word 'Golden.' You may find vases (usually 6" to 6½") marked with the Colorado State Fair stamp and dated 1939. For such a vase, add $10.00 to the suggested values given below.

For further information we recommend *Collector's Encyclopedia of Colorado Pottery, Identification and Values,* by Carol and Jim Carlton, who provide miscellaneous listings. Our Rosebud advisor is Jo Ellen Winther. All are listed in the Directory under Colorado.

Rosebud

Apple baker, w/lid **45.00**
Baker, 11¼" **55.00**
Bean pot, sm **55.00**
Bowl, mixing; 1¾-pt **35.00**
Bowl, mixing; 3-hdld, 1½-pt **40.00**
Bowl, mixing; 3-hdld, 7-pt **80.00**
Bowl, mixing; 8-pt **75.00**
Bowl, oatmeal **25.00**
Cake plate **40.00**
Casserole, Dutch; lg **95.00**
Casserole, str sides, 5" **45.00**
Cookie jar, Deluxe, 8-pt **95.00**
Cream soup **30.00**

Cup & saucer **45.00**
Honey pot w/spoon **250.00**
Muffin set, w/lid, rare **200.00**
Pitcher, w/lid, lg **150.00**
Plate, dinner; 8" **25.00**
Plate, 5" **8.00**
Platter, 9x12" **40.00**
Shirred egg dish **35.00**
Soup plate **35.00**
Sugar shaker **65.00**
Teapot, 6-cup **175.00**
Tumbler, ftd **110.00**
Tumbler, hdl **110.00**
Water server, w/stopper **120.00**

Miscellaneous

Cake knife, Hawthorne, decalcomania **75.00**
Cake plate, Floree, decalcomania **55.00**
Casserole, Coorado, ind, w/lid, 2x2" **45.00**
Casserole, Open window, decalcomania, str sides, w/lid, lg **125.00**
Creamer, Mello-Tone or Rockmount **10.00**
Cup & saucer, Mello-Tone or Rockmount **15.00**
Gravy boat, Mello-Tone or Rockmount **45.00**
Mortar & pestle, cobalt **55.00**
Pie plate, Coorado **55.00**
Pitcher, Open Window, decalcomania, w/lid, lg **125.00**
Plate, dinner; Tulip, decalcomania **75.00**
Shakers, Coorado, gr, pr **65.00**
Shakers, Mello-Tone or Rockmount **15.00**
Teapot, Chrysanthemum, decalcomania **150.00**
Teapot, Tulip, decalcomania **110.00**
Vase, Beehive, orange matt, sm rings, 6" **45.00**
Vase, Brighton, yel matt, bulbous, 8" **70.00**
Vase, bud; yel high gloss, 8" **30.00**
Vase, Empire, yel matt, stepped form, 10" **100.00**
Vase, Florence, bl matt, trumpet neck, uptrn hdls, 12" **125.00**
Vase, Golden, bl matt, integral hdls, 6" **45.00**
Vase, Golden, burgundy high gloss, integral hdls, 6" **45.00**
Vase, Leadville, gr matt, angle hdls, 8" **70.00**
Vase, Matchless, gr matt, emb ribs, 8" **70.00**
Vase, Montrose, bl matt, neck-to-shoulder hdls, 12" **125.00**
Vase, Trinidad, wht matt w/turq int, hdls, 12" **125.00**

Copper

Handcrafted copper was made in America from early in the 18th century until about 1850, with the center of its production in Pennsylvania. Examples have been found signed by such notable coppersmiths as Kidd, Buchanan, Babb, Bently, and Harbeson. Of the many utilitarian items made, teakettles are the most desirable. Early examples from the 18th century were made with a dovetailed joint which was hammered and smoothed to a uniform thickness. Pots from the 19th century were seamed. Coffeepots were made in many shapes and sizes and along with mugs, kettles, warming pans, and measures are easiest to find. Stills ranging in sizes of up to fifty-gallon are popular with collectors today. Our advisor, Mary Frank Gaston, has compiled a lovely book, *Antique Brass and Copper,* with many full-color photos and current market values.

Ale warmer, 12½" **200.00**
Coal hod, helmet shape, 19th C, 20x20", w/shovel **300.00**
Coal/ash box, sq w/pyramid-shaped lid, hinged hdls, 19x17" sq ..**260.00**

Coffeepot, sq hdl, lid attached by brass chain, 13⅜x10¼" 75.00
Colander, punched holes, zinc-coated int, 2 riveted hdls, 17" 60.00
Dipper, dvtl, rolled rim, 3x6⅝"+wrought-iron hdl 85.00
Kettle, apple butter; dvtl, rolled rim, wrought-iron hdl, 17x25" .500.00
Kettle, dvtl, rolled rim, wrought-iron hdl, 10⅝x16¼" 330.00
Kettle, dvtl, wrought-iron hdl mts, iron bail hdl, 9x14" 135.00
Ladle, 3⅜" dia, w/15" wrought-iron hdl 45.00
Measure, ribbon hdl, flared rim, 1-gal, 10½x6¾" dia 40.00
Measure, ribbon hdl, flared rim, 1-qt, 6¼x4⅜" dia 25.00
Sauce pans, CI hdls, tin linings, set of 3: 2⅝", 3¼", 4" 125.00
Teakettle, copper bail hdl, brass hdl mts, CT, 5¼x8⅝" 160.00
Teakettle, dvtl, brass trim, hinged lid, 12" 140.00
Teakettle, dvtl, brass trim, polished, 9½" 105.00
Teakettle, dvtl, gooseneck spout, brass hdl brackets, 8⅜x10" 110.00
Teakettle, dvtl, gooseneck spout, J Kidd, PA, ca 1800, 6½" 990.00
Teakettle, Majestic, brass hdl mts, ebonized finial, 12x13" 55.00
Teapot, gooseneck spout, collar at base, hinged lid, mk, 8½" 110.00
Teapot, gooseneck spout, dvtl sides, 19th C, mini, 5" 200.00
Wash boiler, oblong, tin lid, 17x27x13" 60.00

Copper Lustre

Copper lustre is a term referring to a type of pottery made in Staffordshire after the turn of the 19th century. It is finished in a metallic rusty-brown glaze resembling true copper. Pitchers are found in abundance, ranging from simple styles with dull bands of color to those with fancy handles and bands of embossed, polychromed flowers. Bowls are common; goblets, mugs, teapots, and sugar bowls much less so. It's easy to find, but not in good condition. Pieces with hand-painted decoration and those with historical transfers are the most valuable.

Cup & saucer, House, mini, 1¼" 25.00
Mug, feather designs on gr band, scroll hdl, 5x5¼" 60.00
Pepper pot, yel band, ftd, dome top, 4½", EX 75.00
Pitcher, Faith purple transfer w/mc, pk lustre striping, 4¼" 40.00
Pitcher, mc figures on wide bl band, sq hdl, prof rpr, 7⅛" 100.00
Pitcher, mc floral band, bearded man spout, dolphin hdl, 7" 140.00
Pitcher, mc floral band, scroll hdl, 4⅛" 100.00
Pitcher, mc marbleizing, ftd, scroll hdl, 5½" 75.00
Pitcher, relief figure, mc w/dk bl band, 3½" 30.00
Pitcher, sanded band on neck w/overall lustre, ftd, 4⅜" 35.00
Pitcher, wide cream band w/emb figures, scroll hdl, 4⅝" 30.00
Pitcher, 2-color stripe on cobalt band, scroll hdl, ftd, 4⅛" 50.00
Salt cellar, House band, pk int, ftd 85.00
Teapot, 4-color floral, gallery lid rim, 5⅝" 65.00
Waste bowl, 4-color floral band, ftd, 3x6" dia 30.00

Coralene Glass

Coralene is a unique type of art glass easily recognized by the tiny grains of glass that form its decoration. Lacy allover patterns of seaweed, geometrics, and florals were used, as well as solid forms such as fish, plants, and single blossoms. (Seaweed is most commonly found and not as valuable as the other types of decoration.) It was made by several glasshouses both here and abroad. Values are based to a considerable extent on the amount of beading that remains. Our advisors for this category are Betty and Clarence Maier; they are listed in the Directory under Pennsylvania.

Biscuit barrel, pk Dmn Quilt MOP w/seaweed, SP trim, 7" 800.00
Cruet, turq w/bl-to-yel wheat, frosted hdl, 5", no stopper 350.00

Pitcher, tankard, cased peachblow with gold beading in seaweed motif, camphor handle, numbered base, 9¾", $450.00.

Vase, champagne color w/seaweed, 3⅝x2¼" 135.00
Vase, peachblow w/crystal seaweed, gold trim, 7½" 650.00
Vase, peachblow w/yel seaweed, cylindrical, 8¼" 525.00
Vase, peachblow w/yel seaweed, dbl-branch camphor hdl, 7" 650.00

Cordey

The Cordey China Company was founded in 1942 in Trenton, New Jersey, by Boleslaw Cybis. The operation was small with less than a dozen workers. They produced figurines, vases, lamps, and similar wares, much of which was marketed through gift shops both nationwide and abroad. Though the earlier wares were made of plaster, Cybis soon developed his own formula for a porcelain composition which he called 'Papka.' Cordey figurines and busts were characterized by old-world charm, Rococo scrolls, delicate floral appliqués, ruffles, and real lace which was dipped in liquified clay to add dimension to the work.

Although on rare occasions some items were not numbered or signed, the 'basic' figure was cast both with numbers and the Cordey signature. The molded pieces were then individually decorated and each marked with its own impressed identification number as well as a mark to indicate the artist-decorator. Their numbering system began with 200 and in later years progressed into the 8000s. As can best be established, Cordey continued production until sometime in the mid-1950s. Boleslaw Cybis died in 1957, his wife in 1958. Our advisor for this category is Sharon A. Payne; she is listed in the Directory under Washington.

Key: ff — full figure

#302, lady, ff, flowing dress, 16" 195.00
#304/#305, Grape Harvesters, 16½", pr 225.00
#3241, Oriental duck, wht, 14½" 250.00
#325, Chinese wood duck, intricate base, EX colors, rare 400.00
#343, pheasant, vibrant mc, very early, scarce, 17" 325.00
#4005/#4006, man & lady, ff, pr 300.00
#4129, courting group, man & lady on rnd base, lacy, rare 335.00
#5008, pilgrim, 7" 100.00
#5009, Junior Prom 65.00
#5014, bust of lady 55.00
#5028, bust of lady, textured bonnet & collar, scroll base 90.00
#5029, Elizabeth, high ruffled collar, Raleigh Group, 7½" 85.00
#5034, bust of Raleigh, Raleigh Group, 7½" 85.00
#5043, man, ff, Colonial attire 175.00
#5054, lady, flowers in hair, bustle, skirt forms base, 9¼" 120.00
#5084, lady, Madame, upswept hair, scrolled base, 11¾" 100.00
#6004, bluebird on stump, lg 150.00

#6046, ashtray **22.00**
#6405, lady, flower-trimmed hat, pk & gray dress, 10½" **110.00**
#7004, tray (or shallow bowl), 13x9" **100.00**
#7008, coruncopia, 6½" **135.00**
#7026, bottle, scent; shades of bl, iris-form stopper, 8" **95.00**
#7028, wall shelf, Art Nouveau nude w/cornucopia, 8x6½" **100.00**
#7061, vase, birds on leaf, roses appl ea side, 8¾" **165.00**
#7094 vase, Oriental figures & florals, gourd form, 9x8" **165.00**
#8308, bust, man's, 14¾" **275.00**
#914, clock, mantel; Rococo, Lanshire Electric, 9½" **165.00**
Bowl, w/upright lady's torso & articulated hand, 8", w/wall hanger ...**225.00**
Cat, wht w/gr eyes & pk ears, script mk, 8½" **200.00**
Catalog, factory's; 50-pg **50.00**
Lamp, Chinese Goddess, 12" figure on wooden base, 26" **185.00**
Lamp, lady in dk bl w/much lace (12"), 17" overall **150.00**

Corkscrews

The history of the corkscrew dates back to the mid-1600s, when wine makers concluded that the best-aged wine was that stored in smaller containers, either stoneware or glass. Since plugs left unsealed were often damaged by rodents, corks were cut off flush with the bottle top and sealed with wax or a metal cover. Removing the cork cleanly with none left to grasp became a problem. The task was found to be relatively simple using the worm on the end of a flintlock gun rod. So the corkscrew evolved. Endless patents have been issued for mechanized models. Handles range from carved wood, ivory, and bone to porcelain and repousse silver. Exotic materials such as agate, mother-of-pearl, and gold plate were also used on occasion. Celluloid lady's legs are popular.

In the following descriptions, values are for examples in excellent condition, unless noted otherwise. Our advisor for this category is Roger Baker; he is listed in the Directory under California.

Anheuser-Busch, bottle shape, EX **62.50**
Belgium, Challenge, common type, 1850s, EX **28.00**
Black bulldog, Syroco wood, 1920-30s **52.00**
Champion, CI w/emb vines overall, wood hdl, bar mt **145.00**
England, Lund Patentee London, rack & pinion, Pat 1855, EX ..**315.00**
England, pearl hdls, scent & medicine bottle puller, 3½" **70.00**
England, 4-finger pull, w/button, ca 1895 ....**30.00**
France, iron, octagonal shape, dbl wooden hdl, rnd fr **75.00**
France, Laurent Sibet Rockport, grapevine hdl, EX **20.00**
Germany, legs figural (gr stripes), ca 1910, EX **345.00**
Germany, pocket style, plated lifter & worm, silver sleeve **95.00**
Germany, swivel over collar, rubber ring on lower fr, mid-1900s ..**28.00**
Haff Pat, brass ring mk Pat Appl For, Apr/May 1885 ....**95.00**
Italy, bar man figural, dbl-lever style, 10½" **55.00**
London, John Dewar & Son Distillery, bottle type **40.00**
Man w/straw hat figural, modern dbl lever type, 8½" **23.00**
Monkey (or dog), gold jeweled, corkscrew tail **23.00**
Plastic duplex (dbl worm), picnic type, modern **6.00**
Sommerlier, dbl lever, chrome **35.00**
Thomason, appl bronze crest tablet, bone hdl, Pat 1802, EX **450.00**
US, brass band on boar's tooth hdl, 6", EX **95.00**
US, Clough 1910 Pat, Hennessy advertising on wood sleeve **42.00**
US, H&B Mfg Co, rosewood hdl w/brush & ivory plug on end **58.00**
US, Hollwig, advertising for Pabst Milwaukee, 1891 ....**145.00**
US, NP steel worm, cap lifter & wire breaker, EX **172.50**
US, Roundlet, bullet shape **58.00**
US, staghorn hdl, sterling silver cap ea end, 1900s **140.00**
Walker, 1900 mechanism, wooden hdl **35.00**

Walrus tusk hdl w/sterling ends, SP worm & lifter, Pat 1906 ......**175.00**
Williamson's Pat 1897, self-pulling, EX **35.00**

Cosmos

Cosmos, sometimes called Stemless Daisy, is a patterned glass tableware produced from 1894 through 1915 by Consolidated Lamp and Glass Company. Relief-molded flowers on a finely crosscut background were painted in soft colors of pink, blue, and yellow. Though nearly all were made of milk glass, a few items may be found in clear glass with the designs painted on. In addition to the tableware, lamps were also made.

Bottle, cologne; orig stopper, rare **300.00**
Butter dish, 5x8" **275.00**
Creamer **150.00**
Lamp, banquet, kerosene, 24" **575.00**
Lamp, banquet, slender base, rnd globe, all orig, 16" **525.00**
Lamp, mini, 7½", EX **275.00**
Lamp, parlour; half-shade on matching base, 8" **375.00**
Lamp, 10" **450.00**
Pickle castor, mk SP fr **500.00**
Pitcher, milk; 5" **250.00**
Pitcher, syrup; 6" **300.00**
Pitcher, water **350.00**
Shakers, tall, orig lids, pr **175.00**
Spooner **125.00**
Sugar bowl, open **150.00**
Sugar bowl, w/lid **185.00**
Sugar shaker **400.00**
Tumbler, 3¾" **75.00**

Cottageware

You'll find a varied assortment of novelty dinnerware items, all styled as cozy little English cottages or huts with cone-shaped roofs; some may have a waterwheel or a windmill. Marks will vary. English-made Price Brothers or Beswick pieces are valued in the same range as those marked Occupied Japan, while items marked simply Japan are considerably less pricey. Our advisor for this category is Grace Klender; she is listed in the Directory under Ohio. In the listings that follow, all are English unless noted otherwise.

Pin tray, Price Brothers, 4", $20.00; Teapot, Price Brothers, 6¼", $70.00.

Bank, dbl slot, Price Bros, 4½x3½x5" **85.00**
Biscuit jar, wicker hdl, Maruhon Ware, Occupied Japan, 6½" **65.00**

Bowl, salad; Price Bros 65.00
Butter dish, Price Bros 45.00
Butter pat, emb cottage, rectangular, Occupied Japan 18.00
Chocolate pot, Price Bros 135.00
Condiment set, mustard, 2½" s&p, on 5" hdld leaf tray 75.00
Condiment set, mustard pot, s&p, tray, row arrangement, 6" 45.00
Condiment set, mustard pot, s&p, tray, row arrangement, 7¾" 45.00
Condiment set, 3-part cottage on shaped tray w/appl bush, 4½" ..75.00
Cookie jar, pk/brn/gr, sq, Japan, 8½x5½" 65.00
Cookie jar/canister, cylindrical, Price Bros 125.00
Cookie or biscuit jar, Occupied Japan 85.00
Creamer (post-like hdls) & sugar (no hdls) on 8" tray 65.00
Creamer & sugar bowl, Price Bros, 2½", 4½" 45.00
Cup & saucer, chocolate; str-sided cup: 3½x2¾", saucer 5½" 40.00
Cup & saucer, Price Bros, 2½", 4½" 45.00
Demitasse pot, Price Bros 100.00
Egg cup set, 4 on 6" sq tray, Price Bros 60.00
Grease jar, Occupied Japan, from $25 to 35.00
Marmalade, Price Bros 40.00
Marmalade & jelly, 2 cojoined house, Price Bros 85.00
Mug, Price Bros 50.00
Pitcher, tankard; rnd, Price Bros, 7⅞" 125.00
Pitcher, water; Price Bros 150.00
Platter, England, 11¾" L 45.00
Sugar box (for cubes), Price Bros, 5¾" L 45.00
Tea set, Japan, child's, serves 4 ....150.00
Teapot, Price Bros., rare sz, 7¼" 75.00
Teapot, Keele Street, +cr/sug 95.00
Toast rack, 3-slot, Price Bros, 3½" 65.00
Toast rack, 4-slot, Price Bros, 5½" 75.00
Tumblers, Occupied Japan, 3½" set of 6 ....60.00

Coverlets

The Jacquard attachment for hand looms represented a culmination of weaving developments made in France. Introduced to America by the early 1820s, it gave professional weavers the ability to easily create complex patterns with curved lines. Those who could afford the new loom adaptation could now use hole-punched pasteboard cards to weave floral patterns that before could only be achieved with intense labor on a draw-loom.

Before the Jacquard mechanism, most weavers made their coverlets in geometric patterns. Use of indigo-blue and brightly colored wools often livened the twills and overshot patterns available to the small-loom home weaver. Those who had larger multiple-harness looms could produce warm double-woven, twill-block, or summer-and-winter designs.

While the new floral and pictorial patterns' popularity had displaced the geometrics in urban areas, the mid-Atlantic, and the Midwest by the 1840s, even factory production of the Jacquard coverlets was disrupted by cotton and wool shortages during the Civil War. A revived production in the 1870s saw a style change to a center-medallion motif, but a new fad for white 'Marseilles' spreads soon halted sales of Jacquard-woven coverlets. Production of Jacquard carpets continued to the turn of the century.

Rural and frontier weavers continued to make geometric-design coverlets through the 19th century, and local craft revivals have continued the tradition through this century. All-cotton overshots were factory produced in Kentucky from the 1940s, and factories and professional weavers made cotton-and-wool overshots during the past decade. Many Jacquard-woven coverlets have dates and names of places and people (often the intended owner — not the weaver) woven into corners or borders. In the listings that follow, examples are blue and white

unless noted otherwise. When dates are included, they appear on the coverlet itself as part of the woven design.

Key: mdl — medallion

Jacquard

Washington Hail, red, blue, and green, dated 1869, 76" square, minor discoloration and fringe loss, $575.00.

Floral mdl, Christian/heathen border, 2-pc, 73x73", VG 165.00
Floral mdl w/lg star, eagle corners, 4-color, 1-pc, 78x84", VG 250.00
Floral mdls, lily border, red/bl, 2-pc, 1869, 80x86", NM 990.00
Floral mdls, rose border, 4-color, 2-pc, PA 1843, 70x88", EX 415.00
Floral mdls (4), 1858, 2-pc, dbl weave, 74x84", EX 900.00
Floral mdls/grapes, bl/red/wht, 2-pc, 1860, 72x83", VG 385.00
Floral mdls/pinwheels/roosters, red/bl, 2-pc, 76x82", VG 350.00
Foliage & starflower, 2-pc, single weave, 1851, 72x80", NM 770.00
Geometric floral, blk/wht, 2-pc, dbl weave, 1852, 70x85", NM ..1,100.00
Rose mdls, eagle corners, blk/bl, 2-pc, 1831, 74x92", NM 1,155.00
Rose mdls (4), bird/rose borders, 4-color, 2-pc, 70x91" 660.00
Rose/star mdls, 5-color, single weave, 2-pc, 1841, 71x89", VG ...330.00
Star, floral border, 3-color, dbl weave/1-pc, 1851, 79x99", EX ...650.00
Star mdls, 4-color, 2-pc, single weave, 1867, 76x92", VG 250.00
Vintage, Christian/heathen border, 4-color/1-pc, 1850, 76x90", EX 850.00
Washington portrait/horses/eagle, 3-color, PA, 1869, 75x81", EX 1,150.00

Overshot

Optical, fringe 1 end, 2-pc, 74x74" 150.00
Optical, stains/loss, 84x100" 250.00
Optical, salmon red/blk, bl cotton warp, 2-pc, 82x90", EX 165.00
Optical, 3-color, 2-pc, incomplete fringe, 62x84" 180.00
Stars w/pine tree border, 4-color, 2-pc, 70x92", VG 220.00

Cowan

Guy Cowan opened a small pottery near Cleveland, Ohio, ca 1909, where he made tile and artware on a small scale from the natural red clay available there. He developed distinctive glazes — necessary, he felt, to cover the dark red body. After the war and a temporary halt in production, Cowan moved his pottery to Rocky River, where he made a commercial line of artware utilizing a highly-fired white porcelain. Although he acquiesced to the necessity of mass production, every effort was made to insure a product of highest quality. Fine artists, among them Waylande Gregory, Thelma Frazier, and Viktor Schreckengost, designed pieces which were often produced in limited editions, some of which sell today for prices in the thousands. Most of the ware was marked 'Cowan' or 'Lakewood Ware,' not to be confused with the name of the 1930 mass-produced line called 'Lakeware.' Falling under the crunch of the Great Depression, the pottery closed in 1931.

The use of an asterisk (*) in the listing below indicates a nonfactory name that is being provided as a suggested name for the convenience of present-day collectors. One example is the glaze *Original Ivory, which is a high-gloss white that resembles undecorated porcelain. It was used on many of Cowan's lady 'flower figures' (Cowan's more graceful term for what some collectors call frogs).

Our advisor for this category is Mark Bassett; he is listed in the Directory under Ohio. With Victoria Naumann, Mark is the author of *Cowan Pottery and the Cleveland School*, a detailed history of Cowan Pottery and of Guy Cowan's students, colleagues, and designers. Prices quoted are for examples in mint condition, unless noted otherwise.

Key: Sp/I — Special Ivory

Plate, hand-painted mission scene, F. Luis Mora, 8", $195.00.

Bookends, Camels, Alexander Blazys, #748, Gooseberry, 8" **2,000.00**
Bookends, Sunbonnet Girls, #521, Antique Gr, pr **450.00**
Bowl, Etruscan, #B-6, RG Cowan, Oriental Red...........................**250.00**
Creamer, kitten hdl, Jet or Original Ivory, early mks, ea..............**150.00**
Decanter bookends, King-Queen, #E-4/#E-5, blk, pr **2,000.00**
Flower Frog, Laurel, #721, Orig Ivory, 10" **950.00**
Flower frog, Tambourine Dancer, #805, Sp/I, 10½"..................**2,500.00**
Flower frog, Swan, #F-7, Waylande Gregory, Sp/I........................**950.00**
Nut Dish #788, Clown, Elizabeth Andersen, Turq......................**115.00**
Plaque, Atalanta & Hound, Russet Brn, 15½"...........................**1,200.00**
Sculpture, Woodland Nymph, nude on stump, ltd ed, 14" **3,000.00**
Sculptures, Russian peasants, terra cotta, ltd ed, set of 4...........**5,000.00**
Tea tile, flowers, hexagonal, Raoul Josset, Sp/I **150.00**
Vase, China Bird, #747, RG Cowan, Melon Gr, 11¼".............**1,000.00**
Vase, fan, sea horses & shell, October, 8" **200.00**
Vase, pillow; #649-A, RG Cowan, Marigold, 6½" **65.00**

Cracker Jack

Kids have been buying Cracker Jack since it was first introduced in the 1890s. By 1912 it was packaged with a free toy inside. Before the first kernel was crunched, eager fingers had retrieved the surprise from the depth of the box — actually no easy task, considering the care required to keep the contents so swiftly displaced from spilling over the side! Though a little older, perhaps, many of those same kids still are looking — just as eagerly — for the Cracker Jack prizes. Point of sale, company collectibles, and the prizes as well have over the years reflected America's changing culture. Grocer sales and incentives from around the turn of the century — paper dolls, postcards, and song books — were often marked Rueckheim Brothers (the inventors of Cracker Jack) or Reliable Confections. Over the years the company made some changes, leaving a trail of clues that often help collectors date their items. The company's name changed in 1922 from Rueckheim Brothers & Eckstein (who had been made a partner for inventing a method for keeping the caramelized

kernels from sticking together) to The Cracker Jack Company. Their Brooklyn office was open from 1914 until it closed in 1923 The first time the sailor Jack logo was used on their packaging was in 1919. The sailor image of a Reuckheim child (with red, white, and blue colors) was introduced by these German immigrants in an attempt to show U.S.A. support during the time of heightened patriotism after WW I. For packages and 'point of sale' dating, note that the word 'prize' was used from 1912 to 1925, 'novelty' from 1925 to 1932, and 'toy' from 1933 on.

The first loose-packed prizes were toys made of wood, clay, tin, metal, and lithographed paper. Plastic toys were introduced in 1946. Paper wrapped for safety purposes in 1948, subjects echo the 'hype' of the day — yo-yos, tops, whistles, and sports cards in the simple, peaceful days of our country, propaganda and war toys in the '40s, games in the '50s, and space toys in the '60s. Few of the estimated 15 billion prizes were marked. Advertising items from Angelus Marshmallow and Checkers Confections (cousins of the Cracker Jack family) are also collectible. When no condition is indicated, the items listed below are assumed to be in excellent to mint condition. 'CJ' indicates that the item is marked. Note: An often-asked question concerns the tin Toonerville Trolley called 'CJ.' No data has been found in the factory archives to authenticate this item; it is assumed that the 'CJ' merely refers to its small size. For further information see *Cracker Jack Toys, The Complete, Unofficial Guide for Collectors*, by Larry White. Our advisor for this category is Wes Johnson; he is listed in the Directory under Kentucky. Also look for *The Prize Insider* newsletter listed in the Directory under Clubs, Newsletters, and Catalogs.

Cast Metal Prizes

Badge, shield, CJ Jr Detective, silver, 1931, 1¼" **40.00**
Badge, 6-point star, mk CJ Police, silver, 1931, 1¼" **44.00**
Button, stud bk, Me for Cracker Jack, boy & dog, oval **44.00**
Button, stud bk, Xd bats & ball, CJ pitcher/etc series, 1928 ....**130.00**
Chair, T (Tootsie), 3 different sectional pcs, pnt, mini, ea **12.00**
Coins, Presidents, 31 series, CJ, 1933, ea **8.00**
Dollhouse items: lantern, mug, candlestick, etc; no mk, ea **6.50**
Horse & wagon, CJ, 3-D, silver or gold, early, 2½", ea **250.00**
Pistol, soft lead, inked, CJ on barrel, early, rare, 2⅛" **180.00**
Ring, alphabet letter setting (series), unmk, ea **4.00**
Rocking horse, no rider, 3-D, inked, early, 1⅛" **22.00**
Rocking horse w/boy, 3-D, inked, early, 1½" **29.00**
Spinner, early pkg in center, 'More You Eat...,' CJ, rare **295.00**
Tootsietoy series: boats, cars, animals; '31, ¾"-1½", ea **7.00**

Dealer Incentives and Premiums

Badge, pin-bk, celluloid, lady w/CJ label reverse, 1905, 1¼" **65.00**
Bat, baseball; wood, Hillerich & Bradsby, CJ, full sz **85.00**
Blotter, CJ question mk box, yel, 7¾x3¾" **185.00**
Book, pocket; jester on cover, CJ Riddles **73.00**
Book, pocket; riddle/sailor boy/dog on cover, RWB, CJ, 1919 ......**60.00**
Book, recipe; Angelus, 1930s **22.00**
Book, Uncle Sam Song Book, CJ, 1911, ea **60.00**
Cart w/2 movable wheels, wood dowel tongue, CJ **80.00**
Corkscrew/opener, metal plated, CJ/Angelus, 3" **85.00**
Corkscrew/opener, metal plated, CJ/Angelus, 3¾" tube case **85.00**
Golf tee set, wood tees in paper 'matchbook' folder, CJ, 1920s ...**725.00**
Harmonica, full scale, emb CJ, early, 5⅛" **385.00**
Jigsaw puzzle, CJ or Checkers, 1 of 4, 7x10", in envelope **35.00**
Marbles, Akro set of 12 in box w/instructions, CJ, 1929 ....**950.00**
Mask, Halloween; paper, CJ, series, 10" or 12", ea **22.00**
Match holder, hinged, eng gold-tone case, CJ, 2½x1⅞" **650.00**
Mirror, oval, Angelus (redhead or blond) on box **89.00**
Palm puzzle, mirror bk, CJ, mk Germany/RWB, 1910-14, 1½" ..**110.00**

Pen, ink; w/nib, tin litho bbl, CJ **550.00**
Pencil top clip, metal/celluloid, oval boy & dog logo **220.00**
Pencil top clip, metal/celluloid, tube shape w/package **220.00**
Postcard, bear, 1 of 16, CJ, 1907, ea **37.00**
Puzzle, metal, CJ/Angelus, 1 of 15, '34, in envelope, ea **14.00**
Riddle card, 2 series of 20, w/package/from factory, CJ, '07, ea **8.00**
Tablet, school; CJ, 1929, 8x10" **195.00**
Thimble, aluminum, CJ Co/Angelus, red pnt, rare, ea **165.00**
Wings, air corps type, silver or blk, stud-bk, CJ, '30s, 3", ea **80.00**

Packaging

Box, popcorn; Question Mark box end for CJ 'Toy,' 1923-27 ....**85.00**
Box, popcorn; red scroll border, CJ 'Prize,' 1912-25, ea **95.00**
Box, popcorn; store display, CJ 'Novelty,' 1925-32, ea **90.00**
Canister, tin, CJ Candy Corn Crisp, 10-oz **75.00**
Canister, tin, CJ Coconut Corn Crisp, 1-lb **55.00**
Canister, tin, CJ Coconut Corn Crisp, 10-oz **65.00**
CJ Commemorative canister, mc scene, 1990s, ea **9.00**
CJ Commemorative canister, wht w/red scroll, 1980s, ea **8.00**
Crate, shipping; wood, CJ, Rueckheim Bros Eck, 1902-22, lg **150.00**

Paper Prizes

Point-of-sale store poster, showing package and prizes of the day, Rueckheim Bros & Eckstein (a name that was dropped in 1922 in favor of 'The Cracker Jack Co.'), 1912, $525.00.

Baseball CJ score counter, 3⅜" L **130.00**
Book, Animals (or Birds), to color, Makatoy, unmk, 1949, mini ..**35.00**
Book, Bess & Bill on CJ Hill, series of 12, 1937, mini **95.00**
Book, Birds We Know, CJ, 1928, mini **85.00**
Book, Chaplin flip book, CJ, 1920s, ea **125.00**
Book, drawing w/tracing paper, CJ, 1920s, mini **110.00**
Book, Twigg & Sprigg, CJ, 1930, mini **100.00**
Booklet, stickers/wise cracks/riddles, Borden, CJ, 1965 on **3.00**
Decal, cartoon or nursery rhyme figure, 1947-49, CJ **12.00**
Disguise, ears, red (out of carrier), 1950, pr **30.00**
Disguise, ears, red (still in carrier), CJ, 1950, pr **65.00**
Disguise, glasses, hinged, cello lenses, CJ Where Ever..., '33 ....**125.00**
Disguise, glasses, hinged, w/eyeballs, unmk, 1933 ....**6.00**
Disguise, mustache, blk/brn, in carrier, CJ, 1949 ....**55.00**
Fortune Teller, boy/dog on film in envelope, CJ, '20s, 1¾x2½" ...**75.00**
Fortune wheel, 2-pc litho, turn for fortune, CJ, 1¾" **65.00**
Game, Midget Auto Race, wheel spins, CJ, 1949, 3⅜" H **45.00**
Game spinner, ...baseball at home, rectangle, CJ, 2¾" W **125.00**
Game spinner, ...baseball at home, unmk, 1946, 1½" dia **50.00**
Hat, fold out, More You Eat/More You Want, CJ, early **75.00**
Hat, Indian headdress, CJ, 1931, 2½" H **110.00**
Hat, Indian headdress, CJ, 1950s, 5⅜" H **275.00**

Hat, Me for CJ, early, ea **105.00**
Hat visor, baseball, tie-on string, red or gr, CJ, 1931 ....**110.00**
Magic game book, erasable slate, CJ, series of 13, 1946, ea **35.00**
Movie, boy at blkboard, turn wheel: draws/erases, CJ, '31, 2" **175.00**
Movie, Goofy Zoo, turn wheel(s): change animals, 1939 ....**17.00**
Movie, pull tab for 2nd picture, series, CJ, 1943, 1¼", ea **82.00**
Movie, pull tab for 2nd picture, yel, early, 3", in envelope **125.00**
Sand toy pictures, pours for action, series of 14, 1967, ea **25.00**
Top, golf game, wood stick center, CJ, 1933 ....**57.00**
Top, string; Rainbow Spinner, 2 pcs, cb, different designs, ea **55.00**
Transfer, iron-on, sport figure or patriotic, CJ, 1939, ea **22.00**
Transfer, iron-on, sport figure or patriotic, unmk, 1939, ea **6.00**
Whistle, Blow for More, CJ box/boy/dog, yel, 1931, ea **55.00**
Whistle, Blow for More, CJ/Angelus packages, 1928, '31 or '33, ea .**45.00**
Whistle, pressed paper, series of 10, 1948-49, CJ, 1¼x2", ea **34.00**
Whistle, Razz Zooka, C Carey Cloud design, CJ, 1949 ....**32.00**

Plastic Prizes

Animals, standup, letter on bk, series of 26, Nosco, 1953, ea **4.00**
Animals, standup on base, assorted, Nosco or CJ, 1947 on, ea **2.00**
Baseball players, 3-D, bl or gray team, 1948, 1½", ea **8.00**
Disc, emb comic character, series of 12, 1954, unmk, 1½" **16.00**
Disc, emb fish plaque, oval, series of 10, 1956, unmk, ea **14.00**
Dog, 3-D, hollow base, series of 10, CJCO, 1954, ea **6.00**
Figure, circus; stands on base, 1 of 12, Nosco, 1951-54 ....**2.50**
Figure on rocking base, semi-flat, 1 of 9, Cloud design, '56 ....**4.00**
Fob, alphabet letter w/loop on top, 1 of 26, 1954, 1½" **4.00**
Magnifying glass, many designs/shapes, from 1961, ea **1.00**
Palm puzzle, ball(s) roll into holes, dome or rnd, from 1966 ....**6.00**
Palm puzzle, ball(s) roll into holes, rectangle, CJ, 1920s, ea **55.00**
Palm puzzle, ball(s) roll into holes, sq, CJ, 1920s, ea **45.00**
Pinball game, lever shoots ball/score in holes, 1964 to recent **5.00**
Ships in a bottle, 6 different, 1960, ea **6.00**
Signs, road; Stop, Caution, etc, yel, series of 10, 1954-60, ea **4.00**
Spinner, tops varied colors, 10 designs, from 1948, ea **2.50**
Toys, take apart/assemble, variety, from '62, assembled, ea **2.00**
Toys, take apart/assemble, variety, from '62, unassembled, ea **4.00**
Whistle, tube w/animals on top, CJ, series, 1950-53, 1⅜" **7.00**

Tin Prizes

Badge, boy & dog diecut, complete w/bend-over tab, CJ **150.00**
Badge, boy & dog diecut, w/o tab at top **85.00**
Badge, emb/plated CJ officer, 2⅜" or 1⅝", early, ea **110.00**
Badge, litho, red/wht/bl, boy/dog, CJ, 1920s, 1¼" dia **150.00**
Bank, 3-D book form, red/gr/or blk, CJ Bank, early, 2" **105.00**
Bookmark, dogs, 4 different, 1941, 3", ea **30.00**
Brooch or pin, various designs on card, CJ/logo, early, ea **125.00**
Cash register, litho, More You Eat, CJ, early, 1⅞" **275.00**
Clicker, 'Noisy CJ Snapper,' pear shape, aluminum, 1949 ....**32.00**
Clicker, CJ Telegraph, Pat 1897, inked, 1¾" dia, ea **145.00**
Doll dishes, tin plated, CJ, '31, 1¾", 1⅞", & 2⅛" dia, ea **35.00**
Fortune Wheel, 2-pc litho, CJ, 1939-41, 1¾" **55.00**
Helicopter, yel propeller, wood stick, unmk, 1937, 2⅝" **27.00**
Horse & wagon, litho diecut, CJ & Angelus, 2⅛" **65.00**
Horse & wagon, litho diecut, gray/red mks, CJ, 1914-23, 3⅛" ...**395.00**
Model T Ford, license: NY 1915 #999, blk/wht, CJ, rare, 2" **410.00**
Pocket watch, silver of gold, CJ as numerals, 1931, 1½" **55.00**
Sled, tin plated, CJ, 1931, 2" L **35.00**
Small box shape: electric alarm clock litho, unmk, 1⅛" **85.00**
Small box shape: electric stove litho, unmk, 1⅛" **90.00**
Small box shape: garage litho, unmk, 1⅛" **85.00**
Small box shape: radio litho, bl, unmk, 1⅛" **80.00**

Soldier, litho, die-cut standup, officer/private/etc, unmk, ea **17.00**
Spinner, wood stick, Always on Top, red/wht/bl, CJ, 1½" dia **25.00**
Spinner, wood stick, Fortune Teller Game, red/wht/bl, CJ, 1½" ..**90.00**
Spinner, wood stick, Question Mark Box at center, CJ **50.00**
Spinner, wood stick, 2 Toppers, red/wht/bl, Angelus/Jack, 1½" ...**75.00**
Stand up, comic character, 1 of 10, CJ, 1936-46, ea **105.00**
Stand up, oval Am Flag, series of 4, unmk, 1936-45, ea **35.00**
Stand up, rectangle litho, boy & dog, ca 1916, lg or sm, ea **155.00**
Tall box shape: Frozen Foods locker freezer, '47, unmk, 1¾" **65.00**
Tall box shape: grandfather clock, unmk, 1947, 1¾" **55.00**
Tall box shape: radio, Tune in w/CJ, brn/yel, 1939, 1¾" **120.00**
Tall box shape: refrigerator car, CJ, 1947, 1¾" L **155.00**
Train, engine & tender, litho, CJ Line/512 ....**125.00**
Train, litho coach only, red, unmk, 1941 ....**24.00**
Train, litho engine only, red, 1941, unmk **20.00**
Train, Lone Eagle Flyer cars, unmk **65.00**
Train, Lone Eagle Flyer engine, unmk **60.00**
Tray, emb, litho w/early package, smaller version **115.00**
Tray, emb, litho w/early package, 2¼x1¾" **95.00**
Truck, litho, RWB, CJ/Angelus, 1931, ea **65.00**
Wagon shape: Caterpillar tractor, unmk, 1931, 1¾" L **29.00**
Wagon shape: CJ Shows, yel circus wagon, series of 5, ea **135.00**
Wagon shape: Playtime Trailer (auto trailer), unmk, 1947 ....**40.00**
Wagon shape: tank, orange/red/gr camouflage, unmk **65.00**
Wagon shape: Tank Corps No 57, gr & blk, 1941 ....**30.00**
Wheelbarrow, tin plated, bk leg in place, CJ, 1931, 2½" L **33.00**

Miscellaneous

Ad, comic book, CJ, ea **14.00**
Ad, Saturday Evening Post, mc, CJ, 1919, 11x14" **18.00**
Hat, ball park vendor cap, CJ, 1930s **30.00**
Ink blotter, advertisement **235.00**
Lunch box, tin, 2 hdls, CJ, 1980s, 4½x5x6" **25.00**
Lunch box, tin emb, CJ, 1970s, 4x7x9" **30.00**
Medal, CJ salesman award, brass, 1939, scarce **125.00**
Sign, bathing beauty, 5-color cb, CJ, early, 17x22" **460.00**
Sign, boy or girl w/box of CJ, 5-color cb, early, 17x22", ea **460.00**
Sign, Jack & Bingo, die-cut litho, easel standup, CJ, early **450.00**
Sign, Jack & Bingo, standing on early CJ pkg, mc cb, rare **520.00**
Sign, Santa & prizes, mc cb, Angelus, early, lg **220.00**
Sign, Santa & prizes, mc cb, Checkers, early, lg **1,000.00**
Sign, Santa & prizes, mc cb, CJ, early, lg **265.00**

Cranberry

Cranberry glass is named for its resemblance to the color of cranberry juice. It was made by many companies both here and abroad, becoming popular in America soon after the Civil War. It was made in free-blown ware as well as mold-blown. Today cranberry glass is being reproduced, and it is sometimes difficult to distinguish the old from the new. Ask a reputable dealer if you are unsure.

For further information we recommend *American Art Glass* by John A. Shuman III, available from Collector Books or your local bookstore. See also Cruets; Salts; Sugar Shakers; Syrups.

Basket, appl clear points on body & rim, rope hdl, English, 8" ...**200.00**
Bottle, mc floral, clear cut faceted stopper, 7½x8⅛" **165.00**
Bottle, scent; gold leaves & branches, bubble stopper, 6x3" **195.00**
Bowl, appl bl ruffled rim, foreign coin in center, 2⅜x8" **175.00**
Bowl, appl crystal flowers/ft/finial, 9¼x7½" **660.00**
Bowl, swirled ribs, 3x8" **85.00**
Cruet, Hobnail, Hobbs Brockunier, 7¼x4½" **425.00**

Decanter, enameled German lettering on front, 14¼", $450.00.

Decanter, gold & HP floral decor, clear faceted stopper, 12" **275.00**
Decanter, gold stars, gold-trimmed bubble stopper, 6¼x3" **225.00**
Ewer, hawk figural, clear casing & hdl, brass head lid, 10¾" **275.00**
Night light, Herringbone, ball shape, clear teardrop stem, 6⅜" ..**145.00**
Night light, Swirl, clear columned stem, rnd ft, 7⅜x3½" **175.00**
Night light, wht vintage, rtcl brass rim, ormolu fr, 6¼x3¼" **275.00**
Pitcher, bl & wht florals, int ribs, clear hdl, 11⅜x9" **275.00**
Pitcher, bulbous, ice bladder inside, clear hdl, 10x5" **225.00**
Pitcher, Coin Spot, ruffled rim, clear hdl, 9½" **295.00**
Pitcher, Hobnail, sq mouth, clear hdl, 8¼" **295.00**
Pitcher, Invt T'print, HP florals & bee, 8¾x7" **450.00**
Pitcher, Invt T'print, HP raspberry branches, 8x6" **500.00**
Sugar bowl, clear wafer ft, clear lid w/ball finial, 6⅛x4" **110.00**
Sweetmeat basket, bl & wht forget-me-nots w/gold, ornate hdl/lid ...**295.00**
Vase, HP florals & brn foliage, 8½x4" **145.00**
Vase, jack-in-pulpit; appl wht opal ruffle, Wheeling, 9x5" **225.00**
Vase, mc floral, 6⅜x4⅜" **100.00**
Vase, thorny tree trunk, Victorian novelty, 8¼x2⅛" **140.00**
Vase, wht HP Roman Key & scallop, 6x3" **135.00**

Creamware

Creamware was a type of earthenware developed by Wedgwood in the 1760s and produced by many other Staffordshire potteries, including Leeds. Since it could be potted cheaply and was light in weight, it became popular abroad as well as in England, due to the lower freight charges involved in its export. It was revived at Leeds in the late 19th century, and the type most often reproduced was heavily reticulated or molded in high relief. These later wares are easily distinguished from the originals since they are thicker and tend to craze heavily. See also Leeds; Wedgwood.

Basket, pierced, sm hdls, England, ca 1800, w/11½" tray **860.00**
Bowl, scalloped rim, England, ca 1800, chips, 15" **315.00**
Creamer, HP mc flower, reeded hdl, flower finial, rpr, 5¼" **140.00**
Figurine, racehorse, splashed-on brn, ca 1800-22, 6½" **1,000.00**
Pitcher, Geo Washington transfer, Herculaneum, ca 1800, 7", EX ..**450.00**
Plate, dbl red strawberry w/gr leaves, geometric border, 10" **150.00**
Teapot, floral decor, England, ca 1800, 4", EX **135.00**

Creil

Located in Creil et Montereau, France, the Saint-Cricq-Cazeaux/LeBoeuf & Milliet company produced faience as well as soft paste and porcelain wares. They were in business for only about ten years after their inception in 1795.

Cup & saucer, scenic transfer, old rstr, ca 1800 ....**55.00**
Plate, bl transfer, 8", EX **200.00**

Plate, blk transfers on soft pste, 9¾", EX, 8 for	360.00
Plates, blk transfers, yel rim, 8½", 7 for	350.00
Plates, set of 12 months, blk transfers, 8½", 12 for	1,500.00
Platter, blk transfers, rpr, 14"	175.00
Pot de vereme set, classical scenes, 5 covered pcs on tray	350.00
Soup, blk transfers on soft paste, 9½", 6 for	360.00
Tureen, blk transfer, loop hdls, 8" dia, EX	250.00
Tureen, blk transfers on soft paste, w/ladle, 10¼"	300.00

Crown Ducal

The Crown Ducal mark was first used by the A.G. Richardson & Co. pottery of Tunstall, England, in 1925. The items collectors are taking a particular interest in were decorated by Charlotte Rhead, a contemporary of Suzie Cooper and Clarice Cliff, and a member of the esteemed family of English pottery designers and artists.

Bowl, Deco mc leaves on beige mottle, C Rhead, 3½x10"	235.00
Charger, gr/bl/yel, C Rhead, #3052, 13" dia	450.00
Creamer & sugar bowl, Primula	95.00
Cup, demitasse; Ascot	70.00
Cup & saucer, Florida	145.00
Pitcher, floral on tan, C Rhead, Bursley Ware, 9½"	360.00
Pitcher, leaves, mc on gray w/gr trim, C Rhead, 5¾"	360.00
Plate, Primula, 5" sq	165.00
Plate, tan/orange/dk brn, C Rhead, #4926, 10½"	430.00
Plate, Trellis pattern, sq w/hdls, C Rhead	175.00
Vase, florals & geometrics, C Rhead, Bursley Ware, 9"	440.00
Vase, fruit & flowers, lustre, C Rhead, Bursley Ware, 8"	440.00
Vase, Indian Tree, mc on yel-beige, C Rhead, 5⅛x5"	175.00
Vase, poppies on blk, orange lustre int, 7¾x6⅝"	195.00

Crown Milano

Crown Milano was introduced in 1894 by the Mt. Washington Glass Company of New Bedford, Massachusetts. Along with Burmese, it was their bestselling line. The glass is very pale, almost ivory. It was blown, free-form or in molds, highly decorated with flowers and colored enamels, and fired. Made to compete with the English Porcelain Companies, Crown Milano required only about half as many steps to produce as the porcelain (for which it is often mistaken, especially when viewed from a distance). This enabled Mt. Washington to make very attractive pieces at competitive prices. Some of the very early pieces are referred to as 'Albertine'; these had a glossy finish. Satin pieces were marked 'CM,' and some were shipped with paper labels. One of the most outstanding Crown Milano decorators was Frank Guba, who preferred subjects such as flying ducks or other birds. Pieces decorated by him command very high prices.

In the descriptions that follow, the glassware is assumed to be satin unless noted glossy.

Biscuit jar, acorns/leaves w/gold, silver rim/lid, 6"	900.00
Biscuit jar, bamboo, mc w/gold on pnt burmese, SP trim, 6"	900.00
Biscuit jar, floral, Dresden type, bbl shape, orig hdw	1,450.00
Biscuit jar, mums w/gold on wht, floral emb rim, rope hdl	1,050.00
Bowl, flower bouquets w/gold, tricorner, mk CM 74, 3x9"	1,750.00
Bowl, gold swirls, lilac beads, leafy scrolls, 3¾" H	250.00
Candlesticks, portrait w/gold, Pairpoint base/socket, 8¼", pr	1,750.00
Creamer & sugar bowl, floral, mc w/gold ribbons, w/lid	1,250.00
Mustard, pk coral/gold flowers on wht, thumb-lift lid, 3½"	550.00
Pickle castor, gold branches/mc flowers on Dmn Quilt; SP fr, 10"	1,100.00
Pickle castor, pansies w/gold on wht Dmn Quilt, mk MW 520	1,495.00

Rose bowl, mosaic florals w/gold on yel to wht, 4"	750.00
Sweetmeat, flowers/scrolls/beads on almond, SP lid, 5"	575.00
Sweetmeat, gold starfish/emb stars/jewels on custard, squatty	900.00
Vase, acorn branches in gold/gr/brn, snail hdls, 8¼x9"	2,200.00
Vase, cactus fowers, mc on biscuit w/gold, bulbous, 8½"	1,600.00
Vase, floral w/gold, bulbous swirl mold, unmk, 7x6¾"	2,000.00
Vase, flower opening, gourd base w/turq accents, 13"	1,395.00
Vase, flowering cacti w/gold on beige, unmk, 9¼"	990.00
Vase, ginko, mc on pk, squat, bulbous, 4½x5"	350.00
Vase, gold florals & bl wash, cylindrical, in Pairpoint fr, 7½"	650.00
Vase, gr ivy w/gold trim, w/lid, unmk, 10½"	2,375.00
Vase, Iris gold enamel petit-point on beige, 16x4½"	875.00
Vase, jack-in-pulpit; florals on pnt burmese to peachblow, 9¾"	785.00
Vase, leaves w/gold & jewels, bulbous, 5x7"	1,400.00
Vase, wild roses, gold on peach/yel mottle w/jewels, hdls, 5x7"	1,200.00

Cruets

Cruets, containers made to hold oil or vinegar, are usually bulbous with tall, narrow throats and a stopper. During the 19th century and for several years after, they were produced in abundance in virtually every type of glassware available. Those listed below are assumed to be with stopper and mint unless noted otherwise. Our advisor for this category is Elaine Ezell; she is listed in the Directory under Maryland.

Amber w/HP floral sprays, bubble stopper, 6¼x2½"	110.00
Argonaut Shell, bl opal	475.00
Baby Invt T'print, gr	65.00
Big Button, ruby stain	250.00
Broken Column	95.00
Cathedral, amber	95.00
Challinor's #2 Tree of Life, bl, 5"	195.00
Chrysanthemum Base Swirl, bl opal	395.00
Chrysanthemum Sprig, custard, w/gold & decor, 6¾"	395.00
Circled Scrolls, gr opal	600.00
Column Block, vaseline	295.00
Cranberry w/clear rope hdl	195.00

Croesus, emerald green with gold, fan stopper, 6½", $395.00.

Daisy & Fern, bl	150.00
Daisy & Fern Parian Swirl, bl opal	175.00
Diamond Quilt, yel MOP, Mt WA	750.00
Double Circle, apple gr	225.00
Empress, clear w/gold	145.00
Empress, gr w/gold	350.00
Esther, gr w/gold, lg	395.00
Everglades, vaseline w/gold	595.00
Fern, cranberry opal	650.00
Fluted Scrolls, bl opal w/HP floral decor	225.00
Fluted Scrolls, canary opal w/decor	275.00

Forget-Me-Not, bl, Challinor 125.00
Georgia Gem, custard w/decor 395.00
Hanover, 6½" 30.00
Hobnail, bl, Hobbs 350.00
Intaglio, wht opal 175.00
Invt T'print, amberina, 6" 425.00
Invt T'print, bl, polished pontil, bl cut stopper 195.00
Invt T'print, cranberry 265.00
Jackson, vaseline opal 195.00
Louis XV, gr w/gold 350.00
Medallion Sprig, bl 450.00
Medallion Sprig, rubena 450.00
Millard, etch, amber-stain rim 345.00
Nestor, gr w/gold 275.00
O'Hara's Diamond, ruby stain 295.00
Parian Swirl, cranberry 395.00
Petticoat shape, bl w/HP flowers, bl stopper 165.00
Reverse Swirl, bl opal 350.00
Ribbed Herringbone, wht opal 300.00
Ribbed Lattice, cranberry opal 525.00
Riverside's Ransom, vaseline w/gold 250.00
S Repeat, gr 175.00
Sawtooth Honeycomb 40.00
Scroll w/Acanthus, bl 175.00
Seaweed, bl opal satin 675.00
Seaweed, wht opal 175.00
Shoshone, gr 150.00
Spanish Lace, bl opal 795.00
Swag w/Brackets, gr opal 485.00
Swirl, wht opal, 1960s import 65.00
Thousand Eye, amber, 3-knob 175.00
Tiny Optic, amethyst w/decor 125.00
Tiny Optic, gr, w/decor 125.00
Truncated Cube, ruby stain 285.00
Utopia Optic, gr 150.00
Wide Swirl, bl opal 160.00
Wild Bouquet, bl opal 495.00
X-Ray, gr w/EX gold 225.00

Cup Plates, Glass

Before the middle 1850s, it was socially acceptable to pour hot tea into a deep saucer to cool. The tea was sipped from the saucer rather than the cup, which frequently was handleless and too hot to hold. The cup plate served as a coaster for the cup. It is generally agreed that the first examples of pressed glass cup plates were made about 1826 at the Boston and Sandwich Glass Co. in Sandwich, Cape Cod, Massachusetts. Other glassworks in three major areas (New England, Philadelphia, and the Midwest, especially Pittsburgh) quickly followed suit.

Antique glass cup plates range in size from 2⅝" up to 4¼" in diameter. The earliest plates had simple designs inspired by cut glass patterns, but by 1829 they had become more complex. The span from then until about 1845 is known as the 'Lacy Period,' when cup plate designs and pressing techniques were at their peak. To cover pressing imperfections, the backgrounds of the plates were often covered with fine stippling which endowed them with a glittering brilliance called 'laciness.' They were made in a multitude of designs — some purely decorative, others commemorative. Subjects include the American eagle, hearts, sunbursts, log cabins, ships, George Washington, the political candidates Clay and Harrison, plows, beehives, etc. Of all the patterns, the round George Washington plate is the rarest and most valuable — only four are known to exist today.

Authenticity is most important. Collectors must be aware that contemporary plates which have no antique counterparts and fakes modeled after antique patterns have had wide distribution. Condition is also important, though it is the exceptional plate that does not have some rim roughness. More important considerations are scarcity of design and color.

Our advisor for this category is John Bilane; he is listed in the Directory under New Jersey. The book *American Glass* by George and Helen McKearin has a section on glass cup plates. The definitive book is *American Glass Cup Plates* by Ruth Webb Lee and James H. Rose. Numbers in the listings that follow refer to the latter. When no condition is indicated, the examples listed below are assumed to have only minor rim roughness as is normal. See also Staffordshire; Pairpoint.

Photo courtesy Virgil Scowden Collection

R-645-A, Bunker Hill monument and stars, 53 scallops, Sandwich, 3¾", EX, $170.00.

R-022, VG 30.00
R-027, VG 30.00
R-037, scarce, VG 43.00
R-039, VG 30.00
R-044, scarce, VG 64.00
R-045, scarce, VG 64.00
R-047, G 25.00
R-049, VG 30.00
R-053, scarce, VG 51.00
R-056, scarce, VG+ 52.00
R-062-A, scarce, G 42.00
R-065, scarce, VG+ 52.00
R-079, G 32.00
R-095, VG+ 35.00
R-097, scarce, VG- 48.00
R-101, scarce, G 42.00
R-126-A, rare, G+ 68.00
R-145-C, G+ 30.00
R-149, G 28.00
R-151-A, G- 28.00
R-159-A, scarce, G 39.00
R-159-B, VG 34.00
R-162-A, EX 40.00
R-162-A, VG 35.00
R-165, VG 35.00
R-172-A, EX 40.00
R-177, VG+ 44.00
R-192, VG 26.00
R-208, scarce, VG- 48.00
R-216, bl, 3⅜", VG 1,300.00
R-217-A, G- 45.00
R-233-A, G- 24.00
R-235, VG 35.00

R-242-A, VG 34.00
R-243, VG+ 37.00
R-245, G- 24.00
R-255, VG 20.00
R-257, VG- 32.00
R-258, VG 30.00
R-271, G 24.00
R-272, VG+ 31.00
R-275, VG 34.00
R-291, VG- 26.00
R-311, VG- 20.00
R-313, VG 21.00
R-324, VG 19.00
R-327, G- 12.00
R-332, G 18.00
R-332-B, G- 12.00
R-333, VG 19.00
R-334-A, G 15.00
R-339, VG 19.00
R-340, G 15.00
R-343-B, VG+ 35.00
R-365, VG 16.00
R-367, G- 10.00
R-368, VG 17.00
R-370, EX- 16.00
R-371, VG+ 16.00
R-377-A, VG- 12.00
R-380, VG- 12.00
R-390-A, G+ 11.00
R-391, VG 13.00
R-392, VG- 13.00
R-396, VG 13.00
R-402, VG 14.00
R-417, G+ 12.00
R-425, G+ 23.00
R-440-B, VG 34.00
R-441-A, VG- 32.00
R-447, G 22.00
R-447-A, G+ 23.00
R-455, heart, violet, Sandwich, 3½", VG 750.00
R-458, VG- 28.00
R-465-F, VG 19.00
R-465-H, VG 23.00
R-465-J, VG 19.00
R-465-N, G 16.00
R-467, VG 19.00
R-476, G- 13.00
R-479, VG 20.00
R-499, G 14.00
R-500, VG 55.00
R-508, G+ 15.00
R-516, VG 17.00
R-522, G 10.00
R-531, VG- 20.00
R-537, G 12.00
R-546, G+ 15.00
R-556-A, scarce, G- 33.00
R-562-A, very rare, G 245.00
R-565, G 25.00
R-565-A, G+ 26.00
R-569, VG 43.00
R-576, scarce, G 45.00
R-590, G 28.00
R-595, scarce, G+ 42.00

R-596, VG+ 45.00
R-600C, Log Cabin, 3⅜", EX+ 3,100.00
R-610-A, VG 34.00
R-610-C, VG- 40.00
R-612-A, rare, G 185.00
R-618, VG- 40.00
R-619, G 35.00
R-636, VG- 42.00
R-637, VG- 260.00
R-640, G 17.00
R-642, G+ 18.00
R-643, VG- 24.00
R-643-A, VG 26.00
R-654A, chip, 2⅞" 170.00
R-661, VG 39.00
R-666, VG 35.00
R-666-A, scarce, VG 48.00
R-667-A, G 32.00
R-668, eagle, 3", G+ 150.00
R-671, eagle, 3⅜", NM 330.00
R-676-B, scarce, VG+ 57.00
R-677A, eagel, Midwestern, 3⅛", VG 275.00
R-680, VG 34.00
R-694, beehive, NM 130.00

Cups and Saucers

The earliest utensils for drinking were small porcelain and stoneware bowls imported from China by the East Indian Company in the early 17th century. European and English tea bowls and saucers, imitating Chinese and Japanese originals, were produced from the early 18th century and often decorated with Chinese-type motifs. By about 1810, handles were fitted to the bowl to form the now familiar teacup, and this form became almost universal. Coffee in England and on the continent was often served in a can — a straight-sided cylinder with a handle. After 1820 the coffee can gave way to the more fanciful form of the coffee cup.

An infinite variety of cups and saucers are available for both the new and experienced collector, and they can be found in all price ranges. There is probably no better way to thoroughly know and understand the various ceramic manufacturers than to study cups and saucers. Our advisors for this category, Susan and Jim Harran, have written a book, entitled *Collectible Cups and Saucers, Identification and Values*, published by Collector Books. Over 400 full-color photos fill this exciting new book which is divided into six collectible categories: early years (1700 – 1875), cabinet cups, 19th and 20th century dinnerware, English bone china, miniatures, and figurals. The Harrans are listed in the Directory under New Jersey.

Photo courtesy Susan and Jim Harran

Teacup and saucer, Blue Onion, Meissen, ca 1900, $135.00.

Bouillon, Shamrock & Basketweave, Irish Belleek, ca 1891-1926 ..115.00	
Chocolate, hairbells/holly leaves, Limoges, Pouyat, ca 1895 ....45.00	
Coffee, shell motif, wear on gold band, Meissen, ca 1865 ....115.00	
Demitasse, Begonia, Shelley, ca 1930 ......50.00	
Demitasse, classical figures in relief, Capodimonte style, 1890s ..175.00	
Demitasse, floral, wht on bl, Spode, ca 1955 ......40.00	
Demitasse, HP, molded/3-ftd cup, Limoges, D&Co, ca 1896 ....45.00	

Plate, calender; 10" 17.00
Plate, chop; 11½" 35.00
Plate, chop; 12¼" 35.00
Plate, dinner; 10" 6.00
Plate, luncheon; 9" 18.00
Plate, salad; 7¼" 12.00
Plate, snack; w/cup well, 9" 25.00
Platter, oval, 13" 30.00
Platter, tab hdls, 10½" dia 28.00
Platter, 13" dia 65.00
Saucer, 6⅛" 2.00
Shakers, pr 36.00
Spoon rest, wall hanging 35.00
Sugar bowl, hdld, w/lid 17.00
Sugar bowl, no hdls, flared top 38.00
Sugar bowl, no hdls, w/lid 28.00

Bouillon, Shamrock & Basketweave, Irish Belleek, ca 1891-1926 ..115.00
Chocolate, hairbells/holly leaves, Limoges, Pouyat, ca 1895 ....45.00
Coffee, shell motif, wear on gold band, Meissen, ca 1865 ....115.00
Demitasse, Begonia, Shelley, ca 1930 ......50.00
Demitasse, classical figures in relief, Capodimonte style, 1890s ..175.00
Demitasse, floral, wht on bl, Spode, ca 1955 ......40.00
Demitasse, HP, molded/3-ftd cup, Limoges, D&Co, ca 1896 ....45.00
Sandwich set, Dresden-style floral transfer, Schumann, ca 1930 ..80.00
Tea, bl & wht, unmk (possibly Chinese), ca 1790 ......125.00
Tea, Cupid & woman, mulberry transfer, unmk, 1850s 80.00
Tea, floral, Haviland, Limoges, 1910s, +dessert plate 70.00
Tea, gold floral transfer on aqua, Tuscan China, 1947-60 ......35.00
Tea, Henley, Aynsley, ca 1920 ......40.00
Tea, HP scenes & flowers, Dresden, ca 1905 ......225.00
Tea, Maytime, Crown Staffordshire, ca 1938 ......35.00
Tea, pk floral transfer, Spode, 1950s, mini 130.00
Tea, Queen's Ware, Wedgwood, ca 1960 ......30.00
Tea, rtcl saucer, Fan Crest Fine China, Japan, ca 1950 ......30.00
Tea, Sweet Pea, Chintz, Grimwades, Royal Winton 160.00
Tea, Thistle, Shelley, ca 1930 ......65.00

Currier & Ives by Royal

During the 1950s dinnerware decorated with transfer-printed scenes taken from prints by Currier and Ives was manufactured by Royal China and given as premiums through A&P stores. Though it was also made in pink and green, the blue is by far the most popular. Pie plates in black and brown can be found, but no china sets in these colors have been reported. Today it is readily available at reasonable prices, and it has become a very popular collectible at malls and flea markets around the country. Included in our listings are pieces from hostess sets, which should be of great interest to collectors. New pieces which have been added to the price list include the clock, coffee mug with round handle, tall cup, snack plate, spoon rest/wall plaque, second-type gravy and underplate, and second-type sugar bowl with no handles. Our advisors for this category are Treva and Jack Hamlin; they are listed in the Directory under Ohio. See also Clubs, Newsletters, and Catalogs.

Ashtray, 5½" 18.00
Bowl, cereal; tab hdl, 6¼" 35.00
Bowl, cereal; 6¼" 12.00
Bowl, cereal; 6⅝" 12.00
Bowl, dessert; 5½" 4.00
Bowl, soup; 8" 12.00
Bowl, vegetable; deep, 10" 30.00
Bowl, vegetable; 9" 25.00
Butter dish, Fashionable decal 45.00
Butter dish, Road Winter decal 35.00
Casserole, angle hdls 100.00
Casserole, tab hdls 165.00
Clock, 10" plate, bl #s 75.00
Creamer, angle hdl 6.00
Creamer, rnd hdl, tall 30.00
Cup, angle hdl 4.00
Cup, rnd hdl, tall, 9" 8.00
Gravy boat, pour spout 17.00
Gravy boat, tab hdls 35.00
Ladle, gravy; all wht 40.00
Lamp, candle; w/globe 150.00
Mug, coffee; reg 27.00
Mug, coffee; rnd hdl 27.00
Pie baker, 10 decals, 10" 28.00
Plate, bread; 6½" 4.00

Teapot, sailing ships, lighthouse painted on finial, 4", $150.00.

Teapot 150.00
Tidbit tray, 3-tier, orig only 75.00
Tray, gravy boat; 7¼" 18.00
Tray, gravy; like 7" plate 35.00
Tumbler, iced tea; 12-oz, 5½" 17.00
Tumbler, juice; 5-oz, 3½" 17.00
Tumbler, old-fashion; 7-oz, 3¼" 17.00
Tumbler, water; 8½-oz, 4¾" 17.00

Hostess Set Pieces

Bowl, candy; 7¾" 25.00
Bowl, dip; 4⅜" 18.00
Pie baker, 11" 38.00
Plate, cake; flat, 10" 38.00
Plate, cake; ftd, 10" 75.00
Plate, serving; 7" 18.00
Tray, deviled egg 100.00

Custard

As early as the 1880s, custard glass was produced in England. Migrating glassmakers brought the formula for the creamy ivory ware to America. One of them was Harry Northwood, who in 1898 founded his company in Indiana, Pennsylvania, and introduced the glassware to the American market. Soon other companies were producing custard, among them Heisey, Tarentum, Fenton, and McKee. Not only dinnerware patterns but souvenir items were made. Today custard is the most expensive of the colored pressed glassware patterns. The formula for producing the luminous glass contains uranium salts which impart the cream color to the batch and cause it to glow when it is examined under a black light.

Argonaut Shell, bowl, master berry; gold & decor, 10½" L 275.00
Argonaut Shell, bowl, sauce; ftd, gold & decor 65.00
Argonaut Shell, butter dish, gold & decor 350.00
Argonaut Shell, butter dish, no gold 275.00
Argonaut Shell, compote, jelly; gold & decor, scarce 145.00
Argonaut Shell, creamer, gold & decor 140.00
Argonaut Shell, creamer, no gold 110.00
Argonaut Shell, cruet, gold & decor 775.00
Argonaut Shell, pitcher, water; gold & decor 435.00
Argonaut Shell, shakers, gold & decor, pr 345.00
Argonaut Shell, spooner, gold & decor 140.00
Argonaut Shell, sugar bowl, w/lid, gold & decor 200.00
Argonaut Shell, tumbler, gold & decor 110.00
Bead Swag, bowl, sauce; floral & gold 50.00
Bead Swag, goblet, floral & gold 65.00
Bead Swag, tray, pickle; floral & gold, rare 275.00
Bead Swag, wine, floral & gold 60.00
Beaded Circle, bowl, master berry; floral & gold 245.00
Beaded Circle, butter dish, floral & gold 450.00
Beaded Circle, creamer, floral & gold 180.00
Beaded Circle, pitcher, water; floral & gold 675.00
Beaded Circle, shakers, floral & gold, pr 1,000.00
Beaded Circle, spooner, floral & gold 175.00
Beaded Circle, sugar bowl, w/lid, floral & gold 275.00
Beaded Circle, tumbler, floral & gold, very rare 125.00
Cane Insert, berry set, 7-pc 450.00
Cane Insert, table set, 4-pc 450.00
Cherry & Scales, bowl, master berry; nutmeg stain 130.00
Cherry & Scales, butter dish, nutmeg stain 230.00
Cherry & Scales, creamer, nutmeg stain 115.00
Cherry & Scales, pitcher, water; nutmeg stain, scarce 325.00
Cherry & Scales, spooner, nutmeg stain, scarce 110.00
Cherry & Scales, sugar bowl, w/lid, nutmeg stain, scarce 125.00
Cherry & Scales, tumbler, nutmeg stain, scarce 65.00
Chrysanthemum Sprig, bowl, master berry; gold & decor 275.00
Chrysanthemum Sprig, bowl, master berry; no gold 175.00
Chrysanthemum Sprig, bowl, sauce; ftd, gold & decor 60.00
Chrysanthemum Sprig, butter dish, gold & decor 325.00
Chrysanthemum Sprig, celery vase, gold & decor, rare 600.00
Chrysanthemum Sprig, compote, jelly; gold & decor 145.00
Chrysanthemum Sprig, compote, jelly; no decor 95.00
Chrysanthemum Sprig, creamer, gold & decor 125.00
Chrysanthemum Sprig, cruet, gold & decor, 6¾" 495.00
Chrysanthemum Sprig, pitcher, water; gold & decor 470.00
Chrysanthemum Sprig, pitcher, water; no decor 350.00
Chrysanthemum Sprig, shakers, gold & decor, pr 300.00
Chrysanthemum Sprig, spooner, gold & decor 130.00
Chrysanthemum Sprig, spooner, no gold 75.00
Chrysanthemum Sprig, sugar bowl, gold & decor 225.00
Chrysanthemum Sprig, toothpick holder, gold & decor 325.00
Chrysanthemum Sprig, toothpick holder, no decor 175.00
Chrysanthemum Sprig, tray, condiment; gold & decor, rare 595.00
Chrysanthemum Sprig, tumbler, gold & decor 80.00
Dandelion, mug, nutmeg stain 165.00
Delaware, bowl, sauce; pk stain 65.00
Delaware, creamer, breakfast; pk stain 70.00
Delaware, tray, pin; gr stain 75.00
Delaware, tumbler, pk stain 55.00
Diamond w/Peg, bowl, master berry; roses & gold 225.00
Diamond w/Peg, bowl, sauce; roses & gold 45.00
Diamond w/Peg, butter dish, roses & gold 275.00
Diamond w/Peg, creamer, ind; no decor 30.00
Diamond w/Peg, creamer, ind; souvenir 45.00
Diamond w/Peg, creamer, roses & gold 75.00

Diamond w/Peg, mug, souvenir 50.00
Diamond w/Peg, napkin ring, roses & gold, rare 175.00
Diamond w/Peg, pitcher, roses & gold, 5½" 275.00
Diamond w/Peg, sugar bowl, w/lid, roses & gold 160.00
Diamond w/Peg, toothpick holder, roses & gold 175.00
Diamond w/Peg, tumbler, roses & gold 75.00
Diamond w/Peg, water set, souvenir, 7-pc 650.00
Diamond w/Peg, wine, roses & gold 60.00
Diamond w/Peg, wine, souvenir 50.00
Everglades, bowl, master berry; gold & decor 215.00
Everglades, bowl, sauce; gold & decor 60.00
Everglades, butter dish, gold & decor 395.00
Everglades, creamer, gold & decor 155.00
Everglades, cruet, EX gold & decor 1,595.00
Everglades, shakers, gold & decor, pr 375.00
Everglades, spooner, gold & decor 160.00
Everglades, sugar bowl, w/lid, gold & decor 235.00
Everglades, tumbler, gold & decor 100.00
Fan, bowl, master berry; good gold 160.00
Fan, bowl, sauce; good gold 60.00
Fan, butter dish, good gold 345.00
Fan, creamer, good gold 110.00
Fan, ice cream set, good gold, 7-pc 500.00
Fan, pitcher, water; good gold 285.00
Fan, spooner, good gold 100.00
Fan, sugar bowl, w/lid, good gold 150.00
Fan, tumbler, good gold 75.00
Fan, water set, good gold, 7-pc 725.00
Fine Cut & Roses, rose bowl, fancy int, nutmeg stain 100.00
Fine Cut & Roses, rose bowl, plain int 85.00
Geneva, bowl, master berry; floral decor, ftd, oval, 9" L 110.00
Geneva, bowl, master berry; floral decor, rnd, 9" 130.00
Geneva, bowl, sauce; floral decor, oval 45.00
Geneva, bowl, sauce; floral decor, rnd 45.00
Geneva, butter dish, floral decor 225.00
Geneva, butter dish, no decor 135.00
Geneva, compote, jelly; floral decor 95.00
Geneva, creamer, floral decor 100.00
Geneva, cruet, floral decor 475.00
Geneva, pitcher, water; floral decor 250.00
Geneva, shakers, floral decor, pr 280.00
Geneva, spooner, floral decor 100.00
Geneva, sugar bowl, open, floral decor 85.00
Geneva, sugar bowl, w/lid, floral decor 150.00
Geneva, syrup, floral decor 475.00
Geneva, toothpick holder, floral w/M gold 375.00
Geneva, tumbler, floral decor 60.00
Georgia Gem, bowl, master berry; good gold 135.00
Georgia Gem, bowl, master berry; gr opaque 115.00
Georgia Gem, butter dish, good gold 200.00
Georgia Gem, celery vase, good gold 145.00
Georgia Gem, creamer, good gold 100.00
Georgia Gem, creamer, no gold 60.00
Georgia Gem, cruet, good gold 395.00
Georgia Gem, mug, good gold 45.00
Georgia Gem, powder jar, w/lid, good gold 80.00
Georgia Gem, shakers, good gold, pr 140.00
Georgia Gem, spooner, souvenir 55.00
Georgia Gem, sugar bowl, w/lid, no gold 95.00
Grape (& Cable), bottle, scent; orig stopper, nutmeg stain 600.00
Grape (& Cable), bowl, master berry; nutmeg stain, ftd, 11" 420.00
Grape (& Cable), bowl, nutmeg stain, 7½" 60.00
Grape (& Cable), bowl, sauce; nutmeg stain, ftd 50.00
Grape (& Cable), butter dish, nutmeg stain 275.00

Grape (& Cable), compote, jelly; open, nutmeg stain 145.00
Grape (& Cable), compote, nutmeg stain, 4½x8" 300.00
Grape (& Cable), cracker jar, nutmeg stain 800.00
Grape (& Cable), creamer, breakfast; nutmeg stain 80.00
Grape (& Cable), humidor, bl stain, rare 950.00
Grape (& Cable), humidor, nutmeg stain, rare 900.00
Grape (& Cable), nappy, nutmeg stain, rare 60.00
Grape (& Cable), pitcher, water; nutmeg stain 500.00
Grape (& Cable), plate, nutmeg stain, 7" 50.00
Grape (& Cable), plate, nutmeg stain, 8" 65.00
Grape (& Cable), powder jar, nutmeg stain 350.00
Grape (& Cable), punch bowl, w/base, nutmeg stain 1,900.00
Grape (& Cable), spooner, nutmeg stain 145.00
Grape (& Cable), sugar bowl, breakfast; open, nutmeg stain 75.00
Grape (& Cable), sugar bowl, w/lid, nutmeg stain 195.00
Grape (& Cable), tray, dresser; nutmeg stain, scarce, lg 350.00
Grape (& Cable), tray, pin; nutmeg stain 135.00
Grape (& Cable), tumbler, nutmeg stain 75.00
Grape & Gothic Arches, bowl, master berry; pearl w/gold 200.00
Grape & Gothic Arches, bowl, sauce; pearl w/gold, rare 80.00
Grape & Gothic Arches, butter dish, pearl w/gold 235.00
Grape & Gothic Arches, creamer, pearl w/gold, rare 100.00
Grape & Gothic Arches, favor vase, nutmeg stain 80.00
Grape & Gothic Arches, goblet, pearl w/gold 75.00
Grape & Gothic Arches, pitcher, water; pearl w/gold 300.00
Grape & Gothic Arches, spooner, pearl w/gold 85.00
Grape & Gothic Arches, sugar bowl, w/lid, pearl w/gold 135.00
Grape & Gothic Arches, tumbler, pearl w/gold 65.00
Grape Arbor, vase, hat form 90.00
Heart w/T'print, creamer 85.00
Heart w/T'print, lamp, good pnt, scarce, 8" 435.00
Heart w/T'print, sugar bowl, ind 80.00
Honeycomb, wine 65.00
Horse Medallion, bowl, gr stain, 7" 80.00
Intaglio, bowl, master berry; gold & decor, ftd, 9" 250.00
Intaglio, bowl, sauce; gold & decor 50.00
Intaglio, butter dish, gold & decor, scarce 300.00
Intaglio, compote, jelly; gold & decor 125.00
Intaglio, creamer, gold & decor 125.00
Intaglio, cruet, gold & decor 475.00
Intaglio, pitcher, water; gold & decor 395.00
Intaglio, shakers, gold & decor, pr 235.00
Intaglio, spooner, gold & decor 125.00
Intaglio, sugar bowl, w/lid, gold & decor 165.00
Intaglio, tumbler, gold & decor 85.00
Inverted Fan & Feather, bowl, master berry; gold & decor 275.00
Inverted Fan & Feather, bowl, sauce; gold & decor 75.00
Inverted Fan & Feather, butter dish, gold & decor 350.00
Inverted Fan & Feather, compote, jelly; gold & decor, rare 500.00
Inverted Fan & Feather, creamer, gold & decor 150.00
Inverted Fan & Feather, cruet, gold & decor, scarce, 6½" 1,100.00
Inverted Fan & Feather, pitcher, water; gold & decor 650.00
Inverted Fan & Feather, punch cup, gold & decor 250.00
Inverted Fan & Feather, shakers, gold & decor, pr 750.00
Inverted Fan & Feather, spooner, gold & decor 145.00
Inverted Fan & Feather, sugar bowl, w/lid, gold & decor 250.00
Inverted Fan & Feather, tumbler, gold & decor 100.00
Jackson (Alaska Variant), bowl, master berry; good gold, ftd 135.00
Jackson (Alaska Variant), bowl, sauce; good gold 45.00
Jackson (Alaska Variant), creamer, good gold 85.00
Jackson (Alaska Variant), pitcher, water; good gold 250.00
Jackson (Alaska Variant), pitcher, water; no decor 175.00
Jackson (Alaska Variant), shakers, good gold, pr 195.00
Jackson (Alaska Variant), tumbler, good gold 50.00

Louis XV, bowl, master berry; good gold 250.00
Louis XV, bowl, sauce; good gold, ftd 50.00
Louis XV, butter dish, good gold 250.00
Louis XV, creamer, good gold 80.00
Louis XV, pitcher, water; good gold 250.00
Louis XV, spooner, good gold 80.00

Louis XV, spooner,
worn gold, $70.00.

Louis XV, sugar bowl, w/lid, good gold 165.00
Louis XV, tumbler, good gold 65.00
Maple Leaf, bowl, master berry; gold & decor, scarce 350.00
Maple Leaf, bowl, sauce; gold & decor, scarce 110.00
Maple Leaf, butter dish, gold & decor 350.00
Maple Leaf, compote, jelly; gold & decor, rare 475.00
Maple Leaf, creamer, gold & decor 150.00
Maple Leaf, cruet, gold & decor, rare 3,000.00
Maple Leaf, pitcher, water; gold & decor 400.00
Maple Leaf, shakers, gold & decor, very rare, pr 1,000.00
Maple Leaf, spooner, gold & decor 175.00
Maple Leaf, sugar bowl, w/lid, gold & decor 250.00
Maple Leaf, tumbler, gold & decor 100.00
Panelled Poppy, lamp shade, nutmeg stain, scarce 800.00
Peacock & Urn, bowl, ice cream; nutmeg stain, sm 80.00
Peacock & Urn, bowl, ice cream; nutmeg stain, 10" 350.00
Punty Band, shakers, pr 175.00
Punty Band, spooner, floral decor 100.00
Punty Band, tumbler, floral decor, souvenir 65.00
Ribbed Drape, bowl, sauce; roses & gold 40.00
Ribbed Drape, butter dish, scalloped, roses & gold 375.00
Ribbed Drape, compote, jelly; roses & gold, rare 200.00
Ribbed Drape, creamer, roses & gold, scarce 180.00
Ribbed Drape, cruet, roses & gold, rare 650.00
Ribbed Drape, pitcher, water; roses & gold, rare 365.00
Ribbed Drape, shakers, roses & gold, rare, pr 360.00
Ribbed Drape, spooner, roses & gold 180.00
Ribbed Drape, sugar bowl, w/lid 235.00
Ribbed Drape, toothpick holder, roses & gold 475.00
Ribbed Drape, tumbler, roses & gold 65.00
Ribbed Thumbprint, wine, floral decor 80.00
Ring Band, bowl, master berry; roses & gold 175.00
Ring Band, bowl, sauce; roses & gold 50.00
Ring Band, butter dish, roses & gold 250.00
Ring Band, compote, jelly; roses & gold, scarce 195.00
Ring Band, creamer, roses & gold 115.00
Ring Band, cruet, roses & gold 450.00
Ring Band, pitcher, roses & gold, 7½" 350.00
Ring Band, shakers, roses & gold, pr 155.00
Ring Band, spooner, roses & gold 115.00
Ring Band, syrup, roses & gold 465.00

Ring Band, toothpick holder, roses & gold 135.00
Ring Band, tray, condiment; roses & gold 200.00
Singing Birds, mug, nutmeg stain 75.00
Tarentum's Victoria, bowl, master berry; gold & decor 200.00
Tarentum's Victoria, butter dish, gold & decor, rare 300.00
Tarentum's Victoria, celery vase, gold & decor, rare 275.00
Tarentum's Victoria, creamer, gold & decor, scarce 135.00
Tarentum's Victoria, pitcher, water; gold & decor, rare 375.00
Tarentum's Victoria, spooner, gold & decor 135.00
Tarentum's Victoria, sugar bowl, w/lid, gold & decor 160.00
Tarentum's Victoria, tumbler, gold & decor 75.00
Vermont, butter dish, bl decor 195.00
Vermont, toothpick holder, bl decor 175.00
Vermont, vase, floral decor, jeweled 110.00
Wide Band, bell, roses 195.00
Wild Bouquet, butter dish, gold & decor, rare 700.00
Wild Bouquet, creamer, no gold 145.00
Wild Bouquet, cruet, no decor, w/clear stopper 995.00
Wild Bouquet, sauce, gold & decor 60.00
Wild Bouquet, spooner, gold & decor 160.00
Wild Bouquet, tumbler, no decor 95.00
Winged Scroll, bowl, master berry; gold & decor, 11" L 250.00
Winged Scroll, bowl, sauce; good gold 50.00
Winged Scroll, butter dish, good gold 215.00
Winged Scroll, butter dish, no decor 160.00
Winged Scroll, celery vase, good gold, rare 400.00
Winged Scroll, cigarette jar, scarce 195.00
Winged Scroll, compote, ruffled, rare, 6¾x10¾" 495.00
Winged Scroll, cruet, good gold, rpl clear stopper 375.00
Winged Scroll, hair receiver, good gold 135.00
Winged Scroll, pitcher, water; bulbous, good gold 350.00
Winged Scroll, shakers, bulbous, good gold, rare, pr 400.00
Winged Scroll, shakers, str sides, good gold, pr 195.00
Winged Scroll, sugar bowl, w/lid, good gold 200.00
Winged Scroll, syrup, good gold 450.00
Winged Scroll, tumbler, good gold 75.00

Cut Glass

The earliest documented evidence of commercial glass cutting in the United States was in 1810; the producers were Bakewell and Page of Pittsburgh. These first efforts resulted in simple patterns with only a moderate amount of cutting. By the middle of the century, glass cutters began experimenting with a thicker glass which enabled them to use deeper cuttings, though patterns remained much the same. This period is usually referred to as Rich Cut. Using three types of wheels — a flat edge, a mitered edge, and a convex edge — facets, miters, and depressions were combined to produce various designs. In the late 1870s, a curved miter was developed which greatly expanded design potential. Patterns became more elaborate, often covering the entire surface. The Brilliant Period of cut glass covered a span from about 1880 until 1915. Because of the pressure necessary to achieve the deeply cut patterns, only glass containing a high grade of metal could withstand the process. For this reason and the amount of handwork involved, cut glass has always been expensive. Bowls cut with pinwheels may be either foreign or of a newer vintage, beware! Identifiable patterns and signed pieces that are well cut and in excellent condition bring the higher prices on today's market. See also Dorflinger; Hawkes; Libbey; Tuthill; Val St. Lambert; other specific manufacturers.

Key:
dmn — diamond   X-cut — crosscut
strw — strawberry   X-hatch — crosshatch

Banana bowl, Exquisite Propeller, 11x8" 400.00
Basket, cosmos w/Harvard-type band, 2-notch hdl, 14½x10" 650.00
Basket, flowers & leaves, 2-notch hdl, 21x16" 600.00
Basket, Harvard, carnations & leaves, notched hdl, 18x10" 850.00
Basket, Harvard w/hobstars, low twist hdl, 7½x8½" 200.00
Basket, Harvard w/hobstars & vis-car cuttings, rope hdl, 8x9" ...325.00
Basket, hobstars & brilliant cuttings, ped ft, twist hdl, 13x9" ..1,850.00
Basket, hobstars & fans, twisted rope hdl, 7½x8½" 350.00
Basket, hobstars & florals, sq, 2-notch hdl, 8½x6½" 500.00
Basket, hobstars & pinwheels, 2-notch hdl, 18x12" 1,200.00
Basket, hobstars in steps, 3-notch hdl, serrated rim, 17x11" 2,900.00
Basket, hobstars/dmn points/fans/canes, 3-notch hdl, 6x6" 450.00
Basket, hobstars/fans/strw points, heavy, 10½x10¾" 425.00
Basket, hobstars/fans/X-hatching, notched hdl, Hoare, 9x11" .3,500.00
Basket, hobstars/pinwheels, 2-notch hdl, 21x13¾" 1,500.00
Basket, jeweled roses, buds & sprays, star on base, 18½x12" 550.00
Basket, pinwheels, star-cut base, notched hdl, sgn Frye, 6½" 150.00
Basket, pinwheels & hobstars, rope hdl, 5½x7" 150.00
Basket, plums, leaves & flowers, 2-notch hdl, 14½x10" 750.00
Bonbon, allover cuttings, center stick hdl, Meriden, pr 295.00
Bonbon, flashed hobstars, button vesicas, faceted hdl, 4x6" 75.00
Bonbon, hobstars in arches, buttons, sawtooth rim, cut stem, 4x5" ...135.00
Bottle, cologne; hobstars, rayed base, faceted stopper, 4" 165.00
Bottle, scent; Eggington Lotus, 6½" 375.00
Bowl, Daisy & Button w/3 lg pinwheels, 3¾x8⅜" 60.00
Bowl, flashed hobstars, cane vesicas, shallow, 8" 75.00
Bowl, flowers & leaves, thistle in center, rolled rim, 4½x12" 275.00
Bowl, hobstars, checkerboard, 5½x9" 135.00
Bowl, hobstars, X-hatching, star cutting, 8-lobe, 2x8" 100.00
Bowl, hobstars/nailhead dmn fields & fans, 10" 200.00
Bowl, lg hobstar w/in 8-hobstar band, 3¾x8", EX 110.00
Bowl, Nassau, Hoare, 10" 185.00
Bowl, Pluto, Hoare, 2x9" 225.00
Bowl, Prima Donna, dental edge, heavy blown blank, 8" 185.00
Box, Harvard, oval, hinged lid, 3½x5¼" 475.00
Box, Harvard variant, SP mts, orig mirror-on-swivel lid, 7x7" 750.00
Box, hobstars/fans/stars, hinged mirror lid, CFMCo, 4x8" 750.00
Box, hobstars/X-hatching/fans, bishop's hat form, 4¼x6½" 850.00
Cake stand, hobstars, cut ped ft, 2x9" 325.00
Candlesticks, cut flowers & leaves, hollow center, 12", pr 895.00
Candlesticks, step-cut petticoat base, knobs & prisms, 10", pr 175.00
Candy compote, snowflakes, faceted teardrop stem, 11½" 160.00
Candy compote, Sunburst, 9¼" 160.00
Carafe, hobstars alternate w/flashed stars & fans, cut neck, 7" 155.00
Carafe, pinwheels/fans/miters, notched neck, 7⅝" 55.00
Carafe, Russian, 7½x6", EX, pr 300.00
Celery vase, hobstar center w/buzzstars at sides, 10x4½" 85.00
Celery vase, Russian, scalloped sawtooth rim, 6½" 245.00
Clock, boudoir; buttons & X-hatching, eng satin tulip front 110.00
Compote, Caroline, ruffled, petticoat base, Hoare, 5¼x6½" 145.00
Compote, hobstars/miters/file, hex std, 8½x8" 165.00
Creamer, hobstars/dmns/fans, tankard form, 5" 80.00
Creamer & sugar bowl, Acme, ped ft, Hoare 425.00
Creamer & sugar bowl, hobstars/strw dmns, 3-notch hdls, ped ft 800.00
Creamer & sugar bowl, Hunt's Royal 295.00
Creamer & sugar bowl, Russian, flutes, 3-notch hdl, petite 145.00
Decanter, hobstars & fans, notched hdl, Hoare, 12¾" 150.00
Decanter, hobstars/mitres/file/fans, SP trim, w/stopper, 11x3" sq ..140.00
Decanter, starred buttons/X-hatching, step-cut neck, 13" 295.00
Flowerpot, Florence Hobstar, Meriden plated liner, 4x4" 165.00
Goblet, pyramidal star pattern, star ft, 8¼", 8 for 560.00
Humidor, fans/prisms/hobstars, monogram/dtd Dec 25, 1896 ....450.00
Ice bucket, Carolyn, ftd, Hoare 625.00
Ice bucket, Harvard w/florals, 8-sided, 6½x7" 100.00

Lamp, cut daisies/strawberries/dmns/fans/stars, prisms, 24" **2,000.00**
Lamp, Harvard variant pagoda shade, eng floral base, 19x9" **350.00**
Lamp, hobstars/X-hatching, mushroom shade, Queen base, 23" ...**2,750.00**
Lamp, mushroom shade w/florals & tendrils, stepped cut base, 13" ...**350.00**
Nappy, Expanding Star **135.00**
Pitcher, Conestoga, slim, 15" **475.00**
Pitcher, fans/swags/dmn miters, horizontal seed cut, 7¼x5" **80.00**
Pitcher, hobstars/canes/fans, 2-notch hdl, bulbous, 9" **300.00**
Plate, Stars & Pillar, 24-point star center, 10" **565.00**
Punch bowl, hobstars, 7x14" **550.00**
Punch bowl, hobstars/fans/button banners, 6x10"+base **400.00**
Punch bowl, pinwheels & hobstars, heavy, w/domed base, 11x10" ..**500.00**
Punch cup, Prism & Punty, 5 for **120.00**
Relish, hobstars, intaglio floral & leaf center, 1½x7¼" L **110.00**
Rose bowl, Electric, 3-hdld, Bergen **150.00**
Tankard, Harvard w/flowers, 2-notch hdl, 10", +5 tumblers **300.00**
Tankard, hobstars & dmn points, silver rim, cut hdl, 17¼x7" **700.00**
Tankard, Strw Dmn, 12" **450.00**
Tray, Cane, heavy, 12x8" **400.00**
Tray, ice cream; flowers, sawtooth edge, 15" **250.00**
Tray, ice cream; hobstars, sawtooth edge, 14x7¾" **175.00**
Tray, perfume; Chrysanthemum Variant, oval, 10x7" **225.00**
Tumbler, bird on oak branch & primrose, buttons around base **28.00**
Vase, flowers/leaves, stepped neck, squat, 8¼x10" **165.00**
Vase, flowers/leaves/butterfly cuttings, bulbous, 12" **90.00**
Vase, Gravic, rosebuds & leaves, beaker shape, 8½x6½" **100.00**
Vase, hobstars allover, Maple Leaf mk, 15" **575.00**
Vase, Hunt's Royal, 11½" **375.00**
Vase, Russian, scalloped sawtooth rim, 12x7" **350.00**
Vase, snowflakes & pinwheels, 14" **200.00**
Vase, strw dmns/buzzstars, 12" **150.00**
Wine, hobstars & fans, rayed ft, cut stem, Am, 4¼x3¼" **55.00**
Wine, Honeycomb, flint, 4⅛", 5 for **200.00**

Cut Velvet

Cut Velvet glassware was made during the late 1800s. It is characterized by the effect achieved through the execution of relief-molded patterns, often ribbing or diamond quilting, which allows its white inner casing to show through the outer layer.

Basket, Dmn Quilt, pk, crimped/ruffled, clear loop hdl, 11½" **350.00**
Celery vase, Dmn Quilt, bl, box-pleated rim, Mt WA, 6½" **725.00**
Rose bowl, Dmn Quilt, bl, 6-crimp, 3½x3½" **175.00**
Vase, Dmn Quilt, bl, ruffled top w/crystal edge, 6¼" **195.00**
Vase, Dmn Quilt, bl, stick neck, 5¾" **135.00**
Vase, Dmn Quilt, bl, 6x3⅜" **145.00**
Vase, Dmn Quilt, lt gr, 9" **350.00**
Vase, Dmn Quilt, pale gold, dbl-gourd, Mt WA, 13½" **650.00**
Vase, Dmn Quilt, pk, ruffled rim, 8" **150.00**
Vase, Dmn Quilt, pk, stick neck, 6¼" **195.00**
Vase, Dmn Quilt, teal bl, pleated/scalloped rim, ftd, 9½x5¼" **375.00**
Vase, Dmn Quilt, yel, crimped & folded rim, Mt WA, 9½x6" **375.00**
Vase, Herringbone, bl, ruffled rim, Mt WA, 7½x3½" **445.00**
Vase, Rib, pk, bottle form, 8¾" **195.00**
Vase, Rib, pk, Mt WA, 5½x3", NM **135.00**

Cybis

Boleslaw Cybis was a graduate of the Academy of Fine Arts in Warsaw, Poland, and was well recognized as a fine artist by the time he was commissioned by his government to paint murals in the Polish Pavillion's Hall of Honor at the 1939 World's Fair. Finding themselves stranded in America at the outbreak of WWII, the Cybises founded an artists' studio, first in Astoria, New York, and later in Trenton, New Jersey, where they made fine figurines and plaques with exacting artistry and craftsmanship entailing extensive handwork. The studio still operates today producing exquisite porcelains on a limited edition basis.

Goldilocks and the three Bears (pandas), 6¼", $500.00.

Abigail Adams **750.00**
Apache, Chato **2,000.00**
Ballerina on Cue **400.00**
Barnaby Bear **195.00**
Carmen **1,100.00**
George Washington Bust **225.00**
Hansel **325.00**
Little Bo Peep **275.00**
Marigold **350.00**
Mary, Mary **450.00**
Owl **95.00**
Pegasus **2,250.00**
Peter Pan **650.00**
Romeo & Juliet **1,800.00**
Sebastian Seal **150.00**
Shoshone, Sacajawea **2,250.00**
Sleeping Beauty **800.00**
Yankee Doodle Dandy **250.00**

Czechoslovakian Collectibles

Czechoslovakia came into being as a country in 1918. Located in the heart of Europe, it was a land with the natural resources necessary to support a glass industry that dated back to the mid-14th century. The glass that was produced there has captured the attention of today's collectors, and for good reason. There are beautiful vases — cased, ruffled, applied with rigaree or silver overlay — fine enough to rival those of the best glasshouses. Czechoslovakian art glass baskets are quite as attractive as Victorian America's, and the elegant cut glass perfumes made in colors as well as crystal are unrivaled. There are also pressed glass perfumes, molded in lovely Deco shapes, of various types of art glass. Some are overlaid with gold filigree set with 'jewels.' Jewelry, lamps, porcelains, and fine art pottery are also included in the field.

More than seventy marks have been recorded, including those in the mold, ink stamped, acid etched, or on a small metal nameplate. The newer marks are incised, stamped 'Royal Dux Made in Czechoslovakia' (see Royal Dux) or printed on a paper label which reads 'Bohemian Glass Made in Czechoslovakia.' (Communist controlled from 1948, Czechoslovakia once again was made a free country in December 1989. Today it no longer exists; since 1993 it has been divided to form the world's two newest countries, the Czech Republic and the Slovak Republic.) For a more thorough study of the subject, we recommend you refer to the books *Made in Czechoslovakia* and *Made in Czechoslovakia, Book 2*, by our advisor Ruth A. Forsythe; she is listed in the Directory under Ohio. Another fine book is *Czechoslovakian Glass & Collectibles*, Volumes I and II, by Dale and Diane Barta and Helen M. Rose. In the listings that follow, when one dimension is given, it refers to height; decoration is enamel unless noted otherwise. See also Erphila.

Candy Baskets

Bl mottle w/yel ruffled rim, jet hdl, 8" 250.00
Blk w/silver mica, bl lining, blk hdl, 8" 250.00
Lt gr varicolored, gr hdl, 8" 190.00
Red & gr mottle, crystal twist hdl, 6½" 240.00
Red & yel mottle, crystal arched hdl, 6½" 175.00
Red w/petal-like rim w/blk edge, crystal arched hdl, 6½" 200.00

Cased Art Glass

Candlestick, cameo, floral, brn to orange, 12½" 650.00
Candlestick, HP flower basket on red w/blk trim, slim, 10½" 85.00
Vase, autumn varicolor, bulbous, metalwork at rim, 11" 130.00
Vase, bl, ruffled/pleated rim, crystal hdls, 8¼" 100.00
Vase, bl w/appl red spirals trailing down to form hdls, 8½" 175.00
Vase, bl w/jet ruffled rim, slim, 8¼" 90.00
Vase, bud; blk & silver decor on red, blk ft, 11¼" 110.00
Vase, gr bullet form w/3 dk bl buttressed ft, 8¾" 145.00
Vase, mottled colors, stick form, 8½" 55.00
Vase, pk w/pk crystal angle hdls, scalloped rim, 7½" 95.00
Vase, red & wht mottle w/serpentine, scalloped rim, slim, 8½" ..160.00
Vase, red-orange, stick neck, 10¼" 60.00
Vase, wht w/emb decor, appl crystal pleated rim, 5½" 85.00
Vase, yel w/scalloped rim w/blk edge, slim, 8½" 75.00

Cut Glass Perfume Bottles

Amethyst domed sq w/frosted nude stopper, 6⅝" 800.00
Amethyst stepped sq, pointed amethyst stopper, 4½" 120.00
Bl w/emb figure, clear shield-shape stopper, 5¾" 300.00
Blk opaque w/jeweled shoulders, clear flower stopper, 4⅛" 250.00
Clear body on gr ft, 2-pc, gr frosted flower stopper, 5¾" 300.00
Crystal, shouldered shape, flower clear/frosted stopper, 4¾" 45.00
Crystal domed shape, ornate spherical stopper, 6⅛" 85.00
Crystal domed shape w/frosted figure stopper, 5⅝" 300.00
Crystal sq w/red Triomphe stopper, 3¾" 145.00
Gr ball shape w/emb flowers, gr frosted flower stopper, 5⅛" 155.00
Pk bulb form, simple pk stopper, 4¼" 120.00
Pk ornate ftd form, frosted flowers form stopper, 8" 300.00
Topaz sq w/Witch Hazel on front, 4½" 95.00

Lamps

Lamp, basket form, amber beads, w/mc flowers & fruit, 10" 700.00
Lamp, basket form, crystal beads, mc nuts & fruit, 10¾" 850.00
Lamp, Deco dancing figure beside crystal ball, 9" 900.00
Lamp, lady w/flower dress, Goebel, 10¼" 950.00
Lamp, peacock figural, brass w/beaded tail, onyx base, 12¼" ...1,200.00
Lamp, perfume; cut bl shade, 4" 150.00
Lamp, student; acid-cut shade, 21" 900.00
Lamp, table; Art Deco geometrics on base & cone shade, 9" 900.00
Lamp, table; dk bl lustre, rpl shade, 13¼" 175.00
Yel & bl honeycomb cased, CI/metal mts, 25" overall 200.00

Mold-Blown and Pressed Bottles

Bl opaque w/emb nude & butterfly, fan-shape stopper, 5¼" 600.00
Blk w/wide appl gold band, slim, ftd, atomizer, 9½" 75.00
Clear wide cylinder w/mc daisies, flat stopper, 3⅜" 45.00
Cranberry opal hobnail, bulbous, wht opal stopper, 5½" 85.00
Crystal w/overall jewels, cylindrical, jeweled stopper, 2⅝" 95.00
Gr, appl serpentine, shouldered, ftd, atomizer, 8" 90.00
Gr frosted w/blk & wht Deco-style enamel, 6" 55.00
Gr gourd shape w/red spherical stopper, 7⅛" 40.00
Orange cased, blk stopper & base, 6¼" 55.00
Orange cased w/blk pnt linear decor, atomizer, 5" 55.00
Purple lustre, bulbous, flower stopper, 4½" 140.00

Opaque, Crystal, Colored Transparent Glass

Photo courtesy
Guy S. Forsythe

Dresser set, pink satin glass, powder box, perfume, and atomizer with tray, $2,000.00.

Bowl, pk lustre w/bl lustre King Tut decor, 3½" H 1,800.00
Tumbler, exotic bird HP on dk bl, 5½" 50.00
Tumbler, HP hunt scene on bubbly gr, 5¾" 65.00
Vase, bl opaque, trumpet form, 7" 100.00
Vase, blk w/red mottling, can neck, 4¾" 750.00
Vase, coralene flowers on bl to wht, slim, 7½" 85.00
Vase, crystal w/red spiral threading, ftd cylinder, 8¼" 150.00
Vase, dk bl cut to clear, 10¼" 350.00
Vase, orange w/yel o/l, fan form, 8" 185.00
Vase, red & wht mottle on inverted cylinder, 5⅞" 50.00

Pottery, Porcelain, Semiporcelain

Bowl, Deco floral on blk, wht int, str sides, 3" H 65.00
Canister set, scarlet w/flowers & blk trim, 15-pc 700.00
Creamer, cat hdl, 4⅜" 55.00
Creamer, cow figural, wht w/brn spots, 4¾" 50.00
Creamer, duck figural, mc, 3¾" 35.00
Figurine, Deco lady, wht glossy, 9¾" 250.00
Flower holder, bird on stump form, 5⅜" 40.00
Napkin ring, girl figural, 4" 85.00
Teapot, pk lustre, bulbous, 6⅛" 45.00
Vase, Egyptian figures in band on streaky tan, 9⅛" 300.00
Vase, Peasant Art, fruit & flower, sgn Mrazek, 8½" 200.00
Wall pocket, bird perched beside birdhouse, 5½" 45.00
Wall pocket, woodpecker, 7¾" 65.00

D'Argental

D'Argental cameo glass was produced in France from the 1870s until about 1920 in the Art Nouveau style. Browns and tans were favored colors used to complement florals and scenic designs developed through acid cuttings. Our advisor for this category is Don Williams; he is listed in the Directory under Missouri.

Cameo

Vase, castle scene, 3-color, ca 1900, 5½x5½" 1,950.00
Vase, floral, purple/lav/yel on pk/lav opal w/gold, 4¼x3¼" 700.00
Vase, flowers & leaves, brn on tan, 2⅝x3⅝" 425.00
Vase, morning glories, sepia brn & citron on red-brn, 6¾" 525.00
Vase, trees/lake/sky, golden brn/frosty amber, oviform, 8" 850.00

Daum Nancy

Daum was an important producer of French cameo glass, operating from the late 1800s until after the turn of the century. They used various techniques — acid cutting, wheel engraving, and handwork — to create beautiful scenic designs and nature subjects in the Art Nouveau manner. Virtually all examples are signed. Our advisor for this category is Don Williams; he is listed in the Directory under Missouri.

Cameo

Bottle, scent; berries, cut/pnt on amethyst frost, 2¾" 650.00
Bottle, scent; crocus, cut/pnt, yel/cranberry/opal, 4¾x4" 1,800.00
Bowl, birches/lake/grasses, cut/pnt on bl/gray, ftd, 5⅜" H 2,000.00
Bowl, chestnut/leaves, gr/red/yel, sgn, 5¾x11" 1,650.00
Bowl, grapes, dk bl/red/purple/yel, cluster int, 2½" H 1,600.00
Bowl, orchids, cut/pnt, 3-lobe, SP base, 8⅝" H 4,300.00
Bowl, thistles/leaves, red-amber opal/brn/gold, 2½x4¾" 500.00
Box, floral, cut/pnt, gr/yel/red, 2¾x3½" 1,550.00
Box, flowers/leaves, cut/pnt on mottled frost, 4½x5½" dia 2,850.00
Creamer, trees/lake/sailboats/sky, brn/marmalade, tankard, 4" 450.00
Flask, mistletoe, cut/pnt, gilt metal top, orig stopper, 5¾" 2,050.00
Ice bucket, florals/scrolls, gr/clear w/gold, 5½x5¼" 1,350.00
Jar, poppies, lt & dk bl w/3-color pnt, sterling lid, 2¼x4" 400.00

Lamp, winter scene, dark brown on snowy ground against mottled yellow background, signed AR, marked, 15½", $18,000.00.

Lamp, tulips, yel/gr on rust, domed 11" shade, 19½" 12,650.00
Pitcher, poppies, cut/pnt on apricot opal w/gold, 3x2½" 2,150.00
Rose bowl, snowy woods, cut/pnt, wht on marmalade, 3" 2,600.00
Salt cellar, branches/boughs/cones, cut/pnt, 1¾x2" 1,250.00
Salt cellar, floral on vaseline w/gold, 2⅛" 800.00
Salt cellar, leaves/vines, cut/pnt on gr w/gold, 2½x3½" 650.00
Salt cellar, summer trees & plants, cut/pnt, clear/frost, 2" 1,200.00

Salt cellar, vines/leaves, cut/pnt, vaseline opal w/gold, 3½" 650.00
Sugar castor, poppies, cut/pnt, smoky amethyst, silver mt, 7¼" ..865.00
Vase, birches/branches/grasses, cut/pnt, wht opal, 1¾" 1,000.00
Vase, clematis on lav-pk, turret form, 8" 800.00
Vase, columbines, cut/pnt, amber/wht/burgundy, ovoid, 4⅞" .1,400.00
Vase, dandelions, orange/opal/gr/gray-blk w/gold, 9½" 2,700.00
Vase, dandelions/seeds, gilt on gold-amber opal/lime, 3¼" 1,000.00
Vase, fleur-de-lis, emerald gr w/gold, 13¾x4½" 250.00
Vase, floral, cut/pnt, burgundy/yel mottle/opal/lime, ftd, 4" ...1,750.00
Vase, floral, cut/pnt, yel/pk/gr, mini, 2" 1,050.00
Vase, floral, 5-color, ovoid bulbous base, long neck, 15x6¼" ..4,000.00
Vase, floral/leaves, frost on pk w/gold, dmn form, 4½" 300.00
Vase, irises, pk on pk w/gold, dmn form, 7" 825.00
Vase, jonquils, gr/mustard on mottled frost/mustard, slim, 15" ...4,250.00
Vase, landscape, cut/pnt, yel/frosted, pillow form, 1x2" 1,100.00
Vase, marsh flowers, yel/pk/gr/brn, 13½x2½" 4,100.00
Vase, orchids/bees/web, cut/pnt on yel mottle, trumpet form, 21" ...8,000.00
Vase, parrot tulips, pk on textured frost, 9¾x5½" 1,200.00
Vase, poppies on stems, amber/blk-gr on martele, 8½" 3,250.00
Vase, rain forest, purple on pale pk frost, camphor hdls, 10" ...6,100.00
Vase, rain scene, cut/pnt, frosted clear, 2½" 1,600.00
Vase, snow/forest/sky, cut/pnt, brn-blk/wht/marmalade, 11¾" ...6,000.00
Vase, trees landscape, gr/bl/purple, mini, 3" 1,050.00
Vase, trees/water/sky, yel & lime on frost, 8" 4,500.00
Vase, winter scene, cut/pnt, mustard/clear, ovoid, 5½" 2,600.00
Vase, winter scene, cut/pnt, rare, 2" 1,000.00

Miscellaneous

Bowl, etched horizontal ribs on yel, cone form, 6" H 875.00
Bowl, textured lt gr, encased bubbles, tooled rim, 2½x6" 125.00
Creamer, windmills/sailboats, blk pnt on opal w/gold, 4¼" 2,250.00
Ewer, Dutch seascape/landscape, gray pnt on bl irid, 8" 2,600.00
Lamp, mc mottled domical 12½" shade; 2-light Katona std, 19" ..2,300.00
Lamp, mottled 4-color conical shade; wrought E Brandt std, 20½" ..5,175.00
Pitcher, landscape, blk w/gold on clear, int ribs, hdl, 2½x3" ...2,000.00
Salt cellar, snowy landscape, bucket form, tab hdls, 1¼" 900.00
Vase, aqua frost w/appl frosted coil, ovoid, frosted ft, 21" 1,265.00
Vase, Berluze, red to azure to cobalt, stick neck, 20¼" 800.00
Vase, clear w/appl red lines, blk bands, ftd, 9½" 1,200.00
Vase, etched ribs beneath sqs, lt yel, ftd U-form, 4½" 750.00
Vase, floral, gold sprays on textured frost, 5-peak rim, 6" 700.00
Vase, floral, mc on mottle, tapered cylinder, 12½" 1,100.00
Vase, landscape, HP brn on bright yel, 1¾" 850.00
Vase, lt gr, lobed, many encased bubbles, 10½" 160.00
Vase, mottled fuchsia & plum w/gold foil inclusions, ftd, 14" .1,150.00
Vase, mottled wht, rpt wrought Majorelle, fr w/rtcl base, 12" ..1,955.00
Vase, rust mottle, blown into iron Majorelle scroll fr, 15" 2,860.00
Vase, sailing ships/trees/mtns, purple HP on orange, 2¼x2¼" 900.00
Vase, sailing ships/windmills on opal, globular, 3" 1,095.00
Vase, thistles/leaves, cut on yel opal, 4½x2" 350.00
Vase, tropical island scene, gray/purple/peach, mini, 1¾" 900.00
Vase, violets w/leafy stems on mottled purple & opal, 5" 2,250.00
Vase, wild roses etched on frosted opal, gold rim, 4½x2" 450.00

Davenport

W. Davenport and Company were Staffordshire potters operating in that area from 1793 to 1887, producing earthenware, creamware, porcelain, and ironstone. Many different stamps, all with 'Davenport' were used to mark the various types of ware. See also Mulberry; Flow Blue.

Egg coddler, turq & gilt trim, basketweave base, 6 inserts, hdl ...330.00

Plate, Oriental view, bl transfer, foliate border, mk, 9¾" 35.00
Platter, bird/floral transfer, bl w/mc, ca 1810, 18¼" 230.00
Soup tureen, bird/floral transfer, mc, mask hdls, w/stand, 14" .1,600.00

De Vez

De Vez was a type of acid-cut French cameo glass produced by Cristal-lerie de Pantin in Paris around the turn of the century. Our advisor for this category is Don Williams; he is listed in the Directory under Missouri.

Cameo

Vase, autumn trees/mtns, gr/yel/gold-yel, ftd, 9¼" 1,000.00
Vase, castle/mtn/lake, orange/olive gr/bl/gr, 9½" 1,500.00
Vase, ducks/aquatic plants, cobalt on pk, 7x3" 700.00
Vase, poppies/leaves, wine on citron & red, 5½" 725.00
Vase, trees/cattails fr castle/lake, bl-blk/yel, slim, 6¼" 625.00
Vase, trees/deer/duck, cobalt/yel/pk, 5½x2" 1,200.00
Vase, trees/lakes/mtns, wht/yel/red, ovoid, 5¼" 1,200.00
Vase, trees/waterway/hills, gr/bl/pk, bbl form, 3½" 400.00
Vase, woods/water/meadow, yel/russet, bell form, 8¾" 900.00

De Vilbiss

Perfume bottles, atomizers, and dresser accessories marketed by the De Vilbiss Company are appreciated by collectors today for the various types of lovely glassware used in their manufacture as well as for their pleasing shapes. Various companies provided the glass, while De Vilbiss made only the metal tops. They marketed their merchandise not only here but in Paris, England, Canada, and Havana as well. Their marks were acid stamped, ink stamped, in gold script, molded in, or on paper labels. One is no more significant than another. Our advisor for this category is Randy Monsen; he is listed in the Directory under Virginia.

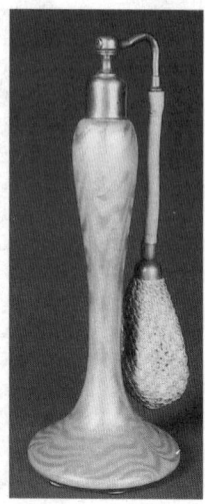

Atomizer, King Tut pattern, blue-green iridescence on green, Durand, original attachments, 7½", $950.00.

Photo courtesy Monsen and Baer

Atomizer, alexandrite, Tiffin, mesh cord & bulb, 6", $275 to 300.00
Atomizer, bl opal, Coin Spot, bulbous 75.00
Atomizer, bl rvpt w/gold o/l, orig mts, lacks cord, 5½" 120.00
Atomizer, bl w/gold, gold metal mts, lacks ball/cord, 5½" 120.00
Atomizer, bl w/4 gold flamingos, 5" 75.00
Atomizer, blk w/crystal stem & ft, 4¼" 65.00
Atomizer, blk w/gold, orig mts, 6¼", in wall-pocket holder 660.00
Atomizer, cranberry, emb swirls, gold metal mts, 7" 285.00
Atomizer, cranberry, gilt mts, rpl ball & tassel, 7" 285.00

Atomizer, cranberry windows, gold encrusted, 7" 250.00
Atomizer, cut birds w/gold, rpl ball & tassel, 7" 715.00
Atomizer, gold Aurene w/rare traces of pk, Steuben, 6" 485.00
Atomizer, gold crackle, beaded flower on top, mk, 4¾" 85.00
Atomizer, gold w/3 cut windows, gold mts, complete, 10" 470.00
Atomizer, pk cone shape, gold mts, complete w/holder, 6" 660.00
Atomizer, pk to bl w/gilt metal & turq stones, Imperial, 7¼" ..1,325.00
Atomizer, silver crackle, w/label 65.00
Atomizer, sky bl pnt, teardrop, complete, 6¼" 165.00
Bottle, blk allover w/gold enamel, glass dauber, 7" 285.00
Bottle, cut crystal, metal stopper, glass dauber, 6½" 200.00
Bottle, irid, blk enamel top, stemmed ft, mk 175.00
Bottle, lt amber, 6-panel, hex ped, w/dropper, 6¼" 145.00
Bottle, lt pk w/dk pk enamel, glass dropper, metal top, 7" 185.00
Bottle, pk enameled w/gold & blk stripes, glass dropper, 4¾" 200.00
Bottle, pk rvpt/pk enamel, glass dropper, silver-metal top, 7" 190.00
Bottle, yel enamel w/blk & gold, bell form, metal lid, 4" 135.00
Bottle, yel w/blk triangles, gold line, clear neck, 4" 85.00
Dresser set, gold enamel w/mc florals, atomizer+2 jars+tray 425.00
Ginger jar, Chinese red w/gold floral 115.00
Lamp, perfume; Fairies at My Garden Gate, brass base, 7¼" 500.00
Lamp, perfume; nude figure on glass insert, 7" 300.00
Pin tray, blk matt w/gold trim 60.00
Vanity set, orange enamel w/blk & gold decor, 3-pc 400.00

Decanters

Ceramic whiskey decanters were brought into prominence in 1955 by the James Beam Distilling Company. Few other companies besides Beam produced these decanters during the next ten years or so; however, other companies did eventually follow suit. At its peak in 1975, at least twenty prominent companies and several on a lesser scale made these decanters. Beam stopped making decanters in mid-1992. Now only a couple of companies are still producing these collectibles.

Liquor dealers have told collectors for years that ceramic decanters are not as valuable, and in some cases worthless, if emptied or if the federal tax stamp has been broken. Nothing is further from the truth. Following are but a few of many reasons you should consider emptying ceramic decanters:

1) If the thin glaze on the inside ever cracks (and it does in a small percentage of decanters), the contents will push through to the outside. It is then referred to as a 'leaker' and worth a fraction of its original value.

2) A large number of decanters left full in one area of your house poses a fire hazard.

3) A burglar, after stealing jewelry and electronics, may make off with some of your decanters just to enjoy the contents. If they are empty, chances are they will not be bothered.

4) It is illegal in most states for collectors to sell a full decanter without a liquor license.

Unlike years ago, few collectors now collect all types of decanters. Most now specialize. For example, they may collect trains, cars, owls, Indians, clowns, or any number of different things that have been depicted on or as a decanter. They are finding exceptional quality available at reasonable prices, especially when compared with many other types of collectibles.

We have tried to list those brands that are the most popular with collectors. Likewise, individual decanters listed are the ones (or representative of the ones) most commonly found. The following listing is but a small fraction of the thousands of decanters that have been produced.

These decanters come from all over the world. While Jim Beam owned its own china factory in the U.S., some of the others have been imported from Mexico, Taiwan, Japan and elsewhere. They vary in size from miniatures (approximately 2 oz.) to gallons. Values range from a few dollars to more than $3,000.00 per decanter.

Most collectors and dealers define a 'mint' decanter as one with no chips, no cracks, and label intact. A missing federal tax stamp or lack of contents have no bearing on value. All values are given for 'mint' decanters. A 'mini' behind a listing indicates a miniature. All others are fifth or 750 ml unless noted otherwise. Our advisor for this category is Roy Willis; he is listed in the Directory under Kentucky.

Aesthetic Specialties (ASI)

Golf, Bing Crosby 39th	30.00
Truck, Ice Cream	90.00
Truck, Telephone	75.00

Beam

Casino Series, Harold's Club Slot Machine, bl	18.00
Casino Series, Harold's Club Slot Machine, gray	15.00
Casino Series, Smith's North Shore	15.00
Centennial Series, Antioch	5.00
Centennial Series, Chicago Fire	22.00
Centennial Series, Dodge City, Boot Hill	10.00
Centennial Series, Laramie	5.00
Centennial Series, Yellowstone	8.00
Executive Series, 1955, Royal Porcelain	250.00
Executive Series, 1957, Royal Dimonte	50.00
Executive Series, 1960, Blue Cherub	75.00
Executive Series, 1968, Presidential	12.00
Executive Series, 1972, Regency	12.00
Foreign Series, Australia, Queensland	24.00
Foreign Series, Australia, Sydney Opera House	24.00
Foreign Series, Australia, Tigers	16.00
Foreign Series, Germany, Hansel & Gretel	10.00
Foreign Series, Germany, Pied Piper	10.00
Foreign Series, Germany, Wiesbaden	10.00
Organization Series, Ducks Unlimited #1, 1974	35.00
Organization Series, Ducks Unlimited #2, 1975	40.00
Organization Series, Ducks Unlimited #3, 1977	40.00
Organization Series, Ducks Unlimited #4, 1978	45.00
Organization Series, Ducks Unlimited #5, 1979	45.00
Organization Series, Fleet Reserve	6.00
Organization Series, Kentucky Colonel	10.00
Organization Series, Marine Corps Emblem	50.00
Organization Series, Pearl Harbor, 1972	18.00
Organization Series, Shriner Indiana	6.00
Organization Series, VFW	8.00
People Series, Buffalo Bill	20.00
People Series, Captain & Mate	10.00
People Series, General Stark	12.00
People Series, Hatfield or McCoy	25.00
People Series, Indian Chief	22.00
People Series, Rocky Marciano	45.00
State Series, Arizona	6.00
State Series, Florida Shell	7.00
State Series, Illinois	8.00
State Series, Michigan	10.00
State Series, Nebraska	8.00
Wheel Series, Army Jeep	48.00
Wheel Series, Cadillac Convertible, 1959, pk	65.00
Wheel Series, Chevy 1957 Belair Convertible, turq & wht	65.00
Wheel Series, Chevy 1957 Belair Hardtop, red & wht	95.00
Wheel Series, Corvette, 1953, wht	175.00
Wheel Series, Corvette, 1957, blk	80.00

Wheel Series, Corvette, 1984, red	85.00
Wheel Series, Corvette, 1984, wht	65.00
Wheel Series, Duesenberg, 1934, lt bl	110.00
Wheel Series, Ford, 1903 Model A, blk or red	55.00
Wheel Series, Ford, 1928 Model A Coupe, gr	75.00
Wheel Series, Ford, 1928 Model A Coupe, gr	75.00
Wheel Series, Ford, 1935 Pickup - Clermont Supply	60.00
Wheel Series, Jewel Tea Wagon	75.00
Wheel Series, Train, Baggage Car	60.00
Wheel Series, Train, Casey Jones Box Car, gr	40.00
Wheel Series, Train, Casey Jones Caboose, red	30.00
Wheel Series, Train, Casey Jones Locomotive w/Tender	30.00
Wheel Series, Train, Casey Jones Tank Car, wht	40.00
Wheel Series, Train, Coal Tender for Grant	65.00
Wheel Series, Train, Dining Car	110.00
Wheel Series, Train, Locomotive, Grant	85.00
Wheel Series, Train, Observation Car	60.00
Wheel Series, Train, Passenger Car	45.00

Brooks

Ontario Racer, Heritage China, dated 1970, 12½" long, $35.00.

American Legion, Hawaii, 1973	16.00
Amvets Polish Legion	10.00
Bareknuckle Fighter	35.00
Basketball Player	18.00
Betsy Ross	10.00
Cardinal, Virginia	15.00
Cards, jack, queen or king	15.00
Clock, Grandfather	10.00
Delta Belle, Riverboat	10.00
Duesenberg	35.00
Equestrienne	12.00
Goldpanner	8.00
Hambletonian	18.00
Harold's Club Dice	15.00
Jayhawk, Kansas	15.00
Kachina #1, Morning Singer	85.00
Kachina #2, Hummingbird	80.00
Kachina #3, Antelope	80.00
Kitten on Pillow	12.00
Lion on Rock	10.00
Owl, Old Ez #1	30.00
Owl, Old Ez #1, mini	20.00
Panda	18.00
Quail	10.00

Dant, J.W.

Fort Sill	8.00
Mount Rushmore	6.00

Paul Bunyon 6.00

Double Springs

Cadillac, 1913 ....38.00
Pierce Arrow, 1915 ....55.00
Stutz Bearcat, 1919 ....40.00

Famous Firsts

Locomotive, Dewitt Clinton 35.00
Racer, Marmon Wasp 75.00
Racer, Marmon Wasp, mini 35.00
Racer, National #8 ....60.00
Racer, National #8, mini 35.00
Spirit of St Louis, lg 150.00
Spirit of St Louis, midi 80.00
Spirit of St Louis, mini 50.00

Hoffman

Betsy Ross 50.00
College Series, Helmet, Gerogia 40.00
College Series, Helmet, LSU 30.00
College Series, Helmet, Nebraska 45.00
College Series, Mascot, Kentucky Football or Basketball 50.00
College Series, Mascot, LSU, Running or Passing 40.00
Mr Lucky Series, Mr Carpenter 35.00
Mr Lucky Series, Mr Carpenter, mini 15.00
Mr Lucky Series, Mr Harpist 25.00
Mr Lucky Series, Mr Harpist, mini 12.00
Mr Lucky Series, Mr Photographer 35.00
Mr Lucky Series, Mr Photographer, mini 18.00
Race Car, Donahue, Sunoco #66 ....125.00
Race Car, Rutherford #3 ....110.00
Wildlife Series, Bobcat & Pheasant 60.00
Wildlife Series, Panda 65.00

Kontinental

Editor 35.00
Editor, mini 20.00
Gunsmith 35.00
Gunsmith, mini 20.00
Innkeeper 30.00
Lumberjack 25.00

Lionstone

Annie Oakley 20.00
Bartender 28.00
Bartender, mini 16.00
Baseball Players 80.00
Basketball Players 60.00
Bath, Saturday Night 75.00
Boxers 75.00
Cowboy 25.00
Cowboy, mini 15.00
Cowgirl 30.00
Custer's Last Stand, set of 4 ....500.00
Fireman #1, red hat 100.00
Fireman #1, yel hat 140.00
Fireman #2, carrying child 90.00
Goldfinch 25.00

Judge Roy Bean 22.00
Laundryman, Chinese 22.00
Madame 45.00
OK Corral Shootout, set of 3 ....475.00
OK Corral Shootout, set of 3, mini 250.00
Oriental Workers, 6 different 35.00
Perfessor 45.00
Perfessor, mini 20.00
Robber, Highway 20.00
Scout, Calvary 20.00
Scout, Calvary, mini 15.00
Telegrapher 25.00
Trapper 25.00

McCormick

Bicentennial Series, Betsy Ross 28.00
Bicentennial Series, Paul Revere 28.00
Bicentennial Series, Spirit of '76 ....50.00
Elvis, Aloha 225.00
Elvis, Aloha, mini 200.00
Elvis, Bust, from $60 to 75.00
Elvis, Gold Tribute, 1979 ....180.00
Elvis, Sergeant 325.00
Ford, Henry 30.00
Ford, Henry; mini 22.00
Grant, US 50.00
King Arthur's Court, Merlin 40.00
King Arthur's Court, Sir Lancelot 35.00
Lindbergh, Charles 40.00
Lindbergh, Charles; mini 18.00
Muhammad Ali 200.00
Roosevelt, Eleanor 25.00
Shrine, Imperial Council 35.00
Shrine, Noble 30.00
Strowger Telephone 35.00
Will Rogers 30.00
Will Rogers, mini 15.00

Old Commonwealth

Boot, Western 25.00
Boot, Western, mini 12.00
Coins of Ireland, 1979 ....25.00
Dogs of Ireland, 1980 ....20.00
Fisherman, A Keeper 50.00
Golden Retriever 30.00
Leprechaun, Elusive, 1980 ....35.00
Leprechaun, Irish Minstrel, 1982 ....35.00
Leprechaun, Lucky, 1983 ....30.00
Princeton University 20.00
Walking Horse, Tennessee 45.00

Old Fitzgerald

Irish Charm, 1977 ....22.00
Irish Counties, 1973 ....20.00
Irish Patriots, 1971 ....18.00
Songs of Ireland, 1974 ....15.00
Sons of Ireland, 1969 ....15.00

Ski Country

Badger Family 55.00

Badger Family, mini	28.00
Barnum, PT	50.00
Barnum, PT; mini	30.00
Bluebirds Wall Plaque	90.00
Bull Rider	75.00
Bull Rider, mini	40.00
Cedar Waxwings	60.00
Cedar Waxwings, mini	25.00
Dove, Peace	65.00
Dove, Peace, mini	32.00
Duck, King Eider	65.00
Duck, King Eider, mini	35.00
Ducks Unlimited #3, Mallard, 1980	75.00
Ducks Unlimited #3, Mallard, 1980, mini	50.00
Ducks Unlimited #4, Canvasback, 1981	60.00
Ducks Unlimited #4, Canvasback, 1981, mini	30.00
Ducks Unlimited #5, Wood Duck, 1982	100.00
Ducks Unlimited #5, Wood Duck, 1982, mini	50.00
Eagle, Bald; On Water	150.00
Eagle, Bald; On Water, mini	50.00
Eagle, Harpy	135.00
Eagle, Harpy, mini	95.00
Flycatcher	130.00
Flycatcher, mini	55.00
Fox on Log	85.00
Fox on Log, mini	160.00
Fox on Log, 1.75 liter	275.00
Indian, End of the Trail	250.00
Indian, End of the Trail, mini	125.00
Indian, Great Spirit	110.00
Indian, Great Spirit, mini	25.00
Indian, Lookout	65.00
Indian, Lookout, mini	35.00
Kestrel Wall Plaque	75.00
Lion, Mountain	50.00
Lion, Mountain; mini	30.00
Lion on Drum	48.00
Lion on Drum, mini	26.00
Owl, Barn	85.00
Owl, Barn; mini	30.00
Owl, Screech Family	110.00
Owl, Screech Family, gal	400.00
Owl, Screech Family, mini	85.00
Raccoon Wall Plaque	95.00
Salmon, Landlocked	50.00
Salmon, Landlocked, mini	30.00
Sea Gull Wall Plaque	60.00
Squirrel Wall Plaque	175.00
Trout, Rainbow	70.00
Trout, Rainbow; mini	35.00
US Ski Team	35.00
US Ski Team, mini	16.00

Wild Turkey

Series I, #1, #2, #3, or #4, mini, ea	18.00
Series I, #1, 1971	250.00
Series I, #2	150.00
Series I, #3	70.00
Series I, #4	70.00
Series I, #5	30.00
Series I, #6	25.00
Series I, #7	25.00
Series I, #8	45.00

Series I, set of #5, #6, #7 & #8, mini	160.00
Series II, Lore #1	25.00
Series II, Lore #2	35.00
Series II, Lore #3	45.00
Series II, Lore #4	50.00
Series III, #1, In Flight	120.00
Series III, #1, In Flight, mini	45.00
Series III, #2, Turkey & Bobcat	140.00
Series III, #2, Turkey & Bobcat, mini	45.00
Series III, #3, Fighting Turkeys	150.00
Series III, #3, Fighting Turkeys, mini	50.00
Series III, #4, Turkey & Eagle	95.00
Series III, #4, Turkey & Eagle, mini	80.00
Series III, #5, Turkey & Raccoon	95.00
Series III, #5, Turkey & Raccoon, mini	45.00
Series III, #6, Turkey & Poults	95.00
Series III, #6, Turkey & Poults, mini	45.00
Series III, #7, Turkey & Red Fox	95.00
Series III, #7, Turkey & Red Fox, mini	50.00
Series III, #8, Turkey & Owl	100.00
Series III, #8, Turkey & Owl, mini	50.00
Series III, #9, Turkey & Bear Cubs	100.00
Series III, #9, Turkey & Bear Cubs, mini	50.00
Series III, #10, Turkey & Coyote	95.00
Series III, #10, Turkey & Coyote, mini	45.00
Series III, #11, Turkey & Falcon	95.00
Series III, #11, Turkey & Falcon, mini	45.00
Series III, #12, Turkey & Skunks	95.00
Series III, #12, Turkey & Skunks, mini	45.00

Decoys

American colonists learned the craft of decoy making from the Indians who used them to lure birds out of the sky as an important food source. Early models were carved from wood such as pine, cedar, balsa, etc., and a few were made of canvas or papier-mache. There are two basic types of decoys: water floaters and shorebirds (also called 'stick-ups'). Within each type are many different species, ducks being the most plentiful since they migrated along all four of America's great waterways. Market hunting became big business around 1880, resulting in large-scale commercial production of decoys which continued until about 1910 when such hunting was outlawed by the Migratory Bird Treaty.

Today decoys are one of the most collectible types of American folk art. The most valuable are those carved by such artists as Laing, Crowell, Ward, and Wheeler, to name only a few. Each area, such as Massachusetts, Connecticut, Maine, the Illinois River, and the Delaware River, produces decoys with distinctive regional characteristics. Examples of commercial decoys produced by well-known factories — among them Mason, Stevens, and Dodge — are also prized by collectors. Though mass produced, these nevertheless required a certain amount of hand carving and decorating. Well-carved examples, especially those of rare species, are appreciating rapidly, and those with original paint are more desirable. Writer Carl F. Luckey has compiled a fully illustrated identification and value guide, *Collecting Antique Bird Decoys*; you will find his address in the Directory under Alabama. In the listings that follow, all decoys are solid-bodied unless noted hollow.

Key:

CG — Challenge Grade	PG — Premier Grade
MDF — Mason's Decoy Factory	RP — repaint
OP — original paint	SG — Standard Grade
ORP — old repaint	WDF — Wildfowler Decoy Factory
OWP — original working paint	WOP — worn original paint

Blk Duck, Crowell, oval brand, EX OP, minor wear o/w EX ...**1,350.00**
Blk Duck, Ed Phillips, 2 sm cracks, minor wear, OP **1,050.00**
Blk Duck, Fitzpatrick, hollow, lowhead, EX OP, 1930s **550.00**
Blk Duck, N Hudson, ½-sz, w/4 ducklings, NM OP, late 1930s .**1,050.00**
Blk Duck, Stevens, scalloped feather pnt, sm crack, NM OP, 1880s ..**1,200.00**
Blk Duck, Tony Bianco, NM OP **275.00**

Bluebill Drake, Mason Decoy Factory, Premier Grade, hollow carved, head turned slightly, NM, $10,000.00.

Bluebill drake, Ed Phillips, OP w/minor wear **1,000.00**
Bluebill drake, Peterson, body WOP, head ORP, 1880s, G **215.00**
Bluebill drake, Stevens, OP, ca 1880, minor wear **1,050.00**
Bluebill hen, MDF, CG, low-head model, EX OP **650.00**
Bluewing Teal drake, MDF, PG, mk BJH, minor WOP, VG **600.00**
Brant, MDF, CG, branded Barron, EX OP, 1910 ....**1,800.00**
Brant, preening; Pete Wilbur, mk CW underside, OP w/minor wear **200.00**
Bufflehead drake, Delaware River area, OP w/minor wear **255.00**
Canada Goose, C Miller, detailed/Xd wing tips/fluted tail, NM OP **2,200.00**
Canada Goose, Crowell, rectagular brand, mini, 1945, NM **650.00**
Canvasback drake, Taylor Boyd, EX OP w/old coat of varnish ...**975.00**
Canvasback hen, MDF, CG, hollow, snakey head trn, EX OP ..**2,100.00**
Canvasbacks, MDF, SG, both RP, structurally VG, pr **210.00**
Coot, Herters, balsa, worn OWP, ca 1946, VG **35.00**
Crow, MDF, crack in 1 side, VG OP **400.00**
Crow, MDF, glass eyes, sm chips, minor WOP **600.00**
Crow (scare), MDF, EX WOP, EX **1,550.00**
Dowitcher w/split tail, MDF, tack eye, shot/rpl bill, WOP **275.00**
Golden Plover, John Dilley, relief wing, detailed, VG OP, EX ..**8,750.00**
Golden Plover, MDF, glass eyes, sm crack, VG WOP **1,550.00**
Goldeneye drake, MDF, tack eye, EX OP **525.00**
Goldeneye drake, Ward Bros, cedar, EX OP & structure, 1940s ..**1,500.00**
Goldeneye pr, WDF, Old Saybrook, VG OP, some RP on head, G ...**160.00**
Mallard drake, MDF, PG, minor WOP, VG **450.00**
Mallard drake, MDF, SG, tack eye, NM OP, rare **500.00**
Mallard hen, MDF, PG, NM OP, unused **2,400.00**
Mallard hen, MDF, SG, putty missing from neck, OP, VG **120.00**
Merganser drake, MDF, PG, HC cvd in bottom, snakey head, WOP, VG ..**1,275.00**
Merganser pr, MDF, CG, EX WOP, sm defect & roughness .**10,500.00**
Old Squaw drake, upper Maine coast, tack eyes, WOP **175.00**
Pintail drake, R Swiderski, hollow, raised V wings, NM OP **700.00**
Pintail hen, John English, hollow, branded Perkins, RP, EX **300.00**
Redbreasted Merganser drake, Gus Wilson, WOP w/some RP, G ..**2,000.00**
Redhead drake, Ed Phillips, orig tape on bill, OP, minor wear ...**900.00**
Redhead drake, John English, U-shaped feather mks, VG OP, 1880s .**8,500.00**
Redhead hen, Crowell, pre-stamp, cvd Xd wing tips, WOP **1,600.00**
Redhead pr, WDF, Old Saybrook, VG OP, oversz **260.00**
Ringneck Pheasant, Crowell, sgn on base, NM OP, EX **475.00**
Robin Snipe, MDF, glass eyes, fall plumage, EX OP **1,050.00**
Ruddy Duck, Crowell, rectangular stamp, EX OP, EX **300.00**
Scooter pr, MDF, SG, tack eyes, EX OP, VG **3,500.00**

Teal, John English, EX in-use RP, ca 1880 ....**700.00**
Wigeon hen, MDF, SG, glass eyes, EX OP, EX **1,350.00**
Wigeon pr, WDF, Old Saybrook, detailed, 1939, EX OP, VG+ .**500.00**
Willet, unknown maker, relief wing, cvd eyes, 2-pc body, NM OP .**2,150.00**
Yellowlegs pr, split tails, MDF, EX OP, minor chips o/w EX ...**2,850.00**

Dedham Pottery

Originally founded in Chelsea, Massachusetts, as the Chelsea Keramic Works, the name was changed to Dedham Pottery in 1895 after the firm relocated in Dedham, near Boston, Massachusetts. The ware utilized a gray stoneware body with a crackle glaze and simple cobalt border designs of flowers, birds, and animals. Decorations were brushed on by hand using an ancient Chinese method which suspended the cobalt within the overall glaze. There were thirteen standard patterns, among them Magnolia, Iris, Butterfly, Duck, Polar Bear, and Rabbit, the latter of which was chosen to represent the company on their logo. On the very early pieces, the rabbits face left; decorators soon found the reverse position easier to paint, and the rabbits were turned to the right. (Earlier examples are worth from 10% to 20% more than identical pieces manufactured in later years.) In addition to the standard patterns, other designs were produced for special orders. These and artist-signed pieces are highly valued by collectors today.

Though their primary product was the blue-printed, crackle-glazed dinnerware, two types of artware were also produced: crackle glaze and flambe. Their notable volcanic ware was a type of the latter. The mark is incised and often accompanies the cipher of Hugh Robertson. The firm was operated by succeeding generations of the Robertson family until it closed in 1943. Our advisor for this category is Dale MacLean; he is listed in the Directory under Massachusetts. See also Chelsea Keramic Art Works.

Dinnerware

Ashtray, Rabbit, flat type, stamped registered, ¾x3¾" **250.00**
Bacon rasher, Swan, stamped registered/imp, 1½x10¼", EX **600.00**
Bacon rasher, Turkey, stamped, 1⅛x9¾" **500.00**
Bowl, Double Blue Band, stamped, 2¾x6" **275.00**
Bowl, mixing; Rabbit, hand thrown, early incised mk, 5¾x12" ..**500.00**
Bowl, nappy, Elephant, med bl, stamped, prof rstr, 1¼x5½" **550.00**
Bowl, Rabbit, dk to med bl, #6, 2x4¼" **225.00**
Bowl, Rabbit, sq w/rnded corners, stamped registered, 7¾" **450.00**
Bowl, Swan, stamped registered, 2x5¼" **425.00**
Bowl, Swan, stamped registered, 3x7¾" **325.00**
Bowl, whipped cream; Azalea, stamped registered, 2½x7½", EX .**250.00**
Candle holder, Elephant & Baby, stamped registered, 1¾x3¼", EX **450.00**
Coaster, Elephant, flared rim, stamped, 4" **450.00**
Creamer, Horse Chestnut, stamped registered, 2x5½" **275.00**
Creamer, Rabbit, dk bl, curved hdl, #13, stamped, 2¾x3" **300.00**
Creamer, Rabbit, spherical, stamped registered/1931, 3x5½" **350.00**
Creamer, Rabbit, stamped, 2¾x3⅛" **350.00**
Creamer, Rabbit, stamped/registered, 3¼x3¾" **400.00**
Cruet, Rabbit, rabbit stopper, rstr, stamped registered, 5" **1,200.00**
Cup, chowder; Rabbit, 2-hdld, stamped registered, w/underplate ..**500.00**
Cup & saucer, bouillon; Rabbit, 2-hdld, stamped registered **300.00**
Cup & saucer, chowder; Rabbit, 2-hdld, stamped registered **500.00**
Cup & saucer, coffee; Horse Chestnut, stamped, EX **250.00**
Cup & saucer, demi; Rabbit, Davenport rebus, stamped **400.00**
Cup & saucer, Duck, stamped/registered, 2x4½", 6" **350.00**
Cup & saucer, Horse Chestnut, stamped, 2⅛x4½", 6" **250.00**
Egg cup, dbl; Elephant & Baby, partial stamp, 3x3" **525.00**
Flower holder, Turtle, figural, stamped registered, 3½" **600.00**

Knife rest, rabbit form, stamped registered, rstr, 2¾x3¼" 400.00
Mug, Double Turtle, stamped, 3½x4¼" 1,000.00
Mug, Elephant, hand-thrown, stamped, 3½x4¼", EX 900.00
Pickle dish, Rabbit, Davenport rebus, stamped, 9½x5¼" 550.00
Pitcher, Rabbit, bulbous, #2, stamped registered, 4¾x6" 500.00
Pitcher, Rabbit, Davenport rebus, stamped, 4½x5", EX 475.00
Plate, Avery Oak, sgn Hugh Robertson, stamped, 8¼" 2,600.00
Plate, Azalea, dk bl, stamped registered, 8¾", EX 300.00
Plate, Bird in Potted Orange Tree, imp, 10" 600.00
Plate, Butterfly, stamped, 6" 450.00
Plate, Clover, stamped registered/imp, 6" 650.00
Plate, Coat of Arms/Fairbanks...Crest, stamped/imp, 8¾", EX ...650.00
Plate, Dolphin & Wave, stamped/registered, 7½" 650.00
Plate, Double Crab, stamped/imp, 8½" 800.00
Plate, Double Scottie Dog, stamped/registered/imp, 8½" 1,800.00
Plate, Double Turtle, stamped/imp, 9¾" 1,000.00
Plate, Double Turtle & Clover, stamped/imp, prof rstr, 9¾" ...1,300.00
Plate, Duck, broad band, stamped/imp, 10" 500.00
Plate, Duck, stamped/registered, 9¾" 500.00
Plate, Elephant, imp, 7½" 350.00
Plate, Elephant, stamped, 7½" 650.00
Plate, Elephant & Baby, stamped registered/imp, 1931, 8½" 750.00
Plate, French Mushroom, cobalt, stamped/imp, 8½", EX 900.00
Plate, Hunter & Bow, registered/imp, prof rstr, 8½" 1,500.00
Plate, Iris, stamped registered/imp, 8½" 300.00
Plate, Landscape, stamped/imp, 6" 400.00
Plate, Lion Tapestry, stamped/imp, 8½" 1,200.00
Plate, Lobster, Davenport rebus, stamped, 5¾" 550.00
Plate, Lobster, stamped, faint peppering, 8½", EX 500.00
Plate, Luna Moth, stamped/imp, 6⅛" 600.00
Plate, Magnolia, stamped/imp, 8½", EX 275.00
Plate, Mushroom, stamped/imp, 8¼" 750.00
Plate, Pineapple, stamped/registered/imp, 8½" 750.00
Plate, Polar Bear, Davenport rebus, stamped/imp, 10", EX 800.00
Plate, Pond Lily, imp, 6" 250.00
Plate, Pond Lily, stamped/imp, 8½", EX 300.00
Plate, Pond Lily & Water, Davenport rebus, stamped/imp, 9¾" .450.00
Plate, Poppy, stamped/imp, 6⅛" 750.00
Plate, Rabbit, Davenport rebus, stamped, 6", EX 275.00
Plate, Rabbit, Davenport rebus, stamped/imp, 10", EX 375.00
Plate, Rabbit, Davenport rebus, stamped/imp, 8½", EX 325.00
Plate, Rabbit, stamped registered, 8½" 250.00
Plate, Seascape, stamped/imp, faint peppering, 6" 375.00
Plate, Snow Tree, stamped/imp, 6" 250.00
Plate, Swan, stamped, 8½" 475.00
Plate, Tufted Duck, imp, 10" 500.00
Plate, Turkey, Davenport rebus, stamped/imp, 6" 400.00
Plate, Turkey, stamped registered, 8½", EX 400.00
Plate, Wild Rose, Davenport rebus, stamped, 6" 1,700.00
Shakers, Rabbit, orig corks, partial bl mk, 3½", EX, pr 450.00
Sherbet, Rabbit, partial bl mk, 3x5½", EX 400.00
Soup, Grape, stamped registered/imp, 1¼x8¼" 275.00
Soup, Rabbit, stamped/imp, 1½x9¼" 250.00
Star dish, Rabbit, stamped registered, 1½x7¼" 500.00
Stein, Rabbit, med bl, stamped/imp, 5x5½", EX 750.00
Sugar bowl, Azalea, registered, 2¾x4", EX 350.00
Sugar bowl, Rabbit, bulbous, #1, stamped, 4½x4½", EX 325.00
Teapot, Rabbit, bulbous, #2, stamped registered, 5⅛x6¼" 1,200.00

Miscellaneous

Vase, dk gr crackle on yel & dk gr glossy, WB, 9x6", EX 500.00
Vase, dripping brn/dk brn/gr flambe, bulbous, 9x7" 700.00
Vase, gr/yel/rouge flambe, baluster, 10x4½", EX 450.00

Degenhart

The Crystal Art Glass factory in Cambridge, Ohio, opened in 1947 under the private ownership of John and Elizabeth Degenhart. John had previously worked for the Cambridge Glass Company and was well known for his superior paperweights. After his death in 1964, Elizabeth took over management of the factory, hiring several workers from the defunct Cambridge Company, including Zack Boyd. Boyd was responsible for many unique colors, some of which were named for him. From 1964 to 1974, more than twenty-seven different moulds were created, most of them resulting from Elizabeth Degenhart's work and creativity, and over 145 official colors were developed. Elizabeth died in 1978, requesting that the ten moulds she had built while operating the factory were to be turned over to the Degenhart Museum. The remaining moulds were to be held by the Island Mould and Machine Company, who (complying with her request) removed the familiar 'D in heart' trademark. The factory was eventually bought by Zack's son, Bernard Boyd. He also acquired the remaining Degenhart moulds, to which he added his own logo.

In general, slags and opaques should be valued 15% to 20% higher than crystals in color.

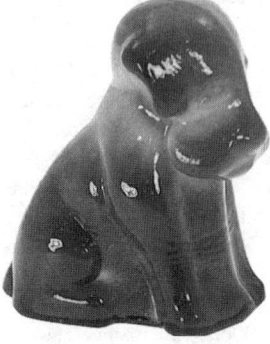

Pooch, Tomato #1, $30.00.

Baby Shoe (Hobo Boot) Toothpick, Pigeon Blood 25.00
Baby Shoe (Hobo Boot) Toothpick, Taffeta 12.00
Basket Toothpick, Cobalt 15.00
Basket Toothpick, Forest Green 15.00
Beaded Oval Toothpick, Aqua 20.00
Beaded Oval Toothpick, Fawn 20.00
Beaded Oval Toothpick, Mulberry 20.00
Bicentennial Bell, Butterscotch 25.00
Bicentennial Bell, Heliotrope 20.00
Bicentennial Bell, Sapphire 8.00
Bird Salt & Pepper Shakers, Antique Blue, pr 35.00
Bird Salt & Pepper Shakers, Forest Green, pr 30.00
Bird Toothpick, Gun Metal 20.00
Bird Toothpick, Lavender Green Slag 35.00
Bird w/Cherry Salt, Bloody Mary 40.00
Bird w/Cherry Salt, Fog 15.00
Bird w/Cherry Salt, Peach Blo 15.00
Bird w/Cherry Salt, Toffee Slag 20.00
Bow Slipper, Bluebell Opal 40.00
Bow Slipper, Gold 17.50
Bow Slipper, Mint Green 15.00
Bow Slipper, Smokey Heather 20.00
Bow Slipper, Wondor Blue 25.00
Buzz Saw Wine, Desert Sun 35.00
Buzz Saw Wine, Pistachio 25.00
Chick Salt, 2", Bittersweet 40.00
Chick Salt, 2", Crown Tuscan 30.00

Chick Salt, 2", Gray Slag 50.00
Chick Salt, 2", Mint or Lime Custard, ea 50.00
Chick Salt, 2", Sapphire 15.00
Colonial Drape Toothpick, Crystal (Frosted) 13.00
Colonial Drape Toothpick, Sunset 20.00
Daisy & Button Creamer & Sugar, Aqua 75.00
Daisy & Button Creamer & Sugar, Pine Green ..75.00
Daisy & Button Hat, Apple Green 15.00
Daisy & Button Hat, Frosty Jade 15.00
Daisy & Button Salt, Amber 8.00
Daisy & Button Salt, Delft Blue 12.00
Daisy & Button Toothpick, Bittersweet 25.00
Daisy & Button Toothpick, Forest Green 15.00
Daisy & Button Wine, Milk Blue 40.00
Elephant Head Toothpick, Amethyst 25.00
Elephant Head Toothpick, Carnival, Ice Blue 35.00
Forget-Me-Not Toothpick, April Green 20.00
Forget-Me-Not Toothpick, Bernard Boyd's Ebony ..25.00
Forget-Me-Not Toothpick, Bluina 40.00
Forget-Me-Not Toothpick, Concord Grape 25.00
Forget-Me-Not Toothpick, Jabe's Amber 20.00
Forget-Me-Not Toothpick, Zack Boyd Slag 50.00
Gypsy Pot, Blue Fire 20.00
Gypsy Pot, Heatherbloom 40.00
Hand, Crystal 5.00
Hand, Lemon Opal 15.00
Heart & Lyle Cup Plate, Blue Green 10.00
Heart & Lyle Cup Plate, Sunset 8.00
Heart Jewel Box, Blue Green Marble 45.00
Heart Jewel Box, Ivory 30.00
Heart Toothpick, Buttercup Slag 25.00
Heart Toothpick, Ivorene 25.00
Hen Covered Dish, 3", April Green 30.00
Hen Covered Dish, 3", Forest Green 35.00
Hen Covered Dish, 3", Sparrow Slag 25.00
High Boots, Champagne 15.00
High Boots, Cobalt 30.00
High Boots, Emerald Green 25.00
Kat Slipper, Bloody Mary 45.00
Kat Slipper, Caramel (dark) 35.00
Kat Slipper, Tiger 40.00
Lamb Covered Dish, 5", Canary 35.00
Lamb Covered Dish, 5", Lavender 75.00
Lamb Covered Dish, 5", Red 75.00
Mini Pitcher, Angel Blue 12.00
Mini Pitcher, Heatherbloom 25.00
Mini Slipper w/o Sole, Honey Amber 15.00
Mini Slipper w/o Sole, Lime Ice 25.00
Mini Slipper w/Sole, Milk White 25.00
Owl, Bittersweet 65.00
Owl, Blue Fire, clear 30.00
Owl, Bluina 225.00
Owl, Cambridge Pink 35.00
Owl, Caramel 75.00
Owl, Carnival, Red 125.00
Owl, Dirty Sally 60.00
Owl, Jim Dandy 175.00
Owl, Lavender Blue 65.00
Owl, Periwinkle 40.00
Owl, Snotty (Snowy) 175.00
Owl, Wanda Blue (Blue Boy) 35.00
Pooch, Autumn 25.00
Pooch, Daffodil Slag 60.00
Pooch, Gun Metal 20.00

Pooch, Teal 15.00
Portrait Plate, Amber 30.00
Portrait Plate, Blue & White Slag, rare 175.00
Portrait Plate, Cobalt 45.00
Portrait Plate, Vaseline 45.00
Pottie Salt, Chocolate Creme Slag 15.00
Pottie Salt, Rose Marie 6.00
Priscilla Doll, April Green 125.00
Priscilla Doll, Baby Green 125.00
Priscilla Doll, Bittersweet Slag 175.00
Priscilla Doll, Heatherbloom 150.00
Priscilla Doll, Powder Blue 125.00
Priscilla Doll, Willow Blue 100.00
Robin Covered Dish, 5", Amethyst Slag 75.00
Robin Covered Dish, 5", Rubina, hand stamped ..225.00
Roller Skate (Skate Shoe), Custard 40.00
Seal of Ohio Cup Plate, Brown 8.00
Seal of Ohio Cup Plate, Persimmon 10.00
Star & Dew Drop Salt, Blue & White Slag 20.00
Star & Dew Drop Salt, Elizabeth's Lime Ice 20.00
Stork & Peacock Child's Mug, Amberina 25.00
Stork & Peacock Child's Mug, Custard 35.00
Texas Boot, Baby Green 15.00
Texas Boot, Sapphire 10.00
Texas Creamer & Sugar, Cobalt 50.00
Texas Creamer & Sugar, Ruby 120.00
Tomahawk, Custard Maverick 75.00
Tomahawk, Dichromatic 45.00
Turkey Covered Dish, 5", Apple Green 65.00
Turkey Covered Dish, 5", Tomato 100.00
Wildflower Candle Holder, Bluebell 25.00
Wildflower Candle Holder, Ruby, pr 150.00
Wildflower Candy Dish, Amberina 40.00
Wildflower Candy Dish, Apple Green 35.00
Wildflower Candy Dish, Milk Opal 25.00

Delatte

Delatte was a manufacturer of French cameo glass. Founded in 1921, their style reflected the influence of the Art Deco era with strong color contrasts and bold design. Our advisor for this category is Don Williams; he is listed in the Directory under Missouri.

Key: fp — fire polished

Cameo

Bowl, fp flowers/foliage, plum on almond, 4-fold rim, 2¾x5" 725.00
Lamp, sea gulls, dk bl on olive, ships on base, 17" 3,500.00
Vase, exotic flowers, maroon on pk mottle, flared, 6½x7½" 700.00
Vase, landscape along river, maroon/rose on wht, hdls, 9" 1,200.00
Vase, tree/sky/water/building, blk/amber/red, hdls, ftd, 15" 1,400.00
Vase, trees/water/sky, brn on yel, invt cone, 8" 1,100.00

Delft

Old Delftware, made as early as the 16th century, was originally a low-fired earthenware coated in a thin opaque tin glaze with painted-on blue or polychrome designs. It was not until the last half of the 19th century, however, that the ware became commonly referred to as Delft, acquiring the name from the Dutch village that had become the major center of its production. English, German, and French potters also produced Delft, though with noticeable differences both in shape and decorative theme.

In the early part of the 18th century, the German potter, Bottger, developed a formula for porcelain; in England, Wedgwood began producing creamware — both of which were much more durable. Unable to compete, one by one the Delft potteries failed. Soon only one remained. In 1876 De Porcelyne Fles reintroduced Delftware on a hard white body with blue and white decorative themes reflecting the Dutch countryside, windmills by the sea, and Dutch children. This manufacturer is the most well known of several operating today. Their products are now produced under the Royal Delft label. Examples listed here are blue on white unless noted otherwise. See also specific manufacturers. Our advisor is Ralph Jaarsma; he is listed in the Directory under Iowa.

Bottle, English, Oriental coast, crimped rim, 1760, 9" 985.00
Bowl, barber's; Dutch, foliate scrolls & flowers, 18th C 215.00
Bowl, fruit; Irish, rock garden/florals, 1750, 9¼" 495.00
Butter tureen, Dutch, chinoiserie, w/lid, 18th C, 13" dia 185.00
Charger, Bristol, floral panels, ca 1740, 13¾" 360.00
Charger, Dutch, foliate devices, 18th C, 13⅛", EX 400.00
Charger, English, Chinaman seated by fence, mc, 1750, rstr, 12" ...385.00
Charger, Frankfort, Oriental decor, 1690, 13½", VG 975.00
Charger, William & Mary, titled portraits, 1690, 13½" 990.00
Cup, English, floral landscape, int: I:S 1712, 2", VG 495.00
Flower brick, Dutch, Chinese figures in landscape, 18th C, 4⅝" ...375.00
Foot warmer, masks, molded scroll hdls, 1770, rstr, 9" 150.00
Jug, Lambeth, floral, bulbous, loop hdl, early 1700s, 5¼" 165.00
Plate, Bristol, Oriental scene, 5-color, floral rim, 8¾" 300.00
Plate, Bristol, 3-color rooster, 1740, rstr, 8½" 1,500.00
Plate, English, floral landscape, lattice rim, 1770, 19¾" 770.00
Plate, English, mc floral, minor chips, 9" 330.00
Plate, Lambeth, mc flowers & birds, rpr, 8⅞" 330.00
Plate, Lambeth, mc landscape, rim chips, 9" 340.00
Vase, Dutch, amorous couple, foo dog finial, 18th C, 20", EX .1,035.00
Vase, Dutch, floral panels/scroll, dome lid, 1780s, 16", EX 1,000.00
Vase, Dutch, goats scene, lid w/lion finial, LPK, 13", VG 800.00
Vase, Swedish, flowers & trees, w/lid, 18th C, 15½", EX 300.00

Denver

The Denver China and Pottery Company began production in 1901 in Denver, Colorado. The founder, William A. Long, used materials native to Colorado to produce underglaze-decorated brownware as well as other artware lines. Several marks were used: an impressed 'Denver' (often with the Lonhuda Faience cipher inside a shield), an imprinted 'Denaura,' and an arrow mark.

•

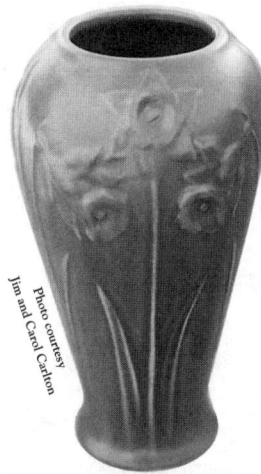

Vase, Denaura, embossed floral on green, attributed to Claude Leffler, dated 1903, 9½", $500.00 minimum value.

Photo courtesy
Jim and Carol Carlton

Bowl/vase, gr, Denaura, 6x7" 250.00
Jug, corn on brn, sgn WA Long, 8x6", minimum value 350.00
Vase, burro on brn, sm rim, 9½x5½" 275.00
Vase, carnations, pk & wht on gray to brn matt, rstr, 8x6" 300.00
Vase, floral on bl, bsk, sgn Leffler, 9½x5", minimum value 650.00
Vase, floral on bl, bsk, sgn w/Long's initials, 9½x5½" 1,000.00
Vase, floral on brn, integral hdls, 6x9" 500.00

Denver Terra Cotta Pottery

While on his honeymoon in Colorado, a young chemist by the name of George Frackt became aware of the natural clay deposits there. As an employee of the St. Louis Terra Cotta Company in Missouri, he was impressed with the samples he had analyzed and decided to establish his own terra cotta plant in Denver.

Within a short time, he opened a two-story plant with twelve employees, where he made finished products in high-gloss colors. The company consolidated with Northwestern Terra Cotta Company in 1924. Artificial stone or concrete came into production in 1925 and continued into the late 1920s. The exact date of closing is unknown. Look for pieces of great weight with high-gloss colors and stamped marks.

Bookends, Liberty Bell form, stamped base, 7x5", pr 195.00
Bookends, owl figural, 7x5", pr, minimum value 225.00
Planter, frog figural, gr, open mouth, stamped mk, 5x4" 125.00
Vase, clear over yel clay, buttresses from rim to ft, 7x6" 125.00

Denver White

In 1894 Frederick and Frank White settled in Denver, Colorado, and formed the F.J. White & Son Pottery Company. They located at 1434 Logan Street. After the death of Frederick in 1919, Frank moved the pottery to 1560 South Logan, where he remained until the company closed. He had a kiln set up at home and worked each day on the pottery, often selling his products in his front yard. On many occasions he was commissioned to produce specialty items for customers.

Each piece is hand thrown and many are dated. They are usually incised with the name Denver and the letter 'W' inside the capital 'D.' Many items are decorated with Colorado scenery. Though most pieces are matt glazed with a glossy interior, some later examples were completely glossy. The Whites would also add a small band to some of the ware, similar to what you see on Wedgwood pottery today. They created a line with swirled colors as well. On March 6, 1960, Frank White died at the age of 91.

Our advisors for this category are Jim and Carol Carlton, authors of *Collector's Encyclopedia of Colorado Pottery*; they are listed in the Directory under Colorado.

Bowl, gray, 3x5" 55.00
Cookie jar, pine cones on brn, squirrel finial, 8x6" 300.00
Pitcher, gr, 4" 65.00
Teapot, turq gloss, squat, rare, minimum value 200.00
Vase, bl, crimped rim, 6" 95.00
Vase, bl & wht swirl, 4", minimum value 150.00
Vase, bl matt w/appl reeding, 5", minimum value 175.00
Vase, deer & mtn scenery, brn tones, sgn Skiff, 10" 500.00
Vase, dk gr, shouldered, 4" 57.00
Vase, mc swirl, classic shape, 6" 150.00
Vase, mc swirl, wide rim, 3" 57.00
Vase, turq gloss, rim-to-shoulder hdls, 12", minimum value 145.00

Depression Glass

Depression glass is defined by Gene Florence, author of several bestselling books on the subject, as 'the inexpensive glassware made primarily during the Depression era in the colors of amber, green, pink, blue, red, yellow, white, and crystal.' This glass was mass produced, sold through five-and-dime stores and mail-order catalogs, and given away as premiums with gas and food products.

The listings in this book are far from being complete. If you want a more thorough presentation of this fascinating glassware, we recommend *The Collector's Encyclopedia of Depression Glass, The Pocket Guide to Depression Glass, Elegant Glassware of the Depression Era,* and *Very Rare Glassware of the Depression Years,* all by Gene Florence, whose address is listed in the Directory under Kentucky.

Key:
AOP — allover pattern   PAT — pattern at top

Adam, bowl, cereal; gr, 5¾" 42.00
Adam, bowl, gr, w/lid 85.00
Adam, bowl, pk, 9" 40.00
Adam, butter dish, gr, w/lid 375.00
Adam, candlesticks, gr, 4", pr 95.00
Adam, candy jar, pk, w/lid, 2½" 90.00
Adam, cup, pk 24.00
Adam, pitcher, gr, 32-oz, 8" 45.00
Adam, plate, dinner; gr, sq, 9" 30.00
Adam, platter, pk, 11¾" 30.00
Adam, relish dish, gr, divided, 8" 25.00
Adam, sugar bowl/candy jar lid, gr 40.00
Adam, vase, pk, 7½" 325.00
Am Pioneer, bowl, crystal, hdls, 9" 22.00
Am Pioneer, candy jar, gr, w/lid, 1-lb 100.00
Am Pioneer, ice bucket, gr, 6" 60.00
Am Pioneer, lamp, crystal, tall, 8½" 100.00
Am Pioneer, pitcher, urn; gr, w/lid, 7" 225.00
Am Pioneer, vase, crystal, 4 styles, 7" 85.00

American Sweetheart, two-tier tidbit, ruby, $225.00.

Am Sweetheart, bowl, console; monax, 18" 450.00
Am Sweetheart, bowl, console; red, 18" 925.00
Am Sweetheart, lamp, floor; cremax, w/brass base 695.00
Am Sweetheart, pitcher, pk, 60-oz, 7½" 825.00
Am Sweetheart, plate, luncheon; smoke & other trims, 9" 40.00
Am Sweetheart, platter, smoke & other trims, oval, 13" 195.00
Am Sweetheart, sugar bowl, red, ftd 125.00
Aunt Polly, bowl, bl, oval, 8⅜" 110.00
Aunt Polly, bowl, bl, 1-hdl, 5½" 22.00
Aunt Polly, butter dish, irid, w/lid 235.00
Aunt Polly, candy dish, gr, hdls, w/lid 75.00
Aunt Polly, pitcher, bl, 48-oz, 8" 175.00
Aunt Polly, shakers, bl, pr 225.00

Aunt Polly, sugar bowl, irid, w/lid 85.00
Aurora, bowl, cobalt, 4½" 55.00
Aurora, creamer, pk, 4½" 25.00
Aurora, tumbler, cobalt, 10-oz, 4¾" 25.00
Avocado, bowl, gr, 3¼x9½" 135.00
Avocado, bowl, pk, hdls, 5¼" 25.00
Avocado, bowl, salad; crystal, 7½" 12.00
Avocado, plate, cake; pk, hdls, 10¼" 35.00
Avocado, tumbler, crystal 35.00
Beaded Block, bowl, crystal, unflared, rnd, 6¾" 10.00
Beaded Block, bowl, ice bl, rnd, 6¼" 28.00
Beaded Block, bowl, red, fluted edges, rnd, 7½" 35.00
Beaded Block, jelly, canary yel, stemmed, 4½" 25.00
Beaded Block, pitcher, wht, jug style, 1-pt, 5¼" 175.00
Block Optic, bowl, pk, 1½x4½" 30.00
Block Optic, candlesticks, gr, 1¾", pr 100.00
Block Optic, candy jar, yel, w/lid, 2¼" 65.00
Block Optic, pitcher, gr, 80-oz, 8" 90.00
Block Optic, pitcher, pk, bulbous, 54-oz, 7⅝" 125.00
Block Optic, plate, dinner; yel, 9" 45.00
Block Optic, sandwich server, gr, center hdl 75.00
Block Optic, shakers, gr, squatty, pr 100.00
Block Optic, shakers, pk, ftd, pr 80.00
Block Optic, tumbler, gr, flat, 15-oz, 5¼" 42.00
Block Optic, vase, gr, blown, 5¾" 295.00
Block Optic, whiskey, pk, 1-oz, 1⅝" 43.00
Bowknot, bowl, berry; gr, 4½" 16.00
Bowknot, cup, gr 8.00
Bowknot, sherbet, gr, low ftd 17.50
Bowknot, tumbler, gr, 10-oz, 5" 22.50
Cameo, bowl, cream soup; gr, 4¾" 130.00
Cameo, cake plate, pk, flat, 10½" 175.00
Cameo, cocktail shaker, crystal, metal lid 750.00
Cameo, decanter, gr, w/stopper, 10" 175.00
Cameo, domino tray, pk, no indention, 7" 250.00
Cameo, ice bowl/open butter, crystal, 3x5½" 265.00
Cameo, pitcher, syrup/milk; yel, 20-oz, 5¾" 2,000.00
Cameo, pitcher, water; crystal, 56-oz, 8½" 500.00
Cameo, plate, grill; gr, closed hdls, 10½" 70.00
Cameo, shakers, pk, ftd, pr 850.00
Cameo, tumbler, gr, ftd, 15-oz, 6⅜" 495.00
Cameo, tumbler, pk, 15-oz, 5¼" 135.00
Cherry Blossom, bowl, berry; Delphite, 4¾" 15.00
Cherry Blossom, bowl, soup; pk, flat, 7¾" 85.00
Cherry Blossom, bowl, vegetable; Delphite, oval, 9" 50.00
Cherry Blossom, butter dish, gr, w/lid 100.00
Cherry Blossom, mug, pk, 7-oz 265.00

Cherry Blossom, pitcher, green, pattern around top, $55.00.

Cherry Blossom, plate, grill; gr, 9" 30.00
Cherry Blossom, platter, pk, oval, 9" 800.00
Cherry Blossom, shakers, gr, scalloped bottom, pr 995.00

Cherry Blossom, tray, sandwich; Delphite, 10½" **22.00**
Cherry Blossom, tumbler, Delphite, AOP, rnd ft, 9-oz, 4½" **22.00**
Cherry Blossom, tumbler, gr, PAT, flat, 4-oz, 3½" **30.00**
Cherry Blossom, tumbler, pk, PAT, flat, 12-oz, 5" **60.00**
Cherryberry, bowl, crystal, 2x6¼" **40.00**
Cherryberry, butter dish, pk, w/lid **175.00**
Cherryberry, pitcher, crystal, 7¾" **160.00**
Cherryberry, sugar bowl, gr, sm **20.00**
Cherryberry, sugar bowl, irid, w/lid **30.00**
Chinex Classic, bowl, brnstone, 11" **17.00**
Chinex Classic, bowl, vegetable; decal decor, 7" **25.00**
Chinex Classic, butter dish, castle decal **150.00**
Chinex Classic, butter dish bottom, decal decor **27.50**
Chinex Classic, sherbet, castle decal, low ftd **25.00**
Circle, bowl, gr or pk, 5¼" **10.00**
Circle, bowl, gr or pk, 9⅜" **20.00**
Circle, pitcher, gr or pk, 80-oz **35.00**
Circle, plate, gr or pk, 9½" **12.00**
Circle, tumbler, gr or pk, flat, 15-oz **22.00**
Circle, tumbler, juice; gr or pk, 4-oz, 3½" **8.00**
Cloverleaf, ashtray, blk, match holder in center, 4" **65.00**
Cloverleaf, bowl, salad; yel, deep, 7" **55.00**
Cloverleaf, creamer, yel, ftd, 3⅝" **18.00**
Cloverleaf, plate, grill; gr, 10¼" **22.00**
Cloverleaf, tumbler, gr, flat, 9-oz, 4" **55.00**
Cloverleaf, tumbler, pk, flat, flared, 10-oz, 3¾" **22.00**
Cloverleaf, tumbler, yel, ftd, 10-oz, 5¾" **35.00**
Colonial, bowl, berry; pk, 3¾" **50.00**
Colonial, bowl, cream soup; gr, 4½" **70.00**
Colonial, butter dish, pk, w/lid **650.00**
Colonial, mug, gr, 12-oz, 4½" **800.00**
Colonial, shakers, pk, pr **140.00**
Colonial, spoon holder, gr, 5½" **125.00**
Colonial, sugar bowl, pk, w/lid, 4½" **85.00**
Colonial, tumbler, crystal, ftd, 5-oz, 4" **22.00**
Colonial, tumbler, gr, 11-oz, 5⅛" **42.00**
Colonial Block, butter dish, pk or gr **45.00**
Colonial Block, candy jar, pk or gr, w/lid **40.00**
Colonial Block, pitcher, pk or gr **45.00**
Colonial Block, tumbler, pk or gr, ftd, 5-oz, 5¼" **25.00**
Colonial Fluted, bowl, berry; gr, 4" **7.50**
Colonial Fluted, bowl, salad; gr, deep, 2½x6½" **25.00**
Colonial Fluted, sherbet, gr **6.00**
Columbia, bowl, crystal, ruffled edge, 10½" **20.00**
Columbia, bowl, soup; crystal, low, 8" **22.00**
Columbia, plate, snack; crystal **30.00**
Columbia, tumbler, water; crystal, 9-oz **30.00**
Coronation, bowl, berry; Royal Ruby, hdls, 4¼" **7.00**
Coronation, bowl, gr, no hdls, 4¼" **45.00**
Coronation, bowl, pk, no hdls, 8" **150.00**
Coronation, pitcher, pk, 68-oz, 7¾" **550.00**
Coronation, tumbler, pk, ftd, 10-oz, 5" **30.00**
Cremax, bowl, soup; bl, 7¾" **20.00**
Cremax, cup, demitasse; cremax **15.00**
Cremax, plate, dinner; bl, 9¾" **10.00**
Cremax, saucer, demitasse; cremax **5.00**
Cube, bowl, salad; pk, 6½" **10.00**
Cube, butter dish, pk or gr, w/lid **65.00**
Cube, pitcher, pk, 45-oz, 8¾" **210.00**
Cube, sugar bowl/candy dish lid only, pk or gr **15.00**
Diamond Quilted, bowl, console; bl, rolled edge, 10½" **60.00**
Diamond Quilted, candlesticks, blk, 2 styles, pr **50.00**
Diamond Quilted, compote, pk, w/lid, 11½" **95.00**
Diamond Quilted, ice bucket, gr **55.00**

Diamond Quilted, punch bowl, pk, w/stand **450.00**
Diamond Quilted, sandwich server, blk, center hdl **50.00**
Diamond Quilted, vase, bl, fan shape, dolphin hdls **75.00**
Diana, candy jar, amber, w/lid, rnd **40.00**
Diana, shakers, crystal, pr **25.00**
Diana, tumbler, pk, 9-oz, 4⅛" **45.00**
Dogwood, bowl, fruit; pk, 10¼" **525.00**
Dogwood, pitcher, gr, decor, 80-oz, 8" **500.00**
Dogwood, platter, pk, oval, rare, 12" **650.00**
Dogwood, saucer, cremax **20.00**
Dogwood, tumbler, gr, decor, 10-oz, 4" **95.00**
Doric, bowl, cream soup; gr, 5" **395.00**
Doric, butter dish, pk, w/lid **70.00**
Doric, candy dish, pk, w/lid, 8" **37.50**
Doric, pitcher, Delphite, flat, 32-oz, 5½" **1,100.00**
Doric, platter, pk, oval, 12" **25.00**
Doric, tray, serving; gr, 8x8" **25.00**
Doric, tumbler, pk, 9-oz, 4½" **65.00**
Doric & Pansy, bowl, berry; gr, 4½" **20.00**
Doric & Pansy, bowl, berry; pk, lg, 8" **25.00**
Doric & Pansy, butter dish lid only, teal **380.00**
Doric & Pansy, shakers, teal, pr **400.00**
Doric & Pansy, sugar bowl, pk, open **75.00**
Doric & Pansy, tray, gr, hdls, 10" **30.00**
English Hobnail, bottle, toilet; turq, 5-oz **50.00**
English Hobnail, bowl, console/flange; pk, 12" **50.00**
English Hobnail, bowl, ice bl, rolled edge, 11" **80.00**
English Hobnail, bowl, nappy; ice bl, rnd, 5" **37.50**
English Hobnail, bowl, rose; gr, 4" **50.00**
English Hobnail, bowl, turq, hdls, hexagonal ft, 8" **110.00**
English Hobnail, candy dish, pk, 3-ftd **55.00**
English Hobnail, compote, sweetmeat; gr, ball stem, 8" **60.00**
English Hobnail, lamp, electric; pk, 6¼" **65.00**
English Hobnail, pitcher, pk, rnd, 38-oz **225.00**
English Hobnail, plate, gr, rnd, 6½" **10.00**
English Hobnail, shakers, gr, flat, pr **125.00**
English Hobnail, sugar bowl, pk or gr, ftd, hexagonal **22.50**
English Hobnail, urn, pk, w/lid, 15" **350.00**
Fire-King Philbe, bowl, cereal; bl, 5½" **65.00**
Fire-King Philbe, bowl, salad; pk, 7¼" **60.00**
Fire-King Philbe, pitcher, crystal, 56-oz, 8½" **395.00**
Fire-King Philbe, plate, grill; gr, 10½" **45.00**
Fire-King Philbe, plate, salver; bl, 10½" **80.00**
Fire-King Philbe, sherbet, pk, 4¾" **450.00**
Fire-King Philbe, tumbler, bl, ftd, 10-oz, 5¼" **95.00**
Fire-King Philbe, tumbler, juice; crystal, ftd, 3½" **40.00**
Floral, bowl, cream soup; pk, rare, 5½" **750.00**
Floral, ice tub, pk, oval, rare, 3½" H **850.00**
Floral, plate, grill; gr, rare, 9" **250.00**
Floral, sherbet, pk **17.50**
Floral, tumbler, water; Delphite, ftd, 7-oz, 4¾" **195.00**
Floral, vase, gr, 8-sided, 6⅞" **435.00**
Floral & Diamond Band, butter dish, pk, w/lid **140.00**
Floral & Diamond Band, compote, gr, 5½" **18.00**
Floral & Diamond Band, pitcher, pk, 42-oz, 8" **95.00**
Floral & Diamond Band, tumbler, iced tea; gr, 5" **45.00**
Florentine No 1, bowl, berry; cobalt, 5" **20.00**
Florentine No 1, bowl, berry; gr, lg, 8½" **25.00**
Florentine No 1, cup, yel **10.00**
Florentine No 1, plate, grill; crystal, 10" **12.00**
Florentine No 1, plate, salad; pk, 8½" **11.00**
Florentine No 1, platter, yel, oval, 11½" **25.00**
Florentine No 1, shakers, yel, ftd **55.00**
Florentine No 1, tumbler, water; pk, ftd, 10-oz, 4¾" **24.00**

Florentine No 2, bowl, berry; pk, lg, 8" 32.00
Florentine No 2, bowl, berry; pk, 4½" 17.00
Florentine No 2, coaster, gr, 3¼" 14.00
Florentine No 2, gravy boat, yel 60.00
Florentine No 2, plate, grill; yel, 10¼" 14.00
Florentine No 2, platter, pk, oval, 11" 16.00
Florentine No 2, sugar bowl, yel, w/lid 36.00
Florentine No 2, tumbler, water; cobalt, 9-oz, 4" 70.00
Flower Garden w/Butterflies, bowl, orange; blk, ftd, 11" 225.00
Flower Garden w/Butterflies, candlestick, amber, 4", pr 42.50
Flower Garden w/Butterflies, comport, pk, 2⅞" 23.00
Flower Garden w/Butterflies, creamer, gr 70.00
Flower Garden w/Butterflies, plate, blk, indented, 10" 100.00
Flower Garden w/Butterflies, powder jar, bl-gr, flat, 3½" 80.00
Flower Garden w/Butterflies, saucer, pk 27.50
Fortune, bowl, pk or crystal, rolled edge, 5¼" 12.00
Fortune, cup, pk or crystal 6.00
Fruits, bowl, berry; gr, 5" 30.00
Fruits, cup, pk 7.00
Fruits, pitcher, gr, flat bottom, 7" 85.00
Fruits, tumbler, juice; gr, 3½" 50.00
Georgian, bowl, gr, deep, 6½" 65.00
Georgian, plate, dinner; gr, 9¼" 25.00
Georgian, platter, gr, closed hdls, 11½" 65.00
Hex Optic, bowl, mixing; gr or pk, 10" 25.00
Hex Optic, butter dish, pk or gr, rectangular, w/lid, 1-lb 85.00
Hex Optic, pitcher, pk or gr, flat, 70-oz, 8" 225.00
Hex Optic, plate, luncheon; pk or gr, 8" 5.50
Hex Optic, refrigerator stack set, pk or gr, 4-pc 60.00
Hex Optic, sugar shaker, pk or gr 195.00
Hex Optic, whiskey, pk or gr, 1-oz, 2" 8.00
Hobnail, decanter, crystal, w/stopper, 32-oz 27.50
Hobnail, tumbler, cordial; crystal, ftd, 5-oz 6.00
Hobnail, tumbler, juice; crystal, 5-oz 4.00
Homespun, bowl, berry; pk or crystal, lg, 8¼" 22.00
Homespun, plate, dinner; pk or crystal, 9¼" 16.00
Homespun, sugar bowl, pk or crystal, ftd 9.50
Homespun, tumbler, pk or crystal, ftd, 5-oz, 4" 7.00
Indiana Custard, bowl, soup; French Ivory, flat, 7½" 32.50
Indiana Custard, creamer, French Ivory 16.00
Indiana Custard, platter, French Ivory, oval, 11½" 35.00
Indiana Custard, sherbet, French Ivory 95.00
Iris, bowl, cereal; crystal, 5" 120.00
Iris, bowl, fruit; irid, ruffled, 11½" 14.00
Iris, bowl, salad; gr or pk, ruffled, 9½" 125.00
Iris, cup, crystal 15.00
Iris, goblet, irid, 8-oz, 5½" 195.00
Iris, goblet, wine; crystal, 3-oz, 4½" 17.00
Iris, plate, sherbet; crystal, 5½" 15.00
Iris, saucer, demitasse; irid 225.00
Iris, sugar bowl, crystal, w/lid 23.00
Iris, tumbler, irid, ftd, 6" 16.00
Jubilee, bowl, pk or yel, 3-ftd, 11½" 250.00
Jubilee, plate, yel, 3-ftd, 14" 200.00
Jubilee, tumbler, water; pk, 10-oz, 6" 75.00
Jubilee, vase, pk or yel, 12" 350.00
Jubilee, yel, stem, cocktail; yel, 3-oz, 4⅞" 150.00
Lace Edge, bowl, pk, 3-leg, 10½" 250.00
Lace Edge, bowl, salad; pk, ribbed, 7¾" 50.00
Lace Edge, plate, luncheon; pk, 8¼" 23.00
Lace Edge, plate, relish; pk, 3-part, 10½" 25.00
Lace Edge, tumbler, pk, ftd, 10½-oz, 5" 80.00
Laced Edge, basket, bowl, opal 225.00
Laced Edge, bowl, opal, divided, oval 115.00

Laced Edge, cup, opal 35.00
Laced Edge, plate, dinner; opal, 10" 85.00
Laced Edge, platter, opal, 13" 175.00
Lake Como, bowl, soup; wht, flat 100.00
Lake Como, cup, St Denis; wht 30.00
Lake Como, plate, dinner; wht, 9¼" 33.00
Lake Como, shakers, wht, pr 42.50
Laurel, bowl, soup; wht opal, Jade Gr or French Ivory, 7⅞" 35.00
Laurel, cheese dish, wht opal or Jade Gr, w/lid 52.50
Laurel, platter, wht opal, Jade Gr or Poudre Bl, 10¾" 25.00
Laurel, sherbet, wht opal or Jade Gr 10.00
Laurel, sugar bowl, Poudre Bl, tall 35.00
Lincoln Inn, cup, colors other than cobalt or red 10.00
Lincoln Inn, tumbler, cobalt or red, ftd, 5-oz 30.00
Lincoln Inn, vase, cobalt or red, 9¾" 135.00
Lorain, bowl, cereal; yel, 6" 65.00
Lorain, bowl, vegetable; crystal or gr, deep, 8" 100.00
Lorain, relish, yel, 4-part, 8" 35.00
Lorain, sherbet, crystal or gr, ftd 23.00
Madrid, bowl, berry; amber or pk, lg, 9⅜" 20.00
Madrid, bowl, vegetable; bl, oval, 10" 40.00

Madrid, butter dish, amber, $70.00.

Madrid, cookie jar, pk, w/lid 30.00
Madrid, gravy boat & platter, amber 1,200.00
Madrid, pitcher, amber, 80-oz, 8½" 60.00
Madrid, plate, sherbet; pk, 6" 3.50
Madrid, platter, pk, oval, 11½" 14.00
Madrid, shakers, bl, ftd, 3½", pr 150.00
Madrid, tumbler, gr, 5-oz, 3⅞" 32.00
Manhattan, ashtray, crystal, rnd, 4" 11.00
Manhattan, comport, pk, 5¾" 35.00
Manhattan, pitcher, pk, tilted, 80-oz 65.00
Manhattan, pitcher, ruby, 24-oz 400.00
Manhattan, plate, dinner; pk, 10¼" 175.00
Manhattan, sherbet, pk 15.00
Mayfair Federal, bowl, vegetable; crystal, oval, 10" 18.00
Mayfair Federal, cup, amber or gr 9.00
Mayfair Federal, plate, dinner; amber, 9½" 14.00
Mayfair Federal, platter, amber or gr, oval, 12" 30.00
Mayfair Federal, sugar bowl, crystal, ftd 11.00
Mayfair Federal, tumbler, amber, 9-oz, 4½" 30.00
Mayfair/Open Rose, bowl, vegetable; bl, 10" 70.00
Mayfair/Open Rose, bowl, vegetable; gr or yel, 7" 150.00
Mayfair/Open Rose, cake plate, pk, ftd, 10" 32.50
Mayfair/Open Rose, candy dish, bl, w/lid 295.00
Mayfair/Open Rose, goblet, gr, 2½-oz, 4⅛" 950.00
Mayfair/Open Rose, pitcher, gr or yel, 60-oz, 8" 525.00
Mayfair/Open Rose, platter, bl, open hdls, oval, 12" 70.00
Mayfair/Open Rose, relish, gr or yel, 4-part, 8⅜" 165.00
Mayfair/Open Rose, shakers, pk, ftd, pr 8,500.00
Mayfair/Open Rose, sherbet, pk or bl, ftd, 4¾" 77.50
Mayfair/Open Rose, tumbler, bl, ftd, 10-oz, 5¼" 130.00

Mayfair/Open Rose, tumbler, water; gr or yel, 11-oz, 4¾" 200.00
Mayfair/Open Rose, vase, sweet pea; pk 145.00
Miss America, bowl, Royal Ruby, shallow, 11" 800.00
Miss America, cake plate, pk, ftd, 12" 45.00
Miss America, goblet, juice; Royal Ruby, 5-oz, 4¾" 255.00
Miss America, pitcher, crystal, 65-oz, 8" 46.00
Miss America, platter, pk, oval, 12¼" 30.00
Miss America, sherbet, Royal Ruby 125.00
Miss America, tumbler, juice; crystal, 5-oz, 4" 16.50
Moderntone, ashtray, cobalt, match holder in center, 7¾" 165.00
Moderntone, bowl, soup; cobalt, 7½" 140.00
Moderntone, plate, dinner; cobalt, 8⅞" 18.00
Moderntone, platter, amethyst, oval, 12" 50.00
Moderntone, sugar bowl, cobalt 11.00
Moderntone, tumbler, amethyst, 12-oz 90.00
Moondrops, bowl, berry; colors other than bl or red, 5¼" 10.00
Moondrops, bowl, bl or red, concave top, ftd, 8⅜" 45.00
Moondrops, butter dish, bl or red, w/lid 440.00
Moondrops, comport, colors other than bl or red, 4" 18.00
Moondrops, decanter, colors other than bl or red, sm, 7¾" 38.00
Moondrops, pitcher, colors other than bl or red, 32-oz, 8⅛" 115.00
Moondrops, plate, luncheon; colors other than bl or red, 8½" 12.00
Moondrops, plate, sherbet; bl or red, 6⅛" 8.00
Moondrops, sugar bowl, bl or red, 3½" 16.00
Moondrops, vase, bud; bl or red, rocket shape, 8½" 265.00
Mt Pleasant, bowl, fruit; amethyst, scalloped, 10" 42.00
Mt Pleasant, candlesticks, dbl; pk or gr, pr 26.00
Mt Pleasant, mint, pk or gr, center hdl, 6" 16.00
Mt Pleasant, plate, cake; pk or gr, hdls, 10½" 16.00
Mt Pleasant, plate, cobalt, hdls, 8" 18.00
Mt Pleasant, tumbler, blk, ftd 23.00
New Century, bowl, berry; gr or crystal, 4½" 20.00
New Century, butter dish, gr or crystal, w/lid 55.00
New Century, plate, dinner; gr or crystal, 10" 18.00
New Century, saucer, pk, cobalt or amethyst 7.50
New Century, tumbler, gr or crystal, 8-oz, 3½" 22.00
New Century, tumbler, pk, cobalt or amethyst, 12-oz, 5¼" 30.00
New Century, whiskey, gr or crystal, 1½-oz, 2½" 20.00
Newport, bowl, berry; cobalt, 4¾" 20.00
Newport, plate, dinner; cobalt, 8¾" 30.00
Newport, plate, luncheon; amethyst, 8½" 12.00
Newport, platter, amethyst, oval, 11¾" 40.00
Newport, tumbler, cobalt, 9-oz, 4½" 40.00
No 610 Pyramid, bowl, master berry; crystal, 8½" 20.00
No 610 Pyramid, pitcher, yel 450.00
No 610 Pyramid, sugar bowl, pk or gr 30.00
No 610 Pyramid, tumbler, pk, ftd, 11-oz 50.00
No 612 Horseshoe, bowl, salad; gr or yel, 7½" 25.00
No 612 Horseshoe, bowl, vegetable; gr, oval, 10½" 25.00
No 612 Horseshoe, pitcher, yel, 64-oz, 8½" 325.00
No 612 Horseshoe, plate, luncheon; yel, 9⅜" 15.00
No 612 Horseshoe, plate, sandwich; gr or yel, 11½" 22.50
No 612 Horseshoe, sherbet, gr 15.00
No 616 Vernon, creamer, crystal, ftd 12.00
No 616 Vernon, plate, sandwich; crystal, 11½" 12.00
No 616 Vernon, sugar bowl, gr or yel, ftd 25.00
No 618 Pineapple & Floral, bowl, cereal; crystal, 6" 28.00
No 618 Pineapple & Floral, cup, crystal 11.00
No 618 Pineapple & Floral, plate, sandwich; crystal, 11½" 17.50
No 618 Pineapple & Floral, sherbet, amber or red, ftd 18.00
No 618 Pineapple & Floral, tumbler, crystal, 12-oz, 5" 45.00
Normandie, bowl, vegetable; pk, oval, 10" 37.50
Normandie, plate, salad; irid, 7¾" 52.50
Normandie, sugar bowl, irid 6.00

Old Cafe, bowl, cereal; crystal or pk, 5½" 20.00
Old Cafe, lamp, crystal or pk 25.00
Old Cafe, pitcher, crystal or pk, 80-oz 100.00
Old Cafe, vase, Royal Ruby, 7¼" 25.00
Old English, candy jar, pk, gr or amber, w/lid 50.00
Old English, creamer, pk, gr or amber 17.50
Old English, pitcher, pk, gr or amber, w/lid 125.00
Old English, sugar bowl, pk, gr or amber, w/lid 52.50
Ovide, candy dish, blk, w/lid 45.00
Ovide, creamer, gr 4.50
Ovide, plate, luncheon; Art Deco, 8" 45.00
Ovide, shakers, blk or gr, pr 27.50
Oyster & Pearl, bowl, crystal or pk, hdls, 5½" 10.00
Oyster & Pearl, candle holders, Royal Ruby, 3½", pr 55.00
Oyster & Pearl, plate, sandwich; crystal or pk, 13½" 20.00
Parrot, bowl, soup; amber, 7" 35.00
Parrot, butter dish, gr, w/lid 365.00
Parrot, pitcher, gr, 80-oz, 8½" 2,700.00
Parrot, plate, dinner; gr, 9" 52.50
Parrot, saucer, gr or amber 15.00
Parrot, tumbler, amber, 10-oz, 4¼" 110.00
Parrot, tumbler, gr, 12-oz, 5½" 160.00
Patrician, bowl, berry; amber or crystal, lg, 8½" 45.00
Patrician, butter dish, pk, w/lid 225.00
Patrician, cookie jar, gr, w/lid 550.00
Patrician, plate, salad; amber or crystal, 7½" 15.00
Patrician, shakers, gr, pr 60.00
Patrician, sugar bowl, pk, w/lid 74.00
Patrician, tumbler, amber or crystal, 14-oz, 5½" 45.00
Patrick, candy dish, pk or yel, 3-ftd 150.00
Patrick, plate, luncheon; yel, 8" 27.50
Patrick, plate, sherbet; pk, 7" 20.00
Patrick, sugar bowl, pk 75.00
Petalware, bowl, berry; cobalt, lg, 9" 45.00
Petalware, plate, dinner; pk, 9" 14.00
Petalware, platter, monax plain, oval, 13" 15.00
Petalware, sherbet, pk, ftd, 4½" 10.00
Petalware, tumbler, red floral trim, 6-oz, 3⅝" 35.00
Primo, bowl, yel or gr, 7¾" 30.00
Primo, coaster/ashtray, yel or gr 8.00
Primo, plate, grill; yel or gr, 10" 15.00
Primo, plate, yel or gr, 7½" 10.00
Primo, sherbet, yel or gr 14.00
Primo, tumbler, yel or gr, 9-oz, 5¾" 22.00
Princess, ashtray, gr, 4½" 70.00
Princess, cookie jar, gr, w/lid 58.00
Princess, cup, gr or pk 12.00
Princess, pitcher, topaz or apricot, 60-oz, 8" 95.00
Princess, plate, grill; gr or pk, 9½" 15.00
Princess, platter, gr or pk, closed hdls, 12" 25.00
Princess, sherbet, gr or pk, ftd 24.00
Princess, tumbler, juice; gr or pk, 5-oz, 3" 30.00
Princess, tumbler, topaz or apricot, ftd, 10-oz, 5¼" 21.00
Queen Mary, bowl, berry; pk, 5" 12.00
Queen Mary, candy dish, pk, w/lid 40.00
Queen Mary, creamer, pk, ftd 40.00
Queen Mary, cup, crystal, sm 8.00
Queen Mary, plate, dinner; pk, 9¾" 60.00
Queen Mary, relish tray, crystal, 4-part, 14" 12.00
Queen Mary, tumbler, pk, ftd, 10-oz, 5" 65.00
Raindrops, sugar bowl, gr, w/lid 47.50
Raindrops, tumbler, gr, 14-oz, 5⅜" 12.00
Raindrops, tumbler, gr, 5-oz, 3⅞" 6.50
Ribbon, bowl, berry; gr, lg, 8" 33.00

Ribbon, plate, luncheon; gr, 8" 5.00
Ribbon, shakers, blk, pr 45.00
Ribbon, tumbler, gr, 10-oz, 6" 30.00
Ring, decanter, crystal, w/stopper 25.00
Ring, goblet, cocktail; w/decor or gr, 3½-oz, 3¾" 18.00
Ring, pitcher, crystal, 80-oz, 8½" 20.00
Ring, shakers, crystal, 3", pr 20.00
Ring, tumbler, crystal, 12-oz, 5⅛" 7.00
Ring, tumbler, old fashion; w/decor or gr, 8-oz, 4" 17.50
Ring, vase, w/decor or gr, 8" 35.00
Rock Crystal, bowl, crystal, scalloped edge, 4" 12.00
Rock Crystal, bowl, relish; red, 2-part, 11½" 75.00
Rock Crystal, butter dish, crystal 335.00
Rock Crystal, cake stand, red, ftd, 2¾x11" 125.00
Rock Crystal, candlesticks, bl, yel or blk, 8", pr 150.00
Rock Crystal, creamer, crystal, ftd, 9-oz 37.50
Rock Crystal, cup, bl, yel or blk, 7-oz 27.50
Rock Crystal, cup, red, 7-oz 70.00
Rock Crystal, goblet, iced tea; red, low ft, 11-oz 67.50
Rock Crystal, pitcher, crystal, ½-gal, 7½" 110.00
Rock Crystal, pitcher, tankard; crystal, fancy 195.00
Rock Crystal, plate, bl, yel or blk, scalloped edge, 10½" 30.00
Rock Crystal, punch bowl, crystal, w/stand, 2 styles, 14" 595.00
Rock Crystal, sandwich server, red, center hdl 145.00
Rock Crystal, shakers, crystal, pr 75.00
Rock Crystal, stem, cocktail; bl, yel or blk, ftd, 3½-oz 21.00
Rock Crystal, sugar bowl, crystal, 10-oz 15.00
Rock Crystal, tumbler, juice; red, 5-oz 57.50
Rock Crystal, tumbler, old-fashioned, red, 5-oz 60.00
Rock Crystal, vase, bl, yel or blk, ftd, 11" 110.00
Rose Cameo, bowl, berry; gr, 4½" 10.00
Rose Cameo, bowl, cereal; gr, 5" 17.00
Rose Cameo, plate, salad; gr, 7" 12.00
Rose Cameo, tumbler, gr, ftd, 2 styles, 5" 22.00
Rosemary, bowl, vegetable; gr, oval, 10" 27.50
Rosemary, cup, pk 10.00
Rosemary, plate, grill; pk 22.00
Rosemary, plate, salad; gr, 6¾" 8.50
Rosemary, platter, gr, oval, 12" 22.00
Rosemary, tumbler, pk, 9-oz, 4¼" 50.00
Roulette, cup, crystal 36.00
Roulette, plate, sandwich; crystal, 12" 11.00
Roulette, tumbler, iced tea; crystal, 12-oz, 5⅛" 16.00
Roulette, tumbler, water; pk or gr, 9-oz, 4⅛" 30.00
Roulette, whiskey, pk or gr, 1½-oz, 2½" 17.00
Round Robin, creamer, irid, ftd 6.50
Round Robin, domino tray, gr 37.50
Round Robin, plate, luncheon; gr or irid, 8" 4.00
Roxanna, bowl, cereal; yel, 6" 17.50
Roxanna, bowl, wht, 4½x2⅜" 15.00
Roxanna, tumbler, yel, 9-oz, 4¼" 20.00
Royal Lace, bowl, berry; pk, rnd, 10" 28.00
Royal Lace, bowl, gr, 3-leg, str edge, 10" 65.00
Royal Lace, bowl, vegetable; bl, oval, 11" 65.00
Royal Lace, cookie jar, crystal, w/lid 35.00
Royal Lace, pitcher, crystal, w/lip, 68-oz, 8" 50.00
Royal Lace, pitcher, pk, w/lip, 96-oz, 8½" 110.00
Royal Lace, plate, dinner; gr, 9⅞" 35.00
Royal Lace, shakers, bl, pr 275.00
Royal Lace, tumbler, bl, 12-oz, 5⅜" 100.00
Royal Lace, tumbler, pk, 5-oz, 3½" 30.00
Royal Ruby, bowl, cereal; 5½" 13.00
Royal Ruby, bowl, hdls, 6½" 12.00
Royal Ruby, candle holders, 3½", pr 55.00

Royal Ruby, cup, rnd 5.50
Royal Ruby, plate, sandwich; 13½" 50.00
Royal Ruby, tray, 6x4½" 12.50
S Pattern, cup, yel, amber or crystal w/trims, thick or thin 4.50
S Pattern, tumbler, crystal, 10-oz, 4¾" 7.00
S Pattern, tumbler, yel, amber or crystal w/trim, 5-oz, 3½" 7.00
Sandwich, basket, amber or crystal, 10" 35.00
Sandwich, candlesticks, amber or crystal, 7", pr 26.00
Sandwich, candlesticks, pk or gr, 3½", pr 45.00
Sandwich, cruet, teal bl, w/stopper, 6½" 135.00
Sandwich, goblet, amber or crystal, 9-oz 13.00
Sandwich, plate, luncheon; red, 8⅜" 20.00
Sandwich, plate, sherbet; teal bl, 6" 7.00
Sandwich, puff box, amber or crystal 16.00
Sandwich, wine, amber or crystal, 4-oz, 3" 6.00
Sharon, bowl, berry; pk, lg, 8½" 32.00
Sharon, bowl, cream soup; amber, 5" 28.00
Sharon, butter dish, gr, w/lid 90.00

Sharon, cup and saucer, pink, $14.00 and $12.00; Creamer and sugar bowl, pink, $18.00 and $14.00.

Sharon, plate, cake; pk, ftd, 11½" 42.50
Sharon, platter, pk, oval, 12½" 30.00
Sharon, tumbler, gr, thin, 12-oz, 5¼" 100.00
Ships, cocktail shaker, bl & wht 35.00
Ships, plate, salad; bl & wht, 8" 25.00
Ships, plate, sherbet; bl & wht, 5⅞" 28.00
Ships, tumbler, iced tea; bl & wht, 12-oz 22.00
Ships, tumbler, whiskey; bl & wht, 3½" 27.50
Sierra, bowl, berry; pk or gr, lg, 8½" 32.00
Sierra, pitcher, pk, 32-oz, 6½" 95.00
Sierra, shakers, pk or gr, pr 40.00
Sierra, sugar bowl, gr 26.00
Spiral, bowl, mixing; gr, 7" 8.50
Spiral, cup, gr 5.00
Spiral, platter, gr, 12" 30.00
Spiral, shakers, gr, pr 35.00
Spiral, tumbler, juice; gr, 5-oz, 3" 4.50
Spiral, vase, gr, ftd, 5¾" 50.00
Starlight, bowl, crystal or wht, 2¾x12" 30.00
Starlight, bowl, pk, closed hdls, 8½" 20.00
Starlight, plate, dinner; crystal or wht, 9" 7.50
Starlight, plate, sandwich; pk, 13" 18.00
Starlight, relish dish, crystal or wht 15.00
Starlight, sherbet, crystal or wht 15.00
Strawberry, bowl, crystal or irid, 2x6¼" 55.00
Strawberry, butter dish, pk or gr, w/lid 150.00
Strawberry, plate, salad; crystal or irid, 7½" 6.50
Strawberry, tumbler, pk or gr, 8-oz, 3⅝" 35.00
Sunburst, bowl, crystal, 11" 22.00
Sunburst, plate, dinner; crystal, 9¼" 20.00
Sunburst, tray, crystal, oval, sm 12.00
Sunflower, cup, opaque 75.00

Sunflower, trivet, pk, turned-up edge, 3-leg, 7" 300.00
Swirl, bowl, salad; pk, 9" 20.00
Swirl, butter dish, ultramarine, w/lid 265.00
Swirl, candle holders, Delphite, single branch, pr 125.00
Swirl, candy dish, pk, w/lid 115.00
Swirl, pitcher, ultramarine, ftd, 48-oz 1,750.00
Swirl, platter, Delphite, oval, 12" 38.00
Swirl, sherbet, ultramarine, low ft 22.50
Swirl, tumbler, pk, 13-oz, 5⅛" 50.00
Tea Room, bowl, celery; pk, 8¼" 27.50
Tea Room, candlesticks, pk or gr, low, pr 50.00
Tea Room, creamer, pk or gr, rectangular 20.00
Tea Room, goblet, gr, 9-oz 75.00
Tea Room, marmalade, pk, notched lid 160.00
Tea Room, shakers, gr, pr 55.00
Tea Room, sherbet, pk, low flared edge 26.00
Tea Room, tumbler, gr, ftd, 12-oz 65.00
Tea Room, tumbler, pk or gr, ftd, 6-oz 35.00
Thistle, bowl, cereal; pk, 5½" 22.50
Thistle, plate, cake; pk, heavy, 13" 135.00
Thistle, plate, grill; gr, 10¼" 25.00
Thistle, plate, luncheon; pk, 8" 15.00
Tulip, candy dish, amber, crystal or gr, ftd, w/lid 50.00
Tulip, decanter, amethyst or bl, w/stopper 95.00
Tulip, sherbet (ivy bowl), amethyst or bl, flat, 3¾" 20.00
Tulip, tumbler, whiskey; amber, crystal or gr 20.00
Twisted Optic, basket, bl, tall, 10" 85.00
Twisted Optic, bowl, canary yel, 4¼x11½" 50.00
Twisted Optic, bowl, salad; pk, 7" 10.00
Twisted Optic, candy jar, bl, ftd, w/lid, tall 75.00
Twisted Optic, candy jar, gr, flat, w/lid 25.00
Twisted Optic, plate, sandwich; pk, 10" 9.00
Twisted Optic, plate, sherbet; canary yel, 6" 4.00
Twisted Optic, tumbler, amber, 9-oz, 4½" 6.00
Twisted Optic, vase, bl, rolled edge, hdls, 7¼" 55.00
US Swirl, bowl, gr, 1-hdl, 5½" 9.50
US Swirl, butter dish, pk or gr, w/lid 110.00
US Swirl, creamer, gr 14.00
US Swirl, shakers, pk or gr, pr 50.00
US Swirl, sugar bowl, pk or gr, w/lid 32.00
Victory, bowl, console; blk or bl, 12" 65.00
Victory, comport, pk, 6x6¾" 15.00
Victory, goblet, blk or bl, 7-oz, 5" 50.00
Victory, platter, blk or bl, 12" 75.00
Vitrock, bowl, cream soup; wht, 5½" 15.00
Vitrock, plate, salad; wht, 7¼" 2.50
Vitrock, plate, soup; wht, 9" 30.00
Vitrock, saucer, wht 2.50
Waterford, ashtray, crystal, 4" 7.50
Waterford, butter dish, pk, w/lid 220.00
Waterford, cup, pk 15.00
Waterford, plate, dinner; crystal, 9⅝" 11.00
Waterford, plate, sandwich; pk, 13¾" 27.50
Waterford, tumbler, juice; pk, Miss America style, 5-oz, 3½" 95.00
Windsor, ashtray, crystal, 5¾" 13.50
Windsor, bowl, cereal; pk, 5⅛" or 5⅜", ea 22.00
Windsor, bowl, fruit console; crystal, 12½" 37.50
Windsor, bowl, gr, hdls, 8" 25.00
Windsor, platter, relish; pk, divided, 11½" 225.00

Derby

William Duesbury operated in Derby, England, from about 1755,

purchasing a second establishment, The Chelsea Works, in 1769. During this period fine porcelains were produced which so impressed the King that in 1773 he issued the company the Crown Derby patent. In 1810, several years after Duesbury's death, the factory was bought by Robert Bloor. The quality of the ware suffered under the new management, and the main Derby pottery closed in 1848. Within a short time, the work was revived by a dedicated number of former employees who established their own works on King Street in Derby.

The earliest known Derby mark was the crown over a script 'D'; however this mark is rarely found today. Soon after 1782, that mark was augmented with a device of crossed batons and six dots, usually applied in underglaze blue. During the Bloor period, the crown was centered within a ring containing the words 'Bloor' above and 'Derby' below the crown, or with a red printed stamp — the crowned Gothic 'D.' The King Street plant produced figurines that may be distinguished from their earlier counterparts by the presence of an 'S' and 'H' on either side of the crown and crossed batons.

In 1876 a new pottery was constructed in Derby, and the owners revived the earlier company's former standard of excellence. The Queen bestowed the firm the title Royal Crown Derby in 1890; it still operates under that name today. See also Royal Crown Derby.

Box, dove, purple and white on brown and tan nest, ca 1880, 7½" long, $800.00.

Coffeepot, rose/multifloral, 1760s, 9½", EX 1,500.00
Cup & saucer, exotic bird, Kakiemon palette, 1815 ....240.00
Figurine, Dr Syntax Tied to a Tree, mc w/gold, ca 1820, 4" 520.00
Figurine, pointer by stump, natural colors, 1795, 6" L 825.00
Figurine, Venus/Cupid on dolphin, 1765, rpr, 10", VG 1,100.00
Garniture, titled scenes, snake hdls, 7½" vase+2 sm vases 1,800.00
Vase, floral, gold trim, bulbous w/slim neck, 11½x4½" 1,100.00

Desert Sands

As early as the 1850s, the Evans family living in the Ozark Mountains of Missouri produced domestic clay products. Their small pot shop was passed on from one generation to the next. In the 1920s it was moved to North Las Vegas, Nevada, where the name Desert Sands was adopted. Succeeding generations of the family continued to relocate, taking the business with them. From 1937 to 1962 it operated in Boulder City, Nevada; then it was moved to Barstow, California, where it remained until it closed in the late 1970s.

Desert Sands pottery is similar to Mission Ware by Niloak. Various mineral oxides were blended to mimic the naturally occuring sand formations of the American West. A high-gloss glaze was applied to add intensity to the colorful striations that characterize the ware. Not all examples are marked, making it sometimes difficult to attribute. Marked items carry an ink stamp with the Desert Sands designation. Paper labels were also used.

Ashtray, 6½" 22.00
Bowl, console; hand thrown, 9½" 45.00
Bowl, incurvate rim, 3" 18.00
Butter dish 50.00
Candle holder, 3" 18.00

Mug **32.00**
Shakers, pr **30.00**
Tumbler **22.00**

Vase, three-color swirl, T
Evans, 4¼", $27.50.

Vase, bulbous, flared rim, 3½" **35.00**
Vase, inverted cylinder, slim, 5" **25.00**
Vase, waisted form, flared rim, 2½" **20.00**

Devon, Crown Devon

Devon and Crown Devon were trade names of S. Fielding and Company, Ltd., an English firm founded after 1879. They produced majolica, earthenware mugs, vases, and kitchenware. In the 1930s they manufactured an exceptional line of Art Deco vases that have recently been much in demand.

Biscuit jar, Windsor, mc flowers, gold trim, rattan hdl, 8¾" **200.00**
Box, dresser; girl holding fishbowl w/gold, newts around base **225.00**
Pitcher, Auld Lang Syne, Scotsman/scenic reliefs, oval **150.00**
Vase, Pegasus, HP on maroon lustre w/gold, 12" **225.00**

Dickota

The Dickota Pottery, a name coined from Dickinsonn, North Dakota, where it was founded as a brickyard, began operations in the early 1930s. In 1934 potters formerly assosciated with the North Dakota School of Mines and Charles Hyten from Niloak began their own operation there. Hyten developed a line of swirled ware which was marked 'Dickota Badlands.' Vases, bowls, and ashtrays in a mottled glaze were also made. A variety of marks were used, all of which contain the Dickota name. The company closed in the late 1930s. For further information we recommend *Collector's Encyclopedia of the Dakota Potteries, Identification & Values*, by Darlene Hurst Dommel (Collector Books).

Ashtray, Marine Bl w/wht flowing overglaze, 2 rests, 4¼" **40.00**
Bowl, Sundogs relief border on glossy blk, 1¾x8½" **75.00**
Figurine, dog, seated, gr, paper label, 2", from $75 to **100.00**
Pitcher, Peacock Bl matt w/wht mottle, tilted ball, 8" **185.00**
Shakers, glossy blk ball shape, 2", from $25 to **45.00**
Teapot, Cableware, glossy blk, 1936, 3¾" **175.00**
Vase, glossy orange w/gold & blk overglaze, flared rim, 4¼" **50.00**
Vase, mc swirl, waisted cylinder, sgn HL (Howard Lewis), 4½" .**135.00**
Vase, Peacock Pk w/wht mottle, flared cylinder, 7½" **75.00**

Documents

Although the word 'document' is defined in the general sense as 'anything printed or written, etc., relied upon to record or prove some-

thing. . .,' in the collectibles market, the term is more diversified with broadsides, billheads, checks, invoices, letters and letterheads, land grants, receipts, and waybills some of the most sought after. Some documents in demand are those related to a specific subject such as advertising, mining, railroads, military, politics, banking, slavery, nautical, or legal (deeds, mortgages, etc.). Other collectors look for examples representing a specific period of time such as colonial documents, Revolutionary or Civil War documents, early western documents, or those from a specific region, state, or city.

Aside from supply and demand, there are five major factors which determine the collector-value of a document. These are

1) Age — Documents from the eastern half of the country can be found that date back to the 1700s or earlier. Most documents sought by collectors usually date from 1700 to 1900. Those with 20th-century dates are still abundant and not in demand unless of special significance or beauty.

2) Region of origin — Depending on age, documents from rural and less-populated areas are harder to find than those from major cities and heavily populated states. The colonization of the West and Mid-West did not begin until after 1850, so while an 1870s billhead from New York or Chicago is common, one from Albuquerque or Phoenix is not, since most of the Southwest was still unsettled.

3) Attractiveness — Some documents are plain and unadorned, but collectors prefer colorful, profusely illustrated pieces. Additional artwork and engravings add to the value.

4) Historical content — Unusual or interesting content, such as a letter written by a Civil War soldier giving an eyewitness account of the Battle of Gettysburg or a western territorial billhead listing numerous animal hides purchased from a trapper, will sell for more than one with mundane information.

5) Condition — Through neglect or environmental conditions over many decades, paper articles can become stained, torn, or deteriorated. Heavily damaged or stained documents are generally avoided altogether. Those with minor problems are more acceptable, although their value will decrease anywhere from 20% to 50%, depending upon the extent of damage. Avoid attempting to repair tears with scotch tape — sell 'as is' so that the collector can take proper steps toward restoration.

Foreign documents are plentiful; and though some are very attractive, resale may be difficult. The listings that follow are generalized; prices are variable depending entirely upon the five points noted above. Values here are based upon examples with no major damage. Common grade documents without significant content are found in abundance and generally have little collector value. These usually date from the late 1800s and early 1900s. It should be noted that the items listed below are examples of those that meet the criteria for having collector value. There is little demand for documents worth less than $5.00. For more information we recommend *Owning Western History* by our advisor Warren Anderson. His address and ordering information may be found in the Directory under Utah.

Key:
illus — illustrated   vgn — vignette

Agreement, NC, widow surrenders slaves to children, 1849, 2-pg .**60.00**
Bill, Savannah, masthead letterhead, rpr of compass, 1862 ....**8.00**
Bill, to Brig Royal Charlotte from metalsmith, 1771, 7x6", EX **28.00**
Billhead, Hart-Parr Co, oil-cooled gas tractors, 1916 ....**8.50**
Billhead, Park Co Milling Co, 1922 ....**8.50**
Certificate, MD, Black man was born free, 1838, 7x4½" **70.00**
Certificate, Missoula Co, bounty for 1 brn bear, 1887 ....**45.00**
Certificate, UT Territory, ore samples tested, 1879, 8x10" **32.00**
Court martial, CA soldier involved in robbery, 1863, 2½-pg **30.00**
Court martial, Fort Keogh, drunken captain on duty, 1878, 10-pg .**17.50**
Currency, 50¢ Confederate note, 1863, EX **30.00**

Deed, manuscript on vellum, Phila, 1824, 27x13", VG **40.00**
Discharge, Iowa soldier, 1866, EX **60.00**
Envelope, Civil War patriotic scene w/log cabin, unused **55.00**
General orders, construction of Fort Assiniboine, 1879, 11-pg **25.00**
General orders, VA City, concerns for dead soldier, 1878 ....**27.50**
Invoice, Civil War, supplies transport & delivery, 8x10" **12.50**
Invoice, Sargeant Drayage Express, Carson City, 1884 ....**30.00**
Land sale, handwritten on vellum, dtd 1650, 5x19" **48.00**
Ledger, drug store sales, cloth & leather covers, 1884-85, 16x11" ..**80.00**
Letter, Civil War, pay due deceased soldier **80.00**
Letter, Confederate soldier to brother, 1862, 1½-pg **90.00**
Letter, demands for tax reduction due to loss of slave, 1865 ....**150.00**
Letter, LA soldier's life in camp/etc, 1862, 4-pg, EX **25.00**
Letter, Union soldier's, describes fighting, 1862, 3-pg **175.00**
List, deeds owned by Cherokee Indians, NC, 1874, 11-pg **15.00**
Mortgage, Dakota Territory, w/seal, 1886, EX **40.00**
Muster roll, Black Infantry, names/rank, Xs for names, 1864 ....**25.00**
Pamphlet, KS as She Is, info to homesteaders, 1870, 64-pg **75.00**
Petition, Galveston Harbor, to congress for lighthouse, 1860 ......**22.50**
Publication, Millenial Star, Morman info, 1852, 16-pg **20.00**
Receipt, CA, Wells Fargo, shipment of freight, 1873, 5x11" **50.00**
Receipt, Confederate Navy receives corn, 1863, 5½x8", EX **40.00**
Receipt, for stores from Brig Charlotte, 1774, 1-pg, 7½x6½" **35.00**
Receipt, Wells Fargo Express, hauling gold bars, 1887 ....**45.00**
Report, lawyer's; annotated, ca 1900 ....**15.00**
Report, MA quartermaster's, supplies & grain, 1863 ....**20.00**
Report, Samoan Islands info to 46th congress, 1879, 29-pg **22.50**
Reunion card, for 88th IN, 1st reunion of 1882, trifold **17.50**
Revolutionary War note, 5 shillings, 1780, EX **55.00**
Speach, on removal of public deposits, JQ Adams, 1834, VG **35.00**
Telegraph, from Gen Bragg to Gen Beauregard, 1864, received copy ..**180.00**
Voucher, paymaster's, Civil War, horses/etc, 1865 ....**50.00**
Voucher invoice, NV, Manhattan Silver Mining Co, 1868 ....**30.00**

Dollhouses and Furnishings

Dollhouses were introduced commercially in this country late in the 1700s by Dutch craftsmen who settled in the East. By the mid-1800s, they had become meticulously detailed, divided into separate rooms, and lavishly furnished to reflect the opulence of the day. Originally intended for the amusement of adults of the household, by the latter 1800s their status had changed to that of a child's toy. Though many early dollhouses were lovingly hand fashioned for a special little girl, those made commercially by such companies as Bliss and Schoenhut are highly valued.

Furniture and furnishings in the Biedermeier style featuring stenciled Victorian decorations often sell for several hundred dollars each. Other early pieces made of pewter, porcelain, or papier-mache are also quite valuable. Certainly less expensive but very collectible, nonetheless, is the quality, hallmarked plastic furniture produced during the '40s by Renwal and Acme, and the 1960s Petite Princess line produced by Ideal. In the listings that follow, dollhouses are litho paper on wood, unless otherwise noted. For more information, see *Schroeder's Collectible Toys, Antique to Modern*. Our advisor for this category is Barbara Rosen; she is listed in the Directory under New Jersey. See also Miniatures.

Furniture

Bed, bl tin w/springs & canvas mattress, gold trim, Marklin, 8" ..**200.00**
Bed, ivory, Plasco, complete **8.00**
Bed, pk w/pk-flocked spread, Tootsietoy **25.00**
Bench, piano; walnut, Strombecker, ¾" scale **30.00**
Buffet, dk brn or marbleized maroon, Ideal, ea **10.00**

Buffet, red, opening drw, Renwal, #D55 ....**12.00**
Chair, caramel w/red bk & seat, Blue Box **3.00**
Chair, guest dining, Ideal Petite Princess, #4414-9 ....**10.00**
Chair, highbk; bl soft plastic, Marx **3.00**
Chair, rocking; red or yel, Renwal, #65, ea **8.00**
China closet, dk marbleized maroon, Ideal **15.00**
Crib, lt bl soft plastic, Marx, ½" scale **3.00**
Cupboard, corner; Jaydon, red-brn **4.00**
Desk, teacher's; brn, Renwal, #34 ....**20.00**
Doll, nurse, flesh, soft plastic, Marx **5.00**
Dresser, gr, long, Imagination **2.00**
Dresser, stained wood, w/mirror, Grand Rapids, 1½" scale **15.00**
Fireplace, brn w/ivory, Renwal, #80 ....**35.00**
Grandfather clock, Ideal Petite Princess, #4423-0 ....**18.00**
Hammock, bl w/red supports, Acme/Thomas **12.00**
Highboy, med brn swirl, Plasco **8.00**
Hutch, maroon, hard plastic, Marx, ¾" scale **5.00**
Nightstand, brn, Ideal **6.00**
Nightstand/end table, lt bl, Renwal, #B84 ....**3.00**

Piano and bench, red, Petite Princess, MIB, $45.00 (as shown, $25.00).

Refrigerator, ivory hard plastic, Marx, ¾" scale **5.00**
Rocker, bentwood; Tomy Smaller Homes **5.00**
Sewing machine, dk marbleized maroon, Ideal **20.00**
Sink, kitchen; hard plastic, Marx, ¾" scale **5.00**
Sofa, 2-tone, Renwal, #78 ....**15.00**
Stove, wht hard plastic, Marx, ¾" scale **5.00**
Swing, gr w/yel ropes & bl supports, Acme/Thomas **15.00**
Table, dining; brn, Tootsietoy **8.00**
Table, dining; Ideal Petite Princess, #4421-4, MIB **15.00**
Table, dressing; w/chair/accessories, Ideal Petite Princess **25.00**
Table, kitchen; aqua, Strombecker, ¾" scale **10.00**
Toilet, red & wht, Allied **4.00**
Toilet, yel soft plastic, Marx, ½" scale **2.00**
Vanity, yel hard plastic, Marx, ¾" scale **5.00**

Houses

Bliss, 2/story, porch w/trn posts/banister, 18", G **750.00**
Fisher-Price, #0250, 3-story/5-room, spiral stars, 1979, M **40.00**
Fisher-Price, 3-story/5-room, spiral stairs, lights, 1981, M **30.00**
Germany, kitchen, wood w/center stove, table/tinware, 12x22", VG ..**700.00**
Germany, 2-story, brick w/gables, porch over door, 1905, 25" .**1,650.00**
Jayline, 2-story/5-room, tin litho, purple roof, 1949, 15x19", VG ..**50.00**
Marx, Newlyweds Parlor #193, tin litho, w/furniture, 1925, MIB .**300.00**
Marx, red siding, gray roof, patio above garage, EX **60.00**
Marx, 2-story, red roof, patio/garage/ABC nursery, ½" scale **50.00**
Schoenhut, 2-story/2-room, brick, red roof, porch, 17x13", G **650.00**
Tootsietoy, 2-story, cb, cream w/red roof, 1951, 16x24x9", VG .**195.00**
Wolverine, Country Cottage #800, 1986, ½" scale, EX **45.00**

Dolls

Collecting dolls of any sort is one of the most rewarding hobbies in the United States. The rewards are in the fun, the search, and the finds — plus there is a built-in factor of investment. No hobby, be it dolls, glass, or anything else, should be based completely on investment; but any collector should ask: 'Can I get my money back out of this item if I should ever have to sell it?' Many times we buy on impulse rather than with logic, which is understandable; but by asking this question we can save ourselves a lot of 'buyer's remorse' which we have all experienced at one time or another.

Since we want to learn to invest our money wisely while we are having fun, we must become aware of defects which may devaluate a doll. In bisque, watch for eye chips, hairline cracks and chips, or breaks on any part of the head. Composition should be clean, not crazed or cracked. Vinyl and plastic should be clean with no pen or crayon marks. Though a quality replacement wig is acceptable for bisque dolls, composition and hard plastics should have their originals in uncut condition. Original clothing is a must except in bisque dolls, since it is unusual to find one in its original costume.

A price guide is only that — a guide. It suggests the average price for each doll. Bargains can be found for less-than-suggested values, and 'unplayed-with' dolls in their original boxes may cost more. Dealers must become aware of condition so that they do not overpay and therefore overprice their dolls — a common occurrence across the country. Quantity does not replace quality, as most find out in time. A faster turnover of sales with a smaller margin of profit is far better than being stuck with an item that does not sell because it is overpriced. It is important to remember that prices are based on condition and rarity. When no condition is noted, dolls are assumed to be in excellent condition with the exceptions of Armand Marseille, Arranbee, and Madame Alexander, which are generally priced in mint condition. Cabbage Patch values are for dolls mint in the box. In relation to bisque dolls, excellent means having no cracks, chips, or hairlines, being nicely dressed, shoed, wigged, and ready to to be placed into a collection. For a more thorough study of the subject, refer to *Modern Collectible Dolls, Volume II* and *Doll Values, Antique to Modern, Second Edition*, by Patsy Moyer; and the many lovely doll books written by authority Pat Smith, available at your favorite bookstore or public library. Several other books are referenced throughout this category.

Key:
bjtd — ball-jointed	OC — original clothes
blb — bent limb body	o/m — open mouth
bsk — bisque	p/e — pierced ears
c/m — closed mouth	pnt — painted
hh — human hair	pwt — paperweight eyes
hp — hard plastic	RpC — replaced clothes
jtd — jointed	ShHd — shoulder head
MIG — Made In Germany	ShPl — shoulder plate
NC — no clothes	SkHd — socket head
o/c/e — open closed eyes	str — straight
o/c/m — open closed mouth	trn — turned

American Character

AC or Petite, baby or mama, compo head & cloth, OC, 14" **175.00**
Betsy McCall, all vinyl, rooted hair, mk McCall 1961, OC, 36" ..**550.00**
Betsy McCall, hp, jtd knees, bathing suit, 1957, EX **100.00**
Bottletot, compo head, cryer, o/c/e, pnt hair, OC, 18" **325.00**
Campbell Kid, compo, jtd limbs, mk A Petite Doll, OC, 12" **335.00**
Carol Ann Bery, compo, o/c/e, c/m, 1935, OC, 13" **400.00**
Eloise, cloth, yarn hair, crooked smile, 1950s, OC, 15" **250.00**

Ricky Jr, vinyl baby boy, 1955-56, OC, 13" **50.00**
Tiny Tears, hp & vinyl, OC, 1955-62, 8" **50.00**
Toodle-Loo, plastic, rooted hair, pnt eyes, c/m, OC, 1961, 18" ..**190.00**
Toodles, vinyl, rooted hair, o/c/e, c/m, OC, 14" **125.00**

Annalee

Barbara Annalee Davis has been making her dolls since 1950. What began as a hobby, very soon turned into a commercial venture. Her whimsical creations range from tiny angels atop powder puff clouds to funky giant frogs, some 42" in height. In between there are dolls for every occasion (with Christmas being her specialty), all characterized by their unique construction methods (felt over flexible wire framework) and wonderful facial expressions. Naturally some of the older dolls are the most valuable (though more recent examples are desirable as well, depending on scarcity and demand), and condition, as usual, is very important. To date your doll, look at the tag. If made before 1986, that date is only the copyright date. (Dolls made after 1986 do carry the manufacturing date.) Dolls from the '50s have a long white red-embroidered tag with no date. From 1959 to '64, that same tag had a date in the upper right-hand corner. From 1965 until '70, it was folded in half and sewn into the seam. In 1970, a satiny white tag with a date preceded by a copyright symbol in the upper right-hand corner was used. In '75, the tag was a long white cotton strip with a copyright date. This tag was folded over in 1982, making it shorter. Our advisor for Annalees is Jane Holt; she is listed in the Directory under New Hampshire.

Photo courtesy Jane Holt

Square Dancers, 1957, 10", minimum value: $950.00 for the pair.

Angel w/instruments, 1982-88, 7" **25.00**
Ballerina Pig, 1981, 7" **75.00**
Bellhop, 1963, 24" **750.00**
Bicentennial Boy & Girl Mice, 1976, 7", pr **300.00**
Boy building boat, 1957, 10" **800.00**
Bride & Groom, 1984-85, 10", pr **200.00**
Bunny w/egg, 1978, 7" **55.00**
Cardplayer Mouse, 1978, 7" **75.00**
Caroller Mouse, wht, 1979 only, 12" **125.00**
Colonial Boy Mouse, 1975-76, 7" **125.00**
Country Cousin Boy & Girl Mice, 1970, 7", pr **250.00**
Duck, wht, w/raincoat & umbrella, 1985-86, 12" **95.00**
Duck head pick, 1973 ....**30.00**
Easter Parade Boy & Girl Bunnies, 1977, 7", pr **65.00**
Easter Parade Boy & Girl Bunnies, 1983, 29", pr **300.00**
Easter Parade Goose, 1988, 24" **50.00**
Elf, red w/blk hair, 1970, 10" **50.00**
Equestrienne Mouse, 1983, 7" **75.00**
Fancy Nancy Cat, yel, wht, or hot pk, 1967, ea **450.00**
Girl Caroller, 1974, 10" **80.00**
Gnome, red, wht or gr, 1978, 12", ea **225.00**

Gnome, 1976, 18" **275.00**
Honey Pot Bear, 1984, 18" **95.00**
Horse, brn w/hearts, 1968, 10" **425.00**
Housewife Mouse, 1981, 7" **50.00**
Jogger Mouse, 1979, 7" **30.00**
Logo Kid w/pin, 1986, 7" **250.00**
Monk, gr robe, carries sm tree in burlap bag, 1966, 10" **250.00**
Nurse Mouse w/needle, 1979, 7" **60.00**
Pilgrim Couple, 1978, 10", pr **160.00**
Reindeer, flat face, 1966, 36" **575.00**
Santa, 1989, 3", in sleigh **35.00**
Santa Frog, 1987, 10" **55.00**
Santa in rocking chair, 1986, 18" **75.00**
Santa on moon, 1983, 7" **50.00**
Santa on Ski-Bob w/sack, 1971, 7" **150.00**
Scarecrow, 1976, 7" **100.00**
Snowman, 1987, 7" **40.00**
Witch Kid Baby, 1987, 3" **100.00**
Yum Yum Bunny, 1966, 12" **550.00**
Yum Yum Bunny, 1966, 7" **300.00**

Armand Marseille

AM, baby, flange neck, 1907, 16" **650.00**
AM, Floradora, SkHd, 12" **150.00**
AM, Floradora 3748, ShHd, 21" **385.00**
AM, Kiddiejoy, ShHd, cloth body, c/m, girl, 20" ...**1,600.00**
AM, Rosebud, ShHd, 1902, 15" **300.00**
AM, SkHd, o/c/e, 7" **185.00**
AM, SkHd, 26" **525.00**
AM 1894, boy, SkHd, brn o/c/e, o/m w/teeth, rprs, RpC, 23" **400.00**
Am 1894, ShPl, 26" **650.00**
AM 1894, SkHd, brn o/c/e, o/m w/teeth, hh wig, 19" **400.00**
AM 252, SkHd, googly eyes, 10" **1,100.00**
AM 253, SkHd, googly eyes, 8" **900.00**
AM 300n, adult, SkHd, 15½" **1,200.00**
AM 310/7/0 Just Me, SkHd, bl o/c/e to side, c/m, 9", EX **1,050.00**
AM 3200, ShHd, some trn, 1898, 14" **265.00**
AM 323, SkHd, googly eyes, 11" **1,200.00**
AM 327, SkHd, 1914, 12" **325.00**
AM 341, My Dream Baby, flange, c/m, wht, 8" **185.00**
AM 341, My Dream Baby, flange, c/m, 21" **625.00**
AM 351, My Dream Baby, flange, o/m, wht, 22" **625.00**
AM 352, Baby Love, flange, 1914, 19" **675.00**
AM 370, 12" **185.00**
AM 390, pnt bsk, 9" **145.00**
AM 390, SkHd, bl o/c/e, o/m w/teeth, jtd compo, Welsh OC, 9" .**375.00**
AM 390, SkHd, brn o/c/e, 21" **750.00**
AM 390, SKhd, o/m w/4 teeth, jtd compo, orig Scottish outfit, 9" .**130.00**
AM 390n, bsk SkHd, brn o/c/e, o/m w/teeth, rpl wig, 30" **400.00**
AM 390n, nun, SkHd, brn o/c/e, o/m w/teeth, OC, 20" **300.00**
AM 390n, 1915, 11" **200.00**
AM 500, Infant Berry, molded hair, 1908, 10" **450.00**
AM 560a, Dorothy, 1912, 15" **350.00**
AM 917, Mobi, baby, Germany, SkHd, 1921, 16" ...**575.00**
AM 975, Sadie, baby, Otto Gans, 1914, 17" **500.00**
AM 985, baby, SkHd, 13½" **400.00**
AM 990, Happy Tot, baby, SkHd, 8" **200.00**
AM 992, baby, SkHd, 1914, 22" **700.00**
AM 996, baby, SkHd, 15" **425.00**
Columbia, ShHd, 1904, 24" **385.00**
Mabel, ShHd, 1898, 15" **300.00**
Queen Louise, SkHd, 1910, 22" **400.00**
Queen Louise, 100, SkHd, 1910, 18½" **425.00**

Arranbee

Baby, compo/cloth, OC, 1930s-40s, 16" **125.00**
Debu-Teen, compo ShHd, mohair or hh wig, c/m, 1940, OC, 12" ..**155.00**
Lil' Imp, hp, red hair, freckles, OC, 1960, 10" **75.00**
My Angel, hp & vinyl, OC, 1961, 22" **70.00**
Nancy, molded hair or wig, o/c/e, o/m, 1930, OC, 17" **300.00**
Nancy Lee, compo, o/c/e, wig, OC, 1939+, 17" **300.00**
Nancy Lee, hp, o/c/e, c/m, mohair wig, 5-pc body, OC, 16" **150.00**
Nannette, hp, o/c/e, c/m, synthetic wig, OC, 1949-59, 14" **250.00**
Sonja Skater, compo, OC, 1945, 10-12", ea **195.00**

Barbie Dolls and Related Dolls

Though the face has changed three times since 1959, Barbie is still as popular today as she was when she was first introduced. Named after the young daughter of the first owner of the Mattel Company, the original Barbie had a white iris but no eye color. These dolls are nearly impossible to find, but there is a myriad of her successors and related collectibles just waiting to be found. When no condition is indicated, the dolls listed below are assumed to be complete and mint in box unless otherwise specified. For further information we recommend *The World of Barbie Dolls* and *The Wonder of Barbie, 1976 – 1986*, by Paris, Susan, and Carol Manos; *The Collector's Encyclopedia of Barbie Dolls and Collectibles* by Sibyl DeWein and Joan Ashabraner; *Barbie Exclusives, Book I* and *II*, by Margo Rana; *A Decade of Barbie Dolls and Collectibles, 1981 – 1991*, by Beth Summers; *Barbie, The First Thirty Years*, by Stefanie Deutsch; *Thirty Years of Mattel Fashion Dolls, The Barbie Doll Book 1986 – 1995, Collector's Encyclopedia of Barbie Doll Exclusives and More*, all by J. Michael Augustyniak; and *Skipper – Barbie Doll's Little Sister*, by Scott Arend, Karla Holzerland, and Trina Kent. *Barbie Fashion, Vol. I, 1959 – 1967*, and *Vol. II, 1968 – 1974*, by Sarah Sink Eames, gives a complete history of the wardrobes of Barbie, her friends, and her family. *Schroeder's Toys, Antique to Modern*, is another good source for current market values.

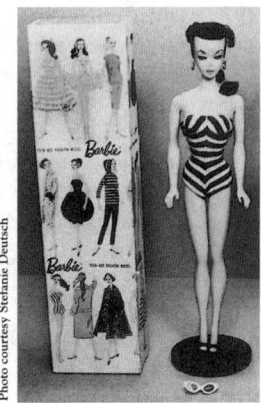

Barbie, 1959-60, #2, brunette, MIB, $7,000.00.

Photo courtesy Stefanie Deutsch

Allan, 1963, pnt red hair, str legs, NRFB **165.00**
Allan, 1963, pnt red hair, str legs, orig trunks & sandals, VG **65.00**
Barbie, #1, 1958-59, blond hair, MIB **9,000.00**
Barbie, #1, 1958-59, brunette hair, MIB **10,000.00**
Barbie, #3, 1960, blond hair, orig swimsuit, NM **950.00**
Barbie, #4, 1960, blond or brunette hair, orig swimsuit, NM **400.00**
Barbie, #5, 1961, blond/hair, MIB **550.00**
Barbie, #5, 1961, red hair, MIB **1,300.00**
Barbie, 1961, Bubble-Cut, blond hair, MIB **500.00**
Barbie, 1961, Bubble-Cut, brunette hair, MIB **250.00**
Barbie, 1961, Bubble-Cut, brunette hair, NM **200.00**
Barbie, 1962-64, Bubble-Cut w/side part, brunette, w/swimsuit, VG **125.00**

Barbie, 1963, Fashion Queen, w/wigs/swimsuit/stand, EX **250.00**
Barbie, 1964, Am Girl, blond, bendable legs, orig swimsuit, M ...**1,300.00**
Barbie, 1966, Color Magic, blond hair, NRFB **1,500.00**
Barbie, 1966, Color Magic, brunette, NRFB **1,800.00**
Barbie, 1968, Truly Scrumptious, NRFB................................**500.00**
Barbie, 1969, Twist 'N Turn, auburn hair, NRFB **700.00**
Barbie, 1970, Standard, blond hair, NRFB **700.00**
Barbie, 1970, Standard, brunette, MIB **550.00**
Barbie, 1971, Hair Happenin's, Sears Exclusive, red hair, MIB ..**1,200.00**
Barbie, 1971, Live Action, NRFB **200.00**
Barbie, 1971, Malibu, orig bl swimsuit, VG **20.00**
Barbie, 1973, Quick Curl, blond hair, orig dress, G **25.00**
Barbie, 1975, Hawaiian, orig outfit, rare, VG **65.00**
Barbie, 1976, Superstar, orig outfit, M **25.00**
Barbie, 1979, Kissing, orig outfit, M **20.00**
Barbie, 1980, Oriental, Dolls of World series, NRFB **95.00**
Barbie, 1981, Eskimo, Dolls of World series, NRFB **75.00**
Barbie, 1982, Pink & Pretty, orig outfit, VG **15.00**
Barbie, 1984, Japanese, Dolls of World series, NRFB **150.00**
Barbie, 1986, Magic Moves, orig outfit, M **20.00**
Barbie, 1987, CA Dream, department store special, NRFB **45.00**
Barbie, 1987, Doctor, department store special, NRFB **35.00**
Barbie, 1988, Frills & Fantasy, Walmart, NRFB **40.00**
Barbie, 1988, Holiday, NRFB **250.00**
Barbie, 1990, Holiday, NRFB **200.00**
Barbie, 1991, Evening Flame, department store special, NRFB ..**200.00**
Barbie, 1992, Benefit Ball, Classique Collection, NRFB **150.00**
Barbie, 1995, Goddess of the Sun, Bob Mackie, NRFB **200.00**
Cara, 1976, Deluxe Quick Curl, MIB **60.00**
Casey, 1990, Malaysian, Dolls of World series, NRFB **60.00**
Chris, 1967-70, brunette, MIB **75.00**
Christie, 1968, Talking, MIB **150.00**
Francie, 1966, blond hair, str legs, MIB **500.00**
Francie, 1970, Growin' Pretty Hair, MIB **200.00**
Ken, 1961, flocked blond or brunette hair, str legs, NM **160.00**
Ken, 1965, pnt brunette hair, bendable legs, orig trunks, M **300.00**
Ken, 1970, Spanish Talking, MIB **200.00**
Ken, 1971, Malibu, orig swimsuit, VG **20.00**
Ken, 1972, Busy, brn pnt hair, orig outfit & accessories, VG **65.00**
Midge, 1963, brunette hair, str legs, orig swimsuit, NM **125.00**
Midge, 1963, str legs, MIB **150.00**
Midge, 1965, red hair, bendable legs, orig swimsuit, EX **300.00**
PJ, 1975, Gold Medal Gymnast, MIB **85.00**
Ricky, 1965, MIB **175.00**
Skipper, 1970, Dramatic New Living, orig swimsuit, M **55.00**
Skipper, 1970, red hair, str legs, MIB **250.00**
Skipper, 1980, Super Teen, MIB **30.00**
Skooter, 1963, brunette hair, str legs, orig swimsuit, NM **65.00**
Stacey, 1968, Talking, blond hair, MIB **385.00**
Stacey, 1969, Twist 'N Turn, blond hair, orig swimsuit, NM **300.00**
Tutti, 1966, blond or brunette hair, MIB **175.00**
Whitney, 1989, Style Magic, orig outfit, VG **35.00**

Barbie Gifts Sets and Related Accessories

When no condition is indicated, the items listed below are assumed to be mint and in the original box or package (if one was issued). Items in only excellent condition may be worth 40% to 60% less.

Animal, Blinking Beauty, horse, 1980, MIB **45.00**
Animal, Dream Horse Prancer, 1984, MIB **30.00**
Animal, Sachi, dog, 1991, MIB **18.00**
Case, blk patent leather, 1963, MIB **100.00**
Case, Fashion Queen, MIB **75.00**

Clothes, Bean Time, 1966, MIP **200.00**
Clothes, Club Meeting, 1966, MIP **250.00**
Clothes, Drum Majorette, 1964, MIP **150.00**
Clothes, Easter Parade, #900 series, 1958, MIP **900.00**
Clothes, Fabulous Fashion, 1966, MIP **500.00**
Clothes, Glowin' Out, 1971, MIP **60.00**
Clothes, Let's Dance, 1960, MIP **125.00**
Clothes, Pajama Party, 1964, MIP **100.00**
Clothes, Winter Holiday, 1959, MIP **175.00**

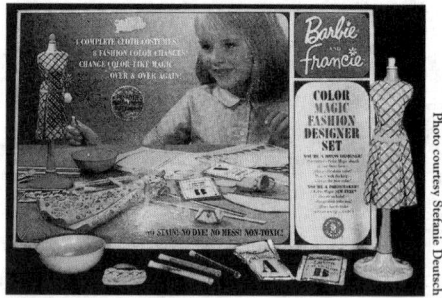

Color Magic Fashion Designer Set, #4040, Sears, 1966, MIB, $500.00.

Furniture, Country Camper, 1971, MIB **35.00**
Furniture, Suzy Goose Wardrobe, ca 1960, MIB **100.00**
Gift set, Color Magic, 1966, Sears, MIB **1,000.00**
Gift set, Hostess, 1965, MIB **2,300.00**
Gift set, Pep Rally, 1964, MIB **700.00**
Gift set, Wedding Party, 1964, MIB **2,000.00**
Vehicle, Dune Buggy, 1970, MIB **200.00**
Vehicle, Sport Plane, 1964, MIB **2,300.00**

Belton

Concave head, 2 or 3 hole, EX bsk, o/c/m or c/m w/wig, 10" ...**1,200.00**
Concave head, 2 or 3 hole, EX bsk, o/c/m or c/m w/wig, 13" ...**1,600.00**
Concave head, 2 or 3 hole, EX bsk, o/c/m or c/m w/wig, 15" ...**1,900.00**
Concave head, 2 or 3 hole, EX bsk, o/c/m or c/m w/wig, 16" ...**2,000.00**
Concave head, 2 or 3 hole, EX bsk, o/c/m or c/m w/wig, 17" ...**2,000.00**
Concave head, 2 or 3 hole, EX bsk, o/c/m or c/m w/wig, 20" ...**2,800.00**
Concave head, 2 or 3 hole, EX bsk, o/c/m or c/m w/wig, 22" ...**3,000.00**
Concave head, 2 or 3 hole, EX bsk, o/c/m or c/m w/wig, 23" ...**3,200.00**
Concave head, 2 or 3 hole, EX bsk, o/c/m or c/m w/wig, 26" ...**3,800.00**
Concave head, 2 or 3 hole, EX bsk, o/c/m or c/m w/wig, 8" **800.00**

Boudoir Dolls

Boudoir dolls, often called flapper dolls, were popular during the 1920s and 1930s, but they continued to be made up into the '40s as well. These dolls are rarely marked, but most were made in the United States, France, Italy, and Germany. Dolls of this type have silk or felt painted face masks, elaborate costumes, and are of excellent quality. The less expensive ones have composition heads and clothes that are stapled or nailed onto the body. Our advisor for this category is Bonnie Groves; she is listed in the Directory under Texas.

Anita, compo head & hands, cloth body, nude, '20s, EX, $50 to ..**85.00**
Anita, compo head & hands, silk floss wig, OC/shoes, VG, $150 to .**200.00**
Black, from $150 to **300.00**
Cloth, music box inside, all orig, Fr, 30", EX, minimum value ...**500.00**
Cloth, silk face, mohair wig, nude, shoes & stockings, 30", VG ...**85.00**
Compo, common carnival type, all orig, 1940s, 28", VG, $50 to .**125.00**

Compo, jtd arms, mk Sterling, all orig, 30", VG 150.00
Compo, sleep eyes, bald, nude, 30", G 50.00
Compo ShPl, compo arms/high-heeled ft, mk WKSMC, EX clothes, 30" ..200.00
Etta, all cloth, all orig, 30", VG, from $95 to 250.00
Finely pnt features, average clothes & quality, 28", from $85 to .125.00
Finely pnt features, average clothes & quality, 32", from $100 to .150.00
Finely pnt features, EX clothes/quality, glass eyes, 28", $145 to ..200.00
Finely pnt features, EX clothes/quality, glass eyes, 32", $150 to ..250.00
Finely pnt features, standard quality, dressed, 16" 125.00
French, silk face/costume, bsk arms & legs, 21", VG, from $150 to .200.00
Glass eyed, 27", EX, from $145 to 200.00
Lenci, 18-26", from $800 to 1,500.00
Smoker, Blosson, Argentine costume, all orig, 30", EX 350.00
Smoker, cloth, 16" 285.00
Smoker, cloth, 25" 475.00
Smoker, compo, 28" 375.00
Smoker, jtd compo, all orig, 25", G 300.00
Smoker, jtd compo, nude, bald, 15", G-, from $50 to 100.00
Smoker, Lenci, all orig, moth damage 500.00

Bru

Br Jne, kid over wood, wood legs, bsk lower arms, 12" **11,500.00**
Brevete, swivel head, kid body, bsk lower arms, 13" **12,500.00**
Brevete, swivel head, kid body, bsk lower arms, 18" **17,250.00**
Bru Jne, kid over wood, wood legs, bsk lower arms, 12" **11,500.00**
Bru Jne, kid over wood, wood legs, bsk lower arms, 14" **13,500.00**
Bru Jne, kid over wood, wood legs, bsk lower arms, 23" **21,500.00**
Bru Jne R, c/m, 19" **3,850.00**
Bru Jne R, o/m, EX bsk, jtd compo body, 12" **1,350.00**
Bru Jne R, o/m, EX bsk, jtd compo body, 19" **3,000.00**
Circle dot or half circle, kid body, bsk lower arms, 13" **14,500.00**
Circle dot or half circle, kid body, bsk lower arms, 19" **21,500.00**
Nursing, turnkey in bk of head, EX quality, 14", minimum **7,000.00**

Cabbage Patch

Babyland General Hospital, A edition (bl), 1978+, minimum .**1,500.00**
Babyland General Hospital, Christmas edition, 1980, minimum .**600.00**
Babyland General Hospital, Oriental edition, 1983 ....850.00
Coleco, astronaut, red signature, 1986, from $50 to 175.00
Coleco, bald baby, powder scent, blk stamp 100.00
Coleco, Black freckled kid, 1983, from $225 to 175.00
Coleco, boy or girl, powder scent, blk signature 95.00
Coleco, Cornsilk Kid, from $30 to 50.00
Coleco, freckled girl or boy, 1983, minimum 35.00
Coleco, gray-eyed girl, 1984-85 ....165.00
Coleco, popcorn curls w/pacifier 65.00
Coleco, popcorn hair, 1986, from $30 to 80.00
Coleco, red fuzzy-haired boys, 1983, from $175 to 300.00
Coleco, single tooth, brunette w/ponytail, 1984-85, minimum ...165.00
Coleco, w/pacifier, from $50 to 75.00
Coleco, World Traveler, bl signature, 1985, from $40 to 45.00
Coleco, 1984-89, minimum 35.00

Cameo Dolls

Annie Rooney, compo, yarn wig, molded shoes, M, minimum value ..475.00
Baby Bo Kaye, bsk/compo/cloth, glass eyes, o/m, 1925, 17", EX .1,875.00
Baby Bo Kaye, celluloid, glass eyes, molded hair, 12", M 400.00
Betty Boop, compo/wood, label on torso, 1932, 11", M 650.00
Giggles, compo w/molded loop for ribbon, 1946, 14", EX 150.00
Ho-Ho, plaster, 5½", EX 20.00
Margie, compo & wood, pnt features, 10", EX 75.00

Newborn, vinyl & hp, 1962, M 40.00
Pretty Bettsie, compo, pnt eyes, o/c/m, pnt clothes, 18", M 500.00
Scootles, Black compo, eyes pnt to side, 15", EX 200.00
Scootles, compo, eyes pnt to side, 1925+, M w/tag 365.00

Celebrity

Lucille Ball, plastic mask face, cloth body, orange yarn hair, apron marked I Love Lucy/Desi 1953, 27", M, $200.00.

Photo courtesy Pat Smith

Andy Gibb, Ideal, 1979, NMIB 45.00
Barbara Eden/I Dream of Jeannie, vinyl, Libby, 1966, EX 300.00
Barry Goldwater, Remco, 1964, NM 45.00
Cher, Mego, 1976, 12", MIB 65.00
Cher, 1st issue, pk dress, 1975, 12¼", MIB (sealed) 70.00
Cheryl Tiegs, Matchbox, 1989, MIB 35.00
Diana Ross, wht & silver dress, Mego, 1977, 12", MIB (sealed) .125.00
Dolly Parton, hp/vinyl, Eegee, 1987, 18", MIB 90.00
Dorothy Hamill, vinyl/plastic, Ideal, 1976, OC, 11½", MIB 75.00
Elvis Presley, Graceland, plastic/vinyl, 12", 1984, MIB 65.00
Farrah Fawcett, vinyl head, pnt gr eyes, Mego, 1976, 12", MIB 60.00
Flip Wilson/Geraldine, talker, Shindana, 1976, 10", MIB 65.00
General MacArthur, compo, all orig, 1930, 19", w/pin 285.00
Jackie Coogan, compo/cloth, Horsman, OC, 1921-22, 13½", NM ..465.00
Julie Andrews (Mary Poppins), Horsman, 1964, w/2 dolls, 10", NRFB .250.00
John Travolta (On Stage...Superstar), Chemtoy, 1977, 12", MIB ..55.00
John Wayne, Effanbee Legend series, cowboy outfit, 17", MIB ...125.00
Laurel & Hardy, Goldberger, 1986, 12", MIB, ea 60.00
Laverne & Shirley, Mego, 1977, 12", MIB (sealed), pr 125.00
Macaully Caulkin (Kevin from Home Alone), vinyl, screams, MIB ..20.00
Mae West, Effanbee Great Legends series, 18", MIB 120.00
Marie Osmond, Mattel, 1976, 11", MIB 50.00
MC Hammer, w/boom box 20.00
Oscar Goldman, MIB 35.00
Sally Field (Flying Nun), Hasbro, 1967, 12", MIB 200.00
Shaun Cassidy (from Hardy Boys), Kenner, 1978, 12", EXIB 50.00
Susan Dey (Laurie Partridge), Remco, 1973, OC, 19", MIB 250.00
Twiggy, Mattel, rare, 1967, 11½", MIB 350.00
Vanna White, Totsy Toys, 1990, MIB (sealed) 100.00
Wayne Gretzky, Mattel, MIB 150.00
WC Fields, compo ShHd, Effanbee, OC, 17½", EX 950.00
6 Million Dollar Man, Bionic Grip, Kenner, 1977, 13", MIB 95.00

China, Unmarked

Adelina Patti, center part, curls at temples, 1860s, 14" 275.00
Adelina Patti, center part, curls at temples, 1860s, 22" 525.00
Biedermeier or Bald Head, takes wig, RpC, 14" 575.00
Brown Eyes (pnt), any hairstyle or date, 16" 575.00
Brown Eyes (pnt), any hairstyle or date, 20" 950.00
Common Hairdo, blond or blk hair, RpC, after 1905, 23" 285.00
Covered Wagon Style, sausage curls, RpC, 1840s-70s, 12" 285.00
Covered Wagon Style, sausage curls, RpC, 1840s-70s, 24" 900.00

Curly Top, loose ringlet curls, RpC, 1845-60s, 20" 700.00
Dolly Madison, modeled ribbon & bow, RpC, 1870-80s, 18" 500.00
Flat Top, blk hair, mid-part/short curls, RpC, ca 1860, 17" 300.00
Flat Top, blk hair, mid-part/short curls, RpC, ca 1860, 20" 350.00
Japanese, blk or blond hair, mk or unmk, RpC, 1910-20s, 14" 185.00
Japanese, blk or blond hair, mk or unmk, RpC, 1910-20s, 17" 250.00
Man or Boy, pnt eyes, side part, RpC, 14", EX 1,200.00
Man or Boy, pnt eyes, side part, RpC, 21½" 2,400.00
Peg Wood Body, early hairdo, 1840s, 16", EX 2,800.00
Pet Name, molded shirtwaist w/name on front, RpC, 1905, 8" ...125.00
Pierced Ears, various hairstyles, RpC, 14" 475.00
Snood/Combs, any appl hair decor, RpC, 14" 650.00
Snood/Combs, any appl hair decor, RpC, 17" 800.00
Spill Curls, w/or w/out head band, RpC, 22" 850.00
Wood Body, articulated/slim hips, RpC, 1840s-50s, 17" 3,500.00
Wood Body, jtd hips, covered-wagon hairdo, 1840s-50s, 12" ..1,000.00

Cloth

A cloth doll in very good condition will display light wear and soiling while one assessed as excellent will be clean and bright. Many cloth dolls are shown in these books: *Black Dolls: 1829 – 1881* and *Black Dolls, Book II*, by Myla Perkins.

Alabama Indestructible Doll, baby, 1900-25, 15", VG 850.00
Alabama Indestructible Doll, child, 1900-25, 22", EX 2,400.00
Art Fabric Mills, Improved Life Sz Doll, printed undies, 20", EX ..275.00
Babyland Rag by Horsman, flat pnt face, 30", VG 540.00
Babyland Rag by Horsman, lithographed face, 14½", VG 175.00
Babyland Rag by Horsman, molded/pnt face, 13", EX 700.00
Bing Art, pnt hair on cloth or felt, 13", VG 275.00
Bing Art, wigged, cloth or felt, 16", EX 650.00
Black Mammy style, pnt or embr features, 1930s, 15", EX, minimum 165.00
Bruckner for Horsman, printed/molded face mask, 1901, 14", EX ...325.00
Chad Valley, Bonzo (dog), pnt eyes, 4", VG 65.00
Columbian Doll, Emma E Adams..., HP features, 15", EX 4,500.00
Mollye, child, 13", EX 130.00
Mollye, lady, long gown, 16", VG 55.00
Pitti Sing, 4 on uncut litho cloth sheet 300.00
Raggedy Ann & Andy, Mollye Goldman, 1920s, OC, 18", pr .1,200.00
Russian, pnt stockinette head, Made in Soviet Union, '20s, 7", EX ...70.00
Wellings, child, pnt eyes, 1926-30, 18", EX 600.00
Wellings, policeman, 1926-30, VG 125.00

Eegee

Andy, vinyl, teen type, pnt/molded hair, pnt eyes, c/m, 1963, M ..35.00
Babette, vinyl & cloth, pnt eyes, rooted hair, 1970, 15", EX 10.00
Baby Luv, vinyl & cloth, rooted hair, pnt eyes, 1973, 14", M 35.00
Barbara Cartland, adult, pnt features, 15", M 52.00
Child, compo, o/m, o/c/e, 14", M 160.00
Flowerkins, hp & vinyl, series of 7, 1973, MIB, ea 60.00
Gigi Perreau, vinyl & hp, o/c smiling mouth, 1951, 17", M 700.00
Miss Charming, compo, Shirley Temple look-alike, 1936, 19", M ...450.00
Shelly, Tammy type w/growing hair, 1964, 12", M 18.00
Tandy Talks, vinyl & hp, pull-string talker, 1961, M 50.00

Effanbee

Bernard Fleischaker and Hugo Baum became business partners in 1910, and after two difficult years of finding toys to buy, they decided to manufacture dolls and toys of their own. The Effanbee trademark is a blending of their names, Eff for Fleischaker and bee for Baum. The company still exists today. For more information we recommend *Effanbee Dolls* by Pat Smith.

Ann Shirley, compo, 1936-40, 18", M 300.00
Baby Cup Cake, plastic/vinyl, o/c/e, dimples, RpC, 12" 20.00
Baby Dainty, compo/cloth, toddler, 1912+, 12", EX 80.00

Dy-Dee Baby, hard rubber swivel head with molded and painted hair, blue sleep eyes, nurser mouth, original clothes and trunk, ca 1934, 21", EX, $475.00.

Baby Evelyn, compo/cloth, ca 1925, 17", EX 75.00
Baby Grumpy, compo/cloth, pnt eyes/hair, pouty, 1915+, 11½", EX 75.00
Baby Tinyette, compo, str or bent legs, OC, 8" 245.00
Baby Wonder, compo, tin o/c/e, o/c/m, holds bottle, OC, 13" 165.00
Barbara Joan, compo, o/m, 1936-39, 15", M 650.00
Barbara Lou, compo, 1936-39, 21", EX 425.00
Button Nose, compo, pnt eyes, molded hair, OC, 8" 185.00
Candy Kid, compo toddler, o/c/e, pnt hair, 1946+, 13½", EX 75.00
Candy Walker, vinyl/hp, head turns, rooted hair, OC, 24" 200.00
Gumdrop, vinyl, jtd toddler, o/c/e, 1962+, 16", M 35.00
Lil Darlin', vinyl/cloth, cry box, o/c/e, OC, 16" 95.00
Louis Armstrong, vinyl, 1984-85, 11", M 150.00
Mary Ann, compo, o/c/e, o/m, 1932, 19", M 350.00
Mary Lee, compo, o/c/e, o/m/teeth/felt tongue, RpC, 16" 265.00
Mary Lee, compo, o/m, on Patsy Joan body, 16", EX 250.00
Merrilee, compo ShHd mama, o/c/e, o/m, 1934, 24", EX 150.00
Patsy, compo/cloth, o/m/teeth, o/c/e, hh wig, 1924, 15", M 300.00
Patsy Ann, jtd vinyl, rooted hair, o/c/e, Scout, 1959, 15", M 200.00
Patsy Baby, compo/cloth/celluloid, o/c/e, OC, 10" 265.00
Patsy Jr, compo, pnt/molded hair, pnt eyes, OC, 11½" 285.00
Patsy Ruth, compo/cloth, brn o/c, hh wig, OC, 27" 850.00
Plymouth Colony Historical, compo, brn pnt eyes, OC, 14" 650.00
Pouting Bess, compo/cloth, pnt eyes, cm, #155 on bk, 1915, 15", EX 85.00
Precious Baby, Limited Edition Club, 1975, MIB 350.00

Half Dolls

Half dolls were never meant to be objects of play. Most were modeled after the likenesses of lovely ladies, though children and animals were represented as well. Most of the ladies were firmly sewn onto pincushion bases that were beautifully decorated and served as the skirts of their gowns. Other skirts were actually covers for items on milady's dressing table. Some were used for parasol or brush handles or for tops to candy containers or perfume bottles. Most popular from 1900 to about 1930, they will most often be found marked with the country of their origin, especially Bavaria, Germany, France, and Japan. You may also find some fine quality pieces marked Goebel, Dressel and Kister, KPM, and Heubach.

Germany, arms & hands attached, common type, 3" 25.00
Germany, arms & hands attached, common type, 5" 35.00
Germany, arms & hands attached, common type, 8" 55.00

Germany, arms & hands completely away, 12", $200 to **950.00**
Germany, arms & hands completely away, 3", $85 to **145.00**
Germany, arms & hands completely away, 5", $100 to **285.00**
Germany, arms & hands completely away, 8", $165 to **650.00**
Germany, arms extended, hands attached, 3" **50.00**
Germany, arms extended, hands attached, 5" **85.00**
Germany, arms extended, hands attached, 8" **125.00**
Japan mk, 3" **20.00**
Japan mk, 5" **30.00**
Japan mk, 8" **50.00**

Handwerck

#189, o/m, RpC, 15" **475.00**
#79 or #u9, c/m, 18", RpC, 18", minimum value **2,000.00**
Bsk ShHd, o/m, kid body, RpC, 18" **350.00**
Child, bsk head, bjtd, set or o/c/e, after 1885, RpC, 15" **375.00**
Child, bsk head, bjtd, set or o/c/e, after 1885, RpC, 24" **650.00**
Child, bsk head, o/c/e, o/m w/4 teeth, RpC, 21" **425.00**
Child, bsk SkHd, bjtd, o/c/e, mold mks, RpC, 31" **1,200.00**

Hertel, Schwab and Company

#119, child, bsk head, glass eyes, jtd compo, RpC, 12" **3,100.00**
#125, Patsy, bsk head, bent limbs, o/c/e, 15" **1,150.00**
#126, Skippy, bsk head, o/c/m, pnt eyes, 16" **1,500.00**
#140, bsk head, pnt eyes, jtd compo, RpC, 12" **2,900.00**
#152, bsk SkHd, o/c/e, o/m w/2 teeth, mohair wig, RpC, 11" **130.00**
#154, bsk head, c/m, RpC, 21" **2,700.00**
#163, googly eyes, wig or molded hair, c/m, att, RpC, 13" **2,800.00**
#169, bsk head, c/m, jtd compo, RpC, 17" **3,200.00**
#208, bsk 1-pc body & head, glass eyes, o/ or c/m, 1920s, 6", M .**325.00**
#217, googly eyes, c/m, wig, RpC, 7½" **875.00**
#222, Our Fairy, molded hair, pnt eyes, RpC, 9" **1,500.00**

Heubach

#1017, baby-faced toddler, bsk head, o/m, RpC, 17" **1,500.00**
#10633, Dainty Dorothy, ShHd, o/c/e, o/m, Sears Roebuck, 25", MIB ...**500.00**
#5636, laughing child, 2 teeth, pnt eyes, RpC, 10" **925.00**
#6692, bsk ShHd, smiling, intaglio eyes, RpC, 16", minimum ..**1,000.00**
#6896, bsk head, pouty, jtd body, RpC, 21" **1,400.00**
#7, pouty character, bsk SkHd, intaglio eyes, c/m, bjtd, 17" **1,000.00**
#7551, squinting eyes, yawning, jtd body, RpC, 16" **3,450.00**
#7602, long face pouty, pnt eyes & hair, c/m, RpC, 16" **2,200.00**
#7603, bsk head, flocked hair, OC, 17½" **1,950.00**
#7616, SkHd or ShHd, molded tongue, glass eyes, RpC, 13" ...**1,600.00**
#8197, ShHd, c/m, molded curls, kid body, RpC, 17", minimum ...**8,700.00**
Character, bl intaglio/e, o/c/m w/teeth, walker, mk, 6" **500.00**
7, SkHd, jtd compo, o/c/e, o/m/2 sq teeth, hh wig, 16½" **1,400.00**

Heubach-Koppelsdorf

#250, jtd body, o/m, o/c or set eyes, after 1888, RpC, 9" **185.00**
#300, baby, 5-pc bent limb body, o/m, o/c/e, RpC, 8" **185.00**
Child, bsk ShHd, kid or cloth body, bsk lower arms, RpC, 15" ...**185.00**
300-14/0, SkHd, o/c/e, o/m w/2 teeth, jtd compo, OC, 10½" **125.00**

Horsman

Angelove, plastic/vinyl, made for Hallmark, 1974, 12", M **22.50**
Baby Butterfly, compo head/limbs, pnt Oriental face, 1914, 12", EX .**65.00**
Betty, vinyl, 1-pc body, 1951, 14", MIB **50.00**
Bright Star, compo, 1937-46, OC, 19", NM **350.00**

Campbell's Kid (boy), compo, pnt eyes, 5-pc body, OC, 12" **200.00**
Campbell's Kids, compo, 5-pc chubby bodies, OC, 12", pr **400.00**
Cindy, hp, jtd waist, 1959, 19", MIB **90.00**
Dolly Rosebud, compo/cloth, dimples, sleep eyes, 1926-30, EX **50.00**
Tiny Baby, vinyl, 1950s, 15", MIB **110.00**

Ideal

Two of Ideal's most collectible lines of dolls are Chatty Cathy and Tammy. For more information, refer to *Chatty Cathy Dolls* by Kathy and Don Lewis, and *Collector's Guide to Tammy, The Ideal Teen*, by Cindy Sabulis and Susan Weglewski.

Betsy McCall, vinyl head, brown sleep eyes, closed mouth, Saran wig, all original, 14", NMIB, $400.00.

Photo courtesy McMasters Auctions

Baby Brother Tender Love, 11½", M **38.00**
Baby Crissy, jtd vinyl, hair grows, pnt teeth, 1973-76, 24", EX **15.00**
Baby Snooks Flexie, wire/compo, OC, 12", minimum value **285.00**
Bamm-Bamm, jtd vinyl, Saran hair, pnt eys, OC, 12", M **20.00**
Betsy Wetsy, vinyl, o/m for bottle, 1983, MIB **35.00**
Bizzie-Lizzie, jtd vinyl, o/c/e, blond hair, 1971-72, 18", M **35.00**
Bonnie Play Pal, vinyl, bl o/c/e, rooted hair, 1959, 24", M **250.00**
Chatty Baby, open speaker, brunette, bl eyes, M **90.00**
Chelsea, posable vinyl, long rooted hair, 1967, 24", M **50.00**
Compo baby, cloth body, c/m, o/c/e, 1930s-40s, OC, 16" **200.00**
Deanna Durbin, jtd compo, o/c/e, o/m, hh, 1938-41, 15", M **500.00**
Dodi, MIB **75.00**
Flexy clown, compo head, wire tubes in legs, OC, 13½", M **225.00**
Flossie Flirt, compo/cloth, tin eyes, crier, 14", M, minimum **225.00**
Grown Up Tammy, MIB **75.00**
Kissy, vinyl, toddler, Saran hair, o/c/e, 1961-64, 22½", M **135.00**
Miss Clairol Glamour Misty, vinyl/hp, blond hair, 1965-66, 12", M .**35.00**
Pos'n Tammy, MIB **95.00**
Sara Ann, hp, Saran wig, 1952 on, OC, 14", minimum value **250.00**
Superman, wood, segmented joints, w/cape, rare **1,695.00**
Tammy, MIB **65.00**
Tammy's Dad, MIB **65.00**
Ted, MIB **65.00**
Tickletoes, compo/rubber/cloth, crier, o/c/e, 1928-29, 14", EX **40.00**
Tiny Chatty Brother, hair parted on side, 1963-64, 15½", M **30.00**
Tippee Toes, battery-op, w/tricycle, 1968-70, 17", M **36.00**

Jumeau

The Jumeau factory became the best known name for dolls during the 1880s and 1890s. Early dolls were works of art with closed mouths and paperweight eyes. When son Emile Jumeau took over, he patented sleep eyes with eyelids that dropped down over the eyes. This model also had flirty (eyes that move from side to side) eyes and is extremely rare. Over 98% of Jumeau dolls have paperweight eyes.

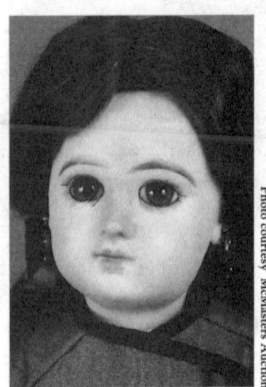

Photo courtesy McMasters Auction

Closed mouth, bisque socket head, brown paperweight eyes, human hair old wig, jointed body, dress possibly original, marked Tete Jumeau, 16", $3,500.00.

Closed mouth, mk EJ (incised) Jumeau, 14" 5,800.00
Closed mouth, mk Tete Jumeau, 10" 3,000.00
Closed mouth, mk Tete Jumeau, 21" 4,800.00
Closed mouth, mk Tete Jumeau, 30" 6,800.00
Jumeau 1907, SkHd, appl ears, o/m, 18" 2,400.00
Long face, c/m, 21" 23,000.00
Open mouth, mk Bebe Jumeau, 27" 2,000.00
Open mouth, mk Jumeau Medaille d'Or, Paris, 20" 1,900.00
Open mouth, mk Tete Jumeau, 10" 2,300.00
Open mouth, mk Tete Jumeau, 21" 3,100.00
Open mouth, mk Tete Jumeau, 30" 4,600.00
Open mouth, mk 1907 Jumeau, 17" 2,500.00
Open mouth, mk 1907 Jumeau, 32" 4,000.00
Portrait Jumeau, c/m, 20" 7,800.00

Kammer and Reinhardt

#100, baby, pnt hair & eyes, o/c/m, 15" 650.00
#101, boy or girl w/pnt eyes, 12" 2,000.00
#101, boy or girl w/pnt eyes, 20" 5,000.00
#109, rare, w/glass eyes, 18" 26,000.00
#109, rare, w/pnt eyes, 18" 22,000.00
#112, rare, w/pnt eyes, 18" 17,000.00
#114, rare, w/pnt eyes, 11" 2,950.00
#114, rare, w/pnt eyes, 18" 5,500.00
#115 or #115a, c/m, 18" 4,900.00
#115 or #115a, o/m, 22" 2,600.00
#116 or #116a, c/m, 18" 3,500.00
#116 or #116a, o/m, 22" 2,600.00
#117a, c/m, 18" 5,400.00
#192 14, SkHd, o/c/e, o/m w/4 teeth, rpl wig, jtd compo, 27" ..1,100.00
#30, bsk SkHd attached to walking mechanism, bl glass eyes, 11½" 575.00
#68, boy or girl, bl o/c/e, o/m, wig, p/e, 27", EX 800.00
#73, SkHd, o/c/e, o/m w/4 teeth, hh wig, jtd compo, RpC, 28" ..600.00
#85, SkHd, o/c/e, o/m w/teeth, p/e, wig, jtd compo, RpC, 33" .2,300.00
Dolly face, o/m, mold #400-403-102, etc, 24" 850.00
Dolly face, o/m, mold #400-403-109, etc, 38" 2,800.00

Kestner

Johannes D. Kestner made buttons at a lathe in a Waltershausen factory in the early 1800s. When this line of work failed, he used the same lathe to turn doll bodies. Thus the Kestner company began. It was one of the few German manufacturers to make the complete doll. By 1860, with the purchase of a porcelain factory, Kestner made doll heads of china and bisque as well as wax, worked-in-leather, celluloid, and cardboard. In 1895 the Kestner trademark of a crown with streamers was registered in the U.S. and a year later in Germany. Kestner felt the mark was appropriate since he referred to himself as the 'king of German dollmakers.'

B/6, ShHd, kid w/bsk ½-arms, o/m/teeth, o/c/e, 19" 685.00
D/8, SkHd & ShHd, kid w/bsk ½-arms, c/m, 15" 800.00
G/11, Hilda, SkHd, o/c/e, o/m/teeth, 1920s, 15" 3,600.00
G11, SkHd, jtd, bl eyes, o/m, mohair wig, 19" 800.00
Hilda, toddler, jtd body, o/m, o/c/e, 1914, rstr, 15" 4,800.00
JDK, bsk head, glass eyes, c/m, appl ears, OC, 20", EX 4,800.00
JDK 12, SkHd, pwt, o/m, bent limbs, RpC, 15", VG 475.00
JDK/Kestner, Oriental, SkHd, o/m, 14" 4,800.00
L/15, SkHd, bsk ShPl, c/m, 21" 3,000.00
10, bsk, o/c/e, orig wig & plaster pate, 22" 995.00
10, SkHd, bsk ShPl, c/m, 21" 2,900.00
11, SkHd, pnt eyes to side, o/c/m, JDK/MIG, 11" 550.00
13, bsk SkHd, bl o/c/e, c/m, rpl mohair wig, Germany, 20" 3,100.00
143, ShHd, jtd compo, o/c/e, o/m, mohair wig, 14", EX 850.00
145 SkHd, c/m, 143/4/0/JDK, 11" 325.00
148, ShHd, kid w/bsk ½-arms, o/m, 7½", 21" 700.00
150 4/0, bsk, pnt bl eyes, c/m, wig, pincushion clothing, 5" 135.00
150 5/0, bsk, brn o/c/e, c/m, mohair wig, JDK, 4½", MIB 275.00
150.41/20, bsk, brn o/c/e, c/m, RpC, 5" 250.00
154, bsk ShHd, brn o/c/e, o/m w/teeth, mohair wig, DEP, 13" 110.00
154, bsk ShHd, brn o/c/e, o/m w/teeth, rpl hh wig, 22", EX 300.00
155, SkHd, brn o/c/e, o/m w/teeth, wig, jtd compo, K, 6¾" 450.00
16, SkHd, o/m, JDK/MIG, 21" 65.00
167, orig pate & wig, bl eyes, 15" 795.00
168, SkHd, o/m, MID/G7, 26" 1,000.00
171, SkHd, jtd compo, o/c/e, o/m, 'Daisy,' F/M110, 18" 700.00
171, SkHd, jtd compo, o/c/e, o/m, hh wig, RpC, 29" 800.00
172, ShHd, c/m, smile, Gibson Girl wig, 6/0 MIG, RpC, 10", EX ..650.00
201, ShHd, celluloid on kid, o/m, set eyes/lashes, JDK, 19" 685.00
221, jtd compo, googly eyes, c/m smile, wig, JDK, 12½" 3,500.00
221, jtd compo, googly eyes, c/m smile, wig, JDK, 15" 5,200.00
245, SkHd, 5-pc baby, G/MIG/11/JDK Jr/1914 Hilda, 14" 3,300.00
245, SkHd, 5-pc baby, H/MIG/12/JDK Jr/1914 Hilda, 16" 3,500.00
257, SkHd, 5-pc baby, o/m, G/JDK, 20" 850.00
260, flirty-eyed toddler, OC, 16" 1,900.00
4 SkHd, bl o/c/e, c/m, mohair wig, jtd compo body, 11½" 1,600.00

Lenci

Characteristics of Lenci dolls include seamless, steam-molded felt heads, quality clothing, childishly plump bodies, and painted eyes that glance to the side. Fine mohair wigs were used, and the middle and fourth fingers were sewn together. Look for the factory stamp on the foot, though paper labels were also used. Dolls under 10" are known as mascots and usually sell for $150.00 to $200.00. The Lenci factory continues today, producing dolls of the same high quality. Values are for dolls in near mint condition — no moth holes, very little fading.

Aviator, girl w/felt helmet, all orig, 18", NM, minimum 3,200.00
Baby, all orig, 15", NM 2,100.00
Boy, side part, all orig, 17", NM, minimum 1,900.00
Child, swivel head, c/m, OC: dress & rain clothes, 16" 800.00
Indian lady w/papoose, all orig, 17", NM 4,200.00
Mascot, all orig, 8", NM 325.00
Shirley Temple type, all orig, 22", NM 1,850.00
Smoking doll, pnt eyes, all orig, 24", NM, minimum 2,000.00
Teenager, long legs, all orig, 15", NM, minimum 1,100.00

Liddle Kiddles

From 1966 to 1971, Mattel produced Liddle Kiddle dolls ranging in size from ¾" to 4". They were all poseable and had rooted hair that could be restyled. There were various series of the dolls, among them Animiddles, Zoolery Jewelry Kiddles, extraterrestrials, and Sweet Treets, as well as many accessories. To learn more about these dolls, we recommend *Liddle Kiddles, Identification and Value Guide,* by our advisor for this category, Paris Langford, who is listed in the Directory under Louisianna. Please send SASE for information.

Babe Biddle, brn hair, yel car, 1966-67, 3", NM complete **55.00**
Beach Buggy, pk plastic & vinyl, 1967, 5½x5x6", NM **25.00**
Beddy-Bye Biddle, w/robe/bed/etc, Sears, 1967, 3", NM **70.00**
Bunson Bernie, fire chief w/engine, 1966-67, 3", NM complete ...**50.00**
Cherry Blossom Skediddle, blk hair, 1969-70, 4", NM complete ..**85.00**
Cinderella Palace Playset, Sears Exclusive, 1967, NM complete .**150.00**
Funny Bunny Kiddle, pk, 1968-69, 3¾", NM complete **20.00**
Greta Griddle, blond, w/table & chairs, 1966, 3½", NM complete ..**55.00**
Heart Necklace, 1½" doll on gold-tone chain, NM complete **100.00**
Heart Pin, 1½" doll w/crown in pin, 1968-70, NM **25.00**
Heather Hiddlehorse, w/horse, 1969-70, 4", NM complete **75.00**
Lady Silver, blond w/cup & saucer, 1970-71, 3½", NM complete ..**100.00**
Lenore Limousine, blond w/car, 1969-70, 2⅞", NM complete **55.00**
Lickety Spliddle & Her Traveliddles, 1968-69, 4", NM complete ..**50.00**
Liddle Biddle Peep, blond w/sheep, 1967-68, 3½", NM complete ..**100.00**
Liddle Diddle, baby in crib, 1955-67, 2⅞", NM complete **50.00**
Liddle Kiddles Club Case, 1966, 12x6x9", NM **25.00**
Liddle Kiddles 3-Story House, 1969, 17x11½x7", NM **45.00**
Liddle Red Riding Hiddle, w/book, 1967-68, 3½", NM complete ..**100.00**
Lolli-Grape Lollipop, 1969-70, 2", NM complete **35.00**
Loretta Locket, gold locket w/bl jewels, 1969, NM complete **25.00**
Lottie Locket, orange fr locket w/pk jewels, NM complete **25.00**
Mattel's Liddle Kiddles Sticker Fun, Whitman, 1966, M **55.00**
Nappytime Baby, 1970, 2½", NM complete **50.00**
Rah-Rah Skediddle, blond, Mattel, 1969-70, 4", NM complete ...**65.00**
Romeo & Juliet, Storybook Sweethearts, 1969-70, NM complete ...**75.00**
Rosebud Kologne, red hair, in bottle, 1968-69, 2", NM complete ...**25.00**
Sheila Skediddle, brn hair, 1968-70, 4", NM complete **25.00**
Shirley Strawberry Kola, w/bottle, 1968-69, 2", NM complete **35.00**
Sizzly Friddle, blond w/barbeque, 1967, 3", NM complete **75.00**
Sleeping Biddle, chaise & story book, '68, 3½", NM complete ..**100.00**
Slipsy Sliddle, blond w/slide & tree, 1968, 3½", NM complete **75.00**
Snap-Happy Patio, 1969, 7-pc set, NM **15.00**
Surfy Skiddle, blond w/surfboard/palm/etc, 1963, 3", NM complete ..**75.00**
Telly Viddle, brunette, w/TV set, 1968, 3½", NM complete **75.00**
Tiny Tiger Animiddle, 2-pc tiger suit, 1969-70, NM complete **30.00**
Train Case, wht vinyl w/zipper, 1966, 5½x3¼x4", NM **25.00**
Trikey Triddle, redhead w/trike, 1967, 2⅞", NM complete **75.00**
Tutti Frutti Kone, w/cone, 1969-70, 2", NM complete **35.00**
Zoolery Kiddles Frame-Tray Puzzle, Whitman, 1969, 14½x11½", M **100.00**

Madame Alexander

Beatrice Alexander founded the Alexander Doll Company in 1923 by making an all-cloth, oil-painted face, Alice in Wonderland doll. With the help of her three sisters, the company prospered; and by the late 1950s there were over six hundred employees making Madame Alexander dolls. The company still produces these lovely dolls today. For more information, refer to *Madame Alexander Collector's Doll Price Guide* by Linda Crowsey.

Active Miss, hp, Violet/Cissy, 1954 only, 18" **850.00**
Agatha, hp, Wendy Ann, blk & floral gown, #00308, 8", minimum .**1,250.00**

Alexander-Kin, str-leg walker, all orig, 1955 only, 7½-8", MIB .**375.00**
Ballerina, compo, Little Betty, 1935-41, 9" **350.00**
Bessy Bell, plastic/vinyl, Mary Ann, #1565, 1988, 14" **70.00**
Bobby, hp, Wendy Ann, #347, 1957 only, 8" **550.00**
Bobby (Bobbie) Soxer, Disney, 1990-91, 8" **165.00**
Bride, hp, Cissette, tulle gown, short veil, 1957, 10" **350.00**
Carmen, compo, Wendy Ann, extra makeup, 1939-42, 21" **1,400.00**
Cinderella, hp, Margaret, 1950-51, 18" **750.00**
Cissette, hp, beauty queen w/trophy, 1961 only, 10-11" **300.00**

Cissy, Queen Elizabeth II, jointed elbows and knees, EX face color, original gown, 20", MIB, $1,000.00.

Photo courtesy McMasters Auctions

Coco, plastic/vinyl, sheath ball gown, 1966, 21", minimum **2,000.00**
Confederate Officer, hp, Wendy Ann, 1990-91, 12" **80.00**
Dionne Quint, compo toddler, 1938-39, 20", single doll **700.00**
Dutch, compo, Tiny Betty, 1935-39, 7" **300.00**
Elise, hp/vinyl, 1-pc arms/legs, jtd ankles/knees, 1961-62, 17" **275.00**
Farmer's Daughter, Enchanted Doll House, 1991, 8" **125.00**
France, compo, Tiny Betty, 1936-43, 7" **275.00**
Godey Bride, hp, Margaret, 1950-51, 18" **1,100.00**
Hawaiian, hp, bend knee, Wendy Ann, #722, 1966-69, 8" **400.00**
Hiawatha, hp, Wendy Ann, #720, 1967-69, 8" **375.00**
Indian Boy, hp, bend-knee, Wendy Ann, #720, 1966 only, 8" ...**400.00**
Italy, hp, bend-knee walker, Wendy Ann, #393, 1961-65, 8" **125.00**
Klondike Kate, hp, Cissette, 1963 only, 10", minimum **1,400.00**
Laurie (Little Men), hp, bend-knee, Wendy Ann, 1966-72, 8" ..**165.00**
Little Devil, hp, 1992-93 only, 8" **60.00**
Little Genius, compo/cloth, 1935-40, 1942-46, 12-14", ea **125.00**
Little Women (Meg, Jo, Amy or Beth), cloth, 1930-36, 16", ea .**625.00**
Madame Butterfly, Marshall Fields, 1990, 10" **125.00**
Maggie, hp, 1948-54, 20-21" **700.00**
Maria of Sound of Music, Elise or Polly, sailor suit, 17" **475.00**
Marilla, Ann of Gr Gables series, #261-168, 10" **85.00**
Melanie, compo, Wendy Ann, 1945-47, 21", minimum **2,300.00**
Melanie, hp/vinyl, Cissy, lace/satin dress, 1961, 21", minimum ..**975.00**
Miss USA, hp, bend-knee, Wendy Ann, #728, 1966-68, 8" **325.00**
Muffin, cloth, 1966 only, 19" **125.00**
Nina Ballerina, compo, Tiny Betty, 1940, 7" **300.00**
Ophelia, Nancy Drew, 1992, 12" **115.00**
Pinky, cloth, 1940s, 16" **475.00**
Pocahontas, hp, Wendy Ann, w/baby, #721, 1967-70, 8" **400.00**
Princess Elizabeth, compo, Tiny Betty, 1937-39, 7" **350.00**
Pumpkin, cloth/vinyl, 1967-76, 22" **125.00**
Quiz-Kin, hp, bald head, Wendy Ann, romper only, 1953, 8" **475.00**
Red Riding hood, compo, Little Betty, 1939-40, 9" **300.00**
Robin Hood, Wendy Ann, #446, 1988-90, 8" **60.00**
Romeo, compo, Wendy Ann, 1949, 18", minimum **1,385.00**
Scarlett O'Hara, compo, Tiny Betty, 1937-42, 7" **450.00**
Scarlett O'Hara, hp, bend-knee, #760, 1963, 8", minimum **650.00**
Sleeping Beauty, compo, Princess Elizabeth, 1938-40, 15-16" **450.00**

So Big, cloth/vinyl, pnt eyes, 1968-75, 22" **225.00**
Special Girl, cloth/compo, 1942-46, 23-34", minimum **500.00**
Sugar Darlin', cloth/vinyl, 1964 only, 14-18", from $75 to **95.00**
Tin Woodsman, #432, 1993, 8" **60.00**
Tippi Ballerina, Collector United, 1988, ltd ed, 8" **400.00**
Tyler, Julia; President's Ladies, Martha, 1979-81 ....**125.00**
Victorian Skater, Cissette, #1155, 10" **125.00**
Wendy's Best Friend Maggie, club members only, 1994, 8" **125.00**
Wilson, Edith; Presidents' Ladies, Mary Ann, 1988 ....**115.00**
Yugoslavia, hp, bend-knee, Wendy Ann, #789, 1968-72, 8" **100.00**

Papier-Mache

Clown, pnt features, 5-pc body, o/ or c/m, OC, 9" **265.00**
French, solid dome, nailed-on wig, teeth, glass eyes, RpC, 15" ..**1,350.00**
French/French type, o/m w/bamboo teeth, glass eyes, RpC, 15" .**1,400.00**
German, molded hair, pnt eyes, c/m, RpC, 1870-1900, 23" **475.00**
M&S Superior, ShHd, molded hair, pnt eyes, RpC, 16" **400.00**
Motschmann type, wood & twill bodies, glass eyes, c/m, RpC, 16" .**700.00**
Trn ShHd, solid dome, glass eyes, c/m, compo lower arms, RpC, 18" ..**775.00**
1840s-50s, wooden limbs, long curls, EX clothes, 14" **650.00**
1920s & on, cloth body, bright coloring, wigged, EX clothes, 9" ..**70.00**

Parian

Bald solid-dome head, ear details, takes wigs, 1850s, RpC, 14" ...**775.00**
Man or boy, parted hair, cloth body, shirt & tie, 16" **900.00**
Molded hat, blond or blk hair, pnt eyes, 15" **2,200.00**
Molded head band, Alice, RpC, 14" **400.00**
Molded necklace, glass eyes, p/e, RpC, 21", minimum **2,500.00**
Plain, no decor in hair or on shoulders, RpC, 10" **175.00**

Schoenhut

Albert Schoenhut left Germany in 1866 to go to Pennsylvania to work as a repairman for toy pianos. He eventually applied his skills to wooden toys and later designed an all-wood doll which he patented on January 17, 1911. These uniquely jointed dolls were painted with enamels and came with a metal stand. Some of the later dolls had stuffed bodies, voice boxes, and hollow heads. Due to the changing economy and fierce competition, the company closed in the mid-1930s.

Baby, bent-limb body, pnt hair, decal eyes, OC, 12" **525.00**
Boy, cvd & pnt hair, bl pnt eyes, c/m, scuffed, RpC, 17" **2,600.00**
Boy, cvd hair, pnt eyes, walker, nude, 16½", VG **2,800.00**
Child, cvd hair, molded ribbon, c/m, OC, 14" **2,500.00**
Compo, molded curls, Patsy-style body, label, OC, 13" **1,600.00**
Dolly face, o/c/m w/teeth, pnt eyes, OC, 14" **675.00**
Girl, brn decal eyes, o/c/m w/4 teeth, RpC, 17", EX **625.00**
Girl, brn pnt eyes, brn hh wig, orig dress, 15", EX **500.00**
Girl, intaglio eyes, pouty mouth, rpl wig, rpt, RpC, 21½" **785.00**
Girl, pnt eyes, 4 pnt teeth, cvd hair, rpt, RpC, 16" **700.00**
Pouty, wooden SkHd, intaglio/e, c/m, rpl wig, Pat...'11, 16" **750.00**
Toddler, OC, 12" **850.00**
Tootsie Wootsie, pnt hair, o/c/m w/tongue/teeth, OC, 14" **2,100.00**
Wood & compo, intaglio eyes, fully jtd, OC, 19", EX **1,400.00**

SFBJ

By 1895 Germany was producing dolls at much lower prices than the French dollmakers could, so to save the doll industry, several leading French manufacturers united to form one large company. Bru, Raberry and Delphieu, Pintel and Godshaux, Fleischman and Bodel, Jumeau, and many others united to form the company Society Francaise de Fabrication de Bebes et Jouets (SFBJ).

Tete Jumeau, p/e, o/m w/teeth, o/c/e, jtd wrists, 22" **2,000.00**
20, molded pnt shoes & eyes, 5-pc body, Paris/12, 10" **365.00**
215, bsk swivel on compo, c/m, inset eyes, 15" **1,800.00**
227, brn swivel closed dome head, animal skin wig, 15" **1,900.00**
227, closed dome, o/m, inset eyes, pnt hair, 15" **2,100.00**
229, compo w/swivel head, o/c/m, inset eyes, 18" **5,000.00**
230, bsk SkHd, pwt eyes, o/m/teeth, jtd wood/compo, wig, RpC, 24" ..**1,000.00**
230, compo walker, p/e, o/m, inset eyes, 16" **1,600.00**
235, closed dome, molded hair, o/c/m & eyes, 16" **1,700.00**
236, laughing Jumeau, o/m, o/c/e, dbl chin, 13" **1,300.00**
236, laughing Jumeau, o/m, o/c/e, dbl chin, 20" **2,200.00**
238, compo w/swivel head, o/m, inset eyes, Paris/6, 15" **3,800.00**
239, Poulbot, c/m, street urchin, red wig, 17" **9,500.00**
245, boy, o/c/m, lg glass googly eyes, pnt shoes, 8" **1,400.00**
247, toddler, o/c/m w/2 inset teeth, 20" **2,900.00**
247, Twirp, SkHd, o/c/m & eyes, 2 teeth, 21" **3,000.00**
252, pouty, c/m, inset eyes, papier-mache body, 11" **2,800.00**
252, pouty, c/m, inset eyes, papier-mache body, 22" **7,800.00**
266, character, bsk head, closed dome, o/c/m, 20" **4,200.00**
301, bsk SkHd on compo, o/m, inset eyes, 22" **1,200.00**
301, bsk SkHd on compo, o/m, inset eyes, 28" **1,700.00**
60, French WWI nurse, 5-pc body, SFBJ/13/0, 8½" **475.00**
60, o/m w/teeth, o/c/e, hh wig, RpC, 12" **450.00**
60, SkHd, compo w/str legs, o/m, curved arms, 15" **650.00**

Shirley Temple

Prices are suggested for dolls complete and in mint conditon. Add up to 25% (depending on her outfit) if mint with box. A played-with doll in only very good condition would be worth only about half of listed values.

Bsk, 6", pnt, molded hair, Japan **250.00**
Celluloid, 5", Japan **185.00**
Celluloid, 8", Japan **245.00**
Compo, 7-8", Japan **300.00**

Photo courtesy McMasters Auctions

Composition, 11", blue tin sleep eyes, open mouth with teeth, five-piece composition body, in original Texas Ranger outfit with replaced pin, $950.00.

Compo, 11", 1934 to late '40s **900.00**
Compo, 13" **700.00**
Compo, 16", Germany, o/c/e, o/m smile, 1936, minimum **600.00**
Compo, 17-18" **950.00**

Compo, 20" 1,100.00
Compo, 25", cowgirl 1,500.00
Plastic/vinyl, 12", 1982-83 ....40.00
Plastic/vinyl, 8", 1982-83 ....30.00
Vinyl, 12", 1950s 225.00
Vinyl, 15", 1950s 265.00
Vinyl, 16", 1973 ....125.00
Vinyl, 17", Montgomery Ward, 1972 ....165.00
Vinyl, 17", 1950s 325.00
Vinyl, 19", 1950s 400.00
Vinyl, 36", 1950s 1,600.00

Simon and Halbig

Simon and Halbig was one of the finest German makers to operate during the 1870s into the 1930s. Due to the high quality of the makers, their dolls still command large prices today. During the 1890s a few Simon & Halbig heads were used by a French maker, but these are extremely rare and well marked S&H.

Baby Blanche, SkHd, o/m baby, S&H, 16" 600.00
Baby Blanche, SkHd, o/m baby, S&H, 21" 950.00
Handwerck, SkHd, o/m, 1893, 16" 450.00
Handwerck, SkHd, o/m, 1895, G/S&H/1, 16" 450.00
Handwerck, SkHd, o/m, 1895, G/S&H/1, 16" 450.00
1079, Skhd, o/c/e, o/m w/4 teeth, SH DEP 15, RpC, 31" 900.00
1080, ShHd, o/c/e, o/m w/4 teeth, p/e, hh wig, SH 12 DEP, 29" ..600.00
1159, SkHd, adult, 1905, G/Simon & Halbig/S&H7, 18" 1,900.00
1159, SkHd, adult, 1905, G/Simon & Halbig/S&H7, 24" 2,600.00
1249, Santa, bsk head, jtd compo, o/m, o/c/e, p/e, 20" 1,400.00
1299, SkHd, o/c/e, o/m w/teeth, jtd compo, S&H 8½, 20½" ..1,200.00
159, SkHd, o/m, Simon & Halbig, 16" 550.00
282, SkHd, o/m, S&H, 18" 650.00
50, SkHd, c/m, Simon & Halbig, 16" 1,800.00
540, SkHd, o/m, G/Halbig/S&H, 16" 600.00
570, SkHd, o/m, Halbig S&H/G, 18" 700.00
670, SkHd, o/m, Simon & Halbig, 16" 600.00
719, SkHd, c/m, S&H DEP, 16" 2,300.00
759, SkHd, o/m, brn, S 10 H, DEP, rare, 20" 8,500.00
939, SkHd, c/m, S 11H DEP, 17" 2,700.00
940, SkHd, closed dome, o/c/m, S 2 H, 26" 3,600.00
945, SkHd, o/m, S 2 H DEP, 16" 2,200.00
949, SkHd, o/c/e, c/m, jtd compo, RpC, 15" 1,900.00

Steiner

Jules Nicholas Steiner established one of the earliest French manufactoring companies (making dishes and clocks) in 1855. He began with mechanical dolls with bisque heads, open mouths with two rows of bamboo teeth, and his patents grew to include walking and talking dolls. In 1880 he registered a patent for a doll with sleep eyes. This doll could be put to sleep by turning a rod that operated a wire attached to its eyes.

A Series, Le Parisien, SkHd, brn set eyes, c/m, p/e, jtd, 11½" .1,850.00
A Series Child, cb pate, c/m, pwt eyes, jtd, RpC, 29" 7,500.00
A Series Child, cb pate, c/m, pwt eyes, jtd, RpC, 9" 3,100.00
A Series Le Parisien, c/m, 1892, RpC, 10" 2,600.00
A Series Le Parisien, o/m, RpC, 23" 2,500.00
B Series, c/m, pwt eyes, jtd, RpC, 29" 8,900.00
Bourgoin, c/m, 1870s, RpC, 17" 5,200.00
Bourgoin, wire-eye, c/m, jtd, RpC, 18" 5,600.00
C Series, o/m w/teeth, pwt eyes, RpC, 23" 6,200.00
Infant, bsk head, molded hair, o/c/e, c/m, 9", EX 250.00

Uneeda

Baby Dollikins, vinyl & hp, jtd body, 1960, 21", MIB 45.00
Blabby, vinyl & hp, 1962+, 14", MIB 28.00
Dollikin, multi-jtd, 1960s, 20", MIB 50.00
Freckles, ventriloquist's doll, vinyl head, 1973, 30", MIB 70.00
Magic Meg, vinyl & plastic, grows hair, 16", MIB 25.00

Vogue

This is the company that made the Ginny doll. Composition was used during the '40s, but vinyl was the preferred material throughout the decade of the '50s. An original mint-condition composition Ginny would be worth a minimum of $450.00 on the market today (played-with about $90.00). The last Ginny came out in 1969. Another Vogue doll that is becoming very collectible is Jill, whose values are steadily climbing. For more information, we recommend *Collector's Guide to Vogue Dolls* by Judith Izen and Carol Stover. Our advisor for Jill dolls is Bonnie Groves; she is listed in the Directory under Texas.

Toddles-Ginny, composition, eyes painted to the side, bent right arm, original tagged clothes, M, $375.00.

Photo courtesy Pat Smith

Baby Dear One, 1973, 25", MIB 175.00
Boy & Girl Toodles, compo, complete & all orig in trunk 450.00
Fairy Godmother, Meyer's Collectibles, 1986, MIB 155.00
Ginny, hp, jtd walker, o/c/e, 1957, 8", M 150.00
Ginny, hp, molded lashes, walker, 1954-57, OC, minimum value ..300.00
Ginny, hp, pnt lashes, strung, ca 1953, 8", MIB 325.00
Ginny, soft vinyl & hp, walker, rooted hair, 1963+, 8", MIB 50.00
Ginny, vinyl by Dakin, 1986+, 8", MIB 50.00
Ginny as Davy Crockett, 1953, 8" 400.00
Ginny Baby, 12", MIB 40.00
Ginny International, vinyl, 1977, OC, minimum value 45.00
Jan, vinyl, basic bra & girdle, VG 54.00
Jan/Jill desk & chair, gr, VG, from $50 to 135.00
Jan/Jill wardrobe, gr, VG, from $50 to 135.00
Jeff, vinyl, bl suit 10", VG 125.00
Jeff, vinyl, in shorts outfit, 10", VG, from $65 to 85.00
Jill, hp, cotton street dress, all orig, 10½", EX, $85 to 135.00
Jill, hp, in formal, 10½", EX, from $150 to 200.00
Jill, hp, leotard, 1957, 10½", MIB 250.00
Jill, hp, nude, haircut, 10½", G- 20.00
Jill, vinyl, History Land, all orig, EX, from $85 to 200.00
Jill bed, VG, from $50 to 85.00
Jill chromium heart pendant, MIP, from $50 to 150.00
Jill cotton dress, EX 35.00
Jill Dream Cozy Bed Set (bedding), MIP, from $35 to 50.00
Jill dress, semiformal, MIP 50.00
Jill shoes, MIP 25.00
Lil Imp, 10½", MIB 65.00
Rose Queen, Modern Doll convention, 1986, MIB 275.00
Toodles, compo, dressed as Hansel, 1940s, 8" 300.00

Toodles Baby, compo, pnt eyes, orig dress/coat/bonnet, 7" **265.00**
Wee Imp, hp, red wig, gr eyes, freckles, 1960, 8", MIB **375.00**
Wee Imp, hp, red wig, OC, 8" **360.00**

Wax, Poured Wax

Alice headband hairdo, RpC, 14" **475.00**
Common type, worn wax, RpC, 12" **150.00**
Lady, poured head & limbs, glass eyes, cloth body, RpC, 24" ..**3,600.00**
Lever-operated eyes, 1850s, RpC, 17" **950.00**
Molded hat, RpC, 16" **3,200.00**
Over compo, sleep eyes, cloth body, wood limbs, 1860s, RpC, 16" ..**850.00**
Poured, bl o/c/e, mohair wig, RpC, 15", EX **400.00**
Poured head & limbs, glass eyes, cloth body, RpC, 16" **1,400.00**
Poured head & limbs, glass eyes, cloth body, RpC, 22" **1,900.00**
Poured over compo, ShHd, brn o/c/e, c/m, wig, OC, 24", EX **300.00**
2-faced, laughing & crying, Bartenstein, 1890s, RpC, 16" **950.00**

Door Knockers

Door knockers, those charming precursors of the doorbell, come in an intriguing array of shapes and styles. The very rare ones come from England. Cast-iron examples made in this country were often produced in forms similar to the more familiar doorstop figures.

Our listings are prices realized at auction. Most were in exceptional condition. To evaluate a doorstoop with only excellent paint, deduct at least 35% from the values given for one in near-mint condition. If the paint is only very good, values drop dramatically.

Butterfly, pnt CI, Judd Co, 4½x4¼", EX **440.00**
Butterfly, pnt CI, Waverly...Pat Apld For, 3½x2¾", NM **440.00**
Butterfly on flowers, CI, mc pnt, 4x2½", NM **635.00**
Cardinal, pnt CI, on twigs, rare, 5x3", M **285.00**
Cherries, pnt CI, leaves bkplate, Judd, #607, 3¼x2⅞", EX **330.00**
Clipper ship, pnt CI, on waves, 3⅞x2⅞", M **100.00**
Colonial woman, pnt CI, Waverly Studios, 4½x2¾", NM **145.00**
Couple kissing against roses, brass, 5½" **65.00**
Daisies tied w/bow, pnt CI, 4½x2¾", VG+ **105.00**
Flattened ball amid scrolls, CI, 18th C, 12¾x9¾", EX **130.00**
Flower basket, pnt CI, country style, unmk, 3½x3", NM **55.00**

Flower basket, multicolor
on white-painted cast iron,
#812, NM, $100.00.

George Washington, pnt CI, Waverly..., 4½x2¾", EX **85.00**
Girl knocking on door, pnt CI, Grace Dayton, Hubley, 3½", EX ...**580.00**
Ivy Pot, pnt CI, Hubley #123, EX **160.00**
Lady's portrait, brass, EX patina, 8" **125.00**
Lady w/bonnet in profile, pnt CI, Judd Co #619, 4x3", M **300.00**
Lion head, bronze, 9" dia **85.00**
Morning glory, pnt CI, Judd Co #608, 3¼x2¾", M **360.00**
Parakeet sitting in circle, CI, gr & yel pnt, EX **135.00**
Parrot, pnt CI, mc pnt, on branch, Hubley, 4¾x2¾", NM **125.00**

Pear, pnt CI, flower bkplate, rare, 4¼x3", M **360.00**
Rooster, pnt CI, realistic, rare, 4½x3", M **495.00**
Rooster, wht variation, 4½x3", EX **330.00**
Rose, pnt CI, detailed, touchup on bkplate, 5x3", NM **495.00**
Roses (3) tied w/bl ribbon, pnt CI, Judd Co, #626, 4x3", EX **55.00**
Victorian cameo, orig pnt on CI, EX **225.00**
Wm Wadsworth bust w/church & poem in bk, brass, 4" **75.00**
Woodpecker, pnt CI, tree bkplate, Hubley #251, 3¾", NM **330.00**
Zinnias, pnt CI, mk Pat Pend LVL, rare, 3¾x2½", NM **550.00**

Doorstops

Although introduced in England in the mid-1800s, cast-iron doorstops were not made to any great extent in this country until after the Civil War. Once called 'door porters,' their function was to keep doors open to provide better ventilation. They have been produced in many shapes and sizes, both dimensional and flat-backed, and in the past few years have become a popular, yet affordable collectible. While cast-iron examples are the most common, brass, wood, and chalk were also used. An average price is in the $100.00 to $200.00 range, though some are valued at more than $400.00. Doorstops retained their usefulness and appeal well into the '30s.

The prices below reflect market values in the East where doorstops are at a premium. For other areas of the country, it may be necessary to adjust prices down about 25%. In the listings below, when no condition code is present, items are assumed to be in excellent original condition, flat-backed unless noted full-figured, and cast iron unless another material is mentioned. For further information we recommend *Doorstops, Identification and Values*, by Jeanne Bertoia.

Key:
B&H — Bradley & Hubbard   ff — full figured

Ann Hathaway Cottage, Hubley, 3-D, 2 joined pcs, M **600.00**
Bathing Beauties, Hubley, sgn by Fish, 10⅞x5¼", EX **1,200.00**
Beagle Pup, ff, realistic, unmk, 8x7½", EX **965.00**
Bellhop, bl suit, Judd Co, 8⅞x4⅝", VG **165.00**
Bird of Paradise, long swirling tail, mk LA-CS 765, 13⅜x7", EX ..**880.00**
Boston Terrier, orig leather collar, 9x8", M **220.00**
Boxer, ff, realistic, Hubley, 8½x9", NM **470.00**
Boy in Tuxedo, wood wedge bk, Judd Co, #1262, 7¼x4⅜", EX .**525.00**
Boy w/Fruit Basket, lav pants & hat, EX **330.00**
Boy Whistling, ff, pot metal/CI, #4298, 10x5½", VG+ **425.00**
Calla Lilies, wht in bl vase, Hubley #343 Made in USA, 7¼", M ..**440.00**
Cape Cod Cottage, Eastern Specialty Mfg, 5¾x8¾", M **330.00**
Cat Scratch Fever, girl w/cat, sgn A Diouhy, Judd #1271, 8¾", EX .**1,200.00**
Charleston Dancers, Deco, sgn Fish, Hubley, 8⅞x5⅝", VG **825.00**
Chicken Snatcher, man running w/chicken, rare, 7½x8¾", EX .**1,350.00**
Clown, wht collar red suit, 2-sided, 10x4½", NM **1,500.00**
Cockatoo, bright colors, unmk, 11¾x5½", M **165.00**
Cockatoo, LACS711, old rpt, 8½x6½" **165.00**
Colonial Lawyer, Waverly Studios, Pat Applied For, 9⅝x5¼", M .**745.00**
Colonial Woman w/Fan, Waverly Studios, Trade WS Mark Pat..., EX **110.00**
Cosmos, pk & bl flowers in wht vase, Hubley, 17¾x10¼", NM .**210.00**
Cottage, 3-D, wht w/red roof, rpt gr base, 4⅝x7½", EX **110.00**
Dancing Girl, skirt held wide, Nat'l Foundry, 9½x6¾", EX **1,200.00**
Deco Lady, holding skirt wide, Judd Co, mk #1251, 9x7½", EX **580.00**
Difficult Lie, overhead swinging golfer, Hubley #238, 10x7", EX ..**745.00**
Duck Pecking Ladybug, wht overpnt, 7½x10½" **250.00**
Ducks, pr preening, sgn Fred Everette, Hubley, 8¼x6¼", EX ...**495.00**
Dutch Girl, wood wedge bk, Judd, #1255, 7⅛x5¾", M **140.00**
Elephant, realistic, B&H #7799, 11¾x10", EX **300.00**
Fawn, Deco style, mk Taylor Cook c 1930 No 6, 10x6", EX **300.00**

Flower, yel mum-like flowers, wedge bk, LVL Pat..., 9¼x6" **465.00**
Flower Basket, lg & heavy w/fine details & pnt, 11x10¾", M .**1,265.00**
Flower Basket, w/angel on basket, fine color, 11½x7", EX **230.00**
Flower Basket w/Bowed Hdl, mc & wht, Judd, 10x6½", EX **330.00**
Flowers, mixed bouquet in wht basket, unmk, 9¾x6¼", NM **415.00**
Footmen, Deco style, sgn Fish, Hubley, 9⅛x6", VG+ **525.00**
Fruit Bowl, Hubley #456, 7x6½", EX **250.00**
Game Cock, ff, Hubley, rare, 6¾x7", M **1,075.00**
Geese, 3 facing left, sgn Fred Everette, Hubley, 8x8", EX **470.00**
Geisha, ff, mc kimono, unmk, 10¼x3½", EX **550.00**
Gladiolus, mc flowers in wht vase, Hubley, #489, 10x8", EX **250.00**
Jonquils, bright colors, Hubley, 7½x8", M **330.00**
Jungle Boy, w/leopard skin & gr turban, 12¾x12", EX **1,595.00**
Lil Bo Peep, ruffled skirt, 6¾x5", EX **275.00**
Little Girl Holding Hat, Pat Appld for Trad WS Mark, M **1,650.00**
Maiden, girl in pk w/flower basket, 8⅞x3¾", EX **200.00**
Mallard Duck, realistic, on rippled water, unmk, 6½x11", EX ...**1,540.00**
Man w/Flowers, chubby, holds 2 bouquets, #821, 9x5¾", NM **440.00**
Messenger Boy, Deco style, sgn Fish, Hubley, 10x5⅜", VG+ ..**1,200.00**
Minuet Girl, pastel clothes, Judd, #1278, 8½x5", EX **195.00**
Narcissus, Hubley #266, 7¼x6¾", NM **385.00**
Old Salt, ff, man in yel slicker, 11x4⅛", M **330.00**
Owl, perched on limb, 8-sided gr base, unmk, 9x5½", EX **550.00**
Parrot, Deco style, Taylor Cook c 1930 No 4, 10½x4⅞", EX **435.00**
Parrot in Medallion, gold scrollwork, #145, 9½x5", EX **120.00**
Pekingese, ff, Hubley, rare, 9x14½", NM **2,850.00**
Penguin, ff, realistic pnt, rare, 9½x4", EX **770.00**
Penguins, Twin; blk & yel, minor touchup, 7¼x7½", EX **495.00**
Persian Cat, ff, Hubley, 8½x6½", VG **195.00**
Pheasant, realistic, sgn Fred Everett, Hubley, 8½x7½", NM **300.00**
Pirate w/Sack, red & blk, 11⅞x9⅝", EX **770.00**
Poinsettia, in ivory pot, 9¾x4⅞", M **275.00**
Poppies in Clay Pot, Hubley #330, M **300.00**
Puppies in Basket, 3 w/paws over side, Wilton...PA, 7x7⅜", EX ..**400.00**
Putting Golfer, brns & grs, Hubley, 8⅜x7", EX **360.00**
Rabbit w/Top Hat, Albany Foundry #94, 9⅞x4¾", M **525.00**
Reaching Child, nude baby's bkside, 17x7", EX **2,300.00**

Rhumba Dancer, EX original paint, 11⅛x6⅝", $475.00.

Roses (3) in Vase, National Foundry, #145, wedge bk, 10½x7", EX **770.00**
Sealyham, ff, realistic, Hubley, 9x14", EX **2,500.00**
Snooper, man w/flashlight & magnifying glass, 2-sided, 13¼", EX ..**825.00**
Spanish Guitarist, ff, mk LVL Pat Pending, EX **800.00**
Swallows, pr on berry branches, Hubley #480, 8½x7½", M **450.00**
Swan, 2-sided, Spencer Guifford CT, rare, 8x13½", EX **3,625.00**
Tiger, man in top hat, sgn Fish, Hubley, rare, 9⅜x4¼", EX **2,300.00**
Tiger Lilies, Hubley, #472, 10½x6", NM **250.00**
Windmill, amid cottages, AM Greenblatt...1926, 9⅞x11½", EX ...**550.00**
Wineman, man w/many bottles, ff, partial rpt, rare, 9½x7" **900.00**

Woman Holding Hat, ff, Southern belle, 8x4½", VG+ **415.00**
Woman w/Muff, bonnet & long coat, unmk, 11½x6½", VG **210.00**
Woman w/Parasol, sgn Sarah Symmons, 12x6¼", EX **495.00**
Yawning Pup, ff, whimsical, unmk, very rare, 7x5", EX **385.00**
Zinnias, Hubley, mk 316 Made in USA, 9¾x8½", M **385.00**

Dorchester Pottery

Taking its name from the town in Massachusetts where it was organized in 1895, the Dorchester Pottery Company made primarily utilitarian wares, though other types of items were made as well. By 1940 a line of decorative pottery was introduced, some of which was painted by hand with scrollwork or themes from nature. The buildings were destroyed by fire in the late 1970s, and the pottery was never rebuilt. In the listings that follow, the decorations described are all in cobalt unless otherwise noted. Our advisor for this category is Dale MacLean; he is listed in the Directory under Massachusetts.

Key: CAH — Charles A. Hill (noted artist)

Bottle, scent; Whale, scroll stopper, CAH, 5" **200.00**
Bowl, Eagle & Star, Nixon Inauguration commemorative, hdls, CAH **275.00**
Bowl, Sea Horse (int), sgn CAH, 2x5½" **125.00**
Candle holder, Half Scroll, ruffled edge, CAH, 5½" **175.00**
Candy dish, Butterfly & Flower, sgn, stamped, 1½x6¼" **240.00**
Candy dish, Clown, striped rim, CAH, 4" dia **150.00**
Casserole, Pine Cone, sgn CAH, 4½x7½" **200.00**
Chamberstick, Pine Cone, sgn CAH, stamped, 1¼x5¾" **150.00**
Creamer & sugar bowl, Blueberry, CAH, 3", 3¼" **150.00**
Creamer & sugar bowl, Whale, CAH, 3", 3½", EX **200.00**
Cup, Happy Day, clown's face, All Gone in bottom, mk, 2¾" ...**100.00**
Cup & saucer, Scroll on yelware, CAH, 2¾", 6½" **75.00**
Mug, Bell, sriped hdl, paper label, 4½x3⅜" **130.00**
Mug, Captain, K Denisons, 4¾", EX **125.00**
Mug, Colonial Lace, J McCune, 4¾" **100.00**
Mug, Eight Bells, K Denisons, flake, 4¾" **125.00**
Mug, Full Scroll, CAH, 4½" **90.00**
Mug, Pine Cone, sgn CAH, stamped, 4½" **75.00**
Nut dish, Striped & Scroll, CAH, 3¾", EX **75.00**
Pitcher, water; Pine Cone, sgn RB, stamped, 7½" **250.00**
Plate, Daffodil, swirled bl ground, CAH, 7¼" **225.00**
Plate, Whale, blended bl waves, CAH, 10½" **275.00**
Plate, Whale, sgn CAH, 10¼" **275.00**
Shot pourer, Rooster, K Denisons, 2½" **75.00**
Soap holder, Colonial Lace, JM/N Ricci, 5½" **200.00**
Star dish, Pine Cone, bsk glaze, CAH, 8", EX **125.00**
Star dish, Star, geometric center, unmk, 7¾" **125.00**
Sugar bowl, Lighthouse, K Denisons, w/lid, 3½" **125.00**
Sugar bowl, Pomegranate, blended bl, sgn K Denisons, EX **125.00**
Sugar bowl, Sacred Cod, med lustre, CAH, 3x4", EX **75.00**
Sugar jar, Lace, bulbous, sgn JM, stamped, 3¼x3" **150.00**
Syrup, Half Scroll, striped hdl, w/lid, sgn, stamped, 4¾" **150.00**
Vase, Pine Cone, trumpet shape, CAH, 3½x3" **100.00**

Dorflinger

C. Dorflinger was born in Alsace, France, and came to this country when he was ten years old. When still very young, he obtained a job in a glass factory in New Jersey. As a young man, he started his own glassworks in Brooklyn, New York, opening new factories as profits permitted. During that time he made cut glass articles for many famous people including President and Mrs. Lincoln, for whom he produced a complete service of tableware with the United States Coat of Arms. In 1863 he sold the New York factories because of ill health and moved to his farm near White Mills, Pennsylvania. His health returned, and he started a plant near his home. It was there that he did much of his best work, making use of only the very finest materials. Christian died in 1915, and the plant was closed in 1921 by consent of the family.

Dorflinger glass is rare and often hard to identify. Very few pieces were marked — many only carried a small paper label which was quickly discarded.

Ice cream tray, fruit cuttings on cranberry to clear, 12", $2,000.00.

Bottle, cut, honeycomb top w/eng florals, sterling lid, 11½" **500.00**
Decanter, gr cut to clear, 6-panel neck, 9½", +4 ftd tumblers **395.00**
Epergne, strawberries/dmns/fans, 3 9" lilies+bowls+baskets, 11-pc .**5,500.00**
Plate, Colonial, 7¼" **120.00**
Vase, Kalana, lilies, 5x2" **140.00**
Vase, Kalana, poppies w/bands, ftd, 8" **265.00**
Vase, Melba w/sawtooth rim, cylindrical, 10" **225.00**

Dragon Ware

Dragon ware is fairly accessible and is still being made today. The new Dragon ware is distinguishable by the lack of detail in the dragon. In the older pieces, much care is given to the slipwork dragon's eyes, scales, and wings. In the new ware, the dragon is flat and lacks detail.

Colors are primary, referring to background color, not the color of the dragon. The primary color of a new piece has more shine than that of the older ware. Old colors are vibrant but for the most part not shiny (except for the lustre colors). New colors include green, lavender, yellow, pink, blue, pearlized, and orange as well as the classic blue/black. Old colors include orange, green, yellow, blue, pearlized, and blue/black. In addition to lustre finishes, you will find some background colors that are applied unevenly (and without shine), producing a cloud effect behind the dragon.

Many Dragon ware cups have lithophanes in the bottoms, often the face of a geisha girl. Nude lithophanes are more scarce but can sometimes be found in cups and saki cups. New pieces may also have lithophanes, but they are lacking in detail and tend to be flat.

Items listed below are unmarked unless noted otherwise. Ranges are given for pieces that are currently being produced. (Be sure to examine unmarked items well, in particular, looking for good detailing in the dragon. Remember, new pieces lack the quality of workmanship evident in items made earlier in the century and should not command the prices of the older ware, so use the low end of the range to evaluate any pieces you feel may be new.) Our advisor for this category is Suzi Hibbard; she is listed in the Directory under California.

Ashtray, tricorner, Nippon mk, 5½" **135.00**
Bowl, dessert; gray, mk Kutani **25.00**
Box, cigarette; mk MIJ **25.00**
Candy dish, orange lustre w/gold, griffin ft, 3-lobe, w/lid **50.00**
Child's cup & saucer, from $5 to **25.00**

Child's set, lustre, 1950s, mk MIJ, 15-pc, in box **125.00**
Chocolate set, bl lustre, 3-pc **55.00**
Condiment set, shakers/mustard/toothpick/plate, red, Nippon ...**175.00**
Creamer & sugar bowl, slip on gray-gr lustre w/gold, souvenir **28.00**
Cup & saucer, demitasse; orange lustre int w/bl irid, Japan **12.50**
Cup & saucer, geisha lithophane **25.00**
Cup & saucer, gr & yel cloud **20.00**
Cup & saucer, gray-bl w/pk highlights, ftd, mini, 3¼" dia **4.50**
Cup & saucer, monk, from $7.50 to **30.00**
Ferner, ftd, scalloped rim, Nippon mk, 7½" **325.00**
Humidor, gray, mk Nippon, 7" **525.00**
Incense jar, bl, mk MIJ, 5" **35.00**
Lamp, gray, 9" **125.00**
Lemon dish, red w/gray & wht dragons, loop hdl, 5½" sq **200.00**
Nut bowl, orange **25.00**
Pitcher, mini; 1¾" **10.00**
Plate, brn edge, twin T/dmn mk, 7½" **8.50**
Plate, brn on beige w/pk & bl, brn rim, Japan, 7" **12.00**
Plate, gold rim, M-in-wreath mk, 7½" **10.00**
Plate, gray w/bl/pk sprays, gold rim/trim, M-in-wreath mk, 7½" **8.50**
Plate, gray w/brn flames, wht beading, Japan, 7½" **8.50**
Plate, wht beads & lav rim, 6" **20.00**
Saki set, gr cloud, +6 cups w/lithophane, mk MIJ **60.00**
Shakers, coffeepot/teapot shape, blk, pr **15.00**
Shakers, sm, pr **12.50**
Tea set, bl/wht, dragon spouts, lithophanes, 21-pc **275.00**
Tea set, demitasse; red cloud, 15-pc **125.00**
Tea set, figures on brn w/gold, lithophane cups, Nippon, 15-pc .**350.00**
Tea set, no mk, 15-pc, from $25 to **125.00**
Teapot, blk/yel, lustre int, +cr/sug **150.00**
Teapot, gray w/dragon spout, mk MIJ **45.00**
Teapot, orange, MIJ, pot+cr/sug **55.00**
Vase, bl cloud, mk Nagoya China, 6½", pr **90.00**
Vase, gray, 6-sided, mk MIJ, 3" **17.50**
Vase, no mk, from $5 to **30.00**
Vase, orange, mk MIJ, 3" **10.00**
Vase, orange lustre int, fancy hdls, Hinode, 9x6x3½" **80.00**
Vase, rectangular, Hinode, 8¼x3½" **80.00**
Vase, sq neck/mouth, orange lustre int, brn rim, Hinode, 8¾" **80.00**
Vase, wht, 8" **25.00**
Watering can, orange, 3" **10.00**

Dresden

The term Dresden is used today to indicate the porcelains that were produced in Meissen and Dresden, Germany, from the very early 18th century well into the next. John Bottger, a young alchemist, discovered the formula for the first true porcelain in 1708 while being held a virtual prisoner at the palace in Dresden because of the King's determination to produce a superior ware. Two years later a factory was erected in nearby Meissen with Bottger as director. There fine tableware, elaborate centerpieces, and exquisite figurines with applied details were produced. In 1731, to distinguish their product from the wares of such potters as Sevres, Worcester, Chelsea, and Derby, the Meissen company adopted their famous crossed swords trademark. During the next century, several potteries were producing porcelain in the 'Meissen style' in Dresden itself. Their wares were often marked with imitations of Meissen's crossed swords.

The Carl Theime factory produced dinnerware as well as decorative pieces in the Meissen style from 1872 until 1972. Openwork pieces were their specialty. Their mark was an intertwined 'SP' with the word Dresden below. Other companies followed suit, and in 1883 began using the crown mark along with the Dresden indication. There were several variations of this mark employed over the years. Many of these companies produced Meissen-type wares well into the 20th century. See also Meissen.

Chocolate pot, floral bouquets/garlands, slim, 11¼" 200.00
Coffeepot, couples reserves, gold leaf/floral decor, 8" 200.00
Compote, couple in garden, appl flowers, rtcl rim, 6¼" 85.00
Compote, floral w/gold, pointed/rtcl rim, 9½" 220.00
Figurine, ballerina, silver gray hair, 6" 150.00
Figurine, courting couple on Fr bench, sgn, 1910, 8x9" 350.00
Figurine, courting couple on rock base w/flower basket, 12" 375.00
Figurine, gentleman in lav coat, 1800s, 8¾" 235.00
Figurine, man & lady, standing, lambs at their ft, 7", pr 400.00
Salad dish, lobster shape, floral w/gold, 2-part 625.00

Dresser Accessories

Dresser sets, ring trees, figural or satin pincushions, manicure sets — all those lovely items that graced milady's dressing table — were at the same time decorative as well as functional. Today they appeal to collectors for many reasons. The Victorian era is well represented by repousse silver-backed mirrors and brushes and pincushions that were used to display ornamental pins for the hair, hats, and scarves. The hair receiver — similar to a powder jar but with an opening in the lid — was used to hold long strands of hair retrieved from the comb or brush. These were wound around the finger and tucked in the opening to be used later for hair jewelry and pictures, many of which survive to the present day. (See Hair Weaving.)

Celluloid dresser sets were popular during the late 1800s and early 1900s. Some included manicure tools, pill boxes, and button-hooks, as well as the basic items. Because celluloid tends to break rather easily, a whole set may be hard to find today. (See also Plastics.) With the current interest in anything Art Deco, sets from the '30s and '40s are especially collectible. These may be made of crystal, Bakelite, or silver, and the original boxes just as lavishly appointed as their contents.

Box, celluloid, w/repousse, pnt lovers scene, hinged lid, sm 60.00
Brush & comb set, Geo Jenson Denmark sterling, 3-pc 400.00

Dresser set, sea green mother-of-pearl box and jar lid, pink satin jar with embossed nudes, $70.00.

Hairbrush, gilt metal w/portrait on bk, +hand mirror 230.00
Set, celluloid, landscape scenes, box+brush+comb+mirror 175.00
Set, china, yel roses, unmk Germany, 5-pc+8x11" tray 275.00
Set, Fr ivory, 10-pc, in faux snake-skin box w/silk lining 110.00
Set, pearlized gr plastic w/blk decor, 9-pc 125.00
Set, pk blown glass w/gold, 2 7" bottles+powder box 95.00
Set, vaseline glass, mk Shari, 4-pc on 2x7" tray 165.00

Dryden

Dryden Pottery was founded fifty years ago in Ellsworth, Kansas, by Jim Dryden, a WWII veteran with financing from a G.I. loan. A mention on the front page of the Wall Street Journal resulted in substantial orders from Macy's of New York and Fred Harvey Restaurants and gift shops in all the stations of the Santa Fe Railroad.

In the late 1940s and early 1950s, some six hundred stores stocked Dryden pottery. Stiff competition from occupied Japan and Europe forced wholesale prices so low that the only profit from the pottery was from direct sales to the traveling public. Tourists watched potters at work. These sales were profitable, but in 1955, the new transcontinental highway 70 through Kansas missed Ellsworth. The pottery had to move. Hot Springs, Arkansas, with its hundreds of thousands of tourists was chosen as the new location.

Since 1970 more and more of the production is wheel thrown and hand sculpted in an all-out attempt to follow the example of the world-famous Rookwood Pottery (1880 – 1967). Beautiful matt and gloss glazes plus one-of-a-kind originals make Dryden Pottery highly collectible.

Ashtray, #110, leaf, gr 20.00
Ashtray, #91, fish, gr 35.00
Ashtray, 3-leaf clover, maroon 18.00
Berry set, #C2, maroon 75.00
Boot, #19, blk & bl 30.00
Buffalo, Abilene KS 95.00
Candle holders, #42, maroon, pr 25.00
Creamer & sugar bowl, #108, Lebanon KS 45.00
Flowerpot, #6E, gr 15.00
Jug, #H3, A 1955, blk 25.00
Jug, #H4, gr 25.00
Jug, #102, Greensburg KS, yel 28.00
Jug, #8, roadrunner, maroon 25.00
Jug, KU, maroon 39.00
Mug, #1, Brookville Hotel, gr 26.00
Mug, #6, Clovis NM, gr 25.00
Pitcher, #H5, Salina KS, blk 35.00
Pitcher, #H8, gr 20.00
Pitcher, #12, Lawrence KS 45.00
Pitcher, #39, bl 30.00
Pitcher, #50, Bridal Cave, maroon 45.00
Pitcher, #8P, bbl, gr 35.00
Planter, #Y, rooster, maroon 35.00
Planter, #87, Madonna, brn 40.00
Shakers, #73, Wichita KS, pr 34.00
Tankard, #49, blk w/6 #4 tumblers 95.00
Vase, #B1, cactus, gr 25.00
Vase, #104, 4-H Shamrock 38.00
Vase, #105, brn 19.00
Vase, #21, donkey, brn 40.00
Vase, #313, elephant, Salina KS, blk 55.00
Vase, #41, gr 35.00
Vase, #6A, maroon 25.00
Vase, #7K, Bridal Cave, yel 25.00
Vase, #88, fish, gr 48.00
Vase, Hot Springs AR, brn, 15" 85.00
Vase, Hot Springs AR, pk, 6" 50.00
Vase, 7M, fish, yel 27.00
Wall pocket, #887, leaf, gr 25.00

Duncan and Miller

The firm that became known as the Duncan and Miller Glass

Company in 1900 was organized in 1874 in Pittsburgh, Pennsylvania, a partnership between George Duncan, his sons Harry and James, and his son-in-law Augustus Heisey. John Ernest Miller was hired as their designer. He is credited with creating the most famous of all Duncan's glassware lines, Three Face. (See Pattern Glass.) The George Duncan and Sons Glass Company, as it was titled, was only one of eighteen companies that merged in 1891 with U.S. Glass. Soon after the Pittsburgh factory burned in 1892, the association was dissolved, and Heisey left the firm to set up his own factory in Newark, Ohio. Duncan built his new plant in Washington, Pennsylvania, where he continued to make pressed glassware in such notable patterns as Bagware, Amberette, Duncan Flute, Button Arches, and Zippered Slash. The firm was eventually sold to U.S. Glass in Tiffin, Ohio, and unofficially closed in August 1955.

In addition to the early pressed dinnerware patterns, today's Duncan and Miller collectors enjoy searching for opalescent vases in many patterns and colors, frosted 'Satin Tone' glassware, acid-etched designs, and lovely stemware such as the Rock Crystal cuttings. Milk glass was made in limited quantity and is considered a good investment. Ruby glass, Ebony (a lovely opaque black glass popular during the '20s and '30s), and, of course, the glass animal and bird figurines are all highly valued examples of the art of Duncan and Miller.

Expect to pay at least 25% more than values listed for other colors, for ruby and cobalt, as much as 50% more in the Georgian, Pall Mall, and Sandwich lines. Pink, green, and amber Sandwich is worth approximately 30% more than the same items in crystal. Milk glass examples of American Way are valued up to 30% higher than color, 50% higher in Pall Mall. Chartreuse Canterbury is worth 10% to 20% more than crystal. Add approximately 40% to 50% to listed prices for opalescent items. Etchings, cuttings, and other decorations will increase values by about 50%. For further study we recommend *The Encyclopedia of Duncan Glass*, by Gail Krause; she is listed in the Directory under Pennsylvania. Several Duncan and Miller lines are shown in *Elegant Glassware of the Depression Era* by Gene Florence. Also refer to *Glass Animals and Figural Flower Frogs of the Depression Era* by Lee Garmon and Dick Spencer; they are both listed under Illinois. See also Glass Animals. Our advisor for this category is Roselle Schleifman; she is listed in the Directory under New York.

Canterbury, blue cup and saucer, $30.00.

Canterbury, crystal, ashtray, 5" 12.00
Canterbury, crystal, bowl, flared, 8x2½" 17.50
Canterbury, crystal, bowl, fruit; nappy, 5" 8.00
Canterbury, crystal, bowl, gardenia; 12x2¾" 30.00
Canterbury, crystal, bowl, rose; 6" 22.50
Canterbury, crystal, cigarette jar, w/lid, 4" 20.00
Canterbury, crystal, cup 10.00
Canterbury, crystal, plate, dinner; 11¼" 27.50
Canterbury, crystal, stem, cocktail; 3½-oz, 4¼" 10.00
Canterbury, crystal, top hat, 3" 15.00
Canterbury, crystal, tumbler, juice; #5115, ftd, 5-oz, 4¼" 7.50
Canterbury, crystal, urn, 4½x4½" 15.00
Canterbury, crystal, vase, oval, 4" 17.50

Caribbean, bl, bowl, hdls, 7" 45.00
Caribbean, bl, bowl, punch; 6¼-qt, 10" 450.00
Caribbean, bl, cocktail shaker, 33-oz, 9" 185.00
Caribbean, bl, ladle, punch 115.00
Caribbean, bl, pitcher, water; w/ice lip, 72-oz, 9" 550.00
Caribbean, bl, plate, 14" 65.00
Caribbean, bl, tumbler, shot glass; 2-oz, 2¼" 55.00
Caribbean, crystal, bowl, finger; 4½" 16.00
Caribbean, crystal, bowl, salad; 9" 30.00
Caribbean, crystal, candelabrum, 2-light, 4¾" 40.00
Caribbean, crystal, pitcher, milk; 16-oz, 4¾" 80.00
Caribbean, crystal, salt cellar, 2½" 10.00
Caribbean, crystal, sugar bowl 11.00
Caribbean, crystal, teacup 10.00
First Love, crystal, bowl, #115, 10x4½" 35.00
First Love, crystal, bowl, #115, 8½x4" 37.50
First Love, crystal, bowl, #6, flared rim, 11x5¼" 67.50
First Love, crystal, bowl, rose; #115, 3x5" 40.00
First Love, crystal, cheese stand, #111, 3x5¼" 25.00
First Love, crystal, comport, #111, w/lid, 8¾x5½" 125.00
First Love, crystal, honey dish, #91, 5x3" 25.00
First Love, crystal, perfume, #5200, 5" 75.00
First Love, crystal, plate, #115, 14" 50.00
First Love, crystal, plate, #30, 8½" 20.00
First Love, crystal, plate, sandwich; #111, hdls, 11" 40.00
First Love, crystal, relish, #115, hdld, 3-part, 8" 25.00
First Love, crystal, stem, cocktail; #115, 3-oz, 4¼" 22.50
First Love, crystal, tray, celery; #91, 8¾" 30.00
First Love, crystal, tray, relish; #115, 11¾" 45.00
First Love, crystal, urn, #525, 5" 37.50
First Love, crystal, vase, #506, ftd, 10" 115.00
Sandwich, crystal, ashtray, rectangular, 2½x3¾" 10.00
Sandwich, crystal, basket, w/loop hdl, 11½" 225.00
Sandwich, crystal, bonbon, ftd, w/lid, 7½" 40.00
Sandwich, crystal, bowl, fruit salad; 6" 12.00
Sandwich, crystal, bowl, nut; cupped, 11" 52.50
Sandwich, crystal, butter dish, w/lid, 1" 37.50
Sandwich, crystal, candlestick, 1-light, 4" 14.00
Sandwich, crystal, candlestick, 2-light, 5" 30.00
Sandwich, crystal, candy jar, ftd, w/lid, 8½" 55.00
Sandwich, crystal, comport, ftd, 4¼" 20.00
Sandwich, crystal, creamer, ftd, 7-oz, 4" 9.00
Sandwich, crystal, plate, deviled egg; 12" 65.00
Sandwich, crystal, stem, goblet; 9-oz, 6" 18.50
Sandwich, crystal, teacup, 6-oz 10.00
Spiral Flutes, amber, gr or pk, bowl, almond shape, 2" 12.00
Spiral Flutes, amber, gr or pk, bowl, console; cupped, 12" 30.00
Spiral Flutes, amber, gr or pk, bowl, grapefruit; 6¾" 9.00
Spiral Flutes, amber, gr or pk, bowl, vegetable; oval, 10" 45.00
Spiral Flutes, amber, gr or pk, candlestick, 11½" 110.00
Spiral Flutes, amber, gr or pk, comport, 6⅝" 17.50
Spiral Flutes, amber, gr or pk, cup, demitasse 25.00
Spiral Flutes, amber, gr or pk, cup, seafood sauce; 3x2½" 25.00
Spiral Flutes, amber, gr or pk, ice tub, hdls 50.00
Spiral Flutes, amber, gr or pk, mug, 9-oz, 7" 35.00
Spiral Flutes, amber, gr or pk, plate, dinner; 10⅜" 22.50
Spiral Flutes, amber, gr or pk, platter, 13" 45.00
Spiral Flutes, amber, gr or pk, stem, parfait; 4½-oz, 5⅝" 17.50
Spiral Flutes, amber, gr or pk, tumbler, flat, 8-oz, 4¼" 30.00
Spiral Flutes, amber, gr or pk, tumbler, ginger ale; 11-oz, 5½" 65.00
Spiral Flutes, crystal, chocolate jar, w/lid 135.00
Spiral Flutes, crystal, fernery (flower box), 4-ftd, 10x5½" 135.00
Tear Drop, crystal, ashtray, ind, 3" 6.00
Tear Drop, crystal, bowl, flower; crimped, 11½" 30.00

Tear Drop, crystal, bowl, flower; ftd, 12" **45.00**
Tear Drop, crystal, bowl, fruit; nappy, 7" **10.00**
Tear Drop, crystal, butter dish, w/lid, hdls, ¼-lb **27.00**
Tear Drop, crystal, candlestick, ball loop center, 2-light, 7" **18.00**
Tear Drop, crystal, candy dish, heart shape, 7½" **22.00**
Tear Drop, crystal, comport, hdls, low ft, 6" **15.00**
Tear Drop, crystal, ice bucket, 5½" **62.00**
Tear Drop, crystal, mustard jar, w/lid, 4¼" **35.00**
Tear Drop, crystal, plate, lazy susan; 18" **75.00**
Tear Drop, crystal, plate, lemon; hdls, 7" **12.50**
Tear Drop, crystal, plate, 4-hdl, 13" **25.00**
Tear Drop, crystal, relish dish, heart shape, 2-part, 7½" **18.00**
Tear Drop, crystal, stem, ale; 8-oz, 6¼" **15.00**
Tear Drop, crystal, stem, sherry; 1¾-oz, 4½" **30.00**
Tear Drop, crystal, sugar bowl, 8-oz **8.00**
Tear Drop, crystal, sweetmeat, center hdl, 6½" **30.00**
Tear Drop, crystal, tray, for shakers, hdls, 6" **12.50**
Tear Drop, crystal, tumbler, whiskey; ftd, 3-oz, 3" **12.00**
Tear Drop, crystal, urn, w/lid, ftd, 9" **115.00**

Durand

Durand art glass was made by the Vineland Flint Glass Works of Vineland, New Jersey. Victor Durand Jr. was the sole proprietor. The division called the 'fancy shop' was geared to the production of fine hand-blown art glass in the style of Tiffany and Steuben. Lustered glass and opal glass were used as a base to create such patterns as King Tut, Heart and Vine, Peacock Feather, and Egyptian Crackle. Cased glass was used to produce cut designs. Production of art glass began in 1924 and continued until 1931. Although most of this art glass was unsigned, when it was, it was generally signed within the pontil 'Durand' or 'Durand' written across the top of a large letter V, all in silver script. The numbers that sometimes appear along with the signature indicate the shape and height of the object. Owner Victor Durand employed the owner and several workers from the failed Quezal Art Glass and Decorating Co. This is why early Durand may sometimes look similar to Quezal art glass. In 1926 Durand art glass was awarded a medal of honor at the Sesquicentennial International Exposition in Philadelphia, Pennsylvania. Our advisor for this category is Edward J. Meschi, author of *Durand — The Man and His Glass,* due out in the fall of 1998 (Antique Publications); he is listed in the Directory under New Jersey.

Ball vase, Egyptian Crackle, opal and blue crackled surface on iridized ambergris base, 9½x10", $1,500.00.

Bonbon, King Tut, bl irid w/coiled wht, amber finial/ft, 4¾" **700.00**
Bowl, centerpiece; cobalt irid, folded rim, #2605, 2¼x14" **750.00**
Bowl, Heart & Vine, bl irid, 2x4½" **500.00**
Bowl, Peacock Feather, wht w/bl border on ambergris, 15" **900.00**
Bowl, red crackle, 4x9", w/14" undertray **700.00**
Bubble vase, yel to royal bl, bubbles, #1710-6, 6¾" **2,250.00**
Candlesticks, emerald gr, 11¾", pr, NM **350.00**

Candlesticks, feathers, wht on bl, flanged rim, 3x5", pr **650.00**
Candlesticks, King Tut, bl irid w/opal, baluster stems, 10", pr .**1,600.00**
Candlesticks, red irid mushroom form, #2044, 3", pr **800.00**
Compote, King Tut, bl irid w/amber ft & finial, 6¼" **750.00**
Compote, King Tut, cobalt w/clear stem, att, 3½x6¾" **475.00**
Console set, feathers, opal on cobalt, yel bases, 3-pc **1,700.00**
Cracker jar, bl irid w/threading, 10" **1,600.00**
Cracker jar, marigold (orange-gold) **1,050.00**
Cup & saucer, feathers, opal on emerald gr **250.00**
Decanter, bl cut to clear, cut stopper, 12" **975.00**
Finger bowl, ruby, ftd, 2½" H, w/6½" scalloped saucer **110.00**
Ginger jar, marigold w/overall threading, 6" **950.00**
Goblet, bl cup w/ambergris stem & ft **225.00**
Goblet, ruby w/yel stem, ruby ft, scalloped, 8½" **350.00**
Lamp, Egyptian Crackle, gr & wht, ginger jar, metal base **1,100.00**
Lamp, feathers, gold w/gold threads on gold base, 10" **600.00**
Lamp, King Tut, opal on bl irid, brass base, 8" **500.00**
Lamp, red cut to clear, 4" **350.00**
Parfait, ruby, ribbed, scalloped, ftd, 5¾" **160.00**
Plate, ambergris w/gr trim, 8" **75.00**
Plate, dinner; bl ribbed, scalloped edge, wht trim, 8" **100.00**
Plate, feathers, opal on cobalt, 8" **225.00**
Plate, ruby w/wht trim, 8" **125.00**
Powder box, bl irid, 3x4½" **700.00**
Rose bowl, gold irid on bl-gold irid base, 5¼" **700.00**
Rose bowl, Heart & Vine, dk bl irid w/silver bl, irid ft, 6" **1,650.00**
Sherbet, emerald gr ribbed, wht trim, w/underplate **175.00**
Tumbler, ruby cut to clear **150.00**
Vase, ambergris (oil glass) w/3 wht opaque arches, 6¾" **460.00**
Vase, bl irid, beehive form, #20177, 6½", pr **2,800.00**
Vase, bl irid, shouldered, 12" **900.00**
Vase, bl irid beehive form, #1978-12, 12½", pr **2,800.00**
Vase, bl irid w/irregular mc lustre, oval sphere, #1995, 3¾" **435.00**
Vase, bl irid w/opal leaves on vertical vines, shouldered, 7" **600.00**
Vase, Coil, bl & marigold on opal, cylindrical, 9" **1,100.00**
Vase, Coil, gr/bl on gold, wide cylinder, unmk, 8" **850.00**
Vase, Coil, opal on gold irid, cylindrical, 10" **550.00**
Vase, dk bl irid w/allover threading, #1710, 8" **850.00**
Vase, Egyptian Crackle, red/wht on gold irid, 6¾" **1,000.00**
Vase, feathers, gr & gold on gold irid w/threading, 9½" **975.00**
Vase, feathers, opal on gold irid w/gold threads, #1710, 10" **1,600.00**
Vase, feathers, opal on marigold, allover threads, #20102, 14" ...**900.00**
Vase, feathers, opal on ruby, ftd trumpet form, 8¾", NM **900.00**
Vase, gold irid, tapered w/beehive shoulder, sgn/#1978, 9" **900.00**
Vase, gold irid w/flared rim, #1770, 8" **700.00**
Vase, Heart & Vine, bl on marigold irid, #1710, 6" **750.00**
Vase, Heart & Vine, bl/gold on opal, gold threads, ftd, 9" **2,100.00**
Vase, Heart & Vine, gr & bl on orange-gold, #1812, 7¾" **1,095.00**
Vase, Heart & Vine, silver-bl on bl irid, gold ft, #2028, 8" **1,200.00**
Vase, Heart & Vine, wht on bl irid, 6½" **865.00**
Vase, King Tut, gold on apple gr, #1722-6, 5½" **1,100.00**
Vase, King Tut, gr on gold irid, ftd, 7" **1,100.00**
Vase, King Tut, opal on bl irid w/caramel inclusions, 7" **1,000.00**
Vase, lt/dk gr melon, hard ribbed, cup neck, 8x11" **1,500.00**
Vase, marigold w/allover threading, #1710, 8" **850.00**
Vase, opal cased to deep Lady Gay Rose, #1730, 6¾" **1,150.00**
Vase, Starburst, emerald cut to clear, #1710, 7" **1,050.00**
Wine, bl cut to clear, 7" **250.00**

Easter

Eggs, bunnies, chicks, and baskets have all become basic elements of Easter celebrations; and the older, more interesting examples are being collected (often for nostalgic reasons) and displayed during the holidays to make the festivities brighter.

Ducks and chicks do not command prices as high as rabbits, and German rabbits with clothes are much more valuable than the plain brown ones. Papier-mache rabbits made in the 1940s – 50s and marked USA are less pricey than composition bunnies made in Germany. Our advisor for this category is Jenny Tarrant; she is listed in the Directory under Missouri.

Wind-up toy, Easter bunny pulling cart, tin litho, Ohio Art, $75.00.

Candy box, Easter design, papier-mache, Germany, 5x7" 8.00
Candy container, boy w/chick, papier-mache, Germany, 6½" 155.00
Candy container, chick, papier-mache, Germany, 6½" 75.00
Candy container, chick in hat/clothes, papier-mache, Germany, 7" .150.00
Candy container, chick w/hat & basket, papier-mache, Germany, 7" 125.00
Candy container, chick w/½-egg, papier-mache, Germany, 4" 80.00
Candy container, dressed rabbit, compo, head removes, Germany, 4½" 295.00
Candy container, duck, papier-mache, egg-shape, W Germany, 6½" ...65.00
Candy container, rabbit in egg, compo, head removes, Germany, 5" .185.00
Candy container, rabbit on egg, plaster/cb, Germany, 4x4", NM ..150.00
Candy container, rabbit w/basket, papier-mache, Germany, 11", NM 340.00
Candy container, rabbit w/basket, papier-mache, Germany, 4¾" .88.00

Egg Cups

Egg cups, one of the fastest growing collectibles of the '90s, have been traced back to the ruins of Pompeii. Since then, they have been made in almost every country and in almost every conceivable material (ceramics, glass, metal, papier-mache, plastic, wood, ivory, even rubber and straw). Popular categories include Art Deco, Black Memorabilia, Chintz, Characters/Personalities, Golliwoggs, Railroadiana, Steamship, Souvenir Ware, etc.

Still being produced today in most countries, egg cups appeal to collectors on many levels. Prices can range from very little to many thousands of dollars. Those made prior to 1840 are scarce and sought after, as are the character/personality egg cups of the 1930s.

For a more thorough study of egg cups we recommend that you refer to *Egg Cups: An Illustrated History and Price Guide* (Antique Publications) by Brenda Blake, our advisor for this category. You will find her address listed in the Directory under Maine.

Key:
bkt — bucket, a single cup without a foot
dbl — 2-sided with small end for eating egg in shell, large end for mixing egg with toast and butter
fig — figural, an egg cup actually molded into the shape of an animal, bird, car, person, etc.
hoop — hoop, a single open cup with waistline
set — tray or cruet (stand, frame, or basket) with 2 to 8 cups
sgl — single, with a foot; goblet shaped

Advertising/Souvenir

Dbl, Hampton Casino, flow bl, Electric Railroad 200.00
Dbl, Haverford School, maroon & gold crest 20.00
Fig, Fanny Farmer, yel rooster, blk tail/wings/ft, gr base 38.00
Sgl, Cambridge, coat of arms, Goss 65.00
Sgl, Euro Disney, Mickey painting, Porzellan, W Germany, 1992 ..22.00
Sgl, Hermitage, red crown, Bauscher Weiden 18.00
Sgl, Laura Second, 2 bunnies 22.00
Sgl, Little Bay Beach Hotel, brn logo w/gilt 16.00
Sgl, Mont St Michel, mc, HP, Fr peasant pottery, 1930s 25.00
Sgl, Nescafe, red, Carlton Ware, 1980s 20.00
Sgl, Paris, La Tour Eiffel, Limoges, 1940s 22.00
Sgl, Revere Beach, transfer, Germany, ca 1900 ....35.00
Sgl, Tower of London, pk lustre, Germany, ca 1900 ....26.00
Sgl, World's Fair St Louis, transfer, 1904 ....130.00

American China/Pottery

Dbl, Chesterton, teal w/wht trim, Harker, 1950s 10.00
Dbl, Deldare, Ye Village Street, artist sgn, Buffalo, ca 1908 ....900.00
Dbl, Frost Flowers, Eva Zeisel design, Hall China, 1950s 25.00
Dbl, Magnolia, cranberry-red floral on tan, Stangl, 1950s 13.00
Dbl, Ming Tree, Lenox, 1930s 45.00
Dbl, Organdie, brn & yel plaid, Vernon Kilns, 1940-58 ....20.00
Dbl, Rabbit, ftd, Dedham, 1897-1929 ....325.00
Dbl, Rainbow, pk, WS George, 1930s 16.00
Dbl, Rooster, folk art, caramel ground, Pennsbury, 1950s 25.00
Dbl, Rooster, yel rim & base, Brock of California, 1950s 10.00
Dbl, Strawberry, Blue Ridge, 1950s 38.00
Sgl, Am Belleek, flower shape, Willets 300.00
Sgl, orange glaze, Jugtown ware, 1930s 48.00
Sgl, Vistosa, mango red, Taylor, Smith & Taylor, ca 1940 ....35.00

Characters/Personalities

Bucket, Beatles egg cups, black and white head and shoulders sketches with first-name signatures printed on rear of cups, Keele St. Pottery, 1960s, $200.00 for the set.

Bkt, Thomas the Tank Engine, Wedgwood, ca 1985 ....15.00
Fig, Mickey Mouse, snouty nose, blk & wht, Japan, 1930s 250.00
Fig, Princess Diana, Spitting Image, Carlton, 1980s 75.00
Fig, Punch, nose & mouth pnt red over glaze 85.00
Fig set, Muppets: Statler/Waldorf/Zoot/Sam, Sigma Tastesetter, '81 .200.00
Fig set, Snow White & 7 Dwarfs stand by their cup, Japan, '37 .1,300.00
Sgl, Buster Brown, Buster & Tige transfer, from breakfast set 135.00
Sgl, Col Baden-Powell, Commander at Mafeking, lustre, ca 1903 ..100.00
Sgl, Garfield, Good Morning series 16.00
Sgl, Major Gen Lord Kitchener of Khartoum, lustre, ca 1903 ....70.00
Sgl, Queen Elizabeth, 70th birthday, Coronet, 1996 ....15.00
Sgl, Queen Victoria, The Queen under portrait, pk lustre, ca 1893 ..250.00

Figurals

Big Feet, blk & wht, Carlton Ware, 1980 ....19.00

Black male, sitting, wht hat, bl jacket, Japan, 1930s **100.00**
Butler serving cup, Silver Crane Co, 1988, 5" **40.00**
Chicks (yel) on seesaw, lt bl cup, emb window, Japan, ca 1930 ....**20.00**
Cottage, boot shape, English, 1950s **11.00**
Financial Times newspaper, soap egg **17.00**
Motorcycle, yel & blk, ca 1940 ....**38.00**
Pirate, blk eye patch, 1980s **12.00**
Quail, bl head, attached to cup w/maroon rim stripe, Occupied Japan .**28.00**
Toby Philpot, wht jacket w/blk trim, hat is cup, late 19th C **58.00**
Volkswagen, Devon Ceramics Ltd, ca 1959 ....**22.00**
Whistler, lustre bear, Foreign in circle **80.00**

Glass

Dbl, Birch Leaf, bl, ca 1878 ....**58.00**
Dbl, Cape Cod, crystal, Imperial Glass Co, ca 1932 ....**38.00**
Dbl, Peloton, bl strings **75.00**
Dbl, Raindrop, amber **38.00**
Dbl, Rock Crystal, ruby, McKee, 1920s **60.00**
Fig, duck, milk glass, Deco, Opalex, 1930s **12.00**
Set, covered hen dish+6 hen's eggs cups+lg salt+tray, Vallerysthal .**475.00**
Sgl, blown, opal w/yel opalescence, appl bl rim, 1790s **285.00**
Sgl, Bristol bl, ca 1820 ....**225.00**
Sgl, Cremax, bl shading, ca 1940 ....**6.00**
Sgl, Hobnail, bl, row of ovals on base, ca 1870 ....**65.00**
Sgl, lacy glass, leaf pattern, ca 1825-40 ....**95.00**
Sgl, mercury glass, etched, gold-wash lining, ca 1900 ....**70.00**
Sgl, purple slag, vertical ribs, scalloped rim **75.00**

Golliwoggs

Bkt, figure at doorway points to display window, English, 1960s ...**55.00**
Fig, Golly Sailor by Sailing Club cup, Silver Crane Co, 1987-94 .**35.00**
Fig, Golly w/afro, stands by orange lustre cup, Japan, 1930s **250.00**

Miniatures

Set, metal-hdld stand w/4 ftd metal cups (1½"), recent **12.00**
Sgl, brn stoneware, Doulton Lambeth, 1880s, ¼" **100.00**
Sgl, porc, romantic scene, Limoges, part of set, 1⅜" **18.00**
Sgl, pressed glass, swirl pattern, ca 1890, 1⅝" **12.00**
Sgl, wooden, ½" **3.00**

Staffordshire

Dbl, Bombay, bl floral, John Maddock **22.00**
Dbl, Jardiniere, mc floral, Masons **16.00**
Dbl, Non-Pareil, flow bl, Burgess & Leigh, ca 1891 ....**200.00**
Dbl, Old Cottage, chintz, Royal Winton **120.00**
Dbl, Old Leeds Sprays, Royal Doulton, 1920s **28.00**
Dbl, Vincent, Wedgwood, ca 1951 ....**22.00**
Sgl, blk basalt, English, 18th C **550.00**
Sgl, geometric Deco design, pewter insert, Shelley, 1930s **80.00**
Sgl, Merryweather, Royal Doulton, 1926 ....**62.00**
Sgl, Mulberry, fluted, ca 1850 ....**240.00**
Sgl, Oriental scene, bl, English, ca 1850 ....**125.00**
Sgl, Scandy, mc peacock design, Devon **65.00**
Sgl, Tower, bl, Copeland Spode, ca 1930 ....**25.00**

Steamship/Cruiseship

Bkt, Maid Line, banner beneath flag & floral garland **20.00**
Dbl, Sitmar Cruises, aqua logo, ca 1980 ....**25.00**
Dbl, US Lines, bl stars & band, Lamberton Sterling China **68.00**

Hoop, Cunard Steamship..., bl floral, lion w/crown/banner, 1890s ..**100.00**
Hoop, SS Hesleyside, bl flag, maroon bands, ca 1890 ....**85.00**
Hoop, White Star Line, maroon banner, ca 1900 ....**120.00**
Sgl, HMS Aquitania, SP, pierced, enameled crest **100.00**

Woodenware

Bkt, HP, bl polka dots, Sweden **7.00**
Fig, Nun, Italy, 1950s **10.00**
Set, fruitwood stand, hdl finial, 6 ftd cups, England, ca 1800 ......**850.00**
Set, Lignum Vitae, rnd hdld stand, 6 ftd cups, 1890s **80.00**
Sgl, gold lcq, floral, Moscow, 1994 ....**10.00**
Sgl, Lehn, pk w/strawberries **875.00**
Sgl, Mauchline, Poland Spring House, Poland Spring ME **58.00**
Sgl, sponge decor, made in PA, 1830s **250.00**
Sgl, Tartan Ware, McDuff plaid, 19th C **150.00**
Sgl, traveler's, hand-trn, 19th C **60.00**

Miscellaneous

Bkt, Friar Tuck, brn robe, Goebel, stylized bee **45.00**
Dbl, Bancroft, Noritake **25.00**
Dbl, rooster, Holt Howard, 1961 ....**20.00**
Hoop, graniteware, wht w/blk rim, 1930s **80.00**
Sgl, bl flower, fluted, Royal Copenhagen, ca 1940 ....**25.00**
Sgl, female peasant, HP Quimper **55.00**
Sgl, Floral Danica (+), Royal Copenhagen, 1990s **500.00**
Sgl, rtcl, mc, gold trim, Fischer, 19th C **200.00**
Sgl, silver, ftd, Spratling, 1930s, 1¼" **115.00**
Sgl, silver egg cutter, w/lid, England, ca 1902 ....**200.00**

Elfinware

Made in Germany from about 1920 until the 1940s, these miniature vases, boxes, salt cellars, and miscellaneous novelty items are characterized by the tiny applied flowers that often cover their entire surface. Pieces with animals and birds are the most valuable, followed by the more interesting examples such as diminutive grand pianos, candle holders, etc. Items covered in 'spinach' (applied green moss) can be valued at 75% to 100% higher than pieces that are not decorated in this manner. See also Salts, Open.

Shoe, green 'spinach' decoration and applied rose, 2¼x4½", $110.00.

Basket, lustre, souvenir of Montreal **280.00**
Basket, moss, mk MIG, 2½x1½" **60.00**
Box, oval, 3x4" **75.00**
Compote, flowers on basket form, mk Germany, 6½x5½" **225.00**
Compote, mc florals, mk Germany, 6½x6½x5½" **235.00**
Place card holder, 8 for **225.00**
Salt cellar, floral sprays w/gold on leaf form, 3½" **15.00**
Shakers, gold & shell lustre, flowers & moss at top, pr **50.00**
Shoe, moss, 1½x4" **110.00**

Vase, 3" 45.00

Epergnes

Popular during the Victorian era, epergnes were fancy centerpieces often consisting of several tiers of vases (called lilies), candle holders, or dishes, or a combination of components. They were made in all types of art glass, and some were set in ornate plated frames.

Bl o/l, ruffled lily w/HP decor, gold trim, 16x10¾" 395.00
Bl satin, 1-lily, NP fr w/lady's head on ea leg, 14½x10" 295.00
Clear w/2 trunk-like apertures, ea w/hanging pk basket, 8½" 350.00
Cranberry, center lily/3 sm lilies/3 canes, 11" bowl, 21" 1,050.00
Cranberry central lily, 2 clear arms w/baskets, 1870s, 22" 600.00
Cranberry w/clear rigaree, 3-lily, ruffled bowl, 16x10" 500.00
Cranberry w/clear rigaree, 3-lily, ruffled bowl, 24x11" 600.00
CW Tuft SP angel w/fancy leaves, 3 glass lilies, 1890s 650.00
Opal & orange w/mc spatter & mica, 3-lily, ruffled bowl, 16" 550.00
Peachblow, 1-lily, ruffled rims, HP berries, SP fr, 14½" 300.00
Peachblow w/lime rigaree, 4-lily, 8" mirror base, 17" 600.00
Pk o/l satin, rstr SP base & vase holder, 1-lily, 18½x12" 495.00
Pk opal, 4-trumpet w/coiled snakes, brass mts, 24" 1,250.00
Vaseline opal, 3-lily, w/rigaree, 18" 495.00
Wht opal center lily w/gr rigaree+3 sm lilies, 12½x10½" 850.00
Wht w/pk int, yel rigaree, 4-lily, 9" mirror base, 14" 625.00

Erickson

Carl Erickson of Bremen, Ohio, produced hand-formed glassware from 1943 until 1960 in artistic shapes, no two of which were identical. One of the characteristics of his work was the air bubbles that were captured within the glass. Though most examples are clear, colored items were also made. Rather than to risk compromising his high standards by selling the factory, when Erickson retired, the plant was dismantled and sold.

Bottle, caramel cased, clear bubble stopper, sgn, 9" 300.00
Candlesticks, gr, controlled bubbles, paperweight, tall, pr 140.00
Compote, smoke, clear paperweight base, 12x6½" 155.00
Decanter, cranberry, w/stopper, unsgn 105.00

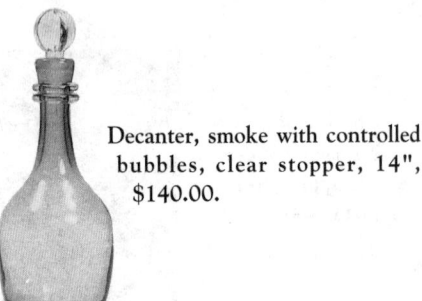

Decanter, smoke with controlled bubbles, clear stopper, 14", $140.00.

Vase, dk gr, hourglass shape, controlled bubbles, 10" 140.00
Vase, gray, controlled bubble base, fan form, unsgn 140.00
Vase, smoky topaz w/triangular crystal control bubble base, 12" .150.00

Erphila

Ebeling and Ruess, an importing company in Philadelphia, began operations in 1886. The acronym 'Erphila' was frequently substituted for the manufacturer's mark on the imported items. It appears that the Erphila mark was used through the late 1930s and then again after WW II on products from U.S. Zone Germany as well as from other areas. The company imported from factories such as Fustenberg, W. Goebel, Villeroy and Boch, Heinrich, Keramos, and Schumann, to name a few. Figurines, art pottery, and some utilitarian items can be found bearing the Erphila mark. Examples are hard to find. Early German marks (those prior to 1900) often contain the word 'Fayence.' After the turn of the century, a rectangular mark in green ink was used. Following WW I, porcelain items were imported from Czechoslovakia. These sometimes carried gold and silver labels. A small variety of marks were used in the 1920s and '30s, but they all contained the name Erphila. Sticker labels were also used. 'Bavaria,' 'Black Forest,' and 'Italy' are sometimes found in combination with 'Erphila.'

Ebeling and Reuss continue the importing business, but it appears that since the 1940s they are also using an 'E' and 'R' on a bell-shaped mark. Because this mark does not contain the name 'Erphila,' we do not consider it to be such. We assume that they stopped using this name sometime in the 1950s.

Box, basket form w/fruit lid, 2 ring hdls, 6¼" 200.00
Box, powder; Madame Pompadour, gr dress, Germany 100.00
Bust, Shakespeare, natural colors, Germany, 2" 35.00
Cake plate, mc roses, Czech, 11½" 38.00
Candlestick, wht w/orange flowers, Czech, 5", pr 75.00
Cigarette holder, dog at point, blk, Germany, 2¾" 60.00
Creamer, lady, wht & orange, Czech 125.00
Creamer, orange flowers, Czech, 4½" 42.50
Dresser doll, Madame Pompadour, yel dress, MIG, 5" 115.00
Figurine, airedale, lg 50.00
Figurine, beagle dog, mk Germany, 9" 52.50
Figurine, bulldog, blk & wht, gr mk, Germany, 3½x6" 75.00
Figurine, cat, sleeping, blk & wht w/mc collar, Germany, 3½" L ..38.00
Figurine, chickens, mc, MIG, 4¾", pr 42.50
Figurine, giraffe, mk Germany, pr 150.00
Figurine, mountain goats, brn & wht, Germany, 8" 95.00
Figurine, rabbit, sitting, natural colors, Germany, 2½" 20.00
Figurine, 2 pheasants on oval base, MIG, 5½" 45.00
Mug, Toby, bl coat, rust hat, Sam Weller, MIG 110.00
Planter, ivory w/3 graduated spheres on ea end, mk, 10" W 50.00
Plate, grapes, majolica, MIG, 7¾" 72.50
Teapot, elephant figural, gray, Germany, 9" 130.00
Urn, cherub transfer scene, gold floral stencil, w/lid, 11" 60.00
Vase, blk silhouette on sand, Czech, 9½" 110.00
Vase, floral w/raised enameling, 11½" 95.00
Wall bust, lady in Tyrolean hat, mk, 11" 60.00

Eskimo Artifacts

While ivory carvings made from walrus tusks or whale teeth have been the most emphasized articles of Eskimo art, basketry and woodworking are other areas in which these Alaskan Indians excel. Their designs are affected through the application of simple yet dramatic lines and almost stark decorative devices. Though not pursued to the extent of American Indian art, the unique work of these northern tribes is beginning to attract the serious attention of today's collectors.

Ball, fox fur w/moose hair embr, mc wool decor, 6" dia 100.00
Basket, brn/cream/blk geometrics connected w/dmns, 3¼x7" 200.00
Carving, figure in parka, dk gr soapstone, 1940s, 8½" 150.00
Carving, figure in sled pulled by dog, soapstone, 3x7½", VG 125.00
Carving, Greenland, flying shaman, bone, 1910s, 8x1" 150.00
Carving, ivory tapalik (shaman figure) w/baby on bk, 1900s, 4½" ...195.00

Cribbage board, from walrus tusk, compartment, much cvg, 15" ..**700.00**
Doll, ivory face, sealskin clothes, 1910s, 14x9" **300.00**
Doll, sealskin pants, cloth parka w/decor, wood sled, 1900, 12" .**145.00**

Face mask, yellow cedar, carved, pierced, and pegged features, multicolor paint and pigment, minor wood loss, EX patination, 10½x8", $8,250.00.

Glasses, cvd bone, snow type, primitive style, ca 1910, 5" **250.00**
Goggles, cvd wooden snow type, 1870s, 5x1" **550.00**
Kayak model, seal skin/wood/hide ties, w/provenance, 1885, 43" ..**1,750.00**
Mask, contorted face w/teeth, thin cvd wood, 1870s, 8½x5" **250.00**
Pants, sealskin w/fur, from Bird expedition, 1880s, 41x15" **75.00**
Puppet, Greenland, bone w/jtd appendages, fur Mukluks, 1910, 9" ...**100.00**
Ulu (knife), lady's, scrimshawed ivory hdl, ca 1850, 5x7" **150.00**
Ulu (knife), NW Coast, slate blade, wood hdl, 1300-1400s, 5x3" .**175.00**

Face Jugs, Contemporary

The most recognizable form of Southern folk pottery is the face jug. Rich alkaline glazes (lustrous greens and browns) are typical, and occasionally shards of glass are applied to the surface of the ware which during firing melts to produce opalescent 'glass runs' over the alkaline. In some locations clay deposits contain elements that result in areas of fluorescent blue or rutile; another variation is swirled or striped ware, reminiscent of 18th-century agateware from Staffordshire. Collector demand for these unique one-of-a-kind jugs is at an all-time high and is still escalating. Choice examples made by Burlon B. Craig and Lanier Meaders often bring over $1,000.00 on the secondary market. If you're interested in learning more about this type of folk pottery, contact the Southern Folk Pottery Collectors Society; their address is in the Directory under Clubs, Newsletters, and Catalogs. Our advisor for this category is Billy Ray Hussey; he is listed in the Directory under North Carolina.

China teeth, pop eyes, incised brows, BB Craig, 5⅜" **250.00**
China teeth, portruded eyes, crude ears, glossy, BB Craig, 9¾" ...**1,600.00**
China teeth, scrolled lines, alkaline, sgn CL, ca 1985, 19" **650.00**
China teeth, short moustache, alkaline, unsgn Reinhardt, 8", EX ...**2,200.00**
China teeth, 1-pc eyebrows/mustache, C Lisk..., 1983, 5" **130.00**
Lion, sgn Owens BH (Billy Ray Hussey), melted glass runs, 8¼" .**325.00**
Mini, orange, dbl-dip blk lead, Celia Cole, 1981, 1" **100.00**
Molded features w/inset eyes, salt glaze, att Westmoore, 4⅞" **175.00**
Naked woman hdl, sgn Owens BH (Billy Ray Hussey), ca 1975, 12" **650.00**
Rnd china teeth, 1-pc brows, mustache, C Lisk Vale NC, 10¾" ...**400.00**

Fairings

Fairings are small, brightly colored 19th-century hard-paste porcelain objects, largely figural groups and boxes. Most figural fairings portray amusing (if not risque) scenes of courting couples, marital woes, and political satire complete with appropriate base captions.

Fairing boxes, also referred to as trinket boxes, sometimes had captions similar to figural fairings, and often there were similar figures on top. It was originally assumed that fairings were made in the Staffordshire area, and for many years, they were referred to as Staffordshire fairings. But soon there were many European makers producing them as well, especially the boxes, since the Europeans could make them more cheaply. England encouraged these makers by not charging import duties. Both the figural fairings and the box fairings (trinket boxes) were made with the same consumers in mind.

Many early fairings were not marked; those that were had only a small incised or painted mark. Before 1850 the makers, especially Conte and Boehme of Possneck, Germany (who became the major maker of the boxes, indicated by 'C&B' in listings), used hand-incised numbers (for one article) and Roman numerals (for the size number). The painter often added his painted-on mark or number. After the 1850s both the article number and the maker's mark were impressed. The Conte and Boehme mark is the most familiar — a bent elbow (arm) holding a sword, laying on a shield. Examples marked 'Conta and Boehme' (words) are post-1890 or newer, possibly even copies.

After 1891 all wares shipped to the U.S. had to be clearly marked by the name of the country. For more information, we recommend *Victorian Trinket Boxes* by Janice and Richard Vogel, published by the authors (see Directory, Florida). Other good references are *Victorian Fairings* by W.S. Bristoe and *Victorian Fairings and Their Value* by Margaret Anderson.

Box, Be Good If You Can't Be Careful **135.00**
Box, boy falls off (log) seesaw/cat at ft, C&B mk, 4½x3", $150 to ...**220.00**
Box, boy seated, crying/feeding cat, C&B mk, 4¾x3x2⅜" **240.00**
Box, cat w/kitten in bed, C&B mk, 4¾x3x2", from $75 to **150.00**
Box, child in bed w/cat at ft, C&B mk, 4⅜x3x2", from $150 to .**200.00**
Box, child in bed w/cat at ft, Germany, ca post-1890, 4⅜x3x2" ...**80.00**
Box, child w/dog, shoe in hand, C&B mk, 4⅝x3⅛x2⅛" **110.00**
Box, dove w/envelope, unmk, 4x3⅛x2½" **70.00**
Box, girl w/kitten in arms, C&B mk, 4¾x3x2⅜" **130.00**
Box, Greenaway-type girls (3), C&B mk, 4¾x3x2" **150.00**
Box, Greenaway-type girls w/muffs, C&B mk, 4⅝x3x2" **150.00**
Box, hand w/ring, floral decor **170.00**
Box, 2 cats w/overtrn bucket, chair shape, C&B mk, 4½" H **190.00**

Fans

The Japanese are said to have invented the fan. From there it went to China, and Portuguese traders took the idea to Europe. Though usually considered milady's accessory, even the gentlemen in 17th-century England carried fans! More fashionable than practical, some were of feathers and lovely hand-painted silks with carved ivory or tortoise sticks. Some French fans had peepholes. There are mourning fans, calendar fans, and those with advertising.

Fine antique fans (pre-1900) of ivory or mother-of-pearl have recently escalated in value. Those from before 1800 often sell for upwards of $1,000.00. Examples with mother-of-pearl sticks are most desirable; least desirable are those with sticks of celluloid. Our advisor for this category is Vicki Flanigan; she is listed in the Directory under Virginia.

Bl satin w/appl lace, bone sticks, ca 1890, 10" **200.00**
Blk gauze w/HP putti, sequins, wooden sticks, 1890s, 13" **300.00**
Blk lace & abalone shell w/inlaid birds on ribs, Fr, 1890s, 27" **250.00**
Blk lace w/sequins, MOP sticks, ca 1890, 12" **480.00**
Brussels lace w/birds/butterflies, MOP sticks, ca 1865, 10" **400.00**
Chickenskin w/HP Roman ruins, pyramids on bk, Italy, 1780s, 11" .**1,000.00**
Courting scenes HP on silk, MOP fr, 19th C, EX **400.00**
Ebony brise, en grisaille roses/buds, palmette shape, 1905, 9" **125.00**
Gauze w/HP birds, MOP sticks, 1890s, 13" **300.00**

HP birds/flowers on silk, Chantilly lace, cvd wooden sticks, 23" ...**385.00**
HP/woodcut fishermen/pheasant/etc, ivory sticks, Japan/1890s, 11" ...**365.00**
Ivory brise, cvd/pierced pagodas & flowers, Canton, 1790s, 11" ..**1,100.00**
Ivory brise w/HP/lacquer figures/ruins, 1730s, in 2-sided case ..**1,800.00**
MOP brise, etched figures/animals/etc, Canton, 1820s, 7" ...**3,600.00**
Peacock feathers w/tortoise shell-type sticks, 8x10½" open **85.00**
Printed/hand-colored paper, cvd bone ribs w/metallic inlay, 19" **300.00**
Printed/hand-colored paper w/abalone shell ribs, eng SP, 19" **325.00**
Red ostrich feathers & satin, gold-trimmed wood sticks **110.00**
Silk w/HP birds/appl feathers, ornate ivory sticks, 1780s, 11" **900.00**
Silk w/HP musicians/reserves/Brussels lace, ivory sticks, 1870s, 12" ..**450.00**
Telescopic, HP figures, lacquer sticks, Canton, ca 1860, 11" **450.00**

Farm Collectibles

Country living in the 19th century entailed plowing, planting, and harvesting; gathering eggs and milking; making soap from lard rendered on butchering day; and numerous other tasks performed with primitive tools of which we in the 20th century have had little first-hand knowledge. Our advisor for this category is Lar Hothem; his address is listed in the Directory under Ohio. See also Cast Iron; Woodenware; Wrought Iron.

Barbed wire stretcher, iron, hinged clamp, ring-shaped hdl, 8¼" ..**10.00**
Bee smoker machine, tin, EX **20.00**
Blueberry picker, tin scoop form, AL Stewart...ME, 6½x8", EX .**120.00**
Book, Humphreys' Veterinary Guide, 1911, 64-pg **8.00**
Booklet, Hanford's Veterinary Hints, 1935, 29-pg **15.00**
Butchering utensils, wrought iron, 3 ladles+spatula, 19th C **575.00**

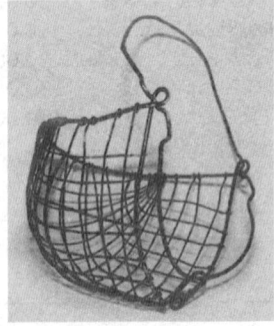

Calf muzzle, wireware restrainer, top loop slips over head, $40.00.

Corn dryer, heavy braided wire, 50 branching prongs, 60" **38.00**
Corn sheller, wooden w/geared mill power train, 20x26½" **140.00**
Cream separator, Sears Farm Master, red porc, manual, 1930s, EX ...**50.00**
Fly switch, leather, for horse or mule **30.00**
Fork, hay, wooden, 4 long wood prongs, iron bracket at bk, 76" ...**90.00**
Fork, shaking; wooden, 3 wood prongs, 61", EX **120.00**
Gauge (plugs & points), Internat'l Harvester, copper/brass, '30s ..**25.00**
Hat, straw, John Deere, pith helmet style, 1940s-50s, EX **45.00**
Hinges, wrought-iron strap type w/horn motifs, 29", pr **25.00**
Husking peg, wood peg w/leather strap **25.00**
Ice creepers, fastens over work boots, 2 straps, EX **75.00**
Implement seat, Buckeye, CI, EX **125.00**
Implement seat, Deering, CI, EX **125.00**
Implement seat, Hoosier, CI, EX **125.00**
Implement seat, no name, CI, ornate casting, EX **140.00**
Implement seat, Parlin & Orendorff Canton IL, CI, EX **125.00**
Implement seat, Rock Island Plow Co, 2 stars, EX **140.00**
Ladle, butchering; wrought iron, 5⅛" dia+16" hdl **20.00**
Lard press, wooden, sawtooth blade adjusts, trn hdls, 31" L **100.00**
Manual, John Deere Model A **25.00**
Manual, McCormick-Deering Cultivator rpr & parts, 1939 ....**2,500.00**

Measure, grain; wood w/pnt traces **65.00**
Planter, corn; Briggs, wood & CI, Pat June 14, 1845, 28" L **180.00**
Planter, seed; wood w/stencil label: Norcross & Boynton..., 40" .**155.00**
Rake, hay; MB Young, 8-prong, arched bentwood braces, 24"+70" hdl ...**35.00**
Sharpening stone, in 12" oak block, grooved sides, old **45.00**
Shovel, grain; cvd wood, 1-pc, 15x17" w/36" hdl, VG **80.00**
Shovel, potato; T Rowland, wrought & CI, 16x13"+40" hdl **55.00**
Textbook, Horseshoeing, illus, 1913, 216-pg, EX **24.00**
Thong maker, works leather, wood & iron, Pat 1867, EX **250.00**
Tractor, Aultman Taylor, 16 horse-power steam engine, 1910, rstr .**1,650.00**
Tractor, Russel, 48 horse-power steam engine, 1916, rstr **2,550.00**
Wagon seat, dbl ladder-bk w/3 slats, splint seat, rpt, 36" **220.00**
Wagon seat, poplar & hardwood, wrought fittings, old pnt, 38" .**140.00**
Yoke, oxen; wooden w/iron ring in center, 25x60", VG **50.00**

Fenton

Frank and John Fenton were brothers who founded the Fenton Art Glass Company in 1906 in Martin's Ferry, Ohio. The venture, at first only a decorating shop, began operations in July of 1905 using blanks purchased from other companies. This operation soon proved unsatisfactory, and by 1907 they had constructed their own glass factory in Williamstown, West Virginia. John left the company in 1909 and organized his own firm in Millersburg, Ohio.

The Fenton Company produced over 130 patterns of carnival glass. They also made custard, chocolate, opalescent, and stretch glass. This company has always been noted for its various colors of glass and has continually changed its production to stay attune with current tastes in decorating. In 1925 they produced a line of 'handmade' items that incorporated the techniques of threading and mosaic work. Because the process proved to be unprofitable, the line was discontinued by 1927. Even their glassware made in the past twenty-five years is already regarded as collectible. Various paper labels have been used since the 1920s; only since 1970 has the logo been stamped into the glass. For information concerning Fenton Art Glass Collectors of America, Inc., see the Clubs, Newsletters, and Catalogs section of the Directory. See also Carnival Glass; Custard Glass; Stretch Glass.

Aqua Crest, plate, 6½" **18.00**
Basket, amethyst carnival w/HP flowers, Louise Piper **150.00**
Basket, candle holders, clear, 3-toed, pr **30.00**
Basket, strawberry, ruby w/wht birds & flowers, Louise Piper **50.00**
Beaded Melon, vase, lt gr o/l, dbl-crimped, #711, 4" **29.00**
Bell, custard satin, HP decor, artist sgn **30.00**
Blue Mist, vase, #6459, 14" **90.00**
Burmese, fairy light, HP roses, #7392 ....**250.00**
Cactus, creamer & sugar bowl, vaseline **150.00**
Candy box, dk carnival, heart shape, #8200 ....**145.00**
Candy Stripe, student lamp, rosalene, #2606, 20" **600.00**
Coin Dot, basket, cranberry opal, #1437, 7" **115.00**
Coin Dot, bowl, cranberry opal, #1427, 7" **85.00**
Coin Dot, candlesticks, cranberry opal, #1524, 5¾", pr **195.00**
Coin Dot, creamer, cranberry opal, #1461, 4" **65.00**
Coin Dot, hat, cranberry opal, #1492, 3¼" **80.00**
Coin Dot, pitcher, cranberry opal, ice lip, #1467, 9½" **375.00**
Coin Dot, pitcher, Fr opal, 9½" **275.00**
Coin Dot, tumbler, cranberry opal, #1449, 12-oz **55.00**
Coin Dot, vase, bl opal, #1458, 8" **90.00**
Coin Dot, vase, bl opal, 6" **30.00**
Coin Dot, vase, cranberry opal, #1457, 7" **150.00**
Coin Dot, vase, Fr opal, #184, 12" **85.00**
Coin Dot, vase, Fr opal, #1925, 6" **55.00**
Daisy & Button, basket, amber, #1936, 6" **55.00**

Daisy & Button, top hat, 4½" 20.00
Daisy & Button, vase, gr pastel, 8½" 45.00
Daisy & Fern, tumbler, cranberry opal, flat, 4" 50.00
Diamond Lace, epergne, aqua crest on Fr opal 315.00
Diamond Lace, epergne, bl opal w/silver crest 300.00
Dolphin, bonbon, aquamarine, cut decor 37.50
Dolphin, bonbon, lt bl 25.00
Dolphin, compote, jade gr, #1533 ....52.00
Dot Optic, creamer, cranberry opal 45.00
Dot Optic, tumbler, cranberry opal, bbl form, 4" 30.00
Dot Optic, vase, cranberry opal, jug form, #192 .....65.00
Emerald Crest, basket, #7237, 7" 97.50
Emerald Crest, bowl, #7330, ftd, sq, tall 75.00
Emerald Crest, comport, 7" 45.00
Emerald Crest, flowerpot, #401, w/saucer 75.00
Emerald Crest, mustard, w/lid & spoon 77.50
Emerald Crest, plate, cake; #7213 (#680), high ftd, 13" 80.00
Emerald Crest, tidbit, #7298, 3-tier plates 77.50
Emerald Crest, vase, bulbous base #186, 8" 62.00
Emerald Crest, vase, 10" 75.00
Florentine, bonbon, gr stretch, w/lid, #643, 5" 55.00
Gold Crest, vase, #1924, 4" 35.00
Hanging Hearts, cruet, custard, #8969, 1976 ....135.00
Hanging Hearts, pitcher, turq, #8964, 1976, 70-oz 350.00
Hobnail, banana bowl, bl opal 115.00
Hobnail, basket, topaz opal, 4½" 95.00
Hobnail, bowl, milk glass, dbl-crimped, 9" 20.00

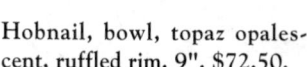

Hobnail, bowl, topaz opalescent, ruffled rim, 9", $72.50.

Hobnail, bowl, topaz opal, 10" 150.00
Hobnail, candlesticks, Fr opal, low, pr 40.00
Hobnail, compote, bl opal, dbl-crimped 50.00
Hobnail, cornucopia, Fr opal, lg, pr 105.00
Hobnail, cruet, Fr opal, 4" 26.00
Hobnail, epergne, plum opal 330.00
Hobnail, epergne, turq, #389, mini, 4-pc 55.00
Hobnail, jam set, bl opal, w/lid, 3-pc 100.00
Hobnail, jam set, Fr opal, w/lid, 3-pc 95.00
Hobnail, jug, cranberry opal, 4¾" 55.00
Hobnail, jug, cranberry opal, 80-oz 285.00
Hobnail, kettle, milk glass, #3990 ....15.00
Hobnail, mayonnaise set, Fr opal, open bowl w/ruffled rim, 3-pc ..90.00
Hobnail, mustard, milk glass, w/lid & wooden spoon ...25.00
Hobnail, perfumer, cranberry opal, flat stopper 75.00
Hobnail, pitcher, milk glass, ice lip 100.00
Hobnail, rose bowl, cranberry opal, 4" 90.00
Hobnail, rose bowl, cranberry opal, 5" 140.00
Hobnail, shakers, bl opal, flat, pr 45.00
Hobnail, shakers, cranberry opal, flat, pr 70.00
Hobnail, shakers, milk glass, flat, pr 20.00
Hobnail, tumbler, Fr opal, flat, 4¼" 18.00

Hobnail, vase, bl opal, #389, 5½" 32.00
Hobnail, vase, bl opal, fan form, 8" 85.00
Hobnail, vase, bl opal, ftd, 4" 28.00
Hobnail, vase, cranberry opal, crimped, #265, 5" 50.00
Hobnail, vase, cranberry opal, dbl-crimped, #3850, 5" 65.00
Hobnail, vase, cranberry opal, 4½" 45.00
Hobnail, vase, Fr opal, #3859, 8½" 145.00
Hobnail, vase, Fr opal, #3958, 8" 65.00
Hobnail, vase, milk glass, #3954, 7" 25.00
Hobnail, vase, plum opal, #3750, 6" 45.00
Honeycomb & Clover, jug, crystal w/gold 135.00
Ivy, vase, #1925, 6¼" 65.00
Ivy, vase, #194, 9" 45.00
Ivy, vase, dbl-crimped, #1924, 3½" 24.00
Jade Green, bud vase, #251, 10" 37.00
Jade Green, lamp, cut, 12", pr 295.00
Jade Green, server, center hdl 55.00
Jade Green, vase, swung; hexagonal base, ftd 75.00
Lamb's Tongue, marmalade, gr pastel 40.00
Lamp, fairy; owl, custard, #5108 ....24.00
Lamp, fairy; owl, Rosalene, #5180 ....55.00
Lamp, student; custard, Hammered Colonial base, HP roses, 20" .250.00
Mikado, compote, Fr opal 140.00
Ming Satin, bowl, pk, oval, #950, 11" 75.00
Orange Tree, mug, marigold carnival, #1430 ....45.00
Orange Tree, mustache mug 62.50
Peach Crest, bowl, dbl-crimped, 4x10¼" 38.00
Peach Crest, vase, hand decor, #186, 8" 52.00
Poppy, basket, bl satin, deep, #9138, 11" 65.00
Poppy, basket, rose satin, #9138, 7" 70.00
Poppy, basket, rose satin, #9138, 7" deep 85.00
Poppy, lamp, gone-w/the-wind; Lime Sherbet, #9202, 24" 350.00
Poppy, vase, Lime Sherbet, #9154, 7" 95.00
Rosalene, candle holders, #8473, pr 65.00
Rose Crest, candlestick, #1523, 5" 25.00
Rose Crest, vase, triple; #36, 6½" 37.50
Rose Mist, vase, fan form, #6457, 7" 60.00
Sheffield, bowl, silver decor at base, #1800, 13" 65.00
Sheffield, vase, bl, ftd 30.00
Silver Crest, banana bowl, low ft, #5824 ....50.00
Silver Crest, bowl, #7330, ftd, tall, 9" sq 67.50
Silver Crest, bowl, ruffled rim, #7224, 10" 40.00
Silver Crest, cake salver, HP violets 70.00
Silver Crest, candle holders, cornucopia; #951, pr 60.00
Silver Crest, candlesticks, #7474, 6", pr 85.00
Silver Crest, epergene, 3-lily, 12" 100.00
Silver Crest, lamp, hurricane; #7398 ....145.00
Silver Crest, pitcher, jug form, #7467, 70-oz 350.00
Silver Crest, plate, torte; 15" 45.00
Silver Crest, relish tray, 2-part 40.00
Silver Crest, sugar bowl, ruffled rim 45.00
Silver Crest, vase, #7450, 10" 110.00
Silver Crest, vase, fan form, 12" 95.00
Silver Crest/Violets in the Snow, basket, 37336, 7" 45.00
Snow Crest, hat vase, gr, #1921, 4" 75.00
Snow Crest, vase, amber, #3005, 7½" 45.00
Snow Crest, vase, emerald gr, dbl-crimped, 4" 34.00
Stretch, bonbon, bl, #634, w/lid 55.00
Stretch, lemon tray, yel, w/decor 35.00
Tear Drop, candy box, milk glass 55.00
Tear Drop, condiment set, milk glass, 4-pc 70.00
Tear Drop, shakers, milk glass, pr 30.00
Vase, Hanging Heart, jade gr opaque w/cobalt rim, 11½x6" ...1,750.00
Vase, Hanging Hearts & Vine, Antique Green, appl hdls, 9" .1,750.00

Vase, jade gr w/ebony base, hand decor, #621, 7" **95.00**
Vase, lilac cased, shell form, #9020, 10" **110.00**
Vase, vaseline w/opal, cobalt hdls & rim, 10x6" **1,650.00**
Velva Rose, epergne, 5-pc **310.00**
Velva Rose Stretch, sugar bowl **25.00**
Waffle, rose bowl, gr opal, 4½" **35.00**
Waffle, vase, swung; gr opal, #6180, 11" **37.00**

Fiesta

Fiesta is a line of dinnerware produced by the Homer Laughlin China Company of Newell, West Virginia, from 1936 until 1973. It was made in eleven different solid colors with over fifty pieces in the assortment. The pattern was developed by Frederick Rhead, an English Stoke-on-Trent potter who was an important contributor to the art-pottery movement in this country during the early part of the century. The design was carried out through the use of a simple band-of-rings device near the rim. Fiesta Red, a strong red-orange glaze color, was made with depleted uranium oxide. It was more expensive to produce than the other colors and sold at higher prices. Today's collectors still pay premium prices for Fiesta Red pieces. During the '50s the color assortment was gray, rose, chartreuse, and dark green. These colors are relatively harder to find and along with Fiesta Red and medium green (new in 1959) command the highest prices.

Fiesta Kitchen Kraft was introduced in 1939; it consisted of seventeen pieces of kitchenware such as pie plates, refrigerator sets, mixing bowls, and covered jars in four popular Fiesta colors.

As a final attempt to adapt production to modern-day techniques and methods, Fiesta was restyled in 1969. Of the original colors, only Fiesta Red remained. This line, called Fiesta Ironstone, was discontinued in 1973.

Two types of marks were used: an ink stamp on machine-jiggered pieces and an indented mark molded into the hollow ware pieces.

In 1986 HLC reintroduced a line of Fiesta dinnerware in five colors: black, white, pink, apricot, and cobalt (darker and denser than the original shade). Since then yellow, turquoise, seafoam green, 'country' blue, lilac, persimmon, and sapphire blue have been added. Collectors have found that the new line poses no theat to their investments.

In the listings below, 'original colors' indicates only three of the original six — light green, turquoise, and yellow (or those remaining after specific original colors have been priced). Red, ivory, and cobalt values are listed separately. Turquoise was the last original color to be introduced, so the items that were discontinued in 1946 are harder to find in that color (since it had a shorter production run), and values fall into the upper price range along with red, cobalt, and ivory. These are designated with an asterisk.

For more information we recommend *The Collector's Encyclopedia of Fiesta, Harlequin, and Riviera* (values updated in 1998) by Sharon and Bob Huxford (Collector Books).

Dinnerware

Ashtray, '50s colors **88.00**
Ashtray, orig colors **47.00**
Ashtray, red, cobalt or ivory **60.00**
Bowl, covered onion soup; cobalt or ivory **750.00**
Bowl, covered onion soup; red **750.00**
Bowl, covered onion soup; turq, minimum value **3,000.00**
Bowl, covered onion soup; yel or lt gr **600.00**
Bowl, cream soup; '50s colors **72.00**
Bowl, cream soup; med gr, minimum value **4,000.00**
Bowl, cream soup; orig colors **42.00**
Bowl, cream soup; red, cobalt or ivory **60.00**

Bowl, dessert; '50s colors, 6" **52.00**
Bowl, dessert; med gr, 6" **475.00**
Bowl, dessert; orig colors, 6" **38.00**
Bowl, dessert; red, cobalt or ivory, 6" **52.00**
Bowl, fruit; '50s colors, 4¾" **40.00**
Bowl, fruit; '50s colors, 5½" **40.00**
Bowl, fruit; med gr, 4¾" **485.00**
Bowl, fruit; med gr, 5½" **75.00**
Bowl, fruit; orig colors, 11¾" **300.00**
Bowl, fruit; orig colors, 4¾" **28.00**
Bowl, fruit; orig colors, 5½" **28.00**
Bowl, fruit; red, cobalt or ivory, 11¾" * **300.00**
Bowl, fruit; red, cobalt or ivory, 4¾" **35.00**
Bowl, fruit; red, cobalt or ivory, 5½" **35.00**
Bowl, ftd salad; orig colors **300.00**
Bowl, ftd salad; red, cobalt or ivory * **350.00**
Bowl, ind salad; med gr, 7½" **105.00**
Bowl, ind salad; red, turq or yel, 7½" **85.00**
Bowl, nappy; '50s colors, 8½" **65.00**
Bowl, nappy; med gr, 8½" **140.00**
Bowl, nappy; orig colors, 8½" **40.00**
Bowl, nappy; orig colors, 9½" **52.00**
Bowl, nappy; red, cobalt or ivory, 8½" * **60.00**
Bowl, nappy; red, cobalt or ivory, 9½" * **65.00**
Bowl, Tom & Jerry; ivory w/gold letters **260.00**
Bowl, unlisted salad; red, cobalt, or ivory **500.00**
Bowl, unlisted salad; yel **105.00**
Candle holders, bulb; orig colors, pr **95.00**
Candle holders, bulb; red, cobalt or ivory, pr * **130.00**

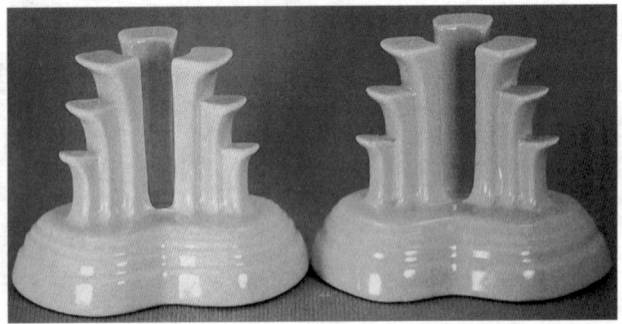

Candle holders, tripod; red, cobalt, or ivory, $600.00 for the pair; Original colors $465.00 for the pair.

Carafe, orig colors **250.00**
Carafe, red, cobalt or ivory * **300.00**
Casserole, '50s colors **300.00**
Casserole, French; standard colors other than yel, minimum **650.00**
Casserole, French; yel **300.00**
Casserole, med gr **725.00**
Casserole, orig colors **150.00**
Casserole, red, cobalt or ivory **200.00**
Coffeepot, '50s colors **350.00**
Coffeepot, demi; orig colors **340.00**
Coffeepot, demi; red, cobalt or ivory * **435.00**
Coffeepot, orig colors **195.00**
Coffeepot, red, cobalt or ivory **245.00**
Compote, orig colors, 12" **148.00**
Compote, red, cobalt or ivory, 12" * **185.00**
Compote, sweets; orig colors **75.00**
Compote, sweets; red, cobalt or ivory * **90.00**
Creamer, '50s colors **40.00**
Creamer, ind; red **250.00**

Creamer, ind; turq or cobalt 345.00
Creamer, ind; yel 70.00
Creamer, med gr 80.00
Creamer, orig colors 22.00
Creamer, red, cobalt or ivory 35.00
Creamer, stick hdld, orig colors 45.00
Creamer, stick hdld, red, cobalt or ivory * 70.00
Cup, demi; '50s colors 350.00
Cup, demi; orig colors 65.00
Cup, demi; red, cobalt or ivory 75.00
Egg cup, '50s colors 160.00
Egg cup, orig colors 58.00
Egg cup, red, cobalt, or ivory 70.00
Lid, for mixing bowl #1-#3, any color, minimum value 785.00
Lid, for mixing bowl #4, any color, minimum value 1,000.00
Marmalade, orig colors 230.00
Marmalade, red, cobalt or ivory * 285.00
Mixing bowl, #1, orig colors 170.00
Mixing bowl, #1, red, cobalt or ivory * 225.00
Mixing bowl, #2, orig colors 110.00
Mixing bowl, #2, red, cobalt or ivory * 125.00
Mixing bowl, #3, orig colors 120.00
Mixing bowl, #3, red, cobalt or ivory * 130.00
Mixing bowl, #4, orig colors 130.00
Mixing bowl, #4, red, cobalt or ivory * 155.00
Mixing bowl, #5, orig colors 155.00
Mixing bowl, #5, red, cobalt or ivory * 185.00
Mixing bowl, #6, orig colors 200.00
Mixing bowl, #6, red, cobalt or ivory * 265.00
Mixing bowl, #7, orig colors 280.00
Mixing bowl, #7, red, cobalt or ivory * 350.00
Mug, Tom & Jerry; '50s colors 100.00
Mug, Tom & Jerry; ivory w/gold letters 65.00
Mug, Tom & Jerry; orig colors 60.00
Mug, Tom & Jerry; red, cobalt or ivory 85.00
Mustard, orig colors 200.00
Mustard, red, cobalt or ivory * 250.00
Pitcher, disk juice; gray, minimum value 2,500.00
Pitcher, disk juice; Harlequin yel 62.00
Pitcher, disk juice; red 450.00
Pitcher, disk juice; yel 45.00
Pitcher, disk water; '50s colors 275.00
Pitcher, disk water; med gr, minimum value 1,150.00
Pitcher, disk water; orig colors 125.00
Pitcher, disk water; red, cobalt or ivory 165.00
Pitcher, ice; orig colors 140.00
Pitcher, ice; red, cobalt or ivory * 160.00
Pitcher, jug, 2-pt; '50s colors 150.00
Pitcher, jug, 2-pt; orig colors 90.00
Pitcher, jug, 2-pt; red, cobalt or ivory 120.00
Plate, '50s colors, 10" 52.00
Plate, '50s colors, 6" 9.00
Plate, '50s colors, 7" 13.00
Plate, '50s colors, 9" 22.00
Plate, cake; orig colors 755.00
Plate, cake; red, cobalt or ivory * 885.00
Plate, calendar; 1954 or 1955, 10" 45.00
Plate, calendar; 1955, 9" 50.00
Plate, chop; '50s colors, 13" 100.00
Plate, chop; '50s colors, 15" 115.00
Plate, chop; med gr, 13" 275.00
Plate, chop; orig colors, 13" 35.00
Plate, chop; orig colors, 15" 48.00
Plate, chop; red, cobalt or ivory, 13" 55.00

Plate, chop; red, cobalt or ivory, 15" 75.00
Plate, compartment; '50s colors, 10½" 75.00
Plate, compartment; orig colors, 10½" 40.00
Plate, compartment; orig colors, 12" 50.00
Plate, compartment; red, cobalt or ivory, 10½" 40.00
Plate, compartment; red, cobalt or ivory, 12" 60.00
Plate, deep; '50s colors 55.00
Plate, deep; med gr 120.00
Plate, deep; orig colors 40.00
Plate, deep; red, cobalt or ivory 60.00
Plate, med gr, 10" 110.00
Plate, med gr, 6" 20.00
Plate, med gr, 7" 32.00
Plate, med gr, 9" 45.00
Plate, orig colors, 10" 32.00
Plate, orig colors, 6" 5.00
Plate, orig colors, 7" 9.00
Plate, orig colors, 9" 12.00
Plate, red, cobalt or ivory, 10" 40.00
Plate, red, cobalt or ivory, 6" 7.00
Plate, red, cobalt or ivory, 7" 10.00
Plate, red, cobalt or ivory, 9" 18.00
Platter, '50s colors 58.00
Platter, med gr 140.00
Platter, orig colors 35.00
Platter, red, cobalt or ivory 45.00
Relish tray, gold decor, complete 250.00
Relish tray base, orig colors 65.00
Relish tray base, red, cobalt or ivory * 85.00
Relish tray center insert, orig colors 42.00
Relish tray center insert, red, cobalt or ivory * 55.00
Relish tray side insert, orig colors 40.00
Relish tray side insert, red, cobalt or ivory * 48.00
Sauce boat, '50s colors 78.00
Sauce boat, med gr 155.00
Sauce boat, orig colors 45.00
Sauce boat, red, cobalt or ivory 75.00
Saucer, '50s colors 6.00
Saucer, demi; '50s colors 95.00
Saucer, demi; orig colors 18.00
Saucer, demi; red, cobalt or ivory 22.00
Saucer, med gr 12.00
Saucer, orig colors 4.00
Saucer, red, cobalt or ivory 5.00
Shakers, '50s colors, pr 45.00
Shakers, med gr, pr 140.00
Shakers, orig colors, pr 22.00
Shakers, red, cobalt or ivory, pr 30.00
Sugar bowl, ind; turq 350.00
Sugar bowl, ind; yel 120.00
Sugar bowl, w/lid, '50s colors, 3¼x3½" 72.00
Sugar bowl, w/lid, med gr, 3¼x3½" 160.00
Sugar bowl, w/lid, orig colors, 3¼x3½" 45.00
Sugar bowl, w/lid, red, cobalt or ivory, 3¼x3½" 55.00
Syrup, orig colors 325.00
Syrup, red, cobalt or ivory * 400.00
Teacup, '50s colors 38.00
Teacup, med gr 58.00
Teacup, orig colors 25.00
Teacup, red, cobalt or ivory 35.00
Teapot, lg; orig colors 185.00
Teapot, lg; red, cobalt or ivory * 220.00
Teapot, med; '50s colors 325.00
Teapot, med; med gr, minimum value 1,000.00

Teapot, med; orig colors	165.00
Teapot, med; red, cobalt or ivory	200.00
Tray, figure-8; cobalt	90.00
Tray, figure-8; turq or yel	350.00
Tray, utility; orig colors	38.00
Tray, utility; red, cobalt or ivory *	42.00
Tumbler, juice; chartreuse, Harlequin yel or dk gr	460.00
Tumbler, juice; orig colors	40.00
Tumbler, juice; red, cobalt or ivory	45.00
Tumbler, juice; rose	65.00
Tumbler, water; orig colors	60.00
Tumbler, water; red, cobalt or ivory *	85.00
Vase, bud; orig colors	80.00
Vase, bud; red, cobalt or ivory *	110.00
Vase, orig colors, 10"	750.00
Vase, orig colors, 12", minimum value	1,000.00
Vase, orig colors, 8"	600.00
Vase, red, cobalt or ivory, 10" *	850.00
Vase, red, cobalt or ivory, 12", minimum value *	1,200.00
Vase, red, cobalt or ivory, 8" *	700.00

Kitchen Kraft

Bowl, mixing; lt gr or yel, 10"	100.00
Bowl, mixing; lt gr or yel, 6"	65.00
Bowl, mixing; lt gr or yel, 8"	82.00
Bowl, mixing; red or cobalt, 10"	120.00
Bowl, mixing; red or cobalt, 6"	75.00
Bowl, mixing; red or cobalt, 8"	92.00
Cake plate, lt gr or yel	55.00
Cake plate, red or cobalt	65.00
Cake server, lt gr or yel	130.00
Cake server, red or cobalt	140.00
Casserole, ind; lt gr or yel	140.00
Casserole, ind; red or cobalt	155.00
Casserole, lt gr or yel, 7½"	85.00
Casserole, lt gr or yel, 8½"	100.00
Casserole, red or cobalt, 7½"	90.00
Casserole, red or cobalt, 8½"	110.00
Covered jar, lg; lt gr or yel	300.00
Covered jar, lg; red or cobalt	320.00
Covered jar, med; lt gr or yel	260.00
Covered jar, med; red or cobalt	280.00
Covered jar, sm; lt gr or yel	270.00
Covered jar, sm; red or cobalt	290.00
Covered jug, lt gr or yel	250.00
Covered jug, red or cobalt	275.00
Fork, lt gr or yel	100.00
Fork, red or cobalt	125.00
Metal frame for platter	26.00
Pie plate, lt gr or yel, 10"	40.00
Pie plate, lt gr or yel, 9"	40.00
Pie plate, red or cobalt, 10"	45.00
Pie plate, red or cobalt, 9"	45.00
Pie plate, spruce gr	290.00
Platter, lt gr or yel	68.00
Platter, red or cobalt	78.00
Platter, spruce gr	350.00
Shakers, lt gr or yel, pr	95.00
Shakers, red or cobalt, pr	105.00
Spoon, ivory, 12", minimum value	500.00
Spoon, lt gr or yel	100.00
Spoon, red or cobalt	125.00
Stacking refrigerator lid, ivory	205.00

Stacking refrigerator lid, lt gr or yel	70.00
Stacking refrigerator lid, red or cobalt	80.00
Stacking refrigerator unit, ivory	195.00
Stacking refrigerator unit, lt gr or yel	45.00
Stacking refrigerator unit, red or cobalt	55.00

Fifties Modern

Postwar furniture design is marked by organic shapes and lighter woods and forms. New materials from war research such as molded plywood and fiberglass were used extensively. For the first time, design was extended to the masses and the baby-boomer generation grew up surrounded by modern shape and color, the perfect expression of postwar optimism. The top designers in America worked for Herman Miller and Knoll Furniture Company. These include Charles Eames, George Nelson, and Eero Saarinen.

Values are given for furnishings in excellent condition; glassware and ceramic items are assumed to be in mint condition. This information was provided to us by Richard Wright. See also Italian Glass.

Key:
lcq — lacquered   vnr — veneer
uphl — upholstered

Chair, Charles Eames/Evans Products, laminated birch with cut-out back, child size, 14x14x11", $6,500.00; Matching stool, 8x14x10", $2,700.00.

Armchair, Breuer/Thonet, tube chrome fr w/leather straps	425.00
Armchair, Girard, wool uphl, splay aluminum legs, U seat	475.00
Armchair, Hoffman/Thonet, blk lcq wood fr, reuphl/rfn, 3 for	200.00
Armchair, Nelson/Miller, oversz/uphl, 1954, +lg ottoman	650.00
Armchair, Robsjohn-Gibbings/Widdicomb, uphl, dowel base, 35"	425.00
Armchair, Wormley/Dunbar, Larson velvet uphl, mahog base, 28", pr	475.00
Armchair, Wormley/Dunbar, uphl, mahog legs w/X stretchers	225.00
Armchair, Wormley/Dunbar, wht leather uphl, oak fr, 35", VG, pr	950.00
Bench, Frankl/Johnson, cork top, mahog legs, 13x72x21", EX	1,500.00
Bench, Nelson/Miller, blond wood slatted top, 48"	550.00
Bench, Nelson/Miller, ebonized slat top & legs, 14x57x19", G	425.00
Bench, Nelson/Miller, ebonized slat top on base, 15x68x19"	375.00
Bench, Wormley/Dunbar, Long John, walnut plank, drw, 54" L	1,200.00
Bookcase, Nelson/Miller, Thin Edge, rosewood vnr, 31x47x18"	1,300.00
Bookcase, Nelson/Miller, walnut vnr, open shelf, 30x34x12", VG	350.00
Bowl, Gambone, abstracts, yel/blk on wheat, 6x12"	425.00
Buffet, Robsjohn-Gibbings/Widdicomb, walnut vnr, 70"	200.00
Bust, Baldelli, lady, bsk w/curls, mahog base, rstr, 12x7"	150.00
Cabinet, display; Nelson/Miller, combed oak vnr, glass doors	550.00
Cabinet, McCobb/Calvin, blond mahog, 4-drw, 34x36x20", VG	550.00
Cabinet, Nelson, combed oak vnr, 3-drw, 1-door, 30x56x19", G	550.00
Cabinet, Nelson/Miller, birch vnr, 4-drw/1-door, 32x56x19"	1,000.00

Cabinet, Nelson/Miller, Thin Edge, oak, 2 drw over 2 doors **950.00**
Cabinet, Nelson/Miller, walnut vnr, 2-door/1-shelf, rfn, 30x34" ...**500.00**
Cabinet, Nelson/Miller, walnut vnr, 5-drw, SP pulls, rfn, 45x34" ...**950.00**
Cabinet, stereo; Nelson/Miller, walnut vnr, aluminum legs **350.00**
Cart, bar; Aalto/Artek, tile top, molded birch fr, 23x36x26" **950.00**
Chair, Aalto/Artek, uphl w/molded birch C fr, 27x30x35", VG ..**2,400.00**
Chair, Bertoia/Knoll, bl wool 'bird' style, wire base, +ottoman ...**475.00**
Chair, blk wire w/wht vinyl reuphl seat, 33x16x16", VG **50.00**
Chair, dining; Nakashima, walnut fr, grass seat, 27", 6 for **3,250.00**
Chair, Eames/Miller, aluminum fr w/chaneled naugahyde, 34x25" ...**240.00**
Chair, Eames/Miller, Eiffel Tower, blk wire/orig leather, 32" **550.00**
Chair, Eames/Miller, red wool, tilting aluminum fr, 36", G **80.00**
Chair, Eames/Miller, uphl w/Eiffel Tower base, 29", 4 for **3,500.00**
Chair, Evans/Miller, molded mahog seat/bk/fr, 27x22x22" **850.00**
Chair, Jacobsen, swan style, shaped fiberglass, new vinyl **650.00**
Chair, Jacobsen/Hanson, uphl fiberglass egg fr, w/ottoman, VG ...**1,800.00**
Chair, Knoll, tufted seat & bk, chrome fr, 32x28", VG, pr **275.00**
Chair, Laverne, clear molded Lucite, orig pillow, 37x29x33" ..**2,500.00**
Chair, lounge; Aalto/ICF, blk lcq molded plywood seat, wood fr **500.00**
Chair, lounge; Eames/Miller #670, leather uphl/aluminum base, G ...**900.00**
Chair, lounge; Robsjohn-Gibbings/Widdicomb, uphl, walnut fr, pr ..**350.00**
Chair, secretarial; Eames/Miller, uphl w/chrome & aluminum fr ..**150.00**
Chair, side; Eames, 1-pc woven-wire shell w/bikini cover **500.00**
Chair, side; Risom/Knoll, woven canvas webbed seat & bk, VG ...**220.00**
Chair, side; Spratling, wooden fr w/leather seat, branded, G **425.00**
Chair, side; Wegner/Hansen, oak/teak, pegged/mortised, pr **425.00**
Chair, Wormley/Dunbar, mahog fr, uphl seat, open arms, 31x22x21" ...**90.00**
Chest, blanket; Nelson/Miller, combed oak vnr, 23x34" sq **300.00**
Chest, Nelson/Miller, Basic Series, walnut, w/drop front, VG **400.00**
Clock, Miller, star, bl/gr/orange/blk arms, wht center, 19" **425.00**
Clock, table; Miller, wood ½-rnd w/rnd face, ball ft, 5x9" **50.00**
Clock, table; Nelson/Miller, rnd bubble face, brass ped base **500.00**
Couch, Luthy/DeSede, leather uphl w/roll pillow, 26x76x37", VG ..**1,800.00**
Credenza, Nelson/Miller, walnut vnr, sliding doors, 56" W **425.00**
Daybed, van der Rohe/Knoll, leather uphl, walnut/steel fr, 78" ...**4,000.00**
Desk, executive; Acton, walnut vnr, chromed trestle base, 72" ...**1,000.00**
Desk, Nelson/Miller, swag-leg, walnut/wht laminate, 39" **2,400.00**
Desk, Nelson/Miller, wht laminate & cast aluminum, 39x50x32" ...**600.00**
Desk, Rohde/Miller, 6-drw, bimorphic Paldao vnr top, 56" W ...**2,400.00**
Dining set, Heywood-Wakefield, table+2 leaves+6 sides, rfn ..**1,600.00**
Figurine, Waylande Gregory, stylized horse, silver, 9" **210.00**
Lamp, bubble; Nelson/Miller, elastic covered wire ball fr, 16" **400.00**
Lamp, desk; aluminum shade, blk enamel base, 9", VG **60.00**
Lamp, desk; Colombo att, metal shade/chrome fr/disk base, 12" .**140.00**
Lamp, desk; Kennedy & Baratelli/Polaroid, Bakelite, indirect **130.00**
Lamp, floor; Arteluce, 3-shade, chrome & blk leather fr, 65" ...**1,400.00**
Lamp, Nelson/Miller, Bubble, saucer shape, hanging, 24" dia **400.00**
Lamp, 9 wht glass ball shades clustered atop wht metal pole **200.00**
Night stand, Deskey/Widdicomb, gr & yel lcq, chrome pull **475.00**
Panel, Waylande Gregory, incised Virgin & Child, 9x6" **350.00**
Rocker, Eames/Miller, fiberglass shell, birch runners, 27" **800.00**
Rocker, Eames/Miller, red fiberglass, birch runners, 37" **850.00**
Screen, Eames/Miller, 8 molded plywood sections, 68x76" **3,750.00**
Sculpture, wall; Seinberg, Swingtime, plaster, 27x39" **550.00**
Server, McCobb/Calvin, 3-shelf, 2-drw, brass fr, 29x30" **150.00**
Sofa, Eames/Miller, Compact, 2-panel fold-down bk, 72" **1,100.00**
Sofa, Knoll, 2-seat, tufted, chrome base, 30x62x33", VG **175.00**
Sofa, Nakashima/Widdicomb, walnut fr, yel uphl, spindle side ..**2,000.00**
Sofa, Nelson, tubular chrome fr, blk leather cushions, 84" **2,600.00**
Sofa, Robsjohn-Gibbings/Widdicomb, reuphl, walnut fr, 72" ..**2,800.00**
Sofa, Wormley/Dunbar, tufted uphl, mahog legs, 26x60x34" ..**1,200.00**
Stool, Girard, 15" rnd uphl seat, splay aluminum legs **750.00**
Table, coffee; Eames/Miller, blk laminate surfboard, 89", VG .**2,400.00**
Table, coffee; Eames/Miller, wht laminate & aluminum, 36" dia ..**170.00**

Table, coffee; Frankl/Johnson, bimorphic cork top, 48" L, VG ..**1,200.00**
Table, coffee; Frankl/Johnson, cork top, mahog legs, 15x48" dia .**1,300.00**
Table, coffee; Fr, 2 glass shelves, steel/brass base, 36" W **1,100.00**
Table, coffee; Knoll, blk & wht laminate, walnut base, 38" L **375.00**
Table, coffee; Mathsson, maple top, beech legs, rfn, 37" sq **375.00**
Table, coffee; Mathsson, teak top, molded ash legs, rfn, 42" dia .**300.00**
Table, coffee; Miller, rnd marble top, wire struts, 16x30" **900.00**
Table, coffee; Nakashima, walnut w/free edge, 14x16x29" **3,750.00**
Table, coffee; Nelson/Miller, blk laminate & aluminum, 28" dia .**210.00**
Table, coffee; Noguchi, free-form glass, 2-pc walnut base, 48" **450.00**
Table, coffee; Ponti/Singer, walnut X base, glass top, 41" dia ..**1,500.00**
Table, coffee; Wormley/Dunbar, Sheaves of Wheat, marble top, 38" **900.00**
Table, conference; Knoll, oval rosewood top, star chrome base ..**850.00**
Table, dining; McCobb/Calvin, walnut vnr, 44" dia+6 leaves **600.00**
Table, dining; Robsjohn-Gibbings/Widdicomb, walnut vnr, 58"+leaf ..**1,800.00**
Table, drop-leaf; Nelson/Miller, blond, #4656, dvtl hinges, 40" ..**1,250.00**
Table, end; Frank/Johnson, triangle cork top, mahog fr, 30", G .**190.00**
Table, folding; Eames/Miller, plywood top, chrome legs, 34" **650.00**
Table, Rhode/Miller, wood top, 3 chrome legs ea side, 19x24" .**1,300.00**
Table, side; Nelson/Miller, walnut plywood, metal base, 18" dia .**400.00**
Vanity, Rhode/Cavalier, 2-tone, 3-drw/2-shelf/mirror, rfn, 65x52" ..**600.00**
Vanity & stool, Haywood-Wakefield, Niagara, wheat finish, G **400.00**
Vase, Gambone, ceramic, blk & wht speckles, 13x8x3" **160.00**
Vase, Waylande Gregory, sgraffito nude/stars, wht on bl, 6" **250.00**

Finch, Kay

Kay Finch and her husband, Braden, operated a small pottery in Corona Del Mar, California, from 1939 to 1963. The company remained small, employing from twenty to sixty local residents who Kay trained in all but the most requiring tasks, which she herself performed. The company produced animal and bird figurines, most notably dogs, Kay's favorites. Figures of 'Godey' type couples were also made, as were tableware (consisting of breakfast sets) and other artware. Most pieces were marked.

After Kay's husband, Brandon, died in 1962, she closed the business. Some of her molds were sold to Freeman-McFarlin of El Monte, California, who soon contracted with Kay for new designs. Though the realism that is so evident in her original works is still strikingly apparent in these later pieces, none of the vibrant pastels or signature curliques are there.

Kay Finch died on June 21, 1993. Prices for her work have been climbing. Our advisor for this category is Jack Chipman, author of *The Collector's Encyclopedia of California Pottery, Second Edition*; he is listed in the Directory under California. Other sources of information include *Collectible Kay Finch* by Richard Martinez, Devin Frick, and Jean Frick (Collector Books) and *Kay Finch Ceramics, Her Enchanted World*, by Mike Nickel and Cynthia Horvath (Schiffer). *Kay Finch Ceramics Identification Guide* (published in 1996), containing many reprints of original catalog pages, is available from Frances Finch Webb; she is also listed in the Directory under California. See also Clubs, Newsletters, and Catalogs. Original model numbers are included in the following descriptions — three-digit numbers indicate pre-1946 models. After 1946 they were assigned four-digit numbers, the first two digits representing the year of initial production.

Figurine, camel, #464,
4½x5½", $450.00.

Cookie jar, Cookie Puss, #4614, 11¾", minimum value **2,500.00**
Creamer & sugar bowl, Briar Rose, w/lid **125.00**
Dish, swan form, #4958, 3½" **75.00**
Figurine, angel, #114A, #114B, or #114C, ea **85.00**
Figurine, bear, #4847, 4½" **275.00**
Figurine, bear, Teddy baby, #4906, 5½" **295.00**
Figurine, birds, Mr & Mrs Bird, #434 & #453, 4½", 3", pr **225.00**
Figurine, bunny, listening, #452, 8½", minimum value **375.00**
Figurine, cat, Ambrosia, #155, 10½", minimum value **600.00**
Figurine, cat, Do No Evil, #4836, 3" **125.00**
Figurine, cat, Jezebel, #5302, 6x9" **350.00**
Figurine, cat, Mehitable, playful, #181 ....**450.00**
Figurine, cats, Muff & Puff, #182 & #183, pr **195.00**
Figurine, cherub head, #212, 2¼" **100.00**
Figurine, chickens, Mr & Mrs Banty, #4843 & #4844, sm, pr **195.00**
Figurine, Chinese Court Lady, #400, 10" **250.00**
Figurine, choir boy, #210, 7½" **150.00**
Figurine, choir boy, kneeling, #211, 5½" **100.00**
Figurine, dog, Afghan, romping, #5554, 5½" **465.00**
Figurine, dog, Afghan angel, wht w/bl wings, #4964, 2½" **365.00**
Figurine, dog, Airedale, standing, #4832, 5x5" **375.00**
Figurine, dog, Boxer, #5025, 5x5" **375.00**
Figurine, dog, Cocker Spaniel, solid blk, #5201, 8" **395.00**
Figurine, dog, Peke, lying down, #156, 2½" **135.00**
Figurine, dog, Poodle, playful, #5203 or #5204, ea **500.00**
Figurine, dog, Vicki (Cocker Spaniel), #455, 11¾" **850.00**
Figurine, dog, Yorky pups, playful, #170 & #171, pr **650.00**
Figurine, donkey, #4768, 4" **120.00**
Figurine, doves, wht w/blk details, #5101 & #5102, pr **325.00**
Figurine, duck, Quacky, #472, 4½" **265.00**
Figurine, ducks, Peep, #178A, & Jeep, #178B, 3", pr **125.00**
Figurine, elephant, Jumbo, #4805, 4" **225.00**
Figurine, elephant, Mumbo, #4804, 4½" **225.00**
Figurine, elephant, Peanuts, #191, 8½" **350.00**
Figurine, elephant, Popcorn, #192, 6¾" **300.00**
Figurine, Godey Couple, #122, 9½", pr **300.00**
Figurine, Godey Couple, #160, 7½", pr **150.00**
Figurine, hippo, #5109, 5" **400.00**
Figurine, lamb, prancing, #168, 10½", minimum value **800.00**
Figurine, lamb, standing, #109, 5½" **125.00**
Figurine, monkey, Jocko, #4841, 4" **250.00**
Figurine, owl, Hoot, #187, 8¾" **225.00**
Figurine, owl, Toot, #188, 5¾" **125.00**
Figurine, owl, Tootsie, #189, 3¾" **65.00**
Figurine, penguin, Pete, #466, 7½" **375.00**
Figurine, pheasant, #5300, 10x10" **550.00**
Figurine, pig, Grumpy, #165, 6x7½" **375.00**
Figurine, pig, Smiley, 6¾x8" **375.00**
Figurine, pig, Winkie, #185, or Sassy, #155, 4" L, ea **150.00**
Figurine, rooster, Chanticleer, #129, 10¾" **500.00**
Figurine, rooster & hen, Butch, #177, & Biddy, #178, he: 8½", pr .**300.00**
Figurine, snail, 6" **100.00**
Figurine, squirrels, #108A & #108B, 3½", pr **225.00**
Mug, Missouri Mule, gold or silver decor, 4½" **350.00**
Planter, Baby Block w/bear, 6½" **150.00**
Plaque, butterfly, #5720, 14" **195.00**
Plaque, Santa face, #5373, 9½" **350.00**
Plate, Corral, prancing horse, #4634, 6½" **100.00**
Vase, simulated wooden ft, #5312, 6" **75.00**

Findlay Onyx and Floradine

Findlay, Ohio, was the location of the Dalzell, Gilmore and Leighton Glass Company, one of at least sixteen companies that flourished there between 1886 and 1901. Their most famous ware, Onyx, is very rare. It was produced for only a short time beginning in 1889 due to the heavy losses incurred in the manufacturing process.

Onyx is layered glass, usually found in creamy white with a dainty floral pattern accented with metallic lustre that has been trapped between the two layers. Other colors found on rare occasions include a light amber (with either no lustre or with gilt flowers), light amethyst (or lavender), and rose. Although old tradepaper articles indicate the company originally intended to produce the line in three distinct colors, long-time Onyx collectors report that aside from the white, production was very limited. Other colors of Onyx are very rare, and the few examples that are found tend to support the theory that production of colored Onyx ware remained for the most part in the experimental stage. Even three-layered items have been found (they are extremely rare) decorated with three-color flowers. As a rule of thumb, using white Onyx prices as a basis for evaluation, expect to pay two to five times more for colored examples.

Floradine is a separate line that was made with the Onyx molds. A single-layer rose satin glassware with white opal flowers, it is usually priced in the general range of colored Onyx.

Chipping around the rims is very common, and price is determined to a great extent by condition. Our advisors for this category are Betty and Clarence Maier; they are listed in the Directory under Pennsylvania.

Floradine

Bowl, fluted, squat bulbous base, 4" **950.00**
Celery vase, fluted cylinder neck, bulbous body, 6½", EX **1,000.00**
Celery vase, NM **1,800.00**
Creamer, bulbous, 4⅝" **950.00**
Mustard pot, NM **1,550.00**
Mustard pot, 3¾", EX **1,000.00**
Spooner **1,000.00**
Sugar bowl, bulbous, w/lid, 5½" **1,200.00**
Sugar shaker **1,500.00**
Syrup pitcher **2,500.00**
Toothpick holder, 2½" **1,500.00**
Tumbler, slightly bulbous, 3⅝" **1,000.00**

Onyx

Covered dish, white with silver decor, 5½", $1,000.00.

Bowl, w/raspberry decor, fluted top, 2½x4½" **2,000.00**
Creamer, wht w/silver decor, opal hdl, 4¾" **525.00**
Mustard, wht w/raspberry decor, hinged metal lid, 3¼" **2,900.00**
Pitcher, water; bulbous, 8" **1,200.00**
Shaker, wht w/silver decor, Pat 3/23/1889, 2⅝" **800.00**
Spooner, wht w/silver decor, 4½x4" **525.00**
Sugar bowl, wht w/silver decor, 5½", EX **475.00**
Sugar shaker, wht w/silver decor, 5½", from $450 to ...**545.00**

Syrup, wht w/silver decor, 7¾", M, from $850 to 1,150.00
Toothpick holder, wht w/silver decor, 2½" 500.00
Tumbler, wht w/silver decor, bbl shape, 3½" 450.00

Fire Marks

The earliest American fire marks date back to 1752 when 'The Philadelphia Contributionship for the Insurance of Houses From Loss By Fire' (the official name of this company, still in business!) used a plaque to identify property they insured. The first fire marks were made of cast iron; later, sheet brass, lead, copper, tin, and zinc were also used. The insignia of the insurance company appeared on each mark, and they would normally reward the volunteer fire department who managed to be the first on the scene to battle the fire. (Altercations occasionally broke out between firefighting companies vying for the chance to earn the reward!)

Fire marks were first used in Great Britain about 1780 and were more elaborate than U.S. marks. The first English examples were made of lead and carried a policy number. They were used to identify insured property to the fire brigades maintained by the insurance companies.

During the latter half of the 19th century, municipalities replaced the volunteer fire companies and fire brigades with paid fire departments. No longer was there a need for fire marks, so the companies discontinued their use. Some companies still use fire marks for advertising purposes. Reproductions may be purchased for decorative purposes. See *The Fire Mark Circle of America,* listed under Clubs, Newsletters, and Catalogs in the Directory.

Assoc Firemen's Insurance Co of Baltimore MD, pnt CI, 11¾" ..**325.00**
FA, hydrant w/hose, minor paint loss, rust, 1860-70, 11¾" **250.00**
Fire Assoc of Phila Penn, CI on wood plaque, 14x10" overall **100.00**
Phoenix, copper, worn **90.00**
United Firemen Ins Co of Phila, steamer, 11½x9¼", VG **100.00**
Valiant Hose No 2, minor pnt loss, 19th C, 10⅝" **400.00**

Firefighting Collectibles

Firefighting collectibles have always been a good investment in terms of value appreciation. Many times the market will be temporarily affected by wild price swings caused by the 'supply and demand principle' as related to a small group of aggressive collectors. These collectors will occasionally pay well over market value for a particular item they need or want. Once their desires are satisfied, prices seem to return to their normal range. It has been noticed that during these periods of high prices, many items enter the market place that otherwise would remain in collections. This may (it has in the past) cause a price depression (due again to the 'supply and demand principle' of market behavior). But when all is said and done, the careful purchase of quality, well-documented firefighting items has been an enjoyable hobby and an excellent investment opportunity.

Today there is a large, active group of collectors for fire department antiques (items over 100 years old) and an even larger group seeking related collectibles (those less than 100 years old). Our advisors for this category (except grenades) are H. Thomas and Patricia Laun; they are listed in the Directory under New York. (SASE required.)

Fire grenades preceded the pressurized metal fire extinguishers used today. They were filled with a mixture of chemicals and water and made of glass thin enough to shatter easily when thrown into the flames. Many varieties of colors and shapes were used. Not all the grenades listed contain salt-brine solution, some, such as the Red Comet, contain carbon tetrachloride, a powerful solvent that is also a health hazard and an environmental threat. (It attacks the ozone layer.) It is best to leave any con-

tents inside the glass balls. The source of grenade prices are mainly auction results; current retail values will fluctuate. Our fire grenades advisor is Larry Meyer; he is listed in the Directory under Illinois.

Key:
ALF — American LaFrance   s&a — soda & acid
CCL4 — carbon tetrachloride

Side lamps, De Voursney Bros...New York, each with two blue, one red, and clear etched (cracked) glass panels, minor dents, late 19th century, 19½", $2,100.00 for the pair. (If panels were perfect and dents were minor, value would be $3,750.00 for the pair.)

Axe, chief's, dtd 1854, 15½x8", EX 120.00
Axe, Viking style, pnt hdl, EX 325.00
Badge, Clerk...Portsmouth FD, eagle/steamer, Sterling, 2¾" 180.00
Badge, Fire Chief on gold-tone shield 65.00
Badge, Long Service NY Fire Patrol, Maltese cross, Tiffany mk .275.00
Badge, presentation; Mayflower...No 1 ENFD...1907, 14k gold ..375.00
Badge, Providence VFA...1881, high eagle/helmet/etc, gold plated ..190.00
Badge, Sr Inspector, LAFD, encased in Lucite, scarce 190.00
Badge, Veteran FA of SF, hook & ladder on sterling shield 125.00
Badge, 1st Prize...1883, hook & ladder, 14k gold, NY, 7½" 600.00
Bag, salvage; linen, stenciled NJ town name, VG 190.00
Bed key, iron, EX 125.00
Bell, apparatus; brass w/iron mt, 6", dia, VG 225.00
Bell, muffin; brass, trn hdl & ring, 3½" dia 220.00
Bell, muffin; brass, trn wood hdl, Pat date on hdl, 6" 325.00
Belt, leather, wht w/red, cut-out letters, brass buckle, PA 70.00
Belt, parade; leather, Liberty, red & wht, PA, EX 85.00
Box, alarm; ...Telegraph Station, Gamewell, CI, empty, 13", w/key ..110.00
Box, alarm; Excelsior, brass, Gamewell 300.00
Box, alarm; Gamewell, aluminum cottage style, red pnt, 17x10½" ..110.00
Box, ballot; walnut, 2-compartment, w/marbles, VG 150.00
Bucket, leather, Cairns, w/cover 110.00
Bucket, leather, early gr & tan rpt: No 15 Academy 1817, 13" ...330.00
Bucket, leather, old blk pnt w/red & yel, 1789, 13½", G 1,200.00
Bucket, leather, worn gr pnt w/traces of decor, 12", G 330.00
Cape, parade; blk leather, Franklin printed along bk 375.00
Extinguisher, apparatus; LaFrance, NP, 2½-gal, VG 150.00
Extinguisher, apparatus; Mack by Childs, NP, VG 230.00
Extinguisher, apparatus; Rough Rider #2, NP, ALF, VG 160.00
Extinguisher, apparatus; Seagrave by Pyrene, NP, s&a, EX 250.00
Extinguisher, Atomizer Fire Powder, tin, dry powder, EX 50.00
Extinguisher, Badger, brass, s&a, pony sz, EX 130.00
Extinguisher, Badger, copper/brass, stored press, H2O, pony sz ...100.00
Extinguisher, Fire Fog, tin tube, dry powder, EX 40.00
Extinguisher, Hanks Celebrated Flamite..., tin, lg, EX 50.00
Extinguisher, Liberty, dry chemical, 3-lb, 22" 45.00
Extinguisher, pump; Carbona paper label on tin, CCL4, EX 60.00
Extinguisher, Red Comet, ceiling mt, metal container, G 15.00
Extinguisher, Shur Spray, ceiling mt, CCL4, 1-gal 80.00
Extinguisher, Shur Stop, frosted glass, CCL4, w/wall bracket, EX ...25.00
Extinguisher, Underwriter's..., copper, s&a, pony sz 125.00
Frontispc, leather, blk w/wht lettering, 8", EX 50.00

Frontispc, leatherete, blk w/wht letters, Boston, 8", EX 110.00
Frontispc, leatherette, blk w/red & wht, 6" shield shape, 6" 60.00
Frontispc, leatherette, Clerk Steamer 1 Everett 120.00
Frontispc, leatherette, red w/wht letters, Asst Foreman #1, VG .100.00
Gauge, water; NP brass, eng steamer, Amoskeag, 1859, 6½" dia .695.00
Gong, apparatus; New Departure, ft-operated, 10" dia, EX 350.00
Gong, brass turtle type, 6", mtd on wood panel, w/key 80.00
Gong, station; Fire Alarm, early hand pull, wood mt, 1863, VG .150.00
Gong, station; Foote-Pierson, 10", in flat-top oak case, EX 800.00
Gong, station; Gamewell, Moses Crane style, 15" 3,300.00
Gong, station; Gamewell, 15", in flat-top oak case, 16x9" 2,750.00
Gong, station; Gamewell, 18", in feather & ball oak case 6,500.00
Gong, station; Gamewell, 8", in feather & ball oak case, VG .1,400.00
Gong, station; Moses Crane, 8", feather & ball walnut case, EX .1,800.00
Grenade, Auto-Fyr-Stop, w/alarm, frosted 25.00
Grenade, Harden's, cobalt, empty, G 125.00
Grenade, Harden's Star, bl, w/paper label & contents, EX 125.00
Grenade, Harden's Star, bl quilted, Pat Aug 14, 83, EX 350.00
Grenade, Harden's Star, turq bl, 7⅞" 150.00
Grenade, Hayward's...NY, cobalt, smooth base, 6⅛", NM 125.00
Grenade, Hayward's...NY, lt gr, w/contents 250.00
Grenade, HS Nutting, yel w/amber tone, smooth base, crude, 7¼" .100.00
Grenade, Magic Fire Extinguisher Co, yel-amber, scarce, 6¼" ...350.00
Grenade, Marvel Kill Fyre 18.00
Grenade, Red Comet Safety Spray Fire..., VG 10.00
Grenade, SF Hayward 407 Broadway..., cobalt, 6⅛" 230.00
Grenade, Shur-Stop, Staten Island, purple (really magenta) 15.00
Helmet, aluminum, high eagle, metal frontispc, VG 200.00
Helmet, aluminum, low front, H&L-WFD, EX 95.00
Helmet, aluminum, low front, Lieutenant..., EX 110.00
Helmet, leather, Boston style, 25 frontispc, VG 150.00
Helmet, leather, Capt #5, Cairns, w/eye shields 180.00
Helmet, leather, high eagle, Anderson/Jones, Asst Chief 600.00
Helmet, leather, high eagle, Charlestown Veteran, EX 425.00
Helmet, leather, high eagle, Chief Engineer, EX 400.00
Helmet, leather, high eagle, Clockford Hose-5-NLFD, VG 450.00
Helmet, leather, high eagle, Excelsior..., Gratacap, VG 400.00
Helmet, leather, high eagle, Foreman Manchester FD, VG 475.00
Helmet, leather, high eagle, gr JJH-13-FD frontispc, VG 400.00
Helmet, leather, high eagle, Peerless-2-MFD frontispc, VG 400.00
Helmet, leather, high eagle, Staff Boston RHB VFA, VG 400.00
Helmet, leather, high eagle, 60-comb, Cairns, Phoenix Engine, EX ...450.00
Helmet, leather, high front w/lion, Anderson & Jones, EX 875.00
Helmet, leather, low front, Arctic-1-MFD frontispc, Cairns, G .175.00
Helmet, leather, low front, Echo Hose-1-Shelton frontispc, G ...165.00
Helmet, leather, New Yorker style, w/HL-1-HFD frontispc, EX .125.00
Helmet, leather, New Yorker style w/ICF-Dist frontispc, G 195.00
Helmet, leather, w/leather eagle frontispc holder, early, EX 475.00
Helmet, plastic, Texaco, stenciled front, VG 50.00
Helmet, presentation; leather, 1st Asst Engineer BFD, Wilson ..1,200.00
Hose, leather w/brass couplings, Lowell MA, 76", EX 520.00
Keg, Hazelton's High Pressure Chemical..., amber glass, empty ..375.00
Lamp, engine; DeVourney Bros CA 1870, 6 eng panels, 20"+base, EX ...2,000.00
Lamp, engine; Frederick Macy-6 on red glass, 15½x4" dia 425.00
Lamp, engine; 6-sided, 2 bl/2 clear/2 red glass panels, 14", VG ..500.00
Lantern, chief's, brass w/clear globe, 10"+hdl, EX 275.00
Lantern, Dietz Chief, brass, cold-blast type, EX 650.00
Lantern, Dietz Fire King, ALF, lt rust 220.00
Lantern, Dietz Queen, brass, scarce, EX 665.00
Lantern, Peter Gray, NP/brass, Boston MA, 10½"+hdl 230.00
Lantern, presentation; SB Underhill NY, NP/brass, eng globe, EX .675.00
Lantern, SP, Adams & Westlake, Skichewaug etch on clear globe, 11" ...650.00
Lantern, wrist; brass, eng name on clear globe, EX 475.00
Match safe, Maltese cross & Baker Fabric Fire Hose, EX 130.00

Medal, FDNY Valor, rescuing child, gold-plated 130.00
Medal, Valor...City of NY, pewter, 3-horse steamer, EX 130.00
Nozzle, ALF, brass, leather hdls, red pnt, 19", EX 265.00
Nozzle, ALF, Foamite Corp, brass, 1½" 45.00
Nozzle, brass & copper, from hand tub, 31" 200.00
Nozzle, chemical apparatus; Foamite Childs...NY, brass, 12" 95.00
Nozzle, foamite airform; ALF...600, brass w/red cord, 36" 65.00
Nozzle, fog; Akron, brass, 1½" 35.00
Nozzle, Larkin, nickel, dtd Jan 1935, Dayton OH, 25", VG 165.00
Nozzle, play pipe; Eastman, leather hdls, complete 200.00
Nozzle, play pipe; WD Allen Chicago, brass w/red cord, 15" 100.00
Nozzle, Powhatan, brass, 1½" 65.00
Nozzle, Seagrave, nickel/brass w/leather hdls, 18", VG 295.00
Nozzle, shut-off; Callahan Co Boston...1885, brass, 6" 65.00
Nozzle, Underwriters, w/shut-off by Wooster Brass Co, 35" 65.00
Play pipe, brass & copper, Powhatan, 2½" 135.00
Play pipe, chrome, w/fire company ID, 31" 145.00
Rattle, alarm; single reed, weighted end, brass caps, VG 110.00
Rattle, alarm; wooden, Bagshaw & Field Phila, VG 50.00
Reel, take-up; Gamewell 100.00
Register, Gamewell, glass panels, 1" hole punch, 7½x4" base 100.00
Register, Gamewell, time & date stamp, no clock, VG 350.00
Register, Gamewell, 4-circuit, VG 150.00
Register, Gamewell Excelsior, Chelsea clock, time/date, early, VG ..850.00
Register, paper tape; Gamewell, 1", w/key, VG 60.00
Shirt, parade; red w/bibbed front, EX 220.00
Siren, Sireno, nickel, electrical, VG 100.00
Siren, Sterling Siren, hand-crank type, EX 450.00
Siren, Sterling 6V w/red light, Model #20, EX chrome finish, VG ..200.00
Torch, apparatus; solid brass, 11½" 150.00
Torch, parade; wood w/brass burner, VG 150.00
Trumpet, presentation; SP w/emb equipment/flowers, 17" 975.00
Trumpet, speaking, NP brass, 8-sided, Cairns, Pat 1877, G 850.00
Trumpet, speaking, SP, eng, 18", w/tassel, EX 750.00

Fireglow

Fireglow is a type of art glass that first appears to be an opaque cafe au lait, but glows with rich red 'fire' when held to a strong source of light.

Vase, stylized multicolored flowers, six relief green rings, 12½", $295.00.

Cruet, mc flowers & St Raphael, frosted hdl, Sandwich, 6¾" 195.00
Ewer, HP decor, mini, 6½" 85.00
Pitcher, bl flowers/rust leaves, ribs, 8", +4 3¾" tumblers 300.00
Vase, brn floral, 9½", NM 150.00

Fireplace Implements

In the colonial days of our country, fireplaces provided heat in the winter and were used year round to cook food in the kitchen. The implements that were a necessary part of these functions were varied and have become treasured collectibles, many put to new use in modern homes as decorative accessories. Gypsy pots may hold magazines; copper and brass kettles, newly polished and gleaming, contain dried flowers or green plants. Firebacks, highly ornamental iron panels that once reflected heat and protected masonry walls, are now sometimes used as wall decorations. By Victorian times the cookstove had replaced the kitchen fireplace, and many of these early utensils were already obsolete; but as a source of heat and comfort, the fireplace continued to be used for several more decades. See also Wrought Iron.

Andirons, brass, acorn finial, trn shaft, ball ft, 19" 375.00
Andirons, brass, ball finials, early 1800s, 17½" 300.00
Andirons, brass, baluster form, scroll legs, ball ft, 1835, 18" 250.00
Andirons, brass, Chpndl style, steeple & urn tops, 31" 500.00
Andirons, brass, Fed, lemon-top style, rprs, 18½" 250.00
Andirons, brass, Neoclassical style, early, pr 360.00
Andirons, brass, steeple top, NY, ca 1800, 18", pr 635.00
Andirons, brass, stylized dolphins, 24", VG 650.00
Andirons, brass, trn spire w/ball tops, ball ft, 1820s, 17" 200.00
Andirons, brass & wrought-iron knife-blade type, 24", pr 1,100.00
Andirons, CI, Black men figural (comic), pitting, 16", pr 275.00
Andirons, CI, Hessian soldiers w/swords & hats, 19x9x1¾" 265.00
Broiler, wrought iron, rotary, ftd, 3½x12½" dia+hdl 140.00
Broiler, wrought iron, rotary, 24½" 175.00
Broiler, wrought iron, rotary w/scroll details, 19" 200.00
Broiler, wrought iron, sq, 20" 100.00
Broiler, wrought iron, 3-leg, 22" dia+hdl 200.00
Coal hod, brass urn shape, paw ft, hawk-head hdls, 15½" 300.00
Coal hod, inlaid mahog w/brass & wood hdls, w/scoop, 15x15" ...300.00
Fan, cast-metal peacock w/feather fan attachment, 18" 150.00
Fender, brass, Regency, gadrooned/floral motifs, 19th C, 40" 250.00
Fender, brass & steel, bow front, 38" L 300.00
Fender, brass & wire, early 19th C, 12x42x11½" 800.00
Fender, brass & wire, Fed style, serpentine form, 40" 350.00
Fender, brass rails, steel wire mesh, 37" 140.00
Fender, pnt sheet metal w/gilt swags & cherubs, CI legs, 19x31" .525.00
Roaster, chestnut; brass, openwork hdl, rtcl cover, 23¼" L 450.00
Screen, brass, tooled & emb sailing ship, EX 135.00
Screen, brass w/stick & ball decor, leather bk, 4 40x17" panels ..350.00
Screen, fruitwood, trestle base, shelf, Fr, 19th C, EX 300.00
Spider pan, bronze, 7¼" w/7½" hdl 150.00
Toaster, wrought iron, rotating, curlicue design, 19" L 200.00
Toaster, wrought iron, twisted, rotating, 3-ftd, 18x13" 225.00
Toaster, wrought iron, twisted hdl, wood grip, 22" L 110.00
Toaster, wrought iron, 13½", 18" hdl 260.00
Wafer iron, CI, rectangular, long hdl, 33" L, VG 85.00
Waffle iron, CI, traditional design, long hdl, 30" L 45.00

Fischer

Ignaz and Emil Fisher were art pottery designers and producers from Hungary. Ignaz Fisher founded a workshop in Budapest, Hungary, in 1866. He had previously worked for M.F. Fisher, owner of the famous Herend factory, also in Hungary. His first products included domestic items that utilized a cream-colored clay; styles were copied from the Herend factory. His ware is recognized by the pale yellow, soft-lead glaze, usually decorated with painted ethnic Hungarian designs.

Emil Fischer took the business over from his father around 1890. The workshop was closed in 1908 and reopened for only a short time. Production from this period was influenced by the high-style designs of the Zsolnay factory in Pécs, Hungary. Unable to compete, they turned

to the manufacture of building materials. Marks (incised and painted): Fisher J. Budapest; initials: F.E. under a crown.

Pitcher, reticulated outer wall, shield-shaped scenic reserve, dolphin handle, 11", $500.00.

Figurine, man w/mandolin, lady w/flowers & bird, 11", pr 320.00
Jug, mc florals, butterflies & fan, Oriental style, 10¾" 200.00
Vase, elaborate floral/bird reserves, rtcl walls, 14½" 435.00
Vase, rtcl w/floral bands, 3 ram heads/hoof ft, w/lid, 14" 345.00

Fisher, Harrison

Harrison Fisher (1875 – 1934), noted illustrator and creator of the Fisher Girl, was the son of landscape artist, Hugh Antoine Fisher. His career began in his teens in San Francisco where he did artwork for the Hearst papers. Later in New York his drawings of beautiful American women attracted much attention and graced the covers of the most popular magazines of the day such as *Puck, Ladies' Home Journal, Saturday Evening Post,* and *Cosmopolitan.* He also illustrated novels, and his art books are treasured. His drawings appeared on thousands of postcards and posters. His creation of the Fisher Girl and his panel of six scenes of the *Greatest Moments in a Woman's Life* made him the most sought-after and well-paid illustrator of his day.

Book, American Beauties, EX 395.00
Book, American Belles, 16 mc plates, 13x9", NM, from $400 to ...450.00
Book, American Girls in Miniature, NM 375.00
Book, Bachelor Belles, 19 mc plates, 1908, 11x7", NM, $250 to ...300.00
Book, Book of Sweethearts, VG 125.00
Book, Dream of Fair Women, EX 360.00
Book, Harrison Fisher Book, EX 295.00
Book, Hiawatha, Indianapolis, 1906, 1st ed, VG 125.00
Book, King Albert's Book, EX 50.00
Book, Wanted Chaperone, Dodd Mead, color plates, 1902, NM ..85.00
Magazine cover, Cosmopolitan, May 1913 ....30.00
Magazine cover, Sunday Magazine, Nov 1906 ....30.00

Fishing Collectibles

Collecting old fishing tackle is becoming more popular every year. Though at first most interest was geared toward old lures and some reels, rods, advertising, and miscellaneous items are quickly gaining ground. Values are given for examples in excellent or better condition and should be used only as a guide. For more information contact our advisor Randy Hilst, an appraiser and collector whose address and phone number are listed in the Directory under Illinois. (SASE required.)

Box, lure; Shur-Strike, 2-pc 10.00
Box, reel; Pflueger Akron #1893 ....15.00
Box, tackle; homemade, cedar, mk Kingfisher, 8½x25", EX 95.00
Casting line spool, JC Higgins 10.00

Catalog, Heddon-Dowagiac Bait-Casting Equip #19, 1922, 9x12", VG .**880.00**
Catalog, Pflueger, 152-pg, 1929, w/cover letter & order form, M ..**160.00**
Catalog, Shakespeare, folding, color covers, 48-pg, 1928, EX **315.00**
Container, split shot; Abercrombie & Fitch, celluloid, rnd, EX .**105.00**
Container, split shot; Selby BB, celluloid, rnd, EX **70.00**
Creel, half-moon; wood & tin, orig blk pnt, early 1800s, 10" **210.00**
Creel, wicker, canvas & leather harness, sliding peg lid latch, EX ..**80.00**
Hooks, Wright & McGill, MIB **10.00**
Knife, fishing; wood hdl, 3" blade, leather sheath, mk Marbles, EX ..**135.00**
Lure, Arbogast Sunfish Tin Liz, glass eyes, 1⅝", VG+ **190.00**
Lure, Arbogast Tin Liz Snake, 2¾", EX **520.00**
Lure, Creek Chub Baby Beetle, blk bug finish, minus 1 eye, o/w VG .**100.00**
Lure, Creek Chub Baby Wigglefish, glass eyes, red finish, NM ...**250.00**
Lure, Creek Chub Injured Minnow, luminous finish, VG **65.00**
Lure, Creek Chub Jointed Husky Pikie, rainbow fire finish, MIB ..**140.00**
Lure, Heddon Little Luny **225.00**
Lure, Heddon Luny Frog, open legs missing hardware **90.00**

Lure, Paw Paw, green and gold with yellow eyes, 3¼", $20.00.

Lure, Shakespeare #64 Musky 5-hook Minnow, glass eyes, 5¼", EX ...**550.00**
Lure, Western Hair Mouse, V671, MIB **80.00**
Net, mk Hardy, aluminum, triangular, belt clip, 24" hdl, VG **85.00**
Reel, bait-casting; Heddon Pal P-41, 1950s, MIB (w/booklet & bag) ...**95.00**
Reel, Defiance #60 ....**20.00**
Reel, fly; Orvis Magnalite Multiplier, exposed rim & drag switch, G .**55.00**
Reel, fly; Shakespeare Kazoo **40.00**
Reel, Johnson #40A, MIB **35.00**
Reel, Johnson #80 ....**20.00**
Reel, Machined Trout Click; JC Arsenault Canada, aluminum, EX .**195.00**
Reel, Martin #63 ....**35.00**
Reel, Pflueger Peerless #700 ....**20.00**
Reel, salmon; Farlow Ambassador, single action, VG **85.00**
Reel, Shakespeare #1740, free spool, Tournament Model FK, M .**195.00**
Reel, South Bend Perfectorene #750 ....**20.00**
Reel, trout; WA Adams, new in leather case **275.00**
Rod, fly; Hardy Palakona, 2-pc, 1-tip, 105", canvas case, VG **330.00**
Rod, fly; Orvis Battenkill, 2-pc, 96", NM (orig bag/tube) **330.00**
Rod, spinning; Gene Edwards, sgn, 2-pc, 78", EX (orig bag/tube) ...**140.00**
Rod, trout; Foster Bros, Ashbourne Manifold, 2-pc, 108", w/case, VG **85.00**
Ruler, wooden; Orvis Impregnated, cane, 2-pc, 7-ft **100.00**
Sign, Simmons Fishing Tackle, oilcloth, ca 1915, 18x36", EX ...**250.00**
Tin, Pflueger split shot **10.00**
Tin, Shurkatch split shot **10.00**
Trap, eel; woven split funnel, 7x21", EX **330.00**
Trap, insect/minnow; lt gr blown glass, emb oval on side, 4x5", EX .**90.00**

Flags of the United States

The brevity and imprecise language of the first Flag Act of 1777 allowed great artistic license for America's early flag makers. This resulted in a rich variety of imaginative star formations which coexisted with more conventional row patterns. In 1912 inviolate design standards were established for the new 48-star flag, but the banners of our earlier history continue to survive:

The 'Great Star' pattern — configured from the combined stars of the union, appeared in various star denominations for about 50 years, then gradually disappeared in the post-Civil War years.

The utilitarian 'scatter' pattern — created through the random placement of stars, is traceable to the formative years of our nation and remained a design influence through most of the 19th century.

The 'wreath' pattern — first appearing in the form of simple single-wreath formations, eventually evolved into the elegant double- and triple-wreath medallion patterns of the Centennial period.

Acquisition of specific star denominations is also a primary consideration in the collecting process. Pre-Civil War flags of 33 stars or less are very scarce and are typically treated as 'blue chip' items. Civil War-era flags of 34 and 35 stars also stand among the most sought-after denominations. Market demand for 36-, 37-, and 38-star flags is strong but less broad-based, while interest in the unofficial 39-, 40-, 41-, and 42-star examples is largely confined to flag aficionados. The very rare 43 remains in a class by itself and is guaranteed to attract the attention of the serious collector.

Row-patterned flags of 44, 45, and 46 stars still turn up with some frequency and serve as a source of more modestly priced vintage flags. Ordinary 48-star flags flood the flea markets and are priced accordingly, while the short-lived 49 is regarded as a legitimate collectible. 13-star flags, produced over a period of more than 200 years, surface in many forms and must be assessed on a case-by-case basis.

Many flag buffs favor sizes that are manageable for wall display while others are attracted to the more monumental proportions. Allowances are typically made for the normal wear and tear — it goes with the territory. But severe fabric deterioration and other forms of excessive physical damage are legitimate points of negotiation.

The dollar value of a flag is by no means based upon age alone. The wide price swings in the listing below have been influenced by a variety of determining factors related to age, scarcity, and aesthetic merit. In fact, almost any special feature that stands out as unusual or distinctive is a potential asset. Imprinted flags and inscribed flags; 8-point stars, gold stars, and added stars; extra stripes, missing stripes, tri-color stripes, and war stripes are all part of the pricing equation. And while political and military flags may rank above all others in terms of prestige and price, any flag with a significant and well-documented historical connection has 'star' potential (pardon the pun). Our advisor for this category is Robert Banks; he is listed in the Directory under Maryland.

11 stars, wreath pattern, hand-sewn flannel, 1840s, 31x40" **650.00**
13 stars, (4-5-4), sea captain's, ca 1860s, 74x140" **500.00**
13 stars, hand/machine sewn, Centennial, 60x86" **250.00**
13 stars, in semi-wreath, hand sewn, 1870s, 54x102" **325.00**
13 stars, printed glazed muslin, 1880s, 7x11" **20.00**
13 stars, 9 stripes, hand sewn, 1860s, 27x50" **700.00**
19 stars, 16 orig+3, sewn scrap fabric, 39x66" **1,500.00**
20 stars, hand-embr into Great Star, rare, 24x32" **1,800.00**
26 stars, Great Star, embr on sewn silk, 30x43" **1,100.00**
29 stars, entirely hand sewn, poor condition, 43x68" **575.00**
30 stars, gold stars/fringe, silk, delicate, 52x68" **550.00**
31 stars, Great Star, Lincoln related, printed, 11x14" **285.00**
31 stars, row pattern, hand-stitched bunting, 104x247" **850.00**
32 stars, dbl wreath of inset stars, hand sewn, 36x48" **700.00**
33 stars, Great Star, hand-sewn muslin, 60x96" **825.00**
33 stars, hand-/machine-sewn wool bunting, 66x92" **600.00**
33 stars, in rows, printed bunting, 28x44", G- **325.00**
34 stars, dbl-wreath pattern, printed silk, 18x28" **300.00**
34 stars, Great Star, mixed fabrics, sewn, 91x154" **1,100.00**
34 stars, printed linen, 3 sewn sections, 22x48" **250.00**

34 stars, random pattern, hand sewn, 66x140" **710.00**
35 stars, dbl-wreath pattern, printed, sized muslin, 19x28" **190.00**
35 stars, recruiting flag, sewn bunting, 50x116" **750.00**
35 stars, row pattern, hand/machine sewn, 96x180" **625.00**
36 stars, cut-in, in rows, machined stripes, 25x50" **300.00**
36 stars, inscr parade flag, muslin print, 6x9" **90.00**
36 stars, sailing ship's, inscr & dtd, 75x142" **375.00**
37 stars, medallion pattern, printed/sewn muslin, 48x87" **280.00**
37 stars, printed silk, 32x40" **85.00**
37 stars, row pattern, hand-sewn silk, poor, 60x80" **230.00**
37 stars, row pattern, stitched bunting, 30x48" **325.00**
38 stars, medallion-wreath pattern, printed cotton, 12x17" **120.00**
38 stars, printed silk w/ribbon ties, 30x47" **100.00**
38 stars, row pattern, clamp dyed in 3 sections, 60x120" **220.00**
38 stars, row pattern, hand/machine-stitched bunting, 71x116" .**250.00**
38 stars, unique wreath pattern, sewn, 89x134" **375.00**
38 stars, 1776-1876 pattern, printed linen, 27½x46" **625.00**
39 stars, Centennial 'International Flag,' 16x24" **90.00**
39 stars, row pattern, all machine-stitched bunting, 40x84" **350.00**
39 stars, row pattern variation, printed silk, 12x24" **85.00**
39 stars (6-5 pattern), printed gauze bunting, 19x34" **70.00**
40 stars, row pattern, hand-sewn bunting, lg, 98x204" **270.00**
40 stars, row pattern, printed/sewn British import, 55x106" **185.00**
41 stars (rare), printed cotton sheeting, 15x24" **140.00**
42 stars, row pattern, printed silk/fringe, poor, 24x36" **70.00**
42 stars, sewn cotton, from Ft Hamilton NY, 120x177" **275.00**
42 stars, 7-row pattern, printed cotton, 27x47" **80.00**
43 stars, machine-sewn bunting, extremely rare, 29x70" **675.00**
44 stars, machine-sewn cotton bunting, 53x82" **90.00**
44 stars, triple-wreath pattern, printed cotton, 23x26" **100.00**
45 stars, HP w/sewn stripes, 38x70" **120.00**
45 stars, machine-sewn cotton bunting, 80x108" **55.00**
45 stars, printed silk w/red ribbon ties, 32x46" **45.00**
45 stars, row pattern variant, printed muslin, 9x13" **25.00**
46 stars, machine-sewn wool bunting, 72x138" **60.00**
46 stars, printed silk, GAR Post in gold, 32x45" **350.00**
47 stars, unofficial, sewn bunting, 108x137" **200.00**
48 stars, all crocheted, dtd 1941, 20x38" **85.00**
48 stars, machine-sewn cotton bunting, 60x96" **30.00**
48 stars, printed cotton w/GAR surprint, 11x16" **25.00**

Photo courtesy Robert Banks

48 stars sewn to form USA, unauthorized WWI, 45x69", $300.00.

48 stars, USN Union Jack, machine-sewn wool, 23x33" **35.00**
48 stars in gold, sewn WWII casket flag, 58x118" **150.00**
49 stars, embr, sewn stripes, 36x60" **45.00**
49 stars, 3 uncut flags, printed cottonsheet, 37x36" **25.00**
50 stars, early prototype 'June 1959,' 52x66" **220.00**
50 stars, hand-knitted coverlet w/fringe, 30x51" **30.00**

51 stars, printed flaglette for DC statehood, 4x6" **15.00**

Florence Ceramics

Figurines marked 'Florence Ceramics' were produced in the '40s and '50s in Pasadena, California. The quality of the ware and the attention given to detail are prompting a growing interest among today's collectors. The names of these lovely ladies, gents, and figural groups are nearly always incised into their bases. The company name is ink stamped. Examples are evaluated by size, rarity, and intricacy of design. For more information we recommend *The Florence Collectibles* by Doug Foland, our advisor for this category. You will find him listed in the Directory under Oregon. Another source is *The Collector's Encyclopedia of California Pottery, Second Edition*, by Jack Chipman; he is listed in the Directory under California.

Adeline, bl or pk **295.00**
Amelia, rust & tan **250.00**
Anna Lisa, from $75 to **125.00**
Ava, flower holder **225.00**
Baby, flower holder, from $75 to **100.00**
Barbara, from $200 to **325.00**
Bea, from $100 to **150.00**
Betsy, youth, from $90 to **100.00**
Blossom Girl, flower holder **125.00**
Blue Boy, from $300 to **350.00**
Bryan, rare, from $200 to **225.00**
Bud (cowboy), 9", from $300 to **350.00**
Camille, Godey style, from $175 to **250.00**
Camille, lamp, from $200 to **500.00**
Carol, rare, from $400 to **500.00**
Caroline, brocade, from $900 to **1,000.00**

Catherine, $575.00 to $700.00.

Photo courtesy Doug Foland

Charles, from $175 to **250.00**
Clarissa, Godey style, from $150 to **175.00**
Darleen, from $250 to **300.00**
David, bust **300.00**
Dear Ruth, lamp, from $950 to **1,200.00**
Deborah, from $475 to **600.00**
Delia, hand showing, from $150 to **200.00**
Delia, lamp, from $200 to **325.00**
Diane, from $175 to **200.00**
Edward, gray w/gr chair, 7" **425.00**
Ellen, from $120 to **125.00**
Fair Lady, rare **1,200.00**
Fern, flower holder, from $200 to **250.00**
Floraline, candy dish, from $75 to **125.00**
Georgette, from $300 to **400.00**
Girl w/pail (Beach Kid), from $300 to **400.00**
Grandmother & I, rare **1,500.00**
Haru & Misha, pr, from $575 to **600.00**
Josephine, from $200 to **250.00**

Joyce, from $200 to 225.00
June, flower holder, from $35 to 40.00
Karla, ballerina, from $200 to 450.00
Lantern Boy, flower holder 125.00
Lavon, rare, from $225 to 250.00
Lillian Russell, brocade, rare 1,200.00
Little Princess, from $150 to 175.00
Love Letter, rare, from $400 to 900.00
Madame Du Barry, rare, from $300 to 450.00
Madame Pompadour, forest gr, 12" 650.00
Madeline, from $200 to 300.00
Madonna & Child, rare 400.00
Marsie, from $175 to 190.00
May, flower holder, from $35 to 40.00
Mikado, from $200 to 350.00
Nancy, from $100 to 135.00
Pat & Mike, pr, from $250 to 500.00
Pinkie, from $300 to 350.00
Prima Donna, from $300 to 500.00
Prom Girl, from $300 to 400.00
Rhett 395.00
Rose Marie, adult, Godey style, 8¼", from $250 to 300.00
Scarlet, hands showing, rare 450.00
Tess Teenager, rare, from $200 to 250.00
Violet, flower holder, from $200 to 250.00
Virginia, brocade, from $600 to 1,200.00
Wood Nymph, from $300 to 450.00
Yulan, flower holder, from $125 to 145.00

Flow Blue

Flow Blue ware was produced by many Staffordshire potters; among the most familiar were Meigh, Podmore and Walker, Samuel Alcock, Ridgway, John Wedge Wood (who often signed his work Wedgewood), and Davenport. It was popular from about 1825 through 1860 and again from 1880 until the turn of the century. The name describes the blurred or flowing effect of the cobalt decoration, achieved through the introduction of a chemical vapor into the kiln. The body of the ware is ironstone, and Oriental motifs were favored. Later issues were on a lighter body and often decorated with gilt.

Our advisor, Mary Frank Gaston, has compiled a lovely book, *The Collector's Encyclopedia of Flow Blue China*, with full-color illustrations and current market values.

Irene, plate, gold trim, Wedgewood, 10¼", $65.00.

Abbey, chamber pot, Geo Jones & Son 300.00
Abbey, plate, Jones, 7¼" 65.00
Abbey, teapot, Jones 245.00
Amoy, creamer, Davenport, 5" 525.00
Amoy, pitcher, Davenport, 8½" 875.00
Amoy, plate, Davenport, 9" 150.00
Amoy, platter, Davenport, 20" 1,195.00

Amoy, teapot, Davenport 1,200.00
Anemone, cupboard sweetmeat jar 395.00
Anemone, platter, 22x17" 895.00
Arabesque, creamer 695.00
Arabesque, gravy boat 475.00
Arabesque, teapot, Mayer, ca 1845, rpr, 8½" 600.00
Argyle, bowl, flanged soup; Grindley, 9" 80.00
Argyle, bowl, 8-sided, w/lid, Grindley 150.00
Argyle, butter dish, w/insert, Grindley 350.00
Argyle, butter pat 40.00
Argyle, cake plate, hdls, Grindley 265.00
Argyle, cup & saucer, coffee; Grindley 90.00
Argyle, gravy boat 140.00
Argyle, plate, gold trim, Grindley, 10" 90.00
Argyle, plate, Grindley, 6" 45.00
Argyle, plate, Grindley, 8¼" 60.00
Argyle, platter, Grindley, 13" 325.00
Argyle, saucer, Grindley, 4½" 25.00
Argyle, sugar bowl, w/lid, Grindley 200.00
Brush Stroke, bud vase 295.00
Brush Stroke, creamer 295.00
Brush Stroke, teapot 825.00
Carlton, sauce ladle, Alcock, 1850s, EX 250.00
Carlton, soup, 10¼" 175.00
Cavendish, biscuit jar 395.00
Cavendish, gravy boat & underplate 350.00
Cavendish, pitcher, Keeling, 7" 195.00
Chapoo, bowl, sauce; Wedge Wood, 5½" 95.00
Chapoo, bowl, vegetable; w/lid, Wedge Wood, rpr, 12x9½" 750.00
Chapoo, bowl, vegetable; w/lid, Wedge Wood, 11¼x9", EX 675.00
Chapoo, bowl, vegetable; Wedge Wood, ca 1850, 9½x7" 275.00
Chapoo, flanged soup, Wedge Wood, 10¾" 145.00
Chapoo, gravy boat, Wedge Wood, ca 1850 ....225.00
Chapoo, pitcher, lighthouse shape, Wedge Wood, rprs, 1850s 600.00
Chapoo, pitcher, milk; Wedge Wood, 6" 600.00
Chapoo, plate, Wedge Wood, 10½", pr 250.00
Chapoo, platter, Wedge Wood, 21¼x15¾", VG 500.00
Chapoo, sauce tureen, 3-pc, Wedge Wood 1,100.00
Chapoo, wash bowl & pitcher, Wedge Wood 2,475.00
Chapoo, waste bowl, 16-panel, Wedge Wood 395.00
Chinese, platter, well & tree; Dimmock, prof rpr, 15¾x12" 350.00
Chinese, sauce tureen, Dimmock 275.00
Chinese, vase, polychromed, Ridgway, 8¼" 275.00
Chusan, cup plate, Clementson 155.00
Colonial, butter pat 38.50
Colonial, plate, 8⅞" 80.00
Conway, bowl, vegetable; 9" 135.00
Conway, platter, 14" 225.00
Conway, soup, 9" 70.00
Conway, waste bowl 125.00
Dundee, creamer 150.00
Dundee, cup & saucer 65.00
Fairy Villas, bowl, Adams, 10" 200.00
Fairy Villas, bowl, Adams, 6½" 50.00
Fairy Villas, plate, Adams, 9" 80.00
Fairy Villas, soup, Adams, 9" 75.00
Fairy Villas, soup tureen, rstr hdl on lid 600.00
Floral, biscuit box, Warwick, 3¾x6¾" 345.00
Floral, plate, 10" 75.00
Florida, bone dish 100.00
Florida, bowl, vegetable; Johnson Bros, w/lid, 12", NM 420.00
Florida, platter, Grindley, 12x8½" 165.00
Formosa, plate, Mayer, 10½" 150.00
Formosa, plate, 12-sided, Mayer, 7½" 125.00

Gironde, gravy boat, Grindley 100.00
Gironde, platter, Grindley, 15" 225.00
Hamilton, butter pat 45.00
Hamilton, sauce ladle 95.00
Hindustan, bowl, vegetable; w/lid, Maddock 650.00
Hindustan, creamer, Maddock 325.00
Holland, soup plate, Johnson, 7½" 45.00
Hong Kong, plate, Meigh, 8" 95.00
Hong Kong, potato bowl, Meigh, 10" 530.00
Hong Kong, teapot, Meigh, ca 1845, rstr, 8½" 600.00
Hong Kong, waste bowl, 8-sided, Meigh 195.00
Idris, creamer, Grindley 195.00
Idris, platter, Grindley, 12" 175.00
Indian, platter, Meigh, 15" 325.00
Indian, platter, Pratt, ca 1840, 16¾x13¼", EX 500.00
Indian, sauce tureen, 4-pc, Pratt, ca 1840 ....1,000.00
Indian, teapot 695.00
Iris, bowl, fruit; gold trim, Wilkinson, 5¼" 28.00
Iris, bowl, vegetable; gold trim, oval, Wilkinson 130.00
Iris, bowl, vegetable; w/lid, Wilkinson, 7½" 290.00
Iris, cup & saucer, Royal Pottery 50.00
Iris, gravy boat, gold trim, Wilkinson 165.00
Iris, plate, bread & butter; gold trim, Wilkinson, 6" ...26.00
Iris, plate, bread & butter; Wilkinson, 6" 20.00
Iris, plate, dinner; gold trim, Wilkinson, 9" 50.00
Iris, platter, gold trim, Wilkinson, 13" 175.00
Iris, platter, polychromed, Wilkinson, 14½x10½" 225.00
Iris, sugar bowl, gold trim, w/lid, Wilkinson 150.00
Iris, waste bowl, gold trim, Wilkinson 120.00
Kelvin, plate, Meakin, 8" 30.00
Kelvin, platter, Meakin, 18" 325.00
Kin Shan, coffeepot 995.00
Kin Shan, gravy boat 475.00
Kyber, plate, Adams, gold trim, 10" 95.00
Kyber, plate, Adams, 10" 125.00
La Belle, bowl, scalloped, oval, 9" 275.00
La Belle, bowl, serving; ruffled rim 225.00
La Belle, bowl, vegetable; w/lid 495.00
La Belle, butter pat 40.00
La Belle, cake tray, gilt raised scrolls, scalloped rim, 10" 235.00
La Belle, celery 295.00
La Belle, charger, 14½" 295.00
La Belle, chocolate pot 995.00
La Belle, ice cream tray, 13" 350.00
La Belle, pitcher, milk; 7" 395.00
La Belle, pitcher, 3-qt, 8" 795.00
La Belle, plate, 7¼" 50.00
La Belle, relish, 8" 250.00
La Belle, sugar bowl, w/lid, 5¼" 495.00
La Belle, wash pitcher, 10½" 1,595.00
La Belle, wash set, minor damage, 6-pc 2,995.00
La Francaise, butter dish, 3-pc 215.00
La Francaise, butter pat, French China 22.00
La Francaise, platter, 15" 165.00
Lonsdale, bowl, vegetable; Ridgway 110.00
Lonsdale, cup & saucer, Ridgway 45.00
Lonsdale, soup, Ridgway, 7½" 75.00
Lorne, bone dish, Grindley 85.00
Lorne, butter pat, Grindley 60.00
Lorne, creamer & sugar bowl 400.00
Lorne, sauce tureen, Grindley 350.00
Lorne, sugar bowl 175.00
Lorne, undertray 165.00
Madras, bowl, vegetable; oval, w/lid, Doulton 325.00

Madras, butter pat, Doulton 60.00
Madras, flanged soup, Doulton 95.00
Madras, plate, Doulton, 10½" 105.00
Madras, plate, Doulton, 6½" 60.00
Madras, plate, Doulton, 9½" 95.00
Madras, platter, Doulton, 17¼" 795.00
Madras, teapot, Doulton 700.00
Madras, tureen, Doulton, w/lid 800.00
Manilla, bowl, vegetable; 9x6¾" 285.00
Manilla, bowl, 2¾x12¼" 395.00
Manilla, pitcher, 8" 650.00
Manilla, platter, 18" 795.00
Manilla, sugar bowl, lion's-head hdls 615.00

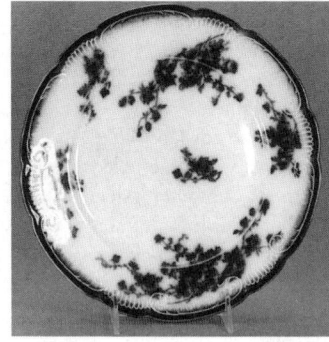

Marchelle Neil, plate, 10", $60.00.

Melbourne, bowl, oval, 10" 95.00
Melbourne, bowl, vegetable; oval, w/lid 375.00
Melbourne, platter, 14" 250.00
Melbourne, platter, 16" 475.00
Melbourne, sauce tureen & undertray 395.00
Melbourne, sugar bowl 295.00
Muriel, plate, Grimwades, 9" 85.00
Muriel, relish dish 45.00
Non-Pareil, bowl, salad; Burgess & Leigh, 8" 100.00
Non-Pareil, bowl, vegetable; rose-bud finial, Burgess & Leigh 600.00
Non-Pareil, butter dish, Burgess & Leigh 395.00
Non-Pareil, butter pat, Burgess & Leigh 50.00
Non-Pareil, cake plate, Burgess & Leigh, 10" 185.00
Non-Pareil, creamer, Burgess & Leigh, 5" 250.00
Non-Pareil, ladle rest, Burgess & Leigh 175.00
Non-Pareil, plate, salad; Burgess & Leigh, 8" 100.00
Non-Pareil, sauce ladle, Burgess & Leigh, EX 200.00
Non-Pareil, sugar bowl, Burgess & Leigh 300.00
Non-Pareil, waste bowl, Burgess & Leigh 225.00
Normandy, bowl, vegetable; Johnson Bros, w/lid 325.00
Normandy, cup & saucer, Johnson Bros 85.00
Normandy, plate, bread & butter; Johnson Bros, 6" 45.00
Normandy, plate, Burgess & Leigh, 9" 65.00
Oregon, bowl, vegetable; ped ft, w/lid, Mayer, 9½x9½" 625.00
Oregon, butter dish, 12-panel lid, Mayer, 1845 ....450.00
Oregon, plate, Mayer, 7½" 75.00
Oregon, platter, Mayer, 18x14" 500.00
Oregon, relish, curled hdl, Mayer, 9" 215.00
Oregon, sauce tureen, 3-pc, Mayer, rstr 600.00
Oregon, teapot, Mayer 895.00
Osborne, bowl, vegetable; oval, w/lid, Grindley 350.00
Osborne, soup, Ridgway 70.00
Oxford, bowl, vegetable; Johnson Bros, 9x7" 95.00
Oxford, gravy boat 95.00
Pagoda, plate, dinner; SK&Co, 10¼" 110.00
Pagoda, teapot, lantern shape, Ridgeway, rstr, 8¾" ...650.00

Paisley, gravy boat 85.00
Paisley, soup, 7½" 70.00
Pansy, bowl, ruffled, Warwick, NM 125.00
Pansy, chocolate pot, Warwick 695.00
Pansy, nut dish, leaf shape, Warwick 150.00
Pansy, pitcher, bulbous, Warwick, 8½" 395.00
Peach Royal, sauce tureen, Johnson Bros 295.00
Peach Royal, soup, Johnson Bros, 7½" 75.00
Pekin, bowl, Royal Staffordshire Burslem, 10" ...150.00
Pekin, butter pat, Jones 45.00
Pekin, creamer, Dimmock 225.00
Pekin, flanged soup, Jones, 9" 65.00
Pekin, gravy boat & tray, Jones 150.00
Pekin, plate, Jones, 10" 70.00
Pekin, platter, Jones, 12½" 145.00
Royal, plate, Furnival, 10" 85.00
Royal, plate, Furnival, 9" 70.00
Sabraon, bowl, dessert; scalloped rim, 5¼" ...125.00
Sabraon, creamer, 5¼" 375.00
Sabraon, waste bowl, 3¾x6" 575.00
Scinde, bowl, vegetable; Alcock, w/lid, 9x11½" ...750.00
Scinde, bowl & pitcher, Alcock 2,250.00
Scinde, butter dish & drainer, Alcock 1,100.00
Scinde, cup plate, Alcock 185.00
Scinde, gravy boat, Alcock 400.00
Scinde, plate, Alcock, 10½" 175.00
Scinde, plate, Alcock, 9½" 135.00
Scinde, platter, Alcock, 15½x12", from $650 to ...700.00
Scinde, platter, Alcock, 18" 900.00
Scinde, relish, Alcock 425.00
Scinde, sauce tureen, Alcock, w/lid & tray ...1,050.00
Scinde, teapot, lighthouse shape, Alcock, prof rpr, 8½" ...650.00
Scinde, teapot, pumpkin shape, Alcock, 1840s, rstr, 8½" ...725.00
Shanghae, plate, Furnival, 9¼" 100.00
Shanghae, sugar bowl, w/lid, Furnival, EX ...250.00
Shanghae, waste bowl, Furnival 195.00
Shanghai, plate, Adams, 10" 140.00
Shanghai, plate, Grindley, 9" 120.00
St Louis, pitcher, 5½", EX 150.00
St Louis, platter, 10½" 155.00
Sutherland, bowl, vegetable; w/lid, Royal Doulton ...325.00
Temple, relish, Podmore Walker 425.00
Temple, sugar bowl, lion-head hdls, Podmore Walker, rstr ...300.00
Tonquin, plate, Adams, 9" 150.00
Tonquin, platter, Heath, 14" 600.00
Tonquin, sauce tureen, w/undertray, Heath ...825.00
Touraine, bone dish, Alcock 85.00
Touraine, bowl, berry; Alcock, sm 55.00
Touraine, bowl, potato; Stanley, 10½" 200.00
Touraine, bowl, vegetable; flanged rim, Alcock, 9½" ...175.00
Touraine, bowl, vegetable; oval, Alcock, 8¾" ...95.00
Touraine, bowl, vegetable; w/lid, Stanley, ca 1898, 11x6½" ...375.00
Touraine, butter dish, Alcock 495.00
Touraine, cake plate, Alcock 285.00
Touraine, coffee cup & saucer 125.00
Touraine, egg cup, Alcock 275.00
Touraine, gravy boat w/undertray, Stanley ...250.00
Touraine, plate, Alcock, 10" 125.00
Touraine, plate, Alcock, 6¼" 38.00
Touraine, plate, Alcock, 8" 65.00
Touraine, plate, Alcock, 9" 95.00
Touraine, platter, Stanley, 10" 165.00
Touraine, platter, Stanley, 14¾x10½" 300.00
Touraine, spooner/toothbrush holder, Alcock ...495.00

Touraine, teapot, Alcock 1,195.00
Vermont, butter pat, Burgess & Leigh 60.00
Vermont, plate, Burgess & Leigh, 8½" 85.00
Waldorf, bowl, New Wharf Pottery, 9" 115.00
Waldorf, creamer, New Wharf Pottery 225.00
Waldorf, plate, New Wharf Pottery, 10" 95.00
Waldorf, plate, New Wharf Pottery, 8" 65.00
Waldorf, sauce dish, New Wharf Pottery 48.00
Watteau, bowl, New Wharf Pottery, 9" 90.00
Watteau, mug, milk; New Wharf Pottery 285.00
Watteau, platter, well & tree; Doulton, ca 1900, 20x16", EX ...750.00
Watteau, punch bowl, ped ft, Doulton, 14" ...1,595.00
Waverly, creamer, Grindley 225.00
Waverly, plate, Grindley, 10" 95.00
Waverly, sugar bowl, w/lid, Grindley 400.00

Flue Covers

When spring housecleaning started and the heating stove was taken down for the warm weather season, the unsightly hole where the stovepipe joined the chimney was hidden with an attractive flue cover. They were made with a colorful litho print behind glass with a chain for hanging. In a 1929 catalog, they were advertised at 16¢ each or six for 80¢. Although scarce today, some scenes were actually reverse painted on the glass itself. The most popular motifs were florals, children, animals, and lovely ladies. Occasionally flue covers were made in sets of three — one served a functional purpose, while the others were added to provide a more attractive wall arrangement. They range in size from 7" to 14", but 9" is the average.

For further information we recommend *Flue Covers, Collector's Value Guide,* by Jim Meckley II, available from Collector Books or your local bookstore.

Dutch scene, reverse painting on glass, 10", $125.00.

Asian Beauty, Japanese lady w/flowers in hair, 7", from $70 to ...80.00
Box of Violets, purple flowers in woven box, 9½", from $75 to ...85.00
Branch of Cherries, Victorian girl w/cherry branch, oval, 7x8½" .80.00
Buddies, 3 Black boys on cotton bale, 9½", from $250 to ...300.00
Czarina, redhead in dk fur & feathered hat, 9½", from $90 to ...100.00
Daddy's Girls, blond & brunette sisters embrace, 9½" ...65.00
Dreaming, lady w/rose, sgn Harrison Fischer, 1910, 9½" ...95.00
Ermine, lady in red w/wht ermine stole, 9½", from $85 to ...95.00
Feeding the Swallows, lady in bl w/wht birds, 8½" ...70.00
Gleaners, figures in harvest scene, 7¾", from $50 to ...60.00
Grandpa's Story, wht-bearded man reads to sm girl, 11¾" ...95.00
Holding Felix, girl holds kitten in apron, 4⅝", from $55 to ...65.00
In the Garden, 2 cherubs kneel in garden, 14", from $90 to ...100.00
Lady in Red, lady in hooded fur-lined red cloak, 14" ...165.00
Peck's Bad Boy, mischievous boy in red cap, 9¾", from $75 to ...85.00
Pink Chapeau, girl in fancy pink hat, 7¾", from $65 to ...75.00
Ready To Pick, lg grape cluster on vine, 9½", from $75 to ...85.00

Rose Bonnet, lady in lovely hat w/red rose band, 9½" **100.00**
Royal Courtship, regal Victorian couple, 9¼", from $85 to **95.00**
Swallows, 3 birds on branch, sepia tones, 9½", from $85 to **95.00**
Teasing Old Nick, 2 boys tease dog, oval, 4x5", from $65 to **75.00**
Teeter-Totter, children w/puppy at play, 9½", from $70 to **80.00**
That Old Gang of Mine, 3 boys walk together, 9½", from $90 to .**100.00**

Folk Art

That the creative energies of the mind ever spark innovations in functional utilitarian channels as well as toward playful frivolity is well documented in the study of American folk art. While the average early settler rarely had free time to pursue art for its own sake, his creative energy exemplified itself in fashioning useful objects carved or otherwise ornamented beyond the scope of pure practicality. After the advent of the Industrial Revolution, the pace of everyday living became more leisurely, and country folk found they had extra time. Not accustomed to sitting idle, many turned to carving, painting, or weaving. Whirligigs, imaginative toys for the children, and whimsies of all types resulted. Though often rather crude, this type of early art represents a segment of our heritage and as such has become valued by collectors.

Values given for drawings, paintings, and theorems are 'in frame' unless noted otherwise. See also Baskets; Decoys; Frakturs; Samplers; Trade Signs; Weather Vanes; Wood Carvings.

Articulated dancer, Black bellhop, orig red/wht/blk pnt, 13½" **80.00**
Ashtray, pop bottle caps strung on wire around tin jar lid, 1940s .**42.00**
Birdhouse, log cabin, 4 windows, shingle roof, 9x8x6" **130.00**
Bust, Chieftan w/full headdress, compo w/mc, glass eyes, 29" ..**1,150.00**
Easter egg, scratch decor on purple, yolk intact, dtd 1863 ....**525.00**
Ferris wheel, wood & metal, electric operated, 19x22x13" **375.00**
Figure, bird, made from branch, tin head & wings, 1930s, 7½" **50.00**
Ink drawing, Black couple courting on bench, sepia, 1900s, 8x6" .**110.00**
Log cabin, pnt logs w/gr & red pnt fr windows, 1930s, 13x8x9" .**145.00**
Oil on board, strawberry basket, gesso fr, 1890s, 16x14" **135.00**
Oil on board, 3 man in boat/icy slopes/polar bear, 1890s, 23x19" ...**225.00**
Painting, US Battleship Oregon on artist board, 15x25" **250.00**
Rooster, pnt/smoke decor on tin, 17⅜x17", EX **550.00**
Ship, match sticks, 3-masted, walnut trim, 1920s, 24x28" **385.00**
Snake, winding root w/lead band rattles/nail eyes/wire tongue ...**140.00**
Spencerian drawing, bird on branch, pen & ink, fr, 12½x11" **110.00**
Spencerian drawing, running horse, pen & ink, 19x23" **330.00**
Theorem on paper, rose watercolor, 9x7¼"+fr **50.00**
Theorem on velvet, bird w/berry, DY Ellinger, orig fr, 10x8" ..**1,150.00**
Whirligig, angel flying, wooden cutout w/mc pnt, 17" L, EX **235.00**
Whirligig, Black lady churning butter, wood/wire/metal, 23x34" .**250.00**
Whirligig, Mammy washerwoman, pnt wood, 1930s, 15x19", EX .**250.00**
Whirligig, man cranking early car, pnt wood, ca 1927, 16x29" **95.00**
Yard ornament, bobbing-head crane, wood/tin, 1930s, 44x13x1" ...**125.00**

Fostoria

The Fostoria Glass Company was built in 1887 at Fostoria, Ohio, but by 1891 it had moved to Moundsville, West Virginia. During the next two decades, they produced many lines of pressed patterned tableware and lamps. Their most famous pattern, American, was introduced in 1915 and was produced continuously until 1986 in well over two hundred different pieces. From 1920 to 1925, top artists designed tablewares in colored glass — canary (vaseline), amber, blue, orchid, green, and ebony — in pressed patterns as well as etched designs. By the late '30s, Fostoria was recognized as the largest produc-

er of handmade glassware in the world. The company ceased operations in Moundsville in 1986.

Many items from both the American and Coin Glass lines are currently being reproduced by Lancaster Colony. In some cases the new glass is superior in quality to the old. Since the 1950s, Indiana Glass has produced a pattern called 'Whitehall' that looks very much like Fostoria's American, though with slight variations. Because Indiana's is not handmade glass, the lines of the 'cube' pattern and the edges of the items are sharp and untapered in comparison to the fire-polished originals. Three-footed pieces lack the 'toe' and instead have a peg-like foot, and the rays on the bottoms of the American examples are narrower than on the Whitehall counterparts. The Home Interiors Company offers several pieces of American look-alikes which were not even produced in the United States. Be sure of your dealer and study the books suggested below to become more familiar with the original line.

Coin Glass reproductions are flooding the market. Among items you may encounter are an 8" round bowl, 9" oval bowl, 8¼" wedding bowl, 4½" candlesticks, urn with lid, 6¼" candy jar with lid, footed comport, sugar and creamer; there could possibly be others. Colors in production are crystal, green, blue, and red. The red color is very good, but the blue is not the original color, nor is the emerald green. Buyer beware!

For further information see *Elegant Glassware of the Depression Era* by Gene Florence; *Fostoria, The Popular Years, Third Edition Price Guide,* by Jo Ann Schliesman; and *Fostoria, Books I and II,* by Ann Kerr. *Glass Animals and Figural Flower Frogs of the Depression Era* by Lee Garmon and Dick Spencer offers an in-depth look at that particular aspect of Fostoria's production. (See also Glass Animals.) Their addresses are listed in the Directory under Illinois. Items with (+) at the end of the lines are currently being reproduced; prices are for original issues. Our advisor is Deborah Maggard; she is listed in the Directory under Ohio.

American, crystal, vase, square sides, footed, 6½", $45.00.

American, crystal, ashtray, 2⅞" sq **7.50**
American, crystal, bottle, cologne; w/stopper, 8-oz, 7¼" **80.00**
American, crystal, bowl, banana split; rare, 9x3½" **350.00**
American, crystal, bowl, bonbon; 3-ftd, 6" **15.00**
American, crystal, bowl, float; oval, 10" **32.50**
American, crystal, bowl, float; oval, 11½" **45.00**
American, crystal, bowl, ftd, 8" **60.00**
American, crystal, bowl, relish boat; 2-pt, 12" **22.00**
American, crystal, bowl, vegetable; oval, 9" **25.00**
American, crystal, bowl, wedding; sq, ped ft, 5¼x6½" **60.00**
American, crystal, candle lamp, w/chimney, 8½" **125.00**
American, crystal, candlestick, bell base, 2-light, 6½" **100.00**
American, crystal, creamer, ind, 4¾-oz **9.00**
American, crystal, fruit; flat, ped ft, 16" **175.00**
American, crystal, goblet, claret; #2056, 7-oz, 4⅞" **50.00**
American, crystal, goblet, sherbet; #2056½, 4½-oz, 4½" **10.00**
American, crystal, ice dish insert **15.00**

American, crystal, marmalade, w/lid & chrome spoon 50.00
American, crystal, mustard, w/lid 30.00
American, crystal, pitcher, ftd, 2-pt, 7¼" 65.00
American, crystal, plate, cake; 3-ftd, 12" 22.50
American, crystal, plate, torte; 24" 225.00
American, crystal, sauce boat, w/liner 50.00
American, crystal, shakers, w/tray, ind, 2" 30.00
American, crystal, sugar shaker 50.00
American, crystal, tray, oval, hdls, 6" 35.00
American, crystal, tray, sandwich; center hdl, 12" 40.00
American, crystal, tumbler, water; #2056, ftd, 9-oz, 4⅞" 18.00
American, crystal, vase, flared, 7" 75.00
American, crystal, vase, str sides, 10" 90.00
American, crystal, vase, w/sq ped ft, 9" 45.00
Baroque, bl, bowl, relish, 3-part, 10" 30.00
Baroque, bl, candelabrum, 3-light, 24-lustre, 9½" 195.00
Baroque, bl, mayonnaise, w/liner, 5½" 55.00
Baroque, bl, plate, cake; 10" 40.00
Baroque, bl, sugar bowl, ind, 3" 27.50
Baroque, bl or yellow, creamer, ftd, 3¾" 14.00
Baroque, crystal, bowl, flared, 12" 21.50
Baroque, crystal, bowl, hdls, 8½" 14.00
Baroque, crystal, bowl, sq, 6" 8.00
Baroque, crystal, pitcher, w/ice lip, 7" 100.00
Baroque, crystal, plate, 9½" 17.50
Baroque, crystal, tray, oval, 11" 15.00
Baroque, yel, bowl, jelly; w/lid, 7½" 55.00
Baroque, yel, candlestick, 2-light, 4½" 50.00
Baroque, yel, shakers, pr 100.00
Buttercup, crystal, bowl, salad; #2364, 9" 50.00
Buttercup, crystal, celery, #2350, 11" 27.50
Buttercup, crystal, comport, #6030, 5" 30.00
Buttercup, crystal, vase, #2614, 10" 120.00
Camelia, crystal, bowl, cereal; 6" 25.00
Camelia, crystal, bowl, ftd, rolled rim, 11" 50.00
Camelia, crystal, tray, muffin; hdls, 9½" 32.50
Century, crystal, basket, wicker hdl, 10¼x6½" 70.00
Century, crystal, butter dish, w/lid, ¼-lb 40.00
Century, crystal, stem, goblet; 10-oz, 5¾" 22.50
Chintz, crystal, plate, cracker; #2496, 11" 40.00
Chintz, crystal, vase, #4131, ftd, 7½" 135.00

Coin, emerald green, jelly compote, $35.00.

Coin, amber, ashtray, #1372/124, 10" 30.00
Coin, amber, cruet, w/stopper, 7-oz 65.00
Coin, amber, lamp, patio; #1372/466, 16⅝" 150.00
Coin, amber, nappy, 1-hdl, #1372/499, 5⅜" 20.00
Coin, bl, cigarette box, w/lid, #1372/374, 5¾x4½" 75.00
Coin, bl, jelly; #1372/448 ....25.00
Coin, bl, pitcher, #1372/453, 32-oz, 6⅜" 105.00
Coin, crystal, candle holders, #1372/326, 8", pr 50.00
Coin, crystal, candle holders, #316, 4½", pr 45.00

Coin, crystal, goblet, #2, 10½" 28.00
Coin, crystal, vase, #1372/818, ftd, 10" 45.00
Coin, emerald gr, red or bl, cigarette urn, #374, w/lid, 5¾" 92.50
Coin, olive gr, stem, wine; #1372/26, 5-oz, 4" 45.00
Coin, olive gr, tumbler, iced tea; #1372/58, 14-oz, 5¼" 40.00
Coin, olive gr or amber, pitcher, #453, 1-qt, 6⅝" 90.00
Coin, ruby, candy box, #1372/354, w/lid, 4⅛" 60.00
Coin, ruby, creamer, #1372/738 ....16.00
Coin, ruby, stem, sherbet; #1372/7, 9-oz, 5¼" 60.00
Colony, crystal, bowl, celery; 11½" 30.00
Colony, crystal, bowl, fruit; 10" 35.00
Colony, crystal, bowl, fruit; 14" 42.00
Colony, crystal, bowl, rnd, 4½" 7.00
Colony, crystal, candlestick, 7" 22.00
Colony, crystal, candy dish, w/lid, 6½" 45.00
Colony, crystal, creamer, 3¾" 7.50
Colony, crystal, pitcher, ice lip, 48-oz 195.00
Colony, crystal, plate, bread & butter; 6" 4.00
Colony, crystal, plate, salver; ftd, 12" 65.00
Colony, crystal, salt shaker, ind, 2½" 12.00
Colony, crystal, tumbler, water; 9-oz, 3⅞" 16.00
Colony, crystal, vase, flared, 7½" 40.00
Corsage, crystal, celery, #2440 ....30.00
Corsage, crystal, ice bucket, #2496 ....65.00
Corsage, crystal, relish, #2496, 3-part 32.50
Corsage, crystal, stem, wine; #6014, 3-oz, 5¼" 30.00
Fairfax, amber, baker, oval, 9" 16.00
Fairfax, amber, bowl, fruit; 5" 8.00
Fairfax, amber, butter dish, w/lid 80.00
Fairfax, amber, plate, chop; 13" 17.50
Fairfax, amber, plate, whipped cream 8.00
Fairfax, gr or yel, bowl, cereal; 6" 12.00
Fairfax, gr or yel, candy dish, w/lid, flat, 3-part 50.00
Fairfax, gr or yel, cup, flat 6.00
Fairfax, gr or yel, relish dish, 3-part, 8½" 12.00
Fairfax, gr or yel, stem, claret; 4-oz, 6" 30.00
Fairfax, gr or yel, vase, 2 styles, 8" 50.00
Fairfax, rose, bl or orchid, bowl, centerpc; oval, 13" 50.00
Fairfax, rose, bl or orchid, bowl, lemon; hdls, 9" 15.00
Fairfax, rose, bl or orchid, creamer, ftd 13.00
Fairfax, rose, bl or orchid, plate, grill; 10¼" 40.00
Fairfax, rose, bl or orchid, sugar pail 55.00
Fairfax, rose, bl or yellow, ice bowl liner 25.00
Heather, crystal, creamer, ind 10.00
Heather, crystal, plate, torte; 14" 45.00
Heather, crystal, tumbler, juice; #6037, 5-oz, 4⅞" 20.00
Hermitage, amber, gr or topaz, bowl, salad; #2449½, 7½" 12.00
Hermitage, amber, gr or topaz, bowl, soup; #2449½, 7" 12.00
Hermitage, amber, gr or topaz, pitcher, #2449, 3-pt 60.00
Hermitage, amber, gr or topaz, plate, sandwich; #2449, 12" 12.50
Hermitage, amber, gr or topaz, stem, claret; #2449, 4-oz, 4⅝" ...15.00
Hermitage, Azure or Wisteria, bowl, fruit; #2449½, 5" 12.00
Hermitage, Azure or Wisteria, coaster, #2449, 5⅝" 11.00
Hermitage, Azure or Wisteria, tumbler, #2449½, 2-oz, 2½" 12.00
Hermitage, Azure or Wisteria, tumbler, #2449½, 5-oz, 3⅞" 12.00
Hermitage, crystal, bowl, salad; #2449½, 6½" 8.00
Hermitage, crystal, candle, #2449, 6" 12.50
Hermitage, crystal, mustard, w/spoon & lid, #2449 ....17.50
Hermitage, crystal, plate, ice dish liner; 7" 4.00
Hermitage, crystal, relish/celery, #2449, 11" 10.00
Hermitage, crystal, tumbler, #2449, ftd, 9-oz, 4⅛" 6.00
Jamestown, amber or brn, tumbler, #2719/64, 12-oz, 5⅛" 9.00
Jamestown, amethyst, crystal or gr, creamer, #2719/681, ftd, 3½" ..16.00
Jamestown, amethyst, crystal or gr, tumbler, #2719/64, 12-oz, 5⅛" ...21.00

Jamestown, bl, pk or ruby, bowl, dessert; #2719/421, 4½" **16.00**
Jamestown, bl, pk or ruby, tumbler, #2719/73, 9-oz, 4¼" **25.00**
June, crystal, bowl, Grecian; 10" **40.00**
June, crystal, comport, #2400, 5" **20.00**
June, crystal, plate, dinner; 10¼" **35.00**
June, crystal, plate, salad; 7½" **5.00**
June, crystal, sugar bowl lid only **50.00**
June, rose or bl, bowl, dessert; hdls, lg **115.00**
June, rose or bl, candlestick, Grecian; 5" **60.00**
June, rose or bl, goblet, cocktail; 3-oz, 5¼" **45.00**
June, rose or bl, plate, cream soup; 7½" **12.00**
June, rose or bl, sherbet, low, 6-oz, 4¼" **25.00**
June, rose or bl, vases, 2 styles, 8", ea **250.00**
June, topaz, bowl, cereal; 6½" **35.00**
June, topaz, bowl, whipped cream **14.00**
June, topaz, candlestick, 2" **22.00**
June, topaz, goblet, claret; 4-oz, 6" **75.00**
June, topaz, platter, 12" **70.00**
Kashmir, bl, bowl, cream soup **25.00**
Kashmir, bl, candlestick, 9½" **60.00**
Kashmir, bl, cup, AD: ftd **55.00**
Kashmir, bl, shakers, pr **150.00**
Kashmir, bl, stem, cordial; ¾-oz **110.00**
Kashmir, bl, stem, ftd, 12-oz **35.00**
Kashmir, bl, stem, sherbet; low, 5-oz **20.00**
Kashmir, yel or gr, bowl, cereal; 6" **30.00**
Kashmir, yel or gr, candlestick, 2" **20.00**
Kashmir, yel or gr, cup **15.00**
Kashmir, yel or gr, plate, grill; 10" **35.00**
Kashmir, yel or gr, saucer, rnd **5.00**
Kashmir, yel or gr, stem, cocktail; 3-oz **22.00**
Kashmir, yel or gr, stem, water; 9-oz **20.00**
Kashmir, yel or gr, sugar bowl lid only **50.00**
Lido, crystal or Azure, bowl, finger; #766 ....**22.00**
Lido, crystal or Azure, plate, 8½" **12.50**
Lido, crystal or Azure, sugar bowl **9.00**

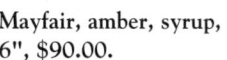

**Mayfair, amber, syrup,
6", $90.00.**

Mayflower, crystal, candlestick, #2560, 4½" **25.00**
Mayflower, crystal, plate, #2560, 9½" **37.50**
Mayflower, crystal, tumbler, juice; #6020, ftd, 5-oz, 4⅞" **17.50**
Meadow Rose, crystal or Azure, bowl, hdls, 8½" **40.00**
Meadow Rose, crystal or Azure, plate, dinner; 9½" **45.00**
Meadow Rose, crystal or Azure, plate, torte; 14" **57.50**
Meadow Rose, crystal or Azure, vase, #2470, ftd, 10" **145.00**
Navarre, crystal, bell, dinner **50.00**
Navarre, crystal, bowl, bonbon; #2496, ftd, 7⅜" **27.50**
Navarre, crystal, candlestick, #2496, 4" **22.00**
Navarre, crystal, comport, cheese; #2496, 3¼" **27.50**
Navarre, crystal, mayonnaise, #2496½, 3-pc **67.50**
Navarre, crystal, plate, bread & butter; #2440, 6" **11.00**
Navarre, crystal, plate, cracker; #2496, 11" **42.50**
Navarre, crystal, plate, luncheon; #2440, 8½" **22.00**

Navarre, crystal, relish, #2496, 3-part, 10x7½" **47.50**
Navarre, crystal, stem, cocktail; #6106, 3½-oz, 6" **25.00**
Navarre, crystal, stem, water; #6106, 10-oz, 7⅝" **30.00**
Navarre, crystal, stem, wine; #6106, 3¼-oz, 5½" **35.00**
Navarre, crystal, tumbler, tea; #6106, ftd, 13-oz, 5⅞" **32.00**
Navarre, crystal, vase, #4121 or #4108, 5", ea **95.00**
Romance, crystal, bowl, baked apple; #2364, 6" **15.00**
Romance, crystal, candlestick, #2594, 3-light, 8" **42.50**
Romance, crystal, shakers, #2364, 2⅝", pr **50.00**
Romance, crystal, vase, #2614, 10" **75.00**
Royal, amber or gr, ashtray, #2350, 3½" **22.50**
Royal, amber or gr, bottle, cologne; #2322, tall **50.00**
Royal, amber or gr, bowl, #2315, ftd, 10½" **45.00**
Royal, amber or gr, bowl, #2324, ftd, 13" **50.00**
Royal, amber or gr, bowl, baker; #2350, oval, 9" **37.50**
Royal, amber or gr, comport, #2358, 8" **30.00**
Royal, amber or gr, egg cup, #2350 ....**27.50**
Royal, amber or gr, pitcher, #1236 ....**365.00**
Royal, amber or gr, plate, dinner; #2350, sm, 9½" **15.00**
Royal, amber or gr, plate, salad; #2350, 7½" **4.00**
Royal, amber or gr, platter, #2350, 10½" **30.00**
Royal, amber or gr, server, #2287, center hdl, 11" **30.00**
Royal, amber or gr, stem, oyster cocktail; #869, 5½-oz **15.00**
Royal, amber or gr, stem, sherbet; #869, high, 6-oz **16.00**
Royal, amber or gr, tumbler, #5000, ftd, 9-oz **16.00**
Royal, amber or gr, tumbler, #859, flat, 9-oz **25.00**
Royal, amber or gr, vase, #2292, flared **90.00**
Seville, amber, bowl, finger; #869/2283, w/6" liner **20.00**
Seville, amber, bowl, fruit; #2350, 5½" **10.00**
Seville, amber, creamer, #2315½, flat, ftd **13.50**
Seville, amber, egg cup, #2350 ....**30.00**
Seville, amber, pitcher, #5084, ftd **235.00**
Seville, amber, platter, #2350, 15" **70.00**
Seville, amber, stem, cordial; #870 ....**65.00**
Seville, amber, tumbler, #5084, ftd, 5-oz **13.50**
Seville, gr, bowl, #2315, low ft, 7" **18.00**
Seville, gr, bowl, console; #2371, oval, 13" **40.00**
Seville, gr, comport, #2327, twisted stem, 7½" **25.00**
Seville, gr, grapefruit, molded, #2315 ....**30.00**
Seville, gr, plate, cream soup liner; #2350 ....**6.00**
Seville, gr, plate, luncheon; #2350, 8½" **6.50**
Seville, gr, stem, oyster cocktail; #870 ....**17.50**
Seville, gr, sugar bowl, #2350½, ftd **13.50**
Seville, gr, tumbler, #5084, ftd, 12-oz **20.00**
Sun Ray, crystal, butter dish, w/lid, ¼-lb **25.00**
Sun Ray, crystal, comport **18.00**
Sun Ray, crystal, nappy, hdl, tricornered **15.00**
Sun Ray, crystal, plate, 9½" **28.00**
Sun Ray, crystal, vase, rose bowl; 5" **30.00**
Trojan, pk, ashtray, #2350, lg **50.00**
Trojan, pk, bowl, whipped cream; #2375 ....**15.00**
Trojan, pk, bowl, combination; #2415, w/candle-holder hdls **195.00**
Trojan, pk, decanter, #2439, 9" **950.00**
Trojan, pk, ice bucket, #2375 ....**100.00**
Trojan, pk, ice dish liner, #2451 ....**29.00**
Trojan, pk, plate, salad; #2375, 7½" **9.00**
Trojan, pk, shaker, #2375, ftd, pr **95.00**
Trojan, pk or yel, sweetmeat dish, #2375 ....**18.00**
Trojan, yel, bowl, #2354, 3-ftd, 6" **35.00**
Trojan, yel, bowl, centerpc; #2394, ftd, 12" **45.00**
Trojan, yel, goblet, water; #5299, 10-oz, 8¼" **27.50**
Trojan, yel, pitcher, #5000 ....**285.00**
Trojan, yel, plate, cake; #2375, hdls, 10" **32.50**
Trojan, yel, sugar bowl, #2375½, ftd **20.00**

Trojan, yel, tumbler, #5099, ftd, 9-oz, 5¼" 17.50
Versailles, bl, bowl, bonbon; #2375 ....25.00
Versailles, bl, comport, #5098, 3" 40.00
Versailles, bl, goblet, wine; #5098 or #5099, 3-oz, 5½" 85.00
Versailles, bl, platter, #2375, 12" 125.00
Versailles, pk or gr, bowl, soup; #2375, 7" 60.00
Versailles, pk or gr, candlestick, #2395, 3" 17.50
Versailles, pk or gr, cup, AD; #2375 ....75.00
Versailles, yel, bowl, #2394, ftd, 12" 45.00
Versailles, yel, candy dish, #2394, w/lid, ¼-lb 195.00
Versailles, yel, creamer, tea; #2375½ 45.00
Versailles, yel, pk or gr, saucer, AD: #2375 ....7.50
Versailles, yel, pk or gr, tumbler, #5098 or #5099, ftd, 2½-oz 40.00

Frakturs

Fraktur is a German style of black letter text type. To collectors the fraktur is a type of hand-lettered document used by the people of German descent who settled in the areas of Pennsylvania, New Jersey, Maryland, Virginia, North and South Carolina, Ohio, Kentucky, and Ontario. These documents recorded births and baptisms and were used as bookplates and as certificates of honor. They were elaborately decorated with colorful folk-art borders of hearts, birds, angels, and flowers. Examples by recognized artists and those with an unusual decorative motif bring prices well into the thousands of dollars, in fact, some have sold at major auction houses in excess of $5,000.00. Frakturs made in the late 1700s after the invention of the printing press provided the writer with a prepared text that he needed only to fill in at his own discretion. The next step in the evolution of machine-printed frakturs combined woodblock-printed decorations along with the text which the 'artist' sometimes enhanced with color. By the mid-1800s, even the coloring was done by machine. The vorschrift was a handwritten example prepared by a fraktur teacher to demonstrate his skill in lettering and decorating. These are often considered to be the finest of frakturs. Those dated before 1820 are most valuable.

The practice of fraktur art began to diminish after 1830 but hung on even to the early years of this century among the Pennsylvania Germans ingrained with such customs. Our advisor for this category is Frederick S. Weiser; he is listed in the Directory under Pennsylvania. (Mr. Weiser has provided our text, but being unable to physically examine the frakturs listed below cannot vouch for their authenticity, age, or condition.) These prices were realized at various reputable auction galleries in the East and Midwest. Unless otherwise noted, values are for examples in excellent condition. Note: Be careful not to confuse frakturs with prints, calligraphy, English-language marriage certificates, Lord's Prayers, etc.

Key:
lp — laid paper   wc — watercolored
pr — printed   wp — wove paper
p/i — pen and ink

Birth Record

P/i/wc, flowers/compote/text, sgn Munch, PA, 1851, 14x18", G- .350.00
P/i/wc, text/flowers/tree/urns/etc, PA, 1847, 5½x8" 2,800.00
P/i/wc/lp, Adam & Eve in garden w/snake/verse, PA, 1838, 17x13" .1,900.00
P/i/wc/lp, cross-legged angel/birds/florals, PA, 1810, 15x13" ...2,300.00
P/i/wc/lp, heart/flowers/scallops/etc, PA, 1815, 15x12" 3,400.00
P/i/wc/lp, ladies/clouds/flowers, sgn, PA, 1864, 16x10" 725.00
P/i/wc/wp, birds/flowers/text/etc, PA, ca 1805, 8x13" 3,100.00
P/i/wc/wp, flowers/text, PA, 1818, 8x13" 400.00
P/i/wc/wp, suns/moons/lions, English text, PA, 1819, 18x21" 715.00

P/i/wc/wp (glued down), angels/birds/etc, PA, 1846, 18x16" 220.00
Pr/p/i/wc, flowers/birds, 5-color, PA, 1801, 13x16"+fr 500.00
Pr/wc, block printed/floral/bird/etc, Heinrich Otto, 1782, 15x13" ..450.00
Pr/wc/lp, birds/angels/cherub/etc, Ritter, PA, 1826, 16x13" 275.00
Pr/wc/lp, flowers, F Krebs, 1809, damage, modern fr: 17x20" 550.00
Pr/wc/lp, heart/eagle/cherub/etc, PA, 1812, 20x16" 475.00

Miscellaneous

Art work, p/i/wc/wp, floral design, PA, ca 1820, 7¾x6½" 625.00
Art work, silhouettes of couple, p/i/wc, early 1800s, 6x7", pr 400.00
Bookplate, p/i/pencil/wc/wp, flowers, PA, 1830, 5⅞x3¾" 660.00
Bookplate, p/i/wc, floral & text, PA, 1890, 3⅝x6¼" 120.00
Bookplate, p/i/wc, florals/hearts/birds, Zink, 1815, 3⅝x6⅜" ...3,600.00
Bookplate, p/i/wc/lp, tulips/heart, PA, 1790, 4¾x2¾"+fr 1,540.00
Family register, p/i/wc/lp, PA, 1850s, 6x9", 2-pg 50.00
House blessing, p/i/wc, text/flowers/birds, PA, 1859, 16x20" 500.00

Frames

Styles in picture frames have changed with the fashion of the day, but those that especially interest today's collectors are the deep shadow boxes made of fine woods such as walnut or cherry, those with Art Nouveau influence, and the oak frames decorated with molded gesso and gilt from the Victorian era. Our advisor for this category is Michael Hinton; he is listed in the Directory under Pennsylvania.

Note: Unless another date is given, mirrors described in the following listings are from the 19th century.

Hand-carved wood, gilded, probably Italian, ca 1900, 13x10", $175.00.

Photo courtesy Michael Hinton

Architectural, cut/cvd pine, fan at top, early 1900s, 18x11" 300.00
Bird's-eye veneer ogee, gilt liner, 33x27" 185.00
Brass filigree, gilt, 5" dia, pr 325.00
Bull's-eye veneer ogee, gilt liner, 33x27" 250.00
Cast brass, Cupid design, 20x12" 200.00
Cast iron, pnt/cast cherubs & flowers, rare, 9½x6½", EX 250.00
Cast iron, pnt/cast flowers on bricked wall, #8957, 10x7¾", EX ..200.00
Cast iron, pnt/cast pheasant & berries, #230, 9x7½" 360.00
Cast iron, pnt/cast woman & flowers, #9016, 11½x8½", EX 300.00
Cherry Empire, half-columns & corner blocks, old pnt, 17x13" .425.00
Cherry w/pearl heart at ea cross corner, folky style, 15x11" 65.00
Chip cvd, old red pnt & natural, easel bk, 7x5" 195.00
Cut brass, filigree, Italian, 1700s, 9x6" 625.00
Laminated mahog/pine, shaped perimeter w/appl bosses, 9x13" ...55.00
Oak & gesso, emb florals, 18x24" 135.00
Silverplate, crown/Cupid crest, scroll ft, easel bk, 8½" 300.00
Sterling, etched flowers ea corner, standing, 2x3" 80.00

Walnut, beveled, 2" molding, 17x14" **150.00**
Walnut, oval liner, incised decor, dtd 1871, 20x30" **975.00**
Walnut Victorian crisscross, cvd leaves at corners, 22x18" **125.00**

Frances Ware

Frances Ware, produced in the 1880s by Hobbs, Brockunier and Company of Wheeling, West Virginia, is either clear or frosted with amber-stained rim bands. The most often found pattern is Hobnail, but Swirl was also made. For more information, refer to *Hobbs, Brockunier & Co. Glass*, by Neila and Tom Bredehoft. Our advisors for this category are Betty and Clarence Maier; they are listed in the Directory under Pennsylvania.

Hobnail, clear; bowl, 7½", from $65 to **75.00**
Hobnail, clear; butter dish, from $80 to **95.00**
Hobnail, clear; creamer, from $50 to **60.00**
Hobnail, clear; finger bowl, 4", from $25 to **35.00**
Hobnail, clear; pitcher, water; from $125 to **175.00**
Hobnail, clear; spooner **45.00**
Hobnail, frosted; bowl, ftd, berry pontil, 6x10" **150.00**
Hobnail, frosted; bowl, oblong, 8" **75.00**
Hobnail, frosted; bowl, sq, 7½" **70.00**
Hobnail, frosted; bowl, 4½" **30.00**
Hobnail, frosted; bowl, 8" dia **75.00**
Hobnail, frosted; bowl, 9" **85.00**
Hobnail, frosted; butter dish, from $80 to **120.00**
Hobnail, frosted; celery vase **75.00**
Hobnail, frosted; chandelier, amber font, brass fr, 14" dia **950.00**
Hobnail, frosted; cruet, from $425 to **500.00**
Hobnail, frosted; pitcher, milk **150.00**
Hobnail, frosted; pitcher, water; sq top, 8½" **175.00**
Hobnail, frosted; plate, sq, 5¾" **25.00**
Hobnail, frosted; sauce dish, sq, 4" **28.00**
Hobnail, frosted; shakers, very rare, pr **300.00**
Hobnail, frosted; sugar bowl, w/lid, from $65 to **80.00**
Hobnail, frosted; syrup, pewter lid **375.00**
Hobnail, frosted; toothpick holder **60.00**
Hobnail, frosted; tray, cloverleaf, 12", from $90 to **125.00**
Hobnail, frosted; tumbler, water **45.00**
Swirl, clear; syrup **90.00**
Swirl, frosted; bowl, 3¾" H **40.00**
Swirl, frosted; cruet **295.00**
Swirl, frosted; mustard jar, from $90 to **125.00**
Swirl, frosted; pitcher, water **250.00**
Swirl, frosted; shakers, pr **165.00**
Swirl, frosted; sugar bowl, w/lid **80.00**
Swirl, frosted; sugar shaker, orig lid **195.00**
Swirl, frosted; syrup, Pat dtd **295.00**
Swirl, frosted; tumbler **45.00**

Franciscan

Franciscan is a trade name used by Gladding McBean and Co., founded in northern California in 1875. In 1923 they purchased the Tropico plant in Glendale where they produced sewer pipe, gardenware, and tile. By 1934 the first of their dinnerware lines, El Patio, was produced. It was a plain design made in bright, attractive colors. El Patio Nouveau followed in 1935, glazed in two colors — one tone on the inside, a contrasting hue on the outside. Coronado, a favorite of today's collectors, was introduced in 1936. It was styled with a wide, swirled border and was made in pastels, both satin and glossy. Before 1940 fif-

teen patterns had been produced. The first hand-decorated lines were introduced in 1937, the ever-popular Apple pattern in 1940, Desert Rose in 1941, and Ivy in 1948. Many other hand-decorated and decaled patterns were produced there from 1934 to 1984.

Dinnerware marks before 1940 include 'GMcB' in an oval, 'F' within a square, or 'Franciscan' with 'Pottery' underneath (which was later changed to 'Ware'). A circular arrangement of 'Franciscan' with 'Made in California USA' in the center was used from 1940 until 1949. At least forty marks were used before 1975; several more were introduced after that. At one time, paper labels were used.

The company merged with Lock Joint Pipe Company in 1963, becoming part of the Interpace Corporation. In July of 1979 Franciscan was purchased by Wedgwood Limited of England, and the Glendale plant closed in October 1984.

Our advisors for this category are Mick and Lorna Chase (Fiesta Plus); they are listed in the Directory under Tennessee. Our Starburst advisor is Karen Silvermintz (under Texas). See also Gladding McBean.

Coronado

Both satin (matt) and glossy colors were made including turquoise, coral, celadon, light yellow, ivory, and gray (in satin); and turquoise, coral, apple green, light yellow, white, maroon, and redwood in glossy glazes. High-end values are for maroon, yellow, redwood, and gray. Add 10 – 15% for gloss.

Coronado, gravy boat, with attached plate, $28.00 to $40.00.

Bowl, casserole; w/lid, from $85 to **125.00**
Bowl, cereal; from $15 to **20.00**
Bowl, cream soup; w/underplate, from $40 to **50.00**
Bowl, fruit; from $12 to **18.00**
Bowl, nut cup; from $16 to **18.00**
Bowl, onion soup; w/lid, from $45 to **60.00**
Bowl, rim soup; from $28 to **32.00**
Bowl, salad; lg, from $35 to **50.00**
Bowl, serving; oval, 10½", from $30 to **45.00**
Bowl, serving; 7½" dia, from $20 to **25.00**
Bowl, serving; 8½" dia, from $18 to **20.00**
Bowl, sherbet/egg cup; from $15 to **18.00**
Butter dish, from $35 to **45.00**
Cigarette box, w/lid, from $75 to **90.00**
Creamer, from $12 to **15.00**
Cup & saucer, demitasse; from $28 to **45.00**
Cup & saucer, jumbo; from $28 to **35.00**
Demitasse pot, from $125 to **195.00**
Fast-stand gravy, from $28 to **40.00**
Jam jar, w/lid, from $65 to **80.00**
Pitcher, 1½-qt, from $35 to **60.00**
Plate, chop; 12½" dia, from $25 to **35.00**
Plate, chop; 14" dia, from $35 to **45.00**
Plate, crescent hostess; w/cup well, no established value
Plate, crescent salad; lg, no established value
Plate, ind crescent salad; from $25 to **35.00**

Plate, 10½", from $20 to 25.00
Plate, 6½", from $6 to 10.00
Plate, 7½", from $9 to 12.00
Plate, 8½", from $12 to 15.00
Plate, 9½", from $15 to 18.00
Platter, oval, 10", from $20 to 25.00
Platter, oval, 13", from $30 to 45.00
Platter, oval, 15½", from $45 to 60.00
Relish dish, oval, from $20 to 35.00
Shakers, pr, from $20 to 35.00
Sugar bowl, w/lid, from $15 to 25.00
Teacup & saucer, from $12 to 15.00
Teapot, from $65 to 95.00
Tumbler, water; no established value
Vase, 8", no established value

Desert Rose

Ashtray, ind 20.00
Ashtray, oval 125.00
Ashtray, sq 295.00
Bell, Danbury Mint 125.00
Bell, dinner 125.00
Bowl, bouillon; w/lid 325.00
Bowl, cereal; 6" 15.00
Bowl, divided vegetable 45.00
Bowl, fruit 12.00
Bowl, mixing; lg 195.00
Bowl, mixing; med 185.00
Bowl, mixing; sm 175.00
Bowl, porringer 295.00
Bowl, rimmed soup 28.00
Bowl, salad; 10" 115.00
Bowl, soup; ftd 32.00
Bowl, vegetable; 8" 32.00
Bowl, vegetable; 9" 40.00
Box, cigarette 125.00
Box, egg 195.00
Box, heart shape 165.00
Box, rnd 165.00
Butter dish 45.00
Candle holders, pr 125.00
Candy dish, oval 295.00
Casserole, 1½-qt 85.00
Casserole, 2½-qt 195.00
Coffeepot 125.00
Coffeepot, ind 395.00
Compote, lg 75.00
Compote, low, no established value
Cookie jar 295.00
Creamer, ind 40.00
Creamer, regular 22.00
Cup & saucer, coffee; no established value
Cup & saucer, demitasse 55.00
Cup & saucer, jumbo 65.00
Cup & saucer, tall 45.00
Cup & saucer, tea 18.00
Egg cup 35.00
Ginger jar 225.00
Goblet, ftd 195.00
Gravy boat 32.00
Heart 145.00
Hurricane lamp, no established value
Jam jar 75.00

Long 'n narrow, 15½x7¾" 495.00
Microwave dish, oblong, 1½-qt 285.00
Microwave dish, sq, 1-qt 215.00
Microwave dish, sq, 8" 245.00
Mug, bbl, 12-oz 50.00
Mug, cocoa; 10-oz 135.00
Mug, 7-oz 32.00
Napkin ring 50.00
Piggy bank 250.00
Pitcher, jug; no established value
Pitcher, milk 95.00
Pitcher, syrup 75.00
Pitcher, water; 2½-qt 125.00
Plate, chop; 12" 75.00
Plate, chop; 14" 175.00
Plate, coupe dessert 75.00
Plate, coupe party 295.00
Plate, coupe steak 50.00
Plate, divided; child's 195.00
Plate, grill 125.00
Plate, side salad 40.00
Plate, TV 175.00
Plate, 10½" 18.00
Plate, 6½" 6.00
Plate, 8½" 18.00
Plate, 9½" 20.00
Platter, turkey; 19" 295.00
Platter, 12¾" 45.00
Platter, 14" 65.00
Porringer 295.00
Relish, oval, 10" 35.00
Relish, 3-section 75.00
Shaker & pepper mill, pr 295.00
Shakers, rose bud, pr 24.00
Shakers, tall, pr 75.00
Sherbet 25.00
Soup ladle, no established value

Desert Rose, soup tureen, flat bottom, $495.00; On 14" chop plate, $175.00.

Sugar bowl, open, ind 125.00
Sugar bowl, regular 32.00
Tea canister 225.00
Teapot 85.00
Thimble 75.00
Tidbit tray, 2-tier 195.00
Tile, in fr 75.00
Tile, rnd, fluted 195.00
Tile, sq 65.00
Toast cover 195.00
Trivet, fluted, rnd 195.00
Tumbler, juice; 6-oz 50.00
Tumbler, 10-oz 32.00
Tureen, soup; flat bottom 495.00
Tureen, soup; ftd, either style 695.00

Vase, bud **75.00**

For other hand-painted patterns, we recommend the following general guide for comparable pieces (based on current values):

Cafe Royal	-20%
Daisy	-20%
October	-20%
Forget-Me-Not	Same as Desert Rose
Meadow Rose	Same as Desert Rose
Desert Rose	Base Line Values
Apple	+10%
Ivy	+40%
Strawberry Fair	+20%
Strawberry Time	+20%
Fresh Fruit	+20%
Bountiful	+20%
Poppy	+50%
Original (small) Fruit	+50%
Wild Flower	+200% or more!

There are several Apple items that are so scarce they command higher prices than fit the above formula. The Apple ginger jar is valued at $600.00+, the 4" jug at $195.00+, and any covered box in Apple is at least 50% more than Desert Rose.

There is not an active market in Bouquet, Rosette, or Twilight Rose, as these are scarce, having been produced only a short time. Our estimate would place Bouquet and Rosette in the October range (-20%) and Twilight Rose in the Ivy range (+40%).

Apple Pieces Not Available in Desert Rose

Bowl, batter; minimum value **450.00**
Bowl, str sides, lg **55.00**
Bowl, str sides, med **45.00**
Casserole, stick hdl & lid, ind **65.00**
Coaster **65.00**
Jam jar, redesigned **425.00**
Shaker & pepper mill, wooden top, pr **395.00**
½-apple baker, from $195 to **225.00**

El Patio, 1934 – 1954

This line includes a few pieces not offered in Coronado and the colors differ, but per piece these two patterns are valued about the same.

Franciscan Fine China

The main line of fine china was called Masterpiece. There were at least four marks used during its production from 1941 to 1977. Almost every piece is clearly marked. This china is true porcelain, the body having been fired at a very high temperature. Many years of research and experimentation went into this china before it was marketed. Production was temporarily suspended during the war years. More than 170 patterns and many varying shapes were produced. All are valued about the same with the exception of the Renaissance group, which is 25% higher.

Bowl, vegetable; serving, oval **50.00**
Cup **20.00**
Plate, bread & butter **18.00**
Plate, dinner **30.00**
Plate, salad **25.00**
Saucer **12.00**

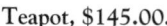

Starburst

Teapot, **$145.00.**

Ashtray, ind **20.00**
Ashtray, oval, lg **50.00**
Bonbon/jelly dish **35.00**
Bowl, crescent salad **40.00**
Bowl, divided, 8" **25.00**
Bowl, salad; ind **25.00**
Butter dish **45.00**
Candlesticks, pr, from $175 to **200.00**
Chop plate, from $55 to **65.00**
Coffeepot **150.00**
Creamer & sugar bowl **25.00**
Gravy boat, from $20 to **30.00**
Jug, water; 10" **90.00**
Mug **60.00**
Oil cruet **75.00**
Pepper mill **150.00**
Pitcher, 7½", from $50 to **75.00**
Plate, dinner **12.00**
Shakers, bullet shape, lg **50.00**
Shakers, sm, pr **20.00**
Snack/TV tray w/cup rest, 12½", from $75 to **100.00**
Tumbler, 6-oz, from $40 to **50.00**
Vinegar cruet **75.00**

Frankart

During the 1920s Frankart, Inc., of New York City, produced a line of accessories that included figural nude lamps, bookends, ashtrays, etc. These white metal composition items were offered in several finishes including verde green, jap black, and gunmetal gray. The company also produced a line of caricatured animals, but the stylized nude figurals have proven to be the most collectible today. With few exceptions, all pieces were marked 'Frankart, Inc.' with a patent number or 'pat. appl. for.' All pieces listed are in very good original condition unless otherwise indicated. Our advisor for this category is Walter Glenn; he is listed in the Directory under Georgia.

Aquarium, 3 kneeling nudes encircle 10" fishbowl, 10½" **950.00**
Ashtray, bk-to-bk nudes hold rack of 4 rnd ashtrays, 8" **450.00**
Ashtray, nude grows from leaves to hold tray above, 25" **900.00**
Ashtray, standing nude leans against circle, tray at ft, 7" **410.00**
Ashtray, stylized pigeon holds insert in wings, 6" **165.00**
Bookends, Indian chief & Indian lady w/papoose, 9½", pr **275.00**
Bookends, kneeling nudes, bks support books, 6", pr **375.00**
Bookends, ladies w/fans support books, 10", pr **450.00**
Bookends, modernistic female heads, 6", pr **325.00**
Bookends, stylized circus ponies, 5", pr **150.00**
Clock, 2 nudes stand either side rectangular glass clock, 10½" .**1,650.00**

Lamp, dancing nude embraces 11" crackle glass cylinder, 12½" .975.00
Lamp, nude as butterfly w/frosted glass wings, 10¼" 1,750.00
Lamp, nude kneels before 4" bubble ball, 8" 850.00
Lamp, nude silhouettes against rectangular glass panel, 11" 950.00
Lamp, standing nude silhouettes against glass panel, 10" 550.00
Lamp, 2 standing bk-to-bk nudes hold skyscraper globe, 21" 975.00
Lamp, 4 standing nudes surround sq glass cylinder, 13" 975.00
Vase, nude caresses sm frosted glass vase, 10" 425.00
Wall plaque, Diana the Huntress, 8" sq 375.00

Frankoma

The Frank Pottery, founded in Oklahoma in 1933 by John Frank, became known as Frankoma in 1934. The company produced decorative figurals, vases, and such, marking their ware from 1936 – 38 with a pacing leopard 'Frankoma' mark. These pieces are highly sought. The entire operation was destroyed by fire in 1938, and new molds were cast — some from surviving pieces — and a similar line of production was pursued. The body of the ware was changed in 1955 from a honey tan (called 'Ada clay,' referring to the name of the town near the area where it was dug) to a red brick clay (known as Sapulpa), and this, along with the color of the glazes (over fifty have been used), helps determine the period of production. A Southwestern theme has always been favored in design as well as in color selection.

In 1965 they began to produce a limited-edition series of Christmas plates, followed by a bottle vase series in 1969. Considered very collectible are their political mugs, bicentennial plates, Teenagers of the Bible plates, and the Wildlife series. Their ceramic Christmas cards are also very popular items with today's collectors.

Frankoma celebrated their 50th Anniversary in 1983. On September 26 of that same year, Frankoma was again destroyed by fire. Because of a fire-proof wall, master molds of all 1983 production items were saved, allowing plans for rebuilding to begin immediately.

Frankoma filed for Chapter 11 in April, 1990, and eventually sold to a Maryland investor in February of 1991, thereby ending the family-ownership era. For a more thorough study of the subject, we recommend that you refer to *Frankoma Treasures* and *Frankoma and Other Oklahoma Potteries* by Phyllis and Tom Bess, our advisors; you will find their address in the Directory under Oklahoma.

Ashtray, red clay, free-form, #30 ....38.00
Bookend, Charger Horse, gr, red clay 75.00

Bookend, Dreamer Girl, Prairie Green, #427, 6", $250.00.

Bookends, Irish setter, Osage Brn, thin neck, pr 150.00
Bookends, Mountain Girl, Ada clay, pr 365.00
Bowl, Royal Bl, oval, Ada clay, #205 ....40.00
Canteen, Thunderbird, Prairie Gr, leather thong, 6¼" 30.00
Casserole, Prairie Gr, Ada clay, #94U, ind 25.00
Christmas card, 1944 ....110.00
Christmas card, 1947-48 ....85.00
Christmas card, 1949 ....65.00

Christmas card, 1950-51 ....75.00
Christmas card, 1952 ....85.00
Christmas card, 1952, Donna Frank 100.00
Christmas card, 1953-56 ....75.00
Christmas card, 1957 ....70.00
Christmas card, 1958-60 ....65.00
Christmas card, 1961-66 ....60.00
Christmas card, 1967-68 ....50.00
Christmas card, 1969-71 ....40.00
Christmas card, 1972 ....35.00
Christmas card, 1973-75 ....30.00
Christmas card, 1976-77 ....25.00
Christmas card, 1980-82 ....25.00
Christmas plate, 1965 ....310.00
Christmas plate, 1967 ....70.00
Christmas plate, 1977-82 ....35.00
Cornucopia, gr, Ada clay, #57 ....45.00
Decanter, Feather design, Prairie Gr, Ada clay, rectangular, 7" 50.00
Mug, Democrat Donkey, Carter/Mondale, 1977 ....35.00
Mug, Democrat Donkey, 1st in series, 1975 ....25.00
Mug, Republican Elephant, Nixon/Agnew, 1969 ....75.00
Mug, Republican Elephant, Reagan/Bush, 1981 or 1985, ea 30.00
Mug, Republican Elephant, 1st of series, 1968 ....85.00
Mug, Uncle Sam, 1976 ....15.00
Pipe rest 140.00
Pitcher, eagle, Dusty Rose 25.00
Pitcher, Guernsey, Prairie Gr, 1940s mk, #93, 6½" 45.00
Pitcher, honey, #831, 16-oz 25.00
Plate, David, Teenager of the Bible, 1974 ....45.00
Plate, Helen Keller 45.00
Plate, Letter Carrier, Desert Gold 75.00
Plate, Wildlife, Prairie Chicken, 1974 ....82.50
Sculpture, Dreamer Girl 250.00
Sculpture, English Setter, mini 70.00
Sculpture, Fan Dancer, gr, red clay, #113, 8½x13½" 250.00
Sculpture, Gardener Girl, bl 95.00
Sculpture, Indian Maiden, #101 ....30.00
Sculpture, Prancing Percheron, Ada clay 375.00
Sculpture, Rearing Clydesdale, flat blk, reissue 175.00
Sculpture, Trojan Horse, mini 65.00
Teapot, Wagon Wheel, Prairie Gr, 2-cup 40.00
Tray, Prairie Green, Ada clay, #206, 5x8" 35.00
Trivet, Governor & Mrs David Boren, 1975 ....20.00
Trivet, Prairie Green, Cattle Brands, red clay 10.00
Vase, bottle; Chinese Red 300.00
Vase, collector; V-1, 1969, 15" 105.00
Vase, collector; V-12, 13" 65.00
Vase, collector; V-13, blk & Terra Cotta, 1981, 13" 65.00
Vase, collector; V-15, Prairie Gr, 2-pc, last of series 80.00
Vase, collector; V-2, turq, 1970, 12" 70.00
Vase, collector; V-4, blk & Terra Cotta, 1972 ....85.00
Vase, collector; V-5, Flame Red, 1973, 13" 85.00
Vase, collector; V-6, Celadon & blk, 13" 85.00
Vase, collector; V-7, 13" 80.00
Vase, collector; V-8, red & wht, red stopper, 13" 75.00
Vase, collector; V-9, blk & wht, w/stopper, 13" 75.00
Vase, mottled, #74 ....70.00
Vase, pillow; Prairie Gr, Ada clay, #63 ....25.00
Vase, pillow; Red Bud, #63, 7" 40.00
Vase, Prairie Gr, scalloped top, Ada clay, #79, 7" 85.00
Vase, Ring, Desert Gold, #500, mini 35.00
Vase, Wagon Wheel, bl, Ada clay 30.00
Wall mask, Phoebe, gr, Ada clay, #730 ....100.00
Wall plaque, Wagon Wheel 40.00

Wall pocket, acorn, gr, Ada clay 30.00
Wall pocket, Wagon Wheel, Red Bud, #510 ....45.00

Fraternal Organizations

Fraternal memorabilia is a vast and varied field. Emblems representing the various organizations have been used to decorate cups, shaving mugs, plates, and glassware. Medals, swords, documents, and other ceremonial paraphernalia from the 1800s and early 1900s are especially prized. Our advisor for Odd Fellows is Greg Spiess; he is listed in the Directory under Illinois. Information on Masonic and Shrine memorabilia has been provided by David Smies, who is listed under Kansas.

Elks

Bookends, bronze, cast elk in high relief, pr 75.00
Cuff links, tooth, 14k mts, pr 75.00
Elks, dbl tooth, w/emblem, 14k cap 45.00
Pendant, bronze, 1868-1968 Centennial, 1¼" dia, EX 25.00
Pin, Woodmen of Am, gold filled, 1916 ....8.00
Tag, ID; metal, Los Angeles 1936 convention 15.00
Tankard, lg elk & BPOE in cobalt on wht ceramic, 12x7" 275.00
Watch fob, gold filled, eagle & claws 195.00

Masons

Uniform, Knights Templar, ca 1890, $175.00.

Photo courtesy
David Smies

Bible, gold letters, ca 1910, 8½x11" 60.00
Books, Encyclopedia of Freemasonry, Mackey, 2-vol set 75.00
Cookie mold, CI, ca 1890, 4⅞" 45.00
Coverlet, Jacquard, eagle/symbols/etc, sgn/dtd 1824, 97x74", VG .250.00
Cupboard, oak, cvd door emblems, 32x24x8" 400.00
Loving cup, Knights Templar, Syracuse NY, 1909 ....50.00
Pocketwatch, Dudley, 19 jewel, gold filled 2,200.00
Working tools, MOP, 1½", 6-pc set 35.00

Odd Fellows

Banner, yel silk w/HP hand w/heart, Unselfishness, 30x18", EX ...110.00
Bookends, bronze, Vergne Artware, ca 1935, 6¼", pr 125.00
Catalog, lodge supplies, Henderson-Ames, 1925 ....30.00
Creed, litho on paper, many vignettes, 19th C, 23x29" 100.00
Mask, Goliath, papier-mache, horsehair beard/mustache, 1900s ...195.00
Pamphlet, IOOF Proceedings, IN 1890, 74-pg, VG 10.00
Pamphlet, Odd Fellows Cemetery Assoc, cremation, 1899, 56-pg .45.00
Ring, 10k gold, std mks on enameled face 125.00
Ring, 10k gold w/hand-eng (fine quality) symbols 175.00
Trivet, brass, hand w/heart, leaf border, 3 circles, 8" L 130.00

Shrine

Circus, porc, McCormick, set of 6 ....200.00
Fez, Isis, pin, long tassel 25.00
Pitcher, cider; Egyptian desert scene, emblem, 1907, +4 mugs ...585.00
Postcard, Shriners 1st pin, comic, 1930 ....10.00

Miscellaneous

Eastern Star, dishes, emblems, 4-place, 16-pc set 50.00
Eastern Star, handkerchief, embr on gold w/wide lace border, M .12.00
Knights of Columbus, pin, Master Counselor, 10k gold 20.00
Knights of Columbus, sword & scabbard, NM 150.00
Order of Eagles, lapel pen, 1898 ....50.00
Pythias, Degree certificate, 1907, in leather pouch 50.00
Pythias, pins on ribbon, 1892 ....45.00
Scottish Rite, supply catalog, Lilley Co, 1920s 30.00

Fruit Jars

As early as 1829, canning jars were being manufactured for use in the home preservation of foodstuffs. For the past twenty-five years, they have been sought as popular collectibles. At the last estimate, over four thousand fruit jars and variations were known to exist. Some are very rare, perhaps one-of-a-kind examples known to have survived to the present day. Among the most valuable are the black glass jars, the amber Van Vliet, and the cobalt Millville. These often bring prices in excess of $3,000.00 when they can be found. Aside from condition, values are based on age, rarity, color, and special features. Our advisor for this category is John Hathaway; he is listed in the Directory under Maine.

Atlas Clover Good Luck, clear, qt 4.00
Atlas E-Z Seal, aqua, ½-pt 20.00
Atlas E-Z Seal, bl, pt 18.00
Atlas E-Z Seal, clear, ½-pt 3.00
Atlas Mason Improved Pat'd, apple gr, qt 30.00
Atlas-Mason's Patent, aqua, qt 4.00
Atlas-Mason's Patent, gr, qt 20.00
Ball (3 L Loop) Mason, lt aquamarine, ½-gal 18.00
Ball Ideal, bl, sq, qt 15.00
Ball Improved, bl, pt 12.00
Ball Mason Patent, clear, qt 5.00
Ball Mason's Improved Pat 1858, aqua, rare, ½-gal 95.00
Ball Perfect Mason, bl, 8 ribs, qt 10.00
Bosco Double Seal, clear, qt 43.00
Boyd Perfect Mason, aqua, qt 5.00
Champion Pat Aug 31 1896, aqua, repro clamp, qt 123.00
Clark's Peerless (in circle), aqua, pt 5.00
Cohansey (arched), aqua, qt 25.00
Columbia, clear, pt 28.00
Daisy Jar (flat emb) 200.00
Double Safety, clear, ½-gal 6.00
Durham (in circle), aqua, pt 25.00
Eureka 8 Pat'd Dec 27th 1864, aqua, repro lid, 1 ½-qt 95.00
Foster Sealfast, base: Foster, clear, ½-pt 10.00
Genuine Mason, aqua, pt 5.00
GJCo, aqua, dome lid, pt 48.00
GJCo, aqua, dome lid, qt 28.00
Globe, amber, qt 70.00
Globe (wide mouth), aqua, orig metal, qt 120.00
Hawley Glass Co Hawley PA on base, qt 9.00
Heroine, aqua, pt, 2-pc zinc lid 120.00

HK Mulford Chemists Philadelphia (vertical), amber, ¼-pt 35.00
Kline's Pat'd Oct 27 63 (on blown stopper), aqua, ½-gal 98.00
Knowlton Vacuum (star), clear, ½-gal 43.00
Lockport Mason, aqua, pt 4.00
Mason (lg letters on slant, no underline), bl, qt 60.00
Mason Arched, aquamarine, ½-gal 24.00
Mason CFJ Improved, reverse: Clyde NY, aqua, midget 48.00
Mason Improved, aqua, pt 8.00
Mason Jar of 1872, aqua, qt 35.00
Mason LGW Improved, lt aqua, qt 20.00
Mason Patent Nov 30th 1858, reverse: circle, aqua, qt 25.00
Mason Root Mold, lt apple gr, qt 32.00
Mason's CFJ Improved, dk amber, ½-gal 150.00
Mason's CFJ Patent Nov 30th 1858, aqua, midget, w/orig lid 35.00
Mason's CFJCo Patent Nov 30th 1858, aqua, qt 4.00
Mason's II Patent Nov 30th 1858, aqua, qt 33.00
Mason's Improved, reverse: CJF, aqua, midget 25.00
Mason's Patent Nov 30th 1859, base: HC&T, aqua, qt 18.00
Mason's Patent Nov 30th 58 (Christmas Mason), aqua, pt 95.00
Mason's 6 Pat Nov 30th 1858, aqua, midget 75.00
Millville WTCo Improved, aqua, qt 68.00
Mission (bell) Made in California, aqua, qt 8.00
New Gem (Gem in script), clear, pt 18.00
Pat'd Feb 9th 1864 WW Lyman Reisd Jan 22nd 1867, aqua, qt 38.00
Poster Sealfast, base: Foster, clear, ½-pt 10.00
Premium Coffeyville Kas, clear, pt 25.00
Protector (arched), aqua, ½-gal 43.00
Puritan TM (sailing ship) Fruit Jar LSCo, aqua, orig clamp, qt ..448.00
Sealtight, base: PA G Co, clear, qt 18.00
Standard (Mason in flag), lt gr, qt 10.00
Sun (in circle w/radiating rays), aqua, pt 150.00
Swayzee's Improved Mason, deep gr, qt 48.00
Swayzee's Improved Mason, med emerald gr, qt 55.00
The Wears Jar (in circle), clear, qt 9.00
TM Lightning, dk amber, pt 90.00
TM Lightning, honey amber, qt 75.00
Trademark Keystone Registered, clear, qt 6.00
Victory in shield on lid, clear, qt 5.00
Whitmore's Pat Rochester NY, aqua, qt 350.00
Winslow Improved Valve Jar, aqua, pt 750.00

Fry

Henry Fry established his glassworks in 1901 in Rochester, Pennsylvania. There, until 1933 when it was sold to the Libbey Company, he produced glassware of the finest quality. In the early years they produced beautiful cut glass; and when it began to wane in popularity, Fry turned to the manufacture of occasional pieces and oven glassware. He is perhaps most famous for the opalescent pearl glass called 'Foval.' It was sometimes made with blue or jade green trim in combination. Because it was in production for only a short time in 1926 and 1927, it is hard to find. Our advisor for this category is Ron Damaska; he is listed in the Directory under Pennsylvania. See also Kitchen Collectibles, Glassware.

Apple baker, Pearl Ovenware, ornate enameled rim, 1937 ....30.00
Aquarium, Golden Glow 150.00
Ashtray, blk, rest at top of ea buttressed ft (4) 25.00
Baker, Pearl Ovenware, 1919, 6" dia 15.00
Bowl, fruit; wht opal, Delft bl ft, #2505, 12" 300.00
Cake pan, Pearl Ovenware, sq 20.00
Cake plate, Sunnybrook, emerald gr, 3-ftd 35.00
Cake server, Foval, jade gr w/wht pearl opal, loop hdl, 7x10" 475.00
Candle holders, amber w/gold trim, orig labels, pr 45.00

Casserole, Pearl Ovenware, eng lid, in metal fr, 1938, 8" 25.00
Compote, Foval, jade gr w/wht pearl, 7x5¾" 275.00
Cream soup & plate, emerald gr, ring hdls 30.00
Cream soup & underplate, Foval, 2 hdls, 1970 ....30.00
Cup & saucer, Fuchsia 15.00
Custard cup, etched leaf design, 1927 ....15.00
Finger bowl, DE 30 Grape pattern, etched 20.00
Ivy bowl, blk bowl & ft, clear swirl connector 85.00
Ivy bowl, emerald gr w/clear swirl connector 65.00
Muffin pan, Pearl Ovenware, 6-compartment, retangular, 9" 35.00
Percolator, Foval, glass insert 400.00
Plate, dinner; Dmn Optic, emerald gr 18.00
Plate, pearl w/jade gr trim, #3101, 7½" 35.00
Plate, Sunbeam, cut, 8" 185.00
Spice tray, Rose (pk), 3-compartment, center fleur-de-lis hdl 35.00
Teapot, Foval, gold enamel trim, #2000, 6-cup 295.00
Teapot, Foval, jade hdl, spout & finial, #2001, 3-cup 200.00
Tumbler, Heart, cut, str sides 65.00
Tumbler, lemonade; Foval, jade hdl, #9416 ....75.00
Vase, Foval w/Delft bl festooning, bl ft/stem, #353, 10" 250.00
Vase, Foval w/Delft bl festooning, invt cylinder, 11" 360.00
Vase, Geneva, cut, chalice form, 10" 210.00
Vase, Golden Glow, fan form, rare, 5½" 95.00
Vase, jack-in-pulpit; Foval, Delft bl trim, 10" 225.00
Vase, Orient cut pattern w/Buzz Star & Zipper neck, sgn, 12" 195.00
Vase, Pershing, cut, flared rim, 14" 360.00

Fulper

Throughout the 19th century (for perhaps as long as one hundred years) the Fulper pottery in Flemington, New Jersey, produced utitarian and commercial wares. But it was during the span from 1909 to 1935 (the Arts & Crafts period in particular) that they became prominent producers of beautifully glazed art pottery. Although most pieces were cast and not hand decorated, their graceful, classical shapes combined with wonderful experimental glaze combinations made each piece a true work of art.

The company also made dolls' heads, Kewpies, figural perfume lamps, and powder boxes. Examples prized most highly by collectors today are those that were produced before the devastating fire of 1929 and the subsequent takeover by Martin Stangl. (See Stangl Pottery.)

Several marks were used: a vertical in-line 'Fulper' being the most common, a horizontal mark, Flemington, Rafco, Prang, and paper labels (on earlier pieces). Most Fulper is marked although unmarked pots that surface can be identified by shape and glaze characteristics. Values are determined by size, desirability of glaze, and rarity of form. Lamps with colored glass inserts are rare and avidly sought by collectors. Our advisor for this category is Douglass White; he is listed in the Directory under Florida.

Bowl, green, blue, and mustard flambe with peacock feather design, incised vertical oval mark, #468, 5¾x9½", NM, $700.00.

Basket, sculptured rose on wht, ribbed, twisted rope hdl, 15" 350.00

Bowl, antique verte w/tan flambe, crystalline int, 18-panel, 3x15" ..**275.00**
Bowl, artichoke form, Leopard Skin crystalline flambe, 5½x8" ..**650.00**
Bowl, bl matt w/Flemington gr int, 3 birds as ft, 5½x11" **600.00**
Bowl, caramel/gr matt, shield decor at rim, 4x9" **200.00**
Bowl, Cat's Eye flambe (tan/brn/cream), ink mk, 2½x10½" **300.00**
Bowl, centerpc; mirror blk, lotus form, ftd, 6x11" **325.00**
Bowl, Chinese bl flambe, ftd, incised vertical mk, 7½" **195.00**
Bowl, Chinese bl flambe (bl/blk/pk), ink mk, 2x9" dia **325.00**
Bowl, cucumber crystalline, scalloped rim, ink mk, 3x15" **350.00**
Bowl, effigy; bl/cream/brn flambe on brn, 3 figures, 7x10½" **425.00**
Bowl, effigy; brn/gr mottle, 3 figures support bowl, 7x10½" **550.00**
Bowl, effigy; butterscotch flambe/mustard, 3-figure, 7½x10¾" ...**800.00**
Bowl, effigy; 3 figures support bowl, bl flambe drip, 7½x10½" **575.00**
Bowl, Famille Rose matt w/royal bl neck, low, ink mk, 10" **220.00**
Bowl, Flemington gr (gr/gray/blk), 3-ftd, label/ink mk, 2x8" **170.00**
Bowl, Flemington gr (lt bl/gray/tan), 2½x11" **260.00**
Bowl, mahog flambe on mustard matt, ped ft, 3x8" **725.00**
Candle sconces, wall mt, brn/gr-mottled matt, 14x5", NM, pr ..**700.00**
Candlesticks, brn to gr flambe, 15x5", pr **1,600.00**
Candlesticks, olive & mint gr crystalline, ink mk, 3½", pr **190.00**
Chamberstick, cucumber gr crystalline, low, mk, 6" L **150.00**
Chamberstick, tan & gunmetal matt, ink mk, 7" **325.00**
Flask, pilgrim; Flemington Gr/gunmetal flambe, scroll hdls, 10" ..**750.00**
Jug, Vasekraft, copper dust crystalline, mk, 12x9" **1,200.00**
Lamp, Cat's Eye lustre flambe, conical shade w/ldgl inlay, 19" ..**15,000.00**
Mug, gray-gr gloss, tapered form, 3½" **125.00**
Tile, flower basket, mc, ca 1910, rare, 6" dia **575.00**
Vase, bl & gr glossy over pk matt, 4½", NM **200.00**
Vase, bl flambe, circular decor at neck, ink mk, 7" **260.00**
Vase, bl glossy over lav matt, 9½" **270.00**
Vase, bl snowflake crystalline base, ring hdls, 13x7¼" **1,200.00**
Vase, blk & silver cucumber crystalline flambe, geometrics, 8x4" ..**475.00**
Vase, blk flambe/copper dust, low angle width, sloped hdls, 9" ...**290.00**
Vase, brn matt, hdls, Prang mk, 4½" **375.00**
Vase, butterscotch flambe on mustard matt, tapered, 12x9" **2,000.00**
Vase, caramel & brn glossy, tiered form w/rnded hdls, mk, 5" **140.00**
Vase, Chinese bl flambe, slightly rolled rim, 6½x7½" **350.00**
Vase, Chinese bl/mirror blk flambe, teardrop w/3 horns, 6½" .**1,100.00**
Vase, copper dust, banded, lg hdls w/3 int lobes, 7x10" **325.00**
Vase, copper dust crystalline, stylized leaves, corseted, 11½" ..**6,000.00**
Vase, cucumber gr w/brn flambe & silver crystals, fan form, 8" ...**175.00**
Vase, deep rose/tan/lt & dk glossy gr, hdls, unmk, 6" **260.00**
Vase, dk bl & gr drips on brn, urn form, #4018, 7¼" **150.00**
Vase, Elephant's Breath flambe, collared, early mk, 4¼x6¼" **450.00**
Vase, Elephant's Breath flambe, sm opening, ovoid, 8x5¼" **800.00**
Vase, EX flambe w/stippled bronze & bl, metallic glaze, 9¾" **425.00**
Vase, EX flambe/crystalline, buttressed hdls, 6½x8¼" **475.00**
Vase, Flemimgton gr flambe, bottle form, early ink mk, 13½x6" .**850.00**
Vase, gr & aqua flambe w/crystalline, baluster, 10½x4¼" **275.00**
Vase, gr & cream flambe on mustard matt, collar rim, 9¾x4" **850.00**
Vase, gr flambe over burgundy, Rafco, early, 4½" **225.00**
Vase, gr metallic/brn microcrystalline, tapered, 8½x2½" **400.00**
Vase, gr/tan/brn flambe, emb mushrooms & lg cutouts, 10x4½" ..**950.00**
Vase, gunmetal crystalline on gr, hdls, ink mk, 4½x6" **350.00**
Vase, gunmetal/gr/bl flambe over caramel, ring hdls, 12½" **450.00**
Vase, hammered frothy mirror bl, hdls, 12x11½" **1,100.00**
Vase, ivory & clear flambe, 4-sided, 4-ftd, unmk, 8¼x3¾" **350.00**
Vase, ivory/mahog/mirror gr flambe, 4-spout flagon, ftd, 8" **700.00**
Vase, Leopard Skin crystalline w/blk metallic & brn flambe, 7" .**425.00**
Vase, lt & cornflower bl/olive crystalline, cylindrical, 11" **325.00**
Vase, lt bl crystalline, short neck, bulbous, #526, 9½" **275.00**
Vase, lt gr crystalline, ribbed, drilled, unmk, 13" **475.00**
Vase, mahog to gr to bl flambe, corseted, early mk, 7½x4" **550.00**
Vase, metallic mahog/Elephant's Breath flambe, bullet form, 6½" .**550.00**

Vase, mirror blk, #604, oval mk/paper label, 8½x11" **675.00**
Vase, mirror blk to copper dust crystaline flambe, 12½x7¾" ..**1,500.00**
Vase, red/bl matt, can neck/rnd body w/rim-to-width hdls, 9" **325.00**
Vase, rose opaque matt, 3 sqd rim-to-shoulder hdls, 4½" **120.00**
Vase, silvery cucumber crystalline, 2 flat hdls, 11½x5" **500.00**
Vase, tan & lt gr crystalline, low form, sq hdls, mk, 7x3½" **180.00**
Vase, violet/dk bl gloss over rose matt, sqd hdls, 4x6" **425.00**

Furniture

American 17th- and 18th-century furniture played an important role in our country's environment. Aside from its utility, furniture was a symbol indicating wealth, taste, and station in life of the owner. Each period brought about distinct design changes that created a recognizable form for that particular time frame. Our earliest furniture was handmade by the cabinetmaker with apprentices and journeymen who learned every phase of the craft of the master cabinetmaker. The end of the Civil War brought the Industrial Revolution and mechanization of furniture manufacturing. With it came the ornate Victorian period and the many revival styles. These were followed in the 20th century by Art Deco and Art Nouveau and more revival of our earliest periods.

It is important for the buyer of antique and collectible furniture to approach each piece from the point of view of the prevailing taste of that particular time frame. Pieces from lesser cabinetmakers should be recognized simply as makers of old furniture, as age alone does not equal value.

The market place is showing a definite recovery from the recession; however, some categories are still selling below their market value. Because of this, items that have sold at auction for at least 25% lower than their normal market values will be designated with (*). Items listed in the lines that are designated with (**) are pieces in the best of form and of museum quality. Traditional mahogany furniture from the 20th century and machine made in the style of Hepplewhite, Sheraton, and Duncan Phyfe is still enjoying great popularity as is its English counterparts. Turn-of-the-century European inlaid and carved furniture is also rising in value. Commonplace oak furniture is still selling well below its highs of a few years ago.

Please note: If a piece actually dates to the period of time during which its style originated, we will use the name of the style only. For example: 'Hepplewhite' will indicate an American piece from roughly the late 1700s to 1815. The term 'style' will describe a piece that is far removed from the original time frame. 'Hepplewhite style' refers to examples from the turn of the century. When the term 'repro' is used it will mean that the item in question is less than thirty years old and is being sold on a secondary market. When only one dimension is given for blanket chests, dry sinks, tables, settees, sideboards, and sofas, it is length.

Condition is the most important factor to consider in determining value. It is also important to remember that *where* a piece sells has a definite bearing on the price it will realize, due simply to regional preference. Our advisor for this category is Suzy McLennan Anderson, ISA, of Heritage Antiques, whose address is listed in the Directory under New Jersey. (Photo and SASE required; no phone appraisals.) To learn more about furniture, we recommend *The Collector's Encyclopedia of American Furniture* (there are three in the series) and *Furniture of the Depression Era* by Robert and Harriet Swedberg; *Heywood-Wakefield Modern Furniture* by Steve and Roger Rouland; *Antique Oak Furniture* by Conover Hill; *American Oak Furniture, Books I* and *II* and *Victorian Furniture, Our American Heritage, Books I* and *II* by Kathryn McNerney; and *Collector's Guide to Oak Furniture* by Jennifer George. See also Fifties Modern; Nutting, Wallace; Shaker; Stickley.

Key:
Am — American
bj — bootjack
Geo — Georgian
grpt — grainpainted

brd — board	hdbd — headboard
Chpndl — Chippendale	hdw — hardware
Co — Country	Hplwht — Hepplewhite
cvd — carved	mar — marriage
cvg — carving	NE — New England
c&b — claw and ball	QA — Queen Anne
do — door	rswd — rosewood
drw — drawer	trn — turning
Emp — Empire	uphl — upholstered/upholstery
Fed — Federal	vnr — veneer
Fr — French	Vict — Victorian
ftbd — footboard	W/M — William and Mary
G — good	: — over (example: 1 do: 2 drw)

Beds

Brass, Aesthetic Movement, roundels, spindles, finials, 62x53" ..880.00
Brass, scrolled horizontal members, bowed ends, Am, 1900s, lg ..400.00
Canopy, birch w/pencil posts, moon cut-out hdbd, 71x50x66" ...1,200.00
Canopy, birch w/pencil posts, shaped hdbd, rprs, 84x77x36" 550.00
Canopy, Fed tall post, finely cvd w/some star punches, 77x48" ..1,500.00
Canopy, hardwood Emp style tall post w/cherry finish, full sz 880.00
Canopy, mahog Fed style, tall reeded posts, full sz 650.00
Canopy, mahog tall post, acanthus cvg, arched cornice 2,475.00
Canopy, tall 4-post w/spire finials, appl acorns, 77x70x52" 650.00
Directoire, mahog, cvd crest, uphl hdbd, trn posts, twin sz 175.00
Empire style, mahog, trn, 81", repro, king sz 550.00
Field, mahog Fed style, shaped hdbd, tall posts 1,200.00
French, walnut w/cvd details, c&b ft, foliage crest, 60x73x34" ...125.00
Hired man's, hardwood w/old red, 28½x74¼" 150.00
Jenny Lind, tall post, poplar/hardwood, rprs, 70x76x42" 110.00
Jenny Lind, walnut, single sz, 43x69" 165.00
Limbert, #473, 5 wide slats:arched toe brd, twin sz, 50x80" 750.00
Murphy, oak, EX orig 2,750.00
Rope, bird's-eye & burl w/figure, rfn, 45x76x52" 300.00
Rope, cherry, trn legs/posts, cannonball finials, 50x76x48" 415.00
Rope, cherry/poplar, scroll/panel hdbd w/trn crest/rail, 52x72x48" ..350.00
Rope, curly maple Co, trn post & crest rails, walnut panel, 42x72x52" ..550.00
Rope, maple w/curly posts, poplar hdbd, 74x48" 220.00
Rope, maple/poplar, rfn, added canopy fr, 57x72x50" 475.00
Rope, maple/poplar, trn posts, orig rails, full sz 225.00
Rope, poplar, trn posts w/acorn finials, shaped hdbd, 52x75" 500.00
Rope, poplar Co, old worn red, trn posts, shaped hdbd, 41x69" ...300.00
Rope, poplar Co, trn posts w/goblet finials, 51x69x50" 100.00
Trundle, cherry, trn ft, low hdbd/ftbd, 16x64x62" 110.00
Vict, Rococo-cvd walnut, paneled hdbd, 1850s, 101x60" 3,575.00
Vict, walnut w/burl vnr, rfn, 83" H, full sz 880.00
4-poster, birch w/grpt, lamb's-tongue detail, shaped hdbd, 84" ...720.00
4-poster, maple Co Emp w/bird's-eye in posts, 60x76x41" 300.00
4-poster, tiger maple, trn, w/lantern finials, full sz 700.00

Benches

Bucket, poplar, cut-out ends, old gr pnt, OH, 36x38x9½" 450.00
Bucket, poplar w/gr wash over gray, wire nails, 36x38x9¼" 525.00
Burled walnut Art Deco, uphl cushion seat, 1930s, 37" 545.00
Cobbler's, hard & soft woods, 2-drw, rprs/rfn, 49" 550.00
Deacon's, Fed, plank seat, str crest rail, trn legs, 1800s 260.00
Fireside, hardwood & pine, high-bk, some age, 72x44" 550.00
Fireside, pine, curved paneled high-bk, brn rpt, 68x72" 825.00
Fireside, pine, high curved bk, 2 do in base, 68x69" 3,200.00
Fireside, pine Co English, curved paneled bk, 73x73" 825.00
Fireside, walnut QA style, cvd shell knees, uphl, repro, 35" 250.00
Lyre shape, cvd fr w/paw ft, reuphl, 20th C, 52" 700.00

Mammy's, 2 baby guards for twins, blk rpt, wear, 79" 335.00
Primitive, pine, cut-out ends mortised through top, rfn, 36" 275.00
Primitive, poplar Co, wire nails, old rpt, age cracks, 60" 300.00
Primitive pine, worn dk finish, legs mortised through top, 66" ...220.00
Settle, arrow-bk, bl rpt, 78" 245.00
Settle, Co, trn legs & rungs, plank seats, spindle-bk, rpt, 97" 525.00
Settle, Co Sheraton, spindled arrow-bk, trn detail, rstr, 75" 990.00
Settle, figured oak English, curved front/flat bk, rprs, 59x47" ..4,475.00
Settle, orig brn pnt w/floral crest, ½-spindle bk, worn, 73" 500.00
Settle, orig grpt w/striping & flower stencil, minor rpr, 80" 2,100.00
Settle, orig yel w/stencil & stripes, ½-spindle bk, 72" 1,325.00
Settle, Sheraton, blk rpt w/stencil, cushion seat, 82" 600.00
Settle, simple trns, plank seat, spindle bk w/arms, 108" 350.00
Settle, spindle bk, dk gr rpt, steel rods added to arms, 68" 500.00
Vict, oak Am Gothic, quatrefoil & foliage-bk fr, 1850s, 56x72x21" .3,300.00
Vict, oak English QA, paneled wainscot bk/cabriole legs, rprs, 73" .360.00
Water, pine Co, mustard rpt, bj ft, 30x31x12" 385.00
Water, pine w/yel wash, 3-shelf, cut-out ft, 42x34x12" 450.00
Water, poplar Co w/red rpt, rprs, 33x38x16" 360.00

Blanket Chests, Coffers, Trunks, and Mule Chests

Cherry Co Chpndl, 2 dvtl drws 2 false drw, rprs, 41x42x20" 500.00
Cherry/poplar, orig gr pnt w/stencil, dtd 1859, 27x48x20" 1,650.00
Cherry/walnut/poplar Co, trn ft/posts, paneled, w/till, 39" 715.00
Oak English Chpndl, 3 raised panels, bracket ft, till, rprs, 45" 825.00
Pine Co Hplwht w/orig grpt, 2-drw, lift lid, 6-brd, 43x42x19" 770.00
Pine Hplwht w/grpt, 2 false:2 dvtl drw, cut-out ft, 39x42" 1,200.00
Pine PA, 2 dvtl drws, bear-trap lock, rfn/rprs, 30x53x23" 550.00
Pine w/brn vinegar grpt on yel w/2-color trim, PA, 49" 1,400.00
Pine w/old red & blk grpt, 2 dvtl drw, 6-brd type, 41x40x18" 440.00
Pine w/orig flame grpt, dvtl case, trn ft, PA, 29x44x22" 440.00
Pine w/orig red & navy flower reserves, dvtl, w/till, 51" 880.00
Pine/poplar PA, brn & bl vinegar grpt w/hearts, w/till, 51" ...22,000.00
Pine/poplar PA Sheraton w/orig grpt, w/till & lock, 47" 1,650.00
Poplar PA w/rpt red & blk vinegar grpt, trn legs, paneled, 43" ...330.00
Poplar w/fruit stencil/1857, 2 dvtl drw/till, 30x47x21" 3,200.00
Poplar w/orig grpt, dvtl case w/till, PA, ca 1816, 26x46x21" 550.00
Primitive, pine w/old red, 6-brd, till, wrought nails, 38" 180.00
Quarter-sawn oak Euro style, tooled hinges, 1900s, 50" 425.00
Walnut w/old gr grpt on wht, dvtl, 28x50" 450.00

Bookcases

Cherry wood bookcase with chevron string inlay, shaped arched panels, scalloped skirt, American, early 1800s, 73x54", $2,400.00.

Cherry, stepbk, 2 15-pane do:4 panel do, rstr cornice, 91x56" ..3,850.00
Golden-oak era, 1 6-pane do, shelves adjust, rfn, 54x32" 440.00
Lifetime #7218, 1-pane do w/10 mullioned sqs at top, 56x28" 2,200.00

Limbert #340, 2 3-pane do, 3 shelves adjust, sgn, 46x32" 2,100.00
Limbert #357, 1 do w/2 vertical glass panels, corbels, 57" 4,000.00
Mahog, cvd details, paw ft, 3-part, 1900s, 68x73" 3,850.00
Quarter-sawn golden-oak era, dbl 1-pane do, 57x44" 350.00
Quarter-sawn oak, 3-part, 48x34x11½" 385.00
Walnut, 4 do:3 drw, cornice w/medallions, 3-part, 54x96" 1,350.00
Walnut, 4-do:drws, shelves adjust, 56x70x14" 1,250.00
Walnut Eastlake Vict, rfn, 62x30x14" 715.00

Bureaus, See Chests

Cabinets

Breakfront, blk pnt Chpndl style w/gilt chinoiserie, repro, 78" .1,375.00
China, Limbert #2425, ebon-oak, shelves adjust, 58x33x16" 4,250.00
China, mahog Hplwht style w/inlay, 2 do:drw:2 do, 91x42x22" ..2,500.00
Curio, cvd walnut w/woman & shell crest, 3-section, 53x50x11" .1,200.00
Curio, gilt Fr style w/mc floral, ormolu, mirror bk, 55x25" 1,200.00
Curio, mahog herringbone vnr Fr style, curved glass, 56x27", pr .990.00
Deco bird's-eye maple, 2-part, 2 lobed do/cornice, 66x55" 4,025.00
Liquor, walnut & mahog Art Deco, mirrored int, 1930s, 65x34" .460.00
Music, hardwood & mahog vnr bow-front w/inlay, 1900s, 46x20x16" ..165.00

Candlestands

Cherry candlestand, shaped top, original
surface, New Hampshire, ca 1810,
28½x14¾" square, $900.00.

Birch Hplwht, tilt top, tripod base, chip-cvd detail, 17x17" 440.00
Cherry Co Hplwht, 1-brd top, tripod base w/spider legs, 28x18" ..385.00
Cherry Hplwht, 1-brd tilt top, tripod base, rprs, 21x16" 600.00
Cherry/birch, trn posts, 3 curved legs, NH, 28x15x16" 800.00
Cherry/maple Co, 1-brd top, trn column, 3-ftd, rfn, 18" dia * 150.00
Cherry/maple Co Chpndl, 1-brd top, snake ft, 38x14x14" 1,100.00
Mahog Emp w/flame vnr tilt top, cvd tripod base, 28x26x17" 440.00
Mahog Fed, tip top, baluster std, curved legs, Am, 1800s * 200.00
Maple Co Chpndl w/some curl, tripod base, rpr, 26x18x19" 660.00
Maple Fed, tilt top, baluster std, Am, early 1800s 300.00
Pnt Fed, decoupage top, vasiform std, curved legs, 1800s 1,725.00
Primitive, hard & soft woods, 1-brd top, 3 trn legs, 24x13" dia ..250.00
Shaker type, chip-cvd at base of post, 3-leg, 1-drw, 28x18x18" ..1,000.00
Shaker type birch, spider legs, rfn/rstr, 28x20x12½" 700.00
Tiger maple w/mahog inlay, tilt top, c&b ft, rfn, 39x26x17" ...3,000.00
Walnut Co Chpndl, 1-brd top, alligatored finish, 39x18" dia 330.00

Chairs

Arm, banister-bk w/half-trn slats, shaped crest & arms, rpt, 47" .660.00
Arm, chestnut Euro, open arms, reuphl, old finish, 37" 990.00
Arm, Fr Deco fruitwood, half-circle open arms, uphl 1,625.00
Arm, hardwood banister-bk, rpl rush seat, blk rpt, 46" 495.00
Arm, japanned Dutch style w/chinoiserie, slip seat, 1880s 660.00
Arm, JM Young #1916, 4-slat bk, reuphl seat, 39" 375.00

Arm, Limbert #588, 5-slat bk w/curved rail, reuphl seat, 38" 450.00
Arm, mahog Chpndl, open arms w/pistol grips, reuphl, 39" 330.00
Arm, mahog Chpndl wing-bk, muslin covered, 44" 2,100.00
Arm, mahog Dutch marquetry w/flower inlay, reuphl, 46" 1,485.00
Arm, mahog English Chpndl style w/cvg, reuphl, 20th C, 39" ...660.00
Arm, maple QA, much cvg, Spanish ft, rush seat, NH, 44" ** .16,500.00
Arm, Potty, walnut QA, deep apron, vase splat, reuphl seat, 41" .1,980.00
Arm, Tobey, leather sling style, 6-leg, 35x46x33" 1,200.00
Arm, walnut Baroque Revival, much cvg, worn uphl, 19th C, 51" .580.00
Arm, walnut Vict w/Minerva-head arms, reuphl/rfn, 44" 660.00
Chaise lounge, tubular chromed & pnt steel, needlework cushion ..460.00
Corner, mahog w/cvd eagle arm terminals, cvd splats, 34½" 650.00
Invalid's, hardwood/wicker/cane, wire wheels, 45" 110.00
Lolling, cherry Chpndl, open arms, reuphl, old rfn, 40" 1,425.00
Lolling, walnut Continental style, open arms, uphl bk/seat, 36" .700.00
Morris, Com-Pact, Mission oak, rpl leather pads, no mk 1,300.00
Recamier, mahog Duncan Phyfe style, ormolu mt, rush seat, 58" L ..1,300.00
Rocker, Limbert #642, 4-slat bk, orig cushion, 33", EX 475.00
Rocker, nursing; 4 arched slats, rush seat, PA, 18th C 350.00
Rocker, platform; walnut Vict, reuphl, rfn, 38½" 235.00
Rocker, sewing; curly maple Emp, cane seat, old finish 150.00
Rocker arm, gr w/freehand & stencil decor, vase splat, 43" 330.00
Rocker arm, Lifetime, 4-slat bk, open arms, cushion seat, 34", G .325.00
Rocker arm, maple/hardwood, 5 arched slats, splint seat, 47" 880.00
Rocker arm, YM Young, 4-slat bk, reuphl seat, 35", EX 350.00
Rocker arm, 4 grad slats, trn legs, shaped arms, 43" 200.00
Rocker arm, 4-slat ladder-bk, splint seat, 45½" 250.00
Side, banister-bk half-spindle, shaped crest, splint seat, 43" 500.00
Side, banister-bk w/half-trn slats, trn finials, rpt, 43" 440.00
Side, Chpndl Spanish ft transitional, vase splat, rush seat, 40" 350.00
Side, Co Windsor, spindled fan-bk w/shaped crest, rfn, 36" 275.00
Side, curly & bird's-eye maple, saber-leg, cane seat, 34" 675.00
Side, Fed, orig grpt w/gold stencil, cane seat, rprs, 31x17" 500.00
Side, hardwood Louis XVI style w/cvg, reuphl, 36" 360.00
Side, hardwood medieval style w/cvg, uphl seat, 32" 440.00
Side, hardwood Moravian, pierced/cvd bk, plank seat, 33" 195.00
Side, Louis XVI style, orig gray-wht pnt, reuphl, 1900s, 37" 360.00
Side, mahog Chpndl, vase splat, shaped yoke, reuphl seat, 38" ...550.00
Side, mahog English Chpndl, pierced splat, reuphl seat, 36" 440.00
Side, mahog Hplwht, shaped seat & bk, reuphl, 36" ** 2,250.00
Side, mahog Hplwht style, velvet reuphl, 37" 220.00
Side, maple Co Chpndl w/some curl, splint seat, 38" 400.00
Side, maple Co QA, vase splat, Spanish ft, rush seat, 41" 1,200.00
Side, rswd Continental w/cvd florals, reuphl seat, 35" 220.00
Side, rswd Vict, finger cvd, reuphl (soiled), 36" 190.00
Side, walnut Baroque Revival, ornate cvg, orig uphl, 49" 660.00
Side, walnut Chpndl, vase splat w/crest, slip seat, rfn, 38" 500.00
Side, walnut English QA, reuphl flame-stitch slip seats, 39" 700.00
Side, walnut QA, vase splat, cabriole legs, reuphl, 39" 3,300.00
Side, walnut Vict w/rswd grpt, reuphl seats, open bks, 35" 85.00
Side, yew English, 6-slat ladder-bk, rush seat, old finish, 40" 300.00
Windsor, bamboo, old blk pnt over red, 34x16" 220.00
Windsor, bamboo spindle fan-bk w/crest, rprs, 35" 300.00
Windsor, continuous-arm, bamboo trn, saddle seat, 35" 550.00
Windsor, fan-bk w/curved crest w/cvd ears, gr rpt, 40" 1,425.00
Windsor, Phila bamboo bow-bk, wht rpt w/striping, 38" 1,200.00
Windsor, 7-spindle bow-bk, old rpt, rprs, 38" 300.00
Windsor, 7-spindle bow-bk, saddle seat, rfn, 35" 825.00
Windsor, 9-spindle bow-bk, saddle seat, rprs, rpt, 37" 385.00
Windsor, 9-spindle brace-bk, continuous-arm, old brn, 36" 3,500.00
Windsor, 9-spindle low-bk, continuous-arm, old rpt, 33" 1,100.00
Windsor ash/poplar/maple sack-bk, CT, 1780s, 36½" 980.00
Wing-bk, QA style, bl leather uphl, Broyhill repro, 46", +ottoman .550.00
Writing arm, half arrow-bk, bamboo trns, red traces, OH, 38" ...825.00

Writing arm Windsor, low-bk, old varnish, handmade repro, 32" .300.00

Chair Sets

Arm, Baker, rswd graining Fr Emp style w/ormolu, reuphl, 4 for ...1,300.00
Arm, Windsow, 7-spindle bow-bk, rfn/rpr, ca 1900, 38", 6 for 825.00
Dining, Hitchcock-type Sheraton, rush seats, rpt, 2arm+6 side ...1,950.00
Dining, Limbert #501, pierced central slat, rpl seats, 4 for 1,600.00
Dining, mahog Deco/Oriental style, uphl seat, 2 arm+6 side 575.00
Dining, mahog Sheraton style, worn brocade seats, 1 arm+5 side ..1,150.00
Side, AG Hibbs, arrow-bk, plank seat, rfn, 32½", 4 for 300.00
Side, bamboo Co Windsor, 6-spindle flat-bk, 34½", 4 for 1,035.00
Side, golden-oak era, laminated curved bks, rfn, 37", 4 for 155.00
Side, ladder-bk, 3 arched slats, splint seats, KY, 38", 6 for 635.00
Side, mahog, 1-slat bk w/crest, reuhpl seat, saber legs, 8 for 1,100.00
Side, Old Hickory, woven bk/seat, twig built, mk, EX, 4 for 1,600.00
Side, PA w/orig grpt, bj splats, wing crests, 33", 4 for 1,200.00
Side, Sheraton Hitchcock type, rpt w/stencil, rush seats, 6 for ...560.00
Side, walnut QA style, reuphl, old dk stain, 1900s, 39", 6 for 525.00
Side, Windsor, 5-spindle bk, shaped seat, youth sz, 30", 4 for 575.00
Side, Windsor, 9-spindle bk, worn blk rpt, 33", arm+4 side 550.00

Chests

Bachelor, Heckman, mahog Chpndl style w/inlay, repro, 30x32", pr .1,100.00
Birch Chpndl bow-front, 4 dvtl drw, oval brasses, rfn, 36x39" ..4,000.00
Birch/cherry/pine QA, 5-drw, dvtl case, rprs, 38x35" 1,750.00

Campaign chest, Late Georgian oak, brass mounts, two short over three long drawers, 19th century, in two parts, 44x39x18", EX, $2,090.00.

Campaign, mahog w/brass corners/flush hdw, 4-drw, 33x33", EX ...850.00
Cherry Chpndl, 4 grad drw, bracket ft, rpr/rpl, 43x41" 525.00
Cherry Chpndl, 5 grad dvtl drw, rprs/rpl/rfn, 50x36" 2,650.00
Cherry Co Chpndl, 4 grad dvtl drw, rfn/rpl/rprs, 44x38x19" 715.00
Cherry Co Emp, rope-cvd pilasters, 4 dvtl drw, rfn, 43x41" 495.00
Cherry Co Emp, trn ft & half-columns, 5-drw, rfn, 45x43" 525.00
Cherry Co Fed, 4 dvtl drw, trn legs, old rfn, 46x42" 550.00
Cherry Co Sheraton, 4 dvtl drw, 1-brd ends, trn ft, rfn, 45x39" .745.00
Cherry Co Sheraton w/walnut band inlay, 2 short:3 drw, 42x40" ..1,375.00
Cherry Emp, 4 dvtl drw w/cockbeading, trn ft, rfn, 48x41" 745.00
Cherry Fed, 6 dvtl drw, reeded half-columns, rfn, 50x41" 500.00
Cherry Fed w/flame grain mahog vnr, 4 dvtl drw, 38x41x17" 750.00
Cherry Hplwht, 5 dvtl drws, Fr ft, rprs/rfn, 41x38" 715.00
Cherry Hplwht style w/inlay, 4 drw:scalloped apron:Fr ft, 37x36" ..850.00
Cherry Sheraton, 4 grad drw w/ivory inlay, rpl/rfn, 37x36" 1,200.00
Cherry Sheraton w/banded vnr, 4 dvtl drw, paneled ends, 45x42" ..1,100.00
Cherry/curly & bird's-eye maple Co Emp, 4-drw, rfn, 52x42" 600.00
Cherry/curly maple Emp, 2 sm drw:3, trn pilasters, 51x43" 990.00
Cherry/curly maple Emp, 4 dvtl drw, rpl crest, 52x43x22" 715.00
Cherry/poplar Emp, trn legs, S-curve pilasters, 4-drw, 44x42" 440.00
Curly maple Hplwht, 4 grad drw, Fr ft, rfn/rpl, 46x42" 4,200.00

Curly maple QA to Chpndl Transitional, 4-drw, rfn, 37x36" ..2,400.00
Curly maple/cherry Co Emp, half-columm pilasters, 4-drw, 45" .600.00
Curly maple/chestnut Chpndl, 8 grad drw, rpl/rfn, 59x34" 7,700.00
Curly maple/pine, 4 dvtl drw w/beading, rpl ft, rfn, 41x39" 1,150.00
Curly/bird's-eye maple Emp, 4-dvtl drw, stepped crest, 56x42" ...715.00
Mahog & bird's-eye maple facade Emp, 6-drw, cvd pilasters, 43x46" ..800.00
Mahog Chpndl, block front, 4 dvtl drw, rpl/rstr, 33x34x21" ..3,300.00
Mahog demilune w/rswd inlay, concave center do, 1800s, 36x41" ..1,600.00
Mahog Emp w/flame vnr, 2 step-bk:5 drw, mirror, 80x43" 600.00
Mahog English, 2 sm:3 grad drw w/beading, rprs, 44x41" 525.00
Mahog English Chpndl, 2 short:2 drw w/beading, 36x36" 775.00
Mahog English Chpndl, 3-drw w/beading, rpl/rfn, 36x36" 660.00
Mahog English Chpndl, 5-drw, old finish, rpl ft, 36x37" 2,035.00
Mahog English Hplwht, bow-front, 2 short drw:3 grad, 41x43" .1,870.00
Mahog English Hplwht, 10 dvtl drw, rpl/rstr, 79x41" 2,200.00
Mahog English Hplwht w/banded inlay, 5-drw, Fr ft, rpl, 42x48" ...660.00
Mahog English Regency, bow-front, 5-drw, rpl/rstr, 41x39" 415.00
Mahog Hplwht serpentine, 4 grad drw, Fr ft, rstr, 36x37" 3,200.00
Mahog Hplwht w/figured vnr, bow-front, 4-drw, rprs, 38x42" .1,425.00
Mahog Hplwht w/flame vnr, bow-front, 4-drw, rpr/rfn, 37x42" .1,875.00
Mahog QA w/cvd bonnet, 2 sm:5 grad:3 sm drw, 1750s, 84" ** .18,000.00
Oak English Jacobean w/quarter-sawn figure, 5-drw, 47x40" ..3,300.00
Pine Co Emp w/flame grpt, 6-drw, crest rpr, 40x42" 660.00
Pine Co QA w/blanket chest top, 3 fake:3 drw, orig pnt, 58x38" .7,700.00
Poplar Emp w/alligatored red, 4-drw, ebonized pilasters, 49x41" ..1,100.00
Tiger maple Chpndl, grad drws, bracket base, 1780s, 42x34x20" .7,500.00
Walnut Chpndl, 4 grad drw, ogee ft, fluted columns, 36x39" ..5,500.00
Walnut Co Sheraton w/curly maple escutcheons, 4-drw, 39x39" ..680.00
Walnut Co Sheraton w/inlay, 4 grad dvtl drw, rprs/frn, 41x40" .2,035.00
Walnut Eastlake Vict, slide lock, sm drw:6, rfn, 63x40" 1,100.00
Walnut Emp w/figure vnr, 4-drw, trn ft, half columns, 47x44" 440.00
Walnut PA Chpndl, 9 grad drws, molded cornice, natural, 61x39" .3,650.00
Walnut Vict bow-front, appl cvgs, 3-drw, marble top, 85x43" 825.00
Walnut/cherry Co Fed, 4 dvtl drw, scrolled crest, 53x43" 600.00

Cupboards (See Also Pie Safes)

Chimney, pine w/worn bl pnt, molded cornice, rprs, 68x23" 400.00
China, faux bamboo/bird's-eye maple, 2-do/4-shelf, 1880s, 84" .3,400.00
Cloak, Shaker type, 2 panel do, red grpt, pegged, 64x52x14" ...4,000.00
Corner, cherry architectural, arched do:2 do, 2-pc, 96x43" ...4,400.00
Corner, cherry architectural w/bbl bk, 1-pc, rfn/damage, 85" ..2,000.00
Corner, cherry Co, 2 raised panel do:2:apron, 1-pc, 85x47" ...1,045.00
Corner, cherry Co, 3-pane dbl do:panel dbl do, 1-pc, 82x48" .2,035.00
Corner, cherry/poplar, brn grpt, 2 panel do, 1-pc, 87x48" 1,300.00
Corner, curly maple Co, 2 panel do, bracket ft, rfn, 77x44" ...2,860.00
Corner, curly maple/poplar, handmade, 2-pc, 80x38" 1,265.00
Corner, curly maple/walnut Co, dbl do:2 drw:dbl do, 89x47" .4,500.00
Corner, hanging; oak English, scalloped shelves, no do, 39x32" ..440.00
Corner, hanging; oak English w/shell inlay medallion, 39x25" .1,550.00
Corner, hanging; pine, old red rpt w/raised chinoiserie, 33x23" .855.00
Corner, hanging; pine Euro, floral pnt decor on red, 82x24" 415.00
Corner, pine Co Irish w/Gothic-style cornice, rprs, 80x49" ...1,750.00
Corner, poplar w/brn grpt, 2 pr panel do, 2-pc, 81x41" 2,145.00
Corner, poplar/pine/oak, open shelves, primitive, 71x33 ....770.00
Corner, walnut architectural, broken-arch top, 2-pc, 102" 5,775.00
Corner, walnut Centennial w/cvg, 2-shelf:dbl do, 95x49" 4,900.00
Court, walnut Continental, cvd detail, inlaid marble, 62x52" ..2,100.00
Dutch, poplar PA w/red traces, 2 do:shelf:2 do, 2-pc, 86x52" ..2,500.00
Jelly, pine, worn bl-gray pnt, 2-brd do, cut-out ft, 47x42" 415.00
Jelly, pine Co, crest:hinged top do:2 do, wire nails, rpt, 73x36" ..1,155.00
Jelly, pine Co, 2 brd & batten do, old salmon red, 56x42" 715.00
Jelly, pine/poplar Co, high ft, 2 panel do, rstr, 67x37" 935.00
Jelly, poplar Co, brd & batten do, 2-drw, worn brn, 50" 580.00

Jelly, poplar Co, panel do, bl pnt over varnish, 39x36" 535.00
Jelly, poplar w/old blk pnt, 2 raised panel do, 71x43" 1,200.00
Jelly, yel pine Co, CI hinges, brd & batten do, 65x38" 350.00
Kitchen, ash/poplar, 2 do:3 drw:2 panel do, rstr, 90x50" 600.00
Pewter, poplar, open step-bk top:shelf:2 do, 1-pc, 75x44" 1,750.00
Pewter, walnut, primitive, 3 open shelves:2 panel do, 79x46" .2,200.00
Step-bk, cherry Co, dbl do:2 raised panel do, cornice, 1-pc, 81" .2,750.00
Step-bk, cherry Co, 2 panel do:2 drw:2 panel do, 1-pc, 82x50" ...1,625.00
Step-bk, pine Co, 2 panel do, scalloped apron, 1-pc, 82x39" ...2,850.00
Step-bk, pine/poplar Co, 2 do:shelf:3 drw:2 do, 2-pc, 84x56" 770.00
Step-bk, poplar, dbl do:pie safe base, mortised & pinned, 83" .2,300.00
Step-bk, walnut Co, dbl do:pie shelf:2 dvtl drw:2 do, 2-pc, 82" .2,975.00
Step-bk, walnut/poplar Co, 2 do:shelf:2 drw:2 do, 2-pc, 79x45" .1,375.00
Wall, ash Co, 2 panel do:2 drw:2 panel do, 1-pc, 77x39" 600.00
Wall, butternut/pine Co, 2 6-pane do:2 drw:2 panel do, 2-pc, 88" .1,975.00
Wall, pine/poplar, dvtl case, 1-brd do, old red, 24x15" 495.00
Wall, pine/poplar, 2 panel do/2 dvtl drw, old mc pnt, 34x22" .1,500.00
Wall, pine/poplar w/old red, dvtl case, 2 1-brd do, 30x30" 825.00
Wall, poplar Co, 2-pc, rfn/rprs, 79x48x20" 660.00
Wall, poplar w/old red, primitive, 2-drw, 2-do, 22x19" 565.00

Desks

Queen Anne cherry slant-lid desk on frame, Connecticut, ca 1750, 45¾x34¾x19¾", $5,465.00.

Butler's, curly maple/mahog Emp, ebonized trim, rfn, 51x43" .1,550.00
Captain, brass-bound rswd, top inlay, 19x12", VG 550.00
Davenport, mahog Geo III, red leather writing surface, 4-drw 1,100.00
Davenport, walnut Emp, paneled do, lift lid, 2-drw, 41x26" 550.00
Kneehole, faux bamboo/bird's-eye maple, 1880s, 34x27" 3,500.00
Mahog Fr Louis XV style w/pnt details, leather top, 3-drw, 45" ...3,100.00
Mahog Hplwht, bow-front w/inlay, 3 dvtl drw, rprs, 30x42" ...2,400.00
Partner's, mahog Chpndl, gadrooned top, c&b ft, 31x54x29", VG ...1,000.00
Pine Co, wht pnt w/gr wash, hinged lid:2 drw, 48x36x18" 500.00
Plantation, cherry/poplar Co, dbl do:dvtl drw, 48x33x26" 600.00
Plantation, cherry/walnut Co, 2 dvtl do, dbl do, rfn, 77x44" 770.00
Plantation, walnut Co, fold-down top, 2-drw, 2-pc, rfn, 92x44" ..1,300.00
Plantation, walnut Co Vict, trn legs, dvtl drw, rfn, 83x43" 935.00
Roll top, oak, S-roll, 8-drw, fitted int, 49x60x35" 1,375.00
Roll top, quarter-sawn golden oak w/figure, S-roll, 7-drw, 55" .1,300.00
Slant front, Cherry Chpndl, cvd fan:4 drw, rfn, 32x36x18" 3,400.00
Slant front, mahog English Chpndl w/oak bands, 3-drw, 39x36" ..855.00
Slant front, mahog Fed, 3 sm drw:slant lid, rstr, 35x30x20" 335.00
Slant front, maple, fitted int, 4 grad drw, NE, 1780s, rprs 2,500.00
Slant front, maple Chpndl, hinged lid:4 grad drw, rfn, 41x36" .5,500.00
Slant front, Oak English Chpndl, 4 dvtl drw, rprs, 42x42" 1,430.00
Slant front, oak w/inlay, 4 grad drw, 8-drw int, 39x42x20" 1,200.00
Slant front, walnut Chpndl, 4 grad drw, rpl ft, rfn, 42x40" 1,320.00
Slant front, walnut Chpndl, 4 grad drw, rstr, late 1700s 1,850.00

Slant front, walnut Co, 2 panel do, scalloped apron, 46x34" 550.00
Slant front, walnut Co Vict, dvtl drw, Huffman...O, 2-pc, 55x35" ...600.00
Slant front, walnut Vict w/burl & bird's-eye maple vnr, 45x40" .450.00
Slant front (oxbow), mahog Chpndl, bandy legs, c&b ft, 42x42" .4,100.00
Walnut Euro Renaissance Revival, 3-drw base, leather top, 54" .1,265.00
Walnut Vict, crest:fold-down lid:dvtl drw:panel do, 55x34" 935.00

Dressers

Ash Vict w/curly ash vnr, 2 sm:3 lg drw, marble top, 40"+mirror ..335.00
Pine/poplar Sheraton w/flame grpt, 3 dvtl drw, NY, 40x36" 1,550.00
Walnut Vict, appl panels & trns, marble insert, crest, rstr, 81" ...330.00
Walnut Vict w/appl trns, 5-drw, lyre-fr mirror, 73x42" 475.00
Walnut Vict w/figured walnut vnr, 5-drw, marble insert, 78x38" ..385.00

Dry Sinks

Pine Co, open base w/cut-out ft, shelf, worn bl pnt, 31x39x18" .775.00
Pine Co, simple cut-out ft, 2 brd & batten do, worn, 32x57x21" .550.00
Pine Fed, 2 batten cabinet do, Am, early 1800s 460.00
Poplar, 2 raised panel do, old grained rpt, rprs, 34x55x21" 525.00
Poplar Co, panel do, dvtl do, crest, pnt int, 34x35x19" 440.00
Poplar Co, 2 panel do, 2-drw, peaked crest, pnt traces, 37x50" ..415.00
Poplar PA, hutch top, worn grained rpt, rpl, 48x66" 2,585.00
Softwood bench-type, bl-gr rpt, PA, ca 1820s, 38x43x16" 4,200.00
Walnut Co, 2 panel do, worn old pnt, rpl hdw, OH, 33x56x18" .1,980.00
Walnut/poplar Co, overhanging top w/gallery:dbl panel do, 30x43" ..825.00
2 raised panel do on cut-out legs, old bl pnt, NY, 34x42x19" 900.00

Hall Piece

Bench, cvd oak-panel bk, open arms, lift seat, ca 1900 ....500.00
Hall tree, cvd/molded mahog, brass trim/marble insert, 85" 1,650.00
Hall tree, mahog English Aesthetic Movement, mirror bk, 1880s, 92" ...1,200.00
Hall tree, quarter-sawn golden oak, rpl pans, lift seat, 70" 470.00
Hall tree, walnut, CI pan for umbrellas, 2-drw, rfn, 91x35" 600.00
Hall tree, walnut Gothic Revival, old rfn, rprs, 82x36" 600.00
Hall tree bench, golden oak, beveled mirror, 4 hooks, 81x42" 880.00

Highboys

Cherry QA, 4 grad dvtl drw:4 w/cvgs, bonnet top, close mar, 78" ..5,500.00
Cherry QA, 4-drw, cvd fans, cabriole legs, rfn/rstr, 78x38" 5,775.00
Curly maple QA, 2 short:3 grad:3 short drw, rfn/rpr, 68x35" ...9,350.00
Curly maple QA, 3-drw base w/fan cvgs, 2-part, 18th C, 67"** .18,000.00
Mahog, c&b ft, broken-arch top, 2-part, 81x38x19", EX 3,850.00
Maple QA, 5 grad drw:3, cabriole legs, cornice, rpl/rfn, 73x39" .7,700.00
Walnut Chpndl, 2 short:3 grad:4 grad base drw, 1790s, 90" ..13,800.00
Walnut English QA w/burl, 3 short:3 grad:3 short drw, 2-pc, 67" .2,200.00
Walnut English QA w/inlay, 2 short:3 grad:3 drw, rpl/rfn, 67" ...3,300.00

Lowboys

Cherry QA, 4 dvtl drw, apron, cabriole legs, att CT, 32x30" 5,450.00
Mahog QA, 3 dvtl drw, cabriole legs, rstr/rpl, 31x34x20" 935.00
Walnut QA, 2 short drw:1, cabriole legs, 18th C, 28x30x19" * .3,500.00
Walnut QA style w/figured vnr, 3 dvtl drw, ca 1900, 39x26x17" ..550.00

Pie Safes

Cherry Fed, shelves:2 drw, apron, Fr ft, early 1900s 1,000.00
Curly maple w/red & gr trim, red punched tin panels, OH, 70x42" ..600.00
Pine Co, nailed, 6 tin panels, old gray over cream, 65x42" 880.00
Pine Fed, 2 punched tin do, early 19th C, sm, EX 400.00

Poplar, dbl do, 2 dvtl drw, 6 punched tin panels, VA, 48x53" .**1,650.00**
Poplar, punchd tin w/Masonic symbols, bl rpt, IN, 63x39x19" .**1,700.00**
Poplar, punched circle tin panels, hanging, PA, 36x39" 1,325.00
Poplar Co, dbl do ea w/3 tin panels, 2 dvtl drw, 53x42", EX 650.00
Poplar Co, red wash, nailed drw, 12 tin panels, IN, 55x41x17" ...550.00
Poplar Co, 2 drw:dbl do, 6 punched tin panels, rprs/rpt, 54x41" ..1,325.00
Poplar w/grpt & gold stencil, Octagon Safe Pat'd 1870, 68x36" .**1,650.00**
Poplar w/rpt, punched tin panels, PA, hanging, 34x28x20" 580.00
Walnut Co, 12 punched tin panels, worn gr pnt, 47x38" 550.00
Walnut w/12 punched tin panels, Shenandoah Valley, 58x41" .**1,200.00**

Secretaries

Birch Hplwht w/bookcase, dvtl drws, slant lid, rfn/rpl, 81x40" .**4,400.00**
Birch w/mahog finish, w/bookcase, mirror, ca 1900s, 74x40" 715.00
Cherry Sheraton style, made from old parts/old wood, 2-pc, 70" .**1,400.00**
Mahog vnr Governor Winthrop style w/bookcase, repro, 76x32" 580.00
Stacked, poplar/mahog, 4-part, Globe Wernicke..., 62x34x12" ..415.00
Walnut Chpndl w/inlay, arched/paneled dbl do:lid:4 drw, 93" * .**17,500.00**
Walnut Eastlake Vict w/burl panels, 2-pc, rprs, 85x41x21" **1,200.00**
Walnut Eastlake Vict w/burl vnr, cylinder top, 2-pc, 97x42" ..**2,100.00**
Walnut Renaissance Revival w/burl, 3-drw base, 1850s, VG ...**1,850.00**
Walnut/walnut burl Vict, cylinder top, appl moldings, 2-pc, 85" .**1,750.00**

Settees

Continental marquetry inlay Rococo style, 19th C, 69" **1,650.00**
Fruitwood Directoire, 3-section w/cvd rosettes on crest, 56" 950.00
Hardwood fr w/trn/cvd details, velvet uphl, 1900s, 59" 275.00
Louis XVI style, orig gray-wht pnt w/gilt, reuphl, 1900s, 53" ...**1,385.00**
Mahog Fr style, reuphl silk brocade, tufted bk, 43" 275.00
Majorelle, floral cvg at bk/front rails, sculpted arms, 61" **4,000.00**
PA orig decor, 3-chair bk, ca 1840 ....**1,250.00**
Walnut Jacobean style, much cvg, uphl 3-chair bk, 52x57" 200.00
Walnut Vict, cvd vintage fr, reuphl, 65" 500.00
Walnut Vict, finger-cvd, medallion bk, reuphl, 60" 450.00
Walnut Vict, finger-cvd, rswd grpt traces, reuphl, 61" 275.00

Shelves

Book, walnut/pine, 3-shelf, cornice, 42x40" 155.00
Bracket, walnut Vict w/cvd fruit scrolls, rprs, 14x19" 265.00
Corner, folky pine w/old dk finish, appl compo florals, 15½" 80.00
Etagere, ebonized/gilt mtd faux bamboo, 3-tiered, 34x16x10" 150.00
Standing, grpt pine step-bk, 8-shelf, skirt, 1850s, 93x48" **2,875.00**
Storage, 9-tier, molded fronts & sides, apron, 88x24x7", EX 500.00
Wall, mahog Wm IV, 4-shelf, trn supports, 1830s, 27x24x7" 250.00
Wall, pine primitive Euro, dvtl w/brackets, towel bar, 28" 125.00
Wall, walnut, pierced/relief-cvd bk w/Masonic signs, rfn, 19" 275.00
Wall, walnut w/alligatored varnish, fan cvgs, PA, 7x14x6" 300.00
Wall, walnut w/whale ends, dvtl, sq nails, 34x24" 55.00
Wall, 3-grad shelves, C scroll supports, gallery, 26x36x13" 375.00

Sideboards

Cherry Emp w/flame mahog facade, 2-dr:2 do, paw ft, 50x55" 700.00
Cherry Sheraton, 3-drw, bksplash, 39x34x20" 800.00
Fr Boule style, pnt w/tortoise shell & brass inlay, marble top, 44" .**1,375.00**
Fruitwood burl Louis XVI, drw:2 panel do, ca 1780, rprs, 51" .**3,200.00**
Huntboard, walnut English QA style, cabriole legs, repro, 72" ...500.00
Limbert #2421¾, ebon-oak, mirrored/slatted bk, 51x49x20" .**3,000.00**
Mahog Am Classical w/vnr, cvd columns, paw ft, 59x72x24" .**1,870.00**
Mahog English Adams style, serpentine case, 5-drw, repro, 69" ..770.00
Mahog Fed style, 3 drw flanked by 2 sm drw/2 panel do, 66" 425.00

Mahogany William IV carved pedestal sideboard, ca 1835, $2,000.00.

Mahog Fed style w/inlay, serpentine 2-do, Am, 1900s 600.00
Mahog Hplwht w/figured vnr, curved front w/2 do/6 drw, 73" ..**4,400.00**
Mahog Sheraton, 3-drw:4 panel do, reeded panels/gallery, 64", G ..700.00
Mahog Sheraton w/inlay, bow-front, 3-drw, 4-do, att MA, 42x66" .**9,125.00**
Mahog/oak English Hplwht w/ebony inlay, cvd details, 38x74" ..**2,000.00**
Oak English Jacobean style, 2-drw, trn legs, old repro, 36x53x19" .440.00
Olivewood vnr Euro w/inlay, marble insert top, 1900s, 82x52" ..825.00
Walnut Continental, panel do, cvd details, 1800s, 35x63x20" ...550.00

Sofas

Bird's-eye maple inlay Sheraton, wht linen uphl, 73" **4,000.00**
Camelbk, mahog fr, 3-cushion, repro 750.00
Camelbk, mahog Hplwht, damask reuphl, rare sz, 59" **3,000.00**
Fainting couch, walnut Eastlake Vict w/burl vnr, reuphl, 74" 660.00
Mahog Chpndl, mortised stretcher, reuphl, rprs, 79" * **9,900.00**
Mahog Chpndl-style camelbk w/Chinese legs, modern repro, 71" ..660.00
Mahog Emp w/detailed cvg, paw ft, lyre arms, reuphl, 89" **1,200.00**
Mahog Fed, cvd winged paw ft, vnr crest, uphl, 88" VG **2,500.00**
Mahog Fed fr w/readed legs & posts, reuphl (soiled), 77" **1,045.00**
Mahog Fed w/eagle-cvd crest, brocade uphl, 38x84x22" **1,100.00**
Mahog Geo III, cvd rosettes, striped uphl, rstr, 28x74" **2,600.00**
Maple Co Emp, trn legs/posts/arms, scrolled bk brd, 71" **1,400.00**
Rswd cvd Vict, crushed velvet uphl, cvd apron, 68", VG 850.00
Walnut Baroque style w/burl vnr, brocade reuphl, 1900s, 85" 440.00
Walnut Emp, lyre fr w/paw ft, cvd crest, horsehair uphl, 66" ...**2,000.00**
Walnut Vict, cvd floral scrolls & bird crest, reuphl, 71" **1,700.00**
Walnut Vict, much cvg, brocade reuphl, rfn, 76" 250.00
Walnut Vict, rose-cvd crest, velvet reuphl, 61", pr 990.00
Walnut Vict w/fruit-cvd crest, rfn/reuphl, 57" 500.00

Stands

Canterbury, mahog, 2-drw, trn finials, 1790s, 19x17x12½" 750.00
Canterbury, rswd, lyre decor, 1-drw, trn posts, 21x23x16" **1,000.00**
Cherry Co Emp, dvtl drw, 2-brd top, trn legs, 29x20x20" 385.00
Cherry Co Hplwht, sq tapered legs, rpl 1-brd top, 27x18x17" 275.00
Cherry Co Sheraton, dvtl drw, 2-brd top, rfn, 37x19x18" 275.00
Cherry Hplwht, tilt top, tripod w/spider legs, 2-brd, 21x16" 415.00
Cherry Sheraton w/figured vnr drw fronts, 2-brd top, 29x23x17" .**1,875.00**
Cherry/mahog Sheraton, rope cvg, 2 dvtl drw, 1-brd top, 28x18x16" ..600.00
Cherry/maple Co, dvtl drw, trn legs, 2-brd top, 38x21x19" 300.00
Cherry/maple Co Sheraton, dvtl drw, 2-brd top, rfn, 30x20x16" ..660.00
Curly maple Sheraton, 6 dvtl drw w/beading, gallery, 32x20x20" ..**7,425.00**
Drop-leaf, walnut Co, pencil-post legs, 30x39x17" 495.00
Hardwood/pine Co QA, cut-out apron, 1-brd top, red stain, 20x21" ...715.00
Lighting, hardwood Windsor, 3 trn legs, old blk rpt, 38½" **2,800.00**
Magazine, Arts & Crafts, 3-shelf, keyed tenons, rfn, 30x17x9" ...120.00
Mahog English Hplwht style, 1-do, gallery w/hdls, 13x13", pr .**1,300.00**
Mahog Louis XV style, marble top, 3-drw, 38x17x12", pr 715.00
Mahog Sheraton style, old lacy pulls, repro, 29x22x17", pr 330.00
Maple Sheraton style, 2 dvtl drw, trn legs, repro, 27x19x14" 500.00
Maple/pine/poplar Co Sheraton, dvtl drw, 2-brd top, 31x22x22" ..**1,045.00**

Pine Co Hplwht, tapered sq legs, old dk brn, 29x19x18" **220.00**
Pine Co Hplwht, yel rpt w/blk stripes & floral stencil, 29x18" ...**250.00**
Plant, Limbert, cruciform base, branded, 36x13x13" **2,500.00**
Poplar Co, old brn flame grpt, nailed drw, 1-brd top, 28x21x22" ..**330.00**
Refectory, oak w/trestle base, worn finish, ca 1900, 72" **275.00**
Telephone, Limbert, arched apron; shelf, brand, rfn, 30x18x15", G ..**400.00**
Tiger maple/cherry, burled drw w/brass pull, 39x17x16" **400.00**
Walnut & cherry Fed, tripod base, S-scroll legs, 1-brd, 29x20x16" ..**470.00**
Walnut OH Hplwht, dvtl drw, 2-brd top, rfn, 26x18x16" **1,265.00**
Work, mahog Sheraton, serpentine front, 2-drw, 29x18x17" ..**2,500.00**

Stools

Footstool, mahog Vict Renaissance Revival w/ebony & gilt, 15" ..**195.00**
Footstool, walnut Vict, floral needlepoint uphl, 17" sq **250.00**
Gout, English mahog, adjusts, uphl leg/ft rest, 19th C, 19x24x17" ..**330.00**
Gout, hardwood English, leather uphl, trn ft, 22" **350.00**
Ottoman, mahog vnr Directoire, chintz uphl, 1820s, 46" W ..**1,500.00**
Potty, mahog Chpndl, scalloped apron, lift lid, rpt, 13x19x16" ..**660.00**
Vanity, Fr style, cream pnt w/gilt trim, 20th C **175.00**

Tables

Banquet, cherry Co Sheraton w/figured apron, open: 81", pr ..**1,100.00**
Breakfast, mahog English Regency, tilt-top, ped base, 29x47" **525.00**
Breakfast, mahog English Regency, tilt-top, 3-part base, 47" **800.00**
Cherry Co Chpndl, dvtl drw, 2-brd breadbrd top, rprs, 27x38x26" ..**990.00**

Classical tiger maple and mahogany veneer dressing table, refinished, ca 1825, 35x36x20", $1,850.00.

Console, mahog English Adams style w/cvg, drw, repro, 44x24" ...**440.00**
Console, rswd Fr Emp w/inlay, marble top, dvtl drw, 36x38x15" ..**2,100.00**
Cricket, pine English Co, folding, shoe ft, 5-brd top, 27x41" **500.00**
Dining, Limbert #2430, ebon-oak, 30x49" dia, w/2 12" leaves ...**4,500.00**
Dining, Limbert #466, rnd top, sq ped w/4 ft, 30x45" dia, VG ...**1,000.00**
Dining, mahog English Adams style w/cvg, 120", w/5 leaves **770.00**
Dining, mahog English Regency w/banded vnr, open: 87" **3,750.00**
Drafting, oak w/CI fr & tripod ft, worn rpt, brd: 21x26" **990.00**
Dressing, mahog Fr Louis XV style w/inlay, 3-drw, mirror, 39x31" ..**600.00**
Dressing, maple Co w/orig grpt/stripes, top case removes, 45" .**1,870.00**
Drop-leaf, curly maple, 6 trn legs, 29x50x21"+leaves **1,875.00**
Drop-leaf, curly maple Co, 1-brd top, stripped, 41"+leaves **500.00**
Drop-leaf, curly maple Co Sheraton, 1-brd top, 38"+leaves **1,045.00**
Drop-leaf, Limbert, gate-leg, drw, branded, 45"+2 13" leaves ..**2,500.00**
Drop-leaf, mahog English Hplwht, drw, rprs, 27x27x18"+leaves ..**1,650.00**
Drop-leaf, mahog English QA, swing legs, oval top, 55"+leaves ..**1,600.00**
Drop-leaf, mahog QA, triangle w/1 leaf, 44" sq open **1,100.00**
Drop-leaf, mahog/oak Sheraton, dvtl drw, rprs, 38"+leaves **990.00**
Drop-leaf, oak, gate-leg, 1 drw, mortised & pinned, 39"+leaves ..**2,000.00**
Drop-leaf, walnut Co Chpndl, swing-leg, c&b ft, rstr, 45"+leaves ..**600.00**
Drop-leaf, walnut QA w/some curl, swing-leg, apron, 42"+leaves ..**1,375.00**
Drop-leaf Pembroke, cherry Co Hplwht, drw, rfn, 36"+leaves **715.00**

Drop-leaf Pembroke, mahog Hplwht w/inlay, dvtl drw, 32"+leaves ..**1,875.00**
Game, mahog Chpndl, sq tapered legs, apron, 39x35x18" **2,900.00**
Game, mahog Hplwht demilune, swing-leg for leaf, 35" W **1,200.00**
Game, mahog Hplwht w/mahog vnr, ovolo cut-out top, 28x36x18" ..**525.00**
Game, mahog Regency w/inlay, flip top, ca 1800, 38x35x18" .**1,100.00**
Game, mahog Sheraton style w/maple vnr, some age, 35x36" **850.00**
Game, walnut English QA, cabriole legs/scrolled apron, 30x15" ..**1,375.00**
Hardwood/pine Co, whittled legs, apron, 3-brd top, rpt base, 44" ..**660.00**
Harvest, David Smith, poplar breadbrd top, blk pnt base, 78" **250.00**
Harvest, drop-leaf, birch/poplar Co, cleaned to old red, 108" ..**3,850.00**
Harvest, drop-leaf, orig grpt, ME, 29x72x60" **7,000.00**
Hutch, hardwood/pine, mortised/pinned, 4-brd top, 60x53" **770.00**
Hutch, pine w/red traces, shoe ft, 3-brd top, repro, 52" dia **775.00**
Library, Limbert, ebon-oak, 1-drw, 3 inlay sqs ea side, sgn **2,400.00**
Library, Limbert #104, ash, 8-sided/4-leg/X-stretchers, 38" dia ...**800.00**
Library, mahog, base shelf/cvd lion-head legs/paw ft, 2-drw, 46" ..**1,200.00**
Limbert #146, oval top, slab sides w/sq cutouts, 30x45x30" **2,300.00**
Limbert #148, 4 splayed legs, stretchers w/cutouts, 29x30" dia ..**3,500.00**
Limbert #158, dbl oval design, cutouts, branded, 29x48x36" ...**11,000.00**
Louis XVI style, orig gilt, wht onyx top, ca 1900, 38x33x25" **660.00**
Low, Art Deco rswd, 4 scroll supports, stepped top, 26x28" dia ..**2,070.00**
Low, Fr Art Deco Circassian walnut, X-form support, 21x26" dia ..**1,035.00**
Marquetry vnr Fr style tiered, glass top, 20th C, 35x32x22" **775.00**
Mixing, maple QA, rpl top, cabriole legs, rprs, 28x30x21" **2,200.00**
Ovolo corner, maple, 4 trn/splayed legs, pad ft, 1740s, 24x26x21" ..**550.00**
Parlor, walnut Eastlake Vict w/burl vnr, granite top, 29x32x22" .**325.00**
Parlor, walnut Rococo Revival w/grpt, cvd squirrel on base, 41" ..**1,875.00**
Parlor, walnut Vict Eastlake, oval marble top, 29x21" **415.00**
Parlor, walnut Vict w/burl vnr, J Moriarty & Bro...O, 30" **715.00**
Parlor, walnut Vict w/burl vnr, wht marble top, 31x21x15" **440.00**
Pier, mahog Vict Rococo Revival, cvd foliage, marble top, 38" ..**660.00**
Pine/poplar Co Hplwht, scrubbed top, red base, 29x38x26" **715.00**
Refectory, walnut early Euro, 4 dvtl drw, cvd apron, 78" **2,000.00**
Side, flame maple top & drw, trn legs, sm **475.00**
Side, Lifetime #930, rnd top, shelf, X-stretchers, 39x18" **950.00**
Tavern, antiqued blk over red, Nelson 1980 repro, 102" **715.00**
Tavern, birch/pine Co QA, dvtl drw, 2-brd top, red traces, 40" .**600.00**
Tavern, cherry Chpndl, 1 sm drw, brass hdls, late 1700s **600.00**
Tavern, cherry/pine Co Hplwht, dvtl drw, breadbrd top, rprs, 44" ...**600.00**
Tavern, chestnut/poplar Co QA, dvtl drw, 2-brd top, 41" **1,600.00**
Tavern, hardwood/pine Co QA, dvtl drw, 2-brd top, 30x36" **880.00**
Tavern, mahog English, triangular base w/shelf, rnd top, 29" **525.00**
Tavern, maple QA, mortised/pinned 1-brd top, blk rpt, 26x32x22" .**2,500.00**
Tavern, walnut/cherry Co, 2-brd top, some age, 39x32x32" **990.00**
Tea, cherry Chpndl, rpl birdcage, tilt top, 27x36" dia **1,875.00**
Tea, cherry Co Emp, tilt top, rfn, 38x34" dia **600.00**
Tea, mahog Chpndl, tilt top, tripod base, rstr birdcage, 30" **500.00**
Tea, mahog English Chpndl, tilt top, tripod base, rprs, 29" dia ..**500.00**
Tea, mahog English Chpndl style, hand cvd, galleried, 1900s, 30" .**500.00**
Tea, mahog English Co Chpndl, tilt top, 3 snake ft, rpl top **600.00**
Tea, maple Chpldl, 2-brd tilt top, 3 snake ft, 35" dia **825.00**
Tea, walnut Chpndl PA, tilt top, tripod base, cvd ft, 2-brd, 36" ..**3,400.00**
Trestle, Lifetime, Prairie design, drw ea end, rfn/rstr, 60" **700.00**
Vanity, English Deco maple/walnut, Bakelite hdls, w/stool **1,265.00**
Vitrine, mahog English Regency w/banded inlay, 32x22x23" **990.00**
Work, curly maple Emp w/mahog trim, mahog ball ft, rfn/rpl, sm ..**1,450.00**
Work, maple Co, trn legs, rebuilt drw, 2-brd top, 43" **715.00**
Work, pine/poplar Co, 2-drw, 4-brd top, old rpt, 29x68x39" **360.00**
Work, pine/poplar Co Hplwht, 1-brd breadbrd top, 42"+leaf **880.00**
Work, poplar Co, 1 drw, 3-brd top, traces of finish, 67" **475.00**
Work, walnut Co, 4 dvtl drw, rnf/rpl top, 31x53x25" **770.00**
Work, walnut Co Hplwht, 1-drw, 2-brd top removes, rfn, 75x43" ..**600.00**
Work, walnut PA, 3 dvtl drw, 4-brd top, rfn/rstr, 66" **990.00**
Work, walnut PA Co QA, 2 dvtl drw, 3-brd top, scrubbed, 66" .**450.00**

Work, walnut Southern Hplwht w/inlay, dvtl drw, 1-brd top: 24x20" .**1,155.00**

Wardrobes

Armoire, fruitwood Louis XV Provincial, cornice:arched do ...**2,300.00**
Armoire, walnut, 2 do w/beveled mirrors, columns/ormolu, 96" **825.00**
Chifferobe, Berkey & Gay, mahog Traditional style, 8-drw, dbl do .**770.00**
English Deco maple/walnut, Bakelite hdls, 70x37" **1,265.00**
Golden oak, quarter-sawn vnr do panels, 2-drw, rfn, 91x54" ...**1,265.00**
Golden oak era, 2-section, 2 dvtl drw, appl cvgs, 87x48x20" **825.00**
Kas, bl & red pnt pine, 2 panel do, fitted int, NY, 77x61" **9,000.00**
Linen press, curly maple Co, 2 panel do:2 drw:apron, 2-pc, 88x52" ..**2,400.00**
Linen press, wavy satin birch, 3-part, 19th C, 80x47x21" **3,250.00**
Pine Co, dbl raised panel do:drw, CI hooks, old pnt, 85x48" **465.00**
Pine Co, 1-brd ends, dbl do:drw, old dk red, damage, 82x43" **415.00**
Pine Shaker style, lg panel do, fitted int, red pnt, 78x48x24" ...**1,750.00**
Walnut Co, cut-out ft, cornice:2 panel do:2 dvtl drw, 88x53" **700.00**
Walnut Vict, panel dbl do, 2 dvtl drw, cornice, 104x52" **825.00**
Walnut Vict w/burl vnr panels, Eastlake detail, 2-drw, 99x55" ..**1,815.00**

Washstands

Ash Vict w/rpl walnut top, 3 dvtl drw, later shelf, 33x31x18" **415.00**
Cherry Emp w/figured vnr, marble top:dvtl drw, 33x40x18" **550.00**
Corner, mahog English Hplwht w/EX detail, dvtl drw & gallery, 41" ..**600.00**
Curly maple/mahog Co Sheraton, 2 dvtl drw in shelf, rpl top, 19x17" **825.00**
Hardwood Co Sheraton w/mahog vnr, dvtl drw, towel bar, 33x27x18" ..**400.00**
Pnt/stenciled Sheraton, 2-tiered w/bksplash, 36x34", EX **425.00**
Poplar Eastlake Vict w/mahog stain, 3 drw:do, 38x30x16" **255.00**
Stenciled/grpt Sheraton, 1-drw, scrolled bksplash, 38x18x14" ...**350.00**
Walnut Co, cut-out scalloped ft, raised panel do, drw, 35x26" ...**385.00**
Walnut Vict, 3-drw & do w/reeded bands, marble top, 27x30x15" ..**300.00**

Miscellaneous

Bin, soft wood, worn gr pnt, 34x30x20" **250.00**
Bin, storage; pine, lift-top, dvtl, trn ft, old gr pnt, 36x35x19" **400.00**
Bin, wood; pine w/worn rpt, primitive, 37x28x17" **385.00**
Gun case, oak English w/brass binding, 30" **440.00**
Ice box, Brunswick, oak, 84x32x26" **3,250.00**
Mantel, quarter-sawn oak dbl-decker, beveled mirror, 85x62" **275.00**
Pulpit, walnut & burl vnr Eastlake, 5-sided front, panel do, 37" .**330.00**
Screen, Arts & Crafts, 4 top-pierced panels w/slag inserts, 70" H ...**950.00**
Screen, Fr style cvd & gilded fr w/tapestry insert, 25x44" **715.00**
Screen, 3 73x20" pnt canvas sections w/leather trim **1,800.00**
Screen, 3-part Fr port panorama (wallpaper), ca 1800, 62x72" ...**1,800.00**
Screen, 4 pnt canvas 70x18" panels on folding wood fr **1,430.00**
Tray, butler's, mahog Fed, mid 1800s **425.00**
Wastebox, Limbert #255, slab sides w/cutouts, 18x11x11" **1,600.00**

Galle

Emile Galle was one of the most important producers of cameo glass in France. His firm, founded in Nancy in 1874, produced beautiful cameo in the Art Nouveau style during the 1890s, using a variety of techniques. He also produced glassware with enameled decoration, as well as some fine pottery — animal figurines, table services, vases, and other objets d' art. In the mid-1880s he became interested in the various colors and textures of natural woods and as a result began to create furniture which he used as yet another medium for expression of his artistic talent. Marquetry was the primary method Galle used in decorating his furniture, preferring landscapes, Nouveau floral and fruit arrangements, butterflies, squirrels, and other forms from nature. It is for his furniture and his cameo glass that he is best known today. All Galle is signed.

In the listings below, 'fp' indicates items that have been fire polished. Our advisor for this category is Don Williams; he is listed in the Directory under Missouri.

Cameo

Atomizer, primroses, butterscotch/wht, SP lid, 8" **980.00**
Bowl, daisies/leaves, cut/pnt on textured gr, SP disk ft, 2x9" ...**1,100.00**
Bowl, floral, gr/frosted gray & pk, 5-point rim/ped ft, 4½x5" **400.00**
Bowl, wisteria, purple on frost, prof rpr to rim, 1½x4¼" **95.00**
Box, apple blossoms, fp, magenta on gold-amber, 2¼x4" **1,750.00**
Compote, vines/pods, wine on yel opal, 5" **1,500.00**
Ewer, grape pods, 4-color on amber mottle, branch hdl, 5½" ..**5,000.00**
Flask, floral, cut/pnt, wht/pk/lime, silver cap, w/shot, 5½" **1,600.00**
Lamp, honeysuckle, apricot/chartreuse/red-brn, floral base, 9" .**1,900.00**
Lamp, perfume; cyclamens, rose/yel frost, 7¼x4" **1,350.00**
Vase, acanthus leaves/flowers, caramel/gr/wht, cylinder, 14½" .**1,265.00**
Vase, apple blossoms, red/apricot/wht, 4½" **230.00**
Vase, bellflowers, lav/gray, baluster, short neck, 12⅜" **1,400.00**
Vase, berry branches, butterscotch/gr/turq, 14¼" **4,025.00**
Vase, bud; poppy, pk/frosted, 4¾x1", EX **550.00**
Vase, clematis, amber on yel frost, mold blown, ovoid, 9½", NM .**6,900.00**
Vase, columbines, clear frosted/yel/lav, 15½x5½" **2,000.00**
Vase, currant branches, red/yel/frosted, 3½x3¼" **650.00**
Vase, ferns, brn/burgundy/crystal/pk/gr, 30½x12" base **8,500.00**
Vase, floral, fuchsia/purple/frosted/yel, banjo form, 7x3½" **800.00**
Vase, floral & leaves, red/amber satin, label, 4⅛" **1,100.00**
Vase, floral clusters, purple on yel to lav, bottle form, 6½" **500.00**
Vase, flowers/pods, dk orange on almond, fp, dbl-gourd, 4¾" ..**1,150.00**
Vase, hydrangeas, lav/dk gr on peach, 12½" **1,350.00**
Vase, hydrangeas, lav/gray-gr/frost/pk, invt trumpet, 5½" **675.00**
Vase, hydrangeas, lav/olive gr on pk/gray, long neck, 10¾" **1,150.00**

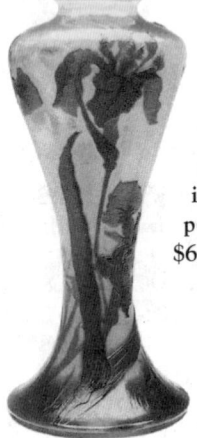

Vase, iris blossoms and leaves, mottled clear and amber overlaid in honey-amber and brown, fire-polished surface, signed, 16", $6,500.00.

Vase, landscape, pk/wht, slim neck, ovoid, ftd, 9¾" **1,500.00**
Vase, leaves & nuts, amber/golden brn on lt bl & frost, 7¼" ...**1,250.00**
Vase, lotus blossoms/pods, pk/olive gr on citron, 10" **15,000.00**
Vase, lotus flowers/pods/plants, brn on citron, bulbous, 6" **675.00**
Vase, mtn landscape, brn/bl/pk/clear, 10½x5½" **3,900.00**
Vase, nasturtiums, gray/pk/pale orange, shouldered, 15x6½" ...**1,550.00**
Vase, pilgrim; pods/leaves, purple-brn on lime frost, 5½" **1,150.00**
Vase, pine cones, frosted/gray/dk to lt brn, str neck, 12½" **800.00**
Vase, pods & leaves, gold-brn/chartreuse on citron, 9" **900.00**
Vase, seed pods, lime gr/orange/gray, waisted cylinder, 22½" ..**2,875.00**
Vase, thistles, med gr on gr mottled frost to apricot blush, 14" .**1,000.00**
Vase, trees/rivers/sky, brn/citron on frost, 9¼" **850.00**

Enameled Glass

Bottle, twigs, blk w/gold & wine insects on clear, 7x6" **2,000.00**
Cordial, amber w/thistles on cup & stem, 3½" **425.00**
Cup, fleur-de-lis on amber, rope hdl, 2x2¾", 4 for **200.00**
Decanter, gilt foliage/floral swags, 7½"+4 lobed glasses **925.00**
Tumbler, motto/whimsical peasant on ribbed clear, 4½" **200.00**
Vase, floral, pk/red/wht w/gold on lt gr, sqd w/rnd ped ft, 2" **350.00**
Vase, floral branches, mc on lt gr w/gold, ftd cylinder, 13¾" ...**2,600.00**
Vase, fuchsia/gilt on gr, cylinder w/disk ft, 17½" **2,200.00**
Vase, orchids/ferns/mushrooms, wht/turq/copper/gilt on gr, 9½" .**2,300.00**

Marqueterie-Sur-Verre

Bowl, tulips/Dutch seascape on gray w/gr streaks, lid, 6" H ...**10,000.00**
Vase, crocuses, mc on bl w/purple streaks, red ft, 8½" **14,000.00**

Marquetry, Wood

Cabinet, mahog, cvd/inlaid florals/scenic, mk, 36x25" **4,500.00**
Stand, Nouveau branch top, 2-tier, spindle sides, 31x26x17" ..**1,550.00**
Table, leaves on scalloped top & sm tier, 3-leg, 32x16" **2,185.00**
Table, tea; orchids on rectangular top, 2-tier, 32x29" **2,500.00**
Table, tea; scalloped top w/floral branch, molded rim, 21x24" .**2,000.00**
Table, 2-tier, butterfly/floral, serpentine legs, 28x25x16" **1,850.00**
Table, 2-tier, jonquils, curved Y-legs, 30x30x20" **2,400.00**

Pottery

Cat, seated, smiling expression, pnt w/hearts, 13" **3,000.00**
Clock, rampant lions support clock w/crown atop, 1890s, 25" ..**5,175.00**
Inkwell, fleur-de-lis shape w/abstract florals, 2x9" **350.00**
Pitcher, serpent spout, ribbed/bulbous, scroll hdl, 9" **900.00**
Plate, landscape w/Oriental, floral border, 9¾", pr **350.00**
Plate, man in ragged cloak, icicle trim, shield form, 7x8½" **225.00**

Gambling Memorabilia

Gambling memorabilia from the infamous casinos of the West and items that were once used on the 'Floating Palace' riverboats are especially sought after by today's collectors.

Ashtray, sterling silver, suits in corners, Armstrong, 3x3", EX **40.00**
Belt buckle, abalone & MOP image of 4 Aces, 2x2½", EX **75.00**
Book, Gambling & Gambling Devices, JP Quinn, 1912, 308-pg, EX **120.00**
Book, Webster's Poker Book, HT Webster, 1925, 126-pg, EX **45.00**
Box, blk lacquer w/4 etched silver cards, 5x6½x1½", EX **100.00**
Caddy, poker chip; brn Bakelite, EX **40.00**
Card press, maple w/turq buttons & beaded rose, VG **275.00**
Card press, rosewood, brass mts, ivory finial, EX **525.00**
Card trimmer, shears style, unmk, ca 1910, 12¾x6½" **1,200.00**
Chips, Carlo, set of 200, in walnut rack & chest **450.00**
Chips, ivory w/fancy numeral cvgs, set of 5 ....**210.00**
Chuck-a-luck cage, 10", w/2 gr die **65.00**
Cover, card table; hand-woven wool, India, 1880, 36x36", EX **90.00**
Craps layout, Caesar's Palace, suede, unused **150.00**
Dice cage, Chuck-A-Luck, w/dice, ca 1930 ....**75.00**
Dice cup, Bakelite, traveling type w/celluloid dice **55.00**
Dice cup, leather **40.00**
Faro casekeeper, rosewood/ivory, Geo Williams NYC, 1860s, NM .**1,050.00**
Game, Put & Take, tin, w/roulette wheel, 1920s, 5" dia, VG **50.00**
Keno cage, NP CI & brass hourglass cage, 18x16x10" **100.00**
Money clip, sterling silver, enameled King of Hearts, ca 1930, EX ...**65.00**

Pillow cover, monkey & dog playing poker, 1910, in fr, 22x26", EX ...**65.00**
Spinner, sterling w/red & blk letters, .12 troy oz, EX **35.00**
Table, bridge; inlaid woods, suit sign in ea corner, 1940s, 31" sq ...**200.00**
Table, gaming; inlaid top & sides, 8-drw, 36" dia, EX **3,250.00**
Watch, roulette; Little Monte Carlo, 1890, EX **475.00**
Watch, roulette; Roulette Ideal, beveled crystal, 1890s, EX **550.00**
Wheel, CI, boy looking at girl in bkground scene, 11½x6", EX .**1,200.00**
Wheel, HC Evans Big 6, horse race, mirrored glass/wood/metal, 60" ...**3,000.00**
Wheel, Lucky Palace, weight balance, HP, 1950s, 60", EX **250.00**
Wheel, wood, #1-30, w/clicker, wall mt, 25" dia **90.00**
Wheel, wood floor model, worn pnt, 73x42" dia, G **300.00**
Whist scorer, MOP w/silver & enamel, 1880s, 2" dia, EX **90.00**

Game Calls

Those interested in hunting and fishing collectibles are beginning to take notice of the finer specimens of game calls available on today's market. Our advisor for this category is Randy Hilst; he is listed in the Directory under Illinois.

Duck call, Trutone, red groove at shoulder, 6¼", $110.00; Goose call, Ken Martin, Idaho Falls, Idaho, wooden mouthpiece on slightly belled body, $75.00; Duck call, C.H. Dittle, metal mouthpiece on graduated body with turned rings, $165.00.

Duck, Chuck Ditto...IL, walnut bbl w/rings, metal stopper **65.00**
Duck, Cochran's Reelfoot style, walnut bbl, metal reed, 7", EX .**165.00**
Duck, E Dennison Reelfoot style, bronze reed, walnut bbl, 6", VG ...**95.00**
Duck, EL Quinn Reelfoot style, cvd dogs/ducks, silver reed, 5" ..**245.00**
Duck, Emory Mitchel, Enticer, walnut bbl, trn rings, 5½" **45.00**
Duck, Fay Holt Reelfoot style, ebony w/metal reed, 6" **160.00**
Duck, Herter's Numara Goose, walnut bbl, plastic stopper, VG ...**30.00**
Duck, Johnny Bill's IL River..., walnut bbl, brass stopper, 4½" ...**45.00**
Duck, McMahon PR III, walnut w/cocobolo stopper, 5", EX **85.00**
Duck, unmk Reelfoot style, maple bbl, cedar stopper, 5", EX **125.00**
Duck, unmk Reelfoot style, walnut bbl, bronze reed, VG **70.00**
Goose, Quinn Call, walnut bbl, dbl band, cedar stopper, 7" **175.00**
Predator, Herter's, walnut bbl, plastic stopper, MIB **20.00**
Quail, Fred Palmer, Trutone, MIB **20.00**
Squirrel, Herter's No 99, MIB **30.00**
Turkey, Herter's Plantation, scratch type, MIB **50.00**
Turkey, Lohman No 110, box type, scuffed **30.00**
Turkey, Lynch's World Champion, box type, EX **75.00**
Turkey, Quaker Bog Easy Yelper, scratch box type, NMIB **15.00**
Turkey, Southland, spring-loaded box type, EX **20.00**

Gameboards

Gameboards, the handmade ones from the 18th and 19th century, are collected more for their folk art quality than their relation to games. Excellent examples of these handcrafted 'playthings' sell well into the thousands of dollars; even the simple designs are often expensive. If you are interested in this field, you must study it carefully. The market is always full of 'new' examples. Well-established dealers are often your best sources; they are essential if you do not have the expertise to judge the age of the boards yourself. Our advisor for this category is Louis Picek; he is listed in the Directory under Iowa.

Checkers, blk/wht pnt wood w/red gallery edge, 15" sq **220.00**
Checkers, blk/wht pnt wood w/silver trim under glass in fr **165.00**
Checkers, dk/lt wood, star inlay corners, inlay border, 23" sq **350.00**
Checkers, maple/cherry/walnut/rosewood inlay sqs, 17" sq **335.00**
Checkers, pine w/old colorful rpt, 19x21" **250.00**
Checkers, pine w/old rpt, recessed tray for checkers, 21" sq **175.00**
Checkers, pnt pine w/leafy border, 2 sm drws, 30x19" **200.00**
Checkers, poplar/walnut, worn 3-color pnt, 18" sq **250.00**
Checkers, pyrographic designs, cvd sqs, 23½x15" **200.00**
Checkers, red/blk pnt pine, age cracks, 31x18", G **360.00**
Checkers, red/blk pnt wood, Am, ca 1900, 14½" sq **650.00**
Checkers, red/blk/gr/yel pnt wood, ca 1900, 15" sq **700.00**
Checkers, red/gr pnt wood, Am, ca 1900, 10" sq **288.00**
Checkers, rvpt (4-color) in wood fr, 29" sq **165.00**
Checkers, whalebone/mahog, ca 1900, 9¼" sq **1,000.00**
Checkers/backgammon, walnut w/cherry/maple inlay, mc pnt, 17" sq **440.00**
Checkers/parcheesi, blk/wht/gr pnt on wood, 20" sq **550.00**
Checkers/parcheesi, pnt wood, Am, ca 1900, 18x10" **975.00**
Checkers/parcheesi, red/gray/gr/bl, Am, ca 1900, 16" sq **550.00**
Checkers/parcheesi, 4-color w/wood graining, 1890s, 23" sq **750.00**
Checkers/unknown, 4-color pnt, brass hanging loop, 1800s, 14" sq **925.00**
Foil/pnt decor wood, glass scrollwork borders, 19th C, 10" sq **500.00**
Unknown game, plywood w/pine fr, mc pnt, 31" sq **415.00**

Games

Collectors of antique games are finding it more difficult to find their treasures at shows and flea markets. Most of the action these days seems to be through specialty dealers and auctions. The appreciation of the art on the boards and boxes continues to grow. You see many of the early games proudly displayed as art, and they should be. The period from the 1850s to 1910 continues to draw the most interest. Many of the games of that period were executed by well-known artists and illustrators. The quality of their lithography cannot be matched today. The historical value of games made before 1850 has caused interest in this period to increase. While they may not have the graphic quality of the later period, their insights into the social and moral character of the early 19th century are interesting.

Games from the 20th-century invoke a nostalgic feeling among collectors who recall looking forward to a game under the Christmas tree each year. They search for examples that bring back those Christmas-morning memories. While the quality of their lithography is certainly less than the early games, the introduction of personalities from the comic strips, radio, and later TV created new interest. Every child wanted a game that featured their favorite character. Monopoly, probably the most famous game ever produced, was introduced during the Great Depression.

For further information, we recommend *Schroeder's Collectible Toys, Antique to Modern*, available from Collector Books. Our advisor for personality-related games is Norm Vigue; he is listed in the Directory under Massachusetts.

Miscellaneous

Admiral Chester's, wooden figures, 1930s, EXIB **150.00**
All American Baseball Game, dvtl box w/tin litho top, EXIB **120.00**
Around the World w/Nelly Bly, McLoughlin Bros, 1890, EXIB .**325.00**
Auto Drome, skill game, Transogram, 1967, NMIB **45.00**

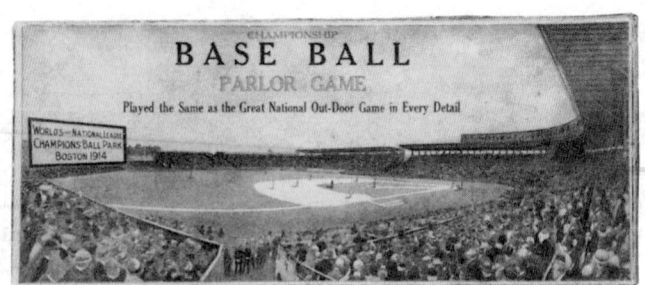

Base Ball, McLoughlin Bros, with instruction booklet, 1886, wooden box, NM in EX box, $2,300.00.

Baseball, Parker Bros, 1950, VG (VG box) **35.00**
Bicycle Race, McLoughlin Bros, VG+ (VG+ wooden box) **500.00**
Blast-Off Globe Game, tin litho, spin globe, EXIB **75.00**
Buying & Selling, Milton Bradley, EXIB.....................................**250.00**
Checkered Game of Life, Milton Bradley, ca 1911, EX (VG box) ...**225.00**
Chiromagica, McLoughlin Bros, question/answer game, EXIB ...**140.00**
Countdown Space Game, Transogram, 1959, VG (VG box) **50.00**
Dominoes, Bakelite, wood slide-top box **60.00**
Electric Football, Tudor, 1964, EX **35.00**
Fang Bang, Milton Bradley, 1967, NMIB **50.00**
Fishing, tin litho fish, wooden pole, Japan, early, MOC **20.00**
Fox & Geese, Milton Bradley, late 1800s, EXIB **250.00**
Game of Authors, JH Singer, card game, EX in Victorian box **35.00**
Game of Checkers, Back-Gammon & Tousel, McLoughlin Bros, EXIB ..**120.00**
Game of Uncle Sam's Mail, McLoughlin Bros, ca 1893, EXIB ...**580.00**
Gee-Wiz, racing game, Wolverine, NMIB **200.00**
Hickman's All Am Action Football Game, Lowell, 1955, EXIB ..**65.00**
Hide & Seek, McLoughlin Bros, ca 1895, EXIB **2,200.00**
Intrigue, Milton Bradley, 1954, VG (VG box) **45.00**
Jolly Marble, paper litho on wood w/clown figures, 1892, EX **440.00**
Junior Auto Race Game, 4 die-cast autos, ca 1926, EXIB **250.00**
Lotto Game, in wood box w/paper label, MIG, 1893, EX **35.00**
Magic Circus Roll Game, tin litho, MIB **50.00**
Mousetrap, Ideal, complete, 1963, EXIB **75.00**
Mr Ree Fireside Detective..., Selchow & Righter, 1937, EXIB **65.00**
Mystic Skull, Ideal, 1964, MIB **75.00**
New Pilgrim's Progress, McLoughlin Bros, 1893, VG (VG box) ...**250.00**
Premium Game of Logomachy, Milton Bradley, 1930s, G (G box) ..**20.00**
Radar Search Game, Ideal, 1969, EXIB **25.00**
Snap, Selchow & Righter, Black boy on box lid, early 1900s **250.00**
Soldier Ten-Pins Game, McLoughlin Bros, 1890s, EX **400.00**
Summit, Milton Bradley, 1960, G (G box) **35.00**
Texas Ranger, All-Fair, 1936, EXIB **55.00**
Thinking Man's Golf, 1966, EXIB **15.00**
Toonerville Trolley, Milton Bradley, 1927, rare, NM (EX box) .**350.00**
Two Game Combination-Baseball & Checkers, Milton Bradley, NMIB **625.00**
Van Loon's Wide World Game, Parker Bros, 1933, EXIB **100.00**
War at Sea, McLoughlin Bros, ca 1898, EXIB **2,100.00**
Wilder's Baseball Game, stand-up grandstand, 1930s, EXIB **165.00**
World Educator, Reed Toy Co...Mass, colorful wooden box, 16" L ..**55.00**

Personalities, Movies, and TV Shows

Addams Family, card game, Filmways, 1965, EXIB **30.00**
Addams Family, 1964, MIB **55.00**
Alfred Hitchcock's Why, NMIB **20.00**
Alley Oop, EXIB **40.00**
Bionic Woman, Parker Bros, 1976, VG (VG box) **30.00**
Blondie, card game, Whitman, 1942, NM (EX box) **50.00**
Buck Rogers Combat, Built-Rite, 1937, EXIB **1,000.00**

Candid Camera, Lowell, 1963, NM (EX box) 70.00
Charlie McCarthy Party Game, EX 55.00
Dick Tracy Bagatell Pinball, Marx, 1960s, NMIB 75.00
Dukes of Hazzard, Ideal, 1981, EXIB 15.00
Eye Guess (Bill Cullen), NMIB 20.00
F-Troop, Ideal, 1965, NM (NM box) 165.00
Game of Li'l Abner, Milton Bradley, 1944, NM (EX box) 70.00
Game of Robin Hood, Parker Bros, 1893, EXIB 235.00
Godfather, 1971, M in violin box 45.00
Gumby Playful Trails, EXIB 40.00
Have Gun Will Travel, Parker Bros, 1959, EX (EX box) 75.00
Hi Yo Silver, Marx, Lone Ranger dbl target game, tin litho, MIB ..175.00
Huckleberry Hound, card game, Ed-U, 1961, MIB 20.00
I Dream of Jeannie, 1965, EX (VG box) 45.00
Johnny Unitas Football, NMIB 40.00
Kukla & Ollie, Parker Bros, 1962, NMIB 40.00
Little House on the Prairie, Parker Bros, 1978, VG (VG box) 20.00
Mandrake the Magician, Transogram, 1966, NM (NM box) 50.00
Mickey Mouse Club Bagatelle, Wolverine, 10x15", EX 200.00
Mickey Mouse Hoop-La, Marks Bros, 1930s, G+ (G box) 260.00
Mickey Mouse Library of Games, Russell, 1960s, MIB 25.00
Mickey Mouse Mix Up Game, Parker Bros, MIB 135.00
Newlywed Game, Hasbro, 1969, NMIB 15.00
Prince Valiant Game of Valor, Transogram, 1957, NM (EX box) ...55.00
Reagonomics, NMIB 20.00
Straight Arrow, Selchow & Righter, 1950s, NM (EX box) 85.00
Swamp Fox, Parker Bros, Walt Disney Productions, 1960, NMIB ...60.00
Thunderball, NMIB 40.00
Tressy Career Girl, NMIB 20.00
Underdog Saves Sweet Molly, Whitman, 1975, NMIB 25.00
Zorro Target, Knickerbocker, 1958, EX+ (EX+ box) 175.00

G. A. R. Memorabilia

The 'The Grand Army of the Republic' was first conceived by Chaplain W.J. Rutledge and Major B.J. Stephenson early in 1864 when they were tent-mates during our own Civil War. These men vowed to each other that if they were spared they would establish an organization that would preserve friendships and memories formed during this time. Shortly after the war ended, Rutledge and Stephenson made their desires a reality. The first National Convention of the Grand Army of the Republic was held in Indianapolis, Indiana, on November 20, 1866. The purpose of the organization was to provide aid and assistance to the widows and orphans of the fallen Union dead and to care for the hospitalized veterans as needed. The last comrade of the G.A.R. died in 1949.

Many items are surfacing from the early encampments which were held on both state and national levels, which resulted in a wide variety of souvenir items having been made.

Walnut pedestal, ornate carvings of cannon, rifles, eagles, etc., ca 1887, 26¾x14½" dia, $865.00.

Badge, Pasadena Sept 9, 1912 ....45.00
Badge, 15th Annual Territorial GAR Reunion, Perry (IN), 1905 ..250.00
Belt, wht canvas, emb metal buckle w/GAR & stars, EX 150.00
Cup, tin, red/wht/bl enamel, 1908 ....95.00
Knife, GAR button end cap, 5½" blade, 10½", G 170.00
Medal, 42nd Nat'l Encampment, Toledo OH, 1908 ....25.00
Pamphlet, Rules & Regulations..., WA DC, 1869, 32-pg 75.00
Ribbon, 9th Annual...15th NY volunteers, w/Custer cello, VG .200.00
Slouch hat w/insignia & braid w/hat band 285.00
Sword, Model 1860 w/GAR eng 195.00
Watch fob, SP canteen form, dtd 1861-65 ....110.00

Gas Globes and Panels

Gas globes and panels, once a common sight, have vanished from the countryside but are being sought by collectors as a unique form of advertising memorabilia. Early globes from the 1920s (some date back to as early as 1912), now referred to as 'one-piece globes,' were made of molded milk glass and were globular in shape. The gas company name was etched or painted on the glass. Few of these were ever produced, and this type is valued very highly by collectors today.

A new type of pump was introduced in the early 1930s; the old 'visible' pumps were replaced by 'electric' models. Globes were changing at the same time. By the mid-teens a three-piece globe consisting of a pair of inserts and a metal body was being produced in both 15" and 16½" sizes. Collectors prefer to call globes that are not one-piece or plastic 'three-piece glass' (Type 2) or 'metal body, glass inserts' (Type 3). Though metal-body globes (Type 3) were popular in the 1930s, they were common in the 1920s, and some were actually made as early as 1915. Though rare in numbers, their use spans many years. In the 1930s Type 2 and Type 3 globes became the replacements of the one-piece globe. The most recently manufactured gas globes are made with a plastic body that contains two 13½" glass lenses. These were common in the '50s but were actually used as early as 1932.

Note: Standard Crowns with raised letters are one-piece globes that were made in the 1920s; those made in the 1950s (no raised letters), though one-piece, are not regarded as such by today's collectors. Our advisor for this category is Scott Benjamin; he is listed in the Directory under Ohio.

Type 1, Plastic Body, Glass Inserts (Inserts 13½"), 1931 – 1950s

Ashland Diesel 275.00
D-X Marine, rare 750.00
Dixie, plastic band 200.00
DX Ethyl 250.00
DX Lubricating Gasoline, tan body 250.00
Falcon 1,000.00
Frontier Gas, Rarin' To Go, w/horse 750.00
Hornet, Capcolite body, 13½", NM 300.00
Kendall Deluxe, Capcolite body w/red pnt, 13½" 250.00
Kendall Polly Power, Capcolite body, 13½" dia, NM 300.00
Marathon, no runner 175.00
Marine, sea horse, EX color 650.00
Never Nox Ethyl 400.00
Shamrock, oval body 300.00
Spur, Oval body 300.00
Texaco Diesel Chief, Capcolite body, 13½", NM 750.00
Texaco Sky Chief 275.00
Viking, pictures Viking ship 650.00
66 Flite Fuel, Phillips, shield shape, all plastic 450.00

Type 2, Glass Frame, Glass Inserts (Inserts 13½"), 1926 – 1940s

Rose Bud Gasoline, milk glass with red and black enameling, 13½", NM, $2,500.00.

Aerio, gr gill ripple body, 13½", NM	5,000.00
Amaco, glass body, 12½", NM	350.00
American, gill body, 12½", NM	375.00
Amoco, gill body, 13½", NM	375.00
Atlantic, glass body, 13½" dia, NM	325.00
Atlantic Imperial, gill body, 13½", EX	400.00
Champlin Preston, 3-pc glass	400.00
Derby	375.00
Esso	325.00
Frontier Gas, Double Refined	350.00
Golden 97 Ethyl, hull glass body, 12½", NM	400.00
Gulf, hull body, 13½", NM	400.00
Guyler Brand, milk glass, EX	700.00
Indian Gas, Red Dot	650.00
Kanotex, w/sunflower, gill body	450.00
Koolmotor, clover shape, gr bkground	1,400.00
Mobil Gas	425.00
Pitman Streamlined, bl gill rippled body, 13½", NM	5,000.00
Pure	400.00
Red Crown, milk glass	350.00
Sinclair Dino, milk glass, EX	250.00
Sinclair Pennant	800.00
Skelly Anomarx w/Ethyl	450.00
Sky Chief, gill body, 13½", NM	400.00
Standard Crown, bl	650.00
Standard Crown, gr or orange, ea	900.00
Standard Flame	400.00
Texaco Diesel Chief	850.00
Texaco Ethyl	1,500.00
Texaco Star, blk outline on 'T'	400.00
White Flash, gill body	375.00
White Rose, boy, glass body	1,250.00
WNAX, w/radio station pictured	1,500.00

Type 3, Metal Frame, Glass Inserts (Inserts 15" or 16½"), 1915 – 1930s

Aero Mobilgas, new metal body, rare, 15", NM	2,200.00
Atlantic Ethyl, 16½"	650.00
Atlantic White Flash, 16½"	500.00
Blue Sunoco, 15"	475.00
Cities Services Oils, 1929, 15" fr	500.00
Crown, crown pictured, 16½", EX	1,200.00
Esso Extra, 15"	425.00
General Ethyl, 15" fr, complete	700.00
Kendal Gasoline, airplane, metal body, rare, 15", NM	5,000.00
Mobil Gas, winged horse, 15" or 16½" metal fr, NM	650.00
Mobilfuel Diesel, lg horse, high profile	800.00
Oil Creek Gas, drake well & derrick, 15", NM	2,500.00

Phillips Benzo, low profile metal body, 15", NM	3,500.00
Pure, porc body, 15"	650.00
Purol Gasoline, w/arrow, porc body	850.00
Purol Pep, porc body	750.00
Red Crown Ethyl	950.00
Richfield, w/eagle	600.00
Rocor, w/eagle	650.00
Signal, old stoplight, 15", VG	3,800.00
Socony, milk glass inserts on metal	1,250.00
Stanolined Aviation, rare, 16½", EX	4,000.00
Sunland Ethyl, 15"	550.00
Texaco Leaded, glass panels, pr	4,000.00
Tidex, 16½"	475.00
Tydol, 16½"	500.00
White Star, 15" fr, complete	850.00

Type 4, One-Piece Glass Globes, No Inserts, Co. Name Etched, Raised or Enameled, 1912 – 1931

Atlantic, chimney cap	3,000.00
Diamond	850.00
Dixie, etched	1,750.00
Iowa Gas	1,800.00
Musgo	4,800.00
Pierce Pennant, etched	2,800.00
Red Crown, rnd, etched	3,500.00
Republic, 3-sided	2,200.00
Shell, rnd, etched	750.00
Sinclair, etched, milk glass	1,100.00
Sinclair Aircraft, etched	4,000.00
Skelly	750.00
Super Shell, clam shape	1,800.00
Super Shell, rnd, etched	3,500.00
Texaco, milk glass, emb letters, brass collar	1,200.00
Texaco Ethyl	2,000.00
That Good Gulf..., emb, orange & blk letters, EX	900.00
White Eagle, some feather detail, 20¾", EX	1,500.00
White Rose, boy pictured, pnt	2,800.00

Gaudy Dutch

Inspired by Oriental Imari wares, Gaudy Dutch was made in England from 1800 to 1820. It was hand decorated on a soft-paste body with rich underglaze blues accented in orange, red, pink, green, and yellow. It differs from Gaudy Welsh in that there is no lustre (except on Water Lily). There are seventeen patterns, some of which are War Bonnet, Grape, Dahlia, Oyster, Urn, Butterfly, Carnation, Single Rose, Double Rose, and Water Lily. For further information we recommend *The Collector's Encyclopedia of Gaudy Dutch & Welsh* by John Shuman, available from Collector Books. Unless otherwise noted, values are given for items with minimal wear and no obvious damage.

Butterfly, cup & saucer, handleless; chip	495.00
Butterfly, cup plate	880.00
Butterfly, pitcher, milk; 4", M	910.00
Butterfly, plate, butterfly on side, 8¼"	900.00
Butterfly, plate, wide spread decor in center, 9⅞", M	1,870.00
Butterfly, waste bowl	1,485.00
Carnation, coffeepot	1,430.00
Carnation, plate, sm feather border, deep, 10"	855.00
Carnation, plate, soup; 8½"	770.00
Carnation, plate, 8⅜", M	855.00
Carnation, teapot	1,485.00

Cybris, plate, toddy; center decor amid sprays, impressed, repro .135.00
Dahlia, cup & saucer, handleless 750.00
Dahlia, plate, 8⅜" 990.00
Double Rose, creamer 660.00
Double Rose, cup & saucer, handleless 580.00
Double Rose, plate, deep, 9¾", M 855.00
Double Rose, plate, toddy; rare, 4½" 825.00
Double Rose, plate, 10", EX 600.00
Double Rose, plate, 10", M 935.00
Double Rose, sugar bowl, w/lid 880.00
Double Rose, waste bowl, 6", M 625.00
Dove, creamer 770.00
Dove, plate, bl band, 8⅛", M 650.00
Dove, plate, plain border, 6¼", M 550.00
Dove, teapot 1,100.00
Dove, waste bowl 770.00
Grape, creamer, M 765.00
Grape, plate, soup; 8¾" 495.00
Grape, plate, 6¼", M 330.00
Grape, plate, 8", M 550.00
Grape, teapot 770.00
Grape, waste bowl 440.00
Leaf, bowl, unusual shape, 8¾" 1,100.00
Leaf, sugar bowl, w/lid, M 1,100.00

**Oyster, sugar bowl, shell and ring handles, with lid, 5½",
VG, $250.00; Cup and saucer, VG, $120.00.**

Oyster, cup & saucer, handleless 385.00
Oyster, plate, orange pattern, 9¾", M 1,430.00
Oyster, plate, 6⅜" 440.00
Oyster, waste bowl, 6¼", M 1,210.00
Primrose, sugar bowl, w/lid 990.00
Primrose, waste bowl 825.00
Single Rose, coffeepot, M 850.00
Single Rose, cup & saucer, handleless; stains 330.00
Single Rose, cup plate 440.00
Single Rose, plate, deep, 8¼", M 440.00
Single Rose, sugar bowl, w/lid 715.00
Single Rose, waste bowl, 6⅛" 605.00
Sunflower, creamer 550.00
Sunflower, cup & saucer, handleless; M 800.00
Sunflower, cup & saucer, handleless; VG 360.00
Sunflower, plate, 8¼", M 700.00
Urn, cup & saucer, handleless; EX 300.00
Urn, cup & saucer, handleless; M 490.00
Urn, plate, toddy; rare, 5¼", M 825.00
Urn, plate, wear, 6½" 500.00
Urn, plate, 8¼", EX 690.00
Urn, plate, 8¼", M 900.00
Urn, waste bowl, 5½", M 850.00
War Bonnet, creamer 660.00
War Bonnet, cup & saucer, 2½", 5¾" 1,000.00

War Bonnet, plate, soup 770.00
War Bonnet, plate, toddy; 5⅛", M 1,045.00
War Bonnet, plate, 7", M 1,000.00
War Bonnet, plate, 8⅛", EX 880.00
War Bonnet, waste bowl, 5", M 1,100.00
Zinnia, plate, 6⅜" 660.00

Gaudy Ironstone

Gaudy Ironstone was produced in the mid-1800s in Staffordshire, England. Some of the ware was decorated in much the same colors and designs as Gaudy Welsh, while other pieces were painted in pink, orange, and red with black and light blue accents. Lustre was used on some designs, omitted on others. The heavy ironstone body is its most distinguishing feature.

Key: ug bl — underglaze blue

Cheese dish, Azalea, floral, cobalt/gold, Woods, w/tray 185.00
Creamer, Morning Glory 160.00
Cup & saucer, handleless; Morning Glory 75.00
Cup & saucer, handleless; Seeing Eye 200.00
Pitcher, Morning Glory, 8" 265.00
Plate, chop; rabbits/frogs/flowers, blk transfer+4 colors, 13" 990.00
Plate, Morning Glory, ug bl, w/lustre, 8⅜" 105.00
Plate, rabbits/cabbages/frogs/trees, blk transfer+4 colors, 9⅜" 385.00
Plate, vintage, ug bl w/red & gr & lustre, 9" 115.00
Platter, floral, bl transfer w/mc, 12¾" 315.00
Platter, Morning Glory, yel transfer w/mc & gilt, 13" 375.00
Platter, Oriental floral, dk bl transfer w/mc, ftd, 12" 155.00
Soup, Oriental floral, ug bl, w/red/pk/gr, Pat Ironstone, 9½" 150.00
Sugar bowl, floral, 3-color, w/lid, 4" 115.00

Gaudy Welsh

Gaudy Welsh was an inexpensive hand-decorated ware made in both England and Wales from 1820 until 1860. It is characterized by its colors — principally blue, orange-rust, and copper lustre — and by its uninhibited patterns. Accent colors may be yellow and green. (Pink lustre may be present, since lustre applied to the white areas appears pink. A copper tone develops from painting lustre onto the dark colors.) The body of the ware may be heavy ironstone, creamware, earthenware, or porcelain; even styles and shapes vary considerably. Patterns, while usually floral, are also sometimes geometric and may have trees and birds. Beware! The Wagon Wheel pattern has been reproduced.

Our advisor for this category is Cheryl Nelson; she is listed in the Directory under Minnesota. For further information we recommend *The Collector's Encyclopedia of Gaudy Dutch & Welsh* by John Shuman, available from Collector Books.

Note: No porcelain Gaudy Welsh was made in Wales.

Aberystwyth, jug, 6" 450.00
Asian, cup & saucer 85.00
Bali, cup & saucer 95.00
Basket of Flowers, jug, 7" 395.00
Brecon, jug, 6" 550.00
Buckle, plate, 7¾" 200.00
Buckle, plate, 10" 135.00
Cherry Tree, plate, 8" 269.00
Conwy, jug, 7" 315.00
Cynon, mug, 2¼" 185.00
Cynon, sugar bowl (open), 2½x4¼" 280.00

Dimity, plate, 10"	235.00
Elfin Cap, plate, 7"	255.00
Gower, jug, 6"	415.00
Gwynedd, jug, 5½"	390.00
Hexagon, oil lamp/stand, 4"	290.00
Honeysuckle, plate, 9½"	245.00
Horton, jug, 5½"	195.00
Leaf, mug, 2½"	235.00
Llanrug, jug, swan hdl, 6"	475.00
Llynfi, jug, 6½"	460.00
Lyre, jug, 4"	225.00
Nebula, sugar bowl, ftd	175.00
Peppermint, cup plate, 3½"	100.00
Ross, jug, gr, rare, 5½"	545.00
Shanghai, jug, 6½"	570.00
Snowdonia, jug, flow, 6½"	450.00
Springtime, jug, flow, 5"	550.00
Tartan, mini jug & bowl, 3½"	290.00
Urn, tureen, ftd, 9½" W	305.00
Victoria & Albert, plate, 10"	400.00
Water Lily, plate, 6"	175.00

Geisha Girl

Geisha Girl Porcelain was one of several key Japanese china production efforts aimed at the booming export markets of the U.S., Canada, England, and other parts of Europe. The wares feature colorful, kimono-clad Japanese ladies in scenes of everyday Japanese life, surrounded by exquisite flora, fauna, and mountain ranges. Nonetheless, the forms in which the wares were produced reflected the late 19th- and early 20th-century Western dining and decorating preferences: tea and coffee services, vases, dresser sets, children's items, planters, etc.

Over a hundred manufacturers were involved in Geisha Girl production. This accounts for the several hundred different patterns, well over a dozen border colors and styles, and several methods of design execution. Geisha Girl Porcelain was produced in wholly hand-painted versions, but most were hand painted over stenciled outlines. Be wary of Geisha ware executed with decals. Very few decaled examples came out of Japan. Rather, most were Czechoslovakian attempts to hone in on the market. Czech pieces have stamped marks in broad, pseudo-Oriental characters. Items with portraits of Oriental ladies in the bottom of tea or sake cups are *not* Geisha Girl Porcelain, unless the outside surface of the wares are decorated as described above. These lovely faces are formed by varying the thickness of the porcelain body and are called lithophanes.

The height of Geisha Girl production was between 1910 and the mid-1930s. Some post-World War II production has been found marked Occupied Japan.

The ware continued in minimal production through the 1980s, but the point of origin was Hong Kong. These productions are discerned by the pure whiteness of the porcelain; even, unemotional borders; lack of background washes and gold enameling; and overall sparseness of detail. A new wave of Nippon-marked reproduction Geisha emerged in 1996. If the Geisha Girl productions of the 1860s – 80s were overly plain, the mid-1990s repros are overly ornate. Original Geisha Girl porcelain was enhanced by brush strokes of color over a stenciled design; it was never the 'color perfectly within the lines' type of decoration found on current reproductions. Original Geisha Girl porcelain was decorated with color washes; the reproductions are in heavy enamels. The backdrop decoration of the current reproductions feature solid, thick colors, and the patterns feature too much color; period Geisha ware had a high ratio of white space to color. The new pieces also have bright shiny gold in proportions greater than most period Geisha ware. The Nippon marks on the reproductions are wrong. Some of the Geisha ware created during the Nippon era bore the small precise decaled green M-in-Wreath mark, a Noritake registered trademark. The reproduction items feature an irregular facsimile of this mark. Stamped onto the reproductions is an unrealistically large M-in-Wreath mark in shades of green ranging from an almost neon to pine green with a wreath that looks like it has seen better days, as it does not have the prefect roundness of the original mark. Reproductions of mid-sized trays, chunky hatpin holders, an ornate vase, a covered bottle, and a powder jar are among the current reproductions popping up at flea and antique markets.

Many of our descriptions contain references to border colors and treatments. This information is given immediately preceding the mark and/or size. Our advisor for this category is Elyce Litts; she is listed in the Directory under New Jersey.

Key:
#2 — Torii Nippon	#42 — Vantine
#4 — T in Cherry Blossom	#68 — SGK China, Occupied
#11 — diaper mk	Japan
#12 — Royal Kaga, Nippon	J #1 — Yachi
#15 — Green, M-in-Wreath,	J #2 — Yachi tsukuru
Nippon	J #6 — Tashiro
#16 — SNB, Nippon	J #16 — Kutani
#19 — Japan	J #19 — Ozan
#20 — Made in Japan	J #36 — Made by Kato
#35 — Plum Blossom	J #46 — Yasutera

Teapot, Mother and Son C, red with gold, 5½", $65.00.

Ashtray, Temple A, heart form, red w/gold, #15	35.00
Basket vase, Bamboo Trellis, gr & brn trim w/gold, 8½", pr	175.00
Biscuit jar, Basket of Mums B, red w/gold, 3-ftd	65.00
Bowl, berry; Boat Festival, cobalt, #35, ind	15.00
Bowl, Feather Fan, pierced hdls, #12, 8"	75.00
Bowl, master nut; Ribbon Parasol, red-orange w/gold	28.00
Bowl, Pointing D, red-orange w/gold buds, 5¼"	14.00
Bowl, Stepping Stones, wavy red w/gold buds, #19, 6¾"	25.00
Box, dresser; Garden Bench B, cobalt w/gold, hexagonal, 6"	48.00
Butter pat, Flower Gathering B, red-orange, 3¼"	12.00
Candlesticks, Temple A, #15, 5¾", pr	250.00
Chocolate pot, River's Edge, red w/gold, J#16	95.00
Chocolate set, Chrysanthemum Garden, cobalt w/gold, #19, 11-pc	125.00
Cocoa set, Bamboo Trellis, gr, 13-pc, serves 6	160.00
Covered dish, Sm Sounds of Summer, red, hdld/3-ftd, J#16, 7½" L	65.00
Creamer, Long-Stemmed Peony, bl w/gold, slim, #20	15.00
Cup, bouillon; Thousand Geisha, cobalt w/gold, J#42, w/lid	65.00
Cup & saucer, chocolate; Garden Bench C, cobalt border	18.00
Cup & saucer, demi; Paper Carp, red-orange, #35	15.00
Cup & saucer, demi; Plum Blossom Branch, red-orange w/gold	20.00
Cup & saucer, tea; Duck Watching B, bl-gr w/wht, #6	15.00
Cup & saucer, tea; Flower Gathering A, bl w/gold lacing	18.00
Cup & saucer, tea; Geisha in Sampan A, gold	15.00
Egg cup, Cherry Blossom Ikebana, red, #20	18.00
Egg cup, dbl; Mother & Son A, bl-gr	20.00
Egg cup, dbl; Temple B, red w/gold	28.00
Hatpin holder, Lantern Dance, red, cylindrical on sm tray	65.00

Jar, condensed milk; Ikebana Party, cobalt w/gold, J#16, 3-pc 85.00
Jar, powder; Processional, mc border, J#16 ....37.00
Jar, powder; Pug, brick red, 4¼" 35.00
Lemonade set, Bellflower, #19, pitcher & 5 mugs 140.00
Mustard, Garden Bench C, cobalt w/gold, #4 ....25.00
Pancake server, So Big, red w/gold lacing, J#16, 9½x3½" 150.00
Plate, Battledore, swirl fluted, scalloped rim, yel-gr, 6" 15.00
Plate, Butterfly Dancers, red w/gold, 7" 28.00
Plate, Duck Watching B, mk, 7" 18.00
Plate, Gardening, red-orange w/gold buds, 6" 10.00
Plate, Visitor to the Court, bl w/gold, #19, 7¼" 22.00
Ramekin, Bamboo Trellis, red, stick hdl 25.00
Shakers, Blind Man's Bluff, lt apple gr, fluted, pr 25.00
Spooner, Vantine's Blue, upright, scalloped edge, #42 ....45.00
Sugar bowl, Boy w/Scythe, cobalt w/gold, #20 ....18.00
Tea strainer, Lady's Lunch, red, very ornate, 2-pc 75.00
Tea strainer, Parasol/Lesson A, red, 2-pc 55.00
Teapot, Garden Bench C, bl w/gold, red spout, #19, 4¾" 30.00
Toothpick holder, 3-patterned on floral/phoenix ground, cobalt ..45.00

German Porcelain

Unless otherwise noted, the porcelain listed in this section is marked simply 'Germany.' Products of other German manufactures are listed in specific categories. See also Bisque; Pink Paw Bears; Pink Pigs; Elfinware.

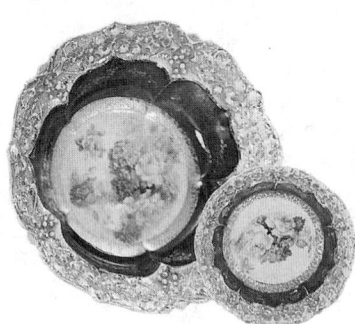

Berry set, roses and lilacs in center, burgundy with ornate gold, 10" bowl with four 5½" individual bowls, $98.00 for the set.

Bowl, berry; classical figures, Kauffmann, 10½"+6 ind 135.00
Bowl, lady sits between 2 lobes, 2 cherubs beside, 9x15x7" 460.00
Bowl, mc flowers, rtcl rim, gold trim, Schumann, 4" 8.00
Cake plate, mixed fruits, emb scrolls, gold trim, 10" 35.00
Figurine, lady in chariot & 4 nude children, gold trim, 8x11x5" ..245.00
Figurine, nude emerging from pearlized conch shell, gold trim 90.00
Figurine, nude standing, fine detail, 3½" 110.00
Figurine, nude standing on rnd turq water base, 3x2¾" 95.00
Pitcher, chrysanthemums w/gold, emb scrolls, 7" 60.00
Plaque, Biblical couple by wall, Thumann, 1790s, 10x12"+fr ..1,750.00
Plaque, lady in wht robe w/gilt fr, HP, 6¾x5⅛" 350.00
Plaque, Ruth's portrait, holds wheat bundle, HP, gold fr, 8x6" ...800.00
Plate, bread; lilies & flowers on mc ground, 9½" 25.00
Teapot, couples & flowers, bird spout, rose finial, older mk 500.00

Gladding McBean and Company

This company was established in 1875 in Lincoln, California. They first produced only clay drainage pipes, but in 1883 architectural terra cotta was introduced, which has been used extensively in the United States as well as abroad. Sometime later a line of garden pottery was added. They soon became the leading producers of tile in the country. In 1923 they purchased the Tropico Pottery in Glendale, Califor-

nia, where in addition to tile they also produced huge garden vases. Their line was expanded in 1934 to included artware and dinnerware.

At least fifteen lines of art pottery were developed between 1934 and 1942. For a short time they stamped their wares with the Tropico Pottery mark; but the majority was signed 'GMcB' in an oval. Later the mark was changed to 'Franciscan' with several variations. After 1937 'Catalina Pottery' was used on some lines. (All items marked 'Catalina Pottery' were made in Glendale.) For further information we recommend *The Collector's Encyclopedia of California Pottery, Second Edition,* by our advisor for this category, Jack Chipman. He is listed in the Directory under California.

Bowl, Avalon, #C703, 15" 45.00
Bowl, Floral Art Ware, coral satin, leaf form, 9x14" 35.00
Candle holder, Tropico Art Ware, wht 30.00
Candlestick, Coronado Art Ware, turq satin, 4" 30.00
Clam shell, giant, #C236, 15x6½" 85.00
Compote, Avalon Art Ware, turq & ivory, #C724, 8" 32.50
Cornucopia, Sea Shell, #C350, 6" 65.00
Cup & saucer, demi; Rancho Ware, turq 20.00
Cup & saucer, Ruby Art Ware 45.00
Head vase, ivory or aqua, cupped hands form opening, 7" 145.00
Lamp base, Ox Blood Art Ware 750.00
Tile, angelfish, 6x6" 75.00
Vase, bud; Encanto Art Ware, celadon, #602 ....65.00
Vase, Catalina Art Ware, coral stain, ribbed, #C312, 7¾" 75.00
Vase, Catalina Artware, ivory, fluted, #C312, 6½" 50.00
Vase, Floral Art Ware, ivory w/peach int, #C338, 11½" 125.00
Vase, Garden Ware, bl-gr w/bead relief at neck, 35" 1,000.00
Vase, Ox Blood Art Ware, #C290, 11" 700.00
Vase, Ox Blood Art Ware, red w/gray crystals, mk, 8" 500.00
Vase, Polynesia Art Ware, Bamboo, ivory/gr, #C387, 8" 100.00
Vase, Saguaro, yel & gr satin, #C252, 5" 55.00

Glass Animals and Figurines

These beautiful glass sculptures have been produced by many major companies in America, in fact, some are still being made today. Heisey, Fostoria, Duncan and Miller, Imperial, Paden City, Tiffin, and Cambridge made the vast majority, but there were many others involved on a lesser scale. Some, but not all, marked their animals.

As many of the glass companies went out of business, molds were often sold to others still active who used them to reproduce their own line of animals. While some are easy to recognize, others can be very confusing. For example, Summit Art Glass now owns Cambridge's 6½", 8½", and 10" swan molds. We recommend *Glass Animals of the Depression Era* by Lee Garmon and Dick Spencer, if you're thinking of starting a collection or wanting to identify and evaluate the glass animals you already have. Both are our advisors for this category and are listed in the Directory under Illinois.

Note: Heisey Collectors of America stopped using the plug horse and have adoped the rabbit paperweight as the new yearly mascot.

Cambridge

Bashful Charlotte, flower frog, crystal, 6½" 100.00
Bashful Charlotte, flower frog, lt emerald, 11½" 350.00
Bashful Charlotte, flower frog, Moonlight Bl, 11½" 525.00
Bashful Charlotte, flower frog, Moonlight Bl satin, 11½" 800.00
Bashful Charlotte, flower frog, Peachblo, 6½" 150.00
Bashful Charlotte, flower frog, pk, 6" 225.00
Bird, crystal satin, 2¾" L 30.00
Bird on stump, flower frog, gr, 5¼" 325.00

Blue jay, flower holder, crystal 125.00
Buddha, amber, 5½" 225.00
Bun Geisha, flower frog, Ritz Bl 1,000.00
Draped Lady, flower frog, amber, 8½" 195.00
Draped Lady, flower frog, crystal frost, 13¼" 175.00
Draped Lady, flower frog, Dianthus frost, 8½" 140.00
Draped Lady, flower frog, Gold Krystol, 8½" 250.00
Draped Lady, flower frog, gr frost, 8½" 125.00
Draped Lady, flower frog, ivory, oval base, 8½" 800.00
Draped Lady, flower frog, lt emerald, 8½" 225.00
Draped Lady, flower frog, Moonlight Bl, 8½" 475.00
Eagle, bookend, crystal, 5½x4x4" 95.00
Frog, crystal satin 25.00
Heron, crystal, sm, 9" 75.00
Lion, bookend, crystal, ea 135.00
Mandolin Lady, flower frog, crystal 250.00
Mandolin Lady, flower frog, dk amber 450.00
Mandolin Lady, flower frog, lt emerald 400.00
Melon Boy, flower frog, pk 425.00
Owl, lamp, ivory w/brn enamel, ebony base, 13½" 1,100.00
Pouter Pigeon, bookend, milk glass, 5½" 95.00
Rose Lady, flower frog, amber, 8½" 200.00
Rose Lady, flower frog, crystal satin, tall base, 9¾" 225.00
Rose Lady, flower frog, Dianthus, 8½" 275.00
Rose Lady, flower frog, dk amber, tall base, 9¾" 275.00
Rose Lady, flower frog, gr, 8½" 200.00
Scottie, bookends, crystal, hollow, pr 175.00
Scottie, frosted, hollow, ea 75.00

Sea Gull, crystal, 10½",
$60.00.

Swan, Apple Gr, #1 style, 13½" 850.00
Swan, candlestick, milk glass, 4½" 175.00
Swan, carmen, #3 style, 8½" 350.00
Swan, Crown Tuscan, 3" 50.00
Swan, Crown Tuscan, 8½" 125.00
Swan, dk gr, #3 style, 8½" 175.00
Swan, ebony, 10½" 250.00
Swan, ebony, 12½" 300.00
Swan, ebony, 8½" 165.00
Swan, emerald, 3" 40.00
Swan, milk glass, 3" 60.00
Swan, milk glass, 6½" 125.00
Swan, punch bowl, Pearl Mist 2,000.00
Swan, yel, 8½" 175.00
Turkey, bl, w/lid 550.00
Turkey, pk, w/lid 400.00
Turtle, flower holder, ebony 225.00
Two Kids, flower frog, amber, oval base, 9¼" 325.00
Two Kids, flower frog, amber satin, 9¼" 400.00
Two Kids, flower frog, crystal, 9¼" 200.00

Duncan and Miller

Bird of Paradise, crystal 700.00

Donkey, cart & peon, crystal, 3-pc set 475.00
Donkey, crystal 120.00
Dove, crystal, head down, 11½" L 175.00
Duck, ashtray, red, 7" 90.00
Duck, cigarette box, red, 6" 170.00
Goose, crystal, fat, 6x6" 375.00
Heron, crystal satin, 7" 120.00
Mallard duck, cigarette box, crystal, #30, w/lid, 3½x4½" 50.00
Ruffled grouse, crystal, very rare 1,750.00
Swan, bl opal, W&F, spread wings, 10x12½" 245.00
Swan, candle holder, red w/crystal neck, 7" 80.00
Swan, chartreuse, open bk, 7" 35.00
Swan, crystal, solid, 3" 25.00
Swan, crystal, solid, 5" 30.00
Swan, crystal, solid, 7" 75.00
Swan, crystal bowl, 7½" 15.00
Swan, dk gr bowl, 10½" 65.00
Swan, milk glass w/red neck, 10½" 450.00
Swan, wheat cutting, 11" 200.00
Swordfish, bl opal, rare 500.00
Swordfish, crystal 275.00
Sylvan swan, bl or pk, 5½" 125.00
Sylvan swan, yel opal, 5½" 120.00
Sylvan swan, yel opal, 7½" 140.00
Tropical fish, candle holder, crystal, 5½" 500.00

Fenton

Airedale, Rosalene 75.00
Alley cat, amethyst carnival, 11" 125.00
Alley cat, pk carnival, mk, 11" 100.00
Bear, blk, sitting on font 38.00
Bear, carnival, sitting 20.00
Boy, blk, praying 12.00
Bunny, pale yel 20.00
Butterfly, candle holder, ruby carnival, 1989 souvenir, 7½" 85.00
Cardinal head, ruby, 6½" 95.00
Elephant, flower bowl, blk satin, 6½x9" 400.00
Elephant, whiskey bottle, periwinkle, 8" 450.00
Fish, paperweight, red carnival, ltd, ed 65.00
Fish, red w/amberina tail & fins, 2½" 55.00
Fish, vase, milk glass w/blk tail & eyes, 7" 425.00
Gazelle, Rosalene 115.00
Happiness Bird, red, 6½" 28.00
Hen, Rosalene 85.00
Rabbit, Rosalene, paperweight 45.00
Turtle, flower block, amethyst, 4" L 85.00

Fostoria

Bird, candle holder, crystal, 1½" 20.00
Cardinal head, Silver Mist, 6½" 125.00
Cat, lt bl, 3¾" 35.00
Chanticleer, blk, 10¾" 600.00
Colts, Silver Mist, standing 45.00
Deer, bl, sitting or standing, ea 55.00
Deer, milk glass, sitting or standing, ea 55.00
Dolphin, bl, 4¾" 25.00
Duck, mama, crystal 30.00
Duck w/3 ducklings, amber, set 50.00
Duckling, crystal, head down (+) 20.00
Duckling, crystal, walking (+) 15.00
Eagle, bookend, crystal, 7½", ea 150.00
Elephant, bookend, ebony, 6½", ea 125.00

Goldfish, crystal, horizontal, rare 125.00
Goldfish, crystal, vertical 95.00
Horse, bookend, crystal, 7¾", ea 45.00
Madonna, Silver Mist, orig issue, 10" (+) 50.00
Madonna, Silver Mist, w/base, orig issue, 11¾" (+) 80.00
Mermaid, crystal, 11½" 125.00
Pelican, amber, 1991 commemorative 55.00
Polar bear, crystal, 4⅝" 65.00
Polar bear, topaz, 4⅝" 125.00
Sea horse, bookend, crystal, 8", ea 125.00
Seal, topaz, 3⅞" 125.00
Squirrel, amber, running 45.00
Squirrel, amber, sitting 45.00
St Francis, Silver Mist, orig issue, 13½" (+) 325.00

Heisey

Flying mare, crystal, $3,000.00.

Airedale, crystal 650.00
Asiatic pheasant, crystal, 7½" L 325.00
Bull, crystal, sgn, 4x7½" 1,700.00
Bunny, crystal, head down, 2½" 200.00
Chick, crystal, head down or up, ea 95.00
Colt, amber, kicking 650.00
Colt, amber, rearing 650.00
Colt, cobalt, kicking 1,500.00
Colt, cobalt, rearing 1,500.00
Colt, cobalt, standing 1,200.00
Colt, crystal, kicking 185.00
Colt, crystal, rearing 200.00
Colt, crystal, standing 100.00
Cygnet, baby swan, crystal, 2½" 210.00
Doe head, bookend, crystal, 6¼" 850.00
Dolphin, candlesticks, crystal, #110, pr 350.00
Donkey, crystal 295.00
Duck, ashtray, crystal 90.00
Duck, ashtray, Marigold 400.00
Duck, flower block, crystal 140.00
Elephant, amber, lg or med 1,850.00
Elephant, amber, sm 1,600.00
Elephant, crystal, lg or med, ea 450.00
Elephant, crystal, sm 225.00
Filly, crystal, head bkwards 1,800.00
Filly, crystal, head forward 1,100.00
Fish, bookend, crystal, ea 135.00
Fish, bowl, crystal, 9½" 525.00
Fish, candlestick, crystal, 5" 210.00
Fish, match holder, crystal, 3x2¾" 175.00
Frog, cheese plate, Flamingo, #1210 ....145.00
Frog, cheese plate, Marigold 285.00
Gazelle, crystal, 10¾" 1,500.00
Giraffe, crystal, head bk 250.00
Giraffe, crystal, head forward 200.00

Giraffe, crystal, head to side 250.00
Goose, crystal, wings down 450.00
Goose, crystal, wings half 100.00
Goose, crystal, wings up 110.00
Horse head, bookend, crystal, ea 175.00
Horse head, bookend, frosted, ea 140.00
Horse head, cigarette box, crystal, #1489, 4½x4" 55.00
Irish setter, ashtray, crystal 30.00
Irish setter, ashtray, Moongleam 55.00
Kingfisher, flower block, Flamingo 225.00
Kingfisher, flower block, Moongleam 250.00
Mallard, crystal, wings down 350.00
Mallard, crystal, wings half 200.00
Mallard, crystal, wings up 200.00
Piglet, crystal, sitting 100.00
Piglet, crystal, standing 100.00
Plug horse, cobalt 1,200.00
Plug horse, crystal 160.00
Pouter pigeon, crystal, 7½" L 800.00
Rabbit, paperweight, crystal, 2¾x3¾" 200.00
Rabbit mother, crystal, 4½x5½" 1,000.00
Ram head, stopper, crystal, 3½" 160.00
Ring-neck pheasant, crystal, 11¾" 160.00
Rooster, amber, 5⅜" 2,500.00
Rooster, crystal, 5½x5" 350.00
Rooster, Fighting; crystal frost, 7½x5½" 200.00
Rooster, vase, crystal, 6½" 110.00
Rooster head, cocktail, crystal 60.00
Rooster head, stopper, crystal, 4½" 45.00
Scotty, crystal 135.00
Sea horse, cocktail, crystal 160.00
Show horse, crystal 1,250.00
Sow, crystal, 3x4½" 750.00
Sparrow, crystal 120.00
Swan, ind nut, crystal, #1503 ....25.00
Swan, master nut, crystal, #1503 ....45.00
Tiger, paperweight, crystal, 2¾x8" 1,100.00
Tropical fish, crystal, 12" 1,800.00
Wood duck, crystal 800.00

Imperial

Angelfish, bookend, amber (crystal or frosted), ea 100.00
Asiatic pheasant, amber 425.00
Bull, amber, very rare 725.00
Bulldog-type pup, milk glass, 3½" 65.00
Champ terrier, caramel slag, 5¾" 95.00
Chick, head down, milk glass 10.00
Clydesdale, Salmon 275.00
Clydesdale, Verde Gr 150.00
Colt, amber, standing 125.00
Colt, caramel slag, balking 140.00
Colt, Horizon Bl, kicking 35.00
Colt, Sunshine Yel, standing 75.00
Cygnet, blk, 2½" 55.00
Cygnet, Horizon Bl 25.00
Dog, Airedale, caramel slag 115.00
Dog, Airedale, Ultra Bl 65.00
Donkey, caramel slag 55.00
Donkey, Meadow Gr carnival 45.00
Duck, Ultra Bl, standing, 2⅝" 45.00
Elephant, caramel slag, med 65.00
Elephant, Meadow Gr carnival, #674, med 75.00
Elephant, Nut Brn, sm 120.00

Filly, head bkward, Verde Gr 155.00
Filly, satin, head forward 85.00
Fish, candlestick, Sunshine Yel, 5" 50.00
Fish, match holder, Sunshine Yel satin, 3" 20.00
Flying mare, amber, NI mk, extremely rare 1,500.00
Gazelle, blk, 11" 350.00
Giraffe, amber, ALIG mk, extremely rare 350.00
Horse head, bookend, pk, rare, ea 300.00
Mallard, caramel slag, wings half 35.00
Mallard, caramel slag, wings up 40.00
Mallard, Horizon Bl, wings down, HCA, 4½" 35.00
Marmote Sentinel (woodchuck), caramel slag, 4½" 60.00
Owl, Hootless; caramel slag 50.00
Owl, jade gr slag, shiny 85.00
Owl, milk glass 48.00
Owl, purple slag, shiny 85.00
Piglet, amber, standing 40.00
Piglet, ruby, standing 35.00
Plug horse, pk, HCA, 1978 ....40.00
Ring-neck pheasant, amber, extremely rare 300.00
Rooster, amber 475.00
Rooster, pk, fighting 175.00
Scottie, milk glass, 3½" 55.00
Swan, purple slag, glossy 95.00
Terrier pup, amethyst carnival, 3½" 45.00
Tiger, paperweight, caramel slag 150.00
Tiger, paperweight, jade marbleized, 8" L 95.00
Wood duck, caramel slag 65.00
Wood duckling, floating, Sunshine Yel satin 20.00
Wood duckling, standing, Sunshine Yel satin 15.00
Wood duckling, standing, Ultra Bl 45.00

L.E. Smith

Cock, Fighting; bl, 9" 45.00
Elephant, crystal, 1¾" 12.00
Goose girl, crystal, orig, 6" 25.00
Goose girl, gr or flame, 6", ea 50.00
Horse, amberina, recumbent, 9" L 150.00
Horse, bookend, crystal, rearing, ea 35.00
Horse, bookend, ruby, rearing, ea 45.00
King fish, aquarium, gr, 7¼x15" 265.00
Rooster, butterscotch slag, ltd ed, #208 ....85.00
Scottie, pipe rest, fired-on blk, 5½" L 10.00
Swan, milk glass w/decor, 8½" 45.00
Thrush, bl frost 20.00

New Martinsville

Bear, baby, crystal, head trn or str, 3" 60.00
Bear, papa, crystal, 4x6½" 250.00
Chick, frosted, 1" 25.00
Eagle, crystal, 8" 85.00
Elephant, bookend, crystal, 5½", ea 90.00
Gazelle, leaping, frosted base, 8¼" 65.00
German shepherd, crystal, 5" 75.00
Horse, crystal, head up, 8" 95.00
Piglet, crystal, standing 125.00
Porpoise on wave, orig 750.00
Rabbit, mama, crystal 350.00
Seal, baby w/ball, crystal 60.00
Seal, candle holders, crystal, pr 125.00
Seal, candlesticks, crystal, lg, pr 150.00
Seal w/ball, candle holder, crystal, 4½" 70.00

Ship, bookend, crystal 45.00
Swan, candle holders, ruby, pr 70.00
Tiger, crystal, head up, 6½" 225.00
Wolfhound, crystal, 7" 95.00
Woodsman, crystal, sq base, 7⅜" 135.00

Paden City

Chinese pheasant, medium blue, 13¾", $150.00.

Bunny, cotton-ball dispenser, bl frosted, ears bk 125.00
Bunny, cotton-ball dispenser, crystal frosted, ears bk 85.00
Bunny, cotton-ball dispenser, milk glass, ears bk 95.00
Bunny, cotton-ball dispenser, pk frosted, ears up 175.00
Dragon swan, crystal, 9¾" L 225.00
Pelican, crystal 600.00
Pheasant, Chinese; crystal, 13¾" 100.00
Pheasant, Chinese; med bl, 13¾" 150.00
Polar bear on ice, crystal, 4½" 65.00
Pony, crystal, 12" 100.00
Pouter pigeon, bookend, crystal, 6¼" 95.00
Rooster, Barnyard; crystal, 8¾" 85.00
Rooster, Chanticleer; crystal, 9½" 75.00
Rooster, Chanticleer; lt bl, 9¼" 200.00
Rooster, Elegant; lt bl, 11" 225.00
Squirrel on curved log, crystal, 5½" 65.00

Tiffin

Cat, blk, glossy, lg 250.00
Cat, Sassy Susie, blk satin w/pnt decor, #9448, 11" 175.00
Fish, crystal, solid, 8¾x9" 350.00
Frog, candlestick, blk satin 115.00
Owl, lamp, cobalt, 1934-29 ....1,250.00

Viking

Angelfish, amber, 7x7" 125.00
Angelfish, milk glass, pr 150.00
Bird, med dk bl, 9½" 35.00
Bird, moss gr, tail up, 12" 40.00
Bird, orange, long tail, 9½" 35.00
Bird, Orchid, 9½" 35.00
Cat, gr, sitting, 8" 55.00
Duck, ashtray, dk bl, 9" 45.00
Duck, crystal, fighting, head up or down, Viking's Epic Line 45.00
Duck, dk teal, Viking's Epic Line, 9" 45.00
Duck, orange, rnd, ftd, 5" 35.00
Duck, ruby, rnd, ftd, 5" 40.00
Duck, vaseline, 5" 35.00
Horse, aqua bl, 11½" 95.00
Jesus, crystal w/crystal mist, flat bk, 6x5" 65.00
Owl, amber, Viking's Epic Line 45.00
Penguin, crystal, 7" 35.00
Rabbit, amber, 6½" 35.00
Rabbit (Thumper), crystal, 6½" 35.00

Rooster, Epic; red, 9½" (+) 60.00
Seal, Persimmon, 9¾" L 25.00
Swan, bowl, amber, 6" 45.00
Swan, orange, fluted, 6½x4" 45.00
Swan, Yel Mist, paper label, 6" 50.00

Westmoreland

Bird in flight, Amber Marigold, wings out, 5" W 35.00
Butterfly, Bl Mist, 2½" 25.00
Butterfly, crystal, 4½" 27.00
Butterfly, Gr Mist, 2½" 25.00
Cardinal, Gr Mist 20.00
Penguin on ice floe, Brandywine Bl Mist 45.00
Pig, amberina 85.00
Pig, milk glass, fired pnt, orig label 37.50
Porky Pig, milk glass, hollow, 3" L 20.00
Pouter pigeon, any color, 2½", ea 30.00
Robin, pk, 5⅛" 25.00
Starfish, candle holders, milk glass, 5", pr 45.00
Turtle, ashtray, crystal 10.00
Turtle, paperweight, Gr Mist, no holes, 4" L 25.00
Wren, Crystal Mist, 2½" 17.50
Wren, pk, 2½" 20.00
Wren, smoke, 2½" 20.00
Wren on perch, lt bl on wht, 2-pc 40.00

Miscellaneous

Federal, Mopey dog, crystal, 3½" 10.00
Haley, horse, crystal, jumping 45.00
Haley, horse, milk glass, jumping 50.00
Haley, Lady Godiva, bookend, crystal, 1940s 40.00
Haley, pheasant, crystal, 1940s, 12" 30.00
Indiana, horse head, bookends, milk glass, 6", pr 45.00
Indiana, panther, amber, walking 225.00
Indiana, panther, bl, walking 250.00
Indiana, pouter pigeon, bookend, crystal, 5½", ea 40.00
Mosser, lady's leg, bookends, custard, pr 175.00
New Martinsville by Mirror Images, baby bear, ruby 75.00
New Martinsville by Mirror Images, baby seal, ruby 75.00
New Martinsville by Mirror Images, mama bear, ruby ..140.00
New Martinsville by Mirror Images, police dog, ruby ...150.00
New Martinsville by Mirror Images, wolfhound, ruby carnival ...125.00

Glass Knives

Glass knives were manufactured from about 1920 to 1950, with distribution at its greatest in the late '30s and early '40s. Colors generally followed Depression glass dinnerware: crystal, light blue, light green, pink (originally called rose), and more rarely amber, forest green, and white (opal). Many glass knives were hand painted in fruit or flower designs. Knife blades were ground to a sharp edge. Today knives are usually found with blades nicked through years of use or bumping in silverware drawers or reground, which is acceptable to collectors as long as the original knife shape is maintained.

Many glass knives were engraved for gift-giving, personalized with the recipient's name and on occasion, with a greeting. Originally presented in boxes, most glass knives were accompanied by a paper insert extolling the virtues of the knife and describing its care.

Boxes printed with World's Fair logos are fun to find, though not rare. Butter knives, which are smaller than other glass knives, typically were made in Czechoslovakia and sometimes match the handle patterns

of glass salad sets. Knife lengths often vary slightly because the knives were snapped off the molded glass during manufacture.

Our advisor for this category is Adrienne Escoe; she is listed in the Directory under California. For information concerning the Glass Knife Collectors' Club, see the Clubs, Newsletters, and Catalogs section of the Directory.

Values reflect knives with minor blade roughness or resharpening.

Aer-Flo (Grid), forest gr, 7½" 250.00
BK Co, gr, 9¼" 40.00
Block, crystal, MIB 20.00
Block, gr, from $30 to 35.00
Butter, gr/crystal, 6¼" 25.00
Dagger, crystal, 9¼", from $75 to 85.00
Dur-X (3-Leaf), bl, 9¼", MIB 20.00
Dur-X (3-Leaf), crystal, 8½" 12.00
Dur-X (5-Leaf), bl, 9¼", MIB 25.00
Dur-X (5-Leaf), crystal, 8½" 12.00
Grid, crystal 30.00
Plain hdl, lt pk, 9" 35.00
Rosespray, crystal 25.00
Steel-ite, crystal, 8½" 25.00
Stonex, gr, 8¼", MIB 70.00
Stonex, opal, 8½" 135.00
Thumbguard, crystal, M in plain box 20.00
Vitex (3-Star), bl, 9¼", MIB, from $28 to 32.00
Vitex (3-Star), crystal, 8½" 10.00
Vitex (3-Star), pk, 9¼" 28.00

Glass Shoes

Little shoes made of glass can be found in hundreds of styles, shapes, and colors. They've been made since the early 1800s by nearly every glasshouse, large and small, in America. To learn more about them, we recommend *Shoes of Glass* (newly updated) by our advisor Libby Yalom, who is listed in the Directory under Maryland. Numbers in the listings refer to her book.

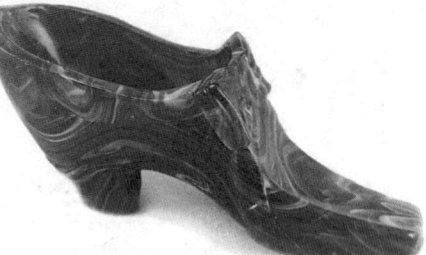

#100, blue and white slag, English Sowerby, 1880s, 2½x5⅞", $170.00.

Photo courtesy Libby Yalom

#101, Cane, crystal, high front, mesh sole, 1880s, 2¼x4⅝" 48.00
#115, half stippled/half plain, crystal, hollow sole, 4¾" 60.00
#127, Daisy & Button boot, crystal, Duncan, 1880s, 4¾" 65.00
#137, cuffed purple & wht slag boot, 1890s, 3¼x4" 75.00
#150, blk amethyst high shoe, stippled top, bow at toe, 4⅛" 80.00
#161, Finecut, bl roller skate, no laces, 1880s, 3x4" 75.00
#170, milk glass high shoe roller skate, ...France, 4x3½" 46.00
#184, Finecut high-button shoe, vaseline, left, B&H, 5½" H 65.00
#289, amethyst high-button shoe, mk Bouquet Holder..., 5½" 80.00
#320, milk glass boot, mc flower/leaves on vamp, 1890, 3¾x4⅞" .150.00
#344, frosted mc millefiori w/crystal heel, Murano label, 5⅝" 90.00
#359, frosted burmese-color, ruffled edge, 2½x6⅜" 98.00
#378, crystal, made as candy dish, mk Baccarat, 1956-70, 10" L .160.00

#385, Dutch shoe, crystal, 3 ridges on vamp, 2 buttons, 7" L 50.00
#395, gr boot match holder, solid glass in ft, ca 1889, 4½" L 45.00
#426, cat in man's shoe, hollow, peacock mk, 1876, 4⅞" L 150.00
#443, amethyst flat boot flask, opal spirals, pontil, 8" 350.00
#471, crystal man's shoe bottle, threaded top, 1870-90, 4⅛" L 55.00
#495, bl w/thimble holder opening, mk B&R, 1890s, 2⅜x4" 95.00
#573, rubena (crystal to cranberry), 6⅜x4⅜" 80.00
#604, Daisy & Button bl cat shoe, gold Kemple label, 1890, 5⅞" .20.00

Glidden

Genius designer Glidden Parker established Glidden Pottery in 1940 in Alfred, New York, having been schooled at the unrivaled New York State College of Ceramics at Alfred University. Glidden pottery is characterized by a fine stoneware body, innovative forms, outstanding hand-milled glazes, and hand decoration which make the pieces individual works of art. Production consisted of casual dinnerware, artware, and accessories that were distributed internationally.

In 1949 Glidden Pottery became the second ceramic plant in the country to utilize the revolutionary Ram pressing machine. This allowed for increased production and for the most part eliminated the previously used slip-casting method. However, Glidden stoneware continued to reflect the same superb quality of craftsmanship until the factory closed in 1957. Although the majority of form and decorative patterns were Mr. Parker's personal designs, Fong Chow and Sergio Dello Strologo also designed award-winning lines.

Glidden will be found marked on the unglazed underside with a signature that is hand incised, mold impressed, or ink stamped. Interest in this unique stoneware is growing as collectors discover that it embodies the very finest of Mid-Century High Style. Our advisor is David Pierce; he is listed in the Directory under Ohio.

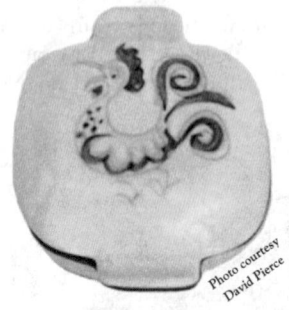

Individual casserole, Menagerie Series, #167, 5¾x4½x2", $20.00.

Photo courtesy David Pierce

Boat, Sandstone, rust/wht/bl, #4034, 10x3½" 120.00
Bowl, Sage & Sand, #17, 4½x8x8" 20.00
Bowl, Turq Matrix, oval, #38, 2x7¼x3¾" 30.00
Box, Afrikans, blk/rust/wht, #223, 2x9x4" 150.00
Canister, Garden, w/cover & bail, #601, 5x5½" dia 60.00
Casserole, Mexican Cock, #163, 5x11x6½" 40.00
Charger, Leaf, cobalt, 368, 15" dia 200.00
Creamer, Pear, 3¼x6x3½" 35.00
Flowerpot, Charcoal & Rice, bird from, 4x5½" 100.00
Flowerpot, Sandstone, rust/wht/bl, #4030, 6" 75.00
Flowerpot, Yellowstone, #218, 3¾x4½x4½" 15.00
Pitcher, Feather, wht, engobe, #616, 2-qt 6.00
Plate, Canine, Great Dane, #35, 5½x5½" 45.00
Plate, Ric Rac, yel, #31-B, 9¾x9¾" 30.00
Plate, Snowdrop, wht/bl, #33, 8x8" 65.00
Plate, Viridian, triangular, #542 ....35.00
Server, Alfred Stoneware, saffron, oak hdl, #805 ....175.00
Teapot, Turq Matrix, #618, 3½x9½x6½" 100.00

Tray, Blackfish, w/metal stand, #200, 8x6" 150.00
Tray, Flourish, cobalt, #32, 9x6¾" 55.00
Vase, cobalt, #2, 9x5" 50.00
Vase, Early Pk, ball form, #62, 4x3¾" 40.00
Vase, Gulfstream, turq/bl/blk, apple form, #4021, 15½x10½" 600.00
Vase, Loop Artware, rust/charcoal, #940, 9x9" dia 500.00
Vase, Turq Matrix, pillow form, #87, 7½x4½x2¾" 35.00

Goebel

F.W. Goebel founded the F&W Goebel Company in 1871, located in Rodental, West Germany. They produced thousands of different decorative and useful items over the years, the most famous of which are the Hummel figurines first produced in 1935 based on the artwork of a Franciscan nun, Sister Maria Innocentia Hummel.

The Goebel trademarks have long been a source of confusion because *all* Goebel products, including Hummels, of any particular time period bear the same trademark, thus leading many to believe all Goebels are Hummels. Always look for the Hummel signature on actual Hummel figurines (these are listed in a separate section).

There are many, many other series — some of which are based on artwork of particular artists such as Disney, Charlot Byj, Janet Robson, Harry Holt, Norman Rockwell, M. Spotl, Lore, Huldah, and Schaubach. Miscellaneous useful items include ashtrays, bookends, salt and pepper shakers, banks, pitchers, inkwells, perfume bottles, etc. Figurines include birds, animals, Art Deco pieces, etc. The Friar Tuck monks and the Co-Boy elves are especially popular.

The date of manufacture of a particular piece is determined by the trademark. The incised date found underneath the base on many items is the *mold copyright* date. Actual date of manufacture may vary as much as twenty years or more from the copyright date.

Most Common Goebel Trademarks and Approximate Date Used:
Crown mark (may be incised or stamped, or both) 1923 – 1950
Full bee (complete bumble bee inside the letter 'V') 1950 – 1957
Stylized bee (dot with wings inside the letter 'V') 1957 – 1964
3-Line (stylized bee with three lines of copyright information to the right of the trademark) 1964 – 1972
Goebel bee (word Goebel with stylized bee mark over the last letter 'e') 1972 – 1979
Goebel (word Goebel only) 1979 – present.

Our advisors for this category are Gale and Wayne Bailey; they are listed in the Directory under Georgia.

Cardinal Tuck (Red Monk)

Mustard, S183, stylized bee, 4" 145.00
Pipe stubber 295.00
Pitcher, S141/0, stylized bee, 4" 135.00
Shakers, P153, stylized bee, 2" 125.00
Sugar bowl, Z37, stylized bee, 4" 135.00

Charlot BYJ Redheads and Blonds

All Gone, BYJ 98 ....65.00
Atta Boy, BYJ 7 ....85.00
Bless Us All, BYJ 16 ....65.00
Captive Audience, BYJ 85 ....125.00
Cheer Up, BYJ 50 ....65.00
Child's Prayer, BYJ 17 ....65.00
Daisies Won't Tell, BYJ 24 ....65.00
Damper on the Camper, BYJ 72 ....125.00

Dealer plaque, BYJ 47	145.00
Dropping In, BYJ 45	90.00
E-ee-eek, BYJ 9	85.00
Evening Prayer, BYJ 38	90.00
Kibitzer, BYJ 23	125.00
Lazy Day, BYJ 78	125.00
Let It Rain, BYJ 51	200.00
Little Prayers Are Best, BYJ 59	125.00
Lucky Day, BYJ 44	75.00
Madonna of the Doves, BYJ 57	225.00
Nurse, BYJ 63	80.00
O'Hair for President, BYJ 8	65.00
Off Key, BYJ 22	95.00
Plenty of Nothing, BYJ 27	75.00
Putting on the Dog, BYJ 25	90.00
Roving Eye, BYJ 2	80.00
Say A-aa-aah, BYJ 68	85.00
Sharing Secrets, BYJ 99	85.00
Sheer Nonsense, BYJ 5	90.00
Sitting Pretty, BYJ 12	90.00
Skater's Waltz, BYJ 52	90.00
Sleepy Head, BYJ 11	80.00
Springtime, BYJ 10	85.00
Stolen Kiss	85.00
Strike, BYJ 1	80.00
This Won't Hurt, blond, BYJ 67	85.00
Trim Lass, BYJ 49	65.00
Way To Pray, BYJ 46	75.00

Co-Boy Figurines

Bert, Jim, Tommy, Bob, Goebel, ea	75.00
Bit, 3-line mk	95.00
Brad Clock, Goebel	225.00
Carol, Jack, or Connie, Goebel, ea	85.00
Gerd the Diver	110.00

Friar Tuck (Brown Monk)

Bank, SD29, full bee	80.00
Condiment set, shakers & mustard on tray, stylized bee	110.00
Cookie jar, full bee	360.00
Egg timer, dbl, E96, stylized bee	125.00
Jug, bl eyes, tiny	75.00
Liquor tot, LKL94, stylized bee	30.00
Mug, T74/0, full bee	35.00
Napkin ring, stylized bee	75.00
Oil & vinegar cruets, 3-line mk, pr	250.00
Shakers, full bee, pr	35.00
Shakers, w/Bible, pr	80.00

Shakers

Cats, P94A&B, pr	40.00
Chipmunks, stylized bee, pr	45.00
Corn, upright, pr	55.00
Duck & drake, pr	35.00
Flower skunks, Disney, pr	165.00
Golfer & ball, pr on tray	150.00
Poodles, blk & wht pr on tray, full bee	85.00
Poodles, full bee, pr	45.00
Squirrel & pine cone, P76A/B, pr	35.00
Turkeys on nests, full bee, pr	45.00
Tyrolean boy & girl, P18/P19, pr	25.00

Miscellaneous

Cookie jar, eagle head	125.00
Figurine, bay thoroughbred	125.00
Figurine, cat, wht, 10"	100.00
Figurine, Dachshund in Tyrolean hat begging, Crown mk	100.00
Figurine, Figaro, full bee	295.00
Figurine, German Shepherd, wht, recumbent, 17"	125.00
Figurine, Great Dane, sitting, 18"	295.00
Figurine, palomino thoroughbred	125.00
Figurine, Persian cat, wht w/gr eyes, 3¼"	30.00
Figurine, Pluto, full bee	295.00
Figurine, Poodle, matt, 7½"	90.00
Figurine, Snow White & 7 Dwarfs, full bee, 1950s	825.00
Figurine, Spaniel, blk & gray glossy, 5"	65.00
Figurine, Springer Spaniel, CH632	65.00
Figurine, Tabby cat, orange, #3103012, 9"	65.00
Figurine, Terrier, #3063509	50.00
Figurine, Thumper's sister, Walt Disney, #36, 1970, 2½"	75.00
Hooks, heart shapes, Crown mk, pr	65.00
Lamp, perfume; dog begging, full bee, 6½"	300.00
Lamp, perfume; fish jumping, 7½"	250.00
Mug, beer; nude hdl, Crown mk	50.00
Mustard, clown	35.00
Nasha lamp, NA 25, full bee	250.00
Ornament, angel, gr, 1977	25.00
Place card holders, Band Members, Crown mk, ea	75.00
Pretzel holder, Tyrolean boy, KF10, full bee	50.00
Vase, 3 gentlemen, VB109, Crown mk	75.00
Wall pocket, liederhosen w/Tyrolean hat, red cherries, 4x4"	45.00

Goldscheider

The Goldscheider family operated a pottery in Vienna for many generations before seeking refuge in the United States following Hitler's invasion of their country. They settled in Trenton, New Jersey, in the early 1940s where they established a new corporation and began producing objects of art and tableware items. (No mention was made of the company in the Trenton City Directory after 1950, and it is assumed that by this time the influx of foreign imports had taken its toll.) In 1946 Marcel Goldscheider established a pottery in Staffordshire where he manufactured bone china figures, earthenware, etc., marked with a stamp of his signature. Larger artist-signed examples are the most valuable with the Austrian pieces bringing the higher prices. Our advisors are Randy and Debbie Coe; they are listed in the Directory under Oregon.

Figurine, dancer wearing top hat, Laurenzal, black stamp mark, #5523/15/7, 13", $1,650.00.

Bust, curly hair, hands by face, Austria, #7653, 15½" **1,250.00**
Bust, lady in lg straw hat w/grapes, mc on terra cotta, 29" **3,745.00**
Bust, Siamese woman, exotic headdress & jewelry, 12¼x8¼" **500.00**
Candy dish, lady figural lid hdl, 9½x7" **275.00**
Figurine, horse, reclining, USA, 12" **145.00**
Figurine, Lady Chrysanthemum, USA, 7" **145.00**
Figurine, lady in bl holding skirt wide, 15" **450.00**
Figurine, Old Virginia, USA, 8½" **125.00**
Figurine, Spanish dancer, skirt held wide, 15¾" **925.00**
Figurines, Royal Blackamoors, B Loveday, full figure, 15", pr **695.00**
Lamp, Aida, lady by lamppost, Austria, #5981, 21" **2,400.00**
Plaque, Madonna & Child, Wien, 14", EX+ **200.00**

Gonder

Lawton Gonder grew up with clay in his hands and fire in his eyes. Gonder's interest in ceramics was greatly influenced by his parents who worked for Weller and a close family friend and noted ceramic authority, John Herold. In his early teens Gonder launched his ceramic career at the Ohio Pottery Company while working for Herold. He later gained valuable experience at American Encaustic Tile Company, Cherry Art Tile, and the Florence Pottery. Gonder was plant manager at the Florence Pottery until fire destroyed the facility in late 1941.

After years of solid production and management experience, Lawton Gonder established the Gonder Ceramic Art Company, formerly the Peters and Reed plant, in South Zanesville, Ohio. Gonder Ceramic Arts produced quality art pottery with beautiful contemporary designs which included human and animal figures and a complete line of Oriental pottery. Accentuating the beautiful shapes were unique and innovative glazes developed by Gonder such as flambe (flame red with streakes of yellow), 24k gold crackle, antique gold, and Chinese crackle.

All Gonder is marked with the company name and mold number. They include 'Gonder U.S.A' in block letters, 'Gonder' in script, 'Gonder Original' in script, and 'Gonder Ceramic Art' in block letters. Paper labels were also used. Some of the early Gonder molds closely resemble RumRill designs that had been manufactured at the Florence Pottery; and because some RumRill pieces are found with similar (if not identical) shapes, matching mold numbers, and Gonder glazes, it is speculated that some RumRill was produced at the Gonder plant. In 1946 Gonder started another company which he named Elgee (chosen for his initials LG) where he manufactured lamp bases until a fire in 1954 resulted in his shifting lamp production to the main plant. Operations ceased in 1957. Our advisor for this category is Ron Hoopes; he is listed in the Directory under Ohio.

Vase, three large leaves, H-67, 9", $35.00.

Basket, shell form, lt yel, #674, 8" **25.00**
Bowl, La Gonda, aqua, 4¼" **10.00**
Candle holders, flower form, #E-14, pr **25.00**

Console bowl, shell form, #505, 8x16" **50.00**
Cookie jar, Ye Olde Oaken Bucket, #974, 8" **65.00**
Creamer, La Gonda, pk, w/lid **22.00**
Ewer, shell & starfish form, dk gr w/brn drip, #508, 13½" **175.00**
Figurine, Chinese girl, #763, 13" **30.00**
Figurine, elephant, stylized, lt gray, #108, 7½x10" **250.00**
Figurine, horse's head, bl & gr onyx, 13" L **45.00**
Planter, gondola, yel & pk **25.00**
Plate, luncheon; pk, 8½" **22.00**
Shakers, La Gonda, aqua, pr **22.00**
Sugar bowl, La Gonda, yel, w/lid **22.00**
Tile, hunting dog decal, sq **20.00**
Vase, aqua, hdls, #E-48, 6½" **30.00**
Vase, fish figural, brn shaded to aqua gr, #422, 9" **60.00**
Vase, gold crackle, hdls, #H-56, 8½" **28.00**
Vase, ribbon candy design, yel w/brn streaking, #517, 10½" **18.00**
Vase, swan form, dk yel w/brn streaks, #802, 10" **35.00**
Vase, trumpet neck, up-trn hdls, gold crackle, #604, 10" **40.00**
Vase, upright cornucopia shape w/integral hdls, #419, 8" **20.00**

Goofus Glass

Goofus glass is American-made pressed glass with designs that are either embossed (blown out) or intaglio (cut in). The decorated colors were aerographed or hand applied and not fired on the pieces. The various patterns exemplify the artistry of the turn-of-the-century glass crafters. The primary production dates were ca 1908 to 1918. Goofus was produced by many well-known manufacturers such as Northwood, Indiana, and Dugan. Our advisor for this categor is Leon Travis of the *Goofus Glass Gazette*; he is listed in the Directory under Virginia. See also Clubs, Newsletters, and Catalogs.

Bonbon, strawberry & flower pod, dome ft, orig pnt, 4" dia **42.50**
Bottle, perfume; Tulips, pk or gr orig pnt, w/stopper, 3½" **35.00**
Bottle, water; Basketweave, amethyst, rose decor, 10" **30.00**
Bowl, Dahlia, scalloped, w/gold, ornate, 4x10" **55.00**
Bowl, Dahlia, 9" **35.00**
Bowl, Dogwood, orig pnt, 3x9½", EX **48.00**
Bowl, field flowers, crimpled & ruffled rim, orig pnt, 3½x8" **45.00**
Bowl, Grape, on amethyst, scalloped, sq, orig pnt, 10", EX **82.00**
Bowl, pears/cherries/plums, crimped rim, EX orig pnt, 4x7" **37.50**
Bowl, reindeer in center, EX **20.00**
Bowl, Wheel & Block, red/gold on opal, scalloped & crimped, 9" ...**45.00**
Box, powder; Basketweave, milk glass, orig pnt, rare, NM **55.00**
Cake plate, acorn & leaf, amethyst, 12" **20.00**
Cake plate, La Belle, orig pnt, 11", EX **47.50**
Cake plate, Rose in Snow, 11" **18.00**
Candy dish, figure-8 design, serrated rim, orig pnt, 8½" **55.00**
Coasters, flowers, orig pnt, rare, 3" dia **12.00**
Compote & saucer set, Poppy, crackle glass, orig pnt, 6", M **40.00**
Decanter, Basketweave, single rose on front, EX orig pnt, 10" **50.00**
Lamp, fairy; Rose, flash-fired gr, 3 holes for smoke, 7" **40.00**
Lamp, oil; Cabbage Rose, amethyst, w/chimney, 15", NM **120.00**
Lamp, oil; Nosegay, #2, EX orig pnt **155.00**
Nut dish, cherries, orig pnt, scalloped rim, 6½" **42.50**
Plate, Gibson Girl, red on gold, 8", EX **55.00**
Plate, Grape, center design, gold trim, orig pnt, 8½" **45.00**
Plate, monk drinking, rose edge, orig pnt, rare, 7", M **125.00**
Plate, Morning Glory, red & gold, rpt, 12" **40.00**
Sauce dish, Rose, crackle glass, orig pnt, 5½" **35.00**
Shakers, Poppy, EX orig pnt, 3", pr **35.00**
Sugar shaker, Grape, gold on milk glass, orig pnt/top, 4½" **37.50**
Tray, bread; Last Supper, red & gold orig pnt, 7x11" **90.00**

Tray, dresser; Cabbage Rose, sq, orig pnt, 6" 32.50
Tumbler, Grape, gold on crackle, orig pnt, 4", NM 50.00
Vase, bird sitting in grapevine, satin glass, 9" 20.00
Vase, Cabbage Rose, EX orig pnt, 7" 25.00
Vase, Dogwood, baluster, orig pnt, 15" 95.00
Vase, Grape, no pnt, crackle, str sides, 9" 15.00
Vase, Irises, orig pnt, 12", EX 125.00
Vase, Lovebirds, orig pnt, 10" 95.00
Vase, mixed fruit, rpt gold on clear, 10" 40.00
Vase, Peacock in a Tree, red/gr/gold, M orig pnt, 15" 225.00
Vase, Rose in Snow, classic form, rpt, 10" 25.00
Vase, Statue of Liberty & Am Eagle, no pnt, 12⅝" 125.00
Vase, Tree Rose, orig pnt, 12", M 55.00
Water bottle, Grape, on crackle, no pnt, 7½" 35.00

Goss and Crested China

William Henry Goss received his early education at the Government School of Design at Somerset House, London, and as a result of his merit was introduced to Alderman William Copeland, who owned the Copeland Spode Pottery. Under the influence of Copeland from 1852 to 1858, Goss quickly learned the trade and soon became their chief designer. Little is known about this brief association, and in 1858 Goss left to begin his own business. After a short-lived partnership with a Mr. Peake, Goss opened a pottery on John Street, Stoke-on-Trent, but by 1870 he had moved to his business to a location near London Road. This pottery became the famous Falcon Works. Their mark was a spread-wing falcon (goss-hawk) centering a narrow, horizontal bar with 'W.H. Goss' printed below.

Many of the early pieces made by Goss were left unmarked and are difficult to discern from products made by the Copeland factory, but after he had been in business for about fifteen years, all of his wares were marked. Today unmarked items do not command the prices of the later marked wares.

Adolphus William Henry Goss (Goss's eldest son) joined his father's firm in the 1880s. He introduced cheaper lines, though the more expensive lines continued in production. Shortly after his father's death in 1906, Adolphus retired and left the business to his two younger brothers. The business suffered from problems created by a war economy, and in 1936 Goss assets were held by Cauldon Potteries Ltd. These were eventually taken over by the Coalport Group, who retained the right to use the Goss trademark. Messrs. Ridgeway Potteries bought all the assets in 1954 as well as the right to use the Goss trademark and name. In 1964 the group was known as Allied English Potteries Ltd. (A.E.P.), and in 1971 A.E.P. merged with the Doulton Group. Now it remains to be seen if Goss ware will ever be produced again. Our advisor for this category is Patrick Herley; he is listed in the Directory under New York.

Plate, unglazed with vine pattern in relief, $110.00.

Abbots cup, Fountains Abbey 7.50
Acanthus rose bowl, Broadstairs 45.00
Beach Head Lighthouse, Brighton crest 29.00
Bowl, Christ Church 13.50
Burns Cottage, sm 115.00
Creamer, Yarmouth, sm 24.00
Dragon beer bowl, Princeton 21.00
Jug, Gloucester 15.00
Jug, Litchfield, St Alban's Abbey 35.00
Leather bottle, Canterbury 18.00
Maltese fire grate, Valleta 20.00
Manx Cottage 95.00
Milk bucket, Swiss, Lucerne crest 18.00
Mortar, Bideford 15.50
Mortar, Hythe Gromwellian 15.00
Pitcher, Devon Oak, Ipwich 35.00
Pot, Roman, Painswick 20.00
Rufus Stone 18.00
Shakespeare bust, colored, sm 45.00
Shrewsbury ewer, Ladysmith crest 9.00
St Nicholas Chapel 170.00
Tobacco jar, terra cotta, 5½" 45.00
Vase, amphora, 1911 Coronation, 4" 42.50
Vase, bud; sm 12.00
Vase, Southwold, 6" 42.50
Welsh Jack, Llanberis, 4" 15.00

Crested China

Arcadian, bottle whiskey; 'I Special Irish,' Arms of Wicklow 25.00
Arcadian, bust, Tommy Atkins, Arms of Foefar crest 27.50
Arcadian, ewer, Wembly 18.00
Arcadian, model figure, baby in bath w/transfer of an insect 85.00
Arcadian, model figure, Black boy in bed 110.00
Arcadian, model figure, comic man at side of ashtray, mc, late 30.00
Arcadian, model figure, man clinging to side of bottle, mc, late ..45.00
Arcadian, model figure, sailor, bl cap/pnt face, 2 szs, ea, $65 to 75.00
Arcadian, model of the Globe, Swanage 25.00
Arcadian, Old Curiosity Shop, wht 35.00
Carlton, bust, Edward VII 75.00
Carlton, figurine, Fisher girl 50.00
Grafton, figurine, baby sitting 10.50
Grafton, Fireman's Helmet, Basingstoke crest 17.50
Shelly, rose bowl, Stafford, silver, #147 ....32.50
Willow, figurine, Burns at the plough 75.00
Willow, model of Hay Castle, 3½" 47.50
Willow, pig, City of St Andrews, 3¼" L 28.00
Wyknot, A Prehistoric Skull, Cheddar 10.00

Gouda

Gouda is an old Dutch market town in the province of South Holland. Famous for its cheese, Gouda's ceramics industry had its beginnings in the early 16th century and was fueled by the growth in the popularity of smoking tobacco. Initally learning their craft from immigrant potters from England who had settled in the area, the clay pipe makers of Gouda were soon regarded as the best. While some authorities give 1889 (the date the Zuid-Holland factory began operations) as the initial date for the manufacturing of decorative pottery in Gouda, C.W. Moody, author of *Gouda Ceramics*, indicates the date was ca 1885. Gouda was not the only town in the Netherlands making pottery; Arnhem, Schoonhoven, and Amsterdam also had earthenware factories, but technically the term 'Gouda pottery' refers only to pieces made within the town of Gouda.

Today, no Gouda-style factories are active within the city's limits, but in the first quarter of the 20th century there were several firms producing decorative pottery in Gouda — the best known being Zuid, Regina, Zenith, Ivora, and Goedewaagen.

This information was provided to us by Adela Meadows; she is listed in the Directory under California.

Urn, floral band with pods and leaves, domed lid, marked DAM III Holland, 16½", NM, $400.00.

Ashtray, Holland America Line, Deco style, set of 6	135.00
Ashtray, Mimi, lg	115.00
Bowl, Damascus, rare	115.00
Bowl, hdls, Corona	115.00
Bowl, mc decor on blk, mk Favorite Korin..., 2½x4¾"	85.00
Bowl, shields, wht & bl on olive w/mc leaves & bl bands, 6¾"	195.00
Bowl vase, floral, mc on blk, wht int, Regina, 6¾x4"	240.00
Box, trinket; AREO, #2614, 1¾x4x3½"	90.00
Candle holder, Dutch, bl floral w/gold, mk, 2½x6½"	110.00
Candlesticks, Nouveau pattern, 4-hdl form, 9", pr	255.00
Candy dish, scalloped, Royal Metz	60.00
Cigarette urn, flat shape	45.00
Cordial bottle, Nouveau design, souvenir, unusual	155.00
Dutch shoe, pastel colors	55.00
Humidor, earth tones	275.00
Inkwell, Rhodian House mk	135.00
Jug, stylized florals, Ivora, 5½"	250.00
Pitcher, Deco design on blk satin, 4x2¼"	55.00
Pitcher, Dutch, floral, mc w/blk trim, 3⅝x2⅝"	50.00
Planter, Veronie, #3	75.00
Plaque, rural autumn scene w/mother & children, fr, 6x12"	425.00
Plate, Deco flowers & foliage on cream w/brn trim, 9⅞"	165.00
Plate, Koningen Wilhelmina 1898-1925, heraldic shield, 12¾"	355.00
Salt or nut dish, Premiere, 4 for	70.00
Smoke set: striker, ashtray & rnd tray, Aurora	125.00
Vase, Deco floral, blk & mc on satin, mk, 6⅛x3¼"	110.00
Vase, floral, mc on blk, bl mk, 6¼"	125.00
Vase, floral on ivory, matt, 9", NM	65.00
Vase, geometrics, mc on blk, House mk, 7x5"	200.00

Graniteware

Graniteware, made of a variety of metals with enamel coatings, derives its name from its appearance. The speckled, swirled, or mottled effect of the vari-colored enamels may look like granite — but there the resemblance stops. It wasn't especially durable! Expect at least minor chipping if you plan to collect.

Graniteware was featured in 1876 at Phily's Expo. It was mass produced in quantity, and enough of it has survived to make at least the common items easily affordable. Condition, color, shape, and size are important considerations in evaluating an item; cobalt blue and white, green and white, brown and white, and old red and white swirled items are unusual, thus more expensive. Pieces of heavier weight, seam con-

structed, riveted, and those with wooden handles and tin or matching graniteware lids are usually older.

For further study we recommend *The Collector's Encyclopedia of Graniteware, Colors, Shapes, and Values*, Books I and II, by our advisor, Helen Greguire. Both are available from the author. For information on how to order, see her listing in the Directory under New York. For the address of the National Graniteware Society, see the section on Clubs, Newsletters, and Catalogs.

Baking pan, bl & wht lg swirl, wht int, molded hdls, oblong, EX	.115.00
Baking pan, brn & wht lg swirl, molded hdls, oblong, NM	295.00
Baking pan, cobalt & wht lg mottle, blk trim, oblong, EX	225.00
Baking pan, mc lg swirl 'end of day,' no hdls, oblong, EX	875.00
Batter jug, gray med mottle, Extra Agate Nickel..., NM	375.00
Bowl, mixing; blk & cream lg swirl, blk trim, rimmed, M	225.00
Bowl, salad/mixing; brn & wht lg swirl, blk trim, M	395.00
Bowl, salad/mixing; cobalt & wht lg swirl, blk trim, EX	350.00
Bowl, vegetable; red & wht lg swirl int/ext w/blk, oblong, '50s, M	.165.00
Bread box, gray & lt gray med mottle, brass hdl & latch, rnd, EX	..155.00
Bread box, wht w/blk trim & letters, vented lid, rnd, EX	125.00
Bread box, wht w/lt bl veins, rnd, EX	395.00
Bread pan, solid bl, wht int, oblong, ring for hanging, EX	75.00
Bucket, blk & wht lg swirl, tin lid, wood bail, lg, M	575.00
Bucket, brn & wht lg swirl w/blk trim, wht int, tin lid, NM	525.00
Bucket, dinner; gray lg mottle, rnd, 4-pc, M	325.00
Bucket, gray med mottle, seamless, tin lid, sm, M	165.00
Bucket, miner's dinner; shaded violet, Thistle Ware, rnd, NM	.395.00
Bucket, wht w/blk trim, matching lid, NM	70.00
Butter dish, wht w/vining bl floral decor, rnd, lg, EX	295.00
Cake pan, gr/wht/blk lg mottle, triple coated, oblong, EX	350.00
Candlesticks, wht on CI, 7⅞x3½", pr, M	495.00
Canister, meal; bl solid w/wht letters, wht int, tub hdls, EX	120.00
Canister, old red & wht lg swirl, mottle int, NM, 3-pc	975.00
Clock, bl Delft-style scene, mk 8 day Germany, M	450.00
Clock, gr & dk gr mottle, mk 8 day Germany, M	325.00
Coaster, gr & wht lg swirl, wht int, blk trim, Emerald Ware, NM	.275.00
Coffee biggin, bl & wht sm mottle, squatty, 3-pc, NM	395.00
Coffee biggin, gray med mottle, 4-pc, weld hdl, M	295.00
Coffee biggin, lt bl & wht lg swirl, blk trim, 3-coated, 3-pc, M	..795.00
Coffee boiler, cobalt & wht lg swirl, M	325.00
Coffee boiler, gr & wht lg swirl, Emerald Ware, NM	950.00
Coffee boiler, lav-bl & wht lg swirl, blk lid, NM	395.00
Coffee flask, brn & wht fine mottle, metal lid, Onyx Ware, NM	..495.00
Coffee flask, gray & wht sm mottle, metal top, 4½", NM	475.00
Coffee flask, solid bl, cork-lined screw top, seamed, NM	285.00
Coffeepot, bl & wht sm mottle w/pewter trim, M	275.00
Coffeepot, lt gr & wht relish pattern, G+	215.00
Coffeepot, red & wht fine mottle, pewter trim, Manning Bowman, NM	.....275.00
Colander, bl & wht lg swirl, blk trim/hdls, ftd, deep, M	395.00
Colander, bl & wht lg swirl, blk trim/hdls, seamed, M	285.00
Colander, sea gr to moss gr, ftd, deep, Shamrock Ware, NM	235.00
Colander, shaded violet, ftd, EX	225.00
Cornstick pan, red solid, cream solid int, CI base, Griswold, M	..345.00
Cream can, bl & wht lg swirl, blk trim, seamless, EX	525.00
Cream can, bl & wht med mottle, seamed, wooden bail, EX	195.00
Creamer, bl & wht lg mottle, bl strap hdl, squat, EX	395.00
Creamer, bl & wht relish, squat, NM	235.00
Creamer, wht w/bl veining, squat, EX	175.00
Cup, brn & wht lg swirl, wht int, blk trim, NM	125.00
Cup, brn & wht sm mottle w/blk trim, Onyx Ware, M	30.00
Cup, custard; Apple Gr w/Tangerine int, Volrath Ware, M	45.00
Cup, custard; cobalt & wht lg swirl, blk trim, NM	195.00
Cup, custard; lt bl & wht lg swirl, wht int, blk trim, NM	135.00
Cup, gray med mottle, riveted hdl, M	95.00

Cup, lt bl, cobalt & wht med mottle, Granite Steel Ware, EX ...115.00
Cup & saucer, wht w/cobalt trim, child sz, EX 50.00
Cuspidor, brn & wht lg swirl, wht int, blk trim, 2-pc, EX 475.00
Dipper, dk bl & wht fine mottle, flared, blk wood hld, EX 95.00
Dipper, gray mottle, hollow hdl appl w/lip-type bracket, NM 40.00
Dipper, suds; gray med mottle, tubular hdl, EX 185.00
Dipper, Windsor; bl & wht lg swirl, blk hollow hdl, EX 95.00
Dishpan, brn & wht lg swirl, brn trim, ltweight, ca 1970, M 55.00
Double boiler, bl & wht lg swirl, Lava Ware, EX 395.00
Double boiler, brn & wht lg swirl, brn trim/hdls, EX 495.00
Double boiler, gr & wht lg swirl, bl trim, Emerald Ware, NM 575.00
Double boiler, gray med mottle, Extra Agate Nickel..., M 265.00
Dust pan, dk bl, seamless, appl blk hdl, NM 225.00
Dust pan, gray & wht med mottle, molded hdl, EX 165.00
Egg poacher, blk & wht lg mottle, tin insert & lid, NM 295.00
Egg separator, cobalt w/fine wht veins, wht int, perforated, EX ..795.00
Egg separator, solid bl int/ext, EX 495.00
Fry pan, bl & wht lg swirl, blk trim & hdl, sm, EX 155.00
Fry pan, brn & wht lg swirl w/blk hdl, wht int, EX 325.00
Fry pan, gr & wht lg swirl, Emerald Ware, NM 425.00
Fry pan, red & wht lg swirl, blk trim & hdl, 1970s, M 125.00
Funnel, bl & wht lg swirl, blk trim & hdl, squat, lg, EX 225.00
Funnel, red & wht snow on the mountain, red trim, EX 275.00
Grater, bl solid, sm, NM 120.00
Grater, gray med mottle, flat, emb Ideal, NM 525.00
Grater, revolving, gray solid, EX 145.00
Gravy boat, bl & wht sm mottle w/cobalt trim, & hdl, ftd, NM ..325.00
Gravy strainer, gray solid, w/kettle hook 150.00
Honey pot, cobalt & wht lg swirl, squat, M 675.00
Kettle, Berlin-style, cobalt & wht chicken wire, Elite, w/lid, NM ..180.00
Kettle, Berlin-style, cobalt & wht lg swirl, w/lid, M 310.00
Kettle, fish; bl & wht fine mottle, dk bl trim/hdls, EX 265.00
Kettle, preserving; bl & wht lg mottle, blk trim, bail hdl, NM ...265.00
Kettle, preserving; cobalt & wht lg swirl, wire bail, M 295.00
Ladle, oyster; gray med mottle, perforated, EX 75.00
Ladle, soup; brn & wht Onyx Ware, blk hdl & trim, NM 55.00
Ladle, soup; cobalt & gray lg mottle, wht int, EX 95.00
Ladle, soup; old red & wht lg mottle, blk hdl, NM 1,250.00
Lady finger pan, cobalt & wht lg swirl, wht int, M 4,975.00
Lady finger pan, gray mottle, Agate Nickel..., M 295.00
Lid, handihook; gray lg mottle, lg, M 75.00
Measure, aqua-gr & wht lg swirl, cobalt trim, 2-cup, EX 325.00
Measure, bl & wht chicken wire, Paragon, NM 210.00
Measure, bl w/wht floral decor, cobalt trim & hdl, EX 75.00
Measure, cobalt & wht lg swirl, blk trim, seamed lip, 2-cup, M ..795.00
Measure, gr & wht lg swirl, bl trim & hdl, Emerald Ware, 2-cup, M ..895.00
Milk can, bl & wht lg swirl, flat ears, tin lid, NM 595.00
Milk can, bl & wht lt mottle, blk trim, flat ears, NM 395.00
Milk can, gr & wht lg swirl, bl trim, Emerald Ware, 2-qt, NM ...1,195.00
Milk can, wht w/dk bl trim, Boston style, EX 125.00
Mold, fluted w/grape imprint, wht, oval, ring, EX 135.00
Mold, melon form, gray solid, tin lid w/hdl 135.00
Mold, tube cake; bl & wht fine mottle, blk trim, M 310.00
Muffin pan, cobalt & wht lg swirl, wht int, blk trim, 8-cup, NM ..595.00
Muffin pan, gray lg mottle, deep, 12-cup, NM 75.00
Muffin pan, gray lg mottle, Turk's head style, 9-cup, NM 145.00
Muffin pan, lt bl & wht lg swirl, 8-cup, EX 295.00
Mug, bl & wht fine mottle, blk trim, short, EX 65.00
Mug, cobalt & wht lg swirl, blk trim, lg bottom, baby sz, M 350.00
Mug, cobalt & wht lg swirl, NM 125.00
Mug, dk gr & wht lg swirl, blk trim, Chrysolite, lg, EX 125.00
Mug, gr & wht lg swirl w/blk trim, wht int, Emerald Ware, lg, G+ ..150.00
Mug, wht & lt gr med mottle, gr trim, mk Elite, EX 45.00
Pail, chamber; wht w/bl lg mottle, matching lid, NM 185.00

Pail, water; bl & wht lg swirl, blk trim, wooden bail, NM 295.00
Pail, water; lt bl & wht lg swirl, blk trim, wooden bail, M 185.00
Pie plate, cobalt & gray lg mottle, gray int, NM 75.00
Pie plate, cobalt & wht lg swirl, blk trim, M 125.00
Pitcher, milk; brn w/wht tiny flecks & fine mottle, Germany, NM .175.00
Pitcher, milk; lt gr & wht relish, bl trim, EX 160.00
Pitcher, molasses; deep shaded violet, enamel lid, NM 265.00
Pitcher, water; bl & wht lg swirl, blk trim, Columbian Ware, M .1,750.00
Pitcher, water; brn/cobalt/wht lg swirl End of Day, seamless, EX ...595.00
Pitcher, water; dk gr & wht lg swirl, bl trim, Chrysolite, EX 595.00
Pitcher & bowl, bl & wht lg mottle w/blk trim, squatty, NM 795.00
Plate, bl, wht & gray lg swirl, wht int, blk trim, NM 125.00
Plate, dessert; aqua & wht lg swirl, cobalt trim, 6½", EX 125.00
Plate, gray lg mottle, lg, M 45.00
Plate, luncheon; yel & wht lg swirl w/blk, ltweight, 1960s, 7¼", M ...35.00
Plate, red-brn & wht fine mottle, wht int, 12-sided, EX 45.00
Pudding pan, blk & wht lg swirl, blk trim, M 225.00
Pudding pan, gray lg mottle, Fayette Quality Ware... label, M 50.00
Roaster, bl & wht fine mottle w/blk, 3-pc, 6½x9", NM 395.00
Roaster, bl & wht lg swirl, blk trim, flat top, 3-pc, NM 375.00
Roaster, brn & wht lg swirl, blk trim, oval, 3-pc, EX 325.00
Rolling pin, wht w/gray screw-on hdls, CI base, M 1,075.00
Salt box, red w/blk trim, NM 145.00

Scoops, gray mottle, 9", EX; 5½", M; 6¾", EX, $195.00 each.

Scoop, spice; gray lg mottle, pieced bk, strap hdl, NM 475.00
Scouring powder holder, Skurepulver, solid red, NM 95.00
Shirred egg plate, lt bl & wht lg swirl, oval, ltweight, M 45.00
Skimmer, bl & wht fine mottle, wht int, perforated/flat, hdld, M ...135.00
Skimmer, blk & wht med mottle int/ext, perforated, hdld, EX 85.00
Skimmer, charcoal gray & wht speckled, perforations, hand type, NM ...350.00
Skimmer, cobalt w/wht int, perforations, hdld, EX 135.00
Slop bucket, pk/gr/wht lg mottle, End of Day, wooden bail, EX .495.00
Soap dish, aqua & wht lg swirl, wall mt, NM 225.00
Spoon, basting; bl & wht lg mottle, wht int, blk hdl, EX 80.00
Spoon, bl & wht lg swirl, wht int, NM 125.00
Spoon, cobalt & wht med mottle, blk hdl, EX 45.00
Spoon, ice cream; gray & wht fine mottle, CI base, wood hdl, EX ...165.00
Spoon, tasting; wht w/fine bl veined int/ext, side hdl, NM 75.00
Strainer, bl & wht lg swirl, wht int, hollow hdl, EX 310.00
Strainer, dk bl & wht med mottle, 8-sided, 3-ftd, M 95.00
Sugar shaker, gray & lt gray fine mottle, Germany, EX 295.00
Sugar shaker, wht w/gr trim, seamless body, cork plug, M 225.00
Syrup, gray lg mottle, pewter trim, squatty, hinged lid, M 1,050.00
Tart pan, bl & wht fine mottle, bl trim, M 65.00
Tea steeper, bl & wht lg swirl, blk trim/hdl, tin lid, M 275.00
Tea steeper, brn & wht relish, dk bl trim, tin lid, EX 195.00
Tea steeper, cobalt & wht lg swirl, blk hdl & trim, M 495.00
Tea steeper, shaded violet, blk hdl, tin lid, Thistle Ware, M 225.00
Tea strainer, wht, screen insert, NM 50.00
Teakettle, bl & wht fine mottle, bail hdl, lg, EX 195.00
Teakettle, bl & wht lg swirl, wht int, bail hdl, EX 395.00
Teakettle, cobalt & wht lg swirl, blk trim, Azurelite, lg, NM 495.00
Teakettle, cobalt solid, wht int, bell shaped, M 195.00
Teakettle, gray med mottle, mk Peerless over orig mk, NM 295.00

Teakettle, oil stove; gray mottle, str spout, Nesco Ware, EX **295.00**
Teakettle, sea gr to moss gr, Shamrock Ware, wire bail, EX **325.00**
Teakettle, yel & wht lg swirl w/blk trim, 1930s, M **195.00**
Teapot, bl & wht fine mottle, brass-plated lid, Pat Pending, VG .**195.00**
Teapot, calla lilies on wht, pewter trim, M **295.00**
Teapot, cobalt, str tubular hdl, NM **240.00**
Teapot, gray lg mottle, pewter trim, Belle shape, M **495.00**
Teapot, heron & rushes on wht, pewter trim, M **550.00**
Tray, bl & wht med mottle, wht int, rectangular, NM **145.00**
Tray, gray med mottle, oval, NM **165.00**
Tray, lt bl & wht lg swirl, wht int, rnd, NM **175.00**
Trivet, aqua-bl on CI, 3 molded ft, W&W ETI, M **75.00**
Trivet, windmill scene, dk bl on wht, rnd, hdls, EX **125.00**
Tumbler, cobalt & wht lg swirl, wht int, blk trim, EX **575.00**
Tumbler, dk solid bl, blk trim, Ski Blu, steel base, M **110.00**
Tureen, soup; cobalt solid, wht int, blk trim, w/lid & ladle, M ...**325.00**
Wash basin, bl & wht lg swirl, wht int, Bl Diamond Ware, lg, NM ..**195.00**
Water cooler, lt bl & wht lg swirl, bail hdl, Lava Ware, EX **795.00**

Green Opaque

Introduced in 1887 by the New England Glass Company, this ware is very scarce due to the fact that it was produced for less than one year. It is characterized by its soft green color and a wavy band of gold reserving a mottled blue metallic stain. It is usually found in satin; examples with a shiny finish are extremely rare.

Bowl, 4x8", M **1,150.00**
Box, powder; NM gold mottling on bowl & lid, 4x6¼" **1,150.00**
Cruet, orig stopper **1,950.00**
Mug, 2¼" **500.00**
Punch cup **550.00**
Punch cup, worn decor, 2½" **225.00**
Shaker, 2½" **400.00**
Toothpick holder, gold trim **1,150.00**
Tumbler, EX gold & mottling, 3½" **665.00**
Tumbler, lemonade; w/hdl, 5" **950.00**
Tumbler, M mottling, 3½" **800.00**
Vase, flared, M gold & mottling, 6" **900.00**
Vase, 14-rib ovoid w/flaring rim, VG gold & mottling, 6" **500.00**

Greenaway, Kate

Kate Greenaway was an English artist who lived from 1846 to 1901. She gained worldwide fame as an illustrator of children's books, drawing children clothed in the styles worn by proper English and American boys and girls of the very early 1800s. Her book, *Under the Willow Tree*, published in 1878, was the first of many. Her sketches appeared in leading magazines, and her greeting cards were in great demand. Manufacturers of china, pottery, and metal products copied her characters to decorate children's dishes, tiles, and salt and pepper shakers as well as many other items. Our advisor is James Lewis Lowe, Director of the Kate Greenaway Society; he is listed in the Directory under Pennsylvania. See also Napkin Rings.

Almanac, Almanack for 1884, London, Routledge, NM **140.00**
Almanac, Almanack for 1888, London, Routledge, 12 illus, NM ...**200.00**
Biscuit jar, ceramic, boy w/tinted features, w/lid **165.00**
Book, Day in Child's Life, Routledge, 1st ed, VG **150.00**
Book, Greenaway's Babies, Saalfield Muslin Book, 1907, G+ **40.00**
Book, Kate Greenaway Pictures, London, 1st ed, 1921, VG w/jacket ...**300.00**
Book, Kate Greenaway's Alphabet, London, 1880, EX **175.00**

Book, Kate Greenaway's Book of Games, Routledge, 1st ed, 1889, NM ..**475.00**
Book, Language of Flowers, Routledge, 1st ed, picture board, VG .**100.00**
Book, Marigold Garden, Warne, no date, early printing, VG+ **45.00**
Engraving, Harper's Bazaar, Jan 1879, full-pg **25.00**
Inkwell, boy & girl, bronze **195.00**
Match holder, ornate SP, girl in fancy clothes, Tufts **195.00**
Pencil holder, pnt porc **20.00**
Pickle castor, bl; SP fr w/2 girls, blown-out florals **455.00**
Salt cellar, Little People, bsk, arms over basket base, 3¾" **110.00**
Scarf, Greenaway illus on silk, early, EX **65.00**

Shakers, boy and girl in coiled baskets, pre-1910, 3", $95.00 for the pair.

Spoons, silver, rare, set of 6 ....**195.00**
Stickpin holder, SP, girl figural, Meriden, 4" **125.00**
Tea set, semiporc, floral motif, 3-pc **70.00**
Toothpick holder, bsk, girl sits on stump, basket on bk **40.00**
Wall pocket, ceramic, 6 girls on open book form, 6x9x3" **125.00**

Greentown Glass

Greentown glass is a term referring to the product of the Indiana Tumbler and Goblet Company of Greentown, Indiana, ca 1894 to 1903. Their earlier pressed glass patterns were #75 (originally known as #11), a pseudo-cut glass design; #137, Pleat Band; and #200, Austrian. Another line, Dewey, was designed in 1898. Many lovely colors were produced in addition to crystal. Jacob Rosenthal, who was later affiliated with Fenton, developed his famous chocolate glass in 1900. The rich, shaded opaque brown glass was an overnight success. Two new patterns, Leaf Bracket and Cactus, were designed to display the glass to its best advantage, but previously existing molds were also used. In only three years Rosenthal developed yet another important color formula, Golden Agate. The Holly pattern was designed especially for its production. The dolphin covered dish with a fish finial is perhaps the most common and easily recognized piece ever produced. Other animal dishes were also made; all are highly collectible. There have been many repros — not all are marked! The symbol (+) at the end of some of the following lines was used to indicate items that have been reproduced.

Our advisors for this category are Jerry and Sandi Garrett; they are listed in the Directory under Indiana. See the Pattern Glass section for clear pressed glass; only colored items are listed here.

Animal dish, bird w/berry, amber (+) **325.00**
Animal dish, bird w/berry, cobalt **650.00**
Animal dish, bird w/berry, emerald gr (+) **325.00**
Animal dish, bird w/berry, Golden Agate **1,750.00**
Animal dish, bird w/berry, Nile Gr **1,950.00**
Animal dish, cat on hamper, canary, low **850.00**
Animal dish, cat on hamper, chocolate, low **700.00**
Animal dish, cat on hamper, chocolate, tall **450.00**
Animal dish, cat on hamper, opaque wht, tall **500.00**
Animal dish, cat on hamper, teal bl, tall **425.00**
Animal dish, dolphin, amber, beaded edge **800.00**
Animal dish, dolphin, amber, sawtooth edge (+) **725.00**

Animal dish, dolphin, chocolate, beaded edge 375.00
Animal dish, dolphin, chocolate, smooth edge 450.00
Animal dish, dolphin, clear, beaded edge 350.00
Animal dish, dolphin, cobalt, sawtooth edge 950.00
Animal dish, dolphin, emerald gr, sawtooth edge (+) 725.00
Animal dish, dolphin, Nile Gr, beaded edge 3,000.00
Animal dish, dolphin, opaque wht, sawtooth edge (+) 750.00
Animal dish, fighting cocks, amber 1,800.00
Animal dish, fighting cocks, cobalt 2,200.00
Animal dish, fighting cocks, emerald gr 1,800.00
Animal dish, hen on nest, cobalt 600.00
Animal dish, hen on nest, emerald gr 225.00
Animal dish, hen on nest, Golden Agate 1,500.00
Animal dish, hen on nest, teal bl 250.00
Animal dish, rabbit, clear 200.00
Animal dish, rabbit, teal bl 225.00
Animal dish, rabbit, wht opaque (+) 225.00
Austrian, butter dish, canary 425.00
Austrian, butter dish, chocolate, child sz 750.00
Austrian, compote, canary, low ped 250.00
Austrian, cordial, emerald gr 260.00
Austrian, creamer, amber, child sz 250.00
Austrian, creamer, canary, no rim, lg 200.00
Austrian, goblet, canary 225.00
Austrian, nappy, canary, w/lid 325.00
Austrian, punch cup, bluish-purple 325.00
Austrian, sugar bowl, chocolate, w/lid, 2½" 185.00
Austrian, vase, canary, 10" 350.00
Austrian, wine, amber 300.00
Beehive, vase, bud; amber 300.00
Brazen Shield, butter dish, bl 265.00
Brazen Shield, compote, bl, w/lid, 6⅜" 225.00
Brazen Shield, sugar bowl, bl, w/lid 225.00
Brazen Shield, tumbler, bl 90.00
Cactus, butter dish, chocolate 200.00
Cactus, celery vase, chocolate, 7½", NM 500.00
Cactus, compote, chocolate, 5¼" dia 165.00
Cactus, compote, chocolate, 9¼" 285.00
Cactus, creamer, chocolate, tankard form, 6" 135.00
Cactus, nappy, chocolate 180.00
Cactus, sugar bowl, chocolate, w/lid, 6" 200.00
Cactus, syrup, chocolate, metal thumblift lid, 6" 225.00
Cactus, toothpick holder, chocolate (+) 95.00
Cactus, tumbler, chocolate, 5" 70.00
Cord Drapery, bowl, bl, hand fluted, ftd, 6¼" 250.00
Cord Drapery, bowl, cobalt, ftd, 6¼" 175.00
Cord Drapery, cake plate, emerald gr, ftd 185.00
Cord Drapery, mug, amber, ftd 175.00
Cord Drapery, pitcher, bl 325.00
Cord Drapery, syrup jug, chocolate 225.00
Cord Drapery, tray, water; amber 280.00
Cupid, spooner, chocolate 375.00
Cupid, spooner, Nile Gr 375.00
Cupid, sugar bowl, wht opaque, w/lid 150.00
Dewey, bowl, berry; chocolate, 8¼" 285.00
Dewey, butter dish, canary, 4" 125.00
Dewey, butter dish, cobalt, 4" 325.00
Dewey, cruet, amber, w/stopper 175.00
Dewey, pitcher, amber 165.00
Dewey, sauce, amber 40.00
Dewey, serpentine tray, emerald gr, sm 60.00
Dewey, spooner, Nile Gr, 5" 285.00
Dewey, sugar bowl, canary, w/lid, 2¼" dia 85.00
Diamond Prisms, tumbler, chocolate 675.00

Early Diamond, dish, cobalt, rectangular, 8x5" 200.00
Early Diamond, tumbler, cobalt bl 200.00
Greentown Daisy, mustard pot, chocolate 230.00
Greentown Daisy, sugar bowl, chocolate, w/lid 240.00
Greentown Daisy, sugar bowl, frosted emerald gr, w/lid 115.00
Herringbone Buttress, bowl, emerald gr, 9¼" 300.00
Herringbone Buttress, cordial, emerald gr, 3" 275.00
Herringbone Buttress, shaker, emerald gr, ea 325.00
Herringbone Buttress, vase, emerald gr, 6" 235.00
Herringbone Buttress, wine, olive gr 210.00
Holly, tumbler, Wht Agate 2,000.00
Holly Amber, bowl, 7½" 675.00
Holly Amber, butter dish, ped ft 2,750.00
Holly Amber, cake stand 2,600.00
Holly Amber, cruet, w/stopper, 6" 2,250.00
Holly Amber, mug, 4" (+) 425.00
Holly Amber, pitcher 3,000.00
Holly Amber, spooner 750.00
Holly Amber, toothpick holder (+) 450.00
Holly Amber, vase, on ped, 8" 2,200.00
Leaf Bracket, butter dish, chocolate 165.00
Leaf Bracket, butter dish, cobalt 1,300.00

Leaf Bracket, cruet, chocolate,
with stopper, $225.00.

Leaf Bracket, sugar bowl, chocolate, w/lid 165.00
Mug, deer & oak tree, chocolate 750.00
Mug, indoor drinking scene, chocolate, 5" 195.00
Mug, Outdoor Drinking, chocolate, 4½" 195.00
Mug, outdoor drinking scene, lt cobalt 350.00
Mug, pepper box, chocolate 350.00
Mug, Serenade, emerald gr, 4¾" 135.00
Novelty, corn vase, amber, 4⅝" 200.00
Novelty, cuff set, teal bl 450.00
Novelty, Dewey bust, wht opaque, w/base 225.00
Novelty, hairbrush, Nile Gr 650.00
Novelty, Scotch thistle, chocolate 1,000.00
Novelty, trunk, chocolate 1,100.00
Pattern #75, bowl, gr, rectangular, 8x6½" 100.00
Pattern #75, toothpick holder, emerald gr 95.00
Pitcher, water; Paneled, chocolate 625.00
Pitcher, water; Ruffled Eye, amber 200.00
Pleat Band, compote, chocolate, plain stem, smooth rim, 4¼" ...175.00
Pleat Band, cordial, canary 250.00
Pleat Band, wine, canary 200.00
Scalloped Flange, vase, Nile Gr 350.00
Shuttle, butter dish, chocolate 1,250.00
Shuttle, mug, cobalt 400.00
Shuttle, mug, gr 450.00
Shuttle, spooner, chocolate 450.00
Shuttle, tumbler, canary 400.00

Teardrop & Tassel, butter dish, cobalt **265.00**
Teardrop & Tassel, compote, Nile Gr, w/lid, 6½" **475.00**
Teardrop & Tassel, shaker, amber, ea **300.00**
Teardrop & Tassel, spooner, chocolate **350.00**
Teardrop & Tassel, spooner, cobalt **165.00**
Toothpick holder, dog's head, bl frost **350.00**
Toothpick holder, picture fr, Nile Gr **425.00**
Toothpick holder, sheaf of wheat, teal bl **275.00**
Tumbler, Paneled, chocolate **500.00**
Tumbler, Sawtooth, chocolate **125.00**
Tumbler, Uneeda Biscuit, chocolate, tall **150.00**

Grueby

William Henry Grueby joined the firm of the Low Art Tile Works at the age of fifteen and in 1894, after several years of experience in the production of architectural tiles, founded his own plant, the Grueby Faience Company, in Boston, Massachusetts. Grueby began experimenting with the idea of producing art pottery and had soon perfected a fine glaze (soft and without gloss) in shades of blue, gray, yellow, brown, and his most successful, cucumber green. In 1900 his exhibit at the Paris Exposition Universelle won three gold medals.

Grueby pottery was hand thrown and hand decorated in the Arts and Crafts style. Vertically thrust stylized leaves and flowers in relief were the most common decorative devices. Tiles continued to be an important product, unique (due to the matt glaze decoration) as well as durable. Grueby tiles were often a full inch thick. Obviously incompatible with the Art Nouveau style, the artware was discontinued soon after 1907. The ware is marked in one of several ways: 'Grueby Pottery, Boston, USA'; 'Grueby, Boston, Mass.'; or 'Grueby Faience.' The artware is often artist signed. Our advisor for this category is David Rago; he is listed in the Directory under New Jersey.

Vase, yellow iris on green, 13", $22,000.00.

Photo courtesy David Rago

Bowl, dk gr, incurvate rim, rpr, 1½x7½" **350.00**
Bowl, gr, spiral decor int, 1½x9½" **450.00**
Bowl, gr, wht crackle int, lotus form, W Post, rstr, 7½" **3,000.00**
Paperweight, scarab, cerulean bl w/lav accents, 1⅛x3¼" **500.00**
Paperweight, scarab, mustard, rpr, mk Faience, 4x2¾" **750.00**
Tile, cherub w/cornucopia, unglazed terra cotta, 6" **175.00**
Tile, cross, dk bl & sand, 3" **70.00**
Tile, cvd vine/branches, foliage reliefs, gr, 6" dia, pr **325.00**
Tile, Eros, oatmeal & soft gr, 6", EX **325.00**
Tile, gr, 4x4" **115.00**
Tile, monk playing cello, unglazed terra cotta, 6" **250.00**
Tile, pine trees & hills, bls & grs, mk MD, 6" **2,000.00**
Tile, pines in landscape, curdled mc, rpr, 6" **2,000.00**
Tile, sailing ship, 8-color, 6" sq **1,250.00**
Tile, star (4 center sqs), dk bl & sand, mk, 3" **70.00**
Tile, 4 penguins on iceberg, mc, label, 4" **600.00**

Vase, bl, cvd/appl leaves on bulbous bottom, mk/label, 12" **2,600.00**
Vase, cucumber gr, textured/mottled, rolled rim, 7½x4¼" **900.00**
Vase, curdled dk bl, circular mk, 4½x4" **550.00**
Vase, curdled gr, leaves & buds, R Erickson, 9x4½", NM **1,600.00**
Vase, dk gr, shouldered, unmk, 3" **250.00**
Vase, experimental gr matt drip on red bsk, #3932, rpr, 9" **600.00**
Vase, gr, cvd panels, shouldered, rpr, 22" **4,250.00**
Vase, gr, cvd panels, 5-lobed bottom, 7½" **1,600.00**
Vase, gr, cvd panels, 7" **895.00**
Vase, gr, cvd/appl leaves, dbl-gourd form, 7½" **3,250.00**
Vase, gr, incurvate rim, 2x3½", NM **200.00**
Vase, gr, leaves & buds on baluster form, R Erickson, 7½" **2,100.00**
Vase, gr, ribbed, bulbous, corseted neck, 3¾x3¼" **500.00**
Vase, gr, rim-to-shoulder hdls, 9½" **2,000.00**
Vase, gr, sculpted/appl leaves, gourd shape, 7" **3,000.00**
Vase, gr, sculpted/appl leaves, paper label/mk, 6" **2,700.00**
Vase, gr, sculpted/appl leaves, shouldered, 10½" **3,500.00**
Vase, gr, sculpted/appl leaves between buds, 10", NM **2,100.00**
Vase, gr, sculpted/appl leaves between buds/stem, rpr, 8½" **425.00**
Vase, gr & oatmeal, leaves at rim, gourd shape, sgn RE, 12½" ..**3,250.00**
Vase, gr & yel, sculpted leaves on body, shouldered, 7" **2,400.00**
Vase, gr w/yel buds among modeled leaves, squat, 7x12" **14,000.00**

Gustavsberg

Gustavsberg Pottery, founded near Stockholm, Sweden, in the late 1700s, manufactured faience, creamware, and porcelain in the English taste until the end of the 19th century. During the 20th century, the factory has produced some inventive modernistic designs, often signed by their artists. Wilhelm Kage (1889 – 1960) is best remembered for Argenta, a stoneware body decorated in silver overlay, introduced in the 1930s. Usually a mottled green, Argenta can also be found in cobalt blue and white. Other lines included Cintra (an exceptionally translucent porcelain), Farsta (copper-glazed ware), and Farstarust (iron oxide geometric overlay). Designer Stig Lindberg's work, which dates from the 1940s through the early 1970s, includes slab-built figures and a full range of tableware. Some pieces of Gustavsberg are dated.

Bowl, Argenta, fish & trailing bubbles, 6" **275.00**
Bowl, Argenta, fish w/bubbles, silver scalloped border, 2x7" **350.00**
Bowl, Argenta, mermaid in center, 11½" **500.00**
Box, Argenta, nude, sgn 1930 RX, 6x4½" **550.00**
Figurine, child w/garland, 6" **500.00**
Jug, Lion, 6½" **450.00**
Plate, Argenta, #939, 4" **45.00**
Tile, King, stylized, bl, 9x9" **220.00**
Vase, Argenta, #A93, 3" **50.00**
Vase, Argenta, #978-0, 5" **165.00**
Vase, Argenta, nude w/flowing drapery, hdls, 10" **1,250.00**
Vase, bl & turq w/cvd leaves, sgn JE, 6" **200.00**
Vase, bud; Bellflower, 8½" **200.00**
Vase, gr/lime leaves, high glaze, 5" **325.00**

Gutta Percha

Gutta percha is the plastic substance from the latex of several types of Malaysian trees. It resembles rubber but contains more resin. Though it was once thought to be the material commonly used for photographic cases, recent research contradicts this assumption. (See Photographia)

Button, coat; profile & beads in relief, dtd 1851, 1½" dia **25.00**

Cuff bracelets, hinged, lg, pr 110.00
Inkwell, Civil War era, lg 35.00
Locket, gold & coral decor 90.00
Snuff box, inlaid pewter top 75.00

Hagen-Renaker

Best known for their line of miniature animal figures, Hagen-Renaker was founded in Monrovia, California, in 1946. It is estimated that perhaps as many as eighty different dogs were produced. In addition to the animals, they made replicas of characters from several popular Disney films under license from the Disney Studio. The firm relocated in San Dimas in 1966, where they remain active to the present time. Their wares are sometimes marked with an incised 'HR,' a stamped 'Hagen-Renaker' or part of the name, or paper labels. For more information, we recommend *The Collector's Encyclopedia of California Pottery, Second Edition,* by Jack Chipman. Another source of information is Hagen-Renaker Collectors' Club (HRCC), listed in the Directory under Clubs, Newsletters, and Catalogs.

Photo courtesy Jack Chipman

**Arabian stallion, 9x11¼", $275.00;
Colt, 6¾x6¼", $150.00.**

Figurine, Adelaide, donkey, hat removes, San Marcos, 5½x6" ...195.00
Figurine, Benny, basset hound, Monrovia, 4½" 85.00
Figurine, Boxing Kitten, #227, 2" 35.00
Figurine, Butch, dog, 1¾" mini or 5¼", ea 125.00
Figurine, Champ II, boxer puppy, 5¼" 85.00
Figurine, Golden Lady, collie, 6" 135.00
Figurine, kitten, recumbent, #529, 1½x3" 50.00
Figurine, Mickey, pomeranian, 3½" 50.00
Figurine, Ming Toy, pekingese, 3" 55.00
Figurine, Moonbeam, Persian kitten, w/label 50.00
Figurine, Mother Goose in bonnet & shawl, 6½" 75.00
Figurine, owl baby, San Marcos, 3" 15.00
Figurine, Patience, deer, orig label, 1953, 4" 60.00
Figurine, Patsy, cocker spaniel, 2¾" 40.00
Figurine, quail mother & baby, San Marcos, 3½", 1½" 30.00
Figurine, Spooky, Dalmatian dog, San Marcos 75.00

Hair Weaving

A rather unusual craft became popular during the mid-1800s. Human hair was used to make jewelry (rings, bracelets, lockets, etc.) by braiding and interlacing fine strands of hair into hollow forms with pearls and beads added for effect. Hair wreaths were also made, often using hair from deceased family members as well as the living. They were displayed in deep satin-lined frames along with mementoes of the weaver or her departed kin. The fad was abandoned before the turn of the century. The values suggested below are for mint condition examples. Any fraying of the hair greatly lowers value. See also Mourning Collectibles.

Bracelet, dbl fancy braid w/15k gold mts & clasp, 6½x½" 380.00
Bracelet, gold mts, gold suspended heart, EX 485.00
Brooch, bow style, eng plaque, gold mts, 1850s 175.00
Brooch, ornate design in crystal case, gold mts, 1870s, 1x1½" 450.00
Brooch, tubular love knot w/14k yg mts, matching earrings 600.00
Brooch, twisted work w/gold mts, w/earrings, MIB 600.00
Charm, cross form, woven over solid core, gold mts, 1870s, 1" 95.00
Cross, sterling & jet w/glass enclosure w/woven hair, 1860s 175.00
Cuff links, pr 125.00
Earrings, 3 woven acorns in dangle style, ca 1850, pr 200.00
Locket, Prince of Wales hair motifs, gold wire & mts, 1x1¼" 450.00
Necklace, brass slide & clip for locket, 1880s, 44" 225.00
Ring, 14k gold band covered in ring-braid design, 1870s 250.00
Ring, 14k gold band w/inset woven heart, 1860s 275.00
Watch chain, 2 interwoven patterns, gold fittings, w/fob 75.00
Wreath, flowers & curls, mc hair, thick, unfr 375.00
Wreath, intricate w/beads, mc hair, full, lg, in shadow box fr 525.00
Wreath, woven hearts, wax flowers, beadwork, 16x12", in fr 375.00

Hall

The Hall China Company of East Liverpool, Ohio, was established in 1903. Their earliest product was whiteware toilet seats, mugs, jugs, etc. By 1920 their restaurant-type dinnerware and cookingware had become so successful that Hall was assured of a solid future. They continue today to be one of the country's largest manufacturers of this type of product.

Hall introduced the first of their famous teapots in 1920; new shapes and colors were added each year until about 1948, making them the largest teapot manufacturer in the world. These and the dinnerware lines of the '30s through the '50s have become popular collectibles. For more thorough study of the subject, we recommend *The Collector's Encyclopedia of Hall China* by Margaret and Kenn Whitmyer; their address may be found in the Directory under Ohio.

Blue Bouquet, casserole, Radiance 35.00
Blue Bouquet, cup & saucer 14.50
Blue Bouquet, gravy boat 30.00
Blue Bouquet, leftover, sq 70.00
Blue Bouquet, plate, D style, 8¼" 10.00
Cameo Rose, bowl, flat soup; 8" 12.00
Cameo Rose, bowl, oval, 10½" 22.00
Cameo Rose, cup & saucer 10.00
Cameo Rose, sugar bowl, w/lid 16.00
Cameo Rose, tidbit tray, 3-tier 42.00
Christmas Tree & Holly, coffeepot 225.00
Christmas Tree & Holly, mug, Irish coffee; 3-oz 22.00
Christmas Tree & Holly, tidbit tray, 2-tier 55.00
Crocus, bowl, fruit; 5½" 7.00
Crocus, butter dish, Zephyr style, 1-lb 650.00
Crocus, cake safe, metal 35.00
Crocus, creamer, Medallion 16.00
Crocus, plate, 9" 16.00
Crocus, platter, oval, 13¼" 30.00
Crocus, soup tureen, Thick Rim 300.00
Game Bird, bowl, oval 35.00
Game Bird, bowl, Thick Rim, 8½" 22.00
Game Bird, cookie jar, Zeisel 180.00
Game Bird, cup 14.00
Game Bird, platter 32.00
Game Bird, teapot, Windshield 165.00
Heather Rose, bowl, salad; 9" 16.00
Heather Rose, platter, oval, 13½" 15.00

Heather Rose, sugar bowl, w/lid 16.00
Homewood, shakers, hdld, pr 36.00
Mums, bowl, rnd, 9¼" 27.00
Mums, bowl, ruffled, tab hdls, Medallion, 9½" 60.00
Mums, plate, 9" 10.00
Mums, pretzel jar 135.00
Mums, sugar bowl, Art Deco, w/lid 30.00
No 488, canister, Radiance 170.00
No 488, coffeepot, Terrace 10.00
No 488, cup & saucer 16.50
Orange Poppy, bowl, cereal; 6" 16.00
Orange Poppy, bread box, metal 50.00
Orange Poppy, pie baker 32.00
Orange Poppy, platter, oval, 11¼" 22.00
Orange Poppy, teapot, Windshield 280.00
Pastel Morning Glory, bowl, oval 25.00
Pastel Morning Glory, bowl, Radiance, 9" 22.00
Pastel Morning Glory, jug, Donut 150.00
Pastel Morning Glory, stack set, Radiance 110.00
Primrose, ashtray 10.00
Primrose, bowl, flat soup; 8" 10.00
Primrose, cake plate 15.00
Primrose, jug, Rayed 16.00
Primrose, plate, 9¼" 6.50
Red Poppy, bowl, oval, 10¼" 125.00
Red Poppy, creamer, Daniel 15.00
Red Poppy, dustpan, metal 40.00
Red Poppy, jug, milk or syrup; Daniel, 4" 47.00
Red Poppy, plate, 6" 5.00
Red Poppy, plate, 9" 11.00
Red Poppy, tablecloth, plastic, 54x100" 110.00
Sears' Arlington, bowl, cereal; 6¼" 5.50
Sears' Arlington, pickle dish, 9" 5.00
Sears' Arlington, plate, 8" 4.50
Sears' Fairfax, bowl, flat soup; 8" 9.00
Sears' Fairfax, plate, 10" 7.00
Sears' Fairfax, plate, 7¼" 4.50
Sears' Monticello, bowl, vegetable; w/lid 32.00
Sears' Monticello, plate, 9¼" 6.00
Sears' Monticello, sugar bowl, w/lid 15.00
Sears' Mount Vernon, bowl, fruit; 5¼" 6.00
Sears' Mount Vernon, coffeepot, all china 135.00
Sears' Mount Vernon, gravy boat & underplate 20.00
Sears' Mount Vernon, platter, oval, 13¼" 16.00
Sears' Richmond/Brown-Eyed Susan, creamer 9.00
Sears' Richmond/Brown-Eyed Susan, French baker, flute 15.00
Sears' Richmond/Brown-Eyed Susan, pickle dish 5.00
Sears' Richmond/Brown-Eyed Susan, plate, 7¼" 5.00
Serenade, bowl, fruit; 5½" 5.50
Serenade, bowl, Radiance, 9" 16.00
Serenade, creamer, New York 14.00
Serenade, gravy boat 25.00
Serenade, sugar bowl, modern, w/lid 15.00
Silhouette, bowl, Medallion, 8½" 22.00
Silhouette, cup 14.00
Silhouette, cup, St Denis 35.00
Silhouette, plate, 6" 6.50
Silhouette, shakers, Five Band, pr 36.00
Silhouette, soap dispenser 45.00
Springtime, cup & saucer 10.00
Springtime, gravy boat 25.00
Springtime, pie baker 20.00
Springtime, plate, 9" 9.50
Teapot, Airflow, cobalt w/gold, 8-cup 95.00

Teapot, Airflow, emerald gr, 6-cup 65.00
Teapot, Airflow, red, 6-cup 145.00
Teapot, Aladdin, gr w/gold, 6-cup 85.00
Teapot, Aladdin, Morning Glory, w/colored infuser 135.00
Teapot, Aladdin, red, oval, 6-cup 145.00
Teapot, Albany, ivory, 6-cup 65.00
Teapot, Automobile, Camelia, 6-cup 675.00
Teapot, Automobile, turq w/platinum trim, 6-cup 600.00
Teapot, Basketball, maroon, 6-cup 625.00
Teapot, Cleveland, emerald gr, 6-cup 65.00
Teapot, Cube, turq, 2-cup 140.00
Teapot, Donut, blk, 6-cup 375.00
Teapot, Donut, red, 6-cup 350.00
Teapot, Dripless, Marine Bl w/gold, 6-cup 85.00
Teapot, Football, rose, 6-cup 650.00
Teapot, Football, Warm Yel, 6-cup 550.00
Teapot, Illinois, Cadet Bl, 6-cup 200.00
Teapot, Kansas, Canary, 6-cup 265.00
Teapot, McCormick, brn w/gold, 6-cup 50.00
Teapot, Melody, gr lustre, 6-cup 200.00
Teapot, Melody, red/Hi-Wht, 6-cup 350.00
Teapot, Moderne, Marine Bl w/gold, 6-cup 40.00
Teapot, Nautilus, pk, 6-cup 250.00
Teapot, Ohio, Chinese Red, 6-cup 400.00
Teapot, Parade, Warm Yel w/gold, 6-cup 40.00
Teapot, Philadelphia, Cadet Bl, 6-cup 35.00
Teapot, Radiance, Cadet Bl, 6-cup 275.00

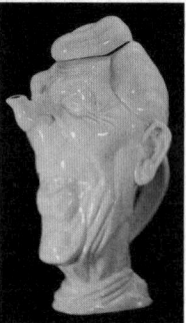

Teapot, Ronald Reagan, $125.00.

Teapot, Rhythm, Delphinium, 6-cup 175.00
Teapot, Sani-Grid, Canary, 6-cup 45.00
Teapot, Star, Delphinium w/gold, 6-cup 75.00
Teapot, Starlight, Lemon Yel, 6-cup 75.00
Teapot, Streamline, emerald gr, 6-cup 75.00
Teapot, Streamline, red, 6-cup 135.00
Teapot, Surfside, emerald w/gold, 6-cup 130.00
Teapot, Surfside, maroon, 6-cup 125.00
Teapot, Thorley Grape, wht w/gold & jewels, 6-cup 135.00
Teapot, Windshield, Chinese Red, 6-cup 300.00
Teapot, Windshield, turq w/gold, 6-cup 55.00
Tulip, bowl, Radiance, 7½" 14.00
Tulip, bowl, Thick rim, 6" 12.00
Tulip, creamer, modern 14.00
Tulip, stack set, Radiance 95.00
Wildfire, bowl, oval 22.00
Wildfire, bowl, Thick Rim, 7½" 18.00
Wildfire, custard 11.00
Wildfire, plate, 7" 7.50
Wildfire, shakers, Pert, pr 60.00
Yellow Rose, coffeepot, Dome 35.00
Yellow Rose, custard 11.00
Yellow Rose, plate, 9" 9.00

Yellow Rose, teapot, New York 85.00

Zeisel Designs, Hallcraft

Century Fern, ashtray 6.00
Century Fern, bowl, vegetable; 10½" 17.00
Century Fern, butter dish 55.00
Century Fern, ladle 10.00
Century Fern, teapot, 6-cup 65.00
Century Sunglow, bowl, divided vegetable 20.00
Century Sunglow, bowl, soup; 8" 9.00
Century Sunglow, plate, 10¼" 9.00
Century Sunglow, plate, 8" 4.50
Century Sunglow, sugar bowl, w/lid 14.00
Tomorrow's Classic Arizona, casserole, 2-qt 35.00
Tomorrow's Classic Arizona, egg cup 27.00
Tomorrow's Classic Arizona, plate, 8" 4.50
Tomorrow's Classic Arizona, vinegar bottle 27.00
Tomorrow's Classic Bouquet, bowl, salad; 14½" 35.00
Tomorrow's Classic Bouquet, creamer 10.00
Tomorrow's Classic Bouquet, gravy boat 27.00
Tomorrow's Classic Bouquet, ladle 16.00
Tomorrow's Classic Bouquet, plate, 8" 7.50
Tomorrow's Classic Bouquet, shakers, pr 22.00
Tomorrow's Classic Buckingham, bowl, coupe soup; 9" 9.00
Tomorrow's Classic Buckingham, bowl, fruit; ftd, lg 37.00
Tomorrow's Classic Buckingham, creamer, AD 12.00
Tomorrow's Classic Buckingham, ladle 20.00
Tomorrow's Classic Buckingham, sugar bowl, w/lid 18.00
Tomorrow's Classic Caprice, bowl, open baker; 11-oz 16.00
Tomorrow's Classic Caprice, candlestick, 8" 30.00
Tomorrow's Classic Caprice, cup 6.00
Tomorrow's Classic Caprice, plate, 8" 6.50
Tomorrow's Classic Caprice, sugar bowl, w/lid 16.00
Tomorrow's Classic Fantasy, bowl, cereal; 6" 7.00
Tomorrow's Classic Fantasy, celery dish, oval 17.00
Tomorrow's Classic Fantasy, creamer w/lid 16.00
Tomorrow's Classic Fantasy, cup 6.00
Tomorrow's Classic Fantasy, plate, 11" 12.00
Tomorrow's Classic Frost Flowers, egg cup 27.00
Tomorrow's Classic Frost Flowers, marmite, w/lid 30.00
Tomorrow's Classic Frost Flowers, platter, 17" 30.00
Tomorrow's Classic Harlequin, butter dish 80.00
Tomorrow's Classic Harlequin, egg cup 25.00
Tomorrow's Classic Harlequin, onion soup, w/lid 27.00
Tomorrow's Classic Harlequin, teapot, Thorley 110.00
Tomorrow's Classic Holiday, bowl, cereal; 6" 8.00
Tomorrow's Classic Holiday, candlestick, 8" 30.00
Tomorrow's Classic Holiday, jug, 3-qt 30.00
Tomorrow's Classic Holiday, plate, 8" 5.00
Tomorrow's Classic Lyric/Mulberry, bowl, coupe soup; 9" ...11.00
Tomorrow's Classic Lyric/Mulberry, casserole, 2-qt 35.00
Tomorrow's Classic Lyric/Mulberry, egg cup 25.00
Tomorrow's Classic Lyric/Mulberry, platter, 15" 25.00
Tomorrow's Classic Peach Blossom, bowl, vegetable; 8¾" sq 16.00
Tomorrow's Classic Peach Blossom, casserole, 2-qt 35.00
Tomorrow's Classic Peach Blossom, plate, 11" 12.00
Tomorrow's Classic Peach Blossom, vase 32.00
Tomorrow's Classic Pinecone, bowl, salad; 14½" 25.00
Tomorrow's Classic Pinecone, casserole, 2-qt 32.00
Tomorrow's Classic Pinecone, creamer 11.00
Tomorrow's Classic Pinecone, plate, 8" 6.50
Tomorrow's Classic Spring, butter dish 80.00
Tomorrow's Classic Spring, egg cup 25.00

Tomorrow's Classic Spring, gravy boat 25.00
Tomorrow's Classic Spring, shakers, pr 18.00

Hallmark

Hallmark introduced a line of artplas (molded plastic) ornaments in 1973 which quickly became popular with collectors. The Hallmark Keepsake Ornament Collectors' Club was organized in 1987 and offered exclusive limited edition ornaments to club members only. Hallmark has produced miniature ornaments since 1988 and added a line of Easter (now known as spring) ornaments beginning in 1991. All these ornaments are very collectibles.

The magazine, *The Ornament Collector,* edited by Rosie Wells, our advisor for this category, is available if you want more information on ornament collecting. Rosie also publishes a yearly official *Secondary Market Price Guide on Hallmark Ornaments.* Her address is listed in the Directory under Clubs, Newsletters, and Catalogs and again under Illinois. Values are for ornaments in mint condition and with their original boxes.

1996, QXM 402-4, Vehicles of Star Wars, Miniature Ornaments, set of 3, MIB, $35.00.

1979, QX 155-9, Here Comes Santa, Santa's Motorcar, MIB 630.00
1980, QX 137-4, Frosty Friends A Cool Yule, 1st in series, MIB ..675.00
1981, QX 422-2, Rocking Horse, 1st in series, MIB 495.00
1982, QCX 460-3, Tin Locomotive, 1st in series, MIB 610.00
1984, QX 448-1, Victorian Dollhouse, 1st in series, MIB 200.00
1984, QX 459-1, Classical Angel, dtd, ltd ed, MIB 100.00
1986, QX 403-3, Christmas Candy Shoppe, 3rd in series, MIB ..300.00
1987, QX481-7, Light Shines at Xmas plate, 1st in series, MIB 75.00
1988, QXC 570-4, Hold On Tight, Keepsake Club mini ornament, MIB .75.00
1988, QXM 563-4, Old English Village...Home, mini ornament, MIB ..45.00
1989, EX 449-2, Baby's 1st Xmas, Teddy Bear Years, MIB 80.00
1991, QLX 719-9, Star Trek Starship Enterprise, MIB 400.00
1991, QX 556-9, Winnie-the-Pooh, MIB 60.00
1991, QXM 582-7, Tiny Tea Party Set, dtd mini porc ornaments, MIB ..175.00
1993, QK 107-2, Santa Claus Folk Art Americana ornament, MIB .220.00
1995, QEO 806-9, Springtime Barbie, 1st in series, MIB 35.00
1996, Qx 631-1, Madame Alexander Cinderella, 1st in series, MIB .40.00
1996, QXC 416-1, Wizard of Oz, Keepsake Club Members only, MIB .45.00
1997, QX 6260-5, Lone Ranger, tin lunch box ornament, MIB, $22 to ...24.00

Halloween

The origin of Halloween can be traced back to the ancient practices of the Druids of Great Britain who began their New Year on the 1st of November. The Druids were pagans, and their New Year's celebrations involved pagan rites and superstitions. They believed that as the old year came to an end, the devil would gather up all the demons and evil in the world and take them back to Hell with him. Witches were women who had sold their souls to the devil and, with their black cat in attendance, flew up through their chimneys on brooms. When the Roman Catholic Church came into power in 700 A.D., they changed the holiday into a religious event called 'All Saints Day,' or 'Allhallows.' The evening before, October 31, became 'Allhallows Eve' or 'Halloween.' Today Halloween is strictly a fun time, and Halloween items are fun to collect. Pumpkin-head candy containers of papier-mache or pressed cardboard, noisemakers, postcards with black cats and witches, costumes, and decorations are only a sampling of the variety available.

Our advisor for this category is Jenny Tarrant; she is listed in the Directory under Missouri. See also Candy Containers.

Candy container, cat pushing pumpkin, both on wheels, hard plastic, orange, black, and green with yellow wheels, 1950s, 6", $120.00.

Photo courtesy Jenny Tarrant

Banner, orange/blk/yel scenes, paper, Germany, '30s, 60", NM ..**185.00**
Candle holder, cat figural, bsk, Germany, 4" **125.00**
Costume, devil, red cotton w/blk appliqued pitch fork, 1930s, EX .**60.00**
Costume, mummy, Ben Cooper, 1963, M **60.00**
Cup & saucer, pumpkin-form cup, gr saucer, bsk, Germany **125.00**
Decoration, cat, orange paper litho, 1930s, 12" **35.00**
Decoration, devil's head, emb cb, Germany, 10" **95.00**
Decoration, devil standing, emb cb, easel bk, Germany, 15" **125.00**
Decoration, jack-o'-lantern, emb cb, Germany, 1930s, 10½" **75.00**
Decoration, owl, emb cb, Germany, 8" **45.00**
Decoration, pumpkin, emb cb, Germany, 10" **45.00**
Decoration, pumpkin man, emb cb, easel bk, Germany, 15" **110.00**
Decoration, scarecrow, emb cb, honeycomb arms, USA, 7¾" **58.00**
Decoration, witch standing, emb cb, easel bk, Germany, 15" **110.00**
Figurine, blk cat, compo, US Zone, 2½", set of 3 ....**45.00**
Figurine, girl w/witch hat on pumpkin, ceramic, Duncan...CA **35.00**
Figurine, jack-o'-lantern on cart, plastic, 1950s, 6", NM **100.00**
Figurine, owl, papier-mache, orange/blk, glass eyes, 10" **110.00**
Figurine, pumpkin-head lady, compo, w/tennis racket, Germany, 5" .**355.00**
Figurine, witch, papier-mache, Germany, 10" **345.00**
Figurine, witch on pumpkin, papier-mache, mc, 5⅝"+stand **250.00**
Horn, cb, cone shape w/shredded paper decor, Germany, 23½" ..**78.00**
Horn, Wizard of Oz characters, US Metal Co, 1940s, 13", NM ..**195.00**
Jack-o'-lantern, cb, w/face insert, Germany, 4" **155.00**
Jack-o'-lantern, common, Cherb, USA, 7" **125.00**
Jack-o'-lantern, devil, orig face, USA, rare, 6" **450.00**
Jack-o'-lantern, orig face, blk wrinkled brow, USA, 6" **125.00**
Jack-o'-lantern, papier-mache, orig face, Germany, 5" **175.00**
Jack-o'-lantern, papier-mache pulp, Cherb, USA, 5" **95.00**
Jack-o'-lantern, papier-mache pulp, Cherb, 6" **110.00**
Jack-o'-lantern, papier-mache pulp, common, orig face, USA, 5" ..**95.00**
Jack-o'-lantern, papier-mache pulp, gr eyebrows, USA, 6½" **185.00**
Jack-o'-lantern, papier-mache pulp, orig face, USA, rare, 8½" ...**255.00**
Jack-o'-lantern, papier-mache pulp, orig face, USA, 4" **90.00**
Lantern, blk cat on fence, egg carton, w/face insert, Am **225.00**
Lantern, cat, cb, blk on orange w/orange tissue, 6½x3½" sq **78.00**
Lantern, cat head, papier-mache, orange, rpl insert **95.00**
Lantern, devil, papier-mache, rpl insert **345.00**
Lantern, devil head, cb or compo, Germany, minimum value **475.00**
Lantern, devil w/long chin, 2-tone, egg carton, face insert, Am .**395.00**
Lantern, watermelon, cb or compo, w/face, Germany, 3-4", min .**450.00**
Noisemaker, children/pumpkins/cats/bats/etc, tin, Chein, NM **55.00**

Rattle, witch w/pumpkin, metal w/wood hdl, Cohn, 2½x5¼" **48.00**
Roly-poly, blk cat w/red top hat, papier-mache, Germany, 8" **455.00**
Saxaphone, papier-mache, pictures blk cat, NM **225.00**
Shakers, devils, pnt plaster, red, Japan, 3", EX, pr **55.00**
Stickpin, blk cat face, compo, Japan, 1930s, rare, EX **45.00**
Tambourine, kids dancing on jack-o'lantern, tin, Chein, EX **60.00**
Tambourine, witch head, tin, J Chein, Kiroff, NM **110.00**
Tinsel picture, boy in costume w/pumpkins/owl/etc, 8x9"+fr **55.00**
Whirligig, witch form, wood, mc pnt, 13½" L **55.00**

Candy Containers

Blk cat w/orange hood, compo, Germany, 1920, 3½", NM **250.00**
Candle face, box w/cb & crepe-paper candle, Japan, 1930s, 3", EX .**100.00**
Cat, blk, papier-mache, Germany, 5" **220.00**
Devil, HP roly-poly style plaster/cb, Germany, 1920s, 5", NM ...**300.00**
Donkey, orange plastic, 1950s, 5" **75.00**
Jack-o'-lantern, plastic, wire bail, 4½" **38.00**
Pumpkin, papier-mache, Germany, 4" **125.00**
Skull head, compo w/mesh clothing, Germany, 1920s, 4½", NM .**350.00**
Vegetable girl in apron, compo, head removes, Germany, 1910, 4", EX .**350.00**
Witch, plastic, USA, 1950s, 4" **35.00**
Witch hat on box, cb & crepe paper, Nippon, 1930s, 2½", EX ..**110.00**
Witch on rocket, plastic, 1950s, 6" **350.00**

Hampshire

The Hampshire Pottery Company was established in 1871 in Keene, New Hampshire, by James Scollay Taft. Their earliest products were redware and stoneware utility items such as jugs, churns, crocks, and flowerpots. In 1878 they produced majolica ware which met with such success that they began to experiment with the idea of manufacturing art pottery. By 1883 they had developed a Royal Worcester type of finish which they applied to vases, tea sets, powder boxes, and cookie jars. It was also utilized for souvenir items that were decorated with transfer designs prepared from photographic plates.

Cadmon Robertson, brother-in-law of Taft, joined the company in 1904 and was responsible for developing their famous matt glazes. Colors included shades of green, brown, red, and blue. Early examples were of earthenware, but eventually the body was changed to semiporcelain. Some of his designs were marked with an M in a circle as a tribute to his wife, Emoretta. Robertson died in 1914, leaving a void impossible to fill. Taft sold the business in 1916 to George Morton, who continued to use the matt glazes that Robertson had developed. After a temporary halt in production during WWI, Morton returned to Keene and re-equipped the factory with the machinery needed to manufacture hotel china and floor tile. Because of the expense involved in transporting coal to fire the kilns, Morton found he could not compete with potteries of Ohio and New Jersey who were able to utilize locally available natural gas. He was forced to close the plant in 1923.

Interest is highest on examples in the monochrome glazes, and it is the glaze, not the size or form, that dictates value. The souvenir pieces are not of particularly high quality and tend to be passed over by today's collectors.

Bowl, gr matt, emb Indian swastika design, 2½x7" **220.00**
Bowl, gr matt, emb water lilies, pk int, 2½x5½" **375.00**
Bowl, gr matt, emb water lilies (bold), #57, 3x9¾" **750.00**
Bowl, gr matt, vertical panels/incised waves, #32, 3¾x8½" **425.00**
Bowl, gr matt w/gray mottle & gr veins, emb crickets, 2¼x5½" .**375.00**
Cabbage bowl, cobalt matt, emb cabbage leaves, 3x4¼" **225.00**
Candle holder, gr matt, drip design at base, hdld, 7½x4¼" **300.00**
Candle holder, gr matt, leaf shape w/rolled-up sides, 3¼x7" **200.00**

Chamberstick, gr matt, hooded, 7" 270.00
Ewer, blk matt w/mc lustre floral, mk, 8" 145.00
Fairy lamp, cobalt matt, inverted mid-section, frosted shade, 5" .325.00
Lamp, gr matt, emb water lilies on gourd shape, 5-hdld, 18½" .1,600.00
Lamp base, gr matt, emb tulips, cutouts, 12"+ldgl shade 4,300.00
Pitcher, gr matt w/gray flecks, JST&Co NH, 5½x5" 200.00
Pitcher, gr matt w/gray mottle, emb leaves, unmk, 8x6¾" 425.00
Pitcher, ivory w/Gen Meade transfer & gold, JST&Co..., 7¾", EX .100.00
Stein, gr matt, emb holly & berries, JST&Co Keene NH, 5½" 175.00
Tumbler, mocha-brn high glaze, emb foliage, JST&Co Keene NH, 4½" .90.00
Vase, aqua matt (textured/mottled), emb tulips, closed rim, 6¾" .500.00
Vase, bl matt, emb leaves, #98, 7½" 600.00
Vase, bl-gr matt, bulbous, 4¼x4¾" 250.00
Vase, blk, emb Greek Key design, #76, rstr, 4⅛x6" 100.00
Vase, cerulean bl w/gray mottle, emb lily buds, #42, 7x5" 900.00
Vase, cobalt lustre, vertical panels, #192, 5¾x6¾", NM 300.00
Vase, cobalt matt, vertical panels, protruding lip, #110, 4½" 250.00
Vase, cocoa-brn matt, trumpet neck, #107, 9¾x6¼" 400.00
Vase, cucumber/olive gr/brn mottle, cylindrical, #188, 8⅛" 425.00
Vase, dbl-drip volcanic look: wht & mocha, #542, 5⅛x5½" 350.00
Vase, forest & cucumber gr matt w/gray mottle, #66, 12" 685.00
Vase, gr matt, emb aspen leaves, 3" 295.00
Vase, gr matt, emb dandelions, open mouth, flat rim, 5¾x5" 700.00
Vase, gr matt, emb foliage, buttressed hdls, #39, 5¾x7¾" 425.00
Vase, gr matt, emb lapping leaves, bulbous, #127, 8½" 895.00
Vase, gr matt, emb slender leaves/buds, #33, 6¾x3½" 475.00
Vase, gr matt, emb tulips, closed rim, 8¾x5½" 1,100.00
Vase, gr matt, gathered cloth form w/flared rim, 11" 475.00
Vase, gr matt, short neck, bulbous, 8½" 475.00
Vase, gr matt, vertical panels, broad shoulders, #129, 5¾x6½" ..650.00
Vase, gr matt, 3-hdld trumpet form, 5x5¼" 225.00
Vase, gr matt & flowing gray, emb geometrics, #11, 3⅛x5¼" ...325.00
Vase, gr matt w/crackled finish, closed flat mouth, #38, 7¼" 275.00
Vase, gr matt w/dk flecks, ovoid, #95, 7¼x4½" 325.00
Vase, gr matt w/dk mottle/gray flecks, ribbon at neck, 10¾" 650.00
Vase, gr matt w/gray flecks, closed mouth, hand-thrown, 6x3¾" .225.00
Vase, gr matt w/gray flecks, short neck, hand-thrown, unmk, 6" ..250.00
Vase, gr matt w/veining, emb corn & husks, short baluster, 5¾" .850.00
Vase, gr/tan/brn/ivory mottle, emb leaves, #86, 7⅛", NM 450.00
Vase, navy matt w/cerulean mottling, trumpet neck, #111, 9x4" .750.00

Handel

Philip Handel was best known for the art glass lamps he produced at the turn of the century. His work is similar to the Tiffany lamps of the same era. Handel made gas and electric lamps with both leaded glass and reverse-painted shades. Chipped ice shades with a texture similar to overshot glass were also produced. Shades signed by artists such as Bailey, Palme, and Parlow are highly valued.

Teroma lamp shades were created from clear blown glass blanks that were painted on the interior (reverse painted), while Teroma art glass (the decorative vases, humidors, etc. in the Handel Ware line) is painted on the exterior. This type of glassware has a 'chipped ice' effect achieved by sand blasting and coating the surface with fish glue. The piece is kiln fired at 800 degrees F. The contraction of the glue during the cooling process gives the glass a frosted, textured effect. Some shades are sand finished, adding texture and depth.

Both the glassware and chinaware decorated by Handel are rare and command high prices on today's market. Many of Handel's chinaware blanks were supplied by Limoges.

Key:
cb — counterbalance   chp — chipped/lightly sanded

Handel Ware

Box, jewelry; carnations on beige, #71/941, 3½x4½" 675.00
Fernery, spider mums, mc on wht, opalware, ftd, 4x9" 1,800.00
Hatpin holder, flowers w/gold, Robscher, 4¾" 425.00
Humidor, brn w/gr highlights, melon ribs, pipe finial, 7¼" 450.00
Humidor, Teroma, Treasure Island, #4204, 9x6½" 2,000.00
Humidor, 2 golfers on gr & brn, Meriden lid, 6x4½" 1,500.00
Humidor, 2 monks & cigars on gr & brn opalware, 6x4¼" 1,400.00
Humidor, 3 dog heads on gr & brn glossy, mk, 7½x5½" 1,100.00
Mug, monk reading newspaper, 5", NM 150.00
Saucer, tulips, pk & gold, 6" 125.00
Tazza, strawberries & blooms on cream to gr opalware, 9x5½" .1,000.00
Vase, Teroma, autumn trees & birds on textured frost, 10½" ..2,450.00

Lamps

Table lamp, reverse-painted 18" chipped ice shade with Roman ruins, palms, and figures, marked Handel #6825 and initialed HB; bronzed metal base with cloth tag, 24", EX, $9,000.00.

Base, birds in flight, 23" 425.00
Base, emb floral baluster stem on rtcl base, 3-socket, 23" 475.00
Base, orange peel on baluster stem, flat disk base, 23" 375.00
Boudoir, rvpt floral shade; bronze rtcl std, 8", pr 1,100.00
Boudoir, rvpt landscape #6155 shade; bronzed trunk std, 14" .3,700.00
Boudoir, rvpt 7" aster #700 shade; label on std, 13½" 1,800.00
Boudoir, rvpt/chp 7x5" windmill scene shade; bronze std, 14" .1,750.00
Boudoir, slag glass w/metal palms o/l shade; baluster std, 14" .2,000.00
Ceiling, 16" alabaster shade w/3 chains, label on center mt 435.00
Desk, bronze spider web & gr glass, cb, 11x6" 800.00
Desk, caramel slag 8" shade w/metal o/l; bronze std, 16" 2,200.00
Desk, rvpt 8" floral band shade; orig sgn base, 14" 1,100.00
Desk, rvpt/chp 10" floral #6573 shade, orig std, 14" 1,300.00
Desk, rvpt/chp 8" Treasure Island shade; #6975 tag on std, 15" .2,350.00
Directoire, rvpt 18" knight & shield shade; #7463 std, 27" 2,500.00
Floor, chp 14" dome #6068½ shade; bronze harp std, 57" 2,700.00
Floor, ldgl 24" tulip dome shade; bronze std 6,500.00
Floor, rvpt #6268 Bailey shade; on #6893 lamp, bronze std, 56" ..3,450.00
Floor, rvpt 10" scenic shade; 3-ftd bronze harp std #6268, 58" ...4,500.00
Hanging, chp 10" birds & branches on bl-gr globe, all mts 3,250.00
Oil, 10" milk glass chrysanthemum shade; bronze 4-toe std, 25" .1,800.00
Piano, filigree pine needles w/gr/amber/wht panels, cast arm, 17" .2,300.00
Sconce, hammered copper, orig patina, #5198, 9x6½" 500.00
Table, ldgl 16" floral-band dome shade; slim std, 24" 3,450.00
Table, ldgl 6" caramel & gr tulip shade, old solder rpr, 15" 600.00
Table, lily, 3 flower shades; CI lily-pad base, mk, 24½" 550.00
Table, rvpt 10" daffodil tam-o'-shanter shade; fluid burner, 19" .1,000.00
Table, rvpt 14" floral #6721 shade; bronzed sgn std, 19" 1,900.00
Table, rvpt 15" palms & ferns #6310 shade; slim std, 21" 5,500.00
Table, rvpt 15" scenic #5813R shade; 3-socket std, 23" 4,900.00

Table, rvpt 16" parrots & roses #6958 shade, ball std, 20" 13,500.00
Table, rvpt 18" autumn landscape #7107 shade; baluster std, 24" .4,600.00
Table, rvpt 18" bird of paradise #7036 shade; 3-column std ..10,500.00
Table, rvpt 18" cherry blossom #7442 shade; paw-ftd std, 26" .3,450.00
Table, rvpt 18" floral-border shade; bronzed sign std, 23" 3,250.00
Table, rvpt 18" landscape #7012 shade; bronze std, 23½" 6,500.00
Table, rvpt 18" landscape #7034 shade; tree trunk std, 25" 5,250.00
Table, rvpt 18" Olympic rain forest shade; bronze std, 26" 10,500.00
Table, rvpt 18" sunset scene #6503 shade; mk vasiform std, 23" .4,000.00
Table, rvpt 7" sunset & trees #6112 shade; bronze std, 14" 1,600.00
Table, rvpt 9" checkerboard ½-rnd #7639 shade; modern std, 12" .925.00
Table, rvpt/chp 10½" floral #6373 shade; bronze std, 14" 1,600.00
Table, rvpt/chp 18" foliage #7918 shade; bronze std, 23" 2,000.00
Table, rvpt/chp 7" bird/floral #6905 shade; unmk std, 13" 3,000.00

Harker

The Harker Pottery was established in East Liverpool, Ohio, in 1840. Their earliest products were yellow ware and Rockingham produced from local clay. After 1900 whiteware was made from imported materials. The plant eventually grew to be a large manufacturer of dinnerware and kitchenware, employing as many as three hundred people. It closed in 1972 after it was purchased by the Jeannette Glass Company. Perhaps their best-known lines were their Cameo wares, decorated with white silhouettes in a cameo effect on contrasting solid colors. Floral silhouettes are standard, but other designs were also used. Blue and pink are the most often found background hues; a few pieces are found in yellow. For further information we recommend *The Collector's Guide to Harker Pottery* by Neva Colbert. Our advisor for this category is Ted Haun, see the Directory under Indiana.

Dealer's sign, very rare, 7", minimum value $250.00.

Amy, bean pot, metal rack 65.00
Amy, bowl, deep, 9" 12.50
Amy, hi-rise jug 22.00
Amy, spoon & fork 34.00
Amy, sugar scoop 36.00
Apple & Pear, platter, 13" 12.50
Apple II, teapot 30.00
Auntie Q, casserole, sq 12.00
Bamboo, plate, luncheon 8.00
Cabbage Rose, dresser tray, turq 100.00
Calender plate, Christmas 1907 ....65.00
Calender plate, Panama Canal, 1915 ....22.00
Calico Ribbon, plate, cake; flat 15.00
Cameo Rose, creamer & sugar bowl 12.50
Cameo Rose, cup & saucer 6.00
Cameo Rose, platter, 14" 12.00
Cameoware, mug, bl, child sz 20.00
Cameoware, plate, cake; bl, crazing 15.00
Cameoware, plate, 6" 3.00
Cherry Blossom, plate, dinner 6.00

Chesterton, cake set, teal gr, 10-pc 27.50
Chesterton, shaker 1.50
Colonial Lady, pie plate, 9" 30.00
Dainty Flower, rolling pin 70.00
Deco Dahlia, bowl, utility 9.00
Deco Dahlia, pie plate, 10" 30.00
Deco Dahlia, shakers, skyscraper shape, pr 15.00
Elk, dresser tray 20.00
Elk, ewer 65.00
Gold Diamonds, creamer & sugar bowl 25.00
Green Rocaille, basin 65.00
Heritance, bowl, divided vegetable 4.00
Mallo, rolling pin 80.00
Melrose, cake lifter 10.00
Modern Tulip, bowl, 6" 5.00
Modern Tulip, custard cup, Zephyr 5.00
Oriental Poppy, platter, Melrose, 15" 18.50
Pastel Posies, bowl, cheese; Zephyr 10.00
Pastel Tulip, gravy boat 14.00
Petit Point, pie plate, 9" 28.00
Petit Point, rolling pin 75.00
Pheasants, platter, signed 30.00
Red Apple, plate, dinner 15.00
Shadow Rose, platter 13.00
White Rose, bowl, soup 12.00
White Rose, cake/pie lifter 12.50
White Rose, tile 25.00
Wood Song, plate, 7" 8.00

Harlequin

Harlequin dinnerware, produced by the Homer Laughlin China Company of Newell, West Virginia, was introduced in 1938. It was a lightweight ware made in maroon, mauve blue, and spruce green, as well as all the Fiesta colors except ivory (see Fiesta). It was marketed exclusively by the Woolworth stores, who considered it to be their all-time bestseller. For this reason they contracted with Homer Laughlin to reissue Harlequin to commemorate their 100th anniversary in 1979. Although three of the original glazes were used in the reissue, the few serving pieces that were made were restyled, and collectors found the new line to be no threat to their investments.

The Harlequin animals, including a fish, lamb, cat, penguin, duck, and donkey, were made during the early 1940s, also for the dime-store trade. Today these are very desirable to collectors of Homer Laughlin china.

In the listings that follow, use the values designated 'high' for all colors other than turquoise and yellow. Unless priced, for medium green, double the 'high' values on all items other than flat items and small bowls. *The Collector's Encyclopedia of Fiesta* (values updated in 1998) by Sharon and Bob Huxford contains a more thorough study of this subject and includes specific pricing for many medium green examples. It is available from Collector Books or your local library.

Animals, maverick, gold trim 55.00
Animals, non-standard color 275.00
Animals, standard color 175.00
Ashtray, basketweave, high 58.00
Ashtray, basketweave, low 35.00
Ashtray, regular, high 53.00
Ashtray, regular, low 38.00
Bowl, '36s oatmeal; high 26.00
Bowl, '36s oatmeal; low 16.00
Bowl, '36s; high 40.00

Bowl, '36s; low 26.00
Bowl, cream soup; high 30.00
Bowl, cream soup; low 22.00
Bowl, cream soup; med gr, minimum value ...600.00
Bowl, fruit; high, 5½" 11.00
Bowl, fruit; low, 5½" 8.00
Bowl, ind salad; high 42.00
Bowl, ind salad; low 28.00
Bowl, mixing; Kitchen Kraft, mauve bl, 8" ...125.00
Bowl, mixing; Kitchen Kraft, red or lt gr, 6", ea 90.00
Bowl, mixing; Kitchen Kraft, yel, 10" 125.00
Bowl, nappy; high, 9" 40.00
Bowl, nappy; low, 9" 26.00
Bowl, oval baker, high 40.00
Bowl, oval baker, low 27.00
Butter dish, cobalt, ½-lb 300.00
Butter dish, high, ½-lb 135.00
Butter dish, low, ½-lb 115.00
Candle holders, high, pr 285.00
Candle holders, low, pr 240.00
Casserole, w/lid, high 160.00
Casserole, w/lid, low 95.00
Creamer, high lip, any color, ea 130.00
Creamer, ind; high 35.00
Creamer, ind; low 20.00
Creamer, novelty, high 40.00
Creamer, novelty, low 28.00
Creamer, regular, high 20.00
Creamer, regular, low 14.00
Cup, demitasse; high 110.00
Cup, demitasse; low 42.00
Cup, lg, any color, ea 180.00
Cup, tea; high 11.00
Cup, tea; low 9.00
Egg cup, dbl, high 28.00
Egg cup, dbl, low 20.00
Egg cup, single, high 35.00
Egg cup, single, low 25.00
Marmalade, high 240.00
Marmalade, low 200.00
Nut dish, basketweave, high 18.00
Nut dish, basketweave, low 13.00
Perfume bottle, any color, ea 120.00

Pitcher, service water; 22-oz. ball jug, High, $105.00; Low, $70.00; Tumbler, High, $58.00; Low, $45.00.

Pitcher, 22-oz jug, high 68.00
Pitcher, 22-oz jug, low 40.00
Pitcher, 22-oz jug, med gr, minimum value 250.00
Plate, deep; high 30.00

Plate, deep; low 20.00
Plate, deep; med gr 75.00
Plate, high, 10" 36.00
Plate, high, 6" 5.50
Plate, high, 7" 8.00
Plate, high, 9" 14.00
Plate, low, 10" 24.00
Plate, low, 6" 4.00
Plate, low, 7" 6.00
Plate, low, 9" 10.00
Platter, high, 11" 25.00
Platter, high, 13" 32.00
Platter, low, 11" 18.00
Platter, low, 13" 22.00
Platter, med gr, 11" 200.00
Platter, med gr, 13" 250.00
Sauce boat, high 35.00
Sauce boat, low 22.00
Saucer, demitasse; high 28.00
Saucer, demitasse; low 15.00
Saucer, demitasse; med gr, minimum value ...125.00
Saucer, high 4.00
Saucer, low 2.00
Saucer/ashtray, high 63.00
Saucer/ashtray, low 50.00
Shakers, high, pr 26.00
Shakers, low, pr 18.00
Sugar bowl, w/lid, high 32.00
Sugar bowl, w/lid, low 20.00
Sugar bowl, w/lid, med gr, minimum value ...100.00
Syrup, red or yel 175.00
Syrup, Spruce Gr or mauve 300.00
Teapot, high 145.00
Teapot, low 85.00
Tray, relish; mixed colors 300.00
Tumbler, car decal 65.00

Hatpin Holders

Most hatpin holders were made from 1860 to 1920 to coincide with the period during which hatpins were popularly in vogue. The taller types were required to house the long hatpins necessary to secure the large hats that were in style from 1890 to 1914. They were usually porcelain, either decorated by hand or by transfer with florals or scenics, although some were clever figurals. Glass examples are rare, and those of slag or carnival glass are especially valuable.

If you are interested in collecting or dealing in hatpins or hatpin holders, you will enjoy *Hatpins and Hatpin Holders*, by Lillian Baker, complete with beautiful color illustrations and current market values. For information concerning the International Club for Collectors of Hatpins and Hatpin Holders, see the Clubs, Newsletters, and Catalogs section of the Directory. Our advisor for this category is Robert Larsen; he is listed in the Directory under Nebraska. (SASE required.)

Adams, jasperware, wht on bl, ca 1891-1914, 4", NM 225.00
Austria, Nouveau floral w/gold, sgn O'Haver, porc, 4¾x2¾" 155.00
Bavaria, silver floral on china, 4¾" 225.00
Bavaria, winter, cottage in snow scene & holly 200.00
Bavarian (unmk), floral, rust on cream, attached saucer, 4¾" ...125.00
Carnival glass, Grape & Cable, marigold, Northwood, 7" 275.00
Celluloid, Viking horn, 2½" 25.00
Egyptian decor on brass, mk Benedict, 4½" 175.00
English (unmk), fruit basket w/butterflies, blk & gold, 5½" 150.00

Germany, wht w/gr & gold trim, porc, open bottom, 5½" 150.00
Japan, bl & wht export, Dutch windmill scene, sgn, 4" 175.00
Nippon, floral on wht w/gr & gold beaded bands, 5¼" 185.00
Nippon, gold moriage butterflies on wht, 5⅛x2¾" 200.00
Pearl lustre w/emb wht lilies 38.00
Royal Bayreuth, clover shape, bl mk, 4½x2¼" 650.00
Royal Bayreuth, Corinthian, bl mk, 4¾", w/4" saucer 495.00
Royal Bayreuth, Nouveau lady figural, bl mk, 4½" 800.00
Royal Doulton, Shakespeare's Ophelia, rare, 5x3½" 325.00
Royal Rudolstadt, wht roses w/gr leaves 125.00
RS Prussia, roses on lustre, scalloped base, mk, 4¾" 325.00
Silver stand w/figural cherub, plush cushion, unmk, ca 1895, 4" ..250.00
WA Pickard-Rosenthal, HP floral w/gold, porc, 4¾" 150.00

Hatpins

A hatpin was used to securely fasten a hat to the hair and head of the wearer. Hatpins, measuring from 4" to 12" in length, were worn from approximately 1850 to 1920. During the Art Deco period, hatpins became ornaments rather than the decorative functional jewels that they had been. The hatpin period reached its zenith in 1913 just prior to World War I, which brought about a radical change in women's headdress and fashion. About that time, women began to scorn the bonnet and adopt 'the hat' as a symbol of their equality. The hatpin was made of every natural and manufactured element in a myriad of designs that challenge the imagination. They were contrived to serve every fashion need and complement the milliner's art. Collectors often concentrate on a specific type: hand-painted porcelains, sterling silver, commemoratives, sporting activities, carnival glass, Art Nouveau and/or Art Deco designs, Victorian Gothics with mounted stones, exquisite rhinestones, engraved and brass-mounted escutcheon heads, gold and gems, or simply primitive types made in the Victorian parlor. Some collectors prefer the long pin-shanks while others select only those on tremblants or nodder-type pin-shanks.

If you are interested in collecting or dealing in hatpins, see the information in the Hatpin Holders introduction concerning a reference book and a national collectors' club. Our advisor for this category is Robert Larsen; he is listed in the Directory under Nebraska. (SASE required.)

Key: cab — cabochon

Hand-painted couple on porcelain with gold trim, European, 1½" dia, on 7½" pin, from $225.00 to $300.00.

Apple blossom, sterling 125.00
Baroque MOP on eng gold strap mt w/red glass, 1½", on pin 150.00
Basse-taille enameled head w/roses & gold, 1½", on 11" pin 175.00
Bezel-set head w/2 topaz-colored stones, 3", on 10" brass pin 275.00
Brass button sleeve-mt porc w/ceramic transfer, 1¼", on pin 200.00
Brass mythological head & ¾" faceted citrine on 7¾" pin 300.00
Brass sphere w/4 coral stones 175.00
Brass-mtd mosaic w/braided trim, 2-pc, 1", rpl steel pin 185.00

Bust of Victorian lady, brass 175.00
Butterfly form w/mc stones, 3⅜", on 9½" steel pin 150.00
Cat's head, brass, red stone eyes 175.00
Cut/blown crystal teardrop shape, 2½", on brass pin 225.00
Garnet cabochon atop 1" head on 5½" gilt pin 175.00
Gibson Girl design, mk Sterling, ca 1900, 1¼", on pin 250.00
Ivory, chrysanthemum & flowers, hollow-cvd, 1", on 7⅜" pin ...185.00
Lt bl topaz stone, cone shape, brass mts 225.00
Nouveau gilt-over-brass openwork w/amethyst stone, 2½" on pin .250.00
Nouveau head, mk sterling, ca 1903, 1", on 9¾" steel pin 200.00
Nouveau oxidized brass w/amethyst brilliant, 3", on 9½" pin 225.00
Nouveau sterling stylized woman w/repousse, 1", on steel pin 250.00
Plique-a-jour Nouveau design w/opal, 1¼x1½", on silver pin 950.00
Rhinestones (prong set) on domed 1¼" brass filigree top 150.00
Sapphire-colored stones w/brilliants, ca 1895, 1½x2", on 8" pin .185.00
Satsuma, birds & leaves, 1½", on 10½" steel pin 325.00
Satsuma, robins among blossoms, 1½", on 8¾" steel pin 350.00
Silver alloy (oxidized) w/faceted amethyst glass, 1900s, 7½" 225.00
Silver lady's portrait, mk silver front, ⅞", on 7½" pin 210.00
Sterling sweet pea form, mk Delamothe, 1¼", on steel pin 200.00
Tortoise shell pear shape, fancy pique work, 1½", on 7" pin 225.00
Vanity, holds str pins, brass mt, ½x½", 8" steel pin 750.00
Vanity, red stone on brass mt, 2x1½", on 11½" pin 900.00
Vanity, sewing kit, brass, 1½x1", 10" pin 1,800.00

Haviland

The Haviland China Company was organized in 1840 by David Haviland, a New York china importer. His search for a pure white, nonporous porcelain led him to Limoges, France, where natural deposits of suitable clay had already attracted numerous china manufacturers. The fine china he produced there was translucent and meticulously decorated, with each piece fired in an individual sagger.

It has been estimated that as many as 60,000 chinaware patterns were designed, each piece marked with one of several company backstamps. 'H. & Co.' was used until 1890 when a law was enacted making it necessary to include the country of origin. Various marks have been used since that time including 'Haviland, France'; 'Haviland & Co. Limoges'; and 'Decorated by Haviland & Co.' Various associations with family members over the years have resulted in changes in management as well as company name. In 1892 Theodore Haviland left the firm to start his own business. Some of his ware was marked 'Mont Mery.' Later logos included a horseshoe, a shield, and various uses of his initials and name. In 1941 this branch moved to the United States. Wares produced here are marked 'Theodore Haviland, N.Y.' or 'Made In America.'

Though it is their dinnerware lines for which they are most famous, during the 1880s and 1890s they also made exquisite art pottery using a technique of underglaze slip decoration called Barbotine, which had been invented by Ernest Chaplet. In 1885 Haviland bought the formula and hired Chaplet to oversee its production. The technique involved mixing heavy white clay slip with pigments to produce a compound of the same consistency as oil paints. The finished product actually resembled oil paintings of the period, the texture achieved through the application of the heavy medium to the clay body in much the same manner as an artist would apply paint to his canvas. Primarily the body used with this method was a low-fired faience, though they also produced stoneware. Numbers in the listings below refer to pattern books by Arlene Schleiger.

Ashtray, Pigall's Paris-Montmartre, well-dressed man, 1920-36 ...65.00
Bonbon basket, floral on wht, Fantaisie Romeo form, 1904-20s .175.00
Bowl, vegetable; sm gold floral on wht, w/lid, 1865-75, 11" 150.00
Bowl, vegetable; sm red roses, ribbon finial & hdls, w/lid 145.00

Butter pat, floral, scalloped rim 45.00
Cake plate, Her Majesty, sgn Fortin, on Satsuma form, 1904-20s .225.00
Candlestick, Ranson, 1888-96, 7" 120.00
Chocolate pot, butterflies/etc on wht, Anchor form, 1876-89, 9" .200.00
Chocolate pot, gold band/hdl/spout on wht, 1893-1930, mini 120.00
Chocolate pot, roses, pk & gr on wht, 1888-96, 10" 250.00
Chocolate set, roses, pk on gr w/gold, mk, 8¾" pot+6 c/s 650.00
Creamer, gold trim on wht, scalloped rim, 1850-65 mk, 5" 60.00
Cup & saucer, Rosalinde 35.00
Gravy boat, Rosalinde 145.00
Hair receiver, floral on wht 4-lobed shape, 1893-1930, 5x4" 165.00
Jardiniere, terra cotta, sculpted flowers, 1873-82 ....2,000.00
Jug, stoneware, floral on brn, Chaplet, 1882-76, 5" 1,000.00
Pitcher, pk roses w/gold rim, corset shape, scalloped ft & hdl 80.00
Plate, dinner; Rosalinde 35.00
Plate, oyster; bl & pastel flowers, 5-section 80.00
Plate, salad; Rosalinde 21.00
Teapot, penguin figural, Sandoz, 5¾" 600.00
Tobacco jar, monkey figural, Sandoz, 7" 850.00
Vase, Marseille, floral on cream bsk, hdls, 1876-1889, 8½" 325.00
Vase, terra cotta, floral on gourd shape, 1873-86 mk, 7¼" 1,100.00

Hawkes

Thomas Hawkes established his factory in Corning, New York, in 1880. He developed many beautiful patterns of cut glass, two of which were awarded the Grand Prize at the Paris Exposition in 1889. By the end of the century, his company was renowned for the finest in cut glass production. The company logo was a trefoil form enclosing a hawk in each of the two bottom lobes with a fleur-de-lis in the center. With the exception of some of the very early designs, all Hawkes was signed. (Our values are for signed pieces.)

Basket, gr w/eng flowers & bow, sterling base, 12x6½" 200.00
Basket, Gravic, dahlias & scrolls, notched hdl, 16x10" 1,800.00
Basket, Gravic, 4-notch hdl resembles snake, 12½x8" 900.00
Bottle, cologne; Venetian, faceted stopper, 8x4½" 495.00
Bowl, Devonshire, early, 9" 225.00
Bowl, Gravic, China asters, 7¾x3½" 450.00
Bowl, Gravic, satin ribbons & medallions w/birds, ped ft, 9" 195.00
Candlesticks, flute cutting, rayed star base, 9", pr 475.00
Candy compote, eng bowl, gr teardrop stem & ft, 6½x7" 95.00
Cocktail shaker, mallard in flight over marsh, SP rim/lid, 12½" .210.00
Cocktail shaker, ovals & bands, silver mts, 11¾x5" 200.00
Compote, cut berries & leaves, hex stem, hobstar base, 5½x7¼" .225.00
Compote, jelly; hobstars, faceted knob, 4¼x4" 225.00
Cruet, hobstars, fluted neck, tricorner rim, faceted stopper, 5½" .160.00
Jar, eng irises, clear ball connector, sterling finial, 10½" 475.00
Pitcher, Jubilee, 10½" 385.00
Tray, hobstars & relief dmn w/decor, 3½x7¼" 175.00
Tray, ice cream; 2 intaglio irises, buds & ferns, 9x12" 300.00
Vase, Brunswick Variant w/hobstar ft, trumpet form, 8" 295.00
Vase, eng dragon w/amber flashing, sterling rim, 10¼" 250.00
Vase, florals & dmn points, 12½x6½" 250.00
Vase, Gladys, 12" 450.00
Vase, iris; Gravic, 11" 495.00
Vase, t'prints & dmns w/X-hatching, bulbous top, cut stem, 11" .550.00

Head Vases

Vases modeled as heads of lovely ladies, delightful children, clowns, Madonnas — even some animals — were once popular as flow-

er containers. Today they represent a growing area of collector interest. Most of them were imported from Japan, although some American potteries produced a few as well.

For more information, we recommend *Head Vases, Identification and Values*, by Kathleen Cole, and *The World of Head Vase Planters* by Mike Posgay and Ian Warner.

Baby, blond hair, lg brn eyes, unmk, 5¼" 25.00
Baby boy in bl cap, blond hair, wht collar, Relpo, 36744, 5½" 45.00
Baby boy in sweater & cap, unmk, 5" 35.00
Baby girl, blond curls, ruffled bonnet, Napco, #C2634B, 5½" 45.00
Baby girl, blond hair w/pk bows, unmk, #TP-2118, 6" 50.00
Baby sucking finger, Relpo, #459B, 5" 45.00
Benjamin Franklin, 6" 125.00
Blond girl in gr bonnet w/lg wht bow, Relpo, #1783, 7½" 250.00
Blond girl w/hand to face, pearls, Relpo, #2055, 6" 100.00
Clown, smiling face, mc on wht, unmk, #9115, 6" 45.00
Clown w/red hair, yel & bl cap & ruffle, Inarco, #E-6730, 5½" 50.00
Geisha girl in bl, gold trim, unmk, #3237, 7½" 85.00
Geisha girl in pk w/fan, unmk, 4¾" 45.00
Girl graduate, Shafford, 4½" 60.00
Girl holding flowers, Delsey (Tissue), Enesco label, 5" 75.00
Girl w/bl bow in blond hair, flower on shoulder, Japan, 5½" 65.00
Girl w/bl bows in blond hair, pearls, Lark, #JN-4112, 5½" 55.00
Girl w/bl headband, pearls, wht collar, Enesco label, 5½" 75.00
Girl w/blond curls & bow, pearl earrings, Inarco, #E3662, 5½" 45.00
Girl w/fancy blond hair, pearls, Eljo label, 6" 60.00
Girl w/flip hairdo, pearl necklace, Relpo, #K1634, 6" 55.00
Girl w/long blond curls, pk flat bow, unmk, 7" 250.00
Girl w/long blond hair, pearl earrings, Inarco, #E6210, 6½" 175.00
Girl w/long brn hair & ruffled bonnet, earring, unmk, 7" 300.00
Girl w/long wht curls, sq neck bodice, Napco, #C5708, 1962, 6" .175.00
Girl w/red telephone receiver, Nancy Pew label, 6" 75.00
Girl w/umbrella, scarf over brn hair, unmk, #S1725A, 5" 75.00
Girl winking, holding fan, unmk, 6" 75.00
Jackie Kennedy Onassis, Inarco, #E1851, 5½" 400.00

Lady in wide-brimmed bonnet, hand to face, Lefton (paper label), #1343B, 6", $95.00; Lady with green hat, bow at chin, Napco, #C4414C, 1959, 6", $65.00.

Lady, ornate Elizabethan collar, flower in hair, unmk, 6½" 60.00
Lady Aileen, jeweled tiara & pendant, Inarco, #E1755, 3½" 60.00
Lady in blk, fancy hat, hand to face, Inarco, #E190 E/L, 8½" 250.00
Lady in blk, flat-rimmed hat, pearls, Inarco, #E190/S, 4¾" 40.00
Lady in blk, flowers on shoulder, blond, Napcoware, #C6431, 6" .50.00
Lady in blk, thick lashes, pearls, Napco, #C4891A, 8½" 250.00
Lady in flower pill box, long wht gloves, Relpo, A-1229, 6½" 65.00
Lady in pk, blond hair, pearl earrings, Vcago, 5¼" 45.00
Lady in pk, feather in hat, earrings, Inarco, #E-191/M/c, 5½" 45.00
Lady in pk, uptrn collar, flat-brimmed hat, unmk, 4½" 35.00

Lady in pk, yel flower on hat & at neck, blk hair, unmk, 5½" 50.00
Lady w/blond flip, wht-gloved hand to face, Lefton's, #2251, 6" ...95.00
Lady w/blond hair, pearls, leaf pin, Napcoware, #C7474, 8" 200.00
Lady w/blond updo, pearls, hand up, Ardco label, 7½" 300.00
Lady w/brn curls, flat-brimmed hat, unmk, 6" 45.00
Lady w/fan, long blond curls, pearl earrings, Inarco, #E1610, 5" ...75.00
Lady w/flower in hair, pearls, wht glove, unmk, 7" 125.00
Lady w/frosted hair, pearls, leaf pin, Napcoware, #C7474, 9" 150.00
Lady w/frosted hair, ruffled wht collar, Relpo, #K1817, 5½" 65.00
Lady w/long curls, ruffled bodice, Napcoware, #C5677, 5½" 45.00
Lady w/pk hood over brn hair, hand up, Inarco, #E1904, 6½" 85.00
lady w/rose at ea shoulder, bonnet w/bl bow, Acme Ware, 6" 50.00
Lady w/rose in up-swept hair, pearls, Inarco, #E193/M, 6" 95.00
Lady w/side-swept blond hair, pearls, hand up, Rubens, #482, 5" .35.00
Lady w/up-do, pearls, hand up, blk bodice, Inarco, #E1753, 6½" ..60.00
Lady w/wht-gloved hands crossed, pearls, Rubens, #495, 5¾" 65.00
Margo, bl & wht plaid bodice w/pansy, pk hat, 6" 35.00
Mary in prayer, Ardalt label, 6" 32.50
Mary Lou, Betty Lou Nichols, 5" 150.00
Mary Lou, Betty Lou Nichols, 7½" 390.00
Mary Poppins, Walt Disney 395.00
Mary w/Christ Child, Napcoware label, #R-7075, 5" 32.50
Native, Dorothy Kindell 95.00
Rose, lady in beige & brn tones, 1978, 7½" 36.50
Teenage girl, yel bow in blk hair, Enesco label, 5½" 55.00
Teenage girl w/blond ponytails, Enesco label, 4½" 40.00
Teenage girl w/gr bows in blond hair, Relpo, #2031, 6" 55.00
Teenage girl w/long hair, 1 pearl earring, Parma, #A-813, 5½" 60.00
Teenage girl w/long hair w/yel bow, Napcoware, #C8493, 5½" 65.00

Heisey

A.H. Heisey began his long career at the King Glass Company of Pittsburgh. He later joined the Ripley Glass Company which soon became Geo. Duncan and Sons. After Duncan's death Heisey became half-owner in partnership with his brother-in-law, James Duncan. In 1895 he built his own factory in Newark, Ohio, initiating production in 1896 and continuing until Christmas of 1957. At that time Imperial Glass Corporation bought some of the molds. After 1968 they removed the old 'Diamond H' from any they put into use. In 1985 HCA purchased all of Imperial's Heisey molds with the exception of the Old Williamsburg line.

During their highly successful period of production, Heisey made fine handcrafted tableware with simple, yet graceful designs. Early pieces were not marked. After November 1901 the glassware was marked either with the 'Diamond H' or a paper label. Blown ware is often marked on the stem, never on the bowl or foot.

Our advisor for this category is Deborah Maggard; she is listed in the Directory under Ohio. For information concerning Heisey Collectors of America, see the Clubs, Newsletters, and Catalogs section of the Directory. See also Glass Animals.

Cabochon, crystal, bowl, dessert; #1951, 4½" 40.00
Cabochon, crystal, butter dish, #1951, ¼-lb 25.00
Cabochon, crystal, plate, sandwich; #1951, 14" 18.00
Cabochon, crystal, tray, pickle; #1951, 8½" 20.00
Cabochon, crystal, tumbler, soda; #6092, blown, 14-oz 11.00
Cabochon, crystal, vase, #1951, flared, 3½" 18.00
Charter Oak, crystal, stem, parfait; #3362, 4½-oz 17.50
Charter Oak, Flamingo, comport, #3362, low ft, 6" 50.00
Charter Oak, Flamingo, tumbler, #3362, flat, 10-oz 18.00
Charter Oak, Hawthorne, candlestick, #129 Tricorn, 3-light, 5" .125.00
Charter Oak, Hawthorne, plate, luncheon; #1246 Acorn & Leaves, 8" ..25.00

Charter Oak, Marigold, stem, goblet; #3362, high ft, 8-oz 60.00
Charter Oak, Marigold, tumbler, #3362, flat, 12-oz 35.00
Charter Oak, Moongleam, comport, #3362, ftd, 7" 60.00
Chintz, crystal, bowl, finger; #4107 ....10.00
Chintz, crystal, platter, oval, 14" 30.00
Chintz, crystal, stem, parfait; 5-oz 17.50
Chintz, crystal, tray, sandwich; center hdl, sq, 12" 35.00
Chintz, Sahara, bowl, jelly; hdls, ftd, 6" 30.00
Chintz, Sahara, comport, oval, 7" 85.00
Chintz, Sahara, mayonnaise, dolphin ft, 5½" 65.00
Chintz, Sahara, plate, dinner; sq, 10½" 85.00
Chintz, Sahara, sugar bowl, 3 dolphin ft 42.50
Chintz, Sahara, tumbler, water; #3389, ftd, 10-oz 25.00
Crystolite, crystal, basket, 6" 450.00
Crystolite, crystal, bottle, bitters; w/short tube, 4-oz 175.00
Crystolite, crystal, bowl, dessert; 5½" 14.00
Crystolite, crystal, bowl, swan nut/ashtray; ind, 2" 18.00
Crystolite, crystal, creamer, reg 30.00
Crystolite, crystal, pitcher, ice; blown, ½-gal 125.00
Crystolite, crystal, plate, mayonnaise liner; oval, 8" 16.00
Crystolite, crystal, plate, shell torte; 13" 90.00
Crystolite, crystal, shakers, pr 35.00
Crystolite, crystal, stem, claret; #5003, wide optic, blown, 3½-oz ..35.00
Crystolite, crystal, sugar bowl, regular 30.00
Crystolite, crystal, tray, relish; oval, 3-part, 12" 35.00
Crystolite, crystal, tumbler, pressed, 10-oz 70.00
Crystolite, crystal, vase, 12" 225.00
Empress, Alexandrite, bowl, floral; dolphin ft, 11" 500.00
Empress, Alexandrite, bowl, nut; dolphin ft, ind 160.00
Empress, Alexandrite, mayonnaise, ftd, w/ladle, 5½" 350.00
Empress, Alexandrite, sugar bowl, 3-hdl, dolphin ft 250.00
Empress, cobalt, bowl, nappy; dolphin ft, 7½" 275.00
Empress, cobalt, candy dish, dolphin ft, w/lid, 6" 450.00
Empress, cobalt, plate, 8" 70.00

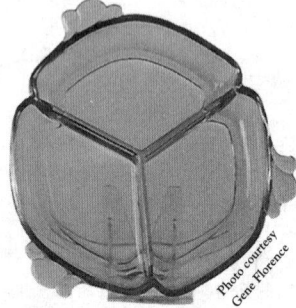

Empress, Flamingo, three-part relish tray, 10", $30.00.

Empress, Flamingo, ashtray 85.00
Empress, Flamingo, bowl, jelly; hdls, ftd, 6" 17.00
Empress, Flamingo, bowl, nappy; 8" 30.00
Empress, Flamingo, candlestick, dolphin ft, 6" 115.00
Empress, Flamingo, marmalade, dolphin ft, w/lid 70.00
Empress, Flamingo, plate, hdls, sq, 13" 40.00
Empress, Flamingo, tumbler, ground bottom, 8-oz 40.00
Empress, Moongleam, bowl, lemon; oval, w/lid, 6½" 90.00
Empress, Moongleam, bowl, vegetable; oval, 10" 55.00
Empress, Moongleam, comport, oval, 7" 75.00
Empress, Moongleam, grapefruit, w/sq liner 35.00
Empress, Sahara, bowl, relish; 3-part, 7" 30.00
Empress, Sahara, creamer, ind 35.00
Empress, Sahara, saucer 14.00
Empress, Sahara, tray, relish; 3-part, 10" 30.00
Greek Key, crystal, bottle, oil; w/#6 stopper, 6-oz 100.00

Greek Key, crystal, bowl, almond shape, ftd, w/lid, 5" 90.00
Greek Key, crystal, bowl, nappy; 6½" 30.00
Greek Key, crystal, bowl, orange; 12" 150.00
Greek Key, crystal, bowl, punch; shallow, 18" 250.00
Greek Key, crystal, bowl, shallow, low ft, 8" 75.00
Greek Key, crystal, comport, 5" 60.00
Greek Key, crystal, egg cup, 5-oz 70.00
Greek Key, crystal, jar, horseradish; w/lid, lg 120.00
Greek Key, crystal, pitcher, jug form, 1-qt 150.00
Greek Key, crystal, plate, 9" 70.00
Greek Key, crystal, sherbet, shallow, high ft, 4½-oz 20.00
Greek Key, crystal, stem, 9-oz 125.00
Greek Key, crystal, tray, celery; oval, 9" 45.00
Greek Key, crystal, tumbler, flared rim, 12-oz 90.00
Greek Key, crystal, tumbler, str sides, 5-oz 40.00
Ipswich, Alexandrite, stem, goblet; knob in stem, 10-oz 750.00
Ipswich, cobalt, candlestick, 1-light, 6" 350.00
Ipswich, crystal, plate, sq, 7" or 8", ea 25.00
Ipswich, pk, tumbler, soda; ftd, 12-oz 65.00
Ipswich, pk or Sahara, creamer 50.00
Ipswich, Sahara, bottle, oil; ftd, w/#86 stopper, 2-oz 175.00
Lariat, crystal, ashtray, 4" 15.00
Lariat, crystal, bottle, cologne 75.00
Lariat, crystal, bottle, oil; oval, 6-oz 75.00
Lariat, crystal, bowl, celery; hdls, 10" 35.00
Lariat, crystal, bowl, cream soup; hdls 45.00
Lariat, crystal, bowl, floral/fruit; 12" 30.00
Lariat, crystal, candlestick, 1-light, ind 20.00
Lariat, crystal, candy dish, w/lid, 7" 90.00
Lariat, crystal, cigarette box 45.00
Lariat, crystal, creamer 20.00
Lariat, crystal, jar, urn shape, w/lid, 12" 175.00
Lariat, crystal, plate, buffet; 21" 70.00
Lariat, crystal, plate, cookie; 11" 25.00
Lariat, crystal, stem, pressed, 9-oz 25.00
Lariat, crystal, stem, sherbet; low, 6-oz 12.00
Lariat, crystal, tray, for creamer & sugar bowl, hdls, 8" 22.00
Lariat, crystal, vase, swung 125.00
Lodestar, dawn, ashtray 90.00
Lodestar, dawn, candlestick, 1-light centerpc, 2" tall, pr 100.00
Lodestar, dawn, relish, 3-part, 7½" 55.00
Lodestar, dawn, sugar bowl, w/hdls 90.00
Lodestar, dawn, tray, celery; 10" 60.00
Minuet, crystal, bowl, sauce; ftd, 7½" 65.00
Minuet, crystal, candlestick, #1511 Toujours, 2-light 145.00
Minuet, crystal, creamer, dolphin ftd 42.50
Minuet, crystal, plate, sandwich; hdls, rnd, 12" 50.00
Minuet, crystal, vase, #1511 Toujours, ftd, 5½" 55.00
New Era, crystal, creamer 35.00
New Era, crystal, plate, 8x10" 40.00
New Era, crystal, saucer, AD 10.00
New Era, crystal, stem, goblet; 10-oz 18.00
New Era, crystal, stem, wine; 3-oz 30.00
New Era, crystal, sugar bowl 35.00
New Era, crystal, tumbler, soda; ftd, 5-oz 12.00
Octagon, crystal, basket, #500, 5" 85.00
Octagon, crystal, cup, #1231 ....5.00
Octagon, crystal, plate, muffin; #1229, sides up, 12" 20.00
Octagon, Flamingo, mayonnaise, #1229, ftd, 5½" 25.00
Octagon, Flamingo, saucer, AD 5.00
Octagon, Flamingo or Sahara, bowl, jelly; #1229, 5½", ea 15.00
Octagon, Hawthorne, cheese dish, #1229, hdls, 6" 15.00
Octagon, Marigold or Hawthorne, bowl, mint; #1229, 6" 30.00
Octagon, Moongleam, bowl, vegetable; 9" 30.00

Octagon, Moongleam, plate, luncheon; 8" 15.00
Octagon, Moongleam, tray, celery; 9" 15.00
Octagon, Sahara, bowl, grapefruit; 6½" 22.00
Octagon, Sahara, plate, cream soup liner 7.00
Old Colony, crystal, bowl, flared, ftd, 13" 30.00
Old Colony, crystal, bowl, salad; hdls, sq, 10" 30.00
Old Colony, crystal, cup, bouillon; hdls, ftd 12.50
Old Colony, crystal, plate, sandwich; hdls, rnd, 12" 31.00
Old Colony, crystal, stem, parfait; #3380, 5-oz 10.00
Old Colony, crystal, stem, water; #3390, low, 11-oz 17.00
Old Colony, crystal, tray, hors d'oeuvre; hdls, 13" 30.00
Old Colony, Flamingo, bowl, mint; dolphin ft, 6" 22.00
Old Colony, Flamingo, comport, ftd, oval, 7" 75.00
Old Colony, Flamingo, plate, sq, 6" 12.00
Old Colony, Flamingo, platter, oval, 14" 35.00
Old Colony, Flamingo, sugar bowl, dolphin ft 30.00
Old Colony, Flamingo, tumbler, bar; #3380, ftd, 2-oz 20.00
Old Colony, Flamingo, vase, ftd, 9" 130.00
Old Colony, Marigold, bowl, finger; #4075 ....20.00
Old Colony, Moongleam, bowl, dessert; hdls, oval, 10" 62.50
Old Colony, Moongleam, stem, champagne; #3390, 6-oz 30.00
Old Colony, Moongleam, stem, cocktail; #3380, 3-oz 40.00
Old Colony, Moongleam, tray, center hdl, sq, 12" 85.00
Old Colony, Sahara, creamer, dolphin ft 45.00
Old Colony, Sahara, ice tub, dolphin ft 115.00
Old Colony, Sahara, plate, rnd, 9" 25.00
Old Colony, Sahara, stem, cocktail; #3390, 3-oz 20.00
Old Colony, Sahara, tray, celery; 10" 25.00
Old Sandwich, cobalt, candlestick, 6" 240.00
Old Sandwich, cobalt, stem, claret; 4-oz 155.00
Old Sandwich, crystal, ashtray, ind 9.00
Old Sandwich, crystal, comport, 6" 40.00
Old Sandwich, crystal, pilsner, 8-oz 16.00
Old Sandwich, crystal, stem, low ft, 10-oz 20.00
Old Sandwich, Flamingo, creamer, 14-oz 175.00
Old Sandwich, Flamingo, mug, beer; 18-oz 400.00
Old Sandwich, Flamingo, plate, ground bottom, sq, 6" 20.00
Old Sandwich, Flamingo, tumbler, bar; ground bottom, 1½-oz ..130.00
Old Sandwich, Flamingo or Sahara, tumbler, 10-oz, ea 40.00
Old Sandwich, Moongleam, bottle, oil; w/#85 stopper, 2½-oz ...140.00
Old Sandwich, Moongleam, bowl, floral; oval, ftd, 12" 80.00
Old Sandwich, Moongleam, stem, cocktail; 3-oz 40.00
Old Sandwich, Moongleam, tumbler, iced tea; ftd, 12-oz 55.00
Old Sandwich, Sahara, bowl, popcorn; cupped, ftd 75.00
Old Sandwich, Sahara, decanter, w/#98 stopper, 1-pt 200.00
Old Sandwich, Sahara, shakers, pr 75.00
Orchid, crystal, ashtray, 3" 30.00
Orchid, crystal, bowl, floral; 13" 110.00
Orchid, crystal, bowl, gardenia; Queen Ann, 9" 70.00
Orchid, crystal, bowl, honey/cheese; Queen Ann, ftd, 6½" 35.00
Orchid, crystal, bowl, mint; Queen Ann, ftd, 8" 60.00
Orchid, crystal, bowl, nappy; Queen Ann, 4½" 37.50
Orchid, crystal, bowl, salad; 7" 45.00
Orchid, crystal, bowl, shallow, rolled edge, 11" 125.00
Orchid, crystal, candlestick, Cascade, 3-light 75.00
Orchid, crystal, candlestick, Mercury, 1-light 40.00
Orchid, crystal, candy dish, w/lid, bow-knot finial, 6" 170.00
Orchid, crystal, cigarette holder, #4035 ....80.00
Orchid, crystal, creamer, ind 35.00
Orchid, crystal, ice bucket, Queen Ann, ftd 400.00
Orchid, crystal, mayonnaise, 1-hdl, 5½" 55.00
Orchid, crystal, mustard, Queen Ann, w/lid 135.00
Orchid, crystal, pitcher, ice tankard; 64-oz 525.00
Orchid, crystal, plate, salad; Waverly, 8" 24.00

Orchid, crystal, plate, sandwich; rnd, hdls, 12" 70.00
Orchid, crystal, saucer, Queen Ann or Waverly, ea 12.50
Orchid, crystal, stem, sherbet; #5022 or #5025, 6-oz 25.00
Orchid, crystal, stem, sherry; #5022 or #5025, 2-oz 120.00
Orchid, crystal, sugar bowl, ind 35.00
Orchid, crystal, tray, celery; 13" 55.00
Orchid, crystal, vase, 14" 650.00
Plantation, crystal, ashtray, 3½" 35.00
Plantation, crystal, bottle, oil; w/#125 stopper, 3-oz 110.00
Plantation, crystal, bowl, celery; 2-part, 13" 50.00
Plantation, crystal, bowl, gardenia; 9½" 85.00
Plantation, crystal, bowl, relish; rnd, 4-part, 8" 70.00
Plantation, crystal, candle block, 1-light 90.00
Plantation, crystal, candy dish, w/lid, ftd, tall, 5" 180.00
Plantation, crystal, comport, w/deep, w/lid, 5" 110.00
Plantation, crystal, plate, salad; 7" 22.00
Plantation, crystal, plate, sandwich; 14" 75.00
Plantation, crystal, stem, blown or pressed, 10-oz, ea 50.00
Plantation, crystal, stem, cordial; 1-oz 130.00
Plantation, crystal, stem, fruit/oyster cocktail; 4-oz 35.00
Plantation, crystal, tumbler, juice; pressed, ftd, 5-oz 50.00
Plantation, crystal, tumbler, pressed, 10-oz 90.00
Plantation, crystal, vase, flared ft, 9" 140.00
Pleat & Panel, crystal, bowl, chow chow; 4" 5.00
Pleat & Panel, crystal, pitcher, 3-pt 45.00
Pleat & Panel, Flamingo, plate, luncheon; 8" 12.50
Pleat & Panel, Moongleam, creamer, hotel 30.00
Pleat & Panel, Moongleam, sherbet, ftd, 5-oz 12.00
Pleat & Panel, Moongleam, vase, 8" 80.00
Provincial, crystal, ashtray, sq, 3" 12.50
Provincial, crystal, bowl, nappy; 4½" 12.00
Provincial, crystal, bowl, relish; 4-part, 10" 40.00
Provincial, crystal, candle block, 1-light 25.00
Provincial, crystal, coaster, 4" 12.00
Provincial, crystal, mustard 110.00
Provincial, crystal, plate, torte; 14" 35.00
Provincial, crystal, stem, sherbet/champagne; 5-oz 7.00
Provincial, crystal, tumbler, iced tea; flat, 13" 20.00
Provincial, limelight gr, creamer, ftd 95.00
Provincial, limelight gr, plate, buffet; 18" 175.00
Queen Ann, crystal, bowl, nappy; 4½" 5.00
Queen Ann, crystal, bowl, vegetable; oval, 10" 27.00
Queen Ann, crystal, candy dish, dolphin ft, w/lid, 6" 40.00
Queen Ann, crystal, cup, bouillon; hdls 16.00
Queen Ann, crystal, mayonnaise, w/ladle, ftd, 5½" 25.00
Queen Ann, crystal, saucer, sq 3.00
Queen Ann, crystal, tray, hors d'oeuvre; 7-part, 10" 50.00
Ridgeleigh, crystal, ashtray, sq 10.00
Ridgeleigh, crystal, bowl, centerpc; 11" 45.00
Ridgeleigh, crystal, bowl, nappy; belled or cupped, 4½" 10.00
Ridgeleigh, crystal, candlestick, bobeche & A prisms, 2-light 75.00
Ridgeleigh, crystal, comport, w/lid, low ftd, 6" 35.00
Ridgeleigh, crystal, plate, sq, 8" 25.00
Ridgeleigh, crystal, tray, celery; 12" 35.00
Ridgeleigh, crystal, tumbler, iced tea; blown, 13-oz 28.00
Ridgeleigh, crystal, vase, 8" 65.00
Rose, crystal, ashtray, 3" 37.50
Rose, crystal, bowl, floral; Waverly, crimped, 9½" 65.00
Rose, crystal, bowl, honey/cheese; Waverly, ftd, 6½" 65.00
Rose, crystal, butter dish, Waverly, w/lid, 6" 185.00
Rose, crystal, cocktail shaker, #4225 Cobel 180.00
Rose, crystal, mayonnaise, Waverly, hdls, 5½" 55.00
Rose, crystal, plate, service; Waverly, 10½" 75.00
Rose, crystal, stem, cocktail; #5072, 4-oz 45.00

Rose, crystal, tray, celery; Waverly, 13" 67.50
Rose, crystal, vase, #4198, 10" 200.00
Saturn, crystal, bowl, nappy; 5" 7.00
Saturn, crystal, comport, 7" 50.00
Saturn, crystal, pitcher, w/ice lip, blown, 70-oz 75.00
Saturn, crystal, tumbler, luncheon; 9-oz 12.00

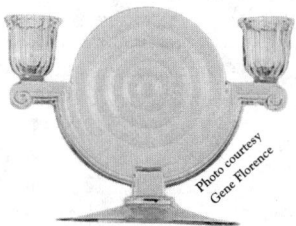

Saturn, limelight green, candelabrum, two-light, $500.00.

Saturn, limelight gr, stem, cocktail; 3-oz 60.00
Saturn, limelight gr, vase, 10½" 230.00
Stanhope, crystal, ashtray, ind 20.00
Stanhope, crystal, bowl, floral; hdls, w/ or w/o T knobs, 11" 60.00
Stanhope, crystal, cup, w/or w/o rnd knob 15.00
Stanhope, crystal, plate, torte; rnd or salad liner, 15" 32.50
Stanhope, crystal, stem, saucer champagne; pressed, 5½-oz 15.00
Stanhope, crystal, vase, ball shape, 7" 60.00
Twist, crystal, baker, oval, 9" 25.00
Twist, gr, bowl, mint; hdls, 6" 18.00
Twist, gr, creamer, zigzag hdls, ftd 50.00
Twist, gr, platter, 12" 60.00
Twist, Marigold or Alexandrite, ice bucket, ea 400.00
Twist, pk, bowl, nut; ind 20.00
Twist, pk, plate, ground bottom, 8" 12.00
Twist, Sahara, bowl, floral; 9" 65.00
Victorian, crystal, bowl, finger 15.00
Victorian, crystal, comport, 3-ball stem, 6" 100.00
Victorian, crystal, shakers, pr 40.00
Victorian, crystal, stem, sherbet; 5-oz 15.00
Victorian, crystal, vase, 4" 40.00
Waverly, crystal, bowl, gardenia; 10" 25.00
Waverly, crystal, bowl, lemon; w/lid, oval, 6" 30.00
Waverly, crystal, butter dish, w/lid, sq, 6" 65.00
Waverly, crystal, cigarette holder 50.00
Waverly, crystal, honey dish, ftd, 6½" 35.00
Waverly, crystal, vase, ftd, 7" 25.00
Yeoman, crystal, ashtray, bow-tie hdls, 4" 10.00
Yeoman, gr, bowl, bonbon; hdls, 6½" 16.00
Yeoman, Hawthorne, plate, cheese; hdls 17.00
Yeoman, pk, cruet, oil; 4-oz 60.00
Yeoman, Sahara, bowl, lemon; w/lid, rnd, 5" 25.00

Herend

Herend, Hungary, was the center of a thriving pottery industry as early as the mid-1800s. Decorative items as well as tablewares were made in keeping with the styles of the times. Items described in the following listings may be marked simply Herend, indicating the city, or with a manufacturer's backstamp.

Bowl, bird on branch & insects w/gold, scalloped, 2x11½" 160.00
Bowl, fruit; bird, mc w/gold, openwork at rim, oval, 10½" 250.00
Bowl, Victoria Butterfly w/gold, rtcl rim, mk, 9½" 235.00
Dish, Rothschild Bird, leaf shape 135.00
Vase, flowers & butterflies w/gold, 7¼x3½" 87.00

Heubach

Gebruder Heubach is a German porcelain company that has been in operation since the 1800s, producing quality figurines and novelty items. They are perhaps most famous for their doll heads and piano babies, most of which are marked with the circular rising sun device containing an 'H' superimposed over a 'C.' Our advisor for this category is Grace Ochsner; she is listed in the Directory under Illinois. See also Dolls, Heubach.

A Dark Secret, two Black children whispering, 7½", $650.00.

Angry baby w/clenched hands sits before open eggshell, 5" 450.00
Baby, lying on bk, ft in air, 4" 300.00
Baby crawling on tummy, wht gown, bsk, 8" 550.00
Baby in highchair, molded clothes, sm 525.00
Baby in wht gown sitting & reaching for toes, 8" 550.00
Baby on bk w/ft up, molded wht bonnet & dress, #89, 4¼" 300.00
Blond girl in pk pleated skirt w/gr sash, 5¾" 375.00
Boy in gr knicker suit w/pocket lining trn out, 9" 425.00
Boy in red hat & eyeglasses sits w/arms Xd on chair bk, 7" 675.00
Boy leans on bicycle, hand to forehead, mk, 12½" 650.00
Bust of Victorian girl leaning on log, mk, 6" 625.00
Dancing girl, gr & aqua dress, mk, 8½x4½" 250.00
Dog on haunches, wht w/tan collar, mk, 9x3⅝" 325.00
Dog-smoking pipe, polka-dot scarf around head, 6¼x8½" 595.00
Dutch boy, seated, yoke on shoulders, basket ea side, 5" 225.00
Dutch boy & girl kissing, 7" 395.00
Dutch girl w/attached basket, flirty pose, mk, 7½" 325.00
Farmer boy & girl, unmk, 12½x5", pr 750.00
Girl w/fruit baskets, unmk, 12½" 265.00
Humidor, Jasper, gr, Indian chief on lid, 5" 275.00
Man w/ax & lady w/baby, bsk, 12½", pr 895.00
Newsboy, 9½" 325.00
Nude boy w/clenched fist, pouty face, vase at bk, 6" 400.00
Plaque, Jasper, Indian on horse attacks bear, wht/lav, 9" L 215.00
Snow baby dressed as bear, seated, 3" 225.00
Soccer player 450.00
Vase, lady's profile w/in Nouveau floral reserve on bl, 4½" 350.00
Vase, roses, pk on gr w/gold, mk, 4x1½" 125.00

Hickman, Royal Arden

Born in Willamette, Oregon, Royal A. Hickman was a genius in all aspects of design interpretation. Mr. Hickman's expertise can be seen in the designs of the lovely Heisey figurines, Kosta crystal, Bruce Fox aluminum, Three Crowns aluminum, Vernon Kilns, and Royal Haeger Pottery, as well as handcrafted silver, furniture, and paintings.

Because Mr. Hickman moved around during much of his lifetime, his influence has been felt in all forms of the media. Designs from his independent companies include 'Royal Hickman Pottery and Lamps'

(sold through Ceramic Arts Inc., of Chattanooga, Tennessee), 'Royal Hickman's Paris Ware,' 'Royal Hickman — Florida,' and 'California Designed by Royal Hickman.' The following listings will give examples of pieces bearing the various trademarks. Our advisor for this category is Doris Frizzell; she is listed in the Directory under Illinois. (SASE required.) See also Royal Haegar; Vernon Kilns, Melinda pattern.

Bruce Fox Aluminum

Banana leaf, sgn Royal Hickman-RH 6, 22½" L 35.00
Dish, lobster, sgn Bruce For-RH #37, lg 85.00
Dish, 3-point leaf, sgn Royal Hickman, 15½" L 30.00
Ivy tray, #362, 13" 25.00
Platter, fish, EX detail, sgn Royal Hickman-RH 3, 13x9" 85.00
Silent butler, dog's head, sgn, 8x5½" 65.00
2-acorn oak tray, 14½" 30.00
5-point leaf tray, 14" 30.00
7-point leaf tray, sgn Royal Hickman, 14" 35.00

California, Designed by Royal Hickman

Bowl, red w/blk highlights, #607, 9½" 50.00
Figurine, deer, apple gr w/wht spots, appl eyes, 15" 45.00
Figurine, giraffe & young, pk w/blk spots 75.00
Gravy boat & leaf tray 75.00
Lamp base, flying geese, 17" 250.00
Punch bowl, Tom & Jerry, w/8 mugs 350.00
Swan, red w/blk highlights, #643, 17" 125.00

Miscellaneous Signatures

Vase, fish figurine, Petty Crystal Glaze, #467 ....45.00
Vase, lg heart, sgn Royal Hickman, Italy, #3774 ....95.00
Vase, rooster figurine, Petty Crystal Glaze, #565 ....125.00
Vase, sea horse shape, sgn Royal Hickman USA, #468, 8" 35.00

Royal Hickman — Florida

Vase, free-form, #578, 14" 50.00
Vase, horse's head, gray w/wht mane, 13¾" 150.00
Vase, pouter pigeon, blk cascade, #599, 8½" 60.00
Vase, swan, head down, blk cascade, #3624-R, 14" 75.00

Royal Hickman — Guadalajara, Mexico

Vase, 3 dolphin figures, 14k gold decor, gold crown label, 13" ...200.00

Higgins

Contemporary glass artists Frances and Michael Higgins have been designing high-quality glassware since the late 1940s. Their designs are often created by fusing layers of glass together, though sometimes colored ground glass is used to 'paint' the decoration onto the surface. Molds are used, and through a process called 'slumping,' the glass is fired to a very high temperature, causing it to soften and take on the predetermined shape. Their work is ultramodern and is more readily found in metropolitan areas.

The earliest mark was an engraved signature on the bottom of the glass — either 'Frances Stewart Higgins' or 'Michael Higgins' or both, which was dropped in favor of just 'Higgins' with a raised 'Higgins Man'. From approximately 1957 to 1964, the Higgins signature was embossed in gold on top. After 1964 up to the present, the signature again appears on the bottom and is engraved in the glass. Our advisor is Dennis Hopp; he is listed in the Directory under Illinois.

Ashtray, bl & yel rays on lt bl, 10x14" 150.00
Ashtray, bl checkerboard, 7x10" 85.00
Ashtray, bl w/pulled feathers, 10x14" 150.00
Ashtray, fish, (5 bl, assorted szs) on clear, 10x14" 85.00
Ashtray, fish, mc on clear, 10x7" 125.00
Ashtray, fish, mc on clear, 14x10" 150.00
Ashtray, Patchwork, bls & wht, 14x10" 140.00
Ashtray, pocket watches, 7x10" 95.00
Ashtray, spikes, purple & gr on clear, 10x14" 50.00
Ashtrays, gray & gold triangles on orange, 10x14", 10x7", 7x5" .125.00
Bow tie dish, blk- & gray-dotted rays, 10" L 175.00
Bowl, bl & lav internal decor w/gold, 6", +underplate 60.00

Bowl, daisies on three diamond-shaped sections, three-footed, signed, 8½", $145.00.

Bowl, pulled feathers, bl, 3-part, ftd, 8½" 85.00
Bowl, pulled feathers, gr on wht, 13" dia 95.00
Bowl, rays, red dotted on clear, 13" dia 95.00
Bowl, rings, brn & purple, 5-corner, 3-ftd, 8½x8" 60.00
Bowl, spikes, bl on bl, 12" 140.00
Bowl, spikes, orange on orange, 8½" 55.00
Bowl, spikes, 2-color on purple, 8½" 85.00
Box, Barbaric jewels in lid 250.00
Charger, Fall Season, autumn trees, 15" dia 550.00
Charger, rays, yel & chartreuse on clear, 17" dia 165.00
Charger, spikes, orange & red on clear, 17" 100.00
Charger, Summer Season, summer-like trees on bl, 15" dia 550.00
Pendant, trees & setting sun, 2x3" 85.00
Platter, red spoke & gold tracery 225.00
Tray, chartreuse & wht stripes w/gold seaweed, 7x14" 125.00
Tray, yel & chartreuse rays w/gold spiral decor, 14x17" 200.00
Wall pocket, fishtail, wht scroll, Francis Higgins, 3-pc, 24" .220.00

Historical Glass

Glassware commemorating particularly significant historical events became popular in the late 1800s. Bread trays were the most common form, but plates, mugs, pitchers, and other items were also pressed in clear as well as colored glass. It was sold in vast amounts at the 1876 Philadelphia Centennial Exposition by various manufacturers who exhibited their wares on the grounds. It remained popular well into the 20th century.

In the listings that follow, L numbers refer to a book by Lindsey, a standard guide used by many collectors. Our advisor for this category is Darlene Yohe; she is listed in the Directory under Arkansas. See also Bread Plates; Pattern Glass.

Bottle, Columbus, lay-down, metal screw lid 350.00
Bottle, Grant's Tomb, milk glass, no stopper 250.00
Bottle, Grover Cleveland bust, clear & frosted, L-318, lg 225.00

Bust, Dewey, Manila 1898, 5" 145.00
Butter dish, American Shield 195.00
Butter dish, Garfield Drape 85.00
Celery, Independence Hall 65.00
Compote, Washington Centennial, ftd, open 40.00
Covered dish, Remember the Maine, gr, L-465 ....115.00
Cup, Harrison & Morton, bl 235.00
Cup plate, Bunker Hill 30.00
Flask, Blaine & Logan, oval, 6¾" 550.00
Flask, John Paul Jones 20.00
Flask, McKinley & Hobart, Distilled Protection, 7" 475.00
Glass, ale; Centennial 55.00
Goblet, 3 Presidents, rare 325.00
Lamp, Emblem, L-62 ....195.00
Mug, Bumper to the Flag, sabers & 35-star flag 235.00
Mug, Christopher Columbus, L-1 ....45.00
Mug, Martyr's Lincoln & Garfield 65.00
Paperweight, Cleveland sulfide medallion, 3½" 195.00
Paperweight, Moses in Bulrushes, frosted center, Gillinder 145.00
Paperweight, Napoleon bust, frosted/clear, L-446 ....295.00
Paperweight, Ruth the Gleaner, frosted, Gillinder 125.00
Paperweight, Shakespeare, frosted, Gillinder 150.00
Pickle dish, E Pluribus Unum 45.00
Pin tray, McKinley bust, frosted base, L-297 ....110.00
Pitcher, Garfield Drape, scarce 145.00
Pitcher, Liberty Bell, John Hancock, milk glass 595.00
Plate, Battleship Maine, openwork border, 5½" 16.00
Plate, Bryan, flag/eagle/star border, milk glass, L-359 ....85.00
Plate, Dewey, clear/frost, sm 15.00
Plate, For President Winfield S Hancock, 8" 110.00
Plate, General Fitzhugh Lee, lattice-work rim, 5½" 110.00
Plate, Indian, milk glass, L-14, 7½" 60.00
Plate, McKinley 35.00
Plate, Pope Leo, milk glass, L-240 ....40.00
Plate, We Mourn Our Nation's Loss, Garfield, w/gold, 11" 55.00
Platter, Constitution, eagle & banner center 75.00
Shot glass, Bryan & McKinley, 1896, NM 130.00
Stein, Centennial 65.00
Syrup, Peace & Plenty, emb sailing ship & anchor, strap hdl ...195.00
Tumbler, America, L-48 ....25.00
Tumbler, eagle/flag/cannon, L-148, 4¾" 125.00
Tumbler, Hobson, in laurel wreath, frosted 60.00
Tumbler, Rock of Ages, L-227 ....25.00
Tumbler, Whittier birthplate etch, waisted, tall 60.00
Wine, Washington Centennial 65.00

Hobbs, Brockunier, & Co.

Hobbs and Brockunier's South Wheeling Glass Works was in operation during the last quarter of the 19th century. They are most famous for their peachblow, amberina, Daisy and Button, and Hobnail pattern glass. The mainstay of the operation, however, was druggist items and plain glassware — bowls, mugs, and simple footed pitchers with shell handles.

For further information we recommend *Hobbs, Brockunier & Co. Glass, Identification and Value Guide,* by Neila and Tom Bredehoft (Collector Books). See also Frances Ware.

Bowl, nut; Leighton, ruby w/crystal rigaree 275.00
Butter dish, Sawtooth, milk glass 50.00
Celery, yacht, Daisy & Button, crystal w/amber stain, 13" 75.00
Celery tray, Daisy & Button, vaseline, 2x14" 125.00
Cheese dish, Polka Dot, canary or crystal 180.00
Creamer, Leighton, ruby w/crystal rigaree 300.00

Finger bowl, Neapolitan, pk satin 150.00
Finger bowl, Venetian, wht loopings w/ruby or bl threads 700.00
Nappy, Maltese & Ribbon, canary, 4" 50.00
Pitcher, milk; Hobnail, wht opal, clear smooth hdl, 5¾x5" 235.00
Spooner, Polka Dot, ruby 120.00
Sugar bowl, Neapolitan, pk satin 350.00
Tumbler, Blackberrry, milk glass, minimum value 100.00

Holt Howard

Novelty ceramics marked Holt Howard represent one of the newest areas of collectibles on today's market, and dealers report a good amount of market activity. Made from the '50s into the '70s, they're not only marked, but most are dated as well. There are several lines to reassemble — the rooster, the white cat, figural banks, Christmas angels, and Santas, to name only a few — but the one that most Holt Howard collectors seem to gravitate toward is the pixie line. For more information see *Garage Sale and Flea Market Annual* (Collector Books). Our advisors for this category are Pat and Ann Duncan; they are listed in the Directory under Missouri.

Sugar bowl, Pixieware, winking head finial on lid, from $75.00 to $100.00; Original carton, from $25.00 to $35.00.

Ashtray, lady w/bottle 110.00
Ashtray, Santa, med 25.00
Ashtray/coaster, mouse 25.00
Bank, Coin Clown, bobbing head, from $150 to 185.00
Bank, Dandy Lion, bobbing head, from $140 to 160.00
Bell, holly decoration 20.00
Butter dish, emb Rooster, ¼-lb 50.00
Butter dish, Kozy Kitten peeking out on side, ¼-lb, rare 150.00
Candle holders, angel figurines, pr 35.00
Candle holders, girl w/reindeer, pr 30.00
Candle holders, Santa w/climbing mouse, pr 35.00
Candle huggers, figural snowman, pr 25.00
Candlestick, Santa handle 25.00
Child's dish, Braille ABCs 25.00
Chocolate pot, emb Rooster on front, tall & narrow w/flaring sides .95.00
Cookie jar, Rooster 200.00
Cookies/candy jar, roly-poly Santa figure, 3-pc 250.00
Cottage cheese keeper, Kozy Kitten on lid 100.00
Cruets, oil & vinegar; Sally & Sam, pr, minimum value 200.00
Decanter, Pixieware, winking head stopper w/Whiskey, minimum value ..200.00
Dish, Santa head w/scalloped beard bowl 25.00
French dressing bottle, Pixieware, minimum value 200.00
Instant coffee jar, Pixieware, scarce, minimum value 250.00
Lipstick holder, Ponytail Girl, from $60 to 75.00

Mayonnaise jar, Pixieware, winking head finial, minimum value 250.00
Mug, Rooster, 3 szs, ea 20.00
Napkin holder, emb Rooster 40.00
Olive jar, Pixieware, winking gr head finial 95.00
Planter, mother deer & fawn, wht w/gold bow 35.00
Plate, Rake 'N Spade, MIB 20.00
Razor bank, barber figure 30.00
Recipe box, wood w/painted-on Rooster 100.00
Sewing box, Kozy Kitten figural w/tape measure tongue on lid ...100.00
Shakers, cat head, pr 20.00
Shakers, Christmas tree w/Santa, pr 25.00
Shakers, full-figure Santa, S or P on tummy, pr 30.00
Spice rack, Kozy Kitten, stacking 175.00
Spoon holder, Rooster 35.00
Spoon rest, apple form 15.00
Tape dispenser, pelican 130.00
Tray, Rooster, facing left 25.00
Trivet, Rooster, tile in iron base 50.00

Homer Laughlin

The Homer Laughlin China Company of Newell, West Virginia, was founded in 1871. The superior dinnerware they displayed at the Centennial Exposition in Philadelphia in 1876 won the highest award of excellence. From that time to the present, they have continued to produce quality dinnerware and kitchenware, many lines of which are becoming very popular collectibles. Most of the dinnerware is marked with the name of the pattern and occasionally with the shape name as well. The 'HLC' trademark is usually followed by a number series, the first two digits of which indicate the year of its manufacture. For further information we recommend *The Collector's Encyclopedia of Fiesta, Eighth Edition,* by Sharon and Bob Huxford; *The Collector's Encyclopedia of Homer Laughlin China* by Joanne Jasper; and *Collector's Guide to Homer Laughlin's Virginia Rose* by Richard G. Racheter (all available from Collector Books). Our advice on the Virginia Rose pattern is from Jack and Treva Hamlin; they are listed in the Directory under Ohio.

Our values are base prices. Very desirable patterns on the shapes named in our listings may increase values by as much as 70%. See also Fiesta; Harlequin; Riviera.

Cavalier, bowl, fruit 6.00
Cavalier, plate, 7" 7.00
Cavalier, sugar bowl, w/lid 16.00
Debutante, casserole, w/lid 35.00
Debutante, coffeepot 55.00
Debutante, nappy, 10" 18.00
Debutante, plate, 10" 9.00
Eggshell Georgian, nappy, 9" 16.00
Eggshell Georgian, plate, 10" 12.00
Eggshell Georgian, teapot 65.00
Eggshell Nautilus, casserole, w/lid 45.00
Eggshell Nautilus, cream soup 15.00
Eggshell Nautilus, plate, rnd, 8" 8.00
Eggshell Nautilus, shakers, Swing, pr 16.00
Empress, cup, bouillon; 6-oz 14.00
Empress, egg cup, Boston 20.00
Empress, plate, coupe; 7" 8.00
Empress, platter, 12" 14.00
Jade, cream soup 20.00
Jade, jug, lg, w/lid 95.00
Jade, plate, 7" 9.00
Jade, tea cup & saucer 16.00

Liberty, baker (oval bowl) **18.00**
Liberty, plate, 8", rare **12.00**
Liberty, teapot **65.00**
Liberty (Historical America), plate, 9" **12.00**
Liberty (Historical America), platter, 11½" **22.00**
Liberty (Historical America), sugar bowl, w/lid **20.00**
Nautilus, baker, 10" **18.00**
Nautilus, plate, 9" **9.00**
Nautilus, sauce boat **20.00**
Nautilus, teacup & saucer **9.00**
Orleans, baker, 9" **20.00**
Orleans, creamer **16.00**
Orleans, plate, 7" **8.00**
Orleans, plate, 9" **14.00**
Swing, casserole, w/lid **45.00**
Swing, cream soup **25.00**
Swing, shakers, pr **18.00**
Swing, utility tray **18.00**
Virginia Rose, bowl, deep, 5" **18.00**
Virginia Rose, jug, 5" **75.00**
Virginia Rose, lug soup **20.00**
Virginia Rose, nappy, 8" **16.00**
Wells, bowl, deep, 6" **18.00**
Wells, bowl, oatmeal **8.00**
Wells, coffee cup, AD **20.00**
Wells, coupe soup **9.00**

Hull

The A.E. Hull Pottery was formed in 1905 in Zanesville, Ohio, and in the early years produced stoneware specialities. They expanded in 1907, adding a second plant and employing over two hundred workers. By 1920 they were manufacturing a full line of stoneware, art pottery with both airbrushed and blended glazes, florist pots, and gardenware. They also produced toilet ware and kitchen items with a white semiporcelain body. Although these continued to be staple products, after the stock market crash of 1929, emphasis was shifted to tile production. By the mid-'30 interest in art pottery production was growing, and over the next fifteen years, several lines of matt pastel floral-decorated patterns were designed, consisting of vases, planters, baskets, ewers, and bowls in various sizes.

The Red Riding Hood cookie jar, patented in 1943, proved so successful that a whole line of figural kitchenware and novelty items was added. They continued to be produced well into the '50s. (See also Little Red Riding Hood.) Through the '40s their floral artware lines flooded the market, due to the restriction of foreign imports. Although best known for their pastel matt-glazed ware, some of the lines were high gloss. Rosella, glossy coral on a pink clay body, was produced for a short time only; and Magnolia, although offered in a matt glaze, was produced in gloss as well.

The plant was destroyed in 1950 by a flood which resulted in a devastating fire when the floodwater caused the kilns to explode. The company rebuilt and equipped their new factory with the most modern machinery. It was soon apparent that the matt glaze could not be duplicated through the more modern processes, however, and soon attention was concentrated on high-gloss artware lines such as Parchment and Pine and Ebb Tide. Figural planters and novelties, piggy banks, and dinnerware were produced in abundance in the late '50s and '60s. By the mid-'70s dinnerware and florist ware were the mainstay of their business. The firm discontinued operations in 1985.

Our advisor, Brenda Roberts, has compiled a lovely book, *The Collector's Encyclopedia of Hull Pottery*, with full-color photos and current values. You will find her address in the Directory under Missouri.

Another informative book is *Collector's Guide to Hull Pottery, The Dinnerware Lines*, by Barbara Loveless Gick-Burke, available from Collector Books or your bookstore.

Special note to Hull collectors: reproductions are on the market in all categories of Hull pottery — matt florals, Red Riding Hood, and later lines including House 'n Garden dinnerware.

Banded, bowl, D-1, 7½" **35.00**
Blossom Flite, bowl, console; ring hdls, boat form, T-10, 16½" ..**145.00**
Blossom Flite, teapot, rope hdl, T-14, 8¼" **145.00**
Bow-Knot, candle holder, bl to gr, 1 low hdl, B-17, 4" **120.00**
Bow-Knot, jardiniere, sm bow hdls, B-19, 9⅜" **1,075.00**

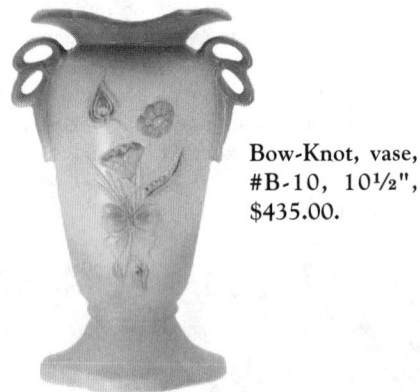

Bow-Knot, vase, #B-10, 10½", $435.00.

Bow-Knot, vase, pk to bl, flared scalloped rim, B-11, 10½" **500.00**
Bow-Knot, vase, pk to gr, hdls, B-7, 8½" **260.00**
Bow-Knot, wall pocket, pitcher form, B-26, 6" **260.00**
Butterfly, ewer, wht & turq matt, sq w/octagonal ft, B-11, 8¾" ..**175.00**
Butterfly, serving tray, wht & turq matt w/gold, B-23, 11½" **115.00**
Butterfly, vase, 3-ftd, B-10, 7" **70.00**
Calla Lily, vase, wht floral on cream, hdls, #560/33, 13" **450.00**
Calla Lily, vase, wht flower on gr to pk, hdls, #540/33, 6" **140.00**
Camellia, basket, pk & yel floral on wht, scalloped, #140, 10½" .**1,150.00**
Camellia, bud vase, pk to bl, low hdls, #129, 7" **135.00**
Camellia, candle holder, bl to pk dove form, #117, 6½" **150.00**
Camellia, ewer, pk & yel floral on wht, flared ft, #106, 13¼" **750.00**
Camellia, vase, pk to bl, flat & ovoid, hdls, #123, 6½" **135.00**
Camellia, vase, pk to bl, low hdls, #130, 4¾" **80.00**
Camellia, vase, swan form, #118, 6½" **175.00**
Cinderella Kitchenware (Blossom), creamer, yel HP floral, #28, 4½" **45.00**
Cinderella Kitchenware (Blossom), pitcher, pk HP floral, #22, 64-oz .**175.00**
Cinderella Kitchenware (Bouquet), bowl, pk/bl/yel HP florals, 9¾" **125.00**
Classic, ewer, flower on creamy wht, #6, 6" **35.00**
Continental, ewer, orange w/yel stripes, #56, 12½" **225.00**
Continental, vase, gr striped, #53, 8½" **45.00**
Crescent Dinnerware, creamer, gr gloss, B-15, 4¼" **22.00**
Crescent Kitchenware, casserole, maroon gloss, #35, w/lid, 11½" ..**65.00**
Crescent Kitchenware, shaker, maroon gloss, B-4, 3½" **20.00**
Dogwood, bowl, console; pk to bl cornucopia form, #511, 11½" ..**435.00**
Dogwood, bowl, low, pk to bl, sm hdls, #521, 7" **180.00**
Dogwood, ewer, pk to bl, ornate hdl & rim, #519, 13½" **900.00**
Dogwood, teapot, #507, 6½" **440.00**
Dogwood, vase, cream to turq, hdls, ftd, #509, 6½" **125.00**
Dogwood, vase, pk to bl, long hdls, #513, 6½" **135.00**
Early Art, jardiniere, emb trees on turq, semiporc, #546, 7" **105.00**
Early Art, vase, pk/bl stripes on turq, stoneware, 5½" **70.00**
Early Utility, bowl, emb ribs on gr, #30, 7" **30.00**
Early Utility, flowerpot, emb bands on gr, w/saucer, #538, 4" **45.00**
Early Utility, pitcher, brn stripe on yel, #107 mk 30, 4¾" **50.00**
Early Utility, spice jar, emb wheat on gr, mk, 3½" **75.00**

Early Utility, stein, Am Legion, brn to yel, #498, 6½" 85.00
Ebb Tide, basket, shell form, E-11, 16½" 230.00
Ebb Tide, creamer, shell form, E-15, 4" 85.00
Ebb Tide, ewer, shell form w/fish hdl, E-10, 14" 260.00
Fiesta, cornucopia, ruffled rim, #49, 8½" 80.00
Fiesta, flowerpot, blk, ruffled rim, #40, 4¼" 30.00
Fiesta, vase, deer & tree in pk panel on wht, #50, 9" 105.00
Floral, bowl, mixing; yel sunflower decor, #40, 5" 25.00
Floral, shakers, #44, 3½", pr 40.00
Imperial, planter, blk gloss w/pk swirl, rectangle, unmk, 6¾" 30.00
Imperial, planter, Carnation Pk, leaf form, F-24, 12½" 32.00
Imperial, vase, Carnation Pk, F-28, 9½" 15.00
Iris, bowl, console; pk to bl, hdls, ftd, #409, 12" L 450.00
Iris, ewer, pk to bl, ornate hdl, ftd, #401, 13½" 675.00
Iris, vase, cream, flared, dbl hdls, #403, 4¾" 95.00
Iris, vase, cream to pk, flared top, hdls, ftd, #402, 8½" 235.00
Magnolia, glossy; sugar bowl, pk floral on bl, H-22, w/lid, 3¾" 40.00
Magnolia, glossy; teapot, bl floral on pk, H-20, 6½" 175.00
Magnolia, glossy; vase, pk floral on pk, fan top, hdls, H-6, 6½" 85.00
Magnolia, glossy; vase, pk floral on pk, gold hdls, H-8, 8½" 125.00
Magnolia, glossy; vase, pk floral on pk, swan hdls, H-16, 12½" ..250.00
Magnolia, glossy; vase, pk floral w/gold on pk, hdls, H-1, 5½" 50.00
Magnolia, matt; candle holder, low hdls, #27, 4" 50.00
Magnolia, matt; ewer, yel, #18, 13½" 380.00
Magnolia, matt; pk floral on bl, dbl cornucopia, #6, 12" 195.00
Magnolia, matt; vase, pk floral on bl, low hdls, #16, 15" 500.00
Magnolia, matt; vase, pk/bl, shoulder hdls, fluted rim, #4, 6¼" 65.00
Magnolia, matt; vase, yel, swan hdls, #17, 12¼" 325.00
Magnolia, matt; vase, yel, tassel open hdls, #21, 12½" 450.00
Mardi Gras, bowl, mixing; cream to pk matt, emb ribs, unmk, 10¼" ..45.00
Mardi Gras, vase, yel gloss cylinder w/emb ribs, unmk, 6" 25.00
Mardi Gras/Granada, ewer, cream to pk matt w/gold, #31, 10" ..275.00
Mardi Gras/Granada, ewer, emb floral on cream to pk matt, #31, 10" ..160.00
Mardi Gras/Granada, vase, wht w/emb decor, hdls, #49, 1947, 9" ..55.00
Mirror Almond, bowl, divided vegetable 30.00
Mirror Almond, bowl, fruit 5.00
Mirror Almond, bowl, soup/salad 7.00
Mirror Almond, bud vase, 9" 20.00
Mirror Almond, casserole, Fr hdl, open 7.00
Mirror Almond, creamer 12.00
Mirror Almond, jug, 2-qt 30.00
Mirror Almond, plate, dinner; 10" 10.00
Mirror Almond, snack set 22.50
Mirror Almond, stein 7.00
Mirror Almond, sugar bowl, w/lid 14.00
Mirror Brown, butter dish, ¼-lb 20.00
Mirror Brown, canisters, stacking, set of 4 ....225.00
Mirror Brown, casserole, duck lid, 2-qt 75.00
Mirror Brown, cheese shaker 22.00
Mirror Brown, coffeepot, 8-cup 35.00
Mirror Brown, deviled egg server, rooster imprint 75.00
Mirror Brown, gingerbread man tray 75.00
Mirror Brown, gravy boat, w/undertray 42.00
Mirror Brown, leaf chip 'n dip, 15" 30.00
Mirror Brown, mug, 9-oz 5.00
Mirror Brown, open baker, incised rooster, 13½" 130.00
Mirror Brown, pie plate, 9¼" 20.00
Mirror Brown, plate, dinner 8.00
Mirror Brown, plate, 8½" 7.00
Mirror Brown, shakers, table sz, pr 20.00
Mirror Brown, spoon rest, oval, 6½" 35.00
Mirror Brown, sugar bowl, 12-oz 14.00
Mirror Brown, vinegar cruet 30.00
Novelty, cat doorstop, hollow int, 7" 320.00

Novelty, dancing girl planter, #955, 7" 60.00
Novelty, giraffe planter, #115, 8" 45.00
Novelty, leaf dish, dk gr & maroon, free-form, #85, 13" 40.00
Novelty, pig dime bank, pk & bl, 3½" 140.00
Novelty, piggy bank, emb florals on bk, cold pnt, USA, 14" 190.00
Novelty, piggy bank, Mirror Brown, #196, 6" 65.00
Novelty, poodle head vase, pk matt, #38, 6¼" 100.00
Novelty, Teddy bear planter, persimmon gloss, #811, 7" 40.00
Novelty, twin geese planter, #95, 7¼" 60.00
Nuline Bak-Serve, pitcher, emb fishscales, pk, C-29, 7" 80.00
Orchid, vase, bl, trumpet neck, hdls, ftd, #301, 10" 410.00
Parchment & Pine, cornucopia, S-2-R, 7¾" 60.00
Parchment & Pine, ewer, S-7, 14¼" 240.00
Parchment & Pine, teapot, S-15, 8" 125.00
Pine Cone, vase, pk, hdls, sm ft, #55, 6½" 185.00
Poppy, basket, cream to pk, flared, scalloped rim, #601, 12" 1,500.00
Poppy, vase, pk to bl, hdls, scalloped rim, ftd, #612, 6½" 150.00
Poppy, wall pocket, cornucopia form, pk to bl, #609, 9" 400.00
Rosella, basket, scalloped rim, R-12, 7" 340.00
Rosella, ewer, R-11, 7" 165.00
Rosella, lamp base, hdls, L-3, 11" 425.00
Rosella, vase, heart form, R-8, 6½" 140.00
Royal Imperial, jardiniere, gray to pk, emb ribs, #75, 7" 55.00
Royal Woodland, basket, aqua, twig hdl, W-9, 8¾" 105.00
Serenade, beverage pitcher, emb birds on yel, S-21, 10½" 220.00
Serenade, candle holders, bl w/yel int, S-16, 6½", pr 140.00
Serenade, sugar bowl, bl, w/lid, S-19, 3¼" 65.00
Sueno Tulip, ewer, pk to bl, ornate hdl, #109-33, 13" 500.00
Sueno Tulip, vase, tulips on cream to bl, hdls, ftd, #106-33, 6" ..125.00
Sunglow, basket, yel, #84, 6½" 90.00
Sunglow, bowl, #50, 9½" 45.00
Sunglow, vase, sm ring hdls, #94, 8" 75.00
Sunglow, wall pocket, pitcher form, #81, 5½" 100.00
Tokay, ewer, pk to gr, branch hdl, #13, 12" 290.00
Tokay, sugar bowl, pk to gr, branch finial, #18 ....75.00
Tokay, vase, pk to gr, branch hdls, #8, 10" 100.00
Tropicana, vase, dancing figure on wht, #54, 12½" 600.00

Tuscany, basket, pink with gray-green decor, #11, 10½", $100.00.

Tuscany, urn, wht w/gr foliage, low hdls, ftd, #5, 5½" 35.00
Tuscany, vase, slim, branch hdls, #12, 12" 95.00
Water Lily, cornucopia, dbl; pk to gr, L-27, 12" 260.00
Water Lily, creamer, apricot to walnut, L-19, 5" 60.00
Water Lily, vase, apricot to walnut, high hdls, L-16, 12½" 550.00
Water Lily, vase, pk to gr, low hdls, L-13, 10½" 255.00
Water Lily, vase, pk to gr, ornate hdls, L-8, 8½" 160.00
Wildflower, candle holder, pk to bl, oval form, unmk, 2½" 45.00
Wildflower, ewer, pk to bl, W-2, 5½" 75.00
Wildflower, ewer, yel, high hdl, W-19, 13½" 450.00
Wildflower, vase, pk to bl, fan form, low hdls, W-15, 10½" 245.00
Wildflower, vase, yel, ornate hdls, scalloped rim, W-9, 8½" 195.00
Wildflower, vase, yel, ornate hdls, W-6, 7½" 80.00

Wildflower (# series), bowl, console; pk to bl, hdls, #70, 12" **425.00**
Woodland, basket, yel to gr matt, twig hdl/flared ft, W-22, 10½" .**975.00**
Woodland, cornucopia, yel to gr matt, W-10, 11" **160.00**
Woodland, ewer, gr gloss, twig hdl, W-24, 13½" **280.00**
Woodland, jardiniere, cream to pk matt, scalloped, hdls, W-7, 5½" .**170.00**
Woodland, matt; vase, gr gloss, low hdls, W-16, 8½" **195.00**
Woodland, vase, bl to gr gloss, twig hdls, W-8, 7½" **145.00**
Woodland, vase, yel to gr matt, low hdls, W-16, 8½" **275.00**

Hummel

Hummel figurines were created through the artistry of Berta Hummel, a Franciscan nun called Sister M. Innocentia. The first figures were made about 1935 by Franz Goebel of Goebel Art Inc., Rodental, West Germany. Plates, plaques, and candy dishes are also produced, and the older, discontinued editions are highly sought collectibles. Generally speaking, an issue can be dated by the trademark. The first Hummels, from 1934 to 1949, were either incised or stamped with the 'Crown WG' mark. The 'full bee in V' mark was employed with minor variations until 1959. At that time the bee was stylized and represented by a solid disk with angled symmetrical wings completely contained within the confines of the 'V.' The three-line mark, 1964 – 1972, utilized the stylized bee and included a three-line arrangement, 'c by W. Goebel, W. Germany.' Another change in 1970 saw the 'stylized bee in V' suspended between the vertical bars of the 'b' and 'l' of a printed 'Goebel, West Germany.' Collectors refer to this mark as the 'last bee' or 'Goebel bee.' The mark in use from 1979 to 1990 omits the 'bee in V.' The current mark in use since 1991 is a small crown with 'WG' initials, a large 'Goebel,' and a small 'Germany' signifying a united Germany. For further study we recommend *Hummel, An Illustrated Handbook and Price Guide*, by Ken Armke; *Hummel Figurines and Plates, A Collector's Identification and Value Guide*, by Carl Luckey; and *The No. 1 Price Guide to M.I. Hummell* by Robert L. Miller. These books are available through your local book dealer. See also Limited Edition Plates.

Key:
ce — closed edition
CM — crown mark
cn — closed number
FB — full bee
NC — new crown mark
SB — stylized bee
LB — last bee
MB — missing bee
oe — open edition
tw — temporarily withdrawn
3L — three-line mark

#700, Annual bell, Let's Sing, 1st edition, 1978, 6", $60.00; #701, Annual bell, Farewell, 2nd edition, 1979, 6", $60.00.

#II/112, Just Resting, table lamp, CM, ce, 7½" **360.00**
#III/57, Chick Girl, box, FB, ce, 6" **380.00**
#1, Puppy Love, FB, ce, 5" **345.00**
#3/II, Book Worm, FB, ce, 8" **1,300.00**
#5, Strolling Along, 3L, ce, 5¼" **200.00**
#7/0, Merry Wanderer, SB, ce, 6" **270.00**
#9, Begging His Share, MB, ce, 5½" **180.00**
#12, Chimney Sweep, CM, ce, 6" **470.00**
#14 A&B, Book Worm, Boy & Girl, bookends, LB, ce, 5½" **305.00**
#16/I, Little Hiker, FB, ce, 5¾" **255.00**
#18, Christ Child, CM, ce, 3¾x6½" **255.00**
#20, Prayer Before Battle, LB, ce, 4¼" **125.00**
#23/III, Adoration, FB, ce, 8¾" **630.00**
#25, Angelic Sleep, candle holder, SB, ce, 3½x5¼" **180.00**
#27/3, Joyous News, SB, ce, 4¼x4¾" **540.00**
#29/0, Guardian Angel, font, SB, ce, 2⅞x6" **685.00**
#30/0 A&B, Ba-Bee-Ring, CM, ce, 4¾x5" **360.00**
#32, Little Gabriel, LB, ce, 5" **110.00**
#33, Joyful, ashtray, MB, TW, 3½x6" **110.00**
#35/I, Good Shepherd, font, CM, ce, 2¾x5¾" **255.00**
#37, Herald Angels, candle holder, 3L, ce, 2¾x4¼" **150.00**
#42/0, Good Shepherd, CM, ce, 6¼" **470.00**
#43, March Winds, LB, ce, 5¼" **115.00**
#44/A, Culprits, table lamp, FB, ce, 9" **290.00**
#46/III, Madonna w/o Halo, CM, colored, ce, 15¾" **290.00**
#47, Goose Girl, CM, ce, 5" **575.00**
#49/I, To Market, FB, ce, 6¼" **865.00**
#51, Village Boy, CM, ce, 8" **615.00**
#53, Joyful, FB, ce, 3¾" **145.00**
#55, Saint George, CM, w/red saddle, ce, 6¾" **1,800.00**
#56/B, Out of Danger, SB, ce, 6½" **290.00**
#57/I, Chick Girl, FB, ce, 4¼" **305.00**
#59, Skier, 3L, ce, 5½" **175.00**
#60 A&B, Farm Boy (A) & Goose Girl (B), bookends, CM, ce, 4¾" **650.00**
#62, Happy Pastime, ashtray, 3L, ce, 3½x6¼" **110.00**
#63, Singing Lesson, FB, ce, 2¾" **145.00**
#65, Farewell, MB, ce, 4¾" **180.00**
#66, Farm Boy, FB, ce, 5¼" **255.00**
#68/0, Lost Sheep, SB, ce, 5½" **205.00**
#70, Holy Child, CM, ce, 7" **430.00**
#71, Stormy Weather, SB, ce, 6½" **360.00**
#73, Little Helper, 3L, ce, 4¼" **95.00**
#74, Little Gardener, CM, ce, 4¼" **215.00**
#78/VIII, Blessed Child, FB, ce, 13¾" **360.00**
#80, Little Scholar, SB, ce, 5½" **215.00**
#81, School Girl, FB, ce, 5¼" **235.00**
#82 2/0, School Boy, CM, ce, 4¼" **290.00**
#84/0, Worship, NC, oe, 5" **115.00**
#85, Serenade, FB, ce, 7¼" **540.00**
#87, For Father, FB, ce, 5½" **255.00**
#89/I, Little Cellist, LB, ce, 5¾" **155.00**
#92, Merry Wanderer, plaque, LB, ce, 4½x5" **110.00**
#94, Surprise, CM, ce, 5¾" **540.00**
#95, Brother, FB, ce, 5½" **235.00**
#97, Trumpet Boy, CM, ce, 4½" **150.00**
#99, Eventide, FB, ce, 4¼x5" **400.00**
#101, To Market, table lamp, FB, ce, 7½" **540.00**
#103, Farewell, table lamp, CM, ce, 7½" **5,760.00**
#106, Merry Wanderer, plaque, CM, ce, 6x6" **3,600.00**
#109/II, Happy Traveler, FB, ce, 7½" **540.00**
#110, Let's Sing, CM, ce, 4" **305.00**
#111 3/0, Wayside Harmony, FB, ce, 3¾" **180.00**
#114, Let's Sing, ashtray, CM, ce, 3½x6¼" **615.00**
#116, Girl w/Fir Tree, Advent candlestick, FB, ce, 3½" **72.00**
#118, Little Thrifty, bank, SB, ce, 5¼" **145.00**
#123, Max & Moritz, CM, ce, 5¼" **430.00**
#125, Vacation Time, plaque, FB, ce, 4⅜x5¼" **255.00**
#127, Doctor, FB, ce, 5" **200.00**
#129, Band Leader, LB, ce, 5½" **150.00**
#131, Street Singer, CM, ce, 5¼" **360.00**
#132, Star Gazer, SB, ce, 4¾" **215.00**
#134, Quartet, plaque, CM, ce, 5½x6¼" **540.00**

#136/I, Friends, FB, ce, 5¼" 270.00
#139, Flitting Butterfly, wall plaque, FB, ce, 2½x 2½" 145.00
#141/V, Apple Tree Girl, LB, ce, 10¼" 885.00
#143, Boots, CM, ce, 6¾" 615.00
#145, Little Guardian, FB, ce, 3⅞" 180.00
#147, Angel Shrine, font, SB, ce, 3x5" 60.00
#150/0, Happy Days, 3L, ce, 5" 255.00
#152 A, Umbrella Boy, 3L, ce, 8" 1,080.00
#154/I, Waiter, FB, ce, 6¾" 325.00
#163, Whitsuntide, CM, ce, 6¾" 720.00
#165, Swaying Lullaby, wall plaque, CM, ce, 4½x5¼" 540.00
#167, Angel Sitting, font, FB, ce, 3¼x4⅛" 110.00
#169, Bird Duet, CM, ce, 3¾" 270.00
#171, Little Sweeper, SB, ce, 4¼" 130.00
#174, She Loves Me, She Loves Me Not, FB, ce, 4¼" 215.00
#178, The Photographer, FB, ce, 5" 325.00
#182, Good Friends, SB, ce, 4" 200.00
#184, Latest News, CM, ce, 5" 540.00
#186, Sweet Music, w/striped slippers, CM, ce, 5" 865.00
#187, MI Hummel Plaque (in English), SB, ce, 5½x4" 360.00
#188, Celestial Musician, FB, ce, 7" 540.00
#193, Angel Duet, candle holder, FB, ce, 5" 360.00
#194, Watchful Angel, SB, ce, 6½" 325.00
#195, Barnyard Hero, FB, ce, 5⅞" 430.00
#197/I, Be Patient, 3L, ce, 6" 235.00
#199/0, Feeding Time, LB, ce, 4⅜" 145.00
#203/I, Signs of Spring, SB, ce, 5¼" 270.00
#204, Weary Wanderer, SB, ce, 5¾" 255.00
#206, Angel Cloud, font, FB, ce, 3¼x4¾" 180.00
#217, Boy w/Toothache, FB, ce, 5⅜" 290.00
#220, We Congratulate (w/base), FB, ce, 3⅞" 215.00
#222, Madonna Plaque (w/metal fr), SB, ce, 4x5" 540.00
#224/I, Wayside Harmony, table lamp, SB, ce, 7½" 275.00
#226, Mail Is Here, FB, ce, 4¼x6" 560.00
#229, Apple Tree Girl, table lamp, SB, ce, 7½" 270.00
#232, Happy Days, table lamp, FB, ce, 9¾" 720.00
#234, Birthday Serenade, table lamp, SB, ce, 7¾" 720.00
#235, Happy Days, table lamp, FB, ce, 7¾" 575.00
#238 A, Angel w/Lute, SB, ce, 2¼" 65.00
#239 B, Girl w/Doll, SB, ce, 3½" 65.00
#240, Little Drummer, FB, ce, 4⅛" 200.00
#241, Angel Lights, candle holder, LB, ce, 10¼x8¼" 215.00
#243, Madonna & Child, font, FB, ce, 3⅛x4" 165.00
#246, Holy Family, font, FB, ce, 3⅛x4½" 165.00
#248/0, Guardian Angel, font, SB, ce, 2⅜x5⅜" 145.00
#252 A&B, Apple Tree Girl & Boy, bookends, SB, ce, 5", pr 255.00
#255, Stitch in Time, SB, ce, 6½" 360.00
#258, Which Hand?, SB, ce, 5⅜" 430.00
#261, Angel Duet, 3L, ce, 5" 430.00
#262, Heavenly Lullaby, LB, ce, 3½x5" 140.00
#266, Globe Trotter, Annual Plate 1973, LB, ce, 7½" 145.00
#270, Apple Tree Boy, Annual Plate 1977, LB, ce, 7½" 60.00
#274, Umbrella Boy, Annual Plate 1981, MB, ce, 7½" 60.00
#286, Shepherd's Boy, Annual Plate 1990, MB, ce, 7½" 165.00
#291, Come Back Soon, Annual Plate 1995, NC, oe, 7½" 180.00
#301, Christmas Angel, MB, ce, 6" 180.00
#304, The Artist, 3L, ce, 5½" 540.00
#306, Little Bookkeeper, SB, ce, 4¾" 720.00
#309, With Loving Greetings (early sample), LB, ce, 3⅜" 720.00
#311, Kiss Me, LB, ce, 6¼" 205.00
#314, Confidentially, 3L, ce, 5½" 650.00
#317, Not for You, SB, ce, 5½" 540.00
#319, Doll Bath, SB, ce, 5" 540.00
#321, Wash Day, SB, ce, 5¾" 400.00
#327, The Run-a-Way, 3L, ce, 5¼" 720.00
#328, Carnival, SB, ce, 5¾" 540.00
#330, Baking Day, NC, oe, 5¼" 200.00
#331, Crossroads, 3L, ce, 6¾" 540.00
#333, Blessed Event, SB, ce, 5⅜" 540.00
#337, Cinderella, 3L, ce, 4½" 865.00
#340, Letter to Santa Claus, 3L, ce, 7¼" 360.00
#343, Christmas Song, MB, ce, 6½" 155.00
#345, A Fair Measure, MB, ce, 5½" 205.00
#346, Smart Little Sister, MB, ce, 4¾" 180.00
#347, Adventure Bound, 3L, ce, 7½x8¼" 2,880.00
#350, On Holiday, LB, ce, 4¼" 1,080.00
#352, Sweet Greetings, NC, oe, 4¼" 145.00
#353/0, Spring Dance, LB, ce, 5¼" 225.00
#356, Gay Adventure, LB, ce, 4¾" 145.00
#357, Guiding Angel, 3L, ce, 2¾" 110.00
#359, Tuneful Angel, 3L, ce, 2¾" 110.00
#361, Favorite Pet, SB, ce, 4½" 720.00
#363, Big Housecleaning, 3L, ce, 4" 720.00
#366, Flying Angel, LB, ce, 3½" 95.00
#367, Busy Student, NC, oe, 4¼" 115.00
#369, Follow the Leader, 3L, ce, 7" 1,080.00
#371, Daddy's Girls, LB, ce, 4¾" 165.00
#373, Just Fishing, NC, oe, 4⅜" 165.00
#374, Lost Stocking, LB, ce, 4½" 105.00
#376, Little Nurse, MB, ce, 4" 175.00
#378, Easter Greetings, 3L, ce, 5" 720.00
#381, Flower Vendor, LB, ce, 5¼" 180.00
#382, Visiting an Invalid, MB, ce, 5" 145.00
#385, Chicken-Licken, 3L, ce, 4¾" 720.00
#387, Valentine Gift, LB, ce, 5¾" 430.00
#388 M, Little Band, candle holder on music box, LB, ce, 3x4¾" ..255.00
#390, Boy w/Accordion, LB, ce, 2½" 65.00
#392, Little Band (on base), 3L, ce, 3x4¾" 180.00
#394, Timid Little Sister, MB, ce, 7" 305.00
#396, Ride Into Christmas, MB, ce, 5¾" 325.00
#399, Valentine Joy, MB, ce, 5¾" 180.00
#403, An Apple a Day, MB, ce, 6½" 200.00
#405, Sing With Me, MB, ce, 5" 240.00
#408/0, Smiling Through, MB, ce, 4¾" 215.00
#410, Little Architect (early sample), LB, ce, 6" 1,440.00
#412, Bath Time, LB, ce, 6¼" 270.00
#414, In Tune, NC, oe, 4" 200.00
#416, Jubilee, MB, ce, 6¼" 255.00
#418, What's New?, MB, ce, 5¼" 200.00
#420, Is It Raining?, MB, ce, 6" 183.00
#421, It's Cold, MB, ce, 5" 215.00

Hutschenreuther

The Porcelain Factory C.M. Hutschenreuther operated in Bavaria from 1814 to 1969. After the death of the elder Hutschenreuther in 1845, his son Lorenz took over operations, continuing there until 1857 when he left to establish his own company in the nearby city of Selb. The original manufactory became a joint stock company in 1904, absorbing several other potteries. In 1969 both Hutschenreuther firms merged, and that company still operates in Selb. They have distributing centers in both France and the United States.

Creamer & sugar bowl, Maple Leaf 45.00
Cup & saucer, Maple Leaf 10.00
Figurine, boxer dog 195.00
Figurine, canary, sgn C Werner, 5½" 160.00

Figurine, colt 110.00
Figurine, dancers, wht & gold, sgn Werner, 1930s, 11½" 600.00
Figurine, dolphin, 4" 125.00
Figurine, elephant, 3½x5" 125.00
Figurine, finch, 3½" 125.00
Figurine, Granger, gray Schnauzer, 6¼x7" 175.00
Figurine, Harlequin Great Dane, blk & wht, 7¼" 48.00
Figurine, lady in yel dancing gown holds skirt wide, 10¼" 250.00
Figurine, lady w/fruit basket, 9½" 165.00
Figurine, Off Season, 3 quail, ltd ed, 8½x15" 2,000.00
Figurine, owl, 2⅝" 125.00
Figurine, panda, 2x3½" 125.00
Figurine, Schnauzer, 5⅞" 150.00
Figurine, 5 flying dolphins, wht, ltd ed 950.00
Figurine, 7 ladies in lav/wht dresses, blk hats, 1886, 5½ 500.00
Plate, dinner; Maple Leaf 10.00
Plate, Pan playing flute, Tutter, 5x4" 275.00

Imari

Imari is a generic term which covers a broad family of wares. It was made in more than a dozen Japanese villages, but the name is that of the port from whence it was shipped to Europe. There are several types of Imari. The most common features a design with panels of birds, florals, or people surrounding a central basket of flowers. The colors used in this type are underglaze blue with overglaze red, gold, and green enamels. The Chinese also made Imari wares which differ from the Japanese type in several ways — the absence of spur marks, a thinner-type body, and a more consistent control of the blue. Imari-type wares were copied on the continent by Meissen and by English potters, among them Worcester, Derby, and Bow. Unless noted otherwise, our values are for Japanese ware.

Bowl, shishi among peonies, deep, 19th C, 16¼" 2,000.00
Bowl, 4 cloud reserves w/lions or people, 19th C, 4¼x9", EX 260.00
Charger, bamboo/peonies/chrysanthemums, 18th C, 18½" 1,500.00
Charger, scenic, bl & rust w/mc, bl & wht reverse, 1830-50, 18" .495.00
Jar, cranes/pines/peonies, 3-lobe collar, late 17th C, 16" 1,000.00

Imperial Glass Company

The Imperial Glass Company was organized in 1901 in Bellaire, Ohio, and started manufacturing glassware in 1904. Their early products were jelly glasses, hotel tumblers, etc., but by 1910 they were making a name for themselves by pressing quantities of carnival glass, the iridescent glassware that was popular during that time. In 1914 NuCut was introduced to imitate cut glass. The line was so popular that it was made in crystal and colors and was reintroduced as Collector's Crystal in the 1950s. From 1916 to 1920 they used the lustre process to make a line called Imperial Jewels. Free-Hand ware, art glass made entirely by hand using no molds, was made from 1922 to 1928.

The company entered bankruptcy in 1931 but was able to continue operations and reorganize as the Imperial Glass Corporation. In 1936 Imperial introduced the Candlewick line, for which it is best known. In the late thirties the Vintage Grape Milk Glass line was added, and in 1951 a major ad campaign was launched, making Imperial one of the leading milk glass manufacturers.

In 1940 Imperial bought the molds and assets of the Central Glass Works of Wheeling, West Virginia; in 1958 they acquired the molds of the Heisey Company; and in 1960 the molds of the Cambridge Glass Company of Cambridge, Ohio. Imperial used these molds, and after 1951 they marked their glassware with an 'I' superimposed over the 'G'

trademark. The company became a subsidiary of Lenox in 1973; subsequently an 'L' was added to the 'IG' mark. In 1981 Lenox sold Imperial to Arthur Lorch, a private investor (who modified the L by adding a line at the top angled to the left, giving rise to the 'ALIG' mark). He in turn sold the company to Robert F. Stahl, Jr., in 1982. Mr. Stahl filed for Chapter 11 to reorganize, but in mid-1984 liquidation was ordered, and all assets were sold. A few items that had been made in '84 were marked with an 'N' superimposed over the 'I' for 'New Imperial.'

For more information, we recommend *Imperial Glass Encyclopedia, Vols I and II*, edited by James Measell. Our advisor is Joan Cimini; she is listed in the Directory under Ohio. See also Candlewick; Carnival Glass; Glass Animals and Figurines; Stretch Glass.

Pitcher, Old Williamsburg, #341, light amber, 1-qt, $80.00; Matching goblet, 9-oz, $12.00; Claret, 4½-oz, $10.00.

Basket, Crocheted, crystal, 12" 60.00
Basket, Crocheted, crystal, 9" 37.50
Basket, ruby slag, #475, mini 55.00
Bowl, berry; Katy, bl opal, flat rim 30.00
Bowl, cereal; Katy, bl opal, deep 65.00
Bowl, console; Crocheted, crystal, 12" 30.00
Bowl, Dmn Quilt, blk, crimped, 7" 20.00
Bowl, Grape, caramel slag, #47c, 10" 90.00
Bowl, jelly; Beaded Block, bl opal, hdld 45.00
Bowl, Katy, gr opal, #749b, 9" 125.00
Bowl, Pillar Flutes, lt bl, 10" 35.00
Bowl, Pipe, ruby slag, #1605, 7½" 40.00
Bowl, Rose, jade slag, #52c, 8" 58.00
Bowl, Rose, jade slag, #62c, 9" 75.00
Bowl, Rose, purple slag, #62c, 9" 54.00
Cake stand, Collector's Crystal, Antique Blue, #505 ....45.00
Cake stand, Crocheted, crystal, ftd, 12" 40.00
Candlesticks, Dolphin, caramel slag, 3779, 5", pr 70.00
Candlesticks, duo; Katy, bl opal, pr 250.00
Candlesticks, Free-Hand, clear w/red knops & threads, 11", pr .1,400.00
Celery tray, Huckabee, pk, oval, 8¼" 32.50
Champagne, Cape Cod, amber, #1602 ....25.00
Claret, Cape Cod, Azalea, #1602 ....20.00
Claret, Cape Cod, crystal, #1602, 5-oz 10.00
Cocktail, Cape Cod, crystal, #160b 12.00
Cocktail, Cape Cod, ruby, #160 ....27.00
Comport, Cape Cod, crystal, #160/48b, ftd, 7" 45.00
Comport, Katy, milk glass, 4¾" 45.00
Cordial, Cape Cod, #1602, ruby, 1½-oz 45.00
Cordial, Collector's Crystal, crystal, #612 ....14.00
Cordial, Decorated Western Apple, crystal, #176, 2-oz 20.00
Cordial, Fancy Colonial, pk, #582, 1-oz 50.00
Creamer, Beaded Block, crystal 20.00
Creamer, Fancy Colonial, pk, hotel, #582 ....35.00
Cruet, Collector's Crystal, caramel slag, #505 ....50.00
Cruet, Octagon, jade, w/stopper 90.00
Cup & saucer, Katy, crystal 15.00
Cup & saucer, Pillar Flutes, lt bl 25.00
Decanter, Big Shots (Shot Gun Shells), red w/EX gold, #711, 40-oz ..210.00
Decanter, Cask #1, Antique Blue 55.00

Decanter, Grape, Heather, #8 ....55.00
Epergne, Crocheted, crystal, ftd, center vase, 11" 130.00
Goblet, Cape Cod, Evergreen, #160, 14-oz 55.00
Goblet, Chroma, burgundy, #123 ....30.00
Goblet, Chroma, ruby, #123 ....30.00
Goblet, Hoffman House, ruby, #46 ....18.00
Hors d'oeuvre dish, Crocheted, crystal, rnd, 4-part, 10½" 30.00
Horseradish jar, Cape Cod, crystal, #160/226 ......70.00
Ivy ball, Reeded (Spun), red, crystal ft, 4" 65.00
Jar, owl form, gr slag 90.00
Jar, vanity; Reeded (Spun), pk, #701, 7⅝" 45.00
Lamp, hurricane; Crocheted, crystal, 11" 35.00
Mayonnaise, Katy, bl opal, w/underplate 120.00
Mayonnaise ladle, Katy, lt bl opal 45.00
Mint dish, Cape Cod, crystal, heart shape 25.00
Nappy, Pansy, caramel slag, hdl, 5" 40.00
Pitcher, Dew Drop, opal, #624, 56-oz 65.00
Pitcher, Windmill, caramel slag, glossy 60.00
Pitcher, Windmill, red slag, satin 55.00
Plate, cheese & cracker; crystal, ftd, 12" 35.00
Plate, Crocheted, crystal, 14" 22.50
Plate, Dmn Quilt, blk, 8" 15.00
Plate, Katy, bl opal, 6" 20.00
Punch bowl, Crocheted, crystal, 14" 65.00
Relish, Crocheted, crystal, 3-part, 11½" 25.00
Shakers, Cape Cod, Fern gr, #160/117, pr 75.00
Shakers, Cape Cod, Sunshine Yel, #160/117, pr 75.00
Sherbet, Huckabee, pk, ftd 30.00
Toothpick holder, Octagon, caramel slag 18.00
Tumbler, juice; Cape Cod, amber, ftd, #1602, 6-oz 20.00
Vase, bud; Free-Hand, hearts/vines, lt gr on opal, 8½" 350.00
Vase, bud; peach & butterscotch w/mirror finish, 10" 225.00
Vase, Free-Hand, Drag Loops, bl on wht, 11½x5" 875.00
Vase, Free-Hand, drape design, brn on gray-gr, 10" 500.00
Vase, Free-Hand, gold w/pk & orange irid, ovoid, 10" 350.00
Vase, Free-Hand, hearts/vines, bl on orange irid, 9" 350.00
Vase, Free-Hand, hearts/vines, gr on opal, orange int, 8¾x2½" 350.00
Vase, Free-Hand, hearts/vines, opal on cobalt, gold int, 10½" 1,300.00
Vase, Free-Hand, hearts/vines, orange on cobalt, bulbous, 6" 600.00
Vase, Free-Hand, hearts/vines, wht on cobalt, label, 4⅝x6" 650.00
Vase, Free-Hand, hearts/vines, wht on orange, 11¼x5" 850.00
Vase, Katy, bl opal, #743b, 5¼" 45.00
Vase, Katy, bl opal, #743n, 5½" 60.00
Vase, Katy, bl opal, #743x, 4½" 45.00
Vase, Katy, cobalt, #743b, 5¼" 65.00
Vase, Katy, red, #743b, 5¼" 65.00
Vase, Loganberry, milk glass, crimped, #356, 10" 35.00
Vase, Reeded, cobalt, squat, 5¾" 65.00
Vase, Reeded (Spun), red, 9" 75.00
Whiskey, Cape Cod, crystal, #160, 2½-oz 12.50

Imperial Porcelain

The Blue Ridge Mountain Boys were created by cartoonist Paul Webb and translated into three-dimensional figurines by the Imperial Porcelain Corporation of Zanesville, Ohio, in 1947. These figurines decorated ashtrays, vases, mugs, bowls, pitchers, planters, and other items. The Mountain Boys series were numbered 92 through 108, each with a different and amusing portrayal of mountain life. Imperial also produced American Folklore miniatures, twenty-three tiny animals one inch or less in size, and the Al Capp Dogpatch series. Because of financial difficulties, the company closed in 1960.

American Folklore Miniatures

Cat, 1½" 50.00
Cow, 1¾" 45.00
Hound dogs 60.00
Plaque, store ad, Am Folklore Porcelain Miniatures, 4½" 450.00
Sow 45.00

Blue Ridge Mountain Boys by Paul Webb

Ashtray, #101, man w/jug & snake 120.00
Ashtray, #103, hillbilly & skunk 120.00
Ashtray, #105, baby, hound dog, & frog 125.00
Ashtray, #106, Barrel of Wishes, w/hound 95.00
Ashtray, #92, 2 men by tree stump, for pipes 125.00
Box, cigarette; #98, dog atop, baby at door, sq 135.00
Dealer's sign, Handcrafted Paul Webb Mtn Boys, rare, 9" 650.00

Decanter, Ma leaning over stump with baby and skunk, #104, $95.00.

Decanter, #100, outhouse, man, & bird 95.00
Decanter, man, jug, snake, & tree stump, Hispch Inc, 1946 ....95.00
Figurine, #101, man leans against tree trunk, 5" 90.00
Figurine, man on hands & knees, 3" 115.00
Figurine, man sitting, 3½" 95.00
Figurine, man sitting w/chicken on knee, 3" 95.00
Jug, #101, Willie & snake 75.00
Mug, #94, Bearing Down, 6" 95.00
Mug, #94, dbl baby hdl, 4¼" 95.00
Mug, #94, ma hdl, 4¼" 95.00
Mug, #94, man w/bl pants hdl, 4¼" 95.00
Mug, #94, man w/yel beard & red pants hdl, 4¼" 95.00
Mug, #99, Target Practice, boy on goat, farmer, 5¾" 95.00
Pitcher, lemonade 200.00
Planter, #100, outhouse, man, & bird 95.00
Planter, #105, man w/chicken on knee, washtub 125.00
Planter, #110, man, w/jug & snake, 4½" 65.00
Planter, #81, man drinking from jug, sitting by washtub 75.00
Shakers, Ma & Old Doc, pr 110.00

Miscellaneous

Items in this section that are designated 'IP' are miscellaneous novelties made by Imperial Porcelain; the remainder are of interest to Paul Webb collectors, though made by an unknown manufacturer. Prints on calendars and playing cards are signed 'Paul Webb.'

Artist board, babies or mtn women, sgn Paul Webb, 30x30" 275.00
Artist board, mtn boys only, sgn Paul Webb, 30x30" 225.00
Calendar, 1954, 12 sgn scenes, Brown & Bigelow, complete 48.00
Figurine, cat in high-heeled shoe, 5½" L 40.00
Hot pad, Dutch boy w/tulips, rnd, IP 30.00
Ink blotters, sgn scenes, ea 12.00

Mug, #29, man hdl, sgn Paul Webb, 4¾" **50.00**
Planter, #106, dog sitting by tub, IP **95.00**
Playing cards, ad: Rafe Oiling Gun, Brown & Bigelow, MIB **75.00**
Shakers, pigs, 5", pr **95.00**
Shakers, standing pigs, IP, 8", pr **95.00**

Indian Tree

Indian Tree is a popular dinnerware pattern produced by various potteries since the early 1800s to recent times. Although backgrounds and borders vary, the Oriental theme is carried out with the gnarled, brown branch of a pink-blossomed tree. Among the manufacturers' marks, you may find represented such notable firms as Coalport, S. Hancock and Sons, Soho Pottery, and John Maddock and Sons.

Oval vegetable bowl, Maddock, 9", $25.00.

Bowl, rim soup; Maddock, 9" **20.00**
Bowl, soup; Johnson Bros, 7¼" **13.00**
Bowl, vegetable; Johnson Bros, 8½" **25.00**
Bowl, vegetable; red, oval, Midwinter, 9" **14.00**
Creamer, Johnson Bros **17.00**
Cup, Myott **3.00**
Cup & saucer, AD; Minton **25.00**
Cup & saucer, yel & gold band, Grosvenor Bone **20.00**
Gravy boat, Maddock **32.00**
Plate, Maddock, 8" **8.00**
Platter, John Maddock & Son, 14" **32.00**
Platter, Johnson Bros, 12¼" **26.00**
Sugar bowl, Johnson Bros, w/lid **22.00**

Inkwells and Inkstands

Receptacles for various writing fluids have been used since ancient times. Through the years they have been made from countless materials — glass, metal, porcelain, pottery, wood, and even papier-mache. During the 18th century, gold or silver inkstands were presented to royalty; the well-known silver inkstand by Philip Syng, Jr., was used for the signing of the Declaration of Independence; and impressive brass inkstands with wells and pounce pots (sanders) were proud possessions of men of letters. When literacy vastly increased in the 19th century, the dip pen replaced the quill pen; and inkwells and inkstands were widely used and produced in a broad range of sizes in functional and decorative forms from ornate Victorian to flowing Art Nouveau and stylized Art Deco designs. However, the acceptance of the ballpoint pen literally put inkstands and inkwells 'out of business.' But their historical significance and intriguing diversity of form and styling fascinate today's collectors.

For further information we recommend *Collector's Encyclopedia to Inkwells, Books I and II*, by Veldon Badders (Collector Books). See also Bottles, Ink.

Brass, polished, concave body, glass insert, ca 1900, 2½x5" **65.00**
Bronze, rooster's head, red fabric comb, neck hinge, 1890s **185.00**
Copper-plated brass, baseball well on base, porc insert, 1913 .....**100.00**
Faience, Chinese Hawthorne style, brass mts, acorn finial, Fr **275.00**
Glass, amber, cut panels, brass mts, hinged top, 4x2⅝" dia **235.00**
Glass, gr, sq cut & polished, dimpled sides, hinged lid, 5x2⅝" ...**235.00**
Glass, gr ball shape w/brass mts, emb ribs at base, 4x3¼" **235.00**
Glass, gr w/emb ripples, brass mts, hinged top, 3¾x3¼" **235.00**
Glass, periwinkle bl, sq w/brass mts, bl ribbed cap, 4¾" **235.00**
Marble, apple shape, ball finial, ca 1900, 2⅝x3" **165.00**
Patinated pot metal, St George's head/dragon, St Louis...1898 ...**185.00**
Porc, bl floral transfer on wht, hinged lid, 1890s, 4⅛x2¾" **115.00**
Porc, gondola form w/wood-look pnt, hinged lid, 1900s, European .**175.00**
Porc, HP landscape w/gold, English, ca 1800s, 3¼x7½" **825.00**
Porc, ovoid urn form w/mc florals & gold, 5-hole, Limoges, 6⅝" L ..**165.00**
Porc, rabbit figural, quill hole in ear, XS 432 DEP, 4½" **350.00**
SP, horseshoe form (rstr), 2 clear wells, 6⅞x7¼" dia **395.00**
SP, revolving dome, 3 paw ft, ca 1900, 3x3¼" **190.00**
SP pot metal, dragoon's helmet form, porc insert, 1880-90 ....**225.00**
Wht metal, crab figural, pottery insert, 1890s, worn, 2⅝" **85.00**
Wood, cvd man w/pipe figural, Am, 19th C, 7" H **860.00**

Insulators

The telegraph was invented in 1844. The devices developed to hold the electrical transmission wires to the poles were called insulators. The telephone, invented in 1876, intensified their usefulness; and by the turn of the century, thousands of varieties were being produced in pottery, wood, and glass of various colors. Even though it has been rumored that red glass insulators exist, none have ever been authenticated. Many insulators are embossed with patent dates.

Of the more than 3,000 types known to exist, today's collectors evaluate their worth by age and rarity of color. Aqua and green are the most common colors in glass, dark brown the most common in ceramic. Threadless insulators (for example, CD #701.1) made between 1850 and 1865, bring prices well into the hundreds, if in mint condition.

In the listings that follow, the CD numbers are from an identification system developed in the late 1960s by N.R. Woodward.

Those seeking additional information about insulators are encouraged to contact Line Jewels NIA #1380 (whose address may be found in the Directory under Clubs, Newsletters, and Catalogs) or attend a club-endorsed show. (For information see Directory under Florida for Jacqueline Linscott.) In the listings that follow those stating 'no name' have no company identification, but do have embossed numbers, dots, etc. Those stating 'no embossing' are without raised letters, dots, or any other markings.

Key:
* (asterisk) — Canadian   RB — rough base
BE — base embossed   RDP — round drip points
CB — corrugated base   SB — smooth base
CD — Consolidated Design   SDP — sharp drip points

Threaded Pin-type Glass Insulators

CD 102, Westinghouse No 3, SB, lt gr **300.00**
CD 112, Lynchburg No 31, RDP, pk **8.00**
CD 112, New England Telegraph and Telephone, SB, gr **90.00**
CD 115, Armstrong No 3, SB, clear **3.00**
CD 115, Hemingray - 10, CB, clear **1.00**
CD 117, no name, SB, dk aqua **25.00**
CD 118, no name, SB, carnival **275.00**

CD 120, CEW, SB, bl	140.00
CD 120, Patent/Dec 19, 1871, SB, ice gr	10.00
CD 121, C&P Tel Co, SB, gr	20.00
CD 122, McLaughlin No 16, RDP, apple gr	35.00
CD 123, EC&M Co, SB, gr-aqua	75.00
CD 127, WU, SB, bl-aqua	250.00
CD 128, Hemingray, E-1, SB, off clear	75.00
CD 128, Hemingray E-14-B, SB, opal	75.00
CD 133, GBM Co, SB, lt purple	75.00
CD 135, Chicago Insulating Co, SB, bl	75.00
CD 137, Hemingray, SB, clear	5.00
CD 138, Brookfield Postal Tel Co, SB, lt aqua	12.00
CD 139.9, McLaughlin USLD, SB, aqua	200.00
CD 142, Hemingray, RDP, carnival	30.00
CD 143, CNR, SB, aqua	10.00
CD 143.5 THE Co, SB, lt gr	125.00
CD 144*, no name, horizontal ridges, SB, gr	125.00
CD 147, Hemingray Pat Oct 8, 1907, SB, aqua	1.00
CD 154, Gayner No 44, SB, bl-aqua	2.00
CD 155, Kerr DB.1, SB, off-clear	2.00
CD 158.1, Chester (inner skirt emb), SB, aqua	2,000.00
CD 160, Armstrong's No 14, SB, clear	15.00
CD 162, Hamilton Glass Co, RDP, lt gr	40.00
CD 163, Armstrong's No 4, SB, clear	1.00
CD 166, California, SB, sage-gr	5.00
CD 168, Hemingray D-510, SB, carnival	30.00
CD 170, no name, SB, gr-aqua	10.00
CD 175, Hemingray - 25, SB, clear	15.00
CD 180, Liquid Insulator, SB, lt aqua	4,000.00
CD 182, Dry Spot No 10, SB, straw	3,000.00
CD 188, B, SB, gr	35.00
CD 196, HGCo, Pat May 2, 1893, SDP, ice aqua	75.00
CD 197, Whitall Tatum No 15, SB, clear	3.00
CD 202, Hemingray 53, SDP, aqua	10.00
CD 206, no name, SDP, straw	350.00
CD 210, Postal, SB, emerald gr	10.00
CD 213, Hemingray 43, RDP, Hemingray bl	15.00
CD 230, Hemingray D-512, SB, lt citrine	20.00
CD 235, Pyrex 662, SB, carnival	30.00
CD 240, Pyrex 131, SB, clear	15.00
CD 245, no name, 9200, SB, gr	300.00
CD 251, NEGM Co, SB, ice bl	20.00
CD 252, M&E, SB, gr	85.00
CD 254, No 3 Cable, SB, lt bl-aqua	75.00
CD 257, Hemingray No 60, RDP, clear	15.00
CD 263, Columbia, SB, lt aqua	200.00
CD 267, NEGM, SB, aqua	450.00
CD 269, Jumbo, SB, dk aqua	300.00
CD 282, Knowles, Boston, SB, aqua	200.00
CD 286, Locke, SB, lt bl	50.00
CD 294, NEGMCo, SB, aqua	40.00
CD 299.1, prism, SB, lt aqua	250.00
CD 306, Lynchburg, SDP, aqua	400.00
CD 317, Chambers, SB, ice gr	300.00
CD 325, Pyrex 401, SB, clear	15.00

Threadless Pin-type Glass Insulators

CD 1038, Cutter, SB, aqua	200.00
CD 724, Chester, SB, dk cobalt	7,500.00
CD 728, no embossing, SB, lt bl	1,250.00
CD 728.8, Boston Bottle Works, SB, lt aqua	4,000.00
CD 734, McMicking, SB, lt aqua	60.00
CD 742, no embossing, SB, lt gr	250.00

Irons

History, geography, art, and cultural diversity are all represented in the collecting of antique pressing irons. The progress of fashion and invention can be traced through the evolution of the pressing iron.

Over seven hundred years ago, implements constructed of stone, bone, wood, glass, and wrought iron were used for pressing fabrics. Early ironing devices were quite primitive in form, and heating techniques relied on inserting a hot metal slug into a cavity of the iron, adding hot burning coals into a chamber or pan, and by placing the iron directly on hot coals or a hot surface.

To the pleasure of today's collectors, some of these early irons, mainly from the period of 1700 to 1850, were decorated by artisans who carved and painted them with regional motifs typical of their natural surroundings and spiritual cultures.

Beginning in the mid-1800s, new cultural demands for fancy wearing apparel initiated a revolution in technology for types of irons and methods to heat them. Typical of this period is the fluter which was essential for producing the ruffles demanded by the 19th-century ladies. Hat irons, polishers, and numerous unusual iron forms were also used during this time, and provided a means to produce crimps, curves, curls and special fabric textures. Irons from this era are characterized by their unique shapes, odd handles, latches, decorations, and even revolving mechanisms.

Also during this time, irons began to be heated by burning liquid and gaseous fuels. Gradually the new technology of the electrically heated iron replaced all other heating methods, except in the more rural areas and undeveloped countries. Even today the Amish communities utilize gasoline fueled irons.

In the listings that follow, prices are given for examples in best possible as-found condition. Damage, repairs, plating, excessive wear, rust, and missing parts can dramatically reduce value. For further information we recommend *Irons by Irons* and *More Irons by Irons* by our advisor Dave Irons; his address and information for ordering these books are given in the Directory under Pennsylvania.

Photo courtesy Dave Irons

Little irons, W.H. Howell Co, Geneva Ill, Pat 11-14-11, burns alcohol (burned entirely before using), 3½", from $200.00 to $300.00; Cast horse, European, late 1800s, 3½" long, minimum value over $750.00.

Ball, European, late 1800s, 1" dia	100.00
Box, decor hdl grip, top lifts off, late 1800s, 5⅞"	200.00
Box, English, str sides, hinged gate, mid-1800s, 5½"	200.00
Charcoal, box, Dutch, brass, openwork sides, mid 1800s, 8½"	375.00
Charcoal, box, European, dolphin posts, iron, ca 1900, 6⅝"	150.00
Charcoal, box, Oriental, characters on hinge, brass, 1900, 8"	150.00
Charcoal, Colebrookdale...#4, tall chimney, late 1800s, 6¾"	200.00
Charcoal, Victoria Registered, trn chimney, late 1800s, 7"	150.00
Cold hdl, Belgian, teardrop style, wood hdl, ca 1900, 7¼"	150.00
Cold hdl, Simplex Sad Iron, twist latch, late 1800s, 6⅜"	200.00
Cold hdl, sleeve, Harper Chicago Navy, ca 1900, 5⅛"	300.00
Combination revolving, Majestic, 4-position hdl, 6¼"	500.00

Drop-in-the-bk, European, pieced, leather hdl, 1700s, 5½" 300.00
Edge/seam, European, thin base, late 1800s, 5½" 150.00
Egg, European, cast egg on rod w/iron hdl, late 1800s, 2¼" 100.00
Flower, Am, brass top, late 1800s, 8¾" 125.00
Flower, G Molla, brass base, iron top, late 1800s, 6¾" 125.00
Fluter, rocker, Geneva Hand...Aug 21 1866, brass plates, 5¾" ...350.00
Fluter, roller, CW Whitfield...Pat 1880, 5½" 150.00
Fluter, roller, Shepard Hardware...1880, hinged base, 7¾" 200.00
Fluter combination, Little Giant, Pat Dec 10 73, 5¼" 350.00
Fluter combination, Myron H Knapp, Pat'd Aug 2 70, 6⅝" 150.00
Fluting scissors, wood grips, ca 1900, 9¼" 100.00
Gasoline, Coleman Model No 5, gr, ca 1930, 7⅝" 300.00
Gasoline, Coleman Model 609, blk, ca 1930, 8⅛" 125.00
Goffering, English, brass, high tripod base, mid 1800s, 10¼" 350.00
Goffering, English, brass, Queen Anne-style tripod, 1850-90s, 10" 250.00
Goffering, English, brass bbl, iron std/base, late 1800s, 10½" 250.00
Goffering, European, wrought, sm monkey tail, tripod, 1800s, 11" ..750.00
Hat, shackle, Am, movable sides, ca 1925, 3¼" 150.00
Hat, tolliker, Fr, all cast, smooth bottom, late 1800s, 5¼" 125.00
Liquid fuel, Grossbar, Pat'd Mar 9 1915, 6⅛" 150.00
Liquid fuel, Matador, ca 1900, 7¼", w/sun-face trivet 300.00
Liquid fuel, revolving, Ellison Bro...1888, tank hdl, 7" 750.00
Little, cast swan form, orig pnt, Am, 1¾" 300.00
Little, cold hdl, Enterprise...No 115, iron, 3⅞" 100.00
Little, cold hdl, Ober, Pat 1895..., removable hdl, 4" 140.00
Little, cylinder grip, mk 0, late 1800s, 3" 110.00
Little, fluter, rocker, Geneva Fluter, Pat'd 1866, 3½" 750.00
Little, slug, Am, brass, lift-up gate, 1⅞" 300.00
Little, slug, European, ca 1900, 3½" 150.00
Little, tri-bump hdl, Am, late 1800s, 3⅜" 50.00
Ox tongue, European, hinged gate, ca 1900, 8" 150.00
Ox tongue, European, some wrought parts, hinged gate, 1700s, 10" ..250.00
Pleating scissors, Am, wrought iron, early 1800s, 10½" 150.00
Polisher, English, W Cross, rnd bottom, late 1800s, 5¼" 100.00
Polisher, Fr, mk 6, rnded bk, late 1800s, 6⅝" 125.00
Polisher, Hoods, soapstone, hound bk, 1867, 2⅝" 350.00
Polisher, Star Polisher, all cast, late 1800s, 4⅞" 110.00
Sad iron, Crown 32, Pat App'd For, CI, late 1800s, 6½" 50.00
Sad iron, H3 (Russian), crossed hammers, late 1800s, 6½" 200.00
Sad iron, Ober #6, Pat Mar 19 '12, CI, 6" 40.00
Sad iron, Wapak #4, cast, ca 1900, 5⅛" 20.00
Sadiron, Fr, brass posts, 1800s, 6½", w/trivet 500.00
Seam, Am, Pat Apd For, hdl opens, late 1800s, 6¾" 300.00
Sleeve, Am, all cast, rope twist hdl, late 1800s, 5⅜" 40.00
Sleeve, Asbestos Sad...May 22nd 1900, long toe, rare, 7¾" 200.00
Sleeve, Sensible No 1, Pat...1887 on hdl, 6⅞" 50.00
Slug, English, brass w/heart cutout under hdl, late 1800s, 7½" ...750.00
Slug, European, iron body, Delft hdl, late 1800s, 8¼" 650.00
Smoother/fluter, NR Streeter, removable hdl, late 1800s, 6⅞" ..300.00

Ironstone

During the last quarter of the 18th century, English potters began experimenting with a new type of body that contained calcinated flint and a higher china clay content, intent on producing a fine durable whiteware — heavy, yet with a texture that would resemble porcelain. To remove the last trace of yellow, a minute amount of cobalt was added, often resulting in a bluish-white tone. Wm and John Turner of Caughley and Josiah Spode II were the first to manufacture the ware successfully. Others, such as Davenport, Hicks and Meigh, and Ralph and Josiah Wedgwood, followed with their own versions. The latter coined the name 'Pearl' to refer to his product and incorporated the term into his trademark. In 1813 a 14-year patent was issued to Charles

James Mason, who called his ware Patented Ironstone. Francis Morley, G.L. Asworth, T.J. Mayer, and other Staffordshire potters continued to produce ironstone until the end of the century. While some of these patterns are simple to the extreme, many are decorated with in-mold designs of fruit, grain, and foliage on ribbed or scalloped shapes. In the 1830s transfer-printed designs in blue, mulberry, pink, green, and black became popular; and polychrome versions of Oriental wares were manufactured to compete with the Chinese trade. See also Mason's Ironstone. Our advice for this category comes from Home Place Antiques, whose address is listed in the Directory under Illinois.

Bowl, sauce; Ceres, Elsmore & Forster, 5" 25.00
Bowl, soup; Full Ribbed, Pankhurst, 8¾" 32.00
Bowl, soup; Mocho, T&R Boote, 8⅝" 30.00
Bowl, vegetable; Fig, Wedgwood, w/lid, med 145.00
Bowl, vegetable; Gothic, w/lid, mk JF, 8¼x11¼x9¾" 165.00
Bowl, vegetable; Wheat & Hops, W Taylor, w/lid, 10¼" L 145.00
Butter dish, Lily of the Valley, Shaw, 3-pc 265.00
Butter dish, President, Edwards, 3-pc 295.00
Chamber pot, Corn & Oats, w/lid 175.00
Coffeepot, Ceres, Elsmore & Forster 265.00
Coffeepot, Lily, H Burgess 295.00
Coffeepot, Wheat & Clover, Tomkinson Bros, 10⅝" 245.00
Compote, New York, 9½" dia 225.00
Creamer, Wheat & Clover, Turner & Tompkinson, 7⅜" 125.00
Cup plate, Fig, Davenport, 4¼" 55.00
Ladle, sauce tureen; Boote's 1851, unmk, 7¼" 60.00
Lazy susan, scalloped Flower Garden border, removable top, 1890s, 18" dia .500.00
Mug, Chinese, Anthony Shaw, 3½" 95.00
Pitcher, Garibaldi, T&R Boote, 8¾" 125.00
Pitcher, milk; Ceres, Elsmore & Forster, 8⅛" 145.00
Pitcher, Panelled Leaves, Meakin, 8¾" 165.00
Pitcher, Potomac, W Baker, 8½" 125.00
Pitcher, Sydenham, 9" 195.00
Plate, Ivy Wreath, J Meir, 9⅝" 36.00
Plate, Laurel Wreath, unmk, 4½" 30.00
Plate, Rolling Star, Edwards, 9½" 27.50
Plate, Sharon Arch, Davenport, 10½" 32.00
Plate, Sydenham, T&R Boote, 9⅛" 25.00

Meat platter, floral pattern, marked BSM, 15", with matching 11" covered casserole, $85.00 for the set.

Platter, De Soto, Thos Hughes, 11⅝x9" 65.00
Platter, Wheat on Ceres shape, Turner, Goddard & Co, 14¾" 60.00
Relish, Ceres, w/rope, Elsmore & Forster 78.00
Soap dish, Block Optic, J&G Meakin, no insert, w/lid 125.00
Sugar bowl, Wheat on Ceres shape, Elsmore & Forster, w/lid, 7¾" .140.00
Tea saucer, Full Ribbed, Pankhurst, 6" 12.00
Teacup & saucer, Baltic, T Hulme 65.00
Teacup & saucer, Leaf & Crossed Ribbon, Livesley Powell 55.00
Toddy bowl, Ceres, open, Elsmore & Forster 350.00
Toothbrush holder, Victory, vase form, Edwards, 5¾" H 85.00
Tureen, sauce; Cable & Ring, Bridgwood, w/underplate/ladle 265.00

Tureen, soup; Fluted Pearl, J Wedgwood, w/underplate/lid **295.00**
Wash bowl & pitcher, Dallas shape, Clementson **450.00**
Wash bowl & pitcher, Hanging Leaves, PB&H **395.00**
Wash pitcher, Hebe, John Alcock, 11⅞" **145.00**
Waste bowl, Ceres, bell shape, Elsmore & Forster (unmk) **120.00**

Patterned Ironstone

Coffeepot, Canella, brn stransfer, Challinor, 14", EX **95.00**
Coffeepot, Cleopatra, bl transfer, 9¼" **195.00**
Coffeepot, Paradise, purple transfer, Livesley Powell, 9", NM **230.00**
Creamer, Cleopatra, bl transfer, 8-sided, 5¾" **95.00**
Cup & saucer, Cleopatra, bl transfer...**60.00**
Cup & saucer, Paradise, purple transfer, Livesley Powell...............**85.00**
Pitcher, milk; floral, purple transfer, unmk, 7⅞" **75.00**
Plate, Cleopatra, bl transfer, 6⅛" **20.00**
Plate, Cleopatra, bl transfer, 9½" **30.00**
Plate, Paradise, purple transfer, Livesley Powell, 8⅝" **100.00**
Plate, Paradise, purple transfer, Livesley Powell, 9½" **25.00**
Sugar bowl, Cleopatra, bl transfer, w/lid, 7¼" **75.00**
Teapot, Hybla, gr, Brougham & Mayer, 8⅞", EX **135.00**
Teapot, Washington Vase, brn transfer, Podmore & Walker, 9", EX ..**125.00**
Waste bowl, Cleopatra, bl transfer, paneled sides, 4x5⅞" **65.00**

Italian Glass

Throughout the 20th century, one of the major glassmaking centers of the world was the island of Murano. From the Stile Liberte work of Artisi Barovier (1890 – 1920s) to the early work of Ettore Sottsass in the 1970s, they excelled in creativity and craftsmanship. The 1920s to '40s featured the work of glass designers like Ercole Barovier for Barovier and Toso and Vittorio Zecchin, Napoleone Martinuzzi, and Carlo Scarpa for Venini. Many of these pieces are highly prized by collectors.

The 1950s saw a revival of Italy as a world-renowned design center for all of the arts. Glass led the charge with the brightly colored work of Fulvio Bianconi for Venini, Dino Martens for Aureliano Toso, and Ercole Barovier for Barovier and Toso. The best of these pieces are extremely desirable. The '60s and '70s have also seen many innovative designs with work by the Finnish Tapio Wirkkala, the American Thomas Stearns, and many other designers.

Unfortunately, amongst the great glass, there was a plethora of commercial ashtrays, vases, and figurines produced that, though having some value, do not compare in quality and design to the great glass of Murano. These pieces are listed as 'Murano' glass rather than by maker.

Venini: The Venini company was founded in 1921 by Paolo Venini, and he led the company until his death in 1959. Major Italian designers worked for the firm, including Vittorio Zecchin, Napoleone Martinuzzi, Carlo Scarpa, and Fulvio Bianconi. After his death, his son-in-law, Ludovico de Santillana, ran the factory and employed designers like Toni Zucchieri, Tapio Wirkkala, and Thomas Stearns. The company is known for creative designs and techniques including Inciso (finely etched lines), Battuto (carved facets), Sommerso (controlled bubbles), Pezzato (patches of fused glass), and Fascie (horizontal colored lines in clear glass). Until the mid-'60s, most pieces were signed with acid-etched 'Venini Murano ITALIA.' In the '60s they started engraving the signatures. The factory still exists.

Barovier: In the late 1920s, Ercole Barovier took over the Artisi Barovier and started designing many different vases. In the 1930s he merged with Ferro Toso and became Barovier and Toso. He designed many different series of glass including the Barbarico (rough, acid-treated brown or deep blue glass), Eugenio (free-blown vases), Efeso, Rotallato, Dorico, Egeo (vases incorporating murrine designs), and Pri-

mavera (white etched glass with black bands). He designed until 1974. The company is still in existence. Most pieces were unsigned.

Aureliano Toso: The great glass designer Dino Martens was involved with the company from about 1938 to 1965. It was his work that produced the very desirable Oriente vases. This technique consisted of free-formed patches of green, yellow, blue, purple, black, and white stars, and pieces of zanfirico canes fused into brilliantly colored vases and bowls. His El Dorado series was based on the same technique but was not opaque. He also designed pieces with alternating groups of black and white filigrana lines. Pieces are unsigned.

Seguso: Flavio Poli became the artistic director of Seguso in the late 1930s and remained until 1963. He is known for his Corroso (acid-etched glass) and his Valve series (elegant forms of two to three layers of colored glass with a clear glass casing).

Archimede Seguso: In 1946 Archimede Seguso left the Seguso Vetri D'Arte to open a new company and designed many innovative pieces. His Merlatto (thin white filigrana suspended three dimensionally) series is his most famous. The epitome of his work is where a colored glass (yellow or purple) is windowed in the merlotti. His Macchia Ambra Verde is yellow and spots on a gold base encased in clear glass. The A Piume series contained feathers and leaves suspended in glass. Pieces are unsigned.

Alfredo Barbini: Barbini was a designer known for his sculptures of sea subjects and his amorphic-shaped vases with an inner core of red or blue glass with a heavy layer of finely incised outer glass. He worked in the 1950s to 1960s, and some pieces are signed.

Vistosi: Although this glassworks was started in the 1940s, fame came in the 1960s and '70s with the birds designed by Allesandro Pianon and the early work of the Memphis school designer, Ettore Sottsass. Pieces may be signed.

AVEM: This company is known for its work in the 1950s and '60s. The designer, Ansolo Fuga, did work using a solid white glass with inclusions of multicolored murrines.

Cenedese: This is a postwar company led by Gino Cenedese with Alfredo Barbini as designer. When Barbini left, Cenedese took over the design work and also used the free-lance designs of Fulvio Bianconi. They are known for their figurines and vases with suspended murrines.

Cappellin: Venini's original partner (1921 – 25), Giacomo Cappellin, opened a short-lived company (1925 – 32) that was to become extremely important. His chief designer was the young Carlo Scarpa who was to create many masterpieces in glass both for Cappellin and then Venini.

Ettore Sottsass: Sottass founded the Memphis School of Design in the 1970s. He is an extremely famous modern designer who designed several series of glass for the Vistosi Glass Company. The pieces were created in limited editions, signed and numbered, and each piece was given a name.

Our advisor for this category is Howard Lockwood, publisher of *Vetri: Italian Glass News.* For further information concerning Mr. Lockwood or this publication, see the Directory under New Jersey.

Venini Glass

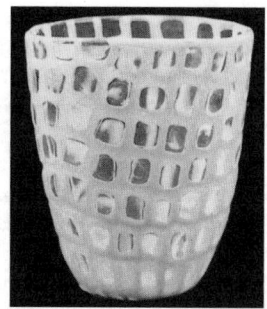

Tobia Scarpa, Occhi vase, murrhina windows, clear in opaque white frames, paper label, 6", $2,000.00.

Bird, Zucchieri A, guinea hen, blk & wht murrines **1,350.00**
Bottle, A Canne, Bianconi, bl/gr/clear, 13½" **935.00**
Bottle, A Canne, Bianconi, wht & gr, w/stopper, 13½" **870.00**
Bottle, Fasce Orizzontali, Bianconi, olive w/3 wht bands **1,920.00**
Bottle, Fasce Orrizontali, Bianconi, blk w/red bands, 18" **2,420.00**
Bottle, Incalmo, Bianconi, red & gr vertical stripes, 19" **1,100.00**
Bottle, Inciso, Venini, lt gr, w/stopper, 10" **550.00**
Bottle, Morandiane, Bianconi, yel canes, 19" **1,210.00**
Bottle, Venini, clear w/swirling amethyst canes, 16" **1,100.00**
Bottle vase, Fasce Orrizontali, Bianconi, red/bl/gr, 17" **1,265.00**
Bowl, Corroso, Scarpa, C; ftd, 5" dia **1,025.00**
Bowl, Inciso, Venini, egg shape, Royal bl, 11½" W **825.00**
Bowl, Murrine, Venini, blk & wht murrines, 3" **2,420.00**

Barovier and Toso, vase, fused red and blue diagonal bands, attributed, ca 1950, 12", $1,800.00; Barovier, vase, green with large feathers of gold leaf and red canes on applied foot, 1930s, 10", $4,200.00.

Chicken, Bianconi, hen, wht w/blk decor **3,575.00**
Decanter, Bianconi, bl w/appl red band, 12½" **1,068.00**
Hourglass, Venini, gr base & red top, 9½" **880.00**
Lamp shade, Vignelli, yel, bulbous, w/metal, 10" H **440.00**
Leaf: Lundgren clear glass w/wht filigrana veins, 9¾" **345.00**
Ovelisk, Venini, clear w/mc spiral threads, 17" **660.00**
Platter, Sommerso, Scarpa C; sqd w/bubbles, 4¼" **230.00**
Tazza, Martinuzzi, clear glass w/mica throughout, 8¼" **1,100.00**
Vase, A Canne, Venini, red/yel/bl/gr/aubergine, 7" **1,265.00**
Vase, A Ritorte, Bianconi, red/bl/gr/clear striped **1,725.00**
Vase, A Spicchi, Bianconi, flared, irregular rim w/vertical bands ...**8,050.00**
Vase, A Spicchi, Bianconi, trapezoidal, mc vertical bands **1,750.00**
Vase, Bianconi, blk w/wht latticino top, fan form, 21" **2,300.00**
Vase, Corroso, Scarpa, C; lt red to burgundy, 4¾" **2,200.00**
Vase, Fasce Murrina, Licata, wht w/center murrine band **6,940.00**
Vase, Fasce Orrizontali, Bianconi, red/bl/gr bands, 19" **4,250.00**
Vase, Fasce Ritorti, Bianconi, red/bl/gr/clear canes, 9" **3,300.00**
Vase, Fasce Verticali, Bianconi, bl/gr/red/tan stripes, 9¼" **4,620.00**
Vase, Fasce Verticali, Bianconi, vase, elliptical, bl/gr/red **4,140.00**
Vase, Fasce Verticali, Bianconi, wide gray/amber bands **1,045.00**
Vase, Incalmo, Bianconi, bl/gray/purple/clear stripes, 9" **1,340.00**
Vase, Incalmo, Licata, bl base, gr top, murrines in middle **7,475.00**
Vase, Inciso, Venini, bl & pk layers, teardrop, 14" **935.00**
Vase, Inciso, Venini, deep amber cased in yel, 4½" **1,210.00**
Vase, Inciso, Venini, flattened ovoid, deep purple, 4½" **1,210.00**
Vase, Laguna, Buzzi, pk opaque, lg, 12¼" **1,870.00**
Vase, Martinuzzi, blk w/mica & red hdls **1,760.00**
Vase, Medusa, Wirkalla, bl w/rolled top & filigrana, 11" **550.00**
Vase, Mosaico Zanfirico, Venini, gray, cigar shape, 14" **6,900.00**
Vase, Occhi, Scarpa, T; sq, reddish brn, 8¾" **3,450.00**
Vase, Pezzato, Bianconi, Am colors, 9" **4,400.00**
Vase, Pezzato, Bianconi, cigar shaped, red/bl/gr/clear, 11" **5,500.00**
Vase, Pezzato, Bianconi, flared, Paris colors, 9½" **4,400.00**
Vase, Pezzato, Bianconi, Istanbul colors, 8" **6,900.00**
Vase, Pezzato, Bianconi, triangular, red/gr/bl/clear, 8¾" **7,187.00**
Vase, Tessuto, Scarpa, C; gr & amethyst, dbl gourd, 12½" **1,725.00**

Vase, Zanfirico, Venini, wht glass, 11½" **440.00**

Non-Venini Glass

Archimede Segus, bookends, bl irid, 2 seated Orientals, 6½" ..**1,955.00**
Archimede Segus, bowl, A Piumme, amber w/7 internal feathers, 9" .**1,340.00**
Archimede Segus, bowl, purple lattice worked w/gold foil, 18" ..**530.00**
Archimede Segus, bowl, yel/red patches outlined in wht **690.00**
Archimede Segus, Cinese Bollicine, vase, red, bubbles, 8½" **230.00**
Archimede Segus, Composizione Latticino, clear w/wht threads ..**5,845.00**
Archimede Segus, headless Harlequin figure, wht latticino, 11½" .**8,625.00**
Aureliano Toso, A Trina, boat-shaped bowl by Martens, 7" L ...**320.00**
Aureliano Toso, A Trina, vase, wht w/gold filigrana, 8½" **220.00**
Aureliano Toso, Bianca/Nera, fan vase, circular ft, 18" **400.00**
Aureliano Toso, Bianca/Nera, vase, ruffled rim, 5" **350.00**
Aureliano Toso, bird, clear w/pk/bl/purple internal specks, 12½" ..**935.00**
Aureliano Toso, bird, wht w/blk & yel filigrana, 10" **745.00**
Aureliano Toso, Eldorado, pierced ewer, appl red hdl, 11½" ...**1,175.00**
Aureliano Toso, Oriente, bowl, triangular, 5¾" **560.00**
Aureliano Toso, Oriente, bowl, 6" L **1,100.00**
Aureliano Toso, Oriente, carafe, appl hdl, 6½" **1,900.00**
Aureliano Toso, Oriente, vase, pinwheel design, 13" **3,040.00**
AVEM, Anse Vilante, pitcher, red irid w/lg hdl, 7½" **1,430.00**
AVEM, vase, cylinder w/red/clear rectangular patches, 12¼" .**2,100.00**
Barbini, dancer, blk w/pk & & bl gold skirt **880.00**
Barbini, Scavo, cranberry w/purple/sand/wht decor, 8" **920.00**
Barbini, Sommerso, lamp base, male figure inside clear, 16½" ...**1,200.00**
Barovier, A Spina, vase, aubergine & opal, 7¾" **1,960.00**
Barovier, Aborigeni, bowl, gr to amber/red, 3½" **880.00**
Barovier, Cordinato D'Oro, vase, pk w/scalloped top, 8½" **300.00**
Barovier, Cordonato D'Oro, vase, purple & clear, 11½" **1,100.00**
Barovier, Eugeneo, bird-shaped pitcher, clear w/gold inclusions .**880.00**
Barovier, Graffito, vase, clear w/wht outlines, 11" **1,380.00**
Barovier, Intarsia, vase, smoky gray w/red triangles, 13¾" **2,400.00**
Barovier, Neolitico, vase, clear w/gold inclusions/internal patch ...**825.00**
Barovier, Primavera, pigeon, blk glass legs, damage, 12¼" **4,300.00**
Barovier, Rosso Corniola, vase, sea-horse hdl, 6½" **3,575.00**
Barovier, Saturneo, vase, 5 rows of teal-gr murrines, 11½" **9,200.00**
Barovier, Tessare, vase, cylinder w/bl/blk/aqua/clear murrines, 9" ..**2,530.00**
Cappellin, Reticello, vase, beaker shape, gr & wht, 9" **1,100.00**
Cenedese, aquarium block, 1 fish, 5x6¾" **550.00**
Cenedese, aquarium block, 3 fish, 5x8¼" **600.00**
Cenedese, bowl, purple/clear/bl, 7¼" **800.00**
Cenedese, Sommerso, vase, fish shape w/internal gr decor, 14½" ...**550.00**
Fontana Arte, Cartoccio, handkerchief vase, gr plate glass, 9" ...**715.00**
Fratelli Toso, Murrine, Stellato vase, bl/red/violet/orange, 14½" .**1,900.00**
Fratelli Toso, Murrine, Terrazza vase, bl/wht/violet **6,000.00**
Fratelli Toso, Murrines, Kiku vase, wht/orange/violet, 8½" **8,000.00**
Mazzega, candlesticks, clear w/gr, organic shape, 28", pr **1,245.00**
Salviati, Discus sculpture by Gaspari, lt brn & bl, 6½" **675.00**
Seguso Vetri, Corroso/Sommerso vase by Poli, bl to clear, 10¼" .**5,750.00**
Seguso Vetri, Siderale by Poli, lt gr/tan bull's-eye, 10½" **8,700.00**
Seguso Vetri, Soffiato, vase, bl, bulbous w/2 appl hdls **1,150.00**
Seguso Vetri, Sommerso, bowl, flaring eggplant w/wavy rim, 5x15" .**1,100.00**
Seguso Vetri, Sommerso, deep purple cased in bright red, 20" ..**1,320.00**
Seguso Vetri, Sommerso, vase, clear w/red & purple layers, 12" .**1,650.00**
Seguso Vetri, Sommerso, vase, elliptical, gr cased in clear, 10" ..**1,475.00**
Seguso Vetri, Sommerso, vase, tall/flared, bl & red layers, 14¾" .**1,360.00**
Sottsass, chalice vase, clear red & blk opaque, 8" **1,725.00**
Sottsass, covered pot, clear amber/red/purple, 10½" **1,725.00**
Sottsass, covered pot, clear yel/gr opaque/blk **1,725.00**
Vistosi, Pulcino: Pianon, cubed olive gr bird w/red & bl **1,725.00**
Vistosi, Pulcino: Pianon, J-shaped bird, 12" **1,040.00**
Vistosi, Pulcino: Pianon, orange spherical bird w/appl prunts .**1,100.00**

Ivory

Technically, true ivory is the substance composing the tusk of the elephant; the finest type comes from Africa. However, tusks and teeth of other animals — the walrus, the hippopotamus, and the sperm whale, for instance — are similar in composition and appearance and have also been used for carving. The Chinese have used this substance for centuries, preferring it over bone because of the natural oil contained in its pores, which not only renders it easier to carve but also imparts a soft sheen to the finished product. Aged ivory usually takes on a soft caramel patina, but unscrupulous dealers sometimes treat new ivory to a tea bath to 'antique' it! A bill passed in 1978 reinforced a ban on the importation of whale and walrus ivory. Our advisor for this category is Robert Weisblut; he is listed in the Directory under Florida.

Buddha w/6 children, red & gr stain in details, China, 10½" **635.00**
Candle screen, European, 19th C, 24" **3,200.00**
Carving, George Washington, 4" **400.00**
Cribbage board, 11" **155.00**
Cricket cage, 5" **350.00**
Dance card, ivory & silver **225.00**
Fantasy cvg, fish/crabs/birds/foliage/etc, China, 14"+stand, pr ..**1,600.00**
Figure w/swords, mc pnt & gold, bl stones, China, rpr, 11½" ..**1,550.00**
Fisherman, child & fishing birds, appl color, China, rpr, 10¼" .**1,100.00**
Fisherman w/child, sgn, China, 6¾" **385.00**
Fisherman w/net, gilt traces, China, old rpr, 10½" **1,045.00**
Inkwell, from whale's tooth **195.00**
Knife, paper; cvd monkey/snakes/etc, pearl inlay, 19th C **800.00**
Ruler, folding, 12" **175.00**
Taoist immortals at table, seal script mk, China, 19", EX **2,500.00**
Tusk section, mammoth's, 48" **850.00**
Vase, China, 20th C, 10" **300.00**
3 figures among plants/trees/etc, brn stain, China, 7¾x11"+stand .**440.00**

Jack-in-the-Pulpit Vases

Popular novelties at the turn of the century, jack-in-the-pulpit vases were made in every type of art glass produced. Some were simple, others elaborately appliquéd and enameled. They were shaped to resemble the lily for which they were named.

Bl Dmn Quilt w/HP floral & gold, ruffled rim, 10¾x5" **195.00**
Blown, gr, polished pontil, tall **55.00**
Butterscotch Raindrop MOP, frosted ruffle, brass ft, 7⅜x3" **225.00**
Cranberry w/wht opal edge, appl clear base, Hobbs, 9x5" **325.00**
Dmn Quilt, sapphire bl w/HP florals & gold trim, 10¾x5" **195.00**
Gr opal Hobnail to clear w/cranberry appl at crimped rim, 7" **60.00**
Maroon to cream o/l, crystal petal ft, 6½x5½" **110.00**
Mc spatter w/silver mica, appl crystal rim, Mt WA, 5½x3½" **250.00**
Pk & wht stripes encased in crystal, Stevens & Wms, 15¼" **300.00**
Purple to clear flower, chartreuse body w/rigaree, 11" **80.00**

Japanese Lustreware

Imported from Japan during the 1920s, novelty tableware items, vases, ashtrays, etc. — often in blue, tan, and mother-of-pearl lustre glazes — were sold through five-and-dime stores or given as premiums for selling magazine subscriptions. The Occupied Japan Club is listed in the Directory under Clubs, Newletters, and Catalogs.

Bookends, Oriental boy & girl sitting, mc lustre, 5½", pr **50.00**
Bowl, pagodas in landscape, mc, orange cat hdl, Goldcastle, 7¼" ..**45.00**
Candlestick, floral medallion on tan lustre, Meito, 8¼" **40.00**
Mayonnaise set, bird on tan band on bl, 3-pc set **45.00**
Salt shaker, bird figural, bl lustre **24.00**
Shakers, chicks, tan w/mc details, in 2-shell bl tray **25.00**
Tea set, pot+cr/sug+4 c/s, child sz **225.00**
Teapot, mc geometrics, 6-sided, 7¾", on bl lustre tile **55.00**
Vase, flower on yel lustre, flared rim, blk mk, 7" **50.00**

Jervis

W.P. Jervis began his career as a potter in 1898. By 1908 he had his own pottery in Oyster Bay, New York. His shapes were graceful; often he decorated his wares with sgraffito designs over which he applied a matt glaze. Many piece were incised 'Jervis' in a vertical arrangement. The pottery closed around 1912.

Pitcher, stylized iris panels, mc w/red clay showing, 4⅛", NM **750.00**
Vase, bronze & copper metallic, stick neck, 5" **320.00**
Wall pocket, calla lilies, wht/gr/dk bl, mk, 6½x6", EX **600.00**

Jewelry

Jewelry as objects of adornment has always been regarded with special affection. Today prices for gems and gemstones crafted into antique and collectible jewelry are based on artistic merit, personal appeal, pure sentimentality, and intrinsic value. Note: In general, diamond prices have gone up more than 20% in the past year, and platinum is becoming popular again, so retail prices are rising. Diamond prices vary greatly depending on cut, color, clarity, etc., and to assess the value of any diamond of more than a carat in weight, you will need to have information about all of these factors. Values given here are for diamond jewelry with a standard commercial grade of diamonds that are most likely to be encountered.

Our advisor for fine jewelry is Rebecca Dodds; her address may be found in the Directory under Florida. If you are interested in collecting or dealing in jewelry, you will find that authority Lillian Baker has several fine books available on the subject — *100 Years of Collectible Jewelry: 1850 – 1950; Art Nouveau and Art Deco Jewelry;* and *Fifty Years of Collectible Fashion Jewelry: 1925 – 1975*. These books are complete with beautiful full-color illustrations and current market values. Other fine sources of information are *Collectible Costume Jewelry* by Cherri Simonds and *Costume Jewelry, a Practical Handbook & Value Guide*, by Fred Rezazadeh (all available from Collector Books). See also Plastics.

Key:
cab — cabochon
ct — carat
dmn — diamond
dwt — penny weight
Euro — European cut
fl — filigree
gf — gold filled
gp — gold plated
grad — graduated
gw — gold washed
k — karat
plat — platinum
r/stn — rhinestone
stn — stone
wg — white gold
yg — yellow gold
ygf — yellow gold filled

Brooch, 14k white gold, three .38 carat diamonds, eighty-eight graduated round diamonds, twenty-four calibre-cut sapphires, Art Deco styling, $2,000.00.

Bar pin, 10k yg arrow w/arrowhead, 7 seed pearls, 2" **45.00**
Bar pin, 10k yg fl, 3 lg garnets, 2½" **215.00**
Belt buckle, Art Nouveau, cut steel butterfly, Fr, ca 1905 ....**45.00**
Bracelet, bangle; 14k yg, eng, hexagonal **375.00**
Bracelet, bangle; 14k yg, flower & leaf emb, ⅜" W **245.00**
Bracelet, charm; 14k yg, 3 gold coins, 4 charms **500.00**
Bracelet, cultured pearls, 3-strand, 87 5.5 mm, 7½" **275.00**
Bracelet, G Jensen, 6 bird-emb ovals, beaded links, 7" **325.00**
Bracelet, pearl, 6mm, 3-strand w/dmn separators, wg clasp **850.00**
Bracelet, plat w/center mtd .35ct dmn+24 tw 2.5ct **4,500.00**
Bracelet, sm brass sea horses on red Bakelite, brass links, France .**150.00**
Bracelet, 14k pk gold, Deco style, 1¼" W, 37dwt **895.00**
Bracelet, 14k wg fl, 6" **225.00**
Bracelet, 14k yg, 2ct tw dmns, 1.5ct tw emeralds **4,750.00**
Bracelet, 14k yg w/enameled charm, 30.7 grams, 8" L **330.00**
Brooch/pendant, cameo, shell, gf rope twist bezel, 1⅝x1⅛" **150.00**
Brooch/pendant, cameo, shell, lady's profile, gold bezel, 1⅝" **450.00**
Brooch/pendant, cameo, wg fl, 1¼x1" **350.00**
Brooch/pin, cameo, carnelian, profile, 14k yg bezel, 1⅛x1" **475.00**
Brooch/pin, G Jensen, silver openwork leaf mt w/7 coral cabs **475.00**
Brooch/pin, Gorham, silver dragonfly, 2½x2½" **175.00**
Brooch/pin, Kalo, lily-of-valley design, brushed silver, #206, 4" .**300.00**
Brooch/pin, onyx w/floral millefiori design in gold fr **350.00**
Brooch/pin, 10k yg, pearls & ornate enamel, chatelaine type **140.00**
Brooch/pin, 14k yg, openwork w/hearts, lg oval citrine, 1½" **350.00**
Brooch/pin, 14k yg w/openwork shell w/7.5mm cultured pearl, 1" **195.00**
Charm, 18k yg gondola, pk stone & quartz **85.00**
Charm, 18k yg horseshoe w/coral & turq stones **90.00**
Charm, 18k yg rtcl fish, gr stone eyes **85.00**
Cuff links, Kalo, geometrics on sterling **140.00**
Earrings, Kalo, flower form, screw bks, pr **150.00**
Earrings, plat sunburst w/23 dmn tw 2.5ct **2,900.00**
Earrings, 14k wg w/.25 tw dmns & sapphires, dangling, 1940s **500.00**
Earrings, 14k wg w/.70ct tw dmns, swirl & leaf shape, pr **1,500.00**
Earrings, 14k yg oak leaves, pierced, 1940s **250.00**
Hair comb, tortoise w/gold pique stud work, 1870s, 6x2¾" **275.00**
Lavaliere, 10kt 2-color gold w/pearl, Edwardian **150.00**
Lavaliere, 14k yg, .12ct emerald **165.00**
Lavaliere, 14k yg w/pearls **135.00**
Locket, ygf, Egyptian princess & snake relief, 1¼" **50.00**
Locket, 14k rose gold w/enamel accents, 1860s **140.00**
Necklace, amethyst grad beads, 3-strand, 14k free-form clasp **475.00**
Necklace, amethyst grad 8-14mm beads, 3-strand, amethyst clasp ..**650.00**
Necklace, Arts & Crafts, clear stone w/3 sm drops, silver chain .**250.00**
Necklace, cameo, shell, lady w/sm dmn, 2¼x⅞", on wg chain ...**300.00**
Necklace, cultured pearls, 1-strand, 48 7.5mm, yg clasp, 15" **440.00**
Necklace, cultured pearls, 1-strand, 52 6-6.5mm, silver clasp, 15" .**165.00**
Necklace, cultured pearls, 1-strand, 96 3-7.5 mm, 18" **250.00**
Necklace, cultured pearls, 1-strand, 98 7mm, wg clasp, 30" **935.00**
Necklace, cultured pearls, 2-strand, 20 5-5.5mm, wg clasp, 15" ..**250.00**
Necklace, freshwater pearl choker w/14k spacers, 16" **60.00**
Necklace, frosted amethyst 8mm beads, hand knotted, 34" **60.00**
Necklace, ivory beads, 11mm, 40" **95.00**
Necklace, Kalo (att), cherries/leaves, silver links, 15" **160.00**
Necklace, Venetian beads w/embedded foils/roses/etc, 28" **110.00**
Necklace, 14k yg links join coral beads, delicate **125.00**
Necklace, 18k yg, hollow beads on 16" chain **265.00**
Pendant, cameo, shell, lady's profile, gold bezel, ⅞x⅝" **125.00**
Pendant, gutta percha w/blk cameo **55.00**
Pendant, 14k wg fl cross w/4 dmns, 1" **250.00**
Pendant, 14k yg w/hanging garnet balls, Victorian **250.00**
Pendant, 14k yg w/lg amethyst flower, Victorian **125.00**
Pendant, 14k yg w/onyx & enameling, Victorian **120.00**
Pendant, 18k yg, lady in relief, floral border, dtd 1901 ....**485.00**

Pendant, 18k yg w/lg fct amethyst, Victorian **225.00**
Ring, man's, heavy gold, eng initials **65.00**
Ring, man's, 14k yg w/3.50ct brilliant cut H-I dmn **22,000.00**
Ring, Peter Lindeman, 14k yg, 3-D fox w/emerald eyes **485.00**
Ring, plat, .25ct dmn, sm dmns at sides, ca 1935 ....**375.00**
Ring, plat w/.80 brilliant cut G color dmns w/4 sm side dmns **1,750.00**
Ring, plat w/.85ct dmn amid 12 sm dmns **2,500.00**
Ring, plat w/14 .02ct single cut dmns **220.00**
Ring, wedding band; 14k wg w/5 dmns tw .80 ....**200.00**
Ring, wg fl w/2 emerald-cut aquamarines, 1920s **250.00**
Ring, yg w/.63ct K color solitaire brilliant cut dmn **600.00**
Ring, yg w/.75 brilliant cut solitaire H color dmn **1,250.00**
Ring, yg w/lg oval amethyst w/sm emeralds **95.00**
Ring, yg w/11x7.5mm emerald cut emerald & 22 .06ct dmns ..**4,400.00**
Ring, 10k wg leaf shape w/1 .12ct dmn & 12 .0075 melee dmns ..**125.00**
Ring, 10k wg w/onyx & sm dmn **50.00**
Ring, 10k yg fl w/sm ruby **145.00**
Ring, 10k yg w/classical cameo in fl mt **250.00**
Ring, 14k rose gold, pearl amid bl turq on wide emb band **95.00**
Ring, 14k wg fl, carnelian cameo of warrior **115.00**
Ring, 14k wg fl w/lg amethyst **75.00**
Ring, 14k wg fl w/5 .10ct dmns in 1" L mt **650.00**
Ring, 14k wg w/.04ct full cut dmn & 2 .01ct & 14 .0075ct dmns .**110.00**
Ring, 14k wg w/cultured pearl & 2 sm dmns **95.00**
Ring, 14k wg w/3ct tw dmn ballerina w/center sapphire **2,500.00**
Ring, 14k yg w/ marquise aquamarine, lg fl mt **195.00**
Ring, 14k yg w/angel-skin coral stone (lg) **300.00**
Ring, 14k yg w/center opal amid 6 .20 tw sapphires **400.00**
Ring, 14k yg w/garnet cluster **70.00**
Ring, 14k yg w/lava cameo **350.00**
Ring, 14k yg w/lg center opal w/dmns tw .9cts **625.00**
Ring, 14k yg w/.45ct I color dmn & pr tiny melee dmns **1,200.00**
Ring, 14k yg w/6x8mm oval emerald, modern **275.00**
Ring, 14k yg w/7 lg fct garnets set in flower form, Victorian **275.00**
Ring, 18k wg fl, .45ct center dmn, 4 sm sapphires, 2 side dmns ..**1,100.00**
Ring, 18k wg w/.75ct dmn+.60ct dmn+6 sm dmns **2,200.00**
Ring, 18k yg, pearl encircled by 18 brilliant cut rubies **500.00**
Stickpin, 14k yg/plat, Euro .94ct dmn in 8-sided fl mt **2,500.00**
Tie bar, cultured pearls, 4 4.5mm on 14k gold bar, 2" **45.00**
Tie pin, 14k wg fl w/2 sm dmns **80.00**

Costume Jewelry

Rhinestone jewelry has become a very popular field of collecting. Copyrighting jewelry came into effect in 1955. Pieces bearing a copyright mark (post-1955) are considered 'collectibles,' while pieces (with no copyright) made before then are regarded as 'antiques.' Rhinestones are foil-backed leaded crystal stones with a sparkle outshining diamonds. Look for signed and well made, unmarked pieces for your collections and preserve this American art form. Our advisor for costume jewelry is Marcia Brown; she is listed in the Directory under Oregon.

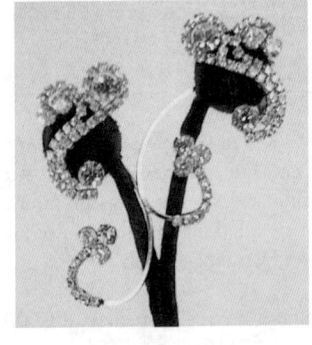

Earrings, unmarked, rhinestones, clip to fasten above ear or completely detach, $80.00.

Belt, celluloid rings w/metal spacers, Deco style, 50" **60.00**
Bracelet, Bakelite bangle, apple juice w/yel r/stns **45.00**
Bracelet, Bakelite bangle, caramel, deep ribs, 1" W **70.00**
Bracelet, Bakelite child's bangle, cvd/cut, 1" W **30.00**
Bracelet, N Rosenstein, gp w/lg r/stns & gp spheres **100.00**
Bracelet, Weiss, Aurora Borealis (3 rows) +cluster earrings **275.00**
Brooch, Alice Caviness, gr & bl pronged stns, 2¼" **85.00**
Brooch, Boucher, cultured pearl/wht r/stns on gp flower form **65.00**
Brooch, Boucher, red-stone pot, clear rim, gold-tone flames, 2"..**75.00**
Brooch, cvd wooden Scotty w/glass eyes **35.00**
Brooch, Danecraft, sterling repousse leaf form, 1940s **55.00**
Brooch, Emmons, gold-tone scarecrow w/faux pearl head, tassel limbs .**35.00**
Brooch, Hattie Carnegie, giraffe running, r/stns on gold-tone **75.00**
Brooch, Judy Lee, starburst w/blk dmn/topaz r/stns, +earrings **30.00**
Brooch, Kramer, gr stns, stacked, 1½x2" **95.00**
Brooch, Lea Stein Paris, celluoid vintage car w/long hood **85.00**
Brooch, Leo Glass, 18 lg purple stones (3 dangle), 1930s **95.00**
Brooch, Miriam Haskell, peacock, bl & gr stones on gold-tone ..**175.00**
Brooch, Orig by Robert, gold-tone Xmas tree w/mc stones **115.00**
Brooch, Pell, turtle, clear stones, bl oval turq on bk, gold-tone **55.00**
Brooch, pk compo leaves w/pk r/stns on silver-tone, 2½" **12.00**
Brooch, Recency, butterfly, bl-gr irid pronged stns, 2" **85.00**
Brooch, Sterling, elephant form, Victorian, 1¼" **32.00**
Brooch, Trifari, gold-tone flower & leaf w/wht cabs, 2" **200.00**
Brooch, Trifari, sterling crown, lg **185.00**
Brooch, Weiss, apple form, blk metal w/red r/stns **75.00**
Brooch, Weiss, mc stns & looped gold-tone wire, 2" dia **55.00**
Brooch, Weiss, poinsettia form, red/gr on gold-tone, +earrings **85.00**
Brooch, Weiss, 3-D wreath w/red berries/gr leaves on gold-tone ...**95.00**
Earrings, Bijoux Cascio, draped rope in brushed gold-tone, 1¼" ..**15.00**
Earrings, Eisenberg, r/stn & rhodium drops, 1950s **85.00**
Earrings, Karu Arke, 3 lg clear r/stns ea, clip bks **10.00**
Earrings, Lerue, floral design w/pastel enamel & r/stns, 2" **17.50**
Earrings, Mazer, r/stns/baguettes on gold-tone drop+pearl drop **35.00**
Earrings, Renoir, copper Art Modern geometric design, 1950s **45.00**
Earrings, Weiss, r/stns w/faux turq drops, clips, 1950s **65.00**
Fur clip, Bakelite, apple juice pineapple scoring, thick, 2½" **55.00**
Fur clip, Bakelite, grasshopper, apple-juice body w/r/stns **250.00**
Necklace, blk fct Bohemian glass woven in bib design, Victorian ..**40.00**
Necklace, Emmons, rhodium cross w/plastic turq/cultured pearls, 24" ..**55.00**
Necklace, Jewelart, choker, roses & leaves, 1930s **60.00**
Necklace, Miriam Haskell, amber beads, 6-strand **175.00**
Necklace, Miriam Haskell, pearl, 2-strand w/rondells **225.00**
Pin, see Brooch
Ring, Eisenberg, sapphire bl r/stns on silver-tone **115.00**
Ring, Miriam Haskell, adjustable, seed pearl cluster **145.00**

Josef Originals

Figurines of lovely ladies, charming girls, and whimsical animals marked Josef Originals were designed by Muriel Joseph George of Arcadia, California, from 1945 to 1985. Until 1960 they were produced in California, but costs were high and copies of her work were being made in Japan. To remain competitive, she and her partner, George Good, contracted with the Katayama Company in Japan to build a factory to produce her designs to her approval. Muriel retired in 1982; however, George Good continued production of her work as well as new ones of his staff's creation. The company was sold in late 1985; the name is currently owned by Applause, and a limited amount of figurines bear the name. Those made during the ownership of Muriel George are the most collectible. They can be recognized by these characteristics: The girls have a high-gloss finish, black eyes, and most are signed. Brown eyes date from 1982 to 85. Applause uses a red-brown eye. The animals were mainly done in a matt finish and have labels. Later ani-

mals have a flocked coat. Prices are given for figurines in perfect condition only. Our advisors, Jim and Kaye Whitaker, are the authors of two books: *Josef Originals, Charming Figurines,* and *Josef Originals, A Second Look.* They are listed in the Directory under Washington.

Angels at various sports, Sports Angels series, Japan, 2¾", ea **35.00**
Birthstone dolls, March Aquamarine & April Dmn, Japan, 3½", ea ..**25.00**
Boxer Dog, Champions series, Japan, 5" **22.00**
Buggy Bugs series, various poses, wire antenna, Japan, 3¼", ea **12.00**
Bunny jumping rope, Bunny Hutch series, Japan, 4" **18.00**
Christmas angel praying by decorated tree night light, 7" **65.00**
Dalmatian, Kennel Club series, Japan, 3½" **18.00**
Elephant, sitting, Japan, 3¾" **20.00**
England, Small World series, brn eyes, w/umbrella, Japan, 4½" **40.00**
Farmers Daughter, girl w/hen & basket of eggs, Japan, 5" **50.00**
First Date, young lady in gr holding fan, Japan, 9" **115.00**
Happiness Is - Mud Pies, girl making mud pies, Japan, 5¼" **45.00**
Hunter, horse standing (beautiful), Japan, 6" **25.00**
It's a Wonderful World series figurines, Japan, 3½", ea **35.00**

Jeanne, Colonial Days series, Japan, 9", $135.00.

Photo courtesy Jim and Kaye Whitaker

Lara's Theme music box, Japan, 6" **85.00**
Love Letter From Love Story, Romance series, Japan, 8" **125.00**
Mary Ann & Mama, California, 4" & 7", pr **145.00**
Melody, Sweet Memories series, lady by Victrola, Japan, 6½" **95.00**
Mice, Christmas, Japan, 2¾", ea **12.00**
Missy, girl in bonnet, several colors, California, 4", ea **45.00**
Monkey dressed as doctor, Japan, 3" **15.00**
Nanette, half doll w/jewels, several colors, California, 5½", ea **65.00**
New Home, Special Occasions series, girl w/key, Japan, 4½" **40.00**
Nurse, Career Girls series, nurse in yel w/baby, Japan, 5¾" **60.00**
Pixie, Christmas Helper, painting toy, Japan, 4¾" **35.00**
Pixies, gr w/red & gold trim, various poses, Japan, 2-3¼", ea **30.00**
Poodle Family, Japan, mini, 3 in set, 1¼-2¼" **15.00**
Puerto Rico, Little International, Japan, 4" **45.00**
Rose, Flower Girl series, girl w/flower hat, Japan, 4¼" **40.00**
Rose Garden series, brn eyes, 6 different, Japan, 5¼", ea **65.00**
Ruby, Little Jewels series, girl w/'ruby' in crown, Japan, 3½" **35.00**
Santa, kiss on forehead, Japan, 4¾" **60.00**
Secret Pal, girl w/fan, various colors, California, 3½" **40.00**
Skunk w/perfume atomizer, Japan, 2½" **18.00**
Warm Hello, Thinking of You series, girl on phone, Japan, 5" **50.00**
Wee Ching & Wee Ling, Chinese children w/dog & cat (copied) ..**75.00**
Wee Folk, various poses, Japan, 4½", ea **20.00**
Wee Three, cats in basket, California, 3" **50.00**
3 Coins in Fountain music box, girl by fountain, Japan, 6¼" **95.00**

Judaica

The items listed below are representative of objects used in both the secular and religious life of the Jewish people. They are evident of a culture where silversmiths, painters, engravers, writers, and metal workers were highly gifted and skilled in their art. Most of the treasures shown in recently displayed exhibits of Judaica were confiscated by the Germans during the late 1930s up to 1945; by then eight Jewish synagogues and fifty warehouses had been filled with Hitler's plunder. Judaica is currently available through dealers, from private collections, and the annual auction held in Israel.

Beaker, wine; Polish silver, chased overall, 19th C, 3¼" **1,800.00**
Challah tray, Austro-Hungarian silver, bread/verse, 1900, 20" ..**1,600.00**
Charity box, Am pewter, tankard form, ca 1900, 4½" **1,500.00**
Charity box, Hungarian silver/wood, synagogue form, 1867, 11" ..**6,000.00**
Charity box, Polish silver, synagogue form, 1868, 5⅝" **3,750.00**
Dowry box, brass & silver, appl bride/groom, M Ende, 1980s, 5⅞" ...**2,200.00**
Etrog container, Continental silver, emb vintage, 1950s, 6½" ...**750.00**
Etrog container, Hungarian silver, oval, florals/doves, 1823, 7" ..**1,300.00**
Etrog container, Hungarian silver, rose clusters, 1890s, 4½" **550.00**
Etrog container, Russian silver, citron form, 1874, 8¼" **2,800.00**
Goblet, German silver, Star of David/etc, 20th C, 6⅜" **500.00**
Goblet, wine; German silver, gilt int, ca 1900, 4⅞" **650.00**
Hannukah lamp, Bohemian pewter, cartouch-form bk plate, 1790s, 8" **750.00**
Hannukah lamp, Dutch copper, punchwork flowers, ca 1860s, 10½" ..**700.00**
Hannukah lamp, E European brass, 8 crowned lions, 1900s, 9⅜" ...**500.00**
Hannukah lamp, German silver, chased roses, 19th C, 11⅜" ...**1,200.00**
Hannukah lamp, German silver, tree-of-life form, 19th C, 10½" .**2,500.00**
Hannukah lamp, Moroccan brass, flowers/birds, late 18th C, 17" ...**650.00**
Hannukah lamp, N African brass, scrolling foliage, 19th C, 9" ..**450.00**
Hannukah lamp, Persian silver, foliate design, 19th C, 10" **1,200.00**
Hannukah lamp, Polish silver, temple style, late 19th C, 23½" ..**700.00**
Hannukah lamp, SP by Shlomo Ohana, architectural, 1930s, 11" ..**700.00**
Havdallah compendium, English Art Deco silver, 1920s, 9¾" **1,000.00**
Havdallah compendium, German silver, late 18th C, 8¼" **4,500.00**
Kiddush beaker, German silver, inscribed, ftd, 1766, 4⅛" **6,000.00**
Kiddush cup, silver, emb fishscale, German, 1770, 2⅞" **1,500.00**
Marriage cup, Austro-Hungarian silver, bbl form, 1880s, 5", pr ..**800.00**
Mezuzzah case, Am silver, Ilya Dschor, NY, 1958, 4¾" **2,000.00**
Passover cup, Germanic-style silver, 20th C, 2¾" **500.00**
Passover Seder compendium, Israel silver, 1940s, 4⅜x10" **1,900.00**
Passover Seder compendium, Palestine wood, tiered, 20th C, 14" ..**1,300.00**
Passover Seder plate, Continental ceramic, late 19th C, 12" **400.00**
Passover Seder tray, Hungarian silver, late 19th c, 20½" **8,000.00**
Purim noisemaker, silver-gilt, M Ende, Jerusalem, 1980s, 6½" ..**2,000.00**
Sabbath candlesticks, German silver, emb floral/lions/etc, 13", pr ..**1,200.00**
Sabbath candlesticks, Polish silver, classic style, 1830s, 9⅜", pr ..**1,800.00**
Sabbath lamp, German brass, star-form oil section, 1800s, 17" ...**600.00**
Spice container, Continental silver, bird form, ca 1800, 7" **700.00**
Spice container, Continental silver, bird form, 20th C, 8" **650.00**
Spice container, Continental silver, fruit form, 19th C, 6¼" **700.00**
Spice container, Dutch silver, fish form, ca 1900, 9¼" **475.00**
Spice container, Polish silver, bird form, 19th C, 5" **1,000.00**
Spice container, Polish silver, dolphin supports, 19th C, 3⅝" **850.00**
Spice container, Russian silver/filigree, locomotive, 1890s, 2⅝" ..**800.00**
Spice tower, Dutch silver, fish form, overall scales, 19th C, 9¼" .**475.00**
Spice tower, German silver, flowers/scrolls, ca 1880s, 8¼" **950.00**
Spice tower, Palestine olivewood, cvd scenes, 1890s, 6¾" **1,000.00**
Spice tower, Polish silver, pierced steeple/pennant, 1880, 9½" ..**1,000.00**
Spice tower, Russian silver, 4 eagles/bells, 1887, 9¾", VG **425.00**
Spice tower, Russian silver & filigree, 5 eagles, 1889, 12" **1,200.00**
Spice tower, silver filigree, Bezalel Jerusalem, ca 1900, 7" **2,100.00**
Spice tower, Spanish silver, pierced/fitted door, ca 1890s, 9" **900.00**
Torah Ark curtain, Calcutta, mc on velvet, 1918, 89x55½" **600.00**
Torah breastplate, Austrian silver, scrolled floral, 1900, 10" ...**1,000.00**
Torah crown, Austria-Hungarian silver w/paste stones, 1880s ..**2,100.00**

Torah crown, Polish silver, emb florals/bells, ca 1900, 13½" **900.00**
Torah crown, Russian silver, w/bells, bird finial, 1882, 16" **2,600.00**
Torah finials, Austro-Hungarian silver, eagle form, 1890s, 12", pr ..**850.00**
Torah finials, Ringnalda silver, 2-tier, 1770s, 17", pr **29,000.00**
Torah pointer, Austrian silver, emb acanthus leaves, 19th C, 11" ..**600.00**
Torah pointer, Austro-Hungarian silver, chased, 1860s, 10½" ..**1,600.00**
Torah pointer, Continental silver, Star of David knop, 19th C, 12" ..**1,300.00**
Torah pointer, cvd ivory, eng star/inscription, 1900s, 15" **900.00**
Torah pointer, European silver filigree, ca 1900, 9¼" **450.00**
Torah pointer, Polish silver, narrow w/spiral middle, 1800s, 7¼" ...**350.00**
Torah pointer, Russian silver & filigree, mk AK, 1885, 10" **900.00**

Jugtown

The Jugtown Pottery was started about 1920 by Juliana and Jacques Busbee, in Moore County, North Carolina. Ben Owen, a young descendant of a Staffordshire potter, was hired in 1923. He was the master potter, while the Busbees experimented with perfecting glazes and supervising design and modeling. Preferred shapes were those reminiscent of traditional country wares and classic Oriental forms. Glazes were various: natural-clay oranges, buffs, 'tobacco-spit' brown, mirror black, white, 'frog-skin' green, a lovely turquoise called Chinese blue, and the traditional cobalt-decorated salt glaze. The pottery gained national recognition, and as a result of their success, several other local potteries were established. Jugtown is still in operation; however, they no longer use their original glaze colors which are now so collectible.

Bowl, Chinese bl, yel & gr crystalline specks inside, 3½x9" **500.00**
Bowl, Chinese bl, 1⅞x4⅜" **225.00**
Bowl, Chinese bl (bl/red/blk), salt glaze ft, 5x5¼" **850.00**
Bowl, Korean, turq w/red, gray salt glaze ft, mk, 3¼x9¼" **750.00**
Covered dish, chicken on nest, cinnamon, C Moore, 1983, 6¾" .**100.00**
Jar, frogskin, w/lid, 6" **120.00**
Jar, red lustre w/Albany slip int, 2-hdld, mk, 1940s, 6¼" **950.00**

Vase, Chinese blue with strong copper red reduction, small handles, attributed to Ben Owen, ca 1920s to early 1930s, 10", $1,700.00.

Jug, frogskin, 6" **175.00**
Vase, Chinese bl (gr/rose/tan/bl), gourd form, mk, 4" **650.00**
Vase, Chinese bl w/multi-reds, mk, 4" **290.00**
Vase, Chinese bl w/some red spots, EX glaze & color, mk, 5" **950.00**
Vase, Chinese red w/bl, 5x7" **525.00**
Vase, Chinese red w/bl & turq splotches, mk, 6" **950.00**
Vase, gr & wht gloss, mk, 5½x7" **230.00**
Vase, Ku, Chinese Translation (red/wht/turq), mk, 3⅝" **700.00**
Vase, oatmeal glossy, pinched/flared rim, 2 sm hdls, 7¾x5¼" **275.00**
Vase, thick wht, 4-hdld, 7" **325.00**
Vase, thick wht gloss, mk, 4x5" **150.00**
Vase, thick wht gloss, shouldered, mk, 7" **250.00**

K. P. M. Porcelain

The original KPM wares were produced from 1823 until 1847 by the Konigliche Porzellan Manfaktur, located in Berlin, Germany. Meissen used the same letters on some of their porcelains, as did several others in the area. In addition to the initials, the mark sometimes contains a crowned eagle with a scepter. Watch for items currently being imported from China; they are marked KPM with the eagle, but the scepter is not present. Our advisor for this category is Don Williams; he is listed in the Directory under Missouri.

Bowl, centerpc; HP florals w/gold (worn), hdls, 6½x14x11" 350.00
Bowl, roses, pk on wht, 4 crimped corners, 3½x8⅞" 375.00
Coffee set, wht w/gold, sceptre mk, 9½" pot+cr/sug 275.00
Cup, opera scene appl to side, w/lid, 19th C, 3¾" 100.00
Figurine, nobleman w/bouquet beside tree, 1720-30, 8¾" 800.00
Lobster dish, dbl shell, pk lustre 150.00

Plaque, Koningin Louise (Queen Louise), R. Dittrich, late 19th century, 13x8", in pierced giltwood 22¼x17½" frame, $7,500.00.

Plaque, after Rapheal's Sistine Madonna, 10x12" 3,000.00
Plaque, Biblical lady w/twin babies, sgn, gold fr, 14x18" 3,000.00
Plaque, Cupid in rose bed w/20 songbirds, gesso fr, 6x9" 5,000.00
Plaque, lady wearing pearls, gilt oval fr, 14½x18" 6,500.00
Plaque, Mid-Eastern lady w/much jewelry, mk, fr, 16x13" 8,500.00
Plaque, sorrowful Magdalene facing heaven, mk, 10½x8½" 3,750.00
Plaque, 20 people outside, wooded mtn beyond, mk, 7½x9⅞" ...4,500.00
Plates, berry or melon center, gold serpentine rim, pr 240.00
Urn, Neoclassical swags on wht, w/lid, late 19th C, 10", pr 700.00

Kayserzinn Pewter

J.P. Kayser Sohn produced pewter decorated with relief-molded Art Nouveau motifs in Germany during the late 1800s and into the 20th century. Examples are marked with 'Kayserzinn' and the mold number within an elongated oval reserve. Items with three-dimensional animals, insects, birds, etc., are valued much higher than bowls, plates, and trays with simple embossed florals, which are usually priced at $100.00 to about $200.00, depending on size.

Bell, cat finial, #4610, 5⅝" 75.00
Bonbon, shell form w/Nouveau nude, sgn/#4136, 8x6¾" 195.00
Candelabrum, 2-arm, T-form std, #4531, 10½" 1,225.00
Egg dish, ftd sq base tray, dome lid, emb design, 10" W 300.00
Gravy boat, floral, #4124 ....95.00
Pitcher, molded irises & face, angular hdl, 12½" 500.00
Platter, floral, #4122, 13" 115.00
Vase, emb vintage, #49, 12" 245.00

Keeler, Brad

Keeler studied art for a time in the 1930s; later he became a modeler for a Los Angeles firm. By 1939 he was working in his own studio where he created naturalistic studies of birds and animals which were marketed through giftware stores. They were decorated by means of an airbrush and enhanced with hand-painted details. His flamingo figures were particularly popular. In the mid-'40s, he developed a successful line of Chinese Modern housewares glazed in Ming Dragon Blood, a red color he personally developed. Keeler died of a heart attack in 1952, and the pottery closed soon thereafter. For more information, we recommend *The Collector's Encyclopedia of California Pottery,* Second Edition, by Jack Chipman.

Bowl, serving; tomato, 12" 50.00
Figurine, canary, male 50.00
Figurine, cat, recumbent, #773, 8" 65.00
Figurine, cockatoo, 6" 75.00
Figurine, fantasy bird, #45 ....155.00
Figurine, Siamese cat, paper label, 9x7" 75.00
Pitcher, fish figural, 8¼" 70.00
Planter, flamingo, #819 ....100.00
Relish, lobster form, divided, #871 ....85.00
Sauce boat w/lid & ladle 70.00
Tray, lobster hdls, 5-part, 17" 100.00
Tray, red pepper in lettuce, 14" 60.00

Keen Kutter

Keen Kutter was the brand name chosen in 1870 by the Simmons Firm for a line of high-grade tools and cutlery. The trademark was first applied to high-grade axes. A corporation was formed in 1874 called Simmons Hardware Company. In 1923 Winchester merged with Simmons and continued to carry a full line of hardware plus the Winchester brand. The merger dissolved, and on July 1, 1940, the Simmons Company was purchased by Shapleigh Hardware Company. All Simmons Hardware Co. trademark lines were continued, and the business operated successfully until its closing in 1962. Today the Keen Kutter logo is owned by the Val-Test Company of Chicago, Illinois. For further study we recommend *Keen Kutter Collectibles,* an illustrated price guide by our advisors for this category, Jerry and Elaine Heuring, available at your favorite bookstore or public library. The Heurings are listed in the Directory under Missouri. See also Knives.

Adz, ship carpenter's; KPS4 ....75.00
Ax, Michigan pattern w/octagon hdl & rnd head, KMA1 ....30.00
Bits, stock drill; K16, 9 bits in orig container 150.00
Brace, K18, 18" sweep 25.00
Brace, ratchet; hand-held 120.00
Butcher knife holder, cb bull stand-up, easel type 1,250.00
Calender, boy fishing, Herron Hardware, 1953 ....150.00
Calender, Lake of the West, 1957 ....150.00
Calender, tin, pad type w/store name & location 100.00
Chisel, socket corner; ¾"-⅞" 40.00
Clippers, horse; L940 ....35.00
Clock, rnd, plastic, yel, wht & red, logo on face, 10" 300.00
Dandelion weeder 40.00
Drill, post; K1902 ....225.00
Fan, fold-up, hand-held, logo on 1 side, floral on other 275.00
Flashlight, D-sz batteries 75.00
Flint paper, KF2 ....25.00
Floral rake, KR8 ....35.00

Food chopper, K23 ....**15.00**
Garden pick, #5 ....**30.00**
Gas cans, 2½-gal capacity, mk w/logo **25.00**
Gauge, marking/mortise; metal bar, dbl-ended, K45 ....**90.00**
Grinder, cornmeal; CI **120.00**
Grinder, meat; sliding base w/thumb screw, family sz, K112 ....**45.00**
Grinder, sickle & tool **65.00**
Grinder, tool; hand powered, mk **75.00**
Hammer, bill posters; K55, 5-oz **50.00**
Handle, plane; replacement **20.00**
Hatchet, flooring; w/nail slot **35.00**
Hay fork, KB304½ **40.00**
Ice shaver, K33 ....**100.00**
Invoice w/window envelope, dtd 1931/1932 ....**30.00**
Knife, bread; K334, 10" blade **20.00**
Knife, cook's; K10, 8" **20.00**
Knife, mincing; dbl-bladed **25.00**
Knife, putty; K75 ....**15.00**
Kraut cutter **75.00**
Letter opener, knife blade w/leather cover **165.00**
Level, adjustable, brass top plate, brass-bound, KK50, 26" **150.00**
Level, nonadjustable, F3-755GK, 28" **45.00**
Mortar hoe, KPM10 ....**30.00**

Padlock, EC Simmons on hasp, brass, 3¾", with original key, **$175.00.**

Pipe cutter, K2, 3-wheel pattern, ¼"-2" capacity **85.00**
Plane, iron block; adjustable knuckle joint, KK18, 6" **65.00**
Plane, iron block; K9½, 6", in orig box **150.00**
Plane, scrub; K240, 9½" **125.00**
Pliers, channel lock; K57 ....**75.00**
Pliers, combination; K160 ....**22.50**
Pliers, combination/pipe wrench; 75 degree angle head, K750 .....**85.00**
Pliers, fence; w/staple puller, K1946, 2⅝" head **35.00**
Punch, revolving, 4-tube, #4, #6, #8 & #10, K44 ....**45.00**
Rasps, wood; ½-rnd, ea from $7 to **12.00**
Razor strap, cushion comb, K50 ....**100.00**
Reamer, K126 ....**30.00**
Rule, folding; boxwood, 4-fold, ½-bound, K840, 24" **60.00**
Safety razor, jr sz, w/metal hdl, in orig box **35.00**
Saw, butcher; K15, 20" blade **40.00**
Saw, crosscut; 1-man, w/emblem on blade, #309 ....**185.00**
Saw, flooring; adjustable **210.00**
Saw, hack; nonadjustable, K188 ....**45.00**
Saw, K88, 20" **55.00**
Saw set, K10, w/Keen Kutter written on **20.00**
Scissors, S128AK, in orig box **75.00**
Screwdriver, brass ferrules, K40, 5" blade **30.00**
Shears, hedge; KS8½ **20.00**
Ship auger car bit, K12, ¾" **12.00**

Shipping tape, roll **100.00**
Showcase, etched logos, floor model, 96" **1,000.00**
Spark plug, made by Val-Test...Chicago, for K17M power mower ..**90.00**
Speed indicator, K40 ....**85.00**
Square, sliding T-bevel, wood hdls, logo on blades, 6" **45.00**
Square, tri; CI hdl, 10" blade **30.00**
Table cutlery, SP, knives & forks, 6 ea, in orig box **80.00**
Tack claw, K5 ....**20.00**
Tape measure, EC Simmons written on tape, K73 ....**90.00**
Tobacco cutter, base mk EC Simmons **375.00**
Vise, KM400, 4" jaws **225.00**
Vise, pipe; KP200, ⅛"-2" capacity, 9¼" H **150.00**
Waffle iron, CI, Keen Kutter logo on 7¼" waffle **175.00**
Weed cutter, KWCS-K **40.00**
Wire gauge **200.00**
Wrench, alligator; dbl-ended, #80, 10" **150.00**
Wrench, automobile; K96, pry end **80.00**
Yardsticks, advertising hardwares, ea **30.00**

Kellogg Studio

Stanley Kellogg (1908 – 1972) opened the Kellogg Studio in Petoskey, Michigan, in 1948. It remained in operation until 1976, producing a wide range of both decorative and functional ceramics including dinnerware, vases, and figurines. Most pieces are glazed in rich, solid colors and are marked 'Petoskey' as well as 'S. Kellogg Studio' or 'Kellogg's.' Stanley Kellogg began as a sculptor, and it was while working on an outdoor monument with the great Swedish-American sculptor, Carl Milles, that Stanley suffered the back injury which forced him to turn to studio work. In addition to naturalistic treatments of Michigan wildlife, Kellogg developed some angular, architectural forms in his molded art pottery. Our coadvisors for this category are Walter P. Hogan and Wendy L. Woodworth; they are listed in the Directory under Michigan.

Bowl, pk w/flower-frog lid, 3¼" dia **30.00**
Figure, Great Horned Owl on branch, brn & ivory, 7¼" **60.00**
Flower-frog vase, gr matt, spherical w/pentagonal rim, 3¼" **30.00**
Jar, rust/brn streaked, flowers etched on lid, rnd, 4" **35.00**
Leaf dish, brn & gr w/raised sides, 8½x4" **35.00**
Pitcher, cobalt w/wht drip at rim, curved hdl, 7½" **50.00**
Plate, maple leaf theme, 10" **10.00**
Table set, sky bl, rnd cr/sug+sq shakers+8x4" rectangular tray **75.00**
Vase, burgundy gloss, narrow hourglass shape, 13" **85.00**
Vase, deep teal, bulbous w/cylindrical top, slanted rim, 5" **25.00**
Vase, speckled sky bl, wide & rnd w/horizontal ribs, 10" **75.00**

Kelva

Kelva was a trademark of the C.F. Monroe Company of Meriden, Connecticut; it was produced for only a few years after the turn of the century. It is distinguished from the Wave Crest and Nakara lines by its unique Batik-like background, probably achieved through the use of a cloth or sponge to apply the color. Large florals are hand painted on the opaque milk glass; and ormolu and brass mounts were used for the boxes, vases, and trays. Most pieces are signed. Our advisors for this category are Dolli and Wilfred Cohen; they are listed in the Directory under California.

Biscuit jar, floral, wht on peach, SP lid & hdl, rare **900.00**
Box, Crown mold, floral w/beadwork, ftd, 6½" dia **995.00**
Box, floral, bl on pk mottle, hexagonal, 3x4", NM **550.00**

Box, floral, mc on gr mottle, SP mts, mk, 3½x6" dia, NM 650.00
Box, floral, pk on bl mottle, raised beading, 4½" dia 575.00
Box, poppies on gr mottle, mk, 3¾x8" dia 1,450.00
Box, wild roses, pk on gr, hinged lid, 2¾x4" sq 495.00

Humidor, cigars and flowers on blue mottle, 5x3½", $995.00.

Humidor, cigars & poppies on gr mottle, 5x3½" dia 795.00
Tray, daisies on maroon, rnd w/emb metal rim, rope hdl, 3½" ... 275.00
Tray, voilets on orange w/gold metal trim, open hdls, 5x6" 350.00
Vase, floral on rose, trumpet form w/4 ormolu ft, 6x2" 525.00
Vase, lilies, mc on gr mottle, brass rim, hdls, 8x3½" 795.00
Whisk broom holder, floral, pk on bl 1,950.00

Kenton Hills

Kenton Hills Porcelain was established in 1940 in Erlanger, Kentucky, by Harold Bopp, former Rookwood superintendent, and David Seyler, noted artist and sculptor. Native clay was used; glazes were very similar to Rookwood's of the same period. The work was of high quality, but because of the restrictions imposed on needed material due to the onset of the war, the operation failed in 1942. Much of the ware is artist signed and marked with the Kenton Hills name or cipher and shape number.

Bowl, console; gray w/brn edge, sgn, 5x15" 300.00
Ginger jar, gr aventurine, w/lid, 9½x6½" 400.00
Vase, clear amber, bulbous, 5½x4" 325.00
Vase, mahog metallic aventurine, baluster, 8½x4" 400.00
Vase, rose, red & yel w/blk leaves on ivory, porc, 7x6" 650.00

Kentucky Derby Glasses

Kentucky Derby glasses are the official souvenir glasses sold at Churchill Downs filled with mint juleps on Derby Day. Many folks who attend the Derby from all over the country take home the souvenir glass, and thus the collecting begins. The first glass (1938) is said to have either been given away as a souvenir or used for drinks among the elite at the Downs. This one, the 1939 glass, two glasses from 1940, the 1940 – 41 aluminum tumbler, the 'Beetleware' tumblers from 1941 – 44, and the 1945 short, tall, and jigger glasses are the rarer, most sought-after glasses, and they command the highest prices. Some 1974 glasses incorrectly listed the 1971 winner Canonero II as just Canonero; as a result, it became the 'mistake' glass for that year. Also, glasses made by the Federal Glass Company (whose logo is a tiny shield with an F inside) were used for extra glasses for the 100th running in 1974. There is also a 'mistake' and a correct Federal glass, making four to collect for that year.

In order to identify the year of a pre-1969 glass, since it did not appear on the front of the glass prior to then, simply add one year to the last date listed on the back of the glass. This may seem to be a confusing practice, but the current year's glass is produced long before the Derby winner is determined. Our advisor for this category is Betty Hornback; she is listed in the Directory under Kentucky.

1940, aluminum 800.00
1941, French Lick 800.00
1941-44, Beetleware, from $2,500 to 4,000.00
1945, jigger 1,000.00
1945, regular 1,200.00
1945, tall 425.00
1946-47, ea 100.00
1948, clear bottom 180.00
1948, frosted bottom 200.00
1949 .... 180.00
1950 .... 425.00
1951 .... 550.00
1952, Gold Cup 190.00
1953 .... 150.00
1954 .... 175.00
1955 .... 135.00
1956, 4 variations, ea from $150 to 250.00
1957, gold & blk on frosted 110.00
1958, Gold Bar 175.00
1958, Iron Leige 185.00
1959-60, ea 80.00
1961 .... 100.00
1962 .... 65.00
1963-64, ea 50.00
1965 .... 70.00
1966 .... 55.00
1967-68, ea 50.00
1969 .... 50.00
1970 .... 55.00
1971 .... 45.00
1972 .... 40.00
1973 .... 45.00
1974, Federal (ea), from $125 to 150.00
1974, mistake 18.00
1974, regular 16.00
1975 .... 12.00
1976 .... 14.00
1976, plastic 12.00
1977 .... 10.00
1978-79, ea 12.00
1980 .... 18.00
1981-82, ea 12.00
1983 .... 9.00
1984 .... 7.00
1985 .... 9.00
1986 .... 10.00
1986 (1985 copy) 18.00
1987-89, ea 9.00
1990-92, ea 7.00
1993-96, ea 5.00
1997-98, ea 3.00

Kew Blas

Kew Blas was a trade name used by the Union Glass Company of Summerville, Massachusetts, for their iridescent, lustered art glass produced from 1893 until about 1920. The glass was made in imitation of Tiffany and achieved notable success. Some items were decorated with pulled leaf and feather designs, while others had a monochrome lustre surface. The mark was an engraved 'Kew Blas' in an arching arrangement.

Compote, gold ribbed bowl, sgn, 4x5½" 325.00
Decanter, gold w/purple-pk irid, ribbed/pnt stopper, 14½x4¾" . 1,450.00

Pitcher, feathers, dk gr/gold on oyster wht, 4½" 725.00
Tumbler, gold irid w/purple irid int, 3½x3" 275.00
Vase, bees cvd on gold, scalloped/waisted cylinder, 9" 725.00
Vase, draped loops, wht on cobalt irid, classic form, 8" 500.00
Vase, feathers, gold irid on opal, bulbous top, 9" 1,200.00
Vase, feathers, gr w/gold irid on oyster wht, 6½x7" 1,450.00
Vase, floriform; red w/purple highlights, 9" 325.00
Vase, gold irid w/gr 'snakeskin,' scalloped, 4½" 675.00
Vase, Honeycomb, emerald gr, purple irid int, 4¼x5¼" 800.00

King's Rose

King's Rose was made in Staffordshire, England, from about 1820 to 1830. It is closely related to Gaudy Dutch in body type as well as the colors used in its decoration. The pattern consists of a full-blown, orange-red rose with green, pink, and yellow leaves and accents. When the rose is in pink, the ware is often referred to as Queen's Rose.

Cake plate, Queen's, floral rim band, rose in center, 10" 165.00
Cup & saucer, handleless; pk border, wear 85.00
Cup & saucer, handleless; red rose, vine border, NM 200.00
Cup & saucer, vine border, EX 120.00
Cup plate, pl lustre & vine decor at rim, 4½" 165.00
Plate, pk border w/dmn designs, 5⅜", EX 55.00
Plate, pk rose, vine border, shaped rim, 7", NM 160.00
Plate, Rogers, 8½" 115.00
Plate, toddy; Queen's, scalloped, 5½" 125.00
Sugar bowl, pk border w/emb dmns, w/lid, rpr, 5½x6¼x4½" 100.00
Teapot, Queen's, 6" 385.00
Waste bowl, solid border, lt wear, 2¾x5⅝" 200.00

Kitchen Collectibles

During the last half of the 1850s, mass-produced kitchen gadgets were patented at an astonishing rate. Most were ingeniously efficient. Apple peelers, egg beaters, cherry pitters, food choppers, and such were only the most common of hundreds of kitchen tools well designed to perform only specific tasks. Today all are very collectible.

For further information we recommend *Kitchen Glassware of the Depression Years* by Gene Florence, and *Kitchen Antiques, 1790 – 1940*, by Kathryn McNerney. See also Appliances; Glass Knives; Molds; Primitives; Reamers; Tinware; Wooden Ware.

Cast Kitchen Ware

Be aware that cast-iron counterfeit production is on the increase. Items with phony production numbers, finishes, etc., are being made at this time. Many of these new pieces are the popular cornstick pans. To command the values given below, examples must be free from damage of any kind or excessive wear and tear. Waffle irons must be complete with all three pieces and the handle. The term 'EPU' in the description lines refers to the **Erie PA, USA** mark. The term 'block mark' refers to the lettering in the large logo that was used ca 1920 until 1940; 'slant logo' refers to the lettering in the large logo ca 1900 to 1920. Victor was Griswold's first low-budget line (ca 1875); skillets #5 and #6 are uncommon, while #7, #8, and #9 are easy to find. For further information contact our advisor, Grant S. Windsor (SASE required); he is listed in the Directory under Virginia. See also Keen Kutter; Clubs, Newsletters, and Catalogs.

Bundt cake pan, Frank Hay 395.00
Bundt cake pan, Griswold 1,100.00
Bundt cake pan, unknown maker 100.00

Cake mold, lamb form, Griswold #866 ....100.00
Cake mold, Santa, Griswold 650.00
Chicken fryer, Wagner #1400, sq, w/lid 125.00

Griswold Crispy Corn Cake Pan, #262, tea size, $75.00. Caution! There are more reproductions of this piece on today's market than originals.

Cornstick pan, Puritan 100.00
Cornstick pan, S&R Co #1270 ....100.00
Dutch oven, Favoriteware #10, w/logo, rolled lid 95.00
Dutch oven, Griswold #8, hinged lid 80.00
Dutch oven, Griswold #10, Tite Top, w/trivet 150.00
Dutch oven, Griswold #12, w/trivet 700.00
Dutch oven, Wagner #6 ....150.00
Dutch oven, Wagner #9, raised letters on lid 50.00
Dutch oven lid, Griswold #9 ....35.00
Egg poacher, Griswold #32, rnd 50.00
Gem pan, unmk, 11 rnd cups 25.00
Gem pan, Wagner D 45.00
Griddle, Griswold #9, Erie/slant logo, oval 175.00
Griddle, Griswold #10, block letters (hdl griddle) 65.00
Griddle, Griswold #108, block letters, smooth bottom (skillet type) .75.00
Hot pot, Wagner #1364, w/lid 150.00
Hot pot, Wagner #1368, w/lid 90.00
Kettle, Griswold #6, flat bottom, w/lid, scarce 650.00
Kettle, Wagner #6, 3-leg 100.00
Muffin pan, GF Filley #5, 8-cup 100.00
Muffin pan, GF Filley #10 ....100.00
Muffin pan, Griswold #10, USN 125.00
Muffin pan, Griswold #21 ....150.00
Muffin pan, Griswold #26 Vienna 200.00
Muffin pan, Griswold #28 ....300.00
Muffin pan, Griswold #140 ....200.00
Muffin pan, Griswold #240 ....475.00
Muffin pan, Griswold #283 ....175.00
Muffin pan, Wagner Q, mk Wagner 55.00
Patty mold, Griswold #1, shallow, MIB 35.00
Patty mold, Griswold #3, combination set, MIB 150.00
Popover pan, Griswold #18, 6-cup 100.00
Roaster, Griswold #5, oval, full writing, w/trivet 525.00
Roaster, Griswold #9, oval, full writing, w/o trivet 700.00
Roaster, Wagner #5, w/trivet 275.00
Roaster, Wagner #7, oval, w/trivet 275.00
Roaster, Wagner #9, oval, w/trivet 350.00
Scotch bowl, Wagner #3 ....35.00
Skillet, breakfast 5 in 1; Griswold 150.00
Skillet, dbl; Wagner, deep 125.00
Skillet, dbl; Wagner #8 (5-star skillet set) 100.00
Skillet, Griswold #4, block logo, no smoke ring 50.00
Skillet, Griswold #5, block letters, w/heat ring 450.00
Skillet, Griswold #6, slant logo, EPU 40.00
Skillet, Griswold #6, Victor (full writing) 350.00

Skillet, Griswold #7, Victor (full writing) 45.00
Skillet, Griswold #11, block letters, w/smoke ring 150.00
Skillet, Griswold #12, block letters, smoke ring 100.00
Skillet, Griswold #12, sm logo 65.00
Skillet, Griswold #15, oval 350.00
Skillet, Wagner #2, smooth, no pattern # 100.00
Skillet, Wagner #4, smooth 35.00
Skillet, Wagner #7, smooth 45.00
Skillet, Wagner #9, smooth 90.00
Skillet, Wagner #11, w/heat ring 100.00
Skillet, Wagner #12, pie logo 100.00
Skillet lid, Griswold #3, high dome, smooth top 275.00
Skillet lid, Griswold #5, low dome, full writing top 500.00
Skillet lid, Griswold #8, high dome, top writing 50.00
Skillet lid, Griswold #9, low dome, full writing top 60.00
Skillet lid, Griswold #12, low dome, full writing top 250.00
Skillet lid, Griswold #769, sq 250.00
Skillet lid, Wagner #5 Drip Drop, outside writing 195.00
Trivet, Griswold #8 Dutch oven 25.00
Trivet, Griswold #10 Dutch oven 50.00
Vienna roll pan, Griswold #2, Vienna Roll/Bread Pan in cups ...800.00
Waffle iron, Andresen, heart shape 125.00
Waffle iron, Griswold #11, sq, high base 150.00
Waffle iron, Griswold #13, hotel 1,000.00
Waffle iron, Griswold #18, hearts & stars 175.00
Waffle iron, Stover #7 ....85.00
Waffle iron, Wagner #9 ....50.00
Yankee bowl, Griswold #3, slant Erie 50.00

Egg Beaters

Egg beaters are an unbeatable collectible. Ranging from hand-helds to rotary cranks, to squeeze power, to Archimedes up-and-down models, egg beaters are America's favorite kitchen gadget. A mainstay of any kitchenware collection, in recent years egg beaters have come into their own — nutmeg graters, spatulas, and can openers will have to scramble to catch up! At the turn of the century, everyone in America owned an egg beater. Every household did its own mixing and baking — there were no pre-processed foods. And every inventor thought he/she could make a better beater. Thus American ingenuity produced more than one thousand egg beater patents, dating back to 1856, with several hundred different models being manufactured over the years. As true examples of Americana, egg beaters have risen in value over the past couple of years, with a half dozen mixers valued at $2,000.00 and more. But the vast majority are under $50.00, while the values of the super rare beaters continue upward. And just when you think you've seen them all, new ones always, always turn up, usually at flea markets or garage sales. For further information, we recommend our advisor (author of the definitive book on egg beaters) Don Thornton, who is listed in the Directory under California (SASE required). See also Clubs, Newsletters, and Catalogs for Kollectors of Old Kitchen Stuff (KOOKS).

Keystone Mfg. Co., Pat. Dec. 15, '85, Philadelphia, PA, wall mount, EX, $425.00.

Photo courtesy Don Thornton

A&J, all metal, sm, 9¾" 15.00
A&J, center drive, pk & gray wooden hdls, 12" 15.00
Aluminum Beauty Pat'd April 20, 1920, rotary crank, 10½" 15.00
Beats Eggs, Cream...No 825 Androck, hand-held fan type, 11" 5.00
Dover...Patd May 6th 1873...1891..., CI rotary crank, 11¼" 55.00
Holt's Egg Beater & Cream Whip, CI, Pat Aug 22 '99-Apr 6 '00, 9" .240.00
Jaquette Phila PA, CI & wire, dbl hdls, Pat No 3, 10½" 750.00
Jiffy Whip...Krasbert & Sons Mfg, rotary crank turbine, 11¾" 25.00
K-C (soap bubble), 1930s, 10" 75.00
Quik Whip Reg US Pat Off...Pending, metal, squeeze power, 11¼" ..295.00
Turbine Beater Androck Made in USA, rotary crank, 11½" 18.00
Vandeusen Egg Whip, CA Chapman...1894, all metal, hand held, 11" 15.00
Whipwell...USA Pat Mch 23 1920..., rotary crank, wood hdl, 11" ..25.00

Glass

Ashtray holder, crystal, Cambridge 35.00
Baker, Sapphire Bl, Fire-King, 1½-qt 12.00
Batter jug, gr, Jenkins 225.00
Batter jug, red, New Martinsville, w/liner, chrome lid 175.00
Bottle, oil/vinegar; Flamingo Pk, Heisey 75.00
Bottle, oil/vinegar; gr, Cambridge, etched pattern 85.00
Bottle, oil/vinegar; gr, Paden City 60.00
Bottle, oil/vinegar; yel or gr, Fostoria 75.00
Bottle, water; Forest Gr, emb penguin 18.00
Bottle, water; gr, Owen-Illinois, emb Juice & Water, metal lid 8.00
Bowl, batter; Fruits decor, Fire-King, Hocking, hdld 20.00
Bowl, beater; Jade-ite, Jeannette, w/metal beater 30.00
Bowl, bl, Banded Dots, Hocking, 8½" 15.00
Bowl, bl, LE Smith, horizontal ribs, 9¼" 75.00
Bowl, blk/gr dots on custard, McKee, w/spout, 9" 25.00
Bowl, mixing; blk/gr dots on custard, McKee, 7" 15.00
Bowl, mixing; gr, Crisscross, Hazel Atlas, 6⅝" 18.00
Bowl, mixing; Turq Bl, Swedish Modern, Fire-King, 3-qt, 11" 20.00
Bowl, red dots on wht, Hazel Atlas, 9" 20.00
Bowl, wht w/apple decor, Hocking, 9½" 15.00
Butter dish, amber, Federal, 1-lb 35.00
Butter dish, custard, McKee, 1-lb 40.00
Butter dish, Delphite Bl, McKee, 1-lb 250.00
Cake pan, Sapphire Bl, Fire-King, deep, 8¾" 22.00
Canister, bl/red dots on custard, McKee, screw lid, 48-oz 75.00
Canister, crystal w/Dutch decal, Hocking, metal lid 20.00
Canister, dots on wht, McKee, rnd, w/lid, 10-oz 15.00
Casserole, Pk Floral on wht, Fire-King, 1-qt 12.00
Creamer, pk, Crisscross, Hazel Atlas 40.00
Cruet, bl, Janice, New Martinsville 65.00
Cruet, vaseline or canary, Imperial 50.00
Cruet, yel, Trojan, Fostoria 250.00
Cup, custard; Jade-ite, McKee 6.00
Decanter, transparent gr, Hocking, pinched-in sides 45.00
Drippings jar, Delphite Bl, Jeannette, w/lid, blk letters 110.00
Gravy boat, dbl; pk, Cambridge, 2-hdld 30.00
Gravy boat, transparent gr, Cambridge, w/underliner 75.00
Grease jar, red dots on wht, Hocking 18.00
Ice bucket, amber, Ring, Hocking 15.00
Ice bucket, gr, Polar Bear decor, Fostoria 35.00
Jug, milk; clear w/bl lid, Paden City 65.00
Ladle, lt bl, Fostoria 40.00
Ladle, Moonlight Bl, Cambridge 40.00
Ladle, pk, Duncan 12.00
Loaf pan, Sapphire Bl, Fire-King, deep, 9⅛" 20.00
Measuring cup, crystal, Heisey, 1-cup 250.00
Measuring cup, Delphite Bl, Jeannette, 1-cup 50.00
Measuring cup, gr, Cambridge, dry measure, 1-cup 250.00

Measuring cup, irid carnival, US Glass, 2-cup **45.00**
Measuring cup, pk, US Glass, 1-cup **60.00**
Measuring cup, wht w/trim, Hazel Atlas, 3-spout, 1-cup **65.00**
Measuring pitcher, blk or red Diamond Check, McKee, 2-cup **30.00**
Measuring pitcher, Delphite Bl, McKee, 2-cup **85.00**
Measuring pitcher, lt Jade-ite, Jeannette, sunflower bottom, 2-cup ..**18.00**
Mug, Forest Gr, Cambridge **45.00**
Mug, gr, Chesterfield, Imperial **25.00**
Mug, red, New Martinsville **25.00**
Mug, Tom & Jerry; custard, McKee, blk letters **15.00**
Mug, wht w/Esso's Tony the Tiger decal, Fire-King **8.00**
Napkin holder, blk, Nar-O-Fold **135.00**
Pitcher, bl, Crisscross, Hazel Atlas, 54-oz **700.00**
Pitcher, bl or red dots on custard, McKee, 2-cup **38.00**
Plate, grill; rose, Fry, 8½" **30.00**
Roaster, Sapphire Bl, Fire-King, 10⅜" **65.00**
Rolling pin, bottle gr glass, Stoddard...Keen NH, 1800s, 16" **310.00**
Rolling pin, clambroth, screw-on hdls **125.00**
Rolling pin, cobalt glass, gold leaves, For My Mother, dtd 1860 .**275.00**
Rolling pin, Delphite Bl, McKee, shaker top end **1,800.00**
Rolling pin, Forest Gr, blown **150.00**
Rolling pin, milk glass, wooden hdls, 17½" **50.00**
Rolling pin, Peacock Bl, wooden hdls attach to metal rod inside ..**275.00**
Salt box, Chalaine Bl, McKee **200.00**
Shaker, cinnamon; crystal, Roman Arch, McKee, blk letters **30.00**
Shaker, crystal w/raised dots, Hocking **5.00**
Shaker, Delphite Bl, Jeannette, sq **75.00**
Shaker, flour or sugar; McKee Roman Arch **25.00**
Shaker, gr, Hocking, rnd **25.00**
Shaker, wht, McKee, sq, 16-oz **45.00**
Skillet, clear, Range Tec, McKee **10.00**
Spoon & fork set, transparent gr, Cambridge **110.00**
Straw holder, blk, metal lid **700.00**
Straw holder, crystal, Heisey, metal lid **275.00**
Sugar shaker, gr, Beehive, Lancaster Glass **175.00**
Sugar shaker, pk or gr, Jeannette, ea **60.00**
Syrup, amber, Cambridge **55.00**
Syrup, clear w/bl lid, Paden City **60.00**
Syrup pitcher, amber, Cambridge, w/lid **50.00**
Syrup pitcher, gr, Paden City, w/lid **35.00**
Syrup pitcher, pk, Imperial, slotted lid **75.00**
Syrup pitcher, Sahara Yel, Heisey, w/lid **85.00**
Tumbler, Jade-ite, Jeannette, 12-oz **15.00**
Tumbler, pk, Crisscross, Hazel Atlas, 9-oz **85.00**
Tumbler, transparent gr, Paden City, ftd **12.00**
Water dispenser, cobalt bl, LE Smith **400.00**
Water dispenser, crystal, McKee, w/ice insert **100.00**
Water dispenser, wht, McKee **110.00**

Miscellaneous

Apple peeler, CI, early half-moon shape, Pat 1863 ....**185.00**
Apple peeler, CI, 5-geared, mk Pat Pending **95.00**
Apple peeler, Goodell's, CI, 1896 ....**85.00**
Apple peeler, Harbster Bros 1868, CI **195.00**
Apple peeler, Hudson Pat 1882, CI **85.00**
Apple peeler, Little Starpat 1885, CI, EX **75.00**
Apple peeler, Lockey & Holland, CI, Pat 1856 ....**95.00**
Apple peeler, Reading Advance Pat 1878, 1883, CI **145.00**
Apple segmenter, Rollman Mfg Co, CI **75.00**
Asparagus buncher, Phila Buncher, iron on wood brd **95.00**
Biscuit cutter, Egg Baking Powder **175.00**
Blueberry scoop, wood & wire w/hdl, sm **95.00**
Bucket, mop wringer, wood & iron, 1892 ....**95.00**

Butter curler, wooden w/sq grooved end **75.00**
Can opener, CI, bull figural, head at blade end, tail hdl, 6½" **35.00**
Can opener, CI, fish figural, 5⅛" **70.00**
Can opener, Del Monico, iron, Feb 11, 1890 ....**30.00**
Can opener, Preston, CI, duck-head form, curved hdl, 5⅝" **160.00**
Cherry seeder, Logan & Strobridge New Brighton, CI **50.00**
Cherry seeder, New Standard, CI **110.00**
Cherry seeder, Rollman #8, CI & wood, clamps on, 12" **65.00**
Chopper, flat steel blade, maple hdl, 8¾", G **45.00**
Chopper, New Standard, sz 00 ....**125.00**
Chopper, P Cutlani, wrought steel, trn wood hdl, 6⅝" W **100.00**
Chopper, ½-moon blade on goal-post shaft, wood hdl, 8" **60.00**
Churn, Dazey #10, beveled edge, 1-qt **1,350.00**
Churn, Dazey #10, bull's-eye, 1-qt **1,300.00**
Churn, Dazey #20 ....**200.00**
Churn, Dazey #30, Pat 1922 ....**225.00**
Churn, Dazey #40 ....**140.00**
Churn, Dazey #400, heavy tin, 4-gal **200.00**
Churn, Elgin, 2-qt **200.00**
Churn, Universal #15, glass container, clamps on, NM **500.00**
Churn, unmk, glass, 1-gal **95.00**
Churn frame, Dazey, 1917 ....**30.00**
Cork press, CI, dog figural hdl, EX **95.00**
Cracker pricker, tin, rnd w/spikes inside **95.00**
Decorker, Yankee #7, clamping type, EX **295.00**
Dough mixer, Landers, geared, crank **85.00**
Doughnut cutter, Dover, dk tin **12.00**
Doughnut cutter, maple wood, 2-part, Pat 3/26/01, 3½" dia **120.00**
Doughnut cutter, Rumford, tin, 3¾x2½" dia **20.00**
Egg poacher, copper, tin lined, 3-compartment **185.00**
Egg poacher, wire, 5-compartment **24.00**
Flour sifter, Brite Pride, aluminum, red hdl **35.00**
Flour sifter, Bromwell, pnt tin, ca 1940s-50s, EX **15.00**
Flour sifter, Duplex, dk tin, red wood center hdl, 1922, 6¾" **50.00**
Flour sifter, Rumford Baking Powder, ca 1950s, scarce, EX **75.00**
Flour sifter, wooden, looks like Bloods, 1861 ....**275.00**
Fly trap, glass, hanging type **35.00**
Fly trap, glass, table model w/3 ft **125.00**
Fly trap, spherical screen **45.00**
Freezer, ice cream; Dazey Whip, up & down dasher, glass base ...**600.00**
Funnel, Dover, tin **12.00**

Photo courtesy Fran Carter

Grater, The Acme Safety Grater, box dated 1933, MIB, $20.00.

Grater, cheese; punched tin & wood, box shape, nailed, 3x16x9" ..**300.00**
Grater, nutmeg; Gem, rotary **135.00**
Grater, nutmeg; Little Rhody **85.00**
Grater, nutmeg; Standard, tin & wood **150.00**
Grater, nutmeg; tin, w/lidded storage compartment, 5", VG **95.00**
Grater, nutmeg; tin & wood cylinder, wire/wood crank, 1877, 6" ..**450.00**
Grater, nutmeg; tin & wood half cylinder, 5¼x3", VG **85.00**

Grinder, food; Griswold #4, CI, w/3 blades **40.00**
Grinder, food; Universal **20.00**
Guardian Service, bacon fryer, aluminum, w/press **95.00**
Guardian Service, chicken fryer, aluminum **85.00**
Guardian Service, coffeepot, aluminum **105.00**
Guardian Service, turkey roaster, aluminum **105.00**
Hot plate & dish lifter, Triumph, Pat 4/14/1868, open: 10x13" **50.00**
Ice shaver, Griswold #1, CI **125.00**
Juicer, Dazey Churn Co, aluminum, wall mt, EX **15.00**
Juicer, Handy Andy, ca 1930 ....**55.00**
Juicer, Orange Flow, iron & aluminum, 1936 ....**40.00**
Kraut cutter, wood w/chip-cvd flowers, wire nails, angle blade, sm ...**250.00**
Lard press, wood w/brass hinges, like lemon squeezer **95.00**
Lemon squeezer, Griswold #2, CI **125.00**
Lemon squeezer, metal box type, Pat May 3, 81, EX **20.00**
Marmalade cutter, Follows & Bate Ltd, CI, EX **135.00**
Mayonnaise maker, Wessen Oil, glass w/emb recipe **45.00**
Meat tenderizer, stoneware head, rpl wood hdl, dtd 1877 ....**50.00**
Mixer, Horlick's Speedy, wire, 2x9½", MIB **50.00**
Mixer, mayonnaise; A&J, NP CI, 10x5" dia **40.00**
Mold, cloverleaf doughnut form, CI, hinged, 1¼x6⅛x5¾" **95.00**
Noodle cutter, 6 adjustable blades, EX **55.00**
Pie crimper, brass **35.00**
Pie crimper, wrought iron w/trn wood hdl, brass collar, 8¾" **120.00**
Pie fly cover, wire screen mesh, 5x8¼" **65.00**
Pie lifter, wood & wire, Farmer's Supply Co **85.00**
Pie tin, Crisco advertising, Pat 5-26 ....**28.00**
Pie tin, Mrs Wagner's Pies **20.00**
Potato baker, stove-top, tin, 1940s **40.00**
Potato peeler, Guaranty **30.00**
Potato peeler, Hamlinite, Pat July 20-20 ....**85.00**
Raisin seeder, Everette, wood & wire, hand held **95.00**
Rice ball, tin w/holes, hasp closure, chain hanger **95.00**
Rolling pin, hdl across top **275.00**
Rolling pin, Krispy Krust, MIB **55.00**
Rolling pin, red pnt hdls **25.00**
Rolling pin, springerle w/24 sqs, 18" **140.00**
Sausage stuffer, tin w/wooden plunger **110.00**
Sieve, Foley Food Mill, tin, EX **12.00**
Slicer, cheese; iron U-shaped fr w/wire blade, 16" W **125.00**
Slicer, vegetable; Catawisa Specialty, wood, 6 metal blades, 1898 ..**45.00**
Slicer, vegetable; wood & steel, half-moon cut-out hdl, 18x8" ...**200.00**
Sprinkler bottle, Chinaman, towel over arm, ceramic **120.00**
Sprinkler bottle, Chinaman holding iron, ceramic **110.00**
Sprinkler bottle, clothespin, aqua, w/smiling face, ceramic **125.00**
Sprinkler bottle, Dutch girl, ceramic **100.00**
Sprinkler bottle, elephant, pk & gray, ceramic **55.00**
Sprinkler bottle, elephant, wht w/pk shamrock on tummy, ceramic **75.00**
Sprinkler bottle, iron, gr plastic **25.00**
Sprinkler bottle, iron w/ivy, ceramic **40.00**
Sprinkler bottle, Merry Maid, wht, plastic, from $15 to **35.00**
Sprinkler bottle, poodle, ceramic **125.00**
Sprinkler bottle, Siamese cat, ceramic **125.00**
Sugar cutter/break, CI, crescent blades, eng stars, 9⅞" **160.00**
Sugar cutter/break, CI, crescent blades, 8⅝" **120.00**
Trivet, Wagner #8, aluminum **35.00**

Knives

Knife collecting as a hobby began in earnest during the 1960s when government regulations required for the first time that knife companies mark their product with the country of origin. The few collectors and dealers cognizant of this change at once began stockpiling the older knives made before this law was enacted. Another impetus to the growing interest in this area came with the Gun Control Act of 1968, which severely restricted gun trading. Frustrated gun dealers transferred their attention to knives. Today there are collectors clubs in many of the states.

The most sought-after pocketknives are those made before WWII. However, Case, Schrade, and Primble knives of a more recent manufacture are also collected. Most collectors prefer knives 'as found.' Do not attempt to clean, sharpen, or in any way 'improve' on an old knife.

The prices quoted here are for knives in mint condition. If a knife has been used, sharpened, or blemished in any way, its value decreases. Knives in excellent condition generally are valued at half the prices listed below. The newer the knife, the greater the reduction in value. For further information refer to *The Standard Knife Collector's Guide, 2nd Edition*, by Ron Stewart and Roy Ritchie, and *Sargent's American Premium Guide to Knives and Razors, Identification and Values, 3rd Edition*, by Jim Sargent. Our advisor for this category is Bill Wright; he is listed in the Directory under Indiana.

Key:
bd — blade   s/b — slant button
imi — imitation   wb — winterbottom
jack — jackknife

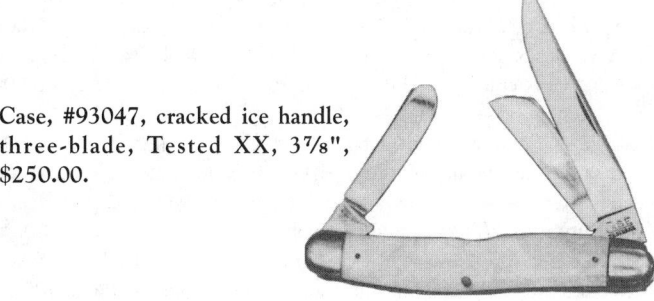

Case, #93047, cracked ice handle, three-blade, Tested XX, 3⅞", $250.00.

Case, B1025, waterfall hdl, 1-bd, Tested XX, 3" **225.00**
Case, C61050 SAB, red bone hdl, 1-bd, XX, 5⅜" **300.00**
Case, GS1097, gold-stone hdl, 1-bd, Tested XX, 1920-30, 5" **400.00**
Case, Maize, walnut hdl, 1-bd, Tested XX, 4" **225.00**
Case, Muskrat, red bone hdl, 2-bd, XX, 1940-64, 3⅞" **175.00**
Case, R1049L, candy-stripe hdl, 1-bd, Tested XX, 1920-30, 4⅛" ...**500.00**
Case, 04247SP, wht compo hdl, 2-bd, USA, 3⅞" **100.00**
Case, 05247SP, stag hdl, 2-bd, Tested XX, 1920-40, 3⅞" **175.00**
Case, 11031SH, walnut hdl, 1 LP bd, USA, 3¾" **110.00**
Case, 2136, slick blk hdl, 1-bd, XX, 1940-55, 4⅛" **150.00**
Case, 2217, slick blk hdl, 2-bd, Tested XX, 3⅞" **250.00**
Case, 42035½LP, wht compo hdl, 2-bd, Case Bradford PA, 3¼" ..**250.00**
Case, 5224½, stag hdl, 2-bd, Tested XX, 3" **175.00**
Case, 5225½, stag hdl, 2-bd, WR Case & Sons, 3" **300.00**
Case, 5265SAB, stag hdl, 2-bd, Tested XX, 1920-40, 5¼" **325.00**
Case, 5364TF, stag hdl, 3-bd, Tested XX, 1920-40, 3⅛" **250.00**
Case, 5488, wb bone hdl, 4-bd, Tested XX, 1920-40, 4⅛" **1,500.00**
Case, 5488, 2nd-cut stag hdl, 4-bd, USA, 1965-69, 4⅛" **500.00**
Case, 61005, gr bone hdl, 1-bd, Tested XX, 1920-40, 3⅜" **450.00**
Case, 61011, Rogers bone hdl, 1-bd, Tested XX, 1920-40, 4" **210.00**
Case, 61049LP, gr bone hdl, 1-bd, Case Tested XX, 4⅛" **325.00**
Case, 6106, gr bone hdl, 1-bd, Case 25¢, 2⅝" **300.00**
Case, 61093, bone hdl, 1-bd, XX, 1940-64, 5" **100.00**
Case, 61213, gr bone hdl, 1-bd, Tested XX, 1920-40, 5⅜" **550.00**
Case, 6172, gr bone hdl, 1-bd, Tested XX, 5½" **1,400.00**
Case, 62009, bone hdl, 2-bd, XX, 3⅜" **50.00**
Case, 62042, stainless hdl, 2-bd, 10 Dot, 1970, 3¼" **200.00**
Case, 6206½, gr bone hdl, 2-bd, Tested XX, 2⅝" **175.00**

Case, 6207, gr bone hdl, 2-bd, Tested XX, 3½" 300.00
Case, 62100, gr bone hdl, 2-bd, WR Case & Sons, 4⅝" 650.00
Case, 62109X, gr bone hdl, 2-bd, Tested XX, 3⅛" 250.00
Case, 6213LP, Rogers bone hdl, 2-bd, WR Case & Sons, 3⅞" ...700.00
Case, 62131, bone hdl, 2-bd, XX, 1964, 3⅝" 250.00
Case, 6214½, red bone hdl, 2-bd, XX, 1940-64, 3⅜" 60.00
Case, 6222LP, gr bone hdl, 2-bd, Tested, 3⅜" 400.00
Case, 6228, gr bone hdl, 2-bd, Tested XX, 1920-40, 3½" 200.00
Case, 6233, gr bone hdl, 2-bd, XX, 1940-55, 2⅝" 150.00
Case, 6250, bone hdl, 2-bd, USA, 1965-69, 4⅜" 250.00
Case, 6250, red bone hdl, 2-bd, XX, 1940-64, 4⅜" 325.00
Case, 6265 SAB, gr bone hdl, 2-bd, Tested XX, 1920-40, 5¼" ...350.00
Case, 6269, bone hdl, 2-bd, 10 Dot, 1970, 3" 35.00
Case, 6288, gr bone hdl, 2-bd, Tested XX, 1920-40, 4⅛" 600.00
Case, 6296XSS, bone hdl, 2-bd, USA, 1965-69, 4¼" 250.00
Case, 6345PU, gr bone hdl, 3-bd, Tested XX, 1920-40, 3⅝" ...250.00
Case, 6347SHPU, bone hdl, 3-bd, XX, 1940-64, 3⅞" 75.00
Case, 6379½F, gr bone hdl, 3-bd, Tested XX, 1920-40, 3¼" ...450.00
Case, 6392PU, gr bone hdl, 3-bd, Tested XX, 4" 200.00
Case, 6445R, rough blk hdl, 4-bd, Tested XX, 1920-40, 3¾" ...200.00
Case, 7197SSP, curly maple hdl, 1-bd, Case XX, 5" 125.00
Case, 72006, tortoise-shell hdl, Case Brad PA, 2⅝" 300.00
Case, 8151LSAB, pearl hdl, 1-bd, Tested XX, 5¼" 1,200.00
Case, 8225LP, pearl hdl, 2-bd, WR Case & Sons Bradford PA, 3" ...350.00
Case, 8233, letter opener, pearl hdl, 2-bd, 6¾" 225.00
Case, 8279F, pearl hdl, 2-bd, Tested XX, 3⅛" 150.00
Case, 83102SS, genuine pearl hdl, 2-bd, XX, 1940-64, 2¾" ...150.00
Case, 92001T, cracked ice hdl, 2-bd, Tested XX, 2⅝" 110.00
Case, 92058, cracked ice hdl, 2-bd, XX, 1940-50, 3¼" 125.00
Case, 9240SP, imi pearl hdl, 2-bd, Tested XX, 1920-40, 4⅜" ...550.00
Keen Kutter, hawkbill, walnut hdl, 1-bd, EC Simmons, 4" 40.00
Keen Kutter, jack, brn bone hdl, 1-bd, EC Simmons, 3¼" 40.00
Keen Kutter, K03706½, dog-leg pen, brn bone hdl, 2-bd, 3¼" ...60.00
Keen Kutter, K100, Texas toothpick, butter/molasses hdl, 1-bd, 5" .150.00
Keen Kutter, K1058, brn bone hdl, 1 lock bd, EC Simmons, 4¼" ...300.00
Keen Kutter, K187, moose, brn bone hdl, 2-bd, 4" 175.00
Keen Kutter, K254, barlow, brn bone hdl, 2-bd, 3⅜" 60.00
Keen Kutter, lobster pen, pearl hdl, 2-bd, EC Simmons, 3" ...45.00
Keen Kutter, peanut, cracked ice hdl, 2-bd, Keen Kutter, 2⅞" ...35.00
Keen Kutter, peanut dog-leg, pearl hdl, 2-bd, EC Simmons, 3" ...50.00
Keen Kutter, sleeveboard pen, pearl hdl, 2-bd, EC Simmons, 2⅞" ..45.00
Keen Kutter, Texas toothpick, candy-stripe hdl, 1-bd, 5" ...175.00
Keen Kutter, trapper, blk imi bone hdl, 2-bd, 3¾" 75.00
Keen Kutter, 801, daddy barlow, brn bone hdl, 1-bd, 5" 125.00
Keen Kutter, 828, barlow, yel bone hdl, 2-bd, 3⅜" 60.00
Queen, 14, peanut, wb bone hdl, 2-bd, 2¾" 25.00
Queen, 20, Texas toothpick, wb bone hdl, 1-bd, Queen Steel, 5" ...85.00
Queen, 22, barlow, brn bone hdl, 2-bd, Queen, 3½" 45.00

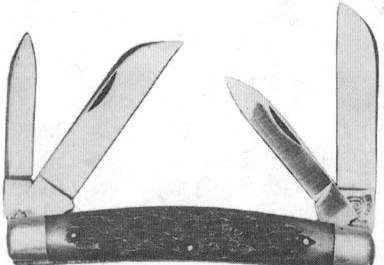

Queen, Congress, #33, Big Q, Rogers bone handle, four-blade, 3½", $120.00.

Queen, 36, lockbk, Rogers bone hdl, 1-bd, Queen, 4½" 75.00
Queen, 61, stockman, wb bone hdl, 3-bd, Queen Steel, 3⅝" ...50.00
Queen, 7, Senator, wb bone hdl, 2-bd, mk Big Q, 2½" 35.00
Remington, moose, brn bone hdl, 2-bd, 4¼" 300.00

Remington, RH73, brn bone hdl, 2-bd, 3⅛" 130.00
Remington, R1103, brn bone hdl, 2-bd, 3⅜" 135.00
Remington, R1173, brn bone hdl, 2-bd, baby bullet shield, 3½" ..2,200.00
Remington, R1285, swell center, tortoise-shell hdl, 2-bd, 3" ...160.00
Remington, R165, jack, yel scale hdl, 2-bd, 3½" 125.00
Remington, R1653, peanut, brn bone hdl, 2-bd, 2⅞" 125.00
Remington, R1783, jack teardrop, brn bone hdl, 2-bd, 3½" ...125.00
Remington, R2215, jack, red & blk pyremite hdl, 2-bd, 3⅜" ...125.00
Remington, R273, brn bone hdl, 2-bd, acorn shield, 4" 200.00
Remington, R3054, stockman, genuine pearl hdl, 3-bd, 4" ...400.00
Remington, R3115, serpentine, imi ivory hdl, 2-bd, 4" 135.00
Remington, R3273, cattle, brn bone hdl, 3-bd, equal end, 3¾" ..250.00
Remington, R3485, gold swirl pyremite hdl, 3-bd, 3⅜" 200.00
Remington, R3513, brn bone hdl, 3-bd, acorn shield, 3⅜" ...150.00
Remington, R3555, stockman, mingled red scale hdl, 3-bd, 4" ...250.00
Remington, R3855, imi ivory hdl, 2-bd, 4" 250.00
Remington, R391, equal-end jack, redwood hdl, 2-bd, 3⅜" ...160.00
Remington, R4336, stag hdl, 3-bd +corkscrew, 3½" 225.00
Remington, R4466, baby muskrat, stag hdl, 2-bd, bullet shield, 3¾" .2,500.00
Remington, R563, brn bone hdl, 2-bd, acorn shield, 3¼" 150.00
Remington, R6104, Congress, pearl hdl, 2-bd, 3⅛" 150.00
Remington, R6225, whittler, gr swirl pyremite hdl, 3-bd, 3¼" ...300.00
Remington, R645, sb, candy stripe hdl, 1-bd, 4" 500.00
Remington, R6465, onyx hdl, 2-bd, 3" 90.00
Remington, R756, genuine stag hdl, 1-bd, 4½" 175.00
Remington, sowbelly, brn bone hdl, 5-bd, 3¾" 2,500.00
Remington, stockman, bone hdl, 3-bd, 3⅜" 175.00
Western States, A100BH, amber cream hdl, 1-bd, 5¼" 125.00
Western States, S203B, gr sparkle hdl, 2-bd w/bail, 2½" 25.00
Western States, 05244, buck horn hdl, 2-bd, 3" 25.00
Western States, 100, Christmas tree hdl, 1-bd, 5¼" 200.00
Western States, 13208, brn & blk swirl compo hdl, 2-bd, 3⅜" ...25.00
Western States, 2106BH, pearl o/l hdl, 1-bd, 5¼" 150.00
Western States, 6111SP, barlow, bone hdl, 1-bd, 3⅜" 100.00
Western States, 6130, bone hdl, 1-bd, oval shield, 4½" 250.00
Western States, 819, lobster, pearl hdl, 2-bd, 2½" 45.00
Winchester, 1950, lockbk, stag hdl, 1-bd, 5¼" 1,200.00
Winchester, 2099, jack, pk celluloid hdl, 2-bd, 3⅜" 150.00
Winchester, 2205, pen, metal hdl, 2-bd, 3¼" 125.00
Winchester, 2608, stabber, cocobolo hdl, 2-bd, 3⅝" 125.00
Winchester, 2690, Texas jack, ebony hdl, 2-bd, 4½" 300.00
Winchester, 2853, gunstock, brn bone hdl, 2-bd, 3½" 400.00
Winchester, 2945, Senator, bone hdl, 2-bd, 3⅜" 100.00

Miscellaneous

Bowie, Randall, brass guard, stag hdl, 9" clip-point bd, G ...425.00
Bowie, 2-pc stag hdl, aluminum pommel, brass guard, Solingen, 6" ..50.00
Butcher, J Russell Gr River, iron bolster, wood hdl, 11⅝" bd ...100.00
Carving, Landers Frary & Clark, Aetna Works, stag hdl, 10" ...25.00
Hunting, Kinfolks, Flame Edge Super, stag hdl, 5½" bd, VG ...65.00
Hunting, Puma White Hunter, stag hdl, 6" bd, EX w/sheath ...85.00
Hunting, US Model 1880, 8½" single edge spear point bd, EX ...400.00
Sailor's, whalebone hdl, 7", +makeshift sheath 125.00
Sheath knife, stag hdl, integral guard, Linder-Forester, 5", M ...50.00
Skinning, Puma #6373, stag hdl, 5" bd, EX w/sheath 50.00
Trench, brass knuckle hdl, mk US 1917, EX 175.00
WWII, handmade w/plexiglass hdl, 8" blade, w/sheath, EX ...125.00

Kosta

Kosta glassware has been made in Sweden since 1742. Today they are one of that country's leading producers of quality art glass. Two of their most important designers were Elis Bergh (1929 – 1950) and Vicke Lindstrand, artistic director from 1950 to 1973. Lindstrand brought to the company knowledge of important techniques such as Graal, fine figural engraving, Ariel, etc. He influenced new artists to experiment with these techniques and inspired them to create new and innovative designs. Today's collectors are most interested in pieces made during the 1950s and '60s. Our advisor for this category is Abby Malowanczyk; she is listed in the Directory under Texas.

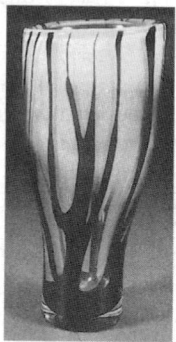

Vase, Trad I Dimma, amorphous aubergine trees in clear walls with white opal fog among branches, Lindstrand/Kosta/LU2005, 1959, 13", $2,990.00.

Vase, clear w/cut decor & purple canes, Lindstrand/#631, 10" ...300.00
Vase, eng fishermen w/nets, conical, Lindstrand/#LG134, 9½" ..465.00
Vase, flattened teardrop on ped base, Lindstrand 1962/63, 5¾" .175.00
Vase, int seaweed/bubbles, teardrop, Lindstrand/ LH 1803, 8" ...195.00
Vase, mauve stripe fishnets, slits simulate fish, LS 612, 5¼" 300.00
Vase, trees/fog, wht semiopaque/blk, Lindstrand, LH 1493, '59, 9" .1,300.00

Kutani

Kutani, named for the Japanese village where it originated, was first produced in the seventeenth century. The early ware, Ko Kutani, was made for only about thirty years. Several types were produced before 1800, but these are rarely encountered. In the nineteenth century, kilns located in several different villages began to copy the old Kutani wares. This later, more familiar type has large areas of red with gold designs on a white ground decorated with warriors, birds, and flowers in controlled colors of red, gold, and black.

Bowl, geishas & medallions, ca 1900, 6½" 230.00
Bowl, trees/boats/houses/etc, w/lid, 1900s, 5x4" 65.00
Charger, figures in scene, gilt border, 12" 285.00
Chocolate pot, flowers & birds in reserve, people/gardens, 8" 150.00
Compote, figures & florals, 1890s, 5½x8" 185.00
Cup, Gods of Good Fortune, inscription, 2" 70.00
Jardiniere, figures in panels, red/navy/gold, 1800s, 14x17" 2,150.00
Teapot, figures in scene, cobalt w/gold, ftd, squat, mk, 8" 650.00

Labels

Before the advent of the cardboard box, wooden crates were used for transporting products. Paper labels were attached to the crates to identify the contents and the packer. These labels often had colorful lithographed illustrations covering a broad range of subjects. Eventually the cardboard box replaced the crate, and the artwork was imprinted directly onto the carton. Today these paper labels are becoming collectible — primarily for the art, but also for their advertising appeal. Our advisor for this category is Cerebro; their address is listed in the Directory under Pennsylvania.

Can, Apollo, goddess playing lyre, fruit, EX 15.00
Can, Blue Banner Malt Syrup, wheat, yel/bl/wht, VG 4.00
Can, Casserole Oysters, bowl of oysters in cream, M 5.00
Can, Cuckoo Brand, singing bird on branch, M 15.00
Can, Dellford White Potatoes, boy w/food basket, sm, M 1.00
Can, Eatmor, waiter w/salmon can on tray, M 8.00
Can, Epicure Elderberries, man w/can, fruits & berries, M 8.00
Can, Ferndell, ferns, lima beans in pods, M 12.00
Can, Garden, red bowl of gr beans, M 1.00
Can, Kamo Shrimp, mallard duck on water, 1923, EX 30.00
Can, La Choy Chow Mein Noodles, Chinese dishes, 1934, EX 7.00
Can, National Dairy Chocolate, happy children, 1950s, EX 5.00
Can, Royal Baker, baker inspecting pie, blackberries, EX 2.00
Can, Shawnee Tomatoes, Indian on horsebk on summit, M 20.00
Cigar box, inner lid; New Day, sunrise/tobacco field, 1935, M 10.00
Cigar box, inner lid; Red Line, red train & caboose, M 200.00
Cigar box, inner lid; Turnover Club, people at table, M 100.00
Cigar box, outer; General Knox, military portrait, M 50.00
Cigar box, outer; Illustrato, painter & 2 women, M 7.00
Cigar box, outer; Kennel Club, dog in coat & scarf, M 25.00
Cigar box, outer; Opera Pony, cameo of woman, cherub, EX 14.00
Cigar box, outer; Supporter, socker player kicking ball, M 15.00
Cigar box, outer; Zurica, tigers & women by torch, M 30.00
Crate, apple, Apple Kids, 2 boys push/pull apple, 1940, M 12.00
Crate, apple, Chief Joseph, Indian, 1940, M 7.50
Crate, apple, Independent, Liberty Bell on bl, 1930, M 4.00
Crate, apple, Laurie, girl reaching for fruit, 1940, M 5.00
Crate, apple, Swan, lg wht swan, 1920, EX 10.00
Crate, apple, Utility Brand, valley view, yel apples, 1920, M 8.00
Crate, California Orange, Cock of the Walk, rooster, 1930, M 50.00
Crate, California Orange, Pine Cone, lg cone/orchard, 1930, M 7.00
Crate, California Orange, Woodlake Gold, tree/lake/mtns, M 6.00
Crate, Florida Citrus, Blue Heron, bird & coast, M 17.50
Crate, Florida Citrus, Florida Cowboy, man on bronco, 1930, M .10.00
Crate, Florida Citrus, Full Ahead, battleship at sea, 7x7", M 1.00
Crate, Florida Citrus, Orange Lake, pineapple, M 1.00
Crate, lemon, Basketball, women playing basketball, 1920, EX 50.00
Crate, lemon, Index, hand pointing at lemons, 1920, M 7.00
Crate, lemon, Montecito Valley, stone litho of grove, 1920, M 24.00
Crate, lemon, Southland Beauties, rose buds, 1950, EX 3.00
Crate, lemon, Vesper, church at dusk, 1930, M 3.00
Crate, pear, B-Wise, owl on bl, 1930, M 16.00
Crate, pear, Pet's Best, smiling boy, M 4.00
Crate, pear, Top Card, ace of spades atop 3 cards, 1940, M 3.00

Labino

Dominick Labino was a glass blower who until mid-1985 worked in his studio in Ohio, blowing and sculpting various items which he signed and dated. A ceramic engineer by trade, he was instrumental in developing the heat-resistant tiles used in space flights. His glassmaking shows his versatility in the art. While some of his designs are free-form and futuristic, others are reminiscent of the products of older glasshouses. Because of problems with his health, Mr. Labino became unable to blow glass himself; he died January, 10, 1987. Work coming from his studio since mid-1985 has been signed 'Labino Studios, Baker,' indicating ware made by his protegee, E. Baker O'Brien. In addition to her own compositions, she continues to use many of the colors developed by Labino.

Bottle, silver schmelz, knopped neck, 1978, 7" 750.00
Cup, smoky w/red rim, 1967, 3½" 450.00
Emergence, dbl veil & encased air, 1976, 6" 6,100.00

Fountain, clear bl w/gold veil & colored design, 1970, 5¾" **3,500.00**
Fountain, pk/purple int emerging forms in clear, 1983, 9" **3,000.00**
Paperweight, bl w/purple clouds, opal/brn swirls, conical, 4" **325.00**
Paperweight, peach w/air bubbles & veil, 1971, lg **400.00**

Pitcher, dark red to brown opaque at top, signed and dated 1968, 7", $550.00; Free-form sculpture titled Iris, cobalt blue, signed and dated 1975, 7½", $1,000.00.

Sea Kingdom, clear w/bl fish, 1979, 4" **4,800.00**
Vase, bl opal w/lt ruby swirls, ovoid, 1971, 5x4" **525.00**
Vase, bud; pk swirled, 1968, 5½" **850.00**
Vase, clear bl-gr, dbl gourd int w/2 bubbles, 1967, 5½" **750.00**
Vase, clear-cased cobalt w/3-color pull-ups, 1979, 5½" **1,200.00**
Vase, cobalt bl w/appl dripping ribs & tooling, 1981, 6½" **450.00**
Vase, copper w/red/bl/wht/orange design, ovoid, 1983, 4½" **500.00**
Vase, owl, clear salmon irid, 1981, 3¾" **325.00**
Vase, silver schmelz w/lav & gr swirls, wide mouth, 1968, 7½" .**1,300.00**
Vase, yel 'ferns' on caramel w/int petal motif, 1982, 5½" **650.00**

Lace, Linens, and Needlework

Two distinct audiences vie for old lace and linens. Collectors seek out exceptional stitchery like philatelists and numismatists seek stamps or coins — simply to marvel at its beauty, rarity, and ties to history. Collectors judge lace and linens like figure skaters and gymnasts are judged: artist impression is half the score, technical merit the other. How complex and difficult are the stitches and how well are they done? The 'users' see lace and linens as recyclables. They seek pretty wearables or decorative materials. They want fashionable things in mint condition, and have little or no interest in technique. Both groups influence price.

Undiscovered and underpriced are the eighteenth-century masterpieces of lace and needle art in techniques which will never be duplicated. Their beauty is subtle. Amazing stitches often are invisible without magnification. To get the best value in any lace, linen, or textile item, learn to look closely at individual stitches, and study the design and technique. The finest pieces are wonderfully constructed. The stitches are beautiful to look at and do a good job of holding the thing together. Our advisor for this category is Elizabeth M. Kurella; she is listed in the Directory under Michigan.

Key: embr — embroidered

Barbe (long tie), Maltese bobbin lace, pearl-wht silk, 8x64" **445.00**
Bed cover, crochet, yarn-woven wooden soldiers in sqs, 48x96" .**115.00**
Bedspread, crochet, ecru, heavy, old, 78x102" **175.00**
Bedspread, Marseilles lace, cutouts for bed posts, full sz **250.00**
Blanket, wool homespun, 3-color plaid, 2-pc, 79x96", EX **200.00**
Bobbin lace, pomegranate design, beige, 5½" **15.00**
Cape, needle lace, wht, late 1800s, 10x50" dia **285.00**
Collar, bobbin lace, geometric design (like Cluny or LePuy), EX .**145.00**
Collar, bobbin lace, wht, lapel style, 19th C, 2½x24" **85.00**
Collar, knotted lace, geometric, Middle-Eastern, 4¼" deep **125.00**
Collar, Maltese bobbin lace, scalloped edge, 5x20" **175.00**

Collar, Maltese bobbin lace, silk, leaves & wheat ears, 7½x17" .**285.00**
Collar, Maltese bobbin lace, silk, medallions/wheat, scallops **355.00**
Comforter, patchwork, mc w/red border, fading, ca 1800, 86x90" .**130.00**
Crewel picture, ship w/9 flags, rose vine border, 15x21", EX ...**1,200.00**
Cuffs, Duchesse bobbin lace, cream wht, 19th C, 8½x3½", pr .**105.00**
Curtain panels, ecru machine lace, rprs, 103x32", EX **150.00**
Doily, Battenberg lace, oval, 9¼x13½" **40.00**
Doily, Battenberg lace, 5¾" sq **15.00**
Doily, chemical (machine) lace, floral (like Duchesse lace), 6" **15.00**
Doily, crochet, dog sitting on porch, 17x12½" **36.00**
Doily, crochet, God Bless Our Home, 9x16" **45.00**
Doily, drawnwork (fine & complex), 6" sq **35.00**
Doily, meandering tape design, Hungarian or E European, 10" **15.00**
Doily, needle design, rose motif, beige, 6" dia **10.00**
Doily, tatted lace, 12" dia **70.00**
Fallcap, Honiton English bobbin lace, mid-19th C, 6½x13" **185.00**
Fichu, Brussels bobbin lace appl on machine net, 19th C, 17x60" .**525.00**
Fichu, Duchesse bobbin lace, flower bouquets, mid-19th C, 13x60" .**525.00**
Fichu, Maltese bobbin lace, silk, tulip design, 13x68" **375.00**
Fichu (sm shawl), machine lace, wht, 19th C, 10½x36", VG **75.00**
Flounce, lace dbl-headed eagles/scrolls/etc, 18th C, 8½x36" **950.00**
Handkerchief, hairpin lace **45.00**
Handkerchief, 5" Point-de-Gaze needle lace, 1870s, 18" sq **350.00**
Jabot, Valenciennes bobbin lace, dbl ruffle, 5x13" **85.00**
Lace fragment, Mechlin bobbin lace, 18th C, 2½x8" **55.00**
Lappet, Brussels bobbin lace, ca 1740, 22" dia, damaged, pr **650.00**
Mantel cloth, embr roses on fine wht linen, Victorian, 26x88" ..**265.00**
Mat, handmade filet, asymmetrical, 9½x5¼" **15.00**
Needle lace fragment, cherubs/bows/flowers/etc, 19th C, 11x14" .**75.00**
Needle lace initial, set in lacy oval, 2x1½" **10.00**
Needlepoint panel, lovebirds among roses, ca 1845, 18x16", EX .**100.00**
Needlework panel, bird & flowers, 1850s, in maple fr: 35x32" ...**375.00**
Needlework panel, couple on beach, floral border, 19th C, 14x17" ..**150.00**
Needlework panel, dog & tree, rose border, sgn/1829, 17x17" ...**375.00**
Needlework panel, embr velvet w/leaves & pods, fringe, 26x14" ...**75.00**
Needlework panel, Napoleon on horsebk, Fr, 1850s, 25x28" ...**165.00**
Needlework panel, parrot on branch, yarn on velvet, fr, 20x14" ..**215.00**
Needlework panel, sailing ship, wool yarn on linen, 28x40" **85.00**
Petite-point panel, cherubs dancing, 19th C, gilt fr, 9x11" **150.00**
Piano shawl, blk silk w/pk roses, chenille work, 18" fringe **150.00**
Pillow, baby's, crochet lace inserts, sm **25.00**
Pillow, embr lady in flower hat on pk organdy, much lace, 24x14" .**70.00**
Pillow case, Irish linen, tatted edge, pr, MIB **45.00**
Pillow top, embr red & pk roses, Victorian **30.00**
Runner, Battenberg, 24x40" **65.00**
Runner, filet lace, cherubs in center, 18x42" **145.00**
Runner, linen w/gold/orange Arts & Craft designs, 48x21", VG ...**100.00**
Shams, cutwork & lace inserts, monogrammed, pr **85.00**
Shams, wht-on-wht floral trapunto w/tied lace border, 39x21", pr .**465.00**
Shawl, machine-made Chantilly lace, ca 1860s, from $45 to **75.00**
Sheet, heavy linen, Italian cutwork baskets, lg, w/pillow covers .**225.00**
Sheet, lace edge, embr & monogram, 84x78" **65.00**
Sheet, much cutwork, inset lace panels w/angel/cherubs, 95x66" ...**175.00**
Show towel, embr birds & flowers on homespun, 1841, 67x18", VG ...**160.00**
Table pc, Battenberg lace, 14" dia **70.00**
Table pc, crochet, Spirit of St Louis & plane in center, 18x25" .**100.00**
Table pc, filet lace, Grecian lady & cherubs, 10x23" **80.00**
Table pc, silk w/embr roses, 45x45"+20" fringe **165.00**
Tablecloth, Battenberg, ecru grape clusters, 104x68", +12 napkins ..**500.00**
Tablecloth, Battenberg vintage pattern, 49" dia **175.00**
Tablecloth, Battenberg 17" vintage border, 65" dia **295.00**
Tablecloth, drawnwork center, machine lace inserts, 68x88" **45.00**
Tablecloth, ecru, ornate cutwork & embr, 65x134", +12 napkins ..**995.00**
Tablecloth, handwoven linen, geometric pattern, 1840s, 45x70" ...**100.00**

Tablecloth, homespun cotton w/stitched wool florals, 36x36" ...**115.00**
Tablecloth, linen, Cluny lace inserts & edge, 92" dia **325.00**
Tablecloth, linen, Italian cutwork, 70x90", +12 napkins **275.00**
Tablecloth, Madeira lace, 72" dia **150.00**
Tablecloth, needle lace, beige, 19th C, 70x104", +10 napkins ...**725.00**
Tablecloth, 5" Cluny lace border, scalloped center, 22" dia **195.00**

Lacy Glassware

Lacy glass became popular in the late 1820s after the development of the pressing machine. It was decorated with allover patterns — hearts, lyres, sheaves of wheat, etc. — and backgrounds were completely stippled. The designs were intricate and delicate, hence the term 'lacy.' Although Sandwich produced this type of glassware in abundance, it was also made by other eastern glassworks as well as in the Midwest. By 1840, its popularity on the wane and a depressed economy forcing manufacturers to seek less expensive modes of production, lacy glass began to be phased out in favor of pressed pattern glass.

When no condition is indicated, the items listed below are assumed to be without obvious damage; minor roughness is normal. See also Salts, Open.

Bowl, Butterfly, ca 1835-50, 1x6¼x4½" **95.00**
Bowl, Eagle, sitting owl in 4 panels, scalloped edge, 6", EX **100.00**
Bowl, Gothic Arch & Pineapple, 10" L, EX **300.00**
Bowl, Industry, 6¼", EX **150.00**
Bowl, nappy, Iron Cross in Heart Box, 1835-50, rare, 2x10" ...**1,000.00**
Bowl, nappy, Princess Feather Medallion, ca 1830-45, 1¼x6" **45.00**
Bowl, nappy, Rayed Peacock Eye, ca 1835-50, 1x8½" **325.00**
Bowl, nappy, Tulip & Acanthus Leaf, plume ft, 5⅛x8½" **400.00**
Bowl, Peacock Eye, bl tinge, ca 1835-50, 1½x6¾" **325.00**
Bowl, Peacock Feather & Dmn, 1830-45, 2x10½x7¾" **800.00**
Bowl, Princess Feather Medallion & Basket of Flowers, 2x10½x8½" ..**350.00**
Bowl, Rayed Peacock Eye, 11" L, VG **100.00**
Bowl, Roman Rosette, ftd, 1835-1850, 6½x10¾", EX **350.00**
Bowl, vegetable; Princess Feather/Basket of Flowers, 10½" **350.00**
Creamer, Heart & Scale, 1838-45, 4½" **350.00**
Creamer, Tulip & Scroll, flake/roughness, mini, 1⅝" **40.00**
Dish, Constitution & Am Eagle, oval, 1830-33, 6⅛", EX **500.00**
Egg cup, Anthemion leaves, scalloped rim, 3⅜", EX **70.00**
Honey dish, Scroll, amethyst, 4½" dia **50.00**
Plate, Pine Tree & Shield, opal, scalloped, 6" **350.00**
Plate, Scroll & Scale, 1835-45, 6⅛" **60.00**
Sugar bowl, Gothic Arch, electric bl, w/lid, 5", EX **2,200.00**
Sugar bowl, Gothic Arch, 5⅛", EX **80.00**
Sugar bowl, scalloped rim, ca 1830s, 5¾", EX **180.00**
Tureen, deep sapphire bl, w/lid, Sandwich, mini, 2x3" **400.00**
Whiskey taster, gray-bl, pontil, 1⅞" **105.00**
Window pane, Ritchie, acorns/leaves surround riverboat, 7x5" ..**10,500.00**

Lalique

Beginning his lengthy career as a designer and maker of fine jewelry, Rene Lalique at first only dabbled in glass, making small panels of cire perdue (wax casting) to use in his jewelry. He also made small flacons of gold and silver with his glass inlays, which attracted the attention of M.F. Coty, who commissioned Lalique to design bottles for his perfume company. The success of this venture resulted in the opening of his own glassworks at Combs-la-Ville in 1909. In 1921 a larger factory was established at Wingen-sur-Moder in Alsace-Lorraine. By the '30s Lalique was world renown as the most important designer of his time.

Lalique glass is lead based, either mold blown or pressed. Favored motifs during the Art Nouveau period were dancing nymphs, fish, dragonflies, and foliage. Characteristically the glass is crystal in combination with acid-etched relief. Later some items were made in as many as ten colors (red, amber, and green among them) and were occasionally accented with enameling. These colored pieces, especially those in black, are highly prized by advanced collectors.

During the '20s and '30s, Lalique designed several vases and bowls reminiscent of American Indian art. He also developed a line in the Art Deco style decorated with stylized birds, florals, and geometrics. In addition to vases, clocks, automobile mascots, stemware, and bottles, many other useful objects were produced. Most items made before his death in 1945 were marked 'R. Lalique'; later the 'R' was deleted even though some of the original molds were still used. Numbers found on the bases of some pieces are catalog numbers. Beware of fraudulent pieces that have begun to surface in increasing numbers. Our advisor for this category is John Danis; he is listed in the Directory under Illinois.

Key:
cl/fr — clear and frosted
L — signed Lalique
LF — signed Lalique France
RL — signed R. Lalique
RLF — signed R. Lalique, France

Statuette, Suzanne, opal, draped nude with outstretched arms, R Lalique, 9¼", $7,500.00.

Annual plate, 1966 through 1969, MIB, ea **75.00**
Annual plate, 1971 through 1975, MIB, ea **50.00**
Atomizer, Nini Ricci, bird motif, gold trim **400.00**
Bookends, Tete D'Aigle, eagle head, fr, stepped base, LF, pr **865.00**
Bottle, scent; Air du Temps, sunburst, cl/fr, LF, 2" **275.00**
Bottle, scent; Ambroise, stepped leaves, fr, RL, 3" **770.00**
Bottle, scent; Amphitrite, cl-gray, nude stopper, RLF, 3¾" **1,000.00**
Bottle, scent; Belle Saison, cl/fr w/enameling, RL, 4", w/box ..**2,500.00**
Bottle, scent; Cinq Fleurs, 5 flowers, cl/fr, RL, 4" **550.00**
Bottle, scent; Coeur Joie, heart form, cl/fr, LF, 3⅜" **385.00**
Bottle, scent; draped woman ea corner, blk, floral stopper, L, 5¼" .**1,000.00**
Bottle, scent; Fille d'Eve, Daughter of Eve, cl/fr apple, L, 2½" ...**300.00**
Bottle, scent; Fleurs de Pommier, gr wash, tiara stopper, RLF, 5½" .**5,000.00**
Bottle, scent; Grecian maidens, cl/fr, brn wash, RL, 6⅛" **1,200.00**
Bottle, scent; Hirondelle, Swallow Sq, cl/fr, bl wash, RL, 3½" ...**1,450.00**
Bottle, scent; maidens w/flowers, amber w/brn wash, 1910, 6" **500.00**
Bottle, scent; Olives, 8 oval cabochons, lt bl wash, RL, 4¾" ...**1,000.00**
Bottle, scent; Pan, satyr's heads, cl/fr, bl patina, RL, 5" **1,550.00**
Bottle, scent; Panier de Roses, pk fr, RL, 4" **2,200.00**
Bottle, scent; Perles, swags, fr w/turq enamel, RL, 8", pr **700.00**
Bottle, scent; Salamandres, lizards, cl/gray-gr wash, RLF, 3¾" ..**1,500.00**
Bottle, scent; Telline, gr semi-opaque, RL, 3¾", NM **3,500.00**
Bottle, scent; Tzigane, gypsy, cl/fr, RL, 4¼" **500.00**
Bottle, scent; Vers le Jour, lt/dk amber w/chevrons, RL, 4¼" ..**1,045.00**
Bowl, birds on branches, fr, sq base, LF, paper label, 5½" H **250.00**
Bowl, Dahlias, fr, RL, ca 1921, 12" **1,800.00**
Bowl, lily of the valley, opal, RL, 12¼" **600.00**
Bowl, lotus blossoms & lily pads, fr, RL, 4½x11" **700.00**

Bowl, Lutteurs, male figures, lt brn enamel, L, 5⅜" 3,450.00
Bowl, Marguerite, daisies, cl/fr, script sgn, low, 12½" dia 450.00
Bowl, Nemours, flowers, cl/blk enamel centers, LF, 4x10" 500.00
Bowl, Pinsons, birds, cl/fr, LF, 3¾x9¼" 250.00
Bowl, Sirene, wht opal, RL, 14⅜" 1,500.00
Bowl, Vernon, sunflowers, opal, RLF, 2⅛x8½" 700.00
Box, powder; swans, LF, 2½x3½" dia 300.00
Burner, perfume; Sirenes, opal/bl wash, orig wick, RLF, 7" 1,200.00
Candlesticks, Tokyo, stylized tree form, RLF, 8¼", pr 1,000.00
Clock, lovebirds, wht opal, domed glass, 10½", EX 1,200.00
Decanter, teardrop, cl, fr grapes stopper, LF, 9½" 250.00
Jar, Dans La Nuit, stars, cl/bl opaque, raised mk, 5" 475.00
Jar, powder; Quatre Scarabees, 4 scarabs, bl fr, RL, 3⅜" 1,950.00
Lamp, boudoir; 2 birds, cl/fr w/bl heads, LF, 12"+shade 1,600.00
Lamp, boudoir; 2 fr doves on base, LF, 8½"+fabric shade 2,750.00
Luminaire, Oiseau de Feu, bird-woman, cl/fr, RLF, 17" 12,000.00
Mascot, Archer, cl/fr, RLF, on NP brass base, 6½" 1,500.00
Mascot, Bison, 31196 ....325.00
Mascot, Chouette, owl, #1193 ....325.00
Mascot, Coq Nain, rooster, #1135 ....395.00
Mascot, eagle's head, cl/fr, RL, 4" 395.00
Mascot, Libellule Grande, dragonfly, cl/fr, RL/RLF, 8½" 5,000.00
Mascot, Saint-Christophe, cl/fr, RLF, 6" 1,000.00
Mirror, Narcisse Couche, fr w/gray wash, nude at hdl, RLF, 12" L 980.00
Paperweight, Levrier, greyhound, cl/fr, RLF, 7⅞" 1,955.00
Paperweight, owl, cl/fr, LF, 3½" 195.00
Paperweight, wart hog, cl/fr, LF, 2¾" 120.00
Pendant medallion, Dans les Fleurs, fr, RL Fioret Paris, 1⅜" 520.00
Shade, chrysanthums/leaves, cl/fr, invt hanging dome, 6x12" 900.00
Statuette, Crucifixion, on heavy lit stand, 20x11" 500.00
Statuette, Hiver Surtout Quatre Saisons, fr, LF, 7¾" 575.00
Statuette, Thais, nude, cl opal, RL, 8½" 7,500.00
Vase, Archers, bl frost, RLF, 10½", NM 16,000.00
Vase, Archers, fr/gray wash, RLF, #893, 10½", NM 2,750.00
Vase, Coqs et Plumes, roosters, fr, RLF, 6¼" 925.00
Vase, Danaides, nudes w/vessels, opal, RFL, #972, 7⅛" 2,500.00
Vase, Domremy, thistles, gray fr w/coral enamel, RLF, 8⅜" 1,800.00
Vase, draped nudes, fr, 8-sided rim, RL, 5½" 700.00
Vase, Eglantines, rose branches, fr, oval, RL, 4½" 400.00
Vase, flowers/leaves/dmns in relief, cl/fr, RL, 5" 225.00
Vase, Formose, gr fr, RLF, 6¾" 3,450.00
Vase, Grignon, feathery leaves, cl/fr, RLF, 7⅛" 450.00
Vase, Gros Scarabees, red, RLF, #892, 11½" 7,000.00
Vase, Ibis, herons amid bamboo, fr/brn wash, RLF, 9½" 1,600.00
Vase, Jafa, petal forms, fr, RLF, 7⅞" 1,950.00
Vase, Malesherbes, overlapping leaves, gray fr, RLF, 9" 1,380.00
Vase, Ondines, nude sea nymphs, 10" 675.00
Vase, Ormeaux, elm leaves, fr, RLF, #984, 6⅝" 500.00
Vase, Ormeaux, elm leaves, gr opaque, RLF, #984, 6⅝" 2,000.00
Vase, Perruches, lovebirds, fr opal, RL, 10" 4,025.00
Vase, Piriac, fish, cl/fr, #1043, 6½" 550.00
Vase, St Marc, cl/fr, ca 1950, 6½" 445.00
Vase, Thibet, recumbent ibex hdls, fr, RLF, 8" 2,300.00
Vase, Tulipes, cl/fr opal, RLF, 8⅛" 1,725.00

Lamps

The earliest lamps were simple dish containers with a wick that hung over the edge or was supported by a channel or tube. Grease and oil from animal or vegetable sources were the first fuels used. Ancient pottery lamps, crusie, and Betty lamps are examples of these early types. In 1784 Swiss inventor Ami Argand introduced the first major improvement in lamps. His lamp featured a tubular wick and a glass chimney. During the first half of the 19th century, whale oil, burning fluid (a highly explosive mixture of turpentine and alcohol), and lard were the most common fuels used in North America. Many lamps were patented for specific use with these fuels.

Kerosene was the first major breakthrough in lighting fuels. It was demonstrated by Canadian geologist Dr. Abraham Gesner in 1846. The discovery and drilling of petroleum in the late 1850s provided an abundant and inexpensive supply of kerosene. It became the main source of light for homes during the balance of the 19th century and for remote locations until the 1950s.

Although Thomas A. Edison invented the electric lamp in 1879, it was not until two or three decades later that electric lamps replaced kerosene household lamps. Millions of kerosene lamps were made for every purpose and pocketbook. They ranged in size from tiny night or miniature lamps to tall stand or piano lamps. Hanging varieties for homes commonly had one or two fonts (oil containers), but chandeliers for churches and public buildings often had six or more. Wall or bracket lamps usually had silvered reflectors. Student lamps, parlor lamps (now called Gone-With-the-Wind lamps), and patterned glass lamps were designed to complement the popular furnishing trends of the day. Gaslight, introduced in the early 19th century, was used mainly in homes of the wealthy and public places until the early 20th century. Most fixtures were wall or ceiling mounted, although some table models were also used.

Few of the ordinary early electric lamps have survived. Many lamp manufacturers made the same or similar styles for either kerosene or electricity, sometimes for gas. Top-of-the-line lamps were made by Pairpoint, Phoenix, Tiffany, Bradley and Hubbard, and Handel. See also these specific sections.

When buying lamps that have been converted to electricity, inspect them very carefully for any damage that may have resulted from the alterations; such damage is very common, and when it does occur, the lamp's value may be lessened by as much as 50%. Lamps seem to bring much higher prices in some areas than others, especially the larger cities. Conversely, in rural areas they may bring only half as much as our listed values. One of our advisors for lamps is Carl Heck; he is listed in the Directory under Colorado. Advice for miniature lamps comes from Bob Culver; he is listed in the Directory under Michigan. See also Stained Glass.

Aladdin Lamps, Electric

From 1908 Aladdin lamps with a mantle became the mainstay of rural America, providing light that compared favorably with the electric light bulb. They were produced by the Mantle Lamp Company of America in over eighteen models and more than one hundred styles. During the 1930s to the 1950s, this company was the leading manufacturer of electric lamps as well. Still in operation today, the company is now known as Aladdin Industries Inc., located in Nashville, Tennessee. For those seeking additional information on Aladdin Lamps, we recommend *Aladdin — The Magic Name in Lamps, Aladdin Electric Lamps,* and *A Collector's Manual and Price Guide,* all written by our advisor for Aladdins, J. W. Courter; he is listed in the Directory under Kentucky. Mr. Courter has also published a book called *Angle Lamps, Collector's Manual and Price Guide.*

Bed, #2021 SS, whip-o-lite shade 75.00
Bedroom, P-55, ceramic 30.00
Bedroom, P-68, ceramic 35.00
Boudoir, G-203R, Alacite 40.00
Boudoir, G-24, Alacite, Cupid, short base 150.00
Boudoir, G-47C, Alacite, Hoppy bullet w/shade 400.00
Boudoir, G-61, moonstone base, 1935 ....75.00
Figurine, G-375, Dancing Ladies Urn 950.00

Figurine, G-70, lady in cape, etched crystal, minimum value ..**1,500.00**
Figurine, G-77, glass, Susie, minimum value **800.00**
Figurine, M-160, horse, metal, minimum value **500.00**
Pin-Up, P-57, ceramic, Gun-n-Holster **125.00**
Ranch House, G-355C, gun in holster wall plaque w/decal **300.00**
Table, #204, Vogue ped, red **475.00**
Table, #785, Lg Vase, gr **225.00**
Table, E-380 ....**140.00**
Table, G-142, etched crystal **175.00**
Table, G-169, crystal **175.00**
Table, G-184, opalique **400.00**

Table lamp, G-195, Alacite, lighted base, whip-o-lite shade and finial, EX, $100.00.

Table, G-199, Alacite, illuminated base **100.00**
Table, G-234, Alacite, pheasant **200.00**
Table, G-243, Alacite, illuminated base **60.00**
Table, G-25, glass **150.00**
Table, G-288, Alacite, illuminated base **60.00**
Table, G-296D, Alacite, classic figures, illuminated base **90.00**
Table, G-329, Alacite **50.00**
Table, G-348, Alacite, world lamp **250.00**
Table, G-49, glass **100.00**
Table, G-85, glass **150.00**
Table, M-476, Abacus, metal **50.00**
Table, M-5, metal **100.00**
Table, MT-407, ceramic, magic touch **350.00**
Table, P-404, ceramic **40.00**
Table, P-424, ceramic **30.00**
TV, TV-380, shell, ceramic **50.00**
TV, TV-385, ceramic **40.00**
Urn, G-376, Alacite, short **100.00**

Aladdin Lamps, Kerosene

Caboose Model C, B-400, aluminum font, w/burner, wht shade .**100.00**
Crystal Vase Model #12, bl Venetian Art-Craft, 10¼" **400.00**
Crystal Vase Model #12, variegated verde, 12" **175.00**
Floor Model #12, blk & gold, #1251 ....**200.00**
Floor Model B, #1258, bronze **150.00**
Floor Model B, B-270, gr & silver, 1936 ....**175.00**
Floor Model B, B-274, oxidized bronze, 1936 ....**175.00**
Floor Model B, B-280, ivory & gold, 1937 ....**200.00**
Floor Model B, B-292, bronze lacquer, 1939-42 ....**150.00**
Floor Model B, B-296, oxidized bronze plated, 1939-40 ....**200.00**
Foreign Model #11, table lamp, London **75.00**
Hanging Model #12, 4-post, parchment shade **300.00**
Hanging Model #6 w/#215 shade, harp w/chimney tube **375.00**
Hanging Model B, outside chain, parchment shade **375.00**
Practicus, table lamp, polished brass **375.00**
Shelf Model B-170, aluminum, blk, 1987-88 ....**50.00**
Student Model #4, Old English **6,000.00**

Table Model #12, str side, bronze or nickel **100.00**
Table Model #23, amber, mk Aladdin 1979 ....**100.00**
Table Model #23, red carnival, mk Aladdin/Fenton 1993, no shade ...**200.00**
Table Model A, Venetian, #102, peach **150.00**
Table Model B, Beehive, B-82L, amber crystal (lt) **150.00**
Table Model B, Cathedral, B-110, wht moonstone **300.00**
Table Model B, Colonial, #106, amber **175.00**
Table Model B, Corinthian, B-102, gr crystal **125.00**
Table Model B, Corinthian, B-116, rose moonstone **250.00**
Table Model B, Majestic, B-122, gr moonstone **350.00**
Table Model B, Orientale, B-133, silver **200.00**
Table Model B, Queen, B-96, wht moonstone, silver base **375.00**
Table Model B, Quilt, B-86, gr moonstone **250.00**
Table Model B, Short Lincoln Drape, B-60, Alacite **475.00**
Table Model B, Simplicity, B-27, Alacite, gold lustre **300.00**
Table Model B, Tall Lincoln Drape, B-75, Alacite, old formula .**200.00**
Table Model B, Tall Lincoln Drape, ruby crystal (deep color) ...**850.00**
Table Model B, Treasure, B-136, chromium **200.00**
Table Model B, Vertique, B-87, rose moonstone **375.00**
Table Model B, Washington Drape, B-41, amber crystal **125.00**
Table Model B, Washington Drape, B-48, gr crystal, bell stem ..**350.00**
Table Model B, Washington Drape, B-52, amber crystal, filigree ..**150.00**
Table Model B, Washington Drape, B-53, clear, plain stem **80.00**
Wall Bracket Model #21C, aluminum font **60.00**
Wall Bracket Model #7 or #8 , w/font & burner, no shade **500.00**

Angle Lamps

The Angle Lamp Company of New York City developed a unique type of kerosene lamp that was a vast improvement over those already on the market; they were sold from about 1896 until 1929 and were expensive for their time. Our Angle lamp advisor is J.W. Courter; he is listed in the Directory under Kentucky. See the narrative for Aladdin Lamps for information concerning popular books Mr. Courter has authored.

Barn lantern, 3115, tin, complete **1,000.00**
Chandelier, #465, 4-arm, polished brass, wired, plain glass **3,500.00**
Hanging, #203, 2-burner, NP tin, wht chimney tops, EX **350.00**
Hanging, #284, antique brass, no glass, EX **500.00**
Hanging, Classic, dbl; Antique Gold, EX **1,400.00**
Hanging, dbl; #203, nickel, old glass, EX **425.00**
Hanging, EG-22, nickel, old glass **550.00**
Hanging, Fleur-de-lis, 4-burner, antique copper, old glass, EX **925.00**
Hanging, 3-burner, emb grapes, nickel, no glass, EX **675.00**
Wall, #102, nickel, old glass **350.00**
Wall, #163, polished brass, old glass, EX **275.00**
Wall, EG-12, nickel, extended grape, no glass, EX **275.00**
Wall, floral pattern, tin, no glass, EX **245.00**
Wall, plain grape, nickel, old glass, EX **425.00**

Chandeliers

Art glass shades w/pulled leaves (7), SP mts, 6-arm, 43½" **1,050.00**
Brass, 2 tiers of arms, 16 electric candles, Dutch, 50x42" **3,950.00**
Bronze d'ore, Louis XV style, 30-light, 1870s, 60x30" **13,200.00**
Cast metal, 4-arm, glass bobeches/cut chimneys, 3 cast cherubs .**950.00**
Cast metal, 5 ivory glass shades, R Wmson Chicago, 24x19" **450.00**
Crystal, 5-light, domical shade above, prisms, 39" **1,100.00**
Crystal, 5-light, scroll arms, prisms, Victorian, 35x32" **990.00**
Irish cut crystal, 6-light, domed shade, prisms, 38" **900.00**
Italian-cvd giltwood, 12-light, ca 1900, electrified, 35x26" **825.00**
Parcel-gilt/patinated wrought iron, 6-light, Poillerat, 32" **4,000.00**
Rice paper & bamboo, varnished/ribbed globular shade, 35x45" ...**860.00**
Venetian glass, bl/clear, pendant drops, 3-tier/6-branch, 40" **500.00**

Wrought iron, 6 candle arms, trn wood center, some age, 20x29" ...**300.00**
Wrought steel w/scrollwork, 16 electric candles, 42x33x47" ...**1,155.00**
Yel/orange 14" shade+3 7" bell shades, wrought arms, Fr, 24" **900.00**
12 lights w/ind glass shades, prisms, 19th C, 46x22" **7,500.00**

Decorated Kerosene Lamps

Bl cut to wht to clear, 3-dolphin base, Sandwich, 12½", EX ...**2,000.00**
Bl cut to wht to clear w/gilt, stepped marble/brass base, 11⅜" **825.00**
Blk base & clear cut font w/cranberry stain, brass collar, 9¾" **275.00**
Brn-lav MOP Swirl, ribbed clambroth ball shade, 21" **795.00**
Clear font w/red & wht loopings, marble base, brass stem, 8" **600.00**
Cobalt cut to clear, marble base, fluted brass stem, 16½" **825.00**
Cranberry & wht latticinio font, brass stem, marble ft, 11" **1,400.00**
Cranberry craquelle w/gilt cut stripes, marble base, 8½" **300.00**
Cranberry o/l & gilt, cut stem & font, marble base, 15" **550.00**
Cranberry w/florals & gold, ruffled shade; metal ft, 12½" **650.00**
Dk bl cut to clear paw prints, brass stem, marble ft, 12" **700.00**
Fiery opal cut to clear, marble base, brass stem, 7¾" **300.00**
Gr opaque acanthus font, fire-gilt std, marble base, 12" **165.00**
Gr to clear w/eng flowers, wht opaque base, brass collar, 12" ...**1,100.00**
Milk glass cut to pk font w/pnt decor, wht marble base, 15" **330.00**
Pk cut to wht to clear, lg wht clambroth base, 13", EX **900.00**
Rubena frost w/floral 6" shade/font; orig burner, NP std, 15" **495.00**
Triple cut o/l butterflies, wht stem, marble base, Sandwich **900.00**
Tulip cuttings, clear/frosted, turned-over rim, Sandwich, 6½" ...**160.00**
Wht cut to clear w/circles, marble base, 9" **265.00**
Wht cut to clear w/t'prints & quatrefoils, marble base, 26" **450.00**
Wht cut to cranberry, brass stem, 2-step marble ft, 12" **1,200.00**
Wht cut to cranberry, stepped marble/brass base, 13" **1,430.00**

Fairy Lamps

Peacock blue satin shade with painted white flowers and leaves, matching 6" saucer, clear Clarke base, 5⅝", EX, $550.00.

Bl Nailsea fairy-sz dome, Clarke base, 4¾", EX **325.00**
Bl opal dome on cream base w/HP roses, Clarke-Tunnicliffe, 4⅛" ..**550.00**
Bl satin o/l, ruffled base, 4¼x5¾", EX **200.00**
Bl/wht/opaque Cleveland swirl w/emb ribs, 5¾", EX **450.00**
Bsk, brick cottage shape w/open windows, 6¾" **600.00**
Bsk, triangular w/mc faces of dog, cat & owl, 3¾" **600.00**
Burmese, Clarke clear glass base, pyramid sz, 4" **350.00**
Burmese, ruffled trn-down rim on base, Webb, 6" **835.00**
Burmese w/gr ivy, floral tapestry ceramic base, pyramid, 5x6" .**1,250.00**
Burmese w/HP florals dome shade on burmese molded base, 5" ..**850.00**
Citron fairy-sz dome on sgn Clarke base, sgn candle cup, 4¾" **225.00**
Citron Nailsea on matching tricorner base, Clarke base, 6¼" **725.00**
Cranberry swirl, appl crystal drips on base, pyramid, 4¼" **420.00**
Gr satin swirl, orig Burglar's Horror candle, pyramid, 3¾" **275.00**
Pk Dmn Quilt MOP pyramid-sz dome, Clarke base, 3¾", EX **150.00**
Pk smocked pyramid-sz dome, Clarke base, 4", EX **100.00**
Pk/wht/opaque Cleveland swirl, Clarke cup, fluted rim, 5⅜" **600.00**
Rose Nailsea dome, Clarke base, 4⅞", EX **300.00**

Wht opaque dog's head figural shade w/bl eyes, 4¼" **450.00**
Wht spatter on chartreuse, swirled ribs, clear candle cup, 5½" ...**580.00**

Gone-With-the-Wind and Banquet Lamps

Amber frost 11" globe w/matching squatty base, 22", EX **600.00**
Bl cut to clear Punty font, 2-step marble base, 20½" **2,550.00**
Cranberry w/cut ovals ball shade, brass/marble stem & base, 22" ..**650.00**
Dahlias emb on red satin, banquet sz **550.00**
Girls transfers on wht w/bl & gold, marble & brass stem, jr sz ...**1,000.00**
Gr, strawberries/dmns/fans, 3-section, att Dorflinger, 9½" dia ..**5,250.00**
Gr frost 11" globe w/matching fabrique textured base, 23" **550.00**
Red satin, roses & ribbons, matching ball shade/base **825.00**
Sapphire bl w/frosted bl verre moire shade, marble/metal base, 21" ...**500.00**
Treenware, trn base, kerosene burner, 21"+cut chimney **200.00**

Hanging Lamps

Bl satin Dmn Quilt MOP, jeweled brass fr, w/bell, EX **3,500.00**
Candle, bl opaline w/gold & jewels, fancy canopy, 6½x12" **400.00**
Cranberry w/wht enameling, brass fr w/shell & drop-in front ..**2,250.00**
Milk glass w/HP scenes, brass fr, prisms, 14" dia **250.00**
Milk glass w/transfer, brass fr, prisms, B&H burner, 36"+chain ..**450.00**
Nouveau CI fr, majolica font, milk glass shade, smoke bell, 21x12" ..**330.00**

Lanterns

Candle, pierced tin, 6-panel sides, 15¼x6¼" dia, EX **875.00**
Copper sphere w/hole in base, punched face, old patina, 22x11" ..**50.00**
Dietz Scout, tin, kerosene burner, Pat July-25-04, 7⅝x3" **55.00**
Hall, gilt brass, 5 curved glass panes, 35x15" dia, EX **770.00**
Lantern, Dietz 330 Beacon light, old gr pnt, EX, pr **230.00**
Nier No 5, tin w/dk red glass globe, MIG, 6⅛x3¼" dia **160.00**
Onion, tin w/red glass globe, brass burner, 10x5⅜", EX **395.00**
Pine w/old blk pnt, glass sides, candle socket, 10" **685.00**
Pine w/tin & wire fittings, pnt traces, rprs, 12" **275.00**
Royal Dietz, clear Popcorn globe, tin w/brass cap, 14¾x7" **120.00**
Sheet metal, glass in 4 sides, hinged bottom, blk rpt, 25" **250.00**
Skater's, Jewel, tin w/clear globe, 7⅛x3", EX **55.00**
Skater's, Orion, brass w/clear globe, MIG, 6⅝x2¾" **230.00**
Skater's, tin w/clear globe, orig burner, wire bail, 7x3" dia **75.00**
Wm Porter's Sons, brass w/clear globe, belled top, 17¼", EX **450.00**
Wood, tin candle socket, hinged door, bail hdl, 12" **450.00**
Wood w/tin door & candle holder, bail hdl, 9" **300.00**

Lard Oil/Grease Lamps

Betty, cast & wrought iron, brass spout extension, H Foker, 4" ..**440.00**
Betty, miner's, wrought iron w/heart finial, pnt, w/hanger, 4" **200.00**
Betty, wrought iron, arched spout & bracket, ca 1800, 5½" **200.00**
Betty, wrought iron, tin lid, rpl hanger, 6" **100.00**
Crusie, dbl, wrought iron, twisted hanger, 6" **125.00**
Crusie, wrought iron w/jam spike of twisted design, 7⅜x4⅝" **70.00**
Kettle, iron/brass, pencil std, 3-ftd saucer vase, 9" **300.00**
Loom, Continental, wrought iron w/brass rooster finial, 18x5¼" ..**350.00**
Rush, wrought iron, w/candle socket counterweight, 9½" **385.00**

Miniature Lamps, Kerosene

Miniature oil lamps were originally called 'night lamps' by their manufacturers. Early examples were very utilitarian in design — some holding only enough oil to burn through the night. When kerosene replaced whale oil in the second half of the nineteenth century, 'mini' lamps became more decorative and started serving other purposes. While mini lamps continue to be produced today, collectors place special value on the lamps of the kerosene era, roughly 1855 to 1910. Four reference books are especially valuable to collectors as they try to identify and value their collections: *Miniature Lamps* by Frank and Ruth Smith, Schiffer Publishing, 1968 (referred to as SI); *Miniature Lamps II* by Ruth Smith, Schiffer Publishing, 1982 (SII); *Miniature Victorian Lamps* by Margorie Hulsebus, Schiffer Publishing, 1996; and *Price Guide for Miniature Lamps* by Marjorie Hulsebus, Shiffer Publishing, 1998 (contains 1998 values for all the above books). References in the following listings correlate with each lamp's plate number in the Smith books. Our advisor is Bob Culver; he is listed in the Directory under Michigan.

Beaded Heart or Sweetheart, SI-109 ....150.00
Beauty Night Lamp, NP, SI-77 ....85.00
Block & Dot, milk glass, SI-191 ....125.00
Bull's Eye, gr glass, SI-110 ....100.00
Cable, flint, orig whale oil burner & cap, hdld 150.00
Cosmos, clear, SI-286 ....75.00
Cosmos, milk glass, SI-286 ....275.00
Cranberry opal swirl, LG Wright, 1960-70s 225.00
Defender, gr milk glass, SI-240 ....320.00
Evening Star emb on clear finger lamp, SI-12C 135.00
Fishscale, amber, SI-116 ....150.00
Handy emb on cobalt, SI-5L 90.00
Little Duchess, cobalt, brass saucer, SI-32 ....110.00
Little Harry's, clear, S-15 ....110.00
Little Harry's, milk glass, stem lamp, SI-17 ....285.00
Little Jewel emb on apple, gr, SI-44 ....110.00
Log Cabin, clear (beware of repros), SI-50 ....325.00
Nelly Bly, complete, SI-219 ....125.00
Noxall emb on clear, SI-22 ....90.00
Nutmeg emb on clear, SI-29 ....50.00
Nutmeg emb on cobalt, SI-29 ....100.00
Swan, pk milk glass, very rare complete, SI-499 ....2,800.00
TE Handy emb on clear, tin burner, SI-5R 65.00
Tulip, red satin, complete, SI-284 ....225.00
Twilight emb on clear stem lamp, SII-45 ....165.00

Motion Lamps

Animated motion lamps were made as early as 1920 and as late as 1980s. They reached their peak during the 1950s when plastic became widely used. They are characterized by action created by the heat of a light bulb which causes the cylinder to revolve and create the illusion of an animated scene. Some of the better-known manufacturers were Econolite Corp., Scene in Action Corp., and LA Goodman Mfg. Co. As with many collectible items, prices are guided by condition, availability, and collector demand. Values are given for lamps in mint condition. Any damage or flaws seriously reduce the price. Our advisors for motion lamps are Kaye and Jim Whitaker; they are listed in the Directory under Washington.

Fountain of Youth, Econolite (Roto-Vue Jr.), 1950, 10", $130.00.

Antique Autos, Econolite, 1957, 11" 110.00
Disneyland Express, Econolite, 1955, 11" 175.00
Elvgrin Pin-up Girls 400.00
Firefighters, LA Goodman, 1957, 11" 195.00
Fireplace, Econolite, 1958, 11" 115.00
Forest Fire, Econolite, 1955, 11" 75.00
Forest Fire, Rotovue Jr, 1949, 10" 75.00
Forest Fire, Scene in Action, 1931, 10" 100.00
Fresh Water Fish, Econolite, 1950s, 11" 95.00
Indian Chief, Gritt Inc, 1920s, 11" 115.00
Indian Maiden, Gritt Inc, 1920s, 11" 120.00
Japanese Twilight, Scene in Action 1931, 13" 150.00
Merry Go Round, Rotovue Jr, 1949, 10" 95.00
Michelob Advertising Lamp, Christmas design, 13" 95.00
Miss Liberty, Econolite, 1957, 11" 225.00
Niagara Falls, Econolite, 1955, 11" 75.00
Niagara Falls, Rotovue Jr, 1949, 10" 75.00
Niagara Falls, Scene in Action, 1931, 10" 100.00
Op Art Lamp, Visual Effects, 1970s, 13" 35.00
Oriental Fantasy, LA Goodman, 1957, 11" 95.00
Oriental Scene, Econolite, 1959, 11" 105.00
Sailboats, LA Goodman, 1954, 14" 110.00
Steamboats, Econolite, 1957, 11" 110.00
The Bar Is Open, Visual Effects, Op Art, 1970s, 13" 35.00
Totville Train, Econolite, 1948, 11" 150.00
Tropical Fish, Econolite, 1954, 11" 95.00
White Christmas, flat front, Econolite, 11" 125.00

Pattern Glass Lamps

Apollo, frosted/clear, Eagle burner, chimney, 21" 70.00
Appleton Plain, QA #2 burner, chimney, 7⅝" 30.00
Aries, brass burner, plain chimney, ftd hand lamp, 12½" 40.00
Beaded Heart, nutmeg burner, chimney mk Germany, 9⅝" 160.00
Blackberry, bl & wht clambroth, Sandwich, stand lamp, 8⅝" .1,100.00
Block & Dot, milk glass, nutmeg burner, clear chimney, 8" 45.00
Bridges Bowl, Venus burner, dtd 1867, hand lamp, 11¾" 40.00
Britannic, Eagle burner, chimney, hand lamp, 12⅛" 50.00
Bull's Eye, cobalt, nutmeg burner, ped ft, 9¼" 80.00
Bull's Eye, turq, nutmeg burner, ped ft, 9¼" 180.00
Bull's Eye Fine Detail, Banner burner, ped ft, chimney, 16" 50.00
Cathedral, amber, uptrn shade, acorn burner, 10⅞" 135.00
Christmas Tree, milk glass, gold ribs, acorn burner, 6½" 90.00
Claudia, Eagle burner, chimney, hand lamp, 13⅛" 55.00
Coin Dot, wht opal, flat base, finger lamp 300.00
Coin Dot #2, amber, complete 375.00
Convex Window, QA burner, chimney, hand lamp, 11½" 45.00
Coolidge Drape, QA burner, chimney, hand lamp, 14" 90.00
Daisy, amber, lg bull's-eye ft & shoulder, Colonial stem, 9" 100.00
Dart, brass burner, ped ft, chimney, 10" 45.00
Dogtooth, brass Eagle burner, plain chimney, hand lamp, 13⅝" ...45.00
Double Arch, Eagle burner, plain chimney, ped ft, 15⅝" 45.00
Drape, pk cased satin, ball shade, nutmeg burner, 10" 190.00
Duncan Bar Rayed Panel, QA burner, chimney, hand lamp, 11¾" ..90.00
Eclipse font, stand lamp, 9½" 125.00
Empress #2, emerald, complete, stand lamp 295.00
Eyebrow, brass collar, Eagle burner, hand lamp, 14" 45.00
Fancy Panel, brass Banner burner, chimney, ped ft, 21½" 100.00
Feathered Cartouche, Eagle burner, chimney, ped ft, 17" 50.00
Fishscale, brass burner, chimney, 18⅜" 60.00
Fishscale, pnt goofus, Eagle burner, chimney, hand lamp, 15⅛" ...80.00
Florette, gr cased, ball shade, nutmeg burner, 7¾" 400.00
Grace, White Flame burner, ped ft, chimney, 15⅞" 50.00
Greek Key, Eagle burner, chimney, hand lamp, 11½" 65.00

Hackle, stand lamp, 8½" **145.00**
Harp, clear flint, hornet burner, 9" **130.00**
Hobbs #1 Snowflake, wht, complete, stand lamp **375.00**
Hobbs Windows, wht opal **260.00**
Invt T'print, bl, flat base, finger lamp **400.00**
Invt T'print, cranberry, ball shade, nutmeg burner, 7¾" **85.00**
Janice, brass burner, ped ft, w/chimney, 17⅜" **55.00**
Lomax, brass burner, kitchen-style hand lamp, ped ft, 13¼" **40.00**
Lomax, Oil Gard Lamp...1870, hand lamp, 14⅛" **70.00**
Melon, hexagonal base, brass collar, 10⅛" **50.00**
Moon, brass Eagle burner, ped base, hand lamp, 14½" **55.00**
Peanut, brass burner, ped ft, chimney, 18⅛" **75.00**
Plain Six Panel, brass burner, chimney, 19" **60.00**
Princess Feather, cranberry spatter swirl, oil burner **80.00**
Princess Feather, QA burner, plain chimney, hand lamp, 13½" .**125.00**
Quartered Block, Eagle burner, ped ft, chimney, 16¾" **60.00**
Quartered Block, ftd finger lamp **200.00**
Rib Scallop, hinged burner mk Pat Apr 7 1866, hand lamp, 12¾" ..**50.00**
Rope Brand, Eagle burner, ped ft, chimney, 15¼" **50.00**
Sharon Panel, brass Banner burner, chimney, 17" **35.00**
Six Panel Fine Cut, brass ABCO burner, chimney, ped ft, 15¾" ..**45.00**
Stippled Fishscale, ped, finger lamp **48.00**
Turkey Foot, P&A Burner, chimney, flat bottom, hand lamp, 10½" **55.00**
Westmoreland, Eagle burner, ped ft, chimney, 18⅛" **100.00**
Wild Iris, milk glass, umbrella shade, fired-on pnt, 9½" **55.00**
Zipper Loop, finger lamp **140.00**

Peg Lamps

Bl Dmn Quilt MOP sq ruffle shade/bulb font; fluted std, 17" **695.00**
Clear w/gold floral shade/font; brass twist stick, 20" **400.00**
Cranberry fluted shade/font, brass base, w/chimney, 15" **335.00**
Pk shaded satin w/emb swirled ribs, pleat-top shade, 11" **450.00**
Pk Swirl MOP fluted shade, gold dore base, 13" **575.00**
Stippled cranberry w/gold cherries on shade/font, 11" **565.00**

Perfume Lamps

One catalog from the 1950s states that a perfume lamp 'precipitates and absorbs unpleasant tobacco smoke in closed rooms; freshens air in rooms, and is decorative in every home — can be used as a night lamp or television lamp.' An earlier advertisement reads 'an electric lamp that breathes delightful, delicate fragrance as it burns.' Perfume-burner lamps can be traced back to the earliest times of man. There has always been a desire to change, sweeten, or freshen air. Through the centuries the evolution of the perfume-burner lamp has had many changes in outer form, but very little change in function. Many designs of incense burners were used not only for the reasons mentioned here, but also in various ceremonies — as they still are to this day. Later, very fine perfume burners were designed and produced by the best glasshouses in Europe. Other media such as porcelain and metal also were used. It was not until the early part of the twentieth century that electric perfume lamps came into existence. Many lamps made by both American and European firms during the '20s and '30s are eagerly sought by collectors.

From the mid-1930s to the '70s there seems to have been an explosion in both the number of designs and manufacturers. This is especially true in Europe. Nearly every conceivable figure has been seen as a perfume lamp. Animals, buildings, fish, houses, jars, Oriental themes, people, and statuary are just a few examples. American import firms have purchased many different designs from Japan. These lamps range from replicas of earlier European pieces to original works. Except for an occasional article or section in reference books, very little has been written on this subject. The information contained in each of these articles generally covers only a specific designer, manufacturer, or country. To date, no formal group or

assocation exists for this area of collecting. Our advisors for this category are Tom and Linda Millman; they are listed in the Directory under Ohio.

Arabian jewel seller, sitting, Goebel, TMK1, 7¾" **450.00**
Bambi on floral & grassy base, Goebel, mk TMK3 DIS 150, 6½" ...**350.00**
Elephant, wht, Aroma #9748, 8½x9" **300.00**
German shepherd, recumbent, realistic, Goebel, TMK3 ET 41, 4¼" **340.00**
German shepherd, sitting, realistic, Goebel, TMK3 #5 34, 9" **340.00**
Hummel-like boy w/musical instrument stands by wall, Irice, 5½" ...**40.00**
Hummel-like girl w/accordion stands against wall, Irice, 5½" **40.00**
Hyacinth bloom in fluted pot, Norcrest, 7" **45.00**
Lady, basket on arm, dog held in other, mc, Irice, 6¾" **60.00**
Lady, basket on arm, 3 lg applied bows on skirt, gold trim, 6¼" ...**45.00**
Lady reads w/child on lap, gold trim base, Ardalt, 7¼" **65.00**
Lady w/basket on right arm, Ardalt, 5¾" **65.00**
Lady w/bouquet, 1 hand at waist, bl dress w/gold, Irice, 7¼" **45.00**
Lady w/fan, Colonial-style dress, silver trim, MIJ, 7" **100.00**
Man w/bouquet, bow tie & spats, Goebel, TMK6 58-071, 9" **380.00**
Night watchman w/weapon & lantern, Goebel, TMK6 58-050-22, 8¼" **370.00**
Oriental ginger jar, water lilies on red, Aerozon, #734, 7⅜" **275.00**
Penguin standing, realistic, Goebel, TMK3 ET 67, 7¼" **355.00**
Swans, 2 on wave base, Irice, 4¼" **20.00**
Table, conical antique auto shade, stepped base, Irice, 5" **20.00**
Table, floral, bl on wht w/gold, brass band, Irice, 5½" **25.00**
Table, floral fluted shade w/gold, bulbous base, Irice, 5¼" **20.00**

Reverse-Painted Lamps

Jefferson, 10" scenic dome #2705 shade, green and black painted metal base, 15", $1,495.00

Jefferson, 16" landscape hex shade; baluster-form std, 22" **2,500.00**
Jefferson, 16" landscape shade; copper-color std, 22" **1,100.00**
Jefferson, 16" rvpt butterflies/ferns shade; bronze std, 22" **1,750.00**
Jefferson type, 14½" roses shade; heavy bronze std, 24" **350.00**
Jefferson type, 18" palms shade, urn-shaped std, 23½" **1,500.00**
Moe Bridges, 15" pines/water/sky shade; sq-ft base, 21" **2,800.00**
Moe Bridges, 8" country scenic shade; brn baluster std, 15" **1,000.00**
Pittsburgh, 14" scenic shade; emb thistles on hammered std ...**1,100.00**
Pittsburgh, 14" scenic shade; orig metal std, 18" **925.00**
Pittsburgh, 16" Lakes of Killarny scene, purple/gr/brn, 19" **850.00**
Pittsburgh, 18" Indian campsite scenic shade; 3-socket std, 22" .**1,950.00**
Unmk, 14" winter domical shade; foliate std, Am, 20½" **1,100.00**
Unmk, 16" fall landscape; urn-form base w/ball stem, 22" **1,500.00**
Unmk, 16" scenic shade; brass-color reeded-column std, 23" **850.00**
Unmk, 16" village scenic shade; Nouveau floral std, 25" **1,000.00**

Student Lamps, Kerosene

Brass, dbl, cased gr shades, electrified, 22½x27", EX **400.00**
Brass, milk glass shade, K Brenner, 18" **365.00**

Brass w/fleur-de-lis on font & reservoir, rpr, 21" **350.00**
NP, Miller syphon-style, wht shade, cut/frosted font, 21" **1,150.00**
NP brass, gr cased shade, 1-light, 20½", NM **675.00**
SP brass, dbl, milk glass shades, Argand/1871, 21x19", EX **800.00**

Whale Oil/Burning Fluid Lamps

Blown, conical amber font on pressed amber base, 1830s, 7" ...**4,100.00**
Blown, mercurial ring decor on clear, ca 1813-30, 9¾", pr **1,700.00**
Pressed, alabaster/clambroth, Paneled Waffle font, Sandwich, 14" .**850.00**
Pressed, amethyst, Ring & Oval font, hex base, Sandwich, 8⅜" .**1,600.00**
Pressed, dk amethyst, Loop font, sq base, Sandwich, 10½" **2,000.00**
Pressed, Dmn Quilted ft, columnar stem, rpl collar, 8¾" **140.00**
Pressed, hex base & font w/Gothic arches, pewter collar, 6¾" ...**140.00**
Pressed, hexagonal w/loop font, 2-pc mold, pewter collar, 9x8¾" ..**195.00**
Pressed, jade gr, Star & Punty font, hex base, Sandwich, 12" ..**5,250.00**
Pressed, lion-head decor, paw ft, blown font, Sandwich, 1820s, 12" ..**288.00**
Pressed, sapphire bl, Loop font, 8-sided stem, Sandwich, 10", pr **4,100.00**
Pressed, sapphire bl w/eng florals, 8-paneled, 2-tube, 10", EX **300.00**
Pressed, sq base, rnd pear-shaped font, pewter collar, 6⅝" **165.00**
Pressed, sq base & font w/eng vintage, brass collar, 7½" **165.00**

Miscellaneous

Argand, bronze w/brass, grape-pattern shades, 1840s, 21", pr ..**1,100.00**
Arsall cameo dome shade; bronze lovers figural std, 29" **3,165.00**
Astral, etched globe, gilt-brass font, prisms, marble base, 27" **865.00**
Bicycle, NP brass w/carbide burner, Lucas, Silver King..., 5" **95.00**
Figural, alabaster maiden by pool, bl glass insert, Italy, 16" **1,600.00**
Figural, alabaster maiden w/post above shoulders, 17x15" dia .**2,250.00**
Glow, ruby w/orig glass burner, 4½", EX **100.00**
Piano, pk glass & gilt metal, tripod base, height adjusts **1,400.00**

Lang, Anton

Anton Lang was a German studio potter and an actor in the Ober-
ammergau Passion Plays early in the 20th century. Because he played
the role of Christ three times, tourists brought his pottery back to the
U.S. in suitcases, which accounts for the prevalence of smaller examples
today. During 1923 – 1924 Anton Lang and the other 'Passion Players'
toured the U.S. selling their crafts. Lang would occasionally throw pottery when the cast passed through a pottery center such as Cincinnati,
where Rookwood was located. His pottery, marked with his name in
script, is fairly scarce and highly valued for its artistic quality. His son
Karl designed most of the Art Deco shapes and conducted glaze experiments. Only pieces bearing a hand-written signature (not a facsimile)
are certain to be Anton Lang originals instead of the work of Karl or
the Langs' assistants. Postcards, programs, and photographs depicting
Lang are also collectible. The pottery is now owned and operated by
Karl's daughter, Barbara Lampe. Our advisor for this category is Clark
Miller; he is listed in the Directory under Minnesota.

Box, brn & orange, 3¾x3¾" **105.00**
Etching, Anton Lang shop, autographed, 1922, 14¾x10½" **200.00**
Figurine, Joseph, Mary & Child, Deco style, mc, 12x8x5" **500.00**
Figurine candle holders, gargoyles, orange, 7½x7½", pr **500.00**
Holy water font, raised dove decor, bl matt, hand sgn, 5½x3½" ...**105.00**
Lamp, Deco style, orange, 9x5½" **225.00**
Vase, bl matt, 2¾x2¾" **35.00**
Vase, bl w/band of mc flowers, 5½x5½" **150.00**
Vase, Deco style, blk w/bl int, 7¾x7¼" **275.00**
Vase, frog skin, 3x2¾" **60.00**
Vase, pine boughs, gr & brn, hand sgn, 3¼x2¾" **65.00**

Vase, turq, 1¾x2½" **32.50**
Wall pocket, Deco style, gr, 7½x3½" **180.00**

Le Verre Francais

Le Verre Francais was produced during the 1920s by Schneider at
Epinay-sur-Seine in France. It was a commercial art glass in the cameo
style composed of layered glass with the designs engraved by acid.
Favored motifs were stylized leaves and flowers or geometric patterns. It
was marked with the name in script or with an inlaid filigrane. Our
advisor for this category is Don Williams; he is listed in the Directory
under Missouri.

**Vases, fuchsia flowers, orange
and cobalt on gray with blue
and yellow mottling, signed,
17¾", $5,000.00 for the pair.**

Cameo

Bowl, centerpc; 5 scarabs/geometrics, orange/aubergine, 10" **635.00**
Coupe, flower, gr mottle/orange/clear/wht, 9½x8¼" **750.00**
Jar, stylized geometrics, wht/amber/burgundy, w/lid, 4x5" **435.00**
Lamp, orange/grapes/geometrics on camphor mushroom shade ...**3,900.00**
Punch bowl, horse chestnut burrs, gray/pk/gr/brn/rust, +base ..**1,600.00**
Vase, apples/leaves, olive gr/brn/pk, 5½x3" **500.00**
Vase, berries/horse chestnut, pale yel frost, 12x7" **600.00**
Vase, daisies, dk purple/clear, wafer base, Charder, 5¾x4¼" **850.00**
Vase, Deco flowers, yel/orange/brn/gr, bulbous, 10x14" **450.00**
Vase, foliage, pastel bl/royal bl, Charder, 12½" **1,150.00**
Vase, leaves/berries, red/yel, Ovington, 11" **1,265.00**
Vase, leaves/berries, red/yel w/purple hdls, Ovington, 12" **1,380.00**
Vase, scarab, orange/aubergine-purple, ovoid, 16½" **1,600.00**
Vase, sunflower, pk/amethyst/purple, Ovington, 10¼" **1,025.00**

Leeds, Leeds Type

The Leeds Pottery was established in 1758 in Yorkshire and under
varied management produced fine creamware, often highly reticulated
and transfer printed, shiny black-glazed Jackfield wares, polychromed
pearlware, and figurines similar to those made in the Staffordshire area.
Little of the early ware was marked; after 1775 the impressed 'Leeds
Pottery' mark was used. From 1781 to 1820, the name 'Hartley Greens
& Co.' was added. The pottery closed in 1898.

Today the term 'Leeds' has become generic and is used to encompass all polychromed pearlware and creamware, wherever its origin.
Thus similar wares of other potters (Wood for instance) is often incorrectly called 'Leeds.' Unless a piece is marked or can be definitely

attributed to Leeds by confirming the pattern to be authentic, 'Leeds-Type' would be a more accurate nomenclature.

Key:
cw — creamware   pw — pearlware

Bowl, cw, emb festoons, pierced/scalloped rim, 9", EX	150.00
Coffeepot, pw, floral, rpl but matching lid, 10½", NM	300.00
Creamer, cw, mc floral, 3½", EX	90.00
Creamer, pw, Oriental decor, 3¼", EX	220.00
Creamer, pw, peafowl in sponged tree, 4-color, rpr, 3½"	140.00
Creamer & sugar bowl, surface granite, w/lid, ca 1800, rprs	550.00
Cup & saucer, handleless; pw, peafowl, mc, bl feather edge	440.00
Pitcher, surface granite, early 19th C, rprs, 6¾"	800.00
Plate, pw, eagle, 4-color, gr feather rim, flakes, 8⅛"	660.00
Plate, pw, peafowl in tree, 5-color, feather edge, 8-sided, 6¼"	660.00
Sugar bowl, pw, floral, mismatched lid, 5½", EX	120.00
Sugar bowl, pw, house & fence, mc, w/lid, 1800s, 4½", NM	575.00
Teapot, cw, mc foliage bands, 6¼x9"	200.00
Teapot, pw, floral, 6½", EX	225.00

Lefton China

The Lefon China Company was the creation of Mr. George Zoltan Lefton who migrated to the United States from Hungary in 1939. In 1941 he embarked on a new career and began shaping a business that sprang from his passion for collecting fine china and porcelains. Though his funds were very limited, his vision was to develop a source from which to obtain fine porcelains by reviving the postwar Japanese ceramic industry, which dated back to antiquity. As a trailblazer, George Zoltan Lefton sooned earned the reputation as 'The China King.'

Counted among the most desirable and sought-after collectibles of today, Lefton items such as Bluebirds, Miss Priss, Angels, all types of dinnerware and tea-related items are eagerly acquired by collectors. As is true with any antique or collectible, prices may vary, dependent on location, condition, and availability. For additional information on the history of Lefton China, its factories, marks, products, and values, readers should consult the *Collector's Encyclopedia of Lefton China, Books I and II*, and the *1998 Lefton Price Guide* by our advisor, Loretta DeLozier, who is listed in the Directory under Iowa.

Angel, musical guardian w/2 children, #06995, 7½"	75.00
Angel, October, #6224, 5"	22.00
Angel, praying, pastel bsk, #931, 4"	35.00
Angel, w/mandolin & song sheet, #00055, 4"	15.00
Animal, Am Blk bear, #789, 6½"	60.00
Animal, camel, Bethlehem Collection, #06117, 6"	32.00
Animal, cat, #80219, 4¾"	30.00
Animal, cat, Siamese, sitting, #4032	12.00
Animal, puppy w/collar, #5221, 12"	125.00
Ashtray, gr w/butterfly & rose, #1237	28.00
Ashtray, w/violets, sponge gold touches, #136, 3½"	15.00
Bank, Clock, gold Rustic Daisy, #6145, 6"	20.00
Bank, kangaroo w/pk bow, #2778, 7¾"	25.00
Basket, White Holly, w/hdl, #6069, 4¾"	24.00
Bird, peacock, #2335, 7¼"	55.00
Bird, pheasant w/open wings, #1547, 8½", pr	250.00
Bookends, tigers, #6664, pr	45.00
Bowl, punch; White Christmas, #1339	75.00
Box, candy; Christy, ftd, #442, 5"	32.00
Box, Eastern Elegance, ftd, #990	55.00
Box, Spring Bouquet, #8134, 4"	35.00
Box, wht milk china w/roses, w/lid, #843, 7"	65.00

Bust, Jefferson, #1136, 5½"	30.00
Butter dish, Celery Line, #1301	25.00
Butter dish, Gingham, w/lid, #3301	30.00

Cookie jar, Miss Priss, #1502, $135.00.

Photo courtesy Loretta DeLozier

Cookie jar, Bloomer Girl, #3966, 10"	275.00
Cookie jar, Bossie the Cow, #6594	150.00
Cookie jar, White Holly, #6054	90.00
Cookie jar, Young Lady, Geo Z Lefton 040A	45.00
Creamer, bluebird, unmk	10.00
Creamer & sugar bowl, Blue Paisley, #1974, w/lid	22.00
Creamer & sugar bowl, Cuddles, #1449	32.00
Creamer & sugar bowl, Dutch Girl, #2698	80.00
Creamer & sugar bowl, Moss Rose, #3167	32.00
Cup & saucer, AD; French Rose on wht swirl, #3450	10.00
Cup & saucer, Brown Heritage Floral, #1883	40.00
Cup & saucer, Eastern Star, #2337	22.00
Cup & saucer, Holly Garland, #1802	32.00
Dish, Americana, 2-compartment, #938	40.00
Dish, Classic Elegance, #4808, 8½"	35.00
Dish, sq nappy, Violets, #2874, 8"	35.00
Figurine, Colonial man & woman, #1065, 14"	450.00
Figurine, doctor, #04422, 8"	38.00
Figurine, Pinkie & Blue Boy, glazed, #3049, 8", pr	125.00
Jar, jam; Americana, #6973	65.00
Jar, jam; Holly Garland, #2039	65.00
Jar, jam; Miss Priss, #1515	75.00
Jar, jam; Poinsettia, #4385, w/tray	35.00
Lamp, Elegant Rose, #931, 13½"	125.00
Lantern, Green Holly, #2694, 8½"	125.00
Mug, Robert E Lee, #2365, 5½"	55.00
Pitcher & bowl, Green Holly, #5174, 4", 5½"	20.00
Pitcher & bowl, Heirloom Elegance, #5522, 3½"	28.00
Pitcher & bowl, Rose Heirloom, #1937	32.00
Planter, angel on cloud, #165	45.00
Planter, Calico Donkey, #5897, 5½"	32.00
Planter, comic bluebird figural, #288	35.00
Planter, fish, #709, 10¼"	28.00
Planter, whiteware, 2 cherubs support bowl, #2313, 8"	45.00
Plaque, Colonial girl, #117, 6¼"	15.00
Plate, Blue Paisley, #2337, 9¼"	25.00
Plate, To a Wild Rose, #2578, 9¼"	28.00
Shakers, forget-me-nots on wht, #4184, pr	9.00
Shakers, Miss Priss, #1521, pr	15.00
Shakers, Rose Chintz, #665, 2¾", pr	18.00
Shakers, Rustic Daisy, #4124, 6¾", pr	25.00
Shakers, swan figural, #2254, 2½", pr	17.00
Snack plate & cup, Rose Chintz, #637	18.00
Teapot, Brown Heritage Floral, musical, #7543	120.00
Teapot, Green Holly, #1357, 6-cup	85.00
Teapot, Hollyberry, #10419	85.00
Teapot, Miss Priss	35.00
Teapot, Poinsettia, #4388, 6-cup, 8"	90.00

Vase, bud; Forget Me Not, 3-hole, #10 ....**65.00**
Vase, cornucopia; gr, 6¼", pr **90.00**
Vase, pk w/gold flowers, #70425 ....**48.00**
Wall plaque, Kitchen, Memories of Home, #00807, 6½" **22.00**
Wall plaque, Rooster, #397, 7", pr **28.00**
Wall plaque, 4 Seasons, #4927, 8½", set of 4 ....**120.00**

Legras

Legras and Cie was founded in St. Denis, France, in 1864. Production continued until the 1930s. In addition to their enameled wares, they made cameo art glass decorated with outdoor scenes and florals executed by acid cuttings through two to six layers of glass. Their work is signed 'Legras' in relief and in enamel. Our advisor for this category is Don Williams; he is listed in the Directory under Missouri.

Cameo

Compote, foliage, gr on clear, etched ft, 10x16" **1,200.00**
Lamp, holly leaves & berries, cut/pnt on yel/orange, 17½x8½" ..**2,800.00**
Vase, apple blossoms, cut/pnt on frost, ovoid, 8" **325.00**
Vase, floral stem, cut/pnt on textured clear, 12½" **850.00**
Vase, grape pods/vines, dk/lt maroon, ribbed cylinder, 10½" **350.00**
Vase, grapevines, cut/pnt, maroon/peach/frost, stick neck, 16" ...**875.00**
Vase, V-shaped band w/birds, brn/wht, cylindrical, 15" **1,250.00**

Enameled Glass

Box, snowy trees/birds pnt on orange sky, cylindrical, 2¾" **785.00**
Vase, harbor/sailing scene, metal Depose #357 base, 11½" **260.00**
Vase, sailboat/lake/trees, gr & bl on orange, sq, 6" **475.00**
Vase, ships/trees, cylindrical w/irregular rim, 5¼" **250.00**
Vase, sunset landscape, yel/orange/gr/brn, 16x4" **500.00**
Vase, winter scene on gr frost, #4114, 9¾x4" **350.00**

Lenox

Walter Scott Lenox, former art director at Ott and Brewer, and Jonathan Coxon founded The Ceramic Art Company of Trenton, New Jersey, in 1889. By 1906 Cox had left the company and to reflect the change in ownership, the name was changed to Lenox Inc. Until 1930 when the production of American-made Belleek came to an end, they continued to produce the same type of high-quality ornamental wares that Lenox and Coxon had learned to master while in the employ of Ott and Brewer. Their superior dinnerware made the company famous, and since 1917 Lenox has been chosen the official White House China. Our advisor for this category is Mary Frank Gaston. See also Ceramic Art Company.

Bowl, The Patriot, 1976 Special Commemorative, gold trim, 9½" .**150.00**
Bud vase, Coral, 4-spout, gr mk, 8½" **95.00**
Chocolate pot, Coral, gr mk **225.00**
Cigarette lighter, pk w/gold trim, Ronson wick, wreath mk, 4" ..**125.00**
Creamer & sugar bowl, much gold decor, gold wreath mk, w/lid ...**100.00**
Cup & saucer, Avon **22.00**
Cup & saucer, Christie **22.00**
Cup & saucer, demitasse; HP floral **100.00**
Cup & saucer, Fantasies **22.00**
Cup & saucer, Flirtation **22.00**
Cup & saucer, Gaylord **22.00**
Cup & saucer, Golden Mood **22.00**
Cup & saucer, Golden Wreath **22.00**
Cup & saucer, Maywood **22.00**

Cup & saucer, Meadowsong **22.00**
Cup & saucer, Merrivale **22.00**
Cup & saucer, Modern Profile **22.00**
Cup & saucer, Rapture **22.00**
Cup & saucer, Sachet **22.00**
Cup & saucer, Temple Blossom **22.00**
Cup & saucer, Tudor **22.00**
Figurine, Am Fashion **110.00**

Figurine, ballerina on base, 6½", $600.00.

Figurine, First Waltz **110.00**
Figurine, Princess Cleopatra **110.00**
Goblet, Midnight Mood (blk) **18.00**
Leaf dish, wht w/much gold, gold wreath mk, #3005, 2x10½" **75.00**
Nut dish, swan figural, wht, gr wreath mk, 3¾x5" **30.00**
Plate, bread & butter; Avon **8.00**
Plate, bread & butter; Desire **8.00**
Plate, bread & butter; Fantasies **8.00**
Plate, bread & butter; Futura **8.00**
Plate, bread & butter; Gaylord **8.00**
Plate, bread & butter; Golden Wreath **8.00**
Plate, bread & butter; Marissa **8.00**
Plate, bread & butter; Meadowsong **8.00**
Plate, bread & butter; Memories **8.00**
Plate, bread & butter; Modern Profile **8.00**
Plate, bread & butter; Oslo **8.00**
Plate, bread & butter; Rhythm **8.00**
Plate, bread & butter; Sachet **8.00**
Plate, bread & butter; Tudor **8.00**
Plate, dinner; Avon **18.00**
Plate, dinner; Desire **18.00**
Plate, dinner; Fantasies **18.00**
Plate, dinner; Futura **18.00**
Plate, dinner; Gaylord **18.00**
Plate, dinner; Golden Mood **18.00**
Plate, dinner; Marissa **18.00**
Plate, dinner; Meadowsong **18.00**
Plate, dinner; Memories **18.00**
Plate, dinner; Oslo **18.00**
Plate, dinner; Rapture **18.00**
Plate, dinner; Rhythm **18.00**
Plate, dinner; Sachet **18.00**
Plate, dinner; Temple Blossom **18.00**
Plate, salad; Avon **13.00**
Plate, salad; Christie **13.00**
Plate, salad; Fantasies **13.00**
Plate, salad; Futura **13.00**
Plate, salad; Gaylord **13.00**
Plate, salad; Golden Mood **13.00**
Plate, salad; Marissa **13.00**
Plate, salad; Meadowsong **13.00**

Plate, salad; Merrivale 13.00
Plate, salad; Oslo 13.00
Plate, salad; Rapture 13.00
Plate, salad; Sachet 13.00
Plate, salad; Tudor 13.00
Toby mug, Wm Penn, gr mk, 6½" 195.00
Vase, emb lilies w/gold, gold wreath mk, 4⅜x4x1⅝" 50.00
Vase, emb vertical lines, gold trim, 8¾" 60.00
Vase, pk orchids, Wm Morey, corseted, gr stamp, 11¾x4½" 850.00
Vase, red rose w/gold leaves, long neck, #27, 8" 65.00

Letter Openers

Made in a wide variety of materials and designs, letter openers make an interesting collection, easy to display and easy on the budget as well. For further information we recommend *Collector's Guide to Letter Openers, Identification & Values*, by Everett Grist (Collector Books); Mr. Grist is listed in the Directory under Tennessee.

Blown glass, Indian Chief, Winnipeg 25.00
Brass, knight in armor hdl 8.00
Brass/SP, cranes & flowers in high relief, artist sgn, 11" 175.00
Bronze, Champion Coal...Pittsburg Coal Co, stainless tip 45.00
Bronze, pheasant figural, tail forms blade 8.00
Bronze, Williams & Peters Pittston Coal, Buffalo 38.00

Carved walnut, one-piece with well carved snake handle, EX patina, 8¾", $85.00.

Photo courtesy Garth's Auction Gallery

Celluloid, elephant head hdl 45.00
Celluloid, W Atlee Burpee & Co, EX 20.00
Ebony w/sterling cap, 14" 195.00
Eskimo ivory, mother seal w/baby, silver ferrule, umbrella hdl 250.00
Ivory, cvd dragon hdl, dbl-sided 55.00
Lucite, reverse cvd & filled rose, Bircraft label 30.00
Metal, Burrough's Adding Machine Co 10.00
Metal cast fish figural, Central Diecasting & Mfg Co 25.00
Plastic, clear bathing beauty figural w/flocked swimsuit 20.00
Plastic, Fuller Brush Man figural, clear 15.00
Plastic, red w/brass shield, magnifier, mk SP, made in USA 6.00
SP, Boston souvenir, Midnight Ride of Paul Revere hdl 10.00
Steel, w/pen knife, Harry Tall, Tailords ad, Cheapside 30.00
Walrus tooth, dagger shape, heavy 175.00
Wood, African head hdl 15.00

Libbey

The New England Glass Company was established in 1818 in Boston, Massachusetts. In 1892 it became known as the Libbey Glass Company. At Chicago's Columbian Expo in 1893, Libbey set up a ten-pot furnace and made glass souvenirs. The display brought them world-wide fame. Between 1878 and 1918, Libbey made exquisite cut and faceted glass, considered today to be the best from the brilliant period. The company is credited for several innovations — the Owens bottle machine that made mass production possible and the Westlake machine which turned out both electric light bulbs and tumblers automatically. They developed a machine to polish the rims of their tumblers in such a way that chipping was unlikely to occur. Their glassware carried the patented Safedge guarantee. Libbey also made glassware in numerous colors, among them cobalt, ruby, pink, green, and amber. Our advisor for this category is Mike Roscoe; he is listed in the Directory under Ohio.

Banana bowl, cut hobstars/canes/trellis, dbl sgn, 6¾x12½" 900.00
Basket, cut, berries & leaves, disk base, cut hdl, 18½x9" 1,000.00
Basket, cut, carnations, cut hdl, 14½x9¾" 275.00
Basket, cut, roses & dmn band, dbl-knotted hdl, sgn, 19½x8¾" ..800.00
Bottle, scent; amberina, oval teardrop stopper, 7" 1,900.00
Bowl, amberina, tricorner, 2¼" H 200.00
Bowl, hobstar center w/hobstars/cane lozenges, prism border, 8" ...500.00
Bowl, Sultana, 8" 295.00
Champagne, squirrel stem, wht opal, 6" 200.00
Claret, bear stem, blk, 5½" 155.00
Claret, bear stem, wht opal 165.00
Compote, amberina, flared rim, #3021, 5x7½" 1,750.00
Compote, clear w/pk loops, flared petal rim, 4x10½" 600.00
Cordial, kangaroo stem, blk 110.00
Cordial, monkey stem, blk 150.00
Cordial, monkey stem, wht opal, 5" 130.00
Cordial, whippet/greyhound stem, wht opal 175.00
Cruet, cut, hobstars/fans, notched hdl, faceted stopper, 5½" 130.00
Flower center, cut, Ellsmere, heavy, 7x10" 1,150.00
Goblet, cat stem, wht opal 200.00
Hair receiver, amberina, partial label, 2-pc, 2x4½" 1,750.00
Lamp, cut, Harvard, 26" Turkish dome shade, SP mts, prisms, 26" 3,750.00
Maize, butter dish, bl husks on irid 650.00
Maize, butter dish lid, gr husks on custard 165.00
Maize, celery vase, clear w/amber staining & bl leaves, 6" 235.00
Maize, celery vase, gr husks on custard 200.00
Maize, condiment set, custard, 3 pcs on tray w/metal lid 600.00
Maize, pickle castor, amber stain 595.00
Maize, pickle castor, gr husks on custard, SP fr 550.00
Maize, pitcher, bl husks on clear w/amber irid, clear hdl, 9" 600.00
Maize, pitcher, clear irid w/amber stain, 8½" 550.00
Maize, shakers, gold-edged bl husks on custard, pr ...250.00
Maize, sugar shaker, yel/gold leaves on custard, 5¾" 345.00
Maize, toothpick holder, gold-edged gr husks on custard 400.00
Maize, tumbler, bl husks on irid 235.00
Maize, vase, yel/gold leaves on custard, 6½" 250.00
Orange bowl, Princess pattern, cradle shape, 11x7½" 310.00
Punch cup, petal form, World's Fair 1893 ....75.00
Rose bowl, cut, pansies on beige w/wht beads, 2½x3½" 525.00
Sherbet, rabbit stem, wht opal, 2½" 160.00
Sherbet, squirrel stem, wht opal, 4" 150.00
Tazza, clear w/opal ft, pk/wht pulled-feather bowl, Nash, 6x7" 150.00
Vase, amberina, shape #3004, sgn, 11" 750.00
Vase, bud; amberina, label, 11½x2½" 950.00

Lightning Rod Balls

Used as ornaments on lightning rods, the vast majority of these balls were made of glass, but ceramic examples can be found as well.

Their average diameter is 4½", but it can vary from 3½" up to 5½". Only a few of the many available pattern and color combinations are listed here. The most common measure 4½" and are found in sun-colored amethyst and milk glass. Our advisor is Rod Krupka, author of a book on this subject. Anyone interested in receiving a hobby-related newsletter may write to him for more information; he is listed in the Directory under Michigan.

Ruby red, Moon and Star, 4⅜", $300.00.

Photo courtesy Norman C. Heckler & Co.

Amber, plain ball shape, crude wavy glass, 3½x3½"	75.00
Bl opaque, Moon & Star, 5⅛x4⅜"	30.00
Bl opaque, National, rnd, 5¼x4½"	35.00
Bl opaque, Quilt-Raised pattern, 5½x5"	80.00
Clear, Ribbed Grape pattern, 5⅛x4⅜"	250.00
Dk bl opaque, pleated pattern, 5x4⅜"	150.00
Gr opaque, Doorknob, 4¼x4"	275.00
Milk glass, Ear of Corn, 3¾x2⅞"	75.00
Milk glass, Mast, emb swirls on ball shape, 5¾x4⅞"	90.00
Red, Electra, cone, 5⅜x4⅝"	230.00
Red flashed, plain rnd shape, 4½" dia	35.00
Silver, WC Shinn, belted ball from, 4¾x4¼"	110.00
Sun-colored amethyst, Swirl pattern, 5½x5"	100.00

Limited Edition Plates

Currently values of some limited edition plates have risen dramatically while others have fallen drastically. Prices charged by plate dealers in the secondary market vary greatly; we have tried to suggest an average.

Bing and Grondahl

1895, Behind the Frozen Window	6,250.00
1896, New Moon	2,250.00
1897, Christmas Meal of Sparrows	1,300.00
1898, Roses & Star	795.00
1899, Crows Enjoying Christmas	1,650.00
1900, Church Bells Chiming	995.00
1901, 3 Wise Men	425.00
1902, Gothic Church Interior	395.00
1903, Expectant Children	425.00
1904, View of Copenhagen From Fredericksberg Hill	225.00
1905, Anxiety of the Coming Christmas Night	215.00
1906, Sleighing to Church	165.00
1907, Little Match Girl	225.00
1908, St Petri Church	110.00
1909, Yule Tree	110.00
1910, Old Organist	110.00
1911, Angels & Shepherds	110.00
1912, Going to Church	110.00
1913, Bringing Home the Tree	110.00
1914, Amalienborg Castle	105.00
1915, Dog on Chain Outside Window	175.00
1916, Prayer of the Sparrows	105.00
1917, Christmas Boat	105.00

1918, Fishing Boat	105.00
1919, Outside the Lighted Window	95.00
1920, Hare in the Snow	95.00
1921, Pigeons	95.00
1922, Star of Bethlehem	95.00
1923, Hermitage	95.00
1924, Lighthouse	105.00
1925, Child's Christmas	105.00
1926, Churchgoers	105.00
1927, Skating Couple	155.00
1928, Eskimos	95.00
1929, Fox Outside Farm	105.00
1930, Tree in Town Hall Square	115.00
1931, Christmas Train	115.00
1932, Lifeboat at Work	115.00
1933, Korsor-Nyborg Ferry	105.00
1934, Church Bell in Tower	105.00
1935, Lillebelt Bridge	105.00
1936, Royal Guard	110.00
1937, Arrival of Christmas Guests	135.00
1938, Lighting the Candles	175.00
1939, Old Lock-Eye, The Sandman	235.00
1940, Delivering Christmas Letters	285.00
1941, Horses Enjoying Meal	325.00
1942, Danish Farm on Christmas Night	275.00
1943, Ribe Cathedral	235.00
1944, Sorgenfri Castle	125.00
1945, Old Water Mill	185.00
1946, Commemoration Cross	115.00
1947, Dybbol Mill	165.00
1948, Watchman	115.00
1949, Landsoldaten	145.00
1950, Kronborg Castle at Elsinore	175.00
1951, Jens Bang	145.00
1952, Old Copenhagen Canals & Thorsvaldsen Museum	155.00
1953, Royal Boat	155.00
1954, Snowman	155.00
1955, Kaulundborg Church	155.00
1956, Christmas in Copenhagen	175.00
1957, Christmas Candles	175.00
1958, Santa Claus	140.00
1959, Christmas Eve	155.00
1960, Village Church	185.00
1961, Winter Harmony	115.00
1962, Winter Night	90.00
1963, Christmas Elf	115.00
1964, Fir Tree & Hare	75.00
1965, Bringing Home the Tree	60.00
1966, Home for Christmas	55.00
1967, Sharing the Joy	49.00
1968, Christmas in Church	35.00
1969, Arrival of Guests	35.00
1970, Pheasants in Snow	32.00
1971, Christmas at Home	30.00
1972, Christmas in Greenland	30.00
1973, Country Christmas	30.00
1974, Christmas in the Village	30.00
1975, The Old Water Mill	30.00
1976, Christmas Welcome	30.00
1977, Copenhagen Christmas	30.00
1978, A Christmas Tale	30.00
1979, White Christmas	30.00
1980, Christmas in the Woods	36.00
1981, Christmas Peace	36.00

1982, The Christmas Tree 45.00
1983, Christmas in Old Town 48.00
1984, Christmas Letter 60.00
1985, Christmas Eve, Farm 48.00
1986, Silent Night 50.00
1987, Snowman's Christmas 65.00
1988, In King's Garden 55.00
1989, Christmas Anchorage 55.00
1990, Changing Guards 75.00
1991, Copenhagen Stock Exchange 85.00
1992, Pastor's Christmas 95.00
1993, Father Christmas in Copenhagen 95.00

M. I. Hummel

The last issue for M.I. Hummel annual plates was made in 1995. Values listed here are for plates in mint condition with original boxes.

1971, Heavenly Angel 475.00
1972, Hear Ye, Hear Ye 55.00
1973, Glober Trotter 85.00

1974, Goose Girl, $50.00.

1975, Ride Into Christmas 55.00
1976, Apple Tree Girl 55.00
1977, Apple Tree Boy 65.00
1978, Happy Pastime 40.00
1979, Singing Lesson 40.00
1980, School Girl 40.00
1981, Umbrella Boy 55.00
1982, Umbrella Girl 85.00
1983, The Postman 165.00
1984, Little Helper 50.00
1985, Chick Girl 75.00
1986, Playmates 140.00
1987, Feeding Time 160.00
1988, Little Goat Herder 100.00
1989, Farm Boy 110.00
1990, Shepherd's Boy 185.00
1991, Just Resting 135.00
1992, Meditation 150.00
1993, Doll Bath 185.00
1994, Doctor 180.00
1995, Come Back Soon 200.00

Royal Copenhagen

1908, Madonna & Child 3,500.00
1909, Danish Landscape 225.00
1910, Magi 170.00
1911, Danish Landscape 180.00

1912, Christmas Tree 175.00
1913, Frederik Church Spire 165.00
1914, Holy Spirit Church 185.00
1915, Danish Landscape 205.00
1916, Shepherd at Christmas 145.00
1917, Our Savior Church 145.00
1918, Sheep & Shepherds 135.00
1919, In the Park 135.00
1920, Mary & Child Jesus 135.00
1921, Aabenraa Marketplace 125.00
1922, 3 Singing Angels 125.00
1923, Danish Landscape 115.00
1924, Sailing Ship 150.00
1925, Christianshavn Street Scene 110.00
1926, Christianshavn Canal 105.00
1927, Ship's Boy at Tiller 175.00
1928, Vicar's Family 115.00
1929, Grundtvig Church 115.00
1930, Fishing Boats 140.00
1931, Mother & Child 145.00
1932, Frederiksberg Gardens 150.00
1933, Ferry & Great Belt 160.00
1934, Hermitage Castle 175.00
1935, Kronborg Castle 235.00
1936, Roskilde Cathedral 215.00
1937, Main Street of Copenhagen 275.00
1938, Round Church of Osterlars 345.00
1939, Greenland Pack Ice 435.00
1940, Good Shepherd 525.00
1941, Danish Village Church 375.00
1942, Bell Tower 415.00
1943, Flight Into Egypt 475.00
1944, Danish Village Scene 325.00
1945, Peaceful Scene 450.00
1946, Zealand Village Church 225.00
1947, Good Shepherd 255.00
1948, Nodebo Church 225.00
1949, Our Lady's Cathedral 255.00
1950, Boeslunde Church 245.00
1951, Christmas Angel 375.00
1952, Christmas in Forest 165.00
1953, Frederiksberg Castle 165.00
1954, Amalienborg Palace 175.00
1955, Fano Girl 215.00
1956, Rosenborg Castle 195.00
1957, Good Shepherd 145.00
1958, Sunshine Over Greenland 145.00
1959, Christmas Night 155.00
1960, Stag 155.00
1961, Training Ship 165.00
1962, Little Mermaid 235.00
1963, Hojsager Mill 95.00
1964, Fetching the Tree 75.00
1965, Little Skaters 74.00
1966, Blackbird 55.00
1967, Royal Oak 52.00
1968, Last Umiak 45.00
1969, Old Farmyard 39.00
1970, Christmas Rose & Cat 52.00
1971, Hare in Winter 32.00
1972, In the Desert 26.00
1973, Train Home Bound 37.00
1974, Winter Twilight 32.00
1975, Queen's Palace 26.00

1976, Danish Watermill 43.00
1977, Immervad Bridge 28.00
1978, Greenland Scenery 28.00
1979, Choosing Tree 60.00
1980, Bringing Home Tree 28.00
1981, Admiring Tree 40.00
1982, Waiting for Christmas 95.00
1983, Merry Christmas 57.00
1984, Jingle Bells 52.00
1985, Snowman 65.00
1986, Wait for Me 62.00
1987, Winter Birds 67.00
1988, Christmas Eve Copenhagen 75.00
1989, Old Skating Pond 85.00
1990, Christmas in Tivoli 120.00
1991, St Lucia Basilica 65.00
1992, Royal Coach 70.00
1993, Arrival Guests by Train 75.00
1994, Christmas Shopping 85.00

Limoges

From the mid-18th century, Limoges was the center of the porcelain industry of France, where at one time more than forty companies utilized the local kaolin to make a superior quality china, much of which was exported to the United States. Various marks were used; some included the name of the American export company (rather than the manufacturer) and 'Limoges.' After 1891 'France' was added. Pieces signed by factory artists are more valuable than those decorated outside the factory by amateurs. The listings below are hand-painted pieces unless noted otherwise.

For a more thorough study of the subject, we recommend you refer to *The Collector's Encyclopedia of Limoges Porcelain, 2nd Edition,* by our advisor, Mary Frank Gaston. Her book has beautiful color illustrations and current market values.

Biscuit jar, overall floral, leaf finial, 7½x5½" dia 145.00
Bowl, centerpc; grapes w/much gold, T&V, 6x10" 350.00
Bowl, wild roses, sgn Thaw, loop hdl, oval, 6½x10¾" 110.00
Box, glove; wht forget-me-nots w/gold, scroll ft, T&V, 13" L 370.00
Box, sm flowers, free-form Art Nouveau, 3½x9x5½" 165.00
Butter dish, carnations on underplate & lower half of lid 75.00
Chamberstick, Deco design w/gold, molded hdl, 5x4", NM 150.00
Chamberstick, flowers w/gold, 2½x5¼" 175.00
Charger, florals w/cobalt & gold, sgn D&C France..., 13½" 250.00
Charger, kingfisher & lotus blossoms, gold border, 13½" 325.00
Chocolate pot, mc mums, gold hdl & finial 175.00
Chocolate pot, pk roses, artist sgn, +6 c/s 525.00
Cup & saucer, country scenes in purple, fluted rim, B&C 45.00
Cup & saucer, demi; pk roses & leaf garlands, gold rim 35.00
Dresser set, lilacs decal w/gold, 4-pc on 11" oval tray 160.00
Ewer, tulips, mc on cobalt, maroon neck, 4-ftd, unmk, 14¼" 610.00
Jar, dresser; holly, T&V France, 5½" 140.00
Jardiniere, mc tulips w/gold, D&C, 9x7" 325.00
Mirror & brush set, violet sprays, brass hdls 250.00
Mug, grapes, gr to tan w/gold hdl, T&V, 5⅝x4" 75.00
Mush bowl & saucer, dk bl to lav w/bl & wht flowers, ca 1908 .....50.00
Pitcher, lemonade; roses, WG & Co 165.00
Pitcher, lg flowers, gold hdl, scalloped base & rim, mk, 8x7" 300.00
Pitcher, mistletoe & leaves, platinum on gray to pk, 6" 175.00
Pitcher, open rose w/bud, pk on brn, basketweave bottom, 7" ...190.00
Pitcher, tankard, vintage w/vine hdl, sgn, T&V, 15½" 475.00
Plaque, gulls & surf, ships & cliffs beyond, crown mk, 11½" 175.00

Plaque, Gypsy woman portrait, beading, 11½" 495.00
Plaque, horse & colt, dog w/pups, sgn Baumy, mk, 12½" 300.00
Plaque, lady's portrait, orange lustre poppies, mk, 1902, 11" 400.00
Plate, blond lady's portrait in bl headdress & jewels, 10" 450.00
Plate, building by seashore, sgn A Rene, mk, 10¼" 120.00
Plate, couple in garden, 1930s, mini, 2½" 25.00
Plate, fruit, gold rococo border, pierced, mk, 12⅜" 225.00
Plate, fruit w/gold rococo rim, sgn Goise, 12¼" 245.00
Plate, game birds, irregular gold rim, 10⅜" 175.00
Plate, quail pr & flowers, pierced, mk, 10½" dia 145.00
Plate, quail pr w/3 babies, pierced, unmk, 14¼" 195.00
Platter, forget-me-nots, Elite Limoges, 16¾" 145.00
Punch bowl, purple flowers, 15" dia, 2-pc 650.00

Tankard, vintage decoration with much gold, 13½", $225.00.

Toothpick holder, florals on blk, gold collar & hdl 35.00
Tray, dresser; windmill/cottage/fisherman/shore, ca 1870 ....165.00
Tray, floral w/cobalt & gold, D&C France, 13½" dia 145.00
Trivet, yel roses, sgn E Thau, T&V, 6½" 36.00
Vase, berries & blossoms, pillow form w/gold twig feet, 9x6½x3" .270.00
Vase, dragons & floral sprays, streaky mc, 17x8¼" 395.00
Vase, roses, artist sgn, gold hdls, 15" 150.00
Vase, roses, red on bl to gr w/gold, rpr, unmk, 12½" 125.00
Vase, wild roses, pk on med bl, squatty, 7½" 95.00
Wastebasket, poppies w/gold, 4 gold ft, loop hdls, 12½x9" 500.00

Lithophanes

Lithophanes are porcelain panels with relief designs of varying degrees of thickness and density. Transmitted light brings out the pattern in graduated shading, lighter where the procelain is thin and darker in the heavy areas. They were cast from wax models prepared by artists and depict views of life from the 1800s, religious themes, or scenes of historical significance. First made in Berlin about 1803, they were used as lamp shade panels, window plaques, and candle shields. Later steins, mugs, and cups were made with lithophanes in their bases. Japanese wares were sometimes made with dragons or geisha lithophanes. See also Dragon Ware; Steins.

Candle shield, lovers in boat, wood-caned fr, 9x7" 450.00
Cup & saucer, pk w/moriage dragon, lady in bottom of cup 45.00
Lamp, fairy; mc landscape w/fox & deer, Clarke cup, 4½" 550.00
Lamp, scenic shade w/lady smoking, converted burner, 19" 1,200.00
Lamp, 5-panel shade, figural cherub std, electrified, 16" 450.00
Lamp shade, 5 scenic panels, metal fr, Schierholz, 6½x9" 385.00
Lamp shade, 6 scenic panels, metal fr, Schierholz, 19th C, 6x10" .440.00
Lantern, 4 mini panes w/children scenes, ea pane: 1x¾" 200.00
Panel, lady by river bank, brass fr, Fr, 4⅜x5¼" 225.00
Panel, man gives lady gift, child sleeps, PPM, 5x4¼" 350.00
Panel, young maiden, KPM, wood fr, 6x4" 200.00

Stein, 2 girls read letter (in base), tavern scene ext, 10" 225.00

Little Red Riding Hood

Though usually thought of as a product of the Hull Pottery Company, research has shown that a major part of this line was actually made by Regal China. The idea for this popular line of novelties and kitchenware items was developed and patented by Hull, but records show that to a large extent Hull sent their whiteware to Regal to be decorated. Little Red Riding Hood was produced from 1943 until 1957. Values have risen sharply over the past several months. For further information we recommend *Collecting Hull Pottery's Red Riding Hood* by Mark Supnick. Our advisors for this category are Rose and Charlie Snyder; they are listed in the Directory under Kansas. Note: Beware of reproductions.

Spice jar, Ginger, square base, $750.00.

Bank, standing 850.00
Bank, wall hanging 2,100.00
Butter dish 550.00
Canister, cereal 1,475.00
Canister, coffee, sugar or flour; ea 850.00
Canister, pretzels (few exist) 7,100.00
Canister, salt 1,200.00
Canister, tea 850.00
Clock 450.00
Cookie jar, closed basket, minimum value 360.00
Cookie jar, open basket 350.00
Cookie jar, open basket, red shoes 850.00
Cookie jar, open basket, stars on apron, minimum value 675.00
Cookie jar, poinsettia 1,050.00
Cookie jar, red spray w/gold bows, red shoes 950.00
Cookie jar, wht 200.00
Cracker jar, unmk 850.00
Creamer, side pour 200.00
Creamer, top pour, no tab hdl 575.00
Creamer, top pour, tab hdl 500.00
Grease jar, flower basket, gold trim 1,100.00
Lamp 2,450.00
Match holder, wall hanging 1,275.00
Match holder, wall hanging, overglaze pnt gone, EX 450.00
Mustard jar, no spoon 350.00
Mustard jar, w/orig spoon 575.00
Pitcher, batter 575.00
Pitcher, milk; standing, 8" 450.00
Planter, hanging 575.00
Shakers, Pat Design 135889, med sz, pr 1,100.00
Shakers, 3¼", pr 195.00
Shakers, 5½", pr 250.00

Spice set, 6-pc 6,400.00
Sugar bowl, crawling 400.00
Sugar bowl, side pour 250.00
Sugar bowl, w/lid 575.00
Sugar bowl lid 325.00
Teapot 365.00
Wall pocket 450.00
Wolf jar, yel base 900.00
Wolf jar, red base............1,400.00

Liverpool

In the late 1700s Liverpool potters produced a creamy ivory ware, sometimes called Queen's Ware, which they decorated by means of the newly perfected transfer print. Made specifically for the American market, patriotic inscriptions, political portraits, or other States themes were applied in black with colors sometimes added by hand. (Obviously their loyalty to the crown did not inhibit the progress of business!) Before it lost favor in about 1825, other English potters made a similar product. Today Liverpool is a generic term used to refer to all ware of this type.

Jug, By Virtue & Valor.../WA w/15 States, blk w/mc, 11¼" ...1,900.00
Jug, East View of Liverpool Lighthouse..., blk w/mc, 4⅞" 600.00
Jug, He in Glory/Am in Tears, Washington profile, blk, 8½", EX .2,200.00
Jug, hunt scenes, 2 blk transfers, old rstr, 9½" 225.00
Jug, John Adams/Plenty/Justice/Cupid, blk w/mc, 9¾" 4,000.00
Jug, May Commerce Flourish/Seal of US, blk, 8¾", EX 1,100.00
Jug, Napoleon/Success to Volunteers, orange, 5¼", VG 130.00
Jug, Plan of City of WA/...Prebles Squadron, blk w/mc, 10⅜" ...2,250.00
Jug, Seal of US/Chain of States, blk, 8¼", EX 750.00
Jug, WA in Glory/Am in Tears/other transfers, blk w/mc, 10¾" ..2,100.00
Plate, Am sailing ship, blk, Herculaneum, 9⅞" 200.00
Plate, British sailing ship, blk w/mc, Neale, 9⅞" 120.00

Lladro

Lladro porcelains are currently being produced in Labernes Blanques, Spain. Their retired and limited edition figurines are popular collectibles on the secondary market.

Attentive Bear, #1204 ....100.00
Ballerina, #1356 ....125.00
Ballet Blue, #1359 ....265.00
Beagle puppy, #1072 ....200.00
Bear, seated, #1206 ....100.00
Beth, #1358 ....180.00
Boy Meets Girl, #1188 ....250.00
Boy w/goat, #2009 ....750.00
Butterfly Girl, #1401 ....395.00
Cinderella, #4828 ....850.00
Clown w/clock, #5056 ....640.00
Country Woman, #353, rare 1,600.00
Daydream, #2062 ....1,500.00
Dog & snail, #1139 ....680.00
Dog in a basket, #1128 ....340.00
Duck, #1263 ....60.00
Ducks flying, #1264 ....50.00
English Lady, #5324 ....400.00
Family Roots 800.00
Garden Song, #7618 ....300.00
Geisha, #4807 ....400.00

Girl w/flowers, #1172, 1971, MIB	285.00
Girl w/pigeons, #4915	300.00
Good Bear, #1205	100.00
Harmony	300.00
In the Garden, #4978	725.00
Lady w/roses, #5127	350.00
Languid Clown, retired, #4924	600.00
Laura, #1360	180.00
Little Bo Peep, retired, #1312	345.00
Loving Mouse, #5883	150.00
Pekingese, sitting, retired, #4641	325.00
Pharmacist, #4844	1,200.00
Socker Player Puppet, #4967	250.00
Sunning, #1481	345.00
Surprised Cat, #5114	40.00
Wedding, #1404	375.00

Lobmeyer

J. and L. Lobmeyer, contemporaries of Moser, worked in Vienna, Austria, during the last quadrant of the 1800s. Most of the work attributed to them is decorated with distinctive enameling; favored motifs are people in 18th-century garb.

Punch set, painted figures and flowers, gold trim, 15¼" jar and four 6" wines, $3,500.00 for the set.

Beverage set, coats of arms, dtd 1860, pitcher+6 tumblers	900.00
Bowl, couple in mc enamel, quatrefoil, 4", +underplate	975.00
Box, intaglio lid w/nude & cornucopias, clear, 6" dia	750.00
Plate, Persian enameling	350.00
Tumbler, lady & florals, 12-panel, sgn	400.00

Locke Art

Joseph Locke already had proven himself many times over as a master glassmaker, working in leading English glasshouses for more than seventeen years. He came to America where he joined the New England Glass Company. There he invented processes for the manufacture of several types of art glass — amberina, peachblow, pomona, and agata among them. In 1898 he established the Locke Art Glassware Co. in Mt. Oliver, Pittsburgh, Pennsylvania. Locke Art Glass was produced using an acid-etching process by which the most delicate designs were executed on crystal blanks. Most examples are signed simply 'Locke Art,' often placed unobtrusively near a leaf or a stem. Other items are signed 'Jo Locke,' some are dated, and some are unsigned. Most of the work was done by hand. The business continued into the 1920s. For further study we recommend *Locke Art Glass, Guide for Collectors*, by Joseph and Janet Locke, available at your local bookstore.

Champagne, Poppy, 6"	140.00

Goblet, Ivy	145.00
Pitcher, Poinsettia, sgn, 8½"	650.00
Sherbet, Grape & Line, ftd, short stem	148.00
Tray, ice cream; eng florals, 16x8"	435.00
Tumbler, Roses, hdl, sgn, 4"	125.00
Tumbler, Vintage, vertical lines, optic ribs, 5"	135.00
Vase, Peonies, ruffled, sgn, 5"	650.00
Vase, Stork, camphor glass, 4½x2¼" sq	275.00

Locks

The earliest type of lock in recorded history was the wooden cross bar used by ancient Egyptians and their contemporaries. The early Romans are credited with making the first key-operated mechanical lock. The ward lock was invented during the Middle Ages by the Etruscans of Northern Italy; the lever tumbler and combination locks followed at various stages of history with varying degrees of effectiveness. In the 18th century the first precision lock was constructed. It was a device that utilized a lever-tumbler mechanism. Two of the best known of the early 19th-century American lock manufacturers are Yale and Sargent, and today's collectors value Winchester and Keen Kutter locks very highly. Factors to consider are rarity, condition, and construction. Brass and bronze locks are generally priced higher than those of steel or iron. Our advisor for this section is Joe Tanner; he is listed in the Directory under Washington.

Key:
bbl — barrel   st — stamped

Brass Lever Tumbler

Anchor, 6-lever, emb, 3⅛"	38.00
Automatic, emb, flat key, 2⅛"	15.00
Belknap, emb, 3⅛"	25.00
Bingham's Best Brand, BBB emb on front, 3¼"	150.00
Blue Grass, emb, 3"	85.00
Chubbs Patent London, st, 6⅛"	350.00
Cotterill, st High Security key, 5⅛x3⅛"	290.00
Cotterill Birmingham Eng, st, 5⅛"	350.00
Crusader, shield, swords emb on body, 2¾"	45.00
Eagle Lock Co, word Eagle emb on front, scrolled, 3"	60.00
Geo B Bahr & Co Lou KY, st, 3⅛"	45.00
Good Luck, emb, 2¾"	45.00
GW Nock, fancy etch, st, 2⅞"	160.00
Jackson's, st Jackson's on front, 2½"	20.00
JWM, emb, bbl key, 2⅝"	25.00
Mercury, Mercury emb on body, 2¾"	75.00
Motor, Motor emb on body, 3¼"	35.00
Our Very Best, OVB emb on body, 2⅞"	150.00
Roeyonoc, Roeyonoc st on body, 3¼"	30.00
Romer & Co, Romer & Co st on dust cover, 3"	55.00
Ruby, Ruby emb in scroll on front, 2¾"	20.00
Siberian, Siberian emb on shackle, 2½"	110.00
Simmons, emb, 2¼"	18.00
Sphinx, sphinx & pharaoh head emb on front, 2¾"	35.00
Tower & Lyon NY, st, 3"	25.00
W Bohannan & Co, SW emb in scroll on front, 2⅜"	30.00
Watch, emb, flat key, 3"	30.00
1898, emb, 2¾"	30.00

Combinations

Chicago Combination Lock Co, st on front, brass, 2¾"	60.00

Clark, st, brass, 2¼" 300.00
Corbin Sesamee 4-Dial Brass Lock, st Sesamee, 2¾" 15.00
Edwards Mfg Co No-Key, st on lock, brass, 2¾" 60.00
Junkunc Bros Mfrs, all st on bk, brass, 1⅞" 30.00
Miller Keyless, st, iron, 3¼" 70.00
Number or letter disk, st, 3-disk, brass, 1½" 100.00
Number or letter disk, st, 3-disk, iron, 2" 20.00
Number or letter disk, st, 4-disk, brass, 3½" 170.00
Number or letter disk, st, 4-disk, iron, 4½" 275.00
Number or letter disk type (4 disks), brass, 2¾" 130.00
Permutation Lock Den Co, emb, brass, 3⅝" 400.00
Sorel Limited Canada, st, brass, 3¼" 200.00
Sq lock case of steel, st Pat Germany, 4-wheel, 3¼" 110.00
Sutton Lock Co st on body, 3" 200.00
Vulcana Push Lock Corp, st on lock case, 3¼" 50.00
WA Harrison, Inc, st, brass, 2½" 60.00

Eight-Lever Type

Blue Chief, st, steel, 4½" 25.00
Electric, steel, Electric st on front 30.00
Excelsior, st, steel, 4¾" 30.00
Mastodon, st, brass, 4½" 30.00
Mastodon, st, steel, 4½" 15.00
Miller, steel, Miller 8-Lever st on front 18.00
Reese, st, steel, 4¾" 15.00

Iron Lever Tumbler

Beta embossed on front, 2⅞", $15.00.

Airplane, st, 2¾" 40.00
Automobile, st, 2⅞" 35.00
Bronco, emb, 3¼" 45.00
Bull, word Bull emb on front, 2⅝" 30.00
Bulldog, word Bulldog & face of dog emb on front, 2¾" 30.00
Dan Patch, Dan Patch emb on front, horseshoe on bk, 2¾" 130.00
Dragon, word Dragon & dragon emb on front, 2⅞" 25.00
Eagle, word Eagle emb on body, 4⅜" 40.00
G Merkel, st, 3" 30.00
HC Jones (trick lock), st, 4¼" 470.00
Indian Head, Indian head emb on front, 3" 90.00
Karo, word Karo emb on front, CI, 3⅛" 25.00
King Korn, words King Korn emb on body, 2⅞" 40.00
Lever Buckle Co, emb, 4½" 45.00
Moose head, emb, 2¾" 20.00
Nineteen O Three, 1903 emb on front, iron, 3⅞" 90.00
Owl, emb, 2¼" 30.00
Rough Rider (horse & rider), emb, 3" 50.00
Rugby, football emb on body, 3" 20.00
S Andrews, st, 2⅝" 200.00
Thoroughbred, emb, 2⅛" 12.00

Unique, word Unique emb on front, 3¼" 120.00
Victory, emb, 3⅛" 45.00
W Hall & Co, st, 4½" 300.00
Woodland, emb, 2⅜" 30.00
Yale & Towne, lion face emb on front, shackle mk Y&T, 3" ...110.00

Lever Push Key

Achilles, emb, iron, 3⅝" 50.00
Aztec, emb 6-lever, 2⅛" 50.00
California, emb, brass, 2½" 20.00
Celtic Cross, emb cross on face, brass, 2¼" 125.00
Champion, emb Champion 6-Lever, brass push-key type, 2¼" 25.00
Climax, emb Climax 6-lever, iron push-key type, 2¼" 35.00
Columbia, emb Columbia 6-Lever, brass push-key type, 2¼" 35.00
Crank, emb, iron, 2⅞" 25.00
Dash, emb Dash 6-Lever, iron push-key type, 2¼" 25.00
Duke, emb 6-Lever, 2⅛" 45.00
Eagle 3-Lever, emb, brass, 2" 50.00
Elm City 4-Lever, emb, brass, 2" 35.00
Empire, emb, 6-lever, brass, 2½" 20.00
Excelsior, emb Excelsior 6-Lever, brass push-key type, 2¼" ..25.00
Harvard, emb Harvard 4-Lever, brass push-key type, 2" 50.00
HS&Co 6-Lever, emb, brass, 2¼" 70.00
IXL, emb IXL on body, 2¼" 75.00
Keystone, emb Keystone 6-Lever, brass push-key type, 2¼" 40.00
McIntosh, emb, 6-lever, iron, 2½" 90.00
McIntosh, emb McIntosh on body, 2¼" 90.00
National Lock Co, emb, brass, 2½" 120.00
Nugget 4-Lever, emb, brass, 2" 50.00
SB Co, emb SB Co on body, 3¼" 60.00
Supplee, emb, iron, 2½" 20.00
Ten Star, emb Ten Star 6-Lever, 2¼" 45.00

Logo — Special Made

Anaconda, st, brass, 2⅞" 60.00
Brass pancake push key emb US Internal Revenue, 2¼" 185.00
City of Boston Dept of Schools, st, brass, 2⅞" 40.00
Coca-Cola, st, brass, 2⅝" 40.00
Conoco, st, brass, 2⅝" 25.00
D&H, emb, brass, 2½" 170.00
Delco Products, st, brass 20.00
Georgia Power Co, st, brass, 3" 15.00
Heart-shape brass lever type emb Shults Co, bbl key, 2¾" 55.00
Heart-shape brass lever type st Board Education, bbl key, 3½" .65.00
International Harvester Co, emb, brass, 2½" 100.00
Lilly, st, brass, 2½" 15.00
Okla State Pen, st, brass, 2⅝" 50.00
Oliver, emb, iron, 2½" 80.00
Property of Syracuse Univ, st, brass, 2⅝" 40.00
Public Service Co, st, brass, 2⅞" 20.00
Sq brass pin-tumbler case st Regd US Mail, int counter, 2¾" .140.00
Sq Yale-type brass pin tumbler, st US/A/tree/Forest Svc, 2⅞" .125.00
Standard Oil Co, st, brass, 2⅝" 25.00
Swift & Co, st, iron, 2¼" 20.00
University of Notre Dame, emb, brass, 2½" 160.00
University of Okla, st, brass, 2⅞" 40.00
USBIA, st, brass, 3¾" 80.00
USBIR, st, brass, 3¾" 80.00
USGS, emb, iron, 2½" 40.00
USMC, st, brass, 2½" 20.00
West Baking Co, emb, brass, 2½" 90.00
Zoo, st, iron, 2½" 25.00

Pin-Tumbler Type

Corbin, brass, Corbin in oval st on body, 3⅝" 25.00
Eagle, brass, Eagle st on body, 2⅞" 20.00
Eagle, emb, iron, 2¾" 20.00
Hickory, emb, iron, 2¾" 60.00
Hope, brass, emb Hope on body, 2½" 20.00
Il-A-Noy, emb, iron, 2¾" 35.00
Pearl, brass, emb Pearl on body, 2⅛" 20.00
Rich-Con, emb, iron, 2⅞" 50.00
Sargent, brass, emb Sargent on body, 3" 15.00
Segal, iron, emb Segal on shackle, 3¾" 30.00
Shapleigh, emb Shapleigh on body, 2⅝" 30.00
Simmons, emb, iron, 2⅝" 30.00
Yale, brass, emb Yale on body, Yale & Towne on shackle, 2⅝" 25.00
Yale, emb, iron, 2½" 20.00

Scandinavian (Jail House) Type

Backalaphknck (Russian), st, iron, 5" 200.00
Corbin, st, brass, 2½" 50.00
JHW Climax Co, iron, 2⅞" 50.00
Pear, emb, iron, 3½" 40.00
R&E Co, emb, iron, 3¼" 40.00
Star, emb line on bottom, iron, 3¾" 100.00
Star, iron, 2½" 70.00
99 Miller, emb 99, brass, 1¾" 80.00

Six-Lever Type

Bon-Ton, st, iron, 3" 15.00
Edwards, iron, Edwards st on body 18.00
Miller Six Lever, st, brass, 3⅞" 20.00
Oak Leaf Six Lever, st, iron, 3¼" 15.00
Safe, brass, Safe st on body 18.00
SHCo Simmon Six Lever, emb, iron, 3⅞" 70.00

Story and Commemorative

AYPEX Seattle (Alaska Yukon Pacific Expo), emb tin/iron, 3" .235.00
Canteen, US emb on lock, lock: canteen shape, 2" 500.00
CI, emb skull/X-bones w/florals, NH Co on bk, 3¼" 200.00
CQD/sinking ship Titanic & SOS waves emb on brass, 2¾" 120.00
Dan Patch, iron, 1⅞" 125.00
Mail Pouch emb on lock, lock in shape of mail pouch, 3⅛" 225.00
Missouri Seal, brass, 2¼" 150.00
National Hardware Co (NHCo), emb, iron, 2½" 200.00
National Hardware Co (NHCo), emb SK, iron, 3½" 425.00
New York to Paris, brass, 2⅝" 200.00
North Pole, brass, 2⅞" 150.00
Russell & Erwin (R&E), emb bird, iron, 2⅞" 400.00
Russell & Erwin (R&E), emb Ganesha form, iron, 3" 325.00
Russell & Erwin (R&E), emb mailbox, iron, 3⅛" 300.00
1901 Pan Am Expo, brass, emb w/buffalo, 2⅝" 175.00
1904 World's Fair, iron & brass, 3⅝" 300.00

Warded Type

Aetna, emb, brass, 2¼" 35.00
Army, iron pancake ward key, emb letters, 2½" 40.00
Cruso Chicken, emb, brass, 2¾" 35.00
Enders, st, brass, 1½" 25.00
Globe, iron sq lock case, emb US on bk, 2⅜" 20.00
Jewel, emb, iron, 2½" 18.00

Kirby, emb, brass, 2¼" 20.00
Lucky, emb, brass, 2½" 45.00
Red Cross, brass sq case, emb letters, 2" 10.00
Red Seal, emb, brass, 2" 20.00
Rex, steel case, emb letters, 2⅝" 18.00
Safe, brass sq case, emb letters, 1⅞" 8.00
Safety First, brass pancake type, emb letters, 2¾" 15.00
Secure, iron pancake type, emb letters, 2⅝" 20.00
Sprocket, brass oval shape, emb letters, 2⅛" 50.00
Texas, emb, brass, 2½" 50.00
Try Me, iron pancake type, emb letters, 2½" 25.00
Van Guard, emb, iron, 2⅞" 18.00
Winchester, brass sq case, st letters, 2¾" 125.00

Wrought Iron Lever Type (Smokehouse Type)

Bramah's Patent VR, 5" 60.00
Improved Warranted, 3½" 35.00
MW&Co, bbl key, 2⅝" 10.00
R&E, 4½" 40.00
S&Co, bbl key, 3" 8.00
VR, 3½" 30.00
WT Patent, 3¼" 20.00

Loetz

The Loetz Glassworks was established in Klostermule, Austria, in 1840. After Loetz's death the firm was purchased by his grandson, Johann Loetz Witwe. Until WWII the operation continued to produce fine artware, some of which made in the early 1900s bears a striking resemblance to Tiffany's, with whom Loetz was associated at one time. In addition to the iridescent Tiffany-style glass, he also produced threaded glass and some cameo. The majority of Loetz pieces will have a polished pontil. Our advisor for this category is Don Williams; he is listed in the Directory under Missouri.

Vase, pulled and trailed ice green iridescent decor on fuchsia, controlled air bubbles, shaped cylinder with flared mouth, 10", $3,700.00.

Basket, clear w/random gr threads, appl hdl & leaves, 6x8" 150.00
Basket, gold mottle, wht int, clear hdl, floral prunts, 16x10" 250.00
Basket, gr w/purple & bl irid, 18¼x11½" 300.00
Basket, raindrops, ruby-brn on wht, Nouveau floral SP fr, 10x7" ..600.00
Basket, red to clear w/gr hooked/pulled design, clear hdl, 18x10" .250.00
Bowl, amberina, gr irid oil spots, ruffled rim, 3½x10" 75.00
Bowl, amethyst irid w/silver bl threads, 4½x9½" 300.00
Bowl, bl irid oil spots, gold web, scroll hdls, 3½x6¼" 650.00
Bowl, clear to ruby, 4-lobed, dimples/striations, 4x8½" 525.00
Bowl, gold-bronze w/purple decor, bronze Nouveau fr, 10x15x10" 1,500.00
Bowl, gr irid w/dimples, crimped rim, 3½x6½" 190.00
Bowl, gr w/appl decor & wht striping, 4½x8" 500.00

Bowl, lt gr irid, spherical w/wide mouth, hdls, 4½x8½" 525.00
Bowl, oil spots, dimpled, folded rim, 12" dia 425.00
Bowl, opal irid w/purple threads, brass acanthus base, 3¼x7" 650.00
Compote, gr Dmn Quilt; Nouveau rtcl metal fr, 9½x10" 300.00
Cracker barrel, oil spots w/rainbow irid, vintage emb lid, 7" 300.00
Dish, gold base, 3 appl pulled-out hdls, 2¾x8½" dia 200.00
Globe, amethyst on wht w/allover threading, 8¾x8" 400.00
Inkwell, cobalt textured & irid, 3¼x4" 300.00
Rose bowl, red craquelle w/golden bl irid, ruffled, 3¼" H 250.00
Salt cellar, bl w/gold oil spots, 1x2¾" 650.00
Shell, bl irid on gr ft, 6½x13½" 2,350.00
Vase, amber w/pulled bl-gold irid design, pinched sides, 4" 1,200.00
Vase, amethyst irid w/random web threading, 10x9" 200.00
Vase, bl/gold irid, pinched, 4¼x4" 300.00
Vase, bl/gold irid w/cobalt vines, twist body, 9½" 1,000.00
Vase, brn irid, ribbed body, appl hdls, 5x3½" 575.00
Vase, dk gr w/bl irid, raised pattern, 4x3" 150.00
Vase, emerald gr, irregular crinkles, ruffled rim, 7" 375.00
Vase, emerald gr w/appl raindrops, 3½" 125.00
Vase, emerald gr w/purple & bl oil spots, waisted, 14½" 425.00
Vase, emerald gr w/silver o/l flowers & raindrops, 5" 550.00
Vase, gold w/bl waves, 4 pinched-in sides, 5x3¼" 550.00
Vase, gr irid, twisted body, pinched top, 10" 325.00
Vase, lt gr irid w/gold scale-like decor, 4x4" 300.00
Vase, lt gr spots on clear w/magenta/gold/bl irid, unmk, 7" 210.00
Vase, Moss Agate type, bulbous, flared rim, 4¾" 250.00
Vase, oil spots, amber/silver-violet, ovoid, ruffled rim, 5" 515.00
Vase, oil spots, bl irid, ruffled/twisted, bulbous, 9¾" 1,100.00
Vase, oil spots, gr irid, ruffled trumpet form, 11¾" 700.00
Vase, oil spots, silver-turq on cobalt, 3-crimp/globular, 4¼" 750.00
Vase, oil spots on yel-amber w/purple irid, globular, 8½" 575.00
Vase, opal irid w/draped decor, shouldered, metal cap, 3½" 50.00
Vase, Owl, bl oil spots, ACB eyes/features w/gold, 5" 2,900.00
Vase, peach-pk w/cobalt waves & bl spots, pinched, 4¼" 2,500.00
Vase, Rainbow swirl, shell hdls, gold trim, 10½x6", pr 675.00
Vase, Raindrop, bronze on bl/gold, dimples, 6x5" 750.00
Vase, Raindrop, purple-bl on purple-brn, 7½x4½" 1,150.00
Vase, red to gr w/silver o/l florals, att, 10½x6½" 325.00
Vase, red w/mc irid, dimpled/swirled, 10¼x5" 400.00
Vase, swirled mc irid, appl threads, ftd, flared rim, 13x3⅝" 950.00
Vase, vaseline w/wht swirl & aventurine, pinched design, 6½x7" ...100.00
Vase, violet irid w/silver o/l tulip & tendrils, 2½" 460.00
Vase, wht frost w/amethsyt Deco-style roses, 6½x4½" 1,000.00
Vase, yel-amber/clear mottle w/purple irid, bl wavy bands, 12¾" ...575.00

Lomonosov Porcelain

Founded in Leningrad in 1744, the Lomonosov porcelain factory produced exquisite porcelain miniatures for the Czar and other Russian nobility. One of the first factories of its kind, Lomonosov produced mainly vases and delicate sculptures. In the 1800s Lomonosov became closely involved with the Russian Academy of Fine Arts, a connection which has continued to this day as the company continues to supply the world with these fine artistic treasures. In 1992 the backstamp was changed to read 'Made in Russia,' instead of 'Made in USSR.' Some dealers may be pricing items marked 'Made in USSR' at 75% to 100% above prices listed below.

Baikal Duck, #3438 ....24.50
Bear, standing, #6448 ....12.50
Chow-Chow, #1841 ....17.50
Donkey, #6498 ....20.00
Elephant, #6573 ....24.50

Giraffe, head raised, #6515 ....92.00
Hippopotamus, #7403, mini 4.50
Lion cub, #6349, lg 12.50
Lynx, #6550 ....33.00
Otter, #6538 ....26.50
Rabbit, wht, #9645, mini 8.50
Rock Partridge, turned, #2632 ....9.00
Snowbird, #6558 ....9.00
Tiger cub, #9424, mini 9.50

Lonhuda

William Long was a druggist by trade who combined his knowledge of chemistry with his artistic ability in an attempt to produce a type of brown-glazed slip-decorated artware similar to that made by the Rookwood Pottery. He achieved his goal in 1889 after years of long and dedicated study. Three years later he founded his firm, the Lonhuda Pottery Company. The name was coined from the first few letters of the last name of each of his partners, W.H. Hunter and Alfred Day. Laura Fry, formerly of the Rookwood company, joined the firm in 1892, bringing with her a license for Long to use her patented airbrush-blending process. Other artists of note, Sarah McLaughlin, Helen Harper, and Jessie Spaulding, joined the firm and decorated the ware with nature studies, animals, and portraits, often signing their work with their initials. Three types of marks were used on the Steubenville Lonhuda ware. The first was a linear composite of the letters 'LPCO' with the name 'Lonhuda' impressed above it. The second, adopted in 1893, was a die-stamp representing the solid profile of an Indian, used on ware patterned after pottery made by the American Indians. This mark was later replaced with an impressed outline of the Indian head with 'Lonhuda' arching above it. Although the ware was successful, the business floundered due to poor management. In 1895 Long became a partner of Sam Weller and moved to Zanesville where the manufacture of the Lonhuda line continued. Less than a year later, Long left the Weller company. He was associated with J.B. Owens until 1899, at which time he moved to Denver, Colorado, where he established the Denver China and Pottery Company in 1901. His efforts to produce Lonhuda utilizing local clay were highly successful. Examples of Denver Lonhuda are sometimes marked with the LF (Lonhuda Faience) cipher contained within a canted diamond form. For further information we recommend *Collector's Encyclopedia of Colorado Pottery* by Carol and Jim Carlton; they are listed in the Directory under Colorado.

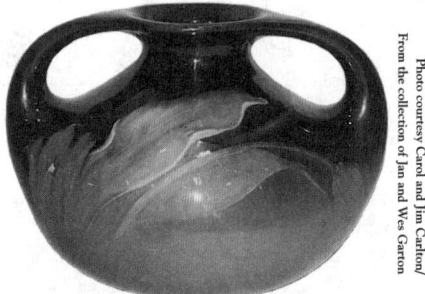

Photo courtesy Carol and Jim Carlton/
From the collection of Jan and Wes Garton

**Vase, tulips on brown, integral handles,
Denver-Lonhuda, 6x9", $650.00.**

Vase, daffodils incised/emb on olive gr, #100, 9" 2,600.00
Vase, dogwood, Eugene Roberts, matt, ovoid, 8¼" 400.00
Vase, mums, yel on brn, Jessie Spalding, 10½x5¾" 250.00
Vase, tulips on brn, integral hdls, Penner, 6x9" 650.00

Lotton

Charles Lotton is a contemporary glass artist. He began blowing glass and developing original designs thirty years ago and now has work on display in many major glass museums and collections, among them the Smithsonian, the Art Institute of Chicago, the Museum of Glass, and the Chrysler Museum. He has become famous for his unique lamps. Every piece is signed and dated. His three sons, David, Daniel, and John, each work in their own studios. All four artists produce distinctive work. They sell their glass at antique shows and in their showroom in Lansing, Illinois. For further information read *Lotton Art Glass* by Charles Lotton and Tom O'Conner; see the Directory under Illinois. The values that follow are actual prices realized from a recent auction.

Bowl, Multi-Flora, cobalt opal w/pk/moss gr, 1995, 9½x10½" ...**1,700.00**
Persian water sprinkler, Mandarin Red, silver-bl feathers, 14" **475.00**
Vase, Cypriot, bl pitted irid w/silver-bl lava rim, '76, 5½" **625.00**
Vase, Multi-Flora, amber w/pk/bl-gr, bulbous, 1985, 6½" **700.00**
Vase, Multi-Flora, autumn gr w/yel/red, 1978, 10¼" **650.00**
Vase, Multi-Flora, cobalt w/opal/gr, 1978, 9½" **350.00**
Vase, Multi-Flora, dbl ruby w/yel-red, 1979, 10" **850.00**
Vase, Multi-Flora, emerald w/pk satin/silver-bl, 1976, 5¼" **300.00**
Vase, Multi-Flora, emerald w/red/tan/silver-gr, 1979, 7" **350.00**
Vase, Multi-Flora, gr w/ruby/tan/gr, bulbous, 1979, 6" **375.00**
Vase, Multi-Flora, irid w/opal/cobalt/purple/bl-gr, 1976, 7" **400.00**

Lotus Ware

Isaac Knowles and Issac Harvey operated a pottery in East Liverpool, Ohio, in 1853 where they produced both yellow ware and Rockingham. In 1870 Knowles brought Harvey's interests and took as partners John Taylor and Homer Knowles. Their principal product was ironstone china, but Knowles was confident that American potters could produce as fine a ware as the Europeans. To prove his point, he hired Joshua Poole, an artist from the Belleek Works in Ireland. Poole quickly perfected a Belleek-type china, but fire destroyed this portion of the company. Before it could function again, their hotel china business had grown to the point that it required their full attention in order to meet market demands. By 1891 they were able to try again. They developed a bone china, as fine and thin as before, which they called Lotus. Henry Schmidt from the Meissen factory in Germany decorated the ware, often with lacy filigree applications or hand-formed leaves and flowers to which he added further decoration with liquid slip applied by means of a squeeze bag. Due to high production costs resulting from so much of the fragile ware being damaged in firing and because of changes in tastes and styles of decoration, the Lotus Ware line was dropped in 1896. Some of the early ware was marked 'KT&K China'; later marks have a star and a crescent with 'Lotus Ware' added. For further information we recommend *Collector's Encyclopedia of Knowles, Taylor & Knowles China* by Mary Frank Gaston, our advisor for this category.

Bottle, scent; pierced/scrolled, twig hdls, folded rim, 3½" **650.00**
Bowl, gold appl florals on tan matt, beaded rim, pk int, 4½" **350.00**
Chocolate jug, emb florals, no enameling or gold, 9" **550.00**
Cup & saucer, AD; Mecca, lt gr geometrics w/gold, 2½", 5" **135.00**
Ewer, pk florals, gold-speckled twig hdl, 6½" **375.00**
Jar, ornate rtcl pattern, rstr finial, hairline, 6¾x6" **1,000.00**
Pitcher, pk floral branches w/gold, bamboo hdl w/gold, 4½" **275.00**
Pitcher, raised net pattern, bamboo hdl, 3½" **185.00**
Rose bowl, lav floral, beaded/ruffled rim, globular, 4" **350.00**
Rose jar, jewel-like garlands/rtcl medallions, w/lid, 7½" **1,700.00**
Rose jar, lt gr & wht accents, rtcl ball form, w/lid, 4" **700.00**

Rose jar, Persian, rtcl, ornamental side mts, w/lid, 7" **1,350.00**
Salt cellar, gold lustre int, ⅜x½" dia **80.00**
Shell tray, gold floral branch, 1905, 5½" dia **150.00**
Syrup, acanthus leaf shoulder, scroll hdl, floral rim, 4½" **225.00**
Teapot, fishnet on wht, 4", +cr/sug, ea 4" **225.00**
Vase, Etruscan, appl flowers, filigree hdls, whtware, 10" **1,350.00**
Vase, yel lily form w/mounded leafy base, gold trim, 8" **225.00**

Lu Ray Pastels

Lu Ray Pastels dinnerware was introduced in the early 1940s by Taylor, Smith, and Taylor of East Liverpool, Ohio. It was offered in assorted colors of Persian Cream, Sharon Pink, Surf Green, Windsor Blue, and Gray in complete place settings as well as many service pieces. It was a successful line in its day and is once again finding favor with collectors of American dinnerware. For further information we recommend *Collector's Guide to Lu Ray Pastels* by Bill and Kathy Meehan. Our advisor for this category is Shirley Moore; she is listed in the Directory under Oklahoma.

Bowl, '36s oatmeal **40.00**
Bowl, coupe soup; flat **15.00**
Bowl, cream soup **55.00**
Bowl, fruit; Chatham Gray, 5" **12.50**
Bowl, fruit; 5" **5.00**
Bowl, lug soup; tab hdld **19.00**
Bowl, mixing; 10" **75.00**
Bowl, mixing; 7" **70.00**
Bowl, salad **50.00**
Bowl, vegetable; oval, 9½" **16.00**
Bowl, 10¼" **85.00**
Bowl, 8¾" **75.00**

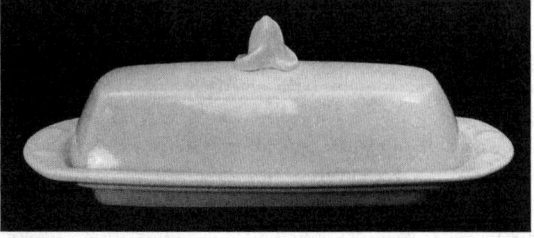

Butter dish, Chatham Gray, rare color, with lid, $90.00.

Calendar plates, 8", 9" & 10", ea **40.00**
Casserole **85.00**
Chocolate cup, AD; str sides **60.00**
Chocolate pot, AD; str sides **360.00**
Coaster/nut dish **65.00**
Coffee cup, AD **20.00**
Coffeepot, AD **160.00**
Creamer **8.00**
Creamer, AD, ind **40.00**
Creamer, AD, ind, from chocolate set **92.00**
Egg cup, dbl **18.00**
Epergne **110.00**
Gravy boat **22.00**
Jug, water; ftd **85.00**
Muffin cover **90.00**
Muffin cover, w/8" underplate **105.00**
Nappy, vegetable; rnd, 8½" **15.00**
Pitcher, any color other than yel, bulbous w/flat bottom **75.00**

Pitcher, juice	150.00
Pitcher, yel, bulbous w/flat bottom	55.00
Plate, cake	63.00
Plate, Chatham Gray, rare color, 7"	16.00
Plate, chop; 15"	25.00
Plate, grill; compartment	22.00
Plate, 10"	20.00
Plate, 6"	3.00
Plate, 7"	8.50
Plate, 8"	15.00
Plate, 9"	10.00
Platter, oval, 11½"	13.50
Platter, oval, 13"	16.00
Relish dish, 4-part	75.00
Sauce boat, fixed stand	23.00
Saucer, coffee; AD	8.50
Saucer, coffee/chocolate	22.50
Saucer, cream soup	22.50
Saucer, tea	3.00
Shakers, pr	13.00
Sugar bowl, AD; w/lid, from chocolate set	92.00
Sugar bowl, AD; w/lid, ind	40.00
Sugar bowl, w/lid	11.00
Teacup	8.00
Teapot, curved spout, w/lid	75.00
Teapot, w/lid, flat spout	125.00
Tray, pickle	24.00
Tumbler, juice	45.00
Tumbler, water	65.00
Vase, bud	215.00

Lunch Boxes

Early 20th-century tobacco companies such as Union Leader, Tiger, and Dixie sold their products in square, steel containers with flat, metal carrying handles. These were specifically engineered to be used as lunch boxes when they became empty. (See Advertising, specific companies.) By 1930 oval lunch pails with colorful lithographed decorations on tin were being manufactured to appeal directly to children. These were made by Ohio Art, Decoware, and a few other companies. In 1950 Aladdin Industries produced the first 'real' character lunch box — a Hopalong Cassidy decal-decorated steel container now considered the beginning of the kids' lunch box industry. The other big lunch box manufacturer, American Thermos (later King Seely Thermos Company) brought out its 'blockbuster' Roy Rogers box in 1953, the first fully lithographed steel lunch box and matching bottle. Other companies (ADCO Liberty; Landers, Frary & Clark; Ardee Industries; Okay Industries; Universal; Tindco; Cheinco) also produced character pails. Today's collectors often tend to specialize in those boxes dealing with a particular subject. Western, space, TV series, Disney movies, and cartoon characters are the most popular. There are well over five hundred different lunch boxes available to the astute collector. For further information we recommend *The Illustrated Encyclopedia of Metal Lunch Boxes* by Allen Woodall and Sean Brickell. Our advisor for this category is Allan Smith; he is listed in the Directory under Texas. In the following listings, lunch boxes are metal unless noted vinyl or plastic, and values include thermoses only when they are mentioned within the descriptions.

Astronaut, dome, 1960, EX-	150.00
Atom Ant, Thermos, 1966, w/thermos, EX	280.00
Beatles, Thermos, yel & pk, wear/scratches, G+	180.00
Boston Red Sox, vinyl, w/generic thermos, 1960, M	95.00
Buck Rogers, w/thermos, hang tags, 1979, M	140.00

Bugaloos, Aladdin, 1971, EX+	130.00
Carnival, 1959, VG+	250.00
Challenger, puffy vinyl, gr, 1986, M	250.00
Circus, oval, 2-hdl, 1930s, EX-	125.00
Color Me Happy, 1984, EX	150.00
Corsage, vinyl, 1970, VG+	100.00
Cracker Jack, w/thermos, 1979, VG+	60.00
Daniel Boone (same front & bk), 1955, VG+	165.00
Disney Firefighter, dome top, 1969, VG+	135.00
Emergency, 1973, EX-	60.00
Evel Knievel, w/thermos, 1974, EX	100.00
Floral, 1970, M	65.00
Goober & the Ghost Chasers, 1974, EX-	70.00
Great Wild West, 1959, VG+	400.00
Green Hornet, 1967, VG+	200.00
Grizzly Adams, dome top, 1977, EX	120.00
Gunsmoke, 1972, VG	85.00
Gunsmoke, 1973, EX-	125.00
Hansel & Gretel, 1982, EX	80.00
Hi-My Lunch, 1977, M	95.00
Jetsons, Aladdin, dome top, 1963, EX	700.00
Lance Link Secret Chimp, 1971, EX	125.00
Legend of Lone Ranger, 1980, VG+	30.00
Leo Lion, vinyl drawstring bag, 1978, NM	145.00
Little Drummer Boy, 1976, M	125.00
Little Orphan Annie, plastic dome, w/thermos, 1973, NM	95.00
Mardi Gras, vinyl, w/thermos, 1971, VG+	100.00
Mighty Mouse, plastic, 1979, EX-	45.00
Monroes, 1967, EX	175.00
Pathfinder, 1959, VG+	350.00
Patriotic Drummer Boy, 1976, M	125.00
Peter Pan, 1969, VG+	65.00
Pink Panther, vinyl, 1980, VG+	65.00
Pit Stop, 1968, NM	375.00
Plaid Scotch, Universal, 1959, EX	40.00
Planet of the Apes, 1974, EX	80.00
Popeye, plastic, 3-D, w/thermos, 1987, M	75.00
Popeye, plastic dome, 1979, EX	65.00
Popeye, 1964, VG+	100.00
Porky's Lunch Wagon, dome, 1959, VG	165.00
Racing Wheels, w/thermos, 1977, EX	55.00
Rambo, w/thermos, 1985, M	45.00
Red Barn, open doors, 1958, EX+	95.00
Return of the Jedi, 1983, VG+	30.00
Rifleman, 1960, VG+, from $200 to	235.00
Roy Rogers, red shirt, 1957, EX	300.00
Sesame Street, vinyl, 1981, EX+	35.00
Snoopy, Peanuts, vinyl brunch bag, 1977, EX	85.00
Snow White, Disney, w/thermos, 1975, EX	75.00

Space: 1999, King-Seeley, 1975, VG/EX, $40.00.

Sports Afield, 1957, EX+	200.00
Star Wars, w/thermos, 1977, EX	75.00

SWAT, plastic dome, 1975, EX 45.00
Three Little Pigs, 1982, EX 80.00
Tropicana Swim Club, vinyl, 1980, EX 50.00
Wonder Woman, vinyl, bl, w/thermos, 1977, EX+ 225.00
Woody Woodpecker, 1972, VG 50.00
Zorro, blk rim, 1958, VG+ 150.00

Lutz

From 1869 to 1888, Nicholas Lutz worked for the Boston and Sandwich Company where he produced the threaded and striped art glass that was so popular during that era. His works were not marked; and since many other glassmakers of the day made similar wares, the term Lutz has come to refer not only to his original works but to any of this type.

Bowl, horizontal ribs, dk bl rim, SP fr w/arched hdl, 6⅝x5⅜" 80.00
Decanter, reverse bl/wht/aventurine swirls, stick neck, 11" 150.00
Finger bowl, bl/wht/gold striping, 5¾", +underplate 110.00
Wine, pk/wht/gold striping, trumpet-shape base, 4⅛" 120.00

Maddux of California

One of the California-made ceramics now so popular with collectors, Maddux was founded in the late 1930s and during the years that followed produced novelty items, TV lamps, figurines, planters, and tableware accessories. Our advisor for this category is Doris Frizzell; she is listed in the Directory under Illinois.

#896, TV lamp, bassett hound, 12", $155.00.

#221, vase, swan, wht, 12" 20.00
#225, vase, horse's head top, str-sided body, aqua, 12" 18.00
#400/401, flamingo, pr 50.00
#510, planter, swan, blk, 11" 18.00
#515, planter, flamingo, pk, 10½" 45.00
#527, Chinese Pheasant, 11½" 20.00
#528, planter, 2 birds in flight, pk & blk, 10" 20.00
#529, vase, 2 flamingos, 5" 40.00
#536, planter, bird in flight, 11½" H 20.00
#627, TV lamp, stallion, Maddux of California, 13" 35.00
#628, swallow planter, pk & gray 35.00
#808, TV lamp, pearltone shell, 13" 40.00
#810, TV lamp, stallion, prancing, on base, 12" 20.00
#826, TV lamp, cockatoos 50.00
#828, TV lamp, swan planter, wht porc, 12½" 20.00
#829, TV lamp, deer (2), running, natural, 10½" 20.00
#839, TV lamp, mallard, flying, natural colors, 11½" 35.00
#841, TV lamp, head of Christ, 3-D planter 25.00
#844, TV lamp, prairie schooner (covered wagon), 11" 30.00
#846, TV lamp, nativity scene, 3-D planter, 12" 25.00

#859, TV lamp, Toro (bull), ft on mound, 11½" 20.00
#887, TV lamp, Persian Glory (horse head), 11½" 20.00
#889, TV lamp, Malibu shell, pearltone, 10¼" 20.00
#892, TV lamp, Colonial ship, 10½" 30.00
#894, TV lamp, Toro (bull), charging, walnut, 11½" 20.00
#895, TV lamp, dbl swan, 11½" 30.00
#897, TV lamp, mare & foal, wht porc 30.00
#907, doe, walnut, wht porc, tangerine, 12½" 15.00
#912/#913, Chinese pheasants, airbrushed colors, 11", pr 30.00
#914, stag, standing, natural colors, 12½" 20.00
#923, swans (2), blk matt, 10½" 25.00
#924, stag, standing, natural colors, 12½" 15.00
#925/926, horses, rearing/charging, pr 20.00
#928/#929, mallards, male/female, natural colors, 9½", pr 40.00
#932, rooster, 10½" 30.00
#969, Early Birds, blk matt, tangerine, 14½", pr 25.00
#970, flamingo, flying, natural colors, 11" 45.00
#971, flamingo, winging, natural colors, 12" 45.00
#972/973, bull, red, head up/head down, 11" L, pr 75.00
#982, horse, prancing 20.00
#984, elephant, sitting, 18" 25.00
#1019, swan console bowl (set), porc wht, 11½" 20.00
#1047, Contempo bowl (set), wht satin, 16½" 15.00
#1051, candlestick, dbl, 12" 25.00
#1067, shell console bowl (set), pk, 16" 15.00
#2015, vase, Antique Gold, hdls, 12" 15.00
#206A, planter, Chinese Bell Tower, 8" 20.00
#2102, bowl, ftd 10.00
#2217, Cream can, Paul Revere Milc Co, Maddux 75.00
#3302, bank, cat, yel 35.00
#3006, TV lamp/planter, half circle 25.00
#3009, serving tray/lazy susan, pearlized, 2-tiered, 6-pc 25.00
#3017, seashell bowl, wht 15.00
#3095A, bowl, ped w/6 ind servers 25.00
#3251-L, tray, serving; 2-tier 20.00
#3275, gr pepper relish, w/lid & side bowls 12.00
#3304, planter, bird 20.00
#7001, ashtray, 12" dia 10.00
#7134, ashtray, fish, 6" L 20.00
#7204, ashtray, pig form, natural color, 7" L 12.00
Ashtray set, yel & red, metal caddy w/6 ind ashtrays 20.00
Bank, smiling piggy, red or gr, 12" L 25.00
Bowl, cabbage leaf design, 4x13" L 30.00
Cats, Deco style, blk matt, 12½", facing pr 50.00
Cockatoo, on branch w/appl flower, 11" 40.00
Cookie jar, Bear, Maddux of Calif c USA #2101 ....75.00
Cookie jar, Beatrix Potter Rabbit, c Maddux of Calif 100.00
Cookie jar, Calory Hippy 300.00
Cookie jar, cat, c Maddux of California 65.00
Cookie jar, Clown, very lg, from $325 to 395.00
Cookie jar, Grape Cylinder 45.00
Cookie jar, Humpty Dumpty, c Maddux of Calif USA #2113 ....300.00
Cookie jar, Koala 75.00
Cookie jar, Queen, #2104, from $125 to 140.00
Cookie jar, Raggedy Andy, #2108, from $250 to 300.00
Cookie jar, Scottie 75.00
Cookie jar, Snowman 75.00
Cookie jar, Squirrel, #2110, Maddux of Calif, C Romanelli 100.00
Cookie jar, Strawberry 35.00
Cookie jar, Walrus 65.00
Cookie jar, 3 baby birds on lid, Maddux of Calif #3233 ......65.00
Ducklings, 3 on grassy base 20.00
Flamingo Line, single flamingo planter, 6" 20.00
Planter, rearing horse, 10x7½" 22.00

Magazines

Magazines are collected for their cover prints and for the information pertaining to defunct companies and their products that can be gleaned from the old advertisements. In the listings that follow, items are assumed to be in very good condition unless noted otherwise. For further information we recommend *Old Magazines Price Guide* (revised prices), by L-W Book Sales. See also Movie Memorabilia; Parrish, Maxfield. Our advisor for this category is Charles Zayic; he is listed in the Directory under Maine.

Key:

M — mint condition, in original wrapper
EX — excellent condition, spine intact, edges of pages clean and straight
VG — very good condition, the average as-found condition

American Weekly, 1950, November, Leyendecker cover, EX 20.00
American Weekly, 1956, April 15, Grace Kelly cover, EX 11.00
American Weekly, 1959, April 26, Audrey Hepburn cover, EX ...11.00
Argosy, 1965, November, Dr Sam Sheppard, EX 7.00
Argosy, 1966, December, Flying Saucers, EX 7.00
Baseball Magazine, 1939, November, DiMaggio & Walters, NM ..100.00
Boy's Life, 1969, June, Mantle & Mickey Jr cover, EX 40.00
Cool & Hep Cats, 1958, October, Elvis Presley cover, EX 24.00
Cosmopolitan, 1922, A Conan Doyle story, NC Wyeth illus, EX ..100.00
Family Circle, 1939, June, Scarlett O'Hara cover, EX 25.00

Fortune, 1946, March, World Rubber cover, EX, $15.00.

Ladies' Home Journal, 1967, June, Twiggy cover 2.00
Ladies' Home Journal, 1973, July, Marilyn Monroe cover, EX 25.00
Ladies' World & Housekeeper, 1913, Harrison Fisher cover, EX ..35.00
Liberty, 1947, August 2, Cary Grant cover, EX 4.00
Life, 1936, November 23, 1st issue, NM 110.00
Life, 1937, January 4, FDR cover 20.00
Life, 1937, May 17, Dionne Quints cover, EX 50.00
Life, 1937, November 8, Garbo cover, EX 30.00
Life, 1938, June 20, Rudolph Valentino cover, EX 25.00
Life, 1938, May 23, Errol Flynn cover, EX 20.00
Life, 1939, December 11, Betty Grable cover, VG 15.00
Life, 1939, May 1, Joe DiMaggio cover, EX 60.00
Life, 1940, September 2, Dionne Quints cover, VG 15.00
Life, 1941, January 6, Katherine Hepburn cover 18.00
Life, 1941, October 13, Turner & Gable cover, EX 20.00
Life, 1943, July 12, Roy Rogers & Trigger, EX 35.00
Life, 1949, August 1, Joe DiMaggio cover, EX 45.00
Life, 1949, October, Princess Margaret cover, EX 15.00
Life, 1949, September, Ben Turpin cover, EX 15.00
Life, 1950, June 12, Hopalong Cassidy cover, NM 45.00
Life, 1950, May, Jackie Robinson cover, EX 45.00
Life, 1953, September 14, Casey Stengel cover, EX 20.00

Life, 1956, April 23, Jane Mansfield cover, EX 28.00
Life, 1958, April 28, Willie Mays cover, VG 15.00
Life, 1958, July, Roy Campanella cover, EX 20.00
Life, 1961, August 18, Mantle & Maris cover, NM 75.00
Life, 1961, January 13, Clark Gable cover, EX 10.00
Life, 1962, April, Burton & Taylor cover, w/inserts, EX 150.00
Life, 1962, June 22, Marilyn Monroe cover, NM, from $24 to 30.00
Life, 1963, April, Burton & Taylor, EX 10.00
Life, 1965, July 30, Mickey Mantle cover, EX 25.00
Look, 1927, December, Shirley Temple/Santa Claus cover, EX 35.00
Look, 1938, Dionne Quints cover, EX 30.00
McCalls, 1937, September, Helen Hayes cover, EX 8.00
McCalls, 1951, June, Greta Garbo cover, EX 10.00
McCalls, 1956, March, Duchess of Windsor cover, EX 8.00
Model Builder, 1939, Vol 3, #18, Joe DiMaggio cover, VG+ 90.00
Newsweek, 1957, July 1, Stan Musial cover 15.00
Photoplay, 1959, June, R Nelson cover, Rock & Roll Yrbook, EX ..11.00
Playboy, 1955, January, Betty Page, NM 275.00
Playboy, 1960, January, Stella Stevens, NM 40.00
Playboy, 1967, February, Kim Farber, NM 15.00
Playboy, 1970, July, Carol Willis, NM 12.00
Playboy, 1979, August, Dorothy Stratten, NM 15.00
Playboy, 1985, January, Joan Bennett, NM 6.00
Redbook, 1954, November, Grace Kelly cover, EX 3.00
Redbook, 1956, March, Frank Sinatra cover, EX 5.00
Redbook, 1956, September, Gina Lollobridgida cover, EX 5.00
Ring, 1976, June, Latin Connection, EX 15.00
Rolling Stone, 1977, September 8, OJ Simpson cover, EX 85.00
Saturday Evening Post, 1903, lady golfer cover, EX 50.00
Saturday Evening Post, 1943, July 31, Hitler cover, M 75.00
Saturday Evening Post, 1946, March 2, N Rockwell cover, EX 10.00
Scientific American, 1887, April 30, 1st Am typewriter, EX 35.00
Scientific American, 1887, December, Edison's Talking Machine ..65.00
Scientific American, 1888, July 14, Tainter's Graphophone, EX ..25.00
Scientific American, 1888, September 15, Kodak Camera, EX 25.00
Sport Life, 1948, November, Ted Williams cover, EX 40.00
Sport Magazine, 1948, August, Stan Musial cover, EX 30.00
Sport Magazine, 1948, May, Babe Ruth cover, EX 30.00
Sport Magazine, 1948, October, Lou Gehrig cover, EX 50.00
Sport Magazine, 1949, August, Robinson cover, EX 30.00
Sport Magazine, 1949, September, Joe DiMaggio cover, EX 65.00
Sport Magazine, 1952, July, Musial cover 20.00
Sport Magazine, 1953, April, Mickey Mantle cover, EX 70.00
Sports Illustrated, 1945, Mickey Mantle cover, EX 35.00
Sports Illustrated, 1957, Sugar Ray Robinson cover, EX 30.00
Sports Illustrated, 1965, Sugar Ray Robinson cover, EX 25.00
Sports Illustrated, 1974, March 18, Babe Ruth cover, EX 45.00
Sports Illustrated, 1976, October 11, George Foster cover, EX 20.00
Time, 1938, March 28, Bette Davis cover, EX- 45.00
Time, 1939, November 6, Tom Harmon cover (b&w) 16.00
Time, 1947, September 22, Jackie Robinson cover, EX 65.00
Time, 1948, May 17, Eddie Arcaro cover, VG+ 25.00
Time, 1949, January 10, Ben Hogan cover, VG+ 45.00
Time, 1950, June 15, world globe drinking Coca-Cola 20.00
Time, 1954, May 31, Native Dancer (race horse) cover, EX 18.00
Time, 1969, September 5, New York Mets cover, EX 22.00
Time, 1973, September 17, McDonald's cover, EX 15.00
TV Guide, 1958, March 15, James Arness & Amanda Blake, NM ...25.00
TV Guide, 1959, December 26, Loretta Young cover, NM 17.50
TV Guide, 1960, March 8, Jay North (Dennis the Menace) cover .6.00
TV Guide, 1960, November 19, Ward Bond cover, NM 10.00
TV Guide, 1961, January 7, Richard Boone cover, EX 17.50
TV Guide, 1962, November 24, Jacqueline Kennedy, NM 25.00
TV Guide, 1964, April 4, Vince Edwards cover, M 8.00

TV Guide, 1969, February 15, Ramond Burr cover, NM 10.00
TV Guide, 1970, February 7, Bewitched cover, NM 35.00
Vogue, 1927, woman in rowboat cover by Lepape, EX 50.00
Woman's Home Companion, 1953, July, Marlene Dietrich cover ..5.00
Youth's Companion, 1898, August 4, Major-General Nelson Miles .12.00
Youth's Companion, 1913, March 27, President Wilson & cabinet .12.00
Youth's Companion, 1926, boys shooting marbles cover 20.00

Majolica

Majolica is a type of heavy earthenware, design-molded and decorated in vivid colors with either a lead or tin type of glaze. It reached its height of popularity in the Victorian era; examples from this period are found in only the lead glazes. Nearly every potter of note, both here and abroad, produced large majolica jardinieres, umbrella stands, pitchers with animal themes, leaf shapes, vegetable forms, and nearly any other design from nature that came to mind. Few, however, marked their ware. Among those who did were Minton, Wedgwood, Holdcroft, and George Jones in England; Griffin, Smith and Hill (Etruscan) in Phoenixville, Pennsylvania; and Chesapeake Pottery (Avalon and Clifton) in Baltimore.

Color and condition are both very important worth-assessing factors. Pieces with cobalt, lavender, and turquoise glazes command the highest prices. For further information we recommend *The Collector's Encyclopedia of Majolica* by Mariann Katz-Marks (see Directory, Pennsylvania). Unless another condition is given, the values that follow are for pieces in mint condition. Our advisor for this category is Hardy Hudson; he is listed in the Directory under Florida.

Bowl, serving; fox w/maple leaves on turq, Geo Jones, sm rpr .1,250.00
Bowl, serving; squirrel w/nut on turq, Geo Jones 1,300.00
Bowl, Shell & Seaweed, Etruscan, 7½" 685.00
Bowl, shell on coral, turq w/pk int, Geo Jones, 8x12" 3,000.00
Butter dish, Shell & Seaweed, w/insert, Etruscan 2,860.00
Butter pat, Begonia Leaf, Etruscan 125.00
Butter pat, Geranium, Etruscan 125.00
Butter pat, leaf on plate, Etruscan 125.00
Butter pat, Shell & Seaweed, Etruscan 200.00
Cache pot, picket fence & vine, sq ft, 9x8x8" 500.00
Cache pot, strawberry, Minton, 8x8" 1,100.00
Cheese keeper, bird on branch on cobalt, 10½" 1,200.00
Cheese keeper, Lily, albino, Etruscan, rare 1,550.00
Cheese keeper, Oak Leaf & Acorn, brn & gr, Sailey, 8x11" 800.00
Cheese keeper, Primrose & Basket w/cobalt, Wedgwood, 10" 3,000.00
Compote, couple on floral tree trunk std, rtcl floral bowl, 17x11" ..785.00
Compote, grapes & leaves, lav & gr on brn, 9½" 300.00
Condiment dish, putti w/turq scarf on pk leaf, 7x11" 1,300.00
Creamer & sugar bowl, Wild Rose on wht, w/lid, Etruscan 325.00
Cup & saucer, Cauliflower, Etruscan 450.00
Cup & saucer, Shell & Seaweed, Etruscan, lg 400.00
Dish, dragonfly on fan shape w/cobalt, Eureka 220.00
Ewer, Renaissance, putto in relief, griffin hdl, Minton, 13½" ..1,200.00

Game dish, basketweave base, game on lid, Minton, 13" L 1,800.00
Game dish, brn, rabbit & game on lid, Wedgwood, 10½" L 1,200.00
Jardiniere, stork in lily pads on cobalt, 10x10" 1,000.00
Match holder, Black boy w/accordion, w/striker 300.00
Match holder, harvester boy w/basket, Minton, 8" 800.00
Match holder, Indian chief seated on rock, mc, w/striker, 8½" ..400.00
Match holder, lady w/basket figural, Minton, 8" 715.00
Match holder, peasant lady at tree stump w/basket on bk, 8½" ..300.00
Match holder, rooster figural, mc, w/striker, 6½" 375.00
Mug, Oak Leaf & Acorn, Etruscan 225.00
Nut dish, squirrel/branch/leaves/acorns on turq, Geo Jones 1,325.00
Pitcher, asparagus form, Fr, 8½" 440.00
Pitcher, Bamboo & Fern, Wardles, 7" 275.00
Pitcher, Dogwood on mottled ground, 10" 275.00
Pitcher, duck figural w/monkey hdl, Brownfield, 14" 1,430.00
Pitcher, fern fronds, mc on bl, pk int, 8¼" 300.00
Pitcher, floral & basketweave, cobalt top, Geo Jones, 6" 375.00
Pitcher, monkey figural w/bamboo hdl, 8½" 700.00
Pitcher, Seaweed & Fishes on cobalt, Shorter, 5" 250.00
Pitcher, Shell & Seaweed, EX color, Etruscan, 6" 550.00
Pitcher, snail shell form, Wedgwood, 9" 1,045.00
Pitcher, Stork in Marsh w/turq & cobalt, 9" 500.00
Pitcher, Sunflower on wht, Etruscan, 5" 465.00
Pitcher, Water Lily & Iris on lav, Geo Jones, 8" 2,500.00
Pitcher, Wild Rose on Tree Bark, 9½" 300.00
Pitcher, Wild Rose on wht, butterfly lip, Etruscan, 8" 400.00
Planter, boy clown riding pig, Continental, 5½" 200.00
Plate, bbl & stave, Geo Jones, 8" 350.00
Plate, Bird & Fan w/cobalt, Wedgwood, 8" 300.00
Plate, bird w/letter in beak, butterfly & flowers, 9" 225.00
Plate, Cauliflower, Etruscan, 9" 350.00
Plate, Cauliflower, Wedgwood, 9" 350.00
Plate, leaves & fern on pk, Geo Jones, 8¼" 360.00
Plate, Ocean w/gr border, Wedgwood, 9" 350.00
Plate, oyster; gray & red dolphins amid wht shells, Wedgwood, 9" .990.00
Plate, oyster; half-moon, lav wells on brn w/gr seaweed 440.00
Plate, oyster; Water Lily, 5 wells, Minton, 9x7½" 990.00
Plate, oyster; 12 wells, dk gr w/turq/yel/gr, St Clements, 15" 660.00
Plate, oyster; 12 wht wells on gr basketweave, Fr, 13" 400.00
Plate, Pineapple, Geo Jones, 9" 300.00
Plate, Pineapple, Wedgwood, 9" 300.00
Plate, Pond Lily, 8" 220.00
Plate, Shell & Seaweed, Etruscan, 9¼" 700.00
Platter, Argenta corn, wheat & floral, Wedgwood, 13" 400.00
Platter, asparagus w/yel basketweave border, mc, Fr, 16" 440.00
Platter, Bird & Fan on wht w/brn rim, Wardles, 13" 350.00
Platter, Shell & Seaweed, Etruscan, 13½x9½" 1,650.00
Sardine box, pelican w/turq & cobalt, Geo Jones 1,600.00
Sardine box, seaweed on brn, overlapping fish on lid 750.00
Sardine box, Swan & Water Lily, Etruscan, rare......................1,650.00
Sardine box, Swan & Water Lily w/cobalt, Etruscan, w/underplate 2,750.00
Spittoon, Lily on wht, Etruscan 600.00
Sugar bowl, Shell & Seaweed, Etruscan, 5" 440.00
Syrup, Bamboo, EX colors, Etruscan 650.00
Syrup, Sunflower on cobalt, Etruscan 650.00
Syrup, Sunflower on wht, Etruscan 500.00
Tankard, figure in relief on cobalt, JM, 15½" 495.00
Teapot, Chinaman figural, much cobalt 900.00
Teapot, fish swallowing fish, 10½" 800.00
Teapot, Isle of Man, rope hdl & base, 10" 880.00
Teapot, monkey & coconut figural, cobalt jacket, Minton, 6x8½" 4,400.00
Teapot, spikey fish figural, over-glaze pnt, Minton, 7½" 2,475.00
Teapot, Wild Rose on cobalt, pewter finial, 6" 500.00
Tray, bread; Oak Leaf, pk border, Etruscan, 12" 400.00

Game pie dish, molded gaming trophies between floral garlands, chick finial, England, 1868, 11", $4,500.00.

Tray, wheat bread; Eat Thy Bread w/Thankfulness 350.00
Vase, Black lady w/basket of fruit figural, 19" 800.00
Vase, Peacock, bl w/mc feathers, 17½" 800.00
Walking stick stand, Stork in Cattails, Minton, 40", EX 20,000.00

Malachite Glass

Malachite is a type of art glass that exhibits strata-like layerings in shades of green, similar to the mineral in its natural form. Some examples have an acid-etched mark of Moser/Carlsbad, usually on the base. However, it should be noted that in the past fifteen years there have been reproductions from Czechoslovakia with a paper label.

Basket, woman w/children in relief, loop hdl, 6½x6" 75.00
Bottle, scent; Birth of Venus, Venus top/fish base, unmk, 7" ...1,450.00
Oil lamp, cut chimney, mini 1,400.00

Vase, draped nude woman each
corner, 10½x7", $750.00.

Vase, dancing nudes w/grapes, ca 1920, 5" 150.00
Vase, 3 nudes w/flowing hair in panels w/grapes, 8¾x4½" 225.00

Mantel Lustres

Mantel lustres are decorative vases or candle holders made from all types of glass, often highly decorated, and usually hung with one or more rows of prisms. In the listings that follow, values are given for a pair.

Cobalt cut to wht opaque w/gold, 12½x6½", pr 250.00
Cobalt w/HP floral urns/fleur-de-lis, spear rims, prisms, 12", pr ..500.00
Pk w/wht florals/gr leaves & gold, 2 rows of prisms, 16", pr 800.00
Ruby w/HP florals & gold, 2 rows of prisms, 14", pr 650.00

Maps and Atlases

Maps are highly collectible, not only for historical value but also for their sometimes elaborate artwork, legendary information, or data that since they were printed has been proven erroneous. There are many types of maps including geographical, military, celestial, road, and railroad. Nineteenth-century maps, particularly of U.S. areas, are increasing in popularity and price. Rarity, area depicted (i.e. Texas is more sought after than North Dakota), and condition are major price factors. Our advisor for this category is Murray Hudson; he is listed in the Directory under Tennessee.

Key:
hc — hand colored

Atlases

Atlas of City of NY..., 45 dbl pgs, Bromley, 1928 ....350.00
Atlas of 11th-17th Wards Philadelphia, 23 dbl pgs, Smith, 1909 ..150.00
CA, Donley, Culver City, 1979, 175-pg, w/jacket, NM 75.00
Chicago Chronicles World Atlas, 1899, lg, G 17.50
Commercial...Marketing Guide, Rand McNally, 81st ed, 1950, G .45.00
Cram's Modern Reference World..., Indianapolis IN, 127 maps, EX ...250.00
FL, Fernald, FL State University, 1981, 800+ maps, NM 55.00
Insurance Maps of City of Phila, Sandborn, 44 dbl pgs, 1929 .....160.00
LG Cram's World, color, EX 185.00
Long's Classical, 1856, leather bound, EX 45.00
Mitchell's New General..., 94 mc litho maps, 1871, EX 400.00
Morse & Gaston's Dmn Atlas, Colby, NY, 1857, 240-pg, VG 375.00
New Universal..., 67 of 73 mc maps, Cowperthwait, 1849, VG ..900.00
New Universal..., 74 mc maps, Cowperthwait, 1852, EX+ 1,500.00
PA, Cuff, Philadelphia, Temple University Press, 1989, 250+ pgs ..72.00
Rand McNally World, pictorial, hardbound, 1935, EX 30.00
Stieler's Hand..., Hermann, lg format, 108 maps, 1938, EX 125.00
Stratigraphy...N & Central Am, Cook, Princeton University, 1975 ....195.00
Topographical...PA, 25 mc maps, Walling & Gray, 1872 ....200.00
Uganda, Downer, Kampala, 2nd ed, 37-pg, 1967, lg format, EX ...95.00
Universel Quillet...Francais, Allain, Paris, 1933, 280+ pgs 225.00
World Maps of 1624, Blaeu & Hondius, Israel, 1977 edition, NM ..150.00

Maps

Am, Lizars, Edinburgh, hc, 1831, 11x9", VG 125.00
AR/KY, Rand McNally, 1889, some color, 13x10½", VG 10.00
AZ&NM, mc, fancy border, Indian tribes shown, 1872, 12x15" ...30.00
Carte des Etats Unis D'Amerique, Thierry, Paris, 1830s, 9x12" 90.00
Chart of Mediterranean Sea, towns & ports, ca 1750, 16x29" 190.00
Chicago & St Louis, Colton, mc, ornate border, 18x15"+fr 55.00
Colton's KY & TN, JH Colton, hc, 1864, 14⅜x17½", EX 125.00
Colton's Traveler's...US, McClellan Bros Litho, 1865, 28x32", G ...750.00
IN, some color, tape rpr, 1897, single fold, 13x17", VG 12.50
Johnson's MO & KS, Johnson & Ward, hc, 1862, 16x22", G 85.00
Johnson's New Military...US, hc, Johnson & Ward, 1864, 17x24" ..250.00
KY & TN Counties, SA Mitchell Jr, Philadelphia, 1862, 9¼x12" .60.00
MO, Colton, mc, St Louis inset, 16x19", EX 40.00
MT, Rand McNalley, mc, 1890s, 9x12" 14.00
NW Montana, color, H Gannett, 1879, 15x22" 35.00
Quebec, inset of Montreal, mc, ornate border, 1872, 15x12" 30.00
Railroad Map of PA, Sutton Wall, hc, 1898, 57x37", EX in case ..110.00
Rand-McNally, Indian watching car on cover, 1926, 72-pg, EX ...15.00
Terra Firma: Guiana & Antilles Islands, London, 1750, 7x10¼" ..100.00
VT/NH, pastels, ornate borders, Mitchell, 1872, 15x12" 35.00
Watson's New Railroad...of US & Canada, hc, 1869, 50x36", VG+ ...170.00

Marblehead

What began as therapy for patients in a sanitarium in Marblehead, Massachusetts, has become recognized as an important part of the Arts and Crafts movement in America. Results of the early experiments under the guidance of Arthur E. Baggs in 1904 met with such success that by 1908 the pottery had been converted to a solely commercial venture. Simple vase shapes were often incised with stylized animal and floral motifs or sailing ships. Some were decorated in low relief; many were plain. Simple matt glazes in soft yellow, gray, wisteria, rose, tobacco brown, and their most popular, Marblehead blue, were used alone or in combination. The Marblehead logo is distinctive — a ship with full sail and the letters 'M' and 'P.' The pottery closed in 1936.

Bowl, bl, 1¾x3½", w/flower frog 165.00
Bowl, centerpc; sky-bl satin w/gr gloss int, 4½x12" 325.00
Bowl, cobalt w/aqua speckled int, ship mk, 3x7¾" 325.00
Bowl, dk bl, minor scratches, 2x8½" 260.00
Bowl, dk bl rim to lt bl interior, 2½x14" 375.00
Bowl, dk gr, 2x8½", +2½" dia flower frog 210.00
Bowl, lotus leaves on dk bl, ship mk, 3¾x8¼" 425.00
Bowl, turq to bl crystalline, mk, 2x14" 450.00
Candlestick, yel (rare color), flared ft, 3x4" 200.00
Chamberstick, bl, hdl, mk, 4" 260.00
Chamberstick, gray, tall curved hdl, 7½" 400.00
Pitcher, bl, AE Baggs, 1933, 8" 425.00
Pitcher, bl w/navy speckles, ribbed body, aqua int, 3⅛" 125.00
Pitcher, lav, ribs, 4¾" 185.00
Tile, flowers in lg vase, A Baggs/H Tutt, 7-color, 5⅞x5⅞" 850.00
Tile, stylized trees, dk gr on olive gr speckles, 6" sq 2,000.00
Tile, trees landscape, gr on amber, oak fr, 4¼" 1,100.00
Vase, bl, flared cylinder, slightly incurvate rim, 12x5" 1,300.00
Vase, bl, flared cylinder, 5" 450.00
Vase, bl, flattened ribbed form w/incised lines, 7x6" 300.00
Vase, bl mottle glossy, incurvate rim, 5" 230.00
Vase, bl w/gray flecks, spherical w/invt base, 4x5¼" 400.00
Vase, bl-gray w/bl int, incurvate rim, 5" dia 220.00
Vase, brn, classic form, mk, 9" 1,800.00
Vase, brn, ftd bowl form, 4½x6" 350.00
Vase, bud; dk bl speckles, incised vertical decor, 4½" 425.00
Vase, bud; dk gray matt w/bl speckles, 6x2½" 175.00
Vase, bud; violet speckled, 4¼x3¼" 250.00
Vase, canary yel, ivory int, 3½x2", NM 150.00
Vase, cobalt to navy, brn int, 4¼x6½" 475.00
Vase, dk gray, glossy aqua int, bulbous, mini, 3⅛x4¼" 350.00
Vase, dk gray w/bl speckles, ovoid, 3¾x3" 200.00
Vase, dragonflies, lt & dk brn on gr, HT, label, 6", NM 4,250.00
Vase, floral cvg, bl on gray, mk, 6" 3,750.00
Vase, geometrics, bl on gray, cylindrical, sgn, mk, 6" 1,300.00
Vase, gr, cylindrical, 7" 425.00
Vase, gr & brn mottle, invt cylinder, 7" 950.00
Vase, gr mottle (unusual glaze), mk, 7" 850.00
Vase, gray, squat, 3½x5" 275.00
Vase, lav, 7" 350.00
Vase, purple, squat, flared rim, 3½" 400.00

Vase, stylized trees in two tones of blue on slate gray ground, 15", $16,000.00.

Vase, stylized thistles incised on mauve, ovoid, 5¼" 1,100.00
Vase, teal gr glossy, hairline, 5½x3½" 200.00
Vase, thick gr on rough textured red clay, mk, 10½" 750.00
Vase, yel, cylindrical, rolled rim, 5¼x4¼" 400.00
Vase, yel, 3½" 375.00

Marbles

Marbles have been popular with children since the mid-1800s. They've been made in many types from a variety of materials. Among some of the first glass items to be produced, the earliest marbles were made from a solid glass rod broken into sections of the proper length which were placed in a tray of sand and charcoal and returned to the fire. As they were reheated, the trays were constantly agitated until the marbles were completely round. Other marbles were made of china, pottery, steel, and natural stones. Below is a listing of the various types, along with a brief description of each.

Agates: stone marbles of many different colors — bands of color alternating with white usually encircle the marble; most are translucent.

Ballot Box: handmade (with pontils), opaque white or black, used in lodge elections.

Bloodstone: green chalcedony with red spots, a type of quartz.

China: with or without glaze, in a variety of hand-painted designs — parallel bands or bull's-eye designs most common.

Clambroth: opaque glass with outer evenly spaced swirls of one or alternating colors.

Clay: one of the most common older types; some are painted while others are not.

Comic Strip: a series of twelve machine-made marbles with faces of comic strip characters, Peltier Glass Factory, Illinois.

Crockery: sometimes referred to as Benningtons; most are either blue or brown, although some are speckled. The clay is shaped into a sphere, then coated with glaze and fired.

End of the Day: single-pontil glass marbles — the colored part often appears as a multicolored blob or mushroom cloud.

Goldstone: clear glass completely filled with copper flakes that have turned gold-colored from the heat of the manufacturing process.

Indian Swirls: usually black glass with a colored swirl appearing on the outside next to the surface, often irregular.

Latticinio Core Swirls: double-pontil marble with an inner area with net-like effects of swirls coming up around the center.

Lutz Type: glass with colored or clear bands alternating with bands which contain copper flecks.

Micas: clear or colored glass with mica flecks which reflect as silver dots when marble is turned. Red is rare.

Onionskin: spiral type which are solidly colored instead of having individual ribbons or threads, multicolored.

Peppermint Swirls: made of white opaque glass with alternating blue and red outer swirls.

Ribbon Core Swirls: double-pontil marble — center shaped like a ribbon with swirls that come up around the middle.

Rose Quartz: stone marble, usually pink in color, often with fractures inside and on outer surface.

Solid Core Swirls: double-pontil marble — middle is solid with swirls coming up around the core.

Steelies: hollow steel spheres marked with a cross where the steel was bent together to form the ball.

Sulfides: generally made of clear glass with figures inside. Rarer types have colored figures or colored glass.

Tiger Eye: stone marble of golden quartz with inclusions of asbestos, dark brown with gold highlights.

Vaseline: machine-made of yellowish-green glass with small bubbles.

Prices listed below are for marbles in near-mint condition unless noted otherwise. When size is not indicated, assume them to be of average size, ½" to 1". Polished marbles have greatly reduced values. (We do not list tinted marbles because there is no way of knowing how much color the tinting has, and intensity of color is an important worth-assessing factor.)

For a more thorough study of the subject, we recommend *Antique and Collectible Marbles, 3rd Edition; Machine-Made and Contemporary Marbles, 2nd Edition;* and *Big Book of Marbles,* all by our advisor, Everett Grist; you will find his address in the Directory under Tennessee.

Agate, contemporary, carnelian, 1¾" 160.00
Banded Opaque, gr & wht, 2" 1,200.00
Banded Opaque, red & wht, 1¾" 1,200.00
Banded Opaque, red & wht, ¾" 95.00
Banded Transparent Swirl, bl, ¾" 75.00
Banded Transparent Swirl, lt gr, 1¾" 750.00
Bennington, bl, 1¾" 40.00
Bennington, bl, ¾" 3.00
Bennington, brn, 1¾" 30.00
Bennington, fancy, 1¾" 80.00
Bennington, fancy, ¾" 5.00
China, decorated, glazed, apple, 1¾" 1,200.00
China, decorated, glazed, rose, 1¾" 2,000.00
China, decorated, glazed, wht w/geometrics, 1¾" 125.00
China, decorated, unglazed, geometrics & flowers, ¾" 200.00
Clambroth, opaque, bl & wht, 1¾" 2,600.00
Clambroth, opaque, bl & wht, ¾" 250.00
Clambroth Swirl, red/wht, Germany, 1900, ⅞" 475.00
Comic, Andy Gump 100.00
Comic, Betty Boop 200.00
Comic, Cotes Bakery, advertising 900.00
Comic, Kayo, rare 300.00
Comic, Little Orphan Annie 100.00
Comic, Moon Mullins 300.00
Comic, set of 12 ....1,500.00
Comic, Skeezix 150.00
Comic, Tom Mix 2,000.00
Cork Screw, machine-made, common, ⅝" 5.00
End of Day, bl & wht, 1¾" 400.00
Goldstone, ¾" 35.00
Indian Swirl, 1¾" 2,500.00
Indian Swirl Lutz-type, gold flakes, ¾" 600.00
Line Crockery, clay, 1¾" 75.00
Mica, bl, ¾" 35.00
Mica, gr, 1¾" 800.00
Onionskin, w/mica, 1¾" 1,500.00
Onionskin, w/mica, ¾" 110.00
Onionskin, 16-lobe, unusual, 1¾" 1,800.00
Onionskin, ¾" 90.00
Onionskin, 4-lobe, 1¼" 450.00
Opaque Swirl, gr, ¾" 75.00
Opaque Swirl Lutz-type, bl, yel, gr, ¾" 325.00
Peppermint Swirl, opaque, red, wht, & bl, 1¾" 2,000.00
Peppermint Swirl, opaque, red, wht, & bl, ¾" 125.00
Pottery, 1¾" 75.00
Ribbon Core Lutz-type, red, 1¾" 1,800.00
Slag, bl, machine-made, sm 3.00
Slag, bl, machine-made, 1½" 150.00
Solid Opaque, gr, 1¾" 800.00
Solid Opaque, ¾" 75.00
Sulfide, alligator, 1¾" 250.00
Sulfide, baboon playing bass fiddle, 2⅛" 1,200.00
Sulfide, bear cub on all 4s, detailed, 1¼", NM+ 400.00
Sulfide, bird, 2", EX 150.00
Sulfide, boar, 1⅞", NM 165.00
Sulfide, camel, 1-hump, on grassy mound, 1½", NM 200.00
Sulfide, child sitting, 1¾" 600.00
Sulfide, child w/sailboat, 1¾" 800.00
Sulfide, circus bear, 2", NM 140.00
Sulfide, crane w/fish, 1¾" 600.00

Sulfide, crucifix, 1¾", NM 600.00
Sulfide, deer, 1¼" 175.00
Sulfide, dog, 1⅜" 175.00
Sulfide, dog howling, 1⅜", M 140.00
Sulfide, dog on grass mound, HP/3-color, pontil, 1¼", NM 3,500.00
Sulfide, dove, 1⅝", M 165.00
Sulfide, eagle w/closed wings, 1⅞" 200.00
Sulfide, elephant w/long trunk, 1¼", NM 140.00
Sulfide, face of angel w/wings, 1¾" 1,000.00
Sulfide, figure-8, 1¾" 400.00
Sulfide, fish, 1¾" 175.00
Sulfide, fox, 1½", EX 130.00
Sulfide, goat, 1¾" 125.00
Sulfide, hen, 1⅛", M 150.00
Sulfide, horse rearing, clear, 1⅞" 175.00
Sulfide, horse standing, 2", EX 130.00
Sulfide, Jenny Lind bust, 1¾" 900.00
Sulfide, lion, standing male, 1½", NM 125.00
Sulfide, monkey, seated on drum, 1⅜", M 200.00
Sulfide, owl, w/closed wings, 1¾" 150.00
Sulfide, papoose, 1¾", M 700.00
Sulfide, pig, 1¾" 150.00
Sulfide, pony, 1¾" 200.00
Sulfide, rabbit running, lg/offset, sm bubble, 1½", M- 110.00
Sulfide, raccoon, 2", M 200.00
Sulfide, razor-bk hog, 1½" 150.00
Sulfide, rooster, 1¾" 150.00
Sulfide, Santa Claus, 1¾" 1,200.00
Sulfide, sheep grazing, 1¼", NM 135.00
Sulfide, squirrel, standing, 1¾", EX 170.00

Marine Collectibles

Vintage tools used on sea-going vessels, lanterns, clocks, and memorabilia of all types are sought out by those who are interested in preserving the romantic genre that revolves around the life of the sea captains, their boats and their crews; ports of call; and the lure of far away islands. See also Steamship Collectibles; Telescopes; Scrimshaw; Tools.

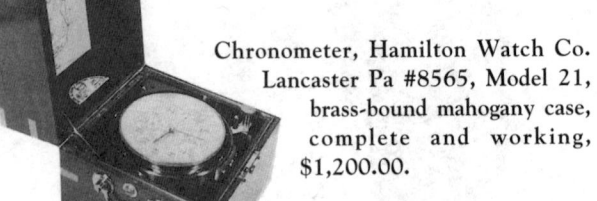

Chronometer, Hamilton Watch Co. Lancaster Pa #8565, Model 21, brass-bound mahogany case, complete and working, $1,200.00.

Bell, ship's; NP, 8½" dia, on stand, VG 250.00
Billethead, cvd wood, 13", EX orig 1,000.00
Binnacle, ES Ritchie & Sons, wood, w/6¾" compass, 12" H 300.00
Binnacle, Oliver of NY, wooden slant top, Pat 1892, 11⅛" 200.00
Binnacle, USN, brass, uses oil/electric compass lights, 1897 ....2,200.00
Calendar, perpetual pocket; German, silver, 1700s, EX 1,500.00
Carving of whale boat, from whale bone, w/tools, 15" L 1,300.00
Chest, brass-bound champhor wood, brass hdls, rfn, 39x19x21" 700.00
Chronometer, brass case, rectangular base w/ball ft, 10", VG 230.00

Chronometer, gimbal; Russian, 56-hr, EX 800.00
Clock, ship's bell; Seth Thomas, brass, EX 600.00
Clock, ship's; Chelsea, Bakelite case, US Navy, 6¾" dia 250.00
Compass, John E Hand..., brass gimbal w/dvtl mahog box 200.00
Compass/sundial, Tho Heath-Fecit, brass, ca 1750, 4¾" dia ...2,700.00
Fog horn, Japanese, WWII, dtd 1943, 39⅜" w/hdl, EX 200.00
Gong, engine room; solid brass, dbl hammer, 18" dia 450.00
Harpoon, dbl-swivel barb, dmn-pointed tip, 27", VG 375.00
Harpoon, early Provincetown type, 26½" 325.00
Harpoon, wrought iron, 45" 275.00
Helmet, diving; Mark V, brass & copper, fine quality 850.00
Helmet, diving; TSK Diving Co (Japan), 3-light, 12-bolt, 1944 .1,450.00
Knife, diver's, steel blade, wood hdl, brass sheath 325.00
Knot board, 30 examples of different knots, 19x34" 325.00
Lamp, galvanized metal & brass, A Ward & Hendrickson, 23" ..140.00
Lantern, Perkins, onion-shaped globes, w/orig burner, 17", pr 450.00
Lantern, Sherwood, brass, clear lens, complete, 11¾" 125.00
Light, masthead; brass & galvanized metal, red/gr lenses, 10½" ..125.00
Light, masthead; WA Robbins of NY, brass, 10" w/hdl, VG 195.00
Log, taffrail; frictionless propeller conical-end, brass, 21", VG ...200.00
Log, Walker's Excelsior III, brass, porc dial, 17x9x5" box+case ..425.00
Mallet, sail maker's, cvd whale bone, trn hdl, 9½" 250.00
Mirror, yacht's, brass, mt bracket adjusts, 7" dia 100.00
Octant, G Heath..., ebony/ivory/brass, EX 600.00
Octant, J Newman...London, ebony/brass/ivory, 1833, 14" 650.00
Octant, Spencer & Browning, ebony/brass, w/step case, VG 575.00
Pantograph, Dollond London, complete, EX in case 400.00
Pantograph, Gilbert & Wright London, brass, ca 1800, EX in case ...575.00
Pistol, flare; European origin, wooden grips, EX 200.00
Pistol, signal; Webly & Scott Model M, VG 90.00
Porthole, brass w/cover, gray pnt, 12" overall 110.00
Protractor, Barnett's Diagraph, Pat July 1860, 9½" 180.00
Protractor, WF Stanley London, precision pin, 6" dia, EX 160.00
Sextant, Mk II, Pioneer Instrument Division, 1941, VG 425.00
Sextant, US Navy Mk II, brass, dtd 1946, EX in case 225.00
Sextant, US Shipping Board-P 949, Heath & Co, silver scales ..375.00
Sextant, W Gerrard Liverpool, brass, 3 lenses, VG, w/case 550.00
Sun dial, Augsburg type, brass, Italian, 18th C, EX w/case 2,750.00
Telegraph, Saura Keiki Japan, brass, wooden base, 40"+hdl 525.00
Telescope, Dollond London, wood, 18th C, 55", EX in case ...2,750.00
Thermometer, Waltham, gimbaled, brass, w/mahog case 200.00
Trumpet, hailing; solid brass, eng name, 17", VG 450.00
Wheel, ship's; wood w/brass hub, 42" dia, VG 550.00
Wheel, wood w/brass hub, brass bound, 12" dia 225.00
Wheel, wood w/brass hub & trim, 20" dia 250.00
Wheel, 60" dia, on 62" stand 4,000.00
Wind speed indicator, Hattori...Japan, brass/iron, 1936, 14½" ...150.00

Markham Pottery

This small business evolved from the hobbies enjoyed by Herman Markham, who used clay from his own property (in Ann Arbor, Michigan) to fashion the planters and pots he used for cultivating flowers. By 1905 he went in to the ceramics business with his son Kenneth, moving to National City, California, in 1913. They were most famous for their glazes, many of which were veined and rough textured. Their ware was marked with an incised script signature. By 1921, operations had ceased.

Vase, acid-etched organic decor, orange/gr, #3678, 6x3¼", NM ..550.00
Vase, acid-etched red/gr/brn matt, ovoid, #2775, 7½x5" 1,300.00
Vase, Arabesque, textured copper glaze, #6365, 7x4" 1,000.00
Vase, gr & brn mottle, tapered form, #2963, 7" 750.00

Martin Bros.

The Martin Bros. were studio potters who worked from 1873 until 1914, first at Fulham and later at London and Southall. There were four brothers, each of whom excelled in their particular area. Robert, known as Wallace, was an experienced stonecarver. He modeled a series of grotesque bird and animal figural caricatures. Walter was the potter, responsible for throwing the larger vases on the wheel, firing the kiln, and mixing the clay. Edwin, an artist of stature, preferred more naturalistic forms of decoration. His work was often incised or had relief designs of seaweed, florals, fish, and birds. The fourth brother, Charles, was their business manager. Their work was incised with their names, place of production, and letters and numbers indicating month and year.

Bird jar, brown, blue, moss green, and gray, mounted on wooden base, 8x3½", $7,475.00.

Bird jar, kingfisher, palm ft, mc matt glazes, 11x5½" 16,250.00
Bird jar, smirking, brn/lt bl/tan, 1898, 14x5½" 22,750.00
Bird jar, tired face, gr/cobalt/tan, 1913, on stand, 8x3½" 7,800.00
Jug, face (expressive), w/blkberries/leaves, brn, 1910, 7x5" 4,550.00
Jug, Renaissance-style animal faces on dk bl, rstr, 6¾" 1,300.00
Jug, storks cvg, beige on brick-red, 3-sided, 9½x4", NM 3,250.00
Jug, toothy fish/creatures, brn on gray, 4-sided, 1900, 12" 3,900.00
Jug, 2-faced (chubby/smiling), gray, 4½x5½", NM 2,300.00
Jug, 2-faced (smiling/pensive), dk brn-gray, rstr, 6½" 4,200.00
Pen stand, open-mouthed fish figural, 2½x4¼", NM 2,600.00
Pen stand, turtle w/gaping mouth figural, 1910, 3½x5" 3,900.00
Pilgrim flask, smiling face, ear hdls, 1900, 9¼x10¼" 7,150.00
Spoon warmer, creature w/long ears/human hands/scales, 1876, 7" L ..6,200.00
Vase, bud; storks cvg, brn on orange, cylindrical, 5x2" 1,300.00
Vase, dbl-owl form, RW Martin, 1892, 8¼x5½" 5,200.00
Vase, dragons cvg, gr/brn on cobalt matt, bulbous, 10x7½" 4,300.00
Vase, grotesque fish, bl on gray, 4-sided, 1901, 3½x2¼" 750.00
Vase, prehistoric fish/jellyfish cvd on brns/grs, 1906, 10x7" 5,000.00
Vase, winged dragons, pearl gray on mustard matt, 9¾x6½", NM 2,900.00

Mary Gregory

Mary Gregory glass, for reasons that remain obscure, is the namesake of a Boston and Sandwich Glass Company employee who worked for the company for only two years in the mid-1800s. Although no evidence actually exists to indicate that glass of this type was even produced there, the fine colored or crystal ware decorated with figures of children in white enamel is commonly referred to as Mary Gregory. The glass, in fact, originated in Europe and was imported into this country where it was copied by several eastern glasshouses. It was popular from the mid-1800s until the turn of the century. It is generally accepted that examples with all-white figures were made in the U.S.A., while gold-trimmed items and those with children having tinted faces or a small amount of color on their clothing are European. Though amethyst is rare, examples in cranberry command the higher prices. Blue ranks next; and green, amber, and clear items are worth the least. Watch for new glass decorated with screen-printed children and a minimum of hand painting. The screen effect is easily detected with a magnifying glass.

Bottle, scent; clear, girl in garden, cut & polished, 5¼x1¾" **175.00**
Bowl, amber, girl fishing, bronze fr w/griffins, 9½x8½" **300.00**
Box, amber, boy w/bird, hinged lid, 3½x3¾" **245.00**
Box, dresser; cranberry, girl, hinged lid, gold tracery **325.00**
Box, glove; sapphire bl, Oriental figures, ornate decor, 11½" ..**1,450.00**
Box, lime gr, girl by fence, 3¾x4½" dia **325.00**
Decanter, amber, girl, amber bubble stopper, 9½" **195.00**
Decanter, cranberry, girl & swan, orig bubble stopper, 9¾" **350.00**
Lamp, amethyst, boy, brass ft, orig burner, 21½x7" **895.00**
Lamp, bl, girl fishing/flowers/scrolls, gold trim, 16¼" **1,500.00**
Lamp, blk amethyst, girl w/flower, milk glass globe, 17½" **1,425.00**
Mug, cranberry, girl, eng name, clear hdl, 3⅝x2⅜" **115.00**
Pitcher, bl, girl w/tinted hair, 10¾" **395.00**
Pitcher, blk amethyst, girl swinging, reed hdl, 9" **530.00**
Pitcher, sapphire bl, girl, appl hdl, 8x3½" **225.00**
Pitcher, sapphire bl, girl w/hat & staff, amber hdl, 12x6½" **400.00**
Tea warmer, ruby, boy & girl, brass fr, w/burner, 5¼" sq **945.00**
Tray, dresser; cranberry, boy & girl in garden, 1½x9½x6¾" **345.00**
Tumbler, bl, girl **135.00**
Vase, amber, boy (girl) making bubbles, ped ft, 13x5", pr **895.00**
Vase, amber, girl, ruffled rim, 8¼x3½" **175.00**
Vase, blk amethyst, girl w/basket, 11½x5" **325.00**
Vase, bud; amber w/wht spatter, girl (boy), 7x2½", pr **550.00**
Vase, cobalt, boy & flowers, crystal shell trim, 7x2⅞" **165.00**
Vase, cranberry, boy, bottle form, 9⅛x3¾" **245.00**
Vase, gr opaque bristol, boy w/flower tray, ruffled, 11⅛x4" **225.00**
Vase, lime gr, girl w/butterfly net, cylindrical, 10⅝x4" **180.00**
Vase, red cased, boy (girl) w/flower chain, 10¾", facing pr **970.00**
Vase, sapphire bl, boy blowing bubbles, ruffled, 10x3⅝" **275.00**
Vase, sapphire bl, boy on his knee beside standing girl, 12" **460.00**

Mason's Ironstone

In 1813 Charles J. Mason was granted a patent for a process said to 'improve the quality of English porcelain.' The new type of ware was in fact ironstone which Mason decorated with colorful florals and scenics, some of which reflected the Oriental taste. Although his business failed for a short time in the late 1840s, Mason re-established himself and continued to produce dinnerware, tea services, and ornamental pieces until about 1852, at which time the pottery was sold to Francis Morley. Ten years later, Geo. L. and Taylor Ashworth became owners. Both Morley and the Ashworths not only used Mason's molds and patterns but often his mark as well. Because the quality and the workmanship of the later wares do not compare with Mason's earlier product, collectors should take care to distinguish one from the other. Consult a good book on marks to be sure. The Wedgwood Company now owns the rights to the Mason patterns and is reproducing Vista. Note: Blue Vista is generally valued at 15% to 20% above prices for pink/red. Our advisor for this category is Susan Hirshman; she is listed in the Directory under Oregon.

Bowl, centerpc; floral, brn w/mc on wht, 1830-35 mk, 9x12½", EX **1,000.00**
Bowl, Flying Bird, mc on wht w/blk transfer, 1890, 10¼" **175.00**
Bowl, Landscape, mulberry w/mc, sq, 10¼" **150.00**
Bowl, serving; Vista, red, scalloped, 1890-1900 mk, 9½x7¼" **100.00**
Bowl, Vista, purple w/mc accents, sq, hdls, 1925-30, 11" **125.00**
Bowl, Watteau, red, dragon hdls, 1925-30, 2¼x10½" **175.00**
Bowl & strainer, Flying Bird, mc on wht, 1855-65 mk, 7¼", 8" ..**175.00**
Casserole, Real Old Canton, Ashworth, w/lid, 6x11x10", EX **250.00**

Chamber pot, Flying Bird, mc, 1830-35 mk, 6x9" **400.00**
Compote, fruit; Vista, red, hdls, 1925-30 mk, 6x9½" **375.00**
Creamer, Am Marine, red, scalloped rim, 1890-1900, 3½x4", EX ...**125.00**
Creamer, Vista, red, sq, 1890-1900 mk, 4½x4", EX **75.00**
Cup & saucer, Am Marine, red, 1890-1900, 3", 7¼", 4 for **200.00**
Cup & saucer, bouillon; Vista, brn, 1925-30, 6", 6½" **50.00**
Cup & saucer, demi; Vista, red, 1890-1900 mk, 2¼", 4¾", pr **70.00**
Display sign, Vista, red, 9¼x6¼", EX **175.00**
Egg cup, Vista, red, 1890-1900 mk, 4x3" **30.00**
Gravy boat, Vista, red, attached plate, 1890-1900 mk, flake **125.00**
Jug, Bandana, blk w/orange on beige, 8-sided, 1851, 8x3½" **375.00**
Jug, Dragon, burnt orange, serpent hdl, 1890, 6¼x4½" **300.00**
Jug, Landscape Scroll, mc on wht, hexagonal, 1835, 5½" **450.00**
Jug, Real Old Canton, bl, Ashworth, 6¾", EX **125.00**
Jug, Regency/Indian Grasshopper, 8-sided, 1920 mk, 5¾", EX ...**200.00**
Jug, Scale, red, 8-sided, 1813-29, 4½" **300.00**
Jug, Vista, bl, 8-sided, 1890-1900, 7" **200.00**
Jug, Vista, red, scalloped rim, 1925-30 mk, 6½x6" **150.00**
Jug, Vista, red, 8-sided, serpent hdl, 1890-1900 mk, 5¼x4" **175.00**
Jug & wash bowl, Dragon, burnt orange, 1890 mk, 11", 15" **800.00**
Jug & wash bowl, Flying Bird, mc, 1855-65 mk, 10½", 16" **850.00**
Plate, Am Marine, bl, scalloped, 1890-1900, 8" **60.00**
Plate, Am Marine, brn, Ashworth, 8", 6 for **150.00**
Plate, Am Marine, brn, 1890, 7½", 7 for **175.00**
Plate, Am Marine, red, scalloped, 1900 mk, 10¼" **100.00**
Plate, Bandana, blk, 1880-1889, 8" **350.00**
Plate, Bandana, blk w/yel & bl, Ashworth, 8" **350.00**
Plate, Bremen Ship commemorative, brn, late mk, 10½" **175.00**
Plate, Dragon, gr, Ashworth, 1890-1900, 8", 3 for **250.00**
Plate, Fruit Basket, mc on wht, 1890-1900, 7¾", 3 for **70.00**
Plate, House, mc w/much cobalt, 1818, 6" **325.00**
Plate, Pagoda Tree, mc on wht, 1890-1900 mk, 10¼" **80.00**
Plate, Persiana, mc on cream, 1930, 10⅝" **80.00**
Plate, soup; floral, bl, flared/scalloped, 1812-15, 9½" **150.00**

Plate, Vista, 1939 World's Fair, blue transfer, 10", $40.00.

Plate, Willow, bl, 1890-1900, 6¼", 4 for **100.00**
Plate, Wood Pigeon, maroon w/mc o/l, 1900-20, 9¼", 5 for **175.00**
Platter, Am Marine, red, 1890-1900, 10½", 4 for **300.00**
Platter, Plank Bridge, 1820 bl mk, 22½x19" **1,200.00**
Platter, Vista, purple, 1890-1900, 12¾" **175.00**
Platter, Vista, red, scalloped, 1925-30 mk, 13", NM **125.00**
Platter, Vista, red, 1890-1900 mk, 13" **250.00**
Platter, Vista, red, 1925-30 mk, 15¼x12½", EX **175.00**
Shakers, Vista, red, 8-sided, 1890-1900 mk, 3¼", pr **70.00**
Slop jar, Dragon, burnt orange, 1890 mk, 11x13" **600.00**
Supper dish, Floral & Vase, mc on cream, 1890-1900 mk, 8½x5" ...**50.00**
Tea caddy, Scale, red w/mc, 1890-1900, 6¾x6¼" **500.00**
Teapot, Vista, red, squatty, late 1800s, 6½", +trivet **325.00**
Teapot, Willow, bl, 1890-1900, 7¼" **300.00**
Tureen stand, Chinese Mtn, maroon w/mc, Ashworth, 7¼" **125.00**
Vase, Landscape Scroll, mc on wht, scalloped, 1835, 6½" **450.00**

Match Holders

John Walker, an English chemist, invented the match more than one hundred years ago, quite by accident. Walker was working with a mixture of potash and antimony, hoping to make a combustible that could be used to fire guns. The mixture adhered to the end of the wooden stick he had used for stirring. As he tried to remove it by scraping the stick on the stone floor, it burst into flames. The invention of the match was only a step away! From that time to the present, match holders have been made in amusing figural forms as well as simple utilitarian styles and in a wide range of materials. Both table-top and wallhanging models were made — all designed to keep matches conveniently at hand.

Caution: as prices for originals continue to climb, so do the number of reproductions. Know your dealer. Our advisor for this category is Ron Damaska; he is listed in the Directory under Pennsylvania. See also Advertising.

Brass, man swinging on fence, desk type with sealing-wax holder, 7x4x5½", $250.00.

Brass, bird & basket, striker on base, 4¼" 135.00
Brass, Colonial man w/musket, deer behind wood pile, 3½" 125.00
Brass, pig figural, short legs, open top, 1800s, 2x4½" 165.00
Bronze, troll figural, 4" 495.00
Bsk, boy w/butterfly net figural 55.00
Cast metal, stag at top, rabbit & game bird below, 1916, 11" 80.00
China, Greek figure in toga w/horn, 5¼" 130.00
China, saucer type, box holder, Mayer 30.00
CI, fly shape, 6-leg, hinged bk, 1¾x4" 115.00
CI, grape cluster form 80.00
CI, grotesque man w/comic nose, hat is lid, old blk pnt, 5¼" 165.00
CI, high-button shoe form, rectangular base, 4x5" 50.00
CI, turtle figural, orig pnt 155.00
CI, urn w/hdls, on sq saucer base, 3" 78.00
CI, 2-tier, 2-lid, self closing, Pat 1870, 1½x3¼x6" 125.00
Jasper, elephant head, hat & eyeglasses, chamberstick shape 105.00
Lead, beetle figural, 4¼" 27.50
Pressed wood, Scottie figural front, wall hanging 30.00
Redware, acorns & leaves, wht & gr, around pocket, 7" dia 170.00
Tin, crest w/crimped & cut-out decor, pnt traces, 4x7", EX 32.50

Match Safes

Before the invention of the safety match in 1855, matches were carried in small pocket-sized containers because they ignited so easily. Aptly called match safes, these containers were used extensively until about 1920, when cigarette lighters became widely availabe. Some incorporated added features (hidden compartments, cigar cutters, etc.), some were figural, and others were used by retail companies as advertising giveaways. They were made from every type of material, but silverplated styles abound. Both the advertising and common silverplated cases generally fall in the $50.00 to $100.00 price range.

Beware of reproductions and fakes; there are many currently on the market. Know your dealer. Our advisor for this category is Ron Damaska; he is listed in the Directory under Pennsylvania. See also Advertising.

Bakelite, top opens, striker on bottom 35.00
Brass, Pan Am Expo, eng buffalo/etc, dtd 1901 ....195.00
German silver, emb Nouveau floral, 2¾" 75.00
Gutta percha, lady's shoe, striker bottom, ca 1870s 125.00
Gutta percha, Queen Victoria funeral memorial, w/striker 225.00
NP, book-shaped vesta box, King Edward coronation, EX 75.00
NP, lady in flower field litho 225.00
NP brass, horse's leg shape 175.00
NP brass, man in outhouse, European, older version w/screw, EX ..300.00
SP, book type w/built-in cutter 54.00
SP, emb sunburst, 3x2½" 55.00
SP, lady smoking, ornate, NM 95.00
SP, Match for World, patriotic, flat, Pairpoint, lg 150.00
SP, Nouveau lady's head & cattails 85.00
SP, Nouveau lady smoking/horse racing, 2 sliding doors 80.00
Sterling, cast w/36 seashells, R Wallace 650.00
Sterling, Home Ins Co NY/firemen w/hose, 2½", VG 275.00

McCoy

The third generation McCoy potter in the Roseville, Ohio, area was Nelson, who with the aid of his father, J.W., established the Nelson McCoy Sanitary Stoneware Company in 1910. They manufactured churns, jars, jugs, poultry fountains, and foot warmers. By 1925 they had expanded their wares to include majolica jardinieres and pedestals, umbrella stands and cuspidors, and an embossed line of vases and small jardinieres in a blended brown and green matt glaze. From the late '20s through the mid-'40s, a utilitarian stoneware was produced, some of which was glazed in the soft blue and white so popular with collectors today. They also used a dark brown mahogany color and a medium to dark green, both in a high gloss. In 1933 the firm became known as the Nelson McCoy Pottery Company. They expanded their facilities in 1940 and began to make the novelty artware, cookie jars, and dinnerware that today are synonomous with 'McCoy.' More than two hundred cookie jars of every theme and description were produced.

More than a dozen different marks have been used by the company; nearly all incorporate the name 'McCoy,' although some of the older items were marked 'NM USA.' For further information consult *The Collector's Encyclopedia of McCoy Pottery* (with recently updated values) by Sharon and Bob Huxford or *McCoy Pottery Collector's Reference & Value Guide* by Margaret Hanson, Craig Nissen, and Bob Hanson (both published by Collector Books). Also available is *Sanford's Guide to McCoy Pottery* by Martha and Steve Sanford (Mr. Sanford is listed in the Directory under California.)

Alert! Stimulated by the high prices commanded by desirable cookie jars, a broad spectrum of 'new' cookie jars are flooding the market place in three categories: 1) Manufacturers have expanded their lines with exciting new designs to attract the collector market. 2) Limited editions and artist-designed jars have proliferated. 3) Reproductions, signed and unsigned, have pervaded the market, creating uncertainty among new collectors and inexperienced dealers. After McCoy closed its doors in the late 1980s, an entrepreneur in Tennessee tried (and succeeded for nearly a decade) to adopt the McCoy Pottery name and mark. This company reproduced old McCoy designs as well as some classic designs of other defunct American potteries, signing their wares 'McCoy' with a mark which very closely approximated the old McCoy mark. Legal action finally put a stop to this practice, though since then this company has used other fradulent marks as well: Brush-McCoy (the compound name was never used on Brush cookie jars) and B.J. Hull.

Cookie Jars

Apollo Age, minimum value, $1,400.00.

Animal Crackers 120.00
Apple, 1950-64 ....65.00
Apple on Basketweave 70.00
Asparagus 50.00
Astronauts 650.00
Bananas 125.00
Barnum's Animals 400.00
Baseball Boy 225.00
Basket of Eggs 60.00
Basket of Potatoes 50.00
Bear, cookie in vest, no 'Cookies' 95.00
Betsy Baker 275.00
Black Kettle, w/immovable bail, HP flowers ...40.00
Black Vase, w/flowers on lid 220.00
Blue Willow Pitcher 50.00
Bobby Baker 100.00
Bugs Bunny, cylinder 225.00
Caboose 165.00
Cat on Coal Scuttle 200.00
Chairman of the Board, minimum value (+) 500.00
Chef 140.00
Chilly Willy 85.00
Chinese Lantern 85.00
Chipmunk 150.00
Circus Horse 250.00
Clown Bust (+) 85.00
Clown in Barrel 150.00
Clyde Dog 200.00
Coalby Cat 450.00
Coca-Cola Can 100.00
Coca-Cola Jug 85.00
Coffee Grinder 45.00
Coffee Mug 45.00
Colonial Fireplace 95.00
Cookie Barrel 45.00
Cookie Boy 225.00
Cookie Cabin 125.00
Cookie Jug, dbl loop 30.00
Cookie Jug, single loop, 2-tone gr rope 25.00
Cookie Jug, w/cork stopper, brn & wht 30.00
Cookie Log 75.00
Cookie Safe 65.00
Cookstove, blk 50.00
Corn 200.00
Covered Wagon 150.00
Cylinder, w/red flowers 45.00
Dalmatians in Rocking Chair (+) 450.00

Dog on Basketweave 90.00
Drum 100.00
Duck on Basketweave 100.00
Dutch Boy 55.00
Dutch Girl, boy on reverse, rare 125.00
Dutch Treat Barn 75.00
Eagle on Basket 35.00
Elephant 200.00
Elephant w/Split Trunk, rare, minimum value ...450.00
Engine, blk 175.00
Flowerpot, plastic flower on top 500.00
Football Boy 225.00
Forbidden Fruit 75.00
Freddy Gleep 500.00
Friendship 250.00
Frog on Stump 45.00
Frontier Family 60.00
Fruit in Bushel Basket 80.00
Gingerbread Boy 75.00
Globe 325.00
Grandfather Clock 80.00
Granny 85.00
Granny, gold trim 125.00
Hamm's Bear 225.00
Happy Face 100.00
Hen on Nest 95.00
Hillbilly Bear, rare, minimum value 900.00
Hobby Horse (+) 175.00
Hocus Pocus, wht 60.00
Honey Bear 120.00
Hot Air Balloon 60.00
Indian (+) 400.00
Jack-O'-Lantern 750.00
Kangaroo, bl 300.00
Keebler Tree House 95.00
Kettle, jumbo sz 60.00
Kissing Penguins 110.00
Kitten on Basketweave 90.00
Kittens (2) on Low Basket, minimum value ...800.00
Kittens on Ball of Yarn 150.00
Kookie Kettle, blk 45.00
Lamb on Basketweave 90.00
Leprechaun, minimum value (+) 1,200.00
Liberty Bell 100.00
Little Clown 100.00
Lollipops 100.00
Mac Dog 95.00
Mammy, Cookies on base (+) 300.00
Mammy w/Cauliflower, G pnt, minimum value (+) ...1,100.00
Modern 50.00
Monk 75.00
Mother Goose 175.00
Mr & Mrs Owl 110.00
Mushroom on Stump 40.00
Nursery, decal of Humpty Dumpty 100.00
Oaken Bucket 35.00
Old Churn 40.00
Owl, #204 USA 45.00
Pears on Basketweave 70.00
Pelican 195.00
Pepper, yel 40.00
Picnic Basket 85.00
Pineapple 100.00
Pineapple, Modern 100.00

Pirate's Chest	110.00
Popeye Cylinder	225.00
Potbelly Stove, blk	40.00
Puppy, w/sign	125.00
Quaker Oats, rare, minimum value	450.00
Red Barn, cow in door, rare, minimum value	350.00
Rooster, wht, 1970-1974	75.00
Rooster, 1955-1957	175.00
Round w/HP Leaves	65.00
Sad Clown	100.00
Snoopy on Doghouse	300.00
Snow Bear	100.00
Spaniel in Doghouse, pup finial	295.00
Stagecoach, minimum value	1,000.00
Strawberry, 1955-57	35.00
Strawberry, 1971-75	60.00
Sweet Notes	750.00
Teapot, 1971	95.00
Tepee, str top (+)	350.00
Tilt Pitcher, blk w/roses	40.00
Timmy Tortoise	35.00
Tomato	55.00
Touring Car	130.00
Traffic Light	65.00
Tudor Cookie House	125.00
Tulip on Flowerpot	225.00
Turkey, gr, rare color	300.00
Upside Down Bear, panda	75.00
WC Fields	250.00
Wedding Jar	125.00
Windmill	150.00
Wishing Well	65.00
Woodsy Owl	300.00
Wren House	175.00
Yosemite Sam, cylinder	250.00

Miscellaneous

Bank, Woodsey Owl, 1974	100.00
Basket vase, metallic glaze, 1970 reissue	65.00
Bean pot, Suburbia, mk, 1964, 2-qt	45.00
Cache pot, bird between 2 flower forms, petal base, mk, 1948	45.00
Casserole, turq w/blk lid, tab hdls, ca 1950s, 1-qt	35.00
Creamer, dog figural, turq, 1950s	150.00
Creamer & sugar bowl, Sunburst Gold, mk, w/lid	70.00
Decanter, Apollo Missile	75.00
Dog's dish, emb bird dog, mk, 1950s	95.00
Dog's dish, To Man's Best Friend, mk	60.00
Dresser caddy, Am Eagle	55.00
Flowerpot, emb lotus decor on gr, #4	35.00
Jardiniere, holly emb on gr, 1935, lg	80.00
Mug, Campbell Kids, mk USA, late	25.00
Pitcher, floral on brn, tilt ball form	50.00
Pitcher, parrot figural, mc, mk, 1952	200.00
Planter, cowboy boots form, blk, mk, 1956	50.00
Planter, dalmatian figural, mk, 1959	75.00
Planter, driftwood form, brn tones, mk, 1957	30.00
Planter, hand figural, gr, USA, 1941	40.00
Planter, rooster figural, mk, 1951	30.00
Planter, stork beside basket, pk, mk, 1956	50.00
Planter, Ye Old Kettle, yel, bail hdl, 1955	40.00
Planter, zebra mother & baby figural, mk, scarce	300.00
Salt & pepper shakers, together form head of cabbage, pr	75.00
Sugar bowl, Grecian, crackle look, w/lid, mk, ca 1958	45.00

Tea set, Ivy, mk, 1950, 3-pc	120.00
Vase, butterflies emb on yel, mk, 1954, 6"	50.00
Wall pocket, banana cluster on leaves, 1953	90.00
Wall pocket, flower form, Rustic	35.00
Wall pocket, flower w/bird atop	55.00
Wall pocket, leaves & berries, late 1940s	300.00
Wall pocket, mail box, 1951	90.00
Wall pocket, Mexican man emb on gr, 1941	60.00
Wall pocket, orange on leaves, 1953	75.00
Wall pocket, umbrella, 1955	75.00

McCoy, J. W.

The J.W. McCoy Pottery Company was incorporated in 1899. It operated under that name in Roseville, Ohio, until 1911 when McCoy entered into a partnership with George Brush, forming the Brush-McCoy Company. During the early years, McCoy produced kitchenware, majolica jardinieres and pedestals, umbrella stands, and cuspidors. By 1903 they had begun to experiment in the field of art pottery and, though never involved to the extent of some of their contemporaries, nevertheless produced several art lines of merit. Their first line was Mt. Pelee, examples of which are very rare today. Two types of glazes were used, matt green and an iridescent charcoal gray. Though the line was primarily mold formed, some pieces evidence the fact that while the clay remained wet and pliable it was pulled and pinched with the fingers to form crests and peaks in a style not unlike George Ohr.

The company rebuilt in 1904 after being destroyed by fire, and other artware was designed. Loy-Nel Art and Renaissance were standard brown lines, hand decorated under the glaze with colored slip. Shapes and artwork were usually simple but effective. Olympia and Rosewood were relief-molded brown-glaze lines decorated in natural colors with wreaths of leaves and berries or simple floral sprays. Although much of this ware was not marked, you will find examples with the die-stamped 'Loy-Nel Art, McCoy,' or an incised line identification.

Vase, Loy-Nel Art, floral, 11", $450.00.

Corn Line, tankard, unmk, 1910	350.00
Loy-Nel Art, jardiniere, Halley's Comet, 1910, 4"	450.00
Loy-Nel Art, spittoon, 1905, 4½"	300.00
Loy-Nel Art, vase, flower, integral hdls, unmk, 8"	300.00
Loy-Nel Art, vase, iris on dk brn, sgn WLK, att, 14½"	425.00
Loy-Nel Art, vase, poppies, orange & gr on dk brn, 3½"	75.00
Marble Ware, jardiniere & ped, unmk, 1910, 39"	800.00
Matt Green, umbrella stand, unmk, 1910, 21"	550.00
Olympia, mug, mk, 1905	200.00
Rosewood, ewer, bulbous, long neck, 1905, 10"	450.00
Rosewood, jardiniere, unmk, pre-1903, 9"	450.00
Rosewood, jug vase, unmk, 1905, sm	275.00

McKee

McKee Glass was founded in 1853 in Pittsburgh, Pennsylvania. Among their early products were tableware of both the flint and non-flint varieties. In 1888 the company relocated to avail themselves of a source of natural gas, thereby founding the town of Jeannette, Pennsylvania. One of their most famous colored dinnerware lines, Rock Crystal, was manufactured in the 1920s. During the '30s and '40s, colored opaque dinnerware, Sunkist reamers, and 'bottoms up' cocktail tumblers were produced as well as a line of black glass vases, bowls, and novelty items. All are popular items with today's collectors. The company was purchased in 1916 by Jeannette Glass, under which name it continues to operate. See also Animal Dishes with Covers; Depression Glass; Kitchen Collectibles; Reamers.

Basket, cut/pressed, bird w/butterfly & flowers, att, 15½x11" **100.00**
Bottoms Down mug, Jade-ite **175.00**
Bottoms Down mug, yel opaque **150.00**
Bottoms-Up coaster, crystal **50.00**
Bottoms-Up tumbler, blk, w/coaster **150.00**
Bottoms-Up tumbler, Jade-ite, w/coaster, rare **175.00**
Bowl, Colonial, Forest Gr, ftd, #1776, 12" **50.00**
Bowl, Colonial, Seville Yel, #1776, 12" **85.00**
Clock, vaseline, Tambour Art Glass, 14" L **450.00**
Jardiniere, blk, 4 buttressed ft, 1931, #25, 5½" **45.00**
Mug, Troubador, bl **70.00**
Pitcher, Sunburst, Prescut **95.00**
Pitcher, Yutec Eclipse, Prescut **45.00**
Rose jar, Colonial, gr, #1776, 10" **85.00**
Tom & Jerry set, wht 11" bowl & 9 mugs w/red lettering **55.00**
Toothpick holder, Britannic, ruby stain **85.00**
Vase, nudes, Jade-ite, 3-sided, 8½" **125.00**

Medical Collectibles

The field of medical-related items encompasses a wide area from the primitive bleeding bowl to the X-ray machines of the early 1900s. Other closely related collectibles include apothecary and dental items. Many tools that were originally intended for the pharmacist found their way to the doctor's office, and dentists often used surgical tools when no suitable dental instrument was available. A trend in the late 1700s toward self-medication brought a whole new wave of home-care manuals and 'patent' medical machines for home use. Commonly referred to as 'quack' medical gimmicks, these machines were usually ineffective and occasionally dangerous. Our advisor for this category is Jim Calison; he is listed in the Directory under New York.

Birthing chair, walnut, legs detach, M **195.00**
Bleeder, Borwick, horn & brass, w/3 graduated steel blades, 3¼" .**75.00**
Bleeder, C Croory on blade, bone over brass hdl, set of 3 ....**265.00**
Bleeder, Proctor, brass, w/3 graduated steel blades, 4" **95.00**
Bleeder, trigger loaded, w/box **350.00**
Book, Atlas of...Nerve Injuries, Lions/Barns, 1st ed, 1949, EX ..**200.00**
Book, Cancer of Stomach, Robson, MY, 1st Am ed, 1907, EX ...**100.00**
Book, Principles...of Obstetrics, Hodge, Phila, 1866, VG **400.00**
Chair, dental; CI w/leather, old gr pnt, early, EX orig **225.00**
Craniotomy set, 1909, MIB **400.00**
Dental cabinet, Ransom & Randolf, oak, EX orig **4,500.00**
Ether mask, silver, foldable **125.00**
Eye cup, cobalt, ped ft, 2½", EX **34.00**
Eye cup, milk glass, paneled side, ped ft, unmk, 3" **22.50**
Hearing aid, brass funnel w/earpc on cord, early, EX **85.00**

Hearing aid, flexible cloth cord w/plastic funnel end, 44" **385.00**
Matriculation ticket, Long Island College Hospital, 1890s **7.00**
Pill maker, brass & wood, 12 slots, Wiegand, 11½x12" **100.00**
Quack machine, Electreat, working **25.00**
Sterilizing kit (instruments), copper, Pat 1876, London, 15" **195.00**
Thermometer, doctor's pocket type, 1930s, in blk/wht Catalin case ...**48.00**
Tooth extractor, turnkey, ivory hdl, R&L, 1800s **395.00**
Tourniquet, brass, no strap, ca 1850 ....**225.00**
Tracheotomy perforator, sterling & agate, 1800s **395.00**

Meissen

The Royal Saxon Porcelain Works was established in 1710 in Meissen, Saxony. Under the direction of Johann Frederick Bottger, who in 1708 had developed the formula for the first true porcelain body, fine ceramic figurines with exquisite detail and tableware of the highest quality were produced. Although every effort was made to insure the secrecy of Bottger's discovery, others soon began to copy his ware; and in 1731 Meissen adopted the famous crossed swords trademark to identify their own work. The term 'Dresden ware' is often used to refer to Meissen porcelain, since Bottger's discovery and first potting efforts were in nearby Dresden. See also Onion Pattern.

Figural dish, modeled in the form of a mermaid emerging from swirling water, blue and white, crossed swords mark, 8½" long, $450.00.

Basket, appl flowers & leaves, rtcl, vine hdl, mk, 4½x12" **400.00**
Bowl, centerpc; center bouquet & emb gold roses, Xd swords mk ..**850.00**
Bowl, potpourri; garlands/ram's heads, openwork lid, 1900s, 12" .**3,100.00**
Cup & saucer, floral sprays on pear shape w/bird's-head hdl **100.00**
Figurine, cherub by floral-draped urn, Je Les Enflamme, 5½" **650.00**
Figurine, cherub w/fish baskets at ft, fish in hand, 3½x5½" **600.00**
Figurine, Cupid fanning flame of lovers' hearts, 1877 mk, 7¼" .**1,350.00**
Figurine, draped nude man w/nude lady on shoulder, 7", EX **775.00**
Figurine, Fall, seminude boy w/wheat sheaf, Xd swords mk, 5¼" .**475.00**
Figurine, girl feeding chickens, Xd swords mk, 4½" **500.00**
Figurine, lady feeding bird in cage, 5½" **900.00**
Figurine, lady seated at table w/wine bottle & fruit bowl, 5" **800.00**
Figurine, peasant lady fills bottle/2 men carry basket, 8", EX ...**1,500.00**
Figurine, peasant lady w/baby rides goat as kid feeds, 6½" **1,500.00**
Figurine, Spring, seminude cherub w/grapes, Xd swords mk, 5" ..**625.00**
Figurine, Winter, seminude boy on skates, Xd swords mk, 5" **525.00**
Jar, pomade; floral, red/bl & gold, 3" **140.00**
Salt cellar, lady reclines w/oval bowl, Xd swords mk, 5½" L **450.00**
Slippers, bl & wht w/red flowers & gold, Xd swords, 2¼x6¼" ..**1,500.00**
Tazza, Indian Purple, Xd swords mk, 12½" dia **550.00**
Vase, floral, mc on wht w/gold, Xd swords mk, 10" **325.00**

Mercury Glass

Mercury glass was made popular during the 1850s when the New England Glass Company displayed an assortment of items at the New York Crystal Palace Exhibition. It enjoyed a short revival at the turn of the century. Mercury glass was made with two thin layers, either blown with a double wall or joined in sections, with the space between the walls of the vessel filled with a mixture of tin, lead, bismuth, and perhaps some mercury, though some authorities say that because mercury was so costly, it was soon replaced with silver nitrate. The opening was sealed to prevent air from dulling the bright color. Though most examples are silver, red, blue, green, and gold can be found on occasion. Remember that the value of this type of glass hinges greatly on the condition of the 'mercury' lining. In the listings that follow, all examples are silver unless noted another color.

Bowl, 3 clear appl ft, 4¾x9½" 120.00
Mug, clear hdl, 3" 30.00
Rose bowl, Czechoslovakia, 10" 200.00
Vase, HP floral sprays in panel, 10", pr 225.00
Wig stand, 2-pc, 10½" 330.00

Merrimac

Founded in 1897 in Newburyport, Massachusetts, the Merrimac Pottery Company primarily produced gardenware. In 1901, however, they introduced a line of artware that is now attracting the interest of collectors. Marked examples carry an impressed die-stamp or a paper label, each with the firm name and the outline of a sturgeon. Merrimac is the Indian word for sturgeon.

Bowl, gr oatmeal gloss w/blk metallic drip, 5¼x8½", NM 800.00
Bowl, lotus blossoms, silvery gr, EB, 5x8¾" 850.00
Stein, textured gr & blk, mk, 4½x5½", NM 325.00

Vase, green matt with hand-applied leaf decoration, ca 1907, 4½x4½", $800.00.

Vase, gr matt, waisted form, att, 6", EX 70.00
Vase, gr matt w/blk striations, unmk, 7½", NM 475.00

Metlox

Metlox Potteries was founded in 1927 in Manhattan Beach, California. Before 1934 when they began producing the ceramic housewares for which they have become famous, they made ceramic and neon outdoor advertising signs. The company went out of business in 1989.

Well-known sculptor Carl Romanelli designed artware in the late 1930s and early 1940s (and again briefly in the 1950s). His work is especially sought after today.

Some Provincial dinnerware lines can be confusing. There are two 'rooster' lines, Red Rooster (red, orange, and brown) and California Provincial (dark green and burgundy), and there are two 'homestead' lines, Colonial Heritage (red, orange, and brown like the Red Rooster pieces) and Heritage Provincial (dark green and burgundy like California Provincial). For further information we recommend *Collector's Encyclopedia of Metlox Potteries* by our advisor Carl Gibbs, Jr.; he is listed in the Directory under Texas.

Cookie Jars

Apple, red, 3½-qt, 9½", from $65 to 75.00

Barrel, w/Cookie lid (Cookie Barrel), 11", from $100 to 125.00
Barrel, w/Pretzel lid (Pretzel Barrel), 11", from $100 to 125.00
Barrel, w/Red Apple lid (Apple Barrel), 11", from $40 to 50.00
Basket, natural, w/Basket lid (Basket), 10½", from $35 to 45.00
Basket, natural, w/Fruit lid (Fruit Basket), 4-qt, from $40 to 50.00
Basket, wht, w/red Apple lid, from $40 to 50.00
Bear, Beau, from $40 to 50.00
Bear, Panda, w/lollipop, minimum value 350.00
Bear, Panda, w/o lollipop, from $100 to 125.00
Bear, Sombrero, Pancho, from $100 to 125.00
Bear, Teddy, wht, 3-qt, from $40 to 45.00
Bear, Uncle Sam, minimum value 950.00
Blue Bird on Pine Cone, stain finish, 3-qt, from $65 to 75.00
Calf, Ferdinand, minimum value (+) 750.00
Cat, Ali, from $175 to 195.00
Cat, Calico, cream w/bl ribbon, from $140 to 150.00
Cat, Katy, from $75 to 95.00
Chickadee, Cookie Creations series, 2-qt, from $65 to 85.00
Clown, yel, 3-qt, from $125 to 150.00
Cookie Girl, bsk, 2½-qt, from $50 to 60.00
Cow, purple, wht flowers, yel butterfly & bell, from $475 to 500.00
Debutante, bl or pk dress, minimum value 600.00
Dina-Stegosaurus, yel, from $150 to 175.00
Dog, Fido, cream, from $150 to 175.00
Dog, Gingham, bl, from $200 to 225.00
Drummer Boy, 2½-qt, minimum value 500.00
Duck, Sir Francis Drake, from $40 to 50.00
Elephant, 11", minimum value 750.00
Goose, Lucy, from $150 to 175.00
Hippo, Bubbles, lt gray & gr, minimum value 500.00
Jolly Chef, blk or bl eyes, 11", from $400 to 425.00
Kitten, says Meow, 2¾-qt, from $100 to 125.00
Lamb, Says Baa, 3½-qt, from $100 to 125.00
Lamb w/Flowers, 2½-qt, from $325 to 350.00
Mammy, Cook, red, from $750 to (+) 850.00
Merry Go Round, red/bl/yel/wht, from $350 to 375.00
Mona Monoclonius, aqua, from $150 to 175.00
Mushroom Cottage, from $300 to 350.00
Nun, minimum value 1,000.00
Owl, wht, 2½-qt, from $65 to 75.00
Parrot, from $325 to 350.00
Pelican, Salty, from $175 to 200.00
Pig, Slenderella, from $125 to 150.00
Pineapple, 3¾-qt, from $70 to 80.00
Pretty Anne, 2½-qt, from $175 to 200.00
Rabbit, Easter Bunny, solid chocolate, minimum value 750.00
Rabbit on Cabbage, 3-qt, 10", from $125 to 150.00
Raccoon, Cookie Bandit, bsk, 2¾-qt, from $75 to (+) 100.00
Rag Doll Girl, 2½-qt, from $175 to 200.00
Rex-Tyrannosaurus Rex, French Bl, from $150 to 175.00
Rose, 2¾-qt, from $400 to 425.00
Santa head, minimum value 400.00
Scout, Brownie, minimum value 750.00
Squirrel on Pine Cone, stain finish, 3-qt, 11", from $65 to 75.00
Sun, from $160 to 175.00
Tulip Time, Cookie Creations series, 2-qt, from $65 to 85.00
Turtle, Flash, minimum value 650.00
Watermelon, from $300 to 325.00
Whale, wht, from $300 to 350.00
Woodpecker on Acorn, 3-qt, from $375 to 400.00

Dinnerware

#200 series/Poppy Trail, butter dish, from $50 to 55.00

#200 series/Poppy Trail, creamer, from $18 to 20.00
#200 series/Poppy Trail, cup, Tom & Jerry; from $15 to 18.00
#200 series/Poppy Trail, cup & saucer, demi; from $28 to 33.00
#200 series/Poppy Trail, mug, ribbed, from $15 to 18.00
#200 series/Poppy Trail, plate, dinner; coupe, 10", from $15 to 18.00
#200 series/Poppy Trail, shakers, S&P shapes, pr, from $20 to 24.00
#200 series/Poppy Trail, teapot, from $40 to 45.00
Antique Grape, butter dish, from $55 to 60.00
Antique Grape, gravy, fast stand, 1-pt, from $35 to 40.00
Antique Grape, pitcher, 1¼-qt, from $45 to 50.00
Antique Grape, plate, salad; 7½", from $10 to 12.00
Antique Grape, platter, oval, 14¼", from $45 to 50.00
Blueberry Provincial, bread server, 9½", from $55 to 60.00
Blueberry Provincial, creamer, 6-oz, from $20 to 22.00
Blueberry Provincial, cup & saucer, from $12 to 14.00
Blueberry Provincial, pitcher, 2¼-qt, from $65 to 70.00
Blueberry Provincial, shakers, pr, from $22 to 24.00
California Aztec, bowl, soup; from $22 to 25.00
California Aztec, butter dish, from $95 to 100.00
California Aztec, chop plate, from $80 to 85.00
California Aztec, creamer, from $22 to 25.00
California Aztec, plate, salad; from $15 to 18.00
California Aztec, tumbler, from $45 to 50.00
California Ivy, barbeque pepper shaker, lg, from $28 to 30.00
California Ivy, bowl, cereal; 6¾", from $15 to 16.00
California Ivy, bowl, vegetable; 9", from $40 to 45.00
California Ivy, buffet server, 13¼", from $60 to 65.00
California Ivy, cup & saucer, from $13 to 15.00
California Ivy, mug, 7-oz, from $25 to 28.00
California Ivy, plate, luncheon; 9¼", from $11 to 12.00
California Ivy, sugar bowl, w/lid, 9-oz, from $25 to 28.00
California Peach Blossom, bowl, soup; from $16 to 18.00
California Peach Blossom, chop plate, from $65 to 75.00
California Peach Blossom, gravy boat, from $40 to 45.00
California Peach Blossom, lug soup, from $22 to 25.00
California Peach Blossom, pitcher, water; from $75 to 85.00
California Peach Blossom, plate, salad; from $11 to 12.00

California Provincial, candle holder, from $50.00 to $55.00; Chop plate, 12¼", from $80.00 to $85.00; Teapot, seven-cup, from $135.00 to $145.00.

California Provincial, bowl, salad; 11⅛", from $90 to 100.00
California Provincial, bowl, vegetable; basket style, 8⅛" 60.00
California Provincial, coaster, 3¾", from $28 to 30.00
California Provincial, cookie jar, from $100 to 110.00
California Provincial, cruet set, 5-pc, complete, from $185 to 200.00
California Provincial, lazy susan, 7-pc, complete, from $225 to ..250.00
California Provincial, plate, dinner; 10", from $18 to 20.00
California Provincial, platter, oval, 11", from $50 to 55.00
California Provincial, server, 3-part, 13¼", from $150 to 165.00
California Provincial, sprinkling can, from $105 to 115.00

California Strawberry, baker, oval, 11", from $40 to 45.00
California Strawberry, salad fork & spoon set, from $50 to 55.00
California Strawberry, soup, 6¾", from $14 to 15.00
Colonial Heritage, platter, oval, med, from $35 to 40.00
Della Robbia, bowl, divided vegetable; 12⅛", from $45 to 55.00
Della Robbia, casserole, 2-qt, from $90 to 95.00
Della Robbia, cup & saucer, from $13 to 16.00
Della Robbia, platter, sm, 9⅝", from $35 to 40.00
Homestead Provincial, bowl, soup; 8", from $28 to 30.00
Homestead Provincial, cigarette box, from $115 to 125.00
Homestead Provincial, creamer, 6-oz, from $30 to 32.00
Homestead Provincial, hen on nest, from $125 to 150.00
Homestead Provincial, kettle casserole warmer, metal, med 40.00
Homestead Provincial, mug, cocoa; 8-oz, from $28 to 30.00
Homestead Provincial, oil cruet, w/lid, 7-oz, from $38 to 40.00
Homestead Provincial, plate, salad; 7½", from $14 to 16.00
Homestead Provincial, platter, oval, 16", from $90 to 95.00
Homestead Provincial, rooster pepper, from $35 to 38.00
Homestead Provincial, shakers, pr, from $28 to 30.00
La Mancha, baker, 10¾", from $35 to 40.00
La Mancha, bowl, divided vegetable; 10¾", from $40 to 45.00
La Mancha, bowl, soup; 8⅛", from $16 to 18.00
La Mancha, gravy boat, 12-oz, from $25 to 28.00
La Mancha, mug, 10-oz, from $18 to 20.00
La Mancha, plate, salad/dessert; 8¼", from $11 to 12.00
La Mancha, platter, lg, 14¼", from $35 to 40.00
La Mancha, teapot, 6-cup, from $85 to 95.00
Lotus, banana leaf, 20", from $80 to 85.00
Lotus, bowl, fruit; 5½", from $14 to 16.00
Lotus, coffeepot, 6-cup, from $135 to 145.00
Lotus, plate, crescent salad; 8", from $35 to 38.00
Lotus, shell chip & dip, from $65 to 70.00
Lotus, sugar bowl, w/lid, 11-oz, from $35 to 38.00
Navajo, baker, oval, from $40 to 45.00
Navajo, bowl, fruit; from $12 to 14.00
Navajo, bowl, salad; 12", from $80 to 90.00
Navajo, chop plate, 13", from $60 to 65.00
Navajo, gravy ladle, from $20 to 22.00
Navajo, mug, espresso; from $18 to 20.00
Navajo, plate, bread & butter; 6½", from $8 to 9.00
Navajo, platter, rectangular, 11", from $35 to 40.00
Navajo, tumbler, 10-oz, from $30 to 32.00
Provincial Blue, bowl, vegetable; 7⅛", from $50 to 55.00
Provincial Blue, coffee canister, w/lid, from $75 to 80.00
Provincial Blue, coffeepot, 7-cup, from $130 to 140.00
Provincial Blue, cup & saucer, from $16 to 18.00
Provincial Blue, egg cup, from $35 to 38.00
Provincial Blue, salt box, from $125 to 135.00
Provincial Blue, sugar bowl, w/lid, from $35 to 38.00
Provincial Blue, turkey platter, 22½", from $275 to 295.00
Red Rooster Provincial, buffet server, 12¼" dia, from $70 to 75.00
Red Rooster Provincial, candle holder, from $45 to 50.00
Red Rooster Provincial, cruet set, 5-pc, complete, from $175 to ...185.00
Red Rooster Provincial, cup & saucer, from $14 to 16.00
Red Rooster Provincial, Flour canister, from $85 to 90.00
Red Rooster Provincial, match box, from $90 to 95.00
Red Rooster Provincial, mug, lg, 1-pt, from $35 to 38.00
Red Rooster Provincial, pitcher, 2½-qt, from $90 to 95.00
Red Rooster Provincial, salt & pepper mill, pr, from $100 to 120.00
Red Rooster Provincial, sugar bowl, w/lid, 8-oz, from $30 to 32.00
Sculptured Daisy, bowl, vegetable; 10" dia, from $40 to 45.00
Sculptured Daisy, plate, bread & butter; 6¼", from $7 to 8.00
Sculptured Daisy, plate, dinner; 10½", from $12 to 13.00
Sculptured Daisy, salad fork & spoon set, from $50 to 55.00

Sculptured Daisy, teapot, 7-cup, from $90 to 100.00
Sculptured Grape, bowl, vegetable; w/lid, 1-qt, from $85 to 90.00
Sculptured Grape, bowl, vegetable; 9½", from $40 to 45.00
Sculptured Grape, cup & saucer, 7-oz, from $14 to 16.00
Sculptured Grape, jam & jelly, 8⅛", from $55 to 60.00
Sculptured Grape, plate, dinner; 10½", from $14 to 15.00
Sculptured Grape, salad fork & spoon, from $60 to 65.00
Sculptured Grape, shakers, pr, from $24 to 26.00
Sculptured Zinnia, bowl, fruit; 6", from $11 to 12.00
Sculptured Zinnia, bowl, vegetable; 9½", from $35 to 40.00
Sculptured Zinnia, coffeepot, 8-cup, from $90 to 100.00
Sculptured Zinnia, plate, dinner; 10½", from $12 to 13.00
Vineyard, bowl, cereal; 6⅞", from $13 to 14.00
Vineyard, bowl, vegetable; w/lid, 9¼", from $75 to 80.00
Vineyard, coffeepot, 8-cup, from $80 to 90.00
Vineyard, jam & jelly, 8¼", from $40 to 45.00
Vineyard, pitcher, 1-qt, from $50 to 55.00
Vineyard, plate, dinner; 10¾", from $12 to 13.00
Vineyard, soup tureen, from $165 to 180.00
Woodland Gold, bowl, cereal; 5⅝", from $13 to 14.00
Woodland Gold, bowl, divided vegetable; 9", from $40 to 45.00
Woodland Gold, butter dish, oval, from $50 to 55.00
Woodland Gold, cup & saucer, from $12 to 14.00
Yorkshire, celery dish, from $20 to 25.00
Yorkshire, plate, salad; from $10 to 12.00
Yorkshire, platter, 11", from $25 to 30.00
Yorkshire, sherbet, from $20 to 22.00
Yorkshire, teapot, sm, from $65 to 70.00
Yorkshire, tumbler, lg, from $20 to 25.00

Disney Figurines

Alice in Wonderland, from $350 to 400.00
Bambi, planter, med, from $275 to 325.00
Bambi, tail up, sm, from $200 to 225.00
Brer Rabbit, planter, from $4,000 to 4,250.00
Cinderella (peasant), from $450 to 500.00
Dachshund (from Lady & Tramp), 1¼", from $200 to 250.00
Donald Duck (3 Caballeros), from $325 to 350.00
Donald Duck w/guitar, from $275 to 300.00
Dumbo (elephant), miniature, 1¾", from $175 to 200.00
Dumbo (elephant), standing, from $200 to 225.00
Dwarf, any, from $200 to 250.00
Faline (deer), from $140 to 165.00
Figaro (cat), standing, from $175 to 225.00
Flower (skunk), sm, from $100 to 125.00
Lady (dog), sitting, 1¾", from $85 to 125.00
Mamma Mouse (from Cinderella), from $175 ....200.00
March Hare, from $325 to 350.00
Mermaid (from Peter Pan), from $450 to 475.00
Mickey Mouse, from $350 to 400.00
Owl (from Bambi), from $175 to 200.00
Pinocchio, from $400 to 450.00
Pluto (dog), sniffing, from $225 to 250.00
Snow White, from $425 to 500.00
Snow White, mini, 3", from $550 to 600.00
Thumper (rabbit), lg, from $85 to 95.00
Timothy Mouse (aka Dumbo Mouse), mini, 1¼", from $200 to .250.00
Tinker Bell, from $450 to 500.00
Tweedle Dum or Tweedle Dee, ea, from $225 to 250.00

Miniatures

Aardvark, from $115 to 125.00

Bear, standing, 6½", from $70 to 75.00
Burro, sitting or standing, 3", ea, from $40 to 45.00

Chimpanzee on all fours, 4½", from $90.00 to $95.00.

Photo courtesy Jack Chipman

Dinosaur, 4½", from $185 to 195.00
Duck, head upright, 3", from $30 to 35.00
Fawn, looking back, from $35 to 40.00
Flamingo, head down, 6¼", from $45 to 50.00
Heron, 6½", from $40 to 45.00
Lizard, 9½", from $90 to 100.00
Penguin, 3", from $45 to 50.00
Squirrel, 2", from $30 to 35.00

Nostalgia Line

Modeled after items reminiscent of the late 19th and early 20th centuries, the Nostalgia line contained models of locomotives, gramaphones, early autos, stage coaches, and baby carriages. There were also wagons and carts pulled by horses or donkeys, sometimes with separate drivers and passengers. The line was produced from the late 1940s through the 1960s.

American Royal Horse, Arabian, 7¾x8¾", from $105 to 115.00
American Royal Horse, colt, standing, 3x4", from $65 to 70.00
American Royal Horse, Dobbin, 11x9", from $95 to 105.00
American Royal Horse, Lg Gaited, 11x9", from $115 to 125.00
Bathtub, 7½" L, from $55 to 60.00
Bob sleigh, 12", from $90 to 100.00
Burro, from $55 to 60.00
Car, Chevrolet, from $75 to 85.00
Drum table, from $40 to 45.00
Fire wagon, from $90 to 100.00
Hitching post boy, from $45 to 75.00
Lyre clock, from $100 to 110.00
Mamma or Papa, ea, from $60 to 65.00
Old Mill ensemble, 2-pc, from $200 to 225.00
Piano & lid, from $75 to 80.00
Pony cart, from $55 to 60.00
Santa, from $90 to 95.00
Stagecoach, from $90 to 100.00
Vanderbilt sleigh, 9", from $65 to 70.00
Watering trough, 15" L, from $90 to 100.00

Poppets

From the mid-'60s through the mid-'70s, Metlox produced a line of 'Poppets,' eighty-eight in all, representing characters ranging from royalty and professionals to a Salvation Army group. They came with a name tag; some had paper labels, others backstamps.

Angelina, angel, 7⅝", from $45 to 55.00
Arnie, golfer, 6½", from $35 to 45.00

Colleen, girl w/coiled hair, 7¼", from $35 to **45.00**
Conchita, Mexican girl, 8¾", from $50 to **60.00**
Dutch girl, 5", from $25 to **35.00**
Eliza, flower vendor, 5⅝", from $45 to **55.00**
Elizabeth, Queen, from $35 to **45.00**
Elliot, boy tennis player, w/4" bowl, from $35 to **45.00**
Mary Lou, seated lady, 9", from $35 to **45.00**
Mike, boy w/pot, 5½", from $25 to **35.00**
Monica, nun, w/4" bowl, from $45 to **55.00**
Myra & Mattie, mother & daughter, 8¼", from $50 to **60.00**
Nellie, girl w/bird, 8⅝", from $45 to **55.00**
Nick, organ grinder, from $45 to **55.00**
Raymond, barrister, w/4" bowl, from $45 to **55.00**
Sarah, choral lady #1, 7¾", from $35 to **45.00**
Schultz, tradesman/grocer, 8½", from $45 to **55.00**

Mettlach

In 1836 Nicholas Villeroy and Eugene Francis Boch, both of whom were already involved in the potting industry, formed a partnership and established a stoneware factory in an old restored abbey in Mettlach, Germany. Decorative stoneware with in-mold relief was their specialty, steins in particular. Through constant experimentation, they developed innovative methods of decoration. One process, called chromolith, involved inlaying colorful mosaic designs into the body of the ware. Later underglaze printing from copper plates was used. Their stoneware was of high quality, and their steins won many medals at the St. Louis Expo and early world's fairs. Most examples are marked with an incised castle and the name 'Mettlach.' The numbering system indicates size, date, stock number, and decorator. Production was halted by a fire in 1921; the factory was not rebuilt.

Key:
L — liter   PUG — print under glaze
POG — print over glaze   tl — thumb lift

#1044/126 and 127, plaques, PUG, hunting dogs, gold rims with some wear, 17", $580.00 for the pair.

#1028, stein, relief: tan & brn, inlaid lid, 5L **145.00**
#1032, coaster, PUG: dwarfs, lt stain, 4¾" **150.00**
#1044, plaque, PUG: Holy Cloth, 10", NM **335.00**
#1044/1325, plaque, PUG: dwarf being attacked, 7¾" **600.00**
#1044/147, plaque, PUG: Lichtenstein, 14" **385.00**
#1044/210, plaque, PUG: Elsass-Lothringen, 12" **230.00**
#1044/9025, plaque, PUG: fish & lobster, 14" **375.00**
#1044/9030, plaque, PUG: ducks, 14½", NM **345.00**
#1044/9032, plaque, PUG: pheasant, 14", NM **425.00**
#1055, stein, etched: repeating design, inlaid lid, ½-L **450.00**
#1215, bowl, etched/glazed: repeating floral, silver trim, rpr, 9" ..**375.00**
#1274, match striker, etched/glazed: repeating design, 2¼" **230.00**

#1476, stein, etched: dwarfs & vineyard, inlaid lid, ½-L **750.00**
#1520, stein, etched: eagle w/cavaliers, pewter lid, ½-L **385.00**
#1526, stein, HP: Caduceus, pewter lid, ½-L **260.00**
#1526, stein, PUG: Munic child, city scenes, pewter lid, ½-L **330.00**
#1526/1281, stein, PUG: hunter, pewter lid, ½-L **230.00**
#1526/1291, stein, PUG: hunter w/dog, pewter lid, ½-L **665.00**
#1526/566, stein, PUG/HP: man w/dogs, inlaid lid, ½-L **425.00**
#1527, stein, etched: drinking scene, inlaid lid, ½-L, NM **350.00**
#1611, vase, relief: lady w/butterfly wings on branch, 25½", EX .**1,250.00**
#1636, vase, etched/glazed: repeating design, 5" **215.00**
#1647, stein, etched: tapestry, man, pewter lid, ½-L **285.00**
#1659, covered dish, etched/glazed, w/lid, 3" **200.00**
#1675, stein, etched: Heidelberg castle, inlaid lid, ½-L, NM **500.00**
#1695, stein, etched: hunter & game panels, inlaid lid, ½-L **725.00**
#1734, stein, etched/glazed: lovers, Warth, inlaid lid, 1.4-L **1,500.00**
#1742, stein, etched: Gottingen & students, inlaid lid, ½-L **935.00**
#1744, stein, etched/threading: verse & leaf design, ½-L **435.00**
#1786, stein, etched/glazed: St Florian, dragon hdl & tl, 1-L ...**1,100.00**
#1856, stein, etched/glazed: eagle & post, pewter lid, ½-L, NM .**900.00**
#1909/1038, stein, PUG: frogs party at pond, pewter lid, ½-L **685.00**
#1909/1074, stein, PUG: man smoking, Schlitt, ½-L **375.00**
#1909/1102, stein, PUG: drunken men, pewter lid, ½-L **300.00**
#1909/1110, stein, PUG: musicians, Schlitt, barmaid lid, ½-L ...**450.00**
#1909/1278, stein, PUG: Dutch children w/cat, ½-L **500.00**
#1909/1539, stein, PUG: animals & dwarf musicians, ½-L **725.00**
#1909/1836, stein, PUG: tennis players, rpr pewter lid, ½-L ...**2,000.00**
#1909/726, stein, PUG: steins walk to be filled, ½-L **700.00**
#1961, vase, etched/glazed: repeating design, 3½" **230.00**
#1995, stein, etched: man drinking, inlaid lid, ½-L **440.00**
#20010-420, mustard pot, transfer/HP: Bavaria, w/lid, 3½" **110.00**
#2005, stein, etched: people at table, inlaid lid, ½-L **700.00**
#2007, stein, etched, blk cat, inlaid lid, ½-L **660.00**
#2009, stein, etched: lovers, inlaid lid, ½-L, NM **525.00**
#2044, stein, etched/glazed: drinking scene, rpr lid, ½-L **495.00**
#2081, plaque, etched: Husaren on horsebk, 15" **1,000.00**
#2093, stein, etched: cards, inlaid lid, sm pewter rpt, ½-L **700.00**
#2255, stein, etched: wedding scene, Etruscan, inlaid lid, 1-L **850.00**
#2271, stein, PUG/HP: Christmas in Mettlach 1916, ½-L **665.00**
#2327, beaker, PUG/HP: Old Vienna Atlantic City, ¼-L **200.00**
#2327, beaker, PUG: Old N Church, Souvenir of Boston, ¼-L .**300.00**
#2327/1200, beaker, PUG: Bremen, ¼-L **100.00**
#2455, stein, etched: Lohengrin, pewter lid, rpr, 6.8-L **2,200.00**
#2530, stein, cameo: boar hunt, Stahl, inlaid lid, 1-L **895.00**
#2542, plaque, etched: Nouveau lady, swans & flowers, 15" **770.00**
#2545, plaque, etched: Nouveau lady, flowers & butterfly, 20" ..**2,100.00**
#2622, plaque, man making toast, sgn EQ, castle mk, 7¾" **275.00**
#2718, stein, etched/glazed: David & Goliath, inlaid lid, ½-L ...**1,985.00**
#2776, stein, etched: man in wine cellar, inlaid lid, ½-L **815.00**
#280, stein: HP: Student Society crest, 1906, pewter lid, ½-L **500.00**
#280/626, stein, PUG: dwarfs drinking, pewter lid, ¼-L **280.00**
#2800, stein, etched: Art Nouveau, inlaid lid, ¼-L, NM **525.00**
#2842/1173, beaker, PUG: dwarf, Schlitt, ¼-L **275.00**
#2846, ashtray/match holder, Nouveau heart shape, rpr, 5" dia ..**275.00**
#285, stein, HP: Student Society Crest, 1904, pewter lid, ½-L ...**375.00**
#2915, planter, etched: Art Nouveau, 4½x14" **1,270.00**
#2936, stein, etched: elks/Art Nouveau, inlaid lid, ½-L **500.00**
#2951, stein, cameo: eagle w/crown, pewter lid, ½-L **415.00**
#3014/5424, vase, Delft: Dutch girl, rpt gold, 11½" **300.00**
#3052, creamer, etched: Art Deco, 4" **175.00**
#3055, tray, etched: Art Deco, 6¼x11½" **450.00**
#3089, stein, etched: Diogenes, Schlitt, inlaid lid, rpr, ½-L **700.00**
#3093, stein, etched: troll, Schlitt, pewter lid, owl tl, ½-L **880.00**
#3185/1282, stein, PUG: men smoking, inlaid lid, ½-L **415.00**
#3192, stein, etched/glazed: man, Ringer, scuffed, ½-L **465.00**

#3225/1290, plaque, PUG: United States, 11x13" 500.00
#3288, stein, etched: Bavaria series, men bowling, ½-L 1,700.00
#335, dish, early style: girl under lg shell, platinum trim, 5" 350.00
#3420, bowl, relief/glazed: repeating design, 3x7" 460.00
#3435, stein, relief: boy dressed as soldier, rpr, ½-L 230.00
#3582, stein, etched: drinking scene, Quidenus, barmaid tl, ½-L ..615.00
#469, mustard pot, relief: early style, inlaid lid, 3", NM 150.00
#5006, stein, Delft: Nurnberg, pewter lid, ½-L, NM 450.00
#5019-5442, stein, faience: cavalier/verse, pewter ring, 1-L 3,575.00
#852, plaque, inlaid (early style): child w/flute, 11½" 440.00

Microscopes

The microscope has taken on many forms during its 250-year evolutionary period. The current collectors' market primarily includes examples from England, those surplused from institutions, and continental beginner and intermediate forms which sold through Sears Roebuck & Company and other retailers of technical instruments. Earlier examples have brass maintubes which are unpainted. Later, more common examples are all black with brass or silver knobs and horseshoe-shaped bases. Early and more complex forms are the most valuable; these always had hardwood cases to house the delicate instruments and their accessories. Instruments were never polished during use, and those that have been polished to use as decorator pieces are of little interest to most avid collectors. Our advisor for this category is Dale Beeks; he is listed in the Directory under Iowa.

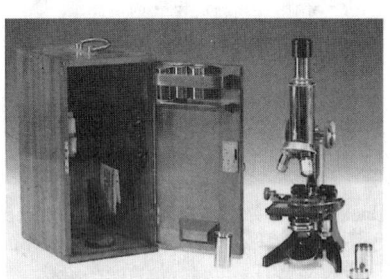

J. Swift & Son, London, brass and steel, late 19th/early 20th century, with all attachments, EX in wooden case, $600.00.

Acme, brass & iron, 14", +case, EX 350.00
Baker, 224 High Holborn London, brass, 1840s, 17" 1,200.00
Bausch & Lomb, all brass, horseshoe base, 1897, 14", EX 350.00
Bausch & Lomb, blk base, brass tube, 1897, 14", EX 275.00
Bausch & Lomb, brass, tripod base, 1876, 16", EX, +case 600.00
Bausch & Lomb, ca 1915, EX orig 200.00
Bausch & Lomb, dissecting, w/filters & holders 200.00
Bulloch, Chicago, brass, complex, Y base, 1880, 15", +case 1,100.00
E Leitz Wetzlar, brass, multi-lens, G, w/orig fitted case, ...150.00
English, professional, brass, 1876, 18", +case/accessories 950.00
English, student, brass, ca 1870, 12", +case/accessories 595.00
French, drum & furnace form, 5", EX, +case 65.00
French, student, ca 1910, 9", G, +case 65.00
Grundlach Manhattan, student, all brass, 11", EX 165.00
Grunow, New York, iron & brass, 15", EX, +case 1,100.00
Hand-held, simple form, 1890, 3", G 45.00
McAllister, chain-drive focus, 14", G, +case 325.00
McIntosh Battery & Optical, brass & iron, 12", G 550.00
Queen, brass & iron, Y base, 14", G, +case 325.00
Spencer Lens Co, brass, horseshoe base, 13", EX 195.00
Tighe, brass, 12", EX, +case 450.00
Tolles, Boston, brass, Y base, ca 1880, 16", G, +case 950.00
Watson, English binoculars form, 1880, 18", EX, +case 1,250.00
Zentmeyer, brass, complex, dbl pillar, tripod base, 18", G 2,250.00

Midwestern Glass

As early as 1814, blown glass was made in Ohio. By 1835 glasshouses in Michigan were producing similar pattern-molded types that have long been highly regarded by collectors. During the latter part of the 19th century, all six of the states of the Northwest Territory were mass producing the pressed-glass tableware patterns that were then in vogue. Various types of art glass were produced in the area until after the turn of the century. Items listed here are attributed to the Midwest by certain physical characteristics known to be indigenous to that part of the country. See also Findlay Onyx; Greentown Glass; Libbey; Zanesville Glass. Our advisor for this category is Mark Vuono; he is listed in the Directory under Connecticut.

Bottle, club; bl-aqua, 30 right-swirl ribs, pontil, 1820s, 8" 110.00
Bottle, pitkin, dk grass gr, 16 broken swirl ribs, 7¼" 300.00
Chestnut flask, lt citron, 24 swirled ribs, pontiled, 5⅜" 150.00
Ewer, 15 vertical ribs, hollow hdl, no stopper, 7¾" 100.00
Nurser, gr-aqua, 18 vertical ribs, pontil, sheared lip, 8" 75.00
Pitcher, appl ribbed hdl, tooled lip, 8" 310.00
Pitcher, 25 ribs, appl hollow hdl, 6" 220.00
Sugar bowl, appl ft, gallery rim, lid w/folded rim, 9" 195.00

Militaria

Because of the wide and varied scope of items available to collectors of militaria, most tend to concentrate mainly on the area or areas that interest them most or that they can afford to buy. Some items represent a major investment and because of their value have been reproduced. Extreme caution should be used when purchasing Nazi items. Every badge, medal, cap, uniform, dagger, and sword that Nazi Germany issued is being reproduced today. Some repros are crude and easily identified as fakes, while others are very well done and difficult to recognize as reproductions. Purchases from WWII veterans are usually your safest buys. Reputable dealers or collectors will normally offer a money-back guarantee on Nazi items purchased from them. There are a number of excellent Third Reich reference books available in bookstores at very reasonable prices. Study them to avoid losing a much larger sum spent on a reproduction. Our advisor for this category is Ron Willis; he is listed in the Directory under Oklahoma.

Key: insg — insignia

East German

Cap, visor, Navy officer, EX 50.00
Cap, visor; Air Force officer, EX 40.00
Cap, visor; Army officer, EX 35.00
Cap, visor; border guard, EX 25.00
Dagger, Army, EX 150.00
Helmet, EX 30.00
Helmet, paratrooper's, plastic, 1st issue 75.00
Helmet, paratrooper's, 2nd issue 50.00

Imperial German

Badge, Prussian Veteran, blk/wht enamel shield w/eagle & ribbon ...25.00
Breast armor, machine gunner's, field gray finish, scarce, EX 895.00
Buckle, Prussian, NP inset on brass field, Gott Mit Uns, EX 30.00
Document, Prussian Honor Cross Award, 1904, EX 35.00
Hat, visor; Prussian officer, gray wool w/red crown, EX 110.00
Helmet, spike; Baden Artillery, blk leather w/brass, 1915, EX 700.00

Helmet, spike; Hessian enlisted, gray metal mts, complete 700.00
Helmet, spike; Prussian Artillery, eagle frontplate, EX 760.00
Jumper, Imperial Navy enlisted, bl wool, dbl-breasted, EX 300.00
Knapsack, Army, gray canvas w/leather straps, dtd 1916, EX 75.00
Light, field map reading; tin rectangular case w/eagle, 6" 65.00
Medal, Iron Cross, 2nd Class, 1914, w/sm ribbon 25.00
Medal, Prussian Army 9 Yr Long Service, gilt bronze, w/ribbon ...25.00
Medal, Southwest Africa Service, gilt brass, w/ribbon, EX 25.00
Pin, Wartime Patriotic, brass brooch w/flags, EX 25.00
Shoulder boards, Bavarian Technical Lieutenant, bl/silver, pr 40.00

Third Reich

Ammunition crate, Army, wooden, 18x13x8", EX 26.00
Badge, Hunting Assoc 50 Yr Commemorative, SP stag's skull 50.00
Badge, Infantry Assault, bronze, stamped, EX 55.00
Badge, Luftwaffe Parachutist Combat, eagle w/gold wash, EX 175.00
Badge, Navy High Seas Fleet, SP ship w/gilt wreath, VG 100.00
Badge, SA Sports, bronze, hallmk 25.00
Badge, Tank Assault, silver, stamped planchet, EX 55.00
Bar, Army Close Combat, bronze clasp, hallmk, EX 65.00
Book, Sword & Swastika, T Taylor, c 1952, illus, EX 20.00
Collar tabs, Customs officer, embr ½-wreath w/single pips on gr ..32.00
Collar tabs, N Caucasians Foreign Volunteer Lieutenant, rare 65.00
Currency, 100 Reichsmark note, dtd 1935, EX 20.00
Dagger, Hitler Youth Leader, eng blade, eagle on scabbard 75.00
Flag pole finial, NP swastika in circle, 8½", EX 50.00
Flight suit, Luftwaffe, summer weight, complete w/headgear 695.00
Gaiters, Army, field gray canvas w/leather straps, pr, VG 20.00
Hat, visor; Veteran Assoc for Kyffauserbund, blk wool, EX 50.00
Helmet, Luftschutz M34 Sq Dip, EX dk bl w/insignia, VG 150.00
Helmet, Reichswer Model 1915, pnt traces, G 70.00
Insignia, breast; Navy enlisted, gold embr eagle on bl wool 25.00
Insignia, sleeve; Army Jager Troops, oak leaves on gr cloth 20.00
Insignia, sleeve; Army Mtn Troop, edelweiss on gr cloth 20.00
Knife, gravity; Luftwaffe Paratrooper, P Weyersberg mk, EX 195.00
Log book, Luftwaffe pilots, 6 months of entries, 1944 ....280.00
Medal, Mother's Cross, silver, w/ribbon fob, EX 45.00
Medal, RAD 4 Yr Long Service, bronze, w/ribbon 60.00
Mittens, Luftwaffe, winter reversible, down filled, EX 65.00
Parachute, Luftwaffe, camo pack, complete w/rigging, EX 425.00
Photograph, Hitler in open car, 3x2" 20.00

Police helmet, leather lining and chin strap, $175.00.

Postcard, Rommel commemorative by Willrich, sepia toned 32.00
Propaganda leaflet, to Am soldiers, EX 80.00
Scope, Field Artillery, gray finish, w/rubber eyepc, EX 400.00
Shoulder boards, Fire Police Major, silver on rose wool 26.00
Shoulder boards, Luftwaffe General, gold/silver on wht wool 175.00
Stationery, Reichsfuhrer-SS Henrich Himmler, unused sheet 80.00

Japanese

Badge, hat; WWII Navy cadet, gilt brass w/anchor, scarce 70.00

Badge, WWII Military veteran, silver w/gilt star, pin-bk, EX 40.00
Badge, WWII pilot, winged, hand embr silver & yel on bl 60.00
Dagger, WWII, 12½" overall, w/wooden resting scabbard 140.00
Helmet, fire; WWII era, riveted compo, front/rear visors, EX 75.00
Helmet, flight; WWII, brn leather, earphone flaps, EX 80.00
Helmet, Jingasa style, blk lacquer w/gold dragons, bronze finial .950.00
Helmet, WWII Army, brn khaki pnt on steel, star missing, G ...115.00
Insignia, visor hat; Police, embr gold wreath on bl, brass mum 25.00
Medal, Red Cross Golden Order of Merit, gilt silver cross 120.00
Medal, WWII, China Incident, bronze, w/ribbon & clasp 42.50

Russia/Soviet

Badge, Imperial Era, Sharpshooter, bronze, Xd rifles, EX 40.00
Badge, KGB Border Guard officer, red/gr on gilt, 1979 ....25.00
Dagger, Army, dbl-sided blade, dtd 1957, yel compo grips, EX ...140.00
Hat, Army, winter style, gray wool, 1980s, M 50.00
Hat, Navy enlisted, blk wool twill, star insg, 1980, EX 40.00
Helmet, Army, gr w/brn leather straps, cloth liner, 1960, EX 35.00
Helmet, Tank Crew, gray cotton, leather chin strap, dtd 1961 .....75.00
Helmet, WWII Model 1936, NM dk khaki finish, w/liner, NM .155.00
Medal, Imperial Era, Bravery, Nicholas II portrait, w/ribbon 70.00
Medal, Imperial Era, Campaigns in Central Asia, bronze, w/ribbon ..110.00
Medal, Navy Nakhimov, bronze planchet, w/ribbon, EX 130.00
Medal, St George Cross, Bravery 4th Class, w/ribbon, EX 90.00
Medal, 50 Yr Anniversary Soviet Armed Forces, red star, w/ribbon ...25.00
Order of Lenin, WWII, EX 650.00
Order of October Revolution, EX 150.00
Order of the Red Banner of Labor, EX 50.00
Shoulder boards, Army enlisted, wine-red wool on khaki, M 20.00
Shoulder boards, Major General, silver star on gold & red wool ...60.00
Shoulder boards, WWII Infantry Colonel, red on khaki, EX 45.00

United States

Backpack, WWII, mk USMC under flap, dtd 1943, EX 48.00
Badge, WWII, Army Combat Infantryman, bl enamel on sterling ..20.00
Badge, WWII aircraft observer, cloth, winged, unissued 20.00
Badge, WWII Army Combat Medical, sterling silver, hallmk 35.00
Belt, money; WWI Army, khaki cotton twill, 3-compartment, VG ...20.00
Blanket, WWII Army, khaki wool, EX 25.00
Boots, combat; WWII Army, 2-buckle, EX 150.00
Boots, Korean War Army Combat, blk leather, buckle tops, EX ..35.00
Boots, WWI Cavalry, high top, brn leather, EX 85.00
Breeches, WWI Army, khaki wool, stamped buttons, EX 35.00
Canteen, Spanish-Am War era, canvas cover on tin body, EX 55.00
Cap, overseas; WWI Army, khaki wool, w/Medical Corps disk, EX ..20.00
Cap, overseas; WWII Army enlisted, khaki wool, EX 25.00
Cap, overseas; WWII Navy aviator, khaki cotton twill, 1942, VG ...30.00
Chevrons, Marine Corps 1st Sergeant, yel stripes on red, 1890s ...35.00
Clip, Thompson submachine gun; WWII, unissued, M 20.00
Coat, dress; Indian War Infantry officer, 27-button, EX 1,450.00
Collar disk, WWI Forestry Service enlisted, bronze, scarce 35.00
Coveralls, WWII, Civil Defense warden, wht w/lettering 65.00
Dress, WWII Army nurse, rayon 85.00
Duffel bag, WWII Army, khaki canvas, EX 20.00
Flagpole finial, WWI era, brass eagle w/outstretched wings, EX ...30.00
Flight overalls, WWII ANS-31 type, khaki wool twill, EX 85.00
Guide, WWII Aircraft Spotter, EX 15.00
Handcuffs, Indian War-era Marine Corps, worn NP, 1880s, EX ...95.00
Hat, WAAC, 1950s 18.00
Helmet, Korean War-era jet pilot, w/liner & strap, VG 85.00
Helmet, pith; WWII Army, khaki cloth cover, 1944, EX 30.00
Helmet, WWI Anti-Aircraft Unit, khaki sand, w/liner & strap ...85.00

Helmet, WWI Army Medical Corps, NM camo, w/liner, EX **245.00**
Helmet, WWI 101 Ammunition Train, dk khaki, w/liner & strap, EX ..**250.00**
Insignia, shoulder; Artillery Pioneer, Xd axes on bl, 1880s, EX **20.00**
Insignia, WWII Lieutenant, gold bars on brn leather, pr **20.00**
Jacket, US Navy GI, leather, VG **200.00**
Jumpsuit, WWII Am League of Para-Nurses, wht **75.00**
Leggings, WWII Army, khaki canvas, w/laces, EX **25.00**
Medal, Coast Guard...Rifleman Marksmanship, bronze, w/ribbon .**20.00**
Medal, WWII, Bronze Star, w/worn ribbon **22.50**
Overcoat, WWI, Army enlisted, VG **25.00**
Shoe buckles, Revolutionary War era, silver on brass, pr **275.00**
Sleeping bag, WWII Army, khaki cotton, down filling, EX **25.00**
Slide rule, Civil War era, ebony rule w/brass pivot, 8¾" L **55.00**
Suit, WWII Wave Navy, cotton, EX **70.00**
Sunglasses, WWII Airforce pilot's, gr tinted lenses, EX **30.00**
Swagger stick, WWII Army, polished oak, brass head/tip, EX **25.00**
Tunic, WWI Army Model 1912, khaki wool, Quartermaster disks, VG ...**45.00**
Tunic, WWII Army enlisted, khaki wool, w/chevrons, EX **35.00**
Uniform, WWI, Army enlisted, w/cap & leggings, no patches ...**120.00**
Uniform, WWI era, US Cavalry, olive drab cotton, 3-pc w/belt ..**750.00**
Uniform, WWI Marine Corps enlisted, dress bls, VG **150.00**

Milk Glass

Milk glass is the current collector's name for milk-white opaque glass. The early glassmaker's term was Opal Ware. Originally attempted in England in the 18th century with the intention of imitating china, milk glass was not commercially successful until the mid-1800s. Pieces produced in the U.S.A., England, and France during the 1870 – 1900 period are highly prized for their intricate detail and fiery, opalescent edges.

For further information we recommend *Collector's Encyclopedia of Milk Glass, An Identification & Value Guide*, by Betty and Bill Newbound. Our advisor for this category is Rod Dockery; he is listed in the Directory under Texas. Several standard collectors' books have been referenced in our listings: Belknap (B), Collector's Encyclopedia by Newbound (CE), Ferson (F), Grist (G), Imperial's Vintage Milk Glass by Garrison (I), Lindsey (L), Millard (M), and Warman (W). See also Animal Dishes with Covers; Bread Plates; Historical Glass; Westmoreland.

Plate, flowers, lattice edge, Atterbury, ca 1880, 10½", B-25, $75.00.

Bowl, lacy edge, B-136, 9½x8½" **60.00**
Bowl, Scroll, rnd ft, B-99, 8½" **60.00**
Bowl, Scroll & Eye, M-70a, 8" **30.00**
Bowl, Wicket, 6½" **24.00**
Cake stand, Grape, I-1950/375 (Pg 52), 10" **45.00**
Compote, Atlas, B-103 ....**80.00**
Compote, Scroll, hexagonal, B-127/F-383 ....**100.00**
Covered dish, Baby Moses, cattail or reed base, CE-162, 6¼" **275.00**
Covered dish, Uncle Sam on battleship, Flaccus, B-189 ....**80.00**
Creamer, Ceres, F-309 ....**95.00**
Creamer, Coreopsis **160.00**
Creamer, Swan, F-235 ....**65.00**

Jar, Queen Victoria, M-259a **150.00**
Match holder, hand w/fan, ped, orig pnt, CE-350 ....**35.00**
Mug, Bird & Wheat, pk, Atterbury, F-486, 3½" **55.00**
Plate, Ancient Castle, B-121 ....**40.00**
Plate, Angel & Harp or w/Mandolin, B-11c/CE-279d **40.00**
Plate, Beaded Loop, Indian Chief, B-8f, 7¼" **40.00**
Plate, Cupid & Psyche, B-6b, 7½" **40.00**
Plate, Diamond & Shell, B-8d **20.00**
Plate, Easter Greeting, w/chick, F-492 ....**50.00**
Plate, Easter Greeting, w/rabbit & egg, B-3c **70.00**
Plate, Easter Opening, B-7d, 7½" **75.00**
Plate, Easter Sermon, B-7c **75.00**
Plate, Fleur-de-Lis, Flag & Eagles **20.00**
Plate, Forget Me Not, 8½" **20.00**
Plate, No Easter Without Us, rooster, CE-268/F-30 ....**55.00**
Plate, Owl Lovers, owls, eagle, frog on pad, moon, w/gold, B-7b ..**65.00**
Plate, pie-crust rim, 8" **15.00**
Plate, Ring & Dot **10.00**
Plate, Serenade, B-9e, 6½" **40.00**
Plate, Square S Repeat, 8½" **20.00**
Plate, Star, lacy edge **15.00**
Plate, Star Variant **15.00**
Plate, Wicket, 7¼" **15.00**
Platter, Retriever, B-53, 13¼x9¾", EX **110.00**
Spooner, Blackberry, F-253 ....**55.00**
Sugar bowl, Blackberry, F-250 ....**70.00**
Sugar bowl, Coreopsis **180.00**
Sugar bowl, Twin Horn, M-207b **45.00**
Sugar shaker, Grape, Imperial, I-1950/167 (Pg 55) **20.00**
Syrup, Tree of Life, w/lid, F-145 ....**110.00**
Tray, Question Mark, 8" **18.00**
Tray, ribbed edge, 3x5" **8.00**
Vase, ear of corn, orig pnt, CE-381a, 4¼" **30.00**

Miniatures

There is some confusion as to what should be included in a listing of miniature collectibles. Some feel the only true miniature is the salesman's sample; other collectors consider certain small-scale children's toys to be appropriately referred to as miniatures, while yet others believe a miniature to be any small-scale item that gives evidence to the craftsmanship of its creator. For salesman's samples, see specific category; other types are listed below. See also Dollhouses and Furnishings; Children's Things.

Andirons, wrought iron, ftd bases, mushroom finials, 4⅛" **275.00**
Blanket chest, walnut, dvtl ft & drw, rpl till lid, 13x28x11" **1,100.00**
Blanket chest, 6-brd construction, worn bl rpt, 15" **425.00**
Box, hat; flower & fruit decor, 3¾", EX **300.00**
Candlestick, canary, hexagonal socket/base, 2", NM **185.00**
Chest, blanket; appl moldings, brass hinges, PA, 8x13x6¾" ...**1,850.00**
Chest, blanket; tiger maple, dvtl, w/key escutcheon, 7x11x6" .**1,600.00**
Chest, Chpndl style, 5 dvtl drw, trn columns, 17x17x7" **360.00**
Chest, mahog Emp, 3 dvtl drw, scroll ft, rprs, 13x14x7" **500.00**
Chest, mahog Hplwht, 3-drw, 12x12¼x5¾", EX **1,400.00**
Chest, pine, 4 grad drw, wood knobs, 13x12x8", G **200.00**
Chest, pine/poplar, 3-drw, sq nails, old brn pnt, 8½x10¼" **415.00**
Chest, walnut European serpentine, 3 dvtl drws, 9x13x8" **475.00**
Chest, walnut Hplwht, Fr ft, 4 dvtl drws, 27x26" **3,575.00**
Desk, maple, slant front, 3-drw, hinged lid, early, 20x19" **1,450.00**
Dresser, mahog Sheraton, 3 sm drws over 3, reeded columns, 14½" ...**1,500.00**
Fireplace, pine, old marbleized pnt, 8¼" **140.00**
Mirror, shaving; pine w/rosewood graining, ebonized posts, 6" .**250.00**

Platter, Donington Park, bl transfer, Staffordshire, 4¼" **125.00**
Saddle, tooled leather, aluminum pummel, 7¾", EX **125.00**
Sap bucket, wood w/wire rings, wire bail, VT, 4¾x5" **75.00**
Table, gate-leg, butterfly supports, repro, 25x24"+leaves **300.00**

Minton

Thomas Minton established his firm in 1793 at Stoke on Trent and within a few years began producing earthenware with blue-printed patterns similar to the ware he had learned to decorate while employed by the Caughley Porcelain Factory. The Willow pattern was one of his most popular. Neither this nor the porcelain made from 1798 to 1805 was marked (except for an occasional number series), making identification often impossible.

After 1805 until about 1816, fine tea services, beehive-shaped honey pots, trays, etc., were hand decorated with florals, landscapes, Imari-type designs, and neoclassic devices. These were often marked with crossed 'L's. It was Minton that invented the acid gold process of decorating (1863), which is now used by a number of different companies. From 1816 until 1823, no porcelain was made. Through the '20s and '30s, the ornamental wares with colorful decoration of applied fruits and florals and figurines in both bisque and enamel were usually left unmarked. As a result, they have been erroneously attributed to other potters. Some of the ware that was marked bears a deliberate imitation of Meissen's crossed swords. From the late '20s through the '40s, Minton made a molded stoneware line (mugs, jugs, teapots, etc.) with florals or figures in high relief. These were marked with an embossed scroll with an 'M' in the bottom curve. Fine parian ware was made in the late 1840s, and in the '50s Minton experimented with and perfected a line of quality majolica which they produced from 1860 until it was discontinued in 1908. Their slogan was 'Majolica for the Millions,' and for it they gained widespread recognition. Leadership of the firm was assumed by Minton's son Herbert sometime around the middle of the 19th century. Working hand in hand with Leon Arnoux, who was both a chemist and an artist, he managed to secure the company's financial future through constant, successful experimentation with both materials and decorating methods. During the Victorian era, M.L. Solon decorated pieces in the pate-sur-pate style, often signing his work; these examples are considered to be the finest of their type. After 1862 all wares were marked 'Minton' or 'Mintons,' with an impressed year cipher.

Many collectors today reassemble the lovely dinnerware patterns that have been made by Minton. Perhaps one of their most popular lines was Minton Rose, introduced in 1854. The company itself once counted forty-seven versions of this pattern being made by other potteries around the world. In addition to less expensive copies, elaborate hand-enameled pieces were also made by Aynsley, Crown Staffordshire, and Paragon China. Solando Ware (1937) and Byzantine Range (1938) were designed by John Wadsworth. Minton ceased all earthenware production in 1939.

Dinnerware values given in the following listings are for items that were produced from 1870 to 1950. Current production pieces bring lower prices on the resale market. See also Majolica; Pate-Sur-Pate.

Bowl, rim soup; Spring Bouquet **55.00**
Coffeepot, Spring Bouquet **180.00**
Creamer, Spring Bouquet **75.00**
Cup & saucer, demitasse; Spring Bouquet **58.00**
Dinner set, Ancestral, serves 12, 49-pc **1,200.00**
Figurine, Canova, parian, ca 1863, 15" **750.00**
Figurine, Shakespeare w/scroll, parian, ca 1865, 17½" **880.00**
Flower box, 6 Idylls of the King tiles in brass fr, pr **1,400.00**
Plaque, cavalier w/sword, buildings beyond, gr-gold, 12x6" **325.00**
Plate, lady's portrait, plique-a-jour border, 9⅛", pr **1,800.00**

Plate, Spring Bouquet, 6½" **25.00**
Sugar bowl, Spring Bouquet **47.00**
Teapot, Spring Bouquet **180.00**
Tile, Gemini, Astrology series by HS Marks, fr, 6" **175.00**
Tile, Othello, Shakespeare series by Moyr Smith, brn/buff, 6" **85.00**
Urn, exotic birds/grapes & fruit, rose/gilt decor, 10½" **575.00**

Mirrors

The first mirrors were made in England in the 13th century of very thin glass backed with lead. Reverse-painted glass mirrors were made in this country as early as the late 1700s and remained popular throughout the next century. The simple hand-painted panel was separated from the mirrored section by a narrow slat, and the frame was either the dark-finished Federal style or the more elegant, often-gilded Sheraton.

Mirrors changed with the style of other furnishings; but whatever type you purchase, as long as the glass sections remain solid, even broken or flaking mirrors are more valued than replaced glass. Careful resilvering is acceptable if excessive deterioration has taken place. In the listings that follow, items are from the 19th century unless noted otherwise. The term 'style' (example: Federal style) is used to indicate a mirror reminiscent of, but made well after, the period indicated. Obviously these retro styles will be valued much lower than their original counterparts. Our advisor for this category is Michael Hinton; he is listed in the Directory under Pennsylvania.

Key:
Chpndl — Chippendale   QA — Queen Anne
Emp — Empire   Vict — Victorian
Fed — Federal   vnr — veneer

Wall mirror, Country Chippendale mahogany, decorative etched border on mirror plate, ca 1900, 18" high, EX, $700.00.

Bird's-eye & curly maple Chpndl-style scroll, 27x18" **225.00**
CI w/bronze pnt traces, 12x10" **150.00**
Co pine, old dk red, rvpt house scene, 23x14" **385.00**
Curly maple Chpndl-style scroll, natural finish, repro, 27" **110.00**
Ebonized QA-style w/chinoiserie decor, arched top, 55x30" **400.00**
Emp 2-part, brass rosettes, worn grpt decor, 29x14" **200.00**
Emp 2-part, mahog, rvpt fruit, 28x15½" **300.00**
Emp 2-part, mahog, rvpt fruit, 38x16" **300.00**
Emp 2-part half-post w/brass/gilt/ebony, rvpt scene, 28x13" **330.00**
Fed style, cherry/mahog, brass rosettes, 37x20" **475.00**
Fed style, mahog, 2-part, rvpt landscape, 33x18" **275.00**
George II, cvd/pierced crest, scrolled ears, 1770s, 27x16" **2,000.00**
Gilded, cvd, marble-top base, Willard & Woodworth NY, 72x60" ...**3,500.00**
Gilded, cvd grapes/basket crest, wine bbl below, 36x24" **1,100.00**
Gilded Emp, split columns, cvd cornucopias, 33x17" **250.00**
Gilded silver & gold, convex, 21¾" dia **220.00**
Gilded split baluster w/Edward Lothrop label, 46x31" **1,000.00**
Gilt gesso Classical, split balusters, 1830s, 33x22" **400.00**

Gilt gesso Fed, appl cornice, rvpt panel, 1815, 44x20" **1,840.00**
Hitchcock-type Sheraton, rvpt sailing scene, wear, 21x11" **200.00**
Mahog & gilt Georgian, broken-arch pediment w/phoenix finial, 55" .**3,000.00**
Mahog & parcel gilt Colonial style, phoenix/scroll top, 53" **500.00**
Mahog Chpndl Revival, brass rosettes, cvd posts, 71x33" **1,500.00**
Mahog Chpndl scroll, gilt eagle, 18x12" **500.00**
Mahog Chpndl scroll, top & bottom crest, rstr, 22x12" **200.00**
Mahog Chpndl scroll on pine, 20x13" **450.00**
Mahog Chpndl scroll on pine w/gilt eagle finial, 48x25" **650.00**
Mahog Chpndl scroll w/gilt, Am, late 1700s, 36x19" **1,500.00**
Mahog Chpndl scroll w/gilt, foliate crest, 18th C, 45x25" **2,500.00**
Mahog Chpndl scroll w/gilt, phoenix crest, 1790s, 31" **1,500.00**
Mahog Chpndl scroll w/gilt & blk decor, 48x24" **700.00**
Mahog Chpndl vnr w/gilt, scrolled crest, Am, 41x22" **1,000.00**
Mahog Chpndl-style scroll, old rprs/dk finish, 25x15" **300.00**
Mahog Chpndl-style scroll w/reeded fr, rvpt scene, 1900s, 48x22" .**225.00**
Mahog QA scroll, rpr crest, 15x9⅝" **385.00**
Mahog QA scroll, rprs, 25x12¾" **600.00**
Mahog scroll w/inlay, some age, rfn, 30x17½" **415.00**
Mahog vnr Chpndl w/shell inlay, ca 1775, old rfn/rprs, 33x18" .**1,000.00**
Neoclassical, gold rpt, 20th C, 45x29" **270.00**
Over-the-mantle, classical detail, gilded, 1900s, 61x23" **365.00**
Over-the-mantle, gilt/gesso on wood w/cartouch, 1870s, 60x50" ..**700.00**
Over-the-mantle, rococo gilt & gesso, 1860s, 61x56" **500.00**
Pier, Eastlake Vict walnut & rosewood, marble shelf, 102" **1,000.00**
Pier, gilt gesso Fed, VG detail, orig glass, 59x35" **2,000.00**
Pier, walnut Vict Eastlake, marble top, appl crest/hooks, 92" **900.00**
Pier, walnut w/stick & ball decor, gray marble top, 95x29" **700.00**
Rosewood w/maple Harlequin decor, appl spool trns, 11x13" **300.00**
Shaving, chinoiserie bow-front, blk rpt w/gilt, dvtl drws, 32" **700.00**
Shaving, mahog Am w/trn columns, swell-front drw, 1830s, 21" ..**225.00**
Shaving, mahog Emp, trn ft, 2 rnded dvtl drws, 27" **300.00**
Shaving, mahog Emp on pine, dvtl drws, trn posts, 23x18" **270.00**
Shaving, mahog w/inlay, beveled mirror, early 1900s, 14¾" **275.00**
Shaving, poplar folky Vict, cvd details, lift lid, 26" **245.00**
Shaving, walnut European Emp w/brass trim, dvtl drw, crest, 31" ..**385.00**
Venetian glass, reverse eng floral scrolls, 27x34" **400.00**
Walnut Chpndl scroll, molded fr w/appl compo eagle on crest, 30" **330.00**
Walnut Chpndl scroll w/gilt, England, 1750s, 36x20" **1,500.00**
Walnut Chpndl scroll w/gilt leaves, phoenix crest, rfn, 44x24" ..**990.00**
Walnut Chpndl scroll w/gilt liner & eagle at crest, 23x12" **525.00**
Walnut George II, cvd crest, molded fr, rpl glass, 34x14" **800.00**

Mocha

Mochaware is utilitarian pottery made principally in England (and to a lesser extent in France) between 1780 and 1840 on the then prevalent creamware and pearlware bodies. Initially, only those pieces decorated in the seaweed pattern were called 'Mocha,' while geometrically decorated pieces were referred to as 'Banded Creamware.' Other types of decorations were called 'Dipped Ware.' During the last thirty to forty years the term 'Mocha' has been applied to the entire realm of 'Industrialized Slipware' — pottery decorated by the turner on his lathe using coggle wheels and slip cups.

Mocha was made in numerous patterns — Tree, Seaweed or Dandelion, Rope (also called Worm or Loop), Cat's-eye, Tobacco Leaf, Lollypop or Balloon, Marbled, Marbled and Combed, Twig, Geometric or Checkered, Banded, and slip decorations of rings, dots, flags, tulips, wavy lines, etc. It came into its own as a collectible in the latter half of the 1940s and has become increasingly popular as more and more people are exposed to the rich colorings and artistic appeal of its varied forms of abstract decoration.

The collector should take care not to confuse the early pearlware

and creamware Mocha with the later kitchen yellow ware, graniteware, and ironstone sporting mocha-type decoration that was produced in America by such potters as J. Vodrey, George S. Harker, Edwin Bennett, and John Bell. This type was also produced in Scotland and Wales and was marketed well into the 20th century.

Bowl, earthworm, 3-color on orange band, brn stripes, 3x5⅝" ...**550.00**
Bowl, mixing; cat's eye, brn on wht band w/bl, 5¾x13", EX ...**1,000.00**
Bowl, mixing; scrolled leaves, bl on wht band, 5½x12¼", EX **450.00**
Jar, earthworm & cat's eyes, 3-color on bl band, rprs, 5" **495.00**
Mug, seaweed, blk/bl stripes on olive-gray band, 3¾" **200.00**
Mustard pot, earthworm, 3-color, tan band, blk stripes, rpr, 2½" .**600.00**
Mustard pot, seaweed, bl & blk stripes, leaf hdl, stripe lid, 3" **330.00**
Pepper pot, bl stripe, narrow cream bands, blk stripes, 4" **450.00**
Pepper pot, cat's eye, mc on dk brn band, ovoid, ftd, 4¾" **1,050.00**
Pepper pot, seaweed, blk on orange band, 2 yel bands, w/lid, 4" .**900.00**
Pepper pot, seaweed, brn on yel band, 3¾", EX **475.00**
Pitcher, milk; cat's eye, wht on bl band, wht stripes, 6⅛" **2,200.00**
Pitcher, milk; earthworm, bl/blk/tan stripes, bl band, 6¾" **1,150.00**
Pitcher, milk; seaweed, blk on brn band w/gr & bl stripes, 6⅝" .**1,500.00**
Pitcher, milk; seaweed, gr & blk on bl-gray band, 4⅝", EX **500.00**
Salt cellar, seaweed, blk on orange band, yel bands, master **650.00**
Salt cellar, wavy lines, wht on gray band w/blk stripes, 2½x3" **330.00**
Shaker, earthworm, 3-color w/blk stripe, bl band & top, 5", EX ..**330.00**
Shaker, seaweed, blk on orange band w/brn stripes, 4⅛", NM **465.00**
Shaker, seaweed, blk w/tan bands, blk strips, 4⅛", EX **220.00**
Tankard measure, seaweed, blk on gray band, blk/bl stripes, pt ..**140.00**
Tankard measure, seaweed, blk on gray band, blk/bl stripes, qt ..**120.00**

Molds

Food molds have become popular as collectibles — not only for their value as antiques, but because they also revive childhood memories of elaborate ice cream Santas with candy trim or barley sugar figurals adorning a Christmas tree. Ice cream molds were made of pewter and came in a wide variety of shapes and styles. Chocolate molds were made in fewer shapes but were more detailed. They were usually made of tin, copper, and occasionally of pewter. Hard candy molds were usually metal, although primitive maple sugar molds (usually simple hearts, rabbits, and other animals) were carved from wood. (Unless otherwise indicated, those in our listings are cast aluminum or stainless steel.) Cake molds were made of cast iron or cast aluminum and were most common in the shape of a lamb, a rabbit, or Santa Claus. Our advisors for this category are Dale and Jean Van Kuren; they are listed in the Directory under New York.

Chocolate Molds

Three different minstrels joined by straps, Germany, ca 1927, 6x9½", $200.00.

Astronaut **75.00**
Bride & Groom, 10", ea **140.00**
Bulldog **35.00**
Bunny pulling cart of eggs, 4" **25.00**

Cartoon cat w/long neck **295.00**
Cat, sitting, much detail, 2-pc w/clamps, 3⅞x3¾" **110.00**
Champagne bottle, Germany, 4¾" **30.00**
Charlie Chaplin **255.00**
Chicken, S&Co #173 ....**55.00**
Chicken on nest, lg **65.00**
Circus elephant, 2-part, 4¼" **160.00**
Easter rabbit, Germany, 2-pc, rpl clips, 20" **175.00**
Easter rabbit, 2-pc, Anton Reiche, Dresden Germany, 18½" **220.00**
Father Christmas on donkey, 2-pc w/clamps, 3⅛x3⅛" **95.00**
Heart w/Cupid, S&Co #1102 ....**40.00**
Hen, 5" **35.00**
Hen on basket, lg **60.00**
Hen on nest, 2¾" **25.00**
Jack-o'-lantern, 2-pc, folding **66.00**
Jeep **85.00**
Lion, 2-pc, 6½" **65.00**
Little Red Riding Hood **175.00**
Model T, Germany, 7½" **175.00**
Pig, standing, 2-pc w/clamps, 6¼x3" **87.00**
Rabbit, Eppelsheimer & Co, lt rust, 11¼" **150.00**
Rabbit, full body, TC Weygandt Co, 2-pc w/clip, EX **30.00**
Rabbit, running, 10½" **75.00**
Rabbit, sitting, 2-pc w/clamps, 7¾x7½" **85.00**
Rabbit, 3-part, tin mold in steel fr, 13½" **220.00**
Rabbit, 6½" **30.00**
Rabbit in convertible **145.00**
Rabbit on stool, 6¼" **30.00**
Rabbit w/basket, 2-pc, Made in Germany, 7½" **105.00**
Rabbit w/umbrella, Dresden, 7¼" **200.00**
Ram **85.00**
Santa, 4" **145.00**
Scottie **65.00**
Shoe, sm **60.00**
Smokey the Bear, metal, 8½" **58.00**
Snowman **65.00**
Train, lg **95.00**
Turkey **95.00**

Hard Candy Molds

Battleship in waves, TM-256, groove for stick, 2½x1¼" **55.00**
Elephant, TM-138, groove for stick, 1¾x1¼" **62.50**
Lion, 3-part, TM-40, groove for stick, 4x5" **115.00**
Locomotive, 3-part, TM-14, groove for stick, 3½x6" **125.00**
Mouse, TM-37, groove for stick, 2¼x1¼" **90.00**
Pipe, TM-88, groove for stick, 3½x¾" **45.00**
Rat, TM-238, groove for stick, 2½x1" **80.00**
Steamboat w/paddle wheel, groove for stick, 1¼x2¼" **90.00**
Teddy bear, walnut, rtcl, 2-part, makes 6, 1½x12" **130.00**

Ice Cream Molds

Airplane **95.00**
Automobile, hinged, unmk, 2¼x4" **30.00**
Bananas, E&Co NY **65.00**
Battleship, hinged, #513, S&Co, 2½x2¼x5⅞" **35.00**
Boy on motorcycle **130.00**
Bull **95.00**
Cardinal bird **75.00**
Chameleon, #576 ....**100.00**
Cogged wheel, hinged, 4¼x3⅞" **10.00**
Donkey, hinged, #630 K, 4⅝x4½" **40.00**
Football **45.00**

Grapes, E&Co NY **65.00**
Mr Mouse **65.00**
O'possum, #616 ....**95.00**
Stork w/baby **125.00**
Toy soldier **130.00**

Maple Sugar Molds

Beaver, hand cvd, EX detail, 5x9" **125.00**
Cow, 2-part, varnished, 4½x7" **95.00**
Fruit & foliage, hardwood, 2-part, 5½x8" **50.00**
Heart & clover, primitive, 5x17½" **75.00**
Heart w/face, hand cvd, in orig tin case, 1800s, 5½" **425.00**

Indian on horse, well carved, two-part, $95.00.

Rabbit sitting, EX cvg, 1¼x6½x5" **75.00**
Strawberry, deeply cvd pine, dvtl, 1830s, 1¾x5½x9" **165.00**

Miscellaneous

Bronze, for cast pewter spoons, 8" **250.00**
CI, fruit, vegetable & leaf designs, hdls, 1½x16x8" **125.00**
Ladyfinger, aluminum, England, 4", set of 6, MIB **15.00**
Pewter, fruit at top, removable base, mk 1-qt, 6⅝" dia **195.00**
Tin, apple/plums/grapes, scalloped sides, 4½x8½" **85.00**
Tin, fish, jumping, 9", w/hanging rings **9.00**
Tin, melon, 2-part, mk Kreamer, 4x5¼x2½" **40.00**
Tin/copper, lion top w/ruffled sides, 8" L **220.00**

Monmouth

The Monmouth Pottery Company was established in 1892 in Monmouth, Illinois. Their primary products were salt-glazed stoneware crocks, churns, jugs, bristol, spongeware, and brown glaze. In 1906 they were absorbed by a conglomerate called the Western Stoneware Company. Monmouth became their #1 plant and until 1930 continued to produce stoneware marked with their maple leaf logo. Items marked 'Monmouth Pottery Co.' were made before 1906. Western Stoneware Co. introduced a line of artware in 1926. The name chosen for the artware was Monmouth Pottery. Some stamps and paper labels add ILL to the name.

Churn, bristol glaze, 2-gal **250.00**
Churn, salt glazed, 3-gal, M **350.00**
Cookie jar **50.00**
Cooler, ice water; bl & wht sponge, w/lid & spigot, 8-gal **2,000.00**
Cow & calf, brn, mk Monmouth Pottery Co, M **2,000.00**
Crock, bristol glaze, 20-gal **100.00**
Crock, bristol glaze, 60-gal, M **700.00**
Crock, bristol & Albany glaze, 1-qt, M **100.00**
Crock, early dull bristol glaze, cobalt stencil **300.00**
Crock, salt glazed, hand decor, base mk, 2-gal, M **125.00**

Pig, brn, mk Monmouth Pottery Co, M **1,000.00**
Snuff or preserve jar, bristol glaze, wax seal, M **350.00**
Water cooler, Ice Water, bl & wht sponge, 5-gal, M **2,000.00**

Monot and Stumpf

The firm of Monot and Stumpf was organized in 1868, the merger of the E.S. Monot and F. Stumpf glassworks. It was located in Pantin, France. They produced fine art glass of various types until ca 1892, when the company reorganized and became known as the Cristallerie de Pantin.

Bowl, pk powl w/gold lustre int, folded in rim, sq, 6" **125.00**
Cheese dish, pk striped opal, gold lustre int, 7½x6¼" **195.00**
Salt cellar, pk opal, gold lustre int, 1¼x2⅞x2¼" **65.00**
Salt cellar, pk opal, gold lustre int, 1½x2⅛x1¾" **65.00**
Salt cellar, wht opal, striped oval w/gold, 1⅛x1¾" **65.00**
Vase, Optic, pk opal, bulbous w/sq top, 4¼x5" **110.00**

Mont Joye

Mont Joye was a type of acid-cut French cameo glass produced by Cristallerie de Pantin in Paris around the turn of the century. It is accented by enamels. Our advisor for this category is Don Williams; he is listed in the Directory under Missouri.

Bowl, iris int, trn-in rim, ftd, 3½x9¾x7" **435.00**
Dish, floral/buds, gold/wht/yel on gray texture, 4-lobe, 6" **400.00**
Pickle castor, frosted w/HP orchids; ornate SP fr & lid **395.00**
Vase, acorns/leaves, gold/silver on textured emerald, 13x9" **1,000.00**
Vase, hollyhock w/gr leaves on golden-brn frost, 10" **1,200.00**
Vase, Nouveau floral, gilt on irid, cylindrical, 11½" **850.00**
Vase, peonies, 4-sided, 8½", EX **750.00**
Vase, thistles/scrolls on ice gr to opaque, shouldered, 12" **1,200.00**
Vase, violets, purple on frost w/gold, 6" **450.00**

Moon and Star

Moon and Star was originally produced in the 1880s by John Adams & Company of Pittsburgh. In the 1960s, Joseph Weishar of Wheeling, West Virginia, owner of the Island Mould & Machine Company, reproduced some of the original molds and incorporated the pattern into approximately forty new and different items. Two of the largest distributors of this line were L.E. Smith of Mt. Pleasant, Pennsylvania, who pressed their own glass, and L.G. Wright of New Martinsville, West Virginia, who had theirs pressed by Fostoria, Fenton, and Westmoreland. Both companies carried a large and varied assortment of shapes and colors. Several other companies were involved in its manufacture as well, especially of the smaller items.

Over the years the glassware has been pressed in amberina (yellow shading to orange- or ruby-red), green, amber, crystal, light blue, and ruby. Pieces in ruby and light blue are most collectible and harder to find than the other colors, which seem to be abundant. Purple, pink, cobalt, amethyst, tan slag, and light green and blue opalescent were made, too, but on a lesser scale.

Current L.E. Smith catalogs contain a small assortment of pieces that are still available in crystal, pink, cobalt (lighter than the old shade), and these colors with an iridized finish. A new color, teal green, was introduced in 1992, a water set in sapphire blue opalescent was pressed in 1993, and the new color in 1994 was cranberry ice. Items are currently being pressed in various colors by the Weishar Company, who

add their mark to the new glassware which is made primarily for collectors. Our values are given for ruby and light blue. For amberina, green, and amber, deduct 20%.

Ashtray, moons at rim, star in base, 6-sided, 8½" **25.00**
Banana boat, allover pattern, scalloped rim, 12" **45.00**
Basket, allover pattern, scalloped rim, solid hdl, 9" **75.00**
Bell, pattern along sides, plain rim & hdl, 6" **40.00**
Butter dish, allover pattern, scalloped rim, star finial, ¼-lb **45.00**
Cake stand, allover pattern, plate removes from std, 11" dia **95.00**
Candle lamp, patterned shade, clear base, 2-pc, 7½" **25.00**
Canister, allover pattern, 1-lb or 2-lb, from $12 to **15.00**
Chandelier, ruffled dome shape w/allover pattern, 10" **100.00**
Cheese dish, patterned base, plain clear lid, 9½" **70.00**
Compote, allover pattern, scalloped ft, patterned lid, 8x4" **40.00**
Creamer & sugar bowl, open, disk ft, sm **28.00**
Cruet, vinegar; 6¾" **75.00**
Decanter, bulbous w/allover pattern, plain neck, 32-oz, 12" **60.00**
Epergne, allover pattern, 1-lily, flared bowl, scalloped ft **95.00**
Lamp, oil; allover pattern, all orig, 10", from $100 to **125.00**

Pitcher, patterned body, straight sides, plain disk foot, one-quart, 7½", $65.00 in ruby or light blue; $50.00 for other colors.

Relish tray, moons form scalloped rim, star base, rectangular, 8" ..**35.00**
Shakers, allover pattern, metal lids, 4x2", pr **25.00**
Soap dish, allover pattern, oval, 2x6" **12.00**
Sugar shaker, allover pattern, metal lid, 4½x3½" **40.00**
Tumbler, iced tea; no pattern at rim or ft, 11-oz, 5½" **20.00**
Tumbler, no pattern at rim or disk ft, 5-oz, 3½" **14.00**
Tumbler, no pattern at rim or disk ft, 7-oz, 4½" **15.00**

Moorcroft

William Moorcroft began to work for MacIntyre Potteries in 1897. At first he was the chief designer but very soon took over their newly created Art Pottery department. His first important design was the Aurelian Ware, part transfer and part hand painted. Very shortly thereafter, around the turn of the century, he developed his famous Florian Ware, with heavy slip, done in mostly blue and white. Since the early 1900s there has been a sucession of designs, most of them very characteristic of the company. Moorcroft left MacIntyre in 1913 and went out on his own. He had already established his name, having won prizes and gold medals at the St. Louis World's Fair as well as in Paris. In 1929 Queen Mary, who had been collecting his pottery, made him 'Potter to the Queen,' and the pottery was so stamped up until 1949. William Moorcroft died in 1945, and his son Walter ran the company until recent years. The factory is still in existence. They now produce different designs but continue to use the characteristic slipwork. Moorcroft pottery was sold abroad in Canada, the United States, Australia, and Europe as well as in specialty areas such as the island of Bermuda.

Moorcroft went through a 'Japanese' stage in the early teens with his lovely lustre glazes, Oriental shapes, and decorations. During the mid-teens he began to produce his most popular Pomegranate Ware, and Wisteria (often called 'Fruit'). Around that time he also designed the popular Pansy line as well as Leaves and Grapes. Soon he introduced a beautiful landscape series called variously Hazeldine, Moonlit Blue, Eventide, and Dawn. These wonderful designs along with Claremont (Mushrooms) seem to be the most sought after by collectors today. It would be possible to add many other designs to this list.

During the 1920s and '30s, Moorcroft became very interested in highly fired Flambe (red) glazes. These could only be achieved through a very difficult procedure which he himself perfected in secret. He later passed the knowledge on to his son.

Dating of this pottery is done by knowledge of the designs, shapes, signatures, and marks on the bottom of each piece; an experienced person can usually narrow it down to a short time frame. Prices escalated for this 'rediscovered' pottery in the late 1980s but has now leveled off. This is true mainly of the pre-1935 designs of William Moorcroft, as it is items from that era that attract the most collector interest. Prices in the listings below are for pieces in mint condition unless noted otherwise; no reproductions are listed here. Advisors for this category are Wilfred and Dolli Cohen; they are listed in the Directory under California.

Bowl, Claremont, toadstools in purple/gr/bl/yel, 12" L **1,995.00**
Bowl, cornflowers, rose/bl/wine on sage gr to bl, ftd, 3x6" **1,350.00**
Bowl, Eventide landscape, imp mk, ca 1925, 8¼" **1,450.00**
Bowl, hibiscus on gr, 1½x3¾" **80.00**
Bowl, pansies on dk bl, mks, ca 1945, 4½" **150.00**
Box, floral bouquet, red/yel/dk bl on shaded bl, label, 4½" dia ...**245.00**
Candlesticks, wisteria, wht/yel/wine/rose on dk bl, 8½", pr **900.00**
Candlesticks, wisteria on bl, pewter bobeches/ft, ca 1925, 6", pr ..**750.00**
Charger, heron & reeds in dk bl against sunset, 14" **220.00**
Cup & saucer, demitasse; 18th-C pattern, MacIntyre **450.00**
Humidor, Florian, poppies on gr & bl, screw-on lid, 3¾" H **1,895.00**
Jar, wisteria, purple/red/yel/br on dk bl, w/lid, #869, 10" **895.00**
Lamp base, pomegranates, wine/purple on dk bl, 13x8", +shade .**1,195.00**
Plate, swans, wht & blk on gr, sgn WM, MIE, 10¼" **85.00**
Sweet dish, Moonlit Bl, Tudric pewter mts, '25, 4½x2¾" **795.00**
Tea set, wisteria, mc w/SP trim, 1925, 4½" pot+cr/sug **1,295.00**
Vase, anemones, purple/bl/red on dk bl/gr, 6" **250.00**
Vase, anemones on bl, bulbous top half, mk, #3, 9⅛" **400.00**
Vase, Aurelian, floral transfer, tapered, hdls, 8" **1,500.00**
Vase, Bermuda Lily, flared cylinder, Royal Warrant label, 14⅝" ..**1,000.00**
Vase, clematis on bright flambe, MIE, 5" **350.00**
Vase, clematis on flambe, classic form, MIE, 12⅛" **500.00**
Vase, clematis on maroon flambe w/snowflake crystals, MIE, 9½" ..**550.00**
Vase, Flaminian, red flambe, shouldered, 6" **750.00**
Vase, landscape, bright colors, MIE, 1980s, 7½" **475.00**
Vase, Lions' Den, rampant lion on cobalt, ltd ed, 1988, 9¾" **600.00**
Vase, Moonlit Bl, trees on dk bl, #M94, bulbous, 8½" **1,950.00**
Vase, Moonlit Bl, turq trees on cobalt, 5x5" **1,495.00**
Vase, orchids on cobalt, MIE, #5, 7⅜" **350.00**
Vase, orchids on cobalt, MIE, #8, 10" **400.00**
Vase, orchids on cobalt & orange, MIE, 5⅝" **400.00**
Vase, orchids on orange (possibly flambe), MIE, 9⅛" **650.00**
Vase, pansies on bl, bulbous upper portion, MIE, 9⅛" **425.00**
Vase, pansies on cobalt, hdls, MIE, #5, 8⅛" **500.00**
Vase, Persian, floral, red/bl/ivory/gr panels on gr, 9½" **2,950.00**
Vase, pomegranates, gourd shape, Royal Warrant label/MIE, 9" ..**650.00**
Vase, pomegranates on cobalt, bottle neck, MIE, 8⅛" **650.00**
Vase, pomegranates on cobalt, bulbous bottom, MIE, 6⅛" **300.00**
Vase, pomegranates on cobalt, flared rim, Burslem, 10¼" **850.00**
Vase, pomegranates on cobalt, hdl, Burslem England, #5, 8¼" ..**700.00**
Vase, spring flowers, mc on pale flambe, can neck, MIE, 7" **650.00**
Vase, swans, wht & blk on gr pond, #187/350, 7" **220.00**
Vase, wisteria on cobalt, stick neck, MIE, 11½" **895.00**

Moravian Pottery and Tile Works

The Moravian Pottery and Tile Works, Doylestown, Pennsylvania, was founded by Dr. Henry Chapman Mercer in 1898. He discovered the art and science of tile making on his own, without training from the existing American or European tile industry. This, along with his diverse talents as an author, anthropologist, historian, and artist, led Dr. Mercer to create something very unique. He approached tile design with an historic point of view, and he created totally new production methods that ultimately became widely accepted by manufacturers of handcrafted tile. The subject matter for the designs he preferred included nature and the arts, colonial tools and artifacts, storytelling, and medieval themes. Both of these 'new' approaches, to design and production, allowed Dr. Mercer to become extremely influential in the development of pottery and tile in the Arts & Crafts Movement in America.

After Mercer's death in 1930, the Tile Works was managed by Frank Swain until 1954. In 1967 it was purchased by the Bucks County Dept. of Parks & Recreation. Tiles are being produced there today in the handmade tradition of Mercer; they are marked with a conjoined MOR and dated. Collectors look for the early tiles (mostly pre-1940), the preponderance of which bear no backstamps. These tiles were made using both red and white clays and are also referred to as 'Mercer' tiles. Our advisor is Karen Guido; she is listed in the Director under Connecticut.

Tile, Mayflower, green and cream with red flush, 4", $85.00.

Tile, artist's palette, w/Latin, bl/cream w/red flush, 3¾", NM **75.00**
Tile, Birds of Tintern Abbey, bl matt, red clay, 5x5¾" **165.00**
Tile, Bounty ship, bl/wht underglazed, filigree border, 4" **65.00**
Tile, Flying Dutchman ship, gr/bl/red flush, high glaze, 4" **75.00**
Tile, La Perouse ship, gr/cream w/red flush, high glaze, 4" **85.00**
Tile, Leo zodiac sm brocade, bl, high glaze **40.00**
Tile, Montezuma (city), bl/cream w/red flush, high glaze, 4" **155.00**
Tile, Quarter Wheel, gr/cream w/red flush, high glaze, 4" **55.00**
Tile, scaled dragon, bl & red clay, unglazed, 2" **40.00**
Tile, St John, gr/cream w/red flush, high glaze, 4" **180.00**
Tile, tulip (1), stove tile, yel/brn, red clay, 5½x7" **265.00**

Morgantown Glass

Incorporated in 1899, the Morgantown Glass Works experienced many name changes over the years. Today 'Morgantown Glass' is a generic term used to identify all glass produced there. Purchased by Fostoria in 1965, the factory was permanently closed in 1971. Our advisor for this category is Jerry Gallagher, longtime researcher of the company and author of *A Handbook of Old Morgantown Glass, Volume I*. He is listed in the Directory under Minnesota. See Clubs, Newsletters, and Catalogs for information concerning The Morgantown Collectors of America (a research society founded by him), and *The Morgantown Newscaster*, a triannual M.C.A. journal with research updates and reports of current trends.

Adair etch, crystal/gold; stem, goblet; #7604½, 10-oz **125.00**

Adam etch, crystal; stem, champagne; #7810 Monaco, 5-oz **38.00**
Adonis etch, crystal; stem, goblet; #7604½ Heirloom, 9-oz **60.00**
Adonis etch, crystal/gr; stem, goblet; #7606½ Athena, 9-oz **120.00**
Adonis etch, rose; stem, goblet; #7604½ Heirloom, 9-oz **75.00**
Adonis etch, topaz; stem, goblet; #7604½ Heirloom, 9-oz **70.00**
Am Beauty etch, crystal; jug, no lid, #2 Arcadia, 54-oz **395.00**
Am Beauty etch, crystal; stem, champagne; #7695 Trumpet, 6-oz ...**48.00**
Am Beauty etch, crystal; stem, wine; #7668 Galaxy, 5-oz **55.00**
Am Beauty etch, crystal; stem, wine; #7695 Trumpet, 2½-oz **70.00**
Am Beauty etch, crystal; stem wine; #7668 Galaxy, 5-oz **55.00**
Am Beauty etch, crystal; tumbler, iced tea; #8701 Garret, 14-oz ..**45.00**
Am Beauty etch, crystal; tumbler, juice; #7668 Galaxy, 6-oz **38.00**
Am Beauty etch, crystal; tumbler, water; #9715 Calhoun, 10-oz ..**45.00**
Am Beauty etch, rose; finger bowl, #2927, 4¼" **95.00**
Am Beauty etch, rose; stem, goblet; #7565 Astrid, 10-oz **125.00**
Am Beauty etch, rose-amber; jug, w/lid, #39 Milton, 54-oz **500.00**
Aquaria etch, crystal; stem, goblet; #7640 Art Moderne **145.00**
Aquaria etch, crystal/gr; stem, goblet; #7643 Oceana, 9-oz **95.00**
Art Moderne, cobalt/crystal; stem, cordial; #7640, 1½-oz **155.00**
Art Moderne, crystal/blk; stem, goblet; #7640, 9-oz **120.00**
Art Moderne, crystal/frost; stem, icer; sgn DC Thorpe, 2-pc **250.00**
Baden etch, blk filament; stem, goblet; #7606½ Athena, 9-oz ...**100.00**
Baden etch, crystal/blk; jug, ftd, #49 Jubilee, 54-oz **500.00**
Baden etch, crystal/blk; tumbler, ftd; #7661 Camilla, 6-oz **60.00**
Barry #37, crystal/rose; jug, hdld/ftd, Palm Optic, 48-oz **500.00**
Barry #37, Meadow Gr/Jade; jug, hdld/ftd, 84-oz **625.00**
Bartley #7637, gr/cased Alabaster/gr; tumbler, ftd, 13-oz **95.00**
Biscayne etch, crystal/gold; tumbler, bar; #9715, 2½-oz **68.00**
Bramble Rose etch, crystal; stem, champagne; #7577 Venus, 5½-oz ..**58.00**
Bramble Rose etch, rose; plate, luncheon; #1500, 8½" **45.00**
Candlespheres, Old Amethyst; #8 Mars, pr **300.00**
Carlton, platinum Marco; bowl, flared, #4355 Janice, 13" **275.00**
Carlton, platinum Marco; stem, goblet; #7653 Cantata, 9-oz **82.00**
Carlton etch, crystal/blk; stem, sherbet; #7606½, 5½-oz **70.00**
Carlton frostie etch, crystal; punch bowl, #21, 12" **650.00**
Carlton Milan, crystal; stem, goblet; #7668 Galaxy, 10-oz **32.50**
Cathay etch, crystal; stem, champagne; #7711, Callahan, 5½-oz .**50.00**
Cherry Blossom etch, topaz; stem, champagne; #7577, 5½-oz **50.00**
Cherry Blossom etch, topaz; stem, goblet; #7577 Venus, 9-oz **75.00**

Circlet, #24, 24-oz decanter with 3-oz. footed bar tumblers, Old Amethyst with platinum decor, rare, $1,200.00 for the set.

Photo courtesy Jerry Gallagher

Corinth etch, crystal/gold; stem, wine; #7654 Lorna, 3-oz **70.00**
Courtney #7637, crystal/DC Thorpe decor; stem, claret; 4½-oz .**280.00**
Crinkle, amethyst; San Juan, tankard, #1962, 54-oz, 9" **100.00**
Crinkle, crystal; Tiajuana, juice/martini, #1962, 34-oz, 6½" **70.00**
Crinkle, gr; Ockner jug, #1962, 54-oz **145.00**
Crinkle, lt bl frosted; tumbler, flat, #1962, 20-oz **38.00**
Crinkle, peacock bl; Ockner jug, #1962, 54-oz **130.00**
Crinkle, peacock bl; tumbler, juice; flat, #1962, 6-oz **26.00**

Crinkle, peacock bl; tumbler, water; flat, #1962, 10-oz **26.00**
Crinkle, ruby; Ockner jug, #1962, 54-oz **145.00**
Crinkle, ruby; Owl tumbler, highball; flat, #1969, 16-oz **135.00**
Eileen etch, crystal/gold #32 band; goblet; #7673 Lexington, 9-oz ...**125.00**
Elizabeth, azure; stem, goblet; #7630 Ballerina, 9-oz **130.00**
Elizabeth, crystal; stem, wine; #7630 Ballerina, 2¾-oz **95.00**
Fairwin, bl filament; stem, goblet; #7673 Lexington, 9-oz **135.00**
Faun etch, crystal/blk; champagne, #7640 Art Moderne, 5½-oz .**160.00**
Faun etch, crystal/blk; stem, goblet; #7640 Art Moderne, 9-oz ...**185.00**
Fernlee, crystal/blk; stem, goblet; #7640 Art Moderne, 9-oz **145.00**
Florence etch, crystal; stem, cocktail; #300 Touraine, 3-oz **45.00**
Floret etch, crystal; stem, goblet; #7684 Yale, 9-oz **110.00**
Floret etch, crystal; stemmed icer & insert; #7589 Laurette **95.00**
Golf Ball, cobalt/crystal; candlesticks, 2 styles, #7643, 4", pr **265.00**
Golf Ball, cobalt/crystal; stem, champagne; #7643, 5½-oz **52.00**
Golf Ball, cobalt/crystal; stem, goblet; #7643, 9-oz **58.00**
Golf Ball, pastel/crystal; stem, goblet; from $48 to **60.00**
Golf Ball, rose/gr finial; candy dish, flat, #2938 Helga, 5" **745.00**
Golf Ball, ruby/crystal; candy dish, #9074 Maureen, 4½" **400.00**
Golf Ball, ruby/crystal; candy dish, flat, #1212 Michael, 7" **525.00**
Golf Ball, ruby/crystal; compote, low, w/lid, #7643 Celeste **500.00**
Golf Ball, ruby/crystal; stem, goblet; #7643, 9-oz **58.00**
Guest set, Anna Rose; Palm optic, #25 Trudy, 2-pc **125.00**
Guest set, Azure; Festoon optic, #25 Trudy, 2-pc **135.00**
Guest set, Baby Bl opaque; Hollyhock decor, #23 Margaret **300.00**
Guest set, Golden Iris; hdls, pulled spout, #23 Margaret **450.00**
Guest set, yel opaque bottle/blk tumbler, #25 Trudy **275.00**
Hollywood, blk band; tumbler, highball; flat, #8701, 12-oz **55.00**
Kyoto etch, crystal/gr; stem, champagne; #7634 Tiburon, 6-oz ...**120.00**
Kyoto etch, crystal/gr; stem, goblet; #7634 Tiburon, 9-oz **150.00**
Labelle etch, crystal/gold band; stem, goblet; #7640 Art Moderne ..**110.00**
Lace Bouquet etch, cyrstal; stem, goblet; #7668 Galaxy, 10-oz **42.00**
LeMons, cobalt/gold; stem, goblet; #7640 Art Moderne, 9-oz **300.00**
LeMons, cobalt/platinum; stem, goblet; #7640 Art Moderne, 9-oz ...**250.00**
LMX (El Mexicano), Hyacinth; Ockner jug, #1933, 54-oz **350.00**
LMX (El Mexicano), Ice; candle holders, bulbous, #1933, 4", pr ...**325.00**
LMX (El Mexicano), Rose Quartz; ice tub, #1933 ....**310.00**
LMX (El Mexicano), Rose Quartz; Ockner jug, #1933, 54-oz **340.00**
LMX (El Mexicano), Rose Quartz; tumbler, ftd, #1933, 13-oz **68.00**
LMX (El Mexicano), Seaweed; decanter, liquor; w/stopper, #1933 .**275.00**
Marilyn etch, crystal/gr; stem, goblet; #7636 Square, 5½-oz **120.00**
Marilyn etch, crystal/rose; stem, champagne; #7636 Square, 5½-oz ..**135.00**
Mayfair etch, crystal; stem, goblet; #7668 Galaxy, 10-oz **38.00**
Maytime etch, topaz; stem, champagne; #7664½ Vernon, 5½-oz **42.00**
Melon, alabaster/cobalt hdl; beverage set, #20069, 7-pc **1,200.00**
Melon, frosted/blk hdl, Aurora etch; jug, #20069 ....**725.00**
Mikado etch, crystal; stem, goblet; #7711 Callahan, 10-oz **45.00**
Monroe #7690, cobalt or ruby/crystal; stem, champagne; 6-oz **75.00**
Monroe #7690, Golden Iris/crystal; stem, cordial; 1½-oz **120.00**
Monroe #7690, Old Amethyst/crystal; stem, cordial; 1½-oz **145.00**
Nantucket etch, crystal; stem, goblet; Queen Anne, 10-oz **95.00**
Nantucket etch, crystal/gr; stem, goblet; #7654 Lorna, 9-oz **85.00**
Nasreen etch, crystal/blk; tumbler, #9074 Belton, 9-oz **58.00**
Nasreen etch, topaz/crystal; stem, claret; #7665 Laura, 5-oz **95.00**
Old Bristol, cobalt w/opal rim; plate, unknown #, 7½" **95.00**
Old English #7678, cobalt/crystal; stem, champagne; 6½-oz **50.00**
Old English #7678, Stiegel Gr/crystal; stem, goblet; 10-oz **58.00**
Old English #7678, Stiegel Gr/crystal; stem, iced tea; 12-oz **58.00**
Palm Optic, Alexandrite; stem, cocktail; #7667 Georgian, 12-oz ..**250.00**
Palm Optic, Anna Rose; stem, goblet; 37477 Venus, 9-oz **95.00**
Palm Optic, Anna Rose/gr; stem, goblet; 37646 Sophisticate, 9-oz ..**90.00**
Palm Optic, Anna Rose/gr; stem, wine; #7614 Hampton, 3-oz **95.00**
Palm Optic, Azure; salver, ftd, unknown #, 7" **235.00**
Palm Optic, Azure; stem, parfait; #7536 Alycia, 5½-oz **50.00**

Palm Optic, crystal/Anna Rose; jug, #37 Barry, 48-oz **385.00**
Palm Optic, Venetian Gr; stem, goblet; #7577 Venus, 9-oz **50.00**
Paragon #7624, crystal/blk; stem, goblet; 9-oz **185.00**
Paragon #7624, crystal/blk; stem, sherbet; 5½-oz **110.00**
Paula #7675, Stiegel gr/crystal; stem, goblet; 10-oz **125.00**
Peacock Optic, gr or rose; stem, goblet; #7638 Avalon, 9-oz **48.00**
Peacock Optic, gr; tumbler, tar; flat, #9051 Zenith, 1½-oz **85.00**
Persian etch, crystal; marmalade jar, glass lid, #106 Willett **175.00**
Picardy etch, crystal; champagne, #7646 Sophisticate, 5½-oz **42.00**
Picardy etch, crystal; stem, goblet; #7646 Sophisticate, 9-oz **60.00**
Pineapple Optic, gr; stem, goblet; #7644½ Vernon, 9-oz **55.00**
Prairie Rose, crystal/gr; stem, goblet; #6046 Kirby **65.00**
Priscilla, blk filament; stem, champagne; #7620 Fontanne, 6-oz .**120.00**
Pygon #7623, crystal/blk; sherbet, 5-oz **110.00**
Pygon #7623, crystal/frosted; champagne, sgn Thorpe, 5½-oz **175.00**
Pygon #7623, frosted; wine, Thorpe HP bird decor, 3½-oz **265.00**
Reyer Thistle, crystal; stem, goblet; #7713 Scotia, 9-oz **45.00**
Reyer Thistle, crystal; stem, wine; #7668 Galaxy, 2½-oz **45.00**
Richmond etch, crystal; stem, goblet; #7570 Horizon, 10-oz **30.00**
Rosalie etch, crystal; bowl, console; #4355 Janice, 13" **260.00**
Rosalie etch, topaz/crystal; stem, goblet; #7662 Majesty, 10-oz ...**110.00**
Rosamonde etch, pnt crystal/Golden Iris; tumbler, #9074, 10-oz ..**165.00**
Saranac etch, crystal; stem, champagne; #7690 Monroe, 5½-oz ...**48.00**
Sea Gulls enamel decor, jug, #545 Pickford, 60-oz **475.00**
Sea Gulls enamel decor, tumbler, ftd, #9093, 12-oz **95.00**
Sharon etch, crystal/platinum; candlespheres, #8 Mars, pr **325.00**
Sharon etch, crystal/platinum; vase, ball shape, #8 Luna **200.00**
Sonoma etch, crystal; stem, goblet; #7659 Cynthia, 10-oz **68.00**
Sonoma etch, topaz; stem, goblet; #7659 Cynthia, 10-oz **90.00**
Square #7636, claret, DC Thorpe decor, 4½-oz **265.00**
Square #7636, crystal; champagne, 5½-oz **170.00**
Superba, blk filament; champagne, #7664 Queen Anne, 6½-oz .**145.00**
Superba, blk filament; goblet, #7664 Queen Anne, 10-oz **230.00**
Tinker Bell, crystal; guest set, #24 Maria, 4-pc, very rare **785.00**
Tinker Bell, gr; vase, bud; ftd, #43 Serenade, 10" **365.00**
Toulon gold stencil, rose; stem, goblet; #7604½, 10-oz **185.00**
Toulon gold stencil, rose; stem, parfait; #7604½, 6-oz **185.00**
Versailles, crystal; stem, goblet; #7711 Callahan, 10-oz **50.00**
Victoria, crystal; goblet; #300 Touraine, 9-oz **60.00**
Virginia etch, amber; stem, goblet; #7614 Hampton, 9-oz **55.00**
Virginia etch, crystal; stem, goblet; #7587 Hampton, 9-oz **45.00**
Yale #7684, cobalt or ruby; stem, goblet; 9-oz **165.00**
Yale #7684, Stiegel Gr; stem, goblet; 9-oz **155.00**

Continental Line

Ashley #4354, Golden Iris/crystal rim; basket, ftd, 10" dia **375.00**
Clayton #4357½, Spanish Red; basket, 10" dia **400.00**
Electra #35½, Spanish Red; vase, flower; hdls, 10" **390.00**
Irene #4356, amber/crystal rim; basket, 8-crimp, 10½" dia **395.00**
Jennie #20, Aquamarine/crystal hdl; basket, bonbon; 4½" dia ...**500.00**
Jupiter #71, Ritz Bl/crystal; vase, flower; Italian base, 6" **380.00**
Lyndale #64, Confetti; kerosene lamp, Italian base, 6" **750.00**
Neopolitan #64, blk, ivy ball, Italian base, 6" **575.00**
Patrick #4358, all crystal; basket, flower; 8-crimp, 6" dia **325.00**
Roma #68, Indian Blk; vase, flower; Italian base, 10" dia **380.00**
Vienna #71, Stiegel Gr; bowl, console; Italian base, 12" **1,000.00**
Ziegfeld #61, Spanish Red; witch ball, Italian base, 8" **900.00**

Silk-Screen Color Printing on Crystal

Manchester Pheasant, cocktail; #7664 Queen Anne, 3½-oz **195.00**
Manchester Pheasant, goblet; #7664 Queen Anne, 10-oz **225.00**
Queen Louise, crystal/rose; stem, cocktail; #7614 Hampton, 6-oz .**195.00**

Queen Louise, crystal/rose; stem, goblet; #7614 Hampton, 9-oz ...**245.00**

Sunrise Medallion Etch

#37 Barry, Azure; jug, ftd, 84-oz **645.00**
#37 Barry, crystal; jug, ftd, 80-oz **635.00**
#45 Catherine, gr or rose; vase, bud; ftd, 10" **460.00**
#53 Serenade, Azure; vase, bud; bulbous, ftd, 10" **480.00**
#7630 Ballerina, Azure; stem, goblet; 9-oz **100.00**
#7630 Ballerina, rose; stem, goblet; 9-oz **85.00**
#7630 Ballerina, topaz; stem, goblet; 9-oz **75.00**
#7654½ Legacy, crystal/Moonstone; stem, cocktail; 3-oz **195.00**
#7654½ Legacy, crystal/Moonstone; stem, goblet; 9-oz **260.00**
#7664 Queen Anne, crystal; stem, goblet; 10-oz **125.00**

Moriage

The term 'moriage' refers to certain Japanese wares decorated with applied slipwork designs. There are several methods used to achieve the characteristic relief effect. The decorative devices may be designed separately and applied to the vessel, piped on in narrow ribbons of clay (slip-trailed), or built up by brushing on successive layers of liquified slip. See also Dragon Ware; Nippon.

Ewer, white stylized flowers on green, 7", $195.00.

Bowl, purple flowers, beading at rim, 3-ftd, 2x6" **75.00**
Chocolate pot, floral in gold-fr reserves, moriage net, 9" **325.00**
Ginger jar, roses, teal w/allover beading, 4-sided **150.00**
Hair receiver, bl flowers w/moriage trim at top & on lid **75.00**
Pitcher, wisteria & vines, bl leaf mk, 10" **375.00**
Vase, roses in reserves, hdls, 9½" **195.00**

Mortars and Pestles

Mortars are bowl-shaped vessels used for centuries for the purpose of grinding drugs to a powder or grain into meal. The masher or grinding device is called a pestle.

Bell metal, 3⅜", w/pestle **70.00**
Brass, cast, mini, 1x1⅛", w/pestle **8.50**
Brass, diagonal zigzags, 3⅜x4⅜", w/7¾" pestle **42.00**
Brass, handmade design on top rim, 5x5", w/pestle **75.00**
Brass, 4", w/well-formed brass 8½" pestle **100.00**
Bronze, old dk patina, 3½x4¼", w/mismatched pestle **50.00**
Burl & poplar, old dark finish, 8", wear to pestle **85.00**
Cast-iron crescent shape, 16" L, wooden hdl on pestle **480.00**
Trn wood, old gray rpt, age cracks, 6¾" +unpnt pestle **30.00**

Mortens Studio

Oscar Mortens was already established as a fine sculptural artist when he left his native Sweden to take up residency in Arizona. During the 1940s he developed a line of detailed animal figures which were distributed through the Mortens Studios, a firm he co-founded with Gunnar Thelin. Thelin hired and trained artists to produce Mortens's line, which he called Royal Designs. More than two hundred dogs were modeled and over one hundred horses. Cats and wild animals such as elephants, panthers, deer, and elk were made, but on a much smaller scale. Bookends with sculptured dog heads were shown in their catalogs, and collectors report finding wall plaques on rare occasions. The material they used was a plaster-type composition with wires embedded to support the weight. Examples were marked 'Copyright by the Mortens Studio' either in ink or decal. Watch for flaking, cracks, and separations. Crazing seems to be present in some degree in many examples. When no condition is indicated, the items listed below are assumed to be in near-mint condition, allowing for minor crazing.

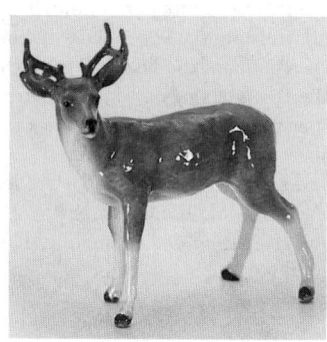

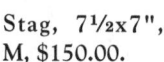
Stag, 7½x7",
M, $150.00.

Beagle, lying down, #554, 2¾" L	55.00
Boston Terrier, sitting, #793, 5½"	70.00
Boxer, fawn, standing, #755, 5½"	75.00
Chow pup, brn, #816, 3"	50.00
Cocker Spaniel, lying down, #516, 4½" L	50.00
Cocker Spaniel pup, golden tan, sitting, #820	40.00
Collie, recumbent, 9½"	125.00
Colt, standing, #714, 5x4½"	65.00
Dachshund, standing, #866, 6" L	65.00
Dachshund head plaque, lg, pr	475.00
Doberman Pinscher, standing, blk & rust, #783, 7¼"	90.00
Filly, chestnut brn, #716, 8½" H	95.00
German Shepherd pup, sitting, #844	55.00
Greyhound, gray, #747, 6¾"	100.00
Horse, blk, running, #112E	100.00
Horse, chestnut, running, #550, 3¾x5½"	85.00
Horse, golden-brn, running, #724, 7" L	100.00
Horse, gray, #652, 4½x5"	85.00
Irish Setter, red, 10½"	150.00
Irish Terrier pup, #814, 3"	50.00
Norwegian Elkhound, gray, #764, 5⅛"	110.00
Stallion, rearing, blk, #662, 4¾"	95.00

Morton Pottery

Six potteries operated in Morton, Illinois, at various times from 1877 to 1976. Each traced its origin to six brothers who immigrated to America to avoid military service in Germany. The Rapp brothers established their first pottery near clay deposits on the south side of town where they made field tile and bricks. Within a few years, they branched out to include utility wares such as jugs, bowls, jars, pitchers, etc. During the ninety-nine years of pottery operations in Morton, the original factory was expanded by some of the sons and nephews of the Rapps. Other family members started their own potteries where artware, gift-store items, and special-order goods were produced. The Cliftwood Art Pottery and the Morton Pottery Company had showrooms in Chicago and New York City during the 1930s. All of Morton's potteries were relatively short-lived operations with the Morton Pottery Company being the last to shut down on September 8, 1976. For a more thorough study of the subject, we recommend *Morton's Potteries: 99 Years, Vols. I* and *II*, by our advisors Doris and Burdell Hall; their address can be found in the Directory under Illinois.

Morton Pottery Works — Morton Earthenware Co. (1877 – 1917)

Acorn bank, brn	50.00
Crock, sauerkraut; Rockingham, w/press, 4-gal	150.00
Cuspidor, Rockingham, 7"	50.00
Jardiniere, cobalt, 7"	60.00
Jug, Rockingham, 8-pt	125.00
Mug, yellowware, banded, 1-pt	85.00
Paperweight, buffalo, brn, w/advertising, 2½"	55.00
Pitcher, mc (gr/brn/yel), #245, 6"	125.00

Cliftwood Art Potteries, Inc. (1920 – 1940)

Ashtray, brn chocolate drip, w/holders for cigarettes & matches	40.00
Bookends, squirrel on log, brn chocolate drip, 5½x5½x3", pr	110.00
Bowl, Viking ship, 14" L, w/dragon candle holder, ivory/turq, 6"	200.00
Compote, mint; bl matt, 3x6¼"	35.00
Creamer, cow figural, brn chocolate drip, 6½x3½x1½"	75.00
Flowerpot, cobalt, 5½"	25.00
Jardiniere, brn chocolate drip, 5½"	35.00
Miniature, elephant, bl/gray, 5½x3x1½"	60.00
Miniature, lion, yel/brn, 6x3¼x1"	70.00
Miniature, lioness, yel/brn, 6¾x3¼x1"	50.00
Stein, bbl shape, German motto on wht, 4½"	30.00
Tray, card; ivory matt w/turq gloss int, 3¾x6½x4"	40.00

Midwest Potteries, Inc. (1940 – 1944)

Ashtray, hand on tray, 14k gold, 4½"	25.00
Creamer, cow figural, wht w/14k gold decor, 5½x7x2"	20.00
Miniature, camel, brn, 2"	10.00
Miniature, lion, brn/wht, 1¾"	12.00
Miniature, polar bear, wht, 2"	10.00
Miniature, turtle, gr, 1"	8.00
Planter, cat holds cactus tail, wht, 4"	12.00
Planter, deer reclining, brn/wht, 6½x5½"	18.00
Shelf sitters, Oriental boy & girl, blk/wht w/gold, 3½", pr	30.00
Vase, bud; hand figural, flesh color, 6½"	20.00
Wall pocket, corner style, underglaze decor	20.00

Morton Pottery Company (1922 – 1976)

Figurine, bison, brn, 7"	75.00
Figurine, Boston Terrier, blk/wht, 7"	25.00
Figurine, elephant, trumpeting, gray, 10"	40.00
Figurine, hound dog plant soaker	18.00
Figurine, seeing-eye dog, blk, 5¾"	20.00
Lamp, Davy Crockett w/bear & tree trunk	125.00
Lamp, Easter bunny w/carrot, male	40.00
Lamp, Easter bunny w/umbrella, female	40.00
Lamp, old woman shoe house	35.00

Lamp, teddy bear 35.00
Political giveaway, ashtray, Dirksen, bl 20.00
Political giveaway, ashtray, Nixon, red 25.00
Political giveaway, elephant, trumpeting, GOP, gr w/bl letters 30.00
Political giveaway, figurine, donkey, Kennedy, brn, 2" 40.00
Political giveaway, figurine, donkey, Tawes, gray, 2" 25.00
Political giveaway, figurine, elephant, misc names, bl or gray, 2" ..20.00
Political giveaway, ring holder, elephant, Dirksen, 4" 30.00
Political giveaway, ring holder, elephant, Nixon, 4" 40.00

American Art Potteries (1947 – 1961)

Figurine, Hampshire hog, natural colors, 5½", $35.00.

Candlestick, blk, 3 cups, #140, 6x7½" 30.00
Candlestick, gr, 3 cups, #141, 8x9" 36.00
Flower frog, bird on stump, #98, 8½" 15.00
Flower frog, frog, #400, 2½" 12.00
Flower frog, turtle, #411, 2" 12.00
Flower frog, turtle, #412, 2½" 16.00
TV lamp, conch shell, mauve/gray, #131, 7¼" 30.00
TV lamp, rearing horse, gr/blk, #327, 9x8x6" 36.00
TV lamp, swordfish, wht, #307, 7½x11" 54.00
Wall pocket, apple & leaf, #127, 6½" 18.00
Wall pocket, dustpan, decor, #81, 8" 25.00
Wall pocket, teapot, decor, #79, 4" 22.00

Moser

Ludwig Moser began his career as a struggling glass artist, catering to the rich who visited the famous Austrian health spas. His talent and popularity grew and in 1857 the first of his three studios opened in Karlsbad, Czechoslovakia. The styles developed there were entirely his own; no copies of other artists have ever been found. Some of his original designs include grapes with trailing vines, acorns and oak leaves, and richly enameled, deeply cut or carved floral pieces. Sometimes jewels were applied to the glass as well. Moser's animal scenes reflect his careful attention to detail. Famed for his birds in flight, he also designed stalking tigers and large, detailed elephants, all created in fine enameling.

Moser died in 1916, but the business was continued by his two sons who had been personally and carefully trained by their father. The Moser company bought the Meyr's Neffe Glassworks in 1922 and continued to produce quality glassware.

When identifying Moser, look for great clarity in the glass; deeply carved, continuous engravings; perfect coloration; finely applied enameling (often covered with thin gold leaf); and well-polished pontils. Our advisor for this category is Don Williams; he is listed in the Directory under Missouri. Items described below are enameled unless noted otherwise.

Basket, cranberry w/wht florals & gold, brass ft, flower hdl, 7½" .200.00
Bottle, scent; gr to clear, intaglio cut, cut stopper, 6¼" 250.00
Bowl, amethyst, mc floral w/gold, ribbed, 5" H 850.00

Bowl, sapphire bl, mc florals, scalloped, brass fr, 5x6¾" 245.00
Casket, burgundy, ormolu ft/brass mts, mc w/gold, 6½x4¾" 625.00
Compote, amber w/bl rigaree border, florals int/ext 450.00
Cordial, cranberry, flowers 145.00
Cruet, ruby w/gold oak leaves & acorns, matching stopper, 10½" ...2,500.00
Cup & saucer, demitasse; floral, gold on amber to wht 100.00
Finger bowl, clear w/mc floral & gold, 2¼" H, +6¾" tray 350.00
Goblet, cranberry to clear w/stylized florals, ftd, 5¼" 120.00
Lamp, cranberry opaque cased, florals w/gold, 1920s, 18" 2,500.00
Pitcher, amber, bl lava rim, alligator-tail bl hdl, 8½x7¼" 1,250.00
Pitcher, cut, gold stylized decor, +8 tumblers 350.00
Ring tree, blk amethyst w/mc foliage & gold, 4x3¾" 110.00
Rose bowl, gr to clear, intaglio lilies, mini, 2½" dia 240.00
Rose bowl, purple to clear, floral intaglio, Karlsbad, 2½x7½" 480.00
Tankard, apple gr to clear, floral intaglio, 12¼" 765.00
Tumbler, clear, cut base, 2 floral ovals & overall decor, 7¼" 300.00
Tumbler, juice; amethyst, 4 appl acorns 585.00
Vase, amethyst, floral intaglio, fan form, 6½x10½" 250.00
Vase, amethyst to clear, sq, bands & tassels, 5x2⅝" 195.00
Vase, birds on branches/scrolls on gold pillow form, hdls, 7½" ..1,200.00
Vase, bl w/floral & grasshopper, 3-hdld, 8¼x6½" 1,200.00
Vase, citron, cut tulip rim w/gold & wht trim, 4" 110.00
Vase, cranberry w/coralene beading, gold leaf & enamel, 10x5" .995.00
Vase, cranberry w/gold lady medallion/berries/etc, 8x3" 195.00
Vase, cranberry w/mc florals & gold, stick neck, 9½" 125.00
Vase, cranberry w/mc florals & leaves, 3-sided, ped ft, 8" 990.00
Vase, custard to bl w/silver floral o/l, shell form, 5¾" 400.00
Vase, gr w/wht o/l, gold border, ca 1890, 12½x5½" 1,075.00
Vase, rubena crystal, stylized enameling, 11¾" 275.00
Wine, clear, florals w/gold, 1880s, 5½" 335.00

Moss Rose

Moss Rose was a favorite dinnerware pattern of many Staffordshire and American potters from the mid-1800s. In America the Wheeling Pottery of West Virginia produced the ware in large quantities, and it became one of their bestsellers, remaining popular well into the '90s.

Bone dish, unmk, gold edge 32.00
Bowl, vegetable; unmk, w/lid 60.00
Cake plate, open hdls, unmk 60.00
Coffee set, pk striping, unmk, 9" pot+cr/sug+6 c&s, EX 175.00
Coffeepot, dolphin hdl, 7" 70.00
Creamer & sugar bowl, unmk 30.00
Cup & saucer, demitasse; ornate hdl & ft 15.00
Gravy boat, Meakin 35.00
Plate, Powell Bishop, 9" 25.00
Plate, unmk, 7½" 10.00
Platter, rectangular, Meakin, 14x10" 38.00
Tea set, Am, 14-pc 125.00
Tea set, child sz, 15-pc 275.00
Toothbrush holder, w/drain 75.00
Tray, tiered, unmk 32.00
Wash set, unmk, 11" pitcher+13½" bowl 300.00

Mother-of-Pearl Glass

Mother-of-Pearl glass was a type of mold-blown satin art glass popular during the last half of the 19th century. A patent for its manufacture was issued in 1886 to Frederick S. Shirley, and one of the companies who produced it was the Mt. Washington Glass Company of New Bedford, Massachusetts. Another was the English firm of Stevens and

Williams. Its delicate patterns were developed by blowing the gather into a mold with inside projections that left an intaglio design on the surface of the glass, then sealing the first layer with a second, trapping air in the recesses. Most common are the Diamond Quilted, Raindrop, and Herringbone patterns. It was made in several soft colors, the most rare and valuable is rainbow — a blend of rose, light blue, yellow, and white. Occasionally it may be decorated with coralene, enameling, or gilt. Watch for 20th-century reproductions, especially in the Diamond Quilted pattern. Our advisors for this category are Betty and Clarence Maier; they are listed in the Directory under Pennsylvania. See also Coralene.

Basket, Dmn Quilt, red, camphor hdl, Mt WA, 11x11" 500.00
Basket, Herringbone, yel, ruffled, frosted hdl, Mt WA, 9½x7½" ...250.00
Bonbon, Dmn Quilt, wht w/clear ribbons, ruffled rim, 8½" 450.00
Bowl, Dmn Quilt, bl, 3 frosted thorny ft, 4½x5⅞" 395.00
Bowl, Dmn Quilt, rainbow, mk Pat; Pairpoint Cupid fr, 6" 725.00
Celery vase, Herringbone, bl, 8 melon ribs, 5x3" 325.00
Creamer, Dmn Quilt, rainbow, sq top, frosted hdl, 2¾x2¾" 950.00
Creamer, Raindrop, bl, rnd mouth, frosted bl hdl, 4½x3⅛" 195.00
Creamer, Ribbon, bl, heart shape, 2⅛x2¾" 245.00
Ewer, Herringbone, apricot, ruffled rim, thorny hdl, 7x4¼" 265.00
Ewer, Herringbone, bl, frosted loop hdl, 3-pour spout, 7½" 375.00
Finger bowl, Dmn Quilt, amberina, 4½", +6½" plate 915.00
Lamp base, Dmn Quilt, pk, w/burner, 3¾x2½" dia 350.00
Pitcher, Dmn Quilt, wht, frosted camphor shell hdl, 6x3" 325.00
Pitcher, Dmn Quilt, yel to wht, sq top, shell hdl, 6½x3" 375.00
Rose bowl, Concentric Circles, rainbow, mk Pat, 2½x4⅜" 850.00
Rose bowl, Dmn Quilt, bl, dimpled sides, 8-crimp, 3⅝x4" 185.00
Rose bowl, Dmn Quilt, bl, pleated top, Stevens & Wms, 3¾x4" .225.00
Rose bowl, Dmn Quilt, brn, 8-crimp, 3x3" 395.00
Rose bowl, Dmn Quilt, lemon yel, 8-crimp, 3½x3⅞" 175.00
Rose bowl, Herringbone, apricot, 6-crimp, 3¾x3¼" 195.00
Rose bowl, Herringbone, bl, 6-crimp, 4x3⅞" 185.00
Rose bowl, Peacock Eye, bl, 3" 175.00
Rose bowl, Ribbon, avocado gr, 9-crimp, 2¾x3½" 245.00
Rose bowl, Ribbon, bl, frosted wafer ft, 8-crimp, 2½x3¼" 185.00
Rose bowl, Ribbon, bl, 3-pinch top, wafer ft, 3⅛x2⅝" 175.00
Rose bowl, Ribbon, bl, 9-crimp, 2⅞x3¾" 245.00
Shade, Dmn Quilt, rainbow, ruffled, 6¼x9¼" 1,250.00
Shaker, Dmn Quilt, pk, orig 2-part lid, 3¼" 550.00
Sugar bowl, Dmn Quilt, pk, stationary hdl, rstr SP, 7½x4½" 450.00
Sweetmeat, Flower & Acorn, red, gold trim, SP mts, 5½x3¼" ...945.00
Tumbler, Dmn Quilt, apricot to pk to wht, 4" 235.00
Tumbler, Dmn Quilt, bl, 4" 165.00
Tumbler, Dmn Quilt, yel, Mt WA, 4" 165.00
Tumbler, Herringbone, bl, 4" 165.00
Tumbler, Herringbone, pk, 3¾x2⅝" 175.00
Tumbler, Rib, bl, air traps resemble raindrops, 3½x2½" 75.00
Tumbler, Verre Moire, bl, 4" 145.00
Vase, Basketweave, bl, Webb, 7x5" 750.00
Vase, Basketweave, brn to tan to gold to cream, Webb, 7x5½" ..850.00
Vase, Coin Spot, pk, 3½x2¼" 350.00
Vase, Dmn Quilt, bl, ruffled rim, 8x4½" 375.00
Vase, Dmn Quilt, bl, 4½x3⅛" 110.00
Vase, Dmn Quilt, bl, 6½x4" 275.00
Vase, Dmn Quilt, chartreuse, bl int, ftd, ruffled, 4¼x5⅛" 375.00
Vase, Dmn Quilt, gr, amber frosted rim, bulbous, 7¼x5¼" 850.00
Vase, Dmn Quilt, rainbow, mk Pat, 7¼x4" 1,250.00
Vase, Flower & Acorn, bl, waisted neck, tricorn top, 7x6" 735.00
Vase, Flower & Acorn, wht w/gold floral, Webb, 3½x5½" 650.00
Vase, Herringbone, pk, bulbous w/fan-shaped ruffled top, 6½" ..175.00
Vase, Herringbone, yel, HP florals, clear frosted hdl, 8⅛" 385.00
Vase, Muslin, bl, 3-petal top, 8x7" 675.00
Vase, Muslin (lg Raindrop), gold, melon ribs, Mt WA, 7¾x7" ..375.00

Vase, Pompeian Swirl, lime gr, bulbous, Stevens & Wms, 10¾" ...850.00
Vase, Pompeian Swirl, pk, Stevens & Wms, 11½x6" 950.00
Vase, Raindrop, bl, ruffled fan form, w/amber edge, 5½x2¾" 150.00
Vase, Ribbon, bl, 3-way top w/pinched-in sides, 4½x5⅝" 395.00
Vase, Ribbon, chartreuse w/gold prunus, scalloped, 4⅛" 395.00
Vase, Ribbon, pk, rectangular top, frosted ft, 3⅛x2¾" 195.00
Vase, Swirl, amberina satin, tapered form, Stevens & Wms, 10" ..1,000.00
Vase, Swirl, gold to pk-wht, Mt WA, 9x3½" 425.00
Vase, Swirl, rubena verde, Stevens & Wms, 9¾" 600.00
Vase, Zipper, bl, 30 ribs, Northwood, 7½x6" 450.00

Mountainside

John Kovaks operated a ceramic studio from the late 1920s until about 1939 in Mountainside, New Jersey, where through extensive experimentation he produced stoneware and earthenware items glazed with colors of his own formulation.

Vase, beehive; dk red w/heavy gold, factory flaws, 10" 150.00
Vase, grn/brn/gray mottle, flared rim, hdls, MP mk, 9" 130.00
Vase, incised flowers on brn, factory flaws, rare, 6" 75.00

Movie Memorabilia

Movie memorabilia covers a broad range of collectibles, from books and magazines dealing with the industry in general to the various promotional materials which were distributed to arouse interest in a particular film. Many collectors specialize in a specific area — posters, pressbooks, stills, lobby cards, or souvenir programs (also referred to as premiere booklets). In the listings below, a one-sheet poster measures approximately 27" x 41", three-sheet: 41" x 81", and six-sheet: 81" x 81". Window cards measure 14" x 22". See also Autographs; Cartoon Art; Paper Dolls; Personalities; Sheet Music.

Lobby card, *Modern Times*, Charlie Chaplin, 1936, 11x14", complete set of eight, $3,000.00.

Book, Giant movie edition, James Dean, Dutch, 1957, w/jacket ..75.00
Film strip, Betty Boop Show Girl, 8mm 20.00
Film strip, Where's the Fire?, Snub Pollard, Hal Roach, 16mm 12.00
Insert card, Bride by Mistake, L Day/A Marshall, RKO, 1944, NM ..40.00
Insert card, Clash by Night, Marilyn Monroe, 1952, EX+ 95.00
Insert card, Cloak & Dagger, Cooper/Palmer, 1946, EX 75.00
Insert card, Dmns Are Forever, S Connery, 1971, M 48.00
Insert card, Gamma People, Paul Douglas, 1956, M 35.00
Insert card, Green Mansions, A Hepburn/A Perkins, 1959, NM ..55.00
Insert card, Iron Petticoat, K Hepburn/B Hope, 1956, NM 37.50
Insert card, Machine Gun Kelly, Charles Bronson, 1958, EX+ 40.00
Insert card, Mad Wednesday, Harold Lloyd, 1950, NM 75.00
Insert card, Pushover, Kim Novak/Fred MacMurray, 1954, NM ...47.50
Lobby card, Bachelor & the Bobby Soxer, EX 45.00
Lobby card, D.O.A., Edmund O'Brien/Pamela Britton, 1950, NM ...32.00

Lobby card, Gay Falcon, George Sanders, 1941, EX **20.00**
Lobby card, Gone w/the Wind, 1947 release **150.00**
Lobby card, Meet the Mummy, Abbott & Costello, EX **75.00**
Lobby card, Misfits, Marilyn Monroe, EX **60.00**
Lobby card, Now & Forever, Gary Cooper/Shirley Temple, 1934, EX ..**160.00**
Lobby card, Picadilly Jim, Robert Montgomery, 1935, EX **25.00**
Lobby card, Range War, Hopalong Cassidy, 1937, EX **45.00**
Lobby card, Star Is Born, Judy Garland, EX **75.00**
Lobby card, Under Capricorn, Ingrid Bergman/M Wilding, 1940, NM ..**28.00**
Lobby card set, Father of Bride, Tracey/Taylor/Bennet, EX **30.00**
Lobby card set, Pride & Prejudice, Olivier/Garson, 1962 reissue, M .**30.00**
Lobby card set, Silver Lining, Maureen O'Sullivan, 1931, NM **35.00**
Magazine, Holly Wood, Dorothy Lamour cover, October, 1937, VG .**25.00**
Magazine, Modern Screen, Judy Garland cover, June, 1943, EX ...**25.00**
Magazine, Modern Screen, Paulette Goddard, July, 1941, EX **22.00**
Magazine, Motion Picture, Barbara Stanwick cover, 1943, EX **20.00**
Magazine, Motion Picture, Joan Crawford cover, 1934, VG+ **30.00**
Magazine, Photoplay, Ann Harding cover, August, 1931, EX **28.00**
Magazine, Photoplay, Irene Dunne cover, October, 1941, EX **20.00**
Magazine, Picture Play, Loraine Day cover, October, 1940, EX **20.00**
Magazine, Screen Great, Clark Gable cover, 1971 Series #3, M **17.50**
Magazine, Screen Great, Marilyn Monroe, 1971 Series #4, M **40.00**
Magazine, Screen Land, Janet Leigh cover, November, 1958, VG .**20.00**
Magazine, Screen Land, Marion Davies cover, June, 1935, EX **25.00**
Magazine, Screen Romances, Ann Sheridan cover, June, 1944, EX .**18.00**
Playbill, Diamond Lil, Mae West, EX **25.00**
Poster, Act of Murder, Fredric March, 1948, 3-sheet, EX **75.00**
Poster, Affairs of Susan, Joan Fontaine, 1945, 3-sheet, EX **90.00**
Poster, Black Doll, Donald Woods, 1946 (reissue), 1-sheet, M **36.00**
Poster, Captain Lightfoot, Rock Hudson, 1955, 1-sheet, EX **38.00**
Poster, Dock Savage, Ron Ely, 1975, 1-sheet, M **25.00**
Poster, East of Eden, James Dean, 1955, 27x41", NM **900.00**
Poster, Enforcer, Clint Eastwood, 1977, 1-sheet, M **50.00**
Poster, Georgy Girl, Lynn Redgrave/James Mason, 1966, 1-sheet, M ..**24.00**
Poster, Guess Who's Coming to Dinner, Hepburn, 1967, 1-sheet, NM .**30.00**
Poster, How To Stuff a Wild Bikini, Funicello, 1965, 1-sheet, M .**32.50**
Poster, Hush Hush Sweet..., Davis/DeHaviland, 1965, 1-sheet, M ..**65.00**
Poster, It Happened...Athens, Mansfield, 1962, ½-sheet, NM **45.00**
Poster, Ivy, Joan Fontaine, 1947, 1-sheet, EX **100.00**
Poster, Jungle Man, Buster Crabbe, 1941, 1-sheet, NM **55.00**
Poster, Love w/Proper Stranger, Natalie Wood, 1963, 3-sheet, NM .**375.00**
Poster, Madame, S Loren, 1962, ½-sheet, M **45.00**
Poster, Mame, Lucille Ball, 1974, 1-sheet, NM **32.00**
Poster, Night at the Opera, Marx Bros, 1930s, 1-sheet, NM **250.00**
Poster, Phantom of the Opera, 1945, mini, NM **50.00**
Poster, Phantom Speaks, Richard Arlen, 1957 reissue, 1-sheet, M ..**22.50**
Poster, Prisoner of War, Ronald Reagan, 1-sheet, VG **40.00**
Poster, Raintree County, E Taylor/M Clift, 1957, 1-sheet, NM ..**120.00**
Poster, Raisin in the Sun, Poitier/Dee, 1961, ½-sheet, NM **50.00**
Poster, Shut My Big Mouth, Joe E Brown, 11x16", VG **25.00**
Poster, Tarzan, Weismuller, 1950s, 1-sheet, EX+ **125.00**
Poster, That Touch of Mink, C Grant/D Day, 1962, ½-sheet, EX ..**40.00**
Poster, Town Like Alice, Finch/McKenna, 1957, ½-sheet, EX **40.00**
Poster, Union Station, Wm Holden, 1-sheet, VG **40.00**
Poster, Untamed, T Power/S Hayward, 1955, ½-sheet, NM **35.00**
Press kit, Panic in the Year Zero, Ray Milland, NM **80.00**
Pressbook, Beatniks, Peter Breck, 1959, EX **25.00**
Pressbook, Black Raven, George Zucco, 1943, M **22.00**
Pressbook, Charlie Chaplin, Economy Novelty, 12x18", EX **550.00**
Pressbook, Golden Earrings, M Dietrich/R Milland, 1947, EX **32.00**
Pressbook, Hopalong Cassidy, EX **50.00**
Program, Hell's Angel, Jean Harlow, hardbound, EX **85.00**
Program, La Dolce Vita, Anita Ekberg cover, late 1950s **30.00**
Program, Private Lives, Tallulah Bankhead, EX **30.00**

Program, Some Like It Hot, Dutch, 1954 ....**50.00**
Souvenir book, Longest Day, John Wayne, ca 1962, EX **40.00**
Title card, Strike Up the Band, Garland/Rooney, 1941, NM **70.00**
Window card, Dangerous Blondes, Evelyn Keys, 1943, NM **35.00**
Window card, Kiss Me Deadly, Ralph Meeker, 1954, NM **45.00**
Window card, Lost World, Claude Rains, 1960, EX **40.00**
Window card, Melody Man, Alice Day/Wm Collier, 1930, EX **75.00**
Window card, Sweepstakes, Eddie Quillan, 1930, NM **50.00**
Window card, 2001: Space Odyssey, 1968, NM **60.00**

Mt. Washington

The Mt. Washington Glass Works was founded in 1837 in South Boston, Massachusetts, but moved to New Bedford in 1869 after purchasing the facilities of the New Bedford Glass Company. Frederick S. Shirley became associated with the firm in 1874. Two years later the company reorganized and became known as the Mt. Washington Glass Company. In 1894 it merged with the Pairpoint Manufacturing Company, a small Brittania works nearby, but continued to conduct business under its own title until after the turn of the century. The combined plants were equipped with the most modern and varied machinery available and boasted a working force with experience and expertise rival to none in the art of blowing and cutting glass. In addition to their fine cut glass, they are recognized as the first American company to make cameo glass, an effect they achieved through acid-cutting methods. In 1885 Shirley was issued a patent to make Burmese, pale yellow glassware tinged with a delicate pink blush. Another patent issued in 1886 allowed them the rights to produce Rose Amber, or amberina, a transparent ware shading from ruby to amber. Pearl Satin Ware and Peachblow, so named for its resemblance to a rosy peach skin, were patented the same year. One of their most famous lines, Crown Milano, was introduced in 1893. It was an opal glass either free blown or pattern molded, tinted a delicate color and decorated with enameling and gilt. Royal Flemish was patented in 1894 and is considered the rarest of the Mt. Washington art glass lines. It was decorated with raised, gold-enameled lines dividing the surface of the ware in much the same way as lead lines divide a stained glass window. The sections were filled in with one or several transparent colors and further decorated in gold enamel with florals, foliage, beading, and medallions.

Our advisors for this category are Betty and Clarence Maier; they are listed in the Directory under Pennsylvania. See also Amberina; Cranberry; Salt Shakers; Burmese; Crown Milano; Mother of Pearl; Royal Flemish; etc.

Biscuit jar, berries and leaves on tan to pink, silverplated rim, lid, and handle, 5", $1,000.00.

Basket, pk satin Herringbone, ruffled, frosted hdl, att, 4½x4" **150.00**
Biscuit jar, Albertine, floral, bl on orange/yel, SP lid, 6" **850.00**
Biscuit jar, daffodils on yel to pk, Pairpoint mts & lid **695.00**
Biscuit jar, floral w/copper enamel, rstr SP fr, unmk **815.00**
Biscuit jar, raspberries/flowers on opal, sea urchin finial **1,000.00**
Biscuit jar, wild roses w/gold, SP rim, gilt lid, 4½" **1,700.00**

Bottle, scent; nasturtiums, mc on opalware, sprinkler top, 5¼" ..**375.00**
Bowl, fruit; Napoli, pond lilies on gr w/gold, +7½" mk base **2,250.00**
Bowl, wht satin hobnail to pk, bl rim, Barbour Bros fr, 8x14" **875.00**
Box, Collars & Cuffs, poppies on opalware w/gold, rare **1,000.00**
Box, Colonial lady's portrait on opalware, rare, 4¾x6½" **1,100.00**
Box, monk drinking, gold-washed SP Pairpoint fr, 3¼x5¼" **550.00**
Box, poppies on emb swirl w/SP & gold trim, 6¼x8" **1,750.00**
Box, windmill scene, Delft Bl, Guba, #d, 4x6" **950.00**
Compote, Napoli, cranberry w/HP peaches, Pairpoint base, 11x10" .**650.00**
Flower frog, mushroom form, daisies on pnt burmese, 3x5½" **250.00**
Flower frog, mushroom form, forget-me-nots, mc on yel/wht, 3" ..**375.00**
Humidor, Prism & Punty, cranberry to clear, SP lid, 6¾x6" **650.00**
Humidor, windmill scene, Delft Bl, Guba, Pairpoint mts, 6x5" ..**1,950.00**
Lamp, chrysanthemums, yel/pk/gold on opal, brass ft, 15x8½" ...**700.00**
Lamp, floral bouquets/birds, pk on wht w/gold, 16x10" **1,000.00**
Lamp, lady w/flower baskets cameo, yel/wht, 21x10" **8,500.00**
Lamp, Lava stem, clear cut font, ornate silver sq base, 16" **550.00**
Mustard pot, floral, mc on melon-ribbed satin, SP lid/hdl, 3¼" ..**175.00**
Plate, floral, violet/gold/gr, mk Asbury Park, 4" **125.00**
Rose bowl, daisies & foliage, mc on wht, crimped rim, 2¾x3¼" ...**410.00**
Rose bowl, vines & berries on crystal, 4x3" **450.00**
Shaker, chick form, pk/burgundy flowers, metal chick head, 2¼" .**650.00**
Shaker, floral, bl & wht on wht opal, fig shape **195.00**
Shaker, floral, wht on cranberry, fig shape **525.00**
Sugar shaker, daffodils, mc on yel to bl, egg form, orig lid, 4" **450.00**
Sugar shaker, floral, mc on wht, tomato shape, 2½" **550.00**
Sugar shaker, wild roses, mc on wht, egg form, orig lid **375.00**
Syrup, cut, strawberry, dmn & fan **165.00**
Vase, Colonial Ware, Persian water jug form, #1022, 12¾" **2,200.00**
Vase, Delft windmill scene on pk opal w/gold, 9x5½" **375.00**
Vase, jack-in-pulpit; Napoli, pansies w/gold, 4x4" **1,800.00**
Vase, Lava, mc flux on glossy blk, 5¼x4½", NM **1,200.00**
Vase, Napoli, frog & bulrushes w/gold, emb ribs, 8½x5" **1,000.00**
Vase, Napoli, spider mums w/gold webbing inside, 10" **1,450.00**
Vase, seaweed enameling on brn to gold, gourd form, 11¼" **285.00**

Mulberry China

Mulberry china was made by many of the Staffordshire area potters from about 1830 until the 1850s. It is a transfer-printed earthenware or ironstone named for the color of its decorations, a purplish-brown resembling the juice of the mulberry. Some pieces may have faded out over the years and today look almost gray with only a hint of purple. (Transfer printing was done in many colors; technically only those in the mauve tones are 'mulberry'; color variations have little effect on value.) Some of the patterns (Corean, Jeddo, Pelew, and Formosa, for instance) were also produced in Flow Blue ware. Others seem to have been used exclusively with the mulberry color. Our advisor for this category is Mary Frank Gaston.

Abbey, pitcher, 8-sided, 7¼" **265.00**
Abbey, platter, 12" **165.00**
Alleghany, plate, 9¼" **75.00**
Alleghany, punch cup, hdld, Goodfellow **95.00**
Alleghany, teapot **295.00**
Argyle, tazza, polychrome, Dimmock **325.00**
Athens, plate, 9¼" **55.00**
Bochara, bowl, vegetable; w/lid **375.00**
Bochara, plate, Edwards, 10¾" **85.00**
Bochara, plate, Edwards, 9" **75.00**
Castle Garden, plate, medallion-floral border, 7⅞" **85.00**
Castle Scenery, pitcher, Furnival, 8" **425.00**
Castle Scenery, sugar bowl, w/lid, Furnival **275.00**
Coburg, shaving mug, Edwards **250.00**
Corea, plate, 6¼" **45.00**
Corea, plate, 7¼" **55.00**
Corean, cup & saucer, handleless **75.00**
Corean, cup plate **65.00**
Corean, plate, 10" **55.00**
Corean, plate, 8" **50.00**
Corean, platter, Podmore Walker, 13½" **225.00**
Corean, tea set, 3-pc **895.00**
Corean, teapot **600.00**
Cyprus, creamer, Davenport **225.00**
Cyprus, cup & saucer, handleless **125.00**
Cyprus, plate, Davenport, 9¼" **45.00**
Cyprus, platter, Davenport, 12½" **175.00**
Flora, platter, Thomas Walker, 15¼x12" **250.00**
Foliage, cup & saucer, handleless **95.00**
Hong, pitcher, 2-qt **500.00**
Jeddo, bowl, vegetable; Adams, 6x7" **200.00**
Jeddo, cup & saucer, Adams **85.00**
Jeddo, gravy boat, Adams **175.00**
Jeddo, plate, Adams, 7½" **38.00**
Jeddo, platter, 13½" **180.00**
Jeddo, sauce bowl **35.00**
Jeddo, sugar bowl, open, Adams **215.00**
Jeddo, waste bowl & pitcher, Adams **750.00**
Marble, pitcher, 8" **325.00**
Nankin, creamer, Davenport **225.00**
Neva, teapot, Challinor, rstr lid **225.00**
Ning-Po, pitcher, ca 1850, 8" **195.00**
Ning-Po, plate, Hall, 9½" **70.00**
Panama, creamer, Challinor **245.00**
Panama, plate, 7¼" **35.00**
Pelew, bowl, vegetable; Challinor, w/lid **420.00**
Pelew, cup & saucer, handleless; Challinor **50.00**
Pelew, pitcher, water **195.00**
Pelew, platter, 13¼" **200.00**
Pelew, sauce plate, 4¼" **55.00**

Rhone Scenery, creamer, $110.00.

Rhone Scenery, platter, 13½" **175.00**
Rhone Scenery, teapot **275.00**
Rose, plate, Walker, 9½" **70.00**
Rose, platter, Challinor, 14x11", EX **185.00**
Savoy, teapot **275.00**
Shapoo, cup plate **65.00**
Shapoo, platter, 14x10" **225.00**
Temple, plate, Podmore Walker, 9¾" **80.00**
Tulip & Fern, tea set, Brushstroke, child sz, 14-pc **2,100.00**
Vincennes, bowl, vegetable; w/lid **325.00**
Vincennes, plate, 10", EX **65.00**
Vincennes, plate, 9½" **75.00**

Washington Vase, creamer, Podmore Walker 225.00
Washington Vase, plate, Podmore Walker, 10" 80.00
Washington Vase, plate, Podmore Walker, 7½" 70.00
Washington Vase, plate, Podmore Walker, 8¾" 75.00
Washington Vase, sugar bowl, prof rstr to lid 225.00
Washington Vase, sugar pot, lion's head hdls 240.00
Washington Vase, teapot 475.00
Washington Vase, waste bowl, Podmore Walker 215.00
Whampoa, sugar bowl 225.00

Muller Freres

Henri Muller established a factory in 1900 at Croismare, France. He produced fine cameo art glass decorated with florals, birds, and insects in the Art Nouveau style. The work was accomplished by acid engraving and hand finishing. Usual marks were 'Muller,' 'Muller Croismare,' or 'Croismare, Nancy.' In 1910 Henri and his brother Deseri formed a glassworks at Luneville. The cameo art glass made there was nearly all produced by acid cuttings of up to four layers with motifs similar to those favored at Croismare. A good range of colors was used, and some later pieces were gold flecked. Handles and decorative devices were sometimes applied by hand. In addition to the cameo glass, they also produced an acid-finished glass of bold mottled colors in the Deco style. Examples were signed 'Muller Freres' or 'Luneville.' Our advisor for this category is Don Williams; he is listed in the Directory under Missouri.

Cameo

Bowl, woods/lake/islands, brn/orange, oblong, 3¾x10¼" 1,200.00
Box, raspberries/flowers, maroon/dusty pk, 2¾" H 550.00
Lamp, wild boars/foliage, red-orange/wine/blk, 25½x11" 10,500.00
Vase, carnations, red-pk/ebony-red on olive/lime/frost, 7" 2,700.00
Vase, iris, gr/wht glossy, 12½x3½" 1,500.00
Vase, landscape, orange/blk, 5¼x5" 1,000.00
Vase, mtns/trees, bl/wht/pk, 6¼x6¼" 1,100.00
Vase, peonies, maroon/cranberry/lt yel opal, 5¼x5½" 1,800.00
Vase, sailboats, cut/pnt, gr/bl/brn/orange, sgn, 6x3" 1,800.00
Vase, trees/mtn/sky, blk/almond/orange/bl-blk, shouldered, 4¼" ..1,500.00

Miscellaneous

Bowl, mottled orange & bl, low, mk, 10" dia 220.00
Chandelier, 4 SP arms, 5 frosted glass shades, 32x30" 800.00
Plaque, emb birds (3) on branch, on base, frosted, 8x14⅜" 1,035.00
Vase, emb flowers/leaves on frost, flat sided, hex base, 12" 400.00

Muncie

The Muncie Pottery was established in Muncie, Indiana, by Charles O. Grafton; it operated there from 1922 until about 1935. The pottery they produced is made of a heavier clay than most of its contemporaries; the styles are sturdy and simple. Early glazes were bright and colorful. In fact, Muncie was advertised as the 'rainbow pottery.' Later most of the ware was finished in a matt glaze. The more collectible examples are those modeled after Consolidated Glass vases — sculptured with lovebirds, grasshoppers, and goldfish. Their line of Art Deco-style vases bears a remarkable resemblance to the Consolidated Glass Company's Ruba Rombic line. Vases, candlesticks, bookends, ashtrays, bowls, lamp bases, and luncheon sets were made. A line of garden pottery was manufactured for a short time. Items were frequently impressed with MUNCIE in block letters. Letters such as A, K, E, or D

and the numbers 1, 2, 3, 4, or 5 often found scratched into the base are finishers' marks.

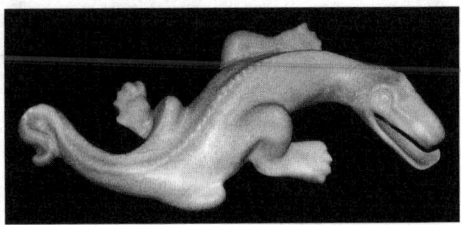

Wall alligator, green/rose matt, 10½" L, $1,050.00.

Deco lamp, 6 nude panels, gr matt, 9¾" 450.00
Goldfish vase, lt bl gloss, 8½" 375.00
Katydid vase, gr matt, 6½" 275.00
Lovebird vase, gr/lav matt, 9" 400.00
Pitcher, juice; orange peel, 6¼" 100.00
Rombic bulb bowl, gr/rose matt, 2½x8" 450.00
Rombic lamp, gr/lav matt, 10" 395.00
Rombic lamp, gr/tan matt, 8" 365.00
Rombic Star vase, gr/tan matt, 4x5" 350.00
Vase, blk gloss, hdls, #143, 7" 95.00
Vase, gr matt, trn/ruffled top, 4" 60.00
Vase, gr/rose matt, ruffled top, hdls, 6" 75.00
Vase, wht/bl matt, corset shape, 9" 115.00

Musical Instruments

The field of automatic musical instruments covers many different categories ranging from watches and tiny seals concealing fine early musical movements to huge organs and orchestrions which weigh many hundreds of pounds and are equivalent to small orchestras. Music boxes, first made in the early 19th century by Swiss watchmakers, were produced in both disk and cylinder models. The latter type employs a cylinder with tiny pins that lift the teeth in the comb of the music box (producing a sound much like many individual tuning forks), and music results. The value of a cylinder music box depends on the length and diameter of the cylinder, the date of its manufacture, the number of tunes it plays (four or six is usually better than ten or twelve), and its manufacturer. Nicole Freres, Henri Capt, LeCoultre, and Bremond are among the most highly regarded, and the larger boxes made by Mermod Freres are also popular. Examples with multiple cylinders, extra instruments (such as bells or an organ section), and those in particularly ornate cabinets or with matching tables bring significantly higher prices. While smaller cylinder boxes are still being made, the larger ones (over 10" cylinders) typically date from before 1900. Disk music boxes were introduced about 1890 but were replaced by the phonograph only twenty-five years later. However, during that time hundreds of thousands were made. Their great advantage was in playing inexpensive interchangeable disks, a factor that remains an attraction for today's collector as well. Among the most popular disk boxes are those made by Regina (USA), Polyphon, Mira, Stella, and Symphonion. Relative values are determined by the size of the disks they play, whether they have single or double combs, if they are upright or table models, and how ornate their cases are. Especially valuable are those that play multiple disks at the same time or are incorporated into tall case clocks.

Player pianos were made in a wide variety of styles. Early varieties consisted of a mechanism which pushed up to a piano and played on the keyboard by means of felt-tipped fingers. These use sixty-five note rolls. Later models have the playing mechanism built in, and most use eighty-eight note rolls. Upright pump player pianos have little value in unrestored condition because the cost of restoration is so high. 'Reproducing' pianos, especially the 'grand' format, can be quite valuable, depending on the make, the size, the condition, and the ornateness of the case. 'Reproducing' pianos have very sophisticated mechanisms and are much more realistic in the reproduction of piano music. They were made in relatively limited quantities. Better manufacturers include Steinway and Mason & Hamlin. Popular roll mechanism makers include Ampico, Duo-Art, and Welte. The market for all types of player pianos has been weak for several years.

Coin-operated pianos (Orchestrions) were used commercially and typically incorporate extra instruments in addition to the piano action. These can be very large and complex, incorporating drums, cymbals, xylophones, bells, and hundreds of pipes. Both American and European coin pianos are very popular, especially the larger and more complex models made by Wurlitzer, Seeburg, Cremona, Weber, Welte, Hupfeld, and many others. These companies also made automatically playing violins (Mills Violin Virtuoso, Hupfeld), banjos (Encore), and harps (Whitlock); these are quite valuable.

Mechanical organs range all the way from parlor pump organs and roll-operated reed organs to band organs found on carousels and giant fairground and dance hall organs. Pump organs made by Estey, Wilcox, and others are often very ornate but also very common and bulky; as a result, the market is very limited. The more sophisticated roll-playing reed organs are collectible but still find a limited market due to the cost of restoration. They are very undervalued and have been for a long time. Carousel-type band organs, especially those made by well-known manufacturers such as Wurlitzer and Artizan, continue to sell well. The highest values are reserved for the larger Welte, Gavioli, Bruder, and other organs used in fairgrounds, dance halls, and private residences that incorporate hundreds of pipes. With a harder-to-find larger instrument, a good supply of rolls contributes much to its value, since in many cases rolls cannot be found.

Unless noted, prices given are for instruments in fine condition, playing properly, with cabinets or cases in well-preserved or refinished condition. In all instances, unrestored instruments sell for much less, as do those with broken or missing parts, damaged cases, and the like. On the other hand, particularly superb examples in especially ornate case designs and those that have been particularly well kept will often command more. Our advisor for mechanical instruments is Martin Roenigk; he is listed in the Directory under Connecticut.

Key:
c — cylinder   d — disk

Mechanical

Box, B&M, 10¾" c, 6-tune 800.00
Box, Baker, Troll & Fils, 17¼" c, 12-tune, 31" case 2,100.00
Box, Criterion 15½", dbl combs, w/matching base, EX 5,500.00
Box, Imperial Symphonion, 17⅝" upright, 2 c, EX 7,000.00
Box, Landgorf Longue Marche, 7 12½" c, EX 12,000.00
Box, Langdorf & Fils, 17¼" c, 6-tune, 29" case 2,700.00
Box, Mandoline Quatuor, 17¼" c, ornate 28" case 5,000.00
Box, Mermod Freres, 11¼" c, 2½" d, 10-tune 1,500.00
Box, Mermod Freres, 17½" c, 8-tune, 35" case 3,200.00
Box, Mermod Freres Interchangeable, 4 13" c, rprs/rstr 5,000.00
Box, Nichole Freres, 13¼" c, 8-tune, ebony wood case 1,700.00
Box, Perfection, 14" single comb, 4 d, EX orig 1,800.00
Box, Regina, 11" d, oak case, VG, +16 d 1,100.00
Box, Regina, 15½" d, mahog, auto change, art glass, 68", rstr ..21,000.00
Box, Regina, 15½" d, single comb, pinstriped case, EX 2,400.00
Box, Regina, 20¾" d, dbl comb, oak desk style, ca 1910 ....14,000.00
Box, Regina, 27" d, automatic changing, walnut case, EX rstr .20,000.00

Box, Regina, 27" d, eng mahog case 12,000.00
Box, Regina Sublima Corona Style #31, 20¾" d, EX 19,000.00
Box, Stella Concert, 15½" d, w/table 4,000.00
Box, Swiss, 11⅛" c, 4-tune, key wind, 1850s 1,700.00
Box, Swiss, 12⅞" c, 4-tune, ca 1850, 21" case 1,600.00
Box, Swiss, 6½" c, 4-tune, veneer 21" case 450.00
Box, Swiss Flutes Voix Celestes, 11" c, 6-tune, 20¾" 2,200.00
Box, Symphonium, 17⅝" d, dbl comb, mahog table model 5,800.00
Box, Troll & Baker, 13" c, brass & silver inlay, 9 bells, EX 4,000.00
Caliola, Wurlitzer, Clancy O'Toole front, rare, EX 14,500.00
Calliope, Tangley, roll operated, EX 7,500.00
Hurdy gurdy, Victor Chlappa, 34-key c (2), EX orig 6,000.00
Nickelodeon, Coinola Cupid, EX orig, rare 15,000.00
Nickelodeon, Coinola CX, walnut case, w/xylophone, EX orig ...7,000.00
Nickelodeon, Cremona G, 29 flute pipes, rstr 12,000.00
Nickelodeon, Seeburg A, w/xylophone, rstr 6,900.00
Nickelodeon, Seeburg C, oak w/beveled glass panels, EX orig .5,000.00
Nickelodeon, Seeburg F, w/xylophone, rstr 8,000.00
Nickelodeon, Seeburg K, eagle front, w/xylophone, rstr 10,000.00
Nickelodeon, Seeburg L, rstr 8,500.00
Nickelodeon, Western Electric, mascot art glass cabinet, rstr .8,000.00
Nickelodeon, Wurlitzer CX, Grecian style, rstr 23,500.00
Nickelodeon, Wurlitzer IX-B, bells/auto roll changer, rstr 16,500.00
Orchestrelle, Aeolian V, oak, EX orig 3,500.00
Orchestrion, Coinola C-2, EX 27,000.00
Orchestrion, Coinola CX, w/11 instruments 18,000.00
Orchestrion, Coinola K Midget, walnut case, violin/flute pipes ...10,000.00
Orchestrion, Coinola Style #0 Midget, oak case, art glass, rstr .15,000.00
Orchestrion, Cremona J, rstr 45,000.00
Orchestrion, Seeburg G, M 60,000.00
Orchestrion, Western Electric, 10-tune G roll, 1920s, rstr 7,500.00
Organ, band; Artisan, 46-key, +15 rolls 16,000.00
Organ, band; Artisan A-1 military, paper roll op, 1920s, 76", G- ...16,000.00
Organ, band; Wurlitzer #125, partially rstr 18,000.00
Organ, band; Wurlitzer #146, rstr 18,000.00
Organ, band; Wurlitzer #153, rstr 42,000.00
Organ, dance; Arburo, rstr 15,000.00
Organ, Dutch street; Limonaire, 34-key, w/music book/1 figure ..22,000.00
Organ, fairground; Gasparini, 52-key, early 1900s, rstr 16,000.00
Organ, fairground; Gavioli, 65-key, 240 pipes, EX 42,000.00
Organ, grand; Kanabe Ampico, 64", EX orig 2,500.00
Organ, monkey; Molinari, 26-key, EX 4,000.00
Organ, monkey; Molinari, 47-key, w/orig cart 11,500.00
Organ, monkey; Molinari & Sons, 7-tune bbl, EX 4,500.00
Organ, player; Aeolian Style #1500, rstr/rfn 1,850.00
Organ, pump; Aeolian Orchestrelle Reed, mahog, '03, EX+, w/rolls ...4,000.00
Organette, Celestina, crank type, EX orig, w/3 rolls 800.00
Organette, Organina, walnut case, paper rolls 375.00
Piano, baby grand; Steinway, Eastlake cvg, 1885, 72" L, EX 2,000.00
Piano, grand; Ampico, art case, 74", EX orig 22,000.00
Piano, grand; Knabe, art case, 68", EX orig 6,500.00
Piano, grand; Marshall & Wendall Ampico, 60", EX orig 1,800.00
Piano, grand; Mason & Hamlin, 1982, 68", M 8,500.00
Piano, grand; Steinway Concert C, pianomation/orchestration, M .16,000.00
Piano, grand; Steinway Louis XV Duo-Art XR, mahog, 73", rstr .18,500.00
Piano, grand; Weber #77755 Model FR, mahog, 1922, 71½", EX ..5,000.00
Piano, grand; Weber Duo-Art, 73", rstr 8,000.00
Piano, grand; Wurlitzer/Apollo Ampico, art case, 73", rstr ...14,000.00
Piano, push-up; Harrand Cecilian, EX 500.00
Piano, upright; Charles Steiff Welte, M orig 1,200.00
Piano, upright; Chickering Ampico, EX orig 1,500.00
Piano, upright; Duo-Art, foot pump, walnut, 1922, EX orig 1,250.00
Piano, upright; Marshall & Wendall Ampico, rstr 2,700.00
Piano, upright; Stroud Duo-Art Style #593, walnut, 1938, rstr .3,800.00

Piano, upright; Symphony, oak/art glass, 10-tune, 61", EX **4,000.00**
Piano/pipe organ, Reproduco, EX orig **6,500.00**
Pianocorder, Marantz, w/50 cassettes, EX **3,000.00**
Violano, Mills Double Vialano, EX **60,000.00**
Violano, Mills Violano Virtuoso, oak case, ca 1920 ....**24,000.00**
Violano, Mills Violano Virtuoso, single violin, rfn, EX **22,500.00**

Non-Mechanical

Bagpipes, Scottish, w/Stewart bag, EX **250.00**
Banjo, English, 5-string, fancy inlays, 1890s, EX, w/case **500.00**
Banjo, Vega, 5-string, EX, w/case **500.00**
Banjo, Vega Senator, 5-string, 1929, 11" rim, EX **770.00**
Baritone horn, Fr, brass, 3 piston valves, ca 1885, EX **155.00**
Cornet, Imperial London, brass, 3 piston valves, 1890s, EX **60.00**
Drum, Excelsior, wood, gut snares, rope tension, 16x10", G **90.00**
Fife, rosewood w/brass ends, Civil War era, EX **70.00**
Flute, Firth Hall & Pond, coccuswood, ivory mts & cap, 21" **600.00**
French horn, C Mahillon Brussels, brass, 3 piston valves, EX **665.00**
Guitar, Danelectro **450.00**
Guitar, Fender Stratocaster, 1962 ....**4,500.00**
Guitar, Gibson, tenor, early 1960s, EX w/case **350.00**
Guitar, Gibson ES-175, sunburst w/inlays, 2PU, 1954, VG+ ..**2,700.00**
Guitar, Gibson ES-335N, 1982 ....**1,650.00**
Guitar, Gibson ES-350N **2,500.00**
Guitar, Gibson ES-5, 1948, sunburst/flame maple, 3PU, NM in case ..**6,500.00**
Guitar, Gibson L-3, reddish sunburst w/inlay, 1930s, EX **2,000.00**
Guitar, Gibson L-50, 1936 ....**1,200.00**
Guitar, Gretsch Acoustic **450.00**
Guitar, lap steel; Gibson **400.00**
Guitar, lap steel; Gibson, 1950s, NM, w/case & amplifier **1,500.00**
Guitar, lap steel; K&F **450.00**
Guitar, lap steel; Rickenbacker **250.00**
Harmonica, Magnus Duo-Tone Giant, 1950s, 9½" **15.00**
Harmonica, Sonora (made in Poland), 7" **35.00**
Harp, Wurlitzer, concert model, gold gilt, ornate, M **6,475.00**
Mandolin, Martin, rosewood, M in case **325.00**
Piano, Am, rosewood, scrolled lyre music rest, 1860s, 38x80⅝" ..**1,650.00**
Piano, grand; Kurtzmann, 1885, EX orig **6,200.00**
Piano, upright; Geo Steck, rosewood, cvd supports, 63x59" **1,000.00**
Pianoforte, English Regency mahog w/ebony bands, 1815, 66" ..**1,500.00**
Pianoforte, Schomacker, rococo rosewood, cvd legs, 44x78", EX ..**3,960.00**
Tambourine, canvas cover w/HP landscape, 10" dia **50.00**
Violin, Am, baroque neck, pnt-on stars, early 1800s, child's **325.00**
Xylophone, JC Deagan, Chicago, dtd 1914, EX **875.00**
Zither, Am Concert, floral marquetry, ca 1890s **365.00**

Mustache Cups

Mustache cups were popular items during the late Victorian period, designed specifically for the man with the mustache! They were made in silverplate as well as china and ironstone. Decorations ranged from simple transfers to elaborately applied and gilded florals. To properly position the 'mustache bar,' special cups were designed for the 'lefties.' These are the rare ones!

Blue Onion, 1800s **95.00**
Floral, bl on wht w/gold trim, Germany **75.00**
Flowers & bird on pk, Limoges, 3⅜", w/6⅝" saucer **110.00**
Knights & angels, gold trim, Royal Bavaria, w/saucer **75.00**
Oriental motif, HP, 2¾x3", w/saucer **65.00**
Pk lustre w/gold leaves **50.00**
Roses, red on gr, Germany **65.00**

SP, cut/beaded decor, Eureka Silver, 1901, w/saucer **80.00**
SP, floral eng, Barbour, EX **90.00**

Nailsea

Nailsea is a term referring to clear or colored glass decorated in contrasting spatters, swirls, or loops. These are usually white but may also be pink, red or blue. It was first produced in Nailsea, England, during the late 1700s but was made in other parts of Britain and Scotland as well. During the mid-1800s a similar type of glass was produced in this country. Originally used for decorative novelties only, by that time tumblers and other practical items were being made from Nailsea-type glass. See also Lamps; Witch Balls.

Bottle, gemel; clear w/wht loopings & rigaree, bl rim, 8" **165.00**
Creamer, aqua opaque w/rose & bl loopings, pour spout, 4⅜" **390.00**
Flask, cranberry w/wht & pk feathering, 6½x5" **100.00**
Flask, pk-red w/red herringbone loopings, English, 6⅜" **165.00**
Flask, wht opal w/cobalt loops, 7¼x4¼", EX **100.00**
Pipe, wht w/red loopings, 13½" **295.00**
Rolling pin, amber w/wht splotches, sheared ends, 1850-70, 14½" ..**95.00**
Rolling pin, red/wht/bl loopings, 15½", EX **500.00**
Vase, clear w/bl opaque loopings, scroll ft, rigaree, 5¾" **100.00**

Nakara

Nakara was a line of decorated opaque milk glass produced by the C.F. Monroe Company of Meriden, Connecticut, for a few years after the turn of the century. It differs from their Wave Crest line in several ways. The shapes were simpler; pastel colors were deeper and covered more of the surface; more beading was present; flowers were larger; and large transfer prints of figures, Victorian ladies, cherubs, etc., were used as well. Ormolu and brass collars and mounts complemented these opulent pieces. Most items were signed; however, this is not important since the ware was never reproduced. Our advisors for this category are Dolli and Wilfred R. Cohen; their address is listed in the Directory under California.

Ashtray, floral, pk on brn, ormolu mts, octagonal, 6" dia **300.00**
Box, Bishop's Hat, apple blossoms on bl, mk, 4x4¼" **495.00**
Box, Bishop's Hat, azaleas on butterscotch, mk, 3¾x5¼" **595.00**
Box, Bishop's Hat, lady's portrait on pk, 4½" **650.00**
Box, Bishop's Hat, roses on gr to pk, wht beads, mk, 4½x6½" ...**750.00**
Box, blown-out pansy on bl lid, 3¾" dia **750.00**
Box, cherubs in reserve on lid, 3¾" dia **495.00**
Box, cherubs, 6" dia **575.00**
Box, courting couple on lid, florals on base, mk, 3½x6" dia **1,000.00**
Box, Crown mold, floral, pk on brn, 8½" dia **1,650.00**
Box, Crown mold, sailing scene panels, HP, ftd, 6½" dia **1,895.00**
Box, Egg Crate, daisies & forget-me-nots, unmk, 5¾x5" dia **750.00**

Box, floral on green, metal finial, 4x8", $1,450.00.

Box, floral, pk on bl, hexagonal, 3x3¼" 400.00
Box, floral, pk on bl reserve, oval, 2¾x5¼" 500.00
Box, Queen Louise portrait on gr to pk, 3¾x8" 1,795.00
Box, ring; Victorian lady's portrait, mk, 2¼x2½" 950.00
Box, Spindrift, floral on cream to bl, 8" dia 1,850.00
Cracker jar, Crackers & florals on pk, fancy lid & hdl 895.00
Hair receiver, floral w/beadwork, orig tiered lid 550.00
Humidor, Cigars & florals on bl to ivory, shelf inside, 5¾", EX ..895.00
Humidor, monk smoking cigar on bbl shape, unmk, 5¼x4¼" 650.00
Humidor, Old Sport, bulldog & mug, SP lid w/pipe, unmk, 7" ...550.00
Humidor, owl on branch, invt pear shape, mk, w/lid, 7½" 1,300.00
Humidor, Tobacco & florals on gr, mk, 5¾x6¼", EX 900.00
Mustard jar, daisies on pnt burmese, metal finial, 4" 475.00
Tray, mums, mc on gr, mk, 2¼x6", NM 250.00
Tray, pin; floral on pk, ormolu rim & hdls, pk wash int 275.00

Napkin Rings

Napkin rings became popular during the late 1800s. They were made from various materials. Among the most popular and collectible today are the large group of varied silverplated figurals made by American manufacturers. Recently the larger figurals in excellent condition have appreciated considerably. Only those with a blackened finish, corrosion, or broken and/or missing parts have maintained their earlier price levels. When no condition is indicated, the items listed below are assumed to be all original and in very good to excellent condition. Check very carefully for missing parts, solder repairs, or marriages.

A timely warning: inexperienced buyers should be aware of excellent reproductions on the market, especially the wheeled pieces. However, these do not have the fine detail and patina of the originals and tend to have a more consistent, soft pewter-like finish. These are appearing at the large, quality shows at top prices, being shown along with authentic antique merchandise. Beware! For further information we recommend *Figural Napkin Rings* (Collector Books) by Lillian Gottschalk and Sandra Whitson. Our advisor for this category is Deborah Maggard; she is listed in the Directory under Ohio.

Key:
gw — gold washed
R&B — Reed & Barton
SH&M — Simpson, Hall, & Miller

Rabbits before barrel ring, New Bedford #89, $385.00.

Acorns at side of ring, rnd base, Meriden #163 ....65.00
Arab kneels, holds torch, oblong base, Tufts #1583 ....250.00
Bird w/long tail on leaf, ring attached to wings 150.00
Boy (Tom Sawyer-type) stands by ring, fancy base, Barbour #8 ..425.00
Boy & girl on seesaw, ring in middle, Simpson #029, minimum .500.00
Boy crawling/carries narrow ring on bk, R&B #480 ....295.00
Boy in harness pulls ring on wheels 595.00
Boy removing socks sits beside ring, Derby #341 ....325.00
Boy w/rope pulls 4-wheeled cart, Rogers #128 ....650.00
Boys kick on ea side of filigree ring, Meriden #332 ....225.00

Bud vase w/spout atop ring, sailor w/anchor, R&B #1357 ....300.00
Bull beside ornate ring, raised oval base, Knickerbocker #1250 ..275.00
Cat & bird heads as bookends of ornate ring, Rogers & Smith #361 ..295.00
Cat hisses at music stand, no ring, Tuft #1609 ....425.00
Cat looks thoughtful & leans against beaded ring 250.00
Cat pulls wheeled base that supports ring 525.00
Chair of tree limbs holds ring, rstr 125.00
Cherries & leaves on side of ring, leafy base, Standard #732 ....95.00
Cherub (lg) beside bbl ring on branch base 325.00
Cherub climbs ladder onto ring, plain base, R&B #1458 ....275.00
Cherub in soldier hat w/sword sits on alligator 425.00
Cherub sits on ea side of bbl-shaped ring, Meriden #147 ....200.00
Cherub twins w/rings on bks, rectangular base, Tufts #1544 ....500.00
Cherubs sit on ring, hold leash of prancing dog, Tufts #1543 .....300.00
Chick on wishbone, rococo base, elevated ring, NM 65.00
Chinese figure beside ring, oval ftd base, Meriden #158 ....395.00
Crocodile carries ring on bk, Meriden #0202 ....225.00
Deer harnessed to ring resting on filigree sled, Toronto #11 ....375.00
Dog on ea side of ring on trunk base, bird atop, Meriden #366 ...200.00
Dog on haunches after bird atop ring, Aurora #27 ....200.00
Dog pulls sled w/running fox decor, ring on sled, Meriden #285 .325.00
Eagle holds knife rest, rectangular base, Rogers & Bros #203 ......350.00
Eagle on side of ring, Meriden 70.00
Fairy w/butterfly, Wilcox #2206 ....300.00
Fans support ring, butterfly below, Meriden #208 ....200.00
Fox on ea side of ring, Rockford #174 ....275.00
Fox runs beside ring, rectangular 4-ftd base, Rogers #882 ....425.00
Foxes on ea side of ring, detailed base, Middletown, #119 ....250.00
Girl by bbl-shaped ring w/in branches w/owl family, #205 ....550.00
Girl in long braids stands beside ring, Meriden #280 ....300.00
Girl teaches lg poodle ABCs, ball-ft base, JW Tufts 500.00
Gnomes carry bbl-shaped ring w/long poles, Simpson #016 ....275.00
Goat on rectangular base beside ring, Knickerbocker #181 ....250.00
Grapes & leaves around ring, leafy base, Standard #701 ....65.00
Greenaway baby on chair & baby in canoe on fork-shaped base ...500.00
Greenaway boy feeds dog on rectangular base, Meriden #199 ....500.00
Greenaway boy w/drumsticks on hands & knees, ring on bk, #243 .350.00
Greenaway boy w/whistle, Tufts #1622 ....400.00
Greenaway girl in bonnet pushes ring, octagonal base, SH&M ..375.00
Greenaway girl sits on sm base beside ring, Derby #316 ....295.00
Greenaway-type boy stands by wooden fence (forms ring), Tufts 1598 ..425.00
Greyhound sits beside ring on oval base, R&B #1485 ....450.00
Horse head on ea side of ped ring w/fancy base, Derby #326 ....300.00
Horse prances w/ring on bk, leafy base, ftd 225.00
Horse stands by fence that juts out from ring, Meriden #0284 ....350.00
Knight, raised arm w/torch, rnd base, Barbour #59 ....150.00
Ladder-bk chair (rustic wood) holds ring in fr 125.00
Lion reclines w/ring on bk 200.00
Lion roars, attached to ring 295.00
Miner w/pick leans against triangular ring 135.00
Napoleon on ring, salt cellar & pepper shaker, Miller 400.00
Oriental fan on ea side w/bee beneath ring, Meriden #208 ....100.00
Palmer Cox Brownie stands by ring, rnd base, Pairpoint #37 ......350.00
Parrot w/glass eyes on loop hdl by ring, #4338 ....225.00
Peacock sits atop decor ring, Meriden #151 ....295.00
Pheasant leans on branch, flat octagonal base, Meriden #246 ....150.00
Reindeer pulls ring on ornate sled, Toronto #1111, minumum ...500.00
Rifles crossed on ea side of ring, Meriden #355 ....200.00
Rip Van Winkle w/rifle, bbl ring on bk, dog beside, Meriden 895.00
Rooster on shovel, flat base, Meriden #181 ....225.00
Sailor boy on triangle base w/poles behind, Tufts #2590 ....350.00
Sled w/ring atop, old-fashion type, Wilcox #01532 ....65.00
Soldier in tunic stands beside ring, Middletown #340 ....195.00
Squirrel w/glass eyes blows horn 250.00

Stork pulls rope attached to ring, oval base, R&B #1126 ....**350.00**
Sunflower base, octagonal, Meriden #37 ....**75.00**
Triangular ring w/Good Luck eng, horseshoe on ea side, Toronto #78 .....**125.00**
Turtle on circular base, supports ring, Meriden-Britania #193 ....**295.00**
Wheelbarrow holds ring, shield-shaped base, Tufts #1537 ....**225.00**

Nash

A. Douglas Nash founded the Corona Art Glass Company in Long Island, New York. He produced tableware, vases, flasks, etc. using delicate artistic shapes and forms. After 1933 he worked for the Libbey Glass Company.

Cordial, Chintz, red w/silver, 4", 6 for **650.00**
Vase, Chintz, gr w/brn/mustard stripes on opal/bl swirls, 8" **800.00**
Vase, Chintz, silver-bl veins on dk red, gourd form, 7½" **1,050.00**
Vase, gold irid flower form, textured calyxes leaves, #551, 5½" ...**1,550.00**
Vase, gold irid to red to bl at top lip, trumpet, #537, 6½" **650.00**
Vase, orange w/cobalt stripes, hourglass form, 13¼x4¼" **395.00**
Vase, red-gold irid, emb leaves, ftd trumpet form, #567, 5" **425.00**
Vase, ribbed amber w/gr zipper-like pattern, att, 6x7" **200.00**

Natzler, Gertrude and Otto

The Natzlers came to the United States from Vienna in the late 1930s. They settled in Los Angeles where they continued their work in ceramics, for which they were already internationally recognized. Gertrude created the forms; Otto formulated a variety of interesting glazes, among them volcanic, crystalline, and lustre. Our advisor for this category is Abby Malowanczyk; she is listed in the Directory under Texas.

Bowl, dk brn metallic w/silvery crystalline, #H270, 2x6½" ...**1,600.00**
Bowl, gr & bl glossy, #E071, 2x6" **1,800.00**
Bowl, wht matt w/red clay showing through, #J491, 2½x6" **1,000.00**
Bowl, 4-color volcanic glaze, 2½x5½" **1,900.00**
Cup, gray opal, 2¼" **175.00**
Cup, gray opal (mottled gray) on thin red clay, mk, 1¾" **150.00**
Vase, brn & gold crystalline, bottle neck, broad form, 6" **2,100.00**
Vase, deep bl nocturne w/silver crystals, teardrop, #K399, 7" ..**6,000.00**
Vase, gray-brn/blk volcanic on red clay, 5x6⅞" **3,200.00**
Vase, lime gr matt w/red clay showing through, 5½x10", NM ..**1,600.00**
Vase, yel matt w/red clay showing through, folded form, 3½x8" .**3,000.00**

New England Glass Works

Founded in 1818 by Deming Jarves in Boston, Massachussetts, the New England Glass Company produced cut, blown three-mold, free-blown, and pressed glass of the highest quality. They were recognized for their fine decorative accomplishments, using etching, gilding, and engraving to emphasize their wares. For more than fifty years, they produced prize-winning pressed glass dinnerware sets. Because they refused to compromise the quality of their product by using the cheaper lime-based glass that flooded the market in the 1860s, the company fell into financial trouble and by 1877 was forced to close. However, William Libbey, who had been the sales manager there since 1870, leased the premises and resumed operations with his father, Edward Drummond Libbey, as full partner. In 1892 the firm became known as The Libbey Glass Company. See also Amberina; Libbey.

Bottle, scent; wht opal, hexagonal, w/stopper, 1869-75, 4½" **150.00**
Creamer, added threading, appl ring/gadrooning, knop stem, 5¼" ..**160.00**

Goblet, Pineapple, pressed, non-flint, 6¼" **25.00**
Pitcher, milk; Pineapple, pressed, solid hdl, 8¼", 1-qt+ **950.00**
Vase, Stork (Joseph Locke design), amberina, 4½x2¼" sq **1,500.00**
Vase, Stork (Joseph Locke design), camphor glass, 4½x2¼" sq ..**385.00**

New Geneva

In the early years of the 19th century, several potteries flourished in the Greensboro, Pennsylvania, area. They produced utilitarian stoneware items as well as tile and novelties for many decades. All failed well before the turn of the century.

Flowerpot, Nannie Cary and vining floral decor, brown on buff clay, 7¾", rim chip, $500.00.

Photo courtesy Garth's Auction Gallery

Pitcher, free-hand floral, brn slip on gray, 5½" **250.00**
Pitcher, free-hand floral, brn slip on tan, 7" **360.00**
Pitcher, stenciled scroll in brn slip, 7" **195.00**

New Martinsville

The New Martinsville Glass Company took its name from the town in West Virginia where it began operations in 1901. In the beginning years, pressed tablewares were made in crystal as well as colored and opalescent glass. Considered an innovator, the company was known for their imaginative applications of the medium in creating lamps made entirely of glass, vanity sets, figural decanters, and models of animals and birds. In 1944 the company was purchased by Viking Glass, who continued to use many of the old molds, the animals molds included. They marked their wares 'Viking' or 'Rainbow Art.' Viking recently ceased operations and has been purchased by Kenneth Dalzell, president of the Fostoria Company. They, too, are making the bird and animal models. Although at first they were not marked, future productions are to be marked with an acid stamp. Dalzell/Viking animals are in the $50.00 to $60.00 range. Values for cobalt and red items are two to three times higher than for the same item in clear. See also Depression Glass; Glass Animals and Figurines.

Candle holders, Radiance, ruby, ball form, 2¾", $90.00 for the pair.

Basket, Janice, crystal, oval, 10x12" **85.00**
Basket, Janice, lt bl, #4552, 11" **295.00**

Bowl, fruit; Janice, crystal, ruffled top, 12" 50.00
Bowl, Prelude, crystal, 3-ftd, 10" 40.00
Bowl, Radiance, lt bl, crimped, #4211, 12" 85.00
Bowl, Radiance, lt bl, etch, ftd, #4218/28, 10" 145.00
Bowl, Radiance ruby w/Prelude etch, 12" 40.00
Candy box, Janice, bl or ruby, w/lid, 5½" 85.00
Candy box, Prelude, crystal, 3-ftd, w/lid, 7" 65.00
Cheese & cracker set, Radiance, lt bl, etch 95.00
Cheese & cracker set, Radiance, red 98.00
Cocktail shaker, Prelude, crystal, w/metal lid 125.00
Condiment set: tray & 2 covered jars, Janice, crystal ...55.00
Cordial, Radiance, red 38.00
Creamer & sugar bowl, Janice, lt bl, ind, w/tray 85.00
Goblet, water; Hilton, clear w/bl band 10.00
Ice pail, Janice, bl or ruby, hdld, 10" 145.00
Ice tub, Janice, bl or ruby, ftd, 6" 225.00
Ivy ball, Janice, lt bl 95.00
Lazy susan, Prelude, crystal, 3-pc set, 18" 125.00
Mint dish, Radiance, lt bl, hdls, #4237, 5" 45.00
Pitcher, berry cream; Janice, bl or ruby, 15-oz 110.00
Pitcher, Oscar, red 95.00
Pitcher, Prelude, crystal, 78-oz 195.00
Plate, Prelude, crystal, 16" 75.00
Platter, Prelude, crystal, 14½" 45.00
Stem, cordial; Prelude, crystal, 1-oz 40.00
Syrup, Janice, crystal, w/drip-cut top 55.00
Treasure jar, Prelude, crystal, w/lid, 8" 65.00
Tumbler, Amy, ftd, #34 ....22.50
Tumbler, Hostmaster (Mildred), ruby, 4¼" 8.50
Vase, Janice, crystal, ball form, 9" 55.00
Vase, Prelude, crystal, ftd, 11" 65.00
Wine, Hostmaster (Mildred), ruby, 4x2¼" 8.50

Newcomb

The Newcomb College of New Orleans, Louisiana, established a pottery in 1895 to provide the students with first-hand experience in the fields of art and ceramics. Using locally dug clays — red and buff in the early years, white-burning by the turn of the century — potters were employed to throw the ware which the ladies of the college decorated. Until about 1910 a glossy glaze was used on ware decorated by slip painting or incising. After that a matt glaze was favored. Soft blues and greens were used almost exclusively, and decorative themes were chosen to reflect the beauty of the South. The year 1930 marked the end of the matt-glaze period and the art-pottery era.

Various marks used by the pottery include an 'N' within a 'C,' sometimes with 'HB' added to indicate a 'hand-built' piece. The potter often incised his initials into the ware, and the artists were encouraged to sign their work. Among the most well-known artists were Sadie Irvine, Henrietta Bailey, and Fannie Simpson.

Newcomb pottery is evaluated to a large extent by two factors: design and condition. In the following listings, items are assumed matt unless noted otherwise. Our advisor for this category is David Rago; he is listed in the Directory under New Jersey.

Bowl, lilies on bl, Anna Simpson, 1922, 5⅝" 865.00
Jar, lilies, 4-color, A Munson, w/lid, #E27, 4½" 2,700.00
Jug, syrup; stylized floral, EHP, #BV10, 1907, 4¾x3¾" 1,400.00
Mug, pine cones, Ada Lonnegan, #R15, 1904, 4¼x5" 750.00
Pitcher, trees, bl/gr on yel to bl, waisted, Bailey, 1909, 8" 5,400.00
Pitcher, vines & leaves, gr/dk bl/tan, SB Levy, DD 93, 5½" 3,500.00
Vase, calla lilies, H Joor, JM/VV37/Q, 1904, 11¼x5¾" 20,000.00
Vase, daffodils, AF Simpson, GJ 66, #150, 8" 3,750.00

Vase, daffodils, cream/gr/bl, A Munson, #236/JM/FZ79, 6½" ..2,700.00
Vase, daffodils, cream/gr/bl, S Irvine, #037/#TS13, 5½" 1,500.00
Vase, floral, pk/gr/bl, S Irvine, #12, SW67, 2x3" dia 850.00
Vase, floral, 3-color, M Sheerer, #FF39, 6" 4,750.00
Vase, floral, 4-color, S Irvine, #QS100, 1928, 4½" 900.00
Vase, floral (stylized), ML Benson, ovoid, 1905, 7½x5½" 4,500.00
Vase, gr & gunmetal drip on cream, hand thrown, mk, 2½" 250.00
Vase, gr w/gunmetal drip on red clay, Meyer, 3½" 425.00
Vase, holly leaves & berries, S Irvine, #LN86, 5" 1,200.00
Vase, irises, rtcl, bl on bl & yel, S Irvine, 1912, 5½" 2,900.00
Vase, moon/moss/oak trees, A Arbo, #T45 F, 6½" 2,500.00
Vase, moon/moss/oak trees, AF Simpson, #161, 8½" 3,500.00
Vase, moon/moss/trees, AF Simpson, #229, 1927, 10x4½" 4,000.00
Vase, moon/moss/trees, AF Simpson, NM/115/LM87, 1921, 12½x5" ..4,500.00
Vase, moon/moss/trees, S Irvine, TU86/HJ/900, 1932, 14x9" .7,000.00
Vase, moss/trees, celadon/bl, S Irvine, 1928, 6¼" 1,800.00
Vase, narcissus, Anna Simpson, #MX46/97, 8¾x3¼" 2,000.00
Vase, organic decor, Sabrina E Wells, 1904, 6¼x3½" 2,600.00
Vase, pine trees, AF Simpson, 1925, #OP39/19/150, 11x5" ...4,000.00
Vase, pine trees, 3-color, AF Simpson, #FV77, 9" 3,500.00
Vase, streaky turq, L Nicholson, early 20th C, 3¼" 575.00
Vase, swirls, gr on bl, S Irvine, #UD8, 1933, 4x4½" 750.00
Vase, swirls, mc on turq, paper label, 6½x6" 650.00
Vase, trees landscape, 3-color, S Irvine, #PT64, 5½" 2,600.00
Vase, trees/moon/hills, AF Simpson, #RD5, 4" 1,800.00
Vase, water lilies, mc on med bl, waisted, S Irvine, 12" 2,587.50
Vase, wild roses, wht on bl, bulbous, 1904, #DD8, 6¼x5" 8,250.00

Newspapers

People do not collect newspapers simply because they are old. Age has absolutely nothing to do with value — it does not hold true that the older the newspaper, the higher the value. Instead, most of the value is determined by the historic event content. In most cases, the more important to American history the event is, the higher the value. In over two hundred years of American history, perhaps as many as 98% of all newspapers ever published **do not** contain news of a significant historic event. Newspapers not having news of major events in history are called 'atmosphere.' Atmosphere papers have little collector value. (See price guide below.)

To learn more about the hobby of collecting old and historic newspapers, be sure to visit our mega-web sight on the Internet at: http://www.historybuff.com/. Within this sight you will find a more extensive price guide to old and historic newspapers; an extensive, searchable, 300,000-word reference library of American history with an emphasis on newspaper publishing speeches; interactive crossword puzzles; regular auctions of ephemera, historic documents, and newspapers; a mall with over one hundred different online catalogs of paper collectibles; and much, much more! The e-mail address for the NCSA is rbrown@tir.com.

1800-1820, Atmosphere editions 7.00
1821-1859, Atmosphere editions 5.00
1836, Texas declares independence 60.00
1845, Annexation of Texas 35.00
1846, Start of Mexican War 30.00
1846-1847, Major battles of Mexican War 20.00
1847, End of Mexican War 30.00
1848, Gold discovered in California 60.00
1859, John Brown's raid on Harper's Ferry 45.00
1860, Lincoln elected 1st term 150.00
1861, Lincoln's inaugural address 175.00
1861-1865, Atmosphere editions: Confederate titles 50.00

1861-1865, Atmosphere editions: Union titles 7.00
1861-1865, Major battles of Civil War 75.00
1862, Emancipation Proclamation 135.00
1863, Gettysburg Address 250.00
1865, April 29 edition of Frank Leslie's 350.00
1865, April 29 edition of Harper's Weekly 300.00
1865, Capture & death of J Wilkes Booth 100.00
1865, Fall of Richmond 100.00
1865, NY Herald, Apr 15 (Beware: reprints abound) 900.00
1865, Titles other than NY Herald, Apr 15 ....400.00
1866-1900, Atmosphere editions 4.00
1876, Custer's Last Stand 150.00
1881, Billy the Kid killed 200.00
1881, Garfield assassinated 50.00
1881, Gunfight at OK Corral 225.00
1882, Jesse James killed 200.00
1898, Sinking of Maine 40.00
1901, McKinley assassinated 60.00
1903, Wright Brother's flight 300.00
1906, San Francisco earthquake, other titles 30.00
1906, San Francisco earthquake, San Francisco title 500.00
1912, Sinking of Titanic 250.00
1915, Sinking of Lusitania 125.00
1927, Babe Ruth hits 60th home run 70.00
1927, Lindbergh arrives in Paris 75.00
1929, St Valentine's Day Massacre 150.00
1929, Stock market crash 90.00
1931, Al Capone found guilty 35.00
1931, Jack 'Legs' Diamond killed 35.00
1933, Machine Gun Kelley captured 35.00
1934, Baby Face Nelson killed 40.00
1934, Bonnie & Clyde killed 125.00
1934, Dillinger killed 150.00
1934, Pretty Boy Floyd killed 35.00
1937, Hindenbergh explodes 65.00
1941, Honolulu Star-Bulletin, Dec 7, 1st extra (+) 600.00
1941, Other titles, Dec 7, w/Pearl Harbor news 35.00
1948, Chicago Daily Tribune, Nov 3, Dewey Defeats Truman ...900.00
1961, Alan Shephard 1st astronaut in space 20.00
1961, Roger Maris hits 61st home run 25.00
1962, Death of Marilyn Monroe 30.00
1962, John Glenn orbits Earth 18.00
1963, JFK assassination, Nov 22, Dallas title 60.00
1963, JFK assassination, Nov 22, titles other than Dallas 8.00
1968, Assassination of Martin Luther King 12.00
1968, Assassination of Robert Kennedy 12.00
1969, Moon landing 22.00
1974, Nixon resigns 12.00

Nicodemus

Chester Nicodemus moved from Dayton, Ohio, to Columbus in 1930 and started teaching at the Columbus Art School. During this time he made vases and commissioned sculptures, water fountains, and limestone and wood carvings. In 1941 Chester left the field of teaching to pursue pottery making full time, using local red clay containing a large amount of iron. Known for its durability, he called the ware Ferro-stone. He made teapots and other utility wares, but these goods lost favor, so he started producing animal and bird sculptures, nativity sets, and Christmas ornaments, some bearing Chester's and Florine's names as personalized cards for his customers and friends. Chester died in 1990.

His glaze colors were turquoise or aqua, ivory, green mottle, pussy willow (pink), and golden yellow. The glaze was applied so that the

color of the warm red clay would show through, adding an extra dimension to each piece. Examples are usually marked with his name incised in the clay, but paper labels were also used. Our advisor for this category is James Riebel; he is listed in the Directory under Ohio.

Ashtray, Indy 500, race car 50.00
Bank, rabbit figural, gr mottle, 4" 350.00

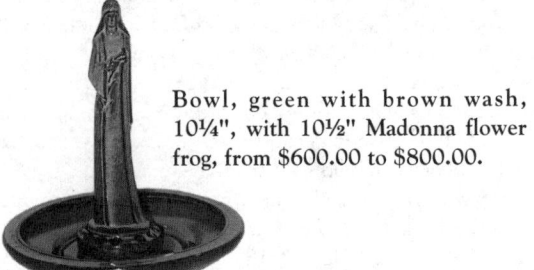

Bowl, green with brown wash, 10¼", with 10½" Madonna flower frog, from $600.00 to $800.00.

Bowl, leaf decor, mustard, 4" 45.00
Candy dish, concentric circles, brn, w/lid, 7½" 300.00
Christmas card/ornament, sleigh motif, 1967 ....85.00
Christmas card/ornament, star, brn, 1963 ....75.00
Creamer, w/lid, 4" 50.00
Figurine, kitten sleeping, sgn EJ, 3" L 150.00
Figurine, robin, 5" 195.00
Figurine, squirrel 135.00
New Year's card, rare, 1977 ....115.00
Pitcher, golden yel, 4" 60.00
Pitcher, turq, 2" 65.00
Planter, squirrel 150.00
Teapot, ind 250.00
Vase, brn, hdls, 4" 110.00
Vase, brn, 3" 65.00
Vase, cornucopia, mustard, 10" 235.00
Vase, gr, dbl twist hdl, 8" 175.00
Vase, gray, 3" 65.00
Vase, gray/brn, hdls, 4" 100.00
Vase, turq, bottle form, 4" 85.00
Vase, yel, 4" 95.00
Vase/cigarette holder (no lid, $60), w/lid 100.00
Wall pocket, dbl cornucopia, mustard, 9" 500.00

Niloak

During the latter part of the 1800s, there were many small utilitarian potteries in Benton, Arkansas. By 1900 only the Hyten Brothers Pottery remained. Charles Hyten, a second generation potter, took control of the family business around 1902. Shortly thereafter he renamed it the Eagle Pottery Company. In 1909 Hyten and former Rookwood potter Arthur Dovey began experimentation on a new swirl pottery. Dovey previously worked for the Ouachita Pottery Company of Hot Springs and produced a swirl pottery there as early as 1906. In March 1910 the Eagle Pottery Company introduced Niloak, kaolin spelled backwards. During 1911 Benton businessmen formed the Niloak Pottery corporation. Niloak, connected to the Arts and Crafts Movement and known as 'mission' ware, had a national representative in New York by 1913. Niloak's production centered on art pottery characterized by accidental, swirling patterns of natural and artificially colored clays. Many companies through the years have produced swirl pottery, yet none achieved the technical and aesthetic qualities of Niloak. Hyten received a patent in 1928 for the swirl technique. Although most examples have an interior glaze, some early Mission Ware pieces have an exterior glaze as well; these are extremely rare. Swirl/Mission Ware production continued steadily until the Depression when hard times and sagging sales caused Hyten to produce more traditional wares. In 1931 Niloak introduced Hywood Art Pottery, a glazed ware (sometimes similar in shape to Weller's Nile) of mostly hand-thrown vases. Soon thereafter, Niloak introduced castware as its primary production and renamed the line Hywood by Niloak. Throughout its existence, the company produced utilitarian items as well as artware. In 1934 Hyten's company found itself facing bankruptcy. Hardy L. Winburn, Jr., along with other Little Rock businessmen, raised the necessary capital and were able to provide the kind of leadership needed to make the business profitable once again. Both lines (Eagle and Hywood) were renamed 'Niloak' in 1937 to capitalize on this well-known name. The pottery continued in production until 1947 when it was converted to the Winburn Tile Company, which exists to this day in Little Rock. Be careful not to confuse the swirl production of the Evans Pottery of Missouri with Niloak. The significant difference is the dark brown matt interior glaze of Evans pottery.

Our co-advisors for this category are Lila and Fred Shrader (see the Directory under California) and David Edwin Gifford (see Arkansas). Mr. Gifford is the author of *Collector's Encyclopedia of Niloak Pottery*, and the editor of the *National Society of Arkansas Pottery Collectors Newsletter*.

Mission Ware

Photo courtesy David Gifford

Vase, spherical, 6½", $200.00; Vase, 6¾", $185.00.

Ashtray, w/fitted metal collar & cigarette holder, unmk, 5½" **135.00**
Ashtray/matchbox holder, 1st art mk+paper sticker, 4¾" **250.00**
Bottle, water; w/tumbler, 2nd art mk, 8¼" **450.00**
Bowl, flower; w/flower-frog rim, 2nd art mk, 4¾x5" **295.00**
Bowl, lily; str sides, flat, early art mk, 2¼x10½" **290.00**
Bowl, paper label, mini, 2¾x2¾" **110.00**
Bowl, powder; str sides, w/lid, 2nd art mk, 5" **350.00**
Bowl, 3-color swirl, Pat Pend'g, 3¼" **125.00**
Bowl/vase, 3-color swirl, 1st art mk, 2½x5" **100.00**
Box, cigar; w/ashtray lid, paper label+2nd art mk, 6½" sq **480.00**
Box, knobbed lid, 2nd art mk, 4½x3½" **265.00**
Candlestick holder, slim w/2¾" W base, early art mk, 6½" **125.00**
Chamberstick, w/finger ring, 5½" **225.00**
Compote, appl ftd stem, invt rim, sticker, 8¼x6" **400.00**
Flower frog, unmk, 1x3½" **75.00**
Humidor, bbl shape, 2nd art mk, 6½" **400.00**
Inkwell, bottle neck, bl & tan swirl, squat, 2½" **150.00**
Inkwell, cap w/orig glass liner, 2nd art mk, 3¼" sq **240.00**
Jar, bulbous, lid w/perforated insert, 2nd art mk, 6½" **460.00**
Jar, bulbous, w/lid, 2nd art mk, 3½" **290.00**
Jardiniere, decor rim, 2nd art mk, 13" **625.00**
Jug, w/finger ring, no stopper, 1st art mk, 6" **400.00**
Lamp base, old metal fittings, obscured mk, 14" **540.00**
Matchstick holder, cylindrical w/flared base, 2nd art mk, 2" **90.00**
Mug, conical, w/hdl, 1st art mk, 4½" **165.00**
Paperweight, state of Arkansas outline on unmk, 4" sq tile **190.00**

Paperweight, 1½" knob on unmk 4" sq tile **190.00**
Pitcher, bulbous, 9" **500.00**
Pitcher, lemonade; 1st art mk, 2-qt+, 6¾" **300.00**
Rose jar, 1st art mk, 8x5¾" **500.00**
Stein, flared base, 1st art mk, 4½" **250.00**
Tile, unmk, 4½" sq **85.00**
Tray, w/raised lip, 1st art mk, 4½" **400.00**
Tumbler, conical, 1st art mk, 4½" **110.00**
Tumbler, 2nd art mk, shot sz **110.00**
Vase, cylindrical w/slight flare at base, 1st art mk, 12" **360.00**
Vase, flared neck, 1st art mk, 6¾" **175.00**
Vase, flared neck, 2nd art mk, 4" **90.00**
Vase, flared rim, Benton Ark mk (die stamp), 8" **225.00**
Vase, flared rim, 2nd art mk,, 4¼" **70.00**
Vase, flat rim, early art mk, 4½" **70.00**
Vase, gourd shape, unmk, 9⅛" **180.00**
Vase, hourglass shape, 2nd art mk, 3½" **95.00**
Vase, incurvate rim, 1st art mk, 7¾" **160.00**
Vase, ovoid w/rolled rim, early art mk, 8½" **250.00**
Vase, rolled rim w/high shoulders, paper label, 4½" **100.00**
Vase, shouldered cylinder, 1st art mk, 10¼" **250.00**
Vase, squat w/sm neck opening, 2nd art mk, 3½x6" **240.00**
Vase, trumpet neck, 1st art mk, 10" **250.00**
Vase, waisted, 2nd art mk, 6¾" **100.00**
Vase, 3-color swirl, bulbous, Patent Pend'g, 5½" **140.00**
Vase, 4-color swirl, 2nd art mk, 3¼" **80.00**
Wall pocket, rolled rim, 2nd art mk, 8½" **295.00**
Water bottle, 1st art mk, 8½" **350.00**

Miscellaneous

Key:
HN — Hywood by Niloak   NB — Niloak (block letters) low-
ht — hand-tooled   relief mark
N — N mark   NI — Niloak (impressed) mark

Ashtray, football w/'A,' 2 rests, gloss, N, 3x4½" **40.00**
Ashtray, wooden shoe, 1 rest, N, 2½x5" **20.00**
Basket, basketweave, w/hdl, matt, N, mini, 3½" **30.00**
Basket, hanging, w/3 sm loops, matt, NI, 4½" dia **35.00**
Basket, w/hdl, gloss, NB, 6x6" **65.00**
Bowl, flower; low, flat, matt, NB, 3x12" dia **65.00**
Bowl, flower; overlapping leaves, matt, NB, 12" dia **75.00**
Bowl, 8 lg scallops, matt, NB, 8" dia **50.00**
Box, recessed-hdl lid, matt, NB, 3½x5" **55.00**
Candlestick, hand-thrown, paper label, matt, 6" **85.00**
Canoe, matt, N, mini, 2x5½" **35.00**
Cigarette holder, elephant w/open saddle, matt, 4" **60.00**
Cigarette holder, Southern Belle, seated w/open basket, 4½" **55.00**
Cornucopia, very graceful lines, gloss, NB, 8½" L **45.00**
Ewer, high-gloss, N, 6½" **25.00**
Figurine, deer in alert position, matt, 10" **95.00**
Figurine, donkey, head turned, facial features, ht, NB, 4" **100.00**
Figurine, donkey, stubborn, facial features, ht, NB, 3" **70.00**
Figurine, elephant, trunk extended lg ears, matt, 8" L **75.00**
Figurine, rabbits (2), ears up, matt, NB, 5½" **45.00**
Figurine, razorbk hog, w/or w/o U of A, matt, 4" **95.00**
Figurine, retriever, sitting, matt, NB, 4½" **45.00**
Figurine, Scottie dog, high-gloss, unmk, 3¼" **40.00**
Figurine, Trojan Horse on brick-like base, matt, 8½" **125.00**
Flower frog, various animals, up to 1½x4½" dia, from $15 to **30.00**
Flowerpot w/saucer, basketweave, gloss, 4½" **35.00**
Jar, strawberry; 4 bud-shape openings, matt, NB, 5½" **35.00**
Jar, strawberry; 6 openings, high-gloss, NB, 9½" **55.00**

Jug, gloss, mini, 3½" **15.00**
Jug, matt, mini, 3½" **25.00**
Jug, w/finger ring & spout, tall, slender, semigloss, NB, 8" **55.00**
Juice set, matt, NB, 7" pitcher+4 4¾" tumblers **60.00**
Matchbook holder, razorbk hog, w/or w/o U of A, matt, 5" **100.00**
Pin dish, open flower shape, matt, 3½" dia **20.00**
Pitcher, Art Deco decor, angular hdl, matt, 7" **85.00**
Pitcher, graceful hdl & spout, matt, mini, 2½" **18.00**
Pitcher, hand-thrown, detail on appl hdl, gloss, 4" **30.00**
Pitcher, hand-thrown, matt, recessed lid, 2nd art mk, 7" **100.00**
Pitcher, syrup-like, glossy, N, 4" **25.00**
Planter, cradle, matt, 4x6" **35.00**
Planter, frog, smiling/seated/arms crossed, glossy, 5½" **30.00**
Planter, parrot on bowl, overglaze decor, NB, matt, 5" **95.00**
Planter, pelican w/overglaze decor, matt, NB, 5½" **95.00**
Planter, polar bear w/attached sq basket, matt, 3½" **75.00**
Planter, pouter pigeon w/fanned wings, matt, NB, 9" **120.00**
Planter, rocking horse, well detailed, matt, 6½" **85.00**
Planter, rooster, crowing, detailed feathers, NB, 9" **45.00**
Planter, Southern belle standing, matt, 11" **135.00**
Planter, swan, high-gloss, NB, 3½" **15.00**
Planter, wishing well, covered, matt, 8½" **45.00**
Shakers, various shapes, matt, from 2-3", pr, from $20 to **35.00**
Tumbler, Art Deco decor, matt, 5½" **28.00**
Vase, bud; matt, HN, 9" **20.00**
Vase, hand-thrown, appl hdls, matt, HN, 9" **100.00**
Vase, hand-thrown, semigloss, HN, 4" **40.00**
Wall pocket, cup & saucer, bouquet decor, pastel matt, NB, 5" **45.00**

Nippon

Nippon generally refers to Japanese wares made during the period from 1891 to 1921, although the Nippon mark was also used to a limited extent on later wares (accompanied by 'Japan'). Nippon, meaning Japan, identified the country of origin to comply with American importation restrictions. After 1921 'Japan' was the acceptable alternative. The term does not imply a specific type of product and may be found on items other than porcelains. For further information we recommend *The Collector's Encyclopedia of Nippon Porcelain* (there are five in the series) by our advisor, Joan Van Patten; you will find her address in the Directory under New York. In the following listings, items are assumed hand painted unless noted otherwise. Numbers included in the descriptions refer to these specific marks:

Key:
#1 — China E-OH
#2 — M in Wreath
#3 — Cherry Blossom
#4 — Double T Diamond in Circle
#5 — Rising Sun
#6 — Royal Kinran
#7 — Maple Leaf
#8 — Royal Nippon, Nishiki
#9 — Royal Moriye Nippon

Ashtray, blown-out reclining dog, 5¾" dia, $465.00.

Photo courtesy Joan Van Patten

Ashtray, autumn leaves in relief, 4-rest, #2, 2½" H **325.00**
Ashtray, Sitting Bull portrait, 3-rest, #2, 5½" **500.00**

Basket vase, mc roses w/heavy gold beads, unmk, 7½" **450.00**
Basket vase, moriage geese on lt bl, integral hdl, unmk, 8½" **700.00**
Beverage set, river scenic, #2, 9½" pitcher+6 4" tumblers **650.00**
Bookends, horses in relief, brn tones, #2, 6", pr **2,200.00**
Bowl, fruit; mc fruit in relief, hdls, #2, 7½" **225.00**
Candlesticks, sailing ships, much gold at top & ft, #2, 9½", pr ...**800.00**
Celery tray, floral reserves on cobalt w/gold, #7, 13¼" L **450.00**
Cheese dish, sampan scenic, slant lid, #5, 7¾" L **185.00**
Chocolate set, gold o/l on wht, bl #7, pot+6 c/s **1,200.00**
Chocolate set, mums, pk on wht w/gold, pot+8 c/s **925.00**
Chocolate set, roses, mc on wht w/much gold, #7, pot+6 c/s **900.00**
Chocolate set, scenic w/cobalt & gold, #7, pot+4 c/s **2,000.00**
Coffeepot, river scenic, earth tones, stick hdl, #7, 6" **150.00**
Compote, roses w/bl Wedgwood-style borders, #2, 4½x8½" **300.00**
Condensed milk container, floral on wht w/cobalt & gold, #6 ...**175.00**
Condensed milk container, gold o/l on wht, #7 ....**175.00**
Cracker jar, lg pk roses, gold trim, 3-ftd, #7, 8" **500.00**
Cruet, rabbit running, earth tones, #2, 5½" **250.00**
Demitasse set, butterflies, blk on wht, pot+cr/sug+6 c/s **300.00**
Ewer, Madame Lebrun reserve on gr w/gold, #7, 12" **1,300.00**
Ferner, Egyptian decor panels, 8-sided, #2, 7" **400.00**
Ferner, fox hunt scene, 4-lobe, ftd, hdls, bl #7", 4" **450.00**
Ferner, river scenic w/cobalt & gold, ftd, hdls, #2, 8¼" **450.00**
Hair receiver, river scenic, 4-ftd, #2, 3" dia **65.00**
Humidor, dogs in relief on brn, #2, 6" **1,100.00**
Humidor, Dutch-type figures w/dog, brn borders, #2, 7" **1,200.00**
Humidor, florals w/moriage, squirrel finial, unmk, 7½" **750.00**
Humidor, lady chasing geese, 8-sided, #2, 8" **950.00**
Humidor, man on camel, earth tones w/gold, #2, 7" **800.00**
Humidor, monk portrait reserve, moriage trim, #7, 8" **1,700.00**
Humidor, playing cards on brn, #2, 7" **800.00**
Inkwell, Deco florals on bl, #2, 4" W **275.00**
Inkwell, Egyptian decor, brn & yel, rnd, gr #2, 4" H **1,200.00**
Jug, whiskey; wht woodland scene w/moriage, bl #2, 7½" **950.00**
Jug, wine; monk drinking, moriage trim, #7, 9½" **2,000.00**
Letter holder, floral on cream, #2, 4½x6" **200.00**
Loving cup, early airplane, angle hdls, #2, 3¾" **225.00**
Loving cup, Wedgwood-style scenic, sm gold hdls, #2, 7¾" **550.00**
Mug, 2 clown children w/rabbit on wht, #5, 3¾" **120.00**
Pitcher, Deco-style mc florals at top on wht, w/lid, #2, 5½" **150.00**
Pitcher, Dutch lady at water's edge, simple hdl, #2, 4½" **350.00**
Plaque, cockatoo on perch, #2, 10" **325.00**
Plaque, lady's portrait, coralene at rim, Kinran mk, 7½" **1,200.00**
Plaque, moose & tree in relief, earth tones, #4, 15" **900.00**
Plaque, still life on table, realistic, #2, 12¼" **450.00**
Plaque, swan scenic, #2, 10" **350.00**
Plaque, windmill scenic, gr #2, 10" **275.00**
Plaque, 3 dogs in relief, brn/wht/blk, smooth rim, #2, 10½" **1,300.00**
Plate, lady's portrait, leaf & floral rim w/gold, #7, 10" **700.00**
Plate, moriage flying geese in sunset, #7, 11" **650.00**
Platter, lobster & fruit, gr & gold border, #2, 16" **850.00**
Relish, Wedgwood type, bl boat form w/uptrn hdls, #2, 7½" **250.00**
Serving dish, floral on cream, center hdl, 3-compartment, #2, 7" .**110.00**
Shaving mug, Indian reserve, ring hdl, #2, 3¾" **325.00**
Shaving mug, roses on wht w/gold, 2-pc, mk, 3½" **350.00**
Sugar bowl, floral band on cream, hdls, w/lid, #2, 6½" dia **80.00**
Sugar cube holder, river scenic, rectangular, hdls, #2, 5½" **125.00**
Sugar shaker, floral band on wht, gold hdl, gr #2, 5¼" **120.00**
Sugar shaker, roses on cobalt w/gold, #7, 4¼" **250.00**
Tankard, gold floral on wht, slim, mk, 16" **800.00**
Tankard, irises, bl & brn tones, ornate hdl, slim, #6, 12¼" **700.00**
Tankard, lg open flowers w/much gold, Oriental China mk, 14" .**575.00**
Tea caddy, roses reserve on gr w/mc enamel beads, mk, 4½" **210.00**
Tea set, boy in sailor suit holds gun, child sz, 15-pc **300.00**

Tea set, woodland scene, brn sky, #7, pot+cr/sug+6 c/s **1,200.00**
Tea strainer, floral & cobalt w/gold, gr #2, 6¼" L **225.00**
Tray, Wedgwood type, bl, sm sq hdls, canted corners, #2, 10" ...**350.00**
Trivet, Black man stands w/camel, 8-sided, #2, 7" **250.00**
Urn, deer at water reserve on wht w/much gold, gr #2, 24" **5,000.00**
Urn, floral reserves on gr w/gold, uptrn hdls, w/lid, #7, 10" **450.00**
Urn, floral w/coralene & gold on gr, mk, w/lid, 15" **1,800.00**
Urn, lady's portrait reserve on red & wht w/gold, #7, 14" **1,600.00**
Urn, man on camel w/gold, ornate hdls, #2, 38" **9,500.00**
Urn, moriage dragon & trim, lg hdls, unmk, 11" **425.00**
Vase, bird on branch, Deco style, hdls, #2, 7½", pr **175.00**
Vase, bird on floral branch, trumpet form, gr #2, 9" **300.00**
Vase, coralene flowers on wht w/gold, shouldered, mk, 6¾" **500.00**
Vase, floral reserve on cobalt w/gold o/l, slim, #7, 18" **2,500.00**
Vase, floral reserves on wht band w/gold, 6-sided, slim, #7, 12" ..**350.00**
Vase, fruit reserve w/moriage trim, ornate hdls, #7, 8" **325.00**
Vase, irises, purple w/gold tracery, slim, unmk, 10¼" **250.00**
Vase, kangaroo scenic, sm gold hdls, mk, 12" **275.00**
Vase, lady's portrait reserve on cobalt w/gold, hdls, #7, 9½" ...**1,400.00**
Vase, man on camel scene, ornate brn hdls, #2, 9¼" **550.00**
Vase, man on camel scene, 3 elephant-head hdls, #2, 6" **375.00**
Vase, man sowing seed in relief, #2, 10½" **2,200.00**
Vase, moriage crane & flowers, ornate hdls, 4-ftd, #7, 8½" **700.00**
Vase, moriage dragon, creature hdls, #7, 9½" **750.00**
Vase, moriage dragon, gourd form w/shaped rim, #7, 8" **350.00**
Vase, mtn scenic on cobalt w/gold, ring hdls, #7, 13½" **3,000.00**
Vase, mums, mc w/gold, slim form, ruffled rim, #6, 11½" **375.00**
Vase, mums, pk on cobalt, classic form, #7, 18" **900.00**
Vase, ocean & gull scene, gold hdls & rim, #2, 8½" **600.00**
Vase, orchid reserve band on cobalt w/gold o/l, hdls, #7, 9" **525.00**
Vase, Oriental floral on wht w/gr & gold, sm hdls, #2, 18" **800.00**
Vase, Oriental-style tapestry on wht w/gold, bulbous, #7, 5½" ...**800.00**
Vase, Queen Louise portrait on turq w/gold, cylinder, #7, 12" ..**1,750.00**
Vase, rose tapestry, gold hdls, bottle neck, #7, 7¾" **900.00**
Vase, roses, mc/lg, gold rim/ft/ring hdls, #7, 12½" **625.00**
Vase, roses on mottle w/gold tracery, cylindrical, #7, 15¼" **700.00**
Vase, roses reserve, mc w/gold, bottle neck, hdls, unmk, 9½" **475.00**
Vase, sampan scenic, tall ft, angular hdls, #2, 6" **150.00**
Vase, scenic reserve on cobalt w/gold o/l, uptrn hdls, #7, 12" **800.00**
Vase, snow scene, silver o/l, akimbo hdls, RC Nippon mk, 9½" .**800.00**
Vase, sunset scenic band, gold hdls, bottle neck, #2, 10½" **375.00**
Vase, swan scenic on cobalt w/much gold, urn form, #7, 24" ...**6,500.00**
Vase, Wedgwood style, bl, sm hdls, sq mouth, gr #2, 7¾" **600.00**
Vase, windmill scene, angle hdls w/rings, ftd, #2, 14" **1,000.00**
Vase, windmill scene, earth tones, hdls, #2, 12¾" **400.00**
Vase, windmill scenic band, 6-sided, #2, 15" **1,200.00**
Vase, woodland scene, brn sky, bottle neck, hdls, #2, 4½" **350.00**
Vase, woodland scene, wht w/moriage, shouldered, #2, 9" **500.00**
Vase, woodland scene w/brn sky, hdls, #2, 10½" **625.00**
Vase, woodland scene w/moriage, 3-ftd, angle hdls, #2, 8¼" **500.00**

Nodders

So called because of the nodding action of their heads and hands, nodders originated in China where they were used in temple rituals to represent deity. At first they were made of brass and were actually a type of bell; when these bells were rung, the heads of the figures would nod. In the 18th century, the idea was adopted by Meissen and by French manufacturers who produced not only china nodders but bisque as well. Most nodders are individual; couples are unusual. The idea remained popular until the end of the 19th century and was used during the Victorian era by toy manufacturers. For further informations we recommend *Figural Nodders, Indentification & Value Guide*, by Hilma R.

Irtz, available from Collector Books or your local bookstore. Our advisor for non-German nodders is Barry Larkins; he is listed in the Directory under Florida.

Blinking boy, compo, 1 glass eye open, Germany, 1910s, 5½", EX .**165.00**
Camel, fabric over papier-mache & wood, 8x6½" **175.00**
Campbell Kid, compo, wood base, G Drayton, Germany, 1910, 6⅛", EX **200.00**
Cockatoo, noods/sticks out tongue, Germany, 1890s, 6⅝" **350.00**
Donald Duck in sailor outfit, WDP, Irwin, 5" **95.00**
Donkey, mc chalkware, 6", EX **45.00**
Elephant, celluloid, pk, German sticker, 1½" **75.00**
Elfin-like figure, compo, cb base, Germany, ca 1910, 5½", EX **70.00**
Falconer by tree-trunk candle holder, Conta & Boehme, #8343, 6½" ..**225.00**
Flapper girl kicks legs in bathtub ashtray, Japan, 5½x5¼" **70.00**
Indian man on nodding elephant, bsk, 4¾" **220.00**
Keystone Cop, compo & wood, Germany, ca 1900, 7⅝", EX **230.00**
Lucky Leo Lion, MIB **25.00**
Old Lady, compo & wood, Germany, ca 1900, 6⅛", EX **220.00**
Oriental lady w/samisen, mc on terra cotta, 3¼" **150.00**
Policeman drawing saber, 2-way swayer, Portugal, 1900s, 9¼" ...**125.00**
Rabbit, life-like, Japan, 1960s, MIB **55.00**

German Comic Characters

During the early 1930s, Germany produced a collection of small figure dolls, approximately 2" to 4" high, representing the most popular comic strip and cartoon characters of that time. They were made of bisque with brightly painted details and clearly stamped with their appropriate names and 'Germany' on their backs. Generally, their movable heads were attached with an elastic string going through their bodies, hence the name 'nodders,' but there were some characters produced earlier that were frozen with no movable parts. The most popular ones came in boxed sets, but the lesser-known characters were sold separately, making them rarer and harder to find today. We have listed the most valuable characters from the series here; those not mentioned below are valued at $125.00 and under. Our advisor for German character nodders is Doug Dezso; he is listed in the Directory under New Jersey. He will answer questions (as long as an SASE is included) on German character nodders only.

Old Timer, $350.00.

Photo courtesy Doug Dezso

Ambrose Potts **350.00**
Auntie Blossom **150.00**
Auntie Mamie & Uncle Willie, ea **350.00**
Bill, Dock, Avery, Max or Pop Jenks, ea **200.00**
Buttercup **250.00**
Chubby Chaney **250.00**
Corky **475.00**
Ferina **350.00**
Grandpa Teen **350.00**
Happy Hooligan **600.00**
Harold Teen **150.00**

Jeff Regus, med or lg, ea 250.00
Jeff Regus, sm 175.00
Junior Nebbs 500.00
Lillums 150.00
Little Annie Rooney, arms move 250.00
Little Egypt 350.00
Lord Plushbottom 150.00
Ma & Paw Winkle, ea 350.00
Marjory, Patsy, Lilacs or Josie, ea 400.00
Mary Ann Jackson 250.00
Min Gump 150.00
Mr Bailey 150.00
Mr Bibb 400.00
Mr Winker 250.00
Mushmouth 200.00
Mutt or Jeff, ea 250.00
Nicodemus 350.00
Pat Finnegan 400.00
Pete the Dog 250.00
Rudy or Fanny Nebbs, ea 250.00
Scraps 250.00
Widow Zander 400.00
Winnie Winkle 150.00

Noritake

The Noritake Company was first registered in 1904 as Nippon Gomei Kaisha. In 1917 the name became Nippon Toki Kabushiki Toki. The 'M in wreath' mark is that of the Morimura Brothers, distributors with offices in New York. It was used until 1941. The 'tree crest' mark is the crest of the Morimura family.

The Noritake Company has produced fine porcelain dinnerware sets and occasional pieces decorated in the delicate manner for which the Japanese are noted. (Two dinnerware patterns are featured below, and a general range is suggested for others.)

Authority Joan Van Patten has compiled two lovely books, *The Collector's Encyclopedia of Noritake, Vols. I* and *II*, with many full-color photos and current prices; you will find her address in the Directory under New York. In the following listings, examples are hand painted unless noted otherwise. Numbers refer to these specific marks:

Key:
#1 — Komaru   #3 — M in Wreath
#2 — M in Wreath

Azalea

The Azalea pattern was produced exclusively for the Larkin Company, who gave the lovely ware away as premiums to club members and their home agents. From 1916 through the '30s, Larkin distributed fine china which was decorated in pink azaleas on white with gold tracing along edges and handles. Early in the '30s, six pieces of crystal hand painted with the same design were offered: candle holders, a compote, a tray with handles, a scalloped fruit bowl, a cheese and cracker set, and a cake plate. All in all, seventy different pieces of Azalea were produced. Some, such as the fifteen-piece child's set, bulbous vase, china ashtray, and the pancake jug, are quite rare. One of the earliest marks was the Noritake 'M in wreath' with variations. Later the ware was marked 'Noritake, Azalea, Hand Painted, Japan.' Our advisor is Peggy Roush; she is listed in the Directory under Florida.

Basket, mint; Dolly Varden, #193 ....195.00
Bonbon, #184, 6¼" 50.00

Bowl, #12, 10" 42.50
Bowl, candy/grapefruit; #185 ....195.00
Bowl, deep, #310 ....68.00
Bowl, fruit; shell form, #188, 7¾" 385.00
Bowl, oatmeal; #55, 5½" 28.00
Bowl, vegetable; divided, #439, 9½" 295.00
Bowl, vegetable; oval, #101, 10½" 60.00
Bowl, vegetable; oval, #172, 9¼" 58.00
Butter chip, #312, 3¼" 145.00
Butter tub, w/insert, #54 ....48.00
Cake plate, #10, 9¾" 40.00
Candy jar, w/lid, #313 ....695.00
Casserole, gold finial, w/lid, #372 ....540.00
Casserole, w/lid, #16 ....115.00
Celery/roll tray, #99, 12" 55.00
Cheese/butter dish, #314 ....135.00
Child's set, #253, 15-pc 2,500.00
Coffeepot, AD; #182 ....595.00
Compote, #170 ....98.00
Condiment set, #14, 5-pc 65.00
Creamer & sugar bowl, #122 ....158.00
Creamer & sugar bowl, #7 ....45.00
Creamer & sugar bowl, AD; open; #123 ....140.00
Creamer & sugar bowl, gold finial, #401 ....155.00
Creamer & sugar bowl, ind, #449 ....395.00
Cruet, #190 ....195.00
Cup & saucer, #2 ....20.00
Cup & saucer, AD; #183 ....150.00
Cup & saucer, bouillon; #124, 3½" 24.50
Gravy boat, #40 ....48.00
Jam jar set, #125, 4-pc 155.00
Mayonnaise set, scalloped, #453, 3-pc 495.00
Mustard jar, #191, 3-pc 60.00
Pickle/lemon set, #121 ....24.50
Pitcher, milk jug; #100, 1-qt 195.00
Plate, #4, 7½" 10.00
Plate, bread & butter; #8, 6½" 10.00
Plate, breakfast; #98 ....28.00
Plate, cream soup; #363 ....175.00
Plate, dinner; #13, 9¾" 28.00
Plate, grill; 3-compartment, #38, 10¼" 165.00
Plate, scalloped sq, salesman's sample 950.00
Plate, soup; #19, 7⅛" 25.00
Platter, #17, 14" 60.00
Platter, #186, 16" 475.00
Platter, #56, 12" 58.00
Platter, cold meat/bacon; #311, 10¼" 215.00
Refreshment set, #39, 2-pc 48.00
Relish, #194, 7⅛" 85.00
Relish, oval, #18, 8½" 20.00
Relish, 2-part, #171 ....58.00
Relish, 2-part, loop hdl, #450 ....425.00
Relish, 4-section, #119, rare, 10" 150.00
Saucer, fruit; #9, 5¼" 10.00
Shakers, bell form, #11, pr 30.00
Shakers, bulbous, #89, pr 30.00
Shakers, ind, #126, pr 27.50
Spoon holder, #189, 8" 115.00
Syrup, #97, w/underplate & ladle 135.00
Tea tile 40.00
Teapot, #15 ....110.00
Teapot, gold finial, #400 ....495.00
Toothpick holder, #192 ....135.00
Vase, bulbous, #452 ....1,150.00

Vase, fan form, ftd, #187 ....**185.00**
Whipped cream/mayonnaise set, #3, 3-pc **38.50**

Tree in the Meadow

Another of their dinnerware lines has become a favorite of many collectors. Tree in the Meadow features a hand-painted scene with a large dark tree in the foreground, growing near a lake. There is usually a cottage in the distance. Sometimes referred to as Tree by the Lake, this line was made during the 1920s and '30s and seems today to be in good supply. Various interesting forms are seen, and reassembling a complete set should be an enjoyable undertaking. Our advisor is Peggy Roush; she is listed in the Directory under Florida.

Basket, Dolly Varden **125.00**
Bowl, cream soup; 2-hdl **35.00**
Bowl, fruit; shell form, #210 ....**300.00**
Bowl, oatmeal **15.00**
Bowl, soup **20.00**
Bowl, vegetable; 9" **35.00**
Butter pat **15.00**
Butter tub, open, w/drainer **35.00**
Cake plate **35.00**
Candy dish, 5½" **400.00**
Celery dish **35.00**
Cheese dish **45.00**
Coffeepot **200.00**
Compote **50.00**
Condiment set, 5-pc **45.00**
Creamer & sugar bowl, demitasse **40.00**
Cruets, vinegar & oil; cojoined, #319 ....**360.00**
Cup & saucer, breakfast **25.00**
Cup & saucer, demitasse **35.00**
Egg cup **30.00**
Gravy boat **50.00**
Jam jar/dish, 4-pc **70.00**
Lemon dish **15.00**
Mayonnaise set, 3-pc **50.00**
Relish, divided **35.00**
Sugar bowl, #204 ....**25.00**
Tea set, 3-pc **100.00**

Miscellaneous

Ashtray, pipe & matches on brn, 4-rest, #2, 4½" sq **80.00**
Ashtray, playing cards on tan, 1-rest, gr #2, 5½" **65.00**
Basket vase, lovebirds on yel w/gold, #2, 5¾" **135.00**
Bowl, exotic bird center, Deco-style band, gr #2, 7¼" **65.00**
Bowl, florals on orange lustre band, hdls, #2, 6¾" **40.00**
Bowl, irises on wht, bl band, gold hdls, #2, 10½" **75.00**
Bowl, lovebirds on branch, yel band, blk hdls, #2, 7" **45.00**
Bowl, parrot on branch, wide blk band, #2, 10" **65.00**
Bowl, roses on ivory, pk scalloped rim, #2, 5" **40.00**
Bowl, sampan scene w/silver o/l trim, #2, 10" **150.00**
Bowl, snow scene, 3 sm integral hdls, red #2, 6½" **55.00**
Bowl, tree landscape on yel, gold angle hdls, #2, 7" **40.00**
Box, elephant w/howdah figural, red #2, 6½" **400.00**
Bread & butter set, floral/orange lustre, #2, lg+6 sm plates **85.00**
Cake plate, flower baskets & swags along rim, hdls, #2, 11" **45.00**
Cake plate, river/sailboat/palms, orange/bl lustre, #2, 9¾" **45.00**
Candlesticks, exotic bird on wht, bl at rim & ft, #2, 8¼", pr **200.00**
Candy dish, Deco lady on red lid, blk base, #2, 6½" dia **350.00**
Celery tray, Deco floral & bluebirds on wht, #2, 11" **50.00**
Chambersticks, flower on orange lustre, ring hdls, #2, 2¼", pr **90.00**

Cheese dish, Deco-style floral band, slant top, gr #2, 4x8x6" **100.00**
Chip & dip set, river scene at sunset, gr #2, 9¾" **80.00**

Chocolate pot, gold decor on white, blue mark, 9¾", $225.00.

Chocolate pot, floral, pastel on wht, 6-sided, #2, +6 c/s **225.00**
Chocolate pot, gold design on wht, gr #2, 9" **110.00**
Chocolate pot, pyramids & palms on yel, #2, 9½", +6 c/s **225.00**
Cigarette holder, floral on bell shape, bird finial, #2, 5" **140.00**
Compote, trees at water's edge, shaped rim, hdls, #2, 9" **60.00**
Condensed milk container, Deco floral on wht w/gold, gr #2, 5¼" .**135.00**
Creamer, Deco flowers on wht w/orange lustre & gold, #2, 5¾" ...**30.00**
Cup & saucer, mustache; river scenic, gr #2, 5¾" dia **100.00**
Demitasse set, river at sunset, #2, pot+cr/sug+6 plates+6 c/s **450.00**
Dresser doll, lady w/fan figural, #2, 6½" **325.00**
Egg cup, river scenic w/sm windmill, gr #2, 3½" **30.00**
Ferner, red leaves & blkberries, triangular, #2, 6" **135.00**
Fish set, fish in water, #2, 16" platter+8 8½" plates **1,100.00**
Flower holder, bird on stump form, orange/bl lustre, #2, 4¾" **200.00**
Game plate, mallards, fruit basket rim, #2, 8½" **90.00**
Humidor, man & woman silhouettes on ivory, gr #2, 6¾" **450.00**
Humidor, river at sunset scene, pipe finial, gr #2, 3¾" **160.00**
Jam jar, strawberries on tan, rose finial, #2, 5½" **100.00**
Jar, potpourri; bl upper third over wht body, rose finial, #2, 6" **85.00**
Jar, potpourri; floral wreath on bl, rose finial, gr #2, 6½" **110.00**
Lemon dish, lemon on ivory, red rim & hdl, #2, 5¾" **40.00**
Mustard jar, scenic in bls & brns on ivory w/gold, gr #2, 2½" **35.00**
Napkin ring, roses, mc on wht, gr #2, 2¼" W **45.00**
Nappy, Deco floral on wht, gold scalloped rim, 1-hdl, #2, 6½" **40.00**
Nut cup, floral, pastel on wht, 3-ftd, #2, ind **12.00**
Plaque, dog at river scene, gr #2, 7½" **175.00**
Plaque, lady on sofa silhouette on ivory, #2, 8½" **275.00**
Plaque, steamship portrait, RC mk, 19" **200.00**
Playing card holder, palm scenic, gr #2, 3¾" **135.00**
Sauce dish, fruit on ivory int, flower form, #2, 4" H **45.00**
Sauce dish, river scenic, earth tones, #2, 3", w/ladle & plate **75.00**
Shaker, river scene w/tree & sailboat, #2, 2½" **10.00**
Spooner, river scene in earth tones w/red, hdls, #2, 8" L **60.00**
Tea tile, river scene, earth tones, canted corners, #2, 5" **45.00**
Teapot, snow scene w/gold, #2, 4¾", +cr/sug+6 plates+6 c/s **250.00**
Tidbit, river scene at sunset, 2-tier, gr #2, 8¾" **80.00**
Toast rack, bl lustre w/red bird finial, #2, 5½" L **95.00**
Toothpick holder, lady w/red fan, bl lustre, 3-hdl, #2, 2¼" **65.00**
Tray, Deco fruit border, gold hdls, red #2, 11" **95.00**
Tray, lady w/ruffled collar & sleeves on gr, #2, 8¼" **300.00**
Tray, river scene, brns & bls, bl #1, 12" **70.00**
Vase, bl Wedgwood type, sm angle hdls, #1, 9½" **425.00**
Vase, floral on ivory, gold trim/hdls, gr #2, 10½" **175.00**
Vase, floral w/bl & orange lustre, 6 birds perched at rim, #2, 7" ..**300.00**
Vase, gr fan form w/wide floral band along rim, #2, 6½" **150.00**
Vase, peacock feathers on tan, slim, ruffled rim, #1, 8", pr **270.00**
Vase, river scene, earth tones, hdls, #2, 7" **100.00**
Vase, river scene reserve on bl, gold rim & hdls, #2, 7¼", pr **340.00**
Vase, sampan scene, gold band & ring hdls, #1, 10" **350.00**

Wall pocket, butterflies on orange lustre, red #2, 8¼" **100.00**
Wall pocket, dbl; Deco florals on ivory, bl lustre band, #2, 8" **150.00**
Wall pocket, swan scene, #2, 8" **110.00**

Various Dinnerware Patterns, ca. 1933 to Present

So many lines of dinnerware have been produced by the Noritake company that to list them all would require a volume in itself. In fact, just such a book is available — *The Collector's Encyclopedia of Early Noritake* by Aimee Neff Alden (Collector Books). And while many patterns had specific names, others did not, so you'll probably need the photographs the book contains to help you identify your pattern. Outlined below is a general guide for the more common pieces and patterns. The high side of the range will represent lines from about 1933 until the mid-'60s (including those marked 'Occupied Japan'), while the lower side should be used to evaluate lines made after that period.

Bowl, berry; individual, from $8 to..**10.00**
Bowl, soup, 7½", from $10 to **15.00**
Bowl, vegetable; rnd or oval, ca 1945 to present, from $25 to........**35.00**
Butter dish, 3-pc, ca 1933-64, from $35 to......................................**50.00**
Creamer, from $15 to **25.00**
Cup, demi; w/saucer, from $10 to **17.50**
Gravy boat, from $35 to..**45.00**
Pickle or relish dish, from $15 to..**25.00**
Plate, bread & butter; from $8 to **12.00**
Plate, dinner; from $15 to **30.00**
Plate, luncheon; from $10 to **18.00**
Plate, salad; from $10 to **15.00**
Platter, 12", from $25 to **40.00**
Platter, 16" (or larger), from $40 to..**60.00**
Shakers, pr, from $15 to..**25.00**
Sugar bowl, w/lid, from $15 to..**30.00**
Tea & toast set (sm cup & tray), from $15 to **25.00**
Teapot, demi pot, chocolate pot, or coffeepot, from $45 to **60.00**

Norse

The Norse Pottery was established in 1903 in Edgerton, Wisconsin, by Thorwald Sampson and Louis Ipson. A year later it was purchased by A.W. Wheelock and moved to Rockford, Illinois. The ware they produced was inspired by ancient bronze vessels of the Norsemen. Designs were often incised into the red clay body. Dragon handles and feet were favored decorative devices, and they achieved a semblance of patina through the application of metallic glazes. The ware was marked with model numbers and a stylized 'N' containing a vertical arrangement of the remaining letters of the name. Production ceased after 1913. Our advisor for this category is John Danis; he is listed in the Directory under Illinois.

Bowl, incised rising sun, dragon head hdls, #50, 7½" L.................**250.00**
Bowl, incised waves, 3-ftd, #55, 2½x4½" **200.00**
Jardiniere, incised snake, 3 Viking head ft, verdigris, #62, 7x9" .**500.00**
Jardiniere, serpent hdls, 3-ftd, #70, 4x6" **500.00**
Mug, incised circles/waves on hdl, verdigris/gold wash, #51 ....**125.00**
Pitcher, 1-stem plant w/incised leaves, gold wash, #90, 12" **300.00**
Vase, geometrics, gold wash, #13, 9½x8" **250.00**
Vase, geometrics, gold wash, w/hdl, #102, 3x4½" **150.00**
Vase, geometrics at shoulder, gold wash, #45, 4¾" **110.00**
Vase, lg lizard on side, gold wash, #25, 12" **1,000.00**
Vase, 2 lions on sides at top, gold wash, flowerpot form, #114, 8" .**1,000.00**
Vase, 4 applied ferns attach to lg rolled-out rim, gold wash, #24, 10" ..**1,200.00**
Vase/lamp base, appl ferns, verdigris, #29L (V if vase), 10" **850.00**

Wall pocket, 2 lg imp lizards, dmn shape, #72, 11" **1,500.00**

North Dakota School of Mines

The School of Mines of the University of North Dakota was established in 1890, but due to a lack of funding it was not until 1898 that Earle J. Babcock was appointed as director, and efforts were made to produce ware from the native clay he had discovered several years earlier. The first pieces were made by firms in the East from the clay Babcock sent them. Some of the ware was decorated by the manufacturer; some was shipped back to North Dakota to be decorated by native artists. By 1909 students at the University of North Dakota were producing utilitarian items such as tile, brick, shingles, etc., in conjunction with a ceramic course offered through the chemistry department. By 1910 a ceramic department had been established, supervised by Margaret Kelly Cable. Under her leadership, fine artware was produced. Native flowers, grains, buffalo, cowboys, and other subjects indigenous to the state were incorporated into the decorations. Some pieces have an Art Nouveau — Art Deco style easily attributed to her association with Frederick H. Rhead, with whom she studied in 1911. During the '20s the pottery was marketed on a limited scale through gift and jewelry stores in the state. From 1927 until 1949 when Miss Cable announced her retirement, a more widespread distribution was maintained with sales branching out into other states. The ware was marked in cobalt with the official seal — 'Made at School of Mines, N.D. Clay, University of North Dakota, Grand Forks, N.D.' in a circle. Very early ware was sometimes marked 'U.N.D.' in cobalt by hand. For more information refer to *Collector's Encyclopedia of Dakota Potteries* by Darlene Hurst Dommel.

Ashtray, pale gr, leaf form, Solee **80.00**
Bowl, burgundy w/squirrel & acorn, hexagonal, McNicol, 1953 .**140.00**
Bowl, centerpc; dusty rose, triangular, ruffled, dbl mkd **265.00**
Bowl, floral checker band on brn, R Rudser, 3½" dia **110.00**
Bowl, gr matt, closed form, 2x8½" **220.00**
Bowl, jonquils, brn & gr on bl, D Kane, 1925, 2½x8", NM **650.00**
Bowl, meadowlarks/rushes emb on lime gr, M Cable, #155, 6¼" .**600.00**
Carafe, deer & oak leaf relief, Ida McNicol, 1950 ....**525.00**
Carafe, Sioux Calendar, turq, Mattson, #199 ....**495.00**
Ginger jar, birds & scrolls, FL Hammers, 1926, 7⅞", NM **300.00**
Humidor, Indian chiefs' profiles on band, M Cable, rpr, 7¾" ..**1,900.00**
Lamp base, gr to brn, sgn Taft, ink mk, 1930, 10" **165.00**
Paperweight, lion, tan gloss, Julia Mattson, 3" **300.00**
Pitcher, floral on tan, sgn, 1949, lg **325.00**
Plaque, Grand Council of Masters, 1933 ....**185.00**
Plaque, Stockwell portrait, bl & wht gloss, J Mattson, 5x3¼" **175.00**
Tile, Conestoga wagon, sgn Huckfield, 4¾" dia **395.00**
Tile, geometric border, orange on cobalt, dtd 1930, 6¼" sq **325.00**
Tile, prairie rose design, #85, mk, 4⅞" dia **150.00**
Tile, Rebekah symbol, bright bl, 3⅝" dia **135.00**

Vase, Bentonite clay body with three pair of buffalo, brown on burgundy, attributed to Julia Mattson, #992, 3¼", $800.00.

Vase, Am Indian cvd/pnt decor, MH Davies, 1934, 4¼" 1,800.00
Vase, bl, M Cable, 8¾" 145.00
Vase, bl gloss, mk, #1269, 3½" 60.00
Vase, coffee brn flowing over bl & gr, sgn LB, #912, 1913, 6¾" ..600.00
Vase, lotus flowers cvd under bl-gray gloss, bulbous, 6½" 750.00
Vase, lt yel w/dk bl int, 3¾" 125.00
Vase, prairie dogs/wheat stalks, brn tones, J Mattson, 5¼" 375.00
Vase, stylized leaves, brn matt, D Obrien, ovoid, 8½x4¾" 500.00
Vase, vertical brn & tan stripes, Mattson, 4½" 250.00
Vase, wheat emb on mulberry, ink mk, 8" 65.00
Vase, 3 birds on floral branch (repeating), bulbous, 9" 775.00

North State

In 1924 the North State Pottery of Sanford, North Carolina, began small-scale production, the result of the extreme fondness Mrs. Rebecca Copper had for potting. With the help of her husband and the abundance of suitable local clay, the pottery flourished and became well known for lovely shapes and beautiful glazes. The pottery was in business for thirty-five years; most of its ware was sold in gift and craft shops throughout North Carolina.

Ewer, gr & wht, 13" 100.00
Pitcher, gr-turq drip w/some red, 3rd stamp, 3¾" 25.00
Pitcher, turq w/dk turq dbl drip, ice lip, att, 6" 65.00
Plate, gr matt on earthenware, 2nd stamp, 1⅛x9⅜" 65.00
Urn, gr matt w/volcanic turq on red clay, 11¾x8" 375.00
Vase, bl mottle, 5" 75.00
Vase, blk-speckled gr w/runs, rolled rim, 1st stamp, 6" 75.00
Vase, gr & gunmetal on red, open hdls, unmk, 9", NM 650.00
Vase, gunmetal blk, hdl, rare color, 5" 135.00
Vase, mc, hdls, 4" 65.00
Vase, mc splotches, celadon int, ftd ovoid, 2nd stamp, 5½x7" ...450.00
Vase, red & pk on gr, mk, 6" 300.00
Vase, red w/gr touches, open hdls, early, 8" 700.00

Northwood

The Northwood Company was founded in 1896 in Indiana, Pennsylvania, by Harry Northwood, whose father, John, was the art director for Stevens and Williams, an English glassworks. Northwood joined the National Glass Company in 1899 but in 1901 again became an independent contractor and formed the Harry Northwood Glass Company of Wheeling, West Virginia. He marketed his first carnival glass in 1908, and it became his most popular product. His company was also famous for its custard, goofus, and pressed glass. Northwood died in 1923, and the company closed. See also Carnival; Custard; Goofus; Opalescent; Pattern Glass.

Louis XV pitcher, green with gold, ca 1898, 7¼", $180.00; Matching tumbler, 4", $50.00.

Bottle, dresser; Leaf Mold, vaseline spatter, shiny 500.00
Bowl, berry; Grape Frieze, gr w/gold, 11" 225.00
Bowl, berry; Leaf Mold, vaseline, lg 150.00
Bowl, berry; Posies & Pods, gr w/gold, lg+6 sm 275.00
Bowl, berry; Royal Ivy, rainbow cased, 8" 245.00
Bowl, berry; Strawberry & Cable, w/ruby & gold, sm 20.00
Bowl, sauce; Leaf Umbrella, bl cased 85.00
Bowl, sauce; Royal Oak, rubena frost 225.00
Butter dish, Cherry & Cable, clear w/gold & ruby 125.00
Butter dish, Grape & Gothic Arches, gr w/gold 95.00
Butter dish, Memphis, gr w/gold 175.00
Butter dish, Royal Oak, rubena 375.00
Butter dish, Royal Oak, rubena satin 425.00
Compote, bl opaque stretch, #637 ....50.00
Compote, jelly; Leaf Medallion, amethyst w/gold 150.00
Creamer, Cherry Thumbprint, w/ruby & gold 50.00
Creamer, Holly & Berry, w/ruby & gold 75.00
Creamer, Invt Fan & Feather, gr w/gold 45.00
Creamer, Leaf Mold base, mc spatter, shiny 185.00
Creamer, Memphis, gr w/gold 85.00
Creamer, Posies & Pods, gr w/gold 70.00
Creamer, Royal Ivy, rubena 175.00
Creamer, Royal Ivy, rubena frost 300.00
Cruet, Leaf Mold, vaseline spatter, shiny 450.00
Cruet, Royal Ivy, rainbow craquelle 725.00
Cruet, Royal Oak, rubena 700.00
Decanter, Cornflower, gr w/gold, orig stopper, +4 wines 125.00
Goblet, Leaf Mold, vaseline, jumbo 1,000.00
Lamp base, Royal Ivy, rubena frost 325.00
Pickle castor, Panelled Sprig, cranberry w/HP decor; SP fr 450.00
Pickle castor, Royal Ivy, rubena; SP fr w/ribbons & bows 425.00
Pickle castor, Royal Oak, rubena frost; SP fr, w/tongs 400.00
Pitcher, water; Leaf Mold, vaseline, +4 tumblers 550.00
Pitcher, water; Leaf Umbrella, cranberry spatter (rose agate) 600.00
Pitcher, water; Leaf Umbrella, vaseline spatter frost 500.00
Pitcher, water; Memphis, gr w/gold, +6 tumblers 385.00
Pitcher, water; Peach, crystal w/ruby & gold 150.00
Pitcher, water; Royal Ivy, cased spatter 250.00
Pitcher, water; Royal Ivy, frosted, no decor 90.00
Pitcher, water; Royal Ivy, rubena craquelle satin 250.00
Punch stand, Grape & Cable, amethyst 65.00
Rose bowl, Leaf Mold, vaseline frost 285.00
Rose bowl, Royal Ivy, rainbow cased 160.00
Rose bowl, Royal Ivy, rubena 150.00
Rose bowl, Royal Ivy, rubena frost 165.00
Shakers, Leaf Mold, vaseline, pr 150.00
Shakers, Royal Ivy, rubena, pr 140.00
Shakers, Royal Oak, rubena, pr 230.00
Shakers, Royal Oak, rubena frost, MOP lids, pr 250.00
Spooner, Grape & Gothic Arches, gr w/gold 50.00
Spooner, Holly & Berry, w/ruby & gold decor 75.00
Spooner, Peach, gr w/gold 95.00
Spooner, Royal Ivy, rubena 110.00
Spooner, Royal Oak, rubena frost 135.00
Sugar bowl, Holly & Berry, w/ruby & gold decor 95.00
Sugar bowl, Royal Ivy, rubena, w/lid 225.00
Sugar bowl, Royal Ivy, rubena frost, w/lid 225.00
Sugar bowl, Teardrop Flower, gr w/gold 125.00
Sugar shaker, Leaf Mold, bl frost 295.00
Sugar shaker, Leaf Mold, cranberry spatter w/mica 360.00
Sugar shaker, Leaf Umbrella, cranberry, orig lid 495.00
Sugar shaker, Parian Swirl, gr opaque 125.00
Sugar shaker, Royal Ivy, rainbow cased 345.00
Sugar shaker, Royal Ivy, rubena 275.00

Syrup, Leaf Mold, vaseline, shiny 475.00
Syrup, Optic Ribbed, rubena 915.00
Syrup, Royal Ivy, rainbow cased 695.00
Syrup, Wild Rose 65.00
Toothpick holder, Leaf Mold, cranberry spatter 275.00
Toothpick holder, Leaf Mold, vaseline 125.00
Toothpick holder, Leaf Mold, yel satin 295.00
Toothpick holder, Leaf Umbrella, cranberry spatter 295.00
Toothpick holder, Royal Ivy, clear & frosted 55.00
Toothpick holder, Royal Ivy, rubena frost 125.00
Tumbler, Invt Fan & Feather, gr w/gold 25.00
Tumbler, Leaf Mold, vaseline frost 100.00
Tumbler, Memphis, gr w/gold 30.00
Tumbler, Royal Ivy, rubena frost 100.00

Norweta

Norweta pottery was produced by the Northwestern Terra Cotta Company of Chicago, Illinois. Both matt and crystalline glazes were employed, and terra cotta vases were also produced. It was made for approximately ten years, beginning sometime before 1907. Not all was marked.

Vase, modeled leaves, green tones, 8", $1,400.00.

Lamp base, cream on terra cotta, F Albert/F Moreau, 1920s, 65" .2,600.00
Vase, gray-bl snowflake crystalline, bulbous, 9¾x6" 1,800.00
Vase, wht w/bl crystals, 4" 375.00

Nutcrackers

The nutcracker, though a strictly functional tool, is a good example of one to which man has applied ingenuity, imagination, and engineering skills. Though all were designed to accomplish the same end, hundreds of types exist in almost every material sturdy enough to withstand sufficient pressure to crack the nut. Figurals are popular collectibles, as are those with unusual design and construction. Patented examples are also desirable. Our advisor for this category is Earl MacSorley; he is listed in the Directory under Connecticut. For more information, we recommend *Ornamental and Figural Nutcrackers* by Judith A. Rittenhouse.

Dog, blk & wht porc enamel-plated CI, Am, 1900s, 5¾x11" 250.00
Elephant figural, CI, worn red & blk pnt, 9¾" 175.00
Elephant w/rider, brass, 1930-50s, 6⅝x2x1" 75.00
Fish, olive wood, Greek, 1950s, 8x2¼x2" 25.00
Lion head, wooden, glass eyes, Swiss or Tyrolean, 1900s, 9" 165.00
Man w/long nose figural, CI, worn gr pnt, 7" 250.00
Naughty Nelly, bronze, English, ca 1900 ....85.00
Nude lady figural, cvd wood, 13" 25.00
Oriental dancers figural, brass, English 125.00

Parrot, CI, w/old red/gr/gold pnt, 5¾" 125.00
Peasant, standing, wooden, attached tray, Am, 1930s, 12" 115.00
Rabbit head, wood/glass, Swiss or Scandinavian, 8¼" 125.00
Rooster head, brass 25.00
Skull & cross-bones, NP CI, mk, English, 1928, 6" 200.00
Squirrel on leaf, aluminum, old blk pnt, 1950s, 12x8x10" 30.00

Nutting, Wallace

Wallace Nutting (1861 – 1941) was America's most famous photographer of the early 20th century. A retired minister, Nutting took more than 50,000 pictures, keeping 10,000 of his best and destroying the rest. His popular and bestselling scenes included exterior scenes (apple blossoms, country lanes, orchards, calm streams, and rural American countrysides), interior scenes (usually featuring a colonial woman working near a hearth), and foreign scenes (typically thatch-roofed cottages). His poorest selling pictures, which have become today's rarest and most highly collectible, are classified as miscellaneous unusual scenes and include categories not mentioned above: animals, architecturals, children, florals, men, seascapes, and snow scenes. Process prints are 1930s machine-produced reprints of twelve of Nutting's most popular pictures. These have minimal value and can be detected by using a magnifying glass.

Nutting sold literally millions of his hand-colored platinotype pictures between 1900 and his death in 1941. He started in Southbury, Connecticut, and later moved his business to Framingham, Massachusetts. The peak of Wallace Nutting picture production was 1915 – 25. During this period Nutting employed nearly two hundred people, including colorists, darkroom staff, salesmen, and assorted office personnel. Wallace Nutting pictures proved to be a huge commercial success and scarcely an American household was without one by 1925.

While attempting to seek out the finest and best early American furniture as props for his colonial interior scenes, Nutting became an expert in early American antiques. He published nearly twenty books in his lifetime, including his 10-volume *State Beautiful* series and various other books on furniture, photography, clocks, stools, chairs, settles, settees, tables, stands, desks, mirrors, beds, chests of drawers, cabinet pieces, and treenware. He made furniture as well, which he clearly marked with a distinctive paper label that was glued directly onto the piece, or a block or script signature brand which was literally branded, into the furniture.

The overall synergy of the Wallace Nutting name — on pictures, books, and furniture — has made anything 'Wallace Nutting' quite collectible.

Our advisor for this category is Michael Ivankovich, author of many books concerning Nutting. Those currently available are *The Collector's Guide to Wallace Nutting Pictures; The Wallace Nutting Expansible Catalog; The Alphabetical and Numerical Index to Wallace Nutting Pictures; The Guide to Wallace Nutting Furniture, Wallace Nutting General Catalog, Supreme Edition; Wallace Nutting: A Great American Idea; Wallace Nutting's Windsors: Correct Windsor Furniture;* and *The Guide to Wallace Nutting-Like Photographers of the Early 20th Century.* Also available through Mr. Ivankovich is *The History of the Sawyer Pictures* by Carol Begley Gray. Mr Ivankovich's address and ordering information are listed in the Directory under Pennsylvania.

Prices below are for pictures in good to excellent condition. Mat stains or blemishes, poor picture color or frame damage can decrease value significantly.

Wallace Nutting Pictures

Affectionately Yours, 14x17" 230.00
Ambush for a Redcoat, 13x15" 770.00
Among Saffron Sails, 11x14" 265.00
Among the Ferns, 14x17" 165.00

August in the Meadow, 12x15" 95.00
Barre Brook, 11x14" 105.00
Better Than Mowing, 16x20" 485.00
Billows of Blossoms, 14x17" 120.00
Blossom Landing, 11x14" 75.00
Blossoms at the Bend, 10x12" 50.00
Bonnie Dale, 10x12" 150.00
Bonnie May, 16x20" 40.00
Bridge & the Elm, 16x20" 105.00
Call for More, 10x13" 330.00
Catskill Summit Blooms, 11x14" 165.00
Chair for John, 12x16" 130.00
Comfort & the Cat, 14x17" 440.00

Photo courtesy Michael Ivankovich

The Coming Out of Rosa, 14x17", $325.00.

Coming Out of Rosa, 16x20" 360.00
Creature Comforts, 16x20" 230.00
Dog-On-It, 7x11" 1,265.00
Evening at the River Bend, 13x22" 75.00
Fleck of Sunshine, 13x17" 155.00
Floral, mini, 4x5" 240.00
Flowery Path, 13x16" 395.00
Glory of Spring, 16x20" 40.00
Greeting, 10x12" 100.00
Guardian Mother, 11x17" 2,970.00
Hint of September, 15x22" 75.00
Honeymoon Shore, 13x16" 160.00
Honeymoon Windings, 12x20" 180.00
Into the Birchwood, 13x16" 165.00
Larkspur, 13x16" 175.00
Lingering Water, 16x20" 100.00
Little River & Mt Washington, 10x16" 138.00
Lough Gill Cottage, 11x14" 165.00
Meandering Battenkill, 10x16" 155.00
Middlesex Glen, 13x15" 120.00
Mills at the Turn, 13x17" 220.00
New Hampshire Roadside, 10x16" 90.00
Old Cabinet Maker, 12x14" 4,500.00
Old Time Friends, 13x16" 220.00
Old Tune Melody, 13x17" 220.00
Overflowing Cup, 13x16" 60.00
Pennsylvania Arches, 14x17" 300.00
Pennsylvania Stream, 13x16" 375.00
Picture Library, 14x17" 185.00
Pink, Blue & Green, 11x14" 145.00
Pride of the Lane, 13x17" 165.00
Providence Pond, 10x12" 240.00
River Meadow, 16x20" 130.00
Rose Gate, 10x12" 130.00
Sheffield Basket, 13x16" 580.00
Slack Water, 9x14" 140.00
Southern Colonial Room, 13x17" 240.00

Spinnet Corner, 13x15" 220.00
Street Border, 12x16" 240.00
Unbroken Flow, 16x20" 90.00
Untitled (birches & country lane), 8x10" 85.00
Untitled (blossoms & house), 20x40" 80.00
Venice's Chief Glory, 14x17" 575.00
Walk Under the Buttonwood, 14x17" 65.00
Watching for Papa, 13x16" 415.00
Water Maples, 14x17" 110.00
Wealth of October, 15x22" 90.00
Whitsunday, 9x16" 85.00
Winslow Water, 14x17" 130.00
Woodland Cathedral, 13x17" 85.00
Zinnias, 13x16" 500.00

Wallace Nutting Books

Cruise of the 800 ....95.00
Furniture of the Pilgrim Century, 1st ed 140.00
Furniture Treasury, Volume III 105.00
Maine Beautiful, 1st ed 45.00
New York Beautiful, 1st ed 85.00
PennsylvanIa Beautiful, 1st ed 45.00
Photographic Art Secrets 28.00
Social Life in Old New England 75.00
Vermont Beautiful, 2nd ed 40.00
Wallace Nutting Biography, w/dust jacket 140.00

Wallace Nutting Furniture

Armchair, mahog chip 1,265.00
Armchair, sack bk 825.00
Candlestand, whirling 500.00
Candlestand, Windsor 460.00
Chair, bedroom; mahog 440.00
Chair, side; mahog chip 1,155.00
Chair, slipper 715.00
Desk, child's 230.00
Hutch table, pine 825.00
Rack, costumer/coat 415.00
Table, crane bracket 715.00
Table, mahog Pembroke 1,450.00
Table, trestle 500.00
Table, trestle, maple 600.00

Major Wallace Nutting-Like Photographers

Although Wallace Nutting was widely recognized as the country's leading producer of hand-colored photographs during the early 20th century, he was by no means the only photographer selling this style of picture. Throughout the country literally hundreds of regional photographers were selling hand-colored photographs from their home regions or travels. The subject matters of these photographers was very comparable to Nutting's, including interior, exterior, foreign and miscellaneous unusual scenes. The key determinants of value include the collectibility of the particular photographer, subject matter, condition, and size. Keep in mind that only the rarest pictures, in the best condition, will bring top prices. Discoloration and/or damage to the picture or matting can reduce value significantly.

Several photographers operated large businesses and, although not as large or well known as Wallace Nutting, they sold a substantial volume of pictures which can still be readily found today. The vast majority of their work was photographed in their home regions and sold primarily to local residents or visiting tourists. It should come as little surprise that three of the major Wallace Nutting-like photographers — David Davidson, Fred Thompson, and the Sawyer Art Co. — each had ties to Wallace Nutting.

David Davidson: Second to Nutting in overall production, Davidson worked primarily in the Rhode Island and Southern Massachusetts area. While a student at Brown University around 1900, Davidson learned the art of hand-colored photography from Wallace Nutting, who happened to be the minister at Davidson's church. After Nutting moved to Southbury in 1905, Davidson graduated from Brown and started a successful photography business in Providence, Rhode Island, which he operated until his death in 1967.

Blossom Lane	35.00
Grandmother's Garden	35.00
Her House in Order	75.00
Home of the Lorelei	30.00
Lamb's May Feast	130.00
Neighbors	170.00
Old Mill	65.00
On a News Hunt	120.00
Porch Beautiful	60.00
Puritan Lady	70.00
Silent Wave	35.00
Snowbound Brook	55.00
Vanity	70.00

Sawyer: A father and son team, Charles H. Sawyer and Harold B. Sawyer, operated the very successful Sawyer Art Company from 1903 into the 1970s. Beginning in Maine, the Sawyer Art Company moved to Concord, New Hampshire, in 1920 to be nearer their primary market of New Hampshire's White Mountains. Charles H. Sawyer briefly worked for Nutting in 1902 – 03 while living in southern Maine. Sawyer's production volume ranks #3 behind Wallace Nutting and David Davidson.

Atumnal Tapestry	70.00
Gosport Church	90.00
Lake George	60.00
Lake Morey	30.00
Majestic Nature	55.00
Original Dennison Plant	100.00
San Juan Capistrano Mission	60.00
Silver Birches, Lake George	50.00
Which Way?	50.00
Winchester Bridge	210.00

Fred Thompson: Frederick H. Thompson and Frederick M. Thompson were another father and son team that operated the Thompson Art Company (TACO) from 1908 to 1923, working primarily in the Portland, Maine, area. We know that Thompson and Nutting had collaborated, because Thompson widely marketed an interior scene he had taken in Nutting's Southbury home. The production volume of the Thompson Art Company ranks #4 behind Nutting, Davidson, and Sawyer.

Brook in Winter,
14x17", $190.00.

Photo courtesy Michael Ivankovich

Apple Tree Road	45.00
Calm of Fall	50.00
Dancing Lesson	80.00
Elms & Apple Blossoms	20.00
Fireside Fancy Work	140.00
High & Dry	45.00
Knitting for the Boys	160.00
Lombardy Poplar	100.00
Nature's Carpet	50.00
Neath the Blossoms	95.00
Old Toll Bridge	130.00
Pasture Apple Blossoms	30.00
Portland Head	240.00
Schooner Lawrence	260.00
Toiler of the Sea	525.00

Charles Higgins: Working out of Bath, Maine, some of Higgins' finest pictures rivaled Nutting's best. No firm connection has been found between Higgins and Wallace Nutting.

Charles R. Higgins, Colonial Stairway	65.00
F Radel, Buckwood Inn, Shawnee-on-the-Delaware	15.00
Farini, In Her Boudoir	30.00
Florence Thompson, Difficult Lesson	60.00
Florian A Baker, Rushing Waters	50.00
Gibson, Mountain Road	20.00
Harris, From Black Bear Mt, Inlet NY	95.00
Haynes, Untitled Waterfalls	20.00

Minor Wallace-Like Photographers

Hundreds of other smaller local and regional photographers attempted to market hand-colored pictures comparable to Nutting's during the 1900 – 30s time period. Although quite attractive, most were not as appealing to the general public as Wallace Nutting pictures. However, as the price of Wallace Nutting pictures has escalated, the work of these lesser-known Wallace Nutting-like photographers have become increasingly collectible.

A partial listing of some of these minor Wallace Nutting-like photographers include Babcock; J.C. Bicknell; Blair; Ralph Blood (Portland, Maine); Bragg; Brehmer; Brooks; Burrowes; Busch; Carlock; Pedro Cacciola; Croft; Currier; Depue Bros; Derek; Dowly; Eddy; May Farini (hand-colored colonial lithographs); Geo. Forest; Gandara; Gardner (Nantucket, Bermuda, Florida); Gibson; Gideon; Gunn; Bessie Pease Gutmann (hand-colored colonial lithographs); Edward Guy; Harris; C Hazen; Knoffe; Haynes (Yellowstone Park); Margaret Hennesey; Hodges; Homer; Krabel; Kattleman; La Bushe; Lake; Lamson (Portland, Maine); M. Lightstrum; Machering; Rossiler Mackinae; Merrill; Meyers; William Moehring; Moran; Murrey; Lyman Nelson; J. Robinson Neville (New England); Patterson; Owen Perry; Phelps; Phinney; Reynolds; F. Robbins; Royce; Fred'k Scheetz (Philadelphia, Pennsylvania); Shelton; Standley (Colorado); Stott; Summers; Esther Svenson; Florence Thompson; Thomas Thompson; M.A. Trott; Sanford Tull; Underhill; Villar; Ward; Wilmot; Edith Wilson; and Wright.

A very general breakdown of prices for works by these minor Wallace Nutting-like photographers would be as follows:

Larger pictures, greater than 14x17", from $75 to over	200.00
Medium pictures, from 11x14" to 14x17", from $50 to	200.00
Smaller pictures, 5x7" to 10x12", from $10 to	75.00

The same pricing guidelines that apply to Wallace Nutting pictures typically apply to Wallace Nutting-like pictures
1.) Exterior scenes are the most common.

2.) Some photographers sold colonial interior scenes as well.

3.) Subject, matter, condition, and size are all important determinants of value.

Miscellaneous Nutting Memorabilia

Catalog, furniture, 1927-28 ....**65.00**
Catalog, Nutting pictures, 1912 ....**110.00**
Catalog, Parke-Bernet Auction **75.00**
Christmas card, 4x5" **150.00**
Silhouette, George and Martha Washington, 3x4" **88.00**
Silhouette, Girl by Cheval Mirror, 4x4" **55.00**
Silhouette, Girl w/Powder Puff, 4x4" **70.00**

Occupied Japan

Items marked 'Occupied Japan' have become popular collectibles in the last few years. They were produced during the period from the end of World War II until April 18, 1952, when the occupation ended. By no means was all of the ware exported during that time marked 'Occupied Japan'; some was marked 'Japan' or 'Made In Japan.' It is thought that because of the natural resentment felt by the Japanese toward the occupation, only a fraction of these wares carried the 'Occupied' mark. Even though you may find identical 'Japan'-marked items, because of its limited use, only those with the 'Occupied Japan' mark are being collected to any great extent. Values vary considerably, based on the quality of workmanship. Generally, bisque figures command much higher prices than porcelain, since on the whole they are of a finer quality.

For those wanting more information, we recommend *The Collector's Encyclopedia of Occupied Japan Collectibles* (there are six in the series) by Gene Florence; he is listed in the Directory under Kentucky. Our advisor for this category is Florence Archambault; she is listed in the Directory under Rhode Island. She represents the Occupied Japan Club, whose mailing address may be found in the Directory under Clubs, Newsletters, and Catalogs. All items described in the following listings are assumed ceramic unless noted otherwise.

Ashtray, antimony, fancy border, 2 rests, oval, 5x3" **5.00**
Ashtray, HP rose spray w/gold trim, 3½x2½" **5.00**
Ashtray, jasper, lt bl, classical figures, 4x3" **10.00**
Ashtray, metal, 2 rests, duck mk, 5x3" **5.00**
Ashtray holder, elephant figural, high gloss brn, w/4 trays **20.00**
Bottle, scent; gr glass, canteen shape, Deco emb, 2¼" **20.00**
Bowl, lacquered wood, Karavan/Hand Turned, 4x11½" **25.00**
Bowl, soup; red roses w/blk & gold, 7½" **5.00**
Bowl, SP, scalloped/pierced rim, lt wear, 4½" **5.00**
Bust, cherub w/music scroll, bl w/pk wings, Lamore, 4" **35.00**
Bust, man in tricorn hat, lady w/pompadour, bsk, 5¾", pr **65.00**
Candy dish, SP, rtcl bowl, fleur-de-lis rim, ped ft, 6¾" dia **12.00**
Cigarette lighter, gr & wht w/much gold, 3½x2¼" **15.00**
Cigarette lighter, metal, grape clusters, cobalt insert **15.00**
Cigarette lighter, SP, cowboy boot form, working **20.00**
Creamer, lemon figural **10.00**
Creamer & sugar bowl, floral sprays & bl lustre band **14.00**
Cup, Father in gold, mc florals, 3½x3¾" **15.00**
Dinnerware set, apples or crab apples, serves 6+gravy+platter **250.00**
Dinnerware set, dogwood on ivory w/gold trim, serves 8 ....**300.00**
Dinnerware set, Livonia (Dogwood), serves 12+casserole+platter ..**450.00**
Dinnerware set, Livonia (Dogwood), serves 6+gravy boat+platter .**250.00**
Dinnerware set, Rochelle, Grace China, serves 4+serving pcs **200.00**
Dinnerware set, simple pattern, serves 4 ....**225.00**
Dinnerware set, simple pattern, serves 8+platter+2 lg bowls **350.00**

Dinnerware set, Wild Rose, Fuji China, serves 8+2 serving pcs ..**300.00**
Fan, floral on paper, bamboo sticks, 8½" **15.00**
Fan, HP flowers on silk, bamboo sticks, 7" **20.00**
Figurine, blowfish, tan w/gold, open mouth, 5" L **22.00**
Figurine, boy by fence, hat w/feather, mc clothes, bsk, 7⅝" **55.00**
Figurine, boy clarinetist, mc, illegible mk, 4¾" **8.50**
Figurine, cherub on sea creature blowing shell horn, 3¾" **30.00**
Figurine, cherubs (2) on shell, mc w/gold, bsk, 7½x8x4¾" **150.00**
Figurine, Colonial man in ruffled shirt, striped pants, 4½" **11.00**

Figurine, couple at harpsicord, marked Mariyama, 4", $30.00.

Figurine, elephant, metal, celluloid tusks, trunk up, 3x4¼" **15.00**
Figurine, figures on coach w/4 horses, pastels w/gold, bsk, 5x9" ..**175.00**
Figurine, girl w/donkey cart, pastels w/gold, bsk, 3x5⅜" **45.00**
Figurine, Hummel-type girl w/flower basket, mc, 6" **25.00**
Figurine, Hummel-type girl w/goose, mc, 5" **20.00**
Figurine, lady w/cello, mc w/gold, 3x3" **10.00**
Figurine, lady w/flower basket, Delft bl, 5" **20.00**
Figurine, lady w/grain sheaf & sickle, bsk, 9" **50.00**
Figurine, lady w/nosegay, ruffled dress, bsk, 4" **10.00**
Figurine, lady w/tambourine, ceramic, Delft Bl, 4¾" **20.00**
Figurine, man in red coat, lady w/bustle, mc, 3½" **10.00**
Figurine, man w/book, lady w/flower basket, seated, 3½" **10.00**
Figurine, man w/flower & cane, mc, 4" **9.00**
Figurine, man w/guitar, lady w/purse, mc, 3¼" **9.00**
Figurine, Oriental musician seated w/flute, 4½" **12.00**
Figurine, reindeer, celluloid, 3½" **15.00**
Figurine, Schnauzer dog, mc, 3¾" **10.00**
Figurine, Spanish dancer, Delft Bl, 5⅜" **20.00**
Incense burner, gold-toned metal, Buddha figural, 4½x4" **22.00**
Leaf dish, gr w/gold veins & trim, Shofu, 3½x3" **6.00**
Leaf dish, lacquered metal, HP bamboo on red, Maruni, 6" **12.00**
Lemon dish, HP flowers, gold trim, loop hdl, 5¾" **12.00**
Lemon dish, HP pansies w/gold, mitered corners, 5½" **8.00**
Mug, hunting/archery scenes, mc, figural hdl, 5¼" **25.00**
Mug, tavern scene relief, mc on cobalt, 6" **20.00**
Parasol, bamboo/tissue paper, 4", M **6.50**
Planter, cherubs by urn w/incised florals, mc, 4x5" **25.00**
Planter, coolie boy beside stump, mc, 5½" **14.00**
Planter, Dutch girl holds wide basket planter, mc, 4½" **10.00**
Planter, horsebk rider before planter, hound at ft, 2⅛" H **5.00**
Planter, man w/donkey & cart, mc, 3x3½" **8.00**
Plaques, Dutch children, traditional clothes, Yameka, 5¼", pr **30.00**
Plate, floral sprays w/gold, Jyoto China/wreath mk, 7½" **8.00**
Plate, ivory band w/gold rim, Meito, 6½" **8.00**
Plate, mc wildflowers at rim w/gold, Kent, 7½" **8.00**
Plate, red lilies w/gold trim, Grace China/Medina, 10¾" **10.00**
Plate, Will Rogers Memorial, Claremore OK, 3⅜" **8.00**
Shakers, hen sitting, rooster standing, mc, 2¼", 3", pr **15.00**
Shell dish, roses w/gold, Berkshire China, 5" **8.50**
Tile, HP maple leaves, 3⅜" sq **18.00**

Toby jug, balding man, graying hair/beard/mustache, 2¼" **12.00**
Toby jug, lady, full figure, mc clothes, 2¾" **20.00**
Toby jug, Old Charlie, 4¾x4" **35.00**
Toby jug, Sairey Gamp, 4½x4" **35.00**
Toby mug, lady, full figure, ruffled cap, flower basket, 3⅛" **12.00**
Toby mug, man scowling, lg mustache, 3" **15.00**
Toby mug, man w/red beard, jeweled cap, 2½" **15.00**
Toby mug, man w/top hat, bl collar, pk tie, 2⅝" **15.00**
Tray, HP rose & bud w/scalloped gold rim, 3¾" dia **6.00**
Tray, papier-mache, mc florals & scrolls, Alcohol Proof, 8" **10.00**
Tray, SP, Chicago souvenir, 5x3" **5.00**
Vase, angelfish relief medallion, mc, 3" **7.00**
Vase, cherub w/shell vase, pastels, bsk, 6x3¾" **50.00**
Vase, compo, mc hunt scene, diapering, hdls, 5x7¼" **12.00**
Vase, flower relief w/gold, shoulder hdls, 2½" **6.00**
Vase, jasper, appl flower, scrolls & leaves, hdls, 2¾" **9.00**
Vase, jasper, man w/grapes in basket, scrolled decor, 2¾" **9.00**
Wall pocket, flying duck, mc, 6½x12½" **75.00**

Ohr, George

George Ohr established his pottery in the 1880s in Biloxi, Mississippi. The first pottery burned down and was subsequently rebuilt. Ohr, among other things, was a master of the wheel. This mastery enabled him to create unique forms of unbelievable thinness, verging at times on abstraction and looking far ahead toward many art movements of the 20th century. In addition to abstraction, by studying Ohr, one can discover elements of Expressionism and Fauvism (the wild use of color often seemingly at odds with the piece being glazed) and Dada (meaning shock the bourgeoisie). An Ohr piece may be rooted in the functional form of a teapot, but following his manipulation it becomes a sculpture for which the functional form serves only as a take-off point for the finished piece. Ohr was also a master of glazes. Highly esteemed are his volcanic and gunmetal glazes. He was not well received in his day and sold few pieces of his art pottery — a van Gogh-like tale. Ohr decorated his pieces with snakes and lizards and sometimes with asymetrical handles. He believed that like all things on earth, no two things should be alike. This dictum was applied to his pottery making. He signed his pieces either in impressed letters or florid script. In the early 1900s Ohr ceased making pottery and became a motorcycle dealer and ultimately sold automobiles. His pottery was stored away to be rediscovered many years later. Ohr died in 1918. Our advisor for this category is Fer-Duc, Inc.; whose address is listed in the Directory under New York.

Bowl, moss green and pink dapple, shouldered cylinder with crimpled rim, earthenware, stamped signature, 8", $1,980.00.

Bowl, brn/gr speckled, undulating oval rim, rstr, 7½x5" **1,400.00**
Bowl, bsk, flared/folded/notched, 2½x5¼" **1,500.00**
Bowl, gr speckled on orange clay, 4-lobed, crimped, 2x3¾" **850.00**
Candle holder, mc mottle, twisted waist, ribbon hdls, 6½", EX .**3,300.00**
Chamberstick, red/gr/yel mottled matt, slit pulls at base, 4" **1,500.00**
Cup, mustache; shirt cuff form, sponged bl, ribbon hdl, 2¾" ..**2,000.00**

Jar, gunmetal/gr drip on raspberry, spherical, w/lid, 4¼x5" **1,500.00**
Pitcher, bsk, brick/putty marbleized, pinched/folded, 4¼x6" ...**1,500.00**
Pitcher, lt & med gr/gunmetal/red flambe, bulbous, 5¼x6" ...**1,700.00**
Pitcher, pk/gr volcanic glaze, pinched hdl, 4x4¼" **2,200.00**
Pitcher, raspberry semigloss w/yel froth, pinched, 4½x8½" **8,500.00**
Pitcher, women & child, bk: floral, blk/gr mottle, 8x7" **800.00**
Vase, bl-gr to raspberry mottle, corseted, flared/folded rim, 4" ..**4,250.00**
Vase, brn/olive speckles, deeply pinched, lobed rim, 3½x4½" ..**2,100.00**
Vase, bsk-fired buff clay, folded/dimpled, 4x5¼" **700.00**
Vase, dk gr/amber/gunmetal mottle, corseted, hdls, 7¾x5½" ..**3,750.00**
Vase, gold speckled, crimped rim, baluster, 9x4" **3,300.00**
Vase, gr w/bl sponging/purple metallic, 3-part bottle form, 7" .**1,200.00**
Vase, gunmetal leather over amber, folded/pinched, 5½x4¼" ..**2,400.00**
Vase, gunmetal over dk gr flambe, crimped/dimpled, 2¼x3¾" .**1,000.00**
Vase, gunmetal/yel blotches on pk matt, hdls, rpr, 3¾x4¾" ...**1,200.00**
Vase, mc mottle, twisted w/cupped top, ribbon hdls, 4¾x4¾" .**4,250.00**
Vase, mc speckled lustre, bottle form, prof rstr, 8½" **1,200.00**
Vase, mc sponging, bulbous w/lobed rim, orig price tag, 3x3½" .**2,600.00**
Vase, mc spots on lav-gray semimatt, corseted, 10¾x5" **900.00**
Vase, mirrored brn & gunmetal, ruffled/pinched/dimpled, 6¾" .**2,750.00**
Vase, mustard & gunmetal gray, twisted/compressed base, 6¾x7" .**4,750.00**
Vase, raspberry/turq/amber, cupped top/in-body twist, 3¾x3¼" .**4,500.00**
Vase, raspbery/purple/cobalt/gr mottle, bottle form, 9¼" **2,500.00**
Vase, red w/mc specks, cylinder neck, conical body, 10½x7" ..**3,080.00**
Vase, semivolcanic gray & pk, folded/dimpled, rpr, 4¾x5" **1,200.00**
Vase, speckled amber & gunmetal, twisted/ruffled/pinched, 6" ..**1,500.00**
Vase, sponged brn/gr w/gunmetal drip, pinched/folded, 3¼x4" ..**2,100.00**
Vessel, gr speckled gloss, dimpled front/folded rim, 5½" **3,000.00**
Vessel, gr/berry/amber gloss, in-body twist/folded rim, 5x3¾" .**3,200.00**
Vessel, gunmetal on raspberry, squat w/tapered neck, 4¼x3¾" .**1,500.00**

Old Ivory

Old Ivory dinnerware was produced during the late 1800s by Herman Ohme, of Lower Salzbrunn in Silesia. The patterns are referred to by the numbers stamped on the bottom of many items. (Though not every piece is numbered, the vast majority bears the tiny blue fleur-de-lis/crown mark with Silesia or Germany beneath. Handwritten numbers signify something other than pattern.) Patterns #16 and #84 are the easiest to find and come in a wide variety of table items. Values are about the same for both patterns. Other floral designs include pink, yellow, and orange roses; holly; and lavender flowers — all on the same soft ivory background. The ware was not widely distributed; its two main distribution points were in Maine and, to a lesser extent, Chicago. Our prices are intended to represent a nationwide average, though you may have to pay a little more in some areas. Novice collectors should be aware of copy-cat versions from the turn of the century that are much heavier and of a coarser material. They are marked 'Old Ivory' without the blue trademark. They are not included in this listing.

For further information we recommend *Collector's Encyclopedia of Old Ivory China, The Mystery Explored*, by Alma Hillman (our advisor), David Goldschmitt, and Adam Szynkiewicz (Collector Books). Ms. Hillman is listed in the Directory under Maine.

Basket, #145, hdld **200.00**
Bonbon (also called nappy), #76 (rare pattern), fancy hdl **150.00**
Bone dish, #11 ....**400.00**
Bowl, berry; #22 (Holly), deep, 9½" **300.00**
Bowl, berry; #27 (rare pattern), 9½" master+10 sm **350.00**
Bowl, berry; #40, ind **35.00**
Bowl, cereal; #16 or #84, 6½" **65.00**
Bowl, cereal; poppies, mc on ivory, 1¾x6", 4 for **125.00**
Bowl, ice cream; #16 or #84, 4½x5" **35.00**

Bowl, serving; #200, 9¼" 100.00
Bowl, soup; #16 or #84, 7½" 150.00
Bowl, vegetable; #16, oval, w/lid 700.00
Butter dish, #84, w/lid & insert, 7½" 700.00
Butter pat, #16 or #84 ....125.00
Cake plate, #62 (Holly) 300.00
Celery tray, #16 or #84, 5½x11" 150.00
Charger, #82, 13" 395.00
Chocolate pot, #11, Clairon, 9½" 450.00
Chocolate set, #15, pot+6 c/s 850.00
Chocolate set, #16 or #84, 9½" pot+6 c/s 850.00
Cracker jar, #16 or #84 ....450.00
Creamer & sugar bowl, #16 or #84, Empire, w/lid 175.00
Cup & saucer, #75 ....75.00
Cup & saucer, #76 ....85.00
Cup & saucer, demi; #15 ....100.00
Demitasse pot, #16 or #84 ....450.00
Gravy boat, #16 or #84, attached base, 8½" L 800.00
Ladle holder, #16 or #84 ....195.00
Mayonnaise & underplate, #73, 6½" 200.00
Mustard pot, #15, w/lid, 3¾" 285.00
Pitcher, water; #28, 8" 900.00
Plate, #15, 7¾" 55.00
Plate, #16 or #84, 6⅛" 35.00
Plate, #16 or #84, 7¾" 55.00
Plate, #16 or #84, 8¼" 60.00
Plate, #82, Silesia, 8½" 85.00
Plate, Holly, 6¼" 75.00
Plate, soup; #16 or #84, 10" 200.00
Porringer, #33 ....95.00
Shakers, #16 or #84, 2½", pr 125.00
Teapot, #15 ....500.00
Toothpick holder, #16 or #84 ....250.00
Toothpick holder, #73 ....265.00
Tray, #16 or #84, rectangular, flat bottom, 12x7" 175.00
Tray, bun; #204, 10" 225.00
Tureen, soup; cut out for ladle, 13" 2,000.00

Old Paris

Old Paris porcelains were made from the mid-18th century until about 1900. Seldom marked, the term refers to the area of manufacture rather than a specific company. In general, the ware was of high quality, characterized by classic shapes, colorful decoration, and gold application.

Garniture vases, pastoral scenes, gilt floral highlights, floral bouquets on reverse, ornate molded handles, pierced rims, ca 1850, 26", $4,000.00 for the pair.

Bottles, scent; lady/gentleman figurals, no stoppers, 11", pr 140.00
Bowl, centerpc; openwork, hdls, gold trim, 1840s, 16½" L 280.00
Cake basket, floral w/gold, pierced hdls, mid-19th C, 12" 110.00
Cake stand, 3 graduated tiers w/floral sprigs 75.00
Candlesticks, gilt florals, circular bobeches, 1850s, 6", pr 165.00

Compote, pierced center, gilt paw ft, ca 1820, 9" dia 85.00
Corbeille, rose cabochon on gr, gold paw ft, early 19th C, 5x9" .990.00
Cup & saucer, mc floral garland w/lacy gold, Love the Giver 85.00
Jar, apothecary; labels/cornucopias/flowers/etc, 9¾", pr 385.00
Pastille burner, octagonal pagoda form, early 1800s, 5¼" 220.00
Plate, dessert; floral cornucopias on bl, 19th C, 6 for 250.00
Plate, James Monroe/President..., blk transfer, 9¼" 6,000.00
Platter, morning glories, oval, 19th C, 15¼" 100.00
Punch bowl, floral sprays w/gold, 3 shell ft, 1850s, 13½" 200.00
Tea set, floral w/much gold, ca 1880s, pot+cr/sug+10 c/s 650.00
Vase, floral w/gold on cream, hdls, 6¾" 70.00
Watch/jewelry holder, doves fr w/dbl dish on base, 1840s, 6" 275.00

Old Sleepy Eye

Old Sleepy Eye was a Sioux Indian chief who was born in Minnesota in 1780. His name was used for the name of a town as well as a flour mill. In 1903 the Sleepy Eye Milling Company of Sleepy Eye, Minnesota, contracted the Weir Pottery Company of Monmouth, Illinois, to make steins, vases, salt crocks, and butter tubs which the company gave away to their customers. A bust profile of the old Indian and his name decorated each piece of the blue and gray stoneware. In addition to these four items, the Minnesota Stoneware Company of Red Wing made a mug with a verse which is very scarce today.

In 1906 Weir Pottery merged with six others to form the Western Stoneware Company in Monmouth. They produced a line of blue and white ware using a lighter body, but these pieces were never given as flour premiums. This line consisted of pitchers (five sizes), steins, mugs, sugar bowls, vases, trivets, and mustache cups. These pieces turn up only rarely in other colors and are highly prized by advanced collectors. Advertising items such as trade cards, pillow tops, thermometers, paperweights, letter openers, postcards, cookbooks, and thimbles are considered very valuable. The original ware was made sporadically until 1937. Brown steins and mugs were produced in 1952. Our advisor for this category is Jim Martin; he is listed in the Directory under Illinois.

Banner, center portrait & western scenes, 22" sq, EX 1,450.00
Barrel, flour; orig paper label, 1920s 1,800.00
Barrel, grapevine-effect banding 3,500.00
Barrel, oak w/brass bands 4,500.00
Butter crock, Flemish bl & gray 750.00
Cabinet, bread display; Old Sleepy Eye etched in glass 950.00
Calendar, 1904, NM 375.00
Calendar, 1904, VG 150.00
Cookbook, EX 185.00
Cookbook, Indian on cover, Sleepy Eye Milling Co, 4¾x4" 300.00
Cookbook, loaf of bread shape, NM 210.00
Cookbook, loaf of bread shape, VG 115.00
Coupon, for ordering cookbook 250.00
Coupon, for ordering pillow top 200.00
Dough scraper, tin/wood, To Be Sure, EX 435.00
Fan, chief cb diecut, minor rub on tassle, EX 210.00
Fan, Indian chief, die-cut metal sign, 1900 ....1,200.00
Flour sack, cloth, mc Indian, red letters 345.00
Flour sack, paper, Indian in blk, blk lettering, NM 125.00
Ink blotter 125.00
Label, bbl end; mc Indian portrait, 16", NM 160.00
Letter opener, bronze 900.00
Match holder, pnt 1,875.00
Match holder, wht 1,050.00
Mug, bl & gray, 4¼" 360.00
Mug, bl & wht, 4¼" 220.00
Mug, verse, Red Wing, EX 1,625.00

Paperweight, bronzed company trademk 560.00
Pillow cover, Sleepy Eye & tribe meet President Monroe 750.00
Pillow cover, trademk center w/various scenes, 22", NM 1,600.00
Pin-bk button, Indian, rnd face 350.00
Pitcher, #1, 4" 300.00
Pitcher, #2 ....350.00
Pitcher, #3 ....315.00
Pitcher, #3, w/bl rim 1,375.00
Pitcher, #4 ....400.00
Pitcher, #5 ....435.00
Pitcher, bl & gray, 5" 325.00
Pitcher, bl on cream, 8", M 345.00
Pitcher, standing Indian, good color, #5 size 1,560.00
Postcard, colorful trademk, 1904 Expo Winner 185.00
Ruler, wooden, 15" 700.00
Salt crock, Flemish bl & gray, 4x6½" 700.00
Sheet music, in fr 300.00
Sign, self-fr tin, Old Sleepy Eye Flour, 20x24" 2,500.00
Sign, tin litho die-cut Indian, ...Flour & Cereals, 13½" 1,650.00
Spoon, demitasse; emb roses in bowl, Unity SP 105.00
Spoon, Indian-head hdl 125.00
Stein, bl & wht, 7¾" 800.00
Stein, brn, 1952, 22-oz 300.00
Stein, brn & wht 1,500.00
Stein, brn & yel, Western Stoneware 1,500.00
Stein, cobalt 1,250.00
Stein, Flemish bl & gray 700.00
Stein, ltd edition, 1979-84, ea 125.00
Sugar bowl, bl & wht, 3" 750.00
Thermometer, front rpl 800.00
Vase, cattails, all cobalt 1,450.00
Vase, cattails, bl & wht, good color, 9" 800.00
Vase, cattails, brn on yel, rare color 1,500.00
Vase, cattails, gr & wht 5,000.00
Vase, Indian & cattails, Flemish bl & gray, 8½" 470.00

O'Neill, Rose

Rose O'Neill's Kewpies were introduced in 1909 when they were used to conclude a story in the December issue of *Ladies' Home Journal*. They were an immediate success, and soon Kewpie dolls were being produced worldwide. German manufacturers were among the earliest and also used the Kewpie motif to decorate chinaware as well as other items. The Kewpie is still popular today and can be found on products ranging from Christmas cards and cake ornaments to fabrics, wallpaper, and metal items.

For further information we recommend *Doll Values, Antique to Modern*, by Patsy Moyer (Collector Books). Our advisor for this category is Kitty Watson; she is listed in the Directory under Oklahoma. In the following listings, 'sgn' indicates that the item is signed Rose O'Neill. © is also a good mark on items. Unsigned items can be of interest to collectors; many are authentic and collectible.

Bell, sterling, figural, sgn, 4" 198.00
Booklet, Jell-O, Yel Jell-O Please, 4x6", M 35.00
Booklet, Jell-O & the Kewpies, 1915, 4½x6" 55.00
Booklet, Jell-O Girl Entertains, 5x7" 65.00
Booklet, Jell-O Girl Gives a Party 55.00
Color book, Adventures & Kewpies, 1962, M, from $65 to 70.00
Coloring book, w/Doodle Dog, 1962, M, from $65 to 70.00
Figurine, bsk, Doodle Dog, sgn, 3", minimum value 1,850.00
Hatpin holder, jasper, bl, Kewpies, Rose O'Neill, NM, minimum .425.00
Kewpie, bean-bag body, sgn, 1970s, 10", M, from $40 to 50.00

Kewpie, bsk, Bell Hop, molded gr jacket & hat, sgn, 4", minimum ..950.00
Kewpie, bsk, Black, Hottentot, sgn, 3½" 425.00
Kewpie, bsk, Blunderboo, falling, sgn, 1¾", from $395 to 425.00
Kewpie, bsk, Bride & Groom, Germany, sgn, 3½" 350.00
Kewpie, bsk, Farmer by vase, sgn, 6½", minimum value 950.00
Kewpie, bsk, Huggers, sgn, 3½", from $300 to 350.00
Kewpie, bsk, Jester, wht hat on head, sgn, 4½", minimum value ...850.00
Kewpie, bsk, jtd hips & shoulders, sgn, 10" 1,000.00
Kewpie, bsk, jtd hips & shoulders, sgn, 5" 525.00
Kewpie, bsk, jtd shoulders, molded clothing, sgn, 2½" 200.00
Kewpie, bsk, jtd shoulders, molded clothing, sgn, 8", minimum .950.00
Kewpie, bsk, jtd shoulders, pnt/molded hair, sgn, 10" 625.00
Kewpie, bsk, jtd shoulders, pnt/molded hair, sgn, 2" 95.00
Kewpie, bsk, kneeling, sgn, 4" 750.00
Kewpie, bsk, Mayor, arms folded, sgn, 6" 600.00
Kewpie, bsk, movable arms, sgn, Fulper, 1920s, 10", minimum ..850.00
Kewpie, bsk, nonjtd, pnt/molded hair, sgn, 2" 110.00
Kewpie, bsk, nonjtd, pnt/molded hair, sgn, 4½" 150.00
Kewpie, bsk, on tummy, arms & legs out, sgn, 4" 450.00
Kewpie, bsk, on tummy, Doodle Dog on bk, sgn, 3½", $2,600 to .3,000.00
Kewpie, bsk, seated in lg fancy gr chair, sgn, 4" 850.00
Kewpie, bsk, seated w/chick, sgn, 2", from $350 to 400.00
Kewpie, bsk, Soldier vase, sgn, 6½", minimum value 950.00
Kewpie, bsk, Soldier w/helmet, arms to side, sgn, 4½", minimum ..850.00
Kewpie, bsk, Traveler, w/umbrella & bag, sgn, 4" (common sz) ...350.00
Kewpie, bsk, w/baby bottle & baby Kewpie, sgn, 3½" 2,000.00
Kewpie, bsk, w/blk cat, sgn, 2¼" 300.00
Kewpie, bsk, w/bouquet/pets Doodle Dog, 4½", rare, $2,200 to .2,600.00
Kewpie, bsk, Writer, pen in hand, sgn, 2", from $350 to 400.00
Kewpie, bsk shoulder head, cloth body, sgn, 7", from $600 to 700.00
Kewpie, carnival chalk, jtd shoulders, sgn, 13", M 165.00
Kewpie, celluloid, Bride & Groom, Japan, sgn, 4" 75.00
Kewpie, celluloid, Bride & Groom, sgn, Germany, 3", M 150.00
Kewpie, celluloid, Japan, sgn, 2", M 45.00
Kewpie, celluloid, jtd arms, heart label, Germany, sgn, 12", minimum ..325.00
Kewpie, celluloid, jtd arms, sgn, Japan, 5½", from $85 to 90.00
Kewpie, cloth, 1-pc, Kreuger, 12", EX w/tag 250.00
Kewpie, compo, Black, Hottentot, jtd arms/heart decal/red wings, 11" ...575.00
Kewpie, compo, jtd arms, sgn, 9" 185.00
Kewpie, compo, jtd body, no wings, sgn, orig tag, 13" 450.00
Kewpie, compo & cloth, jtd forearms, tagged dress, 11" 875.00
Kewpie, compo head, cloth body, 14" 325.00

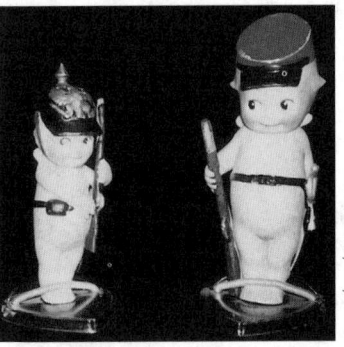

Kewpie: German Soldier, bisque, Kaiser helmet, arms on rifle, signed, 4½", minimum value $850.00; Confederate Soldier, bisque, signed, 5½", $600.00.

Kewpie, hard plastic, jtd neck/shoulders/hips, sleep eyes, sgn, 12" ..435.00
Kewpie, hard plastic, 5-pc body, sgn, 1950, 8½", MIB 325.00
Kewpie, plush, stockinette face, tagged, 8", M 225.00

Kewpie, plush, vinyl mask, Knickerbocker, 1960s, 6" 40.00
Kewpie, vinyl, Baby, hinged joints, 1960s, 15", M w/tag 185.00
Kewpie, vinyl, Black, striped pajamas, 11", MIB 100.00
Kewpie, vinyl, jtd neck, shoulders & hips, sgn, 14" 170.00
Kewpie, vinyl, jtd shoulders only, sgn, 9" 40.00
Kewpie, vinyl, molded in 1 pc, sgn, 9" 25.00
Kewpie, vinyl, Ragsy, 1-pc w/molded clothes, sgn, 8", minimum ..85.00
Kewpie, vinyl, str legs, sgn ft, Cameo, 11", MIP 85.00
Kewpie, vinyl, Thinker, sitting down, orig, sgn, 4" 25.00
Kewpie, vinyl head & limbs, cloth body, sgn, 16" 185.00
Lamp base, Kewpie, metal, cast steel on sq base, sgn, 5½" 850.00
Magazine page, Kewpies & Santa w/verse, R O'Neill, 1914, $30 to ..40.00
Nodder, Kewpie, compo (papier-mache), Japan, 5-5½", ea 85.00
Paper dolls, Kewpiekin, 1962, M, from $65 to 70.00
Paper dolls, 1963, M in folder, from $65 to 70.00
Pincushion, celluloid Kewpie figural 140.00
Place card holder, bsk, Kewpie playing mandolin, 3" 325.00
Scootles, compo head, latex body, orig clothes, 16", minimum ..485.00
Soap figure, w/cotton batting, RO Wilson, 1917, 4", M 110.00
Tea set, Action Kewpies, c O'Neill Wilson, Germany, 22-pc .1,300.00
Tea set, Kewpies, Germany, service for 2, doll sz, MIB 975.00
Tea set, Kewpies w/gold, O'Neill/Bavaria, child's, 15-pc 550.00
Tea set, Royal Rudolstadt, sgn O'Neill Wilson, 12-pc, EX 900.00
Toy, celluloid, Kewpie crawler, w/up, mk Occupied Japan, $185 to 250.00

Onion Pattern

The familiar pattern known to collectors as Onion acquired its name through a case of mistaken identity. Designed in the early 1700s by Johann Haroldt of the Meissen factory in Germany, the pattern was a mixture of earlier Oriental designs. One of its components was a stylized peach, which was mistaken for an onion; as a result, the pattern became known by that name. Usually found in blue, an occasional piece may also be found in pink and red. The pattern is commonly associated with Meissen, but it has been reproduced by many others including Villeroy and Boch and Royal Copenhagen.

Blue Danube is a modern line of Onion-patterned dinnerware produced in Japan and distributed by Lipper International of Wallingford, Connecticut. One hundred twenty five items are available in porcelain; it is sold in most large stores with china departments.

Basket, rtcl, shallow, Meissen, 1890s, 7" 255.00
Bowl, deep, Germany, 9" 60.00
Bowl, Meissen, 6½" 45.00
Bowl, rtcl rim, Meissen, 19th C, 2¼x6" 295.00
Bowl, rtcl rim, ped ft, Meissen, ca 1888, 6x7¼" 400.00
Bowl, scalloped, Meissen Xd swords mk, 8" 245.00
Butter pat, Germany 28.00
Candlesticks, Meissen Xd swords mk, 6", pr 150.00
Candy dish, rolled hdl, Meissen Xd swords mk, 4¾" 75.00
Casserole, domed lid, Meissen, EX 350.00
Chamberstick, 6" 95.00
Cheese dish, Meissen, ca 1900, 7x9" 175.00
Coffeepot, 1800s, 9½" 400.00
Creamer, Meissen, 5¼" 100.00
Cup & saucer, demitasse; Meissen, 1890s 90.00
Cup & saucer, Germany 35.00
Cup & saucer, Meissen, ca 1900 ....135.00
Egg cup, Meissen Xd swords mk, 3½" 75.00
Funnel, loop hdl 125.00
Jar, instant coffee; Japan 24.00
Letter opener, brass blade, Germany 40.00

Pie crimper, wooden hdl 150.00
Plate, Meissen, 10" 75.00
Plate, Meissen, 6" 35.00
Plate, rim soup; Meissen 85.00
Platter, Meissen, 11x8" 175.00
Platter, Meissen, 14" 195.00
Platter, scalloped oval, 1880s, Meissen Xd swords mk, 23x18" ...550.00
Rolling pin, heavy, old, EX quality, 18" 300.00
Salt box, rnd, wood lid, wall mt, Made in Japan, 7" 100.00
Spoon, 10" 95.00
Tray, bread; 16x11" 175.00
Tureen, rnd, w/liner, Japan, 9" 35.00
Vase, ftd, Meissen Xd swords mk, 5" 140.00
Whisk 110.00
Whistle, 12 holes, 6" L, EX 95.00

Opalescent Glass

First made in England in 1870, opalescent glass became popular in America around the turn of the century. Its name comes from the milky-white opalescent trim that defines the lines of the pattern. It was produced in table sets, novelties, toothpick holders, vases, and lamps. Note that American-made sugar bowls have lids; sugar bowls of British origin are considered to be complete without lids. For further information we recommend *The Standard Encyclopedia of Opalescent Glass* by Bill Edwards (Collector Books).

Jewel and Flower, water pitcher, white opalescent with gold trim, 8¾", $225.00.

#220 (Stripe), tumble-up, wht, complete, Fenton 90.00
#950, cornucopia candlestick, amethyst, ea 95.00
Abalone, bowl, bl 35.00
Arabian Nights, tumbler, bl 75.00
Arched Panels, bowl, master berry; vaseline or canary, ea 90.00
Argonaut Shell (Nautilus), spooner, wht 65.00
Ascot, sugar bowl, bl 80.00
Astro, hat whimsey, wht 60.00
Autumn Leaves, bowl, wht 45.00
Barbells, bowl, vaseline or canary, ea 45.00
Basketweave (Open Edge), plate, gr 100.00
Beaded Cable, bowl, gr, ftd 40.00
Beaded Fan, rose bowl, wht, ftd 42.00
Beaded Ovals & Holly, spooner, vaseline or canary, ea 65.00
Beaded Ovals in Sand, butter dish, bl 350.00
Beaded Shell, butter dish, wht 250.00
Beaded Shell, creamer, bl 150.00
Beaded Stars & Swag, plate, bl 45.00
Beads & Bark, vase, gr, ftd 70.00
Beatty Honeycomb, creamer, bl 100.00
Beatty Honeycomb, cruet, wht 175.00
Beatty Honeycomb, mug, bl 55.00
Beatty Swirl, pitcher, bl 180.00
Beatty Swirl, sugar bowl, wht 90.00

Berry Patch, bowl, novelty, bl 50.00
Blooms & Blossoms, nappy, bl, hdld 50.00
Blossom & Palms, bowl, gr 45.00
Blossom & Web, bowl, wht 145.00
Brideshead, creamer, bl 65.00
Broken Pillar, compote, vaseline or canary, ea 55.00
Bull's Eye, shade, bl 60.00
Buttons & Braids, bowl, cranberry 125.00
Carousel, bowl, bl 40.00
Cashews, bowl, wht 30.00
Christmas Pearls, cruet, gr 275.00
Chrysanthemum, bowl, amethyst, ftd, 11" 300.00
Chrysanthemum Base Swirl, butter dish, cranberry 500.00
Chrysanthemum Base Swirl, mustard pot, bl 150.00
Chrysanthemum Swirl Variant, pitcher, wht, rare 235.00
Circled Scroll, cruet, gr 450.00
Cleopatra's Fan (Northwood Shell), vase, novelty, gr 75.00
Colonial Stairsteps, creamer, bl 100.00
Colonial Stairsteps, toothpick holder, bl 195.00
Concave Columns, vase, wht 75.00
Contessa, basket, amber, hdld 250.00
Coral Reef, finger lamp, cranberry 1,650.00
Cornucopia, vase, bl, hdld 75.00
Coronation, tumbler, vaseline or canary, ea 40.00
Criss Cross, toothpick holder, wht 195.00
Crown Jewels, pitcher, bl 195.00
Curtain Optic, guest set, gr, 2-pc 100.00
Daisy & Fern, cruet, cranberry 510.00
Daisy & Fern, finger bowl, gr 85.00
Daisy & Fern, sugar shaker, cranberry 265.00
Daisy & Fern, tumbler, bl 45.00
Daisy & Fern, vase, wht 90.00
Daisy & Greek Key, bowl, sauce; bl, ftd 65.00
Daisy & Plume, rose bowl, wht, ftd 40.00
Daisy in Criss Cross, syrup, cranberry 595.00
Desert Garden, bowl, bl 45.00
Diamond & Daisy, basket, wht, hdld 60.00
Diamond Maple Leaf, bowl, bl, hdld 75.00
Diamond Point & Fleur De Lis, bowl, nut; gr 65.00
Diamond Spearhead, creamer, bl, tall 200.00
Diamond Spearhead, creamer, sapphire, mini 225.00
Diamond Spearhead, tumbler, vaseline or canary, ea 65.00
Diamond Stem, vase, vaseline or canary, 6½", ea 170.00
Diamond Weave, pitcher, amethyst, w/lid 250.00
Dolly Madison, pitcher, wht 195.00
Dolly Madison, spooner, gr 75.00
Dolphin, compote, bl 65.00
Double Greek Key, butter dish, bl 350.00
Double Greek Key, celery vase, wht 135.00
Double Stemmed Rose, bowl, bl, very rare 250.00
Drapery, vase, gr 190.00
Duchess, spooner, bl 85.00
Duchess, toothpick holder, vaseline or canary, ea 150.00
Estate, vase, gr 85.00
Everglades, bowl, master berry; vaseline or canary, oval, ea 195.00
Everglades, spooner, bl, w/lid 250.00
Fancy Fantails, bowl, vaseline or canary, ea 40.00
Feathers, vase, gr 32.00
Fern, bottle, barber; cranberry 295.00
Fern, cruet, cranberry 450.00
Finecut & Roses, rose bowl, wht, rare 35.00
Fish in the Sea, vase, gr 425.00
Fishscale & Beads, bowl, wht 28.00
Flora, cruet, wht 450.00

Flora, sugar bowl, vaseline or canary, ea 125.00
Fluted Scrolls (Klondyke), puff box, bl 45.00
Fluted Scrolls w/Vine, vase, vaseline or canary, ftd, ea 85.00
Four Pillars, vase, bl 65.00
Grape & Cable, bowl, centerpiece; wht 200.00
Grape & Cherry, bowl, gr 90.00
Grapevine Cluster, vase, vaseline or canary, ftd, ea 150.00
Greek Key & Scales, bowl, novelty, bl 85.00
Harrow, wine, vaseline or canary, stemmed, ea 40.00
Heart-Handle Open O's, ring tray, gr 85.00
Hobnail, bowl, sauce; wht, Northwood 30.00
Hobnail, bride's basket, bl, Hobbs 450.00
Hobnail, creamer, bl, Hobbs 90.00
Hobnail, shaker, cranberry, Hobbs 400.00
Hobnail & Panelled Thumbprint, butter dish, wht 140.00
Hobnail in Square, bowl, bl, w/stand 150.00
Hobnail in Square, butter dish, wht 185.00
Hobnail 4-Footed, butter dish, cobalt 210.00
Honeycomb & Clover, pitcher, gr 350.00
Honeycomb & Clover, spooner, wht 110.00
Idyll, tumbler, wht 50.00
Inside Ribbing, butter dish, bl 225.00
Inside Ribbing, creamer, vaseline or canary, ea 80.00
Intaglio, bowl, master; wht, ftd 90.00
Intaglio, cruet, bl 195.00
Intaglio, cruet, wht 125.00
Intaglio, pitcher, wht 135.00
Intaglio Grape, bowl, wht, Dugan 125.00
Interior Panel, vase, fan; amethyst 80.00
Inverted Fan & Feather, bowl, sauce; vaseline or canary, ea 40.00
Inverted Fan & Feather, card tray whimsey, gr 250.00
Inverted Fan & Feather, creamer, bl 225.00
Iris w/Meander, bowl, master berry; wht 70.00
Iris w/Meander, butter dish, bl 295.00
Iris w/Meander, plate, gr 85.00
Jackson, cruet, vaseline 250.00
Jazz, vase, gr 55.00
Jefferson Shield, bowl, bl, rare 250.00
Jefferson Wheel, bowl, bl 55.00
Jewel & Flower, sugar bowl, bl 200.00
Jewelled Heart, bowl, novelty, bl 45.00
Jewels & Drapery, bowl, novelty, gr 50.00
Jolly Bear, bowl, wht 190.00
Keystone (Colonial), compote, bl, hdld 75.00
Lady Chippendale, compote, cobalt, tall 90.00
Lattice (Bubble), bride's basket, cranberry 225.00
Lattice (Bubble), butter dish, bl 200.00
Lattice & Daisy, tumbler, vaseline or canary, scarce, ea 125.00
Lattice & Points, bowl, novelty, wht 55.00
Lattice Medallions, bowl, gr 50.00
Leaf & Beads, rose bowl, gr 70.00
Leaf Mold, creamer, cranberry 170.00
Leaf Rosette & Beads, bowl, bl, scarce 250.00
Little Nell, vase, wht 22.00
Lords & Ladies, butter dish, vaseline or canary, ea 100.00
Lustre Flute, bowl, master; gr 320.00
Lustre Flute, vase, bl 60.00
Many Loops, rose bowl, gr 35.00
Maple Leaf, compote, jelly; gr 100.00
Meander, bowl, novelty, gr 35.00
Melon Swirl, tumbler, bl 75.00
Monkey (Under a Tree), tumbler, wht, rare 500.00
National Swirl, tumbler, gr 45.00
Northern Star, plate, bl 100.00

Northwood Block, celery vase, wht 40.00
Opal Open (Beaded Panels), vase, novelty, bl 40.00
Opal Urn, vase, wht 50.00
Over-All Hob, pitcher, wht 155.00
Overlapping Leaves (Leaf Tiers), plate, wht, ftd, lg 180.00
Palm & Scroll, bowl, vaseline or canary, ftd, ea 60.00
Palm Beach, butter dish, vaseline or canary, ea 285.00
Palm Beach, finger bowl, bl 150.00
Palm Beach, pitcher, bl 395.00
Panelled Flowers, nut cup, wht, ftd 50.00
Panelled Holly, spooner, bl 100.00
Peach Intaglio, plate, wht, Dugan 185.00
Peacocks (On the Fence), bowl, cobalt 350.00
Piasa Bird, rose bowl, bl 55.00
Picadilly, basket, gr, sm 85.00
Pineapple & Fan, vase, vaseline or canary, ea 400.00
Poinsettia, pitcher, water tankard; bl 235.00
Poinsettia, tumbler, cranberry 85.00
Popsicle Sticks, bowl, gr, ftd 50.00
Prince William, creamer, bl 65.00
Princess Diana, plate, bl, crimped 65.00
Princess Diana, water tray, vaseline or canary, ea 50.00
Question Mark, compote, gr 85.00
Quilted Pillar Sham, creamer, vaseline or canary, ea 65.00
Rayed Heart, compote, wht 50.00
Reflections, bowl, gr 50.00
Regal, bowl, berry; bl, 11" 85.00
Regal, butter dish, gr 165.00
Regal, creamer, gr 75.00
Regal, sugar bowl, bl, Northwood 135.00
Reverse Drapery, plate, gr 85.00
Reverse Swirl, cruet, bl 375.00
Reverse Swirl, toothpick holder, cranberry 265.00
Ribbed Coinspot, syrup, cranberry, rare 1,375.00
Ribbed Lattice, cruet, cranberry 550.00
Ribbed Lattice, tumbler, bl 50.00
Ribbed Optic, tumble-up, vaseline or canary, ea 75.00
Ribbed Spiral, toothpick holder, bl 175.00
Richelieu, basket, bl, open 100.00
Richelieu, compote, jelly; wht 55.00
Ring Handle, shakers, bl, pr 100.00
Rococco, bride's bowl, vaseline or canary, ea 300.00
Rose (Rose & Ruffles), compote, bl, tall 95.00
Rose Show, bowl, wht 190.00
Rubina Verde, vase, cranberry 290.00
Ruffles & Rings, rose bowl, wht 30.00
Scottish Moor, cracker jar, wht 210.00
Scroll w/Acanthus, bowl, sauce; bl 25.00
Sea Scroll, compote, vaseline or canary, ea 100.00
Seaspray, whimsey, bl 50.00
Seaweed, creamer, wht 95.00
Seaweed, syrup, bl 175.00
Shell & Dots, bowl, novelty, vaseline or canary, ea 95.00
Sir Lancelot, bowl, gr, ftd 65.00
Somerset, pitcher, juice; bl, 5½" 60.00
Sowerby Salt, salt dish, wht 60.00
Spanish Lace, jam jar, bl 290.00
Spanish Lace, sugar bowl, bl 260.00
Spatter, pitcher, wht 185.00
Stars & Stripes, tumbler, bl 100.00
Stork & Rushes, tumbler, wht 60.00
Stripe, shakers, cranberry, pr 250.00
Sunburst on Shield (Diadem), tumbler, bl 125.00
Swag w/Brackets, cruet, gr 350.00

Swag w/Brackets, cruet, wht 170.00
Swag w/Brackets, spooner, bl 75.00
Swirl, bowl, sauce; cranberry 36.00
Swirl, cruet, bl 75.00
Swirl, cruet, wht 65.00
Swirl, mustard jar, wht 58.00
Swirl, tumbler, bl 125.00
Swirl, vase, gr 65.00
Three Fingers & Panel, bowl, master berry; wht 70.00
Three Fruits w/Meander, bowl, wht, ftd 110.00
Tokyo, pitcher, bl 350.00
Tree Stump, mug, gr 55.00
Trellis, tumbler, vaseline or canary, ea 65.00
Twig, vase, gr, sm, 5½" 75.00
Twisted Ribs, case, wht 30.00
Twister, vase, whimsey; bl 65.00
Venice, oil lamp, wht 340.00
Vintage, bowl, bl, Northwood/Dugan 45.00
Waffle, epergne, olive 750.00
War of the Roses, bowl, vaseline or canary, ea 65.00
Waterlily & Cattails, spooner, amethyst 65.00
Wheel & Block, bowl, novelty, wht 30.00
Wide Stripe, tumbler, wht 40.00
Wild Bouquet, cruet, bl 450.00
Wild Daffodils, mug, wht 30.00
Wilted Flowers, bowl, bl 50.00
Windows (Swirled), creamer, wht 70.00
Winter Cabbage, bowl, bl, ftd 47.00
Winterlily, vase, gr 95.00
Wishbone & Drapery, plate, wht 50.00
Wreath & Shell, butter dish, wht 135.00
Wreath & Shell, celery vase, vaseline or canary, ea 160.00
Wreath & Shell, cracker jar, bl 750.00

Opaline

A type of semiopaque opal glass, opaline was made in white as well as pastel shades and is often enameled. It is similar in appearance to English bristol glass, though its enamel or gilt decorative devices tend to exhibit a French influence.

Bowl 9½", and pitcher 12½", white with gilt bands, French, mid-19th century, $265.00.

Basket, w/appl bl ruffled rim, appl flower, 5¾x9½" 385.00
Bottle, scent; HP floral w/gold butterfly, urn form, 10", pr 120.00
Ring tree, gr w/wht opaque ruffle & gold scrolls, 5⅛x3¼" 110.00
Vase, HP flowers & leaves, tapered, 8" 125.00

Orientalia

The art of the Orient is an area of collecting currently enjoying strong collector interest, not only in those examples that are truly 'antique' but in the 20th-century items as well. Because of the many aspects involved in a study of Orientalia, we can only try through brief comments to acquaint the reader with some of the more readily available examples. We suggest you refer to specialized reference sources for more detailed information. See also specific categories.

Key:
Ch — Chinese	hdwd — hardwood
cvg — carving	Jp — Japan
drw — drawer	Ko — Korean
Dy — Dynasty	lcq — lacquer
E — export	mdl — medallion
FR — Famille Rose	rswd — rosewood
FV — Famille Verte	tkwd — teakwood

Blanc de Chine

Cup, libation; prunus & animal reliefs on wht, Ch, 18th C, EX ..300.00
Figure, Kuan Ti, robes over his armor, 15", +stand 650.00
Figure, Quanyin, standing on self base w/fish basket, 20th C, 14" .125.00
Figure, Quanyin on cushion, hollow molded, 19th C, 8¼" 1,850.00
Teapot, molded as laughing Buddha, Qianlong period, 6" 435.00
Vase, gu form, 8 Daoist immortals/florals, 18th C, 12" 1,775.00

Blue and White Porcelain

Bottle, 3-claw dragon/flaming pearl, Choson Dy, 11" 5,350.00
Bowl, florals/bands/shou medallion, late Choson Dy, 5¼" 1,200.00

Covered jar, warriors in battle reserves, lotus ground, lappet bands, 26", $825.00.

Garden seat, pheasants/peonies/etc, bbl form, Ch 475.00
Jar, pingmei design, dbl ring, no lid, Ch, 18th C, 8" 800.00
Planter, dragon & ornate floral ground, Meiji, 11½" dia 150.00
Tea caddy, Ch silver lid, Ch, ca 1820 ....525.00
Tea caddy, flowers & birds, ca 1775, sm, EX 125.00
Vase, cranes in relief on bl cloud ground, cylindrical, 12" 420.00
Vase, dragon among clouds, ring neck, late Choson Dy, 16½" ..3,800.00

Bronze

Candle holders, dragon & phoenix, lotus drip pan, Jp, 20" 160.00
Crane pr, 2 w/head trn, 2nd w/neck out, detailed, 71", 64" 2,750.00
Figure, Buddha on open throne, Ch, 19th C, 13¾" 200.00
Figure, Lokapala in military garb w/staff & girdle, Ming Dy, 13" ...500.00
Figure, pheasant, pnt decor, on wood base, 25" 425.00
Figure, Sumo wrestler w/hands up holding bowl, 20th C, 19½" .290.00
Koro, twin beast-head hdls, bird reserves, Jp, 16" 250.00
Vase, birds & foliage, baluster, Jp, 14½", pr 260.00
Vase, spherical, bamboo branch hdl w/birds, drilled, Jp, 12" 220.00

Celadon

Brush pot, crackle glaze, ca 1900, 5" 395.00
Charger, peony band, 2 petal rings, 1700s, 16" 475.00
Ewer, 8-lobed melon shape, strapwork hdl, Koryo Dy, 3¾" 1,100.00
Garden seat, keg shape, celadon & wht stripes/bl enamel, 20" ...625.00
Jardiniere, irises on lobed form, flattened rim, 3-ftd, 8" 90.00
Tazza, butterflies, on ornate Fr ormolu holder, 5" dia 245.00
Vase, birds/butterflies/etc, salamander hdls, rstr, 12", pr 650.00

Furniture

Armchair, hdwd, ornate cvg, Ch, 49½" 425.00
Armchair, marble insets, cvd tkwd w/nacre inlay, 39", pr 160.00
Armchair, red lcq in Ch taste, Jp/Meiji, 34½" 350.00
Bed, opium; pnt/gilt decor on blk lcq, Ch trade, 19th C, 83" ..3,000.00
Bench, Ch taste, cvd wood, storage under seat, Ch, 52x48" 1,100.00
Bench, tkwd, dragon/phoenix cvgs, late 19th C, 57" 800.00
Blanket chest, cvd camphorwood, Ch, 40" 95.00
Cabinet, book; mahog w/figured wood panels, 1900s, Ko, 44x23" .190.00
Cabinet, tkwd w/relief cvg, dbl doors/glass door, 72x33x15" 360.00
Cabinet, wall hanging; sliding glass doors, compartments, 23x20" .140.00
Chair, official's, N Ming style, early 19th C, worn lcq, 35" 385.00
Chest, bedding; elm w/brass fittings, 1850s, S Ko, 42x35" 440.00
Chest, bedside; pearwood/burl veneer w/inlay, Ko, 38x35" 415.00
Chest, blanket; pine w/brass mts, fish lock, 1800s, S Ko, child's .195.00
Chest, elm/figured elm root, dbl doors, ca 1900, S Ki, 65x40" .1,540.00
Chest, lady's, pine w/figured veneer on sliding doors, Ko, 22x30 ...330.00
Chest, oak w/burl veneer, brass mts, pine base, Ko, 1800s, 34x37" ...500.00
Chest, rswd w/paktong mts, shell inlay, N Ko, 1800s, 59x35" 470.00
Chest, wedding; pawlonia wood w/appl compo decor, ca 1900, K ..470.00
Chest, wedding; pine w/compo characters, wrought lock, Ko, 24x30" ...300.00
Desk, ornately cvd in Ch taste, 53x47" 1,000.00
Fire screen, cvd tkwd & lcq w/appl ivory/bone, Ch, 1900s, 42" ..200.00
Screen, Coromandel; blk lcq/pnt landscape, 8-panel, Jp, 84x12" .880.00
Screen, landscape on gold paper, 6-fold, Jp, lg, VG 550.00
Screen, MOP/horn florals on kinji ground, 2-fold, Meiji, 18x18" ..13,000.00
Screen, table; brass, wood cvd base w/battle scene, Ch, 28" 200.00
Screen, 4 hinged blk lcq panels: pagoda scene, 19th C, 72x64" ..550.00
Sofa, cvd/inlaid rswd w/pearl inlay, silk cushion, 42x73", EX 900.00
Stand, cvd wood, bamboo-like, hexagonal, Jp, 13" 125.00
Stand, rswd w/marble top, 2-tierd, cvd apron, 32x17x12" 75.00
Table, hdwd, low form, Ch, 17th C, 13x31x21", pr 550.00
Table, tkwd, cvd animal apron, cvd supports, Ch, 40x50x17" 550.00
Table, tkwd w/relief cvgs, brass hdw, dbl doors/drw, 32x15x49" .275.00

Hardstones

Amethyst quartz, foo dog paperweight on sterling base 100.00
Jade, lt gr, plaque, circling dragon, 19th C, 4½" 400.00
Jade, mottled gr, dbl-dragon head bangle, 18th C, 3¼" 400.00
Jade, mottled gr, magnolia bud, on wood stand, 4½" 300.00
Jade, Quanyin figure w/flower & fan, on hdwd stand, 8" 350.00
Jade, wht, coin, Archaic-style knife form 250.00

Lacquer

Lacquerware is found in several colors, but the one most likely to be encountered is cinnabar. It is often intricately carved, sometimes involving hundreds of layers built one at a time on a metal or wooden base. Later pieces remain red, while older examples tend to darken.

Box, aquatic plants, gilt hiramaki-e & aogai, Meiji, 5x9x6" 1,300.00
Box, peacocks on rocks, diapering w/gilt, 1800s, 12½" dia 800.00

Box, scroll; kikko w/jashiji int, rstr, 19th C, 15¾" L 2,100.00
Box, sewing; figures in landscapes, blk/gilt, Jp, 1850s 375.00
Kobako, cranes/pines/Juji in gilt, 19th C, 3¾", NM 2,600.00
Tea caddy, blk/gold w/figural panels, serpentine, 1850s 440.00
Tea safe, E, w/pewter canisters, Ch, 1800s, 11x8" 300.00

Netsukes

A netsuke is a miniature Japanese carving made with two holes called the Himitoshi, either channeled or within the carved design. As kimonos (the outer garment of the time) had no pockets, the Japanese man hung his pipe, tobacco pouch, or other daily necessities from his waist sash. The most highly valued accessory was a nest of little drawers called an Inro, in which they carried snuff or sometimes opium. The netsuke was the toggle that secured them. Although most are of ivory, others were made of bone, wood, metal, porcelain, or semiprecious stones. Some were inlaid or lacquered. They are found in many forms — figurals the most common, mythological beasts the most desirable. They range in size from 1" up to 3", which was the maximum size allowed by law. Many netsukes represented the owner's profession, religion, or hobbies. Scenes from the daily life of Japan at that time were often depicted in the tiny carvings. The more detailed the carving, the greater the value.

Careful study is required to recognize the quality of the netsuke. Many have been made in Hong Kong in recent years; and even though some are very well carved, these are considered copies and avoided by the serious collector. There are many books that will help you learn to recognize quality netsukes, and most reputable dealers are glad to assist you. Use your magnifying glass to check for repairs. In the listings that follow, netsukes are ivory unless noted otherwise; 'stain' indicates a color wash.

Tigress and cub, sepia wash with black pigment, Kyoto School, late 18th century, 1⅜", $6,325.00.

Boys (2) washing hands at tub, blk stain, Homin, 1890s, 1¾" 375.00
Chinese general sharpening sword, Gyokurintei, 1890s, 1¾" 400.00
Farmer by grain-harvesting machine, Seiun, 19th C, 1⅝" 375.00
Hen & chick, boxwood, Gyokurintei, 1890s, lt wear, 1½" 700.00
Momotaro child w/peach/old woodcutter & wife, Seimin, 1¾" ..1,850.00
Ono No Komachi in rags, sepia wash, Chikusai, ca 1890s, 1⅜" ..1,035.00
Puppy crouching, horn inlay, stain, Tomokazu, 19th C, 1¾" 635.00
Sennin & puppy, blk inlay, sepia/blk stain, Yoshitomo, 2½" ...1,100.00
Shiki dragging sack of Oni, sepia wash, Jogyoku, 1890s, 1⅜" ...1,150.00
Shoki & Oni w/demons, sepia wash, Tamayuki, ca 1890s, 1¾" ..700.00

Porcelain

Chinese export ware was designed to appeal to Western tastes and was often made to order. During the 18th century, vast amounts were shipped to Europe and on westward. Much of this fine porcelain consisted of dinnerware lines that were given specific pattern names. Rose Mandarin, Fitzhugh, Armorial, Rose Medallion, and Canton are but a few of the more familiar.

Bowl, E, Mandarin paneled scenes, 3¾x9¼" 400.00

Bowl, E, Mandarin scenes, flower border, rolled rim, 3¾x10" 400.00
Bowl, salad; E, Armorial, early 1800s, 9½" 460.00
Charger, E, FR, late 18th C, 13½" 980.00
Cups, E, mc scenes w/Oriental figures, str sides, ear hdls, 6 for ...330.00
Jardiniere, E, FR, couple in landscape, hexagonal, 9" 320.00
Mug, E, FR, 3 panel flower scenes, 5", NM 350.00
Pitcher, E, mc floral on helmet shape, ca 1800, 5½", EX 75.00
Plate, E, FR, early 19th C, 9¼", EX 230.00
Plate, E, FR, mc butterfly rims w/pagodas, 9½" 120.00
Plate, Thousand Butterfly, mk Made in China, 8½" 200.00
Platter, E, floral spray w/2 mc borders, 16x13½" 725.00
Punch bowl, E, FR, paneled scenes, 6x15" 1,200.00
Teacup, E, Rose Canton, entwined hdl, 6 for 325.00
Teapot, E, Rose Canton, entwined hdl, bud finial, 6¾" 200.00
Vase, E, figural scenes & florals, butterfly hdls, 19th C, 18" 330.00
Vase, E, FR, bird panels, 1830s, 14¾", pr 715.00
Vase, E, FR, 19th C, 13¼", pr 345.00
Vase, E, Mandarin palette, dragon hdls, foo dog finials, 1780s, 15" ..2,000.00

Pottery

Bottle, sake; blk, no decor, teardrop decor, 1800s, 13" 150.00
Bowl, cizhou sgraffito flower deor, Song Dy, 8⅛" 600.00
Bowl, floral, wht on chalky bl, shallow, Ming Dy, 15" 350.00
Brush pot, wht, rtcl wanzi roundel/vajira bolts, Choson Dy, 5" ..2,350.00
Figurine, horse standing on low base, Tang Dy, 14½" 700.00
Figurine, Quanyin, earthenware, gr & brn, 11", EX 200.00
Figurine, Quanyin, tang-style colors, Ch, wood base, 19" 125.00
Teapot, terra cotta, gr enamel spout/hdl, branch on lid, 4x7" 50.00
Teapot, terra cotta, squat melon form w/branch hdl, 1910 ....75.00
Tomb figure, glazed, Ming Dy, 7" 200.00

Rugs

The 'Oriental' or Eastern rug market has enjoyed a renewal of interest in recent years as collectors have become aware of the fact that some of the semiantique rugs (those sixty to one hundred years old) may be had at a price within the range of the average buyer.

Afghan, 4 colors on red-brn, 96x132" 1,750.00
Bakhtiari, mc mdl on bl w/rust corners, 84x121" 950.00
Bidjar, mc floral sprays on bl mdl on wine, bl corners, 85x122" .1,450.00
Caucasian, 3 center mdls/geometrics, bls/red/ivories, 43x59" .1,100.00
Caucasian Kilim, geometric, mc on dk red, 53x185", VG 650.00
Fereghan Sarouk, ivory w/midnight bl border, lt wear, 48x75" .1,300.00
Herez, 3 mdls w/multiple borders, semi-antique, 54x77" 900.00
Kashan, lt bl & ivory spandrels on salmon, bl border, 108x168" ..4,500.00
Kashan, mc on ivory w/red border, lt wear, 42x49" 1,045.00
Kazak, geometrics, 4-color, 68x102", VG 1,100.00
Kazak, rust w/bl border, minor wear, 42x66" 1,300.00
Kerman, red & bl floral sprays on ivory, band border, 112x151" ..750.00
Kirman, mc florals on ivory, wide floral panel border, 117x195" ..2,300.00
Kuba Soumak, dk bl w/brick red border, 48x109" 4,500.00
Mahal, mc floral mdl on wine w/bl & red borders, 84x127" 1,000.00
Nian, overall mc florals, knotted silk, semi-antique, 102x66" .1,750.00
Pakistan Bokhara, mc guls (150) on red w/mc bands, 220x140" .900.00
Pelouchistan prayer, olive w/rust borders, lt wear, 34x62" 330.00
Persian Kashan, center mdl on ivory, 54x84", VG 900.00
Persian Kashan, center mdl/floral, multiple borders, 54x84" 850.00
Sarouk, dk maroon w/midnight bl border, ca 1920, 42x48" 1,265.00
Sarouk, mc florals on wine w/bl floral bands, 122x222" 4,400.00
Sarouk, rust w/ivory border, lt wear, 101x144" 3,025.00
Sarouk, salmon spandrels on ivory, bl border, ca 1880, 102x144" ..7,000.00
Shirvan (Caucasian), ivory w/multiple borders 51x63" 880.00

Shirz, midnight bl w/bl, ivory & red borders, wear, 57x76" **660.00**
Soumak, geometrics, mc on red, 81x136", VG **1,100.00**
Sparta, mc floral mdl on mauve, dk bl geometric bands, 96x156" ...**900.00**
Turkish Ushak, yel-gr ground w/salmon border, wear, 112x136" .**2,900.00**

Snuff Bottles

The Chinese were introduced to snuff in the 17th century, and their carved and painted snuff bottles typify their exquisite taste and workmanship. These small bottles, seldom measuring over 2½", were made of amber, jade, ivory, and cinnabar; tiny spoons were often attached to their stoppers. By the 18th century, some were being made of porcelain, others were of glass with delicate interior designs tediously reverse painted with minuscule brushes sometimes containing a single hair. Copper and brass were used but to no great extent.

Agate, hollow cameo, well cvd bird, 2¼" **125.00**
Bl Peking glass, molded form w/side hdls, orange top, 2¾" **125.00**
Gr jadeite, cvd man on bull on rock w/trees, amethyst top, 2¾" ..**500.00**
Hardstone, blk w/cvd jade insert of immortal & 2 boys, 2½" **150.00**
Ivory, cvd int scene w/figures, w/spoon stopper, 3" **200.00**
Lapis lazuli, cvd florals w/gold inclusions, 2½" **1,500.00**
Porc, traveling sage scene, bl & copper red, Ch, 3½" **125.00**
Red Peking o/l & snowflake glass, cvd fishing scene, 2¾" **300.00**
6-color o/l on milk glass w/mc flowers in basket cvg, 2½" **150.00**

Sumida

Basket, 3 people at front, 1 at open hdl, Gawa, 9" **420.00**
Mug, wise man appl at center, seal signature, Gawa, 5½" **165.00**
Teapot, 2-character Ryosai cartouch in bl w/red & wht **325.00**
Vase, floral branches, ca 1885, 12" **625.00**
Vase, man & flower in relief on brick red, 7¾x3" **125.00**
Vase, 3 emb figures, dk color w/mottling, 12¼x4½" **295.00**

Textiles

Summer robe, Chinese Kesi silk gauze, eight large floral medallions with gold characters in centers, late 1800s, 57", EX, $2,000.00.

Bolt of brocade, mc floral, 26x154", EX **85.00**
Cape, priest's, cranes/clouds embr on peach silk, 1900, 57" **850.00**
Jacket, bl floral center on yel silk, genre/floral bands, 1890s **250.00**
Jacket, bl silk w/appl circles & ribbons, flowing sleeves **85.00**
Panel (orig a battle banner), embr silk, sun & dragon, 40x30" ...**475.00**
Robe, Ch Mandarin, dragons/birds/etc on silk, fringed, 19th C ..**800.00**
Robe, dragons/cranes/clouds/symbols on blk silk, 1920, 58" **550.00**
Robe, gold dragons on bl silk, horse-hoof cuffs, 1800s **1,500.00**

Woodblock Prints, Japanese

Framed prints are of less value than those not framed, since it is impossible to inspect their condition or determined whether or not they have borders or are trimmed.

Autumnal scene, Kyoto Gosho, 1920s, 6½x9¼" **100.00**
Bar, lady w/bottles, sgn Kiyoshi Saito, 20th C, 58¾x43¾" ...**1,750.00**
Jun'ichiro Sekino, Girl w/Cat, 1957, 24½x12" **500.00**
Jun'ichiro Sekino, Portrait of a Man, 1947, 21x17", G **350.00**
Karashishi & pup on rocks, sgn oju Hiroshige hitsu, kakemono-e .**575.00**
Lady in flowing kimono, Kuniyoshi, 19th C, 14½x10" **220.00**
People in pavilion at table, Yoshida, 14½x9½" **350.00**
Pergola & garden, Hasedera Kairo, 1920s, 6½x9" **100.00**
Sand Garden, stone path, sgn Okiie Hasimoto, 1959, 64x54" **885.00**
Women & children on bridge, wisteria, Yoshida, 15½x10½" **450.00**

Miscellaneous

Bowl, Banko, hooded lily pad w/dragonfly/flowers, early, sm **75.00**
Candlestick, soft metal, elephant form, Meiji, 20½" **170.00**
Lantern, iron, hanging, Jp, 19th C, 21" **375.00**
Model, hawk on branch, soft metal, Jp, 32" wingspan **160.00**
Scroll, Empress in colorful costume, remtd on silk, 90x41" **125.00**
Scroll, mtn landscapes & cottages, sgn Nakayama Kimito, 46x12" .**180.00**
Teapot, Banko, elephant & rider figural, mc, M **100.00**
Tsuba, Namban, dragons/ball among scrolls w/gold, 2¾" **300.00**
Tsuba, Namban, dragons/conch shell, gold leaf accents, 2½" **260.00**
Vase, copper, molded lotus & stems, Meiji, 11" **210.00**
Vase, iron, Utsukusima shrine & torii mold, Jp, 18" **500.00**
Vase, soft metal, flowers/birds/fan-like panels, Jp, 30" **200.00**
Wood cvg, group of Quanyin & attendants, mc details, 50½" **325.00**

Orrefors

Orrefors Glassworks was founded in 1898 in the Swedish province of Smaaland. Utilizing the expertise of designers such as Simon Gate, Edward Hald, Vicke Lindstrand, and Edwin Ohrstrom, it produced art glass of the highest quality. Various techniques were used in achieving the decoration. Some were wheel engraved; others were blown through a unique process that formed controlled bubbles or air pockets resulting in unusual patterns and shapes. Our advisor for this category is Abby Malowanczyk; she is listed in the Directory under Texas.

Bowl, Thunderstorm, bl cased to clear, Edward Hald, 1920, 4½x6" .**1,600.00**
Decanter, HP nudes/card suits on topaz, Of LT 63 30, 10" **1,380.00**
Paperweight vase, fish scene in gr, Graal/#1250/ME Hald, 4½" .**585.00**
Vase, Ariel, dove, snake & portrait, #425/Edvin Ohrstrom, 7¼" .**3,335.00**
Vase, Ariel, geometrics, D-167H/Ingeborg Lundin, 4¾x6½" ..**1,200.00**
Vase, Ariel, Ohstrom, mini **450.00**
Vase, bucket form, bl powders/cluthra bubbles/blk rim, Of_70, 9¾" .**230.00**
Vase, bud; oval w/topaz-lined oval pocket, #3538/128, 8¼" **175.00**
Vase, Fish, 1 fish/2 schools, ocean waves, HA 1919, label, 10¼" ..**230.00**
Vase, Graal, gr-brn fish/plants, #313C Edward Hald 1949, 5½" .**575.00**

Ott and Brewer

The partnership of Ott and Brewer began in 1865 in Trenton, New Jersey. By 1876 they were making decorated graniteware, parian, and 'ivory porcelain' — similar to Irish belleek though not as fine and of different composition. In 1883, however, experiments toward that end had reached a successful conclusion, and a true belleek body was introduced. It came to be regarded as the finest china ever produced by an American firm. The ware was decorated by various means such as hand painting, transfer printing, gilding, and lustre glazing. The company closed in 1893, one of many that failed during that depression. In the listings below, the ware is belleek unless noted otherwise. Our advisor for this category is Mary Frank Gaston.

Cup & saucer, bouillon; gold acorns on branch hdls 195.00
Cup & saucer, demitasse; Tridacna, blk mk 145.00
Ewer, gold stylized leaves, cactus hdl, 8½" 1,250.00
Teapot, Tridacna, yel w/gold, wht loop hdl, mk, 4" 400.00
Vase, gold paste on silver gray, crimped, 3 openings, 5" 525.00
Vase, leaves & butterfly, gold paste on matt, hdls, 5½" 600.00
Vase, tree trunk w/floral transfer, red mk, 5x5" 450.00

Overbeck

The Overbeck Studio was established in 1911 in Cambridge City, Indiana, by four Overbeck sisters. It survived until the last sister died in 1955. Early wares were often decorated with carved designs of stylized animals, birds, or florals with the designs colored to contrast with the background. Others had tooled designs filled in with various colors for a mosaic effect. After 1937, Mary Frances, the last remaining sister, favored handmade figurines with somewhat bizarre features in fanciful combinations of color. Overbeck ware is signed 'OBK,' frequently with the designer's and potter's initials under the stylized 'OBK.'

Vase, small girls with large bows, cats and circles, butterscotch matt on teal blue, signed E.F., impressed mark, 11", $4,000.00.

Figurine, chicken (grotesque), mc, rprs, 5" 100.00
Figurine, Colonial man, mc gloss & matt, 5¾", NM 175.00
Figurine, dog, standing w/head up, dk brn matt, OBK, 3¾" 300.00
Figurine, goat (grotesque), 4-color, mk, rprs, 5⅜" 275.00
Figurine, lady w/bonnet & apron carries apple basket, OBK, 4½" ..200.00
Figurine, lady w/bouquet, OBK, 5" 200.00
Figurine, rooster (grotesque) strutting, red/wht/brn, 3¼x1¾" 250.00
Vase, floral cvg on tan/lt orange, E & MF Overbeck, 11⅜" 8,000.00
Vase, hosta flowers/leaves/stems, mc, E & MF Overbeck, 14¼" ..20,000.00
Vase, wizards w/stars in wide band, wht on gr, EF, 7½" 4,750.00

Overlay Glass

Art glass having layers of more than one type or color of glass is sometimes called overlay or cased glass. Very often glassware of this type has applied decorations such as fruit, flowers, leaves, or ruffles (rigaree), such as is commonly identified with Stevens and Williams.

Biscuit jar, lav-pk w/HP decor, SP trim, 6⅝x4¾" 185.00
Bowl vase, rainbow striped w/HP dots & scrolls, 5½x7½" 450.00
Pitcher, orange, ruffled top, readed hdl, 7¼x4¾" 165.00
Pitcher, pk, rnd mouth, clear hdl, 7½x5" 165.00
Vase, opal w/pk spatter flowers, amber branches, egg form, 7" 150.00
Vase, pk, ewer w/frosted hdl, HP flowers w/gold, 9¾x2¾" 125.00

Overshot

Overshot glass is characterized by the beaded or craggy appearance of its surface. Earlier ware was irregularly textured, while 20th-century examples tend to be more uniform.

Basket, cranberry to crystal, thorn hdl, rectangular, 10x7½" 225.00
Bowl, ice cream; wht, 11½", +6 sm 185.00
Ice pail, cranberry w/emb decor, brass rim & hdl, 5¾x5" 145.00
Lamp, gr, uptrn shade, foreign burner, 6½" 800.00
Mug, rubena w/emb pattern, clear ft & hdl, 4⅛x2¾" 95.00
Pitcher, clear, bulbous w/slim neck, 6" 145.00
Pitcher, clear, rope hdl, ruffled rim, Sandwich, 13x6" 215.00
Pitcher, gr to clear, emb swirls, hinged metal lid, 8¾x4" 165.00
Pitcher, tankard, cranberry, lg ice bladder, 9½", $400 to 450.00
Pitcher, tankard, wht, 8⅜" 145.00
Shade, bl to clear, ruffled, 5⅜x7½" 165.00

Owen, Ben

Ben Owen worked at the Jugtown Pottery of North Carolina from 1923 until it closed in 1959. He continued in the business in his own Plank Road Pottery, stamping his ware 'Ben Owen, Master Potter.' His pottery closed in 1972. He died in 1983 at the age of 81.

Candlestick, buff-yel gloss, mk, 1960s, 9¾", EX 45.00
Pitcher, orange, w/lid, 4½" 50.00
Plate, dessert; orange, ¾x6", 8 for 110.00
Plate, dinner; orange, mid-1960s, ¾x10½", 4 for 100.00
Pot, red-orange, 2-hdld, mk, 1960s, 4", NM 75.00

Owens Pottery

J.B. Owens founded his company in Zanesville, Ohio, in 1891, and until 1907, when the company decided to exert most of its energies in the area of tile production, made several quality lines of art pottery. His first line, Utopian, was a standard brown ware with underglaze slip decoration of nature studies, animals, and portraits. A similar line, Lotus, utilized lighter background colors. Henri Deux, introduced in 1900, featured incised Art Nouveau forms inlaid with color. (Be aware that the Brush-McCoy Pottery acquired many of Owens's molds and reproduced a line similar to Henri Deux, which they called Navarre.) Other important lines were Opalesce, Rustic, Feroza, Cyrano, and Mission, examples of which are rare today. The factory burned in 1928, and the company closed shortly thereafter. Values vary according to the quality of the artwork and subject matter. Examples signed by the artist bring higher prices than those that are not signed. For further information we recommend *Owens Pottery Unearthed* by Kristy and Rick McKibben and Jeanette and Marvin Stofft. Mrs. Stofft is listed in the Directory under Indiana.

Alpine, vase, roses, T Steele, bottle shape, 9¾" 650.00
Experimental, vase, floral, yel & bl on bl to orange, unmk, 10" ..400.00
Lightweight, pitcher, clover blossoms, stamped mk, 5½" 175.00
Lotus, pitcher, stylized iris on wht to charcoal 175.00
Lotus, pitcher, wading bird & lotus blossom, #4, 6", NM 450.00
Lotus, pitcher, wading bird & lotus blossom, 8⅝" 600.00
Lotus, vase, fish & seaweed, unmk, 11⅛" 1,200.00
Matt Green, vase, emb geometrics, hdls, bulbous, 8x6" 550.00
Matt Green, vase, Feroza blank, Owensart #1112, 10x9" 650.00
Matt Utopian, vase, cherries, H Eberlein, #817, 7⅞" 350.00
Matt Utopian, vase, wild roses, Tot Steel, #123, 13⅝" 475.00
Soudanese, vase, flower, pk on brn, mk, 4" 325.00
Soudanese, vase, purple blossoms w/gr leaves, squat, 4" 375.00
Tile, floral, 6x6" 175.00
Utopian, candlestick, oak leaves, dk brn-blk, 6" 125.00

Utopian, flower boat, red clovers, ftd crescent, #972, 4¼" 250.00
Utopian, jardiniere, grape decor, 5" 250.00
Utopian, jug, windflowers, mc on brn, torch mk, 6½x5" 300.00
Utopian, mug, blkberries, sgn Tot Steel, 5¼" 150.00
Utopian, vase, blkberries, 6¾", NM 175.00
Utopian, vase, chrysanthemums, S Timberlake, #122, 14x7" 550.00
Utopian, vase, floral, #1048, 5¼" 135.00
Utopian, vase, floral, bulbous, hdls, 5½x3½" 125.00
Utopian, vase, floral, sgn Tot Steel, Owensart #1150, 11" 275.00
Utopian, vase, floral, 8" 165.00
Utopian, vase, horse's head, M Timberlake, pillow form, 12" ..3,500.00
Utopian, vase, leaves, mk, 6¾" 150.00
Utopian, vase, poppies, #1080, 11" 350.00
Utopian, vase, poppies, 17½", NM 650.00
Utopian, vase, portrait, AF Best after Millet, bottle form, 16½" ..1,800.00
Utopian, vase, portrait of Sitting Bull, sgn EBA, 11x5" 3,500.00
Utopian, vase, tiger, sgn CL Leffler, pillow form, sm 1,800.00
Venetian, vase, gypsy on etched gold, bulbous, unmk, 15½x7" ...1,500.00

Pacific Clay Products

The Pacific Clay Products Company got its start in the 1920s as a consolidation of several smaller southern California potteries. The main Los Angeles plant had been founded in 1890 to make kitchen stoneware, ollas, and similar items. Terra cotta and brick were later produced.

In 1932 Hostess Ware, a vividly colored line of dinnerware, was introduced to compete with Bauer's Ring Ware. Coralitos, a lighter-weight, pastel-hued dinnerware line was first marketed in 1937, and a similar but less expensive line called Arcadia soon followed. Art ware including vases, figurines, candlesticks, etc., was produced from 1932 to 1942, at which time the company went into war-related work and pottery manufacture ceased. A limited amount of hand-decorated dinnerware was also made. For further information we recommend *The Collector's Encyclopedia of California Pottery*, Second Edition, by our advisor, Jack Chipman; he is listed in the Directory under California.

Artware vases of the early 1930s: Turquoise, 11½",
$150.00; Green, 8¼", $110.00; Yellow, 7", $125.00.

Bowl, centerpc; bl drip, shell shape, 14" 95.00
Bowl, divided vegetable; apricot 80.00
Bowl, mixing; Apache Red, Hostess Ware, 9½" 75.00
Bowl, Plaid, 15" 125.00
Carafe, red, w/4 tumblers 150.00
Chop plate, wht w/pk border, 13" 95.00
Egg cup, yel, Hostessware 70.00
Figurine, swan, wht, sm 65.00
Jardiniere, gr, #1501 ....35.00
Leaf bowl, pk, #3067 ....30.00
Leaf bowl, turq & wht, #3617 ....35.00
Planter, cameo, lt gr, Artware 45.00

Teapot, yel, 3-ftd 200.00
Vase, bsk, #1100, 28" 500.00

Paden City

The Paden City Glass Company began operations in 1916 in Paden City, West Virginia. The company's early lines consisted largely of the usual pressed tablewares, but by the 1920s production had expanded to include colored wares in translucent as well as opaque glass in a variety of patterns and styles. The company maintained its high standards of handmade perfection until 1949, when under new management much of the work formerly done by hand was replaced by automation. The Paden City Glass Company closed in 1951; its earlier wares, the colored patterns in particular, are becoming very collectible.

Paden City Glass is not always easily recognized by collectors or dealers, as it was almost never marked. It is believed this was so the glass could be sold to decorating companies. The company assigned both line numbers and names to many of its blanks or sets of glassware. Colors were sometimes given more than one name, and etchings were named as well. All this makes identification of items offered for sale through mail order difficult, and labels prepared by dealers are often confusing.

A review of literature available on Paden City reveals the following names for the company's plate etchings: Ardith, California Poppy, Cupid, Delilah Bird (Peacock Reverse), Eden Rose, Frost, Gazebo, Gothic Garden, Lela Bird, Nora Bird, Orchid (three variations), Peacock and Rose (Peacock and Wild Rose), Samarkand, Trumpet Flower, Utopia. Names given to cuttings made on Paden City blanks are Yorktown and Lazy Daisy. It is not clear whether the names originated with Paden City or with secondary decorating companies.

Our advisors for this category are George and Mary Hurney; they are listed in the Directory under Illinois. (Note: their interest is only in Paden City glassware, not the pottery.) See also Glass Animals and Figurines; Kitchen Collectibles, Glass.

This list gives company line numbers with corresponding line names. This information was obtained from Hazel Marie Weatherman's *Price Trends 2* and Jerry Barnett's *Paden City: The Color Company*.

#69, #69½ — Georgian, Aristocrat
#90 — Breton, Chevalier
#154 — Rena
#191 — Party Line
#198 — Ross
#199 — Inna
#202 — Virginia
#203 — Webb
#204 — Etta
#205 — Estelle
#206 — Pineapple
#209 — Edna
#210 — Skidoo, Spire
#215 — Hotcha
#220 — Cantina, Largo
#221 — S.S. Dreamship, Maya
#300 — Archaic
#330 — Luli
#400 — City Lights
#411 — Vaara, Mrs B
#412 — Crow's Foot (Square)
#444 — Vale
#555 — Vermillion
#700 — Simplicity
#701 — Lazy Daisy
#777 — Secrets

#836 — Future
#881 — Wotta Line, Gadroon
#890 — Crow's Foot (Round)
#895 — Lucy
#900 — Nadja
#991 — Penny Line
#994 — Popeye and Olive
#1503 — Trance
#1504 — Chaucer
#2000 — Mystic

And, finally, a listing of colors with alternate names or descriptive phrases:

Amber — (dull)
Cheriglo — (delicate) pink
Cobalt Blue — Royal Blue
Crystal — (clear, no tint)
Dark Green — forest green
Dark Amber — (honey color)
Light Blue — Copen, Neptune

Mulberry — amethyst
Opal — opaque white
Primrose — (amber with reddish tint)
Red — ruby
Rose — (dark pink)
Yellow — (pale, soft)

Ice tubs, Party Line:
Pink, $45.00; Amber,
$35.00.

Ardith, bowl, mayonnaise; blk, ftd	58.00
Ardith, candy dish, yel, w/lid	95.00
Ardith, compote, pk	45.00
Ardith, pitcher, gr, w/6 tumblers	575.00
California Poppy, vase, pk, 12"	275.00
Crow's Foot, bowl, vegetable; oval	45.00
Crow's Foot, gravy boat, red	85.00
Crow's Foot, tumbler, water; bl	90.00
Cupid, creamer, pk	125.00
Cupid, ice tub, gr	350.00
Cupid, mayonnaise & underplate, gr	260.00
Cupid, server, pk, center hdl	140.00
Cupid, sugar bowl, pk	125.00
Gazebo, bowl, crystal w/gold etch, 12"	55.00
Gazebo, plate, crystal w/gold etch, 10½"	85.00
Gazebo, punch cup, crystal	8.00
Gazebo, server, crystal, center hdl, swan neck	75.00
Gothic Garden, bowl, yel, ftd	45.00
Gothic Garden, cake stand, yel	65.00
Gothic Garden, vase, blk, 10"	145.00
Gothic Garden, vase, yel, 9" sq	110.00
Largo, server, red, center hdl	90.00
Lela Bird, server, pk, center hdl	120.00
Lela Bird, vase, blk, 10"	150.00
Lela Bird, vase, blk, 12"	200.00
Lela Bird, vase, gr, 10"	100.00
Lela Bird, vase, pk, 10"	195.00
Lela Bird, vase, pk, 12"	175.00
Orchid, bowl, console; red	250.00
Orchid, candlesticks, red, pr	260.00
Orchid, mayonnaise, red, w/underplate & ladle	150.00
Orchid, server, red, center hdl	175.00

Party Line, cup, red	15.00
Party Line, cup & saucer, amethyst	12.00
Party Line, plate, amethyst, 8"	10.00
Party Line, saucer, red	5.00
Party Line, server, amethyst, center hdl	28.00
Party Line, sherbet, amethyst	12.00
Party Line, sherbet, red	12.00
Party Line, tumbler, iced tea; amethyst	22.00
Party Line, tumbler, water; red	22.00
Peacock w/Rose, bowl, pk, 11"	110.00
Peacock w/Rose, cake plate, pk, low ft	115.00
Peacock w/Rose, cheese plate, pk	50.00
Peacock w/Rose, comport, gr, 7"	55.00
Peacock w/Rose, mayonnaise bowl, pk	45.00
Peacock w/Rose, vase, gr, elliptical	325.00
Peacock w/Rose, vase, gr, 10"	95.00
Utopia, cocktail mixer, crystal	165.00
Utopia, vase, blk, 10"	195.00

Paden City Pottery

Founded in 1907, this company produced many dinnerware and kitchenware lines until they closed in the 1950s. Many were decaled; in fact, this company is credited with originating the underglaze decal process.

One of their most collectible lines is called Caliente. It was Paden City's version of the solid-color dinnerware lines that became so popular in the '30s and '40s. Caliente's shapes were simple and round, but its shell-like finials, handles, and feet did little to enhance its Art Deco possibilities, which the public seemed to prefer at that time. As a result, it never sold in volume comparable to Fiesta or Bauer's Ring, but you should be able to rebuild a set eventually, and your efforts would be well worthwhile. If you'd like to see photographs of this line and many others produced by Paden City, see *The Collector's Encyclopedia of American Dinnerware* by Jo Cunningham.

Bowl, Flaming Rose, LG	15.00
Bowl, Patio decal, oval	20.00
Bowl, Patio decal, sm	6.00
Casserole, Floral, w/lid	18.00
Casserole, Orange Blossom, w/lid, Manning-Bowman metal fr	30.00
Casserole, Patio, w/lid	25.00
Creamer, Shenandoah Ware, Morning Glory	8.00
Creamer & sugar bowl, Acacia Flowers, Shell-Crest shape, w/lid	24.00
Creamer & sugar bowl, Far East, Shell-Crest shape, w/lid	24.00
Creamer & sugar bowl, Jonquil	12.00
Creamer & sugar bowl, Nasturtium decal, Shell-Crest shape, w/lid	26.00
Cup, Springtime, mk	6.00
Cup, Touch of Black, mk	6.00
Cup & saucer, AD; American Beauty	15.00
Cup & saucer, Paden Rose	8.00
Custard, Wild Rose, Princess Line, mk Northern...Chicago, ind	4.00
Gravy boat, Nasturtium decal	17.00
Plate, cartoon; by Peter Arno, Minion shape, from $6 to	10.00
Plate, Far East, Shell-Crest shape, 9"	6.00
Plate, Patio decal, 10"	10.00
Plate, Regina Jonquil, shaped corners, 8"	6.00
Plate, serving; American Beauty, Minion shape	12.00
Plate, Shenandoah Ware, Jonquil, 9"	4.00
Plate, Shenandoah Ware, Morning Glory, 7"	4.00
Plate, Shenandoah Ware, Poppy, 7"	4.00
Plate, Springtime, shaped corners, mk, 10"	10.00
Plate, strawberry; Shenandoah Ware, 8"	4.00
Plate, Touch of Black, shaped corners, mk, 8"	6.00

Plate, Wild Rose, Princess Line, 9" 6.00
Platter, meat; Blossoms, Shell-Crest shape 6.00
Platter, meat; Grandiose, oval 8.00
Platter, Paden Rose, oval 15.00
Platter, Patio decal, Shell-Crest shape 20.00
Shaker, rose decal, rnd, ea 6.00
Sugar bowl, Shenandoah Ware, Morning Glory, w/lid 8.00
Teapot, Shenandoah Ware, Morning Glory, w/lid 35.00
Teapot, Wild Rose, Princess Line, mk Northern Products, Chicago ..30.00

Paintings on Ivory

Miniature works of art executed on ivory from the 1800s are assessed by the finesse of the artist, as is any fine painting. Signed examples and portraits with identifiable subjects are usually preferred.

Baby's portrait, pk & wht, in oval leather case, 4½x3½" 350.00
Geo Washington, red waistcoat, bl frock coat, 3½x2⅛" 500.00
Lady in blk w/wht bonnet & bl ribbon, sgn, 1831, 5x4⅜" 220.00
Lady in lace bonnet, blk lacquer fr w/gilded brass, 4½x4" 275.00
Lady in pk & wht dress, sgn, 3¾x3"+brass fr 275.00
Lady in purple dress w/gold brooch, sgn, 2x1⅛"+ivory fr 330.00
Lady in wht gown, late 19th C, in daguerreotype fr 175.00
Lady w/lacy collar & hat, 1¼x1¾"+ebonized fr 250.00
Lady w/ruffled collar, roses, plumed hat, 3⅝x2"+fr 165.00
Man, blk & gilt brass fr, 4¼x3½" 330.00
Man in blk coat & bow tie, hair locket on bk, 2½x2" 800.00
Napoleon I, sgn FL, gilt-metal bezel, rosewood fr 500.00

Pairpoint

The Pairpoint Manufacturing Company was built in 1880 in New Bedford, Massachusetts. It was primarily a metalworks whose chief product was coffin fittings. Next door, the Mt. Washington Glassworks made quality glasswares of many varieties. (See Mt. Washington for more information concerning their artware lines.) By 1894 it became apparent to both companies that a merger would be to their best interest.

From the late 1890s until the 1930s, lamps and lamp accessories were an important part of Pairpoint's production. There were three main types of shades, all of which were blown: puffy — blown-out reverse-painted shades (usually floral designs), ribbed — also reverse painted, and scenic — reverse painted with scenes of land or seascapes (usually executed on smooth surfaces, although ribbed scenics may be found occasionally). Cut glass lamps and those with metal overlay panels were also made. Scenic shades were sometimes artist signed. Every shade was stamped on the lower inside or outside edge with 1) The Pairpoint Corp., 2) Patent Pending, 3) Patented July 9, 1907, or 4) Patent Applied For. Bases were made of bronze, copper, brass, silver, or wood and are always signed.

Because they produced only fancy, handmade artware, the company's sales lagged seriously during the Depression, and as time and tastes changed, their style of product was less in demand. As a result, they never fully recovered; consequently part of the buildings and equipment was sold in 1938. The company reorganized in 1939 under the direction of Robert Gundersen and again specialized in quality hand-blown glassware. Isaac Babbit regained possession of the silver departments, and together they established Gundersen Glassworks, Inc. After WWII, because of a sharp decline in sales, it again became necessary to reorganize. The Gundersen-Pairpoint Glassworks was formed, and the old line of cut, engraved artware was reintroduced. The company moved to East Wareham, Massachusetts, in 1957. But business continued to suffer, and the firm closed only one year later. In 1970, however, new facilities

were constructed in Sagamore under the direction of Robert Bryden, sales manager for the company since the 1950s.

In 1974 the company began to produce lead glass cup plates which were made on commission as fund-raisers for various churches and organizations. These are signed with a 'P' in diamond and are becoming quite collectible. See also Napkin Rings.

Glass

Basket, cut, ruffled quatrefoil shape, sterling hdl, 14½x7" 450.00
Bowl, console; Flambo Ware, red w/blk ft, 12"+2 candlesticks .1,950.00
Box, roses & scrolls w/gold, ftd metal base, 4x6¾x4¼" 675.00
Candlestick, amethyst, etched/cvd grape pods/vine, 16" 325.00
Candlestick, cobalt stick stem w/ball connector, grape eng, 9¾" .145.00
Candlesticks, peonies on pk-pnt opal, silver o/l, mk, 9½", pr ..1,250.00
Compote, irid swirl bowl on silver std w/3 swans, C-1430 ....250.00
Cracker jar, roses on gold-beige, 16-panel sides, #3932, 5½x6" ..595.00
Panel, rvpt clipper ship, 9½x7½" 700.00

Lamps

Base, brn w/3" emerald Deco band w/enameling, #C3069, 24" ...400.00
Base, gr w/hearts/dmns/red-orange flower band, #C3007, 21" 350.00
Candle, Puffy 4½" poppy shade; orig wood base, 8", EX 1,100.00
Pnt/rvpt 16" wreaths/torches Vienna shade; mk waisted std, 21" ..1,265.00
Puffy 6" rose tree shade w/butterfly; tree trunk std, 11" 8,000.00
Puffy 8" floral-border shade; #C3064 std, 14" 2,600.00
Puffy 8" lotus/dragonflies dome shade; #d baluster std, 16" 1,000.00
Puffy 9" floral Papillon shade; #3057 std, 14" 3,450.00
Puffy 9" floral Papillon shade; gilt baluster #3047½ std 4,600.00
Puffy 9" floral Papillon shade; unmk std, 16" 2,875.00
Puffy 9" floral Stratford shade; mk baluster std, 12¾" 2,600.00
Puffy 9" floral Stratford shade; sgn std, 15", EX 3,100.00
Puffy 10" butterfly shade; acanthus #E3054 std, 14½" 4,800.00
Puffy 10" hollyhock Stratford shade; brass 4-ftd std, 16" 4,800.00
Puffy 12" azalea shade; brass floral #3099 std, 20" 11,000.00
Puffy 12" poppy shade; rstr; sq ftd 2-socket std 4,250.00
Puffy 12" rose bouquet shade; sgn #3054 base, 21", EX 2,300.00
Puffy 14" dogwood dome shade; baluster-form std, 22" 7,500.00
Puffy 14" mixed floral Ravenna shade; foliate std, 24" 7,475.00

Puffy 14" poppy bonnet shade with reverse-painted blossoms, on 12" ring above four blossom supports and pyramidal metal base with molded poppy blossoms, 22", $15,400.00.

Puffy 14" poppy dome shade; #3052 sq std, 21" 11,500.00
Puffy 14" rose/butterfly Papillon shade; #d std, 21" 5,465.00
Puffy 14" vintage dome shade, rpr; #3040 std, 18" 3,450.00
Puffy/rvpt 12" floral Albermarl sq shade; sq mk std, 20" 9,775.00
Rvpt 6½x5" goldenrods dome shade; matching glass base, 11" .1,150.00
Rvpt 8½" winter landscape mk shade; mk std, 15½" 1,500.00
Rvpt 9" floral dome shade; silvered #3064 std, 13" 1,265.00
Rvpt 9" mill/river scenic shade; 4-prong gilt metal std, 15" 5,175.00

Rvpt 9" roses/butterflies Papillon shade; #d paw-ftd std, 15" ...**3,450.00**
Rvpt 12" floral campana-form Cologne shade; #3049 std, 21" .**2,600.00**
Rvpt 13" flower-basket dome shade; urn-form #B 3066 std, 20" .**2,875.00**
Rvpt 14" floral dome shade; gilt metal #3086 std, 22" **4,000.00**
Rvpt 14" floral Venice shade; mk std w/appl lions, 22" **3,165.00**
Rvpt 14" poppies/trellis-work shade; #3085 std, 21" **9,200.00**
Rvpt 15" medallions & garlands urn-shaped shade; #G3067 std, 22" .**2,400.00**
Rvpt 16" clipper ship Directorie shade: 3-dolphin base, 22½" ..**4,000.00**
Rvpt 16" landscape scenic shade; bronzed std, 23", EX **1,100.00**
Rvpt 16" tapestry shade; triple candelabrum #D3099 std, 26" .**2,400.00**
Rvpt 17" chrysanthemums Exeter shade; SP sgn std, 23" **4,700.00**
Rvpt 17" harvest scene shade; SP 2-socket std, 21" **2,875.00**
Rvpt 17" wisteria Berkeley shade; gr-finish glass std **4,000.00**

Pairpoint Limoges

Limoges china blanks were imported from France in strict accordance with Pairpoint specifications. They were decorated by Pairpoint in designs that ranged from simple to elaborate florals and scenics. Called Crown Point French China in old Pairpoint and Mt. Washington catalogs, these are easily identified. Look for the Pairpoint name over a crown with the Limoges name below. You may also find similar ware marked 'Pairpoint Minton.'

Box, boy presents gift to girl/roses, crown mk, 3½x8" L **475.00**
Chocolate pot, floral sprays w/gold, swirled body, 10" **585.00**
Ewer, lotus buds at branch hdl, HP lotus decor, 9x6¼" **850.00**
Gravy boat, mc flowers on wht w/scrolls, w/underplate **175.00**
Vase, girl's portrait reserve on red w/gold (worn), 14" **835.00**
Vase, Persians on carpet/2 camels/Nubian lady w/gold, 13½" .**2,400.00**
Vase, pond lilies, pk on beige w/gr, mk PMC 2004, 7x6¾" **425.00**

Paper Dolls

No one knows quite how or when paper dolls originated. One belief is that they began in Europe as 'pantins' (jumping jacks) and were frequently worn as part of the costume. By the late 1790s, they were being mass produced. During the 19th century, most paper dolls portrayed famous dancers and opera stars such as Fanny Elssler and Jenny Lind. In the late 1800s, the Raphael Tuck Publishers of England produced many series of beautiful paper dolls; retail companies used them as advertisements to further the sale of their products. Around the turn of the century, many popular women's magazines began featuring a page of paper dolls.

Most familiar to today's collectors are the books with dolls on cardboard covers and clothes on the inside pages. These made their appearance in the late 1920s and early '30s. The most collectible (and the most valuable) are those representing celebrities, movie stars, and comic-strip characters of the '30s and '40s.

When no condition is indicated, the dolls listed below are assumed to be in mint, uncut, original condition. Cut sets will be worth about half price if all dolls and outfits are included and pieces are in very good condition. If dolls were produced in die-cut form, these prices reflect such a set in mint condition with all costumes and accessories.

For further information we recommend *A Collector's Guide to Magazine Paper Dolls* (Collector Books) and *Tomart's Price Guide to Lowe and Whitman Paper Dolls*, both by Mary Young, our advisor for this category; she is listed in the Directory under Ohio. We also recommend *Schroeder's Collectible Toys, Antique to Modern* (Collector Books).

Annie Laurie, Lowe #1030, 1941, uncut, M **75.00**
Baby Brother, Saalfield #2783, 1959, uncut, NM **15.00**

Beauty Contest, Lowe #1026, 1941, uncut, M **100.00**
Betty Bonnet, Ladies' Home Journal, 1916, EX **25.00**
Big 'N Little Sister, Merrill #1549, 1951, uncut, NM **35.00**
Bobbsey Twins, Lowe #1254, 1952, uncut, M **75.00**
Carmen Miranda, Whitman #995, 1942, uncut, M **160.00**
Children in the Shoe, Merrill #1562, 1949, uncut, NM **45.00**
Cradle Baby, Saalfield #5214, 1948, uncut, NM **20.00**
Cuddles & Rags, Lowe #1283, 1950, uncut, M **55.00**
Curly-Top, Paper Doll House, Pat 1938, 1939, uncut, NM **25.00**
Debby Dolls, Jaymar Specialty #980, uncut, NM **25.00**
Dionne Quints, Whitman #998, 1935, uncut, M **125.00**
Dionne Quintuplets, Palmolive Giveaway, 1937, uncut, M **75.00**
Dr Kildare Play Book, Lowe #955, uncut, NM **15.00**
Festival Paper Dolls, Saalfield #2431, 1944, uncut **45.00**

Gloria Jean, Saalfield #1661, copyright 1940, uncut, from $85.00 to $125.00.

Goldilocks & 3 Bears, Lowe #2561, 1955, uncut, M **35.00**
Honeymooners, Lowe #2560, 1956, uncut, M **300.00**
Ice Festival, Saalfield #2763, 1957, uncut, NM **25.00**
Improved Paper Doll Outfit, Parker Bros, 1917, uncut, sm, NM ...**50.00**
In Our Backyard, Lowe #1027, uncut, NM **40.00**
Julia, Saalfield #4435, 1968, uncut, M **40.00**
Junior Prom, Lowe #1042, 1942, uncut, M **50.00**
Kathy & Sue, Saalfield #6117, 1958, MIB **30.00**
Laraine Day, Saalfield #2731, 1953, uncut, M **75.00**
Linda Darnell, Saalfield #2733, 1953, uncut, M **100.00**
Lindy-Lou 'N Cindy-Sue, Merrill #2564, 1954, uncut, NM **50.00**
Little Ballerina, Merrill #1542, 1953, uncut, NM **30.00**
Little Polly Dress-Up, Am Colortype #629, NM **40.00**
Little Toddlers, Saalfield #2736, 1954, uncut, NM **20.00**
Little Women, Lowe #1030, 1941, uncut, M **75.00**
My Fair Lady, Ottenheimer #2961-0, 1965, uncut, EX **35.00**
Nurse & Doctor, Saalfield #2613, 1952, uncut, NM **30.00**
Paper Dolls of Early Am, sgn Mary McLain cover, 1975, uncut **18.00**
Partridge Family, Artcraft #5137, 1971, uncut, NM **40.00**
Patti Page, Lowe #2488, 1958, uncut, M **75.00**
Popeye, Whitman #980, 1937, uncut, M **350.00**
Prom Home Permanent, Lowe #1253, 1952, uncut, NM **25.00**
Quiz Kids, Saalfield #2430, 1942, uncut, NM **100.00**
Roy Rogers, Whitman #995, 1948, uncut, M **135.00**
Sally & Dick, Bob & Jean, Lowe #1023, 1940, uncut, NM **40.00**
Sandra the Bride, Avalon Industries #701-3, uncut, M **10.00**
Square Dance, Lowe #968, 1950, uncut, M **25.00**
Storyland, Saalfield #1349, EX **25.00**
Ted & Bob, MA Donohue & Co #81C, uncut, NM **35.00**
Teen Town, Merrill #3443, 1946, uncut, NM **75.00**
Tom the Aviator, Lowe #1074, 1941, uncut, NM **50.00**
Trudy Doll Keepsake Folio, Lowe #2424, 1964, uncut, M **25.00**
Winnie the Pooh, Whitman #947, 1935, uncut, M **100.00**

Paperweights

All paperweights listed here are made totally of glass (including the lampwork flowers, fish, birds, snakes, lizards, and millefiori rods). The only elements that are not glass are the clay sulfides encased within some of the Baccarat and St. Louis weights. Today, antique weights (1845 to ca 1870s) and those made by contemporary artists attract the most attention and are the most expensive. Lower-priced 'gift' weights come from American glasshouses and studios, China, Murano, Italy, and Scotland. But because of the expenses involved in their manufacture (fuel, material, and labor), even they are not cheap. There is an international association of paperweight collectors with many state and regional chapters. (For information see Clubs, Newsletters, and Catalogs in the Directory.) Many books are currently available on the subject of paperweights. For the beginner we recommend *All About Paperweights* by L.H. Selmen.

Probably inspired by the work of Pierre Bigaglia (Venice), the French factories of Baccarat, Clichy, and St. Louis turned their attention to paperweight making in the 1840s. They first made millefiori paperweights, the technique a revival of methods used in Alexandria, Damascus, Rome, and Byzantium before the time of Christ. (This art form had faded out but had been revived in 16th-century Venice.) The French Classic period was 1845 to 1860; English (Whitefriars and Bacchus) and American (Sandwich and New England) glasshouses followed their lead about ten years later. Gradually, as the paperweight's popularity declined, production began to wane; Clichy closed in the 1880s, as did a few American factories. Baccarat made weights as late as 1910; in the '20s and '30s, a worker by the name of Dupont revived the art. Then in the 1950s St. Louis and Baccarat sparked a renewal of interest in weight making that is still going strong today. Some of the most desirable weights from American artists were made by the Banfords, Randall Grubb, Rick Ayotte, Chris Buzzini, Ken Rosenfeld, Gordon Smith, Paul Stankard, Charles Kaziun (d), Del (d) and Debbie Tarsitano, and the Trabuccos. From Scotland, Paul Ysart (d), Perthshire and Caithness/Whitefriars are also well known.

Note: Prices reflect the usual buyer's fee charged by most auction houses. Furthermore, there are many factors which determine value, particularly of antique weights. Auction-realized prices of contemporary weights are usually different from issue price; 'list price' may be for weights issued earlier and reduced for clearance or influenced by market demand and other factors. The competition for antique weights has been increasing dramatically over this decade. New collectors entering the field have greatly influenced prices. As the numbers of collectors increase, available antique weights decrease per capita, forcing prices upwards. Since the 1930s antique paperweights have steadily increased in value, making them one of today's best investments. The dimension given at the end of the description is diameter.

Key:
con — concentric	latt — latticinio
fct — faceted	mill — millefiori
gar — garland	o/l — overlay
grd — ground	(d) — deceased

Ayotte, Rick

Meadowlark on branch on clear grd, 1980, 2½" 385.00
Rose, pk center fades to wht, mini, 2" 350.00
Starthroat hummingbird & honeysuckle flowers, 2½" 350.00
2 parrots on branches on clear grd, compound, 1980, 2¾" 525.00

Baccarat, Antique

Bl & wht Dogrose w/gr leaves, faceted, star-cut base, 3¼" 650.00
Circular mill gar on color grd w/6 rose canes, 2⅞" 2,750.00
Close-pack mill mushroom w/torsade & star-cut base, 3" 1,550.00
Complex cane, mc target canes/wht star canes, dbl trefoil, 3⅛" .900.00
Dtd close-pack mill, cane, sgn B1848, 2¾" 2,200.00
Gr o/l, mill canes form star, silhouettes in center, 3¼" 6,000.00
Spaced mill on muslin w/complex center cane, 2⅛" 975.00

Baccarat, Modern

Aries the Ram, star in base, bl border, 2¾" base 200.00
Con mill w/mc fortress canes, central conical cane, 1¾" 100.00
Entwined dbl gar on lt gr latt, 1988, 3⅛" 300.00
Pansy & bud, star-cut base, 2¾" 715.00
Sulfide, Adlai Stevenson, 2⅝" base 200.00
Wht squirrel con mill w/17 silhouette canes on bl, 1977, 3¼" ...475.00

Banford, Bob

Lilies of the valley w/lg gr leaves, claret base, 3" 600.00
Twin bl-veined wht flowers w/2 buds, gr leaves, 2¾" 300.00
2 dbl clematis & bud on stems w/leaves on wht grd 600.00
5-flower bouquet in fct column, 3¾" 1,100.00

Buzzini, Chris

Bl stickweed flowers, mossy log w/growth rings, ltd ed, 3⅜" 1,200.00
Cornflower/roses/blossoms/etc in bouquet, 3⅜" 1,500.00
Harlequin Lupine w/pk & yel blooms & buds, ltd ed, 3⅜" 850.00
3 Yosemite Aster & 2 buds, brn stem, speckled leaves, ltd ed 850.00

Caithness

Comet, bl, wht & clear on blk grd, 3" 130.00
Deep Sea Diver, diver/fish/ocean scene, W Manson, 3⅜" 995.00
Moonflower, blk grd w/bl, bubbles, 3¼" 65.00
Yel rose on gr, fct, sgn WM, ltd ed, mini, 2¼" 210.00

Clichy, Antique

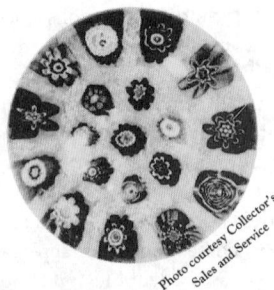

Clichy checquer weight, nineteen multicolor canes with two roses, stars, whorls, and pastry-mold canes, several minute bubbles, 3¼", $2,500.00.

Photo courtesy Collector's Sales and Service

Apple gr grd w/mill circlets, 3½" 825.00
Chequer w/central pk/gr rose cane, 2⅞" 2,475.00
Circular gars w/2 pk/gr rose canes, 3⅛" 1,760.00
Con pk & gr rose cane center w/mc complex canes, 2¾" 850.00
Scramble w/moss/complex & rose canes, 3¼" 1,200.00
Spaced mill w/central pk/gr rose cane, 2½" 1,430.00
Swirl, robin's-egg bl & wht w/complex center cane, 2⅞" 2,100.00
Trefoil w/complex center cane, star & 6 complex canes, 3⅛" 850.00

Deacons, John

Baccarat-type pansy on wht latt w/turq & wht dbl o/l, 3¼" 425.00
Mill butterfly on latt enhanced by dbl trefoil gar, 3⅛" 250.00
Purple & wht primroses, ltd 1980 edition w/D cane 225.00

Donofrio, Jim

Dragon formed by flowering plant root 1,000.00
Gr frog & berries among foliage, 3⅜" 1,000.00
Turtle & plants w/pk blooms on gr grd, 3⅜" 1,200.00
2 salamanders, blooming cactus, Indian pot, 3⅜" 1,000.00

New England Glass, Antique

Con mill on latt, bright colors, 2¾" 880.00
Con mill on latt, off center, 7 running rabbit canes, 2¼" 550.00
Crown w/mc twists, 2⅝" 1,320.00
Fruits in symmetrical form on latt, 2⅞" 1,045.00

Perthshire

Buds & flowers on leafy bed, 1/16 fcts, star-cut base, 3¼" 785.00
Lampwork flower amid mill w/complex canes, ltd ed, 3¼" 285.00
Pk flower & bud w/mc stamens on bl grd, 1/12 fcts, ltd ed, 2¾" .440.00

Rosenfeld, Ken

Dahlia/forget-me-nots/wht flowers/blooms/cherries, ftd 650.00
Mc flower bouquet on clear grd, single fct, 1993, 3½" 400.00
Pk camellia & lt bl flower on rocky floor, 2½" 250.00
Rocks & mc flowers w/grasses on mossy grd, 3½" 800.00
5 wht flowers w/yel centers & gr leaves on bl flash grd, 3⅜" 300.00
6 red cherries/2 flowers/4 buds on branch w/leaves 500.00

St. Louis, Antique

Crown, red & gr, 3⅛" 2,090.00
Flat nosegay bouquet on amber base, 2⅜" 800.00
Jasper grd panel, center, 6 surrounding canes, 2¾" 440.00
Mixed fruit on latt, 2⅞" 1,320.00
Pattern mill gar on latt, 3⅛" 715.00
Plum, royal bl on branch w/2 leaves, fct, star-cut base, 2½" 990.00

Stankard, Paul

Dogwood on bright bl grd, 2¾" 800.00
Morning glory blossoms on bl grd, 1984, 3⅛" 1,980.00
Poinsettia, red/floating, PS cane, 1973, 2¼" 735.00
Sippiwisset bouquet on clear base, 1973, 3" 2,875.00

Tarsitano, Debbie

Lav rose w/bud & wht flowers on cobalt, 3⅜" 925.00
Pansy, lt bl flower & bud, fct, 3½" 950.00
Wht 7-petal flower w/bud & gr leaves, 2¾" 875.00
2 open flowers/2 buds behind bed of purple flowers, 3½" 1,600.00

Whitefriars

Butterfly w/in mc gar, 1 top/6 side fcts, sgn/1982, 2⅞" 165.00
Close mill canes in groups of 4 to 7 enclosing mc canes, 3" 350.00
Con mill w/3 circles of bl/pk/red/wht canes, 2¼" 140.00
Mc patterned mill, 1 top/5 side fcts, 1973, 3" 375.00
Red & wht heart cane amid mc mill canes, sticker, 3¼" 200.00

Ysart, Paul

Gar butterfly on lime opaque grd, PY cane, 3" 775.00
Gr leaves cross on latt, fct, rare, 3½" 2,750.00

Mill & lace pattern, 2⅞" 880.00
Scramble w/geometrically spaced bubbles, H cane, 3" 350.00

Miscellaneous

Grubb, R; violets & yel broom flowers w/in mc mill gar, 3⅛" 650.00
Hansen, E; 2 pk buds, bl flower, wht flower w/mauve, 3" 300.00
Harris, Harv; pk morning glories on dirt grd, 3⅛" 250.00
Harris, Harv; upright bouquet, red/wht/bl flowers, 3" 300.00
Harris, Harv; 3 irises in upright block w/foliage, 3½" 375.00
Jokelson, Paul; lemon gr multi-petal dahlia, sgn, 1970, 3⅛" 300.00
Orient & Flume, Blk-Leg frog on silver pad, D Smallhouse, 3½" .290.00
Smith, Gordon; bl/yel Tang, wht/bl Helipora on gr grd, 3" 325.00

Papier-Mache

The art of papier-mache was mainly European. It originated in Paris around the middle of the 18th century and became popular in America during Victorian times. Small items such as boxes, trays, inkwells, frames, etc., as well as extensive ceiling moldings and larger articles of furniture were made. The process involved building layer upon layer of paper soaked in glue, then coaxed into shape over a wood or wire form. When dry it was painted or decorated with gilt or inlays. Inexpensive 20th-century 'notions' were machine processed and mold pressed. See also Christmas; Candy Containers.

Box, MOP inlay, gilt/pnt decor, English, 1850s, 2x11x8" 330.00
Helmet mask, Head of Goliath, w/pnt & horsehair, 40" dia 150.00

Lap desk, painted floral with mother-of-pearl inlay and gilt tracery, ca 1850, 3¼x12x9", EX, $275.00.

Lap desk, lacquered w/MOP inlay & gilt scrolls, English, 4x13" .525.00
Swan, mc w/gold, feather details, arched neck, lg 65.00
Wig stand, lady's head & torso, orig mc pnt, 14½" 715.00

Parian Ware

Parian is hard-paste unglazed porcelain made to resemble marble. First made in the mid-1800s by Staffordshire potters, it was soon after produced in the United States by the U.S. Pottery at Bennington, Vermont. Busts and statuary were favored, but plaques, vases, mugs, and pitchers were also made.

Bust, Apollo, 19th C, 11¼" 660.00
Bust, Clytie, att Ridgway, Bates & Co, 1856-58, 11¼" 275.00
Commemorative of Prince consort, crest/awards/dates/etc, 9½" .250.00
Creamer, cherub & grapes, wht on bl, Pat Saml A Alcock..., 4½" .135.00
Group, Match Making, owls snuggle on branch, 1871 mk, 7½" .225.00
Group, 5 cherubs pull goddess in carriage, 1890s, 11", EX 450.00
Pitcher, classical figures emb on bl, unmk, 7¾x4½" 175.00
Pitcher, milk; cherubs & grapes in relief, scrolled hdl, 8⅝" 60.00
Pitcher, Naomi, att Alcock, 10" 100.00
Teapot, berries/vines in relief, branch hdl, unmk, 5x7¼" 50.00
Tray, berries & vines in relief, scalloped rim, unmk, 14⅜" 40.00

Vase, cherub among foliage, ped ft, unmk, 10x4¾" 45.00

Parrish, Maxfield

Maxfield Parrish (1870 – 1966), with his unique abilities in architecture, illustrations, and landscapes, was the most prolific artist during 'The Golden Years of Illustrators.' He produced art for more than one hundred magazines, painted girls on rocks for the Edison Mazda division of General Electric, and landscapes for Brown & Bigelow. His most recognized work was *Daybreak* that was published in 1923 by House of Art and sold nearly two million prints. Parrish began early training with his father who was a recognized teacher, studied architecture at Dartmouth, and became an active participant in the Cornish artist colony in New Hampshire where he resided. Due to his increasing popularity, reproductions are now being marketed. Bobby Babcock, our advisor for this category, is listed in the Directory under Texas.

Book, Knave of Hearts, hardbound, 1924, from RKO Pictures library 1,400.00
Book, Knave of Hearts, spiral bound, NM 700.00
Book, Parrish the Early Years, Skeeters, w/dust jacket 225.00
Book, Wonder Book of Tanglewood Tales, Parrish illus, 1910, NM 395.00
Booklet, Joy Be w/You, w/2 Wassail bowl prints 225.00
Brochure, Broadmoor Hotel, mc, w/old photos, EX 175.00
Brochure, Dream Garden, Curtis, Tiffany mural ad, LHJ, 1915 ..150.00
Calendar, Ancient Tree, Brn/Bigelo, 1952, full pad, jumbo 500.00
Calendar, Dodge...Friendship, Jason & Talking Pal, 1925 ....175.00
Calendar, Misty Morn, Brn/Bigelow, 1956, complete, 8x11" 150.00
Calendar, Sunlight, Brn/Bigelow, 1958, complete, 9x12" 275.00
Calendar, Sunlit Valley, 1950, complete, X-lg, 14x22" 450.00
Calendar, Thy Rocks & Rills, Brn/Bigelow, 1944, complete, 5x6¾" 165.00
Calendar top, Ancient Tree, 1952, lt crease, 13x16" 175.00
Calendar top, Ecstasy, Edison Mazda ad, 1930, complete, lg ...1,950.00
Calendar top, Old Glen Mill, 1954, cropped to image, 13x17½" .300.00
Calendar top, The Glen, 1938, med, orig fr 200.00
Calendar top, Twilight, 1937, 23x28", orig full matt & fr 600.00
Calendar top, Valley of Enchantment, 1946, 17½x22", no pad .450.00
Frontispiece, Atlas, Collier's, May 1908 ....60.00
Frontispiece, Bellerphon by Fountain..., Collier's, May 15, 1909 ..70.00
Frontispiece, Fisherman & Genie, Collier's, April 7, 1906 ....60.00
Frontispiece, Queen Gulnare, Collier's, August 3, 1907 ....60.00
Frontispiece, Sugar-Plum Tree, blk/wht, LHJ, December 1902 .....50.00
Label, cigar box; Old King Cole, 1920s 195.00
Lamp tester, Edison Mazda, tin, Knave logo, bulb shape 150.00
Magazine, maid by sundial cover, Scribner's, April 1899, EX 175.00
Magazine ad, Fisk Fit for a King, Life, May 16, 1918 ....95.00
Magazine ad, Magic Shoes, Fisk Tires, Country Life, Sept 1917 .115.00
Magazine ad, Maxwell Coffee, Broadmoor Hotel, mc, July 1925 ..75.00
Magazine cover, Air Castle, LHJ, September 1904 ....175.00
Magazine cover, Botanist, Collier's, July 18, 1908, lt fold 135.00
Magazine cover, Collier's, May, 1913 ....100.00
Magazine cover, Easter, Life, March 29, 1923 ....140.00
Magazine cover, medieval lady, LHJ (1st cover), July 1896 ....190.00
Magazine cover, Old & New Year, Collier's, January 5, 1907 .....100.00
Magazine cover, Outdoor America, Collier's, January 8, 1910 ......75.00
Magazine cover, Penmanship, Collier's, September 3, 1910 ....100.00
Magazine cover, Prospector, Collier's, February 4, 1911 ....165.00
Magazine cover, Shepherd & Wise Men, Scribner's, December 1900 .215.00
Playing cards, Contentment, Edison Mazda, 1928, NM 300.00
Playing cards, In the Mountains, ltd ed, 1972, M 150.00
Postcard, Broadmoor, 1930-60 ....65.00
Poster, Columbia Bicycles, 12½x20" 3,000.00
Poster, 1939 World's Fair, New Hampshire, Winter Paradise 800.00
Print, Circe's Palace, 1908 art print, orig fr, 9x11" 275.00

Print, Daybreak, Reinthal-Newman, 1922, sm, rpl fr 65.00
Print, Daybreak, Reinthal-Newman, 1922, 6x10", M 150.00
Print, Dies Irae, 1914, from King Albert's Book, period fr 65.00
Print, Evening Shadows, 1953, lg, 13x17½", orig fr 295.00
Print, Golden Hours, Edison Mazda, cropped, 14½x22⅝" 600.00
Print, History of Fisherman & Genie, deluxe, orig fr, 1906, 9x11" ...275.00
Print, King of Black Isles, 1907 deluxe art print, orig fr 250.00
Print, Lights of Welcome, 1952, 11x8¼", orig mat & fr 300.00
Print, Prince, 1928, med, 10x12", orig fr 295.00
Print, Queen Gulnare, Collier & Sons, 1907, med 250.00
Print, Thy Templed Hills, 1942, med, orig mat & fr 195.00
Print, Village Church, 1949, 11x15", w/mat & orig fr 220.00
Puzzle, Prince, Jig of Jigs #3, EXIB 250.00
Triptych subscription card, Florentine Fete, VG 150.00

Pate-De-Verre

Simply translated, pate-de-verre means paste of glass. In the manufacturing process lead glass is first ground, then mixed with sodium silicate solution to form a paste which can be molded and refired. Some of the most prominent artisans to use this procedure were Almaric Walter, Daum, Argy-Rousseau, and Decorchemont. See also specific manufacturers.

Bowl, mermaid & crab on edge, Decorchemont, 2x7" 4,250.00
Paperweight, sand dollar, wht opaque matt, Henry Cross, 5" L ..2,000.00
Paperweight, scarab, metallic gray irid, Henry Cross, 3¾" 1,850.00
Pendant, beetle, brn/blk on yel/orange mottle, orig mts, 2" 2,000.00
Tray, flower on lt bl w/lav & gr border, Dammouse, 3¾" 950.00
Vase, flowerheads/stalks, teal w/mc streaks, Decorchemont, 4" .1,150.00

Pate-Sur-Pate

Pate-sur-pate, literally paste-on paste, is a technique whereby relief decorations are built up on a ceramic body by layering several applications of slip, one on the other, until the desired result is achieved. Usually only two colors are used, and the value of a piece is greatly enhanced as more color is added.

Bowl, maidens & cherubs, A Birks, w/lid, ca 1900, 14x10½" ..5,450.00
Compote, Limoges-style foliage, English, late 1800s, w/lid, 9½" .5,175.00
Lamp base, Ronde by Louis Solon, Minton, 1871, 21" 2,100.00
Medallion, Louis Solon self portrait, sgn, 1892, 3⅞" 1,265.00
Plaque, angelic figure among stars, L Solon, 1908, 9½x5½" ..3,735.00
Plaque, Cupid w/hammer & anvil, L Solon, late 19th C, 4¾x6" ..1,840.00
Plaque, Fall of Love, L Solon, 1885, 6x8¼"+fr, pr 5,750.00
Plaque, La Nouvelle Psyche, L Solon, 1870, 11x16" 2,760.00
Plaque, lady w/drinks, cherubs at ft, L Solon, 1908, 11x5" 4,300.00
Plaque, Venus w/mirror, cherubs, L Solon, demilune, 1885, 15" .9,200.00
Plaque, 5 armed females & Cupid, L Solon, 1880, 8½x15½" ..9,200.00
Tray, cherubs at urn, Hildesheim, Solon, 1878 Paris Expo, 13½" .6,300.00
Urn (now lamp), 3 Grecian figures/gold trim, metal hdls, 21" 880.00
Vase, classical figures fishing, Schenk, 1885, 6", pr 1,600.00
Vase, Creation of Earth, L Solon, 1889, 20⅝" 20,700.00
Vase, Cupid chained/Cupid w/broken chain, Solon, 1895, 7½" ..5,465.00
Vase, egrets & foliage, Pillivuyt & Co, 1870, 5⅝" 750.00
Vase, figure at table w/cherubs, mask hdls, L Solon, 10¾", pr .5,750.00
Vase, figure w/book & 3 cherubs, L Solon, 1882, rstr, 20" 2,875.00
Vase, floral, wht on celadon gr, gold serpent hdls, unmk, 7½" ..995.00
Vase, Grecian figures w/horses, ornate rim, G Jones, 4", pr ...1,100.00
Vase, maidens w/lanterns, cherubs, Solon, w/lid, 19th C, 14¾" ..6,000.00
Vase, pilgrim; cherubs/floral borders, att Morgan, 5¼", pr 2,990.00
Vase, Psyche & Mercury, Geo Jones, w/lid, 16½" 3,565.00

Pattern Glass

Pattern Glass was the first mass-produced fancy tableware in America and was much prized by our ancestors. From the 1840s to the Civil War, it contained a high lead content and is known as 'Flint Glass.' It is exceptionally clear and resonant. Later glass was made with soda lime and is known as nonflint. By the 1890s pattern glass was produced in great volume in thousands of patterns, and colored glass came into vogue. Today the highest prices are often paid for these later patterns flashed with rose, amber, canary, and vaseline; stained ruby; or made in colors of cobalt, green, yellow, amethyst, etc. Demand for pattern glass declined by 1915, and glass fanciers were collecting it by 1930. No other field of antiques offers more diversity in patterns, prices, or pieces than this unique and historical glass that represents the Victorian era in America.

Our advisor for this category is Darlene Yohe; she is listed in the Directory under Arkansas. For a more thorough study on the subject, we recommend *The Collector's Encyclopedia of Pattern Glass*, by Mollie Helen McCain, available from Collector Books. See also Bread Plates; Cruets; Historical Glass; Salt and Pepper Shakers; Salts, Open; Sugar Shakers; Syrups; specific manufacturers such as Northwood.

Note: Values are given for open sugar bowls and compotes unless noted 'w/lid.'

Actress, compote, low std, 5" dia 50.00
Actress, sugar bowl, w/lid 110.00
Actress, tray, dresser 65.00
Admiral Dewey, See Dewey; See Also Greentown Dewey
Alabama, celery tray 37.50
Alabama, jelly compote 62.50
Alabama, sugar bowl, mini, w/lid 45.00
Alabama, water tray, 10½" 115.00
Allover Diamond, egg cup 22.00
Allover Diamond, goblet 28.00
Allover Diamond, tumbler 16.00
Almond Thumbprint, champagne, flint 55.00
Almond Thumbprint, decanter, flint 75.00
Almond Thumbprint, tumbler, ftd, flint 38.00
Amazon, butter dish 75.00
Amazon, cake stand, plain, lg 55.00
Amazon, creamer 40.00
Amazon, tumbler, eng 32.00
Amberette, See Klondike
Apollo, compote, w/lid, 6" dia 40.00
Apollo, goblet, frosted 35.00
Apollo, sugar bowl, plain, w/lid 55.00
Arched Ovals, butter dish, gr 48.00
Arched Ovals, pitcher, water; gr 44.00
Argus, celery vase 85.00
Argus, decanter, 1-qt 100.00
Argus, whiskey, appl hdl 72.00
Art, biscuit jar, ruby stain 165.00
Art, creamer 50.00
Art, creamer, ruby stain 95.00
Art, goblet 65.00
Ashburton, claret, 5¼" 55.00
Ashburton, egg cup, dbl 100.00
Ashburton, tumbler, lemonade 62.00
Atlas, cordial 36.00
Atlas, goblet, ruby stain 68.00
Atlas, sugar bowl, w/lid, ruby stain 65.00
Aurora, mug, hdl, ruby stain 65.00
Aurora, pitcher, water 48.00

Aurora, waste bowl 30.00
Austrian, butter dish, canary 325.00
Austrian, compote, low std, canary 145.00
Austrian, tumbler, amber 170.00
Austrian, wine, emerald gr 145.00
Balder, See Pennsylvania
Baltimore Pear, bread plate, 12½" 65.00
Baltimore Pear, creamer 30.00
Bar & Diamonds, shakers, pr 55.00
Bar & Diamonds, tumbler 24.00
Barberry, butter dish, shell finial 48.00
Barberry, creamer 34.00
Barberry, salt cellar, master 15.00
Barley, bowl, oval, 10" 35.00
Barley, platter, oval, 13" 25.00
Barley, sugar bowl, w/lid 40.00
Barrel Huber, See Huber
Basket Weave, cup & saucer, amber 30.00
Basket Weave, pitcher, water; amber 58.00
Basket Weave, wine 20.00
Beaded Band, goblet 34.00
Beaded Band, relish, sm 16.00
Beaded Grape, cake stand, gr, 9" 80.00
Beaded Grape, goblet 32.00
Beaded Grape, tumbler 27.00
Beaded Grape, wine 32.00

Bar Grape Medallion

Beaded Grape Medallion, compote, collared base, w/lid 90.00
Beaded Grape Medallion, sauce bowl 10.00
Beaded Medallion, butter dish 45.00
Beaded Medallion, compote, collared base, w/lid 90.00
Beaded Medallion, goblet 25.00
Beaded Medallion, tumbler 48.00
Beaded Mirror, See Beaded Medallion
Beaded Swirl, compote, high std, gr 50.00
Beaded Swirl, creamer, flat 27.00
Beaded Swirl, mug 14.00
Beaded Tulip, pitcher, water 65.00
Beaded Tulip, plate, 6" 24.00
Beaded Tulip, wine 32.00
Bearded Head, See Viking
Bellflower, bowl, scalloped rim, 4½x8" 78.00
Bellflower, champagne, str sides, plain stem 75.00
Bellflower, creamer, dbl vine, appl hdl 155.00
Bigler, celery vase 90.00
Bigler, salt cellar, master 65.00
Bird & Strawberry, pitcher, water 240.00
Bird & Strawberry, punch cup 20.00
Bird & Strawberry, sugar bowl, w/lid 55.00
Bleeding Heart, bowl, w/lid, 5x7" 95.00

Bleeding Heart, egg cup 45.00
Bleeding Heart, tumbler, flat 95.00
Block & Fan, cake stand, 10" 45.00
Block & Fan, goblet 50.00
Block & Fan, pickle dish 22.00
Blue Jay, See Cardinal Bird
Bohemian, bowl, berry; boat shape, gr 55.00
Bohemian, mug, rose stain w/gold 85.00
Bohemian, tumbler, rose stain 50.00
Bow Tie, butter pat 28.00
Bow Tie, punch bowl 95.00
Bow Tie, tumbler 60.00
Broken Column, butter dish 88.00
Broken Column, carafe 80.00
Broken Column, vase, 6½" 30.00
Buckle, creamer, flint 100.00
Buckle, pickle dish, nonflint 12.50
Buckle, tumbler, flint 50.00
Buckle w/Star, celery vase 32.00
Buckle w/Star, egg cup 185.00
Buckle w/Star, spooner 28.00
Buckle w/Star, whiskey 150.00
Bull's Eye, carafe 50.00
Bull's Eye, cordial 78.00
Bull's Eye, spill holder 88.00
Bull's Eye & Diamond Point, butter dish 235.00
Bull's Eye & Diamond Point, goblet 110.00
Bull's Eye & Diamond Point, tumbler 130.00
Bull's Eye & Fan, relish 24.00
Bull's Eye & Fan, tumbler, pk stain 68.00
Bull's Eye Band, See Reverse Torpedo
Bull's Eye in Heart, See Heart w/Thumbprint
Button Arches, butter dish 58.00
Button Arches, creamer 20.00
Button Arches, match holder, ruby stain, souvenir 15.00
Button Arches, tumbler, frosted band 25.00
Button Band, bowl, 10" 32.00
Button Band, cordial 42.00
Cabbage Rose, butter dish 65.00
Cabbage Rose, compote, high std, 8½" 80.00
Cabbage Rose, tumbler, bar 40.00
Cable, bowl, 9" 55.00
Cable, champagne 235.00
Cable, plate, 6" 80.00
California, See Beaded Grape
Cane, compote, vaseline, low std, 5¾" 36.00
Cane, goblet, amber 35.00
Cane, sugar bowl, w/lid 27.50
Cane, wine, bl 38.00
Cape Cod, goblet 48.00
Cape Cod, marmalade jar 65.00
Cape Cod, plate, 6" 32.00
Cardinal Bird, butter dish, 3 birds on base 125.00
Cardinal Bird, creamer 35.00
Cardinal Bird, sugar bowl, w/lid 60.00
Cathedral, butter dish 45.00
Cathedral, compote, amber, low std, 7" 48.00
Cathedral, spooner, vaseline 40.00
Cathedral, wine 32.00
Chain w/Diamonds, See Washington Centennial
Chain w/Star, goblet 28.00
Chain w/Star, pickle dish, oval 15.00
Chandelier, celery vase 22.00
Chandelier, pitcher, water; etched 150.00

Classic, butter dish, open log ft 245.00
Classic, goblet 285.00
Classic, spooner, log ft 115.00
Coin, See US Coin
Colorado, banana stand 36.00
Colorado, mug, bl 38.00
Colorado, sherbet, gr 48.00
Colorado, wine 25.00
Columbian Coin, bowl, frosted coins, 3x8½" 78.00
Columbian Coin, pitcher, milk; gold coins 200.00
Columbian Coin, tumbler, clear coins 28.00
Comet, butter dish 195.00
Comet, creamer 165.00
Comet, tumbler 100.00
Connecticut, cake stand 42.50
Connecticut, celery vase 28.00
Connecticut, wine 36.00
Cord & Tassel, egg cup 42.00
Cord & Tassel, wine 45.00
Cord Drapery, bowl, 7" 22.50
Cord Drapery, cake stand 45.00
Cord Drapery, pickle dish, amber 80.00
Cord Drapery, sugar bowl 60.00
Cordova, bowl, berry; w/lid 35.00
Cordova, creamer 38.00
Cordova, tumbler 20.00
Cottage, butter dish 50.00
Cottage, champagne 75.00
Cottage, plate, 10" 45.00
Cottage, tumbler 20.00

Croesus

Croesus, bowl, gr, ftd, w/lid, 8" 125.00
Croesus, bowl, purple, ftd, 4x7" 70.00
Croesus, creamer & sugar bowl, gr, w/lid 350.00
Croesus, toothpick holder 27.50
Croesus, tumbler, gr w/gold 65.00
Crow's Foot, See Yale
Crown Jewels, See Chandelier
Crystal Wedding, banana stand 100.00
Crystal Wedding, bowl, sauce; ruby stain 32.00
Crystal Wedding, creamer, etched 60.00
Crystal Wedding, relish, 7½" L 25.00
Cube & Fan, See Pineapple & Fan
Cupid & Venus, bread plate 45.00
Cupid & Venus, cake stand 55.00
Cupid & Venus, creamer 40.00
Currant, butter dish 70.00
Currant, compote, 10½" 55.00
Currant, relish 15.00
Currant, wine 45.00
Currier & Ives, bowl, oval, 10" 36.00
Currier & Ives, cake stand, amber 115.00

Currier & Ives, saucer, bl 80.00
Currier & Ives, tumbler, ftd 42.00
Curtain, creamer 32.00
Curtain, spooner 25.00
Cut Log, cake stand, high std, 10½" 80.00
Cut Log, creamer 38.00
Cut Log, sugar bowl, w/lid 55.00
Dahlia, creamer 22.00
Dahlia, sugar bowl, vaseline, w/lid 70.00
Dahlia, tankard 75.00
Daisy & Button, butter pat, bl 32.00
Daisy & Button, creamer, amber 95.00
Daisy & Button, goblet, bl panels 45.00
Daisy & Button, tumbler, gr 32.00
Daisy & Button w/Crossbars, creamer, ind 22.00
Daisy & Button w/Crossbars, pitcher, milk; amber 95.00
Daisy & Button w/Crossbars, tumbler, vaseline 25.00
Daisy & Button w/Crossbars, wine 27.50
Daisy & Button w/Thumbprint Panels, cake stand 55.00
Daisy & Button w/Thumbprint Panels, creamer, amber panels 70.00
Daisy & Button w/Thumbprint Panels, tumbler 25.00
Daisy & Button w/V Ornament, finger bowl 20.00
Daisy & Button w/V Ornament, mug 25.00
Dakota, basket, etched, 10" 210.00
Dakota, cake stand, 10½" 48.00
Dakota, celery tray, clear 48.00
Dakota, waste bowl, ruby stain 75.00
Deer & Pine Tree, cake stand 125.00
Deer & Pine Tree, celery vase 70.00
Deer & Pine Tree, finger bowl 50.00
Deer & Pine Tree, sugar bowl, w/lid 85.00
Delaware, bowl, 9" 25.00
Delaware, butter dish, rose w/gold 160.00
Delaware, tumbler, gr w/gold 42.00
Delaware, vase, rose w/gold, 9½" 80.00
Dew & Raindrop, bud vase, 6" 27.50
Dew & Raindrop, pitcher, water 55.00
Dewey, butter dish 55.00
Dewey, creamer, w/lid 48.00
Dewey, See Also Greentown, Dewey
Dewey, tumbler 48.00
Diagonal Band, cake stand 40.00
Diagonal Band, celery vase 28.00
Diagonal Band, pitcher, water 45.00
Diamond Horseshoe, See Aurora
Diamond Medallion, See Grand
Diamond Point, compote, nonflint, w/lid, 8" 60.00
Diamond Point, cordial, flint 160.00
Diamond Point, spill holder, gold rim, flint 125.00
Diamond Point, tumbler, ale; flint, 6¼" 88.00
Diamond Quilted, tumbler, amber 32.50
Diamond Thumbprint, butter dish 215.00
Diamond Thumbprint, decanter, 1-qt 235.00
Dinner Bell, See Cottage
Doric, See Feather
Double Leaf & Dart, See Leaf & Dart
Drapery, creamer 34.00
Drapery, goblet 27.50
Egg in Sand, creamer 28.00
Egg in Sand, goblet, bl 45.00
Egg in Sand, platter 44.00
Egyptian, creamer 48.00
Egyptian, pickle dish 22.50
Egyptian, spooner 20.00

Elephant, See Jumbo
Emerald Green Herringbone, see Florida
Empress, pitcher, water; gr w/gold 165.00
Empress, tumbler, gr w/gold 55.00
Esther, bowl, gr w/gold, 8" 75.00
Esther, cracker jar, ruby stain 215.00
Esther, goblet, amber stain 100.00
Esther, spooner, gr 65.00
Etched Dakota, See Dakota
Excelsior, bottler, bar; flint, 1-qt 68.00
Excelsior, champagne 95.00
Eyewinker, banana stand 130.00
Eyewinker, bowl, 6½" 28.00
Eyewinker, goblet 32.00
Eyewinker, tumbler 30.00
Feather, bowl, 7½" 36.00
Feather, compote, low std, 8" 48.00
Feather, sugar bowl, gr 55.00
Festoon, bowl, berry; rectangular, 8" L 24.00
Festoon, butter dish 45.00
Festoon, plate, 9" 45.00
Festoon, waste bowl 55.00
Fine Cut, bowl, 8¼" 12.00
Fine Cut, cake stand 40.00
Fine Cut, pitcher, water; bl 95.00
Fine Cut & Block, champagne, amber 68.00
Fine Cut & Block, cordial 65.00
Fine Cut & Block, punch cup, yel stain 50.00
Fine Cut & Diamond, See Grand
Fine Cut & Feather, See Feather
Fine Cut & Panel, butter dish, vaseline 75.00
Fine Cut & Panel, plate, amber, 6" 28.00
Fine Rib, egg cup, dbl, flint 38.00
Fine Rib, goblet, flint 78.00
Fingerprint, See Almond Thumbprint

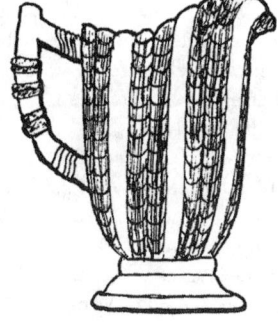

Fishscale

Fishscale, celery vase 32.50
Fishscale, mug 70.00
Fishscale, tumbler 90.00
Flamingo Habitat, butter dish 60.00
Flamingo Habitat, compote, w/lid, 6½" 98.00
Flamingo Habitat, creamer 45.00
Flamingo Habitat, wine 45.00
Florida, goblet, gr, 5¾" 38.00
Florida, nappy 15.00
Florida, pitcher, water 55.00
Florida, spooner 18.00
Flower Pot, butter dish 48.00
Flower Pot, creamer, vaseline 90.00
Flower Pot, spooner 22.50

Frosted Circle, plate, 7" 22.50
Frosted Circle, punch cup 20.00
Frosted Circle, tumbler 25.00
Frosted Leaf, celery vase 125.00
Frosted Leaf, egg cup 98.00
Frosted Lion, See Lion
Frosted Roman Key, champagne, flint 80.00
Frosted Roman Key, sugar bowl, w/lid 88.00
Frosted Stork, platter, oval, 11½" 78.00
Frosted Stork, tray, 15⅛x11" 98.00
Galloway, basket, twist hdl, 10" 65.00
Galloway, creamer, amber stain 15.00
Galloway, mug, 4½" 38.00
Garfield Drape, bowl, 6" 45.00
Garfield Drape, creamer 42.50
Garfield Drape, pitcher, water 105.00
Gem, See Nailhead

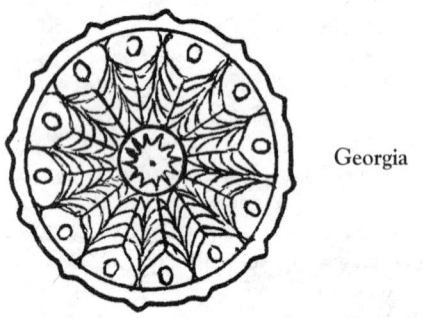

Georgia

Georgia, bonbon 28.00
Georgia, compote, high std, w/lid 37.50
Georgia, plate, 5¼" 17.50
Good Luck, See Horseshoe
Grand, butter dish 45.00
Grand, goblet 32.00
Grand, wine 25.00
Grape & Festoon w/Shield, mug, sapphire bl, 2½" 55.00
Grape & Festoon w/Shield, pitcher, water ...75.00
Grasshopper, butter dish, amber 100.00
Grasshopper, plate, ftd, 10½" 30.00
Grasshopper, salt cellar, master 50.00
Greek Key, goblet, buttermilk 55.00
Greek Key, marmalade 37.50
Greek Key, pitcher, tankard, 1½-qt 245.00
Greek Key, sardine box 38.00
Guardian Angel, See Cupid & Venus
Hairpin, champagne, flint 75.00
Hairpin, tumbler, flint 65.00
Halley's Comet, creamer 42.00
Halley's Comet, goblet 40.00
Halley's Comet, wine 18.00
Hamilton, butter dish 70.00
Hamilton, goblet, flint 55.00
Hand, butter dish 95.00
Hand, claret 80.00
Hand, tumbler, water 95.00
Hawaiian Lei, cup & saucer 40.00
Heart w/Thumbprint, carafe 78.00
Heart w/Thumbprint, cordial, 3" 200.00
Heart w/Thumbprint, finger bowl 42.50
Heart w/Thumbprint, goblet 62.00
Herringbone Buttress, See Greentown, Herringbone Buttress

Hickman, celery tray 17.50
Hickman, creamer, gr 38.00
Hickman, relish, gr 24.00
Hickman, wine 28.00
Hidalgo, butter dish 55.00
Hidalgo, goblet, eng 20.00
Hidalgo, goblet, frosted 24.00
Hidalgo, pitcher, water 45.00
Hinoto, celery vase, amber stain 52.50
Hinoto, egg cup 40.00
Holly, cake stand, 11" 135.00
Holly, egg cup 90.00
Holly, wine 150.00
Holly Amber, See Greentown, Holly Amber
Honeycomb, butter dish, nonflint, clear w/gold 80.00
Honeycomb, champagne, nonflint 32.00
Honeycomb, egg cup, flint 32.00
Honeycomb, tumbler, ftd, flint 38.00
Hops & Barley, See Wheat & Barley
Horn of Plenty, bowl, 7½" 68.00
Horn of Plenty, compote, 6" 78.00
Horn of Plenty, egg cup 45.00
Horseshoe, bowl, oval, 9x6" 32.00
Horseshoe, goblet, plain stem 27.50
Horseshoe, plate, 10" 85.00
Huber, celery vase 38.00
Huber, champagne, flint 34.00
Hummingbird, creamer 48.00
Hummingbird, goblet, bl 68.00
Illinois, creamer, ind 32.00
Illinois, finger bowl 25.00
Illinois, pitcher, tankard, SP rim 90.00
Iowa, decanter 38.00
Iowa, goblet 27.50
Iowa, wine 32.00
Iris w/Meander, See Opalescent Glass
Ivy in Snow, creamer 22.00
Ivy in Snow, goblet 50.00
Ivy in Snow, tumbler 25.00
Jacob's Ladder, compote, 5x10" 45.00
Jacob's Ladder, creamer 38.00
Jacob's Ladder, pitcher, water 190.00
Jacob's Ladder, sugar bowl, w/lid 65.00
Jersey Swirl, butter dish 42.00
Jersey Swirl, goblet, water; bl 42.00
Jersey Swirl, plate, 10" 32.50
Jewel Band, goblet 37.50
Jewel Band, pitcher, milk 48.00
Jewel w/Dewdrop, compote, high std, 8" 80.00
Jewel w/Dewdrop, creamer 38.00
Jewel w/Dewdrop, relish, oval, 8½" 22.00
Jeweled Moon & Star, butter dish 70.00
Jeweled Moon & Star, carafe 37.50
Jeweled Moon & Star, pitcher, water; bl & amber stain 130.00
Job's Tears, See Art
Jumbo, butter dish, frosted elephant finial 675.00
Jumbo, compote, w/lid, 7⅞" 325.00
Jumbo, creamer 255.00
Jumbo, marmalade, frosted elephant finial, head hdls 465.00
Kentucky, cup, gr 22.50
Kentucky, punch cup 17.50
Kentucky, sauce bowl, ftd 10.00
Kentucky, wine 32.00
King's Crown, banana stand, ftd, ruby stained 150.00

King's Crown, butter dish 68.00
King's Crown, pitcher, eng, 13" 125.00
King's Crown, wine, amethyst stain 18.00
Klondike, bowl, frosted w/amber stain, 7" sq 185.00
Klondike, celery vase, amber stained 140.00
Klondike, sugar bowl, amber stain, w/lid, 6¾" 160.00
La Clede, See Hickman
Lace, See Drapery
Lawrence, See Bull's Eye
Leaf & Dart, butter dish, ped ft 88.00
Leaf & Dart, egg cup 20.00
Leaf & Dart, pitcher, milk 140.00
Leaf Bracket, See Greentown, Leaf Bracket
Leaf Medallion, See Northwood, Leaf Medallion
Liberty Bell, bowl, ftd, 8" 100.00
Liberty Bell, butter dish, mini 145.00
Liberty Bell, pitcher, water 800.00
Lily of the Valley, butter dish 100.00
Lily of the Valley, egg cup 45.00
Lincoln Drape, egg cup 70.00
Lincoln Drape, goblet 150.00
Lion, butter dish, frosted lion head finial 95.00
Lion, champagne 195.00
Lion, compote, oval, 7½x7" 130.00
Lion, spooner 85.00

Log Cabin

Log Cabin, butter dish 315.00
Log Cabin, spooner 125.00
Long Spear, See Grasshopper
Loop, cordial, nonflint, 2¾" 35.00
Loop, vase, flint, 9⅜" 80.00
Loop & Dart, goblet 35.00
Loop & Dart, spooner 35.00
Loop & Dart, tumbler, ftd 34.00
Loop w/Stippled Panels, See Texas
Maine, cake stand, gr 60.00
Maine, platter, oval 40.00
Maine, wine, gr 60.00
Manhattan, bowl, 9" 22.50
Manhattan, creamer, ind 25.00
Manhattan, wine 18.00
Maryland, celery vase 32.00
Maryland, compote, high std, w/lid, 7" dia 37.50
Maryland, tumbler 30.00
Mascotte, cake stand, 10" dia 50.00
Mascotte, creamer 35.00
Mascotte, spooner, eng 42.50
Massachusetts, creamer 32.00
Massachusetts, goblet 45.00
Massachusetts, vase, trumpet shape, 9" 35.00

Medallion, cake stand, amber 50.00
Medallion, goblet, amber 48.00
Melrose, compote, 5¾x7½" 27.50
Melrose, plate, 6" 14.00
Michigan, compote, 10" 50.00
Michigan, goblet 37.50
Michigan, mug 30.00
Michigan, sugar bowl, w/lid 70.00
Minerva, compote, 8½x8" 90.00
Minerva, goblet 95.00
Minerva, sugar bowl, w/lid 98.00
Minnesota, basket, reeded hdl 78.00
Minnesota, butter dish 45.00
Minnesota, tumbler 20.00
Minor Block, See Mascotte
Mirror, See Galloway
Missouri, bowl, w/lid, 8" 55.00
Missouri, jelly compote 32.50
Missouri, spooner 25.00
Moon & Star, champagne 70.00
Moon & Star, goblet 42.50
Nail, decanter 37.50
Nail, goblet 48.00
Nail, tumbler, ruby stain 60.00
Nailhead, bowl, 6" 18.00
Nailhead, plate, 7" sq 20.00
Nailhead, wine 38.00
Nestor, sauce dish, gr w/HP decor 40.00
Nestor, tumbler, gr 34.00
New England Pineapple, bar tumbler, flint 130.00
New England Pineapple, champagne, flint 270.00
New England Pineapple, egg cup, flint 55.00
New Jersey, bowl, 9" 30.00
New Jersey, carafe, water 80.00
New Jersey, wine 38.00
O'Hara Diamond, bowl, berry; sm 12.00
O'Hara Diamond, goblet, ruby stain 50.00
Oaken Bucket, See Wooden Pail
One Hundred & One, goblet 50.00
One Hundred & One, pickle dish 22.00
One Hundred & One, sugar bowl, w/lid 48.00
One-O-One, See One Hundred & One
Oregon #1, butter dish, flat 42.00
Oregon #1, cake stand, 8" 40.00
Oregon #1, mug 37.50
Orion, See Cathedral
Palmette, cup plate 57.50
Palmette, goblet 38.00
Palmette, wine 115.00
Panelled Forget-Me-Not, butter dish, w/lid 65.00
Panelled Forget-Me-Not, mustard jar 42.50
Panelled Forget-Me-Not, sugar bowl, w/lid 36.00
Panelled Thistle, basket 75.00
Panelled Thistle, plate, w/bee, 7" sq 28.00
Pavonia, butter dish, eng 88.00
Pavonia, compote, high std, w/lid, 9" dia 58.00
Pavonia, sugar bowl, w/lid 48.00
Pavonia, wine, ruby stain 40.00
Pennsylvania, biscuit jar, gr 135.00
Pennsylvania, celery vase 20.00
Pennsylvania, tumbler, water 22.50
Pigmy, See Torpedo
Pillow Encircled, creamer 26.00
Pillow Encircled, tumbler 30.00

Pillow Encircled, tumbler, ruby stain 40.00
Pineapple & Fan, tumbler, water; gr 58.00
Pineapple & Fan, vase, trumpet form, 10" 35.00
Pineapple Stem, See Pavonia
Pioneer, See Westwood Ho
Pleat & Panel, cake stand, sq, 10" 65.00
Pleat & Panel, goblet 35.00
Pleat & Panel, sugar bowl, w/lid 88.00
Plume, cake stand, high std, 9" 48.00
Plume, celery vase 35.00
Plume, sauce dish 12.00
Polar Bear, goblet 100.00
Polar Bear, tray, water; frosted 230.00
Popcorn, butter dish 58.00
Popcorn, wine 32.50
Portland, cake stand, 10½" 55.00
Portland, celery vase 45.00
Portland, pitcher, water 35.00
Powder & Shot, creamer, flint 110.00
Powder & Shot, honey dish, flint 12.50
Prayer Rug, See Horseshoe
Primrose, pickle dish 25.00
Primrose, pitcher, milk; bl 22.50
Princess Feather, plate, nonflint, 8" 25.00
Princess Feather, sugar bowl, w/lid, nonflint 65.00
Priscilla, bowl, 10½" 37.50
Priscilla, creamer, ind 25.00
Psyche & Cupid, celery vase 32.00
Psyche & Cupid, creamer 65.00
Recessed Pillared Red Top, See Nail
Red Block, cheese dish 132.50
Red Block, creamer, lg 75.00
Red Block, tumbler 32.00
Red Top, See Button Arches
Reverse Torpedo, butter dish 75.00
Reverse Torpedo, goblet 90.00
Reverse Torpedo, sugar bowl, w/lid 75.00

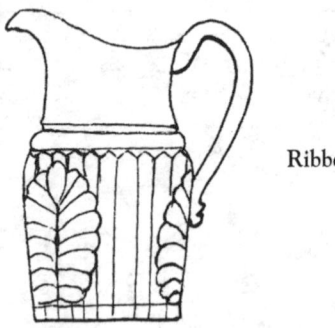

Ribbed Palm

Ribbed Palm, creamer 135.00
Ribbed Palm, goblet 45.00
Ribbed Palm, wine, flint 75.00
Ribbon, compote, w/lid, 8" 95.00
Ribbon, dresser bottle, w/stopper 110.00
Ribbon, ice tub 55.00
Ribbon, plate, 7" 35.00
Ribbon Candy, creamer 32.50
Ribbon Candy, spooner 25.00
Ribbon Candy, wine 98.00
Rochelle, See Princess Feather
Roman Rosette, cordial 50.00
Roman Rosette, relish, 8½" L 12.50

Rose in the Snow, cake stand, 9" 90.00
Rose in the Snow, mug, bl, lg 120.00
Rose in the Snow, sugar bowl, amber, w/lid, rnd 58.00
Rose Sprig, cake stand, 8-sided, 10" 75.00
Rose Sprig, goblet, bl 57.50
Rose Sprig, relish boat, bl 22.00
Rosette, bowl, 7½" 16.00
Rosette, jelly compote 20.00
Royal Ivy, See Northwood
Royal Oak, See Northwood
Ruby Thumbprint, See King's Crown
S-Repeat, butter dish 125.00
S-Repeat, punch cup 15.00
Sandwich Star, butter dish 80.00
Sandwich Star, compote, low std, 8½" 62.50
Sawtooth, champagne, knob stem, flint 60.00
Sawtooth, creamer, flint 75.00
Sawtooth, goblet, plain stem, nonflint 20.00
Sawtooth Band, See Amazon
Scalloped, Daisy Red Top, See Button Arches
Scroll w/Flowers, mustard jar 52.50
Scroll w/Flowers, sugar bowl, w/lid 55.00
Seneca Loop, See Loop
Shell & Jewel, creamer 25.00
Shell & Jewel, pitcher, milk 32.50
Shell & Jewel, tumbler, gr 45.00
Shell & Tassel, bowl, amber, oval, 11½" L 88.00
Shell & Tassel, creamer, rnd 45.00
Shell & Tassel, creamer, sq 60.00
Sheraton, plate, 8½" sq 15.00
Sheraton, relish, hdld, bl 22.50
Shoshone, mug 25.00
Shoshone, wine 22.50
Shuttle, cordial, sm 20.00
Shuttle, mug, amber 325.00
Shuttle, spooner 22.50
Skilton, goblet 35.00
Skilton, pitcher, water 50.00
Skilton, pitcher, water tankard; ruby stain 120.00
Spades, See Medallion
Sprig, bowl, oval, 7" 27.50
Sprig, compote, high std, w/lid 68.00
Sprig, pitcher, water 57.50
Star & Feather, creamer 35.00
Star & Feather, plate, amber, 8" 10.00
Star Rosetted, plate, bl, 7" 15.00
Star Rosetted, plate, 7" 12.00
Stars & Stripes, cordial 20.00
Stars & Stripes, creamer 22.50
States, bowl, 7½" 24.00
States, goblet, clear w/gold 40.00
States, punch bowl, 13" 100.00
States, tumbler 27.50
Stedman, champagne 42.00
Stedman, spooner 17.50
Stippled Chain, cake stand 52.50
Stippled Chain, egg cup 30.00
Stippled Forget-Me-Not, butter dish 50.00
Stippled Forget-Me-Not, cup & saucer 40.00
Stippled Grape & Festoon, goblet 35.00
Stippled Grape & Festoon, pitcher, water 110.00
Stippled Ivy, egg cup 28.00
Stippled Ivy, sugar bowl, w/lid 40.00
Stippled Panelled Flower, See Maine

Strigil, bowl, flared rim, 9"	30.00
Strigil, plate, 11"	28.00
Sunk Honeycomb, cup & saucer, ruby stain	40.00
Sunk Honeycomb, pitcher, water; ruby stain	88.00
Sunken Primrose, See Florida	
Teardrop & Tassel, bowl, 8¼"	57.50
Teardrop & Tassel, compote, 6"	30.00
Teardrop & Tassel, See Also Greentown, Teardrop & Tassel	
Teardrop & Tassel, tumbler	36.00
Tennessee, butter dish	58.00
Tennessee, compote, high std, 8"	42.00
Texas, bud vase, 8"	30.00
Texas, celery tray, ruby stained	55.00
Texas, creamer	50.00
Texas, goblet	95.00
Theatrical, See Actress	
Thousand Eye, cordial, bl	42.50
Thousand Eye, cordial, gr	58.00
Thousand Eye, platter, vaseline, 8x11"	50.00
Thousand Eye, waste bowl	32.00
Three Face, butter dish, eng	230.00
Three Face, claret, eng	260.00
Three Face, goblet	55.00
Three Panel, creamer, bl	45.00
Three Panel, goblet, bl	42.50
Three Panel, tumbler	14.00
Thumbprint, See Argus	
Thumbprint Band, See Dakota	
Thunderbird, See Hummingbird	
Torpedo, bowl, 9½"	45.00
Torpedo, cup & saucer	60.00
Torpedo, tumbler, ruby stain	47.50
Tree of Life, See Portland	
Tree of Life w/Hand, butter dish	135.00
Tree of Life w/Hand, cake stand, frosted base, 11½"	88.00
Tulip w/Sawtooth, creamer, flint	88.00
Tulip w/Sawtooth, salt cellar, petal rim, flint	48.00
Two Panel, bowl, bl, oval, 7¾"	27.50
Two Panel, goblet	22.00
US Coin, butter dish, clear	500.00
US Coin, champagne, flared rim, frosted	795.00
US Coin, cruet, frosted	525.00
US Coin, goblet, frosted, 7"	435.00
Utah, creamer	32.00
Utah, sugar bowl, w/lid	40.00
Valencia Waffle, relish, amber, 9x5⅜"	22.50
Valencia Waffle, spooner, amber	37.50
Vermont, card tray, gold trim	22.00
Vermont, pitcher, water; gr w/gold	130.00
Viking, bowl, 8" sq	48.00
Viking, butter dish	110.00
Viking, spooner	28.00
Viking, sugar bowl, w/lid	68.00
Waffle, egg cup, flint	45.00
Waffle, wine, flint	130.00
Waffle & Thumbprint, goblet, flint	95.00
Waffle & Thumbprint, sweetmeat dish	115.00
Waffle & Thumbprint, wine, flint	98.00
Washington, goblet	115.00
Washington, honey dish, 3½"	32.00
Washington Centennial, egg cup	42.50
Washington Centennial, wine	46.00
Westward Ho, compote, low std, w/lid, 6" dia	125.00
Westward Ho, pickle dish, oval	68.00

Wheat & Barley, creamer	22.50
Wheat & Barley, sauce dish, amber, hdls	12.50
Wheat & Barley, tumbler	22.50
Wildflower, creamer, bl	37.50
Wildflower, tumbler	32.00
Willow Oak, butter dish, bl	75.00
Willow Oak, cake stand, amber, 10" dia	65.00
Willow Oak, tumbler, bl	62.50
Windflower, creamer	38.00
Windflower, egg cup	36.00
Windflower, sugar bowl, w/lid	40.00
Wisconsin, banana stand	72.50
Wisconsin, compote, tricorner top, ftd, 4x7"	27.50
Wisconsin, punch cup	17.50
Wooden Pail, creamer, bl	67.50
Wooden Pail, pitcher	100.00
Wyoming, cake stand, high std, 9"	55.00
Wyoming, creamer	48.00
X-Ray, celery vase, clear w/gold	90.00
X-Ray, marmalade, gr w/gold	75.00
X-Ray, tumbler, amethyst	45.00
Yale, bowl, 10"	34.00
Yale, cake stand, 9"	50.00
Yale, sugar bowl, w/lid	45.00
Zipper, creamer	50.00
Zipper, goblet	25.00
Zipper, relish	17.50

Paul Revere Pottery

The Saturday Evening Girls were a social group of young Boston ladies who met to pursue various activities, among them pottery making. Their first kiln was bought in 1906, and within a few years it became necessary to move to a larger location. Because their new quarters were near the historical Old North Church, they chose the name Paul Revere Pottery. With very little training, the girls produced only simple ware. Until 1915 the pottery operated at a deficit, then a new building with four kilns was constructed on Nottingham Road. Vases, miniature jugs, children's tea sets, tiles, dinnerware, and lamps were produced, usually in soft matt glazes often decorated with incised, hand-painted designs from nature. Examples in a dark high gloss may also be found on occasion.

Several marks were used: 'P.R.P.'; 'S.E.G.'; or the circular device, 'Boston, Paul Revere Pottery' with the horse and rider.

The pottery continued to operate; and even though their product sold well, the high production costs of the handmade ware caused the pottery to fail in 1946.

Bowl, multicolor trees and landscape band on green interior, blue-banded interior, signed SG (Sara Galner), SEG 29.9.12, 1912, 4¼x10¾", $1,150.00.

Bowl, chicory-bl drip on terra cotta, PRP/11-3?/label, 3x6½", EX	50.00
Bowl, deep bl mottle over gray, L Shapiro, 4-sided, PRP, 2¾"	100.00
Bowl, gr/bl mottle, paper label, 5x13"	375.00
Bowl, lotus flowers on bl, Tues/SR, SEG/181-5-10, 2x5"	650.00
Bowl, rooster & chick w/yel sky, SEG/9-18, 8½", EX	750.00

Bowl, tree & landscape, R Bacchini, SEG/11-12, 1½x3¾" 350.00
Bowl, tree & mtn repeats, F Levine, SEG/248-7-22, 1½x4¾" 325.00
Box, trinket; lotus band, S Galner/F Levine, SEG/12-7/12, 2x3" .1,100.00
Box, trinket; tree & landscape at night, SEG/dated, 2x3" dia 550.00
Cake plate, roosters & chicks, cut-out heart hdls, SEG/9-18, 9¼" .1,200.00
Candlesticks, bl/gr mottle, ink mk, 2", pr 160.00
Creamer, mc bands, blk speckles on wht int, SEG, 1¾", EX 60.00
Cup & saucer, demi; tree & landscape, E Brown, PRP/12-28 .....550.00
Cup & saucer, pine cones, mc on ivory, GB, SEG/5-22 ....175.00
Cup & saucer, tree & hill w/layered sky, Brown/Bloom, PRP 375.00
Egg cup, chicks on scarab bl, SEG, mini, 1½" 425.00
Inkwell, banded landscape, rectangular, label, 2¾x4" 1,700.00
Lamp, mottle on bl/gray, SEG, base: 13½", 25" w/metalwork 600.00
Lamp base, cuerda seca w/Queen Anne's Lace, SEG/16-5/SG, 16x9" .15,000.00
Pitcher, buttercup yel lustre, JM, SEG, 4x4" 250.00
Pitcher, chicks, For Barbara's Milk, F Levine, SEG/10-13, 4¼" .1,300.00
Pitcher, cottage & landscape, A Mangini, SEG/11-20, 4¾x6" ...850.00
Pitcher, hare & lettuce pattern on gr, E Geneco, SEG/9-12, 3½" ..800.00
Pitcher, lotus band, wht on speckled bl, AM/1-13/SEG, 4½" 500.00
Pitcher, lotus blossoms, A Mangini, SEG/11-12, 4½x4¾" 600.00
Pitcher, pine cones, GB, SEG/5-22, 4¼x4½", NM 275.00
Plate, cottage & landscape, A Mangini, SEG/7-13, 6¼" 1,200.00
Plate, gr w/blk line & wht border, SEG/4/14, 7½" 125.00
Plate, Greek Key design, S Galner, SEG/2-16, 7¾" 400.00
Plate, pine cones & leaves, brn/gr on cream, SEG/8-17/EG, 7½" ...325.00
Plate, swirled & mottled gr & aqua on steel bl to blk, PRP, 6⅛" ..70.00
Plate, tortoise walking toward bay, DH, SEG/12-19, 6¼" 1,000.00
Plate, tree & landscape, F Levine, SEG/13-1-11, 7¾" 900.00
Plate, wht rosette band, A Mangini, SEG/12-17, 7½" 275.00
Saucer, pine cones w/leaves, brn/gr/cream, SEG/5-22/EB, 5½" ..110.00
Trivet, poplar tree landscape medallion on bl-gr, 1925, 5½" 600.00
Vase, blk glossy, wide mouth, impressed mk, 3½" 70.00
Vase, landscape on bl semigloss, rpr, SEG/L7-22, 8½" 1,700.00
Vase, lotus blossom band, orange & gr on gr, baluster, 7x5¼" .1,300.00

Peachblow

Peachblow, made to imitate the colors of the Chinese Peachbloom porcelain, was made by several glasshouses in the late 1800s. Among them were New England Glass, Mt. Washington, Webb, and Hobbs, Brockunier and Company (Wheeling). Its pink shading was achieved through action of the heat on the gold content of the glass. While New England's peachblow shades from deep crimson to white, Mt. Washington's tends to shade from pink to blue-gray. Many pieces were enameled and gilded. While by far the majority of the pieces made by New England had a satin (acid) finish, they made shiny peachblow as well. Wheeling glass, on the other hand, is rarely found in satin. In the 1950s Gundersen-Pairpoint Glassworks initiated the reproduction of Mt. Washington peachblow using an exact duplication of the original formula. Though of recent manufacture, this glass is very collectible. Our advisors for this category are Betty and Clarence Maier; they are listed in the Directory under Pennsylvania.

Bowl, centerpc; Gundersen, morning-glory form, 4½x10" 850.00
Bowl, New Martinsville, ruffled, sq, 7½" H 140.00
Bowl, Webb, gold prunus & butterfly, 2⅞x4¾" 245.00
Celery vase, Sandwich, Hobnail, 7" 475.00
Creamer, Libbey, 1893 World's Fair souvenir, 2¾x3½" 500.00
Creamer, Wheeling, amber hdl, 4½x4½" 1,265.00
Cruet, Gundersen, shiny, peachblow stopper, 8x3" 570.00
Cruet, NE Glass, satin, orig stopper, 6" 1,950.00
Cup, punch; Gundersen 275.00
Cup & saucer, Gundersen 275.00

Darner, NE Glass, 6x2¼" 125.00
Decanter, Gundersen, Pilgrim Canteen form, raspberry stopper, 10" .950.00
Ewer, Wheeling, pelican form, amber loop hdl, 6½x4½" 4,250.00
Fairy lamp, Webb, HP floral, clear candle cup, 5" 500.00
Finger bowl, Wheeling, 4½" 500.00
Goblet/chalice, Gundersen, shiny, appl burmese base, 7¼x4" 285.00
Jug, Gundersen, bulbous, loop hdl, 4½x4" 450.00
Mustard, Wheeling, bulbous, thumb-lift lid, 3" 500.00
Pear w/stem, NE Glass, 2⅝x4½" 125.00
Pitcher, milk tankard; Gundersen, reeded hdl, 7x4" 675.00
Pitcher, NE Glass, ribbed hdl, 4½" 865.00
Pitcher, water; Wheeling, amber hdl, 8" 2,000.00
Plate, luncheon; Gundersen, 8" 375.00
Shakers, Wheeling, orig lids, 3x2½", pr 1,100.00
Shot glass, NE Glass 225.00
Spittoon, lady's, NE Glass, shiny, waisted w/wavy rim, 2¾x5¼" .775.00
Spooner, NE Glass, sq top 825.00
Toothpick holder, Gundersen, shiny, 2½x1½" 550.00
Tumbler, Wheeling, shiny, 3⅞x3" 465.00
Vase, bud; Wheeling, 8¼" 825.00
Vase, cornucopia; Gundersen, ruffled rim w/curling tip to horn .525.00
Vase, Gundersen, pinched, ruffled rim, 5x6" 525.00
Vase, Gundersen, urn form w/M hdls, sq cut base, 8½x4½" 550.00
Vase, lily; Gundersen, 9x3¼" 425.00
Vase, lily; NE Glass, shiny, 6½x3" 650.00
Vase, lily; NE Glass, shiny, 9x4" 850.00
Vase, Morgan; Wheeling, 7¾", in amber Griffin holder 1,700.00
Vase, Mt WA, gourd shape, 8x4" 2,775.00
Vase, Mt WA, 8 pulled ribs, bulbous, 4½x5½" 4,250.00
Vase, Webb, gold floral w/silver trim, 4¾x3⅛" 425.00
Vase, Webb, pine needles/prunus/butterflies, 11¼x6½" 750.00
Vase, Webb, ruffled top, 4 thorn ft, rigaree, #8919, 10½" 625.00
Vase, Webb, wafer ft, 8½x4", pr 395.00
Vase, Wheeling, stick neck, 10½" 1,275.00
Vase, Wheeling, stick neck, 9" 900.00
Wine, Gundersen, shiny, 5" 175.00

Pearlware

Developed by Wedgwood in the late 1770s primarily for their dinnerware lines, pearlware was soon being made by many other Staffordshire potteries as well. Much of it made for export to America. It is characterized by its blue-white body, similar in appearance to true porcelain. During the first decade of the 1800s, pearlware with chinoiserie decorations and hand-painted flowers became popular. See also Leeds.

Mug, wide multicolor floral band with brown striping, 6x4⅛", $825.00.

Bowl, Oriental landscape, underglaze bl, ca 1790, 3¼x7¼", EX .165.00
Bowl, Oriental landscape, underglaze bl, ftd, 1790s, 2¾x7", EX .170.00
Coffeepot, bl Oriental decor, early 19th C, 9¼", EX 315.00
Coffeepot, blk Oriental transfer, dome top, wear, 11½" 150.00

Coffeepot, mc floral, ftd ovoid, dome lid, 12¼", EX 800.00
Cup & saucer, handleless; bird in tree, mc w/sponged foliage, EX .130.00
Cup & saucer, handleless; mc floral, ftd, 2½", 5¼", EX 275.00
Figurine, crowned lion & tree, bocage, sgn Walton, 6⅜x6" 1,100.00
Figurine, man puts shoe on lady's ft, rstr bocage, 9x6¼" 700.00
Hot water plate, bl feather edge, 10" 250.00
Mug/tankard, Oriental landscape, underglaze bl, 5", EX 170.00
Pitcher, emb hunt scenes in purple & pk lustre w/gr, 6¾" 330.00
Pitcher, gaudy 4-color floral, prof rpr, 6⅝" 110.00
Pitcher, Satyr, knobby form, mc decor, early 19th C, 7" 425.00
Pitcher, water; mc floral, blk stripe at ft, Wm Adams, 10", EX ...160.00
Plate, eagle w/arrows & olive branch, gr shell rim, 7⅜", NM 700.00
Plate, eagle w/shield center, bl shell edge, nicks, 6¼" 700.00
Plate, floral w/gold lustre, red striped scalloped rim, 8½" 70.00
Plate, pk flowers w/pk lustre stems & leaves, 7½" 35.00
Platter, bl feathered edge, unmk, 15x11⅝" 65.00
Sugar bowl, mc floral, flower finial, 4½", EX 75.00
Teapot, mc floral w/blk bands, 6¼", EX 95.00

Peking Cameo Glass

The first glasshouse was established in Peking in 1680. It produced glassware made in imitation of porcelain, a more desirable medium to the Chinese. By 1725 multilayered carving that resulted in a cameo effect lead to the manufacture of a wider range of shapes and colors. The factory was closed from 1736 to 1795, but glass made in Po-shan and shipped to Peking for finishing continued to be called Peking glass. See also Orientalia.

Belt buckle, red o/l, Daoist scene, rectangle, 19th C, 2¾" 860.00
Bottle, scent; floral, turq on wht, disk stopper, 5¼" 150.00
Jar, flowering vines, gr on wht opal, 5x5" 575.00
Rose jar, bird & tree, gr on wht, w/lid, 7½x8" 325.00
Vase, 2 birds/flowering tree, dk bl on wht, late, 10", pr 500.00

Peloton

Peloton glass was first made by Wilhelm Kralik in Bohemia in 1880. This unusual art glass was produced by rolling colored threads onto the transparent or opaque glass gather as it was removed from the furnace. Usually more than one color of threading was used, and some items were further decorated with enameling. It was made with both shiny and acid finishes.

Basket, purple to wht w/mc strings, clear rigaree & ft, sm 195.00
Bowl, pk w/mc strings, pinched middle, 2¾x1¾x3½" 145.00
Bowl, wht w/mc strings, ribbed, 8-pointed star top, 6x6½" 325.00
Pitcher, clear w/mc strings, bulbous, sq top, 6¼x3½" 225.00
Rose bowl, lav w/mc strings, tooled clear base, 2¾" 275.00
Rose bowl/vase, bl w/mc strings, clear edge, ftd, 4x4" 395.00
Sweetmeat, wht w/mc strings, mk Pairpoint SP lid, 2½x5½" 300.00
Vase, clear w/bl strings, mc pnt florals & butterfly, 5x4¾" 250.00
Vase, clear w/cranberry strings, hdls, 4⅛x3" 95.00
Vase, pk w/mc strings, hdls, bulbous, 6x5" 400.00
Vase, pk w/mc strings, 3½x3x3⅞" 225.00
Vase, wht w/mc strings, ruffled, wishbone ft, 6½x4" 400.00

Pennsbury

Established in the 1950s in Morrisville, Pennsylvania, by Henry Below, the Pennsbury Pottery produced dinnerware and novelty items, much of which was sold in gift shops along the Pennsylvania Turnpike. Henry and his wife, Lee, worked for years at the Stangl Pottery before striking out on their own. Lee and her daughter were the artists responsible for many of the early pieces, the bird figures among them. Pennsbury pottery was hand painted, some in blue on white, some in multicolor on caramel. Pennsylvania Dutch motifs, Amish couples, and barbershop singers were among their most popular decorative themes. Sgraffito (hand incising), was used extensively. The company marked their wares 'Pennsbury Pottery' or 'Pennsbury Pottery, Morrisville, PA.'

In October of 1969 the company closed. Contents of the pottery were sold in December of the following year, and in April of 1971, the buildings burned to the ground. Items marked Pennsbury Glenview or Stumar Pottery (or these marks in combination) were made by Glenview after 1969. Pieces manufactured after 1976 were made by the Pennington Pottery. Several of the old molds still exist, and the original Pennsbury Caramel process is still being used on novelty items, some of which are produced by Lewis Brothers, New Jersey. Production of Pennsbury dinnerware was not resumed after the closing. Our advisor for this category is Shirley Graff; she is listed in the Directory under Ohio. Note: prices may be higher in some areas of the country — particularly on the East Coast, the southern states, and Texas.

Wall pocket, lady looking over shoulder, 6½", $150.00.

Ashtray, Amish, rnd 25.00
Ashtray, Don't Be So Dippich, 5" 20.00
Ashtray, Eagle, 7½x5" 40.00
Bowl, divided vegetable; Red Rooster, 9½" 50.00
Bowl, pretzel; Amish Couple 70.00
Bowl, pretzel; Barbershop Quartet 70.00
Bowl, Red Rooster, heart shape, 6" 40.00
Candle holder, Red Berries & Holly, 5" dia 48.00
Candle holder, Red Rooster, 5" dia 45.00
Chip 'n dip, Red Rooster, 11" 85.00
Coaster, Fisherman, 4½" 30.00
Coaster, Gay Ninety, 5" 35.00
Coaster, Horowitz 30.00
Coffeepot, Black Rooster, 6-cup 88.00
Creamer, Amish girl & fence, 2½" 30.00
Creamer, Red Rooster, 4" 30.00
Creamer & sugar bowl, Hex 40.00
Cruet, Amish, pr 100.00
Cup & saucer, Hex 32.00
Figurine, bird of paradise, 10" 700.00
Figurine, bl jay, 10½" 600.00
Mug, beer; Barbershop Quartet, mk, 4¾" 45.00
Mug, beer; Delft Toleware 40.00
Mug, beer; Eagle 42.00
Mug, beer; Fisherman 42.50
Mug, beer; Gay Ninety 45.00
Mug, beer; Red Barn 40.00
Mug, beer; Red Rooster, 4½" 35.00
Mug, beer; Swallow the Insult 42.00

Mug, coffee; Amish Couple, 3¼"	27.50
Mug, coffee; Black Rooster	35.00
Mug, coffee; Sweet Adeline	30.00
Pie plate, Amish couple by tree, 9"	85.00
Pie plate, Red Rooster, 9"	65.00
Pitcher, Amish, 2½"	35.00
Pitcher, Amish Man & heart, 4"	35.00
Pitcher, Black Rooster, 4"	35.00
Pitcher, Black Rooster, 5"	37.50
Plaque, Baltimore & Ohio RR, train, 5¾x7¾"	65.00
Plaque, Central RR of New Jersey, train, 5¾x7¾"	65.00
Plaque, Come in w/o Knocking, Go Out Same Way, 6"	30.00
Plaque, Don't Stand Up While Room Is in Motion, 6"	30.00
Plaque, Eagle, wings wide, 5½x7½"	100.00
Plaque, It Is Whole Empty, 4"	25.00
Plaque, Making Pie, 6" dia	55.00
Plaque, Nat'l & Newark Banking Co	49.00
Plaque, Such Schmootzers, 4"	22.50
Plaque, US Frigate Constitution, 8x11"	90.00
Plate, Black Rooster, 11"	45.00
Plate, Christmas angel, 1970	40.00
Plate, Eagle, pierced for hanging, 8"	45.00
Plate, Green Rooster, 8"	18.00
Plate, Mother's Day, 1972`	22.00
Plate, Red Rooster, 8"	18.00
Platter, Red Rooster, oval, 11"	48.00
Relish, Red Rooster, Christmas tree shape, 14½x11½"	85.00
Shakers, Amish, head figural, pr	45.00
Sugar bowl, Red Rooster, w/lid	30.00
Teapot, Red Rooster, 4-cup	65.00
Teapot, Red Rooster, 6-cup	95.00
Tray, Crested Birds, octagonal, 3x5"	30.00
Tray, Dutch Haven, octagonal, 4"	30.00
Tray, Laurel Ridge, 8½x5¼"	40.00
Tray, Tulip & Heart, 4"	30.00
Wall pocket, bellows, Eagle, 10"	65.00
Wall pocket, clown	75.00
Wall pocket, Red Rooster	55.00
Warming plate, Picking Apples, electric	95.00

Pens and Pencils

The first metallic writing pen was patented in 1809, and soon machine-produced pens with steel nibs gradually began replacing the quill. The first fountain pen was invented in 1830, but due to the fact that a suitable metal for the tips had not yet been developed, they were not manufactured commercially until the 1880s. The first successful commercial producers were Waterman in 1884 and Parker with the Lucky Curve in 1888.

The self-filling pen of 1890 featured the soft, interior sack which filled with ink as the metal bar on the outside of the pen was raised and lowered. Variations of the pumping mechanism were tried until 1932 when Parker introduced the Vacumatic, a sackless pen with an internal pump. Our advisors for this category are Judy and Cliff Lawrence; they are listed in the Directory under Florida. For those seeking additional information, a catalog is published monthly by the Pen Fancier's, whose address can be found in the Directory under Clubs, Newsletters, and Catalogs. In the listings that follow, all pens are lever-filled unless otherwise noted.

Key:
AF — aerometic filler
BF — button filler
HR — hard rubber
LF — lever filler

CPT — chrome-plated trim
ED — eyedropper filler
GFM — gold-filled metal
GFT — gold-filled trim
GPT — gold-plated trim
NPT — nickel-plated trim
PF — plunger filler
TD — touchdown filler
VF — vacumatic filler

Ballpoint Pens

Eversharp, CA, 1946, GFM/GFT, NM	100.00
Reynolds, Rocket, 1946, blk w/CPT, ink dried up, EX	70.00
Reynolds Internat'l, 1945, bl w/CPT, ink dried up, EX	70.00
Tiffany, 1953, sterling, EX	120.00

Fountain Pens

Photo courtesy Judy and Cliff Lawrence

Ideal pen, #412, 1906, sterling filigree, eyedropper filler, initial, EX, $630.00.

Aiken Lambert, Empire, 1920, blk chased HR, GFT, ED, EX	80.00
Blackbird Self-Filling, 1917, blk HR, NPT, LF, EX	90.00
Conklin, #26, 1925, blk chased HR, GFT, LF, NM	145.00
Conklin, #4NL Crescent Filler, 1916, blk chased HR, GFT, EX	350.00
Conklin, #75 Crescent Filer, 1922, blk chased HR, GFT, EX	900.00
Conklin, Crescent Filler, 1923, blk chased HR, GFT, EX	180.00
Conklin, Endura, 1930, gold/blk marbleized, GFT, LF, EX	180.00
Conway Stewart, #475, 1939, bl marbleized, GFT, LF, EX	105.00
Cross, 1935, GFM w/blk ends, Pacard logo on clip, G	450.00
Eversharp, Skyline Presentation, 1945, brn, GFM/GFT, LF, EX	80.00
Mont Blanc, #244, 1946, red, GFT, BF, EX	595.00
Onoto, Self-Filling 1909, blk chased HR, NPT, PF, EXIB	350.00
Parker, #16, 1906, GFM filigree on blk HR, ED, NM	2,250.00
Parker, #51, 1947, blk w/Lustraloy cap, wht GFT, VF, EX	55.00
Parker, Bl Dmn Major Vacumatic, 1941, gold pearl, GFT, VF, EX	170.00
Parker, Bl Dmn Major Vacumatic, 1942, blk, GFT, VF, EX	170.00
Parker, Bl Dmn Maxima, 1940, silver pearl, GFT, VF, G	300.00
Parker, Bl Dmn Splender Maxima, 1940, gr/pearl stripes, GFT, VF, NM	300.00
Parker, Bl Dmn Vacumatic, 1946, emerald/pearl, GFT, VF, M	135.00
Parker, Bl Dmn 51, 1945, gray w/GFM cap, GFT, VF, EX	135.00
Parker, Bl Dmn 51, 1946, bl w/Lustraloy cap, GFT, VF, NM	65.00
Parker, Bl Dmn 51, 1946, blk w/GFM cap, GFT, VF, M	120.00
Parker, Blk Giant, 1915, blk HR, NPT, ED, rare, EX	2,000.00
Parker, Duofold Jr, 1928, Lapis Bl marbleized, GFT, BF, EX	200.00
Parker, Duofold Jr, 1930, Mandarin Yel, GFT, BF, EX	250.00
Parker, Duofold Jr Desk, 1927, Mandarin Yel, GFT, BF, EX	180.00
Parker, Duofold Special, 1930, red, GFT, BF, EX	250.00
Parker, Duofold Sr, 1927, Lapis Bl marbleized, GFT, BF, EX	700.00
Parker, Duofold Sr, 1928, blk, GFT, BF, EX	335.00
Parker, Duofold Sr, 1930, blk, GF, BF, EX	300.00
Parker, Duofold Sr Big Red, 1925, GFT, BF, EX	390.00
Parker, Duofold Sr Big Red, 1928, GFT, BF, EX	390.00
Parker, Lady Duofold, 1926, red, GFT, BF, EX	80.00
Parker, Lady Duofold, 1929, lav-pk marbleized, GFT, BF, NM	350.00
Parker, Lady Duofold, 1933, blk, GFT, EX	72.50
Parker, Lucky Curve, 1922, GFM, GFT, BF, EX	225.00
Parker, Lucky Curve #41, 1905, GFM filigree on blk HR, ED, NM	4,000.00
Parker, Oversz Vacumatic, 1934, gold pearl stripes, GFT, VF, NM	500.00
Parker, Pastel, 1927, mauve or Naples Bl, GFT, BF, EX, ea	110.00
Parker, Vacumatic, 1935, gold pearl stripes, GFT, VF, EX	150.00
Parker, Vacumatic, 1937, silver pearl marbleized, GFT, VF, EX	75.00

Sheaffer, #875, 1939, gold stripes, GFT, LF, EX 80.00
Sheaffer, Lifetime Crest Triumph, 1946, blk, GFM cap, GFT, LF, EX 62.50
Sheaffer, Lifetime Triumph Sentinel, 1946, blk, GFT, PF, EX 90.00
Sheaffer, Lifetime 1000, 1939, blk, GFT, LF, EX 225.00
Sheaffer, Wht Dot Crest Snorkel, 1953, maroon, GFM/GFT, TD, NM ..110.00
Sheaffer, Wht Dot Crest TM, 1951, maroon, GFM cap, GFT, TD, EX 80.00
Wahl, 1926, GFM, GFT, LF, NM 118.00
Wahl-Eversharp, Gold Seal Doric, 1940, blk, GFT, LF, EX 315.00
Wahl-Eversharp, Skyline, 1944, blk, GFT, LF, NM 70.00
Wahl-Eversharp, Skyline, 1944, gr, GFT, LF, NM 80.00
Wahl-Eversharp, Skyline, 1945, brn, gold/blk cap, GFT, LF, EX ..110.00
Wahl-Eversharp, Skyline, 1945, red, red/silver cap, GFT, LF, EX .110.00
Waterman, Hundred Yr, 1940, red, GFT, LF, EX 360.00
Waterman, Ideal #051 1/2 VP, 1911, GFM/GFT, ED, EX 90.00
Waterman, Ideal #0552 1/2V, 1918, GFM/GFT, LF, EX 90.00
Waterman, Ideal #3V, 1932, scarlet marbleized, wht GFT, LF, EX ..65.00
Waterman, Ideal #52, 1926, blk HR, GFT, LF, NM 100.00
Waterman, Ideal #52 1/2V, 1924, red HR, GFT, LF, EX 90.00
Waterman, Ideal #92V, 1921, scarlet marbleized, GFT, LF, EX ...80.00
Waterman, Lady Patricia In View, 1937, scarlet, GFT, EX 110.00
Waterman, Supersz Hundred Yr, 1944, red, GFT, LF, EX 600.00
Williamson, 1910, pearl & gold filigree, ED, EX 900.00

Mechanical Pencils

Eclipse, 1929, red w/blk ends, GFT, M 135.00
Europa, ocean liner inset, 1930, blk HR, EX 80.00
Eversharp, Skyline Presentation Repeater, 1946, blk, GFM/GFT, EX ..27.50
Eversharp, Skyline Repeater, 1945, brn, GFT, M 27.50
Eversharp, Skyline Repeater, 1946, blk w/silver stripe top, GFT, EX .27.50
Eversharp, Skyline Repeater, 1946, brn, GFT, M 36.00
Eversharp, 1925, hand-cvd sterling, EX 70.00
Eversharp, 1928, gr jade marbleized, GFT, EX 45.00
Eversharp, 1928, red chased HR, GFT, EX 65.00
Eversharp, 1928, rosewood HR, GFT, EX 36.00
Eversharp, 1929, red HR, NPT, G 27.00
Eversharp, 64 Repeater, 1945, beige, 14k gold top/trim, M 90.00
Parker, Bl Dmn Vacumatic, 1941, silver pearl, GFT, VF, EX 80.00
Parker, Duofold, 1928, gr jade marbleized, GFT, EX 80.00
Parker, Duofold, 1930, gr jade marbleized, GFT, EX 115.00
Parker, Duofold Deluxe, 1933, Moderne blk/pearl marbleized, GFT, EX ...100.00
Parker, Duofold Jr, 1925, red, GFT, EX 110.00
Parker, Duofold Jr, 1928, Moderne blk & pearl marbleized, EX ..120.00
Parker, Duofold Jr, 1928, red, GFT, G 70.00
Parker, Duofold Jr, 1929, Moderne blk & pearl marbleized, EX ..120.00
Parker, Duofold Sr, 1928, gr jade marbleized, GFT, EX 200.00

Photo courtesy
Judy and Cliff Lawrence

Parker, Duofold Sr, 1929, Moderne Pearl and black marbleized, gold-filled trim, EX, $200.00.

Parker, Duofold Sr, 1930, burgundy red/blk marbleized, GFT, EX ..180.00
Parker, Duofold Sr, 1930, Moderne blk/pearl marbleized, GFT, G .135.00
Parker, Duofold Sr Big Red, 1925, GFT, EX 250.00
Parker, 51, 1951, brn, GFM top, GFT, EX 80.00
Parker, 51 Repeater, 1953, gray w/GFM top, GFT, M 70.00
Parker, 51 Repeater, 1959, gray w/GFM top, GFT, M 80.00
Ronson Penciliter, 1936, rhodium & gr-brn specked, EX 135.00
Sheaffer, Balance, 1932, emerald marbleized, GFT, G 65.00
Sheaffer, Golf, 1933, ebonized pearl marbleized, GFT, EX 90.00

Sheaffer, Lifetime, 1926, gr jade marbleized, GFT, EX 20.00
Sheaffer, Lifetime, 1927, gr jade marbleized, GFT, EX 36.00
Sheaffer, 1933, emerald marbleized, GFT, EX 45.00
Waterman, Ideal, 1925, blk HR, GFT, EX 22.50
Waterman, Ideal, 1930, brn specked pearl, NPT, EX 18.00

Sets

Eversharp, Envoy, 1949, GFM, GFT, LF, NM 150.00
Parker, Bl Dmn 51, 1942, gray w/sterling caps, GFT, VF, EX 200.00
Parker, 51 Demi-Sz, 1947, blk, GFM caps, GFT, VF, M 240.00
Parker, 51 Signet, 1953, GFM, GFT, AF, M 320.00
Sheaffer, Snorkel Admiral, 1953, red, GFT, TD, M 80.00
Sheaffer, Triumph Snorkel, 1953, powder bl, banded caps, GFT, TD, M ..200.00
Sheaffer, Triumph TM Sentinel, 1952, blk, banded caps, GFT, TD, M .110.00
Sheaffer, Triumph Tuckaway, 1948, blk, GFT, PF, M 110.00
Sheaffer Lifetime, 1929, pearl/blk marbleized, GFT, LF, EX 135.00
Swan, 1929, yel & pk GFM, GFT, LF, MIB 250.00
Wahl-Eversharp, 1925, GFM, rare pattern, GFT, LF, EX 160.00
Waterman, Lady Patricia, 1930, onyx marbleized, GFT, LF, NM .150.00

Personalities, Fact and Fiction

One of the largest and most popular areas of collecting today is character-related memorabilia. Everyone has favorites, whether they be comic-strip personalities or true-life heroes. The earliest comic strip dealt with the adventures of the Yellow Kid, the smiling, bald-headed Oriental boy always in a nightshirt. He was introduced in 1895, a product of the imagination of Richard Fenton Outcault. Today, though very hard to come by, items relating to the Yellow Kid bring premium prices.

Though her 1923 introduction was unobtrusively made through only one newspaper, New York's *Daily News*, Little Orphan Annie, the vacant-eyed redhead in the inevitable red dress, was quickly adopted by hordes of readers nationwide, and before the demise of her creator, Harold Gray, in 1968, she had starred in her own radio show. She made two feature films, and in 1977 *Annie* was launched on Broadway.

Other early comic figures were Moon Mullins, created in 1923 by Frank Willard; Buck Rogers by Philip Nowlan in 1928; and Betty Boop, the round-faced, innocent-eyed, chubby-cheeked Boop-Boop-a-Doop girl of the early 1930s. Bimbo was her dog and KoKo her clown friend.

Popeye made his debut in 1929 as the spinach-eating sailor with the spindly-limbed girlfriend, Olive Oyl, in the comic strip *Thimble Theatre*, created by Elzie Segar. He became a film star in 1933 and had his own radio show that during 1936 played three times a week on CBS. He obligingly modeled for scores of toys, dolls, and figurines, and especially those from the '30s are very collectible.

Tarzan, created around 1930 by Edgar Rice Burroughs, and Captain Midnight, by Robert Burtt and Willfred G. Moore, are popular heroes with today's collectors. During the days of radio, Sky King of the Flying Crown Ranch (also created by Burtt and Moore) thrilled boys and girls of the mid-1940s. Hopalong Cassidy, Red Rider, Tom Mix, and the Lone Ranger were only a few of the other 'good guys' always on the side of law and order.

But of all the fictional heroes and comic characters collected today, probably the best loved and most well known is Mickey Mouse. Created in the late 1920s by Walt Disney, Micky (as his name was first spelled) became an instant success with his film debut, *Steamboat Willie*. His popularity was parlayed through wind-up toys, watches, figurines, cookie jars, puppets, clothing, and numerous other products. Items from the 1930s are usually copyrighted 'Walt Disney Enterprises'; thereafter, 'Walt Disney Productions' was used.

For more information we recommend *Schroeder's Collectible Toys, Antique to Modern*, by Sharon and Bob Huxford. For those interested in

Disneyanna, we recommend *Stern's Guide to Disney Collectibles* (there are two in the series), and *The Collector's Encyclopedia of Disneyana* by David Longest and Michael Stern. All are available from Collector Books. Our advisor for this category is Norm Vigue; he is listed in the Directory under Massachusetts. See also Autographs; Banks; Big Little Books; Children's Books; Comic Books; Cookie Jars; Dolls; Games; Lunch Boxes; Movie Memorabilia; Paper Dolls; Pin-Back Buttons; Posters; Puzzles; Rock 'N Roll Memorabilia; Toys.

A-Team, party hat, EX, set of 4 different 8.00
Addams Family, Thing key chain, EX 5.00
Aladdin, PVC figure set, Applause, 1933, set of 4 ....12.00
Alice in Wonderland, wristwatch, pk fabric strap, Ingersoll, EXIB .250.00
Amos 'n Andy, book, All About...& Their Creators, hardbk, 1929, EX 45.00
Archies, tattoos, Topps, 1969, MIP 20.00
Aristocats, Colorforms, 1960s, NM (EX box) 38.00
Bambi, Colorforms, Disney, scarce, complete, 1966, NMIB 35.00
Batman, bank, ceramic nodder, unmk, 5", scarce, NM 450.00
Batman, Batarang, Ideal, 1966, 8", NM 80.00
Batman, bicycle ornament, 1966, 10", EX 45.00
Batman, bread bag, 1960s, M 18.00
Batman, charm bracelet, metal, 1966, M on Batwing card 45.00
Batman, night light, plastic head w/wings, Snap-it, 1966, NM 25.00
Batman, pencil, w/Penguin topper, NM 2.00
Batman, wastebasket, litho scenes on metal, 1966, 10", VG+ 55.00
Battlestar Galactica, wallet, w/Cylon Raider, EX 10.00
Betty Boop, chalkware figure, classic pose, 14", NM 275.00
Betty Boop, clicker, heart shape, Japan, 1930s, EX 150.00
Betty Boop, fan, paper & wood, prewar Japan, 5", M 175.00
Betty Boop, mask, celluloid, 6x6", NM 250.00
Big Bird, doll, talker, Playskool, 1970s, 22", VG 25.00
Black Hole, Colorforms, Disney, 1970s, NM (VG box) 15.00
Bozo the Clown, bendable figure, Lakeside, 1966, 6", EX 10.00
Bozo the Clown, figure, Super Flex, MOC 20.00
Bugs Bunny, cup dispenser, 1989, MIP 8.00
Bugs Bunny, pencil sharpener, figural, NM 15.00
Bugs Bunny, teething ring, rubber, 1966, EX 8.00
Buzz Sawyer, Christmas card, 1950s, unused, NM+ 14.00
Capt Midnight, stamp album of Air Heroes, radio premium 35.00
Captain America, kite, red & bl, Pressman, 1966, EXIP 35.00
Captain Kangaroo, Treasure House tent, canvas, 1958, rare, NM ...75.00
Casper the Ghost, candy bucket, plastic, EX+ 30.00
Casper the Ghost, mobile, fold-out card, Hallmark, 1965, M 20.00

Charlie McCarthy, windup celluloid figure, working, Made in Japan, 7¼", EX in box (not shown), $695.00.

Charlie McCarthy, bubble gum wrapper, ca 1940, VG 12.00
Charlie McCarthy, Mazuma play money, early 1940s, EX 6.00
Charlie McCarthy, pencil sharpener, Bakelite w/decal, 1930s, NM ...85.00
Charlie McCarthy, Radio Party Game, M in mailer 45.00
Charlie's Angels, purse, vinyl box style, names on beige, 8", NM .20.00

Cisco Kid, cowboy hat, 1940s 50.00
Cisco Kid, pin-bk button, Triple-S Safety Club, 1950s, NM 25.00
Cisco Kid, silk tie w/hat slide, 1950s 45.00
Dagwood Bumpstead, sandwich bag, 1952, NM 22.50
Dale Evans, western shirt, fancy, 1950s 120.00
Dale Evans, wristwatch, rnd horseshoe, 1950s, EXIB 275.00
Davy Crockett, bandana, red & blk on yel cloth, 17" sq, EX 20.00
Davy Crockett, flicker key chain, 1950s, EX 18.00
Dick Tracy, Colorforms Adventure Kit, 1962, NMIB 65.00
Dick Tracy, flashlight, bl w/red top, 1950s, EXIB 50.00
Dick Tracy, Secret Code Book, 1938 ....35.00
Dick Tracy, transfer, sheet, 1940s premium, NM 17.00
Dick Tracy, wristwatch, chrome case, New Haven, 1948, VGIB .275.00
Donald Duck, bank, tin litho, Disney, Marx, 1950s, 4", NMIB ..550.00
Donald Duck, bowl, Beetleware 38.00
Donald Duck, charm, enamel, long bill, Disney, 1930s, EX 65.00
Donald Duck, music box, DD as engineer, club song, 1960s, EX .125.00
Donald Duck, pocket watch, British, 1954, NMIB 325.00
Dopey, playing cards, WDE, NM 35.00
Dr Dolittle, card game, Post Cereal premium, NM 15.00
Dr Dolittle, party centerpc, Hallmark, NMIP 20.00
Dr Seuss, book bag, Horton the Elephant, cloth, 12x10", EX+ 50.00
Dukes of Hazzard, wristwatch, LCD Quartz, Unisonic, 1981, MIB ..40.00
Dumbo, pencil sharpener, Bakelite, Disney, 1930s, 1¾", NM 125.00
Elmer Fudd, pencil holder, diecast figure, 1940s, NM 125.00
Elsie, charm w/tag, WWII bond drive, EX 35.00
ET, clothes hamper, MIB 75.00
ET, plush, marble eyes 20.00
ET, sticker sheet, Topps, 1982, uncut, EX 15.00
ET, tray, litho metal, 1982, 17x12", EX 15.00
ET, vinyl figure, Kaymar, EX 35.00
Felix the Cat, bowl, ceramic, Germany, '20s, 6½" 350.00
Felix the Cat, Orange Crush bottle cap, 1930s, EX 28.00
Felix the Cat, tin clicker, Germany, 1920s, EX 85.00
Flash Gordon, beanie, w/fins & goggles, 1950s, NM 400.00
Flash Gordon, compass, silver plastic w/yel band, 1950s, MOC ..55.00
Flintstones, coin purse, 1975, NM 23.00
Flintstones, Dino doll, plush & vinyl, Knickerbocker, 1960s, NM .85.00
Flintstones, Fred pencil holder, plastic, 1974, M 5.00
Garfield, bib, Garfield in sleigh, MOC 2.00
Garfield, book, Scary Tales, Grosset Dunlap 4.00
Garfield, doll, plush, dressed as Santa, orig tag, M 16.00
Garfield, growth chart, 3 sheets, MIB 16.00
Garfield, night light, Off the Wall, Prestigeline PT-5658 ....15.00
Garfield, pencil topper, in Hawaiian shirt w/suitcase, EX 2.00
Garfield, PVC figure, w/suction cup, in football uniform, EX 5.00
Garfield, shakers, Garfield Santa heads, Enesco, 1993, pr 15.00
Garfield, trinket box, Be My Valentine, ceramic, Enesco 30.00
Geppetto, figure, sitting, Disney, Syroco, 6" 155.00
Green Hornet, Humming Bee toy, 1966, NM 22.50
Green Hornet, spoon, SP 15.00
Gremlins, figure, hard rubber, 1984, 4", EX 7.00
Gumby, cowboy outfit, MOC 18.00
Hopalong Cassidy, charm, celluloid, 1940s 35.00
Hopalong Cassidy, record album, contains 2 78s, w/photos 65.00
Hopalong Cassidy, shirt, 1940s, EX 110.00
Hopalong Cassidy, silk tie w/steer-head slide, 1950s 50.00
Howdy Doody, boxing gloves, Parvey, 1950s, M (EX box) 150.00
Howdy Doody, ear muffs, shaped like face, 1950s, EX+ 95.00
Howdy Doody, pen, plastic figure, Leadworks/NBC/KFS, 1988, 6", M ..5.00
Howdy Doody, pencil case, clear vinyl, w/contents, 1950s, VG 45.00
Huckleberry Hound, rug, mc, 1950s, VG 45.00
Huckleberry Hound, squeeze toy, as fireman, vinyl, VG+ 35.00
Huckleberry Hound, Vari-Vue flicker, 1950s, NM 8.00

Incredible Hulk, wallet, vinyl, 1976, unused, NM 18.00
James Bond, tie rack, Agent 007, no mk, NM 40.00
James Bond, transistor tape recorder, Bandai, scarce, NMIB 525.00
Jiminy Cricket, wristwatch, shines in dark, Ingersoll, NMIB 475.00
Jolly Joe Kelly, Radio Club Book, 1938, EX 15.00
Jungle Book, Vulture figure, stuffed cloth, Disney, 1967, M 40.00
King Leonardo, pencil sharpener, vinyl, MIB 20.00
Kliban, coffeepot, wht dbl-breasted jacket, Sigma, 12" 450.00
Kliban, mug, England 30.00
Kliban, pillow, stuffed figural, 22" 22.00
Kliban, teapot, cat in tuxedo, from $175 to 200.00
Laughing Sam, sheet music, 1906, VG+ 65.00
Lion King, PVC figures, Disney/Applause, 1993, set of 5 ....15.00
Little Lulu, jewelry box, Larami, 1973, NMIP (sealed) 12.00
Little Orphan Annie, color book, 1930, EX 65.00
Lone Ranger, wristwatch, flasher image, 1950s, EX 200.00
Lowell Thomas, WWII War map, Sunoco, folded 10.00
Lum & Abner, almanac, 1935 ....40.00
Man From UNCLE, Topps Gum Cards, 1965, complete set (55), NM ..115.00
Mickey Mouse, alarm clock, dial arms, Bayard/France, 5", MIB .330.00
Mickey Mouse, banjo, metal w/wood neck, WDE, 18", NM 650.00
Mickey Mouse, belt, Disney, Pyramid Belt Co, 1978, MIB 30.00
Mickey Mouse, bsk figure, movable arms, Japan, 1930s, 4¾", EX ..475.00
Mickey Mouse, Canasta Junior, Disney, 1950s, EXIB 45.00
Mickey Mouse, costume, WD, 1940s, EXIB 100.00
Mickey Mouse, doll, Knickerbocker, 1930s 575.00
Mickey Mouse, fountain pen, blk & silver MM on clip, 5¼", M ...175.00
Mickey Mouse, gumball machine, head on base, Hasbro, 1968, M .50.00
Mickey Mouse, Inkograph automatic pencil, 1935 ....87.00
Mickey Mouse, magnifier, Disney, Monogram, 1980s, MOC 5.00
Mickey Mouse, paint set, Disney, Transogram, 1952, NM (EX box) 90.00
Mickey Mouse, pencil case, Dixon #2740 ....60.00
Mickey Mouse, planter, Leeds 40.00
Mickey Mouse, playing cards, WDE, 1930s, VG (VG red/wht/bl box) 50.00
Mickey Mouse, pocket watch, Bradley, 1970s, 2", MIB 300.00
Mickey Mouse, pocket watch, w/fob, Ingersoll, 1935, EXIB 1,250.00

Mickey Mouse stuffed figure, Steiff, 1931 – 33, with tag, 7½", M, $2,500.00.

Photo courtesy Dunbar Gallery

Mickey Mouse, squeak toy, Lanco Spain 35.00
Mickey Mouse, swim mask, Disney, Ideal, 1970s, M 40.00
Mickey Mouse, wristwatch, Ingersoll, '50s, NMIB, w/5" plastic MM ..225.00
Mickey Mouse, wristwatch, Ingersoll, 1947, MIB 325.00
Mickey Mouse Club, telescope, WDP, 1970s, 9", MIP 25.00
Mighty Mouse, magic slate, cb w/film sheet, Lowe, '50s, 11x8", NM .30.00
Minnie Mouse, gumball machine, Minnie in pk, WDP, NM 25.00
Minnie Mouse, travel alarm clock, Bradley/WDP, 1970s, MIB 65.00
Mother Goose, dishes, plastic, 1940s, 16-pc set, MIB 135.00
Muhammed Ali, shoe polish tin 15.00
Mummy, figure, Playco, 1991, 10", MIB 12.00
Nightmare on Elm Street, Freddy glove, M (EX+ card) 18.00
OJ Simpson, football game, MIB 60.00
Peanuts, banner, Snoopy, America You're Beautiful, 13x28", M ..20.00
Peanuts, beach bag, Snoopy, Pride of Beach, 2-hdl, EX 8.00

Peanuts, doormat, Snoopy & Woodstock, wht/yel on gray, 14x26", M ..15.00
Peanuts, Linus soap holder, vinyl, no soap, Avon, 1952, EXIB 14.00
Peanuts, Lucy doll, yel dress/red hat, Hungerford, 7", EX 65.00
Peanuts, pajama bag, Snoopy figure, w/button, EX 28.00
Pinky Lee, shoelaces, pk, 1950s, NM w/wrapper 15.00
Pinocchio, knife/fork/spoon set, SP, Disney, 1940s, EX 85.00
Pluto, bank, compo figural, MIB 65.00
Popeye, alarm clock, Smith Alarm/Great Britain, EXIB 440.00
Popeye, bendable figure, Lakeside, 1967, MIP (sealed) 20.00
Popeye, crayon set, Am Crayon, 1933, MIP 80.00
Popeye, pencil sharpener, tin litho stand-up, 1929, 4" 350.00
Popeye, wall sculpture, figural light-up, 24", NM 55.00
Porky Pig, bank, AJ Renzi, rare, 1964, 15½", EX 45.00
Porky Pig, wristwatch, Sheffield, 1960s, MIB 150.00
Radio Orphan Annie, Secret Society membership manual, 1938, EX ..60.00
Radio Orphan Annie, talking stationery, 1937, EX 75.00
Raggedy Ann, bsk figure, 1988, 4", M 15.00
Raggedy Ann, spray starch, 1967 ....85.00
Rat Fink, decal, blk & wht, 1990, 6", NM 5.00
Reddy Kilowatt, Magnepad pot holder, 1950-60s, MIP 30.00
Robin Hood, Colorforms, Disney, 1970s, EX (EX box) 15.00
Rocketeer, tape & book set, Disney, MIP (sealed) 10.00
Rocky & Bullwinkle, Snydley Whiplash bendable figure, Wham-O, EX ..28.00
Scrooge McDuck, bank, money bag, Disney 48.00
Sea Queen, speed boat, 1950s, NM 90.00
Sgt Preston, Big Game Trophies punch-out cards, 1950s, M 60.00
Shmoo, Pendulette alarm clock, Lux, ca 1950, 8", EX+IB 300.00
Simpsons, Bart doll, soft vinyl, Dandee, 10", MIB 10.00
Simpsons, magazine, Simpson Illustrated, Spring 1991, M 10.00
Smokey the Bear, alarm clock, dbl bell, Germany 195.00
Smokey the Bear, hat, felt, EX 12.00
Smokey the Bear, wristwatch, Bradley, 1960s, MIB 170.00
Snow White, pencil sharpener, Bakelite 65.00
Snow White & 7 Dwarfs, bsk figure set, Disney, 1938, 2½", VG+ ..250.00
Snow White & 7 Dwarfs, Doc figure, Enesco, 1960s, 4½", M 50.00
Snow White & 7 Dwarfs, tea set, Marx, 1938, 9-pc, EX 125.00
Spider-Man, book & record set, Peter Pan, 1981, EX 5.00
Spider-Man, comb & brush set, 1970s, MIB 45.00
Spider-Man, wallet, 1978, MOC 25.00
Steve Canyon, helmet, Ideal, EXIB 65.00
Superman, belt, emb images on leather, Pioneer, 1940s, NM 150.00
Superman, Cartoonist Stamp Set, 1966, M (EX+ card) 35.00
Superman, horseshoe set, Super Slim Inc, 1954, EX (VG- box) ...40.00
Superman, poster, Post premium, 1978, EX 12.00
Superman, tote bag, 1982, EX 12.00
Superman, wristwatch, Dabs/DC Comics, 1977, MIB 130.00
Sylvester the Cat, doll, velour, 5", VG 8.00
Tarzan, Colorforms Cartoon Kit, 1966, EXIB 20.00
Tarzan, tennis bag, 1975, EX 30.00
Three Little Pigs, bracelet, enameled brass, 1930s, EX 135.00
Three Little Pigs, switch plate, plastic, 1950s, MIP 35.00
Thumper, planter, w/gold, Leeds 70.00
Tinkerbell, bell, figural hdl, souvenir, '50s, 3", EX 60.00
Tinkerbell, tree topper, Disney 55.00
Tom & Jerry, Jerry ring, cloisonne, 1970s, M 12.00
Tom & Jerry, Jerry squeak toy, as cowboy, Lanco, 1960s, NM 20.00
Tom Mix, photo, blk & wht glossy, 8x10", EX 10.00
Underdog, pillow, wht inflatable vinyl, EX 23.00
Welcome Back Kotter, greeting card, set of 6, MIB (sealed) 25.00
Winnie the Pooh, Piglet PVC figure, 2", EX 3.00
Winnie the Pooh, Roo squeeze toy, NM 28.00
Wizard of Oz, toy watch, Occupied Japan, 1940s, M 50.00
Wizard of Oz, Wicked Witch doll, Presents, 14", MIB 40.00
Wonder Woman, sunglasses, 1976, M (VG card) 15.00

Woody Woodpecker, cloisonne ring, 1970s, M 12.00
Woody Woodpecker, Magnetic Puzzle set, 1973, MOC 14.00
Yogi Bear & Boo Boo, handkerchief, 1960s, 8" sq, EX 10.00

Peters and Reed

John Peters and Adam Reed founded their pottery in Zanesville, Ohio, just before the turn of the century, using the local red clay to produce a variety of wares. Moss Aztec, introduced about 1912, has an unglazed exterior with designs molded in high relief and the recesses highlighted with a green wash. Only the interior is glazed to hold water. Pereco (named for Peters, Reed and Company) is glazed in semi-matt blue, maroon, cream, and other colors. Orange was also used very early, but such examples are rare. Shapes are simple with in-mold decoration sometimes borrowed from the Moss Aztec line. Wilse Blue is a line of high-gloss medium blue with dark specks on simple shapes. Landsun, characterized by its soft matt multicolor or blue and gray combinations, is decorated either by dripping or by hand brushing in an effect sometimes called Flame or Herringbone. Chromal, in much the same colors as Landsun, may be decorated with a realistic scenic, or the swirling application of colors may merely suggest one. Vivid, realistic Chromal scenics command much higher prices than weak, poorly drawn examples. (Brush-McCoy made a very similar line called Chromart. Neither will be marked; and due to the lack of documented background material available, it may be impossible make a positive identification. Collectors nearly always attribute this type of decoration to Peters and Reed.) Shadow Ware is usually a glossy, multicolor drip over a harmonious base color but occasionally seen in overall matt glaze. When the base is black, the effect is often iridescent.

Perhaps the most familiar line is the brown high-glaze artware with the 'sprigged'-type designs. Although research has uncovered no positive proof, it is generally accepted as having been made by Peters and Reed. It is interesting to note that many of the artistic shapes in this line are recognizable as those made by Weller, Roseville, and other Zanesville area companies. Several other lines were produced including Mirror Black, Persian, Egyptian, Florentine, Marbleized, etc., and an unidentified line which collectors call Mottled-Marbleized Colors. In this high-gloss line, the red clay body often shows through the splashed-on colors.

In 1922 the company became known as the Zane Pottery. Peters and Reed retired, and Harry McClelland became president. Charles Chilcote designed new lines, and production of many of the old lines continued. The body of the ware after 1922 was light in color. Marks include the impressed logo or ink stamp 'Zaneware' in a rectangle.

Bowl, Landsun, 10" 70.00
Ewer, Brn Ware, grape clusters, 6" 85.00
Flower frog, Landsun, lily pad, 2x6½" 45.00
Jug, Brn Ware, 4" 55.00
Pitcher, Brn Ware, floral, sq rim, slim, 9" 125.00
Planter, Marbleized, lg 300.00
Umbrella stand, Moss Aztec, sgn Ferrell 650.00
Vase, Brn Ware, crossed leaves, bulbous, sm angle hdls, 10½" ...155.00
Vase, Brn Ware, wreath, 10" 150.00
Vase, bud; Landsun, 9½" 125.00
Vase, Chromal scenic (impressionistic), 11" 400.00
Vase, Chromal scenic (realistic), bulbous, 6" 450.00
Vase, Chromal scenic (realistic), yel sky w/brn, 4½" 300.00
Vase, Chromal scenic (realistic), 11" 900.00
Vase, Landsun, chocolate & gr flames on brn base, 6" 125.00
Vase, Marbleized, blk/bl/yel over red clay, glossy, 9" 125.00
Vase, Moss Azetc, blkberries, unmk, 7¾" 150.00
Vase, Moss Aztec, leaves w/long stems, Ferrell, 8" 175.00
Vase, Moss Aztec, 6" 85.00

Vase, Shadow Ware, brn/yel/bl drip on orange, 9" 250.00
Vase, Shadow Ware, mc drips on brn w/copper dust, Zane mk, 8¼" .225.00
Vase, Wilse Bl, #612, 8½" 80.00
Vase, Wilse Bl, corset shape, 9" 80.00
Vase, Wilse Bl, leaf & branch emb on dk bl gloss, 8" 100.00
Wall pocket, Marbleized, 8" 135.00

Pewabic

The Pewabic Pottery was formally established in Detroit, Michigan, in 1907 by Mary Chase Perry Stratton and Horace James Caulkins. The two had worked together since 1903, firing their ware in a small kiln Caulkins had designed especially for use by the dental trade. Always a small operation which relied upon basic equipment and the skill of the workers, they took pride in being commissioned for several important architectural tile installations.

Some of the early artware was glazed a simple matt green; occasionally other colors were added, sometimes in combination, one over the other in a drip effect. Later Stratton developed a lustrous crystalline glaze. (Today's values are determined to a great extent by the artistic merit of the glaze.) The body of the ware was highly fired and extremely hard. Shapes were basic, and decorative modeling, if used at all, was in low relief. Mary Stratton kept the pottery open until her death in 1961. In 1968 it was purchased and reopened by Michigan State University. Several marks were used over the years: a triangle with 'Revelation Pottery' (for a short time only); 'Pewabic' with five maple leaves; and the impressed circle mark.

Vase, metallic purple with green interior, 2¾", $325.00.

Bowl, gr & purple mottled lustre, ftd, conical, 2¾x6" 300.00
Figurine, girl w/dog, Gwen Lux, gray/gold irid lustre, 11¾" 400.00
Pitcher, gr matt, early maple leaf mk, rpr, 8" 300.00
Vase, bl & gold (lustrous), bottle form, mk/label, 13x6" 2,000.00
Vase, bl & gr metallic, flake, 2½" 200.00
Vase, bl matt, shouldered, 4x5" 375.00
Vase, bl metallic, paper label, 3" 300.00
Vase, bl metallic w/gray highlights, mk, 2" 260.00
Vase, concentric circles of purples/bls/grs, baluster, 7x4½" 600.00
Vase, dk bl to blk metallic, shouldered, mk, 7½" 950.00
Vase, gold & gr irid flambe, rolled rim, ovoid, 6x4" 650.00
Vase, gold & gr lustre, bulbous, 6x4" 600.00
Vase, gold & gr lustre, ovoid, 11½x7" 1,900.00
Vase, gr irid & purple flambe, hand thrown, 6¾x4½" 800.00
Vase, purple/maroon/lt gr metallic, paper label, 6½" 1,000.00
Vase, shaded bl metallic, shouldered, 11" 1,600.00
Vase, turq & purple lustre, mk, 5x6" 450.00
Vase, uneven brn matt, hand thrown, bulbous, label, 5¼x6¾" ..400.00

Pewter

Pewter is a metal alloy of tin, copper, very small parts of bismuth and/or antimony, and sometimes lead. Very little American pewter contained lead, however, because much of the ware was designed to be used as tableware, and makers were aware that the use of lead could result in poisoning. (Pieces that do contain lead are usually darker in color and heavier than those that have no lead.) Most of the fine examples of American pewter date from 1700 to the 1840s. Many pieces were melted down and recast into bullets during the American Revolution in 1775; this accounts to some extent why examples from this period are quite difficult to find. The pieces that did survive may include buttons, buckles, and writing equipment as well as the tableware we generally think of.

After the Revolution, makers began using antimony as the major alloy with the tin in an effort to regain the popularity of pewter, which glassware and china was beginning to replace in the home. The resulting product, known as Britannia, had a lustrous silver-like appearance and was far more durable. While closely related, Britannia is a collectible in its own right and should not be confused with pewter.

Key: tm — touch mark

Basin, Compton tm, 2x8" 220.00
Basin, unmk, 2¼x9" 220.00
Bowl, baptismal; unmk (att Boardman family), polished, 7⅞", pr 880.00
Bowl, Compton, Made in London tm, shallow, wear/pitting, 13¼" ..200.00
Bowl, Townsend & Compton tm, shallow, wear/scratches, 13" ..195.00
Candlesticks, unmk Homan & Co of Cincinnati, 8", pr 220.00
Chalice, unmk (att Boardman family), minor pitting, polished, 5¼" 165.00
Chalice, unmk (att Israel Trask), polished, 5¾" 140.00
Charger, Edward Toms tm, wear/scratches, 14¾" 330.00
Charger, G Lightner Baltimore eagle tm, wear, 13⅛" 770.00
Charger, Robert Bush & Co tm, wear/scratches, 14⅞" 220.00
Charger, Samuel Ellis tms, wear/scratches, 16½" 330.00
Charger, Thomas Townsend Compton tm, wear, 15" 260.00
Charger, unmk (England), polished, 16½" 300.00
Coffeepot, H Homan tm, flower finial, 8¾" 185.00

Flagons: Oliver Trask, Boston, Massachusets, ca 1830, 10⅞", NM, $550.00; William Calder, Providence, Rhode Island, ca 1817 – 56, 11", NM, $850.00.

Lamp, chamber; unmk Am, rpl collar, 5¼", +burner 150.00
Lamp, petticoat; Morey & Smith Warrented tm, 4", +burner, VG ..100.00
Lamp, unmk Am, rpr base, 7¾", +burner w/brass tubes 250.00
Lamp, Yale & Curtis NY tm, 8¼", +burner 220.00
Loving cup, unmk (England), dbl ear hdls, dents/polished, 8" 85.00
Plate, B Barns & eagle tm, wear/dents, 7⅞" 200.00
Plate, Joseph Danforth lion tm, 7⅞" 440.00
Plate, Love tm, wear/dents, 7⅞" 165.00
Plate, S Kilbourn Baltimore eagle tm, minor wear/dents, 7¾" 200.00
Plate, Samuel Danforth eagle tm, wear/pitting, 7⅞" 140.00
Plate, Thomas Danforth Boardman eagle tm, worn SP, 8½" 200.00
Plate, Thomas Danforth I rampant lion tm, 8", EX 220.00
Plate, Thomas Danforth III eagle tm, worn/battered, 7¾" 150.00

Plate, unmk Am, minor wear, polished, 8⅛" 100.00
Plate, Wm Danforth eagle tm, wear/scratches, polished, 8" 200.00
Platter, unmk (England), 19", EX 330.00
Porringer, cast flower hdl, 5½" 148.00
Spoon, John Yates tm, 5¼", set of 6 ....120.00
Sugar bowl, A Griswold eagle tm, 6" 275.00
Sugar bowl, Sheldon & Feltman tm, 7⅝" 95.00
Tall pot, F Porter Westbrook tm, 10⅝" 465.00
Tall pot, G Richardson tm, 10½" 300.00
Teapot, E Smith tm, pear shape, 7¼" 330.00
Teapot, J Danforth tm, wooden wafer finial, polished, 7¼" 225.00
Teapot, Savage #6 tm, some battering, 6¾" 110.00
Teapot, Savage Midd CT tm, 7¾" 260.00
Teapot, unmk Am, 8" 110.00

Pfaltzgraff

Pfaltzgraff has operated in Pennsylvania since the early 1800s making redware at first, then stoneware crocks and jugs, yellow ware and spongeware in the '20s, artware and kitchenware in the '30s, and stoneware kitchen items through the '40s. To collectors, they're best known for their Gourmet Royal (circa 1950s), a high-gloss dinnerware line of solid brown with frothy white drip glaze around the rims, and their giftware line called Muggsy, comic-character mugs, ashtrays, bottle stoppers, children's dishes, pretzel jars, cookie jars, etc. It was designed in the late 1940s and continued in production until 1960. The older versions have protruding features, while the features of later examples were simpy painted on.

For more information on Gourmet Royal dinnerware, we recommend *The Flea Market Trader* and *The Garage Sale and Flea Market Annual*, both by Collector Books.

Dinnerware

Christmas Heritage, bowl, soup/cereal; #009, 5½", from $2 to 3.50
Christmas Heritage, cheese tray, #533, 10½x7½", from $5 to 7.00
Christmas Heritage, mug, ped ft, #290, 10-oz 4.50
Christmas Heritage, plate, dinner; #004, 10", from $4 to 5.50
Gourmet Royale, bean pot, #11-1, 1-qt, from $20 to 22.00
Gourmet Royale, bean pot, #30, w/lid, lg, from $45 to 50.00
Gourmet Royale, bowl, #241, oval, 7x10", from $15 to 18.00
Gourmet Royale, bowl, cereal; #934SR, 5½", from $6 to 8.00
Gourmet Royale, bowl, mixing; 8", from $12 to 14.00
Gourmet Royale, bowl, vegetable; 9¾" 15.00
Gourmet Royale, casserole, ind; #399, stick hdl, 12-oz 12.00
Gourmet Royale, chafing dish, w/hdls/lid/stand, 8x9" 35.00
Gourmet Royale, gravy boat, #426, dbl spout, lg, w/underplate 16.00
Gourmet Royale, ladle, sm, from $12 to 15.00
Gourmet Royale, mug, #391, 12-oz, from $6 to 8.00
Gourmet Royale, plate, grill; #87, 3-section, 11" 20.00
Gourmet Royale, plate, steak; 12", from $15 to 20.00
Gourmet Royale, shakers, #317/#318, 4½", pr 14.00
Gourmet Royale, sugar bowl, from $5 to 7.00
Heritage, au gratin, #265, 9½" 5.00
Heritage, baker, rectangular, #236, 2-qt 12.50
Heritage, bottle, lotion; #313, 6½" 6.50
Heritage, bowl, soup/cereal; #009, 5½" 2.50
Heritage, butter dish, 3002-028, from $6 to 8.00
Heritage, cup & saucer, #002-002, 9-oz 3.00
Heritage, mug, ped ft, #90F, 10-oz 4.50
Heritage, pepper mill, #802 ....7.50
Heritage, pie plate, 9" 7.50
Heritage, plate, luncheon; #005, 8½" 3.00

Heritage, soup tureen, #002-160, 3½-qt, from $25 to 35.00
Heritage, spoon rest, #515, 9" 4.00
Heritage, teapot, #555, 24-oz 13.00
Heritage, utensil crock, 6½ 7.00
Village, baker, #236, rectangular, tab hdls, 2-qt 15.00
Village, beverage server, #490 ....25.00
Village, butter dish, #028 ....8.00
Village, canister set, #520, 4-pc 60.00
Village, cookie jar, #540, 3-qt 20.00
Village, creamer & sugar bowl, #020 ....12.00
Village, picture frame 9.00
Village, pitcher, #416, 2-qt 15.00
Village, plate, dinner; #004, 10¼" 3.00
Village, platter, #016, 14" 14.00
Village, soup tureen, #160, 3½-qt, w/lid & ladle 35.00
Yorktowne, baker, oval, #240 ....4.00
Yorktowne, bowl, mixing; #453, 3-pc set 20.00
Yorktowne, bowl, rim soup; #012, 8¼" 4.50
Yorktowne, bowl, serving; #010, 7" 5.50
Yorktowne, cake/serving plate, #529, 11¼" 10.00
Yorktowne, candlesticks, #564, 3¾", pr 10.00
Yorktowne, corn dish, #046, 8½" 3.00
Yorktowne, gravy boat, w/saucer, #433, 16-oz 10.00
Yorktowne, pitcher, #416, 2-qt 15.00
Yorktowne, plate, dinner; #004, 10¼" 3.00
Yorktowne, shakers, #025, pr 7.00
Yorktowne, trivet, #615, 7½" 6.50

Muggsy Line

Ashtray 125.00
Bottle stopper, head, ball shape 85.00
Canape holder, Carrie, lift-off hat, from $125 to 150.00
Cigarette server 125.00
Clothes sprinkler bottle, Myrtle, Black, from $225 to 260.00
Clothes sprinkler bottle, Myrtle, from $195 to 225.00
Cookie jar, character face, minimum value 250.00
Jar, utility; Handy Harry, hat forms lid 200.00
Mug, action figure, Black 125.00
Mug, action figure (golfer, etc), any from $65 to 85.00
Mug, character face, ea 38.00
Shot mug, character face 50.00
Tumbler 60.00

Stoneware

Bowl, mixing; molded arches, bl stripe, att, mini, 2¾" 130.00
Chamber pot, cobalt stripe on salt glaze, att, mini, 3⅛" 160.00
Crock, bird on branch, cobalt on salt glaze, 10⅝", 3-gal, EX 700.00
Crock, bl mk on front, brn int, unglazed rim, mini, 2⅝", EX 200.00
Crock, floral, cobalt on salt glaze, late 1800s, 12x12⅜", EX 475.00
Crock, floral, cobalt on salt glaze, late 1800s, 7⅞x8", EX 275.00
Crock, floral, cobalt on salt glaze, mk, 1890s, 2-gal, EX 475.00
Jar, tulips, cobalt on salt glaze, late 1800s, 2-gal, EX 700.00
Jug, cobalt on salt glaze, ca 1850-90s, 10⅛x16¾", 1-gal 2,200.00
Jug, Merry Christmas! Happy..., cobalt on salt glaze, att, 4⅛" 200.00
Jug, owl on branch, cobalt on salt glaze, mk, late 1800s, 3-gal .1,800.00
Jug, peony, cobalt on salt glaze, mk, late 1800s, 12⅜x7½" 450.00

Phoenix Bird

Blue and white Phoenix Bird china has been produced by various
Japanese potteries from the early 1900s. With slight variations the

design features the Japanese bird of paradise and scroll-like vines of
Kara-Kusa, or Chinese grass. Although some of their earlier ware is
unmarked, the majority is marked in some fashion. More than one hundred different stamps have been reported, with 'Made in Japan' the one
most often found. Coming in second is Morimura's wreath and/or
crossed stems (both having the letter 'M' within). The cloverleaf with
'Japan' below very often indicates an item having a high-quality transfer-
printed design. Among the many categories in the Phoenix Bird pattern
are several shapes; therefore (for identification purposes), each has been
given a number, i.e. #1, #2, etc. Newer items, if marked at all, carry a
paper label. Compared to the older ware, the coloring of the new is
whiter and the blue more harsh; the design is sparse with more ground
area showing. Although collectors buy even 'new' pieces, the older is, of
course, more highly prized and valued.

For further information we recommend *Phoenix Bird Chinaware,
Books I – IV*, written and privately published by our advisor, Joan
Oates; her address is in the Directory under Michigan. Join Phoenix
Bird Collectors of America (PBCA) and receive the *Phoenix Bird Discoveries* newsletter, an informative publication that will further your
appreciation of this chinaware. See Clubs, Newsletters, and Catalogs for
ordering information.

Stacking tea set, four-piece (counting lid), $150.00;
Tile, $35.00; Sugar bowl, #2, with lid, $45.00.

Bouillon, 2-hdls 15.00
Bowl, rice; all-wht int, sm 8.00
Bowl, vegetable; oval, lg 55.00
Cake tray, #1, rnd 75.00
Coffeepot, #1 ....65.00
Creamer, #9 ....22.00
Cup & saucer, AD/demi; #4-B 15.00
Cup & saucer, for child's play 15.00
Cup & saucer, tea/coffee; border inside, #4 ....15.00
Custard cup, handleless; border inside 15.00
Egg cup, dbl 15.00
Egg cup, single 12.00
Ginger jar, post-1970, w/lid 18.00
Hair receiver, 2-pc 65.00
Pitcher, milk; #3-A 45.00
Plate, breakfast; 9¼" 32.00
Plate, dinner; 9¾" 45.00
Plate, for child's play, 5" 12.00
Platter, oval, 12" 48.00
Platter, oval, 7⅝" 30.00
Teapot, #5, med 65.00

Phoenix Glass

Founded in 1880 in Monaca, Pennsylvania, the Phoenix Glass
Company became one of the country's foremost manufacturers of lighting glass by the early 1900s. They also produced a wide variety of utili-

tarian and decorative glassware, including art glass by Joseph Webb, colored cut glass, Gone-With-the-Wind style oil lamps, hotel and barware, and pharmaceutical glassware. Today, however, collectors are primarily interested in the 'Sculptured Artware' produced in the 1930s and '40s. These beautiful pressed and mold-blown pieces are most often found in white milk glass or crystal with various color treatments or a satin finish.

Phoenix did not mark their 'Sculptured Artware' line on the glass; instead, a silver and black (earliest) or gold and black (later) foil label in the shape of the mythical phoenix bird was used.

Quite often glassware made by the Consolidated Lamp and Glass Company of nearby Coraopolis, Pennsylvania, is mistaken for Phoenix's 'Sculptured Artware.' Though the style of the glass is very similar, one distinguishing characteristic is that perhaps 80% of the time Phoenix applied color to the background leaving the raised design plain in contrast, while Consolidated generally applied color to the raised design and left the background plain. Also, for the most part, the patterns and colors used by Phoenix were distinctively different from those used by Consolidated.

In 1970 Phoenix Glass became a division of Anchor Hocking which in turn was acquired by the Newell Group in 1987. Phoenix has the distinction of being one of the oldest continuously operating glass factories in the United States. For more information refer to *Phoenix and Consolidated Art Glass, 1926 – 1980*, written by our advisor, Jack D. Wilson, who is listed in the Directory under Illinois. See also Consolidated Glass.

Key: mg — milk glass

Ashtray, Phlox, slate bl pearlized **225.00**
Candlestick, Strawberry, tan w/brn shadow **135.00**
Candlesticks, Sawtooth, caramel irid, 6¾", pr **155.00**
Cigarette box, Phlox, brn over mg **175.00**
Compote, Blackberry, pk decor on mg **145.00**
Compote, Lacy Dewdrop, caramel irid, heavy **275.00**
Umbrella vase, Thistle, burgundy pearlized, 18" **580.00**
Vase, Aster, burgundy w/pearlized design, 7" **125.00**
Vase, Bluebell, lt pk w/pearlized design, 7" **110.00**
Vase, Cosmos, bl over mg, 7½" **200.00**
Vase, Dancing Girl, pk shadow, 12" **475.00**
Vase, Diving Girl, brn shadow, 14" L **300.00**
Vase, Fern, pk & gr wash on mg, 7¼" **150.00**
Vase, Flying Geese, mg satin w/pearlized geese, pillow form, 10" .**225.00**
Vase, Freesia, aqua w/frosted design, 8" **140.00**
Vase, Freesia, pk w/frosted design, 8" **150.00**
Vase, Jewel, red pearlized, 4¾" **125.00**
Vase, Lily, purple w/frosted design, 8" **225.00**
Vase, Madonna, lt bl on mg, 10½" **275.00**
Vase, Madonna, slate bl w/wht satin design, 10½" **200.00**
Vase, Madonna, tan w/pearlized design, 10½" **200.00**
Vase, Philodendron, rose shadow, 11½" **250.00**
Vase, Star Flower, coral w/frosted design, 7" **145.00**
Vase, Thistle, plain mg, 18" **180.00**
Vase, Tiger Lily, amethyst frost, 11½" **350.00**
Vase, Tiger Lily, pk frost, 11½" **275.00**
Vase, Tropical Fish, Reuben bl (rare), 9" **630.00**
Vase, Wild Geese, red pearlized, 10" **285.00**
Vase, Wild Rose, aqua wash w/frosted design, 10½" **250.00**
Vase, Zodiac, tan over mg, 10½" **800.00**

Phonographs

The phonograph, invented by Thomas Edison in 1877, was the first practical instrument for recording and reproducing sound. Sound wave vibrations were recorded on a tinfoil-covered cylinder and played back with a needle that ran along the grooves made from the recording, thus reproducing the sound. Very little changed to this art of record making until 1885, when the first replayable and removable wax cylinders were developed by the American Graphaphone Company. These records were made from 1885 until 1894 and are rare today. Edison began to offer musically recorded wax cylinders in 1889. They continued to be made until 1902. Today they are known as brown wax records. The first disc records and disc machines were offered by the inventor Berliner in 1894. They were sold in America until 1900, when the Victor company took over. In the 1890s, all machines played 7" diameter disc records; the 10" size was developed in 1901. By the early 1900s there existed many disc and cylinder phonograph companies, all offering their improvements. Among them were Berliner, Columbia, Zonophone, United States Phono, Wizard, Vitaphone, Amet, and others.

All Victor I's through VI's originally came with a choice of either brass bell, morning-glory, or wooden horns. Wood horns are the most valuable, adding $1,000.00 (or more) to the machine. Spring models were produced until 1929 (and even later). After 1929 most were electric (though some electric-motor models were produced as early as 1910). Unless another condition is noted, prices are for complete, original phonographs in at least fine to excellent condition. Note: Edison coin-operated cylinder players start at $7,000.00 and may go up to $20,000.00 each. All outside-horn Victor phonographs are worth at **least** $1,000.00 or more, if in excellent original condition. Machines that are complete, still retaining all their original parts, and with the original finish still in good condition are the most sought after. Our advisor for this category is J.R. Wilkins; he is listed in the Directory under Texas. Unless noted, values are for examples in excellent condition, sold at popular, repeated buying prices.

Key:
cyl — cylinder   NP — nickel plated
mg — morning glory   rpd — reproducer

Victor I, 8" turntable, 9½" diameter brass bell horn, ca 1903 – 05, EX, $900.00.

Berliner B Ideal, disc, Auto grand rpd, 16" brass bell, oak **1,200.00**
Berliner Trade Mark, disc, Clark-Johnson rpd, brass horn **5,000.00**
Berliner Trade Mark, disc, Johnson rpd, blk bell horn, M **3,750.00**
Bing Kiddyphone, disc, Bing rpd, cone horn, circular case **250.00**
Brunswick, cvd upright case w/moldings, lg **350.00**
Brunswick, plain upright case, sm **200.00**
Busy Bee Grand, disc, orig rpd, red mg horn, w/decal **700.00**
Cameraphone, disc, orig rpd, tortoise-shell resonator, oak **550.00**
Colibiri, disc, box camera type, Colibri rpd, soundbox, w/case ...**350.00**
Columbia A, cyl, eagle rpd, NP bell horn, oak case **500.00**
Columbia AA, cyl, eagle rpd, blk horn, oak **1,000.00**
Columbia AA, cyl, eagle rpd, sm NP horn, sm oak cabinet **500.00**
Columbia AB (McDonald), cyl, eagle rpd, brass horn, 2 mandrels .**1,400.00**
Columbia AH, disc, Columbia rpd, blk/brass repro horn, rear crank ..**700.00**

Columbia AH, disc, Columbia rpd, brass bell horn, no decal ..**1,000.00**
Columbia AJ, disc, Columbia rpd, blk/brass bell horn, top crank .**1,200.00**
Columbia AJ, disc, Columbia rpd, brass bell horn, rear crank **900.00**
Columbia AJ, disc, Columbia rpd, brass bell horn, top crank ..**2,000.00**
Columbia AK, disc, orig rpd, brass bell horn, 7¼" turntable **800.00**
Columbia AO, cyl, D rpd, brass bell horn **500.00**
Columbia AU, disc, rpd attached to horn, openworks, turntable ..**600.00**
Columbia AZ, cyl, Lyric rpd, repro blk/brass horn **500.00**
Columbia B Eagle, cyl, eagle rpd, 7" brass bell, open works **500.00**
Columbia BC 20th C, cyl, 4" Higham rpd, brass bell/5" mandrel .**1,200.00**
Columbia BD Majestic, disc, Columbia rpd, 24" NP horn, mahog ...**1,200.00**
Columbia BE Leader, cyl, Lyric rpd, mg, 6" mandrel, serpentine .**650.00**
Columbia BF Peerless, cyl, Lyric rpd, NP horn, M case **800.00**
Columbia BF Peerless, cyl, Lyric rpd/brass horn/6" mandrel, oak **650.00**
Columbia BG Sovereign, cyl, orig rpd & horn/6" mandrel, mahog ..**900.00**
Columbia BI Sterling, disc, Columbia rpd, oak horn **2,250.00**
Columbia BK Jewel, cyl, Lyric rpd, copper horn, wicker basket ..**460.00**
Columbia BO Invincible, cyl, Lyric rpd, oak horn & case **1,800.00**
Columbia BQ Rex, cyl, Lyric rpd, orig mg horn, oak case **600.00**
Columbia BS Coin-op, cyl, eagle rpd, rpl horn **3,000.00**
Columbia Grafonola, disc, orig rpd, inside horn, mahog, upright ..**200.00**
Columbia Q, cyl, Q rpd, blk cone horn, keywind **300.00**
Columbia Q Busy Bee, cyl, D rpd, 10" blk cone horn, key wind .**300.00**
Columbia Regent Desk, disc, Columbia rpd, inside horn, mahog ..**400.00**
Edison Amberola B-VI, cyl, Dmn B rpd, inside horn, mahog **350.00**
Edison Amberola VI, cyl, Dmn B rpd/inside horn, oak table top .**350.00**
Edison Amberola X, cyl, Dmn B rpd, inside horn, NM **330.00**
Edison Amberola 30, cyl, Dmn C rpd, inside horn, oak, NM **375.00**
Edison Amberola 50, cyl, Dmn C rpd, inside horn, oak case **450.00**
Edison Concert, cyl, D rpd, brass horn/stand, 5" mandrel **2,500.00**
Edison Concert A, cyl, automatic rpd, 36" brass horn, w/stand ..**3,000.00**
Edison Concert C, cyl, R rpd, 30" brass bell, floor stand, M **2,500.00**
Edison Dmn Disc Army-Navy, DD rpd, inside horn, olive drab .**650.00**
Edison Dmn Disc A100, DD rpd, inside horn, Moderne golden oak ...**350.00**
Edison Dmn Disc B80, DD rpd, inside horn, table model **350.00**
Edison Dmn Disc C150, DD rpd, inside horn, Sheridan floor model ...**200.00**
Edison Dmn Disc S19, DD rpd, inside horn, oak, upright **250.00**
Edison Fireside, cyl, H rpd, cygnet horn **1,150.00**
Edison Fireside, cyl, K rpd, blk metal cygnet horn, 2/4 min **850.00**
Edison Fireside A, cyl, Dmn B rpd, oak Music Master horn **2,250.00**
Edison Fireside A, cyl, K rpd, maroon horn/crane **1,000.00**
Edison Fireside B, cyl, Dmn B rpd, blk cygnet horn, 4 min **1,000.00**
Edison Gem A, cyl, B rpd, cone horn, label & decal **400.00**
Edison Gem D Maroon, cyl, K rpd, maroon Fireside horn, w/crane ..**1,800.00**
Edison Gem D Maroon, cyl, K rpd, 20" maroon horn **1,800.00**
Edison Gem E Maroon, cyl, all orig **2,000.00**
Edison Home, cyl, C rpd, 14" brass bell horn, ribbon decal **650.00**
Edison Home, cyl, H rpd, metal cygnet horn, 2/4 min **675.00**
Edison Home A, cyl, C rpd, 14" blk/brass horn, gr oak/banner ...**500.00**
Edison Home A Suitcase, cyl, C rpd, 14" repro horn, decal **550.00**
Edison Home B, cyl, H rpd, lg brass bell, 2/4 min, rfn **550.00**
Edison Home E, cyl, O rpd, oak cygnet horn, oak case **1,800.00**
Edison Opera A, cyl, L rpd, mahog Music Master horn, mahog .**5,000.00**
Edison Standard, cyl, C rpd, brass bell horn **475.00**
Edison Standard A Suitcase, cyl, old-style rpd, 14" brass bell **550.00**
Edison Standard B, cyl, C rpd, rpt mg horn, heavy crane **650.00**
Edison Standard C, cyl, C rpd, mg horn, repeating attachment ..**700.00**
Edison Standard D, cyl, K rpd, blk cygnet horn **1,000.00**
Edison Triumph, cyl, C rpd, 7" brass bell, 2-min **950.00**
Edison Triumph, cyl, O rpd, oak cygnet horn, NM **2,500.00**
Edison Triumph, cyl, O rpd, wood cygnet, 2/4 min repeater **2,800.00**
Edison Triumph D, cyl, H rpd, 23" bell horn, 2/4-min **725.00**
Edison Triumph G, cyl, opera case **4,000.00**
Edison/Amet, spring motor, 1893-95, ea, from $2,500 to **8,000.00**

Excelsior, cyl, aluminum rpd & horn, open works **500.00**
Fern-O-Grand Baby Grand, disc, inside horn, piano shape **950.00**
Kalamazoo Duplex, disc, Kalamazoo rpd, 2 lg horns **3,300.00**
Klingsor, disc, Klingsor rpd, inside horn, stained glass doors ...**2,000.00**
Mae Star Phonograph Doll, cyl, MS rpd, internal horn **500.00**
Montgomery Ward Thornward, cyl, repro rpd, 14" horn, EX ..**1,000.00**
Pathe Actuelle, disc, cone horn, mahog console **1,000.00**
Pathe Actuelle, disc, cone horn, oak console **750.00**
Pathe Coq, cyl, ebonite rpd, aluminum horn, walnut cover **425.00**
Puck Lyre, cyl, floating rpd, red mg horn **400.00**
Puck Lyre, cyl, floating rpd, sm Puck horn **450.00**
Regina Hexaphone #102, cyl, Hexaphone rpd, oak horn, rstr .**7,500.00**
Regina Hexaphone #103, cyl, Hexaphone rpd, oak horn, rstr .**7,500.00**
Regina Hexaphone #104, cyl, Hexaphone rpd, oak horn, rstr .**8,500.00**
Standard A, disc, Standard rpd, bl mg horn, decal **650.00**
Standard A, disc, Standard rpd, red horn **700.00**
Standard X, disc, Standard rpd, blk mg horn, center post **700.00**
Thorens Excelda, disc, Escelda rpd, internal horn, camera type .**285.00**
United Symphony, disc, United rpd, inside horn, table model ...**250.00**
Victor E Monarch Jr, disc, Concert rpd, brass horn, rear mt ...**1,200.00**
Victor E Monarch Jr, disc, Exhibition rpd, brass bell horn **1,100.00**
Victor I, disc, Exhibition rpd, repro brass bell, oak case **1,000.00**
Victor II, disc, Exhibition rpd, metal horn **1,200.00**
Victor II, disc, Exhibition rpd, oak horn & case **2,500.00**
Victor II, disc, Exhibition rpd, 18" brass bell horn, oak **1,000.00**
Victor III, disc, Exhibition rpd, blk mg horn, oak case **1,200.00**
Victor IV, disc, Exhibition rpd, mahog horn & case **2,200.00**
Victor M Monarch, disc, Exhibition rpd, 11" horn, oak/composite ..**1,500.00**
Victor M Monarch, disc, lg brass bell, oak case **1,500.00**
Victor MS Monarch Specialty, disc, Exhibition rpd, oak horn .**2,500.00**
Victor P Premium, disc, Exhibition rpd, 18" brass bell horn **1,000.00**
Victor R Royal, disc, Exhibition rpd, 9½" brass bell, oak **1,000.00**
Victor Schoolhouse XXV, disc, orig oak horn, oak, upright **3,000.00**
Victor VI, disc, Exhibition rpd, mahog horn & case **5,000.00**
Victor VV-IV, disc, Exhibition rpd, inside horn, oak table top **200.00**
Victor VV-VI, disc, Exhibition rpd, inside horn, oak table top ..**200.00**
Victor VV-X, disc, Exhibition rpd, inside horn, table top **500.00**
Victor VV-XII, disc, Exhibition rpd/inside horn/mahog table top ..**550.00**
Victor VV-50, disc, #2 rpd, inside horn, oak portable **150.00**
Victor VV-70, disc, #4 rpd, inside horn, table top **325.00**
Victor VV-8-30, disc, Orthophonic rpd, inside horn, credenza .**1,000.00**
Victrola VV-300, disc, Victrola #2 rpd, inside horn **500.00**
Victrola VV-8-30, disc, Orthophonic rpd, inside horn, credenza .**1,000.00**
Vitaphone, disc, w/horn, minimum value **1,000.00**
Zonophone, disc, front mt w/horn, from $1,000 to **3,000.00**
Zonophone, disc, rear mt, w/horn, from $800 to **1,500.00**
Zonophone A, disc, Concert rpd, brass horn, glass sides **2,500.00**
Zonophone Champion, disc, Exhibition rpd, sm gr mg horn ...**1,200.00**
Zonophone Parlor, disc, brass bell horn, rear crank **1,100.00**

Photographica

Photographic collectibles include not only the cameras and equipment used to 'freeze' special moments in time but also the photographic images produced by a great variety of processes that have evolved since the daguerrean era of the mid-1800s. For the most part, good quality images have either maintained or increased in value. Poor quality examples (regardless of rarity) are not selling well. Interest in cameras and stereo equipment is down, and dealers report that average-priced items that were moving well are often completely overlooked. Though rare items always have a market, collectors seem to be buying only if they are bargain priced.

Our advisor for this category is John Hess; he is listed in the Directory under Massachusetts.

Albumens

Lone Wolf II, Kiowa warrior, eagle feathers, Lenny & Hutchins .200.00
Male acrobat/contortionist performing, tinted, 19th C, 2½x2¼" .75.00
Paddlewheeler Chattanooga on TN River, ca 1864, 9x7½"+fr ...350.00
President Lincoln & Family, based on Carpenter's painting 15.00
To-Wah, Fort Sill, OK Territory, Native Am by canvas tepee ...425.00

Ambrotypes

An ambrotype is a type of photograph produced by an early wet-plate process whereby a faint negative image on glass is seen as positive when held against a dark background.

4th plate, Niagara Falls, Prospect Point 345.00
4th plate, 2 sisters, well dressed, ea w/fan 95.00
4th plate, 3 friends in studio pose (2 seated/1 standing) 60.00

4th plate, four laborers reload cannon on ship's deck, two Naval officers, one with telescope, gilt details, in thermoplastic case, $1,100.00.

6th plate, identified OH couple, ruby, EX 80.00
6th plate, Southern belle, jewelry tinted gold 70.00
6th plate, 2 ladies holding hands, Barnard, NY, EX 25.00
9th plate, Civil War MA Volunteer Militia soldier, w/case 70.00
9th plate, Confederate w/percussion pepperbox, shell jacket 295.00

Cabinet Photos

Amy Arlington holding 2 pythons, Eisemann, VG 32.50
Boxers in ring, spectators & policemen, late 1800s, EX 65.00
Chester A Arthur President from 1881-85, bust portrait 16.50
Edwin Thomas Booth, seated, J Notman, VG+ 32.50
Felix Wehrle Elastic Skin Man, pulling skin, Eisenmann 70.00
Fireman w/fire trumpet, dbl-breasted coat, w/hat, MA 30.00
GAR veteran in uniform w/Kearny medal, ½-view, 1890, VG 30.00
Gen John A Logan, lg mustache, bust portrait, scarce 20.00
Girl holding her push hoop & stick by Victorian chair 12.50
Hunter w/percussion shotgun/powder horn/game in studio pose, VG .12.50
Indian Wars infantryman w/M1840 Civil War musician's sword ..25.00
James A Garfield, bust portrait, Monroe of Rochester NY, VG 12.50
John Greenleaf Whittier, in suitcoat, wht beard/hair 16.50
John Hancock, from Colonial painting, rare 16.50
John L Sullivan in suitcoat, facsimile signature, VG+ 40.00
Lady acrobat in leotard & tights, Wendt, VG 16.50
Lady combing her long hair, Wendt, G+ 16.50
Lillian Russell, Max Platz, Chicago (not tobacco card), 1880s ...140.00
Man seated, elephantitus leg, VG+ 45.00
Miss Millie Lamar Mind Reader, albino lady, Obermuller & Kern ..15.00
Postmortem of baby in flower-draped wicker buggy 90.00
Ralph Waldo Emerson, bust pose, Chas Taber, 1882, VG 16.50
Rossow's Midgets, standing pr w/straw hats & canes, G+ 15.00

US Marine Corps soldier, bust pose, ca 1880s, VG+ 20.00
Waino & Plutaino Wild Men of Borneo..., Obermuller & Kern, VG+ .32.50

Cameras

Antique camera collecting continues to increase in popularity, and values have moved upward as the high-quality items have become increasingly hard to find. Most of the pre-1900 cameras will be found in the large format view cameras or studio-camera types. Well worn examples are not too hard to find, but there is a large difference in the value of those and the high-quality items — the ones that are desirable for display purposes. It is rare indeed to find a very old camera in mint condition. There are many distinct types of cameras — large format, medium format, early folding and box styles, 35mm single-lens-reflex (SLR), 35mm rangefinders, twin-lens reflex (TLR), miniature or subminiature, novelty, and even a few others. Collectors may specialize in a style, in a time period, or even in high-quality pieces of the same camera.

In the 1900 to 1940 period, large quantities of box cameras and folding bed cameras were produced by many manufacturers, and the popular 35mm camera was introduced. Most have low values because they were made in vast numbers, but mint-condition cameras are prized by collectors who are attempting to upgrade. In the 1930 to 1955 period, the famous 35mm rangefinders and the SLR's and TLR's became the cameras of choice. The most prized of these are of German or Japanese manufacture and had interchangeable lenses, built-in rangefinders, and meters. German optics were favored, but following WWII, Japanese cameras and optics improved until they actually surpassed some German cameras in quality as well as quantity.

Today there are thousands of different cameras to choose from, and collectors have many options when selecting categories. The major factor is quality, and values vary widely between cameras with average wear and those in mint condition, still in the original box, and unused. This brief list suggests average prices for good working cameras with average wear. The same camera in mint condition will be valued much higher, while one with excessive wear (scratches, dents, corrosion, poor optics, nonworking meters, or rangefinders) may have little value.

Note: To date, no appreciable collector's market has developed for the older Polaroid cameras or most old movie cameras; however, there are a few collectors of these items, and examples in mint condition may find a market. Also note that fakes and copies abound for many of the classic cameras, such as the German Leica, and caution is advised in purchasing one of these cameras at a price too good to be true. Consult a specialist on high-priced classics if good reference material is not available. Our advisor for this category is Gene Cataldo; he is listed in the Directory under Alabama. (SASE required.)

Agfalex, Models I, II, III, 50/2.8 lens, from $80 to 100.00
Ansco Standard Speedex, f6.3 lens, 1950 ....15.00
Ansco Super Speedex, 75/3.5 lens, 1953-58 ....175.00
Anthony Climax Detective Camera, late 1880s 1,500.00
Asahi Pentax, orig 1957 ....275.00
Asahi Pentax Spotmatic, many models, from $50 to 100.00
Blair Baby Hawk-Eye, 1897 box camera 300.00
Canon IIB, 1949-52, Serenar lenses 250.00
Canon III, 1952, Serenar lenses 300.00
Canon S, 1938-46, w/Nikkor lenses 7,500.00
Conley folding plate cameras, 1900-20, many models, from $75 to ...300.00
Eastman Baby Brownie, NY World's Fair, 1939 ....200.00
Eastman Baby Brownie Special, 1939-54 ....10.00
Eastman Beau Brownie, varied colors, 1930-33, from $50 to 175.00
Eastman Chevron, 1953-56, Ektar 78mm lens 300.00
Eastman Kodak Graflex RB, M in case 400.00
Eastman Kodak No 2C Brownie Box, 1917-34 ....10.00
Eastman Kodax Box, orig, 1888-89 ....3,000.00

Eastman No 1 Kodak Camera, 1889-95 ....**1,200.00**
Eastman Retina, many models, MIG, from $40 to **550.00**
Exakta, German made, various models, 1933-78, from $50 to .**1,000.00**
FED, 35mm Russian-made Leica copies, several models, from $50 to ..**150.00**
Graflex, many models, 1902-73, from $100 to **900.00**
Kodak Brownie Holiday Flash **55.00**
Konica Baby Pearl folding camera, 1934-46 ....**135.00**
Konica II, 35mm rangefinder, 1955 ....**100.00**
Leica II, chrome & blk versions, 1932-48 ....**250.00**
Leica IIIa, 1935-50 ....**275.00**
Leica IIIf, several versions, 1950-56, from $300 to **700.00**
Minolta Autocord, TLR, orig, 1955-65 ....**100.00**
Minolta-Auto, strut folding camera, 1934 ....**300.00**
Minolta-35, 35mm rangefinders, Modela A-F, from $300 to **800.00**
Minox, orig, made in Riga, Latvia **800.00**
Minox B, 1958-71, chrome finish **150.00**
Monox II, made in Wetzlar, Germany, 1949-51 ....**500.00**
Nikon F, 35mm SLR, Photomic-T, 1965 ....**225.00**
Nikon I, rangefinder, 1948, very rare **20,000.00**
Nikon S, rangefinder, w/1.4 lens, 1951-54 ....**500.00**
Olympus Flex A, 3.5 lens, TLR, 1955 ....**135.00**
Olympus Six, folding, 1939 ....**200.00**
Polaroid 195, w/Tominon 114/3.8 lens **200.00**
Polaroid 95, 1948-53, early popular model **20.00**
Praktica FX, 34mm, SLR, 1952 ....**65.00**
Praktica Nova, 1965 ....**55.00**
Rolleicord/Rolleiflex, German made, many models, from $75 to ..**800.00**
Sears (Seroco, Marvel, Perfection, Towers, & others), from $10 to ...**500.00**
Semi-Minolta I, folding camera, 1934 ....**200.00**
Victor Animatograph Model #3 ....**120.00**
Voigtlander Bessa, early folding cameras, 1931-50 ....**40.00**
Voigtlander Bessamatic, 35mm, SLR, 1959 ....**135.00**
Voigtlander Vitessa L, 1954 ....**275.00**
Zeiss Contaflex Super, 1960 ....**120.00**
Zeiss Contax III, 544/24, 1936-42 ....**275.00**
Zeiss Contessa-35, 1950 ....**200.00**
Zeiss Ikoflex 1a, TLR, 1953 ....**135.00**
Zeiss Ikonta A (520), 1933-40, folder **75.00**

Carte De Visites

Among the many types of images collectible today are carte de visites, known as CDVs, which are 2¼" x 4" portraits printed on paper and produced in quantity. The CDV fad of the 1800s enticed the famous and the unknown alike to pose for these cards, which were circulated among the public to the extent that they became known as 'publics.' When the popularity of CDVs began to wane, a new fascination developed for the cabinet photo, a larger version measuring about 4½" x 6½". Note: A common portrait CDV is worth only about 50¢ unless it carries a revenue stamp on the back; those that do are valued at about $1.00 each.

Albino woman, long wht hair, Eisenmann, VG **16.50**
Benjamin Franklin, oval portrait, taken from painting **10.00**
Castle Thunder, Richmond VA, prison scene, VG **25.00**
Cat in close-up on photographer's posing chair **20.00**
Civil War soldier seated w/rifled musket, frock coat, VG **45.00**
Civil War Union Cavalry sergeant stands w/M1860 sword, MA ..**95.00**
Civil War wounded shoulder w/arm in sling, Steiger's, CT, VG ..**85.00**
Dudley Foster (midget) on table, parents beside, Eisenmann, VG .**26.00**
Farmer w/3 Gurnsey bulls, outdoor image, JW Black Boston **20.00**
Gen Geo G Meade, left side profile, Gutenkunst **40.00**
Gen John A Dix in staff frock, w/sword & sash, Brady, 1862 ....**45.00**
Giant Captain Bates & His Manager in Civil War uniform **25.00**

John Stratton, Civil War dbl-arm amputee, seated, NY **95.00**
John Wilkes Booth, 1 hand on hip, cane in other, VG **40.00**
Lady stands & holds gymnastic stick **15.00**
Lieutenant Gen US Grant, ¾-view, frock coat & vest **30.00**
Lucretia Coffin Mott, Quaker-type bonnet, shawl & book in lap .**30.00**
Mary Todd Lincoln, standing, ¾-view, blk dress **55.00**
Miss Jennie Quigley...28", 32 lbs, RH Doane, 1860s, VG **25.00**
Postmortem of child in bed w/handmade afghan, VG **20.00**
Seth Kinman, w/percussion plains rifle in lap, Barker, KS **225.00**
Union enlisted man seated before pnt camp scene, shell jacket **30.00**
Winfield S Hancock, taken for presidential election **22.50**
Zouave cadets standing, fez hats, pantaloons, swords, Boston **95.00**
2 seated gamblers at card game, ca 1864, Roberts, PA **25.00**

Daguerreotypes

Among the many processes used to produce photographic images are the daguerreotypes (made on a plate of chemically treated metal) — the most valued examples being the 'whole' plate which measures 6½" x 8½". Other sizes include the 'half' plate, measuring 4½" x 5½", the 'quarter' plate at 3¼" x 4¼", the 'sixth' plate at 2¾" x 3¼", the 'ninth' at 2" x 2½", and the 'sixteenth' at 1⅜" x 1⅝". (Sizes may vary slightly, and some may have been altered by the photographer.)

Half plate, lady in huge poke bonnet, Philadelphia, 1840s **150.00**
Half plate, lady w/lg book, postmortem mat **75.00**
Half plate, man w/lg cane, elegant attire **75.00**
Half plate, 3 people in formal pose **300.00**
4th plate, husband & wife, well dressed, horizontal, w/case **40.00**
4th plate, lady in blk satin dress & dag case on lap **45.00**
4th plate, man in clerical collar, faces right, w/full case **95.00**
4th plate, postmortem, mother w/child on her lap **250.00**

6th plate, group of carpenters wearing straw hats and aprons, each holds tool, EX, $700.00.

6th plate, girl in print dress w/sm book in lap, 1840s, w/case **22.50**
6th plate, lady in blk w/lace shawl/wht lace bonnet, w/case **22.50**
6th plate, lady seated, frowning, blk lace gloves, w/case **22.50**
6th plate, lady seated, lace collar on dress, w/full case **22.50**
6th plate, man's profile taken from painting, M&P, full case **125.00**
6th plate, man seated, holding pr of wire-fr glasses, VG **22.50**
6th plate, old lady w/hair jewelry pin at neck, w/case **22.50**

Photos

Amelia Earhart w/airplane, EX **8.00**
Cowboy on horse w/pack mule, sagebrush, sepia print, ca 1910 ..**120.00**
Gen US Grant & aides, gelatin print, postwar, EX **275.00**
Man on Indian motorcycle, sepia print, ca 1920s, 3½x5", EX **35.00**
Native Am w/bird wing & pipe, platinum print, 1890s, 8x6" **575.00**
Railway from Vera Cruz to Mexico, 1879 ....**25.00**

Stereoscopic Views

Stereo cards are photos made to be viewed through a device called a stereoscope. The glass stereo plates of the mid-1800s and photo prints produced in the darkroom are among the most valuable. In evaluating stereo views, the subject, date, and condition are all-important. Some views were printed over a thirty- to forty-year period; 'first generation' prices are far higher than later copies, made on cheap card stock with reprints or lithographs, rather than actual original photographs.

It is relatively easy to date an American stereo view by the color of the mount that was used, the style of the corners, etc. From about 1854 until the early 1860s, cards were either white, cream-colored, or glossy gray; shades of yellow and a dull gray followed. While the dull gray was used for a very short time, the yellow tones continued in use until the late 1860s. Red, green, violet, or blue cards are from the period between 1865 until about 1870. Until the late '70s, corners were square; after that they were rounded off to prevent damage. Right now, quality stereo views are at a premium.

Atlantic City Beach, Keystone, ca 1900 ....12.00
Battle of Santiago, destruction of Spanish fleet, Keystone 15.00
Christ Church, Alexandria VA, interior w/pulpit & pews 12.50
Christ Church, WA's Church, Alexandria VA, Phillips & Cole ..12.50
CO & Swimming Pool, hotel & pool, Glenwood Springs, Hook ..25.00
Fidelity Trust Building Tacoma WA 1891, dirt street 18.50
Graff Zeppelin in hanger, Keystone 45.00
Insane Asylum, St Louis 10.00
Interior of Old San Gabriel Mission, alter view, #B68 ....22.50
Labor men marching w/signs: Down w/Coffee Trust, etc, VG 18.50
Old Mission San Gabriel, outdoor view, #B67, Jarvis...CA 20.00
Old Stone House WA's HQ Richmond VA, w/children at play, G+ ..15.00
Orange Picking & Packing, Chinese workers, #B42, Jarvis 20.00
Parade Band & Fraternal Order...Waterville ME, Hodges 22.50
San Diego CA from Upper 7th St, Parker, 1880s 22.50
US Monitar Terror, CH Graves, ca 1910 ....15.00
Waterfront View of 3 Wooden Sailing Ships..., Moore, 1899 ....18.50
West Brighton Beach Hotel, Coney Island 16.00
Zeppelin flying over German town, ca 1915 ....100.00
9 Men at Baseball Outing, ca 1890s, G+ 20.00

Tintypes

Tintypes, contemporaries of ambrotypes, were produced on japanned iron and were not as easily damaged.

4th plate, Union wounded soldier, arm in sling, pnt scene 130.00
5x7", broadside view of open-top carriage & horses, VG 25.00
6th plate, boy seated w/blk & wht dog in posing chair 10.00
6th plate, cowboy w/lg hat/sash/fringed chaps in pnt landscape 22.50
6th plate, fraternal officer stands w/sword, full uniform 16.50
6th plate, girl in wooden-wheeled baby carriage before house, VG .10.00
6th plate, girl w/lg china-head doll, well dressed 16.50
6th plate, horse w/blinders & reigns, VG+ 16.50
6th plate, lady sits on wooden horse, man w/tin feed pail, VG 12.50
6th plate, man seated, holds stereo viewer w/card on slide 30.00
6th plate, man seated, right arm amputated, sleeve folded 10.00
6th plate, man stands/smokes cigar, holds Chinese fan, VG+ 10.00
6th plate, man w/abnormality (no neck, hunched bk), seated 10.00
6th plate, puppy on wooden chair looking right 20.00
6th plate, sm girl w/striped kitten in her lap 18.50
6th plate, Union cavalryman w/saber, Smith & Wesson #1 in belt .235.00
6th plate, Union infantryman stands w/bayonetted musket 150.00
6th plate, Union soldier w/E Whitney pocket-model revolver ...300.00
6th plate, 2 ladies w/tandem bicycle, VG 40.00
6th plate, 2 women exercising w/4 medicine clubs 10.00
6th plate, 5 tradesmen w/tools (possibly carriage makers), VG 12.50
9th plate, Union soldier seated w/bayonetted musket, w/case 195.00

Union Cases

From the mid-1850s until about 1880, cases designed to house these early images were produced from a material known as thermoplastic, a man-made material with an appearance much like gutta percha. Its innovator was Samuel Peck, who used shellac and wood fibers to create a composition he called Union. Peck was part owner of the Scoville Company, makers of both papier-mache and molded leather cases, and he used the company's existing dies to create his new line. Other companies, among them A.P. Critchlow & Company, Littlefield, Parsons & Company, and Holmes, Booth, & Hayden soon duplicated his material and produced their own designs. Today's collectors may refer to cases made of this material as 'thermoplastic,' 'composition,' or 'hard cases,' but the term most often used is 'Union.' It is incorrect to refer to them as gutta percha cases.

Sizes may vary somewhat, but generally a 'whole' plate case measures 7" x 9⅛" to the outside edges, a 'half' plate 4⅞" x 6", a 'quarter' plate 3¾" x 4¾", a 'sixth' 3⅛" x 3⅝", a 'ninth' 2⅜" x 2⅞", and a 'sixteenth' 1¾" x 2". Clifford and Michele Krainik and Carl Walvoord have written a book, *Union Cases*, which we recommend for further study. Another source of information is *Nineteenth Century Photographic Cases and Wall Frames* by Paul Berg. Values are for examples in excellent condition unless noted otherwise.

Half plate, The English Pioneers, EX, $375.00.

Half plate, WA Monument, K-4, couple ambro 450.00
16th plate, Indian Head Penny, K-617, man tintype 200.00
4th plate, Bountiful Harvest, K-47, man portrait ambro 150.00
4th plate, Chasse au Facon, K-32, father & son dags (2) 200.00
4th plate, Cupid & Wounded Stag, K-36, mother/child ambro ..150.00
4th plate, Hanging Bowl of Flowers, K-51, lady's portrait 100.00
4th plate, Roger de Coverly & Gypsies, K-29, couple tintype, VG ..100.00
4th plate, Scroll/Floral, K-76, boy in highchair ambro, VG 125.00
4th plate, Scroll/Geometric, K-74 variant, couple ambro 100.00
4th plate, Scroll/Geometric, K-84, lady dag, VG 250.00
4th plate, Sweet Potato Dinner, K-17, w/couple dag 200.00
4th plate, Union & Constitution, K-27, 2 men in dag 250.00
6th plate, Calmady Children, w/Sioux dag 195.00
6th plate, Chess Players, w/man's portrait dag 175.00
6th plate, Clipper Ship & Fort, K-100, father/daughters ambro ..200.00
6th plate, Deer & Pine Tree, K-167, couple dag 150.00
6th plate, Faithful Hound, K-89, w/4 tintypes 225.00
6th plate, Fireman's Duty, K-118, mother/child ambro 225.00
6th plate, Flower Brier, K-94, w/2 ruby ambros 150.00
6th plate, girl w/flowers, w/4 dags 300.00
6th plate, orange compo (garden scene), w/lady dag 200.00
6th plate, Rebekkah at Well, K-155, man/wife ruby ambros 200.00
6th plate, Scroll, K-95, w/4 dags 225.00
6th plate, Spray of Strawberries, K-93, w/2 ruby ambros 275.00
6th plate, Volunteer Fireman, K-116, couple ruby ambro 250.00
9th plate, Butterfly Chariot, K-339, couple tintype, G 200.00
9th plate, Chess Players, K-338, 2 children tintypes 150.00

9th plate, Cutout (rare), K-335, lady ambro 300.00
9th plate, Eagle & Flag, soldier ambrotype, M 350.00

Miscellaneous

Album, celluloid, classic ladies w/Cupid 155.00
Album, celluloid, Puritan lady front, Victorian, lg 150.00
Case, 4th plate, blk lacquer w/gold florals & MOP inlay, w/ambro ..130.00
Case, 4th plate, blk lacquer w/mc vines, MOP inlay, w/dag 100.00
Case, 6th plate, blk lacquer w/gold floral & MOP inlay, w/dag ..135.00
Case, 6th plate, blk lacquered MOP w/compo florals, rpr, w/2 dags .90.00
Magic lantern, wood/tin, CI ft, kerosene lamp, GVF, 10", EX 150.00
Stanhope, alabaster bbl, Niagara Falls scene 30.00
Stanhope, binoculars, French Expo, EX 75.00
Stanhope, cross, bone, WWI, troups in trenches, ca 1914, EX 50.00
Stanhope, inkwell, ivory, chalet form, German views 50.00
Stanhope, needle case, vegetable ivory, bathing scene 125.00
Stanhope, pen, rhinestones, Lord's Prayer 45.00
Stanhope, pipe, cvd wood, 6 Port Erin views, 1" L, EX 50.00
Stanhope, pipe, rhinestones, Lord's Prayer 45.00
Stanhope, ring, aluminum, nude 65.00
Stanhope, ring, man's, 2 female nude views, EX 295.00
Stanhope, scent bottle, brass, w/neck chain, 6 views, EX 155.00
Stanhope, tape measure, bbl form w/ivory finial, 1 view 65.00
Stereoscope, Paris Unis-France, wood box/binocular type, +slides .275.00

Piano Babies

A familiar sight in Victorian parlors, piano babies languished atop shawl-covered pianos in a variety of poses: crawling, sitting, on their tummies, or on their backs playing with their toes. Some babies were nude, and some wore gowns. Sizes ranged from about 3" up to 12". The most famous manufacturer of these bisque darlings was the Heubach Brothers of Germany, who nearly always marked their product; see Heubach for listings. Watch for reproductions. These guidelines are excerpted from one of a series of informative doll books by Pat Smith, published by Collector Books.

Blk, bsk, 12", EX quality 995.00
Blk, bsk, 12", med quality 495.00
Blk, bsk, 16", EX quality, minimum value 1,085.00
Blk, bsk, 16", med quality 950.00
Blk, bsk, 4", EX quality 425.00
Blk, bsk, 4", med quality 325.00
Blk, bsk, 8", EX quality 525.00
Blk, bsk, 8", med quality 375.00

Bisque, molded hair, unjointed boy in adult boots, molded-on clothes, intaglio eyes, old repairs, 11", VG, $250.00.

Bsk, molded hair, unjtd, molded-on clothes, 12" EX quality 975.00
Bsk, molded hair, unjtd, molded-on clothes, 15", med quality 525.00
Bsk, molded hair, unjtd, molded-on clothes, 4", EX quality 425.00
Bsk, molded hair, unjtd, molded-on clothes, 4", med quality 225.00
Bsk, molded hair, unjtd, molded-on clothes, 8", EX quality 895.00
Bsk, molded hair, unjtd, molded-on clothes, 8", med quality 435.00
Bsk, w/animal/pot/flowers/etc, 12", EX quality 995.00
Bsk, w/animal/pot/flowers/etc, 16", EX quality, minumum value ..1,100.00
Bsk, w/animal/pot/flowers/etc, 4", EX quality 425.00
Bsk, w/animal/pot/flowers/etc, 8", EX quality 615.00

Pickard

Founded in 1895 in Chicago, Illinois, the Pickard China Company was originally a decorating studio, importing china blanks from European manufacturers. Some of these early pieces bear the name of those companies as well as Pickard's. Trained artists decorated the wares with hand-painted studies of fruit, florals, birds, and scenics and often signed their work. In 1915 Pickard introduced a line of 23k gold over a dainty floral-etched ground design. In the 1930s they began to experiment with the idea of making their own ware and by 1938 had succeeded in developing a formula for fine translucent china. Since 1976 they have issued an annual limited edition Christmas plate. They are now located in Antioch, Illinois.

The company has used various marks. The earliest (1893 – 1894) was a double-circle mark, 'Edgerton Hand Painted' with 'Pickard' in the center. Variations of the double-circle mark (with 'Hand Painted China' replacing the Edgerton designation) were employed until 1915, each differing enough that collectors can usually pinpoint the date of manufacture within five years. Later marks included the crown mark, 'Pickard' on a gold maple leaf, and the current mark, the lion and shield. Work signed by Challinor, Marker, and Yeschek is especially valued by today's collectors. For further information we recommend *Collector's Encyclopedia of Pickard China* by Alan B. Reed, available from Collector Books.

Bonbon, violets on airbrushed gr, sgn J Nessy, 1903-05, 9" L 180.00
Bowl, Autumn Blkberries w/gold paste, Goess, 1905-10, 10½" ..265.00
Bowl, Daisy Multi-Flora, sgn Fisher, ftd, 1910-12, 8¼" 200.00
Cake plate, Enchanted Forest, Marker, hdls, 1918-19, 10" 375.00
Candlesticks, Iris Conventional, sgn Lind, 1898-1903, 8¾" 485.00
Chocolate pot, Carnations, Lustre & Matt Gr, sgn Rean, 1910-12 .550.00
Coffee set, Carnation Conventional, sgn Tomas, 1903-05, 3-pc ..435.00
Creamer & sugar bowl, Rose Bower, sgn Leon, 1903-05, w/lid ...200.00
Cup & saucer, Crocus Conventional, 1898-1903 ....165.00
Leaf dish, grapes & much gold, sgn Beutlich, 1905-10, 9½" 155.00
Mug, cherry spray, gold border w/lattice, Beitler, 1903-05, 6" 295.00
Mug, Fishing Boat, Holland 1909, sgn Comyn, 1905-10, 5¼" 700.00
Mug, monk w/tankard & candle, sgn Aldrich, 1898-03, 6" 300.00
Plaque, Moor w/tiger, sgn Kubash, 1903-05, 15½" 1,050.00
Plate, Antique Day Lilies, Leroy, 1903-05, 9" 175.00
Plate, dessert; floral, wht/gr on lav border, 1912-18, 8" 40.00
Plate, floral, wht on gr, sgn Miche, 1905-10, 8¾" 125.00
Plate, Nasturtium Conventional, sgn RH, 1898-1903, 8⅝" 154.00
Plate, Wight Tulips, sgn Wight, 1905-10, 8¾" 125.00
Sugar bowl, violets on yel to bl, sgn Petrykaski, 1898-1902, sm ..100.00
Syrup, Violet Nouveau, gold on wht, sgn Coufall, 1905-10, 5½" .275.00
Vase, Challinor Hollyhocks, Challinor, 1903-05, 7" 465.00
Vase, Easter Lily, sgn Schoner, waisted, 1905-10, 9" 200.00
Vase, Japanese lady w/comb, unsgn, cylindrical, 1903-05, 12" ...1,800.00

Pickle Castors

Pickle castors, which were both functional and decorative, became popular after the Civil War, reaching their peak about 1885. By 1900 they had virtually disappeared from factory catalogs. Numerous styles were available. They consisted of a decorated, silverplated frame that held either a fancy clear pressed-glass insert or one of decorated colored art glass — the latter being popular in the more affluent Victorian households and more desirable with collectors today.

In the listings below, the description prior to the semicolon refers to the jar (insert), and the remainder of the line describes the frame. Unless a color is mentioned, all glassware is clear. When no condition is indicated, the silverplate is assumed to be in very good to excellent condition; glass jars are assumed near-mint. Our advisor for this category is Deborah Maggard; she is listed in the Directory under Ohio.

Key: rsl — resilvered

Amberina, swirled ribs, Libbey; ftd Meriden fr 650.00
Barley; orig SP fr, +tongs 125.00
Cane, bl; ornate SP fr, 11¼", +tongs 300.00
Cane, cranberry; rstr Britannia fr, 10¾x4½" 425.00
Cane & Rosette; rsl fr 175.00
Cobalt, cut & emb florals; ornate orig SP Bridgeport fr 550.00
Cobalt w/mc florals & gold scrolls; SP fr, +tongs 595.00
Cranberry, HP florals w/gold; very ornate SP fr, 10x8" 875.00
Cranberry, HP florals; tall ftd Reed & Barton fr, rstr 425.00
Cupid & Venus; EX SP fr 285.00
Daisy & Button, sapphire bl; orig ftd SP fr 350.00
Daisy & Button w/V Ornament, sapphire bl; ornate SP fr, +tongs ...375.00
Daisy & Button; rstr SP Barbour Bros #117 fr, 9" 250.00
Daisy & Fern, bl opal; SP fr 525.00
Dbl, paneled inserts; unmk rstr SP fr 750.00
Dbl, vertical panels w/eng vines; ornate rstr SP Rogers fr 825.00
Dmn Point; ornate ftd Meriden fr, +tongs 125.00
Dmn Quilt, amber; SP fr, +tongs 195.00
Dmn Quilt, yel satin MOP; SP floral Reed & Barton fr, 11½" ...600.00
Eng flowers in 6 panels; rstr SP Rogers #435 fr, 9" 350.00
Etched herons among cattails; ornate SP Pairpoint fr, 14½" 550.00
Fine Cut, vaseline; EX SP fr 295.00
Florette, pk cased; orig SP fr 395.00
Frosted bbl form w/bl flowers; SP Stevens fr, 9¾" 600.00
Frosted w/HP florals; ftd SP fr w/matching design 225.00
Frosted w/wood texture & flowers; Poole fr, +tongs 350.00
Galloway; orig SP fr & lid 225.00
Hobnail, rubena opal frost; floral SP fr, 12", +tongs 450.00
Hobnail, ruby amberina; quadruplated cherry branches fr, 11" ...750.00
Hobstar, vaseline; mk SP Pairpoint fr, rare 750.00
Invt Peacock Eye, rubena w/coralene; SP leafy fr, 12", +tongs 800.00
Invt T'print, amber w/HP bl berries; SP Meriden fr, 12" 525.00
Invt T'print, bl w/HP floral decor, SP fr, +tongs 600.00
Invt T'print, cranberry w/HP florals; ornate SP fr, +tongs 650.00
Invt T'print, cranberry w/Mary Gregory girl; SP fr/lid, +tongs 695.00
Jacob's Ladder; SP fr, +tongs 225.00
Open Heart & Arches, pigeon blood; EX SP fr 395.00
Optic Rib, cranberry w/HP flowers, corseted; SP Homan fr, tongs .495.00
Optic Rib, pk opal; ftd orig fr, Pairpoint #688 ....650.00
Paneled Cane; SP Roger Bros fr, 9½", EX 100.00
Pigen blood w/mc HP millefiori-style decor; SP fr/lid, +tongs 450.00
Pineapple & Fan, Hobrock; SP fr, +tongs 85.00
Polka Dot, cobalt; EX SP fr 650.00
Raindrop, wht to pk MOP satin; Simpson-Hall-Miller fr, 12" .1,395.00
Robin's-egg bl w/dimpled sides/HP decor; orig SP fr, +tongs 475.00
Shasta daisies, Wave Crest; SP fr & lid, +tongs 495.00
Spatter (cased); ornate Wilcox ftd fr 495.00
Swirl, cranberry w/HP florals; SP Benedict fr 550.00
Swirl, pk satin; SP Pairpoint fr 450.00

Wht satin w/HP apple blossoms; SP fr 325.00
Zipper Slash, amber, etched decor; rstr SP fr 350.00

Pie Birds

A pie bird or pie funnel (pie vent) is generally made of pottery, glazed inside and out. Most are 3" to 5" in height with arches at the base to allow steam to enter. The steam is then released through an exit hole at the top.

The English pie funnel was as tall as the special baking dish was deep and held the crust even with the dish's rim, thereby lifting the crust above the filling so it would stay crisp and firm. These dishes came in several different sizes, which accounts for the variances in the heights of the pie birds.

The first deviations from the basic funnels were produced in the mid-1930s to late 1940s: the Clarice Cliff (signed Midwinter or Newport) pie bird (reg. no. on white base) and the signed Nutbrown elephant. Shortly thereafter (1940s – 1960s), figures of bakers and colorful birds were created for additional visual baking fun. From the 1980s to present, many novelty pie vents have been added to the market for the enjoyment of both the baker and collector. These have been made by commercial (including Far East imorters) and local enterprises in Canada, England, and the United States. A new category for the 1990s includes an array of holiday-related pie vents. Basic tip: older pie vents were airbrushed, not hand painted.

Incense burners (i.e., elephants and Oriental people), one-hole pepper shakers, dated brass toy bird whistle, egg timers (missing glass timer), and ring holders (i.e., elephant with clover on his tummy) should not be mistaken for pie vents. Our advisor for this category is Lillian Cole; she is listed in the Directory under New Jersey.

Servex Chefs: With buttons, marked Holland (inside), 5"; Without buttons, marked Aust. and New Zealand with patent numbers, 4½", $150.00 each.

Photo courtesy Lillian Cole

Aluminum pie funnels, England, ea 25.00
Barn Pottery, England, 2 heads solid yel, body blk, 3¾" 85.00
Bird, all blk or all wht, imported, up to 4" tall 4.00
Bird, bl w/blk speckles, mustard beak 50.00
Bird, blk or wht, wide mouth, mk England 35.00
Bird, mc, Morton Pottery 20.00
Birds on nest, US, copyright mk, 1950s 125.00
Black-faced chef & cook, red, yel, wht pnt, Taiwan, pr 10.00
Boy, gr sombreros, mk pie boy 100.00
Chefs, all wht, pinhole vent, 1995 repros, ea 7.00
Decaled, mk New Devon Pottery, Made in England 50.00
Fred Flour Grader, England, copyright mk on bk if orig 50.00
Funnel, cane color, holes staggered, England, 1980 to present 20.00
Funnel, terra cotta, mk Wales 35.00
Funnels, plain wht, szs vary, ea, from $15 to 25.00
Grimwade funnel, England 50.00
Pie funnel, Pyrex, szs vary, ea, minimum value 15.00
Rooster, mc, mk Cleminson or Cb 28.00

Rowland's Hygienic Patent, England **90.00**
SB mk, England, 1980s to present **30.00**
Tala 1899 emb logo, wht, England, 1996 ....**10.00**
TG gr motif/logo on wht funnel, 1993 to present **15.00**

Pierce, Howard

Howard Pierce opened his studio in Claremont, California, in 1941, where he continued to work until his death on February 28, 1994. He was not only a successful artist but an astute businessman as well.

Howard met Ellen Van Voorhis when he visited National City, California, in 1940. They married and together they immediately set out to create the lines for which they became famous. They knew what the public wanted, and they were careful to keep their prices on a level most could afford. In the beginning, he created small nut dishes and bowls in two-color combinations reminiscent of those he made during his tenure with William Manker (a talented artist, teacher, mentor, and businessman in his own right), with whom he had worked for about three years. Though relatively scarce, they do not command the high prices of Howard's other pieces.

Howard turned his attention toward creating animals, marine life, and establishing himself as an artist. He was one of only a few artists who attempted the use of a variety of mediums. Polyurethane was the only substance that gave him noticeable problems. Though he attempted to make models of birds and roadrunners on bases, an allergic reaction quickly caused him to discontinue the project. Such pieces command high prices on today's market and are considered scarce by collectors.

Howard also produced items (cups and saucers, sugar bowls and creamers, wall pockets, etc.) in a Wedgwood-type Jasper in colors of mint green, blue, pink, and orange. Later he used this material to make porcelain bisque animals and plants (usually horses and various trees) which he attached to open areas in his vases and candle holders.

When Mount St. Helens erupted, a friend sent Howard a small jar of the ash, which he added to a base of various materials, thus creating pieces with a rough texture that the majority of buyers seemed to like. While most of the resulting items are marked with the words 'St. Helens,' some have been found without this designation. The appearance of Mount St. Helen's should not be confused with the 'lava' treatment that Howard also used. Breathtakingly beautiful, 'lava' pieces appear to have a rough surface, though they are smooth to the touch. Mr. Pierce described the lava as 'bubbling up from the bottom.' These items are not readily available.

Howard created two 'gold' lines. His gold leaf was richly elegant and is not easy to find today. The other gold line was commissioned by Sears, Roebuck and Company and was handled through Howard's distributor. Howard was responsible only for the casting. On some of the Sears pieces, red shows through. The majority of these pieces were not marked. Any gold treatment used after his move to Joshua Tree, California, had a more finished look and occasionally such pieces were stamped 'Howard Pierce.' It is difficult to tell which gold Howard created himself, so collectors, especially novices, are often edgy about purchasing a gold piece; but if the price is right and you like the piece, then it's best to purchase it. A marked gold piece is worth about ten to twenty percent less than the same Pierce item in any other glaze.

Experimental glazes are sought by collectors. Some of these colors are deep purple, iridescent green and pink, assorted shades of blue, and even a high-gloss pink with black speckles, which was so commonly used in the 1950s. Howard preferred simple colors — white, gray, or brown, in particular — so most of the experimental glazes were priced less or sold as seconds at the studio. However, today's collector will probably have to pay more for the experimentals than for a like piece in a basic color.

In 1992, due to Howard's failing health, they destroyed all the molds they had created over more than fifty years. Soon, however, Howard found that he missed the work, and in 1993 they purchased a small kiln and created smaller versions of his past products. These pieces are simply stamped 'Pierce.' Even though very few were made, at this time they do not command values as high as comparable pieces marked 'Howard Pierce' or those with experimental glazes.

For further information we recommend *Collector's Encyclopedia of Howard Pierce Porcelain* by Darlene Hurst Dommel (Collector Books). Our advisor for this category is Susan Cox; she is listed in the Directory under California.

Ashtray, experimental gr, trefoil, 1950s mk, 25X, 5" **65.00**
Candle holders, gray, Howard Pierce Porcelains mk, 2¾", pr **75.00**
Creche, Joseph, Mary w/Jesus & lamb, bl, mk, 7½", 4½", 2" **135.00**
Figurine, buffalo, experimental bl & blk, mk, 1993, 2" **55.00**
Figurine, cat, stylized, brn & wht, 8" **50.00**
Figurine, chipmuk, brn, 6" L **35.00**
Figurine, coyote on stepped base, gray, Pierce mk, 1993 ....**125.00**
Figurine, dove, 6" **60.00**
Figurine, gazelle on base, gray, 11¼" **165.00**
Figurine, girl seated w/book, gray w/brn, 6½x3½" **85.00**
Figurine, girl w/goose (1-pc), wht, mk Howard Pierce, 7½" **175.00**
Figurine, horned owl, 8" **100.00**

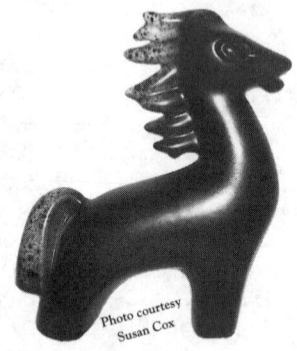

Figurine, horse, dark brown with beige-tipped mane and tail, 1950s, 9", $155.00.

Photo courtesy
Susan Cox

Figurine, Native couple, brn, pr **145.00**
Figurine, owl, 5", 3", pr **70.00**
Figurine, owls (2) in tree, wht, Howard Pierce, 11" (6 variations) ..**225.00**
Figurine, rooster & hen, wht & brn, #251P, pr **165.00**
Figurine, water bird, gr & wht, 5½" **30.00**
Figurine, water bird, 14" **75.00**
Magnet, coyote, brn, no mk, 4¼" **70.00**
Pin, lamb, pewter, mk Howard Pierce, 2¾" **125.00**
Vase, brn, 5x7½" **45.00**
Vase, gondola style, oval, 7½x5" **85.00**
Vase, gr, horse/tree insert, #P-500 ....**100.00**
Wall plaque, modernistic birds, brn tones, cement, 19" L **255.00**

Pigeon Blood

Pigeon blood glass, produced in the late 1800s, may be distinguished from other dark red glass by its distinctive orange tint.

Biscuit jar, Florette, metal lid **310.00**
Biscuit jar, Open Heart Arches **325.00**
Biscuit jar, paneled ribs, SP lid w/bird finial, 8½" **200.00**
Biscuit jar, Torquay **375.00**
Bowl, berry; Open Heart Arches **250.00**
Butter dish, Coreopsis **275.00**
Creamer, arched/pleated base, clear hdl, pontil, 4⅝" **80.00**
Creamer, Beaded Drape **150.00**

Creamer, Bulging Loops **125.00**
Creamer, Florette, satin **195.00**
Cruet, Torquay, shiny **795.00**
Cup, 4" **65.00**
Pitcher, water; Coreopsis, pnt floral, metal lid **400.00**
Toothpick holder, Bulging Loops **225.00**

Pigeon Forge

Douglas J. Ferguson and Ernest Wilson started their small pottery in Pigeon Forge, Tennessee, in 1946. Using red-brown and gray locally dug clay and glazes which they themselves formulate, bowls, vases, and sculptures are produced there. Their primary target is for the tourist trade.

Bowl, Dogwood, floral, wht on pk, 6" **25.00**
Figurine, bear cub, 4" **20.00**
Figurine, bear playing, Fergison, 4½x5" **30.00**

Pilkington

Founded in 1892 in Manchester, England, the Pilkington pottery experimented in wonderful lustre glazes that were so successful that when they were diplayed at exhibition in 1904, they were met with critical acclaim. They soon attracted some of the best ceramic technicians and designers of the day who decorated the lustre ground with flowers, animals, and trees; some pieces were more elaborate with scenes of sailing ships and knights on horseback. Each artist signed his work with his personal monogram. Most pieces were dated and carried the company mark as well. After 1913 the company became known as Royal Lancastrian.

Their Lapis Ware line was introduced in the late 1920s, featuring intermingling tones of color under a matt glaze. Some pieces were very simply decorated while others were painted with designs of stylized leafage, scrolls, swirls, and stripes. The line continued into the '30s. Other pieces of this period were molded and carved with animals, leaves, etc., some of which were reminiscent of their earlier wares.

The company closed in 1938 but reopened in 1948. During this period their mark was a simple P within the outline of a petaled flower shape. Our advisor for this category is David Ehrhard; he is listed in the Directory under California.

Vase, classical maidens rowing single-sail galleons, waves, clouds, gulls, Walter S Mycock, minor restoration, 11", $2,500.00.

Bookends, dolphin, 5½", pr **350.00**
Figurine, bear, Richard Joyce, 3½" **400.00**
Tile, Apache dancer, set of 3 .... **200.00**
Tile, broad leaves, silver on red irid, 6x3"+oak fr **400.00**
Vase, bud; Prussian Bl, 5" **200.00**
Vase, fish/seaweed, gold on bl, Richard Joyce, 6½x5½" **2,200.00**
Vase, gold lustre w/mc highlights, long bottle neck, 7" **350.00**
Vase, matt gr, rnded shoulder, flared neck, emb decor **300.00**

Vase, matt orange, 6" **160.00**

Pillin

Polia Pillin was born in Poland in 1909. She came to the U.S. as a teenager and showed an interest and talent for art which she studied in Chicago. She married William Pillin, who was a poet and potter. They ultimately combined their talents and produced her very distinctive pottery from the 1950s to the mid-1980s. She died in 1993.

Polia Pillin won many prizes for her work, which is always signed Pillin with the loop of the 'P' over the full name. Some undecorated pieces are signed W&P, due to her husband's collaboration.

Her work is prized for its art, not for the shape of her pots, which for the most part are simple vases, dishes, bowls, and boxes. Wall plaques are rare. She pictured women with hair reminiscent of halos, girls, an occasional boy, horses, birds, and fish. After viewing a few of her pieces, her style is unmistakable. Some of her early work is very much like that of Picasso.

Her pieces are somewhat difficult to find, as all the work was done without outside help, and therefore limited in quantity. In the last few years, more and more people have become interested in her work, resulting in escalating prices. Our advisors for this category are Dolli and Wilfred Cohen; they are listed in the Directory under California.

Box, lady w/bird, mc on gr & brn, 2x4" dia **375.00**
Bust, lady w/2 stylized birds, mc **425.00**
Covered dish, lady w/mandolin, mc on shaded bl, 2x4" dia **375.00**
Jug, blistered yel/brn gloss, sgn, 7¾x5" **275.00**
Plate, lady & bird, 7¾" **850.00**
Vase, abstract figure on all 4 sides, 11½x3¾" **975.00**
Vase, birds, mc, 5" **595.00**
Vase, dancing women, mc on mottled pk & yel, 7½" **750.00**
Vase, dbl portraits of girls & rooster on dk yel, pinched, 5" **450.00**
Vase, dk gr/bl crystalline, 1950s, 9¾" **250.00**
Vase, gr/olive matt texture, wide gourd w/tiny neck, 13" **375.00**
Vase, horse & 2 ladies, wht on peacock & rust, 9x7" **850.00**
Vase, horses, lady w/balloons, mc on bl, can form, 4½" **495.00**
Vase, horses, mc on wht to brn, pear form, 6" **550.00**
Vase, horses, 2 frolicking, mk, 4¾" **450.00**
Vase, ladies, mc on bl, rectangular, 9", NM **850.00**
Vase, ladies (2 full length) mc on yel/brn, slim form, 15" **1,500.00**
Vase, ladies (2) seining for fish, bulbous, 4¼" **475.00**
Vase, lady & horse, 6" **625.00**
Vase, lady w/bird, 2 ladies dance, mc on bl, 4½x5" **495.00**
Vase, lady w/birds, ball form, 6" **550.00**
Vase, lt to dk brn crystalline, bulbous w/can neck, 8½" **270.00**
Vase, lt to dk gr gloss, bulbous w/sm opening, 6½" **200.00**
Vase, nudes, 6" **750.00**
Vase, Oriental-look bl & gr glossy w/red highlights, 11½x12" ...**1,000.00**
Vase, rooster on bl, cylindrical, 7" **495.00**
Vase, scarlet flambe gloss, spherical w/short neck, 9½x7" **425.00**
Wine cup, rooster, gr w/mc, 2½" **325.00**

Pin-Back Buttons

Buttons produced up to the early 1920s were made of a celluloid covering held in place by a ring (or collet) to the back of which a pin was secured. Manufacturers used these 'cellos' to advertise their products. Many were of exceptional quality in both color and design. Buttons were produced in sets featuring a variety of subjects. These were given away by tobacco, chewing gum, and candy manufacturers, who often packed them with their product as premiums. Usually the name of the button maker or the product manufacturer was printed on a paper placed in the back of the button. Often these 'back papers' are still in place today. Much of the time the button maker's name was printed on the button's perimeter, and sometimes the copyright was added. Beginning in the 1920s, a large number of buttons were lithographed on tin; these are referred to as tin 'lithos.' Nearly all pin-back buttons are collected today for their advertising appeal or graphic design. There are countless categories to base a collection on.

The following listing contains non-political buttons representative of the many varieties you may find. Our advisor for this category is Michael J. McQuillen; he is listed in the Directory under Indiana.

Bat Man Club, pictures bat, red/wht/blk, litho, '60s, 1½", VG 15.00
Beatles, Harrison portrait, red/wht/blk litho, 1960s, ⅞", NM 10.00
Beatles, Lennon portrait, red/wht/blk, litho, 1960s, ⅞", NM 15.00
Chevrolet, C-Day Is Coming, red/wht/bl litho, 1940s, ⅞", EX 10.00
Danny Thomas, Help Danny Lick Leukemia, blk/wht, 1¼", NM .15.00
Davy Crockett, looking over hill, yel/blk, 1960s, 1½", EX 18.00
Defend Am First, WWII isolationist cause pin, 1940, ⅞", EX 12.00
I Go Pogo, cartoon picture, yel/blk/wht litho, 1956, ⅞", EX 15.00
Jackie Gleason, Loud Mouth/portrait, yel/blk/wht, 2¼", EX 15.00
Lafayette Stock Farm, horses pictured, mc, ca 1900, 1½", EX 125.00
Let's 'Lect Lum, Lum Edwards for President, radio show, ⅞", EX .15.00
Liberty Loan, furled flag, red/wht/bl, 1944, ⅞", NM 10.00
Lion Coffee, lion pictured, mc, 1910s, ⅞", VG 12.00
Lone Ranger, riding horse, mc, 1950s, 1¼", VG 30.00
Lucky Lindy Flexible Flyer, sled, mc, 1930s, ⅞", NM 50.00
Miss Patty Page, portrait, blk/wht, 1½", EX 15.00
Official US Defense Agent, red/wht/bl, 2", EX 18.00
Pat Boone, I Am a Fan, portrait, blk/wht, 1¼", EX 15.00
Remember Pearl Harbor, flag pictured, 1¼", EX 25.00
Rocky Balboa, Contender, portrait, mc, 4", NM 28.00
Roscoe Turner, Corinth Airport Dedication, blk/wht, ⅞", VG 10.00
Santa Claus, Meet Me at Pelletiers, 1940s, 1¼", EX 22.00
Santa Claus, Wolf & Dessauer, mc, 1930s, 1½", VG 45.00
Smokey Bear, Join Smokey's Campaign, mc, 1½", EX 17.00
Star Wars, Darth Vader, mc, 1982, 1½", NM 15.00
Star Wars, Princess Leia, mc, 1982, 1½", NM 15.00
Ted Williams, Boston Red Sox, portrait, blk/wht, 1950s, 1¼", NM .15.00
Waterloo Tractor Co, man on tractor, mc, 1920s, 1¼", EX 125.00
Yankee Doodle, patriotic drummer, scene, 1940s, 1¼", EX 16.00
7-Up, Mark of Zorro, red/wht/blk, 1½", VG 12.00

Pink Lustre Ware

Pink lustre was produced by nearly every potter in the Staffordshire district in the late 18th and first half of the 19th centuries. The application of gold lustre on white or light-colored backgrounds produced pinks, while the same over dark colors developed copper. The wares ranged from hand-painted plaques to transfer-printed dinnerware. Design features in the phrase immediately following the item (i.e. cup, plate, etc.) are in pink lustre unless otherwise specifically described within the line.

Bust, John Wesley, enamel decor, ca 1825, 10½" 1,035.00
Cup & saucer, handleless; floral swags 70.00
Cup & saucer, handleless; House 65.00
Cup & saucer, Temperance Star, purple transfer 110.00
Jug, commemorative; Princess Charlotte/Prince Leopold, 6" 375.00
Mug, shaving; sailboat decor 35.00
Pitcher, blk floral transfer, dolphin hdl, 6⅝" 50.00
Pitcher, Queen Caroline, emb/pnt floral border, 1820, 5¼" 625.00
Sugar bowl, purple transfer genere scene, hdls, w/lid, 4½" 35.00
Watch pocket, 2 columns support shelf w/lion finial, 7½" 800.00

Pink Paw Bears

These charming figural pieces are very similar to the Pink Pigs described in the following category. They were made in Germany during the same time frame. The cabbage green is identical; the bears themselves are whitish-gray with pink foot pads. You'll find some that are unmarked while others are marked 'Germany' or 'Made in Germany.' In theory, the unmarked bears are the oldest, made prior to 1890 when the McKinley Tariff Act required imports to be marked with the country of origin. Those marked 'Made In' were probably produced after the revision of the Act in 1914.

Mama bear with three cubs in cart, The Whole Dam Family, 4¼", $185.00.

1 by bean pot 135.00
1 by graphophone 150.00
1 by honey pot 145.00
1 by top hat 125.00
1 in front of basket 135.00
1 in roadster (car identical to pk pig car) 185.00
1 on binoculars 150.00
1 peaking out of basket 135.00
1 sitting in wicker chair 150.00
2 in hot-air balloon 150.00
2 in purse 165.00
2 in roadster 165.00
2 on pin dish 120.00
2 on pin dish w/bag of coins 145.00
2 peering in floor mirror 150.00
2 sitting by mushroom 125.00
2 standing in wash tub 135.00
3 in roadster 190.00
3 on pin dish 145.00

Pink Pigs

Pink Pigs on cabbage green were made in Germany around the turn of the century. They were sold as souvenirs in train depots, amusement parks, and gift shops. 'Action pigs' (those involved in some amusing activity) are the most valuable, and prices increase with the number of pigs. Though a similar type of figurine was made in white bisque, most serious collectors prefer only the pink ones. They are marked in two ways: 'Germany' in incised letters, and a black ink stamp 'Made in Germany' in a circle.

1 beside gr drum, wall-mt match holder 95.00
1 beside purse 75.00
1 beside shoe 75.00
1 beside stump, camera around neck, toothpick holder 145.00

1 beside wastebasket	75.00
1 coming out of cup	95.00
1 coming out of suitcase	95.00
1 coming through gr fence, post at sides, open for flowers	95.00
1 driving touring car	165.00
1 going through purse	90.00
1 holding cup by fence	140.00
1 in case looking through binoculars	145.00
1 in gr Dutch shoe	75.00
1 in gr suitcase bank, head 1 side, bk other, gold trim	110.00
1 in Japanese submarine, Japan imp on both sides	125.00
1 in money sack bank	85.00
1 in roadster	145.00
1 lg pig sitting behind 3" trough	95.00
1 on binoculars	95.00
1 on binoculars, gold trim	125.00
1 on chair	110.00
1 on gr trinket dish, leg caught in lobster claw	110.00
1 on horseshoe-shaped dish w/raised 4-leaf clover	75.00
1 on keg playing piano	150.00
1 on shoulder of gr ink bottle	115.00
1 playing accordion on side of tray, wht bear ea side	150.00
1 pushing head through wooden gate	95.00
1 putting letter in mailbox	95.00
1 reclining on horseshoe ashtray	70.00
1 riding train, 4½"	150.00
1 sits, holds orange Boston Baked Beans pot match holder	125.00
1 sits by high-top boot	110.00
1 sitting in bathtub	135.00
1 sitting on log, mk Germany	110.00
1 standing in front of cracked open egg	60.00
1 standing in gr tub	95.00
1 w/attached toothpick holder	75.00
1 w/bean pot	85.00
1 w/front ft in 3-part dish containing 3 dice, 1 ft on dice	125.00
1 w/tennis racket stands beside vase, Lawn Tennis, 3¾"	125.00
1 wearing chef's costume, holds frypan, w/basket	125.00

Two, mother and baby by telephone, 4¼", $135.00.

2, mother & baby in bl blanket in tub, rabbit on board atop	110.00
2, mother in tub gives baby a bottle, lamb looks on, 4x3½"	125.00
2, 1 at telephone booth, 1 inside, 4½"	125.00
2 at confession, 4½"	110.00
2 at wishing well	110.00
2 behind trough, unmk	75.00
2 by eggshell	95.00
2 dancing, in top hat, tux & cane	110.00
2 in basket, Merry Squeelers, 3½x3"	135.00
2 in bed, Good Night on footboard, 4x3x2½"	145.00
2 in carriage	115.00
2 in open car	150.00

2 in open trunk, 3¾"	95.00
2 in purse	95.00
2 on basket, head raising lid, plaque on front	110.00
2 on cotton bale, 1 peers from hole, 1 over top	135.00
2 on seesaw on top of pouch bank	90.00
2 on top hat	95.00
2 on tray hugging, 3x4½"	90.00
2 sitting at table playing card game 'Hearts'	170.00
2 under toadstool	125.00
3, 1 on lg slipper playing banjo, 2 dancing on side	145.00
3, 2 sit in front of coal bucket, 3rd inside	125.00
3 at trough, 4½" L	98.00
3 dressed up on edge of dish	80.00
3 sm pigs behind oval trough, mk, 2¾x2½x1¾"	95.00
3 w/baby carriage, father & 2 babies, Wheeling His Own	125.00
3 w/carriage, mother & 2 babies, Germany	95.00

Pisgah Forest

The Pisgah Forest Pottery was established in 1920 near Mount Pisgah in Arden, North Carolina, by Walter B. Stephen, who had worked in previous years at other locations in the state — Nonconnah and Skyland (the latter from 1913 until 1916). Stephen, who was born in the mountain region near Asheville, was known for his work in the Southern tradition. He produced skillfully executed wares exhibiting an amazing variety of techniques. He operated his business with only two helpers. Recognized today as his most outstanding accomplishment, his Cameo line was decorated by hand in the pate-sur-pate style (similar to Wedgwood Jasper) in such designs as Fiddler and Dog, Spinning Wheel, Covered Wagon, Buffalo Hunt, Mountain Cabin, Square Dancers, Indian Campfire, and Plowman. Stephen is known for other types of wares as well. His crystalline glaze is highly regarded by today's collectors.

At least nine different stamps mark his wares, several of which contain the outline of the potter at the wheel and 'Pisgah Forest.' Cameo is sometimes marked with a circle containing the line name and 'Long Pine, Arden, NC.' Two other marks may be more difficult to recognize: 1) a circle containing the outline of a pine tree, 'N.C.' to the left of the trunk and 'Pine Tree' on the other side; and 2) the letter 'P' with short uprights in the middle of the top and lower curves. Stephen died in 1961, but the work was continued by his associates. Our advisor for this category is R.J. Sayers; he is listed in the Directory under North Carolina.

Jar, gr & turq mottle, pk int, D1936, w/lid, 2½"	65.00
Jug, turq & purple, hdld, 1948, 4½"	75.00
Tea set, Cameo, wagon scene on gr, pot+cr/sug	600.00
Vase, Cameo, covered wagon on bl, sgn Stephen, 8½"	500.00
Vase, crystalline, bl & wht snowflake, W Stephen, 1949, 5½"	200.00
Vase, crystalline, Cameo, buffalo hunt band, gr on cream & tan, 7"	450.00
Vase, crystalline, Cameo, pioneer scene band on brn & tan , 12"	800.00
Vase, crystalline, gr on caramel & bl gloss, shouldered, 8"	400.00
Vase, crystalline, metallic brn & cream flambe, 1943, 6x3¾"	100.00
Vase, crystalline, wht on cream, cameo mk, 8", NM	120.00
Vase, crystalline, wht/lt bl/brn/muted gr, 7"	400.00
Vase, crystalline, wht/lt bl/yel, shouldered, 8"	400.00
Vase, pk crackle, aqua int, 1942, 4"	50.00
Vase, turq crackle, bulbous, sgn Stephen, dtd 1948, 7"	95.00

Pittsburgh Glass

As early as 1797, utility window glass and hollow ware were being produced in the Pittsburgh area. Coal had been found in abundance, and it was there that it was first used instead of wood to fuel the glass furnaces. Because of this, as many as 150 glass companies operated there at one time. However, most failed due to the economically disastrous effects of the War of 1812. By the mid-1850s those that remained were producing a wide range of flint glass items including pattern-molded and free-blown glass, cut and engraved wares, and pressed tableware patterns. Our advisor for this category is Mark Vuono; he is listed in the Directory under Connecticut.

Key: strw — strawberry

Bowl, amethyst, 12 molded panels, wear, 3¼x4¾" 700.00
Bowl, appl bl rim, 4⅜x6¼" 415.00
Candlestick, flared rim, 3-knop stem, pressed base, 8⅝" 650.00

Candlesticks, molded hexagonal base, free-blown ring and baluster-form shaft, 1840, 9½", NM, $375.00.

Canister, appl bl rings, clear finial, 11⅛" 775.00
Canister, 2 appl cobalt rings, near-match lid, 10¾" 450.00
Celery vase, cut panels, stars/dmns/fans, scalloped rim, 7¾" 275.00
Compote, appl ft/baluster stem, folded rims on bowl & lid, 12x8" ..385.00
Compote, cut rondels/strw dmns/rays, ftd, 6½x10¼" 100.00
Compote, cut Sheaf of Wheat in bowl, star ft, 7¾x10" 380.00
Compote, galleried rim, knop stem, knop finial, ftd, att, 10" 300.00
Compote, Pillar mold, appl ft & stem, 9x12" 660.00
Decanter, cut flutes/dmn point/strw dmns/panels, 7", +stopper ..110.00
Decanter, cut flutes/strw dmns/etc, 3 appl rings, 9", +stopper 250.00
Decanter, cut panels/fans, 3 appl rings, 8½", +stopper 125.00
Decanter, cut panels/fans/dmn-point roundels, 7",+stopper 220.00
Decanter, cut strw arches w/fans in panels, 8¾", +stopper 220.00
Decanter, cut strw dmns/fans, appl rings/ft, 8", +stopper 250.00
Ewer, Pillar mold, pewter top & hinged lid w/finial, 11¾" 495.00
Goblet, cut strw dmns/fans, star-cut base, knop stem, 5¼" 95.00
Jar, blown, bulbous, for magnifying light, 14½" 250.00
Lamp, sapphire bl, Arch font, tiered stem/base, 10⅜", pr 6,750.00
Pitcher, Pillar mold, appl hdl, tooled lip, 5¾" 300.00
Pitcher, Pillar mold, appl hollow hdl, 8¼" 475.00
Pitcher, 10 panels in base, appl hdl, tooled lip, 7" 300.00
Pitcher, 3 rows of relief cube pattern on body, 9⅛" 200.00
String holder, appl cobalt base ring & finial, 4", NM 330.00
Sugar bowl, Colonial, fiery opal, mold roughness, 9½" 1,700.00
Tumbler, whiskey; gray-bl, plain rim, pontil, att, 2⅛" 190.00
Vase, flared rim, short ribs, wafer stem w/pressed base, 9¼" 2,300.00
Wine, cut strw dmns/fans, appl ft, knop stem, 4⅜" 40.00
Wine rinser, cut strw dmns/fans, 4¼" 170.00

Plastics

The term 'collectible plastics' is defined as those types produced between 1868 (when synthetic plastics were invented) and the period immediately following WWII. There are several, and we shall mention each one and attempt briefly to acquaint you with their characteristics:

1) Pyroxylin (Celluloid, Loalin, French Ivory, Pyralin). Chemical name: cellulose nitrate. Earliest form, invented in 1868 by John Wesley Hyatt; highly flammable; yellows with age; much used in toiletry articles. Fairly lightweight, many articles of pyroxylin were made by heating and molding thin sheets.

2) Cellulose Acetate (Tenite, Similoid). Made in attempt to produce a product similar to cellulose nitrate but without the flammability. Had limited use in the costume jewelry trade; most often encountered as car knobs and handles of the '30s and '40s. Surfaces tend to crack with age and exposure to light. Always molded, never cast. Colors varied; imitation horn and marble were most popular; imitation coral is seen in molded 'floral' jewelry.

3) Casein Plastics (Ameroid, Galalith, Dorcasine, Casolith). Invented in 1904 using milk proteins. Use limited to buttons and buckles due to warping and lengthy curing time. Made in a wide range of colors; very easy to laminate or to carve from stock rods or sheets, but never molded.

4) Phenol Formaldehyde (Bakelite, Catalin, Marblette, Agatine, Gemstone, Durite, Durez, Prystal). Invented by L.H. Baekland in 1908; used extensively in the '30s. There are two major types: cast and molded. Molded types include Durez and Bakelite, dark-toned, wood flour-filled plastics that were used extensively for early telephones (still used when non-conductivity of heat and electricity is vital). The most popular name in cast phenolics was Catalin, trade name of the American Catalin Corporation of New York. Made in a wide range of colors; widely used for costume jewelry, cutlery handles, decorative boxes, lamps, desk sets, etc. Heavyweight material with a slightly 'greasy' feel; very hard but can be carved with files, grinding tools, and abrasive cutters. Buffs to high, durable polish. Cast phenolics were used primarily from 1930 to around 1950 when they proved too labor-intensive to be economical.

5) Urea Formaldehyde (Beetleware, Plaskon, Duroware, Hemocoware, Uralite). Invented around 1929, this was lighter in color than phenol formaldehyde, thus used for injection-molded products in pastel colors. Lightweight, not strong; shiny rather than glossy. It cannot be carved and was used mainly for cheap radio and clock cases, never for jewelry.

The period between the two World Wars produced acrylic resins such as Lucite and vinyl. Polystryene made its appearance then, and furfural-phenols were in use in industrial applications. Though a great future was predicted for ethyl cellulose, by the late '30s it was still in the experimental phase. For most purposes the field of decorative plastics from the first half of the century can be narrowed down to the five major types listed above. Of these, cellulose acetate is rarely encountered. Casein is limited to button and belt buckle manufacture; urea is easily identifiable as a cheap, brittle material. Pyroxylin is the celluloid of which so many vanity sets were made. Molded phenolics such as Bakelite were dark in color and used for utilitarian objects; cast phenolics such as Catalin were used most notably for jewelry (please don't call it Bakelite), cutlery handles, desk sets, and novelties.

Dealers and collectors should be aware of '70s reproduction Marblette animal napkin rings (they have no eye rods and no age patina) and molded acrylic bracelets in imitation of carved Catalin ones (look for a seam line or lack of definition in carved areas). As prices rise, copies become more common. 1986 saw the mass production of inlaid polka-dot bracelets using old-stock findings but without the precision fit (or patina) of the originals.

In 1988 and continuing to the present, a large number of 'collage' pieces appeared in vintage clothing and antique stores on the West and East Coasts. These are over-sized, glued-together assemblages of old Catalin stock parts including buttons with the shanks filed off, poker chips, etc., made into brooches or pendants, sometimes hung on necklaces of re-strung Catalin beads. They can be recognized by their aesthetically jumbled, 'put-together' look; and although some may claim they are old, they are not.

Bakelite

Clock, electric, alarm, Deco design, blk or dk brn 65.00
Inkwell, streamlined, blk, w/lid 25.00
Radio, Majestic #55, dk brn, 1939 ....250.00
Radio, Stewart Warner Varsity College, dk brn, 1938-1939 ....250.00
Roulette wheel, mc Catalin chips, wood rack, w/box, 1930s 200.00

Catalin

Ashtray, marbleized lt gr, sq, 4½" 30.00
Blotter, Carvacraft, Great Britain, amber/blk 45.00
Bracelet, bangle; apple-juice clear, figural bk-cvg 175.00
Bracelet, bangle; apple-juice clear, geometric bk-cvg 130.00
Bracelet, bangle; elaborate floral cvg, narrow 60.00
Bracelet, bangle; lt geometric cvg, narrow 30.00
Bracelet, bangle; novelty, mc, figural or animal cvg 250.00
Bracelet, bangle; scratch cvd, w/rhinestones 35.00
Bracelet, bangle; stylized floral cvg, narrow 28.00
Bracelet, bangle; uncvd, narrow 8.00
Bracelet, bangle; 12 inlaid polka dots, wide 225.00
Bracelet, bangle; 3-color stripes 100.00
Bracelet, bangle; 6 inlaid polka dots, narrow 200.00
Bracelet, clamper; figural, animal, or novelty applique 250.00
Bracelet, clamper; stylized floral cvg 95.00
Bracelet, curved/flat links, deeply cvd 65.00
Bracelet, stretch; orig elastic, Catalin & metal 50.00
Bracelet, stretch; orig elastic, mc, uncvd 50.00
Buckle, latch type, mc, stylized floral or geometric, cvd 40.00
Buckle, latch type, 1-color, novelty or figural 55.00
Buckle, latch type, 1-color, uncvd 8.00
Buckle, slide type, mc, stylized floral or geometric, cvd 35.00
Buckle, slide type, 1-color, stylized floral or geometric, cvd 9.00
Butter mold, gr/amber/brn, floral cvg, 2½" 45.00
Buttons, card of 6, scotty, fruit, or cvd floral figural 28.00
Cake breaker, CJ Schneider, red, gr, or amber hdl 4.00
Carving set, 3-pc w/wood wall rack 40.00
Cheese slicer, scotty hdl, wood & chrome base 20.00
Chopsticks, ivory, pr 5.00
Cigarette box, lt gr, wood bottom, rectangular, 5½x3¾" 40.00
Cigarette holder, long, mc or w/rhinestones 25.00
Cigarette lighter, mc stripes or inlay 45.00
Clock, Sessions, electric alarm, scalloped case, 4¼" dia 60.00
Clock, Westclox, Moonbeam, electric flashing light alarm 90.00
Cocktail recipes, Ben Hur, mtd on drunk, red w/blk base 50.00
Cork, Ben Hur, w/red fighting roosters, blk base 25.00
Corn holder, Kob Knobs, diamond shape or lathe trn, 8 +box 50.00

Crib toy, Black-faced doll, $195.00.

Crib toy, Tykie Toy, clown, Loalin head/Catalin body 195.00
Crib toy, Tykie Toy, 11 mc spools on string, 1940s 100.00

Crib toy, Tykie Toy catalog, 1946 ....35.00
Dice, ivory or red, 2½", pr 15.00
Dice cage, metal/red Catalin, blk Lucite base, w/dice 100.00
Dominoes, ivory or blk, full set, w/wood box 40.00
Drawer pull, 1-color, w/pnt inlay stripe 2.00
Dress clip, mc inlaid Deco design 30.00
Dress clip, scratch cvd 25.00
Dress clip, stylized floral cvg 30.00
Earrings, lg drop style, pr 10.00
Earrings, stylized floral cvg, pr 15.00
Egg beater, red, gr, or amber hdl 16.00
Flatware, chrome plate, 3-pc matched place setting 8.00
Flatware, stainless, 1-color hdl, leatherette box, 36-pc 180.00
Flatware, stainless, 2-color hdl 4.00
Flatware, stainless, 2-color hdl, 3-pc matched place setting 15.00
Gavel, lathe turned, red, blk, & ivory 35.00
Ice cream scoop, stainless, red hdl 20.00
Inkwell, Carvacraft Great Britain, amber, single well 90.00
Lamp base, brass & amber, Deco design, 10" 30.00
Letter opener, blk & amber stripes, Deco design 20.00
Letter opener, marbleized gr, dagger shape 20.00
Memo pad, Carvacraft Great Britain, amber 55.00
Nail brush, marbleized lt gr, 2½x1½" 9.00
Nail brush, Masso, amber octagon, 2" dia 9.00
Nail brush, turtle shape, dark amber, 3½" 20.00
Napkin ring, animal or bird, no inlaid eye or ball on head 30.00
Napkin ring, elephant w/ball on head 35.00
Napkin ring, Mickey Mouse or Donald Duck shape w/decal 60.00
Napkin ring, rocking horse or camel w/inlaid eye rod 72.00
Napkin ring set, 6-colors, 2" band, orig box 40.00
Necklace, cellulose acetate chain, Deco dangling pcs 200.00
Necklace, uncvd gr beads, 20" 40.00
Pencil sharpener, Disney character decal, silhouette shape 55.00
Pencil sharpener, orange, no decal, ¾x1" 8.00
Pencil sharpener, scotty, red, cvd details, blk base 34.00
Pencil sharpener, Trylon & Perisphere, 1939 World's Fair 50.00
Penholder, marbleized amber, Deco design 25.00
Picture frame, amber & red Deco design, 6x7" 45.00
Pin, animal, resin wash w/glass eye, lg 150.00
Pin, animal or vegetable, inlaid or appl in several colors, lg 210.00
Pin, animal or vegetable, 1-color, lg 90.00
Pin, mc Deco design, lg 80.00
Pin, novelty or patriotic figural, resin wash/inlay/appl, lg 200.00
Pin, novelty or patriotic figural, 1-color, lg 95.00
Pin, stylized floral cvg, lg 50.00
Pin, w/danglers, animal or vegetable, resin wash/inlay/appl 200.00
Pin, w/danglers, geometric form, mc 60.00
Pin, w/danglers, novelty or patriotic, resin wash/inlay/appl 250.00
Pipe, amber & gr, bowl lined w/clay 30.00
Pocket watch, Debonaire, yel Deco case, 1⅞" dia 60.00
Poker chip rack, rectangular, w/200 chips, 4" 120.00
Powder box, amber & gr fluted cylinder, 4" 60.00
Ring, stylized floral cvg, 1-color 35.00
Ring, uncvd, 2-color 30.00
Ring case, open-top style, amber, red, or blk, Deco design 90.00
Safety razor, Schick Injector, extra blades, orig box, 1939 ....45.00
Salad servers, chrome, red, gr, or amber hdls, pr 12.00
Shakers, glass, in 3⅛" Catalin holder, pr 30.00
Shakers, stepped cylinder shape, 3½", pr 30.00
Shaving brush, red, gr, or amber 20.00
Spatula, stainless, red, gr, or amber hdl 6.00
Spoon, slotted, stainless, red, gr, or amber hdl 5.00
Stirrer, iced tea; Chase, chrome ball/mint leaf, 6-pc set 35.00
Strainer, red, gr, or amber hdl, 2¾" dia 5.00

Swizzle stick, baseball-bat shape, amber or red 5.00
Thermometer, BT Co, amber & blk, 2¾" dia 45.00
Writing set, blk, amber, or gr marble, Deco, 5-pc, orig box 175.00

Celluloid

Rattle, winking moon face, $260.00.

Bracelet, snake w/inlaid rhinestones 48.00
Bridge pencil holder, animal, pearlescent ivory on blk 70.00
Carving set, ivoroid, knife/fork/steel, eng blade 30.00
Crib toy, TykieToy or similar, man in the moon, Laolin 250.00
Dresser set, ivoroid, 10-pc, w/9" bevel glass mirror 110.00
Flatware, gr pearl on blk hdl, 3-pc set 9.00
Hair receiver, ivoroid, pearlescent or amberoid, w/2-part lid 12.00
Manicure set, ivoroid, pearlescent or amberoid, 10-pc, +case 30.00
Manicure set, 4 mini-tools in coral-color tube, Germany 22.00
Mirror, dresser; ivoroid, cut-out hdl, bevel glass, 8" 25.00
Mirror, dresser; pearlescent or amberoid, bevel glass, 12" 28.00
Powder box, ivoroid, pearlescent or amberoid 15.00

Lucite

Bottle, perfume; w/atomizer, rose inclusion 20.00
Picture frame, Deco, clear, sq, 6" 18.00
Shakers, translucent red, 4", pr 12.00

Playing Cards

Playing cards can be an enjoyable way to trace the course of history. Knowledge of the art, literature, and politics of an era can be gleaned from a study of its playing cards. When royalty lost favor with the people, Kings and Queens were replaced by common people. During the periods of war, generals, officers, and soldiers were favored. In the United States, early examples had portraits of Washington and Adams as opposed to Kings, Indian chiefs instead of Jacks, and goddesses for Queens.

Tarot cards were used in Europe during the 1300s as a game of chance, but in the 18th century they were used to predict the future and were regarded with great reverence.

The backs of cards were of no particular consequence until the 1890s. The marble design used by the French during the late 1800s and the colored wood-cut patterns of the Italians in the 19th century are among the first attempts at decoration. Later the English used cards printed with portraits of royalty. Eventually cards were decorated with a broad range of subjects from reproductions of fine art to advertising.

Although playing cards are becoming popular collectibles, prices are still relatively low. Complete decks of cards printed earlier than the first postage stamp can still be purchased for less than $100.00. In the listings, decks are without boxes unless the box is specifically men-

tioned. Our advisor for this category is Ray Hartz; he is listed in the Directory under Pennsylvania. Another fine source of information is the Antique Deck Collectors' Club, 52 Plus Joker; see Directory under Clubs, Newsletters, and Catalogs.

Key:
AC — ad card
C — complete
cts — courts
J — joker
SC — score card
std — standard
XC — extra card

Advertising

Atwater Kent Radio, turbaned youth, dbl deck, VG+, torn box ...80.00
Better Brushes, pinochle, 1940s, 48+2J+blank, EX, torn box 30.00
Bowlers' Victory Legion, WWII effort, 1944, 52+J+XC, NMIB ...15.00
Enerpac Hydraulic Tools, tool on ea card, 52+2J, M 17.00
Fisk Tires, child in pajamas, 1943, M, sealed in wrapper 26.00
Gilmour Thomson Royal...Whiskey, Waddington, 52+J, VGIB ...40.00
Gold Medal Foods, clown & moon bks, 52, no J, EX- 32.00
Hunter Baltimore Rye, 52+AC, ca 1903, EXIB 47.00
IA State Traveling Men's Assoc, narrow, ca 1925, 52+J+SC, NMIB .65.00
Kinney Tobacco, transformation, 1889, 52, no J, G 350.00

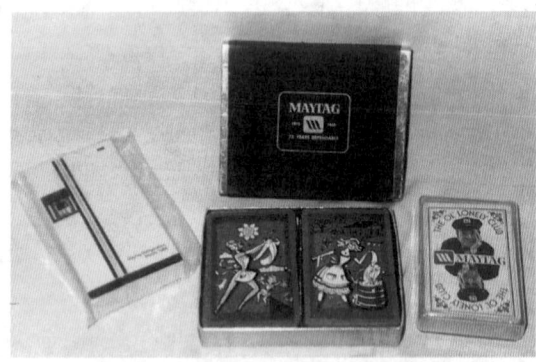

Maytag, assorted decks sold to dealers or employees, MIB, $17.50 each.

Miss Betty Light, Sylvania, dbl, purple/brn bks, ea: EXIB 35.00
Philips Electric, Fr cts, special aces, 52+J, 1930s, VG 60.00
Player's Navy Cut, lady smoking, narrow, Waddington, 52+J, VG ...18.00
President Suspender, Edgarton..., pinochle, 48C, VG+/torn box .300.00
Rigby's Wm Penn, King of...10¢ Cigars, 52+XCs, EX 45.00
Van Camp Packing Co, Indianapolis, 1908, 52+J+SC, VGIB 40.00

Foreign Manufacturers

Austria, Hausermann, aluminum, mc cts, 1925, 52+J, NM 310.00
Canada, Allied Armies I, Montreal, 1916, 52+J, MIB 55.00
Egypt, Tutankhamen, Moharren Press, 52+2J, MIB 12.50
England, Colonials #24, Goodall, red/blk bks, 52+J, NMIB 22.00
England, De La Rue, standard, cotton/rose bks, 1870, 52C, VG ...66.00
England, Dunhill's Sultan, crane/flower bks, 52+J+XC, EXIB 22.00
England, Rameses Fortune..., Goodall, pyramid bks, 1910, NMIB .138.00
France, Jeu Louis XV, Grimaud, 52+J+XC, NMIB 50.00
France, Le Florentin, Philibert, 1955, 52+2J+2XC, NMIB 140.00
France, Memoires de Casanova, Paris, 1960, 52+2J+XC, NMIB .315.00
Germany, Shakespeare Spielkarten, Dondorf, 52+J+XC, EX+, EX box ...275.00
Germany, 4 Continents, Dondorf, late 1800s, 52C, G 140.00
Japan, Japanese Women, erotic bks, Angel, 1985, 52+2J+XC, MIB ..38.50
South Africa, Boer, Cape Times Ltd, 1961, 52+3XC, MIB 80.00
Soviet Union, antireligious, mask bks, 1930, 52+J, NM, torn box ...390.00

Spain, Segundo de Olea, Cadiz, 1893, 48C, EX in torn wrapper ..**130.00**
Switzerland, Swiss Cantons, Wust, 1970, 52C, EX **320.00**

Modern

Adventures of Sherlock Holmes, clues on cards, 52+2J+XC, NMIB ...**15.00**
Aircraft Spotter Cards II, USPC, 1942, 52+J+XC, NMIB **30.00**
Amazing Spider Man, Marvel Comics Group, 1979, MIB, sealed .**10.00**
Bannister Babies I, Brn & Bigelow, 1954, 52+2J, NMIB **30.00**
Classic Playing Cards, Fournier, 1959, 52+2J+SC+booklet, MIB **35.00**
Distant Early Warning, McLuhan, 1969, nonstd cartoon cts, MIB ..**110.00**
Goldwater Campaign, 1966, MIB, sealed **55.00**
Goldwater for President, chemical symbols on bk, 1966, MIB **50.00**
Kennedy Kards, Humor House, bl bks, 1953, M, sealed **28.00**
Oliver North's Pack of Lies, 52+2 liar Js, NM **30.00**
University of AL Crimson Tide, football bks, 1972, MIB, sealed ..**30.00**
Welcome Aboard Air Force Two, dbl deck, ea 52C & NMIB **55.00**

Older Narrow Decks

Celluloid Playing Cards, Whitehead & Hoag, 1920s, 52 no J, VG ..**65.00**
Columbia #133, Nat'l, ca 1900, whist sz, 52+J, VG+, EX box **28.00**
Eagle 5-Suit Bridge, 5th suit is gr eagles, eagle bks, 1938, NMIB ..**16.50**
Gem Squeezers #57, pinochle, angel bks, 1930s, MIB **20.00**
Gibson, Spanish-style Deco bks, 1930s, 52+J+2XC, EX+, rpl box ..**20.00**
Godey's Ladies' Cards, King Press, dbl, 1937, ea: 52 no J, EXIB **22.00**
Ivory Whist #93, USPC, red bks, 1908, 52 no J, EXIB **16.50**
Little Women, RKO movie photo bks, 52+J+SC, VG, G box **22.00**
Mareuerite #130, Harbor, Dougherty, 1919, bridge, MIB, sealed ..**55.00**
New Index, USPC, 1926, 52+J+2XC, VG-, G box **22.00**
Swan, Arrco, pinochle, gr & red bks w/swan, 1930, MIB, sealed ..**15.00**
Trophy Whist #39, 1930s tax stamp, 52+J+2XC, MIB **40.00**
3 Little Pigs, Disney Silly Symphony, 1939, 52+J+XC, VGIB **35.00**

Older Wide Decks

Am Beauty, Std PCC, Chicago, 1927, 52+J, VG, worn box **12.00**
Am Playing Card Co, bl pattern bk, ca 1910, 52+crown J, EX **55.00**
Am Steamboats #99, ca 1890, 52+steamboat J, NM, G box **240.00**
Amerikards, military cts, WWI era, 52+J+XC, EX-, broken box .**635.00**
Apollo #33, National, 4-leaf clover bks, 1895, 52 no J, EX+ **17.50**
Army & Navy #3032, USPC, 1915, 52 no J, EX **50.00**
Bicycle #48, pinochle, nautical bks, 1928, 48C, NMIB **20.00**
Bicycle #808, acorn on red bks, USPC, 52 no J, VG **22.00**
Bicycle #808, thistle on bl bks, USPC, 1914, 52 no J, NMIB **60.00**
Bold Bluff, dogs play poker bks, Brn/Bigelow, 1926, 52+J+2, NM ...**35.00**
Congress #606, Beacon light, 1917 tax stamp, M, sealed **40.00**
Congress #606, Good Night, 1899, 52+J, G **22.50**
Congress #606, Tambourine, 1903, 62+special J, EXIB **42.50**
Dougherty Triplicate, ca 1878, 52 no J, G **35.00**
Eclipse Transformation, FH Lowerre, 1876, 47/52 no J, EX **330.00**
Egyptian Fortune Telling..., Rost, 1898, 52+booklet, NM, G box ..**185.00**
Freedom, bl bks, patriotic cts, 1917, 52 no J, NM, taped box **395.00**
Hungarian #32, A Dougherty, seasons bks, 1910, 32C, EX, torn box ..**55.00**
Lenox #67, National, Oriental gold bks, 52C, EXIB **52.50**
Mascotte #69, fleur-de-lis bks, 1890-1905, 52 no J, VG **35.00**
Peerless Playing Cards, Standard PCC, 1924, 52+SC+XC+J, MIB .**110.00**
Revelation #357, fortunes on cards, 1919, 52+J+SC, EXIB **26.50**
Squared Faro #366, no indices, 1887, 52, G **135.00**
Standard, It Listens Good, lady w/phone bks, 1900, 52+J, EX **45.00**

Pinups and Magic

American Beauties, Elvgren pinups, MIB, sealed **95.00**

Astrological, astrological texts bks, 1933, 50+J+booklet, EXIB **35.00**
Deland's Automatic, SS Adams, 1940 stamp, 52+J, NMIB **28.00**
Deland's Automatic Dollar, mk bks, 1915 to 1940, NMIB **42.00**
Edward D'Anconda, nude behind umbrella bks, 1950s, NM **32.50**
Good Luck, nude color photo bks, Hong Kong, 1950s, 52+2J, NMIB ..**32.00**
Marilyn Monroe, nude photo bks, dbl, ea MIB, sealed **200.00**
Mysto The Magician's Deck, Hart, 51 of 52, EXIB **22.00**
Poker Girls #4151, German, nudes/seminude photo bks, 1970, NMIB ..**45.00**
Vargas, Comme Ci/Comme Ca, mask bks, dbl, 1953, NMIB **250.00**
Vargas Vanities, pinup bks, 52+2J, 1953, MIB **130.00**
Win Lose or Draw, MacPherson, dbl, Brn/Bigelow, EXIB **34.00**
53 Vargas Girls, 1953, 52+2J, NMIB **95.00**

Souvenir, Wide Scenic

Alaska, Puget Sound News Co, 1926, 52+J+XC, NMIB **110.00**
Burro, HH Tammen Curio Co, type A photo bks, 1904, 52+J, NM ...**300.00**
Canada Ocean to Ocean, Goodall, 1915, 52+J+2XC, EX+, G box ..**36.00**
Cleveland Chamber of Commerce, scenic bks, 1940s, 52+2J, MIB ...**15.00**
Cuba, USPC for Roberts & Co, 1915, 52+J+booklet, M, EX box ..**85.00**
East Africa, Nairobi, photo bks, 1957, 52+2J+XC+map, M, G box ...**22.00**
Hawaiian, Wall Nichols, type C photo bks, 1901, 52+J+XC, NMIB .**75.00**
Montreal & Quebec, Goodall, London, 1905, NM, torn box **35.00**
Mountain States, Gray News/USPC, 1914, 52+J, VG-, G box ...**125.00**
Nation's Capital, USPC, gold edge, 52+J+XC, NM, EX box **45.00**
Panama, USPC, 1926, MIB, sealed in wrapper w/booklet **50.00**
Rome, Fotometalgrafica, Bologna, photo bks, 1975, 52+2J+XC, NM ..**17.00**
Vermont, Chisholm Bros, 1915, 52+J+2XC, NMIB **55.00**
Yellowstone Park, geyser bks, gold edges, 1915, 52+J+SC, NMIB .**275.00**

Transportation

United States Lines, S.S. Leviathan, portrait backs, MIB, $17.50.

Along CM & St Paul, Inter-State News, 1912, 52+J, VG-, G box ..**25.00**
C&O Railroad, dbl deck, Chessie/Peake bks, 52+J, MIB **30.00**
C&O Railway, USPC, oval photos, 1900, 52+XC, NM, EX box ..**97.00**
Canadian Nat'l, narrow scenic souvenir, 1935, 52+J+SC, NMIB .**22.00**
Denver Chicago Trucking, dbl, wide, 1950s, ea: 52+2J, NMIB **38.00**
French Line, ocean liner photo bks w/red fr, MIB, sealed **35.00**
Great Northern, dbl, Pinto woman/Middle rider bks, 52+J+XC, EXIB ...**35.00**
Kansas City Southern, bl bks, 1953, MIB, sealed **65.00**
KLM Royal Dutch Airlines, dbl, 1950s, ea: 52+2J & NMIB **40.00**
Southern Pacific, Scenes of Golden West, 52+J+XC, VG, G box .**40.00**
Western Pacific, Van Noy-Inter-State, 1925, 52+J+booklet, NMIB .**57.00**
White Pass & Yukon Route, type A scenes, 1900, 52+J+XC, MIB .**145.00**

Political

The most valuable political items are those from any period which
relate to a political figure whose term was especially significant or marked

by an important event or one whose personality was particularly colorful. Posters, ribbons, badges, photographs, and pin-back buttons are but a few examples of the items popular with collectors of political memorabilia.

Political campaign pin-back buttons were first mass produced and widely distributed in 1896 for the president-to-be William McKinley and for the first of three unsuccessful attempts by William Jennings Bryan. Pin-back buttons have been used during each presidential campaign ever since and are collected by many people. The scarcest are those used in the presidential campaigns of John W. Davis in 1924 and James Cox in 1920.

Contributions for this category were made by Michael J. McQuillen, monthly columnist of *Political Parade*, which appears in *AntiqueWeek* newspapers; he is listed in the Directory under Indiana. Our advisor for this category is Paul J. Longo; he is listed under Massachusetts. See also Autographs; Broadsides; Historical Glass; Watch Fobs.

Pin-back buttons: Nixon in '60, black on white, EX, $45.00; Vote the Kennedy Ticket, red on white, EX+, $315.00; Youth for Kennedy, red, white, and blue, NM, $200.00.

Badge, Democrat Delegate, Truman 50.00
Badge, McKinley/Hobart jugate, portraits, gold wash on brass 75.00
Badge, newsreel operator's; Republican Convention, 1948, EX 50.00
Badge, Roosevelt/Garner portraits, brass, 1" 75.00
Badge, 1908 Republican Nat'l Convention, metal top, ribbon, NM ..85.00
Badge, 1944 IN Republican State Convention, plastic, NM 20.00
Book, McKinley Memorial Edition, 1901, 296-pg, G 25.00
Book, souvenir; Willkie, pictorial, EX 25.00
Bookmark, Willkie/McNary, aluminum, 1940, 6", EX 150.00
Button, Harrison/Reid jugate, celluloid, 1892, on ribbon, EX 100.00
Button, John F Kennedy, celluloid, easel bk, inaugural, 6", M 35.00
Cane, Ford or Carter name, wood w/metal elephant or donkey hdl, ea ..30.00
Coat button, Billy Possum from Taft campaign on brass, ⅞" 35.00
Coin, penny, McClellan campaign, 1864 ....45.00
Coin, Roosevelt/Garner portraits, Good Luck, 1¼" 20.00
Decanter, Robert Kennedy commemorative, colored glass, Wheaton, MIB .12.50
Handbill, Greet President Nixon, 1971, M 3.50
Handkerchief, Hoover 1932 campaign, 17x17", NM 100.00
Invitation, Bush/Quale Inaugural, gold eng, 1989, w/4 enclosures .20.00
Lantern, 4 Yrs More...McKinley/Roosevelt, tin, 8½", EX 500.00
License plate, Goldwater, eagle in corners, 1964, NM 25.00
License plate, Reagan, red/wht/bl, 1981, M 10.00
License plate, Reagan Inaugural, 1981, NM 25.00
Palm puzzle, Vote Republican Ticket 1908, Black man image, 2" dia ..200.00
Pendant, GOP Republican Nat'l Convention, Chicago, 1952 ....25.00
Pennant, Keep Coolidge, 1924, 20x11", EX 150.00
Pennant, Vote Dewey, Republican, gr felt, 1958, 13", VG 30.00
Pin-bk, Henderson for President 15.00
Pin-bk, Hoover, 100% for Hoover, 1932, ⅞", EX 25.00
Pin-bk, I Like Ike & Dick, 1956, ⅞", NM 5.00
Pin-bk, I'm for Nixon, flasher, M 10.00
Pin-bk, Ingalls, celluloid, EX 7.00
Pin-bk, McGovern/Eagleton, NM 5.00

Pin-bk, Roosevelt, Happy Birthday, portrait, 1936, 1¼", EX 40.00
Pin-bk, Tunno Congress, celluloid 3.00
Pin-bk, Vote McGovern, pictures dove, 1972, 1¼", EX 40.00
Pin-bk, Vote Peace Clark President 7.00
Pin-bk, Willkie, Wings for..., pictures plane, 1940, 1¼", EX 15.00
Plate, Cleveland/Thurman, sepia transfer, 8" 95.00
Plate, Dewey, mc transfer, cobalt rim, 8" 50.00
Plate, FD Roosevelt, sepia transfer, w/cobalt & gold, 11" 75.00
Plate, John Hay, sepia transfer, Ohio Society of NY, 1903, 8" 80.00
Plate, Lincoln, mc transfer, advertising, 8" 95.00
Plate, McKinley/Hobart jugate, sepia transfer, 8" 75.00
Plate, Mrs Gladstone, mc transfer, 9½" 45.00
Plate, President & Mamie Eisenhower, portraits, 12", NM 24.00
Postcard, Sure I'm for Roosevelt 20.00
Postcard, Taft/Serman portraits, The Nation's Choice, 1908, EX .20.00
Postcard, Teddy Roosevelt/White House, flasher, Deeks, 1904 ....40.00
Postcard, Wilson, Stand Behind Our President, 1916, mc, used, EX .12.00
Poster, Robert Kennedy, Kennedy for President, 1968, 12x16", NM .35.00
Poster, 1984 Democratic Convention, San Francisco 20.00
Print, Lincoln/Garfield, Our Martyred Presidents, Pites, 1881 ...150.00
Program, John F Kennedy Inaugural, 1961, NM 60.00
Program, Reagan/Bush Inaugural, bl emb cover, 1981, 11x8½", M .12.00
Ribbon, McKinley gubernatorial campaign, late 1800s, EX 100.00
Ribbon, Theodore Roosevelt campaign, 1904 ....110.00
Ribbon, Van Buren campaign, blk print on bl, 1840, 7", EX 500.00
Ribbon, Wm Jennings Bryan/Arthur Sewal jugate, 1896, EX 100.00
Sheet music, Funeral March, Garfield hearse scene cover 40.00
Sheet music, March to Eisenhower, photo cover, 1943, M 25.00
Spoon, Wm McKinley, sterling 25.00
Ticket, 1948 Republican Convention 10.00
Tip tray, Grand Old Party, Taft/Sherman, 1908, NM 175.00
Token, FDR/Chester Arthur, 50 Yrs of Progress, brass, 1¼" 25.00
Token, Stephen Douglas campaign, 1860 ....45.00

Pomona

Pomona glass was patented in 1885 by the New England Glass Works. Its characteristics are an etched background of crystal lead glass often decorated with simple designs painted with metallic stains of amber or blue. The etching was first achieved by hand cutting through an acid resist. This method, called first ground, resulted in an uneven feather-like frost effect. Later, to cut production costs, the hand-cut process was discontinued in favor of an acid bath which effected an even frosting. This method is called second ground. Our advisors for this category are Betty and Clarence Maier; they are listed in the Directory under Pennsylvania.

Bowl, Cornflower, 1st ground, amber stain, 3x4½" 280.00
Bowl, Cornflower, 2nd ground, bl stain, 2½x5½" 225.00
Butter dish, Acanthus Leaf, 1st ground, amber stain, 4½x6" ...1,250.00
Butter dish, Acanthus Leaf, 1st ground, gold stain, 4½x8" ...1,265.00
Celery vase, Acanthus Leaf, 1st ground, gold stain, 6x4½" 550.00
Champagne, 2nd ground, amber stain, 5" 245.00
Creamer & sugar bowl, 2nd ground, amber band at top 300.00
Finger bowl, Cornflower, 2nd ground, amber & bl stain, 2½x5½" .155.00
Mug, Acanthus Leaf, 1st ground, EX stain 120.00
Pitcher, Butterfly & Wheat, 1st ground, bl & amber stain, 12" .1,650.00
Pitcher, lemonade; Riverlet, 2nd ground, EX 185.00
Punch cup, Cornflower, 1st ground, EX color & stain 150.00
Punch cup, Cornflower, 2nd ground, bl stain, appl hdl 145.00
Punch cup, Invt T'print (faint), 1st ground, amber stain 45.00
Toothpick holder, 1st ground, amber stain, tricorner top, 2" 350.00
Tumbler, Cornflower, 2nd ground, amber & bl stain, 3¾" 145.00

Tumbler, Cornflower, 2nd ground, bl stain, 4" 95.00
Tumbler, Dmn Quilt/Cornflower, 2nd ground, bl stain, 4" 950.00
Tumbler, lemonade; Cornflower, 1st ground, amber & bl stain ..365.00
Vase, fan; Invt T'print, 2nd ground, w/stain, 3x6" 150.00

Porcelier

The Porcelier Company, originally from East Liverpool, Ohio, started business in the late 1920s and moved to Greensburg, Pennsylvania, in the early 1930s. The company flourished until the late 1940s and finally closed its doors due to labor disputes in 1954.

They produced an endless line of vitrified porcelain products including furniture coasters, electric appliances, dripolators, and light fixtures. These products were sold in many stores under a variety of names and carried over ten different types of marks and labels.

The prices below are for items in excellent condition. To learn more about this subject, we recommend *Collector's Guide to Porcelier China* by Susan F. Grindberg (Collector Books). If you have any questions or information regarding Porcelier, please contact our advisor, Jim Barker; he is listed in the Directory under Pennsylvania. (Queries require SASE.)

Lavender Bluebell coffee set with platinum trim, three-piece, $165.00.

Photo courtesy
Jim Barker

Canister, flour, sugar or utility; Country Life, ea 35.00
Coasters, set of 4 ....45.00
Coffee urn, Field Flowers, w/creamer & sugar bowl 135.00
Coffeepot, Serv-All Line, #576-D, platinum 65.00
Creamer & sugar bowl, Scalloped Wild Flowers, w/lid 35.00
Double boiler, Rope Bow, w/pot, 8-cup 50.00
Double boiler, Sprig, 6-cup 45.00
Light fixture, dbl ceiling 30.00
Light fixture, triple ceiling 45.00
Light fixture, wall sconce 25.00
Percolator, Silhouette, electric set 125.00
Percolator, Starflower, #120, electric 85.00
Percolator set, Antique Rose 90.00
Pitcher, Beehive Crisscross, ball jug form 70.00
Pitcher, water; Flowers 65.00
Sandwich grill, Basketweave Wild Flowers, from $225 to 275.00
Teapot, American Beauty Rose, 6-cup 45.00
Teapot, Country Life, 6-cup 50.00
Teapot, Flamingo, 6-cup 55.00
Teapot, Leaf & Shadow, 4-cup 45.00
Teapot, Orange Chevron 40.00
Teapot, Oriental Deco, 8-cup 65.00
Teapot, Rooster, 6-cup 55.00
Teapot, Rope Bow, 8-cup 55.00
Urn, Barock-Colonial, #2007, electrical, gold trim 125.00

Postcards

Postcard collecting has overtaken stamp collecting, and there are more collectors in the world seeking out postcards than any other single item. What kind of cards do people collect? A majority collect views of the towns they live in or where their families came from and places they have been. The rest collect subject cards which can include Santa Claus, Art Nouveau, those signed by artists, and cards depicting animals, fire, trains, and ships — the list is inexhaustible. Whatever your interest, it will probably be found on postcards. Values can range from virtually nothing to thousands of dollars. The average older card (modern cards not included) is valued from $2.00 to $4.00 for views, while subject cards with real photos are slightly higher. The golden age of postcards was from 1900 to 1920. Note that cards with tiny images and florals may be old but have almost no value. Our advisor for this category is Pamela E. Apkarian-Russell; she is listed in the Directory under New Hampshire. **Do not** expect a dealer to price cards from a list or written description, as this is not possible. For a dealer list, send an SASE to the International Federation of Postcards Dealers, P.O. Box 1765, Manassas, VA 20108; or Jeff Bradfield, 90 Main St., Dayton, VA 22821, (540)-879-9961.

Key:
p/ — publisher   s/ — signed

Alabama state capital 4.00
Alligator border, Jacksonville scene 25.00
Anti-Axis, Hitler's face in toilet bowl 15.00
Armenial National Anthem 1918, raised gold letters 12.00
Boardwalk, Atlantic City NJ 2.00
Chrome, robin 50
Comic, Bonzo dressed as caveman 16.00
Dental reminder, Peanuts & the gang 2.00
Fantasy, Midsummer Dreams, illus Thomas Maybank, Tuck 25.00
Fantasy, 2 dogs in boxing ring, Dutch 20.00
Hawaii, beautiful colored fish 8.00
Holiday, Christmas, child gives Santa letter, Clapsaddle 10.00
Holiday, Christmas, Santa reading street sign 14.00
Holiday, Easter, elves & giant Easter egg, Fr 6.00
Holiday, New Year's, girl throws snowball, Schmucker, Winch 25.00
Holland America Line DD Nieuw-Amsterdam 9.00
Linen, Anderson's Pea Soup Restaurant 5.00
Linen, Black child on toilet, comic 4.00
Linen, Miami Parrot Jungle 5.00
Man-O'-War & jockey 8.00
Pennsylvania mine interior 4.00
Photo, Amtrack, int view of dining car 6.00
Photo, Ceylon, view of elephants 8.00
Photo, Daytona Beach, 2 cars racing 35.00
Photo, Josephine Baker in banana costume 200.00
Photo, miner in mine, tinted 14.00
Photo, Shirley Temple in bl-tinted dress 22.00
Photo, Stonehenge, close-up view 8.00
Photo, 2 people playing table tennis 20.00
Real photo, Baden Powell & Boy Scouts 15.00
Real photo, Colorado mine 10.00
Real photo, girl by Christmas tree w/teddy, tinted 15.00
Real photo, nude, Fr mk 24.00
Saint Patrick's Day, man dressed in gr w/pig 5.00
Scenic, Alaska, view of totem pole 5.00
Scenic, lighthouse in Portland ME 4.00
Scenic, town view, lobster border 20.00
Scenic, town view, shell border 10.00

Tsar Nicholas of Russia	20.00
Turkey, nicely emb	2.00
View, Chicago IL, downtown	2.00
Wedding, bride & groom #6949, emb, mk PFB	10.00
Whitney Publishing, full-length Santa	10.00
Winch Schmucker, beautiful girl on sea horse	100.00
3-D, butterflies	8.00
3-D, roses	4.00

Posters

Advertising posters by such French artists as Cheret and Toulouse-Lautrec were used as early as the mid-1800s. Color lithography spurred their popularity. Circus posters by the Strobridge Lithograph Co. are considered to be the finest in their field, though Gibson and Co. Litho, Erie Litho, and Enquirer Job Printing Co. printed fine examples as well. Posters by noted artists such as Mucha, Parrish, and Hohlwein bring high prices. Other considerations are good color, interesting subject matter and, of course, condition. The WWII posters listed below are among the more expensive examples; 80% of those on the market bring less than $50.00. See also Movie Memorabilia; Political; Rock 'N Roll.

Advertising

Cognac Briande, lady in grape costume holds bottles, Gaston Stephane, 20th century, 63x47", EX, $2,645.00.

Alba Cigarettes, Black man in yel turban, 47x31", EX	150.00
Am Airlines Over the World, eagle over globe, 39¼x29½", NM-	500.00
Ford, The Universal Car, 4 people grab at car, 63x47", 1910, NM-	1,840.00
Indiana Luxe, Chief on pack w/burning cigar, 50¼x35½", NM	1,610.00
Lily Starch, babies/fairies/gnomes/flowers, 28x12", VG	1,400.00
Olida, salami & utensils, Serven, Paris, 61½x46", NM	450.00

Circus

AG Barnes, Bert Nelson's lion taming act, 27x41", EX	200.00
Clyde Beatty-Cole Bros, Greatest...on Earth, mc, 21x28"	65.00
Clyde Beatty-Cole Bros, lady on elephant, mc, 28x20"	85.00
Clyde Beatty-Cole Bros, lady w/dogs & horses, 28x20"	85.00
Clyde Beatty-Cole Bros, Largest Circus, tiger, 21x28"	110.00
Clyde Beatty-Cole Bros, leaping tiger, 1920s, 21x28", EX	140.00
Cole Bros, mc lettering, 16x29"	120.00
Cole Bros, Ms Jean Allen...Horsewoman, 27x41", EX	200.00
RB B&B, chimps pay elephant nuts for admission, 28x41"	150.00
RB B&B, leaping tiger & lion, 46x27½", EX	150.00
Russell Bros, tigers in the wild, mc, 28x20"	50.00
Russell Bros, 3-ring, dogs doing tricks, mc on wht, 28x20"	55.00
Russell Bros, 3-ring, horses performing, 38x20"	50.00
Wilson Show, clowns/lions/jugglers/etc, 30x40", EX	80.00

Literary

Je Sais Tout/Noel, figure w/globe head, Paris, 55x39", NM	1,100.00
La Reforme/L-Orgueil d'une Mere, couple, 1896, 44x32", NM	925.00
London Handbook, lady w/umbrella, 1897, 29¾x19½", EX	400.00
NY Sunday World Roosevelt's Romance, 1900, 17x22", EX	230.00
What Is That...Lark My Child, mother/child, 1895, 21x15", NM	380.00

Magic

Carter Beats the Devil, magician plays devil in poker, 22x14", NM-	405.00
Carter the Great Coming Soon..., bl/red/wht, Calcutta, 35x30", EX	250.00
Houdini, ca 1925, 72x96", M	8,500.00
Magician by lady in cage, Nat'l Printing Co, 27½x20½"	250.00

Sports

Come to Britain for Golf, autumn golf scene, 29½x19½", EX+	1,500.00
Fun & Snow in Germany, man skiing, 39¾x24¾", EX+	635.00
Grand Prix Monaco, bl/gray car w/skid marks, 1982, 18x27", NM	325.00
Heavyweight Champions, Sullivan through Braddock, VG	75.00
Is He Out-Or Safe?, baseball scene, 28x22", EX+	1,380.00
Jack Johnson, Champion of World, driving car, 1909	600.00
Joe Louis & Jack Sharkey, ea pictured beside name, 22x14", EX	750.00

Theatrical

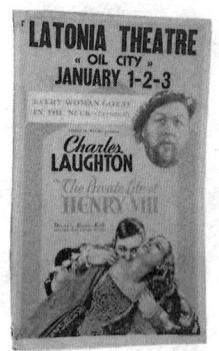

The Private Life of Henry VII, Charles Laughton, Latonia Theatre, color litho, 22x14", VG, $275.00.

Bobino/Josephine, photo in sequins/feathers, 1975, 46x31", M	430.00
Deadline for Murder, Paul Kelly & Kent Taylor, 22x28", VG+	75.00
Gianduja Re DJ Aviator, man on plane, mc, 55x39", EX	430.00
Salle des Capucines, draped butterfly catcher, Willette, 36x25"	350.00
Salon Des Cent, man & woman, mc, Paris, 1897, 22x18", EX	250.00
Sport of Kings/Savoy Theatre, man in stretcher, 30x20", EX	250.00
Theatre Des Nouveautees/Yvette Guilbert, Paris, 46x31", NM	650.00

Travel

Africa by Clipper, leopard head w/African scenes, 42x28", NM	290.00
Agay, beach/water/hills, Lucien Serre, Paris, 1928, 41x30", NM	2,500.00
Air France, winged porter w/cargo cart, 39¾x28", NM	490.00
Australia, lg kangaroo, tan on mc, Mayo, 1954, 40x25", NM	485.00
Fly TWA, plane in sky, 40x25", NM-	500.00
SS United States, ocean liner crossing sea, 30x20", NM-	490.00
Texas, wht monument & bl skies, 24x18", NM	575.00
Vichy Ses Sources, lady golfer, Broders/Paris, '28, 39x24", NM	3,000.00

War

Pre-WWI, US Marine recruiting, 2 Marines, Leyendeck, 36x26", G	250.00
WWI, Armed Marine stands before flag, 40x28", EX+	575.00

WWI, I Want You, Uncle Sam pointing finger, 40x30", NM- .1,800.00
WWI, I Want You for the Navy, gal in uniform, 41x27", EX 430.00
WWI, Is Liberty Worth 25¢...? Uncle Sam w/war stamps, 42x28", NM ..690.00
WWI, Join Air Service, soldiers/plane above, 37x25", EX+ 1,955.00
WWI, Join the Navy, sailor rides torpedo, Babcock, 39x28", EX .700.00
WWI, Put Strength in Final Blow, fight scene, Brangwyn, 60x40", EX ..750.00
WWII, Assurance for Young Men of the Navy, 32x24" 100.00
WWII, Liberty Lives On, ship w/Miss Liberty, 40x26½", NM ...500.00
WWII, US Marines Want You!, full color, 28x18", EX 175.00
WWII, Xmas Overseas..., Santa w/helmet, Graves, 21x17" 20.00
WWII, Your Duty Buy...Bonds, Liberty/immigrants, 20x30", NM .145.00

Pot Lids

Pot lids were pottery covers for containers that were used for hair dressing, potted meats, etc. The most common were decorated with colorful transfer prints under the glaze in a variety of themes, animal and scenic. The first and probably the largest company to manufacture these lids was F. & R. Pratt of Fenton, Staffordshire, established in the early 1800s. The name or initials of Jesse Austin, their designer, may sometimes be found on exceptional designs. Although few pot lids were made after the 1880s, the firm continued into the 20th century.

American pot lids are very rare. Most have been dug up by collectors searching through sites of early gold rush mining towns in California. Minor rim chips are expected and normally do not detract from listed values. When no condition is given, assume that the value is based on an example in such condition.

American

Amadine for Cure & Prevention of Chapped..., blk transfer, 3", EX ..100.00
Areca Nut Tooth Paste...London & NY, blk transfer, 3¼", EX ..210.00
Chlorine Detergent...WE Haga..., brn transfer, 2⅞", EX 350.00
Dr Harvey's Pomade, lizard, blk on wht, chip, 3" 600.00
Holloway's Ointment, brn transfer, 3⅛" 50.00
Jules Hauel..., river scene, blk transfer, 4⅛", EX 900.00
Jules Hauel...Ambrosial Cream, purple transfer, 3½", EX 350.00
Prepared by EH Sargent...Gums, blk transfer, 3⅜", w/base 525.00
Queen, God Bless Her; Jules Hauel Perfumers, mc, rpr, 4¾" 400.00
Taylor's Saponaceous Compound, lav transfer, 4", EX 450.00
Williams Swiss Violet Shaving Cream..., mc transfer, 3¾", EX ..200.00
7 Highest...Worlds Fair 1851, blk transfer, HP & WC Taylor, 4¼" .120.00

English

The Village Wedding, multicolored, Pratt, ca 1857 – 62, 4⅛", $150.00.

Albert Memorial, mc, 4", EX 90.00
Am Indians Hunting Buffalo, mc, Pratt, 4½", EX 260.00
Bear Pit, bldg w/dome roof, World's Fair 1851 ....250.00
Bears on Rock Cliff, mc, Pratt, 3½", EX 110.00
Charing Cross, mc, 4", EX 90.00

Cherry Tooth Paste...John Gosnell, blk transfer, 1¼" 140.00
Children fishing, mc, Pratt, w/base, 4", EX 85.00
Edward Cook's Hygenic..., blk transfer, w/base, 1¾x2⅜"..............90.00
Enthusiast, man fishing, Pratt, mc, fr, 4⅛", EX 110.00
Fish Barrow, mc, fancy emb border, 5" 130.00
Grand Internat'l Bldg 1851 Exhibition..., mc, rare, 5", EX 300.00
Injury, mc transfer, Pratt, dtd 1873 ....190.00
Landing the Catch, mc, 4", EX 70.00
Lobster Sauce, lobster/cat/fish, mc, 4½", EX 135.00
Napoleon III & Empress Eugenia, Pratt, mc, wood fr, 4¾" 260.00
New Saint Thomas's Hospital, Pratt, mc, fr, 4¼", EX 160.00
Room in Which Shakespeare Was Born..., mc, flakes, w/base, 5⅛"...70.00
Room in Which Shakespeare Was Born..., mc, 4", EX 65.00
Royal Harbour Ramsgate, 4", EX 70.00
Shirtlift...Tooth Paste..., blk transfer, rectangular, 3¾" 150.00
Shrimpers, fisherman & children, mc transfer, Pratt, 4⅛" 85.00
St Paul's Cathedral, mc, 4", EX 90.00
Tam O'Shanter & Souter Johnny, mc, rare, 4", EX 150.00
Uncle Toby, man leaning to kiss lady, mc, 4⅛" 110.00
Victor Emmanuel & Garibaldi, mc transfer, Pratt, 4¼", NM 175.00
White Clove Tooth Paste..., floral, blk transfer, 2⅝", EX 150.00
Woods Areca Nut Tooth Paste, blk transfer, 1860-80, 2⅝" 30.00

Powder Horns and Shot Flasks

Though powder horns had already been in use for hundreds of years, collectors usually focus on those made after the expansion of the United States westward in the very early 1800s. While some are basic and very simple, others were scrimshawed and highly polished. Especially nice carvings can quickly escalate the value of a horn that has survived intact to as high as $400.00. Those with detailed maps, historical scenes, etc., bring even higher prices.

Metal flasks were introduced in the 1830s; by the middle of the century they were produced in quantity and at prices low enough that they became a viable alternative to the powder horn. Today's collector regards the smaller flasks as the more desirable and valuable, and those made for specific companies bring premium prices.

Flask, brass, emb eagle/stars/hands/shield, pear shape, 9" 80.00
Flask, brass, G&JW Hawksley Sheffield, emb decor, 8½", EX 90.00
Flask, brass, hunter by gate w/dogs, 8½", EX 80.00
Flask, copper, Am Flask & Cap, emb Indian on horse, 9", EX 225.00
Flask, copper, Hawksley, emb game, 8¼", EX 215.00
Flask, copper w/brass spout, Pease, dtd, 1856, EX 265.00
Flask, Dixon & Sons, hunt scene medallion, 7", EX 100.00
Flask, leather, emb decor, cork stopper, mk 1-lb, 6¼", G 20.00
Flask, tin w/brass cap, flat cylinder, cone top, 1860s, 4½" 50.00
Horn, cvd eagle & shield, inscribed, crack, 8" 150.00
Horn, cvd faceted spout, cvd plug, brass tacks, 17", EX 155.00
Horn, cvd sailing scenes, silver mts, 8", EX 445.00
Horn, eng coat of arm crests & flowers, fat plug, 7" 465.00
Horn, glass, emb game scene, wire hanger, old stopper, 7", EX 50.00
Horn, trn wooden butt, cvd wooden stopper, 1860s, 11x2⅝" 450.00
Horn, trn wooden butt w/iron loop, cvd plug, 11⅜" 165.00
Horn, 2-tier pouring end, wood w/6-pointed star, 17" 200.00

Pratt

Prattware has become a generic reference for a type of relief-molded earthenware with polychrome decoration. Scenic motifs with figures were popular; sometimes captions were added. Jugs are most common; but teapots, tableware, even figurines were made. The term 'Pratt' refers to Wm. Pratt of Lane Delph, who is credited with making the first examples of this type, though similar wares were made later by other Staffordshire potters. Pot lids and other transfer wares marked Pratt were made in Fenton, Staffordshire, by F. & R. Pratt & Co. See also Pot Lids.

Figurine, cat w/farmer, Yorkshire-type palette, 1810s, 6" **1,700.00**
Figurine, Farmer's Wife, mc enamels, 1790s, 4¼", VG **110.00**
Figurine, man holds bottle, sq base, 5½", EX **325.00**
Figurine, Spring, allegorical, mc enamels, 1800s, 7", VG **250.00**
Figurine, women weeping at funerary urn, mc enamels, 9", EX ..**185.00**
Pipe, puzzle; red & bl stripes/dots, 1790s, rpr, 9½" **1,550.00**
Pitcher, children in heart reserves, 5" **375.00**
Plate, brn floral transfer w/mc HP details, scalloped, 8¼" **140.00**
Plate, genre transfer w/mc, emb mc floral/swag border, 7", EX **80.00**
Plate, Now I Have a Sheep & Cow..., pk transfer w/mc, 5½" **80.00**
Sauce boat, fish form orange & gr, ca 1790, 6", EX **375.00**

Precious Moments

Known as 'America's Hummels,' Precious Moments are a line of well-known collectibles created by Samuel J. Butcher and produced by Enesco, Inc. These pieces have endeared themselves to many because of the inspirational messages they portray. Over 300,000 club members have joined the national club in eighteen years.

The collection is twenty years old as of 1998. Each piece is produced with a different mark each year. This mark, not the date, is usually the link to the value of the piece. Most mold changes result in increased values, and when a piece is retired or suspended, its price increases as well. As an example, 'God Loveth a Cheerful Giver' retailed for $9.50 in 1980; it was retired in 1981 and has a secondary market price now of $850.00 to $950.00. The majority of the collection has increased in value from its original retail.

Rosie Wells Enterprises, Inc., our advisor for this category, is in her sixteenth year of publishing *Precious Collectibles,* a Precious Moments collector magazine, as well as a secondary market price guide. She has hosted International Conventions for Precious Moments collectors since 1983. Her address is in the Directory under Clubs, Newsletters, and Catalogs. Items listed below are assumed to be in mint condition with the original box.

Friends Never Drift Apart, #100250, Dove mark, $85.00; Vessel mark, $60.00.

Baby's First Picture, E-2841, retired 1986, Cross mk **185.00**
Baby's First Picture, E-2841, retired 1986, Flower mk **160.00**
Baby's First Trip, #16012, suspended 1989, Dove mk **300.00**

Baby's First Trip, #16012, suspended 1989, Flower mk **265.00**
But Love Goes On..., E-0001, 1991 Club pc, no mk, from $175 to ..**185.00**
But Love Goes On..., E-0001, 1991 Club pc, Triangle mk, $150 to .**165.00**
Come Let Us Adore Him, E-2011, retired 1981, no mk, from $250 to ...**275.00**
I Get a Kick Out of You, E-2827, retired 1986, Olive Branch mk ..**170.00**
I Get a Kick Out of You, E-2827, retired 1986, Fish mk **200.00**
I'm Nuts Over My Collection, BC902, 1990 B'day Club, Dove mk ..**160.00**
I'm Nuts Over My Collection, BC902, 1990 B'day Club, Olive Branch mk ..**135.00**
Love Makes World Go..., #139475, 1985...Exclusive, Ship mk, $450 to ..**500.00**
Make a Joyful Noise, #530322, 9" Easter seals, 1989, Bow/Arrow mk **925.00**
Make a Joyful Noise, goose girl, E-1374G, Cedar Tree mk **35.00**
Make a Joyful Noise, goose girl, E-1374G, no mk **130.00**
Nobody's Perfect, smiling dunce, E-2968, retired 1990, Hourglass mk .**550.00**
Reindeer, ornament, #102466, dtd 1986, missing mk **195.00**
Reindeer, ornament, #102466, dtd 1986, Olive Branch mk **165.00**
Sam Butcher, sign for Sugar Town, #52967, 1992, G-Clef mk, $110 to .**125.00**
Thank You for Coming to My Ade, E-5202, suspended 1984, Cross mk ...**110.00**
Thank You for Coming to My Ade, E-5202, suspended 1984, no mk ...**155.00**
Voice of Spring, #12068, limited to 1985, Cross mk, $250 to **295.00**
Voice of Spring, #12068, limited to 1985, Dove mk **275.00**
Winter's Song, #12092, limited to 1986, Dove mk **130.00**
Winter's Song, #12092, limited to 1986, Flower mk **175.00**

Pre-Columbian Artifacts

The term 'pre-Columbian' loosely refers to some time prior to 1492, when Columbus arrived in America. In particular, it indicates pre-1492 artifacts of Central and South America, some of which can be dated as early as 4000 B.C. Artifacts representing the cultures of the Incan, Mayan, and Aztec Indians are avidly sought by the collector. These may be made of precious metals, hardstones, or pottery. Some were used in rituals and religious rites; some such as bowls and other utensils, though strictly utilitarian, nevertheless convey through form and decoration the craftsmanship of these early tribes.

Bell, copper, Aztec, 1½" **20.00**
Bowl, Colima, blkware, age crack, 7" **140.00**
Carving, stone, human face, 6x4" **80.00**
Carving, stone, human head, 9x5" **150.00**
Ear spool, Mayan, EX **75.00**
Mortar, cvd stone, radiating design, 6x6" **110.00**
Ocarina, terra cotta, bird shape, 1st-5th C AD, EX **125.00**
Pitcher, monkey idol, Chancay, 7" **550.00**
Plate, Colima, eng motif, early AD, 7½" **90.00**
Water bottle, human figure w/EX features, Chancay, Peru, 8" **550.00**

Primitives

Like the mouse that ate the grindstone, so has collectible interest in primitives increased, a little bit at a time, until demand is taking bites instead of nibbles into their availability. Although the term 'primitives' once referred to those survival essentials contrived by our American settlers, it has recently been expanded to include objects needed or desired by succeeding generations — items representing the cabin-'n-cornpatch existence as well as examples of life on larger farms and in towns. Through popular usage, it also respectfully covers what are actually 'country collectibles.'

From the 1600s into the latter 1800s, factories employed carvers, blacksmiths, and other artisans whose handwork contributed to turning out quality items. When buying, 'touchmarks,' a company's name and/or location and maker's or owner's initials, are exciting discoveries. Primitives are uniquely individual. Following identical forms, results more often than not show typically personal ideas. Using this as a guide (combined with circumstances of age, condition, desire to own, etc.) should lead to a reasonably accurate evaluation. For items not listed, consult comparable examples. Authority Kathryn McNerney has compiled several lovely books on primitives and related topics: *Primitives, Our American Heritage; Collectible Blue and White Stoneware;* and *Antique Tools, Our American Heritage.* You will find her address in the Directory under Florida. See also Butter Molds and Stamps; Boxes; Copper; Farm Collectibles; Fireplace Implements; Kitchen Collectibles; Molds; Tinware; Weaving; Woodenware; and Wrought Iron.

Bed warmer, brass, chased decor, trn wood hdl, 43½", EX 150.00
Bed warmer, brass, tooled floral lid, trn wood hdl, rfn, 48" 225.00
Bed warmer, brass w/eng lid, old grpt on trn wood hdl, 41" 260.00
Bed warmer, copper w/tooled star on lid, trn hdl, 43", VG 220.00
Bellows, orig brn w/mc floral stencil, old leather, 17", EX 220.00
Broom, gathered fiber brush, 34" cvd hdl, 48" overall, EX 125.00

Candle mold, wooden frame with eighteen pewter tubes, bootjack ends, original finish, Pennsylvania, light damage, $900.00.

Photo courtesy Aston Macek Auctioneers & Appraisers

Candle mold, pewter, 6-tube, removable threaded tips, 17" 825.00
Candle mold, pewter, 12-tube, dvtl pine fr, rprs, 18x18x5" 600.00
Candle mold, pewter, 21-tube, poplar/pine fr, 13x17x7" 1,500.00
Candle mold, redware, 24-tube, pine fr, 8x24x14", EX 990.00
Candle mold, tin, 1-tube, scrolled braces, sq top pan, 21¼" 225.00
Candle mold, tin, 4 oversz tubes, soldered rpr, 30½" 150.00
Candle mold, tin, 4-tube, ear hdl, lt rust, 5¼" 300.00
Candle mold, tin, 8-tube, ear hdl, curved ft, 11" 260.00
Candle mold, tin, 12-tube, curved base w/conforming ft, 12" 200.00
Candle mold, tin, 12-tube, gallery, strap hdl, 11x11x5" 225.00
Candle mold, tin, 18-tube, dbl-ear hdls, 10½", VG 220.00
Candle mold, tin, 20-tube, pine fr, rust, 12x26x5" 425.00
Candle mold, tin, 24-tube, dbl-ear hdls, 9¾" 300.00
Candle mold, tin, 26-tube, 12x21"+ring hdls 300.00
Candle mold, tin, 48-tube, ear hdl, curved ft, 10½x15" 465.00
Cheese sieve, woven splint, 26" dia 360.00
Churn, wooden Windsor style, drum-type crank, 27" 200.00
Coal tongs, wrought iron, spring mechanism, 14" L 60.00
Cookie board, CI, cornucopia, 3⅞x5¼" 80.00
Cookie board, pine, EX patina, age crack, 16x31" 100.00
Curd separator, wood bench shape w/sm wooden pegs & crank, VG .75.00
Dough box, dvtl poplar, trn legs, 1-brd top, 24x16x39" 245.00
Dough box, dvtl poplar, worn red, 2-brd top, 29x48x26" 1,425.00
Dough box, poplar w/red pnt interior, trn legs, 1-brd top, 39" 330.00
Dough box, walnut, trn legs, rpl top, old dk finish, 31x16x41" ...425.00
Dough scraper, brass & iron blade, Peter Derr, dtd 1854, 3⅛x4" ..470.00
Dough scraper, wrought iron, bell-shaped blade, 4¾x4½" 110.00
Flintlock tinder lighter, brass w/rosewood pistol grip, 5½" 745.00
Foot warmer, punched tin & wood, trn posts at corners 385.00
Foot warmer, punched tin w/circle designs, mortised wood fr, 8" ..150.00
Foot warmer, punched tin w/in wooden fr, old blk rpt, 9" 360.00

Foot warmer, punched tin w/in wooden fr, w/pan, 7x16x11" 275.00
Hourglass, blown glass in pine & oak fr, EX 275.00
Kraut cutter, walnut, sliding hopper, long hdl, 15½x9¾" 75.00
Kraut cutter, walnut w/worn patina, heart cutout, 10" 220.00
Kraut cutter, wood, cut-out heart at top, wrought blade, 18x7" ...150.00
Ladder, herb drying; wood, gr pnt w/red stripe, 28x4" 120.00
Rack, drying; 2-section, folding, old rpt, ea section: 30x46" 125.00
Rug beater, wire evergreen tree form w/trn block hdl, 37" 75.00
Salt box, dvtl pine, drw, hinged lid, rfn/rstr, 10¾" L 300.00
Sock stretchers, wood w/molded edge, child sz, 16x3", pr 30.00
Sugar nippers, wrought iron, simple tooling, 9½" 160.00
Sugar nippers, wrought iron, triangular blades, hinged, 9" 125.00
Tub, staved construction w/cut-out hearts in hdls, rpt, 9¼" 500.00
Washboard, yelware insert w/brn sponging on wood fr, 24x13" ..500.00

Prints

The term 'print' may be defined today as almost any image printed on paper by any available method. Examples of collectible old 'prints' are Norman Rockwell magazine covers and Maxfield Parrish posters and calendars. 'Original print' refers to one achieved through the efforts of the artist or under his direct supervision. A 'reproduction' is a print produced by an accomplished print maker who reproduces another artist's print or original work. Thorough study is required on the part of the collector to recognize and appreciate the many variable factors to be considered in evaluating a print. Prices vary from one area of the country to another and are dependent upon new findings regarding the scarcity or abundance of prints as such information may arise. Although each collector of old prints may have their own varying criteria by which to judge condition, for those who deal only rarely in this area or newer collectors, a few guidelines may prove helpful. Staining, though unquestionably detrimental, is nearly always present in some degree and should be weighed against the rarity of the print. Professional cleaning should improve its appearance and at the same time help preserve it. Avoid tears that affect the image; minor margin tears are another matter, especially if the print is a rare one. Moderate 'foxing' (brown spots caused by mold or the fermentation of the rag content of old paper) and light stains from the old frames are not serious unless present in excess. Margin trimming was a common practice; but look for at least ½" to 1½" margins, depending on print size.

When no condition is indicated, the items listed below are assumed to be in very good to excellent condition. See also Nutting, Wallace; Parrish, Maxfield.

Audubon, John J.

Audubon is the best known of American and European wildlife artists. His first series of prints, 'Birds of America,' was produced by Robert Havell of London. They were printed on Whitman watermarked paper bearing dates of 1826 to 1838. The Octavo Edition of the same series was printed in seven editions, the first by J.T. Bowen under Audubon's direction. There were seven volumes of text and prints, each 10" x 7", the first five bearing the J.J. Audubon and J.B. Chevalier mark, the last two, J.J. Audubon. They were produced from 1840 through 1844. The second and other editions were printed up to 1871. The Bien Edition prints were full size, made under the direction of Audubon's sons in the late 1850s. Due to the onset of the Civil War, only 105 plates were finished. These are considered to be the most valuable of the reprints of the 'Birds of America Series.'

In 1971 the complete set was reprinted by Johnson Reprint Corp. of New York and Theaturm Orbis Terrarum of Amsterdam. Examples of the latter bear the watermark G. Schut and Zonen. In 1985 a second reprint was done by Abbeville Press for the National Audubon Society.

Although Audubon is best known for his portrayal of birds, one of his less-familiar series, 'Vivaparous Quadrupeds of North America,' portrayed various species of animals. Assembled in corroboration with John Bachman from 1839 until 1851, these prints are 28" x 22" in size. Several octavo editions were published in the 1850s. In the following listing, all measurements are actual print size unless stated otherwise.

Am Magpie, #357, Havell, 1837, 38¾x26" **6,500.00**
Antelope Americana Prong-Horned Antelope, #77, Bowen, 21x27" .**3,500.00**
Belted Kingfisher, #77, Havell, 34x25", EX **8,500.00**
Black-Winged Hawk, Bien, 32½x23" **1,500.00**
Burgonmaster Gull, #396, Havell, 26x28½" **3,500.00**
Canis Lupus Red Texas Wolf, #82, Bowen, 1845, 19x25¾" **4,000.00**
Canis Lupus White American Wolf-Male, #72, Bowen, 1845, 21x27" .**3,000.00**
Cardinal, #203, Bowen, 1st edition, 39x26" **900.00**
Common American Skunk, Female/Young, #42, Bowen, 1844, 27x21¼" ..**4,000.00**
Gannet, #326, Havell, 39x26" **12,000.00**
Great American Hen & Young, #6, 26¾x39¾" sheet **30,000.00**

Lepis Artemesia - Worm Wood Hare, hand colored, Imperial Folio Edition, J.T. Bowen, 1845, plate LXXXVIII, NO. 18, 20¼x26", $2,800.00.

Lincoln's Finch, #277, Bien, 18x25" **500.00**
Maryland Marmot, lg folio, 22x27" **1,500.00**
Musk Ox, Males; #111, Bowen, 1847, 21⅝x27⅛" **2,000.00**
Osprey, #381, Amsterdam edition, 39x26" **2,500.00**
Red-Breasted Sandpiper, #315, Havell, 1836, 12¼x19½" **3,000.00**
Swamp Hare, #37, Bowen, 1850s, 7x10" **150.00**
White Ibis, #222, Havell, 1833, 26x28" **18,000.00**
White-Crowned Pigeon, #280, Bien, ca 1858-60, 39x26" **3,500.00**
Whooping Crane, #227, Amsterdam, 37x25" **1,500.00**

Currier and Ives

Nathaniel Currier was in business by himself until the late 1850s when he formed a partnership with James Merrit Ives. Currier is given credit for being the first to use the medium to portray newsworthy subjects, and the Currier and Ives views of 19th-century American culture are familiar to us all. In the following listings, 'C' numbers correspond with a standard reference book by Conningham. Values are given for prints in very good condition; all are colored unless indicated black and white. Unless noted 'NC' (Nathaniel Currier), all prints are published by Currier and Ives. Our advisors for this category are John and Barbara Rudisill (Rudisill's Alt Print Haus); they are listed in the Directory under Maryland.

Abigail, NC, 1846, C-9, sm folio **85.00**
Alnwick Castle, Scotland; undtd, C-87, med folio **125.00**
Am Farm Scenes/No 3, NC, 1853, C-133, lg folio **3,600.00**
Am Fireman, Always Ready; 1858, C-152, med folio **1,300.00**
Am Fireman, Facing Enemy; 1858, C-153, med folio **1,300.00**
Am Fireman, Prompt to Rescue; 1858, C-154, med folio **1,300.00**
Am Prize Fruit, 1862, C-183, lg folio **1,800.00**

Autumn on Lake George, undated, C-324, small folio, $250.00

Bear Hunting, Close Quarters (summer); undtd, C-447, sm folio **750.00**
Beautiful Blonde, undtd, C-452, med folio **90.00**
Beautiful Brunette, undtd, C-453, sm folio **75.00**
Belle of New York, undtd, C-490, sm folio **75.00**
Benjamin Franklin, Statesman...; NC, 1847, C-499, sm folio **500.00**
Black-Eyed Beauty, undtd, C-549, sm folio **65.00**
Black-Eyed Susan, NC, 1848, C-551, sm folio **300.00**
Bombardment & Capture of Fort Henry TN, undtd, C-590, sm folio ...**400.00**
Bombardment of Fort Pulaski...April, 1862; C-595, sm folio **300.00**
Brook Trout Fishing, 1872, C-704, sm folio **900.00**
Burning of Chicago, 1871, C-738, sm folio **450.00**
Burning of Steamship Austria, Sept 13, undtd, C-748, sm folio .**275.00**
Camping Out, Some of Right Sort; NC, 1856, C-777, lg folio .**3,500.00**
Central Park NY, The Bridge; undtd, C-950, sm folio **300.00**
Chicago in Flames, Scene at Randolph...; undtd, C-1027, sm folio ...**600.00**
Children in the Woods, undtd, C-1033, sm folio **150.00**
City of New York, NC, 1855, C-1102, lg folio **3,000.00**
Clipper Ship in a Hurricane, undtd, C-1155, sm folio **650.00**
Clipper Ship in a Snow Squall, undtd, C-1157, sm folio **900.00**
Cork Castle & Black Rock Castle, undtd, C-1253, sm folio **90.00**
Cottage Dooryard, Evening; NC, 1855, C-1265, med folio **250.00**
Cozzen's Dock, West Point; undtd, C-1277, med folio **800.00**
Day Before Marriage, NC, 1847, C-1459, sm folio **100.00**
Destruction of Rebel Monster Merrimac, undtd, C-1572, sm folio ..**500.00**
Distanced, 1878, C-1589, sm folio **225.00**
Dreadful Wreck...Hempstead Beach, NC, undtd, C-1624, sm folio ..**2,500.00**
Dude Belle, 1883, C-1634, sm folio **230.00**
Dutchman & Hiram Woodruff, 1871, C-1640, sm folio **700.00**
Enchanted Isle, 1869, C-1740, sm folio **90.00**
Express Train, 1870, C-1792, sm folio **2,000.00**
Fall of Richmond...April 2..., 1865, C-1822, sm folio **275.00**
First Ride, NC, 1849, C-1987, sm folio **130.00**
Flower Vase, NC, 1848, C-2047, sm folio **135.00**
Fording the River, NC, undtd, C-2081, med folio **550.00**
Fruits of Temperance, 1870, C-2195, sm folio **200.00**
General Shields at the Battle..., 1862, C-2294, sm folio **195.00**
Girl in Love, 1870, C-2376, sm folio **75.00**
Got the Drop on Him, 1881, C-2455, sm folio **250.00**
Grand Pacer Richball, 1890, C-2519, sm folio **300.00**
Great Conflagration at Pittsburgh, NC, undtd, C-2581, sm folio ..**650.00**
Great Fire at Boston, 1872, C-2614, sm folio **350.00**
Great Fire at St John NB, June 20th, 1877; C-2616, sm folio **400.00**
Group of Lilies, undtd, C-2670, sm folio **130.00**
Harbour for the Night, undtd, C-2724, sm folio **300.00**
Henry Clay of Kentucky, NC, undtd, C-2791, sm folio **120.00**
Home of the Deer, undtd, C-2867, med folio **500.00**
Homeward Bound, NC, C-2885, 1845, sm folio **750.00**
Hudson From West Point, 1862, C-2972, med folio **1,050.00**
Impending Crisis, Caught in the Act; 1860, C-3033, med folio .**240.00**
Imported Messenger, 1880, C-3042, sm folio **300.00**
Italian Landscape, undtd, C-3139, sm folio **75.00**
King of the Forest, undtd, C-3333, sm folio **200.00**

Leaders, 1888, C-3471, lg folio **1,000.00**
Life in the Woods, Returning; 1860, C-3513, lg folio **3,500.00**
Life of a Fireman, Ruins; NC, 1854, C-3520, lg folio **2,500.00**
Life of a Hunter, Catching a Tartar; 1861, C-3521, lg folio **5,000.00**
Lincoln Family, 1867, C-3546, sm folio **80.00**
Little Mary & Lamb, 1877, C-3670, sm folio **150.00**
Little Students, undtd, C-3720, sm folio **150.00**
Maggie, undtd, C-3864, sm folio **95.00**
May Queen, NC, undtd, C-4089, sm folio **90.00**
Mink Trapping, Prime; 1862, C-4139, lg folio **10,000.00**
Moonlight the Castle, undtd, C-4183, sm folio **100.00**
Mother's Pet, NC, undtd, C-4237, sm folio **100.00**
Mountain Rumble, undtd, C-4244, sm folio **175.00**
Mrs Lucretia R Garfield, undtd, C-4263, med folio **95.00**
My Little White Kitties Playing Dominoes, undtd, C-4336, sm folio .**150.00**
My Pet Bird, undtd, C-4348, med folio **175.00**
My Three White Kitties, ...Their ABC's; undtd, C-4357, sm folio ..**150.00**
New Suspension Bridge, Niagara Falls; undtd, C-4432, sm folio .**300.00**
Niagara Falls, From Goat Island; undtd, C-4457, med folio **350.00**
Nosegay, 1870, C-4512, sm folio **125.00**
Old Mill in Summer, undtd, C-4571, sm folio **300.00**
Old Oaken Bucket, 1872, C-4577, sm folio **225.00**
On the Coast of California, undtd, C-4598, sm folio **350.00**
On the Owago, undtd, C-4608, sm folio **200.00**
Parson's Colt, 1879, C-4706, sm folio **225.00**
Peaceful River, undtd, C-4736, sm folio **175.00**
Pigeon Shooting, Playing the Decoy; 1862, C-4780, lg folio ...**3,000.00**
Pride of the West, 1870, C-4918, sm folio **75.00**
Prince & Princess of Wales, undtd, C-4926, sm folio **90.00**
Quails, NC, undtd, C-4992, sm folio **350.00**
Rabbits in Woods, undtd, C-5036, sm folio **250.00**
Residence of Lord Byron, Diodati, Italy; undtd, C-5118, sm folio .**90.00**
Roadside Mill, 1870, C-5175 , sm folio **350.00**
Rocky Mountains, undtd, C-5195, sm folio **900.00**
Royal Mail Steamship Persia, NC, 1856, C-5240, lg folio **1,100.00**
See-Saw, undtd, C-5457, med folio **350.00**
Shooting on the Prairie, undtd, C-5498, sm folio **650.00**
Siege & Capture of Vicksburg MS..., undtd, C-5507, sm folio **250.00**
Silver Cascade, White Mountains; undtd, C-5521, sm folio **275.00**
Snipe Shooting, NC, 1852, C-5577, lg folio **3,000.00**
Soldier's Home, 1862, C-5599, sm folio **125.00**
Spring, NC, 1849, C-5671, sm folio **225.00**
Stripped Bass, 1872, C-5844, sm folio **350.00**
Summer Evening, undtd, C-5853, sm folio **175.00**
Summer Ramble, undtd, C-5874, med folio **350.00**
Surrender of General Lee..., 1865, C-5909, sm folio **250.00**
Tomb of Kosciusko, West Point; undtd, C-6103, sm folio **125.00**
Tomb of Washington, Mt Vernon VA; undtd, C-6110, med folio .**175.00**
Tomb of Washington, Mt Vernon VA; undtd, C-6112, sm folio .**125.00**
Trolling for Bluefish, 1866, C-6158, lg folio **10,000.00**
US Frigate Independence, 64 Guns; NC, 1841, C-6307, sm folio ..**465.00**
Vase of Flowers, undtd, C-6363, sm folio **125.00**
Velocipede, 1869, C-6365, sm folio **1,400.00**
View of Astoria, LI; 1862, C-6388, med folio **1,250.00**
View of the Hudson..., 1846, C-6421, sm folio **300.00**
View on Roundout, undtd, C-6451, med folio **600.00**
Village Blacksmith, 1864, C-6462, lg folio **3,000.00**
Virginia Water Windsor Park, undtd, C-6475, sm folio **150.00**
Washington as a Mason, undtd, C-6512, sm folio **150.00**
Washington at Princeton, NC, 1846, C-6518, sm folio **400.00**
Washington Family, undtd, C-6531, sm folio **90.00**
Washington's...at Trenton NJ, NC, 1845, C-6555, sm folio **150.00**
Water Rail Shooting, NC, 1855, C-6567, sm folio **800.00**
West Point Foundry,...Hudson River, NY; 1862, C-6617, med folio .**1,500.00**

Why Don't He Come?..., undtd, C-6653, sm folio **125.00**
Wild Duck Shooting, Good Day's Sport; NC, 1854, C-6670, lg folio .**6,000.00**
Woodcock Shooting, 1870, C-6775, sm folio **550.00**
Woodlands in Summer, undtd, C-6778, sm folio **250.00**
Wreck of the Atlantic, 1873, C-6787, sm folio **290.00**
Yacht Vesta..., undtd, C-6817, sm folio **400.00**
Zachary Taylor, Nation's..., NC, 1847, C-6874, sm folio **150.00**

Fox, R. Atkinson

A Canadian who worked as an artist in the 1880s, R. Atkinson Fox moved to New York about ten years later, where his original oils were widely sold at auction and through exhibitions. Today he is best known, however, for his prints, published by as many as twenty printmakers. More than thirty examples of his work appeared on Brown and Bigelow calendars, and it was used in many other forms of advertising as well. Though he was an accomplished artist able to interpret any subject well, he is today best known for his landscapes. Fox died in 1935. Our advisor for Fox prints is Pat Gibson whose address is listed in the Directory under California.

A Peaceful Summer Day, #223, 9½x7" **80.00**
As the Sun Goes Down, #403, 11x14" **150.00**
By a Winding Stream, #404, 5x7" **100.00**
Forest Ranger, #355, 9x7" **150.00**
Friends, #464, 20x16" **275.00**
Geyser, #382, 11x8" **185.00**
His Last Cartridge, #289, 10x8" **125.00**
Jealousy, unfr, #291, 8½x11½" **145.00**
Nature's Retreat, #97, 24½x16½" **165.00**
Nature's Treasure, #91, 14x22" **125.00**
Poppies, #45, 16x20" **100.00**
Poppies, #45, 18x30" **275.00**
Ready for Anything, #208, 7x9" **200.00**
Shorthorns, #580, 5½x10½" **155.00**
Silver Grandeur, GW Turner, 7x9" **50.00**
Spirit of Youth, #4, 9x15" **75.00**
Thoroughbred, #539, 10x6" **175.00**

Gutmann, Bessie Pease

Delicately tinted prints of appealing children sometimes accompanied by their pets, sometimes asleep, often captured at some childhood activity are typical of the work of Gutmann; she painted lovely ladies as well and was a successful illustrator of children's books. Her career spanned the earlier decades of this century. Our advisor for this category is Earl MacSorley; he is listed in the Directory under Connecticut.

Awakening, #664 ....**75.00**
Butterflies & Daisies, 7½x9½" in oval tin fr **115.00**
Chuckles, #216 ....**60.00**
Daddy's Coming, #644 ....**300.00**
Dreamland's Border, #692 ....**125.00**
Feeling, #118, 1909 ....**125.00**
Good Morning, #801 ....**100.00**
Happy Dreams, #800 ....**125.00**
Harmony, #802 ....**300.00**
His Majesty, #793 ....**185.00**
Homebuilders, #655 ....**150.00**
In Port of Dreams, #214 ....**75.00**
Little Boy Blue, #206 ....**125.00**
Mighty Like a Rose, #642 ....**150.00**
Mine, #798 ....**175.00**
Miss Flirt, #217 ....**60.00**

My Honey, #756 ....700.00
Popularity, #825 ....75.00
Rosebud, #780 ....150.00
Smelling, #18, 1909 ....125.00
Symphony, #702 ....395.00
Winged Aureole, #700 ....350.00

Icart, Louis

Louis Icart (1888 – 1950) was a Parisian artist best known for his boudoir etchings in the '20s and '30s. In the '80s prices soared, primarily due to Japanese buying. The market began to readjust in 1990, and most etchings now sell at retail between $1,400.00 and $2,500.00. Value is determined by popularity and condition, more than by rarity. Original frames and matting are not important, as most collectors want the etchings restored to their original condition and protected with acid-free mats. Beware of the following repro and knock-off items: 1. Pseudo engravings on white plastic with the Icart 'signature.' 2. Any bronzes with the Icart signature. 3. Most watercolors, especially if they look similar in subject matter to a popular etching. 4. Lithographs where the dot-matrix printing is visible under magnification. Some even have phony embossed seals or rubber stamp markings. Our advisor is William Holland, author of *Louis Icart: The Complete Etchings*, and *The Collectible Maxfield Parrish*; he is listed in the Directory under Pennsylvania.

Basket of Apples, 1924, 17¾x13", EX 1,800.00
Bird Bath, 1924, 12½x17¾", EX 980.00
Bubbles, 1930, 17⅜x13⅛"+orig fr 4,600.00
Cinderella, 1927, 15½x19¼", VG 1,800.00
Coursing II, 1929, 16x25⅞", VG 3,900.00
Coursing III, 1930, 16x25⅞"+fr, EX 4,400.00
Don Juan, 1928, 21¼x14⅛", EX 1,150.00
Fair Dancer, 1939, 19⅝x23"+fr, EX 2,000.00
Hydrangeas, 1929, 16⅞x21", EX 2,070.00
Japanese Garden, 1925, 15x18⅛", VG 1,200.00
Joan of Arc, 1929, 21½x15⅛", EX 1,500.00
Lilies, 1934, 38¼x19½", VG 3,800.00
Louise, 1927, 21x14", EX 1,800.00
Madame Butterfly, 1927, 21⅛x14¼", G 1,200.00
Manon, 1927, 20¾x13⅞", EX 1,400.00
My Model, 1933, 21½x16½" 2,860.00
Orchids, 1937, 28⅜x19⅜"+fr, EX 4,800.00
Pals, 1923, 16¾x21¼", VG 3,500.00
Puppies, 1925, 17x22⅛", EX 1,950.00
Sea Gulls, 1926, 21⅛x16¾", EX 1,700.00
Sleeping Beauty, 1927, 15½x19¼", VG 1,800.00
Smoke, 1926, 15x20¼"+orig fr, G 1,400.00
Speed, 1927, 15¼x25½", EX 4,000.00
Speed II, 1933, 15¾x25¼", VG 4,000.00
Spilled Oranges, 1921, 15¾x11¾", VG 1,250.00
Sulking, 1930, 12x17¼", EX 1,600.00
Swallows, 1926, 19⅜x11¾", VG 1,150.00
Tabac Blond, 1940, 19½x8⅜"+fr, EX+ 7,500.00
Waltz Echos, 1938, 19⅜x19½"+fr, EX 4,025.00
Wishing Well, 1925, 17⅝x11⅞", VG 865.00
Wistfulness, 17½x22½" 1,600.00
Youth, 1930, 24½x16"+fr, EX 4,800.00

McKenney and Hall

Louis Kurz founded the Chicago Lithograph Company in 1833. Among his most notable works were a series of thirty-six Civil War scenes and one hundred illustrations of Chicago architecture. His company was destroyed in the Great Fire of 1871, and in 1880 Kurz formed a partnership with Alexander Allison, an engraver. Until both retired in 1903, they produced hundreds of lithographs in color as well as black and white.

Wa-Em-Boesh-Kaa (a Chippewa Chief), hand colored, folio edition, 1836, 18x13", $525.00.

A-Na-Cam-E-Gish-Ca, a Chippewa Chief; 1838, 19½x13¾" 250.00
Chippewa Mother & Child, 1843, sm folio 255.00
Hunting the Buffalo, EC Biddle, 1836, 13¾x19½", G 715.00
Lap Pa Win Soe, a Delaware Chief; 1937, lg folio 200.00
Meta Koosega, a Chippewa Warrior; EC Biddle, 1836, 19½x13¾" ..250.00
Oche-Finceco, Rice & Clark, Phila, 1845, 19½x13¾" 300.00
Ong-Pa-Ton-Ga, Big Elk; EC Biddle, Phila, 1836, 19½x13¾" ...250.00
Pashepaha/Stabber, Sauk & Fox Chief; 1838, lg folio 220.00
Sum-Ma-Nu, a Flat Head Boy; Bowen, 1838, 19½x13¾" 250.00
Waapashaw, a Sioux Chief, Biddle, 1836, lg folio 225.00

Mucha, Alphonse

Mucha became famous for his beautiful Art Nouveau lithographs featuring Sarah Bernhardt and Job cigarette papers, which he issued in the 1890s. Born in Prague in 1860, he studied there as well as in Paris and for a time taught at the New York School of Applied Design for women before returning to Prague.

Daybreak, 1899, 42x15" 6,950.00
Job, brunette w/lit cigarette, 12x9¾" 1,500.00
Laurel, 1901, 15⅜x15¼"+fr, VG 2,300.00
Lefevre-Util, 7¼x7"+fr, EX 635.00
Lorenzaccio, Sarah Bernhardt, 14x5½" 875.00
Repos de la Nuit, 1899, 40⅛x14⅜"+fr, EX 6,325.00
Salome, 1897, 15x11¾" 1,400.00
Tetes Byzantines - Blonde, 1897, 13½x11⅛"+fr 4,000.00

Yard Longs

Values for yard-long prints are given for examples in **near mint** condition, full length, nicely framed, and with the original glass. To learn more about this popular area of collector interest, we recommend *Those Wonderful Yard-Long Prints and More*, *More Wonderful Yard-Long Prints*, Book 2, and *Yard-Long Prints*, Book 3, by our advisors Bill and June Keagy, and Charles and Joan Rhoden. They are listed in the Directory under Indiana and Illinois respectively. A word of caution: watch for reproductions; **know your dealer.**

Am Girl, 1914 Pabst advertising on bk 350.00
Assorted Fruit, Jos Hoover & Son, c 1897 ....200.00
Beauty Among the Roses, Bowles Live Stock Commission Co, 1912 ..400.00
Bridal Favors, Mary E Hart 200.00
Carnations, Grace Barton Allen 200.00
Four Kittens Climbing a Tree, Helena Maguire 275.00
Happy Family, 9 monkeys playing, #1037 by Jos Hoover & Son ..350.00

In Grandmother's Garden, Charles C Curran, 1909	350.00
Kaber orig painting, Diamond Crystal Salt Co, 1913	400.00
Our Feathered Pets, Paul deLongpre	300.00
Pompeian, by Jorbes, sgn Sincerely Mary Pickford, 1916	350.00
Pompeian Bride, sgn Rolf Armstrong, 1927	350.00
Pompeian Liberty Girl by Forbes, 1919	300.00
Selz Good Shoes, lady in bl w/walking stick, 1925	350.00
Spring Is Here, Cambril, c 1907	250.00
Stockman Bride, Nat'l Stockman & Farmer Magazine, 1912	450.00
Study of Chrysanthemums, Paul deLongpre, c 1900	250.00
Tug of War, kittens & puppies	250.00
Yard of Chrysanthemums, Mard Stumm	200.00
Yard of Kittens, CL Vredenburgh	250.00
Yard of Mixed Flowers, Guy Bedford	200.00
Yard of Pansies, V Janus	200.00

Purinton

Founded in 1936 in Wellsville, Ohio, Purinton Pottery relocated in 1941 in Shippenville, Pennsylvania, and began producing hand-painted wares that are today attracting the interest of collectors of 'country-type' dinnerware. Using bold brush strokes of vivid color, simple yet attractive patterns such as Apple, Fruit, Tea Rose, and Pennsylvania Dutch were manufactured in tableware sets and accessory pieces. For more information we recommend *Purinton Pottery* by Susan Morris; she is listed in the Directory under Oregon. Our advisor for this category is Pat Dole; she is listed in the Directory under Alabama.

Ashtray, Apple, center hdl, 2-lobe, 5½"	40.00
Baker, Maywood, 7"	15.00
Baker, Pennsylvania Dutch, 7"	45.00
Basket planter, Blue Pansy, 6¼"	65.00
Basket planter, Mountain Rose, 6¼"	50.00
Basket planter, Palm Tree, 6¼"	100.00
Bowl, cereal; Intaglio, 5¼"	10.00
Bowl, cereal; Normandy Plaid, 5¼"	10.00
Bowl, cereal; Pennsylvania Dutch, 5¼"	20.00
Bowl, dessert; Apple, 4"	8.00
Bowl, dessert; Heather Plaid, 4"	8.00
Bowl, divided vegetable; Apple, 10½" L	35.00
Bowl, divided vegetable; Heather Plaid, 10½" L	30.00
Bowl, fruit; Apple, scalloped border, 12"	40.00
Bowl, fruit; Maywood, 12"	30.00
Bowl, fruit; Normandy Plaid, 12"	20.00
Bowl, fruit; Petals, 12"	50.00
Bowl, fruit; Saraband, 12"	30.00
Bowl, salad; Plaid	45.00
Bowl, spaghetti; Normandy Plaid, 14½" L	55.00
Bowl, vegetable; Heather Plaid, 8½"	20.00
Bowl, vegetable; Intaglio, 8½"	20.00
Bowl, vegetable; Normandy Plaid	18.00
Bowl, vegetable; Tea Rose, 8½"	40.00
Candle holder, Saraband, 2x6"	40.00
Candy dish, Apple, 6¼"	50.00
Canister, Apple, half-oval, 5½"	65.00
Canister, Apple, sq, 7½"	50.00
Canister, Daisy, red trim, 9"	60.00
Canister, Fruit, oval, cobalt trim, 9"	65.00
Canister, Pennsylvania Dutch, sq, 7½"	100.00
Canister set, Fruit, revolves	100.00
Chop plate, Fruit	20.00
Coffee server, Seaform, 9"	125.00
Coffeepot, Chartreuse, 8-cup, 8"	75.00

Coffeepot, Fruit, 8-cup, 8"	50.00
Coffeepot, Ivy, red, 8"	50.00

Cookie jar, Apple, $60.00.

Cookie jar, Fruit, oval, red trim, 9"	60.00
Cookie jar, Heather Plaid, oval, 9½"	60.00
Cookie jar, Pennsylvania Dutch, slant top, wooden lid, 7x7"	125.00
Cookie jar, Petals, 9"	85.00
Cookie jar, Saraband, oval, 9½"	50.00
Covered dish, Mountain Rose, 9" L	75.00
Covered dish, Normandy Plaid, 9" L	55.00
Covered dish, Provincial Fruit, hdls, 9" L	65.00
Covered dish, Saraband, 9" L	35.00
Creamer & sugar bowl, Fruit, mini, 2"	20.00
Creamer & sugar bowl, Intaglio, w/lid, 3½", 5"	25.00
Creamer & sugar bowl, Ivy, w/lid	25.00
Cruets, vinegar/oil; Apple, sq, 5", pr	50.00
Cup & saucer, Apple, set	18.00
Cup & saucer, Maywood, 2½", 5½"	15.00
Cup & saucer, Pennsylvania Dutch, 2½", 5½"	28.00
Cup & saucer, Petals, 2½", 5½"	22.00
Cup & saucer, Provincial Fruit, 2½", 5½"	20.00
Decanter, Intaglio, mini, 5"	35.00
Gravy pitcher, Intaglio, 3¾"	65.00
Grease jar, Fruit, labeled Fats, cobalt trim, 5½"	60.00
Grease jar, Normandy Plaid, 5½"	50.00
Jar, marmalade; Apple, 4½"	50.00
Jar, marmalade; Palm Tree, 4½"	125.00
Jardiniere, Windflower, 5"	30.00
Jug, Dutch; Apple, 5-pt	60.00
Jug, Dutch; Fruit, 2-pt, 5¾"	25.00
Jug, Dutch; Ivy-Red Blossom, 2-pt, 5¾"	45.00
Jug, Dutch; Mountain Rose, 2-pt, 5¾"	85.00
Jug, Dutch; Palm Tree, 2-pt, 5¾"	150.00
Jug, honey; Pennsylvania Dutch, 6¼"	85.00
Jug, honey; Shooting Stars, w/cork	35.00
Jug, Kent; Ivy-Yellow Blossom, 1-pt, 4½"	25.00
Jug, Kent; Maywood, 1-pt, 4½"	25.00
Jug, Kent; Normandy Plaid, 1-pt, 4½"	20.00
Jug, oasis; Fruit, 9½x9½", minimum value	500.00
Mug, Heather Plaid, 8-oz, 4"	25.00
Mug, juice; Fruit, 6-oz, 2½"	15.00
Mug, juice; Intaglio, 6-oz, 2½"	15.00
Mug, juice; Maywood, 6-oz, 2½"	20.00
Pickle dish, Pineapple, sponged edge, 6"	35.00
Pitcher, beverage; Apple, 2-pt, 6¼"	65.00
Pitcher, beverage; Normandy Plaid, 2-pt, 6¼"	55.00
Pitcher, Starflower, 6½"	65.00
Planter, Ming Tree, 5"	40.00
Planter, rum jug; Apple, 6½"	55.00

Plate, breakfast; Crescent Flower, 8½" 35.00
Plate, breakfast; Intaglio, 8½" 10.00
Plate, chop; Apple, scalloped border, 12" 40.00
Plate, chop; Ming Tree, 12" 50.00
Plate, chop; Mountain Rose, 12" 50.00
Plate, dinner; Apple, 9¾" 15.00
Plate, dinner; Maywood, 9¾" 15.00
Plate, dinner; Normandy Plaid 10.00
Plate, dinner; Pennsylvania Dutch, 9¾" 25.00
Plate, dinner; Petals, 9¾" 20.00
Plate, salad; Apple, 6¾" 20.00
Plate, salad; Heather Plaid, 6¾" 10.00
Plate, salad; Saraband, 6¾" 4.00
Plate, tea & toast; Apple, molded cup compartment, 8½" 15.00
Plate, tea & toast; Intaglio, indent for cup, 8½" 15.00
Platter, grill; Apple, 12" 45.00
Platter, grill; Maywood, 12" 35.00
Platter, meat; Intaglio, 12" 30.00
Platter, meat; Provincial Fruit, 11" 40.00
Platter, meat; Tea Rose, 12" 50.00
Relish, Fruit, 3-compartment, center ring hdl, 10" dia 25.00
Relish, Intaglio, 3-compartment, center ring hdl, 10" dia 40.00
Relish, Mountain Rose, 3-compartment, center ring hdl, 10" 75.00
Shakers, Apple, range sz, pr 25.00
Shakers, Apple, stacking, 2¼", pr 35.00
Shakers, Chartreuse, jug-style, mini, 2½", pr 30.00
Shakers, Crescent Flower, rnd, 2¾", pr 65.00
Shakers, Fruit, range style, red trim, 4", pr 25.00
Shakers, Heather Plaid, pour 'n shake, 4¼", pr 60.00
Shakers, Provincial Fruit, stacking, 2¼", pr 25.00
Shakers, Saraband, mini, 2½", pr 20.00
Shakers, Seaform, 3", pr 55.00
Teapot, Apple, 2-cup, 5" 40.00
Teapot, Cherries, 2-cup, 4" 30.00
Teapot, Fruit, w/drip filter, 6-cup, 9" 75.00
Teapot, Fruit, 2-cup, 4" 30.00
Teapot, Intaglio, 6-cup, 6½" 65.00
Teapot, Ivy-Red Blossom, w/drip filter, 6-cup, 9" 75.00
Teapot, Ivy-Red Blossom, 2-cup, 4" 35.00
Teapot, Petals, 2-cup, 4" 45.00
Teapot, Saraband, 6-cup, 6½" 40.00
Tray, roll; Intaglio, 11" L 35.00
Tray, roll; Normandy Plaid 15.00
Tumbler, Apple, 12-oz, 5" 20.00
Tumbler, juice; Apple, 6-oz 20.00
Tumbler, Normandy Plaid, 12-oz, 5" 20.00
Tumbler, Pennsylvania Dutch, 12-oz, 5" 35.00
Vase, cornucopia; Ivy-Red Blossom, 6" 25.00
Vase, Crescent Flower, hdls, 7½" 125.00
Vase, Maywood, pillow form, 6¾" 25.00
Wall pocket, Chartreuse, 3½" 35.00
Wall pocket, Heather Plaid, 3½" 35.00

Purses

Beaded purses and bags represent an area of collecting interest that is very popular today. Purses from the early 1800s are often decorated with small, brightly colored glass beads. Cut steel beads were popular in the 1840s and remained stylish until about 1930. Mesh purses are also popular. In the 1820s mesh was woven. Chain-link mesh came into usage in the 1890s, followed by the enamel mesh bags carried by the flappers in the 1920s. Purses are divided into several categories by (a) construction techniques — whether beaded, embroidered, or a type of needlework; (b)

material — fabric or metal; and (c) design and style. Condition is very important. Watch for dry, brittle leather or fragile material. For those interested in learning more, we recommend *Antique Purses, A History, Identification, and Value Guide, Second Edition*, by Richard Holiner; *More Beautiful Purses*, and *Combs and Purses*, both by Evelyn Haertigi of Carmel, California. An interesting related book is *Vintage Contemporary Purse Accssories* by Roselyn Gerson. Our advisor for this category is Veronica Trainer; she is listed in the Directory under Ohio.

Key: W&D — Whiting & Davis

Beaded, amber, dbl beaded fringe, lg, EX 175.00
Beaded, blk & wht stripes & checks, beaded strap hd, 9x9" 120.00
Beaded, castle, emb sterling fr, Fr, 1880s, 12x7"+fringe 498.00
Beaded, cobalt iridized, metal clasp, 1920s, 6½x5½", EX 95.00
Beaded, cut steel, orange/brn/silver, Fr, 1880s, 4x3" 130.00
Beaded, El Sah style, roses, pk on ivory, W&D fr, 3x7½" 90.00
Beaded, floral, mc on brn metallic, gilt mts, 6x8" +fringe 140.00
Beaded, flower basket on ivory, drawstring, 6½x8" 75.00
Beaded, geometric pattern, SP emb fr, 10½x8¾" 135.00
Beaded, gilt metal w/paste 'jewels,' 6x9" +fringe 100.00
Beaded, lovers in garden scene, jeweled fr, 11x8" 250.00

Beaded, peacock perched among latticework and flower urn, ornate frame, fringed, $425.00.

Beaded, peacock & flowers, mc on blk, SP fr, fringe, 10x7" 100.00
Beaded, roses & bird on blk, metal fr, chain, fringe, 12x8" 240.00
Beaded, roses tapestry, SP emb floral fr, chain, fringe, 14x8" 475.00
Beaded, steel, vegetable-shaped design, mc, sm 160.00
Leather, alligator, 5-pocket classic style, 12x8¼" 50.00
Leather, brn reptile, clutch style, 1940s, 6x10", EX 35.00
Leather, suede w/needlework portrait scene, clutch type 80.00
Leather (gold) box, rhinestone-covered lid, Arnold Scacci, 5x3½" ..60.00
Mesh, blk & pk geometrics, W&D flat fr, fringe, 7x4" 85.00
Mesh, butterfly & flowers on wht, Mandalian, metal fr, 7x4½" ..150.00
Mesh, enameled peacock, Mandalian, SP fr, fringe, 7½x3½" 250.00
Mesh, German silver, emb flat fr, dangles, 7x6½" 100.00
Mesh, gold, clutch style, W&D fr, sm 40.00
Mesh, gold & copper, W&D fr w/chain, 4¾x8¾" 115.00
Mesh, gold & silver geometrics, W&D gold fr w/wht enamel, 6x3½" .85.00
Mesh, landscape scenic, W&D fr w/enameling, chain, 7x4½" ...115.00
Mesh, Nouveau floral, 3-color, gilt fr, Mandalian, 9x4" 170.00
Mesh, silver, SP fr, w/sm compact attached to chain, 5x8" 175.00
Mesh, sterling, emb fr, mesh hdl, fringe, Germany, 8½x3" 185.00
Mesh, sterling, ornate W&D fr, sm dangles, 6x4" 340.00
Plastic, Lucite w/woven brass base, resembles basket 38.00
Plastic, snakeskin-look, Roban by Feiner, NY-Miami, 3½x9" 140.00
Vanity, silver mesh, emb lid, W&D fr, w/chain, 8x5¼" 350.00
Velvet, blk clutch w/gilt beadwork, swag hdl 48.00
Velvet, blk w/ornate brocade design, chain hdl, India, 7x4" 38.00

Puzzles

'Jigsaw' puzzles have been around almost as long as games. The first examples were handcrafted from wood, and they are extremely difficult to find. Most of the early examples featured moral subjects just as the board games did. By the 1890s jigsaw puzzles had become a major form of home entertainment. During the Depression years jigsaw puzzles were set up on card tables in almost every home. The early wood examples are the most valuable.

Cube puzzles, or blocks, were often made by the same companies as the board games. Again, early examples display the finest quality lithography. While all subjects are collectible, some (such as Santa blocks) often command prices higher than games from the same period. Our advisor for this category is Norm Vigue; he is listed in the Directory under Massachusetts.

Personalities, Movies, and TV Shows

Alice in Wonderland, jigsaw, in book-form box 10.00
Alien, jigsaw, HG Toys, 1979, MOC 15.00
Batman, fr-tray, Whitman, 1978, EX 3.00
Black Hole, jigsaw, Whitman/WDP, 1979, 500-pc, MIB (sealed) ..12.00
Buck Rogers, fr-tray, Milton Bradley, 1952, M w/cover sheet 100.00
Bullwinkle & Rocky, fr-tray, Jaymar, 1960s, 10x13", NM 28.00
Charmin' Chatty, fr-tray, 1963, EX 22.50
Cleveland Browns, jigsaw, M 20.00
Davy Crockett, Walt Disney, fr-tray, ca 1955, EX 28.00
Dick Tracy, jigsaw, Bank Holdup, Jaymar, 1950s-50s, NMIB 65.00
Eddie Cantor, jigsaw, 1933, NM 55.00
ET, fr-tray, 1982, M, sealed 12.50
Farrah Fawcett, jigsaw, 1977 .... 35.00
Felix the Cat, fr-tray, Built-Rite, 1949, 9x12", EX 35.00
Fess Parker/Davy Crockett, fr-tray, NM 20.00
Flash Gordon, fr-tray, early image, Milton Bradley, 1951, EX 60.00
Flintstones, fr-tray, Man Called Flintstone, Whitman, 1966, NM .30.00
Gregory Peck, Duel in the Sun, jigsaw, MIB 48.00
Jetsons, fr-tray, Whitman, 1962, EX 32.00
Little Lulu, fr-tray, Whitman, 1959, 11x14", EX 25.00
Little Orphan Annie, Light Up the Candles, jigsaw, EX 65.00
Little Orphan Annie & Sandy, jigsaw, 1935, EX 35.00
Maggie & Jiggs, Bringing Up..., Saalfield, '30s, set of 4, MIB 95.00

Mother Goose Comic Picture Puzzles, Parker Bros., 1950s set of four, MIB, $45.00.

Mr Magoo, fr-tray, Jaymar, 1967, 10x13", EX 18.00
Our Gang, 2-sided jigsaw, Metro Goldwyn Mayer, 1920s, NMIB .175.00
Popeye, fr-tray, Jaymar, 1961, set of 4, 11x14", NMIB 35.00
Rin-Tin-Tin, jigsaw, Whitman, 1950s, NMIB 22.00
Sleeping Beauty, fr-tray, 1958, M, sealed 25.00
Space Kidettes, fr-tray, Whitman, 1967, 14x11", EX 25.00
Spiro Agnew, jigsaw, unopened 25.00

Superman, jigsaw, #1540, 1973, M 8.00
Terrytoons, fr-tray, Jaymar, 1956, complete, 11x14", EX 30.00
Tom Corbett, fr-tray, Saalfield #7320, w/crew at porthole 55.00
Tom Corbett Jr, jigsaw, Saalfield, 1952, NMIB 75.00
Wendy (Casper the Ghost), fr-tray, EX 15.00
Zorro, fr-tray, Jaymar #2311, EX 20.00
101 Dalmatians, fr-tray, Jaymar, 1960s, 3 scenes, EX, ea 18.00

Miscellaneous

Appeal to Great Spirit, jigsaw, 1933, EXIB 15.00
Battle of Manila flagship, jigsaw, EXIB 440.00
Blocks, stack to form obelisk, litho on wood, 8 nesting 550.00
Blocks, Zeppelin/fantasy vehicles, Germany, ½x8x6¾", EXIB ...350.00
Blocks, 6-way, flying machines/Zeppelins, Germany, 1900s, 8x11", EX ..275.00
Carousel Mindflowers, Peter Max, jigsaw, 1967, MIB 40.00
City of Worcester Paddle Wheeler, McLoughlin, ca 1889, EXIB ..990.00
Cubes, Animal Picture Set, litho on cb, McLoughlin, ca 1897, VG ..130.00
Cubes, litho on wood, animal graphics, VGIB 195.00
Cubes, litho on wood, Leibmann, set of 35, VGIB 165.00
Fire Engine Picture Puzzle, McLoughlin 1887, wood & cb box, 12", EX .140.00
Locomotive Picture Puzzle, McLoughlin, 1887, wood/cb box, 12" ..110.00
Locomotive Picture Puzzle, McLoughlin, 1908, wood/cb box, 18" ..325.00
Locomotive Picture Puzzle, Parker Bros, 1894, 8x9½x1", EXIB ..140.00
Mr Pecksniff Leaves for London, wooden jigsaw, Tuck, EXIB 50.00
Picture Puzzle of Pilgrim, McLoughlin, wooden box, 12", VG 70.00

Pyrography

Pyrography, also known as wood burning, Flemish art, or poker work, is the art of burning designs into wood or leather and has been practiced over the centuries in many countries.

In the late 1800s pyrography became the hot new hobby for thousands of Americans who burned designs inspired by the popular artists of the day including Mucha, Gibson, Fisher, and Corbett. Thousands of wooden boxes, wall plaques, novelties, and pieces of furniture that they purchased from local general stores or from mail-order catalogs were burned and painted. These pieces were manufactured by companies such as The Flemish Art Company of New York and Thayer & Chandler of Chicago, who printed the designs on wood for the pyrographers to burn.

This Victorian fad developed into a new form of artistic expression as the individually burned and painted pieces reflected the personality of the pyrographers. The more adventurous started to burn between the lines and developed a style of 'allover burning' that today is known as pyromania. Others not only created their own designs but even made the pieces to be decorated. Both these developments are particularly valued today as true examples of American folk art.

By the 1930s its popularity had declined. Like Mission furniture, it was neglected by generations of collectors and dealers. The recent appreciation of Victoriana, the Arts and Crafts Movement, the American West, and the popularity of turn-of-the-century graphic art has rekindled interest in pyrography which embraces all these styles.

An informative book, *The Burning Passion — Antique and Collectible Pyrography*, by Carole and Richard Smyth, our advisors for this category, is currently available from the authors; they are listed in the Directory under New York.

Key: hb — hand burned

Bedroom set, hb/pnt, Wm Rogers/Forusville PA, 1905-7, 3-pc ..4,000.00
Book rack, hb/pnt girl w/book, 5¾" W, extends to 15¾" L 150.00
Box, flatware; factory burned/pnt poinsettias, Rogers, 9x11x5" ..195.00

Box, floral decor, stamped design, 14½" sq **40.00**
Box, lady w/flowing hair, Flemish Art Co, 1909, 11¾x4¼" **120.00**
Chair-table, hb/pnt poinsettias, Rest-Ye... on chair bk, EX **950.00**
Chest, blanket; hb/pnt swans/lady's head/flowers/etc, ca 1890 ....**850.00**
Coat hanger, hb/pnt poppies & leaves, Mother Dearest **80.00**
Cue holder, hb pool-hall scene, folk art, unique **650.00**
Egg cups, hb/pnt, pr **60.00**
Footstool, hb/pnt allover w/owl/branches/leaves **125.00**
Frame, hb/pnt flower garland, Thayer-Chandler, 8" dia **85.00**
Frame, owls in tree, 2 Is Company, 2 oval cutouts **145.00**
Frame, triple; hb fox/dogs/etc, #3 orig hunt prints, 16x33" **365.00**
Gameboard, hb/pnt ea side/edges, Flemish Art, 15" sq (open) **200.00**
Knife rack, hb Lizzie Borden w/axe, 5 hooks below, rare **550.00**
Magazine stand, 4-shelf, burned/pnt florals, Thayer-Chandler, 48" **800.00**
Medicine chest, hb/pnt Nouveau lady & vines, wall mt **450.00**
Mirror hand; hb/pnt lady's head w/flowing hair, 13¼x6¾" **180.00**
Nut bowl, hb/pnt squirrel on branch, Flemish Art Co #816, 5" **65.00**
Panel, basswood, burned/pnt orange, Thayer-Chandler, 16x30" **465.00**
Panel, hb after pnting: To the Feast, minor gold, 9x34" **500.00**
Pedestal, hb/pnt Nouveau flowers & vines, 45" **400.00**

Photo courtesy
Carole and Richard Smyth

Picture frames, standing type: hand burned and painted cherries, 7½x6", EX, $85.00; Hand burned and painted chrysanthemums, Thayer-Chandler, 10½x8", EX, $85.00.

Plaque, cvd/burned/pnt strawberry basket, 3-ply, 12" dia **70.00**
Plaque, girl bathing puppies, #854, 14½" **125.00**
Plaque, hb orange cat w/bow, paper 1912 calendar, 5¾" dia **50.00**
Plaque, Nouveau lady w/cherries, 19½" **150.00**
Plaque, Victorian couple, Parting by a Wall & flowers **145.00**
Ribbon holder, hb/pnt Sunbonnet babies (3), 5x12" **160.00**
Spoon holder, geometric florals, wall hanging, 1915, 10x8" **45.00**
Tie rack, factory stamp, HP soldier/nurse/sailor, WWI motto **125.00**

Quezal

The Quezal Art Glass and Decorating Company of Brooklyn, New York, was founded in 1901 by Martin Bach. A former Tiffany employee, Bach's glass closely resembled that of his former employer. Most pieces were signed 'Quezal,' a name taken from a Central American bird. After Bach's death in 1920, his son-in-law, Conrad Vohlsing, continued to produce a Quezal-type glass in Elmhurst, New York, which he marked 'Lustre Art Glass.' Examples listed here are signed unless noted otherwise.

Chandelier, leaves, opal on gold, 4-light, 4-arm, 19" H **1,200.00**
Gas shade, feathers, gold on opal irid, gold int, 4" **200.00**
Lamp, orange lustre ribs w/wht lustre int, brass harp std, 57" ..**1,100.00**
Lamp, zippers on 3-lobe shade, metal/brass newell post std, 30" .**500.00**

Lamp base, feathers, gr on bright orange, 15½x8" **1,000.00**
Shades, gr feathers/butterscotch loops/wht ruffles, 5½x6", pr **300.00**
Shades, vines, emerald gr on lt gr w/gold zipper design, 5", pr **300.00**
Vase, feathers, gr & gold on wht, trumpet form, disk base, 7½" .**1,600.00**
Vase, feathers, gr on wht opal w/gold & purple irid, #885, 12" ..**3,500.00**
Vase, feathers, gr on wht w/gold trim, 4¾x5½" **900.00**
Vase, feathers & rickrack, wht on gr, 4¾x3" **2,750.00**
Vase, floral/leaves, silver o/l on rainbow irid, long neck, 10" **950.00**
Vase, jack-in-pulpit; gr/gold feathers on sides, Calcite bk, 11" ..**3,800.00**
Vase, Nouveau leaves silver o/l on rainbow irid, 6½" **950.00**
Vase, red-gold irid, waisted rim, 9½" **600.00**
Vase, scrolls & vines, red-gold on opal, tapered, 11¼" **950.00**

Quilts

Quilts, while made of necessity, nevertheless represent an art form which expresses the character and the personality of the designer. During the 17th and 18th centuries, quilts were considered a necessary part of a bride's hope chest; the traditional number required to be properly endowed for marriage was a 'baker's dozen'! American Colonial quilts reflect the English and French taste of our ancestors. They would include the classifications known as Lindsey-Woolsey and the central medallion appliqué quilts fashioned from imported copper-plate printed fabrics.

By 1829 spare time was slightly more available, so women gathered in quilting bees. This not only was a way of sharing the work but also gave them the opportunity to show off their best handiwork. The hand-dyed and pieced quilts emerged, and they are now known as Sampler, Album and Friendship quilts. By 1845 American printed fabric was available.

In 1793 Eli Whitney developed the cotton gin; as a result, textile production in America became industrialized. Soon inexpensive fabrics were readily available, and ladies were able to choose from colorful prints and solids to add contrast to their work. Both pieced and appliquéd work became popular.

Pieced quilts were considered utilitarian, while appliquéd quilts were shown with pride of accomplishment at the fair or used when itinerant preachers traveled through and stayed for a visit. Today many collectors prize pieced quilts and their intricate geometric patterns above all other types. Many of these designs were given names: Daisy and Oak Leaf, Grandmother's Flower Garden, Log Cabin, and Ocean Wave are only a few. Appliquéd quilts involved stitching one piece — carefully cut into a specific form such as a leaf, a flower, or a stylized device — onto either a large one-piece ground fabric or an individual block. Often the background fabric was quilted in a decorative pattern such as a wreath or medallions.

Amish women scorned printed calicos as 'worldly' and instead used colorful blocks set with black fabrics to produce a stunning pieced effect. To show their reverence for God, the Amish would often include a 'superstition' block which represented the 'imperfection' of Man!

One of the most valuable quilts in existence is the Baltimore Album Quilt. Made between 1840 – 1860 only three hundred or so still exist today. They have been known to fetch over $100,000.00 at prominent auction houses in New York City. Usually each block features elaborate appliqué work such as a basket of flowers, patriotic flags and eagles, the Oddfellow's heart in hand, etc. The border can be sawtooth, meandering, or swags and tassels.

During the Victorian period the crazy quilt emerged. This style became the most popular quilt ever in terms of sheer numbers produced and popularity. The crazy quilt was formed by random pieces put together following no organized lines and was usually embellished by elaborate embroidery stitches. Fabrics of choice were brocades, silks, and velvets.

Another type of quilting, highly prized and rare today, is trapunto. These quilts were made by first stitching the outline of the design onto a solid sheet of fabric which was backed with a second having a much looser weave. White was often favored, but color was sometimes used for accent. The design (grapes, flowers, leaves, etc.) was padded through openings made by separating the loose weave of the underneath fabric; a backing was added and the three layers quilted as one.

Besides condition, value is judged on intricacy of pattern, color effect, and craftsmanship. Examine the stitching. Quality quilts have from ten to twelve stitches to the inch. A stitch is defined as any time a needle pierces through the fabric. So you may see five threads but ten (stitches) have been used. In the listings that follow, examples rated excellent have minor defects, otherwise assume them to be free of any damage, soil, or wear. Values given here are auction results; retail may be somewhat higher. Our advisor is Craig Ambrose; he is listed in the Directory under Iowa.

Key:
hs — hand sewn, sewing   ms — machine sewn
hq — hand quilted, quilting

Amish

Flying Geese, solid dk colors, 90x102", M 895.00
Grandmother's Flower Garden, dk solid colors, 101x103", M 895.00
Gray w/2 bl lines, EX quilting, lt fading, 70x73" 110.00
Lone Star, prints/solids, ms binding, 1850s, 79x89", EX 225.00
Sunshine & Shadow, mc w/bl border, 83x83", EX 715.00
Triple Irish Chain, dk colors, fine hs, 93x105" 895.00

Appliquéd

Appliqué autograph quilt, dated January 10, 1893, light wear, 84x100", $2,500.00.

Cacti, red & gr on wht, red & gr borders, ca 1900, 77x70", EX ..400.00
Crisscrossed tulips (9), tulip border 1 end, mc on wht, 72x78" ...400.00
Dogwood blossoms, mc on wht, lt stains, 82x74" 275.00
Floral medallions (20), vining border, mc on wht, sm rpr, 77x94" ..325.00
Floral medallions (4 lg), red/khaki/goldenrod, 83x85", VG 385.00
Floral medallions (9 puffed), mc on wht, EX hq, 82x86" 825.00
Floral medallions (9), birds & vine border, red & gr, 86" sq 130.00
Floral medallions (9), red/gr/yel on wht, EX hq, 1860s, 86" sq ...385.00
Floral pinwheels, mc on wht, ca 1870s, 73x74", EX 300.00
Floral pinwheels (9), red/gr/wht, sm stain, 83" sq 935.00
Floral wreaths (12), mc on wht, fine hq, PA, 1900s, 90x78" 400.00
Flowering trees (16) & vining border, ca 1870s, 94x93", G 165.00
Foliage pinwheels (4) & floral border, red/gr/wht, 90x92" 1,155.00
Morning glories, mc on wht, embr name/1936, wear, 67x82" 200.00
Orchids & mixed flowers w/ribbon, mc on wht, stains, 73x91" ..115.00
Pinwheel w/corner plumes, pk & wht, fine hq, 77x81" 400.00
Pinwheels (18), red/bl/gr, red & gr border, lg stitches, 90x94" 350.00
Red cross amid flowers, fine quilting, late 1800s, 80" sq, EX 550.00
Star of East variant, mc on wht, pk border, ca 1900, 84x68" 300.00
Thistles (20), scalloped red sawtooth border, 1900s, 96x82" 600.00
Tulips (9), mc on wht w/gr/yel sawtooth border, ca 1900, 86x84" ..950.00

4-part flowers & vining border, 3-color on wht, lt wear, 70x80" ..600.00

Pieced

Basket Squares (36), mc/wht, 72x91", VG 175.00
Baskets, pk calico on cream, trapunto work, 81x98", EX 990.00
Concentric sqs in postage stamp-sz pcs, mc, 88x92", EX 300.00
Crazy, satins/velvets/etc, appliques/embr/pnt, KY, worn, 70x76" ..495.00
Dmns (13), mc on wht, 2-color sawtooth border, ca 1900, 52x50" .1,200.00
Drunkard's Path, dk pk & wht, 1930s, 80x92", EX 300.00
Eagle center w/floral vining border, mc on wht, 80x92", VG 715.00
Fans, mc on 2-tone pk satin, EX hq, some age, 86x94" 350.00
Flower basket, mc calicos on wht w/applique, 1800s, 78x67" 800.00
Flying Geese bands, mc prints & solids w/red calico bars, 88x78" .300.00
Grandmother's Flower Garden, mc on wht, 1950s, 78x90", VG .200.00
Grid, red/bl/wht, EX color, lt wear, 82x91" 325.00
Irish Chain, bl print & wht, lt wear, 74" sq 385.00
Irish Chain, bl prints on wht, fine hq, 69x82", EX 385.00
Irish Chain, red & gr calico on wht, stains, ms, 93x95" 150.00
Leaves, bl & wht, simple border, OH, lt wear, 72" sq 385.00
Lone Star, mc on bl, fine quilting, Mennonite, 76x79", EX 660.00
Lone Star, mc on wht w/lt bl border, hs, 1900s, 88" sq, M 425.00
Pineapple, bl & wht, ms border, worn, 63x74" 275.00
Pinwheel in Sun (9), mc spirals on on bl-gr, 76x74", EX 350.00
Pinwheel medallions (12), 4-color on wht, 60x77", EX 450.00
Pinwheels, red print on wht, fine hq, trapunto borders, 108x112" ..770.00
Sqs, mc prints/wht, pk calico border, ca 1890s, 80x86", EX 415.00
Stars, mc prints w/red & bl calico, 80x82", EX 330.00
Stars on wht sqs, mc on red calico, chintz borders, 92x108" 450.00
Sunbonnet Sue, pk & gr border, 35 sqs, old, EX 145.00
Triangle patches, bl prints, worn/fading, 68x81" 385.00
Vining florals, mc w/trapunto work in corners, 88x102", EX ...1,200.00
Wild Goose Chase, mc calicos, wide border, 1870s-80s, 82x85" ..350.00
Zigzag bars, mc prints, chintz bk, ME, 78x106", EX 165.00

Quimper

Quimper pottery bears the name of the Breton town in northwestern France where it has been made for over three hundred years. Production began in 1690 when Jean-Baptiste Bousquet settled into a small workshop in the suburbs of Quimper, at Locmaria. There he bagan to make the hand-painted, tin enamel-glazed earthenware which we know today as faience. By the last quarter of the 19th century, there were three factories working concurrently: Porquier, de la Hubaudiere (the Grand Maison), and Henriot. All three houses produced similar wares which were decorated with scenes from the everyday life of the peasant folk of the region. Their respective marks are an AP or a P with an intersecting B (similar to a clover), an HB, and an HR (which became HenRiot after litigation in 1922).

The most desirable pieces were produced during the last quarter of the 19th century through the first quarter of the 20th century. These are considered to be artistically superior to the examples made after World War I and II with the exception of the Odetta line, which is now experiencing a renaissance among collectors here and abroad.

Most of what was made was faience, but there was also a history of utilitarian ware having been produced there. In 1922 the Grande Maison HB revitlized this ware and introduced the line called Odetta, examples of which seemed to embody the bold spirit of the Art Deco style. The companion faience pieces of this period and genre are classified as Modern Movement examples and frequently bear the name of the artist who designed the mold.

Currently there are two factories still producing Quimper pottery. La Societe Nouvelle des Faienceries de Quimper is owned by Sarah and

Paul Jenessens along with a group of American investors. Their mark is a stamped HB-Henriot logo. The other, La Faiencerie d'art Breton, is operated by the direct descendents of the HB and Henriot families. Their pieces are marked with an interlocked F and A conjoined with an inverted B. If you care to learn more about Quimper, we recommend *Quimper Pottery: A French Folk Art Faience* by Sandra V. Bondhus, our advisor for this category, whose address can be found in the Directory under Connecticut.

Plate, Decor Riche, bridal couple with acanthus border, HR Quimper, 10", $450.00.

Bannette, facing couple, bl sponged twisted hdls, 12x8" **425.00**
Bannette, market scene/Crest of Brittany, Decor Riche, HRQ, 18" .**1,950.00**
Basket, Breton mother & children wave to ships, crests, PB, 8½" .**925.00**
Bottle, Breton lady, head stopper, Franoir Royale mk, 11" **185.00**
Bottle, snuff; brn frog figural, unmk, sm chip on ft, 3" L **230.00**
Bottle, snuff; fleur-de-lis form, cobalt/yel/gr, 3½" **425.00**
Bottle, snuff; man w/pipe on heart shape, sponging, HBQ **400.00**
Bottle, snuff; peasant man, coquille St Jacques, HRQ, 2¾x2¼" **525.00**
Bottle, snuff; star on donut shape, reverse: flower, unsgn AP, 3½" .**525.00**
Bottle, snuff; 6-pointed star, reverse: man w/pipe, unmk AP, 3" ...**375.00**
Bowl, lady & floral sprays, faience populaire, HR, 3½x10" **160.00**
Cake plate, man w/bagpipes, floral garlands, ped ft, HRQ, 4x9½" ..**350.00**
Cake plate, man w/pipe, garlands on ped base, unmk HR, 8½" ..**300.00**
Candlestick, peasant man, floral sprays, 8-sided base, HRF, 8½" **325.00**
Candlesticks, peasant man/lady, 8-sided base, HQ 116, 5½", pr .**425.00**
Chamberstick, peasant man, bl sponged flowers, AP, 5¼", NM .**425.00**
Charger, Demi-Fantasie lady, panelled/scalloped rim, HQ, 12½" .**350.00**
Charger, mother/4 children/thatched cottage/church, HBQ, 12¼" .**475.00**
Condiment set, attached mustard pot/shakers, man w/pipe, HRQ ...**275.00**
Coupe, couple w/yarn, ermine tails, pierced, PBQ (2nd period), 8½" .**550.00**
Coupe, Demi-Fantasie lady w/jug on head, bl border, HRQ, 8½" **275.00**
Cruets, peasant couple, HQ, on stand w/animal ft, 9" **975.00**
Cup & saucer, Crest of Brittany, shield & lions on saucer, PB, NM ..**330.00**
Dish, dolls, buds & gr lines, orange sponging, HBQ, 2½" **60.00**
Egg cup holder, 6-place, bl flower-form center hdl, HBQ, 5x8" **240.00**
Figurine, Ste Anne w/child Mary, cobalt veil/mantle, HR, 6" **300.00**
Frame, peasant couple/florals/ermine tails, HRQ, 9½x6½" **1,100.00**
Gravy boat, dbl roosters/floral sprays, attached tray, HBQ, 10½" ..**200.00**
Hors d'oeuvre, Breton scenes (3), rope hdl, PB, 12½" dia **1,100.00**
Jardiniere, fairies in glen, lizard hdls, PB, 7½x11" **875.00**
Jardiniere, peasant scenes, fleur-de-lis & ermine tails, HB, 15" .**2,700.00**
Jardiniere, seated couple/Crest of Brittany, HQ, 8x20½"+hdls ...**650.00**
Leaf dish, naive lady, ermine-tail border, pierced, HB, 11" **240.00**
Match/cigarette holder, Rouen pattern, 6-lobed, unmk PB, 3½" .**240.00**
Melonniere, musicians & crest, acanthus rim, hdls, HRQ, 14", NM .**450.00**
Menu holder, bagpipe shape, man w/bagpipe, HRQ, wear, 4" **100.00**
Menu holder, peasant w/bagpipes/Crest of Brittany, PB, rstr, 5½" ..**170.00**
Menu holders, bagpipe form, lady/man, HRQ, rpr, 3½", pr **300.00**
Oil & vinegar, peasant couple/house & tower, HB Quimper, 7" ...**925.00**

Paperweight, fleur-de-lis form, 2-tone, HB, rstr, 3½" **240.00**
Pitcher, AP-style lady & garlands, faience populaire, unmk, 6" ..**160.00**
Pitcher, baby's feeding; a-la-touche florals, mc bands, HRQ, 5½" ..**400.00**
Pitcher, cream; man w/pipe, floral sprays, red clay, HB, 3½" **240.00**
Pitcher, lady seated in grass, flower garland, HRQ, 4" **220.00**
Pitcher, man w/pipe, rstr hdl, HB, 3½" **130.00**
Pitcher, peasant man, floral sprays, HRQ, lt wear, 5" **110.00**
Pitcher, puzzle; grapevines/Buvez je le..., Malicorne, 5" **300.00**
Pitcher, puzzle; lady w/distaff, floral sprays, HR Quimper, 4½" ...**325.00**
Pitcher, Rouen pattern, (1st peroid) PB, 16", NM **1,800.00**
Plate, bird on half sunflower, banded border, HQ, 10" **140.00**
Plate, bird running, a-la-touche florals, unsgn AP, 9" **150.00**
Plate, Breton bride & groom, fleur-de-lis & crests, unmk, 10" **400.00**
Plate, Breton couple, mc pastels, HQ, 10" **350.00**
Plate, couple at stone wall, Decor Riche type, HRQ, 10", NM ...**475.00**
Plate, couple dancing/Crest of Brittany, acanthus rim, HBQ, 9½" ..**550.00**
Plate, facing couple, Crest of Brittany, Decor Riche, HRQ, 10" .**450.00**
Plate, flowering branch & butterfly, PB, 10" **1,700.00**
Plate, hummingbird & wild rose cane, PB, 9½" **1,300.00**
Plate, lady spinning flax, wht hat, unmk, 10", NM **275.00**
Plate, lady w/basket, fruit & floral rim, Malicorne, PBX, 10" **210.00**
Plate, lady w/distaff, floral sprays, bl sponged rim, HRQ, 8½" **375.00**
Plate, lady w/milk pot on head, Demi-Fantasie, HR Quimper, 9½" .**200.00**
Plate, lady w/umbrella, floral border, HBQ, 8¼" **275.00**
Plate, man at fence, fruit garland, Malicorne, PBX, 10", NM **275.00**
Plate, man playing bagpipes, HB, 10", NM **325.00**
Plate, man w/hand in vest, mc clothes, HB/Quimper, 9½" **275.00**
Plate, mixed flowers (bright) & yel border, bl PB, 9½" **1,200.00**
Plate, mother & girl, Malicorne Decor Riche, 19th C, 10" **675.00**
Plate, mums & butterfly, lattice/blossoms, Malicorne, unmk, 10" ..**150.00**
Plate, Porte de Geurande scene, floral border, HB, 10" **525.00**
Plate, primitive lady, concentric mc bands, unmk HR, 9½" **120.00**
Plate, primitive lady & fir tree, faience populaire, HBQ, 9¼" **100.00**
Plate, primitive lady & florals, scalloped, unsgn AP, 8½" **190.00**
Plate, primitive man, faience populaire, HB, 9¼" **160.00**
Plate, stylized starbrust, faience populaire, 8-sided, unmk, 9" **180.00**
Plate, sun face, yel & bl bands, faience populaire, unmk, 9" **375.00**
Plates, lady spinning/man walking, Christmas border, HRQ, 10", pr ..**875.00**
Platter, Bretonne scene at table, acanthus border, PB, 11x11" .**1,800.00**
Platter, man & floral sprays, faience populaire, unmk, 12" **210.00**
Platter, Panier aux Fleurs, faience populaire, HQF, 19¼x9" **400.00**
Platter, peasant couple & fir tree, floral rim, HBA, 10¼x8" **285.00**
Platter, peasant couple/field/church, Malicorne, PBX, 13" **500.00**
Platter, primitive man, buds & ovals, pastels, HB, 11x7½" **250.00**
Platter, 2 couples & wooden fence, Malicorne, unmk, 15½x11" .**1,600.00**
Relish, peasant lady on rock, roses & bluets, HBQ, 8" L **130.00**
Shoe, high-button; peasant lady, sprigs/dots, flake, HB, 3½" **215.00**
Shoe, sabot; mc geometrics & lattice band, unmk, early, 3½" **120.00**
Toby pitcher, man w/pipe on bbl base, HB, 8½", NM **775.00**
Tray, clematis vines, yel rim, 6-lobed, PB, 18½" **1,800.00**
Vase, Breton lady/Crest of Brittany, sgn LD, cylinder, 8½" **250.00**
Vase, couple on crescent moon shape, dolphin ft, HRQ, 6x8", NM ...**525.00**
Vase, lady w/hands in apron, gr sponged hdls, HR Quimper, 9" .**425.00**
Vase, man w/bagpipes in cartouch, yel hdls, HB, 3½" **220.00**
Vase, man w/flute, floral sprays, gr sponged hdls, HR, 9" **425.00**
Vase, man w/flute & floral sprays on tulip form, HRQ, 6" **375.00**
Vase, man w/pipe/Crest of Brittany, Decor Riche, HRQ, 8", EX .**300.00**
Vases, bud; man w/cane, lady w/floral spray, HBQ, 7", pr **190.00**
Vases, Demi-Fantasie man w/pipe & lady w/basket, HQF, 5½", pr .**275.00**
Wall pocket, bagpipe form, man w/flute/floral sprays, HRQ, 4½" ...**170.00**
Wall pocket, basket form, man seated on rock, Malicorne, 7½" .**350.00**
Wall pocket, cornucopia form, lady w/egg baskets, Malicorne, 11" ..**185.00**
Wall pocket, cornucopia form, youth w/cane, Malicorne, PBX, 11" .**140.00**
Wall pocket, dbl cornucopia form, man & lady, AP mk, 4" **375.00**

Wall pocket, slipper form, peasant lady/florals, HQF, 8" 400.00

Radford

Pottery associated with Albert Radford (1882 – 1904) can be categorized by three periods of production. Pottery produced in Tiffin, Ohio (1896 – 1899), consists of bone china (no marked examples known) and high-quality jasperware with applied Wedgwood-like cameos. Tiffin jasperware is often impressed 'Radford Jasper' in small block letters. At Zanesville, Ohio, Radford jasperware was marked only with an incised, two-digit shape number, and the cameos were not applied but rather formed within the mold and filled with a white slip. Zanesville Radford ware was produced for only a few months before the Radford pottery was acquired by the Arc-en-Ciel company in 1903. Production in Zanesville was handled by Radford's father, Edward (1840 – 1910), who remained in Zanesville after Albert moved to Clarksburg, West Virginia, where the Radford Pottery Co. was completed shortly before Albert's death in 1904. Jasperware was not produced in Clarksburg, and the molds appear to have been left in Zanesville, where some were subsequently used by the Arc-en-Ciel pottery. The Clarksburg, West Virginia, pottery produced a standard glaze, slip-decorated ware, Ruko; Thera and Velvety, matt glazed ware often signed by Albert Haubrich, Alice Bloomer, and other artists; and Radura, a semimatt green glaze developed by Albert Radford's son, Edward. The Clarksburg plant closed in 1912.

Pottery marked 'E. Radford, Burslem,' or 'E. Radford, England,' includes a variety of earthenware designed by Edward Radford (1883 – 1968), first for H.J. Wood and later for himself in Burslem (production ending in 1948). A variety of floral patterns, cottage or tavern scenes, and Art Deco motifs distinguish this ware. His father, Edward Thomas Radford, worked at the Pilkington Tile and Pottery Co. in Manchester, England, and appears to have been a brother of Albert Radford. Our advisor for this category is James L. Murphy; he is listed in the Directory under Ohio.

Jasper

Bowl, muses & vintage, fluted rim, imp mk 295.00
Box, figure w/cornucopia on lid, prof rpr, ca 1896, 5⅝" H 500.00
Ewer, grapes/blkberries, lt bl, face on hdl, #17, 9" 300.00
Letter holder, lady w/bow & target scene, bark trim, #61 ....500.00
Mug, vintage, gray, #25, 5" 165.00
Pitcher, tankard, vintage, lt bl, #26, 12" 200.00
Vase, bust of Gladstone ea side, twisted form, 3" 125.00
Vase, bust of Washington, reverse: eagle, bark trim, #12, 7" 265.00
Vase, lady sits, trees & dog, bark trim, #14, 7" 340.00
Vase, lady w/flowers, bk: grapes, #59, 4" 165.00
Vase, running girl, deep bl, flat & twisted, #53, 3½" 100.00

Miscellaneous

Vase, Radura, embossed decor on green matt, three shoulder-to-foot handles, 10", $300.00.

Plate, E Radford, HP floral, gr matt, 5x9" 26.50
Teapot, E Radford, HP floral, gr matt, 4½" 75.00
Vase, Ruko, floral, standard glaze, 15" 325.00
Vase, Thera, floral, bulbous, stamped mk, 12" 700.00
Vase, Thera, nasturtium, A Haubrich, ovoid, 13½", NM 900.00
Vase, Velvety, mums, mc on gr matt, sgn, bottle form, 10¼x3" .550.00

Radios

Vintage radios are very collectible. There were thousands of styles and types produced, the most popular of which today are the breadboard and the cathedral. Consoles are usually considered less marketable, since their size makes them hard to display and store. For those wishing to learn more about antique radios, we recommend *The Collector's Guide to Antique Radios*, Volumes I through IV, by Sue and Marty Bunis, available from your local bookstore or Collector Books. They are also the authors of *A Collector's Guide to Transistor Radios*. For information on novelty radios, refer to *Collector's Guide to Novelty Radios* by Marty Bunis and Robert Breed. Values are given for radios in near mint to mint condition. Our advisor for this category is James Fred; he is listed in the Directory under Indiana.

Key:
BC — broadcast   s/r — slide rule
pb — push button   SW — short wave
phono — phonograph   tbl/m — table model
R/P — radio-phonograph

Philco 37-62, two-tone wood, right front round dial, cloth grill with Deco cutouts, three knobs, 1937, $75.00.

Photo courtesy Sue and Marty Bunis

Admiral, Duet Y3353, plastic, clock face, ftd, AM, AC, 1963 ......15.00
Admiral 6TO6, 2-tone wood, s/r dial, battery, tbl/m, 11946 ....45.00
Airline 04BR-514B, plastic, Deco, s/r dial, 5 pb, tbl/m, 1940 ....90.00
Airline 84WG-2714F, wood, s/r dial, AC, console-R/P, 1948 ......80.00
American Bosch 18, wood, inner dial, console, 1929 ....225.00
American Bosch 565-W, wood, AC, tombstone shape, AC, 1935 ..85.00
Apex 11, wood, upper dial, lower grill, lowboy console, 1930 .....125.00
Arvin 444, metal, midget, BC, AC/DC, 4-tube, tbl/m, 1946 ....85.00
Arvin 618, 2-tone wood, tuning eye, BC/SW, AC, tbl/m, 1937 ...75.00
Atwater Kent 509, wood, clock, BC/SW, AC, console, 1935 .....250.00
Atwater Kent 84, wood, ½-rnd dial, grandfather clock, 1931 .....650.00
Automatic C-65, leatherette, AC/DC/battery, portable, 1942 ......35.00
Bendix 69M9, wood, s/r dial, BC/FM, AC, console-R/P, 1949 .....60.00
Bradford 96651, plastic, 6-tube, AM/FM, AC/DC, tbl/m, 1962 ....15.00
Bulova 400 Series, plastic, clock, ftd, BC, AC, tbl/m 20.00
Clinton 1102, wood, tuning eye, console, 1937 ....150.00
Continental K6, plastic, 3 knobs, BC/SW, tbl/m 40.00
Crosley V, wood, Bakelite panel, lift-top, battery, tbl/m, 1922 ...125.00
Crosley 22, walnut veneer, battery, highboy console, 1929 ....140.00
Crosley 6H2, wood, BC/SW, AC, tombstone shape, 1933 ....110.00
Crosley 66T-T, wood, sq dial, BC/SW, tbl/m, 1946 ....55.00

Delco R-1141, wood, s/r dial, pb, 4 knobs, BC/SW, tbl/m 70.00
Dewald, 562 Jewel, Catalin, s/r dial, hdl, tbl/m, 1941 ....500.00
Earle 4, wood, window dial, BC, AC, tombstone shape 125.00
Emerson AU-213, walnut, ½-rnd dial, tombstone tbl/m, 1938 ...125.00
Emerson CQ-273, wood, 4 pb, 3 knobs, AC/DC, tbl/m, 1939 ......75.00
Emerson M-755, 2-tone burl walnut, cathedral shape, 1932 ....300.00
Emerson 17, plastic, Deco, chrome bars, AC/DC, tbl/m, 1935 ...135.00
Emerson 336, plastic, 5-tube, AC/DC, tbl/m, 1940 ....40.00
Emerson 547A, plastic, s/r dial, BC, AC/DC, tbl/m, 1947 ....40.00
Emerson 641B, plastic, s/r dial, BC, AC/DC, tbl/m, 1951 ....35.00
Fada 31, wood, fold-down front, AC, 3 knobs, console, 1928 .....200.00
Fada 605, plastic, slanted s/r dial, 2 knobs, tbl/m, 1946 ....45.00
Garod 4B-1, plastic, hdl, BC, battery, portable, 1948 ....40.00
General Electric M-42, 2-tone wood, AC, tombstone shape, 1934 ..90.00
Kolster K-120, wood, 8-tube, lowboy console, 1932 ....110.00
Motorola 9A, 2-tone wood, Deco, tuning eye, chair-side, 1937 ..175.00
Philco 18-L, wood, BC/SW, AC, lowboy console, 1933 ....125.00
Philco 54C, walnut w/inlay, top louvers, BC, AC/DC, tbl/m, 1933 ..80.00
Pilot B-3, plastic, s/r dial, BC/SW, AC, tbl/m, 1946 ....40.00
RCA BT42, 2-tone wood, s/r dial, BC, battery, tbl/m, 1940 ....50.00
RCA 1X55, plastic, ½-rnd dial, BC, AC/DC, tbl/m, 1952 ....30.00
RCA 6-T-2, wood, BC/SW, 6-tube, tombstone shape, 1936 ......125.00
RCA 66X12, ivory plastic, s/r dial, BC, AC/DC, tbl/m, 1947 ....45.00
RCA 9T, wood, tuning eye, BC/SW, AC, tombstone shape, 1935 ..165.00
Regal 205, plastic, s/r dial, BC, AC/DC, tbl/m, 1947 ....40.00
Silvertone 215, plastic, BC, AC/DC/battery, portable, 1950 ....30.00
Silvertone 6220A, wood, s/r dial, BC, battery, tbl/m, 1946 ....25.00
Sonora LQ Clipper, plastic, s/r dial, BC, AC/DC, tbl/m, 1942 .....35.00
Sparton 8618, wood, s/r dial, pb, BC/SW, AC, console, 1938 ....150.00
Stewart Warner R-110-A, 2-tone wood, tombstone shape 175.00
Stromberg-Carlson 1204, plastic, s/r, BC/FM, AC/DC, tbl/m, 1948 ..50.00
Trav-ler 5027, leatherette, BC, AC/DC/battery, portable, 1948 ...30.00
Universal 72A6, wood, rnd dial, battery, tombstone shape, 1935 .60.00
Westinghouse WR-21, wood, BC/SW, AC, tbl/m, 1934 ....60.00
Wilcox-Gay A-58, wood, s/r dial, 4-tube, tbl/m, 1940 ....50.00
Zenith B-513V, plastic, BC, AC/DC, tbl/m, 1959 ....20.00
Zenith R-511F, plastic, ½-rnd dial, BC, AC/DC, tbl/m, 1955 ......35.00
Zenith 12, mahog, 6-tube, battery, tbl/m, 1927 ....125.00
Zenith 12-S-267, wood, robot dial, BC/SW, AC, console, 1937 ..350.00
Zenith 4-K-422, plastic, 4-tube, battery, tbl/m, 1940 ....75.00
Zenith 5-S-220, wood, ftd, BC/SW, AC, tbl/m, 1937 ....150.00
Zenith 6-G-560, wood, BC, AC/DC/battery, console, 1941 ....125.00
Zenith 6-V-62, wood, BC/SW, battery, console, 1936 ....150.00

Novelty Radios

Bozo the clown, 5¾x6¾", $85.00.

Bass fiddle, transparent, Radio Shack 60.00
Benson & Hedges cigarette pack, MIB 22.50
Bowling pin, Japan, 3¾x12¼" 125.00
Bud beer bottle, MIB 35.00
Bullwinkle, plastic, 3-D, PAT World Prod, 6¼x11⅞" 250.00
Buster, The Talking Monkey, Stellar #4221, clock, 8x12" 100.00
Cannon on carriage, transistors 40.00
Champion spark plug, 110 volt, 15", MIB 100.00
Coca-Cola vending machine, AM/FM, 1963 ....150.00
Coffee grinder, wood & metal, Nobility, Japan 50.00
Diamond Vogel Paint can, MIB 35.00
Evel Knievel, tire form w/picture, Hong Kong, 6" dia 50.00
Getty gas pump 85.00
Kent cigarette pack, MIB 85.00
Kent Flip-Top cigarette pack, MIB 65.00
Knight on horsebk, VG 30.00
Kraft Macaroni, MIB 35.00
Master Padlock, padlock form, 3x4½" 75.00
Mickey Mouse, sitting in chair, EX 45.00
Mighty Mouse on wedge of cheese, Hong Kong, 1978, 5x4¾" ...150.00
NAPA Batteries, battery shape 35.00
Old World Style globe, Hong Kong, M 50.00
Pepsi-Cola dispenser, Say Pepsi Please on front, 7", MIB 350.00
Pepsi-Cola vending machine, MIB 175.00
Pillsbury Doughboy, behind stove w/clock, Tarcy, 1986, AM/FM ...60.00
Rolls Royce, 1931, EX 35.00
R2-D2 Robot, Kenner #38530, 1978, 2¾x6" 150.00
Schlitz can, GE, Hong Kong 50.00
Sinclair gas pump, transistor, M 45.00
Slot machine, Stellarsonic, Hong Kong, 4¼x5¼" 75.00
Sunkist Orange, MIB 35.00
Sunoco gas pump, yel & bl, 4", M 45.00
Superman in phone booth, plastic, 7" 175.00
Treesweet Orange, MIB 45.00
Wilson Tennis Balls, can form 45.00
Winston cooler, w/FM 25.00

Transistor

Post-World War II baby boomers, now approaching their fiftieth year, are rediscovering prized possessions of youth, their pocket radios. The transistor wonders, born with rock 'n roll, were at the vanguard of miniaturization and futuristic design in the decade which followed their introduction to Christmas shoppers in 1954. The tiny receiving sets launched the growth of Texas Instruments and shortly to follow abroad, Sony and other Japanese giants.

The most desirable sets include the 1954 four-transistor Regency TR-1 and colorful early Sony and Toshiba models. Certain pre-1960 models by Hoffman and Admiral represented the earliest practical use of solar technology and are also highly valued. To avoid high tariffs, scores of two-transistor sets, boys' radios, were imported from Japan with names like Pet and Charmy. Many early inexpensive transistor sets could be heard only with an earphone. The smallest sets are known as shirt-pocket models while those slightly larger are called coat-pockets. Early collectible transistor radios all have civil defense triangle markings at 640 and 1240 on the frequency dial and nine or fewer transistors. Very few desirable sets were made after 1963. Model numbers are most commonly found inside. Our advisor for this category is Mike Brooks; he is listed in the Directory under California and welcomes questions. (Please include a SASE.)

Admiral Y2229 Golden Eagle 30.00
Airline Gen-1207A 30.00
Arvin 62R26 ....15.00

Bulova 640 ....150.00
Bulova 685 ....35.00

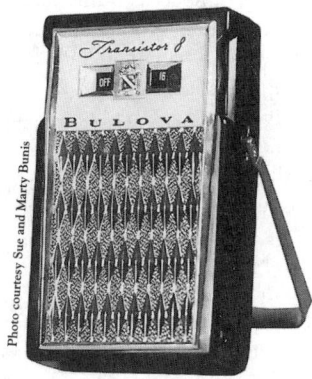

Photo courtesy Sue and Marty Bunis

Bulova Transistor 8, thumbwheel tuning, metal grill with diamond cutouts, swing handle, AM, battery, $60.00.

Commodore TW-66 ....10.00
Crown TRF-1600R 20.00
Echo TRK-225 ....75.00
Emerson 844 ....45.00
General Electric P790B 40.00
General Electric P830E 30.00
Harpers GK900 ....110.00
Heathkit XR-1 ....15.00
Hit Parade, car-phone-only sound 100.00
Hitachi TH-667 ....80.00
Hoffman RP706 Trans Solar 400.00
Juliette SH-516 ....15.00
Jupiter 6T-330 ....225.00
Lafayette KT-116 ....75.00
Lloyd's 6K87B 45.00
Magnovox AM-85 ....25.00
Mantola M4D, red 450.00
MMA F-140 ....15.00
Motorola 6X28B 95.00
NEC NT-61 ....125.00
Norelco L1W32T/02G 25.00
Panasonic DT-495 ....25.00
Panasonic T-22M 35.00
Philco T-9 Trans World 110.00
RCA RLG 12A 10.00
RCA 1-BT-32, w/charger 100.00
Realtone TR-1887 ....15.00
Ross RE-714 ....50.00
Ross 1063 ....15.00
Sharp BH-352 ....175.00
Silvertone 9202 ....40.00
Sony TR55 (1st Sony) 2,000.00
Sony TR8 ....300.00
Standard SR-G430 Micronic Ruby 125.00
Tom Thumb, TT600, w/box 200.00
Tonecrest 1051 ....20.00
Toshiba 5TR193, red lace, w/box 525.00
Toshiba 6TP-385 ....65.00
Toshiba 9TM40 ....400.00
Trancel T-11 ....35.00
Universal YT-161 ....35.00
Westinghouse H-693P8 ....40.00

Windsor 16002 ....30.00
Zenith Royal 130 ....35.00

Railroadiana

Collecting railroad-related memorabilia has become one of America's most popular hobbies. The range of collectible items available is almost endless; not surprising, considering the fact that more than 175 different railroad lines are represented. Some collectors prefer to specialize in only one railroad, while others attempt to collect at least one item from every railway line known to have existed. For the advanced collector, there is the challenge of locating rarities from short-lived railroads; for the novice, there are abundant keys, buttons, and passes. Among the most popular specializations are dining-car collectibles — flatware, glassware, dinnerware, etc., in a wide variety of patterns and styles. Railroad blankets are also starting to gain attention. Most common are Pullman blankets. The early ones had a cross-stitch pattern; these were followed by one in a solid cinnamon color; both are marked clearly with the Pullman name. These are now valued at $125.00 up to $175.00 in good condition. Other railroads had their own 'marked' blankets that are even more desireable, such as the Soo line, the Chessie, and one marked 'Pheasant' (which was a private car on the Milwaukee Line that was reserved to carry special parties for hunting trips).

As is true in most collecting fields, scarcity and condition determine value. There is more interest in some railway lines than in others; generally speaking, it is greater in the region serviced by the particular railroad. Reproductions abound in railroadiana collectibles — from dinnerware and glassware to lanterns, keys, badges, belt buckles, timetables, and much more. Repro hand-executed, reverse-painted glass signs have been abundant throughout the country, most of them read 'Santa Fe,' but some say 'Whites Only.' Beware! Also railroad drumheads are coming out of collections. A drumhead is a large (approximately 24" diameter) glass sign in a metal case. They were used on the back end of all railroad observation cars to advertise a special train or a presidential foray, etc. They're now beginning to surface, and a good one like the Flying Crow from the Kansas City Southern Railroad will go for $2,500.00, as will many others. When items of this value come out, the counterfeiters are right there. It is important to 'know thy dealer.' For a more thorough study, we recommend *Railroad Collectibles, Third Revised Edition*, by Stanley L. Baker. The values noted for most of our dinnerware, glassware, linen, silverplate, and timetables are actual selling prices. However, because prices are so volatile, the best pricing sources are often monthly or quarterly 'For Sale' lists. Two you may find helpful may be ordered from Golden Spike, P.O. Box 422, Williamsville, NY 14221, and Grandpa's Depot and Caboose, 1616 17 St., Suite 264, Denver, CO 80202. Our co-advisors for this category are Fred and Lila Shrader (see Directory, California), and John White (Grandpa's Depot, see Colorado).

Key:
BL — bottom logo	SL — side logo
BS — bottom stamped	SM — side mark
FBS — full back stamp	TL — top logo
NBS — no back stamp	TM — top mark
NTL — no top logo	

Dinnerware

Many railroads designed their own china for use in their dining cars or company-owned hotels or stations. Some railroads chose to use stock patterns to which they added their name or logo; others used the same stock patterns without the added identification.

Ashtray, B&O, Snuf-arette, cobalt, TL, BS 125.00
Ashtray, GN, Mountains & Flowers, 4 rests, BS, 4" dia 85.00
Bowl, ACL, Flora of the South, oval, BS, 6x4¼" 125.00
Bowl, baked apple; PRR, Keystone, NBS, 4x5½" 130.00
Bowl, berry; ATSF, Bleeding Blue, TL, 5¼" 145.00
Bowl, berry; GN, Hill, TM, NBS, 5½" 165.00
Bowl, berry; SP, Prairie Mountain Wildflowers, NBS, 5½" 45.00
Bowl, berry; UP, Challenger, TM, NBS, 5½" 38.00
Bowl, bouillon; Alaska, McKinley, hdls, TL, 3¾" 410.00
Bowl, bouillon; CB&Q, Chuckwagon, SL, 3¾" 95.00
Bowl, bouillon; Feather River, SL, NBS 95.00
Bowl, bouillon; UP, Harriman Blue, BL, 4" W 31.00
Bowl, cereal; Alaska, McKinley, TL, 6¼" 345.00
Bowl, cereal; B&O, Capitol, TL, BS, 6½" 65.00
Bowl, cereal; CRI&P, LaSalle, TM/BS, 6½" 165.00
Bowl, cereal; UP, Circus Series, NBS, 6" 275.00
Bowl, cereal; UP, Desert Flower, BS, 6½" 35.00
Bowl, D&H, Vermont, all gold, oval, 6x5" 110.00
Bowl, GN, Oriental, oval, NBS, 7¾x10" 225.00
Bowl, salad; SP, Prairie Mountain Wildflowers, 3½x9½" 385.00
Butter pat, ACL, Carolina, BS 24.00
Butter pat, ATSF, Mimbreno, BS 110.00
Butter pat, B&O, Capitol, TL 110.00
Butter pat, B&O, Sweetbriar, NBS 48.00
Butter pat, CB&Q, Violets & Daisies, BS 120.00
Butter pat, CMStP&P, Peacock, NBS 125.00
Butter pat, CP, Tremblant, TL 195.00
Butter pat, CRI&P, Golden State, TL 230.00
Butter pat, CRI&P, LaSalle, TL 265.00
Butter pat, D&H, Vermont, all gold, TM, NBS 110.00
Butter pat, Fred Harvey, Trend, NBS, 3" dia 59.00
Butter pat, KCS, Roxbury, NBS 29.00
Butter pat, MKT, Katy Ornaments, NBS 39.00
Butter pat, NYC, Commodore, BS, 3½" sq 23.00
Butter pat, NYC, Depew, BS, 3" sq 185.00
Butter pat, Pullman, Indian Tree, TM 120.00
Butter pat, SP, Prairie Mountain Wildflowers, BS 225.00
Butter pat, UP, Winged Streamliner, NBS 38.00
Chocolate pot, NYC, Mercury, SL, BS 325.00
Coffeepot, MP, Washington, cobalt, SL & pinstripes, gold 280.00
Coffeepot, UP, Portland Rose, FBS 765.00
Compote, CN, Vancouver, TM, NBS, 3½" ped, 6½" dia 45.00
Compote, SP, Hotel Del Monte, BS 235.00
Creamer, ind; ATSF, California Poppy, NBS, 2½" 175.00
Creamer, ind; C&NW, Depot Ornaments, w/hdl, NBS 65.00
Creamer, ind; C&O, George Washington, BS, 2" 245.00
Creamer, ind; FH, Webster, NBS, 2¾" 45.00
Creamer, ind; Inter-State News Co, Interstate, SL, 2¾" 125.00
Creamer, ind; PRR, Purple Laurel, BS, 2" 85.00
Creamer, ind; UP, Desert Flower, NBS, 3½" 165.00

Cup & saucer, ATSF, California Poppy, BS 250.00
Cup & saucer, CMStP&P, Olympian, TM 118.00
Cup & saucer, CMStP&P, Traveler, NBS 145.00
Cup & saucer, demi; C&O, Silhouette, NBS 225.00
Cup & saucer, demi; FH, Webster, NBS 95.00
Cup & saucer, demi; SP, Prairie Mountain Wildflowers, NBS ...225.00
Cup & saucer, demi; UP, Blue & Gold, NBS 49.00
Cup & saucer, Fred Harvey, Trend, NBS 29.00
Cup & saucer, NP, Monad, SL 185.00
Cup & saucer, PRR, Allegheny, BS 425.00
Cup & saucer, PRR, Mountain Laurel, NBS 32.00
Egg cup, CN, Royal York, SM, NBS, 2½" 58.00
Egg cup, dbl; IC, Coral, NBS, 3½" 35.00
Egg cup, dbl; Pullman, Indian Tree, SM, 3½" 165.00
Gravy boat, D&RG, Prospector, SL 245.00
Gravy boat, UP, Desert Flower, BS 145.00
Hot food cover, CMStP&P, Peacock, NBS 165.00
Hot food cover, D&RGW, Blue Adam, NBS, 6" 65.00
Ice cream dish, NYC, Hudson, tab hdl, BS 125.00
Ice cream dish, PRR, Purple Laurel, tab hdl, BL 65.00
Mustard pot, UP, Harriman Blue, w/lid, SM 125.00
Pitcher, B&O, Centenary, BS, 5½" 225.00
Pitcher, NYC, DeWitt Clinton, SL, NBS, 5" 45.00
Plate, ATSF, Griffon, BS, 9½" 355.00
Plate, CMStP&P, Galatea, NBS, 9" 72.00
Plate, CRI&P, LaSalle, NBS, 9½" 165.00
Plate, EH&A, Hampton, TM, NBS, 7" 265.00
Plate, Fred Harvey, Trend, NBS, 6½" sq 10.00
Plate, GM&O, Rose, TL, NBS, 10¼" 285.00
Plate, GN, Glory of the West, BS, 9¾" 225.00
Plate, GN, Mountains & Flowers, BS, 7¼" 110.00
Plate, GN, Rocky (child's ware), TM, 7½" 535.00
Plate, N&W, Coach & Four, NBS, 10" 110.00
Plate, NP, Monad, TL, 9¼" 165.00
Plate, NYNH&H, Merchants, BS, 8½" 135.00
Plate, NYNH&H, Platinum Blue, NBS, 8½" 42.00
Plate, PRR, Broadway, TL, BS, 6½" 45.00
Plate, PRR, Mountain Laurel, BS, 9½" 55.00
Plate, Pullman, Indian Tree, TM, 7½" 45.00
Plate, SP, Sunset, TL, BS, 9¼" 225.00
Plate, T&P, Eagle, TL, BS, 5½" 95.00
Plate, UP, Desert Wildflower, BS, 10½" 85.00
Plate, UP, Zion, BS, 7½" 175.00
Plate, WP, Feather River, TM, NBS, 9½" 275.00
Platter, B&O, Capitol, TL, 11½x8" 345.00
Platter, B&O, Centenary, BS, 11½x8" 185.00
Platter, CM&PS, Puget, TL, 13x9½" 185.00
Platter, CMStP&P, Traveler, BS, 8x6½" 95.00
Platter, DL&H, Anthracite, BS, 13½x9" 285.00
Platter, Erie, Chataqua, TM, 10½x7" 400.00
Platter, KCS, Flying Crow, TL, 11¾x8¼" 655.00
Platter, SAL, Peach Blossom, NTL, BS, 11½x8" 110.00
Platter, UP, Harriman Blue, BL, 11½x7½" 95.00
Platter, WAB, Lafayette, TL, 13x9¼" 275.00
Ramekin, L&N, Regent, NBS, 3½" 85.00
Relish dish, CMStP&P, NBS, 7½x3½" 110.00
Relish dish, NP, Monad, TL, 7½x3½" 195.00
Relish dish, Pullman, Calumet, TM, 11x5½" 225.00
Relish dish, UP, Historical, TL, BS, 7½x3½" 235.00
Sauce boat, NYC, Vanderbilt, NBS 55.00
Sauce boat, PRR, Brown Keystone, SL, NBS 145.00
Service plate, C&O, George Washington, BS 395.00
Service plate, D&H, Ft William Henry, TL, 10" 350.00
Service plate, IC, Panama Ltd, BS 550.00

Cup and saucer, Thomas Viaduct, blue on white, bottom stamp, 1835, 3½", 6⅛", $100.00.

Service plate, MKT, Alamo, cobalt border, BS, 10¾" 395.00
Service plate, MKT, Alamo, gr border, NBS, 10¾" 275.00
Service plate, MP, State Flowers, NBS, 10½" 225.00
Sherbet, ATSF, Mimbreno, ped ft, BS 165.00
Soup plate, NYC, Hyde Park, BS, 8½" 165.00
Soup plate, PRR, Purple Laurel, BS, 9" 85.00
Soup plate, SP, Sunset, BS, 8" 200.00
Sugar bowl, CMStP&P, Galatea, w/lid, NBS 135.00
Sugar bowl, GN, Oriental, w/lid, NBS 110.00
Sugar bowl, UP, Winged Streamliner, w/lid, NBS 95.00
Teapot, B&O, Centenary, BS 395.00
Teapot, GN, Brown Service, BS; silver holder, TM 390.00
Toothpick holder, MKT, Katy Ornaments, NBS 65.00

Glassware

Photo courtesy Stanley Baker

Illinois Central screen-printed glassware: Old-fashioned, Main Line of Mid-America and passenger train, maroon and yellow, 4½", $25.00; Roly-poly, Panama Limited Streamliner, maroon and yellow, 2½", $15.00.

Ashtray, ATSF, Turquoise Room, TM, 4x4¾" 18.00
Ashtray, CMStP&P, Hiawatha, 4 rests, 3½x2½" 15.00
Ashtray, McCloud RR, red logo, 3½" dia 22.00
Ashtray, NP/Yellowstone..., blk & red TL, 4½" sq 23.00
Ashtray, T&P blk logo, 2 rests, oval, 5x3½" 22.00
Bottle, medicine; SP Co Hospital Dept (emb), 5½" 42.00
Bottle, milk; MP buzz-saw logo, qt 65.00
Claret, GN, SM interlocking initials, 5¼" 55.00
Cordial, stem; B&O, SL, 4" 35.00
Cordial, stem; NYC frosted, 3½" 75.00
Cruet, GN, older frosted goat logo 175.00
Goblet, UP, wht enamel shield, SM, ftd, 5½" 13.00
Iced tea, ATSF, cut script+8 parallel lines, 5½" 62.00
Martini set, UP, SM: 5" pitcher+2 sm roly-poly+stirrer 65.00
Mug, coffee; BN in gr w/logo, 1972 ....15.00
Roly-poly, PRR, SM w/red & wht enamel, 2¼" 13.00
Shot glass, UP, wht enamel shield logo, 2¼" 26.00
Tumbler, ATSF, SM, frosted: Santa Fe (script), 5½" 17.00
Tumbler, ATSF, SM Santa Fe cross logo, 4½" 19.00
Tumbler, D&H, The D&H SL in script, 3¾" 45.00
Tumbler, IC, etched SL in box, 8-oz, 4½" 75.00
Tumbler, NYC, SL: Route to the World's Fair..., 4½" 12.00
Tumbler, PRR, gold keystone w/blk & gold locomotives, 3½" 39.00
Tumbler, WAB, emb in bottom: He Man Shot Glass, 3¼" 45.00
Wine, stem, CP script logo w/ornate facets, 4" 39.00
Wine, stem, Fred Harvey, amber, Heisey, 6" 145.00

Keys

Switch keys are brass with hollow barrels and round heads with holes for attaching to a key ring. They were used to unlock the padlocks on track-side switches when the course of the tracks had to be changed. (Switches were padlocked to prevent them from being thrown by accident or vandals, a situation that could result in a train wreck.) A car key, used to open padlocks on freight cars and the like, is very similar to the switch key, except the bit is straighter instead of being specifically curved for a particular railroad and its accompanying switch locks. A second type of 'car' key was used for door locks on passenger cars, Pullmans, etc.; this type was usually of brass, but instead of having a hollow barrel, they were shaped like an old-fashioned hotel door key. In order for a key to be collectible, the head must be marked with a name, initials, or a railroad identification, with 'switch' generally designated by 'S' and 'car' by 'C' markings. Railroad, patina 'not polished,' and the presence of a manufacturer's mark other than Adlake all have a positive affect on pricing and collectibility.

A new precedent was set in 1995 when a Denver and South Park 'car' key went at a Missouri auction for $2,500.00. The key was marked DSP&P (an early Colorado road that stopped running in 1898); it was brass and had a hollow barrel and straight bit. Switch keys that only recently brought $15.00 to $17.00 are now bringing $35.00.

Cab, CNR, Mitchell, hollow bbl, serif letters 20.00
Cabinet, IA Central, brass 50.00
Coach, CNR, Mitchell, long hollow bbl 20.00
Hotel, CPR Empress Hotel, w/Empress tag 17.00
Switch, CPR, brass, serif letters 20.00
Switch, CPR, RMCo, M 20.00
Switch, CRI&P, NP 40.00
Switch, DMCRCo, brass 45.00
Switch, GTR, steel 20.00

Lamps

Berth, Pullman, steel/porc, egg shape, NM, pr 50.00
Caboose bunk, UP, steel/brass, pebbled top globe 45.00
Caboose interior, C&O, 1920s, pr, NM (unused) 400.00
Caboose marker, Armspear, ACL mk, 4-way, complete, scarce ..300.00
Caboose side, C&O, 1920s, unused, pr 350.00
Desk, station; ACL, ornate cast metal & brass, EX 1,000.00
Semaphore, UP, Adlake, electric, dbl bull's-eye lens, NM 90.00
Switch, PRR, Adlake, SM PRR Keystone, 1909, EX 225.00

Lanterns

Before 1920 kerosene brakemen's lanterns were made with tall globes, usually 5⅜" high. These are most desirable to collectors and are usually found at the top of the price scale. Short globes from 1921 through 1940 normally measure 3½" in height, except for those manufactured by Dietz, which are 4" tall. (Soon thereafter, battery brakemen's lanterns came into widespread useage; these are not highly regarded by collectors and are generally not railroad marked.)

All lanterns should be marked with the name or initials of the railroad — look on the top, the top apron, or the bell base (if it has one). Globes may be found in these colors (listed in order of popularity): clear, red, amber, aqua, cobalt, and two-color.

AT&SF, tall clear unmk globe, bell bottom, EX 225.00
B&O, Dietz 999, sm mk globe, EX 65.00
BR&P, CT Ham, clear tall cast globe, bell-bottom, 5⅜" 200.00
BR&P, Dietz #39, rnd top w/Engine on lid, mk globe, bell-bottom ...475.00
Burlington Rte, Handlan, short clear unmk globe, EX 75.00
Conductor's, brass, globe mk P Co, 1864 ....900.00
D&H-CT Ham, clear script logo tall globe, bell-bottom, 5⅜" 275.00
D&SL, Adams & Westlake, emb top, unmk tall globe, Pat 1909 ..350.00

Delaware & Hudson, Adlake, short red unmk globe, EX **70.00**
Erie, Adams & Westlake, tall red globe, wire bottom, 5⅜" **200.00**
Erie RR, Armspeare, tall clear emb globe, EX **225.00**
Frisco, Handlan, clear mk globe, mk apron, drop-in pot, 5⅜" **200.00**
Keystone Casey, Seaboard, tall mk globe, 1903, VG+ **350.00**
LS&MS, Adams & Westlake, tall globe, wire bottom, EX **200.00**
LV, Armspear, 6" bl emb globe, 6" wire bottom, scarce, EX **1,500.00**
NP, flat vertical ribs, tall clear unmk globe, EX **225.00**
NP (on apron), Dressel, short red unmk globe, EX **75.00**
NY Central, Adlake 200, clear short globe, dtd 1923 ....**60.00**
NY Central, Dietz #6, clear emb 6" globe **85.00**
NYLE&W, Adams, Adams & Westlake, clear mk globe, VG **500.00**
NYNH&H, Dietz, short clear unmk globe, EX **65.00**
NYNH&H, Dietz 39 Vulcan, unmk tall globe, wire bottom, 5⅜", EX .**75.00**
P&LE, Dietz, short clear unmk globe, EX **75.00**
PRR, Adlake Reliable, tall etched globe, wire bottom, 5⅜" **100.00**
PRR in Keystone, Adlake Reliable, short clear unmk globe **150.00**
PS&N, Dietz Vulcan, etched globe, twist-off pot, VG **325.00**
Pullman, Adams & Westlake, NP brass, Pat Apr 26, '64, 9⅝x5⅛" **300.00**
Rio Grande, Handlan, mk melon globe, blk pnt, emb apron **350.00**
Rio Grande, Handlan, tall unmk globe, mk apron, no font **175.00**
Santa Fe, tall emb globe, bell-bottom, G **295.00**
ST&SF, Handlan, tall Safety First globe, twist-off pot, G **150.00**

Linens and Uniforms

Apron, bartender's; UP, gray w/Overland logo on plum **22.00**
Blanket, GN, Empire Builder, gr & orange wool, full sz **280.00**
Blanket, GN, woven goat logo center, brn & rose, wool, 67x84" .**275.00**
Blanket, KCS logo woven center, rose, wool, 58x88" **150.00**
Blanket, Pullman in center, wool, full sz **160.00**
Coat, conductor's; NYNH&H brass buttons, 1950s **55.00**
Hand towel, CP woven in center strip, wht-on-wht, 20x12½" **7.00**
Hand towel, CRI&P, lg RI logo, yel waffle weave, 24x15" **16.00**
Hand towel, Pullman, bl center stripe w/date, from $10 to **18.00**
Headrest cover, ACL, beach scene, purple on gray **22.00**
Headrest cover, C&O, The Chessie Route w/cat, 16x23" **38.00**
Headrest cover, CRI&P, orange Rock Island on tan w/stripes **18.00**
Headrest cover, GM&O in winged logo, maroon on tan **24.00**
Headrest cover, L&N red logo on cream, 16x20" **11.00**
Headrest cover, MKT embr on bottom, gr & blk vertical stripes ..**65.00**
Headrest cover, PRR in fancy keystone, 2-button style **25.00**
Headrest cover, UP, yel w/red Streamliner logo **21.00**
Jacket, waiter's; CRI&P, wht w/Rock Island Lines patch **25.00**
Jacket, waiter's; RG&W patch on sleeve, wht w/bl & gold piping .**55.00**
Jacket, waiter's; SP, Sunset logo on lapels, wht **28.00**
Napkin, B&O, Capitol Dome logo, wht-on-wht **27.00**
Napkin, NP/Yellowstone Parke Line logo, wht-on-wht, 22" sq **28.00**
Napkin, NY Central System in center oval, wht-on-wht **30.00**
Napkin, Pullman in center logo, wht-on-wht, 18" sq **25.00**
Napkin, UP, Overland Route TL in wreath, wht-on-wht, 23" sq .**22.00**
Napkin, UP, pk-on-pk w/UP & sm rose in ea corner **35.00**
Shop cloth, dmn logo: IC+safety slogans, 17x30" **7.00**
Shop cloth, Wabash RR Co, 27x16" **10.00**
Tablecloth, ATSF, Santa Fe, script, wht-on-wht, 59x40" **55.00**
Tablecloth, B&O, Capitol Dome logo, wht-on-wht, 54x66" **38.00**
Tablecloth, CA Zephyr, center logo, wht-on-wht, 44" sq **35.00**
Tablecloth, NYC spelled out on corner, wht-on-wht, 45x59" **25.00**
Tablecloth, Prop of AMTRAK, stamped, wht, 50x60" **12.00**
Tablecloth, PRR, keystone ea corner, wht-on-wht, 46x56" **45.00**
Tablecloth, Pullman in center w/florals, wht-on-wht, 43x34" **110.00**
Tablecloth, SOO, center logo, wht-on-wht, 34x44" **65.00**
Tablecloth, ST&SF, Frisco Lines TL, wht-on-wht, 36" sq **55.00**
Tablecloth, UP, pk-on-pk w/UP & sm rose in ea corner **65.00**

Locks

Brass switch locks (pre-1920) were made in two styles: heart-shaped and Keen Kutter style. Values for the heart-shaped locks are determined to a great extent by the railroad they represent and just how its name appears on the lock. Most in demand are locks with large embossed letters; if the letters are small and incised, demand for that lock is minimal. For instance, one from the Union Pacific line (even with heavily embossed letters) may go for only $45.00, while the same from the D&RG railroad could go easily sell for $250.00. Old Keen Kutter styles (brass with a 'pointy' base) from Colorado & Southern and Denver & Rio Grande could range from $600.00 to $1,200.00.

Steel switch locks (circa 1920 on) with the initials of the railroad incised in small letters — for example BN, L&H, and PRR — are usually valued at $20.00 to $28.00.

Lock and key, Illinois Central, brass, Remove Key When Locking embossed on front, $150.00.

Mail, US Mail Bag, stamped steel, no key **20.00**
NKP, Yale & Powine, brass, lg, w/key, scarce **70.00**
NYCS #11, metal, lg, w/mk brass key **80.00**
PRR, metal w/17 brass studs, sm heart shape **45.00**
Signal, C&NW, brass **45.00**
Signal, CRIP, brass, w/2 keys **50.00**
Signal, NIR-CRC, brass **50.00**
Signal, RACO, brass, VG **15.00**
Signal, Rock Island Lines, brass **50.00**
Switch, C&A, Keen Kutter, brass **230.00**
Switch, C&S, Adlake, chrome-plated steel, presentation, w/key ..**60.00**
Switch, CPR, Adlake, cast steel, stamped shank, w/key **30.00**
Switch, CPR, steel, w/key **27.50**
Switch, CR&IP, Adlake **15.00**
Switch, D&RGW, Adlake **20.00**
Switch, Rock Island, Adlake **15.00**
Terminal, NY **40.00**
Western Union Telegraph Co, brass **50.00**
Yard, CM&STP, Baggage Car Cellar, brass **350.00**
Yard, Yale, mk Linen Room **7.00**
Yard, Yale, mk Locker Room **7.00**
Yard, Yale, mk Oil House **7.00**

Silverplate

The value of silverplate, hollow ware, or flatware, is influenced by the location of the logo or railroad name and, of course, by condition. A side- or top-marked piece is preferable to one with a bottom mark. Examine a prospective purchase carefully. Some unmarked flatware has been 'enhanced' with a rather crude stamping of the railroad's name. Authentic railway markings were done at the time of manufacture and were generally executed in a flawless manner.

Butter icer, ATSF, BM, Internat'l, 2-pc **27.00**

Butter icer, SP, Sunset TL, BS, Internat'l, 2-pc 110.00
Butter pat, ATSF, BM, Internat'l, 2¾" sq 39.00
Butter pat, B&A, BM, Reed & Barton, 3¾" 40.00
Butter pat, CA Zephyr, TM, Internat'l, 3¼" 63.00
Butter pat, D&H, BM, Reed & Barton, 3½" sq 45.00
Butter pat, GN, incised G over N, TL, BM, Internat'l, 3½" 48.00
Butter pat, MKT, BM, Wallace, 3½" 38.00
Coffeepot, B&O, hinged lid, BM, Reed & Barton, 10-oz 110.00
Coffeepot, MP, hinged lid, ornate, SL, Internat'l, 8-oz 135.00
Coffeepot, UP System/Overland shield SL, 32-oz 365.00
Corn holders, C&NW, SM, Reed & Barton 75.00
Creamer, B&O, hinged lid, BM, Reed & Barton, 8-oz 135.00
Creamer, CRI&P, Golden Rocket, SM & BS 175.00
Creamer, Fred Harvey, BM, Gorham, 3-oz 75.00
Crumber & scraper, GN, TM/BM, Internat'l, 12" L 325.00
Cup holder w/hdl, MP, SM buzz saw logo & MP, Internat'l 200.00
Finger bowl, NP/YPL, w/underplate, TL & BM, Internat'l, 4½" H ...95.00
Fork, cocktail; MKT, Cromwell, TM, Internat'l 38.00
Fork, dinner; D&H, Royal, TL, BS, Reed & Barton 45.00
Gravy boat, C&NW, BM, Internat'l, 6-oz 85.00
Horseradish bottle holder, CMStP&P, w/glass insert, SL 145.00
Hot food cover, L&N box SL, BM, Internat'l, 6¼" 95.00
Hot food cover, N&W, SL (cursive), Internat'l, 6¼" 195.00
Hot food cover, UP Overland shield TL, Rogers, 6¾" 55.00
Ice cream dish, CRI&P, SM: Golden Rocket, BM, 3" H 145.00
Ice cream fork, SRR, Carlton, TM, Reed & Barton 55.00
Iced-tea spoon, B&O, Cromwell, TM 34.00
Iced-tea spoon, ERIE, Grecian, TM, Internat'l 26.00
Knife, butter; B&O, Clovelly, TM, Reed & Barton 35.00
Knife, butter; GN, Hutton, TM 21.00
Knife, butter; LV, Radisson, TM, Gorham 120.00
Knife, dinner, C&NW, Modern Art, BM 39.00
Knife, dinner; SP, Broadway, BM 26.00
Knife, fruit; ATSF, Cromwell 15.00
Ladle, C&RI, Stanhope, BS, Gorham, 7" L 115.00
Menu holder, GN, w/pencil holders, BS, Internat'l 125.00
Nut pick, FEC, TL, Internat'l, 5" 78.00
Pitcher, Canadian Nat'l in maple leaf SL, Internat'l, 48-oz 270.00
Seafood pick, BS: New Haven RR, w/thumb rests, Internat'l 125.00
Shakers, GN, SM, BM, cone shape, Internat'l, 4", pr 425.00
Shakers, NYC, 20th Century, SM, Internat'l, 3¾", pr 350.00
Sherbet, C&RI, Golden Rocket SL, ped ft, BM, Internat'l, 3" ...135.00
Spoon, bouillon; B&O, Cromwell, TM, Internat'l 25.00
Spoon, bouillon; SP, Broadway, BS, Rogers 12.00
Spoon, demitasse; C&O, Vandome, TM: Homestead, Reed & Barton ...18.00
Spoon, grapefruit; NYC, Century, BS, Internat'l 18.00
Spoon, mustard; GN (ornately mk), Windsor, Meriden 43.00
Spoon, mustard; SP, BS w/Winged Ball logo, Broadway, Internat'l ..28.00
Spoon, serving; ACL, Zephyr, TM, Internat'l 26.00
Spoon, souvenir; GN, Big Baked Potato, sterling 75.00
Sugar bowl, NYC, 20th Century, hinged lid, TM, Internat'l 60.00
Sugar bowl, SRR, hdls, w/lid, SL, Reed & Barton, 9-oz 155.00
Sugar tongs, ACL, Cromwell, SL, Internat'l 118.00
Sugar tongs, CB&Q, Belmont, TM, Reed & Barton 125.00
Sugar tongs, L&N, Cromwell, BS, Internat'l 95.00
Sugar tongs, NYC, Commonwealth, TM 85.00
Syrup pitcher, CN, SL, Internat'l, 8-oz 85.00
Tablespoon, PRR, Kings, TM w/raised keystone, Internat'l 30.00
Tablespoon, SP, Clovelly, TL, Reed & Barton 75.00
Tea strainer, IC, TM, Wallace 165.00
Teapot, ERIE, SM (in script), Wallace, 8-oz 210.00
Teapot, NYNH&H, BS, Meriden, 10-oz 155.00
Teapot, SP, long spout, BS, Reed & Barton, 16-oz 175.00
Teaspoon, T&P, Waverly, TL, Reed & Barton 85.00

Teaspoon, WP, Hutton, BL, Internat'l 25.00
Tray, bread; Fred Harvey, BS, Reed & Barton, 11½x5½" 78.00
Tray, bread; SAL, TM, BS, Internat'l, 11½x5½" 160.00
Tray, CRI&P, oval w/beaded rim, BS, Meriden 65.00
Tray, GN, oval w/beaded rim, BS, Meriden, 7x4" 110.00
Tray, PRR, TL: lg keystone, Internat'l, 14" dia 385.00
Tray, tip; UP, TM: Overland, Rogers, 6" 95.00
Tray, tip; WP, BS, Internat'l, 6½" 75.00
Tureen, MP Buzz-saw SL, hdls, w/lid, BS, Internat'l, 12-oz 125.00

Miscellaneous

  Annual passes continue to be favored over trip and one-time passes. Their value is contingent upon the specific railroad, its length of run, and the appearance of the pass itself. Many were tiny works of art enhanced with fancy calligraphy and decorated with unique vignettes.

  Timetables continue to gain in popularity and offer the collector vast information about the glory days of railroading. Pins and badges bearing the name or logo of a railroad are also popular collectibles. The novice needs to be cautious about signs (metal as well as cardboard) and belt buckles. Reproductions flourish in these areas.

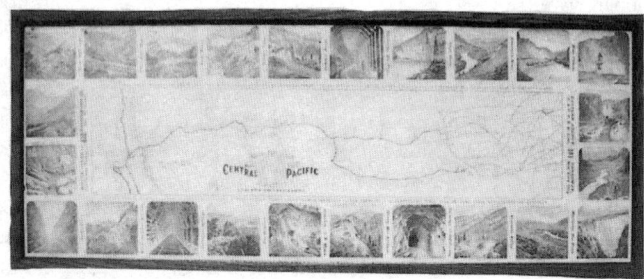

Map/Timetable, Central Pacific, vignettes of Northwest with timetable on reverse, a 1871, 13x36", EX, $550.00.

Ashtray, PRR, Keystone shape, Bakelite, Vespeo 35.00
Ashtray/drink stand, CP logo on base, floor model, Smokador ...340.00
Ashtray/drink stand, SP logo on base, floor model, 27" 630.00
Badge, breast; ACL Police Dept, eagle top, pin clasp, 1¼x1⅞" ..172.00
Badge, cap; ACL Flagman, dome style 85.00
Badge, cap; celluloid & brass-color fr, ornate, 3x1½" 45.00
Badge, cap; PRR Trainman, red enamel keystone logo 75.00
Badge, cap; Yonkers RR Co Conductor, silver, 5½x2½" 52.00
Badge, PRR Police, silver shield w/blk enamel, 2¼x2½" 135.00
Bag, water; UP, canvas over alumimum, rope hdl, 14x12" 35.00
Baggage tag, IC, brass heart shape, 1¾x1¾" 37.00
Baggage tag, PRR, brass, 2¼x1¾" 68.00
Billfold, B&O logo on blk leather w/plastic windows 15.00
Billfold, GN goat logo, gold on leather, in orig box 65.00
Blotter, desk; UP, City of Portland, off-wht, 21x14" 15.00
Blotter, MP, buzz-saw logo, 3x6" 5.00
Blotter, NP, Big Baked Potato, full color, diecut 22.00
Blotter, UP, City of Denver, 3x6" 7.00
Book, Electric Telegraph, Prescott, 1866, 3rd ed, 508-pg 165.00
Book, Freight Traffic Red Book, w/map, 1928, 8th ed, 568-pg 17.00
Book, Locomotive Handbook, Am Locomotive Co, 1917, pocket sz, 195-pg ..24.00
Book, McGraw Electric Ry..., 1919, 274-pg, 4¼x8¼" 86.00
Book, Nothing Could Be Finer, soft cover, Sandknop, 1977 ....30.00
Book, pocket dictionary, SAL, leatherette, 4½x5½", 359-pg 15.00
Book, Signal Dictionary, 1911 ed, illus, 526-pg 158.00
Book, view; SP, Overland Trail, faux leather, 1925, 9x12" 42.00
Book, view; WP, From San Francisco, 18 pictures, 1944, 9x12" ...35.00
Booklet, Pullman Commissary Instructions, 1939, 208-pg 38.00

Booklet, Rocky Mtns of Colorado, string ties, 1913, 11x8½" **12.00**
Booklet, Salt Lake Rte: Sign of Arrowhead, 1910, 25-pg **40.00**
Booklet, SP Lines Scenic Grandeur of West, 1942, 10x8" **13.00**
Button, CP logo, bl enamel on brass, ⅞" **6.00**
Button, Pullman TM, domed, brass, 1912, ⅝", G **3.00**
Button, SP intertwined, brass, ⅞" **5.00**
Calendar, ATSF, Navajo Shepherdess, 1954, 14x24" **75.00**
Calendar, KCS, wall refillable holder, 1970 pad, 7½x12" **67.00**
Calendar, L&N, months fr system map, logo, 22x28" **24.00**
Calendar, perpetual wall; MP, complete w/fr & cards **275.00**
Calendar, PRR, Teller, full pad, 1940s & '50s, 28½" sq, ea **120.00**
Catalog, Am Ry Supply Co, illus (badges/sealers/etc), pre-1915 .**215.00**
Catalog, freight car; Mt Vernon Mfg, drawings/specs, 1921 ....**97.00**
Catalog, truck; Case, Crane & Eng Co, illus, 1924 ....**72.00**
Catalog, Union Switch & Signal Co, VI, '11-'24, 7½x10" **55.00**
Chimes, dining car; w/mallet, 4-tone, Deagan **200.00**
Cigarette lighter, SOO logo ea side, wht on red, Warco **34.00**
Cigarette lighter, WP, steel w/wht enamel: Feather River Rte **55.00**
Coin, ATSF: When the Chips Are Down, plastic (like poker chip) .**6.00**
Coin (lucky), UP, cast aluminum, late '30s-era locomotive, 1¼" ...**5.00**
Cup, collapsible, emb NP on lid, aluminum **35.00**
Cup, collapsible, Rock Island logo on lid, plastic **15.00**
Dipper, water; ATSF, raised SL, tin, 13" **68.00**
Dixie cups, DL&WRR, paper, SM: rte of Phoebe Snow, MIB **10.00**
Dust pan, hooded, raised PRR, hanging loop, 13" W **68.00**
Envelopes, various RR return addresses, 1940s, legal sz, ea **3.00**
Fan, hand; PRR logo on paper w/wood hdl **11.00**
Fan, hand; Wabash, Shriner hat shape w/wood hdl **14.00**
Feather duster, DL&W, paper collar: Lackawanna Line, 36" **85.00**
Fire bucket, SOO, cone shape w/bail hdl, 19" **48.00**
Golf balls, SOO, boxed set of 3 w/logo on ea **18.00**
Hanger, clothes; Pullman, wooden, bottom bar **25.00**
Holster, REA, for Colt 38 revolver, Jos Kantor **85.00**
Jug, Property of Chicago & Northwestern, stoneware, 1-gal **265.00**
Labels, REA, pad of 50, 3x5" **4.00**
Letter opener, NP, Monad logo+Baked Potato both sides, brass .**155.00**
Letter opener, NP Cook Oil Co, tank-car shape, 9" L **23.00**
Magazine cover, Santa Fe (script) on leatherette, old lg LHJ sz **35.00**
Magazine cover, UP, emb Time on leather, 9½x12" **55.00**
Map, wall; CRI&P, USA, schoolroom type, 1928, 59x45" **110.00**
Matchbook, UP logo, red on wht, wide **2.00**
Measuring tape, C&O, TL: Chessie Measures Up, in orig box **28.00**
Menu, C&A, Pioneer Dining Car Line, undtd, very early **29.00**
Menu, CP, Mountaineer, painting of tunnels, 1938, 8-pg **35.00**
Menu, CRI&P, Golden State Ltd, emb oranges, 6x10" folded **27.00**
Menu, Fred Harvey, cover: Arrival of Harvey Girls, 1948 ....**16.00**
Menu, GN, Winold Reis, 1930s **23.00**
Menu, IC, Hawkeye Dinner, 1936, folds to 9x6" **20.00**
Menu, NYC, child's cartoon, diesel diecut, 4½x6" **21.00**
Menu, PRR, Broadway, Ltd, 1949, lg dinner folder **9.00**
Menu, UP, Disneyland cover, City of Los Angeles, 1971 ....**18.00**
Menu, UP, Streamliner, City of Los Angeles, 1954, dinner **11.00**
Napkins, paper, folded, 4½" sq, various railroads, ea **5.00**
Paperweight, B&O, medallion, cast bronze w/trains, 2¾" dia **48.00**
Paperweight, IC, coin-like cast copper w/map, 1½" dia **30.00**
Paperweight, KCS logo on clear Lucite block, 2x2¾" **28.00**
Paperweight, PRR emb, brass w/ball finial, 2½" dia **60.00**
Pass, ATSF, widow's lifetime, gold, orig case **22.00**
Pass, C&S, raised logo, No 87, 1906 ....**150.00**
Pass, CB&Q w/BR logo, 1916 ....**8.00**
Pass, Grand Rapids & IN RR, 1918 ....**15.00**
Pass, Live Oak Perry & Gulf RR, 1930 ....**21.00**
Pass, Louisville, Evansville & StL, w/bank note, 1889 ....**50.00**
Pass, Philadelphia, Wilmington & Baltimore, ornate, 1886 ....**21.00**

Pass, Spokane Internat'l Ry, for wife & maid of RR President, 1927 .**22.00**
Pass, W Jersey & Seashore, ornate, 1905 ....**26.00**
Pass, WP w/Feather River Logo, 1936 ....**9.00**
Pen, ballpoint; ATSF, red on wht **5.00**
Pencil, mechanical; MP, Sunset Special & red logo on pearlized .**28.00**
Pencil, Norther Pacific in blk on red w/eraser, unused **3.00**
Pill box, hospital issue; ATSF, prescription dtd 1942, rnd **18.00**
Playing cards, ACL, Twin Palms, 2¼", emb M box **45.00**
Playing cards, B&O, 4 trains scene, unopened, 2¼" **55.00**
Playing cards, CM&PS, scenic, 2½", G slip case **98.00**
Playing cards, CMStP, Electric, scenic, 2½", G case **125.00**
Playing cards, D&RGW, Seals, scenic, 2½", EX case **80.00**
Playing cards, GN, W Reis Indian, 2 2¼" unopened decks+case ..**62.00**
Playing cards, L&N, Hummingbird, 2 2¼" decks, G box **45.00**
Playing cards, N&W, Rt of Pocahontas..., unopened, 2¼" **135.00**
Playing cards, SP, Sunset Ltd, 2½" deck, M box **65.00**
Pocketknife/money clip, FEC, red on silver color, 2½x2" **35.00**
Pocketwatch, Waltham Premier, 21 jewel, open face **250.00**
Poker chips, GN, goat logo, set of 100, MIB **175.00**
Ruler, C&N logo (front & bk) & train on wood, 15" **22.00**
Ruler, CGW, orange & blk logos on metal, 12" **24.00**
Ruler, M&StL logo & slogans on metal, hanging hole, 12" **45.00**
Scale, counter; Am Express, to 3½-lb, 6" dial, Columbia, 8" **135.00**
Shovel, caboose stove; Burlington Rte raised TM, CI, 22" **145.00**
Sign, Milwaukee Road, reflective pnt on heavy aluminum, 23x16" .**195.00**
Spittoon, SP, bl logo on wht porc over heavy metal **175.00**
Spittoon, UP, blk letters on gr porc over steel, 4½x8" **115.00**
Spittoon, Wabash emb on heavy metal, Handlan-Buck **195.00**
Stool, step; ATSF, SM, Morton, 10½x16x13¾" **235.00**
Stool, step; NP, SM, Morton, 10x15½x13½" **335.00**
Stool, step; T&P, SM, Morton, 10½x14½x9½" **285.00**
Swizzel stick, ATSF, plastic Indian head: The Chief Way **4.00**
Telegram pad, WU, unused blanks, ca 1950s, 40+ sheets **22.00**
Thermometer, GN, full-colored goat on wht enameled tin, 12¾" .**57.00**
Thermos, Pullman, chrome, 11" **75.00**
Timetable, employee's; Alaska RR, system, 1/92 ....**19.00**
Timetable, employee's; B&O, Baltimore Division, 1964 ....**10.00**
Timetable, employee's; CB&Q, Lincoln Division, 1938 ....**25.00**
Timetable, employee's; CB&Q, Lincoln Division, 1966 ....**12.00**
Timetable, employee's; GN, Klamath Division, 1960 ....**15.00**
Timetable, employee's; Santa Fe, 1975 ....**4.25**
Timetable, employee's; Spokane Internat'l, system, 1952 ....**25.00**
Timetable, employee's; Toronto, Hamilton, & Buffalo, system, 1951 ....**22.00**
Timetable, employee's; Wisconsin Central, system, 1990 ....**18.00**
Timetable, public; CN, 3/47, 86 dbl pgs **8.00**
Timetable, public; D&RGW, 10/46, 30-pg **11.00**
Timetable, public; D&RT, 12/12, 32-pg+8-pg map **60.00**
Timetable, public; MStP&SStM, 9/37, 30-pg **27.00**
Timetable, public; Q&CR, 11/02, 20 dbl pgs **80.00**
Timetable, public; 6/1/78, maps & graphics **88.00**
Tongs, 1-man tie; SP on CI, 32" L **48.00**
Tongs, 1-man tie; UP on CI, 28" L **28.00**
Tray, SOO, Opening of Montana Rts, 15x10½" **225.00**
Whistle, PRR emb on brass, police type **70.00**
Whistle, SP emb on blk Bakelite, police type **32.00**

Razors

As straight razors gain in popularity, prices of those razors also increase. This carries with it a lure of investment possibilities which can encourage the novice or speculator to make purchases that may later prove to be unwise. We recommend that before investing serious money in razors, you become familiar with the elements which make a razor valuable. As with other collectibles, there are specific traits which are desirable and which have a major impact on the price of a piece.

The following information is based on the second edition of *The Standard Guide to Razors* by Roy Richie and Ron Stewart (available from R&C Books, P.O. Box 151, Combs, KY 41729, $9.95 +$2.50 S&H, autographed). It describes the elements most likely to influence a razor's collector value and their system of calculating that value. (Their book is a valuable reference guide to both the casual and serious collector of razors.)

There are four major factors which determine a razor's collector value. These are the brand and country of origin, the handle material, the art work found on the handles or blades, and the condition of the razor. Ritchie and Stewart freely admit that there are other factors that may come into play with some collectors, but these are the major players in determining value. They have devised a system of evaluation which is based on these four factors.

The most important factor is the value placed on the brand and country of origin. This is the price of a common razor made by (or for) a particular company. It has plain handles, probably made of plastic, no art work, and is in collectible condition. It is the beginning value. Hundreds (thousands?) of these values are provided in the 'Listings of Companies and Base Values' chapter in the book.

The second category is that of handle material. This covers a wide range of materials, from fiber on the low end to ivory on the high end. The collector needs to be able to identify the different handle materials when he sees them. This often takes some practice, since there are some very good plastics that can mimic ivory quite successfully. Also, the difference between genuine celluloid and plastic can become significant when determining value. A detailed chart of these values is supplied in the book. The listing below can be used as a general guide.

The third category is the most subjective. Nevertheless, it is an extremely important factor in determining value. This category is artwork, which can include everything from logo art to carving and sculpture. It may range from highly ornate to tastefully correct. Blade etching as well as handle artistry are to be considered. Perhaps what some call the 'gotta have it' or the 'neatness' factors properly fall into this category. You must accurately determine the artistic merits of your razor when you evaluate it relative to this factor. Again, the book we referenced earlier provides a more complete listing of considerations than is used here.

Finally, condition is factored in. The book's scales run from 'parts' (10% +/-) to 'Good' (150% +/-). Average (100% +/-) is classified as 'Collectible.'

Samplings from charts:

Chart A: Companies and Base Values:

Abercrombie & Finch, NY	11.00
Aerial, USA	24.00
Boker, Henri & Co, Germany	14.00
Brick, F, England	10.00
Case Mfg Co, Spring Valley, NY	35.00
Chores, James	8.00
Dahlgren, CW; Sweeden	13.00
Diane, Japan	10.00
Electric Co, NY	15.00
ERN, Germany	12.00
Faultless, Germany	11.00
Fox Cutlery, Germany	12.00
Golden Rule Cutlery, Chicago	14.00
Griffon XX, Germany	10.00
Henckels, Germany	15.00
Holley Mfg Co CT	27.00
International Cutlery Co NY/Germany	9.00
IXL, England	14.00

Jay, John; NY	12.00
KaBar, Union Cut Co, USA	28.00
Kanner, J; Germany	10.00
Kern, R&W; Canada/England	9.00
LeCocltre, Jacque; Switzerland	14.00
Levering Razor Co, NY/Germany	18.00
McIntosh & Heather, OH	12.00
Merit Import Co, Germany	9.00
National Cut Co, OH	12.00
Oxford Razor Co, Germany	10.00
Palmer Brothers, Savannah, GA	20.00
Primble, John; India Steel Works, Louisville, KY	24.00
Queen City, NY	30.00
Quigley, Germany	11.00
Rattler Razor Co, USA	25.00
Robeson Cut Co, USA	28.00
Salamander Works, Germany	11.00
Soderein, Ekilstuna, Sweden	14.00
Taylor, LM; Cincinnati, OH	14.00
Tower Brand, Germany	10.00
Ulmer, Germany	10.00
US Barber Supply, TX	14.00
Vinnegut Hdw Co, IN	11.00
Vogel, ED; PA	12.00
Wade & Butcher, England	24.00
Weis, JH; Supply House, Louisville, KY	15.00
Yankee Cutlery Co, Germany	11.00
Yazbek, Lahod, OH	12.00
Zacour Bros, Germany	10.00
Zepp, Germany	9.00

Chart B, as described below, is an abbreviated version of the handle materials list in *The Standard Guide to Razors*. It is an essential category in the use of the appraisal system developed by the authors.

Ivory	550%
Tortoise Shell	500%
Pearl	400%
Stag	400%
Bone	300%
Celluloid	250%
Compostion	150%
Plastic	100%

Chart C deals with the artistic value of the razor. As pointed out earlier, this is a very subjective area. It takes study to determine what is good and what is not. Taste can also play a significant role in determining the value placed on the artistic merit of a razor. The range is from superior to nonexistent. Categories generally are divided as follows:

Exceptional	650%
Superior	550%
Good	400%
Average	300%
Minimal	200%
Plain	100%
Nonexistant	0%

Chart D is also very subjective. It determines the condition of the razor. You must judge accurately if the appraisal system is to work for you.

Good	150%

Does not have to be factory mint to fall within this cagegory. However, there can be no visible flaws if it is to be calculated at 150%.

Collectible 100%
May have some flaws that do not greatly detract from the artwork or finish.

Parts 10%
Unrepairable, valuable as salvageable parts.

Razors may fall within any of these categories, ie. collectible + 112%.

Now to determine the value of your razor, multiply A times B, then multiply A times C. Add your two answers and multiply this sum times D. The answer you get is your collector value. See the example below.

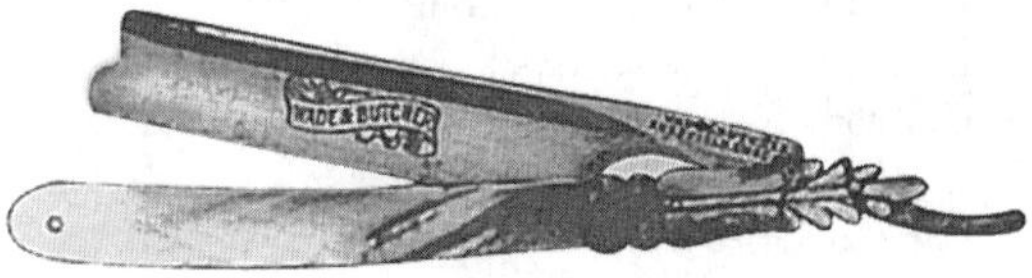

(a) Brand and Origin Base Value	(b) Handle Material % Value	(c) Artwork % Value	(d) Condition % Value	(e) Collector Value
Wade & Butcher England **$24.00**	Iridescent Pearl Handles 24 x400% **$96.00**	Carved handles 24 x 350% **$84.00**	Cracked handle at pin Collectible- 80%	$96+$84=$180 $180 x 80%= **$144.00**

Reamers

The reamer market is very active right now, and prices are escalating rapidly. They have been made in hundreds of styles and colors and by as many manufacturers. Their purpose is to extract the juices from lemons, oranges, and grapefruits. The largest producer of glass reamers was McKee, who pressed their products from many types of glass — custard; Delphite and Chalaine Blue; opaque white; Skokie Green; black; caramel and white opalescent; Seville Yellow; and transparent pink, green, and clear. Among these, the black and the caramel opalescents are the most valuable.

The Fry Glass Company also made reamers that are today very collectible. The Hazel Atlas Crisscross orange reamer in pink is valued at $275.00 to $300.00 or more — the same in blue, $375.00. Hocking produced a light blue orange reamer and, in the same soft hue, a two-piece reamer and measuring cup combination. Both are considered rare and very valuable with currently quoted estimates at $400.00 and up for the former and $800.00 and up for the latter. In addition to the colors mentioned, red glass examples — transparent or slag — are rare and costly. Prices vary greatly according to color and rarity. The same reamer in crystal may be worth three times as much in a more desirable color.

Among the most valuable ceramic reamers are those made by American potteries. The Spongeband reamer by Red Wing is valued in excess of $500.00; Coorsite reamers with gold or silver trim are worth $300.00 and up. Figurals are popular — Mickey Mouse and John Bull may bring $600.00 to $1,000.00. Others range from $55.00 to $350.00. Fine china one- and two-piece reamers are also very desirable and command very respectable prices.

A word about reproductions: A series of limited edition reamers is being made by Edna Barnes of Uniontown, Ohio. These are all marked with a 'B' in a circle. Other repoductions have been made from old molds. The most important of these are Anchor Hocking two-piece two-cup measure and top, Gillespie one-cup measure with reamer top, Westmoreland with flattened handle, Westmoreland four-cup measure embossed with orange and lemons, Duboe (hand-held darning egg), and Easley's Diamonds one-piece.

Our advisor for this category is Dee Long; she is listed in the Directory under Illinois. For more information concerning reamers and reproductions, contact our advisor or the National Reamer Collectors Association (see Clubs, Newsletters, and Catalogs). Be sure to include an SASE when requesting information.

Ceramic

Baby's, chicks jumping rope, pk 150.00
Baby's Orange, red & wht, Japan, 2-pc, 4½" 55.00

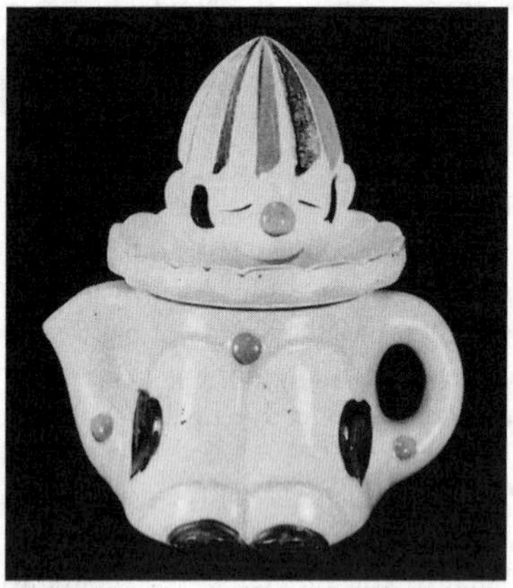

Clown, multicolor on white, Japan turtle mark, $80.00.

Clown, bl/yel/orange, Goebel saucer, 4½" 225.00
Clown, brn body & hat, bl button & collar, 6" 85.00
Clown, lime gr & wht, 4¾" 95.00
Clown, mc Japan, 6½" 75.00
Clown, polka dots, lustre hat, Japan, 4½" 125.00
Clown, Sourpuss, w/saucer, 4¾" 135.00
Clown, various colors, w/neck tie, Japan, 6" 125.00
Clown, wht/blk/red/orange, Japan, 2-pc, 6½" 95.00
Clown, 3-color on wht, Japan, 7½" 80.00
Clown face 'mug' 98.00
Dog, beige w/red & blk trim, 2-pc, 8" 225.00
Duck, sm 95.00
Elephant, mc on wht, Japan, 2-pc, 4¼" 200.00
Floral w/gold, Nippon, 2-pc 195.00
Floral w/gold, Royal Rudolstadt, 2-pc 250.00
Girl face 135.00
House, beige w/tan & orange trim, Japan, 2-pc, 5½" 100.00
Mexican w/cactus figural, Japan 225.00
Moss Rose 50.00
Pail w/hdl form, tan & yel, Japan, 7¾" 70.00
Paisley, wht on bl, England 70.00
Pear, yel & orange w/gr leaves, Japan, 4½" 60.00
Pitcher, blk w/gold wheat, 1960s, 2-pc, 8" 35.00
Pitcher, mc flowers on beige, tan trim at top 50.00
Pitcher form, rust leaves, dk bl trim, 3½" 45.00
Puddinhead, 2-pc, 6¼" 200.00
Rose, pk w/gr leaves, Germany, 1¾" 225.00
Rosebuds on gr, Japan, 2-pc 60.00
Sailboat form, yel or red, 3", ea 125.00
Saucer form, cream w/yel bees, Japan, 3¾" 45.00
Saucer w/head of Black man reamer, Japan, 3½" 325.00
Sleeping Mexican, gr shirt, red pants, gold top, Japan, 2-pc, 4¾" .150.00
Swan, 4" 125.00
Teapot, wht w/bl sailboat, Germany, 2-pc, 3¼" 80.00
Toby-style man figural, gray hair, gr coat, lav hat, 4¾" 175.00
USA, Ade-O-Matic, Genuine Coorsite Porcelain, gr, 9" 150.00
Windmill form, Japan, 4½" 75.00

Glass

Anchor Hocking, crystal, pitcher w/reamer top, 4-cup	35.00
Anchor Hocking, gr, pitcher form, ftd, 4-cup	40.00
Anchor Hocking, gr, panelled	20.00
Cambridge, amber, ear hdl	700.00
Cambridge, gr, ftd, sm	450.00
Cambridge, gr, tab hdl, sm	200.00
Easley's, crystal, chisel cone	75.00

Federal glass, amber, 8" from handle to spout, $35.00.

Federal, pk, ribbed, loop hdl	30.00
Federal, pk, tab hdl	100.00
Fenton, crystal, w/elephant decor on base, 2-pc	75.00
Fenton, red, pitcher w/reamer top	1,200.00
Fleur-de-lis, mustard	600.00
Fleur-de-lis, red	600.00
Fleur-de-lis, wht, emb lettering	85.00
Fry, Azure Bl, str sides, open tab hdl	1,300.00
Fry, Canary Yel, fluted side (Jell-O mold)	275.00
Fry, Emerald Gr, str side	30.00
Hazel Atlas, Crisscross, bl, orange reamer	375.00
Hazel Atlas, Crisscross, gr, lg	32.00
Hazel Atlas, Crisscross, pk, lemon reamer	325.00
Hazel Atlas, Crisscross, pk, orange reamer	300.00
Hazel Atlas, pk, orange reamer	225.00
Hazel Atlas, yel, pitcher w/reamer top, 2-cup	300.00
Hocking, Vitrock, loop hdl, orange reamer	30.00
Indiana, amber, hdld, spout opposite	300.00
Jeannette, Delphite, sm	110.00
Jeannette, gr, tab hdl, 5"	15.00
Jeannette, pk, Hex Optic, bucket reamer	45.00
Jeannette, pk, tab hdl, 5⅞"	40.00
Jeannette, ultramarine	75.00
Jenkins, gr, 2-pc	150.00
LE Smith, pk, 2-pc, baby sz	150.00
LE Smith, pk or gr, 2-pc, ea	275.00
Lindsay, gr	450.00
Lindsay, pk	475.00
McKee, blk, grapefruit reamer	925.00
Mckee, Delphite, sm, rare	645.00
Morgantown, gr, pitcher w/reamer top, 2-cup	250.00
Orange Juice Extractor, pk, unemb	60.00
Paden City, amber, Party Line, cocktail shaker/reamer	110.00
Paden City, blk, Party Line, pitcher w/reamer top, 2-cup	550.00
RADNT, pk	450.00
RE-GO, gr	600.00
Sunkist, blk	600.00
Sunkist, caramel	400.00
Sunkist, Chalaine Bl	275.00
Sunkist, chocolate	600.00

Sunkist, Crown Tuscan	400.00
Sunkist, Crown Tuscan, milk glass	300.00
Sunkist, Jade-ite	65.00
Sunkist, milk glass, Westmoreland	25.00
Sunkist, Skokie Gr, pointed cone, 5¼"	55.00
Sunkist, wht, emb McK	20.00
Tufglas, gr	150.00
Unmk, cobalt, tab hdl, sm	275.00
US Glass, amber, pitcher w/reamer top, 4-cup	550.00
US Glass, gr, slick hdl, grapefruit reamer	450.00
US Glass, pk, tub form w/reamer top, 4-pc	220.00
US Glass, wht, pitcher w/reamer top, 2-cup	150.00
US Glass, yel, pitcher form	500.00
Westmoreland, amber, 2-pc, baby sz	195.00
Westmoreland, crystal w/decor, 2-pc	40.00
Westmoreland, crystal w/oranges decor, flattened loop hdl, ea	65.00
Westmoreland, pk, 2-pc	175.00

Records

Records of interest to collectors are often not the million-selling hits by 'superstars.' Very few records by Bing Crosby, for example, are of any more than nominal value, and those that are valuable usually don't even have his name on the label! Collectors today are most interested in records that were made in limited quantities, early works of a performer who later became famous, and those issued in special series or aimed at a limited market. Vintage records are judged desirable by their recorded content as well; those that lack the quality of music that makes a record collectible will always be 'junk' records in spite of their age, scarcity, or the obsolescence of their technology.

Records are usually graded visually rather than by audio quality, since it is seldom if ever possible to first play the records you buy at shows, by mail, at flea markets, etc. Condition is one of the most important value-assessing factors. For example, a truly mint-condition Elvis Presley 45 of Milk Cow Blues (Sun 215) has a potential value of over $1,000.00. If that same 45 had a sticker on it that was one-eighth of an inch square, it could lose up to half of that value! To be judged mint, a record and sleeve must be in original, unsealed condition. It must show absolutely no evidence of use. Excellent condition is a rating applied to a record that may show slight signs of wear and use but will have almost no audible defect.

While the value of most 78s does not depend upon their being in appropriate sleeves or jackets (although a sleeveless existence certainly contributes to damage and deterioration!), this is not the case with many 45s, most EPs (extended play 45s) and LPs (long-playing 33⅓s). Often, common and otherwise minimally valued 45s might be collectible if they are in appropriate 'picture sleeves' (special sleeves that depict the artist/group or other fanciful or symbolic graphic and identify the song titles, record label, and number), e.g. many common records by Elvis Presley, The Beatles, and The Beach Boys. In order for most EPs and LPs to be saleable, they *must* be in their original jackets and in nice condition — indeed, excellent or better — unless they are very scarce and sought after. Sleeves may show marginal deterioration but no repairs, pen or pencil marks, stickers, or physical damage. A Good record has both visual and audible distractions but is still playable. Sleeves will show ring wear but will not be physically damaged, and Fair indicates a record that is both visually and audibly distracting, one that has obvious damage — no skips, but possibly 'play through' scratches. It can still be usable. Sleeves will show heavy ring wear and some minor physical damage. A Poor record may or may not play. Sleeves are faded, torn, marked, or otherwise damaged beyond pleasurable viewing.

Many promo records being discarded by radio stations today are finding their way into collections. These may say 'Not for Sale,' 'Audition Copy,' 'D.J.,' etc. These radio station versions are sometimes different than commercial issues and sometimes more sought after than their commercial twins. Promos by certain 'hot' artists, such as Elvis Presley and The Beach Boys are usually premium disks.

Our advisor for this category is L.R. Docks, author of *American Premium Record Guide*, which lists 60,000 records by over 7,000 artists, now in its fifth edition. He is listed in the Directory under Texas. In the listings that follow, prices are suggested for records that are in excellent condition. 45 rpm records are with sleeves. Records are 78 rpm unless noted otherwise.

Key:
Bru — Brunswick   Para — Paramount
Ch — Champion   Orch — Orchestra
Col — Columbia   Vi — Victor
Edi — Edison   Vo — Vocalion

Edison (special) record pressed for Edison dealers, Christmas season 1924, features the voice of Thomas Edison, excellent condition in original sleeve, $100.00 or more.

Blues, Rhythm and Blues, Rock 'N Roll, Rockabilly

Adams, Charlie; Pistol Packin' Mama..., Co 21445, 45 rpm 8.00
Anderson, Maybelle; Moanful Wailin' Blues, Supertone 9429 ...200.00
Angel, Johnny; Baby I'm Confessin', Excello 2077, 45 rpm 15.00
Bachelors, Delores, Earl 101, 45 rpm 30.00
Barron, Lonnie; Teenage Queen, Sage 230, 45 rpm 12.00
Beasley, Jimmy; Fabulous, Crown CLP 5014, LP 30.00
Beatnicks, Blue Angel, Key-Lock 913, 45 rpm 15.00
Bennett, Will; Railroad Bill, Vo 1464 ....150.00
Berry, Chuck; Johnny B Goode, Chess 1691, 45 rpm 10.00
Blue Belles, Story of a Fool, Atlantic 987, 45 rpm 8.00
Boyd, Eddie; Cool Kind Treatment, Chess 1523, 45 rpm 20.00
Boyd, Robert; East St Louis Baby, Wasco 201 ....20.00
Brown, Charles; Educated Fool, Ace 561, 45 rpm 10.00
Buck, Peter; That's Enough, Drew-Blan 1005, 45 rpm 10.00
Burston, Clara; Try That Man O' Mine, Ch 16125 ....250.00
Cadets, Do You Wanna Rock, Modern 971, 45 rpm 15.00
Carl, Steve; Curfew, Meteor 6046, 45 rpm 40.00
Carter, Charlie; Long Lost John, Broadway 5076 ....50.00
Carter, Harry; Jump Baby Jump, Mar-Vel 1300, 45 rpm 20.00
Chantels, I Love You So, End 1015, 45 rpm 8.00
Charles, Bobby; Later Alligator, Chess 1609, 45 rpm 15.00
Chuckles, On Street Where You Live, West Side 1019, 45 rpm ...10.00
Cochran Brothers, Walkin' Stick Boogie, Cash 1021, 45 rpm 30.00
Collins Kids, Beetle Bug Bop, Co 21470, 45 rpm 15.00
Country Jim, Rainy Morning Blues, Imperial 5062 ....10.00
Crain, Jimmy; Shig-A-Shag, Spangle 2009, 45 rpm 15.00
Crickets (w/Buddy Holly), That'll Be the Day, Bru 55009, 45 rpm .10.00
Curry, Earl; Try & Get Me, R&B 1313, 45 rpm 15.00
Darin, Bobby & Jaybirds; Splish Splash, Atco 6117 ....25.00
Davis, Link; Bon Ton Rula, All Star 7171, 45 rpm 7.00

Davis, Walter; Moonlight Is My Spread, Bluebird 6167 ....15.00
Dee, Ronnie; Action Packed, Back Beat 522, 45 rpm 10.00
Derringers, Sheree, Capitol 4532, 45 rpm 10.00
Dominoes, Sixty Minute Man, Federal 12022, 45 rpm 50.00
Down South Boys, Down on My Bended Knees, Varsity 6019 ......20.00
Duffill, Tam; Cooly Dooly, Groove 58-0004, 45 rpm 12.00
Earls, Remember Then, Old Town 1130, 45 rpm 8.00
Enchanters, True Love Gone, Coral 62756, 45 rpm 8.00
Fairburn, Werly; Good Deal Lucille, Capitol 2770, 45 rpm 10.00
Feathers & Frogs, How You Get That Way, Para 12812 ....200.00
Five Jets, I Am in Love, De Luxe 6018, 45 rpm 40.00
Ford, Tennessee Ernie; Ol' Rockin' Ern, Capitol 888, LP 20.00
Fuller, Jerry; Blue Memories, LIN 5011, 45 rpm 12.00
Garland, Hattie; Strange Woman's Dream, Black Patti 8005 .....200.00
Gibson, Clifford; Jive Me Blues, Vo 1246 ....100.00
Glad Rags, My China Doll, Excello 2121, 45 rpm 15.00
Gulf Coast Quartet, Alabama Blues, Co 14012-D 30.00
Gypsies, Why, Atlas 1073, 45 rpm 20.00
Harper, Sonny; Lonely Stranger, Ball 1011, 45 rpm 8.00
Hill, Charlie; Papa Charlie Hill Blues, Gennett 6904 ....600.00
Holly, Buddy; Peggy Sue, Coral 61885, 45 rpm 10.00
Hooker, John Lee; High Priced Woman, Chess 1505, 45 rpm 100.00
Hot Shot Love, Wolf Call Boogie, Sun 196, 45 rpm 150.00
Howlin' Wolf, Mr Highway Man, Chess 1510, 45 rpm 100.00
Huff, Willie B; Operator 209, Big Town 105 ....15.00
Hunter, Alberta; Bleeding Heart Blues, Para 12021 ....50.00
Jan & Dean, There's a Girl, Dore 531, 45 rpm 12.00
Johnson, Edna; I'm Drifting From You Blues, Gennett 5367 ....50.00
Johnson, Ruth; Rockin' Chair, Para 13060 ....75.00
Jones, George; Salutes Hank Williams, Mercury 20596, LP 30.00
King, BB; Singing the Blues, Crown 5020, LP 30.00
Lane, Ernest; Prowlin' Ground Hog, Talent 805 ....50.00
Leaders, Stormy Weather, Glory 235, 45 rpm 12.00
Louisiana Johnny, Policy Blues, Vo 02980 ....40.00
Mac Sales, Gal Named Joe, Meteor 5022, red label, 45 rpm 30.00
Majestics, How Long Will It Last, Bim 1, 45 rpm 12.00
Martells, Forgotten Spring, Cessna 477, 45 rpm 20.00
McCoy, William; Mama Blues, Co 14302-D 40.00
Memphis Mose, Billie the Grinder, Bru 7143 ....150.00
Mickey & Sylvia, Love Is Strange, Groove 18, EP 40.00
Mississippi Mudder, Candy Man Blues, Decca 7036 ....50.00
Mitchell, Billy; Bald Head Woman, Atlantic 974, 45 rpm 20.00
Moore, Monette; Memphis Blues, Ajax 17124 ....50.00
Nelson, Ricky; Songs by Ricky, Imperial 9082, LP 40.00
Nugrape Twins, The Road Is Rough & Rocky, Co 14251-D 30.00
Parakeets, Teenage Rose, Atlas 1071, 45 rpm 20.00
Pentagons, To Be Loved, Donna 1337, 45 rpm 10.00
Pinetop, Workhouse Blues, Bluebird 6041 ....50.00
Premiers, Jolene, Alert 706, 45 rpm 20.00
Pruitt, Lewis; Pretty Baby, Peach 703, 45 rpm 30.00
Rafferty, Carl; Mr Carl's Blues, Bluebird 5429 ....100.00
Reeves, Jim; Girls I Have Known, RCA 1685, LP 15.00
Rockettes, I Can't Forget, Parrot 789, 45 rpm 200.00
Scare Crow, Easy Creeping Mama, Ch 16014 ....200.00
Silhouettes, Bing Bong, Ember 1037, 45 rpm 15.00
Sloppy Henry, Canned Heat Blues, Okeh 8630 ....100.00
Smith, Bessie; After You've Gone, Co 14197-D 50.00
Smith, Trixie; Triflin' Blues, Black Swan 14149 ....30.00
Snow, Hank; Country Guitar, RCA Victor 3267, LP 25.00
Sunny Jim & Whistlin' Joe, Black Snake Blues, Ch 15361 ....200.00
Supremes, I Want a Guy, Tamla 54038, 45 rpm 30.00
Taylor, Ethel; Empty Bed Blues, Supertone 9285 ....100.00
Temptations, Letter of Devotion, Goldisk 3007, 45 rpm 10.00
Travis & Bob, We're Too Young, Sandy 1017, 45 rpm 10.00

Tucker, Bessie; Bogy Man Blues, Bluebird 5128 ....100.00
Vaughn, Bobby; Good Good Lovin', Whiz 503, 45 rpm 12.00
Washington, Booker T; Just Want To Think, Bluebird 8352 ....20.00
Whitmire, Margaret; Tain't a Cow in Texas, Bru 7024 ....75.00
Yates, Blind Richard; Sore Bunion Blues, Gennett 6104 ....75.00

Country and Western

Allen Brothers, Pile Drivin' Papa, Vi 23578 ....50.00
Asparagus Joe, Asleep at the Switch, Ch 15709 ....10.00
Baker, Buddy; Box Car Blues, Vi 21549 ....15.00
Barlow, Jerry; Louisiana Baby, OT 103 ....7.00
Boone County Entertainers, Arkansas Traveler, Supertone 9163 ...8.00
Bowers & Lewis, Put on Your Old Gray Bonnet, Superior 2659 ...25.00
Cain, Albert; Runnin' Wild, Okeh 45567 ....40.00
Carolina Tar Heels, My Mamma Scolds Me, Vi 21193 ....50.00
Carter, Floyd; Flemington Kidnap Trial, Oriole 8847 ....10.00
Carter Family, Keep on the Sunny Side, Bluebird 5006 ....12.00
Childre, Lew; Moonshine Blues, Ch 16011 ....50.00
Crowder Brothers, Got No Use for Women, Vo 03030 ....15.00
Foley, David; I'll Never Be Yours, Challenge 393 ....12.00
Freed & Moore, Harmonica Blues, Vo 14865 ....10.00
Green, Amos; Memphis Yodel, Supertone 9671 ....18.00
Hackberry Ramblers, Dobie Shack, Bluebird 2019 ....12.00
Hart & Cates, In Valley of Broken Hearts, Okeh 45499 ....20.00
Hickory Nuts, Louisville Burglar, Okeh 45169 ....15.00
Horton, Johnny; Birds & Butterflies, Abbot 103 ....12.00
Hutchins, John; Preacher & Bear, Ch 15414 ....10.00
Johnson, Edward; Sand Cave, Ch 15048 ....7.00
Justice, Dick; Brown Skin Blues, Bru 336 ....20.00
Lambert & Hillpot, My Carolina Home, Para 3013 ....7.00
Lonesome Cowboy, Memphis Gal, Ch 16767 ....75.00
Mack, Bill; Play My Boogie, Imperial 8174 ....10.00
Major, Jack; Tenenssee Mountain Girl, Bru 252 ....20.00
Martin, John; Railroad Blues, Superior 2626 ....30.00
McGuire, Leon; When Blue Eyes Meet Brown, Vo 5393 ....10.00
Means, Grace; Your Mother Still Prays for You, Supertone 9244 ...8.00
Morris, Frank; Old Brown Pants, Para 3070 ....10.00
Mountain Dew Dare, Don't Love a Smiling..., Okeh 45170 ....12.00
Nichols Brothers, She's Killing Me, Vi 23582 ....100.00
Oaks, Charlie; Old Cottage Home, Vo 15346 ....8.00
Parker, Dan & Bill; Carry Me Back to Mountains, Crown 3279 ...15.00
Pine Ridge Boys, Ramblin' Reckless Hobo, Ch 15610 ....15.00
Prairie Ramblers, Go Easy Blues, Vi 23856 ....100.00
Red Headed Fiddlers, Fatal Wedding, Bru 460 ....20.00
Reinhart, Dick; Rambling Lover, Bru 386 ....15.00
Rice, Edd; Cricket on the Hearth, Vo 5220 ....15.00
Rodgers, Jimmie; Old Love Letters, Bluebird 6198 ....20.00
Scroggins, Liston; Goodby to Friends & Home, Bru 378 ....12.00
Shelton, BF; Cold Penitentiary Blues, Vi V40107 ....50.00
Steen, Joe; Railroad Jack, Ch 16258 ....15.00
Stone, Jimmy; Midnight Boogie, Imperial 8137 ....10.00
Sweet Brothers, I Got a Bull Dog, Gennett 6620 ....30.00
Thompson, Bud; Five Cent Cotton, Crown 3418 ....12.00
Turner, Jack; Honey Stay in Your Own Back Yard, Gennett 7305 .30.00
Virginia Dandies, God's Getting Worried, Crown 3145 ....20.00
Weber, Sam; My Ozark Mountain Home, Superior 2822 ....50.00
Weston, Don; That Old Feather Bed on the Farm, Ch 16748 ......20.00
Williams, Marc; Cowboy's Last Wish, Bru 377 ....12.00
Wyoming Cowboy, Utah Carroll, Ch 16724 ....30.00

Jazz, Dance Bands, Personalities

Al Lynn's Music Masters, Indian Butterfly, Edison 51952 ....12.00

Alabama Fuzzy Wuzzies, Congo Stomp, Ch 15415 ....260.00
Andrews Sisters, Just a Simple Melody, Decca 1496 ....12.00
Arcadian Serenaders, Fidgety Feet, Okeh 40272 ....40.00
Armstrong, Louis; You're Driving Me Crazy, Vo 3216 ....8.00
Auburn, Frank & Orch; Peach of a Pair, Clarion 5180-C 12.00
Bailey's Dixie Dudes, I'm Satisfied, Gennett 5577 ....10.00
Barbecue Pete, Avenue Strut, Ch 15904 ....50.00
Beale Street Five, Waitin' Around, Lincoln 2219 ....8.00
Ben's Bad Boys, Wang Wang Blues, Vi 21971 ....15.00
Bobby's Revelers, Heebie Jeebies, Sivertone 3551 ....75.00
Broadway Broadcasters, Do Something, Cameo 9158 ....8.00
Buck & Bubbles, Rhythm for Sale, Co 2873-D 30.00
Calloway, Cab & Orch; Little Town Gal, Vi 24494 ....12.00
Cardinal Dance Orch, My Mammy Knows, Cardinal 504 ....20.00
Carter, Benny & Orch; Devil's Holiday, Co 2898-D 30.00
Charleston Chasers, Delirium, Co 1076-D 20.00
Cincinnati Jug Band, Newport Blues, Para 12743 ....300.00
Coleman, EL; Steel String Blues, Okeh 8216 ....50.00
Cookie's Gingersnaps, High Fever, Okeh 8369 ....200.00
Cotton Pickers, Railroad Man, Romeo 852 ....15.00
Crosby, Bing; Star Dust, Bru 6169 ....12.00
Cummins, Bernie & Orch; Out-O'-Town Gal, Bru 3952 ....8.00
Davis, Genevieve; I've Got Something, Vi 20648 ....100.00
Dixie Jazz Band, Missouri Squabble, Challenge 952 ....12.00
Dixie Washboard Band, My Own Blues, Co 14141-D 40.00
Down Home Serenaders, Cootie Crawl, Ch 15399 ....200.00
Eaton, Charlie; Bucket of Blood, Herwin 93017 ....150.00
Ellington, Duke & Orch; Birmingham Breakdown, Bru 3480 ....15.00
Etting, Ruth; Close Your Eyes, Bru 6657 ....12.00
Fields, Buddy & Orch; Lovable & Sweet, Romeo 1068 ....10.00
Frisco Syncopators, Forgetful Blues, Claxtonola 40291 ....50.00
Garland, Judy; Stompin' at the Savoy, Decca 848 ....10.00
Gold, Lou & Orch; Luscious, Harmony 616-H 8.00
Goodman, Benny & Orch; Not That I Care, Co 2542-D 25.00
Gotham Stompers, Did Anyone Ever Tell You, Variety 541 ....12.00
Gray, Russell & Orch; Sugar, Okeh 40938 ....60.00
Hall's Jazz Band, Say It Again, Emerson 3007 ....10.00
Happiness Boys, In Sweet Onion Time, Cameo 707 ....8.00
Harmonians, Some Sweet Day, Harmony 863-H 10.00
Herwin Hot Shots, Salty Dog, Herwin 93015 ....300.00
Hines, Earl & Orch; Panther Rag, QRS 7039 ....200.00
Hudson Trio, Twelfth Street Rag, Famous 3024 ....10.00
Imperial Orchestra, Sing Me a Baby Song, Bell 534 ....10.00
Jelly Whippers, SOB Blues, Herwin 92018 ....200.00
Johnston, Grace; Them There Eyes, Melotone 12032 ....12.00
Jones, Hank & His Ginger; Ash Can Stomp, Ch 15437 ....200.00
Kaufman, Irving; St Louis Blues, Banner 6323 ....12.00
Kentucky Blowers, Choo Choo, Gennett 5602 ....12.00
King, Frances; She's Got It, Okeh 40854 ....15.00
La Palina Broadcasters, Sweetness, Perfect 15203 ....10.00
Langford, Frances; Moon Song, Bluebird 5016 ....12.00
Lenox Dance Orch, Me Neenyah, Perfect 14394 ....15.00
Locke Bros' Rhythm Orch, Sills Stomp, Bluebird 6288 ....30.00
Lumberjacks, Black Beauty, Cameo 8352 ....10.00
Marlow, Earl & Orch; Sing Song Girl, Parlophone PNY-34178 ...35.00
McKinney's Cotton Pickers, Cherry, Vi 21730 ....30.00
Meyers, Ken; Stampede, Regal 8183 ....12.00
Miller, Ray & Orch; Come On Red, Bru 2606 ....8.00
Mississippi Trio, Doin' That Thing, Supertone 9528 ....100.00
Moonlight Revelers, Baby Knows How, Grey Gull 1767 ....30.00
Morton, Benny & Orch; Get Goin', Co 2902-D 40.00
Mound City Blue Blowers, One Hour, Bluebird 6456 ....10.00
Noble, Ray & Orch; Crazy Rhythm, Bru 8098 ....10.00
NY Military Band, At a Georgia Campmeeting, Edison 50636 .....10.00

Original Atlanta Footwarmers, Hot Licks, Bell 585 ....50.00
Original Jazz Hounds, Cannon Ball Blues, Co 14124-D 100.00
Paramounteers, I Have To Have You, Publix 2008-P 15.00
Porter's Blue Devils, Steamboat Sal, Gennett 5249 ....15.00
Queen City Blowers, Stomp Off, Let's Go, Ch 15030 ....75.00
Red Onion Jazz Babies, Terrible Blues, Gennett 5607 ....150.00
Rhythm Wreckers, Wabash Blues, Vo 3390 ....8.00
Rocky Mountain Trio, Freakish Blues, Gennett 3002 ....15.00
Rose Room Orch, Glorianna, Banner 6205 ....15.00
Selvin, Ben & Orch; Betty, Bru 3172 ....8.00
Shawne, Ted & Orch; Rockin' Chair, Parlophone PNY-34027 ....50.00
Shreveport Sizzlers, Zonky, Okeh 8918 ....75.00
Smith, Kate; Dinah Lee From Tennessee, Clarion 5278-C 15.00
South Street Ramblers, Endurance Stomp, QRS 7019 ....150.00
Stompin' Six, Jimtown Blues, Sunset 1098 ....300.00
Tennessee Ten, Down Hearted Blues, Vi 19094 ....8.00
Tucker, Sophie; Some of These Days, Co 826-D 10.00
Vallee, Rudy & CT Yankees; Lazy Bones, Bluebird 5114 ....12.00
Victor Orchestra, Black & White Rag, Vi 16350 ....10.00
Washboard Rhythm Band, Going Going Gone, Co 14680-D 75.00
Whistler & His Jug Band, Pig Meat Blues, Okeh 8816 ....150.00
Wiley, Lee; I've got Five Dollars, Gala 2 ....10.00
Williams, Sidney; Mississippi Shivers, Ch 15372 ....60.00
Young, Margaret; Papa Better Watch Your Step, Bru 2459 ....8.00

Red Wing

The Red Wing Stoneware Company, founded in 1878, took its name from its location in Red Wing, Minnesota. In 1906 the name was changed to the Red Wing Union Stoneware Company after a merger with several of the other local potteries. For the most part they produced utilitarian wares such as flowerpots, crocks, and jugs. Their early 1930s catalogs offered a line of art pottery vases in colored glazes, some of which featured handles modeled after swan's necks, snakes, or female nudes. Other examples were quite simple, often with classic styling. After the addition of their dinnerware lines in 1935, 'Stoneware' was dropped from the name, and the company became known as Red Wing Potteries, Inc. They closed in 1967.

Our artware advisors are Wendy and Leo Frese (Three Rivers Collectibles); they are listed under Texas. For further study we recommend *Red Wing Stoneware, An Identification and Value Guide*, and *Red Wing Collectibles* by Dan and Gail DePasquale and Larry Peterson; and *Red Wing Art Pottery, Book I* and *Book II*, by B.L. Dollen. All are published by Collector Books. Another good reference is *Red Wing Art Pottery* by Ray Reiss (privately published).

Commercial Art Ware and Miscellaneous

Bowl, burnt orange w/lime gr int, cloverleaf shape, #1412, 8" 30.00
Bowl, Classic, lt pk semimatt, wht int, silver label, #279, 9" 50.00
Bowl, console; Textura, gray gloss w/pk int, #B2110, 14½" L 35.00
Bowl, console; wht w/silver wing label, scalloped, #1620, 10" 40.00
Bowl, Renaissance, emb feathers, brn stain on ivory, #526, 12" 55.00
Candle holder, English Garden, floral, brn on ivory, #1190, 6" 25.00
Candle holders, wht teardrop form w/gr int, #B1409, 5", pr 22.00
Compote, wht semimatt, contemporary style, low ft, #M5006, 11" ..24.00
Compote, wht w/gr int, fluted/ribbed, #690, 6x9" 35.00
Ewer, #184, 7" 55.00
Figurine, giraffe, 1995 convention commemorative 90.00
Jardiniere, Brushware, emb leaves, walnut gr, 9x10" 125.00
Jardiniere, Brushware, emb lilies & cattails, unmk, 15" 275.00
Pitcher, Vintage, brn stain on wht, long neck, #616, 11" 100.00
Pitcher vase, Magnolia, brn stain on ivory, #1012, 7" 35.00

Planter, deer form, turq gloss, #1338, 5½" 35.00
Planter, gr semimatt rectangle w/emb grid, #1616, 7½" L 25.00
Planter, violin form, Zephyr Pk fleck, w/strings, #M1484, 13" 50.00
Planter, wht w/gr int, flower hdls, #1195, 5" 35.00

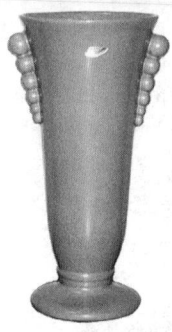

Vase, Neoclassic, light blue, #666, $175.00.

Vase, Athenian, nude, cobalt, #349, circle mk, 11" 2,640.00
Vase, Brushware, cattails in band, gr, cylindrical, 10" 150.00
Vase, burnt orange gloss, contemporary styling, #B1425, 8" 30.00
Vase, cattails emb on lemon yel, gray int, #410, 7½" 35.00
Vase, cornucopia; floral emb on wht, gr int, #1097, 5¾" 35.00
Vase, floral emb on gr semimatt, wht int, hdls, #1360, 7½" 30.00
Vase, hdls, #1376, 11½" 45.00
Vase, Tropicana, Shell Ginger, gunmetal/pea gr, #B2001, 8" 40.00
Vase, vines emb on pea gr, integral vine hdls, #1162, 9" 35.00
Vase, wht ftd form w/brass hdls, #M1609, 10" 45.00
Vase, wht semimatt, fan shape, #946, 6" 22.50
Vase, wht w/gr int, sawtooth design, #1170, 6¾" 40.00

Cookie Jars

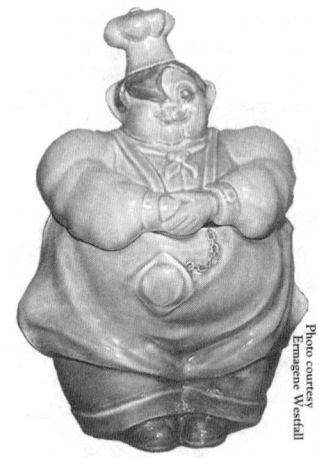

Pierre (chef), green, unmarked, $350.00. (Watch for reproductions.)

Bob White, unmk 125.00
Carousel, unmk 900.00
Crock, wht 80.00
Dutch Girl, yel w/brn trim (+) 140.00
Friar Tuck, cream w/brn, mk 195.00
Friar Tuck, gr, mk 295.00
Friar Tuck, yel, unmk 175.00
Grapes 250.00
Grapes, cobalt or dk purple, ea 350.00
Jack Frost, unmk, 2 styles, ea 750.00
King of Tarts, mc, mk 1,100.00
King of Tarts, pk w/bl & blk trim, mk 1,000.00
King of Tarts, wht, unmk 750.00
Peasant design, emb/pnt figures on brn 85.00

Pierre (chef), brn, unmk (+)	195.00
Pierre (chef), pk, mk	350.00
Pineapple, yel	200.00
Queen of Tarts, mk	550.00

Dinnerware

Dinnerware lines were added in 1935, and today collectors scramble to rebuild extensive table services. Although interest is obvious, right now the market is so volatile, it is often difficult to establish a price scale with any degree of accuracy. Asking prices may vary from $50.00 to $200.00 on some items, which indicates instability and a collector market trying to find its way. (One guide currently on the market, for instance, lists Midnight Rose dinner plates at $15.00 to $20.00, while another terms them 'rare,' and values them at $145.00 each.) Sellers seem to be unfamiliar with pattern names and proper identification of the various pieces of each line. There were many hand-decorated lines; among the most popular are Bob White, Tropicana, and Round-up. But there are other patterns that are just as attractive and deserving of attention. The Dollen books referenced above both have dinnerware sections, and Ray Reiss has published a book called *Red Wing Dinnerware, Price and Identification Guide*, which shows nearly one hundred patterns on its back cover alone.

Town and Country, designed by Eva Zeisel, was made for only one year in the late 1940s. Today many collectors regard Zeisel as one of the most gifted designers of that era and actively seek examples of her work. Town and Country was a versatile line, adaptable to both informal and semiformal use. It is characterized by irregular, often eccentric shapes, and handles of pitchers and serving pieces are usually extensions of the rim. Bowls and platters are free-form comma shapes or appear tilted, with one side slightly higher than the other. Although the ware is unmarked, it is recognizable by its distinctive shapes and glazes. White (often used to complement interiors of bowls and cups), though an original color, is actually more rare than Bronze (metallic brown, also called gunmetal), which enjoys favored status; Gray is unusual. Other colors include Rust, Dusk Blue, Sand, Chartreuse, Peach, and Forest Green. Pieces have also shown up in Mulberry and Ming Green and are considered quite rare. (These are Red Wing Quartelle colors!) Note: Eva Zeisel recently gave permission to reissue a few select pieces of Town and Country; these are being made by World of Ceramics. In 1996 salt and pepper shakers were reproduced in **new** colors not resembling Red Wing colors. In 1997 the mixing bowl and syrup were reissued. All new pieces are stamped EZ96 or EZ97 and are visibly different from the old, as far as glaze, pottery base, and weight.

Our advisor for the general dinnerware lines is Doug Podpeskar; he is listed in the Directory under Minnesota. Karen Silvermintz (see Texas) and Charles Alexander (see Indiana) advise on the Town and Country dinnerware.

Bob White, beverage server, w/stopper	90.00
Bob White, bowl, cereal	22.00
Bob White, bowl, divided vegetable	32.00
Bob White, bowl, salad; 12"	50.00
Bob White, casserole, 2-qt	45.00
Bob White, casserole, 4-qt	55.00
Bob White, cocktail tray	75.00
Bob White, creamer	30.00
Bob White, cup & saucer	20.00
Bob White, gravy boat, stick hdl, w/lid, from $40 to	60.00
Bob White, hors d'oeuvres bird	50.00
Bob White, mug	40.00
Bob White, pitcher, water; 60-oz	50.00
Bob White, plate, 10½"	12.50

Bob White, plate, 6"	7.00
Bob White, plate, 8"	8.00
Bob White, platter, lg, 20", w/metal stand w/ceramic hdls	95.00
Bob White, platter, 13"	45.00
Bob White, platter, 20"	67.50
Bob White, relish, 3-part	30.00
Bob White, shakers, tall, pr	35.00
Bob White, sugar bowl, w/lid	20.00
Bob White, teapot	100.00
Bob White, teapot, w/stand	125.00
Bob White, trivet, ceramic	100.00
Lotus, beverage server	45.00
Lotus, bowl, divided vegetable	24.00
Lotus, butter dish	28.00
Lotus, cup & saucer	10.00
Lotus, plate, 10½"	10.00
Lotus, shakers, pr	20.00
Lotus, sugar bowl, w/lid	20.00
Morning Glory, bowl, cereal	10.00
Morning Glory, bowl, rim soup	14.00
Morning Glory, celery tray	18.00
Morning Glory, creamer	12.50
Morning Glory, plate, 10½"	10.00
Morning Glory, teapot	65.00

Normandy, Creamer and sugar bowl, $50.00 for the pair; Plate, 10¼", $12.00; Cup and saucer $20.00.

Random Harvest, bowl, cereal	17.50
Random Harvest, bowl, salad; 12"	45.00
Random Harvest, creamer	22.00
Random Harvest, cup & saucer	15.00
Random Harvest, plate, 8½"	12.00
Random Harvest, teapot	85.00
Round-Up, beverage server	225.00
Round-Up, bowl, divided vegetable	95.00
Round-Up, bowl, sauce	25.00
Round-Up, bread tray, 24"	150.00
Round-Up, casserole, 2-qt	95.00
Round-Up, creamer	50.00
Round-Up, cup & saucer	55.00
Round-Up, jug, 60-oz	130.00
Round-Up, plate, 10½"	50.00
Round-Up, plate, 6½"	18.50
Round-Up, platter, 13"	90.00
Round-Up, relish, 3-part	125.00
Round-Up, sugar bowl	40.00
Smart Set, bowl, salad; 10½", from $45 to	75.00
Smart Set, bowl, soup	17.50
Smart Set, casserole, 2-qt	60.00
Smart Set, creamer	17.50

Smart Set, cup & saucer 38.00
Smart Set, plate, 10½" 35.00
Smart Set, plate, 6½" 7.50
Smart Set, relish, 3-part 45.00
Smart Set, teapot, from $65 to 110.00
Tampico, beverage server, w/lid 67.50
Tampico, bowl, cereal 16.00
Tampico, bowl, fruit; sm 15.00
Tampico, bowl, vegetable; 8" 17.50
Tampico, butter dish, ¼-lb 32.00
Tampico, cake stand 50.00
Tampico, cup & saucer 15.00
Tampico, gravy boat w/stand 50.00
Tampico, mug, coffee 50.00
Tampico, plate, 10" 20.00
Tampico, plate, 6" 9.00
Tampico, relish 25.00
Tampico, sugar bowl 22.50
Tampico, trivet, 6½" 75.00
Town & Country, bean pot, rust, w/lid, minimum value 400.00
Town & Country, bowl, mixing; dusk bl 125.00
Town & Country, bowl, vegetable; sand, 8" 35.00
Town & Country, bowl, 5" 15.00
Town & Country, casserole, marmite, chartreuse, ind 35.00
Town & Country, casserole, stick hdl, w/lid, lg 125.00
Town & Country, creamer & sugar bowl, w/lid, minimum value .60.00
Town & Country, cruets, mixed colors, orig stoppers, pr 160.00
Town & Country, cup & saucer, forest gr w/wht int 35.00
Town & Country, mug, coffee 75.00
Town & Country, pitcher, peach, 3-pt 150.00
Town & Country, plate, bronze, 10½" 45.00
Town & Country, plate, gray, 8" 20.00
Town & Country, plate, rust, 6½" 10.00
Town & Country, plate, 10½" 30.00
Town & Country, platter, peach, comma shape, 9" 35.00
Town & Country, shakers, Shmoo shape, mixed colors, pr 75.00
Town & Country, sugar bowl, bronze, w/lid 65.00
Town & Country, syrup, chartreuse 110.00
Town & Country, teapot, sand 275.00

Stoneware

Key:
c/s — cobalt on stoneware   RW — Red Wing
MN — Minnesota   RWUS — Red Wing Union
NS — North Star   Stoneware

Baking dish, red & bl sponging on wht, unmk 275.00
Bean cup, Albany slip, RW 60.00
Bean pot, Albany slip, Boston style, RWUS, 1-gal 250.00
Bean pot, Albany slip, short neck, NS, 1-gal 140.00
Bean pot, Albany slip, str sides, MN, ½-gal 150.00
Bean pot, brn & wht, bail hdl, RWUS, 1-qt 95.00
Bowl, cap; full panels & ridges, red & bl sponging on wht, mk, 7" .325.00
Bowl, paneled, red & bl spatter on wht, 5" 450.00
Bowl, Sponge Band on wht, RWUS, 4" 375.00
Bowl, wht w/bl bands, unmk, 12" 95.00
Casserole, Sponge Band, RWUS, sm 400.00
Chamber pot, Albany slip, MN 275.00
Chamber pot, wht, fancy hdl, RW 125.00
Churn, #10/2 birch leaves, c/s, RWUS, 10-gal 1,000.00
Churn, #2/red wing on wht, RWUS, 2-gal 275.00
Churn, #4/P, c/s, RW, 4-gal 950.00
Churn, #6/butterfly, c/s, RW, 6-gal 1,500.00

Churn, #8/dbl leaves, c/s, unmk, 8-gal 800.00
Churn, molded seam, #3/leaf on wht, MN, 3-gal 1,100.00
Combinette, emb lily on wht, bl bands, complete, unmk 275.00
Cooler, #25/Ice Water/birch leaves, c/s, RWUS, 25-gal 600.00

Cooler, #6/butterfly, cobalt on salt glaze, RW, 6-gallon, $2,400.00.

Photo courtesy DePasquale and Peterson

Cooler, #6/Ice Water/detailed flower, c/s, RW, 6-gal 8,000.00
Cooler, #8/daisy, c/s, RW, 8-gal 2,000.00
Cooler, Water Cooler/red wing/bl bands on wht, RWUS, 2-gal .1,600.00
Crock, #2/dbl P, c/s, MN, 2-gal 200.00
Crock, #2/target, c/s, RW, 2-gal 200.00
Crock, #20/elephant ear leaves, c/s, MN, 20-gal 250.00
Crock, #3/dbl P, c/s, unmk, 3-gal 200.00
Crock, #3/drop 8, c/s, RW, 3-gal 450.00
Crock, #30/butterfly, c/s, stenciling, RW, 30-gal 2,200.00
Crock, #30/lily, c/s, stenciling, RW, 30-gal 2,400.00
Crock, #4/dbl P, c/s, MN, 4-gal 600.00
Crock, #4/elephant ear leaves, c/s, MN, 4-gal 125.00
Crock, #5/leaf, c/s, RW, 5-gal 500.00
Crock, #8/red wing on wht, RWUS, 8-gal 85.00
Crock, butter; low style, salt glaze, RW, 10-lb 80.00
Crock, cooking; Albany slip, bail hdl, RW 200.00
Crock, red wing on wht, 1-gal 500.00
Cuspidor, brn & wht, MN, lg 450.00
Cuspidor, molded seam, brn & wht, unmk 200.00
Custard cup, bl shading to wht, unmk 175.00
Flowerpot, Albany slip, repeating pattern along band, MN 350.00
Jar, butter; Albany slip, high style, MN, 1-gal 70.00
Jar, butter; Albany slip, high style, NS, ½-gal 150.00
Jar, butter; Albany slip, low style, MN, 10-lb 100.00
Jar, butter; Albany slip, low style, RW, 1-lb 80.00
Jar, butter; wht, low style, MN, 10-lb 50.00
Jar, butter; wht, low style, RW, 5-lb 40.00
Jar, packing; wht, bail hdl, MN, 3-lb 80.00
Jar, packing; wht, bail hdl, RW, 5-lb 75.00
Jar, preserve; Albany slip, RW, 1-gal 500.00
Jar, preserve/snuff; Albany slip, MN, 2-gal 150.00
Jar, preserve/snuff; Albany slip, RW, 2-gal 150.00
Jar, preserve/snuff; wht, MN, 1-qt 100.00
Jar, preserve/snuff; wht, RW, 1-gal 70.00
Jar, wax sealer; Albany slip, MN, 1-gal 125.00
Jar, wax sealer; Albany slip, RW, 1-qt 60.00
Jug, beehive threshing; #5/red wing on wht, RWUS, 5-gal 1,000.00
Jug, beehive; #3/birch leaves, c/s, RWUS, 3-gal 350.00
Jug, beehive; #3/red wing on wht, RWUS, 3-gal 350.00
Jug, beehive; #4/birch leaves, c/s, hand-trn, RWUS, 4-gal 425.00
Jug, beehive; #5/birch leaves, c/s, RWUS, 5-gal 325.00
Jug, beehive; #5/elephant-ear leaves, wht, Union oval, 5-gal ..1,500.00
Jug, beehive; #5/leaf, c/s, RW, 5-gal 2,400.00
Jug, beehive; Albany slip, #5 etched in glaze, RW, 5-gal 900.00

Jug, bl bands on wht, cone top, RW, 1-gal **450.00**
Jug, bl bands on wht, standard top, MN, 1-qt **425.00**
Jug, common, Albany slip, dome top, MN, 1-gal **75.00**
Jug, common, Albany slip, funnel top, MN, 1-gal **175.00**
Jug, common, Albany slip, standard top, MN, 1-qt **100.00**
Jug, common, wht, MN, 1-gal **70.00**
Jug, fancy, wht w/brn ball top, red wing, 2-gal **750.00**
Jug, fancy, wht w/brn ball top, RW, 1-qt **200.00**
Jug, fancy, wht w/brn ball top, RW, ½-pt **175.00**
Jug, fancy, wht w/brn ball top, RW, 2-gal **275.00**
Jug, fancy; wht w/brn ball top, MN, ⅛-pt **225.00**
Jug, molded seam, Albany slip, 'bird' in bottom mk, RW, 2-gal ..**225.00**
Jug, molded seam, Albany slip, bail hdl, MN, 1-gal **300.00**
Jug, molded seam, wht, bail hdl, MN, 1-gal **125.00**
Jug, molded seam, wht, bail hdl, RW, 1-gal **150.00**
Jug, molded seam, wht, bail hdl, RW, 1-qt **125.00**
Jug, molded seam, wht, bail hdl, wide mouth, MN, ½-gal **100.00**
Jug, shoulder; #3/birch leaves, c/s, standard top, MN, 3-gal **175.00**
Jug, shoulder; #4/red wing on wht, dome top, RWUS, 4-gal **110.00**
Jug, shoulder; Albany slip, cone top, RW, 2-gal **650.00**
Jug, shoulder; brn & salt glaze, ball top, RW, 1-gal **225.00**
Jug, shoulder; brn & salt glaze, cone top, RW, ½-gal **375.00**
Jug, shoulder; brn & salt glaze, cone top, RW, 2-gal **350.00**
Jug, shoulder; brn & salt glaze, dome top, MN, ½-gal **200.00**
Jug, shoulder; brn & salt glaze, dome top, MN, 2-gal **175.00**
Jug, shoulder; brn & salt glaze, funnel top, M, 1-gal **125.00**
Jug, shoulder; brn & salt glaze, funnel top, MN, 2-gal **175.00**
Jug, shoulder; brn & salt glaze, pear top, NS, 1-gal **375.00**
Jug, shoulder; brn & salt glaze, standard top, RW, 1-gal **150.00**
Jug, shoulder; brn drips & salt glaze, pear top, NS, 2-gal **875.00**
Jug, shoulder; red wing on wht, brn top, 2-gal **500.00**
Jug, shoulder; wht, cone top, RW, ½-gal **95.00**
Jug, shoulder; wht, cone top, RW, 2-gal **60.00**
Jug, shoulder; wht, funnel top, MN, 2-gal **75.00**
Jug, shoulder; wht, standard top, MN, 1-gal **50.00**
Jug, shoulder; wht, standard top, MN, 2-gal **75.00**
Jug, shoulder; wht, standard top, RW, ½-gal **50.00**
Jug, shoulder; wht, standard top, RW, 2-gal **75.00**
Jug, shoulder; wht, standard top, short, MN, 1-qt **150.00**
Jug, shoulder; wht, standard top, wide mouth, MN, 1-gal **75.00**
Jug, syrup; wht, cone top, MN, 1-gal **70.00**
Jug, syrup; wht, pour spout, MN, 1-gal **60.00**
Jug, wide mouth; Albany slip, MN, ½-gal **75.00**
Jug, wide mouth/molded seam; wht, MN, 1-gal **70.00**
Jug, wide mouth/molded seam; wht, RW, 1-qt **70.00**
Pipkin, Albany slip, unmk, 2-pt **85.00**
Pipkin, brn & wht, MN, 1-pt **275.00**
Pipkin, brn & wht, MN, 4-pt **300.00**
Pitcher, Albany slip w/emb irises, RW **175.00**
Pitcher, bl mottled, fancy hdl, RWUS, ½-gal **450.00**
Pitcher, mustard; wht, RW, 1-qt **90.00**
Pitcher, Russian milk; Albany slip, unmk, ½-gal **100.00**
Pitcher & bowl, emb lily on wht w/pale bl at top & rim, RW **850.00**
Spittoon, bl bands on salt glaze, German style, MN **800.00**
Spittoon, bl bands on wht, incised decor, German style, unmk ..**500.00**
Spittoon, bl sponging on wht, unmk **550.00**
Spittoon, salt glaze, unmk **250.00**
Success filter, bands, c/s, incised decor, MN, 4-gal **850.00**
Umbrella stand, red & bl sponging on wht, unmk **1,300.00**

Redware

The term redware refers to a type of simple earthenware produced by the Colonists as early as the 1600s. The red clay used in its production was abundant throughout the country, and during the 18th and 19th centuries redware was made in great quantities. Intended for utilitarian purposes such as everyday tableware or use in the dairy, redware was simple in design and decoration. Glazes of various colors were used, and a liquid clay referred to as 'slip' was sometimes applied in patterns such as zigzag lines, daisies, or stars. Plates often have a 'coggled' edge, similar to the way a pie is crimped or jagged, which is done with a special tool. In the following listings, EX (excellent condition) indicates only minor damage. Our advisor for this category is Barbara Rosen; she is listed in the Directory under New Jersey.

Photo courtesy Aston Macek, Auctioneers & Appraisers

Pastry molds, carved animals, flowers, figures, musical instruments, etc., G, $525.00 each.

Bank, apple shape, dk red pnt, slot in top, 2¾x3¼", EX **220.00**
Bank, Empire bureau shape, 4-drw, paw ft, 5⅝x6¼x3⅝", EX **120.00**
Bank, mug shape, red pnt w/gold top, arched hdl, 4x2¾" **150.00**
Bank, onion shape, paper label, unglazed, 3x3" dia **150.00**
Bowl, Cake in yel slip, coggled rim, wear, 12" **275.00**
Bowl, gr-orange w/manganese splotches, incised lines, 3x5¾" **700.00**
Bowl, orange-brn w/manganese mottling/splotches, 2⅛x4¼" **300.00**
Bowl, simple yel slip line, orange-brn int, 3⅝x9⅜" **250.00**
Bowl, yel slip w/Lucia, European, lt wear, 3¼x8½" **70.00**
Charger, yel slip w/dk overglaze, coggled rim, 12", EX **195.00**
Colander, orange-brn w/manganese streaks, arched hdls, 10⅛" ..**110.00**
Creamer, brn mottled, bulbous, flared rim, 2⅞" **45.00**
Creamer, cream slip w/brn, strap hdl, minor flakes, 3½" **200.00**
Creamer, orange w/incised lines, C hdl, 2⅞x2⅜", EX **300.00**
Crock, brn, flat bottom, 3⅜x3⅜", NM **95.00**
Dish, letter V in brn slip, coggled rim, 7¾", EX **140.00**
Dish, yel slip decor w/dk orange, coggled rim, 7¼" dia **165.00**
Flowerpot, orange w/brn mottled band below rim, 5x6¾", EX **50.00**
Jar, gr tint, ovoid w/ribbed strap hdl, 9", EX **220.00**
Jar, ovoid, John Bell Waynesboro, 7½", EX **140.00**
Jar, storage; dk w/manganese splotches, unglazed ext, 14x9" **425.00**
Jug, clear w/blk splotches, ovoid, strap hdl, 8", EX **110.00**
Jug, water; primitive, bulbous, strap hdl, 10¾x7½" **50.00**
Loaf pan, 3-line yel slip, coggled rim, wear, 11¾" **175.00**
Milk pan, amber w/brn splotches, wear/sm chip, 13½" **355.00**
Mold, ear of corn, arched sides, crimped edge, sponging at rim, 8" .**440.00**
Mold, fish form, orange-brn w/brn mottling, 2⅛x11¾x4½" **280.00**
Mold, pineapple in bottom, brn w/splotches, 2⅜x5⅛x4¼" **450.00**
Mold, Turk's head, brn sponging, mk John Bell..., 8¼" **1,200.00**
Mold, Turk's head, gr-orange w/manganese stripes, 5½", EX **200.00**
Mug, brn w/manganese mottling, C hdl, 4x4¾", rprs **75.00**
Mug, orange w/manganese mottling, C hdl, 4⅛x4", EX **125.00**
Mug, orange w/vertical manganese stripes, C hdl, 3⅝", NM **400.00**
Pie plate, orange int, unglazed ext, flat bottom, 5⅞" **170.00**
Pie plate, orange-brn w/gr traces, 7¾" **85.00**

Pie plate, orange-brn w/manganese splotches, unglazed ext, 6" ..175.00
Pie plate, yel slip, minor chips, 7½" 275.00
Pie plate, yel slip wavy lines w/gr, chips, 7⅜" 275.00
Pie plate, 3-line yel slip, coggled rim, wear, 8¾" 110.00
Pie plate, 3-line yel slip, coggled rim, wear, 9½" 250.00
Pie plate, 3-line yel slip, coggled rim, 10¼" 330.00
Plate, orange w/gr tint, unglazed bottom, 9¾", pr 150.00
Plate, yel slip crow's foot on orange-brn, mini, 4" 625.00
Plate, yel slip dbl crow's ft, coggled rim, 5½", EX 275.00
Plate, yel slip dbl music note, feathery designs, coggled rim, 8" ..400.00
Plate, yel slip entwined lines, coggled rim, 9" 550.00
Plate, yel slip lines on orange brn, coggled rim, 8", EX 550.00
Plate, yel slip pinwheel, old flake, 7½" 140.00
Plate, yel slip spatters, coggled rim, 1⅜x7⅞" 325.00
Plate, 3-color sgraffito floral, blk inscription on rim 660.00
Plate, 3-line yel slip, serrated rim, 8", EX 175.00
Plate, 4-line yel slip, wear/chips, 7½" 165.00
Salt cellar, orange-brn w/manganese splotches, 1½x3⅞" 325.00
Umbrella stand, Albany slip, vertical pleating, 34x13", EX 300.00

Regal China

Located in Antioch, Illinois, the Regal China Company opened for business in 1938. Products of interest to collectors are James Beam decanters, cookie jars, salt and pepper shakers, and similar novelty items. The company closed its doors sometime in 1993. The Old Mac-Donald Farm series listed below is especially collectible, so are the salt and pepper shakers.

Note: Where applicable, prices are based on excellent gold trim. (Gold trim must be 90% intact or deductions should be made for wear.) See also Decanters.

Alice in Wonderland

Cookie jar 3,200.00
Creamer, White Rabbit 600.00
Pitcher, King of Hearts, milk sz 650.00
Shakers, matching colors, rare, pr 675.00
Shakers, Tweedledee & Tweedledum, pr 850.00
Shakers, wht w/gold trim, pr 675.00
Sugar bowl, White Rabbit, w/lid 600.00
Teapot, Mad Hatter 2,500.00

Cookie Jars

Abe Lincoln, nodder 375.00
Cat 425.00
Churn Boy 275.00
Clown, gr collar 675.00
Davy Crockett 550.00
Diaper Pin Pig 795.00
Dutch Girl 675.00
Dutch Girl, peach trim 800.00
Fifi Poodle 650.00
Fisherman 650.00
French Chef 375.00
Goldilocks (+) 375.00
Harpo Marx 1,200.00
Hobby Horse 250.00
Hubert Lion 775.00
Humpty Dumpty, red 325.00
Little Miss Muffett 385.00
Majorette 675.00

Oriental Lady w/Baskets 600.00
Peek-a-Boo (+) 1,500.00
Quaker Oats 125.00
Three Bears 285.00
Toby Cookies 750.00
Tulip 300.00
Uncle Mistletoe 850.00

Old McDonald's Farm

Butter dish, cow's head, $220.00.

Canister, flour, cereal, coffee; med, ea 220.00
Canister, pretzels, peanuts, poopcorn, chips, tidbits; lg, ea 300.00
Canister, salt, sugar, tea; med, ea 220.00
Cookie jar, barn 275.00
Creamer, rooster 110.00
Grease jar, pig 175.00
Pitcher, milk 400.00
Shakers, boy & girl, pr 75.00
Shakers, churn, gold trim, pr 90.00
Shakers, feed sacks /wsheep, pr 195.00
Spice jar, assorted lids, sm, ea 100.00
Sugar bowl, hen 125.00
Teapot, duck's head 250.00

Shakers

A Nod to Abe, 3-pc 250.00
Bendel, bears, wht w/pk & brn trim, pr 100.00
Bendel, bunnies, wht w/blk & pk trim, pr 135.00
Bendel, kissing pigs, gray w/pk trim, lg, pr 375.00
Bendel, love bugs, burgundy, lg, pr 165.00
Bendel, love bugs, gr, sm, pr 65.00
Cat, pr 225.00
Clown, pr 450.00
Dutch Girl, pr 275.00
Fifi, pr 450.00
Fish, C Miller, pr 60.00
French Chef, wht w/gold trim, pr 175.00
Humpty Dumpty, pr 140.00
Peek-a-Boo, peach trim, rare, lg, pr 575.00
Peek-a-Boo, red dots, lg, pr (+) 500.00
Peek-a-Boo, red dots, sm, pr 220.00
Peek-a-Boo, w/burgundy trim, rare, sm, pr 350.00
Peek-a-Boo, wht solid, lg, pr 400.00
Peek-a-Boo, wht solid, sm, pr 200.00
Peek-a-Boo, wht w/gold trim, lg, pr 450.00
Pig, pk, mk C Miller, 1-pc 95.00
Tulip, pr 50.00
Van Telligen, bears, brn, pr 20.00
Van Telligen, boy & dog, wht, pr 60.00
Van Telligen, bunnies, solid colors, pr 22.00
Van Telligen, ducks, pr 30.00

Van Telligen, Dutch boy & girl, pr 40.00
Van Telligen, Mary & lamb, pr 55.00
Van Telligen, sailor & mermaid, pr 195.00
Vermont Leaf People, 3-pc 150.00

Relief-Molded Jugs

Early relief-molded pitchers (ca 1830s – 40s) were made in two-piece molds into which sheets of clay were pressed. The relief decoration was deep and well defined, usually of animal or human subjects. Most of these pitchers were designed with a flaring lip and substantial footing. Gradually styles changed, and by the 1860s the rim had become flatter and the foot less pronounced. The relief decoration was not as deep, and foliage became a common design. By the turn of the century, many other types of pitchers had been introduced, and the market for these early styles began to wane.

Watch for recent reproductions; these have been made by the slip-casting method. Unlike relief-molded ware which is relatively smooth inside, slip-cast pitchers will have interior indentations that follow the irregularities of the relief decoration. Values below are for pieces in excellent condition. Our advisor for this category is Kathy Hughes; she is listed in the Directory under North Carolina.

Key: Reg — Registered

Apostle, wht, Meigh, 1842, 9⅞" 565.00
Ariadne, Samuel Alcock & Co, ca 1850, 9" 525.00
Bacchanalian Dance loving cup, bl/wht parian, Meigh, 6½" 675.00
Distin family/instruments, bl smear/gilt, Alcock, 1840s, 7" 525.00
Eglington Tournament, buff, Ridgway, 1840, 7¼" 375.00
Gipsy, lav on parian, Alcock, 1842, 4¾" 375.00
Ivy creamer w/mc enameled trim, S Alcock, 5½" 600.00
Naomi & daughter-in-Law, lav on parian, Alcock, 1847, 8¾" ...375.00
Pan, buff, w/lid, Wm Ridgway, 1830s, 7¼" 275.00
Rose, parian, unmk, ca 1850, 6½" 175.00
Silenus, gr, Minton, 1845, 9" 425.00

Slavery scenes on white body in raised relief, Ridgway and Abington, Hanley, January 1, 1855, 7⅞", minimum value, $1,100.00.

Tam O'Shanter, glazed bl, Ridgeway, 1835, 8¼" 295.00
Toby Philpot, tan, 8" 395.00
Two Drivers, gray, Minton, ca 1849, 7⅞" 575.00

Restraints

Since the beginning of time, many things from animals to treasures have been held in bondage by hemp, bamboo, chests, chains, shackles, and other constructed devices. Many of these devices were used to hold captives who awaited further torture, as if the restraint wasn't torturous enough. The study and collecting of restraints enables one to learn much about the advancement of civilization in the country or region from which they originated. Such devices at various times in history were made of very heavy metals — so heavy that the wearer could scarcely move about. It has only been in the last sixty years that vast improvements have been made in design and construction that afford the captive some degree of comfort. Our advisor for this category is Joseph Tanner; he is listed in the Directory under Washington.

Key:
bbl — barrel
d-lb — double lock button
K — key
Kd — keyed

lc — lock case
NST — non-swing through
ST — swing through
stp — stamped

Foreign Handcuffs

Australian, Saf Lock, ST, takes pin-tumbler K in side, stp 145.00
Czechalaviak, ST, Ralken flat key, modern swing through 90.00
Deutsche Polizei, ST, middle hinge, folds, takes bbl-bit K 80.00
East German, aluminum, single lg hinge, ST, bbl key 60.00
East German, heavy steel, NP single lg hinge, NST, bbl key 90.00
English, Chubb, NST, hi-security 10-slider lock mechanism 275.00
English, Chubb Arrest, steel, ST, multi-bit solid K 225.00
English, Latrobe, aluminum alloy, center chain, ST, dbl-bit K ...160.00
French Lapegy, ST, aluminum alloys, takes flat bitted K 75.00
French Revolved, oval, ST, takes 2 Ks: bbl & pin tumbler 150.00
German, 3-lb steel set, 2⅝" thick, center chain, bbl K 175.00
German Clejuso, oval design, ST, dbl-cuff weight, 22-oz 100.00
German Clejuso, sq lc, adjusts/NST, d-lb on side, bbl K 100.00
German Darby, adjusts, well finished, NST, sm 120.00
German Hamburg 8, non-adjust NST, center bar/post w/K-way ..250.00
Hiatt, English Darby, like US CW Darby, stp Hiatt & #d 75.00
Hiatt, solid state, 2 separate cuffs joined bk to bk, stp/#d 165.00
Hiatt English non-adjust screw K Karby style, uses screw K 100.00
Hiatt Figure 8, swings open to insert/withdraw wrists 125.00
Italian, stp New Police, modern Peerless type, ST, sm bbl K 35.00
Plug 8, remove plug before inserting external threaded K 200.00
Russian modern ST, blued bbl key, unmk, crude 80.00
Spanish, stp Alcyon/Star, modern Peerless type, flat K 65.00
Spanish, stp Alcyon/Star, modern Peerless type, ST, sm bbl K 45.00

Foreign Leg Shackles

East German, aluminum, lg hinge, cable amid 4 cuffs, bbl key 80.00
German Clejuso, sq lc, adjusts/NST, d-bl on side, bbl K 125.00
German Clejuso Darby type, adjusts/NST/plated, uses screw K ..160.00
Hiatt English combo manacles, handcuff/leg irons w/chain 275.00
Hiatt English non-adjust screw K Darby style, uses screw K 100.00
Hiatt Plug leg irons, same K-ing as Plug-8 cuffs, w/chain 225.00

U.S. Handcuffs

Adams, teardrop lc, bbl Kd, NST, usually not stp 170.00
American Munitions, modern/rnd, sm bbl Kd, ST bow, stp 45.00
Bean Giant, sideways figure 8, solid center lc, dbl-bit K 400.00
Bean Patrolman, kidney-bean form, d-lb on lc, NST, stp T 100.00
Bean-Cobb, sm rnd lc, removable cylinder, d-lb, NST, 1899 ....80.00
Cavenay, looks like Marlin Daley but w/screw K, NST 160.00
Civil War padlocking type, various designs w/loop for lock 170.00
Colt, modern ST bow, sm bbl Kd, stp w/Colt & Co name 160.00
Flash Action Manacle, like Bean Giant w/ST, K-way center 225.00
Flexibles, steel segmented bows, NST Darby type, screw K 150.00
H&R Super, ST, shaft-hinge connector takes hollow titted K ...100.00
Harvard, takes sm bbl K, ST, stp Harvard Lock Co 65.00

Judd, NST, used rnd/internally triangular K, stp Mattatuck 120.00
Lilly Hand Iron, 2" strap iron (8" L), oval bands, NST, sq K 400.00
Marlin Daley, NST, bottle-neck form, neck stp, dbl-titted K 200.00
Mattatuck, NST, propeller-like K-way, stp Mattatuck/etc 90.00
Palmer, 2" steel bands, 2 K-ways (top & center), NST stp 300.00
Peerless, ST, takes sm bbl K, stp Mfg'ered by Peerless Co 40.00
Peerless, ST, takes sm bbl K, stp Mfg'ered by S&W Co 75.00
Peerless Big Guy, modern ST, bbl key 50.00
Phelps, NST, twist chain between cuffs, Tower look-alike 225.00
Pratt combo, 1 cuff connects w/nipper/claw, ST, mk Pratt 250.00
Providence Tool Co, stp, NST, Darby screw K style 120.00
Rankin, steel NST, mk screw K 225.00
Romer, NST, takes flat K, resembles padlock, stp Romer Co 250.00
S&W 94 Maximum Security, ST, takes Ace-type K, stp S&W 90.00
Strauss, ST, takes lg solid bitted K, stp Strauss Eng Co 85.00
Tower, NST, bottom K, solid/flat-fitted K goes in cuff edge 100.00
Tower bar cuffs, cuffs separate by 10-12" steel bar 120.00
Tower Dbl Lock, NST, takes bbl-bitted K, usually stp Tower 60.00
Tower Detective Pinkerton, NST, sq lc, bbl-bitted K, no stp 120.00
Tower Single Lock, NST, bbl-bit K, K-way slanted on lc, sm 70.00
Tower-Bean, NST, sm rnd lc, takes tiny bbl-bitted K, stp 75.00
Tri-lock, heavy polymer & stainless steel, ST, triple lock 60.00
Walden 'Lady Cuff,' NST, takes sm bbl K, lightweight, stp 250.00

U.S. Leg Shackles

American Munitions, as handcuffs 55.00
Civil War or prison ball & chain, padlocking or rivet type 250.00
Cloc spike, 30" L opening for ankle w/padlock & 2 spikes 500.00
H&R Supers, as handcuffs 400.00
Harvard, as handcuffs 75.00
Judd, as handcuffs 135.00
Leg lock brace, metal brace, ankle to knee, lever locked 225.00
Oregon boot, break-apart shackle on above ankle support 400.00
Palmer, as handcuffs but w/detachable chain, NST 400.00
Peerless Big Guy, modern ST, bbl key 60.00
Providence Tool Co, stp, NST 150.00
Strauss, as handcuffs 125.00
Tower, bottom K, as handcuffs 100.00
Tower ball & chain, leg iron w/chain & 6-lb to 50-lb ball 250.00
Tower Dbl-Lock, as handcuffs 90.00
Tower Detective, as handcuffs 150.00

Various Other Restraining Devices

African slave Darby-style cuffs, heavy iron/chain, handmade 130.00
African slave Darby-style leg shackles, heavy/hand forged 160.00
African slave padlocking or riveted forged iron shackles 135.00
Argus iron claw, twist T to open & close 40.00
Darby neck collar, rnd steel loop opens w/screw K 150.00
English figure-8 nipper, claws open by lifting top lock tab 80.00
Gale finger cuff, knuckle duster, non-K, mk GFC 125.00
German nipper, twist hdl opens/closes cuff, stp Germany/etc 75.00
Jay Pee, thumb cuffs, mk solid body, bbl K 15.00
Mighty-Mite, thumb cuffs, solid body, ST, mk, bbl K 75.00
Phillips nipper, claw, flip lever on top to open 80.00
Thomas Nipper, claw, push button top to open 80.00
Tower Lyon, thumb cuffs, solid body, NST, dbl-bit center K 150.00

Reverse Painting on Glass

    Verre eglomise is the technique of painting on the underside of glass. Dating back to the early 1700s, this art became popular in the 19th century when German immigrants chose historical figures and beautiful women as subjects for their reverse glass paintings. Advertising mirrors of this type came into vogue at the turn of the century.

A Jackson, colorful uniform, some fading, orig fr, 13⅜x10½" .1,100.00
Daniel Webster, bl & blk coat, wear/flakes, orig fr, 12x9½" 1,100.00
Fanny, colorful clothes, flowers in hair, flakes, fr, 15x12" 330.00
H Clay, bl coat, gr bkground, wht border, wear/flakes, fr, 12x9" ..770.00
Lady in flowered hat, orig fr, 12x9" 385.00
Lady in gr dress, bl bkground, orig fr, 9x6⅝" 220.00
Lady in red coat w/fur, orig fr, some rpt, 12x9½" 200.00
Louise, colorful clothes, minor flaking, orig fr, 15x12" 500.00
Man in bl coat w/red collar, flaking, orig, fr, 8x5⅝" 195.00
Nicholas on horse, EX color, minor flakes, orig fr, 15x12" 600.00
Tavern scene by river, dtd 1859, flakes, 13½x16½"+fr 275.00
Washington, colorful uniform, orig fr, 12x9⅜" 2,475.00
Washington, portrait in shadowbox fr, 22x18" 275.00

Richard

    Richard, who at one time worked for Galle, made cameo art glass in France during the 1920s. His work was often multilayered and acid cut with florals and scenics in lovely colors. The ware was marked with his name in relief. Our advisor for this category is Don Williams; he is listed in the Directory under Missouri.

Cameo

Vase, house among trees, blue on orange, incurvate scalloped rim, blue foot, signed, 7¾", $1,500.00.

Bowl, foliage, brn on poppy red, 2¾x6" 450.00
Vase, floral, purple-brn on lt bl, 6¼" 600.00
Vase, hops on vine, chocolate brn on orange, stick neck, 8¼" ...400.00
Vase, mtn/lake landscape, orange/cobalt, 13½x8" 2,500.00
Vase, mtns/village/water, brn on yel, brn-blk hdls, 7¼" 1,200.00
Vase, orchids/leaves, bl-blk/orange, 7¾" 600.00

Riviera

    Riviera was a line of dinnerware introduced by the Homer Laughlin China Company in 1938. It was sold exclusively by the Murphy Company through their nationwide chain of dime stores. Riviera was unmarked, lightweight, and inexpensive. It was discontinued sometime prior to 1950. Colors are mauve blue, red, yellow, light green, and ivory. On rare occasions, dark blue pieces are found, but this was not a standard color. For further information we recommend *The Collector's Encyclopedia of Fiesta* (1998 values) by Sharon and Bob Huxford, available from Collector Books.

Batter set, complete 285.00
Batter set, ivory, w/decals, complete 170.00

Bowl, baker; 9" 28.00
Bowl, cream soup; w/liner, ivory 95.00
Bowl, fruit; 5½" 12.00
Bowl, nappy; 7¼" 28.00
Bowl, oatmeal; 6" 40.00
Bowl, utility; ivory 50.00
Butter dish, cobalt, ¼-lb 250.00
Butter dish, colors other than cobalt or turq, ¼-lb 135.00
Butter dish, turq, ¼-lb 290.00
Butter dish, ½-lb 140.00
Casserole 110.00
Creamer 12.00
Cup & saucer, demitasse; ivory 80.00
Jug, open, ivory, 4½" 95.00
Jug, w/lid 130.00
Pitcher, juice; mauve bl 210.00
Pitcher, juice; yel 120.00
Plate, deep 24.00
Plate, 10" 55.00
Plate, 6" 8.00
Plate, 7" 12.00
Plate, 9" 18.00
Platter, closed hdls, 11¼" 28.00
Platter, cobalt, 12" 70.00
Platter, 11½" 25.00
Platter, 15" 60.00
Sauce boat 27.00
Saucer 4.00
Shakers, pr 20.00
Sugar bowl, w/lid 20.00
Teacup 11.00
Teapot 145.00
Tidbit, ivory, 2-tier 75.00
Tumbler, hdl 75.00
Tumbler, hdl, ivory 145.00
Tumbler, juice 52.00

Robineau

After short-term training in ceramics in 1903, Adelaide Robineau (with the help of her husband Samuel) built a small pottery studio at her home in Syracuse, New York. She was adept in mixing the clay and throwing the ware, which she often decorated by incising designs into the unfired clay. Samuel developed many of the glazes and took charge of the firing process. In 1910 she joined the staff of the American Women's League Pottery at St. Louis, where she designed the famous Scarab Vase. After this pottery failed, she served on the faculty of Syracuse University. Her work was and is today highly acclaimed for the standards of excellence to which she aspired.

Vase, bl & tan crystalline glossy, ball form, 4x4½" 3,750.00
Vase, brn & robin's-egg bl crystalline, slim, 6x2" 6,500.00
Vase, oxtail mottle, spherical, dtd 1920, 3½x4" 4,500.00
Vessel, lime & celadon microcrystalline, spherical, 3¾x4" 5,000.00

Robj

Robj was the name of a retail store that operated in Paris for only a few years, from about 1925 to 1931. Robj solicited designs from the best French artisans of the period to produce decorative objects for the home. These were executed mostly in porcelain but there were glass and earthenware pieces as well. The most well known are the figural

bottles which were particularly popular in the United States. However, Robj also promoted tea sets, perfume lamps, chess sets, ashtrays, bookends, humidors, powder jars, cigarette boxes, figurines, lamps, and milk pitchers. Robj objects tend to be whimsical, and all embody the Art Deco style. Items listed below are ceramic unless noted otherwise. Our advisors for this category are Randall Monsen and Rod Baer; their address is listed in the Directory under Virginia.

Perfume burner, Oriental man sitting on stepped platform, marked, 8¼" (small lid missing, otherwise M), $550.00.

Atomizer, 4 Seasons, glass, eng gilt top, ca 1925, 6" 600.00
Bottle, French priest, blk hat forms stopper, 10½x4" 375.00
Bottle, scent; sitting Oriental, no lid 65.00
Bottle, Scotsman in uniform, mc, 10½" 350.00
Decanter, musical, Russian man, hat forms stopper, 12" 375.00
Decanter, Professor 360.00
Figurine, Deco lady seated, 1 knee bent, gray, 11x10" 750.00
Inkwell, Blackamoor in gold/wht robe holds well, no lid, 6" 275.00
Jar, powder; lady in tiered gown, yel/blk, mk, 5½x5⅜" 375.00

Rock 'N Roll Memorabilia

Memorabilia from the early days of Rock 'n Roll recalls an era that many of us experienced firsthand; these listings are offered to demonstrate the many and various aspects of this area of collecting. Items indicated by this symbol (+) have been reproduced. Beware! Many are so well done even a knowledgeable collector will sometimes be fooled.

Our advisor for Elvis memorabilia is Rosalind Cranor, author of *Elvis Collectibles* and *Best of Elvis Collectibles* (Overmountain Press); she is listed in the Directory under Virginia. The remainder is under the advisement of Bob Gottuso, author of Beatles and Kiss sections in *Garage Sale Gold* by Tomart; see Pennsylvania.

Beatles, belt buckle, group photo, 1964, M 50.00
Beatles, book, Fun-Kit, 1964, M 65.00
Beatles, book, Hard Day's Night, Dell, softcover, orig 12.00
Beatles, book, In His Own Right, Lennon, hardbk, 1964, #2 & up .60.00
Beatles, book, Lennon Remembers, hardbk, 1971, NM 35.00
Beatles, book, Love Letters to the Beatles, hardcover, NM 25.00
Beatles, book, True Story of..., Bantam paperbk, 1964, M 12.00
Beatles, books, ...Illus Lyrics, Aldridge, hardbk, '70, 2-pc set 90.00
Beatles, Booty Bag, orig paper insert, M 160.00
Beatles, cake decoration, pressed group image, Canada 80.00
Beatles, calendar, John & Yoko, 1970, blk/wht images, w/record, NM ..25.00
Beatles, charms, blk plastic records, 1964, set of 4 (+) 24.00
Beatles, concert ticket, unused, Boston, w/letter of authenticity ..75.00
Beatles, eyeglasses case, John, facsimile signature, England 75.00
Beatles, Fan Club membership card, 1964 ....39.00
Beatles, game, Flip Your Wig, MIB 180.00
Beatles, guitar pins, NEMS, 1964, M set of 4 on M cards (+) 140.00
Beatles, Halloween mask, John Lennon 125.00

Beatles, Life magazine, 1971, Paul & Linda on cover, NM 18.00
Beatles, lobby card, Help!, M (+) 60.00
Beatles, Mod Fashion cards, 8x5½", pr 8.00
Beatles, pin, Help!, cloisonne, 1990s 6.50
Beatles, pin-bk, flasher, M 20.00
Beatles, pin-bk, I'm an Official Beatles Fan, gr duck, 2" 20.00
Beatles, plate, luncheon; Washington Pottery 90.00
Beatles, record sleeve, Can't Buy Me Love, rare, M 525.00
Beatles, ring, group photo, brass, NEMS 75.00
Beatles, sheet music, I Want To Hold Your Hand, 1968 ....20.00
Beatles, sheet music, Paperbk Writer, c 1965 ....20.00
Beatles, story cards, Holland, set of 100 ....50.00
Beatles, throw blanket, Sgt Pepper, 53x65", M 60.00
Beatles, ticket, Candlestick Park, 1966 ....250.00
Beatles, tie tac set, NEMS, 1964, MOC (+) 65.00
Beatles, wallpaper, complete roll, M 185.00
Canned Heat, concert poster, 1967 ....40.00
Country Joe & The Fish, poster, Rick Griffin art, 1967, M 135.00
Donovan, poster, 1967, 1-sheet 50.00
Doors, postcard, 1967, M 25.00

KISS, Donruss cards, 1st series, M set 65.00
KISS, Donruss cards, 2nd series, M set 65.00
KISS, photo, group, all 4 orig members, w/autographs, 8x10" 150.00
KISS, pin-bk button, '76 KISS Army 15.00
KISS, pin-bk button, KISS w/Ace & Eric Together 25.00
KISS, printer's proof record slick, Solo albums, 1977 ....65.00
KISS, sheet music, Love Gun 10.00
KISS, T-shirt, orig logo, 1st available, M 45.00
KISS, T-shirt, 1979 tour, long sleeve 45.00
KISS, T-shirt, 1983 Tour, Eric & Vinnie, scarce, M 65.00
Michael Jackson, belt, leather, licensed 1984, M 14.00
Moby Grape, concert poster, 1967 ....40.00
Monkees, ballpoint pen, 1967, M 65.00
Monkees, charm bracelet, Hey-Hey, MOC 55.00
Monkees, Monkeemobile, Corgi, UK, 5", MIB 300.00
Pat Boone, pin-bk, Pat Boone Fan Club 12.50
Paul Revere & the Raiders, photos in album, w/1966 ticket stub .50.00
Rolling Stones, poster, Oakland Coliseum, silver & blk, 1969 ...175.00
Rolling Stones, VariVue display card, M 125.00

Rockingham

In the early part of the 19th century, American potters began to prefer brown- and buff-burning clays over red because of their durability. The glaze favored by many was Rockingham, which varied from a dark brown mottle to a sponged effect sometimes called tortoise shell. It consisted in part of manganese and various metallic salts and was used by many potters until well into the 20th century. Over the past two years, demand and prices have risen sharply, especially in the East. For further information we recommend *Collector's Guide to Rockingham, The Enduring Ware*, by Mary Brewer. See also Bennington.

Bowl, custard; heavy glaze, thick body, 3" H 35.00
Bowl, mixing; sm ft, plain styling, 10½" 85.00
Butter crock, bulbous, thin walls, missing lid, 4¼" H 100.00
Figurine, dog sitting, lock around collar, Bennington type, 11" ..250.00
Figurine, spaniel, seated, dtd Nov 19 18_1, 9½x6½" 395.00
Frame, brn mottle on wht base, oval, 9x7", EX 225.00
Jar, fruit; 1870s, ½-gal, 7¾" 135.00
Milk boiler, emb bands, dk glaze, att Rapp Bros, 4½" 55.00
Mold, Turk's head, dk brn, heavy, 11" dia 165.00
Nappy, red-brn, 3½x13½" 200.00
Pie plate, completely glazed ea side, 12" 165.00

Elvis Presley, ankle bracelet, dog tag type, Elvis Presley Enterprises, late 1950s, $45.00.

Elvis Presley, ballpoint pen, From Elvis & Colonel, Las Vegas 25.00
Elvis Presley, belt buckle, pewter, 1935-1977 ....20.00
Elvis Presley, book, Illustrated Elvis, soft cover, 1976, M 15.00
Elvis Presley, book, Meet EP, Friedman, paperbk, '71, 1st print, M ..30.00
Elvis Presley, charm bracelet, Loving You, EP Enterprises, 1956 ..40.00
Elvis Presley, Christmas postcard, full color, 1975, 5x7" 20.00
Elvis Presley, concert pin, bk converts to easel, 6" 24.00
Elvis Presley, earrings, Loving You, 1956, MOC 45.00
Elvis Presley, figurine, Avon, 1987, MIB, from $50 to 70.00
Elvis Presley, menu, poster bk, blk & wht, 1971, 11x14", M 75.00
Elvis Presley, pennant, bl/blk felt, Am Knitwear, '70s, 11½x5" 8.00
Elvis Presley, photo, blk & wht promo, matt, ltweight, 8x10" 15.00
Elvis Presley, photo, in uniform, RCA, blk & wht, 8x10" 75.00
Elvis Presley, photo bonus from Harem Scarum album, color, M ..40.00
Elvis Presley, playing cards, 1972 Las Vegas souvenir deck, M 10.00
Elvis Presley, pressbook, Speedway, M 25.00
Elvis Presley, record case, pk-tan w/blk & wht, c 1956, 7⅝" 575.00
Elvis Presley, shirt decal, King Forever, mc picture, 1977, M 8.00
Elvis Presley, souvenir program, TX concert, 1956, NM 175.00
Elvis Presley, Teddy Bear perfume, tall bottle, wht top, '57, M ...250.00
Janice Joplin, postcard, 1969 ....30.00
Janice Joplin, poster, blk & wht, 1969 ....30.00
Jefferson Airplane, postcard, M 20.00
Jefferson Airplane, poster, Avalon Ballroom w/nudes, 1967 ....40.00
Jefferson Airplane/Grateful Dead, concert poster, 1967, 1-sheet ..65.00
KISS, belt buckle, logo, 1977 ....20.00
KISS, book, music; Originals, Destroyer, Love Gun, ea 30.00
KISS, book, Reunion Tour 20.00
KISS, decal sheet, 1977 ....10.00
KISS, display ad, cb, for Dynasty album, 3x5" 125.00
KISS, display box, 1st/2nd series Donruss cards, ea 45.00

Pitcher, swan among cattails and large heart-shaped leaves in relief, 8½", $125.00.

Pitcher, emb foliage, 9⅛" 150.00
Pitcher, emb game in wreath, 1890s, 1½-gal, 8½" 215.00
Pitcher, emb hunter w/dog & game, minor crazing, 9⅛" 200.00
Pitcher, emb peacocks, lt glaze, CC Thompson, 1870-84, 8" 160.00
Pitcher, emb turkey/running stag, pear shape, hound hdl, 9" 525.00

Shaving mug, Toby ea side, branch hdl, att Bennett Bros, 4" 400.00

Rogers, John

John Rogers (1829 – 1904) was a machinist from Manchester, New Hampshire, who turned his hobby of sculpting into a financially successful venture. From the originals he meticulously fashioned of red clay, he had bronze master molds made from which plaster copies were cast. He specialized in five different categories: theatrical, Shakespeare, Civil War, everyday life, and horses. His large detailed groupings portrayed the life and times of the period between 1859 and 1892. In the following listings, examples are assumed to be in very good to excellent condition. Our advisor for this category is George Humphrey; he is listed in the Directory under Maryland.

The Photographer, marked John Rogers/New York/1878, 18¾", $2,000.00.

Bubbles 2,000.00
Bushwacker 2,000.00
Checkers Up at Farm 450.00
Chess 400.00
Coming to the Parson 375.00
Council of War 1,100.00
Country Post Office 750.00
Fairy's Whisper, ca 1881 ....1,400.00
Favored Scholar 400.00
Fetching the Doctor 750.00
Going for the Cows 450.00
Madam, Your Mother Craves a Word w/You 700.00
Mail Day 2,000.00
Neighboring Pews 475.00
Parting Promise 475.00
Peddler at the Fair, rstr 300.00
Playing Doctor 500.00
Rip Van Winkle - At Home 425.00
Rip Van Winkle - Returned 425.00
Rip Van Winkle on the Mountain 425.00
Speak for Yourself John 500.00
Tap on the Window 525.00
Village Schoolmaster 850.00
Watch on the Santa Maria 1,000.00
Wounded to the Rear - One More Shot 550.00

Rookwood

The Rookwood Pottery Company was established in 1879 in Cincinnati, Ohio. Its founder was Maria Longworth Nichols Storer, daughter of a wealthy family who provided the backing necessary to make such an enterprise possible. Mrs. Storer hired competent ceramic artisans and artists of note, who through constant experimentation developed many lines of superior art pottery. While in her employ, Laura Fry invented the airbrush-blending process for which she was issued a patent in 1884. From this, several lines were designed that utilized blended backgrounds. One of their earlier lines, Standard, was a brown ware decorated with underglaze slip-painted nature studies, animals, portraits, etc. Iris and Sea Green were introduced in 1894 and Vellum, a transparent mat-glaze line, in 1904. Other lines followed: Ombroso in 1910 and Soft Porcelain in 1915. Many of the early artware lines were signed by the artist. Soon after the turn of the 20th century, Rookwood manufactured 'production' pieces that relied mainly on molded designs and forms rather than freehand decoration for their esthetic appeal. The Depression brought on financial difficulties from which the pottery never recovered. Though it continued to operate, the quality of the ware deteriorated, and the pottery was forced to close in 1967.

Unmarked Rookwood is only rarely encountered. Many marks may be found, but the most familiar is the reverse 'RP' monogram. First used in 1886, a flame point was added above it for each succeeding year until 1900. After that a Roman numeral added below indicated the year of manufacture. Impressed letters that related to the type of clay utilized for the body were also used — G for ginger, O for olive, R for red, S for sage green, W for white, and Y for yellow. Artware must be judged on an individual basis. Quality of the artwork is a prime factor to consider. Portraits, animals, and birds are worth more than florals; and pieces signed by a particularly renowned artist are highly prized. Our advice for this category comes from Fer-Duc Inc., whose address is listed in the Directory under New York.

Aerial Blue

Vase, tree & lake, H Strafer, 1895, #744C/#273, 7⅞" 4,000.00

Aventurine

Vase, birds in foliage, L Epply, 1920, #356F, 5½", NM 600.00
Vase, emb ducks, bl/gr/yel, 1937, #6550, 6⅛" 350.00
Vase, floral on apple gr flambe, L Epply, #2136, 6¼x3" 1,900.00
Vase, florals atop panels, porc, S Sax, 1922, #1873, rstr, 6" 300.00

Black Opal

Vase, floral (Deco), S Sax, 1929, #614C, 12¾" 8,000.00
Vase, peacock feathers, S Sax, 1928, #2933, 12" 8,000.00

Cameo

Bowl, apple blossoms, H Wilcox, 1890, #431 W, 9⅜" 400.00
Chocolate pot, apple blossoms, A Van Briggle, 1888, #251, 7¾" ..900.00
Honey pot, floral, AB Sprague, 1887, #341/#7W, 3" 375.00
Jar, floral w/gold, G Young, 1889, #479, 6" 475.00
Mustard jar, clovers, OG Reed, 1891, #341 W, w/spoon 450.00
Pitcher, apple blossoms, M Daly, 1887, #182, 7⅛" 850.00
Pitcher, floral branches, H Wilcox, 1887, #211, 3½", EX 100.00
Plate, fruit blossoms, MA Daly, 1886, #317 R, 10¼" 200.00
Teapot, daisies on peach, H Wilcox, 1890, #554 W, 4⅜" 400.00

Iris

Vase, autumn leaves on blk, S Sax, 1903, #907A, 8¾x3½" 1,900.00
Vase, clovers, E Diers, 1902, #922D W, 6⅞" 1,300.00
Vase, crocuses, C Schmidt, 1909, #1655D W, 9½" 3,100.00
Vase, daffodils, C Lindeman, 1903, #117C W, 8" 1,300.00
Vase, daffodils, H Wilcox, 1899, #829, 9" 5,000.00
Vase, daffodils, S Coyne, 1907, #907DD W X, 9⅝" 700.00

Vase, daisies, I Bishop, 1903, #904E, 6¾" **1,000.00**
Vase, daisies, OG Reed, 1903, #821C W, 10¼" **2,500.00**
Vase, daisies (Nouveau), F Rothenbusch, 1904, #614E W, 8⅛" .**2,700.00**
Vase, dogwood blossoms, C Baker, 1901, #922C, 8x4" **900.00**
Vase, fish swimming, JD Wareham, 1896, #765E W, 5⅜" **1,500.00**
Vase, floral, S Sax, 1906, #925C W, 9½" **7,250.00**
Vase, floral on blk to gold, S Sax, 1902, #926E, 5⅞" **1,000.00**
Vase, fruit blossoms, C Lindeman, 1908, #531E W, 5¾" **1,000.00**
Vase, grapevines on blk, S Sax, 1907, #913D W, 7¼" **4,400.00**
Vase, grouse on branch on blk, C Schmidt, 1909, #1369B, 14⅛" ...**42,000.00**
Vase, irises, C Schmidt, 1911, #1357D W, 8⅞", NM **2,500.00**
Vase, irises, L Asbury, 1905, #951E W, 7" **2,000.00**
Vase, irises (EX art), C Schmidt, 1910, #1667 W, 10½" **13,000.00**
Vase, irises (EX art), OG Reed, 1902, #614E W, 8" **4,850.00**
Vase, mistletoe (EX art), S Sax, 1904, #943F W, 4½" **1,700.00**
Vase, mushrooms, C Schmidt, 1901, #903C W, 8⅛" **4,300.00**
Vase, orchids, C Schmidt, 1900, #892C W, 8⅝" **1,200.00**
Vase, pansies, S Sax, 1902, #745B W, prof rpr, 8" **750.00**
Vase, parrot tulips, Caroline Bonsall, 1904, #938C, 8¼" **2,700.00**
Vase, poppies, F Rothenbusch, 1904, #833W, 9½x4½" **3,900.00**
Vase, poppies (wht/Nouveau), S Sax, 1903, #932CC W, 9¼" ...**4,000.00**
Vase, poppies on blk, S Sax, 1904, #925CC W X, 8⅝" **9,500.00**
Vase, sweet peas, C Schmidt, 1907, #482S, 10x3¼" **3,700.00**
Vase, thistles, A Valentien, 1904, #879B, prof rpr, 14½" **7,000.00**
Vase, thistles, F Rothenbusch, 1903, #932W, 9¾x4" **1,300.00**
Vase, trees & lake, L Asbury, 1911, #951E, 7½x3" **800.00**
Vase, tulips, M Nourse, 1904, #926C, 8¼" **1,400.00**
Vase, tulips, OG Reed, 1903, #922CC W, 9¾" **2,500.00**
Vase, water lilies, L Asbury, 1908, #917C W, 7½" **1,800.00**
Vase, wild roses, I Bishop, 1903, #918 W, 5⅝" **850.00**
Vase, wild roses, I Bishop, 1903, #918 W, 6⅞" **1,400.00**
Vase, wild violets, F Rothenbusch, 1904, #939D W, 7" **650.00**

Vase, wisteria branches on green to peach to gray, Ed Diers, #950D, 1909, 9", $3,250.00.

Vase, 11 sm fish, ET Hurley, 1904, #938C, 7½", NM **1,300.00**
Vase, 4 geese in takeoff, OG Reed, 1896, #808 W, 7½" **3,000.00**

Limoges

Jug, perfume; butterfly & grasses, A Velentien, 1883, #123 G, 9" **375.00**
Lamp base, dragonfly grasses, MA Daly, 1883, #97, 5¾" **200.00**

Mat

Note: Both incised mat and painted mat are listed here. Incised mat descriptions are indicated by the term 'cvd' within the line; the others are for the hand-painted mat ware.

Jug, whiskey; cherries, S Toohey, 1905, #889C, 6¾" **700.00**

Mug, incised lines, C Duell, 1909, #587NB X, 5¾" **250.00**
Vase, acorn & oak leaves, S Coyne, 1904, #922E, 5½" **550.00**
Vase, cvd floral, C Todd, 1914, #932E, 7¾x3¼" **750.00**
Vase, cvd floral, C Todd, 1918, #1873, 5x3¾" **550.00**
Vase, cvd floral, E Lincoln, 1918, #943C, uncrazed, 10x5" **1,600.00**
Vase, cvd grapes, C Todd, 1913, #1871, 6½x3" **475.00**
Vase, cvd peacock feathers, S Sax, 1919, #1905, 8" **200.00**
Vase, cvd/emb cattails, A Pons, 1906, #80E, 8x4" **1,200.00**
Vase, cvd/pnt fish, JD Wareham, 1903, #940B, 12¼" **3,400.00**
Vase, cvd/pnt flowers, C Todd, 1913, #2669, 8" **550.00**
Vase, cvd/pnt leaves, bl/gr on maroon, Hentschel, 1910, #789, 4" ..**800.00**
Vase, cvd/pnt leaves, brn w/lt purple, 1910, #952E, X, 6" **500.00**
Vase, cyclamen (EX art), H Wilcox, 1902, #194CZ, 9½x4" ...**7,500.00**
Vase, ferns on pk to gr, K Shirayamadani, 1915, #1374, 8", EX ..**200.00**
Vase, floral, E Lincoln, 1919, #112, 7x7½" **950.00**
Vase, floral, E Lincoln, 1926, #2900, 9⅝" **800.00**
Vase, floral, E Lincoln, 1926, #905F, 6" **375.00**
Vase, floral, Shirayamadani, rose crystalline, #2691, 1923, 6¾" ..**600.00**
Vase, floral, WE Hentschel, 1913, #494A, 9½x5" **550.00**
Vase, floral, 4 buttresses, A Munsen, 1931, #2324, 8" **210.00**
Vase, floral (abstract), E Barrett, 1924, #295D, 8⅞", NM **475.00**
Vase, floral (Deco), E Barrett, crystalline, 1929, #30F, 6¾" **450.00**
Vase, floral (EX art), M McDonald, 1929, #906D, 5⅜" **1,000.00**
Vase, floral (EX art), WE Hentschel, 1921, #924, 6" **750.00**
Vase, floral on pumpkin, V Tischler, 1924, #2499A, 18⅛" **3,800.00**
Vase, floral shoulder band, CS Todd, 1915, #1348, 3½" **300.00**
Vase, flower shoulder band, K Jones, 1924, #614E, 8⅞" **1,000.00**
Vase, grapes, J Harries, 1929, #2182, 5¼" **500.00**
Vase, jonquils, J Jensen, 1929, #907D, cobalt int, 11½" **1,000.00**
Vase, lotus blossoms, S Coyne, 1925, #1358B, 13¼" **1,100.00**
Vase, nasturtiums, E Lincoln, 1930, #1918, 8½" **650.00**
Vase, peacock feathers, C Todd, 1914, ovoid, #939D, 7½x3½" .**800.00**
Vase, poppies, LN Lincoln, 1926, #900A, 13" **1,800.00**
Vase, poppies, Shirayamadani, 1940, #2996, 8½" **3,000.00**
Vase, purple w/incised sm decor at top, AD, 1901, #120EZ, 4" ..**325.00**
Vase, repeating design at rim, CS Todd, 1918, #2118, 7⅜" **275.00**
Vase, Virginia Creepers, E Lincoln, 1922, #900A, 12⅝", NM ..**1,900.00**
Vase, wild roses, M McDonald, 1929, #2254E, 4⅜", EX **350.00**
Vase, wild roses, M McDonald, 1940, #6311, 7⅜" **850.00**
Vase, wisteria, 3-color, A Pons, #948B, 12x6" **1,000.00**

Porcelain

Charger, Russian peasants, Jewel, J Jensen, 1946, #2813C, 13" ..**750.00**
Flower holder, nude w/peacock, EB Haswell, 1915, #2270, 10¼" ...**175.00**
Jar, temple; floral, CJ McLaughlin, high glaze, #S 1968, 10¾" ..**1,000.00**
Vase, cobalt w/maroon int, 1923, #2260, 4⅜" **850.00**
Vase, daffodils, Jewel, K Shirayamadani, 1944, #6869, 9x5" **1,600.00**
Vase, fish, wht/brn on cream & bl, J Jensen, 1943, #6148, 5½" ..**1,000.00**
Vase, floral, Jewel, E Barrett, 1945, #907E, 7½x3¼" **600.00**
Vase, geometrics repeat at rim, A Conant, 1917, #2240 P, 6⅜" ..**1,400.00**
Vase, robin's egg bl, no decor, 1915, #126B, 9¼" **325.00**
Vase, vining floral, H Wilcox, 1921, #2544, 8" **1,800.00**
Vase, wisteria & vines, Ed Diers, 1924, #1781, 6" **1,400.00**

Sea Green

Vase, cvd/pnt chrysanthemums, M Daly, 1900, #886C G, 10⅝" .**11,000.00**
Vase, cvd/pnt/electroplated fruit, unknown, 1901, #531E, 6" .**3,500.00**
Vase, fish, ET Hurley, 1898, #808, 7⅜", NM **1,700.00**
Vase, geese flying, S Laurence, 1900, #829 G, 9⅛" **6,000.00**
Vase, hydrangeas, A Valentien, 1895, #604C, hdls, 9⅛" **4,500.00**
Vase, lotus blossoms, S Coyne, 1903, #938C G, 7½" **3,500.00**
Vase, pine cones/boughs, copper o/l, Fechheimer, 1900, #909, 8⅛" ...**9,000.00**

Vase, poppies (yel), C Baker, 1904, #938C G, 7½" 6,250.00
Vase, swallows in flight, B Horsfall, 1896, #605, 5¼x3¼" 2,100.00
Vase, wht clovers, S Coyne, 1905, #950E G, 6⅞" 1,100.00

Standard

Floor vase, lady in caftan, iris blossoms and clouds, Matthew Daly, #787A, 1896, 18x10", $4,500.00.

Basket, frog on lotus blossom, A Valentien, 1887, #360S, 7½" ...6,000.00
Coffeepot, violets, I Bishop, 1901, #528 V, 8⅛" 750.00
Ewer, honeysuckle w/silver o/l, J Zettel, 1893, #468CC, 8¼" ..1,900.00
Ewer, iris (1 lg), A Sprague, 1890, #433 W L, 6¾" 500.00
Ewer, oak leaves & acorns, E Lincoln, 1900, #433B, 8⅛" 450.00
Ewer, rose hips, G Young, 1895, #578D, prof rprs, 10⅜" 250.00
Ewer, tulips, S Coyne, 1897, #779B, 9⅛" 475.00
Ewer, wild roses, M Daly, 1896, #495A, 9¾" 1,000.00
Jug, corn, L Asbury, 1903, #512B, 10x5" 550.00
Match holder, floral, E Diers, 1898, #855, 1⅞" 200.00
Mug, Am Indian, S Laurence, 1898, #830E, 3-hdld, 4¾" 1,000.00
Mug, bulldog's face, ET Hurley, 1899, #837 X, 5⅛" 375.00
Sugar bowl, floral, unknown artist, 1893, #692 X, 3⅜", EX 100.00
Teapot, floral w/silver o/l, unknown, 1892, #615 W, 6⅜" 1,800.00
Urn, tulips & leaves, S Toohey, hdls, 1900, #800A, 12½x11" ...800.00
Vase, Am Indian, G Young, 1901, #900B, 1904 expo sticker, 8⅞" ...12,500.00
Vase, Am Indian portrait w/metal o/l, MA Daly, 1899, #538C, 12" .12,500.00
Vase, cherry blossoms, L Fry, 1886, #216, 12½x4½" 850.00
Vase, chrysanthemums, Shirayamadani, 1895, #S1183, rpr, 17¼" .2,800.00
Vase, daisies, C Steinle, 1895, #T999 (trial), 3⅜" 250.00
Vase, floral, H Altman, 1903, #917#, 5⅝" 375.00
Vase, floral, L Lindeman, 1905, #924, 5⅝" 325.00
Vase, floral (bright bl), H Altman, 1904, #932F, 6" 700.00
Vase, floral w/silver o/l, R Fechheimer, 1895, #716C, 9½x5" ..1,900.00
Vase, foliage & birds, A Valentien, 1885, #141W, 11" 800.00
Vase, geese among cattails, A Sprague, 1893, #534C R, 6⅞" ..1,800.00
Vase, grapes, L Van Briggle, 1903, #938D, 6⅛" 450.00
Vase, jonquils, E Felten, 1903, #932E X, 7⅜" 250.00
Vase, jonquils, J Zettel, 1897, #642, 10¼" 850.00
Vase, nasturtiums, A Van Briggle, 1892, #573C L, 12½", NM ...800.00
Vase, nasturtiums, L Fry, 1886, #292 A W LY, 16⅞" 850.00
Vase, nasturtiums, Wm Klemm, 1900, #657D, 6" 300.00
Vase, orchids, A Valentien, 1897, #664B, 10¼" 3,300.00
Vase, pansies w/Gorham silver o/l, C Baker, 1892, #941W, 8¼" ..1,700.00
Vase, poppies, L Asbury, 1900, #821C, 10¼x3½" 600.00
Vase, poppies, M Nourse, 1903, #932CC, 9⅞" 1,500.00
Vase, poppies, Shirayamadani, 1899, #792B, Paris expo label, 15" .11,500.00
Vase, rose hips, E Lincoln, 1902, #715E, 4⅞" 350.00
Vase, rose hips, R Fechheimer, 1902, #796B, 9⅞" 375.00
Vase, roses, A Van Briggle, 1890, #77A, 8¼x4½" 800.00
Vase, roses & leaves, A Valentien, 1889, #139a, 19½x10" 3,000.00
Vase, snarling leopard, ET Hurley, 1897, #707B X249X, 5⅞" 750.00
Vase, trumpet creeper flowers, L Perkins, 1898, #715D, 7¼" 325.00
Vase, tulips & leaves, E Lincoln, 1907, #950C, 10x4¼" 500.00

Vase, wisteria, A Valentien, 1893, #S 1055 W, rpr, 17¾" 3,300.00

Vellum

Bowl, floral, L Epply, 1909, #124 V, 6⅜" 275.00
Jar, sea horses (12), ET Hurley, 1911, #1349 V, 3½", w/lid 1,000.00
Plaque, fir trees/mtns, S Coyne, 1913, V, 8x4⅛"+fr 1,000.00
Plaque, lake scene at twilight, L Asbury, 1919, 7¼x9⅛" 2,600.00
Plaque, moonlit swamp, F Rothenbusch, 1918, #464, 7¼x5¾" ...2,500.00
Plaque, mtn scene w/lake, S Sax, 1912, 14¼x9"+oak fr 11,000.00
Plaque, scenic, ET Hurley, 1921, label, 3⅞x5⅝" 1,700.00
Vase, Arts & Crafts scenic, S Sax, 1913, #901C V, rpr, 9¾" 475.00
Vase, banded landscape, F Rothenbusch, 1912, #217C, 8¼x4¼" ..1,000.00
Vase, berries & leaves, S Sax, 1917, #932D, 9¾x3¾" 1,700.00
Vase, berries & vines, OG Reed, 1912, #901D V, 7¾" 400.00
Vase, cherry blossom band, ET Hurley, 1945, #6640/#5034, 6⅜" ...850.00
Vase, church winter scenic, E Diers, 1921, #654E V, 3⅞" 2,000.00
Vase, columbines, E Diers, 1912, #2039CV, 11½x4¾" 2,200.00
Vase, dogwood, CJ McLaughlin, 1915, #30F V, 7" 300.00
Vase, dogwood, peach on cream, Valentien, 1905, #902D, 8" .2,100.00
Vase, fish swimming, K Shirayamadani, 1906, #951B, 12½" ...5,250.00
Vase, floral, A Caven, 1917, #614F, 7" 500.00
Vase, floral, E Lincoln, 1910, #952F V, 6¼" 275.00
Vase, floral, S Sax, 1915, #917B V, drilled, 10¼" 450.00
Vase, floral (Nouveau), L Epply, 1908, #952E V, 7⅝" 2,500.00
Vase, floral branches, F Rothenbusch, 1909, #1553C, 11x5½" ..1,000.00
Vase, floral shoulder band, M McDonald, 1916, #942D, 5⅞" 225.00
Vase, floral shoulder band, MG Denzler, 1925, V X, 5½" 425.00
Vase, grapes, L Asbury, 1934, #1667 V, 11" 3,000.00
Vase, hyacinths, E Lincoln, 1906, #932E V, 7⅝" 600.00
Vase, irises, C Schmidt, 1925, #1358D V X, 8¾" 2,300.00
Vase, irises (lg), Sallie Coyne, 1904, #904 C V, 12⅛" 1,900.00
Vase, Oriental landscape, L Asbury, 1912, #950D, 9x4" 1,000.00
Vase, sailboats in harbor, S Coyne, 1913, #1920, 9¾" 2,300.00
Vase, scenic, Ed Diers, 1925, #1358D, 8¾" 3,600.00
Vase, scenic, ET Hurley, 1920, #1658E V X, 8⅛" 800.00
Vase, scenic, F Rothenbusch, 1922, #904D V, 9⅛" 1,600.00
Vase, sea horses, E Lincoln, 1908, #900D, 7x3¾" 950.00
Vase, sea horses, K Shirayamadani, 1907, #950D V, prof rpr, 9" ..1,200.00

Vase, snow scene, Sallie Coyne, 1919, 10", $4,250.00.

Vase, summer landscape, E Diers, 1920, #1871 V, 6½" 950.00
Vase, trees landscape, CJ McLaughlin, 1915, #1279F V, 7⅝" ...2,900.00
Vase, trees/grasses, ET Hurley, 1915, #1122B V, 8⅞" 900.00
Vase, woodland scenic, E Diers, 1919, #2039E V, 7¾" 900.00
Weed pot, daisies, C Steinle, 1910, #750C V X, 5⅝" 650.00

Wax Mat

Bowl, floral, 3-color, E Lincoln, 1925, #2697, 3¼x9¼" 600.00

Vase, berries & leaves, E Lincoln, 1926, #913F, 5½x3¼" 600.00
Vase, berries on bl, K Jones, 1927, #926E, 6¼x3½" 450.00
Vase, bud; floral, mc on pk, S Coyne, 1930, #2307, 7¼x3¼" 500.00
Vase, clematis blossoms, MH McDonald, 1927, #925D, 8½x4¼" ..700.00
Vase, floral, bl/gr on yel, S Coyne, 1931, #1369E, 7x4" 650.00
Vase, floral, E Lincoln, 1920, #18763V, 6x3½" 600.00
Vase, floral, mc on bl to purple, Shiraymadani, 1938, 7½x4" ..1,100.00
Vase, floral, mc on mustard, C Crofton, 1923, #605, 5¼x3½" ...550.00
Vase, floral, mc on pk to bl, MH McDonald, 1931, #915E, 6x4¼" ..700.00
Vase, floral, V Tischler, 1923, #2545, 10¾x3" 800.00
Vase, gooseberries, E Lincoln, 1926, #2900, 9½x5½" 900.00
Vase, poppies, S Coyne, 1931, #6194D, uncrazed, 6x5" 800.00
Vase, thistles, E Lincoln, 1928, #1369B, 15x8" 1,900.00

Miscellaneous

Bookends, #2274, 1922, rook, brn mat, 6½", pr 900.00
Bookends, #2275, 1925, rook, Wm McDonald, gr-blk mat, 5¼", pr 600.00
Bookends, #2445, 1925, peacock, yel mat, 4⅞", pr 450.00
Bookends, #2603, 1924, frog, mottled bl-gr mat, 4½", pr 1,200.00
Bookends, #2657, 1922, kingfisher, brn/tan mottle, 5⅛", pr 400.00
Bookends, #2837, 1929, flower basket, mc, 5⅞", pr 800.00
Bowl, #1214, 1908, pine cones/needles on pk to gr, 2x7½" 650.00
Bowl, #1929, 1913, bl mat, 3-lobe top, 4½x7" 650.00
Doorstop, #2637, 1924, cat, cobalt bl, rpr, 7¾" 2,200.00
Figurine, #6166, 1930, camel, Louise Abel, tan mat, 6½" 1,600.00
Figurine, #6972, 1954, bird (crane) 170.00
Figurine, #7024, cocker spaniel, 4" 275.00
Frieze, 3 tiles form landscape w/trees/house/water/sky, 6x18" ..4,250.00
Paperweight, #1855, 1933, goose, wht mat, 4⅛" 200.00
Paperweight, #6665, 1954, lamb, gunmetal blk, 5⅛" 275.00
Sconce, #1760, 1915, Glasgow roses, 8½x4½" 500.00
Tile, flower w/geometrics & border, 3-color, 4" sq+fr 425.00
Tile, grapes & leaves, brn/gr, faience, #1146Y/#1147Y, 6", 6 for .1,300.00
Tile, leaf design, gray/bl/brn, 4" 250.00
Tile, rose & leaves in vase, pk/bl/tan/brn, mk, 4" sq 450.00
Tile, rose surrounded by leaves, 4-color, 4" 400.00
Tile, trees beside water, 4-color, C Duell, 8" sq+fr 2,700.00
Trivet, #1794, 1925, rook, blk/bl/wht, 5⅝" sq, EX 300.00
Trivet, #1984, 1918, flowering tree/rabbits, porc, 5⅜" 375.00
Vase, #1253D, 1912, geometrics on gr & brn, 9" 550.00
Vase, #1297, 1907, poppies (well defined), 8x4" 750.00
Vase, #1298, 1913, lotus flowers on gr to pk, 6" 325.00
Vase, #1722, 1910, floral branches, gr mat, 9" 400.00
Vase, #1825, 1923, panels & dmns on gr mat, 5" 240.00
Vase, #1907, 1921, floral on purple mat, flaw in making, 5" 475.00
Vase, #2108, 1922, floral on bl matt, 6½" 250.00
Vase, #2126, 1924, yel mat, 3 sm hdls, 9" 300.00
Vase, #2323, 1921, thick rose matt, flaw in making, 8" 210.00
Vase, #2413, 1928, mistletoe, bulbous, cylindrical neck, 8x5" 325.00
Vase, #2476, 1931, daffodils on long stems, yel mat, 8½" 900.00
Vase, #389B, 1910, geometrics at neck on gr to brn, hdls, 13" ..1,600.00
Vase, #390Z, 1902, gr, Arts & Crafts decor at shoulder, 7" 475.00
Vase, #6146, 1943, orchids/etc, Jensen, butterfat glaze, 5⅝" 600.00
Vase, #63, 1926, rose matt, hdls, 4½" 160.00
Vase, #6317C, 1932, Randy Gray/Riley Bl/Ralphie Brn, 6¾" 500.00
Vase, #6487, 1934, fish & waves, variegated bl, 4½" 550.00
Vase, #704, 1914, gr matt w/maroon, shoulder decor, 9" 750.00
Vase, #806 GZ, 1901, yel & brn mottle, 3½" 200.00

Rose Mandarin

Similar in design to Rose Medallion, this Chinese Export porcelain features the pattern of a robed mandarin, often separated by florals, ladies, genre scenes, or butterflies in polychrome enamels. It is sometimes trimmed in gold. Elaborate in decoration, this pattern was popular from the late 1700s until the early 1840s.

Bowl, scalloped rim, 9½" 385.00
Bowl, serving; 19th C, 9⅞", NM 360.00
Plate, 8⅜", 4 for 350.00
Platter, 16¼" 375.00

Platter, 19th century, 17¾" long, $500.00.

Sauce boat, intertwined hdl, 8¼" 300.00
Shaped dish, 19th C, 10¾" L 175.00
Soup plate, 9¾", 6 for 400.00
Tureen, gilt hdls & finial, 11¼x13¾" 1,100.00
Umbrella stand, wrapped bamboo form, 19th C, 24" 1,495.00

Rose Medallion

Rose Medallion is one of the patterns of Chinese export porcelain produced from before 1850 until the second decade of the 20th century. It is decorated in rose colors with panels of florals, birds, and butterflies that form reserves containing Chinese figures. Pre-1850 ware is unmarked and is characterized by quality workmanship and gold trim. From about 1850 until circa 1860, the kilns in Canton did not operate, and no Rose Medallion was made. Post-1860 examples (still unmarked) can often be recognized by the poor quality of the gold trim or its absence. In the 1890s the ware was often marked 'China'; 'Made in China' was used from 1910 through the 1930s.

Basket, fruit; rtcl, 19th C, 9¾", w/undertray 750.00
Bowl, hot water; w/lid, 10" dia, EX 330.00
Bowl, rice; scalloped rim, 4⅝", 4 for 110.00
Bowl, scalloped rim, ca 1875, 9½", NM 295.00
Bowl, scalloped rim, mid-1800s, 9¾" 700.00
Bowl, scalloped rim, much underside decor, 2x8½" 350.00
Bowl, vegetable; flower & bird panels w/gold, w/lid, 9" L 400.00
Bowl, w/lid, 19th C, 9¼", EX, pr 750.00
Bowl, 3 figures, Made in China, 2⅝x6" 48.00
Box, divided int, 19th C, 2½x7½x3¾", NM 600.00
Brush box, lady w/golden hair, w/lid, 7½x3½" 400.00
Butter dish, 8-sided, 3-pc 250.00
Chop plate, mk China, ca 1895, 11" 225.00
Chop plate, 13¼" 360.00
Chop plate, 16¼" 550.00
Creamer & sugar bowl, w/lid, Made in China, 5½" 115.00
Cup & saucer, birds & people, China 30.00
Cup & saucer, bouillon 55.00
Cuspidor, sm flakes, 6½x9" 355.00
Garden seat, 19th C, lt wear, 18¾" 1,725.00
Oil lamp, gilt-metal mts, 19th C, 13" 430.00
Plate, canted corners, Made in China, 5" sq 35.00

Plate, dinner; 19th C, 9⅝", 10 for 600.00
Plate, Made in China, 6" 17.00
Plate, Made in China, 7½" 30.00
Plate, Made in China, 9½" 50.00
Plate, soup; 19th/20th C, 9¾", 10 for 520.00
Platter, mid-1800s, 18" 1,250.00
Platter, tree & well; rpr rim, 16½" 330.00
Platter, 19th C, 10" 195.00
Platter, 19th C, 13½" 330.00
Platter, 19th C, 14⅛" 285.00
Platter, 19th C, 18⅜" 400.00
Punch bowl, birds & butterflies, 6x14½" 600.00
Punch bowl, late 19th C, 15", EX 900.00
Punch bowl, late 19th C, 16" 1,035.00
Sconces, brass mts, electrified, 19th C, 8¼", pr 975.00
Sugar bowl, birds & people, bulbous, Made in China, 4x6" 85.00
Teapot, domed lid, 8½" 660.00
Teapot, mandarin scenes, in wicker cozy, 5¼" 185.00
Teapot, 19th C, 9¼" 375.00
Tray, quatrefoil, 8¼x10½" 200.00
Tray, trefoil, 9⅞x10¼" 175.00
Tureen, soup; 19th C, 11x14" 2,185.00
Vase, baluster, 19th C, 13½" 315.00
Vase, dbl gourd form, 19th C, 12¼" 800.00
Vase, foo dog hdls, appl serpents, figures in panels, 13", pr 900.00
Vase, trumpet form, 19th C, 13", EX 325.00

Roselane

Founded in California in 1938 by William and Georgia Fields, the Roselane company at first produced only figurines for the local florist. But by the '40s they offered candle holders, wall pockets, vases, and a line of modernistic animals mounted on wooden bases. In the '50s their 'Sparklers' became popular — small stylized animal and bird figures with rhinestone eyes. (Today these are worth from $10.00 to $25.00, depending on size.) The company closed in 1977. A variety of marks was used; all incorporate the Roselane name. Our advisor for this category is Susan Cox; she is listed in the Directory under California.

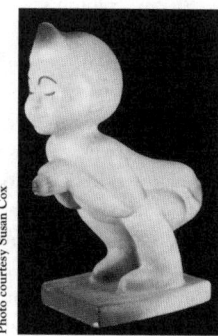

Figurine, Lo Diver (boy), beige and brown satin matt, 3½", $25.00.

Photo courtesy Susan Cox

Bowl, console; pk & gray, A-20, 20" L 38.00
Bowl, gray w/dk gr int, Chinese Modern, 6¼" 29.00
Bowl, sgraffito snowflakes, scroll mk, #A9, 9" 65.00
Candle holders, Chinese Modern, dove gray gloss, pr 82.50
Candle holders, sq center base, ribbed, #C1, pr 55.00
Figurine, Bali male dancer, 11" 60.00
Figurine, boy w/dog, 5½" 30.00
Figurine, cockatoo, cream w/brn tones, 9¾" 60.00
Figurine, deer, Sparkler, plastic eyes, brn & wht, 4" 20.00
Figurine, deer (2) standing on oval base, lt bl, 5" 35.00

Figurine, elephant, stylized, brn lustre, wood base, 8" 150.00
Figurine, giraffe, seated, #264, ca 1960, 9" 65.00
Figurine, goose, bk view, wings open, head over wing, 5" 21.00
Figurine, owl, sgraffito feathers on tan, 6½" 60.00
Figurine, pheasant, brn & wht matt, tail up, 7¾" 40.00
Planter, coolie atop rectangular planter 24.00
Sign, dealer, scroll design, gray, 12½" L 225.00
Vase, Chinese Modern, emb decor base, ftd, 9¾" 40.00

Rosemeade

Rosemeade was the name chosen by Wahpeton Pottery Company of Wahpeton, North Dakota, to represent their product. The founders of the company were Laura A. Taylor and R.J. Hughes, who organized the firm in 1940. It is most noted for small bird and animal figurals, either in high gloss or a Van Briggle-like matt glaze. The ware was marked 'Rosemeade' with an ink stamp or carried a 'Prairie Rose' sticker. The pottery closed in 1961. Our advisor for this category is Bryce L. Farnsworth; he is listed in the Directory under North Dakota. For more information we recommend *Collector's Encyclopedia of the Dakota Potteries* by Darlene Hurst Dommel.

Ashtray, Sauk Centre, S Lewis, Main Street 450.00
Ashtray, Wahpeton National Bank 40.00
Ashtray, Wisconsin, state shape 45.00
Bank, rhino 550.00
Bookends, wolfhounds, pr 340.00
Butter dish, pk 200.00
Butter dish, wht 150.00
Candleholders, Prairie Rose, pr 200.00
Cotton holder, rabbit figural 235.00
Figurine, buffalo, lg 290.00
Figurine, horse, blk 460.00
Figurine, mice, mini, pr 17.50
Figurine, Perching Bird, finch 235.00
Figurine, Perching Bird, robin 175.00
Figurine, pheasant, rooster, 12½" 250.00
Figurine, pheasant, rooster, 14½" 450.00
Figurine, roadrunner 225.00
Flower frog, heron 50.00
Honey pot 27.50
Mug, Indian head, hdld 325.00
Mug, Indian head, no hdl 200.00
Paperweight, Minnesota Centennial 200.00
Pitcher, Art Deco style 40.00
Planter, swan figural 45.00
Shakers, bluebirds, pr 425.00
Shakers, Bob White, pr 40.00
Shakers, brussel sprouts, pr 50.00
Shakers, buffalo, pr 140.00
Shakers, chickadees, pr 300.00
Shakers, corn ears, pr 45.00
Shakers, coyotes, howling, pr 250.00
Shakers, cucumbers, pr 47.50
Shakers, dog heads, bloodhounds, pr 75.00
Shakers, dog heads, bulldog, pr 150.00
Shakers, dog heads, chihuahuas, pr 500.00
Shakers, dog heads, English setters, pr 50.00
Shakers, dog heads, greyhounds, pr 75.00
Shakers, ducklings, pr 80.00
Shakers, elephants, pr 80.00
Shakers, gophers, upright, sm, pr 70.00
Shakers, mallards, hen & drake, pr 80.00

Shakers, mountain goats, pr 275.00
Shakers, parrots, pr 140.00
Shakers, Paul Bunyan & Babe 150.00
Shakers, pheasants, crouching, pr 150.00
Shakers, pheasants, tails down, pr 90.00
Shakers, pheasants, tails up, pr 40.00
Shakers, potatoes, lg, pr 200.00
Shakers, rabbits, running, sm 90.00
Shakers, raccons, pr 210.00
Shakers, skunks, lg 60.00
Shakers, swans, pr 95.00
Shakers, turkeys, lg 75.00
Shakers, turkeys, mini, pr 170.00
Spoon rest, cactus 50.00
TV Lamp, blk panther 650.00
TV Lamp, horse, palomino 450.00
Vase, ball shape, holes for flower frog 35.00
Vase, deer, tall, standing, glossy 47.50
Vase, free-form, chartreuse 30.00
Vase, lovebirds 40.00
Vase, tulip shape, rose bowl 45.00
Vase, wheat design, cylindrical, sm 45.00
Wall pocket, moon, sm 55.00

Rosenthal

In 1879 Phillip Rosenthal established the Rosenthal Porcelain Factory in Selb, Bavaria. Its earliest products were figurines and fine tablewares. The company has continued to operate to the present decade, manufacturing limited edition plates. Our advisor for this category is Raphael Wise; he is listed in the Directory under Florida.

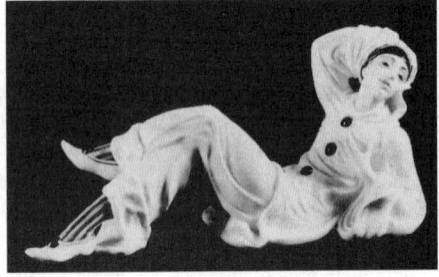

Figurine, Pierrot reclining in dramatic pose, professional repair, $300.00.

Coffee set, Helena, serves 6, 15-pc 165.00
Cup & saucer, bouillon; Ivory Rose (Pompadour) 25.00
Cup & saucer, demi; Die Fledermaus 55.00
Cup & saucer, demi; Victorian portrait 100.00
Cup & saucer, Linnie Lee, ivory 38.00
Figurine, bird, #1647 ....75.00
Figurine, bird on branch, artist sgn, 6" 135.00
Figurine, boy w/lamb, #16665 ....145.00
Figurine, Brittany Spaniel, 5½x9" 550.00
Figurine, dachshund, recumbent, 10x6" 425.00
Figurine, dachshund, standing, 4¾" 125.00
Figurine, dachshund on hind legs, 9½x3½" 370.00
Figurine, fox, #76 ....165.00
Figurine, Harlequin Great Dane, 8x9¼" 650.00
Figurine, horse, standing, bsk, Hussman, #16101/1, 11x18" 450.00
Figurine, musicians (3) on base, 8¼x3" dia 1,000.00
Figurine, nude, sgn Ernst Wenck, lg 550.00
Figurine, Pan seated on column playing pipes, lizard at base 345.00
Figurine, pointer, 5x10½" 500.00
Figurine, poodle, wht, 8½x9½" 300.00

Figurine, princess w/crowned frog at hem, Friedrich-Groneau, 10" ..265.00
Figurine, Victorian lady w/wolfhound (Borzoi), pastels, 11x7" ...950.00
Figurine, wolfhound (Borzoi), wht, head up, recumbent, 9¼x4½" ..380.00
Figurine, 2 nudes playing instruments, wht porc, 13" 3,165.00
Plate, Delft windmills, horses, wagon, fancy mold, 10½" 150.00
Tureen, soup; Ivory Rose (Pompadour), 4-qt 145.00
Vase, conch form, artist sgn 150.00
Vase, flower panels, mc w/gold, sgn, gr mk, 6¼" 190.00
Vase, gold & wht leaf design, M Hildebrand, 7" 45.00
Vase, landscape, artist sgn, pillow form, 8x5" 275.00
Vase, Madeira, sgn Yang, 4½", w/matching ashtray 40.00
Vase, maid dancing, diaphanous gown, soft gr irid, 12" 600.00
Vase, Studio Line, artist sgn, 10" 225.00
Vase, stylized bird & cage, charcoal, 1950s, 8" 65.00

Roseville

The Roseville Pottery Company was established in 1892 by George F. Young in Roseville, Ohio. Finding their facilities inadequate, the company moved to Zanesville in 1898, erected a new building, and installed the most modern equipment available. By 1900 Young felt ready to enter into the stiffly competitive art pottery market. Roseville's first art line was called Rozane. Similar to Rookwood's Standard, Rozane featured dark blended backgrounds with slip-painted underglaze artwork of nature studies, portraits, birds, and animals. Azurean, developed in 1902, was a blue and white underglaze art line on a blue blended background. Egypto (1904) featured a matt glaze in a soft shade of old green and was modeled in low relief after examples of ancient Egyptian pottery. Mongol (1904) was a high-gloss oxblood red line after the fashion of the Chinese Sang de Boeuf. Mara (1904), an iridescent lustre line of magenta and rose with intricate patterns developed on the surface or in low relief, successfully duplicated Sicardo's work. These early lines were followed by many others of highest quality: Fudjiyama and Woodland (1905 – 06) reflected an Oriental theme; Crystalis (1906) was covered with beautiful frost-like crystals. Della Robbia, their most famous line (introduced in 1906), was decorated with designs ranging from florals, animals, and birds to scenes of Viking warriors and Roman gladiators. These designs were worked in sgraffito with slip-painted details. Very limited but of great importance to collectors today, Rozane Olympic (1905) was decorated with scenes of Greek mythology on a red ground. Pauleo (1914) was the last of the artware lines. It was varied — over two hundred glazes were recorded — and some pieces were decorated by hand, usually with florals.

During the second decade of the century until the plant closed forty years later, new lines were continually added. Some of the more popular of the middle-period lines were Donatello, 1915; Futura, 1928; Pine Cone, 1931; and Blackberry, 1933. The floral lines of the later years have become highly collectible. Pottery from every era of Roseville production — even its utility ware — attest to an unwavering dedication to quality and artistic merit.

Examples of the fine art pottery lines present the greatest challenge to evaluate. Scarcity is a prime consideration. The quality of artwork varied from one artist to another. Some pieces show fine detail and good color, and naturally this influences their values. Studies of animals and portraits bring higher prices than the floral designs. An artist's signature often increases the value of any item, especially if the artist is one who is well recognized. The market is literally flooded with imposter Roseville that is coming into the country from China. An experienced eye can easily detect these fakes, but to a novice collector, they may pass for old Roseville. Study the marks. If the USA is missing or appears only faintly, the piece is most definitely a reproduction. Also watch for lines with a mark that is not correct for its time frame; for example Luffa with the script mark, and Woodland with the round Rozane stamp from the 1917 line. For further information consult *The Collector's Encyclopedia of Roseville Pottery, First* and *Second Series*, by Sharon and Bob Huxford (Collector Books), and *Collector's Compendium of Roseville Pottery, Volumes I* and *II*, by R.B. Monsen (see Directory, Virginia). Note: Reference names in the Futura descriptions that follow have developed via communication among collectors (Monsen follows up on this in Volume I). The values we list for that line were prices realized at auction. Futura prices tend to be volatile, and only when there were multiple sales for a particular piece did we choose to include it here.

Apple Blossom, bowl, #326-6, 2½x6½" 95.00
Apple Blossom, vase, #390-12, 12½" 250.00
Apple Blossom, vase, cornucopia; #381, 6" 110.00
Artwood, planter, #1055-9, 7x9½" 95.00
Azurean, vase, nasturtiums, sgn Leffler, #822/7, 15½" 1,150.00
Azurean, vase, scenic, shouldered, unmk, 9" 2,250.00
Baneda, bowl, hdls, unmk, 3½x10" 400.00
Baneda, candle holder, 6-sided base, 4½" 275.00
Bank, beehive, unmk, 2½" 175.00
Bank, monkey, unmk, 6" 150.00
Bank, pig, unmk, 4x5½" 200.00
Bittersweet, basket, #807-8, 8½" 150.00
Bittersweet, candlestick, #851-3, 3" 60.00
Bittersweet, vase, #884-8, 8" 150.00
Bittersweet, vase, #972, 5" 125.00
Blackberry, candle holders, 4½", pr 400.00
Blackberry, jardiniere, sm hdls, paper label, 4" 250.00
Blackberry, vase, bulbous, sm hdls, 4" 300.00
Blackberry, vase, sm hdls, paper label, 6" 350.00
Bleeding Heart, bowl vase, #651-3, 3½" 95.00
Bleeding Heart, candlesticks, #1139-4½, paper label, 5", pr 175.00
Bleeding Heart, ewer, #963, 6" 175.00
Bleeding Heart, plate, #381-10, 10½" 175.00
Blended, jardiniere, emb pea pods, unmk, 4¼" base dia 75.00
Blended, jardiniere & pedestal, #414, 28" 600.00
Blended, umbrella stand, #132, 21½" 400.00
Burmese, wall pocket, wht, #82-B, 7½" 250.00
Bushberry, bowl, #411, 4" 85.00
Bushberry, bud vase, dbl; #148-4½, 4½" 125.00
Bushberry, pitcher, cider; #1325, 8½" 350.00
Bushberry, umbrella stand, #779-20, 20½" 700.00
Bushberry, vase, #157-8, 8" 150.00
Capri, Late Line; basket, #510-10, 9" 150.00
Capri, Late Line; bowl, #527-7, 7" 25.00
Capri, Late Line; leaf, #532-16, 16" 35.00
Carnelian (spongeware), candle holder, wide flared base, 3" 75.00
Carnelian (spongeware), shaving mug, unmk, 4" 75.00
Carnelian (spongeware), wash bowl & pitcher, unmk, 15½", 12" ..450.00
Carnelian I, vase, bulbous, angle hdls, ink stamp, 10" 200.00
Carnelian I, wall pocket, ink stamp, 9½" 200.00
Carnelian II, bowl, ftd, angle hdls, unmk, 3x8" 100.00
Carnelian II, ewer, wide flared base, unmk, 12½" 600.00
Carnelian II, vase, flared rim, tub hdls, unmk, 12" 550.00
Cherry Blossom, bowl vase, 6" 350.00
Cherry Blossom, hanging basket, unmk, 8" 500.00
Cherry Blossom, wall pocket, silver paper label, 8" 700.00
Chloron, sconce, figure in relief, unmk, 17" 1,500.00
Chloron, wall pocket, boy, unmk, 9½" 1,250.00
Clemana, flower frog, #23, 4" 175.00
Clemana, vase, #750-6, 6½" 250.00
Clematis, basket, #389, 10" 200.00
Clematis, bowl, #445, 4" 60.00
Clematis, candle holder, #1155-2, 2½" 60.00
Clematis, flower arranger, #102-5, 5½" 75.00

Clematis, vase, #102-6, 6½" 85.00
Columbine, bowl, #401, 6" 135.00
Columbine, vase, #17-7, 7½" 150.00
Columbine, vase, cornucopia; #149-6, 5½" 95.00
Corinthian, bowl, ftd, unmk, 4½" 70.00
Corinthian, candlestick, 8" 85.00
Corinthian, jardiniere, ink stamp, 7" 100.00
Cosmos, bowl vase, #376, 6" 200.00
Cosmos, flower frog, unmk, 3½" 125.00
Cosmos, vase, #375-4, 4" 175.00
Cosmos, vase, #905-8, 8" 150.00
Cosmos, wall pocket, #1285, 6½" 200.00
Creamware, sugar bowl, Gibson girls, w/lid, unmk, 4" 110.00
Creamware, teapot, forget-me-nots, unmk, 6½" 200.00
Cremona, vase, angle hdls, 10" 175.00

Crocus vase, dark green, signed PD, 9", $475.00.

Dahlrose, vase, sm angle hdsl, paper label, 6" 125.00
Dahlrose, vase, sq sides, paper label, 6" 150.00
Dahlrose, window box, unmk, 16" L 275.00
Dawn, bowl, #3187-14, 16" 175.00
Dawn, ewer, #834-16, 16" 550.00
Dawn, vase, #828, 8" 200.00
Della Robbia, tankard, A Chirping Cup..., Rozane Ware seal, 10½" 1,550.00
Della Robbia, teapot, sgn EB, Rozane Ware seal 1,300.00
Display sign, Roseville, blended, 2x6" 1,500.00
Display sign, Roseville, pk, 5x8" 2,250.00
Dogwood I, hanging basket, unmk, 7" 150.00
Dogwood I, jardiniere, ink stamp, 6" 115.00
Dogwood II, bud vase, dbl; unmk, 8" 135.00
Dogwood II, bud vase, 9" 85.00
Dogwood II, wall pocket, unmk, 9" 250.00
Donatello, ashtray, unmk, 3" 150.00
Donatello, bowl, unmk, 3x8" 120.00
Donatello, jardiniere, 8½" 150.00
Donatello, jardiniere & pedestal, unmk, 23½" 600.00
Dutch, humidor, unk, 5" 300.00
Dutch, pitcher, unmk, 7½" 225.00
Dutch, tumbler, unmk, 4" 150.00
Earlam, bowl, hdls, unmk, 3x11½" 160.00
Earlam, umbrella stand, #741, paper label, 20" 600.00
Earlam, vase, sq incurvate rim, unmk, 9" 375.00
Earlam, wall pocket, paper label, 6½" 350.00
Early Pitcher, Grape, unmk, 6" 150.00
Early Pitcher, Iris, unmk, 7" 250.00
Early Pitcher, Mill, unmk, 8" 325.00
Early Pitcher, Owl, unmk, 6½" 400.00
Early Pitcher, Poppy, #11, 9" 175.00
Egypto, circle jug, seal mk, 11" 700.00
Egypto, creamer, 3-way, seal mk, 3½" 200.00

Egypto, oil lamp, seal mk, 5" 450.00
Falline, comport, #727-10, 4½x10½" 125.00
Falline, vase, bulbous, hdls, silver label, 6" 425.00
Ferella, candlesticks, brn, unmk, 4½", pr 500.00
Ferella, vase, brn, rtcl rim & ft, unmk, 8x6" 500.00
Florane, bowl, bulbous, sm angle hdls, ink stamp, 5" 50.00
Florane, bud vase, dbl; ink stamp, 5" 60.00
Florane, Late Line; bowl, 10" 35.00
Florane, Late Line; planter box, #92-6, 6" 30.00
Florane, Late Line; sand jar, #52-12, 12" 135.00
Florane, Late Line; vase, #81, 7" 85.00
Florentine, bowl, sm angle hdls, unmk, 7" 60.00
Florentine, bud vase, dbl; ink stamp, 6" 110.00
Florentine, candlestick, ink stamp, 10½" 125.00
Florentine, jardiniere, ink stamp, 5" 110.00
Forest, basket, tall hdl, unmk, 12" 325.00
Forest, vase, sm angle hdls, #121-15, 15" 500.00
Foxglove, conch shell, #425, 6" 150.00
Foxglove, tray, integral hdls, mk, 15" 160.00
Foxglove, vase, #58-14, 14" 450.00
Foxglove, vase, low hdls, #47-8, 8½" 150.00
Freesia, bud vase, #195, 7" 95.00
Freesia, candlesticks, #1160-2, 2", pr 110.00
Freesia, ewer, #19, 6" 165.00
Freesia, flowerpot, attached saucer, 3670-5, 5½" 150.00
Freesia, vase, #124-9, 9" 150.00
Fuchsia, bowl vase, #346, 4" 175.00
Fuchsia, candlesticks, #1132, 2", pr 150.00
Fuchsia, vase, #893-6, 6" 150.00
Fuchsia, vase, #898-8, 8" 275.00
Fudji, vase, butterflies, bowl form, ink stamp, 9" 1,350.00
Fudji, vase, floral, slim cylinder, ink stamp, 15" 1,250.00

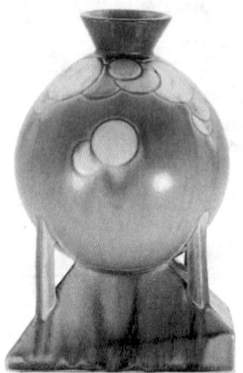

Futura, vase, Balloons Globe, #404-8, from $1,000.00 to $1,300.00.

Futura, vase, Arches, #411-14, from $2,400 to 2,800.00
Futura, vase, Balloons Globe, #404-8, from $1,000 to 1,300.00
Futura, vase, Bamboo Leaf Ball, #387-7, from $600 to 800.00
Futura, vase, Beehive, #406-8, from $600 to 700.00
Futura, vase, Beer Mug, #381-6, from $250 to 325.00
Futura, vase, Big Blue Triangle, #388-9 ....450.00
Futura, vase, Black Flame, #391-10, from $650 to 850.00
Futura, vase, Bomb, #394-12, from $1,000 to 1,100.00
Futura, vase, Bottle, #384-8 ....435.00
Futura, vase, Chinese Pillow, #430-9, from $1,000 to 1,300.00
Futura, vase, Christmas Tree, #390-10, from $450 to 500.00
Futura, vase, Cone, #401-8 ....450.00
Futura, vase, Egg w/Leaves, #428-8, from $400 to 500.00
Futura, vase, Emerald Urn, #398-9 ....600.00
Futura, vase, Football Urn, #409-9, from $1,000 to 1,200.00
Futura, vase, Jukebox, #386-8 ....600.00

Futura, vase, Mauve Thistle, #427-8, from $850 to 1,000.00
Futura, vase, Pink Twist, #425-8, from $450 to 550.00
Futura, vase, Red V (Victory), #399-7, from $350 to 450.00
Futura, vase, Sand Toy, #189-4-6, from $400 to 500.00
Futura, vase, Sea Gull, #408-10, from $1,000 to 1,200.00
Futura, vase, Shooting Star, #392-10, from $800 to 1,100.00
Futura, vase, Space Capsule, #432-10, from $600 to 650.00
Futura, vase, Spittoon, #403-7, from $700 to 900.00
Futura, vase, Square Cone, #397-6, from $325 to 365.00
Futura, vase, Telescope, #382-7, from $350 to 400.00
Futura, vase, Tombstone, #426-6, from $275 to 375.00
Futura, vase, Twist, #398-6½, from $300 to 350.00
Futura, vase, 2-Pole Pink Bud, #84-4, from $275 to 375.00
Futura, vase, 4-Ball, #393-12, from $650 to 850.00
Futura, wall pocket, 8", from $475 to 550.00
Gardenia, hanging basket, 6" 225.00
Gardenia, tray, #631-14, 15" 165.00
Glossy Utility Line, bowl, RUSA #10-6, 7" 40.00
Glossy Utility Line, teapot, RUSA #14, 6½" 110.00
Imperial I, basket, #7, 9" 125.00
Imperial I, basket, unmk, 13" 250.00
Imperial I, vase, bulbous, angle hdls, unmk, 10" 175.00
Imperial II, vase, globular, unk, 4" 200.00
Iris, basket, #354, 8" 275.00
Iris, vase, #358-6, 6½" 200.00
Iris, vase, #917-6, 6½" 125.00
Iris, vase, #924-9, 10" 250.00
Ivory Florentine, umbrella stand, #298, 18½" 350.00
Ivory II, candlestick, ball on flared ft, mk, 2½" 35.00
Ivory II, hanging basket, 7" 100.00
Ivory II, vase, cornucopia; 5½x12" 60.00
Ixia, candle holder/bud vase, #1128, 5" 150.00
Ixia, candlestick, dbl; #1127, 3" 95.00
Jonquil, bowl, hdls, 4" 175.00
Jonquil, candlestick, wide flared rim, unmk, 4" 125.00
Jonquil, crocus pot, attached saucer, hdls, unmk, 7" 400.00
Juvenile, creamer, Santa Claus, ink mk, 3½" 400.00
Juvenile, plate, chicks on gr band, unmk, 7" 125.00
Juvenile, plate, divided; Fancy Cat, ink stamp, 8½" 500.00
Juvenile, sugar bowl, nursery rhyme, unmk, 3" 150.00
La Rose, bowl, sm hdls, ink stamp, 6" 75.00
La Rose, vase, sm uptrn hdls, ink stamp, 4" 110.00
La Rose, wall pocket, unmk, 9" 200.00
Landscape, sugar bowl, sailboat scene, w/lid, unmk, 3½" 85.00
Laurel, bowl, paper sticker, 7" 200.00
Laurel, bowl, sm hdls, unmk, 3½" 225.00
Laurel, vase, stepped neck, sm hdls, paper label, 9½" 300.00
Lombardy, wall pocket, matt, paper label, 8" 300.00
Lotus, bowl, #L6-9, 3x9" 135.00
Lotus, planter, #L9-4, 3½x4" 100.00
Luffa, lamp base, bl/gr, angle hdls, unmk, 9½" 600.00
Luffa, vase, angle hdls, unmk, 8" 250.00
Magnolia, ewer, #13, 6" 135.00
Mara, vase, slim neck, flared rim, unmk, 13½" 3,000.00
Matt Green, hanging basket, unmk, 9" 200.00
Matt Green, jardiniere, #456, 5½" 250.00
Matt Green, wall pocket, unmk, 11" 275.00
Mayfair, bowl, shell shape, mk, 7" 30.00
Mayfair, flowerpot, #71-4, 4½" 45.00
Mayfair, jardiniere, #1109-4, 4" 40.00
Mayfair, planter, #1113, 8" 60.00
Ming Tree, hanging basket, USA, 6" 250.00
Ming Tree, vase, #584-12, 12½" 250.00
Ming Tree, window box, #569-10, 4x11" 150.00

Mock Orange, bowl, #900, 4" 85.00
Mock Orange, vase, #973-8, 8½" 115.00
Mock Orange, window box, #956-8, 4½x8½" 95.00
Moderne, candle holder, triple; #1112, 6" 225.00
Moderne, comport, #295, 5" 125.00
Mongol, mug, 3-hdl, seal mk, 6" 580.00
Mongol, vase, slim cylinder, unmk, 10½" 950.00
Monticello, vase, hdls, 9" 700.00
Morning Glory, bowl vase, 4" 350.00
Morning Glory, candlestick, flared ft, sm hdls, unmk, 5" 200.00
Morning Glory, vase, pillow form, low hdls, paper label, 7" 275.00
Moss, bud vase, triple; #1108, 7" 400.00
Moss, candle holders, #1107, 4½", pr 200.00
Moss, vase, #290-6, 6" 225.00
Mostique, bowl, incurvate rim, unmk, 7" 75.00
Mostique, vase, cylindrical, 6" 100.00
Mostique, vase, shouldered, unmk, 10" 225.00
Mostique, wall pocket, unmk, 9½" 250.00
Novelty Stein, No Vacation in This Business, 4½" .. 250.00
Novelty Stein, Try It on the Dog, 5" 250.00
Olympic, vase, flared cylinder, ftd, ink mk, 13" 3,000.00
Orian, candle holder, unmk, 4½" 95.00
Orian, vase, #733-6, 6" 125.00
Orian, vase, low hdls, paper label, 7" 175.00
Panel, bud vase, dbl; ink stamp 150.00
Pasadena, planter, #L-17, 3½x9" 45.00
Pauleo, vase, berries & leaves on gray lustre, unmk, 17" 1,200.00
Pauleo, vase, bulbous, unmk, 9" 600.00
Pauleo, vase, gold mottling on classic form, unmk, 17½" 1,200.00
Peony, basket, #379-12, 11" 275.00
Peony, bookends, #11, 5½", pr 220.00
Peony, bowl, #427, 4" 125.00
Peony, planter, #388-6, 8½" 95.00
Pine Cone, basket, #353-11, 11" 425.00
Pine Cone, console, #323, 15" 450.00
Pine Cone, pitcher, #485-10, 10½" 375.00
Pine Cone, planter, #124, 5" 225.00
Pine Cone, window box, #431-15, 3½x15½" 400.00
Poppy, basket, #347, 10" 275.00
Poppy, bowl, #336-10, 12" 175.00
Poppy, ewer, #880-18, 18½" 750.00
Poppy, vase, #870-8, 8" 200.00
Primrose, vase, #765, 8" 225.00
Raymor, bowl, divided vegetable; #165, 13" 65.00
Raymor, bowl, salad; #161, 11½" 40.00
Raymor, casserole, w/lid, #183, 11" 85.00
Raymor, gravy boat, #190, 9½" 35.00
Raymor, pitcher, water; #189, 10" 150.00
Rosecraft, flower frog, bl, ink stamp 15.00
Rosecraft, vase, bl, sm angle hdls, ink stamp, 10" .. 200.00
Rosecraft, vase, blk, rim-to-hip hdls, paper label, 9" 175.00
Rosecraft Hexagon, bowl vase, ink stamp, 4" 325.00
Rosecraft Hexagon, candlestick, ink stamp, 8" 250.00
Rosecraft Hexagon, vase, ink stamp, 6" 225.00
Rosecraft Vintage, bowl, ink stamp, 3" 125.00
Rosecraft Vintage, vase, shouldered, narrow rim, 5" 125.00
Rosecraft Vintage, window box, ink stamp, 11½x6" .. 275.00
Royal Capri, Late Line; vase, #583-9, 9" 275.00
Rozane, Light; teapot, sgn Rhead, #60, 8" 1,750.00
Rozane Royal, bud vase, floral, #841/3, 7½" 175.00
Rozane Royal, tankard, sgn J Imlay, Royal seal mk, 11½" 800.00
Rozane Royal, vase, angle hds, Royal seal mk, 4" .. 200.00
Rozane 1917, basket, bl, ink stamp, 11" 175.00
Rozane 1917, candlestick, ivory, 6" 125.00

Rozane 1917, comport, tall ped, unmk, 8" 125.00
Rozane 1917, jardiniere & pedestal, ink stamp, 35" .. 600.00
Rozane 1940s, vase, #10-12, 12" 125.00
Rozane 1940s, vase, #5-8, 8½" 95.00
Russco, vase, flared rim, ftd, unmk, 7" 150.00
Russco, vase, triple cornucopia; silver paper label, 8x12½" 250.00
Silhouette, box, #740, 4½" 125.00
Silhouette, vase, #780-6, 6" 85.00
Silhouette, vase, nude panel, #787-10" 500.00
Silhouette, wall pocket, #766, 8" 175.00
Snowberry, candlesticks, #ICS-2, 4½", pr 150.00
Snowberry, console, #1BL1, 10" 115.00
Snowberry, vase, #1RB-6, 6" 125.00
Snowberry, vase, #1UR-8, 8½" 165.00
Sunflower, candlesticks, unmk, 4", pr 450.00
Sunflower, vase, bulbous, unmk, 7" 500.00
Sunflower, vase, bulbous, 5½" 400.00
Teasel, vase, #881-6, 6" 110.00
Teasel, vase, #888-12, 12" 275.00
Thorn Apple, bowl vase, #305-6, 6½" 175.00
Thorn Apple, vase, #816-8, 8½" 225.00
Thorn Apple, vase, cornucopia; 6" 100.00
Topeo, bowl, console; shaped rim, unmk, 13" 250.00
Topeo, vase, waisted, paper label, 7" 200.00
Tourmaline, ginger jar, paper label 175.00
Tourmaline, vase, ftd bowl form, unmk, 5½" 100.00
Tourmaline, vase, pillow form, unmk, 6" 125.00
Tuscany, flower arranger, low hdls, unmk, 5½" 125.00
Tuscany, vase, bulbous, closed rim, sm hdls, unmk, 6" 115.00
Velmoss, bowl, angle hdls, unmk, 3x11" L 200.00
Velmoss, vase, flared ft, angle hds, unmk, 14½" ... 450.00
Velmoss Scroll, bowl, #C7, unmk, 3" 100.00
Velmoss Scroll, candlestick, 9" 200.00
Velmoss Scroll, vase, shouldered, unmk, 10" 200.00
Water Lily, flower frog, #48, 4½" 95.00
Water Lily, vase, #75, 7" 125.00
Water Lily, vase, #78-9, 9" 225.00
White Rose, candle holder, dbl; #1143, 4" 150.00
White Rose, candlestick, #1142-4½, 4½" 75.00
White Rose, vase, #978-4, 4" 90.00
White Rose, vase, cornucopia; #143, 6" 125.00
Wincraft, basket, #210-12, 12" 300.00
Wincraft, bookends, #259, 6½", pr 175.00
Wincraft, vase, #272, 6" 59.00
Wincraft, vase, cornucopia; #221-8, 5x9" 95.00
Windsor, basket, fan form, integral hdl, paper label, 4½" 350.00
Windsor, console/planter, w/frog, paper sticker, 16" .. 300.00
Windsor, lamp base, bulbous, hdls, umk, 7" 600.00
Wisteria, vase, bowl form, unmk, 5" 350.00
Wisteria, vase, bulbous, sm angle hdls, 7½" 600.00
Wisteria, vase, waisted, low hdls, paper label, 10" . 550.00

Woodland vases: high-glaze mistletoe on gray bisque, twisted shape, 8½", $750.00; high-glaze floral on cream bisque, twisted shape, 10½", $900.00.

Woodland, vase, shouldered, slim, Rozane seal mk, 10" 900.00
Woodland, vase, shouldered, unmk, 6½" 650.00
Zephyr Lily, bowl, #671, 4" 110.00
Zephyr Lily, console bowl, #479-14, 16½" 200.00
Zephyr Lily, vase, #202-8, 8½" 150.00
Zephyr Lily, vase, fan form, #205-6, 6½" 115.00

Rowland and Marsellus

Though the impressive back stamp seems to suggest otherwise, Rowland and Marsellus were not Staffordshire potters but American importers who commissioned various English companies to supply them with the transfer-printed historical ware that had been a popular import commodity since the early 1800s. Plates (both flat and with a rolled edge), cups and saucers, pitchers, and platters were sold as souvenirs from 1890 through the 1930s. Though other importers — Bawo & Dotter, and A. C. Bosselman & Co., both of New York City — commissioned the manufacture of similar souvenir items, by far the largest volume carries the R. & M. mark, and Rowland and Marcellus has become a generic term that covers all 20th-century souvenir china of this type. Their mark may be in full or 'R. & M.' in a diamond. Though primarily made with blue transfers on white, other colors may occasionally be found as well.

Key:
r/e — rolled edge   v/o — view of
s/o — souvenir of

Plate, Porfirio Diaz, Mexican General, rolled rim, 10", $75.00.

Cup & saucer, Alaska-Yukon-Pacific Expo, 1909 ....95.00
Cup & saucer, Chicago, s/o 95.00
Cup & saucer, farmer's 65.00
Cup & saucer, Lenox MA, s/o 85.00
Cup & saucer, Niagara Falls NY, s/o 95.00
Pitcher, Discovery of Am, lt bl, 7½" 275.00
Plate, Albany (NY), s/o, State Capital, r/e, 10" 70.00
Plate, Bethleham PA, Moravian College, v/o, 9" 35.00
Plate, Biltmore House, Asheville NC, fruit & flower border 70.00
Plate, Bunker Hill Monument, Ye Olde Historical Pottery, 9" 50.00
Plate, Cincinnati OH, s/o, State Capital, r/e, 10" 65.00
Plate, coupe; Am Poets, 7 portraits, v/o, 10" 60.00
Plate, coupe; Denver, v/o, 10" 60.00
Plate, coupe; Early Missions of CA, s/o, Parmelee/Dorhman, 6" ...40.00
Plate, coupe; Salem, v/o, witch & 5 scenes, Daniel Low, 6" 60.00
Plate, Denver CO, s/o, Capitol Building, r/e, 10" 70.00
Plate, Famous Musicans & Composers (9), 10" 85.00
Plate, Henry Addressing VA Assembly, fruit/flower border, 9¾" ...60.00
Plate, Jackson MS, s/o, New Capitol Building, r/e, 10" 65.00
Plate, Lookout Mountain TN, s/o, r/e, 10" 70.00
Plate, Nashville, v/o, State Capitol, r/e, 10" 80.00
Plate, Waltham Watch factory, fruit & flower border 70.00
Plate, Whirlpool Rapids, fruit & flower border, 9¾" 55.00
Tumbler, Fall River MA, v/o 85.00

Tumbler, Ottawa Canada 85.00
Tumbler, Thousand Islands, v/o 85.00
Tumbler, Views of Plymouth, 1906 ....65.00

Royal Bayreuth

Founded in 1794 in Tettau, Bavaria, the Royal Bayreuth firm originally manufactured fine dinnerware of superior quality. Their figural items, produced from before the turn of the century until the onset of WWI, are highly sought after by today's collectors. Perhaps the most abundantly produced and easily recognized of these are the tomato and lobster pieces. Fruits, flowers, people, animals, birds, and vegetables shapes were also made. Aside from figural items, pitchers, toothpick holders, cups and saucers, humidors, and the like were decorated in floralsand scenic motifs. Some, such as the very popular Rose Tapestry line, utilized a cloth-like tapestry background. Transfer prints were used as well. Two of the most popular are Sunbonnet Babies and Nursery Rhymes (in particular, those decorated with the complete verse).

Caution: Many pieces were not marked; some were marked 'Deponiert' or 'Registered' only. While marked pieces are the most valued, unmarked items are still very worthwhile. Our advisors for this category are Larry Brenner from New Hampshire and Dee Hooks from Illinois; they are listed in the Directory under their home states.

Figurals

Ashtray, elk, bl mk 185.00
Ashtray, lobster claw, bl mk 100.00
Ashtray, oyster & pearl, bl mk 195.00
Basket, Art Nouveau lady, bl mk/Deponiert, 3x3½", NM 1,300.00
Bowl, grapes, bl mk, lg 265.00
Bowl, radishes, gr leaf edge, bl mk, 2½x5" 200.00
Bowl, salad; lobster, bl mk, lg 325.00
Box, card; Devil & Cards, bl mk 500.00
Box, stamp; Devil & Cards, bl mk 600.00
Candle holder, bassett hound, bl mk 465.00
Candlestick, Devil & Cards, bl mk 350.00
Candlestick, elk, bl mk, 3x7" 450.00
Candy dish, lobster, bl mk, 5½" 180.00
Candy dish, poppy, gr stem hdl, bl mk, 1½x5½" 75.00
Card dish, Devil & Cards, bl mk 100.00
Celery tray, lobster, bl mk 150.00
Chamberstick, shell, MOP, saucer base, unmk, 6½x5½" 600.00
Chocolate pot, poppy, stem hdl, bl mk, 8x7" 900.00
Cracker jar, poppy, stem finial, bl mk, 7x7½" 1,100.00
Cracker jar, strawberry, bl mk 600.00
Cracker jar, tomato w/gr leaf, stem finial, bl mk, 6¼" 500.00
Cup, demitasse; Devil & Dice, bl mk 175.00
Cup, demitasse; rose, bl mk 525.00
Cup, demitasse; spikey shell, bl mk 55.00
Cup & saucer, demitasse; apple, bl mk 135.00
Gravy boat & undertray, tomato, bl mk 335.00
Hatpin holder, poppy, wht, bl mk 500.00
Humidor, man's head w/turban, bl mk 550.00
Marmalade, grape, bl mk 400.00
Match holder, Devil & Cards, bl mk, wall hanging 600.00
Match holder, Devil & Cards (full body), bl mk, 5¼x4" 4,500.00
Match holder, Santa w/bag, red suit, bl mk/Deponiert, 5¼" 4,500.00
Mustard, apple, bl mk 200.00
Mustard, lobster, bl mk 125.00
Mustard, poppy, red, bl mk 225.00
Mustard, shell, bl mk 100.00
Nut dish, poppy, red, bl mk, sm 75.00

Pitcher, alligator, bl mk, milk sz 495.00
Pitcher, apple, gr, bl mk, cream sz 285.00
Pitcher, apple, red, bl mk, cream sz 150.00
Pitcher, apple, red, bl mk, water sz 695.00
Pitcher, Art Nouveau lady, bl mk, milk sz 1,400.00
Pitcher, bellringer, bl mk, cream sz 325.00
Pitcher, bird of paradise, bl mk, cream sz 450.00
Pitcher, bull, brn, bl mk, cream sz 425.00
Pitcher, butterfly, closed wings, bl mk, cream sz 375.00
Pitcher, butterfly, open wings, bl mk, cream sz 375.00
Pitcher, cat hdld, bl, bl mk, cream sz 395.00
Pitcher, coachman, bl mk, cream sz 300.00
Pitcher, coachman, bl mk, milk sz 400.00
Pitcher, coachman, bl mk, water sz 1,200.00
Pitcher, cockatoo, bl mk, cream sz 375.00
Pitcher, crow, blk, bl mk, cream sz 200.00
Pitcher, crow, brn beak, bl mk, cream sz 175.00
Pitcher, dachshund, bl mk, cream sz 350.00
Pitcher, dachshund, bl mk, milk sz 595.00

**Pitcher, duck figural, blue
Registered mark, water size,
6¾", $895.00.**

Pitcher, Devil & Cards, bl mk, cream sz 275.00
Pitcher, duck, bl mk, cream sz 300.00
Pitcher, eagle, bl mk, cream sz 350.00
Pitcher, eagle, bl mk, milk sz 450.00
Pitcher, elk, bl mk, cream sz 200.00
Pitcher, elk, bl mk, milk sz 350.00
Pitcher, elk, bl mk, water sz 600.00
Pitcher, fish head, bl mk, cream sz 325.00
Pitcher, fish head, mk, milk sz 395.00
Pitcher, fish head, unmk, cream sz 295.00
Pitcher, frog, bl mk, cream sz 150.00
Pitcher, girl w/basket, bl mk, cream sz 595.00
Pitcher, grapes, bl, bl mk, cream sz 175.00
Pitcher, grapes, wht satin, bl mk, water sz 550.00
Pitcher, Ibex stirrup, bl mk, cream sz 750.00
Pitcher, lemon, bl mk, cream sz 250.00
Pitcher, lobster, bl mk, milk sz 225.00
Pitcher, lobster, bl mk, water sz 500.00
Pitcher, maple leaf, bl mk, cream sz 400.00
Pitcher, melon, bl mk, cream sz 300.00
Pitcher, milkmaid, bl mk, cream sz 650.00
Pitcher, monkey, bl mk, cream sz 450.00
Pitcher, monkey, gr, bl mk, cream sz 575.00
Pitcher, mountain goat, bl mk, cream sz 335.00
Pitcher, oak leaf, bl mk, cream sz 300.00
Pitcher, Old Man of the Mountain, bl mk, cream sz 150.00
Pitcher, orange, bl mk, cream sz 240.00
Pitcher, owl, bl mk, cream sz 450.00
Pitcher, oyster & pearl, bl mk, cream sz 200.00
Pitcher, pansy, bl mk, cream sz 325.00

Pitcher, parakeet, bl mk, cream sz 350.00
Pitcher, parakeet, bl mk, milk sz 495.00
Pitcher, pear, bl mk, cream sz 400.00
Pitcher, pelican, bl mk, cream sz 350.00
Pitcher, perch, bl mk, cream sz 650.00
Pitcher, pig, gray, bl mk, cream sz 600.00
Pitcher, platypus, bl mk, cream sz 1,275.00
Pitcher, poodle, gray, bl mk, cream sz 375.00
Pitcher, poppy, red, bl mk, cream sz 225.00
Pitcher, poppy, wht, bl mk, cream sz 300.00
Pitcher, robin, gray, bl mk, cream sz 275.00
Pitcher, rooster, blk, bl mk, cream sz 325.00
Pitcher, shell, bl mk, milk sz 195.00
Pitcher, shell, low, bl mk, cream sz 175.00
Pitcher, shell, mc, coral hdl, unmk, water sz, 6½x8½" 350.00
Pitcher, shell, tall, bl mk, cream sz 180.00
Pitcher, shell w/lobster hdl, unmk, milk sz 250.00
Pitcher, snake, gr & wht w/gold scales, pearlized, water sz, rare ...5,000.00
Pitcher, spikey shell, bl mk, cream sz 200.00
Pitcher, St Bernard, bl mk, cream sz 400.00
Pitcher, St Bernard, bl mk, milk sz 550.00
Pitcher, strawberry, bl mk, cream sz 250.00
Pitcher, water buffalo, blk, bl mk, cream sz 250.00
Pitcher, watermelon, bl mk, cream sz 395.00
Pitcher, watermelon, bl mk, milk sz 525.00
Relish, radish, bl mk 350.00
Salt cellar, lobster, bl mk 45.00
Shakers, grapes, purple, bl mk, pr 200.00
Shakers, pepper, red, bl mk, pr 275.00
Shakers, radish, bl mk, pr 350.00
Shaving mug, elk, bl mk 450.00
Sugar bowl, lemon, bl mk 250.00
Sugar bowl, lobster, bl mk, lg 175.00
Sugar bowl, lobster, bl mk, sm 140.00
Sugar bowl, poppy, bl mk 200.00
Sugar bowl, rose, bl mk, rare 595.00
Sugar bowl, shell, bl mk 175.00
Tea strainer, apricot, bl mk 395.00
Teapot, lemon, bl mk 650.00
Teapot, orange, bl mk 375.00
Teapot, pansy, purple, bl mk 625.00
Teapot, poppy, red, bl mk 425.00
Teapot, strawberry, bl mk 385.00
Tray, dresser; clown, red, bl mk, rare 1,050.00
Tray, pin; Santa sitting, red, bl mk, 4" 3,500.00
Wall vase, grapes, wht, bl mk 295.00

Nursery Rhymes

Bell, Jack & Beanstalk, w/rhyme, w/clapper, bl mk 350.00
Bowl, Jack & the Beanstalk, w/verse, bl mk, ftd, sm 285.00
Candlestick, Jack & Jill, w/verse, bl mk, ring hdl 235.00
Candlestick, Jack & Jill, w/verse, bl mk, w/underplate 325.00
Cup & saucer, Jack & the Beanstalk, w/verse, bl mk 235.00
Pitcher, Jack & Jill, w/verse, bl mk, cream sz 225.00
Pitcher, Little Boy Blue, w/verse, bl mk, 3½" 200.00
Pitcher, Little Jack Horner, w/verse, bl mk, milk sz 235.00
Plate, Little Bo Peep, no verse, bl mk, 6¼" 115.00
Plate, Ring Around the Rosies, no verse, bl mk, 6" 125.00
Sugar bowl, Little Boy Blue, no verse, bl mk 215.00
Tea set, child's, Boy Blue etc/verse, Emery Bird...'03, bl mk, 11-pc ..850.00

Scenics and Action Portraits

Ashtray, sheep in meadow, bl mk 65.00
Bell, Beach Babies, wooden clapper, bl mk 325.00
Bowl, fighting cocks, fancy, bl mk 265.00
Box, musicians, unmk, 2x4" dia 110.00
Cake plate, Arab, bl mk, 10½" 200.00
Candle holder, Brittany Girl, shield bk, bl mk 350.00
Candle holder, musician, shield bk, bl mk 350.00
Coffeepot, Brittany girl w/draft horse, bl mk, 8" 600.00
Hatpin holder, hunt scene w/horses & dogs, rtcl base, bl mk 325.00
Humidor, ship scene, bl mk 255.00
Match holder, stork, yel, wall hanging, bl mk, 4¼" 300.00
Pitcher, Arab on horse, gold hdl, bl mk, 3⅛" 100.00
Pitcher, Blk Corinthian w/gold trim, tankard, unmk, 6⅞" 120.00
Pitcher, cavalier, bl mk, water sz 250.00
Pitcher, fox hunt, bl mk, cream sz 125.00
Pitcher, ship scene, bl mk, water sz, 8" 265.00
Plate, jester, bl mk, 1968 ltd ed, 9½" 35.00
Plate, man fishing, bl mk, 8" 125.00
Tea set, child's, pot+cr/sug+6 c/s+2 rtcl bowls, unmk, MIB (mk Tettau) 500.00
Tea tile, Snow Babies, bl mk 145.00
Tray, girl w/geese, gold trim, bl mk, 12¼x9" 320.00
Vase, cows, tab hdls, bl mk, 3¼x1⅞" 125.00

Sunbonnet Babies

Candle holder, fishing, shield bk, bl mk 675.00
Candlestick, cleaning, bl mk, 4⅛x2⅞" 325.00
Creamer & sugar bowl, bl mk 600.00
Feeding dish, bl mk 425.00

Pitcher, babies sewing, blue mark, 4½", $395.00.

Pitcher, sewing, bl mk, cream sz 250.00
Plate, mending, bl mk, 4¼" 100.00
Plate, washing, bl mk, 7½" 175.00
Plate, washing, bl mk, 9" 240.00
Sugar bowl, fishing, w/lid, bl mk 300.00
Toothpick holder, sewing, bl mk, 3-ftd, pie-crust edge, unmk, 2½" 600.00

Tapestries

Basket, Rose Tapestry, 3-color, bl mk, 4¾x5¼" 395.00
Basket, Rose Tapestry, 3-color, openwork at ft, bl mk, 5¼x5" 660.00
Bell, Rose Tapestry, pk, bl mk 545.00
Biscuit jar, lady w/horse, bl mk 850.00
Box, dresser; Rose Tapestry, 3-color, bl mk 350.00
Box, jewel; Rose Tapestry, pk, clam shape, bl mk, 2x5¼" 450.00
Box, Rose Tapestry, 3-color, dome lid, bl mk 400.00
Cake plate, Rose Tapestry, 3-color, open hdl, bl mk, 10" 395.00
Candle holders, Rose Tapestry, 3-color, bl mk, #1251, pr 750.00
Clock, Rose Tapestry, 3-color, bl mk, rpl works 850.00
Flowerpot, Rose Tapestry, 3-color, w/liner, bl mk, 3x4" 295.00
Haptin holder, Rose Tapestry, 2-color, shape #197, bl mk 550.00
Hatpin holder, lady w/horse, bl mk 750.00
Match holder, Rose Tapestry, 3-color, wall hanging, bl mk 450.00

Match holder, sheep, wall hanging, bl mk, #1059 ....485.00
Pitcher, highland goats in field, pinched spout, bl mk, 5" 400.00
Pitcher, Rose Tapestry, pk, pinched spout, bl mk, 4" ...285.00
Pitcher, Rose Tapestry, 2-color, bl mk, cream sz 385.00
Pitcher, Rose Tapestry, 3-color, gilt hdl, bl mk, 5" 320.00
Pitcher, sheep scenic, bl mk, 4" 355.00
Plate, Rose Tapestry, 3-color, bl mk, 7½" 190.00
Powder box, Rose Tapestry, 3-color, ftd, bl mk 350.00
Relish, Rose Tapestry, open hdls, bl mk, 8" 250.00
Relish, Rose Tapestry, 3-color, open hdl, bl mk, 8x4" ..275.00
Shoe, Rose Tapestry, 3-color, bl mk 570.00
Sugar bowl, Rose Tapestry, pk, shape #1310 ....250.00
Toothpick holder, castle scene, bl mk, rare 500.00
Toothpick holder, musicians, cylindrical, bl mk 300.00
Tray, dresser; Prince & His Lady, bl mk, 7x9¼" ...?.......500.00
Vase, cottage by waterfall, bl mk, shape #1015 ....365.00
Vase, Rose Tapestry, w/shadow ferns, bl mk, 6½" 400.00
Vase, The Bathers, bl mk, 8¼" 525.00

Royal Bonn

    Royal Bonn is a fine-paste porcelain, ornately decorated with scenes, portraits, or florals. The factory was established in the mid-1800s in Bonn, Germany; however, most pieces found today are from the latter part of the century.

Biscuit jar, floral on cream, emb scrolls, SP trim, 6⅝x5¼" 195.00
Clock, La Orp, porc, open escapement, VG 750.00
Ewer, floral tapestry & brick fence w/gold, 6½" 150.00
Ewer, red & pk flowers w/gold, ornate hdl, 10⅜" 75.00
Plaque, musician w/mandolin, cobalt trim, rtcl rim, mk, 14" 100.00
Vase, bird & purple orchids, HP, 11" 150.00
Vase, floral coralene decor, 11½" 125.00
Vase, lady in pk, artist sgn, gold trim & hdls, 6" 650.00
Vase, lady's portrait, sgn H Kamp, #2932, mk, 8x5" 600.00
Vase, lady's portrait reserve on pk w/gold, 14" 1,150.00
Vase, mums w/gold o/l on red, 5¾" 295.00
Vase, Nouveau ladies/poppies, Art Nova 221...3838/5 22, 12⅝" .700.00

Royal Copenhagen

    The Royal Copenhagen Manufactory was established in Denmark in about 1775 by Frantz Henrich Muller. When bankruptcy threatened in 1779, the Crown took charge. The fine dinnerware and objects of art produced after that time carry the familiar logo, the crown over three wavy lines. For further information we recommend *Royal Copenhagen Porcelain, Animals and Figurines*, by Robert J. Heritage (Schiffer). See also Limited Edition Plates.

Bowl, vegetable; Frijsenburg, #910/1622 ....110.00
Cream soup, Frijsenburg, #910/1812, w/#1626 underplate 75.00
Cup & saucer, Frijsenburg, #310/1870 ....75.00
Decanter, Egeskov Castle, bl & wht, 12¼" 50.00
Figurine, bassett pup, #1204 ....150.00
Figurine, bird, #1519 ....55.00
Figurine, boy & girl kiss, #2162, 8" 180.00
Figurine, boy w/calf, #772 ....290.00
Figurine, child, sitting, #1517 ....125.00
Figurine, children playing, #1568, 4½" 200.00
Figurine, desert fox pr, #319 ....195.00
Figurine, foal, recumbent, #5691 ....150.00
Figurine, girl knitting, #1314, 6" 195.00

Figurine, girl w/butterfly, #1495 ....180.00
Figurine, girl w/doll, #3539, 5½" 150.00
Figurine, girl w/teddy bear, #1879, 5⅛" 350.00
Figurine, goose girl, #528, 7½" 225.00
Figurine, milkmaid, #899 ....325.00
Figurine, mouse on corncob, #512 ....65.00
Figurine, October, #4532 ....275.00
Figurine, Pan, #2609, ca 1930, 6½x5" 150.00
Figurine, Pan on column w/rabbit looking up from base, #456, 8½" .275.00
Figurine, Pan w/goat, youthful, #1012/498, 5" 265.00
Figurine, parakeet on purple eggplant, #4682 ....165.00
Figurine, penguin pr, #1190 ....100.00
Figurine, pig, #1400, sm 65.00
Figurine, polar bear, #321, 6" 95.00
Figurine, Siamese cat, seated, #3281, 7¾" 145.00
Figurine, squirrel pr, #416 ....400.00
Plaque, angel/2 sleeping babies/owl in relief, wht parian, 6" 17.00
Plate, Frijsenburg, #910/#1624, 8" 50.00
Plate, Shenandoah, Nat'l Park series 50.00
Plate, Yellowstone, Nat'l Park series, MIB 60.00
Platter, Frijsenburg, #910/1556, 14½" 140.00
Tile, Piet Hein verse, drawing, 1948, 6½x5½" 35.00
Vase, faience, Thorsson, 7x5½" 100.00
Vase, magnolia branch, #2629/2129, 11" 175.00
Vase, stylized cobalt florals, 1950s, 10" 150.00
Vase, windmill, #4568 ....100.00

Royal Copley

Royal Copley is a decorative type of pottery made by the Spaulding China Company in Sebring, Ohio, from 1942 to 1957. They also produced two other major lines — Royal Windsor and Spaulding. Royal Copley was primarily marketed through five-and-ten cent stores; Royal Windsor and Spaulding were sold through department stores, gift shops, and jobbers. Items trimmed in gold are worth 25% to 50% more than the same item with no gold trim.

For more information we recommend *Royal Copley* and *More About Royal Copley* by Leslie and Marjorie Wolfe, edited by our advisor for this category, Joe Devine; he is listed in the Directory under Iowa.

Planter, rooster and wheelbarrow, rare, 8", from $110.00 to $125.00.

Ashtray, affectionate birds, emb mk, 5½" 45.00
Ashtray, bow & ribbon, emb mk, 5" 25.00
Bank, blk & wht teddy bear, paper label, 7½" 100.00
Bank, pig, paper label, sm, 4½" 45.00
Coaster, Dutch paintings, paper label, 4⅝" 25.00
Creamer & sugar bowl, leaf hdls, emb mk, 3" 25.00
Figurine, canary, paper label, 5½" 40.00
Figurine, cockatoos, emb mk, 8¼" 45.00
Figurine, dog pulling a 'Flyer' wagon, paper label, 5¾" 45.00

Figurine, flycatcher/thrasher, paper label, 8½" 30.00
Figurine, hen, blk & wht, gr base, paper label, 5½" 90.00
Figurine, Hunt's swallow, paper label, 8" 70.00
Figurine, kingfisher, paper label, 5" 30.00
Figurine, sparrow, paper label, 5½" 28.00
Figurine, woodpeckers, gr stamp or emb mk, 6¼" 18.00
Figurine, wren, paper label, 3½" 18.00
Lamp, clown, paper label, 7½" 95.00
Pitcher, Floral Beauty, gr stamp or emb mk, 8" 45.00
Pitcher, Pome Fruit, gr stamp, 8" 45.00
Planter, Balinese girl, paper label, 8½" 28.00
Planter, bird tracks, paper label, 3¼" 12.00
Planter, boy w/bucket, paper label, 6¼" 30.00
Planter, cat & cello, paper label, 7½" 95.00
Planter, cocker spaniel, paper label, 7" 30.00
Planter, cocker spaniel w/basket, paper label, 5½" 20.00
Planter, dog in picnic basket, paper label, 7¾" 75.00
Planter, duck w/wheelbarrow, paper label, 3¾" 20.00
Planter, Dutch boy w/bucket, paper label, 6" 20.00
Planter, elephant w/ball, paper label, sm, 6" 30.00
Planter, girl leaning on barrel, paper label, 6¼" 25.00
Planter, Indian boy w/drum, paper label, 6½" 25.00
Planter, kitten & birdhouse, paper label, 8" 125.00
Planter, kitten in cradle, paper label, 7½" 95.00
Planter, poodle begging, paper label, 7" 35.00
Planter, poodle resting, paper label, 6½x8½" 60.00
Planter, pouter pigeon, paper label, 5¾" 20.00
Planter, rooster walking, wht, emb mk, 5½" 45.00
Planter, salmon jumping, paper label, 6½x11½" 75.00
Planter, Siamese cats, paper label, 9", from $95 to 150.00
Planter, teddy bear w/concertina, paper label, 7½" 75.00
Planter, trailing leaf & vine, paper label, 4x7½" 15.00
Planter, window box; gr ivy on cream, paper label, 4x7" 12.00
Planter/plaque, Holland scenes, emb mk, 8" 60.00
Planter/vase, little deer head, paper label 28.00
Planter/vase, Palomino horse head, gr stamp or paper label, 6¼" .38.00
Planter/wall pocket, Chinese boy w/big hat, emb mk, 7½" ...30.00
Razor blade receptacle, barber pole, paper label, 6¼" 60.00
Vase, Oriental fish, ftd, paper label, 5½" 15.00
Wall pocket, bamboo, paper label, 7" 45.00
Window box, Harmony, paper label, 4½" 15.00

Royal Crown Derby

The Royal Crown Derby company can trace its origin back to 1848. It first operated under the name of Locker & Co. but by 1859 had become Stevenson, Sharp & Co. Several changes in ownership occured until 1866 when it became known as the Sampson Hancock Co. The Derby Crown Porcelain Co. Ltd. was formed in 1876, and these companies soon merged. In 1890 they were appointed as a manufacturer for the Queen and began using the name Royal Crown Derby.

In the early years, considerable 'Japan ware' decorated in Imari style, using red, blue, and gold in Oriental patterns was popular. The company excelled in their ability to use gold in the decoration, and some of the best flower painters of all time were employed. Nice vases or plaques signed by any of these artists will bring thousands of dollars: Gregory, Mosley, Rouse, Gresley, and D'esir'e Leroy. We have observed porcelain plaques decorated with flowers signed by Gregory selling at auction for as much as $12,000.00. If you find a signed piece and are not sure of its value, if at all possible, it would be best to have it appraised by someone very knowledgeable regarding current market values.

As is usual among most other English factories, nearly all of the vases produced by Royal Crown Derby came with covers. If they are missing, deduct 40% to 45%. There are several well illustrated books available from antique book sellers to help you learn to identify this ware. The back stamps used after 1891 will date every piece except dinnerware. The company is still in business, producing outstanding dinnerware and Imari-decorated figures and serving pieces. They also produce custom (one only) sets of table service for the wealthy of the world.

Soup plate, floral band, ca 1891+, 10½", $75.00.

Ewer, floral w/gold, rtcl hdl, 13½x6" **395.00**
Plate, Aves, red, 8½" **2,250.00**
Vase, floral on pk, 3 gold foliate hdls, red mk, 8¾x4½" **350.00**

Royal Doulton, Doulton

The range of wares produced by the Doulton Company since its inception in 1815 has been vast and varied. The earliest wares produced in the tiny pottery in Lambeth, England, were salt-glazed pitchers, plain and fancy figural bottles, etc. — all utility-type stoneware geared to the practical needs of everyday living. The original partners, John Doulton and John Watts, saw the potential for success in the manufacture of drain and sewage pipes and during the 1840s concentrated on these highly lucrative types of commercial wares. Watts retired from the company in 1854, and Doulton began experimenting with a more decorative product line. As time went by, many glazes and decorative effects were developed, among them Faience, Impasto, Silicon, Carrara, Marqueterie, Chine, and Rouge Flambe. Tiles and architectural terra cotta were an important part of their manufacture. Late in the 19th century at the original Lambeth location, fine artware was decorated by such notable artists as Hannah and Arthur Barlow, George Tinworth, and J.H. McLennan. Stoneware vases with incised animal drawings, gracefully shaped urns with painted scenes, and cleverly modeled figurines rivaled the best of any competitor.

In 1882 a second factory was built in Burslem which continues even yet to produce the famous figurines, character jugs, series ware, and table services so popular with collectors today. Their Kingsware line, made from 1899 to 1946, featured flasks and flagons with drinking scenes, usually on a brown-glazed ground. Some were limited editions, while others were commemorative and advertising items. The Gibson Girl series, twenty-four plates in all, was introduced in 1901. It was drawn by Charles Dana Gibson and is recognized by its blue and white borders and central illustrations, each scene depicting a humorous or poignant episode in the life of 'The Widow and Her Friends.' Dickensware, produced from 1911 through the early 1940s, featured illustrations by Charles Dickens, with many of his famous characters. The Robin Hood series was introduced in 1914; the Shakespeare series #1, portraying scenes from the Bard's plays, was made from 1914 until World War II. The Shakespeare series #2 ran from 1906 until 1974 and was decorated with featured characters. Nursery Rhymes was a series that was first produced in earthenware in 1930 and later in bone china. In 1933 a line of decorated children's ware, the Bunnykin series, was introduced; it continues to be made to the present

day. About 150 'bunny' scenes have been devised, the earliest and most desirable being those signed by the artist Barbara Vernon. Most pieces range in value from $60.00 to $120.00.

Factors contributing to the value of a figurine are age, color, and detail. Those with a limited production run and those signed by the artist or marked 'Potted' (indicating a pre-1939 origin) are also more valuable. After 1920 wares were marked with a lion — with or without a crown — over a circular 'Royal Doulton.' Our advisor for this category is Nicki Budin; she is listed in the Directory under Ohio.

Animals and Birds

Three dogs in a basket, 3", $115.00.

Airedale, HN1028	155.00
Alsation, HN1117	175.00
Antelope, HN1157, gr matt	565.00
Baltimore Oriole, HN2542	250.00
Bull Terrior, K14	325.00
Bulldog, HN1074	175.00
Bulldog, K-1	125.00
Calf, HN1146, gr matt	525.00
Cat, Lucky, K12	135.00
Chestnut Mare & Foal, HN2522	475.00
Chow, K-15	130.00
Cocker Spaniel, HN1036	125.00
Cocker Spaniel, HN1187	150.00
Dachshund, HN1128	150.00
Dalmatian, HN1114	295.00
Drake, HN907, color	100.00
Duck, HN2591	110.00
Duck, HN806, wht	100.00
Elephant, HN2644	150.00
Fox on rock, HN147	325.00
Great Dane, HN2602	700.00
Greyhound, HN1065	550.00
Hare, K-39, ears up	160.00
Irish Setter, HN1056	165.00
Labrador Retriever, HN2667	135.00
Lamb, HN2505, wht	220.00
Peacock, HN2577	250.00
Penguin, K21	250.00
Penguin, K22	225.00
Poodle, HN2631	155.00
Robin, HN2617	165.00
Scottish Terrier, K18	125.00
Spaniel, HN2516	265.00
Yel Bird, HN145	265.00
Yel-Throated Warbler	270.00

Bunnykins

Collector's sign	50.00

Egg cup, ped ft, sgn 110.00
Figurine, Ace 165.00
Figurine, Aerobic 225.00
Figurine, Astro 'Rocket Man' 125.00
Figurine, Be Prepared 65.00
Figurine, Bogey, D832 ....95.00
Figurine, Brownie 65.00
Figurine, Busy Needles 95.00
Figurine, Cook 75.00
Figurine, Cooling Off, BK1 ....145.00
Figurine, Family Photograph, BK2 ....95.00
Figurine, Fisherman 65.00
Figurine, Grandpa's Story 375.00
Figurine, Happy Christmas, BK2 ....40.00
Figurine, Jogger 95.00
Figurine, Master Potter, D8131 ....115.00
Figurine, Mr Easter Parade 50.00
Figurine, Mrs Easter Parade 50.00
Figurine, Partners in Collecting, Michael Doulton, club pc 95.00
Figurine, Playtime, BK2 ....65.00
Figurine, Prince Fredrick 75.00
Figurine, Princess Beatrice 85.00
Figurine, Ringmaster 235.00
Figurine, Santa 40.00
Figurine, Sleepy Time, BK2 ....65.00
Figurine, Storytime, BK2 ....30.00
Figurine, Susan Bunnykins as Queen of May 115.00
Figurine, Tally Ho, BK3 ....70.00
Figurine, Wizard 295.00
Plate, SF13 ....25.00
Saucer, SF10, gr mk 30.00

Character Jugs

'Arriet, tiny 190.00
'Arry, lg 165.00
Airman, sm 85.00
Aramis, mini 50.00
Aramis, sm 65.00
Arry, mini 75.00
Auld Mac, D5823, A, lg 135.00
Bacchus, mini 50.00
Bacchus, sm 65.00
Baseball Player, sm 75.00
Buz Fuz, sm 95.00
Capt Ahab, mini 55.00
Capt Hook, lg 475.00
Capt Morgan, lg 125.00
Cardinal, mini 75.00
Catherine Parr, lg 145.00
Cavalier, lg 145.00
Cavalier, sm 80.00
Clown, brn hair, lg 3,200.00
Clown, wht hair, lg 950.00
Collector, lg 195.00
Dick Turpin, horse hdl, earthenware, lg 125.00
Dick Turpin, mini 60.00
Don Quixote, mini 55.00
Falconer, mini 50.00
Falstaff, lg 135.00
Falstaff, mini 50.00
Farmer John, sm 80.00
Fat Boy, odd sz 220.00
Fat Boy, sm 125.00

Fat Boy, tiny 95.00
Gardener, 2nd version, sm 60.00
Gondolier, D6592, sm 365.00
Gone Away, mini 60.00
Granny, A, sm 60.00
Gulliver, mini 425.00
Jane Seymour, lg 145.00
Jarge, lg 350.00
Jester, sm 125.00
Jockey, earthenware, lg 395.00
Jockey, 2nd version, sm 50.00
John Barleycorn, mini 85.00
John Peel, mini 85.00
John Peel, sm 85.00
John Peel, tiny 195.00
Lawyer, lg 125.00
Lobster Man, D6617, lg 125.00
Lobster Man, sm 65.00
Lord Nelson, lg 375.00
Lumberjack, sm 65.00
Mephistophles, w/verse, lg 2,750.00
Merlin, sm 65.00
Mr Micawber, mini 75.00
Mr Pickwick, odd sz 190.00

Neptune, D6552,
mini, $70.00.

Neptune, sm 80.00
North American Indian, mini 50.00
North American Indian, sm 65.00
Old Charlie, tiny 95.00
Old King Cole, sm 95.00
Old King Cole, tiny 95.00
Paddy, tiny 95.00
Parson Brown, sm 75.00
Pearly King, sm 65.00
Pearly Queen, sm 65.00
Poacher, lg 125.00
Poacher, sm 65.00
Ringmaster, lg 140.00
Rip Van Winkle, sm 65.00
Robin Hood, 1st version, mini 75.00
Romeo, lg 125.00
Sailor, sm 65.00
Sairey Gamp, D6688, lg 125.00
Sairey Gamp, mini 55.00
Sairey Gamp, tiny 95.00
Sam Johnson, lg 325.00
Sam Weller, lg 165.00
Sam Weller, mini 60.00
Sam Weller, sm 75.00
Samuel Johnson, lg 325.00
Sancho Panza, mini 65.00
Scaramouche, 2nd version, lg 135.00

Simon Cellarer, earthenware, lg	135.00
Smuggler, sm	70.00
Snooker Player, sm	75.00
Soldier, sm	65.00
St George, lg	295.00
Tam-O'-Shanter, sm	75.00
Touchstone, lg	275.00
Trapper, lg	145.00
Trapper, sm	65.00
Uncle Tom Cobbleigh, lg	395.00
Vicar of Bray, lg	225.00
Viking, D6526, mini	125.00
Viking, earthenware, lg	185.00
Walrus & Carpenter, sm	75.00
Yachtsman, 2st version, lg	125.00

Figurines

Abdullah, HN2104	450.00
Afternoon Tea, HN1747	500.00
Apple Maid, HN2160	425.00
Balloon Man, HN1954	250.00
Bell of the Ball, HN1997	350.00
Belle, HN2340	90.00
Biddy Pennyfarthing, HN1843	225.00
Blithe Morning, HN2021	200.00
Bluebeard, HN2105	450.00
Bo Peep, M-82, rare	850.00
Boatman, HN2417	180.00
Bride, HN2166	225.00
Bridesmaid, HN2874	90.00

Carrie, HN2800, $175.00.

Cavalier, HN2716	195.00
Cellist, HN2226	425.00
Centurian, HN2726	250.00
Chief, HN2892	225.00
Chloe, HN1765	425.00
Christine, HN2792	265.00
Christmas Morn, HN1992	225.00
Christmas Time, HN2110	450.00
Clarinda, HN2724	175.00
Clarissa, HN2345	180.00
Clown, HN2890	235.00
Cobbler, HN1706	250.00
Cookie, HN2218	175.00
Coralie, HN2307	175.00
Country Lass, HN1991	150.00
Curly Locks, HN2049	450.00
Daffy Down Dilly, HN1712	375.00
Darby, HN1427	315.00

Daydreams, HN1731	225.00
Debbie, HN2385	90.00
Delight, HN1772	195.00
Delphine, HN2136	295.00
Diedre, HN2020	345.00
Dimity, HN2169	250.00
Dinky Doo, HN1678	125.00
Duke of Edinburgh, HN2386	425.00
Easter Day, HN2039	350.00
Eleanor of Provence, HN2009	625.00
Elegance, HN2264	155.00
Elyse, HN2429	280.00
Embroidering, HN2855	195.00
Enchantment, HN2178	175.00
Ermine Coat, HN1981	275.00
Eventide, HN2814	180.00
Falstaff, HN2054	175.00
Farmer's Wife, HN2069	470.00
Favorite, HN2249	195.00
Fiona, HN2694	195.00
First Dance, HN2803	225.00
First Waltz, HN2862	225.00
Folly, HN1335	2,350.00
Fragrance, HN2334	180.00
Francine, HN2402	95.00
Friar Tuck, HN2143	475.00
Genevieve, HN1962	275.00
Good Catch, HN2258	170.00
Good King Wenceslaus, HN2118	395.00
Goody Two Shoes, HN2037	100.00
Gypsy Dance, HN2230	295.00
Harlequin, HN2186	250.00
Hazel, HN1797	560.00
Hilary, HN2335	150.00
Honey, HN1909	450.00
Invitation, HN2170	140.00
Irene, HN1621	460.00
Jane, HN2806	180.00
Janet, HN1916	210.00
Jean, HN2032	375.00
Jennifer, HN2392	275.00
Jersey Milk Maid, HN2057	345.00
Jill, HN2061	150.00
Jovial Monk, HN2144	275.00
Judge, HN2443	175.00
Julia, HN2705	180.00
Kate, HN2789	165.00
Kirsty, HN2381	185.00
Koko, HN2898	600.00
Laird, HN2361	200.00
Leisure Hour, HN2055	425.00
Lilac Time, HN2137	320.00
Lily, HN1798	125.00
Lisa, HN2310	180.00
Lobster Man, HN2317	135.00
Loretta, HN2337	180.00
Lunchtime, HN2485	180.00
Lydia, HN1908	140.00
Madonna on the Square, HN2034	950.00
Margaret Anjou, HN2012, rare	795.00
Marguerite, HN1928	350.00
Market Day, HN1991	345.00
Mask Seller, HN2103	240.00
Masquerade, HN2259	290.00

Master, HN2325 ....195.00
Matilda, HN2011 ....625.00
Maureen, HN1770 ....350.00
Melanie, HN2271 ....250.00
Melissa, HN2467 ....180.00
Merely a Minor, horse, HN2531, 12" 650.00
Milkmaid, HN2057 ....195.00
Minuet, HN2019 ....265.00
Monica, HN1458 ....450.00
My Love, HN2339 ....225.00
New Bonnet, HN1728 ....650.00
Newsboy, HN2244 ....450.00
Nina, HN2347 ....185.00
Noelle, HN2179 ....365.00
Old Balloon Seller, HN1315 ....155.00
Orange Lady, HN1759, purple dress 250.00
Paisley Shawl, HN1988 ....225.00
Parisian, HN2445 ....180.00
Penelope, HN1901 ....375.00
Penny's Worth, HN2408 ....165.00
Philippa Hainault, HN2008 ....625.00
Piper, HN2907 ....250.00
Potter, HN1493 ....450.00
Premier, HN2343 ....165.00
Prince of Edinburgh, HN2386 ....425.00
Prince of Wales, HN2383 ....425.00
Prized Possessions, HN2942 ....450.00
Prue, HN1996 ....350.00
Rest Awhile, HN2728 ....165.00
Reverie, HN2306 ....285.00
Rhapsody, HN2267 ....215.00
Romance, HN2430 ....180.00
Rose, HN1368 ....95.00
Roseanna, HN1921, gr, rare 1,000.00
Roseanna, HN1926, red 425.00
Royal Governor's Cook, HN2233 ....475.00
Sabbath Morn, HN1982 ....300.00
Sandra, HN2275 ....180.00
Santa Claus, HN2725 ....215.00
Sara, HN2265 ....225.00
Sea Harvest, HN2257 ....175.00
Secret Thoughts, HN2382 ....275.00
Silversmith, HN2208 ....200.00
Simone, HN2378 ....165.00
Skater, HN2117 ....395.00
Southern Belle, HN2229 ....260.00
Southern Belle, HN2361 ....270.00
Southern Belle, HN2425 ....150.00
Stephanie, HN2807 ....150.00
Stop Press, HN2683 ....165.00
Susan, HN2952 ....180.00
Sweet Anne, HN1496 ....195.00
Sweet Dreams, HN2380 ....155.00
Sweet Suzy, HN1918 ....895.00
Sweeting, HN1935 ....140.00
Taking Things Easy, HN2677 ....180.00
Teresa, HN1682 ....1,100.00
Thanks Doc, HN2731 ....180.00
Thanksgiving, HN2446 ....200.00
Tinkerbelle, HN1677 ....100.00
Top o' the Hill, HN1834 ....300.00
Town Crier, HN2119 ....270.00
Valeria, HN2107 ....125.00
Veneta, HN2772 ....175.00

Veronica, HN1517 ....425.00
Victoria, HN2471 ....275.00
Votes for Women, HN2816 ....275.00
Washington at Prayer, HN2861, sgn Ispanky, ltd ed 3,500.00
Wigmaker, HN2239 ....200.00
Wizard, HN2877 ....220.00
Young Master, HN2872 ....225.00

Flambe

Biscuit jar, Sung, elephant finial 2,200.00
Figurine, bunny, ear up 165.00
Figurine, cat, seated, 11" 250.00
Figurine, fish, Veined Sung, 12" 1,200.00
Figurine, fox, sitting 160.00
Figurine, rhinoceros, #615, 9x17" 875.00
Figurine, salmon, leaping, 12" 430.00
Figurine, Samurai, ltd ed 500.00
Figurine, tiger, Noke, 9" 1,150.00
Figurine, tiger, rouge flambe, 14" 375.00
Vase, bud; Sung, bl & red mottle, Noke/Allen, 1930s, 6¼" 575.00
Vase, dbl-gourd w/flame decor, Hilda Lindop, ca 1910, 12" 230.00
Vase, Moorish Sung, Arabian scene, blk over ruby red, 13x8½" ..1,100.00
Vase, red w/silver o/l leaves at base & Greek Key at neck, 10" ...920.00
Vase, Sung, berries/vines, orange/blk on red to gr, Noke, 5½" ...1,035.00
Vase, Sung, bl & red mottle, Noke/Allen, 11¼" 400.00
Vase, Sung, peacock & bubbles, C Noke, #3124E, 1930s, 6½" .1,500.00
Vase, Sung, red & cobalt lustre flambe, Noke, 10½x4¾" 600.00
Vase, Sung, sgn Fred Moore, melon shaped top, 7½" 550.00
Vase, Veined, sgn Noke, 6" 475.00
Vase, Veined, textured/mottled red/bl/gr veins, 9½" 175.00
Vase, village scene, sgn HE, #7681, 6⅛" 175.00

Series Ware

Bread tray, Falstaff, man with sword in woods, 14¼", $95.00.

Bowl, Coaching Days, men, carriage & horses, #d, 1½x7¾" 85.00
Creamer & sugar bowl, Kingsware, Pied Piper, silver mts 460.00
Ewer, Babes in Woods, mk, 9" 1,250.00
Flask, Kingsware, Sporting Squire, Dewar's, 8½" 475.00
Loving cup, 3 Musketeers, Noke/H Fenton, #406, ltd ed, 9¾" ...1,250.00
Pitcher, Babes in Woods, girl, winter scene, flow bl, 9" 1,250.00
Plaque, Babes in Woods, girl w/basket, P Jones, 9¾x7¾" 1,525.00
Plaque, Babes in Woods, 2 girls w/pixie man, 7½x9½" 1,500.00
Plate, Babes in Woods, mk, 10" 450.00
Plate, Dickensware, Cap'n Cuttle, 10" 125.00
Plate, Dickensware, Mr Squeers, early mk, 10½" 175.00
Plate, Doctor, 10" 95.00
Plate, Falconer, 10" 95.00
Plate, Gibson Girl, 1904, 10½" 130.00
Plate, Historical England, Francis Drake at Plymouth, D5940 .....85.00
Plate, Jack of the Bushveld, 10" 110.00

Plate, Moreton Hall, Queen Elizabeth at Old Moreton, 10" 110.00
Plate, Old English Coaching Scenes 110.00
Plate, Roger Solem El Cobler, 10" 110.00
Plate, Sketches From Jediers, 10" 95.00
Plate, Where Are You Going My Pretty Maid, 8" 95.00
Tray, Dickensware, Cap'n Cuttle, 10½x5⅝" 125.00
Tray, Dickensware, David & His Aunt, mk, 4½x8⅝" 85.00
Vase, Babes in Woods, children at hide 'n seek, 9½" 950.00
Vase, Babes in Woods, children in garden, 5½" 650.00
Vase, Babes in Woods, children w/dogs, mk, 4½" 275.00
Vase, Babes in Woods, girl picks flowers, hexagonal, #1359, 10" ..300.00
Vase, Babes in Woods, girl picks flowers, sq, #1289 ....195.00
Vase, Babes in Woods, girl walking, #1304, 6½" 475.00
Vase, Babes in Woods, mother & child, #9889, 12" 1,075.00
Vase, Babes in Woods, mother & child in snow, mk, 11½" 1,575.00
Vase, Babes in Woods, mother & child walking, #L6659, 18" 760.00
Vase, Babes in Woods, 2 children look in tree, 10" 750.00
Vase, Babes in Woods, 2 girls under tree, mk, L-9036, 12" 875.00
Vase, Blue Children, 3 girls outdoors, 8x8½" 675.00
Vase, Coaching Days, ovoid, 2¼x3¼" 85.00
Vase, Kingsware, squire at table, 6-line verse, hdls, 10½" 450.00

Stoneware

Foot warmer, advertising, Lambeth, 10" 275.00
Jug, incised scrolled leaves in bl, Barlow, Lambeth, 5½" 325.00
Jug, Neptune spout, brn/tan, Lambeth oval stamp 175.00
Soap dish, dragonfly, Wrights' Coal Tar Soap, 1½x4¼x5¾" 135.00
Vase, cows frieze, floral borders, Hannah Barlow, 16¼", NM 635.00
Vase, owl frieze & leaves, sgn FEB & FAB, Lambeth, 21½" 1,150.00
Vase, sheep frieze, leaf borders, Hannah Barlow, rpr, 10½" 500.00
Vase, stylized floral/leaves, cylindrical, ca 1900, 10½", pr 300.00
Vase, 2-color floral, ear hdls, Slater's Pat, 5x3" 225.00

Toby Jugs

Ben Franklin, sm 80.00
Buz Fuz 150.00
Capt Ahab, sm 65.00
Capt Bligh 120.00
Capt Cuttle 150.00
Churchill 100.00
Cornell, bl or brn 450.00
Custer & Sitting Bull, Antagonists Collection, ltd ed, 6¾" 250.00
Geo Washington 120.00
Happy John 100.00
Huntsman 100.00
Seated Jester 100.00

Royal Dux

The Duxer Porzellan Manufactur was established by E. Eichler in 1860. Located in what is now Duchcov, Czechoslovakia, the area was known as Dux, Bohemia, until WWI. The war brought about changes in both the style of the ware as well as the mark. Prewar pieces were modeled in the Art Nouveau or Greek Classical manner and marked with 'Bohemia' and a pink triangle containing the letter 'E.' They were usually matt glazed in green, brown, and gold. Better pieces were made of porcelain, while the larger items were of pottery. After the war the ware was marked with the small pink triangle but without the Bohemia designation; 'Made in Czechoslovakia' was added. The style became Art Deco, with cobalt blue a dominant color.

Figurine, antelope, wht, 4x3" 50.00
Figurine, Arabic man w/water jug in basket, mc, 28x9" 950.00
Figurine, bird dog w/pheasant, 20" L 695.00
Figurine, cockatoo on branch w/bl flower, 2 mks 175.00
Figurine, Deco lady in bl gown w/gold sits on cushion, triangle mk ..450.00
Figurine, elephant, pk triangle mk, 6" 95.00
Figurine, elephant, trunk up, 10x13" 200.00
Figurine, fisher boy w/bag & hat, bronze & gold, triangle mk, 21" ...750.00
Figurine, German shepherd, sitting 50.00

Figurine, girl in flowing gown reading book, brown, tan, and white with gold, #2374, 16", NM, $800.00.

Figurine, Harlequin & Columbine, cobalt & wht, 19½" 850.00
Figurine, lady in sedan chair, 2 courtiers, hound, 14x9x16" 800.00
Figurine, lady w/basket, ivory w/gold, 19th C, 19", pr 1,800.00
Figurine, retriever w/duck in jaws, matt, 14" L 400.00
Figurine, shepherd w/pipes & dog, triangle mk, 1885, 20" 800.00
Vase, appl roses & buds, yel & mc on gr irid, 4 loop hdls, 9¾" ...160.00
Vase, blackberries & vines, baluster, 20½x7½" 365.00
Vase, maiden w/urn beside tree trunk, gold highlights, 17" 850.00
Vase, 2 figural ladies climbing shoulder, #3705, att, 23" 1,000.00
Vase, 2 nymphs, porc, 10x12" 750.00

Royal Flemish

Royal Flemish was introduced in the late 1880s and was patented in 1894 by the Mt. Washington Glass Company. Transparent glass was enameled with one or several colors and the surface divided by a network of raised lines suggesting leaded glasswork. Some pieces were further decorated with enameled florals, birds, or Roman coins. Our advisors for this category are Betty and Clarence Maier; they are listed in the Directory under Pennsylvania.

Ewer, heavy gilding over surface with rampant lion decoration and double-headed black phoenix shield trademark, rope handle, 12", $6,000.00.

Cracker jar, Roman coins on shaded ground, ornate mts, 8½" ...1,700.00
Cracker jar, thistle blossoms, earth tones & gold, SP rim, 7½" ..1,750.00
Lamp, Guba Duck base, abalone shell 13" dia shade, 23" 2,000.00
Tumbler, scrolls, pk on wht, gold wild roses, 4¼" 2,200.00
Vase, geese in flight/blazing sun, silver-gray/gold, 14¼" 5,750.00

Vase, pansy bouquets & gold sun rays, gold leaf hdls, global, 5½" ..2,500.00
Vase, 3 ebony scrolled medallions/gold asters, stick neck, 12½" 3,500.00

Royal Haeger, Haeger

In 1871 David Henry Haeger, a young son of German immigrants, purchased a brick factory at Dundee, Illinois, and began an association with the ceramic industry that his descendants have pursued to the present time. David's bricks rebuilt Chicago after their great fire in 1871. By 1914 the company had ventured into the field of commercial artware. Vases, figurines, lamp bases, and gift items in pastel matt glazes were marked with the logo of the company name written over the bar of an 'H.' From 1929 to 1933, they produced dinnerware which they marketed through Marshall Fields. Items produced before the mid-'30s are sometimes found with a paper label; such pieces are of special interest. 'Royal Haeger,' their premium line designed in 1938 by Royal Hickman, is highly regarded by collectors today. The mark 'Royal Haeger' (in raised lettering) was used during the '30s and '40s; later a paper label in the shape of a crown was used.

Fast becoming popular is the Earth Graphic Wraps line, first introduced in the mid-'70s. These one-of-a-kind pieces are decorated with raised free-form designs on backgrounds of marigold, white, fern, and brown, in both matt and glossy finishes.

The Macomb plant, built in 1939, primarily made vases and planters for the florist trade. A second plant, built there in 1969, produces lamp bases. For more information we recommend *Haeger Potteries Through the Years* by David Dilley (L-W Books). You may also contact Doris Frizzell, our advisor for this category; she is listed in the Directory under Illinois. (SASE required.)

Ashtray, panther seated in center, R-632, $60.00.

#3010, fountain, 3 mermaid pumps, portable/electric, 17", minimum ..800.00
#3063, dbl football candle holders, Pigskin Brown, pr 75.00
#312-H, swan bowl, 18" 40.00
#3208, flying fish vase, 5¾x6" 35.00
#3266, donkey planter 25.00
#3289, crying girl planter 35.00
#3290, Madonna planter, 9½" 30.00
#3306, horsehead vase, 8¾" 45.00
#3314, horse planter, 7½" 55.00
#3315, elephant planter 55.00
#3318, colonial girl planter 35.00
#4103, pitcher vase, peasant, olive, 18" 45.00
#5025, Playful Critter stoneware elephant 75.00
#503-H, dolphin planter, 19x17" 400.00
#601-H, poodle, 18½" 200.00
#6093, half moon planter lamp, 26" 100.00
#6140, sailfish TV lamp 65.00
#990, Madonna, lg, 13" 50.00
R-G1, window box, 16" 35.00
R-G25, gladiola vase, 13" 35.00
R-G42, pitcher, 10" 35.00

R-10, ashtray trio (nest 3 szs), 8½", 6½", 4½" 30.00
R-1095, Lincoln ashtray, 7" 30.00
R-1155, abstract bird ash bowl, 8" L 25.00
R-1168, sailfish vase, lg, 12½" 195.00
R-1190, pine cone vase, 12" 55.00
R-122, free-form console bowl, 14" 35.00
R-1224, Gypsy girl, 16½", minimum value 150.00
R-1231, St Francis figurine, 10½" 45.00
R-1232, St Francis bowl, 14" 35.00
R-1239, bronco TV planter 125.00
R-127, bowl, floral cutouts, lg, 14" W 175.00
R-134, moon fish planter bookend, 10" 90.00
R-1360, shell bowl, 15" L 30.00
R-1378, free-form floor ashtray w/wrought-iron stand 65.00
R-1440, poodle figurine, 8" 55.00
R-157, angelfish, head up, lg 100.00
R-159, Inebriated Duck, leaning, 10" 75.00
R-164, hen pheasant, 6" 75.00
R-166, greyhound, head down, 9" 125.00
R-167, greyhound, head up, 9" 125.00
R-169, cornucopia, basketweave, 18½" L 125.00
R-1747, jack rabbit planter, oyster color 35.00
R-1748, donkey planter, oyster color 35.00
R-175, Oriental head, woman, ¾-face view, 11" 200.00
R-176, Oriental head, man, ¾-face view, 11" 200.00
R-1761, turkey planter, 11x10x10" 195.00
R-179, bowl, daisy decor, low, oblong 30.00
R-1856, ashtray, state of Michigan, 10" 45.00
R-186, Bird of Paradise vase, 12¾" 50.00
R-1918, swan, 10½" 45.00
R-20, cut-out bowl, rnd, 16" 75.00
R-203, fish candle holder, dbl; 5" 45.00
R-224, Daisy bowl, 12" W 65.00
R-241, Yacha vase, 15" 40.00
R-256, jardiniere, curled edge, 12", minimum value 800.00
R-277, Spiral Plume dish, sm, 6" W 30.00
R-278, Spiral Plume dish, lg, 9" W 45.00
R-310, swan bowl, lg, 13" L 45.00
R-319, Russian Wolfhound, head up, 7" L 125.00
R-34, fan vase, dbl leaf design, 14" 40.00
R-340, pedestal bowl, ftd 25.00
R-361, 3 birds on branch block, 7" 90.00
R-370, Dutch cup bowl, 19" L 30.00
R-386, basket vase, 13¼" L 75.00
R-422, cornucopia vase, 6" 75.00
R-427, sitting horse vase, emb Royal Haeger by Royal Hickman, 11" ..150.00
R-434, hen pheasant, 12" L 75.00
R-444, upright leaf vase, 6½" 25.00
R-451, mare & foal, standing, 13½" L 150.00
R-467, flying goose vase, 16¼" 95.00
R-472, Russian lady's head, 12" 125.00
R-477, modernistic lady's head, 13½", minimum value 150.00
R-510, dolphin bowl, sm, 15" W 35.00
R-534, horn of plenty, 18" L 45.00
R-616, tulip vase, 8" 20.00
R-635, Pei Tung planter, 15" L 35.00
R-648, leopard, sitting, 6" 45.00
R-657, gondolier planter, w/inserts & paddle, 19½" L 75.00
R-659, alligator vase, 14½" 40.00
R-683, panther, 18" L 70.00
R-690, sq Chinese candle holder, 5" W, ea 15.00
R-695, lion figurine 150.00
R-730, flower block 20.00
R-788, jockey flower block 150.00

R-819, acanthus leaf bowl, 14" L 25.00
R-866, lily bowl 25.00
R-883, dbl racing horses planter, 18" L 125.00
R-891, conventional bud vase, 12" 25.00
R-898, cat, sitting, 6" 35.00
R-967, starfish bowl, 14" W 65.00
R-987, basket vase w/hdl, 15½" 75.00
R-992, dog, standing, 7" 25.00
S-3669, goose, 4½" 100.00
S-3670, peasant girl w/geese, 17½", minimum value 200.00
S-3671, goose, 7" 100.00
S-473, pitcher, lg, 17" 75.00
Sign, Haeger logo w/cut-out letters, gold 75.00

Royal Rudolstadt

The hard-paste porcelain that has come to be known as Royal Rudolstadt was produced in Thuringia, Germany, in the early eighteenth century. Various names and marks have been associated with this pottery. One of the earliest was a hay-fork symbol associated with Johann Frederich von Schwarzburg-Rudolstadt, one of the first founders. Variations, some that included an 'R,' were also used. In 1854 Earnst Bohne produced wares that were marked with an anchor and the letters 'EB.' Examples commonly found today were made during the late 1800s and early 1900s. These are usually marked with an 'RW' within a shield under a crown and the words 'Crown Rudolstadt.' Items marked 'Germany' were made after 1890.

Celery dish, pk roses, pierced hdls, mk 35.00
Dresser set, pk roses, tray/hair receiver/box/pin tray 200.00
Ewer, floral w/gold, artist sgn, twig hdl, 11" 235.00
Plate, daisies & foliage, sgn Bach, gold rim, Thuringia, 8½" 12.00
Teaset, Happifats, pot+cr/sug+4 c/s+4 sm plates, child sz 350.00
Vase, floral bouquets on pk to cream, pierced hdls, 14¼" 395.00
Vase, floral on beige, gold scroll hdls, 9½" 125.00
Vase, floral on cream w/peach satin, mk, 8¾" 135.00
Vase, floral w/gold & jewels, scrolled hdls, 10x6¾" 190.00
Vase, poppies on brn to gr, yel at ft, rtcl rim, 7x2½" 85.00

Royal Vienna

In 1719 Claude Innocentius de Paquier established a hard-paste porcelain factory in Vienna where he made highly ornamental wares similar to the type produced at Meissen. Early wares were usually unmarked; but after 1744, when the factory was purchased by the Empress, the Austrian shield (often called 'beehive') was stamped on under the glaze. In the following listings, values are for hand-painted items unless noted otherwise. Decal-decorated items would be considerably lower.

Note: An influx of Japanese reproductions on the market have influenced values to decline on genuine old Royal Vienna. Buyer beware! On new items the beehive mark is over the glaze, the weight of the porcelain is heavier, and the decoration is obviously decaled. Our advisor for this category is Madeleine France; she is listed in the Directory under Florida.

Bowl, flower & scroll mold, heart shape, 3x10½" 185.00
Cake plate, 3 ladies & Cupid w/harp, Carlsbad, 11¼" 215.00
Ferner/centerpc, 2 ladies' portraits, sgn, much gold, 4x7¾" 425.00
Figurine, Victorian couple on common base, beehive mk, 3½" ..200.00
Plaque, scene from Tannhauser, Wagner, gilt fr, rpr, 14x12¼" ..625.00
Plate, lady, Wagner, mc floral border w/gold, 10" 1,350.00

Plate, lady & flowers, cobalt & gold, beehive mk, 15", pr 3,200.00
Plate, lady w/scarf & roses, beehive mk, 8" 160.00
Plate, 3 maidens, Kauffmann, 8¾" 165.00
Plate, 3 maidens dancing, Mignon, beehive mk, 8½" 75.00
Plate, 3 maidens/chariot/Cupid, Kauffmann, mk, 9½" 300.00

Urn, Kuche, Toast und Musik, signed Lefler, gilt arabesques, reticulation, domed lid, beehive mark, 14½", $1,500.00.

Vase, lady on maroon w/gold, turq beading, 9¾" 895.00
Vase, maidens dance w/Cupid, beehive mk, 8" 175.00

Roycroft

Near the turn of the century, Elbert Hubbard established the Roycroft Printing Shop in East Aurora, New York. Named in honor of two 17th-century printer-bookbinders, the print shop was just the beginning of a community called Roycroft, which came to be known worldwide. Hubbard became a popular personality of the early 1900s, known for his talents in a variety of areas from writing and lecturing to manufacturing. The Roycroft community became a meeting place for people of various capabilities and included shops for the production of furniture, copper, leather items, and a multitude of other wares which were marked with the Roycroft symbol, an 'R' within a circle below a stylized cross. Hubbard lost his life on the Lusitania in 1915; production in the community continued until the Depression.

Interest is strong in the field of Arts and Crafts in general and in Roycroft items in particular. Copper items are evaluated to a large extent by the condition of the original patina that remains. In the listings that follow, values reflect the worth of items retaining their original dark brown patina unless condition is otherwise described. Our advisor for this category is Bruce Austin; he is listed in the Directory under New York.

Key: h/cp — hammered copper

Armchair rocker, mahog, corseted slat bk, uphl seat, #39, 35" 900.00
Book, Justinian & Theodora, suede cover, color photos, 1906, EX ...45.00
Bookends, h/cp, emb floral, EX patina, 8¼x6" 250.00
Bookends, h/cp, emb poppies, riveted edges, dk patina, 5¼x5" ..550.00
Bookends, h/cp, fleur-de-lis, brass wash, heavy, 5x5" ...175.00
Bookends, h/cp, floral, brass wash, EX patina, 5x3½" 200.00
Bookends, h/cp, owl design, rolled edge, riveted base, mk, 5" 400.00
Bookends, h/cp, tree design, 4x7" 165.00
Bookends, hammered brass arc on ftd base, 4x7" 140.00
Books, Little Journeys, 14-volume set, M 200.00
Books, Selected Writings, E Hubbard, 14-volume complete set .200.00
Box, h/cp, emb flower, EX new dk patina, 1½x7x3½" 325.00
Box, h/cp, poppy design on lid, cleaned patina, 4x7", VG 750.00
Candlesticks, h/cp w/orig silver wash, mk, 8", VG, pr 250.00

Catalog, Book of the Copper Shop, Roycrofters, 1920s, VG **55.00**
Chair, side; #030, corset-shaped bk, uphl seat, 44", VG **850.00**
Chair, side; 4 vertical slats, rpl leather, #25, 38", pr **1,000.00**
Chair, straddle; 2-slat bk, elbow rest, narrow seat, #29, 34" **1,000.00**
Chamberstick, h/cp, fine orig patina, mk, 1½x5½" **100.00**
Desk set, smooth copper w/leaf design, 5-pc, VG **350.00**
Footstool, recovered cushion, orig finish, 12x14x14", VG **1,200.00**
Frame, NP h/cp, rolled edge, orig patina, 11x9", VG **250.00**
Humidor, h/cp, ltly cleaned, orb mk, 3½x5", VG **450.00**
Jug, ceramic, brn glaze, 4" **40.00**
Lamp, desk; h/cp w/etched brass finish, orb mk, rpl shade, 10x5" ...**550.00**
Lamp, table; copper/mica, 4-sided stem, sq base, 14½x7½" **1,600.00**
Letter opener, copper, mk **85.00**

Magazine rack, mahogany, arched gallery top with plank sides, three graduated shelves, #078, ca 1907, 38x18x16", $1,600.00.

Match holder, h/cp, orig patina, mk, 1½x2¼x1" **225.00**
Pedestal, mahog, 4-shelf, splayed slab sides, 50x29x18" **4,750.00**
Plate, h/cp w/etched silver wash, orb mk, 7" **375.00**
Sconce, h/cp, spade-shaped bk, EX patina, mk, 8x3¼", pr **425.00**
Shaker, geometric decor, china, 4" **700.00**
Stand, Little Journeys, 2-shelf, trestle sides, tag, 14x26x26" **600.00**
Tray, h/cp, 5-hdld, EX recent patina, 19" dia **550.00**
Tray, serving; h/cp, hdls, orig dk brn patina, 10" dia **300.00**
Tray, silver over copper, emb floral, mk, 21½x9½" **325.00**
Trivet, h/cp w/star cutouts, 5-ftd, cleaned patina, 1x4" dia **260.00**
Vase, bud; h/cp, flared base w/glass tube, EX patina, 5x2¾" **150.00**
Vase, bud; h/cp, lotus-shaped base holds glass tube, 7½x2½" **150.00**
Vase, bud; h/cp supports slim glass tube, orb mk, 8½" **150.00**
Vase, h/cp, Am Beauty, rivet design, cleaned patina, 21" **1,600.00**
Vase, h/cp, Am Beauty, riveted base, new dk patina, 22½x8" .**2,000.00**
Vase, h/cp, flared rim, soft shoulders, ca 1910-15, 8½x3¾" **500.00**
Vase, h/cp, incised band at rim, EX patina, mk, 4¾x3½" **500.00**
Vase, h/cp, rolled/crimped rim, brass wash, 1915-38, 5½x2¼" ...**225.00**
Vase, h/cp, stylized dmn-shaped flowers, brass wash, 10x3" **1,200.00**
Vase, h/cp w/appl decor, cylindrical, 6" **550.00**
Vase, h/cp w/nickel o/l, cleaned patina, some wear, 5" **425.00**
Walking stick, fine orig finish, missing strap, orb mk, 35" **375.00**

Rubena

Rubena glass was made by several firms in the late 1800s. It is a blown art glass that shades from clear to red. See also Art Glass Baskets; Cruets; Sugar Shakers; Salts; specific manufacturers.

Bowl, appl chartreuse pulled rim, rigaree collar, 3½x9½" **75.00**
Cruet, gold ribbon streamers w/enameling, clear bubble top, 11⅜" .**195.00**
Jug, liqueur; emb swirls w/gold, SP hinged top & hdl, 7⅝" **175.00**
Pitcher, Invt T'print, Hobbs & Brockunier #0, 4" **150.00**

Pitcher, melon ribs, clear hdl, rnd mouth, 8⅝x5⅛" **175.00**
Shaker, Coquette, bbl shape, 2-part lid, 3" **150.00**
Slipper, appl yel flowers, cut band, clear heel, gold trim **195.00**
Vase, gold scrolls & urn, wht florals, clear hdls, 13x8" **350.00**

Rubena Verde

Rubena Verde glass was introduced in the late 1800s by Hobbs, Brockunier, and Company of Wheeling, West Virginia. Its transparent colors shade from red to green. Our advisor for this category is Mike Roscoe; he is listed in the Directory under Michigan. See also Art Glass Baskets; Cruets; Sugar Shakers; Salts.

Basket, mottled, amber hdl, 4¾x6½" **75.00**
Basket, pk & wht morning glories, cut-away top, gr hdl, 10x5" ..**300.00**
Bottle, whiskey; Invt T'print, 10" **275.00**
Bowl, Hobnail, ruffled rim, 5" **150.00**
Bowl, ruffled rim, heavy SP base, 12¾x10⅛" **395.00**
Butter dish, knob hdl, 5x7" **650.00**
Cruet, gold ribbon streamers, clear stopper, 11⅜x3⅝" **195.00**
Cruet, Invt T'print, rnd body, vaseline hdl & stopper, 6½" **535.00**
Cup, Invt T'print, HP florals, bulbous, 3½" **65.00**
Lamp, peg; HP floral fonts/shade, candlestick std, 1895, 22", pr .**440.00**
Pitcher, Hobnail, appl hdl, 4" **325.00**
Pitcher, water; Hobbs Hobnail, wht opal hobnails **495.00**
Punch bowl, gr hdls & ft, mc floral w/gold, w/lid, 9¾x7¼" **550.00**
Rose bowl, Coin Spot, opal, 3½" **80.00**
Rose bowl, Invt T'print, 4½" **185.00**
Tumbler, Hobnail, 3⅞" **110.00**
Vase, jack-in-pulpit; pulled/folded rim, rigaree on stem, 11½" ...**160.00**
Vase, mc florals & butterfly w/gold, 10x5" **300.00**
Vase, Optic, sq fluted top, HP florals, 8x3¾" **225.00**

Ruby Glass

Produced for over one hundred years by every glasshouse of note in this country, ruby glass has been used to create decorative items such as one might find in gift shops, utilitarian bottles and kitchenware, figurines, and dinnerware lines such as were popular in the Depression era. For further information and study, we recommend *Ruby Glass of the 20th Century* by our advisor, Naomi Over; she is listed in the Directory under Colorado.

Banana boat, Moon & Star, LG Wright, 1974-81, 12" **45.00**
Basket, Daisy & Button, oval, Fenton **18.00**
Bowl, cereal; Old Cafe, Anchor Hocking, 1940s, 5½" **13.50**
Bowl, scalloped, 4-toed, Cambridge, 6" **65.00**
Cake plate, Sandwich, Indiana, 1960s-70s, 13" **92.50**
Candlesticks, metal stem, 8½", pr **100.00**
Candy dish, Sweetheart, LG Wright, 3¾" **22.50**
Creamer & sugar bowl, rnd, Anchor Hocking, 1940s **12.00**
Cup, measuring; 16-oz **30.00**
Figurine, bird, Swedish Glass, 4" **16.50**
Finger bowl, 4¾", +saucer **28.00**
Lamp, fairy; Sweetheart, LG Wright, 1974-81, 4¼" **16.50**
Marmalade, Eyewinker, LG Wright, 1974-81, 8¾" **35.00**
Nappy, Royal Ruby, Anchor Hocking, 6½" **9.00**
Paperweight, pear, Viking, 8½" **45.00**
Pickle dish, Anchor Hocking, 1940s, 6" **16.50**
Pitcher, Blenko, #3750, 16-oz **22.50**
Pitcher, hostess; Roly Poly, MacBeth-Evans, 32-oz **72.50**
Pitcher, HP scrolls & roses w/gold, appl hdl, 2¼x2⅛" **125.00**
Pitcher, reeded, Imperial, 80-oz **100.00**

Platter, Oyster & Pearl, Anchor Hocking, 13½" 45.00
Saucer, American, MacBeth-Evans, 1930-36, scarce 28.00
Sherbet, Anchor Hocking 7.50
Syrup, Moon & Star, LG Wright, 1981, 4-oz 75.00
Tumbler, Hobnail, Anchor Hocking, 1930s, 4½" 9.00
Vase, Heirloom, pitcher form, 9" 55.00
Vase, Rachel, Anchor Hocking, 1940s, 10" 45.00

Ruby-Stained Glass

Ruby-flashed or ruby-stained glass was made through the application of a thin layer of color over clear. It was used in the manufacture of some early pressed tableware and from the Victorian era well into the 20th century. These items were often engraved on the spot with the date, location, and buyer's name. Our advisors for this category are Bill and Marilyn Moore; they are listed in the Directory under Washington.

Creamer, Broken Column 125.00
Decanter, Loop & Block 135.00
Goblet, Duncan Block 38.00
Goblet, Invt T'print, Merry Christmas...1893 ....100.00
Goblet, Red Block 30.00
Goblet, Sawtooth 20.00
Pitcher, Block & Lattice, water sz 130.00
Punch cup, Broken Column 60.00
Spill hold, gold trim, 5¼" 50.00
Spooner, Red Block 28.00
Sugar bowl, Block & Lattice 75.00
Sugar shaker, Late Block, lt wear 165.00
Tankard, Pioneer Victoria 155.00
Toothpick holder, crystal Vs, gold border 35.00
Toothpick holder, King's Crown 37.00
Tumbler, Dakota 25.00

Wine glasses, Baby Thumbprint and Sunk Honeycomb patterns, etched names, example on right dated 1897, $30.00 each.

Wine, Homer MI 42.00
Wine, Rainbow 30.00
Wine, Red Block 30.00
Wine, Shoshone 17.00

Rugs

Hooked rugs are treasured today for their folk-art appeal. Rug making was a craft that was introduced to this country in about 1830 and flourished its best in the New England states. The prime consideration to consider when evaluating one of these rugs is not age but artistic appeal. Scenes with animals, buildings, and people; patriotic designs; or whimsical themes are preferred. Those with finely conceived designs, great imagination, interesting color use, etc., demand higher prices. Condition is, of course, also a factor. Marked examples bearing the stamps of 'Frost and Co.,' 'Abenakee,' 'C.R.,' and 'Ouia' are highly prized. Note: the rugs listed here are made of rag unless noted otherwise. See also Orientalia, Rugs.

Bird on branch, 6-color, 26x40" 250.00
Birds & flowers w/flower border, mc on dk ground, 30x41" 225.00
Cats & birds (primitive style), mc on bl, fr, 16x37" 700.00
Checkerboard w/flower border, 5-color on gray, 22x32" 330.00
Compass star, 5-color, lt wear, 55" dia 415.00
Deer in landscape w/floral cornucopias, mc, rprs, 27x62" 580.00
Dogs in landscape, mc, lt wear, 40x49" 510.00
Floral bouquet w/in vining border, mc, fr, 24x42" 150.00
Flowers in compote (folky), mc on dk ground, rpr, 33x49" 600.00
Geometric floral in pastel colors on beige, 64x100" 415.00
Grenfell, sailboat, mc, minor wear/stains, 10½x9" 225.00
Horse & bird, blk/red/lt brn, 22x31" 300.00
Horse in harness, 4-color, irregular border, 25x29" 165.00
Penny, mc wool circles on wht flannel, tab border, 28x52" 165.00
Recumbent lion among flowers & leaves, mc, 32x63", EX 800.00
Rooster crowing at sunrise, bright colors, 19x33½" 220.00
Saddle horse on variegated gr, mc, mtd, 19th C, 31x51" 2,185.00
Stag in reserve w/oak leaves/acorns in border, mc, 34x60" 330.00
Stag w/acorn & leaf border, folky style, 30x57" 250.00
7 family members & dog, sgn EBM (Barbara Merry), 42x23", G 600.00

RumRill

George Rumrill designed and marketed his pottery designs from 1933 until his death in 1942. During this period of time, four different companies produced his works. Today the most popular designs are those made by the Red Wing Stoneware Company from 1933 until 1936 and Red Wing Potteries from 1936 until early 1938. Some of these lines include Trumpet Flower, Classic, Manhattan, and Athena, the Nudes.

For a period of months in 1938, Shawnee took over the production of RumRill pottery. This relationship ended abruptly and the Florence Pottery took over and produced his wares until the plant burned down. The final producer was Gonder. Pieces from each individual pottery are easily recognized by their designs, glazes, and/or signatures. It is interesting to note that the same designs were produced by all three companies. They may be marked RumRill or with the name of the specific company that made them. You will find information on RumRill in these books: *Red Wing Art Pottery, Books I* and *II,* by B.L. and R.L. Dollen (Collector Books). Our advisors for this category are Wendy and Leo Frese; they are listed in the Directory under Texas.

Bowl, #524, Pompeian 45.00
Bowl, #526, Pompeian, w/deer 60.00
Bowl, console; #RW 62014 ....55.00
Bowl, console; #271, wht 60.00
Bowl, console; #271, wht & gr 45.00
Bowl, nut; #I-11, 2-tier, gr & brn 30.00
Candlesticks, #397, Pompeian, pr 60.00
Candlesticks, #529, wht, pr 40.00
Cornucopia, #413, Pompeian 30.00
Ewer, #H34, bl & pk, Ohio 25.00
Ewer, #455 ....95.00
Ewer vase, #J54 (Gonder shape), wht 45.00
Log, pk 55.00
Urn, #277, ivory 35.00
Urn, #638, wht & gr 50.00
Vase, #H54, bl 25.00
Vase, #M8, peach 70.00
Vase, #242, jade 25.00
Vase, #271, wht w/gr int 95.00

Vase, #313, beige w/brn interior, 10½" **90.00**
Vase, #355, Ripe Wheat **50.00**
Vase, #450, pk glossy **85.00**
Vase, #491, trumpet flower, 10" **185.00**
Vase, #500, gr & ivory **45.00**
Vase, #504, wht **25.00**
Vase, #525, ivory, 8" **80.00**
Vase, #633, bl mottle **55.00**
Vase, #637, bl, 7½" **65.00**
Vase, bud; #329 ....**30.00**
Wall pocket, well, gr **70.00**

Ruskin

This English pottery operated near Birmingham from 1989 until 1935. Its founder was W. Howson Taylor, and it was named in honor of the renowned author and critic, John Ruskin. The earliest marks were 'Taylor' in block letters and the initials 'WHT,' the smaller W and H superimposed over the larger T. Later marks included the Ruskin name.

Bowl, lav gloss w/mc irid, mks, 1925, 3x8½", NM **95.00**
Bowl, pk lustre, low ft, 8" **140.00**
Bowl, red/purple/gray gloss, 1924, 1½x5" **100.00**
Pedestal, red/purple/gray gloss, mks, 2½x4" **300.00**
Vase, aqua crystalline drip on orange matt & cream gloss, 6" ...**375.00**
Vase, bl crystalline on tan/orange/mint gr gloss, 1932, 5½" **475.00**
Vase, bl w/mc irid, long neck, 1910, 11" **425.00**
Vase, blk/gr/tan glossy mottle, waisted, 1906, 7" **650.00**
Vase, cream & bl crystalline gloss, mks, 1930, 5" **210.00**
Vase, gr/tan/wht/red matt mottle, shouldered, 1905, 8" **1,100.00**
Vase, lt bl w/mc irid, shouldered, mks, 1925, 8½" **290.00**
Vase, lt bl/purple/cream/dk gr glossy mottle, bulbous, 1909, 3" ...**325.00**
Vase, purple & wht glossy, flared cylinder, 1923, 7½" **450.00**
Vase, purple/red/wht glossy mottle, gourd form, 4½" **375.00**
Vase, purple/wht/bl glossy mottle, flared cylinder, 1928, 8" **500.00**
Vase, purple/wht/gr gloss (fine), shouldered, 7½" **750.00**
Vase, red & gray gloss, bulbous base, mks, no date, 6½", EX **450.00**
Vase, red & wht gloss, mks, 1922, rpr, 9½" **400.00**
Vase, red flambe w/gr & bl spots, shouldered, on stand, 11" ...**1,725.00**
Vase, red/wht/bl glossy mottle, shouldered, 1922, 3½" **1,600.00**
Vase, red/wht/purple gloss, gourd form w/1 hdl, 1933, 8½" **300.00**
Vase, yel lustre, shouldered, 1916, minor scratches, 14" **325.00**

Russel Wright Dinnerware

Russel Wright, one of America's foremost industrial designers, also designed several lines of ceramic dinnerware, glassware, and aluminum ware that are now highly sought-after collectibles. His most popular dinnerware then and with today's collectors, American Modern, was manufactured by the Steubenville Pottery Company from 1939 until 1959. It was produced in a variety of solid colors in assortments chosen to stay attune with the times. Casual (his first line sturdy enough to be guaranteed against breakage for ten years from date of purchase) is relatively easy to find today — simply because it has held up so well. During the years of its production, the Casual line was constantly being restyled, some items as many as five times. Early examples were heavily mottled, while later pieces were smoothly glazed and sometimes patterned. The ware was marked with Wright's signature and 'China by Iroquois.' It was marketed in fine department stores throughout the country. After 1950 the line was marked 'Iroquois China by Russel Wright.' For those wanting to learn more about the subject, we recom-

mend *The Collector's Encyclopedia of Russel Wright, Second Edition*, by our advisor, Ann Kerr. She is listed in the Directory under Ohio.

American Modern

To calculate values for American Modern, double the values listed for these colors: Canteloupe, Glacier Blue, Bean Brown, and White. Chartreuse is represented by the low end of our range; Cedar, Black Chutney, and Seafoam by the high end; and Coral and Gray near the middle.

Bowl, divided vegetable; from $85 to **120.00**
Bowl, lug soup; from $12 to **15.00**
Bowl, salad; from $85 to **110.00**
Carafe, from $160 to **200.00**
Celery dish, from $25 to **30.00**
Chop plate, from $30 to **45.00**

Covered ramekin, $185.00 to $225.00; Divided relish, 10", $150.00 to $175.00; Coffeepot, 8", $200.00 to $250.00; Icebox jar, $175.00 to $200.00.

Cup & saucer, from $10 to **12.00**
Gravy boat, 10½", from $15 to **30.00**
Hostess set, plate & cup, from $100 to **125.00**
Pickle dish, from $15 to **18.00**
Pitcher, water; from $95 to **150.00**
Plate, dinner; 10", from $8 to **10.00**
Plate, salad; 8", from $12 to **15.00**
Teapot, 6x10", from $85 to **100.00**
Tumbler, child's, from $60 to **80.00**

Casual

To price Brick Red, Aqua, and Canteloupe, double our values; for Avocado, use the low end of the range. Oyster and Charcoal are valued at 50% more than the prices listed.

Bowl, fruit; restyled, 5¾", from $10 to **15.00**
Bowl, gumbo, flat, from $45 to **55.00**
Butter dish, ½-lb, from $75 to **100.00**
Carafe, from $155 to **200.00**
Casserole, deep, 4-qt, 8", from $150 to **200.00**
Cookware, 6-qt, from $200 to **225.00**
Cup & saucer, AD; from $80 to **90.00**
Cup & saucer, coffee; from $12 to **14.00**
Gravy bowl, 12-oz, 5¼", from $12 to **15.00**
Gravy stand, 7½", from $15 to **18.00**
Lid for water pitcher, from $30 to **45.00**
Lid for 4-qt casserole, from $20 to **25.00**
Pepper mill, from $175 to **225.00**
Pitcher, water; restyled, 2-qt, from $150 to **200.00**
Plate, luncheon; 9½", from $6 to **10.00**
Plate, party; w/cup, from $85 to **100.00**
Platter, 14½", from $35 to **40.00**
Shaker, redesigned, ea, from $100 to **150.00**
Shakers, stacking, pr, from $20 to **22.00**

Sugar bowl, stacking, 4", from $15 to 18.00

Glass

Unless otherwise described, values are given for glassware in coral and seafoam; other colors are 10% to 15% less.

American Modern, chilling bowl, 12-oz, 3x5½", from $100 to ...150.00
American Modern, cocktail, 3-oz, 2½", from $25 to 35.00
American Modern, cordial, 2", from $50 to 55.00
American Modern, dbl old-fashioned, rare, from $40 to 50.00
American Modern, dessert dish, 2", from $35 to 40.00
American Modern, goblet, 4", from $40 to 45.00
American Modern, pilsner, rare, 7", from $125 to 150.00
American Modern, sherbet, 2½", from $25 to 30.00
American Modern, tumbler, iced tea; 13-oz, from $25 to 30.00
American Modern, tumbler, juice; 4", from $20 to 25.00
American Modern, tumbler, water; 4½", from $25 to 30.00
American Modern, wine, 3", from $25 to 30.00
Eclipse, old-fashioned, from $18 to 20.00
Eclipse, shot glass, from $20 to 22.00
Flair, tumbler, iced tea; 14-oz, from $50 to 65.00
Flair, tumbler, juice; 6-oz, from $45 to 50.00
Flair, tumbler, water; 11-oz, from $50 to 65.00
Pinch, tumbler, iced tea; 14-oz, from $35 to 45.00
Pinch, tumbler, juice; 6-oz, from $30 to 40.00
Pinch, tumbler, red, any sz, from $100 to 125.00
Pinch, tumbler, water; 11-oz, from $35 to 40.00
Snow Glass, bowl, salad/vegetable; rnd, from $175 to 250.00
Snow Glass, plate, salad; from $150 to 200.00
Snow Glass, tumbler, iced tea; 14-oz, from $150 to 200.00

Highlight

Bowl, soup/cereal; Citron or Nutmeg, 2 szs, ea, from $30 to 35.00
Bowl, vegetable; White, Pepper or Blueberry, rnd, from $60 to 80.00
Butter dish, Citron or Nutmeg, no established value
Creamer, Citron or Nutmeg, ea, from $40 to 50.00
Cup, White, Pepper or Blueberry, from $25 to 35.00
Lid for soup, White, Pepper or Blueberry, no established value
Plate, dinner; Pepper, Blueberry, Nutmeg or Green, from $30 to .35.00
Plate, dinner; White, Pepper or Blueberry 30.00
Platter, Citron or Nutmeg, rnd, sm 55.00
Relish server, Citron or Nutmeg, ea, from $45 to 65.00
Relish server, White, Pepper or Blueberry, no established value
Shakers, White, Pepper or Blueberry, pr, from $75 to 100.00

Spun Aluminum

Russel Wright's aluminum ware may not have been especially well accepted in its day — it tended to damage easily and seems to have had only limited market appeal — but today's collectors feel quite differently about it, as is apparent in the suggested values noted in the following listings.

Baine Marie server, from $400 to 600.00
Beverage set, from $400 to 500.00
Candelabrum, from $225 to 250.00
Casserole, from $100 to 150.00
Cheese board, from $85 to 100.00
Gravy boat, from $150 to 200.00
Humidor, sandwich; from $160 to 175.00
Ice bucket, from $75 to 100.00
Muddler, from $75 to 100.00
Muffin warmer, wire insert, w/lid, from $100 to 125.00

Peanut scoop, from $75 to 100.00
Pitcher, sherry; from $185 to 250.00
Punch set, from $1,000 to 1,500.00
Serving accessory, sm, from $115 to 150.00
Smoking stand, from $450 to 900.00
Spaghetti set, 3-pc, from $500 to 600.00
Vase/flowerpot, sm, from $115 to 125.00
Wastebasket, from $125 to 150.00

Sterling

Bowl, bouillon; 7-oz, from $15 to 18.00
Bowl, onion soup; 10-oz, from $20 to 22.00
Bowl, soup; 6½" 15.00
Coffee bottle, from $115 to 150.00
Creamer, ind, 3-oz 12.00
Cup & saucer, demitasse; 3½-oz, from $55 to 65.00
Pitcher, water; restyled, 2-qt, from $150 to 165.00
Plate, bread & butter, 6¼", from $5 to 8.00
Plate, dinner; 10¼", from $12 to 16.00
Platter, oval, 10½", from $18 to 25.00
Teapot, 10-oz, from $100 to 125.00

Miscellaneous

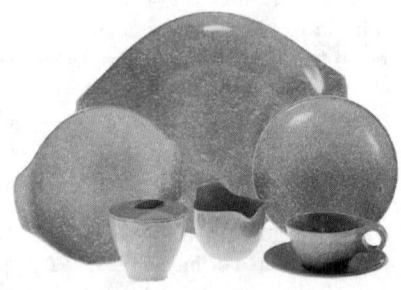

Residential Melmac: Shallow vegetable bowl, $15.00 to $20.00; Platter, $20.00 to $25.00; Creamer and sugar bowl with lid, $25.00 to $30.00; Salad plate, $4.00 to $5.00; Cup and saucer, $10.00 to $12.00.

Bauer, candle-holder bowl, wht, cup ea end, 18" W, from $1,000 to ...2,000.00
Bauer, pillow vase, #1A, from $850 to 1,000.00
Bauer, vase, #2A, 8½", from $500 to 700.00
Bauer, vase, blk metallic (rare glaze), ovoid, 5x4", from $450 to ...700.00
Bauer, vase/planter, #16A, 7½", from $600 to 625.00
Circus animal, ea, from $800 to 1,500.00
Display sign, Iroquois Cookware, minimum, EX, from $300 to ...400.00
Flair, creamer, from $10 to 12.00
Flair, lug soup, from $12 to 15.00
Flair, tumbler, from $15 to 18.00
Frosted Oak, bowl, serving; from $300 to 400.00
Harker White Clover, creamer, clover decor 14.00
Harker White Clover, gravy boat, clover decor 25.00
Harker White Clover, plate, jumbo; clover decor, 10" 16.00
Home Decorated, covered onion soup, from $16 to 20.00
Home Decorator, creamer, from $10 to 12.00
Home Decorator, lug soup, from $12 to 15.00
Home Decorator, sugar bowl, w/lid, from $20 to 25.00
Ideal Adult Kitchen Ware, bowl, salad; from $20 to 25.00
Ideal Adult Kitchen Ware, butter dish, from $45 to 85.00
Ideal Adult Kitchen Ware, decanter, juice; from $30 to 35.00
Ideal Adult Kitchen Ware, jug water; lg; from $50 to 55.00
Ideal Children's Toy Dishes, boxed set, from $200 to 250.00

Ideal Children's Toy Dishes, serving items, ea, from $20 to **22.00**
Knowles, plate, dinner; 10¾", from $15 to **18.00**
Knowles, platter, 13", from $25 to **45.00**
Linen, napkin, from $15 to **18.00**
Linen, tablecloth, from $50 to **100.00**
Mary Wright, Country Garden, plate, from $100 to **150.00**
Mary Wright, wooden cheese board, from $150 to **200.00**
Meladur, cup, 7-oz, from $8 to **10.00**
Meladur, plate, compartmented, 9½", from $12 to **15.00**
Oceana serving item, Buella shell bowl, from $600 to **800.00**
Oceana serving item, starfish relish, from $450 to **500.00**
Oceana serving item, Wave bowl, salad; from $700 to **800.00**
Price list of American Modern, from $55 to **60.00**
Residential, bowl, fruit; from $13 to **15.00**
Stainless, knife, from $100 to **110.00**
Stainless, soup spoon, from $70 to **90.00**
Theme Formal, mug, from $100 to **150.00**
Theme Formal, tumbler, from $250 to **400.00**

Russian Art

Before the Revolution in 1917, many jewelers and craftsmen created exquisite marvels of their arts, distinctive in the extravagant detail of their enamel work, jeweled inlays, and use of precious metals. These treasures aptly symbolized the glitter and the romance of the glorious days under the reign of the Tsars of Imperial Russia. The most famous of these master jewelers was Carl Faberge (1852 – 1920), goldsmith to the Romanovs. Following the tradition of his father, he took over the Faberge workshop in 1870. Eventually Faberge employed more than five hundred assistants and set up workshops in Moscow, Kiev, and London as well as in St. Petersburg. His specialties were enamel work, clockwork automated figures, carved animal and human figures of precious or semiprecious stones, cigarette cases, small boxes, scent flasks, and his best-known creations, the Imperial Easter Eggs — each of an entirely different design. By the turn of the century, his influence had spread to other countries, and his work was revered by royalty and the very wealthy. The onset of the war marked the end of the era. Very little of his work remains on the market, and items that are available are very expensive. But several of his contemporaries were goldsmiths whose work can be equally enchanting. Among them are Klingert, Ovchinnikov, Smirnov, Ruckert, Loriye, Cheryatov, Kuzmichev, Nevalainen, Adler, Sbitnev, Third Artel, Wakewa, Holmstrom, Britzin, Wigstrom, Orlov, Nichols, and Plincke. Most of them produced excellent pieces similar to those made by Faberge between 1880 and 1910.

Perhaps the most important bronze Russian artist was Eugenie Alexandrovich Lanceray (1847 – 87). From 1875 until 1887, he modeled many equestrian groups of falconers and soldiers ranging in height from about 20" to 30". Some of them bear the Chopin foundry mark; they are presently worth from $4,000.00 up. Other excellent artists were Schmidt Felling (19th century), who specialized in mounted figures of cossacks wearing military uniforms, and Nicholas Leiberich (late 19th century), who also specialized in equestrian groups. Most of the pieces made by the above artists were signed and had the foundry mark (Chopin, Woerfell, etc.).

Russian porcelain is another field where Imperial connections have undoubtedly added to the interest of collectors and museums worldwide. The most important factories were Imperial Russian Porcelain, St. Petersburg (or Petrograd or Leningrad, 1744 – 1917); Gardner, Moscow (1765 – 1872); Kuznetsoff, St. Petersburg and Moscow (1800 – 1900); Korniloff, St. Petersburg (1800 – 1900); and Babunin, St. Petersburg (1800 – 1900).

Wedding icons, Kazan Mother of God and Christ as Lord Almighty, overlaid with silver-gilt riza, hallmarked Moscow 84, gilt frame, 19th century, 19x17", $3,300.00.

Bottle, cobalt glass w/gilt decor, faceted stopper, 19th C, 7½" ...**275.00**
Censor, silver, cross finial, bell ft, P Mulikov, ca 1900, 25" **500.00**
Charka, porc, mc flowers w/gold, Gardner, Moscow, 1910, 2½" .**100.00**
Ciborium set, E Fontikov, Moscow, ca 1880s, complete, 4½x2½" ..**300.00**
Cigar case, silver & niello, romantic scene, AI, 1888, 4¼" **275.00**
Cigarette case, silver, much eng, DN, ca 1897-1917, 4½" **550.00**
Cigarette case, silver, proposal scene, Moscow, ca 1905-17 ....**550.00**
Cigarette case, silver, romantic scene, Moscow, 19th C, 4½" **385.00**
Cigarette case, silver, Sadko w/Neptune's daughter, 19th C, 4½" ..**440.00**
Cross, altar; polished brass, 2-pc construction, 10x6" **550.00**
Cross, priestal; cast silver, on 22" silver chain, 1878 ....**715.00**
Cross, wall; cast brass & enamel, 19th C, 8x4½" **125.00**
Easter egg, arms of Moscow on wht, Imperial Porc, 1875-90, 2½" ..**450.00**
Easter egg, mc flower on gr, Imperial Porc, 1875-90, 4" **500.00**
Easter egg, mc flowers & gold scrolls, Imperial Porc, 1875-90, 3" .**450.00**
Easter egg, violets on bl, Imperial Porc, 1875-90, 3" **450.00**
Etrog container, silver, mk GC (Russian), dtd 1829, 7" W **3,250.00**
Eucharist box, silver-gilt, eng decor, FR, Moscow, 1894, 12½" .**1,000.00**
Goblet, wine; silver, emb vintage, Riedel, 1876, 8⅛" **800.00**
Icon, Annunciation, tempera on wood, early style, 19th C, 12x10" **950.00**
Icon, Kazan Mother of God, oil on wood w/silver-gilt, 1900, 11x9" .**3,575.00**
Icon, Mary, tempera on wood, 19th C, 14x12" **440.00**
Icon, Prophet Elijah, cast brass w/enamel, 19th C, 4x5" **275.00**
Icon, St Nicholas, tempera on wood, 19th C, 10½x8½" **385.00**
Icon, St Stephen of Perm, gilt/mc pnt on wood panel, 1700s, 13x9" ..**660.00**
Locket, enameled silver-gilt Easter egg w/cross, 1900s, ½" **200.00**
Match safe, gilt bronze, bear chained to tree form, 1875, 4" **500.00**
Salt cellar, gold washed w/mc enameling, AK 84 Khlebrikoff **550.00**
Samovar, brass urn form on dome base, wood hdls, 1900s, 18½" ...**500.00**
Samovar tray & waste bowl, silver, A Stepanovich Bragin, 79-oz ..**21,000.00**
Spoon, cloisonne on silver, Klingert, 84 hallmk, 7½" **250.00**
Tea set, porc, bl & wht w/gold trim, Made in USSR, 16-pc **415.00**
Wine, silver ped ft, cut decor, 84AA, 1888, 3¾" **125.00**

Sabino

Sabino art glass was produced by Marius-Ernest Sabino in France during the 1920s and '30s. It was made in opalescent, frosted, and colored glass and was designed to reflect the Art Deco style of that era. In 1960, using molds he modeled by hand, Sabino once again began to produce art glass using a special formula he himself developed that was characterized by a golden opalescence. Although the family continued to produce glassware for export after his death in 1971, they were never able to duplicate Sabino's formula.

Bottle, scent; bathing nude, w/stopper, 4¼" **100.00**
Bottle, scent; orchid blossoms, tapered, 4½" **100.00**
Figurine, angelfish, 4¾x4", pr **200.00**

Figurine, bass, 2¼", pr **155.00**
Figurine, bear on bk, playful, 3" **135.00**
Figurine, birds on limb **170.00**
Figurine, bluegill fish, 3¼x4¾" **105.00**
Figurine, cat, seated, 3¾" **85.00**
Figurine, dove, lg **245.00**
Figurine, egret **175.00**
Figurine, elephant w/trunk up, 2¼" **85.00**
Figurine, elephant w/trunk up, 4½" **120.00**
Figurine, gazelle, leaping, 4¼" **120.00**
Figurine, hen, 3⅝" **40.00**
Figurine, nude female w/floor-length hair, 6¾" **145.00**
Figurine, squirrel, 3" **55.00**
Plate, Christmas, 1st edition **50.00**
Sconce, frosted feather blades in quiver SP base, 28", pr **9,200.00**
Vase, clambroth opal, 8 flower panels in relief, 8" **1,200.00**
Vase, elongated leaves & berries, 6¼" **95.00**
Vase, Les Abeilles, globe shape, #7004, 1925 ....**325.00**

Salesman's Samples and Patent Models

Salesman's samples and patent models are often mistaken for toys or homemade folk art pieces. They are instead actual working models made by very skilled craftsmen who worked as model makers. Patent models were made until the early 1900s. After that, the patent office no longer required a model to grant a patent. The name of the inventor or the model maker and the date it was built is sometimes noted on the patent model. Salesman's samples were occasionally made by model makers, but often they were assembled by an employee of the company. These usually carried advertising messages to boost the sale of the product. Though they are still in use today, the most desirable examples date from the 1800s to about 1945.

Many small stoves are incorrectly termed a salesman's sample; remember that no matter how detailed one may be, it must be considered a toy unless accompanied by a carrying case, the indisputable mark of a salesman's sample.

Bank, parlor stove, CI, Vermont Casting **60.00**
Boot & shoe fastenings, leather/fabric, SE Thecker, 1880, 9x4" .**345.00**
Bowl, Cook-Rite, pottery, 3" **10.00**
Burglar alarm, wood/brass, Kislingbury, 1879, 12x3½x12" **690.00**
Coffee roaster, wood/tin/brass, Tinsley/Hackman, IA, 1877, 8x10" .**230.00**
Cook stove, Home Comfort, wht enamel, in case **3,200.00**
Dust pan, tin, D Colby, WA DC, 1869, 10x9x1½" **365.00**
Exhaust system for locomotives, brass, J Barney, 1859, 5x3x3" ...**460.00**

Holland furnace, cast iron and sheet metal, with accessories, VG in case, $100.00.

Furnace, Holland, CI/sheet metal, w/accessories, VG in case **100.00**
Loom, weaver's, oak, natural patina **325.00**
Milk can, Borden's, rare **100.00**

Pew book holder, wood & brass, NA Wright, 1867, 8x7x1" **58.00**
Potato steamer, tin funnel-like device, McDonald/Dewees, 1974 .**138.00**
Safe, Melink Mfg Co...OH, on wheels, 20x13½x16" **685.00**
Showcase, German silver, curved glass, 9x6x5½", EX **7,500.00**
Uterine supporter, brass, JS Shannon, Chicago, 8x5" **750.00**
Valances, 4 sm/5 lg panels, Viking-Celoglace Valances, MIB **465.00**
Washing machine, Double Washer, oak, natural finish, 18" **250.00**

Salt Shakers

The screw-top salt shaker was invented by John Mason in 1858. In 1871 when salt became more refined, some ceramic shakers were molded with pierced tops. 'Christmas' shakers, so called because of their December 25, 1877, patent date, were fitted with a rotary agitator designed to break up any lumps in the salt. There are four types: Christmas Barrel (rare in cranberry and amethyst); Christmas Panel (rare in colors); Christmas Pearl (opaque, pearly white with painted decor); and Octagon Waffle (clear, thick glass made in three sizes with a rotary agitator, sometimes having undated tops). The dated tops and patented agitators were produced by Dana K. Alden of Boston, who contracted with various glasshouses to make the glass bodies. The Christmas Barrel and Christmas Panel patterns were produced by Boston and Sandwich (though the Christmas Barrel was made elsewhere as well). Alden contracted with Mt. Washington to make the Christmas Pearl pattern, and Waffle Octagon was made by several glass factories, McKee and Federal among them. Both of the latter patterns were made as late as 1900. Identical shakers which have no agitator or dated top are the companion peppers; these fetch about 30% less than the salts on today's markets.

Today's Victorian salt shaker collectors' interests primarily encompass art glass, decorated cranberry and ruby glass, and custard and colored opalescent glass examples. (See also specified categories.) If you would like to learn more abut Victorian glass salt shakers, we recommend *The World of Salt Shakers, Second Edition* (updated in 1996), by Mildred and Ralph Lechner; their address may be found in the Directory under Virginia. Be sure to watch for their upcoming Volume III. (Mildred and Ralph deal only in Victorian shakers. Please do not contact them with questions pertaining to novelty types; queries require SASE.) In the following listings, prices are for single shakers unless noted 'pair.' Values are for old, original shakers. Some of these may have been reproduced, and this will be noted in the description.

Alden (Sheaf & Block), ruby stain, ca 1893, 3" **48.00**
Amberette, amber stain, ca 1885, 2¾" **60.00**
Babe Ruth figural, gold & red pnt, ca 1924-32, 5" **790.00**
Beaded Dahlia, pk cased, ca 1894-1900, 2⅝" **85.00**
Beads & Bulges, cranberry, ca 1894-1900, 3⅜" **100.00**
Benjamin Franklin, figural, 1875-80, 3¾" **250.00**
Block & Star, bl opaque, heavy, ca 1955-56, 2¾" **28.00**
Bow & Flower, wht opaque opal, HP gilt decor, 1901-08, 2¾" **25.00**
Bulging Leaf, pk opaque, ca 1894-1896, 2", pr **88.00**
Bulging Lobes, wht opaque opal w/HP brn decor, 1904-10, 2⅞" ..**25.00**
Bulging Nine-Leaf Variant, wht opaque, ca 1897-1900, 3" **36.00**
Caramel Cactus, chocolate opaque, ca 1902, 2⅞" **120.00**
Carmen, amber stain, ca 1896, 3⅛" **36.00**
Christmas Panel, electric bl, ca 1877, 3⅞" **150.00**
Chrysanthemum Sprig, bl opaque **450.00**
Columbian Coin, gold coins, ca 1891, 2⅞" **55.00**
Corn, custard opaque, ca 1894-1901, 3⅛" **65.00**
Cotton Bale, bl opaque, ca 1894-95, 2⅝" **42.00**
Delaware (4-Petal Flower), rose flashed w/gold, ca 1899, 2⅝" **125.00**
Doodad, gr opaque, ca 1896-1902, 3⅝" **40.00**
Double Deck, wht opaque, ca 1897-1902, 2¾" **50.00**
Double Leaf, purple variegated opaque, ca 1895-1901, 3⅝" **110.00**

Eagle's Forget-Me-Not, wht opaque opal, ca 1901, 2⅜" **32.00**
Empress, emerald gr w/gold, ca 1898-99, 3¼" **85.00**
Epaulette, wht opaque opal w/gold, ca 1900-05, 2⅜" **15.00**
Eye Winker, ca 1889-95, 3" (+) **36.00**
Fandangle, gr opaque, ca 1895-98, 2⅝" **48.00**
Fish, gr cased, 1894-1900, 3⅛" **60.00**
Flora, emerald gr w/gold, ca 1895, 3⅛" **92.00**
Flower & Pleat, clear & frosted, ruby stain, ca 1892-93, 3⅛" **56.00**
Flower Band, pigeon blood satin, 1901-02, 2⅝" **72.00**
Flower Bouquet, bl opaque, ca 1891, 3" **38.00**
Forget-Me-Not, pk variegated, ca 1887-91, 2" **42.00**
Gargoyle, wht opaque opal, ca 1905, 2¼" **45.00**
Geranium, ornate decor on opal, 1884-90, 3" **700.00**
Half Cone, pk cased satin, ca 1895-1900, 2⅛" **95.00**
Heart, pk to wht variegated, ca 1894-97, 2⅞" **72.00**
Heavy Gothic, ruby stain, ca 1892, 2¾" **65.00**
Hobnail in Square, crystal & wht opal, ca 1887, 2⅞" **72.00**
Imperial's Grape, pigeon blood, 1965-70, 3⅜" **28.00**
Jeweled Moon & Star, amber stain, bl HP star, ca 1896, 3" **50.00**
Lacy Scroll, yel cased, 2-pc metal lid, ca 1895, 3⅜" **175.00**
Lantern, wire-hdld metal lid, ca 1904, 4" **48.00**
McKee's Flower Panel, gr opaque, ca 1904-10, 2¾" **32.00**
Nine-Rib Melon, cranberry, ca 1895-1900, 1⅞" **220.00**
Overlapping Leaf, pk variegated opaque, ca 1896-1900, 1⅞" **78.00**
Paneled Four Dot, pk-to-wht variegated opaque, 1894-96, 2¼" ...**60.00**
Paneled Shell, pk triple cased, ca 1894-1900, 3" **78.00**

Paneled Sprig, North-wood, clear opal, $110.00 for the pair.

Paneled Teardrop, gr opaque cased, 1905-08, 3⅛" **125.00**
Peachbloom, shaded cased glass, 3¼" **725.00**
Pineapple, pk & wht variegated opaque, ca 1894-98, 3" **60.00**
Pleated Skirt, pk opaque, ca 1891, 1¾" **50.00**
Quilt, bl opaque, ca 1894-98, 2½" **50.00**
Radiance, ruby, 1936-39, 2½", pr **65.00**
Reverse Swirl, cranberry opal, orig screw-on lid, 2½" **95.00**
Rhea-D (Protruding Panels), wht opaque opal, ca 1889-1900, 2¾" ..**45.00**
Rib & Swirl, wht opaque opal, ca 1878-1887, 4" **60.00**
Ring Band, custard opaque w/gold, ca 1901, 2⅞" **80.00**
Ring Neck, pk & wht swirl w/gold mica, ca 1889-90, 3" **160.00**
Scroll & Net, wht opaque opal, ca 1897-1903, 3" **60.00**
Scroll in Scroll, custard, ca 1896-01, 2¼" **60.00**
Spirea Band, dk amber, ca 1886-91, 3" **36.00**
Square S, bl opaque, ca 1890, 3¼" **55.00**
Star of Bethlehem (Nearcut Star), ruby stain, ca 1909, 2⅞" **72.00**
Swag w/Brackets, amethyst w/gold, ca 1904, 3" **85.00**
Tarentum's Atlanta (Diamond & Teardrop), 1894, 3" **40.00**
Thousand Eye, vaseline, ca 1875-80, 2¾" **60.00**
Thrush, wht opaque opal, ca 1890, 2¾" **150.00**
Tiny Thumbprint, amber, sq base, rnd shoulder, 2-pc lid, 2½" ...**135.00**
Tiptoe (Ramona), ca 1904, 3⅛" **30.00**
Twisted Scroll, wht opaque opal w/HP mc decor, 1899-1904, 3¼" ..**50.00**
Vermont, custard w/decor, ca 1899, 2⅜" **125.00**

Wide Diagonal Swirl, bl opaque, ca 1894-96, 2⅜" **55.00**
X-Ray, emerald gr w/gold, ca 1896-99, 2¾" **80.00**

Novelty Salt Shakers

Those interested in novelty shakers will enjoy *Salt and Pepper Shakers, Volumes I, II, III,* and *IV,* by Helene Guarnaccia, and *The Collector's Encyclopedia of Salt and Pepper Shakers, Figural and Novelty, Volumes I* and *II,* by Melva Davern. Both are available at your local library or from Collector Books. Note: 'Mini' shakers are no taller than 2". Instead of having a cork, the user was directed to 'use tape to cover hole.' Our advisor for novelty salt shakers is Judy Posner; she is listed in the Directory under Pennsylvania. See also Regal; Rosemeade; Occupied Japan; Shawnee; other specific manufacturers.

Advertising, Texaco gas pumps, silver and red plastic, 3", MIB, $85.00 for the pair.

Advertising, Bert & Harry for Piels Beer, 1950s, 4", pr **225.00**
Advertising, Chicken of the Sea Tuna, Am pottery, pr **18.00**
Advertising, Dairy Queen girls, flat on bks, 1960s, 4", pr **195.00**
Advertising, Ft Pitt beer bottles, pr **15.00**
Advertising, Hershey's Chocolate ice cream sodas, 3½", pr **29.00**
Advertising, Ken L Ration cat & dog, plastic, F&F, pr **28.00**
Advertising, Max & Ray, Camel Cigarettes, hard plastic, 1993, pr ..**75.00**
Advertising, Nugget Sam for Nugget Casino, Japan, 1950s, 4", pr ..**125.00**
Advertising, Slate Belt Dairy milk bottles, 1930s, 3¼", pr **45.00**
Advertising, Sunshine Bakers, porc, Japan, 2¾", pr **29.00**
Advertising, Tappan Chefs, vintage Japan, 4¼", pr **25.00**
Advertising, Westinghouse washer & dryer, plastic, 1950s, pr **25.00**
Animals, cat & ball of yarn, Norcrest foil label, 3", pr **28.00**
Animals, mermaids, bsk, Florida emb on tail, Kenmar, 3½", pr **49.00**
Animals, mice dressed up, Twin Winton, 5½", pr **39.00**
Animals, monkeys in fancy clothes, Japan, 2¾", pr **16.00**
Animals, sad-eye pup & garbage can, 1960s, unmk, 5", pr **35.00**
Animals, squirrels dressed for ice skating, Japan, 3¾", pr **24.00**
Anthropomorphic, corn fellows, Japan, 1950s, 3½", pr **35.00**
Anthropomorphic, scarecrow couple, Am pottery, 3", pr **28.00**
Anthropomorphic, spoon & fork people, Japan, 5", pr **35.00**
Character, Gen MacArthur's pipe & hat, vintage Am pottery, 1¾", pr .**15.00**
Character, Jerry Colonna, Made in Japan label, 5", 3-pc set **95.00**
Character, Popeye & Olive Oyl, bsk, unmk, 1960s, 6", pr **125.00**
Character, Shmoo, porc, Japan, 1950s, 4¼", pr **250.00**
Character, Smiley faces, Have a..., TreasureCraft USA, 4", pr **29.00**
Comic, happy smiley feet, 1960s era, unmk, 3½", pr **22.00**
Comic, lady w/poodle & man w/packages, Japan, 5", pr **90.00**
Disney, Figaro the Cat, Nat'l Porc, 1940s, 2", pr **125.00**
Disney, Pinocchio, porc, mc w/gold, 1940s, 5", pr **165.00**
Disney, Silly Symphony Pigs, 1930s, Japan, 3", pr **65.00**
Disney, Snow White's Happy, 3¼", scarce, pr **250.00**
Food, chocolate & strawberry ice cream cones, 1950s, Am, 3½", pr ..**14.00**
Inanimate objects, binoculars & case, unglazed bottoms, 3", pr **15.00**
Inanimate objects, fireplace & logs, unglazed bottom, 2½", pr **18.00**

Inanimate objects, gun & bullet, unmk, 4", pr **24.00**
Mini, drum & bugle, Arcadia, 2", pr **45.00**
Mini, McGuffey's reader & school bell, Arcadia, pr **28.00**
Mini, paint can & paint brush, 1950s, can: 1½", pr **24.00**
Mini, squirrel w/acorn, Arcadia, 2", pr **45.00**
Nursery rhyme, Humpty Dumpty, plastic, hair forms lid, 4½", pr ..**22.00**
People, boxing men, vintage pottery, unglazed bottoms, 3½", pr ..**49.00**
People, child in top hat, stacking, Japan, 5", pr **45.00**
People, Colonial couple, Japan, 3½", pr **17.00**
People, Strasburg railroad engineer & conductor, Japan, 4¼", pr .**35.00**

Salts, Open

Before salt became refined, processed, and free-flowing as we know it today, it was necessary to serve it in a salt cellar. An innovation of the early 1800s, the master salt was placed by the host and passed from person to person. Smaller individual salts were a part of each place setting. A small silver spoon was used to sprinkle it onto the food.

If you would like to learn more about the subject of salts, we recommend *5,000 Open Salts,* written by William Heacock and Patricia Johnson, with many full-color illustrations and current values. Our advisor for this category is Chris Christensen; he is listed in the Directory under California. In the listings below, the numbers refer to *Open Salts* by Johnson and Heacock and *Pressed Glass Salt Dishes* by L.W. and D.B. Neal. Lines with 'repro' within the description reflect values for reproduced salts.

Key:
EPNS — electroplated nickel silver HM — hallmarked

Animals, Figurals, and Novelties

Bird & Berry, amber or bl, McKee, HJ-931M, old, ea **65.00**
Bird & Berry, mk Degenhart, HJ-932, colors, minimum value **25.00**
Bird & Berry, unmk Degenhart, HJ-933, colors, minimum value .**15.00**
Chicken, covered, milk glass, Westmoreland, HJ-949 ....**25.00**

Donkey with salts on sides, green and black with gold trim, France, #318, 3½", $125.00.

Duck, covered, clear, red beak, HJ-1012 ....**45.00**
Duck, pressed, heavy, HJ-4677 ....**45.00**
Elk pulling sleigh, mk 800 silver **595.00**
Rabbit, covered, clear, mk Vallerystahl, HJ-3750 ....**55.00**
Sleigh, Fostoria, HJ-3735, ca 1940 ....**55.00**
Squirrel on stump, various colors, Boyd, HJ-929/HJ-930, repro **10.00**
Swan, Crown Tuscan, Cambridge, HJ-936 ....**45.00**
Swan, str neck, Crown Tuscan, Cambridge, HJ-935 ....**110.00**
Swan, str neck, gr, pk or amber, Cambridge, HJ-935, ea **45.00**
Swan pulling cart, bl carnival, HJ-941, 1970s repro **40.00**
Swan pulling cart, clear, HJ-941 shape, ca 1890 ....**75.00**
Turtle, amber, bl or milk glass, HJ-4475, 3¼", ea **65.00**
Wheelbarrow, chocolate, Greentown, HJ-4669 ....**800.00**

Art Glass

Crown Milano, HJ-46 ....**200.00**
Daum Nancy, flowers, mk, HJ-11 ....**900.00**
English Victorian, bl ruffled rigaree, SP fr, HJ-96 style **250.00**
English Victorian, cranberry ruffled, clear rigaree, HJ-312 ...**150.00**
Millefiori, rnd, HJ-609, ca 1890 ....**350.00**
Monot Stumpf, HJ-19 to HJ-22, M **125.00**
Mt Washington, decor, HJ-35 to HJ-44, ea **150.00**
Quezal, mk, HJ-18, 1" dia **295.00**
Steuben, bl, mk Aurene, HJ-14, 2" dia **450.00**
Steuben, Calcite, ped, HJ-34 ....**325.00**
Tiffany, ruffled, bl, HJ-30 or HJ-31, ea **500.00**
Tiffany, ruffled, gold, sgn LCT Favrille, HJ-32 ....**200.00**
Webb, bl, lily design, HJ-85 ....**1,200.00**
Webb, cranberry, acorn design, HJ-84 ....**1,400.00**
Webb, 3-color, HJ-27 ....**1,500.00**

China and Porcelain

Austrian, HP, mk, HJ-1272 ....**15.00**
Elfinware, allover florals, German, HJ-1270 ....**35.00**
French, mk Sampson, HJ-1786, ca 1880, repro of Chinese **125.00**
Goss, mini ancient salt cellar, HJ-2029 ....**45.00**
Haviland, factory decor, HJ-1397 ....**35.00**
KPM, dbl, boy between 2 bowls, HJ-1155 or HJ-1156, ea **325.00**
KPM, dbl, w/cherub, mk, HJ-1107 ....**325.00**
Lenox, silver o/l, HJ-1815 ....**60.00**
Limoges, HP, mk, HJ-1275 ....**15.00**
Meissen, scroll ft decor, HJ-1812 to HJ-1814, ea **125.00**
Meissen, sq, HJ-1595, ind **60.00**
Nippon, HP, HJ-1358 to HJ-1364, ind, ea **15.00**
Nippon, HP, ped ft, HJ-1484 or HJ-1485, ea **18.00**
Nippon, HP buckets, HJ-1446 to HJ-1457, ind, ea **15.00**
Pickard, sq, HJ-1569 ....**75.00**
Royal Bayreuth, HJ-1669 ....**125.00**
Royal Bayreuth, sheep, ped ft, HJ-1666 ....**125.00**
Royal Berlin, HJ-1155 or HJ-1156, 5", ea **275.00**
Royal Copenhagen, oval, HJ-1672, ca 1920 ....**45.00**
Royal Worcester, HJ-1861, ca 1870 ....**150.00**

Cut Glass

Amber flashed, ped ft, hdls, English, HJ-2060, master **150.00**
Amethyst, etched, Hawkes, HJ-2038 ....**75.00**
Bl cut to clear, ped ft, HJ-67 ....**150.00**
Clear, etched, rnd, Hawkes, HJ-3268 to HJ-3269, ea **35.00**
Clear, oval, Hawkes, HJ-3209 ....**55.00**
Clear, oval on ped, shell shape, French, HJ-3717, 4⅞" **195.00**
Clear, ped ft, mk Libbey **85.00**
Clear, rnd, nappy style, HJ-3170 ....**54.00**
Cranberry, rnd, Moser type, HJ-305 ....**85.00**
Cranberry, serrated top edge, rnd, HJ-304 ....**65.00**
Daisy & Button, oval, HJ-3214 ....**20.00**
Daisy & Button, rnd tub, HJ-2853 ....**25.00**
Fan & Diamond, HJ-3416 or HJ-3417, ea **15.00**
Heart, club, spade, diamond, HJ-3033 to HJ-3034, 4 for **195.00**
Zippered, HJ-3088 or HJ-3089, ea **15.00**

Lacy Sandwich Glass

Avon, HJ-3506, repro **10.00**
French, amber, HJ-2117, ca 1900, repro, VG **85.00**
Lafayette Boat, sgn Pairpoint, ca 1980, repro **25.00**

Metro Museum of Art, vaseline, bl, etc, repro, ea 25.00
Neal BF-1C, very rare, HJ-3462 ....195.00
Neal BS-2, fiery opal, scarce, 3¼", EX 85.00
Neal BS-2, fiery opal, scarce, 3¼", NM 275.00
Neal BS-3, violet-bl, 3" L, EX 235.00
Neal BT-5, bl opal, 3⅝" L, EX 900.00

Neal CD-2B, clear, with lid, attributed to Sandwich, extremely rare, EX, $1,800.00.

Neal CN-1A, cobalt, rprs, 3⅛" L 195.00
Neal CN-1A, minor chips, scarce, 3⅛" L 125.00
Neal EE-1A, sm chips, 3" L 125.00
Neal EE-3B, Scrolled Eagle, 3¼" L 150.00
Neal EE-3B, Scrolled Eagle, fiery opal, 3¼" L, EX 450.00
Neal MV-3 variant, chips, rare, 2⅝" 300.00
Neal NE-3, rare, 3" L 175.00
Neal RP-18A, cobalt (unlisted), sm chips/check, 3" 150.00
Neal SD-4E, 3⅛" L 175.00
Neal SL-1, cobalt, sm chips, rare, 3" L 275.00
Neal SN-1, cobalt, edge flakes, scarce, 3" L 150.00

Pottery and Faience

Adams, HM, HJ-1849, ca 1902 ....110.00
Niloak, rnd, mk, HJ-1735, 1½" 45.00
Quimper, dbl w/dog, HJ-1134 ....115.00
Quimper, pr shoes, HJ-1162, ca 1940 ....45.00
Royal Doulton, HP animals, HJ-1859, ca 1890 ....85.00
Royal Doulton, pyramid shape, HJ-1870, ca 1873 ....140.00
Satsuma, various shapes, HJ-1931 to HJ-1933, ca 1970s, ea 20.00
Wedgwood, HM, HJ-1871, ca 1900 ....125.00

Pressed Pattern Glass, Clear

Amazon, HJ-2568, ind 12.00
American, HJ-2574, ind 10.00
Applied Bands, HJ-2934 ....30.00
Arched Leaf, HJ-3530 ....35.00
Atlanta, HJ-2758, ind 60.00
Banded Star, HJ-2939 ....60.00
Beaded Acorn Medallion, HJ-3533 ....45.00
Bearded Head, HJ-3636 ....60.00
Bow Tie, HJ-2548, ind 25.00
Candlewick, HJ-2642 ....12.00
Diamond Point Discs, HJ-2930 ....20.00
Diamond Rosettes, HJ-3407 ....35.00
English Hobnail, master 15.00
Fancy Arch, HJ-3058 ....30.00
Fandango, HJ-2673 ....25.00
Frosted Eagle, HJ-2967, ind 45.00
Grasshopper, HJ-3573 ....45.00
Hartford, HJ-2972, ind 25.00
Hawaiian Lei, HJ-2577, ind 12.00

Jersey Swirl, HJ-3397, ind 12.00
Lady Hamilton, HJ-2954, M 20.00
Liberty Bell, HJ-2689 ....65.00
Loop & Dart, ped ft, HJ-2955 ....45.00
Mardi Gras, HJ-2534 ....12.00
Marjorie, HJ-2676 ....15.00
Moon & Star, ped ft, ind 45.00
Noonday Sun, HJ-2591, ind 22.00
Picket, HJ-2792 ....20.00
Pillows, HJ-2697 ....45.00
Scroll w/Flowers, HJ-3352 ....35.00
Snail, HJ-2656, ind 25.00
Sprig in Snow, HJ-2966 ....30.00
Stippled Scroll, HJ-3538 ....40.00
Tree of Life, 'Salt,' ped ft, HJ-3581 ....125.00
Urn, Heisey, HJ-2969, ind 50.00
Urn, Heisey, master 65.00
Washington Centennial, HJ-3510 ....45.00
3 Face, HJ-4428, old 50.00
3 Face, HJ-4430 to HJ-4431, repro, ea 15.00

Pressed Pattern Glass, Colored

Applied Bands, amber flashed, HJ-2100 ....55.00
Atterbury, color repro 6.00
Bagware, HJ-449 ....20.00
Basketweave, milk glass, mk Atterbury, HJ-4466, master 50.00
Basketweave, milk glass, mk Atterbury, HJ-4482, ind 50.00
Beatty Rib, bl opal, HJ-196 ....35.00
Beatty Rib, wht opal, HJ-196 ....25.00
Brazilian, gr, HJ-335 ....55.00
Chippendale, amber, ped ft, HJ-596 ....35.00
Eye Winker, repro 8.00
Fish figural, milk glass, HJ-4464, master 125.00
Flemish, amber or gr, HJ-507, ea 25.00
Gr opaline, sgn Baccarat, HJ-491 ....75.00
Illinois, ruby stained, HJ-298 ....65.00
King's Crown, ruby stained, HJ-2776 ....65.00
Lady Caroline, bl, English, HJ-127 ....135.00
Leaf & Rib, HJ-505, ind 25.00
Lords & Ladies, bl, English, HJ-137 ....75.00
Lords & Ladies, canary, English, HJ-137 ....65.00
Moon & Star, all colors are repros 8.00
Square Hobnail, canary opal, HJ-197 ....65.00
Tree of Life, bl, HJ-2952, ind 45.00
Tree Stump, Xd logs, milk glass, HJ-4473 ....55.00
Triangle, bl, gr, amethyst, or canary, HJ-442, ea 30.00
William & Mary, rose, English, HJ-568 ....55.00
Wreath & Shell, bl opal, HJ-444 ....110.00
3-Panel, bl, HJ-429, ind 18.00
3-Panel, canary or gr, HJ-564, ea 25.00

Silverplate

Babies, Art Nouveau, gold-washed bowl, English, HJ-4283 ....160.00
Boat shape on ped ft, cobalt liner, Am, HJ-661, VG 55.00
Crackle glass, cranberry flashed, Victorian fr, VG 150.00
Crackle glass in Victorian holder, HJ-4215 to HJ-4217, VG, ea 85.00
Dolphin holds shell, Pairpoint, HJ-4382, master, VG 115.00
Heart shape, 3 ball ft, Wilcox, worn, HJ-4067 ....18.00
Lattice holder, clear liner, ind 12.00
Lattice holder, cobalt liner, HJ-653, ind 20.00
Oval, cranberry liner, ftd lattice holder, HJ-317, VG 75.00
Oval, 4-ftd, clear liner, English, HJ-3945, VG 40.00

Oval lattice, gr liner, Derby, HJ-378, VG 95.00
Overshot cranberry liner, sq fr, HJ-4215 to HJ-4217, ea 85.00
Rams' heads, rnd, Whiting, HJ-4252, VG 65.00
Rnd bowl w/kangaroo, EPNS Australia, HJ-4305, VG 35.00
Shell w/dolphin legs, HJ-4278, VG 20.00
Tulip on leaf, American, HJ-4155, VG 35.00
Victorian holder, clear liner, hdl, HJ-3918, EX 75.00
Wolf-like dogs w/bowl on bk, Meriden, HJ-4322, VG 150.00

Sterling

Albert Cole, medallion, HJ-4208, ca 1850 ....250.00
American, Lenox insert, lattice holder, HJ-3856 ....45.00
Austria-Hungary, cut/flashed bowl, sterling ped, HJ-106 ....225.00
Austria-Hungary, wht opal cut-bk bowl, sterling ped, HJ-138 ....150.00
Chinese, mini house w/shaker set, HJ-4743 ....225.00

Continental silver gold-washed bowl on dolphin pedestal, ca 1810, 2½", $150.00; Sterling shell on pedestal base, bird atop shell, 3", $50.00.

English, boxed set of 2, apostle spoon, HJ-4794 ....200.00
French, ornate, HM, matching spoon, HJ-3937, ind 125.00
German, basket, ped ft, HM 800, HJ-4228 ....110.00
German, cobalt liner, oval, ftd, HJ-724 ....85.00
German, elk pulling sleigh, HM 800, 6" 526.00
German, swan, HM 800, matching spoon, HJ-4299, ca 1890 ....95.00
Gorham, medallion, ped ft, HJ-3976, ca 1870 ....150.00
Gorham, rnd, ornate lattice, cranberry liner, HJ-323, 1890s 160.00
Kerr, Art Nouveau, ped ft, cobalt liner, HJ-702, 1880 ....95.00
Reed & Barton, ped ft, HJ-4226, ca 1900, master, pr 95.00
Russian, chair, HM, dtd, HJ-4737 ....500.00
Russian, HP over sterling, 3 ball ft, HJ-2004 ....650.00
Russian, rnd, ftd, HM, HJ-4053, ca 1893, ind 85.00
Steiff, chased, w/pepper, HJ-4385, ca 1918, pr 125.00
Tiffany, fish, matching spoon, HJ-2002 to HJ-2005, ea 125.00

Other Types

Bl opal, dbl, ped ft, French, HJ-144, ca 1910 ....95.00
Bl slag, tureen shape, Sowerby, HJ-385 ....85.00
Intaglio, HP animals/etched butterfly, HJ-156 or HJ-157, ea 65.00
Intaglio, pnt animal center, HJ-160 ....65.00
Intaglio, 2 in jeweled tree holder, HJ-90 ....145.00
Plique-a-jour, Viking HM, HJ-83 ....950.00
Shell on sterling ped, English HJ, HJ-202 ....35.00
Threaded glass, gr, 'Salt,' sterling rim, HJ-377 ....125.00
Venetian glass, swans 35.00

Samplers

American samplers were made as early as the colonial days; even

earlier examples from 17th-century England still exist today. Changes in style and design are evident down through the years. Verses were not added until the late 17th century. By the 18th century, samplers were used not only for sewing experience but also as an educational tool. Young ladies, who often signed and dated their work, embroidered numbers and letters of the alphabet and practiced fancy stitches as well. Fruits and flowers were added for borders; birds, animals, and Adam and Eve became popular subjects. Later houses and other buildings were included. By the 19th century, the American Eagle and the little red schoolhouse had made their appearances.

Many factors bear on value: design and workmanship, strength of color, the presence of a signature and/or a date (both being preferred over only one or the other, and earlier is better), and, of course, condition.

ABCs, homespun, sgn, dtd 187-, 8¾x10¾" 220.00
ABCs (3 styles)/trees/flowers/etc, PA, 1796, 15x11"+old fr 950.00
ABCs (4 styles) in 4 lines/verse/house/etc, PA, 1834, 15x16" .1,000.00
ABCs/animals/people/lobster, homespun, 1769, stains, 21x10" ..935.00
ABCs/bird, homespun, wear/stains, fr, 8½x17" 770.00
ABCs/borders/#s/Xmas 75, cotton, fr, 13½x13½" 365.00
ABCs/flowers/birds/vines/people, homespun, 1844, 15x14", G ...350.00
ABCs/flowers/borders/crown, homespun, sgn/1822, fr, 15x15" ...500.00
ABCs/flowers/geometrics, homespun, 1739, fr, 15x11⅝" 1,000.00
ABCs/flowers/inscription, homespun, sgn/1770, 10x7"+fr 1,725.00
ABCs/flowers/trees, homespun, sgn, 19x15" 275.00
ABCs/hearts/sheep/etc, EX colors, no date, 18x9" 225.00
ABCs/house/birds/etc, silk on cotton, sgn/1868, 10x8½" 385.00
ABCs/numerals/flowers/etc, homespun, 1826, stain, 24x19" 385.00
ABCs/verse, homespun, sgn/1731, wear/fading, fr, 14x5½" 600.00
ABCs/verse/flowers, homespun, sgn/1831, 15x12½" 1,380.00
ABCS/verse/potted flowers/birds, 1808, 12x12" 375.00
ABCs/verse/trees/ducks/pagoda/pyramids, homespun, 1765, 17x10" .700.00
ABCs/verse/trees/house/etc, sgn/1814, 19x14", VG 440.00
ABCs/verse/urns/willow/etc, homespun, sgn, 1835, rprs, 18x19" .275.00
Angels/flowers/birds/etc, homespun, sgn/1799, fr, 15" sq 600.00
Family record, homespun, early 1800s, 17x17" 415.00
Front View of Temple of Solomon.../verses, 1846, 23x25" 865.00
Verse/Adam & Eve in garden/animals, sgn/1834, 15x12", EX 980.00
Verse/flowers, homespun, sgn/1792, MA, 16x14", NM 7,475.00
Verse/flowers/bird, silk on gauze, sgn/1818, orig fr, 14x11" 500.00
Verse/flowers/birds/animals/etc, homespun, 1835, rprs, 19x18" ..350.00
Verse/flowers/birds/crowns/animals, homespun, sgn/1844, 23x20" .550.00
Verse/flowers/birds/etc, homespun, sgn/1812, fr, 16x13", G 385.00
Verse/flowers/dogs, homespun, sgn/1794, stains, 12x10" 500.00
Verse/flowers/house, homespun, sgn/1845, 20x22", G 525.00
Verse/flowers/house/trees, homespun, sgn/1829, 18x13"+fr 1,000.00
Verse/flowers/trees/etc, homespun, sgn/1824, 19x15"+fr 750.00
Verse/flowers/trees/windmill/men, fine gauze, 12x11" 900.00

Sandwich Glass

The Boston and Sandwich Glass Company was founded in 1820 by Deming Jarves in Sandwich, Massachusetts. Their first products were simple cruets, salts, half-pint jugs, and lamps. They were attributed with being one of the first to perfect a method for pressing glass, a step toward the manufacture of the 'lacy' glass which they made until about 1840. Many other types of glass were made there — cut, colored, snakeskin, hobnail, and opalescent among them. After the Civil War, profits began to dwindle due to the keen competition of the Western factories which were situated in areas rich in natural gas and easily accessible sand and coal deposits. The end came with an unreconcilable wage dispute between the workers and the company, and the factory closed in 1888. See also Cup Plates; Lacy Glass; Salts, Open; other specific types of glass.

Basket, Tomato, yel exterior, thorn hdl, 5½" **250.00**
Bottle, bellows; clear w/red & wht loopings, 13½" **750.00**
Bottle, scent; Baby T'print, vaseline, orig stopper **395.00**
Bottle, scent; canary yel, corset waist, smooth base, 4⅞" **1,450.00**
Bottle, scent; cobalt, 12-sided, sloped shoulders, 7¼" **150.00**
Bottle, scent; purple amethyst, corset waist, 8-sided, 4⅛" **180.00**
Bowl, free-blown opal center w/gr threading at ruffle, 8" **295.00**
Candlestick, alabaster/clambroth, petal socket/dolphin stem, 10" .**550.00**
Candlestick, amethyst, hex socket/stem/base, 8⅜", NM **600.00**
Candlestick, bl opaque petal socket, clambroth Loop base, 7" **200.00**
Candlestick, bl opaque socket, wht dolphin stem, hex base, 9½" .**1,900.00**
Candlestick, bl socket w/6 dolphins, wht dolphin base, 9½" ...**3,000.00**
Candlestick, wht opaque, petal & loop variant, 7½" **100.00**
Candlesticks, canary, hex sockets/stems/bases, pr, 8", EX **375.00**
Cigar holder, pk to wht to clear, rare, 2¾" **60.00**
Vase, emerald gr, tulip form, 1845-65, 10⅛", NM **1,500.00**
Vase, gr, flared rim, polished pontil, wafer connector, att, 4½" **85.00**
Vase, sapphire bl, slim, tooled scalloped rim, 1840-60, 9½", NM .**1,400.00**

Sarreguemines

Sarreguemines, France, is the location of Utzschneider and Company, founded in 1770, producers of majolica, transfer-printed dinnerware, figurines, and novelties which are usually marked 'Sarreguemines.'

Figurine, fox, wht, #5548, 10x18" **195.00**
Figurine, Madonna, creamware, tall **35.00**
Humidor, man at bbl figural, #350, 7x8" **330.00**
Humidor, man in blk top hat, #3338, 7" **580.00**

Pitchers: Man's smiling face and man's winking face, 8½", from $275.00 to $300.00 each.

Pitcher, brn & tan crystalline, imp mk, 7" **150.00**
Pitcher, John Bull's face, #3257, 6½" **330.00**
Pitcher, judge's face, #4502, 6½" **550.00**
Pitcher, man's face, blk beard/mustache, purple hat, rpr, 8½" **275.00**
Pitcher, man's face, brn w/red int, #653, 6½" **45.00**
Pitcher, man's face, bulging eyes, red hat, #8715, 5½" **440.00**
Pitcher, man's face, gr hat, ribbon & bow, 5½" **77.00**
Pitcher, man's face, red hat, #7891, 7½" **120.00**
Pitcher, man's face, rosy cheeks & chin, #3818, 6" **195.00**
Pitcher, man's face w/teeth, #3181, 8½" **275.00**
Pitcher, pig figural, 9½" **330.00**
Plaque, man at desk, lady w/basket, flowers, #2058, 11½x11" **130.00**
Plate, oyster; gray & salmon shells on wht, 9¼", NM **100.00**
Plates, man & lady on bl, #3424/#3425, pierced to hang, 9½", pr .**220.00**
Platter, lg flowers on dk gr, 13½" **75.00**
Platter, mc fruits, 12½" **75.00**
Platter, oyster; 12 gray & salmon wells on wht, 15" **300.00**

Vase, Black man w/banjo figural, several signs, #1845, 12½" ..**2,300.00**
Vase, 2 elephant heads on sides, mc, turq int, 12½", EX **330.00**
Water cooler, shell w/gr seaweed, wall hanging, 19" **880.00**

Satin Glass

Satin glass is simply glassware with a velvety matt finish achieved through the application of an acid bath. This procedure has been used by many companies since the 20th century, both here and abroad, on many types of colored and art glass. See also Mother-of-Pearl; Webb.

Shell pattern, pink with hand-painted decoration, left to right: Biscuit jar, $235.00; Creamer and sugar bowl, $245.00 set.

Biscuit jar, tan w/wine flowers, metal rim, twist bail, 6" **145.00**
Mug, loopings, pk & gold on wht, frosted hdl, 3½" **175.00**
Rose bowl, bl w/HP birds, 4-crimp, 2⅞x2¾" **85.00**
Vase, bl verre moire, wht opaque pull-ups, fluted rim, 3¾" **170.00**
Vase, butterscotch to wht, stick-neck gourd form, 15" **195.00**
Vase, yel cased, stick neck, 7½x3½" **145.00**

Satsuma

Satsuma is a type of fine cream crackle-glaze pottery or earthenware made in Japan as early as the 17th century. The earliest wares, made at the original kiln in the Satsuma province, were enameled with only simple florals. By the late 18th century, a floral brocade (or nishikide design) was favored, and similar wares were being made at other kilns under the direction of the Lord of Satsuma. In the early part of the 19th century, a diaper pattern was added to the florals. Gold and silver enamels were used for accents by the latter years of the century. During the 1850s, as the quality of goods made for export to the Western world increased and the style of decoration began to evolve toward becoming more appealing to the Westerners, human forms such as Arhats, Kannon, geisha girls, and samurai warriors were added. Today the most valuable pieces are those marked 'Kinkozan,' 'Shuzan,' 'Ryuzan,' and 'Kozan.' The genuine Satsuma 'mon' or mark is a cross within a circle — usually in gold on the body or lid, or in red on the base of the ware. Character marks may be included.

Caution: Much of what is termed 'Satsuma' comes from the Showa Period (1926 to the present); it is not true Satsuma but a simulated type, a cheaper pottery with heavy enamel. Collectors need to be aware that much of the of the 'Satsuma' today is really Satsuma style and should not carry the values of true Satsuma.

Bowl, costumed figures/flowers/jewels, 1" rim band, 7x9" **100.00**
Bowl, Thousand Butterflies, scalloped rim, gold trim, 3" **300.00**
Bowl, 10 female musicians, 8-sided, 1890s, 8" **190.00**
Ewer, dragon, blk w/red on dk brn w/flowers, mk, 13x10½" **500.00**

Jar, arhats on gold ground, ftd base, Meiji, w/lid, 22" **2,100.00**
Jar, Thousand Butterflies, gold trim, w/lid, 2¾x3" **350.00**
Vase, chrysanthemums & irises, red/bl/violet, 1890s, 4¾", pr **100.00**
Vase, floral, mc on gr to brn, hdls, flared rim, 12½" **170.00**
Vase, florals & geometrics, animal hdls, pillow form, 9½" **170.00**
Vase, florals & geometrics, dolphin hdls, rtcl neck, 16¼" **395.00**
Vase, gardenias w/gold, jeweled diaper pattern, 9½x4½" **95.00**
Vase, geishes & flowers w/gold & jewels, hdls, 12", pr **185.00**
Vase, samurai reserve, mc w/gold, floral shoulder, hdls, 18¼" **100.00**
Vase, Thousand Butterflies, mini, 2" **125.00**
Vase, 4 arhats w/much gold, gold mk, 6x3⅝" **75.00**

Scales

In today's world of pre-measured and pre-packaged goods, it is difficult to imagine the days when such products as sugar, flour, soap, and candy first had to be weighed by the grocer. The variety of scales used at the turn of the century was highly diverse; at the Philadelphia Exposition in 1876, one company alone displayed over three hundred different weighing devices. Among those found today, brass, cast-iron, and plastic models are the most common. Fancy postal scales in decorative wood, silver, marble, bronze, and mosaic are also to be found.

A word of caution on the values listed: these values range from a low for those items in fair to good condition to the upper values for items in excellent condition. Naturally, items in mint condition could command even higher prices, and they often do. Also, these are **retail** prices that suggest what a collector will pay for the object. When you sell to a dealer, expect to get much less. These estimated values have been prepared by a committee of the International Society of Antique Scale Collectors under the direction of Robert Stein and George Mallis. The values noted are averages taken from various auction and other catalogs in the possession of the Society members. Among these, but not limited to, are the following: Joel L. Malter & Co., Inc., Encino, CA; *Collectors' Journal of Ancient Art*, Joel L. Malter & Co., Inc.; Nobody's Bizness But Our Own, Storrs, CT; Craig A. Whitford Numismatic Auctions; *Auktion Alt Technic*, Auction Team, Koln, Germany; *Waaqgen Auktion Essen*, Auktion Karla W. Schenk-Behrens, Essen, Germany.

Those seeking additional information concerning antique scales are encouraged to contact the International Society of Antique Scale Collectors, whose address can be found in the Directory under Clubs, Newsletters, and Catalogs.

Key:

ap — arrow pointer	hcp — hanging counterpoise
bal — balance	hh — hand held
bm — base metal	l+ — label with foreign coin
br — brass	values
Brit — British	lb w/i — labeled box with
h — hanging	instructions
Can — Canadian	lph — letter plate or holder
Col — Colonial	pend — pendulum
CW — Civil War	PP — Patent Pending
cwt — counterweight	st — sterling
Engl — English	tt — torsion type
eq — equal arm	ua — unequal arm
Euro — European	wt — weight
FIS — Fairbanks Infallible Scale Co.	

Analytical (Scientific)

Am, eq, mahog w/br & ivory, late 1800s, 14x16x8", $200 to **400.00**

Assay

Am, eq, mahog box w/br & ivory, plaque/drw, 1890s, $250 to ...**350.00**

Coin: Equal Arm Balance, American

Blk japanned metal, eagle on lid, late 19th C, $125 to **225.00**
Col, oak 6-part box, Col moneys, Boston, 1720-75, $600 to ...**1,200.00**
Post Col to CW, oak 6-part box, l+, 1843, $400 to **1,000.00**

Coin: Equal Arm Balance, English

Charles I, wooden box w/11 Brit wts, 1640s, $900 to **1,500.00**
1-pc wood box, rnd wts, label, Freeman, 1760s, $250 to **450.00**
6-pc oak box, coin wts label, Thos Harrison, 1750s, $200 to **450.00**

Coin: Equal Arm Balance, French

Solid wood box, 12 sq wts, J Reyne, Bourdeau, 1694, $400 to .**1,000.00**
Solid wood box w/recesses, 5 sq wts, A Gardes, 1800s, $250 to ..**800.00**
1-pc oval box, nested/fractional wts, label, 18th C, $250 to **400.00**
1-pc oval box, no wts, label of Fr/Euro coins, 18th C, $150 to **250.00**
1-pc walnut box, nested wts, Charpentier label, 1810, $275 to ..**675.00**

Coin: Equal Arm Balance, Miscellaneous

Amsterdam, 1-pc box, 32 sq wts, label, late 1600s, $850 to **2,500.00**
Cologne, full set of wts & full label, late 1600s, $1,200 to **2,800.00**
German, wood box, 13+ wts beneath main wts, label, 1795, $650 to .**900.00**

Counterfeit Coin Detectors, American

Allender Pat, lb w/i, cwt, Nov 22, 1855, 8½", $350 to **650.00**
Allender PP, rocker, labeled box, cwt, 1850s, 8½", $450 to **750.00**
Allender PP, rocker, no box or cwt, 1850s, 8½", $250 to **375.00**
Allender PP, space for $3 gold pc, lb w/i, cwt, 1855, $350 to **750.00**
Allender PP, space for $3 gold pc, no box or cwt, 1855, $275 to **375.00**
Allender Warranted, rocker, no box or cwt, 1850s, 8½", $350 to ..**475.00**
McNally-Harrison Pat 1882, rocker, cwt, JT McNally, $275 to ..**500.00**
McNally-Harrison Pat 1882, rocker, cwt & box, FIS, $400 to **750.00**
McNally-Harrison...1882, rocker, CI base, no cwt/box, $250 to .**400.00**
Thompson, Z-formed rocker, Berrian Mfg, 1877 Pat, $175 to **350.00**

Counterfeit Coin Detectors, Dutch

Rocker, Ellinckhuysen, brass, +copy of 1829 Patent, $150 to **165.00**

Counterfeit Coin Detectors, English

Folding, Guinea, self-rising, labeled box, 1850s, $175 to **225.00**
Folding, Guinea, self-rising, wood box/label, ca 1890s, $125 to ..**175.00**
Folding, Guinea, self-rising, wooden box, pre-1800, $175 to **275.00**
Rocker, simple, no maker's name or cb, end-cap box, $85 to **125.00**
Rocker, w/maker's name & cb, end-cap box, $120 to **150.00**

Postal

In the listings below an asterisk (*) was used to indicate that any one of several manufacturers' or brand names might be found on that particular set of scales. Some of the American-made pieces could be marked Pelouze, Lorraine, Hanson, Kingsbury, Fairbanks, Troemner, IDL, Newman, Accurate, Ideal, B-T, Marvel, Reliance, Victor, Liberty, Gem, Superior, Landers-Frary-Clark, Chatillon, Triner, American Bank Service, or Weiss. European/U.S.-made scales marked with an asterisk

(*) could be marked Salter, Peerless, Pelouze, Sturgis, L.F.&C., Alderman, G. Little, or S&D. English-made scales with the asterisk (*) could be marked Josh. & Edmd. Ratcliff, R.W. Winfield, S. Mordan, STS (Samuel Turner, Sr.), W.&T. Avery, Parnall & Sons, S&P, or H.B. Wright. There may be other manufacturers as well.

Brit/Can Bal, eq, br or CI on base, *, 4"-15", $100 to **750.00**
Engl Bal, eq/Roberval, gilt or st, on stand, *, 3"-8", $500 to **2,500.00**
Engl Bal, eq/Roberval, plain to ornate, *, 3"-8", $100 to **2,500.00**
Engl Spring, candlestick, br or st, *, 3½"-15", $100 to **500.00**
Engl Spring, CI, br or NP fr, Salter, ozs/lbs, 7"-10", $25 to **200.00**
Engl Steelyard, ua, 1- or 2-beam, h lph, *, 4"-15", $100 to **1,500.00**
Euro pend, gravity, br, CI or NP fr on base, oz/grams, $75 to **350.00**
Euro pend, gravity, 2-arm, bm, br or NP, *, 6"-9", $50 to **300.00**
Euro/US Spring, br or NP, pence/etc, h or hh, *, 4"-17", $10 to ..**100.00**
US Pend, gravity, metal, pnt face, ap, hcp, sm, $20 to **100.00**
US Spring, pnt base metal, *, 2½"-8", $10 to **80.00**
US Spring, pnt bm, *, mtd on inkstand, 2½"-8", $75 to **250.00**
US Spring, pnt bm, rnd glass-covered face, *, 8"-10", $25 to **100.00**
US Spring, SP, oblong base, *, 2½"-8", $100 to **200.00**
US Spring, st, oblong base, *, 2½"-8", $200 to **500.00**
US Steelyard, ua, CI, *, 5"-13" beam, 4½"-12" base, $25 to **100.00**

Schafer and Vater

Established in 1890 by Gustav Schafer and Gunther Vater in the Thuringia region of southwest Germany, by 1913 this firm employed over two hundred workers. The original factory burned in 1918 but was restarted and production continued until WWII. In 1972 the East German government took possession of the building and destroyed all of the molds and the records that were left.

You will find pieces with the impressed mark of a nine-point star with a script 'R' inside the star. On rare occasions you will find this mark in blue ink under glaze. The items are sometimes marked with a four-digit design number and a two-digit artist mark. In addition or instead, pieces may have 'Made in Germany' or in the case of the Kewpies, 'Rose O'Neill copyright.' The company also manufactured items for sale under store names, and those would not have the impressed mark.

Schafer and Vater used various types of clays. Items made of hard-paste porcelain, soft-paste porcelain, jasper, bisque, and majolica can be found. The glazed bisque pieces may be multicolored or have an applied colored slip wash that highlights the intricate details of the modeling. Gold accents were used as well as spots of high-gloss color called jewels. Metallic glazes are coveted. You can find the jasper in green, blue, pink, lavender, and white. New collectors gravitate toward the pink and lavender shades.

Since Schafer and Vater made such a multitude of items, collectors have to compete with many cross-over collections. These include shaving mugs, hatpin holders, match holders, figurines, figural pitchers, Kewpies, tea sets, bottles, naughties, etc.

Reproduction alert: In addition to the crudely made Japanese copies, some English firms are beginning to make figural reproductions. These seem to be well marked and easy to spot. Our advisor for this category is Joanne M. Koehn; she is listed in the Directory under Minnesota.

Ash/match holder, smiling feet w/holes in tips of toes, 3¼" H ...**255.00**
Ashtray, tiger's head **85.00**
Bottle, A Little Scotch **145.00**
Bottle, bearded man w/bowling ball, 9" **340.00**
Bottle, bearded monk, bl **250.00**
Bottle, Drinkometer (Your Health) **135.00**
Bottle, man holding bottles, mk Prohibition **175.00**
Bottle, old woman w/long neck, fringed shawl, 5¾" **125.00**

Bottle, Prohibition Lady, bl **175.00**
Bottle, Scotsman, mk Scotch Whiskey **150.00**
Bottle, skeleton, bl, tall **250.00**
Bottle, Turkey Trot (dancers) **225.00**
Box, dresser; cherub, jeweled **75.00**
Box, powder; nymph dancing w/frog, pk w/gold **55.00**
Chamberstick, owls **125.00**
Condiment set, man on bbl w/knife & fork, 3¾x4¾" **225.00**
Decanter, Butcher Boy, w/music box, bl **500.00**
Decanter, Never Drink Water, boy & frogs, 5½" **150.00**
Figurine, boy & girl, googly eyes, Everybody's Doing It, bsk, 3¾" .**125.00**
Figurine, comical dog on rectangular base, mk, 5½x2⅜x3" **135.00**
Figurine, man in top hat w/monocle, wood stick legs, NM **165.00**
Figurine, Mr Tenor **145.00**
Flask, Ape Waiter, mc **275.00**
Flask, devil, mc, curved neck **325.00**
Flask, Farm Relief, mc **175.00**
Flask, girl in hand, mc **150.00**
Flask, Pain Expeller, mc **250.00**
Flask, sailor w/life preserver, cm **265.00**
Flask, Santa, mc, curved neck **250.00**
Flask, Turkey Trot, mc **275.00**
Hatpin holder, cameo, bl & gray on pk bsk **325.00**
Hatpin holder, geisha girl, lav **125.00**
Hatpin holder, lady's head w/jewels, lav jasper **185.00**
Incense burner, dancing lady & elephant heads, tan, w/lid **165.00**
Jam pot, jasper, med bl, classical ladies, mk, 5¼x3¾" **95.00**

Match holder, man with umbrella and dog beside tray, Scratch My Back, #8205, 4", $150.00.

Match striker, cat & kitten **100.00**
Mug, elk, 3¼" **45.00**
Nodder, Scotsman playing bagpipes **175.00**
Pitcher, bear w/muff, 5" **165.00**
Pitcher, boy, bl, lg cream sz **175.00**
Pitcher, boy w/umbrella on bk, kneeling, cream sz **100.00**
Pitcher, clown **125.00**
Pitcher, cow, cream sz **135.00**
Pitcher, dressed bull, cobalt w/some wht, 6" **165.00**
Pitcher, girl w/fan, kneeling, cream sz **100.00**
Pitcher, goat, bl, cream sz **145.00**
Pitcher, jester, bl, cream sz **100.00**
Pitcher, lady w/fan & pointed hat, bl, 4" **135.00**
Pitcher, maid w/jug & keys, mc, 3½" **90.00**
Pitcher, milkmaid, bl, cream sz **100.00**
Pitcher, Mrs Goose, cream sz **150.00**
Pitcher, Oriental man w/goose, cream sz **100.00**
Pitcher, smiling apple w/leaves, cream sz **110.00**
Pitcher, Welsh woman, cream sz **195.00**
Pitcher, 3 faces, bl, cream sz **110.00**
Sugar bowl, smiling pear **100.00**
Teapot, jasper, gr, winged female/Cupid/etc, +cr/sug **315.00**

Vase, jewels pnt on pk, bronze bottom half, 6" **85.00**
Vase, lav/gr jasper, cameos: 2 women, jewels, hdls, 4½" **150.00**

Scheier

The Scheiers began their ceramics careers in the late 1930s and soon thereafter began to teach their craft at the University of New Hampshire. After WWII they cooperated with the Puerto Rican government in establishing a native ceramic industry, an involvement which would continue to influence their designs. In the '50s, they retired and moved to Mexico; they currently reside in Arizona.

Bowl, etched faces of mother & daughter, Mexican style, 10½" .**375.00**
Bowl, gr to brn flambe w/speckles, emb swirls, 2¼x12½" **175.00**
Bowl, lav/gray/gr bands, man & fish scene, 1⅛x6½" **225.00**
Bowl, lt bl & buff over red-brn, 4x9" **350.00**
Bowl, mocha brn w/speckles, emb ribs, 2¼x12" **100.00**
Bowl, mottled bl to gray, hdls, 1949, 4¾" H **175.00**
Bowl, 2 bluebirds in tree, 12" **375.00**
Cup & saucer, teal w/brn speckles, brn int w/wht center **50.00**
Pitcher, brn-speckled gloss, crimped mouth, 10⅛x7" **200.00**
Pitcher, deer leaping plants, dk on lt gray, 1949, 9½" **300.00**
Pitcher, gr glossy, strap hdl, 5¼" **185.00**
Plate, aqua w/cobalt speckled gloss, 7½", pr, NM **200.00**
Vase, caramel w/mahog & blk accents, ivory at neck, 5½x3¾" ..**225.00**
Vase, ivory to tan w/brn speckles, fish scene, 5½x4¾" **400.00**

Schlegelmilch Porcelain

Authority Mary Frank Gaston, who is our advisor, has completed four volumes of *The Collector's Encyclopedia of R.S. Prussia* with full-color illustrations and current values. Mold numbers appearing in some of the listings refer to these books.

Key:
BM — blue mark   SM — steeple mark
GM — green mark   RM — red mark

E.S. Germany

Fine chinaware marked 'E.S. Germany' or 'E.S. Prov. Saxe' was produced by the E.S. Schlegelmilch factory in Suhl in the Thuringia region of Prussia from sometime after 1861 until about 1925.

Basket, orchids int/ext, gold trim, GM, 5x3" **75.00**
Bowl, floral w/gold, rtcl rim, open hdls, 3x12x7½" **110.00**
Bowl, jonquils w/gold, beaded edge, unmk **400.00**
Box, 3 maidens & man w/harp, sgn Kauffmann, brass closure, mk .**80.00**
Cake plate, ships & lighthouse, dk sky, mk, 9" **85.00**
Celery tray, roses & snowballs w/gold, cobalt border, jewel mold ..**275.00**
Chocolate set, mc roses w/gold, lustre finish, mk, 10-pc **550.00**
Creamer & sugar bowl, Napoleon & Hortense, mk **300.00**
Cup & saucer, lady w/roses, MOP lustre, fancy ft, unmk **175.00**
Cup & saucer, Madam Recamier, mk **150.00**
Cup & saucer, Napoleon, mk **125.00**
Match holder, lady w/daisy crown, hanging, unmk **125.00**
Plate, Grecian ladies & Cupid, gold beading, Kauffmann, mk **145.00**
Plate, Madame Dubarry portrait, 4 cameos, lustre border, 10½" .**400.00**
Platter, maidens in center, Kauffmann, gold trim, mk, 14½" **210.00**
Syrup, Deco swan, satin finish, RM **250.00**
Tray, dresser; lady's portrait, mk **95.00**
Urn, lady's portrait on maroon, w/lid, 13" **375.00**

Vase, mill scene, RM, 8" **275.00**
Vase, Nouveau lady & peacock w/pearl lustre & gold, mk, 7½" .**395.00**

R.S. Germany

In 1869 Reinhold Schlegelmilch began to manufacture porcelain in Suhl in the German province of Thuringia. In 1894 he established another factory in Tillowitz in upper Silesia. Both areas were rich in resources necessary for the production of hard-paste porcelain. Wares marked with the name 'Tillowitz' and the accompanying 'R.S. Germany' phrase are attributed to Reinhold. The most common mark is a wreath and star in a solid color under the glaze. Items marked 'R.S. Germany' are usually more simply decorated than R.S. Prussia. Some reflect the Art Deco trend of the 1920s. Certain hand-painted floral decorations and themes such as 'Sheepherder,' 'Man With Horses,' and 'Cottage' are especially valued by collectors — those with a high-gloss finish or on Art Deco shapes in particular. Not all hand-painted items were painted at the factory. Those with an artist's signature but no 'Hand Painted' mark indicate that the blank was decorated outside the factory.

Ashtray, orange poppies, mk **75.00**
Basket, floral, scallop & fan mold, gold trim, 3-hdld, mk, 4¾" ...**250.00**
Bottle, scent; pk & wht roses, mk **75.00**
Bowl, floral, mc on pearl lustre, icicle border, unmk, 12" **325.00**
Bowl, wht roses, mk, 9¼" **65.00**
Box, man's trinket; collar shape, gold trim **45.00**
Cake plate, cottage, maiden & 2 oxen, mk, hdls, 10" W **235.00**
Celery dish, mc roses w/gold swags, peach rim, 15¼x5¼" **145.00**
Celery set, azaleas on gr w/tan & gold borders, 7-pc **175.00**
Charger, magnolias w/gold on gray-gr, mk, 11" **95.00**
Cup & saucer, Art Deco dancing lady, mk, 2¼", 3½" dia **88.00**
Cup & saucer, chocolate; sweet peas & gold bands, mk **30.00**
Cup & saucer, demi; roses on pastel w/gold trim, 8-sided **32.00**
Ewer, lady in gr w/Cupid, gold trim, pillow shape, mk, 6x5½" **195.00**
Mustard pot, Calla Lily, mk **40.00**
Nappy, heart shape w/parrot hdl **30.00**
Olive dish, poppies, red on gr w/gold, GM, 9x4¼" **40.00**
Pin dish, lady w/fan, RM **150.00**

Plate, Indians on horses in landscape, Indian head at handle, 8¼", $425.00.

Plate, lilacs w/gold, mk, 11¼" **110.00**
Plate, orange blossoms on pale gr to rose, 8½" **30.00**
Plate, peonies, cut-out hdls, mk, 9¾" **65.00**
Plate, roses, red/yel on pastel w/ornate gold trim, 6¼" **18.00**
Sugar bowl, roses, pk on wht w/gr leaves, gold trim, mk, 3x5" **25.00**
Toothpick holder, apple blossoms, swirl mold, RM **135.00**
Toothpick holder, wht floral, stipple mold, RM **135.00**
Vase, cottage scene w/farmer, mk, salesman's sample, 3½" **145.00**
Vase, 5 draped nudes, Tiffany finish, much gold, mk, 7x4" **245.00**

R.S. Poland

'R.S. Poland' is a mark attributed to Reinhold Schlegelmilch's factory in Tillowitz, Silesia. It was in use for a few years after 1945.

Bowl, crowned cranes, 5¾"	465.00
Server, lav & pk roses w/gold, center hdl, mk, 8x11" dia	515.00
Shaving mug, daffodils & tulips	150.00
Vase, crowned cranes, salesman's sample, mk, 3½"	800.00

R.S. Prussia

Art porcelain bearing the mark 'R.S. Prussia' was manufactured by Reinhold Schlegelmilch from the late 1870s to the early 1900s in a Germanic area known until the end of WWI as Prussia. The vast array of mold shapes in combination with a wide variety of decorations is the basis for R.S. Prussia's appeal. Themes can be categorized as figural (usually based on a famous artist's work), birds, florals, portraits, scenics, and animals.

Chocolate set, floral on white, pot with four cups and saucers, red star mark, $1,200.00.

Bell, floral, unmk, 3½"	135.00
Bell, purple & wht flowers, ruffled edge, unmk, 3½"	285.00
Biscuit jar, hidden image, mold #515, mk, 7x6"	700.00
Bowl, bluebird & 4 swans, RM, lg berry	525.00
Bowl, cobalt w/blown-out gold roses at border, RM, 10"	595.00
Bowl, floral, gr & wht on satin, mold #207, RM, 10½"	230.00
Bowl, floral, mc on satin, mold #82, mk, 10½"	325.00
Bowl, floral, 5-petal-shaped lobes, emb rim, RM, 10¼"	280.00
Bowl, floral w/gold, emb scrolls, 4-lobed, unmk, 11"	195.00
Bowl, jonquils, mc on cobalt w/gold, mk, 10½"	650.00
Bowl, lady w/bl hair, hidden image, iris mold, mk, 10"	550.00
Bowl, lilies, dbl-scalloped rim, purple/orange lustre, RM, 3x11"	350.00
Bowl, lilies reflecting in water, mold #404, RM, 10¾"	325.00
Bowl, Madame LeBrun, emb poppies, gold rim, unmk, sm berry	200.00
Bowl, mums, mc w/gold on turq, unmk, 9" dia	150.00
Bowl, nut; roses w/gold lustre, point & clover mold, mk, 6½"	185.00
Bowl, pheasants scene, oval, RM, 2⅜x8½x10⅛"	165.00
Bowl, poppies & daisies on gr, iris mold, RM, 10½"	300.00
Bowl, poppies w/gold, blown-out sunflowers, mk, 3x10½"	250.00
Bowl, roses, icicle mold, RM, 11"	275.00
Bowl, roses, iris variation mold, gold trim, unmk, 9¾"	255.00
Bowl, roses, pk & wht w/gr leaves & shadows, mold #252, 10¼"	230.00
Bowl, roses, pk w/gold, hdls, oval, mk, 2x10x6¾"	275.00
Bowl, roses & daisies w/gold, scalloped, RM, 10½"	225.00
Bowl, roses & lilies-of-valley w/gold on satin, RM, 10½"	225.00
Bowl, Summer season, prof rpr, RM, 9¾"	800.00
Bowl set, floral w/gold, leaf mold, mk, lg+6 sm	650.00
Bowl set, poppies & daisies, iris panels, RM, lg+6 sm	500.00
Bowl set, roses, acorn mold, RM, lg+6 sm	350.00
Bowl set, roses, iris mold, 9", +6 5½" bowls	500.00
Box, pin; magnolias on leaf form, 4½"	180.00
Cake plate, castle scene, fleur-de-lis mold, RM, 10¼"	795.00
Cake plate, castle scene, hdls, mk, 10¼"	700.00

Cake plate, floral w/gold on pastel, fleur-de-lis mold, RM, 11"	350.00
Cake plate, hidden images, mk	375.00
Cake plate, Nouveau flowers, pk lustre rim & gold trim, unmk, 11"	200.00
Cake plate, roses & daisies, fleur-de-lis mold, mk, 10¼"	325.00
Cake plate, roses on gr & wht, mold #259	175.00
Cake plate, roses w/gold, 6-point & clover mold, mk, 10"	298.00
Cake plate, roses w/gr & gold, carnation mold, mk	225.00
Cake plate, swans on lake, icicle mold, RM	295.00
Celery tray, floral w/gold, open hdls w/gold, RM, 12½"	225.00
Chocolate pot, pk poppies	395.00
Chocolate pot, roses, pk on gr, mk	325.00
Chocolate pot, swans, unmk, 9½"	750.00
Compote, lilacs, mk, 7"	135.00
Cracker jar, roses, lily mold, prof rstr, unmk	300.00
Cracker jar, roses, mc on satin, squat, ftd, mk	525.00
Cracker jar, swan scene, icicle mold, RM	540.00
Creamer, mill scene, mold #501, RM	175.00
Creamer & sugar bowl, floral w/gold & stencil, unmk	200.00
Creamer & sugar bowl, roses, steeple finial, RM	165.00
Creamer & sugar bowl, roses & leaf garlands w/gold, unmk	200.00
Creamer & sugar bowl, swan scene, icicle mold, RM	675.00
Cup & saucer, demitasse; pansies	75.00
Cup & saucer, demitasse; swan scene w/lustre, tall, RM	175.00
Ferner, lilies of the valley w/gold, dbl-scalloped rim, RM, 4x8"	275.00
Ferner, water lilies, 3-ft, pie-crust rim, w/liner, mk, 6¾"	275.00
Hair receiver, roses, Tiffany trim, mk, 4½" dia	185.00
Luncheon set, rose decor, 26-pc	2,500.00
Plate, Dice Throwers, gr & gold, mk, 8½"	725.00
Plate, poppies, gr border, mk, 8¾"	150.00
Plate, roses, yel on pk, shiny yel rim, 8¾"	150.00
Plate, Spring portrait, RM, 9¾"	1,500.00
Relish, basket of roses, shadow flowers, fleur-de-lis mold, 8"	115.00
Relish, mc carnations, jewels, mold #82, unmk, 4¾x9½"	115.00
Relish, mc floral/rose border, open hdls, lily mold, unmk, 9½" L	125.00
Shaving mirror, mc roses w/gold, mold #525, unmk, 3½x4½"	200.00
Shaving mug, duck in evergreen, RM	300.00
Syrup, swan scene on satin, mold #542, RM	325.00
Syrup pitcher, Spring season, iris mold, RM	495.00
Tankard, floral on gr, gold hdl (some wear), RM, 11½"	550.00
Tankard, hanging baskets, mk, 10"	725.00
Tankard, poppies, rtcl arched base, mold #486, RM, 11½x8½"	550.00
Tankard, roses, stipple mold, unmk, 13¼"	625.00
Tea set, floral, mc on wht to gr, mold #632, RM, pot+cr/sug	500.00
Toothpick holder, apple blossoms, stippled floral mold, RM	175.00
Toothpick holder, magnolias, stippled floral mold, RM	175.00
Toothpick holder, roses, mold #509, 3-hdld, unmk	175.00
Toothpick holder, roses, ribbed hexagon, hdls, RM	265.00
Tray, dresser; mums on gr, mold #343, unmk	135.00
Tray, swan scene, icicle mold, RM	650.00
Vase, cottage scene, RM, 7"	300.00
Vase, floral, hdls, RM, 6"	150.00
Vase, lovers scene, sgn Boucher, RM, 6⅜x3"	325.00
Vase, Melon Boy, sgn Murillo, lustre & gold trim, RM, 6⅜"	325.00
Vase, mill scene, dk gray, squatty, RM, 4"	375.00
Vase, parrots on wht satin, unmk, 8"	1,800.00
Vase, roses, pk on Tiffany finish, salesman's sample, RM, 4½"	275.00
Vase, swan scene, mk, 7½"	350.00

R.S. Suhl, Suhl

Porcelains marked with this designation are attributed to Reinhold Schlegelmilch's Suhl factory.

Box, floral, w/beveled mirror, mk	220.00

Cup & saucer, couple scene, flower hdl, gold trim, mk 125.00
Teapot, dogwood, +cr & sug 335.00
Vase, Melon Eaters, mk, 9" 660.00
Vase, sunflowers on brn, hdls, mk, 6¾" 250.00

R.S. Tillowitz

R.S. Tillowitz-marked porcelains are attributed to Reinhold Schlegelmilch's factory in Tillowitz, Silesia.

Bowl, pheasants, scalloped rim, open hdls, oval, mk, 10" 265.00
Creamer & sugar bowl, roses on cream to gr, w/lid 65.00
Pitcher, floral garland at neck on wht, mk, 8½" 80.00
Plate, peafowl, mk, 8" 125.00
Plate, stylized butterfly border w/gold, gold hdls, mk, 7" 45.00
Vase, pheasants, mk, 6" 250.00

Schneider

The Schneider Glass Company was founded in 1914 at Epinay-sur-seine, France. They made many types of art glass, some of which sandwiched designs between layers. Other decorative devices were appliqué and carved work. These were marked 'Charder' or 'Schneider.' During the '20s commercial artware was produced with Deco motifs cut by acid through two or three layers and signed 'LeVerre Francais' in script or with a section of inlaid filigrane. Our advisor for this category is Don Williams; he is listed in the Directory under Missouri. See also Le Verre Francais.

Vase, multicolor splotches and swirls in clear to blue at foot, footed baluster form, 24", $800.00; Pitcher, multicolor mottle with applied black amethyst handle, Ovington, 15", $750.00; Centerpiece compote, expanded bright Yellow 21 with cobalt blue mottled rim, black amethyst pedestal foot and stem, 4¼x15¼", $650.00.

Night light, orange/purple art glass shade, 7¾x5" 900.00
Night light, yel to bl spatter globe on butterfly pewter base, 5" ..650.00
Tazza, lemon yel & opal top w/orange mottled base, 3½x12½" .500.00
Tazza, yel/orange/purple spattering, short purple ped, 15½" 800.00
Vase, bl-gr irid w/allover webs, pewter fr, 7x7" 250.00
Vase, clear to yel translucent, urn form w/air traps, 11¾" 725.00
Vase, leaves, dk amethyst on pk to yel mottle, appl decor, 9¾" ..700.00
Vase, lt/dk orange spatter w/purple at base, gourd form, 6¾" 700.00
Vase, mc mottle, lg orange grape pods, burgundy rim, hdls, 21" ..3,400.00

Schoolhouse Collectibles

Schoolhouse collectibles bring to mind memories of a bygone era

when the teacher rang her bell to call the youngsters to class in a one-room schoolhouse where often both the 'hickory stick' and an apple occupied a prominent position on her desk. Our advisor for this category is Kenn Norris; he is listed in the Directory under Texas.

Bell, bell metal, curly maple hdl, 10¼" 385.00
Bell, master's, brass 65.00
Book, Before We Read, 1940, EX 38.00
Book, Dick & Jane, New Work & Play, 1956, 64-pg, VG 65.00
Book, Dick & Jane New Basic Reader, 1962, EX 30.00
Book, Elsen Basic Reader, 1930, EX 50.00
Book, Fun w/Dick & Jane, hardcover, 1946-47, VG 125.00
Book, Fun w/Our Friends, Dick & Jane, 1965, VG 45.00
Book, mathematics exercises, pen & ink on ledger paper, 1830s ...330.00
Book, McGuffey's Eclectic Reader, revised edition, 1920, EX 35.00
Book, McGuffey's Eclectic Spelling, EX 10.00
Book, McGuffey's 5th Eclectic Reader, 1907, VG 18.00
Book, Ray's Elementary Arithmetic, 1907, EX 12.00
Desk, master's, pine, slant lid w/crest, rprs/rstr/rfn, 34" 260.00
Desk, master's, pine w/old red, nailed apron, drw, 39x42" 220.00
Desk, master's, pine/poplar w/orig grpt, drw, rprs, 36"+crest 750.00
Desk, master's, poplar, slant lid, dvtl, gallery, rfn, 38" 550.00
Desk, master's, walnut, slant lid, fitted int, rfn, 38x39" 825.00
Globe, Kittinger, 12", on trn wood stand, 36" overall H 350.00
Globe, Phillips, mahog shaft & base, 19th C, 12" dia, EX 990.00
Globe, Phillips Popular Celestial..., 19th C, table sz, 5½" 850.00
Globe, Rand McNalley, on brass ftd base, dtd 1916 ....260.00
Globe, Weiland-Weimar, cracked-paper surface, 1838, 4" dia 850.00
Lunch box, pail type, metal, bail hdl, 4x4¼" 18.00
Pencil sharpener, Boston Bulldog, Mod L, 1940s, MIB 65.00
Pencil sharpener, saxaphone, CI, Germany, 1⅝" 40.00
Pencil sharpener, US Automatic, wood box 225.00
Pointer, whalebone & ivory w/cvd eagle's head hdl, 24" 975.00
Slate, bentwood oak fr, bottom tacked together, 7⅝x11" 85.00
Workbook, Beginning Arithmetic, 1951, EX 8.00

Pencil Boxes

Among the most common of school-related collectibles are the many classes of pencil boxes. Generally from the period of the 1870s to the 1940s, these boxes were made in hundreds of different styles. Materials included tin, wood (thin frame and solid hardwood), and leather; fabric and plastics were later used. Most pencil boxes were in a basic, rectangular configuration, though rare examples were made to resemble other objects such as rolling pins, ball bats, nightsticks, etc. They may still be found at reasonable prices, even though collectors have recently taken a keen interest in them. All boxes listed below are in very good to near-mint condition. Our advisors for pencil boxes are Sue and Lar Hothem, authors of School Collectibles of the Past; they are listed in the Directory under Ohio.

Lithographed paper on cardboard, Reg'lar Fellers, Eagle Pencil Co., contains pencils, G, $20.00.

Butternut w/orig orange-red pnt, dvtl, sliding lid **140.00**
Cb tube w/wooden ends, metal twist caps, advertising, 1x9⅞" **28.00**
Fabric, slide drw, Am, 1940s, 8¼x5x⅞" **15.00**
Plastic, pistol shape, 8x4⅝x1½" **28.00**
Plastic, 3-color, #555 Sterling Multiplier, w/sharpener, 7⅞" **12.00**
Tin, Jackie Coogan, smiling face, 7⅞x2¼x1⅝" **55.00**
Tin, Scholar's Companion, Pat 1874, 7¼x3x1" **85.00**
Tin, sliding lid, 1-compartment, dk bl w/sm pnt flowers, 7⅝" **30.00**
Wooden, slide-top, advertising, 9" ruler, str-edge, 9¼" **45.00**
Wooden, 4-level, 1 compartment per level, floral decal, 9¼" **95.00**
Wooden ball bat, World's Champion, 11" **55.00**

Schoop, Hedi

Swiss-born Hedi Schoop started her ceramics business in North Hollywood in 1940. With a talented crew of about twenty decorators, she produced figurines, figure-vases, console sets, TV lamps, and other decorative housewares — much of which was accented with gold or platinum trim. Schoop's pottery closed after a fire destroyed the building in 1958. Marks are impressed or printed. For further information we recommend *The Collector's Encyclopedia of California Pottery* by our advisor, Jack Chipman; he is listed in the Directory under California.

Bowl, Oriental style w/dragons **65.00**
Bowl, shell form, pk w/gold trim, 12" **50.00**
Cookie jar, Queen, rare **1,200.00**

Figurines, Oriental dancer and musician black and white (known as Young China), 10", $200.00.

Figurine, clown w/cello, platinum overglaze, 1943, 12½" **150.00**
Figurine, Conchita, scarf over hat, baskets on side, 12½" **125.00**
Figurine, girl w/accordion, 11" **120.00**
Figurine, girl w/basket & poodle, bl & gray, mk, 10" **160.00**
Figurine, Josephine, holds flower bowl, 1943, 13" **225.00**
Figurine, peasant lady, red scarf, bl flowing skirt, 13" **165.00**
Figurine, Toy & Ming, w/buckets, pr **150.00**
Plate, French poodle, sq **50.00**
TV lamp, Comedy & Tragedy, rare, 11x13" **400.00**
Vase, cactus shape, much color, 6x8" **120.00**
Vase, girl w/eyes open, 8" **95.00**
Vase, rooster, gr w/gold, 14", pr **245.00**
Vase, stylized chicken, 9", pr **155.00**
Vase/planter, lady in long gown w/basket, appl flowers, 12½" **135.00**
Wall pocket, girl angel w/fingers to lips, gr bow in hair **130.00**

Scouting Collectibles

Scouting was founded in England in 1907 by a retired Major General, Lord Robert Baden-Powell. Its purpose is the same today as it was then — to help develop physically strong, mentally alert boys and to teach them basic fundamentals of survival and leadership. The move-ment soon spread to the United States, and in 1910 a Chicago publish-er, William Boyce, set out to establish Scouting in America. The first World Scout Jamboree was held in 1911 in England. Baden-Powell was honored as the Chief Scout of the World. In 1926 he was awarded the Silver Buffalo Award in the United States. He was knighted in 1929 for distinguished military service and for his Scouting efforts. Baden-Powell died in 1941. For more information you may contact our advisor, R.J. Sayers, author of *Guide to Scouting Collectibles,* whose address (and ordering information regarding his book) may be found in the Directory under North Carolina. (Correspondence other than book orders require SASE please.)

Boy Scouts

Badge, BSA Tenderfoot, long knot, 1912-17 era **50.00**
Bar pin, Eagle Scout, w/device, wide bar variation, 1934 ....**25.00**
Book, Boy's Life Library, Outer Space Stories, 1964, EX **6.50**
Book, Boy Scout Firefighters, Crump, EX **4.00**
Book, Boy Scouts of Berkshire, Eaton, Wilde, 1912, EX **8.50**
Book, Handbook for Boys, 1948, EX **8.00**
Book, History of BSA, WD Murry, NY, 21st Anniversary, w/jacket .**3.00**
Book, Midshipman in Pacific, Brady, Every Boy's Library, VG **14.00**
Book, Philmont Scout Handbook, 1958, M **10.00**
Calendar, 1967 World Jamboree, 42x22", complete **20.00**
Certification card, BSA Scoutmaster, trifold, w/sleeve, 1924 ....**10.00**
Cigarette card, Baden-Powell, Adkin & Sons **7.50**
Diary, BS Official, #3012, 1912-17 era, 176-pg, EX **50.00**
Drum, tin w/japanned band, Boy Scout Band, rprs, 12" dia **150.00**
Field glasses, BSA Official, 1933-37 ....**20.00**
Fire-making kit, BSA Official, bow/thong/wood, #1532, 1925-32 .**15.00**
Handbook, BSA, 1917, VG **35.00**
Handbook, Order of the Arrow, 1959, EX **20.00**
Jacket, BS Official, 4-billows pocket, #583, 1918-24 era, EX **50.00**
Literature, How To Organize a Troop, 1925-32 ....**3.00**
Magazine, Scouting, 1913-16 issues, ea **12.00**
Morse code set, early, complete in box **20.00**
Neckerchief, BSA 69 Jamboree, M **10.00**
Neckerchief slide, Geo Washington & scouts emb on brass, 1930s .**5.00**
Note paper, BSA Official, w/letterhead, #5018, 1918-24 era **10.00**
Patch, BSA Eagle, tan, type 1, for 1924 World Jamboree **275.00**
Patch, BSA Official, silk bk, 1929 World Jamboree **90.00**
Patch, BSA Official, solid emblem, 1982 Nat'l Jamboree **4.50**
Patch, Build-Serve-Achieve Roundup, 1961 ....**3.00**
Patch, Eagle Scout, on tan sq, w/BSA, 1918-24 era **150.00**
Patch, Patrol Leader, 2 gr felt bars on tan sq, 1918-24 era **10.00**
Patch, Tenderfoot Air Scout Candidate, tan sq, 2-prop, 1937-45 .**30.00**
Patch, 50th Jubilee **15.00**
Pin, Baden-Powell, 8-point star, bl celluloid, on ribbon **75.00**
Pin, Lone Scout Tribe Chief, 1915-24 ....**75.00**
Pin-bk, BSA Pilgrimage, 1931 ....**15.00**
Plaque, award, 1960, 6x9" **8.00**
Pocketknife, Landers, Frary & Clark, #1585, 4-blade, 1930-40 .....**75.00**
Pocketknife, NY Knife Co, #1005, 2-blade, ebony hdl, 1911-15 ..**250.00**
Pocketknife, Remington, #1496, 4-blade, bone hdl, 1927-28, lg ..**70.00**
Pocketknife, Remington, #1564, 3-blade, bone hdl, w/tools **50.00**
Pocketknife, Schrade, #1066, leader's, 2-blade, blk hdl, 1975-80 ....**5.00**
Pocketknife, Ulster, #1513, 3-blade, stag hdl, 1923-36 ....**20.00**
Pocketknife, Ulster, #1996, 4-blade, blk hdl, 1960-70 ....**6.00**
Poster, 1935 Nat'l Jamboree, Rockwell art, 20x30" **100.00**
Report, US Government Printing Office, 1939 ....**5.00**
Ring, 1950, Jamboree cover, EX **40.00**
Scarf, Nat'l Jamboree, Valley Forge, 1957 ....**12.00**
Twin signal set, BSA Official, MIB **30.00**
Yearbook, Official BSA, 1st edition, 1915, EX **17.50**

Girl Scouts

Collecting Girl Scout memorabilia is a hobby that is growing nationwide. When Sir Baden-Powell founded the Boy Scout Movement in England, it proved to be too attractive and too well adapted to youth to limit its great opportunities to boys alone. The sister organization, known in England as the Girl Guides, quickly followed and was equally successful. Mrs. Juliette Low, an American visitor to England and a personal friend of the father of Scouting, realized the tremendous future of the movement for her own country, and with the active and friendly cooperation of the Baden-Powells, she founded the Girl Guides in America, enrolling the first patrols in Savannah, Georgia, in March 1912. In 1915 national headquarters were established in Washington, D.C., and the name was changed to Girl Scouts. The first national convention was held in 1914. Each succeeding year has shown growth and increased enthusiasm in this steadily growing army of girls and young women who are learning in the happiest ways to combine patriotism, outdoor activities of every kind, skill in every branch of domestic science, and high standards of community service. Today there are over 400,000 Girl Scouts and more than 22,000 leaders. Mr. Sayers is also our Girl Scout advisor.

Badge, First Class, khaki twill 7.00
Badge, Golden Eaglet, 1st issue, eagle w/ribbon, 1916 ....600.00
Badge, proficiency; 1917 era, average value of ea 5.00
Camera, Official GSA, Univex, 1937 ....50.00
Catalog, Official GSA Uniform, 1930 era 15.00
Certificate, Brownie Law, emb, 1920 ....15.00
Cookie cutters, GSA, gr hdl, 1950, complete set 12.00
Cross, Life Saving, cloverleaf type, Maltese Cross, 1917 ....150.00
Doll, Patsy Ann in GS Uniform, fully jtd, Effanbee, 1959, 15" ..100.00
Doll, Terri Lee, GSA Official Uniform Doll, 1956-58, 16" 200.00
Emblem, collar; GSA, brass, 1918 ....10.00
Handbook, Official Leader's, tan cover, 1920 ....30.00
Magazine, Am Girl, 1920-30 era, ea 7.00
Medal, Merit, gilt w/cloverleaf & knot, 1916 ....300.00
Medal, Merit, GSA, 1920, w/ribbon 75.00
Patch, Patrol Leader, khaki twill, 2 chevrons, 1920s 20.00
Pin, GSA Community Service, gr enamel, 1922-31 ....75.00
Pin, GSA Tenderfoot, 1923-34 ....4.00
Pin, Mariner, 1940 ....15.00
Pin, World's Fair GSA Service, 1939 ....200.00
Signal flag, GSA Official, wooden hdl, 1920 ....15.00
Uniform, adult, coat-style dress, w/belt, 1939-48 ....45.00
Uniform, GS-Brownie, middy & bloomers, 1918 ....200.00
Uniform, Senior GS, blouse/slacks/beret, gabardine, 1942-48 ......50.00
Wings, Brownie, 1926 ....15.00

Scrimshaw

The most desirable examples of the art of scrimshaw can be traced back to the first half of the 19th century to the heyday of the whaling industry. Some voyages lasted for several years, and conditions on board were often dismal. Sailors filled the long hours by using the tools of their trade to engrave whale teeth and make boxes, pie crimpers (jagging wheels), etc., from the bone and teeth of captured whales. Eskimos also made scrimshaw, sometimes borrowing designs from the sailors who traded with them.

Beware of fradulent pieces; fakery is prevelant in this field. Many carved teeth are of recent synthetic manufacture (examples engraved with information such as ship's or captain's names, dates, places, etc., should be treated with extreme caution) and have no antique or collectible value. A listing of most of these plastic items has been published

by the Kendall Whaling Museum in Sharon, Massachusetts. If you're in doubt or a novice collector, it's best to deal with reputable people who **guarantee** the items they sell. Our advisor for this category is John Rinaldi; he is listed in the Directory under Maine. See also Powder Horns.

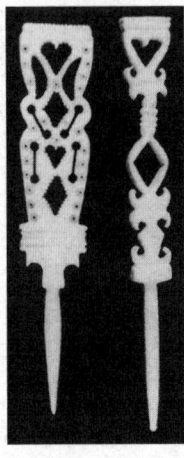

Bodkins: Carved bone with openwork of varied designs, framed, 5", $600.00; Carved bone with openwork, 6", $110.00.

Bodkin, swan's head form w/tortoise shell inlay, 5½" 275.00
Bodkin, 3 openwork hearts, whalebone, 5¼" 220.00
Busk, Cupids w/love potions/arrows/maidens/lovebirds, 15x2" .1,200.00
Busk, foliage/geometrics/circles, 12¼" 300.00
Cane, whalebone w/rope twists, ivory hdl, ebony/silver inlay ..5,950.00
Carving, penguin, from tooth, EX patina, 1920s-30s, 4½" 215.00
Corset, linen w/baleen stays, cvd busk w/figures & flowers 225.00
Crimper, dbl cutting wheel, 3-tine fork, swirl-cvd hdl, 7¾" 325.00
Crimper, sea horse form, 2-parts, ebony separator, VG 1,600.00
Crimper, whale tooth ivory w/ebony separator, 1850s, 4" 550.00
Fid, clenched fist form, whale ivory, 3⅝" 150.00
Fid, cvd ropework, 7½" 275.00
Fid, turk's head knot, spiral rope cvg, 4-pc 500.00
Knitting needles, ebony/bone separators, tooth hdls, 12", pr 800.00
Pie crimper, open cvd hdl, 8¼" L 2,875.00
Rule, carpenter's, whalebone, 18x2", VG 400.00
Seam rubber, tortoise separator, 3½", EX 750.00
Seam rubber, whale ivory w/tortoise & ebony spacers, 1840s, 4½" .825.00
Tooth, bearded man's portrait, mc stain, 19th C, 6", EX 1,350.00
Tooth, classic whaling scene, bk: ship, 6" 3,950.00
Tooth, English ship starbrd view/thistle border, bk: palm, 6" ..1,850.00
Tooth, port view/mtns/coast full-length scene, 1850s, 8½" 6,450.00
Tooth, sailor farewell scene, bk: soldier & 2 ladies, 5½" 3,200.00
Tooth, whaling scene/ship/whales/long boats/island/etc, 6½" 950.00
Tooth, 3 well-dressed ladies in bonnets, 19th C, 6½" 1,975.00
Tusk, detailed whaling scene/Eskimo scenes/animals/totems, 18" ...550.00
Yarn winder, whalebone, trn ivory base clamp & cushion, 16" ..1,400.00

Sebastians

Sebastian miniatures were first produced in 1938 by Prescott W. Baston in Marblehead, Massachusetts. Since then more than six hundred have been modeled. These figurines have been sold through gift shops all over the country, primarily in the New England states. In 1976 Baston withdrew his Sebastians from production. Under an agreement with the Lance Corporation of Hudson, Massachusetts, one hundred designs were selected to be produced by that company under Baston's supervision. Those remaining were discontinued. In the time since then, the older figurines have become very collectible. Price is determined by three factors: 1) in production/out of production; 2) labels — color of oval label, i.e. red, blue, green, etc.; Marblehead label, a green and silver palette-shaped label used until 1977; or no label; 3) condition. If there is no label and the varnish coat is quite yellowed, then it is considered to be of the Marblehead era. Dates are merely copyright dates and have no particular significance in regard to value. A signature of 'P.W. Baston' should only have impact on price when it is an actual autograph. Most pieces are manufactured with an imprinted 'P.W. Baston' on the base. Baston died in 1984; the miniatures are now being done by P.W. Baston, Jr.

Andrew Jackson **95.00**
Candy Store **180.00**
Cavalry **500.00**
Christmas Morning **35.00**
Clown **100.00**
Colonial Watchman **65.00**
Darned Well He Can **275.00**
Diedrich Knickerbocker, Marblehead era **50.00**
Doctor **75.00**
Family Feast **135.00**
Farmer **35.00**
Farmer's Wife **30.00**
Gathering Tulips **110.00**
George Washington **35.00**
Grocery Store, Marblehead era **65.00**
House of 7 Gables, Marblehead era **65.00**
JF Kennedy **60.00**
Jimmy Fund III, Ice Hockey **40.00**
Johnny Appleseed, State Farm Insurance ltd ed, 1985 ....**85.00**
Little Sister, bl label **40.00**
Mark Twain, blk & silver label **95.00**

Mr. Obocell, Marblehead, 4⅜", $55.00.

Old North Church, autographed Woody Baston, bl **45.00**
Old Salt **75.00**
Paul Bunyan, Masons **245.00**
Paul Revere **45.00**
Pilgrims, Marblehead label **60.00**
Robert E Lee & Traveler, Marblehead era **95.00**
Ronald Regan, Young Republican **85.00**
Sampling the Stew, Marblehead era **50.00**
Son of the Desert **225.00**
Uncle Sam, Marblehead era **50.00**
Weaver & Loom, Marblehead label **65.00**

Sevres

Fine-quality porcelains have been made in Sevres, France, since the early 1700s. Rich ground colors were often hand painted with por-

traits, scenics, and florals. Some pieces were decorated with transfer prints and decalcomania; many were embellished with heavy gold. These wares are the most respected of all French porcelains. Their style and designs have been widely copied, and some of the items listed below are Sevres-type wares.

Bowl, centerpc; mc vignettes on yel, hdls, mk, 6x13x8" **1,500.00**
Box, trinket; musical, cobalt w/gilt metal fr, 4¼x3¾" sq **550.00**
Egg casket, HP decor panels w/gilt, ormolu fr, hinged lid, 11", NM ...**300.00**
Figurine, couple dressed for masquerade ball, ca 1800, 22", pr .**4,400.00**
Urn, Cupid & maiden, bk: romantic landscape, gold scrolls, 27" .**1,980.00**
Urn, lady/2 youths/lake scene, leaf hdls, fruit finial, 18" **700.00**
Vase, floral, purple & gr w/gold, Belet, 1911, 9¼x3¾" **1,100.00**

Sewer Tile

Whimsies, advertising novelties, and other ornamental items were sometimes made in potteries where the primary product was simply tile.

Bank, pig form, 8⅜" **170.00**
Candelabrum, appl flowers/birds/leaves, 12⅜" **75.00**
Figurine, bulldog pup on rectangular base, 3¾" **150.00**
Figurine, cat, seated, solid, 7" **165.00**
Figurine, dog, seated, free-standing front legs, solid, 10¼" **220.00**
Figurine, duck, tooled details, 5½" **125.00**
Figurine, raccoon, wht slip details, gr pnt eyes, 15" **165.00**
Figurine, squirrel, yel slip eyes, solid, CM1980, 6¾" **28.00**

Sewing Items

Sewing collectibles continue to intrigue collectors, and fine 19th-century and earlier pieces are commanding higher prices due to increased demand and scarcity. Complete needlework boxes and chatelaines in original condition are rare, but even incomplete examples can be considered prime additions to any collection, as long as they meet certain criteria: boxes should contain fittings of the period; the chains of the chatelaine should be intact and contemporary with the style; and the individual holders should be original and match the brooch. As 19th-century items become harder to find, new trends in collecting develop. Needlebooks, many of which were decorated with horses, children, beautiful ladies, etc., have become very popular. Some were giveaways printed with advertisements of products and businesses. Even early pins are collectible; the first ones were made in two parts with the round head attached separately. Pin disks, pin cubes, and other pin holders also make interesting additions to a sewing collection.

Tape measures are very popular — especially Victorian figurals. These command premium prices. Early wooden examples of transferware and Tunbridge ware have gained in popularity, as have figurals of vegetable ivory, celluloid, and other early plastics. From the 20th century, tatting shuttles made of plastics, bone, brass, sterling, and wood decorated with Art Nouveau, Art Deco, and more modern designs are in demand — so are darning eggs, stillettos, and thimbles. Because of the decline in the popularity of needlework after the 1920s (due to increased production of machine-made items), novelty items were made in an attempt to regain consumer interest, and many collectors today also find these appealing.

Watch for reproductions. Sterling thimbles are being made in Holland and the U.S. and are available in many Victorian-era designs. But the originals are usually plainly marked, either in the inside apex or outside on the band. Avoid testing gold and silver thimbles for content; this often destroys the inside marks. Instead, research the manufacturer's mark; this will often denote the material as well. Even though the reproductions are well finished, they do not have manufacturers' marks. Many thimbles are being made specifically for the collectible market; reproductions of porcelain thimbles are also found. Prices should reflect the age and availability of these thimbles. Our advisor for this category is Marjorie Geddes; she is listed in the Directory under Oregon.

Sewing notion, carved vegetable ivory, cushion top, with tape measure, 3½", $125.00.

Box, cherry, sq corner posts, drw, doweled lid, 1870s, 9" 200.00
Box, hardwood, dvtl w/fitted int & mirror, 10⅝" 300.00
Box, mahog veneer on pine, fitted int, 11" 95.00
Box, softwood, pnt floral decor, cloth lined, 1800s, 8¾" sq 625.00
Box, wood w/sailing ship inlaid lid, dtd 1877, 13x9½x5½" 900.00
Buttonhole cutter, iron & brass, box joint, 6⅝" L 80.00
Buttonhole cutter, iron & brass, Reliance...NJ, 10¼" 30.00
Darner, blown, milk glass 25.00
Darner, burl wood, w/needle storage 48.00
Darner, ebony w/ornate sterling hdl 75.00
Darner, maple, dbl-ended, trn center, 18th C 65.00
Darner, milk glass w/clear & maroon loopings, 7¼" 325.00
Hem gauge, sterling 85.00
Kit, burl wood acorn 110.00
Lace maker's pillow, w/wooden bobbins 165.00
Measure, aluminum, Buckeye Disc Drill, EX 60.00
Measure, bone china, lady figural 40.00
Measure, celluloid, baseball player figural 250.00
Measure, celluloid, bear cub on platform 110.00
Measure, celluloid, Billiken figural 200.00
Measure, celluloid, covered wagon form, EX 55.00
Measure, celluloid, elephant figural 60.00
Measure, celluloid, fish figural, souvenir of Catalina Island 90.00
Measure, celluloid, fruit basket form, Germany 85.00
Measure, celluloid, hen w/chick on its bk 45.00
Measure, celluloid, Indian lady figural, 2½" 85.00
Measure, celluloid, jester's head form 110.00
Measure, celluloid, kangaroo & baby figural 120.00
Measure, celluloid, Mead Johnson, Deca Vitamins 27.00
Measure, celluloid, ocean scenery, Fab, dtd 1917 ....49.00
Measure, celluloid, pig in red hat figural 55.00
Measure, celluloid, pig w/flowers figural 40.00
Measure, celluloid, S&H Green Stamps, push-button, EX 50.00
Measure, celluloid, ship form, red & wht, 2x2¼" 125.00
Measure, celluloid, sunflower form 125.00
Measure, ceramic, wht cat on pk pillow (pin box), Napco, 4" 85.00
Measure, cloth, puppy figural 30.00
Measure, leather, book form 100.00
Measure, metal, turtle figural, pull head 120.00
Measure, metal, Whirlpool advertising 20.00
Measure, metal, woodpecker figural 200.00
Measure, plastic, apple form 25.00
Measure, plastic, dressmaker's dummy form 45.00

Measure, porc, egg & fly form, Germany 25.00
Measure, porc, girl & cherries figural, Germany 85.00
Measure, porc, monkey figural, Germany, 3" 55.00
Measure, vegetable ivory, bbl form, NM 100.00
Measure, vegetable ivory, egg form 50.00
Measure/pincushion, celluloid, dress form, pk 45.00
Measure/pincushion, compo, Red Riding Hood nodder 65.00
Needle case, Boye, w/needle tin, 1902 ....18.00
Needle case, wooden bbl, top rotates, advertising, Germany, 2½" ...65.00
Needle sizer kit, Piccadilly..., bbl shape 80.00
Pincushion, ceramic, beadwork on red, scalloped, Victorian, 8½" ..60.00
Pincushion, CI on ped, ornate, Victorian 40.00
Pincushion, compo, Scottish child's head, fly on face 125.00
Pincushion, Indian beadwork, bird form, wall hanging, 8" L 90.00
Pincushion, Indian beadwork, rnd, Victorian, 7" 40.00
Pincushion, leather Victorian shoe w/beaded trim 38.00
Pincushion, metal, globe form 55.00
Pincushion, metal, pedestal, early, EX 85.00
Pincushion, pot metal, sedan 35.00
Pincushion, velvet/organza eggplant form, 8" 35.00
Pincushion, wooden baby bootie, MOP inserts 75.00
Sewing bird, brass clamp, dtd 1853, 2x3½" 250.00
Sewing bird, stamped metal w/cushion above wings, 5x4" 100.00
Sewing kit, Lydia Pinkham, purse form 40.00
Thimble, Austria, aluminum w/stone top 4.00
Thimble, Brogan, sterling, fleur-de-lis 50.00
Thimble, Germany, sterling, leaf border 35.00
Thimble, Haviland, china 15.00
Thimble, Italy, Murano glass 10.00
Thimble, Ketchum & McDougal, sterling w/gold-plated band 40.00
Thimble, Muhr, gold, faceted rim 100.00
Thimble, Simons, sterling, Columbian Expo 300.00
Thimble, Simons, sterling, mk Priscilla 40.00
Thimble, Simons, sterling, target band 25.00
Thimble, Simons, sterling, 10 panels 30.00
Thimble, Simons, 14k gold 110.00
Thimble, Simons Bros, 10k gold 85.00
Thimble, unmk, base metal 5.00
Thimble, unmk, brass 10.00
Thimble, unmk English, sterling, zipper pattern 30.00
Thimble, Wedgwood, Jasperware 25.00
Thimble case, cvd vegetable ivory, w/thimble 115.00
Thimble holder, Atlanta Expo, sailboat w/sailor, 1895 ....150.00
Thread holder, ivory, hole at side for needles, Victorian, 4" 45.00
Thread holder/pincushion, metal, lazy susan type 50.00

Sewing Machines

The fact that Thomas Saint, an English cabinetmaker, invented the first sewing machine in 1790 was unknown until 1874 when Newton Wilson, an English sewing machine manufacturer and patentee, chanced upon the drawings included in a patent specification describing methods of making boots and shoes. By the middle of the 19th century, several patents were granted to American inventors, among them Isaac M. Singer, whose machine used a treadle. These machines were ruggedly built, usually of cast iron. By the 1860s and '70s, the sewing machine had become a popular commodity, and the ironwork became more detailed and ornate.

Though rare machines are costly, many of the old oak treadle machines (especially these brands: Davis, Home, Household, National, New Home, Singer, Weed, Wheeler & Wilson, and Willcox & Gibbs) have only nominal value. Machines manufactured after 1875 are generally very common as most were mass produced. Values for these later sewing machines range from $50.00 to $100.00. Refer to *Toy and Miniature Sewing Machines (Books I and II)* by Glenda Thomas for more information. Our advisor for this category is Peter Frei; he is listed in the Directory under Massachusetts. In the listings that follow, unless noted otherwise, values are suggested for machines in excellent working order.

Child's, KAYanEE Sew Master, hand operated, wood base, 7½x5x9¾", $50.00.

Photo courtesy Glenda Thomas

Baby, CI, w/finger protector, 1890s, 6½x2⅛x5¾", +box **250.00**
Child's, Betsy Ross, 1949, 6¼x7¾x4½" **100.00**
Child's, Britain's Petite, pk plastic, 1980s, 8¾x10⅛x8¾" **40.00**
Child's, Casige Our Pet, sheet metal, pre-WWII, 5x5x2" **135.00**
Child's, Casige Sew-O-Matic, sheet metal, post-WWII, 6¾" L ..**100.00**
Child's, Cornet, heavy metal, wht rabbit in circle, 9" L **170.00**
Child's, Gloria, Deco decor, MIG-British Zone, post-WWII, 8½" L .**135.00**
Child's, Holly Hobbie, manual or battery-op, 1977-82, 9¼" L **25.00**
Child's, Ideal, CI & oak treadle type, 30½", G **1,200.00**
Child's, Little Mary Mix Up, sheet metal, 1930s, 7¾" L **75.00**
Child's, Little Modiste, electric, wood base, 1950s, 7" L **60.00**
Child's, Little Mother, Artcraft, 1940s, 8x8¼x4⅛" **85.00**
Child's, Little Worker, New Home, hand-op, 1910s, 10½" L **150.00**
Child's, Muller #19, cast metal, floral trim, pre-WWII, 10" L **225.00**
Child's, Sew-Ette, bl-crinkle metal, battery, 1960s, 7⅞" L **50.00**
Child's, Sew-n-Play, plastic, battery or hand-op, 9½" L **25.00**
Child's, Strawberry Shortcake, pk plastic, 1980s, 8¼" L **45.00**
Eldredge Automatic, 1880s, complete, EX **145.00**
Essex, highly chromed, wood base, 1940s-50s, 8" L **130.00**
Florence, CI, belt driven, Pat Nov 12, 1850, 16" L, EX **260.00**
Grover & Baker, last Pat May 27, 1856 ....**1,200.00**
Singer, leather sewing, floor model, heavy, EX **300.00**
Singer, Pat 1846, MOP inlay in head, walnut fold-out case **800.00**
Singer Featherweight #210, w/attachments, EX in case **465.00**
Singer Featherweight #221-1, blk/gold, w/case & attachments ...**300.00**
Wheeler & Wilson, 625 Broadway, EX **125.00**

Shaker Items

The Shaker community was founded in America in 1776 at Niskeyuna, New York, by a small group of English 'Shaking Quakers.' The name referred to a group dance which was part of their religious rites. Their leader was Mother Ann Lee. By 1815 their membership had grown to more than one thousand in eighteen communities as far west as Indiana and Kentucky. But in less than a decade, their numbers began to decline until today only a handful remain. Their furniture is prized for its originality, simplicity, workmanship, and practicality. Few pieces were signed. Some were carefully finished to enhance the natural wood; a few were painted.

Although other methods were used earlier, most Shaker boxes were of oval construction with overlapping 'fingers' at the seams to prevent buckling as the wood aged. Boxes with original paint fetch triple the price of an unpainted box; number of fingers and overall size should also be considered.

Although the Shakers were responsible for weaving a great number of baskets, their methods are not easily distinguished from those of their outside neighbors, and it is nearly impossible without first-hand knowledge to positively attribute a specific example to their manufacture. They were involved in various commercial efforts other than woodworking — among them sheep and dairy farming, sawmilling, and pipe and brick making. They were the first to raise crops specifically for seed and to market their product commercially. They perfected a method to recycle paper and were able to produce wrinkle-free fabrics. Our advisor for this category is Nancy Winston; she is listed in the Directory under New Hampshire. Standard two-letter state abbreviations have been used throughout the following listings.

Key:
bj — bootjack	PH — Pleasant Hill
CB — Canterbury	ML — Mt. Lebanon
EF — Enfield	SDL — Sabbathday Lake
NL — New Lebanon	WV — Watervliet

Basket, ash w/wood button, iron nails, swing hdl, 7½x11" **315.00**
Basket, blk ash, rectangular bottom, wrapped rim, 5¾x17x12" ..**460.00**
Basket, splint, bentwood rim hdls, natural, 5x12" **300.00**
Basket, splint w/pin-type anchors, swing hdls, 7x11½" dia **400.00**
Basket, utility; ash, ear hdls, wrapped rim, 10½x23½" **430.00**
Bench, meeting house, plank seat, bj cutouts, red pnt, 84", VG ..**1,000.00**
Bench, pine, red on gr grpt, 1-brd seat, bj ft, 16x81x9" **550.00**
Bootjack, natural Y form w/chamfered edges, old red, 21" **90.00**
Box, pantry; 2-finger, 3x6½" **350.00**
Box, seed; dvtl pine, paper label, 4x24x12" **1,500.00**
Box, sewing; cherry/maple/mahog, drw in base, compartment, 6" ..**135.00**
Box, 2-finger, lt brn finish, 8" **250.00**
Box, 3-finger, copper tacks, orig gr pnt, 4½x12x8¼" **1,650.00**
Box, 3-finger, copper tacks, pnt pastoral scene, 1868, 2x4x3" .**1,500.00**
Box, 3-finger, gr-brn pnt traces, ML, old renailing, 4½" dia **300.00**
Box, 3-finger, Harvard type, old gr, wrought-iron tacks, 6" **305.00**
Box, 3-finger, natural w/gr traces, iron nails, 7" **115.00**
Box, 3-finger, pine/maple, orig yel-gr pnt, 4⅝x12x8" **2,000.00**
Box, 3-finger, red & blk grpt, pincushion top, 5x7¼x4¾" **450.00**
Box, 3-finger, 19th C, 4⅜x9⅞" L **1,500.00**
Box, 4-finger, beech/pine, old gr rpt over bl, tacks, 12½" L **1,200.00**
Box, 4-finger, maple/pine, orig pnt, 9⅝" L, from $1,500 to **2,000.00**
Box, 4-finger, pine/maple, brn stain, married lid, 9x13x5⅜" **700.00**
Bucket, bl rpt wood, trn wood & wire bail hdl, 4½x5½" **225.00**
Bucket, old yel pnt, hdl held by rivets, metal straps, 8x10½" **900.00**
Bucket, pine staves, iron hoops, brn stain, NL, 9½x12" **300.00**
Carrier, 3-finger, pine/maple, yel pnt, CB, 1840s, 13" L **2,000.00**
Carrier, 4-finger, pine/maple/ash, yel pnt, 3⅝x11x8" **1,500.00**
Chair, side; #3, old dk brn w/gold stencil label, ML, 33¾" **275.00**
Chair, side; maple, 3-slat bk, mc tape seat, rprs, CB **800.00**
Chair, side; 3-slat bk, tape seat, ML, ca 1930s, 40½", pr **800.00**
Chair, side; 3-slat ladder-bk, splint seat, 39¼" **600.00**
Chair, side; 3-slat ladder-bk w/trn finials, tape seat, 40" **400.00**
Chest, 4 grad drws, natural finish, dvtl, CB, 37x30x16", EX ...**1,000.00**
Counter, tailor's, 6 dvtl drws, orig iron supports, 38x72x40", EX ...**21,000.00**
Cupboard, butternut/pine, 4-door, 3-shelf, 1860s, 60x49" **2,000.00**
Cupboard, mustard stain, raised panel door, hanging, 19x24x10" ...**225.00**
Cupboard, pine, door over door, red wash, ML, 1940s, 77x50" ..**17,250.00**
Desk, sewing; pine, old salmon pnt, gallery w/2 drws, CB, 1840s ...**10,000.00**
Desk, sewing; 6-drw top w/central do, 3-drw/1-drw base, rfn ..**10,000.00**
Dipper, wood, trn hdl w/copper tacks, old staining, 7¼" dia **250.00**
Dust pan, metal w/folded corners, birch hdl, CB, 1880, 13" **300.00**

Foot warmer, soapstone w/cotton cover, CB, 10x12x6½" 300.00
Hamper, picnic; woven, dbl-lid top, 16x17½x10½", VG 200.00
Level, surveyor's, brass fittings & plate, tapered legs, 69" 475.00
Mall, wood, head w/beveled sides, 28" hdl, 33½" L 225.00
Peg rack, red stain traces, wall hanging, early, 15½x31" 800.00
Quilt rack, mortised/pinned, nailed top rail, att, 38x48" 330.00
Rocker, #3, slat bk, rush seat, dk brn finish, ML, 34½" 400.00
Rocker, armchair; #3, 3-slat bk, rpl reed seat, rpr, ML, 35" 330.00
Rocker, armchair; #6, mushroom-type arms, rpl seat, 42", EX 850.00
Rocker, armchair; ML type, rfn/rstr taped seat, 38" 275.00
Rocker, maple, 3-slat bk, rush seat, acorn finials, NY, 40" 400.00
Rocker, 3 grad/curved slats, old splint seat, dk over red, 37" 300.00
Shovel, cvd from 1 pc of wood, 35½x11¼" 325.00

Side chair, maple, old brown stain, cane seat, replaced tilters, graduated slats, Canterbury, ca 1840, 40¾", $1,500.00.

Spool rack, maple/fruitwood, 9 trn spools, CB, 4x7½x3" 300.00
Stand, elder's, tiger maple sq lift top, pegged, 28x19x18" 800.00
Stool, 2-step; pine, red pnt, nailed, 14¾x12⅝x11" 125.00
Stove, CI box shape w/4 slip-in legs, serrated decor, VG 200.00
Strainer, punched-screen bottom, pnt hdl, CB, 4¼" dia 85.00
Swift, umbrella type, collapsing, Hancock form, 18x16", EX 300.00
Table, maple/oak, rpl drw, 19⅝x13¼x23⅛" 250.00
Table, work; 1-drw, 2-brd top, rfn w/old red traces, 34" L 3,500.00
Table, 1-drw, tapered legs, old red pnt, 29x43x28" 1,500.00
Tray, cherry sorting; cut-out hdls, 4-sided, 4½x33x20" 150.00
Wheelbarrow, gr-pnt wood, 8-spoke wooden wheels, 81x33x27" ..850.00

Shaving Mugs

Between 1865 and 1920, owning a personalized shaving mug was the order of the day, and the 'occupationals' were the most prestigious. The majority of men having occupational mugs would often frequent the barber shop several times a week, where their mugs were clearly visible for all to see in the barber's rack. As a matter of fact, this display was in many ways the index of the individual town or neighborhood.

During the first twenty years, blank mugs were almost entirely imported from France, Germany, and Austria and were hand painted in this country. Later on, some china was produced by local companies. It is noteworthy that American vitreous china is inferior to the imported Limoges and is subject to extreme crazing.

Artists employed by the American barber supply companies were for the most part extremely talented and capable of executing any design the owner required, depicting his occupation, fraternal affiliation, or preferred sport. When the mug was completed, the name and the gold trim were always added in varying degrees, depending on the price paid by the customer. This price was determined by the barber

who added his markup to that of the barber-supply company. As mentioned above, the popularity of the occupational shaving mug diminished with the advent of World War I and the introduction by Gillette of the safety razor. Later followed the blue laws forcing barber shops to close on Sundays, thereby eliminating the political and social discussions for which they were so well noted.

Occupational shaving mugs are the most sought after of the group which would also include those with sport affiliations. Fraternal mugs, although desirable, do not command the same price as the occupationals. Occasionally, you will find the owner's occupation together with his fraternal affiliation. This combination could add anywhere between 25% to 50% to the price, which is dependent on the execution of the painting, rarity of the subject, and detail. Some subjects can be done very simply; others can be done in extreme detail, commanding substantially higher prices. It is fair to say, however, that the rarity of the occupation will dictate the price. Mugs with heavily worn gold loose between 20% and 30% of their value immediately. This would not apply to the gold trim around the rim, but to the loss of the name itself. Our advisor for this category is Burton Handelsman; he is listed in the Directory under New York.

Decorative, cottage & church scene, much gold, 3⅝" 200.00
Decorative, lady's portrait in reserve, gold trim, 3½" 325.00
Decorative, Nouveau lilies & leaves, SP w/matching brush 225.00
Decorative, 2 horse heads, Koken, 4" 230.00
Figural, Black man w/hat, EX 450.00
Figural, cabbage & leaf 145.00
Figural, elk, matching brush 525.00
Figural, fish in basket 165.00
Figural, fish w/open mouth 90.00
Figural, fish walking 85.00
Figural, lady, majolica 185.00
Figural, pig's head, EX 325.00
Figural, sailing ship in relief 150.00
Figural, snake wrapped around tree trunk 365.00
Figural, witch/hag 600.00
Fraternal, Brotherhood of RR Trainmen, emblem, 4" 130.00
Fraternal, Fraternal Order of Eagles, Pabst & Koler, 3¾" 140.00
Fraternal, Order of the Chosen Friends 325.00
Fraternal, Woodsmen of World, Germany, 3⅝" 230.00
Occupational, baker, 3 men working in bakery, M gold, 3⅞" 350.00
Occupational, bartender, bar room scene w/customers, 3⅝" 350.00
Occupational, baseball player at bat 2,200.00
Occupational, blacksmith, shoeing horse, worn gold 350.00
Occupational, butcher, shop scene, name in gold 180.00
Occupational, cabinetmaker, man w/wood, T&V Limoges 325.00
Occupational, car salesman, rpr 875.00
Occupational, conductor, hat, EX 525.00
Occupational, conductor, train passenger car #8 ....575.00
Occupational, drum major, in uniform, w/baton 2,700.00
Occupational, horse breeder, horse trotting, Austria, 3½", EX ...220.00
Occupational, iceman, block of ice & tongs, T&V Limoges, EX .425.00
Occupational, liveryman, stable scene, prof rpr, 3¾" 625.00
Occupational, pharmacist, skull & crossbones 625.00
Occupational, printer, printing press, T&V Limoges, 3⅝" 500.00
Occupational, sailboat scene w/gulls & shore, name in gold 135.00
Occupational, storekeeper, hardware store scene, 3⅝", EX 235.00
Occupational, telegrapher, telegraph key & flowers, M gold 450.00

Shawnee

The Shawnee Pottery Company operated in Zanesville, Ohio, from 1937 to 1961. They produced inexpensive novelty ware (vases, flowerpots, and figurines) as well as a very successful line of figural cookie jars, creamers, and salt and pepper shakers.

They also produced three dinnerware lines, the first of which, Valencia, was designed by Louise Bauer in 1937 for Sears & Roebuck. A starter set was given away with the purchase of one of their refrigerators. Second and most popular was the King Corn line. It was produced from 1946 to 1954, when the colors were changed to a lighter yellow for the kernels and darker green for the shucks. This variation was called Queen Corn. (Our values are for yellow corn prices unless white is noted in the description.) Their third dinnerware line, produced after 1954, was called Lobsterware. It was made in either black, brown, or gray; lobsters were usually applied to serving pieces and accessory items.

For further study we recommend these books: *The Collector's Guide to Shawnee Pottery* by our advisors, Janice and Duane Vanderbilt, who are listed in the Directory under Indiana; and *Shawnee Pottery, An Identification and Value Guide*, by Jim and Bev Mangus, who are listed in Ohio.

Cookie Jars

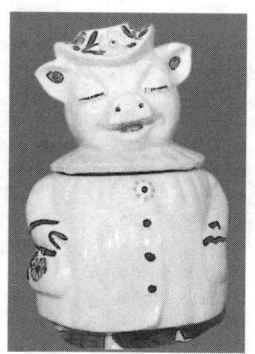

Winnie the Pig, coral collar, marked USA, minimum value, $350.00. (Watch for reproductions.)

Cottage, mk USA 6, minmum value	1,350.00
Drum Major, mk USA, minimum value	425.00
Dutch boy, cold pnt, mk USA, minimum value	50.00
Dutch boy, patches, gold trim, mk USA, minimum value	475.00
Dutch boy, stripes/gold/decals, mk USA, minimum value	375.00
Dutch girl, gold trim & decals, mk USA, minimum value	325.00
Dutch girl, pnt under glaze, mk USA, minimum value	100.00
Fruit basket, gold trim, mk Shawnee 84, minimum value	225.00
Hexagon-Basketweave, mk USA, minimum value	50.00
Jug, flowers pnt over glaze, mk USA, minimum value	100.00
Little Chef, wht w/gold trim, mk USA, minimum value	275.00
Muggsy, decals & gold, mk Pat Muggsy USA, minimum value +	850.00
Octagon, Fernware, emb ferns on bl, mk USA, minimum value	75.00
Owl, gold trim, mk USA, from $295 to	325.00
Puss 'n Boots, gold & decals, mk Pat Puss'n Boots, minimum +	625.00
Puss 'n Boots, tail over ft, mk Pat Puss'n Boots, minimum value +	185.00
Sailor boy, blk hair, gold trim, mk USA, minimum value +	900.00
Sitting elephant, cold pnt, mk USA, minimum value	125.00
Sitting elephant, fly on tusk, gold & decals, mk USA, minimum	500.00
Smiley the Pig, chocolate base, Shawnee Smiley #60, minimum +	350.00
Smiley the Pig, clover bud, mk Pat Smiley USA, minimum value +	500.00
Smiley the Pig, decals & gold trim, mk USA, minimum value +	400.00
Smiley the Pig, plums, mk USA, minimum value +	450.00
Snowflake, bean pot shape, mk USA, minimum value	50.00
Winnie the Pig, bl collar w/gold trim, mk USA, minimum value +	400.00
Winnie the Pig, bl collar, mk USA, minimum value +	325.00
Winnie the Pig, red collar, gold trim, mk USA, minimum value +	650.00

Corn Line

Bowl, cereal; mk #94	45.00

Bowl, fruit; mk #92	40.00
Bowl, mixing; mk #5, 5"	25.00
Bowl, mixing; mk #6, 6"	30.00
Bowl, vegetable; mk #95	45.00
Butter dish, mk #72	50.00
Casserole, mk #73, w/lid, sm, from $60 to	100.00
Casserole, mk #74, w/lid, lg	40.00
Cookie jar, mk #66, from $250 to	300.00
Corn holder, #79	40.00
Creamer, gold trim, mk USA, from $65 to	90.00
Creamer, mk #70	25.00
Cup, mk #90	30.00
Mug, mk #69	45.00
Pitcher, mk #71, lg	65.00
Pitcher, mk USA, wht corn w/gold trim	140.00
Plate, mk #68, 10"	35.00
Plate, mk #93, 8"	25.00
Platter, mk #96, 12"	50.00
Relish dish, mk #79	32.00
Saucer, mk #91	12.00
Shakers, Indian corn, pr	65.00
Shakers, lg, pr	30.00
Shakers, sm, pr	25.00
Shakers, wht corn, lg, pr	30.00
Shakers, wht corn, sm, pr	25.00
Sugar bowl, mk #70	35.00
Sugar bowl, wht corn, gold trim, mk USA	75.00
Sugar shaker, wht corn	60.00
Teapot, mk #65, 10-oz	175.00
Teapot, mk #75, gold trim, 30-oz	175.00
Teapot, mk #75, 30-oz	75.00

Kitchenware

Casserole, Fruit, w/lid, mk Shawnee #83	70.00
Coffeepot, Pennsylvania Dutch, mk USA #52	150.00
Creamer, elephant, gold & decals, mk Pat USA	200.00
Creamer, Smiley, bl & yel, mk Shawnee #86	50.00
Creamer, Snowflake, mk USA	17.00
Creamer, Tulip, ball jug form, mk USA	75.00
Lobster, creamer jug, #921	80.00
Lobster, French casserole, #900, 10-oz	20.00
Lobster, patio plate & mug set, #913, 8-pc	575.00
Lobster, shakers, claw, #905, pr	35.00
Lobster, shakers, full body, #933, pr	175.00
Lobster, spoon holder, dbl; #935	200.00
Pitcher, Bo Peep, lav bonnet, mk Pat Bo Peep	95.00
Pitcher, Bo Peep, mk Shawnee #47, sm	80.00
Pitcher, Charlie Chicken, gold & decals, mk Chanticleer	275.00
Pitcher, Octagon Jug, Fernware, mk USA	50.00
Pitcher, Sunflower, mk USA	80.00
Shakers, Bo Peep & Sailor boy, sm, pr	24.00
Shakers, Charlie Chicken, lg, pr	40.00
Shakers, Dutch boy & girl, gold & decals, lg, pr	135.00
Shakers, Flower & Fern, sq, lg, pr	28.00
Shakers, flowerpot, gold trim, sm, pr	55.00
Shakers, milk can, paper stickers, sm, pr	30.00
Shakers, Muggsy, gold trim, lg, pr	265.00
Shakers, owl, gr eyes, sm, pr	30.00
Shakers, Puss'n Boots, sm, pr	48.00
Shakers, Smiley, gr bib, lg, pr	135.00
Shakers, sunflower, lg, pr	50.00
Shakers, Winnie & Smiley, sm, pr	55.00
Teapot, bl leaves on wht, mk USA	45.00

Teapot, elphant, gr or yel, no decor, mk USA, 5-cup 135.00
Teapot, Granny Ann, mk USA 130.00
Teapot, Pennsylvania Dutch, mk USA #27, 27-oz 80.00
Teapot, Tom Tom, mk Tom the Piper's Son Pat USA 70.00
Utility jar, Bl Basketweave, w/gold & decals, mk USA 115.00
Valencia, ashtray 17.00
Valencia, bowl, mixing; 8" 20.00
Valencia, carafe, 3-pt 55.00
Valencia, chop dish, 13" 32.00
Valencia, coffee cup, AD 37.00
Valencia, cookie jar 100.00
Valencia, pie server, 9" 30.00
Valencia, punch/salad bowl, 12" 47.00
Valencia, vase, 12" 22.00

Miscellaneous

Ashtray, Contemporary Line, boomerang shape, mk USA #300, 11" .12.00
Ashtray, shell form, mk USA #204 ....25.00
Bank, Howdy Doody, mk USA Bob Smith 500.00
Bookends, dog's heads, mk USA, pr 75.00
Bowl, console; emb ribs, integral hdls, oval, mk USA, 4x10" 20.00
Candle holders, cornucopia form, 3½", pr 18.00
Candle holders, magnolia blossoms w/gold, mk USA, 3", pr 30.00
Centerpiece planter, Cameo, mk USA #2503, 10" 15.00
Figurine, bear, tumbling, w/gold & decals 110.00
Figurine, frog, unmk, sm 20.00
Figurine, Orientals playing mandolins, lg, pr 40.00
Figurine, pekingese, sm 60.00
Figurine, squirrel, sm 60.00
Flower frog, dolphin figural, low base, unmk, 3½" 35.00
Flower frog, turtle figural, unmk, 4x5" 35.00
Flowerpot, attached saucer, mk Shawnee USA #533, 3" 8.00
Flowerpot, emb geometric design, attached saucer, mk USA, 2½" .8.00
Jardiniere, emb bamboo, mk USA #4055, 5" 12.00
Jardiniere, emb leaves, mk USA, 3½" 8.00
Jardiniere, emb tulips, mk USA, 3½" 10.00
Jardiniere, Tiara, crown form, mk Shawnee USA #3505, 8" 18.00
Lamp, wall; vegetables in basket, unmk 60.00
Lamp base, Champ the Dog 20.00
Lamp base, clown figural, cold pnt, unmk 55.00
Lamp base, duck, cold pnt, unmk 55.00
Plant waterer, fish form, mk USA 40.00
Planter, Chantilly, mk USA #1804, 5" sq 10.00
Planter, circus wagon, mk USA 50.00
Planter, coal car, mk USA #551 ....50.00
Planter, donkey & cart, mk USA 12.00
Planter, Dutch girl & sprinkler, mk USA 12.00
Planter, gazelle, gold trim, mk USA #614 ....80.00
Planter, globe, gold trim, mk Shawnee USA 55.00
Planter, gondola, mk USA 25.00
Planter, mallard, flying on cube shape, mk Sawnee USA #820 .....20.00
Planter, top hat, mk USA 12.00
Tankard, Bronze Medallion, mk USA #990 ....60.00
Urn planter, Pastel Medallion, mk #1501, 5" 22.00
Vase, Basketweave, mk Shawnee #842, 6½" 12.00
Vase, Confetti, mk Kenwood USA #2103, 10" 14.00
Vase, Conventional, mk USA #2012, 8" 16.00
Vase, cornucopia; wht, mk USA, 3½" 12.00
Vase, emb wheat, gold trim, mk USA, 5" 22.00
Vase, irises emb on fan form, mk USA, 6" 18.00
Wall pocket, Little Jack Horner, mk USA #585 ....30.00
Wall pocket, telephone, gold trim, mk USA #529 ....50.00
Window box, Fairy Wood, mk Shawnee USA #1206, 12" L 12.00

Shearwater

Since 1928 generations of the Peter, Walter, and James McConnell Anderson families have been producing figurines and artwares in their studio at Ocean Springs, Mississippi. Their work is difficult to date. Figures from the '20s and '30s won critical acclaim and have continued to be made to the present time. Early marks include a die-stamped 'Shearwater' in a dime-sized circle, a similar ink stamp, and a half-circle mark. Any older item may still be ordered in the same glazes as it was originally produced, so many pieces on the market today may be relatively new. However, the older marks are not currently in use. Currently produced Blacks and pirates figurines are marked with a hand-incised 'Shearwater' and/or a cypher formed with an 'S' whose bottom curve doubles as the top loop of a 'P' formed by the addition of an upright placed below and to the left of the S. Many are dated, '93, for example. These figures are generally valued at $35.00 to $50.00 and are available at the pottery or by mail order. New decorated and carved pieces are very expensive, starting at $400.00 to $500.00 for a 6" pot.

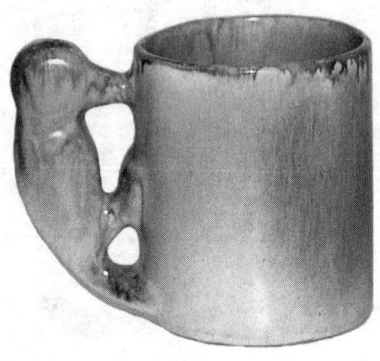

Mug, green flambe, bird handle, die stamp, $65.00.

Bowl, bl & gr flambe, mk, 9" sq 100.00
Figurine, bird, cream 200.00
Figurine, Don Quixote 150.00
Pitcher, dusty gr & gunmetal, 5" 85.00
Pitcher, gr drip, bulbous, lg 75.00
Plate, HP duck motif, stamped mk, WI Anderson, 1½x8¼" ...3,300.00
Vase, gr, cylindrical, thrown, 12" 100.00
Vase, pelicans flying/swimming, mc on cream gloss, 3½x7", NM ...300.00
Vase, turq over cream, mk, 6x8" 185.00

Sheet Music

Sheet music is often collected more for its colorful lithographed covers, rather than for the music itself. Transportation songs (which have pictures or illustrations of trains, ships, and planes), ragtime and blues, comic characters (especially Disney), sports, political, and expositions are eagerly sought after. Much of the sheet music on the market today is valued at under $5.00; some of the better examples are listed here. For more information refer to *Sheet Music Reference and Price Guide, Second Edition*, by Anna Marie Guiheen and Marie-Reine A. Pafik. Values are given for examples in excellent to near-mint condition unless otherwise noted.

After You're Gone, by Waldron & Duke, transportation, 1926 ....10.00
All American Girl, photo cover: Ted Fiorito, 1932 ....10.00
Am I Blue, movie: On With the Show, 1929 ....8.00
Angelina, photo cover: Louis Prima, 1944 ....5.00
Arkansas Traveler, photo cover: Patsy Montana, 1941 ....5.00
Auto Race, by Percy Wenrich, transportation, 1908 ....15.00

Bagdad, by Harold Alleridge & Al Jolson, 1918 ....**10.00**

Beautiful Sahara, photo cover: Louise Glaum, 1919 ....**10.00**

Beware, movie: Call Out the Marines, 1942 ....**5.00**

Blue Skies of Normandie, photo cover: Edith Clifford, 1921 ....**5.00**

Brave Jennie Creek, by Newkirk, transportation, 1895 ....**25.00**

Butcher Rag, by Louis Mentel, 1914 ....**10.00**

Caprola, by Schultz, cover artist: Pfeiffer, 1918 ....**15.00**

Checkers Rag, by Harry J Lincoln, rag, 1913 ....**15.00**

Close, by Cole Porter, movie: Rosalie, 1937 ....**5.00**

Coming Home, by Wilmot & Willeby, WWI, 1914 ....**10.00**

Cup Hunters, by Julius Lenzberg, sports, 1915 ....**15.00**

Darling I, musical: Buddies, WWI, 1919 ....**10.00**

Delightful Rag, by Lester Sell, 1914 ....**15.00**

Don't Cry Baby, photo cover: Guy Lombardo, 1928 ....**5.00**

Down in the Depths, by Cole Porter, Movie: Red, Hot & Blue, 1936 ...**5.00**

Dreaming, photo cover: Kitty Gordon, 1911 ....**5.00**

Entertainer's Rag, by Jay Roberts, 1912 ....**20.00**

Fairy Tales, by BC Hilliam, musical: Buddies, 1919 ....**10.00**

Five More Minutes, photo cover: Bob Crosby, 1946 ....**5.00**

Ford, by Zickel, transportation, 1908 ....**20.00**

GI Jive, by Johnny Mercer, cover artist: Holley, WWII, 1942 ......**10.00**

Girl From Paree, musical: The Girl Who Smiles, 1915 ....**10.00**

God Save America, by Arthur West, WWI, 1918 ....**15.00**

Good Gravy Rag, photo cover: Miss Mike Berkin, 1913 ....**15.00**

Gypsy Blues, musical: Shuffle Along, 1921 ....**8.00**

Hats Off to the Red White & Blue, by Ralph Beegan, WWI, 1918 ..**15.00**

He's So Unusual, movie: Sweetie, photo cover: Helen Kane, 1939 ...**5.00**

Heartbroken, photo cover: Judy Garland, 1953 ....**10.00**

Ho Ho Song, photo cover: Red Buttons, 1953 ....**5.00**

How Deep Is the Ocean, by Irving Berlin, 1932 ....**5.00**

I Beg of You, by Elvis Presley, 1957 ....**20.00**

I'd Be Proud To Be a Mother of a Soldier, WWI, 1918 ....**15.00**

I Double Dare You, photo cover: Rudy Vallee, 1937 ....**5.00**

I Have a Big Jazz Band, by Bowers, 1918 ....**10.00**

I'll Have Vanilla, photo cover: Eddie Cantor, 1934 ....**10.00**

I Love My Wife So Keep Away, musical: Ziegfeld Follies, 1909 ....**10.00**

I'm an Indian Too, movie: Annie Get Your Gun, 1946 ....**5.00**

I'm Happy That's All, cover artist: Pfeiffer, 1911 ....**15.00**

I'm Not Your Steppin' Stone, Monkees, 1966 ....**5.00**

I Surrender Dear, photo cover: Bing Crosby, 1931 ....**5.00**

I've Got a Tooth Bothering Me, Irving Berlin, 1916 ....**10.00**

I Went to Your Wedding, photo cover: Patti Page, 1952 ....**5.00**

If I Had My Way, photo cover: Woody Herman, 1913 ....**5.00**

Ike, Mr President, photo cover: White House, political, 1953 ......**25.00**

In a World of Our Own, movie: Alice in Wonderland, Disney, 1951 ..**10.00**

In the Middle of the Dream, photo cover: Tommy Dorsey, 1939 ....**5.00**

Iron Division, Dedicated to 28th Division, WWI March, 1919 ....**20.00**

It Might Have Been, Cole Porter, movie: Something...About, 1943 ..**5.00**

It's Pretty Things You..., photo cover: Little Amy Butler, 1908 ....**15.00**

Jesse James, by Jerry Livingston, photo Eileen Barton, 1954 ....**5.00**

Just an Echo in Valley, sgn photo cover: Bing Crosby, 1932 ....**30.00**

Kansas City Rag, by James Scott, 1907 ....**10.00**

La Brasiliana Tango, cover artist: Starmer, 1913 ....**10.00**

Lady Bird, Cha, Cha, Cha, cover artist: Norman Rockwell, 1968 ..**25.00**

Lavender Blue, movie: So Dear to My Heart, Disney, 1948 ....**10.00**

Let's Go, by Braley & Kern, musical: Toot Toot, 1918 ....**8.00**

Little Bo Peep Has Lost Her Jeep, Transportation, 1942 ....**10.00**

Little Mother, musical: Four Sons, photo cover: Bob Olsen, 1928 .**10.00**

Lord Is Good to Me, movie: Melody Time, Disney, 1948 ....**10.00**

Love's Golden Dream, advertising: Bromo Seltzer, 1907 ....**15.00**

Magna Carta, by John Phillips Sousa, 1927 ....**20.00**

Man in Love, Ira & Geo Gershwin, movie: Rhapsody in Blue, 1945 ..**10.00**

Massa's in the Cold Cold Ground, by Stephen Foster, 1852 ....**50.00**

Memphis Blues, by WC Handy, 1913 ....**10.00**

My Best Girl's a Corker, photo cover: Washburn Sisters, 1895 .....**15.00**

My Mobile Gal, by MacConnell, transportation, 1900 ....**15.00**

No Strings, Irving Berlin, photo cover: Astaire & Rogers, 1935 ...**10.00**

Oh! Susanna, by Stephen Foster, cover: Black Face, 1848 ....**35.00**

On the Street Where You Live, movie: My Fair Lady, 1956 ....**5.00**

Painting the Roses Red, movie: Alice in Wonderland, Disney, 1951 ..**10.00**

Policemen's Ball, Irving Berlin, musical: Miss Liberty, 194 ....**10.00**

Praise the Lord...Ammunition, by Frank Loesser, WWII, 1942 ....**15.00**

Ragtime Dance, by Scott Joplin, 1906 ....**50.00**

Rose of the Morning, musical: The Passing Show, 1923 ....**10.00**

Say It With Music, by Irving Berlin, musical: Box Revue, 1921 ...**10.00**

Silver Moon, musical: My Maryland, 1927 ....**5.00**

So This Is Love, movie: Cinderella, Disney, 1949 ....**10.00**

Son of the Sheik, photo cover: Rudolph Valentino, 1926 ....**15.00**

Song of the South, movie: Song of the South, Disney, 1946 ....**10.00**

Sugar, sgn photo: Little Jack Little, cover artist: Leff, 1931 ....**5.00**

Teenager's Mother, photo cover: Bill Haley, 1958 ....**5.00**

Then I'd Be Satisfied With You, George M Cohan **15.00**

Thunder Over Paradise, movie: Rose of the Rancho, 1935 ....**5.00**

Tulips, by Walter E Miles, cover artist: Jaroushek, 1916 ....**10.00**

Turn on Heat, photo cover: Janet Gaynor, 1929 ....**15.00**

Underneath Hawaiian Skies, musical: Passing Show 1921, 1921 ..**10.00**

Washington Post March, John Phillips Sousa, 1889 ....**30.00**

What Did You Do in the Infantry, by Frank Loesser, WWII, 1943 .**5.00**

When Johnny Comes Marching Home Again, by Louis Lambert, 1863 ...**45.00**

Where in the World, photo cover: Mindy Carson, 1950 ....**5.00**

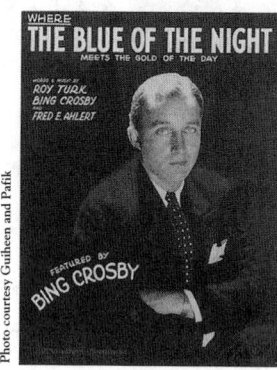

Where the Blue of the Night Meets the Gold of the Day, by Turk, Crosby, and Ahlert, Bing Crosby photo cover, 1931, $15.00.

Will You Be My Teddy Bear, photo Anna Held, 1907 ....**25.00**

Yankee Doodle Blues, George Gershwin, 1922 ....**10.00**

You're on Top, by Cole Porter, movie: Anything Goes, 1934 ....**5.00**

You Said Something, musical: Have a Heart, 1916 ....**10.00**

Shelley

In 1872 Joseph Shelley became partners with James Wileman, owner of Foley China Works, thus creating Wileman & Co. in Stoke-on-Trent. Twelve years later James Wileman withdrew from the company, though the firm continued to use his name until 1925 when it became known as Shelley Potteries, Ltd. Like many successful 19th-century English potteries, this firm continued to produce useful household wares as well as dinnerware of considerable note. In 1896 the beautiful Dainty White shape was introduced, and it is regarded by many as synonymous with the name Shelley. In addition to the original Dainty (6-flute) design, other lovely shapes were produced: Ludlow (14-

flute), Oleander (petal shape), Stratford (12-flute), Queen Anne (with 8 angular panels), Ripon (with its distinctive pedestal), and the 1930s shapes of Vogue, Eve, and Regent.

Though often overlooked, striking earthenware was produced under the direction of Frederick Rhead and later Walter Slater and his son Eric. Many notable artists contributed their talents in designing unusual, attractive wares: Rowland Morris, Mabel Lucie Attwell, and Hilda Cowham, to name but a few.

In 1966 Allied English Potteries acquired control of the Shelley Company, and by 1967 the last of the exquisite Shelley China had been produced to honor remaining overseas orders. In 1971 Allied English Potteries merged with the Doulton group. Reports of Shelley China currently being produced have not been verified. Some Shelley patterns (Dainty Blue, Bridal Rose, and Blue Rock) have been seen on Royal Albert and Queensware pieces. Both of these companies are part of the Doulton Group. Our advisors for this category are Lila and Fred Shrader; they are listed in the Directory under California.

See also Attwell, Mabel Lucie.

Key:
LE — Linda Edgerton   QA — Queen Anne
FMN — Forget-Me-Not   W — Wileman, pre-1910

Trio, Violets, six-flute: Plate, 8", $55.00; Cup and saucer, $58.00.

Ashtray, Dainty Mauve, 3½" dia 45.00
Ashtray, Dainty Pink, 5" dia 55.00
Ashtray, Melody (Chintz), 4½" dia 75.00
Ashtray, Treanor's 101, blk on wht earthenware, 5¾" sq 49.00
Biscuit jar, cloisonne w/brass collar & bail, 7½" 375.00
Bowl, cereal; Harebell, Oleander shape, 6½" 39.00
Bowl, cream soup; Duchess, Gainsborough shape, hdls, w/tray 45.00
Bowl, cream soup; Harebell, Oleander shape, hdls, w/tray 72.00
Bowl, cream soup; Stocks, Dainty shape, hdls, w/tray 89.00
Bowl, flat soup; Dainty Blue, 7½" 110.00
Bowl, fruit; Morning Glory, Dainty shape, 5½" 38.00
Bowl, rimmed soup; Dainty Blue, 8¼" 125.00
Bowl, vegetable; Bridal Rose, hdls, domed lid, 9½" 395.00
Bowl, vegetable; Dubarry, oval, 10x7" 55.00
Bowl, vegetable; Primrose, Dainty shape, oval, 10x7" 225.00
Bowl, vegetable; Spurge, Mode shape, w/lid, 9" 195.00
Box, floral w/gold, Late Foley, 1x2¾" dia 79.00
Butter dish, Harmony Drip Ware, 3½x7x7" 245.00
Butter dish, Rose & Red Daisy, Dainty shape, ¼-lb 155.00
Butter dish, Wildflowers, Dainty shape, 7½" dia 180.00
Butter pat, Dainty Mauve 110.00
Butter pat, England's Charm (scenic) 49.00
Butter pat, Rosebud 45.00
Butter pat, Wild Anenome, Dainty shape 65.00
Butter tub, Harmony Ware, w/lid & underplate.............................110.00
Cake plate, Crabtree, QA shape, ped ft, 8½" dia 165.00
Cake plate, Melody (Chintz), tab hdls, lt gr center, 8" sq 175.00
Cake plate, Rambler Rose, Dainty shape, tab hdls, 8" sq 135.00

Cake plate, rich gold, Empire shape, Wileman, ped ft, 8"dia 255.00
Cake plate, Rock Garden (Chintz), chrome 2½" ped, 8" sq 165.00
Candle holder, Stocks, Dainty shape, brass mt, 6" drilled plate 55.00
Candlestick, Indian Peony, 5½x4" 95.00
Candy dish, Celandine, Ludlow shape, 4½" dia 50.00
Candy dish, Dainty Pink, tab hdls, 5" sq 56.00
Candy dish, Rose, Pansy FMN, Dainty shape, tab hdls, 5" sq 45.00
Candy dish, Rose & Red Daisy, Chicago shape, 5¾" 65.00
Chamber set, earthenware, pitcher+bowl+soap dish+lid+chamberstick ..300.00
Chamberstick, Summer Glory (Chintz), w/finger ring, 5½" W ..225.00
Cheese dish, Dainty Pink, oblong, w/domed lid, 7¼" L 465.00
Children's ware, baby dish, Festival of Empire series, 8" dia 225.00
Children's ware, baby dish, Robinson Crusoe, oval, 7½" 85.00
Children's ware, egg cup, Teddy Bear 72.00
Children's ware, plate, LE, Little Red Riding Hood & Wolf, 6½" ..110.00
Chop plate, Heavenly Blue, Dainty shape, 12" dia 395.00
Cigarette set, Rosebud, Dainty shape, ashtray & cigarette holder .65.00
Coffeepot, Deco, angular open hdl, Mode shape, 8-cup 585.00
Coffeepot, Harmony Drip Ware, Mode shape, 6-cup 345.00
Coffeepot, Heather (scenic), Richmond shape, 6-cup 265.00
Coffeepot, Melody (banded Chintz), Henley, 8-cup 395.00
Coffeepot, Sheraton, Gainsborough shape, 8-cup 350.00
Commemorative cup & saucer, Elizabeth II coronation, Ripon shape ...75.00
Commemorative plate, Elizabeth/Phillip's Canadian Tour 65.00
Creamer, Duchess, Gainsborough shape, 5" 45.00
Creamer & sugar bowl, Bridal Rose, Dainty shape, med 95.00
Creamer & sugar bowl, Heather, w/lid, lg 135.00
Creamer & sugar bowl, Lily of Valley, Dainty, med, +oval tray ..135.00
Creamer & sugar bowl, Maytime...160.00
Creamer & sugar bowl, Primrose Chintz, Richmond shape, med .135.00
Creamer & sugar bowl, Scilla, Bute shape, 3½x2½" 95.00
Creamer & sugar bowl, Spurge, Oxford shape, lg 79.00
Creamer & sugar bowl, Violets, Dainty shape, ind 85.00
Crested ware, hatpin holder, Manchester crest, Dainty shape 75.00
Crested ware, horn w/o hand, Tynemouth, Wileman 68.00
Crested ware, teapot, Turnridge Well, mini, 3" 90.00
Cup & saucer, Begonia, Blue Rock or Rosebud, Dainty shape, ea .58.00
Cup & saucer, Begonia, Cambridge shape 55.00
Cup & saucer, Black Leafy Tree, mc enamel & gold, QA shape .165.00
Cup & saucer, Charm, Henley shape 57.00
Cup & saucer, chocolate; Baker's lady logo, gold trim 125.00
Cup & saucer, Dainty, floral hdl & panels of colors 235.00
Cup & saucer, demi; Campanula, Ludlow shape 60.00
Cup & saucer, demi; Daffodil Time, Cambridge shape 55.00
Cup & saucer, demi; Dainty Blue 65.00
Cup & saucer, demi; Maytime 115.00
Cup & saucer, Hampton Court, QA shape 88.00
Cup & saucer, Harebell w/in cup (bl w/o), bl saucer, Oleander 72.00
Cup & saucer, Honeysuckle, Oleander shape 80.00
Cup & saucer, Mallards in Flight, Cambridge shape 52.00
Cup & saucer, Maytime w/in cup (pk w/o), pk saucer, Oleander ..85.00
Cup & saucer, Shamrock, farmer sz (12-oz) 75.00
Cup & saucer, solid color w/rich gold inside cup, QA shape 125.00
Cup & saucer, Stocks, Henley shape 55.00
Cup & saucer, Summer Glory (Chintz), Ripon shape w/gold ft/hdl .95.00
Cup & saucer, Sunrise & Trees, QA shape 85.00
Cup & saucer, Wildflower, Ripon shape w/bl ft & hdl 65.00
Egg cup, Begonia, Blue Rock or Regency, Dainty shape, lg, ea 75.00
Egg cup, Blue Rock or Bridal Rose/Rose Spray, Dainty shape, sm, ea 65.00
Egg cup, Indian Peony, lg 50.00
Gravy boat, Lilac Time, Dainty shape, w/undertray 175.00
Gravy boat, Rosebud, Dainty shape, w/undertray 165.00
Hatpin holder, bl flowers on wht w/gold, Late Foley, 6½" 110.00
Heraldic ware, ashtray, crested shield shape, W, 2½x3"................20.00

Horn (tumbler), Charm, w/hdl, 4½" 50.00
Horn (tumbler), Japan w/rich gold, Wileman, no hdl, 4¾" 135.00
Horn (tumbler), Lily of the Valley, Dainty shape, w/hdl, 4¼" 125.00
Hot-water pot, Bramble, Dainty shape, 4-cup 235.00
Jam/honey pot, Cleopatra, slotted lid, 3¾" 60.00
Jam/honey pot, Stocks, Dainty shape, slotted lid, 3" 110.00
Menu plaque, garden scene w/flowers & birds, 5x7" 110.00
Mould, food; nesting hen, med, 16-oz 145.00
Mould, food; Queens w/6-petal flower supported by swirls, lg, 20+ oz 110.00
Muffin, Morning Glory, Dainty shape, w/lid, 8" dia 185.00
Mustard, Campanula, slotted lid & underplate, 2¼" 135.00
Mustard, Dainty Ornge, slotted lid, 2¼" 95.00
Napkin ring, Blue Rock, Bridal Rose or Celandine, mk, ea 72.00
Napkin ring, Dainty Blue, unmk (Royal Albert?) 35.00
Pin dish, Maytime 50.00
Pitcher, Countryside (Chintz), gold hdl, 5½" 155.00
Pitcher, Dainty White (no gold), w/lid, 7½" 82.00
Plate, Blue Daisy or Green Daisy (banded Chintz), 8" 50.00
Plate, Dainty Blue or Heavenly Blue, Dainty shape, 8" 62.00
Plate, Drifting Leaves, Serenity, Duchess or Sheraton, 6" 22.00
Plate, Glorious Devon, Oleander shape, gold trim, 8" 55.00
Plate, Green or Blue Daisy (Chintz), 8", ea 65.00
Plate, Harebell, Oleander shape, 10½" 85.00
Plate, Heather, Old Mill or Woodland, Cambridge shape, 6", ea 22.00
Plate, Indian Peony, Sheraton, DuBarry, or Serenity, 10½", ea 55.00
Plate, Lily of the Valley or Rose & Red Daisy, Dainty, 6", ea 35.00
Plate, Melody, 8" 125.00
Plate, Regency (Dainty White w/gold trim), 10½" 85.00
Plate, Summer Glory (Chintz), 7" 85.00
Plate, Thistle, lg Pansy, Begonia, or Primrose, Dainty shape, 8" 55.00
Plate, wide cobalt band w/emb gold bands & center flower, 10½" 75.00
Platter, Dainty Blue or Heavenly Blue, 10½x8½" 240.00
Platter, Harebell or Bridal Rose, Oleander shape, 12½x10" 225.00
Platter, Rosebud or Rose Pansy FMN, Dainty shape, 15x12" 295.00
Platter, wht w/gold trim, Oleander shape, 12½x10" 195.00
Powder jar, matt w/gold decor, bud finial, 6" dia 125.00
Relish dish, Blue Rock, Dainty shape, 6x3½" 95.00
Tea & toast set, Bridal Rose/Rose Spray, Ludlow, cup+8" plate 70.00
Tea & toast set, Rose, Pansy FMN, Dainty shape, cup+5x8" plate 90.00
Teapot, Begonia or Regency, Dainty shape, 8-cup 325.00
Teapot, Crochet, Henley shape, 6-cup 210.00
Teapot, Lord Salisbury, earthenware, 4¾" 550.00
Teapot, pastel color (solid), Dainty shape, 4-cup 255.00
Teapot, turq to wht shaded, Shell shape, Wileman, 6¾" 280.00
Toast rack, Charm, 3-bar, 2¾x3" 100.00
Toast rack, Harmony Drip Ware, 5-bar, 8x5" 165.00
Toast rack, Melody (Chintz), 3-bar, 2¾x3" 195.00
Toast rack, wht utility ware, 5-bar, 8x4¼" 39.00
Tray, sandwich; Dainty Blue, tab hdls, 8½x4½" 175.00
Tray, sandwich; Meissenette, Dainty shape, tab hdls, 11½x4½" 165.00
Tray, sandwich; Phlox, Regent shape, tab hdls, 11½x4½" 145.00
Tray, triple; Bridal Rose, Dainty shape, long pk petal hdl, 12½" 345.00
Vase, bud; Moonlight coastle scene w/boats, Wileman, 6½" 79.00
Vase, Moresque, earthenware, stylized pnt decor, conical, 8" 165.00
Vase, pansy ring; Melody (Chintz), 6½" dia 200.00
Vase, Poppy Spray, enamel on blk matt, cylindrical, 5x3½" 65.00
Vase, storks, yel on orange matt, 8" 110.00

Silhouettes

Silhouette portraits were made by positioning the subject between a bright light and a sheet of white drawing paper. The resulting shadow was then traced and cut out, the paper mounted over a contrasting color and framed. The hollow-cut process was simplified by an invention called the Physiognotrace, a device that allowed tracing and cutting to be done in one operation. Experienced silhouette artists could do full-length figures, scenics, ships, or trains freehand. Some of the most famous of these artists were Charles Peale Polk, Charles Wilson Peale, William Bache, Doyle, Edouart, Chamberlain, Brown, and William King. Though not often seen, some silhouettes were completely painted or executed in wax. Examples listed here are hollow-cut unless another type is described and assumed to be in excellent condition unless noted otherwise.

Key:
bk — backing
c/p — cut and pasted
fl — full length
p — profile
wc — watercolor

Andrew Jackson, President of US, p, gilt & blk ink, fr, 10x9" 800.00
Child, p, ink details, blk lacquer w/gilt fr, 5⅝x5" 135.00
Child w/doll, fl, sm stain, gilt fr, 7⅜x5⅛" 330.00
Girl, p, ink details on hair & torso, gilt-brass fr, 5x4¾" 330.00

Lady on horseback, full-length profile on collage and wash background, Edouart, 1834, 12x9", $1,400.00.

Lady, ink details, beveled fr, 5x4" 140.00
Lady, p, c/p, blk lacquer fr w/gilt brass trim, 6⅜x5½" 88.00
Lady, p, c/p, identified, 19th C, bird's-eye veneer fr, 7x6" 225.00
Lady, p, gilt details, orig blk lacquer fr w/brass, 6x5" 600.00
Lady, p, gilt fr, 6¾x6¾" 195.00
Lady, p, identified/dtd 1871, modern fr, 6x5" 415.00
Lady, p, ink details, bl crepe bodice, 5⅝x5" 160.00
Lady, p, ink details, blk paper bking, old gilt fr, 4x3" 140.00
Lady, p, ink details, sgn, fr, 5x4" 330.00
Lady in bonnet, p, ink & ink wash, fr, 4½x4¼" 220.00
Major Zackary (sic) Taylor 1836, p, ebony fr w/brass liner, 7x6" 415.00
Man, fl, identified, Eduoart, 1829, fr, 12x7¾" 220.00
Man, fl, scratched details, shadowbox fr, 8½x6½" 165.00
Man, p, c/p, blk lacquered fr w/gilt brass trim, 6x5" 115.00
Man, p, dtd 1857, old blk & gilt fr, 6½x5½" 165.00
Man, p, eglomise glass & old blk molded fr, 6x5¼" 130.00
Man, p, gilt details, rosewood veneer ogee fr, 12x11" 175.00
Man, p, ink details, blk reed fr w/label, 4¾x3¾" 500.00
Man, p, ink details, sgn, 1837, shadowbox fr, 8⅜x6⅞" 575.00
Man, p, ink details, shadowbox fr, 6½x5¾" 300.00
Man, p, ink details & wht highlights, oval brass fr, 4½x4" 150.00
Man, p, pencil details, reeded fr: 7¼x5⅜" 100.00
Man, p, trn rnd fr w/old blk pnt, 5⅛" 140.00
Man & lady, p, c/p, identified, 1795, fr, 7x9" 770.00
Man & lady, p, ink & ink wash, fr, 6x4", pr 440.00
Man & lady, p, ink details, mahog veneer fr: 6⅝x10¼" 440.00
Man & lady, p, sgn, mc details, modern frs, 5½x4½", pr 715.00
Man in chair, fl, gilt details, ink wash ground, Medford, 12x10" 440.00

Man in chair reading, fl, separate stand, Edouart, 1828, 10x9" .1,200.00
Man in long robe, fl, gilt details, 1890s, stain, fr, 12x7" 150.00
Man in top hat, fl, gilt details, ink-wash ground, 13x10⅝" 330.00
Man w/scroll of paper, fl, c/p, pnt details, WH Brn/1845, 13x11" .770.00
Man w/top hat, fl, wht details, sgn/1827, 9⅜x7" 250.00
Youth w/book, gilt details, Hubbard, fr, 11¼x8" 635.00

Silver

Coin Silver

During colonial times in America, the average household could not afford items made of silver, but those fortunate enough to have accumulations of silver coins (900 parts silver/100 parts alloy) took them to the local silversmith who melted them down and made the desired household article requested. These pieces bore the owner's monogram and often the maker's mark, but the words 'Coin Silver' did not come into use until 1830. By 1860 the standard was raised to 925 parts silver/75 parts alloy and the word 'Sterling' was added.

Key:
fh — flat handle   hh — hollow handle
gw — gold washed

CF Hills, Hartford; tablespoon, 1850 ....30.00
Coin & pseudo hallmks, teaspoon, 1830s, 10 for 140.00
Cup, chased flowers, cast ear hdl, child sz, 2⅝" 250.00
Cup, repousse floral medallion, dtd Dec 25, 72, 3⅛" 220.00
E&D Kinsey, Newport KY; teaspoon, ca 1840 ....15.00
Eleazer Wyer Jr, Portland ME; teaspoon, ca 1810, 7 for 110.00
G Welsh, master salt cellar, pr 50.00
Gale, Wood & Hughes, NY; teaspoon, ca 1838, 3 for 40.00
George Hoyt, Albany; sauce ladle, ca 1822 ....45.00
Henry Harper, ladle, pierced 95.00
JC, teaspoon, ca 1830, 5 for 60.00
JW Tucker, San Francisco; master butter, beaded, ca 1850 ....35.00
New Orleans, cup, chased floral w/Bettie, dents, 4⅜" 415.00
R&W Wilson, Phila; dinner fork, shell pattern, 1840, 5 for 150.00
R&W Wilson, Phila; pitcher, chased floral rococo, 7⅝" 525.00
S Boardman, teaspoon, ca 1820-30, 6 for 70.00
S Richards, Phila; dessert spoon, ca 1791 ....45.00
S Wilmot, Charleston; gravy ladle, ca 1830 ....75.00
Wm Hackle, Baltimore; teaspoon, ca 1763, 3 for 95.00

Flatware

Silver flatware is being collected today either to replace missing pieces of heirloom sets or in lieu of buying new patterns, by those who admire and appreciate the style and quality of the older ware. Prices vary from dealer to dealer; some pieces are harder to find and are therefore more expensive. Items such as olive spoons, cream ladles, lemon forks, etc., once thought a necessary part of a silver service, may today be slow to sell; as a result, dealers may price them low and make up the difference on items that sell more readily. Many factors enter into evaluation. Popular patterns may be high due to demand though easily found, while scarce patterns may be passed over by collectors who find them difficult to reassemble. If pieces are monogrammed, deduct 25% (for rare, ornate patterns) to 30% (for common, plain pieces). Place settings generally come in three sizes: dinner, place, and luncheon, with the dinner size generally more expensive. In general, dinner knives are 9½" long, place knives, 9" to 9⅛", and luncheon knives, 8¾" to 8⅞" long. Dinner forks measure 7⅜" to 7½", place forks, 7¼" to 7⅜", and luncheon forks, 7" to 7¼" long. Our advisors for this category are Jo

Killmer and Rick Spencer; they are listed in the Directory under Utah. See also Tiffany, Silver.

Francis I, partial flatware service, 111 pieces totalling 131 troy ounces weighable silver, $3,025.00 at auction.

Acanthus, G Jensen, oval soup 92.00
Acanthus, G Jensen, salad fork 95.00
Acanthus, G Jensen, tablespoon 125.00
Aegean Weave, Wallace, bonbon server 33.00
Aegean Weave, Wallace, gravy ladle 59.00
Aegean Weave, Wallace, sugar spoon 30.00
Aegean Weave, Wallace, teaspoon 18.00
Afterglow, Oneida, master butter, fh 28.00
Afterglow, Oneida, 4-pc set, place sz 75.00
Autumn Leaves, Reed & Barton, fruit spoon 30.00
Autumn Leaves, Reed & Barton, ice cream fork 32.00
Autumn Leaves, Reed & Barton, iced tea spoon 38.00
Autumn Leaves, Reed & Barton, olive fork 30.00
Autumn Leaves, Reed & Barton, tablespoon, pierced 68.00
Belle Rose, Oneida, sauce ladle 33.00
Belle Rose, Oneida, 4-pc set, place sz 75.00
Blossom Time, International, cocktail fork 24.00
Blossom Time, International, cream soup 24.00
Blossom Time, International, jelly server 34.00
Blossom Time, International, 4-pc set, dinner sz 110.00
Burgundy, Reed & Barton, cold meat fork 69.00
Burgundy, Reed & Barton, mustard ladle 43.00
Burgundy, Reed & Barton, salt spoon 20.00
Burgundy, Reed & Barton, 4-pc set, dinner sz 138.00
Burgundy, Reed & Barton, 4-pc set, lunch sz 110.00
Burgundy, Reed & Barton, 4-pc set, place sz 115.00
Cactus, G Jensen, salad fork 140.00
Cactus, G Jensen, teaspoon 84.00
Chapel Bells, Alvin, cream soup 21.00
Chapel Bells, Alvin, ind butter spreader, hh 23.00
Chapel Bells, Alvin, 4-pc set, dinner sz 85.00
Colfax, Durgin, dinner knife 39.00
Colfax, Durgin, gravy ladle 68.00
Colfax, Durgin, tablespoon 65.00
Colonial Fiddle, Tuttle, demi spoon 32.00
Colonial Fiddle, Tuttle, oval soup 45.00
Colonial Fiddle, Tuttle, 4-pc set, dinner sz 150.00
Colonnade, Manchester, cream soup 22.00
Colonnade, Manchester, 4-pc set, luncheon sz 62.00
Copenhagen, Manchester, baby fork 22.00
Copenhagen, Manchester, gumbo soup 24.00
Copenhagen, Manchester, lemon fork 22.00

Copenhagen, Manchester, youth knife 25.00	Les Six Fleurs, Reed & Barton, place spoon 45.00
Copenhagen, Manchester, 4-pc set, dinner sz 72.00	Les Six Fleurs, Reed & Barton, salad serving set 395.00
Debussy, Towle, cheese server 42.00	Les Six Fleurs, Reed & Barton, tablespoon, pierced 75.00
Debussy, Towle, pie/cake server 50.00	Les Six Fleurs, Reed & Barton, 4-pc set, dinner sz 145.00
Debussy, Towle, salad fork 36.00	Lotus, Watson, berry server 70.00
Debussy, Towle, tablespoon, pierced 74.00	Lotus, Watson, 4-pc set, place sz 79.00
Delores, Shreve & Co, berry server 62.00	Love Disarmed, Reed & Barton, asparagus fork 245.00
Delores, Shreve & Co, cocktail fork 17.00	Love Disarmed, Reed & Barton, infant feeder 40.00
Delores, Shreve & Co, sauce ladle 29.00	Love Disarmed, Reed & Barton, salad serving spoon 225.00
Dupleix, Christofle, dinner fork 58.00	Love Disarmed, Reed & Barton, spaghetti server 265.00
Dupleix, Christofle, dinner knife 42.00	Love Disarmed, Reed & Barton, 4-pc set, dinner sz 240.00
Dupleix, Christofle, salad fork 39.00	Marie Antoinette, Gorham, oval soup 36.00
El Grandee, Towle, youth fork 28.00	Marie Antoinette, Gorham, tablespoon 60.00
El Grandee, Towle, 4-pc set, place sz 120.00	Mayflower, Kirk, gravy ladle 85.00
Eloquence, Lunt, baby cup 65.00	Mayflower, Kirk, luncheon fork 37.00
Eloquence, Lunt, fish server 130.00	Melrose, Gorham, fruit spoon 36.00
Eloquence, Lunt, gravy ladle 72.00	Melrose, Gorham, olive fork 34.00
Eloquence, Lunt, place fork 44.00	Melrose, Gorham, 4-pc set, dinner sz 126.00
Eloquence, Lunt, place spoon 42.00	Minuet, International, steak carving set, 2-pc 65.00
Faneuil, Tiffany, cocktail fork 36.00	Minuet, International, sugar spoon 27.00
Faneuil, Tiffany, dessert knife 44.00	Minuet, International, tablespoon, pierced 58.00
Faneuil, Tiffany, fruit spoon 47.00	Minuet, International, 4-pc set, place sz 80.00
Faneuil, Tiffany, tablespoon, pierced 98.00	Moonbeam, Rogers, cold meat fork 55.00
Fiddle Shell, Frank Smith, iced teaspoon 42.00	Moonbeam, Rogers, ind butter, fh 19.00
Fiddle Shell, Frank Smith, pie/cake server 48.00	Moonbeam, Rogers, 4-pc set, place sz 75.00
Fiddle Shell, Frank Smith, strawberry fork 33.00	Newport Scroll, Gorham, 4-pc set, place sz 115.00
Florentine Lace, Reed & Barton, candlesticks, 8", pr ...395.00	Normandie, Wallace, 4-pc set, luncheon sz 75.00
Florentine Lace, Reed & Barton, gravy ladle 74.00	Norse, International, salad serving set 135.00
Florentine Lace, Reed & Barton, place fork 39.00	Norse, International, 4-pc set, dinner sz 75.00
Florentine Lace, Reed & Barton, teaspoon 32.00	Old Maryland, Kirk, baby food pusher 45.00
French Regency, Wallace, master butter, hh 32.00	Old Maryland, Kirk, bacon server 85.00
French Regency, Wallace, place spoon 35.00	Old Maryland, Kirk, berry server 135.00
French Regency, Wallace, steak knife 40.00	Old Maryland, Kirk, candlesticks, pr 195.00
Georgian Maid, International, 4-pc set, dinner sz 75.00	Old Maryland, Kirk, iced tea spoon 41.00
Grand Duchess, Towle, bonbon server 45.00	Old Maryland, Kirk, luncheon fork 49.00
Grand Duchess, Towle, sauce ladle 42.00	Parma, Buccellati, casserole spoon 200.00
Greenbriar, Gorham, cream soup 22.00	Parma, Buccellati, cracker scoop, pierced 250.00
Greenbriar, Gorham, jelly server 29.00	Parma, Buccellati, oval soup 65.00
Greenbriar, Gorham, 4-pc set, luncheon sz 79.00	Parma, Buccellati, soup ladle 300.00
Hampton Court, Reed & Barton, salad serving fork 120.00	Parma, Buccellati, 4-pc set, dinner sz 220.00
Hampton Court, Reed & Barton, 4-pc set, place sz 110.00	Pointed Antique, Reed & Barton, bouillon spoon 30.00
Hannah Hull, Tuttle, boullion soup 35.00	Pointed Antique, Reed & Barton, fish fork, hh 32.00
Hannah Hull, Tuttle, salad serving set 139.00	Pointed Antique, Reed & Barton, lemon fork 29.00
Horizon, Easterling, sugar spoon 20.00	Pointed Antique, Reed & Barton, tea set, 5-pc 1,750.00
Horizon, Easterling, tomato server 60.00	Pointed Antique, Reed & Barton, 4-pc set, luncheon sz ...110.00
Horizon, Easterling, 4-pc set, luncheon sz 62.00	Processional, Fine Arts, 4-pc set, place sz 72.00
John & Priscilla, Westmoreland, gumbo soup 32.00	Puritan, Stieff, 4-pc set, luncheon sz 74.00
John & Priscilla, Westmoreland, master butter, fh 26.00	Queen Elizabeth, Towle, cold meat fork 75.00
John & Priscilla, Westmoreland, plastic salad set 44.00	Queen Elizabeth, Towle, place spoon 36.00
John & Priscilla, Westmoreland, tablespoon 45.00	Queen Elizabeth, Towle, steak knife 39.00
John & Priscilla, Westmoreland, 4-pc set, luncheon sz ..70.00	Queen's Lace, International, 4-pc set, dinner sz 98.00
King Albert, Whiting, bouillon spoon 20.00	Queen's Lace, International, 4-pc set, place sz 79.00
King Albert, Whiting, ice cream fork 22.00	Rondo, Gorham, demi spoon 24.00
King Albert, Whiting, luncheon fork 24.00	Rondo, Gorham, teaspoon 20.00
King Edward, Gorham, ind butter, hh 34.00	Rose Mary, Easterling, 4-pc set, luncheon sz 59.00
King Edward, Gorham, steak carving set, 2-pc 90.00	Rosepoint, Wallace, butter pick 26.00
King Edward, Gorham, 4-pc set, dinner sz 120.00	Rosepoint, Wallace, ramekin fork 32.00
Lady Clair, Stieff, cream soup spoon 45.00	Rosepoint, Wallace, sugar tongs 38.00
Lady Clair, Stieff, 4-pc set, luncheon sz 125.00	Rosepoint, Wallace, tea strainer 95.00
Laura, Buccellati, cream soup 64.00	Rosepoint, Wallace, 4-pc set, dinner sz 115.00
Laura, Buccellati, dinner fork 115.00	Rosepoint, Wallace, 4-pc set, luncheon sz 79.00
Laura, Buccellati, salt spoon 25.00	Rosepoint, Wallace, 4-pc set, place sz 89.00
Les Cinq Fleurs, Reed & Barton, pie/cake server 55.00	Savannah, Reed & Barton, pastry server, hh 45.00
Les Cinq Fleurs, Reed & Barton, teaspoon 24.00	Savannah, Reed & Barton, steak knife 40.00

Savannah, Reed & Barton, tomato server 75.00
Sceaux, Christofle, oval soup 44.00
Sceaux, Christofle, 4-pc set, dinner sz 130.00
Shell & Thread, Tiffany, demi spoon 44.00
Shell & Thread, Tiffany, ind paddle butter, hh 59.00
Shell & Thread, Tiffany, oval soup 89.00
Southern Charm, Alvin, tablespoon 49.00
Southern Charm, Alvin, 4-pc set, luncheon sz 75.00
Stieff Rose, Kirk, lettuce fork 75.00
Stieff Rose, Kirk, tablespoon, pierced 68.00
Torchon, Buccellati, oval soup 98.00
Torchon, Buccellati, 4-pc set, dinner sz 369.00
Troubadour, Frank Whiting, cream soup 32.00
Troubadour, Frank Whiting, ind butter, fh 24.00
Troubadour, Frank Whiting, teaspoon 20.00
Troubadour, Frank Whiting, 4-pc set, luncheon sz 95.00
Versailles, Gorham, cream soup 52.00
Versailles, Gorham, tablespoon 90.00
Versailles, Gorham, 4-pc set, dinner sz 245.00
Wild Rose, International, cream soup 34.00
Wild Rose, International, 4-pc set, place sz 98.00
Young Love, Oneida, infant feeder 24.00
Young Love, Oneida, lemon fork 22.00
Young Love, Oneida, 4-pc set, place sz 70.00

Hollow Ware

Until the middle of the 19th century, the silverware produced in America was custom made on order of the buyer directly from the silversmith. With the rise of industrialization, factories sprung up that manufactured silverware for retailers who often added their trademark to the ware. Silver ore was mined in abundance, and demand spurred production. Changes in style occurred at the whim of fashion. Repousse decoration (relief work) became popular about 1885, reflecting the ostentatious preference of the Victorian era. Later in the century, Greek, Etruscan, and several classic styles found favor. Today the Art Deco styles of this century are very popular with collectors.

In the listings that follow, manufacturer's name or trademark is noted first; in lieu of that information, listings are by country. Weight is given in troy ounces. See also Tiffany, Silver.

Key: t-oz — troy ounce

Am, sugar urn w/lid, bright-cut borders, 10", 15-t-oz 1,150.00
Ball Black & Co, NY; milk jug, repousse floral, 6", 12-t-oz 260.00
Boudo, tray, gadrooned edge, 10⅜" 1,650.00
Cellini, bowl, 5 lobes, mk S4, 2x9" 350.00
Chester, 1800; pitcher, Geo III, chased/eng/repousse, 3¾" 275.00
DeMatteo, bowl, openwork, ped base, acorn finial lid, 5½" H 300.00
Dominick & Haff, coffee set, Virginia, 1912, 5-pc 1,200.00
Dominick & Haff, tray, Virginia, 1912, 14" dia 350.00
Durgin, cream pitcher, appl parcel gilt floral 950.00
F Spiegelhalder, Louisville; julep, eng, ca 1840s, 3¾" 350.00
Fletcher & Gardiner, cup, hammered finish, ca 1815, 3" 220.00
G Eoff, coffeepot, melon ribs, floral bands, eagle spout, 10½" 990.00
Geo Jensen, bowl, berries/leaves openwork stem, 8", 26-t-oz 2,875.00
Geo Jensen, tea set, ebony hdld pot+cr/sug, all mk #456, EX 1,600.00
Geo Jensen, tray, Danish floral hdls, 13¼", 20-t-oz 2,500.00
German, jardiniere, Neoclassical style, 7½x18x8", 41-t-0z 2,800.00
Gorham, bud vase, Neoclassic, 1868 ....495.00
Gorham, coffeepot, Persian, hammered/repousse, 1881 ....2,400.00
Gorham, pitcher, floral repousse, decor hdl, 9", 33-t-oz 825.00
Gorham, sandwich tray, scalloped, ftd, 8½", 12½-t-oz 220.00
Gorham, tea set, 8-side urn forms, 5-pc, 68-t-oz 675.00

Grogan & Co, vase, flower form, 8-panel, 26-t-oz 850.00
Heather, tea/coffee service, chased florals, 6-pc/tray, 309-t-oz 2,100.00
Howard & Co, water pitcher, chased florals 1,800.00
IHR (John H Russell), creamer, urn form w/eng medallion, 7⅜" 715.00
IL, pitcher, Geo III, urn form, chased/eng florals, 4½" 225.00
International, bowl, lotus form, 9⅛", 12-t-oz 125.00
International, bread tray, Royal Danish 245.00
International, compote, Royal Danish, med 195.00
International, goblet, Wedgwood 225.00
International, service plate, Wedgwood 325.00
International, tea set, Royal Danish, 4-pc 1,500.00
International, tray, serpentine rim, 17x12", 32-t-oz 200.00
J McMullin, Phila; cake stand, reeded band, 1800s, 19-t-oz 1,550.00
JC Klinkosch, candelabra, 800 fine, 10¼", 42-t-oz, pr 2,645.00
Kirk, salver, repousse, claw ft, 12" 1,200.00
Kirk, service plate, repousse 395.00
Kirk, sugar shaker, repousse, 11-t-oz 450.00
Kirk & Son, butter dish, floral repousse, 11½-t-oz 260.00
Kirk & Son, coffee set, AD; floral repousse, 4-pc, 20-oz 650.00
Kirk & Son, gravy boat, floral repousse, w/ladle, 9-t-oz 300.00
LeBolt, pitcher, hinged lid, #185, 3¾", +5" plate 425.00
London, salver, Greek Key border, 4-ftd, oval, 7x5¼", 4-t-oz 360.00
London hallmk for 1721, castor, baluster, low dome lid, 3¼" 200.00
London hallmk for 1759, pitcher, Geo II, pear form, 4", 3-t-oz 325.00
Merriman, punch ladle, eng CABS, rattail hdl, 13" 385.00
Mexican, platter, well & tree, early 1900s, 72-t-oz 385.00
Mulholland, bowl, hand-wrought, oval, 10" 450.00
Peter L Kreder, goblet, 6⅜", 1850s 160.00
Randahl, bowl, appl & rtcl hdls, mk, 2½x12½" 400.00
Randahl, presentation tray, plain molded border, 45-t-oz 280.00
Reed & Barton, bowl, centerpc; Floral (pierced & appl), heavy, 19" 2,500.00
Reed & Barton, candelabra, Francis I, 3-tier, X5691, 14", pr 4,500.00
Reed & Barton, lady's flask, cherub/florals, hinged lid, 5½" 525.00
Reed & Barton, serving tray, Hampton Court, 27¼x17" 1,400.00
Robert Garrard, coffeepot, Geo III, pearwood hdl, 20-oz 600.00
Rogers 1847, bread tray, Springtime, 1957, 13x8" 50.00
Samuel Hennell, teapot, Late Geo III, bird's head spout, 21-oz 600.00
Samuel Williamson, Phila, bowl, ftd, eng medallion, 5⅝x6½" 1,100.00
Shiebler, nut dish, Poppy 95.00
Thomas Meriton, London, 1810; pap boat, Geo III, 2-t-oz 275.00
Wallace, bread tray, Poppy 225.00
Wallace, creamer & sugar bowl, Grande Baroque 350.00
Wallace, tazza, Stradivari pattern, 10¼", 14½-t-oz 1,350.00
Whiting, bowl, seafood serving; appl crayfish hdls & birds 2,800.00

William Hattersley or William Hewitt, London, tea and coffee service, 12" coffeepot, teapot, creamer, and sugar bowl, 79 troy ounces, $1,750.00.

Wm Gale & Son, NY, ewer, chased decor w/vintage, 1823, 13½" ..**1,425.00**
Wm Kingdom, 1834; castor, Wm IV, urn form, dome lid, 2-t-oz ..**150.00**
Wm Spratling, box, trunk form w/dome lid, 2¼x3¼" **800.00**
Wm Spratling, creamer & sugar bowl, ball finial, 3¼" **800.00**
Wm Spratling, salt cellars, mk Sterling, 1⅜", 12 for **920.00**
Wm Spratling, sauce ladle, hammered, rosewood hdl, 8x3½" **500.00**
Wm Spratling, tea set, ebony hdls & finials, pot+cr/sug+tray, EX .**3,750.00**
Wood & Hughes, cake basket, Renaissance Revival, female masks ..**1,850.00**
Wood & Hughes, cup, child's; Egyptian Revival, Pharaoh head .**950.00**
Wood & Hughes, shakers, hand-chased allover repousse, pr **325.00**

Silver Lustre and Silver Resist

Much of the ware known as silver lustre was produced in the 1800s in Staffordshire, England. This type of earthenware was entirely covered with the metallic silver glaze. It was most popular prior to 1840 when the technique of electroplating was developed and silverplated wares came into vogue. Later in the century, artisans used silver lustre to develop designs on vases and other decorative ware.

The process for decorating pottery with the silver-resist method involved first coating the design or that portion of the pattern that was to be left unsilvered with a water-soluble solution. The lustre was applied to the entire surface of the vessel and allowed to dry. Before the final firing, the surface was washed, removing only the silver from the coated areas. This type of ware was produced early in the 1800s by many English potteries, Wedgwood included.

Creamer, emb strawberry band, rectangular, scroll hdl, 4" **55.00**
Jug, sporting; bl transfer w/mc, ca 1815, 5½", EX **600.00**
Pitcher, farmer's arms, blk transfer w/mc, rpr, 5⅝" **220.00**
Pitcher, floral w/dalmatian & bird, wear, 5⅝" **125.00**
Shaker, Toby figural, minor wear, 5" **110.00**
Teapot, bird-head terminal hdl, ribbed bottom, 6x10" **265.00**

Silver Overlay

The silver overlay glass made since the 1880s was decorated with a cut-out pattern of sterling silver applied to the surface of the ware.

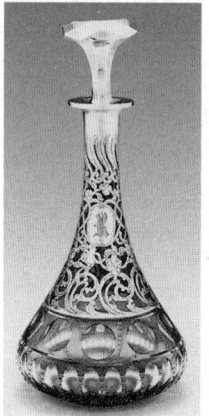

Decanter, engraved floral and scroll-work overlay on cranberry, Black Starr & Frost, 12½", $770.00.

Bottle, scent; clear w/floral o/l, 4½x3½", from $300 to **400.00**
Decanter, cranberry cut to clear w/roses o/l, Alvin, 12" **850.00**
Tankard, cranberry, grapes o/l, clear hdl, 10¾x6" **750.00**
Vase, amber irid w/floral & scroll o/l, L Sterling, 2½" **325.00**
Vase, blk w/bubble ball stem, allover Deco o/l, 13" **550.00**
Vase, cobalt/wht opal cased, floral & scroll o/l, Sterling, 6" **450.00**
Vase, gr w/roses & lattice o/l, baluster form, 10¼x4½" **850.00**

Silverplate

Silverplated flatware is fast becoming the focus of attention for many of today's collectors. Silver prices rose to over $7.00 an ounce in 1998, causing a slight increase in both sterling and silverplate prices on the secondary market. Demand is strong for early, ornate pieces, and prices have continued to rise steadily over the past five years. Our values are based on pieces in excellent or restored/resilvered condition. Serving pieces are priced to reflect the values of examples in complete original condition, with knives retaining their original blades. If pieces are monogrammed, deduct from 30% (for rare, ornate patterns) to 40% (for common, plain pieces). Our advisors for this category are Jo Killmer and Rick Spencer; they are listed in the Directory under Utah. See also Railroadiana, Silverplate.

Key:
fh — flat handle
hh — hollow handle

Flatware

Affection, 1960, Oneida Community, fruit spoon **6.00**
Affection, 1960, Oneida Community, gravy ladle **10.00**
Affection, 1960, Oneida Community, pie server, pierced **10.00**
Affection, 1960, Oneida Community, 3-pc youth set **26.00**
Chester, 1888, Towle, beef fork **20.00**
Chester, 1888, Towle, luncheon fork **9.00**
Clairhill, 1978, Wm A Rogers, gumbo soup spoon **6.00**
Clairhill, 1978, Wm A Rogers, steak knife **8.00**
Clairhill, 1979, Wm A Rogers, 5-pc place setting **28.00**
Countess, 1969, Internat'l, demitasse spoon **4.00**
Countess, 1969, Internat'l, salad fork **7.00**
Countess, 1969, Internat'l, 5-pc place setting **36.00**
Distinction, 1951, Prestige Plate, cream soup spoon **6.00**
Distinction, 1951, Prestige Plate, jelly server **7.00**
Distinction, 1951, Prestige Plate, tomato server **16.00**
Distinction, 1951, Prestige Plate, 3-pc steak carving set **54.00**
Dundee, 1886, 1847 Rogers, cocktail fork **9.00**
Dundee, 1886, 1847 Rogers, gravy ladle **24.00**
Dundee, 1886, 1847 Rogers, salad serving fork **30.00**
Eastlake, 1882, Rogers & Bros, dessert fork, 3-tine **15.00**
Embossed, 1882, 1847 Rogers, dinner knife **20.00**
Embossed, 1882, 1847 Rogers, oval soup spoon **12.00**
Embossed, 1882, 1847 Rogers, sugar spoon **10.00**
Embossed, 1882, 1847 Rogers, teaspoon **8.00**
Gay Adventure, 1955, Prestige Plate, ind butter spreader **6.00**
Gay Adventure, 1955, Prestige Plate, pastry fork **9.00**
Gay Adventure, 1955, Prestige Plate, pickle fork **9.00**
Gay Adventure, 1955, Prestige Plate, 2-pc salad serving set **28.00**
Gem, 1871, Reed & Barton, mustard ladle **24.00**
Gem, 1871, Reed & Barton, soup ladle **75.00**
Gothic, 1874, Rogers, dinner fork **9.00**
Grand Elegance, 1959, Rogers & Bros, bonbon server **8.00**
Grand Elegance, 1959, Rogers & Bros, luncheon knife, hh **5.00**
Grand Elegance, 1959, Rogers & Bros, sauce ladle **8.00**
Grand Elegance, 1959, Rogers & Bros, 5-pc place setting **38.00**
Hiawatha, 1886 Holmes & Edwards, dinner fork **12.00**
Hiawatha, 1886 Holmes & Edwards, tablespoon **14.00**
Interlude, 1971, Internat'l, fruit spoon **6.00**
Interlude, 1971, Internat'l, olive fork **7.00**
Interlude, 1971, Internat'l, oval soup spoon **7.00**
Interlude, 1971, Internat'l, teaspoon **4.00**
Japanese, Holmes Booth & Hayden, dinner fork **16.00**

Japanese, Holmes Booth & Hayden, master butter knife **12.00**

Japanese, Holmes Booth & Hayden, mustard ladle **28.00**

Japanese, Holmes Booth & Hayden, oyster/pickle fork **10.00**

Kings, 19th C, various manufacturers, cocktail fork **9.00**

Kings, 19th C, various manufacturers, cream soup spoon **8.00**

Kings, 19th C, various manufacturers, dinner knife, hh **15.00**

Kings, 19th C, various manufacturers, salad fork **14.00**

Kings, 19th C, various manufacturers, salad serving set **25.00**

Kings, 19th C, various manufacturers, sauce ladle **20.00**

Kings, 19th C, various manufacturers, teaspoon **7.00**

Laurel, 1878 Rogers, demitasse spoon **8.00**

Laurel, 1878 Rogers, dessert fork **15.00**

Lorne, 1878, 1847 Rogers, cocktail fork **10.00**

Lorne, 1878, 1847 Rogers, nut pick **7.00**

Lorne, 1878, 1847 Rogers, sugar tongs **15.00**

Lorne, 1878, 1847 Rogers, tablespoon **10.00**

Medallion, Hall & Elton 1867, Victorian pie knife **48.00**

Modern Baroque, 1969, Community Plate, curved baby spoon **12.00**

Modern Baroque, 1969, Community Plate, dinner knife, hh **9.00**

Modern Baroque, 1969, Community Plate, fish knife **9.00**

Modern Baroque, 1969, Community Plate, pie/cake server **22.00**

Newport-Chicago, 1879, 1847 Rogers, dinner knife, solid hdl **65.00**

Newport-Chicago, 1879, 1847 Rogers, nut pick **8.00**

Newport-Chicago, 1879, 1847 Rogers, pie server **42.00**

Newport-Chicago, 1879, 1847 Rogers, soup ladle **78.00**

Newport-Chicago, 1879, 1847 Rogers, teaspoon **8.00**

Norman, 1903, Tiffany, luncheon fork **10.00**

Olive, 19th C, various manufacturers, berry spoon **25.00**

Olive, 19th C, various manufacturers, dinner fork **8.00**

Olive, 19th C, various manufacturers, master salt spoon **12.00**

Olive, 19th C, various manufacturers, oyster ladle **42.00**

Olive, 19th C, various manufacturers, pastry server **27.00**

Olive, 19th C, various manufacturers, serving fork, pierced **18.00**

Olive, 19th C, various manufacturers, sugar spoon **10.00**

Orleans, 1964, Internat'l, berry spoon **13.00**

Orleans, 1964, Internat'l, cold meat fork **12.00**

Orleans, 1964, Internat'l, iced beverage spoon **9.00**

Orleans, 1964, Internat'l, tablespoon, pierced **10.00**

Princess Louise, 1881 Gorham, entre server **85.00**

Princess Louise, 1881 Gorham, soup ladle **80.00**

Shell, 19th C, various manufacturers, berry spoon **24.00**

Shell, 19th C, various manufacturers, crumber, fh **32.00**

Shell, 19th C, various manufacturers, dinner knife, fh **6.00**

Shell, 19th C, various manufacturers, fruit knife, fh **7.00**

Shell, 19th C, various manufacturers, ind butter spreader **8.00**

Shell, 19th C, various manufacturers, tablespoon **9.00**

Silver Fashion, 1957, Holmes & Edwards, berry spoon **13.00**

Silver Fashion, 1957, Holmes & Edwards, cheese server, fh **6.00**

Silver Fashion, 1957, Holmes & Edwards, dinner knife, hh **7.00**

Silver Renaissance, 1971, 1847 Rogers, master butter, hh **8.00**

Silver Renaissance, 1971, 1847 Rogers, sugar shell **6.00**

Silver Renaissance, 1971, 1847 Rogers, teaspoon **4.00**

Tipped, 19th C, various manufacturers, luncheon fork **4.00**

Tipped, 19th C, various manufacturers, master butter spreader **6.00**

Tipped, 19th C, various manufacturers, sugar shell **7.00**

Tipped, 19th C, various manufacturers, tablespoon **6.00**

Whittier, 1907, Tiffany, teaspoon **8.00**

Wisteria, 1966, Reed & Barton, iced beverage spoon **7.00**

Wisteria, 1966, Reed & Barton, master butter knife **8.00**

Wisteria, 1966, Reed & Barton, oval soup spoon **6.00**

Hollow Ware

Box, jewel; emb reserves, Fr taste, ca 1900, 3x8x5½" **110.00**

Bread tray, Eternally Yours, 1847 Rogers, 17x7½" **85.00**

Cake plate, Bird of Paradise, Community, oval, 1926, 12x9" **55.00**

Candelabra, English Regency, 2-light, 19th C, 18¼", pr **2,200.00**

Candy dish, Aniversary Rose, leaf shape, Internat'l, 1962 ....**28.00**

Candy dish, Countess, Internat'l, 1969 ....**30.00**

Chafing dish, Gorham, horn finial & hdl, on stand, 10x10" **355.00**

Coasters, wine bottle; vintage & pierced decor, pr **475.00**

Coffee set, Countess, Internat'l, 1969, 5-pc set **450.00**

Coffee/tea set, Eternally Yours, 1847 Rogers, 4-pc **650.00**

Coffee/tea set, Reed & Barton, Rococo style, 6-pc **330.00**

Coffee/tea set, Springtime, 1847 Rogers, 1957, 4-pc **275.00**

Compote, Walker/Hall, grapes, ornate stem & base **165.00**

Crumb set, Derby, lady figural, ca 1890 ....**165.00**

Crumb set, Forbes, grapes, vine hdls **150.00**

Entree dishes, English Georgian style, w/lids, 11", 9", pr **400.00**

Gravy boat & tray, Eternally Yours, 1847 Rogers **160.00**

Knife rest, dolphin, 1" **65.00**

Muffin dish, Birk-Ellis, dbl lids: engr dome & pierced, 10" **200.00**

Pitcher, water; Remembrance, 1847 Rogers **140.00**

Platter, well & tree; Daffodil, 1847 Rogers, 1950 ....**175.00**

Punch bowl, Birmingham Silver CT, chased foliage, 12x16" **525.00**

Spoon holder, Simpson-Hall-Miller, w/servant's bell, rstr, 12" ...**235.00**

Tray, Camille, hdls, 1847 Rogers, 1971, 24" **200.00**

Tray, Geo III style, vintage pattern, 12" dia **100.00**

Tray, Gorham, pierced gallery, ball ft, 1910, 3¼x16x23" **385.00**

Tray, Martin Hall & Co/Hopkins & Hopkins, Dublin, rtcl, 27x17" .**440.00**

Unmk English, potato dish, lion's heads, vintage border, 10" ..**1,700.00**

Vase, Meriden, folded-up edges, ornate, 1920s, 10" **165.00**

Wine cooler, Italian, Neoclassical urn, shell decor, 58-t-oz **1,400.00**

Sheffield

Bowl, centerpc; floral/cartouch repousse, ring hdls, oval **175.00**

Bowl, vegetable; removable lid finial, 12" L **250.00**

Bowl, vegetable; w/warming reservoir, wood hdls, 13" **275.00**

Bucket, champagne; lt wear, 9½" **110.00**

Cake basket, gadroon edge, bail hdl, wirework body, 1820, 11" ..**100.00**

Candelabra, telescoping bases, dbl socket inserts, 14", pr **145.00**

Candelabra, 2-arm, 3-socket, 12½", pr **200.00**

Candelabra, 3-arm, old rpr, 19¼", pr **550.00**

Candelabra, 4-arm, 5-socket, 17¾", pr **500.00**

Candelabrum, 4 curved/scrolled arms, bobeches, 33" **1,950.00**

Candlesticks, fluted shafts, thread mold, oval base, 7½", pr **220.00**

Candlesticks, Geo III, in Adam taste, 1790s, 12", 4 for **1,550.00**

Candlesticks, sq tapered shafts, bellflowers, 12¼", pr **325.00**

Candlesticks, vasiform shafts & bases, 10¼", pr **400.00**

Coaster, wine bottle; wooden bottom, 6½" **95.00**

Coffee urn, EX detail, lt wear 16" **495.00**

Coffee urn w/burner, sm rpr, 16¾", EX **330.00**

Hot water urn, classic form, sq base w/ball ft, 19", EX **200.00**

Hot water urn, Regency, lion's head hdls, 1820s, 16½" **990.00**

Spooner, shell form, rustic plinth **225.00**

Taper jack, old rprs, 5" **195.00**

Tea caddy, simple style **24.00**

Tea set, 6-pc, +24" tray **770.00**

Tray, Georgian, floral cartouch, fluted edge, hdls, 20x26" **935.00**

Tray, tea; beads/garlands/openwork, leaf hdls, 30" **275.00**

Tureen, eng dog on lid, EX detail, 15" **385.00**

Wine coolers, uptrn hdls, ornate rim & ft, 10½", pr **1,430.00**

Sinclaire

In 1904 H.P. Sinclaire and Company was founded in Corning,

New York. For the first sixteen years of production, Sinclaire used blanks from other glassworks for his cut and engraved designs. In 1920 he established his own glass-blowing factory in Bath, New York. His most popular designs utilize fruits, flowers, and other forms from nature. Most of Sinclaire's glass is unmarked; items that are carry his logo: an 'S' within a wreath with two shields.

Compote, Colonial Blue, ftd, #11901, 13¾" 225.00
Compote, Pillar Optic, amber, ftd, #11900, 14" 125.00
Jug, whiskey; cut decor, salesman's sample, 4" 160.00
Tazza, topaz, cut & eng, 4x8" 110.00
Tray, overall floral eng, sgn, 14½x11¼" 325.00
Vase, intaglio flower form, 14" 875.00
Vase, Nubian Black, ACB dragons/scrolls/etc, tapered, 8½" 850.00

Sitzendorf

The Sitzendorf factory began operations in East Germany in the mid-1800s, adopting the name of the city as the name of their company. They produced fine porcelain groups, figurines, etc., in much the same style and quality as Meissen and the Dresden factories. Much of their ware was marked with a crown over the letter 'S' and a horizontal line with two slash marks.

Box, 2 putti appl to lid, ca 1900, 4" dia 150.00
Figurine, girl on goat & boy playing instrument, wht, 6¼" 650.00
Figurine, Mary of Burgundy, 8" 150.00
Figurine, monkey playing trumpet, 5½" 150.00
Figurine, polar bear, EX details on face, mk, 8½x4" 300.00
Urn, draped cherubs & appl florals, floral lid, mk, 8¼" 325.00
Vase, appl flowers, twig hdls, w/lid, ca 1887, 4¼" 150.00

Skookum Dolls

Representing real Indians of various tribes, stern-faced Skookum dolls were designed by Mary McAboy of Missoula, Montana, in the early 1900s. The earliest of McAboy's creations were made with air-dried apple faces that bore a resemblance to the neighboring Chinook Indian tribe. The name Skookum is derived from the Chinook/Siwash term for large or excellent (aka Bully Good) and appears as part of the oval paper labels often attached to the feet of the dolls.

In 1913 McAboy applied for a patent that described her dolls in three styles: a female doll, a female doll with a baby, and a male doll. In 1916 George Borgman and Co. partnered with McAboy, registered the Skookum trademark, and manufactured these dolls which were distributed by the Arrow Novelty Co. of New York and the HH Tammen Co. of Denver. The Skookum (Apple) Packers Association of Washington state produced similar 'friendly faced' dolls as did Louis Ambery for the National Fruit exchange.

The dried apple faces of the first dolls were replaced by those made of a composition material. Plastic faces were introduced in the 1940s, and these continued to be used until production ended in 1959. Skookum dolls were produced in a variety of styles, with the most common having stern, lined faces with small painted eyes glancing to the right, colorful Indian blankets pulled tightly across the straw- or paper-filled body to form hidden arms, felt pants or skirts over wooden legs, and wooden feet covered with decorated felt suede or masking tape.

Skookums were produced in sizes ranging from a 2" souvenir mailer with a cardboard address tag to 36" novelty and advertising dolls. Collectors highly prize 21" to 26" dolls as well as dolls that glance to their left. Felt or suede feet predate the less desirable brown plastic feet of the

late 1940s and '50s. Our advisor is Glen Rairigh; he is listed in the Directory under Michigan.

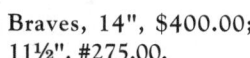

Braves, 14", $400.00; 11½", #275.00.

Photo courtesy Glen Rairigh

Baby, looks left, cradle brd, beaded body/head covering, 10½" ..1,100.00
Baby, mc blanket, leather headband w/pnt decor, 4" 30.00
Baby, wrapped in mc blanket, feather in headband, 3½x3" 200.00
Baby mailer, 1½¢ postcard attached, feather/ribbon binding, 4" ...100.00
Baby mailer, 1½¢ postcard attached, rattan binding, 4" 105.00
Baby/child in loop basket, blanket wrap, unbraided hair, 12" 225.00
Baby/child in loop basket, blanket wrap, necklace, 14" 200.00
Boy, brn ft w/pnt decor, Bully Good label, 6½" 100.00
Boy, brn suede ft w/decor, headband, 10" 150.00
Boy, mc blanket, felt pants, leather shoes, 6½", VG 50.00
Boy, w/blanket/felt pants, brn plastic ft w/mk, wood beads, 9½" ..85.00
Chief w/headdress, tan/gr attire, paper shoes w/decor, 12½" 250.00
Family, chief w/mc feathers, 15", female w/baby, clothes match, 14" ...600.00
Family, man w/exposed right arm, 13½", female w/baby, 12½" ..900.00
Family, w/blankets/clothes/beads, 35", 33" w/10" baby in arms ..5,900.00
Female w/baby, floral skirt, glass bead necklace, 11½" 300.00
Female w/baby, w/blanket, purple felt ft/skirt, necklace, 11½" ...200.00
Female w/baby, w/blanket, worn paper ft, 12½", VG 150.00
Girl, cotton-wrapped legs, beaded ft decor, headband, 9½" 150.00
Girl, cotton-wrapped legs, pnt suede ft covers, Bully Good, 6½" ...100.00
Girl, w/blanket, felt skirt, decor felt ft, bandana, 10" 85.00
Girl, w/blanket/skirt, leather shoes, feather, label, 6½" 125.00
Mailer, baby in bl & yel cotton, Grand Canyon 10-1-52 ....25.00
Mailer, baby in patterned cotton on yel cb 25.00
Mailer, baby in red bandanna on yel cb 55.00
Mailer, clay child in leather pouch, Yel Stone Park 6-22-39 ....35.00

Slag Glass

Slag glass is a marbleized opaque glassware made by several companies from about 1870 until the turn of the century. It is usually found in purple or caramel (see Chocolate Glass), though other colors were also made. Pink is rare and very expensive. It was revived in recent years by several American glassmakers, L.E. Smith, Westmoreland, and Imperial among them. The listings below reflect values for items with excellent color. Our advisor for this category is Sharon Thoerner; she is listed in the Directory under California.

Blue, basket, cherries/leaves in relief, crimped/ruffled, 9" 75.00
Blue, humidor, drum shape, cap-shaped finial, 6½x5¼" 250.00
Pink, Invt Fan & Feather, bowl, master berry 800.00
Pink, Invt Fan & Feather, butter dish, 7x7⅝" 1,300.00

Pink, Invt Fan & Feather, creamer 425.00
Pink, Invt Fan & Feather, cruet 1,400.00
Pink, Invt Fan & Feather, jelly compote, scalloped, 4½x5" 550.00
Pink, Invt Fan & Feather, pitcher, 7½" 1,200.00
Pink, Invt Fan & Feather, punch cup 315.00
Pink, Invt Fan & Feather, sauce dish, ball ft, 2½x4½" 265.00
Pink, Invt Fan & Feather, sauce dish, shell ft, 2⅜x4" 600.00
Pink, Invt Fan & Feather, shakers, rare, pr 1,200.00
Pink, Invt Fan & Feather, spooner, 4¼" 425.00
Pink, Invt Fan & Feather, sugar bowl, w/lid, 7¼" 900.00
Pink, Invt Fan & Feather, toothpick holder 650.00
Pink, Invt Fan & Feather, tumbler, average color, 4" 250.00
Pink, Invt Fan & Feather, tumbler, EX color, 4" 435.00
Purple, Beads & Bark, vase, novelty 85.00
Purple, cake stand, Dart Bar, 6x11" 225.00
Purple, candy dish, Indiana Glass, ftd 55.00
Purple, Flute, celery vase 85.00
Purple, Jenny Lind, compote, 7¾x8½" 165.00
Purple, Notched Daisy, platter, oval 75.00
Purple, oil lamp, emb spears, clear font, 13" 250.00
Purple, Oval Medallion, spooner 85.00
Purple, Panel & Waffle mold, compote, w/lid, 8x8" 125.00
Purple, Panel & Waffle mold, vase, ftd, scallopoed, 8" 90.00
Purple, plate, lattice edge, 13" 125.00
Purple, Scroll w/Acanthus, creamer & sugar bowl 100.00
Purple, Scroll w/Acanthus, spooner 75.00
Purple, Shell w/Acanthus, jelly compote 85.00
Purple, Tam O'Shanter & Southbar Johnny, platter, oval 150.00
Purple, vase, paneled sides, 8" 150.00
Red, vase, HP flowers & butterfly, banjo shape on ped 100.00
Red, vase, mc/gold decor at top, 7" 60.00

Smith Bros.

Alfred and Harry Smith founded their glassmaking firm in New Bedford, Massachusetts. They had been formerly associated with the Mt. Washington Glass Works, working there from 1871 to 1875 to aid in establishing a decorating department. Smith glass is valued for its excellent enameled decoration on satin or opalescent glass. Pieces were often marked with a lion in a red shield. Our advisors for this category are Betty and Clarence Maier; they are listed in the Directory under Pennsylvania.

Photo courtesy John A. Shumann III

Covered jar, pansies on pale beige, melon ribs, rampant lion mark, 3½" high, $600.00.

Atomizer, daisies, mc w/gold on wht opal, orig mts/bulb, 7x3½" .750.00
Biscuit jar, crabs, gold & gr, swirled blank, SP mts, 9x5" 2,000.00

Biscuit jar, pansies, bl on cream, swirled ribs, 8¾x4¾" sq 715.00
Biscuit jar, pansies, mc w/gold on beige, metal lid, 7x5" 750.00
Bowl, gold prunus, wht beads, melon ribs, 2¾x6" 380.00
Bowl, Moss Rose, pk on beige, melon ribs, wht beaded rim, 4x9" ...675.00
Creamer & sugar bowl, violets, mc on bl to beige, SP mts 750.00
Humidor, pansies, bl on cream, melon ribs, 6½x4" 850.00
Plate, Santa Maria, ship scene, 7¾" 595.00
Rose bowl, asters, mc on cream, pk swirls/wht beaded top, 4x5½" ...295.00
Rose bowl, asters, mc on cream, 2¼x3" 285.00
Rose bowl, daisies on beige, beaded top, bulbous, 4½" 325.00
Rose bowl, gold prunus w/jewels on cream, gold beads, 2¼x3" ...285.00
Rose bowl/vase, gold iris & beading on pale beige, 3¾" 375.00
Salt cellar, floral, mc on wht satin, melon ribs, 1¼x2" 80.00
Salt cellar, gold prunus, beaded rim, 1¼x2¼", 6 for 650.00
Shaker, violets on pk, melon ribs, SP lid, low 120.00
Toothpick holder, wild roses on wht, bl beaded rim, 2¼" 250.00
Vase, apple blossoms on pk-beige gloss, 10x8" 595.00
Vase, pond lilies (inverted), maroon trim, 7", pr 375.00
Vase, storks, mc on pk, 5½", pr 850.00
Vase, wisteria, wht on pnt apricot w/gold, pinched, 5¼x3½" ...375.00
Vase, wisteria w/gold, bk: harbor scene, dbl-canteen form, 7x8" ...2,500.00
Vase/rose bowl, daisy-like flowers on beige, beaded top, 4½" 325.00

Snow Babies

During the last quarter of the 19th century, snow babies — little figurals in white snowsuits — originated in Germany. They were made of sugar candy and were often used as decorations for Christmas cakes. Later on they were made of marzipan, a confection of crushed almonds, sugar, and egg whites. Eventually porcelain manufacturers began making them in bisque. They were popular until WWII. These tiny bisque figures range in size from 1" up to 7" tall. Quality German pieces bring very respectable prices on the market today. Beware of reproductions. Our advisor for this category is Linda Vines; she is listed in the Directory under New Jersey.

Photo courtesy Linda Vines

Two babies play on a WWI tank, Germany, 2", $200.00.

Adult skier, mica coat & hat, blk pants, Germany, 2½" 65.00
Babies, no snow, 2 atop snowball, Am flag, Germany, 3" 150.00
Babies, 3 on sled, Germany, 3" L 250.00
Baby, jtd shoulders & hips, Germany, 5" 250.00
Baby, playing musical instrument, Germany, 2" 125.00
Baby, sitting or standing, Germany, 1" 40.00

Baby, standing on wooden skis, Germany, 3" 175.00
Baby kicking ball w/blk dog, Germany, 2" 165.00
Baby pulling smaller baby on sled, Germany, 2" 175.00
Baby riding on red plane, Germany, 1½" 150.00
Baby riding on snow bear, Germany, 2½" 165.00
Baby riding on snow bear, Japan, 2½" 45.00
Baby w/medicine ball, Germany, 2" 165.00
Baby w/seal & red ball, Germany, 2½" 165.00
Children (2, no snow) sitting on sled, Germany, 2½" ...75.00
Doll, bsk shoulderhead & limbs, cloth body, Germany, 5" 275.00
Pixie hiding from witch around snow-covered house, Germany, 2½" ..175.00
Pixies (2) riding mule w/blk dog, Germany, 2" 150.00
Santa atop snow bear, Germany, 2½" 200.00
Santa climbing over log fence, Germany, 2" 110.00
Santa in yel train, toys in bk, Germany, 3" 200.00
Santa riding in sled pulled by huskies, Germany, 2" 165.00
Santa riding motorcycle, pixie on bk, Germany, 2" 165.00
Snow bear, standing or walking, Germany, 2" 75.00
Snow dog, standing, blk muzzle, Germany, 2" 90.00
Snowman, standing, blk hat & cigar, Germany, 1½" 65.00

Snuff Boxes

As early as the 17th century, the Chinese began using snuff. By the early 19th century, the practice had spread to Europe and America. It was used by both the gentlemen and the ladies alike, and expensive snuff boxes and bottles were the earmark of the genteel. Some were of silver or gold set with precious stones or pearls, while others contained music boxes. In the following listings, the dimension noted is length. See also Orientalia, Snuff Bottles.

Continental ivory and tortoise shell with gold-plated bands and lady's portrait inset beneath glass panel, mid-1800s, 3" dia, $500.00.

Agate top, enameled top, oval, chased ormolu mts, 3" 165.00
Brass, oval, eng name, dtd 1882, 2½" 110.00
Burl w/scratch-cvd initials, 3⅞", EX 92.50
Geo IV silver-gilt, eng crest, appl foliage, 1825, 3½" 1,380.00
Horn w/eng flowers/couple/inscription, oval, 3" 175.00
Niello on 800 silver w/strapwork on lid, 'wicker' sides, 3" 345.00
Papier-mache, revelers in gentlemen's club, English, 4¼" dia 725.00
Pewter, eng florals, JP Jennson, lt wear, 3½" 165.00
Regency silver, presentation, appl mts & thumbpc, 1819, 3¼" ..975.00
Sterling, incised design, NM London, 1813, ¾x1¾x3" 260.00
Victorian silver, presentation, eng crest, bombe sides, 1840 ....925.00
Victorian silver, presentation, eng fr, appl thumbpc, 1854, 2⅝" 550.00
Wm IV parcel-gilt silver, presentation, appl borders, 1835, 3½" ..1,500.00
Wm IV silver, presentation, appl scrolls, 1837, 3¼" 700.00

Soap Hollow Furniture

In the Mennonite community of Soap Hollow, Pennsylvania, the women made and sold soap; the men made handcrafted furniture. Rare today, these pieces were stenciled, grain painted, and beautifully decorated with inlaid escutcheons. These pieces are becoming very sought after. When well kept, they are very distinctive and beautiful. The items described in these listings were recently sold through Merle S. Mishlers Auctions, RD 2, Hollsopple, Pennsylvania. All are in excellent condition unless otherwise noted. Our advisor for this category is Anita Levi; she is listed in the Directory under Pennsylvania.

Chest, blanket; feathers on mustard & brn, MB/1897, EX 1,100.00
Chest, blanket; grpt w/blk lid, fruit/florals w/gold, 1882 ....2,900.00
Chest, blanket; maroon w/gold stencil, rnd escutcheon, 1856 .2,000.00
Chest, blanket; poplar, orig red pnt w/blk/gold, att, 22x42" ...3,850.00
Chest, blanket; red w/floral stencils, rpl hinges, FJ/1892, VG ..3,800.00
Chest, blanket; rose decals, blk & brn graining, LK/1890, EX .5,000.00
Chest, 4 lg/2 sm drws w/decor, enamel pulls, sgn, 1851, EX+ ..4,600.00
Chest, 4 lg/3 sm drws, stencil, enamel pulls, sgn, 1883, EX+ ...5,400.00
Chest, 6-drw, brn w/mustard & decals, blk top/sides, Sala, EX .1,900.00
Chest, 6-drw, no pnt or decor, EX wood, G 475.00
Chest, 7-drw, maroon w/blk top/sides, rpt CKM/1879, G 550.00
Chest of drws, bk brd, hidden lock, stencil, HS/1879, EX 5,500.00
Chest of drws, brn grpt w/stencil, pnt pulls, 1883, EX+ 5,400.00
Chest of drws, floral decals/fruit gilt stencil/grpt, MH/1879, EX ..2,750.00
Chest of drws, redwood, 1841, EX 750.00
Chest of drws, stenciling w/decals, dk brn, fancy bk brd, EX ...7,200.00
Cradle, gilt stencils, mustard trim, maroon grpt, EX 1,100.00
Cupboard, corner; maroon w/blk, stencil, 1856, EX 11,500.00
Cupboard, Dutch; 4 doors/2 drws, stencil/old rpt, 1875, 84x65" ..6,000.00
Dresser, Emp style, columns on 3 drws, HF/1874, EX 2,200.00
Frame, gilt eagles, stenciled, blk, EX 1,050.00
Rope bed, cherry, red & brn finish, rare, EX 2,300.00
Stand, bedside; rpt mustard brn, EX 400.00

Soapstone

Soapstone is a soft talc in rock form with a smooth, greasy feel from whence comes its name. (It is also called Soo Chow Jade.) It is composed basically of talc, chlorite, and magnetite. In colonial times it was extracted from out-croppings in large sections with hand saws, carted by oxen to mills, and fashioned into useful domestic articles such as footwarmers, cooking utensils, inkwells, etc. During the early 1800s, it was used to make heating stoves and kitchen sinks. Most familiar today are the carved vases, bookends, and boxes made in China during the Victorian era.

Bookends, elephant, pr 750.00
Cigarette/match holder, phoenix birds/eng, red, 3½x4" 70.00
Foot warmer, 6x9x3" 75.00
Toothpick holder, tan/wht, cylindrical, 2" 28.00
Vase, monkey 1 end, bird at other, lt gray w/rust, 9" L 85.00
Wax seal, oxen, head bent down, brn, rstr, 2½" 165.00

Soda Fountain Collectibles

The first soda water sales in the United States occurred in the very late 1790s in New York and New Haven, Connecticut. By the 1830s soda water was being sold in drug stores as a medicinal item, especially the effervescent mineral waters from various springs around the country. By this time the first flavored soda water appeared at an apothecary shop in Philadelphia.

The 1830s also saw the first manufacturer (John Matthews) of devices to make soda water. The first marble soda fountain made its appearance in 1857 as a combination ice shaver and flavor-dispensing apparatus. By the 1870s the soda fountain was an established feature of the neighborhood drug store.

The fountains of this period were large, elaborate marble devices with druggists competing with each other for business by having fountains decorated with choice marbles, statues, mirrors, water fountains, and gas lamps.

In 1903 the fountain completed its last major evolution with the introduction of the 'front' counter service we know today. (The soda clerk faced the customer when drawing soda.)

By this time ice cream was a standard feature being served as sundaes, ice cream sodas, and milk shakes. Syrup dispensers were just being introduced as 'point-of-sale' devices to sell various flavorings from many different companies. Straws were commonplace, especially those made from paper. Fancy and unusual ice cream dippers were in daily use, and they continued to evolve reaching their pinnacle with the introduction of the heart-shaped dipper in 1927.

This American business has provided collectors today with an almost endless supply of interesting and different articles of commerce. One can collect dippers, syrup dispensers, glassware, straw dispensers, milk shakers, advertising, and trade catalogs. (Note: The presence of a 'correct' pump enhances the value of a syrup dispenser by 25%.)

Collectors need to be made aware of decorating pieces that are fantasy items: copper ice cream cones, a large copper ice cream dipper, and a copper ice cream soda glass. These items have no resale value. Our advisors for this category are Joyce and Harold Screen; they are listed in the Directory under Maryland. See also Advertising; Coca-Cola.

Calendar, Cherry Smash, 1912, girl w/fan on swing, complete, EX ...575.00
Canteen, Bardwell's Root Beer, Whites Utica Pottery 800.00
Dipper, Bohlig 1,250.00
Dipper, cone holder, HS Geer, Pat 11/19.1912, from $2,000 to ..2,500.00
Dipper, DanDee, ice cream sandwich, 1920s 1,000.00
Dipper, Dover, slicer, dbl trigger 800.00
Dipper, Erie Specialty, aluminum, rnd bowl, from $100 to 125.00
Dipper, Gilchrist #31, rnd bowl, szs 6 & 40, ea 175.00
Dipper, Gilchrist #31, rnd bowl, szs 8 to 30, ea, from $25 to 50.00
Dipper, IcyPi, ice cream sandwich, from $150 to 250.00
Dipper, J Manos, heart shape 5,000.00
Dipper, Meyers, ice cream sandwich, curved 175.00
Dipper, rnd bowl, point on top of bowl 750.00
Dipper, sq 100.00
Dispenser, Beefmalt, hot bouillon, w/bull's head & lid 600.00
Dispenser, Birchola, emb leaves & nuts, orig pump 1,500.00
Dispenser, Buckeye, brn tree stump, orig mk pump 600.00
Dispenser, Buckeye, dancing centaurs, orig unique pump 2,500.00
Dispenser, Buckeye, urn shape, wht or blk, orig mk pump 850.00
Dispenser, Cherry Smash, 5¢ over soda glass, orig mk pump ...2,500.00
Dispenser, Cherry Smash, 5¢ on 2 sides, orig mk pump 1,500.00
Dispenser, Dr Swett's, ceramic, tree stump, wht bkground 6,500.00
Dispenser, Ginger Mint Julep, ceramic bbl form, orig pump 700.00
Dispenser, Hires, ceramic, hourglass w/orig mk pump 700.00
Dispenser, Hires, ugly kid, tall bowl w/lid, Mettlach 48,000.00
Dispenser, Hires, wooden bbl, tall, w/carbonator 1,000.00
Dispenser, Howell's Cherry Julep, orig ball pump 900.00
Dispenser, Indian Rock Ginger Ale, w/orig pump 2,000.00
Dispenser, Johnson's Hot Fudge 125.00
Dispenser, Liberty Cherry 8,500.00
Dispenser, Liberty Root Beer, wood bbl, 2 spigots, no carbonator ..400.00
Dispenser, Liggett's Grape Juice, 2 parts, colorful 1,500.00

Dispenser, Middleby Root Beer, mug form, brn glass, w/base & lid ..700.00
Dispenser, Mission, pk or gr crackle glass on base, w/lid 200.00
Dispenser, Nestle Hot Fudge, tin & chrome 125.00
Dispenser, Orange Julep, w/orig ball pump 1,000.00
Dispenser, Pepsi, outboard style, 1950s, working rstr 500.00
Dispenser, Verba, urn shape, orig pump 1,500.00
Dispenser, Ward's Lemon Crush, lemon form, w/orig ball pump .2,000.00
Dispenser, Ward's Lime Crush, lime form, w/orig ball pump ...2,500.00
Dispenser, Ward's Orange Crush, orange shape, orig ball pump ..1,500.00
Fountain glass, Allen's Red Tame Cherry 100.00
Fountain glass, Bludwine, acid etched, w/syrup line 100.00
Fountain glass, Bromo Seltzer, bl 30.00
Fountain glass, Cherry Smash, w/syrup line 250.00
Fountain glass, Fox's Cherry, modified flared top, fluted 125.00
Fountain glass, Green River, yel w/syrup line 65.00
Fountain glass, Howell's Orange Julip, milk glass goblet 175.00
Fountain glass, ice cream soda, pk, Tea Room pattern 150.00
Fountain glass, Julep, yel or gr, ea 75.00
Fountain glass, Keodinger's Ginger Ale 100.00
Fountain glass, Mission, flared, w/syrup line 45.00
Fountain glass, Modox, glass mug, Indian chief 175.00
Fountain glass, Nehi, w/syrup line 25.00
Fountain glass, Nesbitt's 30.00
Fountain glass, Orange Crush, wht letters, w/syrup line 100.00
Fountain glass, Pur-ox 50.00
Fountain glass, Richardson's Real Orangeade, goblet 100.00
Fountain glass, Seven-Up, gr, sq logo 30.00
Fountain glass, TJ Clement, Atlantic City, orange juice 125.00
Fountain glass, Vernon's Ginger Ale 50.00
Fountain glass, Zipp's Grape-O 125.00
Ice cream cone holder, rnd glass w/metal lid, 10x14" 400.00

Ice cream dish, heart shaped with vine pattern, marked JM Pat Pend., 3¼", $250.00.

Ice cream measure, tin, conical, 1-qt 75.00
Jar, Fox's Hot Chocolate powder, red ceramic, orig lid 250.00
Jar, Horlick's Malted Milk, label under glass, w/glass lid 400.00
Jar, malted milk container, Borden's, aluminum lid 400.00
Malted milk container, Borden's, aluminum 50.00
Mixer, milk shake; Hamilton Beach, polished brass 275.00
Mixer, milk shake; Hamilton Beach, wht porc base 250.00
Mixer, milk shake; Hamilton Beach, 3 heads, gr porc 350.00
Mixer, milk shake; Horlick's, lighted base 1,000.00
Mixer, milk shake; Myers, twin units 500.00
Mug, A&W Root Beer, emb glass 20.00
Mug, Armour's Hot Bouillon, wht china w/carnations 40.00
Mug, Buckeye Root Beer, centaur hdl 100.00
Mug, Dove Brand Ginger Ale, brn pottery 125.00
Mug, Dr Swett's Root Beer, bl & brn pottery 300.00

Mug, Hires, ugly kid, Mettlach #3021 ....**250.00**
Mug, Lash's Root Beer, plain pottery **100.00**
Mug, Richardson's Liberty Root Beer, pottery, short **150.00**
Mug, Richardson's Root Beer, emb clear glass **30.00**
Mug, Zipp's Root Beer, clear glass **150.00**
Pitcher, Henderson's Wild Cherry, 9½" **250.00**
Pitcher, Hires Root Beer, ugly kid, Mettlach **25,000.00**
Postcard, int view of fountain, color, pre-1920 ....**25.00**
Sign, cb hanger, Cherry Smash, cherries w/sundae, 1920s, 6x11" ...**500.00**
Soda fountain, RM Green, marble/SP base, Oracle model, 1880s ..**8,000.00**
Soda fountain, Tufts, marble/SP brass, Cottage model, 1880s .**8,000.00**
Straw jar, clear cut glass, sq, Near Cut pattern **700.00**
Straw jar, clear glass w/hinged metal lid, 5x11" **250.00**
Syrup bottle, Ginger Mint Julep, rvpt glass label, w/cap, EX **400.00**
Syrup bottle, Hires Root Beer, red rvpt glass label, w/cap, EX **500.00**
Syrup bottle, Stromeyer's Grape Punch, rvpt glass label, w/cap ..**450.00**
Syrup jug, Cherry Smash, invt paper label w/mansion scene **50.00**
Syrup jug, S&H Root Beer, 12", NM **125.00**
Tape measure, Abbott's Ice Cream **100.00**
Tray, Nehi, tin, bathing beauty in ocean wave **150.00**
Tray, Nu-Grape, tin, hand holds bottle against oval, EX **125.00**
Watch fob, brick ice cream shape, mc enamel **150.00**
Watch fob, Cherry Smash, celluloid, 1912 ....**275.00**
Watch fob, Lippencott Soda Fountain Co **125.00**

Spangle Glass

Spangle glass, also known as Vasa Murrhina, is cased art glass characterized by the metallic flakes embedded in its top layer. It was made both abroad and in the United States during the latter years of the 19th century, and it was reproduced in the 1960s by the Fenton Art Glass Company.

Vasa Murrhina was a New England distributor who sold glassware of this type manufactured by a Dr. Flower of Sandwich, Massachusetts. Flower had purchased the defunct Cape Cod Glassworks in 1885 and used the facilities to operate his own company. Since none of the ware was marked, it is very difficult to attribute specific examples to his manufacture. See also Art Glass Baskets; Fenton.

Bowl, cranberry w/silver mica, melon ribs, ped ft, 3¾x5" **115.00**
Cruet, sapphire bl w/gold aventurine, bl stopper, 9½x3½" **165.00**
Pitcher, rose cased w/silver mica, bulbous, Hobbs Brockunier, 8" .**500.00**
Rose bowl, mc spatter w/mica, clear ft, 3¾x3½" **110.00**
Rose bowl, pk spatter w/mica, clear petal ft, 3¾x3½" **110.00**
Rose bowl, pk w/silver mica, wht int, 8-crimp, 3¾x3⅜" **110.00**
Rose bowl, rose w/mica, wht int, ruffled, 3¾x3¼" **110.00**
Tumbler, orange & opaque spatter w/mica, Invt T'print, 3¾" **40.00**
Vase, cobalt w/silver mica, HP flowers & birds, ftd, 13½" **375.00**
Vases, bl o/l w/coral-like mica, 7⅜x3", pr **295.00**

Spatter Glass

Spatter glass, characterized by its multicolor 'spatters,' has been made from the late 19th century to the present by American glasshouses as well as those abroad. Although it was once thought to have been made entirely by workers at the 'end of the day' from bits and pieces of leftover scrap, it is now known that it was a standard line of production. See also Art Glass Baskets.

Creamer, mc/cranberry spatter, crimped rim, melon ribs, 5¼" **165.00**
Pitcher, water; 4-color, clear hdl, pinched spout, 9⅜" **110.00**
Ring tree, orange & wht w/mc enameled dots & gold, 3½x3¼" ...**65.00**
Underplate, amethyst w/pk/yel/red, 1x6⅛" **5.00**

Vase, jack-in-pulpit; amber/red/wht, blown, 4¾x7¾x6¼" **85.00**
Vase, mc on wht, wht int, 7½x3⅜" **110.00**
Vase, pk & brn w/crimped & ruffled rim w/amber trim, 10" **135.00**

Spatterware

Spatterware is a general term referring to a type of decoration used by English potters beginning in the late 1700s. Using a brush or a stick, brightly colored paint was dabbed onto the soft-paste earthenware items, achieving a spattered effect which was often used as a border. Because much of this type of ware was made for export to the United States, some of the subjects in the central design — the schoolhouse and the eagle patterns, for instance — reflect American tastes. Yellow, green, and black spatterware is scarce and highly valued by collectors.

In the descriptions that follow, the color listed after the item indicates the color of the spatter. The central design is identified next, and the color description that follows that refers to the design. Our advisor is Diane Patalano; she is listed in the Directory under New Jersey.

Pomegranate, 4-color: Sugar bowl, with lid, repaired, $525.00; Plate, 8⅝", $735.00; Plate, 7¾", $700.00; Plate, Meakin, 6¾", NM, $375.00.

Bowl, gr, Peafowl, 3-color, deep, 4¾", EX **330.00**
Bowl, red, Thistle, 3-color, flared rim, ftd, 9⅛" **575.00**
Bowl, sauce; gr, Peafowl, 4-color, 4½" **200.00**
Bowl, vegetable; bl, Fort, 4-color, rpr, 10½" L **550.00**
Creamer, bl, Cluster of Buds, 2-color, 4" **150.00**
Creamer, bl, Fort, 4-color, rpr, 4½" **200.00**
Creamer, bl, Peafowl, 4-color, 8-sided, 5½" **330.00**
Creamer, bl, Windmill, 4-color, rpr, 4½" **495.00**
Creamer, purple, Adam's Rose, 3-color, 5⅛" **300.00**
Creamer, purple, Star, bl, minor stains, 4½" **770.00**
Cup, handleless; brn, Tree, 2-color, mini **275.00**
Cup, handleless; red, Primrose, 4-color **145.00**
Cup, handleless; red, Schoolhouse, 4-color, rpr **275.00**
Cup & saucer, handleless; bl, Dove, 4-color **835.00**
Cup & saucer, handleless; bl, Flower (4-petal), red & gr **635.00**
Cup & saucer, handleless; bl, Peafowl, 4-color, flakes **660.00**
Cup & saucer, handleless; bl, Star, 3-color, lt stain **330.00**
Cup & saucer, handleless; bl, Tulip, 3-color, flakes **495.00**
Cup & saucer, handleless; bl, Tulip, 4-color **350.00**
Cup & saucer, handleless; brn, Thistle, 3-color **1,300.00**

Cup & saucer, handleless; gr, Peafowl, 4-color 600.00
Cup & saucer, handleless; gr, Peafowl, 5-color 1,600.00
Cup & saucer, handleless; gr multi-point Star border, minor wear ...550.00
Cup & saucer, handleless; maroon, Eagle & Shield, bl, EX 140.00
Cup & saucer, handleless; purple, Thistle, 2-color 525.00
Cup & saucer, handleless; red, Cock's Comb, 3-color, EX 990.00
Cup & saucer, handleless; red, Dahlia, 4-color, EX 275.00
Cup & saucer, handleless; red, Eagle & Shield, gr 300.00
Cup & saucer, handleless; red, Hollyberry, 3-color 550.00
Cup & saucer, handleless; red, Peafowl, 4-color, EX 385.00
Cup & saucer, handleless; red & gr, Christmas Balls, EX 1,045.00
Cup & saucer, handleless; red & yel Rainbow, Thistle, red & gr ..2,200.00
Cup & saucer, handleless; yel, Thistle, 2-color, rpr 1,045.00
Cup plate, bl & purple, Rainbow w/Bull's-Eye center, 4⅛" 215.00
Cup plate, purple, Eagle & Shield, bl, 3⅞" 300.00
Cup plate, red, children playing leap frog, blk transfer, 3½" 195.00
Cup plate, red, 2 boys at fence, purple transfer, 3½" 400.00
Mug, bl, Peafowl, 3-color, 3½x3⅜", NM 1,350.00
Pitcher, bl, Eagle & Shield, bl, hexagonal, 6¼", EX 300.00
Pitcher, bl, Oriental men at table, bl, 8-sided, 10¼", EX 200.00
Pitcher, lt bl, House, 3-color, gr hdl, 5⅛" 3,100.00
Plate, bl, Bird in Fountain, bl, stains, 10⅜" 200.00
Plate, bl, Eagle, brn, 8" 360.00
Plate, bl, Peafowl, 4-color, molded rim, 8½" 550.00
Plate, bl, Peafowl, 4-color, 14-sided, 9½" 550.00
Plate, bl, Peafowl (unusual style), 4-color, 8¾" 1,100.00
Plate, bl, Pomegranate, 4-color, 8½", EX 385.00
Plate, bl, Pomegranate, 5-color, wear, 8⅝" 470.00
Plate, bl, Primrose, 4-color, 8⅝" 495.00
Plate, bl, Schoolhouse, 4-color, 6¼" 500.00
Plate, bl, Star, 3-color, 6⅜" 390.00
Plate, bl, Tulip, 4-color, 7¼", EX 385.00
Plate, bl, Tulip, 4-color, 8⅞" 385.00
Plate, bl & purple Rainbow w/Bull's-Eye center, stain, 8¼" 500.00
Plate, gr, Peafowl, 4-color, flakes, 8¼" 500.00
Plate, gr, Vine & Berry, red & yel, 8⅜", NM 1,000.00
Plate, gr & bl, Tulip, 3-color, 8⅜", EX 125.00
Plate, red, Cowboy, red, stains, 9½" 70.00
Plate, red, Oriental scene, bl, 9½" 50.00
Plate, red, Peafowl, 3-color, 9½" 550.00
Plate, red, Peafowl, 4-color, wear, 8⅛" 440.00
Plate, red, Peafowl, 4-color, 6⅞", NM 385.00
Plate, red, Peafowl, 4-color, 9½" 700.00
Plate, red, Schoolhouse, 3-color, rpr, 10¼" 1,450.00
Plate, red, Thistle, 2-color, pnt touchup, 8¼" 350.00
Plate, red, Tulip, 3-color, 9⅛" 935.00
Platter, bl, Rainbow, Cowboys, red, 12½" EX 275.00
Platter, purple, Eagle & Shield, bl, sm stain, 15½" 525.00
Relish tray, bl, Peafowl, 3-color, Adams, rprs, 1½x9x5" 775.00
Saucer, gr, Schoolhouse, red & gr, 6" 475.00
Saucer, red, Schoolhouse, 3-color, rpr 250.00
Soup plate, bl, Dahlia, 3-color, 9⅜" 450.00
Soup plate, bl, Peafowl, 4-color, 10½" 2,100.00
Sugar bowl, bl, Tulip, 4-color, 5¼", EX 250.00
Sugar bowl, red, Thistle, 2-color, rpr, 4½" 440.00
Teapot, bl, Horses, bl, 6¼" 550.00
Teapot, bl, Thistle, red & gr, near-match lid, 6⅛" 550.00
Teapot, bl, Tree, 2-color, flower finial, 6" 330.00
Teapot, purple, Eagle, brn-blk, 8-sided, rpr, 9" 575.00
Teapot, red, Florets, red & gr, 5½" 200.00
Teapot, red, Peafowl, 4-color, chips/rpr, 7¼" 1,650.00
Wash bowl & pitcher, bl, Memorial Tulip, 5-color, 11", 14", EX+ ...3,800.00
Waste bowl, bl, House, 4-color, 3x5¾" 1,375.00
Waste bowl, bl, Peafowl, 3-color, 2⅞x5½" 75.00

Cut-Sponge

Cup & saucer, blk, leaf band, wide red band on rim, gr stripe 65.00
Cup & saucer, red & bl, florets w/red dots & stripes 75.00
Plate, bl, snowflake, mk SN & SC, 8⅞", NM 70.00
Plate, gray-bl florets & chaplets, Mayer, 7¾" 15.00
Plate, 8-pointed star w/mc sawtooth bands, 7⅞", NM 130.00

Spelter

Spelter items are cast from commercial zinc and coated with a metallic patina. The result is a product very similar to bronze in appearance, yet much less expensive.

Candelabra, 2-light, putti std, base w/3 kneeling boys 17" 575.00
Figurine, young shepherd, reumbent, staff & horn aside, 13" 225.00
Lamp, peasant girl w/flower basket on head, oil burner, 13" 75.00
Statue, La Melodie, lady w/harp, 21" 750.00

Spode-Copeland

The Spode Works was established in 1770 in England by Josiah Spode I and continued to operate under that title until 1843. Their earliest products were typical underglaze blue-printed patterns. After 1790 a translucent porcelain body was the basis for a line of fine enamel-decorated dinnerware. Stone China was introduced in 1805, often in patterns reflecting an Oriental influence. In 1833 William Taylor Copeland purchased the company, having been Spode's business partner. Copeland continued the business in much the same tradition as the Spode-Copeland partnership. Spode was the Royal Potter for years, providing many exquisite items for the Royal Families. They employed paintresses to decorate the merchandise by hand. Most of the Spode-Copeland wares were marked with one of several variations that incorporate the firm's name, making identification possible. The Spode Company merged with Worcester Royal Porcelain Company in 1976 and became Royal Worcester Spode Limited. This company was then purchased by Derby International in 1988. The two firms separated in 1989. The holding company is the Porcelain and Fine China Companies Limited, a division of Derby International. Spode china is still being manufactured today at exactly the same location where Josiah Spode I began in 1770. Robert Copeland, a descendent of William Taylor Copeland, resides in England. He writes books and gives lectures on Spode. Our advisor for this category is Don Haase; he is listed in the Directory under Washington.

Blue Tower: Dinner plate, $45.00; Creamers, large, $75.00 each; Cup, from $25.00 to $30.00.

Bouillon cup & saucer, Blue Italian	45.00
Bread & butter, Cowslip, 5½"	23.00
Bread & butter, Gainsborough, 6½"	25.00
Bread & butter, Tower, pk, 6¼"	28.00
Butter pat, Blue Tower	32.00
Butter pat, Chelsea Wicker	22.00
Butter pat, Mayflower	35.00
Butter pat, Pink Camilla	25.00
Butter pat, Wicker Lane	25.00
Butter pat, Wildflower	38.00
Cake plate, Blue Tower, 11" sq	185.00
Cake plate, Pink Tower, 11"	185.00
Cereal, Blue Tower, 6¼"	28.00
Cereal, Florence	28.00
Chocolate cup & saucer, Blue Italian	65.00
Chop plate, Mayflower, 15" dia	325.00
Coffeepot, Cowslip, 6-cup	175.00
Coffeepot, Mayflower, 6-cup	365.00
Coffeepot, Pink Tower, 6-cup	295.00
Coffeepot, Wicker Lane, 6-cup	185.00
Comport, Cairo	145.00
Comport, Florence	135.00
Comport, Ruins	165.00
Comport, Wickerdale	125.00
Cream soup, Blue Tower, w/saucer	130.00
Cream soup, Gainsborough, w/saucer	120.00
Creamer, Blue Jasperware, 4"	95.00
Creamer, Bridal Rose, bone	125.00
Creamer, Buttercup, 4"	110.00
Creamer, Pink Tower	120.00
Creamer, Wicker Lane, lg	65.00
Demitasse cup & saucer, Mayflower	55.00
Demitasse cup & saucer, Pink Tower	45.00
Demitasse cup & saucer, Rosebud Chintz	40.00
Dessert plate, Blue Camilla, 8"	39.00
Dessert plate, Carnelia, bone china	45.00
Dessert plate, Chelsea Garden, bone china	65.00
Dessert plate, Wicker Lane, 8"	30.00
Dinner plate, Billingsley Rose	39.00
Dinner plate, Bridal Rose	69.00
Dinner plate, Buttercup, 10½"	35.00
Dinner plate, Filigree (1830)	165.00
Dinner plate, Pink Tower	45.00
Dinner plate, Shima, 10"	45.00
Dinner plate, Wicker Lane	35.00
Egg cup, Buttercup, dbl-ended	35.00
Fish sauce, Blue Tower	295.00
Footed salad, Blue Tower	625.00
Footed salad, Mayflower	695.00
Footed salad, Ruins	595.00
Fruit, Blue Tower, 5"	28.00
Fruit, Dimity, bone china	39.00
Fruit, Pink Tower	28.00
Jubilee dish, Blue Camilla	165.00
Jubilee plate, Buttercup, scalloped edge	165.00
Jug, Blue Tower, bbl form, 4"	125.00
Jug, Blue Tower, bbl form, 5"	145.00
Jug, Blue Tower, bbl form, 6"	165.00
Jug, Pink Tower, 7"	185.00
Luncheon plate, Blue Tower, 8½" sq	45.00
Luncheon plate, Mayflower, 7½" sq	42.00
Luncheon plate, Mayflower, 9"	45.00
Luncheon plate, Old Salem, 9"	42.00
Luncheon plate, Patricia, 9"	48.00
Luncheon plate, Pink Tower, 7½" sq	39.00
Luncheon plate, Pink Tower, 8¼" sq	45.00
Luncheon plate, Rosebud Chintz, 7½" sq	42.00
Luncheon plate, Wicker Rose, 8½" sq	42.00
Luncheon plate, Wickerdale, 8½" sq	42.00
Platter, Aster, 11"	125.00
Platter, Blue Tower, 11"	135.00
Platter, Blue Tower, 13"	145.00
Platter, Gainsborough, 14½"	145.00
Platter, Pink Tower, 15"	175.00
Platter, Pink Tower, 24"	695.00
Platter, Trophies, 15"	165.00
Punch bowl, Blue Tower, lg	695.00
Punch bowl, Mayflower, sm	495.00
Rim soup, Blue Tower, 8½"	45.00
Rim soup, Blue Tower, 9¼"	75.00
Rim soup, Buttercup, 8½"	42.00
Rim soup, Canton, 10½"	75.00
Rim soup, Gainsborough, 7½"	35.00
Rim soup, Old Salem, 7½"	35.00
Rim soup, Pink Camilla, 8½"	42.00
Rim soup, Rosalie, 7½"	32.00
Rim soup, Ruins, 10½"	75.00
Rim soup, Wickerdale, 10½"	45.00
Salad plate, Bridal Rose, bone	45.00
Salad plate, Buttercup	28.00
Salad plate, Lady Ann	28.00
Salad plate, Pink Tower	32.00
Sauce boat, Pink Tower, w/underplate	145.00
Sauce tureen, Pink Tower, w/underplate	395.00
Soup tureen, Blue Camilla, w/ladle, lg	1,395.00
Soup tureen, Blue Tower, w/ladle, lg	1,565.00
Soup tureen, Pink Tower, oval, w/ladle & underplate	1,450.00
Soup tureen, Rosalie, w/ladle, lg	1,095.00
Sugar bowl, Bridal Rose, bone, w/lid, lg	125.00
Sugar bowl, Gainsborough, w/lid, lg	65.00
Supper set, Pink Tower	1,495.00
Syrup, Black Herring Hunt, 6"	135.00
Syrup, Gainsborough, 6"	75.00
Tea tile, Blue Tower	145.00
Tea tile, Chinese Rose	125.00
Tea tile, Irene	195.00
Tea tile, Rosalie	125.00
Teacup & saucer, Bridal Rose	69.00
Teacup & saucer, Buttercup	39.00
Teacup & saucer, Chelsea Garden, bone, low	69.00
Teacup & saucer, Cowslip, tall	39.00
Teacup & saucer, Patricia, low	51.00
Teacup & saucer, Valencia, low	39.00
Teapot, Buttercup, 6-cup	195.00
Teapot, Chelsea Garden, bone, 6-cup	395.00
Teapot, Cowslip, 6-cup	195.00
Teapot, Dresden Rose Savoy, 8-cup	450.00
Teapot, Irene, 8-cup	395.00
Teapot, Mayflower, 6-cup	365.00
Teapot, Pink Tower, 6-cup	265.00
Teapot, Pink Tower, 8-cup	325.00
Vegetable, Blue Seasons, covered/ftd, 11"	265.00
Vegetable, Blue Tower, 8" sq	165.00
Vegetable, Blue Tower, 9" sq	185.00
Vegetable, Castle, sq	275.00
Vegetable, Mayflower, covered/ftd, 9"	345.00
Waste bowl, Blue Tower, 5"	45.00
Waste bowl, Buttercup, 4½"	28.00

Waste bowl, Old Salem, 5½" 45.00

Spongeware

Spongeware is a type of factory-made earthenware that was popular during the last quarter of the 19th century. It was decorated by dabbing color onto the drying ware with a sponge, leaving a splotched design at random or in simple patterns. Sometimes a solid band of color was added. The vessel was then covered with a clear glaze and fired at a high temperature. Blue on white is the most preferred combination, but green on ivory, orange on white, or those colors in combination may also occasionally be found. For further informaton we recommend *Collector's Encyclopedia of Salt Glaze Stoneware* by Terry Taylor, our advisor for this category, and Terry and Kay Lowrance, available from Collector Books.

Water cooler, blue overall, No. 7 stenciled on side, brass spigot, 1880 – 1900, 13", EX, $525.00.

Baking dish, patterned bl, wire hdl, str rim, 3⅞x8⅜" 200.00
Bean pot, bl/wht, emb children, Boston Baked Beans, 7½" 450.00
Bowl, flowing bl sponging, vertical ribs, 4x10⅛" 95.00
Bowl, gray/bl/wht, hairlines, 4x9½" 55.00
Bowl, patterned bl, arched panels, 4¾x10⅛", NM 175.00
Bowl, patterned bl, arched panels, 5¾x12", NM 275.00
Bowl, patterned bl, flattened rim, 3¾x10¼", EX 180.00
Bowl, vegetable; flowing bl sponging, oval, 2⅛x10x6¾" 50.00
Butter crock, bl/wht, Village Farm Dairy stencil, no lid, 4x5½" .150.00
Butter crock, bl/wht, wire bail & wood hdl, no lid, 5¼" 220.00
Butter tub, patterned bl w/Butter, bail hdl, lid, 8½" dia, EX 420.00
Chamber pot, Thundermug sponge w/bl stripe, no lid, 5x8½" 250.00
Cooler, bl/wht, brn Albany slip int, blk #15 enamel label, 10" ...110.00
Creamer, bl/wht, emb ear of corn, 5" 110.00
Creamer, brn & bl on wht, 3⅛" 150.00
Crock, bl/wht, wire bail hdl, chips & cracks, 8" 85.00
Crock, milk; patterned bl, bail/wood hdl, 6x5⅝", EX 375.00
Flowerpot, bl/wht, crimp rim attached saucer, 4⅝", EX 330.00
Jug, bl/wht, emb label, wire bail, 7¾", EX 660.00
Jug, bl/wht, emb leaf detail, 5½" 770.00
Mug, bl/wht, 4½" 180.00
Mush dish, patterned bl, flat rim, 3⅛x10¼", EX 225.00
Pitcher, bl/wht, bulbous, 7½" 195.00
Pitcher, bl/wht, emb horizontal ribs, hairline, 9" 195.00
Pitcher, bl/wht, str sided, 8⅜" 250.00
Pitcher, bl/wht chickenwire sponging, str sided, 9" 550.00
Pitcher, bl/wht w/Albany slip int, 8¾" 750.00
Pitcher, Garden Rose in sponge allover 800.00
Pitcher, Leaping Deer, rare 1,200.00
Pitcher, Wild Rose, bl/wht sponge top & bottom 500.00
Pitcher & bowl, bl/wht, bl stripes, 12", 14½" dia 650.00
Platter, bl/wht, oval, 13" 260.00
Platter, flowing bl sponging, emb scrolls, scalloped, 13⅜", EX .110.00

Salt box, bl/wht, wooden lid, 3⅜x3" dia, EX 325.00
Soap dish, sponging allover 120.00
Teapot, bl/wht, prof rpr, 4¼" 580.00
Vase, bl/wht, cylindrical w/emb ribs & zigzags at rim, 8¾" 415.00
Wash bowl, bl/wht, bl ext stripes, 5x14" 75.00
Wash bowl & pitcher, earthworm sponge, 5½x15", 10x8½" ...1,200.00
Wash bowl & pitcher, variegated bl & brn, 7¾", 11" 375.00

Spoons

Souvenir spoons have been popular remembrances since the 1890s. The early hand-wrought examples of the silversmith's art are especially sought and appreciated for their fine craftsmanship. Commemorative, personality-related, advertising, and those with Indian busts or floral designs are only a few of the many types of collectible spoons. In the following listings, spoons are sorted by city, character, or occasion. Our advisor for this category is Margaret Alves; she is listed in the Directory under Connecticut.

Key:
B — bowl
BR — bowl reverse
emb — embossed
eng — engraved

ff — full figure
GW — gold wash
H — handle
HR — handle reverse

Aberdeen SD High School in B; girl graduate ff H 25.00
Atlanta GA Terminal Station in B; Georgia state seal H 22.00
Atlantic City on H; scene in B; teaspoon 60.00
Bartlesville OK in B; oil gusher H 28.00
Carlsbad NM in B; girl w/apples ff H 40.00
Catalina Island, Avalon Bay in B; bathing beauty ff H 45.00
Catholic Church, Coeur D'Alene ID on H; plain B 10.00
Chicago Masonic Temple in B; scroll H; demi 12.00
Chicago World's Fair, 1892 ....40.00
Cliff House San Francisco in B; emb floral H & HR 18.00
CO in gw B; ornate scene on H & HR 30.00
Colorado/miner/mule/etc on H; Garden of Gods in B; floral HR ..18.00
Concord MA & minuteman cut-out on H; plain B; demi 9.00
Denver State Capitol in B; mule/flower on H; floral HR; demi 10.00
Detroit eng in B; state seal on H; demi 7.50
Empire State Building 12.00
Fiji Islands, enameled B & H 45.00
Galesburg IL in B; scroll hdl, demi 10.00
Hollywood CA & cutout of NBC Studios on H; plain B; demi 8.00
Kalispell MT in H; Indian ff H 18.00
Kansas City MO in B; cut-out H 24.00
Lake George NY on H; Fort Wm Henry Hotel in B 35.00
Lincoln on H; memorial on HR 45.00
Los Angeles in B; bathing beauty cutout on H 42.00
Mt Pleasant IA in B; ornate poppy H 17.50
Muncie IN Courthouse etched in B; floral H 14.00
Natatorium, Boise ID in B; jester & mandolin H 15.00
NY & Brooklyn Bridge on H; Statue of Liberty in B 40.00
Omaha NE on H; 1898 Horticultural Building in B 25.00
Pasadena CA on H: Hotel Raymond in B 35.00
Pittsburg KS in B; kaola bears climbing tree of H 25.00
Round Oak etc in B; Indian ff H 89.00
Sacramento State Capitol in B; ornate H; demi 10.00
Salem witch in B; broom H; Daniel Low, teaspoon 155.00
San Diego CA in B; floral H; demi 7.00
San Francisco in B; miner & gold pan ff H 40.00
St Louis in B; cutout St Louis on horse bk at H finial 21.00
Wallace ID in B; state seal on H; Indian/tepee/canoe HR 12.50

Sporting Goods

When sports cards became so widely collectible several years ago, other types of related memorabilia started to interest sports fans. Now they search for baseball uniforms, autographed baseballs, game-used bats and gloves, and all sorts of ephemera. Although baseball is America's all-time favorite, other sports have their own groups of interested collectors. Our advice for this category comes from Paul Longo Americana. Mr. Longo is listed in the Directory under Massachusetts. See also Target Balls.

Baseball, red & bl stitching, Am League, game used, early **65.00**
Baseball, sgn by Catfish Hunter **30.00**
Baseball, sgn by Dave Winfield **30.00**
Baseball, sgn by Mickey Mantle **175.00**
Baseball, sgn by Nolan Ryan, M on stand **55.00**
Baseball, sgn by 1985 World Champion Mets team **175.00**
Baseball bat, imprinted Hank Aaron, H&B Pro Motel Bats Clemente ..**80.00**
Baseball bat, imprinted Jackie Robinson **80.00**
Baseball bat, imprinted Mickey Mantle **100.00**
Baseball bat, imprinted Willie Mays, EX **65.00**
Baseball bat, Jackie Robinson **75.00**
Baseball glove, sgn Eddie Collins **800.00**
Blotter, Reach ad, oversz baseball, game pictured, 1899 ....**75.00**
Book, Athletic Sports in Am, England &..., Palmer, 1899, 1st ed ..**250.00**
Book, Wrestling & Jujitsu, Liederman, many photos, 1925 ....**30.00**
Clock, Joe Louis statue, EX patina **475.00**
Guide, Barne's Baseball, 1946 ....**18.00**
Key chain, Arnold Palmer, problem dialer, lg **25.00**
Letter, Dodgers, scout tryouts, 1946 ....**50.00**
Letterhead, St Louis Cardinals, mc, 1940s **40.00**
Pennant, Brooklyn Dodgers, Dem Bums, felt, sm, EX **50.00**
Pennant, Superbowl, NY Giants/Buffalo Bills, 1991 ....**20.00**
Photo, football player, cabinet type, early uniform, ca 1900 ....**45.00**
Pin-bk, Mohammed Ali, I'm The Greatest, 1971, 3½" **10.00**
Pin-bk, Willie Mays Say Hey Daily News, NM **15.00**
Poster, Cy Young, autographed by Jim Lonborg & Roger Clemens ..**90.00**
Poster, Spaulding, standard sports dimensions, 1930s, 1-sheet **150.00**
Program, Indianapolis Speedway, 1973, NM **25.00**
Program, 1960 Olympic Winter Games, Squaw Valley CA, w/inserts ..**40.00**
Ray-o-view card, Lou Gehrig, 1930 ....**150.00**
Record album, Baseball: First 100 Yrs, Jimmy Stewart, 1976 ....**15.00**
Score card, Dodgers/Phillies, 1946 ....**15.00**
Score card, Rochester/Syracuse, 1954 ....**10.00**
Shoes, baseball, Joe DiMaggio, youth sz, MIB w/image of Joe **300.00**
Skiis, wooden w/old bl-gray pnt, early 20th C, 70" L **85.00**
Ticket stub, 1942 Yankees World Series **100.00**
Vase, Olympiad 1928 Amsterdam, glass soccer ball form **195.00**
Wastebasket, Jets, Namath & team pictured, 1950s, M **50.00**
Wristwatch, Harlem Globetrotters, animated hands, 1960s, rare .**75.00**
Yearbook, Harlem Globetrotters, 1964, NM **35.00**
Yearbook, Street & Smith's Baseball, Mantle cover, 1956, EX **65.00**

St. Clair

The St. Clair Glass Company began as a small family-oriented operation in Elwood, Indiana, in 1941. Most famous for their lamps, the family made numerous small items of carnival, pink and caramel slag, and custard glass as well. Later, paperweights became popular production pieces; many command relatively high prices on today's market. Weights are stamped and usually dated, while small production pieces are often unmarked. Lamps are in big demand (prices depend on size

and whether or not they are signed) as are items signed by Paul or Ed St. Clair. For further information we recommend *St. Clair Glass Collector's Book* by Bonnie Pruitt, available from our advisor, Ted Pruitt, who is listed in the Directory under Indiana.

Perfume bottle, white flowers in clear, $95.00.

Bell, carnival glass, from $90 to **100.00**
Bell, Christmas, from $100 to **125.00**
Bird, bl & clear, lg, from $75 to **95.00**
Bowl, pk slag, ped ft, from $150 to **175.00**
Candle holder, mc floral, sulfide, from $75 to **85.00**
Cordial, any color, from $50 to **65.00**
Covered dish, Reclining Colt, cobalt custard, from $135 to **160.00**
Creamer & sugar bowl, Grape & Cable, red carnival, from $150 to ..**200.00**
Doll, any color, from $30 to **40.00**
Goblet, Wild Flower, bl carnival, from $35 to **40.00**
Insulator, red, red carnival or marigold carnival, ea **110.00**
Lamp, glass shade, gr/wht pear weight, Pop St Clair, complete .**2,000.00**
Paperweight, butterfly, controlled bubble, etched, from $250 to ..**350.00**
Paperweight, cameo, windowed, from $250 to **300.00**
Paperweight, Kewpie, windowed, from $175 to **200.00**
Paperweight, strawberry, from $75 to **100.00**
Paperweight, sulfide, assassinated president, set of 4 ....**525.00**
Paperweight, sulfide, Betsy Ross, Joe St Clair **350.00**
Paperweight, sulfide, flower, windowed, Ed St Clair **300.00**
Paperweight, sulfide, flower, windowed, Paul St Clair **200.00**
Paperweight, sulfide, frog, from $140 to **165.00**
Paperweight, sulfide, James Madison on cobalt bl, 1971 ....**150.00**
Paperweight, sulfide, kitten, from $140 to **165.00**
Paperweight, sulfide, rose, windowed, from $1,000 to **1,200.00**
Plate, Lyndon B Johnson, from $20 to **25.00**
Plate, Mt St Helen, from $20 to **25.00**
Plate, Reagan/Bush, any color, from $30 to **35.00**
Ring holder, teapot form, from $75 to **85.00**
Statue, Scottie dog, blk amethyst, sgn Maude St Clair, minimum ..**300.00**
Statue, Scottie dog, custard or caramel, sgn Maude St Clair, ea .**150.00**
Toothpick holder, Bicentennial sq, any color, from $27.50 to **30.00**
Toothpick holder, Cactus, any color, from $25 to **30.00**
Toothpick holder, Indian, bl & wht slag, sgn Joe St Clair **75.00**
Toothpick holder, Shriner's hat (fez), red, from $125 to **150.00**
Toothpick holder, sulfide, flower, from $65 to **75.00**
Toothpick holder, Swans, any color, from $35 to **45.00**
Toothpick holder, Witch, chocolate, from $50 to **75.00**
Tumbler, Holly Band, marigold carnival, from $30 to **35.00**
Vase, paperweight base, clear trumpet neck, from $75 to **85.00**
Wine, Hobstar, crystal carnium, from $40 to **45.00**

Staffordshire

Scores of potteries sprang up in England's Staffordshire district in the early 18th century; several remain to the present time. Figurines and groups were made in great numbers; dogs were favorite subjects. Often they were made in pairs, each a mirror image of the other. They varied in heights from 3" or 4" to the largest, measuring 16" to 18". From 1840 until about 1900, portrait figures were produced to represent specific characters, both real and fictional. As a rule these were never marked.

The Historical Ware listed here was made throughout the district; some collectors refer to it as Staffordshire Blue Ware. It was produced as early as 1820, and because much was exported to America, it was very often decorated with transfers depicting scenic views of well-known American landmarks. Early examples were printed in a deep cobalt. By 1830 a softer blue was favored, and within the next decade black, pink, red, and green prints were used. Although sometimes careless about adding their trademark, many companies used their own border designs that were as individual as their names.

This ware should not be confused with the vast amounts of modern china (mostly plates) made from early in the century to the present. These souvenir or commemorative items are usually marketed through gift stores and the like. (See Rowland and Marcellus.) See also specific manufacturers.

Key:
blk — black   l/b — light blue
gr — green   m/b — medium blue
d/b — dark blue   m-d/b — medium dark blue

Figures and Groups

Whippets by tree-trunk vase, gray, tan, and green, 1800s, 11½", $375.00.

Bust, John Wesley, mc, detailed, 1870-80, 11⅞", NM **350.00**
Bust, Lord Wellington portrait in relief on ebonized panel **165.00**
Couple by fence pour water from well, 9½" **195.00**
Dogs, spaniels, copper over pk lustre, 10", pr....................**415.00**
Garibaldi, man w/scroll, gold trim, 19" **325.00**
Highland lad & lassie & fawn by tree, spill vase, 7" **250.00**
Hunter w/quail in hand & at ft, 15½" **200.00**
Lady w/bouquet in lap kisses bird on hand, 7¼" **200.00**
Lord & Lady Stanhope drawing water, 9" **350.00**
Lovers by tree & trellis w/dog, spill vase, 13", EX **275.00**
Man seated w/rooster & dog, mc on cream, 9¾", NM **120.00**
Poodles (3) on dk bl ground w/single gold band, 4" **350.00**
Prince of Wales astride, wht w/flesh tones, 12" **365.00**
Shakespeare, ermine cape & manuscript, 11½", EX **300.00**
Sheep (2) on mc base, rstr, 5¼" **385.00**
Spaniel, gr lustre, 10½", pr......................................**235.00**
Spaniel, rust mottle, 12", pr.....................................**175.00**
Vase, spill; Rebecca at well, 19th C, 12" **150.00**
Wedding couple beneath grape arbor, gold trim, 14x9" **150.00**

Historical

Basket, Shepherd Piping, m/b, att Riley, w/undertray, 3x10½" ..**1,100.00**

Basket, Tunbridge Castle..., d/b, openwork, Stevenson, 11½" ...**1,200.00**
Basket, West Point Military Academy, d/b, openwork, Wood, 11" .**2,250.00**
Bowl, Shells, d/b, beaded, Stubbs & Kent, 9⅞" **350.00**
Bowl, Shield of US, l/b, line border, mini, 3⅝" **120.00**
Bowl, vegetable; States...Castle w/Flag, d/b, Clews, 11⅛" **1,000.00**
Creamer, Lafayette at Tomb of Franklin, d/b, Phillips **575.00**
Cup & saucer, floral, d/b, Rogers, NM **60.00**
Cup & saucer, Log Cabin, pk, Ridgway, NM **155.00**
Cup & saucer, Yale College...CT, brn, rare **80.00**
Cup plate, Canova, lav, Mayer, 4", pr.............................**375.00**
Cup plate, Castle Garden Battery, d/b, Wood, 3¾" **190.00**
Cup plate, Columbus GA, l/b, Wood's Celtic China series, 4" ...**180.00**
Cup plate, English Manor, d/b, Wood's grapevine border, 3⅝" ..**120.00**
Cup plate, Hunter, Dog & Pheasant, d/b, Wood, 3⅝" **170.00**
Cup plate, Hyena, d/b, Hall Quadrupeds series, 4" **200.00**
Cup plate, Near Sandy Hill..., red, Clews, 8¾", NM **70.00**
Cup plate, States...3-Story Mansion, d/b, Clews, 4½" **325.00**
Custard cup, Game Birds, d/b, hdld, Stubbs, 2¼" **60.00**
Ladle, Upper Ferry Bridge..., d/b, Stubbs, rstr, 6½" **350.00**
Ladle, Utica, lt bl, Meigh Am Cities & Scenery series, 11½" **150.00**
Leaf dish, unidentified view (college), d/b, Ridgway, 5¾" **225.00**
Pitcher, City Hall NY/Hospital NY, d/b, RSW, 7⅛" **1,000.00**
Pitcher, Dam & Waterworks Phila (sidewheeler), d/b, 6½" **2,400.00**
Pitcher, Franklin's Tomb, d/b, Wood, rstr, 10¼" **425.00**
Pitcher, Lafayette at Tomb..., d/b, urn shape, 7¾" **1,100.00**
Pitcher, View of St Lawrence/Indian Encampment, l/b, Morely, 6" ..**180.00**
Plate, Am & Independence, man w/net, d/b, Clews, 10⅝", EX ..**300.00**
Plate, Am & Independence, men w/net, m/b, 10½", NM **450.00**
Plate, Angus Seats...Unidentified View, d/b, 7⅛" **80.00**
Plate, B&O Railroad (incline), d/b, Wood, 9½" **770.00**
Plate, B&O Railroad (straight), d/b, Wood, 10¼", EX **825.00**
Plate, Battery NY, red, Jackson, 8", NM **140.00**
Plate, Boston State House, m/b, Wood & Sons, 10¼" **165.00**
Plate, British America - Montreal, brn, Davenport, 6¾" **145.00**
Plate, British Views, d/b, openwork, unmk, 7¼", NM **200.00**
Plate, British Views, d/b, 9¾" **200.00**
Plate, Bunker Hill Monument, purple, Jackson, 6¼" **185.00**
Plate, Cadmus, d/b, Wood's irregular shell border, 10" **475.00**
Plate, Caledonia, purple, Adams, 9¼" **85.00**
Plate, Capitol Washington, d/b, Wood's shell border, 7⅝" **935.00**
Plate, castle & cows, m/b, 9¾", NM **75.00**
Plate, Castle of Lavenza, d/b, Wood, 10⅛" **160.00**
Plate, Chinoiserie, d/b, 9¼" **60.00**
Plate, Christ Church Oxford, d/b, Ridgway College series, 10" ..**135.00**
Plate, Church in City of NY, d/b, Stubbs' eagle border, 6⅛" **400.00**
Plate, City Hall NY, d/b, Beauties of Am, Ridgway, 9⅞" ....,**150.00**
Plate, City Hall NY, d/b, Stubbs' eagle border, 6¾" **135.00**
Plate, Columbian Star...Side View, brn, Ridgway, 10" **150.00**
Plate, Commodore MacDonnough's Victory, d/b, Wood, 9½" ...**385.00**
Plate, Constitution & Guerriere, d/b, Wood, 10¾", NM **1,760.00**
Plate, Dam & Water Works Phila, m/b, 9⅞" **440.00**
Plate, Deaf & Dumb Asylum Phila, red, Jackson, 7", EX **50.00**
Plate, Eashing Park Surrey, d/b, 7½", NM **120.00**
Plate, Eastern Palace, d/b, unmk, 10⅜" **145.00**
Plate, Eastern Scenery, m-d/b, Wood, 9⅞" **90.00**
Plate, Entrance of Erie Canal Into Hudson..., d/b, 6" **700.00**
Plate, Falls of Killarney, d/b, 10" **70.00**
Plate, Fort Montgomery Hudson River, l/b, Clews, 5¾" **50.00**
Plate, Gem, d/b, Hammersley, 8¾" **250.00**
Plate, Girard's Bank Phila, mulberry, Jackson, 6¼" **80.00**
Plate, Grecian Scenery, m/b, wht emb border, Wood, 10½" **90.00**
Plate, Hartford CT, blk, Jackson Am Scenery series, 10¼" **120.00**
Plate, Harvard College, m/b, 10⅛", VG **110.00**
Plate, Hudson River, d/b, Wood's shell border, 5⅝" **775.00**

Plate, hunter & fox, d/b, Wood Zoological series, 8½" 300.00
Plate, Junction of Sacandaga & Hudson Rivers, blk, 7", NM 100.00
Plate, Junction of Sacandaga & Hudson Rivers, pk, Clews, 6¾" .100.00
Plate, Kingsweston Gloucestershire, d/b, Riley, 8¾" 110.00
Plate, Knighthood Confer'd on Don Quixote, d/b, 10" 250.00
Plate, Landing of Gen Lafayette, d/b, Clews, 10¼" 360.00
Plate, Landing of Gen Lafayette, d/b, 8⅜", NM 300.00
Plate, Legend of Montrose, l/b, Davenport, 9⅛" 90.00
Plate, Lion, d/b, Hall Quadrupeds series, 9¾" 300.00
Plate, Mastiff (guard dog), d/b, Hall's Quadrupeds series, 7¼" 150.00
Plate, Mitchell & Freeman's...Boston, d/b, Adams, 10¼" 715.00
Plate, Muhammadan Mosque & Tomb, d/b, Hall, 9⅞" 120.00
Plate, Near Fishkill Hudson River, blk, Clews, 10¼" 100.00
Plate, Otter, d/b, Hall's Quadrupeds series, 8⅝", NM 200.00
Plate, Park Theatre NY, d/b, 10⅛" 330.00
Plate, Peace Plenty, d/b, Clews, 10¼" 465.00
Plate, Peaches & Cherries, d/b, 10" 225.00
Plate, Picturesque Views Near Fishkill..., purple, 10⅝" 110.00
Plate, Pittsfield Elm, d/b, Clews, 8¾" 275.00
Plate, President's House, Washington, Jackson, purple, 10⅜" 275.00
Plate, Residence of Richard Jordan..., brn, 9", EX 250.00
Plate, River Fishing, d/b, Meir, 6⅜" 110.00
Plate, Sancho Panza's Debate w/Teresa, d/b, Davenport, 9" 255.00
Plate, Shannondale Springs, red, Adams, 8" 20.00
Plate, Sheltered Peasants, d/b, 10" 160.00
Plate, Shirely House Surrey, d/b, Wood's grapevine border, 6⅜" ..85.00
Plate, Signing of Magna Charta, m/b, Jones & Son, 10¼" 180.00
Plate, Springer Spaniel, d/b, Stevenson, 9¾", NM 275.00
Plate, St George's Chapel..., d/b, Wood's Regents Park series, 10" ..165.00
Plate, Steam Dredge, d/b, Diorama series, unmk, 8" 325.00
Plate, toddy; Setter, d/b, Hall's Quadrupeds series, 5⅛" 250.00
Plate, Trenton Falls, red, Wood's Celtic China series, 7¾" 120.00
Plate, two-pony cart, m/b w/floral border, 9¾", NM 180.00
Plate, Tyrolean, l/b, Ridgway, 10⅜" 60.00
Plate, Union, d/b, Wood's irregular shell border, 10" 450.00
Plate, Upper Ferry Bridge...Schuylkill, m-d/b, Stubbs, 8⅞" 250.00
Plate, View of Liverpool, d/b, Wood's irregular shell border, 10" ...900.00
Plate, Villa in Regent's Park London, d/b, Adams, 10¼" 275.00
Plate, Welcome Lafayette...Country's Glory, d/b, Clews, 7⅝" .1,155.00
Plate, Woodman, d/b, Stubbs, 6⅜" 170.00
Plate, York Minster, d/b, Hanshall's fruit/flower border, 10", NM ..300.00
Plate, Zebra, d/b, Rogers, 10" 170.00

Platter, America and Independence, states names form border, mansion and lake with swans in center, dark blue, Clews, 17", NM, $4,000.00.

Platter, Archipelago, l/b, Ridgway, 13", EX 100.00
Platter, Baltimore, l/b, Meigh, 16", EX 160.00
Platter, Boston & Bunker Hill, l/b, Mellor Venables, rstr, 17⅝" ...95.00
Platter, Calecionia, purple, Adams, 12¼" 300.00
Platter, Cambrian, Phillips, brn, 19" 415.00
Platter, Chinese Marine Scene, d/b, 16¼", +13⅜" strainer 650.00
Platter, Delhi, brn, unmk, 19⅝" 425.00

Platter, Highlands, Hudson River, d/b, Wood, 12½" L 1,650.00
Platter, Highlands, Hudson River, l/b, Wood, 12½", NM 185.00
Platter, Italian, m-d/b, 11½" 95.00
Platter, Ladies Cabin (Boston Mails), blk, 15½", EX 325.00
Platter, Landing of Gen Lafayette, d/b, Clews, 15¼" 1,700.00
Platter, Landing of Gen Lafayette, d/b, Clews, 17", EX 1,300.00
Platter, London Views, St George's Chapel..., d/b, Wood, 16⅝" .660.00
Platter, Moditonham Hall, d/b, Henshall's fruit/flower rim, 15" ..650.00
Platter, Palestine, l/b, Adams, 17" 300.00
Platter, Ponte Rotto, d/b, unmk, 12¾" 500.00
Platter, Residence of...Richard Jordan, red, unmk, 15⅞" 715.00
Platter, Sandusky, d/b, 16⅝", NM 8,525.00
Platter, States...Castle w/Flag, d/b, Clews, 12⅞", NM 1,100.00
Platter, Tyrolean, l/b, Ridgway, 19" 325.00
Platter, Upper Ferry Bridge..., red, Jackson, 9¾", EX 500.00
Platter, View From Fort Putnam, l/b, Ridgway, 15¼" 350.00
Platter, View From Port Putnam, blk, Ridgway, 15¼", EX 145.00
Platter, View of Capitol at WA, l/b, Ridgway, rstr, 19¼" 250.00
Platter, well & tree; Ruins w/Horseman in Foreground, m-d/b, 21" .1,100.00
Platter, well & tree; Upper Ferry Bridge...Schuylkill, d/b, 18½" .950.00
Platter, well & tree; Upper Ferry...Schuylkill, d/b, Stubbs, 18¾" ..1,000.00
Punch bowl, Arms of NY, d/b, Mayer, rstr, 4½x10¾" 3,300.00
Sauce boat, Fruit & Flowers, d/b, 7⅞", EX 330.00
Sauce boat, Yangeusian Conflict, d/b, unmk Davenport, NM 350.00
Sauce tureen, Fort Ticonderoga NY, blk, Jackson, rpr 180.00
Sauce tureen, Landing of Lafayette, d/b, Clews, w/lid & tray ..1,100.00
Sauce tureen, Upper Ferry Bridge..., d/b, Stubbs, w/lid, 5¾x8¼" ..900.00
Saucer, early railroad w/engine & 1 car, d/b, floral border, 6" 275.00
Soup, Bisham Abbey Berkshire, lt m/b, Davenport, 9½" 110.00
Soup, Bridge of Lucano, d/b, Wood's Italian Scenery series, 10" ...145.00
Soup, Harvard College, d/b, acorn & leaf border, 10" 300.00
Soup, llama, d/b, Hall's Quadrupeds series, 10" 300.00
Soup, Octagon Church Boston, m-d/b, Ridgway, 9⅞" 330.00
Soup, Picturesque Views, Hudson, Hudson River, blk, Clews, 10½" ..140.00
Soup, Picturesque Views, Pittsburgh PA, blk, Clews, 10½", EX .330.00
Soup, President's House WA, blk, Jackson, 10½", NM 150.00
Soup, Shells, d/b, Stubbs & Kent, 9¾" 425.00
Soup, Thorton Castle..., d/b, Wood's grapevine border, 10" 250.00
Soup, Thrybergh Yorkshire, d/b, Wood's grapevine border, 10¼" ..275.00
Soup, tureen, Birds & Fruit, d/b, w/lid, Stubbs, rstr, 9¼x14" ...1,300.00
Soup, Veranda, brn, Hall, 10½" 100.00
Soup, Winter View of Pittsfield Mass, d/b, Clews, 10⅜" 440.00
Soup tureen, Caledonia, purple, ftd, Adams, w/lid, 9¾x14" 600.00
Soup tureen, Florence, d/b, acanthus hdls, rose finial, 12x15" .3,750.00
Sugar bowl, Water Girl, m/b, Spode, w/lid, 4½" dia 165.00
Tea bowl, ducks, m/b, unmk, 2⅝x4¼" 65.00
Tea bowl & saucer, Couple at Franklin's Tomb, d/b, Phillips 240.00
Tea bowl & saucer, flower in vase, d/b, Clews, EX 100.00
Tea bowl & saucer, MacDonnough's Victory, d/b, Wood 600.00
Teapot, Harp, d/b, Stevenson, rstr spout, 8¼" 375.00
Teapot, Residence of...Richard Jordan..., brn, rpr, 8¼" 715.00
Tray, Dulwich College Essex, d/b, Stevenson's rose border, 10¼" ..570.00
Wash bowl, Upper Ferry Bridge...Schuylkill, d/b, Stubbs, 12⅝" .550.00
Wash pitcher, Near Weehawken, blk, 12¾", EX 375.00

Stained Glass

There are many factors to consider in evaluating a window or panel of stained glass art. Besides the obvious factor of condition, intricacy, jeweling, beveling, and the amount of selenium (red, orange, and yellow) present should all be taken into account. Remember, repair work is itself an art and can be very expensive. Our advisor for this category is Carl Heck; he is listed in the Directory under Colorado.

Lamps

Duffner-Kimberly, att; 20" acorn/leaf shade; split std, 24" 5,000.00
Duffner-Kimberly, 21" heraldic element shade; bronze std, 24" ...4,600.00
Duffner-Kimberly, 22½" hollyhock shade; bronze std, 30" 6,000.00
Duffner-Kimberly, 22½" roses dome shade; bronze std, 30" 5,000.00
Duffner-Kimberly, 24" floral shade; bronze lobed std, 26" 7,500.00
Gorham, 19" poppy shade w/apron; bronze std, 24" 6,000.00
Suess, 25" floral shade; mk 6-socket tree trunk std, 28" 8,500.00
Wilkinson, 20" apple blossom shade; 3-socket std, 27½" 3,200.00
Williamson, 20" tulip shade, 4-socket floral std, rstr, 25" 4,250.00
Williamson, 22" slag shell-border shade; 3 paw ft, 62" 8,000.00
Williamson, 3 5" bell-form shell-border shades; hanging, 5" ...5,000.00

Windows

Stained and faceted jewel window, exceptional glass and jewelwork, from St. Joseph, Missouri, ca 1888, 26½x34", $1,850.00.

Bull's-eye panes (5) surrounded by geometrics, 41x21" 250.00
Center medallion w/beveled oval clear glass, 48x26", EX 350.00
Florals & cut jewels in amber slag field, wood fr, 19x51" 550.00
Nouveau tulips on bl & caramel slag, 2-pane, 39x26", EX 450.00
Prairie School, stylized flowers, arched top, 45x13", VG 1,100.00

Stanford

The Stanford Pottery Co. was founded in 1945 in Sebring, Ohio. One of the founders was George Stanford, a former manager at Spaulding China (Royal Copley). They continued in operations until the factory was destroyed by a fire about 1961. They produced a Corn Line, similar to that of the Shawnee Company, that is today very collectible. Most examples are marked (either Stanford Sebring Ohio or with a paper label), so there should be no difficulty in distinguishing one line from the other.

In addition to their Corn Line, they produced planters and figurines, many of which were black trimmed with gold, made to be sold as pairs or sets. Wall pockets and vases were made as well. In 1949 they introduced a line called Tomato Ware, consisting of a cookie jar, grease jar, salt and pepper shakers, creamer and sugar bowl, mustard jar, marmalade jar, etc. These were shaped as bright red tomatoes with green leaves and stems (often used as lid finials), and were marketed under the name 'The Pantry Parade.' Our advisor for this category is Joe Devine; he is listed in the Directory under Iowa.

Ashtray, free-form, orange w/wht 'stucco,' #270-D, mk, 10x7" 12.00
Corn Line, butter dish 45.00
Corn Line, casserole, 8" L 35.00

Corn Line, creamer & sugar bowl 45.00
Corn Line, pitcher, 7½" 55.00
Corn Line, plate, 9" L 30.00
Corn Line, relish tray 35.00
Corn Line, shakers, sm, pr 25.00
Corn Line, shakers, 4", pr 25.00
Corn Line, spoon rest 25.00
Corn Line, teapot 60.00
Planter, drum major or majorette, ea 15.00
Planter, Dutch boy or girl by tulip, blk w/gold trim, ea 15.00
Planter, teddy bear, wht w/pk & bl trim, paper label, 7" 28.00
Tomato Ware, casserole, w/lid, 6x9" 55.00
Tomato Ware, cookie jar, 8" 60.00
Tomato Ware, creamer 25.00
Tomato Ware, grease jar, w/lid 30.00
Tomato Ware, marmalade jar 25.00
Tomato Ware, mustard jar 25.00
Tomato Ware, pitcher, 6½" 50.00
Tomato Ware, sugar bowl 25.00
Wall pocket, bird, bl & cobalt w/gold trim 28.00
Wall pocket, cherry branch, red pie-crust edge, #299, mk, 6¼" 20.00

Stangl

Stangl Pottery was one of the longest existing potteries in the United States, having as its beginning in 1814 the Sam Hill Pottery, becoming the Fulper Pottery which gained eminence in the field of art pottery (ca. 1860), and then coming under the aegis of Johann Martin Stangl. The German-born Stangl joined Fulper in 1910 as chemical engineer, left for a brief stint at Haeger in Dundee, Illinois, and rejoined Fulper as general manager in 1920. He became president of the firm in 1928. Although Stangl's name was on much of the ware from the late '20s onward, the company's name was not changed officially until 1955. J.M. Stangl died in 1972; the pottery continued under the ownership of Wheaton Industries until 1978, then closed. Stangl is best known for its extensive Birds of America line, styled after Audubon; its brightly colored, hand-carved, hand-painted dinnerware; and its great variety of giftware, including its dry-brushed gold lines. For more information we recommend *Stangl Pottery* by Harvey Duke; for ordering information refer to the listing for Nancy and Robert Perzel, Popkorn Antiques (our advisors for this category), in our Directory under New Jersey.

Birds

#3250E, Drinking Duck 125.00
#3274, Penguin 500.00
#3275, Turkey 475.00
#3276, Bluebird, 5" 100.00
#3276D, Bluebirds, 8" 180.00
#3285, Rooster, wht & blk w/red & yel, early version, 4½" 100.00
#3286, Hen, late version 50.00
#3400, Lovebird, old version, 4½" 100.00
#3400, Lovebird, revised version 60.00
#3401, Wren, brn, revised version, 5" 60.00
#3401, Wren, tan, old version 250.00
#3401D, Wrens, brn, revised version, 6" 125.00
#3401D, Wrens, early version, 6½" 250.00
#3402D, Orioles, old version, 6½" 225.00
#3402D, Orioles, revised version 125.00
#3404, Lovebirds Kissing 350.00
#3404D, Lovebirds, revised version, 6" 125.00
#3405, Cockatoo, sm, 6½" 60.00
#3405D, Cockatoos, old version, 10" 190.00

#3405D, Cockatoos, revised version, 9½" 150.00
#3406, Kingfisher, bl or teal 75.00
#3406D, Kingfishers, bl or teal, 5" 135.00
#3407, Owl 350.00
#3408, Bird of Paradise, 5" 125.00
#3443, Flying Duck, bl, 9" 275.00
#3443, Flying Duck, teal gr 300.00
#3444, Cardinal, dk red matt, 7" 135.00
#3444, Cardinal, pk, revised, 7" 100.00
#3444, Cardinal (female), pk, orig version, 6½" 100.00
#3445, Rooster, gray, 10" 250.00
#3445, Rooster, lt yel 175.00
#3446, Hen, gray 200.00
#3446, Hen, yel & brn, 7" 165.00
#3447, Prothonatary Warbler, yel & gr, 5" 85.00
#3448, Blue-headed Vireo 85.00
#3449, Parrot, dk gr w/mc, 5½" 165.00
#3450, Passenger Pigeon 1,200.00
#3452, Painted Bunting, 5" 125.00
#3454, Key West Quail Dove, both wings up 750.00
#3454, Key West Quail Dove, single wing up, 10" 300.00
#3455, Shoveler Duck, rare, 12½x14" 1,200.00
#3456, Cerulean Warbler, 4" 65.00
#3458, Quail, 7½" 1,200.00
#3490D, Redstarts, 9½" 225.00
#3491, Pheasant Hen 200.00
#3492, Cock Pheasant 200.00
#3518D, White-Crowned Pigeons 750.00
#3580, Cockatoo, med, 9" 150.00
#3581, Chickadees, blk & wht 275.00
#3581, Chickadees, brn & wht 225.00
#3582D, Parakeets, bl 275.00
#3583, Parula Warbler, 4½" 60.00
#3584, Cockatoo, 11⅜" 300.00
#3585, Rufus Hummingbird, mc, 3½" 75.00
#3589, Indigo Bunting, 3½" 85.00
#3590, Carolina Wren 165.00
#3591, Brewer's Blackbird, 4" 130.00
#3592, Titmouse, 3" 65.00
#3593, Nuthatch, 3" 65.00
#3594, Red-Faced Warbler, 3" 85.00
#3596, Grey Cardinal, 5" 90.00
#3597, Wilson Warbler, yel & blk, 3" 60.00
#3598, Kentucky Warbler, 3½" 60.00

#3599D, Hummingbird pair, $300.00.

#3626, Broadtail Hummingbird, bl flowers, 6½" 150.00
#3627, Rivoli Hummingbird, w/pk flower 150.00
#3628, Reiffer's Hummingbird, 4½x6½" 125.00
#3629, Broadbill Hummingbird 125.00
#3634, Allen Hummingbird, 4" 85.00
#3635, Gold Finches (group) 200.00
#3715, Blue Jay w/peanut, 10" 675.00

#3716, Blue Jay w/leaf 675.00
#3750, Western Tanager, 8½" 275.00
#3752D, Red-Headed Woodpeckers, pk gloss, 8½" 325.00
#3752D, Red-Headed Woodpeckers, red matt 350.00
#3754, White-Wing Crossbill 2,250.00
#3757, Scissor-Tailed Flycatcher, 11" 600.00
#3758, Magpie-Jay, 11x7" 1,200.00
#3810, Blackpoll Warbler 175.00
#3811, Chestnut-Backed Chickadee, 5" 125.00
#3812, Chestnut-Sided Warbler, 4½" 125.00
#3813, Evening Grosbeak, 5" 135.00
#3814, Black-Throated Green Warbler, 3" 135.00
#3815, Western Bluebird 400.00
#3848, Golden-Crowned Kinglet, 4½" 110.00
#3852, Cliff Swallow, 3½" 125.00
#3853, Golden-Crowned Kinglets, 5½x5" 600.00
#3922, European Finch 1,000.00
#3924, Yellow-Throated Warbler, 6" 425.00

Dinnerware

Amber Glo, plate, 10" 8.00
Amber Glo, plate, 12½" 15.00
Amber Glo, plate, 6" 3.00
Amber Glo, shakers, pr 12.00
Antique Gold, bud vase, #3981, 6¾" 20.00
Antique Gold, pitcher, #4056, 8⅜" 25.00
Antique Gold, server, center hdl, 10" 13.00
Antique Gold, vase, tulip form, #5144, 4" 15.00
Apple Delight, bowl, cereal 12.00
Apple Delight, bowl, fruit; 5½" 10.00
Apple Delight, bowl, 10" 30.00
Apple Delight, coupe soup, 7½" 15.00
Apple Delight, cup & saucer 11.00
Apple Delight, liner for gravy 8.00
Apple Delight, plate, 10" 15.00
Apple Delight, plate, 6" 3.50
Apple Delight, plate, 8" 9.00
Apple Delight, tea tile 14.00
Bittersweet, cup & saucer 11.00
Bittersweet, pitcher, 2-qt 40.00
Bittersweet, plate, 10" 13.00
Blueberry, butter dish 40.00
Blueberry, gravy boat 25.00
Blueberry, plate, 10" 22.00
Blueberry, server, center hdl, 10⅛" 15.00
Blueberry, shakers, pr 20.00
Colonial, chop plate, Persian Yel, 12½" 16.00
Colonial, grill plate, 11⅝" 25.00
Concord, bowl, fruit; 5⅛" 10.00
Concord, bowl, soup; 8⅛" 14.00
Concord, cup, 2⅜" 11.00
Concord, plate, bread & butter; 6" 7.00
Concord, plate, 10" 18.00
Concord, plate, 11¼" 20.00
Concord, plate, 8⅛" 12.00
Concord, saucer 4.00
Country Garden, bowl, cereal 18.00
Country Garden, bowl, fruit 15.00
Country Garden, bowl, salad; 10" 50.00
Country Garden, bowl, 8" 30.00
Country Garden, bread tray 45.00
Country Garden, chop plate, 12" 40.00
Country Garden, chop plate, 14" 55.00

Country Garden, creamer & sugar bowl	27.50
Country Garden, gravy boat	25.00
Country Garden, mug	40.00
Country Garden, pitcher, 1-qt	40.00
Country Garden, plate, 10"	18.00
Country Garden, plate, 6"	6.00
Country Garden, plate, 8"	12.00
Country Garden, relish	30.00
Country Life, bowl, coupe soup; mallard, single	100.00
Country Life, bowl, fruit; w/pony	75.00
Country Life, bowl, salad; pig	125.00
Country Life, bowl, vegetable; mallard	130.00
Country Life, cake stand, 10" rooster plate, 4½" H	100.00
Country Life, chop plate, farmhouse	250.00
Country Life, coaster, duckling	40.00
Country Life, creamer	40.00
Country Life, cup & saucer	65.00
Country Life, plate, farmer's wife, 10"	180.00
Country Life, plate, pig at fence	90.00
Country Life, plate, rooster, 10"	80.00
Country Life, plate, rooster, 6"	15.00
Country Life, shakers, pr	60.00
Cranberry, bowl, flat soup	22.00
Cranberry, bowl, fruit; 5½"	15.00
Cranberry, plate, 10"	18.00
Cranberry, plate, 6"	8.00
Cranberry, saucer	5.00
Cranberry, sugar bowl, w/lid	15.00
Flora, saucer	5.00
Flora, teapot, ind, 5¾"	40.00
Flora, teapot, 6-cup	60.00
Fruit, bowl, soup; 7½"	20.00
Fruit, chop plate, 12½"	45.00
Fruit, chop plate, 14½"	55.00
Fruit, creamer & sugar bowl	30.00
Fruit, egg cup	15.00
Fruit, plate, dinner	22.00
Fruit, relish tray	40.00
Fruit, server, center hdl	12.00
Fruit & Flowers, bowl, divided vegetable	50.00
Fruit & Flowers, bowl, flat soup	25.00
Fruit & Flowers, bowl, vegetable; 8"	40.00
Fruit & Flowers, cake stand, 10" plate w/wht ped	35.00
Fruit & Flowers, chop plate, 14"	70.00
Fruit & Flowers, cup & saucer	20.00
Fruit & Flowers, plate, 10"	22.00
Fruit & Flowers, plate, 6"	10.00
Fruit & Flowers, plate, 8"	18.00
Fruit & Flowers, platter, oval	65.00
Fruit & Flowers, shakers, pr	24.00
Fruit & Flowers, sugar bowl	18.00
Garden Flower, coaster	16.00
Garden Flower, egg cup	15.00
Garden Flower, pitcher, 1-qt	35.00
Garden Flower, plate, 8"	13.00
Garden Flower, plate, 9½"	14.00
Golden Blossom, cup & saucer	10.00
Golden Blossom, egg cup	12.00
Golden Blossom, platter, 12" dia	20.00
Golden Grape, bowl, 12"	28.00
Golden Grape, server, center hdl	8.00
Golden Harvest, bowl, divided vegetable	30.00
Golden Harvest, chop plate, 12"	20.00
Golden Harvest, cup & saucer	10.00

Golden Harvest, plate, 10"	12.00
Golden Harvest, shakers, pr	15.00
Jonquil, plate, bread & butter	6.00
Jonquil, plate, dinner	15.00
Kiddieware, cup, ABCs	50.00
Kiddieware, cup, Ginger Cat	180.00
Kiddieware, cup, Indian Campfire	100.00
Kiddieware, cup, Little Boy Blue	40.00
Kiddieware, dish, ABCs, divided, whiteware	80.00
Kiddieware, dish, ABCs, 3-part	100.00
Kiddieware, dish, Ducky Dinner, 3-part, w/cup	180.00
Kiddieware, dish, Kitten Kapers, 3-part	100.00
Kiddieware, dish, Mealtime Special, 3-part	90.00
Kiddieware, dish, Our Barnyard Friends, 3-part	100.00
Kiddieware, plate, Circus Clown, pk whiteware	80.00
Kiddieware, plate, Little Quackers	165.00
Kiddieware, plate, Peter Rabbit, Terra Rose	195.00
Kiddieware, plate, Pink Fairy	180.00
Magnolia, bowl, divided vegetable	28.00
Magnolia, bowl, 8"	25.00
Magnolia, butter dish	30.00
Magnolia, candle warmer	20.00
Magnolia, chop plate, 12½"	28.00
Magnolia, chop plate, 14¼"	40.00
Magnolia, creamer & sugar bowl, w/lid	22.00
Magnolia, cup & saucer	12.50
Magnolia, gravy boat	15.00
Magnolia, plate, 10"	15.00
Magnolia, plate, 6"	5.00
Magnolia, plate, 8"	9.50
Magnolia, platter, Casual	28.50
Magnolia, saucer	4.00
Magnolia, shakers, pr	20.00
Magnolia, sugar bowl, w/lid	12.00
Orchard Song, bowl, fruit; 5½"	9.00
Orchard Song, bowl, 12"	45.00
Orchard Song, bread tray	28.00
Orchard Song, coaster, 5"	4.00
Orchard Song, plate, snack; 10", w/cup	15.00
Orchard Song, plate, 12"	24.00
Orchard Song, plate, 6"	4.50
Orchard Song, plate, 8"	8.00
Orchard Song, server, center hdl	8.00
Provincial, bowl, lug soup; 5½"	12.00
Provincial, butter dish	35.00
Provincial, cup & saucer	12.50
Provincial, plate, luncheon; 8"	10.00
Provincial, plate, 10"	15.00
Provincial, relish tray, 10½"	20.00
Provincial, sugar bowl, w/lid	12.50
Rooster, cup & saucer	20.00
Rooster, plate, 10"	25.00
Sculptured Fruit, bowl, 8"	30.00
Sculptured Fruit, cup & saucer	15.00
Sculptured Fruit, mug	20.00
Sculptured Fruit, plate, 10"	14.00
Sculptured Fruit, saucer	5.00
Thistle, bowl, divided vegetable; 7½"	40.00
Thistle, bowl, fruit; 5½"	12.00
Thistle, bowl, lug soup	15.00
Thistle, coffeepot, 8-cup	70.00
Thistle, cup & saucer	11.00
Thistle, plate, 10⅛"	18.00
Thistle, plate, 6¼"	6.00

Thistle, shakers, pr 18.00
Thistle, sugar bowl, w/lid 12.00
Town & Country, bowl, cereal/soup; bl 30.00
Town & Country, butter dish, w/lid, ¼-lb 50.00
Town & Country, casserole, w/lid, 2-qt 80.00
Town & Country, coffeepot 85.00
Town & Country, creamer 25.00
Town & Country, mug 40.00
Town & Country, pitcher, 2½-pt 65.00
Town & Country, pitcher, 2½-qt 80.00
Town & Country, pitcher & bowl, lg 285.00
Town & Country, pitcher & bowl, sm 160.00
Town & Country, plate, 10" 35.00
Town & Country, plate, 8" 20.00
Tulip, bowl, fruit; 5½" 15.00
Tulip, cookie jar/bean pot 60.00
Tulip, gravy tray 15.00
White Dogwood, cup & saucer 15.00
White Dogwood, plate, dinner 12.00
White Dogwood, plate, 8" 6.00
Wild Rose, bowl, divided vegetable 45.00
Wild Rose, bowl, flat soup 22.00
Wild Rose, bowl, fruit; 5½" 15.00
Wild Rose, bowl, salad; 12" 75.00
Wild Rose, bread tray 45.00
Wild Rose, chop plate, 14½" 55.00
Wild Rose, coffeepot 75.00
Wild Rose, condiment tray 25.00
Wild Rose, creamer 15.00
Wild Rose, cup 8.50
Wild Rose, gravy boat 25.00
Wild Rose, gravy boat stand 15.00
Wild Rose, pitcher, ½-pt 20.00
Wild Rose, plate, 10" 18.00
Wild Rose, plate, 11¼" 35.00
Wild Rose, plate, 6" 7.00
Wild Rose, plate, 8" 15.00
Wild Rose, saucer 6.00
Wild Rose, sugar bowl, w/lid 15.00

Miscellaneous

Ashtray, Blue-Wing Teal 60.00
Cigarette box, apple tree, w/1 ashtray 60.00
Cigarette box, fruit, w/1 ashtray 60.00
Cigarette box, hummingbird, #3842, 5⅝x4½", NM ...65.00
Cigarette box, pheasant 85.00
Cigarette box, tropic flower, w/1 ashtray 60.00
Dealer sign, Indian Summer 125.00
Fish vase, Terra Rose, gr, #3569 ....200.00
Vase, Terra Rose, mountain goat, gr & mauve, #3708 ....450.00
Wig stand, blond, wood base 375.00
Wig stand, brunette, wood base 350.00

Stanley Tools

The Stanley company was founded in Connecticut in 1854, and over the years has absorbed more than a score of tool companies already in existence. By the second decade of the 20th century, having long since solidified their position as *the* source for tools of the highest grade, the company enjoyed worldwide prestige. Through both World Wars, they were recognized as one of the nation's premier producers of wartime goods. Industrial arts classes introduced baby boomers to Stan-

ley tools and provided yet another impetus to expansion and recognition. Overall, the company's growth and development has kept an easy pace along with the economy of the nation, and it continues today as a leader in the field of tool production.

Two factors to consider when evaluating a tool are age and condition. One of their earliest trademarks (1854 – 1857) is 'A. Stanley,' found only on rulers. In the early '20s, their now-familiar 'sweetheart' trademark, the letters SW and a heart shape within the confines of a modified rectangle, was adopted. They continued to use this trademark until it was discontinued in 1933. Many other variations were used as well, some of which contain a patent date. A study of these marks will help you determine the vintage of your tools. Condition is extremely important, and though a light cleaning is acceptable, you should never attempt to 'restore' a tool by sanding, repainting, or replacing parts that may be damaged or missing. Tools listed below are for those in average 'as found' condition, ranging from very good to excellent.

For more information, we recommend *Antique and Collectible Stanley Tools*, written by our advisor, John Walter, who is listed in the Directory under Ohio.

Combination plane, Miller's 1870 Pat., Type 3, No. 41 (reverse side), 1874 – 1897, from $800.00 up to $1,600.00 depending on condition.

Axe, 4-sq; japanned steel, hickory hdl, 1925-30, 18" 50.00
Bench bracket, #203 ....45.00
Brace, spofford; #112, NP, wood head & hdl, 1920-42, 12" 100.00
Chisel, socket; #446, set of 6, ¼"-1½" W, 1927-35, EX 175.00
Chisel set, #750C, ½", ¾", & 1", NMIB 295.00
Drill, hand; #612, japanned steel, 1925-35, 12" 25.00
File, mill; steel, smooth or bastard cut, 1930s-40s, 8"-14" 3.00
Gauge, marking; #61, beech, boxwood screws, 1859-1984, 8" 15.00
Hammer, ball pein; #3008, 4-oz head 85.00
Hammer, shoemaker's; #6, CI, walnut infill, 1872, 12" 175.00
Level, hexagon; #31 ....50.00
Level, pocket; CI, polished, brass top plate, 1871, 3" 75.00
Leveling stand, #338 ....250.00
Mallet, #14, hickory hdl, iron rings, 1863-1923, 13" L, 6" head 20.00
Mitre box, #109, japanned CI, cuts 4" metal, 1929-34, 20" 175.00
Nail pinchers, japanned steel, 1920s-40s, mk Stanley, 7" 55.00
Nosing tool, #5 ....125.00
Plane, bench; Bedrock, #604 ....150.00
Plane, circular; #113, NM 350.00
Plane, jack; #26, type 12 ....200.00
Plane, jointer; #8C, corrugated bottom, 1898-1984 ....125.00
Plane, plow; #50, MIB (tin box) 400.00
Plane, plow; Miller's 1872 Pat 15,000.00
Plane, smooth; #3C 140.00
Pliers, battery; #1, polished steel, 1934, 7" 50.00
Router, #271, M in EX box 65.00
Rule, carpenter's; boxwood, brass trim, 2-ft, 2-fold, 1854-59 ......450.00

Rule, school; maple, brass trim, vertical figures, 1934-61, 12" **15.00**
Screwdriver, flashlight; #1021 ....**300.00**
Spoke shave, dbl cutter; NM **75.00**
Tool chest, #801 ....**275.00**
Wrench, pipe; #10, adjustable, steel, wood hdl, 1923-42, 10" **75.00**

Statue of Liberty

Long before she began greeting immigrants in 1886, the Statue of Liberty was being honored by craftsmen both here and abroad. Her likeness was etched on blades of the finest straight razors from England, captured in finely detailed busts sold as souvenirs to Paris fairgoers in 1878, and presented on colorfully lithographed trade cards, usually satirical, to American shoppers. Perhaps no other object has been represented in more forms or with such frequency as the universal symbol of America. Liberty's keepsakes are also universally accessible. Delightful souvenir models created in 1885 to raise funds for Liberty's pedestal are frequently found at flea markets, while earlier French bronze and terra cotta Liberties have been auctioned for over $100,000.00. Some collectors hunt for the countless forms of 19th-century Liberty memorabilia, while many collections were begun in anticipation of the 1986 Centennial with concentration on modern depictions. Our advisor for this category is Mike Brooks; he is listed in the Directory under California.

Booklet, Rays From Liberty's Torch, 1890 ....**30.00**
Bookmark, fabric, Bartholdi Souvenir, 1886 ....**25.00**
Bottle, milk glass, pewter lid, 10" **235.00**
Bottler, seltzer, etched Liberty, A Doeink, Liberty NY **35.00**
Box, Liberty Hair Clipper, 1930s **25.00**
Candy container, glass miniature w/metal statue top, 1920s **130.00**
Card, admission to inauguration, 1886 ....**70.00**
Card, eng, Visit to Gauthier et Cie, Paris Foundry, 1883, VG **75.00**
Charm bracelet, NY World's Fair **40.00**
Cigar box label, Victory Day, WWI **6.00**
Clock, figural, United, animated, very rare **350.00**
Cup, pewter, Germany, ca 1904 ....**60.00**
Cup, sterling, Windsor Club, 1907, 2" **22.00**
Doorknob, brass, Liberty in high relief, ca 1900 ....**90.00**
Envelope, NY World newspaper, postmk 1885, Liberty logo **55.00**
Flier, Statue of Liberty steamboat excursions, 1890s **25.00**
Hanukkah menorah, Liberty-featured candle holders, M Anson ..**1,800.00**
Harper's Weekly, various litho prints, 1880s, ea, from $10 to **25.00**
Invitation to inauguration, by President Cleveland **150.00**
Letter, teen to military father re: parade on Broadway, 1886 ....**95.00**
Letter opener, Tat Hosiery Mills, 1930s **35.00**
Magic lantern side, harbor scene **30.00**
Medal, central Valley Nat'l Bank **18.00**
Medal, Democratic National Convention, NY, 1924 ....**30.00**
Medal, Tasset, Paris, 1876 (earliest known) **100.00**
Napkin holder, sterling **15.00**
Paperweight, rnd, ca 1880s **100.00**
Photo, Liberty sketch, Centennial Photographic Co, 1876, VG ...**40.00**
Photo album, celluloid image on front, velvet bk, 10x8" **275.00**
Pin, enamel, 77th Div, WWI **12.00**
Pin-bk buttons, Liberty Centennial, enamel, various, ea, $5 to **15.00**
Pipe, glazed clay, 1880s **90.00**
Plate, Austrian, various NY scenes, ca 1900 ....**45.00**
Plate, glass, eng statue, heart shape **22.00**
Plate, World Wide Art Studio, 1985, 8½" **10.00**
Plates, various makers, 1980s, ea, from $10 to **20.00**
Playing cards, Allied Nations, WWI, complete deck **20.00**
Postcards, hold-to-light, various, ea, from $40 to **75.00**
Radio speaker stand, wht metal casting, Palcone, 17" **175.00**

Snow dome, glass w/wood base, fancy, contemporary **40.00**
Spoon, figural stem, sterling, Shiebler **75.00**
Statue, cast metal on marble base, June 13, 1885 ....**1,000.00**
Stereo card, head of Liberty, Paris, 1878 ....**80.00**
Straight razor, Liberty-etched blade, Sheffield, ca 1880 ....**75.00**
Tapestry, w/NY Harbor scene, 24x48" **85.00**
Trade card, satirical, A&C Hams **70.00**
Trade card, satirical, Moline Plow **30.00**
Vase, frosted Liberty hand, Gillinder, 1876 Centennial **70.00**
Watercolor, View of Liberty, JW Goppard, 21x15" **220.00**

Steamship Collectibles

For centuries, ocean-going vessels with their venturesome officers and crews were the catalyst that changed the unknown aspects of our world to the known. Changing economic conditions, unfortunately, have now placed the North American shipping industry in the same jeopardy as the American passenger train. They are becoming a memory. The surge of interest in railroad collectibles and the railroad-related steamship lines has lead collectors to examine the whole spectrum of steamship collectibles. Our advisors for this category are Lila and Fred Shrader; they are listed in the Directory under California.

Key:
BS — back stamped   SM — side mark
NBS — no back stamp   TL — top logo
SL — side logo   TM — top mark

Dinnerware

Bowl, berry; Alaska SS, The Alaska Line, TM, 5½" **49.00**
Bowl, berry; New England SS Co, TM, 6x4½" **50.00**
Bowl, flat soup; Am Export, turq & silver pinstripes, BM, 9½" **40.00**
Bowl, flat soup; Nippon Yusen Kaisha Line, flag TL/pinstripe, 7½" **30.00**
Butter pat, CA Navigation & Improvement Co, TL, CN&ICo flag .**165.00**
Butter pat, Cunard, shell shape w/gold, BM **22.00**
Butter pat, Merchants & Miners Trans Co, TM, M&MMTCo flag ..**135.00**
Butter pat, Nippon Yusen Kaisha Line, Mt Fuji, BM w/house flag ...**35.00**
Butter pat, States Steamship Co, States sea horse TL **55.00**
Compote, Savannah Line w/TL Co flag, ped ft, 2¾x7" **235.00**
Creamer, Canadian Pacific BC SS, Empress, logo BM **35.00**
Cup, Ward Line, Mexico, TM: NY&CMSSCo+Ward Line flag ..**67.00**
Cup & saucer, Am Mail Line, Island Mail, SL/TM **68.00**
Cup & saucer, demi; Am Mail Line, SL/TL **85.00**
Cup & saucer, Interlake SS Co, ICSS TL, gr on wht **58.00**
Cup & saucer, souvenir; Queen Mary, Long Beach CA, 1980s **8.00**
Egg cup, dbl; Admiral Line, gr on wht, SL, BM **44.00**
Egg cup, dbl; Los Angeles SS Co, flag in circle SL, BM **135.00**
Gravy boat, Moore McCormack Lines, Rio, BM **38.00**
Hot food cover, Greek Line, cobalt TL **18.00**
Oyster plate, Northern SS Co, TL N inside star w/gold trim, 9½" ...**245.00**
Pitcher, Texaco, gr & red star, SL, 7" **185.00**
Plate, Am Export Lines, colorful flags on rim, BM, 8" **28.00**
Plate, Am Mail Line, TL w/house flag, 7½" **48.00**
Plate, Chesapeake & Ohio, train/ferry, TM, 10" **85.00**
Plate, Dollar Line, TL $-sign house flag, 9" **75.00**
Plate, Eastern SS w/E flag enclosed in ring, TL, 11½" **65.00**
Plate, souvenir; Georgian Bay Line, SS So Am, 9" **18.00**
Plate, souvenir; Swedish-Am, early ship w/rich gold, BS, 8" **11.00**
Platter, Great North Pacific SS, Pacific Coast, TL, 7½x6" **110.00**
Platter, Munson SS Lines, bl TL w/chain & rope decor, 9" **49.00**
Relish dish, Elders & Fyffes, TM w/E&F flag & name, 5x8½" **48.00**
Saucer, C&B Line in TL shield w/vine & leaves, BM **22.00**

Teapot, Cunard, tan/blk stripes on tan cube form, BM, 5" sq 195.00

Glassware

Ashtray, Bergen Line Meteor Cruises, silvered, 4½" free-form 13.00
Carafe, cut, Hamburg Am Line, SL, 8¼" 225.00
Cocktail, stem; Matson, SL in wht enamel 18.00
Cordial, stem; North German Lloyd, cut SL & bands, fancy stem ...75.00
Tumbler, souvenir; Cunard, Countess, 5½" 6.00
Tumbler, Swedish-Am Line, SL, old picture of Drottingham, 1940s ...15.00

Linens

Bath towel, Dollar Line w/red $-sign woven logo 75.00
Blanket, Admiral Line, bl on gray center logo, wool, 48x80" 195.00
Hand towel, bl stripe w/woven Admiral Line on wht, 15x28" 15.00
Hand towel, red stripe w/woven Canadian SS Lines, 16x30" 15.00
Hand towel, Rotterdam Lloyd, damask bl on beige, 18x28" 22.00
Napkin, Carnival Cruise Line, tan/brn 4.00
Napkin, Old Dominion SS, wht-on-wht flag logo in ship's wheel ...24.00
Napkin, Rotterdam Lloyd, wht-on-wht w/logo & date, 1940 .....12.00
Tablecloth, US Lines, gr & wht w/corner-stitched name 25.00

Silverplate

Ashtray/matchbox holder, Union Castle, portrait Europa, BM 85.00
Butter pat, Eastern SS Lines, BM, International 11.00
Champagne bucket w/bail hdl, Great Northern SS, BM, 8¼" 385.00
Coffee service, brass, E Asiatic SS Line, SM pot+cr/sug+TM tray 165.00
Coffeepot, Savannah Line, SM, Reed & Barton, ind sz 165.00
Compote, Canadian Nat'l SS, ped, TL, Elkington, 2¾x8" 135.00
Creamer, Delta Lines, SL w/flag, open style, Internat'l, 4-oz 49.00
Creamer, Great Northern SS, SM, Reed & Barton, 3-oz 68.00
Crumber & scraper, Am Export Lines BM, ornate, Internat'l 122.00
Fork, dinner; Holland-Am Line, TM: NASM 12.00
Gravy boat, New England SS, BM: SS Massachusetts, Internat'l, 16-oz ...110.00
Iced-tea spoon, Dollar Line, TM 28.00
Knife, dinner; P&O, TL, ornate scrolls 16.00
Knife, dinner; PSS Co, Belmont, TM, Reed & Barton 12.00
Knife, fruit; Dollar SS Lines, $-sign house flag TL, Internat'l 29.00
Loving cup, Holland-Am w/colored enamel cartouch, 6" 25.00
Sherbet, Peninsular & Occidental SS Co, ped ft, BM w/dmn logo .125.00
Spoon, demi; sterling; Holland-Am, Nieuw Amsterdam 39.00
Spoon, souvenir; sterling, Alaska SS, TL house flag 55.00
Spoon, souvenir; sterling, Princess of Victoria w/pnt portrait 59.00
Sugar bowl, Alaska SS SL & BM, w/lid, Reed & Barton, 9-oz 135.00
Tablespoon, Cunard, BM, Meat written in English & Hebrew 28.00
Teaspoon, Am Presidential Lines, Priscilla, BM, Internat'l 10.00
Tray, Canadian Nat'l, TM, Elkington, 12" dia 35.00

Miscellaneous

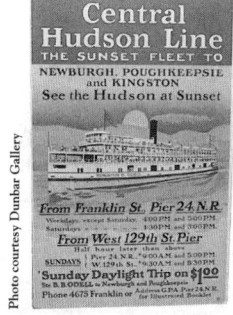

Poster, Central Hudson Line, Sunday Daylight Trip on $1.00, multicolor on cardboard, 47x29", NM, $250.00.

Ashtray, Alaska SS, stamped copper w/logo & slogan, 3" sq 38.00
Ashtray, Daido Line w/TL house flag, bl & gold on wht, 5¾" 18.00
Ashtray, Ile de France, TL, Premiere Classe, 1978 BM, china, 5" .19.00
Award medallion, employee; Hol-Am, 40,000 sea miles, w/ribbon ..45.00
Baggage sticker, Am President Line, gr & yel 6.00
Baggage sticker, Union Castle, blk & orange Art Deco, 3½" dia ..10.00
Baggage tag, Block Island steamer, brass, 1½x1¾" 38.00
Baggage tag, Los Angeles SS Co, celluloid w/leather strap, oval ...45.00
Bell, souvenir; Holland-Am, Volendam, blk enamel on brass 12.00
Book, Titanic, Sinking of..., mc portrait cover, 1912, 350-pg 65.00
Book, Titanic Memorial, by Christian Herald, 1912, 230-pg 45.00
Bottle opener, souvenir; Delta SS Lines, church key-like w/TL 5.00
Bridge pad w/vinyl cover, French Line, TM Antilles, '50s 9.00
Brochure, Am President Lines, 1960s, 4 panels 2x5½" 9.00
Brochure, Clyde Line, Algonquin, 1940, 3 panels, 3x5" 9.00
Brochure, Cunard, Franconia, world cruise, full color, 1930, 63-pg ..35.00
Brochure, N German Lloyd, Bremen mc interiors, deck plans, '30 ...24.00
Brochure, Royal Caribbean..., Song of Norway, info+deck plans, '70 ..6.00
Brochure, TT, Boston & Hingham Steamboat Co, int views, 1881 ...18.00
Button, Anchor Line, brass, ⅝" 3.00
Button, President Lines, brass, ⅝" 6.00
Button, US Maritime Service, brass, ⅞" 8.00
Button, White Star Line, brass, ¾" 16.00
Callendar, wallet; Prudential Lines, Santa Magdelena, celluloid ..18.00
Candy tin, Cunard's Queen Mary, Benson's ship portrait, 4½x6" .45.00
Charm, Cunard, Queen Elizabeth II, sterling silver ship, ¾" 39.00
Clock, wind-up alarm; Cunard, Mauretania, Deco chrome, '30s ..125.00
Coaster, paper, w/ship or line's name &/or flag, from $1 to 3.00
Compact, souvenir; Furness Line, Q of Bermuda pnt on metal 42.00
Cuff links, Italian Line, Andrea Doria, line flag, orig box 26.00
Deck plans, Greek Line, Olympia, tissue in red & blk emb folder ...18.00
Diary, traveler's, aboard Queen Mary, describes trip, 1930s 50.00
Doll, Hamburg Am Line, German peasant dress, 1920s, 10" 44.00
Doll, Holland Am Line, plastic head, sailor suit, 1980s, 8" 16.00
Hanger, clothes; US Lines w/7 ships' names & portraits 25.00
Lantern, ship's; brass, kero, wall mt, bail hdl, w/chimney, 15" 310.00
Letter opener, Savannah Line, copper, SS decor, 8" 65.00
Life jacket, Queen Mary, navy & orange canvas, adult sz 175.00
Life ring, Lumber Lady, 39" dia 150.00
Life ring, souvenir; Castle Line, Roslin Castle HP, wood, 7" 85.00
Lighter, Zippo, Matson Line, SS Mariposa, SL name & flag, enamel 19.00
Menu, Alaska SS, Crumrine sled dog portraits, '40s, 5½x8½", ea ...28.00
Menu, Alaska SS, dinner on SS Denali, photo scenic cover, 1953 ..18.00
Menu, Am Export, SS Constitution, 1955, folded: 8x11" 6.00
Menu, French Line's Ile de France, music decor, 1955, 9½x13" 14.00
Menu, Hamburg-Amerika Line, SS NY, 1937, 5x8½" 12.00
Mug, beer; N German Lloyd, SM house flag, stoneware, 5¼" 43.00
Newspaper account of Lusitania disaster, 1915, folded 25.00
Newspaper account of Titanic disaster, 1912, folded 63.00
Note pad, N German Lloyd TM logo, brass fr w/pencil, 2x3" 65.00
Notebook, Hamburg-Amerika Lines, leather, w/orig pencil, 1930s ..35.00
Paperweight/bank, Cunard, ceramic Queen Mary shape, mc, 1930s, 7" 65.00
Pass, annual; Hudson River Day Line, Mrs B Harrison & son, '12 ...38.00
Pass, annual; Panama RR/SS Line, 1936 .....18.00
Passenger list, Am President Line, President Wilson, 1969 .....4.00
Pen, ball-point; Cunard, Countess, oil-filled w/ship 8.00
Pencil, mechanical; Interlake SS Co, SM wht on blk Bakelite 16.00
Pencil, souvenir; Queen Mary, 1980s 1.00
Pennant, felt; Eastern SS Lines, Southern Cross, 16" 18.00
Photograph, Hamburg AM HAPAG Captain w/medals, autographed .16.00
Photos, Cunard's Queen Mary, souvenir type, 12 in orig envelope .27.00
Playing cards, Am Mail Line, Oriental lady, logo S-ace, TL box ..28.00
Playing cards, Cunard, TL, CWS, ship's portrait on box 25.00
Playing cards, Royal Caribbean..., ship & anchor crown logo, mk case ...9.00

Postcard, Am President Line, SS President Wilson, 1966 ....**3.00**
Poster, Cunard, Queen Mary, 1930s, fr, 28x48½" **235.00**
Puzzle, jigsaw; Cunard, Queen Mary, wooden, 1930s, 150-pc, orig box ..**85.00**
Puzzle, Titanic, 1500 pcs, 1980, MIB (sealed) **18.00**
Ship model, agent's; Holland Am, brass, lighted, 50" L **750.00**
Ship model, agent's; Italian Line, Andrea Doria, wood, 25½" L .**250.00**
Ship model, Cunard, Mauretania, plastic, 15" L **55.00**
Ship model, NYK, Hikawa Maru waterline model, 9" **50.00**
Ship model, SS France, plastic on wood base w/brass plaque, 18" ...**185.00**
Ship model kit, French Line, Normandy, balsa, MIB (sealed) **55.00**
Ship model kit, Titanic, plastic, 1950s, 16" completed, MIB **65.00**
Soap, Cunard, Mauretania, ind sz, wrapped **4.00**
Spittoon, Pacific Mail SS, PMSS TM, wht enamel on steel **165.00**
Stationery, sheet & envelope; Cunard, Queen Elizabeth, 1950s ...**22.00**
Swizzle stick, Grace Lines, gr plastic, ear shape **2.00**
Visor, sun; Royal Caribbean..., plastic w/ship's name **4.00**
Whistle, ship's, CI/brass, Lunkenheimer, 18", +brass/copper stand ..**200.00**

Steins

Steins have been made from pottery, pewter, glass, stoneware, and porcelain, from very small up to the four-liter size. They may be decorated by etching, in-mold relief, decals, and occasionally they may be hand painted. Some porcelain steins have lithophane bases. Collectors often specialize in a particular type — faience, regimental, or figural, for example — while others limit themselves to the products of only one manufacturer. See also Mettlach.

Key:
L — liter   PUG — print under glaze
lith — lithophane   tl — thumb lift
POG — print over glaze

Anheuser Busch by Ceramarte, Budweiser label, .5L **525.00**
Anheuser Busch by Ceramarte, Endangered Species, Bald Eagle, .5L .**445.00**
Anheuser Busch by Ceramarte, German City series, Munchen, .5L ...**550.00**
Anheuser Busch by Ceramarte, History of Brewing #1, .5L **140.00**
Anheuser Busch by Ceramarte, US of Am 200 Yrs, .5L **350.00**
Anheuser Busch by Ceramarte, Venator, tan, 1L **235.00**
Anheuser Busch by Thewalt, lovers, A & eagle on lid, .5L **155.00**
Bl salt glaze, etched: leaping deer, pewter lid, .5L **250.00**
Bl salt glaze, relief: hunt scene, horse head tl, .5L **130.00**
Bl salt glaze, relief: hunter & bear, pewter lid, .5L **115.00**
Bl/gr/purple salt glaze: hunting scene, Dumler/Brieden, .5L **115.00**
Bl/purple salt glaze, relief: stag/deer/dog, Gerz #660, 2L, NM **220.00**
Character, artillery shell, stoneware, hairline, .5L **265.00**
Character, Bismark, porc, Schierholz, porc lid, rpr, .3L **575.00**
Character, Bock, porc, Schierholz, inlaid lid, .5L **550.00**
Character, cat w/hangover, porc, Shierholz, .5L **670.00**
Character, dog w/pipe, porc, Schierholz, .5L **2,600.00**
Character, drunken monkey, porc, Schierholz, .5L **570.00**
Character, fraternity student w/pipe, pottery, inlaid lid, .5L **415.00**
Character, Frauen Kirche Tower, porc, inlaid lid, Pauson, 1L .**1,750.00**
Character, Fraunkirche Munchen, pewter, pewter lid, 4½" **500.00**
Character, Grethl, stoneware, Ringer, Reinemann, 4½" **800.00**
Character, Happy Radish, porc, inlaid lid, Schierholz, .3L **475.00**
Character, high-wheel bicycle, porc, Schierholz, lith, .5L **440.00**
Character, Hops Lady, porc, Schierholz, porc lid, .5L **700.00**
Character, Iron Maiden, stoneware, inlaid lid, mk TW, .5L **415.00**
Character, money bag, porc, Bohne & Son, chip, .5L **1,550.00**
Character, monk, porc, red robe, inlaid lid, lith, .5L **180.00**
Character, monk, pottery, tan & brn, inlaid lid, #572, .5L **245.00**

Character, Munich Child, porc, porc lid, lith, Mayer, .5L **665.00**
Character, Munich Child on bbl, pottery, inlaid lid, .5L **230.00**
Character, nun, porc, blk robe, inlaid lid, lith, .5L **180.00**
Character, nun, stoneware, inlaid lid, .5L **300.00**
Character, Nurnberg Tower/Father John, pottery, Ostermayer, .5L ..**500.00**
Character, owl, porc, glass eyes, Bohne & Son, .5L **1,675.00**
Character, pig singing, porc, Schierholz, .5L **575.00**
Character, pixie on bbl, porc, Schierholz, musical, .5L **2,550.00**
Character, radish w/Munich child face on front, porc, lith, .5L .**950.00**
Character, rich man, stoneware, inlaid lid, #8667, .5L **400.00**
Character, Sad Radish, porc, inlaid lid, Schierholz, .3L **400.00**
Character, skull, porc, inlaid lid, E Bohne & Son, .25L **420.00**
Character, skull on book, porc, Bohne & Son, .3L **700.00**
Character, skull w/lg jaw, porc, Bohne & Son, .3L **700.00**
Character, skull w/lg jaw, porc, Bohne & Son, inlaid lid, .5L **950.00**
Character, snake & apple, porc, rpl lid, Bohne & Son, .3L **575.00**
Faience, bl floral on wht, pewter base & lid, 1960s, 8½" **180.00**
Glass, blown, amber, ornate pewter o/l & hdl, griffin tl, .5L **365.00**
Glass, blown, appl gr glass knobs, pewter lid, dwarf tl, 2L **1,150.00**
Glass, blown, cobalt, pewter lid, closed hinge, ca 1850, 3¾" **260.00**
Glass, blown, cut florals, pewter lid dtd 1896, .5L, NM **100.00**
Glass, blown, cut florals, prism inlaid lid, 1870s, .5L **110.00**
Glass, blown, drunken man figural, porc lid, rpr, 1850s, .5L **500.00**
Glass, blown, eng: deer/forest, red stain, inlaid lid, .5L **245.00**
Glass, blown, eng: dog, purple o/l on clear, 1850s, .5L **750.00**
Glass, blown, eng: spa scenes, glass inlaid lid, brass mts, .5L **670.00**
Glass, blown, eng: stag scene, cut base panels, .5L **140.00**
Glass, blown, HP children on amber, pewter lid & base, .5L **500.00**
Glass, blown, HP decor/appl glass bands on amber, inlaid lid, .5L ..**500.00**
Glass, blown, HP floral/Friendship, pewter base & lid, 1L, NM .**425.00**
Glass, blown, HP food & verse, pewter lid, .5L, NM **175.00**
Glass, blown, HP Nouveau florals, Gambrinus pewter lid, .5L ...**1,300.00**
Glass, blown, HP Prussian eagle, pewter lid, .5L, NM **215.00**
Glass, blown, HP scene/cutwork w/gold, pk o/l on clear, .5L ...**1,000.00**
Glass, blown, HP target/rifles/goblet, Gambrinus lid, .5L **385.00**
Glass, blown, Nouveau pewter o/l on amber, floral lid, .5L **330.00**
Glass, blown, transfer/HP: Curhaus Bad Hall, pewter lid, .5L **130.00**
Glass, pressed, fluted, wooden lid, pewter finial, .5L **220.00**

Glass stein, stag and doe, blown, faceted, and deeply engraved, porcelain lid with farmer and cows, horn thumb lift, pewter foot ring, 2.5-L, $1,700.00.

Military, porc, Western Area Command Blood Bank, w/lid, .5L .**165.00**
Military, relief: train scenes/winged wheel, wheel tl, .5L **300.00**
Occupation, porc, HP: belt maker, scratched pewter lid, .5L **770.00**
Occupation, porc, HP: lion & shield, pewter lid, rpr, .5L **600.00**
Occupation, porc, HP: waitress, pewter lid, lith, 1L, NM **950.00**
Occupation, porc, transfer/HP: brewer, dtd 1896, rpr, 1L **575.00**
Occupation, porc, transfer/HP: jockey, pewter lid, .5L **800.00**

Occupation, porc, transfer/HP: milk wagon driver, lith, .5L **750.00**
Occupation, pottery, transfer/HP: farmer, dtd 1905, 1L, NM **460.00**
Occupation, stoneware, transfer/HP: machinist, flake, 1L **715.00**
Pewter, relief: men & women, shooting target lid, .5L **180.00**
Porc, transfer/HP: deer, pewter lid, dog tl, lith, .5L, EX **200.00**
Porc, transfer/HP: Greetings from Augsburg/floral, lith, .5L **90.00**
Porc, transfer/HP: hunters/deer, jeweled lid, lith, .5L **175.00**
Porc, transfer/HP: Kaiser Wilhelm II, lith, pewter lid, .5L **300.00**
Pottery, etched/HP: barmaid/men, inlaid lid, Gerz, #1322, .4L ...**165.00**
Pottery, etched/HP: people toasting, gold-pnt lid, #749, 1L **125.00**
Pottery, etched: cards, tans, pewter lid, #1255A, .5L **110.00**
Pottery, etched: castle & lake, Hauber/Reugher #443/55, .5L **275.00**
Pottery, etched: Kochelbrau Munchen, pewter lid, .4L **450.00**
Pottery, gr glaze, jug form, Hafner, pewter lid, 1.5L, NM **115.00**
Pottery, HP: Nouveau floral, Bonn, #2568, scratches, .5L **265.00**
Pottery, relief/etched: Diana huntress, inlaid lid, JWR, .5L, NM ..**300.00**
Pottery, relief/threading: couple bicycling, mc, #412, 2L **470.00**
Pottery, relief: anti-Semitic scenes, Dumler & Breiden, .5L, rpr ...**1,150.00**
Pottery, relief: bicycle scene, tans, no lid, .5L **100.00**
Pottery, relief: deer, pewter lid, #16368, .5L **115.00**
Pottery, relief: dogs & deer, inlaid lid, fox hdl, .3L, NM **85.00**
Pottery, relief: Gasthause scene in tans, pewter lid, 1L **55.00**
Pottery, relief: Heidelberg scene, armor hdl, pewter lid, .5L **550.00**
Pottery, relief: HP boar hunt, fox relief lid, recent, .5L **85.00**
Pottery, relief: HP clown/jester, inlaid lid, #11166, 2L **255.00**
Pottery, relief: knights, figural lid, Thewalt #3617, 3L **200.00**
Pottery, relief: man on high-wheel bicycle, Merkelbach, .5L **330.00**
Pottery, relief: music box (tans), Hauber & Reuther, .5L **175.00**
Pottery, relief: musical design in tans, pewter lids, #965, 1L **100.00**
Pottery, relief: Romans meet Germans, pewter lid, #445, .5L **325.00**
Pottery, relief: souvenir of WA, inlaid eagle lid, #6090, .5L **230.00**
Pottery, transfer: HP Shubert Club...1903, .5L **75.00**
Regimental, porc, Kgl Sachs...1905-08, Saschen tl, .5L **1,000.00**
Regimental, porc, V Matrosen Art...1908-11, eagle tl, .5L **2,000.00**
Regimental, porc, 1 Foot Artillery...1901-03, lion tl, .5L **675.00**
Regimental, porc, 10 Field Artl...1903-05, female tl, .5L **500.00**
Regimental, porc, 115 Infantry...1901-03, lion tl, .5L, EX **300.00**
Regimental, porc, 126 Infantry Strassburg 1900, stanhope tl, .5L ...**990.00**
Regimental, porc, 15 Infantry...1897-99, rpl pewter lid, .5L **240.00**
Regimental, porc, 3 Eisenbahn...1912-14, eagle tl, lith, .5L **775.00**
Regimental, porc, 4 Garde Field...1904-07, stanhope tl, lith, .5L ...**700.00**
Regimental, pottery, Dienstz...1912, lion tl, stanhope, .5L **2,195.00**
Regimental, pottery, infantry/Ludwig II, 1930s, .5L, NM **300.00**
Regimental, pottery, 15 Husar...1910-13, glass lid, lion tl, 1L .**1,100.00**
Regimental, stoneware, SMS Danzig, servicemen photo, .5L ..**1,900.00**
Stoneware, etched: dwarfs & frog band, Hauber & Reugher, .5L ..**550.00**
Stoneware, relief: cats, monkey w/boot lid, #940, .5L, NM **370.00**
Stoneware, relief: Gasthaus scene, Whites, pewter lid, 1L, NM .**210.00**
Stoneware, relief: man by high-wheel bicycle, .5L **400.00**
Stoneware, relief: Sioux Chief & artifacts, Gerz #025, .5L **370.00**
Stoneware, transfer/HP: Brauerei Zett, pewter lid, .5L, NM **65.00**
Stoneware, transfer/HP: chemical scene w/verse, Ringer, .5L **425.00**
Stoneware, transfer/HP: Expo of Bavarian Handwerker 1927, 1L ..**465.00**
Stoneware, transfer/HP: Hofbrauhaus, pewter lid/lion tl, .5L **395.00**
Stoneware, transfer/HP: Hofbrauhaus Munchen, Munich child lid, .5L ..**350.00**
Stoneware, transfer/HP: Lowenbrau Keller, lion tl, 1L **925.00**
Stoneware, transfer/HP: Regensburg, pewter lid, .5L, NM **80.00**
Stoneware, transfer/HP: waitress, Ringer, pewter lid, .5L **350.00**
Stoneware, transfer/HP: 4 Munich breweries, dtd 1906, .5L **550.00**

Steuben

Carder Steuben glass was made by the Steuben Glass Works in Corning, New York, while under the direction of Frederick Carder from 1903 to 1932. Perhaps the most popular types of Carder Steuben glass are Gold Aurene which was introduced in 1904 and Blue Aurene, introduced in 1905. Gold and Blue Aurene objects shimmer with the lustrous beauty of their metallic iridescence. Carder also produced other types of 'Aurenes' including Red, Green, Yellow, Brown, and Decorated, all of which are very rare. Aurene also was cased with calcite glass. Some pieces had paper labels.

Other types of Carder Steuben include Cluthra, Cintra, Florentia, Rosaline, Ivory, Ivorene, Jades, Verre de Soie; there are many more.

Frederick Carder's leadership of Steuben ended in 1932, and the production of colored glassware soon ceased. Since 1932 the tradition of fine Steuben art glass has been continued in crystal.

Our advisor for this category is Thomas P. Dimitroff; he is in the Directory under New York. In the following listings, examples are signed unless noted otherwise.

Key: ACB — acid cut back

Atomizer, Blue Aurene, eng floral/jeweled top/orig mts, 9¾" .**1,200.00**
Basket, Blue Aurene on calcite, loop hdl, 15⅜x10" **3,500.00**
Basket, Blue Aurene w/purple irid, #455, 19x12" **5,250.00**
Basket, Gold Aurene, bl/gold hdl, berry prunt, #453, 9½x8" ..**1,800.00**
Basket, Gold Aurene, loop hdl, berry prunts, #453, 6¾x6¼" ..**1,750.00**
Basket, Gold Aurene on calcite, bl-gr appl hdl, 9½x8" **1,300.00**
Basket, Verre-De-Soire, ruffled rim, EX color, 13x8" **750.00**

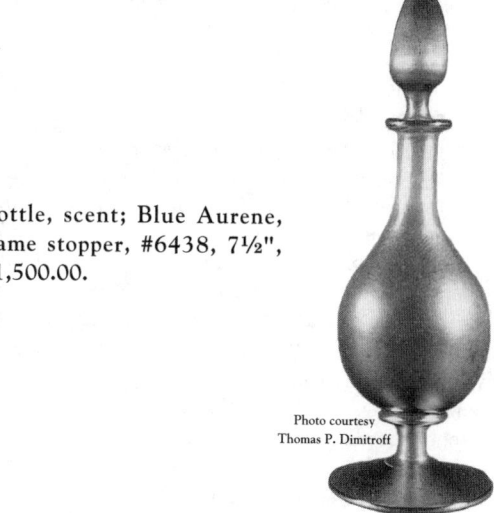

Bottle, scent; Blue Aurene, flame stopper, #6438, 7½", $1,500.00.

Photo courtesy
Thomas P. Dimitroff

Bottle, scent; Blue Aurene, teardrop stopper, #1414, 7½" **1,200.00**
Bottle, scent; Blue Aurene, Oriental shape #6233, 4¼" **1,600.00**
Bottle, scent; Gold Aurene, melon ribs, squatty, #1355, 4½" ..**1,000.00**
Bottle, scent; Verre-De-Soie w/bl threading, bl stopper, #6619 ..**475.00**
Bowl, Blue Aurene, ped ft, #2799, 4x5" **900.00**
Bowl, Blue Aurene, rolled-in rim, appl ft, #2586, 2¾x8" **750.00**
Bowl, Blue Aurene on calcite, #2687, 3" H **900.00**
Bowl, bubbly clear, gr threads at rim, 2x12" +gr frog **375.00**
Bowl, Canton, Plum Jade to Alabaster, etched, #2687, 4x7¾" ..**2,500.00**
Bowl, Gold Aurene on calcite, ftd, 11½" dia **525.00**
Bowl, Gold Aurene on calcite, stretched rim, 2½x5½" **450.00**
Bowl, Gold Aurene on calcite, wrought-iron fr, 12" **395.00**
Bowl, Gold Aurene on calcite, 14" dia **825.00**
Bowl, Grotesque, crystal, 6x12x7" **357.00**
Bowl, Grotesque, gr to clear open flower form, 6x11" **550.00**
Bowl, Ivorene Grotesque, #7535, 12" **650.00**

Bowl, Mirror Black w/wide ribs, 4-scallop top, 4¾x8" 450.00
Bowl, Verre-De-Soie, pinched rim, #2775, 3x8" 265.00
Candlesticks, amber, dbl twisted stem, 10", pr 495.00
Candlesticks, Celeste Blue, optic ribbed, hollow, 15", pr 800.00
Candlesticks, Pomona Green, mushroom form, 3¾x4⅛", pr 250.00
Champagne, Opal w/Cintra twist stem, 5½" 275.00
Champagne, Oriental Jade, #6464 ....350.00
Compote, Blue Aurene, #2642, 8" 1,000.00
Compote, Blue Aurene w/purple irid, #2760, 5x6" 1,100.00
Compote, Celeste Blue w/crystal stem, #3234, 10" 250.00
Compote, Topaz w/Pomona Green stem, Optic Ribbed, #6044 ..435.00
Compote, Yellow Jade, #3234 tall variant, 4¼x10" 650.00
Compote/tazza, Gold Aurene on calcite, ACB lilies, 7x12½" ..1,750.00
Cornucopia, Green Jade, Alabaster domed ft, 8¼x4½", pr 1,150.00
Figurine, angelfish, crystal, 10½x10" 750.00
Figurines (bookends), Art Deco gazelles, frosted, #7399, 6½", pr .1,700.00
Finger bowl, Gold Aurene, #2361, 2¼" H, +plate 325.00
Flower frog, butterfly form, Blue Aurene, 2-tier, 2¾x4¼" 300.00
Goblet, Gold Aurene, ½-twist stem, #2361, 6", +5¾" tray 500.00
Goblet, Opal w/Cintra twist stem, 7" 350.00
Goblet, Oriental Poppy, Pomona Green stem, 8¼" 500.00
Jar, potpourri; Gold Aurene, #3812, w/lid 875.00
Jar, powder; clear w/gr threading, mk 300.00
Lamp, Alabaster/bl & pk feathers/Gold Aurene, #2806, 13½" .2,875.00
Lamp, Amethyst Cintra w/ACB chrysanthemum, block shape, 18½" ..975.00
Lamp, Rose on Alabaster, cut decor, sq rtcl metal base, 15", NM ..950.00
Lamp, Rose Quartz frosted Matsu-No-Ke w/ACB floral, gold ft, 12" ..2,250.00
Lamp, Rose Quartz w/ACB gr floral, #8514, metal base, 24" ..3,000.00
Lamp base, Green Jade on Alabaster w/ACB, SP mts, 25x5½" ..750.00
Loop dish, Blue Aurene w/Gold Aurene ring hdl, #3997, ½x4" .950.00
Luminor, crystal pineapple w/controlled bubbles, #6971, 8" 750.00
Plate, Rouge Flambeau, 16 vertical ribs, 8½" 2,500.00
Salt cellar, Rosalene & Alabaster, ped ft 250.00
Shade, calcite w/ACB, #2938, 16" 400.00
Shade, feathers, gr on oyster wht, gr int, 2¼x5½", 3 for 550.00
Shade, red-gold irid, like #3243, 3½x7" 275.00
Sherbet, Gold Aurene on calcite, 3¾" 250.00
Sherbet, Oriental Poppy, pk w/gr ft, 2¼", +8¼" plate 650.00
Sherbet & underplate, Gold Aurene, #2361, 3¼", 6½" 400.00
Tumbler, Verre-De-Soie, F Carder, flared rim, 4x3¼" 450.00
Vase, Amethyst Cluthra w/opal 'M' hdls, 10" 2,800.00
Vase, amethyst swirl, #6031, acid stamp, 7" 350.00
Vase, Black Jade, 3-prong, #6873, 10", NM 600.00
Vase, Blue Aurene, ribbed morning-glory form, 5½" 1,000.00
Vase, Blue Aurene, stick form, w/verdigris 3-figure holder, 13" ...1,300.00
Vase, Blue Aurene, 3-part tree trunk form, #2744, 6" 865.00
Vase, Blue Aurene w/mc irid, #2413, 6½x10" 1,500.00
Vase, Gold Aurene, ruffled rim, #162, 3⅜x4½" 650.00
Vase, Gold Aurene, 3-part tree trunk form, 6¼x6½" 550.00
Vase, Gold Aurene on calcite, ACB Easter lilies, 7x12½" 2,200.00
Vase, Gold Aurene on calcite, flared trumpet form, 6x5¼" 550.00
Vase, Gold Aurene w/mc irid, 4 swirled/twisted ribs, #135, 6¾" ..1,175.00
Vase, Gold Aurene w/purple irid, #723, 8¾x9½" 800.00
Vase, Green Aurene, Gold Aurene decor, style D, #506, 10" ..5,200.00
Vase, Green Aurene w/gold floral, #244, 10½x5" 4,000.00
Vase, Green Cluthra, crystal hdls, random bubbles, 12½x10½" ...2,450.00
Vase, Green Jade, stick neck, #2556 ....375.00
Vase, Green Jade, urn form w/Alabaster 'M' hdls, #2939, 9¾" ...900.00
Vase, Green Jade & Alabaster, 5-prong, #7063, 11½" 900.00
Vase, green w/gold decor over Alabaster, #500, 8½" 7,000.00
Vase, Grotesque, amethyst to clear, #7090, ca 1920, 11" 525.00
Vase, Grotesque, amethyst to clear, 19½x7½" 1,000.00
Vase, Grotesque, clear, #7535 ....250.00
Vase, Grotesque, Flemish Blue border on crystal, #7090, 9½" 500.00

Vase, Ivorene, classic form, #5133, 10½" 750.00
Vase, Ivorene, classic form, 8" 650.00
Vase, Ivorene, handkerchief top, ftd, 37490, 9¼" 650.00
Vase, Ivorene, ruffled rim, ftd, 10¼" 570.00
Vase, Ivorene, 3-lily form on disk ft, #7566, 12" 900.00
Vase, Lace Cintra, blk & wht stripes, #7197, 8x6¼" 4,890.00
Vase, Mirror Black above etched Alabaster, #T133, 6" 1,000.00
Vase, Pink Cluthra, classic form, fleur-de-lis mk, 6" 1,025.00
Vase, Platinum Aurene, hearts/vines/millefiori flowers, #599, 6" ...2,500.00
Vase, Pomona Green Cluthra, classic form, 8" 1,300.00
Vase, Pomona Green swirl, ftd, 7" 200.00
Vase, Red Aurene w/Gold Aurene feathers, #522, 10" 8,500.00
Vase, Rosalene cut to Alabaster, birds on branches, #938, 9" ..1,500.00
Vase, Rose to Alabaster, Oriental floral, 4½" 1,300.00
Vase, Roseline on Alabaster ACB, Sea Holly, #6087, 6½x7½" ..1,600.00
Vase, Selenium Red, dome ft, rolled rim, 6x4" 450.00
Vase, Tyrian, gray-gr irid w/wine blush, HP, #2139, 7¾" 8,500.00
Vase, Verre-de-Soie, melon ribs at base, ormolu top, 9x4", pr 400.00
Vase, Verre-de-Soie, oval urn form w/ball stem, disk ft, 12" 230.00
Vase, White Cluthra, classic form, 6¼" 750.00
Vase, Wisteria, appl hdls, #7208, 10½" 800.00
Vase/lamp base, Mirror Black/Flint White etched dragons, 8½" ...2,500.00
Wine, Gold Aurene, twist stem, 4" 250.00
Wine, Rosalene & Alabaster, twist stem 200.00

Stevengraphs

A Stevengraph is a small picture made of woven silk resembling an elaborate ribbon, created by Thomas Stevens in England in the latter half of the 1800s. They were matted and framed by Stevens, usually with his name appearing on the mat or, more commonly, the trade announcement on the back of the mat. He also produced silk postcards and bookmarks, all of which have 'Stevens' woven in silk on one of the mitered corners. Anyone wishing to learn more about Stevengraphs is encouraged to contact the Stevengraph Collectors' Association, whose address can be found in the Directory under Clubs, Newsletters, and Catalogs.

The Finish, original mat and frame, NM, $250.00.

Called to the Rescue, Heroism at Sea, EX 250.00
Columbus Leaving Spain, G 225.00
Crystal Palace (inside), orig mat, G 385.00
Death of Nelson, G 195.00
Dick Turpin's Last Ride on His Black Bess, Hogarth, VG 150.00
First Innings, G 325.00
First Train Built by Geo Stephenson in 1825, 8⅞x11⅝" 150.00
Full Cry, w/mat 120.00
Grace Darling, EX 200.00
Landing of Columbus, NM 250.00
London & York Mail Coach, 1879 Expo 120.00

Mrs Cleveland, VG **135.00**
Park in Coventry **75.00**
Present Time, 60 Miles an Hour, Lord Howe, orig mat, EX **175.00**
Start, NM **175.00**
Wellington & Blugher, EX **300.00**

Miscellaneous

Bookmark, Behold the Man, blk fr, G **50.00**
Bookmark, Geo Washington, made for Philadelphia Expo, 12x2" ...**175.00**
Bookmark, Home Sweet Home, VG **65.00**
Bookmark, Love's Remembrance, VG **75.00**
Bookmark, Remember Me, VG **65.00**
Bookmark, To My Sons, G **40.00**
Postcard, Ann Hathaway's Cottage **40.00**
Postcard, RMS Lusitania, VG **75.00**

Stevens and Williams

Stevens and Williams glass was produced at the Brierly Hill Glassworks in Stourbridge, England, for nearly a century, beginning in the 1830s. They were credited with being among the first to develop a method of manufacturing a more affordable type of cameo glass. Other lines were also made — silver deposit, alexandrite, and engraved rock crystal, to name but a few. Our advisor for this category is Don Williams; he is listed in the Directory under Missouri.

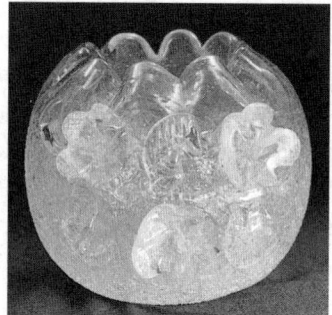

Rose bowl, rubena overshot with applied floral decoration, 5" with 3" diameter opening at incurvate ruffled rim, $250.00.

Basket, amber w/appl amber apples w/gr leaves, 7½x6" sq **150.00**
Basket, Arabesque on clear, 7 cranberry & yel bands, 14x8¾" ...**125.00**
Basket, pk o/l w/appl amber to cranberry leaf, amber hdl, 7½" ...**225.00**
Basket, wht hobnail, pk int, amber trim & hdl, 13x10½" **175.00**
Basket, wht w/pk int, amber ft/cranberry rigaree/mc leaves, 10" .**400.00**
Biscuit jar, swirling bl/wht/crystal stripes, 8" to top of hdl **420.00**
Bottle, Pompeian Swirl, gold & brn, turq int, cut top, 6½x4" **895.00**
Cruet, Arabesque, wht opaque w/amber beneath, amber stopper, 8" ..**165.00**
Epergne, 3 pk bowls w/Matsu-No-Ke flowers, mirror base, 8x15" .**600.00**
Finger bowl, emerald gr, grapes intaglio, 4¾", +6⅜" plate **295.00**
Match holder, cameo flowers, red cut to wht, 2¼x2½" **650.00**
Pitcher, wht w/appl flowers, cornucopia form w/amber ft, 11" ...**300.00**
Pitcher, yel & pk opal stripes on clear, reeded shell hdls, 6x5" **225.00**
Ramekin, Jewel, golden red, ruffled rim, 2" H, +4¾" plate **175.00**
Vase, amber w/appl turq bow tie & prunts, 10" **350.00**
Vase, cameo flower clusters, wht/pk on yel, 5¾" **2,000.00**
Vase, cream opaque o/l, appl flower w/mc leaves, amber ft, 6½" ...**295.00**
Vase, jack-in-pulpit; wht opaque w/cranberry rim, clear base **335.00**
Vase, Matsu-No-Ke rosettes on peachblow, shell-like rigaree, 6" ..**750.00**
Vase, pk o/l w/appl florals, amber rim/branches/hdls, 10¾x5" **495.00**
Vase, Pompeian Swirl, amber to pk, tapered stick neck, 9¼" **450.00**
Vase, Pompeian Swirl, amber to red, wht cased, stick neck, 11x6" .**950.00**
Vase, Pompeian Swirl, bl & brn, yel int, gourd form, 12x6½" .**1,750.00**

Vase, Pompeian Swirl, brn to gold, bl int, ruffled, 5x5½" **850.00**
Vase, Pompeian Swirl, rose, wht int, bulbous base, 8x4½" **575.00**
Vase, Swirl, pk & yel stripes on frost, 36-rib, 7½x5" **425.00**

Stickley

Among the leading proponents of the Arts and Crafts Movement, the Stickley brothers — Gustav, Leopold, Charles, Albert, and John George — were at various times and locations separately involved in designing and producing furniture as well as decorative items for the home. (See Arts and Crafts for further information.) The oldest of the five Stickley brothers was Gustav; his work is the most highly regarded of all. He developed the style of furniture referred to as Mission. It was strongly influenced by the type of furnishings found in the Spanish missions of California — utilitarian, squarely built, and simple. It was made most often of oak, and decoration was very limited or non-existent. The work of his brothers displays adaptations of many of Gustav's ideas and designs. His factory, the Craftsman Workshop, operated in Eastwood, New York, from the late 1890s until 1915, when he was forced out of business by larger companies who copied his work and sold it at much lower prices. Among his shopmarks are the early red decal containing a joiner's compass and the words 'Als Ik Kan,' the branded mark with very similar components, and paper labels.

The firm known as Stickley Brothers was located first in Binghamton, New York, and then Grand Rapids, Michigan. Albert and John George made the move to Michigan, leaving Charles in Binghamton (where he and an uncle continued the operation under a different name). After several years John George left the company to rejoin Leopold in New York. (These two later formed their own firm called L. & J.G. Stickley.) The Stickley Brothers Company's early work produced furniture featuring fine inlay work, decorative cutouts, and leaned strongly toward a style of Arts and Crafts with an English influence. It was tagged with a paper label 'Made by Stickley Brothers, Grand Rapids,' or with a brass plate or decal with the words 'Quaint Furniture,' an English term chosen to refer to their product. In addition to his furniture, he made metal accessories as well.

The workshops of the L. & J.G. Stickley Company first operated under the name 'Onondaga Shops.' Located in Fayetteville, New York, their designs were often all but copies of Gustav's work. Their products were well made and marketed, and their business was very successful. Their decal labels contained all or a combination of the words 'Handcraft' or 'Onondaga Shops,' along with the brothers' initials and last name. The firm continues in business today. Our advisor for this category is Bruce Austin; he is listed in the Directory under New York. Note: When only one dimension is given for tables, it is length. Cleaning diminishes values; ours are for furniture and metals with excellent original finishes unless noted otherwise.

Key: h/cp — hammered copper

Gustav Stickley

Armchair, #56, willow, bbl form, cutouts in bk, pnt wht, 33" **750.00**
Armchair, child's; 3-slat bk, recent finish, unmk, 26", G **130.00**
Armchair, dbl-rail bk w/3 slats, copper/pewter/wood inlay, VG ..**8,000.00**
Bed, #923, 5 wide slats under peaked top rail, full sz **4,500.00**
Bed, maple w/pewter/wood inlay, cane panel, 40x79x46", VG ..**2,100.00**
Bookcase, #716½, 5-shelf, through tenons, decal, 56x42", NM .**8,000.00**
Bookcase, #717, 2 8-pane doors, branded, recoated finish, 56" .**5,000.00**
Bookcase, #719, 2 12-pane doors, slab sides, decal, 56x60" **7,000.00**
Bookrack, slides to adjust width, 3 slats ea end, 7x20" **800.00**
Bowl, h/cp, 3 riveted ft, att, cleaned, 4x8½" **475.00**
Bowl, h/cp, 3 riveted ft, att, 2½x4", VG **500.00**

Bowl, h/cp, 3 riveted ft, att, 3x6½", VG 550.00
Box, shirtwaist; #95, paneled lid, 11-spindle sides, 16x30x16" ..7,000.00
Box, stamp; h/cp, cleaned patina, 2x4" L, VG 260.00
Buffet, #955, 2 short drws/1 long, open shelf, 1901, 44x60x24" .15,000.00
Cabinet, china; #820, 12-pane door, 4 panes ea side, 63x36" ..5,000.00
Cabinet, china; 12-pane door, red decal, ca 1901, 67x36", VG ..24,000.00
Cabinet, smoker's; flip top, 1 drw over panel door, 30x20x16" ...11,000.00
Calendar holder, h/cp, cleaned patina, mk, 4½x5½", VG 200.00
Chair, #348½, 3-slat bk, rpl leather seat, brand, 36" 500.00
Chair, H-bk w/recovered leather seat, rfn, unsgn, 40", VG 500.00
Chair, Morris; #336, bow arms, bk adjusts, rpl leather, 44" 4,750.00
Chair, Morris; #346, open arms, leather cushions, red decal, 42" .2,000.00
Chair, Morris; #369, slant arms, 5-slat sides & bk, no mk, VG .6,000.00
Chairs, dining; #354, 5-slat V bk, 6 sides+1 arm 10,000.00
Chamberstick, h/cp, loop hdl, spade design, 9", VG 350.00
Coal bucket, #350, h/cp, iron hdl, minor rstr patina, 19x13" ..4,000.00
Costumer, #52, tapered form, iron hooks, unmk, 72x23x23", VG ...600.00
Costumer, #53, 2-post, shoe ft, decal, recoated, 71" 1,900.00
Crib settle, #173, 13-slat canted bk, 4-slat canted ends, 71" 8,500.00
Desk, #709, 5-drw, central cut-bk shelf, red decal/label, VG ...1,600.00
Desk, chalet; narrow form w/panel door, keyed tenons, 46x20x10" ...1,600.00
Desk, chalet; #505, paneled front, shelf, keyed tenons, 46x24" ...1,800.00
Dresser, #625, 2 half drws over 2 long, mirror, 64x42x22" 4,700.00
Footstool, #300, rpl leather, red decal, ca 1904, 15x20x16" 950.00
Gong, dinner; tapered posts, arched top rail, rpl gong, 37x24" ...5,000.00
Inkwell, h/cp, glass insert, 2x5½" dia, VG 260.00
Lamp, #609, 12" wicker/copper/silk shade; copper/wood std, 22" .2,600.00
Lamp, #625, 18" h/cp shade w/amber panels; 3-socket std, 25" ..3,500.00
Letter opener, h/cp, cleaned patina, 8½", VG 160.00
Plaque, #345, h/cp, swirling pods, recent patina, 20" dia 4,500.00
Rocker, #337, 3-slat bk, rstr seat, arched seat rails, 34" 500.00
Settee, #212, V-bk top over 10 slats, rstr leather cushion, 48" ...1,500.00
Settle, #172, leather uphl, keyed tenons, 1907, 55" L 3,500.00
Settle, #208 (but higher), even arm, 8-slat bk, rpl seat, 39" 5,000.00
Settle, #225, 5-slat even arms, recovered cushion, 78" 6,000.00
Settle, #226, 5-slat even arms, 1-brd bk, rpl leather seat 6,500.00
Sideboard, #814, 3 sm drws between 2 doors, 1 long drw, 49x66" ...7,000.00
Sideboard, #814½, 3 drws amid 2 doors over long drw, 56" 4,250.00
Stand, Bombay plant; #8, hex top w/Grueby tile inset, 21x18" ..14,000.00
Stand, plant; #660, apron, 4 splayed legs, brand/label, 18" sq .3,500.00
Table, #601, X-stretchers, red decal, 16x14" dia 600.00
Table, #603, notched X-stretchers, needs rfn, 20x18" dia 650.00
Table, #667, rnd top, X-stretcher base, branded/label, 30x38" ..3,000.00
Table, child's; #648, rnd 24" top, X-stretchers, wear 1,000.00
Table, dining; #634, 5-leg, thru tenons, rfn, 29x60" dia, VG ..7,000.00
Table, dining; #634, 5-leg, X-stretcher, 7 skirted leaves 15,000.00
Table, library; #616, 2-drw, corbel legs, thru tenons, 54" 1,000.00
Table, library; #650, 1-drw, low shelf, branded/label, rfn, VG 800.00
Table, lunch; #424, keyed stretcher, red decal, 38x41x28", VG ..1,600.00
Table, trestle; #637, thick shelf, shoe-ft base, 30x48x30" 2,500.00
Tray, #355, h/cp, oval w/2 appl hdls, recent patina, 23x11" 800.00
Tray, h/cp, cleaned patina, rectangular, 10" L, VG 200.00
Umbrella stand, #54, 4-post, copper pan, decal, 34x12" 1,000.00

L. & J.G. Stickley

Bookcase, #643 (but wider), 2 12-pane doors, no mk, 55x47", NM ..1,600.00
Cabinet, china; #746, 2 doors, ea w/6 sm panes over lg, 62x40" ..6,500.00
Cabinet, smoker's; #26, 1-drw, panel do, decal, 29x20x15" 3,250.00
Chair, #1260 (similar), open arms, 3-slat bk, cushion, G 180.00
Chair, Morris; #470, bk adjusts, rstr cushions, unmk, 40" 3,750.00
Chair, Morris; #830, open arms, rpl cushions, 41" 1,000.00
Chair, side; #370, 4 slat bk, rpl rush seat, 35x17x16, VG 170.00
Chairs, side; #384, 8-spindle bks, rush seats, 36", 6 for 4,750.00

Costumer, dbl-pole form w/6 hooks, shoe ft, mk, 72x32", VG ...1,900.00
Daybed, #292, 4 slats ea end, leather cushion, Handcraft, 81" ..2,900.00
Daybed, 4 wide slats ea end, spring cushion, att, 30x79x36" ..2,000.00
Desk, chalet; #395, Onondaga Shops, rfn, 48x33x15" 1,900.00
Dresser, #90, 2 half drws over 4, Handcraft, 53x34" 1,500.00
Footstool, #1292, 7-spindle sides, arched rails, rpl seat, 18" L 700.00
Footstool, #394, curved aprons, tacked (rpl) uphl, rfn, 20" 500.00

Mantel clock, acid-etched copper face, square peg details, #85, unmarked, 22x16x8", $8,500.00.

Magazine stand, #45, 4-shelf, arched supports, Handcraft, 21" ...2,000.00
Pedestal, #27, long corbel under 19" sq top, no mk, rfn, 36" ...1,900.00
Settle, #225, 13-slat U-bk, drop arms, orig seat, Handcraft 1,300.00
Settle, #275, paneled form, leather cushion, brand, 40x84x32" ..13,000.00
Settle, #385, Davenport bed, 7-slat bk, even arms, 70" 5,500.00
Stand, drink; #22, leather top, 4-leg w/X-stretcher, 28x18" dia ...2,600.00
Stand, drink; #587, horizontal stretcher, 27x16" sq 750.00
Table, #559, 8-sided, through-post legs, X-stretcher, 18" dia ...1,200.00
Table, #574, cut-corner top, shelf, rfn, 29x18x18" 850.00
Table, #599, mouse-hole slab sides w/keyed tenon, 48" W 5,000.00
Table, dressing; #87, 2-drw, recessed shelf, mirror, 55x44" 1,700.00
Table, library; #1152, mahog, 2-drw, keyed-tenon stretcher, VG ..1,500.00

Stickley Bros.

Armchair, #705, oversz, 3-slat arms, reuphl seat/bk, 38" 550.00
Armchair, att, 5 vertical slat bk, open arms, old cushion, 39" 850.00
Bookstand, #4611, V-shaped trough, 1 shelf, unmk, 34x30x10" .500.00
Cabinet, china; #8544, dbl doors, 3-shelf, Quaint tag, VG 1,200.00
Candlesticks, #177, copper w/shaped brass supports, 10½", pr 800.00
Desk, fruitwood inlay, 2-drw, slatted bksplash, 47x39x27" 2,400.00
Footstool, #5674, leather cushion top, through tenons, 9x19x12" ..500.00
Lamp, att, glass/copper fr 20" 4-pane shade, copper vase std 2,800.00
Magazine stand, #4602, 5-shelf, 2-slat sides/bk, label, VG 700.00
Magazine stand, #4706, 4-shelf/3-spindle sides/bksplash, 40x27x13" .1,100.00
Magazine stand, #7473, 5-shelf, center slat, label, 42x14" 550.00
Magazine stand, 5-shelf, rnd cutouts, unmk, 49x14x12" 1,000.00
Mirror, hall; #7555, orig iron hooks, chain supports, 32x41" ...1,100.00
Pitcher, att, h/cp, riveted hdl, stovepipe neck, 18x14" 1,300.00
Rocker, #472½, high 4-slat bk, rstr cushion, rfn, 46", G 550.00
Rocker, child's; #380, open arm, drop-in seat, reuphl 300.00
Table, #2500, 4-leg, through tenons, unmk, 29x24" dia, G 450.00
Table, #2676, gate-leg, slab sides, 9" drop leaves, 29x39" 1,000.00
Table, #2828, sq top, shelf, splayed legs, Quaint, 32x18x18" 550.00
Table, #2864, X-stretcher, label, rfn 38" dia top, VG 1,000.00
Table, #314½, 3 splayed legs, flush tenons, 18x15" dia 1,000.00
Table, drink; #2684, rnd copper top, splayed legs, 26x25", VG ..850.00
Table, library; #253, 2-drw, shelf, Quaint, 39x48x28" 700.00
Table, side; #2882, 3-slat sides, narrow stretcher, rstr, 30" 850.00
Table, tea; #2506, octagonal, lower shelf, 26x30" dia 800.00
Umbrella stand, #167, h/cp hexagonal form, recent patina, 27" ..900.00

Stiegel

Baron Henry Stiegel produced glassware in Pennsylvania as early as 1760, very similar to glass being made concurrently in Germany and England. Without substantiating evidence, it is impossible to positively attribute a specific article to his manufacture. Although he made other types of glass, today the term Stiegel generally refers to any very early ware made in shapes and colors similar to those he is known to have produced — especially that with etched or enameled decoration. It is generally conceded, however, that most glass of this type is of European origin. Our advisor for this category is Mark Vuono; he is listed in the Directory under Connecticut.

Bottle, amethyst, expanded diamonds, sheared lip and pontil, 5⅜", very rare, $4,000.00.

Bottle, Dmn Daisy, amethyst, squat, pontiled base, 5¼" **3,300.00**
Bottle, pocket; dk amethyst (blk), 20 vertical ribs, pontil, 4¾" ...**2,000.00**
Salt cellar, cobalt, 16 ribs, appl ft, galleried rim, 2¾" **330.00**
Tumbler, mc floral enamel w/bird, 3⅝" **415.00**

Stocks and Bonds

Scripophily (scrip-awfully), the collecting of 'worthless' old stocks and bonds, gained recognition as an area of serious interest around the mid-1970s. Today there are an estimated 5,000 collectors in the United States and 15,000 worldwide. Collectors who come from numerous business fields mainly enjoy its hobby aspect, though there are those who consider scripophily an investment. Some collectors like the historical significance that certain certificates have. Others prefer the beauty of older stocks and bonds that were printed in various colors with fancy artwork and ornate engravings. Even autograph collectors are found in this field, on the lookout for signed certificates.

Many factors help determine the collector value: autograph value, age of the certificate, the industry represented, whether it is issued or not, its attractiveness, condition, and collector demand. Certificates from the mining, energy, and railroad industries are the most popular with collectors. Other industries or special collecting fields include banking, automobiles, aircraft, and territorials. Serious collectors usually prefer only issued certificates that date from before 1910. Unissued certificates are usually worth one-fourth to one-tenth the value of one that has been issued. Inexpensive issued common stocks and bonds dated between the 1930s and 1980s usually retail between $1.00 to $10.00. Those dating between 1890 and 1930 usually sell for $10.00 to $50.00. Those over one hundred years old retail between $25.00 and $100.00 or more, depending on the quantity found and the industry represented. Some stocks are one of a kind while others are found by the hundreds or even thousands, especially railroad certificates. Autographed stocks normally sell anywhere from $50.00 to $1,000.00 or more. A formal collecting organization for scripophilists is known as The Bond and Share Society with an American chapter located in New York City.

Our advisor for this category is Warren Anderson; he is listed in the Directory under Utah. In many of the following listings, two-letter state abbreviations immediately follow company name. All are in fine condition unless noted otherwise.

Key:
cp — coupon   U — unissued
I/C — issued/cancelled   vgn — vignette
I/U — issued/uncancelled

ACF-Brill Motors, DE/1955, wheel w/logo & men, I/U **35.00**
Adventure Consolidated Copper Co, MI/1909, elk/shield vgn, I/C ...**5.00**
Albany Insurance, NY/1904-22, 3 vgns, I/C **50.00**
Am Express, NY/1870s, Type VI, sgn Wm Fargo/J Knapp/A Holland **425.00**
Am Telephone & Telegraph, NY, 1950s, gold/4 handsets vgn, U ..**3.00**
Annie C Gold Mining Co, NE/1896, 3 vgns, ornate banner, I/U .**60.00**
Black Hills Copper Co Ltd, AZ Territory/1905, miners vgn, I/U ..**35.00**
Burlington & Northwestern Rwy, IA/1877, emb seal, vgn, I/CI/C ..**35.00**
Chester River Steamboat Co, MD/18__, boats vgn, U **17.50**
Chester Street Rwys, PA/1921-28, streetcar vgn, I/C **25.00**
Chicago/St Louis/Pittsburgh RR, IN/IL/1887, train vgn, I/C **25.00**
Chrysler, DE/1920s, hood ornament/cars/etc, I/C **75.00**
Coca-Cola, DE/1929, bl borders, minor pinholes **650.00**
Elgin Nat'l Watch, IL/1925-30, woman w/wheat vgn, I/C **15.00**
First Nat'l Bank of Brooklyn, NY/1863-71, 6 vgns, I/C **75.00**
Fort Wayne & Chicago RR, 1853, shares, train/steamboat vgn, I/C ..**45.00**
Golden Sun Mining & Milling, WY/1904, gold border, vgn, I/C ...**35.00**
Harvard Gold Mining Co, CO/1896, eagle vgn, orange banner, I/U ...**45.00**
Henrietta Gold Mining, CO/1895-99, factory vgn, 100 shares, I/C ..**65.00**
Herschell-Spillman Motor, MA/1919, orange, preferred, I/C **125.00**
Highland Chief Consolidated Mining, CO/1879, miners vgn, I/C ..**100.00**
Home Fire Security, NY/1931, house on island/cherubs vgns, I/U ..**20.00**
Homestake Mining Co, CA/1910s, Indians/mining camp vgn, I/U .**15.00**
IA Homestead Co, IA/18__, eagle vgn, U **5.00**
KY & Great Eastern Railway, 1972, $1,000 bond, vgn, coupons, U ..**65.00**
Lily Mfg Co, District of Columbia/1906, Capitol vgn, I/U **10.00**
Lincoln Nat'l bank of Bath, ME/1888-1903, US Capitol vgn, I/C ..**20.00**
Moonlight Mining, CA/1881, 500 shares, silver foil moon, I/C .**150.00**
Nat'l Tea Co, IL, reclining girl w/book vgn, U **2.00**
New England Telephone & Telegraph, NY/1960s, 6 state shields, I/C ...**3.00**
Newark Athletic Club, NJ/1922, mortgage gold bond, bl, series D, U ..**40.00**
NY $1,000 Bounty Bond, 1866, Columbia/Liberty vgns, I/C **75.00**
NY Central & Hudson River RR, NY/1898, Gold Bond, 10x16", I/C ..**30.00**
Oil Lease Development Co, DE/1923, eagle vgn/banner, I/U **10.00**
PA Salt Mfg, PA/1940s, PA silhouette in keystone, U **2.00**
Peerless Motor Car, VA/1927-29, brn, 3 vgns, Am Bank Note, I/C ..**20.00**
People's Telephone, NY/1887, allegorical figures, I/C **125.00**
Pepsi-Cola...Bottlers, NY/1964, 100 shares, allegorical vgns, I/C ..**20.00**
Phila Traction Co, PA/1907, street railway vgn, I/C **9.00**
Progressive Placer Co, AZ/1913, Miss Liberty vgn/banner, I/U **20.00**
Pure Gold Mines Co, AZ Territory/1904, 3 vgns/artwork, I/U **30.00**
Republic of Bolivia, 1870, 100 pesos, bl w/40 coupons, vgn, unsgn .**25.00**
Sentinel Remedies, DE/1915, shares, gr w/eagle vgn, I/C **45.00**
Tenderfoot Mining, CO/1896, brn w/miners vgn, I/C, VG **40.00**
Toledo Milling Machine, DE/1920, eagle on shield, preferred, I/C ...**15.00**
Tonopah Belmont Development, NJ/1928, miners vgns, I/U **15.00**
Traders Gold Mining Co, CO/1896, Liberty vgn, ornate banner, I/U .**45.00**
Trinity Goldbar Mining Co, NV/1933, mining vgn+6 miners, I/U ..**15.00**
United Stores Corp, DE/1921, angels vgn, logo, I/U **2.00**
UT Bingham Mining Co, ME/1906, miners vgn, bold title, I/U **25.00**
VA State College for Negroes, VA/1937, $1,000 revenue bond, I/C **50.00**
Weems Steamboat...Baltimore City, MD/189_, steamer vgn, U ...**20.00**

Westchester & Phila RR, PA/1858, blk on bl, 6x13", I/U **15.00**
Winchester Repeating Arms, DE/1929, orange, Am Bank Note, I/C .**40.00**
Woman's Gold Mining, CO/1894, brn w/gold seal, miners vgn, I/C ...**90.00**
Woolworth Co, NY/1970, brn w/woman vgn, I/C **2.50**

Stoneware

There are three broad periods of time that collectors of American pottery can look to in evaluating and dating the stoneware and earthenware in their collections. Among the first permanent settlers in America were English and German potters who found a great demand for their individually turned wares. The early pottery was produced from red and yellow clays scraped from the ground at surface levels. The earthenware made in these potteries was fragile and coated with lead glazes that periodically created health problems for the people who ate or drank from it. There was little stoneware available for sale until the early 1800s, because the clays used in its production were not readily available in many areas and transportation was prohibitively expensive. The opening of the Erie Canal and improved roads brought about a dramatic increase in the accessibility of stoneware clay, and many new potteries began to open in New York and New England.

Collectors have difficulty today locating earthenware and stoneware jugs produced prior to 1840, because few have survived intact. These ovoid or pear-shaped jugs were designed to be used on a daily basis. When cracked or severely chipped, they were quickly discarded. The value of handcrafted pottery is often determined by the cobalt decoration it carries. Pieces with elaborate scenes (a chicken pecking corn, a bluebird on a branch, a stag standing near a pine tree, a sailing ship, or people) may easily bring $1,000.00 to $12,000.00 at auction.

After the Civil War there was a need and a national demand for stoneware jugs, crocks, canning jars, churns, spittoons, and a wide variety of other pottery items. The competition among the many potteries reached the point where only the largest could survive. To cut costs, most potteries did away with all but the simplest kinds of decoration on their wares. Time-consuming brush-painted birds or flowers quickly gave way to more quickly executed swirls or numbers and stenciled designs. The coming of home refrigeration and Prohibition in 1919 effectively destroyed the American stoneware industry.

Investment possibilities: 1) Early 19th-century stoneware with elaborate decorations and a potter's mark is expensive and will continue to rise in price. 2) Late 19th-century hand-thrown stoneware with simple cobalt swirls or numbers is still reasonably priced and a good investment. 3) Mass-produced stoneware (ca. 1890 – 1920) is available in large quantities, inexpensive, and has been slowly increasing in price over the last ten years.

Skillfully repaired pieces often surface; their prices should reflect their condition. Look for a slight change in color and texture. The use of a black light is also useful in exposing some repairs. Buyer beware! Hint: Buy only from reputable dealers who will guarantee their merchandise.

In the following listings, 'c/s' means 'cobalt on salt glaze'; all decoration described before this abbreviation is in cobalt. See also Bennington, Stoneware.

Churn, #3/bird on twig, c/s, Whites Utica, rstr, 14½" **625.00**
Churn, #3/flower (dbl), c/s, EA Mantell Olean NY, spider, 16" .**635.00**
Churn, #4/bird running, c/s, S Hart Fulton, orig guide, 16" **900.00**
Churn, #4/flower, c/s, N Clark...Lyons, 18", NM **300.00**
Churn, #5/bird on leaf, c/s, J Burger Jr..., rstr, 18½" **415.00**
Churn, #5/floral spray, c/s, NA White & Son, tight line, 17" **475.00**
Churn, #5/partridge/branch, c/s, T Harrington Lyons, rstr, 19" ...**1,025.00**
Churn, #6/polka-dot lion, c/s, hairline, 18½" **6,000.00**
Cooler, #6/dotted bird & 1860, c/s, Geddes NY, 15", NM **6,000.00**
Cream pot, #2, dbl brushed flower, c/s, N Clark Jr, 9½", EX **210.00**

Cream pot, flower (dbl), c/s, John Burger, 1865, 3-gal, 12" **880.00**
Crock, #1/bird running, c/s, Whites Utica, ca 1870, 7", EX **550.00**
Crock, #1/flower, c/s, AO Whittemore, ca 1870, 7½", EX **150.00**
Crock, #1/flower, c/s, John Burger..., semi-ovoid, 6½" **360.00**
Crock, #1/oak leaf (slip), c/s, Whites Utica, ca 1865, 7", EX **200.00**
Crock, #1/orchid, c/s, NA White & Son, ca 1885, 7", VG **200.00**
Crock, #1/orchid, c/s, Whites Utica NY, 1870s, 7", EX **185.00**
Crock, #2/bird, c/s, Whites Utica, chip/line, 10" **125.00**
Crock, #2/bird on floral branch, c/s, W Roberts...NY, 9", EX **690.00**
Crock, #2/chicken pecks corn, c/s, Brady/Ryan, ca 1885, 9½", EX ..**900.00**
Crock, #2/flower, c/s, J Mantell Penn Yan, stains, 9½" **185.00**
Crock, #2/flower (dbl), c/s, HM Whitman, Havana NY, 9½", EX ...**190.00**
Crock, #2/flower & urn, c/s, Whites Utica, ca 1850, 8", EX **375.00**
Crock, #2/long-tailed bird, c/s, Haxstun & Ottman, 1880s, 9½" ..**1,200.00**
Crock, #2/paddletail bird, c/s, NA White & Son, rstr, 9" **300.00**
Crock, #2/parrot, c/s, FB Norton...MA, ca 1870, 11", EX **1,500.00**
Crock, #2/smiley-face flower, c/s, J Burger...NY, 8½" **1,155.00**
Crock, #3/bird on fence, c/s, unsgn, ca 1885, lines, 10" **990.00**
Crock, #3/chickens/trees/grass, c/s, N Clark, ca 1892, 10", EX ...**1,800.00**
Crock, #3/flower, c/s, Harrington & Burger, ca 1852, 10¼", EX ...**500.00**
Crock, #3/flower, c/s, West Troy NY, ca 1880, 10½", EX **440.00**
Crock, #3/flower (stylized), c/s, Bullard & Scott..., 11", EX **300.00**
Crock, #3/flower/bird, c/s, Charleston, 11½", EX **440.00**
Crock, #3/flowers & leaves, c/s, NA White, ca 1885, 10", VG ...**200.00**
Crock, #4/bird on flower w/ribs, c/s, J Burger Jr..., 11" **1,075.00**
Crock, #4/hen pecks corn, c/s, Brady & Ryan...NY, 11", EX **770.00**
Crock, #4/stag & ground cover, c/s, Ft Edward, rstr, 11½" **3,500.00**
Crock, #5/signature wreath, c/s, Burger & Lang, 14", EX **330.00**
Crock, #5/triple flower, c/s, N Clark & Co, 12", VG **135.00**
Crock, #6/daisy/leaves (fancy), c/s, unsgn, 1870s, 13½", EX **330.00**
Crock, #6/dog w/basket, c/s, S Hart Fulton NY, rstr, 13" **2,000.00**
Crock, Albany slip, I Seymour Troy, ca 1850, 7", EX **45.00**
Crock, bird on stump/dog, c/s, Brady & Ryan, 1880s, 11", EX **900.00**
Jar, #1/flamingo, c/s, Whites Utica, ca 1865, 9½", EX **330.00**
Jar, #2/deer, c/s, Edmands & Co, prof rstr, ca 1870, 12" **1,500.00**
Jar, #2/ferns, c/s, John Burger, spider, ca 1865, 10" **275.00**
Jar, #2/flower (lg/elaborate), c/s, Edmands & Co, 1870, 12", EX ...**385.00**
Jar, #2/ribbed floral, c/s, Edmands & Co, 1870s, 12", EX **200.00**
Jar, #2/wreath, c/s, CW Braun...NY, 1880s, 11½", EX **300.00**
Jar, #3/eagle on flag, c/s, Edmands & Co, prof rstr, 13" **1,870.00**
Jar, #3/tornado, c/s, J Burger Jr, 13", VG **275.00**

Jar, #5/bird within floral wreath, cobalt on salt glaze, C Clark & Co., Lyons, 13¾x11⅞", EX, $3,100.00.

Jar, preserve; #2/bird on twig, c/s, Whites Utica, 10½", VG **450.00**
Jar, preserve; #2/bird on twig, c/s, Wm Dornat...NY, 11½", NM ...**635.00**
Jar, preserve; #2/flower (triple), c/s, chip, ca 1870, 11½" **250.00**
Jar, preserve; #2/flowers (closed), c/s, N Clark, 1850, 11½", EX .**650.00**
Jar, preserve; #2/leaves (3), c/s, John Burger, 11½", EX **325.00**
Jar, preserve; #3/bird, c/s, NY...Ft Edward NY, 13", EX **440.00**
Jar, preserve; #3/triple flower, c/s, Edmands & Co, 13½", VG **200.00**

Jar, preserve; #4/flowers (lg/stylized), c/s, West Troy..., 14" **415.00**
Jar, preserve; cornstalk/coiled snake, c/s, w/lid, 8⅜" **1,265.00**
Jug, #1/bird on twig, c/s, West Troy, ca 1870, 11½", EX **475.00**
Jug, #1/flamingo, c/s, Whites Utica, 1870s, 11", EX **450.00**
Jug, #1/flower, c/s, Cowden & Wilcox, ca 1870, 11", EX **675.00**
Jug, #1/leaf, c/s, Fulper Bros Flemington NJ, 11" **190.00**
Jug, #1/name/accents, c/s, AE Smith Norwalk, ovoid, 11" **200.00**
Jug, #1/pine tree, c/s, NA White & Son Utica NY, 1885, 11", EX .**200.00**
Jug, #1/1876 in script, c/s, West Troy, rstr, 12" **220.00**
Jug, #2, c/s, C Boynton & Co, ca 1825, 13", EX **220.00**
Jug, #2/bird, c/s, Ft Edward..., advertising, 1870s, 13½" **375.00**
Jug, #2/bird (paddletail), c/s, NA White & Son, 14½", EX **2,400.00**
Jug, #2/bird on floral branch, c/s, W Roberts Binghamton NY, 14" .**500.00**
Jug, #2/bird on plume, c/s, NY Stoneware..., ca 1870, 13½", NM **600.00**
Jug, #2/cherries, c/s, Cowden & Wilcox...PA, rpr, 14" **550.00**
Jug, #2/dbl bud flower, c/s, Burger & Lang, spider, 1871, 14½" ..**200.00**
Jug, #2/flower (brushed), c/s, unsgn, cvd stopper, 1830s, 13" **525.00**
Jug, #2/flower (triple), c/s, Cowden & Wilcox...PA, 14" **385.00**
Jug, #3 & accents, c/s, J Fisher, ca 1885, 15½", EX **165.00**
Jug, #3/bird (plump), c/s, Whites Utica, ca 1865, 15", EX **440.00**
Jug, #3/bird singing, c/s, NY Stoneware...Ft Edward NY, 16", EX ...**440.00**
Jug, #3/daffodil, c/s, N Clark & Co, ca 1850, 17", EX **2,700.00**
Jug, #3/flower (brushed, dbl), c/s, unsgn, 1880s, 16½", EX **330.00**
Jug, #3/flower (dbl), c/s, G Adley & Co, ca 1860, 15", EX **330.00**
Jug, #4/flower basket, c/s, Satterlee & Morey..., 17½", EX **525.00**
Jug, incised eagle/shield on olive branch, c/s, rstr hdl, 14" **385.00**
Jug, ribbed flower, c/s, CW Braun, ca 1860, 13½", EX **500.00**
Pail, #2/flowers & accents, c/s, H&G Nash Utica, 12½", EX **400.00**
Pail, batter; brushed bl on spout/hdls, W Roberts..., 6-qt **265.00**
Pitcher, Albany slip/lt brn, Wm E Warner West Troy, 1-gal, EX ..**110.00**
Pitcher, flower, c/s, John Burger, rstr, 10½" **440.00**
Pitcher, tulip, c/s, Burger & Lang, ca 1872, 1-gal, 10", EX **300.00**

Store

Perhaps more so than any other yesteryear establishment, the country store evokes feelings of nostalgia for folks old enough to remember its charms — barrels for coffee, crackers, and big green pickles; candy in a jar for the grocer to weigh on shiny brass scales; beheaded chickens in the meat case outwardly devoid of nothing but feathers. Today mementos from this segment of Americana are being collected by those who 'lived it' as well as those less fortunate! Our advisor for this category is Charles Reynolds; he is listed in the Directory under Virginia. See also Advertising; Scales.

Display case, walnut and nickel, bowed front, Excelsior Showcase Works, Quincy, Illinois, ca 1900, 37x36", EX original, $915.00.

Bill clip, brass, horseshoe shape, 2½x4" **25.00**
Bill clip, brass w/Acanthus leaf & flower relief, Parker, 4½" **175.00**
Bill clip, bronze finish, heavily emb, Pat 1871 & 1874 ....**32.00**
Bill hook, celluloid, Eagle Paint ad w/eagle, EX **110.00**
Bill hook, emb iron, Pat 1872 ....**30.00**
Bin, apple; slatted wood, stenciled letters, 35x31x31", EX **525.00**
Bin, coffee; pine w/red stencil, Jersey Coffee, 32x22x20" **330.00**
Cabinet, ribbon; oak, int racks, metal decal, 49x27x23", VG **350.00**
Case, collar button; curved glass front, oak fr, 15x7", EX **600.00**
Case, display; dvtl case w/10-pane hinged lid, 10x23x44" **200.00**
Case, display; pine, glass window, lift-off lid, 12x12x8" **215.00**
Case, hardwood fr w/curved glass, door in bk, rprs, 10x16x32" ...**110.00**
Case, JS Fry Chocolates, wall mt **250.00**
Case, oak fr w/curved glass in lid & on ends, 16x36x18" **165.00**
Check writing machine, Paymaster Series 700, M **22.00**
Cheese cutter, pnt CI, dial adjustment on bk, Enterprise, 30" **350.00**
Counter, pine w/marble top, 96" **2,850.00**
Credit coin, Finder Please Return to...PA emb on German silver ...**12.50**
Dispenser, Heinz Oven-Baked Beans, ceramic, M **275.00**
Fan, ceiling; Hunter Fan & Ventilating Co, 4-blade, 36" dia **600.00**
Grinder-grater, Fripu-Germany, CI, 4 grating inserts, EX **24.00**
Jar, candy; clear glass, tilts forward, hinged & latched lid, lg **95.00**
Jar, clear glass, emb Licorice Y&S Lozenges, metal lid, 9¼" **65.00**
Mannequin, compo lady, dress & pnt shoes, w/stand, 1940s, 24" .**250.00**
Mannequin shoes, high-button, CI, ca 1890, 7x7½x2½" **230.00**
Paper spindle, iron base, desk type **10.00**
Price marker, Monarch, Deco style **90.00**
Rack, broom; CI, on castors, Pat 1885, 28x12", EX **265.00**
Rack, broom; rnd, hanging, holds about 15 brooms, early **175.00**
Sieve, tin, Foley Food Mill, EX **10.00**
Sign, cash register; Get a Receipt, brass, 2-sided, 6x14", EX **165.00**
Till, Tucker, wooden w/hidden mechanisms & alarm, 1890s **220.00**
Wire measurer **400.00**
Wrapping paper, waxed (for bread), 1945 Ward Bakery **40.00**

Stoves

Antique stoves' desirability is based on two criteria: their utility and their decorative value. It's the latter that adds an 'antique' premium to the basic functional value that could be served just as well by a modern stove. Sheer age is usually irrelevant. Decorative features that enhance desirability include fancy, embossed ornamentation, nickel-plated trim, mica windows, ceramic tiles, and (in cooking stoves) water reservoirs and high warming closets rather than mere high shelves. The less sheet metal and the more cast iron, the better. Look for crisp, sharp designs in preference to those made from worn or damaged and repaired foundry patterns. Stoves with a pastel porcelain finish can be very attractive; blue is a favorite, white is least desirable. Chrome trim, rather than nickel, dates a stove to circa 1933 or later and is a good indicator of a post-antique stove. Though purists prefer the earlier models trimmed in nickel rather than chrome, there is now considerable public interest in these post-antique stoves as well, and some people are willing to pay a good price for these appliance-era 'classics.' (Note: remember, not all bright metal trim is chrome; it is important to learn to distinguish chrome from the earlier, more desirable nickel plate.)

Among stove types, base burners (with self-feeding coal magazines) are the most desirable. Then come the upright, cylindrical 'oak' stoves, kitchen ranges, and wood parlors. Cannon stoves approach the margin of undesirability; laundries and gasoline stoves plunge through it.

There's a thin but continuing stream of desirable antique stoves going to the high-priced Pacific Coast market. Interest in antique stoves is least in the Deep South. Demand for wood/coal stoves is strongest in areas where firewood is affordable and storage of it is practical. Demand for antique gas ranges has become strong, especially in metropolitan markets, and interest in antique electric ranges is starting to surface. The market for antique stoves is so limited and the variety so bewildering that a consensus on a going price can hardly emerge. They are only worth something to the right individual, and prices realized depend very greatly on who happens to be in the auction crowd. Even an expert's appraisal will usually miss the realized price by a substantial percent.

In judging condition look out for deep rust pits, warped or burntout parts, unsound firebricks, poorly fitting parts, poor repairs, and empty mounting holes indicating missing trim. Search meticulously for cracks in the cast iron. Our listings reflect auction prices of completely restored, safe, and functional stoves, unless indicated otherwise.

Base Burners

Acme Sunburst #112, Wehrle Co, Newark OH, M **3,200.00**
Art Amherst #15, NP trim, tiles, 11" urn, 50x25x18" **12,875.00**
Favorite #30, Piqua OH, fancy CI, mica windows, 52"+14" urn ...**2,000.00**
Ransom Art Denmark 315, Albany NY, tiles/NP/mica, 1887, VG ...**4,500.00**
Waverly #12, Thos Caffney & Co, Boston MA, 40x20x22" **1,500.00**
Weir Glenwood #6, NP trim, mica, windows, 1909, 68" **875.00**

Box Stoves

A Belanger Barge #34, scrollwork, CI, 1905, sm **200.00**
BF&M Co #1, front load, early legs, 1800s, 17x13x24" **125.00**
Bussey & McLeod Ajax 18, ornate CI, 1897, 53-lb, very sm **250.00**
E Eaton #24, Amherst NH, schoolhouse type, 24x38x16" **435.00**
Shaker, 1-pc cast body, wrought latch, 1800s, 21x35x14" **345.00**
Unknown, parlor type, reeded-column sides, 1830s, 25x37x17" ..**500.00**
Walker & Pratt Laconia, ornate CI, NP ft rail, 1860s, 35" **125.00**

Franklin Stoves

Acme #18 Orient 1890, 6 tiles, mica windows, fancy **375.00**
Atlanta Franklin #8M, CI, 2-burner, coal/wood, EX **150.00**
Barstow #137 Orient 1886, CI fireplace, coal, 37"+6" urn **995.00**
C Newcomb & Co Worcester, fireplace, ca 1800, 38x24x30" .**1,450.00**
Muzzy & Co Villa Franklin, folding doors, 1830s, 30"+4" urn **175.00**
SH Ransom Ben Franklin Air Tight, Pat 1850, 33x22x34" **265.00**
Southard Robertson Sunny Hearth #2, 1850s, 35x20x29½" **275.00**
Sunny Hearth #2, CI fireplace, 1850s, 11x18x18" **950.00**
Walker/Pratt Berkeley #3, fancy CI fireplace, 42" **825.00**

Parlor Stoves

The term 'parlor stove' as we use it here is very general and encompasses at least eight distinct types recognized by the stove industry: cottage parlor, double-cased airtight, circulator, cylinder, oak, base burner, Franklin, and the fireplace heater.

Anthony Davy & Co Lady Washington, Pat 1848, 26"+7" urn ..**295.00**
Bangor Comfort #23, oval w/dome top, Pat 1875, 33"+10" urn ..**185.00**
Beckwith Air Tight #18, NP trim & rail, 1880s, 48x23x21" **365.00**
Burdette Smith & Co #44, sq, tiles, mica door, 38"+8" urn **350.00**
C&EL Granger #1, 2-column, sheet metal top, 1830s, 26" **365.00**
Cooperative Cycle #12, 6-panel mica door, 1890s, 46"+10" urn ..**475.00**
Cooperative Foundry Sylvan Red Cross #45, Pat 1899, 52" **300.00**
Ilion #3, ornate CI, rnd body, claw ft, 1853, 27"+11" urn **600.00**
J Petree Excelsior #5, ornate CI, side door, 27"+12" urn **250.00**
Johnson, Geer & Cox #4, CI, 4-column, 56" **1,000.00**
Oak Peninsular #216, coal burner, 48"+11" urn **885.00**
Pratt & Wentworth Peerless, tip-up dome, 1840s, 37x19x25" **135.00**
Tropic Crawford #114, mica windows, NP trim, 1890s, 60" **150.00**

Union Airtight, Pat 1851, Victorian styling, 26x18x24" **300.00**
Wood/Bishop Sunrise-Sunshine #23, 1870s, 28"+10" dome/urn ...**325.00**

Ranges (Gas)

Cribben-Sexton Universal, 4-burner, gr/cream, high oven,'27, VG ...**375.00**
Magic Chef, 6-burner/2-oven, warming closet, 1932, EX **2,500.00**
Magic Chef, 6-burner/2-oven, warming closet, 1937, rstr **6,000.00**
Weir Insulated Glenwood, 6-burner/2-oven, wht, 1932, rstr ...**4,125.00**

Ranges (Gas, Wood, and Coal Combination)

Kalamazoo, tan enamel, 1937, EX **315.00**
Magee New Republic, 1929, M, rstr **5,000.00**
Taunton Quaker Standard 8-20, NP trim, trivets/shelf, 1890s **850.00**
Wier Glenwood C #280, 2-shelf bk, no trivets, 1900s **1,000.00**
Wood/Bishop Low Clarion #8, low closet, 1882, 32x28x46" ...**1,875.00**

Ranges (Wood and Coal)

Atlantic Grand, Portland, ornate bk shelf, 12x2018", EX **1,985.00**
Lakeside Eastern Windsor, warming oven/reservoir, 1908, lg **475.00**
South Bend #818, Malleable Range Co, South Bend, M **1,500.00**
Walker & Pratt Village Crawford Royal, NP trim, 1910s **725.00**
Weir Modern Glenwood Home Grand #280, NP trim, 1910, lg .**725.00**

Stove Manufacturers' Toy Stoves

Buck's Jr Range, St Louis MO, new body/pnt/recast parts, 26" ...**850.00**
Charter Oak #503, GF Filley, St Louis MO, 14x12x25", EX ...**2,050.00**
Dainty, Reading Stove Works, PA, 7x13x8", VG **150.00**
Estate Fresh Air Oven, blk/wht enamel, NP, working gas range, 15" **2,400.00**
Karr, Qualified, bl porc w/NP, Belleville IL, 1925, EX **2,500.00**
Karr Range, Belleville IL, bl porc, old model, 21½x13x9" **3,100.00**
Little Eva T Southard, NYC, 8½x14x11", G **350.00**
Little Fanny, CI, minor rust, EX **300.00**
Royal American, Bridgeford, Louisville KY, 14x12x10", G **950.00**

Toy Manufacturers' Toy Stoves

Arcade Hotpoint Range, pnt CI, tan & gr, VG **150.00**
Arcade Roper range, pnt CI, gas type, door opens, 4½", EX **70.00**
Bing, cookstove, bl steel, brass trim, 16½", VG **600.00**
Crescent, cookstove, plated CI & steel, 4-burner, 11½", EX **230.00**
Eagle, Hubley, Lancaster PA, NP, recast parts **450.00**
Eclipse, CI, EX **175.00**
Kenton Royal, CI & steel, 4-burner, ornate, 10", VG **100.00**
Little Giant, unmk/unidentified, 7½x8½x11", EX orig **675.00**
Novelty, Kenton Hdwe, bl pnt/NP trim, rfn, 13x6½x8½" **600.00**
Pet, The; Young Bros, Albany NY, 10½x6x8½" **165.00**
Rival, J&E Stevens, Cromwell CT, 14x9x16", M, +2 kettles ..**1,350.00**
Royal, plated CI, stovepipe, shield shape, 16", G **85.00**
Triumph, Kenton Hdwe, OH, 14x8½x19", G **195.00**

Stretch Glass

Stretch glass, produced from 1916 until after 1930, was made in an effort to emulate the fine art glass of Tiffany and Carder. The glassware was sprayed with a metallic salts mix while hot, then reshaped, causing a stretch effect in the iridescent finish. Pieces which were not reshaped had the iridized finish without the stretch, as seen on Fenton's #222 lemonade set and #401 guest set. Northwood, Imperial, Fenton, Diamond, Lancaster, and the United States

Glass Company were the largest manufacturers of this type of glass. See also specific companies.

Bonbon, Diamond, pk, 3-toed, Dugan 135.00
Bowl, bl, Northwood, #617, 3¾x8" 85.00
Bowl, bl, 3-ftd, Fenton, 9" 135.00
Bowl, tangerine, Fenton, #857, 11" 95.00
Bowl, topaz, Northwood, #660 ....65.00
Candle bowl, Diamond, gr, Dugan 85.00
Candlestick, Diamond, bl, Dugan, #900 ....60.00
Candlestick, topaz, gold decor, Northwood, #695, 8½" 40.00
Candlestick, wht, Imperial, #635, 8½" 50.00
Candy jar, bl, Northwood, #636 ....55.00
Candy jar, pk, Fenton, #835, ½-lb 50.00
Candy jar, pnt wht/floral, Lancaster, 5¼x7" 40.00
Cheese/cracker set, Diamond, gr, Dugan 90.00
Compote, pnt gr/floral, Lancaster 45.00
Compote, purple, sq ft, Northwood, 4x6¾" 75.00
Compote, topaz, Northwood, #637 ....50.00
Creamer & sugar bowl, topaz, Northwood 125.00
Guest set, gr, Fenton, #401 ....75.00
Pitcher, Diamond, bl, w/lid, Dugan 200.00
Plate, amberina, Imperial, #6724, 6" 45.00
Plate, Octagon, purple, Fenton, 7" 45.00
Plate, salad; bl, Northwood 22.00
Plate, wht, Imperial, 8" 16.00
Tumbler, iced tea; topaz, Fenton 35.00
Vase, Diamond Optic, topaz, Northwood, #613 ....125.00
Vase, wht, Fenton, #950 ....95.00

String Holders

Today, if you want to wrap and secure a package, you have a variety of products to choose from: cellophane tape, staples, etc. But in the 1800s, string was about the only available binder; thus the string holder, either the hanging or counter type, was a common and practical item found in most homes and businesses. Chalkware and ceramic figurals from the 1930s and '40s contrast with the cast and wrought-iron examples from the 1800s to make for an interesting collection. Our advisor for this category is Charles Reynolds; he is listed in the Directory under Virginia. See also Advertising.

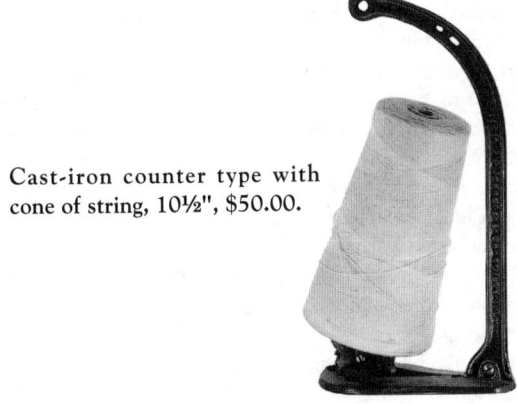

Cast-iron counter type with cone of string, 10½", $50.00.

Acorn, wooden 60.00
Apple w/Blackberries, chalkware 50.00
Baby face, chalkware, rare, EX 240.00
Beehive shape, CI, Pat April 21, 1865, 5¼x6½" 125.00
Bellhop, Black, FAP 285.00

Black girl, chalkware face 300.00
Chef, chalkware 50.00
Chef w/rolling pin, full figure, chalkware 60.00
Chinaman's head, chalkware 265.00
Duck w/scissors, ceramic 75.00
Dutch boy on swing, Cornell White Lead Paint, 30", EX 2,450.00
Dutch girl's head, chalkware 50.00
Housewife, chalkware, MIB 60.00
I Hate Housework, ceramic 160.00
Indian chief, chalkware 300.00
Kangaroo, ceramic 125.00
Kitten on ball of yarn, ceramic, from $50 to 70.00
Mammy face, Ty Me, chalkware 395.00
Owl, pottery 175.00
Peasant lady knitting, ceramic 200.00
Poncho Villa, chalkware 350.00
Witch, Fitz & Floyd 45.00
Worm & apple, chalkware, EX 100.00

Sugar Shakers

Sugar shakers (or muffineers, as they were also called) were used during the Victorian era to sprinkle sugar and spice onto breakfast muffins, toast, etc. They were made of art glass, in pressed patterns, and in china. See also specific types and manufacturers. Our coadvisors for this category are Jeff Bradfield and Dale MacAllister; they are listed in the Directory under Virginia.

Acorn, blk amethyst 275.00
Acorn, wht opaque 120.00
Alba, bl opaque 180.00
Argus Swirl, wht opaque w/decor 125.00
Coinspot, 9-Panel 125.00
Coinspot, 9-Panel, bl 165.00
Coinspot, 9-Panel, gr 175.00
Colorature, vaseline & wht spatter 225.00
Cone, bl 125.00
Cone, bl satin 200.00
Cone, pk opaque 175.00
Daisy & Fern, cranberry opal, Northwood mold 350.00
Florette, pk satin cased 275.00
Forget Me Not, bl 175.00
Forget Me Not, chartreuse 225.00
Forget Me Not, pk 175.00
Gargoyle, milk glass 100.00
Hobbs Optic, rubena 175.00
Hobnail, amber 95.00
Leaning Pillar, amber 85.00
Leaning Pillar, bl opaque 110.00
Medallion Sprig, amethyst to clear 300.00
Melon, bl floral, Gillinder 240.00
Panelled Teardrop, yel custard 195.00
Parian Swirl, bl satin 210.00
Parian Swirl, cranberry 275.00
Parian Swirl, gr opaque w/decor 185.00
Quilted Phlox, gr transparent 175.00
Quilted Phlox, pk cased 250.00
Reverse Swirl, cranberry opal 275.00
Reverse Swirl, wht opal 150.00
Ribbed Lattice, bl opal 225.00
Ribbed Lattice, cranberry opal 275.00
Snail, clear pattern glass 125.00
Venetian Diamond, cranberry 185.00

West Virginia Optic, milk glass w/decor 110.00
Windemere Fan, peachbloom w/HP floral 295.00
Wisconsin, clear pattern glass 100.00

Sunderland Lustre

Sunderland lustre was made by various potters in the Sunderland district of England during the 18th and 19th centuries. It is often characterized by a splashed-on application of the pink lustre, which results in an effect sometimes referred to as the 'cloud' pattern. Some pieces are transfer printed with scenes, ships, florals, or portraits.

Chamber pot, verse 'Marriage'/other blk transfers w/mc, EX 565.00
Creamer, emb floral w/mc decor, copper lustre band, 3⅜" 160.00
Pitcher, Battle of Wasp & Reindeer/Constitution, 6½", VG 350.00
Pitcher, rococo form, blk fruit & flower transfer, 6½" 125.00
Plaque, Thou God Seest..., blk transfer, wear, 6" dia 200.00
Sugar bowl, comic blk transfers w/mc, unmk, late, w/lid, 4⅜" 65.00
Wine, wht band w/mc florals, copper lustre trim, wear, 4" 125.00

Surveying Instruments

The practice of surveying offers a wide variety of precision instruments primarily for field use, most of which are associated with the recording of distance and angular measurements. These instruments were primarily made from brass; the larger examples were fitted with tripods and protective cases. These cases also held accessories for the instruments, and these can sometimes play a key part in their evaluation. Instruments in complete condition and showing little use will have much greater values than those that appear to have had moderate or heavy use. Instruments were never polished during use, and those that have been polished as decorator pieces are of little interest to most avid collectors. Our advisor for this category is Dale Beeks; he is listed in the Directory under Iowa.

Alidade, coast-survey style high-post, CL Berger & Sons, '32 ....650.00
Clinometer, Watkin Clinometer J Iticks...1896, 9½" case 230.00
Compass, GM Pool...MA, brass, 6" dial, w/tripod & case, G 800.00
Compass, Knox & Shain, Phila, brass cased, w/2 sights, 14" 775.00
Compass, S Thaster & Son Boston, brass, 1850s, 3" dia, VG 175.00
Compass, WL Potts NJ, decor on dial, brass case, 14¾" 1,500.00
Level, combination, AS Aloe MO, 1930, 11¼" scope, 5" vial 350.00
Level, hand, peep, 6" L w/bubble, w/leather case 35.00
Level, surveyor's, Aloe & Co St Louis, blk enamel, w/tripod & case ..330.00
Level, wye, architect's, L Black Detroit, 1920s, 11" scope 250.00
Level, wye, Stackpole & Brother NY, 1875, 17½" 320.00
Level & sight, Keuffel & Esser NY, orig leather holders, G 100.00
Level/transit, builder's, CL Berger & Sons, '40, 10½" 125.00

Photo courtesy Dale Beeks

Plane compass, early 19th century, English, VG, $800.00.

Rod, #d stick, brass plate w/blk #s & letters, 0 in red, 81x2" 50.00
Rod, 2-part stick w/blk #s, blk & wht target, 84x1½" 75.00
Staff, instrument; trn oak rod, brass end, iron drive point, 57" ...100.00
Transit, David White WI, ca 1953, 11½" scope, 6¼" 275.00
Transit, Keuffel & Esser NY, ca 1908, 11" scope, 5" vial 400.00
Transit, mountain; Eugene Dietzgen Chicago IL, 1927, 5¼" 375.00
Transit, Stackpole & Brother NY, ca 1855, 10½" scope, 6" 600.00

Swarovski Crystal

The Swarovski family has been perfecting the glassmaker's art in Wattens, Austria, since 1895. Collectible figurines and desk items were introduced in 1977, and the Swarovski Collectors Society (SCS) was created in 1987. Featuring lead content of 30%+, these 'Silver Crystal' limited edition decorative accessories have attracted a following of over 200,000 dedicated collectors worldwide. Some designs were distributed regionally, making persuit of retired items an interesting challenge that spans the globe. Most items have an etched mark on the underside. The first mark was a block-style SC. In 1989 the mark was changed to a Swan. Marks on larger items also include the name Swarovski. SCS figurines are further identified with the year and designer's initials. As the vigilance of Swarovski collectors has grown, their interest in all items of Swarovski manufacture has increased. In addition to Swarovski Silver Crystal, collectors also seek Trimlite, Giftware Suite, Swarovski Selections, Ebeling & Reuss, and private label productions by the Swarovski company. Prices listed below reflect the presence of complete original packing and enclosures, without which prices are compromised 10% to 35%.

d01x861, lovebirds, 1987 annual edition, from $4,750 to 5,000.00
d01x881, woodpeckers, 1988 annual edition, from $1,650 to ..1,750.00
d01x881cb, woodpeckers, clear base, 1988 annual edition 3,250.00
d01x891, turtledoves, 1989 annual edition, from $1,080 to 1,200.00
d01x901, dolphins, 1990 annual edition, from $1,050 to 1,080.00
d01x911, seals, 1991 annual edition, from $480 to 540.00
7515nr000003, beaver (recumbent baby), from $70 to 90.00
7601nr000001, eagle, edition of 10,000, from $7,800 to 8,600.00
7616nr000001, beaver mother, from $140 to 155.00
7617nr043000, kiwi, from $65 to 80.00
7619nr000003, poodle 170.00
7621nr000003, owl, from $200 to 235.00
7622nr70, rhinoceros, lg, from $115 to 140.00
7626nr65, hippopotamus, lg, from $125 to 130.00
7629nr70v1, fox, frosted nose, from $155 to 180.00
7630nr30, hedgehog, sm, from $480 to 550.00
7630nr60, hedgehog, king sz, from $780 to 850.00
7632nr40, turtle, giant, from $2,200 to 3,500.00
7633nr160000, swan, maxi 3,400.00
7634nr028000, kitten, from $80 to 90.00
7634nr52, cat, med, from $570 to 600.00
7634nr70, cat, lg, from $150 to 160.00
7635nr70, dog (Pluto), from $140 to 150.00
7636nr46, owl, sm, from $90 to 105.00
7637nr112, bear, giant, from $2,400 to 3,000.00
7637nr54, bear, sm, from $80 to 100.00
7637nr92, bear, king sz 2,600.00
7639nr55br, butterfly, blk & rhodium 450.00
7639nr55cg, butterfly, crystal & gold, from $300 to 435.00
7640nr55, elephant, lg, from $270 to 280.00
7642nr48b, prince frog, blk eyes, from $155 to 165.00
7645nr100v2, falcon head, variant 2, lg 1,975.00
7647nr80, mallard, from $160 to 170.00
7648nr30, snail, from $80 to 95.00
7651nr20, chicken, mini, from $75 to 95.00

7653nr45, duck, mini, from $90 to **100.00**
7657nr27c, pig, crystal tail, mini, from $90 to **105.00**
7670nr32, bear, mini, from $240 to **300.00**
7672nr042, dachshund, frosted tail, mini, from $90 to **110.00**
7673nr40r, koala, right, from $120 to **130.00**
7677nr055, fox, running, mini, from $70 to **85.00**

Syracuse

Syracuse was a line of fine dinnerware and casual ware which was made for nearly a century by the Onondaga Pottery Company of Syracuse, New York. Early patterns were marked O.P. Company. Collectors of American dinnerware are focusing their attention on reassembling some of their many lovely patterns. In 1966 the firm became officially known as the Syracuse China Company in order to better identify with the name of their popular chinaware. Many of the patterns were marked with the shape and color names (Old Ivory, Federal, etc.), not the pattern names. By 1971 dinnerware geared for use in the home was discontinued, and the company turned to the manufacture of hotel, restaurant, and other types of commercial tableware.

Arcadia, cup & saucer, demitasse **30.00**
Arcadia, plate, dinner; 9¾" **26.00**
Bombay, cup & saucer, gold trim **30.00**
Bombay, teapot, gold trim **98.00**
Briarcliff, cream soup **25.00**
Briarcliff, creamer **32.00**
Clover, bowl, cereal; 5½" **16.00**
Compote, floral garlands w/portrait medallions, 3⅝x7" **11.00**
Coronet, plate, salad **20.00**
Governor Clinton, bowl, cereal **20.00**
Jefferson, cup & saucer **32.00**
Jefferson, platter, 14" **78.00**
Jefferson, rim soup **26.00**
Lyric, cup & saucer **32.00**
Lyric, plate, dinner **26.50**
Minuet, bowl, cereal; w/hdls **26.00**
Minuet, bowl, vegetable; oval **50.00**
Minuet, creamer **40.00**
Minuet, cup & saucer **32.00**
Minuet, plate, bread & butter **10.00**
Minuet, plate, salad **17.50**
Minuet, platter, lg **100.00**
Minuet, platter, med **82.50**
Nordic, creamer & sugar bowl **30.00**
Olive dish, urn medallions/florals/geometrics **5.00**
Orchard, plate, dinner **25.00**
Pitcher, Herbert Hoover figural, ltd ed, 6¾x5¾" **67.00**
Rosalee, platter, 16" **50.00**
Rosalee, soup tureen, w/lid **75.00**
Sharon, creamer **32.00**
Sharon, plate, dinner **27.50**
Sherwood, creamer **15.00**
Sherwood, cup & saucer **18.00**
Sherwood, nappy **22.00**
Sherwood, plate, bread & butter **6.00**
Sherwood, platter, 12" **45.00**
Sherwood, platter, 16"rim, brass mts **35.00**
Sherwood, sugar bowl, w/lid **25.00**
Singing Cowboys, mug **25.00**
Singing Cowboys, plate, 6½" **15.00**
Stansbury, cream soup, w/underplate **30.00**
Stansbury, platter, 12" **50.00**

Suzanne, bowl, Federal shape, oval, 10½" **50.00**
Suzanne, bowl, Federal shape, 5" **15.00**
Suzanne, cup & saucer, Federal shape **25.00**
Suzanne, plate, Federal shape, 10" **25.00**
Suzanne, plate, Federal shape, 6½" **12.00**
Suzanne, plate, Federal shape, 8" **10.00**
Suzanne, platter, Federal shape, 14" **50.00**
Sweetheart, creamer **37.50**
Sweetheart, cup & saucer **26.00**
Sweetheart, plate, dinner; 10¼" **24.00**
Sweetheart, plate, salad; 8" **14.00**
Sweetheart, sugar bowl, w/lid **45.00**

Syrups

Values are for old, original syrups. Beware of reproductions and watch handle area for cracks! See also various manufacturers and specific types of glass. Our coadvisors are Jeff Bradfield and Dale MacAllister; they are listed in the Directory under Virginia.

Flower and Pleat, ca 1895, $185.00.

Acorn, bl opaque **225.00**
Alba, wht milk glass w/decor **80.00**
Brittanic, clear pattern glass **85.00**
Buckle w/Star **95.00**
Bulging Loops, pk cased **325.00**
Button Arches, ruby stain **275.00**
Coin Spot & Swirl, bl opal **200.00**
Coin Spot & Swirl, wht opal **150.00**
Coreopsis, milk glass w/decor **185.00**
Corona, ruby stain, sm **185.00**
Flat Flower, milk glass **140.00**
Florette, pk satin **300.00**
Forget-Me-Not, bl opaque **200.00**
Forget-Me-Not, pk opaque **225.00**
Guttate, robin's-egg bl, dtd, tall **400.00**
Hercules Pillar, amber **175.00**
Hexagon Block, ruby flashed **225.00**
Inside Ribbed, bl **175.00**
Inside Ribbed, vaseline **195.00**
Jewelled Moon & Star, w/decor **295.00**
Medallion Sprig, gr **350.00**
Missouri, gr, rare **195.00**
Polka Dot, bl opal, bulbous **450.00**
Reverse Swirl, bl opal **325.00**
Ribbed Lattice, cranberry opal **475.00**
Ring Band, custard, souvenir decor, Heisey **275.00**
Seaweed, wht opal **275.00**
Tall Cone, pk cased **325.00**
Tall Stripe, bl opal **325.00**

Thousand Eye, amber **150.00**	Shotshell loader, rosewood/brass, Parker Bros, Pat 1884 ....**50.00**
Thousand Eye, clear **125.00**	Target, Am sheet metal, rod ends mk Pat Feb 8 '21, set **25.00**
Thousand Eye, lt gr **175.00**	Target, blk japanned sheet metal, Bussey Patentee, London **50.00**
Valencia Waffle, amber **135.00**	Target, BUST-O, blk or wht breakable wafer **20.00**
Zippered Borders, clear **85.00**	Trap, DUVROCK, w/blk pitch birds **250.00**
Zippered Borders, ruby stain **300.00**	Trap, MO-SKEET-O, w/birds **150.00**

Target Balls

Prior to 1880 when the clay pigeon was invented, blown glass target balls were used extensively for shotgun competitions. Approximately 2¾" in diameter, these balls were hand blown into a three-piece mold. All have a ragged hole where the blowpipe was twisted free. Target balls date from approximately 1840 (English) to World War I, although they were most widely used in the 1870 – 1880 period. Common examples are unmarked except for the blower's code — dots, crude numerals, etc. Some balls were embossed in a dot or diamond pattern so they were more likely to shatter when struck by shot, and some have names and/or patent dates. When evaluating condition, bubbles and other minor manufacturing imperfections are acceptable; cracks are not. The prices below are for mint condition examples.

Amber w/emb ribs, horizontal or vertical **150.00**
Bogardus' Glass Ball Pat'd April 10 1877, amber, Am **350.00**
Bogardus' Glass Ball Pat'd April 10 1877, other than amber, Am ..**800.00**
CTB Co, blk pitch, Pat dates on bottom, Am **250.00**
Dmn Quilt w/o center band, yel-amber, 2¾" **210.00**
Dmn Quilt w/plain center band, cobalt, 2⅝" **250.00**
Dmn Quilt w/plain center band, ground top, Am **150.00**
Dmn Quilt w/shooter emb in 2 panels, clear, English **300.00**
Dmn Quilt w/shooter emb in 2 panels, gr or purple, English **300.00**
EE Eaton Guns & C 53 State St Chicago, golden yel-amber, 2⅝" .**1,000.00**
Flesschenfabriek Boers & CP Delft, emb dmns, lt olive, 2⅝" **300.00**
For Hockey's Pat Trap, gr, English **500.00**
Glashuttenewotte Un Charlottenburg, clear, emb dmns, 2⅝" ..**1,800.00**
Glashuttenewotte Un Charlottenburg, med yel-olive, 2⅝" **1,000.00**
Great Western Gun Works, Pittsburgh, amber, Am **900.00**
Gurd & Son, London, Ontario, amber, Canadian **500.00**
Ilmenau (Thur) Sophiehutte, amber, Dmn Quilt, Germany **425.00**
Ira Paine's Filled Ball Pat Oct 23 1877, amber, Am **250.00**
Ira Paine's Filled Ball Pat Oct 23 1877, other than amber, Am ..**800.00**
Man shooting, clear, 2⅝" **150.00**
NB Glass Works Perth, other than pale gr, English **200.00**
NB Glass Works Perth, pale gr, English **100.00**
Plain, amber w/mold mks **65.00**
Plain, clear w/mold mks **1,000.00**
Plain, cobalt w/mold mks **150.00**
Plain, dk teal gr w/mold mks, 2¾" **375.00**
T Jones, Gunmaker, Blackburn, pale bl, English **150.00**
Van Cutsem A St Quentin, cobalt, 2¾" dia **150.00**
WW Greener, St Mary's Works, various colors, English, ea **250.00**

Related Memorabilia

Ball thrower, dbl; old red pnt, ME Card, Pat...78, 79, VG **900.00**
Clay birds, Winchester, Pat May 29 1917, 1 flight in box **100.00**
Pitch bird, blk DUVROCK **1.00**
Shell, dummy, w/single window, any brand **35.00**
Shell, dummy shotgun, Winchester, window w/powder, 6" **125.00**
Shell set, dummy, Gamble Stores, 2 window shells, 3 cut out **125.00**
Shell set, dummy, Winchester, 5 window shells **175.00**
Shell set, dummy shotgun, Peters, 6 window shells+full box **175.00**

Tea Caddies

Because tea was once regarded as a precious commodity, special boxes called caddies were used to store the tea leaves. They were made from various materials: porcelain, carved and inlaid woods, and metals ranging from painted tin or tole to engraved silver. Our advisor for this category is Tina Carter; she is listed in the Directory under California.

Burl veneer w/banded inlay, dmn escutcheon, rpr, 7½" **220.00**
Burl yewwood w/ebony inlay, fitted int, 5½x12x6", EX **500.00**
Mahog casket form, lid w/brass bail, ca 1820s, English, 9" **700.00**
Mahog Hplwht w/inlay, rprs, 4¼x3¾x4⅛" **330.00**
Mahog veneer w/inlaid shell/fan/flowers, 3-compartment, 11" ...**165.00**
Mahog veneer w/line & floral inlay, rpr, 4½" **150.00**
Regency rosewood casket form w/pearl inlay, early, 14", EX **350.00**
Regency rosewood casket w/MOP inlay, ivory ball ft, 12x6" **575.00**
Rosewood veneer, lift top w/storage space, MOP escutcheon, 9" .**150.00**
Satinwood, boxwood/hardwood inlaid garlands, England, 1790 ..**1,750.00**
Satinwood & mahog w/acorn & leaf medallions, brass ft, 8¼" ...**450.00**

Tea Leaf Ironstone

Tea Leaf Ironstone became popular in the 1880s when middle-class American housewives became bored with the plain white stone china that English potters had been exporting to this country for nearly a century. The original design has been credited to Anthony Shaw of Longport, who decorated the plain ironstone with a hand-painted copper lustre design of bands and leaves. Originally known as Lustre Band and Sprig, the pattern has since come to be known as Tea Leaf Lustre. It was produced with minor variations by many different firms both in England and the United States. By the early 1900s, it had become so commonplace that it had lost much of its appeal.

Items marked Red Cliff are reproductions made from 1950 until 1980 for this distributing and decorating company of Chicago, Illinois. Hall China provided many of the blanks.

Our advice for this category comes from Home Place Antiques, whose address is listed in the Directory under Illinois.

Doughnut stand, Alfred Meakin, 4½x8", $280.00.

Bone dish, scalloped, Meakin **75.00**
Bone dish, scalloped, Wilkinson **75.00**
Bowl, high crimped rim, Wilkinson, 3⅜x9½" **75.00**

Bowl, vegetable; Cable, w/lid, Burgess **235.00**
Bowl, vegetable; Fish Hook, bracket ft, w/lid, Meakin, 11x7" **195.00**
Bowl, vegetable; Hexagon Sunburst shape, w/lid, Shaw, 11½" ...**295.00**
Butter dish, Fish Hook, Meakin, w/drain **175.00**
Butter dish, sq, leaf finial, vertical ribs, w/drain, Mellor Taylor ..**165.00**
Butter dish, sq, Wedgwood, 5½", w/drain **165.00**
Butter pat, Meakin, 2¾" sq **14.00**
Butter pat, Meakin, 3¼" **15.00**
Butter pat, scalloped edge, ribbed, sq, Mellor Taylor **16.00**
Coffeepot, Bamboo, Meakin, 9" **225.00**
Creamer, Bamboo, Meakin, 6½" **195.00**
Creamer, Wedgwood, 5¼" **165.00**
Cup & saucer, Adams Microtex **35.00**
Cup & saucer, Chelsea type, Johnson Bros, 2⅝", 3½" **85.00**
Cup & saucer, handleless; Meakin, 3", 3½" **100.00**
Cup & saucer, Lily of the Valley, Shaw **125.00**
Cup & saucer, Morning Glory, Tunstall **125.00**
Cup plate, unmk, 3½" **60.00**
Cup plate, Wilkinson, 3¼" **60.00**
Gravy boat, Alfred Meakin **65.00**
Gravy boat, Fish Hook, Meakin, 2¾x8" **75.00**
Gravy boat, simple sq, unmk **65.00**
Pitcher, milk; Bamboo, Meakin, 7½" **265.00**
Plate, gold lustre variant, Buford's Porcelain, 7½" **12.50**
Plate, Meakin, 7⅞" **14.00**
Plate, Meakin, 9" **35.00**
Plate, Morning Glory, 9¾" **45.00**
Plate, Red Cliff, 8¼" **22.00**
Plate, Teaberry, 8" **35.00**
Plate, Wedgwood, 8¼" **18.00**
Platter, rectangular, Meakin, 14" **75.00**
Platter, rectangular, ribbed, Wedgewood, 12" **75.00**
Sauce dish, rnd, Meakin, 4¾" **18.00**
Shaving mug, leaf at hdl, Shaw **200.00**
Shaving mug, Meakin, 3¼x3½" **185.00**
Soap dish, gold lustre, Powell & Bishop **110.00**
Soup, flanged, Meakin, 8¾" **30.00**
Sugar bowl, Bamboo, Grindley **95.00**
Sugar bowl, Fish Hook, w/lid, Meakin, 6½" **95.00**
Sugar bowl, Lily of the Valley, Shaw, 5½x6½" **145.00**
Teapot, Fish Hook, Meakin, 8½" **225.00**
Toothbrush holder, Meakin, 5" **165.00**
Wash bowl & pitcher, Lily of the Valley, Shaw, +2 pcs **675.00**

Teapots

Teapots have become popular collectibles in recent years with a surge in tea shops featuring tea and teapots, and serving afternoon tea. Collectors should be aware of modern teapots which imitate older similar versions. Study the types of pottery, porcelain, and china, as well as the marks. Multicolored, detailed marks over the glaze represent modern pieces. Teapots made in the last thirty years are quite collectible but generally don't demand the same prices as their antique counterparts.

A wide range of teapots can be found by the avid collector. Those from before 1880 are more apt to be found in museums or sold at quality auction houses. Almost every pottery and porcelain manufacturer in Asia, Europe, and America have produced teapots. Some are purely decorative and whimsical, while others are perfect for brewing a pot of tea. Tea drinkers should beware of odd-shaped spouts which sputter and drip. Reproductions to be aware of: majolica styles with modern marks, Blue Willow which has been made continuously for almost two centuries, and those marked Made in China (older teapots have 'chop marks' in Chinese).

Refer to various manufacturers' names for further listings. Our advisor for this category is Tina M. Carter, listed in the Directory under California. Her book, *Teapots*, is available at bookstores or direct from the author.

ALB, dripless, mottled, England, ca 1920 ....**52.00**
Anniversary, 50th; floral, Price Kensington **48.00**
Automobile, silver lustre, Carlton Ware, England **495.00**
Ballerina, music box & movement, Japan, ca 1960 ....**30.00**
Barge, brn, emb mk, Derbyshire, England, lg **75.00**
Barge, emb floral decor, A Present..., ca 1800s **1,000.00**
Basket, picnic teapot & 2 cups, hinged lid, padded, China **100.00**
Belleek, Am, ornate detail, palette mk, ca 1900 ....**850.00**
Ben Franklin figural, ceramic w/metal hdl **65.00**
Beswick Ware, Dicken's characters, England, ca 1930 ....**75.00**
Boston Tea Party, commemorative, Davison Newman, +cr/sug **45.00**
Cast metal, scenes, octagonal, China, ca 1920 ....**65.00**
Charles & Diana, brn pottery, Wales CM, 2½" **78.00**
Cloisonne, animal or designs, China, mini **35.00**
Copper, Art Deco style, enamel decor, ball ft, China **38.00**
Crinoline Lady, Made in Czechoslovakia **75.00**
Crinoline Lady (Cinderella), Sadler, England, ca 1930 ....**65.00**
Cube, fleur-de-lis, Royal Crownford, England **25.00**
Cube, HP, Made in Japan, ca 1940 ....**20.00**
Cube, Los Angeles Steamship Co, Clews, England **38.00**
Duck, Peking; HP, wicker hdl, no mk, China, ca 1920 ....**75.00**
Edward VII commemorative, pk lustre, England, 2-cup **250.00**

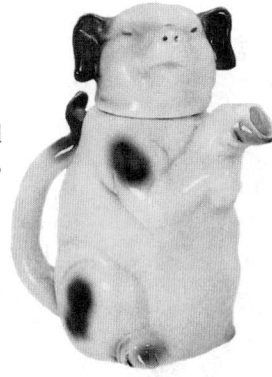

German pig figural teapot, marked PK, #722, 7½", $65.00.

Granny, mc, Lingard or HJ Wood, England, 1930 ....**55.00**
Granny, Queensware, modern **35.00**
Iced tea dispenser, USA, 2-pc, lg **175.00**
Jim Beam, characters, ltd ed, Wade **48.00**
Lefton, cozy set, violets, ca 1950 ....**32.00**
Lipton's, oval, ribbed, Fraunfelter, ca 1930 ....**35.00**
Lipton's, rnd, various colors, Hall China Co **30.00**
Man in tux forms hdl, lady forms pot, ceramic, unmk, modern **35.00**
Meakin, Alfred; blk trim, china relief, England **38.00**
Pewter, New Amsterdam Silver Co, USA **35.00**
Pottery, pk, mk Ford, USA, 1-cup **25.00**
Rough glaze, buff sharkskin, tan, slip decor, Japan, 1920s **28.00**
RS Prussia, scalloped hdl/edge, HP decor, unmk **75.00**
Sadler, folklore, Robin Hood/King Arthur/etc, ca 1990 ....**35.00**
Salada Tea, promotional item, USA, 1-cup **25.00**
Silverplate, Rococo style, Community **70.00**
Snow White w/Dwarfs, musical, Walt Disney Prod **75.00**
Spode's Tower, bl/wht transfer, London shape, England, VG **58.00**
Tiffin, tea liqueur, depot decanter, Germany, 1960 ....**95.00**
WWII, Esc to US by Royal Navy or Allied Fleets, brn, England ..**45.00**
Yxing, padded box, chop mk, China repro **45.00**

Teco

Teco artware was made by the American Terra Cotta and Ceramic Company, located near Chicago, Illinois. The firm was established in 1886 and until 1901 produced only brick, sewer tile, and other redware. Their early glaze was inspired by the matt green made popular by Grueby. 'Teco Green' was made for nearly ten years. It was similar to Grueby's, yet with a subtle silver-gray cast. The company was one of the first in the United States to perfect a true crystalline glaze. The only decoration used was through the modeling and glazing techniques; no hand painting was attempted. Favored motifs were naturalistic leaves and flowers. The company broadened their lines to include garden pottery and faience tiles and panels. New matt glazes (browns, yellows, blue, and rose) were added to the green in 1910. By 1922 the artware lines were discontinued; the company was sold in 1930.

Values are dictated by size and shape, with architectural and organic forms being more desirable. Teco is usually marked with a vertical impressed device comprised of a large 'T' to the left of the remaining three letters.

Jar, gr, ribbed cylinder, w/lid, 5¼x4½" 600.00
Jardiniere, gr, water lilies & leaves, 8 leaf hdls, rstr, 10x10" 7,500.00
Jardiniere, lt & med gr, broad shoulders, #144, 10½x15", EX 700.00
Pitcher, lt gr matt, divided hdl, mks, 8½" 550.00
Stein, gr matt w/emb cattails, 2 mks, 6x4½" 300.00
Tea set, gray-beige, emb Nouveau decor, pot+cr/sug+lemon pot ..650.00
Vase, brn/orange crystalline, long neck, bulbous, 5⅜" 350.00

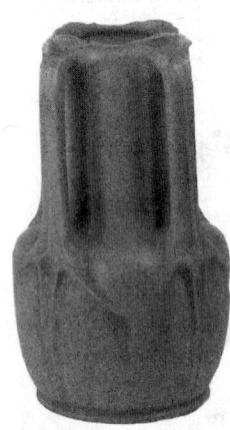

Vase, green matt with charcoaling, four rim-to-hip handles, superior molding, 15", NM, $3,250.00.

Vase, gr, bulbous, 3¾x4" 375.00
Vase, gr, dimpled sides, #201A, 3" 240.00
Vase, gr, emb foliage, rtcl body/rim, 4-hdld, #113, 6¼" 1,900.00
Vase, gr, emb leaves above low buttresses, #87, 12" 1,600.00
Vase, gr, flared cylinder, 13x4¼" 650.00
Vase, gr, fluted/ribbed neck, bulbous, F Albert, #182, 16x7½" ...1,500.00
Vase, gr, gourd shape, open sq hdls, 5½" 900.00
Vase, gr, hdls, mk, 9" 650.00
Vase, gr, linear decor, H Garden, #252, 11½", EX 2,000.00
Vase, gr, lotus top w/4 vertical buttresses, 12x6" 2,400.00
Vase, gr, ovoid, paper label, 4¼x3½" 425.00
Vase, gr, slightly bulbous, sm rim, 5" 375.00
Vase, gr, tulip shape w/buttresses, gunmetal delineation, 12¼" ..3,500.00
Vase, gr, 2 integral hdls w/flared lip, mk, 5½x9" 650.00
Vase, gr, 2 sm closed sq hdls, mks, 7" 950.00
Vase, gr, 3 protrusions, 3 legs, 3x5" 270.00
Vase, gr, 3 rim-to-ft buttresses, waisted, WD Gates, 155, 8½" .2,200.00
Vase, gr w/charcoal, 2 buttressed hdls, Mundie, #266, 11½" ...1,300.00
Vase, gr w/charcoal, 2 open buttresses, WD Gates, #432, 11½" ..1,900.00

Vase, gr w/charcoal, 4 buttresses, WD Gates, #436, 7", NM 1,000.00
Vase, gr w/charcoal, 4-hdld, rpr drill hole, #223, 14x7½" 4,500.00
Vase, mustard, rtcl top, F Albert, #113, 6x5½" 2,400.00
Vase, orange/yel/red/blk crystalline, mk, 8⅛" 850.00
Vase, Pompeian, gr, flared rim, shouldered, mk, 7½" 550.00
Vase, sage gr w/oatmeal texture, sgn MI, 7x7¼" 700.00
Vase, yel-gr, 3-sided, #336, 7⅝" 450.00
Wall pocket, gr, emb florals (unusual), 5½x9", NM 425.00

Teddy Bears

The story of Teddy Roosevelt's encounter with the bear cub has been oft recounted with varying degrees of accuracy, so it will suffice to say that it was as a result of this incident in 1902 that the teddy bear got his name. These appealing little creatures are enjoying renewed popularity with collectors today. To one who has not yet succumbed to their obvious charms, one bear seems to look very much like another. How to tell the older ones? Look for long snouts, jointed limbs, large feet, felt paws, long curving arms, and glass or shoe-button eyes. Most old bears have a humped back and are made of mohair stuffed with straw or excelsior. Cute expressions, original clothes, a nice personality, and, of course, good condition add to their value. Early Steiff bears in mint condition may go for a minimum of $100.00 per inch (for a small bear) up to $200.00 per inch (for one 20" high or larger). These are easily recognized by the trademark button within the ear. Our advisor for this category is Candace Gunther; she is listed in the Directory under California. For further information we recommend *Teddy Bears, Annalee's & Steiff Animals,* by Margaret Fox Mandel, available from Collector Books. See also Toys, Steiff.

Key: jtd — jointed

Am, mohair w/felt pads, shoe-button eyes, jtd, 1905, 12", VG ...460.00
Am, mohair w/hump, felt pads, embr face, jtd, 1915, worn, 25" ...260.00
Bing, brn/wht frosted, shoe-button eyes, rpr pads, 24", EX 2,850.00
Chad Valley, gold mohair, glass eyes, straw stuffed, 11", EX 250.00
German, brn mohair, glass eyes, pnt details, 1927, 15", EX 350.00
German, caramel mohair, shoe-button eyes, long snout, 1900s, 12" 1,250.00
German, gold mohair, glass eyes, loosely jtd, 1940s, 15", EX 200.00
German, growler, gold mohair, glass eyes, unshaved snout, 11", EX ...300.00
Hermann, beige wooly plush, glass eyes, 1950s, 13½", EX 175.00
Hermann, growler, beige mohair, glass eyes, 14", EX 165.00
Hermann, Zotty, 15" 165.00
Ideal, gold, ca 1908, 14½", EX 850.00
Schuco, AJ, brn, 3½", M 150.00
Schuco, AJ, gold, metal eyes, lg ears, 2¼" 150.00
Schuco, champagne, orig ribbon, ca 1950, 3½" 195.00
Schuco, gold mohair, 1930s, 17", M 550.00
Schuco, Tricky, yes/no, lt wear, in cowboy outfit, 8" 650.00
Schuco, yes/no, tan, glass eyes, rpl tail, 5", EX 450.00
Steiff, brn plush, linen pads, w/button, 1920s, 17", M 3,900.00
Steiff, cinnamon long mohair, shoe-button eyes, ca 1907, 20", NM 6,800.00
Steiff, Cosy Teddy, dk brn, tag/button/ribbon, 1960, 8", M 175.00
Steiff, early bendy type, caramel, all ID, 1950s, mini, M 125.00
Steiff, lt cinnamon, prof rpr pads, ca 1907, 24", EX 5,500.00
Steiff, Orig Teddy, caramel, chest tag/ribbon, 1950s, 13", NM ...500.00
Steiff, Orig Teddy, chocolate, button/tag, 1950s, 13½", M 700.00
Steiff, Orig Teddy, chocolate curly mohair, button, 1950s, 24", NM ...2,800.00
Steiff, Orig Teddy, gold, all ID, 1950s, 3½", M 325.00
Steiff, Orig Teddy, gold, w/all ID, 1950, 11", NM 675.00
Steiff, Orig Teddy, tan, w/button, ca 1950, 3½", NM 235.00
Steiff, Orig Teddy, wht silky mohair, w/button, 20", NM 1,650.00
Steiff, Petsy bear, gold, #025479, limited edition, 7" 100.00

Steiff, Somersault Bear, wht tag, 11", MIB 295.00
Steiff, Teddy Baby, honey, collar/bell, button, 1950s, 11", NM ..900.00
Steiff, Teddy Baby, wht, #029522, limited edition, 6" 95.00
Steiff, wht, glass eyes, w/button, 1920s, 5", NM 1,100.00
Steiff, wht w/rust nose, shoe-button eyes, button, 1908, 12", M ...2,400.00
Steiff, Zotty, complete ID, 1960, 6½", M 185.00
Steiff, Zotty, w/button & ribbon, ca 1950, 8", NM 225.00
Unmk, blk mohair, swivel head, glass eyes, 5-pc body, 13", EX ..400.00
Unmk, blond mohair, swivel head, squeaker, long pads, 12", EX 175.00
Unmk, frosted mohair, glass eyes, open mouth, 1940s, 21", NM 265.00
Unmk, mohair, modified hump, glass eyes, jtd, 1930s, 18", VG .485.00
Unmk (Ideal?), gold mohair, swivel head, button eyes, jtd, 18", EX ...2,500.00
Unmk Am, gold mohair, swivel head, glass eyes, oversz ears, 23", EX ...300.00
Unmk Am, gold mohair plush, glass eyes, oversz ears, 15", EX ...260.00

Telephones

Since Alexander Graham Bell's first successful telephone communication, the phone itself has undergone a complete evolution in style as well as efficiency. Early models, especially those wall types with ornately carved oak boxes, are of special interest to collectors. Also of value are the candlestick phones from the early part of the century and any related memorabilia.

Long Distance Telephone, table model, golden oak, glass panel allows view of works, 40" high, $2,750.00.

Am Electric, str shaft desk stand, 1903, 11", VG 150.00
Automatic Electric, str-shaft upright desk stand, dial, NM 250.00
Automatic Electric monophone, Bakelite, cradle type, 1920s, EX ..85.00
Cracraft, oak, wall type, complete 250.00
French, w/eavesdropper 60.00
Gray #50, pay phone, blk 400.00
Kellogg, candlestick, Bakelite & metal, blk finish, 12" 110.00
Kellogg Redbar 50.00
Leich Magneto 30.00
Manhattan Electric Intercom, walnut, 1899, 5¾x5x3½", EX 150.00
North Electric H-6, blk, 'Bogart phone,' EX 85.00
Pay phone, chrome 250.00
Stromberg, tapered desk stand, ca 1900, EX 650.00
Stromberg-Carlson, candlestick, NP head 125.00
Stromberg-Carlson intercom, blk Bakelite, EX 50.00
Stromberg-Carson, desk type, 1930s, EX 40.00
Table model, golden oak, metal plate: Long Distance, 40", EX ..2,650.00
Viaduct Mfg, 3-box wall type, Blake transmitter, 1883, EX 1,800.00
Western Electric, dial, desk stand, 1920s, 12", EX 250.00
Western Electric, oak, wall style, EX orig 275.00
Western Electric #202, blk metal cradle type, 1931, EX 120.00
Western Electric #300, red, cradle type, NM 265.00
Western Electric #500, blk cradle type, 1950s, EX 20.00
Western Electric Interphone, wall type, watch case receiver 95.00

Novelty Telephones

AC Sparkplug, figural 35.00
Airplane, Northern Telecron, 1970s 85.00
Alvin 60.00
Bart Simpson, MIB 35.00
Bozo the Clown, 1980s, MIB 75.00
Buzz Lightyear, movable arms, 16", MIB 125.00
Crest Sparkle, NMIB 50.00
Keebler Elf, NM 100.00
Kermit the Frog, touchtone, 1970s, EX 160.00
Lazy Pig, MIB 65.00
Little Green, Sprout 75.00
Mickey Mouse, Western Electric, 1976 ....175.00
Oscar Mayer Weiner, EX 65.00
Popeye figural 150.00
Snoopy, Western Electric, 1976 ....175.00
Snoopy as Joe Cool, 1980s, MIB 55.00
Super Bowl XIX, full sz football w/hand set, NM 70.00
Superman, dial, early version, M 500.00
Winnie the Pooh, sq base, M 250.00

Blue Bell Paperweights

First issued in the early 1900s, bell-shaped glass paperweights were used as 'give-aways' and/or presented to telephone company executives as tokens of appreciation. The paperweights were used to prevent stacks of papers from blowing off the desks in the days of overhead fans. Over the years they have all but vanished — some taken by retiring employees, others accidently broken. The weights came to be widely used for advertising by individual telephone companies; and as the smaller companies merged to form larger companies, more and more new paperweights were created. They were widely distributed with the opening of the first transcontinental telephone line in 1915. The bell-shaped paperweight embossed 'Opening of Trans-Pacific Service, Dec. 23, 1931,' in peacock blue glass is very rare, and the price is negotiable. In 1972 the first Pioneer bell paperweights were made to sell to raise funds for the charities the Pioneers support. This has continued to the present day. These bell paperweights have also become 'collectibles.' For further study we recommend *Blue Bell Paperweights, 1992 Revised Edition*, and its accompanying *1995 Addendum* by Jacqueline C. Linscott; she is listed in the Directory under Florida.

ABA National Convention/25th Anniversary, cobalt 200.00
Bell System, Peacock 225.00
Bell System (front/bk), Michigan Bell Telephone, Ocean Bl 35.00
Bell System (front/bk), Region 12 (base emb), ruby red 40.00
Bell System (front/bk), TPA (base emb), cobalt 35.00
Bell System (front/bk), TPA Region 12 (base emb), red carnival 50.00
Bell System (front/bk), TPA Region 15 (base emb), cobalt 40.00
Commemorating Florida's 1,000,000 Telephone, cobalt 175.00
Compliments of Clarion Kiwanis Club, ice bl ....open
Compliments of Millville Kiwanis Club, ice bl 900.00
Nebraska Telephone Co, Peacock 375.00
Nevada Bell, blk glass & etched in silver 75.00
North Louisiana Telephone Co, Peacock ....open
Opening of Trans-Pacific Service Dec 23, 1931, Peacock ....open
West Virginia Centennial 1863-1963, cobalt 160.00
Western Electric Co, (inkwell), cobalt 200.00

Related Memorabilia

Almanac, Bell Telephone, 1950 ....10.00
Booth, wood w/windows, seat, ledge, metal panels, lamp, 1950s .400.00

Coin saver, Bell Telephone, early attachment **75.00**
Phone booth, walnut **1,250.00**
Shade, pnt glass bell shape, Telephone, wht w/bl, 14", EX **300.00**

Telescopes

Antique telescopes were sold in large quantities to sailors, astronomers, voyeurs, and the military but survive in relatively few numbers because their glass lenses and brass tubes were easily damaged. Even scarcer are antique reflecting telescopes, which use a polished metal mirror to magnify the world. Telescopes used for astronomy give an inverted image, but most old telescopes were used for marine purposes and have more complicated optics that show the world right-side up. Spyglasses are smaller, hand-held telescopes that collapse into their tube and focus by drawing out the tube to the correct length. A more compact instrument, with three or four sections, is also more delicate, and sailors usually preferred a single-draw spyglass. They are almost always of brass, occasionally of nickel siver or silver plate; and usually covered with leather, or sometimes a beautiful rosewood veneer. Solid wood barrel spyglasses (with a brass draw tube) tend to be early and rare. Before the middle of the 1800s, makers put their names in elaborate script on the smallest draw tube, but as 1900 approached, most switched to plain block printing. From the WWII era, British instruments by a variety of makers are commonly found, sharing a format of a 2" objective, 30" long with three draws extended, a tapered main tube, and sometimes having low- and high-power oculars and beautiful leather cases. U.S. Navy WWII spyglasses are quite common but have outstanding optics and focus by twisting the eyepiece, which makes them weather-proof. The Quartermaster (Q.M.) 16x spyglass is 31" long, with a tapered barrel and a 2½" objective. The Officer of the Deck (O.D.D.) is a 23" cylinder with a 1½" objective. Very massive, short, brass telescopes are usually gunsights or ship equipment and have little interest to most collectors. World War II marked the first widespread use of coated optics, which can be recognized by a colored film on the objective lens. Collectible post-WWII telescopes include early refractors by Unitron or Fecker and reflectors by Cave or Questar. Modern spotting scopes often use a prism to erect the image and are of great interest if made by the best makers, including Nikon and Zeiss. Several modern makers still use lacquered brass, and many replica instruments have been produced.

A telescope with no maker's name is much less interesting than a signed instrument, and 'Made in France' is the most common mark on old spyglasses. Dollond of London made instruments for two hundred years and this is probably the most common name on antiques; but because of their important technical innovations and very high quality, Dollond telescopes are always valuable. Bardou, Paris, telescopes are also of very high quality. Bardou is another relatively common name, since they were a prolific maker for many years and their spyglasses were sold by Sears. Alvin Clark and Sons were the most prolific early American makers, in operation from the 1850s to the 1920s, and their astronomical telescopes are of great historical import.

Spyglasses are delicate instruments that were subject to severe use under all weather conditions. Cracked or deeply scratched optics are impossible to repair and lower the value considerably. Most lenses are doublets, two lenses glued together, and deteriorated cement is common. This looks like crazed glaze and is fairly difficult to repair. Dents in the tube and damaged or missing leather covering can usually be fixed. The best test of a telescope is to use it, and the image should be sharp and clear. Any accessories, eyepieces, erecting prisms, or quality cases can add significantly to value. The following prices assume that the telescope is in very good to fine condition and give the objective lens (obj.) diameter, which is the most important measurement of a telescope.

Our advisor for this category is Peter Abrahams, who studies and collects telescopes and other optics. Please contact him, especially to exchange reference material. Mr. Abrahams is listed in the Directory under Oregon. (Please include SASE with questions.)

Key:
obj — objective lens   ODD — Officer of the Deck

Typical 3" telescope, ca. 1850 – 1930, depending on name, from $800.00 to $3,500.00.

Adams, George; 2" dia, reflecting, brass cabriole tripod **2,700.00**
Bardou & Son, Paris, 4 draw, 50mm obj, 36", leather **220.00**
Bausch & Lomb, 1 draw, 17", 45mm obj, wrinkle pnt **90.00**
Brashear, brass, 3½" obj, tripod, w/eyepcs **4,000.00**
Brass, no name, spyglass, 2" obj, leather cover, $150 to **300.00**
Brass, no name, 2" obj, stand w/cabriole legs **1,200.00**
Brass, US military, complex housing, very heavy, from $100 to .**300.00**
Cary, London (script), 2" obj, tripod, w/3 eyepcs **2,200.00**
Clark, Alvan; 4" obj, 48", iron mt on wooden legs **5,000.00**
Criterion RV-6 Dynascope, 6" reflector, 1960s **500.00**
Dallmeyer, London (script), 5 draw, 2½" obj, SP, 49" **450.00**
Dollond, London (block), 2 draw, 2" obj, leather cover **270.00**
Dollond, London (script), 2 draw, 2" obj, leather cover **200.00**
Dollond, London (script), 2 draw, 2" obj, leather cover **340.00**
France or Made in France, 30mm obj, 3 draw, lens cap **80.00**
McAlister (script), brass, 3½" obj, 45", tripod **3,000.00**
Mogey, brass, 3" obj, 40", on tripod, w/4 eyepcs **2,400.00**
Negretti & Zambra, 2½" obj, 36", equatorial mt, tripod **2,200.00**
Plossl, Wien, 2½" obj, 24", table-top tripod, Dialytic optics ...**3,000.00**
Queen & Co (script), wood veneer, 70mm obj, 6 draw, 50" **650.00**
Questar, reflecting, 3½" dia, on astro mt, 1950s **1,900.00**
R&J Beck, 2" obj, 24", table-top tripod, cabriole legs **2,000.00**
Short, James; 3" dia, reflecting, brass cabriole tripod **3,000.00**
Tel Sct Regt Mk 2 S, (many makers' names), UK, WWI **120.00**
Unitron, wht, 4" obj, 60", on tripod, w/many accessories **1,800.00**
US Navy, Bu Ships, Mk II, 10-Power, 1943, (ODD) **125.00**
US Navy, QM Spyglass, 16X, MK II, in box **220.00**
Vion, Paris, 40 Power, 3 draw, 21", 40mm obj, leather **110.00**
Wollensak Mirroscope, 2" dia, 12" L, 1950s, leather case **200.00**
Wood bbl, rnd taper, 1½" obj, sgn, 1800s **300.00**
Wood bbl, 8-sided, 1½" obj, 1700s, 30" **1,500.00**
Zeiss, brass w/eps & porro prism, 60mm bbl, tripod **1,400.00**
Zeiss Asiola, 60mm obj prism spotting scope, pre-WWII **450.00**

Televisions

Many early TVs have escalated in value over the last few years. Pre-1943 sets (usually with only one to five channels) are often worth $500.00 to $5,000.00. Unusually styled small-screen wooden 1940s TVs are 'hot'; but most metal, Bakelite, and large-screen sets are still shunned by collectors. 1950s color TVs with 16" or smaller tubes are valuable; larger color sets are not. One of our advisors for this category is Harry Poster, author of *Poster's Radio & Television Price Guide 1920 – 1990, 2nd Edition*; he is listed in the Directory under New Jersey.

Key: t/t — table-top

Admiral, 1911, Bakelite, w/Chinese grill, 7" t/t, 1948	200.00
Ansley, 1949, 12" wooden t/t, continuous tuner	65.00
Arvin, #2160, simple console version of #2161, 1950	25.00
Arvin, #4080T, metal w/mahog front, 8" t/t, 1950	150.00
Automatic, TV-1649-1650, sq lines, 1950s, 16", ea	50.00
Bendix, #2001, rnded corners, 3 knobs, 1950, 10" t/t	100.00
Bush (English), w/magnifier, 1948	500.00
CBS-Columbia, #20T, wooden t/t version of #20C, 1950s	25.00
Cleervue, Regency, console w/15" tube, 4 knobs, dbl doors, 1947	75.00
Crosley, #EU-30, 30" console (actually a DuMont RA-119)	250.00
Crosley, #G-17TO, Super V, sq-lined wooden t/t, 1955	20.00
Crosley, #9-425, 7" portable, 1949	175.00
Daven, Essential TV kit, complete, 1931	1,000.00
DuMont, #RA 119, Royal Sovereign, FM radio, 30" screen, 1951	300.00
DuMont, #180-183, 14" prewar t/t, 4-channel tuner, 1937, ea	2,500.00
DuMont, Chatham, 12" trapezoidal t/t, w/radio, 1947	145.00
Emerson, #644, porthole-type screen, 12" t/t	75.00
Emerson, #662, rectangular picture tube, 14" Bakelite t/t, 1950	25.00
Fada, #965, 16" console version of model #930	55.00
General Electric, #HM-185, 5" console, 3-channel tuner, 1938	4,000.00
General Electric, #835, 10" t/t, metal mesh grill	50.00
General Electric, #901, projection TV, radio, phono, 18x24", 1946	300.00
Hallicrafters, #T505, blond ext, 7" screen, 1947	150.00
Hallicrafters, #860, 16" combination w/dbl doors, 1950, lg	50.00
HMV (English), #907, radio, 9" screen, minimum value	4,000.00
Motorola, #VF-103, 10" combination, 12-channel tuner, 1948	100.00
Motorola, #VT-71, 7" wooden t/t, ltweight, 1948	75.00
Motorola, #19P1 Astronaut, all transistor, 19" screen, 1961	150.00
Motorola, #21P1, 21" metal t/t, flip-up controls on top, 159	35.00
National, #TV 7M, 7" metal t/t, 6 knobs, 1949	225.00
Olympic, #TV-947, 16" console, dbl doors, 1950	25.00
Philco, #H-2010 Safari, 1st transistor, 2" screen, 1960	150.00
Philco, #49-702, 7" wooden t/t, peaked cabinet	175.00
RCA, #TLS-86, projection TV, tube/controls on top, 1946	150.00
RCA, #TT5, 5" t/t, 5-channel tuner, no sound, 1939	3,500.00
RCA, #621 TS, walnut cabinet, 7" screen, 1946	400.00
RCA, #630 TS, 1st postwar set mass produced, 10 screen, 1946	250.00
RCA, #8T270, 1st 16" t/t, 1949	50.00
Scott, #6T11, projection TV, 1949	300.00
Sentinal, #431-CV, console, dbl doors, 1951	15.00
Silvertone, #101, 12" t/t, sq-lined cabinet, 1950	35.00
Sparton, #4964, 16" picture tube, dbl-door console, 1949	50.00
Stromberg Carlson, #TC 10H, Manhattan porthole, 10" screen, 1958	125.00
Stromberg Carlson, #TC-125-LA, 12" console, 1949	85.00
Sylvania, #245, 12" console, 4 low knobs, 1950	35.00
Western Television, #V-00151, scanning disk, 1928, minimum value	2,500.00
Westinghouse, #H-181, 10" dbl-door highboy, 4-leg, 1948	125.00
Zenith, #27F20, Broadmoor, 12" screen, 1948	200.00

Philco Predictas and Related Items

In the late 1950s Philco needed to give consumers a compelling reason to buy a new television set. By adding the atom-age styling of the day, the Predicta line of televisions was born. Made in the years between 1958 – 1960, the Philco Predicta has become the icon for television of the modern age. Predicta televisions feature swivel or separate picture tubes and very radical designs. The values given here are for as-found, average, clean, complete, unrestored sets, running or not, that have good picture tubes. Picture tubes that can not be proven good or

are known to be bad can cost up to $375.00 to replace. Predictas that have damaged viewing screens or missing parts will have a lower value. Our advisor for Predicta televisions is David Weddington; he is listed in the Directory under Tennessee.

G4242 Holiday, 21" table-top, wood cabinet with mahogany finish, $325.00.

Photo courtesy David Weddington

G4242 Holiday, 21" t/t, wood cabinet, blond finish	375.00
G4654 Barber-Pole, 21" console, bomerang front leg, mahog	500.00
G4654 Barber-Pole, 21" console, boomerang front leg, blond	600.00
G4710 Tandem, 21" separate screen w/25' cable, blond finish	525.00
G4720 Stereo Tandem, 21" separate screen, 4 brass legs, mahog	600.00
G4720 Stereo Tandem, 21" w/matching 1606S phono/amp, mahog	900.00
H3406 Motel, 17" t/t, metal cabinet, cloth grill, no antenna	275.00
H3408 Debutante, 17" t/t, cloth grill, antenna, UHF, charcoal	300.00
H3410 Princess, 17" t/t, metal grill, plastic tuner window	325.00
H3410 Princess, 17" t/t, orig metal stand, brn finish	400.00
H3412 Siesta, 17" t/t, w/clock-timer above tuner, gold finish	400.00
H4730 Danish Modern, 21" console, 4 fin-shaped legs, mahog finish	700.00
H4730 Danish Modern, 21" console, 4 fin-shaped legs, walnut finish	750.00
H4744 Townhouse, 21" room-divider, walnut shelves, brass finish	850.00
Stand, orig, for 17" t/t, brass finish w/blk wood shelf	125.00
Stand, tubular steel, for 21" t/t, brass finish	125.00
Stand, wood, for 21" t/t, mahog finish	150.00
17 DRP4 picture tube, 17" t/t Predicta replacement, MIB	125.00
21EAP4 or 21FDP4 picture tube, 21" Predicta replacement, MIB	175.00

Teplitz

Teplitz, in Bohemia, was an active art pottery center at the turn of the century. The Amphora Pottery Works was only one of the firms that operated there. (See Amphora.) Art Nouveau and Art Deco styles were favored, and much of the ware was hand decorated with the primary emphasis on vases and figurines. Items listed here are marked 'Teplitz' or 'Turn,' a nearby city. Our advisor for this category is Jack Gunsaulus; he is listed in the Directory under Michigan.

Basket, floral on bl irid, dbl hdls, Stellmacher, #d, 4¼"	150.00
Basket, floral on gr w/gold, dbl hdls, ornate, 6x8"	295.00
Bust, Cancan dancer, porc, realistic, 19½"	600.00
Bust, lady, beige & tans, rtcl at shoulders, sgn, mk, 14"	1,800.00
Bust, lady w/long hair on cobalt & gold floral base, 23", EX	1,500.00
Bust, lady w/upswept hair, lace/ribbons/gold trim, red mk, 14"	1,400.00
Chocolate pot, emb tomatoes, Ernst Wahliss	295.00
Compote, draped women w/fruit basket, 2-pc, mk, 15x10"	550.00
Ewer, mums w/gold, dragon hdl, pear shape, 16x8"	630.00
Ewer vase, mc florals w/gold, goldfish lip, beaded hdl, 11x5"	380.00
Vase, bird pecking at web, gold leaves, dolphin hdls, 9½", EX	100.00

Vase, floral, rtcl rim & hdls, waisted, mk, 9½x5", pr, EX **400.00**
Vase, floral on bl, 9½" **70.00**
Vase, florals w/gold on pastel, bullet shape, mk, 13x4½" **325.00**
Vase, lady, gold on turq flower form, Wahliss, 12½" **865.00**
Vase, lady's portrait on bl/gr/purple irid, 9" **385.00**
Vase, pk bouquet, cut-out leaf rim, gold scroll hdls, 8½" **325.00**
Vase, poppies/flowers, branch hdls, cobalt at shoulder, 9½" **100.00**

Terra Cotta

Terra cotta is a type of earthenware or clay used for statuary, architectural facings, or domestic articles. It is unglazed, baked to durable hardness, and characterized by the color of the body which may range from brick red to buff.

Sculpture, draped nude on craggy pedestal, signed Moreau, 1880, 34", $1,500.00.

Bust, Classical maiden, WW Ines, London/1826, 27" **2,000.00**
Bust, Louis XVI, Fr, 18th C, 22" **1,500.00**
Humidor, devil bust on bbl, mk JM 3465, 7½" **350.00**
Jar, storage; incised geometrics at rim, 20x26" **110.00**
Jar, storage; overall banding, 35x22" **175.00**
Jar, storage; 3 wide hdls, banding at center, 25x27" **155.00**
Match box, African head form, worn mc pnt, w/lid, rpr, 5" **110.00**
Sculpture, man sitting, multi-tone brn matt, unmk, 12x12", EX ...**200.00**
Sculpture, man struggling w/boulder, H Bargas, 12x20" **1,600.00**
Sculpture, putto, A Bruges, unglazed in skin tones, 10" **425.00**
Shelves, gr glaze, Baroque taste, mermaid supports, 20", pr **745.00**
Tile, roof; modeled w/classical head, 9½" H, pr **165.00**
Urn, bl glazed, fleur-de-lis in relief, borders, 32x31", pr **2,200.00**

Thermometers

Few objects man has invented have been so eloquently expressed both functionally and artistically as the ubiquitous thermometer. Developed initially by Galileo as a scientific device, thermometers slowly evolved into decorative objet d'art, functional household utensils, and eye-catching advertising specialties. Most American thermometers manufactured early in the 20th century were produced by Taylor (Tycos), and today their thermometers remain the most plentiful on the market. Decorative thermometers manufactured before 1800 are now ensconced in the permanent collections of approximately a dozen European museums. Because of their fragility, few devices of this era have survived in private collections. Nowadays most antique thermometers find their way to market through estate sales.

Insofar as sheer beauty, uniqueness, and scientific accuracy, decorative thermometers are far superior to the ordinary and inexpensive versions which carry advertising. Decorative thermometers run the gamut from plain tin household varieties to the highly ornate creations of Tiffany and Bradley and Hubbard. They have been manufactured from nearly every conceivable material — oak, sterling, brass, and glass being the favorites — and have tested the artistry and technical skills of some of America's finest craftsmen. Ornamental models can be found in free-hanging, wall-mounted, or desk/mantel versions.

Since 1994 prices have been escalating at a rate of 35% annually. This is due to their relative scarcity, infrequent trading, and absence of a 'knock-off' (retro) market. Look for this trend to continue indefinitely.

Thermometer prices are based on age, ornateness, and whether mercury or alcohol is used as the filler in the tube. A broken or missing tube will cut at least 40% off the value. Virtually all American-made thermometers available today as collectors' items were made between 1875 and 1940. The Golden Age of decoratives ended in the early 1940s as modern manufacturing processes and materials robbed them of their natural distinctiveness.

Key:
br — brass
Cen — Centigrade
Fah — Fahrenheit
mrc — mercury in tube
pmc — permacolor
R — rare
Rea — Reaumer
sc — scale
stl — stainless
strl — sterling
VR — very rare

Amadio, Fah, Corn Hill, desk, ivory pillar/compass, mrc, 1890, 10" **850.00**
Anonymous, cvd wood squirrel, glass Rea sc, mrc, 1905, 10" **800.00**
Anonymous, desk, br conquistador figural, br sc, mrc **650.00**
Anonymous, desk, love scene, silver metal, br Rea/Cen sc, mrc, 8" **830.00**
Anonymous, wall, giltwood fr, ivory, Fah sc, mrc, 1790, 10x3½" **3,100.00**
Blk/Starr/Frost, desk, barometer, stl, Fah/Cen, mrc, '10, 11" **2,200.00**
Bradley & Hubbard, desk, br fr & Fah sc, mrc, 1895, 13x6" **2,800.00**
Calley, desk, strl inkwell fr, porc Rea sc, mrc, 1899, 5x6" **3,200.00**
Capendium, desk, handmade br/porc fr, Fah/Cen sc, rnd mrc, 4" ..**850.00**
Carpenter & Westley, desk, ivory w/glass dome mrc, 1880, 6" ...**950.00**
Casella London, wall, maxi/minimum, 2 units, wood, plastic sc .**430.00**
Cheshire Silversmiths, desk, br candelabra, mrc, 1875, 10" **4,500.00**
Chevallier, L'ingre, wall, ivory/mahog, Rea/Cen sc, 1880, 11x3" ..**2,350.00**
Clark, desk, ivory ped, crown, mrc, 1904, 7" **400.00**
Cloister, inkwell, stl bk & base w/angels at side, 1901 ....**1,050.00**
Creswel, travel, ivory case/mirror, removable sc, mrc, 2½" **2,800.00**
CW Wilder...NH, desk, Deco women, br Fah sc, mrc, R, 8" ...**1,300.00**
Desk, cvd walrus tusk, 2-tier disk base, inlay sc, 1860, 9" **430.00**
Diamond, wall, br Fah sc on wood, R, 7½x1½" **525.00**
Dixie, W (London); desk, gilt/br, Gothic, SP sc, mrc, 8" **790.00**
Dollard London, desk, strl, br sc, mrc, 1908, R, 6" **750.00**
Dollard London, hanging, mahog fr, strl sc, mrc, 1810, 18" **4,600.00**
Dring & Fage, desk, marble, ivory sc, mrc, 1880, 6" **1,500.00**
Farley, travel, walnut base mt, ivory Fah/Cen sc, mrc, 5" **900.00**
Freeborn, desk, bronze w/3 lead decor, br sc, mrc, 8" **180.00**
G Cooper, desk, bell shape w/cupola, strl, dial, 2x3" **400.00**
Gilbert & Co, travel, silver eng sc, mrc, 1850, 8" **630.00**
Gloucenter Scientific, stl case, glass front, pmc, 42" **1,500.00**
Heath & Wing, figural calendar, br w/porc sc, mrc, 1870 ....**930.00**
J Waldstein, wall, br Rea sc on wood, mrc, 1900s, VR, 10½" **920.00**
Kendal, desk, strl obelisk, br Fah sc, mrc, 1890, 8", $1,350 to .**1,850.00**
Moreau, desk, mahog, Rea/Cen, spiral tube, mrc, 1860, 6½x5½" .**1,725.00**
Pairpoint, desk, strl picture fr, mrc, 1907, 5" **650.00**
Reau, desk, sq incline base, floral top, mrc, 1895 ....**180.00**
Rowley & Sons, travel, ivory sc, mrc, 1894, 4", +case **350.00**
Standard, wall, ivory Fah sc on ebony, mrc, 9" **750.00**
Standard..., wall, br fr, enamel dial Fah sc, 1885, 9" dia **950.00**
Taylor, ped, 3-sided, Fah sc, alcohol, 1900, R, 6" **3,200.00**
Thermindex Switzerland, desk, Bakelite stand, Fah sc, 5" **725.00**
Tiffany, desk, strl tetrahedron fr & Fah sc, mrc, 1910, 2x4" **4,000.00**
Tiffany, gr glass w/pine needles, br sc/mrc, '02, 8x12" **2,800.00**

Tycos, maxi/minimum, japanned tin/br, mrc, T-5452, 8" **125.00**
Unknown, cvd wood squirrel, glass Rea sc, mrc, 1905, VR, 10" ..**800.00**
Unknown, desk, alabaster w/eagle, Rea/Cen sc, mrc, 1895 ....**875.00**
Unknown, desk, br conquistador figural, br sc, mrc **650.00**
Unknown, desk, love scene, silver metal, br Rea/Cen sc, mrc, 8" ...**830.00**
Unknown, Engalnd, wall, br game bag fr, Fah sc, mrc, 1890, 9x5" .**1,650.00**
Unknown, England, desk, glass obelisk/8-sided, br Fah sc, mrc, 1880 ..**1,259.99**
Unknown, England, desk, marble ped fr, Cen, mrc, 1885, 6½" ..**930.00**
Unknown, England, wall, rect wood fr, porc Cen sc, mrc, 1905, 5" ..**1,350.00**
Unknown, pendant, strl case, ivory Fah sc, mrc, 1880, 5" ..**1,250.00**
Unknown, wall, giltwood fr, ivory Fah sc, 1790, 10x3½" **3,100.00**
VJD Inc, wall, clip Fah br sc, mrc, VR, 4" **1,650.00**
W Pratt, desk, wood inlays, ivory sc, mrc, 1900, 6" **350.00**
Warren Foundries, wall, umbrella w/dragon hdl, br sc, mrc, 12" .**220.00**
West, desk, Gothic design, br, 1900, 12" **1,360.00**
WG Loveday, wall, Clearside, Fah sc, 5" dia **725.00**
Whitehead & Hoag, Lambrecht's Polymeter, mrc, 9" **1,200.00**
Zeradatha, desk, cast metal w/rotate sc, 1926, 7" **140.00**

1000 Faces China

So named because of its many hand-painted faces, much of this chinaware was made during the '30s through the '50s (some even earlier). Though many pieces are unmarked, others are marked 'Made in Japan.' There are two primary patterns, 'Black Face' and the 'Gold' pattern, and variations exist. Both designs employ many colors. Dinner plates usually are decorated with an outer-most 'ring of color' (two or three hues) containing a simple design which is often flowers. The inner ring is usually comprised of many colors radiating from the center circle which may be done in a primary color (red, for instance) with a design such as a dragon or clouds painted in gold. 'Black Face' is distinguishable by its range of colors — primarily red, white, and yellow with some green and blue — and the black hand-painted faces. The 'Gold' pattern is also multicolored but is dominated by the gold throughout the design, and the faces themselves are gold as well. Other variations include '1000 Men in Robes' and '1000 Faces' with black or blue rims on the saucers and cups. These pieces seem to be very scarce. In the listings that follow, all items are marked 'Made in Japan' (MIJ) unless noted otherwise. Our advisor for this category is Suzi Hibbard; she is listed in the Directory under California.

Bowl, gold faces, petal shape, 6" **20.00**
Cup & saucer, blk faces **40.00**
Cup & saucer, demitasse; gold faces **25.00**
Cup & saucer, gold faces, from $30 to **50.00**
Cup & saucer, 1000 Geishas, MIJ **40.00**
Egg cup, bl faces **20.00**
Ginger jar, gold faces, from $75 to **100.00**
Lamp, gold faces, 8" vase base **125.00**
Plate, blk/gold, 6" **10.00**
Salt cellar, bl faces, from $5 to **10.00**
Shakers, bl faces, pr **20.00**
Shakers, gold faces, pr **20.00**
Snack set, blk faces, kidney shape **45.00**
Sweetmeat, blk faces, 9-pc set in lacquer box **175.00**
Sweetmeat set, gold faces, 15-pc, serves 6 ....**175.00**
Tea set, blk faces, 15-pc, serves 6 ....**175.00**
Tea set, demitasse; bl faces, 15-pc **125.00**
Tea set, gold faces, 21-pc, MIJ **225.00**
Teapot, gold faces, dragon spout, 7" **50.00**
Teapot, Men in Robes, 6-sided, Japanese mk **45.00**
Teapot, 1000 Geishas, dragon spout **55.00**
Vase, blk faces, MIJ, 8" **60.00**

Vase, gold, 8", from $75 to **100.00**

Tiffany

Louis Comfort Tiffany was born in 1848 to Charles Lewis and Harriet Young Tiffany of New York. By the time he was eighteen, his father's small dry goods and stationery store had grown and developed into the world-renowned Tiffany and Company. Preferring the study of art to joining his father in the family business, Louis spent the next six years under the tutelage of noted artists. He returned to America in 1870 and until 1875 painted canvases that focused on European and North African scenes. Deciding the more lucrative approach was in the application of industrial arts and crafts, he opened a decorating studio called Louis C. Tiffany and Co., Associated Artists. He began seriously experimenting with glass, and eschewing traditionally painted-on details, he instead learned to produce glass with qualities that could suggest natural textures and effects. His experiments broadened, and he soon concentrated his efforts on vases, bowls, etc., that came to be considered the highest achievements of the art. Peacock feathers, leaves and vines, flowers, and abstracts were developed within the plane of the glass as it was blown. Opalescent and metallic lustres were combined with transparent color to produce stunning effects. Tiffany called his glass Favrile, meaning handmade.

In 1900 he established Tiffany Studios and turned his attention full time to producing art glass, leaded-glass lamp shades and windows, and household wares with metal components. He also designed a complete line of jewelry which was sold through his father's store. He became proficiently accomplished in silverwork and produced such articles as hand mirrors embellished with peacock feather designs set with gems and candlesticks with Favrile glass inserts.

Tiffany's work exemplified the Art Nouveau style of design and decoration, and through his own flamboyant personality and business acumen he perpetrated his tastes onto the American market to the extent that his name became a household word. Tiffany Studios continued to prosper until the second decade of this century when due to changing tastes his influence began to diminish. By the early 1930s the company had closed.

Serial numbers were assigned to much of Tiffany's work, and letter prefixes indicated the year of manufacture: A – N for 1896 – 1900, P – Z for 1901 – 1905. After that, the letter followed the numbers with A – N in use from 1906 – 1912; P – Z from 1913 – 1920. O-marked pieces were made especially for friends and relatives; X indicated pieces not made for sale.

Our listings are primarily from the auction houses in the East where Tiffany sells at a premium. All pieces are signed unless noted otherwise.

Glass

Snuff box, vertically striped and iridized amber with shoulder loops, matching glass stopper, copper-colored metal rim and hinged lid, #09105 and paper label on base, 3", $1,955.00.

Basket, gr w/wht opal Dmn Quilt, vaseline base, HP decor, 7x8" ...**1,000.00**
Bottle, scent; King Tut, gold on ivory w/bl irid, gold lid, 7½" **950.00**

Bowl, amber w/violet irid, ribbed, scalloped, sm ft, 6⅜" **400.00**
Bowl, bl irid, yel-gr int w/lime opal vines, #5016M, 11" **1,250.00**
Bowl, canary yel to wht opaque to clear, ribbed, low ft, 8⅛" **975.00**
Bowl, gold & bl irid to clear w/overall dimples, 2¼x6¾" **400.00**
Bowl, gold w/mc irid, twisted rim, 3x8" **400.00**
Bowl, gold w/mc irid, twisted wide rim, 3½x10", NM **650.00**
Bowl, intaglio ivy vines, bl/pk/gold irid, 7" **900.00**
Bowl, lemon yel w/wht opal pulls to center, 2½x8½" **635.00**
Bowl, peacock bl irid, ribbed, #X308, 1¼x6½" **450.00**
Bowl, red-gold w/stretch rim, gold bronze ft, #500, 11½" **1,000.00**
Box, blown artichoke style, gold irid w/bl-purple irid, 5¼" **300.00**
Candlestick/vase, lt gr, hollow-blown paperweight type, 10½" ..**450.00**
Candlesticks, gr opal w/wht opal striped base, 6x3¾", pr **2,250.00**
Candlesticks, gr slag w/vintage metal o/l, 10½", pr **300.00**
Candlesticks, pk pastel, reeded opal stems, 7", pr **950.00**
Champagne, gold irid, thin stem, 5½" **285.00**
Champagne, vintage cuttings, gold w/bl irid, 3½x4" **350.00**
Champagne, yel to dk gr opal irid, #1806, 5x4", NM **350.00**
Compote, amber w/violet irid, shallow, scalloped, 4¼" **750.00**
Compote, gold irid, ribbed base, rolled rim, #1847, 4x8½" **950.00**
Compote, gold irid w/bl/purple irid, mirror base, 2x6" **550.00**
Compote, nut; gold irid, gold stretched ruffle, baluster stem **500.00**
Compote, pastel pk irid w/opal leaves, #1700, 3¼x5¼" **750.00**
Cup & saucer, gold irid, 7 lg appl lily pads & stems at ft **425.00**
Decanter, Flemish, amber w/violet irid, slim neck, #R3331, 8" ..**400.00**
Finger bowl, gold irid, w/underplate, 3x6½" **575.00**
Letter seal, scarab w/initial on hdl, gold w/bl irid, 1½" L **150.00**
Plate, gr pastel irid, stretched edge, 10½" **600.00**
Salt cellar, gold w/purple/bl irid, 1¼x2" **225.00**
Shot glass/toothpick holder, rose gold irid, dimpled, 1¾" **135.00**
Tazza, peacock bl w/purple irid, domed ft, 5½x10" **2,250.00**
Vase, amber w/textured & spotted surface, #8343, 4" **1,000.00**
Vase, bl irid, shouldered ovoid, #5378, 12" **2,585.00**
Vase, bl irid, w/lid, #6988N, 9" **1,200.00**
Vase, butterfly bl irid, gourd shape, #6333G, 4¼x4" **800.00**
Vase, emerald gr w/yel-almond int, #118L, 10" **1,350.00**
Vase, feathers, jade gr on gold w/purple irid, #2413, 3¼" **1,250.00**
Vase, feathers, red on bottle gr, #X1284, stain, 6x4¼" **1,000.00**
Vase, feathers, yel/gr/orange w/mc irid, copper base, 16" **1,600.00**
Vase, floriform; gold irid, #4008B, label, 10½x5" **2,650.00**
Vase, floriform; gold irid, tricorner rim, #CT112, 14¾" **3,000.00**
Vase, floriform; leaves, gr on gold irid, #W3254, 10½" **3,750.00**
Vase, flowers, wht opal/caramel on gold w/purple irid, #1570B, 7" **4,300.00**
Vase, gild irid, bulbous, 4¾x3½", NM **400.00**
Vase, gold irid, full sgn, 2½x1¾" **300.00**
Vase, gold irid, ruffled/stretched rim, 4 pulled ft, #7633A, 3½" ..**350.00**
Vase, gold irid millefiori/opal flowers/gr leaves, #W3926, 3½" ..**1,550.00**
Vase, gold irid trumpet form, #5780, 11" **700.00**
Vase, gold irid w/20 heart-shaped gr leaves, #4112, 3x3½" **900.00**
Vase, gold w/mc irid, ribbed bottle form, #W7609, 7¼x3½" **725.00**
Vase, gold w/violet irid, swollen ovoid w/short neck, #1051, 20" .**3,450.00**
Vase, gold w/violet irid, waisted baluster, #1974, 12⅜" **1,600.00**
Vase, gr/wht/gray granite w/gr/irid/gold streaks, #R1773, 3⅜" .**3,565.00**
Vase, intaglio ivy & insect, gr on amber irid, #6542, 9¼" **2,185.00**
Vase, jack-in-pulpit; gold irid, #Y946, 15½" **5,500.00**
Vase, jack-in-pulpit; leaves, opal on red-gold, #W7296, 15", NM ..**3,000.00**
Vase, leaf tips, gr & gold on gold irid, cast stem, #1043, 12" **2,185.00**
Vase, leaves at base, dk gr on gold, #621J, 7¾" **750.00**
Vase, mustard yel opal, ovoid w/int ribs, 10x5" **800.00**
Vase, pastel oyster wht to pale vaseline, 2x2½" **575.00**
Vase, peacock bl, ribbed trumpet form, #1528 972N, 16½" **2,500.00**
Vase, peacock eyes on purple/gr/bl irid, #L645, 7x5½" **2,400.00**
Vase, peonies/leaves, burgundy/gr on frosted, ovoid, 9⅞" **10,350.00**
Vase, pulled decor, dk gr/gold on gr irid, mushroom form, 2¼" ..**900.00**

Vase, wht opal irid, 2 pulled hdls, #8094A/label, 3¼x3½" **700.00**
Vase, yel & wht stripes, flared rim, #1886, 9½" **550.00**
Whiskey taster/toothpick holder, gold w/purple irid, 1¾x1½" ...**200.00**
Wine, gold irid, cut/notched base/stem/bowl, 3¾", 4 for **1,150.00**

Lamps

Lamp prices seem to be getting stronger, especially for leaded lamps with lighter colors (red, blue, purple). Bases that are unusual or rare have brought good prices and added to the value of the more common shades that sold on them. Bases with enamel or glass inserts are very much in demand. Our advisor for Tiffany lamps is Carl Heck; he is listed in the Directory under Colorado.

Key: c-b — counter-balance

Table lamp, 16" dogwood flower-band shade signed Tiffany Studios; three-arm Nouveau #25778 standard with original green-brown patina, 18", EX, from $10,000.00 to $12,000.00.

Boudoir, 9" yel-amber linenfold dome shade; disk std, 18" **3,750.00**
Candle, bl butterfly shade; 3-part, 11½", EX **1,850.00**
Candle, gold, honeycomb gold irid shade, gr/wht column, 14½" ..**1,600.00**
Candle, gr/bl ruffled shade, bl base, gr/wht brass column, 14" .**2,000.00**
Candle, mica/metal pine needle shade; glass stem, sgn std, 16" ..**3,750.00**
Chandelier, 4 tulip shades; brass fixture, 14x9" **2,300.00**
Desk, damascene mc swirl 7⅛" shade; c-b bronzed std, 12½" ..**6,500.00**
Desk, ldgl Nautilus shade; mk bronze std, 13", EX **6,000.00**
Floor, damascene 10" shade; #682 harp std, 56" **6,850.00**
Floor, gold 10" shade w/pk irid; gold dore std, 56" **4,000.00**
Floor, wht frosted shade w/purple threads; leafy c-b std, 54" **2,600.00**
Mini, gold irid w/wht & gr bands, electric, sgn, 10½x6" **2,550.00**
Table, cased 10" red w/silver feathers shade; matching base, 16" **13,500.00**
Table, ldgl 14" acorn-band shade; mk std, 18½", EX **6,000.00**
Table, ldgl 14" daffodil shade; mk mushroom std, 18" **17,000.00**
Table, ldgl 15" spider web #1424 shade; mushroom std, 18" ..**20,500.00**
Table, ldgl 16" acorn-band dome shade; urn-form std, 22" **6,500.00**
Table, ldgl 16" apple blossom shade; tapered #584 std, 21" ...**16,000.00**
Table, ldgl 16" crocus mk shade; repro #6846 std, 21" **8,625.00**
Table, ldgl 16" geometric shade; #444 std, 21¼" **3,165.00**
Table, ldgl 16" gridwork panels w/geometric border; mk std, 22" ..**5,000.00**
Table, ldgl 16" pansy shade; 3-arm #26530 std, 19" **27,500.00**
Table, ldgl 16" pomegranate #1457 shade; #534 baluster std, 23" **7,000.00**
Table, ldgl 16" pomegranate border shade; #538 std, 22" **5,500.00**
Table, ldgl 16" swirling leaf shade; #444 std, 22" **7,000.00**
Table, ldgl 18" lemon-leaf shade; jonquil base mk Grueby, 22" ...**10,000.00**
Table, ldgl 18" swirling leaf #1474 shade; #440 urn std **8,625.00**
Table, ldgl 21½" Harvard emblems shade; 4 Virtues std, 24" ..**3,500.00**
Table, linenfold 14" gr frosted shade; #585 std, 20", EX **2,300.00**

Table, linenfold 19" yel-amber conical shade; #534 std, 22" ...**6,500.00**

Metal Work

Items are bronze unless noted otherwise.

Blotter, gr & bl jewels, #1628, 5½x2¾", EX **175.00**
Blotter, Zodiac, 5½x2¾" **175.00**
Bookends, owl heads, mk, cast by Griffoul Newark NY, 5⅛", pr ...**550.00**
Box, jewel; Chinese, gr-brn patina, mirror in lid, 2½" **1,200.00**
Box, Treasure Chest, domed hinged lid, gold dore, #1666, 8" **950.00**
Candelabrum, brn patina, 2-socket w/gr glass inserts, mk, 9" ..**3,565.00**
Candlestick, bud-like cup w/gr opaque insert, #1301, 20" **1,380.00**
Candlestick, root-form base w/glass balls at rim, #1228, 14½" ..**4,600.00**
Candlesticks, bud-like cup w/gr opaque insert, 18", pr **1,800.00**
Candlesticks, gr blown cups on gr-brn stem, #1213 base, 17", pr ..**2,200.00**
Cigarette/match holder, emb sailing ships, brass ped, #302, 5½" ..**100.00**
Desk pcs, Zodiac, lg inkstand & paper rack, #1073/#1009 ....**525.00**
Desk set, Adam, rack/2 blotter ends, HP decor, 3-pc **575.00**
Desk set, Pine Needle, inkwell/box/fr/blotter/tray/etc, 7-pc **1,250.00**
Desk set, Zodiac, tray/inkstand/bookends +8 pcs **1,950.00**
Figurine, bulldog, prone w/ears up, #933, 2" **345.00**
Frame, Chinese pattern, 9x6¾" **900.00**
Frame, Grapvine, dbl, hinged, ea fr: 9¼x8" **975.00**
Frame, Grapevine on gr, 2 oval openings, 7½x10¼" **1,700.00**
Frame, Pine Needle on mc mottled glass, #916, 14x12" **2,000.00**
Frame, spider web on gr glass, 7½x6½" **1,100.00**
Frame, Zodiac, cleaned patina, #942, 8x7", VG **600.00**
Inkstand, red-brn patina w/cut-out floral/gr glass, #d, 4x7" **2,500.00**
Inkstand, Venetian, ermine border, 2⅝x3x3" **400.00**
Inkwell, bronze filigree branch & leaf, gr slag insert, 3¾x4¼" **400.00**
Inkwell, Grapevine, gr slag inserts, hinged cap, #843, 3x3¼" **500.00**
Inkwell, Zodiac, heavy scrollwork, glass liner, #1072, 3¾x7" **425.00**
Letter opener, bronze blade, bl irid glass hdl **235.00**
Match stand, Zodiac, on disk tray, #1041, 4" H **200.00**
Paper clip, Southwest Indian influence, rectangular, 4x2½" ...**2,000.00**
Paper rack, Zodiac, 3-tier, 8⅜x12¼" **430.00**
Trays, ribbed nesting group of 4, lg: 3½x5½" **865.00**

Silver

Bowl, branch-form base, 4x8½", 24-t-oz **1,100.00**
Bowl, scalloped edge, hammered finish, 2x7¼", 14-troy-oz **700.00**
Coffee set, neoclassical taste, ca 1900, 3-pc+teapot/waste bowl **6,000.00**
Dessert spoons, Olympian, vermeil, 15 for **920.00**
Dessert stand, grapes/roses, monogram, ftd, 1875-91, 4¾x10" **925.00**
Dish, Indian Basket, cast & chased, 6" **1,750.00**
Flatware, Flemish, monogram, 120 place pcs+4 serving pcs **5,175.00**
Flatware, Old English w/Bright Cut decor, vermeil, 47-pc **1,725.00**
Tazza, Japanese taste, gilt bowl on ped, appl bands, 5½x13" ...**1,500.00**

Tiffin Glass

The Tiffin Glass Company was founded in 1887 in Tiffin, Ohio, one of the many factories composing the U.S. Glass Company. Its early wares consisted of tablewares and decorative items such as lamps and globes. Among the most popular of all Tiffin products was the black satin glass produced there during the 1920s. In 1959 U.S. Glass was sold, and in 1962 the factories closed. The plant was re-opened in 1963 as the Tiffin Art Glass Company. Products from this period were tableware, hand-blown stemware, and other decorative items.

Those interested in learning more about Tiffin glass are encouraged to contact the Tiffin Glass Collectors' Club, whose address can be found in the Directory under Clubs, Newsletters, and Catalogs. See also Black Glass; Glass Animals.

Water set, aquamarine craquelle, 7-piece set, $165.00.

Ashtray, Fuchsia, w/cigarette rest, 2¼x3¾" **30.00**
Ashtray, Twilight, cloverleaf form, #9123/96, 3" **25.00**
Ashtray, Twilight, cloverleaf form, #9123/97, 5" **45.00**
Basket, Twilight, 9x5½" **295.00**
Bowl, bouillon; Flanders, hdls **40.00**
Bowl, Cellini, crystal & bl, cut, #6067, 6" **175.00**
Bowl, centerpc; Fontaine, gr, 13" **90.00**
Bowl, Classic, hdls, 8x9¼" **110.00**
Bowl, console; amber, #15328, w/pr 8" candlesticks **100.00**
Bowl, cream soup; Cadena **30.00**
Bowl, finger; Cherokee Rose, 5" **35.00**
Bowl, finger; June Night, 5" **30.00**
Bowl, Flanders, hdls #5831, 8⅜" **55.00**
Bowl, June Night, crimped, 12" **75.00**
Bowl, pickle; Cadena, pk or yel, 10" **35.00**
Bowl, salad; Cherokee Rose, deep, 10" **65.00**
Bowl, wishbone; Twilight, ftd, 6½" **135.00**
Cake plate, Cherokee Rose, center hdl, 12½" **125.00**
Candlesticks, #6460, 13½", pr **150.00**
Candlesticks, bl & crystal, low, #17350, pr **75.00**
Candlesticks, Cellini, bl & crystal, #17423, pr **125.00**
Candy comport, #6355 ....**95.00**
Candy jar, Cellini, #17423 ....**125.00**
Candy jar, Flanders, pk, w/lid, flat **325.00**
Celery, June Night, oblong, 10½" **45.00**
Comport, Fuchsia, #5831, 6¼" **125.00**
Comport, Persian Pheasant, blown, 6" **100.00**
Cornucopia, Twilight, Swirl, #6041 ....**245.00**
Creamer, Classic, pk, flat **55.00**
Creamer, Flanders, yel, flat **80.00**
Creamer & sugar bowl, Kilarney & crystal, #6259 ....**175.00**
Creamer & sugar bowl, plain, #5811 ....**45.00**
Cup, Cadena **25.00**
Cup & saucer, Flanders, pk **125.00**
Cup & saucer, Fontaine, Twilight, blown **125.00**
Jug, martini; Twilight, 11½" **350.00**
Lamp, hurricane; Twilight, #17430 ....**250.00**
Magnum, Paulina, #14199 ....**22.00**
Nut cup, Flanders, pk, ftd, blown **65.00**
Pitcher, Cadena, pk or yel, ftd **250.00**
Pitcher, crystal & cut, bubble ball stem, #5961, rare **195.00**
Pitcher, Enchanted, #17477, water sz **18.00**
Pitcher, Twilight, milk sz **250.00**
Plate, bread & butter; Fuchsia, #5902, 6¼" **10.00**
Plate, bread & butter; La Fleur, topaz, 6" **9.00**
Plate, champagne liner; Classic, 6⅜" **10.00**
Plate, dinner; Cadena, yel, 9¼" **40.00**
Plate, dinner; Fuchsia, #5902, 9½" **55.00**

Plate, dinner; Juno, yel, 9½" 40.00
Plate, lily; Cerise, 13" 65.00
Plate, luncheon; Cherokee Rose, 8" 18.50
Plate, luncheon; Flanders, pk, 8" 20.00
Plate, luncheon; Fontaine, pk, 8" 22.50
Plate, luncheon; Julia, amber, 8½" 10.00
Plate, luncheon; June Night, 8" 10.00
Plate, luncheon; La Fleur, topaz, 8½" 14.00
Plate, salad; La Fleur, yel, 7¼" 15.00
Relish, Fuchsia, #5902, hdld, 3-part, 10½x12½" 60.00
Rose bowl, Twilight, ftd 225.00
Sherbet, Byzantine, low 12.00
Sherbet, Classic, short, 6½-oz, 3⅛" 27.50
Sherbet, Cordelia, 3¾" 8.00
Sherbet, Fontaine, pk 22.00
Sherbet, Wisteria, #17477 ....18.00
Stem, champagne; Fontaine, pk 32.50
Stem, champagne; Persian Pheasant, 5½-oz 30.00
Stem, claret; Persian Pheasant 55.00
Stem, cocktail; Adam 17.00
Stem, cocktail; Cadena, pk or yel, 5¼" 25.00
Stem, cocktail; Classic, 4-oz, 4⅞" 27.50
Stem, cocktail; Cordelia 13.00
Stem, cocktail; Fountaine, pk 25.00
Stem, cordial; Persian Pheasant 55.00
Stem, oyster cocktail; Flanders, yel, 4½" 35.00
Stem, parfait; Cadena, 8-oz, 6⅜" 25.00
Stem, parfait; Cherokee Rose, 4½-oz 48.00
Stem, parfait; Flanders, 5⅝" 30.00
Stem, saucer champagne; Classic, pk, 7½-oz, 6" 32.50
Stem, saucer champagne; Fuchsia, #17453, 7-oz, 5⅝" ...30.00
Stem, sherry; Cherokee Rose, 2-oz 35.00
Stem, sherry; Cherokee Rose, 2-oz 45.00
Stem, sherry; June Night, #17403, 2-oz 45.00
Stem, water; Flanders, #15047, 8¼" 45.00
Stem, water; Persian Pheasant 30.00
Stem, water; Twilight, #17492 ....35.00
Stem, wine; Byzantine 18.00
Sugar bowl, Cadena, pk or yel 30.00
Tumbler, Flanders, yel, ftd, 10-oz, 4¾" 28.00
Tumbler, Fontaine, pk, ftd 45.00
Tumbler, iced tea; Classic, pk, ftd, 13-oz, 6" 45.00
Tumbler, iced tea; Flying Nun, crystal w/gr base, ftd, #185 ...60.00
Tumbler, iced tea; La Fleur, ftd 26.00
Tumbler, juice; Byzantine, ftd 18.00
Tumbler, juice; Classic, 5-oz, 3½" 17.50
Tumbler, juice; Fuchsia, flat, 4⅞" 25.00
Tumbler, juice; June Night, ftd, 5-oz 25.00
Vase, bud; Isabella, #9780, 10" 95.00
Vase, bud; June Night, 10" 35.00
Vase, Dahlia, blk satin, gold decor, flared rim, 8" ...125.00
Vase, upright cornucopia, crystal w/Kilarney, #6301 ...200.00
Vase, upright cornucopia, crystal w/paperweight base, #6301 ...150.00

Tiles

The history of tile making dates back to ancient Egypt and Assyria. For centuries tiles have played an important role as a decorative art form, as well as having a utilitarian function. Places such as palace walls, Islamic mosques, Roman floors, and medieval English churches were all adorned with tiles or glazed ceramic surfaces. Remnants of these tile installations can still be seen throughout the world.

The heyday of tile making in England and the United States dates back to circa 1860 through 1930 and envelops the Victorian, Art Nou-

veau, and Arts & Crafts Movements in both countries. These tiles comprise most of those seen on today's market.

Tiles are being collected today as individual art objects and are increasingly used as decorative accessories. They are also sought in order to restore homes, buildings, and furniture to original period condition. Many people are now incorporating antique and collectible tiles into their home-rebuilding projects for gardens, kitchens, bathrooms, fireplaces, stair risers, and floors.

Tiles must be judged on an individual basis. The condition of the tile face; the quality of the design; the rarity of the artist, company, or series; and the size of the tile or tile panel are just some of the factors to consider when assessing value. People, animals, and scenes are generally more desirable than florals and geometrics. Some glaze colors, such as true pale pink or bright red majolica, add value to Victorian tiles. Tiles may be more difficult to find than many other antiques or collectibles, partly because many were permanently installed. Unfortunately many installations have been destroyed. These factors all have influence on the tile market, and it is not unusual for prices to vary greatly. See also American Encaustic Tiling Co.; Batchelder; Moravian; Grueby; Rookwood; other specific manufacturers. Our advisor for this category is Karen Guido; she is listed in the Directory under Connecticut.

Key:
bkg — background
geo — geometric
maj — majolica glaze
plych — polychrome

pr mld — press molded
srs — series
tbld — tube lined
tp-transfer printed

American

Atlantic, lamb representing Christ, plych matt & maj, 8¼" ...650.00
CA Art Tile, floral, salmon/bl/grays, semimatt, 6", NM ...120.00
CALCO, geo, cobalt/orange/yel semimatt, unmk, 4" ...55.00
Claycraft, flower basket, mc high glaze, mk, 8" ...375.00
Emp, geo, self-fr, mc matt, imp mk, 6", G ...75.00
Enfield, fish, turq & gold semimatt, 6x4" ...80.00
Flint Faience, fleur-de-lis, gr/buff/orange, semimatt, 6" ...120.00
Flint Faience, silver crystalline, imp mk, 4" ...35.00
Franklin Faience, geo bl/mustard/brn semimatt, 6" ...45.00
Handcraft, forest scene, keystone, grs, 11x12" ...395.00
Hartford Faience, pr mld Celtic knots, matt brn & gr, 4¾", VG ...225.00
Kraftile, geo, mc semimatt, cuerda seca, 6" ...75.00
Low, Ben Franklin, bl, sgn Osborne, 6", NM ...425.00
Malibu, floral border, mc, unmk, 4" ...75.00
Matawan, octagonal geo design, mc, 6" ...65.00
Mosaic, rtcl grill tile, mustard yel matt, 6" ...75.00
Muresque, village scene, mc matt, mc, horizontal, 4x8" ...265.00
Pewabic, bird w/branch, bl & gr matt, 1924, 2¾" ...95.00
Providential, portrait fr, gr w/heavy crackle, 4" ...95.00
Providential, Rampant lion w/branches, maj mottle, pr mld, 6" .175.00
Solon & Schemmel, floral & geo floor tile, mc, 6" ...70.00
Trent, woman w/scarf, dk bl, unmk, 3⅛" dia, EX ...85.00
Unmk southern CA, geo, mc semimatt, ca 1930, 6" ...55.00
US Encaustic, gr on gr, maj, pr mld sunflower, 6" ...35.00
Volkmar, lt bl & wht, column base & leaves, pr mld, 6" ...65.00
Wheeling, tennis player, mc, pr mld, 6" ...95.00

English

Godwin, encaustic, cloverleaf, bl/brn/gold, 6", VG ...85.00
Maw, poppies, pr mld, high relief, brn maj, 4" ...30.00
Minton Hollins, Arts & Science srs, Navigator, brn & wht tp, 6" ...125.00
Minton Hollins, Fairy Tale srs, Blue Beard, bl & wht, 6" ...150.00
Minton Hollins, flying birds, blk & wht tp, 6" ...65.00

Mintons Ch Wks, encaustic, mc geo, high glaze, 6" 60.00
Mintons Ch Wks, Minots Light House, brn & wht tp, 6" 100.00
Pilkingtons, floral pr mld, mc maj, ca 1900, 6" 85.00
Sherwin & Cotton, barbotine maj flower, olive gr, 6" 100.00
Sherwin & Cotton, tbld sailing ship, mc maj, 6" 125.00
Webbs Tileries, hopps flowers, mc, 2 6" tiles in fr 145.00
Wedgwood, musicians in orange grove, brn & wht tp, 6" 100.00

Other Countries

Cantagalli Firenze, plaque, woman's profile, wht on bl, 5x8½" ..120.00
Delft Dutch scene, HP plych, ca 1850, 6", VG 100.00
Portuguese, rampant lion, mc cuenca, ca 1930, 6" 55.00
Tunisian, daisy in quatrefoil, mc semimatt, ca 1940, 4" 45.00
Villeroy & Boch, Mettlach, house along canal, bl & wht, 6" 45.00

Tinware

In the American household of the 17th and 18th centuries, tinware items could be found in abundance, from food containers to foot warmers and mirror frames. Although the first settlers brought much of their tinware with them from Europe, by 1798 sheets of tin plate were being imported from England for use by the growing number of American tinsmiths. Tinwares were often decorated either by piercing or painted designs which were both freehand and stenciled. (See Toleware.) By the early 1900s, many homes had replaced their old tinware with the more attractive aluminum and graniteware.

In the 19th century, tenth wedding anniversaries were traditionally celebrated by gifts of tin. Couples gave big parties, dressed in their wedding clothes, and reaffirmed their vows before their friends and family who arrived bearing (and often wearing) tin gifts, most of which were quite humorous. Anniversary tin items may include hats, cradles, slippers and shoes, rolling pins, etc. See also Primitives and Kitchen Collectibles.

Anniversary, top hat, 6¼" 300.00
Ash protector, punched/pierced crescent shape w/C hdl, 5x12x8" 2,600.00
Butter press, long tube, open star design, wooden pusher 75.00
Can, pouring spigot on top, strap hdl, 4¾" 200.00
Candle box, cylindrical, punched lid & ends, hanging 265.00
Candle snuffer, cone shape, stationary ring at top 60.00
Cheese mold, heart shape, handmade, early 295.00
Cheese mold, heart shape w/sieve holes, resoldered, 4½" 250.00
Cheese strainer, brass hanging loop, 2¾x6⅝" dia 125.00
Cheese strainer, heart shape, 3-ftd, ribbon hdl, 19th C, 6⅜" 550.00
Cheese strainer, pierced, wire ring, 1¼x6⅜" dia 110.00
Cheese strainer, pierced, 3-ftd, arched ribbon hdl, 4x5x6½" 475.00
Coffeepot, gooseneck, punched band on hinged lid, 11" 190.00
Coffeepot, 2-pc w/drip top, cast leaf & ring hdl, 14" 90.00
Colander, strap hdls, brass screen, attached rim base, sm 45.00
Cookie press, tube shape, wooden pusher w/heart design 125.00
Dinner horn, oval strap hdl, 54½" L 125.00
Egg coddler, holds 2 tiers of 4 eggs, ftd, side hdls 285.00
Ladle, cup shape w/pour spout, long hook hdl, early 30.00
Ladle, rnd stick hdl w/hook end, 3½" dia, 11½" hdl 32.00
Matchbox holder, punched floral, 4¾x2¾x1⅝" 45.00
Measure, raised rings, 1-pt 30.00
Measure, raised rings, 1-qt 32.00
Measure, 1-cup, VG 12.00
Milk pan, Shaker style, minor rpr to lip, 6x16" 25.00
Oil lamp filler, squatty funnel shape 75.00
Pan, muffin; Self Rising Up & Up Cake Flour, 6-hole 30.00
Pie crimper, wooden hdl, 6¾" 35.00
Pie pan, sunburst design in bottom & initials HM 15.00
Rack, potato baking; 6 rnded points, dtd 1909, 2¼x13½" 45.00
Skimmer, molasses; wood & dk tin, 10x5¾"+4" hdl 50.00
Strainer, soldered seams, brass screen, 3" legs, 6x9½" 56.00
Teakettle, stick spout, strap hdl, handmade, early, 5½" dia 80.00
Teapot, pewter finial, 8" 105.00

Tobacciana

Tobacciana is the generally accepted term used to cover a field of collecting that includes smoking pipes, cigar molds, cigarette lighters, humidors — in short, any article having to do with the practice of using tobacco in any form. Perhaps the most valuable variety of pipes is the meerschaum, hand carved from hydrous magnesium, an opaque white-gray or cream-colored mineral of the soapstone family. (Much of this is today mined in Turkey which has the largest meerschaum deposit in the world, though there are other deposits of lesser significance around the globe.) These figural bowls often portray an elaborately carved mythological character, an animal, or a historical scene. Amber is sometimes used for the stem. Other collectible pipes are corn cob (Missouri meerschaum) and Indian peace pipes of clay or catlinite. (See American Indian Art.)

Chosen because it was the Indians who first introduced the white man to smoking, the cigar store Indian was a symbol used to identify tobacco stores in the 19th century. The majority of them were hand carved between 1830 and 1900 and are today recognized as some of the finest examples of early wood sculptures. When found they command very high prices.

For further information on lighters, refer to *Collector's Guide to Cigarette Lighters* by James Flanagan. Our advisor for this category is Chuck Thompson; he is listed in the Directory under Texas. See also Advertising; Snuff Boxes.

Cigarette case, burl with Bakelite inlaid scenes, exterior with parson ringing bell, naughty lady inside, 3¾x4¾", $495.00.

Ashtray, copper, man lifting lady's skirt on bk, 3½x5½" 90.00
Box, cigarette, leather book form, Philip Morris 16.00
Cabinet, pipe; walnut, holds 6, w/shelf & hidden compartment .165.00
Cheroot holder, meerschaum, cvd eagle 85.00
Cheroot holder, meerschaum, cvd nude woman, 1880s, M 575.00
Cigar box opener, Chancellor 30.00
Cigar box opener, Charles Derby 25.00
Cigar box opener, Faust 35.00
Cigar box opener, John Ruskin 20.00
Cigar box opener, RG Sullivans 4-20-4 Cigar w/bottle opener 45.00
Cigar box opener, Sullivan 40.00
Cigar perforater, Souvenir of Louisiana Expo...1904 ....195.00
Cigarette case, chrome & wood w/base, gold cougar on lid, 4¼" ..50.00
Cigarette holder, ivory, 3½" 40.00
Cigarette package, Black Cat, VA, unopened 150.00
Cutter, cigar; brass scissors type, vest pocket sz 45.00
Cutter, cigar; brass-plated w/emb floral & deer, table-top 135.00
Cutter, cigar; Cressmann's, counter-top, wind-up 765.00
Cutter, cigar; curved horn 165.00
Cutter, cigar; gold-filled, entwined snake 195.00

Cutter, cigar; gold-filled, w/bl sapphire 165.00
Cutter, cigar; gold-filled, winged dragon figural 285.00
Cutter, cigar; gold-filled gargoyle figural 250.00
Cutter, cigar; New Currency 5 Cents 450.00
Cutter, cigar; Perforator 65.00
Cutter, cigar; Smoke the Eagle, counter-top 350.00
Cutter, cigar; sterling w/eng florals 195.00
Cutter, cigar; Upmann's Extra Five...1891, counter-top, 3x4½" .365.00
Cutter, cigar; whale's tooth w/scrimshawed eagle's head 275.00
Cutter, cigar; 10k gold w/eng florals 265.00
Cutter, plug; Arrow 125.00
Cutter, plug; Champion 135.00
Cutter, plug; Cremo, CI V shape, 5¾x5½" 55.00
Cutter, plug; Empire, Quebec 150.00
Cutter, plug; Standard 65.00
Figure, Indian brave, fine cvg & pnt, ca 1850-90s, 88", EX ...21,000.00
Figure, Indian chief, cvd wood, EX details & pnt, 1920s, 84" ..3,850.00
Figure, Indian chief, cvd wood, headdress/feathered skirt, 28" ...2,850.00
Figure, Indian chief, cvd wood, mc pnt, EX details, 81" 4,000.00
Figure, Indian chief, cvd wood, 1880s, EX pnt & condition 6,875.00
Figure, Indian princess w/headdress, EX mc pnt, 1880s, 80" ..17,250.00
Humidor, bsk, lady w/bandanna over hair, brn face, 4¾x3¾" 135.00
Humidor, ceramic, Turkish man, ¾-figure, mc, Japan 95.00
Humidor, mahog, brass bound, dtd 1919 ....750.00
Humidor, majolica, Arab, mc, 6½" 300.00
Humidor, majolica, bowler figural, ¾-figure, bl & wht, 6" 300.00
Humidor, majolica, Irish jockey figural, mc, 5" 195.00
Humidor, majolica, Scotsman, mc, #d base, 6½" 195.00
Humidor, pewter, claw & ball ft, 7½" 75.00
Humidor, porc, man's head, brn & flesh tones, #d, 6" 65.00
Humidor, pottery, monk figural, brn & tan, 9" 195.00
Lighter, Camel, brass plated 12.50
Lighter, cigar; hammered SP globe w/dragon hdl 175.00
Lighter, Evans, Am cut glass & silver, 1920s 85.00
Lighter, Evans, Limoges china, wht/gold, gas 25.00
Lighter, Evans, magic lamp, gold metal 30.00
Lighter, Evans, sterling goblet shape 45.00
Lighter, gold-pnt metal, man w/hunting dog, counter-top, 1880s ..2,500.00
Lighter, golf ball on tee w/turf base 20.00
Lighter, Hamilton, chrome ship's wheel 50.00
Lighter, risque dancer on ped, 1880s, 15" 2,950.00
Lighter, Ronson, Queen Anne, silver, much eng, 3" 195.00
Lighter, Ronson, Royal Crown Derby, Imari pattern 95.00
Lighter, Ronson, silver pencil, table model, 1930s 95.00
Lighter, Ronson Gem, rhinestones on front 85.00
Lighter, SP, armored car form, 1930s 160.00
Lighter, sterling, fancy eng, 4x2¾" 185.00
Lighter, Wedgwood, bl jasper, United insert 40.00
Lighter, Zippo type, rebel flag/soldier, Forget Hell, Japan, MIB 30.00
Photo, cigar store int, 1895, EX 12.50
Pipe holder, bone, cvd horse's head, flowing mane, realistic, EX ...115.00
Tag, Lorillard Mechanic's Delight, carpenter & blacksmith, tin ...20.00
Token, Ace Cigar Store 25¢ 3.00

Pipes

Blown glass, cranberry, England 125.00
Briar, bull's head shape w/horn & glass eyes 75.00
Clay, French lady w/lg hat, 1860s, 4¼" 45.00
Meerschaum, bearded Arab's head, 4½", EX in case 175.00
Meerschaum, boxer dogs cvg, rpl stem, EX 100.00
Meerschaum, eagle holding egg, amber mouthpc, 6½" 175.00
Meerschaum, eagle in eagle claw, 1880s, 6¾", EX in case 425.00
Meerschaum, head of Pan, 6⅝", EX in case 420.00

Meerschaum, horn stem, Bakelite mouthpc, 8½" 75.00
Meerschaum, horse's head cvg, amber stem 275.00
Meerschaum, prospector & dog, 4⅝", VG in case 550.00
Meerschaum, stag & doe scene, amber stem, EX 175.00
Meerschaum, Winston Churchill bust bowl, amber stem, '40s ...375.00
Wood, bull's head cvg, ivory horns, amber eyes, 1950s 85.00
Wood, fox head cvd at bowl, red glass eyes, mk JKM 185.00

Toby Jugs

The delightful jug known as the Toby dates back to the 18th century, when factories in England produced them for export to the American colonies. Named for the character Toby Philpots in the song *The Little Brown Jug*, the Toby was fashioned in the form of a jolly fellow, usually holding a jug of beer and a glass. The earlier examples were made with strict attention to details such as fingernails and teeth. Originally representing only a non-entity, a trend developed to portray well-known individuals such as George II, Napoleon, and Ben Franklin. Among the most valued Tobies are those produced by Ralph Wood I in the late 1700s. By the mid-1830s Tobies were being made in America. See also Doulton; Lenox; Occupied Japan.

Man with warty face sits and holds jug, pink coat, spotted waistcoat, striped stockings, Staffordshire, early 19th century, 10", EX, $300.00.

Admiral Beatty, Dread Naught, Wilkinson, 1917, 10½" 700.00
Admiral Jelhoe, Hell Fire Jack, Wilkinson, 1918, 10" 575.00
Black slave, crabstock hdl w/gold, England, 1850s 2,600.00
Field Marshall Haig, Push & Go, Wilkinson, ca 1917, 10¾" 460.00
Geo Whitefield, hat in hand, mc, early 19th C, rprs, 8¾" 260.00
HM King George V, Pro Patria, Wilkinson, 1919, 12" 430.00
Lord Kitchener, Bitter for the Kaiser, Wilkinson, 1918, 9¾" 700.00
Marshall Foch, Au Diable Le Kaiser, Wilkinson, 1918, 11¾" 350.00
Marshall Joffre, seated, 75mm Ce que Joffre, Wilkinson, 1918, 10" 350.00
Martha Gunn, translucent mc on pearl body, 1780s, rpr, 9¼" ..1,265.00
Pratt type, mc on pearlware, ca 1800, 9¼", EX 400.00
President Wilson, Welcome! Uncle Sam, Wilkinson, 1918, 10¾" ..980.00
Ralph Wood type, translucent glazes, England, 1770s, 9¾", EX .1,035.00
Winston Churchill, Clarice Cliff design, Wilkinson, 1941, 12" ..1,380.00
Yorkshire type, caryatid-form hdl, early 19th C, rstr, 7¾" 750.00
Yorkshire type, sponged base, early 19th C, rstr, 4⅝" 230.00

Toleware

The term 'toleware' originally came from a French term meaning 'sheet iron.' Today it is used to refer to paint-decorated tin items, most popular from 1800 to 1850s. The craft flourished in Pennsylvania, Connecticut, Maine, and New York state. Early toleware has a very distinctive look. The surface is dull and unvarnished; background colors range from black to cream. Geometrics are quite common, but florals and fruits were also favored. Items made after 1850 were often stenciled, and gold trim was sometimes added.

American toleware is usually found in practical, everyday forms —

trays, boxes, and coffeepots are most common — while French examples might include candlesticks, wine coolers, jardinieres, etc. Be sure to note color and design when determining date and value, but condition of the paint is the most important worth-assessing factor. In the listings that follow, the dimension given for boxes and trays indicates length. Unless noted otherwise, values are for examples with average wear.

Bowl, floral, mc on blk w/gold, swan neck hdls, France, 17" **400.00**
Candle floor light, dbl; floral, etched globe, 59", EX **600.00**
Candle lamp, brn japanning w/gold stripes, 19", w/orig snuffer ..**935.00**
Coal hod, floral, mc on blk, urn shape, 18x23" **800.00**
Coal hod, gr & gold apples, lion finial, paw ft, Fr, 1820s, 25" **650.00**
Coffeepot, floral, mc on blk, gooseneck spout, worn, 10¼" **225.00**
Coffeepot, floral, mc on blk, stick spout, hinged lid, 10" **2,900.00**
Coffeepot, floral, mc on blk, stick spout, hinged lid, 9" **1,600.00**
Deed box, floral, mc on blk, wire hdl, worn, 3x4¼x3" **130.00**
Deed box, floral, mc on red w/blk veins, hinged lid, 5x9x5" **2,400.00**
Deed box, plums & flowers, mc on blk, 6¼x9½", VG **200.00**
Deed box, rosettes & peonies, mc on blk, 7½x10x6⅝", VG **650.00**
Sconce, floral, mc on blk w/gold, crimped crest, 14", EX **200.00**
Sugar bowl, plum & floral, mc on blk, worn, w/lid, 3⅝x4" **220.00**
Syrup, floral, mc on blk, cylindrical, hinged lid, 4x3" **475.00**
Tea caddy, floral, mc on blk, 4¼x3½x2⅝" **400.00**
Tea caddy, floral, mc on red, oval shape, worn, 4x3⅜x2⅝" **110.00**
Tray, bread; floral, mc on blk, EX color, lt wear, 12½" **360.00**
Tray, courting couple, border scenes on mustard, 1800s, 30x23", VG .**650.00**
Tray, foliage & vintage, gold on blk, lt wear, 22x30" **220.00**
Tray, Fr scenes/events around border on yel, 26½x19½", G- **175.00**
Tray, leaf border, gr on cranberry red, early 1800s, 24x28", G **125.00**
Tray, plum & floral, mc on blk, worn, 2¾x12½x7¾" **75.00**
Tray, tulip & fruit on blk w/crystalline, open hdls, 13x8" **900.00**
Urn, floral, gold on blk, tin & pewter w/brass base, 15", EX **470.00**

Tools

Before the Civil War, tools for the most part were handmade. Some were primitive to the point of crudeness, while others reflected the skill of those who took pride in their trade. Increasing demand for quality tools and the dawning of the age of industrialization resulted in tools that were mass produced. Factors important in evaluating antique tools are scarcity, usefulness, and portability. Those with a manufacturer's mark are worth more than unmarked items. When no condition is indicated, the items listed here are assumed to be in excellent condition. Our advisor for this category is Jim Calison; he is listed in the Directory under New York. See also Keen Kutter; Stanley; Winchester.

Block plane, carved whalebone with cast-steel angled bit, ship carpenter's, 19th century, 4¾x10⅜x¾", EX, $1,875.00.

Axe, grubbing; 2-head, hand forged **40.00**
Barking spud, spoon type, used for peeling bark **125.00**
Baseball stitching vise, locking lever **75.00**
Bitstock, coachmaker's, metal w/wood fixtures **85.00**
Broadaxe, goosewing, minimum value **550.00**
Calipers, iron w/brass joiner **35.00**
Cradle scythe, 4-finger bow, metal blade, minimum value **175.00**

Cutter, burley tobacco **42.50**
Flagging iron **150.00**
Hammer, carenter's, burl **68.00**
Hatchet, earliest factory-made type, ca 1845 ....**48.00**
Hoof scraper, wooden hdl, steel files **22.00**
Jointer, barrel maker's, 6' **175.00**
Level, cherry, brass throat, 1867 ....**80.00**
Log tongs **45.00**
Mallet, wooden burl, 5¾" dia, 14" hdl **60.00**
Maul, burl; wht oak hdl, 18th C, minimum value **55.00**
Measure, Master #306 ....**12.50**
Plane, Bedrock #605 ....**49.00**
Plane, moulding; maple **40.00**
Plane, plow; cherry w/brass fittings, 1850-60, minimum value **150.00**
Plane, rabbet; maple, wide eye **65.00**
Plane, thumb; mahog, sm, 3¾" **65.00**
Ruler, Lufkin, solid brass, folding, 24" **64.00**
Ruler, wood, brass fixtures, 4-fold **50.00**
Saw, ice; horse drawn **350.00**
Saw, trenching; maple, 1840 ....**85.00**
Scraper, cooper's, pull type, maple hdl, brass ferrule **40.00**
Scribe, walnut, adjustable, 1800s, 28¾" L **160.00**
Stitching horse, hickory, vise mortised into seat, 1840s **225.00**
Straight edge, walnut w/heart cutouts, 1800s, 21¾" L, EX **800.00**
Tongs, button **35.00**
Tool belt, leather, Leather Guild Co, brass buckle, EX **40.00**
Trammel, wood & brass, 1890 ....**100.00**
Wagon jack, Conestoga, dtd 1806, 21" block **165.00**
Wagon jack, wood & iron, New England origin **125.00**
Witchet, hardwoods, brass-lined throat, dbl blades, 1840 ....**250.00**
Wrench, steamboat's engineer's **55.00**

Toothbrush Holders

Most of the collectible toothbrush holders were made in prewar Japan and were modeled after popular comic strip, Disney, and nursery rhyme characters. Since many were made of bisque and decorated with unfired paint, it's not uncommon to find them in less-than-perfect paint, a factor you must consider when attempting to assess their values. Our advisor for this category is Marilyn Cooper, author of *Pictorial Guide to Toothbrush Holders*; she is listed in the Directory under Texas.

Aviator, celluloid, 1 hole, tray, stands, 6⅛" **135.00**
Baby Bunting, shaker top, Germany, 6¾" **395.00**
Bear w/scarf & hat, 2 holes, tray at ft, hangs, Japan, 5½" **95.00**
Big Bird, 2 holes, no tray, stands, Taiwan, 4½" **80.00**
Boy on elephant, 3 holes, tray at ft, hangs, Japan, 6¼" **95.00**
Carousel, 4 holes, no tray, hangs, Crown mk, 5" **125.00**
Clown w/bug on nose, 3 holes, w/tray, hangs, Japan, 5⅛" **150.00**
Clown w/fancy vest, lustre, 2 holes, no tray, hangs, Japan, 6⅝" **85.00**
Cowboy, lustre, 1 hole, w/tray, stands, Japan, 4½" **95.00**
Doc (dwarf), Brush Your Teeth Snow White, WDP, stands, 4¼" ..**110.00**
Donald Duck, bsk, long bill, Disney, late 1930s, EX **250.00**
Donald Duck Siamese Twins, bsk, c WED, 2 holes, hangs, 5¼" .**300.00**
Frog w/mandolin, 2 holes, tray, stands, Goldcastle, 6" **95.00**
Indian Chief (bust), 2 holes, tray, hangs, Japan, 4½" **250.00**
Sailors on anchor, 2 holes, tray, hangs, Japan, 5½" **70.00**
Skippy w/jtd arm, bsk, arm holds brush, no tray, stands, 5⅝" **125.00**

Toothpick Holders

Once common on every table, the toothpick holder was relegated to the china cabinet near the turn of the century. Fortunately, this contributed to their survival. As a result, many are available to collectors today. Because they are small and easily displayed, they are very popular collectibles. They come in a wide range of prices to fit every budget. Many have been reproduced and, unfortunately, are being offered for sale right along with the originals. These 'repros' should be priced in the $10.00 to $30.00 range. Unless you're sure of what you're buying, choose a reputable dealer. In addition to pattern glass, you'll find examples in china, bisque, art glass, and various metals. Toothpick holders in the listings that follow are glass unless noted otherwise. Values here are for originals. Our advisor for this category is Judy A. Knauer; she is listed in the Directory under Pennsylvania.

Acanthus, bl w/gold 295.00
Alabama 65.00
Arched Ovals 20.00
Atlas, milk glass 48.00
Banded Portland, cranberry stain 55.00
Bead & Scroll, clear w/gold 25.00
Beatty Honeycomb, wht opal 40.00
Beveled Star, gr 125.00
Blazing Cornucopia, amethyst stain 55.00
Button & Bulge, pk w/floral decor 45.00
Button Arches, clambroth, souvenir 30.00
Button Arches, ruby flash (+) 32.00
Button Panel, Duncan 35.00
Carmen 55.00
Church Windows, lg 24.00
Coal Hod, amber 40.00
Colorado, clear w/gold 25.00
Cone, pk satin, scarce 85.00
Cord Drapery, rare 125.00
Daisy & Button w/V Ornament 35.00
Diamond Spearhead, vaseline opal 65.00
Diamond w/Peg, ruby stain 45.00
Feather, gr, NM 395.00
Galloway 30.00
Gathering Knot, purple, Imperial 45.00
Georgia Gem, gr opaque 80.00
Gonterman Swirl, yel opal 295.00
Harvard, gr, souvenir 45.00
Hickman, amber stain 80.00
Illinois 30.00
Illinois, clear w/gold 35.00
Intaglio Flower 35.00
Invt T'print, amberina 275.00
Invt T'print, cranberry 95.00
Iris w/Meander, gr opal 80.00
Iris w/Meander, purple w/gold 55.00
Iris w/Meander, wht opal 60.00
Jefferson Optic, bl w/wht decor 65.00
Jefferson Optic, gr w/HP flowers 45.00
Kansas 60.00
Kemple's Pansy, milk glass 35.00
Kentucky, gr 145.00
King's Crown, ruby stain 30.00
Ladder 25.00
Lone Star 35.00
Lucerne 35.00
Majestic, ruby stain 135.00
Manhattan, gold trim 32.00
Mardigras 45.00
Michigan 45.00
Mikado, bl 75.00

Minnesota, clear w/gold 20.00
Model Peerless 50.00
National's Eureka 35.00
National's Eureka, ruby stain 80.00
New Hampshire, clear w/etched advertising .45.00
One-O-One, gr opaque 100.00
Owl on branch before egg-shaped holder, SP .85.00

Paddlewheel and Star with gold trim, $32.00.

Panelled Grape 45.00
Pearls & Shells, milk glass 28.00
Pennsylvania, clear w/gold 40.00
Pennsylvania, gr 85.00
Pillar, pk & wht spatter 75.00
Pleating, ruby stain 50.00
Punty Band, custard, beaded top, souvenir, Heisey .65.00
Punty Band, ruby stain, scalloped top 65.00
Queen's Necklace 40.00
Reverse 44, clear w/platinum 95.00
Ribbed Lattice, bl opal 245.00
Rising Sun 40.00
Scroll w/Cane Band, ruby stain 110.00
Shoshone, clear w/gold 30.00
Sunbeam, gr w/gold 80.00
Swag w/Brackets, gr opal (+) 75.00
Swirl, amber stain & enamel 75.00
Swirled Windows, cranberry opal 275.00
Tacoma, amber stain 195.00
Tarentum's T'print, clear w/HP flowers, souvenir .40.00
Tarentum's T'print, custard, souvenir 55.00
Uncle Sam's Hat, milk glass, no pnt (+) 32.00
Union's Radiant, amethyst stain 250.00
Windsor Anvil, bl 35.00
Winged Scroll, custard w/gold 140.00
York Herringbone Swirl, ruby stain 75.00
3 Dolphins 50.00

Torquay Pottery

Torquay is a unique type of pottery made in the South Devon area of England as early as 1867. At the height of productivity, at least a dozen companies flourished there, producing simple folk pottery from the area's natural red clay. The ware was both wheel turned and molded and decorated under the glaze with heavy slip resulting in low-relief nature subjects or simple scrollwork. Three of the best known of these potteries were Watcombe (1867 – 1962); Aller Vale (in operation from the mid-1800s, producing domestic ware and architectural products); and Longpark (1890 until 1957). Watcombe and Aller Vale merged in 1901 and operated until 1962 under the name of Royal Aller Vale and Watcombe Art Pottery.

A decline in the popularity of the early classical terra-cotta styles (urns, busts, figures, etc.) lead to the introduction of painted and glazed terra-cotta wares. During the late 1880s, white clay wares, both turned and molded, were decorated with colored glazes (Stapleton ware, grotesque molded figures, ornamental vases, large jardinieres, etc.). By the turn of the century, the market for art pottery was diminishing, so the potteries turned to wares decorated in colored slips (Barbotine, Persian, Scrolls, etc.).

Motto wares were introduced in the late 19th century by Aller Vale and taken up in the present century by the other Torquay potteries. This eventually became the 'bread and butter' product of the local industry. This was perhaps the most famous type of ware potted in this area because of the verses, proverbs, and quotations that decorated it. This was achieved by the sgraffito technique — scratching the letters through the slip to expose the red clay underneath. The most popular patterns were Cottage, Black Cockerel, Multi-Cockerel, and a scroll-work design called Scandy. Other popular decorations were Kerswell Daisy, ships, kingfishers, applied bird decorations, Art Deco styles, Egyptian ware, and many others. Aller Vale ware may sometimes be found marked 'H.H. and Company,' a firm who assumed ownership from 1897 to 1901. 'Watcombe Torquay' was an impressed mark used from 1884 to 1927.

Our advisors for this category are Jerry and Gerry Kline; they are listed in the Directory under Ohio. If you're interested in joining a Torquay club, you'll find the address of The North American Torquay Society under Clubs, Newsletters, and Catalogs.

Art Pottery

Ashtray, Polka Dot, Watcombe, 3¼" sq 27.50
Bottle, scent; Devon Violets, crown stopper, unk, 2½" 50.00
Bowl, stylized leaves, mc on bl, cream int, ped ft, 3x4" 75.00
Candlestick, Bl Scroll, Aller Vale, wht clay, 4¼" 120.00
Candlestick, Tintern Abbey, Longpark, 8½x5" 250.00
Candlesticks, Bl Scroll, Longpark Tormohun, 5½" 250.00
Chamberstick, Persian, Aller Vale, wht clay, 2½x6¾" L 350.00
Egg cup & saucer, Polka Dot, Sandygate 40.00
Jug, Rosy Sunset, Royal Torquay, 8 ....395.00
Jug, Sea Gull, Babbacombe, 3½" 35.00
Mug, Scrolls, Brannum, 3-hdld, 'Be Aisy If Ye...,' 2" 70.00
Pitcher, Bl Scroll, side spout, unmk Exeter, 4" 69.00
Pitcher, colored scrolls, Aller Vale, pinched spout, A-1 ....200.00
Salt cellar, Polka Dot, unmk 35.00
Sugar bowl, faience, bridge w/trees, Watcombe, 1½" 50.00
Teapot, Widecombe Fair, Dartmouth, men on horse & signpost, 5½" ...125.00
Vase, Rusticware, appl flowers, Longpark, 1914-23, 5" 130.00

Devon Motto Ware

Ash receiver, Cottage, 'I'll Take Care of the Ashes' 50.00
Ashtray, Cottage, Watcombe, 'Better To Smoke Here...,' 3¼x5" .34.00
Ashtray, Cottage, Watcombe, 'I'll Take...,' 4½" dia 65.00
Ashtray, Cottage, Watcombe, 'Who Burnt the Tablecloth,' 3¼" .34.00
Ashtray, Shamrock, unmk Watcombe, 'Ireland Paddy...,' 3¾" sq .60.00
Beaker, Scandy, unmk Exeter, 'Shut Mouth...,' 3¾" 60.00
Biscuit barrel, Cottage, Watcombe, 'May the Hinges...' 245.00
Bowl, Cottage, Aller Vale, twist hdl, 'Guid Things...,' 3x5¼" .135.00
Bowl, Cottage, Watcombe, ruffled rim, 'There's More...,' 6½" ...100.00
Butter dish, Cottage, Longpark, 'Help Yourself...,' 5½" 95.00
Butter dish, Scandy, Longpark, 'Minehead 'Elp...,' 4" H 80.00
Butter dish, Watcombe, 'Help Yourself,' 4¼" dia 105.00
Butter shovel, Cottage, Watcome, 'Cum Me Artiez...' 78.00
Butter tub, Cottage, Watcombe, 'To Say Well...,' 3¾" 85.00
Butter tub, Shamrock, Longpark, 'From Killarney,' 4½" dia 65.00
Candlestick, Cottage, Watcombe, 'Blessed Are Drowsy...,' 5½" .155.00

Candlestick, Scandy, Aller Vale, 'Many Are Called...,' 4¼" 97.50
Candlestick, Scandy, Tormohun Ware, 'Last in Bed...,' 6" 120.00
Candy dish, Cottage, Watcombe, 'Where Friends...,' 5" 47.50
Cauldron, Cottage, unmk Hart & Moist, 'Strive To Learn...,' 3¾" ...85.00
Chamberstick, Cottage, Longpark, 'Towyn, Hear All...' 110.00
Chamberstick, Cottage, Watcombe, Aladdin lamp form, w/motto ..140.00
Chamberstick, Scandy, Aller Vale, 'Be the Day...,' 5¼" 125.00
Chamberstick, Scandy, Aller Vale, 'Many Are Called...,' 5¾" ...150.00
Chamberstick, Shamrock, Longpark, 'From Youghal...,' 2½" 85.00
Chamberstick, Ship, unmk, 'Don't Burn the Candle...,' 5" 90.00
Cheese dish, Cottage, Dartmouth, w/motto 60.00
Cheese server, Snow on Roof, Royal Watcombe, 'No Road Long...' ..420.00
Coffeepot, Cottage, Watcombe, 'Take a Cup...,' 7" 150.00
Coffeepot, Scandy, unmk, 'Due'e Have a...,' 6½" 140.00
Condiment set, Cottage, Watcombe, 'There's No Fun...' 175.00
Creamer, Cottage, snow scene, Royal Watcombe, w/motto, 2½" .125.00
Creamer, Double Cottage, Watcombe, 'Make Thisen...,' 2¼" 45.00
Creamer, Multi-Cockerel w/baby chick, 'Where's Mother...' 150.00
Cup & saucer, Cottage, w/motto, 4½x5¼", 8" dia 125.00
Cup & saucer, Scandy, Watcombe, 'Daunt'u Be Fraid...,' over sz ..150.00
Dresser tray, Black Cockerel, Watcombe, 'Life Is Mostly...,' 10x7" ..325.00
Dresser tray, Cottage, 'The Oldest Chemist Shop...,' 14x10" 440.00
Dresser tray, Dbl Scandy, 'Do Not Hurry, Flurry...,' lg 275.00
Egg cup, Cottage, Babbacombe, 'Fresh Today,' 2¾" 30.00
Fish ashtray, Black Cockerel, Watcombe, 'A Plaice for Ashes...' 130.00
Gypsy pot, Scandy, Longpark, 'If You Can't...,' 3" 75.00
Hair tidy, Scandy, unmk, 'Hair Tidy' 85.00
Hatpin holder, Scandy, Aller Vale, 'Place for...,' 4½" 150.00
Hatpin holder, Scandy, Long Park, 'Keep Me on the...,' 5" 145.00
Inkwell, Blue Thistle, unmk, 'Dip Deep,' 2" 90.00
Inkwell, Multi-Cockerel, Tormohun, 'Us Be Always Glad...' 96.00
Jug, barrel; Scandy, unmk, 'Take Thy Calling...,' 4½" 85.00
Jug, milk; Cottage, Watcombe, 'Greatest Troubles...,' 6½" 120.00
Jug, puzzle; Cottage, Watcombe, 'Here Gent...,' 6¾" 395.00
Jug, Scandy, Longpark, 'Do All Tha Gud E Yu...,' mini, 1¾" 65.00
Jug, Scandy, unmk Exeter, 'Be Slow To Promise...,' 5¾" 90.00
Jug, Shamrock, Longpark, bbl form, 'From Cushendall...,' 3½" 70.00
Match holder, Scandy, Longpark Tormohun, 'A Match for...,' 3¼" ...100.00

Meat platter, Scandy, impressed Watcombe Torquay, with motto, 10x13¾", $400.00.

Mug, amber, Exeter, 2-hdld, 'Who Makes His Bed...,' 3½" 75.00
Mug, Cottage, Humpty Dumpty, unmk, child sz, 3½" 75.00
Mug, Cottage, Royal Watcombe, wide mouth, 'Up to the Lips...,' 4½" 90.00
Mug, Scandy, Watcombe, 'Blackgang Work on Hope...,' 6" 180.00
Mug, Shamrock, Royal Watcombe, 'The Green...,' 2½" 45.00
Mustard pot, Cottage, Longpark, 'A Light Heart,' 2½" 80.00
Pen tray, Scandy, Watcombe, 'If You Can't Be Aisy...,' 9" L 110.00
Pepper pot, Scandy, Aller Vale, 'Ca Canny Wi the...,' 2¾" 35.00
Pin dish, Shamrock, Longpark, 'None of Your...,' 4" 45.00
Pin tray, Cottage, 'Every Why Hath a...,' 1920s, 5½" 47.50
Pin tray, Portland Lighthouse, Watcombe, oval, w/motto, 4¾" L 38.00
Pitcher, hot water; Scandy, Aller Vale, 'In Trouble...,' 5½" 155.00
Pitcher, hot water; Shamrock, Aller Vale, 'There's a Dear...,' 6½" .125.00

Pitcher, house, Dartmouth, 'Guid Volks Be...,' 5½x5" 100.00
Pitcher, Kerswell Daisy, Aller Vale, 'A Man May Travel...,' 4⅛' .175.00
Pitcher, Kerswell Daisy, Aller Vale, 7¾" 250.00
Pitcher, Scandy, Aller Vale, 'Do Not Stain...,' 4½" 100.00
Pitcher, Scandy, Aller Vale, side spout, 'Du'ee Mak...,' 4" 70.00
Pitcher, Scandy, Aller Vale, side spout, 'Every Blade...,' 3" 60.00
Plate, Cottage, Dartmouth/Devon, 10" 75.00
Plate, Cottage, Royal Watcombe, 'Fairest Gems...,' 4¾" 65.00
Plate, Cottage, Watcombe, 'Better Wait...,' 8¼" 125.00
Plate, Cottage, Watcombe, 'Masters Two Will Never Do,' 5" 50.00
Plate, Shamrock, Longpark, 'From Sligo Ould...,' 5" 48.00
Salt cellar, Cottage, Longpark, 'Be Aisy w/tha Salt,' 1½" 50.00
Salt cellar, Scandy, Aller Vale, 'Help Yersel...,' 1½" H 60.00
Salt cellar, Scandy, unmk Aller Vale, ftd, 'Elp Yerzel...,' mini 60.00
Shaker, Cottage, unmk, 'There's No Fun Like...' 35.00
Shaving mug, Cottage, Watcombe, 'A Present for Friend...,' 4½" ..175.00
Stein, Scandy, Aller Vale, 'A Heart To Feel...,' 4½" 90.00
Sugar bowl, Scandy, Aller Vale, 'Tak What Yu Want,' 2" 40.00
Sugar bowl, Shamrock, Longpark, 'Ould Ireland's...' 35.00
Sugar cauldron, Scandy, Watcombe, 'Take a Little...,' 2¼" 60.00
Sugar shaker, Scandy, Longpark, 'Be Aisy...,' rare, 4" 120.00
Teapot, Burns Cottage, 'When Freens Meet...,' 5½" 220.00
Teapot, Cottage, 'We'll Take a Cup o' Kindness' 125.00
Teapot, Cottage, Longpark, 'Dauntee Be Fraid...,' 4x4¾" 125.00
Teapot, Cottage, Rugby, 'Tea Seldom Spoils...,' 4x4" 85.00
Teapot, Cottage, Watcombe, 'A Cup...Very Refreshing,' rstr, 4½" .130.00
Teapot, Scandy, Aller Vale, 'Droon Your Sorrows,' mini, 3" 165.00
Tyg, Shamrock, Longpark, 'Ould Ireland's...,' 3-hdl, mini, 2" 65.00
Vase, Scandy, Watcombe, 3-hdl, 'Time & Tide Wait...,' 2¼" 65.00
Wall pocket, Aller Vale, 1891-1902, 8" 280.00

Toys

Toys can be classified into at least two categories: early collectible toys with an established history, and the newer toys. The antique toys are easier to evaluate. A great deal of research has been done on them, and much data is available. The newer toys are just beginning to be studied; relative information is only now being published, and the lack of production records makes it difficult to know how many may be available. Often warehouse finds of these newer toys can change the market. This has happened with battery-operated toys and to some extent with robots. Review past issues of this guide. You will see the changing trends for the newer toys. All toys become more important as collectibles when a fixed period of manufacture is known. When we know the numbers produced and documentation of the makers is established, the prices become more predictable.

The best way to learn about toys is to attend toy shows and auctions. This will give you the opportunity to compare prices and condition. The more collectors and dealers you meet, the more you will learn. There is no substitute for holding a toy in your hand and seeing for yourself what they are. If you are going to be a serious collector, buy all the books you can find. Read every article you see. Knowledge is vital to building a good collection. Study all books that are available. These are some of the most helpful: *Collecting Toys, Collecting Toy Soldiers,* and *Collecting Toy Trains, An Identification & Value Guide #3,* by Richard O'Brien; and *Toys of the Sixties, A Pictorial Guide,* by Bill Bruegman. Other informative books (published by Collector Books) are *Schroeder's Collectible Toys, Antique to Modern,* by Sharon and Bob Huxford; *Collector's Guide to Tinker Toys* by Craig Strange; *Classic Plastic Model Kits* by Rick Polizzi; *The Golden Age of Automotive Toys, 1925 – 1941,* by Ken Hutchinson and Greg Johnson; *Motorcycle Toys, Antique & Contemporary,* by Sally Gibson-Downs and Christine Gentry; *Collector's Encyclopedia of Disneyana* by David Longest and Michael Stern; *Stern's Guide to*

Disney Collectibles, Vol I – 3, by Michael Stern; *Modern Toys, American Toys, 1830 – 1980,* by Linda Baker; *Antique and Collectible Toys, 1970 – 1950,* and *Toys, Antique & Collectible,* both by David Longest; *Collector's Guide to Tootsietoys* by David Richter; *Collectible Action Figures* by Paris and Susan Manos; *Collectible American Yo-Yos* by Christopher Cook; *Breyer Animal Collector's Guide* by Felicia Browell; *Collector's Guide to Battery Toys, Identification & Values* by Don Hultzman; *Collector's Guide to TV Memorabilia, 1960s & 1970s,* by Greg Davis and Bill Morgan; *Matchbox Toys, 1948 – 1993, Matchbox Toys, 1974 – 1996, Second Edition,* and *Diecast Toys and Scale Models,* all by Dana Johnson.

Our advisor for all toys except Farm Toys, Guns, Schoenhut, Steiff, Toy Soldiers, and Trains is Jon Thurmond; he is listed in the Directory under Missouri. In the listings that follow, toys are listed by manufacturer's name if possible, otherwise by type. Measurements are given when appropriate and available; if only one dimension is noted, it is the greater one — height if the toy is vertical, length if it is horizontal. See also Children's Things; Personalities. For toy stoves, see Stoves.

Key:
b/o — battery operated	NP — nickel plated
cl — celluloid	w/up — wind-up
jtd — jointed	

Company or Country of Manufacture

Photo courtesy Dunbar Gallery

Buddy L, Express Body Truck, black, red spoke wheels, 1920s, 24", EX, $1,500.00.

Alps, Balloon Blowing Monkey, b/o, 1950s, 11", MIB 225.00
Alps, Cola Drinking Bear, b/o, rare yel version, 1950s, NMIB ...185.00
Alps, Television Car, tin litho, friction, 6", EX (VG box) 260.00
Alps, Whirly Twirly Rocket Ride, b/o, tin litho, 13", NM 325.00
Arcade, Caterpillar Ten Tractor, pnt CI w/NP, 7½", EX 700.00
Arcade, Ford Dump Truck, pnt CI, NP spoke wheels, 1929, 7", EX ..360.00
Arcade, Ford Touring Car, blk pnt CI, NP driver, 6½", EX+ ..1,100.00
Arcade, Gas Pump, pnt CI, dial revolves, rope hose, 6", NM ..2,600.00
Auburn, De Soto Airflow Car, red/wht tires, 1937, 5", VG 35.00
Auburn, Krazy Tow Set, rubber, 8" truck/7" car, 1950s, NMIB 75.00
Aurora, Thunderjet Cougar Slot Car #1389, gr, EX 30.00
Aurora AFX, Blazer Flame-thrower Slot Car #1984, NM 18.00
Aurora AFX, Roarin' Rolls Slot Car, wht & blk, EX 15.00
Aurora Cigarbox, Ford J Car, die-cast, blk rubber tires, M 18.00
Bandai, Ford Mustang Coupe, friction, litho int, 1965, 8", NM .200.00
Bandai, Mercedes 219 Sedan, friction, bl/chrome, 8", NM 235.00
Bing, Gunboat Mars, pnt tin/live steam, 2-mast, 1908, 24", NM ..7,150.00
Bing, Limousine Saloon Taxi, w/up, 13", M 3,300.00
Bing, Steam Engine, brass/tin on CI base, steam driven, 17", G .360.00
Breyer, Andalusian Foal, matt dk chestnut, 1973-93 ....15.00
Breyer, Bucking Bronco, gray matt, 1961-67, from $150 to 200.00
Breyer, Man O' War, 1969-95 ....18.00
Buddy L, Aerial Ladder Truck, mk BLFD, 2 ladders, 1960, 24", EX ..100.00
Buddy L, Baby Truck, red, spoke wheels, 1920s, 24", G 750.00
Buddy L, Greyhound Bus, MIB, from $550 to 600.00

Buddy L, Pile Driver, #260, 1924-27, 19", G 425.00
Buddy L, US Mail Truck, Buy Defense Bonds decal, 21", M 850.00
Chein, Cathedral Organ, tin litho, crank for music, 9½", NMIB ..175.00
Chein, Drummer boy, tin litho, w/up, 1930s, 9", NM 275.00
Chein, Greyhound Bus, tin litho, w/up, 9", EX 325.00
Chein, Rabbit w/Cart, tin litho, w/up, 8", NM, from $125 to 150.00
Corgi, Batcopter, die-cast, #925, MIB 60.00
Corgi, Ferrari Formula I, die-cast, #154, MIB 50.00
Corgi, Fort GT70, die-cast, #316, MIB 50.00
Corgi, James Bond's Aston Martin, die-cast, #271, MIB 90.00
Corgi, Radio Rescue Rover, die-cast, bl, #416, MIB 125.00
Corgi, Studebaker Golden Hawk, die-cast, 3211, MIB 100.00
Cragstan, Concrete Mixer Truck, tin, friction, 8", VGIB 50.00
Cragstan, Moon City, b/o, 1970, MIB 250.00
Cragstan, Rambler Classic Sedan, friction, 1960s, 8", MIB 75.00
Creation, Chinese Man Pulling Rickshaw, compo/tin, w/up, 6½", NMIB ..400.00
Dakin, Baby Puss, Hanna-Barbera, 1971, EX+ 100.00
Dakin, Deputy Dawg, Terrytoons, 1977, EX 50.00
Dakin, Hoppy Hopperoo, Hanna-Barbera, 1971, EX+ 100.00
Dakin, Popeye, King Features, cloth clothes, 1974, MIP 50.00
Dent, Fire Ladder Wagon, pnt CI, 3 blk horses/2 men, 28", EX .715.00
Dinky, Guy Van, Lyons, die-cast, #514, MIB 2,000.00
Dinky, Hudson Commodore Sedan, die-cast, #139b, MIB 225.00
Dinky, Leyland Comet Wagon, die-cast, #933, MIB 200.00
Dinky, Lotus Racer, die-cast, #241, MIB 80.00
Dinky, Rolls Royce Silver Shadow, die-cast, #158, MIB 100.00
Dinky, Triumph TR2, die-cast, #111, MIB 160.00
Distler, Jazzi Jim, w/concertina, tin litho, w/up, 7½", EXIB 3,100.00
Distler, Monkey Drummer, tin litho, w/up, 7½", EX 400.00
Duncan, Beginner Yo-Yo, wood, #1044 or #44, MIP, ea 25.00
Duncan, Glow Imperial Yo-Yo, red letters, early 1970s, MIP 800.00
Duncan, Peg Top Chicago Twister #329, wood, MIP 20.00
Duncan, Shrieking Sonic Satellite Yo-Yo, #500, MIP 35.00
Emenee, accordion, plastic, 18 keys, 52 reeds, 1957, NM in case .50.00
Fischer, Riverboat, tin litho, w/pilot, 7½", EX 950.00
Fisher-Price, Chuggy Pop-Up, #0616, 1955, EX 100.00
Fisher-Price, Granny Doodle, #0101, 1321, EX 800.00
Fisher-Price, Piggy Bank, pk plastic, #0166, 1981-82, EX 20.00
Fisher-Price, Play Family Hospital, complete, #0931, 1976-78, EX ..125.00
Fisher-Price, Popeye Spinach Eater, #0488, 1939, EX 600.00
Fisher-Price, Running Bunny Cart, #0304, 1957, EX 75.00
Fisher-Price, Talking Donald Duck, #0765, 1955, EX 125.00
Fisher-Price, Teddy Bear Parade, limited edition, #6592, 1991, EX ..70.00
Fleischmann, Battleship, tin litho, w/up, 4 flags, 14", EX 775.00
Gibbs, See-Saw Motion Toy, 2 figures spin on pole, 14", EX 250.00
Gilbert, Erector Set #4, complete, VG (VG box) 125.00
Gund, Pluto hand puppet, cloth & vinyl, squeaker, MIP 50.00
Guntherman, Beetle Crawling, w/up, 7½", NMIB 350.00
Hartland Plastics, Bat Masterson, standing figure, NMIB 500.00
Hartland Plastics, Commanche Kid, NM 150.00
Hartland Plastics, General Custer, NMIB 200.00
Hartland Plastics, Matt Dillon, w/tag, NMIB 275.00
Hasbro, Autobot Car #TF1061, Powerdasher #1, jet, mail-in, MIP ..15.00
Hasbro, Autobot Minicar #TF1883, Hubcap, metallic, MIP 10.00
Hasbro, Decepticon Jet #TF1191, Thrust, maroon jet, MIP 30.00
Hasbro, Glow Action Yo-Yo, 1968, MOC, from $10 to 15.00
Hasbro, Monsterbot #TF1461, Grotusque, tiger, MIP 30.00
Hubley, Air Ford Monoplane, pnt CI w/NP, 1930s, 4", EX 185.00
Hubley, Attack Bomber #326, red plastic, 8" W, NM (EX box) .165.00
Hubley, Monocoupe, pnt CI w/NP, 8½", EX 500.00
Hubley, Motorcycle, pnt CI, b/o lights, rubber wheels, 6", EX 520.00
Ideal, Bamm-Bamm hand puppet, cloth/vinyl, 1966, EX+OC 45.00
Ideal, Dukes of Hazzard Slot Car Set, MIB 85.00
Ideal, Famous Frontier Am, Roy Rogers, plastic figure, 5", M 10.00

Ideal, Underwater Adventure Diver, red plastic figure, M 5.00
Irwin, Taxi Cab, friction, yel/red plastic, 12", EXIB 175.00
Ives, Dancing Couple, spinning CI figures, 3½", EX 135.00
Kenner, Girder & Panel Constructioneer Set #8, VG (VG box) ..85.00
Kenner, Give-a-Show Projector, 1963, complete, NM (VG box) ..55.00
Kenner, Imperial TIE Fighter, Micro Collection, NM 30.00
Kenner, Luke Skywalker, Empire Strikes Bk, blond, 3¾", MOC .125.00
Kenner, Stormtrooper, Return of Jedi, 3¾", MOC 35.00
Kenton, Overland Circus Calliope Truck, pnt CI, no driver, 9", G ..850.00
Kenton, Stake Truck, CI, gr pnt, rpl tires, 8", NM 365.00
Keystone, Bluebird Racer, w/up, rpt, 19", G 400.00
Keystone, Dump Truck, hydraulic lift, 1920s, 28", VG 1,250.00
Keystone, Steam Shovel, open sides w/corrugated roof, G 250.00
Kilgore, Coupe, pnt CI, NP spoke wheels/2 passengers, 6¼", EX ..400.00
Kilgore, Cris-Craft Commuter, pnt CI, 1930, 11", EX 6,820.00
Kingsbury, Aerial Ladder Truck, pnt steel, CI seat, 35", VG 750.00
Kingsbury, Chrysler Airflow, pnt steel, w/up, b/o lights, 14", EX ..575.00
Kingsbury, Stake Truck, pnt steel, w/up, w/driver, 9", VG 400.00
Knickerbocker, Laurel & Hardy hand puppets, 1965, NM, pr 70.00
Lehmann, Auto Post, tin litho, driver in mail van, 5", VG 1,100.00
Lehmann, Climbing Monkey, litho face, 1903, 7½", M 200.00
Lehmann, Lolo Automobile, w/driver, tin litho, 4", EX 700.00
Lehmann, Titania Sedan, tin litho, electric headlights, 10", VG .2,500.00
Lehmann, Tut-Tut, driver in open auto, litho/pnt tin, 6½", EX ..1,200.00
Lesney, Matchbox Car Transporter, clear windows, K-10C, NM 8.50
Lesney, Matchbox Diesel Road Roller, #01-A, 1953, NM 43.00
Lesney, Matchbox Lincoln Continental, #31-C, 1-75 Series, M ..12.00
Lindstrom, Mammy, tin litho, w/up, 8", G 125.00
Linemar, Drumming Mickey Mouse, b/o, remote control, NM (EX box) 1,200.00
Linemar, Hoop Clown, tin litho, w/up, 4", NMIB 850.00
Linemar, Mickey Mouse Xylophone Player, tin litho, w/up, 7", VG ..425.00
Linemar, Smoking Spaceman, b/o, eyes light up, moves, 12", EX ..1,800.00
Linemar, Telephone Bear, b/o, plush/tin, 1950s, 7½", MIB 375.00
Linemar, Uncle Scrooge, tin litho, w/up, 6", EX 350.00
LJN, Emergency Rescue Truck, red plastic, 1975, 14", MIB 135.00
Marklin, Fire Pumper, tin/CI, steam driven, ca 1900, 11", EX ..11,000.00
Martin, Boy Pushing Cart, pnt tin, w/up, 8", EX 1,000.00
Martin, Bull Fighter, rubber-band drive, 8", EXIB 1,320.00

Martin, Delivery Boy, tinplate cloth-dressed boy pushes cart, wind-up, complete, 7½", EX in original box, $1,300.00.

Martin, Fisherman, pnt tin, w/up, 7", EX 1,825.00
Marusan, SSN 571 Skate Submarine, tin litho, b/o, 19", EXIB ..250.00
Marx, Barney Rubble, plastic figure, Hanna-Barbera, 60mm, NM ..4.00
Marx, Ben Hur Series 2000 Playset, complete, MIB 2,000.00
Marx, Campus Cuties Dinner for Two, plastic figure, M 8.00
Marx, Cape Canaveral Playset #2656, complete, MIB 900.00
Marx, Climbing Fireman, plastic/tin, w/up, VG 200.00
Marx, Disneykings Pecos Bill, plastic figure, 1960s, NMIB 22.00
Marx, Funny Tiger, tin litho, w/up, 7", VG (VG box) 200.00
Marx, General Lee, Civil War plastic figure 6.00
Marx, Mr Mercury, tin/plastic, b/o, remote control, 13", EX 350.00
Marx, Nellybelle Jeep, pressed steel, complete, 11", MIB 400.00

Marx, Old Mother Goose, tin litho, w/up, 1930, NM (VG box) ..1,925.00
Marx, Phantom of the Opera, orange plastic figure, NM 20.00
Marx, Steam Roller, tin litho, w/up, w/flat figure, 8½", EX+ 250.00
Mattel, Flipper Music Box, plastic Flipper pops up, 1960s, VG 15.00
Mattel, guitar, Mother Goose Graphics, NM 60.00
Mattel, Hot Wheels Baja Breaker, red line tires, 1989, MOC 44.00
Mattel, Hot Wheels Greased Gremlin, blk walls, 1982, MOC 25.00
Mattel, Hot Wheels Thor Van, blk walls, 1979, M (VG card) 15.00
Mattel, Ringling Bros Toy Circus, MIB 85.00
Mattel, Sizzler Ferrari 512DS, red, decal, NM 30.00
Mego, USS Enterprise Bridge Playset, 1975, MIB 125.00
Parker Bros, Toy-Town Telegraph Office Playset, VG (VG box) ..100.00
Remco, Gallant Gladiator Warship Playset, EXIB 235.00
Remco, Lost in Space Robot, plastic, 1966, 12", EX (EX+ box) .500.00
Remco, Mighty Mike Action Track Set, NMIB 100.00
Richter, Anchor Stone Fortress Set #406, VG 500.00
Schuco, Bigo-Bello Dog, orig clothes, 14", NM 175.00
Schuco, BMW Convertible, w/up, #1048, 4½", NM 225.00
Schuco, BMW Turbo Coupe, die-cast, orange, #613, M 25.00
Schuco, Coupe 3000, w/up, w/accessories, 4", EX+ (G box) 150.00
Schuco, Micro Racer, red, w/up, #1042, 3", EX 300.00
Schuco, Tabby Cat, Noah's Ark, orig ribbon, 1950s, 3", M 265.00
Schuco, Telesteering Car, tin litho, w/up, #3000, MIB 225.00
Schuco, Yes/No Tricky Monkey, US Zone tag, ribbon, 13", NM ..450.00
Schwinn, bicycle, Black Phantom, boy's, rstr 850.00
Steelcraft, Little Jim/JC Penney Mack Dump Truck, 22", G- 300.00
Steelcraft, US Mail Plane #NS-131, pressed steel, 23", VG 850.00
Strauss, Dandy Jim Clown Dancer, tin litho, w/up, 1921, 10" 600.00
Strauss, Leaping Lena Car, tin, w/up, 1930, VG, from $400 to ...450.00
Strauss, Red Flash Racer, tin litho, w/up, #31, 9½", EX 650.00
Strauss, Yell-O-Taxi, tin litho, w/up, w/driver, #59, 8", VG 425.00
Structo, Cattle Truck, pressed steel, red/wht, #708, MIB 225.00
Structo, Earth Mover, pressed steel, red pnt, 20", EX 75.00
Structo, Ready Mix Cement Mixer, pressed steel, #700, NMIB .250.00
Structo, Taxicab, pressed steel, early 2-tone 4-door, 11", G 250.00
Structo, Truck Fleet Set, pressed steel, #725, NMIB 550.00
Sturditoy, Wrecker, pnt steel, doorless cab, 30½", EX 1,050.00
Sun Rubber, Bobtail Racer, gr/wht, 4", VG 15.00
Tekno, Cooper Norton #1, silver, #812, EX 60.00
Tekno, Corvair Monza Coupe, chrome, #930S, M 45.00
Tekno, Ford VB Garbage Truck, #423, gr/red, G 45.00
Tekno, Scania Vebis Ladder Truck, red, #445, EX 100.00
TN, Bobo the Magician, tin litho, w/up, 9", NM (EX box) 500.00
TN, Cadillac Sedan, friction, cream/yel w/chrome, 1950s, 13¼", M ..300.00
TN, Clown Magician, tin w/cloth clothes, w/up, 7", NMIB 425.00
TN, Piston Action Robot, b/o, remote control, 8", NMIB 1,600.00
TN, Red Rosco Astronaut, b/o w/flashing lights, 13", EX 1,400.00
Tonka, CAT Cement Mixer, yel, M 40.00
Tonka, Farm Truck, w/stock rack, 1957, EX 375.00
Tonka, Hi-Way Custom Mixer, 1957, VG+ 185.00
Tonka, Lumber Changeable Flatbed Truck, 1955, EX 325.00
Tonka, Service Truck, bl, 1959, EX 185.00
Tonka, Wheaton Van Lines Truck, 1956, G 450.00
Tootsietoy, Battleship, silver/red, #1034, 1940s, 6", NM 30.00
Tootsietoy, Chevy Fastback, red, rubber tires, 1947-49, 4", EX 35.00
Tootsietoy, Ford Texaco Oil Truck, red, 1949-52, 6", NM+ 65.00
Tootsietoy, Mack Transport, red w/3 mc Buicks, #0190, 8½", NM+ ..210.00
Tootsietoy, Playtime Set, #5031, 1920s, M (EX box) 1,450.00
Tootsietoy, US Army Armored Car, tan/gr, #4635, 4", M 55.00
TPS, Mama Kangaroo & Playful Baby, tin litho, w/up, 6½", MIB ...200.00
Tyco, A-Team Van Slot Car, blk w/red stripe, EX 38.00
Tyco, Lamborghini Slot Car, wht w/blk letters, EX 10.00
Unique Art, Hee Haw, tin litho, w/up, 1930, 10¼", VG 225.00
Unique Art, Rodeo Joe, tin litho, w/up, 7", NM (EX box) 375.00

US Zone, Bully Bulldog, tin litho, w/up, 8", NMIB 450.00
Vindex, Whitewater Farm Wagon, pnt CI, 2 blk horses, 7½", EX ..2,425.00
Wilkins, Doctor's Buggy, pnt CI/red spoke wheels, 10½", EX 600.00
Wolverine, canister set, tin, MIB 130.00
Wyandotte, Boat-Tail Racer, red, w/wheel covers, 8½", G 175.00
Wyandotte, Dump Truck, yel/red/blk, 16", VG 100.00
Wyandotte, Gr Valley Ranch Semi, red, open stake bed, VG 100.00
Wyandotte, Tank Truck, gr, wooden wheels, 1930s, 10", EX 115.00
Y, Atomic Robot, tin litho/plastic, w/up, 6", EX (EX box) 675.00
Y, Bubble Blowing Musician, b/o, 1950s, 11", NMIB 175.00
Y, Deluxe Open Zephyr, tin, friction, 1950s, 11", EXIB 275.00
Y, Magic Bulldozer, b/o, bump-&-go, w/driver, 5", MIB 175.00

Farm Toys

Tractor, Kilgore No. T-83, cast-iron take-apart type with nickel wheels and bucket, molded driver, 1930s, 3½", NM, $115.00.

Barge wagon, John Deere, Ertl, 1/64th scale, #5586, MIB 2.50
Combine, John Deere 12-A, Ertl, Collectors Edition, 1/16th scale, MIB ..44.00
Disk harrow, Ertl, 4½" 35.00
Disk harrow, Tru Scale, #D405, red, MIB 50.00
Rake, Ford New Holland, Ertl, 1/64th scale, #369, MIB 3.00
Skid steer loader, John Deere, Ertl, 1/16th scale, #569, MIB 18.00
Threshing machine, McCormick-Deering, CI, rpt, Arcade, 12" L .165.00
Tractor, Allis-Chalmers, Arcade, NP driver, 7", NM 925.00
Tractor, Case IH w/End Loader, Ertl, 1/64th scale, #212, MIB 5.00
Tractor, Case L, Ertl, 1/43rd scale, #2554, MIB 5.50
Tractor, Fordson, Arcade, gr spoke wheels, driver, 5½", EX+ 385.00
Tractor, John Deere Model A, Ertl, 1/16th scale, #539, MIB 18.00
Tractor, John Deere Model L1, Ertl, 1/16th scale, #21056, MIB ...38.00
Tractor, John Deere 3010, 1/16th scale, #5635, MIB 20.00
Tractor, Massey-Ferguson 555, Ertl, 1/16th scale, #1105, MIB 22.00
Tractor, Massey-Harris 55 Wide Front, Ertl, 1/16th scale, MIB 20.00
Tractor, McCormick-Deering WD-40, gray/red, 1/16th scale, MIB 265.00
Tractor, McCormick-Deering 10-20, Arcade, w/driver, 7", G 250.00
Tractor, Oliver 1555 Diesel, Ertl, 1/16th scale, #2223, MIB 22.00
Truck, CI, red rpt, unknown mfg, 7⅛" 95.00
Wagon, pnt tin, Tru Scale, 7½", EX 18.00
Wagon w/horse & driver, CI, worn pnt, Arcade, 6½x5¼", G 85.00

Guns: Cast-Iron Cap Guns (Caution: Some reproductions exist.)

In years past, virtually every child played with toy guns, and the survival rate of these toys is minimal, at best. The interest in these charming toy guns has recently increased considerably, especially western styled, as collectors discover their scarcity, quality, and value. Toy gun collectibles encompass the early and the very ornate figural toy guns and bombs through the more realistic ones with recognizable character names, gleaming finishes, faux jewels, dummy bullets, engraving, and colorful grips. This section will cover some of the most popular cast-iron and die-cast toy guns from the past one hundred years.

Our advisor is James Schleyer, internationally recognized collector and appraiser of toy guns. He has authored numerous books, articles, and newsletters on antique toy guns and holsters. He is the former editor for *Toy Gun Purveyors*, an international newsletter that fostered the collecting of these valuable and rare toys. His current book, *Backyard*

Buckaroos — Collecting Western Toy Guns, contains nearly 2,500 photographs. Toy gun inquiries that include a SASE will be gracious answered. Send to: Toy Guns, Box 243-E, Burke, VA 22015.

American, Kilgore, cylinder revolves, 1940, 9⅜", EX 450.00
Army 45 Auto, Hubley, 1945, 6½", M 150.00
Atta Boy, Hubley, single shot, 1935, 4", G- 50.00
Bango, Stevens, engr/jewels, 1940, 7½", VG 100.00
Big Bill, Kilgore, single shot, 1935, 4⅞", M 65.00
Big Horn, Kilgore, cylinder revolves, 1940, 8⅝", M 550.00
Big Scout, Stevens, single shot, 1930, 9⅜", VG 165.00
Billy the Kid, Stevens, single shot, 1940s, 6¾", G- 145.00
Border Patrol, Kilgore, automatic, 1935, 4½", VG 85.00
Buc-A-Roo, Kilgore, single shot, 1940, 7¾", M 135.00
Buffalo Bill, Kenton, single shot, 1930, rare, 13½", VG 550.00
Buffalo Bill, Stevens, single shot, 1890, rare, 11¾", G- 250.00
Bull's Eye, Kenton, engr, 1940, 6½", M 450.00
Bulldog, Hubley, single shot, 1935, 6", G 35.00
Bunker Hill, National, single shot, 1925, 5¼", M 100.00
Captain, Kilgore, automatic, 1940, 4¼", VG 85.00
Champ, Hubley, automatic, Star Medallion, 1940, 5", EX 100.00
Chief, Dent, single shot, 1935, 7½", VG 85.00
Colt, Stevens, single shot, 1900, 5½", EX 65.00
Cowboy, Hubley, 1940, 8", VG 120.00
Cowboy King, Stevens, 1940, 9", M 350.00
Dick, Hubley, automatic, 1930, 4⅛", VG 45.00
Doughboy, Kilgore, automatic, 1920, 4⅞", VG 125.00
Eagle, Hubley, single shot, 1935, 8½", VG 150.00

Gene Autry, Kenton, cast iron, dummy variety with scalloped hammer, $350.00.

Gene Autry, Kenton, engr, 1940, rare, 6½", VG 500.00
Gene Autry, Kenton, repeater, nickel, 1940, 8⅜", VG 250.00
Guard, Kilgore, bl finish, 1935, 6¼", EX 100.00
Invincible, Kilgore, 1935, 5¼", G- 45.00
Lasso Em Bill, Kilgore, cylinder revolves, 1930, 9", EX 250.00
Lawmaker, Kenton, nickel, 1940, rare, 8⅜", M 300.00
Lone Eagle, Kilgore, cylinder revolves, 1930, 5¼", EX 150.00
Lone Ranger, Kilgore, nickel, 1940, rare, 8¼", M 345.00
Long Boy, Kilgore, single shot, 1920, 11⅛", VG 135.00
Long Tom, Kilgore, cylinder revolves, 1940, rare, 10⅜", M 650.00
Mohican, Dent, single shot, 1930, 6¼", EX 100.00
National Auto, National, 1915, 3¾", G- 25.00
Officers Pistol, Kilgore, automatic, 1940, rare, 6", M 400.00
Patrol, Hubley, 1935-40, 6", M 85.00
Pawnee Bill, Stevens, 1940, 7⅝", VG 235.00
Peacemaker, Stevens, gold, 1940, 8½", M 155.00
Pirate, Hubley, dbl bbl, 1940, 9⅜", M 125.00
Police Chief, Kenton, plastic grip, 1940, 4⅝" 145.00
Presto, Kilgore, automatic, 1940, 5⅛", VG 65.00
Rodeo, Hubley, single shot,1940, 7", EX 45.00
Scout, Stevens, single shot, 1890, 7", VG 75.00
Six Shooter, Kilgore, cylinder revolves, 1940, 6½", VG 85.00
Spitfire, Kilgore, automatic, 1940, 4⅝", EX 90.00
Texan, Hubley, cylinder revolves, NPCI, 1940, 9¼", M 165.00

Texan Jr, Hubley, CI, 1940, 8⅛", VG 85.00
Trooper Safety, Kilgore, repeater, 1925, 10¼", M 145.00
Two Time, Kenton, rubber band, 1929, 9¼", VG 155.00
Warrior, Kilgore, repeater, nickel, 1920s, 9", EX 175.00
Wild West, Kenton, single shot, 1920s, rare, 11½", M 275.00
101 Ranch, Hubley, single shot, 1930, 11½", VG 245.00
2 In 1, Stevens, rubber band, 1930, 9¼", VG 150.00
49-er, Stevens, 1940, 9", M 325.00

Guns: Die-Cast and Miscellaneous Toy Guns

Alan Ladd, Geo Schmidt, rare, 10¼", EX 325.00
Army 45 Auto, Hubley, compo, nonworking, 1940 .... 75.00
Army 45 Auto, Hubley, dull gray finish, 6½", M 85.00
Atomic Disintegrator, Hubley, space gun, 8", VG 345.00
Bonanza, Leslie-Henry 44, cylinder revolves, 10½", M 185.00
Bronco, Kilgore, cylinder revolves, 9¼", VG 75.00
Buck'n Bronc, Geo Schmidt, 10½", EX 115.00
Buckle Gun, Mattel, derringer, 3", VG 95.00
Champion, Leslie-Henry, 9", VG 100.00
Colt, Hubley Snub Nose Detective, mini, M 30.00
Colt .45, Hubley, cylinder revolves, bullets, 14", VG 150.00
Cowboy, Hubley, cylinder revolves, gold, rare, 12", EX 250.00
Cowboy, Hubley, cylinder revolves, 12", M 165.00
Cowhand 250, Nichols, 8½", VG 70.00
Coyote, Hubley, 8¼", M 85.00
Dale Evans, Geo Schmidt, jewels, rare, 10½", VG 400.00
Davy Crockett, Hubley, Flintlock Buffalo Rifle, 25", EX 175.00
Deputy-BB, Schmidt, copper grips, sm, 8½", EX 75.00
Dick Tracy Squad Shotgun, Mattel, cap & water, pump 125.00
Eagle, Kilgore, nickel, cylinder revolves, 8", M 125.00
Fanner 'Shootin' Shell,' Mattel, bullets, 9", M 150.00
Fanner 45 'Shootin' Shell,' Mattel, rare, 11¼", EX 325.00
Fanner 50, Mattel, nickel, cylinder revolves, 10⅝", EX 145.00
Flip Rifleman Ring Rifle, Hubley, 32", VG 275.00
G-Man, Marx, Sparkling Machine Gun, tin, 26", VG 175.00
G-Man, Marx, tin clicker pistol w/jewel, 1935, M 75.00
Gene Autry, Leslie-Henry, nickel, 9", M 175.00
Gene Autry, Leslie-Henry 44, cylinder revolves, bullets, 11", EX ... 165.00
Gray Ghost, Lone Star, nickel, silver grips, rare, 9", EX 400.00
Grizzly, Kilgore, gold, cylinder revolves, 10¼", M 275.00
Hawkeye, Kilgore, automatic, 4¼", M 45.00
Hopalong Cassidy, Geo Schmidt, cameo grips, 9", EX 325.00
Hopalong Cassidy, Wyandotte, gold, 9", M 650.00
Hopalong Cassidy, Wyandotte, nickel, 9", VG 350.00
Indian Scout Rifle, Mattel, bullets, 30", M 210.00
Lone Ranger, Actoy, antique bronze, 10", VG 175.00
Lone Ranger, Marx, tin clicker w/jewel, 8", M 95.00
Marshal, Halco, cylinder revolves, bullets, 10½", M 175.00
Maverick, Leslie-Henry, 10½", VG 130.00
Maverick 45, Halco, cylinder revolves, 11", M 325.00
Me & My Buddy, Wyandotte, tin clicker, 1935-40, VG 125.00
Model 61, Nichols, chrome finish, cylinder revolves, rare, M ... 425.00
Model 61, Nichols, steel-bl finish, cylinder revolves, rare, M ... 365.00
Mountie, Kilgore, automatic, 6", M 45.00
Mustang 500, Nichols, nickel, 12¼", EX 165.00
Pal, Kilgore, nickel, sm single shot, 1945-60, M 10.00
Paladin, Leslie-Henry, nickel, repeater, rare, 9", EX 250.00
Pet, Hubley, nickel, 1945-60, M 10.00
Pioneer, Hubley, blk grips w/compass, 10¼", EX 130.00
Pioneer, Hubley, nickel, amber grips, 10¼", M 115.00
Pirate, Hubley, over-under bbls, 1960, VG 45.00
Pony Boy, Esquire-Actoy, nickel, 10", EX 85.00
Rebel Scattergun, Marx, dbl bbl, rare, 21", M 800.00

Red Ranger, Wyandotte, 7¾", VG **45.00**
Remington 36, Hubley, cylinder revolves, bullets, 8¼", EX **75.00**
Ric-O-Shay, Hubley, cylinder revolves, bullets, 12¼", M **125.00**
Roy Rogers, G Schmidt, copper grips, 10¼", EX **225.00**
Roy Rogers, Kilgore, die cast, cylinder revolves, engr, 10", M **385.00**
Roy Rogers, Leslie-Henry, gold, 9", EX **350.00**
Scout Rifle, Hubley, nickel, lever, 1960, EX **125.00**
Sharps Carbine, Marx, Civil War Model, 1960, rare, EX **200.00**
Stallion .32, Nichols, 8", VG **35.00**
Stallion 38, Nichols, cylinder revolves, bullets, 9½", EX **115.00**
Stallion 45 Mk II, Nichols, cylinder revolves, bullets, 12", M **300.00**
Star, Hubley, nickel, single shot, 7", MIB **25.00**
Sure Shot, Hubley, nickel, 8", EX **30.00**
Texan, Hubley, die cast, gold, cylinder revolves, 9½", M **175.00**
Texan Jr, Hubley, die cast, side opener, 9½", M **65.00**
Texan Jr, Hubley, die cast, 9", VG **50.00**
Thundergun, Marx, nickel, engr, 12½", M **225.00**
Trooper, Hubley, nickel, snub nose, 1950-60, EX **30.00**
US Marshal, Leslie-Henry, antique bronze, 11¼", VG **130.00**
Wagon Train, Leslie-Henry 44, antique bronze, 11¼", VG **135.00**
Wells Fargo, Actoy, nickel, 11", M **155.00**
Western, Hubley, nickel, 9", M **70.00**
Wild Bill Hickok, Leslie-Henry, 9", VG **125.00**
Wild Bill Hickok, Leslie-Henry 44, 11¼", EX **165.00**
Winchester Carbine, Mattel, Shootin' Shell, 26", M **165.00**
Winchester Saddle Gun, Mattel, 33", M **185.00**
Wyatt Earp, Actoy, Buntline Special, 11", M **155.00**
Wyatt Earp, Hubley, nickel, log bbl, 11", M **175.00**
2 in 1, Hubley, 2 interchanging bbls, 6", EX **50.00**
45 Colt, Hubley, nickel/ivory grips, cylinder revolves, 14", VG .**125.00**

Guns: Early-Style Figural Guns and Bombs (Caution: Reproductions exist.)

Admiral Dewey Bomb, CI, Grey Iron, 1900, 1¾", EX **345.00**
Butting Match, CI, Ives, 1885, 5", EX **500.00**
Cannon, Kenton, CI, 1900, 4⅞", VG **450.00**
Chinese Must Go, CI, Ives, 1880, 4¾", G- **400.00**
Clown on Powder Keg, CI, Ives, 1890s, 3¾", VG **435.00**
Devil's Head Bomb, Ives, CI, .22 blank, 1880, 2¼", VG **300.00**
Dog's Head Bomb, Ives, CI, 1880, 2⅛", EX **265.00**
Double-Face Man, Ives, CI, 1890, 1⅝", VG **165.00**
George Washington Bomb, CI, 1900, 1¼", EX **350.00**
Hobo Bomb, Ideal, CI, 1890s, 2", G- **135.00**
Liberty Bell Bomb, CI, 1876, 2⅜", EX **195.00**
Lightning Express, Kenton, CI, 1900, 5", EX **750.00**
Punch & Judy, Ives, CI, 1880s, 5¼", VG **850.00**
Sea Serpent, Stevens, CI, 1890, 3½", EX **975.00**
Yellow Kid Bomb, Grey Iron, CI, 1900, 1½", VG **200.00**

Models

Addar, Jaws, Diorama #S31, 1975, MIB (sealed) **70.00**
Addar, Planet of Apes, Dr Zira #105, 1974, MIB **70.00**
Airfix, Bristol Bloodhound, #M01703, 1/75, MIB **15.00**
Airfix, Lunar Module #3013, 1981, 1/72, MIB **16.00**
Airfix, Russian Vostok, #5172, 1/144, 1991, MIB **20.00**
AMT, Airwolf Helicopter #6680, 1984, 1/48, MIB **40.00**
AMT, Flintstones Sportscar #495, 1974, MIB **40.00**
AMT, Star trek, USS Enterprise #917, 1967, orig issue, MIB **190.00**
AMT/Ertl, Star Trek Klingon Cruiser, 1991, MIB **6.00**
Articles & Objects, Firefox Jet #FF-01, 5", MIB **20.00**
Aurora, Buccaneer, Pirate Ship #429, 1959, MIB **100.00**
Aurora, Comic Scenes, Spider-Man #182, 1974, 1/12, MIB **170.00**

Aurora, Elfred E Neuman, #802, 1965, M (NM box) **60.00**
Aurora, Frankenstein, #449, 1/8, 1972, MIB **150.00**
Aurora, Godzilla #466, 1969, 1/600, MIB **320.00**
Aurora, Super Boy, #478, 1/8, 1964, MIB **350.00**
Bandai, EDF Unmanned Battleship #36135, 1/1220, MIB **40.00**
Billiken, Mechanic Kong, 1987, vinyl, MIB **180.00**
Lunar Models, Batmobile #SF039, 1/25, MIB **90.00**
Monogram, De Havilland Mosquito, NMIB **12.00**
Monogram, Elvira Mobile #2783, 1/24, MIB (sealed) **30.00**
Monogram, Space Taxi, #45, 1/48, 1959, MIB **155.00**
MPC, Ironside Van #3012, 1970, 1/20, MIB **100.00**
Renwal, Apollo Lunar Module #1861, 1975, 1/48, MIB (sealed) ..**50.00**
Revell, Botany Science, 1964, M (NM box) **35.00**
Revell, Dr Seuss, Game of Yertle #2100, 1960, EXIB **125.00**
Revell, Jupiter C, #1819, 1/96, 1958, MIB **270.00**

Pedal Cars and Ride-On Toys

Chevrolet 1955 Bel Air convertible, fiberglass body with Indianapolis 500 decals, rubber tires, chain drive, EX, $4,500.00.

Airplane, Murray-Otto, silver w/bl & red, decals, 45", EX **3,500.00**
American National Ford fire truck, 1938, EX orig **2,950.00**
Chrysler Airflow fire engine, 2 wooden ladders, rstr, 50" **1,150.00**
Chrysler car, Steelcraft, bl w/wht & chrome, 1941, EX **2,500.00**
GMC cab over body, EX **150.00**
Irish Mail Racer, Frank Taylor Mfg, ca 1930, 60", EX **400.00**
Locomotive, Pioneer, pressed steel/wood, wire wheels, rpt, 54", G **935.00**
National car, hand brake, horn, windshield, 46", EX+ orig **3,600.00**
Packard, 1927, M orig **10,500.00**
Packard Fire Chief, open roadster car, red w/blk & yel, 28", EX ...**8,000.00**
Racer, Garton, gr metal w/yel trim, spoked tires, 33½", G+ **650.00**
Racer #9, Am Nat'l, metal w/wood spoke wheels, bell, 42", VG+ ...**2,550.00**
Sad Face dump truck, 1950s, M **1,800.00**
Steelcraft Chief of Police Squad car, red w/yel stripes, 34", EX .**2,500.00**
Stutz car, w/oil can, bulb horn, windshield/etc, rstr, 53" L **3,000.00**
Torpedo Convertible, Murray, wht & red w/chrome, 1949, rstr ...**2,500.00**
Tractor, 1948 Farmall H, closed grill, G **900.00**
Yellow Cab, 1960s, EX **295.00**

Penny Toys

Auto, tin litho, Japanese people graphics, Japan, 2¾", EX **360.00**
Baby carriage, mc pnt, Made in Germany, 3½", VG **250.00**
Biplane, tin litho, Germany/Distler, EX **700.00**
Butting goat, tin litho, head moves, Germany, EX **220.00**
Carousel, 3 chairs w/riders, mc pnt, 4¼", EX **440.00**
Chinaman w/parasol, tin litho, Germany/Distler, EX **1,200.00**
Dancer w/hand crank, mc pnt, Johann Distler, 3¾", EX **300.00**
Delivery truck, tin litho, spoke wheels, Germany/Fischer, EX **250.00**
Double swing, mc pnt, Johann Meier, 3¼", EX **200.00**
Fire truck, mc pnt, w/up w/key, Made in Germany, 4¼", EX **440.00**
Gnomes cutting wood, tin litho, Germany/Meier, EX **415.00**
Goose, tin litho, spoked wheels, neck moves, Germany, EX **525.00**

Horse-drawn ambulance, tin litho, Germany/Meier, EX **220.00**
Horse-drawn plantation cart, tin litho, Germany/Meier, VG **155.00**
Hose-Reel Wagon, tin litho, Germany/Meier, VG **185.00**
Pool player at table, mc pnt, Kellerman, 4", EX **250.00**
Saloon car, tin litho, spoked wheels, Germany/Fischer, EX **175.00**
Sedan, tin litho, bl & wht, Germany, EX **145.00**
Sedan w/driver, mc pnt, GF (Georg Fischer), 4½", VG **140.00**
Touring car w/driver, mc pnt, GF (Georg Fischer), 4", VG **140.00**
Train & 3 cars, mc pnt, mk JLH 100, 12" **275.00**
Truck w/canvas cover & driver, mc pnt, JD (Distler), MIG, 3⅝" ...**415.00**
Whistle, w/squirrel in cage, mc pnt, 4¾" **195.00**

Pull Toys

Pipsqueak toys were popular among the Pennsylvania Germans. The earliest had bellows made from sheepskin. Later cloth replaced the sheepskin, and finally paper bellows were used.

Rich's Milk Wagon, paper litho on wood horse, tin litho wagon, 20" long, NM, $450.00.

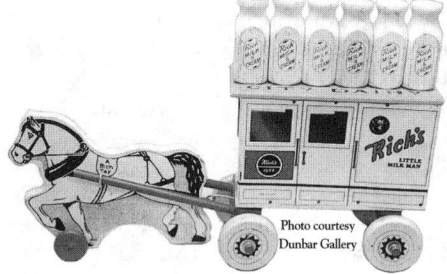

Photo courtesy Dunbar Gallery

Duck on wheels, USA, mohair duck, CI wheels, 1912, 9", VG ..**125.00**
Horse & jockey on platform, Althof-Bergmann, pnt tin, 4", EX ...**650.00**
Horse-drawn bakery wagon, trotting horse, tin, 8½", EX **600.00**
Horse-drawn cart, Geo Brown, pnt tin, 1 horse, 1870s, 14", EX .**400.00**
Horse-drawn circus wagon, Arcade, steel/wood, 2 blk horses, 14", G ...**385.00**
Horse-drawn doctor's buggy, Geo Brown, pnt tin, 13", G **855.00**
Horse-drawn Hansom cab, European, pnt tin/CI, 9", VG+ **575.00**
Horse-drawn milk wagon, Rich Toys, closed door, 20", EX **330.00**
Mule bell ringer, Gong Bell, pnt CI, 8", EX+ **880.00**
Wild Mule Jack, Gong Bell, pnt CI, 8", VG **470.00**

Humpty Dumpty Circus Clowns and Other Personel

Our advisor for Schoenhut Toys is Keith Kaonis, who has collected these toys for twenty years. Because of his involvement with the publishing industry (currently *Collectors' Eye, Antique DOLL Collector*, and during the '80s, *Collectors' SHOWCASE*), he has visited collections across the United States, produced several articles on Schoenhut toys, and served a term as president of the Schoenhut Collectors' Club. Keith is listed in the Directory under New York.

The listings below are for Humpty Dumpty Circus pieces. All rating conditions that follow are based on good to very good condition, i.e., very minor scratches and wear, good original finish, no splits, chips, no excessive paint wear or cracked eyes, and of course completeness.

Clowns with two-part heads (a cast face applied to a wooden head) were made from 1903-1915 and are most desirable — condition always is important. There have been nine distinct styles in fourteen different costumes recorded. Only eight costume styles apply to the two-part headed clowns. The later clowns had one-part heads whose features were pressed, and the costumes on the later ones, circa 1920, were no longer tied at the wrists and ankles.

Black Dude, reduced sz, from $250 to **600.00**

Black Dude, 1-part head, purple coat, from $250 to **800.00**
Black Dude, 2-part head, blk coat, from $500 to **700.00**
Chinese Acrobat, 1-part head, from $200 to **500.00**
Chinese Acrobat, 2-part head, rare, from $400 to **1,000.00**
Clown, early, G, from $150 to **500.00**
Clown, reduced sz, 1925-35, from $75 to **150.00**
Gent Acrobat, bsk head, rare, from $300 to **600.00**
Gent Acrobat, 2-part head, very rare, from $600 to **1,500.00**
Hobo, reduced sz, from $300 to **600.00**
Hobo, 1-part head, from $200 to **500.00**
Hobo, 2-part head, curved-up toes, from $500 to **1,000.00**
Hobo, 2-part head, facet toe ft, from $400 to **800.00**
Lady Acrobat, bsk head, from $300 to **600.00**
Lady Acrobat, 1-part head, from $200 to **400.00**
Lady Rider, bsk head, from $250 to **500.00**
Lady Rider, 1-part head, from $200 to **400.00**
Lady Rider, 2-part head, very rare, from $600 to **1,200.00**
Lion Tamer, bsk head, rare, from $350 to **750.00**
Lion Tamer, 1-part head, from $250 to **600.00**
Lion Tamer, 2-part head, early, very rare, from $600 to **1,200.00**
Ring Master, bsk, ca 1912-14, from $400 to **650.00**
Ring Master, 1-part head, from $200 to **450.00**
Ring Master, 2-part head, early, very rare, from $500 to **1,200.00**

Humpty Dumpty Circus Animals

Humpty Dumpty Circus animals with glass eyes, ca. 1903 – 1914, are more desirable and can demand much higher prices than the later painted-eye versions. As a general rule, a glass-eye version is 30% to 40% more than a painted-eye version. (There are exceptions.) The following list suggests values for both GE (glass-eye) and PE (painted-eye) versions and reflects a low PE price to a high GE price.

There are other variations and nuances of certain figures: Bulldog — white with black spots or brindle (brown); open- and closed-mouth zebras and giraffes; ball necks and hemispherical necks on some animals such as the pig, leopard, and tiger, to name a few. These points can affect the price and should be judged individually. Condition and rarity affect the price most significantly.

Alligator, GE/PE, from $200 to **500.00**
Arabian Camel, 1 hump, GE/PE, from $250 to **750.00**
Bactrian Camel, 2 humps, GE/PE, from $200 to **1,500.00**
Brown Bear, GE/PE, from $200 to **900.00**
Buffalo, cloth mane, GE/PE, from $300 to **1,000.00**
Buffalo, cvd mane, GE/PE, from $200 to **900.00**
Bulldog, GE/PE, from $400 to **1,600.00**
Burro (made to go w/chariot & clown), GE/PE, from $200 to **700.00**
Cat, GE/PE, rare, from $600 to **2,500.00**
Cow, GE/PE, from $250 to **900.00**
Deer, GE/PE, from $300 to **1,000.00**
Donkey, GE/PE, from $75 to **200.00**
Donkey w/blanket, GE/PE, from $90 to **400.00**
Elephant, GE/PE, from $90 to **300.00**
Elephant w/blanket, GE/PE, from $200 to **600.00**
Gazelle, GE/PE, rare, from $700 to **3,000.00**
Giraffe, GE/PE, from $200 to **800.00**
Goat, GE/PE, from $150 to **400.00**
Goose, PE only, from $200 to **600.00**
Gorilla, PE only, from $1,200 to **2,500.00**
Hippo, GE/PE, from $300 to **900.00**
Horse, brn, saddle & stirrups, GE/PE, from $150 to **400.00**
Horse, wht, platform, GE/PE, from $125 to **400.00**
Hyena, GE/PE, very rare, from $1,000 to **3,700.00**
Kangaroo, GE/PE, from $400 to **1,200.00**

Lion, cloth mane, GE, from $500 to **1,200.00**
Lion, cvd mane, GE/PE, from $250 to **900.00**
Monkey, 1-part head, PE only, from $250 to **450.00**
Monkey, 2-part head, wht face, from $300 ....**900.00**
Ostrich, GE/PE, from $200 to **750.00**
Pig, 5 versions, GE/PE, from $200 to **700.00**
Polar Bear, GE/PE, from $500 to **1,200.00**
Poodle, cloth mane, GE only, from $300 to **500.00**
Poodle, GE/PE, from $125 to **300.00**
Rabbit, GE/PE, very rare, from $1,000 to **3,000.00**
Rhino, GE/PE, from $250 to **1,000.00**
Sea lion, GE/PE, from $400 to **1,200.00**
Sheep (lamb) w/bell, GE/PE, from $200 to **700.00**
Tiger, GE/PE, from $250 to **800.00**
Wolf, GE/PE, very rare, from $600 to **4,000.00**
Zebra, GE/PE, from $250 to **800.00**
Zebu, GE/PE, rare, from $1,000 to **2,500.00**

Humpty Dumpty Circus Accessories

There are many accessories: wagons, tents, ladders, chairs, pedestals, tightropes, weights, and more.

Menagerie tent, early, ca 1904, from $1,500 to **2,500.00**
Menagerie tent, later, ca 1914-20, from $1,200 to **2,000.00**
Oval litho tent, 1926, from $2,000 to **4,000.00**
Sideshow panels, 1926, pr, from $2,000 to **4,000.00**

Steiff

Margaret Steiff began making her stuffed felt toys in Germany in the late 1800s. The animals she made were tagged with an elephant in a circle. Her first teddy bear, made in 1903, became such a popular seller that she changed her tag to a bear. Felt stuffing was replaced with excelsior and wool; when it became available, foam was used. In addition to the tag, look for the 'Steiff' ribbon and the button inside the ear. For further information we recommend *Teddy Bears and Steiff Animals*, a full-color identification and value guide by Margaret Fox Mandel, available from Collector Books or your public library. See also Teddy Bears.

Bear, on all 4s, mohair, collar/bell, chest tag, 1950, 5½", M **175.00**
Bendy Bear, caramel, chest tag, 1960, 3", M **125.00**
Bison, mohair, felt horns, chest tag, 1950, 8", M **225.00**
Camel, all ID, 1950s, 6", NM **125.00**
Cosy Camel, Dralon, all ID, 1968, 10½", M **125.00**
Grizzly Donkey, dralon, all ID, 1968, 9½", M **100.00**
Kangoo Kangaroo, mohair, w/joey, all ID, 1950, 6½", M **125.00**
Leo Lion, standing, script button/stock tag, 1968, 4½", M **125.00**
Lion, standing, growler, glass eyes, button, 15x36x12", EX **425.00**
Peacock, all ID, 1980s, M **1,000.00**
Peggy Penguin, all ID, 1959, 5", M **125.00**
Renny Reindeer, all ID, 1959, 4½", NM **185.00**
Snucki Ram, tan mohair, blk face/ft, chest tag, 1950s, 5", NM ...**145.00**
Tabby Cat, wht w/blk stripes, ribbon/bell, chest tag, 4½", NM ..**125.00**
Tiger Cub, chest tag, 1950, 4", NM **125.00**
Turkey, raised script button, 1950s, 4¼", M **285.00**
Woolie Chick, plastic ft, script button, stock tag, 2", M **45.00**
Xorry Desert Fox, all ID, 1950, 4½", M **145.00**

Toy Soldiers and Accessories

Among the better-known manufacturers of 'dimestore' soldiers are Barclay, Manoil, and Jones, all of whom made hollow cast-lead figures; Gray Iron, who used cast iron; and Auburn, who made theirs of rubber.

They all measured about 3" to 3½" tall, and often accessories such as trucks, tanks, and airplanes were designed to add to the enjoyment of staging mock battles, parades, encampments, etc.

Britains is a very popular line, smaller and usually more detailed than the 'dimestores.' They've been made in England since 1893, and most of their boxed sets sell for a minimum of $100.00.

Some examples are very rare and therefore expensive, but condition is the driving force in making a value assessment. Percentages in the description lines refer to the amount of original paint remaining. Our advisors for this category are Stan and Sally Alekna; they are listed in the Directory under Florida. To learn more about this subject, we recommend *Toy Soldiers* by Richard O'Brien (Books Americana).

Auburn Rubber, machine gunner charging, early sm version, 99% **84.00**
Auburn Rubber, observer w/binoculars, 97% **20.00**
Barclay, aviator, khaki, 98% **22.00**
Barclay, fireman w/axe, 97% **28.00**
Barclay, mechanic w/plane engine, scarce, 98% **68.00**
Barclay, sailor, flag bearer, 97% **39.00**
Barclay, solder marching w/rifle, cast helmet, 99% **39.00**
Britains, #1284, Royal MArines, 16-pc, G-EX (G box) **275.00**
Britains, #147, Zulus of Africa, 8-pc, EXIB **275.00**
Britains, #1901, Capetown Highlanders, 8-pc, EX-M (G box) ...**100.00**
Britains, #2, Royal Guardsmen, 16-pc, EX-M **200.00**
Britains, #33, 16th Lancers, 1900, 4-pc (partial set), G **200.00**
Britains, #48, Egyptian Camel Corps, 3-pc, EX-M (EX box) **225.00**
Britains, #88, Seaforth Highlanders Charging, 16-pc, VGIB **375.00**
Britains, #9184, US Sailors Marching, 7-pc, MIB **100.00**
Grey Iron, conductor, 98% **12.00**
Grey Iron, Indian on horse, scarce, 88% **41.00**
Grey Iron, milkman, scarce, 98% **24.00**
Grey Iron, trooper, mounted, EX **9.00**
Grey Iron, US Doughboy, grenade thrower, 97% **39.00**
Jones, calf, #236, 93% **10.00**
Jones, farmer's wife, 98% **18.00**
Jones, soldier, AA gunner, kneeling, brn, scarce, NM **115.00**
Jones, soldier, wounded, prone, scarce, 98% **145.00**
Manoil, aviator, holding bomb, 94% **34.00**
Manoil, hostess in gr, scarce, 8% **72.00**
Manoil, soldier, AA gunner, w/range finder, 97% **59.00**
Manoil, soldier, flag bearer, 3rd version, NM **33.00**
Manoil, soldier, marching, thin, 98% **41.00**
Mignot, Austrian Infantry, 16-pc, EX **550.00**
Mignot, Fr Military Napoleonic Artillery & Infantry, 14-pc, M .**350.00**
Mignot, Fr Boy Scouts Marching, 12-pc, M (EX box) **275.00**
Mignot, Italian Dragoons, 16-pc, M (EX box) **460.00**
Mignot, Russian Imperial Guard (1900), #0235, 5-pc, M (G box) ..**315.00**

Trains

Electric trains were produced as early as the late 19th century. Names to look for are Lionel, Ives, and American Flyer. Identification numbers given in the listings below actually appear on the item.

Lionel #4083 electric locomotive, Standard gauge, 1927 – 36, 16½" long, NMIB, $2,500.00; Lionel #213 cattle car, Standard gauge, 1926 – 40, 12½", MIB, $600.00.

Am Flyer, #21551 Northern Pacific A-Unit Locomotive, NM ...**375.00**
Am Flyer, #24222 Domonio Sugar Hopper, 1963-64, VG+ **400.00**
Lionel, #11745 Navy Set, LTI, 1987-96, NMIB **190.00**
Lionel, #2243 AB Santa Fe Locomotive, postwar, VG **275.00**
Lionel, #2367C Wabash B-Unit Locomotive, postwar, VG **175.00**
Lionel, #2452X PRR Gondola Car, postwar, EX **20.00**
Lionel, #422 Blue Comet Observation Car, prewar, MIB **1,725.00**
Lionel, #433E Tender, gray, prewar, VG **1,300.00**
Lionel, #52 Fire Car, postwar, EX **190.00**
Lionel, #6361 Timber Car, postwar, MIB **135.00**
Lionel, #6557 Smoking Caboose, postwar, NMIB **400.00**
Lionel, #700E Hudson Locomotive, prewar, VG+ **3,000.00**
Lionel, #8602 PA 4-4-2 Steam Locomotive, LTI, 1987-96, NMIB .**120.00**
Lionel, #87405, PRR Gondola Car, LTI, 1987-96, NMIB **25.00**
Lionel, #8850 Pen Central GG-1 Locomotive, MPC, 1970-86, NM ...**460.00**
Lionel, #9186 Conrail Caboose, lighted, MPC, 1970-86, NMIB ..**50.00**
Lionel, #9413 Naperville Boxcar, LTI, 1987-96, NMIB **15.00**
Marklin, #3024 Locomotive, bl w/silver roof, NMIB **300.00**
Marklin, G800 Locomotive, blk & red, VG+ **160.00**
Williams, #5200 PRR B6SB 0-6-0 Steam Locomotive, MIB **375.00**
Williams, #6013 Southern PS-4 4-6-2 Locomotive, NM **460.00**
Williams, Amtrak Amfleet Set, 4 cars, MIB **210.00**
Williams, Lackawanna Trainmaster Locomotive, MIB **290.00**
Williams, PRR E6S-4-4-2 Locomotive & Tender, MIB **345.00**
Williams, Tucsan SD-45 Diesel Locomotive, MIB **175.00**

Trade Signs

Trade signs were popular during the 1800s. They were usually made in an easily recognizable shape that one could mentally associate with the particular type of business it was to represent, especially appropriate in the days when many customers could not read!

Barber, flat brd w/red/wht/bl pnt stripes, primitive, 37" **495.00**
Bootmaker, boots, red & blk pnt wood, 19th C, 36", EX **475.00**
Cabinetmaker, 2-sided, pnt letters on wood, 14x38", G **250.00**
Hand points to Lunch, gold-leaf letters on blk glass, fr, 8x16" ...**325.00**
Hat shop, top hat, blk-pnt CI w/gold letters, hanging **1,500.00**
Locksmith, blk letters on yel w/mc borders, 19th C, 84x25" **800.00**
Pocketwatch, cast metal, 28x30" dia **350.00**
Slide rule, pnt wood, 13x77x2", VG **200.00**
Tavern, Independence & eagle pnt on wood panel, 1800s, 41x31" .**17,250.00**
Tavern, Royal Gorge, pnt wood, sailing ship, 19th C, 65x36x9" ...**880.00**

Tramp Art

'Tramp' is considered a type of folk art. In America it was primarily made from the end of the Civil War through the 1930s though it employs carving and decorating methods which are much older, originating mostly in Germany and Scandinavia. 'Trampen' probably refers to the itinerant stages of Middle Ages craft apprenticeship. The carving techniques were also used for practice. Tramp art was spread by soldiers in the Civil War and primarily practiced where there was a plentiful and free supply of materials such as cigar boxes and fruit crates. The belief that this work was done by tramps and hobos as payment for room or meals is generally incorrect. The larger pieces especially would have required a lengthy stay in one place.

There is a great variety of tramp art, from boxes and frames which are most common to large pieces of furniture and intricate objects. The most common method of decoration is chip carving with several layers built one on top of another. There are several variations of that form as well as others such as 'Crown of Thorns,' an

interlocking method, which are completely different. The most common finishes were lacquer or stain, although paints were also used. The value of tramp art varies according to size, detail, surface, and complexity. The new collector should be aware that tramp art is being made today. While some sell it as new, others are offering it as old. In addition, many people mistakenly use the term as a catchall phrase to refer to other forms of construction — especially things they are uncertain about.

For further information we recommend *Tramp Art, One Notch at a Time*, a coffee-table book by Clifford Wallace (published by David Irons, who is listed in the Directory under Pennsylvania). Our advisor is Matt Lippa; he is listed in the Directory under Alabama.

Box, appl dbl horseshoes & birds, chip cvd, hinged, 7x10x6", EX ...**350.00**
Box, chip cvd, dk gr pnt, hinged top, 1900s, 7x9x5½", EX **200.00**
Box, sewing, chip cvd, dbl ped, 5-drw, 1900s, 18x11x17", EX **795.00**
Box, tiered, pyramidal legs, sliding top, gold pnt, 10x7x7" **250.00**
Box, trinket; 2-drw, simple chip cvg, 7x2½x9" **250.00**
Cabinet, apothecary; 3 long/8 short drws, canted case, 1900s, 30" .**1,150.00**
Cabinet, cornice, 2 hinged/molded drws, 2 doors, 1900s, 69x41" .**1,725.00**
Cabinet, cottage form, 2 dormers, shelves, 1900s, 66x28" **2,070.00**
Cabinet, cvd rosettes/dmns/gallery, drw/door, 1900s, 49x24" ..**3,450.00**
Cathedral, 3 cvd towers, pierced scrollwork, masks, 1900s, 40x19" .**1,850.00**
Clock, mantel; scrolled steeple, spandrels w/bird, 1929, 25" **850.00**
Clock, mantel; 3-part, steeple, stepped bosses, 1900s, 25x35" .**2,000.00**
Cradle, chip cvd, leaf designs, orig pnt, 1900s, doll sz, EX **250.00**
Diorama, box w/pyramidal roof, hinged door, stain, 1900s, 18x18" **700.00**
Dresser, chip cvd (5 to 6 layers), 4-drw, wht pnt, 1910 ....**3,000.00**
Dresser, chip cvd (5 to 8 layers), porc pulls, 1900s, 28x12" **800.00**
Dresser, stepped/cvd top, hinged mirror, 3-drw, 1890s, 24" **600.00**
Frame, bold chip-cvd layers w/appl corners, varnish, 21x10½" ...**325.00**
Frame, chip cvd, heart shapes, fence-like border, 20x18" **350.00**
Frame, chip cvd layers, lt & dk wood, 8-sided, 19x13x2" **345.00**
Frame, chip-cvd pyramids, red & silver pnt, 14x12", 1¾" W **295.00**
Matchbox holder/ashtray, chip cvd, gold pnt, '20s, 10x3x3" **150.00**
Mirror, hand; 5 chip-cvd layers, 1800s, 11x7x5½" **165.00**
Planter, 16-layer ped base, 8-sided (9-layer), 1900, 10x8" **500.00**
Shelf, pine, scalloped, chip cvd w/appl cvd flowers, 9x16x17" **250.00**
Shrine, chip-cvd star & cross, dmn shapes, 2-tier base, 15x7x5" ...**325.00**

Traps

Though of interest to collectors for many years, trap collecting has gained in popularity over the past ten years in particular, causing prices to appreciate rapidly. Traps are usually marked on the pan as to manufacturer, and the condition of these trademarks are important when determining their value. Grading is as follows:

Good: one-half of pan legible.
Very Good: legible in entirety, but light.
Fine: legible in entirety, with strong lettering.
Mint: in like-new, shiny condition.

Our advisor for this category is Boyd Nedry; he is listed in the Directory under Michigan. Prices listed here are for traps in fine condition.

Adirondack Instant Death, trip wire **325.00**
Allsteel #0, single long spring **125.00**
Anti-Cat, automatic mousetrap **60.00**
Arrow #1, single under spring **50.00**
Aurouze Rat Trap, wire cage **45.00**
Austin Humane, killer **30.00**
Baker's Automatic, tin & wood, mousetrap **100.00**
Blizzard, wood snap, mousetrap **15.00**
Bonanza Self-setting Mousetrap **55.00**

Buffalo Bill, wood snap, rat trap 20.00
Clayton, killer trap 325.00
Clincher #1, single long spring 75.00
Cyclone, wire mousetrap 65.00
Cyclone Rat Trap, wood snap 20.00
Diamond #H22, dbl long spring 160.00
Diamond #34, dbl coil spring 35.00
Dodd Hair Trigger, wood snap, mousetrap 35.00
Economy #1½, single long spring 22.00
Ejector, wood snap, mousetrap 15.00
Elgin, metal, rat trap 20.00
Epp, chain trap 300.00
Everset, self-setter, drowner, mousetrap 80.00
Fairy Revolving, mousetrap 85.00
Fatal Grip, single long spring, killer 35.00
Faultless Rat Trap, wood snap 15.00
Gabriel Fish & Game Trap 100.00
Gibbs #3 Dope Trap 450.00
Gibbs Live Muskrat Trap 265.00
Gibbs Two Trigger #1 ....10.00
Gurney's Gopher Trap 18.00
Hawley Norton, #0 single long spring 50.00
Hawley Norton #4, dbl long spring 40.00
Hellcat, metal, mousetrap 15.00
Henderson Mole Trap, spear type 35.00
Herters #0 single long spring 95.00
Hotchkiss #1, single long spring 120.00
Ideal Claw, gopher trap 85.00
Intruder, gray plastic, mousetrap 12.00
Jack Frost Killer 25.00
Joker, wood snap, mousetrap 15.00
Kiser's Clean Kill, mousetrap 10.00
Kliflock #1, killer 40.00
Kompakt #0, under spring 35.00
Kompakt #4, under spring 45.00
Lastword, wood snap, mousetrap 15.00
Lic-Lure, metal snap, rat trap 18.00
McGill Can't Miss, metal, mousetrap 6.00
Miles Standish #3, dbl long spring 600.00
Montgomery #2, dbl coil spring 8.00
Muscatine, L shape, rat trap 25.00
Nash, mole choker 10.00
Newhouse #150, bear trap 395.00
Newhouse #2½, single long spring 60.00
Newhouse #50, bear trap 395.00
Newhouse Gopher Trap 25.00
Nip-It, sq, wood, 3-hole, mousetrap 22.00
Nisbit #3½, w/teeth, single long spring 60.00
Northwoods #3, dbl coil spring 12.00
Nox, wood snap, mousetrap 10.00
Oneida #13, dbl under spring 40.00
Oneida #2, dbl under spring 25.00
Out-O-Sight, mousetrap 15.00
Pat Trap, metal box w/snap trap inside, mousetrap 35.00
Prott #1¼, single long spring 35.00
PS Mfg Co #2, dbl long spring 55.00
PS&W Hector #3, dbl long spring 45.00
Reddick Mole Trap, spear type 10.00
Roy Mole Trap 15.00
Runway, metal, mousetrap 35.00
Sabo, den trap 485.00
Sargent #23, w/teeth, dbl long spring 175.00
Schroder's, spear type, mole trap 35.00
Snap Shot, wooden, 2-hole, mousetrap 22.00

Stop Thief #3, wire killer 22.00
Taylor Spec #2, dbl long spring 22.00
True Value #1, single long spring 18.00
Tu-Wa, wood snap, mousetrap 20.00
Union Hardware Co #1, single long spring 55.00
Victor #40, 2 traps in 1, long spring 150.00
Victor Double Shot, long spring 30.00
Victor Red Tread, wood snap, mousetrap 12.00
Webley #2, dbl long spring 15.00
Western Exterminator, mousetrap 15.00
White House, wood snap, rat trap 15.00
Woods & Waters, killer 12.00

Trenton

Trenton, New Jersey, was an area that supported several pottery companies from the mid-1800s until the late 1960s. A consolidation of several smaller companies that occured in the 1890s was called Trenton Potteries Company. Each company produced their own types of wares independent of the others.

Planter, seashell, lt bl, glossy, 7" 20.00
Tableau, Venetian gondolier scene, CB Upgon, 1906, 6-tile, EX .3,100.00
Tile, sailboats, 9x3" in fr 135.00
Vase, aqua, scalloped rim, 4" 24.00
Vase, cornucopia; lt bl, glossy, 6" 20.00

Trivets

Although strictly a decorative item today, the original purpose of the trivet was much more practical. They were used to protect table tops from hot serving dishes, and irons heated on the kitchen range were placed on trivets during use to protect work surfaces. The first patent date was 1869; many of the earliest trivets bore portraits of famous people or patriotic designs. Florals, birds, animals, and fruit were other favored motifs. Watch for remakes of early original designs. Some of these are marked Wilton, Emig, Wright, Iron Art, and V.M. for Virginia Metalcrafters. However, many of these reproductions are becoming collectible in the '90s. Expect to pay considerably less for these than for the originals, since they are abundant.

Brass

Brass & wrought iron, applewood trn hdl, 10x15x6½" 200.00
Club, heart & dmn cutout, ftd, 7x4⅜" 65.00
Compass design, 3-ftd 120.00
Heart shape w/3 stars, no hdl 85.00
Musical note 75.00
Pierced top, brass & steel, cabriole legs, 11x13x13" 375.00
Shield shape w/openwork, English, rosewood hdl, 13½" L 100.00
Thistle design, 4-ftd, 7½x5½" 85.00
2 fish in circle, 3-ftd, 3¼" dia 75.00

Cast Iron

Circle, 4 paw ft 30.00
Colt logo, pierced/ftd shield form, VG 60.00
Crown & cross 32.00
Daisy design, 4¼" 20.00
Oak tree & acorn, trunks extends through hdl, 8¼x4¼" 170.00
Oval w/2 hearts, 5" 45.00
Scrolled heart in center of arched design, 6" dia+10½" hdl 150.00

Spoke design **35.00**
Star, 2¼x4⅝" dia **40.00**
Star & Heart, 4⅝" **35.00**
Williams on face **24.00**

Wrought Iron

Snake form, coiled body forms trivet, snake head handle, 11",
$550.00.

Circle, 3-legged, 1830s, 34x25x22" **270.00**
Circle w/bar across center, 3-ftd, 6⅜" dia **100.00**
Circle w/X in center, 4-ftd, mk GPK **30.00**
Clover shape, 3-ftd, 6¼x6x5" **88.00**
Rectangular, 4 legs w/penny ft, wood hdl, 14x11" **75.00**
Shield shape w/3 crimped/flared rods in center, wood hdl, 10", EX ...**120.00**
Triangular, high legs w/paw-like ft, 9" **45.00**
5-bar rectangle, 16x13x15" **100.00**

Trolls

The first trolls to come to the United States were molded after a
1952 design by Marti and Helena Kuuskoski of Tampere, Finland. The
first trolls to be mass produced in America were molded from wood
carvings made by Thomas Dam of Denmark. As the demand for these
trolls increased, several U.S. manufacturers were licensed to produce
them. The most noteworthy of these were Uneeda Doll Company's
Wishnik line and Inga Dykin's Scandia House True Trolls. Thomas
Dam continued to import his Dam Things line. Today trolls are enjoying a renaissance as baby boomers try to recapture their childhood. As a
result, values are rising.

The troll craze from the '60s spawned many items other than troll
dolls such as wall plaques, salt and pepper shakers, pins, squirt guns,
rings, clay trolls, lamps, Halloween costumes, animals, lawn ornaments,
coat racks, notebooks, folders, and even a car.

In the '70s, '80s, and '90s new trolls were produced. While these
trolls are collectible to some, the avid troll collector still prefers those
produced in the '60s. Remember, trolls must be in mint condition to
receive top dollar. For more information we recommend *Collector's
Guide to Trolls, ID and Values,* by Pat Peterson. Our advisor for this category is Roger Inouye; he is listed in the Directory under California.

Army soldier, tagged clothes, all orig, Dam, 12" **125.00**
Astronaut, yel mohair, orig silver suit, unmk, 2½" **20.00**
Batman, bl mohair, orig cape & cowl, unmk Sheri, 2¾" **35.00**
Black Playboy Bunny, yel mohair, orange eyes, Thomas Dam, 7" **200.00**
Bride, gr mohair, orig clothes, Scandia House Ent, 2¾" **20.00**
Cow, magenta hair, amber glass eyes, bell, unmk Thomas Dam, 6" **200.00**
Cowgirl w/molded clothes, pk synthetic hair, Creative Mfg, 9" **30.00**
Double-headed, Lucky Shnooks, Uneeda Wishnik, 3", MIB **40.00**
Fox, wht mohair, aqua eyes, pnt tail, felt coat, unmk, 6½" **65.00**
Frankenstein, hard gr plastic, blk mohair, pnt features, unmk, 3" **50.00**
Grandma, peach mohair, plastic eyes, all orig, Uneeda Wishnik, 5½" ..**35.00**
Grandpa, wht mohair & beard, gr eyes, rpl clothes, Dam Things, 11" ...**100.00**

Hard plastic w/wooly mohair, pin eyes, orig clothes, unmk, 2½" ..**20.00**
Hobo, wht/blk mohair, glass eyes, orig clothes, Dam Things, 12" **150.00**
Horse, lav mohair, gr spiral eyes, felt saddle, Dam Things, 2½" **35.00**
King Kong, fur pate on blk 2-pc plastic body, unmk, 3½" **15.00**
Marine, wht mohair, bl eyes, Thomas Dam, 1961, 7" **60.00**
Mouse, short brn hair, glass eyes, felt clothes, Dam, 1967, 5" **75.00**
Nurse, wht mohair, 1-pc uniform, all orig, Scandia House Ent, 2¾" ..**18.00**
Pig, Norfin, flesh-tone vinyl, felt clothes, Thomas Dam, 6½" **75.00**
Playboy Bunny, red mohair, orig clothes, Dam Things, 12" **175.00**
Porcu-Pen, brn eyes, mk Dam Nitusch R ...1986, 3¼" **35.00**
Rabbit fur on head & body, thin vinyl head, unmk, 4" **20.00**
Red mohair w/pk bow & dress, dbl-horseshoe mk, Wishnik, 2¾" .**12.00**
Rooted long blond hair & skirt, unmk, 7¼" **40.00**
Rooted long hair, pk rhinestone eyes, nude, Uneeda Wishnik, 5½" ..**25.00**
Rooted orange hair, plastic eyes, orig clothes, unmk, 2¾" **10.00**
Santa, wht mohair & beard, orig clothes, Dam Things, 7½" **100.00**
Santa, wht mohair & beard, orig clothes, Thomas Dam, 5½" **45.00**
Saran hair, bl eyes, 1-pc vinyl nude body, unmk Marx, 3" **10.00**
Skateboarder, hard plastic gr body, mohair, pinhead eyes, unmk, 3" ..**30.00**
Squirrel, bank, mk Thomas Dam, 6½" **75.00**
Superman, wht mohair, gold plastic eyes, Uneeda Wishnik, 5½" ..**65.00**
Vampire, wht rabbit fur on head, orange 2-pc body, Japan, 3" **15.00**
Viking, brn mohair beard, glass eyes, rubber hat, unmk, 3" **25.00**
WAC, yel mohair, orig clothes, Dam Things, 1964, 12" **175.00**

Trunks

The first use of the term 'trunk' can be traced back to Egyptian times,
when hollowed-out tree sections were used to transport goods of commerce. In the the days of steamboat voyages, stagecoach journeys, and railroad travel, trunks were used to transport clothing and personal belongings.

The most desirable trunks are flat-tops, 24" to 38" long, from the
late 1800s, preferably in restored condition. Embossed dome-tops
(rounded on top to better accommodate milady's finery) from the
1880s, 24" to 38" long, in complete original condition are very desirable
as well. On the other hand, ca 1870s flush tin trunks, even in mint condition, inspire very little collector interest.

Unless the trunk is complete (retaining all original trays and compartments), its value is considerably lessened. If parts are absent or broken, the trunk is judged incomplete. All interiors differ; some had
upper-lid compartments, others did not. Our advisor is Doris Harroff;
she is listed in the Directory under Indiana.

Dome-top, emb decor, 1880s, 24" to 38", complete, from $75 to .**175.00**
Dome-top, top & front pnt w/mc flowers on blk, mid-1800s, complete **2,000.00**
Flat-top, orig, 1880-1900, complete, rstr, from $300 to **425.00**
Flat-top, orig, 1880-1900, 24" to 38", complete, from $75 to **125.00**
Leather trim w/brass tacks on pine, 19x10x9" **110.00**
Stagecoach, flat or dome, pre-1860s, 24" to 38", rstr, up to **475.00**

Tucker

Chinaware marked 'William Ellis Tucker' or 'Tucker & Hulme'
was made in Philadelphia, Pennsylvania. They used other marks as well
that are more difficult to recognize, one a large script 'W.' The small
firm specialized in painted porcelain wares and was in business for only
a short time, closing ca. 1838.

Pitcher, floral bouquets w/gold, reeded base, 9¼" **1,100.00**
Pitcher, floral bouquets w/gold, urn form, 9¼", NM **3,200.00**
Pitcher, Grecian shape, mc flowers w/gold, prof rpr **800.00**
Pitcher, mc floral w/gold, pear form, mk/1828, 7¼" **2,800.00**

Pitcher, sepia landscape reserves w/gold, urn shape, 9⅞" 825.00
Pitcher, urn form w/loop hdl, gold band decor, 5¾" 250.00
Plate, center monogram, gold & peach border, 10" 625.00
Plate, mc floral w/gold, scalloped, 8¾", pr 675.00
Plate, Monroe portrait, blk transfer w/gold, 9¼" 2,300.00
Tea set, gold trim, bird's head spout, pot+cr/sug+4 c/s, mini ...1,800.00

Tuthill

The Tuthill Glass Company operated in Middletown, New York, from 1902 to 1923. Collectors look for signed pieces and those in an identifiable pattern. Condition is of utmost importance, and examples with brilliant cutting and intaglio (natural flowers and fruits) combined fetch the highest prices.

Vase, Primrose, star-cut base, 14", $1,000.00.

Basket, wild rose intaglio, appl crystal hdl, sgn, 5½x6" 1,125.00
Bonbon, notching, eng flowers/leaves, star center, 8-sided 95.00
Bowl, cosmos/hobstars, 3¼x8" 165.00
Bowl, multiple fruit intaglio, Daisy & Button rim, att, 8" dia 265.00
Compote, floral intaglio, 6" dia 225.00
Plate, wild rose intaglio, 8¼" 285.00
Tazza, Evening Primrose, allover intaglio, 5x7" 335.00
Vase, 3 fruits/geometrics intaglio, waisted/3-ftd, 12½" 625.00

Twin Winton

Twin brothers Don and Ross Winton started this California-based company during the mid-1930s. It became a major producer of cookie jars, kitchenware, and household items until it closed in 1977. Besides their extensive line of very collectible cookie jars, they're also well known for their Hillbilly line — mugs, pitchers, bowls, lamps, ashtrays, decanters, and other novelty items modeled after the mountain boys in Paul Webb's cartoon series. To learn more about this subject, we recommend *The Collector's Guide to Don Winton Designs* (Collector Books), by our advisor, Mike Ellis; he is listed in the Directory under California.

Bank, Dobbin, wood stain w/HP details or gray, ea 50.00
Bank, elf on stump, wood stain w/HP details or gray, ea 40.00
Bank, foo dog, wood stain w/HP details or gray, ea 50.00
Bank, Friar, wood stain w/HP details or gray, ea 40.00
Bank, lamb, wood stain w/HP details or gray, ea 50.00
Bank, poodle, wood stain w/HP details or gray, ea 40.00
Bank, shoe, wood stain w/HP details or gray, ea 50.00
Bronco Group, ashtray, cowboy on saddle 65.00
Bronco Group, pitcher, bronco on side, cowboy hdl 150.00
Bronco Group, stein, steer opposite cowboy hdl 150.00

Candy jar, bear w/lollipop on stump, wood stain w/HP details 85.00
Candy jar, Candy House, wood grain w/HP details or gray, ea 65.00
Candy jar, elf on stump, wood stain w/HP details or gray, ea 65.00
Canister set, house forms, 5-pc 450.00
Canister set, Pot O'Canister, 5-pc 175.00
Cookie jar, Collector Barn, Collector Series, fully pnt 175.00
Cookie jar, Cookie Catcher, wood stain w/HP details or gray, ea .80.00
Cookie jar, cop, wood stain w/HP details or gray, ea 100.00
Cookie jar, Dutch Girl, Collector Series, fully pnt (+) 250.00
Cookie jar, Gorilla, wood stain w/HP details, minimum value ...350.00
Cookie jar, Hobby Horse, Collector Series, fully pnt 250.00
Cookie jar, Ole King Cole, wood stain w/HP details, minimum .450.00
Cookie jar, Persian Cat, wood stain w/HP details 140.00
Cookie jar, Pirate Fox, Collector Series, fully pnt 250.00
Cookie jar, Potbellied Stove, avocado gr, orange or red, ea 85.00
Cookie jar, Raggedy Ann (Mopsy), Collector Series, fully pnt (+) ..250.00
Cookie jar, Rooster, Collector Series, fully pnt 100.00
Cookie jar, Sheriff Bear, Collector Series, fully pnt 200.00
Cookie jar, Teddy Bear, wood stain w/HP details 85.00
Cookie jar, Tug Boat, wood stain w/HP details 250.00
Creamer & sugar bowl, cow & bull, wood stain w/HP details 200.00
Men of Mountains, cigarette box, outhouse 75.00
Men of Mountains, ice bucket, bathing in bbl, wood stain w/HP ...250.00
Men of Mountains, pitcher w/hillbilly hdl 75.00
Men of Mountains, punch cup w/hillbilly hdl 15.00
Napkin holder, butler, wood stain w/ HP details 100.00
Napkin holder, cocktail, rabbit holds bottle, wood stain w/HP ..100.00
Napkin holder, cow, wood stain w/HP details 85.00
Napkin holder, Hotei, avocado gr, pineapple yel, or orange, ea 85.00
Napkin holder, squirrel, wood stain w/HP details 60.00
Planter, Bambi deer, wood stain w/HP details 65.00
Planter, cat & boat, wood stain w/HP details 65.00
Planter, Ranger bear, wood stain w/HP details 65.00
Planter, squirrel & stump, wood stain w/HP details 65.00
Shakers, bucket, avocado gr or orange, pr 30.00
Shakers, Dobbin, wood stain w/HP details or gray, pr 45.00
Shakers, elf on stump, pineapple yel orange, pr 40.00
Shakers, Indian, wood stain w/HP details, pr 60.00
Shakers, owl, wood stain w/HP details or gray, pr 30.00

Typewriters

The first commercially successful typewriter was the Sholes and Glidden, introduced in 1874. By 1882 other models appeared, and by the 1890s dozens were on the market. At the time of the First World War, the ranks of typewriter-makers thinned, and by the 1920s only a few survived.

Collectors informally divide typewriter history into the pioneering period, up to about 1890; the classic period, from 1890 to 1920; and the modern period, since 1920. There are two broad classifications of early typewriters: (1) Keyboard machines, in which depression of a key prints a character and via a shift key prints up to three different characters per key; (2) Index machines, in which a chart of all the characters appears on the typewriter; the character is selected by a pointer or dial and is printed by operation of a lever or other device. Even though index typewriters were simpler and more primitive than keyboard machines, they were none the less a later development, designed to provide a cheaper alternative to the standard keyboard models that were selling for upwards of $100.00. Eventually second-hand keyboard typewriters supplied the low-price customer, and index typewriters vanished except as toys. Both classes of typewriters appeared in a great many designs.

It is difficult, if not impossible, to assign standard market prices to early typewriters. During the past decade, competition from a handful of wealthy overseas collectors has drastically affected the American market, and prices have become inflated on the rarer models. Some auction-realized prices have been astronomical. It is predicted that the market will drop again when this small group of collectors are satisfied and this atypical activity subsides. For now, we have updated values to reflect current market activity. Also, condition is a very important factor, and typewriters can vary infinitely in condition. A third factor to consider is that an early typewriter achieves its value mainly through the skill, effort, and patience of the collector who restores it to its original condition, in which case its purchase price is insignificant. Some unusual looking early typewriters are not at all rare or valuable, while some very ordinary looking ones are scarce and could be quite valuable. No general rules apply.

For further information we recommend *Antique Typewriters & Office Collectibles* by Darryl Rehr (Collector Books). When no condition is indicated, the items listed below are assumed to be in excellent, unrestored condition. Our advisor for this category is Mike Brooks; he is listed in the Directory under California.

American, CI pointer	175.00
Bennet, w/case	95.00
Bing #2, 1926	135.00
Blickensderfer #6, oak case	200.00
Blinkensderfer Electric, 1903, extremely rare	7,000.00
Blinksensderfer #5, dtd 1892	110.00
Boston, index	13,000.00
Crandall	1,000.00
Crown, index	1,000.00
Fitch	1,500.00
Hall, index	250.00
Hammond Multiplex, for all languages, w/accessories, M	265.00
Keystone	1,000.00
Niagara, index	3,500.00
Oliver Standard Visible #9, VG	60.00
Pittsburgh Visible #10, in case	435.00

Smith #1 Premier, EX, $115.00.

Smith-Corona #4, portable, 1920s, in case	50.00
Standard Visible Writer, old upright keys, NM	85.00
Underwood Standard, dtd 1912	28.00
Victor, index	700.00
World, index	250.00

Uhl Pottery

Founded in Evansville, Indiana, in 1849 by German immigrants, the Uhl Pottery was moved to Huntingburg, Indiana, in 1908 because of the more suitable clay available there. They produced stoneware — Acorn Ware jugs, crocks, and bowls — which were marked with the acorn logo and 'Uhl Pottery.' They also made mugs, pitchers, and vases

in simple shapes and solid glazes marked with a circular ink stamp containing the name of the pottery and 'Huntingburg, Indiana.' The pottery closed in the mid-1940s. Those seeking additional information about Uhl pottery are encouraged to contact the Uhl Collectors' Society, whose address is listed in the Directory under Clubs, Newsletters, and Catalogs.

Birdhouse, #525	270.00
Casserole, bl or pk, w/lid, ea	50.00
Churn, 3-gal, w/lid	125.00
Dutch pot, w/acorn	170.00
Jug, Egyptian, bl, #162	50.00
Jug, Evansville, 5-gal	120.00
Jug, polar bear, pk, w/stopper	375.00
Jug, purple, med	90.00
Jug, purple, mini	150.00
Jug, Xmas 1930	800.00
Jug bank, bl	220.00
Mug, brn, mini	70.00
Mug, tan bbl form, mini	90.00
Pitcher, grape, brn, 1-qt	20.00
Pitcher, Lincoln, brn, lg	300.00
Pitcher, sponged, bulbous, lg	475.00
Teapot, pk, lg	160.00
Teapot, yel, #131, sm	70.00
Teapot, yel, med	125.00

Ungemach Pottery Company

Fred Ungemach began his career as a boy, jiggering for the Nelson McCoy Pottery of Roseville, Ohio. Later he worked for Thomas Watt in Hawthorne, Pennsylvania; then he returned to Roseville to work for the Ransbottom Pottery. In 1938 with the help of his daughter Mary who was an employee of the Brush Pottery, he opened his own company in Roseville. The business was first known as the South Fork Pottery, but after several years and a number of expansions, the name was changed to the Ungemach Pottery Company (UPCO).

In June 1950 a flood demolished the plant, but it reopened in three weeks and continued to expand. In April 1966 the plant was struck by lightning and destroyed again, but by September of the same year they were back in production. Then in 1984 the pottery was sold to Friendship Pottery of Roseville, Ohio.

Ungemach produced a full line of wares including kitchen items, planters, vases, and novelty pieces. During the 1940s and '50s they obtained an exclusive contract with Walt Disney Productions, Burbank, California, to produce Disney character planters. These pieces were marked with Disney copyrights only. Their other production pieces are marked in a variety of ways — 'Ungemach, UPCO, Roseville.' A few are not marked at all. Our advisors for this category are Brenda and Jerry Siegel; they are listed in the Directory under Missouri.

Bowl, brn, fluted, rnd, #762	7.00
Bowl, fruit; yel, #779, 7"	8.00
Bowl, wht w/bl/yel/red rings, UPCO, #741, 4½x7⅞"	10.00
Bread server, brn, mk Roseville, #630, 10"	8.00
Bread server, rust & brn, oval, #797	9.00
Candy server, bl, 10"	11.00
Lamp, blk cat, stylized, cut-out eyes/ears/etc, unmk, 11½"	30.00
Lamp, Santa head, wht ceramic, cold pnt, unmk, 9"	40.00
Lamp, snowman's head, blk, red & gr pnt, unmk, 8½"	24.00
Planter, bonsai, wht, #289, 9x6x3½"	10.00

Planter, cactus, yel, 8" 8.00
Planter, chalice, brn, mk Floral Plant UPCO, rare, 8" 16.00
Planter, dk yel w/brn shading, oval, fluted, unmk, #720, 4½" 10.00
Planter, floral relief on sides, dk gr, ped ft, mk UPCO, 5¼" 12.00
Planter, fluted star, tan, 5" 6.00
Planter, hand thrown, gr, #489, 8" 9.00
Planter, lt yel w/brn speckles, rnd, ftd, UPCO, #401, 6⅝" 10.00
Planter, octagonal, tan, #755 ....6.00
Planter, rnd, tan, 6½" 4.00
Planter, rnd, wht, #610, 4½" 4.00
Strawberry pot, gr, 4" 6.00

Unger Brothers

Art Nouveau silver items of the highest quality were produced by Unger Brothers, who operated in Newark, New Jersey, from the early 1880s until 1909. In addition to tableware, they also made brushes, mirrors, powder boxes, and the like for milady's dressing table as well as jewelry and small personal accessories such as match safes and flasks. They often marked their products with a circle seal containing an intertwined 'UB' and '925 fine sterling.' In addition to sterling, a very limited amount of gold was also used. Note: This company made no pewter items; Unger designs may occasionally be found in pewter, but these are copies. Items dated in the mark or signed 'Birmingham' are English (not Unger).

Thimble case, 1⅛x1" diameter, $195.00; Thread/spool case, 1¼x1⅛" diameter, $190.00; Needle case, 2⅛" long, $150.00.

Ashtray, smoking lady 375.00
Bowl, Floral, rnd 475.00
Box, hinged lid, Unger/#B-2649, 1x4½", EX 180.00
Brooch, lady w/hat & flowing hair, minimum value 195.00
Coffee set, demitasse; Floral, 3-pc 1,000.00
Dresser set, Loves Dream, 5-pc 950.00
Dresser set, Secret of the Flowers, 7-pc 1,200.00
Flask, knight's head 795.00
Hatpin, Art Nouveau 225.00
Match safe, Art Nouveau 275.00
Smoking tray, Douvaine, lady in pipe smoke, sm 550.00
Thread case, ornate, mk 190.00
Tray, bread; Floral, oval 450.00
Vanity set, He Loves Me, 1904, 5-pc 950.00
Vanity set, lady w/flowing hair & Cupid, 9-pc 850.00

Universal

Universal Potteries Incorporated operated in Cambridge, Ohio, from 1934 to 1956. Many lines of dinnerware and kitchen items were produced in both earthenware and semiporcelain. In 1956 the emphasis was shifted to the manufacture of floor and wall tiles, and the name was changed to the Oxford Tile Company, Division of Universal Potteries. The plant closed in 1976. Our advisor for this category is Ted Haun; he is listed in the Directory under Indiana.

Shakers, Fruit, 4", $20.00 for the pair.

Ballerina, creamer 10.00
Ballerina, egg cup 12.00
Ballerina, gravy boat 12.00
Ballerina, mug 12.50
Ballerina, plate, hdls, 12" 8.00
Ballerina, plate, luncheon; 9¼" 6.00
Ballerina, platter, rnd, tab hdls, 11½" 14.00
Calico Fruit, bowl, serving; tab hdls 12.00
Calico Fruit, bowl, soup; tab hdls 6.00
Calico Fruit, custard cup, 5-oz 6.00
Calico Fruit, plate, 6" 4.00
Calico Fruit, plate, 9" 8.00
Calico Fruit, refrigerator jar, w/lid, 4" 10.00
Calico Fruit, refrigerator jar, w/lid, 5" 15.00
Calico Fruit, shakers, utility; pr 24.00
Cattail, batter jug, metal lid, part of set 80.00
Cattail, butter dish, w/lid, 1-lb 45.00
Cattail, cookie jar, tab hdld 85.00
Cattail, creamer, Laurella 16.00
Cattail, jug, canteen; angle hdl 30.00
Cattail, kitchen scales 37.00
Cattail, pitcher, glass w/ice lip 100.00
Cattail, pitcher, milk/utility 25.00
Cattail, plate, Old Holland, Wheeling, 6" 6.00
Cattail, plate, serving; early, mk Universal Potteries 35.00
Cattail, salad set, bowl, fork & spoon 50.00
Cattail, saucer, Old Holland, mk Wheelock 6.00
Cattail, shaker set, glass, 2 tall, 2 short, red metal lids & rack 40.00
Cattail, shakers, 3 styles, ea pr 12.00
Cattail, teapot, w/lid 35.00
Cattail, tumbler, iced tea; glass 35.00
Circus, shaker 8.00
Circus, teapot, wht over bl, w/lid 32.00
Criss Cross, bowl, mk Made Especially for Blair 20.00
Holland Rose, plate, Old Holland 4.00
Iris, casserole, w/lid 22.00
Iris, jug, canteen refrigerator 18.00
Iris, pie baker 17.00
Kitchenware, bean pot, red & wht, hdld 32.00
Kitchenware, pitcher, red & wht, tilted ball jug 35.00
Kitchenware, syrup pitcher, metal lid, red & wht 35.00
Kitchenware, teapot, red & wht, w/lid 40.00
Largo, creamer 6.00
Largo, pie baker, 10" 12.00
Largo, plate, dessert; 6" 3.00
Largo, shakers, pr 6.00
Largo, sugar bowl, no lid 4.00
Rambler Rose, bowl, flat, sm 6.00
Rambler Rose, plate, 9" 6.00
Red Poppy, plate, utility; tab hdls, 11½" 12.00
Refrigerator ware, bowl set, bl & wht, 3 pc w/lids 27.00
Refrigerator ware, canteen jug, bl & wht, cork stopper 20.00

Refrigerator ware, canteen jug, bl & wht, various decals, ea 20.00
Refrigerator ware, syrup, bl & wht, God Bless Am, w/red lid 35.00
Windmill, bowl, utilty; w/lid 8.00
Windmill, shakers, pr 12.00
Woodvine, bowl, soup; flat 4.00
Woodvine, cup & saucer 8.00
Woodvine, gravy boat 12.00
Woodvine, plate, 6" 3.00
Woodvine, plate, 9" 6.00
Woodvine, shakers, pr 12.00
Woodvine, tray, utility; tab hdls 15.00

Val St. Lambert

Since its inception in Belgium at the turn of the 19th century, the Val St. Lambert Cristalleries has been involved in the production of high-quality glass, producing some cameo. The factory is still in production. Our advisor for this category is Don Williams; he is listed in the Directory under Missouri.

Cameo

Box, bl opaque w/fiery opal, basketweave, sgn, 3¾x4" 100.00
Sherbet, children & animals, gold & bl on clear 225.00
Tankard, floral, amethyst on frost, clear base, notched hdl 1,275.00
Tumbler, classic figures, cranberry on clear w/gold, 5½" 250.00
Vase, fern fronds, cranberry on textured frost, tapered, 7" 475.00
Vase, poppies, wine frost on frost, glossy wavy collar, 7" 350.00

Miscellaneous

Bottle, scent; frosted sapphire bl w/allover patterning, 5½" 75.00
Candlesticks, full-length cut panels, hex base, 9", pr 200.00

Valentines

These valentine listings have been separated into the following styles of cards: booklet, dimensional, flat, greeting, honeycomb paper puff, mechanical, and mechanical flat. All categories come in these styles.

The number preceding the dimensional cards is very important when determining the value of this type of card, along with the height, width, and depth.

As always, please remember the seven specifications when evaluating your card: condition, category, manufacturer, artist signature, age, and geographical location. Our advisor for this category is Katherine Kreider; she is listed in the Directory under California and Pennsylvania.

Key:
AS — artist signed   HCPP — honeycomb paper puff

Four-door sedan with open driver cab, dimensional, spoked wheels, accented with red honeycomb paper puff and Victorian scraps, 1920s, 6½x11¾x2", EX, $125.00.

Booklet, Jack in the Beanstalk, 1940s, VG 10.00
Booklet, Mary Had a Little Lamb, 1940s, EX 25.00
Dimensional, 1-D, Love's Auto, easel bk, 10x7", EX 175.00
Dimensional, 2-D fountain, ca 1930s, 7x6x3", VG 25.00
Dimensional, 2-D harp, ca 1910, 5x3x1", VG 25.00
Dimensional, 3-D Dove Cote, ca 1910, 9x5x3", EX 125.00
Dimensional, 3-D Victorian boy w/violets, 7x4x2", NM 50.00
Dimensional, 4-D angel w/doves, 1930s, 9x5x3", EX 100.00
Dimensional, 4-D child on bike, 1930s, 9x6x3", EX 125.00
Flat, big-eared golfer, 9x5", NM 75.00
Flat, child w/tulips, Louis Prang, ca 1900s, 5x5", VG 25.00
Flat, deck of cards, Carrington Co, 4x6", EX 25.00
Flat, Dutch maiden, Tuck & Sons, ca 1900s, 8x5", EX 50.00
Flat, Fr bulldog, ca 1900s, MIG, 4x4", EX 35.00
Flat, monoplane, AS, MIG, ca 1915, 3x3", NM 45.00
Flat, unicycle, MIG, 5x3", NM 25.00
Flat, Valentine Police, Carrington Co, 7x5", EX 25.00
Gift-giving card, w/fingernail file, Volland, EX 35.00
Gift-giving card, w/linen hankie, 1920s, 9x12", EX 75.00
Gift-giving card, w/lollipop, 1930s, 5x5", EX 25.00
Greeting card, Art Nouveau artistry, 9x7", EX 75.00
Greeting card, cherub in slipper, ca 1890, 6x4", EX 35.00
Greeting card, heart shaped, ca 1910, 4x4", VG 5.00
Greeting card, My Heart Beets, paper can, 4x3", EX 20.00
Greeting card, w/cat, chromolitho, ca 1890, 5x4", VG 10.00
Greeting card, w/orig mirror, Dobbs, ca 1860, EX 125.00
Greeting card, Whitney, 3x3", EX 2.00
Greeting card, Whitney, 8x6", EX 15.00
HCPP, basket w/hdl & hearts, ca 1920s, 9x8", EX 75.00
HCPP, mushroom type, ca 1920s, 5x3", EX 10.00
HCPP, Wheel of Love, ca 1920s, 9x6", EX 75.00
Heart made of parchment, easel bk, 7x7", EX 45.00
Mechanical, Boy Scout, ca 1940s, 4x6", NM 25.00
Mechanical, child w/vibrating belt, ca 1940, MIG, 5x4" 5.00
Mechanical, monkey agent w/gr lobster, MIG, 7x5", EX 35.00
Mechanical, snowman, AS, easel bk, ca 1930, 7x5", EX 20.00
Mechanical-Flat, Ace of Hearts, MIG, 7x5", EX 45.00
Mechanical-Flat, Bonnet Lady, MIG, 5x4", EX 25.00
Mechanical-Flat, Buster Brown, MIG, 9x6", NM 125.00
Mechanical-Flat, Goose, MIG, 7x3", VG 5.00
Novelty, Button Boy, flat, 4x4", VG 5.00
Novelty, cowboy finger puppet, Ameri-card, 6x3", EX 10.00
Paper doll card, all intact, 1950s, 6x6", NM 25.00
Penny Dreadful, Blundering Fireman, VG 5.00
Penny Dreadful, Lawyer, ca 1920s, EX 25.00
Penny Dreadful, Penny Pincher, ca 1940s, EX 15.00
Penny Dreadful, Politician, EX 25.00
Penny Dreadful, Woman Golfer, ca 1920s, EX 35.00
Rapunzal valentine accented w/HCPP, 7x5", VG 5.00
Theorem valentine, flat, ca 1840s, 11x10", EX 400.00

Van Briggle

The Van Briggle Pottery of Colorado Springs, Colorado, was established in 1901 by Artus Van Briggle, whose early career had been shaped by such notables as Karl Langenbeck and Maria Nichols Storer. His quest for several years had been to perfect a completely flat matt glaze, and upon accomplishing his goal, he opened his pottery. His wife, Anne, worked with him, and they, along with George Young, were responsible for the modeling of the wares. Their work typified the flow and form of the Art Nouveau movement, and the shapes they designed played as important a part in their success as their glazes. Some of their most famous pieces were Despondency, Lorelei, and Toast Cup. Increasing demand for their work soon made it necessary to add to their quarters as well as their staff. Although much of the ware was eventually made from molds, each piece was carefully trimmed and refined before the glaze was sprayed on. Their most popular colors were Persian Rose, Ming Blue, and Mustard Yellow.

Van Briggle died in 1904, but the work was continued by his wife. New facilities were built; and by 1908, in addition to their artware, tiles, gardenware, and commercial lines were added. By the '20s the emphasis had shifted from art pottery to novelties and commercial wares. Reproductions of some of the early designs continue to be made. The double AA mark has always been in use, but after the 1920s the dates and/or shape numbers were dropped. Our advisor for this category is Michelle Ross; she is listed in the Directory under Michigan.

Vases: embossed violet iris blossoms with blue-green leaves on light green, #161, 1903, 9½x3¾", $4,000.00; Lorelei, embossed form-fitting woman on oviform body, yellow matt, repair, #17, 1907 – 12, 9½x3¾", $3,750.00; Spiderwort flowers and flowing leaves (exceptionally sharp modeling) on bottle form, green matt, #26, 1901 (very rare date), 4½x2¾", M, $5,750.00 (more than double its pre-sale estimate).

Bookends, owls on open book, Mtn Craig Brn, 1910s, rpr, 5", pr ..165.00
Bookends, polar bear, turq & bl, mid to late teens, pr 330.00
Bowl, acorns, wine matt w/gr spray, #670, 1915, 5½" 195.00
Bowl, console; Lady of the Lake, turq/bl, 1940s, mk, 10x15x11"...295.00
Bowl, dragonflies, mulberry w/bl spray, low, 1923-26, 9" dia 225.00
Bowl, floral, navy & lt bl matt, 1920s, 4x7½" 200.00
Bowl, floral, red & bl matt, 1930s, 5½x7½" 225.00
Bowl, leaves (spade shaped), wine w/bl spray, 1923-26, 10½" 250.00
Bowl, leaves (stylized), Persian Rose, 1940s, 6" dia 70.00
Bowl, leaves (stylized), wine & bl, #510, 1923-26, 8" 165.00
Bowl, leaves & berries, bl matt, #678, ca 1907-12, 2x3½" 160.00
Bowl, leaves at shoulder, pierced rim, turq, 1930s, 4" 75.00
Bowl, maroon/bl matt on acorn form, 3x6½" 60.00
Candle shield, acanthus leaf form, burgundy, electrified, 6" 200.00
Dish, stylized spider, blk on gr, #491, 1906, 5½" dia 550.00
Figurine, elephant, gr w/purple spray, 1940s, 8" L 110.00
Figurine, elephant, turq, 1940s-50s, 8" L 95.00
Figurine, Indian maiden grinding corn, turq, 1940s, 5½" 85.00
Flower frog, turtle figural, turq & bl, 1930s, 6" 75.00
Jug, firewater; Indian designs in relief, dk gr matt, 1902, 6½" .1,875.00
Lamp, 3-hdld, bulbous, ftd, turq, 1940s, orig shade, 12" 165.00
Paperweight, elephant, turq, 1930s, 3½" L 85.00
Paperweight, rabbit crouching, maroon & blk, 2¼x2½" 200.00
Planter, swan (leaves on bk), ftd, brn & gr, 1930s, 9½" L 275.00
Plaque, praying hands over cross, aqua to bl matt, 14½x9¾" 140.00
Plate, central leaf, turq & bl, 1907-12, 6¼" 195.00
Plate, grape cluster, rose w/lt overspray, #15, 1910, 8½" 300.00
Tile, geese (3), 5-color, 6" sq 850.00
Vase, arrowhead leaves, bl, bulbous, 1904, 5x5½" 800.00

Vase, bl matt, #119, ca 1907-12, 4⅞" 200.00
Vase, butterfly, turq & bl, 1940s, 3" 40.00
Vase, dandelions, curdled gr on lt gr, hdls, #756, 7⅝" 800.00
Vase, dandelions on maroon matt, #135, 1903, 10" 650.00
Vase, Dos Cabezas, 2 ladies, mulberry w/bl spray, 1919, 7¾" ...2,975.00
Vase, floral, bl & gr matt, post-1920, 14½" 350.00
Vase, floral, lt gr & bl, #503, 1923-26, 10" 275.00
Vase, floral, mulberry, 4-hdld, 1930s, 3¾" 70.00
Vase, floral, turq, trumpet neck, 1960s, 5½" 40.00
Vase, floral, 2-tone bl matt, hdls, post-1920, 14" 375.00
Vase, floral (incised), mulberry & bl, open hdls, 1920, 6½" 275.00
Vase, floral (stylized), gr matt w/lav spray, 1907, 5½" 850.00
Vase, floral (stylized), mulberry w/bl spray, #654, 1930, 3¾" 150.00
Vase, floral (stylized), turq, 1930s, 9½" 65.00
Vase, floral (stylized), wine w/bl spray, #135, 1915, 10½" 360.00
Vase, gr & gunmetal mottle, bulbous, 1905, 7" 375.00
Vase, gr & gunmetal mottle, shouldered, 1904, 9x6½" 230.00
Vase, gray-bl w/exposed red clay, bulbous, ca 1906, 5x3¼" 400.00
Vase, iris, cobalt gloss, 1980, 10½" 90.00
Vase, iris (stylized), dk mulberry & bl, #503, 1930s, 10" 225.00
Vase, leaves, bl & lt gr, 1917, 4½" 330.00
Vase, leaves, gunmetal & dk gr matt, closed rim, 1914, 5¾x4" ..400.00
Vase, leaves (spade-like), bl, bottle shape, 1907-12, 7x5" 550.00
Vase, leaves (stylized), gr matt, #657, 1907-12, 3" 295.00
Vase, leaves (stylized), turq & lt gr, #681, 3" dia 195.00
Vase, leaves at shoulder, wine w/bl-gr spray, #780, 1920s, 7½" ..330.00
Vase, lime gr w/wine curdling at top & int, #209B, 1904, 6½" ...600.00
Vase, linear decor, shaded mulberry, #838, 1930, 6" 165.00
Vase, lizards & flowers, tobacco brn/gr matt, drilled, 12", EX 550.00
Vase, Lorelei, lt bl & gr matt, post-1940, 10" 325.00
Vase, Lorelei, mulberry matt w/bl spray, 1920s, 10" 700.00
Vase, peacock feathers, bl on med gr, #62, 1903, 12x3½" 1,600.00
Vase, poppies, gr over deep red, #143, 1903, 9½" 4,250.00
Vase, poppies, 2-tone bl matt, mks, 1920s, 8" 230.00
Vase, poppy pods, bl matt w/red clay spots, #173, 1905, 9½" ..1,800.00
Vase, spiderwort, gr matt w/mulberry spray, #381, 1907-12, 9¼" ..375.00
Vase, thistle, yellow & ochre, #380, 1906, 8x4" 1,200.00
Vase, thistles, leathery bl-gr, #380, 1905, 8¼x4" 950.00
Vase, turq to dk bl, slim, flared ft, 1920s, 9½" 95.00
Vase, twisted panels, pinched rim, turq, 1940s, 5" 60.00
Vase, yucca leaves, turq, 1930s, 4½" 80.00

Vance Avon

Although pottery had been made in Tiltonville, Ohio, since about 1880, the ware manufactured there was of little significance until after the turn of the century when the Vance Faience Company was organized for the purpose of producing quality artware. By 1902 the name had been changed to the Avon Faience Company, and late in the same year it and three other West Virginia potteries incorporated to form the Wheeling Potteries Company. The Avon branch operated in Tiltonville until 1905 when production was moved to Wheeling. Art pottery was discontinued.

From the beginning, only skilled craftsmen and trained engineers were hired. Wm. P. Jervis and Fredrick Hurten Rhead were among the notable artists reponsible for designing some of the early artware. Some of the ware was slip decorated under glaze, while other pieces were molded with high-relief designs. Examples with squeeze-bag decoration by Rhead are obviously forerunners of the Jap Birdimal line he later developed for Weller. Ware was marked 'Vance F. Co.'; Avon F. Co., Tiltonville'; or 'Avon W. Pts. Co.'

Pitcher, cat figural, brn, sgn Lorber in mold, 1901, 10" 700.00

Tankard, peasants planting border, Avon bkstamp, 14" **125.00**
Vase, flowers & stems, mc on bl, waisted, mk, 8⅜", NM **850.00**
Vase, squeeze-bag leaves & blossoms, mc on gr, waisted, 9", NM ..**325.00**
Vase, stylized floral trees, A Cusick, shouldered, 11⅛", EX **1,600.00**

Vaseline

 Vaseline, a greenish-yellow colored glass produced by adding uranium oxide to the batch, was produced during the Victorian era. It was made in smaller quantities than other colors and lost much of its popularity with the advent of the electric light. It was used for pressed tablewares, vases, whimseys, souvenir items, oil lamps, perfume bottles, drawer pulls, and doorknobs. Pieces have been reproduced, and some factories still make it today in small batches. Vaseline glass will fluoresce under an ultraviolet light.

Bowl, dmn pattern w/cut fans at rim 3½x8" **865.00**
Box, shell pattern lid, dolphin legs **45.00**
Candlestick, flint, Sandwich or NE Glass, 10½x5" **140.00**
Candlesticks, flint, ca 1820, 7", pr **495.00**
Card holder, hands **40.00**
Celery yacht, Daisy & Button, Hobbs & Brockunier, 2x14" **125.00**
Coaster, starfish form **30.00**
Compote, T'print w/Lattice **95.00**
Cuspidor **120.00**
Dish, opal, heart shape w/ruffle, appl hdl, 1¼x7½x6½" **75.00**
Eye cup, satin **35.00**
Mug, Cat & Dog **35.00**
Mug, Ceron, child sz **35.00**
Slipper, Daisy & Button, satin **35.00**
Spoon holder, Moon & Star **50.00**
Sugar bowl, Gothic Arch w/acanthus leaf lid, 8-sided, 5⅜" **550.00**
Sweetmeat, appl ruby loop edge, metal fr, 8x10" **125.00**
Toothpick holder, Bird, satin **30.00**
Tumbler, Hobnail, 10-row, pontil **115.00**
Vase, vaseline opal w/twist stem, England, 1890s, 10" **1,195.00**
Wine, Rose, satin **35.00**

Verlys

 Verlys art glass, produced in France after 1931 by the Holophane Company of Verlys, was made in crystal with acid-finished relief work in the Art Deco style. Colored and opalescent glass was also used. In 1935 an American branch was opened in Newark, Ohio, where very similar wares were produced until the factory ceased production in 1951. French Verlys was signed with one of three mold-impressed script signatures, all containing the company name and country of origin. The American-made glassware was signed 'Verlys' only, either scratched with a diamond-tipped pen or impressed in the mold. There is very little if any difference in value between items produced in France and America. Though some seem to feel that the French should be higher priced (assuming it to be scarce), many prefer the American-made product.

 In June of 1955, about sixteen Verlys molds were leased to the A.H. Heisey Company. Heisey's versions were not signed with the Verlys name, so if an item is unsigned it is almost certainly a Heisey piece. The molds were returned to Verlys of America in July 1957. Fenton now owns all Verlys molds, but all issues are marked Fenton. Our advisor for this category is Don Frost; he is listed in the Directory under Washington.

Bowl, Cupid, clear frosted, 2x6" **145.00**
Bowl, Orchid, frosted opal, 1½x4" **250.00**
Bowl, Pine Cone, bl, 6" **185.00**

Bowl, Pine Cone, opal **225.00**
Bowl, Poppies, shallow, ftd, mk, 13½" **300.00**
Bowl, Tassels **150.00**
Bowl, Thistle, crystal etched, 9" **195.00**
Bowl, Thistle, topaz **250.00**
Bowl, Water Lily, Dusty Rose (rare color) **500.00**
Bowl, Wild Duck, 2½x13½" **275.00**
Candlesticks, Eagle, crystal etched, 3½x2⅜", pr **500.00**

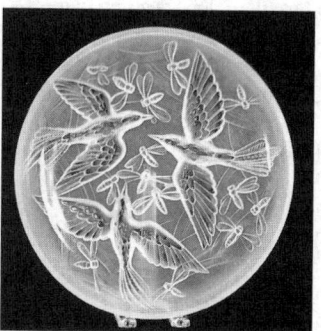

Charger, Birds and Bees, clear and frosted, 11½", $250.00.

Vase, Alpine Thistle, topaz, 9x9" **450.00**
Vase, Gems **200.00**
Vase, Gems, amber, w/frog, 6½x6½" **350.00**
Vase, Grasshopper, base chip **125.00**
Vase, Lovebirds, clear frosted, 4½x6½" **175.00**
Vase, Mandarin, clear frosted, script mk, 9¼" **500.00**
Vase, Seasons, 8x5½" **800.00**

Vernon Kilns

 Vernon Potteries Ltd. was established by Faye G. Bennison in Vernon, California, in 1931. The name was later changed to Vernon Kilns; until it closed in 1958, dinnerware, specialty plates, and figurines were their primary products. Among its wares most sought after by collectors today are items designed by such famous artists as Rockwell Kent, Walt Disney, Don Blanding, Jane Bennison, and May and Vieve Hamilton. Our advisor is Maxine Nelson, author of *Collectible Vernon Kilns* (now out of print); you will find her listed in the Directory under Arizona.

Anytime, bowl, chowder **8.00**
Anytime, plate, 10" **7.00**
Anytime, relish **20.00**
Anytime, tumbler **20.00**
Brown-Eyed Susan, bowl, chowder; tab hdl, 6" **12.00**
Brown-Eyed Susan, bowl, fruit; 5½" **6.00**
Brown-Eyed Susan, bowl, serving; 9" **20.00**
Brown-Eyed Susan, carafe, 8" **30.00**
Brown-Eyed Susan, chop plate, 12⅜" **25.00**
Brown-Eyed Susan, creamer & sugar bowl, w/lid **25.00**
Brown-Eyed Susan, cup & saucer **10.00**
Brown-Eyed Susan, custard cup **25.00**
Brown-Eyed Susan, plate, bread & butter; 6" **5.00**
Brown-Eyed Susan, plate, 9¾" **9.00**
Calico, bowl, divided vegetable **40.00**
Calico, bowl, fruit; 5½" **9.00**
Calico, creamer **20.00**
Calico, cup & saucer, jumbo **42.00**
Calico, plate, bread & butter; 6½" **7.50**
Calico, plate, dinner; 10½" **18.00**
Calico, shakers, pr **25.00**
Calico, sugar bowl **18.00**

Fantasia, bowl, goldfish, #121 ....375.00
Fantasia, bowl, mushroom, pk, #120 ....225.00
Fantasia, bowl, satyr, #124 ....250.00
Fantasia, bowl, sprite, HP, #125 ....325.00
Fantasia, cup & saucer, demi 225.00
Fantasia, figurine, Nubian Centaurette 1,475.00
Fantasia, vase, Pegasus, bl, #127 ....700.00
Fantasia, vase, winged nymph, HP, #123 ....450.00
Hawaiian Flowers, chop plate, 12" 55.00
Hawaiian Flowers, chop plate, 14" 75.00
Hawaiian Flowers, coffeepot 125.00
Hawaiian Flowers, plate, dinner; 10¼" 30.00
Hawaiian Flowers, shakers, pr 35.00
Homespun, chop plate, 12" 20.00
Homespun, creamer & sugar bowl 25.00
Homespun, pitcher, 2-qt 47.50
Homespun, plate, 6" 5.00
Homespun, syrup, drip-cut 55.00
Lei Lani, chop plate, 12" 85.00
Lei Lani, chop plate, 17" 195.00
Lei Lani, creamer 35.00
Lei Lani, cup & saucer, demitasse 35.00
Lei Lani, plate, 10¼" 45.00
Lei Lani, plate, 9¼" 35.00
Lei Lani, shakers, ultra shape, pr 45.00
Lei Lani, sugar bowl, w/lid 40.00
Lei Lani, tumbler 65.00
Linda (#838), bowl, chowder; tab hdl 16.00
Linda (#838), cup & saucer 12.00
Linda (#838), teapot 45.00
May Flower, bowl, vegetable; 9" 25.00
May Flower, chop plate, 14" 40.00
May Flower, cup & saucer 12.00
May Flower, gravy boat 25.00
May Flower, plate, dinner; 10¼" 15.00
May Flower, plate, salad; 7½" 9.00
May Flower, platter, 14" 40.00
May Flower, shakers, pr 18.00
Moby Dick, chop plate, 12" 125.00
Moby Dick, jam jar, notched lid 195.00
Moby Dick, mug, maroon 75.00
Moby Dick, pitcher, brn, 2-qt 245.00
Moby Dick, plate, 10½" 55.00
Moby Dick, plate, 7½", in Farberware fr 210.00
Modern California, bowl, fruit; 5½" 9.00
Modern California, pitcher, 1-pt 25.00
Organdie, bowl, fruit; 5½" 5.00
Organdie, bowl, lug chowder 10.00
Organdie, bowl, vegetable; rnd 18.00
Organdie, cup & saucer 7.00
Organdie, plate, bread & butter 3.00
Organdie, plate, luncheon; 9½" 8.00
Organdie, plate, salad; 7½" 6.00
Organdie, platter, 12½" 15.00
Organdie, shakers, pr 12.00
Plate, Alaska, Scrimshaw, artist sgn, 10½" 65.00
Plate, Bits of the Old South, Down on the Levee, 14" 95.00
Plate, Boeing Aircraft, 10½" 65.00
Plate, Edvard Grieg, Composer, 8½" 25.00
Plate, Grand Canyon Nat'l Park, red, 10½" 12.00
Plate, Historic Baltimore, John's Hopkins Hospital, 8½" 20.00
Plate, Idaho, mc, 10½" 15.00
Plate, Moor Mans, advertising, 10½" 45.00
Plate, My Maryland, 10½" 9.00

Plate, United States Map, 10½" 35.00
Salamina, bowl, fruit; 5½" 55.00
Salamina, bowl, serving; 9" 150.00
Salamina, chop plate, 12" 285.00
Salamina, chop plate, 14" 325.00
Salamina, chop plate, 17" 500.00
Salamina, cup & saucer 100.00
Salamina, pitcher, 2-qt 775.00
Salamina, plate, bread & butter; 6½" 55.00
Salamina, plate, dinner; 10½" 125.00
Salamina, plate, luncheon; 9½" 95.00
Salamina, plate, salad; 7½" 75.00

Tam O'Shanter, Carafe, $45.00; Pitcher, 11", $45.00; Tumbler, straight sides, 5", $20.00.

Tickled Pink, bowl, chowder 12.00
Tickled Pink, bowl, divided vegetable 20.00
Tickled Pink, bowl, vegetable; 8" 12.00
Tickled Pink, bowl, vegetable; 9" 14.00
Tickled Pink, butter dish 35.00
Tickled Pink, coffeepot 45.00
Tickled Pink, creamer 12.00
Tickled Pink, cup & saucer 10.00
Tickled Pink, gravy boat 18.00
Tickled Pink, pitcher, 1-qt 25.00
Tickled Pink, plate, dinner; 10" 9.00
Tickled Pink, plate, salad; 7½" 7.00
Tickled Pink, platter, 11" 18.00
Tickled Pink, platter, 13½" 22.00
Tickled Pink, sugar bowl, w/lid 18.00
Vernon 1860, chop plate, 14" 50.00
Vernon 1860, coffeepot 75.00
Vernon 1860, shakers, pr 20.00
Vernon 1860, teapot 65.00
Winchester 73, cup & saucer 75.00
Winchester 73, mug 45.00
Winchester 73, plate, dinner; 10" 75.00
Winchester 73, platter, 12½" 130.00
Winchester 73, salt cellar & pepper mill, pr 125.00
Winchester 73, tumbler 45.00

Villeroy and Boch

The firm of Villeroy and Boch, located in Mettlach, Germany, was brought into being by the 1841 merger of three German factories — the Wallerfangen factory, founded by Nicholas Villeroy in 1787; and Boch's father's factory in Septfontaines, established in 1767. Villeroy and Boch produced many varieties of wares, including earthenware with printed under-glaze designs which carried the well-known castle mark with the name 'Mettlach.' See also Mettlach.

Charger, sunflowers & gr leaves, majolica, 11¾" 175.00
Charger, wht flower w/purple & gr, majolica, mk, 11¾" ...175.00

Plate, children cameo, bl on wht, child sz, 7½" 45.00
Tile, anchor w/rope, wht & lt gr, vertical panel, 6x18" 295.00
Vase, cherubs & flowers, rtcl lattice rim, 4-ftd low ped, 11" 335.00

Vistosa

Vistosa was produced from about 1938 through the early '40s. It was Taylor, Smith, and Taylor's answer to the very successful Fiesta line of their nearby competitor, Homer Laughlin. Vistosa was made in four solid colors: mango red, cobalt blue, light green, and deep yellow. 'Pie crust' edges and a dainty five-petal flower molded into handles and lid finials made for a very attractive yet nevertheless commercially unsuccessful product. For further information, we recommend *Collector's Guide to Lu-Ray Pastels* by Kathy and Bill Meehan (Collector Books). Our advisor for this category is Ted Haun; he is listed in the Directory under Indiana.

Bowl, coupe soup; from $20 to 25.00
Bowl, fruit; from $10 to 15.00
Bowl, nappy; from $40 to 50.00
Bowl, salad; ftd, 12", from $175 to 200.00
Bowl, soup; lug hdld, from $25 to 30.00
Chop plate, 12" 40.00
Chop plate, 15", from $40 to 50.00
Coffee cup, AD; from $30 to 35.00
Coffee saucer, AD; from $15 to 20.00
Creamer 20.00
Egg cup, ftd, from $25 to 35.00
Jug, water; 2-qt 85.00
Plate, 10", from $50 to 60.00
Plate, 6", from $10 to 15.00
Plate, 7", from $12 to 18.00
Plate, 9", from $15 to 20.00
Sauce boat, from $125 to 150.00
Shakers, pr 32.00
Sugar bowl, w/lid 25.00
Tea saucer, from $5 to 7.00
Teacup, from $10 to 15.00
Teapot, 6-cup 125.00

Volkmar

Charles Volkmar established a workshop in Tremont, New York, in 1882. He produced artware decorated under the glaze in the manner of the early barbotine work done at the Haviland factory in Limoges, France. He relocated in 1888 in Menlo Park, New Jersey, and together with J.T. Smith established the Menlo Park Ceramic Company for the production of art tile. The partnership was dissolved in 1893. From 1895 until 1902, Volkmar located in Corona, New York, first under the name Volkmar Ceramic Company, later as Volkmar and Cory, and for the final six years as Crown Point. During the latter period he made art tile, blue under-glaze Delft-type wares, colorful polychrome vases, etc. The Volkmar Kilns were established in 1903 in Metuchen, New Jersey, by Volkmar and his son. Wares were marked with various devices consisting of the Volkmar name, initials, or 'Crown Point Ware.'

Mug, boxer dog, gr & brn, corseted, 5¾x5¼" 200.00
Pitcher, dk gr matt, hand thrown, bulbous, ribbon hdl, 5x4" 75.00
Plaque, Mt Vernon/DAR, bl & wht, 1890, 11½" 300.00
Tile, men fishing at river, bl & wht, 8" sq+fr 650.00
Tile, stylized duck, gr matt & blk, 8" sq 450.00
Vase, bl feathered matt, cylindrical neck, 7½x5¼" 500.00

Vase, brn & gr flames, Crown Point Ware, 10" 150.00
Vase, trumpet flowers, mc on shaded ground, pillow form, 9¾" .600.00

Wade

The Wade Group of Potteries originated in 1810 with a small, single-oven pottery near Chesterton, just west of Burslem, England. This pottery, first owned by a Henry Hallen, was eventually taken over by George Wade who had opened his own pottery in the latter part of the 19th century on Hall Street, Burslem. In the early 19th century, George Wade combined the two businesses into one pottery — the George Wade Pottery, located on High Street, Burslem. This pottery was named the Manchester Pottery; it still stands and is in business today.

Both the original Hallen Pottery and the newer George Wade Pottery specialized in pottery items for the textile industry, then booming in northern England. In 1906 Wade's son, George Albert Wade, joined the company, and in 1919 the pottery name was changed to George Wade and Son Ltd.

George Wade's brothers, Albert and William, had interests in two other potteries, Wade Heath & Co. Ltd., founded in 1867 as Wade, Colclough and Lingard (changed to Wade & Co. in 1887 and to Wade Heath & Co. Ltd. in 1927) and J.& W. Wade & Co., founded in the late 19th century with a name change also in 1927, to A.J. Wade & Co. Together the potteries manufactured decorative tiles, teapots, and other related dinnerware. In 1938 Wade Heath took over the Royal Victoria Pottery, also in Burslem, and began producing a wide range of figurines and other decorative items. The A.J. Wade & Co. pottery ceased production in 1970, but the main building was not sold and has reopened recently as The Pottery Store. The Royal Victoria Pottery is still in production but is now referred to as Hill Top.

In 1947 a new pottery was opened in Portadown, Northern Ireland, to produce both industrial ceramics and Irish porcelain giftware. In 1958 all the Wade potteries were amalgamated, becoming the Wade Group of Potteries. The most recent addition to the group is Wade (PDM) Limited, a marketing arm for the advertising ware made by Wade Heath at the Royal Victoria Pottery. Wade (PDM) Limited was incorporated in 1969. In 1989 the Wade Group of Potteries was bought out by Beauford Engineering. With this takeover, Wade Heath and George Wade & Son Ltd. were combined to form Wade Ceramics. Wade (Ireland) Ltd. and Wade (PDM) Ltd. became subsidiaries of Wade Ceramics. In 1990 Wade (Ireland) Ltd. changed its name to Seagoe Ceramics Limited. In April 1993, Seagoe Ceramics Limited ceased the production of table and gifware to concentrate on industrial ceramics. The pottery, although still owned by Beauford, is no longer part of the Wade Group.

For those interested in learning more about Wade pottery, we recommend *The World of Wade* and *The World of Wade Book 2* by Ian Warner and Mike Posgay; Mr. Warner is listed in the Directory under Canada.

Pitcher, spatter decoration, shape #92, mark type 5, 8¼", $60.00.

Animal Figure, Baby Panda 170.00
Animal Figure, Dachshund 155.00
Animal Figure, Playful Lamb, from prewar Geo Wade mold 155.00
Aquarium Set, Diver, 2¾" 20.00
Aquarium Set, Mermaid, 2½" 50.00
Basket, Gothic, 7½" 150.00
Cellulose Figurine, Carnival, 7" 275.00
Cellulose Figurine, Jeanette, 6½" 300.00
Creamer & sugar bowl, Basket Ware 38.00
Disney Blow-Up, Scamp, 4⅛x5" 235.00
Disney Blow-Up, Si, 5½x6" 200.00
Disney Series, Baby Pegasus, 1¾" 75.00
Disney Series, Big Mama, 1¾" 37.00
Disney Series, Dumbo, 1⅜" 85.00
Disney Series, Sgt Tibbs, 2" 100.00
Disney Series, Thumper, 1⅞" 35.00
Everlasting Candles, pr 145.00
Hanna-Barbera Cartoon Character, Huckleberry Hound, 2⅜" ...125.00
Hanna-Barbera Cartoon Character, Yogi Bear, 2½" 140.00
Happy Family, Frog Baby, ⅝" 10.00
Happy Family, Frog Parent, ⅞" 15.00
Happy Family, Rabbit Baby, 1⅛" 12.00
Happy Family, Rabbit Parent, 2" 15.00
Ice bucket, Bombay London Dry Gin 45.00
Irish Porcelain, child's tankard 20.00
Irish Porcelain, serpent urn, 11½" 75.00
Lucky Leprechauns, Larry & Lester, ea 70.00
Money bank, Percy 145.00
Money bank, Thomas 150.00
Money box, JW Thornton's Delivery Van 60.00
Nursery Favourite, Bo-Peep, 2⅞" 65.00
Nursery Favourite, Jack & Jill, 2⅞", pr 90.00
Nursery Favourite, King Cole, 2½" 50.00
Nursery Favourite, Queen of Hearts, 2⅞" 55.00
Nursery Rhyme Figure, Blynken, 2" 195.00
Nursery Rhyme Figure, Butcher, 3¼" 350.00
Nursery Rhyme Figure, Goldilocks, 4" 240.00
Nursery Rhyme Figure, Thief, 3" 200.00
Pet dish, fawn, kitten, or horse, ea 25.00
Posy bowl, Barge, 1970s 30.00
Posy bowl, w/rabbit 20.00
Red Rose Tea (US), Beaver, 1¼" 6.00
Red Rose Tea (US), Gorilla, 1½" 5.50
Red Rose Tea (US), Koala Bear, 1⅜" 5.00
Shaving mug, Steam Coach 20.00
Teapot, Bramble Ware 90.00
Teapot, Donald Duck 850.00
Teapot, Old English Castle 120.00
Tortoise Ashbowl, lg, 2x7¼" 50.00
Tortoise Ashbowl, sm, 1⅝x5¾" 30.00
Wall plate, Romance 75.00
Water jug, Wade PDM, Dewar's Whiskey 30.00
Water jug, Wade PDM, VJ Dry Gin 25.00
Whimsie-Land, Lion, 1¼x1⅞" 16.00
Whimsie-Land, Pony, 1½x1½" 15.00
Whimsie-Land, Retriever, 1¼x1⅝" 12.00
Whimsie-Land, Rooster, 2x1⅛" 24.00

Wallace China

Dinnerware with a Western theme was produced by the Wallace China Company, who operated in California from 1931 until 1964. Artist Till Goodan designed three lines, Rodeo, Pioneer Trails, and Boots and Saddle, which they marketed under the package name Westward Ho. When dinnerware with a western theme became so popular just a few years ago, Rodeo was reproduced, but the new trademark includes neither 'California' or 'Wallace China.'

Our advisor for this category is Marv Fogleman; he is listed in the Directory under California. If you'd like to learn more about this company, we recommend *The Collector's Encyclopedia of California Pottery* by Jack Chipman.

Boots and Saddle, shaker, 5¼", $45.00.

Boots & Saddle, bowl, oval, 12" 250.00
Boots & Saddle, bowl, vegetable 285.00
Boots & Saddle, chop plate, 13" 295.00
Boots & Saddle, plate, dinner 125.00
Boots & Saddle, platter 300.00
Chuck Wagon, platter, 12" 75.00
El Rancho, grill plate 100.00
Little Buckaroo, plate 150.00
Longhorn, stacking bowl set, 5-pc 1,850.00
Pioneer Trails, chili bowl, 5½" 45.00
Rod's Steak House, disk pitcher 350.00
Rodeo, bowl, chili 65.00
Rodeo, bowl, ice cream 38.00
Rodeo, bowl, serving; 9" 160.00
Rodeo, chop plate, 13" 295.00
Rodeo, cup & saucer 65.00
Rodeo, cup & saucer, lg 100.00
Rodeo, pitcher 425.00
Rodeo, plate, child's 165.00
Rodeo, plate, rare, 6¼" 150.00
Rodeo, plate, 10½" 90.00
Rodeo, plate, 7¼" 60.00
Rodeo, plate, 9" 60.00
Rodeo, platter, 15" 300.00
Rodeo, sugar bowl, w/lid, lg 125.00
Westward Ho, shakers, 4", pr 125.00

Walrath

Frederick Walrath was a studio potter who worked from around the turn of the century until his death in 1920. He was located in Rochester, New York, until 1918 when he became associated with the Newcomb Pottery in New Orleans, Louisiana.

Bowl, leaves, olive on dk mustard, 1912, 1½x5" 195.00
Chamberstick, gr, 7" 400.00
Chamberstick, gray, 5" 300.00
Figurine, mountain lion, gr & brn matt, 1919, 3½x3¾" 450.00
Mug, stylized leaves, lt gr on brn matt, 5¼x6" 500.00
Vase, pendant berries & leaves, olive/pk on dk gr, 5½" 3,500.00

Walter, A.

Almaric Walter was employed from 1904 through 1914 at Verreries Artistiques des Freres Daum in Nancy, France. After 1919 he opened his own business where he continued to make the same type of quality objets d'art in pate-de-verre glass as he had earlier. His pieces are signed A. Walter, Nancy H. Berge Sc.

Bowl, gr ribs on wht frost w/turq/amber/bl at base, 7" **1,850.00**
Bowl, scarab beetles, brn on bl-gr to yel & gr, Cayette, 4x8¾" .**4,600.00**
Box, yel mottle w/bright gr/brn/blk moth on lid, 2½x4" **2,750.00**
Dish, moth, bl on yel-orange & bl ground, 6" L **2,500.00**
Inkwell, beetle, blk & brn w/orange & yel, dbl, 3x6½" **4,500.00**
Paperweight, beetle, yel w/brn & blk, EX detail, 2x2" **2,700.00**
Paperweight, chameleon, teal-blk w/red dots, 3½x3¼" **3,300.00**
Paperweight, lizard, brn & blk on bl & gr base, 3¾x3½" **5,250.00**
Paperweight, moth, bl/blk/brn on yel & gr base, 1½x4" **2,200.00**
Paperweight, snail, brn on gr & bl base, 2½x3½" **2,500.00**
Tray, butterfly relief, emerald gr on royal bl, ¾x5x6" **3,450.00**
Tray, fantailed goldfish, yel-brn on mottled yel, 2½x5" dia **3,500.00**
Vide poche, fish & seaweed, mauve/amber/brn/gray/teal, 9½" ...**2,875.00**

Warwick

The Warwick China Company operated in Wheeling, West Virginia, from 1887 until 1951. They produced both hand-painted and decaled plates, vases, teapots, coffeepots, pitchers, bowls, and jardinieres featuring lovely florals or portraits of beautiful ladies done in luscious colors. Backgrounds were usually blendings of brown and beige, but ivory was also used as well as greens and pinks. Various marks were employed, all of which incorporate the Warwick name. For a more thorough study of the subject, we recommend *Warwick, A to W*, a supplement to *Why Not Warwick* by our advisor, Donald C. Hoffmann, Sr.; his address can be found in the Directory under Illinois. In an effort to inform the collector/dealer, Mr. Hoffmann now has a video available that identifies the company's decals and their variations by number.

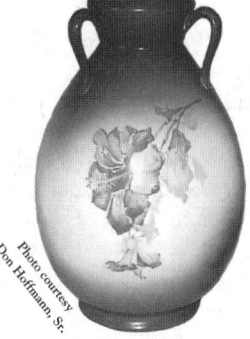

Vase, Regency, russet to white to russet, floral, A-27, 11½x9", $325.00.

Photo courtesy Don Hoffmann, Sr.

Vase, A Beauty, wht, rose, D-2, 15" 330.00
Vase, Albany, tan matt, nuts, M-64, 7" 230.00
Vase, Alexandria, red, poinsettia, E-2, 12½" 330.00
Vase, Bonnie, wht, roses, F-2, 10¼" 290.00
Vase, Bouquet #1, charcoal, floral, C-6, 11½" 280.00
Vase, Bouquet #1, red, orchid, E-2, 11½" 300.00
Vase, Bouquet #2, Bonfits, hair up, A-17, 10½" 290.00
Vase, Bouquet #2, brn, gypsy, A-17, 10½" 240.00
Vase, Bouquet #2, brn, lady w/sunflower in hair, A-17, 10½" 325.00
Vase, Bouquet #2, brn, Madame Recamier, A-17, 10½" 280.00
Vase, Bouquet #2, brn, redhead, A-17, 10½" 280.00

Vase, Bouquet #2, brn, sgn Carreno, A-33, 10½" 325.00
Vase, Bouquet #2, brn, sm roses, A-23, 10½" 250.00
Vase, Bouquet #2, charcoal, sgn Carreno, A-33, 10½" 300.00
Vase, Bouquet #2, gr, Madame Le Brun (child), F-3, 10½" 290.00
Vase, Bouquet #2, matt gr to tan, floral, M-15, 10½" 280.00
Vase, Carnation, gr, roses, B-30, 9" 190.00
Vase, Carnation, pk, lady w/boa, H-1, 9" 220.00
Vase, Carnation, red, poinsettias, E-2, 9" 290.00
Vase, Carnation, yel/gr, portrait, K-1, 9" 280.00
Vase, Carol, pk, lady w/boa, H-1, 8" 300.00
Vase, Chrys #1, brn, floral, A-40, 15" 185.00
Vase, Chrys #2, charcoal, floral, C-6, 13" 190.00
Vase, Clematis, wht, birds, D-1 ....290.00
Vase, Cloverleaf, red, floral, poinsettias, E-2 ....285.00
Vase, Maria, brn, floral, A-40, 10½" 210.00
Vase, Maria, pk, Hilda type w/flower, H-1, 10½" 265.00
Vase, Monroe, brn, Anna Potaka, A-17, 10½" 265.00
Vase, Narcis #1, brn, floral, A-27, 8½" 220.00
Vase, Narcis #1, charcoal, nude, C-1, 8½" 285.00
Vase, Narcis #2, red, floral, E-2, 6¾" 240.00
Vase, Orchid, pk, portrait, H-1, 10¼" 290.00
Vase, Oriental, charcoal, floral, C-6, 11" 295.00
Vase, Pansy, brn, floral, A-23, 4" 100.00
Vase, Pansy, red, floral, E-2, 4" 95.00
Vase, Parisian, charcoal, nude, C-1, 4" 255.00
Vase, Peerless, brn, floral, A-40, 9½" 230.00
Vase, Penn, brn, floral, A-40, 9½" 230.00
Vase, Poppy, brn, floral, A-27, 10½" 260.00
Vase, Poppy, wht, w/roses, no RLC, 10½" 285.00
Vase, President, matt, pine cones, M-64, 11½" 260.00
Vase, Regency, brn, floral, A-27, 11½" 275.00
Vase, Regency, russet, floral, 11½" 290.00
Vase, Roberta, tan matt, acorns, M-4, 10" 310.00
Vase, Rosalie, brn, floral, A-27, 9½" 200.00
Vase, Rosalie, charcoal, floral, C-6, 9½" 230.00
Vase, Rosalie, pk, portrait, H-1, 9½" 275.00
Vase, Rose, brn, floral, A-6, 8" 150.00
Vase, Rose, red, portrait, E-1, 8" 190.00
Vase, Royal #2, brn, floral, A-27, 8" 285.00
Vase, Senator #1, matt, nut, M-4, 15" 215.00
Vase, Senator #2, brn, floral, A-23, 13½" 200.00
Vase, Senator #2, pk, Hilda type, H-1, 13½" 290.00
Vase, Tobio Jug #1, brn, floral, A-027, 7¾" 140.00
Vase, Tobio Jug #1, brn, monk, A-36, 7¾" 135.00
Vase, Tobio Jug #1, wht, birds, D-1, 7¾" 215.00
Vase, Tobio Jug #2, brn, floral, A-6, 7" 145.00
Vase, Verbinia #2, charcoal, portrait, Carreno, C-1 ....230.00
Vase, Verona, brn, floral, A-16 ....175.00
Vase, Violet, brn, floral, A-27 ....115.00
Vase, Virginia, matt, nuts, M-4 ....180.00
Vase, Warwick, brn, floral, A-40 ....290.00
Vase, Warwick, pk, portrait, H-1 ....315.00
Vase, Windsor, brn, nuts, A-64 ....285.00
Vase, Windsor, pk, portrait, H-1 ....330.00

Wash Sets

Before the days of running water, bedrooms were standardly equipped with a wash bowl and pitcher as a matter of necessity. A 'toilet set' was comprised of the pitcher and bowl, toothbrush holder, covered commode, soap dish, shaving dish, and mug. Some sets were even more elaborate. Through everyday usage, the smaller items were often broken, and today it is unusual to find a complete set.

Porcelain sets decorated with florals, fruits, or scenics were produced abroad by Limoges in France; some were imported from Germany and England. During the last quarter of the 1800s and until after the turn of the century, American-made toilet sets were manufactured in abundance. Tin and graniteware sets were also made.

England, exotic bird and flower decals, gold trim, 12" pitcher, 5¾" H bowl, EX, $125.00.

Bridgewood & Sons (England), floral on wht, 7-pc set 750.00
Clews, Staffordshire, floral transfer, bowl, 4x12", EX 470.00
Gr-striated opal glass, 19th C, pitcher+bowl+2 pcs 660.00
Homer Laughlin, floral on wht, 7-pc set 850.00
Ironstone, Greek Key & vase transfer, pitcher+bowl, 13", 16" ...150.00
Minton, child's, gr ivy on cream, 7" pitcher, 9½" bowl 250.00
Minton, Flow Blue, pitcher+bowl+pot+toothbrush holder+soap dish ...3,800.00
Paris, porc, floral on blk w/gold, 8-side, pitcher+bowl 825.00

Watch Fobs

Watch fobs have been popular since the last quarter of the 19th century. They were often made by retail companies to feature their products. Souvenir, commemorative, and political fobs were also produced. Of special interest today are those with advertising, heavy equipment in particular. Some of the more pricey fobs are listed here, but most of those currently available were produced in such quantities that they are relatively common and should fall within a price range of $3.00 to $10.00. Our advisor for this category is Tony George; he is listed in the Directory under California.

Abraham Fur Co...MO, arrowhead shape 85.00
Acme Cement 30.00
Am Institute of Banking, New Orleans LA, enamel, 1919 ....70.00
Am Road Congress, shape of Texas, 1913 ....45.00
Avery, bulldog 80.00
Avery, tractor 115.00
Budweiser, horseshoe & eagle, red porc 160.00
Bulldog Cylinders 110.00
Car on shield & winged tire 40.00
Case Cross, engine 125.00
Cat 60 ....45.00
DeLaval, brass & blk enamel 50.00
Duhamel Saddles, leather, 2¼" 135.00
Fechheimer Uniforms, metal & celluloid 65.00
Fordson, tractor 80.00
French Lick Pluto Water, red & wht porc 250.00
GM Engines, Diesel Power, OK City, Tulsa, brass 35.00
Good Roads 95.00
Green River Whiskey, orig leather strap 250.00
IL Boys' State Fair School, 1924 ....40.00
Indian bust on arrowhead 20.00
Jersey Cream, rectangle 80.00

John's Leather Shop, Denver, saddle shape 80.00
Keystone Boss Watch Cases, IA 20.00
Komi Tommy, HI, pineapple shape w/red & gr enamel 36.00
Lawson, engine 125.00
Lindbergh, w/compass 85.00
Malleable Steel Ranges, South Bend IN 50.00
Man o' War, leather, 2¼" dia 40.00
Marion Steam Shovel, emb machine 30.00
NY to Paris 95.00
Old Style Lager, metal, man w/beer 65.00
Peter Weatherbird Shoes 225.00
Public Golf Course, Fairmount Park, Phila, 1927 ....40.00
Rock Island Plow 110.00
RT Frazier, Pueblo Co, Famous Pueblo Saddles, brass saddle 125.00
Sharples Separator Co, lady & Indian 85.00
Sharples Separator Co, lady in front of cabin 90.00
Sheboygen Water 125.00
Silver w/1910 imbedded penny 22.00
Texas Cowboy Reunion, Stamford TX, 1930 ....125.00
Tyler Equipment Corp, MA, metal, loader shape 20.00
Winchester Sporting Goods, catcher's glove/ball/bats, copper 165.00

Watch Stands

Watch stands were decorative articles designed with a hook from which to hang a watch. Some displayed the watch as the face of a grandfather clock or as part of an interior scene with figures in period costumes and contemporary furnishings. They were popular products of Staffordshire potters and silver companies as well.

Bronze, Nouveau lady by arched case, after Burschner, 8" 750.00
CI, leafy scrollwork w/eagle, blk pnt traces, lt rust, 10¼" 85.00
Cvd bone, floral w/mc highlights, 19th C, 12" 750.00
Pk lustre, clock form amid 2 cherubs, Dixon Austin, 1820-26 .1,300.00
Staffordshire, Scottish couple w/hound, 19th C, 8½" 160.00
Whalebone & cherry wood, scrolled crest, 19th C, 9⅛" 700.00

Watches

First made in the 1500s in Germany, early watches were actually small clocks, suspended from the neck or belt. By 1700 they had become the approximate shape and size we know today. The first watches produced in America were made in 1810. The well-known Waltham Watch Company was established in 1850. Later, Waterbury produced inexpensive watches which they sold by the thousands.

Open-face and hunting-case watches of the 1890s were often solid gold or gold-filled and were often elaborately decorated in several colors of gold. Gold watches became a status symbol in this decade and were worn by both men and women on chains with fobs or jeweled slides. Ladies sometimes fastened them to their clothing with pins often set with jewels. The chatelaine watch was worn at the waist, only one of several items such as scissors, coin purses, or needle cases, each attached by small chains.

Most turn-of-the-century watch cases were gold-filled; these are plentiful today. Sterling cases, though interest in them is on the increase, are not in great demand. Our advice for this category comes from Maundy International Watches, Antiquarian Horologists, price consultants, and researchers for many watch reference guides and books on horology. Their firm is a leading purveyor of antique watches of all kinds. They are listed in the Directory under Kansas. For character-related watches, see Personalities.

Key:

adj — adjusted	k/s — key set
brg — bridge plate design	k/w — key wind
d/s — double sunk dial	l/s — lever set
fbd — finger bridge design	mvt — movement
g/f — gold-filled	o/f — open face
g/j/s — gold jewel setting	p/s — pendant set
h/c — hunter case	r/g/p — rolled gold plate
HCI#P — heat, cold,	s — size
isochronism & position	s/s — single sunk dial
adjusted	s/w — stem wind
j — jewel	w/g/f — white gold-filled
k — karat	y/g/f — yellow gold-filled

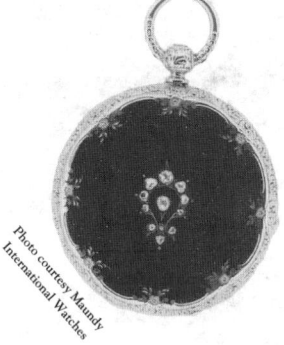

Swiss, 18k, lady's enamel pocketwatch, open face, key-wind, ca 1860, $800.00.

Photo courtesy Maundy International Watches

Am Watch Co, 0s, 7j, #1891, 14k, h/c, Am Watch Co 500.00
Am Watch Co, 12s, 17j, #1894, 14k, o/f, Royal 350.00
Am Watch Co, 12s, 21j, #1894, 14k, h/c 575.00
Am Watch Co, 16s, 11j, #1872, p/s, silver h/c, Park Road 575.00
Am Watch Co, 16s, 15j, #1899, y/g/f, h/c 265.00
Am Watch Co, 16s, 16j, #1884, 5-min, 14k, Repeater 5,850.00
Am Watch Co, 16s, 17j, #1888, Railroader 975.00
Am Watch Co, 16s, 19j, #1872, 14k, h/c, Am Watch Woerd's Pat .4,200.00
Am Watch Co, 16s, 21j, #1888, o/f, 14k, Riverside Maximus .1,675.00
Am Watch Co, 16s, 21j, #1899, y/g/f, l/s, o/f, Crescent St 425.00
Am Watch Co, 16s, 21j, #1908, y/g/f, o/f, Grade #645 ....325.00
Am Watch Co, 16s, 23j, #1908, o/f, 18k, Premier Maximus, MIB 12,000.00
Am Watch Co, 16s, 23j, #1908, y/g/f, o/f, adj, RR, Vanguard 375.00
Am Watch Co, 16s, 23j, #1908, y/g/f, o/f, Vanguard Up/Down ..825.00
Am Watch Co, 18s, #1857, silver h/c, Samuel Curtiss k/w 4,000.00
Am Watch Co, 18s, 11j, #1857, k/w, 1st run, PS Barlett, M ..3,500.00
Am Watch Co, 18s, 11j, #1857, silver h/c, k/w, DH&D 1,600.00
Am Watch Co, 18s, 11j, #1857, silver h/c, k/w, s/s, Ellery, M 500.00
Am Watch Co, 18s, 15j, #1877, k/w, RE Robbins, M 500.00
Am Watch Co, 18s, 15j, #1883, y/g/f, 2-tone, Railroad King 700.00
Am Watch Co, 18s, 17j, #1883, y/g/f, o/f, Crescent Street 175.00
Am Watch Co, 18s, 17j, #1892, HC, Canadian Pacific Railway ...950.00
Am Watch Co, 18s, 17j, #1892, y/g/f, o/f, Sidereal, rare 2,400.00
Am Watch Co, 18s, 17j, 25-yr, y/g/f, o/f, s/s, PS Bartlett 180.00
Am Watch Co, 18s, 21j, #1892, y/g/f, o/f, d/s, Crescent St 400.00
Am Watch Co, 18s, 21j, #1892, y/g/f, o/f, Grade #845 ....375.00
Am Watch Co, 18s, 21j, #1892, y/g/f, o/f, Pennsylvania Special .3,000.00
Am Watch Co, 18s, 7j, #1857, silver case, k/w, CT Parker 2,800.00
Am Watch Co, 6s, 7j, #1873, y/g/f, h/c, Am Watch Co 95.00
Auburndale Watch Co, 18s, 7j, k/w, l/s, Lincoln 1,500.00
Aurora Watch Co, 18s, 11j, k/w, silver h/c 300.00
Aurora Watch Co, 18s, 15 ruby j, y/g/f, s/w, 5th pinion 1,400.00
Ball (Elgin), 18s, 17j, o/f, silver, Official RR Standard 550.00
Ball (Hamilton), 16s, 21j, #999, g/f, o/f, l/s, M 500.00
Ball (Hamilton), 16s, 23j, #998, y/g/f, o/f, Elinvar, M 1,300.00
Ball (Hamilton), 18s, 19j, #999, g/f, o/f, l/s 550.00

Ball (Hampden), 18s, 17j, o/f, adj, RR, Superior Grade 1,500.00
Ball (Illinois), 12s, 19j, w/g/f, o/f 250.00
Ball (Waltham), 16s, 17j, y/g/f, o/f, RR, Commercial Std 300.00
Ball (Waltham), 16s, 21j, o/f, Official RR Standard 500.00
Columbus, 18s, 11-15j, k/w, k/s 500.00
Columbus, 18s, 15j, o/f, l/s 300.00
Columbus, 18s, 15j, y/g/f, o/f, Jay Gould on dial 950.00
Columbus, 18s, 21j, y/g/f, h/c, train on dial, Railway King 700.00
Columbus, 18s, 23j, 14k h/c, Columbus King 2,400.00
Columbus, 6s, 11j, 14k h/c 360.00
Cornell, 18s, 15j, s/w, JC Adams 575.00
Cornell, 18s, 15j, silver h/c, k/w, John Evans 700.00
Dudley, 12s, #1, 14k, o/f, flip-bk case, Masonic 2,600.00
Elgin, 10s, 18k, h/c, k/w, k/s, s/s, Gail Borden 650.00
Elgin, 12s, 15j, 14k, h/c 425.00
Elgin, 12s, 17j, 14k, h/c, GM Wheeler 350.00
Elgin, 16s, 15j, doctor's, 4th model, 18k, 2nd sweep hand, h/c ..1,400.00
Elgin, 16s, 15j, 14k, h/c 500.00
Elgin, 16s, 21j, g/f, 3 fbd, grade #91, scarce 2,400.00
Elgin, 16s, 21j, y/g/f, g/j/s, o/f, BW Raymond 350.00
Elgin, 16s, 21j, y/g/f, g/j/s, 3 fbd 450.00
Elgin, 16s, 21j, y/g/f, o/f, l/s, RR, Father Time 400.00
Elgin, 16s, 23j, up/down indicator, BW Raymond 1,300.00
Elgin, 17s, 7j, k/w, orig silver case, Leader 150.00
Elgin, 18s, 11j, silver, h/c, k/w, gilded, MG Odgen 225.00
Elgin, 18s, 15j, o/f, d/s, k/w, silveroid, RR, BW Raymond 1st run, M .1,500.00
Elgin, 18s, 15j, silver, k/w, k/s, h/c, HL Culver 350.00
Elgin, 18s, 15j, silver h/c, Penn RR dial, BW Raymond k/w mvt, M ..4,500.00
Elgin, 18s, 17j, silveroid, BW Raymond, M 200.00
Elgin, 18s, 21j, y/g/f, o/f, Father Time 400.00
Elgin, 18s, 23j, y/g/f, o/f, 5-position, RR, Veritas 525.00
Elgin, 6s, 11j, 14k, h/c, M 300.00
Elgin, 6s, 15j, 20-yr, y/g/f, h/c, s/s, EX 80.00
Fredonia, 18s, 11j, y/g/f, h/c, k/w 450.00
Hamilton, #4992B, 16s, 22j, o/f, steel case, M 325.00
Hamilton, #910, 12s, 17j, 20-yr, y/g/f, o/f, s/s, EX 70.00
Hamilton, #912, 12s, 17j, y/g/f, o/f, adj, EX 60.00
Hamilton, #920, 12s, 23j, 14k, o/f, M 600.00
Hamilton, #922MP, 12s, 18k case, Masterpiece (sgn), M 1,200.00
Hamilton, #925, 18s, 17j, y/g/f, h/c, s/s, l/s, M 200.00
Hamilton, #928, 18s, 15j, y/g/f, o/f, s/s, EX 175.00
Hamilton, #933, 18s, 16j, h/c, nickel plate, low serial # 700.00
Hamilton, #938, 18s, 17j, y/g/f, adj, M 650.00
Hamilton, #940, 18s, 21j, nickel plate, coin silver, o/f 350.00
Hamilton, #946, 18s, 23j, y/g/f, o/f, g/j/s, M 800.00
Hamilton, #947 (mk), 18s, 23j, 14k, h/c, orig/sgn, M 6,500.00
Hamilton, #950, 16s, 23j, y/g/f, o/f, l/s, sgn d/s, M 1,200.00
Hamilton, #965, 16s, 17j, 14k, p/s, h/c, brg, scarce 800.00
Hamilton, #972, 16s, 17j, y/g/f, g/j/s, o/f, d/s, l/s, adj 225.00
Hamilton, #974, 16s, 17j, 20-yr, y/g/f, o/f, s/s 150.00
Hamilton, #992, 16s, 21j, y/g/f, o/f, adj, d/s, dbl roller 350.00
Hamilton, #992B, 16s, 21j, y/g/f, o/f, l/s, Bar/Crown 475.00
Hampden, 12s, 17j, w/g/f, o/f, thin model, Aviator, M 200.00
Hampden, 16s, 17j, o/f, adj, EX 60.00
Hampden, 16s, 17j, y/g/f, h/c, s/w, M 150.00
Hampden, 16s, 21j, g/j/s, y/g/f, NP, h/c, Dueber, ¾-mvt, M 280.00
Hampden, 16s, 21j, o/f, adj, dbl roller, Special Railway 400.00
Hampden, 16s, 7j, gilded, nickel plate, o/f, ¾-mvt, EX 85.00
Hampden, 18s, 15j, k/w, mk on mvt, Railway 1,000.00
Hampden, 18s, 15j, s/w, gilded, JC Perry 175.00
Hampden, 18s, 15j, silver, k/w, h/c, Hayward 240.00
Hampden, 18s, 15j, y/g/f, damascened, h/c, Dueber 150.00
Hampden, 18s, 21j, y/g/f, g/j/s, h/c, New Railway 325.00
Hampden, 18s, 21j, y/g/f, o/f, d/s, l/s, N Am Railway 400.00

Hampden, 18s, 23j, y/g/f, o/f, d/s, adj, New Railway 425.00
Hampden, 18s, 23j, 14k, h/c, Special Railway 950.00
Hampden, 18s, 7-11j, k/w, gilded, Springfield Mass 195.00
Howard, E; 16s, 15j, s/w, 14k h/c, Series V, L sz 1,450.00
Howard, E; 18s, 15j, h/c, silver case, k/w, Series I, N sz 3,200.00
Howard, E; 18s, 15j, 18k h/c, k/w, Series II, N sz 3,950.00
Howard, E; 18s, 17j, 25-yr, y/g/f, o/f, orig case 800.00
Howard, E; 6s, 15j, s/w, 18k h/c, Series VIII, G sz, M 1,475.00
Howard (Keystone), 12s, 23j, 14k, h/c, brg, Series 8 ....700.00
Howard (Keystone), 16s, 17j, y/g/f, o/f, Series 9 ....240.00
Howard (Keystone), 16s, 21j, y/g/f, o/f, RR Chronometer II 525.00
Howard (Keystone), 16s, 23j, y/g/f, o/f, Series 0, jeweled bbl 725.00
Illinois, 0s, 7j, 14k, l/s, h/c 350.00
Illinois, 12s, 17j, y/g/f, o/f, d/s dial 95.00
Illinois, 16s, 17j, y/g/f, o/f, d/s, Bunn, EX 225.00
Illinois, 16s, 19j, y/g/f, o/f, d/s, 60-hr, Sangamo Special 1,500.00
Illinois, 16s, 21j, g/j/s, h/c, Burlington 295.00
Illinois, 16s, 21j, o/f, d/s, Santa Fe Special 550.00
Illinois, 16s, 21j, y/g/f, o/f, d/s, Bunn Special, M 425.00
Illinois, 16s, 23j, y/g/f, stiff bow, o/f, Sangamo Special, EX 900.00
Illinois, 18s, 11j, #1, silver, k/w, Alleghany 190.00
Illinois, 18s, 11j, #3, o/f, s/w, l/s, Comet 250.00
Illinois, 18s, 11j, Forest City 225.00
Illinois, 18s, 15j, #1, adj, y/g/f, k/w, h/c, gilt, Bunn 775.00
Illinois, 18s, 15j, #1, k/w, k/s, silver hunter, Stuart 675.00
Illinois, 18s, 15j, k/w, k/s, gilt, Railway Regulator 800.00
Illinois, 18s, 15j, s/w, silveroid 95.00
Illinois, 18s, 17j, g/j/s, adj, B&O RR Special (Hunter), h/c 1,650.00
Illinois, 18s, 17j, h/c, s/w, nickel plate, coin silver, Bunn 350.00
Illinois, 18s, 17j, o/f, d/s, adj, silveroid case, Lakeshore 225.00
Illinois, 18s, 17j, o/f, s/w, 5th pinion, Miller 300.00
Illinois, 18s, 21j, g/j/s, g/f, o/f, A Lincoln 340.00
Illinois, 18s, 21j, g/j/s, o/f, adj, B&O RR Special 1,900.00
Illinois, 18s, 21j, 14k, g/j/s, h/c, Bunn Special 1,100.00
Illinois, 18s, 23j, g/j/s, Bunn Special 750.00
Illinois, 18s, 24j, g/j/s, adj, o/f, Chesapeake & Ohio 2,400.00
Illinois, 18s, 24j, g/j/s, Bunn Special 825.00
Illinois, 18s, 26j, g/j/s, o/f, Ben Franklin USA, M 7,400.00
Illinois, 18s, 26j, 14k, Penn Special 6,300.00
Illinois, 18s, 7j, #3, Interior 150.00
Illinois, 18s, 7j, #3, silveroid, America 100.00
Illinois, 18s, 9-11j, o/f, k/w, s/s, silveroid case, Hoyt 150.00
Illinois, 8s, 13j, ¾-mvt, Rose LeLand, scarce 275.00
Ingersoll, 16s, 7j, wht base metal, Reliance 60.00
Lancaster, 18s, 7j, o/f, k/w, k/s, eng silver case 225.00
Marion US, 18s, h/c, k/w, k/s, ¾-plate, Asa Fuller, M 500.00
Marion US, 18s, 15j, nickel plate, h/c, s/w, Henry Randel 400.00
Melrose Watch Co, 18s, 7j, k/w, k/s 375.00
New York Watch Co, 18s, 7j, silver, h/c, k/w, Geo Sam Rice 375.00
New York Watch Co, 19j, low sz #, wolf's teeth wind 1,850.00
Patek Philippe, 12s, 18j, 18k, o/f 2,000.00
Patek Philippe, 16s, 20j, 18k, h/c 3,300.00
Rockford, 16s, 17j, y/g/f, h/c, brg, dbl roller 295.00
Rockford, 16s, 21j, #515, y/g/f 450.00
Rockford, 16s, 21j, g/j/s, o/f, grade #537, rare 1,500.00
Rockford, 16s, 23j, 14k, o/f, mk Doll on dial/mvt 2,400.00
Rockford, 18s, 15j, o/f, k/w, silver case 360.00
Rockford, 18s, 17j, silveroid w/M mc dial, fancy mvt/hands 700.00
Rockford, 18s, 17j, y/g/f, o/f, Winnebago 375.00
Rockford, 18s, 21j, o/f, King Edward, M 600.00
Seth Thomas, 18s, 17j, #2, g/j/s, adj, Henry Molineux 625.00
Seth Thomas, 18s, 17j, Edgemere 100.00
Seth Thomas, 18s, 25j, g/j/s, g/f, Maiden Lane 2,450.00
Seth Thomas, 18s, 7j, ¾-mvt, bk: eagle/Liberty model 200.00

South Bend, 12s, 21j, dbl roller, Grade #431 ....225.00
South Bend, 12s, 21j, orig o/f, d/s, Studebaker 250.00
South Bend, 18s, 21j, g/j/s, h/c, Studebaker 1,200.00
South Bend, 18s, 21j, 14k, h/c 850.00
Swiss, 18s, 18k, h/c, 1-min, Repeater, High Grade, M 4,500.00

Waterford

The Waterford Glass Company operated in Ireland from the late 1700s until 1851 when the factory closed. One hundred years later (in 1951) another Waterford glassworks was instituted that produced glass similar to the 18th-century wares — crystal, usually with cut decoration. Today Waterford is a generic term referring to the type of glass first produced there.

Guild bowl, 1986 limited edition, 5½x5½", $1,000.00 to $1,200.00.

Atomizer, Lismore 70.00
Biscuit barrel, Lismore 195.00
Bottle, perfume; Lismore 98.00
Bowl, Moon Dance, 6" 50.00
Bowl, salad; Lismore, 8" 198.00
Box, Heart 68.00
Box, Nocturn, 4" 48.00
Brandy, Colleen, balloon type, sm 75.00
Brandy, Lismore, balloon type, 12-oz 75.00
Brandy, Lismore, balloon type, 6-oz 65.00
Candlesticks, Nocturn, 3", pr 68.00
Carafe, Lismore 169.00
Champagne flute, Colleen, tall 79.00
Champagne flute, Kildare 55.00
Champagne flute, Lismore 55.00
Champagne flute, Sheila 85.00
Christmas bell, 1984 ....85.00
Claret, Colleen, tall 77.00
Claret, Lismore 55.00
Claret, Sheila 85.00
Clock, heart shaped 99.00
Compote, Colleen, ftd, lg 99.00
Compote, Lismore 105.00
Compote/candy dish, Glandore, stemmed, 5½" 98.00
Cordial, Colleen 50.00
Decanter, Lismore, 13" 298.00
Decanter, ship's, Colleen 298.00
Decanter, wine; Colleen 298.00
Dinner bell, Lismore 85.00
Goblet, water; Castletown 185.00
Goblet, water; Colleen 79.00
Goblet, water; Kildare 55.00
Goblet, water; Lismore 55.00
Goblet, water; Sheila 85.00
Hock, Colleen 80.00
Hock, Lismore 70.00

Liqueur glass, Lismore **45.00**
Old-fashioned, dbl, Lismore **65.00**
Paperweight, heart **89.00**
Shakers, Glandore, pr **110.00**
Sherbet, Lismore **65.00**
Sherry, Colleen **59.00**
Sherry, Lismore **49.00**
Tumbler, Lismore, 12-oz **50.00**
Vase, Noah, sgn/#d, 11" **1,500.00**
Vase, ornate cuttings, scalloped top, 9½" **395.00**
Vase, Rock of Cashel **325.00**
Wine, Castletown **185.00**
Wine, Kildare **55.00**
Wine, Lismore **55.00**

Watt Pottery

The Watt Pottery Company was established in Crooksville, Ohio, on July 5, 1922. From approximately 1922 until 1935, they manufactured hand-turned stone containers — jars, jugs, milk pans, preserve jars, and various sizes of mixing bowls, usually marked with a cobalt blue acorn stamp. In 1936 production of these items was discontinued, and the company began to produce kitchen utility ware and ovenware such as mixing bowls, spaghetti bowls and plates, canister sets, covered casseroles, salt and pepper shakers, cookie jars, ice buckets, pitchers, bean pots, and salad and dinnerware sets. Most Watt ware is individually hand painted with bold brush strokes of red, green, or blue contrasting with the natural buff color of the glazed body. Several patterns were produced: Apple, Autumn Foliage, Cherry, Dutch Tulip, Morning Glory, Rio Rose, Rooster, Tear Drop, Starflower, and Tulip, to name a few. Much of the ware was made for advertising premiums and is often found stamped with the name of the retail company.

Tragedy struck the Watt Pottery Company on October 4, 1965, when fire completely destroyed the factory and warehouse. Production never resumed, but the ware they made has withstood many years of service in American kitchens and is today highly regarded and prized by collectors. The vivid colors and folk art-like execution of each cheerful pattern create a homespun ambiance that will make Watt pottery a treasure for years to come.

For further study we recommend *Watt Pottery, An Identification and Price Guide,* by our advisors for this category, Sue and Dave Morris; they are listed in the Directory under Oregon. For the address of the *Watt's News* newsletter, see the section on Clubs, Newsletters, and Catalogs.

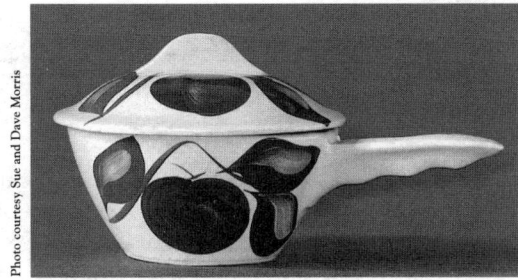

Photo courtesy Sue and Dave Morris

Apple individual French-handled casserole, #18, $225.00.

Apple, beanpot, w/lid, #76 ....**175.00**
Apple, bowl, mixing; deep, #64 ....**60.00**
Apple, bowl, ribbed, #06 ....**50.00**
Apple, bowl, salad; #73 ....**85.00**
Apple, bowl, spaghetti; #39 ....**175.00**

Apple, cookie jar, w/lid, #503 ....**450.00**
Apple, creamer, w/advertising, #62 ....**110.00**
Apple, grease jar, w/lid, #01 ....**375.00**
Apple, mug, #121 ....**185.00**
Apple, pie plate, w/advertising, #33 ....**150.00**
Apple, pitcher, #15 ....**75.00**
Apple, shakers, hourglass form, pr **250.00**
Autumn Foliage, bowl, ribbed, #604 ....**55.00**
Autumn Foliage, pitcher, #15 ....**65.00**
Autumn Foliage, platter, #31 ....**110.00**
Banded, bowl, gr/wht bands, 7" dia **25.00**
Banded, casserole, bl/wht bands, w/lid, 8" dia **45.00**
Basketweave, bowl, mixing; gr, #8 ....**30.00**
Brn glaze, dog dish, #7 ....**145.00**
Butterfly, bowl, #7 ....**275.00**
Cherry, bowl, berry; #4 ....**45.00**
Cherry, casserole, w/lid, #3/19 ....**175.00**
Cherry, pitcher, w/advertising, #15 ....**175.00**
Cherry, salt shaker, barrel-shaped **90.00**
Dogwood, platter, 15" **110.00**
Double Apple, baker, w/lid, wire stand, #96 ....**250.00**
Double Apple, bowl, ribbed, #07 ....**75.00**
Dutch Tulip, bowl, mixing; #7 ....**100.00**
Dutch Tulip, casserole, French hdld, ind, w/lid, #18 .....**275.00**
Dutch Tulip, pitcher, #16 ....**250.00**
Dutch Tulip, refrigerator pitcher, sq, #69 ....**600.00**
Eagle, bowl, mixing; ribbed, #6 ....**125.00**
Goodies jar, w/lid, #59 ....**350.00**
Kitch-N-Queen, bowl, mixing; #12 ....**60.00**
Kitch-N-Queen, cookie jar, #503 ....**225.00**
Kitch-N-Queen, pitcher, w/ice lip, #17 ....**200.00**
Morning Glory, bowl, mixing; #6 ....**85.00**
Morning Glory, sugar bowl, #98 ....**250.00**
Rio Rose, bowl, serving; bull's eye pattern, 15" **100.00**
Rio Rose, casserole, 4-hdld, #8 ....**90.00**
Rio Rose, cup & saucer, cut-leaf **90.00**
Rio Rose, pitcher, #17 ....**225.00**
Rio Rose, plate, dinner; cut-leaf, 8½" **55.00**
Rooster, baker, w/lid, #67 ....**200.00**
Rooster, bowl, salad; #73 ....**145.00**
Rooster, ice bucket, w/lid **275.00**
Rooster, pitcher, #15 ....**145.00**
Starflower, baker, w/lid & wire warming stand, #96 ......**150.00**
Starflower, bean server, ind, #75 ....**45.00**
Starflower, mug, barrel-shaped, #501 ....**100.00**
Starflower, pitcher, #15 ....**65.00**
Tear Drop, bowl, ribbed, #06 ....**40.00**
Tear Drop, pitcher, #15 ....**60.00**
Tulip, bowl, mixing; deep, #64 ....**85.00**
Tulip, cookie jar, w/lid, #503 ....**375.00**
Tulip, creamer, #62 ....**225.00**
White Daisy, plate, bread; 6½" **65.00**

Wave Crest

Wave Crest is a line of decorated opal ware (milk glass) patented in 1892 by the C.F. Monroe Co. of Meriden, Connecticut. They made a full line of items for every room of the house, but they are probably best known for their boxes and vases. Most items were hand painted in various levels of decoration, but more transfers were used in the later years prior to the company's demise in 1916. Floral themes are common; items with the scenics and portraits are rarer and more highly prized. Many pieces have ornately scrolled ormolu and brass handles, feet and rims attached. Early pieces were often signed with a black mark; later a red banner mark was used, and occasionally a paper label may be found. However, the glass is quite distinctive and has not been reproduced, so even unmarked items are easy to recognize. Our advisors for this category are Dolli and Wilfred Cohen; they are listed in the Directory under California. Note: There is no premium for signatures on Wave Crest. Values are given for hand-decorated pieces (unless noted 'transfer') that are *not* worn.

Ashtray/match holder, floral, mc on wht, ftd, mk, 6x3" **695.00**
Biscuit jar, floral transfer, rococo leaves, unmk, 5½x7½" **250.00**
Box, apple blossoms on bl, rococo, 3x3¼" dia, EX **350.00**
Box, Collars & Cuffs, mums & daisies on tan, mk, 7½x7" dia ..**1,350.00**
Box, Double Shell, shells & flowers, mc on wht, sgn, 3" dia **295.00**
Box, Egg Crate, floral, autumn tones, mk, 5¼x6¾" dia **1,050.00**
Box, floral, pk on wht, mk, 2½x2½" dia **175.00**
Box, glove; roses, mc on yel, ormolu ft, mk, 5½x9½x5¾" **1,550.00**
Box, Puffy, lilies, yel on wht w/lav & gold, 6½x6¾" sq **1,095.00**
Box, shadow flowers & wht beads on gr, 8-sided, 4½x6¾" dia ...**700.00**
Box, Spindrift, pansies on pk to wht, ftd, mk, 6¾x8" dia **2,500.00**
Box, Swirl, floral, mc on pk to wht, unmk, 2¾x4½" dia **175.00**
Box, Swirl, lily of the valley, mc on wht, unmk, 4½x6" dia **450.00**
Box, Swirl, roses, wht on dk gr w/lav trim, unmk, 4x7" **700.00**
Broom holder, pansies, mc w/wht beads on ivory, 10½x7" **2,100.00**
Cigar holder, forget-me-nots on wht, unmk, 3¾x4" at hdls **295.00**
Clock, mantel; Waterbury, cherubs, Wavecrest floral finial, 14" .**1,950.00**
Comb & brush holder, asters, bl & purple on wht, mk, 4½x9" ..**2,050.00**
Creamer, Swirl, mushroom garden decor, mk **75.00**
Humidor, Cigars & daisies, blown-out shell lid, mk, 6x4¼" **850.00**
Humidor, Swirl, daisies on pk to yel, Souvenir, 7" **850.00**
Jar, daisies on wht, melon ribs, Souvenir on swirl lid, mk, 5x6" ..**325.00**
Lamp, boudoir; forget-me-nots on bl to wht, socket base, 7" **500.00**
Letter holder, Puffy, floral, mc on wht, unmk, 4x5½" **475.00**
Match holder, floral w/beading, 4 gold ft **250.00**
Paperweight, forget-me-nots, bl on wht, 8-sided, 3x3¼" **600.00**
Plaque, nasturtiums & buds on pk to wht, 10x8"+fr **3,750.00**
Plaque, trees/rocks/mtns, gr border, ornate metal fr, 8x10½" ...**4,250.00**
Playing card holder, roses, pk on bl to wht, mk, 2½x4x1¼" **350.00**
Shakers, asters, bl on wht to pk, sq, unmk, 2¾x1¼", pr, NM **150.00**
Shakers, asters, mc on beige to wht, lids w/agitators, 4", pr **150.00**
Shakers, Swirl, floral, mc on yel, pewter lids, 2¼", pr **250.00**
Sugar bowl, bluebird on fence, SP lid & bail, unmk, 4" **100.00**
Toothpick holder, apple blossoms on wht w/gold, unmk, 2⅛" **250.00**
Tray, floral, mc on bl to wht, mirror top, 4½x4" dia **595.00**
Vase, daisies on russet, gilt metal mts/hdls at rim, 9½" **1,000.00**
Vase, daisies on wht to gr, gilt-metal mts, mk, 4¾x3¼" **350.00**

Weapons

Among the varied areas of specialization within the broad category of weapons, guns are by far the most popular. Muskets are among the earliest firearms; they were large-bore shoulder arms, usually firing black powder with separate loading of powder and shot. Some ignited the charge by flintlock or caplock, while later types used a firing pin with a metallic cartridge. Side arms, referred to as such because they were worn at the side, include pistols and revolvers. Pistols range from early single-shot and multiple barrels to modern types with cartridges held in the handle. Revolvers were supplied with a cylinder that turned to feed a fresh round in front of the barrel breech. Other firearms include shotguns, which fired round or conical bullets and had a smooth inner barrel surface, and rifles, so named because the interior of the barrel contained spiral grooves (rifling) which increased accuracy. For further study we recommend *Modern Guns,*

Twelfth Edition, by Russell Quertermous and Steve Quertermous, available at your local bookstore. All weapons but swords are under the advisement of Steve Howard, see the Directory under California. See also Militaria.

Key:
bbl — barrel	mag — magazine
cal — caliber	mgn — magnum
conv — conversion	mod — modified
cyl — cylinder	oct — octagon
f/l — flintlock	o/u — over/under
f/s — full stock	p/b — patch box
ga — gauge	perc — percussion
hdw — hardware	/s — stock
h/s — half stock	

Carbines

Burnside Civil War, 54 cal, 21" bbl w/M blueing **2,500.00**
Colt CAR-15 semi auto, 223 cal, SP1 shorty, retractable/s, EX ..**500.00**
Enfield Jungle, 303 British cal, dtd 1947, EX **225.00**
Inland M-1, 30 cal, bbl dtd 12-42, 20-rnd mag, EX+ **300.00**
Inland M-1A1 Paratrooper, 30 carb cal, folding stock, 1944, EX+ .**1,100.00**
Japanese Type 44, 6.5 Japanese cal, folding bayonet, EX **150.00**
Marlin 1894SRC, 44 mgn cal, ramp front/open rear sights, EX ..**175.00**
Marlin 336, 34REM cal, pistol grip/s, strap, EX **175.00**
Remington 742 Deer & Bear, 30.06 cal, w/2.5X8 scope, EX, $300 to ...**400.00**
Ruger semiauto, 44 mgn cal, Wms peep sight, EX **300.00**
Saginaw M1, 30 cal, w/20-rnd mag, EX+ **375.00**
Savage 99 lever action, 303SAV cal, 20" rnd bbl, EX **500.00**
Sharps 1863 cartridge conv, iron mtd, 2-pc walnut/s, VG **2,000.00**
Spencer M 1865, not fitted w/Stabler cutoff, military mks, M .**3,750.00**
Spencil Civil War, complete & orig, VG **2,000.00**
Thompson 1927A3 semiauto, 22LR cal, 20" finned bbl, MIB **400.00**
US 1863 Springfield, Plains Indian brass tack decor, G **900.00**
Winchester M-1, 30 cal, pushbutton safety, ramp sight, EX **500.00**
Winchester 1866 Henry, 44RF cal, 24" oct bbl, walnut/s, VG ...**4,500.00**
Winchester 1866 Saddle Ring Henry, 44RF cal, 20" rnd bbl, G ...**4,500.00**
Winchester 1873 Saddle Ring, 32WCF cal, 20" rnd bbl, EX, $4,000 to ..**5,000.00**
Winchester 1876 NWMP Saddle Ring Model 2, 45-75 cal, VG .**3,000.00**
Winchester 364, 30-30 cal, lever action, postwar, EX **225.00**
Winchester 64 Deluxe, 30WCF cal, 20" bbl, ¾ mag, EX **550.00**
Winchester 94 Flatband, 32 cal, lever action, 1940s, NM **225.00**

Muskets

Winchester M.1873 musket, 44 caliber, standard type with 30" barrel, modified carbine buttstock with straight grip, with bayonet, EX, from $2,400.00 to $2,750.00.

Brown Bess, sea service, f/l, 75 cal, brass plates, 36" bbl, EX **4,250.00**
Brown Bess 3rd Model, ca 1812, 39" bbl, VG **1,550.00**
Harper's Ferry 1816, walnut/s, stamped mks, 38⅝" bbl, EX **1,750.00**
M 1816 Contract, tang dtd 1836, mk lockplate, w/bayonet, EX ..**1,000.00**
New England Militia, perc conv, walnut f/s, brass hdw, 39" bbl **325.00**
Parker Field & Co, Indian trade, 52 cal smooth bore, 30" bbl, G ...**1,700.00**
Prussian perc, 70 cal, walnut/s, iron butt plate, G- **150.00**
Sharps Military, 45 cal conv, std military stock, 28" bbl **925.00**

Springfield, Maynard primer feature, 1858, cut down to 24" **200.00**
US Trenton, perc lock dtd 1864, 40" rnd bbl, G **600.00**

Pistols

Allen & Wheelock, 31 cal, center hammer, 4" oct bbl, G **80.00**
Browning 1955 semiauto, 380 cal, 3½", M **225.00**
Colt combat Commander semiauto, 45 cal, 4¼" bbl, M **500.00**
Colt Mk IV Series 80 Lt Weight Commander semiauto, 45-cal, NM ..**325.00**
Colt Pre-Series 70 semiauto, 38 super cal, compo grips, NM **600.00**
Colt 1903 Pocket, 38 rimless/smokeless cal, rubber grips, NM **400.00**
Colt 1911A1 semiauto, 45 cal, re-Parkerized, rpl bbl, VG **325.00**
Colt 1911A1 US Army semiauto, 45 cal, 5" bbl, NM **400.00**
CYQ P38 semiauto, 9 mm cal, rfn slide & grips, EX **275.00**
Luger Black Widow semiauto, 9mm cal, 1939 on chamber, NM .**435.00**
Luger 1908 semiauto, 42 code on link, chamber dtd 1940, EX .**1,750.00**
Luger 42 Code semiauto, 9mm cal, dtd 1940 on chamber, EX **600.00**
Mauser 1896 Broomhdl, late type, NM **600.00**
Mauser 1896 Broomhdl, 9mm cal, shoulder stock, 5½" bbl, EX ..**1,700.00**
Mauser 1914 semiauto, 32 cal, rpl mag, wood grips, VG **200.00**
Norwegian 1927 semiauto, 11.25mm cal, 5" bbl, VG **450.00**
Remington 1911 semiauto, 45 cal, rfn, rpl grips/mag, VG **325.00**
Semmerling LM-4 Mag, 45ACP cal, dbl action, 3⅝" bbl, M ..**2,750.00**
Smith & Wesson str-line target, 22LR cal, 10" ribbed bbl, MIB ...**1,300.00**
Smith & Wesson 3rd Model, 22LR cal, single shot, 10" bbl, NM **350.00**
Springfield Armory 1911A1 semiauto, 45 cal, 5" bbl, EX **250.00**
Stevens Dmn 43 2nd issue, 22 cal, sm fr, 10" oct bbl, NM **400.00**
Swiss 1900 Luger semiauto, 30 cal, DWM on link, rfn, M **675.00**
Walther PPK Party Leader semiauto, swastika grips, NMIB **3,250.00**
Walther P38 semiauto, 9mm cal, rpl grips, EX in holster **350.00**

Revolvers

Bacon Mfg Co pocket perc, 31 cal, 5-shot, walnut grips, G **225.00**
Colt .22 open top, NP, ivory grips, 2⅜" bbl, NM, $300 to **600.00**
Colt Army, 45 cal, single action, dtd 1926, 7½" bbl, EX **4,250.00**
Colt Army single action, 45 cal, NP, ivory grips, 7½" bbl, EX ..**3,300.00**
Colt Bisley flat-top target, 6-shot, 7½" bbl, EX **8,000.00**
Colt Frontier Six Shooter, 44-40 cal, single action, NM **3,250.00**
Colt London 1849 pocket perc, 31 cal, 5-shot, 6" bbl, MIB **4,250.00**
Colt M 1849, factory eng/ivory grips, NM in case w/accessories ..**9,000.00**
Colt M 1860 Army, walnut grips, all orig, EX+ **6,250.00**
Colt Navy pocket, cartridge conv, 38RF cal, 5-shot, EX **600.00**
Colt New Service, 44-40 cal, 4½" bbl, lanyard ring, G **350.00**
Colt Peacemaker, 22 cal, w/extra 22 mgn cyl, 4¾" bbl, MIB **350.00**
Colt 1849 pocket perc, 31 cal, 4" bbl, G in repro box **300.00**
Colt 1849 pocket perc, 31 cal, 5-shot, 4" bbl, VG **550.00**
Colt 1851 Navy, iron trigger guard/bkstrap, G **975.00**
Colt 1860 Army perc, 44 cal, lt cyl scene, EX **1,600.00**
Colt 2nd Generation 1st Model Dragoon perc, MIB **325.00**
Eli Whitney Navy, 36 cal, 6-shot, 7½" oct bbl, EX **900.00**
Eli Whitney 2nd Model pocket perc, 31 cal, 5-shot, EXIB **450.00**
JM Cooper 1st Model pocket, 31 cal, SP trigger, 4" oct bbl, G ...**375.00**
Manhattan Firearms Co Navy, 36 cal, 5-shot, 6½" oct bbl, G **550.00**
Manhattan Series II pocket, 6-shot, eng fr, 4" bbl, EX **715.00**
Remington New Model Army, 44 cal, 2-pc walnut grips, EX **500.00**
Rogers & Spencer perc, 44 cal, 6-shot, 7½" oct bbl, VG **650.00**
Savage Revolving Firearms Navy, 36 cal, 6-shot, 7⅛" oct bbl, EX ..**850.00**
Smith & Wesson #2 Army, 32RF cal, 6-shot, 6" oct bbl, VG **400.00**
Smith & Wesson 1950, 45 cal, target sights/hammer, 6½" bbl, NM ..**300.00**

Rifles

British Enfield Sniper, 303 Brit cal, w/scope, EX+ **950.00**

Colt-Burgess lever action, 44-40 cal, 25½" oct bbl, G **750.00**
German G41 semiauto, 8X57 cal, AC43 code Walther, EX **1,750.00**
Hecker & Koch HK91, 308 cal, 30 rnd mag, synthetic/s, M **1,050.00**
Henry, 44RF cal, full mag, 24" oct bbl, VG **4,200.00**
Henry 1st Model, 44RRF cal, 24" oct bbl, brass plate, G **10,500.00**
Marlin 1893 SRC, 3030 cal, full mag, str/s, ladder sight, EX ...**1,000.00**
Marlin 1895 Deluxe, 40-82 cal, full mag, ½-oct 26" bbl, EX ...**3,250.00**
Savage 1899C lever action, 30-30WIN cal, 26" rnd/oct bbl, EX ..**400.00**
Saver 1895 lever action, 303SAV cal, str/s, 28" oct bbl, EX **450.00**
Springfield 1873 trap door, 45-70 cal, dtd 1881, VG **400.00**
US 1898 Krag, 30-40 cal, walnut/s, 30" rnd bbl, EX **325.00**
Winchester 1873 Indian 2nd Model, 44 cal, full mag, oct bbl, G- .**2,650.00**
Winchester 1873 lever action, 32WCF cal, 30" rnd bbl, VG ..**1,800.00**
Winchester 1873 lever action, 38WCF cal, 24" oct bbl, EX ...**1,750.00**
Winchester 1873 3rd Model, 44WCF cal, full mag, 24" oct bbl, VG **1,050.00**
Winchester 1876 lever action, 45-60 cal, 28" oct bbl, EX **2,000.00**
Winchester 1886 lever action, 40-82 cal, 26" rnd bbl, EX **2,500.00**
Winchester 1892 Deluxe, 32WCF cal, pistol grip, oct bbl, EX ..**1,300.00**
Winchester 1892 takedown lever action, 44 cal, 24" oct bbl, NM ...**6,000.00**
Winchester 1894 lever action, 32-40 cal, full mag, G **650.00**

Shotguns

Alfred Woodhill pin fire, 12 ga, 30" dbl bbls, EX **300.00**
Baretta ASE90 o/u, 12 ga, 28" ribbed bbl, skeet bore, MIB **6,000.00**
Beretta S686 Silver Perdiz o/u, 12-ga, 29½" bbls, M **950.00**
Beretta 686EL Superposed, 12 ga, 28" bbls, NM **700.00**
Browning Model 42 pump, 410 cal, 26" full choke bbl, MIB **400.00**
Ithica 37 Featherlight pump, 12 ga, 38" poly-choke bbl, EX **150.00**
Ithica 37 police riot, 12 ga, 20" plain bbl, extended mag, EX+ ...**200.00**
JP Clabrough dbl bbl, 12 ga, 30" Damascus bbls, G **650.00**
Marlin pump, 12-ga, 30" matted top bbl, str/s, VG **170.00**
Nikko 550 Eagle Grade o/u, 12 ga, 2¾" chamber, 27½" bbls, M ..**950.00**
Parker VHE dbl bbl, 12 ga, 30" bbl, pistol grip/s, VG **900.00**
Remington #9, 12 ga, 28" steel single bbl, walnut grip/s, VG **100.00**
Remington 1881 dbl-bbl, 12 ga, Damascus bbls, pistol grip, G ...**275.00**
Remington 1893, 16 ga, single 30" rnd bbl, iron fr, VG **100.00**
Remington 870 deer pump, 12 ga, 20" smooth bore, EX **165.00**
W&C Scott & Son sidelock dbl bbl, 10 ga, 30" Damascus bbls, EX **750.00**
Winchester Model 12 Deluxe pump, 12 ga, 30" full choke bbl, NM ..**1,500.00**
Winchester 101 o/u, 20 ga, 28" full/mod bbls, EX **800.00**
WW Greener dbl bbl, 10 ga, 30" bbls, G **375.00**

Swords

All swords listed below are priced 'with scabbard' unless otherwise noted.

Confederate Artillery short sword, crude brass hilt, 19" blade .**1,200.00**
German 3rd Reich officer's, P guard, 32" unmk curved blade, EX .**225.00**
Japanese, sharkskin covered hdl w/blossom decor, 27"+scabbard .**275.00**
Royal Canadian Regimental, 24" str dbl-edged blade, brass hilt .**125.00**
Spanish Lt Cavalry, 30" single-edged blade mk Toledo 1887, G ..**85.00**
US 1833 Foot Artillery, 19" dbl-edged blade, crude hilt **300.00**
US 1840 Heavy Cavalry, unmk German, 36" single-edged blade, G .**225.00**
US 1850 foot officer's, European import, no scabbard, VG **300.00**
US 1860 Lt Cavalry, Emerson & Silver NJ, dtd 1864, 35" blade, VG .**450.00**
US 1860 Naval Cutlass, Ames, 25" curved blade dtd 1861, EX ..**800.00**
USN 1841, NP Ames Springfield MA, dtd 1843, VG **450.00**
185-Pattern Naval officer's, 31½" etched blade, EX **400.00**

Weather Vanes

The earliest weather vanes were of handmade wrought iron and were generally simple angular silhouettes with a small hole suggesting an eye. Later copper, zinc, and polychromed wood with features in relief were fashioned into more realistic forms. Ships, horses, fish, Indians, roosters, and angels were popular motifs. In the 19th century, silhouettes were often made from sheet metal. Wooden figures became highly carved and were painted in vivid colors. E.G. Washburne and Company in New York was one of the most prominent manufacturers of weather vanes during the last half of the century. Two-dimensional sheet metal weather vanes are increasing in value due to the already heady prices of the full-bodied variety. Originality, strength of line, and patination help to determine value. When no condition is indicated, the items listed below are assumed to be in excellent condition.

Key:
fb — full-bodied   f/fb — flattened full-bodied

Bird with fancy tail, wrought iron, paint traces, original V mount, 37⅝" overall, bullet holes, $1,000.00.

Bird silhouette, tin, dbl cone base, 25¼" H 465.00
Bust of Columbia, cast zinc, ca 1900, imperfections, 17" 550.00
Cockerel, sheet metal/CI/zinc, red tin tail, 32x31½" 1,500.00
Eagle, copper, imperfections, 20" 1,095.00
Eagle, gilt copper, late 19th C, 38x44" 4,000.00
Eagle, molded copper, old gold finish, 33" wingspan 650.00
Eagle on arrow, copper, JW Fiske NY, late 19th C, 49½" L 3,500.00
Fish on spire std, wooden, weathered gray patina, 67" H 440.00
Grasshopper, copper repro, EX patina, 20th C, 32" L, EX 250.00
Horse, sheet metal, primitive, blksmith rivets, ca 1900, 30" 150.00
Horse & sulkey w/jockey, pnt CI, 33" 2,750.00
Horse running, cast head, copper body, lt gr pnt, 20" L, G 700.00
Horse running, gilt copper, lead solder, EX patina, 24" L 990.00
Horse running, gilt copper w/verdigris traces, 1880s, 16x26" ...1,495.00
Horse running, zinc, fb, gilt traces, rpr shaft, 23x54" 1,750.00
North Wind, copper banneret, att Fiske, late 19th C, w/base .13,800.00
Pig, zinc, on CI arrow, 20¾" L 415.00
Rooster, copper, hollow body, tooled details, 24" H 1,045.00
Rooster, copper & cast metal, EX patina, 20½x20" 1,300.00
Rooster, sheet iron, primitive silhouette, pitting, 14" 300.00
Rooster, sheet steel, pnt traces, 1900s, 24x21" +modern base 360.00
Salmon, cvd wood, artist sgn, worn pnt, 39" L 300.00
Sheep, copper w/verdigris, rpr bullet holes/dents, 19th C, 30" ..5,750.00
Stag leaping, gilt copper, att Harris & Co, 1880s, 25x30" 13,800.00
Stallion, AB & WT Westervelt...NY, 1883, 22x26", EX 6,000.00
Swordfish, pnt wood & CI, weathered, 19th C 1,150.00
Tut-Tut figure in auto on arrow, sheet metal, 1970s, 35x74", VG ...1,350.00

Weaving

Early Americans used a variety of tools and a great amount of time to produce the material from which their clothing was made. Soaked and dried flax was broken on a flax brake to remove waste material. It

was then tapped and stroked with a scutching knife. Hackles further removed waste and separated the short fibers from the longer ones. Unspun fibers were placed on the distaff on the spinning wheel for processing into yarn. The yarn was then wound around a reel for measuring. Three tools used for this purpose were the niddy-noddy, the reel yarn winder, and the click reel. After it was washed and dyed, the yarn was transferred to a barrel-cage or squirrel-cage swift and fed onto a bobbin winder.

Today flax wheels are more plentiful than the large wool wheels since they were small and could be more easily stored and preserved. The distaff, an often-discarded or misplaced part of the wheel, is very scarce. French spinners from the Quebec area painted their wheels. Many have been stripped and refinished by those unaware of this fact. Wheels may be very simple or have a great amount of detail, depending upon the owner's ethnic background and the maker's skill.

Bobbin rack, hardwood, mortised, shoe ft, w/spools, 29" 250.00
Flax break, 21½" 22.00
Hackle, wooden base w/7 iron spikes, dtd 1823, 4x12x3⅛" 50.00
Niddy noddy, trn center shaft, cvd ends, 17¼" 200.00
Spinning wheel, hardwood w/dk finish, slender trn legs, 62" 200.00
Spinning wheel, hardwoods, trn legs & details, 45" dia 165.00
Spinning wheel, hardwoods w/red stain, rprs, 34" 220.00
Spinning wheel, oak & hardwood w/trn detail, rprs/rfn, 36" 300.00
Spinning wheel, Shaker type, red pnt, lg yarn holder, 44½" ...1,200.00
Spool winder, dbl; wood pinned construction, table-top, 14x10" ..275.00
Swift, mc pnt w/floral decor, table-top style, 23", EX 500.00
Swift, whalebone & ivory, fastened by silver pins, 19" L 1,100.00
Swift, whalebone & ivory w/red & blk inscribed lines, 19th C, 23" ...920.00
Yarn winder, clock gear, pnt decor, simple trnings, 42", EX 150.00
Yarn winder, pegged wood, quality trnings, typical style, VG 110.00
Yarn winder, 2-part, 3-leg, 4-arm top, adjusts to 25½", 8" H 300.00

Webb

Thomas Webb and Sons have been glassmakers in Stourbridge, England, since 1837. Besides their fine cameo glass, they have also made enameled ware and pieces heavily decorated with applied glass ornaments. The butterfly is a motif that has been so often featured that it tends to suggest Webb as the manufacturer. Our advisor for this category is Don Williams; he is listed in the Directory under Missouri. See also specific types of glass such as Alexandrite, Burmese, Mother of Pearl, and Peachblow.

Cameo

Bottle, scent; wild roses (detailed), wht/citron, SP lid, 5½" 1,500.00
Bowl, floral/butterfly, lav/wht on red, 2½x5¼" 1,400.00
Finger bowl & saucer, floral/butterfly, cranberry/clear 550.00
Finger bowl & saucer, prunus blossoms, cranberry/clear 550.00
Jug, claret; glorinias & leaves, wht on bl, SP trim 1,300.00
Vase, anemones/ferns, wht on red, tapered, 6¾" 950.00
Vase, cherry blossom branches, wht on rose, ovoid base, att, 10" .1,265.00
Vase, clematis, wht on citron, 4" 1,100.00
Vase, crested parrot on pine bough, wht on gr, Gem mk, 3" 3,200.00
Vase, floral, shaded ivory, dimpled, hexagonal top, 5¼" 1,025.00
Vase, floral vine, wht on textured confetti, 3¼" 550.00
Vase, floral w/leaves, cvd band, citron on clear, 5¼x4" 1,240.00
Vase, honeysuckle/butterflies, wht on red, ftd, 5¾" 2,100.00
Vase, lady's portrait medallion, wht on citron w/gold, 4" 1,200.00
Vase, narcissus/leaves, acanthus leaf rim, wht on citron, 5¼" 900.00
Vase, orchid & leaves, wht on peachblow, 4¼" 1,750.00
Vase, wild roses & butterfly, bl/wht, pillow form, 7½x6½" 2,700.00

Miscellaneous

Bowl, butterfly & flowers, gold & silver on bl to cream, 7x13x5" **650.00**
Creamer, flowers & butterfly, gold on lt/dk butterscotch, 3¼" ...**200.00**
Ewer, apple branches, gold on gr to wht, ivory hdl, 9x4" **425.00**
Pitcher, brn satin, cream int, frosted hdl, 3¾x2½" **195.00**
Potpourri jar, floral, mc on wht opal w/gold, brass base, 5½" **615.00**
Rose bowl, gold prunus & dragonfly, 6-crimp, 3⅝x5" **495.00**
Vase, azaleas, mc w/gold on gr, banjo form, dome ft, hdls, 20" ...**900.00**
Vase, berries & leaves, mc w/gold on bl, wht int, 7x4" **450.00**
Vase, bird in flight/butterfly/floral on bl satin, 8¼x6¼" **425.00**
Vase, butterfly & floral, gold on ivory opaque, 4x2⅜" **165.00**
Vase, butterfly & leaves, gold on gold satin, 5¼x2⅝" **245.00**
Vase, floral, bl w/gold on bl cased, 4¾x4¼" **175.00**
Vase, floral, gold on orange cased, appl hdls, 7½x5⅝" **245.00**
Vase, jack-in-the-pulpit; pk & wht stripes, bulbous, 6x5" **380.00**
Vase, pk & wht stripes, ruffled rim, bulbous, 8x4" **425.00**
Vase, pk satin cased, ruffled top, dome ft, 10x4" **275.00**
Vase, plum leaves/floral inclusions on wht w/gold, global, 6" **175.00**
Vase, prunus, gold on brn satin, 5½x5¼" **495.00**
Vase, yel to wht satin, gourd shape, 10½" **285.00**

Wedgwood

Josiah Wedgwood established his pottery in Burslem, England, in 1759. He produced only molded utilitarian earthenwares until 1770 when new facilities were opened at Etruria for the production of ornamental wares. It was there he introduced his famous Basalt and Jasperware. Jasperware, an unglazed fine stoneware decorated with classic figures in white relief, was usually produced in blues, but it was also made in ground colors of green, lilac, yellow, black, or white. Occasionally three or more colors were used in combination. It has been in continuous production to the present day and is the most easily recognized of all the Wedgwood lines. Jasper-dip is a ware with a solid-color body or a white body that has been dipped in an overlay color. It was introduced in the late 1700s and is the type most often encountered on today's market.

Though Wedgwood's Jasperware was highly acclaimed, on a more practical basis his improved creamware was his greatest success. Due to the ease with which it could be potted and because its lighter weight significantly reduced transportation expenses, Wedgwood was able to offer 'chinaware' at affordable prices. Queen Charlotte was so pleased with the ware that she allowed it to be called 'Queen's Ware.' Most creamware was marked simply 'Wedgwood.' ('Wedgwood & Co.' and 'Wedgewood' are marks of other potters.) From 1769 to 1780, Wedgwood was in partnership with Thomas Bentley; artwares of the highest quality may bear the 'Wedgwood & Bentley' mark indicating this partnership. Moonlight Lustre, an allover splashed-on effect of pink intermingling with gray, brown, or yellow, was made from 1805 to 1815. Porcelain was made, though not to any great extent, from 1812 to 1822. Bone china was produced before 1822 and after 1872. These types of wares were marked 'WEDGWOOD' (with a printed 'Portland Vase' mark after 1872). Stone china and Pearlware were made from about 1820 to 1875. Examples of either may be found with a printed or impressed mark to indicate their body type. During the late 1800s, Wedgwood produced some fine parian and majolica. Creamware, hand painted by Emile Lessore, was sold from about 1860 to 1875. From the 20th century, several lines of lustre wares — Butterfly, Dragon, and Fairyland (designed by Daisy Makeig-Jones) — have attracted the collector and, as their prices suggest, are highly sought after and admired.

Nearly all of Wedgwood's wares are clearly marked. 'WEDGWOOD' was used before 1891, after which time 'ENGLAND' was added. Most examples marked 'MADE IN ENGLAND' were made after

1905. A detailed study of all marks is recommended for accurate dating. See also Majolica.

Key:
WW — Wedgwood
WWE — Wedgwood England
WWMIE — Wedgwood Made in England

Game pie dish, Caneware, hare finial, fruiting grapevines and game on oval form, WWE, 9½", $490.00.

Basket, Creamware, Twig w/brn enameling, w/underplate, WW, 11" .**750.00**
Basket, potpourri; Caneware, basalt grapevines, WW, 4¼" **575.00**
Basket, Queensware, pierced gallery, WW, 9", w/undertray **300.00**
Bidet, Queensware, WW, early 1800s, in mahog stand, 22" **400.00**
Biscuit jar, Jasper, dk bl, baluster shape, WW, 1870, 5¼" **250.00**
Biscuit jar, Jasper, dk bl, ladies/cherubs, SP trim/lid, WW, 6¾" .**235.00**
Biscuit jar, Jasper, gr, melon shape, WW, ca 1870, 6" **275.00**
Bowl, Butterfly Lustre, Byerly shape, WWE, 4½" **350.00**
Bowl, Creamware, salmon, Victoria Ware, SP rim, WW, 9½" dia ..**650.00**
Bowl, Dragon Lustre, WWE, 2½" dia **225.00**
Bowl, Fairyland Lustre, 8-sided, WW, 9" **3,825.00**
Bowl, Hummingbird Lustre, Empire shape, WWE, 4½" **425.00**
Bowl, Jasper, lt bl, WWE, 4½" dia **100.00**
Bowl, Jasper, lt gr, Dancing Hours, MIE, ca 1958, 10" dia **800.00**
Box, Basalt, Cupid Sharpening Arrow in gold, WWE, 1½x2" **100.00**
Box, Basalt, Nefertiti in gold, scalloped, WWE, ca 1978, 3½" ...**145.00**
Box, Bone China, Wild Strawberry, hexagonal, WWE, ca 1981 ..**50.00**
Box, Creamware, lt bl, fish, WWE, 3½x5" **95.00**
Box, Jasper, lilac, pentagonal, scalloped, WWE, ca 1960 ....**95.00**
Box, Jasper, lilac, rnd, WWE, mini **75.00**
Box, Jasper, lt bl, Portland Vase, WWE, mini, 1¼" dia **95.00**
Box, Jasper, lt bl, scalloped, WWE, 5" dia **95.00**
Box, Jasper, Royal Blue, WWE, 1⅜x4⅝" **125.00**
Box, Jasper, 3-color, Jupiter, WWE, ca 1995 ....**50.00**
Box, pomade; Jasper, dk bl, WW, ca 1850, 3¼" **175.00**
Bust, Abraham Lincoln, Basalt, WWE, 8½", MIB **275.00**
Bust, Dwight Eisenhower, Basalt, WWE, 8½", MIB **225.00**
Bust, Locke, Basalt, WW, ca 1865, 7¾" **520.00**
Bust, Matthew Prior, Rosso Antico, WW, late 1700s, rstr, 7¼" .**400.00**
Bust, Minerva, Basalt, WW, 19th C, mtd as lamp, 18" **1,600.00**
Bust, Pinder, Basalt, raised base, WW/Bentley, 1775, 4" **750.00**
Bust, Robert Burns, Basalt, circular base, WW, 7½" **500.00**
Bust, Robert Burns, Basalt, WW, mid-19th C, 8" **500.00**
Bust, Wesley, Basalt, mid-19th C, WW, 8" **500.00**
Cameo, Jasper, blk, WW, in 18k brooch **225.00**
Cameo, Jasper, lt bl, WW, in sterling pendant **125.00**
Cameo, Jasper, lt bl, WW, 2¼x1⅞" **95.00**
Candlestick, Agate w/swags, Basalt base, WW/Bentley, 6½" **1,500.00**
Candlestick, Jasper, crimson, WWE, ca 1910, 7" **835.00**
Candlesticks, Basalt, Triton w/swirled sconce, WW, 9¾", pr ..**2,400.00**
Candlesticks, Creamware, bl figural, WW, ca 1872, 10", pr **850.00**
Celery dish, Bone China, gold dmns, WW 1st period, 1820s, 10" ..**250.00**
Cheese keeper, Jasper, dk bl, England, ca 1900, 6½x8¼" **850.00**
Chess piece, Drabware, King, WW, early 19th C, 4½" **700.00**
Chess piece, Jasper, wht, after Flaxman, unmk, 19th C, 2⅛", EX .**70.00**
Coffeepot, Jasper, dk bl, Muses, WWE, ca 1900, 5½" **350.00**

Coffeepot, Moonlight Lustre, WW, 1810, 5½", EX 700.00
Compact, Jasper, gr, WWE 95.00
Comport, Jasper, terra cotta, WWE, 3¾x6" 195.00
Creamer, Creamware, Eastern Flowers, WW, ca 1860 ....78.00
Creamer, Drabware, bl vintage band, WW, ca 1830 ....150.00
Creamer, Drabware, emb roses/thistles, WW, ca 1840, 2½x5" ...175.00
Creamer, Jasper, dk bl, Domestic Employment, WWE, 2⅝x3½" .75.00
Creamer, Jasper, dk bl, mythological scenes, WWE, 2⅝x2⅛" 88.00
Creamer & sugar bowl, Jasper, terra cotta, WWE, 2½" 200.00
Crocus pot, Basalt, hedgehog figural, WW, ca 1800, 9¾" 920.00
Cup, custard; Creamware, armorial decor, WW, ca 1800 ....100.00
Cup, custard; Jasper, lilac, lattice, teardrop shape, WW 800.00
Cup, custard; Jasper, lt bl, lattice, comma shape, WW, 1790 .....835.00
Cup & saucer, AD; Jasper, dk bl, Boston shape, WWE, ca 1930 ..95.00
Cup & saucer, AD; Jasper, terra cotta, WWE 125.00
Cup & saucer, Basalt, Nova Scotia coat of arms, WWE 95.00
Cup & saucer, Creamware, Fallow Deer, WWE 100.00
Cup & saucer, Jasper, dk bl, pear shape, WWE 95.00
Cup & saucer, Pearlware, Strawberry Lustre, WWE, ca 1900 ....95.00
Ewer, Basalt, Triton at shoulders/monster at spout, WW, 15", pr .3,335.00
Figurine, baby reclining, Basalt, WW, 1850s, 5⅛", EX 700.00
Figurine, Cupid & Psyche, Basalt, WW, 19th C, 8" 1,500.00
Figurine, Hercules, Basalt, WWE, ca 1978, 11½" 425.00
Figurine, Raven by Light, Basalt, glass eyes, WWE, ca 1915 ....435.00
Figurine, toucans (pr), Basalt, glass eyes, WW, 1913, 5¼" 1,380.00
Flower bowl, Basalt, vintage, shallow, MIE, 12" dia 350.00
Flowerpot, Jasper, dk bl, WW, ca 1870, 2¾" 195.00
Flowerpot, Jasper, dk bl, WWE, 2¾x3" 120.00
Incense burner, Basalt, 3 dolphins, WW, 1805, rstr, 5½" 1,600.00
Jar, Bone China, red printed decor, apple finial, WW, ca 1880 ..225.00
Jar, cigarette; Jasper, lt bl, WWE, ca 1956 ....100.00
Jar, cigarette; Jasper, lt gr, WWE 125.00
Jardiniere, Creamware, leaves relief, WW, 8⅝", w/stand 515.00
Jardiniere, Jasper, cobalt, Muses, WWE, ca 1900, 6⅛x7" 300.00
Jardiniere, Jasper, red, WWE, ca 1910, 6½x7½" 1,250.00
Match/toothpick holder, Jasper, dk bl, ladies/cherubs, WWE, 2⅛" .95.00
Matchbox holder, Jasper, olive gr, WWE, ca 1910, 3½" 300.00
Matchbox/striker, Jasper, lt bl, oblong, WW, ca 1850 ....265.00
Medallion, dk bl, Petrarch, unmk, 19th C, 5x3¼" 200.00
Medallion, Jasper, lt gr, Admiral Howe, WW, 3½x4¼" 260.00
Medallions, Jasper, lt gr, Jervis/Nelson, WW, 3⅜x4⅜", pr 550.00
Mold, Creamware, corncob form, WW, ca 1825 ....275.00
Mortar & pestle, vitreous stoneware, WW, 1850s, 3⅛", 6" 200.00
Mug, Creamware, Chaucer, WWE, ca 1977 ....75.00
Mug, Jasper, lt bl, mythological scenes, WWE, 1⅜x1⅜" 145.00
Napkin rings, Bone China, Clementine, WWE, set of 4 ....75.00
Nautilus shell, Bone China, on coral stand, WW, ca 1878, 4" ...225.00
Paperweight, Jasper, blk, Liberty Bell, WWE, ca 1975 ....95.00
Pie dish, Caneware, leaf molded, WW, 1863, 12" L 750.00
Pipe holder, Jasper, cobalt, WW, 19th C 300.00
Pitcher, Dutch jug, Jasper, gr, WW, ca 1875, 5½" 225.00
Pitcher, Jasper, dk bl, couple w/dogs, WW, 2¾x1¾" 195.00
Pitcher, Jasper, dk bl, Cupid & Psyche, WW, ca 1850, 8" 350.00
Pitcher, Jasper, dk bl, mythological scenes, WWE, 2⅝x2⅛" 100.00
Pitcher, Jasper, dk bl, Washington & Franklin, England, 4" 300.00
Pitcher, Oenochoe jug, Jasper, lt bl, mask hdls, WW, rprs, 7½" .575.00
Pitcher, salt glaze, Bacchanalian Boys, WW, 1820, 9", EX 275.00
Pitcher, tankard, dk bl, WW, ca 1880, 4½" 100.00
Pitcher, tankard, Jasper, dk bl, MIE, ca 1900, 8¼" 300.00
Pitcher, tankard, Jasper, olive gr, WWE, ca 1910, 7¼" 250.00
Plaque, Basalt, Death of Roman Warrior, WW, rstr, 11x19" ...2,875.00
Plaque, Jasper, blk, Choice of Hercules, WW, 1805, 6x17½" .1,500.00
Plate, Bone China, Black Hawk, MIE, ca 1975, 8" 145.00
Plate, calendar; Creamware, December, WW, ca 1895 ....225.00

Plate, Creamware, Anticipation..., Lessore, WW, 9⅛" 425.00
Plate, Creamware, Buns! Buns! Buns!, sgn Lessore, WW, 9⅛" ...425.00
Plate, Creamware, Duke University, MIE, ca 1930, 10½" 40.00
Plate, Creamware, Japanese, WW, ca 1872, 9" 125.00
Plate, Creamware, owl pnt on shell shape, WW, ca 1876, 8½" ..175.00
Plate, dessert; Basalt, WW, 19th C, 6" dia 100.00
Plate, Jasper, lt bl, Statue of Liberty 1886-1986, WWE, 6¾" 75.00
Plate, Queensware, landscape, oak leaf border, WW, 1872, 9" ...315.00
Platter, Queensware, mc bird & floral, WW, 1871, 20⅜x15¾" .375.00
Posy pot, Jasper, lt gr, Seasons, WWE, ca 1958, 3½" 85.00
Potpourri, Creamware, Worcester-style decor, w/lids, WW, 1880s ..750.00
Roast dish & drainer, Creamware, puce/yel decor, WW, 11½" dia ..300.00
Shell, Moonlight Lustre, WW, 1½x8¼" 365.00
Sugar bowl, Jasper, lt gr, WWE, w/lid, 3" 130.00
Sugar bowl, Jasper, terra cotta, WWE, w/lid 140.00
Sweetmeat, Jasper, dk bl, classical ladies, SP trim, WWE, 4x3¼" ..145.00
Syrup, Bone China, HP flowers & birds, SP lid, WWE 145.00
Tea bowl & saucer, Jasper, lt bl, Bacchanalian, WW 1,100.00
Tea set, Bone China, Liberty, WWE, ca 1919, 11-pc 1,500.00
Tea set, Jasper, Royal Blue, MIE, ca 1953, 3-pc 650.00
Teakettle, Creamware, prunus w/gold, WW, ca 1874 ....450.00
Teapot, Basalt, Capri, WW, ca 1840, lg 650.00
Teapot, Caneware, grapevine relief, WW, ca 1830, 7", EX 375.00
Teapot, Drabware, spaniel finial, WW, ca 1840, lg 295.00
Teapot, Jasper, dk bl, England, 4x6½" 225.00
Teapot, Jasper, dk bl, St Louis shape, WWE 250.00
Teapot, Jasper, lilac, Brewster, WW, ca 1870 ....445.00
Teapot, Jasper, Royal Blue, Coronation, WWE, ca 1953 ....375.00
Teapot, Moonlight Lustre, drum form, WW, 1810, rpr, 3" 575.00
Teapot, Pearlware, knot emblems, WW, 1850, rstr, 18½" 1,380.00
Teapot, wht stoneware w/bl vintage band, WW, ca 1810 ....250.00
Tray, dresser; Jasper, dk bl, WW, ca 1880, 3x8½" 130.00
Tray, Jasper, lt bl, Churchill, MIE, 4¼" 78.00
Tray, Jasper, lt bl, Josiah Wedgwood, WW Collector's Society 50.00
Tray, Jasper, lt bl, Spade, WWE 42.50
Tray, Jasper, sage gr, Cupid, wavy rim, WWE, ca 1963, 4x4" 38.00
Tray, pin; Basalt, Capri, WW, ca 1840, 8" L 450.00
Urn, Basalt, pierced disk lid, mc florals, WW, 19th C, rstr, 12" .1,265.00
Vase, Agate w/Sybil finial, blk base, WW/Bentley, 1770, 9½" ...3,750.00
Vase, Basalt, Capri, 2-hdl, WW, ca 1840, 5¼" 650.00
Vase, Basalt, swags, w/lid, WW/Bentley, rpr, 7" 1,150.00
Vase, Basalt, Venus & Cupid, hdls, WW/Bentley, rstr, 14" 1,725.00
Vase, bud; Jasper, dk bl, cameo, MIE, ca 1937, 5" 120.00
Vase, bud; Jasper, lt gr, WWE, ca 1900, 5" 120.00
Vase, bud; Jasper, Portland Blue, Seasons, WWE, ca 1972, 5⅜" ...95.00
Vase, Creamware, slip decor, WW, Marsden's Pat, 6x9" dia ...1,200.00
Vase, Jasper, dk bl, Aurora, WW, ca 1870, rpr, 10" 625.00
Vase, Jasper, dk bl, stick neck, WW, ca 1867, 7¼" 175.00
Vase, Jasper, lt bl, Cupid finial, w/lid, WW, ca 1825, 9" 1,225.00
Vase, Jasper, lt bl, 3 Graces, MIE, 1967, 2" 120.00
Vase, potpourri; Pearlware, slip decor, pierced lid, WW, rstr, 7" .230.00
Vase, spill; Jasper, cobalt, Bellflower, WW, ca 1870, 5½" 300.00
Vase, spill; Jasper, cobalt, sterling top, WW, ca 1870, 6½" 225.00
Wine cooler, Redware, fruited vine, mask hdls, WW, 10", EX ...550.00

Weil Ware

Max Weil came to the United States in the 1940s, settling in California. There he began manufacturing dinnerware, figurines, cookie jars, and wall pockets. American clays were used, and the dinnerware was all hand decorated. Weil died in 1954; the company closed two years later. The last backstamp to be used was the outline of a burro with the words 'Weil Ware — Made in California.' Many unmarked pieces found today originally carried a silver foil label; but you'll often find a four-digit handwritten number series, especially on figurines. For further study we recommend *The Collector's Encyclopedia of California Pottery* by our advisor, Jack Chipman. He is listed in the Directory under California.

Creamer and sugar bowl, brown roses on yellow, with lid, $25.00.

Ashtray, Bamboo, 5"	10.00
Bowl, cream soup; Rose	15.00
Butter dish, Blossom, ¼-lb	30.00
Butter dish, Rose	28.00
Cup & saucer, Rose	15.00
Dish, Dogwood, divided, sq, 10½"	22.00
Figurine, boy w/wheelbarrow, #4005	45.00
Plate, Bamboo, dinner sz	12.00
Plate, Rose, 10"	10.00
Vase, bud; Ming Tree, w/coralene, #946, 6"	30.00
Vase, girl, ½-rnd flower vase ea side, appl roses, 10"	45.00
Vase, girl in bl dress, pk shawl, 10½"	45.00
Vase, girl in gr dress sits between 2 bud vases	32.00
Vase, sailor boy w/flowers before wht vase, 10¾"	48.00
Wall pocket, Oriental girl	45.00

Weller

The Weller Pottery Company was established in Zanesville, Ohio, in 1882, the outgrowth of a small one-kiln log cabin works Sam Weller had operated in Fultonham. Through an association with Wm. Long, he entered the art pottery field in 1895, producing the Lonhuda Ware Long had perfected in Steubenville six years earlier. His famous Louwelsa line was merely a continuation of Lonhuda and was made in at least five hundred different shapes until 1924. Many fine lines of artware followed under the direction of Charles Babcock Upjohn, art director from 1895 to 1904: Dickens Ware (1st Line), under-glaze slip decorations on dark backgrounds; Turada, featuring applied ivory bands of delicate openwork on solid dark brown backgrounds; and Aurelian, similar to Louwelsa, but with a brushed-on rather than blended ground. One of their most famous lines was 2nd Line Dickens, introduced in 1900. Backgrounds, characteristically caramel shading to turquoise matt, were decorated by sgraffito with animals, golfers, monks, Indians, and scenes from Dickens novels. The work is often artist signed. Sicardo, 1903, was a metallic lustre line in tones of rose, blue, green, or purple with flowing Art Nouveau patterns developed within the glaze.

Frederick Hurten Rhead, who worked for Weller from 1903 to 1904, created the prestigious Jap Birdimal line decorated with geisha girls, landscapes, storks, etc., accomplished through application of heavy slip forced through the tiny nozzle of a squeeze bag. Other lines to his credit are L'Art Nouveau, produced in both high-gloss brown and matt pastels, and 3rd Line Dickens, often decorated with Cruikshank's illustrations in relief. Other early artware lines were Eocean, Floretta, Hunter, Perfecto, Dresden, Etched Matt, and Etna.

In 1920 John Lessel was hired as art director, and under his supervision several new lines were created. LaSa, LaMar, Marengo, and Besline attest to his expertise with metallic lustres. The last of the artware lines and one of the most sought after by collectors today is Hudson, first made during the early 1920s. Hudson, a semimatt glazed ware, was beautifully artist decorated on shaded backgrounds with florals, animals, birds, and scenics. Notable artists often signed their work, among them Hester Pillsbury, Dorothy England Laughead, Ruth Axline, Claude Leffler, Sarah Reid McLaughlin, E.L. Pickens, and Mae Timberlake.

During the '30s Weller produced a line of gardenware and naturalistic life-sized figures of dogs, cats, swans, geese, and playful gnomes. The Depression brought a slow, steady decline in sales, and by 1948 the pottery was closed. For a more thorough study we recommend *The Collector's Encyclopedia of Weller Pottery* by Sharon and Bob Huxford, available at your local library or from Collector Books.

Alvin, vase, tree trunk form w/4 openings, unmk, 8½"	75.00
Ardsley, vase, irises & leaves form body, mk, 7"	300.00
Ardsley, wall pocket, dbl; cattails & leaves, mk, 11½"	275.00
Athens, vase, cat's heads & swags on brn, unmk, 10"	650.00
Atlas, star dish, #C-2, mk, 2"	45.00
Atlas, vase, 5-pointed star top, mk, 10½"	115.00
Aurelian, ewer, floral, sgn MP, slim neck, mk, 6"	275.00
Aurelian, vase, floral, brn tones, sgn TJW, cylindrical, 16"	1,750.00
Auroro, vase, goldfish, Hattie Mitchell, bulbous, mk, 9"	1,750.00
Baldin, vase, apples along shoulder, mk, 7"	200.00
Baldin, vase, apples branch along bottom, unmk, 11"	500.00
Barcelona, ewer, stylized flower, bulbous, mk, 9½"	275.00
Barcelona, vase, stylized flower, rim-to-hip hdls, mk, 6½"	225.00
Besline, vase, floral, shouldered, unmk, 12"	550.00
Blo' Red, vase, hdls, mk, 3½"	50.00
Blo' Red, vase, shouldered, label, 9½"	140.00
Blossom, vase, floral, gourd shape, mk, 9½"	60.00
Blossom, vase, floral, pk on bl, hdls, mk, 6"	45.00
Blue Drapery, jardiniere, roses on bl, unmk, 5"	95.00
Blue Drapery, vase, roses on bl, unmk, 4"	60.00
Blue Ware, comport, fruit swags, mk, 5½"	225.00
Blue Ware, jardiniere, 2 angels, unmk, 8½"	300.00
Blue Ware, vase, classical figure, mk, 8½"	250.00
Bonito, candle holders, stylized floral, mk, 1½", pr	100.00
Bonito, vase, stylized floral, sgn NC, sm angle hdls, mk, 10"	400.00
Bouquet, vase, floral, scalloped rim, ftd, B-5, mk, 5½"	45.00
Breton, bowl, emb floral on blk, invt rim, unmk, 4"	95.00
Brighton, crow on base, unmk, 6½"	900.00
Brighton, kingfisher on stump, mk, 9"	400.00
Brighton, parrot on base, mk, 7½"	700.00
Brighton, woodpecker on base, unmk, 6½x3"	400.00
Burntwood, vase, floral, shouldered, unmk, 7"	150.00
Burntwood, vase, floral, unmk, 12"	275.00
Burntwood, vase, stylized floral, 6-sided, mk, 5"	125.00
Cactus, figurine, camel, mk, 4"	100.00
Cactus, figurine, Glouster Woman, mk, 11½"	750.00
Camelot, vase, geometric decor, bulbous, unmk, 8"	250.00
Cameo, hanging basket, floral, wht on bl, unmk, 6"	90.00
Cameo, vase, floral, wht on gr, low hdls, mk, 7"	45.00
Cameo Jewel, jardiniere, portrait cameos & jewels, mk, 8"	375.00
Cameo Jewel, umbrella stand, portrait cameos & jewels, 22"	1,000.00
Candis, ewer, ivory w/floral teardrop-shaped panel, mk, 11"	110.00
Candis, hanging basket, gr & ivory w/emb scrolls, unmk, 5½"	125.00
Chase, vase, fox hunt scene, cream on tan, mk, 10½"	500.00
Chase, vase, fox hunt scene, wht on bl, bulbous, mk, 6½"	350.00
Chengtu, ginger jar, mk, 12"	225.00
Chengtu, vase, bulbous, paper label, 3½"	55.00
Chengtu, vase, sq sides, rnd rim, ink mk, 11"	150.00

Classic, window box, openwork at rim, mk/label, 4" 70.00
Claywood, candle holder, floral, flared ft, unmk, 5" 85.00
Claywood, mug, floral, unmk, 5" 100.00
Claywood, spittoon, floral, unmk, 4½" 150.00
Colored Glaze, jardiniere, squirrels, unmk, 8" 275.00
Coppertone, basket, emb flowers, integral branch hdl, unmk, 8½" ..225.00
Coppertone, frog, unmk, 4½" 400.00
Coppertone, pitcher, fish hdl, mk, 7½" 950.00
Coppertone, vase, frog hdls, mk, 8" 900.00
Copra, vase, floral, ring hdls, mk, 10" 275.00
Creamware, bowl, lady's portrait in cameo, hdls, unmk, 2½" 60.00
Creamware, mug, HP floral, unmk, 5" 125.00
Creamware, planter, Coat of Arms, mk, 3½" sq 65.00
Creamware, teapot, decalcomania, unmk, 5½" 125.00
Darsie, vase, tassels, flared rim, mk, 5½" 50.00
Dickens I, jardiniere, trumpet flowers on brn, mk, 9" 400.00
Dickens I, mug, floral, flared base, mk, 7" 225.00
Dickens I, pillow vase, lady's portrait, mk, 7" 2,250.00
Dickens I, vase, cherubs, ftd/bottle neck, mk, 11½" 1,250.00
Dickens II, ewer, mermaid, unmk, 10½" 700.00
Dickens II, pillow vase, Old North Church..., 7x8" 2,250.00
Dickens II, vase, Bald Eagle, sgn A Dautherty, 9" 2,000.00
Dickens II, vase, Indian portrait, sgn, HS, cylindrical, 11" 1,100.00
Dickens II, vase, men drinking, sgn (illegible), 13" 1,750.00
Dickens II, vase, swordsmen, sgn LJB, hdls, 5½" 600.00
Dickens III, ewer, gremlin, mk, 3½" 225.00
Dickens III, ewer, Squeers, sgn LM, slim, mk, 12½" 750.00
Dickens III, teapot, Captain Cuttle/Florence Dombey, #5055, 7" ..750.00
Dickens III, vase, man's portrait, 2-hdld, unmk, 4" 300.00
Dickens III, vase, Wilkins Micauber..., sgn LS, 10½" 800.00
Dupont, bowl, flower basket panels, Roma glaze, unmk, 3" 50.00
Dupont, planter, potted plants, mk, 5" sq 75.00
Elberta, bowl, 3-part, mk, 3½" 75.00
Elberta, cornucopia vase, mk, 8" 85.00
Eocean, basket, floral, unmk, 6½" 450.00
Eocean, Late; bud vase, floral, unmk, 6½" 125.00
Eocean, vase, floral, flared cylinder, unmk, 9" 325.00
Eocean, vase, floral branches, sgn JLB, bulbous, 13" 1,100.00
Etna, jardiniere, roses, mk, 9½' 400.00
Etna, pitcher, floral, mk, 6" 175.00
Etna, vase, floral, curved hdls, mk, 9" 500.00
Etna, vase, floral, waisted, 5½" 176.00
Etna, vase, forg & snake on gourd form, mk, 6½" 800.00
Etna, vase, grapes, shouldered, mk, 15" 650.00
Evergreen, console bowl, scalloped, flared ft, mk, 7½x14" 45.00
Evergreen, pelican, open bk, mk, 7½" 125.00
Fairfield, bowl, cherubs band, unmk, 4½" 90.00
Fairfield, vase, cherubs band, unmk, 9½" 125.00
Flask, Dust Remover, whisk broom form, unmk, 6" 195.00
Flask, Never Dry, unmk, 6" 235.00
Flask, Suffer-E-Get, figural, unmk, 6" 275.00
Flemish, jardiniere, floral panels, unmk, 7½" 150.00
Flemish, jardiniere, lg florals w/long leafy stems, mk, 8" 350.00
Flemish, tub, roses, rnd bowl w/hdls, unmk, 3½" 85.00
Flemish, umbrella stand, vining floral panels, mk, 21½" 400.00
Flemish, vase, floral, shape #8, mk, 10" 250.00
Fleron, vase, flat flared rim, hdls, mk, 19½" 750.00
Fleron, vase, ruffled rim, mk, 9" 175.00
Florala, candle holder, floral panels, 6-sided, mk, 5" 150.00
Floretta, ewer, grapes emb on brn, mk, 10½" 225.00
Floretta, tankard, fruit branch, sgn CD, matt, ummk, 13½" 550.00
Floretta, vase, floral on brn to pk, mk, 19" 950.00
Forest, hanging basket, unmk, 8" 200.00
Forest, jardiniere, sq sides, unmk, 8½" 450.00

Forest, teapot, glossy, mk, 4½" 250.00
Forest, vase, inverted cylinder, unmk, 13½" 375.00
Fruitone, vase, sq sides, rnd rim, unmk, 5½" 50.00
Fruitone, vase, 6-sided, mk, 8" 150.00
Garden ornament, gnome, mk, 14" 2,500.00
Garden ornament, Pan w/fife, mk, 16½" 3,000.00
Glendale, bird on nest, classic form, label/mk, 12" 700.00
Glendale, vase, bird beside nest in involved landscape, mk, 13" ...1,250.00
Glendale, vase, bird in flight, unmk, 6½" 450.00
Gloria, ewer, floral, G-12, mk, 9" 70.00
Gloria, vase, floral, low hdls, ornate ft, G-14, mk, 6½" 60.00
Greenbriar, ewer, marbleized, 2-loop hdl, unmk, 11½" 250.00
Greenbriar, vase, marbleized, bulbous, unmk, 8½" 200.00
Greora, strawberry pot, marbleized, mk, 8½" 175.00
Hobart, candle holder, kneelng girk at side, unmk, 6" 300.00
Hobart, figurine, girl w/flowers, bl, unmk, 8½" 350.00
Hobart, figurine, nude on base, wht, unmk, 8½" 350.00
Hudson, Blue & Decorated; vase, floral band, mk, 7½" 225.00
Hudson, Light; vase, floral, bulbous, mk, 4½" 175.00
Hudson, Light; vase, floral, sgn HP, mk, 9" 450.00

Hudson vase, multicolor orchids on blue to creamy white (very rare glossy glaze), Timberlake, 27x11", $21,850.00.

Hudson, vase, floral, hdls, mk, 13½" 1,750.00
Hudson, vase, floral, sgn Axline, cylindrical, mk, 8½" 550.00
Hudson, vase, irises, sgn McLaughlin, classic form, mk, 15" ...1,600.00
Hudson, vase, irises, sgn Pillsbury, classic form, mk, 15" 2,000.00
Hudson, vase, mtn & water scenic, sgn Pillsbury, mk, 8" 1,600.00
Hudson, vase, sailboat scenic, cylindrical, mk, 8½" 1,500.00
Hudson, vase, scenic, sgn Pillsbury, bulbous, mk, 8" 2,500.00
Hudson, vase, scenic, sgn Timberlake, cylindrical, mk, 8½" 800.00
Hudson, vase, tiger in tall grass, mk, 8" 2,250.00
Hudson, vase, trees/mtn/water scenic, sgn Pillsbury, mk, 12" ..3,250.00
Hudson, Wht & Decorated; bowl, floral band at rim, unmk, 4" .200.00
Hudson, Wht & Decorated; vase, birds on floral branch, mk, 15" .1,800.00
Hudson-Perfecto, vase, berry & leaf band, shiny, mk, 6" 300.00
Hudson-Perfecto, vase, floral, bulbous, mk, 5½" 400.00
Hudson-Perfecto, vase, lg flowers, sg Leffler, mk, 13½" 1,400.00
Hunter, vase, duck, brn tones, jug form, mk, 7" 575.00
Hunter, vase, gulls on brn, sgn UJ, shouldered, #413, 7½" 950.00
Ivory (Clinton Ivory), leafy panels, cylindrical, mk, 10" 85.00
Ivory (Clinton Ivory), planter box, scenic, unmk, 5" sq 130.00
Ivory (Clinton Ivory), umbrella stand, floral, unmk, 19½" 250.00
Ivory (Clinton Ivory), window planter, floral, mk, 6x15½" 225.00
Jap Birdimal, mug, Oriental figure, Weller Rhead Faience, 5" .1,000.00
Jap Birdimal, oil pitcher, floral, sgn HMR, 10½" 1,000.00
Jap Birdimal, vase, fish, bl on lt gr, F Rhead, 6" 650.00
Jap Birdimal, vase, landscape w/trees (bl), mk, 14" 1,200.00
Jap Birdimal, vase, Oriental figure, sgn VMH, 13" 2,000.00
Jewell, vase, floral w/jewel centers, mk, 10½" 500.00
Kenova, vase, emb floral, 6½" 400.00

Klyro, bowl, flowers & berries, mk, 3½" 85.00
Klyro, wall pocket, flowers & berries, openwork at top, mk, 7½" ..150.00
Knifewood, bowl, daisies & butterflies, mk, 3" 100.00
Knifewood, vase, daisies & butterflies, unmk, 8" 250.00
Knifewood, vase, squirrel & acorn branches, unmk, 11" 700.00
L'art Nouveau, bank, ear of corn form, unmk, 8" 550.00
L'art Nouveau, bud vase, flower-form top, unmk, 7½" 575.00
L'art Nouveau, vase, grapes, flared cylinder, mk, 16" 600.00
L'art Nouveau, vase, lady's portrait, glossy, mk, 12" 525.00
Lamar, vase, palm trees, shouldered, unmk, 6" 200.00
Lamar, vase, scenic, classic form, unmk, 11½" 375.00
LaSa, vase, floral, bulbous, mk, 3½" 150.00
LaSa, vase, floral, shouldered, mk, 6" 165.00
LaSa, vase, landscape, pyramidal form, unmk, 6½" 200.00
Lebanon, vase, man on camel, unmk, 8" 1,500.00
Lorbeek, vase, pleated futuristic shape, mk, 7" 115.00
Lorbeek, wall pocket, pleated futuristic shape, mk, 7½" 150.00
Louella, hair receiver, floral on drapery, mk, 3" 95.00
Louwelsa, Blue; vase, bulbous, single integral hdl, mk, 3" 500.00
Louwelsa, Blue; vase, floral, cylindrical, mk, 10½" 1,100.00
Louwelsa, Blue; vase, floral, sgn LM, slim, mk, 10" 1,000.00
Louwelsa, candle holder, floral, sgn HL, slim, mk, 9" 250.00
Louwelsa, jardiniere, floral on brn, ruffled rim, 9½" 325.00
Louwelsa, mug, floral on brn, str sides, mk, 4½" 125.00
Louwelsa, vase, fish, classic form, mk H Pillsbury, 14" 1,500.00
Louwelsa, vase, floral, sgn AH, integral hdls, #820, 4½" 250.00
Louwelsa, vase, floral, sgn CL, bulbous, mk, 16" 1,500.00
Louwelsa, vase, floral, sgn CT, shouldered, 5" 225.00
Louwelsa, vase, floral, V Adams, rim-to-shoulder hdls, mk, 10" ...350.00
Louwelsa, vase, lady's portrait, sgn RGT, bulbous, mk, 11" ...1,500.00
Louwelsa, vase, pansies w/silver o/l, mk, 6½" 3,000.00
Louwelsa, vase, stylized floral, flared cylinder, mk, 12" 550.00
Lustre, basket, unmk, 6½" 95.00
Lustre, candlestick, flared ft, mk, 8" 75.00
Lustre, vase, invt rim, cylindrical, unmk, 8½" 65.00
Malverne, jardiniere & ped, leafy branches, unmk, 29½" 550.00
Malverne, vase, leaves & buds, gourd shape, mk, 5½" 85.00
Malverne, wall pocket, leaves & buds, unmk, 11" 200.00
Mammy Line, creamer, nude child figural hdl, mk, 3½" 400.00
Mammy Line, teapot, Mammy figural, mk, 8" 900.00
Manhattan, pitcher, emb florals on gr, cylindrical, mk, 10" 100.00
Manhattan, vase, emb florals on gr, mk, 5½" 35.00
Marbleized, bowl, invt rim, mk, 1½x7" 50.00
Marbleized, jardiniere, invt rim, mk, 10" 350.00
Marbleized, vase, bulbous, mk, 4½" 85.00
Marbleized, vase, squat, mk, 4½" 175.00
Marengo, vase, stylized tree/mtns, 6-sided, unmk, 8" 300.00
Marengo, wall pocket, stylized tree/mtns, unmk, 8½" 250.00
Marvo, bud vase, dbl; flower & leaf design, unmk, 5" 95.00
Melrose, console bowl, rose branch, scalloped, hdls, mk, 5x8½" ...125.00
Melrose, vase, rose branch, hdls, unmk, 5" 85.00
Minerva, planter, mythological creatures, mk, 12x16" 850.00
Minerva, vase, trees scenic, shouldered, mk, 13½" 850.00
Mirror Black, bud vase, dbl; mk, 9" 80.00
Mirror Black, bud vase, flared rim, unmk, 5½" 50.00
Mirror Black, strawberry jar, unmk, 6½" 85.00
Muskota, bowl w/goose at rim, mk, 4½" 375.00
Muskota, elephant, mk, 7½x12½" 1,500.00
Muskota, gate w/pots & cats, mk, 7" 600.00
Muskota, girl w/flowers & hat, unmk, 9" 450.00
Muskota, nude on rock, mk, 8" 325.00
Noval, bowl, appl apples form hdls, unmk, 3½x9½" 80.00
Noval, comport, appl apple hdls, unmk, 5½" 95.00
Novelty, ashtray, kangaroo w/open pouch, unmk, 5½" 95.00

Novelty, ashtray, sitting dog (howling) at side, mk, 5" 110.00
Novelty, butterfly, bl, unmk, 2¼" 175.00
Novelty, butterfly, pk w/dk flecks, unmk, 3" 175.00
Novelty, dragonfly, unmk, 3½" 175.00
Novelty, red bird, wings outspread, unmk, 2½" 200.00
Novelty, wall vase, teapot form, mk, 9" 150.00
Oak Leaf, basket, branch hdl, G-1, 7½" 100.00
Oak Leaf, basket vase, hdl joins at center from 4 corners, 9½" 95.00
Panella, bowl, floral, ftd, mk, 3½" 40.00
Panella, cornucopia, floral, mk, 5½" 50.00
Paragon, vase, cvd flowers & leaves, mk, 7½" 200.00
Parian, vase, floral tile-like design, unmk, 8½" 125.00
Parian, wall pocket, floral tile-like design, unmk, 10" 250.00
Patra, basket, stylized floral hdl, mk, 5½" 175.00
Patricia, vase, duck-head hdls, mk, 4" 75.00
Patricia, vase, emb leaves, duck-head hdls, mk, 7" 65.00
Pearl, candle holders, roses & pearls on cream, mk, 8½", pr 225.00
Pearl, vase, roses & pearls on cream, unmk, 7" 125.00
Perfecto (Matt Louwelsa), ewer, corn, A Haubrich, #580/4, 12" ...850.00
Perfecto (Matt Louwelsa), ewer, floral, #580/2, unmk, 12" 550.00
Pumilla, bowl, lotus flower form, mk, 3½" 35.00
Pumilla, vase, leaves form ruffled rim, mk, 9½" 125.00
Ragenda, vase, draped swag on pk, shouldered, mk, 6½" 75.00
Roba, ewer, floral on swirled body, twig hdl, mk, 6" 75.00
Roba, vase, floral, sm hdls, 13" 200.00
Roma, bud vase, dbl; floral, mk, 8½" 115.00
Roma, candlestick, floral, 3-light, unmk, 9" 200.00
Roma, comport, floral swags, rtcl sq rim, mk, 9½" 150.00
Roma, console bowl, grapes, w/liner, unmk, 6½x18" 250.00
Roma, jardiniere, flower basket reserves, unmk, 10½" 275.00
Roma, vase, floral panels, sq, shouldered, mk, 8½" 125.00
Rosemont, jardiniere, fruit bowl reserves, unmk, 8" 200.00
Rosemont, jardiniere & ped, floral panels on brn, mk, 25½" 550.00
Rosemont, vase, bird on leafy branch, mk, 10½" 500.00
Sabrinian, vase, shell body, sea horse hdls, mk, 12" 350.00
Sabrinian, window box, shells form sides, mk, 3½x9" 225.00
Senic, vase, palm tree, scalloped rim, S-2, 6½" 40.00
Senic, vase, river scene, sm hdls, S-4, mk, 5½" 75.00
Sicardo, figurine, Tambourine Boy, unmk, 9½" 5,000.00
Sicardo, pillow vase, floral, hdls, mk, 6½x10" 1,200.00

Sicardo vase/lamp base, sylized florals on purple lustre, drilled, 22", $2,850.00. (Value if not drilled: $5,000.00 to $6,000.00.)

Sicardo, vase, floral, shouldered, mk, 10½" 1,500.00
Sicardo, vase, floral, trumpet neck, mk, 15½" 1,700.00
Sicardo, vase, floral, unmk, 4½" 400.00
Silvertone, basket, grapes, branch hdl, mk, 13" 450.00
Silvertone, vase, floral, angular rim-to-hip hdls, mk, 10" 275.00
Silvertone, vase, flowers & butterflies, ruffled rim, hdls, 12" ...600.00
Softone, bud vase, dbl; pastel pk, mk, 9" 28.00
Softone, ewer, pastel pk, mk, 9½" 35.00
Souvenir, mug, St Louis LPE, 1904, unmk, 3½" 275.00
Souvenir, vase, Indian portrait, St Louis World's...1904, 6½" ...600.00
Souvenir, vase, St Louis 1904, unmk, 3" 250.00

Stellar, vase, stars on blk, bulbous, mk, 5" **500.00**
Sydonia, console bowl, mottled bl, mk, 6x17" **80.00**
Sydonia, vase, dbl; mottled bl, mk, 10½" **100.00**
Teakwood, umbrella stand, emb lion band, mk, 21" **750.00**
Trellis, wall shelf, unmk, 10½" **200.00**
Turada, lamp base, appl filigree on brn, 4-ftd, mk, 8" **1,000.00**
Turada, mug, appl filigree, #562/7 on base, 6" **325.00**
Turada, umbrella stand, appl filigree on brn, mk, 21" ...**1,250.00**
Turkis, vase, angle hdls, mk, 5½" **125.00**
Turkis, vase, ruffled rim, flared ft, mk, 8" **150.00**
Tutone, vase, floral, bulbous, 4-ftd, mk, 4" **70.00**
Tutone, vase, floral, flared ft, mk, 12½" **250.00**
Velva, vase, floral panel, sm uptrn hdls, ftd, mk, 9" **75.00**
Velva, vase, floral panel, sm uptrn hdls, mk, 6" **50.00**
Voile, fan vase, fruit tree, unmk, 8" **150.00**
Voile, jardiniere, flowering trees, unmk, 6" **150.00**
Warwick, jardiniere, floral branch on trunk form, mk, 7" **150.00**
Warwick, vase, flower branch on trunk form, hdls/ftd, mk, 4½" ...**85.00**
Wild Rose, vase, open flower, hdls, mk, 9½" **60.00**
Wild Rose, vase, open flower, sm hdls, mk, 6½" **30.00**
Woodcraft, basket, acorn form w/branch hdl, mk, 9½" **400.00**
Woodcraft, bowl, emb fruit, unmk, 3" **95.00**
Woodcraft, candle holder, stump form, mk, 8½" **125.00**
Woodcraft, lamp, owls on stump form, mk, 12½" **350.00**
Woodcraft, vase, fruit branch emb on stump form, unmk, 13" **275.00**
Woodcraft, wall vase, tree trunk form, mk, 9" **150.00**
Woodrose, vase, roses on brn tub form, tub hdls, mk, 4" **50.00**
Zona, baby plate, squirrels, ABCs on rolled rim, unmk, 7½" **135.00**
Zona, pitcher, fruit branch, branch hdl, mk, 6" **85.00**
Zona, pitcher, strutting duck, mk, 7" **140.00**
Zona, platter, fruit branches, unmk, 12" dia **80.00**
Zona, umbrella stand, ladies w/flower swags, glossy, 20½" **1,500.00**

Western Americana

The collecting of Western Americana encompasses a broad spectrum of memorabilia. Examples of various areas within the main stream would include the following fields: weapons, bottles, photographs, mining/railroad artifacts, cowboy paraphernalia, farm and ranch implements, maps, barbed wire, tokens, Indian relics, saloon/gambling items, and branding irons. Some of these areas have their own separate listings in this book. Western Americana is not only a collecting field but is also a collecting *era* with specific boundries. Depending upon which field the collector decides to specialize in, prices can start at a few dollars and run into the thousands.

Our advisor for this category is Bill Mackin, author of *Cowboy and Gunfighter Collectibles* (order from the author); he is listed in the Directory under Colorado.

Book, Buffalo Bill's...Story, Wm Cody, Farran & Rinehart, 1920 .**45.00**
Branding iron, circle 3, hand forged **85.00**
Bridle, leather w/brass tacks, old curb bit, ca 1920, 27x6" **70.00**
Bridle & quirt, horsehair, prison made, EX **4,000.00**
Chaps, child's, leather, EX **150.00**
Chaps, leather, batwing type w/conchos, ca 1935, 37" L, EX **175.00**
Chaps, wooly style, ca 1900, 29x15", EX **900.00**
Gauntlets, Indian beadwork on leather, fringed, ca 1900 ....**425.00**
Hat rack, buffalo horns **125.00**
Ingot weight, Wells Fargo, NP counterbalance, well mk, ca 1852 ..**475.00**
Medal, Cheyenne WY Frontier Day 1898, bronze, emb scenes, 1½" .**90.00**
Mittens, horsehide, lined w/mattress ticking, 1880s, 16", pr **60.00**
Pin, Daughters of CA, 1900s, w/ribbon **200.00**
Saddle, leather w/tooled swastikas, Porter, ca 1906-30, child's ...**325.00**

Spurs, Buermann, CA chased dropshank w/chains, pr **375.00**
Spurs, Buermann, silver mtd stars, dropshank, pr **375.00**
Spurs, Buermann, str shank, X design, pr **165.00**
Wax seal, Wells Fargo No 1219, brass **250.00**

Western Pottery Manufacturing Company

This pottery was originally founded as the Denver China and Pottery Company; William Long was the owner. The company's assets were sold to a group who in 1905 formed the Western Pottery Manufacturing Company, located at 16th Street and Alcott in Denver, Colorado. By 1926, One hundred eighty-six different items were being produced, including crocks, flowerpots, kitchen items, and other stoneware. The company dissolved in 1936.

Seven various marks were used during the years, and values may be higher for items that carry a rare mark. Numbers within the descriptions refer to specific marks, see the line drawings. Prices may vary depending on demand and locale. Our advisors for this category are Cathy Segelke and Pat James; they are listed in the Directory under Colorado.

Churn, #2, hdl, 4-gal, M **75.00**
Churn, #2, hdl, 5-gal, M **65.00**
Churn, #2, no lid, 5-gal, G **80.00**
Crock, #4, bail lip, 4-gal, G **55.00**
Crock, #4, hdl, no lid, 8-gal, M **90.00**
Crock, #4, ice water; bl/wht sponge pnt, 3-gal, NM **30.00**
Crock, #4, 6-gal, EX **72.00**
Crock, #4b, 20-gal, M **200.00**
Crock, #4b, 22x17½", 15-gal, NM **150.00**
Crock, #5, bail lip, 1½-gal, M **45.00**
Crock, #5, no lid, 6-gal, M **70.00**
Crock, #6, wire hdl, 10-gal, NM **100.00**
Crock, #6, 3-gal, M **40.00**
Crock, #6, 4-gal, M **50.00**
Crock, #6, 5-gal, NM **60.00**
Foot warmer, #6, M **60.00**
Jug, #6, brn/wht, 1-gal, EX **25.00**
Jug, #6, brn/wht, 5-gal, M **75.00**
Rabbit feeder, #1, EX **25.00**
Rabbit waterer, #1, M **25.00**

Western Stoneware Co.

The Western Stoneware Co., Monmouth, Illinois, was formed in

1906 as a merger of seven potteries: Monmouth Pottery Co., Monmouth, IL; Weir Pottery Co., Monmouth, IL; Macomb Pottery Co. and Macomb Stoneware Co., Macomb, IL; D. Culbertson Stoneware Co., Whitehall, IL; Clinton Stoneware Co., Clinton, MO; and Fort Dodge Stoneware Co., Fort Dodge, IA.

Western Stoneware Co. manufactured stoneware, gardenware, flowerpots, artware, and dinnerware. Some early crocks, jugs, and churns are found with a plant number in the Maple Leaf logo. Plants 1 through 7 turn up. In 1926 an artware line was introduced as the Monmouth Pottery Artware. One by one each branch of the operation closed and today one branch remains. Western Stoneware Co. is still in operation in Monmouth on the site of the Weir Pottery Co. Our advisor for this category is Jim Martin; he is listed in the Directory under Illinois.

Ashtray, Cardinal Brand Flower Pots 150.00
Birdbath, brn glaze 250.00
Churn, flowers on side, 3-gal 200.00
Churn, Maple Leaf mk, mini 600.00
Churn, Maple Leaf mk, 2-gal 175.00
Cigar humidor, cobalt bl 300.00
Crock, Maple Leaf mk, 60-gal 600.00
Crock, Plant 1 mk, 5-gal 75.00
Jardiniere, Egret pattern, brushed gr 75.00
Jardiniere, Egyptian motif, brn-glazed int, 7" 75.00
Jug, Plant 3, 5-gal 200.00
Pitcher, bl & wht, sq, 1-qt 100.00
Pitcher, Cattail, bl & wht, 1-qt 150.00
Pitcher & bowl, Memphis pattern, bl & wht 350.00
Vase, Etruscan pattern, gr & wht 45.00
Water cooler, Cupid, bl & wht 550.00
Water cooler, Egyptian motif, 9¼x11", M 300.00

Westmoreland

Originally titled the Specialty Glass Company, Westmoreland began operations in East Liverpool, Ohio, producing utility items as well as tableware in milk glass and crystal. When the company moved to Grapeville, Pennsylvania, in 1890, lamps, vases, covered animal dishes, and decorative plates were introduced. Prior to 1920 Westmoreland was a major manufacturer of carnival glass and soon thereafter added a line of lovely reproduction art glass items. High-quality milk glass became their speciality, accounting for about 90% of their production. Black glass was introduced in the 1940s, and later in the decade ruby-stained pieces and items decorated in the Mary Gregory style became fashionable. By the 1960s colored glassware was being produced, examples of which are very popular with collectors today. Early pieces were marked with a paper label; by the 1960s the ware was embossed with a superimposed 'WG.' The last mark was a circle containing 'Westmoreland' around the perimeter and a large 'W' in the center. The company closed in 1985, and on February 28, 1996, the factory burned to the ground. See also Animal Dishes with Covers; Carnival Glass. Note: Though you may find pieces very similar to Westmoreland's, their Della Robbia has no bananas among the fruits relief.

Ashtray, Beaded Grape, milk glass, 6½" sq 12.00
Basket, English Hobnail, amber or crystal, hdld, tall, 6" 35.00
Basket, Panelled Grape, milk glass, oval, 6½" 22.00
Basket, Panelled Grape, milk glass, ruffled, 8" 65.00
Bottle, oil-vinegar; English Hobnail, amber or crystal, 6-oz 30.00
Bottle, toilet; Panelled Grape, milk glass, 5-oz 62.50
Bowl, Beaded Grape, milk glass, ftd, w/lid, 7" 30.00
Bowl, English Hobnail, amber or crystal, bell shape, 11" 30.00
Bowl, English Hobnail, amber or crystal, ftd, 8" 25.00

Bowl, English Hobnail, amber or crystal, oval, crimped, 10" 35.00
Bowl, fruit; Old Quilt, milk glass, 3¼" 22.00
Bowl, Old Quilt, milk glass, crimped skirt, 9" 48.00
Bowl, Old Quilt, milk glass, flat, 4" 22.00
Bowl, Old Quilt, milk glass, ftd, 5¼" 15.00
Bowl, Old Quilt, milk glass, 8" 30.00
Bowl, Panelled Grape, milk glass, hdls, 5" 20.00
Bowl, Panelled Grape, milk glass, 3⅛" high, 6½x12½" 110.00
Bowl, punch; English Hobnail, amber or crystal 175.00
Bowl, punch; Panelled Grape, milk glass, bell shape or flared, 13" .450.00
Bowl, Ring & Petal, milk glass, sq 35.00
Box, Beaded Grape, milk glass, ftd, w/lid, 4" sq 22.00
Box, chocolate; Panelled Grape, milk glass, 6½" 40.00
Box, cigarette; Beaded Grape, milk glass, w/lid, 4x6" 40.00
Cake salver, Beaded Grape, milk glass, 11" 64.00
Cake salver, Panelled Grape, milk glass, skirted 75.00
Cake stand, Ring & Petal, milk glass, w/skirt 45.00
Candelabrum, Panelled Grape, milk glass, 3-light, ea 225.00
Candlestick, English Hobnail, amber or crystal, rnd base, 9" 22.50
Candlesticks, Beaded Grape, milk glass, 4", pr 25.00
Candlesticks, Dolphin, milk glass, 4", pr 35.00
Candlesticks, Old Quilt, milk glass, 4", pr 18.00
Candlesticks, Ring & Petal, milk glass, pr 22.00
Candy dish, Panelled Grape, milk glass, ruffled, 3-ftd, 8" 35.00
Canister, Panelled Grape, milk glass, 11" 250.00
Celery bowl, English Hobnail, amber or crystal, 9" 15.00
Celery vase, Old Quilt, milk glass, ftd, 6½" 15.00
Cheese dish, Panelled Grape, milk glass 60.00
Compote, Dolphin, milk glass, shell form, milk glass, 8" 65.00
Compote, Old Quilt, antique bl opaque, low ft, w/lid 35.00

Compote, milk glass, openwork at rim and foot, $45.00.

Compote, Panelled Grape, milk glass, 7" 25.00
Compote, sweetmeat; English Hobnail, amber, ball stem, 8" 35.00
Creamer, Beaded Edge, milk glass, ftd 11.00
Creamer, Blackberry, milk glass, 4½" 25.00
Creamer, Panelled Grape, milk glass, #135 ....22.50
Creamer & sugar bowl, Beaded Grape, milk glass 25.00
Creamer & sugar bowl, Old Quilt, milk glass, lg 30.00
Cup & saucer, Panelled Grape, milk glass 18.00
Decanter, English Hobnail, amber or crystal, 20-oz 65.00
Decanter, wine; Panelled Grape, milk glass 145.00
Egg plate, Panelled Grape, milk glass, 12" 100.00
Epergne, Panelled Grape, milk glass, 12" bowl, 8½" vase 185.00
Goblet, water; Old Quilt, milk glass, ftd 16.00
Goblet, water; Panelled Grape, milk glass, ftd 13.00
Honey dish, Roses & Bows, milk glass, pnt decor 40.00
Ivy ball, Panelled Grape, milk glass 47.50
Jardiniere, Panelled Grape, milk glass, cupped, 6½" 30.00
Ladle, punch; Panelled Grape, milk glass 47.50
Marmalade, Panelled Grape, milk glass, w/ladle & lid 40.00

Nappy, Beaded Edge, milk glass w/red edge, crimped, oval, 6" **10.00**
Nut bowl, Panelled Grape, milk glass, 6½" **17.00**
Pitcher, English Hobnail, amber or crystal, str sides, 64-oz **75.00**
Pitcher, Old Quilt, milk glass, 8½" **30.00**
Pitcher, Panelled Grape, milk glass, 16-oz **35.00**
Planter, Panelled Grape, milk glass, 8" **25.00**
Planter, wall; Panelled Grape, milk glass, lg, 8" **125.00**
Plate, dinner; Della Robia **18.00**
Plate, English Hobnail, amber or crystal, rnd, 3-ftd, 8" **12.50**
Plate, Panelled Grape, milk glass, 14½" **125.00**
Plate, Panelled Grape, milk glass, 18" **165.00**
Plate, torte; Beaded Edge, milk glass w/decor, 15" **50.00**
Plate, torte; English Hobnail, amber or crystal, rnd, 20½" **50.00**
Platter, Beaded Edge, milk glass w/decor, w/tab hdls, oval, 12" **45.00**
Relish, Old Quilt, milk glass, 3-part, 9" **35.00**
Shakers, Beaded Edge, milk glass, pr **18.00**
Shakers, Beaded Grape, milk glass, pr **15.00**
Soap dish, Panelled Grape, milk glass **65.00**
Spooner, Blackberry, milk glass, 4½" **18.00**
Sugar bowl, Beaded Edge, milk glass w/red edge, w/#108 lid, ftd ...**12.00**
Tidbit, English Hobnail, amber or crystal, 2 tier **22.50**
Tidbit, Panelled Grape, 2-tier, dinner & breakfast plates **100.00**
Tray, Panelled Grape, milk glass, oval, 13½" **100.00**
Tumbler, iced tea; Panelled Grape, milk glass **15.00**
Urn, English Hobnail; amber or crystal, w/lid, 11" **30.00**
Vase, flip; English Hobnail, amber or crystal, 7½" **25.00**
Vase, Old Quilt, milk glass, fan form, 9" **20.00**
Vase, Panelled Grape, milk glass, hand blown, 12" **150.00**
Vase, Roses & Bows, milk glass, pnt decor, 9" **35.00**
Vase (straw jar), English Hobnail, amber or crystal, 10" **57.50**
Wine, English Hobnail, lt bl, ftd, 2-oz, 4½" **15.00**

Wheatley, T. J.

In 1880 after a brief association with the Coultry Works, Thomas J. Wheatley opened his own studio in Cincinnati, Ohio, claiming to have been the first to discover the secret of under-glaze slip decoration on an unbaked clay vessel. He applied for and was granted a patent for his process. Demand for his ware increased to the point that several artists were hired to decorate the ware. The company incorporated in 1880 as the Cincinnati Art Pottery, but until 1882 it continued to operate under Wheatley's name. Ware from this period is marked 'T.J. Wheatley' or 'T.J.W. and Co.,' and it may be dated.

Matt green pieces dominate today's market place and will bring much more than the decorated pieces. The matt green pieces are seldom, if ever, marked or dated.

Vase, impasto flowers, three-legged, 5½", NM, $500.00.

Lamp, gr matt, cvd floral 8½", +7x14" ldgl shade **3,000.00**
Pitcher, gr matt w/emb grape clusters & leaves, #087, 8" **500.00**

Vase, cafe-au-lait brn, leaves & buds, bat-wing hdls, 10⅝" **5,250.00**
Vase, gr matt, belted, unmk, 5⅝" **375.00**
Vase, gr matt, geometrics, rolled rim, 8¾x6½" **750.00**
Vase, gr matt, overlapping leaves at base, buds at neck, 7¾" **900.00**
Vase, gr matt, 3 angular hdls, unmk, 4½" **300.00**
Vase, gr matt w/appl leaves, dbl-gourd form, 12½", NM **4,000.00**
Wall pocket, tulip buds w/stems & leaves, unmk, 17½x7½", pr ..**3,200.00**

Whieldon

Thomas Whieldon was regarded as the finest of the Staffordshire potters of the mid-1700s. He produced marbled and black Egyptian wares as well as tortoise shell, a mottled brown-glazed earthenware accented with touches of blue and yellow. In 1754 he became a partner of Josiah Wedgwood. Other potters produced similar wares, and today the term Whieldon is used generically.

Jug, sporting dogs, bk: long-haired dog, mc, 5¼" **450.00**
Plate, dk brn tortoise-shell mottle, flake, 9¼" **130.00**
Plate, mocha & creme tortoise-shell mottle, 8-sided, 8⅝" **250.00**

Wicker

Wicker is the basket-like material used in many types of furniture and accessories. It may be made from bamboo cane, rattan, reed, or artificial fibers. It is airy, lightweight, and very popular in hot regions. Imported from the Orient in the 18th century, it was first manufactured in the United States in about 1850. The elaborate, closely woven Victorian designs belong to the mid- to late 1800s, and the simple styles with coarse reedings usually indicate a post-1900 production. Art Deco styles followed in the '20s and '30s. The most important consideration in buying wicker is condition — it can be restored, but only by a professional. Age is an important factor, but be aware that 'Victorian-style' furniture is being manufactured today.

Key: HB — Heywood Bros.

Armchair, crisscross bk, horizontal-weave arms, McHugh, 45" ...**900.00**
Armchair, fan bk w/crisscross design, natural, McHugh, 40x39" ..**1,200.00**
Armchair, oversz wing type, dk stain, 48", pr **1,600.00**
Armchair rocker, bk resembles scallop shell, wooden seat, 35" ...**325.00**
Baby buggy, fancy curved hdls & ft, wire wheels, Victorian, EX .**265.00**
Baby buggy, Heywood-Wakefield, wht, EX+ **700.00**
Basket, sewing; tight weave, 2-door, wht pnt, EX **235.00**
Chair, corner; fancy scrollwork, cane seat, HB, 1890s, EX **765.00**
Chair, photographer's; tight weave, birdcage details, 1910s **520.00**
Chair, side; crisscross bk, tight-weave seat, apron, McHugh **1,000.00**
Chair, side; curlicues on bk & apron, high bk, cushion, 43" **295.00**
Chair, side; machine loomed, tight weave, wht pnt, 32x20" **215.00**
Chair, side; scrolls & curlicues on rnd bk & legs, 32x29" **275.00**
Chair, side; tight weave bk w/dmns, X-stretchers, cushion, 37" ..**165.00**
Cradle, loose weave, braid trim, wood rockers, 1920s, doll sz **110.00**
Cradle, swings in fr, ca 1900, EX **1,350.00**
Highchair, fine-weave bk, wooden tray & footrest, 1900s **385.00**
Lamp, floor; Eiffel tower form, 62", w/26" dia wicker shade **425.00**
Lamp, table; tight weave, wicker dome shade, 22" **170.00**
Lounge, tight weave, bk & armrest, cushions **450.00**
Planter, 26" dia bowl w/4-leg scroll-support base, 44" **365.00**
Porch swing, continuous arms, hooks from base, 75" **850.00**
Potty chair, orig finish, w/play tray **195.00**
Potty chair, tight-weave skirt, continuous arms, 1900s, 18" **185.00**

Rickshaw, wood hdl, metal undercarriage, rubber wheels, doll sz .**175.00**
Rocker, platform; open dmn weave, cushion seat, 36" **585.00**
Rocker, sewing; tight weave, side pocket, 34" **165.00**
Settle, crisscross bk design, tight-weave arms, McHugh, 69" ...**1,000.00**
Sofa, tight weave w/dmns, 3-cushion, flat arms, 1910s, EX **1,875.00**
Table, dining; fine-weave skirting under wood top, ped ft, 42" ...**550.00**
Table, library; tight-weave apron & end panels, 30x46x18" **350.00**
Table, parlor; tight-weave oval top, X-stretchers, 25x28x20" **135.00**
Tea cart, tight weave, bottom shelf, front wheels, top tray **300.00**
Vanity, tight weave, wht pnt, child sz, EX **225.00**

Will-George

In 1934, after years of working in the family garage (in Los Angeles, California), William and George Climes founded the Will-George Company. They manufactured high quality artware of porcelain and earthenware. Both brothers, motivated by their love of art pottery, had completed extensive education and training in manufacturing and decoration. In 1940 actor Edgar Bergen, a collector of pottery, developed a relationship with the brothers and invested in their business. With this new influx of funds, the company relocated to Pasadena. There they produced an extensive line of art pottery, but it was the bird and animal figurines they created that made them so well known. In addition they molded a large line of human figurines similar to Royal Doulton. The brothers, now with a staff of decorators, precisely molded their pieces with great care. They placed added emphasis on originality and detail, and as a result the products they created were high quality works of art that were only carried by exclusive gift stores.

In the late 1940s, after a split with Bergen, the company moved to San Gabriel to a larger, more modern location and renamed themselves The Claysmiths. There they mass produced many items, but due to the cheap, postwar imports from Italy and Japan that were then flooding the market, they liquidated the business in 1956. Our advisor for this category is Marty Webster. He is listed in the Directory under Michigan.

Bird figurine, Baltimore Oriole **155.00**
Bird figurine, cardinal on branch, 10" **75.00**
Bird figurine, cardinal on branch, 12½" **150.00**
Bird figurine, eagle on rock, wht/brn, 10" **150.00**
Bird figurine, flamingo, head up, looking bk, 7½" **50.00**
Bird figurine, flamingo, looking bk, 10" **75.00**
Bird figurine, Mallard duck w/spread wings, 7x11" **95.00**
Bird figurine, parrot (mc) on branch, 15" **200.00**
Bird figurine, pheasant hen **110.00**
Figurine, artist holding a palette, mc, 8" **95.00**
Figurine, boy holding a frog on base, mc, 9" **95.00**
Figurine, girl holding a doll on base, mc, 9" **125.00**
Figurine, hula dancer, wht skirt, 12" **155.00**
Figurine, monk, brn bsk, 4½" **50.00**
Figurine, monk, brn bsk, 5½" **75.00**
Pitcher, chicken figural, mc, 7" **125.00**
Tumbler, chicken figural, mc, 4½" **50.00**
Wine, chicken figural, mc, 5" **55.00**

Willets

The Willets Manufacturing Company of Trenton, New Jersey, produced a type of belleek porcelain during the late 1880s and 1890s. Examples were often marked with a coiled snake that formed a 'W' with 'Willets' below and 'Belleek' above. Not all Willet's is factory decorat-

ed. Items painted by amateurs outside the factory are worth considerably less. High prices usually equate with fine artwork. In the listings below, all items are belleek unless noted otherwise. Our advisor for this category is Mary Frank Gaston.

Bowl, allover gold & bl flowers, 2¼x3¼" **45.00**
Bowl, gold grapes & vines, 3x8" **95.00**
Bowl, roses, artist sgn, ruffled, shallow, 8¾" **325.00**
Bowl, vintage, gold on wht, 3x8" **190.00**
Cider set, fruit/foliage/flowers, 14½" tankard+6 mugs **700.00**
Cup & saucer, demitasse; silver deposit decor, ped ft **75.00**
Egg cup, petal design w/gold trim, mk, 2¾" **195.00**
Mug, berries & vines, dragon hdl, mk **275.00**
Mug, no decor except for lizard hdl, 5½" **95.00**
Pitcher, lemonade; mc lilies w/gold trim & scrolls, 7x8" **275.00**
Vase, lg flowers at top, gold banding, mk, 12½" **240.00**
Vase, mc roses, sgn Hamilton, urn form, 14" **350.00**
Vase, pansies, 13½" **295.00**
Vase, 2 egrets on pk & blk, tapering shape, 11⅝" **350.00**

Willow Ware

Willow Ware, inspired no doubt by the numerous patterns of the blue and white Nanking imports, has been popular since the late 18th century and has been made in as many variations as there were manufacturers. English transfer wares by such notable firms as Allerton and Ridgway are the most sought after and the most expensive. Japanese potters have been producing Willow-patterned dinnerware since the late 1800s, and American manufacturers have followed suit. Although blue is the color most commonly used, mauve, black, and even multicolor Willow Ware may be found. Complementary glassware, tinware, and linens have also been made. For further study we recommend the book *Blue Willow,* with full-color photos and current prices, by Mary Frank Gaston. In the following listings, if no manufacturer is noted, the ware is unmarked. See also Buffalo.

Ashtray, Royal China, 5½" **12.00**
Bowl, Petrus, 6" **50.00**
Bowl, Petrus, 9¼" **75.00**
Bowl, Royal China, 6½" **4.00**
Bowl, soup; Bennett, 7½" **14.00**
Bowl, soup; John Maddocks & Sons, 8⅝" **16.00**
Bowl, soup; Maddock, 8⅞" **12.00**
Bowl, soup; Royal, 8½" **10.00**
Bowl, vegetable; Brown & Steventon, w/lid, 9" **155.00**
Bowl, vegetable; Occupied Japan, mc w/gold trim, 11x7½" **35.00**

Butter dish, English, marked, 8" diameter, $150.00.

Butter dish, Royal China, ¼-lb **55.00**
Cheese dish, Mason **200.00**
Chop plate, Buffalo, 11¾" **150.00**
Cosy pot, stack set **120.00**

Creamer, Shenango 22.00
Creamer, thick 4.00
Creamer & sugar bowl, Japan, oval 40.00
Cruets, oil & vinegar; Japan, tall 90.00
Cup, England 12.00
Cup & saucer, Buffalo 30.00
Cup & saucer, giant, 3⅜x4", 6½" 47.00
Cup & saucer, handleless; Buffalo 50.00
Cup & saucer, Johnson Bros 12.50
Cup & saucer, USA, stacking 6.00
Garlic keeper, Mahling England 385.00
Gravy boat, Allerton, w/attached underplate 150.00
Gravy boat, Royal China 15.00
Krispy Kan, EX 45.00
Mug, Doulton, 4x4" 75.00
Mug, Japan 15.00
Mug, Japan, inside decal 20.00
Mug, Royal Doulton, 4x4" 90.00
Pie plate/shallow bowl 40.00
Pitcher, iced tea; Japan, ice lip, tall 115.00
Pitcher & bowl, Wedgwood 1,450.00
Plate, Adams, 12½" 30.00
Plate, Adams & Sons, 10½" 24.00
Plate, Buffalo, 5" 20.00
Plate, coupe shape, 6" 8.00
Plate, grill; Occupied Japan, 10½" 30.00
Plate, Ironstone China/Occupied Japan, 6⅜" 14.00
Plate, Japan, 9½" 15.00
Plate, Maastricht, 6" 10.00
Plate, Maastricht, 8" 12.00
Plate, Maddock & Son, 8" 18.00
Plate, Made in Japan, 8¾" 14.00
Plate, Occupied Japan, 9" 24.00
Plate, rolled rim, 7⅛" 12.00
Plate, rolled rim, 9⅛" 16.00
Plate, Royal China, 12" 22.00
Plate, Royal China, 6⅜" 3.00
Plate, Royal China, 9" 10.00
Plate, Shenango China, 9" 35.00
Platter, Aldine China/Occupied Japan, 12" 55.00
Platter, Aldine China/Occupied Japan, 16" 75.00
Platter, Baker...England, 9⅛x7¼" 50.00
Platter, New Wharf Pottery, 11¾" 60.00
Platter, Stone Ware, lt bl, ribbon mk, 12¼x9¾" ...65.00
Platter, Stone Ware, lt wear, 15¾" 75.00
Platter, Stone Ware, 16x12½" 115.00
Platter, Wedgwood, 11x9" 45.00
Pudding mold, Made in England, 3⅝x5¾" 55.00
Shaker, Japan, bbl form, ea 10.00
Teapot, Allerton 175.00
Teapot, Royal China 65.00
Tray, Allerton 45.00
Tumbler, glass 18.00

Winchester

The Winchester Repeating Arms Company lost their important government contract after WWI and of necessity turned to the manufacture of sporting goods, hardware items, tools, etc., to augment their gun production. Between 1920 and 1931, over 7,500 different items, each marked 'Winchester Trademark U.S.A.,' were offered for sale by thousands of Winchester Hardware stores throughout the country. After 1931 the firm became Winchester-Western. Collectors prefer the prewar items

such as we have listed below. Unless noted otherwise, values are for examples in excellent condition. Our advisor for this category is James Anderson; he is listed in the Directory under Minnesota. See also Knives.

Ad booklet, 'New Model 63 Speed King,' form #1250, 6x3¼" closed .29.00
Ad sheet, You Too Can Powder 'Em... w/a Model 21, 1945, VG ..30.00
Ax, boy's, orig #d hdl, VG 130.00
Baseball, G 260.00
Baseball bat 295.00
Baseball glove, 2 fingers torn, G- 250.00
Baseball uniform shirt, w/label, EX 550.00
Bayonet, for model 1873 rifle, EX 195.00
Brace, #W410, 10", VG 110.00
Bullet mold, 38 S&W 65.00
Bullet mold, 38 WCF cal, wood hdl, 95% finish, EX 85.00
Catalog, #72 rifles, shotguns & ammo, 1905, EX 90.00
Chisel, #4841, orig wood hdl, discolored blade,¼", VG 40.00
Display, counter; horse & rider, bronzed metal 275.00
Drill bit, #1205 ....15.00
Flashlight, bronze, mk Bronzelite, w/trademk, G 30.00
Flashlight, NP, 5-cell, trademk 75.00
Fly rod, bamboo, 3-pc, 108", EX in orig cloth bag 350.00
Grease gun tube, gr/red/lt gr, about full, VG 25.00
Guide, Fisherman's Pocket, 46-pg 45.00
Hammer, ball pein, EX+ 125.00
Hammer, machinist's ball pein, #6203, orig hdl, 12-oz, VG/EX ..130.00
Hat, straw, lady's 190.00
Hockey puck 160.00
Hockey stick, 1920s, EX 500.00
Ice skates, factory eng 475.00
Ice skates, leather uppers, Barney & Berry, sz 5, VG 100.00
Knife, beef slicer; 12" blade 95.00
Knife, butcher; #1107, hickory hdl, logo, 10", VG 45.00
Knife, carving; #5176, stag hdl, nickel-silver pommel, logo, VG+ ...70.00
Level, wood; #9815, 28" 100.00
Level, wood; brass ends & hardware, decal logo, 24", VG 85.00
Line, braided silk, on orig spool 55.00
Loading tool, 38 WCF, Pat 1874 & 82 ....55.00
Marble, blk, 1866-1966 Centennial w/gold Rider logo, EX 30.00
Meat grinder, #W-12, 90% finish, VG+ 85.00
Paint brush, 4", G 60.00
Paperweight, marble, horse, rider & model 94, dtd 1910, MIB ...100.00
Pin-back, Junior Rifle Corps, mc w/gold wreath border, EX 40.00
Plane, hand; #3011, rpt removed, orig wood, blade #12, 15", G 125.00
Plate, We Recommend & Sell...Cartridges & Guns, brass, 4½x2" ..60.00
Pliers, bent-nose combination 95.00
Pliers, end cutting; G- 60.00
Plug, Winchester, 3-hook 400.00
Poster, cartridge board; reissue, heavy cb, 1950s, 36x52", VG+ ..160.00

Poster, Winchester Big Game Rifles and Ammunition, hunter and mountain sheep, 1904, EX, $2,500.00.

Photo courtesy James Anderson

Print, duck camp scene, 1954, 28x20½" 100.00
Printer's block, says 'Happy Hunting,' 3x6" 50.00
Radio, floor type 1,200.00
Radio battery, #5116-B 160.00
Razor strop, #8383, G 250.00
Reel, brass, #1218, sm, M 95.00
Reel, casting; NP, #2442, med 140.00
Reel, fly; #1335, skeleton spool, blk finish, NM 130.00
Ruler, Winchester Store, wood, 12" 125.00
Rust remover, lt gr/red/dk gr, about full, bent corners, VG 30.00
Sad iron, electric, EX 285.00
Saw, crosscut 145.00
Saw, keyhole 125.00
Saw, meat; G 110.00
Screwdriver, mk Special, 4" 30.00
Sharpening steel, #1757, blk pnt wood hdl, slightly discolored, VG .50.00
Sign, hounds, Winchester For Sale Here on orig fr, EX 3,000.00
Spinner, trolling; willow leaf, #9781 ....75.00
Tennis racket, Ranger, As Good As the Gun, EX 375.00
Varnish, pt can 80.00
Wagon, wooden, G- 1,400.00
Wrench, brake adjusting 110.00
Wrench, monkey; Coe's pattern, wood hdl, #1004, 12" 95.00
Wrench, pipe; steel hdl, #1033, 14" 95.00
Wrench, pipe; wood hdl, #1020, 6" 85.00

Windmill Weights

Windmill weights made of cast iron were used to protect the windmill's plunger rod from damage during high winds by adding weight that slowed down the speed of the blades.

Bull, old wht, pnt, 18x24½" 600.00
Crescent, Eclipse B13, Fairbanks Morse Co, Chicago, pnt, 10¾" .415.00
Hanchett Bull, Simpson, full body, 2-part casting, rpt, 13" 500.00
Horse, bobtail, pnt traces, ca 1910, 17x17" 300.00
Horse, Demster, old rpt, 17x16½" 300.00
Horse, long-tailed, mc layers of old pnt, ca 1910, 17x17" 400.00
Letter W, Althouse Wheeler...WI, 16¾" 365.00
Rooster, Elgin, old rpt, 16" 660.00
Rooster, Hummer, Elgin Wind Power..., 13½"+wood base 600.00
Rooster, Hummer #184, Elgin, worn rpt, 9¼"+wooden base 330.00
Squirrel, Elgin, old dk tan pnt, lt rust, 17½" 1,650.00
Star, H37 Halladay Standard, worn wht pnt, 14" 660.00

Wire Ware

Very primitive wire was first made by cutting sheet metal into strips which were shaped with mallet and file. By the late 13th century, craftsmen in Europe had developed a method of pulling these strips through progressively smaller holes until the desired gauge was obtained. During the Industrial Revolution of the late 1800s, machinery was developed that could produce wire cheaply and easily; and it became a popular commercial commodity. It was used to produce large items such as garden benches and fencing as well as innumerable small pieces for use in the kitchen or on the farm. Beware of reproductions. Our advisor for this category is Rosella Tinsley; she is listed in the Directory under Kansas.

Basket, bread; wire in sm sqs, oval, 2 hdls 75.00
Basket, calling card; heart-shaped hdls, glass plate, 7¼" 110.00
Basket, calling card; heart-shaped hdls, w/majolica plate, 3x8½" ..105.00

Basket, ornate twisted wire, ftd, 1850s, 5" 110.00
Basket, potato; sm dmn designs, bail hdl, ½-bushel 50.00
Bottle carrier, circular, top hdl, ftd 37.50
Bottle carrier, holds 6, twisted hdl, 4x9x14" 50.00

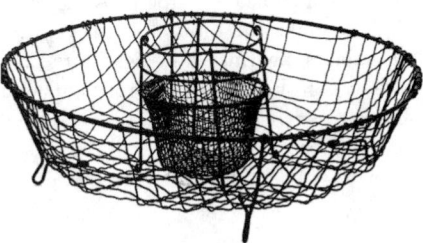

Dish rack, ca 1890 – 1920, 16" diameter, $75.00.

Egg cooker, 6-compartment, simple style 35.00
Fly cover, screen wire, wooden knob, 6½" 55.00
Hanger, heavy wire & wood, PA advertising 50.00
Napkin ring, twisted wire, fancy design, pr 115.00
Pie rack, heavy wire, for 6 pies 125.00
Rolling pin holder, heavy wire, hangs vertically, rare 65.00
Rug beater, wood hdl mk Kleen-e-ze Bristol Eng...1928, 21" 20.00
Soap dish, twisted wire, fancy wire bk w/hanging loop 75.00
Toaster, Maltese cross design, wood hdl 55.00
Trivet, tea; twisted wire, 6½" dia 45.00
Trivet, triangular, dbl wire at sides, loop hdl, 3-ftd 40.00
Whisk, fancy twisted stem, target-shaped base, 1870s, 11½" 70.00
Whisk, tined loops w/twisted hdl, Germany, 8", EX 25.00

Wisecarver, Rick

Rick Wisecarver is a contemporary ceramic artist from Ohio who is well known not only for his renderings of Indian portraits and brown-glaze ware reminiscent of similar lines made by earlier Ohio potteries but for his figural cookie jars as well, most of which have a Black theme.

Cookie jar, Black Santa & child, sgn, 1984 ....300.00
Cookie jar, Christmas Day, from $200 to 225.00
Cookie jar, Cookstove Mammy, from $150 to 200.00
Cookie jar, Hill Folk, from $200 to 225.00
Cookie jar, Mammy w/Cookies, pk, sgn 165.00
Cookie jar, Snow White, from $200 to 250.00
Vase, deer in snow, 18x10" 295.00
Vase, Indian, 13" 350.00

Witch Balls

Witch balls were a Victorian fad touted to be meritorious toward ridding the house of evil spirits, thus warding off sickness and bad luck. Folklore would have it that by wiping the dust and soot from the ball, the spirits were exorcised. It is much more probable, however, considering the fact that such beautiful art glass was used in their making, that the ostensive Victorians perpetrated the myth rather tongue-in-cheek while enjoying them as lovely decorations for their homes.

Amethyst, 6½", w/matching free-blown trumpet vase, 16½" ..9,000.00
Clear w/fiery opal loopings, open pontil, 6", +11" vase 3,900.00
Milk glass w/red & bl loopings, sheared end, Am, 3¼" 400.00
Red honey-amber, open pontil, 4" 250.00
Smoky sapphire bl, sheared end, Am, 4⅝" 160.00

Wood Carvings

Wood sculptures represent an important section of American folk art. Wood carvings were made not only by skilled woodworkers such as cabinetmakers, carpenters, etc., but by amateur 'whittlers' as well. They take the form of circus-wagon figures, carousel animals, decoys, busts, figurines, and cigar store Indians. Oriental artists show themselves to have been as proficient with the medium of wood as they were with ivory or hardstone. See also Carousel Animals; Decoys; Tobacciana.

Photo courtesy Dunbar Gallery

Jointed man, 9½", $300.00.

Am eagle, stained, fine detail, 20½" 250.00
Bear, varnished, fine dust added when wet for fur, ca 1920s, 4½" .85.00
Bird, wings closed, glass eyes, little detail, gold rpt, 5¼" 40.00
Buddha sitting, gold gilt, 3 garnets in forehead, late 1700s, 13" ...1,400.00
Cowboy & horse in relief, ca 1930, 12x5½" 110.00
Diety in headdresss, scrollwork bocage, on base, India, 72x16" ..550.00
Eagle, pine w/worn brn & gilt, glass eyes, rprs, 13" 275.00
Eagle, w/shield & arrows, pnt traces, 20th C, 44" W 935.00
Eagle on ped, EX patina, made in 5 pcs, 15", 15" wingspan 300.00
Eve, nude on rock w/lg leaf, varnished, 1930s, 12½" 125.00
Figure, articulated, appl eyes & nose, 1940s, 5¼x2¼x1¼" 85.00
Goose w/head raised, detailed mc pnt, Glatfelter, 1932, 10⅛x6" .950.00
Peasant lady on bench w/beer mug & broom, mc pnt, Carli, 3¾x5" 475.00
Rooster, splotchy mc pnt, PA, late 1800s, 3¾x2⅝x1⅛" 2,000.00
Woodcutter w/bundle & ax, seated on bench, mc pnt, Carli, 6½" 400.00

Woodenware

Woodenware (or treenware, as it is sometimes called) generally refers to those wooden items such as spoons, bowls, food molds, etc., that were used in the preparation of food. Common during the 18th and 19th centuries, these wares were designed from a strictly functional viewpoint and were used on a day-to-day basis. With the advent of the Industrial Revolution which brought with it new materials and products, much of the old woodenware was simply discarded. Today original handcrafted American woodenwares are extremely difficult to find. See also Primitives.

Bowl, ash burl, boat shape, cut-out hdls, EX figure, 9½x18" ...4,500.00
Bowl, ash burl, EX patina & figure, 5½x10¼" 475.00
Bowl, ash burl, filled crack, 3x12" 275.00
Bowl, ash burl, naturally shaped, dtd 1840, 2½x7x5½" 275.00
Bowl, ash burl, trn, shiny, 2⅝x4½" 215.00
Bowl, ash burl, worn surface, old varnish, 7½x16" 770.00
Bowl, ash burl w/striped figure, EX color, 4⅜x12" 1,155.00
Bowl, ash burl w/tight figure, worn varnish, 3¾x11" 900.00
Bowl, birch, edge damage, rpr, old dk finish, 6x20x18" 165.00
Bowl, poplar w/worn brn finish, tight age cracks, 6" 165.00
Bowl, scrubbed patina, pnt traces to bottom, 5x16" 125.00
Bucket, Lehnware, pnt pussy willows, w/lid, 9⅜" 825.00
Bucket, bentwood, hinged arched hdl, mustard pnt, 1800s, 6x11½" ..300.00
Bucket, gr pnt, metal bands, bail hdl, late 1800s, 7½" dia 225.00
Bucket, Lehnware, sponged orange, metal bands, 9x11½" 1,025.00
Bucket, mahog w/brass bands/insert/bail, English, 12x10x13" 880.00
Butter paddle, old dk patina, minor wear from use, 8⅝" 360.00
Canister, mustard pnt, 1800s, 6⅜x4" dia 400.00
Chalice, ash burl, 3 trn pcs, minor age cracks, 5x4¼" 75.00
Chalice, Lehnware, worn orig pnt w/mc decor, rstr cup, 3" 220.00
Churn, staved, metal bands, old rfn, turned lid, dasher: 21½" 200.00
Cup, Lehnware, pnt floral, rnd ft, 3⅛x2½" 875.00
Cup, Lehnware, pnt floral on yel, w/lid, 4⅝" 625.00
Cup, Lehnware, pnt peonies & pussy willows on yel, 5¾" 300.00
Cup, Lehnware-type, initials on yel, ftd, w/lid, 2½x4¾" 325.00
Cup & saucer, Lehnware, pnt strawberries/leaves on yel, sgn/1887 ...2,800.00
Cup & saucer, pnt strawberries & bl stripes, EX 775.00
Cutting board, pine, 1-brd, arched end w/lg hole to hang, 36" ...165.00
Dipper, ash burl, tab hdl, worn finish, 4" 325.00
Dipper, cvd horse-head hdl, worn patina, 5½" 230.00
Egg cup, Lehnware-type, pnt strawberries, 1¾x1¾", EX 350.00
Egg cup, Lehnware-type, pnt strawberries (crude), 2⅞" 100.00
Egg cup, Peaseware, flared opening on ped, 3" 60.00
Firkin, Lehnware, horizontal iron bands, 9½x7¼" 4,100.00
Firkin, mc pnt, bentwood bands, arched wood hdl, 1800s, 10¼" dia ..200.00
Jar, Pease, old soft finish, age cracks, 5⅝" 215.00
Measure, metal bands, salmon pnt, 5x9½", EX 150.00
Measure, old bl-gray pnt, 3 old tin bands, 7x11½" 145.00
Measure, orange pnt, 3 iron bands, 1800s, 9¾x9¼" 250.00
Measures, softwood dvtl box shapes, gr pnt, graduated set of 3 ..1,300.00
Noggin, worn patina, short age crack, 4⅞" 120.00
Pie board, pod-shaped hdl, old rpr, 18⅜" dia, 23½" L 125.00
Salt cellar, ash burl, trn rings, EX figure, 3⅛x3" dia 165.00
Spoon, cvd, woman figural hdl, sm chip, 12" 225.00
Tray, dough; mustard pnt, appl base, nailed, 1800s, 8x18x11" ...2,050.00
Tray, dough; mustard pnt, nailed butt joints, w/lid, mini, 14" L ..2,850.00

Woodworking Machinery

Vintage cast-iron woodworking machines are monuments to the highly skilled engineers, foundrymen, and machinists who devised them, thus making possible the mass production of items ranging from clothespins, boxes, and barrels to decorative moldings and furniture. Though attractive from a nostalgic viewpoint, many of these machines are bought by the hobbyist and professional alike, to be put into actual use — at far less cost than new equipment. Many worth-assessing factors must be considered; but as a general rule, a machine in good condition is worth about 65¢ a pound (excluding motors). A machine needing a lot of restoration is not worth more than 35¢ a pound, while one professionally rebuilt and with a warranty can be calculated at $1.10 a pound. Modern, new machinery averages over $3.00 a pound. Two of the best sources of information on purchasing or selling such machines are *Vintage Machines — Searching for the Cast Iron Classics* by Tom Howell, and *Used Machines and Abused Buyers* by Chuck Seidel from *Fine Woodworking*, November/December 1984. Prices quoted are for machines in good condition, less motors and accessories. Our advisor for this category is Mr. Dana Martin Batory, author of *Vintage Woodworking Machinery, An Illustrated Guide to Four Manufacturers*. See his listing in the Directory under Ohio for further information. No phone calls, please.

American Saw Mill Machinery Company, 1931

Band saw, Monarch Line, #X25, 30" built-in ball-bearing motor .770.00
Jointer, Monarch Line, #XII, ball-bearing, 16" 1,200.00
Mortiser, Monarch Line, #XI, hollow chisel, motorized 345.00
Planer, Monarch Line, single surface, 30" 2,600.00
Sander, Monarch Line, #X8, ball-bearing drum & disk 560.00
Table saw, Monarch Line, #X24, tilting arbor, 16" 425.00

Blue Star Products, 1939

Band saw, #1200, 12" floor model 85.00
Lathe, #1001, 72" bed, 12" swing 60.00
Table saw, #800, 8" 95.00

Boice-Crane Power Tools, 1937

Band saw, #800, 14" 100.00
Drill press, #1600, 15" 75.00
Lathe, #1100, gap bed 50.00
Scroll saw, #900, 24" 75.00

Crescent Machine Company, 1921

Band saw, 36" 975.00
Mortiser, hollow chisel 525.00
Universal Wood-Worker, #59, 5 machines in 1 ....2,050.00

Defiance Machine Works, 1910

Band saw, 28" 520.00
Table saw, #2, hand feed, 20" 650.00
Table saw, #2, power feed, 20" 1,100.00

F.H. Clement Company, 1896

Band saw, 28", Improved 1,040.00
Band saw, 30" 555.00
Band saw, 34", Patent Improved 635.00
Band saw, 36", Patent Improved 815.00
Band saw, 42" 1,430.00
Boring machine, Post, #2 ....325.00
Jointer, Perfection, 30" 1,690.00
Jointer, Perfection, 8" 620.00
Mortising & boring machine, No 1 ....520.00
Planer, #2½, dbl belted, Improved, 24" 1,465.00
Planer, #3, dbl belted, Improved, 20" 2,015.00
Planer, #3, dbl surface, 26" 3,000.00
Ripsaw, #2, iron fr, 16" 585.00
Sand belt machine, Improved 425.00
Sand-papering machine, #2, Universal 585.00
Sander, #1, spindle & drum 520.00
Sander, #3, dbl spindle 585.00
Sanding machine, surface; Improved 650.00
Shaper, #1, reversible, Improved 650.00
Shaper, variety, #3, heavy, dbl spindle 1,300.00
Slitting saw, #1, iron fr/wood top, 12" 325.00
Table saw, dbl arbor, Improved, 16" 815.00
Table saw, variety, #1, 15" 585.00

Gallmeyer & Livingston Company, 1927

Band saw, Union, 20" 390.00
Jointer, Union, motor on arbor, 8" 370.00

Table saw, Union #7, 7" 210.00

G.N. Goodspeed Company, 1876

Boring machine, upright 225.00
Planer, New & Improved, Pony, 24" 900.00
Table saw, 12" 200.00

Greenlee Bros. & Company, 1925

Tenoner, #530, sash, door & cabinet, ball-bearing 1,530.00

Hoyt & Brother Company, 1888

Band saw & resawing machine, #1194, 20" 1,700.00
Cut-off saw, overhung, traversing, 14" 650.00
Jointer, Perfection, 8" 450.00
Mortiser & borer, #2 ....780.00
Planer, matcher & surfacer, New Combined, #2, 24" 5,200.00
Planing & matching machine, #7, 13" 3,250.00
Sandpapering machine, The Boss, #5, 24" 1,600.00
Scroll saw, #1 ....300.00
Shingle machine, Grand Mogul, 2-block, automatic feed 2,210.00
Table saw, #2, 14" 800.00
Tenoning machine, #2 ....650.00
Wood shaper, dbl spindle 850.00

J.A. Fay & Egan Company, 1900

Jointer, New #2, 16" 1,550.00
Jointer, New #2, 20" 1,625.00
Jointer, New #2, 24" 1,700.00
Jointer, New #2, 30" 1,820.00
Jointer, New #4, extra heavy, 16" 1,625.00
Jointer, New #4, extra heavy, 20" 1,690.00
Jointer, New #4, extra heavy, 24" 1,885.00
Jointer, New #4, extra heavy, 30" 2,275.00
Molder, #1½, 4-sided, 4" 1,050.00
Molder, #2, 4-sided, 6" 1,500.00
Molder, #2½, 4-sided, 7" 2,100.00
Mortiser, #2, hollow chisel, automatic horizontal 1,500.00
Mortiser, #5, dbl hollow chisel, horizontal 1,100.00
Planer, #2½, dbl-belted surface, med sz, 26" 1,850.00
Saw, rip; #2, Improved Standard 1,175.00
Saw, rip; #2, self-feeding, lg 1,775.00
Saw, rip; #3, self-feeding, X-lg 2,400.00

J.D. Wallace Company, 1940s

Band saw, 16" 210.00
Grinder & sander, disk; Wonder, 16" 165.00
Jointer, 4" 15.00
Lathe, 6x24" 115.00
Saw, circular (table saw); Universal, 7" 75.00

L. Power & Company, 1888

Mortiser & borer, #2 ....780.00
Shaper, single spindle, reversible 585.00
Table saw, self feed, 14" 715.00

Ober Manufacturing Company, 1889

Rip saw, self feed, 14" 725.00

Saw, swing cut-off, 18" 275.00
Shaper, saw & jointer combination 400.00

Oliver Machinery Company, 1922

Band saw, #17, 30" 925.00
Shaper, #483, high speed, dbl spindle 1,300.00
Table saw, #32, Variety, 12" 500.00

Parks Ball Bearing Machine Company, 1925

Jointer, H-133, Ideal, 12" 400.00
Sanding machine, H-165, Economy, 24" 230.00
Saw, H-97, swing cut-off, Alert, 12" 225.00

P.B. Yates Machine Company, 1917

Planer, #160, dbl surface, 20" 1,235.00
Saw, #232, swing cut-off, 16" 260.00

Powermatic, Inc., 1965

Band saw, #141, 14" 145.00
Band saw, #81, 20" 500.00
Jointer, #50, 6" 110.00
Jointer, #60, 8" 170.00
Lathe, #45, 12" 230.00
Lathe, #90, 12" 360.00
Mortiser, #10, hollow chisel 375.00
Mortiser, #15, chain saw 390.00
Planer, #100, 12" 200.00
Planer, #160, 16" 650.00
Planer, #180, 18" 685.00
Planer, #221, 20" 725.00
Planer, #225, 24" 1,600.00
Sander, #300-01, 12" disk & 6" belt combination 95.00
Sander, #33, 6" belt 90.00
Sander, #35, 12" disk 55.00
Scroll saw, #95, 24" 100.00
Shaper, #26, single spindle 240.00
Table saw, #62, 10" 135.00
Table saw, #66, 10" 230.00
Table saw, #72, 12" 515.00
Tenoner, #2-A, single end 620.00

S.A. Woods Machine Company, 1876

Circular resawing machine, Joslin's Improved, 50" 2,275.00
Planer, panel; Improved, 20" 520.00
Planer, surface; Pat Improved, 30" 1,430.00

Sprunger Power Tools, 1950s

Band saw, 14" 60.00
Jigsaw, 20" 40.00
Lathe, gap bed, 10" 50.00
Table saw, tilt arbor, 10¼" 75.00

Worcester Porcelain Company

The Worcester Porcelain Company was deeded in 1751. During the first or Dr. Wall period (so called for one of its proprietors), porcelain with an Oriental influence was decorated in underglaze blue. Useful tablewares represented the largest portion of production, but figurines and decorative items were also made. Very little of the earliest wares were marked and can only be identified by a study of forms, glazes, and the porcelain body, which tends to transmit a greenish cast when held to light. Late in the '50s, a crescent mark was in general use, and rare examples bear a facsimile of the Meissen crossed swords. The first period ended in 1783, and the company went through several changes in ownership during the next eighty years. The years from 1783 to 1792 are referred to as the Flight period. Marks were a small crescent, a crown with 'Royal,' or an impressed 'Flight.' From 1792 to 1807 the company was known as Flight and Barr and used the trademark 'F&B' or 'B,' with or without a small cross. From 1807 to 1813 the company was under the Barr, Flight, and Barr management; this era is recognized as having produced porcelain with the highest quality of artistic decoration. Their mark was 'B.F.B.' From 1813 to 1840 many marks were used, but the most usual was 'F.B.B.' under a crown to indicate Flight, Barr, and Barr. In 1840 the firm merged with Chamberlain, and in 1852 they were succeeded by Kerr and Binns. The firm became known as Royal Worcester in 1862. The production was then marked with a circle with '51' within and a crown on top. The date of manufacture was incised into the bottom or stamped with a letter of the alphabet, just under the circle. In 1891 Royal Worcester England was added to the circle and crown. From that point on, each piece is dated with a code of dots or other symbols. After 1891 most wares had a blush-color ground. Prior to that date it was ivory. Most shapes were marked with a unique number.

During the early years they produced considerable ornamental wares with a Persian influence. This gave way to a Japanesque influence. James Hadley is most responsible for the Victorian look. He is considered the 'best ever' designer and modeller. He was joined by the finest porcelain painters. Together they produced pieces with very fine detail and exquisite painting and decoration. Figures, vases, and tableware were produced in great volume and are highly collectible. During the 1890s they allowed the artists to sign some of their work. Pieces signed on the face by the Stintons, Baldwyn, Davis, Raby, Austin, Powell, Sedgley, and Rushton (not a complete list) are in great demand. The company is still in production. There is an outstanding museum on the company grounds in Worcester, England.

Note: most pieces had lids or tops (if there is a flat area on the top lip, chances are it had one), if missing deduct 30% to 40%.

Vase, pyriform in Mid-Eastern taste, three paneled sides, three handles, pierced domical lid, ca 1887, 18¼", $1,350.00.

Basket, bl & wht w/emb floral, rtcl, Dr Wall period, 3½x9" 1,000.00
Basket, woven oval, floral sprays, mk/#1012, 7" 135.00
Cracker jar, floral sprays w/gold, crown mk, 6½x6" dia 495.00
Cracker jar, potato form, oval w/gilt rim, mk, 5" 200.00
Creamer, floral sprays, gold reeded hdl, mk, #1094 ....60.00
Cup & saucer, Gold Chantilly 28.00
Ewer, floral bouquets w/gold, lion masks, scroll/pillar hdl, 16½" ...350.00

Ewer, gold floral vine, squatty, dragon hdl, mk, #1048, 4" **120.00**
Figurine, angelfish, bl, sgn/dtd **375.00**
Figurine, Bal Masque, CM Parnell, costumed lady, #3111, 9" **495.00**
Figurine, Bulldog, Doris Lindler, 7¾x9½" **350.00**
Figurine, Capt Raimondo (horse) **995.00**
Figurine, draped nude drinks from shell, ivory w/pnt details, 14" ..**375.00**
Figurine, Grandmother's Dress, pk w/gold, #3081, 6⅜" **130.00**
Figurine, horse, Marion Coates w/Stroller **995.00**
Figurine, horse, Percheron **1,095.00**
Figurine, horse, Royal Canadian Mounted **895.00**
Figurine, maiden w/creel by wall, fitted as lamp, 18" **260.00**
Figurine, Peter Pan, modeled by F Gertner, #3011, 7¾" **310.00**
Figurine, Woodland Dance, girl & animals, #3076, 4x4" **380.00**
Figurines, 4 seasons, blanc de chine, gilt bases, 40", 4 for **990.00**
Mug, Wednesday's Child, MIB **25.00**
Pitcher, cantaloupe form, gold leaves, vine hdl, #1111, 6½" **200.00**
Pitcher, cranes in moonlight, horn hdl, #1116, 10" **495.00**
Pitcher, floral sprays, gold reeded hdl, mk, #1094, 6" **90.00**
Pitcher, floral w/gold, horn form, antler hdl, #1116, 8" **60.00**
Pitcher, flowers & gold, rtcl neck, #G713/1914, 5x8" **295.00**
Plate, dinner; Silver Chantilly **25.00**
Rose bowl, pheasants, sgn Stinton **175.00**
Shell dish, tan to cream w/gold, serrated edge, ca 1907, 4x4½" **50.00**
Tray, floral branches, maroon mk/Ovington Bros, 9x16" **95.00**
Vase, floral, mc w/gold, long neck, 10¼" **325.00**
Vase, floral sprays, emb fleur-de-lis, rtcl neck, 8x5" **325.00**

World's Fairs and Expos

Since 1851 and the Crystal Palace Exhibition in London, World's Fairs and Expositions have taken place at a steady pace. Many of them commemorate historical events. The 1904 Louisiana Purchase Exposition, commonly known as the St. Louis World's Fair, celebrated the 100th anniversary of the Louisiana Purchase agreement between Thomas Jefferson and Napoleon in 1803. The 1893 Columbian Exposition, known as The Chicago World's Fair, commemorated the 400th anniversary of the discovery of America by Columbus in 1492. (Both of these fairs were held one year later than originally scheduled.) The multitude of souvenirs from these and similar events have become a growing area of interest to collectors in recent years. Many items have a 'crossover' interest into other fields: i.e., collectors of postcards and souvenir spoons eagerly search for those from various fairs and expositions. For additional information collectors may contact World's Fairs Collectors Society (WFCS), whose address is in the Directory under Clubs, Newsletters, and Catalogs, or our advisor, D.D. Woollard, Jr. His address is listed in the Directory under Missouri.

Key:
T&P — Trylon & Perisphere   WF — World's Fair

1876 Centennial, Philadelphia

Charm, Liberty 1886/Liberty Bell 1776, bronze, EX **30.00**
Cup, Centennial Memorial Building, mc on china, 3½" dia **100.00**
Medal, Liberty w/sword/13 stars, Official Expo, gilt bronze, 38mm ...**20.00**
Medal, simulated half-cent, Liberty Head/13 stars, brass, 23mm ...**16.00**
Mug, Liberty & the Republic, amber glass, 5" **60.00**
Silk, Memorial Hall, bl, woven **85.00**
Stud, brass, emb Art Gallery 1876, 1" dia **22.50**

1893 Columbian, Chicago

Book, History of WF, Ben C Truman, illus, 549-pg, EX **27.50**

Goblet, gr etched glass, WF 1893 & lady's name, 3" **60.00**
Invitation, Dedication Ceremonies **35.00**
Match safe, Ferris Wheel design emb on NP **100.00**
Medal, Columbus portrait by Saint-Gaudens, copper, 38mm, NM ...**28.00**
Medal, Machinery Hall, WF...1893, gilt bronze, 24mm, EX+ **10.00**
Paperweight, glass w/sepia view of Ferris wheel, rnd, EX **75.00**
Stick pin w/medal, Columbus, World's...Expo 1893, gilt metal, 19mm ...**11.00**
Watch case opener, Keystone Watch..., copper-nickel, 25x36mm .**18.00**

1901 Pan American

Elongated cent, Mfg & Liberal Arts..., rolled on 1894 cent **10.00**
Medal, US Government Building, Pan-Am...1901, brass, EX **10.00**
Napkin ring, buffalo emb/florals eng on aluminum, 1½" dia **25.00**
Pin-bk, robed female figures, celluloid, Whitehead & Hoag, NM .**17.50**
Ribbon, woven silk, 5x3½" on orig 6x8" mat, EX **65.00**
Spoon, Indian/falls/Pan Am 1904 on hdl, emb view in bowl, 4¼" .**20.00**
Token, World's Greatest Wonder Niagara Falls, aluminum **10.00**
Tumbler, Liberal Arts Building etched on glass, gold rim 3½" **35.00**

1904 St. Louis

Mug, Machinery Building, multicolor transfer on white, Victoria Carlsbad, Austria, 3¼", $150.00.

Ax, Peace & Prosperity emblem emb on glass, 9½" **75.00**
Cigar case, leather slipcase w/burned-in design, 3¼x5¼", EX **35.00**
Napkin ring, emb Cascade Gardens on wht metal, 1¾", EX **15.00**
Napkin ring, WF...1904 & flower pattern, aluminum, 1⅝" dia **25.00**
Paperweight, Fair building, mc, glass, 3" **75.00**
Paperweight, sea shells encased in glass, 3½" dia **25.00**
Pin tray, Louis IX emb on pewter, 5½" dia, EX **55.00**
Pocket mirror, US Government Building, mc on celluloid **100.00**
Pocketknife, Cascade Gardens/etc, 2-blade, aluminum fr, 2¾" **70.00**
Spoon, cherub rings bells on hdl, scene in bowl, SP, demi **18.00**

1905 Lewis and Clark

Handkerchief, wht w/mc embr Foreign Exhibits Building, VG **10.00**
Pin-bk, JI Case Threshing Machines, Fair logo, mc cello, EX **55.00**
Punch tag, cut-out star, Portland Fair 1905 in center, EX **15.00**
Stickpin, Liberty embracing Louis & Clark, SP brass, 2½" **17.50**
View book, Sights & Scenes at..., 94 pgs of photos, 7x5", EX **25.00**

1909 Alaska Yukon Pacific

Fob, totem design ea side, WF mks, silver, EX **35.00**
Label, Expo Brand Lemons, Johnston Fruit Co, mc, 8¼x12¼", EX .**5.00**
Pin-bk, AYP cutout/interlocking letters, gilt brass **10.00**
Postcard, Carnation Milk Modern Milkman, mc, used, EX **25.00**
Ribbon, Japan Day, September 4, 1904, wht silk, 7½", EX **27.50**

1915 Panama Pacific

Book, Boy Scouts at...Expo, Payson, hardcover, 303-pg, VG **28.00**
Indian-head penny, Pan-Am...1915, state seal/etc, 38mm, NM ...**25.00**
Pennant, bear & pick, IOOF...Lodge, PPIE 1915, bl on wht, 8½" .**25.00**

Pin-bk, Liberty Bell, celluloid, Am flag suspended below, EX **30.00**
Spoon, Tower of Jewels on hdl, building in bowl, SP, 6", EX **10.00**
Watch fob, 1915 in cut-out #s, heavy brass, NM **35.00**

1926 Sesquicentennial

Ashtray, bell in relief, leafy border, lead, 5¼", EX **10.00**
Bookends, Liberty Bell/Independence Hall, brass, wood bases, pr .**30.00**
Compact, Liberty Bell w/mc rhinestones on gold-tone, 2½" **22.50**
Pin-bk, Treasure Island Doubloon..., gilt brass, 26mm **15.00**

1933 Chicago

Playing cards, Century of Progress, Avenue of Flags, gold edges, standard bridge deck, EXIB, $25.00.

Blotter, Johnson Gasoline ad, Fair building pictured, mc **15.00**
Book, Official Book of the Fair, illus, 1933, 104-pg **22.50**
Book, Official Guide, illus, 1933, 176-pg **20.00**
Bookmark, Comet logo/Chicago/scrollwork, enamel on brass, 4¼" ...**13.50**
Handkerchief, Mt Fugiyama on bl silk, Japan, 11" sq, NM **24.00**
Mailer, fold-out postcards, mc views, set of 18, M **10.00**
Medal, Good Luck (symbols), Century of Progress..., bronze, NM ..**5.00**
Menu, Pabst Bl Ribbon Casino, w/Ben Bernie autograph **35.00**
Miniature, toy wagon, Radio Flyer, wht rubber tires, 4x2" **100.00**
Pin-bk, World Champion Log Rollers, 1" **20.00**
Ring, comet design, silver on bl, adjustable **10.00**
Wooden nickel, laughing chief/Comet logo, Century of..., 25mm, M .**12.50**

1935 California Pacific

Book, Official Guide, illus, 56-pg **20.00**
First Day cover, Exposition Station cancel 5/29/35 ....**20.00**
Mailer, fold-out postcards, 18 different views w/history, M **10.00**
Medal, buildings & San Diego on banner, aluminum, 25mm, M **5.00**
Tile, Exposition Building emb, yel/orange, ceramic, 6" **60.00**

1939 New York

Ashtray, Syrocco, T&P in center, NY WF, 4-rest, 3½" sq, NM ...**28.00**
Bandana, Boy Scouts Service Camp 1939, 30" sq **100.00**
Book, Official Guide, illus, 1st ed, 1939, 256-pg **25.00**
Book, Official Guide...WF of 1940 in NY, softcover, 160-pg, NM ..**17.50**
Booklet, Futurama, illus, 24-pg **20.00**
Booklet, 1001 Facts About WF & NY, Dreier Hotels, 96-pg, EX .**15.00**
Game, Going to WF, mc gameboard, EX in G 9½x19" box **100.00**
Jacket, NY WF, gray gabardine, Expo buttons, EX **200.00**
Medal, brass, T&P, Metropolitan Life Ins tower, 1¼" **7.50**
Medal, brass, T&P w/1939, Souvenir of 150th Anniv..., 1¼" **10.00**
Pin-bk, Gas Wonderland **12.50**
Pin-bk, I Have Seen the Future, 1" **15.00**
Playing cards, T&P, NY WF in bl, world globe, EX in case **40.00**
Postcards, NY WF views, set of 20, M in orig sleeve **50.00**
Poster, For Peace & Freedom, mc, 13x20", EX **125.00**

Sheet music, Yours for a Song, Rose/Fetter, T&P cover, NM **30.00**
Ticket, flags w/T&P, Guest of Internat'l...Machines, 4½" **20.00**
Ticket, type found in school child's ticket booklet, 1x2¼" **2.00**
Vase, ruby-stained souvenir, NY WF 1940, T&P, gold trim, 3¾" .**25.00**

1939 San Francisco

Bath towel, Golden Gate.../Bridge/etc, terry cloth, 44", NM **55.00**
Bookmark, clear plastic w/scenes, butterfly shape, M in mailer **35.00**
Catalog, Art Exhibition by CA Artists, softbound, 44-pg, NM **12.50**
Comb, amber plastic, in emb gold-tone case w/brass medallion, EX **30.00**
Pathegram viewer, blk/red plastic, NMIB w/many extra views **70.00**
Pin-bk, Tower of Sun & bridge at sunset, brass, NM **15.00**
Thermometer, celluloid key shape, gold-plated metal, 8½x3", NM .**40.00**
Wallet, leather, Columbus & ship, Golden Gate..., 3½x4¼" **35.00**
Wooden shoes, Golden Gate.../Tower of Sun, 2", pr, M w/tag **28.00**

1962 Seattle

Bottle opener, Space Needle shape, enamel on steel, MIB **30.00**
Pennant, Space Needle, red & blk felt, 7¾", EX **7.50**
Plate, Seattle WF, overhead view, ceramic, 5", NM **8.00**
Token, Good for $1, Space Needle/etc, gilt brass, 39mm dia, M **3.50**
Tray, Space Needle & Fair scenes, mc on bl, tin, 11" dia, EX **20.00**
Tumbler, Century 21 Expo, bl on clear glass, 4¾" **10.00**

1964 New York

Coaster set, wood w/mc views, 4" dia, set of 6, MIP **15.00**
Fan, Zephyr, battery powered, steel, EXIB **12.50**
Medallion, Unisphere/Man's Achievements..., bronze, 63mm, M ..**18.00**
Plate, Unisphere & views, mc, ceramic, 7¼" **14.00**
Ring, gold-tone w/mc flasher front, Unisphere/fireworks, EX **15.00**
Token, transit; Unisphere, Long Island Rail Road, brass, 25mm **2.50**
Tray, Unisphere, NY WF...Peace...Understanding, metal, 11¾" ..**10.00**

Wright, Frank Lloyd

Born in Richland Center, Wisconsin, in 1869, Wright became a pioneer in architectural expression, developing a style referred to as 'prairie.' From early in the century until he died in 1959, he designed houses with rooms that were open, rather than divided by walls in the traditional manner. They exhibited low, horizontal lines and strongly projecting eaves, and he filled them with furnishings whose radical aesthetics complemented the structures to perfection. Several of his homes have been preserved to the present day, and collectors who admire his ideas and the unique, striking look he achieved treasure the stained glass windows, furniture, chinaware, lamps, and other decorative accessories made by Wright.

Chair, dressing table; spindle bk, drop-in seat, rfn, 27", VG **4,000.00**
Chair, plywood, low folding form for Unitarian Church, 28", VG **650.00**
Chair, side; spindle bk, worn drop-in seat, 42", VG **1,300.00**
Chair, steel w/perforated grid bk & seat, Van Dorn Iron Wks, 39" ..**1,200.00**
Dresser, Heritage Henredon, 3-section, 27x60x20", VG **1,200.00**
End table, Heritage Henredon, drw between upper & lower shelf, VG **750.00**
Headboard, Heritage Henredon, Taliesin edge, king sz, 39x38" .**500.00**
Modular system, 4-pc, case+2 bookcases+6-door/2-drw base, 78" ..**3,500.00**
Seat, theatre; angular metal fr w/uphl seat & bk, 34x21x23" **550.00**
Sofa, Heritage Henredon, mahog fr w/Taliesin edges, reuphl, 52" ..**800.00**
Sofa, Heritage Henredon, 3-sided angular form, reuphl, 95" ...**1,000.00**
Table, dining; Heritage Henredon, copper inlay, 54", +4 chairs ..**2,200.00**
Table, dining; Heritage Henredon, Taliesen edge, 78"+leaves .**3,250.00**

Tile, geometric relief decor, 4x4", EX, 4 for 1,200.00

Wrought Iron

Until the middle of the 19th century, almost all the metal hand forged in America was made from a material called wrought iron. When wrought iron rusts it appears grainy, while the mild steel that was used later shows no grain but pits to an orange-peel surface. This is an important aid in determining the age of an ironwork piece.

Beam hook, long spike w/hook & curlicue top, 8¼x6½" 300.00
Fork, meat; 2-tine, flattened hdl, 17" 170.00
Fork, meat; 2-tine, self-loop hdl, 17" L 75.00
Fork, meat; 3-tine, scrolled end, 13" 220.00
Hinges, ram's horn style, strap type w/old red pnt, 24", pr 180.00
Hook, 3-prong, ca 1830, 6x5" 40.00
Kettle stand, flat apron w/decor, penny ft, 12x8x10" 200.00
Ladle, flattened hdl w/pinched-in center & curl, 15½" 150.00
Peel, ram's horn hdl, 33" 110.00
Pipe tongs, EX detail, 19½" 400.00
Rack, pipe-drying; for holding 4 new clay pipes, 12" 385.00
Rack, utensil; scrolled details, 5-hook, 18x24" 440.00
Rack, utensil; tulip-shaped ends, arched top w/scrolls, 11x17" ..2,600.00
Roasting fork, w/rest 125.00
Skewer, twisted hdl w/hook, 30" 65.00
Skewer holder, punched hearts, 5½x6½" 180.00
Spatula, flattened tapered section at base of flat hdl, 11⅜" 65.00
Tripod, 3 rnd splayed legs w/pad-like ft, 7⅝x13¼" 75.00

Yellow Ware

Ranging in color from buff to deep mustard, yellow ware which almost always has a clear glaze can be slip banded, plain, Rockingham decorated, flint enamel glazed, or mocha glazed. Mocha-decorated pieces, especially those which are red or black decorated, are usually the most expensive and desirable pieces to own. The majority of pieces are plain and do not bear a manufacturer's mark. Yellow ware which was primarily produced in the United States, England, and Canada was popular from the mid-19th century to the early 20th century. A utilitarian ware, it was first domestically produced in New York, Pennsylvania, and Vermont. With more than thirty active potteries, East Liverpool, Ohio, became the center for yellow ware production. Although other wares have become more popular, yellow ware is still being produced today in both England and the United States. Because of advanced collectors attempting to complete their collections, prices continue to rise. Note: Because this is a utilitarian ware, it is often found with damage and heavy wear; this would of course decrease its value. For further information we recommend *Collector's Guide to Yellow Ware* by Lisa S. McAllister and *Collecting Yellow Ware, An Identification and Value Guide*, written by our advisor, John Michel and Lisa S. McAllister. Mr. Michel's address is in the Directory under New York.

Baker, plain, oval, 12" dia 150.00
Bowl, batter; emb decor, wht int, JE Jeffords/Phila, 9" 250.00
Bowl, batter; emb floral design, wht int 185.00
Bowl, batter; 3 brn slip bands, w/hdl 105.00
Bowl, seaweed band, 1850-90s, Am or Canadian, from $295 to .450.00
Butter crock, 3 bl bands, matching lid, 4¾" 235.00
Colander, pie plate; plain, 9½" 450.00
Colander, pie plate; Rockingham decorated, 9¾" 425.00

Cup & saucer, handleless; England, ca 1900, demitasse 150.00
Custard cup, cone shaped, thin, ca 1880-1920 ....35.00
Figurine, dog seated, EX molding, mc mottle, 10", EX+ 4,400.00
Flask, fish-shape, English manufacturer 900.00
Flower pot, bl mocha on wht slip band 800.00
Foot warmer, plain, sloping rectangular shape 100.00
Funnel, plain 400.00
Funnel, Rockingham decoration 450.00
Jar, octagonal, scarce, from $200 to 250.00
Jar, storage; plain, w/lid, ca 1890-1920, 5", $150 to 185.00
Milk pan, rolled rim, Am, 1840-70, 8-15", ea, from $150 to 225.00
Mini-mold, fluted & heart-shaped 200.00
Mold, fig figural 300.00
Mold, fish form, ca 1850-1900, 12", from $450 to 550.00
Mold, Turk's head form, Am, ca 1860-1900, 5-12" dia, from $95 to .225.00
Nappy, plain w/plain rim, 10¾" dia 165.00
Pepper pot, bl bands, English, ca 1870-1900, from $450 to 550.00
Pepper pot, bl mocha on wht slip 595.00
Pitcher, bl & red mocha on wht ship, 10¾" 950.00
Pitcher, emb basketweave, rope hdl, att Jeffords 375.00
Pitcher, emb cows, 8¾" 175.00
Pitcher, emb hunt scene, hound hdl, 4½" 475.00
Pitcher, emb hunt scene, 7½" 300.00
Pitcher, emb peacock design, 9½" 375.00
Pitcher, water; Earthworm, mc w/wht band/brn stripes, C hdl, 7⅝" ..950.00
Punch cup or syllabub 95.00
Rolling pin, plain, wooden hdls 200.00
Rolling pin, 3 wht bands at ea end, wooden hdls 575.00
Salt cellar, Seaweed, bl on wht band, flared rim, master, 3" 625.00
Soap dish, oval, 1 hole 300.00
Soap dish, rectangular, multiple holes 325.00
Teapot, emb floral, 8-sided, Am Pottery...Jersey City, 1½-cup ...950.00

Zanesville Glass

Glassware was produced in Zanesville, Ohio, from as early as 1815 until 1851. Two companies produced clear and colored hollow ware pieces in five characteristic patterns: 1) diamond faceted, 2) broken swirls, 3) vertical swirls, 4) perpendicular fluting, 5) plain, with scalloped or fluted rims and strap handles. The most readily identified product is perhaps the whiskey bottles made in the vertical swirl pattern, often called globular swirls because of their full, round bodies. Their necks vary in width; some have a ringed rim and some are collared. They were made in several colors; amber, light green, and light aquamarine are the most common. Our advisor for this category is Mark Vuono; he is listed in the Directory under Connecticut.

Bottle, globular, 24 swirled ribs, yellow-olive (rare), pontil scar, rolled rim, 8⅜", $2,200.00 (Amber value: $400.00 to $600.00).

Bottle, globular, aqua, 24 right-swirl ribs, 8¾" **225.00**
Bottle, globular, deep amber, 24 swirled ribs, 7⅞" **465.00**
Chestnut flask, amber, 24 vertical ribs, 4¾" **250.00**
Chestnut flask, aqua, 24 swirled ribs, pontiled, stain, 7" **150.00**
Chestnut flask, aqua, 24 vertical ribs, 4½" **200.00**
Chestnut flask, clear, long neck, 24 ribs, lt wear, 5⅛" **70.00**
Chestnut flask, clear, 24 swirled ribs, minor wear, 7" **195.00**
Chestnut flask, golden amber, 24 vertical ribs, pontiled, 5⅜" **300.00**
Flask, GIV-32, Shepards & Co...Masonic, deep amber, bruise, 6⅝" ..**385.00**

Zell

The Georg Schmider United Zell Ceramic Factories has a long and colorful history. Affectionately called 'Zell' by those who are attracted to this charming German-Dutch type tin-glazed earthenware, this type of ware came into production in the latter part of the last century.

While Zell has created some lovely majolica-like examples, it is the German-Dutch scenes that are collected with such enthusiasm. Typical scenes are set against a lush green background with windmills on the distant horizon. Into the scenes appear typically garbed girls (long dresses with long white aprons and lowland bonnet head gear) being teased or admired by little boys attired in pantaloon-type trousers and short rust-colored jackets, all wearing wooden shoes. There are variations on this theme, and occasionally a collector may find an animal theme or even a Kate Greenaway-like scene.

A similar ware in theme, technique, and quality but bearing the mark Haag or Made in Austria is included in this listing.

While Zell produced a wide range of wares and even quite recently (1970s) introduced an entirely hand-painted hen/rooster line, it is this early charming German-Dutch theme pottery that is coveted and collected in increasing numbers by devoted collectors. Our advisors for this category are Fred and Lila Shrader; they are listed in the Directory under California.

Key:
KG — Kate Greenaway style   MIA — Made in Austria

Bowl, boy & girl w/cat, low flared ped, Zell, 3x5¼" **39.00**
Bowl, oval w/brass rtcl 2" fr, boy & girl strolling, Haag, 8x6" **175.00**
Bowl, porridge; frightened chickens, MIA, 1½x3½" **28.00**
Bowls, mixing; boys & girls feed animals, Zell, set of 3, to 11" **285.00**
Cake plate, flared copper ped & rtcl fr, boy/girl kiss, 6x12" **225.00**
Creamer, boy & windmill, 6-oz **45.00**
Creamer, boy/girl stroll, hdl at right angle to spout, Zell, 6-oz **56.00**
Creamer, girls strolling w/boys teasing, Zell, 6-oz **48.00**
Cup & saucer, tea; boys stroll, scenic bkground saucer, Zell **45.00**
Lamp base, kerosene; old brass fittings, boys w/dog, Zell, 9½" **175.00**
Mug, well-dressed baby plays w/rabbit, Zell, child sz, 2½" **55.00**
Pitcher, cats play in garden, Zell, 6½" **75.00**
Plaque, boy & girl arm-in-arm, brass rtcl fr, 7½" dia **95.00**
Plate, child holding doll/pushing cart, Haag, 7" **56.00**
Plate, grandpa w/wheelbarrow/child tills garden, KG, Zell, 8" **72.00**
Sugar bowl, chickens peck corn, Haag, 1½x3½" **30.00**
Tumbler, boy strolling/boats beyond, hdl, Zell, 8-oz, 5½" **55.00**
Vase, children stroll on path, slim, Haag, 7" **45.00**

Zsolnay

Only until the past decade has the production of the Zsolnay factory become more correctly understood. In the beginning they produced

only cement; industrial and kitchen ware manufacture began in the 1850s, and in the early 1870s a line of decorative architectural and art pottery was initiated which has continued to the present time.

The city of Pécs (pronounced Paach) is the major provincial city of southwest Hungary close to the Yugoslav border. The old German name for the city was Funfkirchen, meaning 'Five Churches.' (The 'five-steeple' mark became the factory's logo in 1878.)

Although most Americans only think of Zsolnay in terms of the bizarre, reticulated examples of the 1880s and '90s and the small 'Eosine' green figures of animals and children that have been produced since the 1920s, the factory went through all the art trends of major international art potteries and produced various types of forms and decorations. The 'golden period,' circa 1895 – 1920, is when its Art Nouveau (Sezession in Austro-Hungarian terms) examples were unequaled. Vilmos Zsolnay was a Renaissance man devoted to innovation, and his children carried on the tradition after his death in 1900. Important sculptors and artists of the day were employed (usually anonymously) and married into the family, creating a dynasty.

Nearly all Zsolnay is marked, either impressed 'Zsolnay Pécs' or with the 'five steeple' stamp. Variations and form numbers can date a piece fairly accurately. For the most part, the earlier ethnic historical-revival pieces do not bring the prices that the later Sezession and second Sezession (Deco) examples do. Our advisor for this category is John Gacher; he is listed in the Directory under Rhode Island.

Jardiniere, multicolor thistles, majolica, form #5454, ca 1899, 18", NM, $6,500.00.

Bowl, mc flower & leaf decor, 4-ftd, full rtcl, 5x7½" **260.00**
Cache pot, 2 figures in garden, att Klein, Pécs/HP mk, 1880s, 6¾" ..**1,650.00**
Chalice, Sezession, emb floral/4 stem hdls, rpr, #5668, 1899, 6" ...**1,650.00**
Figure, bust of Lenin, gr Eosin glaze, 10¼" **350.00**
Figure, Elvis, gr Eosin glaze, ca 1983, 15¾" **500.00**
Figure, frog, gr Eosin glaze, ca 1971, 6¼" **150.00**
Figure, hedgehog, gr Eosin glaze, 3¼" **75.00**
Figure, The Thinker, gr Eosin glaze, ca 1963, 9" **250.00**
Flask, Old Ivory Ware, mk, #2902, ca 1899, 14" w/stopper **750.00**
Jardiniere, thistles, majolica, #5454, ca 1899, 18", NM **6,500.00**
Jug, 6 appl/rtcl medallions on gr, gold trim, #763, 9¼" **260.00**
Tray, Crayfish & Snake re-release, Eosin glaze, 6" dia **150.00**
Vase, bl/red/purple metallic, Pécs/Made in Hungary, 7¾" **375.00**
Vase, designed by Eva Zeisel, gr Eosin glaze, 10" **800.00**

Advisory Board

The editors and staff take this opportunity to express our sincere gratitude and appreciation to each person who has in any way contributed to the preparation of this guide. We believe the credibility of our book is greatly enhanced through their efforts. See each advisor's Directory listing for information concerning their specific areas of expertise.

You will notice that at the conclusion of some of the narratives the advisor's name is given. This is optional and up to the discretion of each individual. Simply because no name is mentioned does not indicate that we have no advisor for that subject. Our board grows with each issue and now numbers nearly 450; if you care to correspond with any of them or anyone listed in our Directory, you must send a SASE with your letter. If you are seeking an appraisal, first ask about their fee, since many of these people are professionals who must naturally charge for their services. Because of our huge circulation, every person who allows us to publish their name runs the risk of their privacy being invaded by too many phone calls and letters. We are indebted to every advisor and very much regret losing any one of them. By far, the majority of those we lose give that reason. Please help us retain them on our board by observing the simple rules of common courtesy. Take the differences in time zones into consideration; some of our advisors tell us they often get phone calls in the middle of the night. For suggestions that may help you evaluate your holdings, see the Introduction.

AAA Antique Shop
Nappanee, Indiana

Peter Abrahams
Lake Oswego, Oregon

Charles and Barbara Adams
Middleboro, Massachusetts

Geneva D. Addy
Winterset, Iowa

Stan and Sally Alekna
Jacksonville, Florida

Charles Alexander
Indianapolis, Indiana

Margaret Alves
Shelton, Connecticut

Craig Ambrose
Des Moines, Iowa

James Anderson
New Brighton, Minnesota

Suzy McLennan Anderson
Holmdel, New Jersey

Tim Anderson
Provo, Utah

Warren R. Anderson
Cedar City, Utah

Dorothy Malone Anthony
Fort Scott, Kansas

Pamela Apakarian-Russell
Winchester, New Hampshire

John Apple
Racine, Wisconsin

Una Arnbal
Ames, Iowa

Bruce A. Austin
Pittsford, New York

Bobby Babcock
Austin, Texas

Veldon Badders
Hamlin, New York

Rod Baer
Vienna, Virginia

Wayne and Gale Bailey
Dacula, Georgia

Roger Baker
Woodside, California

Robert Banks
Brookeville, Maryland

Jim Barker
Bethlehem, Pennsylvania

Kit Barry
Brattleboro, Vermont

Henry Bartsch
Rockaway, Oregon

Mark Bassett
Lakewood, Ohio

Dana Martin Batory
Crestline, Ohio

D.R. Beeks
Mt. Vernon, Iowa

Scott Benjamin
LaGrange, Ohio

Phyllis and Tom Bess
Tulsa, Oklahoma

Robert Bettinger
Mt. Dora, Florida

John E. Bilane
Union, New Jersey

Brenda Blake
York Harbor, Maine

Clarence H. Bodine, Jr.
New Hope, Pennsylvania

Sandra V. Bondhus
Unionville, Connecticut

Clifford Boram
Monticello, Indiana

Jeff Bradfield
Dayton, Virginia

Larry Brenner
Manchester, New Hampshire

William J. Brinkley
McLeansboro, Illinois

Mike Brooks
Oakland, California

Jim Broom
Effingham, Illinois

David L. Brown
Victoria, British Columbia, Canada

Marcia Brown
White City, Oregon

Rick Brown
Newspaper Collector's Society of America
Lansing, Michigan

Nicki Budin
Worthington, Ohio

Richard M. (Dick) Bueschel
Mt. Prospect, Illinois

Robert C. Butz
Newbury Park, California

Jim Calison
Wallkill, New York

Carol and Jim Carlton
Englewood, Colorado

Tina M. Carter
El Cajon, California

Gene Cataldo
Huntsville, Alabama

Cerebro
East Prospect, Pennsylvania

Mick and Lorna Chase
Cookeville, Tennessee

Jack Chipman
Venice, California

Pat and Chris Christensen
Costa Mesa, California

Joan Cimini
Belmont, Ohio

Debbie and Randy Coe
Lafayette, Oregon

Wilfred and Dolli Cohen
Santa Ana, California

Lillian M. Cole
Flemington, New Jersey

Marilyn Cooper
Houston, Texas

J.W. Courter
Kevil, Kentucky

Susan Cox
El Cajon, California

Rosalind Cranor
Blacksburg, Virginia

Bob Culver
Northville, Michigan

Ron Damaska
New Brighton, Pennsylvania

John Danis
Rockford, Illinois

Patricia M. Davis
Portland, Oregon

Richard K. Degenhardt
Hendersonville, North Carolina

Loretta DeLozier
Bedford, Iowa

Joe Devine
Council Bluffs, Iowa

Doug Dezso
Maywood, New Jersey

Thomas P. Dimitroff
Corning, New York

Ginny Distel
Tiffin, Ohio

Rod Dockery
Ft. Worth, Texas

L.R. 'Les' Docks
San Antonio, Texas

Rebecca Dodds
Ft. Lauderdale, Florida

Maryanne Dolan
Pleasant Hill, California

Pat Dole
Birmingham, Alabama

Ron Donnelly
Tuscaloosa, Alabama

Robert A. Doyle, C.A.I., I.S.A.
Fishkill, New York

James Dryden
Hot Springs National Park, Arkansas

Louise Dumont
Coventry, Rhode Island

Pat and Ann Duncan
Cape Fair, Missouri

Ken and Jackie Durham
Washington, DC

William Durham
Belvidere, Illinois

Rita and John Ebner
Columbus, Ohio

Bill Edwards
Madison, Indiana

Auction Houses

We wish to thank the following auction houses whose catalogs have been used as sources for pricing information. Many have granted us permission to reproduce their photographs as well.

A-1 Auction Service
P.O. Box 540672, Orlando, FL 32804;
407-839-0004. Specializing in American antique sales

A&B Auctions, Inc.
17 Sherman St., Marlboro, MA
01752; 508-480-0006 or Fax 508-460-6101. Specializing in English and
Mason's Ironstone

Absolute Auction & Realty, Inc./
Pleasant Valley Auction Hall
Robert Doyle
P.O. Box 658, 348 Main St., Beacon,
NY 12524. Antique and estate auctions
every month at their Beacon gallery,
twice a month at Pleasant Valley Auction Hall; Free calendar of auctions;
Web site: www.auctionweb.com/aar-ny

Alex G. Malloy, Inc.
P.O. Box 38, South Salem, NY 10590;
203-438-0396. Specializing in ancient and
medieval coins, antiquities, numismatic
literature; four mail bid auctions per year

America West Archives
Anderson, Warren
P.O. Box 100, Cedar City, UT 84721;
435-586-9497; Publishes 26-page
illustrated catalog six times a year that
includes auction section of scarce and
historical early western documents,
letters, autographs, stock certificates,
and other important ephemera, Subscription: $15 per year

Americana Auctions
c/o Glen Rairigh
12633 Sandborn, Sunfield, MI 48890.
Specializing in Skookum dolls

Andre Ammelounx
The Stein Company
P.O. Box 136, Palatine, IL 60078; 708-991-5927 or Fax 708-991-5947. Specializing in steins, catalogs available

Anthony J. Nard & Co.
U.S. Rt. 220, Milan, PA 18831; 717-888-9404 or Fax 717-888-7723

Arman Absentee Auctions
16 Sixth St., Stamford, CT 06905;
203-928-5838. Specializing in American glass, Historical Staffordshire,
English soft paste, paperweights

The Arts & Crafts Emporium
434 N. La Brea Ave., Los Angeles,
CA 90036; 213-935-3777

Aston Macek Auctioneers and Appraisers
2825 Country Club Rd., Endwell, NY
13760-3349; Phone/Fax 607-785-6598. Specializing in and appraisers of
Americana, folk art, other primitives,
furniture, fine glassware and china

Bill Bertoia Auctions
2413 Madison Ave., Vineland, NJ
08360; 609-692-4092 or Fax 609-692-8697. Specializing in toys, dolls,
advertising, and related items

Bider's
241 S. Union St., Lawrence, MA
01843; 508-688-4347 or 508-683-3944. Antiques appraised, purchased,
and sold on consignment

Brian Riba Auctions Inc.
P.O. Box 53, Main St., S. Glastonbury, CT 06073; 203-633-3076

Butterfield & Butterfield
220 San Bruno Ave., San Francisco, CA
91043; 415-861-7500 or Fax 415-861-8951. Also located at 7601 Sunset Blvd.,
Los Angeles, CA 90046; 213-850-7500
or Fax 213-850-5843. Fine Art Auctioneers and Appraisers since 1865

Cerebro
P.O. Box 327, E. Prospect, PA
17317-0327; 717-252-2400 or 800-69-LABEL. Specializing in antique
advertising labels, especially cigar
box labels, cigar bands, food labels,
firecracker labels; Holds semiannual
auction on tobacco ephemera; Consignments accepted;
E-mail: Cerebro@Cerebro.com

Charles E. Kirtley
P.O. Box 2273, Elizabeth City, NC
27096; 919-335-1262. Specializing in
World's Fair, Civil War, political, advertising, and other American collectibles

Cincinnati Art Gallery
635 Main St., Cincinnati, OH 45202;
513-381-2128. Specializing in American art pottery, American and European fine paintings, watercolors

Col. Doug Allard
P.O. Box 460, St. Ignatius, MT
59865-0460; 406-745-2951 or
Fax 406-745-2961

Collector's Auction Services
R.D. 2, Box 431, Oil City, PA 16301;
814-677-6070. Specializing in advertising, oil and gas, toys, rare museum
and investment-quality antiques

Collector's Sales & Service
P.O. Box 4037, Middletown, RI
02842; 401-849-5012 or
Fax 401-846-6156

Country Girls Estate & Appraisal Service
Diane Patalano
P.O. Box 144, Saddle River, NJ 07458

Dargate Auction Galleries
5607 Baum Boulevard, Pittsburgh, PA
15206; 412-362-3558 Specializing in
porcelain, furniture, lighting, silver, glass,
art, jewelry and Orientalia

David Rago
20th Century Design
Auction hall: 333 N. Main, Lambertville, NJ 08530; 609-397-7330;
Gallery: 17 S. Main St., Lambertville,
NJ 08530. Specializing in American
art pottery and Arts & Crafts

Dunbar's Gallery
Leila and Howard Dunbar
76 Haven St., Milford, MA 01757;
508-634-8697 or Fax 508-634-8698

Dunning's
755 Church Rd., Elgin, IL 60123;
708-741-3483 or 312-664-8400

Dynamite Auctions
Franklin Antique Mall & Auction Gallery
1280 Franklin Ave., Franklin, PA
16323; 814-432-8577 or 814-786-9211

Du Mouchelles
409 Jefferson Ave., Detroit, MI 48226

Early American Numismatics
Dana Linett, President
P.O. Box 2442, La Jolla, CA 92038

Early Auction Co.
123 Main St., Milford, OH 45150

Flying Deuce Auctions & Antiques
1224 Yellowstone Ave., Pocatello, ID
83201; 208-237-2002 or Fax 208-237-4544; E-mail: flying2@nicoh.com or
Web site: www.flying2.com

Frank's Antiques & Auctions
222 S. Kings Rd., Hilliard, FL 32046;
904-845-2870 or Fax 904-845-4000.
Specializing in antique advertising,
country store items, rec room and
restaurant decor as well as sporting
collectibles, pottery and stoneware;
catalogs issued

Freeman Fine Arts
1808 Chestnut St., Philadelphia, PA
19103; 215-563-9275 or Fax 215-563-8236

Full House
Gene Willett
9090 Cherokee, Clarkston, MI 48348;
248-394-0313. Specializing in mail-bid playing card auctions

Garth's Auctions Inc.
2690 Stratford Rd., Box 369,
Delaware, OH 43015; 614-362-4771

Glass-Works Auctions
James Hagenbuch
102 Jefferson, East Greenville, PA
18041; 215-679-5849. America's leading auction company in early American bottles and glass

Hake's Americana & Collectibles
Specializing in character and personality collectibles along with all artifacts of popular culture for over 20
years. To receive a catalog for their
next 3,000-item mail/phone bid auction, send $5 to Hake's Americana,
P.O. Box 1444M, York, PA 17405.

Hanna-Whysel Auctioneers & Appraisers
Steven Whysel
3403 Bella Vista Way, Bella Vista,
AR, 72714; 501-855-9600. Antiques
and art auctions

Harmer Rooke Galleries 32 E. 57th
St, 11th Floor, New York, NY 10022;
212-751-1900 or Fax 212-758-1713

Henry/Pierce Auctioneers
1456 Carson Court, Homewood, IL
60430; 708-798-7508. Specializing in
bank auctions.

Horst Auctioneers
Horst Auction Center
50 Durlach Rd. (corner of Rt. 322 &
Durlach Rd., West of Ephrata),
Ephrata, Lancaster County, PA
17522; 717-859-1331 or 717-738-3080. Voices of Experience

Jack Sellner
Sellner Marketing of California
P.O. Box 308, Fremont, CA 94536;
415-745-9463

Jackson's, Auctioneers & Appraisers
of Fine Art
2229 Lincoln St., Cedar Falls, IA
50613; 319-277-2256 or Fax 319-277-1252. Specializing also in art pottery,
jewelry, and decorative arts

James D. Julia
P.O. Box 210, Showhegan Rd.,
Fairfield, ME 04937

James R. Bakker Antiques, Inc.
James R. Bakker
370 Broadway, Cambridge, MA
02139; 617-864-7067. Specializing in
American paintings, prints, and decorative arts

John Toomey Gallery
818 North Blvd., Oak Park, IL 60301;
708-383-5234 or Fax 708-383-4828.
Specializing in furniture and decorative
arts of the Arts & Crafts, Art Deco,
and Modern Design movements; Modern Design Expert: Richard Wright

Joy Luke Fine Arts Brokers and Auctioneers
The Gallery
300 East Grove St., Bloomington, IL
61701; 309-828-5533

Ken Farmer Realty & Auction Company
1122 Norwood St., Radford, VA 24141;
703-639-0939 or Fax 703-639-1759

Kerry & Judy's Toys
7370 Eggleston Rd., Memphis, TN
38125-2112; 901-757-1722. Specializing in toys, 1900 – 1960s; Consignments always welcome.

Kit Barry Ephemera Auctions
88 High St., Brattleboro, VT 05301;
802-254-3634. Tradecard and ephemera auctions, fully illustrated catalogs with prices realized; Consignment inquiries welcome.

Kurt R. Krueger
160 N. Washington St., P.O. Box
275, Iola, WI 54945-0275

L.R. 'Les' Docks
Box 691035, San Antonio, TX 78269-1035. Providing occasional mail-order record auctions, rarely consigned. The only consignments considered are exceptionally scarce and unusual records.

Liberty Historic Manuscripts
300 Kings Hwy. East, Haddonfield,
NJ 08033

Litchfield, Auction Gallery
425 Bantam Rd., P.O. Box 1337,
Litchfield, CT 06759; 203-567-3126
or Fax 203-567-3266

Lloyd Ralston Toys
447 Stratford Rd., Fairfield, CT 06432

Manion's International Auction
House, Inc.
P.O. Box 12214, Kansas City, KS
66112; 913-299-6692 or Fax 913-299-6792; E-mail: manions@qni.com
URL: www.manions.com
Specializing in international militaria, particularly the U.S., Germany, and Japan. Extensive catalogs in antiques and collectibles, sports, transportation, political and advertising memorabilia, and vintage clothing and denim. Publishes nine catalogs for each of the five categories per year. Request a free sample of past auctions, 1 issue of current auction for $7 or a 6-catalog subscription for $35.

Maritime Auctions
R.R. 2, Box 45A, York, ME 03909;
207-363-4247

Michael Ivankovich Auctions, Inc.
P.O. Box 2458, Doylestown, PA, 18901;
215-345-6094. Specializing in early hand-colored photography and prints. Auction held four times each year, providing opportunity for collectors and dealers to compete for the largest variety of Wallace Nutting and Wallace Nutting-Like pictures available anywhere.

Michael John Verlangieri
20th Century Arts & Design
P.O. Box 844, Cambria, CA 93428;
805-927-4428. Specializing in fine mid-century California pottery; holds cataloged auctions (video tapes available); E-mail: INTERNET:
71332.3017@compuserve.com

McMasters Doll Auctions
P.O. Box 1755, 5855 Glenn Highway
Rd., Cambridge, OH 43725; 614-432-4320 or Fax 614-432-3191

Mid-Hudson Auction Galleries
One Idlewild Ave., Cornwall-on-Hudson, NY 12520; 914-534-7828 or
Fax 914-534-4802

Monsen & Baer, Annual Perfume
Bottle Auction
Randall Monsen and Rod Baer
Box 529, Vienna, VA 22183; 703-938-2129 or Fax 703-242-1357. Cataloged auctions of perfume bottles; Will purchase, sell, and accept consignments; Specializing in commercial, Czechoslovakian, Lalique, Baccarat, Victorian, crown top, factices, miniatures

Neal Auction Company
4038 Magazine St., New Orleans, LA
70115; 504-899-5329 or 1-800-467-5329 or 504-897-3803

Noel Barrett Antiques & Auctions
P.O. Box 1001, Carversville, PA 18913;
215-297-5109 or Fax 215-297-0457

New England Absentee Auctions
16 6th St., Stamford, CT 06905; 203-975-9055. Specializing in Quimper pottery

Norman C. Heckler & Company
79 Bradford Corner Rd., Woodstock
Valley, CT 06282; 860-794-1634 or Fax
860-974-2003. Auctioneers and appraisers specializing in early glass and bottles

Nostalgia Co.
21 S. Lake Dr., Hackensack, NJ
07601; 201-488-4536

Past Tyme Pleasures
Steve Howard
101 1st St., Suite 404, Los Altos, CA
94022; 510-484-4488 or Fax 510-484-2551. Offers two absentee auction catalogs per year pertaining to old advertising items

Phillips
406 E. 79th St., New York, NY 10021

Postcards International
P.O. Box 2930, New Haven, CT
06515-0030; 203-865-0814 or Fax
203-495-8005

Rafael Osona, Auctioneer & Appraiser
P.O. Box 2607, Nantucket, MA
02584; 508-228-3942. Specializing in Americana, Fine Arts, Continental & Marine Antiques

Refinders
737 Barberry Rd., Highland Park, IL
60035; 708-831-1102 or 708-831-1160. Refinders will find your wants from 1860 to 1960

Rex Stark Auctions
49 Wethersfield Rd., Bellingham, MA
02019

Richard A. Bourne Co. Inc.
Estate Auctioneers & Appraisers
Box 141, Hyannis Port, MA 02647;
617-775-0797

Richard Opfer Auctioneering, Inc.
1919 Greenspring Dr., Timonium,
MD 21093; 301-252-5035

Roan, Inc.
Box 118, R.D. 3, Cogan Station, PA
17728

Schoolmaster Auctions and Collectibles
Kenn Norris
P.O. Box 4830; 513 N. 2nd St., Sanderson, TX 79848; 915-345-2640. Specializing in school-related items, barbed wire and related literature, and L'il Abner

Shot Glass Exchange
P.O. Box 219, Western Springs, IL,
60558; 706-246-1559. Publishes mail-auction catalog twice yearly

Skinner, Inc.
Auctioneers & Appraisers of Antiques
and Fine Arts
The Heritage on the Garden, 63 Park
Plaza, Boston, MA 02116; 617-350-5400
or Fax 617-350-5429. Second address:
357 Main Street, Boston, MA 01740;
508-779-6241 or Fax 508-779-5144

Smith & Jones, Inc.
12 Clark Lane; Sudbury, MA 01776;
508-443-5517 or Fax 508-443-8045.
Specializing in Dedham dinnerware,
Buffalo china, and important American
art pottery; Full-color catalogs available

Soldiers Trunk
60 Craigs Rd., Windsor, CT 06095;
203-688-0580. Specializing in American and foreign military items; four
catalog issues for $20

Sotheby Parke Bernet, Inc.
980 Madison Ave., New York, NY
10021

Stanton's, Auctioneers & Realters
144 S. Main St., P.O. Box 146, Vermontville, MI 49096; 517-726-0181 or
Fax 517-726-0060. Specializing in all
types of property, at auction, anywhere

Steffen Historical Militaria
Roger S. Steffen
14 Murnan Rd., Cold Springs, KY
41076; 606-431-4499. Specializing in
quality militaria, military art, rare
books, antique firearms

Three Rivers Collectibles
Wendy and Leo Frese
P.O. Box 551542, Dallas, TX 75355;
214-341-5165. Annual Red Wing and
RumRill pottery and stoneware auctions

Toy Scouts, Inc.
137 Casterton Ave., Akron, OH
44303; 330-836-0668 or Fax 330-869-8668; Specializing in baby-boom era
collectibles. E-mail:
toyscout@newreach.net or Web site:
http://www.csmonline.com/toyscouts/

Tradewinds Auctions
Henry and Nancy Taron
P.O. Box 249, Manchester-by-the-Sea, MA 01944-0249; 508-768-3327

Treadway Gallery, Inc.
2029 Madison Rd., Cincinnati, OH
45208; 513-321-6742 or Fax 513-871-7722. Specializing in American Art
Pottery; American and European art
glass; European ceramics; Italian glass;
fine American and European paintings
and graphics; and furniture and decorative arts of the Arts & Crafts, Art
Nouveau, Art Deco, and Modern
Design Movements. Modern design
expert: Thierry Lorthioir. Members:
National Antique Dealers Association,
American Art Pottery Association,
International Society of Appraisers,
American Ceramic Arts Society, Ohio
Decorative Arts Society, Art Gallery
Association of Cincinnati

Vicki and Bruce Waasdorp
P.O. Box 434; 10931 Main St.;
Clarence, NY 14031; 716-759-2361.
Specializing in decorated stoneware

Weschler's
Adam A. Weschler & Son
905 E. St. N.W., Washington, DC 20004

Willis Henry Auctions
22 Main St., Marshfield, MA 02050

Directory of Contributors

When contacting any of the buyers/sellers listed in this part of the Directory by mail, you must include an SASE (stamped, self-addressed envelope) if you expect a reply. As hectic as our lifestyles are, the time it saves them is probably worth more to them than the price of a stamp. Not only that, but trying to decipher someone's handwritten name and address can be very frustrating. Sometimes even zip codes are unreadable, and even more time is required to double check zip code numbers. And in the end, if 'Rosen' becomes 'Rirer' and 'Ave. 5' becomes 'Ave. S,' even if the person you contacted was gracious enough to answer you, you probably won't ever know he did. Many of these people are professional appraisers and there will be a fee for their time and service. Find out up front. Include a clear photo if you want an item identified. Most items cannot be described clearly enough to make an identification without a photo.

If you call and get their answering machine, when you leave your number so that they can return your call, tell them to call back collect. And please take the differences in time zones into consideration. 7:00 AM in the Midwest is only 4:00 AM in California! And if you're in California, remember that even 7:00 PM is too late to call the East Coast. Most people work and are gone during the daytime. Even some of our antique dealers say they prefer after-work phone calls. Don't assume that a person who deals in a particular field will be able to help you with related items. They may seem related to you when they are not.

Please, we need your help. This book sells in such great numbers that allowing their names to be published can create a potential nightmare for each advisor and contributor. Please do your part to help us minimize this, so that we can retain them on our board and in turn pass their experience and knowledge on to you through our book. Their only obligation is to advise us, not to evaluate your holdings. Many of our people tell us that even with the occasional problem, they feel that the good outweighs the bad and makes all their hard work worthwhile.

Alabama

Cataldo, Gene
Gene's Cameras
2603 Artie St., S.W., Ste. 16,
Huntsville, 35805; 205-536-6893.
Specializing in classic and used cameras

Dole, Pat
9825 Red Mill Rd., Birmingham,
35215; 205-833-9853. Specializing in
Purinton pottery

Donnelly, Ron
Saturday Heroes
6302 Championship Dr., Tuscaloosa,
35405. Specializing in Big Little Books,
movie posters, premiums, western
heroes, Gone With the Wind, character
collectibles, early Disney; Inquiries
require SASE; No free appraisals

Lippa, Matt; and Schaaf, Elizabeth
Artisans
P.O. Box 256, Mentone, 35984; 256-
634-4037. Specializing in folk art,
quilts, painted and folky furniture,
tramp art, whirligigs, windmill
weights; Further contacts:
http://www.folkartisans.com or
artisans@folkartisans.com

Luckey, Carl
Carl F. Luckey Communications
1973 Lingerlost Trail, Killen, 35645.
Free-lance writer specializing in art,
antiques, and collectibles. No
telephone calls will be accepted;
SASE required for correspondence.

Walthall, Judith and Robert
P.O. Box 4465, Huntsville, 35815; 256-
881-9198. Judith founded Peanut Pals
in 1978. Robert is serving second term
as president of Peanut Pals. Specializing
in Planters Peanuts memorabilia; also
Old Crow collectibles

Arizona

Nelson, Maxine
7657 E. Hazelwood St., Scottsdale,
85251. Specializing in Vernon Kilns;
Author of Collectible Vernon Kilns (out of
print). SASE appreciated for inquiries.

Webb, Maret
Vehr/Webb Studio Architects
4118 E. Vernon Ave., Phoenix,
85008-2333; 602-957-0653 or Fax
602-957-1631. Specializing in
Swarovski crystal; Founder of Swan
Seekers Network

Arkansas

Dryden, James
Dryden Pottery
P.O. Box 603, Hot Springs National
Park, 71902; 501-627-4201.
Specializing in hand-thrown artware
vases, mugs, ovenware, etc.

Gifford, David Edwin
P.O. Box 7617, Little Rock, 72217;
501-664-0902. Author of Collector's
Encyclopedia of Niloak Pottery (out of
print) and The Collector's Encyclopedia of
Camark Pottery, Volume 1 (early art
pottery production); Autographed copies
of Camark book available from author
for $25 ppd.

Musgrave, Marge
Look Nook Antiques
10757 Hwy. 5-S, Salesville, 72653-
9698; 870-499-5283. Specializing in
colored Victorian and art glass

Yohe, Darlene
Timberview Antiques
P.O. Box 343, Stuttgart, 72160; 870-
673-3437. Specializing in American
pattern glass, historical glass,
Victorian pattern glass, carnival glass,
and custard glass

California

Aldrich, Jon Wm.
Jon Aldrich Antique Aero
P.O. Box 706, Groveland, 95321; 209-
962-6121. Specializing in vintage aviation

Baker, Roger
Baker's Lady Luck Emporium
Box 620417, Woodside, 94062.
Specializing in Saloon Americana —
advertising, gambling, bar bottles, cigar
lighters, match safes, bowie knives
(1830 – 1900), dirks, daggers, cowboy
hats, spurs, chaps, saddles, barber
items: bottles, shaving mugs, razors

Berg, Paul
P.O. Box 8895, Newport Beach, 92620.
Author of Nineteenth Century
Photographica Cases and Wall Frames

Brooks, Mike
7335 Skyline, Oakland, 94611; 510-
339-1751 (evenings). Specializing in
typewriters, transistor radios, early
televisions, Statue of Liberty

Bueschel, Richard M.
414 N. Prospect Manor Ave., Mt.
Prospect, 60056-2046; 847-253-0791.
Specializing in saloon, coin-operated
machines, trade catalogs

Butz, Robert C.
Collector's Wedgwood
P.O. Box 462, Newbury Park, 91319.
Specializing in Wedgwood; SASE
required for reply

Carter, Tina M.
882 S. Mollison, El Cajon, 92020; 619-
440-5043. Specializing in teapots, tea-
related items, tea tins, children's and toy
tea sets, plastic cookie cutters, etc. Book
on teapots available. Send $16 (includes
postage) or $17 for CA residents,
Canada: add $5, to above address.

Chipman, Jack
California Spectrum
P.O. Box 1079, Venice, 90294-1079.
Specializing in California ceramics;
author of Collector's Encyclopedia of
California Pottery, and Collector's
Encyclopedia of Bauer Pottery,
autographed copies available from
author; either book: $28.45 ppd.,
+(CA) tax of $2.35

Christensen, Pat and Chris
1067 Salvador St., Costa Mesa,
92626. Specializing in open salts

Cohen, Wilfred and Dolli
Antiques & Art Glass
P.O. Box 27151, Santa Ana, 92799;
714-545-5673. Specializing in Wave
Crest (C.F. Monroe); Victorian-era art
and pattern glass (salt shakers,
toothpick holders, syrups, cruets, sugar
shakers, tumblers, biscuit jars, table
and pitcher sets); art glass and cameo
glass open salts; custard and ruby-
stained glass; burmese, peachblow, and
amberina glass; pottery by Moorcroft
(pre-1935 only); Buffalo (Deldare and
Emerald ware); Polia Pillin; Shelley
China; Chintz China; and Clarice
Cliff. Please include SASE for reply.

Cox, Susan N.
237 E. Main St., El Cajon, 92020;
619-447-0800. Specializing in
California pottery and Frankoma

Dolan, Maryanne
138 Belle Ave., Pleasant Hill, 94523.
Specializing in and author of several
informative books on vintage clothing;
E-mail: 72144,1353@compuserve.com

Ehrhard, J. David
Psycho-Ceramic Restorations
7212 Valmont St., Tujunga, 91042.
Specializing in restoration of
ceramics, collects Susie Cooper and
other British pottery, Mabel Lucie
Attwell, 'Old Bill' china by Grimades,
etc., Artist: Bruce Bairnsfather

Ellis, Mike
266 Rose Ln., Costa Mesa, 92627;
714-645-4697. Author (Collector
Books) of *Collector's Guide to Don
Winton Designs, Identification &
Values*; Specializing in Twin Winton

Enge, Delleen
Franciscan Dinnerware Matching
Service
323 E. Matilija, Ste. 112, Ojai, 93023.

Escoe, Adrienne S.
4448 Ironwood Ave., Seal Beach,
90740-2926; 562-598-1585.
Specializing in glass knives; E-mail:
escoebliss@earthlink.net

Fogleman, Marv
Marv's Memories
1814 W. Carriage Dr., Santa Ana, 92704.
Specializing in Western Dinnerware,
Metlox, Mikasa, and Franciscan

George, Tony
22431-B160 Antonio Pkwy., #252,
Rancho Santa Margarita, 92688; 714-
589-6075. Specializing in watch fobs

Giacomini, Mary Jane
P.O. Box 404, Ferndale, 95536-0404.
Author of *American Bisque, A
Collector's Guide With Prices*;
Specializing in American Bisque
Pottery, cookie jars; E-mail:
Giaco@humboldt1.com

Gibson, Pat
38280 Guava Dr., Newark, 94560; 510-
792-0586. Specializing in R.A. Fox

Gunther, Candace (Candelaine)
Specializing in Steiff and Schuco
bears and animals; Phone 616-796-
4568; Fax 626-796-7172; E-mail:
candelain@aol.com

Harrison, Gwynne
P.O. Box 1, Mira Loma, 91752-0001;
909-685-5434. Specializing in
Autumn Leaf (Jewel Tea)

Hibbard, Suzi
WanderWares
2570 Walnut Blvd. #20, Walnut
Creek, 94596. Specializing in
Dragonware, 1000 Faces china, other
Orientalia. Inquiries should be
accompanied by LSASE. Also
available at: HMBK24A@Prodigy.com

Howard, Steve
Past Tyme Pleasures
101 1st St., Suite 404, Los Altos,
94022; 510-484-4488 or Fax 510-484-
2551. Specializing in antique
American firearms, bowie knives,
Western Americana, old advertising,
and vintage gambling items

Inouye, Roger
2622 Valewood Ave, Carlsbad,
92008-7925. Specializing in trolls

Main Street Antique Mall
237 E Main St., El Cajon, 92020; 619-
447-0800

Maurer, Oveda L.
Oveda Maurer Antiques
34 Greenfield Ave., San Anselmo,
94960; 415-454-6439. Specializing in
18th-century and early 19th-century
American furniture, lighting, pewter,
hearthware, glass, folk art, and paintings

The Meadows Collection
Mark and Adela Meadows
P.O. Box 819, Carnelian Bay, 96104;
530-546-5516. Specializing in Gouda
and Quimper; lecturers, authors of
*Quimper Pottery, A Guide to Origins,
Styles, and Values*, serving on the
board of directors of the Associated
Antiques Dealers of America

Pardini, Dick
3107 N. El Dorado St., Dept. SAPG,
Stockton, 95204-3412; 209-466-5550
(recorder may answer). Specializing in
California Perfume Company items
dating from 1886 to 1928 and 'go-
with' related companies: buyer and
information center. Not interested in
items that have Avon, Perfection, or
Anniversary Keepsake markings.
California Perfume Company
offerings must be accompanied by a
photo, Xerox copy, or sketching along
with a condition report and, most
importantly, price wanted. Inquiries
require large SASE and must state
what information you are seeking; not
necessary if offering items for sale.

Roller, Gayle
P.O. Box 222, San Marcos, 92079-
0222. Specializing in Hagen-Renaker

Sanford, Steve and Martha
230 Harrison Ave., Campbell, 95008;
408-978-8408. Authors of two books, on
Brush-McCoy and *Sanford's Guide to
McCoy Pottery* (available from the
authors)

Shrader, Fred and Lila
Shrader Antiques
2025 Hwy. 199, Crescent City, 95531;
707-458-3525. Specializing in railroad,
steamship, and other transportation
memorabilia; Shelley china (and its
predecessor, Foley China); Buffalo
china and Buffalo Pottery including
Deldare; Niloak, and Zell (and Haag)

Stella's Collectibles
Pieces of the Past
19032 S. Vermont Ave., Torrance
(Space 11), 90503; 310-316-7198;
Julie's Antiques, Long Beach (Space
24); Westchester Faire Mall (Space
320); Enchanted Treasures, Lake
Elsinore (Space 25). Specializing in
quality glass and china

Thoerner, Sharon
15549 Ryon Ave., Bellflower, 90706;
562-866-1555. Specializing in covered
animal dishes, powder jars with
animal and human figures, slag glass

Thornton, Don
1345 Poplar Ave., Sunnyvale, 94087.
Specializing in egg beaters; author of
Beat This: The Eggbeater Chronicles
(out of print, new edition coming in
1999); and *Apple Parers* ($59 ppd.).

Webb, Frances Finch
1589 Gretel Lane, Mountain View,
94040. Specializing in Kay Finch ceramics

Zeder, Audrey
6755 Coralite St. S., Long Beach, 90808
(appointment only). Specializing in
British Royal Commemorative
Souvenirs (mail-order catalog available);
Author (Wallace-Homestead) of *British
Royal Commemoratives*

Canada

Brown, David L.
Stevengraph Collectors Assn.
2103-2829 Arbutus Rd., Victoria,
British Columbia, V8N 5X5; 250-477-
9896. Specializing in Stevengraphs

Melis, Mirko
Marcelle Antiques
P.O. Box 53039, 5100 Erin Mills
Pkwy., Mississauga, Ontario, L5M 4Z5;
905-689-1648. Specializing in
American and European art glass,
Russian works of art (enamels,
porcelains, silver, etc.), English and
Continental glass and china; Member
of Antique Appraisal Association of
America, Inc., and AADA (Associated
Antique Dealers of America, Inc.)

Warner, Ian
P.O. Box 93022, 499 Main St. S.,
Brampton, Ontario, L6Y 4V8; 905-453-
9074 or Fax 905-453-2931. Specializing
in Wade porcelain and Swankyswigs;
Author of *The World of Wade, The World
of Wade Book 2, Wade Price Trends*, and
The World of Head Vase Planters, Co-
author: Mike Posgay

Colorado

Carlton, Carol and Jim
8115 S. Syracuse St., Englewood,
80112; 303-773-8616. Specializing in
Broadmoor, Coors, and other
Colorado pottery

Heck, Carl
Carl Heck Decorative Arts
Box 8416, Aspen, 81612; Phone/Fax
970-925-8011. Specializing in original
Tiffany lamps, art glass, windows, and
chandeliers; Also reverse-painted and
leaded-glass table lamps, stained and
beveled glass windows, bronzes, paintings,
etc.; Buy and sell; Fee for written
appraisals. Please include SASE for reply.

Mackin, Bill
Author of *Cowboy and Gunfighter
Collectibles*; available from author: 1137
Washington St., Craig, 81625; 970-824-
6717; Paperback: $25; Other titles
available; Specializing in old and fine
spurs, guns, gun leather, cowboy gear,
Western Americana (Collection in the
Museum of Northwest Colorado, Craig)

Over, Naomi L.
8909 Sharon Lane, Arvada, 80002;
303-424-5922. Specializing in ruby
glassware, author of *Ruby Glass of the
20th Century*, available from author
for $24.50 softbound or $32.50 hardbound, ppd. Naomi will attempt to
make photo identifications for all who
include a SASE with correspondence.

Segelke, Cathy; and James, Pat
970-847-3759 (Pat). Specializing in
crocks, Western Pottery Mfg. Co.
(Denver, CO)

Toohey, Marlena
703 S. Pratt Pky., Longmont, 80501;
303-678-9726. Specializing in black
glass (buy, sell, or trade); Book
available from author for $20 ppd.

White, John 'Grandpa'
Grandpa's Depot
1616 17th St., Suite 267, Denver,
80202; 303-628-5590 or Fax 303-628-
5547. Specializing in railroad-related
items; Catalogs available

Winther, Jo Ellen
8449 W. 75th Way, Arvada, 80005;
800-872-2345 or 303-421-2371.
Specializing in Coors

Connecticut

Alves, Margaret
Spoonville Scoop
84 Oak Ave., Shelton, 06484; 203-
924-4768. Specializing in spoons:
plated, sterling, silver, pre-1920s

Bondhus, Sandra V.
Box 100, Unionville, 06085; 860-678-
1808. Author of *Quimper Pottery: A
French Folk Art Faience*; Specializing
in Quimper pottery

FDS Antiques, Inc.
62 Blue Ridge Dr., Stamford, 06903-
4923. Publishes *The 'No Nonsense'
Antique Mall Directory*, a directory of
antique malls, centers, and multi-
dealer co-ops; Over 4,700 listings
listed according to state

Guido, Karen M.
Karen Michelle
P.O. Box 489, Bridgewater, 06752.
Specializing in tiles; Buy & sell; Books
on tiles available, many out of print;
Fee for written appraisal. Please
include SASE for inquiries.

Kilbride, Mrs. Richard J.
81 Willard Terrace, Stamford, 06903;
203-322-0568. Has available for sale:
*Art Deco Chrome, The Chase Era, and
Art Deco Chrome, Book 2, A
Collector's Guide, Industrial Design in
the Chase Era*

MacSorley, Earl
823 Indian Hill Rd., Orange, 06477;
203-387-1793 (after 7:00 p.m.).
Specializing in nutcrackers, Bessie Pease
Gutmann prints, figural lift-top spittoons

Postcards International
Shapiro, Marty
P.O. Box 2930, New Haven, 06515-
0030; 203-865-0814 or Fax 203-495-
8005. Specializing in vintage picture
postcards

Roenigk, Martin
Mechantiques
26 Barton Hill, E. Hampton, 06424;
800-671-6333. Specializing in
mechanical musical instruments, music
boxes, band organs, musical clocks and
watches, coin pianos, orchestrions,
monkey organs, automata, mechanical
birds, and dolls, etc.

Thalberg, Bruce
Mountain View Dr., Weston, 06883;
203-227-8175. Specializing in canes
and walking sticks: novelty, carved,
and Black

Van Deusen, Hobart D.
28 The Green, Watertown, 06795;
860-945-3456. Specializing in
Canton. SASE required when
requesting information.

Vuono, Mark
16 6th St., Stamford, 06905; 203-357-
0892 (10 a.m. to 5:30 p.m. E.S.T.).
Specializing in historical flasks, blown
three-mold glass, blown American glass

District of Columbia
Durham, Ken and Jackie (By appointment)
909 26 St. N.W., Suite 502,
Washington, D.C. 20037. Specializing
in counter-top arcade machines, trade
stimulators, and vending machines;
16-page illustrated list: $2. Send
SASE for free list of books on coin-
operated machines. Web:
http://www.GameRoomAntiques.com

Nelson, Scott
1636 Nicholson St. N.W.,
Washington, D.C. 20011; Specializing
in African Art

Florida

Alekna, Stan and Sally
4724 Kernan Mill Lane East;
Jacksonville, 32224; 904-992-9525.
Specializing in toy soldiers

Bettinger, Robert
P.O. Box 333, Mt. Dora, 32756; 352-
735-3575. Specializing in American
art pottery

Cohen, Joel
Cohen Books & Collectibles
P.O. Box 810310, Boca Raton, 33481;
407-487-7888. Specializing in Disneyana

Kamm, Dorothy
P.O. Box 7460, Port St. Lucie, 34985-
7460; 561-465-4008 or Fax 407-460-
9050. Specializing in American
painted porcelain; Author of
*American Painted Porcelain:
Identification & Value Guide* (Collector
Books); Publishes *Dorothy Kamm's
Porcelain Collector's Companion*
bimonthly newsletter, subscription:
$28 per year

Dodds, Rebecca
Silver Flute
Box 480644, Ft. Lauderdale, 33348.
Specializing in jewelry

Elsner, Dr. Robert
29 Clubhouse Lane, Boynton Beach,
33436; 561-736-1362. Specializing in
antique barometers and nautical
instruments

France, Madeleine
P.O. Box 15555, Ft. Lauderdale,
33318; 305-584-0009. Specializing in
top-quality perfume bottles: Rene
Lalique, Steuben, Czechoslovakian,
DeVilbiss, Baccarat, Commercials;
French dore bronze and decorative arts

Hudson, Hardy
Our Antiques Market
5453 Lake Howell Rd., Winter Park,
32792; 407-657-2100 from 11:00 a.m. to
6:00 p.m. Specializing in majolica,
American art pottery (buying one piece or
entire collections); Also buying Weller
(garden ornaments, birds, Hudson, Sicard,
Sabrinian, Glendale, or animal related),
Roseville, Grueby, Newcomb, Overbeck,
Kay Finch, Clewell, Tiffany, etc.

Kuritzky, Louis
4510 NW 17th Place, Gainesville,
32605; 352-377-3193. Author
(Collector Books) of *Collector's Guide
to Bookends*

Lawrence, Judy and Cliff
1169 Overcash Dr., Dunedin, 34698.
Specializing in fountain pens and
mechanical pencils

Linscott, Jacqueline C.
Line Jewels
3557 Nicklaus Dr., Titusville, 32780.
Specializing in glass insulators and
other telephone items. Distributor of
the only known set of books dealing
with insulators, *North American Glass
Insulators* (2 volumes), and
accompanying price guide. LSASE
required for information.

McNerny, Kathryn
118 Creek Hollow Lane, Middleburg,
32068. Author (Collector Books) on blue
and white stoneware, primitives, tools

New World Maps, Inc.
Charles R. Neuschafer
1123 S. Broadway, Lantana, 33462-
4522; 407-586-8723. Buys and sells
antique and collectible maps,
specializing in 20th-century road maps;
Columnist for *Paper Collectors
Marketplace* and member of
International Map Dealers Association

Posner, Judy
October – May: P.O. Box 2194 SC,
Englewood, FL 34295; Fax 941-475-
2645. Specializing in Disneyana, Black
memorabilia, salt and pepper shakers,
souvenirs of the USA, character and
advertising memorabilia, figural
pottery; Buy, sell, collect; Informal
appraisals: $5+LSASE and photo of
item. E-mail: judyandjef@aol.com

Roush, Peggy E.
Peggy's Matching Service
P.O. Box 476, Ocala, 34478; 352-629-
3954. Specializing in discontinued
Noritake patterns; E-mail:
Pegsmatch@aol.com

Supnick, Mark
2771 Oakbrook Manor, Ft.
Lauderdale, 33332; Author of
*Collecting Hull Pottery's Little Red
Riding Hood* ($12.95 ppd.);
Specializing in American pottery

Vogel, Janice and Richard
4720 S.E. Fort King St., Ocala,
34470-1501. Authors of *Victorian
Trinket Boxes*

White, Douglass
Classic Interiors & Antiques
2042 N. Rio Grande Ave., Suite E,
Orlando, 32804; 407-839-0004.
Specializing in Fulper, Arts & Crafts
furniture (photos helpful)

Whysel, Steven
7867 N.W. 11th St., Plantation, 33322;
954-382-0008. Specializing in Art
Nouveau, 19th- and 20th-century art

Wise, Raphael C.
The Collector's Stop
12018 Suellen Circle, West Palm Beach,
33414; 561-793-0986. Specializing in
Wedgwood Jasper Ware, Rosenthal,
Moorcroft, Buffalo Deldare, and Emerald
Ware, Heisey, contemporary
paperweights, English porcelains

Georgia

Bailey, Wayne and Gale
P.O. Box 173, Dacula, 30019; 770-
963-5736. Specializing in Goebels
(Friar Tuck)

Glenn, Walter
Geode Ltd.
3393 Peachtree Rd., Atlanta, 30326;
404-261-9346. Specializing in Frankart

Joiner, John R.
Aviation Collectors
173 Green Tree Dr., Newnan, 30265;
770-502-9565. Specializing in
commercial aviation collectibles

Illinois

Ammelounx, Andre
The Stein Auction Company
P.O. Box 136, Palatine, 60078; 708-
991-5927 or Fax 708-991-5947.
Specializing in steins, catalogs available

The Barrel Antique Mall
5850 S St. Road, I-55 Exit 90,
Springfield, 62707; 217-585-1438

Brinkley, Wm. J.
Brinkley Galleries
401 S. Washington Ave.,
McLeansboro, 62859. Specializing in
Meissen, Dresden, European porcelains,
American porcelains (Cybis)

Broom, Jim
Box 65, Effingham, 62401. Specializing
in opalescent pattern glassware

Bueschel, Richard M. (Dick)
414 N. Prospect Manor Ave., Mt.
Prospect, 60056-2046; 847-253-0791
or Fax 847-253-7919. Specializing in
coin machines, trade catalogs, pre-
prohibition saloon, prohibition
speakeasy, screen doors, fretwork,
advertising folding chairs, food can
openers; Author of books relating to
coin-operated machines and saloon
collectibles (available from author)

Danis, John
11028 Raleigh Ct., Rockford, 61115;
815-877-6004 or Fax 815-877-6042.
Specializing in R. Lalique, Norse
pottery; E-mail: danis6033@aol.com

Feldman, Arthur M.
Arthur M. Feldman Gallery
1815 St. Johns Ave., Highland Park,
60035; 847-432-8858 or Fax 847-266-
1199. Specializing in Judaica, fine art,
and antiques

Frizzell, Doris
5687 Oakdale Dr., Springfield, 62707;
217-529-3873. Specializing in Royal
Haeger and Haeger and Royal
Hickman; Co-author (Collector Books)
of Royal Haeger book

Garmon, Lee
1529 Whittier St., Springfield, 62704;
217-789-9574. Specializing in Royal
Haeger, Royal Hickman, glass
animals; Co-author (Collector Books)
of *Glass Animals and Figural Flower
Frogs of the Depression Era*

Griffith, Woody
4132 N. Clarenden Ave., Chicago, 60613; 773-975-1957. Specializing in DeVilbiss perfumes and perfume lamps of the Deco period

Hall, Doris and Burdell
B&B Antiques
210 W. Sassafras Dr., Morton, 61550-1245. Authors of *Morton's Potteries: 99 Years* (Vols. I and II); Specializing in Morton pottery, American dinnerware, early American pattern glass, historical items

Hastings, Mary Jane
310 West 1st South, Mt. Olive, 62069; Phone/Fax 217-999-1222. Specializing in Chintz dinnerware

Hilst, Randy
1221 Florence #4, Pekin, 61554; 309-346-2710. Specializing in general line including fishing and hunting collectibles

Hoffmann, Pat and Don, Sr.
1291 N. Elmwood Dr., Aurora, 60506; 630-859-3435. Authors of *Warwick, A to W*, a supplement to *Why Not Warwick?*; video regarding Warwick decals currently available. P.C.: http://www.skognet.com/nwarwick/ or E-mail: warwick@skognet.com

The Home Place Antiques
Durham, William; Galaway, William
615 S. State St., Belvidiere, 61008; 815-544-0577. Specializing in Tea Leaf ironstone and white ironstone

Hooks, Dee
Dee's China Shop
P.O. Box 142, Lawrenceville, 62439-0142; 618-943-2741. Specializing in R.S. Prussia, Royal Bayreuth, Haviland, other fine china

Hopp, Dennis Carl
Midcentury
Chicago, 773-935-7872. Specializing in 20th-century design, glass, pottery, enamels, metal, art

Hurney, George and Mary
Glass Connection (mail-order only)
312 Babcock Dr., Palatine, 50067; 847-359-3839. Specializing in Depression glass and Paden City glass (not advising on pottery); E-mail: glasscon@starnetusa.com

The Illinois Antique Center
320 S.W. Commercial St., Peoria, IL 61602

International Society of Antique Scale Collectors
Bob Stein, President
300 W. Adams, Suite 821, Chicago, 60606; 312-263-7500. Publishes *Equilibrium Magazine*; President's newsletter; Annual membership directory; Out-of-print catalogs; Annual convention

John Toomey Gallery
818 N. Blvd, Oak Park, 60301

Long, Dee
112 S. Center, Lacon, 61540. Specializing in reamers

Lotton, Charles
Lotton Art Glass
1938 177th St., Lansing, 60438; 708-474-4022. Specializing in art glass

Lubliner, Larry
Refinders mail/telephone auction
737 Barberry Rd., Highland Park, 60035; 708-831-1102 or 708-831-1160. Refinders will find your wants from 1860 – 1960

Martin, Jim
R.R. 1, 1091 215th Ave., Monmouth, 61462; 309-734-2703. Specializing in Old Sleepy Eye, Monmouth pottery, Western Stoneware

Meyer, Larry
4001 Elmwood, Stickney, 60402; 708-749-1564. Specializing in fire grenades and extinguishers

Miller, Larry; and Strickfaden, Dick
218 Devron Circle, E. Peoria, 61611-1605. Specializing in German and Czechoslovakian Erphila

Ochsner, Grace
Grace Ochsner Doll House
1636 E. County Rd. 2700, Niota, 62358; 217-755-4362. Specializing in piano babies, bisque German dolls

Owen, Larry and Sally
Specializing in Morten Studio dogs, etc.

Randy's Ol' Time Collectibles
Illinois Antique Center
308 S.W. Commercial, Peoria, 61602; 309-346-2710. Specializing in general line, including hunting and fishing collectibles

Rastello, Lisa
Milkweed Antiques
5N531 Ancient Oak Lane, St. Charles, 60175; 708-377-4612. Specializing in Depression-era collectibles

Rhoden, Joan and Charles
Memories/Rhoden's Antiques
605 N. Main, Georgetown, 61846; 217-662-8046. Specializing in Heisey and other Elegant Glassware, general line antiques. Co-authors of *Those Wonderful Yard-Long Prints and More*, and *More Wonderful Yard-Long Prints, Book II*, and *Yard-Long Prints, Book III*, illustrated value guides

Rodgers, Joanne
Stretch Glass Society
P.O. Box 573, Hampshire, 60140. Membership: $18 per year; Quarterly newsletter with color photos; Annual spring convention

Spencer, Dick
Glass and More (Shows only)
1203 N. Yale, O'Fallon, 62269; 618-632-9067. Specializing in Cambridge, Fenton, Fostoria, Heisey, etc.

Spiess, Greg
230 E. Washington, Joliet, 60433; 815-722-5639. Specializing in Odd Fellows lodge items

Stifter, Donna & Craig
P.O. Box 6514, Naperville, 60540; 630-789-5780; Specializing in Coca-Cola, Pepsi-Cola, Orange Crush, Dr. Pepper, Hires, and other soda-pop brand collectibles; E-mail: cocacola@enteract.com

TV Guide Specialists
Box 20, Macomb 61455; 309-833-1809

Waite, Jim
112 N. Main St., Farmer City, 61842; 800-842-2593. Specializing in Sebastians

Wells, Rosalie J. 'Rosie'
22341 E. Wells Rd. S, Canton, 61520; 1-800-445-8745. Publishes *Collectors' Bulletin*, four magazines in one, including Precious Collectibles, The Ornament Collector, Collectors' Bulletin, and Beanie Digest, and annual price guides for Precious Moments Collectibles, Hallmark Ornaments, Merry Miniatures and Kiddie Car Classica, Boyds Bears and Friends, The Enesco Cherished Teddies Collection, Precious Moments Company's Dolls, and Beanie Babies! Check out Rosie's Internet site! http:/www.RosieWells.com. Rosie has hosted eight International Conventions for Precious Moments Collectors, hosts the semiannual Midwest Collectibles Fest, held in Westmont, IL, each March and October, and hosts the largest Beanie shows in the world! For hot tips and to record voice ads Rosie offers a touch-tone 900 line (1-900-740-7575). Send for a category list or see our web site! Call Rosie at 800-445-8745 for information on limited edition collectibles. E-mail: Rosie@RosieWells@aol.com

Wilson, Jack D.
P.O. Box 81974, Chicago, 60681-0974; 773-282-9553. Specializing in Phoenix and Consolidated glass; Buying Ruba Rombic; Author of *Phoenix & Consolidated Art Glass: 1926 – 1980*; E-mail: jdwilson@earthlink.net; Web site: http://home.earthlink.net/~jdwilson1/

Yester-Daze Glass
c/o Illinois Antique Center
320 S.W. Commercial St., Peoria, 61604; 309-347-1679. Specializing in glass from the 1920s, '30s, and '40s; Fiesta; Hall; Pie Birds; Sprinkler Bottles; and Florence figurines

Indiana

AAA Antique Shop
U.S. 6 West, Nappanee, 46550; 219-773-4912. Specializing in trunks

Alexander, Charles
221 E. 34th St., Indianapolis, 46205; 317-924-9665. Specializing in American dinnerware

Boram, Clifford
Antique Stove Information Clearinghouse
Monticello. Free consultation by phone only: 219-583-6465

Crossroads Antique Mall
311 Holiday Square, Seymour, 47274; 812-522-5675. Open 7 days a week

Edwards, Bill
620 W. 2nd, Madison, 47250. Author (Collector Books) on carnival glass

Fred, James A.
Antique Radio Labs
5355 So. 275W, Cutler, 46920; 765-268-2214. Specializing in radios made from 1922 to 1950

Garrett, Jerry and Sandi
Jerry's Antiques (Shows only)
1807 W. Madison St., Kokomo, 46901; 765-457-5256. Specializing in Greentown glass, old postcards

Gilley's Antique Mall and Collectibles
1209 W. Main (U.S. 40), Plainfield, 46168; 317-839-8779. Open daily from 10 a.m. to 5 p.m., features booths with over 250 dealers; Outdoor summer weekend flea market

Haun, Ted
2426 N. 700 East, Kokomo, 46901; 765-628-7028. Specializing in American pottery and china, '50s items, Russel Wright designs

Highfield, James
1601 Lincoln Way East, South Bend, 46613; 219-288-0300. Specializing in Capo-di-Monte-style porcelain (Doccia, Ginori, and Royal Naples). Look for upcoming book.

Heiss, Virginia
7777 N. Alton Ave., Indianapolis, 46268; 317-875-6797. Specializing in Muncie, AMACO, Brandt Steele, Marblehead, Kenton Hills

Keagy, William and June
P.O. Box 106, Bloomfield, 47424; 812-384-3471. Co-authors of *Those Wonderful Yard-Long Prints and More*, *More Wonderful Yard-Long Prints, Book II*, and *Yard-Long Prints, Book III*, illustrated value guides

Leslie, Beverly
Secretary/Treasurer of Uhl Collectors Society
801 Poplar St., Boonville, 47601; 812-897-3681. Contact for newsletter and membership information.

McQuillen, Michael J. and Polly
McQuillen's Collectibles
P.O. Box 11141, Indianapolis, 46201; 317-322-8518. Writer of column, Political Parade, which appears monthly in *AntiqueWeek* newspapers; Specializing in political campaign memorabilia, Kentucky Derby items, sports memorabilia; Buys and sells

Old Storefront Antiques
P.O. Box 357, Dublin, 47335; 317-478-4809. Specializing in country store items, tins, primitives, pharmaceuticals, advertising, etc.; Active in mail order with catalogs available. Information requires LSASE.

Pruitt, Ted
3350 W. 700 N., Anderson, 46011. *St. Clair Glass Collector's Book*, available ($15 ea) from Ted at above address

Scowden, Virgil
Williamsport, 47993; 317-762-3408 or 317-762-3178. Antiques museum, general line, tours

Slater, Thomas D.
Slater's Americana
1325 W. 86th St., Indianapolis, 46260; 317-257-0863. Specializing in political and sports memorabilia

Stofft, Jeanette
Marnette Antiques
Tell City, 47586; 812-547-5707. Specializing in Ohio art pottery, buy and sell; No phone appraisals; SASE required

Swayzee Antique Mall
115 N. Washington St., Swayzee, 46986; 317-922-7903

Vanderbilt, Duane and Janice
4040 W. Over Dr., Indianapolis, 46268; 317-875-8932. Authors (Collector Books) of *Collector's Guide to Shawnee Pottery*

Webb's Antique Mall
over 400 Quality Dealers
200 W. Union St., Centerville, 47330

Wright, Bill
325 Shady Dr., New Albany, 47150. Specializing in knives: Bowie, hunting, military, and pocketknives

Iowa

Addy, Geneva D.
P.O. Box 124, Winterset, 50273; 515-462-3027

Ambrose, Craig
Box 41338, Des Moines, 50311; 515-256-0339. Specializing in quilts; Author of *Picture Book and Price Guide to Antique Quilts*, available from author for $45+postage

Arnbal, Una
Woodland Antiques
242 Trail Ridge Rd., Ames, 50014; 515-292-1005. Specializing in china, glass, Lomonosov figurines, Danish collector plates

Beeks, Dale
P.O. Box 117, Mt. Vernon, 52314; 319-895-0506. Specializing in instruments of science technology and medicine, also surveying instruments and microscopes

Bilsland, William M., III
P.O. Box 2671, Cedar Rapids, 52406; 319-363-1193 or 319-368-0658 (message). Specializing in American art pottery

DeGood, Hal and Meredith
The Baggage Car
3100 Justin Dr., Suite B, Des Moines, 50322; 515-270-9080. Specializing in Hallmark collectibles; publishers of Hallmark newsletter

DeLozier, Loretta
1101 Polk St., Bedford, 50833; Monday – Friday: 9:00 a.m. to 4:00 p.m., 712-523-2289 or Fax 712-523-2624. Author (Collector Books) of *Collector's Encyclopedia of Lefton China, Identification & Values, Books I and II* and the *1998 Lefton Price Guide*; Specializing in Lefton China; Buy, sell & consign; Fee for written appraisals; Price list available for each pattern or series; E-mail: Leftonlady@AOL.com

Devine, Dennis; Norman; and Joe
D & D Antique Mall
1411 3rd St., Council Bluffs, 51503; 712-323-5233 or 712-328-7305. Specializing in furniture, phonographs, collectibles, general line. Joe Devine: Royal Copley collector

Jaarsma, Ralph
De Pelikaan Antieks
812 Washington St., c/o Red Ribbon Antique Mall, Pella, 50219. Specializing in Dutch antiques

Picek, Louis
Main Street Antiques
110 W. Main St., Box 340, West Branch, 52358. Specializing in folk art, country Americana, the unusual

Westmoreland Glass Society
Jim Fisher, President
513 5th Ave., Coralville, 52241; 319-354-5011. Membership: $15 (single) or $25 (household)

Kansas

Anthony, Dorothy Malone
World of Bells Publications
2401 S. Horton, Fort Scott, 66701; 316-223-3404. Specializing in publishing and selling books on all types of small bells

Hartl, Jeff; and Davis, Ann
Pigeon West
24 S. Silver, Paola, 66071; 913-294-9094. Specializing in Haeger

Maundy International
P.O. Box 13028-GG, Shawnee Mission, 66282; 1-800-235-2866. Specializing in watches — antique pocket and vintage wristwatches

Old World Antiques
4436 State Line Rd., Kansas City, 66103; 913-677-4744 or Fax 913-677-4879. Specializing in 18th- and 19th-century furniture, paintings, accessories, cocks, chandeliers, sconces, and much more.

Rash, Jim
135 Alder Ave., Pleasantville, 08232; 609-646-4125. Specializing in advertising, cereal, and cartoon figures

Smies, David
Pops Collectibles
Box 522, 315 So. 4th, Manhattan, 66502; 913-776-1433. Specializing in coins, stamps, cards, tokens, Masonic collectibles

Snyder, Charlie and Rose
Charlie's Collectables
R.R. 4, Box 79, Independence, 67301; 316-331-6259. Specializing in cookie jars and accessories, salt and pepper shakers, pottery

Street, Patti
Currier & Ives (China) Newsletter
P.O. Box 504, Riverton, 66770; 316-848-3529

Tinsley, Rosella
105 15th St., Osawatomie, 66064; 913-755-3237. Specializing in primitives, kitchen, farm, woodenware, and miscellaneous (phone calls only, no letters please)

Kentucky

Courter, J.W.
3935 Kelley Rd., Kevil, 42053; 502-488-2116. Specializing in Aladdin lamps; Author of *Aladdin — The Magic Name in Lamps, Revised Edition*, hardbound, 304 pages; and *Aladdin Electric Lamps*, softbound, 229 pages

Florence, Gene
Box 7186H, Lexington, 40522. Author (Collector Books) on Depression glass, occupied Japan; Elegant glass, kitchen glassware

Hornback, Betty
Betty's Antiques
707 Sunrise Lane, Elizabethtown, 42701; Specializing in Kentucky Derby glasses

Johnson, Wes, Sr.
RFD, Glenview, 40025. Specializing in Cracker Jack: toys, point of sale, packages, etc.; Checkers Confection, Schoenhut toys, Victor Toy Oats, Universal Theatre (Chicago), old toys. Please include SASE.

Ritchie, Roy B.
P.O. Box 384, Hindman, 41822; 606-785-5796. Co-author of *Standard Knife Collector's Guide* and *Standard Guide to Razors*; Specializing in razors and knives, all types of cutlery

Stewart, Ron
P.O. Box 151, Combs, 41729; 606-435-2412. Co-author of *Standard Knife Collector's Guide* and *Standard Guide to Razors*; Specializing in razors and knives, all types of cutlery

Willis, Roy M.
Heartland of Kentucky Decanters and Steins
P.O. Box 428, Lebanon Jct., 40150. Huge selection of limited edition decanters and beer steins — open showroom. Include large self-addressed envelope (two stamps) with correspondence. Fee for appraisals. Decanter price guide (listings only, no pictures, information on marketing decanters): $9.50 ppd. Web site: www.ka.net/heartlandky

Louisiana

Langford, Paris
Kollecting Kiddles
415 Dodge Ave., Jefferson, 70121; 504-733-0667. Specializing in all small vinyl dolls of the '60s and '70s; Author of *Liddle Kiddles Identification and Value Guide* (Collector Books)

Maine

Blake, Brenda
Box 555, York Harbor, 03911; 207-363-6566. Specializing in egg cups; E-mail: Eggcentric@AOL.com

Hathaway, John
Hathaway's Antiques
3 Mills Rd., Bryant Pond, 04219; 207-665-2124. Specializing in fruit jars; Mail order a specialty

Hillman, Alma
Antiques at the Hillman's
362 E. Main St., Searsport, 04974; 207-548-6658. Co-author (Collector Books) of *Collector's Encyclopedia of Old Ivory China, the Mystery Explored, Identification & Values*; Specializing in Old Ivory China

Rinaldi, John
Nautical Antiques and Related Items
Box 765, Dock Square,
Kennebunkport, 04046; 207-967-
3218. Specializing in nautical
antiques, scrimshaw, naval items,
marine paintings, naval items, etc.;
Fully-illustrated catalog: $5

Zayic, Charles S.
Americana Advertising Art
P.O. Box 57, Ellsworth, 04605; 207-667-
7342. Specializing in early magazines,
early advertising art, illustrators

Maryland

Banks, Robert
18901 Gold Mine Court, Brookeville,
20833. Specializing in American flags
of historical significance and
exceptional design

Ezell, Elaine; & Newhouse, George
Cruets Cruets Cruets
P.O. Box 1609, Pasadena, 21123-
1609; 410-255-6777. Specializing in
cruets, glass, porcelain, and pottery

Humphrey, George C.
4932 Prince George Ave., Beltsville,
20705; 301-937-7899. Specializing in
John Rogers groups

Katz, Jerome R., Vice President
International Society of Antique
Scale Collectors
1108 Pipestem Place, Rockville,
20854. Please include SASE when
requesting information.

Meadows, John, Jean and Michael
Meadows House Antiques
919 Stiles St., Baltimore, 21202; 410-
837-5427. Specializing in antique
wicker, furniture (rustic, twig, and old
hickory), quilts, and tramp art

Rudisill's Alt Print Haus
Rudisill, John and Barbara
P.O. Box 199, Worton, 21678; 410-
778-9290. Specializing in Currier &
Ives

Screen, Harold and Joyce
2804 Munster Rd., Baltimore, 21234;
410-661-6765. Specializing in soda
fountain 'tools of the trade' and paper:
catalogs, *Soda Fountain Magazine*, etc.;
E-mail: hscreen@home.com

Weisblut, Robert
International Ivory Society
11109 Nicholas Dr., Wheaton, 20902;
301-649-4002. Specializing in ivory
carvings and utilitarian objects

Welsh, Joan
7015 Partridge Pl., Hyattsville, 20782;
301-779-6181; Specializing in Chintz;
Author of *Chintz Ceramics*

Yalom, Libby
The Shoe Lady
P.O. Box 7146, Adelphi, 20783; 301-
422-2026. Specializing in glass and
china shoes: Author of book

Massachusetts

Adams, Charles and Barbara
Middleboro, 02346; 508-947-7277.
Specializing in Bennington (brown only)

Dunbar's Gallery
Leila and Howard Dunbar
76 Haven St., Milford, 01757; 508-
634-8697 or Fax 508-634-8698.
Specializing in advertising and toys

Frei, Peter
P.O. Box 500, Brimfield, 01010; 1-
800-942-8968. Specializing in sewing
machines (pre-1875, non-electric
only), adding machines, typewriters,
and hand-powered vacuum cleaners;
SASE required with correspondence

Hess, John A.
Fine Photographic Americana
P.O. Box 3062, Andover, 01810.
Specializing in 19th-century photography

Longo, Paul J.
Paul Longo Americana
Box 5510, Magnolia, 01930; 978-525-
2290. Specializing in political pins,
ribbons, banners, autographs, old
stocks and bonds, baseball and sports
memorabilia of all types

MacLean, Dale
183 Robert Rd., Dedham, 02026; 781-
326-3010 or 781-329-1303
(evenings). Specializing in Dedham
and Dorchester potteries

Mallis, A. George
208 Reeds Landing, 807 Wilbraham
Rd., Springfield, 01109-2055.
Specializing in antique scales

Morin, Albert
668 Robbins Ave. #23, Dracut, 01826;
978-454-7907. Specializing in
miscellaneous Akro Agate and Westite

Owings, K.C., Jr.
Antiques Americana
Box 19, N. Abington, 02351; 617-
857-1655. Specializing in Civil War,
Revolutionary War, autographs,
documents, books, antiques

Vigue, Norm
62 Bailey St., Stoughton, 02072; 781-
344-5441. Buying and selling TV,
western, cartoon-show collectibles,
animation art and 1-sheets, radio
cereal premiums, board games, and
1930s through 1950 space (including
Buck Rogers, Flash Gordon, Captain
Video, Tom Corbett, etc.)

Wellman, BA
P.O. Box 673, Westminster, 01473-
0673. Specializing in all areas of
American ceramics, dinnerware,
figurines, and art pottery; E-mail:
BAWELLMAN@NET1PLUS.COM

Michigan

Brown, Rick
Newspaper Collector's Society of
America
Lansing, 517-887-1255. Specializing
in newspapers;
HTTP: //www.historybuff.com or
E-mail: rbrown@tir.com

Culver, Bob
Night Light Club
38619 Wakefield Ct., Northville,
48167; 248-473-8575. Specializing in
miniature oil lamps

Gunsaulus, Jack
Gray's Gallery/Jack's Corner
Bookstore
583 W. Ann Arbor Trail, Plymouth,
48170. Specializing in porcelain,
books, jewelry, glass

Haas, Norman
264 Clizbe Rd., Quincy 49802; 517-
639-8537. Specializing in American
art pottery

Hogan & Woodworth
Walter P. Hogan and Wendy L.
Woodworth
520 N. State, Ann Arbor, 48104;
313-930-1913. Specializing in Kellogg
Studio

Iannotti, Dan
212 W. Hickory Grove Rd., Bloomfield
Hills, 48302-1127S. Specializing in
modern mechanical cast-iron banks;
Member of The Mechanical Bank
Collectors of America

Krupka, Rod
2615 Echo Lane, Ortonville, 48462;
248-627-6351. Specializing in
lightning rod balls

Kurella, Elizabeth M.
The Lace Merchant
Box 222, Plainwell, 49080; 616-685-
9792. Publisher of newsletter and
books on lace and linens; Specializing
in lace and linens

Marsh, Linda K.
1229 Gould Rd., Lansing, 48917.
Specializing in Degenhart glass

Nedry, Boyd W.
728 Buth Dr., Comstock Park, 49321;
616-784-1513. Specializing in traps
(including mice, rat, and fly traps)
and trap-related items

Nickel, Mike
A Nickel's Worth
P.O. Box 456, Portland, 48875; 517-
647-7646. Specializing in Roseville art
pottery and juvenile pieces, Weller,
Rookwood, Kay Finch, Ceramic Arts
Studio, Josef, and Florence figurines

Oates, Joan
685 S. Washington, Constantine,
49042; 616-435-8353. Specializing in
Phoenix Bird chinaware

Rairigh, Glen
Americana Auctions
12033 Sandborn, Sunfield, 48990;
800-919-1950. Specializing in
Skookum dolls

Ross, Michelle
P.O. Box 102, Sodus, 49126; 616-925-
1604. Specializing in Van Briggle pottery

Webster, Marty
6943 Suncrest Drive, Saline, 48176;
313-944-1188. Specializing in
California porcelain and pottery,
Orientalia

Minnesota

Anderson, James
Box 120704, New Brighton, 55112;
612-484-3198. Specializing in old
fishing lures and reels, also tackle
catalogs, posters, calendars,
Winchester items

Gallagher, Jerry
420 1st Ave. N.W., Plainview, 55964;
507-534-3511. Specializing in
Morgantown research; Matching service
for Morgantown, Heisey, Fostoria,
Cambridge, Duncan, and Tiffin; Publisher
of *A Handbook of Old Morgantown Glass
and Price Guide* (currently out of print),
and *The Morgantown Newscaster*,
triannual research journal of the
Morgantown Collectors of America, Inc.
(subscription: $18 per year)

Harrigan, John
1900 Hennepin, Minneapolis, 55403;
612-660-2794 or (in winter) 561-732-
0525. Specializing in Battersea
(English enamel) boxes, Moorcroft,
and Toby jugs

Hoppe, Gordon and Sue
10120 32nd Ave. N., Plymouth,
55441; 612-546-7461. Specializing in
Roseville; American art pottery

Ketcham, Steve
Steve Ketcham Antiques (Shows and
mail order only)
Box 24114, Edina, 55424; 612-920-
4205. Specializing in and buying early
American bottles; Red Wing
stoneware (no dinnerware);
advertising signs, trays, trade cards,
pocket mirrors, etched beer and shot
glasses. Please include SASE for reply.

Koehn, Joanne M.
Temple's Antiques
PO Box 46237, Eden Prairie, 55344;
612-941-7641. Specializing in
Victorian glass and china.

Miller, Clark
4444 Garfield Ave., Minneapolis,
55409-1847; 612-827-6062.
Specializing in Anton Lang pottery,
American art pottery, Scandinavian
glass and pottery

Nelson, C.L.
Box 222, Spring Park, 55384; 612-
473-5625. Specializing in 18th-, 19th-
and 20th-century English pottery and
porcelain, among others: Gaudy
Welsh, ABC plates, relief-molded
jugs, Staffordshire transfer ware

Podpeskar, Doug
624 Jones St., Eveleth, 55734-1631.
Specializing in Red Wing dinnerware;
Prefers letters with clear photos of
items to be identified along with
LSASE for return; E-mail:
thepods@northernnet.com

Schoneck, Steve
Handicraft Guild, Minneapolis
P.O. Box 56, Newport, 55055; 612-
459-2980

Missouri

Duncan, Pat and Ann
Box 175, Cape Fair, 65624; 417-538-
2311. Specializing in Holt Howard,
Roseville, Lefton

Heuring, Jerry
R.R. 1, Box 1110, Scott City, 63780;
573-264-3947. Specializing in Keen
Kutter

International Rose O'Neill Club
Contact Karen Stewart
P.O. Box 668, Branson, 65616. Dues:
$7 (single) or $10 (family) includes
newsletter Kewpiesta Kourier,
published quarterly

Roberts, Brenda
Country Side Antiques
R.R. 2, Marshall, 65340. Specializing
in Hull pottery and general line;
Author of Collector's Encyclopedia of
Hull Pottery, Roberts' Ultimate
Encyclopedia of Hull Pottery, and The
Companion Guide to Robert's Ultimate
Encyclopedia of Hull Pottery, all with
accompanying price guides; SASE
required

Siegel, Brenda and Jerry
Tower Grove Antiques
3308 Meramec, St. Louis, 63118; 314-
352-9020. Specializing in Ungemach
pottery

Scott, John and Peggy
Scotty's Antiques
4640 S. Leroy, Springfield, 65810;
417-887-2191. Specializing in
Depression-era glassware and pottery,
Florence figures

Smith, Pat
Independence
Author (Collector Books) of doll
book series

Tarrant, Jenny
Holly Daze Antiques
4 Gardenview, St. Peters, 63376.
Specializing in early holiday items,
Halloween, Christmas, Easter, etc.;
Always buying Halloween collectibles
(except masks and costumes) and
German rabbits and Santas; E-mail:
JennyJOL@aol.com

Wiesehan, Doug
D & R Farm Antiques
4535 Hwy. H, St. Charles, 63301.
Specializing in salesman's samples and
patent models, antique toys, farm toys,
metal farm signs

Williams, Don
P.O. Box 147, Kirksville 63501; 660-
627-8009 (between 8 a.m. and 6
p.m.). Specializing in art glass; SASE
required with all correspondence

Winslow, Ralph
Box 1175, Laurie, 65038. Specializing
in Dryden Pottery

Woollard, D.D., Jr.
11614 Old St. Charles Rd., Bridgeton,
63044; 314-739-4662. Specializing in
World's Fair & Exposition
memorabilia

Nebraska

Larsen, Robert V.
3214 19th St., Columbus, 68601.
Specializing in old hatpins and hatpin
holders. Please include SASE when
requesting information.

Neely, Nancee P.
16592 Hascall, Omaha, 68130; 402-
330-7033. Specializing in Fairing boxes

New Hampshire

Apakarian-Russell, Pamela
Halloween Queen Antiques
P.O. Box 499, Winchester, 03470;
Specializing in Halloween (and other
holidays) and postcards

Brenner, Larry
Brenner Antiques
1005 Chestnut St., Manchester,
03104; 603-625-8203. Specializing in
Royal Bayreuth

Holt, Jane
Jane's Collectibles
P.O. Box 115, Derry, 03038.
Specializing in Annalee Mobilite
Dolls; List sometimes available

Snyder, Eileen; and Kuperman, Keith
Snyder's Antiques
131 D.W. Highway #119, Nashua,
03060; 716-885-3403. Specializing in
Royal Haeger

Winston, Nancy
Willow Hollow Antiques
648 1st N.H. Turnpike, Northwood,
03261; 603-942-5739. Specializing in
Shaker baskets, primitives, country
smalls, paper Americana, iron, and
copper

New Jersey

Anderson, Suzy McLennan
Heritage Antiques & Appraisal
Services
65 E. Main St., Holmdel, 07733; 908-
946-8801 or Fax 908-946-1036.
Specializing in American furniture
and decorative accessories. Please
include photo and SASE when
requesting information; appraisals and
identification are impossible to do
over the phone.

Bilane, John E. (Mail order only)
2065 Morris Ave., Apt. 109, Union,
07083. Specializing in antique glass
cup plates

Cole, Lillian M., Editor of Piebirds
Unlimited Newsletter
14 Harmony School Rd., Flemington,
08822; 908-782-3198. Specializing in
pie birds, pie funnels, pie vents

Dezso, Doug
864 Paterson Ave., Maywood, 07607-
2119; 201-488-1311. Specializing in
nodders (comic German), glass candy
containers, Tonka; SASE required for
information

Doorstop Collectors of America
Doorstopper newsletter
Jeanie Bertoia
2413 Madison Ave., Vineland, 08630;
609-692-4092. Membership: $20 per
year, includes two newsletters and
convention. Send 2-stamp SASE for
sample.

George, Dr. Joan M.
ABC Collector's Circle
67 Stevens Ave., Old Bridge, 08857;
Fax 732-679-6102. Specializing in
educational china (particularly ABC
plates and mugs); E-mail:
drgeorge@nac.net

Harran, Jim and Susan
208 Hemlock Dr., Neptune, 07753;
908-922-2825. Specializing in English
and Continental porcelains with
emphasis on antique cups and saucers;
Author of Collectible Cups and
Saucers, Identification and Values
(Collector Books); Available for
$20.95 ppd.

Litts, Elyce
P.O. Box 394, Morris Plains, 07950;
201-361-4087. Author (Collector
Books) of Collector's Encyclopedia of
Geisha Girl Porcelain. (Out of print.
Ask your reference librarian or used
bookstore to secure you a copy.)

Lockwood, Howard J.; Publisher
Vetri: Italian Glass News
Box 191, Fort Lee, 07024; 201-969-
0373. Specializing in Italian glass of
the 20th century

Meschi, Edward J.
129 Pinyard Rd., Monroeville, 08343;
Phone/Fax 609-358-7293. Specializing
in Durand art glass, Icart etchings,
Maxfield Parrish prints, Rookwood
pottery, occupational shaving mugs, oil
paintings, and other fine arts; Author
of Durand — The Man and His Glass,
due out October 1998

Patalano, Diane. I.S.A.
Appraisals, Liquidations, and Auctions
P.O. Box 144, Saddle River, 07458.
Specializing in banks, Black
Americana, furniture, spatterware,
various antiques and collectibles

Perzel, Robert and Nancy
Popkorn
4 Mine St. (near Main St.), P.O. Box
1057, Flemington, 08822; 908-782-
9631. Specializing in Stangl
dinnerware, birds, and artware;
Depression Glass

Poster, Harry
Vintage TVs
Box 1883, S. Hackensack, 07606;
Days: 201-794-9606; 24-Hour Fax
201-794-9553. Writes Poster's Radio
and Television Price Guide; Specializes
in vintage televisions, transistor
radios, 3-D stereo cameras

Rago, David
17 S. Main St., Lambertville, 08530;
609-397-9374. Specializing in Arts &
Crafts, art pottery

Rash, Jim
135 Alder Ave., Egg Harbor
Township, 08234; 609-646-4125.
Specializing in advertising dolls

Rosen, Barbara
6 Shoshone Trail, Wayne, 07470.
Specializing in figural bottle openers
and antique dollhouses

Vines, Linda L.
Yesterday Once More
P.O. Box 43721, Upper Montclair,
07043; 973-748-4990. Specializing in
Snow Babies, all holidays (Christmas,
Easter, Halloween), dolls, toys, and Steiff

Visakay, Stephen
Vintage Cocktail Shakers (by
appointment)
P.O. Box 1517, W. Caldwell, 07007-
1517. Specializing in vintage cocktail
shakers

New Mexico

Hardisty, Don
Artistic Restorations
3020 E. Majestic Ridge, Las Cruces,
88011; For information and questions,
505-522-3721, Fax 505-522-7909.
Specializing in Bossons, Hummels,
postcards, rare coins. Don's Collectibles
carries a full line of current issues and
most discontinued Bossons and
Hummel figurines of all marks. Postcard
inventory includes over 500,000 with
many original photo cards and all
current issues of Legend. When mail
ordering, you may dial toll free 800-267-
7667. E-mail: donbossons@zianet.com/
or Visit Don's web page:
http://www.zianet.com/donsbossons/

Manns, William
P.O. Box 6459, Santa Fe, 87502; 505-
995-0102. Co-author of *Painted Ponies*,
hardbound (226 pages), available from
author for $49.95 ppd.; Specializing in
carousel art and cowboy antiques

Moyer, Patsy
Box 311, Deming, 88031; 505-546-
4019 or 505-546-2525; Fax 505-546-
2500. Collector Books author on
dolls; E-mail: sctrading@zianet.com

New York

Austin, Bruce A.
1 Hardwood Hill Rd., Pittsford, 14534;
716-387-9820 (evenings); 716-475-
2879 (week days). Specializing in
clocks and Arts & Crafts furnishings
and accessories including medalware,
pottery, and lighting; E-mail:
BAAGLL@RIT.EDU

Badders, Veldon
692 Martin Rd., Hamlin, 14464; 716-
964-3360. Author (Collector Books)
of *Collector's Guide to Inkwells,
Identification & Values*; Specializing in
inkwells

Calison, Jim
Tools of Distinction
Wallkill, 12589; 914-895-8035.
Specializing in antique and collectible
tools, buying and selling

Dimitroff, Thomas P.
Dimitroff's Antiques (Appointment
only)
140 E. First St., Corning, 14830; 607-
962-6745. Specializing in Steuben
and cut glass

Doyle, Robert A.
Absolute Auction & Realty,
Inc./Pleasant Valley Auction Hall
P.O. Box 658, 348 Main St., Beacon
12524. Antique and estate auctions every
month at their Beacon gallery, twice a
month at Pleasant Valley Auction Hall;
Free calendar of auctions available; Web
site: www.auctionweb.com/aar-ny

Endter, Barbara
29 Sandalwood Dr., Rochester,
14616-1513; 716-621-1433.
Specializing in Chase Brass & Copper
Company

Fer-Duc Inc.
Ferrara, Joseph
433 West 21st St #7F, New York,
10011-2906; 212-627-5023.
Specializing in American art pottery
(Ohr and Rookwood), 19th- and
20th-century American paintings

Gerson, Roselyn
P.O. Box 40, Lynbrook, 11563; 516-
593-8746. Author/collector
specializing in unusual, gadgetry,
figural compacts, vanity bags and
purses, solid perfumes and lipsticks

Greguire, Helen
Helen's Antiques
103 Trimmer Rd., Hilton, 14468; 716-
392-2704. Specializing in graniteware
(any color), carnival glass lamps and
shades, carnival glass lighting of all
kinds; Author (Collector Books) of
*The Collector's Encyclopedia of
Graniteware, Colors, Shapes & Values*,
(updated values, $28.45 ppd.); Second
book on graniteware now available
with prices updated to 1997 (same
price); Also available is *Carnival in
Lights*, featuring carnival glass, lamps,
shades, etc. ($13.45 ppd.); and
*Collector's Guide to Toasters and
Accessories, Identification & Values*,
($21.95 ppd.); All available from
author. Please include SASE when
requesting information.

Handelsman, Burton
18 Hotel Dr., White Plains, 10605;
914-428-4480 (home) and 914-761-
8880 (office). Specializing in
occupational shaving mugs, accessories

Herley, Patrick J.
P.O. Box 606, E. Setauket, Long
Island, 11733; 516-928-6052.
Specializing in Goss china; E-mail:
PHERLEY@CCMAIL.SUNYSB.EDU

Jordan, Ruth E.
Meridale, 13806; 607-746-2082.
Specializing in cut glass, American
Brilliant period

Kaonis, Keith; Publisher
Collectors Eye and Antique Doll
Collector Magazines
60 Cherry Lane, Huntington, 11743;
516-351-0982. Specializing in
Schoenhut toys

Laun, H. Thomas and Patricia
Little Century
215 Paul Ave., Syracuse, 13206; 315-
437-4156. Summer residence: 35109
Country Rte. 7, Cape Vincent, 13618;
315-654-3244. Specializing in
firefighting collectibles. All free
appraisals require SASE.

Malitz, Lucille
Lucid Antiques
Box KH, Scarsdale, 10583; 914-636-
7825. Specializing in lithophanes,
kaleidoscopes, stereoscopes, medical
and dental antiques

Malloy, Alex G.
Alex G. Malloy, Inc.
P.O. Box 38, South Salem, 10590;
203-438-0396. Specializing in ancient
and medieval coins; antiquities,
numismatic literature

Michel, John and Barbara
Americana Blue
200 E. 78th St., 18E, New York City,
10021; 212-861-6094. Specializing in
yellow ware, cast iron, and tramp art

Owens, Lowell
Owens' Collectibles
12 Bonnie Ave., New Hartford,
13413. Specializing in beer advertising

Rifken, Blume J.
Author of *Silhouettes in America —
1790-1840 — A Collector's Guide*;
Specializing in American antique
silhouettes from 1790 to 1840

Safir, Charlotte F.
1349 Lexington Ave., 9-B, New York
City, 10128-1513; 212-534-7933.
Specializing in cookbooks, children's
books (out-of-print only)

Schleifman, Roselle
Ed's Collectibles/The Rage
16 Vincent Rd., Spring Valley, 10977;
914-356-2121. Specializing in Duncan
& Miller, Elegant glass, Depression glass

Smyth, Carole and Richard
Carole Smyth Antiques
P.O. Box 2068, Huntington, 11743.
Authors of *The Burning Passion —
Antique and Collectible Pyrography*,
available from authors at above address
for $22.95 ppd. (New York: add $1.74
state sales tax), and *Neptune's
Treasures, a Study and Value Guide on
Antique Shell Decorated Love Tokens,
Souvenirs, Whimsies*, call for price

Steinbock, Nancy
Nancy Steinbock Posters
518-438-1577. Specializing in posters:
travel, war, literary, advertising

Tuggle, Robert
105 W. St., New York City, 10023;
212-595-0514. Specializing in John
Bennett, Anglo-Japanese china

Van Kuren, Jean and Dale
Ruth's Antiques, Inc.
P.O. Box 152, Clarence Center,
14032; 716-741-8001. Specializing
chocolate molds, Buffalo pottery
Deldare ware

Van Patten, Joan F.
Box 102, Rexford, 12148. Author
(Collector Books) of books on
Nippon and Noritake

North Carolina

Degenhardt, Richard K.
Carriage Park
302 High Point Lane, Hendersonville,
28791; 704-696-9750. Author of
*Belleek, The Complete Collectors' Guide
and Illustrated Reference*, 1st and 2nd
editions; Specializing in Belleek. (The
only Belleek is the Irish, established
by legal action in 1929.)

Hughes, Kathy (Mrs. Paul)
Tudor House Galleries
1401 E. Blvd., Charlotte, 28203; 704-
377-4748. Specializing in relief-
molded jugs, 18th- and 19th-century
English pottery and 19th-century oil
paintings

Hussey, Billy Ray and Susan
01828 N. Howard Mill Rd., Robbins,
27325. Specializing in Southern folk
pottery contemporary face jugs

Iannantuoni, Jean-Paul
P.O. Box 563072, Charlotte, 28256-
3072; 704-547-9951 (Monday –
Thursday: 7:00 p.m. to 10:00 p.m.
E.S.T., Saturday and Sunday: 1:00
p.m. to 8:00 p.m.). Specializing in
Royal Doulton secondary market

Kirtley, Charles E.
P.O. Box 2273, Elizabeth City, 27096;
919-335-1262. Specializing in
monthly auctions and bid sales
dealing with World's Fair, Civil War,
political, advertising, and other
American collectibles

Newbound, Betty
2206 Nob Hill Dr., Sanford, 27330.
Author (Collector Books) on Blue
Ridge dinnerware, milk glass, wall
pockets, and figural planters and
vases; Specializing in collectible china
and glass

Sayers, R.J.
Southeastern Antiques & Appraisals
P.O. Box 629, Brevard, 29812.
Specializing in Boy Scout collectibles,
Pisgah Forest pottery, primitive
American furniture; Author of *Guide to
Scouting Collectibles,* Revised 1996
Edition, available from author for
$32.95 ppd.; Member NEAA Appraisers

Taylor, Terry
3648 Prides Rd., East Bend, 27018. Co-
author of *Collector's Encyclopedia of Salt
Glaze Stoneware* (Collector Books);
Specializing in salt glaze stoneware

North Dakota

Farnsworth, Bryce
1334 14½ St. South, Fargo, 58103;
701-237-3597. Specializing in
Rosemeade pottery. If writing for
information, please send a picture if
possible, also phone number and best
time to call.

Ohio

Bassett, Mark
P.O. Box 771233, Lakewood, 44107;
216-221-6025. Author of *Cowan
Pottery and the Cleveland School,*
researcher with specialties in American
art pottery, Cleveland artists, Art Deco,
and other 20th Century design
movements and designers

Batory, Mr. Dana Martin
402 E. Bucyrus St., Crestline, 44827.
Specializing in antique woodworking
machinery, old and new woodworking
machinery catalogs; Author of *Vintage
Woodworking Machinery, an Illustrated
Guide to Four Manufacturers,* currently
available from Astragal Press, P.O. Box
239, Mendham, NJ 07945 for $25.45
ppd. In order to prepare a difinitive
history on American manufacturers of
woodworking machinery, Dana is
interested in acquiring by loan, gift, or
photocopy, any and all documents,
catalogs, manuals, photos, personal
reminiscences, etc., pertaining to
woodworking machinery and/or their
manufacturers. Also available for $7.50
money order: 30+ page list of catalogs,
owner's manuals, parts lists, company
publications, etc. (updated quarterly).
No phone calls please.

Benjamin, Scott
411 Forest St., LaGrange, 44050; 440-
355-6608. Specializing in gas globes;
Co-author of *Gas Pump Globes* and
several other related books, listing
nearly 4,000 gas globes with over 400
photos, prices, rarity guide, histories,
and reproduction information
(currently available from author);
Also available: *Petroleum Collectibles
Monthly* magazine, please inquire

Blair, Betty
Golden Apple Antiques
216 Bridge St., Jackson, 45640; 614-
286-4817. Specializing in art pottery,
Watt, cookie jars, chocolate molds,
Beanie Babies general line

Budin, Nicki
Curio Cabinet
679 High St., Worthington, 43085;
614-885-1986. Specializing in Royal
Doulton

Business Recollections, Antiques and
Collectibles
Nada Sue Knauss
1211 Potter Rd., Weston, 43569; 419-
669-4735. Specializing in pottery,
postcards

China Specialties, Inc.
Box 471, Valley City, 44280.
Specializing in Autumn Leaf

Cimini, Joan
67183 Stein Rd., Belmont, 43718.
Specializing in Imperial glass;
Candlewick matching service

Cincinnati Auction Gallery
635 Main St., Cincinnati, 45202;
513-381-2128. Specializing in
American art pottery (especially
Rookwood), American and European
fine paintings, watercolors

Collectors of Findlay Glass
P.O. Box 256, Findlay, 45840. An
organization dedicated to the study
and recognition of Findlay glass; *The
Melting Pot Newsletter* published
quarterly; Convention held annually;
Membership: $10 per year

Distel, Ginny
Distel's Antiques
4041 S.C.R. 22, Tiffin, 44883; 419-
447-5832. Specializing in Tiffin glass

Ebner, Rita and John
Cracker Barrel Antiques
4540 Helen Rd., Columbus, 43232.
Specializing in door knockers, cast-
iron bottle openers, Griswold

Ferguson, Maxine
1380 Bussemer, Zanesville, 43701.

Forsythe, Ruth A.
Box 327, Galena, 43021. Author of
Made in Czechoslovakia, books I and
II; SASE required

Graff, Shirley
4515 Grafton Rd., Brunswick, 44212.
Specializing in Pennsbury pottery

Guenin, Tom
Box 454, Chardon, 44024.
Specializing in antique telephones
and antique telephone restoration

Hamlin, Jack & Treva
145 Township Rd. 1088, Proctorville,
45669; 740-886-7644. Specializing in
Currier and Ives by Royal China Co.;
Buy and sell

Hothem, Lar
Hothem House
Box 458, Lancaster, 43130.
Specializing in books about Indians
and artifacts

Kao, Fern Larking
P.O. Box 312, Bowling Green, 43402;
419-352-5928. Specializing in jewelry,
sewing implements, ladies' accessories

Kerr, Ann
P.O. 437, Sidney, 45365; 937-492-6369.
Author (Collector Books) of *Collector's
Encyclopedia of Russel Wright Designs;*
Specializing in work of Wright;
Interested in 20th-century decorative arts

Kier, Don and Anne
2022 Marengo St., Toledo, 43614;
419-385-8211. Specializing in general
glass and china, 19th-century antiques,
autographs, Brownies, Royal Bayreuth

Kitchen, Lorrie
Toledo, 419-478-3815. Specializing in
Depression-era glass, Hall china,
Fiesta, Blue Ridge, Shawnee

Klender, James and Grace
Town & Country Antiques &
Collectibles
P.O. Box 447, Pioneer, 43554; 419-
737-2880. Specializing in Depression
glass, and general line

Kline, Mr. and Mrs. Jerry and Gerry
Members of North American Torquay
Society and Torquay Pottery
Collectors' Society
604 Orchard View Dr., Maumee,
43537; 419-893-1226. Specializing in
collecting Torquay pottery

Maggard, Deborah
P.O Box 211, Chagrin Falls, 44022;
440-247-5632. Specializing in elegant
glassware, china, and Victorian art
glass; E-mail:
debmaggard@worldnet.att.net

Mathes, Richard
P.O. Box 1408, Springfield, 45501-
1408; 513-324-6917. Specializing in
buttonhooks

Millman, Tom and Linda
231 S. Main St., Bethel, 45106;
Phone/Fax 513-734-6884 (after 9
p.m.). Specializing in perfume lamps,
other antique and unique lighting

Moore, Carolyn
445 N. Prospect, Bowling Green, 43402.
Specializing in primitives, yellow ware,
graniteware, collecting stoneware

Murphy, James L.
1023 Neil Ave., Columbus, 43201;
614-297-0746. Specializing in
Radford, Vance Avon

National Imperial Glass Collectors'
Society, Inc.
P.O. Box 534, Bellaire 43906. Dues:
$15 per year (plus $1 for each
additional member in the same
household); Quarterly newsletter;
Convention every June

Pierce, David
27544 Black Rd., P.O. Box 248,
Danville, 43014; 614-599-6394.
Specializing in Glidden pottery; Fee
for appraisals

Rees, Debbie
Zanesville. Specializing in Watt,
Roseville juvenile and other Roseville
pottery, Zanesville area pottery,
cookie jars, and Steiff

Riebel, James; Krause, Terry
Pottery Peregrinators
Zanesville, 740-452-7687.
Specializing in American art pottery,
Nicodemus, and carnival glass;
Promoter Zanesville's Voyage through
the Past, Antique Pottery Show &
Sale, 2nd to 3rd weekend in July

Roscoe, Mike
3351 Lagrange, Toledo, 43608; 419-
244-6935. Specializing in toys,
advertising, coin-operated machines,
furniture, and miscellaneous

Trainer, Veronica
Bayhouse
Box 40443, Cleveland, 44140; 216-
871-8584. Specializing in beaded and
enamelled mesh purses

Tucker, Dan
Toledo, 419-478-3815. Specializing in
Depression-era glass, Hall china,
Fiesta, Blue Ridge, Shawnee

Walter, John
The Old Tool Shop
208 Front St., Marietta, 45750; 740-
373-9973. Specializing in all types of
antique tools; For detailed
information on Stanley tools, *John
Walter's Antique & Collectible Stanley
Tools Guide to Identity and Value* is
highly recommended, 885 pages, over
1500 crisp photos and engravings,
current values, softcover: $35 ppd.,
hardcover: $45 ppd.; 1998 *Stanley
Pocket Price Guide:* $12 ppd.

Whitmyer, Margaret and Kenn
Box 30806, Gahanna, 43230. Authors
(Collector Books) on children's
dishes. Specializing in Depression-era
collectibles

Wilkins, Juanita
The Bird of Paradise
Lima. Specializing in R.S. china, Old Ivory china, colored pattern glass, lamps, and jewelry

Young, Mary
Box 9244, Wright Brothers Branch, Dayton, 45409; 937-298-4838. Specializing in paper dolls; Author of several books

Oklahoma

Bess, Phyllis and Tom
14535 E. 13th St., Tulsa, 74108; 918-437-7776. Authors of *Frankoma Treasures*, and *Frankoma and Other Oklahoma Potteries*. Specializing in Frankoma and Oklahoma pottery

Klein, Bob and Dondee
1002 Walnut Court, Guthrie, 73044; 405-282-6545. Specializing in Tamac pottery

Moore, Art and Shirley
4423 E. 31st St., Tulsa, 74135; 918-747-4164 or 918-744-8020. Specializing in Lu Ray Pastels, Depression glass

Scott, Roger R.
4250 S. Oswego, Tulsa, 74135; 918-742-8710 or Fax 918-583-1226. Specializing in Victor and RCA Victor trademark items along with Nipper

Watson, Kitty
Kitty's Kewpie-Corner
201 Dena Dr., Guthrie, 73044; 405-282-2287. Specializing in Rose O'Neill items; Kewpies, Scootles, and other related works

Willis, Ron L.
2110 Fox Ave., Moore, 73160. Specializing in militaria

Oregon

Abrahams, Peter
1948 Mapleleaf Rd., Lake Oswego, 97034; 503-636-2988. Specializing in telescopes, binoculars, microscopes. Peter studies and collects optics: telescopes, binoculars, hand magnifiers, and microscopes and especially seeks reference material on these subjects, including books, catalogs, repair manuals, and histories. E-mail: telscope@europa.com.

Bartsch, Henry
Antique Registers
Box 444, Rockaway, 97136; 503-355-2932. Specializing in servicing antique cash registers (by appointment)

Brown, Marcia
Sparkles
P.O. Box 2314, White City; 97503; 541-826-3039 or Fax 541-830-5385. Specializing in rhinestone jewelry

Coe, Debbie and Randy
Coe's Mercantile
Lafayette School House Mall #2, 748 3rd (Hwy. 99W), Lafayette, 97127. Specializing in Elegant and Depression glass, art pottery

Davis, Patricia M.
Antique and personal property appraisals
4326 NW Tam-O-Shanter Way, Portland, 97229-8738; 503-645-3084

Foland, Doug
1811 N.W. Couch #303, Portland, 97209. Author of *The Florence Collectibles, an Era of Elegance,* available at your local bookstore or from Schiffer publishers

Geddes, Marjorie
5955 W.W. 179th Ave., Beaverton 97007; 503-649-1041. Specializing in sewing items, open salts, Florence ceramics, California figurines, tea-related items, miscellaneous small and elegant collectibles; In space 21, Lafayette Schoolhouse Antique Mall, 503-864-2720

Hirshman, Susan and Larry
Everyday Antiques
2011 E. Main St., Medford, 97504. Specializing in china, glassware, kitchenware

Main Antique Mall
30 N. Riverside, Medford, 97501
Quality products and services for the serious collector, dealer, or those just browsing

Medford Antique Mall
Jim & Eileen Pearson, Owners
1 West 6th St., Medford 97501

Miller, Don and Robby
541-535-1231. Specializing in milk bottles, TV Siamese cat lamps, seltzer bottles, red cocktail shakers

Morris, Sue and Dave
3388 Merlin Rd., Suite 351
Grants Pass, 97526. Specializing in Watt pottery and Purinton pottery; Author of *Watt Pottery — An Identification and Value Guide,* and *Purinton Pottery — An Identification and Value Guide*

Morris, Thomas G.
Prize Publishers
P.O. Box 8307, Medford, 97504. Author of *The Carnival Chalk Prize, Books I and II,* pictorial price guides on carnival chalkware figures with brief histories and values for each; E-mail: chalkman@cdsnet.net

Ringering, David
4063 Durbin Ave SE, Salem, 97301; pager 503-588-3747. Specializing in Roland & Marsellus

Roberts, Fred and Marilyn
Bah Humbug Collectibles
2663 Aldersgate Rd., Medford, 97504; Specializing in Hummels; E-mail: bahhumbug@juno.com

Pennsylvania

Barker, Jim
Toastermaster Antique Appliances
P.O. Box 41, Bethlehem, 18016; 610-439-0751. Specializing in early electric toasters and fans, Porcelier and Royal Rochester; Unusual electric toasters always wanted

Barrett, Noel
Rosebud Antiques
P.O. Box 1001, Carversville, 18913; 215-297-5109. Specializing in toys

Bodine, Clarence H., Jr., Proprietor
East/West Gallery
41B Ferry St., New Hope, 18938. Specializing in antique Japanese woodblock prints, netsuke, inro, porcelains

Cerebro
P.O. Box 327, East Prospect, 17317-0327; 717-252-2400 or 800-69-LABEL; Fax 717-252-3685. Specializing in antique advertising labels, especially cigar box labels, cigar bands, food labels, firecracker labels; E-mail: Cerebro@Cerebro.com

Damaska, Ron
738 9th Ave., New Brighton, 15066; 724-843-1393. Specializing in Fry cut glass, match holders. SASE required when requesting information.

Garvin, Joann
P.O. Box 182, Beaver Falls, 15010; 412-843-3999. Specializing in Fiesta

Gottuso, Bob
Bojo
P.O. Box 1403, Cranberry Township, 16066-0403; Phone/Fax 724-776-0621. Specializing in Beatles, Elvis, KISS, Monkees, licensed Rock 'n Roll memorabilia

Goyda, Cheryl
Box 192, E. Petersburg, 17520; 717-569-7149. Specializing in SMF/Wheelock Black Forest and Czechoslovakian pottery

Hagenbuch, James
Glass-Works Auction
102 Jefferson, East Greenville, 18041; 215-679-5849. America's leading auction company in early American bottles and glass

Hain, Henry F., III
Antiques & Collectibles
2623 N. Second St., Harrisburg, 17110; 717-238-0534. Lists available of items for sale

Hartz, Ray
120 Amberwood Ct., Bethel Park, 15102; 412-833-6777. Specializing in old, unusual playing cards: U.S. and Foreign, war, transformation, advertising; E-mail: rhartz@bellatlantic.net

Hinton, Michael C.
246 W. Ashland St., Doylestown, 18901; 215-345-0892. Owns/operates Bucks County Art & Antiques Company and Chem-Clean Furniture Restoration Company; Specializing in quality restorations of a wide range of art and antiques from colonial to contemporary; Also owns Trading Post Antiques, 532 Durham Rd., Wrightstown, PA, 18940, a 50-dealer antiques co-op with 15,000 square feet — something for everyone in antiques and collectibles

Holland, William
William Holland Fine Arts
1554 Paoli Pike, West Chester, 19380; 610-344-9848 or Fax 610-344-0651. Specializing in Louis Icart etchings and oils, Art Nouveau and Art Deco items; Author of *Louis Icart: The Complete Etchings* and *The Collectible Maxfield Parrish*; Website: www.hollandarts.com

Irons, Dave
Dave Irons Antiques
223 Covered Bridge Rd., Northampton, 18067; 610-262-9335 or Fax 610-262-2853. Author of *Irons by Irons* and *More Irons by Irons* (both soft-cover), available from author (both contain pictures of over 1,600 irons, current information and price ranges, collecting hints, news of trends, and information for proper care of irons); Specializing in pressing irons, country furniture, primitives, quilts, accessories

Ivankovich, Michael
Michael Ivankovich Auctions, Inc.
P.O. Box 2458, Doylestown, 18901. Specializing in early 20th-century hand-colored photography and prints; Author of *The Collector's Value Guide to Popular Early 20th Century American Prints* (1998) $19.95; *The Collector's Guide to Wallace Nutting Pictures,* $17.95; *The Wallace Nutting Expansible Catalog,* $14.95; *The Alphabetical and Numerical Index to Wallace Nutting Pictures,* $14.95; and *The Guide to Wallace Nutting Furniture,* $14.95 Also available: *Wallace Nutting General Catalog, Supreme Edition* (reprint), $13.95; *Wallace Nutting: A Great American Idea* (reprint), $13.95; and *Wallace Nutting's Windsor's: Correct Windsor Furniture* (reprint), $13.95. Related books available are: *The Guide to Wallace Nutting-Like Photographers of the Early 20th Century,* $13.95; and *The History of Sawyer Pictures* by Carol Begley Gray, $14.95. All these books are currently available at the above address. Shipping is $3.75 for the first item ordered and $1.50 for each additional item.

Knauer, Judy A.
National Toothpick Holder
Collectors Society
1224 Spring Valley Lane, West Chester,
19380-5112; 610-431-3477. Specializing
in toothpick holders and Victorian glass

The Krauses
Krause, Gail
97 W. Wheeling St., Washington,
15301; 412-228-5034. Author of book
on Duncan glass

Kreider, Katherine
Kingsbury Antiques
P.O. Box 7957, Lancaster, 17604-7957;
717-892-3001. Author of *Valentines with
Values*, available post-paid by sending
$22.90 ($24.09 Pennsylvania residents).
No free appraisals. Stop by Booth #315
at Black Angus, in Adamstown (new
section) and talk about valentines.

Levi, Anita
Allegheny Mountain Antique Gallery
5151 Clear Shade Dr., Windber, 15963;
814-467-8539. Specializing in novelty
clocks, advertising tins, primitives,
holiday decorations, quilts, purses,
Black memorabilia, linens, stoneware,
Roseville, kitchenware, Art Deco

Lindsay, Ralph
P.O. Box 21, New Holland, 17557.
Specializing in target balls. SASE
required with correspondence.

Lowe, James Lewis
Kate Greenaway Society
P.O. Box 8, Norwood, 19074;
Specializing in Kate Greenaway; E-
mail: JLewisLowe@juno.com

Maier, Clarence and Betty
Mail order: The Burmese Cruet
Box 432, Montgomeryville, 18936;
215-855-5388. Specializing in
Victorian art glass

Marks, Mariann Katz
1416 Main, Honesdale, 18431. Author
(Collector Books) of *Majolica Pottery*,
Second Series; Specializing in collecting,
buying, and selling American and English
majolica of the Victorian period; LSASE
required for mail-order list; Enclose photo
and price wanted with offers to sell

Merchants Square Mall
Jim & Annetta Vitez, Managers
1901 S. 12th St., Allentown, 18103;
610-797-7743

Posner, Judy
June – September: R.D. 1 Box 273 SC,
Effort 18330; Fax 717-629-0521.
Specializing in Disneyana, Black
memorabilia, salt and pepper shakers,
souvenirs of the U.S.A., character and
advertising memorabilia, figural pottery;
Buy, sell, collect; Informal appraisals, $5
LSASE and photo of item; E-mail:
judyandjef@aol.com
Rosso, Philip J. and Philip Jr.

Wholesale Glass Dealers
1815 Trimble Ave., Port Vue, 15133;
412-678-7352. Specializing in
Westmoreland glass

Weiser, Pastor Frederick S.
55 Kohler School Rd., New Oxford,
17350; 717-624-4106. Specializing in
frakturs and other Pennsylvania
German documents

Rhode Island

Dumont, Louise
579 Old Main St., Coventry, 02816;
Alternative address: 319 Hawthorne
Blvd, Leesburg, FL 34748.
Specializing in cookie jars, Abingdon

Gacher, John
The Zsolnay Store
152 Spring St., Newport, 02840; 401-
841-5060. Specializing in Zsolnay,
Fischer, Amphora, and Austro-
Hungarian art pottery; On the Web:
http://www.drawrm.com

The Occupied Japan Club
c/o Florence Archambault
29 Freeborn St., Newport, 02840-
1821. Publishes bimonthly newsletter,
*The Upside Down World of an O.J.
Collector*; SASE required when
requesting information

South Carolina

Roerig, Fred and Joyce
R.R. 2, Box 504, Walterboro, 29488;
803-538-2487. Specializing in cookie
jars; Authors of *Collector's
Encyclopedia of Cookie Jars* (series of
three), *an Illustrated Value Guide*,
publishers of *Cookie Jarrin' with Joyce:
The Cookie Jar Newsletter*

Tennessee

Chase, Mick and Lorna
Fiesta Plus
380 Hawkins Crawford Rd.,
Cookeville, 38501; 931-372-8333.
Specializing in Fiesta, Harlequin,
Riviera, Franciscan, Metlox, other
American dinnerware

Grist, Everett
P.O. Box 91375, Chattanooga,
37412-3955; 423-510-8052.
Specializing in covered animal dishes
and marbles

Hudson, Murray
Murray Hudson Antiquarian Books & Maps
109 S. Church St., Box 163, Halls,
38040; 901-836-9057 or 800-748-
9946; Fax 901-836-9017. Specializing
in antique maps, globes and books with
maps, atlases, explorations, travel
guides, geographies, surveys, etc.
Weddington, David

Predicta Sales & Service
2702 Albany Ct., Murfreesboro,
37129; 615-890-7498. Specializing in
vintage Philco Predicta TVs

Texas

Babcock, Bobby
Jubilation Antiques
5108 Saddleridge Cove, Austin,
78759; 512-258-2272. Specializing in
Maxfield Parrish, Black memorabilia,
and brown Roseville Pine Cone

Cooper, Marilyn
8408 Lofland Dr., Houston, 77055; 713-
465-7773. Specializing in figural
toothbrush holders, Pez, candy containers

Dockery, Rod
4600 Kemble St., Ft. Worth, 76103;
817-536-2168. Specializing in milk glass;
SASE required with correspondence

Docks, L.R. 'Les'
Shellac Shack; Discollector
Box 691035, San Antonio, 78269-1035.
Author of *American Premium Record
Guide*; Specializing in vintage records

Fer-Duc Inc.
Joseph D. Ferrara
2814 College Plaza #5112, Dallas, 78205;
214-368-1113. Specializing in American
art pottery (Ohr and Rookwood), 19th-
and 20th-century paintings

Frese, Leo and Wendy
Three Rivers Collectibles
Box 551542, Dallas, 75355; 214-341-
5165. Specializing in RumRill, Red
Wing pottery, and stoneware

Gibbs, Carl, Jr.
P.O. Box 131584, Houston, 77219-1584;
713-521-9661. Author of *Collector's
Encyclopedia of Metlox Potteries*,
autographed copies available from
author for $27.95 ppd.; Specializing in
American ceramic dinnerware

Groves, Bonnie
402 North Ave. A, Elgin, 78621.
Specializing in boudoir dolls

Malowanczyk, Abby and Wlodek
Collage-20th Century Classics
2820 N. Henderson, Dallas, 75206;
Phone/fax 214-828-9888; Also may be
reached at 3017-B Routh St., Dallas,
75201; 214-880-0020. Specializing in
architect-designed furniture and
decorative arts from the modern
movement

Norris, Kenn
Schoolmaster Auctions and
Collectibles
P.O. Box 4830, 513 N. 2nd St.,
Sanderson, 79848; 915-345-2640.
Specializing in school-related items,
barbed wire, related literature, and L'il
Abner (antique shop in downtown
Sanderson)

Pringle, Joyce M.
Antiques and Moore
3708 W. Pioneer Pkwy., Arlington,
76013. Specializing in Boyd, Summit,
and Mosser glass;
www.Antiquesandmoore.com/glas/ or
chip@antiquesandmoore.com

Silvermintz, Karen
6164 Ravendale Lane, Dallas, 75214;
214-826-1107. Specializing in
American dinnerware

Smith, Allan
1806 Shields Dr., Sherman, 75092;
903-893-3626. Specializing in
children's lunch boxes, Coca-Cola,
Dr. Pepper, Pepsi Cola, RC Cola,
western stars' items, character tin
windup toys, and most character
collectibles

Thompson, Chuck
Chuck Thompson & Associates
10802 Greencreek Dr., Suite 703,
Houston, 77070. Send LSASE for free
list of Chuck's tobacciana
publications. Thompson is writing a
book of Cowboy fables. His latest
pamphlet is *Cowboy Tobacciana*.

Tucker, Richard and Valerie
Argyle Antiques
P.O. Box 262, Argyle, 76226; 940-
464-3752. Specializing in windmill
weights, shooting gallery targets,
figural lawn sprinklers, cast-iron
advertising paperweights and other
unusual figural cast iron; E-mail:
lead1234@gte.net orrtucker@jw.com

Turner, Danny and Gretchen
Running Rabbit Video Auctions
P.O. Box 701, Waverly, 37185; 615-
296-3600. Specializing in marbles

Waddell, John
2903 Stan Terrace, Mineral Wells,
76067. Specializing in buggy steps

Wilkins, James R.
Olden Year Musical Museum
Box 381951, Duncanville, 75138-
1951; 972-298-5587. Specializing in
music boxes, phonographs, grind
organs, nickelodeons

Utah

Anderson, Tim
Box 461, Provo, 84603. Specializing
in autographs; Buys single items or
collections — historical, movie stars,
US Presidents, sports figures, and pre-
1860 correspondence. Autograph
questions? Please include photocopies
of your autographs if possible and
enclose a SASE for guaranteed reply.

Anderson, Warren R.
America West Archives
P.O. Box 100, Cedar City, 84721;
435-586-9497. Specializing in old
stock certificates and bonds, western
documents and books, financial
ephemera, autographs, maps, photos;
Author of *Owning Western History*,
with 75+ photos of old documents
and recommended reference guide
(available for $18 (soft cover) or $28
(hardback) ppd., from author)

Killmer, Jo
P.O. Box 1424, Provo, 84603; 801-
375-1211. Specializing in silverplate
patterns, also sterling, china, general
line of antiques, Roseville

Spencer, Rick
Salt Lake City, 801-973-0805.
Specializing in silverware, silverplate,
hollow ware, Shawnee, Van Telligen,
salt and pepper shakers. No free
appraisals.

Vermont

Barry, Kit
88 High St., Brattleboro, 05301; 802-
254-3634. *Author of Reflections 1* and
Reflections 2, reference books on
ephemera; Specializing in advertising
trade cards and ephemera in general

Marie Miller's American Quilts
P.O. 968, Dorset, 05251; 802-867-
5969

Virginia

Bradfield, Jeff
Jeff's Antiques
90 Main St., Dayton, 22821; 540-879-
9961. Also located in Pat's Antique
Mall (I-81), Exit 227, Verona, and
Rolling Hills Antique Mall, I-81, Exit
247B, Harrisonburg. Specializing in
candy containers, toys, postcards,
sugar shakers, lamps, furniture,
pottery, and advertising items

Cranor, Rosalind
P.O. Box 859, Blacksburg, 24063.
Specializing in Elvis collectibles;
Author of *Elvis Collectibles and Best of
Elvis Collectibles*, available from
author for $21.70 each (ppd.)

Flanigan, Vicki
Flanigan's Antiques
P.O. Box 1662, Winchester, 22604.
Specializing in antique dolls, hand
fans, and Hawaiian dolls

Friend, Terry
839 Glendale Rd., Galax, 24333; 540-
236-9027 after 9:30 p.m. E.S.T.
Specializing in coffee mills; SASE
required; E-mail: friend@tcia.net

Haigh, Richard
10607 Baypines Lane, Richmond,
23233; 804-741-5770. Specializing in
Locke Art, Steuben, Loetz, California
pottery

Lechner, Mildred and Ralph
Box 554, Mechanicsville, 23111; 804-
737-3347. Author (Collector Books)
on glass salt shakers; Specializing in art
and pattern glass salt shakers circa 1870
– 1940; Directors of Antique and Art
Glass Salt Shakers Collectors' Society
Club, 1991 – 92. Please note: Mildred
and Ralph have absolutely no
involvement or dealings concerning
novelty salt shakers or their values.

MacAllister, Dale
P.O. Box 46, Singers Glen, 22850.
Specializing in sugar shakers and
syrups

Monsen, Randall; and Baer, Rod
Monsen & Baer
Box 529, Vienna, 22183; 703-242-
1357. Specializing in perfume bottles,
Roseville pottery, Art Deco

Reynolds, Charles
Reynolds Toys
2836 Monroe St., Falls Church,
22042; 703-533-1322. Specializing in
limited-edition mechanical and still
banks, figural bottle openers

Schleyer, Jim
Box 243-E, Burke, 22015. Former
editor of the newsletter, *Toy Gun
Perveyors* and author of *Backyard
Buckaroos — Collecting Western Toy
Guns*, which contains nearly 2,500
photographs and value guide. Toy gun
inquiries that include a SASE will be
graciously answered.

Travis, Leon
Goofus Glass Gazette
9 Lindenwood Ct., Sterling, 20165.
Specializing in Goofus glass

Tutton, John
1967 Ridgway Rd., Front Royal,
22630; 540-635-7058. Specializing in
milk bottles

Windsor, Grant S.
P.O. Box 3613, Richmond, 23235-
7613; 804-320-0386. Specializing in
Griswold cast-iron cookware. SASE
required for inquiries. Grant currently
has a reprint of Griswold Catalog S,
dated November 1, 1895, 20 pages. It
contains much information and
illustrations of several items not seen
in catalogs previously known.
Information is revealed which
specifically dates the 'World's Fair'
griddle; Currently available for $11.50
each, (ppd.); For orders of 10 or more:
$7.50 each (ppd.).

Washington

Frost, Donald M.
Country Estate Antiques
(Appointment only)
14800 N.E. 8th St., Vancouver,
98684; 360-604-8434. Specializing in
art glass and earlier 20th-century
American glass

Haase, Don (Mr. Spode)
D&D Antiques
P.O. Box 818, Mukilteo, 98275; 425-
348-7443. Specializing in Spode-
Copeland China; E-mail:
mrspode@aol.com or Web page:
www.collectoronline.com/booths/
booth-85

Jackson, Denis C., Editor
The Illustrator Collector's News
P.O. Box 1958, Sequim, 98382; 206-
683-2559. Copy of recent sample: $3;
Specializing in old magazines &
illustrations such as Rose O'Neill,
Maxfield Parrish, pinups, Marilyn
Monroe, Norman Rockwell, etc.

Moore, Bill and Marilyn
Mukilteo, 296-290-9055. Specializing
in ruby-stained glass

Payne, Sharon A.
Antiquities & Art
9104. 163rd Ave. NE, Granite Falls,
98252; 360-691-4847. Specializing in
Cordey; E-mail: sharpay@gte.net

Rothe, Linda
10020A, Main St. #422, Bellevue,
98004. Specializing in Black Americana

Weldin, Bob
Miner's Quest
W. 3015 Weile, Spokane, WA 99208;
509-327-2897. Specializing in mining
antiques and collectibles (mail-order
business)

Wheeler-Tanner Escapes
Tanner, Joseph and Pamela
3024 E. 35th Ave., Spokane, 99223;
509-448-8457. Specializing in
handcuffs, leg shackles, balls and
chains, restraints and padlocks of all
kinds (including railroad) locking and
non-locking devices; Also Houdini
memorabilia: autographs, photos,
posters, books, letters, etc.

Whitaker, Jim and Kaye
Eclectic Antiques
P.O. Box 475 Dept. S, Lynnwood,
98046. Specializing in Josef Originals
and motion lamps; SASE required

West Virginia

Fostoria Glass Society of America, Inc.
Box 826, Moundsville, 26041.
Specializing in Fostoria glass

Wisconsin

Antique Associates Mall
220 Walnut St.; Suite #1, Spooner,
54801; 715-635-6666. Furniture,
glassware & china, quilts, dolls, toys,
books, pottery, primitives, lamps;
Open: Mon. – Sat. 10 a.m. – 5 p.m.;
Sunday by chance

Apple, John
John Apple Antiques
1720 College Ave., Racine, 53403;
414-633-3086. Specializing in brass
cash registers and parts

Helley, Phil
Old Kilbourne Antiques
629 Indiana Ave., Wisconsin Dells,
53965; 608-254-8770. Specializing in
premiums, German and Japanese tin
toys, Cracker Jack, toothbrush
holders, radio premiums, pencil
sharpeners, and comic strip toys

Knapper, Mary
Phoneco, Inc.
207 E. Mill Rd., P.O. Box 70,
Galesville, 54630; 608-582-4124.
Specializing in telephones, antique to
modern

Matzke, Gene
Gene's Badges & Emblems
2345 S. 28th St., Milwaukee, 53215;
414-383-8995. Specializing in police
badges, leg irons, old police photos,
fire badges (old), patches, old
handcuffs, and memorabilia

Rice, Ferill J.
302 Pheasant Run, Kaukauna, 54130.
Specializing in Fenton art glass

Clubs, Newsletters, and Catalogs

ABC Collectors' Circle (Quarterly newsletter)
Dr. Joan M. George
67 Stevens Ave., Old Bridge, NJ 08857.
Specializing in ABC plates and mugs

Abingdon Pottery Collectors Club
Elaine Westover, Membership and Treasurer
210 Knox Hwy. 5, Abingdon, IL 61410; 309-462-3267. Specializing in collecting and preservation of Abingdon pottery

ACME (Association of Coffee Mill Enthusiasts)
c/o Terry Friend
839 Glendale Rd., Galax, VA 24333; 540-236-9027 after 9:30 p.m. EST; e-mail: friend@tcia.net

Akro Agate Collectors Club *Clarksburg Crow* Newsletter
Roger Hardy
10 Bailey St., Clarksburg, WV 26301-2524; 304-624-4523 (evenings) or West End Antiques, 97 Milford St., Clarksburg, WV 26301; 304-624-7600 (weekdays). Annual membership fee: $20

The Akro Arsenal quarterly catalog
Larry D. Wells
6301 Walnut Valley Dr., Ft. Wayne, IN 46818; 219-489-5842

The Aluminist
Dannie Woodard, Publisher
P.O. Box 1346, Weatherford, TX 76086. Subscription: $12 (6 issues)

America West Archives
Anderson, Warren
P.O. Box 100, Cedar City, UT 84721; 435-586-9497. Twenty-six page illustrated catalogs issued six times a year; Has both fixed-price and auction sections offering early western documents, letters, stock certificates, autographs, and other important ephemera; Subscription: $15 per year

American Antique Deck Collectors
52 Plus Joker Club
Clear the Decks, quarterly publication
Ray Hartz, Past President
Rhonda Hawes, Membership
204 Gorham Ave., Hamden, CT 06514 ($25 in U.S. and Canada, $35 foreign). Specializing in antique playing cards

American Bell Association, Int., Inc.
c/o The Bell Tower
P.O. Box 19443, Indianapolis, IN 46219. Dorothy Malone Anthony, Past President

American Hatpin Society
Virginia Woodbury, President
20 Montecillo, Rolling Hills Estates, CA 90274; 310-326-2196. Newsletter published quarterly; Meetings also quarterly

Antique and Art Glass Salt Shaker Collectors' Society (AAGSSCS)
17460 Caloosa Trace Circle, Ft. Meyers, FL 33912

Antique & Collectors Reproduction News
Antiques Coast to Coast
c/o Lorna Bambrook
Box 71174, Des Moines, IA 50325; 515-270-8994 or (subscriptions only) 800-227-5531. Monthly newsletter, subscription: $32 per year in US; $41 in Canada

Antique Advertising Association of America (AAAA)
P.O. Box 1121, Morton Grove, IL 60053; 708-466-0904. Publishes *Past Times* Newsletter; Subscription: $35

Antique Bottle & Glass Collector Magazine
Jim Hagenbuch, Publisher
102 Jefferson St., P.O. Box 180, East Greenville, PA 18041. Published monthly for $3 per copy and $19 annual subscription ($22 in Canada)

Antique Bowie Knife Collectors Assn.
Roger Baker, Member
Box 620417, Woodside, CA 94062

Antique Comb Collectors Club International
Antique Comb Collector Newsletter
Belva Green, Editor
3748 Sunray Dr., Holiday, FL 34691-3239; 813-942-7554

Antique Journal
Michael F. Shores, Publisher
Jeffrey Hill, Editor/General Manager
1684 Decoto Rd., Suite #166, Union City, CA 50191-8592

Antique Purses Catalog: $4
Bayhouse
P.O. Box 40443, Cleveland, OH 44140; 216-871-8584. Includes colored photos of beaded and enameled mesh purses.

Antique Souvenir Collectors' News
Gary Leveille, Editor
P.O. Box 562, Great Barrington, MA 01230

Antique Stove Association
Clifford Boram, Secretary
417 N. Main St., Monticello, IN 47960. Inquiries should be accompanied by SASE and marked 'Urgent' in red.

Antique Telephone Collectors Association
Box 94, Abilene, KS 67410; 913-263-1757. An international organization associated with the Museum of Independent Telephony

Antique Trader Weekly
Julie Hoppensteadt, Editor
P.O. Box 1050, Dubuque, IA 52004-1050. Featuring news about antiques and collectibles, auctions, and events; Listing over 165,000 buyers and sellers in every edition; Subscription: $32 (52 issues) per year; Toll free for subscriptions only: 800-334-7165

Antique Wireless Association
Ormiston Rd., Breesport, NY 14816

Appraisers National Association
120 S. Bradford Ave., Placentia, CA 92670; 714-579-1082. Founded in 1982 by Dr. David Long, Ph.D., President of the College for Appraisers, to provide for a standardization of educational requirements for certification of its appraiser members and assure the public that A.N.A. appraisers not only have a broad range of knowledge in personal property valuation, but are held to the highest ethical and professional standards in the industry

Alex G. Malloy, Inc.
P.O. Box 38, South Salem, NY 10590; 203-438-0396. Specialized catalogs on antiquities, and ancient and medieval coins

Arkansas Pottery Collectors' Society
P.O. Box 7617, Little Rock, AR 72217

Arts & Crafts Quarterly/Style: 1900
17 S. Main St., Lambertville, NJ 08530; 609-397-9374

Ashtray Collectors Directory
Chuck Thompson
10802 Greencreek Dr., Suite 703, Houston, TX 77070. Annual publication listing all known ashtray collectors with addresses and specialties, $9.95 postage paid

Association of Coffee Mill Enthusiasts
c/o John E. White, Treasurer
5941 Wilkerson Rd., Rex, GA 30273. Annual dues: $30, covers cost of quarterly newsletter and copy of membership roster

Autograph Times
2303 N. 44th St., #225, Phoenix, AZ 85008; 602-947-3112 or Fax 602-947-8363. Subscription: $15 (U.S.) per year

Autographs of America
Tim Anderson
P.O. Box 461, Provo, UT 84603; 801-226-1787 (please call in the afternoon). Free sample catalog of hundreds of autographs for sale

Autumn Leaf
Bill Swanson, Editor
807 Roaring Springs Dr., Allen, TX 75002-2112; 972-727-5527
Gwynne Harrison, Club Member
P.O. Box 1, Mira Loma, CA 91752-0001; 909-685-5434

Avon Times (National Newsletter Club)
c/o Dwight or Vera Young
P.O. Box 9868, Dept P., Kansas City, MO 64134. Inquiries should be accompanied by LSASE.

Beatlefan
P.O. Box 33515, Decatur, GA 30033. Subscription: $15 (U.S.) for 6 issues or $18 (Canada and Mexico)

The Beer Stein Journal
Gary Kirsner, Publisher
P.O. Box 8807, Coral Springs, FL 33075; 305-344-9856 or Fax 305-344-4421. Published quarterly; Subscriptions $20 per year in USA

Black Memorabilia Illustrated Sales List ($2 and LSASE)
Judy Posner
June – September: R.D. 1, Box 273 SC, Effort, PA 18330; Fax 717-629-0521; October – May: P.O. Box 2194 SC, Englewood, FL 34295; Fax 941-475-2645. Buy-Sell-Collect; E-mail: judyandjef@aol.com or URL: http://www.judyposner.com

Bojo
P.O. Box 1403, Cranberry Township, PA 16066-0403. Send $3 for 38 pages of Beatles, toys, dolls, jewelry, autographs, Yellow Submarine items, etc.

Bookend Collector Club
c/o Louis Kuritzky, M.D.
4510 NW 17th Place, Gainesville, FL 32650; 352-377-3193.
lkuritzky@aol.com

Boyd's Art Glass Collectors Guild
P.O. Box 52, Hatboro, PA 19040-0052

Boyd's Crystal Art Glass
Jody & Darrell's Glass Collectibles Newsletter
P.O. Box 180833, Arlington, TX 76096-0833. Publishes six times a year. Subscription includes an exclusive glass collectible produced by Boyd's Crystal Art Glass; LSASE for current subscription rates; Sample copy of newsletter: $3

British Royal Commemorative Souvenirs Mail Order Catalog
Audrey Zeder
6755 Coralite St. S, Long Beach, CA 90808

Buckeye Marble Collectors Club
437 Meadowbrook Dr., Newark, OH
43055

The Buttonhook Society
Box 287, White Marsh, MD 21162.
Publishes bimonthly newsletter *The Boutonneur*, which promotes collecting of buttonhooks and shares research and information contributed by members

California Perfume Company
For information contact Dick Pardini
3107 North El Dorado St., Dept.
SAPG, Stockton, CA 95204-3412.
Information requires large SASE; not necessary when offering items for sale.

Candy Container Collectors of America
The Candy Gram newsletter
Joyce L. Doyle
P.O. Box 426; North Reading, MA
01864-0426. Send SASE for application

The Cane Collector's Chronicle
Linda Beeman
15 2nd St. N.E., Washington, D.C.
20002. $30 for 4 issues

The Carnival Pump
International Carnival Glass Assoc., Inc.
Lee Markley
Box 306, Mentone, IN 46539. Dues: $15 per family per year payable each July 1st

The Carousel News & Trader
87 Parke Ave. W., Suite 206, Mansfield, OH 44902. A monthly magazine for the carousel enthusiast; Subscription: $22 per year; Sample: $3

The Carousel Shopper Resource Catalog
Box 47, Dept PC, Millwood, NY
10546. Only $2 (+50¢ postage); A full-color catalog featuring dealers of antique carousel art offering single figures or complete carousels, museums, restoration services, organizations, full-size reproductions, books, cards, posters, auction services, and other hard-to-find items for carousel enthusiasts

Cast Iron Marketplace
P.O. Box 16466, Saint Paul, MN
55116. Available to hobbyists/dealers on a monthly basis to buy/sell/trade products made by the great foundries from our industrial past; Subscription: $30 per year (includes free ads up to 200 words per issue)

Central Florida Insulator Collectors
557 Nicklaus Dr., Titusville, FL 32780

Ceramic Arts Studio Catalog Reprints
BA Wellman
P.O. Box 673, Westminster, MA
01473-0673. Also offers many other catalog reprints from dinnerware to art pottery; Specializing in all areas of American ceramics, art pottery, dinnerware and figurines; E-mail:
BAWELLMAN@NET1PLUS.COM

Ceramic Arts Studio Collector's
Association
P.O. Box 46, Madison, WI 53701;
608-241-9138. Publishes newsletter, *CAS Collector*, a 22-page bimonthly; Annual membership: $15; Sample copy: $3; Inventory record and price guide also available

Character and Advertising Collectibles Illustrated Sales List ($2 and LSASE)
Judy Posner
June – September: R.D. 1, Box 273
SC, Effort, PA 18330, Fax 717-629-0521; October – May: P.O. Box 2194
SC, Englewood, FL 34295, Fax 941-475-2645. Buy-Sell-Collect; E-mail:
judyandjef@aol.com or URL:
http://www.judyposner.com

Chicagoland Antique Amusements Slot Machine & Jukebox Gazette
Ken Durham, Editor
909 26 St., N.W., Suite 502, Washington, DC 20037. Twenty page newspaper published twice a year; Subscription: four issues for $10; Sample: $5; Send SASE for free list of books; Web site: http://www.GameRoomAntiques.com

China Specialties, Inc.
Fiesta Collector's Quarterly Newsletter
P.O. Box 471, Valley City, OH 44280

Chintz Connection Newsletter
P.O. Box 222, Riverdale, MD 20738.
Dedicated to helping collectors share information and find matchings; Subscription: four issues per year for $25

Coin-Op Newsletter
Ken Durham, Publisher
909 26th St. N.W., Suite 502, Washington, D.C. 20037. Subscription: $15 per year; Sample: $5; Send SASE for free list of books; Web site: http://www.GameRoomAntiques.com

The Cola Clan
Alice Fisher, Treasurer
2084 Continental Drive N.E.,
Atlanta, GA 30345

Collectors of Findlay Glass
P.O. Box 256, Findlay, OH 45840.
An organization dedicated to the study and recognition of Findlay glass; Newsletter *The Melting Pot*, published quarterly; Annual convention; Membership: $10 per year

The Compact Collectors Chronicles
Roselyn Gerson
P.O. Box S, Lynbrook, NY 11563.
Publishes *Powder Puff* Newsletter, which contains articles covering all aspects of compact collecting, restoration, vintage ads, patents, history, and articles by members and prominent guest writers; Seeker and sellers column offered free to members

Cookie Crumbs
Cookie Cutter Collectors Club
Ruth Capper, Secretary/Treasurer
1167 Teal Road S.W., Dellroy, OH
44620. Subscription $12 per year (4 issues); Payable to CCCC

Cookie Jars and Go Withs Sales List
($2 and LSASE)
Judy Posner
June – September: R.D. 1, Box 273
SC, Effort, PA 18330; Fax 717-629-0521; October – May: P.O. Box 2194
SC Englewood, FL 34295; Fax 941-475-2645. Buy-Sell-Collect; E-mail:
judyandjef@aol.com or URL:
http://www.judyposner.com

Cookie Jarrin' With Joyce: The Cookie Jar Newsletter
R.R. 2, Box 504, Walterboro, SC 29488

Cookies
Rosemary Henry
9610 Greenview Lane, Manassas, VA
20109-3320. Subscription: $12 per year (6 issues); Payable to Cookies

The Copley Courier
1639 N. Catalina St., Burbank, CA 91505

Cowan Pottery Museum Associates
Annual dues: $35. Newsletter being developed; includes subscription to biannual *Cowan Pottery Journal*. For information write Mark Bassett, CPMA Secretary, P.O. Box 771233; Lakewood, OH 44107; or contact Victoria Naumann Peltz, Curatorial Associate, Cowan Pottery Museum at Rocky River Public Library, 1600 Hampton Rd., Rocky River, OH 44116; 440-333-7610, ext. 214.

Cracker Jack® Collector's Assoc.
The Prize Insider Newsletter
Larry White
108 Central St., Rowley, MA 01969;
508-948-8187. Subscription/membership: $18 per year (single) or $24 (family)

Creamers (Quarterly newsletter)
P.O. Box 11, Lake Villa, IL 60046-0011. Subscription: $5 per year

Currier & Ives Catalog
Rudisill's Alt Print Haus
P.O. Box 199, Worton, MD 21678.
Please include LSASE.

Currier & Ives China by Royal Newsletters
c/o Jack and Treva Hamlin for information
145 Township Rd. 1088, Proctorville, OH 45669; 614-886-7644. Two different newsletters and a book now available (over 100 pages). There is also a collector club.

Currier & Ives (China) Quarterly Newsletter
c/o Patti Street
P.O. Box 504, Riverton, KS 66770;
316-848-3529. Subscription: $12 per year (includes 2 free ads); Holds annual reunion

Czechoslovakian Collectors Guild International
P.O. Box 901395, Kansas City, MO 64190

The Dedham Pottery Collectors Society Newsletter
Jim Kaufman, Publisher
248 Highland St., Dedham, MA
02026; 800-283-8070

Depression Glass Daze
Teri Steel, Editor/Publisher
Box 57, Otisville, MI 48463; 810-631-4593. The nation's market place for glass, china, and pottery

Disneyana Illustrated Sales List
($2 and LSASE)
Judy Posner
June – September: R.D. 1, Box 273
SC, Effort, PA 18330, Fax 717-629-0521; October – May: P.O. Box 2194
SC, Englewood, FL 34295, Fax 941-475-2645. Buy-Sell-Collect; E-mail:
judyandjef@aol.com or URL:
http://www.judyposner.com

Docks, L.R. 'Les'
Shellac Shack
Box 691035, San Antonio, TX
78269-1035. Send $2 for a 72-page catalog of 78s that Docks wants to buy, the prices he will pay, and shipping instructions.

Doorstop Collectors of America
Doorstopper Newsletter
Jeanie Bertoia
2413 Madison Ave., Vineland, NJ
08630; 609-692-4092. Membership:
$20 per year, includes two newsletters and convention; Send two-stamp SASE for sample

Dorothy Kamm's Porcelain Collector's Companion
P.O. Box 7460, Port St. Lucie, FL
34985-7460; 407-465-4008 or Fax
407-460-9050. Published bimonthly; Subscription: $28 per year

Dragonware Club
c/o Suzi Hibbard
2570 Walnut Blvd. #20, Walnut Creek, CA 94596. Inquiries should be accompanied by long SASE. All contributions welcome. HMBK24A@Prodigy.com

Drawing Room of Newport
Gacher, John
152 Spring St., Newport, RI 02840; 401-841-5060. Book on Zsolnay available; On the Web: http://www.drawrm.com

Eggcup Collector's Corner
67 Stevens Ave., Old Bridge, NJ
08857. Issued quarterly; Subscriptions:
$18 per year (payable to Joan George); Sample copies: $5

The Elegance of Old Ivory Newsletter
Box 1004, Wilsonville, OR 97070

Fenton Art Glass Collectors
of America, Inc.
Williamstown, WV 26187

Fiesta Club of America
P.O. Box 15383, Loves Park, IL,
61132-5383; 815-282-2585

Fiesta Collector's Quarterly Newsletter
P.O. Box 471, Valley City, OH
44280. Subscription: $12 per year

Figural Bottle Opener Collectors
Linda Fitzsimmons
9697 Gwynn Park Dr.
Ellicott City, MD 21042; 301-465-
9296. Please include SASE when
requesting information.

Fire Mark Circle of Americas
Glen Hartley, Sr.
2859 Marlin Dr., Chamblee, GA
30341-5119; 404-451-2651. Specializing in fire marks, Methodist, Masonic,
Foremost Dairies, Goodyear

Florence Collector's Club Newsletter
Rita Bee, Editor; Beth Dunigan, Pub-
lisher; c/o Florence Collector's
Club Membership Chairman
P.O. Box 122, Richland, WA 99353.
6 issues per yr for $20

Fostoria Glass Society of America, Inc.
P.O. Box 826, Moundsville, WV 26041

Frankoma Family Collectors Association
c/o Nancy Littrell
P.O. Box 32571, Oklahoma City, OK
73123-0771. Membership dues: $25;
Includes quarterly newsletter, Annual
convention

Friar Tuck Collectors Club
Bob Furman
P.O. Box 262, Oswego, NY 13827.
Quarterly newsletter, annual conven-
tion. Write for membership applica-
tion and information.

Friends of Degenhart
c/o Degenhart Museum
P.O. Box 186, Cambridge, OH 43725;
614-432-2626. Membership: $5 ($10
for family) includes *Heartbeat*
Newsletter (printed quarterly) and
free admission to museum

H.C. Fry Society
P.O. Box 41, Beaver, PA 15009.
Founded in 1983 for the sole purpose
of learning about Fry glass; Publishes
Shards, quarterly newsletter

GAB! *(Glass Animal Bulletin!)*
P.O. Box 143, N. Liberty, IA 52317.
Subscription: $16 for 12 monthly
issues, ads free to subscribers

The Glass Post, monthly newsletter
P.O. Box 205, Oakdale, IA 52319;
Phone/Fax 319-626-3216. Subscription:
$25 per year, ads free to subscribers

The Glass Menagerie, bimonthly newsletter
Susan Candelaria, Editor
5440 El Arbol, Carlsbad, CA 92008

Gonder Pottery Collectors' Newsletter
c/o John and Marilyn McCormick
P.O. Box 3174, Shawnee, KS 66226

Glass Knife Collectors' Club
Adrienne Escoe
4448 Ironwood Ave., Seal Beach, CA
90740; 562-430-6479. SASE for information

Grandpa's Depot
John 'Grandpa' White
1616 17th St., Suite 267, Denver, CO
80202; 303-628-5590 or Fax 303-628-
5547. Publishes catalogs on railroad-
related collectibles

Griswold & Cast Iron Cookware
Association
Grant Windsor
P.O. Box 3613, Richmond, VA
23235; 804-320-0386. Membership:
$15 per individual or $20 per family (2
members per address) payable to club

Haeger Pottery Collectors of America
Lanette Clarke
5021 Toyon Way, Antioch, CA
94509; 510-776-7784. Monthly
newsletter available

*The Hagen-Renaker Collector's Club
Newsletter*
c/o Jenny Palmer
13975 Litzen Rd., Copemish, MI
49625. Subscription: $20 per year;
Sample copy: $4

Hake's Americana & Collectibles
Specializing in character and personality collectibles along with artifacts
of popular culture for over twenty
years. To receive a catalog for their
next 3,000-item mail/phone bid auction, send $3 to: Hake's Americana;
P.O. Box 1444M, York, PA 17405.

Hall China Collector's Club Newsletter
P.O. Box 360488, Cleveland, OH
44136

Head Hunters Newsletter
c/o Maddy Gordon
P.O. Box 83H, Scarsdale, NY 10583.
Subscription: $20 yearly for four quar-
terly issues

Homer Laughlin Eagle
c/o Richard Racheter
1270 63rd Terrace South, St. Petersburg, FL 33705

*How to Open and Operate a Home-
Based Antiques Business; How to Rec-
ognize and Refinish Antiques for
Pleasure and Profit*
Jacquelyn Peake, author
Globe Pequot Press
P.O. Box 833, Old Saybrook, CT
06475 or any book store

Ice Screamer
c/o Duvall Sollers
P.O. Box 132, Monkton, MD 21111.
Published quarterly; Dues: $15 per
year; Annual convention held in late
June in Lancaster, PA

The Illustrator Collector's News (TICN)
Denis C. Jackson, Editor
P.O. Box 1958, Sequim, WA 98382; Fax
206-683-2559. Subscription: $17 per
year; $3 for sample copy of bimonthly
publication; Publishes price and identification guides on various illustrators and
magazines, write for further information

Indiana Historical Radio Society
245 N. Oakland Ave., Indianapolis,
IN 46201

International Association of Calcula-
tor Collectors, *International Calcul
ator Collector* Newsletter
Guy Ball, Co-Editor
P.O. Box 345, Tustin, CA 92781-
0345. Subscription: $16 per year ($20
foreign); Sample copy: $3; E-mail:
mrcalc@usa.net

International Club for Collectors of
Hatpins and Hatpin Holders (ICC
of H&HH)
Audrae Heath, Managing Editor
P.O. Box 1009, Bonners Ferry, ID
83805-1009. Bimonthly *Points*
newsletter and *Pictorial Journal*

International Association of R.S.
Prussia, Inc.
Frances Coy, Secretary
212 Wooded Falls Rd., Louisville, KY
40243. Membership: $20 per house-
hold; Yearly convention

International Ivory Society
Robert Weisblut, Co-Founder
11109 Nicholas Dr., Wheaton, MD
20909; 301-649-4002. $10 annual mem-
bership fee includes four newsletters

International Nippon Collectors Club
(INCC)
c/o Phil Fernkes
112 Oak Ave N., Owatonna, MN
55060. Publishes newsletter six times
a year; Holds annual convention

International Perfume and Scent Bot-
tle Collectors Association
Randall B. Monsen, President
P.O. Box 529, Vienna, VA 22183 or
Fax 703-242-1357. Membership: $35
(U.S.A.) or $48 (Foreign); Newsletter
published quarterly

International Rose O'Neill Club
Contact Karen Stewart
P.O. Box 668, Branson, MO 65616.
Publishes quarterly newsletter *Kewpi-
esta Kourier*; Dues: (includes newslet-
ter) $7 (single) or $10 (family)

International Society of Antique
Scale Collectors
Bob Stein, President
300 West Adams, Suite 821, Chicago, IL
60606; 312-263-7500. Publishes *Equilibrium*
Magazine; Quarterly President's Newsletter;
Annual membership directory and out-of-
print scale catalogs; Annual convention

Iron Talk
Jimmy Walker, Editor
P.O. Box 68, Waelder, TX 78959. Journal
of antique pressing irons; News of prices,
patents, markets, collectibles, collectors,
history, reference, advice, and much more;
One-year bimonthly subscription: $25 in
U.S. (Texans add $1.94 tax); $30 foreign

Josef Originals Newsletter
Jim and Kaye Whitaker
P.O. Box 475, Dept. S, Lynnwood,
WA 98046. Subscription (four issues):
$10 per year

Kitchen Antiques & Collectibles News
Newsletter
Kollectors of Old Kitchen Stuff
Dana & Darlene DeMore, Editors
4645 Laurel Ridge Dr., Harrisburg, PA
17110; 717-545-7320. Subscription:
$24 per year for six issues of *Kitchen
Antiques & Collectibles News*

The Lace Merchant
Elizabeth M. Kurella, Publisher
Box 222, Plainwell, MI 49080; 616-
685-9792

The Laughlin Eagle
Joan Jasper, Publisher
Richard Racheter, Editor
1270 63rd Terrace S., St. Petersburg,
FL 33705. Subscription: $14 (4 issues)
per year; Sample: $4

License Plate Collectors Hobby Magazine
Drew Steitz, Editor
P.O. Box 222, East Texas, PA 18046;
Phone/Fax 610-791-7979. Bimonthly
publication with many photographs,
classifieds, etc.; $18 per year (1st class,
U.S.); Sample: $2

Line Jewels, NIA #1380
3557 Nicklaus Dr., Titusville, FL 32780

Mabel Lucie Attwell Catalogs
J. David Ehrhard
7212 Valmont St., Tujunga, CA 91042

Majolica International Society
Suite #103, 1275 First Ave., New
York, NY 10021. Dues: $30 per year,
entitles member to attend annual
meeting and to receive the quarterly
newsletter *Majolica Matters*

Majolica Mail Order Catalog
Items from the collection of Mariann
Katz Marks
P.O. Box 750, Honesdale, PA 18431.
Please send LSASE for majolica listing.

Marble Collectors' Society of America
Claire Block, Secretary
P.O. Box 222, Trumbull, CT 06611.
Publishes *Marble Mania*; Gathers and
disseminates information to further
the hobby of marbles and marble collecting; $12 adds your name to the
contributor mailing list ($21 covers
two years)

Marble Collectors Unlimited
P.O. Box 206, Northboro, MA 01532

Martha's Kidlit Newsletter
Martha Rasmussen, Editor and Publisher
Box 1488, Ames IA 50014; 515-292-
9309. For children's booklovers and
collectors; Subscription: $30 for U.S.
subcribers, all others: $31; E-mail:
mart515@aol.com

Mid-West Open Salt Society
Dave Dillingham
2620 Middlebelt Rd., W. Bloomfield,
MI 48324. Dues: $6 per year

Midwest Sad Iron Collector Club
c/o Dave Irons
223 Covered Bridge Rd., Northampton, PA, 18067; 610-262-9335 or Fax
610-262-2853

Mike's General Store
52 St. Anne's Rd., Winnepeg, Mani-
toba, Canada R2M 2Y3; 204-255-
3464. Catalog subscription: $6 per
issue or next four issues for $20

Miniature Bottle Club of the Great Lakes
39145 Marne, Sterling Heights, MI
48313; 810-566-0891. Dues $5 per
year; four meetings per year

Morgantown Collectors of America
Jerry Gallagher
420 1st Ave. N.W., Plainview, MN
55964; 507-534-3511. *The Morgantown Newscaster,* triannual journal for
research of Morgantown Glass only;
affiliated with no club; Subscription:
$18 per year; *A Handbook of Old Mor-
gantown Glass, Volume I* (A Guide to
Identification and Shape): 256 pages,
includes eight color plates, 1,800+
illustrations, and price guide, currently out of print; SASE required for
answers to queries

Mt. Washington Art Glass Society
P.O. Box 24094, Fort Worth, TX
76124-1094. Publishes *MWAGS
Review,* to educate, inform, and provide helpful information to anyone
interested in art glass; Holds annual
convention; Subscription/member-
ship: $20 per individual or $25 for two
persons in one household

Murray Hudson Antiquarian Books
and Maps
109 S. Church St., Box 163, Halls, TN
38040; 800-748-9946 or 901-836-9057;
Fax 901-836-9017. Buyer and seller of
antiquarian maps (especially pocket, wall,
U.S. Civil War, and railroad maps) and
books with maps (atlases, travel guides,
geographies, gazetteers, explorations, land
surveys, etc.), especially of Southeastern
and Southwestern U.S. prior to 1900; Also
world globes, map jigsaw puzzles and gameboards prior to 1950; Contact for catalog

Mystic Lights of the Aladdin Knights
bimonthly newsletter
c/o J.W. Courter 3935 Kelley Rd.,
Kevil, KY 40253; 502-488-2116.
Information requires LSASE

National Association of Avon Collectors
c/o Connie Clark
6100 Walnut, Dept. P, Kansas City, MO
64113. Information requires LSASE

National Association Breweriana
Advertising
2343 Met-To-Wee Lane, Wauwatosa,
WI 53226; 414-257-0158. Member-
ship: $20 (U.S.), $30 (Canada) or $40
(Overseas); Publishes *The Breweriana
Collector* and Membership Directory;
Holds annual convention

National Association of Miniature
Enthusiasts (N.A.M.E.)
Box 2621, Anaheim, CA 92804-0621;
714-871-NAME

National Association of Watch &
Clock Collectors, Inc. (NAWCC)
514 Poplar St., Columbia, PA 17512-
2130 (Headquarters, Museum, Library).
Featured on national live FX Collector's
program 1/24/96; Information/member-
ship application available; Dues $40 per
year, $50 outside U.S.; Benefits include
subscriptions to two publications; Listed
in *Maloney's Directory*

National Autumn Leaf Collectors' Club
c/o Gwynne Harrison
P.O. Box 1, Mira Loma, CA 91752-
0001; 909-685-5434

National Blue Ridge Newsletter
Norma Lilly
144 Highland Dr., Blountville, TN
37617. Subscription: $15 per year (six
issues)

National Bobbin Heads Club
Larkins, Barry
P.O. Box 9297, Daytona Beach, FL
32120; 904-253-7040

National Cambridge Collectors, Inc.
P.O. Box 416, Cambridge, OH 43725

National Depression Glass Association
Anita Woods
P.O. Box 69843, Odessa, TX 79769;
915-337-1297. Publishes *News and Views*

National Graniteware Society
P.O. Box 10013, Cedar Rapids, IA 52410

National Greentown Glass Association
1807 W. Madison, Kokomo, IN 46901

National Imperial Glass Collectors'
Society, Inc.
P.O. Box 534, Bellaire, OH 43906.
Dues: $15 per year (+$1 for each addi-
tional member of household); Quarter-
ly newsletter; Convention every June

National Insulator Association
1315 Old Mill Path, Broadview
Heights, OH 44147

National Milk Glass Collectors' Society
Opaque News, quarterly newsletter
c/o Helen D. Storey
46 Almond Dr., Cocoa Townes, Hershey, PA 17033. Please include SASE.

National Reamer Association
c/o Debbie Gillham
47 Midline Ct., Gaithersburg, MD 20878

National Shaving Mug Collectors
Association
Penelope G. Nader, Treasurer
320 S. Greenwood St., Allerton, PA
18104; 610-437-2534. To stimulate the
study, collection, and preservation of
shaving mugs and all related barbering
items; Provides quarterly newsletter,
bibliography, and directory; Holds two
meetings per year; Dues: $15 per year

National Society of Arkansas Pottery
Collectors
P.O. Box 7617, Little Rock, AR
72217. Quarterly newsletter dealing
with Arkansas' three early pottery
companies (Ouachita, Niloak, and
Camark); Membership: $20 per year

National Society of Lefton Collectors
c/o Loretta DeLozier
1101 Polk St., Bedford, IA 50833;
712-523-2289 (Mon. – Fri. 9:00 a.m. –
4:00 p.m.). Quarterly newsletter,
annual convention; Dues: $25 per year

National Toothpick Holder Collectors Society
Toby Shugart, Membership
P.O. Box 417, Safety Harbor, FL
34695-0417. Dues: $15 (single) or $20
(couple); Includes 10 *Toothpick Bulletin* newsletters per year; Annual convention held in August; Exclusive
toothpick holder annually

National Valentine Collectors Association
Evalene Pulati
P.O. Box 1404, Santa Ana, CA
92702; 714-547-1355. Specializing in
Valentines and love tokens

The Nelson McCoy Express
Carol Seman
7670 Chippewa Rd., Ste. 406,
Brecksville, OH 44141-2320

New England Society of Open Salt
Collectors
Chuck Keys
21 Overbrook Lane, East Greenwich,
RI 02818; Dues: $7 per year

New York Decorative Ceramic Society
17 S. Main St., Lambertville, NJ
08530. Meetings held 4 – 6 times a
year in New York and New Jersey,
at museums, galleries, and collectors' homes

Newspaper Collector's Society of America
Rick Brown
Lansing, MI 48901; 517-887-1255 or
HTTP://www.historybuff.com or E-
mail: rbrown@tir.com

Night Light Club
Culver, Bob
38619 Wakefield Ct., Northville, MI
48167; 248-473-8575. Specializing in
miniature oil lamps

North American Torquay Society
Jerry and Gerry Kline, Archivists
604 Orchard View Dr., Maumee, OH
43537. Quarterly newsletter sent to
members; Information and membership form requires #10 SASE

North American Trap Collectors'
Association
c/o Tom Parr
P.O. Box 94, Galloway, OH 43119-
0094. Dues: $15 per year; Publishes
bimonthly newsletter

Nutcracker Collectors' Club and
Newsletter
Susan Otto, Editor
12204 Fox Run Dr., Chesterland, OH
44026. $10 for membership and quar-
terly newsletters, free classifieds for
members

The Occupied Japan Club
c/o Florence Archambault
29 Freeborn St., Newport, RI 02840-
1821. Publishes *The Upside Down
World of an O.J. Collector,* a
bimonthly newsletter; Information
requires SASE

Old Sleepy Eye Collectors Club of
America, Inc.
P.O. Box 12, Monmouth, IL 61462.
Membership: $10 per year with addi-
tional $1 for spouse (if joining)

Old Stuff
Donna and Ron Miller, Publishers
336 N. Davis, P.O. Box 1084,
McMinnville, OR 97128. Published
six times annually; Copies by mail: $3
each; Annual subscription: $12 ($20
in Canada)

On the LIGHTER Side Newsletter
(bimonthly publication)
International Lighter Collectors
Judith Sanders, Editor
136 Circle Dr., Quitman, TX 75783;
903-763-2795 or Fax 903-763-4953.
Annual convention held in different
cities in the U.S.; Subscription fees:
Overseas rate, U.S., and Canada rate,
and a Junior and Senior Citizen rate.
Please include SASE when requesting
information.

Open Salt Collectors of the Atlantic
Regions (O.S.C.A.R.)
Wilbur Rudisill, Secretary
1844 York Rd., Gettysburg, PA
17325. Dues: $5 per year

Open Salt Seekers of the West,
Northern California Chapter
Sara Conley
84 Margaret Dr., Walnut Creek, CA
94596. Dues: $7 per year

Open Salt Seekers of the West,
Southern California Chapter
Janet Hudson
2525 E. Vassar Court, Visalia, CA
93292. Dues: $5 per year

Pacific Northwest Fenton Assoc.
P.O. Box 881, Tillamook, OR 97141;
503-842-4815. Newsletter subscription: $20 per year (published quarter-
ly, includes annual piece of glass made
only for subscribers)

Paper Collectors' Marketplace
P.O. Box 128, Scandinavia, WI
54977-0128; 715-467-2379 or Fax
715-467-2243 (8:00 a.m. to 5:00 p.m.,
Mon. – Fri.). Subscription: $19.95 per
year in U.S. (12 issues)

Paper Pile Quarterly Magazine
Ada Fitzsimmons, Editor
P.O. Box 337, San Anselmo, CA
94979; 619-322-3525. Sales and features magazine serving paper collectors and dealers since 1980, quarterly
cataloged sales, large advertising section; Subscription: $17 per year
(shipped 1st class)

Paperweight Collectors' Association, Inc.
P.O. Box 1263, Beltsville, MD 20704;
410-828-5722. Membership: $15 per
person or $25 per couple; Publishes
five newsletters a year; Biannual conventions to promote and study paperweights; Annual bulletin not
included with dues

Peanut Pals
Robert Walthall, President
P.O. Box 4465, Huntsville, AL
35815; 205-881-9198.
Associated collectors of Planters
Peanuts memorabilia, bimonthly
newsletter *Peanut Papers*; Annual directory sent to members; Annual convention and regional conventions; Dues:
$20 per year (+$3 for each additional
household member); Membership information: P.O. Box 652, St. Clairsville,
OH, 43950; Sample newsletter: $2

Pen Collectors of America
P.O. Box 821449, Houston, TX
77282-1449; Phone/Fax 713-496-
2290. Published quarterly newsletter,
Pennant; Annual membership fee: $25
(includes publication and access to
extensive reference library)

Pen Fancier's Club
1169 Overcash Dr., Dunedin, FL
34698. Publishes bimonthly catalog of
vintage pens and mechanical pencils,
books, parts, and information; Subscription: $20 per year; Sample: $4

Pepsi-Cola Collectors Club Express
Bob Stoddard, Editor
P.O. Box 1275, Covina, CA 91723

Petroleum Collectibles Monthly
Scott Benjamin and Wayne Henderson, Publishers
411 Forest St., LaGrange, OH 44050;
440-355-6608. Suscription: $29.95
per year (Samples $5). Scott advises
on Gasoline Globes and is devoted to
gas and oil collectibles.

Phoenix and Consolidated Glass Collectors' Club
Tom Jiamachello, Secretary
41 River View Drive, Essex Junction,
VT 05452; 802-878-2682. E-mail:
TOPofVT@aol.com. Membership:
$25 for single, $35 for family membership per year. Please make checks
payable to club.

Phoenix Bird Collectors of America (PBCA)
685 S. Washington, Constantine, MI
49042; 616-435-8353. Membership:
(payable to Joan Oates) $15 per year,
includes *Phoenix Bird Discoveries*, published three times a year; Also available:
1996 Updated Value Guide to be used in
conjunction with Books I – IV: $6 (ppd.)

Pickard Collectors Club, Ltd.
Membership office: 300 E. Grove St.,
Bloomington, IL 61701; 309-828-5533
or Fax 309-829-2266. Membership:
$20 a year (single) or $25 (family);
Membership includes club newsletter

Piebirds Unlimited Newsletter
Lillian M. Cole
14 Harmony School Rd., Flemington,
NJ 08822; 908-782-3198. Specializing
in pie birds, pie funnels, pie vents

*The Prize Insider Newsletter for Cracker
Jack Collectors*
Larry White
108 Central St., Rowley, MA 01969;
508-948-8187

Political Collectors of Indiana Club
Michael McQuillen
P.O. Box 11141, Indianapolis, IN 46201;
317-322-8518. Official APIC (American
Political Items Collectors) Chapter comprised of over 100 collectors of presidential and local political items

The Political Gallery
Thomas D. Slater
1325 W. 86th St., Indianapolis, IN
46260; 317-257-0863. Specializing in
political and sports memorabilia

Porcelain Collector's Companion
c/o Dorothy Kamm
P.O. Box 7460, Port St. Lucie, FL
34985-4760; 561-464-4008 or Fax
561-460-9050

Porcelier Collectors Club
21 Tamarac Swamp Rd., Wellingford,
CT 06492. Publishes *Porcelier Paper*
Newsletter; $2.50 for sample copy
which contains much information
and classified ads

Pottery Today
Bimonthly publication by Paradise
Publications, P.O. Box 221, Mayview,
MO 60471. Subscription: $15 (6
issues) per year

Powder Puff Compact Collectors'
Chronicle
P.O. Box 40, Lynbrook, NY 11563;
516-593-8746

Purinton Pastimes
P.O. Box 9394, Arlington, VA 22219.
Newsletter for Purinton pottery
enthusiasts; Subscription: $10 per year

R. Lalique
John Danis
11028 Raleigh Ct., Rockford, IL
61115; 815-877-6004 or Fax 815-877-
6042; E-mail: danis6033@aol.com

Red Wing list of related clubs, publications, and websites contact:
Doug Podpeskar
624 Jones St., Eveleth, MN 55734-
1631. Please include LSASE when
requesting information.

Ribbon Tin News Newsletter
(quarterly publication)
Hobart D. Van Deusen, Editor
28 The Green, Watertown, CT
06795; 203-945-3456

Rosevilles of the Past Newsletter
Jack Bomm, Editor
P.O. Box 656, Clarcona, FL 32710-
0656. $19.95 per year for six to 12
newsletters

Rosie Wells Enterprises, Inc.
22341 E. Wells Rd. S., Canton, IL
61520. Write for free literature; Publishes secondary market price guides for Precious Moments ® collectibles, Hallmark
ornaments, Boyds Bears & Friends,
Cherished Teddies, Precious Moments
Company's Dolls, and Beanie Babies.
Check out Rosie's internet site!
http://www/RosieWells.com. Rosie has
hosted International Conventions for
Precious Moments Collectors, hosts the
semiannual Midwest Collectibles Fest
(both held in Westmont, IL), and the
largest exclusive Beanie shows in the
world! For Hot Tips and to record Voice
Ads, Rosie offers a touch-tone 900 line
(1-900-740-7575). Send for a category
list or see our web site! Call Rosie at
800-445-8745 for information on limited edition collectibles. E-mail:
RosieWells@aol.com

Salt & Pepper Illustrated Sales List
($2 and LSASE)
Judy Posner
June – September: R.D. 1, Box 273
SC, Effort, PA 18330; Fax 717-629-
0521; October – May: P.O. Box 2194
SC, Englewood, FL 34295, Fax 941-
475-2645. Buy-Sell-Collect; E-mail:
judyandjef@aol.com or URL:
http://www.judyposner.com

Salt & Pepper Novelty Shakers Club
Irene Thornburg
581 Joy Road, Battle Creek, MI 49017;
616-963-7953. Publishes quarterly
newsletter; Holds annual convention;
Dues: $20 per year in U.S., Canada
and Mexico ($5 extra for couple)

Schoenhut Collectors Club
c/o Pat Girbach
1003 w. Huron St., Ann Arbor, MI
48103-4217 for membership information

Shawnee Pottery Collectors' Club
P.O. Box 713, New Smyrna Beach, FL
32170-0713. Monthly nation-wide
newsletter; SASE (c/o Pamela Curran)
required when requesting information;
$3 for sample of current newsletter

Shelley National China Club
c/o LaDonna Douglass
P.O. Box 580, Chokoloskee, FL 34138.
Membership: $25 per year; four quarter-
ly newsletters, plus many other benefits
and publications; eight years old, 500
members and growing, 1998 National
convention in Minneapolis, next year
in Atlanta; Building large Shelley
database and links to international
Shelley clubs; E-mail: cleiser@com-
puserve.com

Society of Inkwell Collectors
5136 Thomas Ave. South, Minneapolis, MN 55410. Membership: $22.50
per year, includes subscription to *The
Stained Finger*, a quarterly publication

Southern California Marble Club
18361-1 Strothern St., Reseda, CA 91335

Southern Folk Pottery Collectors Society
Newsletter
c/o Billy Ray & Susan Hussey
1828 N. Howard Mill Rd., Robbins,
NC 27325; 910-454-3961 or Fax 910-464-2530; Wednesday – Saturday
10:00 – 5:00 or by appointment; Dues:
$25 per year; Membership includes
biannual absentee auction catalogs,
access to member pieces, opportunities
to meet potters, participate in events,
newsletter information, and more

Southern Oregon Antiques & Collectibles Club
P.O. Box 508, Talent, OR 97540; 541-535-1231 or Fax 541-535-5109. Meets
1st Wednesday of the month; Promotes
two shows a year in Medford, OR

Stangl/Fulper Collectors Club
P.O. Box 538, Flemington, NJ 08822.
Yearly membership: $25 (includes
quarterly newsletter); Annual auction
in June; American pottery and dinnerware show and sale in October

Stevengraph Collectors Assn.
David L. Brown
2103-2829 Arbutus Rd., Victoria,
British Columbia, Canada, V8N 5X5;
250-477-9896

Still Bank Collectors Club of America
c/o Larry Egelhoff
4175 Millersville Rd., Indianapolis,
IN 46205. Membership: $35 per year

Stretch Glass Society
P.O. Box 573, Hampshire, IL 60140.
Membership: $18; Quarterly newsletter with color photos; Annual spring
convention

Style: 1900 The Quarterly Journal of
the Arts & Crafts Movement
David Rago
17 S. Main st., Lambertville, 07606;
609-397-9374

Surveyors Historical Society Identification Committee
D.R. Beeks
P.O. Box 117, Mt. Vernon, IA 52314;
391-895-0506

Susie Cooper Catalogs
J. David Ehrhard
7212 Valmont St., Tujunga, CA 91042

Swan Seekers Network
9470 Campo Rd., Suite 134, Spring
Valley, CA 91977; 619-462-5517;
Business hours: 10:00 a.m. – 4:00 p.m.
Pacific Time, Monday – Thursday.
Publishes *Swan Seekers News* and
Swan Seekers Marketplace periodicals
($28 per year U.S., $38 foreign); Specializing in Swarovski crystal; E-mail:
jimer@swanseekers.com or Web page:
www.swanseekers.com

Table Toppers
1340 West Irving Park Rd., P.O. Box
161, Chicago, IL 60613; 312-769-3184. Membership: $18 (single) per
year, which includes *Table Topics*, a
bimonthly newsletter for those interested in table-top collectibles

The Tanner Restraints Collection
3024 E. 35th, Spokane, WA 99223;
509-448-8457. Forty-page catalog of
magician/escape artist equipment from
trick and regulation padlocks, handcuffs, leg shackles, and straight jackets
to picks and pick sets; Books on all of
the above and much more; Catalog: $3

Tarrant, Jenny
Holly Daze Antiques
4 Gardenview, St. peters, MO 63376.
Send large SASE for monthly holiday
lists; all illustrated photos of antique
holiday items

Tea Leaf Club International
222 Powderhorn Dr., Houghton Lake,
MI 48629. Publishes *Tea Leaf Readings*
Newsletter; Membership: $20 (single)
or $25 (couple) per year

Tea Talk
Tina M. Carter, Teapot Columnist
Diana Rosen and Lucy Roman, Editors
P.O. Box 860, Sausalito, CA 94966;
415-331-1557

The TeaTime Gazette
Linda Ashley Leamer
P.O. Box 40276, St. Paul, MN 55104

Texas Gun Collectors Assn.
Roger Baker, Member
Box 620417, Woodside, CA 94062

Thermometer Collectors' Club of
America
Richard Porter, Vice President
P.O. Box 944, Onset, MA 02558

Thimble Collectors International
6411 Montego Rd., Louisville, KY 40228

Three Rivers Depression Era Glass Society
Meetings held 1st Monday of each month
at DeMartino's Restaurant, Carnegie, PA
For more information call: Edith A.
Putanko at John's Antiques & Edie's
Glassware
Rte. 88 & Broughton Rd., Bethel
Park, PA 15102; 412-831-2702

Tiffin Glass Collectors
P.O. Box 554, Tiffin, OH 44883.
Meetings at Seneca City; Museum on
second Tuesday of each month

Tins 'n Signs
Box 440101, Aurora, CO 80044. Subscription: $25 per year

Tobacco Antiques and Collectibles Market
Chuck Thompson, Publisher
P.O. Box 11652, Houston, TX 77293.
Subscription: $9.95 (12 issues); $19.95
in Canada and Mexico; All other foreign countries: $30 for six issues

Tops & Bottoms Club (Rene Lalique
perfumes only)
c/o Madeleine France
P.O. Box 15555, Ft. Lauderdale, FL 33318

Toy Gun Collectors of America Newsletter
Jim Buskirk, Editor & Publisher
3009 Oleander Ave. San Marcos, CA;
619-599-1054. Published quarterly, covers
both toy and BB guns; Dues: $17 per year

Uhl Collectors' Society
Beverly Leslie, Secretary/Treasurer
801 Poplar St., Boonville, IN, 47601;
812-897-3681

Dave and Donna Swick, Newsletter
506 Martin St., Newton, IL 62488;
618-783-3455

Vaseline Glass Newsletter
Jerry Chambers
2163 Pomona Place, Fairfield, CA 94533;
707-425-6166 after 4:30 p.m. P.S.T.

Vernon Views, newsletter for Vernon
Kilns collectors
P.O. Box 945, Scottsdale, AZ 85252.
Published quarterly beginning with
the spring issue, $10 per year

Vetri: Italian Glass News
Howard Lockwood, Publisher
P.O. Box 191, Fort Lee, NJ 07024;
201-969-0373. Quarterly newsletter
about 20th-century Italian glass

Vintage Fashion & Costume Jewelry
Newsletter/Club
P.O. Box 265, Glen Oaks, NY 11004;
718-969-2320 or 718-939-3095. Year's
subscription (four issues): $15 in U.S.;
$20 in Canada; $25 International;
Back issues available at $5 each

Vintage TVs
Harry Poster
Box 1883, S. Hackensack, 07606;
Days: 201-794-9606; 24-hour Fax
201-794-9553. Specializes in vintage
TVs, transister radios, 3-D stereo cameras; Catalog available online:
www.harryposter.com

Visakay, Stephen
P.O. Box 1517, W. Caldwell, 07007.
Writes monthly column for cyberspace magazine: *Shaken Not Stirred*, at
http://www.martinis.com/key/

The Wade Watch
Collector's Corner
8199 Pierson Ct., Arvada, CO 80005;
303-421-9655 or 303-424-4401; Fax
303-421-0317. Year's subscription
(four issues): $8 in U.S.; $10 International; Articles and photos welcome,
but if to be returned, enclose SASE

Walking Stick Notes
Cecil Curtis, Editor
4051 E. Olive Rd., Pensacola, FL
32514. Quarterly publication with
limited distribution

The Wallace Nutting Collector's Club
P.O. Box 22475, Beachwood, OH 44122.
Established in 1973, holds annual conventions, usually in the northeastern portion of the country. Generally recognized
national center of Wallace Nutting-like
activity are Michael Ivankovich's Wallace Nutting & Wallace Nutting-Like
Specialty Auctions, held four times each
year. These auctions provide the opportunity for collectors and dealers to compete for the largest variety of Wallace
Nutting and Wallace Nutting-Like pictures available anywhere. These auctions
also give sellers the opportunity to place
their items in front of the country's leading enthusiasts. When writing for information please enclude a close-up
photograph which includes the picture's
frame, and a SASE.

Watt's News Newsletter
c/o Watt Collectors Association
P.O. Box 1995, Iowa City, IA 52240.
Subscription: $12 per year; quarterly
newsletter, annual convention

The Wedgwood Society of New York
5 Dogwood Court, Glen Head, NY 11545.
Membership: $27.50 (individual) or
$32.50 (family); Publishes newsletter (6
times per year) and a scholarly magazine
of original articles published by the Society; six meetings per year

Westmoreland Glass Collector's Newsletter
P.O. Box 143, North Liberty, IA
52317. Subscription: $16 per year.
This publication is dedicated to the
purpose of preserving Westmoreland
Glass and its history.

Westmoreland Glass Society
Jim Fisher, President
513 5th Ave., Coralville, IA 52241;
319-354-5011. Membership: $15 (single) or $25 (household)

The Whimsey Club
c/o Christopher Davis
522 Woodhill, Newark, NY 14513.
Whimsical Notions, quarterly newsletter;
Dues: $5 per year; Annual meeting in
Rochester, NY, in April during Genessee
Valley Bottle Collectors' Show

The White Ironstone China Association, Inc.
c/o Jimm Kerr, Membership Committee
R.D. #1, Box 23, Howes Cave, NY
12092. Newsletter available for: $25 (sin-
gle) or $30 (2 individuals at same address)

The Willow Word
Mary Lina Berndt, Publisher
P.O. Box 13382, Arlington, TX 76094.
Each bimonthly issue contains twenty
pages of articles, photographs and full-color
'centerfold'; Subscription: $20 in U.S., $22
in Canada, $25 overseas (U.S. funds only)

World's Fair Collectors' Society, Inc.
Fair News Newsletter (monthly publication for members)
Michael R. Pender, Editor
P.O. Box 20806, Sarasota, FL 34276-
3806; 941-923-2590. Dues: $17 per year
in U.S., $18 in Canada, and $27 overseas

The Zsolnay Store
152 Spring St., Newport, RI 02840;
401-841-5060. Zsolnay book available; On the Web:
http://www.drawrm.com

Invention Patents

Invention patents cover the unique mechanical workings of inventions which produce utilitarian results.
An invention patent is in effect, with exclusive rights for the inventor, for 17 years from date of issuance.

A GUIDE FOR DATING INVENTION PATENT NUMBERS

Patent Numbers		Date	Patent Numbers		Date	Patent Numbers		Date
1 through	109	1836	236,137	251,684	1881	1,568,040	1,612,789	1926
110	545	1837	251,685	269,819	1882	1,612,790	1,654,520	1927
546	1,060	1838	269,820	291,015	1883	1,654,521	1,696,896	1928
1,061	1,464	1839	291,016	310,162	1884	1,696,897	1,742,180	1929
1,465	1,922	1840	310,163	333,493	1885	1,742,181	1,787,423	1930
1,923	2,412	1841	333,494	355,290	1886	1,787,424	1,839,189	1931
2,413	2,900	1842	355,291	375,719	1887	1,839,190	1,892,662	1932
2,901	3,394	1843	375,720	395,304	1888	1,892,663	1,941,448	1933
3,395	3,872	1844	395,305	418,664	1889	1,941,449	1,985,877	1934
3,873	4,347	1845	418,665	443,986	1890	1,985,878	2,026,515	1935
4,348	4,913	1846	443,987	466,314	1891	2,026,516	2,066,308	1936
4,914	5,408	1847	466,315	488,975	1892	2,066,309	2,104,003	1937
5,409	5,992	1848	488,976	511,743	1893	2,104,004	2,142,079	1938
5,993	6,980	1849	511,744	531,618	1894	2,142,080	2,185,169	1939
6,981	7,864	1850	531,619	552,501	1895	2,185,170	2,227,417	1940
7,865	8,621	1851	552,502	574,368	1896	2,227,418	2,268,539	1941
8,622	9,511	1852	574,369	596,466	1897	2,268,540	2,307,006	1942
9,512	10,357	1853	596,467	616,870	1898	2,307,007	2,338,080	1943
10,358	12,116	1854	616,871	640,166	1899	2,338,081	2,366,153	1944
12,117	14,008	1855	640,167	664,826	1900	2,366,154	2,391,855	1945
14,009	16,323	1856	664,827	690,384	1901	2,391,856	2,413,674	1946
16,324	19,009	1857	690,385	717,520	1902	2,413,675	2,433,823	1947
19,010	22,476	1858	717,521	748,566	1903	2,433,824	2,457,796	1948
22,477	26,641	1859	748,567	778,833	1904	2,457,797	2,492,943	1949
26,642	31,004	1860	778,834	808,617	1905	2,492,944	2,536,015	1950
31,005	34,044	1861	808,618	839,798	1906	2,536,016	2,580,378	1951
34,045	37,265	1862	839,799	875,678	1907	2,580,379	2,624,045	1952
37,266	41,046	1863	875,679	908,435	1908	2,624,046	2,664,561	1953
41,047	45,684	1864	908,436	945,009	1909	2,664,562	2,698,433	1954
45,685	51,783	1865	945,010	980,177	1910	2,698,434	2,728,912	1955
51,784	60,657	1866	980,178	1,013,094	1911	2,728,913	2,775,761	1956
60,658	72,958	1867	1,013,095	1,049,325	1912	2,775,762	2,818,566	1957
72,959	85,502	1868	1,049,326	1,083,266	1913	2,818,567	2,866,972	1958
85,503	98,459	1869	1,083,267	1,123,211	1914	2,866,973	2,919,442	1959
98,460	110,616	1870	1,123,212	1,166,418	1915	2,919,443	2,966,680	1960
110,617	122,303	1871	1,166,419	1,210,388	1916	2,966,681	3,015,102	1961
122,304	134,503	1872	1,210,389	1,251,457	1917	3,015,103	3,070,800	1962
134,504	146,119	1873	1,251,458	1,290,026	1918	3,070,801	3,116,486	1963
146,120	158,349	1874	1,290,027	1,326,898	1919	3,116,487	3,163,864	1964
158,350	171,640	1875	1,326,899	1,364,062	1920	3,163,865	3,226,728	1965
171,641	185,812	1876	1,364,063	1,401,947	1921	3,216,729	3,295,142	1966
185,813	198,732	1877	1,401,948	1,440,361	1922	3,295,143	3,360,799	1967
198,733	211,077	1878	1,440,362	1,478,995	1923	3,360,800	3,419,096	1968
211,078	223,210	1879	1,478,996	1,521,589	1924	3,419,907	3,487,469	1969
223,211	236,136	1880	1,521,590	1,568,039	1925	3,487,470	3,551,908	1970

Design Patents

Design patents cover unique, ornamental exterior shapes or structures of an invention. A design patent is in effect, with exclusive rights for the inventor, for 14 years from date of issuance.

A GUIDE FOR DATING DESIGN PATENT NUMBERS
Design patent numbers are preceded with the letters D or DES

Patent Numbers		Date	Patent Numbers		Date	Patent Numbers		Date
1 through	14	1843	16,451	17,045	1886	77,347	80,253	1929
15	26	1844	17,046	17,994	1887	80,254	82,965	1930
27	43	1845	17,995	18,829	1888	82,966	85,902	1931
44	102	1846	18,830	19,552	1889	85,903	88,846	1932
103	162	1847	19,553	20,438	1890	88,847	91,257	1933
163	208	1848	20,439	21,274	1891	91,258	94,178	1934
209	257	1849	21,275	22,091	1892	94,179	98,044	1935
258	340	1850	22,092	22,993	1893	98,045	102,600	1936
341	430	1851	22,994	23,921	1894	102,601	107,737	1937
431	539	1852	23,922	25,036	1895	107,738	112,764	1938
540	625	1853	25,037	26,481	1896	112,765	118,357	1939
626	682	1854	26,482	28,112	1897	118,358	124,502	1940
683	752	1855	28,113	29,915	1898	124,503	130,988	1941
753	859	1856	29,916	32,054	1899	130,989	134,716	1942
860	972	1857	32,055	33,812	1900	134,717	136,945	1943
973	1,074	1858	33,813	35,546	1901	136,946	139,861	1944
1,075	1,182	1859	35,547	36,186	1902	139,862	143,385	1945
1,183	1,365	1860	36,187	36,722	1903	143,386	146,164	1946
1,366	1,507	1861	36,723	37,279	1904	146,165	148,266	1947
1,508	1,702	1862	37,280	37,765	1905	148,267	152,234	1948
1,703	1,878	1863	37,766	38,390	1906	152,235	156,685	1949
1,879	2,017	1864	38,391	38,979	1907	156,686	161,403	1950
2,018	2,238	1865	38,980	39,736	1908	161,404	165,567	1951
2,239	2,532	1866	39,737	40,423	1909	165,568	168,526	1952
2,533	2,857	1867	40,424	41,062	1910	168,527	171,240	1953
2,858	3,303	1868	41,063	42,072	1911	171,241	173,776	1954
3,304	3,809	1869	42,073	43,414	1912	173,777	176,489	1955
3,810	4,546	1870	43,415	45,097	1913	176,490	179,466	1956
4,547	5,451	1871	46,098	46,812	1914	179,467	181,828	1957
5,452	6,335	1872	46,813	48,357	1915	181,829	184,203	1958
6,336	7,082	1873	48,358	50,116	1916	184,204	186,972	1959
7,083	7,968	1874	50,117	51,628	1917	186,973	189,515	1960
7,969	8,883	1875	51,629	52,835	1918	189,516	192,003	1961
8,884	9,685	1876	52,836	54,358	1919	192,004	194,303	1962
9,686	10,384	1877	54,359	56,843	1920	194,304	197,268	1963
10,385	10,974	1878	56,844	60,120	1921	197,269	199,994	1964
10,975	11,566	1879	60,121	61,747	1922	199,995	203,378	1965
11,567	12,081	1880	61,748	63,674	1923	203,379	206,566	1966
12,082	12,646	1881	63,675	66,345	1924	206,567	209,731	1967
12,647	13,507	1882	66,346	69,169	1925	209,732	213,083	1968
13,508	14,527	1883	69,170	71,771	1926	213,084	216,418	1969
14,528	15,677	1884	71,772	74,158	1927	216,419	219,636	1970
15,678	16,450	1885	74,159	77,346	1928			

Index